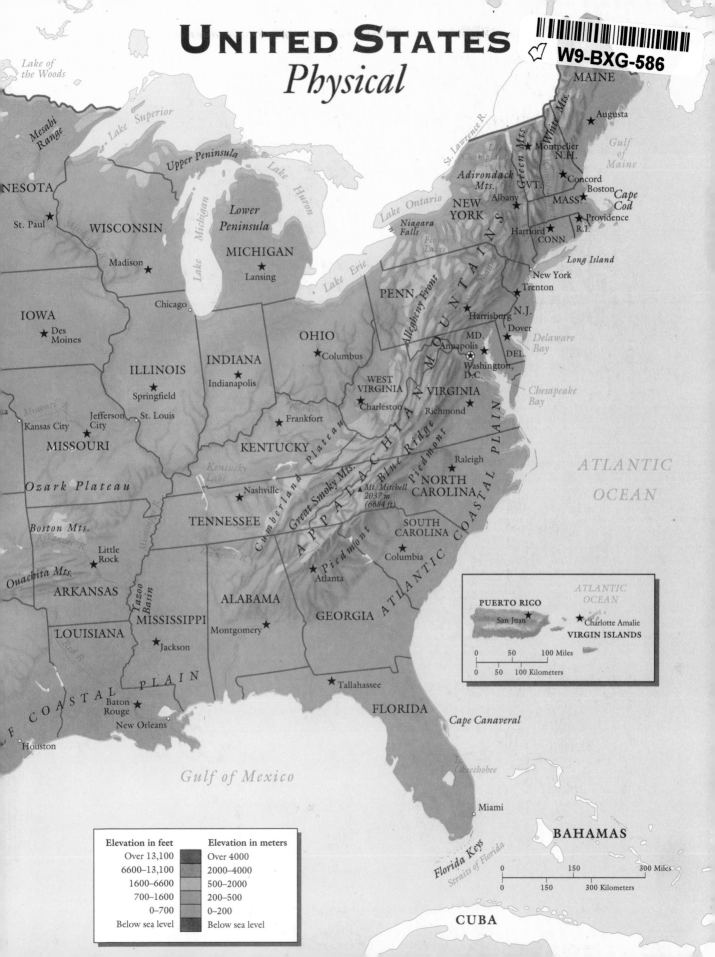

UNITED STATES
Physical

Lake of the Woods

MAINE

Augusta

Gulf of Maine

Mesabi Range

Lake Superior

Upper Peninsula

Lake Huron

St. Lawrence R.

White Mts.

Montpelier
N.H.

Adirondack Mts.

Green Mts.

VT.

Concord
Boston
Cape Cod

MINNESOTA

WISCONSIN

Lake Michigan

Lower Peninsula

NEW YORK

Albany

MASS.

St. Paul

Madison

MICHIGAN

Lansing

Niagara Falls

Lake Ontario

Hartford
CONN.

Providence
R.I.

Lake Erie

Finger Lakes

Long Island

Chicago

New York
Trenton

IOWA

Des Moines

ILLINOIS

INDIANA

OHIO

Columbus

Allegheny Front

PENN.

Harrisburg
N.J.

Dover

MD.

Delaware Bay

Springfield

Indianapolis

Annapolis

DEL.

Jefferson City
St. Louis

WEST VIRGINIA

VIRGINIA

Washington, D.C.

Chesapeake Bay

Kansas City

Frankfort

Charleston

Richmond

MISSOURI

KENTUCKY

Missouri R.

Ohio R.

Cumberland Plateau

Blue Ridge

Piedmont

ATLANTIC OCEAN

Ozark Plateau

Kentucky Lake

Nashville

Great Smoky Mts.

Mt. Mitchell 2037 m (6684 ft)

NORTH CAROLINA

Raleigh

Boston Mts.

TENNESSEE

APPALACHIAN MOUNTAINS

SOUTH CAROLINA

Little Rock

Ouachita Mts.

Tennessee R.

Piedmont

Columbia

ATLANTIC COASTAL PLAIN

ARKANSAS

Yazoo Basin

Piedmont

Atlanta

ATLANTIC OCEAN

PUERTO RICO

San Juan

Charlotte Amalie
VIRGIN ISLANDS

0   50   100 Miles

0   50   100 Kilometers

LOUISIANA

MISSISSIPPI

ALABAMA

Montgomery

GEORGIA

Jackson

Red R.

COASTAL PLAIN

Tallahassee

Baton Rouge

New Orleans

FLORIDA

Cape Canaveral

Houston

Gulf of Mexico

Okeechobee

Miami

BAHAMAS

Florida Keys

Straits of Florida

0   150   300 Miles

0   150   300 Kilometers

CUBA

Elevation in feet	Elevation in meters
Over 13,100	Over 4000
6600–13,100	2000–4000
1600–6600	500–2000
700–1600	200–500
0–700	0–200
Below sea level	Below sea level

LIBERTY
EQUALITY
POWER

LIBERTY
EQUALITY
POWER

A HISTORY OF THE AMERICAN PEOPLE

THIRD EDITION

John M. Murrin   *Princeton University*

Paul E. Johnson   *University of South Carolina*

James M. McPherson   *Princeton University*

Gary Gerstle   *University of Maryland*

Emily S. Rosenberg   *Macalester College*

Norman L. Rosenberg   *Macalester College*

WADSWORTH

™

THOMSON LEARNING

Australia • Canada • Mexico • Singapore • Spain •
United Kingdom • United States

WADSWORTH

THOMSON LEARNING ™

Executive Editor: David Tatom
Development Editor: Margaret McAndrew Beasley
Marketing Manager: Steve Drummond
Project Editor: Elizabeth Cruce Alvarez
Print/Media Buyer: Vanessa Manning Jennings
Permissions Editor: Shirley Webster
Production Manager: Diane Gray

Art Designer: Sue Hart
Photo Researcher: Lili Wiener
Copy Editor: Karen Keady
Cover Printer: Lehigh Press, Inc.
Compositor: TSI Graphics
Printer: R.R. Donnelley Willard

3 4 5 6 7 048 05 04 03 02

For more information about our products, contact us at:
Thomson Leaning Academic Resource Center
1-800-423-0563
For permission to use material from this text, contact us by:
Phone: 1-800-730-2214 **Fax:** 1-800-730-2215
Web: http://www.thomsonrights.com

Library of Congress Catalog Card Number: 2001090210
ISBN: 0-15-508568-9

Asia
Thomson Learning
60 Albert Street, #15-01
Albert Complex
Singapore 189969

Australia
Nelson Thomson Learning
102 Dodds Street
South Melbourne, Victoria 3205
Australia

Canada
Nelson Thomson Learning
1120 Birchmount Road
Toronto, Ontario M1K 5G4
Canada

Europe/Middle East/Africa
Thomson Learning
Berkshire House
168-173 High Holborn
London WC1 V7AA
United Kingdom

Latin America
Thomson Learning
Seneca, 53
Colonia Polanco
11560 Mexico D.F.
Mexico

Spain
Paraninfo Thomson Learning
Calle/Magallanes, 25
28015 Madrid, Spain

The author team (from left): Norman Rosenberg, Emily Rosenberg, Paul Johnson, Gary Gerstle, John Murrin, and Jim McPherson.

JOHN M. MURRIN
Princeton University

John M. Murrin, a specialist in American colonial and revolutionary history and the early republic, is the author of chapters 1–6. He has edited one multivolume series and five books, including two co-edited collections, *Colonial America: Essays in Politics and Social Development*, Fifth Edition, (2001) and *Saints and Revolutionaries: Essays in Early American History* (1984). His own essays on early American history range from ethnic tensions, the early history of trial by jury, the rise of the legal profession, and the political culture of the colonies and the new nation, to the rise of professional baseball and college football in the 19th century. Professor Murrin served as president of the Society for Historians of the Early American Republic in 1998–99.

PAUL E. JOHNSON
University of South Carolina

Paul E. Johnson authored chapters 7–12. A specialist in early national social and religious history,

he is also the author of *A Shopkeeper's Millennium: Society and Revivals in Rochester, New York, 1815–1837* (1978); coauthor (with Sean Wilentz) of *The Kingdom of Matthias: Sex and Salvation in 19th-Century America* (1994); and editor of *African-American Christianity: Essays in History* (1994). He has been awarded the Merle Curti Prize of the Organization of American Historians (1980), a John Simon Guggenheim Memorial Fellowship (1995), and the Gilder Lehrman Fellowship (2001).

JAMES M. MCPHERSON
Princeton University

James M. McPherson is the author of chapters 13–19. A distinguished Civil War historian, he won the 1989 Pulitzer Prize for his book *Battle Cry of Freedom: The Civil War Era*. His other publications include *Marching Toward Freedom: Blacks in the Civil War*, Second Edition, (1991); *Ordeal by Fire: The Civil War and Reconstruction*, Third Edition, (2001); *Abraham Lincoln and the Second American Revolution*

(1991); and *For Cause and Comrades: Why Men Fought in the Civil War* (1997), which won the Lincoln Prize for 1998. In addition he is, along with Gary Gerstle, a consulting editor of *American Political Leaders: From Colonial Times to the Present* (1991) and *American Social Leaders: From Colonial Times to the Present* (1993).

GARY GERSTLE
University of Maryland

Gary Gerstle is the author of chapters 20–25. A specialist in labor, immigration, and political history, he has published four books: *Working-Class Americanism: The Politics of Labor in a Textile City, 1914–1960* (1989); *The Rise and Fall of the New Deal Order, 1930–1980* (1989); *American Crucible: Race and Nation in the Twentieth Century* (2001); and *E Pluribus Unum: Immigrants, Civic Culture, and Political Incorporation* (2001). His articles have appeared in the *American Historical Review*, *Journal of American History*, *American Quarterly*, and other journals, and he is a consulting editor, along with James M. McPherson, of *American Political Leaders: From Colonial Times to the Present* (1991) and *American Social Leaders: From Colonial Times to the Present* (1993). He has been awarded many honors, including a National Endowment for the Humanities Fellowship for University Teachers and a John Simon Guggenheim Memorial Fellowship, and he directs the Center for Historical Studies at the University of Maryland.

EMILY S. ROSENBERG
Macalester College

Emily S. Rosenberg is coauthor, along with Norman L. Rosenberg, of chapters 26–31. She specializes in United States foreign relations in the 20th century and is the author of the widely used books *Spreading the American Dream: American Economic and Cultural Expansion, 1890–1945* (1982) and *Financial Missionaries to the World: The Politics and Culture of Dollar Diplomacy* (1999). Her other publications include (with Norman L. Rosenberg) *In Our Times: America Since 1945*, Fifth Edition, (1995) and numerous articles on subjects such as international finance, gender issues, and foreign relations. She has served on the board of the Organization of American Historians, on the board of editors of the *Journal of American History*, and as president of the Society for Historians of American Foreign Relations.

NORMAN L. ROSENBERG
Macalester College

Norman L. Rosenberg is coauthor, along with Emily S. Rosenberg, of chapters 26–31. He specializes in legal history with a particular interest in legal culture and First Amendment issues. His books include *Protecting the "Best Men": An Interpretive History of the Law of Libel* (1990) and (with Emily S. Rosenberg) *In Our Times: America Since 1945*, Fifth Edition, (1995). He has published articles in the *Rutgers Law Review*, *Constitutional Commentary*, *Law & History Review*, and many other legal journals.

LIBERTY EQUALITY POWER

A Student's Guide to Learning from This Textbook

As the year 1860 began, the Democratic Party was one of the few national institutions left in the country. The Methodists and Baptists had split into Northern and Southern churches in the 1840s over the issue of slavery; several voluntary associations had done the same; the Whig Party and the nativist American Party had been shattered by sectional antagonism in the mid-1850s. Finally, in April 1860, even the Democratic Party, at its national convention in Charleston, South Carolina, split into Northern and Southern camps. This virtually ensured the election of a Republican president. Such a prospect aroused deep fears among southern whites that a Republican administration might use its power to bring liberty and perhaps even equality to the slaves. When Abraham Lincoln was elected president exclusively by northern votes, the lower-South states seceded from the Union. When Lincoln refused to remove U.S. troops from Fort Sumter, South Carolina, the new Confederate States army opened fire on the fort. Lincoln called out the militia to suppress the insurrection. Four more slave states seceded. In 1861, the country drifted into a civil war whose immense consequences no one could foresee.

This chapter will focus on the following major questions:

- Why did political leaders in the lower South think that Lincoln's election made secession imperative?
- Why did compromise efforts to forestall secession fail, and why did war break out at Fort Sumter?
- What were Northern advantages in the Civil War? What were Southern advantages?
- How did these advantages manifest themselves in the military campaigns and battles in 1861–62?

THE ELECTION OF 1860

A hotbed of southern-rights radicalism, Charleston turned out to be the worst possible place for the Democrats to hold their national convention. Sectional confrontations took place inside the convention hall and on the streets. Since 1836 the Democratic Party had required a two-thirds majority of delegates for a presidential nomination, a rule that in effect gave southerners veto power if they voted together. Although Stephen A. Douglas had the backing of a simple majority of the delegates, southern Democrats were determined to deny him the nomination. His opposition to the Lecompton

In writing this textbook, the authors—all students and teachers of history themselves—have given careful consideration to students and how they use textbooks. As part of the effort to write the clearest, most complete, and most accurate history possible, they have included study aids to help you interpret and relate to the stories of the past. The following pages show examples of the various features in your textbook and provide tips on how to get the most from your reading.

New chapter outlines and focus questions set up the framework and guide you through the major points within each chapter. In addition to helping you see where the chapter is leading before you read, these features may also be used to review the material in preparation for a test.

been dulled by his 1936 victory. His inflated sense of power infuriated many who had previously been New Deal enthusiasts. Although working-class support for Roosevelt remained strong, many middle-class voters turned away from the New Deal. In 1937 and 1938 a conservative opposition took shape, uniting Republicans, conservative Democrats (many of them southerners), and civil libertarians determined to protect private property and government integrity.

Ironically, Roosevelt's court-packing scheme may have been unnecessary. In March 1937, just one month after he proposed his plan, Supreme Court Justice Owen J. Roberts, a former opponent of New Deal programs, decided to support them. In April and May, the Court upheld the constitutionality of the Wagner Act and Social Security Act, both by a 5-to-4 margin. The principal re-

forms of the New Deal would endure. Roosevelt allowed his court-reform proposal to die in Congress that summer. Within three years, five of the aging justices had retired, giving Roosevelt the opportunity to fashion a court more to his liking. Nonetheless, Roosevelt's reputation had suffered.

THE RECESSION OF 1937–1938

Whatever hope Roosevelt may have had for a quick recovery from the court-packing fiasco was dashed by a sharp recession that struck the country in late 1937 and 1938. The New Deal programs of 1935 had stimulated the economy. In 1937 production surpassed the highest level of 1929, and unemployment fell to 14 percent. Believing that the depression was easing at last, Roosevelt began to scale back relief programs. New payroll taxes took two

UNEMPLOYMENT IN THE NONFARM LABOR FORCE, 1929–1945

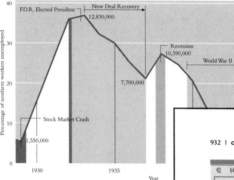

Source: Data from *Historical Statistics of the United States, Colonial Times to 1970* (p. 126.

> Graphs, charts, and tables help to summarize and visually illustrate trends and changes discussed in the text.

CHRONOLOGY

1946 Baruch plan for atomic energy proposed • Employment Act passed • Republicans gain control of Congress in November elections

1947 Truman Doctrine announced • HUAC begins hearings on communist infiltration of Hollywood • George Kennan's "Mr. X" article published • National Security Act passed (CIA and NSC established) • Marshall Plan adopted • Truman's loyalty order announced • Taft-Hartley Act passed over Truman's veto • Jackie Robinson and Larry Doby break major league baseball's color line

1948 Berlin Airlift begins • Truman wins reelection • The Kinsey Report and Dr. Benjamin Spock's *Baby and Child Care* published

1949 NATO established • China "falls" to communism • NSC-68 drafted • Soviet Union explodes atomic device • Truman unveils his Fair Deal

1950 Korean War begins • Senator Joseph McCarthy charges communist infiltration of State Department • McCarran Internal Security Act passed

1951 Truman removes General MacArthur as commander in Korea

1952 GI Bill of Rights passed • Dwight Eisenhower elected president

1953 Korean War ends • Julius and Ethel Rosenberg executed • *Playboy* magazine debuts

1954 Joseph McCarthy censured by U.S. Senate • Communist Control Act passed

States and the Soviet Union steadily degenerated into a cold war of suspicion and growing tension.

ONSET OF THE COLD WAR

Historians have discussed the origins of the cold war from many different perspectives. The traditional interpretation, which gained new power after the collapse of the Soviet Union in 1989, focuses on Soviet expansionism, stressing a traditional Russian appetite for new territory, an ideological zeal to

spread international communism, or some interplay between the two. The United States, proponents of this view still insist, needed to take as hard a line as possible. Other historians—generally called revisionists—argue that the Soviet Union's obsession with securing its borders was an understandable defensive response to the invasion of its territory during both world wars. The United States, in this view, should have tried to reassure the Soviets by seeking accommodation, instead of pursuing policies that intensified Stalin's fears. Still other scholars maintain that assigning blame obscures the clash of deep-seated rival interests that made postwar tensions between the two superpowers inevitable.

In any view, Harry Truman's role proved important. His brusque manner, in sharp contrast to Franklin Roosevelt's urbanity, brought a harsher tone to U.S.–Soviet meetings. Truman initially hoped that he could somehow cut a deal with Soviet Premier Joseph Stalin, much like his old mentor, "Boss" Tom Pendergast, struck bargains with rogue politicians back in Missouri. "I like Stalin," Truman once wrote his wife. "[He] knows what he wants and will compromise when he can't get it." However, as disagreements between the two former allies mounted, Truman came to rely on advisers hostile to Stalin's Soviet Union.

The atomic bomb provided an immediate source of friction. At the July 1945 Potsdam Conference Truman had casually remarked to Stalin, "We have a new weapon of unusual destructive force." Calmly, Stalin had replied that he hoped the United States would make "good use" of it against Japan. Less calmly, Stalin immediately ordered a crash program to develop nuclear weapons of his own. After atomic bombs hit Japan, Stalin reportedly told his scientists that "the equilibrium has been destroyed. Provide the bomb. It will remove a great danger from us." Truman hoped that the bomb would scare the Soviets, and it did. Stalin grew even more concerned about Soviet security. Historians still debate whether "wearing the bomb ostentatiously on our hip," as Secretary of War Henry Stimson put it, frightened the Soviets into more cautious behavior or made them more fearful and aggressive.

In 1946 Truman authorized Bernard Baruch, a presidential adviser and special representative to the United Nations, to offer a proposal for the

> Chronologies, now located near the opening of each chapter, provide a quick overview of major events and movements of that period.

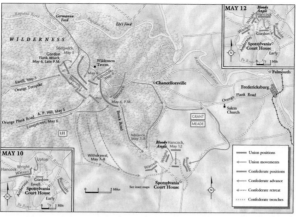

MAY 12

MAY 10

BATTLE OF THE WILDERNESS AND SPOTSYLVANIA, MAY 5–12, 1864

quick, decisive victory in 1864. The mood ...
Grant's appointment as general-in-chief ...
Grant decided to remain in Virginia with ...
of the Potomac and to leave Sherman in co...
the Union forces in northern Georgia, N...
expected these two heavyweights to ...
Confederacy with a one-two punch. Li...
alarmed by this euphoria. "The people ar...
guine," he told a reporter. "They expect t...
once." Disappointment might trigger desp...

Lincoln was nearly proved right. Gra...
gic plan was elegant in its simplicity. Wh...
Union armies in peripheral theaters c...
auxiliary campaigns, the two principal ...
Virginia and Georgia would attack ...
Confederate forces under Lee and ...
Convinced that in years past Union armi...
ous theaters had "acted independently an...
concert, like a balky team, no two ever p...

...MERICAN POPULATION, 1910

...ed. Their belongings were locked up ... them from running away. Although ...ally was less severe among other ...oyers of black laborers, blacks often ...h the dirtiest and most grueling jobs. ...w" laws passed by every southern ...e in the 1890s legalized this rigid ...he black and white races (see chap-

...rthern states had no Jim Crow laws, ...orsening racial climate adversely af-...n blacks who came north. Industrial-...refused to hire black migrants for ... jobs, preferring the labor of Euro-...nts. Only when those immigrants ...did employers turn to African Amer-

icans. Black workers first gained a foothold in the Chicago meatpacking industry in 1904, when 28,000 ethnic packinghouse workers walked off their jobs. Employers hoped that the use of black strikebreakers would inflame racial tensions between white and black workers and thus undermine labor unity and strength.

African Americans who had long resided in northern urban areas also experienced intensifying discrimination in the late 19th and early 20th centuries. In 1870 about a third of the black men in many northern cities had been skilled tradesmen: blacksmiths, painters, shoemakers, and carpenters. Serving both black and white clients, these men enjoyed steady work and good pay, but by 1910 only 10 percent of black men made a living in this way.

Maps are tools that historians use to help tell the story. This textbook includes several different types of maps to illustrate different types of information. Maps of the entire United States, as shown above, use color, shading, or symbols to highlight information such as territorial boundaries and shifts in population or voting patterns. Whereas maps of smaller areas such as battle locations, as shown at top, "zoom in" on a specific site and include topographical markings indicating mountains, lakes, or even trees to help you envision the landscape and understand the role that geography may have played in the outcome of the battle.

New "History Through Film" features highlight films relating to the chapter material. These essays examine how historical events and figures have been portrayed—accurately or inaccurately—through the lens of the camera and the vision of the director. The authors selected films ranging from classics such as *Gone with the Wind*, *Invasion of the Body Snatchers*, and *Star Wars* to recent box-office draws such as *Beloved* and *Saving Private Ryan* (see the Table of Contents for a complete listing of films featured). Enjoy the movie, read the feature, and, in the process, gain new perspectives on the past.

The Patriot (2000)
Directed by Roland Emmerich. Starring Mel Gibson (Benjamin Martin), Jason Isaacs (Colonel Tavington), Heath Ledger (Gabriel Martin), and Joely Richardson (Charlotte Selton).

Hollywood has a poor record of depicting the American Revolution. First, nearly every screenplay simplifies the issues until the complexities of slavery and abolition disappear altogether. Second, the leading patriots become filiopietistic caricatures of the fascinating men they actually were (the portrayal of George Washington in *Lafayette*, 1962, is an excellent example). *The Patriot* fails on both of these counts. Although the cinematography is superb and the battle scenes are compelling, Robert Rodat's screenplay falls sadly short of his accomplishment in *Saving Private Ryan* (1998).

At the outset, the film shows promise. Mel Gibson portrays Benjamin Martin, a widower with seven children and a prosperous farmer in the South Carolina backcountry. A veteran of the French and Indian War, Martin supports the colonial constitutional position against Great Britain but opposes the resort to arms. His oldest son disagrees and enlists in the Continental Army. Then the war invades Martin's family. After a losing confrontation with the redcoats, some wounded Americans take refuge at the Martin farm. The British find them there, and Col. Tavington (Jason Isaacs) executes another of Martin's sons. With two of his small boys and an armload of muskets, Mar-

tin pursues the British column, ambushes it, and the three Martins kill about 20 redcoats. Up to this point the drama is intense and almost believable, but it soon deteriorates.

In *The Patriot*, South Carolina has almost no loyalists, and Martin owns no slaves but has a free black as a friend and neighbor, all but impossible for that time and place. As the colonists take up arms, they recruit blacks, which in fact South Carolina adamantly refused to do. The film even depicts a free black (or "Maroon") community, presumably of escaped slaves, leading an idyllic life on the Atlantic coast, where it would have had no chance whatever of surviving. In the film's climactic battle, General Nathanael Greene's army smashes the British army of Charles, Earl Cornwallis (Tom Wilkinson) and drives it off the field, something that never happened in the entire southern campaign.

Emmerich, the director, grew up in Germany, where he acquired a laudable hatred for the Nazis. Unfortunately, he also seems to believe that no foe can be credible unless it becomes as loathsome as the Nazis were. In his biggest hit, *Independence Day* (1996), the earth-invading aliens have no redeeming qualities of

any kind. They intend to obliterate the human race, loot the planet of all of its resources, and then move on. Emmerich's Col. Tavington, loosely modeled on Banastre Tarleton, is almost as despicable. In one scene, he locks Martin's neighbors, nearly all women and children, in a church and burns them alive, an

atrocity familiar to the Nazis in the Russian campaign, but one that had no counterpart in the Revolutionary War. Naturally, Martin must kill Tavington in hand-to-hand combat during the final battle. Such overexertions make *The Patriot*, for all of its sweeping battle scenes, just another lost opportunity.

The Patriot falls short of portraying the reality and complexity of the American Revolution.

In October 1780, Congress sent Nathanael Greene to the Carolinas with a small Continental force. When Sumter withdrew for several months to nurse a wound, Francis Marion took his place. A much abler leader, Marion (who became known as the Swamp Fox) operated from remote bases in the swampy low country. Yet Greene's prospects seemed desperate. The ugliness of the partisan war—the mutilation of corpses, killing of prisoners, and wanton destruction of property—shocked him. The condition of his own soldiers appalled him. Yet Greene and Marion devised a masterful strategy of partisan warfare that finally wore out the British.

In the face of a greatly superior enemy, Greene ignored a standard maxim of war and split up his force of 1,800 Continentals. In smaller bands they would be easier to feed, but Greene's decision involved more than supplies. He sent 300 men east to bolster Marion and ordered Daniel Morgan and 300 riflemen west to threaten the British outpost of Ninety-Six. Tarleton urged Cornwallis to turn and crush the 1,000 men still with Greene, but Greene had no intention of engaging a superior force. Cornwallis, worried that after King's Mountain Morgan

might raise the entire backcountry against the British, divided his own army. He sent Tarleton with a mixed force of 1,100 British and loyalists after Morgan, who decided to stand with his back to a river at a place called Cowpens, where a loyalist kept cattle. Including militia, Morgan had 1,040 men.

Tarleton attacked on January 17, 1781. In another unorthodox move, Morgan sent his militia out front as skirmishers. He ordered them to fire two rounds and then redeploy in his rear as a reserve. Relieved of their fear of a bayonet charge, they obeyed. As they pulled back, the British rushed forward into the Con-

tinentals, who also retreated at first, then wheeled and discharged a lethal volley. After Morgan's cavalry charged into the British left flank, the militia returned to the fray. Although Tarleton escaped, Morgan annihilated his army. For the first time in the war, an American force had clearly outfought a British army without an advantage of numbers or terrain.

As Morgan rejoined Greene, Cornwallis staked everything on his ability to find Greene and crush him, precisely what he had failed to do to Washington after Trenton and Princeton four years earlier. But Greene outthought him. He placed flatboats in

Images of Men and Women in the Great Depression

Women played an important role in the New Deal. Eleanor Roosevelt set the tone through her visible involvement in numerous reform activities. She met with many different groups of Americans, including the miners depicted in the first photo, seeking to learn more about their condition and ways that the New Deal might assist them. But women also found their activism limited by a widespread hostility toward working women, who were thought to be taking scarce jobs away from men. In the popular movie, *Mr.*

Smith Goes to Washington (1939), Jefferson Smith (Jimmy Stewart) helps a hardboiled career secretary, Clarissa Saunders (Jean Arthur), to realize that work has damaged her sweet, womanly soul. By movie's end, Saunders is ready to leave her job and become Smith's wife and homemaker. Many other movies of the period also conveyed the sentiment that women belonged in the home.

Men, for their part, responded enthusiastically to the hypermasculinism that characterized much of the

decade's mass culture. Images of strong, muscled workers (such as in the portrait below of a working man in front of the White House) were popular with trade unionists who feared that the Depression would strip them of their manly roles as workers and breadwinners. Boys and male adolescents, meanwhile, found a new hero in Superman, the "man-of-steel" comic-book hero who debuted in 1938. Superman's

strength, unlike that of so many men in the 1930s, could not be taken away—except by Kryptonite and Lois Lane, that "dangerous" working woman.

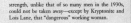

on "protective legislation"—laws that safeguarded female workers, whom they considered more fragile than men. Those who insisted that women needed special protections could not easily argue that women were the equal of men in all respects.

Even so, feminism was hemmed in on all sides by a male hostility that the depression had only intensified. Men had built their male identities on the value of hard work and the ability to provide eco-

nomic security for their families. For them, the loss of work unleashed feelings of inadequacy. Male vulnerability increased as unemployment rates of men—most of whom labored in blue-collar industries—tended to rise higher than those of women, many of whom worked in white-collar occupations less affected by job cutbacks. Many fathers and husbands resented wives and daughters who had taken over their breadwinning roles.

This male anxiety had political and social consequence. Several states passed laws outlawing the hiring of married women. New Deal relief agencies were reluctant to authorize aid for unemployed women. The labor movement made protection of the male wage earner one of its principal goals. The Social Security pension system left out waitresses, domestic servants, and other largely female occupations. Some commentators even proposed ludi-

crous gender remedies to the problem of unemployment. Norman Cousins of the *Saturday Evening Post*, for example, suggested that the depression could be ended simply by firing 10 million working women and giving their jobs to men. "Presto!" he declared. "No unemployment, no relief roles. No Depression."

Many artists introduced a strident masculinism into their painting and sculpture. Mighty *Superman*,

Each chapter includes an "American Album," a brief essay illustrated with historic photos or artwork that offers a visual excursion into fascinating moments from the American past. Often connected to the themes of liberty, equality, and power, these features explore intriguing subjects such as the environment, gender roles, religion, popular and material culture, war, and race. We hope that the American Albums will tempt you to leaf through the textbook, much as you would leaf through a family album, and that your interest in and understanding of American history will deepen and diversify as a result. A complete list of American Album features follows the Table of Contents.

not only as owner but also as paternal protector and lawgiver. Yet both slaveholders and slaves knew that slaves could not be treated like farm animals or little children. Wise slaveholders learned that the success of a plantation depended less on terror and draconian discipline (though whippings—and worse—were common) than on the accommodations by which slaves traded labor and obedience for some measure of privilege and autonomy within the bounds of slavery. After achieving privileges, the slaves called them their own: holidays, garden plots, friendships, and social gatherings both on and off the plantation; hunting and fishing rights; and so on. Together, these privileges provided some of the ground on which they made their own lives within slavery.

THE SLAVE FAMILY

The most precious privilege was the right to make and maintain families. As early as the Revolutionary War era, most Chesapeake slaves lived in units consisting of mother, father, and small children. On Charles Carrol's Maryland farms in 1773, for example, 325 of the 400 slaves lived in such families. At Thomas Jefferson's Monticello, most slave marriages were for life, and small children almost always lived with both parents. The most common exceptions to this practice were fathers who had married away from their own plantations and who visited "broad wives" and children during their off hours. In Louisiana between 1810 and 1864, half the slaves lived in families headed by both parents; another one-fourth lived in single-parent families. Owners encouraged stable marriages because they made farms more peaceful and productive and because they flattered the owners' own religious and paternalistic sensibilities. For their part, slaves demanded families as part of the price of their labor.

Yet slave families were highly vulnerable. Many slaveholders assumed that they had the right to coerce sex from female slaves; some kept slaves as concubines, and a few even moved them into the main house. They tended, however, to stay away from married women. While the slave community—in contrast to the whites—seldom punished sex before marriage, it took adultery seriously. Slaveholders knew that violations of married slave women could be enormously disruptive and strongly discouraged

them. A far more serious threat to slave marriages was the death, bankruptcy, or departure of the slaveholders. Between one-fifth and one-third of slave marriages were broken by such events.

Slaveholders who encouraged slave marriages—even perhaps solemnizing them with a religious ceremony—knew that marriage implied a form of self-ownership that conflicted with the slaves' status as property. Some conducted ceremonies in which couples "married" by jumping over a broomstick; others had the preacher omit the phrases "let no

"Dear Husband I write you a letter to let you know of my distress my master has sold Albert to a trader on Monday court day and myself and other child is for sale also and I want you to let [me] hear from you very soon before next cort if you can I don't know when I don't want you to wait till Christmas I want you to tell Dr. Hamilton your master if either will buy me then can attend to it know and then I can go afterwards

"I don't want a trader to get me they asked me if I had got any person to buy me and I told them no they told me to the court house too they never put me up A man buy the name of brady bought albert and is gone I don't know whare they say he lives in scottsville my things is in several places some is in stanton and if I would be sold I don't know what will become of them I don't expect to meet with the luck to get that way till I am quite heart sick nothing more I am and ever will be your kind wife Marie Perkins"

MARIE PERKINS
a slave mother writing to her husband, Richard Perkins, Charlottesville, Virginia, 1852

Through selected boxed quotations you can listen to voices of the past—from ordinary citizens to prominent figures. These quotations—such as the example from an enslaved woman to her husband—bring to life moments of triumph and tragedy from the surrounding text.

militia. The free states filled their quotas immediately. More than twice as many men volunteered as Lincoln had requested. Recognizing that the 90 days' service to which the militia were limited by law would be too short a time, Lincoln, on May 3, issued a call for three-year volunteers. Before the war was over, more than two million men would serve in the Union army and navy.

The eight slave states still in the Union rejected Lincoln's call for troops. Four of them—Virginia, Arkansas, Tennessee, and North Carolina—soon seceded and joined the Confederacy. Forced by the outbreak of actual war to choose between the Union and the Confederacy, most residents of those four states chose the Confederacy. As a former Unionist in North Carolina remarked, "The division must be made on the line of slavery. The South must go with the South. . . . Blood is thicker than Water."

Few found the choice harder to make than Robert E. Lee of Virginia. One of the most promising officers in the United States Army, Lee believed that southern states had no legal right to secede. General-in-Chief Winfield Scott wanted Lee to become field commander of the Union army. Instead, Lee sadly resigned from the army after the

LINK TO THE PAST

The Valley of the Shadow: Two Communities in the Civil War

http://valley.vcdh.virginia.edu

This site contains a wealth of data for two counties from the late 1850s through the end of the war: newspapers, tax lists, manuscript census returns, regimental records, official reports, soldiers' and civilians' letters and diaries, interactive maps, and more. The counties are Augusta County, Virginia, and Franklin County, Pennsylvania. Both are in the same valley (called the Shenandoah Valley in Virginia and Cumberland Valley in Pennsylvania), and their county seats, Staunton, Virginia, and Chambersburg, Pennsylvania, are less than 150 miles apart. Except for slavery, the counties had similar socioeconomic, cultural, ethnic, and political structures, yet their people fought on opposite sides in the war.

1. Analyze the principal newspapers in each county for a selected period (for example, 1860–61) to determine what issues were most important in shaping political allegiances.

2. Using the maps and regimental records, follow the troop movements of three Augusta County Confederate regiments and three Cumberland County Union regiments as they fought in the major campaigns and battles in the Eastern theater, sometimes against each other.

3. In July 1864 Confederate troops burned Chambersburg, and in October of the same year Union troops destroyed crops and other property in Augusta County. Using letters, diaries, newspapers, and other relevant sources, describe how the respective civilian populations reacted to these events.

4. Compare the home-front activities of women in support of the war effort in the two counties.

New "Link to the Past" Internet features in each chapter highlight Web sites related to interesting historical events and figures discussed in the text. Following a brief description of the site, the authors guide you, through a set of questions, toward interesting online resources that will enhance your understanding of that period in U.S. history. Whether assigned specifically by your instructor or left for you to explore on your own, these links provide valuable portals to the past.

We are pleased to present the third edition of *Liberty, Equality, Power*. Like the first two editions, this one captures the drama and excitement of America's past, from the pre-Columbian era through our own time. It integrates social and cultural history into a political story that is organized around the themes of liberty, equality, and power, and synthesizes the finest older historical scholarship with the best of the new to create a narrative that is balanced, lively, and accessible to a broad range of students.

THE *LIBERTY EQUALITY POWER* APPROACH

In this book we tell many small stories, and one large one: how America transformed itself, in a relatively brief era of world history, from a land inhabited by hunter-gatherer and agricultural Native American societies into the most powerful industrial nation on earth. This story has been told many times before, and those who have told it in the past have usually emphasized the political experiment in liberty and equality that took root here in the 18th century. We, too, stress the extraordinary and transformative impact that the ideals of liberty and equality exerted on American politics, society, and economics during the American Revolution and after. We show how the creation of a free economic environment—one in which entrepreneurial spirit, technological innovation, and industrial production has flourished—underpinned American industrial might. We have emphasized, too, the successful struggles for freedom that, over the course of the last 225 years, have brought—first to all white men, then to men of color, and finally to women—rights and opportunities that they had not previously known.

But we have also identified a third factor in this pantheon of American ideals—that of power. We examine power in many forms: the accumulation of vast economic fortunes that dominated the economy and politics; the dispossession of American Indians from land that they regarded as theirs; the enslavement of millions of Africans and their African American descendants for a period of almost 250

years; the relegation of women and of racial, ethnic, and religious minorities to subordinate places in American society; and the extension of American control over foreign peoples, such as Latin Americans and Filipinos, who would have preferred to have been free and self-governing. We do not mean to suggest that American power has always been turned to these negative purposes. Subordinate groups have themselves marshaled power to combat oppression, as in the abolitionist and civil rights crusades, the campaign for woman suffrage, and the labor movement. The state has used its power to moderate poverty and to manage the economy in the interests of general prosperity. And it has used its military power to defeat Nazi Germany, World War II Japan, the cold war Soviet Union, and other enemies of freedom.

The invocation of power as a variable in American history forces us to widen the lens through which we look at the past and to complicate the stories we tell. Ours has been a history of freedom and domination; of progress toward realizing a broadly democratic polity and of delays and reverses; of abundance and poverty; of wars for freedom and justice and for control of foreign markets. In complicating our master narrative in this way, we think we have rendered American history more exciting and intriguing. Progress has not been automatic, but the product of ongoing struggles.

In this book we have also tried to capture the diversity of the American past, both in terms of outcomes and in terms of the variety of groups who have participated in America's making. American Indians, in this book, are not presented simply as the victims of European aggression but as a people remarkably diverse in their own ranks, with a variety of systems of social organization and cultural expression. We give equal treatment to the industrial titans of American history—the likes of Andrew Carnegie and John D. Rockefeller—and to those, such as small farmers and poor workers, who resisted the corporate reorganization of economic life. We celebrate the great moments of 1863, when African Americans were freed from slavery, and of 1868, when they were made full citizens of the United States. But we also note how a majority of African Americans had to wait another 100 years, until the civil rights movement of the 1960s, to gain full access to American freedoms. We tell similarly complex stories about women, Latinos, and other groups of ethnic Americans.

Political issues, of course, are only part of America's story. Americans have always loved their leisure and have created the world's most vibrant popular culture. They have embraced technological innovations, especially those promising to make their lives easier and more fun. We have, therefore, devoted considerable space to a discussion of American popular culture, from the founding of the first newspapers in the 18th century and the rise of movies, jazz, and the comics in the early 20th century, to the cable television and Internet revolutions in recent years. We have pondered, too, how American industry has periodically altered home and personal life by making new products—such as clothing, cars, refrigerators, and computers—available to consumers. In such ways we hope to give our readers a rich portrait of how Americans lived at various points in our history. See A Student's Guide to Learning from This Textbook for descriptions of study aids to help you get the most out of your reading.

NEW TO THE THIRD EDITION

The second edition won praise for its successful integration of political, cultural, and social history, its thematic unity, its narrative clarity and eloquence, its extraordinary coverage of pre-Columbian America, its attention to war and conquest, its extended treatment of the Civil War, its history of economic growth and change, and its excellent map and illustration programs. It also received high marks for its 31 richly illustrated American Albums, brief features on fascinating and important topics of the American past, and for the new introductions and conclusions that graced the beginning and end of each chapter. And, judging by their comments, users were pleased to see that we maintained and even improved our high quality map and illustration programs. We have preserved and enhanced all the strengths of the second edition in the third.

In preparing for this revision, we solicited feedback from professors and scholars throughout the country, many of whom have used the second edi-

tion of *Liberty, Equality, Power* in their classrooms. Their comments proved most helpful, and many of their suggestions have been incorporated into the third edition. For example, we have introduced, for the first time, chapter outlines and focus questions at the opening of each chapter to guide students through the material and to help them review for tests. Also in response to reviewer comments, we have moved the Chronology boxes from the end to the beginning of each chapter so that students can note, at a glance, the important events and individuals they will be learning about in each week's assignment. We hope that students and their teachers find these study aids useful.

In addition to these pedagogical changes, we scrutinized each page of the textbook, making sure our prose was clear, the historical issues well presented, and the scholarship up to date. This review, guided by the scholarly feedback we received, caused us to make numerous revisions and additions. A list of notable substantive changes appears below. Finally, we have brought this textbook to the present, so that students can learn about the last years of the Clinton presidency and about the first president of the new century, George W. Bush, and the forces that propelled him to victory in 2000.

New to this edition as well are two features that meet the high standard of historical interest and pedagogical utility set by our celebrated American Album series. The first, History Through Film, discusses 31 films, mostly produced in Hollywood, that treat important aspects of the American past. Some of these films, such as *Birth of a Nation*, *Wilson*, and *Malcolm X*, are self-consciously historical in that they attempt to present interpretations of actual historical events and personalities. Others, such as *Tarzan*, *Invasion of the Body Snatchers*, and *Star Wars*, were never intended to offer accounts of the American past but are nevertheless revealing historical documents about the cultural and political attitudes of the period in which they were made. We offer summaries of the films, note the interesting historical questions that they intentionally or unintentionally raise (and that students can fruitfully discuss), and offer a commentary on the accuracy or inaccuracy of historical figures and events as seen through the lens of the camera and the vision of the director.

We believe that students will respond well to this feature, especially given the important role that film, video, and digitized images already play in their lives. We hope that instructors will find this feature a useful way to integrate film into their courses and to encourage in hard-to-reach students a new sense of excitement about studying the American past. In choosing the 31 films, we have been careful to select only those available on video, so as to make viewing them feasible for anyone with access to a VCR and monitor.

The second new feature, Link to the Past, places a customized Web-based lesson plan in each textbook chapter. It uses clear instructions and the best technology currently available to encourage students to visit Web sites where they can examine issues in-depth that are raised in the textbook. In each chapter, a Link to the Past feature introduces students to a Web site carefully chosen by the authors to illuminate a particular theme discussed in the text. The feature lists the URL where that Web site can be found, offers instructions on how to find specific historical documents on that Web site, and asks a series of questions that students can keep in mind while examining the documents themselves. Instructors can make this lesson a formal part of their teaching plans for the week or they can simply encourage students to explore the featured Web sites on their own. In either case, we believe that this feature does a great deal to integrate Web-based learning directly into a survey course.

SPECIFIC REVISIONS TO CONTENT AND COVERAGE

Chapter 1 New explanations of (1) how lack of domestic animals left the Indians vulnerable to Eurasian diseases and (2) why Eurasia expanded at the expense of sub-Sahara Africa and the Americas.

Chapter 2 New material on religious struggles within New Netherland, the founding of Roanoke and Jamestown, the abandoned Sagadahoc colony (1607–1608), and the founding of Pennsylvania. New American Album feature entitled, "The Prince, the Quaker, and the Middle Colonies."

Chapter 3 More material on the Glorious Revolution in New England and on the Salem witch trials.

Chapter 4 New material on the cruelty and arbitrary nature of the punishments inflicted on slaves in South Carolina and Virginia, on 18th-century land banks, and on Commodore Anson's circumnavigation of the globe for Britain, 1740–44.

Chapter 5 Expanded discussion of Phillis Wheatley's poems and of the Declaration of Independence.

Chapter 6 New material on the impact of smallpox in several military campaigns during the Revolution, the constitutional powers of New York governors after 1777, the Iroquois Confederation during and after the war, and the tragic role of South Carolina slaves in developing cotton as a new staple crop.

Chapter 8 New material on the trial of Aaron Burr and Justice Marshall's strict constructionism in limiting the definition of treason.

Chapter 10 Revised section on *Uncle Tom's Cabin*.

Chapter 11 Additional material on Northern blacks' involvement in the abolitionist movement and the fight against discrimination (including David Walker, Harriet Tubman, Sojourner Truth, and Frederick Douglass) and the connection between the abolitionist movement and the Seneca Falls Convention.

Chapter 17 Expanded section on the woman suffrage movement and the split over the 15th Amendment.

Chapter 18 New material on Helen Hunt Jackson and American Indian reform.

Chapter 21 New material on gender, race, and progressive reform, especially in regard to the Mann Act, prostitution, and Black Clubwomen.

Chapter 24 New material on women and work and on "The Age of Celebrity Culture" (Babe Ruth, Jack Dempsey, and Charles Lindbergh).

Chapter 25 Revised section on the limitations of New Deal Reform.

Chapter 26 Revisions and updates, including a new paragraph on codebreaking.

Chapter 27 Sharpened treatment of the cold war at home and abroad in light of newly declassified documents and recent scholarship.

Chapter 30 Tightened and updated section on media and on racial and ethnic movements of the late 20th century.

Chapter 31 Includes full history of the Clinton administration and a new section on the election of 2000 ("The Long Election"). Updated and thoroughly revised coverage of recent changes in demographic and economic trends includes careful attention to new immigration and technological change. New American Album feature, "Cityscapes." New set of five charts showing the dramatic economic expansion of the late 20th century.

SUPPLEMENTS FOR THE INSTRUCTOR

Instructor's Resource Manual The Instructor's Resource Manual, revised by Janet Brantley of Texarkana College, is a comprehensive teaching tool that includes chapter summaries; Thematic Braid discussions of the interconnected themes of liberty, equality, power; identification items; chronologies; geography objectives; topics for classroom and group activities; detailed lecture outlines; discussion questions; suggested essay and paper topics; new suggested Web activities for the classroom; an audiovisual bibliography, and the instructor's guide to the Core Concepts video package. The Instructor's Resource Manual is free to instructors with adoption.

Test Bank The Test Bank, prepared by B. Jane England of North Central Texas College, includes more than 2,650 test items. The printed Test Bank includes new map questions that can be photocopied for use as quizzes or as part of an exam (the map questions are also available as part of the Overhead Transparency set). It contains a wide variety of question styles with graded levels of difficulty. Some questions emphasize critical thinking skills while others test general recall. The Test Bank offers chapter learning objectives, multiple-choice, true/false, fill-in, identification, short and long essay questions, and map questions. The Test Bank is available free to instructors with adoption.

Full Color Overhead Transparency Package This package contains nearly 200 color transparencies that include many of the text's excellent maps, charts, graphs, new mapping questions for use in quizzing and testing, and political cartoons from the text, as well as other sources. The transparencies are keyed to chapters of the text for ease in lecture planning.

Online Resources Visit the *Liberty*, *Equality*, *Power* Web site to access a wealth of online resources for instructors and students. Resources include a syllabus generator, downloadable overhead transparencies and Instructor's Manual, and an exciting new set of group projects that bring history to life in the classroom. Current projects available:

Recreating the '60s: Teaching History Through Teach-Ins
This unique project examines a turbulent decade of social and political change in American history. Students stage a '60s-style teach-in by recreating the arguments, visions, and experiences of key groups that were actively involved in the causes. This model provides complete instructions for professors and a free, convenient download for students.

Commemorating the Boston Massacre: Teaching History Through Public Memory
Students examine the Boston Massacre from the perspectives of six different historical groups involved in the event. In the context of a modern "town hall" meeting, students present their ideas for a new public memorial, and they debate

which proposed monument represents the best interpretation of the pivotal event of March 5, 1770. Complete instructions are provided.

Reconstruction and the Meaning of Freedom: Teaching History Through Public Debate
In the context of a public debate, four major groups active during the Reconstruction era examine what "freedom" should mean for the newly freed after the Civil War. Complete instructions are provided for group and individual projects.

Find the new group projects and many other resources at *Liberty, Equality, Power* Web site: www.harcourtcollege.com/history/murrin

U.S. History PowerPoint Slide Archive CD-ROM
The PowerPoint Lecture Presentations, developed by Raymond M. Hyser and J. Christopher Arndt of James Madison University, feature 31 text-based outlines plus a collection of more than 600 images—maps, graphs, and illustrations. Available free to instructors with adoption.

Computerized Test Bank The EXAMaster system simplifies test generation and allows instructors the flexibility to add or edit questions, select test items by learning objectives or level of difficulty, and incorporate maps, graphs, and charts. Available in Macintosh® and Windows™ formats.

The American History CD-ROM The American History CD-ROM is an interactive learning tool providing a vast library of pictures, film clips, sound recordings, and maps. It is indexed and organized in a unique, flexible format that makes it easy to explore U.S. history from ancient times through the 1990s. Features include: *Overviews*, narrated by Charles Kuralt; thousands of captioned illustrations; 68 motion pictures; dozens of brief sound clips; self-assessment quizzes; and *The Histriopix Game*, designed to test students' recall of key concepts and information conveyed through the images. Useful for independent study or creation of lessons, lesson plans, or presentations. Adoption requirements apply.

Second World War Photo CD-ROM The Second World War CD-ROM is a three-disc set that features selections from the National Archives. It in-

cludes more than 900 black and white images taken during the war that are accompanied by historically accurate captions. Adoption requirements apply. The set is also available for purchase.

Core Concept Lecture Launcher Videos The Core Concept video package was created exclusively for *Liberty, Equality, Power* by Films for the Humanities. Each video contains eight segments that include introductions by the respective author, concept clues, brief video segments, and concluding questions that take the student from image to text. Video segments are arranged chronologically and relate to topics of importance in the text. The video package is available free to instructors and may be purchased by students for independent study.

U.S. History Videos/Films for the Humanities Contact your local sales representative for a complete listing of the many videos available from the Films for the Humanities American History catalog. Adoption requirements apply.

U.S. History Videos/Arts and Entertainment Many outstanding U.S. history selections are available from the Arts and Entertainment video library. Choose from *American Revolution, Civil War Journal, The Real West, Mike Wallace's The Twentieth Century*, and selections from A&E's extensive *Biography* collection. Adoption requirements apply.

SUPPLEMENTS FOR THE STUDENT

United States History Atlas An invaluable collection of more than 50 clear and colorful historical maps covering all major periods in American history. Available to kit with the textbook. Please contact your local sales representative for information.

Study Guide The Study Guide is a thorough student resource prepared by Mary Jane McDaniel of the University of North Alabama. It provides both review and critical thinking opportunities for students. New "What If" questions challenge students to imagine themselves back in a particular moment in time and to think through the issues from the perspective of the historical figure(s) involved. Completion exercises, multiple-choice, matching, essay, and analysis questions allow students to test their comprehension of the material. Other features include an in-depth chronological overview, a glossary of important terms, and a crossword puzzle.

U.S. History Documents Package The Documents Package, edited by Mark W. Beasley of Hardin-Simmons University, has been expanded to include more than 250 primary source documents interspersed with political cartoons and advertisements. Chapter openers and notes for each selection introduce the documents, provide essential background, and tie in the themes of liberty, equality, and power. Chapter discussion questions ask students to think critically about the ways that documents relate to each other and the text. The two-volume package is available to kit with the textbook or for individual purchase by students.

Guide to America's Historical Geography This mapping workbook, revised by Timothy J. McMannon of Highline Community College, provides students with a variety of challenging and innovative geography exercises. In addition to labeling and locating exercises, the guide includes fill-in and essay questions that ask students to relate historical events to their geographic contexts. The workbook is available to kit with the textbook or for individual purchase by students.

Online Resources Visit the *Liberty, Equality, Power* Web site at www.harcourtcollege.com/history/murrin to access a wealth of online student resources and study aids, including annotated primary sources, chapter summaries, interactive self-assessment quizzes, Web activities, and additional history-related links.

ACKNOWLEDGMENTS

In the 15-year life of this textbook, the authors have been fortunate to work with an unusually stable, expert, and committed staff at Harcourt College Publishers. Drake Bush, Sue Lister, Lynne Bush, Everett Sims, Lili Weiner, Ruth Steinberg, and Bernard Sinsheimer made invaluable contributions to the first edition, and the book still owes a large debt to their hard work and influence. A new team, led by Executive Editor David Tatom, took up where the old one left off seven years ago. A model of professionalism and a wise counselor, David has repeatedly impressed us with his sage advice and his deep commitment to this book. His willingness to bring the author team together for brainstorming sessions and convivial dinners has done wonders for our esprit and has ensured a constant flow of smart suggestions for textbook revision and improvement. We also have been blessed these last two editions with an extraordinary developmental editor, Margaret McAndrew Beasley, whose standards of organization, diligence, and patience are incomparable. Against great odds, she has kept us on schedule and in good cheer. Together, David and Margaret have helped us to achieve many of the original ambitions we had for this book and to develop new goals. Project Editor Beth Alvarez expertly managed the manuscript through production while Sue Hart, senior art director, made lovely adjustments to the book's visual appearance. Diane Gray, our production manager, brought the same high level of skill and dedication to this edition as she did to the second and somehow kept this project on track even as we repeatedly missed deadlines. Steve Drummond, executive marketing strategist, has worked hard and imaginatively to promote this book and has been a vital source of good advice on how to structure our revisions so as to meet the needs of the book's users. We were delighted to work a third time with Lili Weiner, our imaginative freelance photo editor, and appreciate her undiminished willingness to track down photos and illustrations that matched our (not always reasonable) specifications. To the many editorial and production assistants with whom we did not work directly but who contributed significantly to this textbook, we express our hearty thanks. A special thanks, too, to the numerous Harcourt sales representatives who have done such a good job presenting our book to potential users and who have provided us with a steady stream of valuable feedback from the field.

We have also benefited greatly from the many historians—some of whom have used the second edition of *Liberty, Equality, Power* in their classrooms—who have reviewed the second edition and provided suggestions for this revision. We would like to thank each of them by name:

William Allison, Weber State University
Angie Anderson, Southeastern Louisiana University
Paul R. Beezley, Texas Tech University

David Bernstein, California State University at
  Long Beach
Michael R. Bradley, Motlow College
Betty Brandon, University of South Alabama
Daniel Patrick Brown, Moorpark College
Ronald G. Brown, College of Southern Maryland
Phil Crow, North Harris College
Lorenzo M. Crowell, Mississippi State University
Thomas M. Deaton, Dalton State College
Norman C. Delaney, Del Mar College
Ted Delaney, Washington and Lee University
Andrew J. DeRoche, Front Range Community
  College
Bruce Dierenfield, Canisius College
Maura Doherty, Illinois State University
R. Blake Dunnavent, Lubbock Christian
  University
Eileen Eagan, University of Southern Maine
Derek Elliott, Tennessee State University
B. Jane England, North Central Texas College
Van Forsyth, Clark College
Michael P. Gabriel, Kutztown University of
  Pennsylvania
Gary Gallagher, Pennsylvania State University
Gerald Ghelfi, Santa Ana College
David E. Hamilton, University of Kentucky
Michael J. Haridopolos, Brevard Community
  College
Mark Harvey, North Dakota State University
Samuel C. Hyde, Jr., Southeastern Louisiana
  University
Michael Kazin, American University
Michael King, Moraine Valley Community
  College
Frank Lambert, Purdue University
Jan Leone, Middle Tennessee State University
Craig Livingston, Montgomery College
Robert F. Marcom, San Antonio College
Suzanne Marshall, Jacksonville State University
Jimmie McGee, South Plains College
Jerry Mills, Midland College
Charlene Mires, Villanova University
Rick Moniz, Chabot College
Michael R. Nichols, Tarrant County College,
  Northwest
Linda Noel, University of Maryland
Richard B. Partain, Bakersfield College
William Pencak, Penn State University,
  University Park Campus

David Poteet, New River Community College
Roy Scott, Mississippi State University
Reynolds J. Scott-Childress, University of
  Maryland
Siegfried H. Sutterlin, Indian Hills Community
  College
Xiansheng Tian, Metro State College of Denver
Vernon Volpe, University of Nebraska
Harry L. Watson, The University of North
  Carolina at Chapel Hill
Laura Matysek Wood, Tarrant County College,
  Northwest

In addition, each of us would like to offer particular thanks to those historians, friends, and family members who helped to bring this project to a successful conclusion.

John M. Murrin Mary R. Murrin has read each chapter, offered numerous suggestions, and provided the kind of moral and personal support without which this project would never have been completed. James Axtell and Gregory Evans Dowd saved me from many mistakes about Indians. John E. Selby and the late Eugene R. Sheridan were particularly helpful on what are now chapters 5 and 6. At an early phase, William J. Jackson and Lorraine E. Williams offered some very useful suggestions. Fred Anderson and Virginia DeJohns Anderson offered many acute suggestions for improvement. I am deeply grateful for their advice. Several colleagues and graduate students also have contributed in various ways, especially Stephen Aron, Ignacio Gallup-Diaz, Evan P. Haefeli, Geoffrey Plank, Nathaniel J. Sheidley, Jeremy Stern, and Beth Lewis Pardse.

Paul E. Johnson My greatest debt is to the community of scholars who write about the United States between the Revolution and the Civil War. Closer to home, I owe thanks to the other writers of this book—particularly to John Murrin. The Tanner Humanities Center and the Department of History at the University of Utah provided time to work, while my wife, Kasey Grier, and a stray dog we named Lucy provided the right kinds of interruptions.

James M. McPherson My family provided an environment of affection and stability that contributed immeasurably to the writing of my chapters, while undergraduate students at Princeton University who have taken my courses over the years provided feedback, questions, and insights that helped me to understand what students know and don't know, and what they need to know.

Gary Gerstle I would like to thank a number of people who provided me with invaluable assistance. My work benefited enormously from the input of Roy Rosenzweig and Tom Knock, who gave each of my chapters an exceptionally thorough, thoughtful, and insightful critique. Kathleen Trainor was a gifted research assistant: She researched subjects I knew too little about, contributed to the design of charts and maps, checked facts, and solved countless thorny problems. To all these tasks she brought imagination, efficiency, and good cheer. Jerald Podair helped me to compile chapter bibliographies, offered me excellent ideas for maps and tables, and, on numerous occasions (and at all hours of the day and night), allowed me to draw on his encyclopedic knowledge of American history. Christopher Gildemeister dropped his own work at short notice to help me out with a difficult map problem. Elliott Shore graciously shared his time and expert librarian skills to help me locate obscure information for maps and illustrations. Our trip with Maria Sturm to locate a little-known Ben Shahn mural was a true

adventure. Finally, a special thanks to Kelly Ryan and Daniel Levi for helping me to assemble the Link to the Past features for this edition.

Emily and Norman Rosenberg We would like to thank our children—Sarah, Molly, Ruth, and Joe, who provided expert assistance on our charts. Students at Macalester College also deserve thanks, especially Sonya Michlin, Lorenzo Nencioli, Katie Kelley, Justin Brandt, Jessica Ford, and Mariah Howe. Paul Solon, a colleague at Macalester, provided his expertise in commenting on the maps. We also want to acknowledge all of the people who offered their responses to the first edition, including the historians who adopted the book and the students, especially those at San Diego State University, who read and evaluated it. Gary Gerstle, our collaborator, the late Richard Steele, a colleague at San Diego State, and Bruce Dierenfield provided wonderfully critical readings, and this edition is much better for their assistance.

John M. Murrin
Paul E. Johnson
James M. McPherson
Gary Gerstle
Emily S. Rosenberg
Norman L. Rosenberg

CONTENTS IN BRIEF

CONTENTS IN DETAIL

MAPS

AMERICAN ALBUMS

HISTORY THROUGH FILM

LINKS TO THE PAST

To the Student: Why Study History?

Why take a course in American history? This is a question that many college and university students ask. In many respects, students today are like the generations of Americans who have gone before them: optimistic and forward looking, far more eager to imagine where we as a nation might be going than to reflect on where we have been. If anything, this tendency has become more pronounced in recent years, as the Internet revolution has accelerated the pace and excitement of change and made even the recent past seem at best quaint, at worst uninteresting and irrelevant.

But it is precisely in these moments of great change that a sense of the past can be indispensable in terms of guiding our actions in the present and future. We can find, in other periods of American history, moments, like our own, of dizzying technological change and economic growth, rapid alterations in the concentration of wealth and power, and basic changes in patterns of work, residence, and play. How did Americans at those times create, embrace, and resist these changes? In earlier periods of American history, the United States was home, as it is today, to a remarkably diverse array of ethnic and racial groups. How did earlier generations of Americans respond to the cultural conflicts and misunderstandings that often arise from conditions of diversity? How did immigrants perceive their new land? How and when did they integrate themselves into American society? To study how ordinary Americans of the past struggled with these issues is to gain perspective on the opportunities and problems that we face today.

History also provides an important guide to affairs of state. What should the role of America be in world affairs? Should we participate in international bodies such as the United Nations or insist on our ability to act autonomously and without the consent of other nations? What is the proper role of government in economic and social life? Should the government regulate the economy? To what extent should the government enforce morality regarding religion, sexual practices, drinking and drugs, movies, TV, and other forms of mass culture? And what are our responsibilities as citizens to each other and to the nation? Americans of past generations have debated these issues with verve and conviction. Learning about these debates and how they were resolved will enrich our understanding of the policy possibilities for today and tomorrow.

History, finally, is about stories—stories that we all tell about ourselves, our families, our communities, our ethnicity, race, region, and religion, and our nation. They are stories of triumph and tragedy, of engagement and flight, and of high ideals and high comedy. When telling these stories, "American history" is often the furthest thing from our minds. But, often, an implicit sense of history informs what we say about grandparents who immigrated many years ago, the suburb in which we live, the church, synagogue, or mosque that we attend, or the ethnic or racial group to which we belong. But how well do we really understand these individuals, institutions, and groups? Do we tell the right stories about them, ones that capture the complexities of their past? Or have we wittingly or unwittingly simplified, altered, or flattened them? A study of American history first helps us to ask these questions and then to answer them. In the process, we can engage in a fascinating journey of intellectual and personal discovery and situate ourselves more firmly than we had ever thought possible in relation to those who came before us. We can gain firmer self-knowledge and a greater appreciation for the richness of our nation and, indeed, of all humanity.

LIBERTY
EQUALITY
POWER

CHAPTER 1

WHEN OLD WORLDS COLLIDE: CONTACT, CONQUEST, CATASTROPHE

HISTORY ON CANVAS

Cortés Scuttles Ship (left), by O. Graeff, circa 1805. Nezahualcoyotzin (right), ruler of Texcoco from approximately 1431 to 1472, painted in battle array by a late 16th- or early 17th-century Mexican Indian who had mastered European artistic techniques.

When Christopher Columbus crossed the Atlantic, he did not know where he was going, and until his death he never figured out where he had been. Yet he changed history forever. In the 40 years after 1492, European navigators mastered the oceans of the world, joining together societies that had lived in isolation for thousands of years. European invaders conquered the Americas, not just with sails, gunpowder, and steel, but also with their plants and livestock and, most of all, their diseases. They brought staple crops and slavery with them as well. By 1600 they had created the first global economy in the history of mankind and had inflicted upon the native peoples of the Americas—unintentionally, for the most part—the greatest known catastrophe that human societies have ever experienced.

In the 15th century, when all of this started, the Americas were in some ways a more ancient world than Western Europe. For example, the Portuguese, Spanish, French, and English languages were only beginning to assume their modern forms during the century or two before and after Columbus's voyage. Centuries earlier, when Rome was falling into ruins and Paris and London were little more than hamlets, huge cities were thriving in the Andes and Mesoamerica (the area embracing Central America and southern and central Mexico). Which world was old and which was new is a matter of perspective. Each already had its own distinctive past.

This chapter will focus on the following major questions:

- What enabled relatively backward European societies to establish dominance over the oceans of the world?
- Why were the native peoples of the Americas extremely vulnerable to European diseases, instead of the other way around?
- Why did Western Europe, a free-labor society, generate systems of unfree labor overseas?
- What was the Columbian Exchange and how important has it been?

PEOPLES IN MOTION

Like all other countries of North and South America, the United States is a nation of immigrants. Even the native peoples were once new settlers in a strange land.

Long before Europeans discovered and explored the wide world around them, many different peoples

C H R O N O L O G Y

50,000–40,000 B.C. Possible early migration across Beringia to America

23,000–10,000 B.C. Migration across Beringia to America

14,000 B.C. Meadowcroft (Pennsylvania) site inhabited

9000 B.C. Shenandoah Valley occupied

9000–7000 B.C. Most large American mammals become extinct

5000–700 B.C. Cultures of the Red Paint People and the Louisiana mound builders thrive

1600 B.C. Polynesian migrations begin (reaching Hawaii by A.D. 100)

500 B.C.–A.D. 400 Adena-Hopewell mound builders emerge in Ohio River valley

874 Norsemen reach Iceland

900–1250 Toltecs dominate the Valley of Mexico • Cahokia becomes largest Mississippian mound builders' city • Anasazi culture thrives in American Southwest

982 Norse settle Greenland

1001–14 Norse found Vinland on Newfoundland

1400s Incas begin to dominate the Andes; Aztecs begin to dominate Mesoamerica (1400–50) • Cheng Ho makes voyages of exploration for China (1405–34) • Portuguese begin to master the Atlantic coast of Africa (1434) • First Portuguese slave factory established on African coast (1448) • Dias reaches Cape of Good Hope (1487) • Columbus reaches the Caribbean (1492) • Treaty of Tordesillas divides non-Christian world between Portugal and Spain (1494) • da Gama rounds Cape of Good Hope and reaches India (1497–99)

1500s Portuguese discover Brazil (1500) • Balboa crosses Isthmus of Panama to the Pacific (1513) • Magellan's fleet circumnavigates the globe; Cortés conquers the Aztec empire (1519–22) • de Vaca makes overland journey from Florida to Mexico (1528–36) • Pizarro conquers the Inca empire (1531–32) • de Soto's expedition explores the American Southeast (1539–43) • Coronado's expedition explores the American Southwest (1540–42) • Jesuit mission established at Chesapeake Bay (1570–71) • Philip II issues Royal Order for New Discoveries (1573) • Philip II unites Spanish and Portuguese empires (1580)

had migrated thousands of miles over thousands of years across oceans and continents. Before Columbus sailed west from Spain in 1492, five distinct waves of immigrants had already swept over the Americas. Three came from Asia. The fourth, from the Pacific Islands, or Oceania, may have just brushed America. The last, from northern Europe, decided not to stay.

FROM BERINGIA TO THE AMERICAS

Before the most recent Ice Age ended about 12,000 years ago, glaciers covered huge portions of the Americas, Europe, and Asia. The ice captured so much of the world's water that sea level fell drastically. Twice it dropped more than 200 feet, enough to create a land bridge 600 miles wide across the Bering Strait between Siberia and Alaska. For several thousand years about 50,000 B.C., and again for more than 10,000 years after 23,000 B.C., this exposed area—geographers call it Beringia—was dry land on which plants, animals, and humans could live. People drifted in small bands from Asia to North America. No doubt many generations lived on Beringia itself, although the harsh environment of this land on the edge of the Arctic Circle would have required unusual skills just to survive. These first immigrants to the Americas hunted animals for meat and furs and probably built small fishing vessels that could weather the Arctic storms. Faced with impassable glaciers to the north and east, they made snug homes to keep themselves warm through the fierce winters. Their numbers were, in all likelihood, quite small.

Exactly when they arrived remains controversial. Many archaeologists believe that humans crossed Beringia and began spreading through the Americas more than 40,000 years ago. Canadians digging at the Old Crow site in the Yukon claim they have found evidence of human habitation that may be 50,000 years old. A French team working in northeastern Brazil, thousands of miles from Beringia, is examining a site that may be 48,000 years old. That site may provide the strongest evidence yet found for very early settlement of the Americas. Other experts remain skeptical, however. Until the Brazilian find, which is still being evaluated, all very old sites have had something wrong with them, archaeologically speaking. For example, natural forces might have disturbed the setting or carried the artifacts away

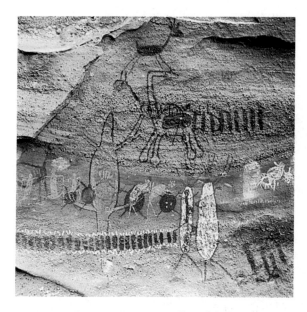

AN INDIAN WALL PAINTING Found in northeastern Brazil, this painting may be 32,000 years old. If so, it is one of the oldest in the world.

from their original environment. A bone that looks to one scholar as though it had been shaped into a tool strikes another as merely the product of some natural accident, perhaps of an animal breaking its leg. Finally, no evidence has yet been found that humans were living in eastern Siberia—where the settlers would have originated—as far back as 30,000 years ago. Even if some people did make it to the Americas at that time, they multiplied quite slowly.

The record becomes clearer toward the end of the last Ice Age, about 12,000 years ago. By then, humans definitely were living in eastern Siberia, western Alaska, and Beringia. (Because Beringia is once again under water, it cannot easily be studied, although fossils of mammoths have been found on the ocean floor.) As the glaciers receded for the last time, these people spread throughout the Americas. By 8000 B.C. they had reached all the way to Tierra del Fuego off the southern tip of South America. Near the eastern coast of North America, the Meadowcroft site in Pennsylvania may be 16,000 years old, and the Thunderbird dig in Virginia's Shenandoah Valley shows signs of continuous human occupation from before 9000 B.C. until the arrival of Europeans.

These Asians probably came in three waves. Those in the first wave, which began more than 14,000 years ago, spread over most of the two continents and spoke "Amerind," the forerunner of the vast majority of American Indian languages on both continents. The Algonquian, Iroquoian, Muskogean, Siouan, Nahuatl (Aztec), Mayan, and all South American tongues derive from this source. Those in the middle wave, which came a few thousand years later, spoke what linguists call "Na-Déné," which eventually gave rise to the various Athapaskan languages of the Canadian Northwest as well as the Apache, Navajo, and related tongues in the American Southwest. The last to arrive, the ancestors of the Inuits (called Eskimos by other Indians), crossed after 7000 B.C., when Beringia was again under water. About 4,000 years ago, these people began to migrate from the Aleutian Islands and Alaska to roughly their present sites in the Americas. Unlike their predecessors, they found the Arctic environment to their liking and migrated across the northern rim of North America and then across the North Atlantic to Greenland, where they encountered the first Europeans migrating westward—the Norsemen. Somehow, the Inuits maintained at least limited contact with one another across 6,000 miles of bleak Arctic tundra. The Thule, or final pre-Columbian phase of Inuit culture, which lasted from A.D. 1000 to 1700, sustained similar folkways from Siberia to Greenland.

THE GREAT EXTINCTION AND THE RISE OF AGRICULTURE

As the glaciers receded and the climate warmed, the people who had wandered south and east found an attractive environment teeming with game. Imperial mammoths, huge mastodons, woolly rhinoceroses, a species of enormous bison, and giant ground sloths roamed the plains and forests, along with camels and herds of small horses. These animals had thrived in a frigid climate, but they had trouble adjusting to hot weather. They also had no instinctive fear of the two-legged intruders, who became ever more skillful at hunting them. A superior spear point, the Clovis tip, appeared in the area of present-day New Mexico and Texas some time before 9000 B.C., and within a thousand years its use had spread throughout North and South America. As it spread, the big game died off along with horses, which were small and valued only as food. Overhunting cannot explain the entire extinction, but it was a

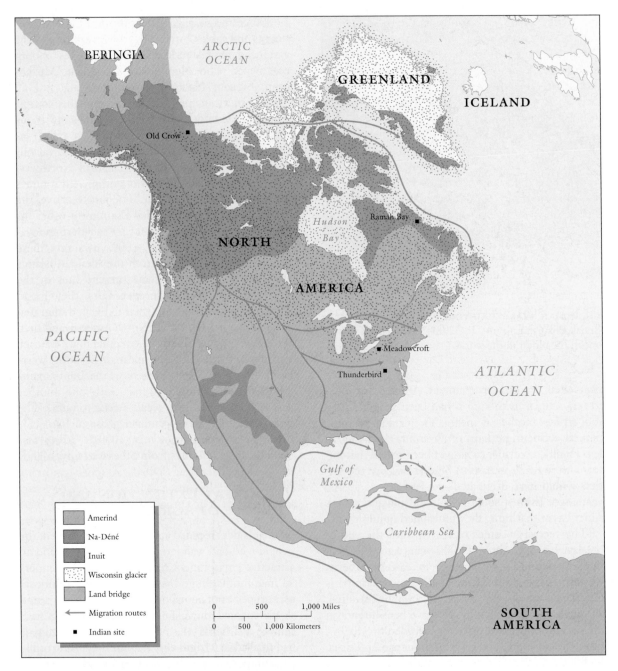

INDIAN SETTLEMENT OF AMERICA

major factor, along with climatic change. Mammoths, for example, survived until 2000 B.C. on uninhabited Wrangell Island near Alaska. Most large animals of the Americas disappeared about 9,000 years ago.

Their passing left the hemisphere with a severely depleted number of animal species. Nothing as big as the elephant survived. The largest beasts left were bears, buffalo, and moose; the biggest cat was the jaguar. The human population had multiplied and spread with ease so long as the giant species lasted. Their extinction probably led to a sharp decline in population as people scrambled for new sources of food. Some Indians raised guinea pigs, turkeys, or ducks, but apart from dogs on both continents, they domesticated no large animals except in South America, where they used llamas to haul light loads in mountainous terrain and raised alpacas for their wool. In Eurasia, with its numerous domesticated animals, the killer diseases such as smallpox and bubonic plague took hold first among domestic animals and then spread among humans. Disease by disease, the survivors developed immunities over a long period of time. No comparable process occurred in the Americas, where few animals were domesticated.

One North American culture, adapting to the new demands of a world with few large animals, displayed an energy that archaeologists are only now beginning to recognize. About 5000 B.C., along the northeast coast, a gifted maritime people emerged who ventured onto the Atlantic to catch swordfish and, probably, whales. They carried on a vigorous trade from Labrador to Maine and perhaps as far south as New Jersey, spanning a coastline of more than 1,500 miles. They are sometimes called the Red Paint People (a more technical term is Maritime Archaic) because of their use of red ocher in funeral ceremonies. Their burial mounds are the oldest yet found in America. They lived in multiroom houses up to 100 yards long. Most remarkable of all, the motifs on their religious monuments—mounds and stone markers—resemble others found in Brittany and Norway, but the American monuments are several hundred years older than the most ancient ones yet found in Europe. It is just possible that these North American seafarers followed the Gulf Stream across the Atlantic to Europe thousands of years before Europeans voyaged to America. This culture collapsed 4,000 years ago. No one knows why.

Some native peoples settled down without becoming farmers. Those in the Pacific Northwest developed complex art forms that fascinate modern collectors and sustained themselves through fishing, hunting, and the gathering of nuts, berries, and other edible plants. Men fished and hunted; women gathered. California peoples sustained some of the densest populations north of Mexico by collecting acorns and processing them into meal, which they baked into cakes. In the rain forests of Brazil, in south and central Florida, and in the cold woodlands of northern New England, hunter-gatherers also got along without becoming farmers.

Most North Americans could not depend solely on hunting and gathering food, however. In a few places some of them, probably women, began to plant and harvest crops instead of simply gathering and eating what they found. In Asia and Africa, this practice was closely linked to the domestication of animals and happened quickly enough to be called the Neolithic (new or late Stone Age) revolution. But in the Americas the rise of farming had little to do with animals, occurred gradually, and might better be termed the Neolithic *evolution*. For the first 3,500 years, farming supplemented a diet that still depended mostly on fishing and hunting, though now of smaller animals. Somewhere between 4000 and 1500 B.C., permanent farm villages began to dominate parts of Peru, south-central Mexico, northeast Mexico, and the southwestern United States. Their crops were different from those of Europe, the Middle East, or East Asia. The first American farmers grew amaranth (a cereal), manioc (familiar to modern Americans as tapioca), chili peppers, pumpkins, sweet potatoes, several varieties of beans, and, above all, maize, or Indian corn, which became a staple throughout most of the Americas. Indians also raised white potatoes and tomatoes. The spread of these crops launched another population surge great enough to support cities in some areas.

THE POLYNESIANS AND HAWAII

Asians migrating across Beringia were not the only people on the move. Polynesians sailed out from Southeast Asia into the Pacific about 1600 B.C. and during the next 2,000 years settled hundreds of islands scattered across more than 30 million square miles of ocean. Their ability to carry families and plants safely across thousands of miles of open sea in what were essentially large dugout canoes with sails and attached outriggers was the greatest maritime feat of the era. Nearly all of their settlements were on tropical islands. By the first century A.D., Fiji had become a kind of cultural and linguistic center, and the Polynesians had reached as far as Hawaii, nearly

2,500 miles to the northeast. By A.D. 300 they had colonized Easter Island, more than 4,000 miles to the east and only 2,000 miles off the coast of South America. Before A.D. 1000 they had also settled New Zealand, far to the south of Fiji. Hawaii's population, organized into stratified societies and multiple chiefdoms, would grow to 800,000 before the first Europeans arrived in the 1770s.

Did Polynesians ever reach the American mainland in prehistoric times? It seems hard to believe that such daring mariners would not have sailed on beyond Hawaii and Easter Island. And yet, if some of them did reach the Americas, they left no discernible influence on the Indian societies already there. Someone—either an Indian or a Polynesian—must have brought the sweet potato from South America to Easter Island. Yet the culture of Easter Island was Polynesian, while that of South America remained thoroughly Indian.

THE NORSEMEN

About the time that Polynesians were settling Easter Island, Europeans also began trekking long distances. Pushed by fierce invaders from central Asia, various Germanic tribes overran the western provinces of the Roman Empire. The Norse, a Germanic people who had occupied Scandinavia, were among the most innovative of these invaders. For centuries their Viking warriors raided the coasts of the British Isles and France. Their sleek longboats, propelled by both sails and oars, enabled them to challenge the contrary currents of the north Atlantic. Some of them began to gaze westward across the ocean.

Beginning in A.D. 874, Vikings occupied Iceland. In 982 and 983 Erik the Red, accused of manslaughter in Norway and outlawed for committing more mayhem in Iceland, led his Norse followers farther west to Greenland. There the Norse made Europe's first contact with Inuits and established permanent settlements.

Leif, Erik's son, sailed west from Greenland in 1001 and began to explore the coast of North America. He made three more voyages, the last in 1014, and started a colony that he called "Vinland" on the northern coast of Newfoundland at a place now named L'Anse aux Meadows. The local Indians (called "Skrellings" by the Norse, which means

MUMMY OF A 6-MONTH-OLD INUIT CHILD, CIRCA 1475 This well-preserved mummy has recently been discovered in Greenland. Because the remains show no sign of disease or injury, the child may have been smothered and then buried with his mother when she died. Arctic societies could not always care for an orphaned infant.

"barbarians" or "weaklings") resisted vigorously. In one engagement, just as the Norse were about to be routed, Freydis, the bastard daughter of old Erik, and the first European woman known to North American history, saved the day by baring her breasts, slapping them with a sword, and screaming ferociously. Awed, the Skrellings fled. Nevertheless, the Norse soon quarreled among themselves and destroyed the colony. During the 1014 voyage, Freydis and her husband murdered her brother and seized his ship. When Leif found out, he cursed Freydis's offspring, who, Norse poets assure us, never amounted to anything after that. The Norse abandoned Vinland, but they continued to visit North America for another century, probably for wood. A 12th-century Norse coin, recovered from an Indian site in Maine, gives proof of their continuing contact with North America.

About 500 years after Erik the Red's settlement, the Norse also lost Greenland. There, not long before Columbus sailed in 1492, the last Norse settler died a lonely death. In the chaos that followed the Black Death in Europe and Greenland after 1350, the colony had suffered a severe population decline, gradually lost regular contact with the homeland, and slowly withered away. Despite their spectacular exploits, the Norse had no impact on the later course of American history. They had reached a dead end.

EUROPE AND THE WORLD IN THE 15TH CENTURY

Nobody in the year 1400 could have foreseen the course of European expansion that was about to begin. Europe stood at the edge, not the center, of world commerce.

CHINA: THE REJECTION OF OVERSEAS EXPANSION

By just about every standard, China under the Ming dynasty was the world's most complex culture. In the 15th century the government of China, staffed by well-educated bureaucrats, ruled 100 million people, a total half again as large as the combined populations of all European states west of Russia. The Chinese had invented the compass, gunpowder, and early forms of printing and paper money. Foreigners coveted the silks, teas, and other fine products available in China, but they had little to offer in exchange. Most of what Europe knew about China came from *The Travels of Marco Polo*, a merchant from the Italian city-state of Venice who at age 17 journied overland with his father and uncle to the Chinese court, which he reached in 1271 and then served the emperor, Kublai Khan, for the next 20 years. This "Great Khan is the mightiest man, whether in respect of subjects or of territory or of treasure, who is in the world today or who ever has been, from Adam our first parent down to the present moment," Marco assured Europe. The Khan's capital city (today's Beijing) was the world's largest and grandest, Marco insisted, and received 1,000 cartloads of silk a day. In brief, China outshone Europe and all other cultures.

The Chinese agreed. Between 1405 and 1434 a royal eunuch, Cheng Ho, led six large fleets from China to the East Indies and the coast of East Africa, trading and exploring along the way. His biggest ships, 400 feet long, displaced 1,500 tons and were certainly large enough to sail around the southern tip of Africa and "discover" Europe. Had China thrown its resources and talents into overseas expansion, the subsequent history of the world would have been vastly different, but most of what the Chinese learned about the outside world merely confirmed their belief that other cultures had little to offer their Celestial Kingdom. No one followed Cheng Ho's lead after he died. Instead, the emperor banned the construction of oceangoing ships and later forbade anyone to own a vessel with more than two masts. China, a self-contained economic and political system, turned inward. It did not need the rest of the world.

EUROPE VERSUS ISLAM

Western Europe was a rather backward place in 1400. Compared with China or the Islamic world, it suffered severe disadvantages. Its location on the Atlantic rim of the Eurasian continent had always made access to Asian trade difficult and costly. Islamic societies controlled overland trade with Asia and the only known seaborne route to Asia through the Persian Gulf. As of 1400, Arab mariners were the world's best.

Europeans desired the fine silks of China. They also coveted East Indian spices to enliven their food and help preserve it through the long winters. But because Europeans produced little that Asians wished to buy, they had to pay for these imports with silver or gold. Both were scarce.

In fact, while Europe's sphere of influence was shrinking and while China seemed content with what it already had, Islamic states were well embarked on another great phase of expansion. Europe's mounted knights in heavy armor failed to stop the Ottoman Turks, who took Constantinople in 1453, overran the Balkans by the 1520s, and even threatened Vienna. The Safavid Empire in Iran (Persia) rose to new splendor at the same time. Other Moslems carried the Koran to Indonesia and northern India, where their powerful Mogul empire formed the basis for the modern states of Pakistan and Bangladesh.

CHARTING HEAVENLY BODIES The astrolabe was invented in the 14th century to calculate the position of celestial bodies. This example was used at the Collegium Maius, Cracow, Poland, when Nicolas Copernicus, the great astronomer, studied there, around 1500.

Yet Europe had certain advantages, too. The European economy had made impressive gains in the Middle Ages, primarily owing to agricultural advances, such as improved plows, that also fostered rapid population growth. By 1300, more than 100 million people were living in Europe. Europe's farms could not sustain further growth, however. Lean years and famines ensued, leaving people undernourished. In the late 1340s, the Black Death (bubonic plague) reduced the population by more than a third. Recurring bouts of plague kept population low until about 1500, when vigorous growth resumed. But during the long decline of the 15th century, overworked soil regained its fertility, and per capita income rose considerably among people who now had stronger immunities to disease.

By then European metallurgy and architecture were quite advanced. The Renaissance, which revived interest in the literature of ancient Greece and Rome, also gave a new impetus to European culture, especially after Johannes Gutenberg invented the printing press and movable type in the 1430s. Soon information began to circulate more rapidly in Europe than anywhere else in the world. This revolution in communications permitted improvements in ship design and navigational techniques to build on each other and become a self-reinforcing process. The Arabs, by contrast, had borrowed block printing from China in the 10th century, only to give it up by 1400.

Unlike China, none of Europe's kingdoms was a self-contained economy. All had to trade with one another and with the non-Christian world. Although in 1400 this need was a drawback, between the 15th and 17th centuries it slowly became an asset. No single state had a monopoly on the manufacture of firearms or on the flow of capital, and European societies began to compete with one another in gaining access to these resources and in mastering new maritime and military techniques. European armies were far more formidable in 1520 than they had been in 1453, and by then European fleets could outsail and outfight all rivals.

THE LEGACY OF THE CRUSADES

Quite apart from the Norse explorers, Europe had a heritage of expansion that derived from the efforts of the crusaders to conquer the Holy Land from Islam. Crusaders had established their own Kingdom of Jerusalem, which survived for more than a century but was finally retaken in 1244. Thereafter, while a new wave of Islamic expansion seemed about to engulf much of the world, Christian Europe gained only a few Mediterranean and Atlantic islands before 1492 but learned some important lessons in the process. To make Palestine profitable, the crusaders had taken over sugar plantations already there and had worked them with a combination of free and slave labor. After they were driven from the Holy Land, they retreated to the Mediterranean islands of Cyprus, Malta, Crete, and Rhodes, where they used slaves to grow sugar cane or grapes.

Long before Columbus, these planters had created the economic components of overseas expansion. They assumed that colonies should produce a staple crop, at least partly through slave labor, for

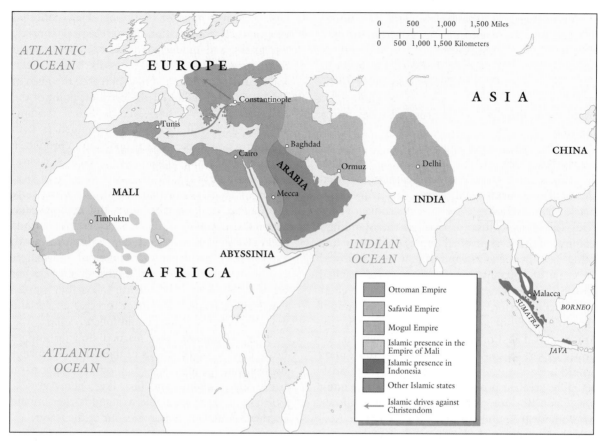

EXPANSION OF ISLAM

sale in Europe. The first slaves were Moslem captives. In the 14th and 15th centuries, planters turned to pagan Slavs (hence the word "slave") from the Black Sea area and the Adriatic. Some black Africans were also acquired from Arab merchants who controlled the caravan trade across the Sahara Desert, but these early plantations never exploited their laborers with the intensity that would later become routine in the Americas.

The crusades also left a cultural legacy in the legend of Prester John. For centuries after the loss of Jerusalem, many Europeans still cherished the hope of linking up somewhere deep in the African interior with this mythical Christian king, whose legend reflected the garbled information that Europe had acquired about the Coptic Christian kingdom of Ethiopia. As late as the 15th century, Euro-

peans still hoped to inflict a mortal blow upon Islam by uniting with the descendants of that powerful prince.

THE UNLIKELY PIONEER: PORTUGAL

It seemed highly improbable in 1400 that Europe was standing on the threshold of a dramatic expansion. That Portugal would lead the way seemed even less likely. Portugal, a small kingdom of fewer than a million people, had been united for less than a century. Lisbon, with 40,000 people, was the only city of any size. Portugal's maritime traditions lagged well behind those of the Italian states, France, and England. Its merchant class was tiny, and it had little capital.

Yet Portugal had some advantages. It enjoyed internal peace and an efficient government at a time when its neighbors were beset by war and internal upheaval. Moreover, Portugal's location at the intersection of the Mediterranean and Atlantic worlds prompted its mariners to ask how they could transform the Atlantic from a barrier into a highway.

At first, they were interested in short-term gains, rather than in some all-water route to Asia. The Portuguese knew that Arab caravans crossed the Sahara to bring gold, slaves, and ivory from black Africa to Europe. Arab traders spoke of how King (or *Mansa*) Musa (d. 1332) of the Mandingo empire of Mali controlled more gold than any other ruler in the world and of how he could field an army of 100,000 men. These reports reached Europe, where Musa was described as "the richest and most noble lord of all this region on account of the abundance of gold which is gathered in his kingdom." The Portuguese believed that an Atlantic voyage to coastal points south of the Sahara would undercut Arab traders and bring large profits. The greatest problem they faced in this quest was Cape Bojador, with its treacherous shallows, awesome waves, and strong northerly winds. Several bold captains had sailed around the cape. None had returned.

A member of the Portuguese royal family, Prince Henry, challenged this barrier. In 1420 he became head of the crusading Order of Christ and used its revenues to sponsor 15 voyages along the African coast. In 1434 one of his captains, Gil Eannes, finally succeeded. After passing the cape and exploring the coastline, Eannes sailed west into the Atlantic beyond the sight of land until he met favorable winds and currents that carried him back to Europe. Having launched Portugal's era of expansion, Henry soon lost interest in it. While he indulged in costly and futile crusades against Morocco, less exalted men pushed farther south along the African coast. Only after they made it beyond the Sahara did their efforts begin to pay off.

During the 15th century Portugal vaulted past all rivals in two major areas—the ability to navigate the high seas beyond sight of land, and the capacity to defeat any non-European fleet on the world's oceans. Portuguese (and later Spanish) navigators mapped the prevailing winds and currents on the high seas over most of the globe. They collected geographical information from classical sources, foreigners, and modern navigators. They studied the superior designs of Arab vessels, copied them, and improved on them. They increased the ratio of length to beam (width at the broadest point of the hull) from 2:1 to 3:1, borrowed the lateen (triangular) sail from the Arabs, and combined it with square rigging in the right proportion to produce a superb oceangoing vessel, the caravel. A caravel could make from 3 to 12 knots and could beat closer to a head wind than any other sailing ship. Portuguese captains also used the compass and adopted the Arabs' astrolabe, a device that permits accurate calculation of latitude, or distances north and south. (The calculation of longitude—distances east and west—is much more difficult and was not mastered until the 18th century.) As they skirted the African coast, they made precise charts and maps that later mariners could follow.

The Portuguese also learned how to mount heavy cannon on the decks of their ships—a formidable advantage in an age when others fought naval battles by grappling and boarding enemy vessels. Portuguese ships were able to stand farther off and literally blow their opponents out of the water.

As the 15th century advanced, Portuguese mariners explored ever farther along the African coast, looking for wealth, news of Prester John, and eventually a direct, cheap route to Asia. South of the Sahara they found the wealth they had been

THE CARAVEL: A SWIFT OCEANGOING VESSEL This caravel is a modern reconstruction of the 15th-century *Niña*, which crossed the Atlantic with Columbus in 1492.

seeking—gold, ivory, and slaves. These riches kept the enterprise alive.

AFRICA, COLONIES, AND THE SLAVE TRADE

West Africa was inhabited by a mostly agricultural population that also included skilled craftsmen. West Africans probably learned how to use iron long before Europeans did, and they had been supplying Europe with most of its gold for hundreds of years through indirect trade across the Sahara. West Africa's political history had been marked by the rise and decline of a series of large inland states. The most recent of these, the empire of Mali, was already in decline by 1450. As the Portuguese advanced past the Sahara, their commerce began to pull trade away from the desert caravans, which further weakened Mali and other interior states. By 1550, the empire had fallen apart.

The Portuguese also founded offshore colonies along the way. They began to settle the uninhabited Madeira Islands in 1418, took possession of the Azores between 1427 and 1450, occupied the Cape Verde group in the 1450s, and took over São Tomé in 1470. Like exploration, colonization also turned a profit. Lacking investment capital and experience in overseas settlement, the Portuguese drew on Italian merchants for both. In this way, the plantation complex of staple crops and slavery migrated from the Mediterranean to the Atlantic. Beginning in the 1440s, Portuguese island planters produced sugar or wine, increasingly with slave labor imported from nearby Africa. Some plantations, particularly on São Tomé, kept several hundred slaves at work growing and processing sugar.

At first the Portuguese acquired their slaves by landing on the African coast, attacking agricultural villages, and carrying off everyone they could catch, but these raids enraged coastal peoples and made other forms of trade more difficult. In the decades after 1450, the slave trade assumed its classic form. The Portuguese established small posts, or "factories," along the coast or, ideally, on small offshore islands, such as Arguin Island near Cape Blanco, where they built their first African fort in 1448. Operating out of these bases, traders would buy slaves from the local rulers, who usually acquired

LINK TO THE PAST

Pictorial Images of the Transatlantic Slave Trade

http://gropius.lib.virginia.edu/SlaveTrade/index.html

This site, put together by Jerome S. Handler and Michael L. Tulte, is the first large collection of visual resources for the Atlantic slave trade ever compiled. It presents these materials under nine categories, including Africa: Society, Polity, Culture; Slave Capture and Coffles; Slave Sales on the Coast; Forts, Castles, & Factories; and Slave Ships & the Middle Passage.

1. Go to the collection on the middle passage. How might we explain the sheer brutality at the heart of this commerce?

2. Visit the images in the "Slave Capture and Coffles" and "Slave Sales on the Coast" sections. How deeply were Africans implicated in this whole process?

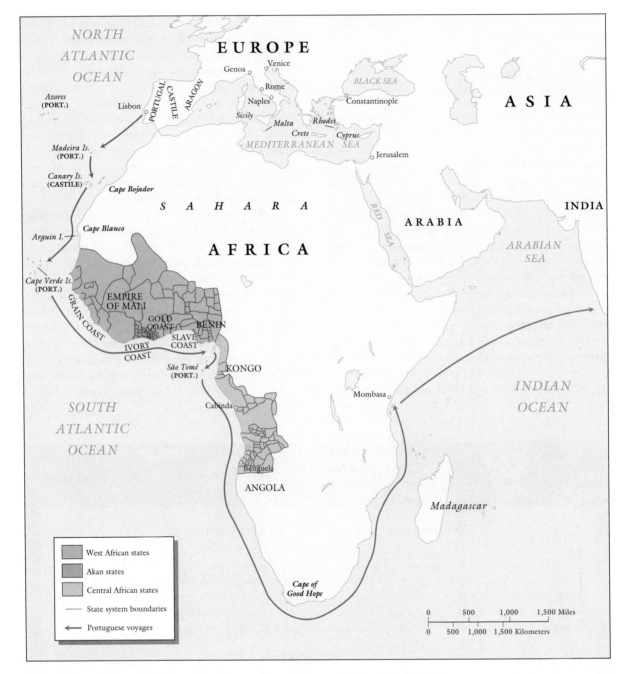

AFRICA AND THE MEDITERRANEAN IN THE 15TH CENTURY

them by waging war. During the long history of the Atlantic slave trade, nearly every African shipped overseas had first been enslaved by other Africans.

Slavery had long existed in Africa, but in a form less brutal than that which the Europeans would impose. When the Atlantic slave trade began, no African middleman could have foreseen how the enslavement of Africans by Europeans would differ from the enslavement of Africans by Africans. The differences were crucial. In Africa, slaves were not

THE PORTUGUESE SLAVE-TRADING FORTRESS OF ELMINA Located on the Gold Coast of West Africa, the fortress was built in 1481.

forced to toil endlessly to produce staple crops, and their descendants often became fully assimilated into the captors' society. Slaves were not isolated as a separate caste. By the time African middlemen learned about the cruel conditions of slavery under European rule, the trade had become too lucrative to stop, although several African societies tried. They discovered, however, that those who refused to participate in the trade were likely to become its victims. When the rulers of the Kongo embraced Catholicism in the 16th century, they protested against the Atlantic slave trade, only to see their own people become vulnerable to enslavement by others. The non-Christian kingdom of Benin learned the same lesson.

The Portuguese made the slave trade profitable by exploiting rivalries among the more than 200 small states of West and Central Africa. This part of Africa was divided into more language groups and small states than Europeans would find anywhere else in the world. And despite many cultural similarities among these groups, West Africans had never thought of themselves as a single people. Nor did they share a universal religion that might have restrained them from selling other Africans into slavery. Moslems believed it sinful to enslave a fellow believer. Western Europeans, although they were quite capable of waging destructive wars against one another, strongly believed that enslaving fellow Christians was immoral. Enslaving pagan

IVORY SALT CELLAR FROM BENIN The Portuguese certainly aroused much curiosity in West Africa. This ivory salt cellar depicts a Portuguese nobleman. The lid is surmounted by a caravel.

or Moslem Africans was another matter. Some Europeans even persuaded themselves that they were doing Africans a favor by buying them and making their souls eligible for salvation.

PORTUGAL'S ASIAN EMPIRE

Portuguese exploration continued, paying for itself through gold, ivory, and slaves. In the 1480s the government decided to support the quest for an all-water route to Asia. In 1487 Bartolomeu Dias reached the Cape of Good Hope at the southern tip of Africa and headed east toward the Indian Ocean, but his crew rebelled in those stormy waters, and he turned back. Ten years later Vasco da Gama led a small fleet around the Cape of Good Hope and sailed on to the Malibar Coast of southwestern India. In a voyage that lasted more than two years (1497–99), he bargained and fought for spices that yielded a 20-to-1 profit for his investors.

Da Gama opened the way for Portugal's empire in the East. To secure their Asian trade, the Portuguese established a chain of naval bases that extended from East Africa to the mouth of the Persian Gulf, then to Goa on the west coast of India, and from there to the Moluccas, or East Indies. Portuguese missionaries even penetrated Japan. The Moluccas became the Asian center of the Portuguese seaborne empire, with their spices yielding most of the wealth that Portugal extracted from its eastern holdings. As early as 1515, African and Asian trade was providing two-thirds of Portugal's state revenues.

Beyond assuring its continued access to spices, Portugal made little effort to govern its holdings, and thus its eastern empire never became colonies of settlement. In all their Asian holdings, the Portuguese remained heavily outnumbered by native peoples. Only in the western hemisphere—in Brazil, discovered accidentally by Pedro Álvares Cabral in 1500 when he was blown off course while trying to round the Cape of Good Hope—had settlement become a major goal by the late 16th century.

EARLY LESSONS

As the Norse failure showed, the ability to navigate the high seas, though an impressive feat in itself, gave no guarantee of lasting success. Sustained expansion overseas required the support of a home government and ready access to what other states had learned. Italian merchants in nearby Rhodes or Cyprus passed their experiences on to the Portuguese to be applied in the Atlantic islands of Madeira or the Azores. And the lessons learned there were then relayed to distant Brazil. The Portuguese drew on Italian capital and maritime skills, as well as on Arab learning and technology, in launching their ventures. Spaniards, in turn, would learn much from the Portuguese, and the French, Dutch, and English would borrow from Italians, Portuguese, and Spaniards.

The economic impulse behind colonization was thus in place long before Columbus sailed west.

The desire for precious metals provided the initial stimulus, but staple crops and slavery kept that impetus alive. Before the 19th century, more than two-thirds of the people who crossed the Atlantic were slaves, brought to America to grow sugar or other staples. The Atlantic slave trade was not some unfortunate exception to a larger story of liberty. For three and a half centuries, it was the norm.

Few Europeans who crossed the ocean expected to work. Early modern Europe was a hierarchical society in which men with prestige and wealth did virtually no physical labor. Upward social mobility meant advancing toward the goal of "living nobly," without the need to labor. In both Portugal and Spain, the social barriers between aristocrats and commoners had been flexible for some time. Professional men, famous soldiers, and rich merchants could acquire titles and begin to "live nobly." The opening of the Americas offered even greater possibilities for men to succeed by forcing others to toil for them.

SPAIN, COLUMBUS, AND THE AMERICAS

While the Portuguese surged east, Spaniards moved more sluggishly to the west. Just as Portugal gained experience by colonizing Madeira and the Azores, the Spanish kingdom of Castile sent its first settlers to the Canary Islands shortly after 1400. They spent the last third of the 15th century conquering the local inhabitants, the Guanches, a Berber people who had left North Africa before the rise of Islam and had been almost completely cut off from Africa and Europe for a thousand years. By the 1490s the Spanish had all but exterminated them, the first people to face virtual extinction in the wake of European expansion.

Except for seizing the Canaries, the Spaniards devoted little attention to exploration or colonization. Instead, for most of the 15th century the Iberian kingdoms of Aragon and Castile warred with other powers, quarreled with each other, or dealt with internal unrest. But in 1469 Prince Ferdinand of Aragon married Princess Isabella of Castile. They soon inherited their respective thrones and formed the modern kingdom of Spain, which had a population of about 4.9 million by 1500. Aragon, a

Mediterranean society, had made good an old claim to the Kingdom of Naples and Sicily and thus already possessed a small imperial bureaucracy with experience in administering overseas possessions. Castile, landlocked on three sides, was larger than Aragon but in many ways more parochial. Its people, though suspicious of foreigners, had turned over much of their small overseas trade to merchants and mariners from Genoa in northern Italy who had settled in the port of Seville. Crusading Castilians, not traders, had taken the lead in expelling the Moors from the Iberian peninsula. Castilians, who were more likely than the Portuguese to identify expansion with conquest instead of trade, would lead Spain overseas.

In January 1492 Isabella and Ferdinand completed the reconquest of Spain by taking Granada, the last outpost of Islam on the Iberian peninsula. Flush with victory, they gave unconverted Jews six months to become Christians or be expelled from Spain. Just over half of Spain's 80,000 Jews fled, mostly to nearby Christian lands, including Portugal, that were more tolerant than Spain. A decade later Ferdinand and Isabella also evicted all unconverted Moors. Spain entered the 16th century as Europe's most fiercely Catholic society, and this attitude accompanied its soldiers and settlers to America.

COLUMBUS

A talented navigator from Genoa named Christopher Columbus promptly sought to benefit from the victory at Granada. He had served the Portuguese Crown for several years, had engaged in the slave trade between Africa and the Atlantic islands, had married the daughter of a prominent Madeira planter, and may even have sailed to Iceland. He had been pleading for years with the courts of Portugal, England, France, and Spain to give him the ships and men to attempt an unprecedented feat: He believed he could reach eastern Asia by sailing west across the Atlantic.

Columbus's proposed voyage was controversial, but not because he assumed the earth is round. Learned men at that time agreed on that point, but they disagreed about the earth's size. Columbus put its circumference at only 16,000 miles. He pro-

posed to reach Japan or China by sailing west a mere 3,000 miles. The Portuguese scoffed at his reasoning. They put the planet's circumference at about 26,000 miles, and they warned Columbus that he would perish on the vast ocean if he tried his mad scheme. Their calculations were, of course, far more accurate than those of Columbus; the circumference of the earth is about 25,000 miles at the equator. Even so, the fall of Granada gave Columbus another chance to plead his case. Isabella, who now had men and resources to spare, grew more receptive to his request. She appointed him "Admiral of the Ocean Sea" in charge of a fleet of two caravels, the *Niña* and the *Pinta*, together with a larger, square-rigged vessel, the *Santa María*, which Columbus made his flagship.

Columbus's motives were both religious and practical. He believed that the world was going to end soon, perhaps in 1648, but that God would make the Gospel available to all mankind before the last days. As the "Christ-bearer" (the literal meaning of his first name), Columbus was convinced that he had a role to play in bringing on the Millennium, the period at the end of history when Christ would return and rule with his saints for 1,000 years. However, he was not at all averse to acquiring wealth and glory along the way.

Embarking from the port of Palos in August 1492, Columbus headed south to the Canaries, picked up provisions, and sailed west across the Atlantic. He kept two ship's logs, one to show his men, in which he underestimated the distance they had traveled, and the other for his eyes only. (Ironically, the false log turned out to be more accurate than the official one.) He promised a prize to the first sailor to sight land. Despite his assurances that they had not sailed far, the crews grew restless in early October. Columbus pushed on. When land was spotted, on October 12, he claimed the prize for himself. He said he had seen a light in the distance the previous night.

The Spaniards splashed ashore on San Salvador, now Watling's Island in the Bahamas. (A few historians argue for Samana Cay, 60 miles south of San Salvador, as the site of the first landfall.) Convinced that he was somewhere in the East Indies, near Japan or China, Columbus called the local inhabitants "Indians," a word that meant nothing to them but one that has endured. When the peaceful Tainos (or Arawaks) claimed that the Carib Indians on nearby islands were cannibals, Columbus interpreted their word for "Carib" to mean the great "Khan" or emperor of China, known to him through Marco Polo's *Travels*. Columbus set out to find the Caribs. For several months he poked about the Caribbean, mostly along the coasts of Cuba and Hispaniola. Then, on Christmas, the *Santa María* ran onto rocks and had to be abandoned. A few weeks later Columbus sailed for Spain on the *Niña*. Some historians speculate that he had arranged the Christmas disaster as a way of forcing some of the crew to stay behind as a garrison on Hispaniola, but by then even the gentle Tainos had seen enough. By

the time Columbus returned on his second voyage in late 1493, they had killed every man he had left.

The voyage had immediate consequences. In 1493 Pope Alexander VI (a Spaniard) issued a bull, *Inter Caeteras*, which divided all non-Christian lands between Spain and Portugal. A year later, in the Treaty of Tordesillas, the two kingdoms adjusted the dividing line, with Spain eventually claiming most of the western hemisphere, plus the Philippines, and Portugal most of the eastern, including the African coast, plus Brazil. As a result, Spain never acquired direct access to the African slave trade.

Columbus made three more voyages in quest of China and also served as governor of the Spanish

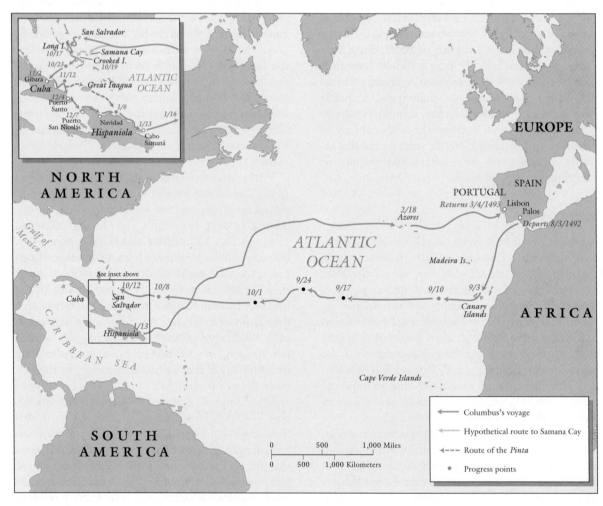

COLUMBUS'S FIRST VOYAGE, 1492

Indies. But Castilians never really trusted this Genoese opportunist, who spoke their language with a Portuguese accent and was a poor administrator to boot. The colonists often defied him, and after his third voyage they shipped him back to Spain in chains in 1500. Although later restored to royal favor, he died in 1506, a bitter, disappointed man.

SPAIN AND THE CARIBBEAN

By then overseas settlement had acquired a momentum of its own as thousands of ex-soldiers, bored *hidalgos* (minor nobles with little wealth), and assorted adventurers drifted across the Atlantic. They carried with them seeds for Europe's cereal crops and livestock, including horses, cows, sheep, goats, and pigs. On islands without fences, the animals roamed freely, eating everything in sight, and soon threatened the Tainos' food supply. Unconcerned, the Spaniards forced the increasingly malnourished Indians to work for them, mostly panning for gold. Under these pressures, even before the onset of major infectious diseases, the native population declined catastrophically throughout the Caribbean. By 1514 only 22,000 able-bodied adults remained on Hispaniola, from an initial population of perhaps one million. The native people disappeared even more rapidly than the meager supply of placer gold. This story was soon repeated on Cuba, Jamaica, and other islands. A whole way of life all but vanished from the earth to be replaced by sugar, slaves, and livestock as the Spaniards despaired of finding other forms of wealth. African slaves, acquired from the Portuguese, soon arrived to replace the dead Indians as a labor force.

The Spaniards continued their New World explorations: Juan Ponce de León tramped through Florida in quest of a legendary fountain of youth, shrewdly calculating that such an elixir would bring a handsome price in Europe. Vasco Núñez de Balboa became the first European to reach the Pacific Ocean, after crossing the Isthmus of Panama in 1513. Even so, as late as 1519—a full generation after Columbus's first voyage—Spain had gained little wealth from these new possessions, whatever and wherever they turned out to be. One geographer concluded that Spain had found a whole new continent, which he named "America" in honor of his informant, the explorer Amerigo Vespucci. For

those who doubted, Ferdinand Magellan, a Portuguese mariner serving the king of Spain, settled the issue when his fleet sailed around the world between 1519 and 1522. Magellan himself never completed the voyage. He was killed in the Philippines.

During the same three years, Hernán Cortés sailed from Cuba, conquered Mexico for Spain, and found the treasure that Spaniards had been seeking. In 1519 he landed at a place he named Vera Cruz ("The True Cross") and over the next several months succeeded in tracking down the fabulous empire of the Aztecs, high in the Valley of Mexico. When his small army of 400 men first laid eyes on the Aztec capital of Tenochtitlán (a metropolis of 200,000, much larger than any city in Western Europe), they wondered if they were dreaming. But they marched on. Moctezuma, the Aztec "speaker," or ruler, sent rich presents to persuade the Spaniards to leave, but the gesture had the opposite effect. "They picked up the gold and fingered it like monkeys," an Aztec later recalled, " . . . Their bodies swelled with greed, and their hunger was ravenous. . . . They snatched at the golden ensigns, waved them from side to side and examined every inch of them." Cortés had stumbled upon a wholly different world in the Americas, one with its own long and varied past.

THE EMERGENCE OF COMPLEX SOCIETIES IN THE AMERICAS

The high cultures of the Americas had been developing for thousands of years before Cortés found one of them. Their ways were ancient, and they were proud of their past. Their wealth fired the imagination of Europe and aroused the envy of Spain's enemies. The fabulous Aztec and Inca empires became the magnets that turned European exploration into rival empires of permanent settlement.

THE RISE OF SEDENTARY CULTURES

After 4000 B.C., agriculture transformed the lives of most Indians. As farming slowly became the principal source of food in the Americas, settled villages in a few locations grew into large cities. Most of them appeared in the Valley of Mexico, Central America,

Global Empire and the Aesthetics of Power

The Portuguese Empire brought together peoples who, in the past, had interacted only through numerous intermediaries. Thus, after Vasco da Gama's 1497–99 voyage to India, the Portuguese also reached China, the East Indies, and Japan and became the means through which other Europeans obtained goods from the Far East. The Spanish explorers, by contrast, established contact with peoples that Europeans had never heard of—and who knew nothing of Europeans, Asians, or Africans. When King Philip II of Spain took over the Portuguese throne in 1580, he united the two empires. His overseas possessions stretched from the Philippines and the Spice Islands in the Far East to a string of bases in Japan and India, to the Portuguese slave factories in West Africa and Angola, and on to the West Indies, Mexico, and Peru. Only Spain's American silver permitted Europe to pay for the silks and spices it imported from the Far East.

Even in colonial Mexico, far from the seats of imperial power in Seville and Madrid, Spanish artists knew that they were part of a global empire without precedent in the history of the world. Juan Correa, a Mexican artist born sometime between 1645 and 1650 and who died in 1716, borrowed the *biamba*, or folding-screen, from Japan and painted majestic scenes on each side to celebrate Spain's great triumph. One side depicts *The Encounter of Cortés and Moctezuma*. The other displays *The Four Continents* (Europe, Asia, Africa, and America) drawn together by Spain's heroic exploits.

or the Andes. For centuries, however, dense settlements also thrived in Chaco Canyon in present-day New Mexico and in the Mississippi River valley. Meanwhile, farming continued to spread. By the time Columbus sailed, the great majority of Indians were raising crops.

Indians became completely sedentary (nonmigratory) only in the most advanced cultures. Most of those north of Mexico lived a semisedentary life—that is, they were migratory for part of each year. After a tribe chose a site, the men chopped down some trees, girded others, burned away the underbrush, and often planted tobacco, a mood-altering sacred crop grown exclusively by men. Burning the underbrush fertilized the soil with ash and gave the community years of high productivity. Meanwhile, women erected the dwellings (longhouse, wigwam, tepee) and planted and harvested food crops, especially corn. Planting beans among the corn helped to maintain good crop yields. In the fall, either the men alone or entire family groups went off hunting or fishing.

Under this "slash and burn" system of agriculture, farming became women's work, beneath the dignity of men, whose role was to hunt and make war. Because this system slowly depleted the soil, the whole tribe had to move to new fields after a decade or two, often because accessable firewood had been exhausted. In this semisedentary way of life, few Indians cared to acquire more personal property than the women could carry from one place to another, either during the annual hunt or when the whole community had to move. This limited interest in consumption would profoundly condition their response to capitalism after contact with Europeans.

Even sedentary Indians did not own land as individuals. Clans or families guarded their "use rights" to land that had been allocated to them by their chiefs. In sedentary societies both men and women worked in the fields, and families accumulated surpluses for trade. Not all sedentary peoples developed monumental architecture and elaborate state forms. The Tainos of the Greater Antilles in the Caribbean were fully sedentary, for example, but they never erected massive temples or created powerful states. But, with a few striking exceptions, such examples of cultural complexity emerged primarily

LONGHOUSE, WIGWAM, AND TEPEE The longhouse (top right), made from bark or mats stretched over a wooden frame, was the standard communal dwelling of the Iroquois and Huron peoples. Most Algonquian peoples of the eastern woodlands lived in wigwams (top left), such as this undated Winnebago example. Wigwams were made by bending the boughs of trees into a frame to be covered with animal skins. West of the Mississippi, most Plains Indians lived in small but strong tepees (bottom left), which were usually made from poles covered with buffalo hides. All of these dwellings were constructed by women.

among sedentary populations. In Mesoamerica and the Andes, intensive farming, cities, states, and monumental architecture came together at several different times to produce distinctive high cultures.

The spread of farming produced another population surge among both sedentary and semisedentary peoples. Estimates vary greatly, but according to the more moderate ones, at least 50 million people were living in the western hemisphere by 1492—and perhaps as many as 70 million, or one-seventh of the world's population. High estimates exceed 100 million. The Valley of Mexico in 1500 was one of the most densely inhabited regions on earth.

Despite their large populations, even the most complex societies in the Americas remained Stone Age cultures in their basic technology. Indeed, the urban societies of Mesoamerica and the Andes became the largest and most complex Stone Age cultures in the history of the world. The Indians made some use of metals, although more for decorative than practical purposes. This metalworking skill originated in South America and spread to Mesoamerica a few centuries before Columbus. By 1520 Indians had amassed enough gold and silver to provide dozens of plundering Europeans with princely fortunes. As far north as the Great Lakes, copper had been mined and fashioned into fishing tools and art objects since the first millennium B.C. Copper was traded over large areas of North America, but Indians had not learned how to make bronze (a compound of copper and tin), nor found any use for iron. Nearly all of their tools were made of stone or bone, and their sharpest weapons were made from obsidian, a hard, glassy, volcanic rock. Nor did they use the wheel or devices based on the wheel, such as pulleys or gears. They knew how to make a wheel—they had wheeled toys—but they never found a practical purpose for this invention, probably because North America had no draft animals, and South Americans used llamas mostly in steep mountainous areas where wheeled vehicles would have made no sense.

THE ANDES: CYCLES OF COMPLEX CULTURES

Despite these technological limitations, Indians accomplished a great deal. During the second millen-

INDIAN WOMEN AS FARMERS In this illustration, a French artist depicted 16th-century Indian women in southeastern North America.

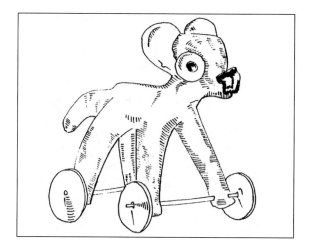

MESOAMERICAN TOY DEER This sketch of a toy deer shows that Mesoamerican people did understand the principle of the wheel, but they found no practical use for it.

societies devised extremely productive agricultural systems at 12,000 feet above sea level, far above the altitude at which anyone else has ever been able to raise crops. In the 1980s, when archaeologists rebuilt part of the prehistoric Andean irrigation system according to ancient specifications, they discovered that it was far more productive than a system using modern fertilizers and machines. The Andean system could produce 10 metric tons of potatoes per hectare (about 2.4 acres), as against 1 to 4 tons on nearby modern fields. Lands using the Andean canal system never had to lie fallow. This type of irrigation took hold around Lake Titicaca about 1000 B.C. and spread throughout the region. It was abandoned around A.D. 1000, apparently in response to a monster drought that endured, with only brief intermissions, for two centuries.

Monumental architecture and urbanization appeared in the Andes even before the canal system at Lake Titicaca was created. Between 3000 and 2100 B.C., both took hold along the Peruvian coast and in the interior. The new communities were built around a U-shaped temple about three stories high. Some of the earliest temples were pyramids, the oldest of which are as ancient as those of Egypt. In later centuries, as more people moved into the

nium B.C., elaborate urban societies began to take shape both in the Andes and along Mexico's gulf coast. Because no Andean culture had become literate before the Europeans arrived, we know much less about events there than we do about Mesoamerica, but we do know that ancient Andean

COMPLEX CULTURES OF PRE-COLUMBIAN AMERICA

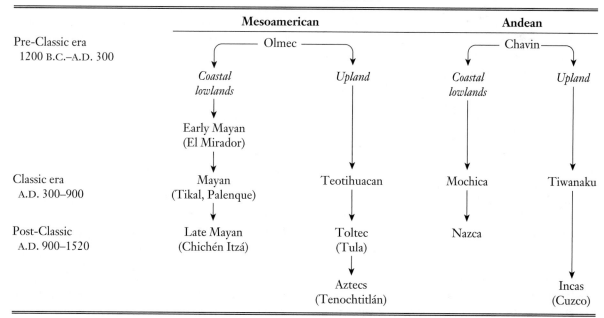

	Mesoamerican		Andean	
Pre-Classic era 1200 B.C.–A.D. 300	— Olmec —		— Chavin —	
	Coastal lowlands	*Upland*	*Coastal lowlands*	*Upland*
	Early Mayan (El Mirador)			
Classic era A.D. 300–900	Mayan (Tikal, Palenque)	Teotihuacan	Mochica	Tiwanaku
Post-Classic A.D. 900–1520	Late Mayan (Chichén Itzá)	Toltec (Tula)	Nazca	
		Aztecs (Tenochtitlán)		Incas (Cuzco)

TERRACED AGRICULTURE OF THE ANDES This example is from the Incas, but the technology was much older than the Inca civilization.

mountains, some pyramids became immense. The one at Sechin Alto near Lima, more than 10 stories high, was built between 1800 and 1500 B.C. Eventually these accomplishments merged into what archaeologists call the "Pre-Classic" Chavin culture, which was well established by 1000 B.C., only to collapse suddenly about 300 B.C. In all probability, no single state ever dominated this culture.

Chavin culture had two offshoots, one on the coast, one in the mountains. Together they constitute the "Classic" phase of pre-Columbian history in South America. The Mochica culture, which emerged about A.D. 300 on the northwest coast of Peru, produced finely detailed pottery, much of it erotic, and built pyramids as centers of worship. At about the same time, another Classic culture arose in the mountains around the city of Tiwanaku, 12,000 feet above sea level. The people of this society grew a great variety of food plants, both tropical and temperate. Terraces, laid out at various altitudes on the mountainside, enabled the community to raise crops from different climatic zones, all a few hours distant from one another. At the lowest levels, Tiwanakans planted cotton in the hot, humid air. Farther up the mountain, they raised maize (corn) and other crops suitable to a temperate zone. At still higher elevations, they grew potatoes and grazed their alpacas and llamas. They even invented freeze-dried food by carrying it far up the mountains to take advantage of the frost that fell most nights of the year.

The Tiwanaku Empire, with its capital on the southern shores of Lake Titicaca, flourished until even its sophisticated irrigation system could not survive the horrendous drought that began at the end of the 10th century A.D. The Classic Andean cultures collapsed between the 6th and 11th centuries A.D., possibly after a conquest of the Mochica region by the Tiwanakans, who provided water to the coastal peoples until they too were overwhelmed by the drought.

The disruption that followed this decline was temporary, for complex Post-Classic cultures soon thrived both north and west of Tiwanaku. The coastal culture of the Nazca people has long fascinated both scholars and tourists because of its exquisite textiles, and above all because of a unique network of lines that they etched in the desert. Some lines form the outlines of birds or animals, but others simply run straight for miles until they disappear at the horizon. Only from the air are these patterns fully visible.

INCA CIVILIZATION

About A.D. 1400 the Inca (the word applied both to the ruler and to the empire's dominant nation) emerged as the new imperial power in the Andes. They built their capital at Cuzco, high in the mountains. From that upland center, the Incas controlled an empire that eventually extended more than 2,000 miles from south to north, and they bound it together with an efficient network of roads and suspension bridges. Along these roads the Incas maintained numerous storehouses for grain. They had no written language, but high-altitude runners, who memorized the Inca's oral commands with perfect accuracy, raced along the roads to relay their ruler's decrees over vast distances. The Incas also invented a decimal system and used it to keep accounts on a device they called a *quipu*. By 1500 the Inca empire ruled perhaps 8 to 12 million people. No other nonliterate culture has ever matched that feat.

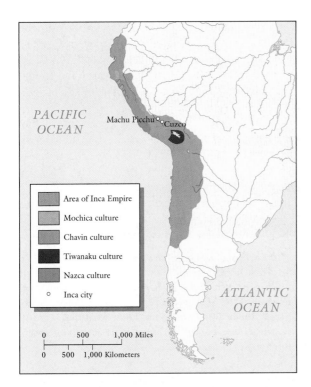

INCA EMPIRE AND PRINCIPAL EARLIER CULTURES

MESOAMERICA: CYCLES OF COMPLEX CULTURES

Mesoamerica experienced a similar cycle of change, but over a somewhat shorter period of time. Its own Pre-Classic, Classic, and Post-Classic cultures also comprised both upland and lowland societies.

The Olmecs, who appeared along the Gulf Coast about 1200 B.C., became the parent culture for the region. It centered on three cities. The oldest, San Lorenzo (names are modern, as is "Olmec," which means "people of rubber," for the rubber trees that thrive in this tropical region), flourished from 1200 to 900 B.C., when it was conquered by invaders. Olmec influence reached its zenith during the domination of La Venta, which became an urban center about 1100 B.C., reached its peak 300 years later, and declined. After La Venta was demolished between 500 and 400 B.C., leadership passed to the city of Tres Zapotes, which thrived for another four centuries.

These three Olmec centers, with permanent populations of only about 1,000, were too small to sustain large armies. The colossal stone heads that honored their rulers were the most distinctive Olmec artifacts, but they appeared only in the homeland. Other aspects of Olmec culture became widely diffused throughout Mesoamerica. The

INCA *QUIPU* The accounting device pictured here is based on a decimal system developed by the Incas.

OLMEC STONE HEAD This giant head of stone is 9 feet 4 inches tall.

Olmecs built the first pyramids and the first ball-parks in Mesoamerica. Their game, played with a heavy rubber ball, spread into what is now the southwestern United States. The losers were, at least on certain religious occasions, beheaded.

The Olmecs also learned how to write and developed a dual calendar system that endured through the Aztec era. At the end of a 52-year cycle, the first day of the "short" calendar would again coincide with the first day of the "long" one. Olmecs faced the closing days of each cycle with dread, lest the gods allow the sun and all life on earth to be destroyed—something that, Olmecs believed, had already happened several times. They believed that the sacrifice of a god had been necessary to set the sun in motion in each new creation cycle, and that only the blood of human sacrifice could placate the gods and keep the sun moving.

EL CARACOL, A LATE MAYAN OBSERVATORY AT CHICHÉN ITZÁ Astronomy was highly developed in all of the pre-Columbian high cultures of Mesoamerica. However, if the Mayans used any specialized instruments to study the heavens, we do not know what they were.

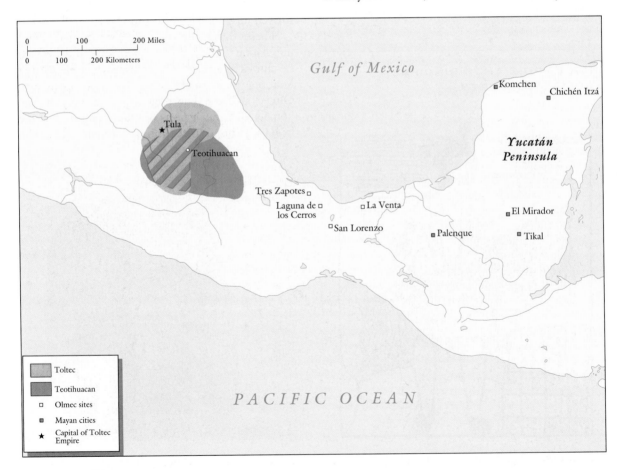

ANCIENT MESOAMERICA

These beliefs endured in Mesoamerica for perhaps 3,000 years, regardless of the rise and fall of empires and cities. The essentials may even be older than Olmec culture. The creation myths of both Mesoamerican and Andean peoples are similar, which may suggest a common origin in the distant past, perhaps as far back as Beringia where the sun did disappear for part of each year. Olmec beliefs retained immense power. The arrival of Cortés created a religious as well as a political crisis, because 1519 marked the end of a 52-year cycle.

The Olmecs were succeeded by two Classic cultures, both of which created great cities and studied the heavens. The city and empire of Teotihuacan emerged in the mountains not far from modern Mexico City. Mayan culture took shape mostly in the southern lowlands of Yucatán.

Teotihuacan was already a city of 40,000 by A.D. 1 and grew to five times that size over the next three centuries. Its temples included enormous pyramids, but its most impressive art form was its brightly painted murals, of which only a few survive. Teotihuacan invested resources in comfortable apartment dwellings for ordinary residents, not in monuments or inscriptions to rulers. It probably had a form of senate government, not a monarchy. The city extended its influence throughout Mesoamerica and remained a powerful force until its sudden destruction about A.D. 750, apparently by conquest, for its shrines were toppled and the city was abandoned. In all likelihood, Teotihuacan's growth had so depleted the resources of the area that the city could not have sustained itself much longer. Modern beliefs to the contrary, Indians enjoyed no mystical protection from ecological disasters.

In the lowlands, Classic Mayan culture went through a similar cycle from expansion to ecological crisis. It was also urban but less centralized than that of Teotihuacan, although some Mayan temples were just as monumental. For more than 1,000 years, Mayan culture rested upon a network of competing city-states which, as in ancient Greece, shared similar values. One of the largest Mayan cities, Tikal, arose on the plateau separating rivers flowing into the Caribbean from rivers emptying into the Gulf of Mexico. It controlled commerce

THE TEMPLE OF THE SUN AT TEOTIHUACAN The giant, stepped pyramid shown here is one of pre-Columbian America's most elegant pyramids.

with Teotihuacan. Tikal housed 100,000 at its peak before A.D. 800. Twenty other cities, most about one-fourth the size of Tikal, flourished throughout the region. Mayan engineers built canals to water the crops needed to support this urban system, which was well established by the 1st century B.C. The Danta pyramid, completed in the 2nd century B.C. at the Pre-Classic city of El Mirador, was probably the most massive architectural structure in pre-Columbian Mesoamerica. El Mirador declined before the Classic era began.

The earliest Mayan writings date to 50 B.C., but few survive from the next 300 years. About A.D. 300, Mayans began to record their history in considerable detail. Since 1960 scholars have deciphered most Mayan inscriptions, which means that

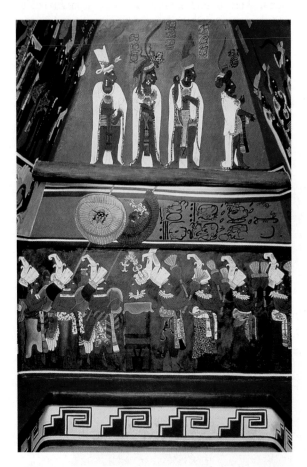

WALL PAINTINGS AT BONAMPAK The wall paintings at Bonampak from the Teotihuacan era are a spectacular example of pre-Columbian art.

the Classic phase of Mayan culture is completing a shift from a prehistoric to a historic (or written) past. Mayan texts are now studied much like those of Europe. Mayan art and writings reveal the religious beliefs of these people, including the place of human sacrifice in their cosmos and the role of ritual self-mutilation, particularly among the elite, in their worship. Scholars have learned, for example, about the long reign of Pacal the Great, king (or "Great Sun") of the elegant city of Palenque, who was born on March 26, 603, and died on August 31, 683. His sarcophagus lists his ancestors through six generations. Other monuments tell of the Great Suns of other cities whom Pacal vanquished and sacrificed to the gods.

Classic Mayan culture began to collapse about 50 years after the fall of Teotihuacan, which disrupted Mayan trade with the Valley of Mexico. The crisis spread rapidly. Palenque and a half-dozen other cities were abandoned between 800 and 820. The last date recorded at Tikal was in 869; the last in the southern lowlands came 40 years later. The Mayan aristocracy had grown faster than the commoners could support it, until population outstripped local resources and generated irreversible ecological decay. Frequent wars hastened the decline. Trade with the Valley of Mexico, though diminished, shifted north to other cities. With the collapse of the southern cities, the population of the region fell drastically, partly through emigration northward.

After A.D. 900, the Post-Classic era saw a kind of Mayan renaissance in the northern lowlands of the Yucatán, where many refugees from the south had fled. Chichén Itzá, a city that had existed for centuries, preserved many distinctive Mayan traits but merged them with new influences from the Valley of Mexico, where the Toltecs had become dominant in the high country and may even have conquered Chichén Itzá. The Toltecs were a fierce warrior people whose capital at Tula, with 40,000 people, was one-fifth as large as Teotihuacan at its peak. They prospered from the cocoa trade with tropical lowlands but otherwise did nothing to expand the region's food supply. They controlled the Valley of Mexico for almost three centuries, until about A.D. 1200 when they too declined. They left a legacy of conquest to later rulers in the valley, all of whom claimed descent from Toltec kings.

MAYAN SACRIFICIAL VICTIM Human sacrifice played a major role in Mesoamerican religion. The artist who crafted this disemboweled man recognized the agony of the victim.

THE AZTECS AND TENOCHTITLÁN

By 1400 power in the Valley of Mexico was passing to the Aztecs, a warrior people who had migrated from the north about two centuries earlier and had settled, with the bare sufferance of their neighbors, on the shore of Lake Texcoco. They built a great city, Tenochtitlán, out on the lake itself. Its only connection with the mainland was by several broad causeways. The Aztecs raised their agricultural productivity by creating highly productive *chinampas*, or floating gardens, right on the lake. Yet their mounting population strained the food supply. In the 1450s the threat of famine was severe.

Tenochtitlán, with a population of something over 200,000, had forged an alliance with Texcoco and Tlacopan, two smaller lakeside cities. Together

they dominated the area, but by the second quarter of the 15th century, leadership was clearly passing to the Aztecs. As newcomers to the region, the Aztecs felt a need to prove themselves worthy heirs to Teotihuacan, Tula, and the ancient culture of the Valley of Mexico. They adopted the old religion but practiced it with a terrifying intensity. They waged perpetual war, usually with neighboring cities, to gain captives for their ceremonies. They built and constantly rebuilt and enlarged their Great Pyramid of the Sun. At its dedication in 1487, they sacrificed—if we can believe later accounts—about 14,000 people in a ceremony that went on for four days until the priests dropped from exhaustion. Each captive climbed the steep steps of the pyramid and was held by his wrists and ankles over the sacrificial slab while a priest cut open his breast, ripped out his heart, held it up to the sun, placed it inside the statue of a god, and then rolled the carcass down the steps so that parts of the body could be eaten, mostly by members of the captor's family, but never by the captor himself. He fasted instead, and mourned the death of a worthy foe.

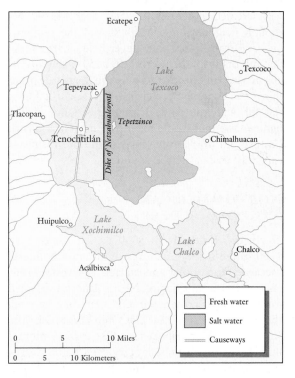

VALLEY OF MEXICO, 1519

THE CHACMOOL The Chacmool, a glowering statue at Tula, was a huge receptacle for the hearts of sacrificial victims. It became the most distinctive contribution of the Toltecs to Mesoamerican art. The Mayans copied it at Chichén Itzá, as did the Aztecs at Tenochtitlán.

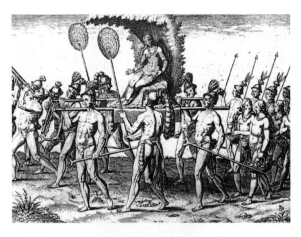

WOODCUT OF A QUEEN, OR THE WIFE OF A "GREAT SUN" OF THE MISSISSIPPI MOUND BUILDERS, BEING CARRIED ON A LITTER This 16th-century engraving is by Theodore de Bry.

Human sacrifice was an ancient ritual in Mesoamerica, familiar to everyone, but the Aztecs practiced it on a scale unparalleled anywhere else in the world. The need for thousands of victims each year created potential enemies everywhere. Although neighboring peoples shared the religious beliefs of the Aztecs, they nevertheless hated these conquerors from the north. After 1519, many Indians in Mesoamerica would help the Spaniards bring down the Aztecs. By contrast, the Spanish found few allies in the Andes, where resistance in the name of the Inca would persist for most of the 16th century and would even revive in the late 18th century, 250 years after the conquest.

NORTH AMERICAN MOUND BUILDERS

North of Mexico, from 3000 B.C. to about A.D. 1700, three distinct cultures of "mound builders" succeeded each other and exerted a powerful influence over the interior of North America. Named for the huge earthen mounds that they erected, these cultures arose near the Ohio and Mississippi Rivers and their tributaries. The earliest mound builders became semisedentary even before learning to grow crops. Fish, game, and the lush vegetation of the river valleys sustained them for most of the year and enabled them to erect permanent dwellings.

The oldest mound-building culture appeared among a preagricultural people in what is now northeastern Louisiana about 3400 B.C., at a site called Watson Break. Later, just 40 miles away, early mound builders flourished from 1500 B.C. to 700 B.C. at Poverty Point (named for a 19th-century plantation), a center that contained perhaps 5,000 people at its peak about 1000 B.C. The second mound-building culture, the Adena-Hopewell, emerged between 500 B.C. and A.D. 400 in the Ohio River valley. Its mounds were increasingly elaborate burial sites, indicating belief in an afterlife. Mound-building communities participated in a commerce that spanned most of the continent between the Appalachians and the Rockies, the Great Lakes and the Gulf of Mexico. Obsidian from the Yellowstone Valley in the Far West, copper from the Great Lakes basin, and shells from the Gulf of Mexico have all been found buried in the Adena-Hopewell mounds. Both the mound building and the long-distance trade largely ceased after A.D. 400, for reasons that remain unclear. The people even stopped growing corn for a few centuries. Yet the mounds were so impressive that when American settlers found them after the Revolution, they refused to believe that "savages" could have built them.

Mound building revived in a third and final Mississippian phase between A.D. 1000 and 1700. This culture dominated the Mississippi River valley from modern St. Louis to Natchez, with the largest center at Cahokia in present-day Illinois, and another important one at Moundville in Alabama. Ordinary people became "stinkards" in this culture, while some families had elite status. The "Great Sun"

ruled with authority and was transported by litter from place to place. When he died, some of his wives, relatives, and retainers even volunteered to be sacrificed at his funeral and join him in the afterlife. Burial mounds thus became much grander in Mississippian communities. The Indians topped the mounds in which their rulers were interred with elaborate places of worship and residences for

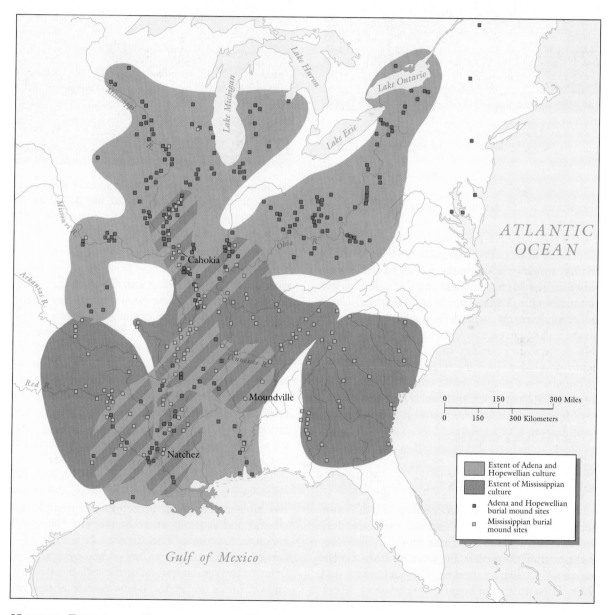

MOUND-BUILDING CULTURES OF NORTH AMERICA

CAHOKIA Lloyd Kennett Townsend's modern depiction of Cahokia at the height of its power, in the 12th or 13th century.

MODERN RESTORATION OF AN ANASAZI *KIVA* This kiva, or meeting room of the Anasazi, was located underground and was accessed by ladder through a hole in the ceiling.

the priests and Great Suns of these highly stratified societies.

The city of Cahokia, near modern St. Louis, flourished from A.D. 900 to 1250 and may have had 30,000 residents at its peak, making it the largest city north of Mexico and almost as populous as the contemporary Toltec capital at Tula. Cahokia's enormous central mound, 100 feet high, is the world's largest earthen work. Similarities with Mesoamerican practices and artifacts have led many scholars to look for direct links between the two cultures. Yet although it was possible to travel between Mesoamerica and the Mississippi valley, no Mesoamerican artifacts have been found in the southeastern United States.

URBAN CULTURES OF THE SOUTHWEST

Other complex societies emerged in North America's semiarid Southwest—among them the Hohokam, the Anasazi, and the Pueblo. The Hohokam Indians settled in what is now central Arizona somewhere between 300 B.C. and A.D. 300. Their irrigation system, consisting of several hundred miles of canals, produced two harvests a year. They wove cotton cloth and made pottery

with a distinctive red color. They traded with places as distant as California and Mesoamerica and even imported a version of the Mesoamerican ball game. Perhaps because unceasing irrigation had increased the salinity of the soil, this culture, after enduring for more than 1,000 years, had gone into irreversible decline by 1450.

Even more tantalizing and mysterious is the brief flowering of the Anasazi (a Navajo word meaning "the ancient ones"), a cliff-dwelling people who have left behind some remarkable artifacts at Chaco Canyon in New Mexico, at Mesa Verde in Colorado, and at other sites. In their caves and cliffs they constructed apartment houses five stories high with as many as 500 dwellings and with elegant and spacious *kivas*, or meeting rooms for religious functions. The Anasazi were superb astronomers. Through an arrangement of rock slabs, open to the sun and moon at the mouth of a cave, and of spirals on the interior wall that plotted the movement of the sun and moon, they created a calendar that could track the summer and winter

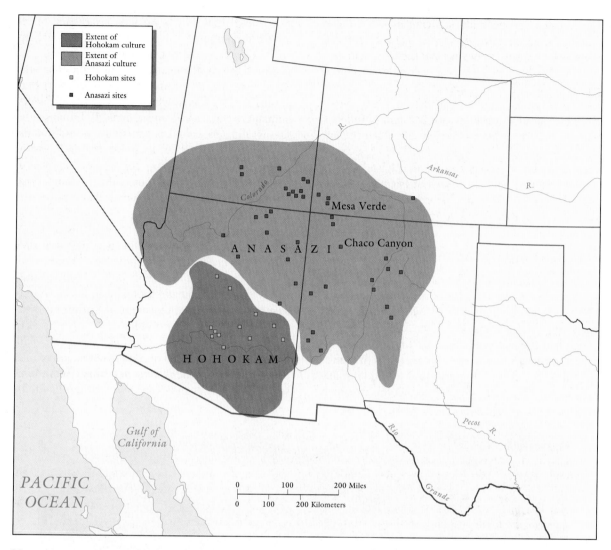

HOHOKAM AND ANASAZI SITES

solstices and even the 19-year cycles of the moon, an astronomical refinement Europeans had not yet achieved. They traveled to their fields and brought in lumber and other distant supplies on a network of roads that ran for scores of miles in several directions. They achieved most of these feats over a period of about two centuries, although Anasazi pottery has been found that dates from much earlier times. In the last quarter of the 13th century, apparently overwhelmed by a prolonged drought and by hostile invaders, they abandoned their principal sites. Pueblo architecture resembles that of

the Anasazi, and the Pueblo Indians claim descent from them.

CONTACT AND CULTURAL MISUNDERSTANDING

After the voyage of Columbus, the peoples of Europe and America, both with ancient pasts, confronted each other. Mutual understanding was unlikely except on a superficial level. Nothing in the histories of Europeans or Indians had prepared either of them for the encounter. The humanists of

Renaissance Europe, avidly studying ancient Greece and Rome, were uncovering the huge differences between those pagan cultures and the Christian values of the Middle Ages and were developing a strong sense of history, an awareness that their past had been quite different from their present. They were also used to dealing with Moslem "infidels," whom they regarded as terribly alien but whose monotheistic beliefs were not all that different from their own. They also understood that East Asia was neither classical nor Christian, not Islamic or "barbaric." Even so, none of this experience prepared them for what they found in America.

RELIGIOUS DILEMMAS

Christians had trouble understanding how Indians could exist at all. The Bible, they were certain, recorded the creation of all mankind, but it never mentioned the Indians. From which of the sons of Noah had they descended? Were they the "lost 10 tribes" of Israel, perhaps? This idea was first suggested by Spanish missionaries and would later appeal to British Protestants. Some theologians, such as Spaniard Juan Ginés de Sepúlveda, tried to resolve this dilemma by arguing that Indians were animals without souls, not human beings at all. The pope and the royal courts of Portugal and Spain listened instead to a Dominican missionary, Fray Bartolomé de Las Casas, who insisted on the Indians' humanity. But, asked Europeans, if Indians (and Asians) did possess immortal souls, would a compassionate God have left them in utter darkness for centuries without making the Gospel known to them? Rejecting that possibility, some early Catholic missionaries concluded that one of the apostles must have visited America (and India) and that the Indians must have rejected his message. The Portuguese announced in the 1520s that they had discovered the tomb of St. Thomas the Doubter in India, and then in 1549 a Jesuit claimed to have found Thomas's footprint in Brazil. If only to satisfy the spiritual yearnings of Europeans overseas, St. Thomas got around!

To Europeans, the sacrificial temples, skull racks, and snake motifs of Mesoamerica led to only one conclusion: The Aztecs worshiped Satan himself. Their statues and even their writings had to be

AZTEC SKULL RACK ALTAR This rack held the skulls of hundreds of sacrificial victims and shocked the invading Spaniards.

destroyed. Human sacrifice and ritual cannibalism were indeed widespread throughout the Americas, although nowhere else on the two continents did the scale approach that practiced by the Aztecs. The Incas, whose creation myth resembled that of Mesoamerica, offered an occasional victim to the sun or to some other god. The Indians of eastern North America frequently tortured to death their adult male captives, and every Indian warrior learned from boyhood how to endure such torments. Christians were shocked by human sacrifice and found cannibalism revolting, but Indians regarded certain European practices with equal horror. Between 1500 and 1700, Europeans burned or hanged up to 100,000 people, usually old women, for conversing with the wrong spirits—that is, for witchcraft. The Spanish Inquisition burned thousands of heretics. To the Indians, such executions looked like human sacrifices to placate an angry Christian God.

The dilemma that Indians posed for Europeans emerged almost at once. On his second voyage, Columbus brought the first missionaries to the Americas. After one of them preached to a group of Tainos and presented them with some holy images, the Indians, records relate, "left the chapel, . . . flung the images to the ground, covered them with a heap of earth, and pissed upon it." The governor, a brother of Columbus, had them burned alive. The Indians probably saw this punishment as a form of human sacrifice to a vengeful god. They had no way of grasping the Christian distinction between human sacrifice and punishment for desecration.

Even the Christian's moral message was ambiguous. Missionaries eagerly brought news of the Christ, how he had died to save mankind from sin. Catholic worship, then as now, centered on the Mass and the Eucharist, in which a priest transforms bread and wine into the literal body and blood of Christ. "Except ye eat the flesh of the Son of man, and drink his blood," Jesus told his disciples (John 6:53), "ye have no life in you." Most Protestants also accepted this sacrament but interpreted it symbolically, not literally. To the Indians, Christians seemed to be a people who ate their own god but grew outraged at the lesser matter of sacrificing a human being to please an Indian god.

When Europeans tried to convert Indians to Christianity, the Indians concluded that the converts would spend the afterlife with the souls of Europeans, separated forever from their own ancestors, whose memory they revered. Neither side fully recognized these obstacles to mutual understanding. Although early Catholic missionaries converted thousands of Indians, the results were, at best, mixed. Some Indians willingly abandoned their old beliefs, while others resisted Christian doctrines. Most converts adopted some Christian practices and continued many of their old rituals, often in secret.

WAR AS CULTURAL MISUNDERSTANDING

Such misunderstandings multiplied as Indians and Europeans came into closer contact. Both waged war, but with different objectives. Europeans tried to settle matters on the battlefield and expected to kill many enemies. Indians fought mostly to obtain captives, whether for sacrifice (as with the Aztecs) or to replace tribal losses through adoption (as with the Iroquois). To them, massive deaths on the battlefield were almost a blasphemy, an appalling waste of life that could in no way appease the gods. Europeans and Indians also differed profoundly on what acts constituted atrocities. The torture and ritual sacrifice of captives horrified Europeans; the slaughter of women and children, which Europeans brought to America, appalled Indians.

GENDER AND CULTURAL MISUNDERSTANDING

Indian social organization also differed fundamentally from that of Europeans. European men owned almost all property, set the rules of inheritance, farmed the land, and performed nearly all public functions. Among many Indian peoples, especially those first encountered by Europeans north of Mexico, descent was matrilineal (traced through the maternal line) and women owned nearly all movable property. European men felt incomplete unless they acquired authority over other people, usually the other members of their households. Indian men had none of these patriarchal ambitions. Women did the farming in semisedentary Indian cultures, and they often could demand a war or try to prevent one, although the final decision rested with men. When Europeans tried to change warriors into farmers, Indian males protested that they were being turned into women. Only over fully sedentary peoples could Europeans impose direct rule by building upon the social hierarchy, division of labor, and system of tribute already in place.

CONQUEST AND CATASTROPHE

Spanish *conquistadores*, or conquerors, led small armies that rarely exceeded 1,000 men. Yet they subdued two empires much larger than Spain itself and then looked around for more worlds to overrun. There, beyond the great empires, Indians had more success in resisting them.

THE CONQUEST OF MEXICO AND PERU

When Cortés entered Tenochtitlán in 1519, he seized Moctezuma, the Aztec ruler, as prisoner and hostage. Though overwhelmingly outnumbered, Cortés and his men began to destroy Aztec religious objects, replacing them with images of the Virgin Mary or other Catholic saints. In response,

while Cortés was away, the Aztecs rose against the intruders, Moctezuma was killed, and the Spaniards were driven out with heavy losses. But then, the smallpox the Spaniards left behind soon began killing Aztecs by the thousands. Cortés found refuge with the nearby Tlaxcalans, a proudly independent people who had never submitted to Aztec rule. With thousands of their warriors, he returned the next year, built several warships armed with cannon to dominate Lake Texcoco, and destroyed Tenochtitlán. He had hoped to leave the great city intact, not wreck it, but he and the Aztecs found no common understanding that would enable them to stop fighting before the city lay in ruins. "We have chewed dry twigs and salt grasses," mourned one Aztec poet after the fall of the city; "we have filled our mouths with dust and bits of adobe; we have eaten lizards, rats and worms." With royal support from Spain, the *conquistadores* established themselves as new imperial rulers in Mesoamerica, looted all the silver and gold they could find, and built Mexico City on the ruins of Tenochtitlán.

Rumors abounded about an even richer civilization far to the south, and in 1531 and 1532 Francisco Pizarro finally located the Inca empire high in the Andes. Smallpox had preceded him and had

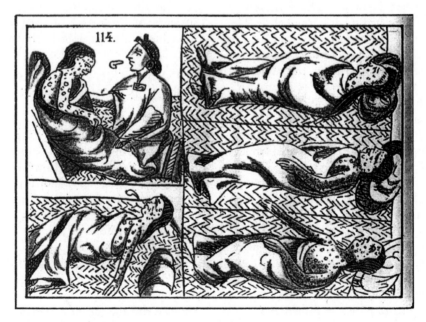

THE RAVAGES OF SMALLPOX These drawings show the devastation of smallpox among the Aztecs, as depicted in the Aztec Codex, one of the few surviving collections of Aztec writing.

TRIBUTE LABOR (*MITA*) IN THE SILVER MINES The silver mines of Potosí, in the Andes, are about two miles above sea level. The work, as depicted in this 1603 engraving by Theodore de Bry, was extremely onerous and often dangerous.

killed the reigning Inca. In the civil war that followed, Atahualpa had defeated his brother to become the new Inca. Pizarro captured Atahualpa, held him hostage, and managed to win a few allies from among the Inca's recent enemies. Atahualpa filled his throne room with precious metals as a truly royal ransom, but Pizarro had him strangled anyway. Tens of thousands of angry Indians besieged the Spaniards for months in Cuzco, the Inca capital, but Pizarro, though vastly outnumbered, managed to hold out and finally prevailed. After subduing the insurgents, the Spanish established a new capital at Lima on the coast.

In a little more than 10 years, some hundreds of Spanish soldiers with thousands of Indian allies had conquered two enormous empires with a combined population perhaps five times greater than that of all Spain. But only in the 1540s did the Spanish finally locate the bonanza they had been seeking. The fabulous silver mines at Potosí in present-day Bolivia and other smaller lodes in Mexico became

the source of Spain's wealth and power for the next 100 years. So wondrous did the exploits of the *conquistadores* seem by then that anything became believable, including rumors that cities of pure gold lay somewhere in the interior of North America.

NORTH AMERICAN *CONQUISTADORES* AND MISSIONARIES

Alvar Núñez Cabeza de Vaca was one of four survivors of Pánfilo de Narváez's disastrous 1528 expedition to Florida. Cabeza de Vaca made his way back to Mexico City in 1536 after an overland journey that took him from Florida through Texas and northern Mexico. In a published account of his adventures, he briefly mentioned Indian tales of great and populous cities to the north, and this reference soon became stories of "golden cities." Hernando de Soto landed in Florida in 1539 and roamed through much of the southeastern United States in

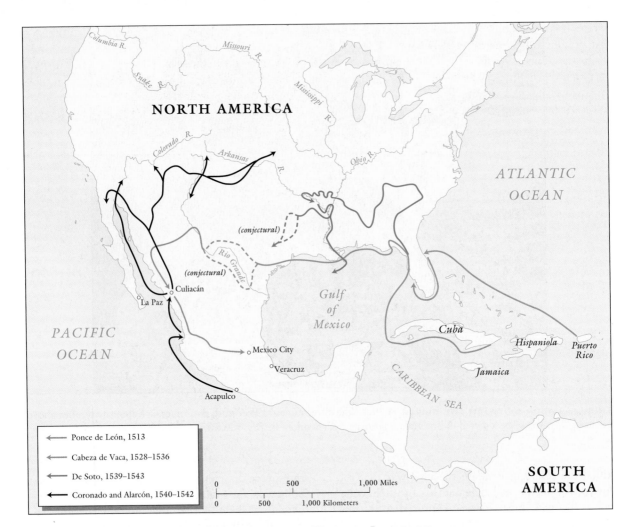

PRINCIPAL SPANISH EXPLORATIONS OF NORTH AMERICA

quest of these treasures, leaving disease and mayhem in his wake. He crossed the Mississippi in 1541, wandered through the Ozarks and eastern Oklahoma, and marched back to the great river. He died there in 1542. His companions continued to explore for another year before returning to Spanish territory. Farther west, Francisco Vasquez de Coronado marched into New Mexico and Arizona, where he encountered several Pueblo towns but no golden cities. The expedition reached the Grand Canyon, then headed east into Texas and as far north as Kansas before returning to Mexico in 1542. North of Mexico, Indians menaced and sometimes even defeated Spanish soldiers, who finally gave up, but left their diseases behind. There were no cities of gold.

After the *conquistadores* departed, Spanish priests did their best to convert thousands of North American Indians to the Catholic faith. These efforts extended well north of New Spain (Mexico). In 1570 the Jesuits even established a mission in what is now Virginia. When some Spaniards reconnoitered Chesapeake Bay at midcentury, they took the young son of a local chief back to Spain, where he was baptized as Don Luis and given a European education. He later returned to his people to assist at the new mission. When he celebrated his homecoming in 1571 by taking several wives, the Jesuits reproached him for his sin. He retaliated by wiping out the mission. Historian Carl Bridenbaugh has argued that Don Luis' Indian name became Opechancanough (which means "he whose soul is white"), the war chief who later attacked the English at Jamestown (see chapter 2). More likely, Don Luis was an uncle or cousin of that famous warrior.

After the failure of the Jesuit mission in 1571, Spain decided to treat the Indians of Florida and New Mexico with decency and fairness and eventu-ally came to rely on these missions for protection against English and French intruders. The Jesuits withdrew and Franciscans took their place. In 1573 King Philip II issued the Royal Orders for New Discoveries, which made it illegal to enslave Indians or even attack them. Instead, unarmed priests were to

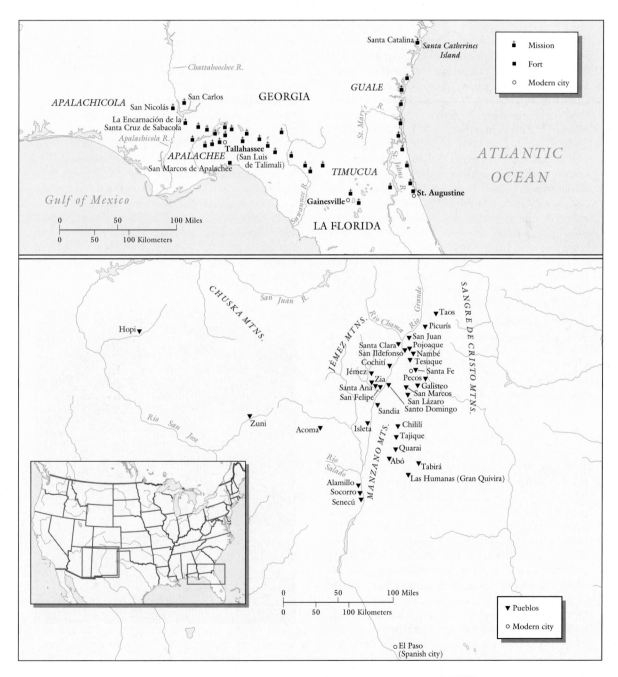

SPANISH MISSIONS IN FLORIDA AND NEW MEXICO, CIRCA 1675

The Mission (1986)
Directed by Roland Joffé. Starring Jeremy Irons (Father Gabriel), Robert De Niro (Mendoza), and Liam Neeson (Father Fielding).

This film passionately portrays the destruction of the Jesuit missions in 18th-century Paraguay. Their success and communal prosperity (which included abolishment of private property) aroused the envy and the enmity of neighboring Portuguese settlers. Some of their churches were as large and as beautifully adorned as European cathedrals. When the Crown of Spain transferred the Guaraní territory to the Crown of Portugal in a 1750 treaty, the settlers and the government of Brazil got their chance to move against the missions. Loosely based on the Portuguese war against the Guaraní in the 1750s, the film is really a tribute to the dedication and sincerity of the Jesuit order, the colonial era's most successful missionary organization in either North or South America.

The screenplay by Robert Bolt, well known for his play and film of *A Man for All Seasons* (1966) and his film script for *Dr. Zhivago* (1965), telescopes the events of one and a half centuries into what seems to be only a year or so. In the 17th century Portuguese slavers raided even Jesuit missions and carried off thousands of Indians to a life of toil in Brazil. The Guaraní War was not about enslavement but about the campaign to seize the native inhabitants' land and communal property. Bolt puts both events in the 18th century and provides a dramatic climax.

The film stars Jeremy Irons as Gabriel, a Spanish Jesuit missionary who uses the Guaraní Indians' love of music as a means of converting them. Robert De Niro plays Mendoza, a reformed slaver who has killed his own brother in a lovers' quarrel and then repents by joining Father Gabriel's mission. When the European courts and even the Jesuit order command the missionaries not to resist the Portuguese takeover, the missionaries refuse to leave their people but split over how to resist. Gabriel chooses nonviolence. Mendoza and Father Fielding (Liam Neeson) take up arms. All of them are killed. Jesuit involvement in the Guaraní War gave the Catholic monarchs of Europe the excuse they need to expel the Jesuits from their kingdoms and then to persuade the pope to disband the order.

By telescoping events that occurred decades apart into a short period of time, Bolt intensifies the drama but also suggests that some Europeans, especially Jesuits, did consistently and over a long period of time place the welfare of Indians above all other values. In a poignant final scene, many mission children, now completely naked, are rowing back into the wilderness to escape enslavement. The settlers, Bolt insists, would not allow them to become civilized.

Filmed on location above and below magnificent Agazzu Falls, one of the most spectacular sights in South America, the film won the 1986 Cannes Film Festival's award for best picture and an Oscar for best cinematography. British director Roland Joffé had already earned acclaim for *The Killing Fields* (1983), a stark depiction of the near-genocidal atrocities in Cambodia after the Vietnam War. He later directed *Fatman and Little Boy* (1989), a dramatization of the birth of the atomic bomb.

In this scene, Father Gabriel plays the flute to attract a Guaraní audience.

bring them together in missions and convert them into peaceful Catholic subjects of Spain. The Franciscans quickly discovered that, without military support, they were more likely to win martyrdom than converts. They reluctantly accepted military protection, but they took care that none of the few soldiers who accompanied them behaved like *conquistadores*.

Missionary work demanded commitment and faith. The Franciscans had both. A belief in miracles also sustained them. In 1631 a mystical nun in Castile, María de Jesús de Agreda, claimed that angels had carried her across the Atlantic where she preached to Indians in their own languages. When Pueblo Indians reported that a "Lady in Blue" once preached to them, the Franciscans put the two accounts together into a miraculous event that enchanted thousands for a century, even though the nun retracted most of her story in 1650.

Franciscans had no success among the nomadic residents of central and southern Florida. They had to build their missions within the permanent villages of northern Florida or the Pueblo communities of New Mexico. At first Indian women willingly supplied the labor needed to build and sustain these missions. By 1630 about 86,000 Pueblo,

Apache, and Navajo Indians of New Mexico had accepted baptism. They lived in a chain of missions north and south of Santa Fe, 1,500 arduous and dusty miles from the colonial capital at Mexico City. By midcentury 30 missions in Florida contained about 26,000 baptized Indians and covered an area extending some 250 miles from the Atlantic coast of what is now Georgia westward into the Florida panhandle. The Franciscans also urged their converts, with limited success, to wear European clothing. In 1671, when a bishop counted 4,081 newly converted women in Florida who went about topless and with their lower legs exposed, he ordered them to cover up.

THE SPANISH EMPIRE AND DEMOGRAPHIC CATASTROPHE

By the late 16th century, the Spanish Empire had emerged as a system of direct colonial rule in Mexico and Peru, protected by a strong defensive perimeter in the Caribbean, and surrounded by a series of frontier missions, extending in the north into Florida and New Mexico. The Spaniards also brought new systems of labor and new religious institutions to their

INTERIOR VIEW OF SAN JOSE DE GRACIA, AN 18TH-CENTURY CHURCH IN TRAMPAS, NEW MEXICO The Spanish built elegant and graceful churches, even on the far northern perimeter of their American empire.

overseas colonies, although in time both were altered by local conditions.

The first Spanish rulers in Mexico and Peru relied on a form of labor tribute that had helped to depopulate the West Indies. Called *encomienda*, this system permitted the holder, or *encomendero*, to claim labor from an Indian district for a stated period of time. *Encomienda* worked because it resembled the way the Aztecs and the Incas had routinely levied labor for their own massive public buildings and irrigation projects. In time, the king intervened to correct abuses and to limit labor tribute to projects that the Crown initiated, such as mining and the construction of churches or other public buildings. Spanish settlers resisted the reforms at first but slowly shifted from demanding labor to claiming land. In the countryside the *hacienda*, a large estate with its own crops and herds, became a familiar institution.

Although the Church never had enough clergy to meet its needs, it became a massive presence during the 16th century. Yet America changed it, too. As missionaries acquired land and labor, they began to exhibit less zeal for Indian souls. The Franciscans—in Europe, the gentlest of Catholic religious orders—brutally and systematically tortured their Mayan converts in the 1560s whenever they caught them worshiping their old gods. To the Franciscans, the slightest lapse could signal a reversion to Satan worship, with human sacrifice a likely consequence. They did not dare to be kind.

Most important of all, the Spaniards brought deadly microbes with them. Smallpox, which could be fatal but which most Europeans survived in childhood, devastated the Indians, who had almost no immunity to it. Even measles could be fatal, and common colds easily turned into pneumonia. When Cortés arrived in 1519, the native population of Mexico probably exceeded 15 million. In the 1620s, after waves of killing epidemics, it bottomed at 700,000 and did not regain its pre-Spanish level until the 1950s. Peru suffered nearly as horribly. Its population fell from about 10 million in 1525 to 600,000 a century later. For the hemisphere as a whole, any given region probably lost 90 or 95 percent of its population within a century of sustained contact with Europeans. Lowland tropical areas usually suffered the heaviest casualties; in some of these places, all the Indians died. Highland areas and sparsely settled regions fared somewhat better.

The Spanish Crown spent much of the 16th century trying to keep abreast of these changes, but eventually it imposed administrative order on the unruly *conquistadores* and brought peace to its colonies. At the center of the imperial bureaucracy, in Seville, stood the Council of the Indies. The council administered the three American viceroyalties of New Spain, Peru, and eventually New Granada, which were further subdivided into smaller *audiencias*, executive and judicial jurisdictions supervised by the viceroys. The Council of the Indies appointed the viceroys and other major officials, who ruled from the new cities that the Spaniards built with local labor at Havana, Mexico City, Lima, and elsewhere. Although centralized and autocratic in theory, the Spanish Empire allowed local officials a fair degree of initiative, if only because months or even years could elapse in trying to communicate across its immense distances. "If death came from Spain," mused one official, "we should all live long lives."

BRAZIL

Portuguese Brazil was theoretically autocratic, too, but it was divided into 14 "captaincies," or provinces, and thus was far less centralized. The Portuguese invasion did not lead to the direct rule of native societies, but to their displacement or enslavement. After the colonists on the northeast coast turned to raising sugar in the late 16th century, Brazilian frontiersmen, or *bandeirantes*, foraged deep into the continent to enslave more Indians. They even raided remote Spanish Andean missions, rounded up the converts, and dragged them thousands of miles across mountains and through the jungle to be worked to death on the sugar plantations. On several occasions, while Brazil was ruled by Spain (see the discussion that follows), outraged missionaries persuaded the king to abolish slavery altogether. Not even absolutism could achieve that goal. Slavery continued without pause, and Africans gradually replaced Indians as the dominant labor force. Brazil was the major market for African slaves until the 1640s, when demand in West Indian sugar islands became even greater.

GLOBAL COLOSSUS, GLOBAL ECONOMY

American silver made the king of Spain the most powerful monarch in Christendom. Philip II (1556–98) commanded the largest army in Europe, held the Turks in check in the Mediterranean, and tried to crush the Protestant Reformation in northern Europe (see chapter 2). He had other ambitions as well. In 1580, when the king of Portugal died with no direct heir, Philip claimed his throne, thus uniting under his own rule Portugal's Asian empire, Brazil, Spain's American possessions, and the Philippines. This colossus was the greatest empire the world had ever seen. It also sustained the first truly global economy, because the Portuguese used Spain's American silver to pay for the spices and silks they imported from Asia. The union of Spain and Portugal lasted until the 1640s, when Portugal revolted and regained its independence.

The Spanish colossus became part of an even broader economic pattern. Serfdom, which tied peasants to their lords and to the land, had been Europe's predominant labor system in the early Middle Ages. Although peasants could not move, neither could they be sold; they were not slaves. Serfdom had been declining in Western Europe since the 12th century and was nearly gone by 1500. A system of free labor arose in its place, and overseas expansion strengthened that trend within western Europe. Although free labor prevailed in the western European homeland, unfree labor systems took root all around Europe's periphery, both overseas and in eastern Europe, and the two systems were structurally linked. In general, free labor reigned where populations were dense and still growing. Large pools of labor kept wages low, but around the periphery of western Europe, where land was cheap and labor expensive, coercive systems became the only efficient way for Europeans to extract from those areas the goods they desired.

The forms of unfree labor varied greatly across space and time, from slavery to less brutal systems. In New Spain, as the native population dwindled, the practice of *encomienda* slowly yielded to debt peonage. Unpayable debts kept Indians tied to the *haciendas* of the countryside. The mining of precious metals, on the other hand, was so dangerous and unpleasant that it almost always required a large degree of physical coercion, a system of labor tribute called *mita* in the Andes. Similarly, any colonial

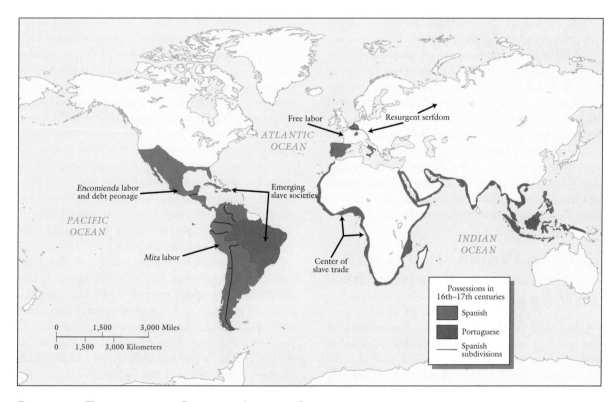

SPANISH EMPIRE AND GLOBAL LABOR SYSTEM

region that devoted itself to the production of staple crops for sale in Europe also turned to unfree labor and eventually to overt slavery. Sugar production first reduced Indians to bondage in the Caribbean and Brazil and later, as they died off, led to the importation of African slaves by the millions. Other staples—tobacco, rice, cotton, coffee—later followed similar patterns. At first these crops were considered luxuries and commanded high prices, but as they became widely available on the world market, their prices fell steeply, profit margins contracted, and planters turned overwhelmingly to coerced labor. Even in eastern Europe, which began to specialize in producing cereal crops for sale in the more diversified West, serfdom vigorously revived. In Russia, where the Orthodox Church never condemned the enslavement of fellow Christians, the condition of a serf came to resemble that of a slave in one of the Atlantic empires. Some serfs were even bought and sold.

Spain's rise had been spectacular, but its empire was vulnerable. Although silver from the Americas vastly enhanced the Crown's ability to wage war, the costs of continuous conflict, the inflation generated by a steady influx of silver, and the need to defend a much greater perimeter absorbed Spain's new resources and a great deal more. Between 1492 and 1580 Spain's population grew from 4.9 million to 8 million, but over the course of the following century, it fell by 20 percent, mostly because of the escalating costs, both financial and human, of Spain's wars. As population declined, taxes rose. Castile grew poorer, not richer, in its century and a half of imperial glory. Most of the wealth of the Indies went elsewhere to pay for goods or services that Spain failed to provide for itself—to merchants in Genoa, to manufacturers in Lombardy and the Low Countries, and to bankers in Augsburg.

EXPLANATIONS: PATTERNS OF CONQUEST, SUBMISSION, AND RESISTANCE

By the middle of the 18th century, Europeans who thought seriously about the discovery of America and its global implications generally agreed that the whole process had been a moral outrage, possibly the worst in history. Conquest and settlement had killed millions of Indians, had enslaved millions of

Africans, and had degraded Europeans. The benefits seemed small by comparison, even though economic gains were undeniably large by 1750. If the cruelest of the conquerors had been able to foresee the results of this process, asked the Abbé Raynal, would he have proceeded? "Is it to be imagined that there exists a being infernal enough to answer this question in the affirmative!" The success of the American Revolution, with its message of freedom and human rights, quieted such thinking for a time, but the critique has revived in recent years, especially in the developing world.

Modern historians, less moralistic than Raynal, also realize that he considerably underestimated the death toll. Even so, they are more interested in asking how and why these things happened. One major reason is geographical. The Eurasian land mass, the world's largest, follows an east-west axis that permits life forms and human inventions to travel immense distances without going through forbidding changes of climate. Chinese inventions eventually reached Europe. By contrast, the Americas, and sub-Saharan Africa, lie along north-south axes that do impose such barriers. Another compelling explanation for European success focuses on the prolonged isolation of the Americas from the rest of the world. If two communities of equal ability are kept apart, that with the larger and more varied population will be more inventive than the other and its people will learn more rapidly from one another over time. For example, the use of iron spread gradually through nearly all of Asia, Africa, and Europe. And even though Europeans knew little about China, they slowly acquired Chinese inventions such as paper, the compass, and gunpowder. More than any other technological edge, far more than firearms or even horses, steel made military conquest possible. European armor stopped enemy spears and arrows, and European swords killed opponents swiftly without any need to reload.

The biological consequences of isolation were even more momentous than the technological. The devastation European microbes inflicted upon the Indian population is the greatest tragedy in the history of mankind. The Indians' genetic makeup was more uniform than that of Europeans, Africans, or Asians. Indians were descended from a rather small sample of the total gene pool of Eurasia. Centuries spent in frigid Beringia had weeded out weaker people and killed the microbes that produce most diseases. The Indians first encountered by Europeans were bigger, stronger, and—at first contact—healthier than the newcomers, but they died in appalling numbers because they had almost no resistance to European diseases.

European plants also thrived at the expense of native vegetation. For example, when British settlers first crossed the Appalachian mountains, they marveled at the lush Kentucky bluegrass. They did not realize that they were looking at an accidental European import that had conquered the landscape even faster than they had. European animals also prevailed over potential American rivals. Horses multiplied at an astonishing rate in America, and wild herds moved north from Mexico faster than the Spaniards, transforming the way of life of the Apaches and the Sioux. The lowly sparrow never had it so good until someone turned a few loose in North America. But some life-forms also moved from the Americas to Europe, Asia, and Africa. Indians probably gave syphilis to the first Europeans they met. Other American exports, such as corn, potatoes, and tomatoes, were far more benign and have enriched the diet of the rest of the world. Historian Alfred W. Crosby has called this larger process "the Columbian exchange." It ranks as one of the most important events of all time.

CONCLUSION

Americans like to believe that their history is a story of progress. They are right about its European phase. After its tragic beginnings in conquest, depopulation, and enslavement, things had to improve.

For thousands of years the Americas had been cut off from the rest of the world. The major cultures of Eurasia and Africa had existed in relative isolation, engaging in direct contact with only their immediate neighbors. Islamic societies that shared borders with India, the East Indies, black Africa, and Europe, had been the principal mediators among these cultures and, in that era, were more tolerant than most Christian societies.

In just 40 years, daring European navigators, supported by the Crowns of Portugal and Spain, joined the world together and challenged Islam's mediating role. Between 1492 and 1532 Europe, Africa, Asia, the Spice Islands, the Philippines, the Caribbean, Aztec Mexico, Inca Peru, and other parts of the Americas came into intense and often violent contact with one another. A few individuals gained much, and Spain acquired a military advantage within Europe that endured into the 1640s. Nearly everybody else suffered, millions horribly, especially in the Americas and Africa. And Spain spent the rest of the 16th century trying to create an imperial system that could impose order on this turbulent reality.

But Spain had many enemies. They too would find the lure of wealth and land overseas irresistable.

IROQUOIS INDIANS PLAYING LACROSSE Lacrosse originated among North American Indians. This 1908 drawing by Jesse Cornplanter, an Iroquois, shows a game in action.

Suggested Readings begin on page SR-1.
For Web activities and resources
related to this chapter, go to
http://www.harcourtcollege.com/history.murrin

CHAPTER 2

THE CHALLENGE TO SPAIN AND THE SETTLEMENT OF NORTH AMERICA

ARCHITECTURAL CONTRASTS

A modern view of Mexico City (left) captures its historical evolution from the Aztec ruins of Tlatelolco (foreground) to the Spanish church and modern high-rise apartment buildings. The grandeur of the 16th-century Spanish cathedral contrasts sharply with the Hingham meetinghouse (right), typical of the simple architecture of the English colonies during the same period.

Catholic France and two Protestant countries, the Dutch Republic and England, challenged Spanish power in Europe and overseas. None of them planted a permanent settlement in North America before 1600. In the quarter-century after 1600, they all did. The French converted thousands of Indians. The French and Dutch brought Indian hunters into the world market by trading European goods for their furs. By 1700 the English, who coveted the land itself, had founded 12 permanent colonies in North America and others in the West Indies.

These American colonies differed as much from one another as they did from their parent cultures in Europe. Europeans, Indians, and Africans interacted in contrasting ways in this strange "new world." In Mexico and Peru, the Spaniards had set themselves up as a European ruling class over a much larger Indian population of farmers, artisans, and miners. Spain's rivals created colonies of different kinds. Some, such as Virginia and Barbados, grew staple crops with indentured servants and African slaves. New France and New Netherland developed a prosperous trade with the Indians without trying to rule them. In New England, the Puritans relied on free labor provided by hardworking family members. After 1660 the English state conquered New Netherland, and English Quakers created another free-labor society in the Delaware valley, dedicated more than any of the others, to human equality and complete religious liberty.

This chapter will focus on the following major questions:

- Why were Catholics generally more successful than Protestants in their efforts to convert Indians?
- Why did Englishmen, crossing the Atlantic at nearly the same time, create such radically different societies in the Chesapeake colonies and New England?
- How did England's Restoration colonies differ from those founded before 1660?
- If Pennsylvania really was the political failure described by many contemporaries, how could it have become such a spectacular economic success?

THE PROTESTANT REFORMATION AND THE CHALLENGE TO SPAIN

Spain, the most militantly Catholic society in Europe, did its best to crush the Protestant Reformation.

C H R O N O L O G Y

1517 Luther begins the Protestant Reformation

1577–80 Drake circumnavigates the globe

1580s Gilbert claims Newfoundland for England (1583) • Ralegh twice fails to colonize Roanoke Island (1585–87) • England repels attack by the Spanish Armada (1588)

1607 English settlement established at Jamestown

1608 Champlain founds Quebec

1609 Virginia receives sea-to-sea charter

1613–14 Rolfe grows tobacco, marries Pocahontas

1618 Sandys implements London Company reforms

1619 More Africans arrive in Virginia • House of Burgesses and Headright system created

1620s Pilgrims adopt Mayflower Compact, land at Plymouth (1620) • Dutch West India Company chartered (1621) • Opechancanough launches war of extermination in Virginia (1622) • King assumes direct control of Virginia (1624) • Minuit founds New Amsterdam (1626)

1630s Puritans settle Massachusetts Bay (1630) • Maryland chartered (1632) • Williams founds Providence; Hooker founds Hartford (1636) • Anne Hutchinson banished to Rhode Island; Minuit founds New Sweden (1638) • New Haven Colony founded (1639)

1640s Massachusetts "Body of Liberties" passed (1641) • English civil wars begin (1642) • Pavonia Massacre in New Netherland (1643) • Charles I beheaded (1649)

1655 New Netherland conquers New Sweden • Quakers invade New England

1660s Charles II restored to English throne (1660) • Puritans institute Half-Way Covenant (1662) • First Carolina charter granted (1663) • New Netherland surrenders to the English (1664) • New Jersey becomes a separate colony (1665) • Carolina's Fundamental Constitutions proposed (1669)

1670s First permanent English settlement established in South Carolina (1670) • Dutch retake New York (1673–74) • West New Jersey approves Concessions and Agreements (1677)

1680s Charleston founded (1680) • Pennsylvania charter granted (1681) • New York and Pennsylvania each adopt a Charter of Liberties (1683)

1705 Virginia adopts comprehensive slave code

Many of Spain's European enemies became Protestants during the 16th century and had strong religious motives for exposing Spanish "cruelties" in the Americas. Most Protestants, however, proved no more humane than the Spaniards in their own dealings with Indians.

By the time Spain's enemies felt strong enough to challenge Spain overseas, the Protestant Reformation had shattered the religious unity of Europe. In November 1517, not long before Cortés landed at Vera Cruz, Martin Luther nailed his 95 Theses to the cathedral door at Wittenberg in the German electorate of Saxony and touched off the Reformation. No human act, or "good work," Luther insisted, can be meritorious in the sight of God. Salvation comes through faith alone, and God grants saving faith only to those who hear his Word preached to them, struggle to understand it, and admit that, without God's grace, they are damned. Within a generation, the states of northern Germany and Scandinavia had embraced Lutheranism, but the Lutheran Church never played a major role in founding colonies overseas. Calvinism did.

John Calvin, a French Protestant, also embraced justification by faith alone and put his own militant principles into practice in the Swiss canton of Geneva. The Huguenot movement in France, the Dutch Reformed Church in the Netherlands, and the Presbyterian Kirk (or Church) of Scotland all embraced Calvin's principles, as set forth in *The Institutes of the Christian Religion* (1536). In England the Anglican Church adopted Calvinist doctrines (but not liturgy), a compromise that prompted the Puritan reform movement toward a more thoroughly Calvinist Church of England. Calvinists won major victories over Catholics in Europe in the last half of the 16th century. After 1620 Puritans carried their religious vision across the Atlantic to New England.

Calvinists rejected papal supremacy, the seven sacraments (they kept only baptism and the Lord's Supper), clerical celibacy, veneration of the saints, and the acts of charity and the penitential rituals by which Catholics tried to earn grace and store up merits. They denounced these rites as "work righteousness." Calvin gave central importance to predestination. According to that doctrine, God decreed, even before creating the world, who will be saved and who will be damned. Christ died, Calvin insisted, not for all humankind, but only for God's

SPANIARDS TORTURING INDIANS, AS DEPICTED BY THEODORE DE BRY, LATE 16TH CENTURY Among Protestants in northern Europe, images such as this one merged into a "black legend" of Spanish cruelty—which in turn helped to justify their own challenge to Spanish power overseas. But in practice, the behavior of Protestant settlers toward Indians was often as harsh as anything the Spaniards had done.

elect. Calvinists kept the Lord's Supper, but in denying that Christ is actually present in the bread and wine, they broke with Luther as well as with Rome. Because salvation and damnation were beyond human power to alter, Calvinists—especially English Puritans—felt a compelling inner need to find out whether they were saved. They struggled to recognize in themselves a conversion experience, the process by which God's elect discovered that they had been chosen.

France, the Netherlands, and England, all with powerful Protestant movements, challenged Spanish power in Europe. Until 1559 France was the main threat, with Italy as the battleground, but Spain won that phase. In the 1560s, with France embroiled in its own Wars of Religion, a new challenge came from the 17 provinces of the Netherlands, which Spain ruled. The Dutch rebelled against the heavy taxes and severe Catholic orthodoxy imposed by Philip II. As Spanish armies put down the rebellion in the 10 southern provinces (modern Belgium), merchants and Protestants fled north. Many went to Amsterdam, which replaced Spanish-controlled Antwerp as the economic center of northern Europe. The seven northern provinces gradually took shape as the Dutch Republic, or the United Provinces of the Netherlands. The Dutch turned their resistance into a war for independence from Catholic Spain. The conflict lasted 80 years until 1648, drained Spanish resources, and spread to Asia, Africa, and America. England long remained on the edges of this European struggle, only to emerge in the end as the biggest winner overseas.

NEW FRANCE

About 16 million people lived in France in 1500, more than three times the population of Spain. The French made a few stabs at overseas expansion before 1600, but with little success. "The sun shines for me as for the others," growled King Francis I (1515–47) when reminded that the pope had divided all non-Christian lands between Spain and Portugal. "I should like to see the clause of Adam's will which excludes me from a share of the world."

EARLY FRENCH EXPLORERS

In 1524 Francis sent Giovanni da Verrazano, an Italian, to America in search of a northwest passage to Asia. (Magellan's voyage had shown how difficult it was to sail around South America and across the Pacific.) Verrazano explored the North American coast from the Carolinas to Nova Scotia and noted Manhattan's superb potential as a harbor but found no passage to Asia. Between 1534 and 1543, Jacques Cartier made three voyages to North America. He sailed up the St. Lawrence River in search of Saguenay, a wealthy kingdom rumored to be in the interior. Instead he discovered the severity of a Canadian winter and gave up. For the rest of the century, the French ignored Canada, except for a few fur traders and for fishermen who in growing numbers descended on Newfoundland each year. By the 1580s, the Canadian fisheries rivaled New Spain in the volume of shipping they employed.

After 1550 the French turned to warmer climates. Some Huguenots briefly challenged the Portuguese in Brazil. Others sacked Havana, prompting Spain to turn it into a fortified, year-round naval base under

Black Robe (1991)

**Directed by Bruce Beresford. Starring Lothaire Bluteau (Father Laforgue),
Aden Young (Daniel), Jean Brusseau (Samuel de Champlain), and Sandrine Holt (Annuka).**

In *Black Robe* director Bruce Beresford has given us the most believable film portrayal of 17th-century North America—both the landscape and its peoples—yet produced. This Canada-Australia co-production won six Genie Awards (Canada's equivalent of the Oscar), including best picture, best director, and best cinematography. The film is based on Brian Moore's novel of the same title, and Moore wrote the screenplay. It was filmed on location amidst the spectacular scenery in the Lac St. Jean/Saguenay region of Quebec.

In New France in the 1630s Father Laforgue (Lothaire Bluteau), a young Jesuit, and Daniel (Aden Young), his teenaged assistant and translator, leave on Laforgue's first mission assignment. Samuel de Champlain (Jean Brusseau), the governor of the colony, has persuaded the Algonquin tribe to convey the two to their mission site among the Hurons, far in the interior. Before long Daniel falls in love with Annuka (Sandrine Holt), the beautiful daughter of Algonquin chief Chomina (August Schellenberg). When the priest inadvertently watches the young couple making love, he knows that, according to his faith, he has committed a mortal sin. From that point his journey into the North American heartland threatens to become a descent into hell.

The Algonquins, guided by a dream quest, pursue a logic that makes no sense to the priest. Conversely, his religious message baffles them. Even so, when Chomina is wounded and Laforgue and Daniel are captured by the Iroquois, Annuka seduces their lone guard, kills him, and enables all four of them to escape. Chomina dies of his wounds, politely but firmly rejecting baptism until the end. What Indian, he asks, would want to go to the Christian heaven, populated by many black robes but none of his ancestors?

With the priest's approval, Daniel and Annuka go off by themselves. Laforgue reaches the mission, only to find many of the Indians dead or dying from some European disease. As the film closes, we learn that smallpox would devastate the mission in the following decade, and the Jesuits would abandon it in 1649.

Brian Moore's realism romanticizes nobody but treats both the Jesuits and the Algonquins with great

the command of Admiral Pedro Menéndez de Avilés. Still others planted a settlement on the Atlantic coast of Florida. Menéndez attacked them in 1565, talked them into surrendering, and then executed every man who refused to accept the Catholic faith.

In France the Wars of Religion blocked further efforts at expansion for the rest of the century. King Henry IV (1589–1610), a Protestant, converted to Catholicism and granted limited toleration to Huguenots through the Edict of Nantes in 1598, thus ending the civil wars for the rest of his reign. Henry was a *politique;* he insisted that the survival of the state take precedence over religious differences. Moreover, he believed in toleration for its own sake. Another *politique* was the Catholic soldier and explorer, Samuel de Champlain.

MISSIONS AND FURS

Champlain, whose mother may have been a Huguenot, believed that Catholics and Huguenots could work together, Europeanize the Indians, convert them, and even marry them. Before his death in 1635, he made 11 voyages to Canada. During his second trip (1604–06), he planted a predominantly Huguenot settlement in Acadia (Nova Scotia). In 1608 he sailed up the St. Lawrence River, established friendly relations with the Montagnais, Algonquin, and Huron Indians, and founded Quebec. "Our sons shall wed your daughters," he told them, "and we shall be one people." Many Frenchmen cohabited with Indian women, but only 15 formal marriages took place between

respect. The screenplay drew criticism for its harsh depiction of the Iroquois, but it portrayed them through the eyes of the people they planned to torture. A smaller criticism is that Laforgue is the lone priest on the journey during which he commits the sin of watching Daniel and Annuka make love. Jesuits, however, traveled in pairs precisely so that they would always be accompanied by someone who could hear their confessions.

Bruce Beresford, an Australian, directed *Breaker Morant* (1979), a highly acclaimed film set in the Boer War a century ago, and also *Driving Miss Daisy* (1989).

Black Robe, based on Brian Moore's novel of the same title, is set in 17th-century North America.

them in the 17th century. Champlain's friendliness toward the Indians of the St. Lawrence valley also had some unpleasant consequences. It drew him into their wars against the Iroquois Five Nations farther south. At times, Iroquois hostility almost destroyed New France.

Champlain failed to unite Catholics and Protestants in mutual harmony. Huguenots in France were eager to trade with Canada, but few settled there. Their ministers showed no interest in converting the Indians, whereas Catholic priests became zealous missionaries. In 1625 the French Crown declared that only the Catholic faith could be practiced in New France, thus ending Champlain's dream of a colony more tolerant than France. Acadia soon became Catholic as well.

Early New France is a tale of missionaries and furs, of attempts to convert the Indians and of efforts to trade with them. The career of Etienne Brûlé, the first French *coureur de bois* (roamer of the woods), illustrates how incompatible these goals could be. Champlain left this teenage lad with the Indians in the winter of 1610 to learn their languages and customs. Brûlé absorbed more than that. He enjoyed hunting, the sexual permissiveness of Indian culture, and the chance to go where no European had ever gone before. He soon forgot most of his Christian training. Once, when he was about to be tortured to death by Indians, he tried to cry out to God, but the only prayer he could recall was, ominously, grace before meals. Desperate, he flashed a religious medal, and, when a thunderclap

SAMUEL DE CHAMPLAIN'S DRAWING OF AN EARLY BATTLE WITH THE IROQUOIS Champlain, a French Catholic, befriended the Indians of the St. Lawrence River valley, who were enemies of the Iroquois. Eventually, he was drawn into their battles, as depicted in this drawing.

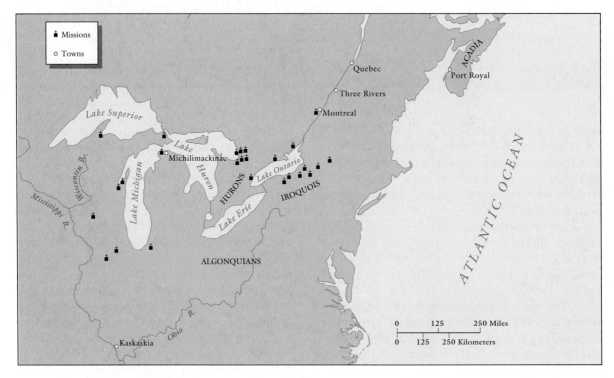

NEW FRANCE AND THE JESUIT MISSIONS

signaled divine approval, the Indians released him. Brûlé apparently learned little from that experience. In 1632 he was caught robbing an Indian grave and was executed and eaten by the offended tribe. *Coureurs de bois*, such as Brûlé, did much for the fur trade but made life difficult for the missionaries.

After 1630 Jesuit missionaries made heroic efforts to bring Christ to the wilderness. The Society of Jesus, or Jesuits, emerged in the 16th century as the Catholic Church's best-educated and most militant religious order. Uncompromising in their opposition to Protestants, Jesuits proved remarkably flexible in dealing with non-Christian peoples, from China to North America. Other missionaries insisted that Indians must be Europeanized before they could be converted, but the Jesuits disagreed. They saw nothing contradictory about a nation of Christians that retained its Indian customs. The Jesuits also tried to protect their converts from contamination by the *coureurs de bois*.

After learning to speak several Algonquian and Iroquoian dialects, the Jesuits began to convert the five confederated Huron nations and baptized several thousand of their members. The Jesuits mastered Indian languages, lived in Indian villages, accepted most Indian customs, and converted 10,000 Indians in 40 years, but this success antagonized Indians who were still attached to their own rituals. When smallpox devastated the Hurons in the 1640s, Jesuits baptized hundreds of dying victims to ensure their salvation. Many of the Indian survivors noticed that death usually followed this mysterious rite, and their resistance grew stronger. A second disaster occurred when the Iroquois attacked, defeated, and scattered the Hurons. Despite these setbacks, the Jesuits' courage remained strong. They were the only Europeans who measured up to Indian standards of bravery under torture. Some of them, such as Isaac Jogues and Jean de Brebeuf, died as martyrs. Even so, their efforts slowly lost ground to the fur trade, especially after the Crown assumed control of New France in 1663.

NEW FRANCE UNDER LOUIS XIV

Royal intervention transformed Canada after 1663 when Louis XIV and his minister, Jean-Baptiste Colbert, took charge of the colony and tried to turn it into a model absolutist society—peaceful, orderly, deferential. Government was in the hands of two appointive officials, a governor-general responsible for military and diplomatic affairs, and an *intendant* who administered justice. Justice was made affordable to everyone, partly by banning lawyers. The people paid few taxes, and the church tithe was set at half its rate in France.

The governor appointed all militia officers and granted promotion through merit, not by selling commissions. When the Crown sent professional soldiers to New France after 1660, the governor put them under the command of Canadian officers, who knew the woodlands—a decision that had no parallel in the English colonies. Colbert also sent 774 young women to the St. Lawrence, to provide brides for settlers and soldiers. He offered bonuses to couples who produced large families and fined fathers whose children failed to marry while still in their teens. Between 1663 and 1700, the population of New France increased from 3,000 to about 14,000 even though close to 70 percent of 10,000 immigrants throughout the colonial era went back to France, usually to claim a tiny inheritance. About one-fourth of the population concentrated in three cities—Quebec, Three Rivers, and Montreal. Montreal, the largest, became the center of the fur trade.

Farming took hold in the St. Lawrence valley, and by the 1690s Canada was growing enough wheat to feed itself and to give its *habitants*, or settlers, a level of comfort about equal to that of contemporary New Englanders. A new class of *seigneurs*, or gentry, claimed most of the land between Quebec and Montreal, but they had few feudal privileges and never exercised the kind of power wielded by aristocrats in France. Few of them even became militia captains, an office open to *habitants*. Yet when the Church was also the *seigneur*, as often happened near Quebec and Montreal, the obligations imposed on farmers could be heavy.

Colbert even tried to ban Frenchmen from Indian territory by limiting the fur trade to annual fairs at Montreal and Quebec, thus bringing the Indians to the settlers, not the settlers to the Indians. Still, he failed to rein in the *coureurs de bois*, although a stint in the forests was becoming something a man did just once or twice in his youth, before settling down. Colbert's policy failed and, by 1700, even led to a quiet rebellion in the west. Hundreds of Frenchmen settled in the Mississippi River valley between the missions of Cahokia and Kaskaskia in what became the Illinois country. By 1750 these communities contained 3,000 residents.

The settlers rejected *seigneurs*, feudal dues, tithes, and compulsory militia service. They did, however, import African slaves from Louisiana. Most settlers prospered as wheat farmers, and many married Christian Indian women from the missions.

But Canada did not long remain the center of French overseas activity. Like other Europeans, most of the French who crossed the Atlantic preferred the warmer climes of the Caribbean. At first the French in the West Indies joined with other enemies of Spain to prey upon Spanish colonies and ships, contributing the word "buccaneer" (*boucanier*) to the English language. Then they transformed the island colonies of Saint-Domingue (modern Haiti), Guadeloupe, and Martinique into centers of sugar production, where a small planter class prospered from the labor of thousands of slaves. The sugar islands were worth far more than Canada. In the late 18th century, Saint-Domingue became the world's richest colony.

THE DUTCH AND SWEDISH SETTLEMENTS

For most of the 17th century, the Dutch were more active overseas than the French. In alliance with France during Europe's Thirty Years' War (1618–48), the Dutch wore down and finally destroyed Spain's bid for "universal monarchy" in Europe. The Netherlands, the most densely populated part of Europe, surpassed northern Italy in manufacturing and moved ahead of all competitors in finance, shipping, and trade. The Dutch Republic, with a population of two million by 1600, offered an ideological as well as a political challenge to Spanish absolutism.

In contrast to Spain, which stood for Catholic orthodoxy and the centralizing tendencies of Europe's "new monarchies," Dutch republicanism emphasized local liberties, prosperity, and, in major centers such as Amsterdam, religious toleration. Political power was decentralized to the cities and their wealthy merchants, who favored religious toleration, tried to keep trade as free as possible, and resisted the monarchical ambitions of the House of Orange. The prince of Orange usually served as *stadholder* (captain general) of Holland, the richest province, and commanded its armies.

The Dutch Republic—with Protestant dissenters from many countries, a sizable Jewish community, and a Catholic minority that approached 40 percent of the population—was actually a polyglot confederation. Amsterdam's merchant republicanism competed with the Dutch reformed church for the allegiance of the people. Only during a military crisis could the prince of Orange mobilize the Dutch Reformed clergy and impose something like Calvinist orthodoxy, even on the cities. The States General, to which each province sent representatives, became a weak central government for the republic. The broader public did not vote or participate actively in public life. The tension between tolerant merchant republicanism and Calvinist orthodoxy carried over into New Netherland.

Profit was the dominant motive in Dutch expansion overseas. By 1600 Dutch commercial assets were already enormous. The Bank of Amsterdam, founded in 1609, was the most important financial institution in Europe for the next century. By 1620 Dutch foreign trade probably exceeded that of the rest of Europe combined. Even during the long war with Spain, the Dutch traded with Lisbon and Seville for products from the East Indies and America. This effrontery so annoyed Philip II that he twice committed a grave blunder in the 1590s, when he confiscated all the Dutch ships crowding his ports. The Dutch retaliated by sailing into the Atlantic and Indian Oceans to acquire colonial goods at the source. Spanish power finally crumbled. The Dutch threat forced Spain to use expensive convoys to protect the silver fleets crossing the Atlantic. Spain's supply of precious metals, after peaking in the 1590s, fell sharply in the 1630s, as the rapidly declining Indian population reduced the labor supply for the silver mines.

THE EAST AND WEST INDIA COMPANIES

In 1602 the States General chartered the Dutch East India Company, the richest corporation the world had yet seen. It pressured Spain where it was weakest, in the Portuguese East Indies. Elbowing the Portuguese out of the Spice Islands and even out of Nagasaki in Japan, the Dutch set up their own capital at Batavia (now Jakarta) on the island of Java.

The Atlantic and North America also attracted the Dutch, though never as strongly as did the East Indies. In 1609, during a 12-year truce between Spain and the Netherlands, Henry Hudson, an Englishman in Dutch service, sailed up what the Dutch called the North River (the English later renamed it the Hudson) and claimed the whole area for the Netherlands. In 1614 some Lutheran refugees from Amsterdam built a fort near modern Albany to trade with the Mahicans and Iroquois for furs, but they did not occupy the site on a year-round basis.

In 1621, when the truce expired between the Netherlands and Spain, the States General chartered the Dutch West India Company and gave it jurisdiction over the African slave trade, Brazil, the Caribbean, and North America. The West India Company harbored strong Orangist sympathies and even some Calvinist fervor, sustained by refugees fleeing from the Spanish army. Within the company, other activities—such as Piet Heyns's capture of the entire Spanish treasure fleet in 1627—were more attractive than opportunities in North America. The company took over Portugal's slave-trading posts in West Africa and for a while even dominated Angola. It also occupied the richest sugar-producing region of Brazil until the Portuguese took it back, as well as Angola, in the 1640s.

In North America the Dutch claimed the Delaware, the Hudson, and the Connecticut river valleys. The company put most of its effort, and some of its religious fervor, into the Hudson valley. The first permanent settlers arrived in 1624. Two years later, Deacon Pierre Minuit, leading 30 Walloon (French-speaking) Protestant refugee families, bought Manhattan Island from the Indians and founded the port of New Amsterdam. The Dutch established Fort Orange (modern Albany) 150 miles upriver for trade with the Iroquois. Much like New France, New Netherland depended on the goodwill of nearby Indians, and the fur trade gave the colony a similar urban flavor. But unlike the settlers of New France, few Dutchmen ventured into the deep woods. There were no *coureurs de bois*, and hardly any missionaries. The Indians brought their furs to Fort Orange and exchanged them for firearms and other goods that the Dutch sold more cheaply than anyone else.

In other ways, New Netherland resembled New France. In the 1630s, decades before the French created *seigneuries* in the St. Lawrence valley, the Dutch established "patroonships," vast estates under a single landlord, mostly along the Hudson. But patroonships never thrived, largely because few Dutch settlers had much interest in becoming peasants. The one excep-tion was Rensselaerswyck, a gigantic estate on both banks of the Hudson above and below Fort Orange, which exported wheat and flour to the Caribbean.

NEW NETHERLAND AS A PLURALISTIC SOCIETY

New Netherland became North America's first ex-periment in ethnic and religious pluralism. The Dutch themselves were a mixed people with a Flemish majority and a Walloon minority. Both came to the colony. So did Danes, Norwegians, Swedes, Finns, Germans, and Scots. One observer in the 1640s counted 18 languages spoken by the 450 inhabitants of New Amsterdam.

The government of the colony tried to utilize this diversity by drawing upon two conflicting prece-dents from the Netherlands. On the one hand, it ap-pealed to religious refugees by emphasizing the company's Protestant role in the struggle against Spain. This policy, roughly speaking, reflected the Orangist position in the Netherlands. On the other hand, the West India Company sometimes recog-nized that acceptance of religious diversity might stimulate trade. The pursuit of prosperity through toleration was the normal role of the city of Amster-dam in Dutch politics. Minuit and Pieter Stuyvesant represented the religious formula for unity, and they resisted toleration even in the name of commerce.

After Minuit returned to Europe in 1631, the em-phasis shifted rapidly from piety to trade. The Dutch sold muskets to the Iroquois to expand their own ac-cess to the fur trade. They began to export grain to the Caribbean, a more elusive goal in which the pa-troonships were supposed to give the colony a strong agricultural base. In 1643, however, Willem Kieft, a stubborn and quarrelsome governor, slaughtered a tribe of Indian refugees to whom he had granted asy-lum from other Indians. This Pavonia Massacre, which took place across the Hudson from Manhat-tan, set off a war with nearby Algonquian nations that nearly destroyed New Netherland. By the time Stuyvesant replaced Kieft in 1647, the colony's pop-ulation had fallen to about 700 people. An autocrat, Stuyvesant made peace and then strengthened town governments and the Dutch Reformed Church. During his administration, the population rose to more than 6,000 by 1664, twice that of New France. Most newcomers arrived as members of healthy families who reproduced readily, enabling the population to double once every generation.

SWEDISH AND ENGLISH ENCROACHMENTS

Minuit, back in Europe, organized another refugee project, this one for Flemings who had been uprooted by the Spanish war. When Dutch authorities refused to back him, he turned for support to the Protestant kingdom of Sweden. Financed by private Dutch capital, he returned to America in 1638 with Flemish and Swedish settlers to found New Sweden, with its capital at Fort Christina (modern Wilmington) near the mouth of the Delaware River, on land claimed by New Netherland. After Minuit died on his return trip to Europe, the colony became less Flemish and Calvinist and more Swedish and Lutheran, at a time when Stuyvesant was trying to make New Netherland an orthodox Calvinist society. The Swedes and Dutch lost another common bond in 1648 when their long war with Spain finally ended. In 1654 the Swedes seized Fort Casimir, a Dutch post that provided access to the Delaware. In response, Stuyvesant took over all of New Sweden the next year, and Amsterdam sent over settlers to guarantee Dutch control. Stuyvesant actively persecuted Lutherans in New Amsterdam but had to tolerate them in the Delaware Valley settlements. Orthodoxy and harmony were not easily reconciled.

The English, already entrenched around Chesapeake Bay to the south and New England to the east (discussed in the next section), threatened to overwhelm the Dutch as they moved from New England onto Long Island and into what is now Westchester County, New York. Kieft welcomed them in the 1640s and gave them local privileges greater than those enjoyed by the Dutch, in the hope that their farms and herds would give the colony valuable exports to the Caribbean. Stuyvesant regarded these "Yankees" (a Dutch word that probably meant "land pirates") as good Calvinists, English-speaking equivalents of his Dutch Reformed settlers. They agitated for a more active role in government, but their loyalty was questionable. If England attacked the colony, would these Puritans side with the Dutch Calvinists or the Anglican invaders? Which ran deeper, their religious or their ethnic loyalties? Stuyvesant learned the unpleasant answer when England attacked him in 1664.

THE CHALLENGE FROM ELIZABETHAN ENGLAND

England's interest in America emerged slowly, even though ships from Bristol may have reached North America several years before Columbus's first voyage. If so, the English did nothing about it. In 1497 Henry VII (1485–1509) sent Giovanni Cabato (John Cabot), an Italian mariner who had moved to Bristol, to search for a northwest passage to Asia. Cabot probably reached Newfoundland, which he took to be part of Asia. He sailed again in 1498 with five ships but was lost at sea. Only one vessel returned, but Cabot's voyages gave England a vague claim to portions of the North American coast.

THE ENGLISH REFORMATION

When interest in America revived during the reign of Elizabeth I (1558–1603), England was rapidly becoming a Protestant kingdom. Elizabeth's father, Henry VIII (1509–47), desperate for a male heir, had broken with the pope to divorce his queen and had remarried. He proclaimed himself the "Only Supreme Head" of the Church of England, confiscated monastic lands, and opened the way for serious Protestant reformers. Under Elizabeth's younger brother Edward VI (1547–53), the government embraced Protestantism. When Edward died, Elizabeth's older sister Mary I (1553–58) reimposed Catholicism, burned hundreds of Protestants at the stake, and drove thousands into exile, where many of them became Calvinists. Elizabeth, however, accepted Protestantism, and in her reign the exiles returned. The Church of England, as reconstituted under Elizabeth, became an odd compromise—Calvinist in doctrine and theology, still largely Catholic in structure, liturgy, and ritual. By the time of Elizabeth's death, England's Catholics were a tiny, persecuted minority, but one with powerful allies abroad, especially in Spain.

Some Protestants demanded a fuller reformation—the eradication of Catholic vestiges and the replacement of the Anglican Book of Common Prayer with sermons and psalms as the dominant mode of worship. These "Puritans" resisted any relaxation of Calvinist rigor and played a major role in English expansion overseas. More extreme Protestants, called Separatists, denied that the Church of England was a true church and began to set up independent congregations of their own. Some of them would found the small colony of Plymouth.

HAWKINS AND DRAKE

In 1560 England was a rather backward country of three million people. Its chief export was woolen cloth, most of which was shipped to the Netherlands, where the Dutch turned it into finished textiles. During the 16th century the numbers of both people and sheep grew rapidly, and they sometimes competed for the same land. When farms were enclosed for sheep pasture, laborers were set adrift, creating the impression that England was overpopulated. Even without the enclosures, internal migration was becoming routine for a great many people. Thousands headed for London. Although deaths greatly outnumbered births in London, new arrivals lifted the city's population from 50,000 in 1500 to 200,000 in 1600 and, including the suburbs, to 575,000 by 1700. By then London was the largest city in western Europe, containing more than 10 percent of England's population of five million. After 1600 internal migration fueled overseas settlement. Before then interest in America centered not in London, but in the southwestern ports already involved in the Newfoundland fisheries.

Taking advantage of friendly relations that still prevailed between England and Spain, John Hawkins of Plymouth made three voyages to New Spain between 1562 and 1569. On his first trip he bought slaves from the Portuguese in West Africa and sold them to the Spaniards in Hispaniola where, by paying all legal duties, he tried to set himself up as a legitimate trader. Spanish authorities disapproved, and on his second voyage he had to trade at gunpoint. On his third trip, the Spanish viceroy, in command of a much larger fleet, trapped his six vessels in a Mexican port. After promising Hawkins quarter, the viceroy sank four of his ships. Hawkins and his young kinsman Francis Drake escaped, both vowing vengeance.

Drake even began to talk of freeing slaves from Spanish tyranny. His most dramatic exploit came between 1577 and 1580 when he rounded Cape Horn and plundered Spanish possessions along the undefended Pacific coast of Peru. Knowing that the Spaniards would be waiting for him if he returned by the same route, he sailed north, explored San Francisco Bay, and continued west around the world to England—the first circumnavigation since

Magellan's voyage more than half a century earlier. Elizabeth rewarded him with a knighthood.

GILBERT, IRELAND, AND AMERICA

By the 1560s the idea of permanent colonization intrigued several Englishmen. England had a model close at hand in Ireland, which the English Crown had claimed for centuries. As of 1560, however, England had achieved little direct control over Ireland, except around Dublin. After 1560 the English tried to impose their agriculture, language, local government, legal system, aristocracy, and religion upon the clan-based, mostly pastoral and Gaelic-speaking Irish. The Irish responded by becoming more intensely Roman Catholic than ever.

The English formed their preconceptions about American Indians largely from contact with the Irish who, claimed one Elizabethan, "live like beasts, void of law and all good order" and are "more uncivil, more uncleanly, more barbarous and more brutish in their customs and demeanors, than in any part of the world that is known." The English tried to conquer Ulster in the northeast and Munster in the southwest, the most Gaelic provinces. In Ulster the Protestant invaders drove out most of the residents and took over the land. In Munster they ejected the Catholic leaders and tried to force the remaining Catholic Irish to become tenants under Protestant landlords. Terror became an acceptable tactic, as when the English slaughtered 200 Irish at a Christmas feast in 1574.

Sir Humphrey Gilbert, a well-educated humanist, was one of the most brutal of Elizabeth's captains in the Irish wars of the 1560s. "He thought his dogs' ears too good to hear the speech of the greatest nobleman amongst them," one admirer noted. In subduing Munster in 1569, Gilbert killed nearly everyone in his path and destroyed all the crops, a strategy that the English later employed against Indians. Massacring women and children "was the way to kill the men of war by famine," explained one apologist. For 80 years after 1560, Ireland attracted more English settlers than all American and Caribbean colonies combined. Only after 1641, when the Irish rose and killed thousands of English settlers, did the Western Hemisphere replace Ireland as a preferred site for English colonization.

Fresh from his Irish exploits, Gilbert began to think about colonizing America. In an essay titled

SOUTHEASTERN INDIANS AT WORK Jacques Le Moyne, an artist who accompanied the French Huguenot expedition to Florida in 1564, painted this scene of Indians in a canoe loaded with produce. They are rowing past one of their capacious storehouses. Engraving by Theodore de Bry.

"A Discourse How Her Majesty May Annoy the King of Spain" (1577), he proposed that England grab control of the Newfoundland fisheries, a nursery of seamen and naval power. He urged the founding of settlements close enough to New Spain to provide bases for plundering. He obtained a royal patent in 1578 and sent out a fleet, but his ships got into a fight somewhere short of America and limped back to England. He tried again in 1583. This time his fleet sailed north to claim Newfoundland. The crews of 22 Spanish and Portuguese fishing vessels and 18 French and English ships listened in astonishment as he read his royal patent to them, divided up the land among them, assigned them rents, and established the Church of England among this mostly Catholic group. He then sailed away to explore more of the American coast. His own ship went under during a storm.

RALEGH, ROANOKE, AND WAR WITH SPAIN

Gilbert's half-brother, Sir Walter Ralegh (or Raleigh), obtained his own patent from the queen and tried twice to plant a colony in North America. In 1585 he sent a large expedition to Roanoke Island in Pamlico Sound, but the settlers planted no crops and exasperated the Indians with demands for food during a time of drought. In June 1586 the English killed the local chief, Wingina, whose main offense was apparently a threat to resettle his people on the mainland and leave the colonists to starve—or work. Days later, when the expected supply vessels failed to arrive on schedule, the colonists sailed back to England on the ships of Sir Francis Drake, who had just burned the Spanish city of St. Augustine with the support of Florida Indians, whom he freed from service to the Spanish.

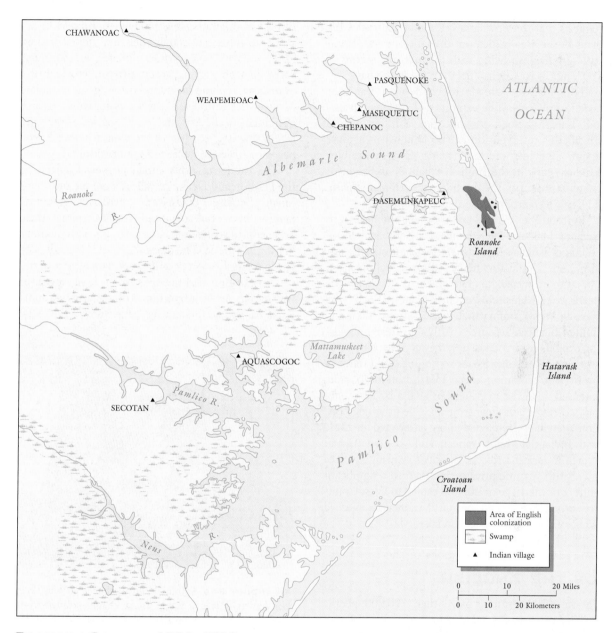

ROANOKE COLONY, 1584–1590

The supply ships reached Roanoke a little later, only to find the site abandoned. They left a small garrison there and sailed off in quest of Spanish plunder. The garrison was never heard from again.

Ralegh sent a second expedition to Roanoke in 1587, one that included some women—an indication that he envisioned a permanent colony, not just an outpost for raiding New Spain. When Governor John White went back to England for more supplies, his return to Roanoke was delayed by the assault of the Spanish Armada on England in 1588. By the time he reached Roanoke in 1590, the settlers had vanished, leaving a cryptic message—"CROA-TOAN"—carved on a tree. The colonists may have settled among the Chesapeake nation of Indians near the entrance to Chesapeake Bay. Sketchy evidence suggests that the Powhatans, the most powerful Indians in the area, wiped out the Chesapeakes, along with any English living with them, in the spring of 1607, just as an English fleet arrived in the bay.

The Spanish Armada touched off a war that lasted until 1604. The exploits of Hawkins, Drake, and Ralegh helped provoke this conflict, as did Elizabeth's intervention in the Dutch war against Spain. The loss of the Armada, first to nimbler English ships in the English Channel and then to fierce storms off the Irish coast, crippled Spain. The war also strained England's resources.

By 1600 Richard Hakluyt the elder and his cousin Richard Hakluyt the younger were publishing accounts of English exploits overseas and offering advice on how to make future colonization efforts more successful. The Hakluyts celebrated the deeds of Hawkins, Drake, Gilbert, and Ralegh, who were all West Country men with large ambitions and limited financial resources. Although their plundering exploits continued to pay, they could not afford to sustain a colony like Roanoke until it could return a profit. But beginning in the 1590s, London became intensely involved in American affairs by launching privateering fleets against Spain. Even though London merchants remained more interested in trade with India, the Mediterranean, and Muscovy than in North American projects, the city's growing involvement with Atlantic privateering marked a significant shift. The marriage of London capital to West Country experience would permit Virginia to succeed where earlier settlements had failed.

THE SWARMING OF THE ENGLISH

In the 17th century, more than 700,000 people sailed from Europe or Africa to the English colonies in North America and the Caribbean. Most of the European migrants were unmarried younger sons. With no inheritance at home, they hoped to improve their lot in a warmer climate. Instead, most spent their time trying to stay alive under the threat of malaria, typhoid fever, and other lethal maladies. Most of the Europeans arrived as servants. At first even many of the Africans were regarded as servants rather than slaves. Most of the men, whether Europeans or Africans, never fathered children.

The Europeans who settled in New England or the Hudson and Delaware valleys were the most fortunate. Because Puritans and Quakers migrated as families into wholesome and healthy regions, their population expanded at a rate far beyond anything known in Europe. The descendants of this small, idealistic minority soon became a substantial part of the total population, and they played a role in American history far out of proportion to their original numbers. As the accompanying table shows, the New

AN INDIAN GOD A John White painting called *Their Idol* depicts Kewás, a statue four feet high, carved from wood by the Indians on the island of Roanoke. Engraving by Theodore de Bry.

THE PATTERN OF SETTLEMENT IN THE ENGLISH COLONIES UP TO 1700

	Who Came (in thousands)		Population in 1700 (in thousands)	
Region	*Europeans*	*Africans*	*Europeans*	*Africans*
West Indies	220 (29.6%)	316 (42.5%)	33 (8.3%)	115 (28.8%)
South	135 (18.1%)	30 (4.0%)	82 (20.5%)	22 (5.5%)
Mid-Atlantic	20 (2.7%)	2 (0.3%)	51 (12.8%)	3 (0.8%)
New England	20 (2.7%)	1 (0.1%)	91 (22.8%)	2 (0.5%)
Total	395 (53.1%)	349 (46.9%)	257 (64.4%)	142 (35.6%)

England and Middle Atlantic colonies together attracted only 5.4 percent of the immigrants, but by 1700 they contained 37 percent of all the people in the English colonies and 55 percent of the Europeans.

THE CHESAPEAKE AND WEST INDIAN COLONIES

In 1606 King James I of England (1603–25) chartered the Virginia Company with authority to colonize North America between the 34th and 45th parallels. The company had two headquarters. One, in the English city of Plymouth, raised only a small amount of capital but won jurisdiction over the northern portion of the grant. Known as the Plymouth Company, it carried on the West Country expansionist traditions of Gilbert and Ralegh. In 1607 it planted a colony at Sagadahoc on the coast of Maine. But the colonists found the cold winter intimidating, and when the Abenaki Indians refused to trade with them, they abandoned the site in September 1608. The Plymouth Company ran out of money and gave up.

The other branch, which had its offices in London, decided to colonize the Chesapeake Bay area. In 1607 the London Company sent out three ships carrying 104 settlers. They sailed up the Powhatan River (which they renamed the James), landed at a defensible peninsula, built a fort and other crude buildings, and called the place Jamestown. The investors hoped to find gold or silver, a northwest passage to Asia, a cure for syphilis, or other valuable products for sale in Europe. The settlers expected to persuade or compel local Indians to work for them, much as the Spanish had done. If the Indians proved hostile, the settlers were told to form alliances with more distant Indians and subdue those who resisted. Company officials did not realize that a war chief named Powhatan ruled virtually all of the Indians below the fall line.[1] He had no rival within striking distance. The company's other expectations proved equally skewed.

THE JAMESTOWN DISASTER

Jamestown was a deathtrap. Every summer the James River became contaminated around James-

---

[1] The *fall line*, defined by the first waterfall encountered on each river by a vessel sailing inland from the sea, marked a significant barrier to penetration of the continent. In the South, the area below the falls is called the *tidewater*. The land between the falls and the Appalachians is called the *piedmont*.

CAPTAIN JOHN SMITH SUBDUING OPECHANCANOUGH, THE WARRIOR CHIEF OF THE PAMUNKEY INDIANS, 1608 Note the difference in height between Opechancanough and Smith, even as depicted by a European artist.

town and sent out killing waves of dysentery and typhoid fever. Before long malaria also set in. Only 38 of the original 104 settlers survived the first year. Of the 325 who came before 1609, fewer than 100 remained alive in the spring of that year.

The survivors owed their good fortune to the resourcefulness of Captain John Smith, a soldier and adventurer who outmaneuvered other members of the colony's ruling council and took charge. When his explorations uncovered neither gold or silver nor any quick route across the continent to Asia, he concentrated instead on sheer survival. He tried to awe Powhatan, maintain friendly relations with him, and buy corn. Through the help of Pocahontas, Powhatan's 12-year-old daughter, he avoided war. Though Smith gave conflicting versions of the story later on, he clearly believed that Pocahontas saved his life in December 1607. But food remained scarce. The colony had too many gentlemen and specialized craftsmen (including a perfumer) who considered farming beneath their dignity. Over

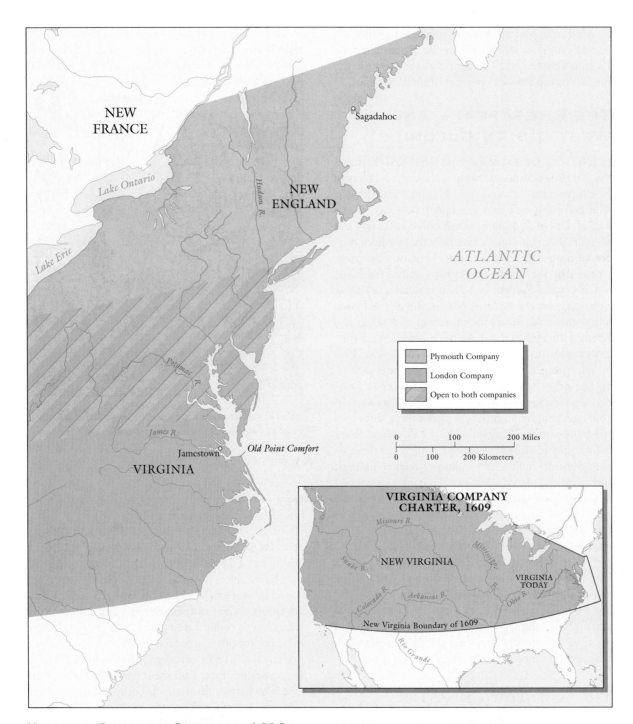

VIRGINIA COMPANY CHARTER, 1606

their protests, Smith set them to work raising grain for four hours a day.

In 1609 the London Company sent out 600 more settlers under Lieutenant Governor Thomas Gates,

but his ship ran aground on Bermuda, and the crew spent a year building another vessel. About 400 new settlers reached Virginia before Gates arrived. Smith, after suffering a severe injury in an explosion, was shipped back to England, and the colony lacked firm leadership for the next year. Wearying Powhatan with their endless demands for corn at a time of severe drought, the settlers provoked the Indian war that Smith had avoided. They almost starved during the winter of 1610. One settler was executed for cannibalizing his wife. Two were tied to posts and left to starve to death for raiding company stores. Some escaped to the Indians, but those who were caught fleeing were executed.

When Gates finally reached Jamestown with 175 colonists in June 1610, he found only 60 settlers alive (plus a garrison at Point Comfort) and the food supply nearly exhausted. Gates despaired, packed everyone aboard ship, and started downriver. Virginia was going the way of Roanoke and Sagadahoc, despite its greater resources. Instead, the small fleet came abreast of the new governor, Thomas West, baron de la Warr, sailing up the James with 300 new colonists. They all went back to Jamestown, and the colony managed to survive.

De la Warr and Gates found themselves in the middle of the colony's first Indian war, which lasted from 1609 to 1614. Powhatan's warriors picked off any settlers who strayed far from Jamestown. The English retaliated by slaughtering whole villages and destroying crops, as they had in Ireland. In August 1610, for example, Commander George Percy attacked the Paspahegh Indians, who had refused to give the colonists more corn and had sheltered runaways. He burned the Paspahegh's crops, massacred most of them, captured the "queen" and her children, and started back to Jamestown by boat. When the soldiers murmured because "the queen and her children were spared," Percy had the children thrown overboard and let his men shoot "out their brains in the water." At Jamestown, a settler suggested burning the queen alive. Percy, feeling merciful, had her put to the sword instead. Percy's strategy was terroristic. The slaughter of one tribe might intimidate others. The war finally ended after the English captured Pocahontas and used her as a hostage to negotiate peace.

THE CAPTURE OF POCAHONTAS This engraving by an unknown artist shows Pocahontas being lured aboard an English ship by an Indian named Iopassus whose animal skins and feathers are worn in a way that makes him resemble a devil. The artist clearly sympathizes with Pocahontas.

She converted to Christianity and in 1614 married John Rolfe, a widower who had fallen in love with her.

Despite the Indian war, the colony's prospects improved after 1610. The governors imposed martial law on the settlers and sent some of them to healthier locations, such as Henrico, 50 miles upstream. Through the efforts of John Rolfe, the colony began to produce a cash crop. In 1613 Rolfe imported a mild strain of tobacco from the West Indies. It brought such a good price in England that the king—who had insisted no one could build a colony "upon smoke"—was proved wrong. Soon, settlers were even growing tobacco in the streets of Jamestown.

REORGANIZATION, REFORM, AND CRISIS

In 1609 a new royal charter extended Virginia's boundaries to the Pacific. A third charter in 1612 made the London Company a joint-stock company. It resembled a modern corporation except that each stockholder had only one vote regardless of how many shares he owned. The stockholders met quarterly in the company's General Court but entrusted everyday management to the company's treasurer, who until 1618 was Sir Thomas Smyth, a wealthy London merchant. The lack of profits led to turmoil among the stockholders, who replaced Smyth in 1618 with Sir Edwin Sandys, the Puritan son of the archbishop of York.

In 1618 the company adopted an ambitious reform program for Virginia. It encouraged economic diversification, such as glassblowing, planting grape vines, and raising silkworms. English common law replaced martial law. The settlers were allowed to elect their own assembly, the House of Burgesses, to meet with the governor and his council and to make local laws. Finally—the most popular reform—settlers were permitted to own land. Under this "headright" system, a colonist received 50 acres for each person whose passage to Virginia he financed. By 1623 Sandys had shipped 4,000 settlers to Virginia, but the economic diversification program failed. Only tobacco found a market. Corn still provided

THE OPECHANCANOUGH MASSACRE OF 1622 This famous event, as portrayed in an engraving from the workshop of Theodore de Bry, depicts the warriors as treacherous, bloodthirsty savages and the settlers as innocent victims.

most of the food. Instead of growing silkworms and grapes, Virginians raised Indian crops with Indian methods, which meant using hoes instead of plows.

The flood of newcomers strained the food supply and soured relations with the Indians, especially after Powhatan died and was succeeded by his militant brother, Opechancanough. On Good Friday in March 1622, the new chief launched an attack intended to wipe out the whole colony. Without a last-minute warning from a friendly Indian, Jamestown might not have survived. As it turned out, 347 settlers were killed that day, and most of the outlying settlements were destroyed. Newcomers who arrived in subsequent months had nowhere to go and, with food again scarce, hundreds died over the winter. "Oh, that you did see my daily and hourly sighs, groans, and tears, and thumps that I afford my own breast, and rue and curse the time of my birth, with holy Job," complained Richard Frethorne, a servant, to his parents a year after the massacre, "I thought no head had been able to hold so much water as hath and doth daily flow from mine eyes."

Back in London, Smyth and his allies turned against Sandys, withdrew their capital, and asked the king to intervene. A royal commission visited the colony and found only 1,200 settlers alive out of the 6,000 sent over since 1607. In 1624 the king declared the London Company bankrupt and assumed direct control of Virginia, making it the first royal colony, with a governor and council appointed by the Crown. The London Company had invested some £200,000 in the enterprise, equal to £1,400 or £1,500 for every surviving settler, at a time when skilled English craftsmen were lucky to earn £50 a year. Such extravagance guaranteed that future colonies would be organized in different ways.

TOBACCO, SERVANTS, AND SURVIVAL

Between Opechancanough's 1622 attack and the 1640s, Virginia proved that it could survive. Despite an appalling death rate, about a thousand new settlers came each year, and population grew slowly, to 5,200 by 1634 and 8,100 by 1640. For 10 years the settlers warred against Opechancanough. In 1623 they poisoned 200 Indians they had invited to a peace conference. In most years they attacked the Indians just before harvest time, destroying their crops and villages. By the time both sides made peace in 1632, all Indians had been expelled from the peninsula between the James and York Rivers below Jamestown.

That area became secure for tobacco, and the export of tobacco financed the importation of indentured servants, even after the price of tobacco fell sharply in the 1630s. Most servants were young men who agreed to work for a term of years in exchange for the cost of passage, for bed and board during their years of service, and for modest freedom dues when their term expired. Those signing indentures in England usually had valuable skills and negotiated terms of four or five years. Those arriving without an indenture, most of whom were younger and less skilled, were sold by the ship captain to a planter. Those over age 19 served five years. Those under 19 served until age 24. The system turned servants into freemen who hoped to prosper on their own. Most former servants became tenants for several years while they tried to save enough to buy their own land. Better tobacco prices enabled many to succeed between 1640 and 1660, but those who imported the servants were always in a stronger economic position, collecting the headright of 50 acres for each one. Because deaths still outnumbered births, the colony needed a steady flow of newcomers to survive.

In 1634 Virginia was divided into counties, each with its own justices of the peace, who sat together as the county court and, by filling their own vacancies, soon became a self-perpetuating oligarchy. Most counties also became Anglican parishes, with a church and a vestry of prominent laymen, usually the justices. The vestry managed temporal affairs for the church, including the choice of the minister. Though the king did not recognize the House of Burgesses until 1639, it met almost every year after 1619 and by 1640 was well established. Before long, only a justice could hope to be elected as a burgess.

Until 1660 many former servants managed to acquire land, and some even served on the county courts and in the House of Burgesses. As tobacco prices fell after 1660, however, upward mobility became more difficult. Political offices usually went to the richest 15 percent of the settlers, those able to pay their own way across the Atlantic. They, and eventually their descendants, monopolized the posts of justice of the peace and vestryman, the pool from which burgesses and councillors were normally chosen. Virginia was becoming an oligarchy.

MARYLAND

Maryland had different origins but became much the same kind of society as Virginia. It grew out of

the social and religious vision of Sir George Calvert and his son Cecilius, both of whom became Catholics and looked to America as a refuge for persecuted English and Irish people of that faith. Sir George, a prominent officeholder, had invested in the London Company. When he resigned his royal office because of his Catholicism, King James

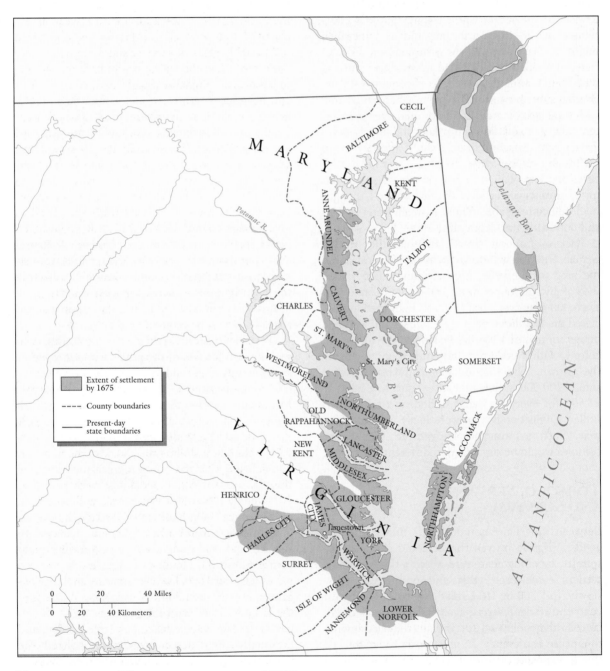

VIRGINIA AND MARYLAND, CIRCA 1675

I made him baron Baltimore in the Irish peerage. Both James and Charles I (1625–49) encouraged his colonial projects.

The Maryland charter of 1632 made Baltimore "lord proprietor" of the colony. It came close to making Baltimore king within Maryland, the most sweeping delegation of power that the Crown could make. After 1630 most new colonies were proprietary projects, often with the Maryland charter as a model. Many of them embodied the distinctive social ideals of their founders.

George Calvert died as the Maryland patent was being issued, and Cecilius inherited Maryland and the peerage. Like Champlain, he believed that Catholics and Protestants could live in peace in the same colony, but he expected the servants, most of whom were Protestants, to continue to serve the Catholic gentlemen of the colony after their indentures expired. Baltimore made the gentlemen manor lords, with the power to preside over courts leet and courts baron, feudal tribunals that were nearly obsolete in England.

Those plans were never fulfilled. The condition of English Catholics improved under Charles I and his queen, Henrietta Maria, a French Catholic for whom the province was named. Because few Catholics emigrated, most settlers were Protestants. The civil war that erupted in England in 1642 (see below) soon spread to Maryland. Protestants overthrew Lord Baltimore's regime several times between 1642 and 1660, but the English state always sided with him, even when the Puritans were in power there. During these struggles, Baltimore conceded a bicameral legislature to the colony, knowing that Protestants would dominate the elective assembly and that Catholics would control the appointive council. He also approved the Toleration Act of 1649, which granted freedom of worship to Christians (but not to Maryland's tiny Jewish minority).

The manorial system did not survive these upheavals. Protestant servants, after their indentures expired, acquired their own land rather than become tenants under Catholic manor lords, most of whom died or returned to England. When Maryland's unrest ended around 1660, the colony was raising tobacco, corn, and livestock and was governed by county courts similar to those in Virginia. If anything, the proprietary family's Catholicism and its claims to special privileges made the Maryland assembly more articulate than the Virginia House of Burgesses in demanding the liberties of Englishmen. Otherwise religion provided the biggest difference between the two colonies. Virginia was Anglican, but Maryland had no established church and no vestries. Most Maryland Protestants had to make do without ministers until the 1690s.

CHESAPEAKE FAMILY LIFE

At first, men outnumbered women in Virginia and Maryland by 5 to 1. Among new immigrant servants as late as the 1690s, the ratio was still 5 to 2. Population became self-sustaining about 1680, when live births finally began to outnumber deaths. Among adults this transition made little difference before 1700. Until then, most prominent people were immigrants.

Life expectancy slowly improved as the colonists planted orchards to provide wholesome cider to drink, but it still remained much lower than in England, where those who survived childhood could expect to live into their fifties. The Chesapeake immigrants had survived childhood diseases in Europe, but men at age 20 could expect to live only to about 45, with 70 percent dead by age 50. Women died at even younger ages, especially in areas ravaged by malaria, a dangerous disease for pregnant women. In those places women rarely lived to age 40. England's patriarchal families found it hard to survive in the Chesapeake. About 70 percent of the men never married or, if they did, produced no children. Most men waited years after completing their service before they could marry. Because women could not marry until they had finished their indentures, most spent a good part of their childbearing years unwed. About one-fifth had illegitimate children, despite severe legal penalties, and roughly one-third were pregnant on their wedding day. Virtually all women married, most as soon as they could.

In a typical Chesapeake marriage, the groom was in his thirties and the bride eight or ten years younger. Though men outlived women, this age gap meant that the husband usually died before his wife, who then quickly remarried. In one Virginia county, three-fourths of all children lost a parent, and one-third lost both. Native-born settlers married at a much earlier age than immigrants; women were often in their middle to late teens when they wed. Orphans were a major community problem. Stepparents were common; surviving spouses with property usually remarried.

Few lived long enough to become grandparents. By the time the oldest child in a household was 20, the husband and wife, because of successive remarriages, might not even be that child's blood relatives.

Under these circumstances, family loyalties tended to focus on other kin—on uncles, aunts, cousins, older stepbrothers or stepsisters—thus contributing to the value that Virginia and Maryland placed upon hospitality. Patriarchalism remained weak. Because fathers died young, even members of the officeholding elite that took shape after 1650 had difficulty passing on their status to their sons. Only toward the end of the century were the men holding office likely to be descended from fathers of comparable distinction.

THE WEST INDIES AND THE TRANSITION TO SLAVERY

Before 1700, far more Englishmen went to the West Indies than to the Chesapeake. Between 1624 and 1640 they settled the Leeward Islands (St. Christopher, Nevis, Montserrat, and Antigua) and Barbados, tiny islands covering just over 400 square miles. In the 1650s England seized Jamaica from Spain, increasing this total by a factor of 10. At first English planters grew tobacco, using the labor of indentured servants. Then, beginning around 1645 in Barbados, sugar replaced tobacco, with dramatic social consequences. The Dutch, who were then being driven from Brazil by the Portuguese, provided some of the capital for this transition, showed the English how to raise sugar, introduced them to slave labor on a massive scale, and for a time dominated the exportation and marketing of the crop. Sugar became so valuable that planters imported most of their food from North America rather than divert land and labor from the cash crop.

Sugar required a heavy investment in slaves and mills, and large planters with many slaves soon dominated the islands. Ex-servants found little employment, and most of them left after their terms expired. Many joined the buccaneers or moved to the mainland. Their exodus hastened the transition to slavery. In 1660 Europeans outnumbered slaves in the islands by 33,000 to 22,000. By 1700, the white population had stagnated, but the number of slaves had increased sixfold. By 1775 they would triple again. Planters appropriated about 80 percent of their slaves' labor for their own profit, a rate of exploitation that had probably never been reached anywhere else. They often worked their slaves to death and then bought others to replace them. Of the 316,000 Africans imported before 1700, only 115,000 remained alive in that year.

Observers were depressed by the moral climate on the islands, where underworked and overfed planters arrogantly dominated their overworked and underfed slaves. Some of the islands were "of no advantage," remarked one governor, who thought they

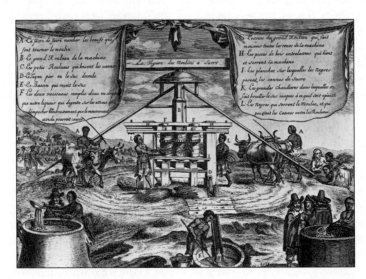

SUGAR MILL This 1665 engraving shows an animal-powered sugar mill, worked by African slaves, in one of the French West Indian islands.

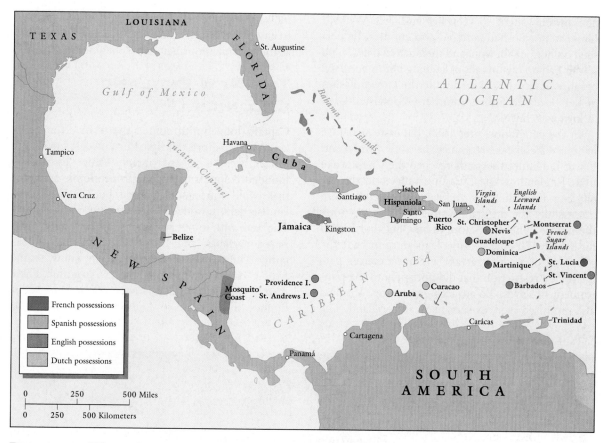

PRINCIPAL WEST INDIAN COLONIES IN THE 17TH CENTURY

were "better under water than above." In 1671 another governor canvassed 40 parishes in the Leeward Islands and found just "one drunken orthodox [Anglican] priest, one drunken sectary priest, and one drunken parson." Yet the islands generated enormous wealth for the English empire, far more than the mainland colonies well into the 18th century.

THE RISE OF SLAVERY IN NORTH AMERICA

Africans appeared in Virginia even before 1619 when, John Rolfe reported, a Dutch ship "sold us twenty Negars." Their status remained ambiguous for decades, even after slavery had been sharply defined in the West Indies. In the Chesapeake some Africans were treated as servants and won their freedom after several years. In Virginia, one "Anthony Johnson Negro" even became the master of other Africans, one of whom complained that John-

son held him beyond the term of his indenture. (The court backed Johnson.) But other Africans in the early years were already serving for life, a pattern that finally prevailed.

This uncertainty about status is understandable. Because the English had no experience with slavery at home, a rigid caste system took time to crystallize. When Hugh Davis was whipped in 1630 "for abusing himself to the dishonor of God and shame of Christians, by defiling his body in lying with a negro," his offense may have been sodomy rather than miscegenation. The record is unclear. Fifty years later when Katherine Watkins, a white woman, accused John Long, a mulatto, of raping her, the neighbors (both men and women) blamed her, not him, for engaging in seductive behavior, which they described in lurid detail. The case of Elizabeth Key, a mulatto, a Christian, and the bastard daughter of Thomas Key, shows similar ambiguity. In 1655 when she claimed her freedom, her new owner fought to keep her enslaved. William Greensted, who had fathered two children by her, sued on her behalf, won, and then married her. One settler had no qualms about keeping her in bondage because of her dark skin, despite the known wishes of her deceased father. Another—Greensted—fell in love with her.

In the generation after 1680, the caste structure of the Chesapeake colonies became firmly set. Fewer indentured servants reached the Chesapeake from England, as the Delaware valley and the expanding English army and navy competed more successfully for the same young men. Slaves took their place. They cost more to buy, but they served for life. In 1705 the Virginia legislature forbade the whipping of a white servant without a court's permission, a restriction that did not apply to the punishment of slaves. To attract more whites, Virginia also promised every ex-servant 50 acres of land. The message was obvious. Every white was now superior to any black. Racial caste was replacing opportunity as the organizing principle of Chesapeake society.

THE NEW ENGLAND COLONIES

Captain John Smith coined the term "New England" years before the first Puritans left for America. It became an apt phrase. Other Europeans founded colonies to engage in economic activities they could not pursue at home, but the New England settlers reproduced the mixed economy of old England, with minor variations. Their family farms raised livestock and European grains, as well as corn. Their artisans specialized in many crafts, from carpentry and shipbuilding to printing. Their quarrel with England was over religion, not economics. They came to America, they insisted, to

---

LINK TO THE PAST

Jamestown Historic Briefs

http://www.nps.gov/colo/Jthanout/JTBriefs.html

The National Park Service has put together this site, which provides access to many themes in early Virginia history, including 14 items under "Historical Significance," five timelines, five biographical essays, and three specialized bibliographies.

1. Under "Historical Significance," click on the "Role of Women at Jamestown." What does their presence tell you about the London Company's intentions for the Colony?

2. Also under "Historical Significance," read the section entitled "Jamestown vs. Plymouth." After a brief description of the beginnings of both colonies, the essay uses eight categories to compare and contrast the two settlements. Are you more impressed with the similarities or the differences? As of 1630 Plymouth seemed more successful than Jamestown, but by 1700 Plymouth Colony would be absorbed by Massachusetts Bay, while Virginia was becoming the most populous and, arguably, the most important English colony in North America. How do you account for these differences? What, if anything, surprises you about the origins of the Thanksgiving tradition?

Note: For material related to chapter 3, you may wish to follow the link to "Bacon's Rebellion."

worship as God commanded, not as the Church of England required. That imperative made them critical of other English practices as well. Driven by a radical communitarian vision, the first settlers created towns, congregations, and law courts well suited to Puritan purposes while changing the English models on which they drew. Later generations were less certain of their place in the world, less eager to question English ways, and more inclined to drift back toward English models. They wanted to preserve what had already been accomplished. They became conservative communitarians.

THE PILGRIMS AND PLYMOUTH

As mentioned earlier in this chapter, the Pilgrims were Separatists who left England for the Netherlands between 1607 and 1609, convinced that the Church of England was no true daughter of the Reformation. They hoped to worship freely in Holland. After 10 years there, they realized that their children were growing up Dutch, not English. That fear prompted a minority of the congregation to move to America. After negotiating rather harsh terms with the London Company, they sailed for Virginia on the *Mayflower*. But the ship was blown off course late in 1620, landing first on Cape Cod, and then on the mainland well north of the charter boundaries of Virginia, at a place they named Plymouth. Two-thirds of the settlers were not Separatists; they had been added to the passenger list by London investors. Before landing, the 100 passengers agreed to the Mayflower Compact, which bound them all to obey the decisions of the majority, an essential precaution in a colony with uncertain legal status.

Short on supplies, the colonists suffered keenly during the first winter. Half of them died, including the governor. His successor was William Bradford, who would be reelected annually for all but five years until his death in 1656. The settlers fared much better when spring came. The Patuxet Indians of the area had been wiped out by disease in 1617, but their fields were ready for planting. Squanto, the only Patuxet to survive, had been kidnapped in 1614 by coastal traders and carried to England. He had just made his way home and showed up at Plymouth one day in March 1621. He taught the settlers Indian methods of fishing and

growing corn. He also introduced them to Massasoit, the powerful Wampanoag sachem (or chief), whose people celebrated the first thanksgiving feast with the settlers after the 1621 harvest. After a decade the settlers numbered about 300. By paying off their London creditors, they gained political autonomy and private ownership of their flourishing farms. During the 1630s they founded several new towns and sold their surplus crops to the colonists flooding into Massachusetts.

COVENANT THEOLOGY

A much larger Puritan exodus settled Massachusetts Bay between 1630 and 1641. The best-educated English group yet to cross the Atlantic, 130 of them had attended a university, most often Cambridge, a Puritan center. Puritans distrusted Charles I and his courtiers, especially William Laud, archbishop of Canterbury, whom they accused of Catholic sympathies and of "Arminianism," a heresy named for a Dutch theologian who had challenged strict Calvinists a generation earlier. To Puritans the stakes were high indeed by the late 1620s. During that early phase of the Thirty Years' War (1618–48), Catholic armies seemed about to crush the German Reformation. Charles I blundered into a brief war against both Spain and France, raised money for the war by dubious methods, and dissolved Parliament when it protested. Puritans complained that Laud punished them for their piety but left blatant sinners alone. God's wrath would descend on England, they warned.

These matters were of genuine urgency to Puritans, who embraced what they called "covenant theology." According to this system, God had made two personal covenants with humans, the covenant of works and the covenant of grace. In the covenant of works God had promised Adam that if he kept God's law he would never die—but Adam ate of the forbidden fruit, was expelled from the Garden of Eden, and died. All of Adam's descendants remained under the same covenant, but because of his Fall would never be capable of keeping the law. All humans deserved damnation, but God was merciful and answered sin with the covenant of grace. God would save his chosen people: "I will be their God, and they shall be my people" (Jeremiah 31:34). Everyone else would be damned: "Saith the Lord:

yet I loved Jacob, and I hated Esau" (Malachi 1:3). Even though the covenant of works could no longer bring eternal life, it remained in force and established the strict moral standards that every Christian must strive to follow, before and after conversion. A Christian's inability to keep the law usually triggered the conversion experience by demonstrating that only faith, not works, could save.

At this level, covenant theology merely restated Calvinist orthodoxy, but the Puritans gave it a novel social dimension by pairing each personal covenant with a communal counterpart. The social equivalent of the covenant of grace was the church covenant. Each congregation organized itself into a church, a community of the elect. The founders, or "pillars," of each church, after satisfying one another of their own conversions, agreed that within their church the Gospel would be properly preached and discipline would be strictly maintained. God, in turn, promised to bestow saving grace within that church—not to everyone, of course, but presumably to most of the children of the elect. The communal counterpart of the covenant of works was the key to secular history. Puritans called it the "national" covenant. It determined not who was saved or damned, but the rise and fall of nations or peoples. As a people, New Englanders agreed to obey the law, and God promised to prosper them. They, in turn, covenanted with their magistrates to punish sinners. If magistrates enforced God's law and the people supported these efforts, God would not punish the whole community for the misdeeds of individuals. But if sinners escaped public account, God's anger would be terrible toward his chosen people of New England. God gave them much and expected much in return.

For New Englanders the idea of the covenant became a powerful social metaphor, explaining everything from crop failures and untimely deaths to Indian wars and political contention. Towns and militia companies used covenants to organize themselves. If only because a minister could always think of something that had missed proper correction, the covenant generated almost an automatic sense of moral crisis. It had a built-in dynamic of moral reform that was becoming obvious even before the migrants crossed the ocean.

In England the government had refused to assume a godly role. Puritans fleeing to America hoped to escape the divine wrath that threatened England and to create in America the kind of churches that God demanded. A few hoped to erect a model "city upon a hill" to inspire all humankind. Governor John Winthrop developed this idea in a famous sermon of 1630, but this theme seldom appeared in the writings of other founders. It became more common a generation later when, ironically, any neutral observer could see that the rest of the world no longer cared what New Englanders were doing.

MASSACHUSETTS BAY

In 1629 several English Puritans obtained a charter for the Massachusetts Bay Company, a typical joint-stock corporation except for one feature: The charter did not specify where the company was to be located. Puritan investors going to New England bought out the other stockholders. Led by Winthrop, they carried the charter to America, beyond the gaze of Charles I. They used it not to organize a business corporation, but as the constitution for the colony. In the 1630s the General Court created by the charter became the Massachusetts legislature.

New England settlers came from the broad middle range of English society, few rich, few very poor. Most had owned property in England. When they sold it to go to America, they probably liquidated far more capital than the London Company had invested in Virginia. A godly haven was expensive to build.

An advance party that sailed in 1629 took over a fishing village on the coast and renamed it Salem. The Winthrop fleet brought 1,000 settlers in 1630. In small groups they scattered around the bay, founding Dorchester, Roxbury, Boston, Charlestown, and Cambridge. Each town formed around a minister and a magistrate. The local congregation was the first institution to take shape. From it evolved the town meeting, as the settlers began to distinguish more sharply between religious and secular affairs. Soon the colonists were raising European livestock and growing English wheat and other grains, along with corn. Perhaps 30 percent of them perished during the first winter. A few hundred others grew discouraged and returned to England. Conditions after that rapidly improved, as they had at Plymouth a decade earlier. About 13,000 settlers came to New England by 1641, most as families—a unique event in Atlantic empires to that time.

Settlers did a brisk business selling grain to the newcomers arriving each year. When the flow of immigrants ceased in 1641, that trade collapsed, creating a crisis that ended only as Boston merchants opened up West Indian markets for New England grain, lumber, and fish. New Englanders possessed this flexibil-

ity because they had started to build ships in 1631, and shipbuilding soon became a major industry. The economic success of the region depended on its ability to ship food and lumber products to colonies that grew staple crops. The very existence of colonies committed to free labor was an oddity. To prosper, they had

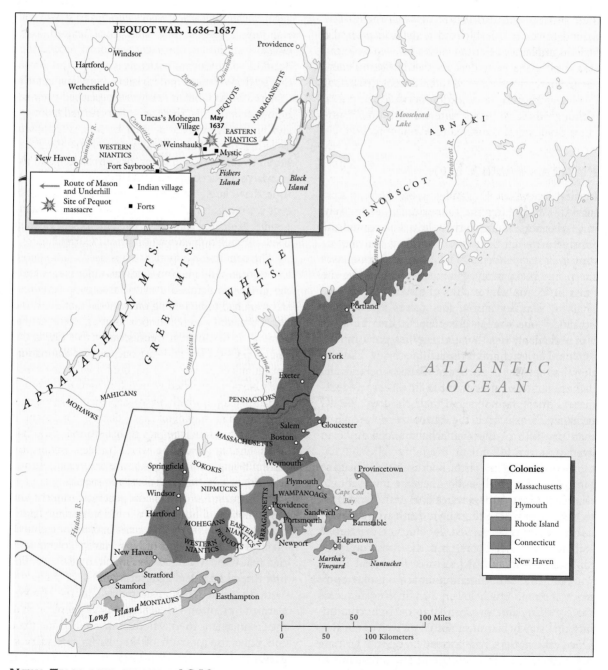

NEW ENGLAND IN THE 1640s

to trade with more typical colonies, the societies elsewhere in the hemisphere that raised tobacco and sugar with unfree labor.

The region's economy imperiled Puritan orthodoxy. Few Boston merchants and almost no fishermen could meet the religious standards of a Puritan society. Although few of these men became church members in the first generation, the colony needed their services and had to put up with them. The fishing towns of Marblehead and Gloucester did little to implement Puritan values or even to found churches in the early decades, while Boston merchants increasingly favored toleration of Protestant dissenters because it would be good for business. Although these contrasts softened with time, Puritan orthodoxy was mostly a rural phenomenon.

PURITAN FAMILY LIFE

In rural areas, New Englanders soon observed a remarkable fact. After the first winter, deaths were rare. Mariners sailing to the Chesapeake noted the contrast between the sickly Virginians and the robust New Englanders. "The air of the country is sharp, the rocks many, the trees innumerable, the grass little, the winter cold, the summer hot, the gnats in summer biting, the wolves at midnight howling," one woman complained. But the place was undeniably healthy, and families grew rapidly as 6 or even 10 children reached maturity. The settlers had left most European diseases behind and had encountered no new ones in the bracing climate. For the founders and their children, life expectancy far exceeded the European norm. More than one-fifth of the men who founded Andover lived past age 80. Infant mortality fell, and few mothers died in childbirth. Because people lived so long, New England families became intensely patriarchal. Many fathers refused to grant land titles to their sons before their own deaths. In the early years settlers often moved, looking for the richest soil, the best neighbors, and the most inspiring minister. By about 1645 most of them had found what they wanted. Migration into or out of country towns became much lower than in England, and the New England town settled into a tight community that slowly became an intricate web of cousins. Once the settlers had formed a typical farming town, they grew reluctant to admit "strangers" to their midst. New Englanders largely avoided slavery, not out of sympathy for Africans or hatred of the institution, but to keep outsiders from contaminating their religion.

CONVERSION, DISSENT, AND EXPANSION

Among serious Puritans, competing visions of the godly society became divisive enough to spawn several new colonies. The vital force behind Puritanism was the quest for conversion. Probably because of John Cotton's stirring sermons in Boston, the settlers crossed an invisible boundary in the mid-1630s. As Cotton's converts described their religious experiences, their neighbors turned from analyzing the legitimacy of their own conversions to assessing the validity of someone else's. Churches began to test for regeneracy, or conversion, and the standards of acceptance escalated rapidly. "These times have lately shown . . . more false hearts than ever we saw before," noted one minister. Too many people "expected to believe by some power of their own, and not only and wholly from Christ."

The conversion experience was deeply ambiguous to a Puritan. Anyone who found no inner trace of saving grace was damned. Anyone absolutely certain of salvation had to be relying on personal merit and was also damned. Conversion took months, even years to achieve. It began with the discovery that one could not keep God's law and that one *deserved* damnation, not for an occasional misdeed, but for what one was at one's best—a wretched sinner. It progressed through despair to hope, which always arose from passages of scripture that spoke to that person's condition. A "saint" at last found reason to believe that God had saved him or her. The whole process involved a painful balance between assurance and doubt. A saint was sure of salvation, but never too sure.

This quest for conversion generated dissent and new colonies. The founders of Connecticut feared that Massachusetts was too strict in certifying church members. The founders of New Haven Colony worried that the Bay Colony was much too lenient. The first Rhode Islanders disagreed with all of them.

In the mid-1630s, Reverend Thomas Hooker, alarmed by Cotton's preaching, led his people west to the Connecticut River where they founded Hartford and other towns south of the charter boundary of Massachusetts. John Winthrop, Jr., built Saybrook Fort at the mouth of the river, and it soon merged with Hooker's towns into the colony of Connecticut. In 1639 an affluent group planted New Haven Colony on Long Island Sound. The leaders were Theophilus Eaton, a wealthy London merchant, and Reverend John Davenport, who imposed the most severe requirements for church membership in New England. New Hampshire and Maine had independent origins under their own charters, but when England fell into civil war after 1642, Massachusetts took control of both of them for most of the 17th century.

The residents of most towns agreed on the kind of worship they preferred, but some settlers, such as Roger Williams and Anne Hutchinson, made greater demands. Williams, who served briefly as Salem's minister, was a Separatist who refused to worship with anyone who did not explicitly repudiate the Church of England. Nearly all Massachusetts Puritans were Nonseparatists who claimed only to be reforming the Anglican Church. In 1636, after Williams challenged the king's right as a Christian to grant Indian lands to anyone at all, the colony banished him. He fled to Narragansett Bay with a few disciples and founded Providence. He developed eloquent arguments for religious liberty

and the complete separation of church and state.

Anne Hutchinson, a merchant's wife and an admirer of John Cotton, claimed that virtually all other ministers were preaching only the covenant of works, not the covenant of grace, and were leading people to hell. She won a large following in Boston. At her trial there, she claimed to have received direct messages from God (the "Antinomian" heresy). Banished in 1638, she and her followers also fled to Narragansett Bay, where they founded Newport and Portsmouth. These towns united with Providence to form the colony of Rhode Island and accepted both the religious liberty and the separation of church and state that Williams advocated.

Much of this territorial expansion reflected not just religious idealism, but a quest for more land that threatened the neighboring Indians. Connecticut and Massachusetts waged a war of terror and annihilation against the Pequot Indians, who controlled the fertile Thames River valley in Connecticut. In May 1637 New England soldiers debated with their chaplain which of two Pequot forts to attack, the one held by warriors or the one with women, children, and the elderly. He probably told them to remember Saul

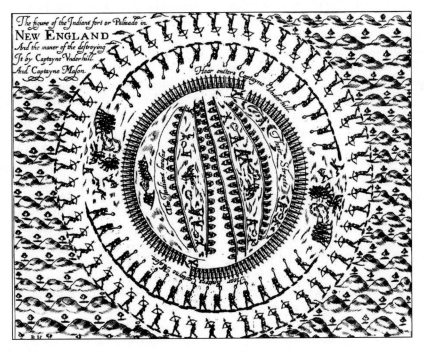

THE PURITAN MASSACRE OF THE PEQUOT INDIANS, 1637 The massacre took place at what is now Mystic, Connecticut. Most of the victims were women and children. The Indians shown in the outer circle were Narragansett allies of the settlers and were appalled by the carnage.

and the Amalekites because, with horrified Narragansett Indians looking on as nominal allies of the settlers, the Puritan army chose the second fort, set fire to all the wigwams, and shot everyone who tried to flee. The godly had their own uses for terrorism.

CONGREGATIONS, TOWNS, AND COLONY GOVERNMENTS

These struggles helped to shape New England's basic institutions. Congregations abolished the distinctive rites of Anglicanism—vestments, incense, the Book of Common Prayer, church courts, bishops. The sermon became the center of worship, and each congregation chose and ordained its own minister. No singing was permitted, except of psalms, with each worshiper warbling in his or her own key. Congregations sometimes sent ministers and laymen to a synod, but its decisions were advisory, not binding. A 1648 synod issued the Cambridge Platform, which defined "Congregationalist" worship and church organization.

By then the town had become something distinct from the congregation. Some towns chose independent farms at the outset, but many adopted a medieval system that appeared nowhere else in colonial America, open-field agriculture. In that system farmers owned scattered strips of land within a common field, and the town decided what crops to grow. Although this emphasis on communal cooperation may have appealed to the founders, who were also short of oxen and plows at first and had to share them, the open-field system did not survive the first generation.

Town meetings decided who got how much land. It was distributed broadly but never equally. In Springfield, at one extreme, the Pynchon family controlled most of the land and most of the labor as well. In other towns, such as Dedham, the distribution was much more equitable. In some villages, town meetings occurred often, made most of the decisions, and left only the details to a board of elected "selectmen." In others the selectmen did most of the governing. All adult males usually participated in local decisions, but Massachusetts and New Haven restricted the vote for colonywide offices to men who were full church members, a decision that greatly narrowed the electorate by the 1660s.

Massachusetts had a bicameral legislature by the 1640s. Voters in each town chose representatives

NEW ENGLAND IRON WORKS A modern drawing by Edwin Tunis of what the iron works on the Saugus River in Massachusetts may have looked like about 1650.

who met as the Chamber of Deputies, or lower house. Voters also elected the governor and the magistrates, or upper house (the Council or, in its judicial capacity, the Court of Assistants). The magistrates also staffed the county courts. The Court of Assistants heard appeals from the counties and major criminal cases. Final appeals were heard by the General Court, with both houses sitting together to decide judicial questions.

Massachusetts defined its legal system in the "Body of Liberties" of 1641 (which may actually be history's first bill of rights) and in a comprehensive law code of 1648 that was widely imitated in other colonies. Massachusetts sharply reduced the number of capital offenses under English law and listed them in the order of the Ten Commandments. Unlike England, Massachusetts seldom executed anyone for a crime against property. Other distinctive features of the legal system included an explicit recognition of the liberties of women, children, servants, foreigners, and even "the Bruite Creature," or animals; a serious effort to ban professional lawyers; and the swift punishment of crime.

New England also transformed the traditional English jury system. New Haven abolished juries altogether because the Bible does not mention them. But the other colonies vastly expanded the role of civil (noncriminal) juries, using them even to decide appeals, something that never happened in England. Except in capital trials, however, the criminal jury—a fixture of English justice—almost disappeared in New England. The punishment of sin involved fidelity to the covenant and was too important to leave to 12 ordinary men. This system worked well because even sinners shared its values. Most offenders appeared in court and accepted their punishments. Acquittals were rare, almost unheard of in New Haven. Yet hardly anyone ran away to avoid trial or punishment.

INFANT BAPTISM AND NEW DISSENT

Although most of the founders of the New England colonies became church members during the fervor of the 1630s, their children had trouble achieving conversion. They had never lived as part of a beleaguered minority in England, nor had they experienced the joy of joining with other holy refugees in founding their own church. They had to find God on their own and then persuade their elders—on guard because leniency had let Williams, Hutchinson, and other deviants through—that their conversions were authentic. Most failed. They grew up, married, and requested baptism for their children. The Cambridge Platform declared that only "saints" (the converted) and their children could be baptized. But what about the grandchildren of the saints if their own parents had not yet experienced conversion? By 1660 this problem was becoming acute.

Dissenters offered two answers, the ministers a third. In the 1640s some settlers became Baptists. Noting that scripture contains no mandate to baptize infants, they argued that only converted adults should receive that rite. Their position challenged the logic of a covenanted community by implying that New England was no different from Europe. The community was a mass of sinners from whom

God would randomly choose a few saints. Samuel Gorton, a Baptist expelled from Massachusetts and Plymouth (he denounced the magistrates as "just asses"), founded Warwick, Rhode Island, in the 1640s. When Massachusetts arrested him, accused him of blasphemy, and put him on trial for his life, the legislature banished him instead, but Gorton appealed to Parliament in England, and Massachusetts backed down. Baptist principles also attracted Henry Dunster, the able president of Harvard College, which had been founded in 1636 to educate ministers and magistrates for a Puritan society. When the courts began to harass Baptists, Dunster left for more tolerant Plymouth.

Even more alarming to the Puritan establishment were the Quakers, who invaded the region from England in the 1650s (to be discussed later in the chapter). Quakers found salvation within themselves—through God, the Inner Light present in all people if they will only let it shine forth. To Puritans the Quaker answer to the conversion dilemma seemed blasphemous and Antinomian. Massachusetts hanged four Quakers who refused to stop preaching, including Mary Dyer, once a disciple of Anne Hutchinson.

The clergy's answer to the lack of conversions, worked out at a synod in 1662, became known as the Half-Way Covenant. Parents who had been baptized but had not yet experienced conversion could bring their children before the church, "own the covenant" (that is, subject themselves and their offspring to the doctrine and discipline of the church), and have their children baptized. In practice, women often experienced conversion before age 30, men closer to 40, but many never did. In most churches women also began to outnumber men as full members. For 15 or 20 years after 1662, most churches were still dominated by the lay members of the founding generation. Despite the urging of the clergy (by then most ministers were young Harvard graduates, not venerable saints), aging church members resisted the Half-Way Covenant. But as the founders died off in the 1670s and 1680s, it took hold and soon led to something like universal baptism. Almost every child had an ancestor who had been a full church member.

Dissent persisted anyhow. The orthodox colonies were divided over whether to persecute or to ignore their Baptist and Quaker minorities. Ministers

The Prince, the Quaker, and the Middle Colonies

Two Englishmen profoundly affected the middle colonies in the 17th century: James, duke of York, and William Penn. James became king, Penn a Quaker. Though they hailed from quite different backgrounds, they learned to like and trust each other.

Born in 1633 as the second son of King Charles I, James fled into exile as a teenager when his father lost the Civil War to Parliament and was then beheaded in 1649. James spent most of the next decade in France where he acquired immense respect for the French court and for the Catholic religion. In the 1650s France was the most tolerant Catholic society in Europe, and when James returned to England in the Restoration of 1660, he brought back with him a conviction that Catholics and Protestants could live together harmoniously under the same government, preferably under an absolute monarch who had enough power to keep his subjects from quarreling openly about religion. When he founded his own colony (New York) in 1664, he gave it an absolute government that provided freedom of worship for all Christians and that also tolerated New York's tiny Jewish minority.

William Penn was born 11 years later than James. The son of an admiral who fought for the English Commonwealth that executed Charles I, he was proud enough of this heritage as a young man to be painted in a suit of armor in 1666 by an unknown artist (right). But then he converted to the Society of Friends and was almost disowned by his father. Imprisoned for blasphemy in a bleak room of the Tower of London from December 1668 to July 1669 (see illustration), he too insisted on freedom of worship. When Quakers decided to colonize the Delaware Valley, he made "soul liberty" a central principle of his own province of Pennsylvania and drew upon his friendship

with James to overcome resistance from the Lords of Trade, who tried to block the whole project.

The support of James made Pennsylvania's success possible, not just in the tempestuous world of English politics, but also in North America. The governors of New York negotiated what they called the "Covenant Chain" of peace with the Iroquois Five Nations, providing, in effect, a northern shield that could protect Penn's colony from Indian wars so long as the settlers dealt fairly with the local Delaware, or Lenni Lenape

preached "jeremiads," shrill warnings against any backsliding from the standards of the founding generation. Many laypeople disliked the persecution of conscientious Protestants, however. By the 1670s, innovation seemed dangerous and divisive, but the

past was also becoming a burden that no one could shoulder. As towns buried the founders, they began to move their cemeteries from outlying fields to meetinghouse hill. John Winthrop's city upon a hill was becoming a city of the dead.

Indians. Pennsylvania benefited more than New York. By 1700 Pennsylvania's population exceeded New York's even though it had been founded half a century later.

James openly professed the Catholic faith in the mid-1670s. After he became King James II in 1685 (see portrait by Sir Peter Lely), he issued a Declaration of Indulgence granting toleration to both Catholics and Protestant dissenters. Because Louis XIV revoked the Edict of Nantes in the same year and launched a vicious persecution of French Huguenots, most English dissenters interpreted the Declaration of Indulgence as a cynical move to bring Catholics back into power. Penn was one of the few Protestants who believed James and supported him openly. In the Glorious Revolution of 1688-89, James lost his throne and, for two years, Penn lost control of Pennsylvania. He was never again as influential as he had been in the 1680s, but he and James had already made a permanent contribution to North American history. Religious liberty continued to flourish in the middle Colonies to a degree not matched in any other part of any European empire in the Americas.

THE ENGLISH CIVIL WARS

The 1640s were a critical decade in England and the colonies. From 1629 to 1640 Charles I governed without Parliament, but when he tried to impose the Anglican Book of Common Prayer on Presbyterian Scotland, his Scottish subjects rebelled and even invaded England. Needing revenue, Charles summoned two Parliaments in 1640 only to find that many of its members, especially the Puritans, sympathized with the Scots. In 1641 Irish Catholics launched a massive revolt against the Protestant colonizers of their land. King and Parliament agreed that the Irish must be crushed, but neither dared trust the other with the men and resources to do the job. Instead, they began to fight each other.

In 1642 the king and Parliament raised separate armies and went to war. Parliament gradually won the military struggle and then had to govern most of England without a king. In January 1649, after its moderate members had been purged by its own "New Model Army," Parliament beheaded Charles, abolished the House of Lords, and proclaimed England a Commonwealth (or republic). Within a few years Oliver Cromwell, Parliament's most successful general, dismissed Parliament, and the army proclaimed him "Lord Protector" of England. He convened several of his own Parliaments, including one that consisted entirely of godly men, but these experiments failed. The army, even when it drafted a written constitution for England, could not win legitimacy for a government that ruled without the ancient trinity of "King, Lords, and Commons." Cromwell also faced a challenge outside Parliament from "levelers," "diggers," and "ranters" who claimed to speak for "the people" while demanding sweeping social reforms.

Cromwell died in September 1658, and his regime collapsed. Part of the army invited Charles II (1660–85) back from exile to claim his throne. This "Restoration" government, after 20 years of turmoil, did its best to restore the old order. It brought back the House of Lords. The Church of England was reestablished under its episcopal form of government. The English state, denying any right of dissent, persecuted both Catholics and Protestant dissenters: Presbyterians, Congregationalists, Baptists, and Quakers. This persecution drove thousands of Quakers to the Delaware valley after 1675.

THE FIRST RESTORATION COLONIES

England had founded six of the original 13 colonies before 1640. Six others were founded or came under English rule during the Restoration era (1660–88). The last, Georgia, was settled in the 1730s (see chapter 4). Most of the new colonies shared certain common features and also differed in some respects from earlier settlements. All were proprietary in form. As with Maryland earlier, a proprietary charter enabled the organizers to pursue daring social experiments. Except for Pennsylvania, the Restoration colonies were all founded by men with big ideas and small purses. The proprietors tried to attract settlers from the older colonies because importing them from Europe was too expensive.

The most readily available prospects were servants completing their indentures in the West Indies and being driven out by the sugar revolution. The most prized settlers, however, were New Englanders. Although the proprietors distrusted their politics, New Englanders had built the most thriving colonies in North America. Cromwell had tried but failed to attract New Haven settlers to Jamaica. Few New Englanders would go farther south than New York or New Jersey. Settlers from the West Indies populated South Carolina.

The Restoration colonies made it easy for settlers to acquire land, and they competed with one another by offering newcomers strong guarantees of civil and political liberties. They all promised either toleration or full religious liberty, at least for Christians. Whereas Virginia and New England (except Rhode Island) were still homogeneous societies, the Restoration colonies all attracted a mix of religious and ethnic groups. None of them found it easy to translate this human diversity into political stability.

Most of the new proprietors were "cavaliers" who had supported Charles II and his brother James, duke of York, during their long exile. Charles owed them something, and a colonial charter cost nothing to grant. Many proprietors took part in more than one project. The eight who obtained charters for Carolina in 1663 and 1665 were also prominent in organizing the Royal African Company, which soon made England a major participant in the African slave trade. Two of the Carolina proprietors obtained a charter from the duke of York for New Jersey as well. William Penn, although the son of a Commonwealth admiral, became a friend of James and invested in West New Jersey before acquiring Pennsylvania from the king.

Far more than New England or Virginia, the Restoration colonies foreshadowed what the United

States would become in later centuries. In the 1790s South Carolina became the first home of the cotton kingdom. The Middle Atlantic provinces eventually stamped their character on the Midwest.

CAROLINA, HARRINGTON, AND THE ARISTOCRATIC IDEAL

In 1663 eight courtiers obtained a charter by which they became the board of proprietors for a colony to be founded south of Virginia. Calling their province "Carolina" in honor of the king, they tried to colonize the region in the 1660s but achieved little success until the following decade. Most of the settlers came from two sources. Former servants from Virginia and Maryland, many in debt, hoped that they would be left alone if they claimed land around Albemarle Sound in what eventually became North Carolina. Another wave of former servants came from Barbados. They settled the area that became South Carolina, 300 miles south of Albemarle, and began to export grain and meat to the West Indies.

To the proprietors in England, these scattered settlements made up a single colony called Carolina. Led by Anthony Ashley-Cooper, later the first earl of Shaftesbury and the principal organizer of England's Whig Party, the proprietors drafted the Fundamental Constitutions of Carolina in 1669, an incredibly complex plan for organizing the new colony. Philosopher John Locke, Shaftesbury's young secretary, helped write the document.

The Fundamental Constitutions drew on the work of Commonwealth England's most prominent republican thinker, James Harrington, author of *Oceana* (1656). He tried to design a republic that could endure—unlike ancient Athens or Rome, which had finally become despotic states. Harrington argued that how land was distributed ought to determine whether power should be lodged in one man (monarchy), a few men (aristocracy), or many (a republic). Where ownership of land was widespread, he insisted, absolute government could not prevail. He proposed several other devices to prevent one man, or a few, from undermining a republic, such as frequent rotation of officeholders (called "term limits" today), the secret ballot, and a bicameral legislature in which the smaller house would propose laws and the larger house approve or reject

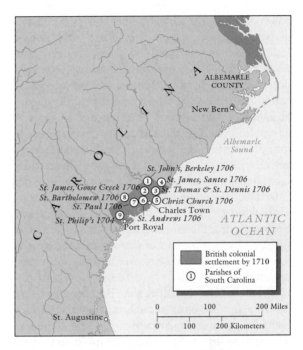

EARLY CAROLINA, CIRCA 1710

them. Harrington had greater impact on colonial governments than any other thinker of his time.

Shaftesbury believed that Harrington had uncovered the laws of history. By emphasizing Henry VIII's confiscation of monastic lands and their sale to an emerging gentry, Harrington seemed to have an explanation for the decline of the monarchy, England's civil wars, and the execution of Charles I—an explanation that was anathema to the king because, if Harrington was correct, the dynasty was still in trouble. English writers dared not discuss these ideas openly in the 1660s, but by applying Harrington's principles at a safe distance of 3,000 miles, the Carolina proprietors could choose the kind of society they desired and devise institutions to ensure its success. Well aware that the House of Lords had been abolished for 11 years after 1649, they were not yet certain whether the English aristocracy could survive at home. In Carolina they hoped to create a thriving aristocratic society.

The Fundamental Constitutions proposed a government far more complex than any colony could sustain. England had three supreme courts; Carolina would have eight. A Grand Council of proprietors and councillors would exercise executive power and propose all laws. Their bills would have to pass a Parliament of commoners and nobles (called "landgraves" and "casiques"). The nobles would control 40 percent of the land. In a later version of the text, a noble who lost his land or permanently left the colony would forfeit his title, an application of Harrington's warning not to divorce power from land. A distinct group of manor lords would also have large estates. The document guaranteed religious toleration to all who believed in God, but everyone had to join a church or lose his citizenship. The document also envisioned a class of lowly whites, "leetmen," who would live on small tracts and serve the great landlords—and it accepted slavery. "Every Freeman of Carolina shall have absolute Power and Authority over his Negro Slaves," declared Article 110.

Conditions were bleak on Barbados for ex-servants, but not bleak enough to make the Fundamental Constitutions attractive to the Barbadians who settled in Carolina. Between 1670 and 1700, the proprietors tried several times, without success, to win their approval of the document. In the 1680s, weary of resistance from the predominantly Anglican Barbadians, the proprietors shipped 1,000 dissenters from England and Scotland to South Carolina. These newcomers formed the nucleus of a proprietary party in South Carolina politics and made religious diversity a social fact, but their influence was never strong enough to win approval for the Fundamental Constitutions. The Barbadians remained in control.

Carolina presented its organizers with other unanticipated obstacles to these aristocratic goals. The proprietors assumed that land ownership would be the key to everything else, including wealth and status, but many settlers prospered in other ways. Some of them, especially in Albemarle, exploited the virgin forests all around them to produce masts, turpentine, tar, and pitch for sale to English shipbuilders. Other settlers raised cattle and hogs by letting them run free on open land. Some of South Carolina's early slaves were probably America's first cowboys. The settlers also traded with the Indians, usually for deerskins, often acquired west of the Appalachians. As in New France and New Netherland, the Indian trade sustained a genuine city, Charleston, the first in the American South, founded in 1680 at the confluence of the Ashley and Cooper Rivers. The Indian trade also became something more dangerous than hunting or trapping animals. Carolina traders allied themselves with some Indians to attack others and drag the captives, mostly women and children, to Charleston for sale as slaves.

In the early 18th century, South Carolina and North Carolina became separate colonies, and South Carolina's economy moved in a new direction. For two decades, until the mid-1720s, a parliamentary subsidy sustained a boom in the naval stores industry, which in turn stimulated a large demand for slaves, but Charleston merchants increasingly invested their capital, acquired in the Indian trade, in rice plantations. In the 1690s planters learned how to grow rice from slaves who had cultivated it in West Africa. It quickly became the staple export of South Carolina and triggered a massive growth of slavery. In 1700 more than 40 percent of the colony's population of 5,700 were African or Indian slaves engaged in a wide variety of activities. By 1730 two-thirds of the colony's 30,000 people were African slaves, most of whom toiled on rice plantations.

NEW YORK: AN EXPERIMENT IN ABSOLUTISM

In 1664 James, duke of York, obtained a charter from his royal brother for a colony between the Delaware and Connecticut Rivers. Charles II claimed that the territory of New Netherland was rightfully England's because it was included in the Virginia charter of 1606. James sent a fleet to Manhattan, and the English settlers on Long Island rose to support his claim. Reluctantly, Stuyvesant surrendered without resistance. The English renamed the province New York. New Amsterdam became New York City, and Fort Orange became Albany. The Dutch ceded New Netherland with few regrets. It had never been profitable anyway. New York took over all of Long Island, most of which had been ruled by Connecticut, but never made good its claim to the Connecticut River as its eastern boundary.

New York also inherited New Netherland's role as mediator between the settlers and the Iroquois Five Nations. In effect the duke of York's autocratic colony assumed most of the burdens of this relationship while unintentionally conferring most of the benefits upon the Quakers who would begin to settle the Delaware Valley a decade later. The shield provided by New York and the Iroquois would make the Quaker experiment in pacifism a viable option.

Richard Nicolls, the first English governor of New York, planned to lure Yankees to the Jersey coast as a way of offsetting the preponderance of Dutch settlers in the Hudson valley. Although English soldiers abused many Dutch civilians, official policy toward the Dutch was conciliatory. Those who chose to leave could take their property with them. Those who stayed retained their property and were assured of religious toleration. Most stayed. Except in New York City and the small Dutch portion of Long Island, Dutch settlers still lived under Dutch law. Dutch inheritance practices, which were far more generous to women than English law, survived in New York well into the next century. England also expected to take over the colony's trade with Europe, but New York's early governors realized that a total ban on commerce with Amsterdam could ruin the colony. Under various legal subterfuges, they allowed this trade to continue.

The duke boldly tried to do in New York what he and the king did not dare attempt in England—to govern without an elective assembly. This policy upset English settlers on Long Island far more than the Dutch, who had no experience with representative government. Governor Nicolls compiled a code of laws ("the Duke's Laws") culled mostly from New England statutes. With difficulty, he secured the consent of English settlers to this code in 1665, but thereafter he taxed and governed on his own, seeking only the advice and consent of his appointed council and of a somewhat larger court of assize, also appointive, that dispensed justice, mostly to the English settlers.

This policy made it difficult to attract English colonists to New York, especially after New Jersey became a separate proprietary colony in 1665. The two proprietors, Sir George Carteret and John, baron Berkeley, granted settlers the right to elect an assembly, which made New Jersey far more attractive to English settlers than New York. The creation of New Jersey also slowed the flow of Dutch settlers across the Hudson and thus helped to keep New York Dutch.

The transition from a Dutch to an English colony did not go smoothly. James expected his English invaders to assimilate the conquered Dutch, but the reverse was more common for two or three decades. Most Englishmen who settled in New York after the conquest married Dutch women (few unmarried English women were available) and sent their children to the Dutch Reformed Church. In effect, the Dutch were assimilating the English. Nor did the Dutch give up their loyalty to the Netherlands. In 1673 when a Dutch fleet threatened the colony, the Dutch refused to assist the English garrison of Fort James at the southern tip of Manhattan. Eastern Long Island showed more interest in reuniting with Connecticut than in fighting the Dutch. Much like Stuyvesant nine years earlier, the English garrison gave up without resistance. New York City now became New Orange and Fort James was renamed Fort William, both in honor of young William III of Nassau, Prince of Orange, the new *stadholder* (military leader) of the Dutch Republic in its struggle with France. Thus James and William became antagonists in New York 15 years before the Glorious Revolution, in which William would drive James from the English throne (see chapter 3).

New Orange survived for 15 months, until the Dutch Republic again concluded that the colony was not worth what it cost and gave it back to England at the end of the war. The new governor, Major Edmund Andros, arrested seven prominent Dutch merchants and tried them as aliens after they refused to swear an oath of loyalty to England that might oblige them to fight other Dutchmen. Faced with the confiscation of their property, they gave in. Andros also helped secure bilingual ministers for Dutch Reformed pulpits. These preachers made a great show of their loyalty to the duke, a delicate matter now that James, back in England, had openly embraced the Catholic faith. Ordinary Dutch settlers looked with suspicion on the new ministers and on wealthier Dutch families who socialized with the governor or sent their sons to New England to learn English.

English merchants in New York City resented the continuing Amsterdam trade and the staying power of the Dutch elite. They believed the colony had to become more English to attract newcomers. When Andros failed to renew the colony's basic

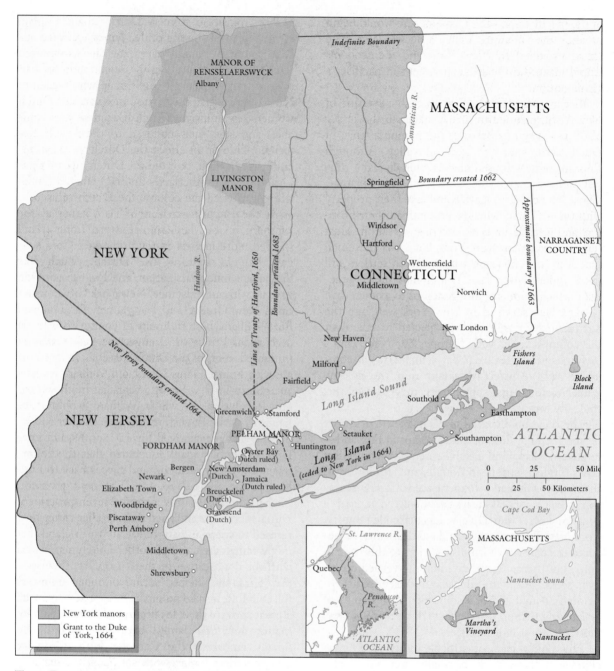

THE DUKE OF YORK'S COLONIAL CHARTER

revenue act before returning to England in 1680, the merchants refused to pay any duties not voted by an elective assembly. The court of assize, supposedly a bastion of absolutism, supported the tax strike, convicted the duke's customs collector of usurping authority, and sent him to England for punishment where, of course, James exonerated him. The justices also fined several Dutch officeholders for failing to respect English liberties. The English (but not Dutch) towns on Long Island joined in the demand for an elective assembly, an urgent matter now that William Penn's much freer colony on the Delaware threatened to drain away the small English population of New York. Several prominent merchants did move to Philadelphia.

The duke finally relented and conceded an assembly. When it met in 1683, it adopted a Charter of Liberties that proclaimed government by consent. It also imposed English law on the Dutch parts of the province. Although the drain of English settlers to Pennsylvania declined, few immigrants came to New York at a time when thousands were landing in Philadelphia. Philadelphia's thriving trade cut into New York City's profits. New York remained a Dutch society with a Yankee enclave, governed by English intruders. In 1689, when James and William fought for the English throne, their struggle would tear the colony apart.

BROTHERLY LOVE: THE QUAKERS AND AMERICA

The most fascinating social experiment of the Restoration era took place in the Delaware valley where Quakers led another family-based, religiously motivated migration of more than 10,000 people between 1675 and 1690. Founded by George Fox during England's civil wars, the Society of Friends expanded dramatically in the 1650s as it went through a heroic phase of missionaries and martyrs, including the four executed in Massachusetts. After the Restoration, Quakers faced harsh persecution in England and finally began to seek refuge in America.

QUAKER BELIEFS

Quakers infuriated other Christians. They insisted that God, in the form of the Inner Light, is present in all people, who can become good—even perfect—if only they will let that light shine forth. They took literally Jesus' advice to "Turn the other cheek." They became pacifists, enraging Catholics and most other Protestants, all of whom had found ways to justify war. Quakers also obeyed Jesus's command to "swear not." They denounced oath-taking as sinful. Again, other Christians reacted with horror because their judicial systems rested on oaths.

Although orderly and peaceful, Quakers struck others as dangerous radicals whose beliefs would bring anarchy. For instance, slavery made them uncomfortable, although the Friends did not embrace abolitionism until a century later (see chapter 5). Further, in what they called "the Lamb's war" against human pride, Quakers refused to doff their hats to social superiors. More than any other simple device, hats symbolized the social hierarchy of Europe. Every man knew his place so long as he understood whom to doff to, and who should doff to him. Quakers also refused to accept or to confer titles. They called everyone "thee" or "thou," familiar terms used by superiors when addressing inferiors, especially servants.

Although Quakers disliked theological speculation, the implications of their beliefs appalled other Christians. Without the bother of a refutation, the Inner Light seemed to obliterate predestination, original sin, maybe even the Trinity. Quakers had no sacraments, not even an organized clergy. They denounced Protestant ministers as "hireling priests," no better than the "papists." Other Protestants retorted that the Quakers were conspiring to return the world to "popish darkness" by abolishing a learned ministry. (The terms "papists" and "popish" were abusive labels applied to Catholics by English Protestants.) Quakers also held distinctive views about revelation. If God speaks directly to Friends, that Word must be every bit as inspired as anything in the Bible. Quakers compiled books of their "sufferings," which they thought were the equal of the "Acts of the Apostles," a claim that seemed blasphemous to others.

Contemporaries expected the Society of Friends to fall apart as each member followed his or her own Light in some unique direction. However, it did nothing of the kind. In the 1660s Quakers found ways to deal with discord. The heart of Quaker worship was the "weekly meeting" of the local congregation. There was no sermon or liturgy. People spoke whenever the Light inspired them. But because a few men and women spoke often and with great effect, they became recognized as "public friends," the closest the Quakers came to having a clergy. Public friends occupied special, elevated seats in some meetinghouses, and many went on missionary tours in Europe or America. The weekly meetings within a region sent representatives to a "monthly meeting," which resolved

HEXAGONAL QUAKER MEETING HOUSE This unique design emphasizes the Quaker belief in the fundamental equality of all souls under God. The interior has no altar or pulpit, no front or back. All worshippers are equally close to God.

questions of policy and discipline. The monthly meetings sent delegates to the "yearly meeting" in London. At every level, decisions had to be unanimous. There is only one Inner Light, and it must convey the same message to every believer. This insistence on unanimity provided strong safeguards against schism.

QUAKER FAMILIES

Quakers transformed the traditional family as well. Women enjoyed almost full equality, and some of them, such as Mary Dyer, became exceptional preachers, even martyrs. Women held their own formal meetings and made important decisions about discipline and betrothals. Quaker reforms also affected children, whom most Protestants saw as tiny sinners whose wills must be broken by severe discipline. But once Quakers stopped worrying about original sin, their children became innocents in whom the Light would shine if only they could be protected from worldly corruption. In America, Quakers created affectionate families,

built larger houses than non-Quakers with equivalent resources, and worked hard to acquire land for all their children. Earlier than other Christians, they began to limit family size to give more love to the children they did have. After the missionary impulse declined, Quakers seldom associated with non-Quakers, and the needs of their own children became paramount. To marry an outsider meant expulsion from the Society, a fate more likely to befall poor Friends than rich ones. Poor Quakers had difficulty finding spouses precisely because their children might never receive the advantages that most Friends had come to expect.

Persecution in England helped to drive Quakers across the ocean, but the need to provide for their children was another powerful motive for emigration. By 1700, about half of the Quakers in England and Wales had moved to America.

WEST NEW JERSEY

In 1674 the New Jersey proprietors split their holding into two colonies. Sir George Carteret claimed what he now called East New Jersey, a province near New York City with half a dozen towns populated by Baptist, Quaker, Puritan, and Dutch Reformed settlers. Lord Berkeley claimed West New Jersey and promptly sold it to the Quakers, who then founded two colonies in America: West New Jersey and Pennsylvania. In the 1680s, when Quakers bought out the proprietor of East New Jersey and also gained power in Delaware (formerly New Sweden), they seemed poised to dominate the entire region between Maryland and New York. The West Jersey purchasers divided their proprietary into 100 shares. Two of them were Edward Byllinge, a former "leveler," and William Penn, an admirer of Harrington. They revived in West Jersey many radical ideals of the English Commonwealth era.

In 1676 Byllinge drafted a document, the West Jersey Concessions and Agreements, which was approved by the first settlers in 1677. It lodged legislative power in a unicameral assembly, elected by secret ballot, and it empowered voters to instruct their representatives. In the court system, juries would decide both fact and law. Judges would merely preside over the court and, if asked by a juror, offer advice. Although the document was never fully implemented, it made West Jersey the most radical political experiment attempted in America before the Revolution. West Jersey Quakers believed that godly people could live together in love—without war, lawyers, or internal conflict. They kept government close to the people, made land easy to acquire, and promised freedom of worship to everyone. In the 1680s lawsuits often ended with one litigant forgiving the other, and criminal trials sometimes closed with the victim embracing the perpetrator. But as social and religious diversity grew, the system broke down. Non-Quakers increasingly refused to cooperate. In the 1690s the courts became impotent, and Quaker rule collapsed some years before the Crown took over the colony in 1702.

PENNSYLVANIA

By 1681 Quaker attention was already shifting to the west bank of the Delaware River. There William Penn launched a much larger, if rather more cautious, "holy experiment" in brotherly love. The son of a Commonwealth admiral, Penn grew up surrounded by privilege. He knew well both Charles II and the duke of York, attended Oxford and the Inns of Court (England's law schools), went on the grand tour of Europe, and began to manage his father's Irish estates. Then something happened that embarrassed his family. "Mr. William Pen," reported a neighbor in December 1667, " . . . is a Quaker again, or some very melancholy thing." Penn often traveled to the continent on behalf of the Society of Friends, winning converts and recruiting settlers in the Netherlands and Germany. In England he was jailed several times for his beliefs, and in the so-called Penn-Meade trial of 1670 he challenged a judge's right to compel a jury to reconsider its verdict. In a landmark decision, a higher court vindicated him.

A gentleman and a Quaker, Penn was no ordinary colonizer. Using his contacts at court, he converted an old debt (owed to his father by the king)

***PENN'S TREATY WITH THE INDIANS*, BY BENJAMIN WEST** This 1771 painting celebrates William Penn's efforts, nearly a century earlier, to establish peaceful relations with the Delaware Indians.

into a charter for a proprietary colony that Charles named "Pennsylvania" in honor of the deceased admiral. The emerging imperial bureaucracy disliked the whole project and, after failing to block it, inserted several restrictions into the charter. Penn agreed to enforce the Navigation Acts (see chapter 3), to let the Crown approve his choice of governor, to submit all legislation to the English Privy Council for approval, and to allow appeals from Pennsylvania courts to the Privy Council in England.

Contemporaries said little about the most striking innovation attempted by the Quaker colonists. They entered America unarmed. Pennsylvanians did not even organize a militia until the 1740s. Friendly relations with Indians were essential to the project's success, and Penn was careful to deal fairly with the Lenni Lenape, or Delaware Indians. They liked him and called him "Miquon," their word for "quill" and thus a pun on "Penn."

More thought went into the planning of Pennsylvania than into the creation of any other colony. Twenty drafts survive of Penn's First Frame of Government, his 1682 constitution for the province. His plan evolved from what was roughly a larger version of the West Jersey Concessions and Agreements into something more Harringtonian but still quite liberating. The settlers would elect a council of 72 men to staggered three-year terms. The council would draft all legislation and submit copies to the voters. In the early years the voters would meet to approve or reject these bills in person, Penn anticipated that as the province expanded, such meetings would become impractical. Voters would then elect an assembly of 200, which would increase gradually to 500, about the size of the House of Commons, though for a much smaller population. Government would still remain close to the people. Penn gave up the power to veto bills but retained control of the distribution of land. Capital punishment for crimes against property and most other offenses, except murder, was abolished. Religious liberty, trial by jury, and habeas corpus all received strong guarantees.

Settlers had been arriving in Pennsylvania for a year when Penn landed in 1682 with his First Frame of Government. Some lived in caves along the river. Others, imitating the nearby Swedes, built log cabins. The colonists persuaded Penn that the First Frame was too cumbersome for a small colony, and the first legislature worked with him to devise a sim-

pler government. In what became known as the Second Frame, or the Pennsylvania Charter of Liberties of 1683, the council was reduced to 18 men and the assembly to 36. The assembly's inability to initiate legislation soon became a major grievance.

Penn laid out Philadelphia as "a green country town" and organized other settlements. Then, in 1684, he returned to England to answer Lord Baltimore's complaint that Philadelphia fell within the charter boundaries of Maryland, a claim that was soon verified. This dispute troubled the Penn family until the 1760s, when the Mason-Dixon line finally established the modern boundary.

In England, persecution had kept Quaker antiauthoritarianism in check, at least in relations with other Friends. In the colony these attitudes soon became public. Penn expected his settlers to defer to the leaders among them. He created the Free Society of Traders to control commerce with England and gave high offices to its members. From the start, however, wealth in Pennsylvania rested on

EARLY PENNSYLVANIA AND NEW JERSEY, CIRCA 1700

trade not with England, but with other colonies, especially in the Caribbean. That trade was dominated by Quakers from Barbados, Jamaica, New York, and Boston. These men owed little to Penn and became an opposition faction in the colony. They and others demanded more land, especially in Philadelphia. They claimed that they could not afford to pay Penn's quitrents,[2] and quarreled more often than was seemly for men of brotherly love.

In exasperation, Penn finally appointed John Blackwell, a friend and old Cromwellian soldier, as governor in 1688, ordering him to end the quarrels and collect quitrents but to rule "tenderly." Boys jeered Blackwell as he tried to enter Penn's Philadelphia house, and the council refused to let him use the colony's great seal. Debate in the legislature became angrier than ever. After 13 months, Blackwell resigned. Each Quaker, he complained, "prayed for the rest on the First Day [of the week], and preyed on them the other six." The local mosquitoes, he added, "were worse than armed men but not nearly so nettlesome as the men without Armes."

In 1691, the Society of Friends suffered a brief schism in the Delaware valley. A Quaker schoolteacher, George Keith, urged all Quakers to systematize their beliefs and even wrote his own catechism, only to encounter the opposition of the public friends, who included the colony's major officeholders. When he attacked them directly, he was convicted and fined for abusing civil officers. He claimed that he was being persecuted for his religious beliefs, but the courts insisted that his only crime was his attack on public authority. In contrast to Massachusetts in the 1630s, no one was banished, and Pennsylvania remained a haven for all religions. The colony's government changed several more times before 1701, when Penn and the assembly finally agreed on the Fourth Frame, or Charter of Privileges, which gave Pennsylvania a unicameral legislature, but its politics remained turbulent and unstable into the 1720s.

Despite these controversies, Pennsylvania quickly became an economic success, well established in the Caribbean trade as an exporter of wheat and flour. Quaker families were thriving, and the colony's policy of religious freedom attracted thousands of outsiders. Some were German pacifists who shared the major goals of the Society of Friends. Others were Anglicans and Presbyterians who warned London that Quakers were unfit to rule—anywhere.

CONCLUSION

In the 16th century, France, the Netherlands, and England all challenged Spanish power in Europe and across the ocean. After 1600 all three founded their own colonies in North America and the Caribbean. New France became a land of missionaries and traders and developed close ties of cooperation with most nearby Indians. New Netherland also was founded to participate in the fur trade. Both colonies slowly acquired an agricultural base.

The English, by contrast, desired the land itself. They founded colonies of settlement that threatened nearby Indians, except in the Delaware valley where Quakers insisted on peaceful relations. The southern mainland and Caribbean colonies produced staple crops for sale in Europe, first with the labor of indentured servants and then with enslaved Africans. The Puritan and Quaker colonies became smaller versions of England's mixed economy, with an emphasis on family farms. Maintaining the fervor of the founders was a problem for both. After conquering New Netherland, England controlled the Atlantic seaboard from Maine to South Carolina, and by 1700 the population of England's mainland colonies was doubling every 25 years. England was beginning to emerge as the biggest winner in the competition for empire.

---

[2] A feudal relic, a *quitrent* was an annual fee, usually small, required by the patent that gave title to a piece of land. It differed from ordinary rents in that nonpayment led to a suit for debt, not ejection from the property.

Suggested Readings begin on page SR-1.
For Web activities and resources
related to this chapter, go to
http://www.harcourtcollege.com/history.murrin

CHAPTER 3

ENGLAND DISCOVERS ITS COLONIES: EMPIRE, LIBERTY, AND EXPANSION

THE KINGFISHER ENGAGING THE BARBARY PIRATES ON 22 MAY, 1681, BY WILLEM VAN DE VELDE THE YOUNGER

By the end of the 17th century, England had become the greatest naval power in the world, a position that Great Britain would maintain until overtaken by the United States in the Second World War.

In 1603, when James VI of Scotland ascended the throne of England as King James I (1603–25), England was still a weak power on the fringes of Europe with no colonies except in Ireland. By 1700 England was a global giant, able to tip Europe's balance of power. It possessed 20 colonies in North America and the Caribbean, controlled much of the African slave trade, and had muscled its way into distant India. Commerce and colonies had vastly magnified England's power in Europe.

This transformation occurred during a century of political and religious upheaval at home. King and Parliament fought over their respective powers—a long struggle that led to civil war and the execution of one king in 1649 and to the overthrow of another in 1688. The result was a unique constitution that rested upon parliamentary supremacy and responsible government under the Crown.

This upheaval produced competing visions of politics and the good society. At one extreme, the ruling Stuart dynasty often seemed to be trying to create an absolute monarchy, similar to that of Spain or France. Opponents of absolutism groped for ways to guarantee government by consent without undermining public order. England's colonies shared in the turmoil. Yet by 1700 all of them had begun to converge around the newly defined principles of English constitutionalism. All adopted representative government at some point during the century. All affirmed the values of liberty and property under the English Crown.

England also quarreled with the colonies, whose sheer diversity daunted anyone who hoped to govern them. The colonies formed not a single type, but a spectrum of settlement with contrasting economies, social relationships, and institutions. Yet by 1700 England had created a system of regulation that respected colonial liberties while asserting imperial power.

This chapter will focus on the following major questions:

- What were the major colonial goals of English mercantilists and how close to success did they come?
- What enabled the Middle Colonies to avoid the Indian wars that engulfed New England and Virginia in the mid-1670s?
- On what common principles did English political culture begin to converge in both the mother country and the colonies after the Glorious Revolution?

• What enabled sparsely settled New France to resist British expansion with great success for over half a century, while Spanish Florida seemed almost helpless against the same threat?

THE ATLANTIC PRISM AND THE SPECTRUM OF SETTLEMENT

Over thousands of years, the Indians of the Americas, at first a fairly homogeneous people, had become diversified into hundreds of distinct cultures and languages. The colonists of 17th-century North America and the Caribbean were following much the same course. America divided them. The Atlantic united them. Their connection with England gave them what unity they could sustain.

As long as population remained small, no colony could duplicate the complexity of England. The settlers had to choose what to bring with them and what to leave behind, what they could provide for themselves and what they would have to import—

THE SPECTRUM OF SETTLEMENT: DEMOGRAPHY, ETHNICITY, ECONOMY, 1650–1700

Category	West Indies	Lower South	Chesapeake	Mid-Atlantic	New England	New France
Life expectancy for men, age 20	40	42	45	60+	late 60s	60s
Family Size	Below replacement rate	About two children	Rising after 1680	Very large	Very large	Very large
Race and Ethnicity	Black majority by circa 1670s	Black majority by circa 1710	Growing black minority	Ethnic mix, NW Europe, English a minority	Almost all English	Almost all French
Economy	Sugar	Rice, 1690s ff	Tobacco	Furs, farms	Farms, fishing, shipbuilding	Furs, farms

THE SPECTRUM OF SETTLEMENT: RELIGION AND GOVERNMENT, CIRCA 1675–1700

Category	West Indies	Lower South	Chesapeake	Mid-Atlantic	New England	New France
Formal religion	Anglican Church establishment	Anglican Church establishment by circa 1710	Anglican Church establishment (after 1692 in Md.)	Competing sects, no established church	Congregational Church established	Catholic Church established
Religious tone	Irreverent	Contentious	Low-church Anglican	Family-based piety, sectarian competition	Family-based piety, intensity declining	Intensely Catholic
Local government	Parish	Parish and phantom counties (i.e., no court)	County and parish	County and township	Towns and counties; parishes after 1700	Cities
Provincial government	Royal	Proprietary	Royal (Va.), proprietary (Md.)	From proprietary to royal, except in Pa.	Corporate, with Mass. and N.H. becoming royal	Royal absolutism

choices dictated both by their motives for crossing the ocean and by what the new environment would permit. The colonists sorted themselves out along a vast arc from the cold North to the subtropical Caribbean. If we can imagine England as a source of white light and the Atlantic as a prism refracting that light, 17th-century America becomes a spectrum of settlement, with each color merging imperceptibly into the shade next to it. Each province had much in common with its neighbors, but shared few traits with more distant colonies. At the extremes, the sugar and slave society of Barbados had almost nothing in common with Puritan Massachusetts. Nor did Canada with the French West Indies.

DEMOGRAPHIC DIFFERENCES

The most pronounced differences involved life expectancy, the sex ratio (the ratio of men to women in any society), and family structure. At one extreme were the all-male, multiethnic buccaneering societies in the Caribbean that lived only for plunder. In the sugar colonies, European men often died by age 40, and slaves even sooner. Because women settlers were scarce at first, the family itself seemed an endangered institution. Even when the sex ratio evened out and families began to emerge, couples had few children. Life expectancy in early South Carolina was slightly better than in the islands, slightly lower than in the Chesapeake Bay area. In the Chesapeake colonies men who survived childhood diseases lived to an average age of about 45 years during the last half of the 17th century, still less than in England, where life expectancy exceeded 50. In Virginia and Maryland, as natural increase replaced immigration as the main source of population growth after 1680, women became more numerous, married much earlier, and raised larger families.

The northern colonies were much healthier. In the Delaware valley, a man who reached adulthood could expect to live past 60. In New Netherland, life expectancy and family size exceeded Europe's by 1660, and men outnumbered women among the newcomers by only 2 to 1. On Long Island in the 1680s, one woman claimed that she had more than 300 living descendants. New England was one of the healthiest places in the world. Because the sex

CHRONOLOGY

1642 Civil war erupts in England • Miantonomo abandons planned war of extermination

1643 New England Confederation created

1644 Opechancanough's second massacre in Virginia

1649 England becomes a commonwealth

1651 Parliament passes first Navigation Act

1652–54 First Anglo-Dutch War

1660 Charles II restored to English throne • Parliament passes new Navigation Act

1662 Charles II grants Rhode Island Charter

1663 Staple Act passed • Charles II grants Connecticut Charter

1664 English conquest of New Netherland

1670 First permanent English settlement established in South Carolina

1673 Plantation Duty Act passed • Dutch retake New York for 15 months

1675 Lords of Trade established • Metacom's War breaks out in New England

1676 Bacon's Rebellion breaks out in Virginia

1678 "Popish Plot" crisis begins in England

1680 Pueblos revolt in New Mexico

1684 Massachusetts Charter revoked

1685 Louis XIV revokes Edict of Nantes

1686 Dominion of New England established

1688–89 Glorious Revolution occurs in England

1689 Anglo-French wars begin • Glorious Revolution spreads to Massachusetts, New York, and Maryland

1691 Leisler executed in New York

1692 19 witches hanged in Salem

1696 Parliament passes comprehensive Navigation Act • Board of Trade replaces Lords of Trade

1699 French establish Louisiana • Woolens Act passed

1701 Iroquois make peace with New France

1702–04 Carolina slavers destroy Florida missions

1707 Anglo-Scottish union creates kingdom of Great Britain

1713 Britain and France make peace

1714 George I ascends British throne

1715 Yamasee War devastates South Carolina

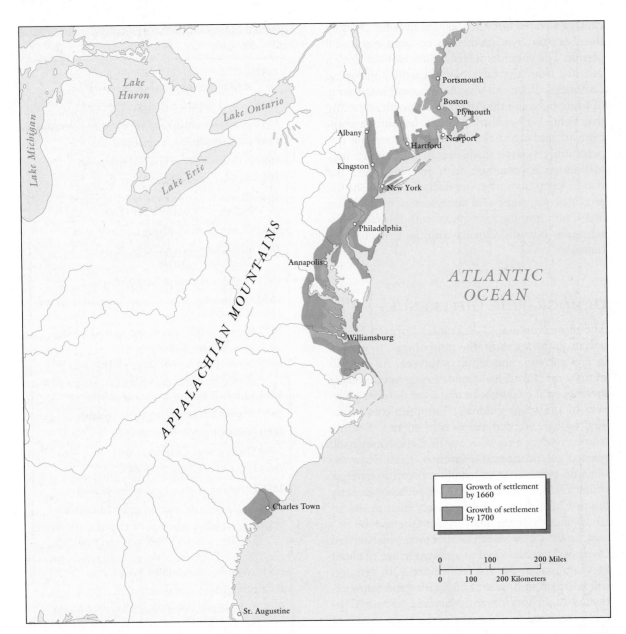

AREA OF ENGLISH SETTLEMENT BY 1700

ratio rapidly approached equality and because the thriving economy permitted couples to marry perhaps two years earlier than in England, population growth exploded. Canada followed a similar pattern. In the late 17th century, the birthrate in New France caught up with New England's, and population grew at a comparable pace.

These demographic differences had significant consequences. For example, the Caribbean and southern colonies were youthful societies in which men with good connections could expect to achieve high office while in their thirties, or even their twenties. By contrast, the New England colonies gradually became dominated by grandfathers. A man rarely became even a selectman before his forties. Magistrates were even older. Simon Bradstreet was 90 when he completed his last term as governor of Massachusetts in 1692. Despite the appalling death rate in the sugar and tobacco colonies, young men remained optimistic and upbeat, as they looked forward to challenging the world and making their fortunes. But in New England, people grew ever more despondent as the century progressed, even though they lived much longer. The typical sermon was a gloomy jeremiad that deplored the failings of the rising generation.

RACE, ETHNICITY, AND ECONOMY

The degree of racial and ethnic mixture also varied from region to region, along with economic priorities. The West Indies already had a large slave majority by 1700 and were well on their way to becoming a New Africa, except that the European minority had a firm grip on wealth and power. In 1700 English settlers were still a clear majority in the southern mainland colonies, but African slaves became a majority in South Carolina around 1710 and were increasing rapidly. They would comprise 40 percent of Virginia's population by the 1730s. Africans were less numerous in the Delaware and Hudson valleys, although slavery became deeply entrenched in New York City and parts of New Jersey.

In the Middle Atlantic region, settlers from all over northwestern Europe were creating a new ethnic mosaic, especially in New Jersey and Pennsylvania. English colonists were probably always a minority, outnumbered at first by the Dutch, and later by Germans, Scots, and Irish. But New England was in every sense the most English of the colonies. In ethnic composition, it may have been more English than England, which by 1700 had sizable Dutch Reformed, French Huguenot, and Scottish Presbyterian minorities. New France was as French as New England was English. The farther south one went, the more diverse the population; the farther north, the more uniform.

Slavery and staple crops went together. The slave societies raised sugar, rice, or tobacco for sale in Europe. General farming and family labor also went together. By 1700 the Middle Atlantic was the wheat belt of North America. The New Englanders farmed and exported fish and lumber to the West Indies.

RELIGION AND EDUCATION

With the exception of Spanish Florida, the intensity of religious observance varied immensely across the spectrum of settlement, ranging from irreverence and indifference in the West Indies to intense piety in New England and New France. Because formal education in the 17th century nearly always had a religious base, literacy followed a similar pattern. Colonists everywhere tried to prevent slaves from learning to read, and low literacy prevailed wherever slavery predominated. Chesapeake settlers provided almost no formal schooling for their children prior to the founding of the College of William and Mary in 1693 and of a Latin grammar school in Annapolis at about the same time. Even some of the justices of the peace in Maryland and Virginia were unable to write. By contrast, the Dutch maintained several good schools in New Netherland. Massachusetts founded Harvard College in 1636 and in 1642 required every town to have a writing school, and larger towns to support a Latin grammar school, in order to frustrate "ye old deluder Satan," as a 1647 school law phrased it. The Jesuits founded a college (actually more akin to a secondary school) in Quebec a few years before Harvard opened. France sent a bishop to Quebec in 1659, and he established a seminary (now Laval University) in the 1660s. Along the spectrum, piety, literacy, and education all grew stronger from south to north, although laymen in New France never became as literate as in New England.

Public support for the clergy followed the same pattern. By 1710 the established church of the mother country was the legally established church in the West Indies and in the southern mainland colonies. Establishment and dissent fought to a standstill in the Middle Atlantic, with toleration claiming the real victory in New York and full religious liberty in Pennsylvania. In New England, Old World dissent became the New World establishment. Public support for the clergy was much greater in the north than in the south. The sugar islands had the most wealth, but they maintained only one clergyman for every 3,000 to 9,000 people, depending on the island. In the Chesapeake the comparable ratio was about one for every 1,500 people by 1700. It was perhaps one for every 1,000 in New York, one for every 600 in New England, and still lower in New France.

Moral standards also rose from south to north. New Englanders boasted that they were far more godly than all other colonists. The Puritans "give out that they are Israelites," reported a Dutch visitor to Connecticut, "and that we in our colony are Egyptians, and that the English in the Virginias are also Egyptians." As early as 1638 one Marylander quipped that a neighbor deserved to be "whippt at virginea" or "hanged in new England."

LOCAL AND PROVINCIAL GOVERNMENTS

Forms of government also varied. Drawing on their English experience, settlers could choose from among parishes, boroughs (towns), and counties. A colony's choices depended on its location along the spectrum of settlement.

The only important local institution in the sugar islands and in South Carolina was the parish, which took on many secular functions, such as poor relief. The Chesapeake colonies relied primarily on the county but also made increasing use of the parish. Few parishes were ever organized in the Middle Atlantic colonies, but the county as a form of government arrived with the English conquest of New Netherland in 1664 and became a powerful institution. Townships also appeared. New England's most basic local institution was the town. Massachusetts created counties in the 1640s, followed 20 years later by Connecticut and in the 1680s by Plymouth. Rhode Island and New Hampshire waited until the 18th century before creating counties. After 1700, towns large enough to support more than one church also adopted the parish system. In local government as in its economy, New England's use of the full range of parishes, towns, and counties made the region more fully English than other colonies.

The West Indian colonies all had royal governments by the 1660s (see the subsection "The Lords of Trade and Imperial Reform" later in this chapter). Proprietary forms dominated the mainland south of New England, except for royal Virginia.

Until the 1680s New England relied on corporate forms of government in which all officials, even governors, were elected. This system survived in Connecticut and Rhode Island until independence and beyond.

UNIFYING TRENDS: LANGUAGE, WAR, LAW, AND INHERITANCE

Despite all this diversity, the 17th century produced a few trends toward greater homogeneity. For instance, language became more uniform in America than in England. True, the New England dialect derived mostly from East Anglia, the southern accent from southern and western England, and Middle Atlantic speech from north-central England. But Londoners went to all the colonies (in England, people went to London), and London English affected every colony and softened the contrasts among the emerging regional dialects.

Another area of uniformity was the manner in which the settlers waged war: They did it in their own way, not with the professional armies that were just taking hold in Europe, but with short-term volunteers for whom terror against Indian women and children was often the tactic of choice. Europe was moving toward limited wars; the colonists demanded quick and total victories.

In the colonies, law became a simpler version of England's complex legal system. Justice was local and uncomplicated—in fact, an organized legal profession did not emerge until the 18th century. The absence of lawyers pleased most settlers.

Finally, no mainland American colony rigidly followed English patterns of inheritance. Instead, the colonies were developing their own practices. Some women had a chance to acquire property, usually by inheritance from a deceased husband, particularly in the Chesapeake colonies during the long period when men greatly outnumbered women. The single women who crossed the Atlantic as servants were desperate people who had hit bottom in England. Those who survived enjoyed a fantastic chance at upward mobility. Many won a respectability never available to them in England. In every colony younger sons also found their situation improved. They played a huge role in settling the colonies, especially among the Chesapeake elite, and they showed little inclination to preserve institutions that had offered them no landed inheritance in England. Most families made no distinction between the eldest and other sons, except in New England. The Puritan colonies honored a biblical mandate to give the eldest son a double share. That practice strengthened patriarchy in the region, but it was much less discriminatory than primogeniture, which in England gave all land to the eldest son.

THE BEGINNINGS OF EMPIRE

In the chaotic 1640s, the English realized that their colonies overseas were bringing them few benefits. England had no coherent colonial policy.

UPHEAVAL IN AMERICA: THE CRITICAL 1640S

England's civil wars rocked its emerging empire, politically and economically. As royal power collapsed in the 1640s, the West Indian colonies demanded and received elective assemblies. The Dutch, taking advantage of the chaos in England, helped finance the sugar revolution in Barbados and seized control of trade in and out of England's West Indian and Chesapeake colonies. By 1650 most sugar and tobacco exports were going to Amsterdam, not London.

During the civil wars, nobody in England exercised effective control over the colonies. The king had declared that their trade was to remain in English hands, but no agency existed to enforce that claim. The new elective assemblies of Barbados and the Leeward Islands preferred to trade with the Dutch, even after the English Crown took over those colonies in 1660. The mainland colonies had been organized by joint-stock companies or proprietary lords under royal charters, but there the colonists governed themselves. As the New England settlements expanded, the new colonies of Connecticut, Rhode Island, and New Haven did not even bother to obtain royal charters. On the mainland, only Virginia had a royal governor.

The chaos of the 1640s gave Indians a unique opportunity to resist the settlers. As civil war disrupted trade with England and threatened to cut off regular supplies of muskets and gunpowder, the Indians gained a powerful advantage over the settle-

> "*Our fathers had plenty of deer and skins, our plains were full of deer, as also our woods, and of turkies, and our coves full of fish and fowl. But these English have gotten our land, they with scythes cut down the grass, and with axes fell the trees; their cows and horses eat the grass, and their hogs spoil our clam banks, and we shall be starved; therefore. . . . When you see the three fires that will be made forty days hence, in a clear night, then do as we, and the next day fall on and kill men, women, and children, but no cows, for they will serve to eat till our deer be increased again.*"
>
> **MIANTONOMO**
>
> *Sachem of the Narragansetts, urging all Indians to unite and destroy all New England settlers, 1642*

ments. That danger seemed so ominous that Rhode Island ordered young men to learn how to use bows and arrows. Although the Indians of the eastern woodlands never united into an effective league, many of them, such as Miantonomo in New England and Opechancanough in Virginia, began to think of driving the Europeans out altogether.

Indians greatly outnumbered settlers, except in eastern New England and the Virginia tidewater. Between 1643 and 1647, the Iroquois nearly wiped out New France, and the Hudson valley Algonquians almost destroyed New Netherland. Maryland, beset by conflicts with Susquehannock Indians and by civil war among its colonists, nearly ceased to exist. The number of settlers there may have fallen to 300 by 1648. In Virginia the aging warrior Opechancanough staged another massacre, killing 500 settlers without warning on a holy day in 1644. This time the settlers recovered more quickly, took Opechancanough prisoner in 1646, and murdered him. They broke up his chiefdom and made its member tribes accept treaties of dependency.

Only New England avoided war with the Indians—just barely. Miantonomo, sachem of the Narragansetts, called for a war of extermination against the settlers, to be launched by a surprise attack in 1642. He abandoned the plan when settlers got wind of it. The colonists created their own defensive alliance in 1643, the New England Confederation, which united the four orthodox colonies of Massachusetts, Plymouth, Connecticut, and New Haven. Rhode Island was not invited to join. The confederation persuaded the Mohegans to kill Miantonomo, and tensions with the Narragansett Indians remained high. The Narragansetts controlled some of the finest land in New England. Massachusetts, Plymouth, and Connecticut all wanted that land, but the Narragansetts were still too powerful to intimidate. When threatened, they withdrew into inaccessible places that terrified most of the settlers. After the Narragansetts made it clear that they would fight if they had to, the Puritans backed down.

What happened in the colonies seemed of little interest to the English people in the turbulent 1640s. Later, as the debris of civil war was cleared away and the extent of Dutch commercial domination became obvious, the English turned their eyes westward once again. In a sense, England first discovered its colonies and their importance around 1650.

MERCANTILISM AS A MORAL REVOLUTION

During the 17th century, most of the European powers adopted a set of policies now usually called "mercantilism." The decline of the Spanish Empire persuaded many observers that the power of a state depended more on its underlying economy than on armies or the silver that paid for them. Mercantilists argued that power derived ultimately from the wealth of a country, that the increase of wealth required vigorous trade, and that colonies had become essential to that growth. Clearly, a state had to control the commerce of its colonies. Mercantilists, however, disagreed over the best ways to promote economic growth. The Dutch favored virtual free trade within Europe. England preferred some kind of state regulation of the domestic and imperial economy.

After a century of religious wars, neither Catholics nor Protestants had won a decisive victory in Europe. To European statesmen of the time, these conflicts merely confirmed their belief that governments reflected the passions of men. Philosophers agreed that the major passions are glory, love, and greed. Glory seemed nobler than carnal love, and love more inspiring than greed, which in any case was beneath the dignity of a gentleman. Still, the endless wars, driven by the quest for glory and the love of holy causes, had crippled Spain, killed one-third of the German people, and nearly destroyed the English state.

As time passed, statesmen began to look more favorably upon greed, a passion in which they found interesting properties. The pursuit of glory or love inspires intense but unpredictable activity, followed by relaxation or even exhaustion. Greed, because it is insatiable, fosters *predictable* behavior—namely, the pursuit of self-interest. By creating economic incentives, then, a state could induce its people to work to increase not only their own wealth and power but that of the whole country. Likewise, by imposing import duties and other disincentives, the state could discourage actions detrimental to its power.

At first these ideas were as gloomy as the world in which they arose. Early mercantilists assumed that the world contained a fixed supply of wealth. A state, to augment its own power, would have to expropriate the wealth of a rival. Trade wars would replace religious wars, though presumably they would be less destructive, which they usually were. Gradually, however, a more radical idea took hold: The growth of trade might multiply the wealth of the whole world, with all nations benefiting and becoming so interdependent that war between them would be recognized as suicidal. That vision of peace and unending growth has never been realized, but it still inspires people today.

Mercantilism marked a major breakthrough toward modernity. It gradually became associated with the emerging idea of unending progress, and it made statesmen rethink the role of legislation in their societies.

Europeans were already familiar with two kinds of progress, one associated with Renaissance humanism, the other explicitly Christian. The opening of the Americas had already reinforced both visions. Humanists knew that the distant ancestors of Europeans had all been "barbarians" who had advanced over the centuries toward "civility." Their own encounters with the indigenous peoples of Africa, Ireland, and America underscored this dual-

A PICTISH MAN HOLDING A HUMAN HEAD, BY JOHN WHITE, LATE 16TH CENTURY In the ancient world, the Picts were among the ancestors of the English and the Scots. John White, who painted many Indian scenes on Roanoke Island in the 1580s, believed that the English had been "savages" not all that long ago and that American Indians, like the English, could progress to "civility." America made him think of "progress."

istic view by revealing new "savages" who seemed morally and culturally inferior to the "civilized" colonists. Most Christians shared these convictions, but they also believed that human society was progressing toward a future Millennium in which Christ will return to earth and reign with his saints in perfect harmony for 1,000 years. To missionaries, both Catholic and Protestant, the discovery of millions of "heathens" in the Americas stimulated millennial thinking. God had chosen this moment to open a new hemisphere to Christians, they explained, because the Millennium was near. Both the humanist and the Christian notions of progress

were static concepts, however. Humanity would advance to a certain level, and progress would cease. Mercantilism, by contrast, marked a revolution of the human imagination precisely because it could arouse visions of endless progress.

Mercantilism also promoted a more modern concept of law. In the past, most jurists believed that legislation merely restated natural laws or immemorial customs in written form. Mercantilists, on the other hand, saw law as an agent of change. They intended to modify behavior, perhaps even transform society. They had no illusions about achieving perfection, however. At first, they probably considered anything a triumph that made their exhausted world less terrible. But as the decades passed, mercantilists became more confident of their ability to improve society.

THE FIRST NAVIGATION ACT

English merchants began debating trade policy during a severe depression in the 1620s. They agreed that a nation's wealth depended on its balance of trade, that a healthy nation ought to export more than it imports, and that the difference—or balance—could be converted into military strength. They also believed that a state needed colonies to produce essential commodities unavailable at home. And they argued that a society ought to export luxuries, not import them. English merchants observed Dutch commercial success and determined that it rested on a mastery of these principles. For England to catch up, Parliament would have to intervene.

With the close of the Thirty Years' War in Europe in 1648, the three major Protestant powers—Sweden, the Netherlands, and England—no longer had reason to avoid fighting one another. England reacted quickly after the execution of Charles I. London merchants clamored for measures to stifle Dutch competition. Parliament listened to them, not to Cromwell and other Puritans who regarded war between two Protestant republics as an abomination. The merchants got their Navigation Act—and their war.

In 1650 Parliament banned foreign ships from English colonies. A year later, it passed the first comprehensive Navigation Act, aimed at Dutch competition. Under this act, Asian and African goods could be imported into the British Isles or the colonies only in English-owned ships, and the master and at least half of each crew had to be Englishmen. European goods could be imported into Britain or the colonies in either English ships or the ships of the producing country, but foreigners could not trade between one English port and another.

This new attention from the English government angered the colonists in the West Indies and North America. Mercantilists assumed that the colonies existed only to enrich the mother country. Why else had England permitted them to be founded? But the young men growing sugar in Barbados or tobacco in Virginia intended to prosper on their own. Selling

THE COFFEHOUS MOB This engraving appeared in Edward Ward, *Vulgus Britannicus*, or the British *Hudibras* (1711). By the 18th century, colonial products were transforming social life in London. Ward depicts this coffeehouse as a scene of disorder.

their crops to the Dutch, who offered the lowest freight rates, added to their profits. Although New England produced no staple that Europeans wanted except fish, Yankee skippers cheerfully swapped their fish or forest products in the Chesapeake for tobacco, which they then carried directly to Europe, usually to Amsterdam.

Barbados greeted the Navigation Act by proclaiming virtual independence. Virginia recognized Charles II as king and continued to welcome Dutch and Yankee traders. In 1651 Parliament dispatched a naval force to America. It compelled Barbados to submit to Parliament and then sailed to the Chesapeake, where Virginia and Maryland capitulated in 1652. In return, the Virginians received the right to elect their own governor, a privilege that the Crown revoked in 1660. Without resident officials to enforce English policy, however, trade with the Dutch continued.

By 1652 England and the Netherlands were at war. For two years the English navy, trim and efficient after a decade of struggle against the king, dealt heavy blows to the Dutch. Finally, in 1654, Cromwell sent Parliament home and made peace. A militant Protestant, he preferred to fight Catholic Spain rather than the Netherlands. In the tradition of Drake, Gilbert, and Ralegh, he sent a fleet to take Hispaniola. It failed in that mission but it seized Jamaica in 1655.

RESTORATION NAVIGATION ACTS

By the Restoration era, mercantilist thinking had become widespread. Although the new royalist Parliament invalidated all legislation passed during the Commonwealth period, these "Cavaliers" promptly reenacted and extended the original Navigation Act in a series of new measures. The Navigation Act of 1660 required that all colonial trade be carried on English ships (a category that included colonial vessels but now excluded the Scots), but the master and *three-fourths* of the crew had to be English. The act also created a category of "enumerated commodities," of which sugar and tobacco were the most important, permitting these products to be shipped from the colony of origin *only* to England or to another English colony—the intent being to give England a monopoly over the export of major staples from every English colony to Europe and to the rest of the world. The colonists could still export nonenumerated commodities elsewhere. New England could send fish to a French sugar island, for example, and Virginia could export wheat to Cuba, provided the French and the Spanish would let them.

In a second measure, the Staple Act of 1663, Parliament regulated goods going to the colonies. With few exceptions, products from Europe, Asia, or Africa had to land in England before they could be delivered to the settlements.

A third measure, the Plantation Duty Act of 1673, required captains of colonial ships to post bond in the colonies that they would deliver all enumerated commodities to England, or else pay on the spot the duties that would be owed in England (the "plantation duty"). This measure, England hoped, would eliminate all incentives to smuggle. To make it effective, England for the first time sent customs officers to the colonies to collect the duty and prosecute all violators. Because the only income of these officials came from fees and from their share of condemned vessels, their livelihood was precarious. At first colonial governments regarded customs collectors as parasites. Maryland officials even murdered one of them in the 1680s.

Parliament intended nothing less than a revolution in Atlantic trade. Properly enforced, the Navigation Acts would dislodge the Dutch and establish English hegemony over Atlantic trade, and that is what happened by the end of the century. In 1600, about 90 percent of England's exports consisted of woolen cloth. By 1700, colonial and Asian commerce accounted for 30 to 40 percent of England's overseas trade, and London had become the largest city in western Europe. As the center of England's colonial trade, its population tripled during the 17th century.

Enforcement long remained uneven, but in the 1670s a war between France and the Netherlands diverted critical Dutch resources from trade to defense, thus helping England catch up with the Dutch. The British navy soon became the most powerful fleet in the world. By 1710 or so, virtually all British colonial trade was carried on British ships. Sugar, tobacco, and other staple crops all passed through Britain on their way to their ultimate destination. Nearly all of the manufactured goods consumed in the colonies were made in Britain. Most products from Europe or Asia des-

tined for the colonies passed through Britain first, although some smuggling of these goods continued.

Few government policies have ever been as successful as England's Navigation Acts, but England achieved these results without pursuing a steady course toward increased imperial control. For example, in granting charters to Rhode Island in 1662 and to Connecticut in 1663, Charles II approved elective governors and legislatures in both colonies. (The Connecticut charter also absorbed the New Haven Colony into the Hartford government.) These elective officials could not be dismissed or punished for failure to enforce the Navigation Acts. Moreover, the Crown also chartered several new Restoration colonies (see chapter 2), whose organizers had few incentives to obey the new laws. Making the empire work would take time.

INDIANS, SETTLERS, UPHEAVAL

As time passed, the commercial possibilities and limitations of North America were becoming much clearer. The French and Dutch mastered the fur trade because they controlled the two all-water routes to the interior, via the St. Lawrence system and the Hudson and Mohawk valleys. South Carolinians could go around the southern extreme of the Appalachians. They all needed Indian trading partners.

As of 1670, no sharp boundaries yet existed between Indian lands and colonial settlements. Boston, the largest city north of Mexico, was only 15 miles from an Indian village. Connecticut valley towns were surrounded by Indians. The outposts on the Delaware River were islands in a sea of Indians. In the event of war, nearly every European settlement was vulnerable to attack.

INDIAN STRATEGIES OF SURVIVAL

By the 1670s most of the coastal tribes in regular contact with Europeans had already been devastated by disease or soon would be. European diseases, by magnifying the depleted tribes' need for captives, also increased the intensity of wars among Indian peoples, probably to their highest point ever. The Iroquois, for example, although hard hit by smallpox and other ailments, acquired muskets from the

Dutch and used them, first to attack other Iroquoian peoples, and then Algonquians. These "mourning wars" were often initiated by the widow or bereaved mother or sister of a deceased loved one. She insisted that her male relatives repair the loss. Her warrior relatives then launched a raid and brought back captives. Adult male prisoners, who might take revenge if allowed to live, were usually tortured to death. Most women and children were adopted and assimilated. Adoption worked because the captives shared the cultural values of their captors. They became Iroquois. As early as the 1660s, a majority of the Indians in the Five Nations were adoptees, not native-born Iroquois. In this way the confederacy remained strong while its rivals declined. In the southern piedmont, the warlike, Sioux-speaking Catawba Indians also assimilated thousands from other tribes. Further into the southern interior, the Creeks assimilated adoptees from a wide variety of ethnic backgrounds. They and other southern nations also became adept at playing off the Spaniards against the English (and later the French).

In some ways, America became as much a new world for the Indians as it did for the colonists. European cloth, muskets, hatchets, knives, and pots were welcomed among the Indians and spread far into the interior, but they came at a price. Indians who learned to use them gradually abandoned traditional skills and became increasingly dependent on trade with Europeans, a process not complete until the 19th century. Alcohol, the one item always in demand, was also dangerous. Indian men drank to alter their mood and achieve visions, not for sociability. Drunkenness became a major, if intermittent, social problem.

Settlers who understood that their future depended on the fur trade, as in New France, tried to stay on good terms with the Indians. Pieter Stuyvesant put New Netherland on such a course, and the English governors of New York after 1664 followed his lead. Edmund Andros, governor from 1674 to 1680, cultivated the friendship of the Iroquois League, in which the five member nations had promised not to wage war against one another. In 1677 Andros and the Five Nations agreed to make New York the easternmost link in what the English called the "Covenant Chain" of peace, a huge defensive advantage for a lightly populated colony. Thus, while New England and Virginia fought bitter Indian wars in the 1670s, New York avoided conflict.

The Covenant Chain later proved flexible enough to incorporate other Indians and colonies as well.

Where the Indian trade was slight, war became more likely. In 1675 it erupted in both New England and the Chesapeake. In the 1640s Virginia had negotiated treaties of dependency with the member nations of the Powhatan chiefdom, in the hope of keeping them loyal in the event of war with other Indians. The New England colonies had similar understandings with the large non-Christian nations of the region. But the Puritan governments placed even greater reliance on a growing number of Christianized Indians.

PURITAN INDIAN MISSIONS

Serious efforts to convert Indians to Protestantism began in the 1640s on the island of Martha's Vineyard under Thomas Mayhew, Sr., and Thomas Mayhew, Jr., and in Massachusetts under John Eliot, pastor of the Roxbury church. Eliot tried to make the nearby Indian town of Natick into a model mission community.

The Mayhews were more successful than Eliot, although he received most of the publicity. They worked with local sachems and challenged only the tribal powwows (prophets or medicine men) and even converted some of them when they proved unable to cure smallpox. The Mayhews encouraged Indian men to teach the settlers of Martha's Vineyard and Nantucket how to catch whales, an activity that made them a vital part of the settlers' economy without threatening their identity as males. Eliot, by contrast, attacked the authority of the sachems as well as the powwows, challenged the traditional tribal structure, and insisted on turning Indian men into farmers, a female role in Indian society. Yet he did translate the Bible and a few other religious works into the Massachusett language.

By the early 1670s more than 1,000 Indians, nearly all of them survivors of coastal tribes that had been decimated by disease, lived in a string of seven "praying towns," and Eliot was busy organizing five more, mostly among the Nipmucks of the interior. By 1675 about 2,300 Indians, perhaps one-quarter of all those living in southeastern New England, were in various stages of conversion to Christianity. But only 160 of them had achieved the kind of conversion experience that Puritans required for full membership in a church. Indians did not share the Puritan sense of sin. They could not easily grasp why their best deeds should stink in the nostrils of the Lord. The more powerful nations felt threatened by this pressure to convert, and resistance to Christianity became one cause of the war that broke out in 1675. Other causes were the settlers' lust for Indian lands and the fear, especially among younger warrior-hunters, that their whole way of life was in danger of extinction.

Metacom (whom the English called King Philip) was one of those Indians. He was sachem of the Wampanoags and the son of Massasoit, who had celebrated the first thanksgiving feast with the Pilgrims. Metacom once remarked that if he became "a praying sachem, I shall be a poor and weak one, and easily be trod upon."

METACOM'S (OR KING PHILIP'S) WAR

War broke out shortly after Plymouth executed three Wampanoags accused of murdering John Sassamon, a Harvard-educated Indian preacher who may have been spying on Metacom. The fighting began in the frontier town of Swansea in June 1675, after settlers killed an Indian they found looting an abandoned house. When the Indians demanded satisfaction the next day, the settlers laughed in their faces. The Indians took revenge, and the violence escalated into war.

The settlers, remembering their easy triumph over the Pequots a generation earlier (see chapter 2), were confident of victory. But, since the 1630s, the Indians had acquired firearms. They had built forges to make musket balls and repair their weapons. They had even become marksmen with the smoothbore musket by firing several smaller bullets, instead of a single musketball, with each charge. The settlers, who had usually paid Indians to do their hunting for them, were terrible shots. In the tradition of European armies, they discharged volleys without aiming. To the shock of the colonists, Metacom won several engagements against Plymouth militia, usually by ambushing the noisy intruders. He then escaped from Plymouth Colony and headed toward the upper Connecticut valley, where he burned five Massachusetts towns in three months.

Massachusetts and Connecticut joined the fray. Rather than attack Metacom's Wampanoags they went after the Narragansetts, who were trying hard

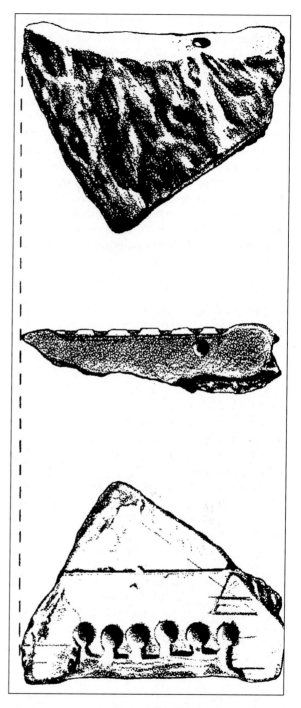

BULLET MOLD IN USE AMONG NEW ENGLAND INDIANS, CIRCA 1675 Indians could make bullets and repair muskets, but they remained dependent on Europeans for their supply of gunpowder. In early 1676, the Indian leader Metacom ran out of gunpowder after failing to acquire more from New France. Over the next several months, he lost the war.

to remain neutral but whose fertile lands many settlers dreamed of acquiring. In the Great Swamp Fight of December 1675, a Puritan army, with the aid of Indian guides, attacked an unfinished Narragansett fort and massacred hundreds of Indians, most of them women and children, but not before the Indians had picked off a high percentage of the officers. The surviving warriors joined Metacom and showed that they too could use terror. They torched more frontier settlements. Altogether about 800 settlers were killed, and two dozen towns were destroyed or badly damaged in the war.

Atrocities were common on both sides. When one settler boasted that his Bible would save him from harm, the Indians disemboweled him and stuffed the sacred book in his belly. At least 17 friendly Indians were murdered by settlers, some in cold blood before dozens of witnesses, but for more than a year New England juries refused to convict anyone. On one occasion, when some Maine Indians were brought to Marblehead as prisoners, the women of that fishing village literally tore them to pieces with their bare hands.

Frontier settlers demanded the annihilation of all nearby Indians, even the Christian converts. The Massachusetts government, shocked to realize that it could not win the war without Indian allies, did what it could to protect the "praying" Indians. The magistrates evacuated them to a bleak island in Boston harbor where they spent a miserable winter

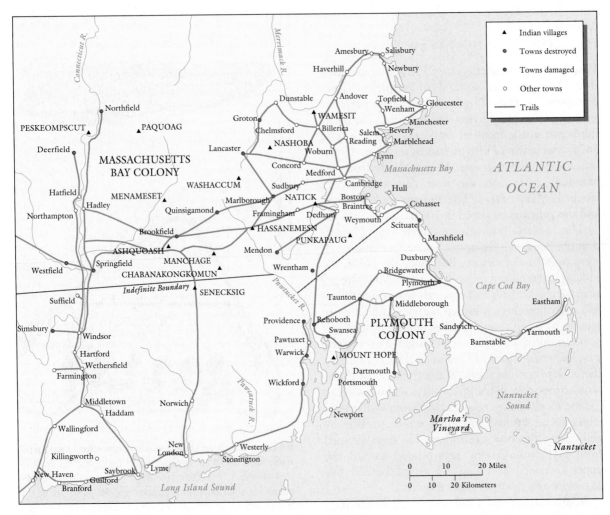

NEW ENGLAND IN METACOM'S WAR, 1675–1676

of privation but then enlisted to fight against Metacom in the spring campaign. Some settlers may even have tried to assassinate Eliot by ramming his boat in Boston harbor. The accused men, who insisted that the collision was accidental, were acquitted.

The war nearly tore New England apart. It split the clergy. Increase Mather, a prominent Boston minister, saw the conflict as God's judgment on a sinful people and warned that no victory would come until New England repented and reformed. At first the Massachusetts General Court agreed. It blamed the war on young men who wore their hair too long, on boys and girls who took leisurely horse rides together, on people who dressed above their station in life, and on blaspheming Quakers. Another Boston minister, William Hubbard, insisted that the war was only a brief testing time, after which the Lord would lead his saints to victory over the heathen. To Daniel Gookin, a magistrate committed to Eliot's mission work, the war was an unspeakable tragedy for both settlers and Indians.

Despite their disagreements, the settlers pulled together and won the war in 1676. Governor Andros of New York persuaded the Mohawks to attack Metacom's winter camp and disperse his people, who by then were short of gunpowder. The New Englanders, working closely with Mohegan and Christian Indian allies, then hunted down Metacom's war parties, killed hundreds of Indians, including Metacom, and sold hundreds more into West Indian slavery. Some of those enslaved had not even been party to the conflict and had actually requested asylum from it. As the tide turned, the Massachusetts government sided with Hubbard by ordering a day of thanksgiving, but Increase Mather's church observed a fast day instead. The colony had not reformed adequately, he explained.

VIRGINIA'S INDIAN WAR

In Virginia, Governor Sir William Berkeley, who had led the colony to victory over Opechancanough 30 years earlier, rejoiced in the New Englanders' woes. Metacom's War was the least they deserved for the way the Puritans had ripped England apart and executed Charles I during the civil wars. Then Virginia began to have troubles of its own.

In 1675 the Doegs, a dependent Indian nation in the Potomac valley, demanded payment of an old debt from a local planter. When he refused, they ran off some of his livestock. After his overseer killed one of them, the others fled but later returned to ambush and kill the man. The county militia mustered and followed the Doegs across the Potomac into Maryland. At a fork in the trail, the militia split into two parties. Each found a group of Indians in a shack a few hundred yards up the path it was following. Both parties fired at point-blank range, killing 11 at one cabin and 14 at the other. One of the bands was indeed Doeg; the other was not: "Susquehannock friends," blurted one Indian as he fled.

The Susquehannocks were a strong Iroquoian-speaking people with firearms; they had moved south to escape Iroquois attacks. At Maryland's invitation, they had recently occupied land north of the Potomac. Berkeley, still hoping to avoid war, sent John Washington (ancestor of George) with some Virginia militia to investigate the killings and, if possible, to set matters right.

Washington preferred vengeance. His Virginia militia joined with a Maryland force, and together they besieged a formidable Susquehannock fort on the north bank of the Potomac. The fort was too strong to take without artillery even though the attackers had a huge edge in numbers. When the Indians sent out five or six sachems to negotiate, the militia murdered them and then laid siege to the fort for the next six weeks. The Indians, short of provisions, finally broke out one night with all their people, killing several militiamen. After hurling taunts of defiance and promises of vengeance, they disappeared into the forest. Apparently blaming Virginia more than Maryland, they killed more than 30 Virginia settlers in January 1676. The colonists began to panic.

Berkeley favored a defensive strategy against the Indians; most settlers wanted to attack. In March 1676 the governor summoned a special session of the Virginia legislature to approve the creation of a string of forts above the fall line of the major rivers, with companies of "rangers" to patrol the stretches between them. Berkeley also hoped to maintain a distinction between the clearly hostile Susquehannocks and other Indians who might still be neutral or friendly. Frontier settlers demanded war against them all. Finally, to avoid further provocation, Berkeley restricted the fur trade to a few of his close associates. To the men excluded from that circle, his actions looked like favoritism. To new settlers in frontier counties, whose access to land was blocked by the Indians and who now had to pay higher taxes, Berkeley's strategy seemed intolerable, ineffective, and needlessly expensive.

In both the Second (1665–67) and Third (1672–74) Anglo-Dutch Wars, Berkeley had built costly forts to protect the colony from the Dutch navy, but Dutch warships had sailed around the forts and mauled the tobacco fleet anyway. Accordingly, colonists denounced the building of any more forts and demanded an offensive campaign waged by unpaid volunteers, who would take their rewards by plundering and enslaving Indians. In April the frontier settlers found a reckless leader in Nathaniel Bacon, a young newcomer to the colony with a scandalous past and £1,800 to invest. Using his po-

litical connections (he was the governor's cousin by marriage), he managed an appointment to the council soon after his arrival in the colony in 1674. Bacon, the owner of a plantation and trading post in Henrico County at the falls of the James River (now Richmond), was one of the men excluded from the Indian trade under Berkeley's new rules.

BACON'S REBELLION

Ignoring Berkeley's orders, Bacon marched his frontiersmen south in search of the elusive Susquehannocks. After several days his weary men reached a village of friendly Occaneechees, who offered them shelter, announced that they knew where to find a Susquehannock camp, and even offered to attack it. The Occaneechees surprised and defeated

CRUDE HOUSING FOR SETTLERS IN NORTH AMERICA When the first settlers came to North America, their living quarters were anything but luxurious. The crude housing shown in this modern reconstruction of Jamestown remained typical of Virginia and Maryland through the 17th century.

the Susquehannocks and returned with their captives to celebrate the victory with Bacon. But after they had fallen asleep, Bacon's men massacred the Occaneechees and seized their furs and prisoners. On the return to Henrico in May, the Baconians boasted of their prowess as Indian killers.

By then, Berkeley had outlawed Bacon, dissolved the legislature, and called the first general election since 1661. He asked the burgesses to bring their grievances to Jamestown for redress at the June assembly. "How miserable that man is," he complained, "that Governes a People where six parts of seaven at least are Poore Endebted Discontented and Armed."

Henrico's voters elected Bacon to the House of Burgesses. Berkeley had him arrested when he reached Jamestown and made him go down on his knees before the governor and council and apologize for his disobedience. Berkeley then forgave him and restored him to his seat in the council. By then, even the governor had abandoned his effort to distinguish between hostile and friendly Indians, but he still favored a defensive war. While the burgesses were passing laws to reform the county courts, the vestries, and the tax system, Bacon slipped away to Henrico, summoned his followers again, and marched on Jamestown. At gunpoint, he

forced Berkeley to commission him as general of volunteers and compelled the legislature to authorize another expedition against the Indians.

Berkeley retreated down river to Gloucester County and mustered its militia, but they refused to follow him against Bacon. They would fight only Indians. Mortified, Berkeley fled to the eastern shore, the only part of the colony that was safe from Indian attack and thus still loyal to him. Bacon hastened to Jamestown, summoned a meeting of planters at the governor's Green Spring mansion, made them swear an oath of loyalty to him, and ordered the confiscation of the estates of Berkeley's supporters. Meanwhile, Berkeley raised his own force on the eastern shore by promising the men an exemption from taxes for 21 years and the right to plunder the rebels.

Royal government collapsed. During the summer of 1676, hundreds of settlers set out to make their fortunes by plundering Indians, other colonists, or both. Bacon's Rebellion was the largest upheaval in the American colonies before 1775. Later legends to the contrary, it had little to do with liberty.

Bacon never did kill a hostile Indian. While he was slaughtering and enslaving the unresisting Pamunkeys along the frontier, Berkeley assembled a small fleet and retook Jamestown in August. Bacon rushed east, exhibiting his Indian captives along the

HENRY LATROBE'S SKETCH OF GREEN SPRING, THE HOME OF GOVERNOR SIR WILLIAM BERKELEY, AT THE TIME OF BACON'S REBELLION Green Spring was one of the first great houses built in Virginia. Latrobe made this drawing in the 1790s.

way, and laid siege to Jamestown. He captured the wives of prominent Berkeley supporters and forced them to stand in the line of fire as he dug his trenches closer to the capital. After suffering only a few casualties, the governor's men grew discouraged, and in early September the whole force returned to the eastern shore. Bacon then burned Jamestown to the ground. He also boasted of his ability to hold off an English army, unite Virginia with Maryland and North Carolina, and win Dutch support for setting up an independent Chesapeake republic. Instead he died of dysentery in October.

Berkeley soon regained control of Virginia. Using the ships of the London tobacco fleet, he overpowered the plantations that Bacon had fortified. Then, in January 1677 a force of 1,000 redcoats arrived, too late to help but in time to strain the colony's depleted resources. Ignoring royal orders to show clemency, Berkeley hanged 23 of the rebels. A new assembly repudiated the reforms of 1676, and in

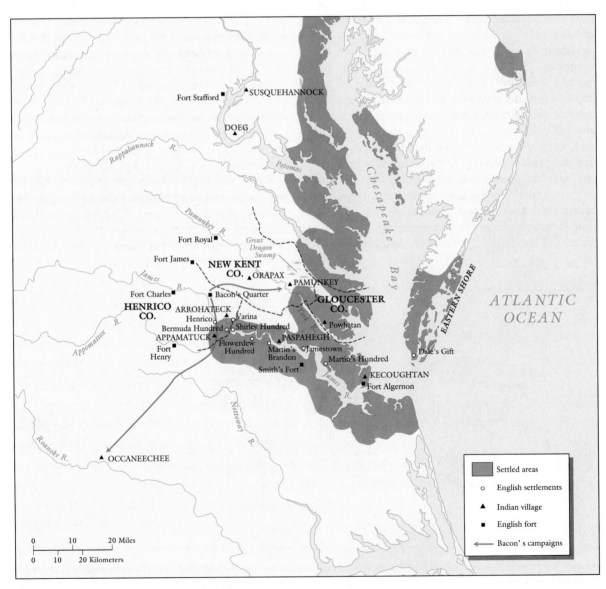

BACON'S REBELLION IN VIRGINIA, 1676

many counties the governor's men used their control of the courts to continue plundering the Baconians through confiscations and fines. Berkeley, summoned to England to defend himself, died there in 1677 before he could present his case.

CRISIS IN ENGLAND AND THE REDEFINITION OF EMPIRE

Bacon's Rebellion helped trigger a political crisis in England. Because Virginia produced little tobacco in 1676 during the uprising, English customs revenues fell sharply, and the king was obliged to ask Parliament for more money. Parliament's response was tempered by the much deeper problem of the royal succession. Charles II had fathered many bastards, but his royal marriage was childless. After the queen reached menopause in the mid-1670s, his brother James, duke of York, became his heir. By then James had become a Catholic. When Charles dissolved the Parliament that had sat from 1661 until 1678, he knew he would have to deal with a new House of Commons terrified by the prospect of a Catholic king.

THE POPISH PLOT, THE EXCLUSION CRISIS, AND THE RISE OF PARTY

In this atmosphere of distrust, a cynical adventurer, Titus Oates, fabricated the sensational story that he had uncovered a sinister "Popish Plot" to kill Charles and bring James to the throne. In the wake of these accusations, the king's ministry fell, and the parliamentary opposition won majorities in three successive elections between 1678 and 1681. Organized by Lord Shaftesbury (the Carolina proprietor), the opposition demanded that James, a Catholic, be excluded from the throne in favor of his Protestant daughters, Mary and Anne. It also called for a guarantee of frequent elections and for an independent electorate not under the influence of wealthy patrons. The king's men began castigating Shaftesbury's followers as "Whigs," the name of an obscure sect of Scottish religious extremists who favored the assassination of both Charles and James. Whigs in turn denounced Charles's courtiers as "Tories," a

term for Irish Catholics who murdered Protestant landlords. Like "Puritan," "Quaker," "Papist," and other terms of abuse, both words stuck.

England's party struggle reflected a deep rift between "Court" and "Country" forces. As of 1681 Tories were a Court party. They favored the legitimate succession, a standing army with adequate revenues to maintain it, the Anglican Church without toleration for Protestant dissenters, and a powerful monarchy. The Whigs were a Country opposition that stood for the exclusion of James from the throne, a decentralized militia rather than a standing army, toleration of Protestant dissenters but not of Catholics, and an active role in government for a reformed Parliament. During this struggle, James fled to Scotland in virtual exile. But Charles, after getting secret financial support from King Louis XIV of France, dissolved Parliament in 1681 and ruled without one for the last four years of his reign.

THE LORDS OF TRADE AND IMPERIAL REFORM

English politics of the 1670s and 1680s had a profound impact on the colonies. The duke of York emerged from the Third Anglo-Dutch War as the most powerful shaper of imperial policy. At his urging the government created a new agency in 1675, the Lords Committee of Trade and Plantations, or more simply, the Lords of Trade. This agency, a permanent committee of the Privy Council, enforced the Navigation Acts and administered the colonies. Although Virginia was the oldest royal colony, the West Indies became the object of most of the new policies, simply because the Caribbean remained a much more important theater of international competition. The instruments of royal government first took shape in the islands and were then extended to the mainland.

In the 1660s the Crown took control of the governments of Barbados, Jamaica, and the Leeward Islands. The king appointed the governor and upper house of each colony; the settlers elected an assembly. The Privy Council in England reserved to itself the power to hear appeals from colonial courts and to disallow colonial legislation after the governor had approved it. The Privy Council also issued a formal commission and a lengthy set of instructions to each royal governor. In the two or

Religious Strife, Liberty, and the Clash of Empires

When Europeans thought about liberty in the 17th century, they nearly always placed the idea in a religious context. France, the Netherlands, and England all had developed traditions of religious liberty. France was the only European country that permitted both Catholics and Protestants to worship in public, even though for Huguenots that privilege was confined to certain specified parts of the kingdom. Because France had also intervened to prevent Spain from reconquering the Netherlands, the French monarchy was widely admired among educated Dutchmen. Although the Dutch forbade Catholics to worship openly, they "connived" at private worship by residents who remained peaceful and otherwise obeyed the law. The Netherlands attracted numerous Protestant dissenters and many Jews, mostly refugees from the Portuguese Empire after Spain assumed control there.

In France the toleration of Protestants rested on the power of the state to restrain an otherwise hostile Catholic majority. King Louis XIV destroyed that arrangement, first by invading the Netherlands in 1672, and then by persecuting the Huguenots, a campaign that led to the revocation of the Edict of Nantes in 1685 and provoked a massive flight of Huguenots

out of France. Louis's militant Catholicism transformed the diplomacy of Europe. The French cartoon shown below, "Calvinism on Its Deathbed," reflected the king's point of view. The Dutch replied elo-

three decades after 1660, these documents became standardized, especially after the Lords of Trade began to apply the lessons learned in one colony to problems anticipated in others.

The king's commission defined a governor's powers. From the Crown's point of view, the commission *created* the constitutional structure of each colony, a claim that few settlers accepted. The colonists believed they had an inherent right to constitutional rule even without the king's explicit warrant.

Written instructions told each royal governor how to use his broad powers. They laid out what he must do, such as command the militia, and what he must avoid, such as approving laws detrimental to English trade. Despite some confusion at first,

Crown lawyers eventually agreed that these instructions were binding only on the governor, not on the colony as a whole. In other words, royal instructions never acquired the force of law.

London also insisted that each colony pay the cost of its own government. This requirement, ironically, strengthened colonial claims to self-rule. After a long struggle in Jamaica, the Crown imposed a compromise in 1681 that had broad significance for all the colonies. The Lords of Trade threatened to make the Jamaica assembly as weak as the Irish Parliament, which could debate and approve only those bills that had first been adopted by the English Privy Council. Under the compromise, the Jamaica assembly retained its power to initiate and amend legisla-

quently with a portrayal of Death as "Le Roy de France" ("The King of France"), shown at right. Between 1652 and 1674 the English and Dutch had fought three wars, but Louis's policies drew the two Protestant countries together and made the Glorious Revolution possible in England. The Dutch print below, titled *The Flight of Popery out of England*, celebrated the accession of William III of Orange, the Dutch *stadholder*, to the throne of England. In the Anglo-French wars that began in 1689, nearly all Englishmen agreed that only Protestants could truly be free.

LE ROY DE FRANCE.
l'Home immortel Chef de la S.te Ligue.

Mon soleil par sa force eclaira l'heretique.
Il chassa tout d'un coup les brouillards de Calvin:
Non pas par un Zele divin.
Mais afin de cacher ma fine Politique.

tion, in return for agreeing to a permanent revenue act, a measure that freed the governor from financial dependence on the assembly.

Metacom's War and Bacon's Rebellion lent urgency to these reforms and speeded up their use in the mainland colonies. The Lords of Trade ordered soldiers to Virginia along with a royal commission to investigate grievances there. In 1676 they also sent an aggressive customs officer, Edward Randolph, to Massachusetts. His lengthy reports recommended that the colony's charter be revoked. The Lords of Trade viewed New England and all proprietary colonies with deep suspicion, although they failed to block the founding of Pennsylvania as a new proprietary venture. They had reason for concern. As late

as 1678, Virginia remained the only royal colony on the mainland. The Lords of Trade might enforce compliance with the Navigation Acts elsewhere, but they possessed no effective instruments for punishing violators in North America. The king could demand and reprimand, but not command.

The Jamaica model assumed that each royal governor would summon an assembly on occasion, though not often. In the 1680s the Crown imposed a similar settlement on Virginia—an occasional assembly with full powers of legislation in exchange for a permanent revenue act. Although New York had been an experiment in autocracy since the English conquest of 1664, James conceded an assembly to that colony, too, in exchange for a permanent revenue act in 1683. The Jamaica model was becoming the norm for the Lords of Trade. James's real preference emerged after the English Court of Chancery revoked the Massachusetts Charter in 1684. Charles II died and his brother became King James II in early 1685. The possibility of a vigorous autocracy in America suddenly reappeared.

THE DOMINION OF NEW ENGLAND

Absolutist New York now became the king's model for reorganizing New England. James disallowed the New York Charter of Liberties of 1683 (see chapter 2) and abolished the colony's assembly but kept the permanent revenue act in force. In 1686 he sent Sir Edmund Andros, the autocratic governor of New York from 1674 to 1680, to Massachusetts to take over a new government called the Dominion of New England. James added New Hampshire, Plymouth, Rhode Island, Connecticut, New York, and both Jerseys to the Dominion. Andros governed this vast domain through an appointive council and a superior court that rode circuit dispensing justice. There was no elective assembly. Andros also imposed religious toleration on the Puritans, even forcing one Boston church to let Anglicans use its meetinghouse for public worship for part of each Sunday.

At first, Andros won support from merchants who had been excluded from politics by the Puritan requirement that they be full church members, but his rigorous enforcement of the Navigation Acts soon alienated them. When he tried to compel New England farmers to take out new land titles that included annual quitrents, he enraged the whole countryside. His suppression of a tax revolt in Essex County, Massachusetts, started many people thinking more highly of their rights as Englishmen than of their peculiar liberties as Puritans. By 1688, government by consent probably seemed more valuable than ever.

THE GLORIOUS REVOLUTION

Events in England and France undermined the Dominion of New England. James II proclaimed toleration for Protestants and Catholics and began to name Catholics to high office, in violation of recent laws. In 1685 Louis XIV revoked the 1598 Edict of Nantes that had granted toleration to Protestants, and he launched a vicious persecution of the Huguenots. About 160,000 fled the kingdom, the largest forced migration of Europe's early modern era. Many went to England; several thousand settled in the English mainland colonies. James II tried to suppress the news of Louis's persecution, which made his own professions of toleration seem hypocritical, even though his commitment was probably genuine. In 1688 his queen gave birth to a son who would clearly be raised Catholic, thus imposing a Catholic *dynasty* on England. Several Whig and Tory leaders swallowed their mutual hatred and invited William of Orange, the *stadholder* of the Netherlands, to England. The husband of the king's older Protestant daughter Mary (by James's first marriage), William had become the most prominent Protestant soldier in Europe during a long war against Louis XIV.

William landed in England in November 1688. Most of the English army sided with him, and James fled to France in late December. Parliament declared that James had abdicated the throne and named William III (1689–1702) and Mary II (1689–94) as joint sovereigns. It also passed a Toleration Act that gave Protestant dissenters (but not Catholics) the right to worship publicly, and a Declaration of Rights that guaranteed a Protestant succession and condemned as illegal many of the acts of James II. This "Glorious Revolution" also brought England and the Netherlands into war against Louis XIV, who supported James.

THE GLORIOUS REVOLUTION IN AMERICA

The Boston militia overthrew Andros on April 18 and 19, 1689, even before they knew whether William had succeeded James. Andros's attempt to suppress the news that William had landed in England convinced the Puritans that he was part of a global "Popish Plot" to undermine Protestant societies everywhere. After some hesitation, Massachusetts resumed the forms of its old charter government. The other New England colonies followed its example.

In May and June, the New York City militia took over Fort James at the southern tip of Manhattan and renamed it Fort William. To hostile observers, this action seemed almost a replay of the events of 1673, when the Dutch had reconquered New York and renamed the fort for William. Francis Nicholson, lieutenant governor in New York under Andros, refused to proclaim William and Mary as sovereigns without direct orders from England and soon sailed for home. The active rebels in New York City were nearly all Dutch who had little experience with traditional English liberties. Few had held high office. Their leader, Jacob Leisler, dreaded conquest by Catholics from New France and began to act like a Dutch *stadholder* in a nominally English colony.

Military defense became Leisler's highest priority, but his demands for supplies soon alienated even his Yankee supporters on Long Island. Although he summoned an elective assembly, he made no effort to revive the Charter of Liberties of 1683 while continuing to collect duties under the permanent revenue act of that year. He showed little respect for the legal rights of his opponents, most of whom were English or were Dutch merchants who had served the Dominion of New England. He jailed several Anti-Leislerians for months without bringing them to trial, and when his own assembly raised questions about their legal rights, he sent it home. Loud complaints against his administration reached the Crown in London.

In Maryland, Protestants overthrew Lord Baltimore's Catholic government in 1689. The governor of Maryland had refused to proclaim William and Mary, even after all the other colonies had done so. To Lord Baltimore's dismay, the messenger he sent from London to Maryland with orders to accept the new monarchs died en route. Had he arrived, the government probably would have survived the crisis.

THE ENGLISH RESPONSE

England responded in different ways to each of these upheavals. The Maryland rebels won the royal government they requested from England and soon established the Anglican Church in the colony. Catholics could no longer worship in public, hold office, or even expect toleration. Most prominent Catholic families, however, braced themselves against the Protestant storm and remained loyal to their faith.

In New York, the Leislerians suffered a deadly defeat. Leisler and his Dutch followers, who had no

THE FORT PROTECTING NEW YORK CITY, AS SEEN FROM BROOKLYN HEIGHTS, 1679 This sketch, probably by Jasper Danckaerts or Peter Sluyter, two Dutch visitors, shows the fort at the southern tip of Manhattan Island. When the English conquered New Netherland in 1664, the fort was renamed for James, the lord proprietor of what now became New York. When the Dutch retook the fort in 1673, they changed its name to Fort William (for William of Orange). When the English regained control in 1674, they again renamed it Fort James, but when James II was overthrown in the Glorious Revolution of 1688–89, the settlers named it for William once again. Thereafter, the fort took the name of the reigning British monarch.

Three Sovereigns for Sarah (1986)
Directed by Philip Leacock. Starring Vanessa Redgrave (Sarah Cloyse), Phyllis Thaxter (Rebecca Nurse), and Kim Hunter (Mary Easty).

This film, originally a PBS American Playhouse miniseries, is the most powerful and effective dramatization ever made of the Salem witch trials of 1692. The three principal actresses were all previous Academy Award winners. When this series appeared, British director Philip Leacock was perhaps best known in the United States for *The War Lover* (1962) and *The Daughters of Joshua Cabe* (1972).

The screenplay by Victor Pisano, who also produced the film, concentrates on the three Towne sisters: Sarah Cloyse (Vanessa Redgrave), Rebecca Nurse (Phyllis Thaxter), and Mary Easty (Kim Hunter). Rebecca Nurse's ordeal became the major turning point in the Salem tragedy. Hers was one of the early trials, and at first the jury acquitted her, only to be urged by the judges to reconsider the verdict. They did, and she was hanged. After this reversal, no one else was acquitted. Mary Easty, after she too had been convicted, sent a petition to the magistrates, one of the most eloquent documents ever written in colonial America. As a committed Christian, she accepted her own death, but she urged the judges to reconsider their procedures because she knew that she was innocent, and so must be many of the other condemned witches. She was hanged.

Of the three sisters, only Sarah Cloyse survived the trials. The film focuses on Cloyse's life-long efforts to vindicate the reputations of her two sisters. Vanessa Redgrave's portrayal of her suffering and her resistance to the whole appalling affair is one of the most compelling performances of Redgrave's long and distinguished career.

The screenplay, by concentrating on the three sisters and their families, brings home the human tragedy that the trials became. This emphasis forced Pisano to leave out other important victims. For example, the Reverend George Burroughs, the only minister executed in the trials (or in any New England colony in the 17th century, for that matter), is not even mentioned. In addition, Pisano never explains that Sarah Cloyse survived because the grand jury refused to indict her. Because grand juries were exempt from explaining their decisions to anyone else, we do not know why she became an exception, but evidently the jurors believed that she was too dedicated a Christian woman to sell her soul to the devil.

Three Sovereigns for Sarah is a grim, compelling, relentless drama. It romanticizes nothing and makes clear, unlike some Hollywood depictions of these events, that nothing about the trials was sexy. The accusation scenes, dominated by girls, convey the madness of the whole affair. Most of those accused and executed were grandmothers. When they are turned off the ladder, their bodies bounce as the nooses take hold. This film is a cinematic triumph.

Three Sovereigns for Sarah brings home the human tragedy of the Salem witch trials of 1692.

significant contacts at the English court, watched helplessly as their enemies, working through the imperial bureaucracy that William inherited from James, manipulated the Dutch king of England into undermining his loyal Dutch supporters in New York. The new governor, Henry Sloughter, named prominent Anti-Leislerians to his council, arrested Leisler and his son-in-law in 1691, tried both for treason, and had them hanged, drawn, and quartered. The assembly elected that year was controlled by Anti-Leislerians, most of whom were English. It passed a modified version of the Charter of Liberties of 1683, this time denying toleration to Catholics. Like its predecessor, it was later disallowed. Bitter struggles between Leislerians and Anti-Leislerians would characterize New York politics until after 1700.

Another complex struggle involved Massachusetts. In 1689 Increase Mather, acting as the colony's agent in London, failed to persuade Parliament to restore the charter of 1629. Over the next two years he negotiated a new charter, which gave the Crown what it had been demanding since 1664—the power to appoint governors, justices, and militia officers, and the power to veto laws and to hear judicial appeals. The 1691 charter also granted toleration to all Protestants and based voting rights on property qualifications, not church membership. In effect, liberty and property had triumphed over godliness.

While insisting on these concessions, William also accepted much of the previous history of the colony, even if it did not augur well for the emerging model of royal government. The General Court, not the governor as in other royal colonies, retained control over the distribution of land. The council remained an elective body, although it was chosen annually by the full legislature, not directly by the voters. The governor could veto any councillor. Massachusetts also absorbed the colonies of Plymouth and Maine. New Hampshire regained its autonomy, but until 1741 it usually shared the same royal governor with Massachusetts. Rhode Island and Connecticut resumed their charter governments.

THE SALEM WITCH TRIALS

When Mather sailed into Boston harbor with the new charter in May 1692, he found the province besieged by witches. The accusations arose in Salem Village (modern Danvers) among a group of girls, most of whom had been orphaned during the Indian wars and had been adopted into households more pious than those of their original families. Uncertain whether anyone was responsible for finding husbands for them, they probably asked Tituba, a Carib Indian slave in the household of Reverend Samuel Parris, to tell their fortunes. This occult activity imposed a heavy burden of guilt on the girls, and they broke under the strain, beginning with the youngest two, a 9-year-old daughter and 12-year-old niece of Parris. The girls howled, barked, and stretched themselves into frightful contortions. At first Parris treated the outbursts as cases of demonic possession, but after weeks of prayer sessions brought no improvement, he accepted a diagnosis of witchcraft. With adult encouragement, the girls accused many of their neighbors of witchcraft. The accusers came from families that strongly supported Parris. Most of the accused were old women in families that had opposed his appointment as village minister.

In June the trials began in Salem Town. The court, composed mostly of judges who had compromised their Puritanism through willing service to the Dominion of New England, hanged 19 people, pressed one man to death because he refused to stand trial, and allowed several other people to die in jail. Most of those hanged were grandmothers, several quite conspicuous for their piety. One victim was a former minister at Salem Village who had become a Baptist. The governor finally halted the trials after the girls accused his wife of being a witch.

The witch trials provided a bitter finale to the era of political upheaval that had afflicted Massachusetts since the loss of the colony's charter in 1684. Along with the new charter, the trials brought the Puritan era to a close.

THE COMPLETION OF EMPIRE

The Glorious Revolution killed absolutism in English America and guaranteed that royal government would be representative government in the colonies. Both Crown and colonists took it for granted that any colony settled by the English would elect an assembly to vote on all taxes and consent to all local laws. Governors would be appointed by the Crown or a lord proprietor. (Governors were elected in Connecticut and Rhode Island.) But royal government soon became the norm, especially after the New Jersey proprietors surrendered their powers of government in 1702, and the Carolina proprietors followed suit after their last governor was deposed by the settlers in 1719. On the other hand, the Crown restored proprietary rule in Maryland in 1716, after the fifth Lord Baltimore converted to the Church of England. By the 1720s, however, Maryland and Pennsylvania (along with Delaware, which became a separate colony under the Penn proprietorship in 1704) were the only surviving proprietary provinces on the mainland, and their proprietors were usually careful to abide by the rules of imperial administration.

This transition to royal government seems smoother in retrospect than it did at the time. London almost lost control of the empire in the 1690s. Overwhelmed by the pressures of the French war, the Lords of Trade could not keep pace with events in the colonies. When French privateers disrupted the tobacco trade, Scottish smugglers stepped in and began to divert it to Glasgow in defiance of the Navigation Acts. New York became a haven for pirates. The northern colonies could not cooperate effectively in the war against New France. Parliament, suspecting William of favoring Dutch interests over English, even threatened to take control of the colonies away from the king.

William took action in 1696. With his approval Parliament passed a new, comprehensive Navigation Act that plugged several loopholes in earlier laws and extended to America the English system of vice admiralty courts, which dispensed quick justice without juries. When the new courts settled routine maritime disputes or condemned enemy merchant ships captured by colonial privateers, their services were highly regarded by the settlers. But when the courts tried to assume jurisdiction over the Navigation Acts, they aroused controversy.

William also replaced the Lords of Trade in 1696 with a new agency, the Board of Trade. Its powers were almost purely advisory. It corresponded with governors and other officials in the colonies, listened

LINK TO THE PAST

Witchcraft in Salem Village

http://etext.virginia.edu/salem/witchcraft/

This site, created with the cooperation of half a dozen scholarly archives and institutions, makes available many documents, both published and manuscript, from the most famous series of trials held in colonial America.

1. Go to the collection of maps of Salem Village, compiled by several 19th-century historians. You can view them at three different levels of magnification. Then view the "Map of Salem Village 1692" alongside its Index, which tells you where to find the location of every known resident in the village at the outbreak of the crisis. What use might historians make of this kind of visual evidence?

2. In what ways might the geography of this community have affected the pattern of accusations and trials?

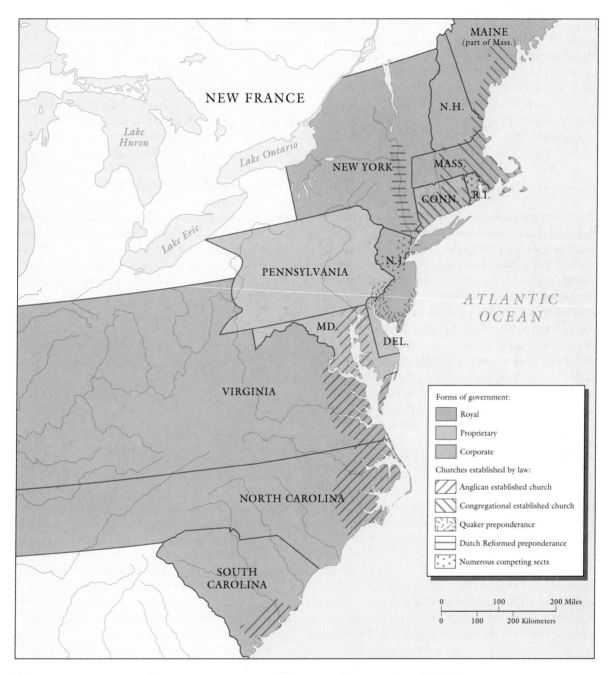

GOVERNMENT AND RELIGION IN THE BRITISH COLONIES, 1720

to lobbyists in England, and made policy recommendations to appropriate governmental bodies, whether Parliament, the Treasury, or a secretary of state. The board tried to collect information on complex questions and to offer helpful advice. It was, in short, an early attempt at government by experts. John Locke, England's foremost philosopher and an able economist, was one of the board's first members.

Another difficult problem was resolved in 1707 when England and Scotland agreed to merge their separate parliaments and become the single kingdom of Great Britain. At a stroke, the Act of Union placed Scotland inside the Navigation Act system, legalized Scottish participation in the tobacco trade, and opened numerous colonial offices to ambitious Scots. By the middle of the 18th century most of Scotland's growing prosperity derived from its trade with the colonies. In a very real sense, the tobacco trade built Glasgow.

IMPERIAL FEDERALISM

The transformations that took place between 1689 and 1707 defined the structure of the British Empire until the American Revolution. Although Parliament claimed full power over the colonies, in practice it seldom regulated anything colonial except Atlantic commerce. Even the Woolens Act of 1699, designed to protect the English woolens industry from Irish and colonial competition, did not prohibit the manufacture of woolen textiles in the colonies. It simply prohibited their export. The Hat Act of 1732 was similarly designed, except for a clause limiting the number of apprentices or slaves a colonial hatter could maintain. Nobody enforced that provision.

When Parliament regulated oceanic trade, its measures were usually enforceable. But compliance was minimal to nonexistent when Parliament tried to regulate inland affairs through statutes protecting white pines (needed as masts for the navy) or through the Iron Act of 1750, which prohibited the erection of certain types of new iron mills. To get things done within the colonies, the Crown had to win the settlers' agreement through their lawful assemblies and unsalaried local officials. In effect, the empire had stumbled into a system of de facto federalism, an arrangement that no one could quite explain or justify. Parliament exercised only limited powers, and the colonies controlled the rest. What seemed an arrangement of convenience in London soon acquired overtones of right in America, the right to consent to all taxes and local laws.

THE MIXED AND BALANCED CONSTITUTION

The Glorious Revolution transformed British politics in a way that profoundly affected the colonies after 1700. To Europe's surprise, Britain, whose government had seemed wildly unstable for half a century, quickly became a far more powerful state under its limited government after 1689 than the Stuart kings had been able to sustain with their pretensions to absolute monarchy. The British constitution, which made ministers legally responsible for their public actions, proved remarkably stable. Before long many Englishmen were celebrating this achievement as the wonder of the age. In the ancient world, as had been pointed out by republican thinker James Harrington (see chapter 2), free societies had degenerated into tyrannies. Liberty had always been fragile and was easily lost. Yet England had retained its liberty and grown stronger in the process. England had defied history.

The explanation, everyone agreed, lay in England's "mixed and balanced" constitution, which embraced Harrington's ideas about republican liberty but absorbed them into a monarchical framework. Government by "King, Lords, and Commons" mirrored society itself—the monarchy, aristocracy, and commonality—and literally embodied all three in its very structure. As long as each freely consented to government measures, English liberty would be secure because each had voluntarily placed the public good ahead of its own interests. But if one of the three acquired the power to dominate or manipulate the other two, English liberty would be in peril. That danger fueled an unending dialogue in 18th-century Britain. The underlying drama was always the struggle of power against liberty, and liberty usually meant a limitation of governmental power.

Power had to be controlled, or liberty would be lost. Nearly everyone agreed that a direct assault on Parliament through a military coup was highly unlikely. The real danger lay in corruption, in the ability of Crown ministers to undermine the independence and integrity of the House of Commons.

The wars with France made Britain a great power, but they also aroused acute constitutional anxieties. After 1689 England raised larger fleets and armies than it had ever mobilized before. To support them the kingdom created for the first time a funded national debt, in which the state agreed to pay the interest due to its creditors ahead of all other obligations. This simple device gave Britain enormous borrowing power. In 1694 the government created the Bank of England to facilitate its own finances; the London Stock Exchange also emerged in the 1690s. Parliament levied a heavy land tax on the gentry and excises on ordinary people to meet wartime expenses. Together, debt, bank, stock market, and new sources of revenue added up to a financial revolution that enabled England to outspend France, despite having only one-fourth of France's population. These resources and a sharp expansion of offices during the wars vastly increased patronage. By giving offices to members of Parliament, Crown ministers were almost assured of majority support for their measures.

As during the controversy over the Popish Plot, public debates still pitted Court against Country. The Court favored policies that strengthened its war-making capabilities. The Country stood for liberty. Each of the parties, Whig and Tory, had Court and Country wings. Between 1680 and 1720, however, they reversed their polarities. Although the Tories had begun as Charles II's Court party, by

1720 most of them were a Country opposition. Whigs had defended Country positions in 1680, but by 1720 most of them were strong advocates for the Court policies of George I (1714–27). Court spokesmen defended the military buildup, the financial revolution, and the new patronage as essential to victory over France. Their Country opponents denounced standing armies, attacked the financial revolution as an engine of corruption, favored an early peace with France, demanded more frequent elections, and tried to ban "placemen" (officeholders who sat in Parliament) from the House of Commons.

Court Whigs emerged victorious during the long ministry of Sir Robert Walpole (1721–42), but their opponents were more eloquent and controlled more presses. By the 1720s, the opposition claimed many of the kingdom's best writers, especially Tories Alexander Pope, Jonathan Swift, John Gay, and Henry St. John, viscount Bolingbroke. Their detestation of Walpole was shared by a smaller band of radical Whigs, including John Trenchard and Thomas Gordon, who wrote *Cato's Letters*, four volumes of collected newspaper essays. The central theme of the opposition was corruption—the indirect and insidious means by which ministers threatened the independence of Parliament and thus English liberty. This debate over liberty soon

HAMPTON COURT PALACE This elegant palace near London was one of Queen Anne's residences. Court architecture and protocol were hierarchical and designed to be awesome.

VIEW OF THE HARVESTING FIELD OF JAMES HIGFORD'S MANOR, DIXTON, GLOUCESTERSHIRE (CIRCA 1725–35) The Country wing of British politics was dominated by landed gentlemen who owned great estates. The men who actually worked their fields seldom had a voice in politics.

reached America. *Cato's Letters* were especially popular in the northern colonies, while Bolingbroke won numerous admirers among the gentry in the southern colonies.

CONTRASTING EMPIRES: SPAIN AND FRANCE IN NORTH AMERICA

After 1689, Britain's enemies were France and Spain, Catholic powers with their own American empires. Until 1689 the three empires had coexisted in America without much contact among them, but Europe's wars soon engulfed them all. Spain and France shared a zeal for converting Indians that exceeded anything displayed by English Protestants, but their American empires had little else in common.

THE PUEBLO REVOLT

In the late 17th century, the Spanish missions of North America entered a period of crisis. Franciscan zeal began to slacken, and fewer priests took the trouble to master Indian languages, insisting instead that the Indians learn Spanish. For all of their good intentions, the missionaries regarded Indians as children and often whipped or even shackled them for minor infractions. They refused to trust them with firearms. Disease also took a heavy toll. A declining Indian population led to more pressing labor demands by missionaries, and despite strong prohibitions, some Spaniards enslaved some Indians in Florida and New Mexico. After 1670 Florida also feared encroachments by English Protestants out of South Carolina, eager to enslave unarmed Indians, whether or not they had embraced Christianity. By 1700, the European refusal to enslave other Christians protected only white people.

The greatest challenge to the Spanish arose in New Mexico, where the Pueblo population had fallen from 80,000 to 17,000 since 1598. A prolonged drought, together with Apache and Navajo attacks, prompted many Pueblos to abandon the Christian God and resume their old forms of worship. Missionaries responded with whippings and even several executions in 1675. Popé, a San Juan Pueblo medicine man who had been whipped for his beliefs, moved north to Taos Pueblo, where he

organized the most successful Indian revolt in American history. In 1680, in a carefully timed uprising, the Pueblos killed 400 of the 2,300 Spaniards in New Mexico and destroyed or plundered every Spanish building in the province (see the chapter 1 map, "Spanish Missions in Florida and New Mexico, circa 1675"). They desecrated every church and killed 21 of New Mexico's 33 missionaries. "Now," they exulted, "the God of the Spaniards, who was their father, is dead," but the Pueblos' own god, whom they obeyed, "[had] never died." Spanish survivors fled from Santa Fe down the Rio Grande to El Paso.

Popé lost his influence when the traditional Pueblo rites failed to end the drought or stop the attacks of hostile Indians. When the Spanish returned in the 1690s, this time as conquerors, the Pueblos were badly divided. Most villages yielded without much resistance, and Spain accepted their submission, but Santa Fe held out until December 1693. When it fell, the Spanish executed 70 men and gave 400 women and children to the returning settlers as their slaves. The Hopi Indians to the west, however, never again submitted to Spanish rule.

Before these crises, missionaries in both Florida and New Mexico had often resisted the demands of Spanish governors. By 1700 the state ruled, and missionaries obeyed. Spain's daring attempt to create a demilitarized Christian frontier was proving a tragic failure for both Indians and Franciscans.

NEW FRANCE AND THE MIDDLE GROUND

A different story unfolded along the western frontier of New France over the same decades. There the Iroquois menace made possible an unusual accommodation between the colony and the Indians of the Great Lakes region. The survival of the Iroquois Five Nations depended on their ability to assimilate captives seized from other nations through incessant warfare. Their raiders, armed with muskets, terrorized western Indians, carried away thousands of captives, and left behind grisly trophies of their cruelty to discourage revenge. The Iroquois wars depopulated nearly all of what is now the state of Ohio and much of the Ontario peninsula. The Indians around Lakes Erie and Huron either fled west to escape these horrors or were absorbed by the Iroquois. The refugees, mostly Algonquian-speaking peoples, founded new communities farther west. Most of these villages contained families from several different tribes, and village loyalties gradually supplanted older tribal (or ethnic) loyalties, which often broke down under Iroquois pressure. When the refugees disagreed with one another or came into conflict with the Sioux to their west, the absence of traditional tribal structures made it difficult to resolve their differences. Over time, French soldiers, trappers, and missionaries stepped in as mediators.

The French were not always welcome. In 1684, the only year for which we have a precise count, the Algonquians killed 39 French traders. Yet the leaders of thinly populated New France were eager to erect an Algonquian shield against the Iroquois and, in later decades, against the British. They began by easing tensions among the Algonquians while supplying them with firearms, brandy, and other European goods. In fact, to the exasperation of missionaries, brandy became the lubricant of the fur trade by keeping the warriors hunting for pelts and dependent on French traders. New France, in turn, provided the resources that the Algonquians needed to strike back against the Iroquois. By 1701 Iroquois losses had become so heavy that the Five Nations negotiated a peace treaty with the French and the western Indians. The Iroquois agreed to remain neutral in any war between France and England. France's Indian allies, supported by a new French fort erected at Detroit in 1701, began returning to the fertile lands around Lakes Erie and Huron. That region became the Great Lakes "Middle Ground" over which no one could wield sovereign power, although New France exercised great influence within it. France always ran a deficit in supporting the fur trade but kept the trade going mostly to block British expansion.

France's success in the interior rested more on intelligent negotiation than on force. Officials who gave orders instead of fostering negotiations merely alienated France's Indian allies. Blind obedience to commands, grumbled the warriors, was slavery. Hugely outnumbered, the French knew that they could not impose their will on the Indians. Indians respected those Frenchmen who honored their ways. The French conducted diplomacy according to Indian, not European rules. The governor of New France became a somewhat grander version of a traditional Indian chief. Algonquians called him Onontio ("Great Mountain"), the supreme alliance chief who won cooperation through persuasion and who had learned that, among the Indians, persuasion was always accompanied by gifts. The respect accorded to peacetime chiefs was roughly proportionate to how much they gave away, not to how much they accumulated. The English, by contrast, tried to "buy" land from the Indians and regarded the sale of both

IROQUOIS WARRIORS LEADING AN INDIAN PRISONER INTO CAPTIVITY, 1660s Because Indian populations had been depleted by war and disease, a tribe's survival became dependent on its ability to assimilate captives. This is a French copy of an Iroquois pictograph.

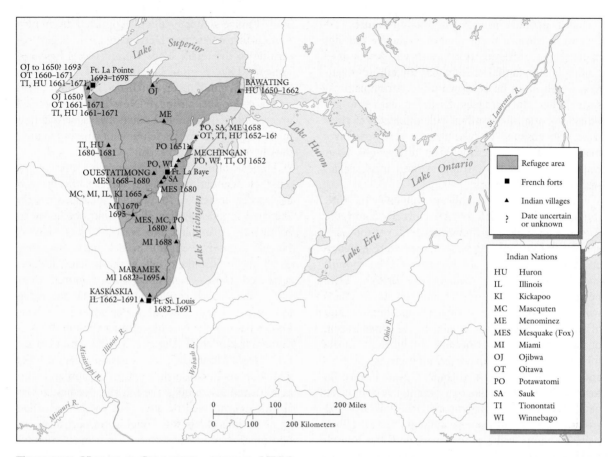

FRENCH MIDDLE GROUND, CIRCA 1700

the land and of the Indians' right to use it as irrevocable. The French understood that this idea had no place in Indian culture. Agreements were not final contracts but required regular renewal, always with an exchange of gifts. The strongest party had to be more generous than all others.

FRENCH LOUISIANA AND SPANISH TEXAS

The pattern worked out by the French and the Indians on the Great Lakes Middle Ground also took hold, though in a more fragile form, in the lower Mississippi valley. In quest of a passage to Asia, Father Jacques Marquette and trader Louis Joliet paddled down the Mississippi to its juncture with the Arkansas River in 1673. But once they became convinced that the Mississippi flowed into the Gulf of Mexico and not the Pacific, they turned back. Then,

in 1682, René-Robert Cavelier, *sieur* de La Salle traveled down the Mississippi to its mouth, claiming possession of the entire area for France and calling it Louisiana (for Louis XIV). But when La Salle returned in 1684 by way of the Gulf of Mexico to plant a colony there, he overshot the mouth of the Mississippi, landed in Texas, and wandered around for three years in search of the great river until his exasperated men murdered him.

In 1699, during a brief lull in the wars between France and England, the French returned to the Gulf of Mexico. Pierre le Moyne d'Iberville, a Canadian, landed with 80 men at Biloxi, built a fort, and began trading with the Indians. In 1702 he moved his headquarters to Mobile, closer to the more populous nations of the interior, especially the Choctaws, who were looking for allies against the English. The Choctaws could still field 5,000 warriors but had suffered heavy losses from slaving

LA SALLE AND FATHER HENNEPIN ON THE MISSISSIPPI After La Salle and his party traveled down the Mississippi to its mouth, he claimed possession of the entire area for France. Father Louis Hennepin made this drawing in about 1683.

raids organized by South Carolinians and carried out mostly by that colony's Chickasaw and Creek allies. About 1,800 Choctaws had been killed and 500 enslaved during the preceding decade. Using the Choctaws to anchor their trading system, the French created a weaker, southern version of the Great Lakes Middle Ground, acting as mediators and trading brandy, firearms, and other European products for furs and food. Often, during the War of the Spanish Succession (1702–13), the French received no European supplies, and they remained heavily outnumbered by the Indians. Although European diseases had been ravaging the area since the 1540s, the Indians of the lower Mississippi valley still numbered about 70,000. In 1708 the French numbered fewer than 300, including 80 Indian slaves. The French were lucky to survive at all.

Spain, alarmed at any challenge to its monopoly on the Gulf of Mexico, founded Pensacola in 1698, more to counter the English than the French. Competition from France prompted the Spanish to move into Texas in 1690, where they established missions near the modern Texas-Louisiana border. At first, the missionaries were cordially received by the Tejas (Texas) Indians, but they brought smallpox with them. The Indians rejected their explanation that the epidemic was God's "holy will" and told the missionaries to get out or be killed. They departed in 1693, leaving Texas to the Indians for 20 more years.

AN EMPIRE OF SETTLEMENT: THE BRITISH COLONIES

By 1700 250,000 settlers and slaves were already living in England's mainland colonies and the population was doubling every 25 years. New France matched that pace, but with only 14,000 people in 1700, it could not close the gap. By contrast, the population of the Spanish missions continued to decline. In the struggle for empire, a growing population became Britain's greatest advantage.

THE ENGINE OF BRITISH EXPANSION: THE COLONIAL HOUSEHOLD

Virginia's Robert "King" Carter, who died in 1730, became the first settler to acquire a thousand slaves and several hundred thousand acres of land. His household differed strikingly from that of an ordinary Pennsylvania or New England farmer, but both had something in common that distinguished them from households in England. With few exceptions, colonial families rejected the English customs of entail and primogeniture. Entail prohibited a landowner, or his heir, from dividing up his landed estate (that is, selling part of it) during his lifetime. Primogeniture obliged him to leave all of his land to his eldest surviving son. Under this system, younger sons clearly ranked below the oldest son, and daughters ranked behind both.

Primogeniture and entail became more common in the 18th-century colonies than they had been before, but until the late colonial period they failed to structure social relations the way they did in England. A Virginia planter, for example, might entail his home plantation (the one on which he had erected his big house) and bequeath it to his oldest son, but he would also leave land and slaves, sometimes whole plantations, to his other sons. The primacy of the eldest son was far more sentimental than structural. By contrast, the patriarchs of colonial households tried to pass on their status to all their sons, and to provide dowries that would enable all their daughters to marry men of equal status. Until 1750 or so, these goals were usually realistic.

For younger sons, then, the colonies presented a unique opportunity. Benjamin Franklin began his *Autobiography*, colonial America's greatest success story, by boasting that he was "the youngest Son of the youngest Son for 5 Generations back." Despite those odds, Franklin became a gentleman with an international reputation. He made enough money to retire as a printer, commissioned a genteel portrait of himself, engaged in scientific experiments, and entered public life. He no longer worked with his hands.

English households had become "Americanized" in the colonies during the earliest years of settlement, as soon as Virginia and Plymouth made land available to nearly all male settlers. By the mid-18th century, the question was whether that system could survive the pressures of a rising population. Social change began to drive American households back toward English practices. Only continual expansion onto new lands would allow the colonial household to provide equal opportunity for all sons, much less for all daughters.

Colonial households were patriarchal. The father expected to be loved and revered by his wife and children but insisted on being obeyed. A man's standing in the community depended on his success as a master at home. A mature male was expected to be the master of others. In New England and Pennsylvania typical householders probably thought they

were the rough equals of most other householders. Above all, a patriarch strove to perpetuate the household itself into the next generation and to preserve his own economic "independence," or autonomy. Of course, complete independence was impossible. Every household owed small debts or favors to its neighbors, but these obligations seldom compromised the family's standing in the community.

Although farmers rarely set out to maximize profits, they did try to grow an agricultural surplus, if only as a hedge against drought, storms, and other unpredictable events. For rural Pennsylvanians this surplus averaged about 40 percent of the total crop. With the harvest in, farmers marketed their produce, often selling it to merchants in Boston, New York, or Philadelphia for local consumption or for export to the West Indies or Europe. Farmers used the proceeds to pay taxes or their ministers' salaries and to buy British imports. Although these arrangements sometimes placed families in short-term debt to merchants, most farmers and artisans managed to avoid long-term debt. Settlers accepted temporary dependency among freemen—of sons on their parents, indentured servants on their masters, or apprentices and journeymen on master craftsmen. Sons often worked as laborers on neighboring farms, as sailors, or as journeymen craftsmen, provided that such dependence was temporary. A man who became permanently dependent on others lost the respect of his community.

THE VOLUNTARISTIC ETHIC AND PUBLIC LIFE

Householders carried their quest for independence into public life. In entering politics and in waging war, their autonomy became an ethic of voluntarism. Few freemen could be coerced into doing something of which they disapproved. They had to be persuaded or induced. "Obedience by compulsion is the Obedience of Vassals, who without compulsion would disobey," explained one essayist. "The Affection of the People is the only Source of a Cheerful and rational Obedience." Local officials serving without pay frequently ignored orders contrary to their own interests or the interests of their community.

Most young men accepted military service only if it suited their future plans. They would serve only under officers they knew, and then for only a single campaign. Few reenlisted. To the exasperation of professional British soldiers, provincials, like Indians, regarded blind obedience to commands as slavery. They did not enlist in order to become soldiers for life. After serving, they used their bonus and their pay, and often the promise of a land grant, to speed their way to becoming masters of their own households. Military service, for those who survived, could lead to land ownership and an earlier marriage. For New England women, however, war reduced the supply of eligible males and raised the median age of marriage by about two years, which meant, in effect, one fewer pregnancy per marriage.

THREE WARRING EMPIRES, 1689–1716

When the three empires went to war after 1689, the Spanish and French fought mostly to survive. The British fought to expand their holdings. None of them won a decisive advantage in the first two wars, which ended with the Treaty of Utrecht in 1713.

Smart diplomacy with the Indians protected the western flank of New France, but the eastern parts of the colony were vulnerable to English invasion. The governors of New France knew that Indian attacks against English towns would keep the English colonies disorganized and make them disperse their forces. Within a year after the outbreak of war between France and England in 1689, Indians had devastated most of coastal Maine and parts of New Hampshire and had attacked the Mohawk valley town of Schenectady, carrying most of its inhabitants into captivity.

In each of the four colonial wars between Britain and France, New Englanders called for the conquest of New France, usually through a naval expedition against Quebec, combined with an overland attack on Montreal. In King William's War (1689–97), Sir William Phips of Massachusetts forced Acadia to sur-

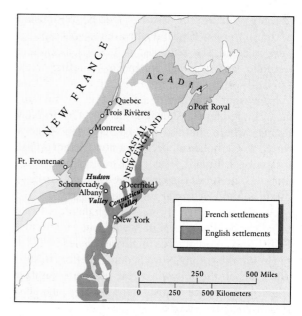

NORTHEASTERN THEATER OF WAR, 1689–1713

render in 1690 (although the French soon regained it) and then sailed up the St. Lawrence. At Quebec, he was bluffed into retreating by the French governor, the comte de Frontenac, who kept marching the same small band of soldiers around his ramparts until the attackers became intimidated and withdrew. The overland attack on Montreal collapsed amid intercolonial bickering and an outbreak of smallpox. French attacks, with Indians providing most of the fighters, continued to ravage the frontier.

In 1704, during Queen Anne's War (1702–13), the French and Indians destroyed Deerfield, Massachusetts, in a winter attack and marched most of its people off to captivity in Canada. Hundreds of New Englanders spent months or even years as captives. One of them was Eunice Williams, young daughter

BRITISH WARS AGAINST FRANCE (AND USUALLY SPAIN), 1689–1763

European Name	American Name	Years	Peace
War of the League of Augsburg	King William's War	1689–97	Ryswick
War of the Spanish Succession	Queen Anne's War	1702–13	Utrecht
War of Jenkins's Ear, merging with		1739–48	
War of the Austrian Succession	King George's War	1744–48	Aix-la-Chapelle
Seven Years' War	French and Indian War	1754–63*	Paris

*The French and Indian War began in America in 1754 and then merged with the Seven Years' War in Europe, which began in 1756.

of John Williams, the pastor of Deerfield. Refusing to return to New England when the town's captives were released, she remained in Canada, became a Catholic, and married an Indian. Another New England woman who refused to return was Esther Wheelwright, daughter of a prominent Maine family. Captured by the Abenakis, she was taken to New France, where she also refused repatriation, converted to Catholicism, became a nun (Esther Marie Joseph de L'Enfant Jésus), and finally emerged as mother superior of the Ursuline Order in Canada—surely an unlikely career for a Puritan girl!

As the war dragged on, New Englanders twice failed to take Port Royal in Acadia, but a combined British and colonial force finally succeeded in 1710, renaming the colony Nova Scotia. An effort to subdue Quebec the following year met with disaster when many of the British ships ran aground in a treacherous stretch of the St. Lawrence River.

Farther south, the imperial struggle was grimmer and even more tragic. The Franciscan missions of Florida were already in decline, but mission Indians still attracted Carolina slavers, who invaded Florida between 1702 and 1704 with a large force of Indian allies, dragged off 4,000 women and children as slaves, drove 9,000 Indians from their homes, and wrecked the missions. The invaders failed to take the Spanish fortress of St. Augustine, but slaving raids spread devastation as far west as

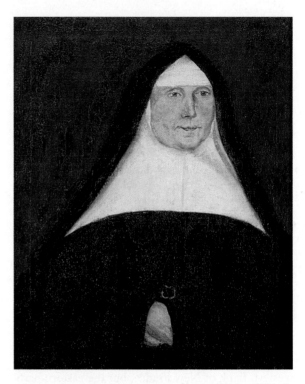

PORTRAIT OF ESTHER WHEELWRIGHT Esther Wheelwright (1696–1780), an English Puritan who was captured by the French and Indians during Queen Anne's War, converted to Catholicism and became Sister Esther Marie Joseph de L'Enfant Jésus and eventually mother superior of the Ursuline nuns in New France.

the lands of the Choctaws and far south along the Florida peninsula.

South Carolina's greed for Indian slaves finally alienated the colony's strongest Indian allies, the Yamasees, who, fearing that they would be the next to be enslaved, attacked South Carolina in 1715 and almost destroyed the colony before being thrust back and nearly exterminated. Some of the Yamasees and a number of escaped African slaves fled as refugees to Spanish Florida.

The wars of 1689–1716 halted the movement of British settlers onto new lands in New England and the Carolinas. Only four Maine towns survived the wars; after half a century, South Carolina still had only 5,200 settlers (and 11,800 enslaved Africans and Indians) in 1720. In Pennsylvania, Maryland, and Virginia—colonies that had not been deeply involved in the wars—the westward thrust continued.

CASTILLO OF SAN MARCOS AT ST. AUGUSTINE, FLORIDA Although South Carolina tried several times to overrun Spanish Florida, the castle always held out and preserved Spanish rule until 1763.

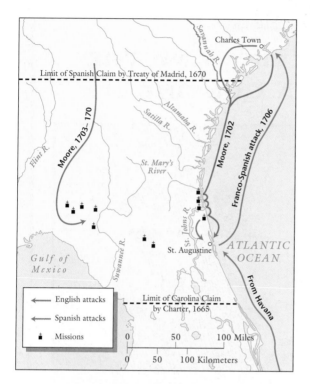

SOUTHEASTERN THEATER OF WAR, 1702–1713

SOUTH CAROLINA COLONISTS ENSLAVING AN INDIAN The colony enslaved thousands of Indians from 1680 through 1715, a practice that touched off the Yamasee War, which nearly destroyed the settlement.

CONCLUSION

The variety and diversity of the colonies posed a huge challenge to the English government. After 1650 it found ways to regulate their trade, mostly for the mutual benefit of both England and the colonies. The colonies, beset by hostile Indians and internal discord, began to recognize that they needed protection that only England could provide. Once the Crown gave up its claims to absolute power, the two sides discovered much on which they could agree.

Political values in England and the colonies began to converge during the Glorious Revolution and its aftermath. Englishmen throughout the empire insisted that the right to property was sacred, that without it liberty could never be secure. They celebrated liberty under law, government by consent, and the toleration of all Protestants. They barred Catholics from succession to the throne and loaded them with severe disabilities of other kinds. In an empire dedicated to "liberty, property, and no popery," Catholics became big losers.

By the 18th century, the British colonists had come to believe they were the freest people on earth. They attributed this fortune to their widespread ownership of land and to the English constitutional principles that they had incorporated into their own governments. When George I became king in 1714, they proudly proclaimed their loyalty to the Hanoverian dynasty that guaranteed a Protestant succession to the British throne. In their minds, the British Empire had become the world's last bastion of liberty.

Suggested Readings begin on page SR-1.
For Web activities and resources
related to this chapter, go to
http://www.harcourtcollege.com/history.murrin

CHAPTER 4

PROVINCIAL AMERICA AND THE STRUGGLE FOR A CONTINENT

WATSON AND THE SHARK

John Singleton Copley's 1778 painting, dramatically depicting a young man's rescue from shark attack, began the democratization of heroism. Note that a black man holds the traditional central and elevated place of honor in the painting, and that only one person on the rescue boat is a "gentleman." In this work, Copley announced that ordinary men can be heroes.

The British colonists believed they were the freest people on earth. Yet during the 18th century they faced a dilemma peculiarly their own. To maintain the opportunity that settlers had come to expect, the colonies had to expand onto new lands. But, more and more, provincial society also emulated the cultural values of Great Britain—its architecture, polite learning, evangelical religion, and politics. Relentless expansion made this emulation difficult because the two often worked at cross purposes: An anglicized province would become far more hierarchical than the colonies had so far been and might not even try to provide a rough equality of opportunity. The settlers tried to sustain both, an effort that brought brutal conflict with their neighbors—the Indians, the Spanish, and the French.

When the British again went to war against Spain and France after 1739, the settlers joined in the struggle and declared that liberty itself was at stake. Less fortunate people among them disagreed. Slaves in the southern colonies saw Spain, not Britain, as a beacon of liberty. In the eastern woodlands, most Indians identified France, not Britain, as the one ally genuinely committed to their survival and independence.

This chapter will focus on the following major questions:

- Why was it difficult to sustain both continual expansion and the anglicization of the colonies in the eighteenth century?
- How were the colonists able to embrace both the enlightenment and evangelical religion at the same time?
- How could both the royal governors and the colonial assemblies grow stronger at the same time?
- What made the War for North America (1754–63) so much more decisive than the three earlier Anglo-French conflicts?

EXPANSION VERSUS ANGLICIZATION

In the 18th century, as the British colonists sought to emulate their homeland, many of the institutions and material goods they had left behind in the 17th century began to reappear. After 1740, for example, imports of British goods grew spectacularly, even faster than population. The gentry dressed in the latest London fashions and embraced that city's

C H R O N O L O G Y

1690	Massachusetts invents fiat money
1704	Boston *News-Letter* founded
1712	Slaves revolt in New York City
1716	Spanish begin to settle Texas
1718	Beginning of Scots-Irish emigration to North America
1721	Boylston introduces smallpox inoculation in Boston
1732	Georgia charter granted by Parliament
1733	Molasses Act passed
1734	Edwards launches massive religious revival in the Connecticut valley
1735	Zenger acquitted of seditious libel in New York
1738	Spanish found Mose in Florida
1739	Slaves revolt in Stono, South Carolina
1739–41	Whitefield launches Great Awakening
1741	New York slave conspiracy trials lead to 35 executions
1745	New England volunteers take Louisbourg
1747	Ohio Company of Virginia founded • Anti-impressment rioters in Boston resist Royal Navy
1750	Massachusetts converts from paper money to silver
1754	Washington attacks French patrol near the forks of the Ohio River • Albany Congress proposes plan for colonial union
1755	Braddock suffers disaster near Fort Duquesne • British expel Acadians from Nova Scotia
1756–57	Loudoun antagonizes the colonies as commander in chief
1756	French take Oswego
1757	French take Fort William Henry • Pitt becomes Britain's war minister
1758	British take Fort Duquesne • British take Fortress Louisbourg and Fort Frontenac • French repel British attack at Ticonderoga
1759	British take Ticonderoga and Crown Point • Wolfe dies taking Quebec; Montcalm also killed
1760	Montreal falls; Canada surrenders to the British
1760–61	Cherokee War devastates South Carolina backcountry
1762	Spain enters war, loses Havana and Manila
1763	Peace of Paris ends Seven Years' War

standards of taste and elegance. Between 1720 and 1750 wealthy settlers built handsome mansions in the older portions of the colonies. Virginia planters erected "big houses," such as Mount Vernon, built by Lawrence Washington and bequeathed to his half-brother George. In Boston, on Beacon Hill, the merchant Thomas Hancock built a stylish residence that later passed to his nephew John. Newspapers and learned professions based on English models proliferated after 1700, and colonial seaports began to resemble Bristol and other provincial cities in England.

But the population of British North America doubled every 25 years. Each new generation required twice as many colleges, ministers, lawyers, physicians, craftsmen, printers, sailors, and unskilled laborers as the preceding generation. Without them, standards of "civility" would decline. None of these institutions could meet colonial needs unless it continued to grow. As the 18th century progressed, the colonies became the scene of a contest between the unrelenting pace of raw expansion and these newer, anglicizing tendencies.

Colonies that looked only to England, or even Europe, to satisfy their needs for skilled talent could no longer attract as many people as they needed. In 1700, for example, Oxford and Cambridge Universities in England had managed to fill the colonies' needs for Anglican clergymen by sending over those graduates who were unable to find parishes at home. Most of them went to the southern colonies. By 1750 the colonial demand far exceeded what Oxford and Cambridge could supply, and the colonies were also trying to attract Scottish and Irish clergymen. Before long those sources also proved inadequate. By contrast, northern colonies founded their own colleges and trained their own ministers, lawyers, and doctors, as well as their own printers, shipwrights, and other skilled craftsmen. Although still colonies, they were becoming America's first modernizing societies. They learned to do for themselves what Britain had to do for the southern colonies.

Much of this change occurred during prolonged periods of warfare. War interrupted expansion, which then resumed at an even more frantic pace with the return of peace. By midcentury, the wars were becoming a titanic struggle for control of the North American continent. Gradually Indians realized that they would be the ultimate victims of British victory. Constant expansion for British settlers meant unending retreat for them.

THREATS TO HOUSEHOLDER AUTONOMY

As population rose, some families acquired more prestige than others. Although the status of "gentleman" was less rigid in the colonies than in Britain, it usually implied a man who performed no manual labor, and such men began to dominate public life. Before 1700 ordinary farmers and small planters had often sat in colonial assemblies. In the 18th century the assemblies grew much more slowly than the overall population. In the five colonies from New York to Maryland, they remained almost unchanged in size despite enormous population growth. The men who took part in public life above the local level came, more and more, from a higher social status. They had greater wealth, a more impressive lineage, and a better education than ordinary farmers or craftsmen. Unlike their counterparts in England, however, few colonial gentlemen enjoyed a patron-client relationship with the voters. In England, one or two families dominated each of the "pocket boroughs" that elected most members of Parliament. In the colonies, most voters remained independent.

By midcentury, despite the high value that colonists placed on householder autonomy, patterns of dependency were beginning to emerge. In tidewater Virginia by 1760, about 80 percent of the land was entailed. Younger sons had to look west for an inheritance. In one Maryland county, 27 percent of the householders were tenants who worked small tracts of land without slaves, or were men who owned a slave or two but had no claim to land. Such families could not satisfy the ambitions of all their children. In Pennsylvania's Chester County, a new class of married farm laborers arose. Their employers, without granting them title or lease, would let them use a small patch of land on which they could build a cottage and raise some food. Called "inmates" in Chester County records (or "cottagers" in England), such people made up 25 percent of the county population. Tenants on New York manors had to accept higher rents and shorter leases after 1750. In Chebacco Parish in Ipswich,

Massachusetts, half of the farmers had land enough for only some of their sons by 1760.

Families that could not provide for all of their children reverted to English social norms. A father favored his sons over his daughters, unless he could marry a daughter to a wealthy suitor. In Connecticut, from the 1750s to the 1770s, about 75 percent of eligible sons inherited some land, but for daughters the rate fell from 44 to 34 percent. When a father could not support all his sons, he favored the eldest over the younger sons. The younger sons, in turn, took up a trade or headed for the frontier. To increase their resources, many New England farmers added a craft or two to the household. The 300 families of Haverhill, Massachusetts, supported 44 workshops and 19 mills by 1767. In Northampton more than one-third of all the farming families also practiced a craft. Families in the town of Lynn began making shoes in quantity, many for export. Most families added a craft in order to sustain household autonomy. The goal of independence continued to exercise great power, but it was under siege. The fear of imperiled independence energized the whole westward movement (see chapter 7).

ANGLICIZING THE ROLE OF WOMEN

The changing role of women provides a dramatic example of the anglicizing tendencies of the 18th century. When they married, most women received a dowry from their father, usually in cash or goods, not land. Under the common law doctrine of coverture, married women could not make a contract. The legal personality of the husband "covered" the wife, and he made all legally binding decisions. If he died first, his widow was entitled to dower rights, usually one-third of the estate, which passed, after her death, to the couple's surviving children.

Women in many, perhaps most, households, had to work harder to maintain the family status—at the spinning wheel, for example. In a sense, women were becoming more English, thus reversing some earlier trends. Until 1700 many Chesapeake widows inherited all of their husbands' property and administered their own estates. After 1700 such arrangements were rare. In the Hudson valley, Dutch law had been much more generous than

English common law in bestowing property rights on women, but during the 18th century English law gradually prevailed. In New England, too, as Puritan intensity waned, women suffered losses. Before 1700, courts had routinely punished men for sexual offenses, such as fornication, and many men had pleaded guilty and accepted their sentence. After 1700 almost no man would plead guilty to a sexual offense, except perhaps to making love to his wife before their wedding day. However, to avoid a small fine, some husbands humiliated their wives by denying that charge, even if their wives had already pleaded guilty after giving birth to a child that had obviously been conceived before marriage. Courts rarely convicted men of sex offenses, not even serious crimes such as rape. The European double standard of sexual behavior, which punished women for their indiscretions while tolerating male infractions, had been in some jeopardy under the Puritan regime. It now revived.

EXPANSION, IMMIGRATION, AND REGIONAL DIFFERENTIATION

The end of the wars encouraged renewed expansion. After 1715, the settled portions of North America enjoyed their longest era of peace since the arrival of Europeans. The wars had emptied the borderlands of most of their inhabitants. Until midcentury, people poured into these areas without provoking the strong Indian nations of the interior. As they expanded, the colonies fitted, more or less snugly, into distinct regions, although only New Englanders had acquired a self-conscious sense of regional identity before independence.

EMERGENCE OF THE OLD SOUTH

Renewed immigration, free and unfree, drove much of the postwar expansion. After 1730 the flow became enormous. In that year, about 630,000 settlers and slaves lived in the mainland colonies. By 1775 another 248,000 Africans and 284,000 Europeans had landed, including 50,000 British convicts, shipped mostly to Maryland and Virginia, where they served long indentures. During this period, the African slave trade to North America

reached its peak. Most of the 210,000 voluntary immigrants settled in the middle or southern colonies. Free migration decisively outweighed the influx of slaves only after 1763.

Almost 90 percent of the slaves went to the southern colonies. At least 84,000 slaves went to Charleston, 70,000 to Virginia, and 25,000 to Maryland. One-eighth of the slaves went to northern colonies. New England had 15,000 blacks by 1770, New York 19,000, and New Jersey, Pennsylvania, and Delaware had a combined total of 16,000. About 80 percent of the slaves arrived from Africa on British-owned vessels. Most of the rest came, a few at a time, from the West Indies on New England ships.

This massive influx of slaves created the Old South, a society consisting of wealthy slaveholding planters, a much larger class of small planters, and thousands of slaves. By 1720 slaves made up 70 percent of South Carolina's population. By 1740 they made up 40 percent of Virginia's and 30 percent of Maryland's. Slaves performed most of the manual labor in the southern colonies.

Their arrival transformed the social structure of the southern colonies. In 1700 most members of Virginia's House of Burgesses were small planters who raised tobacco with a few indentured servants and perhaps a slave or two. After 1730 the typical burgess was a great planter who owned at least 20 slaves. And by 1750 the rice planters of South Carolina were richer than any other group in British North America. Tobacco and rice planters had few contacts with each other, except in North Carolina where they seldom got along well. They did not yet think of themselves as "southerners."

The life of slaves in the upper South (Maryland, Virginia, and the Albemarle region of North Carolina) differed considerably from the life of slaves in the lower South (from Cape Fear in North Carolina through South Carolina and eventually Georgia). The Chesapeake tobacco planters organized their slaves into gangs, supervised them closely, and kept them in the fields all day, weather permitting. To make their plantations more self-sufficient, they also trained perhaps 10 percent of their slaves as blacksmiths, carpenters, coopers, or as other skilled artisans. The planters, who saw themselves as benevolent paternalists, also encouraged family life among their workers, who by the 1720s were beginning to achieve a rate of reproduction that almost

THE GOLD COAST OF AFRICA AT THE HEIGHT OF THE SLAVE TRADE This 18th-century view of the Gold Coast shows five European slaving posts, including "Mina" or Elmina, the Portuguese fortress built in 1481 and captured by the Dutch in the 17th century.

equaled that of the settlers. Slaveholders even explained brutal whippings as fatherly efforts to correct the behavior of members of their household.

South Carolina planters began with similar paternalistic inclinations, but the rice swamps and mosquitoes defeated them. "Carolina is in the spring a paradise, in the summer a hell, and in the autumn a hospital," claimed one visitor. Whites who supervised slave gangs in the rice fields quickly caught malaria. Although malaria was seldom fatal, it left its victims vulnerable to other diseases that often killed them. Many rice planters relocated their big houses to higher ground, at a safe distance from their rice fields.

Africans fared much better than whites in the marshy rice fields. (According to modern medicine, many Africans possess a "sickle cell" in the blood that grants them protection against malaria but can also expose their children to a deadly form of inherited anemia.) As the ability of Africans to resist malaria became evident, Carolina planters seldom ventured near the rice fields and became less paternalistic than their Virginia counterparts except toward their household servants. After midcentury, many of them chose to spend their summers in Charleston or else found summer homes on high ground in the interior. Others vacationed in Newport, Rhode Island.

This situation altered work patterns. To produce a crop of rice, planters devised the task system, in which the slaves had to complete certain chores each day, after which their time was their own. Slaves used their free time to raise crops, hunt, or fish, activities that enabled them to create a largely invisible economy of their own. The South Carolina planters relied on a large class of white artisans in Charleston for local manufacturing such as blacksmithing, coopering, and carpentry.

Thus, while many Chesapeake slaves were acquiring the skills of artisans, Carolina slaves were heading in the other direction. Before rice became the colony's staple, they had performed a wide variety of tasks. But the huge profits from rice now condemned nearly all of them to monotonous, unpleasant labor in the swamps, even though they were freed from the direct oversight of their masters. Rice culture also left Africans with low rates of reproduction. Yet because the task system gave them more control over their own lives, slaves preferred it to gang labor.

This freedom meant slower assimilation into the British world. African words and customs survived longer in South Carolina than in the Chesapeake colonies. Newly imported slaves spoke Gullah, originally a pidgin language (that is, a simple second language for everyone who spoke it). Gullah began with a few phrases common to many West African languages, gradually added English words, and became the natural language of subsequent generations. Modern black English, which developed from Gullah, was born in the Carolina rice fields.

The South Carolina slave population failed to grow by natural increase until perhaps the 1770s, a half century later than in the tobacco colonies. Even South Carolina planters had difficulty replacing themselves before 1760. But by the Revolution, the American South was becoming the world's only self-sustaining slave society. Nowhere else could staple colonies reproduce their labor force without continuous imports from Africa.

Everywhere that slavery took hold the system required a great deal of brute force to maintain. Slaves convicted of arson were often burned at the stake, an unthinkable punishment to inflict on a white person. Whippings were frequent, and the master or overseer determined the number of stripes. In South Carolina one overseer killed five slaves in two or three years before 1712. When one slave fell asleep and lost a parcel of rice in the river, he chained him, whipped him twice a day, refused to give him food, and confined him at night in a "hellish Machine contrived by him into the Shape of a Coffin where [he] could not stir." The victim finally obtained a knife from one of his children and committed suicide.

If extreme cruelty of this sort was rare, random acts of violence were common and, from a slave's perspective, unpredictable. In Virginia William Byrd II was one of the most refined settlers in the colony and owned its largest library. His diary reveals that when he and his wife, Lucy, disagreed, the slaves could suffer. "My wife and I had a terrible quarrel about whipping Eugene while Mr. Mumford was there but she had a mind to show her authority before company but I would not suffer it,

ENTRANCE HALL TO "CARTER'S GROVE," JAMES CITY COUNTY, VIRGINIA The wealthiest family in Virginia in the first half of the 18th century, the Carters celebrated their status by erecting a stylish big house with the grandest entrance hall in the colony.

which she took very ill." On that occasion, Eugene was spared, but slaves were not always so lucky. One day "My wife caused Prue to be whipped violently notwithstanding I desired not, which provoked me to have Anaka whipped likewise who had deserved it much more, on which my wife flew into such a passion she hoped she would be revenged of me." This time both slaves were whipped, apparently for minor infractions. The Byrds also quarreled about whether Lucy could beat Jenny with the fire tongs. House servants must have dreaded the days that Byrd spent in Williamsburg, leaving Lucy in charge of the plantation.

The southern colonies prospered in the 18th century by exchanging their staple crops for British imports. By midcentury much of this trade had been taken over by Scots. Glasgow became the leading tobacco port of the Atlantic. Although tobacco profits remained precarious before 1730, they improved in later decades, partly because Virginia guaranteed a high-quality leaf by passing an inspection law in 1730 (Maryland followed suit in 1747), and partly because a tobacco contract between Britain and France brought lucrative revenues to both governments and opened up a vast continental market for Chesapeake planters. By 1775, more than 90 percent of their tobacco was re-exported to Europe from Britain.

Other exports and new crafts also contributed to rising prosperity. South Carolina continued to export provisions to the sugar islands and deerskins to Britain. Indigo, used as a dye by the British textile industry, received a cash bounty from Parliament and emerged at midcentury as a second staple crop, pioneered by a woman planter, Eliza Lucas Pinckney. North Carolina, where the population increased fivefold between 1720 and 1760 and more than doubled again by 1775, sold naval stores (pitch, resin, turpentine) to British shipbuilders. Many Chesapeake planters turned to wheat as a second cash crop. Wheat required mills to grind it into flour, barrels in which to pack it, and ships to carry it away. It did for the Chesapeake what tobacco had failed to do. It created cities. Norfolk and Baltimore had nearly 10,000 people by 1775, and smaller cities, such as Alexandria and Georgetown, were also thriving. Shipbuilding, closely tied to the export of wheat, became an important Chesapeake industry.

THE MID-ATLANTIC COLONIES: THE "BEST POOR MAN'S COUNTRY"

The Mid-Atlantic colonies had been pluralistic societies from the start. Immigration added to this ethnic and religious complexity after 1700. The region had the most prosperous family farms in America and, by 1760, the two largest cities, Philadelphia and New York. Pennsylvania outpaced New York in the competition for immigrants. New York governors had granted enormous manors to political supporters, mostly in the 1680s and 1690s, which dominated the Hudson valley and discouraged immigration. As late as 1750, the small colony of New Jersey had as many settlers as New York, but fewer slaves. Pennsylvania's growth exploded, driven by both natural increase and a huge surge of immigration. The 12th colony to be founded out of the original 13, Pennsylvania was the second most populous by 1770, surpassed only by Virginia.

After 1720 Ireland and Germany replaced England as the source of most free immigrants. About 70 percent of Ireland's emigrants came from Ulster. They were Presbyterians whose forebears had come to Ireland from Scotland in the 17th century. (Historians now call them the Scots-Irish, a term seldom used at the time.) Most of them left for America to avoid an increase in rents and to enjoy greater trading privileges than the British Parliament allowed Ireland. The first Ulsterites sailed for New England in 1718. They expected a friendly reception from fellow Calvinists, but the Yankees treated them with suspicion. Some of them stayed and introduced linen manufacturing in New Hampshire, but after 1718 most immigrants from Ulster headed for the Delaware valley. About 30 percent of Irish immigrants came from southern Ireland. Most of these were Catholics, but perhaps a quarter were Anglicans. They too headed for the Mid-Atlantic colonies. Altogether, some 80,000 Irish reached the Delaware valley before 1776.

About 70,000 of the free immigrants were Germans. Most of them arrived as families, often as "redemptioners," a new form of indentured service attractive to married couples because it allowed them to find and bind themselves to their own masters. Families could stay together. After redemptioners completed their service, most of them streamed into the interior of Pennsylvania, where Germans outnumbered the original English and Welsh settlers by 1750. In an outburst that he later regretted, Benjamin Franklin complained that German "boors" were taking over the colony. Other Germans moved to the southern backcountry with the Irish. The Mid-Atlantic colonies, already North America's breadbasket, were the favored destination of free immigrants because the expanding economies of the region offered many opportunities. These colonies grew excellent wheat and built their own ships to carry it abroad. At first New York flour outsold Pennsylvania's, but Pennsylvania gained the edge in the 1720s after it instituted a new system of public inspection and quality control. When Europe's population started to surge, after 1740, the middle colonies began to ship flour across the Atlantic. Before 1760 both Philadelphia and New York City overtook Boston's stagnant population of 15,000. Philadelphia, with 32,000 people, was the largest city in British North America by 1775.

THE BACKCOUNTRY

Many of the Scots-Irish, together with some of the Germans, pushed west into the mountains and up the river valleys into the interior parts of Virginia and the Carolinas. In South Carolina, about 100 miles of pine barrens stood between these backcountry settlements and the rice plantations along the coast. Most of the English-speaking colonists were immigrants from Ulster, northern England, or lowland Scotland who brought their folkways with them and soon gave the region its own distinctive culture. Although most of them farmed, many turned to hunting or raising cattle. Unlike the coastal settlements, the backcountry showed few signs of anglicizing. It had no newspapers, few clergymen or other professionals, and little elegance. Some parts, especially in South Carolina, had almost no government. A visiting Anglican clergyman bemoaned "the abandon'd Morals and profligate Principles" of the settlers. In 1768 he preached to a gathering who had never before heard a minister, or even the Lord's Prayer. "After the Service," he wrote, "they went out to Revell[in]g, Drinking, Singing, Dancing and Whoring, and most . . . were drunk before I quitted

the Spott." Refined easterners found the backcountry more than a little frightening.

Backcountry settlers were clannish and violent. They drank heavily and hated Indians. After 1750 the situation became quite tense in Pennsylvania, where the Quaker legislature insisted on handling differences with the Indians through peaceful negotiation, even though few Quakers lived on the frontier. (The Moravian Brethren, a pacifist German sect, maintained Indian missions in Pennsylvania and North Carolina but had little impact on other colonists.) Once fighting broke out against the Indians, most backcountry residents demanded their extermination. Virginia and South Carolina faced the same problem.

NEW ENGLAND: A FALTERING ECONOMY AND PAPER MONEY

New England was a land of farmers, fishermen, lumberjacks, shipwrights, and merchants and still considered itself more pious than the rest of the British Empire. But the region faced serious new problems. Few immigrants, either slave or free, went there. In fact, since about 1660 more people had been leaving the region, mostly for New York and New Jersey, than had been arriving.

New England's relative isolation in the 17th century began to have negative social and economic effects after 1700. Life expectancy declined as diseases from Europe, especially smallpox and diphtheria, invaded the region by way of Atlantic commerce. The first settlers had left these diseases behind in Europe, but lack of exposure in childhood made later generations vulnerable. When smallpox threatened to devastate Boston in 1721, Zabdiel Boylston, a self-taught doctor, began inoculating people with the disease on the theory that healthy people would survive the injection and become immune. Although the city's leading physicians opposed the experiment as too risky, it worked and soon became a regular feature of public health in many colonies. Even so, a diphtheria epidemic in the 1730s and high military losses after 1740 reduced population growth. New England's rate of growth fell behind that of other regions.

After the wars ended in 1713, New England's economy began to weaken. The region had prospered in the 17th century, mostly by exporting cod, grain, and barrel staves to the West Indies. After 1700, however, Yankees had trouble feeding themselves, much less others. A blight called the "wheat blast" first appeared in the 1660s and slowly spread until cultivation of wheat nearly ceased. Because Yankees preferred wheat bread to corn bread, they had to import flour from New York and Pennsylvania and, eventually, wheat from Chesapeake Bay. Poverty became a huge social problem in Boston, where by the 1740s about one-third of all adult women were widows, mostly poor. Poor relief became a major public expense.

After grain exports declined, the once-profitable West Indian trade barely broke even. Yet its volume remained large, especially after enterprising Yankees opened up new markets in the lucrative French sugar islands. Within the West Indian market, competition from New York and Philadelphia grew almost too severe for New Englanders to meet, because those cities had flour to export and shorter distances over which to ship it. Mostly, the Yankees shipped fish and forest products to the islands in exchange for molasses, which they used as a sweetener (cheaper than sugar) or distilled into rum. Rum joined cod and lumber as a major export. British West Indian planters, alarmed by the flood of cheap French molasses, urged Parliament to stamp out New England's trade with the French West Indies. Parliament passed the Molasses Act of 1733, which placed a prohibitive duty of six pence per gallon on all foreign molasses. Strictly enforced, the act would have strangled New England trade; instead it gave rise to bribery and smuggling, and the molasses continued to flow.

Shipbuilding gave New England most of its leverage in the Atlantic economy. Yankees made more ships than all the other colonies combined, although the Chesapeake colonies and the Delaware valley were closing the gap by the 1760s. New England ships earned enough from freight in most years to offset losses elsewhere, but Boston merchants often had to scramble to pay for their imports. New England ran unfavorable balances with nearly every trading partner, especially England. Yankees imported many British products but produced little that anybody in Britain wanted to buy. Whale oil, used in lamps, was an exception. A prosperous whaling industry emerged on the island of Nantucket, where surviving Indians taught set-

tlers how to use harpoons and actively participated in the trade until they were decimated by disease. But the grain trade with the Mid-Atlantic and Chesapeake colonies was not profitable. Settlers there eagerly bought rum and a few slaves from Yankee vessels that stopped on their way back from the West Indies. Newport even became deeply involved in slave trading along the African coast. Although that traffic never supplied a large percentage of North America's slaves, it contributed to the city's growth.

New England's experience with paper money illustrates these economic difficulties. In response to a military emergency in 1690, Massachusetts invented fiat money—that is, paper money backed, not by silver or gold, but only by the government's promise to accept it in payment of taxes. It worked well enough until serious depreciation set in after the Treaty of Utrecht. The return of peace in 1713 meant that nearly all paper money would be retired within a few years through taxes already pledged for that purpose. To sustain its paper currency, the Massachusetts legislature created four land banks between 1714 and 1728. Settlers could borrow paper money using their land as security and pay off the debt over 10 years at 5 percent interest. But when the value of New England's currency declined steadily in relation to the British pound, most Boston merchants turned against paper money. They sold many of their wares on credit only to be repaid in depreciated paper. Farmers, who had originally been suspicious of land banks, became strong advocates after they discovered that they could benefit as debtors. When Britain forbade the governor to consent to any new land banks, the countryside organized a private land bank that issued huge amounts of paper in 1741, provoking a major political crisis. Parliament quickly intervened to crush the bank. But as the bank's supporters pointed out, land banks worked quite well in colonies outside New England, such as Pennsylvania where Franklin became an eloquent supporter.

The declining value of money touched off a fierce debate that raged from 1714 until 1750. Creditors attacked paper money as fraudulent: Only gold and silver, they claimed, had real value. Defenders retorted that, in most other colonies, paper was holding its value. The problem, they insisted, lay with the New England economy, which could not generate enough exports to pay for the region's imports. The elimination of paper, they warned, would only deepen New England's problems. War disrupted shipping in the 1740s, and military expenditures sent New England currency to a new low. Then, in 1748, Parliament agreed to reimburse Massachusetts for these expenses at the 1745 exchange rate. Governor William Shirley and House Speaker Thomas Hutchinson, an outspoken opponent of paper money, barely persuaded the legislature to use the grant to retire all paper and convert to silver money. That decision was a drastic example of anglicization. Although fiat money was the colony's own invention, Massachusetts repudiated its own offspring in 1750 in favor of orthodox methods of British public finance. As Hutchinson's critics had warned, however, silver gravitated to Boston and back to London to pay for imports. New England's economy entered a deep depression in the early 1750s from which it did not revive until after 1755, when the wars resumed.

ANGLICIZING PROVINCIAL AMERICA

What made these diverse regions more alike was what they retained or acquired from Britain, not what they found in America. Although each exported its own distinctive products, their patterns of consumption became quite similar. In the 18th century, printing and newspapers, the learned professions, and the intellectual movement known as the Enlightenment all made their mark on British North America. The new colony of Georgia was in many ways a byproduct of the English Enlightenment. A powerful transatlantic religious revival, the Great Awakening, swept across Britain and the colonies in the 1730s and 1740s. And colonial political systems tried to recast themselves in the image of Britain's mixed and balanced constitution.

THE WORLD OF PRINT

Few 17th-century American settlers owned books, and except in New England, even fewer engaged in the intellectual debates of the day. For most of the century, only Massachusetts had printing presses, first in Cambridge to serve Harvard College, the clergy, and the government, and then in Boston beginning in 1674. For one hundred years, Boston was the printing capital of North America. In the 1680s, William Bradford became Philadelphia's first printer, but after a Quaker controversy drove him from the colony, he moved to New York. By 1740 Boston had eight printers; New York and Philadelphia each had two. No other community had more than one.

Not surprisingly, Boston also led the way in newspaper publishing. John Campbell, the city's postmaster, established the Boston *News-Letter* in

A NEW ENGLAND TRADING BRIG, CIRCA 1750 Modern drawing by Edwin Tunis.

WOODEN PRESS IN A COLONIAL PRINT SHOP Modern drawing by Edwin Tunis.

1704, only a few years after provincial newspapers had begun to appear in England. By the early 1720s two more papers had opened in Boston, and Philadelphia and New York City had each acquired one. The *South Carolina Gazette* was founded in Charleston in 1732 and the *Virginia Gazette* at Williamsburg in 1736. By then, Boston had added several more. Benjamin Franklin took charge of the *Pennsylvania Gazette* in 1729, and John Peter Zenger launched the controversial *New York Weekly Journal* in 1733. In 1735, after attacking Governor William Cosby, Zenger won a major victory for freedom of the press when a jury acquitted him of "seditious libel," the crime of criticizing government officials.

These papers were weeklies that devoted nearly all of their space to European affairs. Before mid-century, they rarely reported local news because they assumed their readers already knew it. At first, they merely reprinted items from the *London Gazette*. Beginning in the 1720s, however, the *New England Courant*, under James Franklin (with Benjamin, his younger brother and apprentice), also began to reprint Richard Steele's essays from the *Spectator*, Joseph Addison's pieces from the *Tatler*, and the angry, polemical writings, mostly aimed at religious bigotry and political and financial corruption, of "Cato," a pen name used jointly by John Trenchard and Thomas Gordon. *Cato's Letters*, which Gordon later published in four volumes, became immensely popular among colonial printers and readers. In short, newspapers began to spread the English Enlightenment throughout the North American colonies.

Benjamin Franklin personified the Enlightenment values that the newspapers were spreading. As a boy, although raised in Puritan Boston, he skipped church on Sundays to read Addison and Steele and to perfect his prose style. As a young printer with the *New England Courant* in the 1720s, he helped to publish the writings of John Checkley, an Anglican whom the courts twice prosecuted in a vain attempt to silence him. Franklin joined the Church of England after moving to Philadelphia. In 1729 he took over the *Pennsylvania Gazette* and made it the best-edited paper in America. It reached 2,000 subscribers, four times the circulation of a Boston weekly.

Franklin was always looking for ways to improve society. In 1727 he and some friends founded the Junto, a debating society that met Friday evenings to discuss literary and philosophical questions. It later evolved into the American Philosophical Soci-ety, which still thrives near Independence Hall. Franklin was a founder of North America's first Masonic lodge in 1730, the Library Company of Philadelphia a year later, the Union Fire Company in 1736, the Philadelphia Hospital in 1751, and an academy that became the College of Philadelphia (now the University of Pennsylvania) in the 1750s. His greatest fame came from his electrical experiments during the 1740s and 1750s, which brought him honorary degrees from Harvard, Yale, William and Mary, Oxford, and St. Andrews University in Scotland. He invented the Franklin stove (much more efficient than a fireplace) and the lightning rod. By the 1760s he had become the most celebrated North American in the world and was thinking of retiring to England.

THE ENLIGHTENMENT IN AMERICA

The English Enlightenment, which rejected a vengeful God and exalted man's capacity for knowledge and social improvement, grew out of the rational and benevolent piety favored by Low

LINK TO THE PAST

Benjamin Franklin and the Colonial Enlightenment

http://tlc.ai.org/franklin.htm

Put together by the Access Indiana Teaching and Learning Center, this site makes accessible most major aspects of the life and accomplishments of Benjamin Franklin, prerevolutionary America's most famous person. The section on "Scientist & Inventor" allows one to explore his contribution to our understanding of electricity, including his invention of the lightning rod.

1. Find the section on *The New-England Courant*, the first literary journal published in the colonies. The *Courant* was founded in 1721 by James Franklin, Benjamin's older brother, and Benjamin, an apprentice, also contributed to it, sometimes without James's knowledge. Read an issue or two and then under Contents, follow the link to "The Little-Compton Scourge: Or, The Anti-Courant" and read it. What made the *Courant* controversial? Is this attack effective or merely pedantic?

Church (latitudinarian) Anglicans in Restoration England. These Anglicans disliked rigid doctrine, scoffed at conversion experiences, attacked superstition, and rejected all "fanaticism," whether that of High Church Laudians, who had brought on England's great crisis of 1640–42, or that of the Puritans, who had dismantled the monarchy. High Church men, a small group after 1689, stood for orthodoxy, ritual, and liturgy.

Enlightened writers greeted Sir Isaac Newton's laws of motion as one of the greatest intellectual achievements of all time, joined the philosopher John Locke in looking for ways to improve society, and began to suspect that moderns had surpassed the ancients in learning and wisdom. John Tillotson, archbishop of Canterbury until his death in 1694, embodied this "polite and Catholick [that is, universal] spirit." He preached morality rather than dogma and had a way of defending the doctrine of eternal damnation that left his listeners wondering how a merciful God could possibly have ordained such a cruel punishment.

Enlightened ideas won an elite constituency in the mainland colonies even before newspapers began publishing and circulating these new views. Tillotson had a huge impact on America. His sermons appeared in numerous southern libraries and made a deep impression at Harvard College, beginning with two young tutors, William Brattle and John Leverett, Jr. After Leverett replaced Increase Mather as college president in 1707, Tillotson's ideas became entrenched in the curriculum. For the rest of the century most Harvard-trained ministers, although still claiming to be Calvinists, embraced Tillotson's latitudinarian piety. They stressed the similarities, not the differences, between Congregationalists and Anglicans and favored broad religious toleration. After 1800 most Harvard-educated ministers became Unitarians who no longer believed in hell or the divinity of Jesus.

In 1701, largely in reaction against this trend at Harvard, a new college was founded as a bastion of orthodoxy in Connecticut. When it finally settled in New Haven, it was named Yale College in honor of a wealthy English benefactor, Elihu Yale, who donated his library to the school. Those Anglican books did to the Yale faculty, and to several nearby ministers, what Tillotson had done at Harvard—and more. At the commencement of 1722, Yale's

THE REDWOOD LIBRARY, NEWPORT, RHODE ISLAND Designed by architect Peter Harrison and erected between 1748 and 1750, this elegant building was named for Abraham Redwood, who donated £500 for the purchase of books in 1747.

small faculty, except for a 19-year-old tutor, Jonathan Edwards, announced their conversion to the Church of England. They sailed for England to be ordained by the bishop of London. Their leader, Timothy Cutler, became the principal Anglican spokesman in Boston. Samuel Johnson, another defector, became the first president of King's College (now Columbia University) in New York City in the 1750s and won a considerable reputation as a moral philosopher.

LAWYERS AND DOCTORS

The rise of the legal profession helped to spread Enlightenment ideas. Before 1700 most colonists despised lawyers as men who took advantage of the misery of others and who deliberately stirred up discord. Virginia and Massachusetts briefly abolished the legal profession. Only in Maryland did it take firm hold before 1700, but then it began to spread everywhere. In 1692 three English lawyers handled nearly all the cases in the province of New York; by 1704 there were eight. In Boston, the legal profession seemed disreputable as late as 1720. Three British immigrants, all of them Anglicans, handled most cases. When a Congregational clergyman resigned his Connecticut pulpit and moved to

Boston to practice law, he too joined Anglican King's Chapel. Benjamin Gridley, a Harvard man famous for his impiety, took up law and wrote enlightened essays for Boston newspapers in the 1730s, turned his office into an informal law school, and set up a debating society, the Sodalitas, in which students disputed legal questions within the context of contemporary oratory and philosophy. By then, a college education was almost a prerequisite to a legal career in New England.

Most Massachusetts lawyers before 1760 were either Anglicans or young men who had rejected the ministry as a career. Some were scoffers and skeptics, and most probably thought of themselves as a new learned elite. By the 1790s, lawyers saw themselves as the cultural vanguard of the new republic. Poet John Trumbull, playwright Royall Tyler, and novelist Hugh Henry Brackenridge all continued to practice law while writing on the side. Others turned from the law to full-time writing, including poet William Cullen Bryant, writer Washington Irving, and novelist Charles Brockden Brown. Clearly, law and the Enlightenment rode together in 18th century America.

Medicine also became an enlightened profession, with Philadelphia setting the pace. William Shippen earned degrees at Princeton and Edinburgh, the best medical school in the world at the time, before returning to Philadelphia in 1762, where he became the first American to lecture on medicine, publish a treatise on chemistry, and dissect human cadavers—a practice that shocked the unenlightened. His student John Morgan became the first professor of medicine in North America when the College of Philadelphia established a medical faculty a few years later. Benjamin Rush, who also studied at Princeton and Edinburgh, brought the latest Scottish techniques to the newly founded Philadelphia Hospital. He too became an enlightened reformer. He attacked slavery and alcohol and supported the Revolution. Many colonial physicians embraced radical politics.

GEORGIA: THE FAILURE OF AN ENLIGHTENMENT UTOPIA

In the 1730s Anglican humanitarianism and the Enlightenment belief in the possibility of social improvement converged in Britain to provide support for the founding of Georgia, named for King George II (1727–60). The sponsors of this project had several goals. They hoped to create a society that could make productive use of England's "worthy" poor (but not the lazy or criminal poor). Believing that South Carolina might well be helpless if attacked by Spain, they also intended—with no sense of irony—to shield that colony's slave society from Spanish Florida by populating Georgia with disciplined, armed free men. The founders of Georgia were appalled by what cheap English gin was doing to the sobriety and industry of the working people of England. They hoped to produce silk and wine, items that no other British colony had yet succeeded in making. They prohibited hard liquor and slavery. Slaves would make Georgia a simple extension of South Carolina, with all of its vulnerabilities.

A group of distinguished trustees, including members of both houses of Parliament, set themselves up as a nonprofit corporation and announced that they would give land away, not sell it. Led by James Oglethorpe, the trustees obtained a 20-year charter from Parliament in 1732, raised money from Anglican friends, and launched the colony on land claimed by both Spain and Britain. The trustees recruited foreign Protestants, including some Germans who had just been driven out of Salzburg by its Catholic bishop, a small number of Moravian Brethren (a German pacifist sect, led by Count Nicholas von Zinzendorf), and French Huguenots. In England, they interviewed many prospective settlers to distinguish the worthy poor from the unworthy. They engaged silk and wine experts and recruited Scottish Highlanders as soldiers.

But the trustees refused to consult the settlers on what might be good for them or for Georgia. As refined men of the Enlightenment, they believed they knew what the colony needed. They created no elective assembly, nor did they give the British government much chance to supervise them. Under their charter, Georgia laws had to be approved by the British Privy Council. Therefore the trustees passed only three laws during their 20 years of rule. One laid out the land system, and the others prohibited slavery and hard liquor. The trustees governed through "regulations" instead of laws. An elective assembly, the trustees promised, would come later, after Georgia's character had been firmly set.

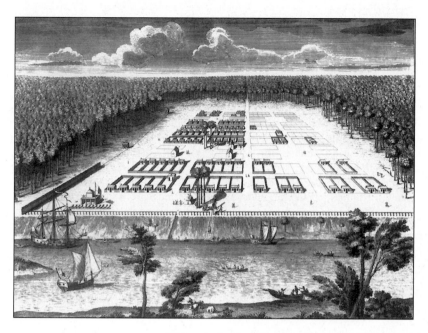

A VIEW OF SAVANNAH ON MARCH 29, 1734 This painting by Peter Gordon emphasizes the wide streets and spacious atmosphere of this planned city.

In 1733 the first settlers laid out Savannah, a town with spacious streets. Within 10 years, 1,800 charity cases and just over 1,000 self-supporting colonists reached Georgia. The most successful were the Salzburgers, who agreed with the prohibitions on slavery and alcohol and built a thriving settlement at Ebenezer, farther up the Savannah River. The Moravian Brethren left for North Carolina after five years rather than bear arms. A group of Lowland Scots known as the Malcontents grew disgruntled, and after Oglethorpe ignored their complaints, left for South Carolina.

The land system never worked as planned. The trustees gave 50 acres to every male settler whose passage was paid for out of charitable funds. Those who paid their own way could claim up to 500 acres. Ordinary farmers did poorly; they could not support a family on 50 acres of the sandy soil around Savannah. Because the trustees envisioned every landowner as a soldier, women could not inherit land, nor could landowners sell their plots.

The settlers were unable to grow grapes or to persuade the sickly worms that survived the Atlantic crossing to make silk out of mulberry leaves. They clamored for rum, smuggled it into the colony when they could, and insisted that Georgia would never thrive until it had slaves. By the mid-1740s, enough people had died or left to reduce the population by more than half, and by 1752 the population had dropped below the 2,800 who had first settled the colony.

Between 1750 and 1752 the trustees gave up. They dropped their ban on alcohol, allowed the importation of slaves, summoned an elective assembly (but only to consult, not legislate), and finally surrendered their charter to Parliament. The establishment of royal government in 1752 at last gave Georgia an elective assembly with full powers of legislation, and Georgia became what it was never meant to be, a smaller version of South Carolina, producing rice and indigo with slave labor. By then, however, in one of the supreme ironies of the age, the colony had done more to spread religious revivalism than to vindicate Enlightenment ideals. Georgia helped to turn both John Wesley and George Whitefield into the greatest revivalists of the century.

THE GREAT AWAKENING

Between the mid-1730s and the early 1740s, an immense religious revival, the Great Awakening, swept

The Refined and the Crude

In the 17th century, few colonists placed much value on elegance or refinement. Most families ate from wooden bowls with wooden spoons and usually sat on crude benches rather than chairs. After 1700 that pattern began to change. Families hoping to achieve

prominence cultivated a genteel style in their homes, their possessions, their clothing, their manners, and their way of speaking. While Benjamin Franklin worked in his Philadelphia print shop, he had ink on his hands, probably rolled up his sleeves on the job, and declined to serve in public office because men who did manual labor were not gentlemen. When he retired about 1747, however, he acquired a wig, a ruffled shirt, and an expensive greatcoat and had Robert Feke paint his portrait (left). Franklin now thought of himself as a gentleman and dedicated his life to scientific research and public service. Refined colonists set aside

across the Protestant world. Within the British Empire, it affected some areas more intensely than others. England, Scotland, Ulster, New England, the Mid-Atlantic colonies, and for a time South Carolina responded warmly to emotional calls for a spiritual rebirth. Southern Ireland, the West Indies, and the Chesapeake colonies remained on the margins until Virginia and Maryland were drawn into a later phase of revivalism in the 1760s and 1770s. The Great Awakening shattered some denominational loyalties in the colonies and enabled the Methodists and the Baptists to surge ahead of all Protestant rivals in the generation after 1780.

ORIGINS OF THE REVIVALS

Some of the earliest revivals arose among the Dutch in New Jersey. Guiliam Bertholf, a farmer and cooper (barrelmaker), was a lay reader who had been ordained in an obscure corner of the Netherlands in 1694 (Amsterdam did not approve) and returned to preach to his former neighbors in

whole rooms in their homes for genteel pursuits, such as visiting and polite conversation. The sitting room of the Verplanck family in its Wall Street residence in New York City, as reconstructed and shown here at the left, reflects the opulence of wealthy urban families by the 1760s. Everything depicted here was actually in the house at that time. The exterior of gentry homes also made a social and cultural statement.

The gentility of the leisured few acquired its full force only in contrast with the crude sensibilities of the many who worked hard for a living. The painting at bottom, John Greenwood's *Sea Captains Carousing in Surinam* (circa 1750), suggests that working men, when not kept busy, would drink themselves into oblivion. Only the favored few could achieve true refinement.

Hackensack and Passaic. His emotional piety won many adherents. After 1720 Theodorus Jacobus Frelinghuysen sparked several revivals in his congregation in New Brunswick, New Jersey. The local Presbyterian pastor, Gilbert Tennent, watched and learned.

Tennent was a younger son of William Tennent, Sr., a Presbyterian minister from Ulster who had moved to America. At Neshaminy, Pennsylvania, he set up the Log College, where he trained his sons and other young men as evangelical preachers.

The Tennent family dominated the Presbytery of New Brunswick, used it to ordain ministers, and sent them off to any congregation that requested one, even in other presbyteries. That practice angered the Philadelphia Synod, the governing body of the Presbyterian church in the colonies. Most of its ministers emphasized orthodoxy over a personal conversion experience. In a 1740 sermon, *The Dangers of an Unconverted Ministry*, Gilbert Tennent denounced those preachers for leading their people to hell. His attack split the church. In 1741 the

THE SYNOD OF PHILADELPHIA BY 1738 *In actuality, some presbyteries had more churches than others. Arrows indicate descending lines of authority.*

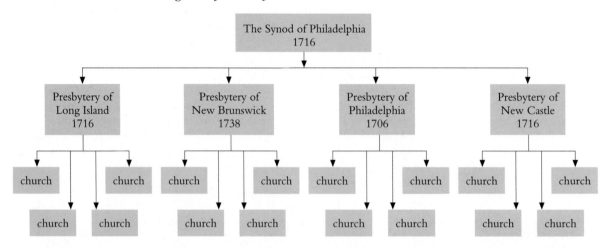

outnumbered revivalists withdrew and founded their own Synod of New York.

In New England, Solomon Stoddard of Northampton presided over six revivals, which he called "harvests of souls," between the 1670s and his death in 1729. Jonathan Edwards, his grandson and successor—the only member of the Yale faculty who had not defected to the Anglicans in 1722—touched off a revival in 1734 and 1735 that rocked dozens of Connecticut valley towns. It ended suddenly when a prominent man, overwhelmed by the burden of his sins, slit his own throat. Edwards's *A Faithful Narrative of the Surprising Work of God* (1737) explained what a revival was—an emotional response to God's Word that brought sudden conversions to scores of people. He described these conversions in acute detail and won admirers in Britain as well as in New England.

In England, John Wesley and George Whitefield set the pace. At worldly Oxford University, Wesley and his brother Charles founded the Holy Club, a High Church society whose members fasted until they could barely walk. One even lay prostrate for hours on the frigid earth, lost in prayer while his hands turned black. These methodical practices prompted scoffers to call them "Methodists." Still dissatisfied with the state of his soul, Wesley went to Georgia as a missionary in 1735, an unhappy experience for him. He fell in love with a woman who did not return his affection, and the settlers rejected his ascetic piety. In 1737, on the return voyage to England, some Moravians convinced him that, for all his zeal, he had never grasped the central Protestant message, justification by faith alone. Some months later he was deeply moved by Edwards's *Faithful Narrative*. Soon, Wesley found his life's mission, the conversion of sinners, and it launched him on an extraordinary preaching career of 50 years.

George Whitefield, who had been a talented amateur actor in his youth, joined the Holy Club at Oxford and became an Anglican minister. He followed Wesley to Georgia, founded an orphanage, then returned to England and preached all over the kingdom to raise money for it. He had the power to move masses of people through a single sermon, and he too began to preach the "new birth"—the necessity of a conversion experience. When many pastors banned him from their pulpits, he responded by preaching in open fields to anyone who would listen. Newspapers reported the controversy, and soon Whitefield's admirers began to notify the press where he would be on any given day. Colonial newspapers, keenly sensitive to the English press, also reported his movements.

WHITEFIELD LAUNCHES THE TRANSATLANTIC REVIVAL

In 1739 Whitefield made his second trip to America, ostensibly to raise funds for his orphanage at

Bethesda, Georgia. Everyone knew who he was from newspaper accounts, and thousands flocked to hear him preach. After landing in Delaware, he preached his way northward through Philadelphia, New Jersey, and New York City, and then headed south through the Chesapeake colonies and into South Carolina. In September 1740 he sailed to Newport and for two months toured New England. During his travels he met Benjamin Franklin, Gilbert Tennent, and Jonathan Edwards. In the cities he sometimes attracted as many as 30,000 people, or twice the population of Boston. His voice was so musical, claimed one observer, that he could seduce a crowd just by the way he said "Mesopotamia." Using his acting skills, he imitated Christ on the cross, shedding "pious tears" for poor sinners. Or he became God at the Last Judgment, thundering: "Depart from me ye accursed into everlasting fire!" When he wept, his audience wept with him. When he condemned them, they fell to the ground in agony.

Although Whitefield wore the surplice of an Anglican minister and carried the *Book of Common Prayer* when he preached, Anglicans treated him with reserve or hostility. In Charleston and New York City, the official spokesmen for the bishop of London denounced him, but Presbyterians, Congregationalists, and Baptists embraced him, at least until some of them began to fear that he was doing more harm than good. To many he embodied the old nonseparatist ideal that all English Protestants were really members of the same church.

DISRUPTIONS

When other preachers tried to take up Whitefield's role after he moved on, they aroused fierce controversy. In South Carolina Hugh Bryan, a Savannah River planter, began preaching the evangelical message to his slaves. In 1742, not long after a major slave revolt had rocked the colony, he denounced slavery as a sin and warned that God would pour out his wrath on the planters unless they rejected it. Proclaiming himself an American Moses, he attempted to part the waters of the Savannah River and lead the slaves to freedom in Georgia. Instead, he almost drowned. He then confessed publicly that he had been deluded. This fiasco discredited evangelicalism among the planters

of the lower South for another generation, but Bryan and his family continued to convert their own slaves. African American evangelical piety, including some of the first black preachers, took root from these efforts.

Whitefield's successors caused severe disturbances in New England. Gilbert Tennent preached there for months. Lacking Whitefield's musical voice and Oxford diction, Tennent spoke with a Scottish burr and specialized in "Holy Laughter," the scornful peals of a triumphant God as sinners tumble into hell. He abandoned the usual garb of a minister for a robe and sandals and let his hair grow long, thereby proclaiming himself a new John the Baptist heralding the Second Coming of Christ. Many ecstatic followers believed that the biblical Millennium was at hand.

James Davenport, who succeeded Tennent, denounced unregenerate ministers by name. He liked to preach by eerie candlelight, roaring damnation at his listeners, even grabbing Satan and wrestling him back to hell. He advised his admirers to drink rat poison rather than listen to another lifeless sermon. In 1743 he established the "Shepherd's Tent" in New London to train awakened preachers. This outdoor school abandoned the classical curriculum of colleges and insisted only on a valid conversion experience. He organized a book-burning (in which titles by Increase Mather and other New England dignitaries went up in flames) and threw his britches on the fire, declaring them a mark of human vanity. A New England grand jury, asked to indict him, proclaimed him mad instead. Like Bryan in South Carolina, he repented and claimed that he had been deluded. The Shepherd's Tent collapsed.

LONG-TERM CONSEQUENCES OF THE REVIVALS

The revivals had dramatic consequences. As time passed, they feminized evangelical churches. Amid the enthusiasm of Whitefield's tour, more men than usual had joined a church, but after another year or two, men became hard to convert. The number of women church members began to soar, however, until by 1800 they often formed a majority of 3 or 4 to 1, and in some congregations acquired an informal veto over the choice of the minister.

"The God that holds you over the pit of hell, much as one holds a spider, or some loathsome insect over the fire, abhors you, and is dreadfully provoked: his wrath towards you burns like fire; he looks upon you as worthy of nothing else, but to be cast into the fire; . . . you are ten thousand times more abominable in his eyes than the most hateful venomous serpent is in ours. You have offended him infinitely more than ever a stubborn rebel did his prince; and yet it is nothing but his hand that holds you from falling into the fire this very moment. . . . There is no other reason to be given why you have not gone to hell, since you have sat here in the house of God, provoking his pure eyes by your sinful manner of attending his solemn worship. . . .

"You hang by a slender thread, with the flames of divine wrath flashing about it, and ready every moment to . . . burn it asunder; and you have no interest in any Mediator, and nothing to lay hold of to save yourself, nothing to keep off the flames of wrath, nothing that you have ever done, nothing that you can do, to induce God to spare you one moment."

JONATHAN EDWARDS
in Sinners in the Hands of an Angry God, *1741*

Partly in reaction to the revivals, thousands of men became Freemasons, often instead of joining a church. After 1730 the Masons made some headway among the merchants and professionals of Philadelphia and Boston, but during and after the Revolution their membership grew spectacularly. They appealed to men of all denominations, accepting even a few Catholics, Jews, and Indians. Artisans began to dominate city lodges, and the Masons penetrated deeply into the countryside as well. They very nearly turned their order into a religion of manliness, complete with secret and mysterious rituals. They extolled sobriety, industry, brotherhood, benevolence, and citizenship. At first most clergymen saw Masons as a force for good, but by the 1820s the order would be drawing angry criticism.

The revivals shattered the unity of New England's Congregational Church. Evangelicals seceded from dozens of congregations to form their own "Separate" churches. Many of those that survived went Baptist by the 1760s, thereby gaining protection under the toleration statutes of the New England colonies. In the middle colonies, the revivals strengthened denominational loyalties and energized the clergy. In the 1730s most people in the region, particularly in New Jersey and Pennsylvania, had never joined a church. The revivals prompted many of them to become New Side (evangelical) Presbyterians, Old Side (antirevival) Presbyterians, or nonevangelical Anglicans. Similar cleavages ran through the German population. The southern colonies were less affected, although evangelical Presbyterians made modest gains in the Virginia backcountry after 1740. Finally, in the 1760s, the Baptists began to win thousands of converts, as did the Methodists after 1776, whose numbers surpassed the Baptists a few decades later.

The revivals broke down localism by creating new cosmopolitan links with Britain and between colonies. Whitefield ran the most efficient publicity machine in the Atlantic world. In London, Glasgow, and Boston, periodicals called the *Christian History* carried news of revivals occurring anywhere in the empire. For years, London evangelicals held regular "Letter Days," at which they read accounts of revivals in progress. Revivalists wrote often to one another. When fervor declined in New England, Jonathan Edwards organized a Concert of Prayer with his Scottish correspondents, setting regular times for them all to beseech the Lord to pour out his grace once more. As Anglicans split into Methodists and Latitudinarians, Congregationalists into New Lights (prorevival) and Old Lights (antirevival), and Presbyterians into comparable New Side and Old Side synods, evangelicals discovered that they had more in common with revivalists in other denominations than with antire-

A REVIVAL IN LATE 18TH-CENTURY VIRGINIA Religious revivals spread throughout the colonies during the Great Awakening. Note how many of the participants shown are women.

vivalists in their own. When New Side Presbyterians chose a new president of the College of New Jersey in 1757, they saw nothing strange in naming a Congregationalist, Jonathan Edwards.

Edwards was the ablest apologist for revivals in Britain or America and probably the most profound theologian that North America has yet produced. When Boston's Charles Chauncy (very much a man of the Enlightenment) attacked the revivals as frauds because of their emotional excesses, Edwards replied with *A Treatise concerning Religious Affections* (1746), which displayed his own mastery of Enlightenment sources, including Newton and Locke. Although admitting that no emotional response, however intense, was proof by itself of the presence of God in a person's soul, he insisted that intense feeling must always accompany the reception of divine grace. That view upset people who believed that a rational God must have established a polite and genteel religion. For Edwards, an unemotional piety could never be the work of God. In effect, Ed-

wards countered Chauncy's emotional defense of reason with his own rational defense of emotion.

NEW COLLEGES

The Great Awakening also created several new colleges. Each was set up primarily by a single denomination, but all admitted other Protestants. In 1740 North America had only three colleges: Harvard, William and Mary, and Yale. Although Yale eventually embraced the revivals, all three opposed them at first. In 1746 middle colony evangelicals, eager to show their commitment to classical learning after the fiasco of the Shepherd's Tent, founded the College of New Jersey. It graduated its first class in 1748 and settled in Princeton in 1756. Unlike the older colleges, it drew students from all 13 colonies and sent its graduates throughout America, especially to the middle and southern colonies. It also reshaped the Presbyterian Church. When Presbyterians healed their schism and reunited in

1758, the New Siders set the terms. Outnumbered in 1741, they held a large majority of ministers by 1758. Through control of Princeton, their numbers had increased rapidly. The Old Side, still dependent on the University of Glasgow in Scotland, could barely replace those who died.

New Light Baptists founded the College of Rhode Island (now Brown University) in the 1760s. Dutch Reformed revivalists established Queens College (now Rutgers University) in New Jersey, mostly to train evangelical ministers who could preach in English. Eleazer Wheelock opened an evangelical school for Indians in Lebanon, Connecticut. After his first graduate, Samson Occum, raised £12,000 in England for the school, Wheelock moved to New Hampshire and used most of the money to found Dartmouth College instead. By 1790 Dartmouth was turning out more graduates, and far more ministers, than any other American college.

In the 1750s Anglicans countered with two new colleges of their own: the College of Philadelphia (now the University of Pennsylvania), which also had Old Side Presbyterian support, and King's College (now Columbia University) in New York. Their undergraduate programs remained small, however, and few of their students chose a ministerial career. In the competition for student loyalties, nonevangelicals could not yet compete effectively with revivalists.

THE DENOMINATIONAL REALIGNMENT

The revivals transformed American religious life. In 1700, the three strongest denominations had been the Congregationalists in New England, the Quakers in the Delaware valley, and the Anglicans in the South. By 1800 all three had lost ground to newcomers: the Methodists, who grew at an astonishing rate as the Church of England collapsed during the Revolution; the Baptists, who leaped into second place; and the Presbyterians. Methodists and Baptists did not expect their preachers to attend college, and they recruited ministers from a much broader segment of the population than their rivals could tap. Although they never organized their own Shepherd's Tent, they embraced similar principles, demanding only personal conversion, integrity, knowledge of the Bible, and a talent for preaching. Antirevivalist denominations, especially Anglicans and Quakers, lost heavily. New Light Congregationalists made only slight gains because, when their people left behind the established churches of New England and moved west, they usually joined a Presbyterian church, which provided a structure and network of support that isolated congregations in a pluralistic society could not sustain.

POLITICAL CULTURE IN THE COLONIES

In politics as in other activities, the colonies became more like Britain during the 18th century. A quarter-century of warfare after 1689 convinced the settlers that they needed the protection of the British state and strengthened their admiration for its parliamentary system. Most colonial voters and assemblymen were more "independent" than their British counterparts, who lived in a hierarchical world of patrons and clients. Still, provincial politics began to absorb many of the values and practices that had taken hold in Britain after the Glorious Revolution.

THE SPECTRUM OF COLONIAL POLITICS

Constitutional Type	Successful	Unsuccessful
Northern "Court"	New York, circa 1710–28 New Hampshire after 1741 Massachusetts after 1741 New Jersey after 1750	New York after 1728 Pennsylvania (successful in peace, ineffective in war)
Southern "Country"	Virginia after 1720 South Carolina after 1730 Georgia after 1752	Maryland North Carolina

Connecticut and Rhode Island never really belonged to this system.

Colonists agreed that they were free because they were British, because they too had mixed constitutions that united monarchy, aristocracy, and democracy in almost perfect balance.

By the 1720s every colony except Connecticut and Rhode Island had an appointive governor, either royal or proprietary, plus a council and an elective assembly. The governor stood for monarchy and the council for aristocracy. In Massachusetts, Rhode Island, and Connecticut the council or upper house was elected (indirectly in Massachusetts). In all other colonies except Pennsylvania, an appointive council played an active legislative role. The office of councillor was not hereditary, but many councillors served for life, especially in Virginia, and some were succeeded by their sons.

THE RISE OF THE ASSEMBLY AND THE GOVERNOR

In all 13 colonies, once the Crown took over Georgia, the settlers elected the assembly, which embod-

ied a colony's "democratic" elements. The right to vote in the colonies, although narrowing as population rose, was more widely shared than in England, where two-thirds of adult males were disfranchised, a ratio that continued to rise. By contrast, something like three-fourths of free adult white men could vote in the colonies, and a fair number of those ineligible at any given time would win that right by acquiring property as they grew older. The frequency of elections varied—every seven years in New York (from the 1740s on) and Virginia, as well as in Britain; every three years in New Hampshire, Maryland, and South Carolina; irregular but fairly frequent by midcentury in New Jersey, North Carolina and Georgia; and at least once a year in the other five colonies. As the century advanced, legislatures sat longer and passed more laws. The lower house—the assembly—usually initiated major bills. The rise of the assembly was a major political fact of the era. It made most of its gains at the expense of the council.

Every royal colony except New York and Georgia already had an assembly with a strong sense of its

THE GOVERNOR'S PALACE AT WILLIAMSBURG, VIRGINIA The governor's palace was built during the term of Governor Alexander Spotswood (1710–22) and restored in the 20th century. For Spotswood, the palace was an extension of royal might and splendor across the ocean. He set a standard of elegance that many planters imitated when they built their own great houses in the second quarter of the 18th century.

own privileges when the first royal governor arrived, but the governors in most colonies also grew more effective as time passed. Because the governor's instructions usually challenged some existing practices, clashes often occurred in which the first royal governors never got all of their demands. Nevertheless, they did win concessions and became much more effective over the years. In almost every colony the most successful governors were men who served between 1730 and 1765. Most of them had learned by then that their success depended less on their prerogatives (specific royal powers embodied in their commissions) than on their ability to win over the assembly through persuasion or patronage.

Early in the century, conflicts between the governor and an assembly majority tended to be legalistic. Each side cited technical precedents to justify the governor's prerogatives or the assembly's traditional privileges. Later on, when conflict spilled over into pamphlets and newspapers, it often pitted an aggrieved minority (unable to win a majority in the assembly) against both governor and assembly. These contests were ideological. The opposition accused the governor of corruption, of threatening the colonists' liberties, and he denounced the opposition as a "faction." Everyone condemned factions, or political parties, as self-interested and destructive. "Party is the madness of many for the gain of a few," declared poet Alexander Pope. Hardly anyone claimed to be a party leader; the other side was the faction.

"COUNTRY" CONSTITUTIONS: THE SOUTHERN COLONIES

Although the colonies were all aware of the ideological currents in British politics, they reacted to them in different ways. In most southern colonies, the "Country" principles of the British opposition (see chapter 3) became the common assumptions of public life, acceptable to both governor and assembly, typically after a failed attempt to impose the "Court" alternative. When a governor, such as Virginia's Alexander Spotswood (1710–22), used his patronage to fill the assembly with his own "placemen," the voters turned them out at the next election. Just as Spotswood learned that he could not manipulate the house through patronage, the assembly discovered that it could not coerce a governor who had a permanent salary. Accordingly, Virginia and South Carolina cultivated a "politics of harmony," a system of ritualized mutual flattery. Governors found that they could accomplish more through persuasion than through patronage, and the assemblies responded by showing their appreciation. The planters of Virginia and South Carolina concluded that their societies embodied almost exactly what British opposition writers had been demanding. Factions disappeared, allowing the governor and the assembly to pursue the common good in an atmosphere free of rancor or corruption. Georgia adopted the same practices in the 1750s.

This system worked well because the planters were doing what Britain wanted them to do: shipping staple crops to Britain. Both sides could agree on measures that would make this process more efficient, such as the Virginia Tobacco Inspection Act of 1730. In Virginia, public controversy actually ceased. Between 1720 and 1765, particularly during the able administration of Sir William Gooch (1727–49), the governor and House of Burgesses engaged in only one public quarrel, an unparalleled record of political harmony. South Carolina's politics became almost as placid from the 1730s into the 1760s, but harmony there masked serious social problems that were beginning to emerge in the unrepresented backcountry. By contrast, the politics of harmony never took hold in Maryland, where the lord proprietor always tried to seduce assemblymen with his lavish patronage, nor in factional North Carolina, where the tobacco and rice planters continually wrangled, and the backcountry disliked both.

"COURT" CONSTITUTIONS: THE NORTHERN COLONIES

With many economic interests and ethnic groups to satisfy, the northern colonies often produced political factions. Governors with a large vision of the public welfare could win support by using patronage to reward some groups and to discipline others. William Shirley, governor of Massachusetts from 1741 to 1756, used judicial and militia appointments and war contracts to build a majority in the assembly. Like Sir Robert Walpole in Britain, he was a master of "Court" politics. In New Hampshire, Benning Wentworth created a political machine that rewarded just about every assemblyman between 1741 and 1767. An ineffective opposition in both colonies accused the governors of corrupting the assembly, but Shirley and Wentworth each claimed that their actions were essential to their colony's needs. Both governors remained in tight control.

The opposition, though seldom able to implement its demands at the provincial level, was important nonetheless. It kept settlers alert to any infringements on their liberties. It dominated the town of Boston from 1720 on, and it reminded people that resistance to authority might be the only means to preserve liberty. Boston artisans engaged in ritualized mob activities that had a sharp political edge. Every year on Guy Fawkes Day (November 5) a North End mob and a South End mob bloodied each other for the privilege of burning effigies of the pope, the devil, and the Stuart pretender to the British throne. These men celebrated liberty, property, and no popery—the British constitution as they understood it. The violence made many wealthy merchants nervous, and by 1765 some of them would become its targets.

New York's governors, particularly Robert Hunter (1710–19), achieved great success even before 1720, mostly by playing off one faction against another in a colony that had been fiercely divided since Leisler's rebellion of 1689. Hunter's salary and perquisites became more lucrative than those attached to any other royal office in North America, and after 1716 he and his successor were so satisfied with their control of the assembly that they let 10 years pass without calling a general election. During the 25 years after 1730, later governors lost these advantages, primarily because London gave the governorship to a series of men eager to rebuild their tattered fortunes at New York's expense. This combination of greed and need gave new leverage to the assembly, which attacked many royal prerogatives during the 1740s. Of the mainland colonies, only the governor of New York emerged weaker by 1760 than he had been in 1730.

Pennsylvania, by contrast, kept its proprietary governor weak well into the 1750s. After three decades of factionalism, a unified Quaker Party won undisputed control of the assembly during the 1730s. The governor, who by this time was never a Quaker, had a lot of patronage to dispense. He found it useless in controlling the Quaker assemblymen, who had lost interest in becoming judges if that meant administering oaths. Nor could he win these pacifists over with military commissions or contracts, no matter how lucrative.

The colonists, both north and south, absorbed the ideology of the British opposition, which warned that those in power were always trying to destroy liberty and that corruption was power's most dangerous weapon. By 1776 that view would justify independence and the repudiation of a "corrupt" king and Parliament. Before the 1760s, however, it served different purposes. In the south, this ideology celebrated both the political success of Virginia and South Carolina and Anglo-American harmony. In the north, it replicated its role in Britain and became the language of frustrated minorities unable to defeat the governor or control the assembly.

THE RENEWAL OF IMPERIAL CONFLICT

A new era of imperial war began in 1739 and continued, with only a brief interruption, until 1763. The British colonies, New Spain, and New France all became involved, and eventually so did all the Indians of the eastern woodlands. By 1763 France had been expelled from North America. Britain controlled the continent east of the Mississippi, and Spain claimed the land west of it.

CHALLENGES TO FRENCH POWER

In the decades of peace after 1713, the French tried, with mixed results, to strengthen their position in North America. At great cost, they erected the continent's most formidable fortress, Louisbourg, on Cape Breton Island. The naval force stationed there could protect the French fishery and guard the approaches to the St. Lawrence River. The French also built Fort St. Frédéric, (the British called it Crown Point) on Lake Champlain and maintained their Great Lakes posts at Forts Frontenac, Michilimackinac, and Detroit. To bolster its weak hold on the Gulf of Mexico, France created the Company of the Indies, which shipped 7,000 settlers and 2,000 slaves to Louisiana between 1717 and 1721 but then failed to supply them. By 1726 half had starved to death or had fled. Another 5,000

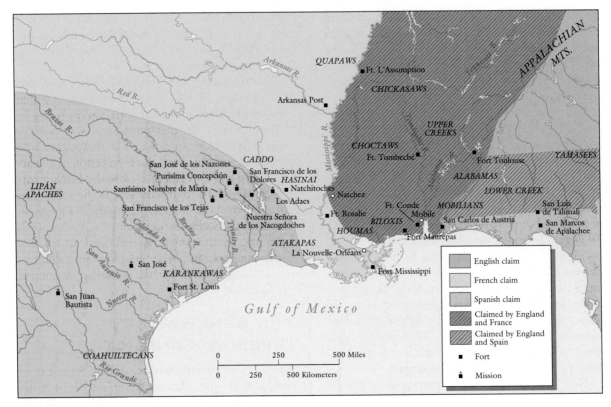

FRENCH LOUISIANA AND SPANISH TEXAS, CIRCA 1730

slaves, but few settlers, reached the colony by 1730. The French founded New Orleans, which became the capital of Louisiana in 1722.

Despite these efforts, the French hold on the interior began to weaken, both north and south. From all points of the compass, Indians returned to the Ohio valley, mostly to trade with pacifist Pennsylvania or with Fort Oswego, a new British post on Lake Ontario. Compared with the French, the British were often clumsy in their dealings with Indians, but they had one advantage: British goods were cheaper than French trade goods, although no better in quality. Many of the Indians founded what the French disparagingly called "republics," villages outside the French alliance system that were willing to trade with the British. The chiefs at Venango, Logstown, and other "republics" accepted people from all tribes—Delawares from the east, Shawnees from the south and east, Mingoes (Iroquois who had left their homeland) from the north, and other Algonquians of the Great Lakes region to the west. Because the inhabitants of each new village had blood relatives living among all the nearby nations, the chiefs hoped that none of their neighbors would attack them and welcomed Pennsylvania traders.

Sometimes even the French system of mediation broke down. In the northwest from 1712 to 1737, the French and their Algonquian allies fought a long, intermittent war with the Fox nation. In the southwest an arrogant French officer decided to take over the lands of the Natchez Indians (the last of the Mississippian mound builders) and ordered them to move. While pretending to comply, the Natchez planned a counterstroke and on November 28, 1729, killed every French male in the vicinity. In the war that followed, the French and their Choctaw allies destroyed the Natchez as a distinct people, although some Natchez refugees found homes among the Chickasaws or the Creeks.

During the war, in 1730, the French barely averted a massive slave uprising in New Orleans. To

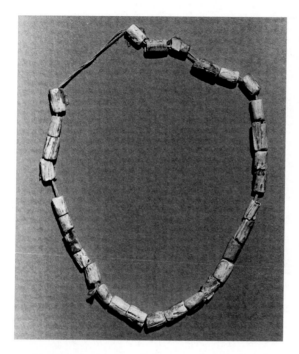

A STRING OF WAMPUM Indians made wampum from conch and clam shells found along the Atlantic Coast. It served as the currency of the fur trade and as a mark of status. Wampum belts preserved communal memories and conveyed messages. Wampum necklaces were buried with prominent Indians in much the same manner that Europeans decorated the coffins of kings and nobles with gold, silver, and jewels. After Indians were driven from the Atlantic Coast, Dutch settlers took over the manufacture of wampum in the 18th century.

stir up hatred between Indians and Africans, the French turned over some of the African leaders of the revolt to the Choctaws to be burned alive. They also encouraged hostilities between the Choctaws and the Chickasaws, largely because they could not afford enough gifts to hold an alliance with both nations. This policy did serious damage to the French. Instead of weakening the pro-British Chickasaws, it touched off a civil war among the Choctaws, and France lost both influence and prestige.

THE DANGER OF SLAVE REVOLTS AND WAR WITH SPAIN

To counter the French, Spain sent missionaries and soldiers into Texas between 1716 and 1720 and founded a capital at Los Adaes, a few miles from the French trading post at Natchitoches. To prevent smuggling, Spain refused to open a seaport on the Gulf Coast. As a result, its tiny outposts had to depend on French trade goods for supplies, sometimes even for food. The Texas missions won few converts and suffered frequent depredations by Indians carrying French muskets. In 1719 the survivors of these attacks abandoned their missions in eastern Texas and fled west to San Antonio, which eventually became the capital.

The Spanish presence in Florida proved troublesome to the British, especially in South Carolina. In the 16th century, Francis Drake had proclaimed himself a liberator when he attacked St. Augustine and promised freedom to Indians and Africans groaning under Spanish tyranny (see chapter 2). By the 1730s the roles had been reversed. On several occasions after 1680, Spanish Florida had promised freedom to any slaves who escaped from Carolina and were willing to accept Catholicism. In 1738 the governor established, just north of St. Augustine, a new town, Gracia Real de Santa Teresa de Mose (or Mose for short, pronounced Moe-shah). He put a remarkable African in charge, a man who took the name Francisco Menéndez at baptism. He had escaped from slavery, had fought with the Yamasees against South Carolina in 1715, and had fled to Florida, only to be enslaved again. Yet he became literate in Spanish and, while still a slave, rose to the rank of militia captain. After winning his freedom, he took charge of Mose in 1738 and made it the first community of free blacks in what is now the United States. The very existence of Mose acted as a magnet for Carolina slaves.

In 1739, the governor of Spanish Florida offered liberty to any slaves from the British colonies who could make their way to Florida. This manifesto, and rumors about Mose, touched off the Stono Rebellion in South Carolina, the largest slave revolt in the entire history of the 13 colonies. Some of the rebellion's leaders were Catholics from the African Kingdom of the Kongo, which Portuguese missionaries had converted in the 16th century.

On Sunday morning, September 9, 1739, a force of 20 slaves attacked a store at Stono (south of Charleston), killed the owner, seized weapons, and moved on to assault other houses and to attract new recruits. Heading toward Florida, they killed about 25 settlers that day and nearly captured Lieutenant

CHRISTIAN BURIAL IN THE KONGO, 18TH CENTURY At least some of the Africans who organized the Stone rebellion in South Carolina in 1739 were Catholics from the kingdom of the Kongo.

Governor William Bull, who happened to be riding by and just managed to gallop away. When the rebels reached the Edisto River, they stopped, raised banners, and shouted "Liberty," hoping to begin a general uprising. There the militia caught them and killed about two-thirds of the growing force. In the weeks that followed, the settlers killed another 60. None of the rebels reached Florida, but, as the founders of Georgia had foreseen, South Carolina was vulnerable in any dispute with Spain.

In 1739, at almost the same moment, the War of Jenkins's Ear, derisively named for a ship captain who displayed his severed ear to Parliament as proof of Spanish cruelty, broke out between Britain and Spain. The war cost Britain dearly because Spanish defenses held everywhere. Some 3,000 men from the 13 colonies, eager for plunder, joined expeditions in 1741 and 1742 against the seaport of Cartagena, New Granada, (now Colombia), and against Cuba and Panama. All were disasters (see map on p. 155). Most of the men died of disease; only 10 percent of the volunteers returned home. But one of the survivors, Lawrence Washington, so admired the British naval commander, Edward Vernon, that he named his Virginia plantation Mount Vernon. Britain also experienced a surge of patriotic fervor from the war. Both "God Save the King" and "Rule Britannia" were written during the struggle.

Georgia was supposed to protect South Carolina. General Oglethorpe, its governor, retaliated against the Spanish by invading Florida in 1740. He dispersed the black residents of Mose and occupied the site, but the Spaniards mauled his garrison in a surprise counterattack. Oglethorpe retreated without taking St. Augustine and returned to Georgia with disturbing reports. Spain, he said, was sending blacks into the British colonies to start slave uprisings. And Spanish priests in disguise were intermingled with the black conspirators and would try to destroy British fortifications. This news set off panics in the rice and tobacco colonies, but it had its biggest impact in New York City.

Back in 1712 a slave revolt had shaken the city. After setting fire to a barn one night, slaves had shot 15 settlers who rushed to put out the blaze, killing nine. Twenty-one slaves were executed, some after gruesome tortures. By 1741 New York City's 2,000 slaves were the largest concentration of blacks in British North America outside of Charleston. On March 18, Fort George burned down in what was probably an accident, but when a series of suspicious fires broke out, the settlers grew nervous. Some of the fires probably provided cover

SAVAGES OF SEVERAL NATIONS, NEW ORLEANS, 1735 This painting by Alexandre de Batz depicts a multiethnic Indian village near New Orleans. The woman at lower left was a Fox Indian who had been captured and enslaved. The African boy was an adoptee.

for an interracial larceny ring that operated out of the tavern of John Hughson, a white man. When the New York Supreme Court offered freedom to Mary Burton, a 16-year-old Irish servant girl at the tavern, in exchange for her testimony, she swore that the tavern was the center of a hellish "popish plot" to murder the city's whites, free the slaves, and make Hughson king of the Africans. Several free black Spanish sailors, who had been captured and enslaved by privateers, also were accused, though apparently their only crime was to insist that they were free men. After Oglethorpe's warning reached New York in June, the number of the accused escalated, and John Ury, a recently arrived High Churchman and a Latin teacher, was hanged as the likely Spanish priest.

The New York conspiracy trials, which continued from May into August of 1741, reminded one observer of the Salem witch frenzy of 1692, in which the testimony of several girls had led to 19 hangings. The toll in New York was worse. Four whites and 18 slaves were hanged, 13 slaves were burned alive, and 70 were banished to the West Indies. The judges spoke pompously about the sacred rights of Englishmen, again in danger from popish conspirators, and grew enraged at any African who

dared to imperil what the colony would not let him share.

In 1742 King Philip V of Spain nearly accomplished what Oglethorpe and the New York judges dreaded. He sent 36 ships and 2,000 soldiers from Cuba with orders to devastate Georgia and South Carolina, "sacking and burning all the towns, posts, plantations, and settlements" and freeing the slaves.

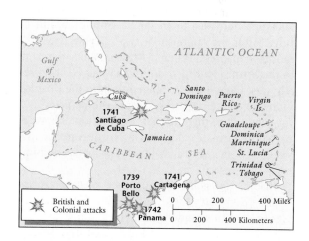

CARIBBEAN THEATER OF WAR, 1739–1742

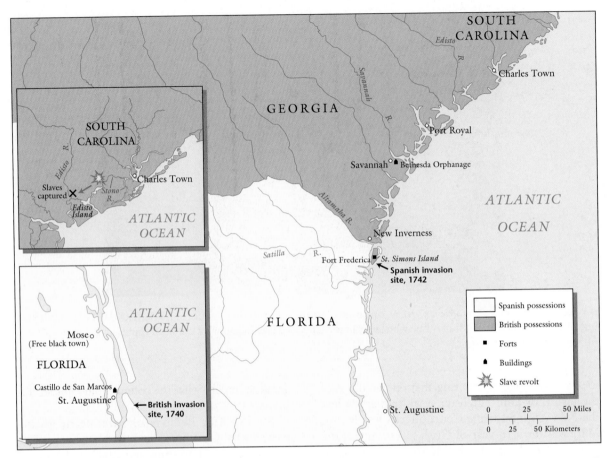

SOUTHEASTERN THEATER OF WAR, 1739–1742

Although the invaders probably outnumbered the entire population of Georgia, Oglethorpe raised 900 men and met them on St. Simons Island in July. After he ambushed two patrols, Spanish morale collapsed. When a British soldier deserted to the Spanish with word of how weak Georgia really was, Oglethorpe arranged to have the Spanish intercept a letter that implicated the deserter as a spy sent to lure them to their destruction. They departed in haste, leaving British North America as a safe haven once more for liberty, property, no popery—and slavery.

Britain did achieve one other success against Spain. Between 1740 and 1744, Commodore George Anson rounded Cape Horn, plundered and burned a small port in Peru, captured several prizes, and then sailed across the Pacific where he captured the Manila galleon, a ship loaded with sil-

ver that sailed annually from Mexico to the Philippines. Anson completed his circumnavigation of the globe and returned to England with 1.3 million pieces of eight and more than 35,000 ounces of silver. Even though only one of Anson's six ships completed the voyage, his success alarmed the Spanish about the security of their lightly defended Pacific possessions. Spain would be reluctant to challenge Britain in the next war.

FRANCE VERSUS BRITAIN: KING GEORGE'S WAR

In 1744 France joined Spain in the war against Britain. The main action then shifted to the north. When the French laid siege to Annapolis Royal, the capital of Nova Scotia, Governor William Shirley of Massachusetts intervened just in time to save the small garrison, and the French withdrew. Shirley then planned his own offensive, a rash attack on Fort Louisbourg on Cape Breton Island. With only a few lightly armed Yankee vessels at his disposal, he asked the commander of the British West Indian squadron, Sir Peter Warren, for assistance. But Shirley's expedition, which included about one-sixth of all the adult males of Massachusetts, set out before Warren could respond. With no heavy artillery of his own, Shirley ordered the expedition to take the outer batteries of the fortress, capture their guns, and use them to knock down its walls. Had the Yankees met a French fleet instead of the Royal Navy, which arrived in the nick of time, nearly every family in New England might have lost a close relative. The most amazing thing about this venture is that it worked. The British navy drove off the French, and untrained Yankee volunteers subdued the mightiest fortress in America with its own guns. Louisbourg fell on June 16, 1745.

After that, however, nothing went right. Hundreds of volunteers died of various afflictions before regular troops arrived to take over. Elaborate plans to attack Quebec by sea in 1746 and 1747 came to nothing because no British fleet appeared. French and Indian raiders devastated the weakly defended frontier while Shirley held back most of his men for a Canada offensive that never took place. Bristol County farmers rioted against high taxes. When the Royal Navy finally docked at Boston in late 1747, its commander sent gangs of sailors ashore to compel anyone they could seize into serving with the fleet. An angry crowd descended on the sailors, took some officers hostage, and controlled the streets of Boston for three days before the naval commander relented and released all the Massachusetts men he had impressed. (The rioters let him keep outsiders.) Finally, Britain had to return Louisbourg to France under the Treaty of Aix-la-Chapelle, which ended the war in 1748. New England had suffered enormous losses and had gained nothing except pride. Yet well into 1747, public opinion had strongly supported the war. The clergy, in particular, saw it as an apocalyptic struggle of free British Protestants against popish tyranny.

THE IMPENDING STORM

The war had driven back the frontiers of British settlement in North America, but the colonies had promised land grants to many volunteers. Thus peace touched off a frenzy of expansion that alarmed Indians and French alike. The British,

THE *BETHEL* This ship belonged to a new class of large privateering vessels launched in the 1740s. After it captured a lucrative Spanish treasure ship, the owners commissioned this painting in 1748.

aware that their hold on Nova Scotia was feeble, recruited 2,500 Protestants from the continent of Europe to populate the colony and sent four regiments of redcoats to accompany them. In 1749 they founded the town of Halifax, which became the new capital of Nova Scotia. The governor also emphasized that his colony would be European, not Indian, by offering bounties for Indian scalps even though the war had ended. When the Micmac Indians, who had lived in peace with the Acadians for more than a century, turned to them for support, the British relented. The Acadians were still too numerous to challenge.

In the 13 colonies, settlers eagerly pressed on to new lands. Yankees swarmed north into Maine and New Hampshire and west into the middle colonies, creating serious tensions. By refusing to pay rent to the manor lords of the Hudson valley, they sparked a tenant revolt in 1753 that the wealthy Livingston family had difficulty subduing. A year later, Connecticut's delegation to the Albany Congress (discussed in the next section) used bribes to acquire an Indian title to all of northern Pennsylvania, which Connecticut claimed on the basis of its sea-to-sea charter of 1663. The blatant encroachments of New York speculators and settlers on Mohawk lands west of Albany so infuriated the Mohawks' Chief Hendrik that he bluntly told the governor of New York in 1753, "the Covenant Chain is broken between you and us [the Iroquois League]. So brother you are not to hear of me any more, and Brother we desire to hear no more of you." New York, Pennsylvania, and Virginia competed for trade with the new Indian "republics" between Lake Erie and the Ohio River. The expansionist thrust pitted colony against colony, as well as settler against Indian, and British against French.

Virginians, whom the Indians called "long knives," were particularly aggressive. Citing their own 1609 sea-to-sea charter (see the chapter 2 map, "Virginia Company Charter, 1606"), they organized the Ohio Company of Virginia in 1747 to settle the Ohio valley and established their first outpost at the place where the Monongahela and Allegheny Rivers converge to form the Ohio River (the site of modern Pittsburgh). The company hired George Washington as a surveyor. Farther south, encroachments upon the Cherokees almost flared into war with South Carolina in 1750.

PORTRAIT OF CHIEF HENDRIK OF THE MOHAWKS
Hendrik's ultimatum to New York in 1753 precipitated the summoning of the Albany Congress a year later.

The French response to these intrusions verged on panic. The fall of Louisbourg had interrupted the flow of French trade goods to the Ohio country for several years, and the men who had long been conducting Indian diplomacy had either died or left office by the late 1740s. Authoritarian newcomers from France replaced them and began giving orders to Indians instead of negotiating with them. The French did, however, make some constructive moves. They rebuilt Louisbourg and erected Fort Beauséjour on the neck that connects mainland Canada to Nova Scotia. In 1755 they erected Fort Carillon (Ticonderoga to the British) on Lake Champlain to protect Crown Point.

Far more controversial was the new French policy in the area between the Great Lakes and the Ohio. Without trying to explain themselves to the Indians, they launched two expeditions into the area. In 1749 Pierre-Joseph Céloron de Blainville led several hundred men down the Allegheny and the Ohio, then up the Miami and back to Canada. He ordered western Indians to join him, but most of them refused. To them, the French were acting like British settlers, intruding on their lands. Along the way Blainville buried plaques, claiming the area for France. The Indians removed them. Marquis Duquesne sent 2,000 Canadians, with almost no Indian support, to erect a line of posts from Fort Presque Isle (now Erie, Pennsylvania) to Fort Duquesne (now Pittsburgh).

The object of this activity was clear enough. The French intended to prevent British settlement west of the Alleghenies. Duquesne thought this policy so obviously beneficial to the Indians that it needed no explanation. Yet the Mingoes warned him not to build a fort in their territory, and a delegation of Delawares and Shawnees asked the Virginians if they would be willing to expel the French from the Ohio country and then go back home. The Indians did not like Virginia's response. In 1753 Virginia sent Washington to the Ohio country to warn Duquesne to withdraw, and a small Virginia force began building its own fort at the forks of the Ohio. Washington was not the man to win over the Indians, who, he declared, had "nothing human except

the shape." Duquesne ignored Washington, advanced toward the Ohio, expelled the Virginians, took over their site, and finished building the fort. Virginia sent Washington back to the Ohio in 1754. On May 28, after discovering a French patrol nearby, Washington launched an attack. That order set off a world war.

THE WAR FOR NORTH AMERICA

Beginning in 1755, the modernizing British state with its professional army came into direct contact with the householder society and the voluntaristic ethic of the colonists. The encounter was often unpleasant, but the gap between the two sides lessened as each became more familiar with the other. At first, the war with France generated fierce tensions between Britain and the colonies, but both sides learned to cooperate effectively until together they achieved victory.

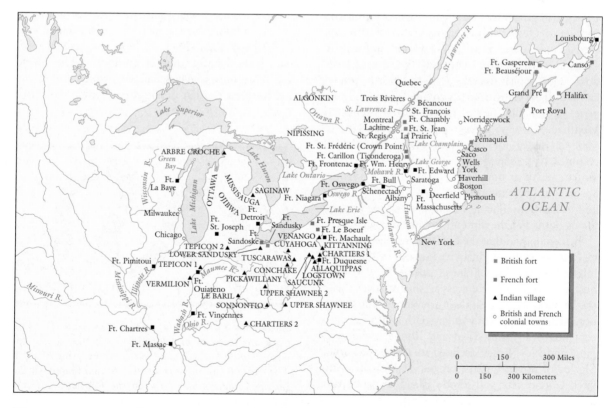

FRANCE VERSUS BRITAIN IN NORTH AMERICA BY 1755

Of the four wars fought between Britain and France from 1689 to 1763, only the last began in America. That conflict, popularly known as the French and Indian War, was also the biggest and produced the most sweeping results. Among all of America's wars from 1750 to the present, according to unpublished calculations by Thomas L. Purvis, it achieved the fourth highest rate of mobilization and, measured by casualties per capita (excluding Indians), it was the third bloodiest contest Americans have ever fought. Only World War II, the Civil War, and the Revolution put a higher percentage of men under arms. Only the Civil War and the Revolution killed a higher percentage of those mobilized.

THE ALBANY CONGRESS AND THE ONSET OF WAR

In the spring of 1754 both New France and Virginia were expecting a limited clash at the forks of the Ohio. Neither anticipated the titanic struggle that encounter would set off, nor did the French and British governments, which hoped to limit any conflict to a few strategic points in North America. New Englanders, however, saw an apocalyptic struggle in the making between "Protestant freedom" and "popish slavery," with the North American continent as the battleground. The only purpose of all the new French forts, suggested Jonathan Mayhew, a Boston preacher, must be to serve as bases for the conquest of the British colonies: "The slaves [that is, the French] are content to starve at home in order to injure freemen abroad, and to extend their territories by violence and usurpation. The continent is not wide enough for us both, and they intend to have the whole."

Britain, fearful that the Six Nations (the Tuscaroras had joined the original Five Nations by the 1720s) might side with New France, ordered New York to host an intercolonial congress at Albany to meet with the Iroquois and redress their grievances. The governor invited every colony as far south as Virginia, except nonroyal Connecticut and Rhode Island. Virginia and New Jersey declined to attend. Governor Shirley of Massachusetts, on his own initiative, invited Connecticut and Rhode Island to participate, and the Massachusetts legislature instructed its delegates to work for a plan of intercolonial union.

In Philadelphia, Benjamin Franklin too was thinking about colonial union. On May 9, 1754, his *Pennsylvania Gazette* printed the first political cartoon in American history, with the caption, "Unite or die." A month later he drafted his "Short Hints towards a Scheme for Uniting the Northern Colonies," which he presented to the Albany Congress in June. His plan called for a "President General" to be appointed by the Crown as commander in chief and to administer the laws of the union, and for a "Grand Council" to be elected for three-year terms by the lower houses of each colony. Deputies would be apportioned according to tax receipts. The union would have power to raise soldiers, build forts, levy taxes, regulate the Indian trade when it touched the welfare of more than a single colony, purchase land from the Indians, and supervise western settlements until the Crown organized them as new colonies. To take effect, the plan would require approval by the Crown and by each colonial legislature and presentation to Parliament for its consent. The Albany Congress adopted an amended version of Franklin's proposal.

Both Shirley and Franklin were far ahead of public opinion. Newspapers did not even discuss the Albany Plan. Every colony rejected it, most with little debate, some unanimously. The voting was close only in Massachusetts, which had borne the heaviest burden in the three earlier wars with

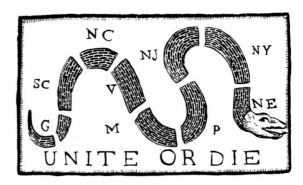

BENJAMIN FRANKLIN'S SNAKE CARTOON The first newspaper cartoon in colonial America, this device appeared in the *Pennsylvania Gazette* in the spring of 1754. The cartoon called for colonial union on the eve of the Albany Congress and drew on the folk legend that a snake, cut into pieces, could revive and live if it somehow joined its severed parts together before sundown.

New France. As Franklin later explained, the colonies feared that the president general might become too powerful. But they also distrusted one another. Despite the French threat, they were not ready to patch up their differences and unite. They did not yet see themselves as "Americans."

The Board of Trade responded by drafting its own plan of union. Its plan resembled Franklin's, except that the Grand Council could only requisition—instead of tax—and colonial union would not require Parliament's approval. After news arrived that Washington had surrendered his small force to the French at Great Meadows in July 1754, Britain decided that the colonies were incapable of uniting in their own defense. Even if they could, the precedent would be dangerous. London sent redcoats to Virginia instead—two regiments, commanded by Edward Braddock. For Britain, colonial union and direct military aid were policy *alternatives*. Although military aid was more expensive to the British government than the proposed union, it seemed the safer choice. By the winter of 1754–55, colonial union was a dead issue on both sides of the ocean.

Yet the Albany Congress achieved one major objective. Sympathizing with Iroquois grievances against New York, it urged the Crown to take charge of relations with all western Indians. London responded by creating two Indian superintendencies—one south of the Ohio, which went first to Edmund Atkin and then John Stuart; and one north of the Ohio, which went to William Johnson, an Irish immigrant to New York who had influence with the Mohawks. These offices would survive the war.

BRITAIN'S YEARS OF DEFEAT

In 1755, London hoped that a quick victory by Braddock at the forks of the Ohio would keep the war from spreading. Braddock's regiments landed in Virginia, a signal that London probably intended to let Virginia, rather than Quaker Pennsylvania, control the upper Ohio valley, including what is now Pittsburgh. At a council of high officials called by Braddock at Alexandria, Virginia, Governor Shirley persuaded him to accept New England's much broader war objectives. Instead of a single expedition aimed at one fort, to be followed by others if time permitted, the campaign of 1755 became four distinct offensives designed to crush the outer

defenses of New France and leave it open to British invasion. Braddock was so impressed with Shirley that he named him second in command of the British army in North America, not bad for an English lawyer with no military training who had arrived almost penniless in Boston 25 years earlier.

Braddock and Shirley tried to make maximum use of both redcoats and provincials. The redcoats were highly disciplined professional soldiers who served long terms and had been trained to fight other professional armies. Irregular war in the forests of North America made them uncomfortable. Provincial soldiers, by contrast, were recruited by individual colonies. They were volunteers, often quite young, who usually enlisted only for a single campaign. They knew little about military drill, expected to serve under the officers who had recruited them, and sometimes refused to obey orders that they disliked. Provincials admired the courage of the redcoats but were shocked by their irreverence and by the brutal discipline imposed on them by their officers. Nevertheless, several thousand colonists also enlisted in the British army, providing up to 40 percent of its strength in North America by 1760.

Under the enlarged plan for 1755, the redcoats in Nova Scotia together with New England provincials would assault Fort Beauséjour, where the Acadian peninsula joins mainland Canada. New England and New York provincials would attack Crown Point, and Shirley, commissioned as a British colonel, would lead two regiments of redcoats (recently recruited in New England) to Niagara and cut off New France from the western Indians. Braddock, with the strongest force, would attack Fort Duquesne.

Instead, Braddock alienated the Indians and marched to disaster on the Monongahela. In April the western Delawares asked him whether their villages and hunting rights would be secure under British protection. He replied, "No Savage Should Inherit the Land." The chiefs retorted that "if they might not have Liberty To Live on the Land they would not Fight for it." Braddock declared that he "did not need their Help." It took Braddock several months to hack a road through the wilderness wide enough for his artillery. He took care to prevent ambushes at two fords of the Monongahela, but as he crossed that stream on July 9, he thought he had overcome all obstacles and pushed on confidently.

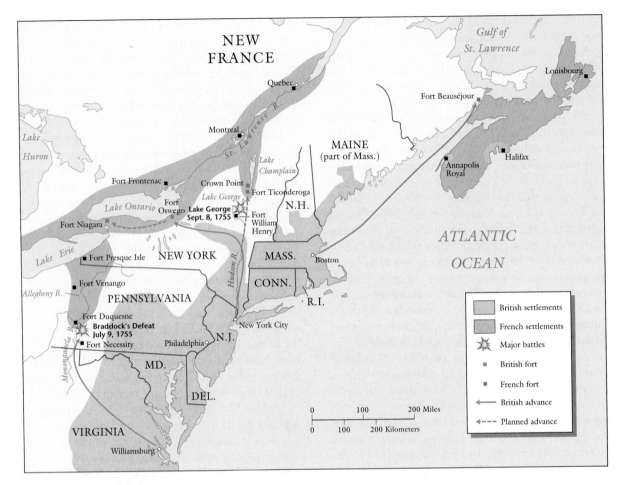

BRITISH OFFENSIVES, 1755

At Fort Duquesne the French commander, Liénard, *sieur* de Beaujeu, could muster only 72 French, 146 Canadians, and 637 Indians against the 1,400 regulars under Braddock and 450 Virginia provincials. Beaujeu had planned to attack the British at the fords of the Monongahela, but the Indians thought such an assault would be suicidal and refused. "Will you allow your father to act alone?" he finally asked melodramatically. "I am sure to defeat them." As Beaujeu marched out, the reluctant Indians followed. Too late to attack at the fords, the French ran into the British vanguard a few miles southeast of the fort. They clashed along a narrow path with thick forest and brush on either side. Beaujeu was killed at once, and his men almost broke, but they rallied and took cover on the British flanks. Braddock's rear elements rushed toward the sound of the guns and

there, massed together, the redcoats formed a gigantic bull's-eye. The Indians and the French poured round after round into them, while the British fired wild volleys at the invisible enemy. The British lost 977 killed or wounded, along with their artillery. Braddock was killed. Only 39 French and Indians were killed or wounded. The redcoats finally broke and ran. Washington, who had fought as a Virginia volunteer, reported that offensive operations would be impossible for the rest of the year. Braddock's road through the wilderness now became a highway for the enemy. For the first time in the history of Quaker Pennsylvania, its settlers faced the horrors of a frontier war.

In Nova Scotia, Fort Beauséjour fell on June 17, 1755. Then the commanders did something to indicate that this war would not be a conventional, limited struggle. When the Acadians refused to take an oath that might have obliged them to bear arms against other Frenchmen, the British and Yankees responded with an 18th-century version of ethnic cleansing. They rounded up between 6,000 and 7,000 Acadians, forced them aboard ships, and expelled them from the province, to be scattered among the 13 colonies, none of which was prepared for the influx. A second roundup in 1759 caught most of the families that had evaded the first one. The British also resumed their merciless war against the Micmac Indians.

The officers who organized these expulsions insisted that they had found a humane way of compelling French Catholics to assimilate with the Protestant majority. Reasoning also that the Acadians were not British subjects because they had not taken the oath, and that only British subjects could own land in a British colony, the government of Nova Scotia confiscated the land the Acadians had farmed for generations and redistributed it to Protestant settlers, mostly from New England. About 3,000 of the Acadian refugees, after spending miserable years as unwanted Catholic exiles in a Protestant world, finally made it to French Louisiana, where their descendants became known as Cajuns. Others went to France, and some even made their way back to Nova Scotia or what later became New Brunswick. Few remained in the 13 colonies.

In the principal northern theater of war in 1755, William Johnson led his provincials against Crown Point. The French commander, Jean-Armand, baron Dieskau, hoping to repeat the French success against Braddock, attacked a body of provincials on September 8 and drove it back in panic to its base camp, the improvised Fort William Henry near Lake George. French regulars assailed the fort but were driven off with heavy losses in a six-hour struggle. Colonial newspapers proclaimed the battle a great victory because the provincials had not only held the field but had also wounded and captured Dieskau. Johnson probably could have taken poorly defended Crown Point, but he too had been wounded and was content to hold Fort William Henry and nearby Fort Edward at the headwaters of the Hudson. It took a more professional eye than his to distinguish the carnage of victory from the carnage of defeat.

Further west, Shirley's Niagara campaign reached Oswego on Lake Ontario and then stopped

GENERAL JOHNSON SAVING A WOUNDED FRENCH OFFICER [BARON DIESKAU] FROM THE TOMAHAWK OF A NORTH AMERICAN INDIAN, BY BENJAMIN WEST, CIRCA 1762–1766 The setting of this painting is the 1755 Battle of Lake George. Obviously West intended to contrast the civility of Europeans, both British and French, with the savagery of Indians, including those allied with the British. In fact, this incident never happened. When the French retreated, according to Dieskau's own account, he had been shot in the thigh and the knee and was left on the battlefield, propped sitting against a tree. When a British colonist approached, Dieskau tried to signal his surrender, but was shot again in the hip. Only then was he carried before the wounded William Johnson, where he formally surrendered.

for the winter, held in check by the French at Fort Frontenac on the lake's northern shore. Oswego was soon cut off by heavy snows. Malnutrition and disease ravaged the garrison.

A WORLD WAR

With the death of Braddock and the capture of Dieskau, military amateurs took over both armies:

Shirley in the British colonies and Governor-General Pierre de Rigaud de Vaudreuil in New France. Vaudreuil, a Canadian, understood his colony's weakness without Indian support. First, the white population of the 13 colonies outnumbered that of New France by 13 to 1; Massachusetts alone had nearly three times as many settlers as New France. Second, Vaudreuil knew that if the redcoats and the British colonies could concentrate their resources in a few places, they had a good chance of overwhelming New France. Therefore, a frontier war that pitted New France primarily against ordinary settlers—horrible though it was—remained the most effective way to force the British colonies to scatter their resources over a vast area.

As long as Vaudreuil was in charge, New France kept winning. Indian attacks devastated frontier settlements, especially in Pennsylvania, a pacifist colony without even a militia when the war began. Even so, the French government decided that New France needed a professional general and sent Louis-Joseph, marquis de Montcalm, in 1756. Shocked and repelled by the brutality of frontier warfare, Montcalm tried to turn the conflict into a traditional European struggle of sieges and battles in which the advantage (as Vaudreuil well understood) would pass to the British. Nevertheless he won several major successes. Oswego fell in the summer of 1756. When Fort William Henry surrendered to him a year later, he promised the garrison the honors of war, which meant that it could keep its property and march unmolested to Fort Edward. But France's Indian allies considered this agreement a betrayal of their customs. They killed or carried off 308 of the 2,300 prisoners, an event that colonial newspapers called the Fort William Massacre. Most of those killed were trying to save their property, which the Indians considered their rightful plunder. Montcalm lost heavily at Fort William Henry. He never again managed to raise sizable bodies of Indian allies, and because the British blamed him for the "massacre," they refused to grant the honors of war to any French force for the rest of the conflict.

Meanwhile, Braddock's defeat, combined with the British loss of Minorca in the Mediterranean, convinced the British government that the struggle with France could not be limited to a few outposts. Britain declared war on France in 1756, and the French and Indian War in the colonies merged with a general European struggle—the Seven Years' War (1756–63)—involving France, Austria, and Russia against Prussia, which was heavily subsidized by Britain. Although religion had little to do with anyone's war aims in Europe, the Seven Years' War aligned coalitions of Protestant states against Catholic states in a way not seen in Europe for a century. To many North American clergymen, a Protestant victory might well herald the onset of the Millennium. The conflict spread even to India, where British forces expelled the French from nearly all of that vast subcontinent.

Reluctant to challenge Britain, Spain remained neutral for most of the war, unwilling to challenge Britain, a choice that had huge implications within North America. In the previous war, Spain had been able to turn the slaves of South Carolina against their masters and to create unrest even in New York. At a minimum, Spanish hostilities early in the war would have forced the British to fight in another theater of conflict. Instead, Spain's neutrality permitted Britain to concentrate its resources against New France. By 1762, when Spain finally entered the war in a vain effort to prevent a total British victory, the French had already surrendered Canada, and Britain's seasoned army and navy easily rolled over Spain's less experienced forces.

IMPERIAL TENSIONS: FROM LOUDOUN TO PITT

In 1755 London, to its dismay, realized that Shirley, an amateur, had taken command of the British army in North America. The government dispatched an irascible Scot, John Campbell, earl of Loudoun, to replace him and began pouring in reinforcements. Loudoun had a special talent for alienating provincials. Colonial units did not care to serve under his command and sometimes bluntly rejected his orders. Provincial volunteers believed they had a contractual relationship with *their* officers; they had never agreed to serve under Loudoun's professionals. They refused to serve beyond their term of enlistment, most of which expired on November 1 or December 1 of each year. Even when the British ordered them to stay longer, many of them defiantly marched home.

In fact, many British officers despised the provincials, especially their officers. "The Americans are in general the dirtiest most contemptible cowardly dogs that you can conceive," snarled General James Wolfe; " . . . They fall down dead in their own dirt and desert by battalions, officers and all." General John Forbes was usually more positive, but he too once suggested "shooting dead a Dozen of their cowardly Officers at the Head of the Line." Other British officers held more favorable opinions. Horatio Gates, Richard Montgomery, Hugh Mercer, and Arthur St. Clair all remained in America after the war and became generals in the American army during the Revolution. Colonel Isaac Barré praised American courage in the House of Commons in 1765 and even coined the phrase "Sons of Liberty," to describe them—a label instantly adopted by men who resisted Britain's postwar policies.

As the new commander in chief, Loudoun faced other problems—the quartering (or housing) of British soldiers, the relative rank of British and provincial officers, military discipline, revenue, and smuggling. He tried to impose authoritarian solutions on them all. When he sent redcoats into a city, he demanded that the assembly pay to quarter them or else he would take over buildings by force. He tried to make any British captain superior in rank to any provincial officer, a rule that antagonized such veteran New England wilderness fighters as General John Winslow and his six colonels. Loudoun ordered New England troops to serve directly under British officers and to accept the harsh discipline of the British army, an arrangement that New Englanders thought violated the terms of their enlistment. They refused to cooperate. When some colonial assemblies refused to vote adequate supplies, Loudoun urged Parliament to tax the colonies directly. Shocked that the molasses trade with the French West Indies was proceeding as usual, he urged the navy to stamp it out and sometimes imposed embargoes on colonial shipping, an action that punished fair traders as well as smugglers. Loudoun did build up his forces, but otherwise he accomplished little.

In 1757 William Pitt came to power as Britain's war minister and found workable voluntaristic solutions to the problems that had defeated Loudoun's authoritarian methods. Pitt understood that consent worked better than coercion in the colonies. Colonial assemblies built barracks to house British soldiers. Pitt declared that every provincial officer would rank immediately behind the equivalent British rank but above all lesser officers, British or provincial. He then promoted every British lieutenant colonel to the rank of "colonel in America only." That decision left only about 30 British majors vulnerable to being ordered about by a provincial colonel, but few of them had independent commands anyway. Provincial units under the command of their own officers cooperated with the British army, and the officers began to impose something close to British discipline on them, including hundreds of lashes for routine offenses. Rather than impose a parliamentary tax, Pitt set aside £200,000 beginning in 1758 (later reduced to £133,000) and told the colonies that they could claim a share of it in proportion to their contribution to the war effort. In effect, he persuaded the colonies to compete voluntarily in support of his stupendous war effort. The subsidies covered something less than half of the cost of fielding 20,000 provincials each year from 1758 to 1760, and rather smaller numbers in 1761 and 1762 as operations shifted to the Caribbean. Smuggling angered Pitt as much as it did anyone else, but British conquests soon reduced that problem. By 1762 Canada, Martinique, and Guadeloupe, as well as Spanish Havana, were all in British hands. Few places were any longer worth smuggling to, except Saint-Domingue.

Pitt had no patience with military failure. After Loudoun called off his attack on Louisbourg in 1757, Pitt replaced him with James Abercrombie. He also put Jeffrey Amherst in charge of a new Louisbourg expedition, with James Wolfe as one of his brigadiers. By 1758 the British Empire had finally put together a military force capable of overwhelming New France and had learned how to use it. In the last years of the war, cooperation between redcoats and provincials became routine and devastatingly effective.

THE YEARS OF BRITISH VICTORY

By 1758 the Royal Navy had cut off Canada from reinforcements and even from routine supplies. Britain had sent more than 30 regiments to North America. Combined with 20,000 provincials, thousands of bateau men rowing supplies into the interior, and swarms of privateers preying on French commerce, Britain had mustered perhaps 60,000

The Last of the Mohicans (1992)

Directed by Michael Mann. Starring Daniel Day-Lewis (Hawkeye),
Russell Means (Chingachgook), Eric Schweig (Uncas), Steven Waddington (Major Heyward),
Madeleine Stowe (Cora), Jodhi May (Alice), and Wes Studi (Magua).

This movie, the most recent and most effective film version of James Fenimore Cooper's immensely successful 1826 novel of the same title, centers on the siege and capture of Fort William Henry in 1757, an event that had enormous consequences for everyone involved. During the Seven Years' (or French and Indian) War, the French, accompanied by a huge contingent of Indian allies, besiege this British fort at the northern tip of Lake George in New York. Hawkeye (Daniel Day-Lewis) is a frontiersman reared among Indians, who include his two closest friends, Chingachgook (Russell Means) and Chingachgook's son Uncas (Eric Schweig). The trio are escorting to the fort a party that includes British Major Hayward (Steven Waddington) and Cora (Madeleine Stowe) and Alice (Jodhi May), the two daughters of Colonel Munro (Maurice Reyes), the commander of the fort. Heyward plans to marry Cora. Through the treachery of another Indian, Magua (Wes Studi), the party is ambushed, but the trio of escorts rescue the major and the two women and lead them safely to the fort just as the siege begins.

Fort William Henry soon falls to the French. General Montcalm (Patrick Chereau) accepts the formal surrender of the British garrison and promises them the "honors of war, " the right to march away with their unloaded muskets and personal possessions. Instead, Magua defies Montcalm and leads a murderous assault against the column as it tries to retreat to Fort Edward at the head of the Hudson River. In a climactic action sequence, Heyward is captured and is being tortured to death when Hawkeye shoots him to end his misery. Alice leaps off a cliff rather than submit to Magua, who has already killed Uncas. Chingachgook then kills Magua. Along with Hawkeye and Cora, Chingachgook survives, thus becoming the last of the Mohicans.

Cooper gave the Iroquois the role of the attacking Indians, probably because most of them did side with the British during the American Revolution. But in the Seven Years' War, most of those who fought were on the British side. The film version addresses this problem by making the Hurons, by then a minor nation, into the pro-French Indians, thereby providing a rare example of a movie being more accurate historically than the novel on which it rests. The film, like Cooper, makes the massacre far more destructive than it actually was. Most of the settlers killed or captured that day were trying to protect their personal property, which the Indians regarded as their rightful plunder. The French had traditionally raised Indian forces with the promise of loot and captives. Montcalm's attempt to impose European standards of war

men in North America and in nearby waters. Most of them now closed in on the 75,000 people of New France. Montcalm, who in any case was running out of goods for use in the Indian trade, refused to encourage more Indian attacks on the frontier and prepared to defend the approaches to Canada at Forts Duquesne, Niagara, Frontenac, Ticonderoga, Crown Point, and Louisbourg.

Spurred on by Quaker mediators, the British and colonial governments came to terms with the western Indians in 1758, promising not to seize their lands after the war and arranging an uneasy peace. Few settlers or officials had yet noticed a new trend that was emerging during the conflict: Before the 1750s, Indian nations had often waged terrible wars against one another. Now, however, few Indians in the northeastern woodlands were willing to attack others. In 1755, for example, some Senecas fought with New France and some Mohawks with the British, but they maneuvered

on his allies by intervening on the soldiers' and settlers' behalf meant that he broke faith with his Indian allies and was never again able to raise a force of comparable size. That the massacre occurred at all meant that he had lost credibility with the British and the settlers. For the rest of the war, the British never again granted a French force the honors of war. Montcalm's great victory became, in the long run, a severe defeat for France.

In 1979 director Michael Mann won an award as best director from the Directors' Guild of America for *The Jericho Mile*.

The Last of the Mohicans tells of the siege and capture of Britain's Fort William Henry in 1757, during the French and Indian War.

carefully to avoid confronting each other. This Iroquois sense of solidarity was beginning to spread. Iroquois and western Algonquians, once deadly enemies, saw real advantages in cooperation. A sense of pan-Indian identity was beginning to emerge. Although most Indians regarded the French as far less dangerous than the British and even fought alongside the French, they were never French puppets. They fought, negotiated, and made peace in 1758 to preserve their own hold on the land.

Peace with the western Indians in 1758 permitted the British to revive the grand military plan of 1755, except that this time the overall goal was clear—the conquest of New France. Amherst and Wolfe, with 9,000 regulars and 500 provincials, besieged Louisbourg for 60 days. It fell in September, thus adding Cape Breton Island to the British province of Nova Scotia. A force of 3,000 provincials under Colonel John Bradstreet advanced to Lake Ontario, took Fort Frontenac, and began

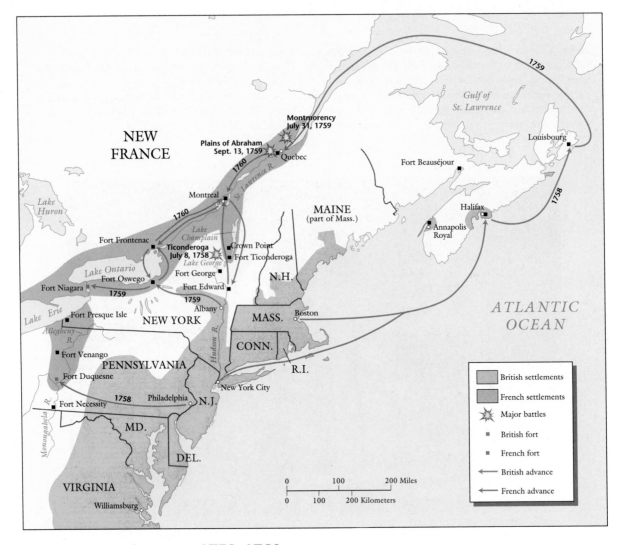

CONQUEST OF CANADA, 1758–1760

building a fleet. This victory cut off the French in the Ohio valley from their supplies. A powerful force of regulars under John Forbes and provincials under Washington marched west, this time through Pennsylvania, to attack Fort Duquesne, but the French blew up the fort and retreated north just before they arrived. The British erected Fort Pitt on the ruins.

The only British defeat in 1758 occurred in northern New York when Abercrombie sent 6,000 regulars and 9,000 provincials against Ticonderoga (Carillon), defended by Montcalm and 3,500 troops. Instead of waiting for his artillery to arrive

or trying to outflank the French, Abercrombie ordered a frontal assault against a heavily fortified position. His regulars were butchered by the withering fire, and after watching the carnage for several hours, the provincials fled. Like Indians, they regarded such attacks as sheer madness. When Pitt heard the news, he sacked Abercrombie, put Amherst in charge of the New York theater of war, and left Wolfe at Louisbourg to plan an attack up the St. Lawrence against Quebec.

In 1759, while the provincials on Lake Ontario moved west and took Niagara, Amherst spent the summer cautiously reducing Ticonderoga and

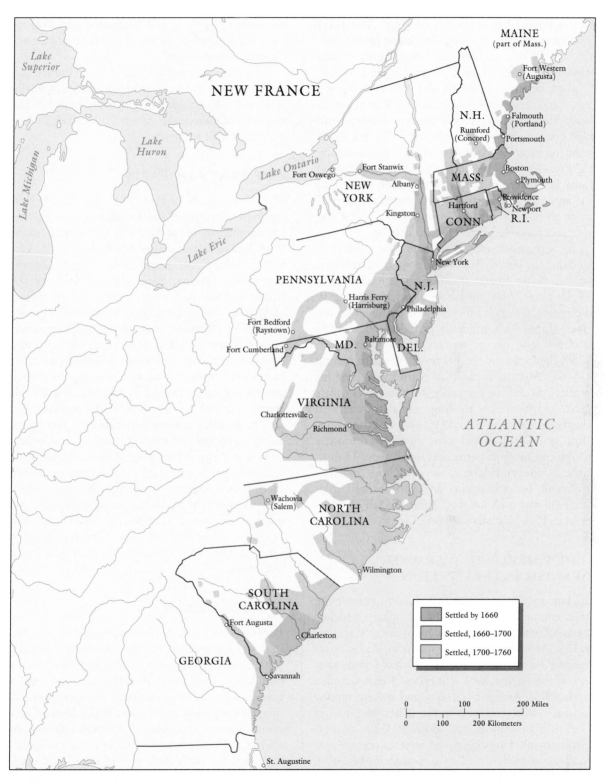

Lake Superior

NEW FRANCE

Lake Michigan

Lake Huron

Lake Ontario

Lake Erie

MAINE
(part of Mass.)

Fort Western
(Augusta)

N.H.

Falmouth
(Portland)

Rumford
(Concord)

Portsmouth

Fort Stanwix

Boston

Fort Oswego

Albany

MASS.

Plymouth

NEW
YORK

Hartford

Providence

Newport

Kingston

CONN.

R.I.

New York

PENNSYLVANIA

N.J.

Harris Ferry
(Harrisburg)

Philadelphia

Fort Bedford
(Raystown)

Baltimore

Fort Cumberland

MD.

DEL.

VIRGINIA

Charlottesville

Richmond

ATLANTIC
OCEAN

Wachovia
(Salem)

NORTH
CAROLINA

Wilmington

SOUTH
CAROLINA

Fort Augusta

Charleston

GEORGIA

Savannah

	Settled by 1660
	Settled, 1660–1700
	Settled, 1700–1760

0   100   200 Miles

0   100   200 Kilometers

St. Augustine

GROWTH OF POPULATION TO 1760

Crown Point. (Pitt expected him to reach Montreal.) The most dramatic campaign occurred farther east. In June, Wolfe ascended the St. Lawrence with 8,000 redcoats and colonial rangers and laid siege to Quebec, defended by Montcalm with 16,000 regulars, Canadian militia, and Indians. When an attack below the city failed, Wolfe mounted howitzers on high ground across the river from Quebec and began reducing most of the city to rubble. Frustrated by the French refusal to come out and fight, he turned loose his American rangers ("the worst soldiers in the universe," he boasted), who ravaged and burned more than 1,400 farms. Anyone who resisted was shot and scalped. Still the French held out.

By September both Wolfe and Montcalm realized that the British fleet would soon have to depart or risk being frozen in during the long winter. Wolfe made a last desperate effort, preferring to die rather than fail. His men silently sailed up the river, climbed a formidable cliff above the city in darkness, and on the morning of September 13, 1759, deployed on the Plains of Abraham behind Quebec. Montcalm panicked. Instead of using his artillery to defend the walls from inside (Wolfe's force had been able to drag only two guns with them), he marched out of Quebec onto the plains. Both generals now had what they craved most, a set-piece European battle that lasted about 15 minutes. Wolfe and Montcalm were both mortally wounded, but the British drove the French from the field and took Quebec. After the fall of Montreal in 1760, Canada surrendered.

THE CHEROKEE WAR AND SPANISH INTERVENTION

In January 1760, as the British were completing their triumph over France, the Cherokees, who had been allies and trading partners of South Carolina, reacted to a long string of violent incidents by attacking backcountry settlers. Within a year, they drove the settlers back 100 miles. South Carolina appealed to Amherst for help, and he sent regular soldiers who laid waste the Cherokee Lower Towns in the Appalachian foothills. When that expedition failed to bring peace, another one the next year devastated the Middle Towns farther west, while Virginia threatened the Overhill Towns. The Cherokees made peace in December 1761, but the

backcountry settlers, left brutalized and lawless, soon became severe political problems for South Carolina's government.

Only then, in January 1762, after the French and the Cherokees had been defeated, did Spain finally enter the war. British forces quickly took Havana and even Manila in the distant Philippines. France and Spain sued for peace.

THE PEACE OF PARIS

In 1763 the Peace of Paris ended the war. Britain returned Martinique and Guadeloupe to France. France surrendered to Great Britain several minor West Indian islands and all of North America east of the Mississippi, except New Orleans. In exchange for Havana, Spain ceded Florida to the British and also paid a large ransom for the return of Manila. To compensate its Spanish ally, France gave all of Louisiana west of the Mississippi and New Orleans to Spain. Most of the Spanish and African occupants of Florida withdrew to other parts of the Spanish Empire, but nearly all French settlers remained behind in Canada, the Illinois country, and what was now Spanish Louisiana.

The British colonists were jubilant. The age of warfare and frontier carnage seemed over at last. Britain and the colonies could now develop their vast resources in an imperial partnership and would share unprecedented prosperity. But the western Indians angrily rejected the peace settlement. No one had conquered them, and they denied the right or the power of France to surrender their lands to Great Britain. They began to plan their own war of liberation.

CONCLUSION

Between 1713 and 1754, expansion and renewed immigration pushed the edge of North American settlement ever farther into the interior. With a population that doubled every 25 years, many householders no longer enjoyed the opportunity to give all their sons and daughters the level of economic success that they themselves enjoyed. By midcentury many families took up a trade or looked westward for what their old neighborhood could not provide. Women had to work harder just to sustain levels of opportunity for their households.

Many families had to favor sons over daughters and the eldest son over his younger brothers, reluctantly following the practice in England.

The colonies anglicized in other ways as well. Newspapers and the learned professions spread the English Enlightenment to the colonies. English revivalists, especially George Whitefield, had a tremendous impact in North America. The northern colonies borrowed "Court" politics from Walpole's Britain, while most southern colonies favored politics as envisioned by the "Country" opposition in Britain. Both considered themselves the freest people on earth. When expansion and imperial rivalries again led to war after 1739, the colonists discovered that enslaved Africans associated Spain with liberty, while most eastern woodland Indians looked to New France for support. The threat of internal upheaval kept King George's War indecisive in the 1740s. Taking advantage of Spain's neutral position when Britain and France went to war after 1754, the British Empire mobilized its full resources and conquered New France.

The French and Indian War left behind vivid memories. Provincials admired the courage of the redcoats and the victories they won but hated their brutal discipline and arrogant officers. British officials greatly exaggerated what military force alone could accomplish and underestimated colonial contributions to the imperial cause. The concord and prosperity that were supposed to follow Britain's great triumph yielded instead to bitter strife.

Suggested Readings begin on page SR-1.
For Web activities and resources
related to this chapter, go to
http://www.harcourtcollege.com/history.murrin

CHAPTER 5

REFORM, RESISTANCE, REVOLUTION

A VIEW OF THE SOUTH PART OF LEXINGTON, APRIL 19, 1775

This painting by Ralph Earl, done in 1775, shows the retreat of the British toward Boston, under heavy fire, on the first day of the Revolutionary War.

Britain left an army in North America after 1763 and taxed the colonies to pay part of its cost. The colonists agreed that they should contribute to their own defense but insisted that taxation without representation violated their rights as Englishmen. During the next 12 years, three successive crises shattered Britain's Atlantic empire.

In the first, the Stamp Act crisis, the colonists began by petitioning for a redress of grievances. When that effort failed, they nullified the Stamp Act and continued their resistance until Parliament repealed the tax in 1766. The jubilant colonists celebrated their victory. In the second, the Townshend crisis of 1767–70, Parliament imposed new taxes on certain imported goods. The colonists petitioned and resisted simultaneously, mostly through an intercolonial nonimportation movement. The British sent troops to Boston. After several violent confrontations, the soldiers withdrew, and Parliament modified but did not repeal the Townshend Revenue Act. The duty on tea remained. Repeal of the other duties broke the back of the nonimportation movement, but nobody celebrated the gains. The third crisis began with the Tea Act of 1773 and quickly escalated. Boston destroyed British tea without bothering to petition first. When Parliament responded with the Coercive Acts of 1774, the colonists created the Continental Congress to organize further resistance. Neither side dared back down, and the confrontation careened toward military violence. The war broke out in April 1775. Fifteen months later the colonies declared their independence.

This chapter will focus on the following major questions:

- Why, in 1766, did the colonists stopped resisting and rejoice over the repeal of the Stamp Act, even though the Revenue Act of 1766 continued to tax molasses?
- Why did the colonists start a revolution after the government lowered the price of tea through the Tea Act of 1773?
- In 1775 Lord North promised that Parliament would not tax any colony that paid its share of the costs of imperial defense and gave adequate salaries to its civil officers, but the Second Continental Congress rejected the proposal out of hand. Had George Grenville offered something of the kind between 1763 and 1765, could Britain have averted the Revolution?

CHRONOLOGY

1745–55 Land riots rock New Jersey

1760–61 Cherokee War occurs in South Carolina

1760 George III becomes king of Great Britain

1761 Pitt resigns as war minister

1763 Grenville ministry takes power • Wilkes publishes *North Briton* No. 45 • Pontiac's War begins • King issues Proclamation of 1763

1764 Parliament passes Currency and Sugar Acts

1765 Parliament passes Quartering Act • Stamp Act passed and nullified • Rockingham replaces Grenville as prime minister

1766 Parliament repeals Stamp Act, passes Declaratory Act and Revenue Act of 1766 • Chatham (Pitt) ministry takes power

1767 Parliament passes New York Restraining Act and Townshend Revenue Act

1768 Massachusetts assembly dispatches Circular Letter • Wilkes elected to Parliament • Massacre of St. George's Fields occurs in England • Massachusetts refuses to rescind Circular Letter • Liberty riot occurs in Boston • Governors dissolve assemblies that support Circular Letter • Redcoats sent to Boston

1769 Nonimportation becomes effective • Regulators achieve major goals in South Carolina

1770 North becomes prime minister • Boston Massacre • Townshend Revenue Act partially repealed • Nonimportation collapses

1771 North Carolina regulators defeated at Alamance Creek

1772 *Gaspée* affair in Rhode Island increases tensions

1772–73 Twelve colonies create committees of correspondence

1773 Tea Act passed • Boston Tea Party protests tea duty • Wheatley's poetry published in London

1774 American Quakers prohibit slaveholding • Parliament passes Coercive Acts and Quebec Act • First Continental Congress convenes in Philadelphia

1775 Revolutionary War begins at Lexington and Concord • Second Continental Congress creates Continental Army • George III issues Proclamation of Rebellion

1775–76 Americans invade Canada

1776 Paine publishes *Common Sense* • British evacuate Boston • Continental Congress approves Declaration of Independence

• How and why did a resistance movement, dedicated to protecting the colonists' rights as Englishmen, end by proclaiming American independence instead?

IMPERIAL REFORM

In 1760 George III (1760–1820) inherited the British throne at the age of 22. The king's pronouncements on behalf of religion and virtue at first won him many admirers in North America, but the political coalition leading Britain to victory over France fell apart. The king's new ministers set out to reform the empire.

THE BUTE MINISTRY

The king, along with his tutor and principal adviser, John Stuart, earl of Bute, feared that the Seven Years' War would bankrupt Britain. From 1758 on, while London celebrated one victory after another, George and Bute grew more and more despondent. When William Pitt, the king's war minister, urged a preemptive strike on Spain before Spain could attack Britain, Bute forced him to resign in October 1761, even though Pitt had become the most popular official of the century. Bute soon learned that Pitt had been right. Spain entered the war as an ally of France in January 1762 as soon as the annual treasure fleet from America reached Seville.

In May 1762, Bute forced Thomas Pelham-Holles, duke of Newcastle and the most powerful politician of the previous 25 years, to resign as first lord of the treasury. To economize, Bute next reduced Britain's subsidies to Prussia, its only major ally in Europe. So eager were the king and Bute to end the war that they gave back to France the wealthy West Indian islands of Guadeloupe and Martinique; they might even have returned Canada, but France never asked for it.

The British press, much of it subsidized by Pitt, Newcastle, and even King Frederick the Great of Prussia, harshly denounced Bute. As soon as Parliament approved the Treaty of Paris, Bute dismayed the king by resigning. He had had enough. Thus in April 1763, George Grenville (Pitt's brother-in-law) became first lord of the treasury, though the king distrusted him and found him only marginally acceptable. Pitt and Newcastle, who blamed Grenville for having sided with Bute against them, would have nothing at all to do with him.

THE GRENVILLE MINISTRY

Grenville spent most of his first year coping with a crisis at home that later dovetailed with events in the colonies. John Wilkes, a radical journalist, questioned the king's integrity in the 45th number of the *North Briton*, a newspaper founded to vilify Bute, a Scot (a "North Briton"). The government used a general warrant (one that specified neither the person nor place to be searched) to invade the newspaper's offices and arrest Wilkes, a member of Parliament as well as a journalist. He was charged with publishing a seditious libel. But Chief Justice Charles Pratt, an admirer of Pitt, declared general warrants illegal and freed Wilkes. The government promptly arrested Wilkes on a special warrant, but Pratt again freed him, declaring that parliamentary privilege extended to seditious libels. London artisans lustily embraced the cause of "Wilkes and Liberty!" Grenville had given the opposition two popular issues, and its leaders fully expected to overturn him during the winter session of Parliament. Grenville triumphed, however. A reading of Wilkes's pornographic *Essay on Woman* to a shocked and amused House of Lords mustered Grenville enough votes in the Commons for an unexpectedly huge victory on parliamentary privilege. Months later, after the shock had faded, Grenville also managed a narrow win on general warrants. Wilkes fled to France and was outlawed in Britain, but "45" became a symbol of liberty on both sides of the ocean.

As the Wilkes affair subsided, Grenville turned his attention to the colonies. Britain's national debt had nearly doubled during the last war with France and stood at £130 million. Interest on the debt absorbed more than half of annual revenues, and Britain was already one of the most heavily taxed societies in the world. The sheer scale of Britain's victory required more revenue just to police the conquered colonies. In 1762 and 1763 Bute and Grenville decided to leave 20 battalions with about 7,000 men in America, mostly in Canada and Florida, with smaller garrisons scattered throughout

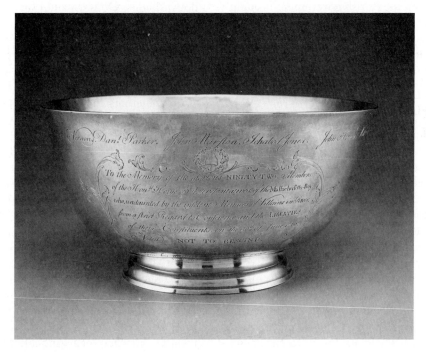

SILVER BOWL BY PAUL REVERE Like many patriots, Revere admired John Wilkes. In 1768 Revere crafted this silver bowl celebrating the *North Briton No. 45*.

Indian territory. Because the colonists would receive the benefit of this protection, Grenville argued, they ought to pay a reasonable portion of the cost, and eventually all of it. He never asked the settlers to contribute anything to Britain's national debt or to Britain's heavy domestic needs, but he did insist that the colonies begin to pay toward their own defense.

Instead of building on the voluntaristic measures that Pitt had used to win the war, Grenville reverted to the demands for coercive reforms that had crisscrossed the Atlantic during Britain's years of defeat from 1755 to 1757. London, he believed, must gain effective centralized control over the colonies. To the settlers, victory over France would mean new burdens, not relief.

To Grenville, the willing cooperation of the colonies after 1758 reflected the empire's weakness, not its strength. He thought Britain had won the war, not with the cooperation of the colonies, but despite their obstruction. He believed that the British government must act quickly to establish its authority before the colonies, with their astonishing rate of growth, slipped completely out of control. In effect, he set in motion a self-fulfilling prophecy in which the British government brought about precisely what it was trying to prevent. Nearly every step it took undermined the colonies' loyalty to Britain.

INDIAN POLICY AND PONTIAC'S WAR

The king's Proclamation of 1763 honored wartime commitments to the western Indians and established governments in Canada, Florida, and other conquered colonies. It tried to set the pace of western settlement by laying out the so-called Proclamation Line along the Appalachian watershed. No settlements could be planted west of that line unless Britain first purchased the land by treaty from the Indians. Settlers would be encouraged to move instead to Nova Scotia, northern New England, Georgia, or Florida. Because most Iroquois land lay east of the line, the Six Nations felt threatened by the new policy, even though Sir William Johnson, the northern superintendent, upheld their claims. General Amherst's decision in 1760 to cut back sharply on gifts to Indians angered many of them.

His contempt for Indian customs deprived the government of its major leverage with Indians, at a time when their ability to unite had become stronger than ever.

In 1761 Neolin, a western Delaware, reported a vision in which God commanded Indians to return to their ancestral ways. Neolin called for an end to Indian dependence on the Anglo-Americans, although he did accept Christian ideas of heaven and hell. European vices, he said, especially drinking rum, blocked the path to heaven. "Can ye not live without them?" he asked. God was punishing Indians for accepting European ways: "If you suffer the English among you, you are dead men. Sickness, smallpox, and their poison will destroy you entirely." Neolin stopped short of condemning the French who were still living in the Great Lakes region. Indeed, many of his followers hoped that their display of unity would attract the support of King Louis XV of France (1715–74), restore the friendly relations of the past, and halt British expansion.

With a unity never seen before, the Indians struck in 1763. The conflict became known as "Pontiac's War," named for an Ottawa chief. Senecas, Mingoes, Delawares, Shawnees, Wyandots, Miamis, Ottawas, and other nations attacked 13 British posts in the West. Between May 16 and June 20, all of the forts fell except Niagara, Pitt, Detroit, and a tiny outpost on Green Bay that the Indians did not bother to attack. For months the Indians kept Forts Detroit and Pitt under close siege, something Indians were supposed to be incapable of doing. They hoped to drive British settlers back to the eastern seaboard.

These Indian successes enraged Amherst. In retaliation, he ordered Colonel Henry Bouquet, commander at Fort Pitt, to distribute smallpox-infested blankets among the western nations, touching off a lethal epidemic in 1763 and 1764. "You will do well to try to Inoculate the Indians by means of Blankets," he wrote to Bouquet, "as well as to Try Every other Method that can serve to Extirpate this Execrable Race." Not until 1764 did British and provincial forces end resistance and restore peace. The British then reluctantly accepted the role that the French had played in the Great Lakes region by distributing gifts and mediating differences.

By then, 10 years of conflict had brutalized the frontiersmen. Perhaps sensing the Indians' growing

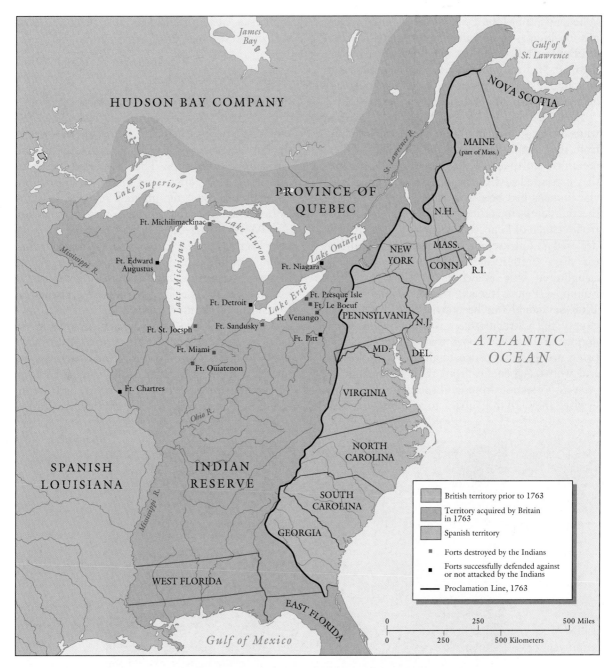

PONTIAC'S WAR AND THE PROCLAMATION LINE OF 1763

revulsion against warring with one another, many settlers began to assume that all Indians must be the enemies of all whites. In December 1763 the Scots-Irish of Paxton Township, Pennsylvania, unable to find the elusive warriors who were striking at their settlements, murdered six unarmed Christian Indians—two old men, three women, and a child—at nearby Conestoga. Two weeks later the "Paxton Boys" slaughtered 14 more Christian Indians who had been brought to Lancaster for protection.

When Governor John Penn removed 140 Moravian mission Indians to Philadelphia for safety, the Paxton Boys marched on the capital determined to kill them all. "If I tho't that any of their Colour was to be admitted to the Heavenly World," explained one insurgent, "I would not desire to go there myself."

Denouncing the Paxton Boys as "Christian white Savages," Benjamin Franklin led a delegation from the assembly that met the marchers at Germantown and persuaded them to go home after they presented a list of their grievances. The Moravian Indians had been spared. All efforts to bring the murderers to justice failed, however, and the frontiersmen of Pennsylvania and Virginia virtually declared an open season on Indians that continued for years. Settlers in Augusta County, Virginia, slaughtered nine Shawnees in 1765. Frederick Stump, a Pennsylvanian, murdered 10 more in 1768 but could not be convicted in his frontier county. Such atrocities kept western Indians smoldering. London had hoped that its officials would bring evenhanded justice to the frontier. Indians had won real benefits from the superintendents, such as protection from land speculators, but otherwise they found little to choose between Amherst's smallpox blankets and the murderous rage of the Paxton Boys.

THE SUGAR ACT

In a step that settlers found ominous, Grenville's Sugar Act of 1764 proclaimed it "just and necessary, that a revenue be raised . . . in America for defraying the expenses of defending, protecting, and securing" the colonies. The act placed duties on Madeira wine, coffee, and other products, but Grenville expected the greatest revenue to come from the molasses duty of three pence per gallon. The Molasses Act of 1733 had been designed to keep French molasses out of North America by imposing a prohibitive duty of six pence per gallon. Instead, by paying a bribe of about a penny a gallon, merchants got French molasses certified as British. By 1760, more than 90 percent of all molasses imported into New England came from the French islands. Planters in the British islands gave up, lost interest in New England markets, and turned their molasses into quality rum for sale in Britain and Ireland. Nobody, in short, had any interest in stopping the trade in French molasses.

ANTI-FRANKLIN CARTOON Pontiac's War and the Paxton riots inspired this anti-Franklin cartoon in which Quakers and Franklin protect Indians from settlers instead of settlers from Indians.

New England merchants said they were willing to pay a duty of one pence (the current cost of bribes), but Grenville insisted on three. He hoped to raise £100,000 per year from the molasses duty, although in public he seldom put the figure above £40,000.

The Sugar Act also launched Grenville's war against smugglers. It vastly increased the amount of paperwork required of ship captains and permitted seizures of ships for what owners considered mere technicalities. In effect, Grenville tried to make it more profitable for customs officers to hound the merchants than to accept bribes from them. The Sugar Act encouraged them to prosecute violators in vice admiralty courts, which did not use juries, rather than in common law courts, which did. Prosecutors were virtually immune from any suit for damages, even when the merchant won an acquittal, so long as the judge certified "probable cause" for the seizure.

THE CURRENCY ACT AND THE QUARTERING ACT

Grenville passed several other imperial measures. The Currency Act of 1764 responded to wartime protests of London merchants against Virginia's paper money, which had been issued for the colony's defense. (That money had lost almost 15 percent of its value between 1759 and 1764.) The Currency Act forbade the colonies to issue any paper money as legal tender. The money question had become urgent because the Sugar Act (and, later, the Stamp Act) required that all duties be paid in specie (silver or gold). Supporters of those taxes argued that the new duties would keep the specie in America to pay the army, but the colonists replied that the drain of specie from some of the colonies would put impossible constraints on trade. Boston and Newport, for instance, would pay most of the molasses tax, but the specie collected there would follow the army to Quebec, New York, the Great Lakes, and Florida. Grenville saw "America" as a single region in which specie would circulate to the benefit of all. The colonists knew better. As of 1765, "America" existed only in British minds, not yet in colonial hearts.

Another reform measure was the Quartering Act of 1765, requested by Sir Thomas Gage, Amherst's successor as army commander. Gage asked for par-

liamentary authority to quarter soldiers in private homes, if necessary, when on the march and away from their barracks. Grenville turned the problem over to Thomas Pownall, the governor of Massachusetts during its 1757 quartering crisis, which had been resolved by building the barracks that Gage now feared might not be adequate. Pownall came up with a bill that addressed the old problem, not the new one. It ordered colonial assemblies to vote specific supplies, such as beer and candles, for the troops, which the assemblies were willingly doing already. It also required the army to quarter its soldiers only in public buildings, such as taverns, which existed in large numbers only in cities. The Quartering Act solved no problems, but it created several new ones.

THE STAMP ACT

When Parliament passed the Sugar Act early in 1764, Grenville announced that it might also be necessary to impose a stamp tax on legal documents and publications in the colonies. The army in North America was costing Britain £225,000 a year. Other expenses, including the navy, transport, and Indian gifts, brought the annual total closer to £400,000. Grenville needed more revenue, and a stamp tax seemed the best way to raise it.

No one in the House of Commons, he declared, doubted Parliament's right to impose such a tax. Because Parliament had never imposed a direct tax on the colonies, however, he also knew that he must persuade the settlers that a stamp tax would not be an innovation. His supporters insisted that the measure did not violate the principle of no taxation without representation. Each member of Parliament, they argued, represented the entire empire, not just a local constituency. The colonists were no different from the large nonvoting majority of subjects within Great Britain. All were "virtually" represented in Parliament. Grenville also denied that there was any legal difference between external taxes (port duties, such as that on molasses) and internal (or inland) taxes, such as the proposed stamp tax.

Grenville put off passage of the Stamp Act while he collected more complete information about legal forms in the colonies. He also indicated that, if the colonies could devise a revenue plan better than a stamp tax, he would listen. His offer created confusion and, finally, a public relations disaster for the government. In response, all 13 colonial assemblies drafted petitions objecting to the Stamp Act as a form of taxation without representation. Most of them also attacked the duties imposed by the Sugar Act. Like Grenville, they rejected the distinction between internal and external taxes. Both kinds, they declared, violated the British constitution. While agreeing that they ought to contribute to their own defense, they urged the government to return to the traditional method of requisitions, in which the Crown asked a colony for a specific sum, and the assembly decided how (or whether) to raise it. Colonists feared that taxation by Parliament might tempt Britain to rule them without consulting their assemblies.

But when these petitions began to reach London early in 1765, Parliament refused to receive them, citing a standing rule that prohibited petitions against money bills, and declaring that any petition challenging the right of Parliament to pass such a tax was inadmissible on those grounds alone. To Grenville, requisitions were not a better idea. They had often been tried, had never worked efficiently, and never would. He rejected the petitions with a clear conscience. But to the colonists, he seemed to have acted in bad faith all along. He had asked their advice and had then refused even to consider it.

The Stamp Act passed in February 1765, to go into effect on November 1. Grenville believed it would almost enforce itself. Under this law, all contracts, licenses, commissions, and most other legal documents would be void unless they were executed on officially stamped paper. Law courts would not recognize any document that lacked the proper stamp, and the colonists would quietly if grudgingly accept Parliament's power to tax them. A stamp duty was also put on all newspapers and pamphlets, a requirement likely to anger every printer in the colonies. Playing cards and dice were also taxed.

When the Stamp Act became law, most colonial leaders resigned themselves to a situation that seemed beyond their power to change. Daniel Dulany, a Maryland lawyer who did more than any other colonist to refute the argument for virtual representation, drew a line short of overt resistance. "I am upon a Question of *Propriety*, not of

Power," he wrote; " . . . at the same Time that I invalidate the Claim upon which [the Stamp Act] is founded, I may very consistently recommend a Submission to the Law, whilst it endures." But ordinary settlers were less fatalistic than their leaders, and some of them began to take direct action to prevent the implementation of the act.

THE STAMP ACT CRISIS

Resistance to the Stamp Act began in the spring of 1765 and continued for nearly a year, until it was repealed. Patrick Henry, a newcomer to the Virginia House of Burgesses, launched the first wave by introducing five resolutions on May 30 and 31, 1765, after most of the other members had gone home. His resolves passed by margins ranging between 22 to 17 and 20 to 19; one was rescinded and expunged from the record the next day. Henry had two more in his pocket that he decided not to introduce.

Over the summer the *Newport Mercury* printed six of Henry's seven resolutions, and the *Maryland Gazette* printed all of them. Neither paper reported that some of the seven had not passed. To other colonies, Virginia seemed to have taken a far more radical position than it actually had. The last two resolves printed in the *Maryland Gazette* claimed that Virginians "are not bound to yield Obedience to any Law . . . designed to impose any Taxation upon them" except those passed by their own assembly, and that anyone defending Parliament's right to tax Virginia "shall be Deemed, an Enemy to this his Majesty's Colony."

In their fall or winter sessions, eight colonial legislatures passed new resolutions condemning the Stamp Act. Nine colonies sent delegates to the Stamp Act Congress, which met in New York in October. It passed resolutions affirming colonial loyalty to the king and "all due subordination" to Parliament but condemned the Stamp and Sugar Acts. By 1765 nearly all colonial spokesmen agreed that the Stamp Act was unconstitutional, that colonial representation in Parliament (urged by a few writers) was impractical because of the distance and the huge expense, and that therefore the Stamp Act must be repealed. They accepted the idea of virtual representation *within* the colonies—their assemblies, they said, represented both voters and nonvoters—but the colonists ridiculed the argument

> "*I regard with inexpressible Detestation and Abhorrence the Notion of the Colonies becoming independent. Not that I doubt in the least, that the Attempt may be executed whenever it is made. The Strength of the Colonies, their Distance, the Wealth that would pour into them on opening their Ports to all Nations, the Jealousy entertained of Great Britain by some European Powers, and the peculiar Circumstances of that Kingdom, would insure Success. But what, sir, must be the Consequences of that Success? A Multitude of Commonwealths, Crimes, and Calamities, of mutual Jealousies, Hatreds, Wars and Devastation; till at last the exhausted Provinces shall sink into Slavery under the yoke of some fortunate Conqueror. History seems to prove that this must be the deplorable Fate of these Colonies whenever they become independent.*"

JOHN DICKINSON

to William Pitt, on the perils of independence, December 21, 1765

when it was applied across the Atlantic. A disfranchised Englishman who acquired sufficient property could become a voter, pointed out Daniel Dulany, in a pamphlet widely admired, even in Britain. But, Dulany explained, no colonist, no matter how wealthy he became, could vote for a member of Parliament. Members of Parliament paid the taxes that they levied on others within Britain, but they would never pay any tax imposed on the colonies.

NULLIFICATION

No matter how eloquent, resolutions and pamphlets alone could not defeat the Stamp Act. Street violence might, however, and Boston showed the way, led by men calling themselves "Sons of Liberty." On August 14 the town awoke to find an effigy of Andrew Oliver, the stamp distributor, hanging on what became the town's Liberty Tree (the gallows on which enemies of the people deserved to be hanged). The sheriff admitted that he dared not remove the effigy. After dark a crowd of men roamed the streets, shouted defiance at the governor and council, and demolished a new building Oliver was erecting that "they called "the Stamp Office," according to the governor's report. The men beheaded and burned Oliver's effigy and finally invaded Oliver's home "declaring they would kill Him." Oliver had already fled to a neighbor's home. Thoroughly cowed, he resigned.

On August 26 an even angrier crowd all but demolished the elegant mansion of Lieutenant Governor Thomas Hutchinson, hated by many for leading the fight to replace paper money with silver in 1749. Most Bostonians also believed that, in letters to British friends, Hutchinson had defended and even helped to draft the Stamp Act. In fact, he had opposed it, although quietly. Shocked by the destruction of property, the militia finally appeared to police the streets, but when Governor Sir Francis Bernard tried to arrest those responsible for the first riot, he got nowhere. Bostonians deplored the events of August 26 but approved those of August 14. No one was punished for either event, although the whole city knew that Ebenezer McIntosh, a poor shoemaker and a leader of the annual Pope's Day (Guy Fawkes Day) processions, had organized both riots.

Everywhere except Georgia, the stamp master was forced to resign before the law took effect on November 1. With no one to distribute the stamps, the act could not be implemented. Merchants adopted nonimportation agreements to pressure the British into repeal. Following Boston's lead, the Sons of Liberty took control of the streets in other cities. After November 1, they agitated to open the ports and courts, which had closed down rather than operate without stamps. Neither the courts nor the customs officers had any stamps to use because nobody dared distribute them. As winter gave way to spring, most ports and some courts resumed business. Only Newport matched Boston's level of violence, but in New York City a clash between the

LORD BUTE AND GEORGE GRENVILLE HANGED IN EFFIGY, 1765 OR 1766 Bute and Grenville were always unpopular in the colonies, but even more so after passage of Grenville's Stamp Act. This image, which shows both men (Bute wears a kilt) chained to the devil, borrowed from the popular rites of Pope's Day (Guy Fawkes Day), November 5. Especially in Boston, images of the pope, the Stuart pretender to the British throne, and the devil were destroyed each year on this day. Bute was especially vulnerable because his family name was Stuart.

Sons of Liberty and the British garrison grew ugly and almost escalated into an armed encounter. Violent resistance worked. The Stamp Act was nullified—even in Georgia, eventually.

REPEAL

Clearly, the next move was up to Britain. For reasons that had nothing to do with the colonies, the king dismissed Grenville in the summer of 1765 and replaced his ministry with a narrow coalition organized primarily by William Augustus, duke of Cumberland, the king's uncle. An untested young nobleman, Charles Watson-Wentworth, marquess of Rockingham, took over the treasury. This "Old Whig" ministry had to deal with the riots in America, and Cumberland—the man who had sent Braddock to America in the winter of 1754–55—may have favored a similar use of force in late 1765. If so, he never had a chance to issue the order. On October 31, minutes before an emergency cabinet meeting on the American crisis, he died of a heart attack, leaving Rockingham in charge of the government. At first, Rockingham favored amending the Stamp Act, but by December he had decided on repeal. He faced resistance from the other ministers, the king, and Parliament. To win them over would demand great skill.

To Rockingham, the only alternative to repeal seemed to be a ruinous civil war in America. Only massive force, he believed, could reclaim the cities from the rioters. Even so, as the king's chief minister, he could hardly tell Parliament that the world's greatest empire must yield to unruly mobs. He needed a better reason for repeal. On December 6, even before the first American nonimportation agreements were printed in London on December 12 (New York City's) and December 26 (Philadelphia's), he began to mobilize "public opinion"—specifically, the British merchants and manufacturers who traded with America. They petitioned Parliament to repeal the Stamp Act. They condemned the Grenville program as an economic disaster, and their arguments gave Rockingham the leverage he needed.

Rockingham won over the other ministers by promising to support a Declaratory Act affirming Parliament's sovereignty over the colonies. When William Pitt eloquently demanded repeal in the House of Commons on January 14, 1766, Rockingham gained a powerful, though temporary, ally. "I rejoice that America has resisted," declared Pitt. "Three millions of people, so dead to all the feelings of liberty, as voluntarily to submit to be slaves, would have been fit instruments to make slaves of the rest." Parliament "may bind [the colonists'] trade, confine their manufactures, and exercise every power whatsoever," Pitt declared, "except that of taking their money out of their pockets without their consent."

Rockingham still faced resistance from the king, who hinted that he favored "modification" rather than repeal. George III appeared willing to repeal all the stamp duties except those on dice and playing cards, the two levies most difficult to enforce. Only Grenville, however, was ready to use the army to enforce even an amended Stamp Act. Rockingham brought the king around by threatening to resign, which would have forced the king to bring back Grenville, whom he hated. Many pro-American witnesses appeared before Parliament to urge repeal, including Benjamin Franklin, who gave a masterful performance. Slowly, Rockingham put together his majority.

Three pieces of legislation ended the crisis. The first repealed the Stamp Act because it had been "greatly detrimental to the commercial interests" of the empire. The second, the Declaratory Act, affirmed that Parliament had "full power and authority to make laws and statutes of sufficient force and validity to bind the colonies and people of America . . . in all cases whatsoever." Rockingham resisted pressure to insert the word "taxes" along with "laws and statutes." That omission permitted the colonists, who drew a sharp distinction between legislation (which, they conceded, Parliament had a right to pass) and taxation (which it could not), to interpret the act as an affirmation of their position,

while nearly everyone in Britain read precisely the opposite meaning into the phrase "laws and statutes." Old Whigs hoped that Parliament would never again have to proclaim its sovereign power over America. Like the royal veto of an act of Parliament, that power existed, explained Edmund Burke; and like the veto, which had not been used for 60 years, it should never again be invoked. The colonists agreed. They read the Declaratory Act as a face-saving gesture that made repeal of the Stamp Act possible.

The third measure, the Revenue Act of 1766, reduced the duty on molasses from three pence per gallon to one penny, but imposed the duty on all molasses, British or foreign, imported into the mainland colonies. Although the act was more favorable to the molasses trade than any other measure yet passed by Parliament, it was also, beyond any doubt, a revenue measure, and it generated more income for the empire than any other colonial tax. Few colonists attacked it for violating the principle of no taxation without representation. In Britain it seemed that the colonists objected to internal taxes but would accept external duties.

Against the advice of British friends, the colonists greeted repeal with wild celebrations. Over the next decade many communities observed March 18 as the anniversary of the Stamp Act's repeal. Neither

"THE REPEAL OR THE FUNERAL OF MISS AMERIC-STAMP" This London cartoon of 1766 shows George Grenville carrying the coffin of the Stamp Act with Lord Bute behind him. Contemporaries would easily have identified the other personalities.

side fully appreciated the misunderstandings that had made repeal possible, or their significance.

In the course of the struggle, both sides, British and colonial, had rejected the distinction between "internal" and "external" taxes. They could find no legal or philosophical basis for condemning the one while approving the other. Hardly anyone except Franklin noticed in 1766 that the difference was quite real and that the crisis had in fact been resolved according to that distinction. Parliament had tried to extend its authority over the internal affairs of the colonies and had failed, but it continued to collect port duties in the colonies, some to regulate trade, others for revenue. Although no one knew how to justify this division of authority, the internal-external cleavage marked, even defined, the power axis of the empire, the boundary between what Parliament could do on its own and what the Crown could accomplish only with the consent of the colonists.

Another misunderstanding was equally grave. Only the riots had created a crisis severe enough to push Parliament into repeal. Both sides, however, preferred to believe that economic pressure had been decisive. For the colonies, this conviction set the pattern of resistance for the next two imperial crises.

THE TOWNSHEND CRISIS

The goodwill created by repeal was brief. In 1766 the king again replaced his ministry. This time he persuaded William Pitt, the popular war minister in the struggle against France, to form a government. He and Pitt shared a contempt for the aristocratic families that had governed Britain since 1714, most of whom were now Rockingham Whigs. Both the king and Pitt considered factions immoral and put their faith in a government of "measures, not men." Pitt appealed to men of good will from all parties, but few responded. His ministry, which included many supporters of the Grenville program, faced serious opposition within Parliament. Pitt compounded that problem by accepting a peerage as earl of Chatham, a decision that removed his magnificent oratory from the House of Commons and, after several months, left Charles Townshend as his spokesman in that chamber. A witty, extemporaneous speaker, Town-

shend had betrayed every leader he ever served. The only point of real consistency in his political career had been his hard-line attitude toward the colonies.

THE TOWNSHEND PROGRAM

New York had already created a small crisis for the new earl of Chatham by objecting to the Quartering Act as a disguised form of taxation without consent. Under the old rules, when the army had asked for quarters and supplies and the assembly had voted them, consent had been an integral part of the process. Now one legislature (Parliament) was telling others (the colonial assemblies) what they must do. New York refused. In 1767 Parliament passed the New York Restraining Act, which forbade New York's governor from signing any law until the assembly complied with the Quartering Act. The crisis fizzled out when the governor bent the rules and announced that the assembly had already complied with the substance (if not all the specifics) of the Quartering Act before the Restraining Act went into effect. In the end, instead of helping the army, the Quartering Act weakened colonial loyalty to Britain.

Chatham, who announced that he would meet Britain's revenue needs by extracting millions from the East India Company, soon learned that he could not control the House of Commons from his position in the House of Lords. His East India bill got tied up in committee with no chance of passage. During the Christmas recess of 1766–67, Chatham saw the extent of his failure and began to slip into an acute depression that lasted more than two years. He refused to communicate with other ministers or even with the king. The colonists, who admired him more than any other Englishman of the day, expected sympathy from his administration. Instead they got Townshend, who took charge of colonial policy in the spring of 1767.

As chancellor of the exchequer, Townshend presented the annual budget to the House of Commons. A central aspect of that year's budget, the Townshend Revenue Act of 1767, imposed new duties in colonial ports on certain imports that the colonies could legally buy only from Britain: tea, paper, glass, red and white lead, and painter's colors. At the same time, Townshend removed more

"THE TRIUMPH OF AMERICA" This 1766 London cartoon suggests that the pro-American attitudes of William Pitt, earl of Chatham, will drive Britain over a precipice. Chatham is depicted as the coachman, and America has taken over the British coach. Each horse represents a different minister, some rushing eagerly to destruction, others more hesitant. Instead of this scenario, Charles Townshend led the Chatham administration into renewed conflict with the colonies.

duties on tea within Britain than he could offset with the new revenue collected in the colonies. Revenue, clearly, was not his object. The statute's preamble stated his real goal: to use the new American revenues to pay the salaries of governors and judges in the colonies, thereby freeing them from dependence on the assemblies. This rather devious strategy aroused suspicions of conspiracy in the colonies. Many sober provincials began to believe that, deep in the recesses of the British government, men really were plotting to deprive them of their liberties.

Other measures gave appellate powers to the vice admiralty courts in Boston, Philadelphia, and Charleston and created a separate American Board of Customs Commissioners to enforce the trade and revenue laws in the colonies. The board was placed in Boston, where resistance to the Stamp Act had been fiercest, rather than in Philadelphia, which had been rather quiet in 1765 and would have been a much more convenient location. Townshend was eager for confrontation.

The British army also began to withdraw from nearly all frontier posts and concentrate near the coast. Although the primary motive was to save money, the implications were striking. It was one

thing to keep an army in America to guard the frontier and then ask the colonists to pay part of its cost, but an army far distant from the frontier presumably existed only to police the colonists themselves. Why should they pay any part of its cost if its role was to enforce policies that would deprive them of their liberties?

Townshend ridiculed the distinction between internal and external taxes, a distinction that he attributed to Chatham and the colonists, but he declared that he would honor it anyway. After winning approval for his program, he died suddenly in September 1767 and passed on to others the dilemmas he had created. Frederick, Lord North, became chancellor of the exchequer. Chatham resigned, and Augustus Henry Fitzroy, duke of Grafton, became prime minister.

RESISTANCE: THE POLITICS OF ESCALATION

The internal-external distinction troubled the colonists. Since 1765 they had objected to all taxes for revenue, but in 1766 they had accepted the penny duty on molasses with few complaints. Defeating the Revenue Act of 1767 would prove tougher than nullifying the Stamp Act. Parliament had never been able to impose its will on the internal affairs of the colonies, as the Stamp Act fiasco demonstrated, but it did control the seas. Goods subject to duties might arrive aboard any of hundreds of ships from Britain each year, but screening the cargo of every vessel threatened to impose an enormous, perhaps impossible burden on the Sons of Liberty. A policy of general nonimportation would be easier to implement, but British trade played a bigger role in the colonial economy than North American trade did in the British economy. To hurt Britain a little, the colonies would have to harm themselves a lot.

Faced with these difficulties, the colonists divided over strategies of resistance. On August 31, 1767, the radical *Boston Gazette* proclaimed the death of liberty in America and called for complete nonimportation of all British goods. The merchants' paper, the *Boston Evening Post*, disagreed. In October, the Boston town meeting temporized by encouraging greater use of home manufactures. Boston also authorized voluntary nonconsumption of British goods. Even so, no organized resistance formed against the new measures, and for months little happened. The Stamp Act had been nullified before it could go into effect, but the Townshend duties became operative in November 1767 with little opposition. A month later, John Dickinson, a Philadelphia lawyer writing as a Pennsylvania farmer, tried to rouse his fellow colonists to action through 12 urgent letters printed in nearly every colonial newspaper. These *Letters from a Farmer in Pennsylvania* denied the distinction between internal and external taxes, insisted that all parliamentary taxes for revenue violated the colonists' rights, and speculated darkly about Townshend's real motives.

Massachusetts again set the pace of resistance. In February 1768 its assembly petitioned the king, not Parliament, against the new measures. Without waiting for a reply, it also sent a Circular Letter to the other assemblies, urging them to pursue "constitutional measures" of resistance against the Quartering Act, the new taxes, and the use of Townshend revenues to pay the salaries of governors and judges. The implication was that, because Britain responded only to resistance, the colonies had better work together.

The British ministry got the point but did not like it. Wills Hill, earl of Hillsborough and secretary of state for the American colonies (an office created in 1768), responded so sharply that he turned tepid opposition into serious resistance. He told the Massachusetts assembly to rescind the Circular Letter and ordered all governors to dissolve any assembly that dared to accept it. The Massachusetts House voted 92 to 17 in June 1768 not to rescind, and the Sons of Liberty castigated the minority as enemies of the people. Most other assemblies had shown little interest in the Townshend program, particularly in the southern colonies where governors already had fixed salaries. Even so, they bristled at being told what they could or could not debate. All of them took up the Circular Letter or began to draft their own. One by one, the governors dissolved their assemblies until government by consent did indeed seem endangered.

The next escalation again came from Boston. On March 18, 1768, the town's celebration of the anniversary of the Stamp Act's repeal grew so raucous that the governor and the new American Board of Customs Commissioners asked Hillsborough for troops. He ordered General Gage, based in New York, to send two regiments from Nova Scotia to Boston. On June 10, before Gage could respond, a riot broke out in Boston after customs collectors seized John Hancock's sloop *Liberty* for having smuggled Madeira wine (taxed under the Sugar Act) on its *previous* voyage. By waiting until the ship had a new cargo, informers and customs officials would split larger shares when the sloop was condemned. Terrified by the furious popular response, the commissioners fled to Castle William in Boston harbor and again petitioned Hillsborough for troops. He sent two more regiments from Ireland.

At about this time, nonimportation at last began to take hold. Two dozen Massachusetts towns adopted pacts in which they agreed not to consume British goods. Boston merchants drafted a nonimportation agreement on March 1, 1768, conditional on its acceptance by New York and Philadelphia. New York agreed, but Philadelphia balked, preferring to wait and see whether Parliament would make any effort to redress colonial grievances. There the matter rested until the *Liberty* riot prompted most Boston merchants to agree to nonimportation, effective January 1. New York again concurred, but Philadelphia held out until early

1769 when it became obvious that Parliament would make no concessions.

Spurred on by the popular but mistaken belief that the nonimportation agreements of 1765 had forced Parliament to repeal the Stamp Act, the colonists again turned to a strategy of economic sanctions. Nonimportation affected only imports from Britain. Tea, consumed mostly by women, was the most objectionable import of all. No one tried to block the importation of West Indian molasses, which was essential to the rum industry of Boston and Newport and which brought in about £30,000 a year under the Revenue Act of 1766. Rum was consumed mostly by men. Some women resented the disproportionate sacrifices they were asked to make. On the other hand, the Sons of Liberty knew that virtually all molasses came from the French islands, and that nonimportation would injure only French planters and American manufacturers and consumers and put no pressure on Parliament or British merchants. The only proven way to resist the penny duty was through smuggling.

Believing that he held the edge with the army on its way, Governor Bernard leaked this news in late August. The public response flabbergasted him. The Boston town meeting asked him to summon the legislature, which Bernard had dissolved in June after it stood by its Circular Letter. When Bernard refused, the Sons of Liberty asked the other towns to elect delegates to a "convention" in Boston. The convention contained most of the radical members of the House of Representatives but not the conservatives. It had no legal standing in the colony's royal government. Boston, professing alarm over the possibility of a French invasion, urged its citizens to arm themselves. When the convention met, it accepted Boston's definition of colonial grievances but refused to sanction violence. Boston had no choice but to go along. It could not call the shots for the whole colony. Instead, the *Boston Gazette* portrayed the city as an orderly community (which it usually was) that had no need of British troops.

AN EXPERIMENT IN MILITARY COERCION

The British fleet entered Boston harbor in battle array by October 2, 1768, and landed 1,000 soldiers, sent by General Gage from Nova Scotia.

They soon discovered that their most troublesome enemy was not the Sons of Liberty but the Quartering Act, which required that British soldiers be lodged in public barracks where available. Massachusetts had built such barracks—in Castle William, miles away on an island in Boston harbor, where the soldiers could hardly function as a police force. According to the act, any attempt to quarter soldiers on private property would expose the officer responsible to being cashiered from the army, after conviction before any two justices of the peace. And several prominent patriots, such as John Adams and James Otis, Jr., were justices. The soldiers pitched their tents on Boston Common. Seventy men deserted in the first week, about 7 percent of the force. Eventually the soldiers took over a building that had been the Boston poorhouse. The regiments from Ireland joined them later.

To warn the public against the dangers posed by a standing army in time of peace, the patriots compiled a "Journal of the Times" describing how British soldiers were undermining public order in Boston—clashing with the town watch, endangering the virtue of young women, disturbing church services, and picking fights. The "journal" always appeared first as a newspaper column in some other city, usually New York. Only later was it reprinted in Boston, after memories of any specific incident had grown hazy. Yet violence against customs officers ceased for many months. John Mein (pronounced "mean"), loyalist editor of the *Boston Chronicle*, caricatured leading patriots (John Hancock's generosity, for example, made him "the milch-cow of the disaffected") and began to publish customs records that exposed merchants who were violating the nonimportation agreement. This information could undermine intercolonial resistance by discrediting its Boston leaders. Yet Britain's experiment in military coercion seemed successful enough to justify withdrawal of half the soldiers in the summer of 1769.

Meanwhile, when news of the Massachusetts convention of towns reached Britain, the House of Lords promptly escalated the crisis another notch by drafting a set of resolutions calling for the deportation of colonial political offenders to England for trial. Instead of quashing dissent, this threat to colonial political autonomy infuriated the southern colonies, which had not been deeply involved in resistance to the Townshend duties. Virginia,

PAUL REVERE'S ENGRAVING OF THE BRITISH ARMY LANDING IN BOSTON, 1768 The navy approached the city in battle array, a sight familiar to veterans of the French wars. To emphasize the peaceful, Christian character of Boston, Revere exaggerated the height of the church steeples.

Maryland, and South Carolina now adopted non-importation agreements. In the Chesapeake, the movement had more support among planters than among tobacco merchants, most of whom were Scots loyal to their parent firms. No enforcement mechanism was ever put in place. Charleston, however, took nonimportation seriously. Up and down the continent, the feeble resistance of mid-1768 was becoming formidable by 1769.

THE SECOND WILKES CRISIS

In 1768, just as the Townshend Crisis was brewing up, George III dissolved Parliament and issued writs for the usual septennial elections. John Wilkes, an outlaw since 1763, returned from France and won a seat for the English county of Middlesex. He then received a one-year sentence in King's Bench Prison. Hundreds of supporters gathered to chant "Wilkes and Liberty!" or even "No Wilkes, No King!" On May 10, 1768, as the new Parliament convened, Wilkites just outside the prison clashed with soldiers who fired into the crowd, killing six and wounding 15. Wilkes denounced "the massacre of St. George's Fields."

The House of Commons expelled Wilkes and ordered a new election, but the voters chose him again. Two more expulsions and two more elections took place the next year, until April 1769 when, after Wilkes won again by 1,143 votes to 296, the exasperated House of Commons voted to seat the loser.

Wilkes had created a constitutional crisis. His adherents founded "the Society of Gentlemen Supporters of the Bill of Rights," which raised money to pay off his huge debts and organized a national campaign on his behalf. About one-fourth of the voters of the entire kingdom signed petitions demanding a new general election. Wilkites called for a reduction of royal patronage and major reforms of the electoral system. They also began the regular publication of parliamentary debates and sympathized openly with North American protests. Colonial Sons of Liberty began to identify strongly with Wilkes. If he lost, they warned, their own liberties would be in danger. The Wilkite number "45" (issue number of the *North Briton* in which his notorious anti-Bute essay had appeared), often combined with the number "92" (number of members in the Massachusetts House who stood by the Circular Letter), became sacred in America. Boston even printed a Wilkite parody of the Apostles' Creed. It began: "I believe in Wilkes, the firm patriot, maker of number 45. Who was born for our good. Suffered under arbitrary power. Was banished and imprisoned." It ended with a hope for "the resurrection of liberty, and the life of universal freedom forever. Amen."

In South Carolina, Wilkes was hailed as the "unshaken colossus of freedom; the patriot of England, the rightful and legal representative of Middlesex; the favourite of the people; the British Hercules, that has cleaned a stable fouler than the Augean." In 1769 the South Carolina assembly borrowed £1,500 sterling from the colony's treasurer and donated it to Wilkes. When the assembly passed an appropriation to cover the gift, the council rejected the bill. Because neither side would back down, the assembly voted no taxes after 1769 and passed no laws after 1771. Royal government broke down over the Wilkes question.

The Townshend crisis and the Wilkite movement became an explosive combination. For the first time, many colonists began to question the decency of the British government and its commitment to liberty. That a conspiracy existed to destroy British and colonial liberty began to seem quite credible to sober observers.

THE BOSTON MASSACRE

In late 1769, the Boston Sons of Liberty turned to direct confrontation with the army, and the city again faced a serious crisis. The redcoats had intimidated Boston for nearly a year. Now Boston reciprocated. The town watch clashed with the army's guard posts because the watch, when challenged by the redcoats' call "Who goes there?" refused to give the required answer: "Friends." Under English common law, soldiers could not fire on civilians without an order from a civil magistrate, except in self-defense when their lives were in danger. By the fall of 1769 no magistrate dared issue such a command. Clashes between soldiers and civilians grew frequent, and justices of the peace singled out the soldiers for punishment. At one point, when town officials tried to arrest a British officer who was commanding the guard at Boston Neck, Captain Ponsonby Molesworth intervened to confront a stone-throwing crowd. Molesworth ordered the soldiers to bayonet anyone throwing stones who moved too close. Later, a

Boston justice told him that under common law a bayonet thrust was not an act of self-defense against a stone, which was not a lethal weapon. Had a soldier killed anyone, Molesworth could have been tried for his life for issuing the order.

By 1770 the soldiers often felt under siege. When rioters drove editor John Mein out of town, the army offered him no protection. "Go, Mein, to some dark corner of the world repair," mocked one poet, "And spend thy life in horror and despair." Once again the Sons of Liberty freely intimidated merchants who violated nonimportation. They nearly lynched Ebenezer Richardson, a customs informer who fired shots from his home into a stone-throwing crowd and killed an 11-year-old boy. The lad's funeral on February 26, 1770, became an enormous display of public mourning. Several hundred schoolboys marched ahead of the bier, which was carried by six youths and followed by 30 coaches and thousands of mourners. Richardson, although convicted of murder, was pardoned by George III.

After the funeral, tensions between soldiers and citizens reached a fatal climax. Off-duty soldiers tried to supplement their meager wages with part-time employment, a practice that angered local artisans who resented the competition in the city's depressed economy. On Friday, March 2, 1770, three soldiers came to John Hancock's wharf looking for work. "Soldier, will you work?" asked Samuel Gray, a rope maker. "Yes," replied one. "Then go and clean my shit house," sneered Gray. The soldiers attacked him but were repelled. They returned with 10 others but were again repulsed. Forty soldiers had no better luck. Gray's employer finally persuaded Colonel William Dalrymple to confine his men to barracks. Peace prevailed through the Puritan sabbath that ran from Saturday night to sunrise on Monday, but everyone expected trouble on Monday, March 5.

After dark on Monday, fire bells began ringing throughout the town, and civilians and soldiers clashed at several places. A crowd hurling snowballs and rocks closed in on the lone sentinel guarding the hated customs house, where the king's revenue was stored. The guard called for help. A corporal and seven soldiers, including two who had participated in the wharf brawl, rushed to his aid and loaded their weapons. Captain Thomas Preston took command and ordered the soldiers to drive the attackers slowly back with fixed bayonets. The crowd taunted the soldiers, daring them to fire. One soldier apparently slipped, discharging his musket into the air as he fell. The others then fired into the crowd, killing five and wounding six. One of the victims was Samuel Gray; another was Crispus Attucks, a sailor of African and Indian ancestry.

With the whole town taking up arms, the soldiers were withdrawn to Castle William in Boston harbor where, the Sons of Liberty insisted, they had always belonged. Preston and six of his men stood trial for murder and were defended, brilliantly, by two radical patriot lawyers, John Adams and Josiah Quincy, Jr., who believed that every accused person ought to have a proper defense. Preston and four of the soldiers were acquitted. The other two were convicted only of manslaughter, which permitted them to plead a legal technicality called "benefit of clergy." They were branded on the thumb and released.

The Boston Massacre, as the Sons of Liberty called this encounter, became the colonial counterpart to the Massacre of St. George's Fields in England. It marked the failure of Britain's first attempt at military coercion.

PARTIAL REPEAL

March 5, 1770, the day of the massacre, marked a turning point in Britain as well, for on that day Lord North asked Parliament to repeal the Townshend duties, except the one on tea. North regarded the duties as an antimercantile restriction on Britain's own exports and wanted them all repealed. But the cabinet had rejected complete repeal by a 5-to-4 vote back on May 1, 1769. As with the Stamp Act, Britain had three choices: enforcement, repeal, or modification. The ministry feared that Parliament would lose all credibility in North America if it retreated as far as it had in 1766. In effect, North chose the middle ground that had been rejected in 1766—modification instead of full repeal or enforcement. In public, he claimed to be retaining only a preamble without a statute, a vestige of the Townshend Revenue Act, while repealing the substance. In fact, he did the opposite. Tea provided nearly three-fourths of the revenue under the act. North kept the substance but gave up the shadow.

"THE COLOSSUS OF THE NORTH; OR THE STRIDING BOREAS" This print was an opposition cartoon condemning the corruption of Lord North's ministry while Britannia complains that "Those that should have been my Preservers have been my Destroyers."

IMPORTS IN £000 STERLING FROM ENGLAND AND SCOTLAND TO THE AMERICAN COLONIES, 1766–1775

Colony	1766	1767	1768	1769	1770	1771	1772	1773	1774	1775
New England	419	416	431	224	417	1,436*	844	543	577	85.0
New York	333	424	491	76	480	655*	349	296	460	1.5
Pennsylvania	334	383	442	205	140	747*	526	436	646	1.4
Chesapeake†	520	653	670	715	997*	1,224*	1,016	589	690	1.9
Lower South‡	376	292	357	385*	228	515*	575*	448	471	130.5
Totals	1,982	2,168	2,391	1,605	2,262	4,577*	3,310	2,312	2,844	220.3

Average total imports, 1766–68 = £2,180
1769 = 73.6 percent of that average, or 67.1 percent of 1768 imports
1770 = 103.8 percent of that average, or 94.6 percent of 1768 imports

*These totals surpassed all previous highs
†Chesapeake = Maryland and Virginia
‡Lower South = Carolinas and Georgia

This news reached the colonies just after nonimportation had achieved its greatest success in 1769 (see the accompanying table). The colonies reduced imports by about one-third from what they had been in 1768, but the impact on Britain was slight, partly because Britain had found a lucrative market for textiles by selling new uniforms to the entire Russian army. North had hoped that partial repeal, although it would not placate all the colonists, would at least divide them. It did. Most merchants favored renewed importation of everything but tea, while the Sons of Liberty, most of whom were artisans, still supported complete nonimportation, a policy that would increase demand for their own manufactures.

Resistance to the Townshend Act collapsed first in Newport, where smuggling had always been the preferred method of challenging British authority. It spread to New York City, where the boycott on imports had been most effective. Soon Philadelphia caved in, followed by Boston in October 1770. By contrast, nonimportation had hardly caused a ripple in the import trade of the Chesapeake colonies. North's repeal was followed everywhere by an orgy of importation of British goods, setting record highs in all the colonies.

DISAFFECTION

Repeal in 1770 lacked the impact that it had in 1766. There was no public rejoicing, not even when Lord North's government (he had become prime minister in January 1770) took further steps to reduce tension. The Quartering Act expired quietly in 1770; some of the more objectionable features of the vice admiralty courts were softened; and the Currency Act of 1764 was repealed in stages between 1770 and 1773, as even London began to recognize that it was harming trade. Yet North failed to achieve reconciliation. He had not restored confidence in the justice and decency of the British government. To a degree hard to appreciate today, the empire ran on voluntarism, on trust, or what people at the time called "affection." Its opposite, *dis*affection, had a more literal and dangerous meaning to them than it does now.

Many colonists blamed one another for failing to win complete repeal of the duties. A Philadelphian attacked the "little dirty colony of Rhode Island" for yielding first. Bostonians lamented the "immortal shame and infamy" of New Yorkers for abandoning resistance: "Let them . . . be despised, hated, detested, and handed down to all future ages as the betrayers of their country." A New Yorker retaliated by calling Boston "the common sewer of America into which every beast that brought with it the unclean thing has disburthened itself."

These recriminations, gratifying as they must have been to British officials, actually masked a vast erosion of trust in the imperial government. The colonists were angry with one another for failing to appreciate how menacing British policy still was. The tea duty still proclaimed Parliament's sovereignty over the colonies. It remained a sliver in a wound that would not heal.

That fear sometimes broke through the surface calm of the years from 1770 to 1773. Rhode Islanders had often clashed with customs officers and had even fired on the king's ships once or twice without stirring much interest in other colonies. Then, in 1772, a predatory customs vessel, the *Gaspée*, ran aground near Providence while pursuing some peaceful coastal ships. After dark, men with blackened faces boarded the *Gaspée*, wounded its captain, and burned the ship. Britain sent a panel of dignitaries to the colony with instructions to send the perpetrators to England for trial. The inquiry failed because no one would talk.

Twelve colonial assemblies considered this threat so ominous that they created permanent committees of correspondence to keep in touch with one another and to *anticipate* the next assault on their liberties. Even colonial moderates now believed that the British government was conspiring to destroy liberty in America. When Governor Hutchinson announced in 1773 that, under the Townshend Act, the Massachusetts Superior Court justices would receive their salaries from the imperial treasury, Boston created its own committee of correspondence and urged other towns to do the same. Boston's role in the "patriot" cause had grown dramatically since the convention of 1768, and Bostonians such as John Adams had become the major spokesmen for the resistance movement. A plot to destroy their liberties now seemed plausible to many colonials. Hutchinson, amused at first, grew alarmed when most towns of any size followed Boston's lead.

The Boston Massacre trials and the *Gaspée* affair convinced London that it was pointless to prosecute individuals for politically motivated crimes. Whole communities would have to be punished. That choice brought the government to the edge of a precipice. Was the empire held together by law and consent, or only by force? The use of force against entire communities could lead to outright war, and war is not and cannot be a system of justice. The spread of committees of correspondence within Massachusetts and throughout the colonies suggested that settlers who had been unable to unite against New France at Albany in 1754 now deemed unity against Britain essential to their liberties. By 1773 several New England newspapers were calling on the colonies to create a formal union.

In effect, the Townshend crisis never ended. With the tea duty standing as a symbol of Parliament's right to tax the colonies without their consent, genuine imperial harmony was becoming impossible. North's decision to retain the tea tax in 1770 did not guarantee that armed resistance would break out five years later, but it severely narrowed the ground on which any compromise could be built. The price of miscalculation had grown enormously.

INTERNAL CLEAVAGES: THE CONTAGION OF LIBERTY

Any challenge to British authority carried high risks for prominent families in the colonies. They depended on the Crown for their public offices, official honors, and government contracts, which in turn ratified their status at the top of society. Since the Stamp Act crisis, these families had faced a dilemma. The Hutchinsons of Massachusetts kept on good terms with Britain while incurring the scorn and even hatred of many of their neighbors. John Hancock, the Livingstons of New York, and most of the great planters in the southern colonies championed the grievances of their communities but alienated British authorities. The Townshend crisis was a far more accurate predictor of future behavior than response to the Stamp Act had been. Nearly everyone had denounced the Stamp Act, including such future loyalists as Daniel Dulany of Maryland. By contrast, the merchants and lawyers who resisted nonimportation in 1768 were likely to become loyalists by 1775. Artisans, merchants, and lawyers who supported the boycotts, especially those who favored continuing them past 1770, became patriots.

But the patriot leaders also faced challenges from within their own ranks. Artisans, who had mobilized to resist Britain in 1765 and 1769, demanded more power, and tenant farmers in the Hudson valley protested violently against their landlords. Discontent ran high in Boston, where the economy had been faltering since the 1740s while taxes remained high; Britain's policies bore hard on the town and gave an angry edge to its protests. Boston set the pace of resistance in every imperial crisis. In New York City, Philadelphia, and Charleston, artisans began to play a much more assertive role in public affairs. Could the new and fragile social hierarchy of the 18th century withstand these strains?

THE FEUDAL REVIVAL AND RURAL DISCONTENT

Tensions increased in the countryside as well as in the cities. Three processes intensified discontent in rural areas: a revival of old proprietary charters, massive foreign immigration, and the settlement of the backcountry.

Between about 1730 and 1750, the men who owned 17th-century proprietary or manorial charters began to see, for the first time, the prospect of huge profits by enforcing these old legal claims. These demands profoundly affected every colony from New York to North Carolina. The great estates of the Hudson valley had attracted few settlers before the mid-18th century, and those who arrived first had received generous leases. By the 1750s, however, a typical manor lord was taking in between £1,000 and £2,000 a year, while the Livingston and Van Rensselaer families did much better. As leases became more restrictive and as New Englanders swarmed into New York, discontent increased. In 1753 the proprietor of Livingston Manor had difficulty putting down Yankee rioters, and discontent spread through the Hudson valley over the next decade. In 1766 several thousand angry farmers, inspired by the Stamp Act riots, took to the fields and the roads to protest the terms of their leases. They threatened to kill the lord of Livingston Manor or to pull down the mansions of absentee landlords in New York City. The colony called in redcoats to suppress them. But when New York landlords also tried to make good their claims to the upper Connecticut valley, the Yankee settlers utterly defied them, set up their own government and, after a long struggle, ultimately became the independent state of Vermont.

The proprietors of East New Jersey claimed much of the land being worked by descendants of the original settlers of Newark and Elizabethtown, who thought they owned their farms. The proprietors, in firm control of the law courts, planned to sell or lease the land, either to the current occupants or to newcomers. After they expelled several farmers and replaced them with tenants, the farmers retaliated. A succession of land riots, in which farms were burned and jails were broken open, rocked

much of northern New Jersey for 10 years after 1745. The proprietary intruders were driven out, and the riots stopped, but tensions remained high.

Maryland and Pennsylvania had brought few returns to the Calvert and Penn families before 1730, but over the next three or four decades both families organized land sales much more carefully and began to collect quitrents. Frederick, seventh and last Lord Baltimore, milked Maryland for the princely income of £30,000 sterling per year until his death in 1771. The Penns enjoyed similar gains in Pennsylvania, though more slowly. Their landed income rose to about £15,000 or £20,000 in the 1760s and then soared to £67,000 in 1773, only to fall sharply as the Pennsylvania government disintegrated over the next three years. With more than half of their land still unsettled, they seemed about to turn their colony into the most lucrative piece of real estate in the Atlantic world. Their reluctance to contribute to the war effort in the 1750s had so angered Benjamin Franklin at the time, however, that, with the assembly's support, he went to London to urge the Crown to make Pennsylvania a royal colony. This effort weakened the colony's resistance to both the Stamp Act and the Townshend Act. Meanwhile Connecticut settlers, who claimed they had bought the Wyoming valley from the Indians at the Albany Congress of 1754, rejected the Penns' authority, claimed all of northern Pennsylvania on the basis of Connecticut's sea-to-sea charter and, aided by the Paxton Boys, set off a small civil war in the 1770s.

In Virginia, Thomas, sixth baron Fairfax, acquired title to the entire northern neck of the colony (the land between the Potomac and the Rappahannock Rivers), which Charles II had granted to two courtiers in the mid-17th century. By 1775, the Fairfax estate's five million acres contained 21 counties. He received £5,000 a year from his holdings, but he muted criticism by moving to the colony and setting himself up as a great planter.

In North Carolina, John Carteret, earl of Granville—the only heir of the original Carolina proprietors, who refused to sell his share to the Crown in the 1720s—consolidated his claim as the Granville District after 1745. Although still living in England, he received an income of about £5,000 per year. The Granville District embraced more than half of North Carolina's land and two-thirds of its population, deprived the colony of revenue from land sales and quitrents within the district, and

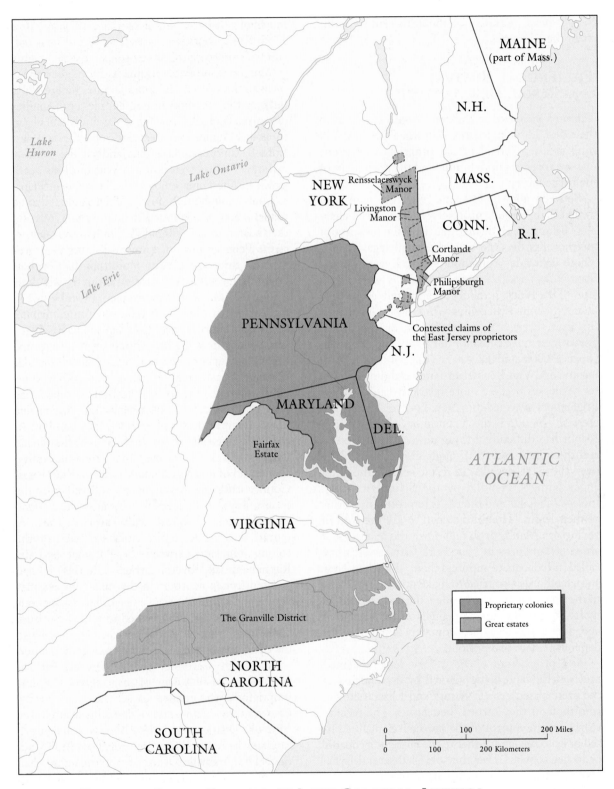

FEUDAL REVIVAL: GREAT ESTATES OF LATE COLONIAL AMERICA

forced North Carolina to resort to direct taxation. For several years after Granville's death in 1763, his land office remained closed. Disgruntled settlers, unable to gain title to their lands, often rioted.

Taken together, the New York manor lords, the New Jersey proprietors, and the Penn, Baltimore, Fairfax and Granville claims blanketed the colonies from New York to North Carolina. They were the biggest winners in America's "feudal revival," the use of old charters to pry income from the settlers.

THE REGULATOR MOVEMENTS IN THE CAROLINAS

Massive immigration from Europe, mostly through Philadelphia, and the settlement of the backcountry created severe social tensions. Most immigrants were Scottish or Scots-Irish Presbyterians, Lutherans, or German Reformed Protestants. They were dissenters from the prevailing faith in the colonies they entered, whether it was the Quaker religion in Pennsylvania or the Church of England from Maryland to Georgia. They angered Indians by squatting on their land and, quite often, by murdering those who were in their way—behavior that the Paxton Boys' march on Philadelphia in 1763 attempted to justify. In the Carolina backcountry, the newcomers provoked the Cherokee War of 1760–61, which in turn brutalized and demoralized the whole region.

Following the Cherokee War, backcountry South Carolina faced an enormous crime problem. Great bands of outlaws, men who had been dislocated by the war, began roaming the countryside, plundering the more prosperous farmers and often raping their wives and daughters. As the violence peaked between 1765 and 1767, the more respectable settlers organized themselves as "regulators" (a later generation would call them "vigilantes") to impose order in the absence of any organized government. Although South Carolina claimed jurisdiction over the backcountry, the colony's law courts were located in Charleston, more than 100 miles to the east. The Anglican parish system, which provided what little local government there was, barely reached into the backcountry. Even though most of the white settlers now lived in the backcountry, they elected only 2 of the 48 members of South Carolina's assembly. In effect, they had no local government.

After obtaining commissions from Charleston as militia officers and justices of the peace, the regulators chased the outlaws out of the colony, many of them into North Carolina. They then imposed order on what they called the "little people," poor settlers who often made a living as hunters, many of whom may have aided the outlaws. The discipline imposed by the regulators, typically whippings and forced labor, outraged their victims, who organized as "moderators" and got their own commissions from the governor. With both sides claiming legality, about 600 armed regulators confronted an equal force of moderators at the Saluda River in 1769. Civil war was avoided only by the timely arrival of an emissary from the governor bearing a striking message: South Carolina would finally bring government to the backcountry by providing a circuit court system for the entire colony. Violence ebbed, but tensions remained. Eastern planters, by now a very wealthy group, continued to distrust western settlers, at least until cotton plantations and slavery made the two regions more alike toward the end of the century.

In North Carolina, the backcountry's problem was corruption, not the absence of government. The settlers, mostly immigrants pushing south from Pennsylvania, found the county courts under the control of men with strong blood or business ties to powerful families in the eastern counties. Because county officials were appointed by the governor, political success required gaining access to his circle. These justices, lawyers, and merchants seemed to regard county government as an engine for fleecing farmers through regressive poll taxes, fees, and court costs, and through suits for debt. North Carolina's regulator movement arose to reform these abuses. The backcountry counties contained more than half the colony's population, but they elected only 17 of the 78 assemblymen.

In 1768 the regulators refused to pay taxes in Orange County, which was part of the Granville District. Governor William Tryon mustered 1,300 eastern militiamen, one-sixth of whom were officers, including more than half of the assemblymen from the eastern counties. With 8 generals and 14 colonels, and led by an elite unit of Gentlemen Volunteer Light Dragoons, this force overawed the regulators for a time. Then, in a bid for a voice in the 1769 assembly, the regulators managed to capture six seats. These new assemblymen called for the secret ballot, fixed salaries (instead of fees) for justices and other officials, and a land tax rather than poll taxes. But they were outvoted by the eastern majority. After losing ground in the 1770 election, they stormed into Hillsborough, closed the Orange County Court, and whipped Edmund Fanning, a Yale graduate whose lust for fees had made him the most detested official in the backcountry. They also seized the court docket and scribbled unflattering comments next to many of the names of their creditors. Tryon responded by marching 1,000 militiamen westward, who defeated a force of more than 2,000 poorly armed regulators in early 1771 at the battle of Alamance Creek. Seven regulators were hanged, and many fled the colony. North Carolina entered the struggle for independence as a bitterly divided society.

SLAVES AND WOMEN

In Charleston, South Carolina, in 1765, the Sons of Liberty marched through the streets chanting "Liberty and No Stamps." To their amazement, slaves organized a parade of their own, shouting, "Liberty! Liberty!" Merchant Henry Laurens tried to convince himself that they probably did not know the meaning of the word.

About the middle of the 18th century, slavery came under attack for the first time. An antislavery movement arose on both sides of the Atlantic and attracted both patriots and loyalists. Quakers led the assault in America. In the 1740s and 1750s, Benjamin Lay, John Woolman, and Anthony Benezet urged fellow Quakers to free their slaves. In the 1750s the Quaker Yearly Meeting placed the slave trade off limits and finally, in 1774, forbade slaveholding altogether. Any Friend who failed to comply by 1779 was disowned. Britain's Methodist leader John Wesley, in almost every other respect a social conservative, also attacked slavery, as did several colonial disciples of Jonathan Edwards. Two and three decades after the Great Awakening, many evangelicals began to agree with the message of Hugh Bryan in 1742, that slavery was a sin.

By the 1760s, for the first time, supporters of slavery found that they had to defend the institution. Hardly anyone had bothered to do so earlier, because a social hierarchy seemed necessary and inevitable, and slavery was merely an extreme example of that pattern. As equal rights became a popular topic, however, some began to suggest that *all* peo-

"Here lies the body of John Jack, a native of Africa . . .
Tho' born in a land of slavery
He was born free.
Tho' he lived in a land of liberty,
He lived a slave.
Till by his honest, tho' stolen labor,
He acquired the source of slavery,
Which gave him his freedom;
Tho' not long before
Death, the grand tyrant,
Gave him his final emancipation,
And set him on a footing with Kings.
Tho' a slave to vice,
He practiced those virtues
Without which Kings are but slaves."

EPITAPH FOR JOHN JACK
written by Daniel Bliss, a Massachusetts loyalist, 1772

ple could claim these rights, and slavery came under attack. In Scotland, Adam Smith, the most original economist of the age, praised African slaves for their "magnanimity," which, he claimed, "the soul of the sordid master is scarce capable of conceiving." Arthur Lee, a Virginian, defended the character of his fellow planters against Smith's charge but discovered that he could not justify slavery, "always the deadly enemy to virtue and science." Patrick Henry agreed. Slavery, he wrote, "is as repugnant to humanity as it is inconsistent with the Bible and destructive of liberty." He himself kept slaves, but only because of "the general inconvenience of living without them. I will not, I cannot justify it." In England, Granville Sharp, an early abolitionist, brought the Somerset case before the Court of King's Bench in 1771 and compelled a reluctant Chief Justice William Murray, baron Mansfield, to declare slavery incompatible with the "free air" of England. That decision gave England's 10,000 or 15,000 blacks a chance to claim their freedom. With the

"A SOCIETY OF PATRIOTIC LADIES AT EDENTON IN NORTH CAROLINA" This 1775 London cartoon satirized the active role of women in resisting British policies.

courts challenging slavery in Britain, with Quakers taking steps against it in the Mid-Atlantic colonies, and with even great planters expressing doubts about it, New Englanders began to move as well.

Two women, Sarah Osborn and Phillis Wheatley, played leading roles in the movement. Osborn, an English immigrant to Newport, Rhode Island, and a widow, opened a school in 1744 to support her family. A friend of revivalist George Whitefield, she also taught women and blacks and began holding evening religious meetings, which turned into a big local revival. At one point in the 1760s, about one-sixth of Newport's Africans were attending her school. That made them the most literate African population in the colonies, although they were living in the city most deeply involved in the African slave trade. Osborn's students supported abolition of the slave trade and, later, of slavery itself. She sent two of her African pupils to Princeton to be tutored in classics by John Witherspoon, president of the College of New Jersey. They almost became the

first black college students in American history, but the Revolutionary War disrupted their plans.

Meanwhile, an eight-year-old girl who would become known as Phillis Wheatley arrived in Boston from Africa in 1761; she was purchased by wealthy John Wheatley as a servant for his wife, Susannah, who treated her more like a daughter than a slave, taught her to read and write, and emancipated her when she came of age. In 1767 Phillis published her first poem in Boston, and in 1773 a volume of her poetry was printed in London, making her a transatlantic celebrity by age 20. Her poems deplored slavery but rejoiced in the Christianization of Africans. Some of them supported the patriot cause, but she withheld those from the London edition.

Soon many of Boston's blacks sensed an opportunity for emancipation. On several occasions in 1773 and 1774, they petitioned the legislature or the governor for freedom, pointing out that, although they had never forfeited their natural rights, they were being "held in slavery in the bowels of a free and Christian Country." When the legislature passed a bill on their behalf, Governor Hutchinson vetoed it. Boston slaves made it clear to General Gage, Hutchinson's successor, that they would serve him as a loyal militia in exchange for their freedom. In short, they offered allegiance to whichever side supported their emancipation. Many patriots began to rally to their cause. "If we would look for Liberty ourselves," the town of Medfield declared in 1773, ". . . we ought not to continue to enslave others but immediately set about some effectual method to prevent it for the future."

The patriots could look to another group of allies, as well. Many women became indispensable to the broader resistance movement. They could not vote or hold office, but without their willing support nonimportation would have been not just a failure, but a fiasco. In thousands of households, women joined the intense discussions about liberty and agreed to make homespun clothing to take the place of imported British textiles.

Freedom's ferment made a heady wine. After 1773, any direct challenge to British power would trigger enormous social changes within the colonies.

THE LAST IMPERIAL CRISIS

The surface calm between 1770 and 1773 ended when Lord North moved to save the East India

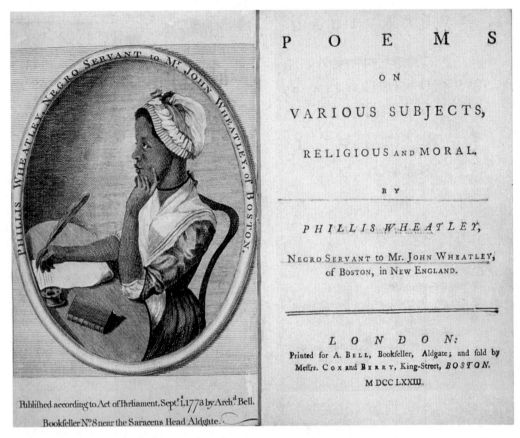

PHILLIS WHEATLEY Engraving of Phillis Wheatley opposite the title page of her collected poems, published in 1773.

Company, Britain's largest corporation, from bankruptcy. Southeastern England and the colonies were buying low-priced smuggled Dutch tea, which left the East India Company's warehouses bulging with millions of unsold pounds of tea. North's main concern was the company, not colonial resistance to Townshend's tea duty. Without solving the company's problems, he threw North America into a crisis too big for Britain to handle.

THE TEA CRISIS

North decided to rescue the East India Company by empowering it to undersell its rivals, the smugglers of Dutch tea. Benjamin Franklin, still in London as a colonial agent, reminded North that he could achieve that goal in the colonies by repealing the Townshend duty for sound economic reasons. North rejected that idea. The settlers, he thought, would hardly revolt if he somehow managed to give them cheap tea.

His Tea Act of 1773 repealed import duties on tea in England but retained the Townshend duty in the colonies. In both places, North estimated, legal tea would be cheaper than anyone else's. The company would be saved, and the settlers, by willingly buying legal tea, would accept Parliament's right to tax them.

Another aspect of the Tea Act antagonized most merchants in the colonies. The company had been selling tea to all comers at public auctions in London, but the Tea Act gave it a monopoly on the shipping and distribution of tea in the colonies. Only company ships could carry it, and a few consignees in each port would have the exclusive right to sell it. The combined dangers of taxation and monopoly again forged the coalition of artisans and merchants that had helped to defeat the Stamp Act by 1766 and to resist the Townshend Act by 1769. Patriots saw the Tea Act as a Trojan horse that would destroy liberty by seducing the settlers into accepting Parliamentary sovereignty. Unintentionally, North gave a tremendous advantage to those determined to resist the Tea Act. He had devised an oceanic, or "external," measure that the colonists could actually nullify despite British control of the seas. No one would have to police the entire waterfront looking for tea importers. The patriots had only to wait for the specially chartered tea ships and prevent them from landing their tea.

Direct threats usually did the job. As the first tea ship approached Philadelphia, the Sons of Liberty greeted the skipper with a rude welcome: "What think you Captain, of a halter around your neck— ten gallons of liquid tar decanted on your pate— with the feathers of a dozen wild geese laid over that to enliven your appearance? Only think seriously of this—and fly to the place from whence you came—fly without hesitation—without the formality of a protest—and above all, . . . let us advise you to fly without the wild geese feathers." The ship quickly departed.

Similar scenes took place in every port except Boston. There, Governor Hutchinson, whose sons were the local tea consignees, decided to face down the radicals. He refused to grant clearance papers to three tea ships which, under the law, had to pay the Townshend duty within 21 days of arrival or face seizure. Hutchinson meant to force them to land the tea and pay the duty. This timetable led to urgent mass meetings for several weeks and generated a major crisis. Finally, convinced that they had no other way to block the landing of the tea, Boston radicals disguised themselves as Indians and threw 342 chests of tea, worth about £11,000 sterling (more than $700,000 in 2001 dollars), into Boston harbor on the night of December 16, 1773.

BRITAIN'S RESPONSE: THE COERCIVE ACTS

This willful destruction of private property shocked both Britain and America. The news reached Parliament in January. Convinced that severe punishment was essential to British credibility, Parliament passed four Coercive Acts during the spring of 1774. The Boston Port Act closed the port of Boston until Bostonians paid for the tea. A new Quartering Act allowed the army to quarter soldiers on civilian property if necessary. The Administration of Justice Act (a response to the Boston Massacre trials) permitted a British soldier or offi-

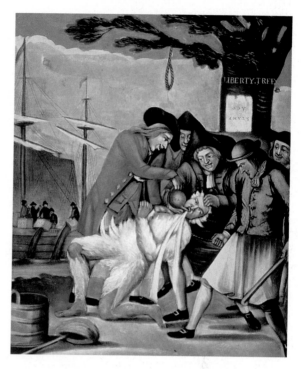

"THE BOSTONIANS PAYING THE EXCISE-MAN, OR TARRING AND FEATHERING" This London cartoon of 1774 satirizes the Sons of Liberty.

cial who was charged with a crime while carrying out his duties to be tried either in another colony or in England. Most controversial of all was the Massachusetts Government Act. It overturned the Massachusetts Charter of 1691, made the council appointive, and restricted town meetings. In effect, it made Massachusetts like other royal colonies. Before it passed, the king named General Gage, already the commander of the British army in North America, as the new governor of Massachusetts, with the clear implication that he could use military force against civilians.

Parliament also passed a fifth law, unrelated to the Coercive Acts but significant nonetheless. The Quebec Act established French civil law and the Roman Catholic Church in the Province of Quebec, provided for trial by jury in criminal but not in civil cases, gave legislative power (but not the power to tax) to an appointive governor and council, and extended the administrative boundaries of Quebec to the area between the Great Lakes and the Ohio River, saving only the legitimate charter claims of other colonies. Historians now regard the act as a

American Artists and the Revolution in Painting

Protestant England sustained few painters before the 18th century, when William Hogarth and Sir Joshua Reynolds established international reputations for their highly original creations. They were soon joined by several North Americans. Benjamin West, a self-taught Pennsylvanian, established his own studio in Philadelphia in the 1750s, then went to Italy from 1760 to 1763 to study the Renaissance masters before settling in London, where Reynolds gave him strong encouragement. Until West's arrival, heroic contemporaries were always depicted in classical grab. West's *Death of General Wolfe* (1771) depicts James Wolfe after he has fallen on the

farsighted measure that gave French Catholics the toleration that the empire had denied to Acadians 20 years earlier. Settlers from New England to Georgia were appalled. Instead of conciliation and toleration, they saw a deliberate revival of the power of New France and the Catholic Church on their northern border, this time bolstered by Britain's naval and military might. The Quebec Act added credibility to the fear that evil ministers in London were conspiring to destroy British and colonial liberties. Many British colonists suspected that the autocratic government of Quebec might become a model for restructuring their own provinces. The settlers lumped the Quebec Act together with the

battlefield of the Plains of Abraham outside Quebec in 1759. All the participants are wearing their appropriate uniforms. George III spent hours studying the painting and was so impressed that he created a special position for West as historical painter to the royal court. West's breakthrough soon established a new tradition. He was joined by John Singleton Copley, a Bostonian, who painted *The Death of the Earl of Chatham* (1781), which portrays the collapse of Chatham (William Pitt) on the floor of the House of Lords in 1778 after giving his last speech, an impassioned appeal not to drive the colonies into complete independence.

West and Copley were both moderate loyalists, although West did, on occasion, quietly donate money to American prisoners of war who had escaped and were trying to return home. The two painters also attracted patriots as students. John Trumbull of Connecticut, who had fought on the American side in the Revolution, began studying with West before the war was over and painted *Death of General Warren at Bunker's Hill* (1786). Trumbull also painted scenes of other battles and of the signing of the Declaration of Independence, as well as numerous portraits, including George Washington's. Transcending the bitterness of the war, these Americans transformed painting in their own day, the greatest cultural accomplishment of any American artist thus far in any field—literature, music, architecture, sculpture, or painting.

Coercive Acts and coined their own name for all of them: the Intolerable Acts.

THE RADICAL EXPLOSION

The interval between passage of the Boston Port Act in March 1774 and passage of the Massachusetts Government Act in May 1774 permits us to compare the response that each provoked. The Port Act was quite enforceable and immune to nullification by the colonists. It led to another round of nonimportation and to the summoning of the First Continental Congress. But the Government Act *was* nullified by the colonists. It led to war. The soldiers marching to

"The Able Doctor, or America Swallowing the Bitter Draught" This 1774 engraving by Paul Revere used "The Bostonians Paying the Excise-Man" as a model but turned it into a patriot statement. In Revere's version, the British are forcing tea down the throat of America (represented by a ravished lady, Liberty). The British also are imposing martial law in Boston.

Concord on April 19, 1775, were trying to enforce it against settlers who absolutely refused to obey it.

By the king's appointment, Gage took over the governorship of Massachusetts in May 1774, before Parliament passed the Massachusetts Government Act. In June he closed the ports of Boston and Charlestown, just north of Boston. The navy gave him more than enough power to do so. At first, Boston split over the Port Act. Many merchants wanted to abolish the Boston Committee of Correspondence and pay for the tea to avoid an economic catastrophe, but they were badly outvoted in a huge town meeting. Boston then called for a colonial union and for immediate nonimportation and nonconsumption of British goods. By then some radicals were losing patience with nonimportation as a tactic. Parliament had already shut Boston down.

Discouraging news arrived from elsewhere. A mass meeting in New York City rejected immediate nonimportation in favor of an intercolonial congress. Philadelphia followed New York's lead. In both cities, cautious merchants hoped that a congress might postpone or prevent radical measures of resistance.

This was only a momentary success. North assumed that the Coercive Acts would isolate Boston from the rest of the province, Massachusetts from the rest of New England, and New England from

the other colonies, a goal that Britain would pursue through 1777. Instead, contributions began pouring in from all the colonies to help Boston survive. The Stamp Act crisis and the Townshend crisis had been largely urban affairs. The Intolerable Acts politicized the countryside on a scale never seen before. When royal governors outside Massachusetts dismissed their assemblies to prevent them from joining the resistance movement, colonists there did what Massachusetts had done in 1768: They elected "provincial congresses," or conventions, to organize resistance. These bodies were much larger than the legal assemblies that they displaced, and they mobilized far more people. As the congresses took hold, royal government began to collapse almost everywhere.

Numerous calls for a continental congress made the movement irresistible. By June it was obvious that any congress would adopt nonimportation. Except for some details, that issue had been settled, even before the congress met, by mandates that the delegates brought with them.

Despite these signs of disaffection, Gage remained optimistic through most of the summer. Then news of the Massachusetts Government Act arrived on August 6. Gage's authority disintegrated when he tried to enforce the act, which marked the most dramatic attempt yet made by Parliament to control the internal affairs of the colonies. The "mandamus councillors," whom Gage appointed to the new upper house under the act, either resigned their seats or fled to Boston to seek the protection from the army. The Superior Court could not hold its sessions, even in Boston under the guns of the army, because jurors refused to take an oath under the new act. At the county level (the real center of royal power in the colony), popular conventions closed the courts and took charge in August and September. Gage was beginning to realize that none of his major objectives was achievable.

Before this explosion of radical activity, Gage had called for a new General Court to meet in Salem in October. Many towns sent representatives, but others followed the lead of the Worcester County Convention, which in August urged all towns to elect delegates to a provincial congress in Concord, 17 miles inland, out of range of the navy. Although Gage revoked his call for a General Court, about 90 representatives met at Salem anyway. When Gage refused to recognize them, they adjourned to Concord in early October and joined the 200 delegates already gathered there as the Massachusetts Provincial Congress. That body became the de facto government of the colony and implemented the radical demands of the Suffolk County Convention (representing Boston and its hinterland), which included a purge of unreliable militia officers, the creation of a special force of armed "minutemen" able to respond rapidly to any emergency, and the payment of taxes to the congress in Concord, not to Gage in Boston. The Provincial Congress also collected military stores at Concord and created an executive arm, the Committee of Public Safety. North assumed that Gage's army would uphold the new Massachusetts government. Instead, Gage's government survived only where the army could protect it. That excluded Salem, which was supposed to remain Gage's capital until Boston paid for the tea.

The alternative to government by consent was becoming no British authority at all in the colony. For example, in the predawn hours of September 1, Gage dispatched soldiers to confiscate 250 half-barrels of gunpowder stored a few miles outside Boston. He got the powder, but the foray started one-third of the militia of New England marching toward Boston. They turned back when assured that no one had been killed. In later raids on other stores, the colonists always beat the redcoats to the

"THE BOSTONIANS IN DISTRESS" This cartoon appeared in London in November 1774 to celebrate the success of the Boston Port Act. The city has become a cage hanging from the Liberty Tree while other settlers try to feed fish to the residents.

powder. By October, Gage's power was limited to the Boston area, which the army held. Unable to put his 3,000 soldiers to any positive use, he wrote North on October 30 that "a small Force rather encourages Resistance than terrifys." He then stunned North by asking for 20,000 redcoats, as many as had been needed to conquer Canada.

THE FIRST CONTINENTAL CONGRESS

From 1769 into 1774, colonial patriots had looked to John Wilkes in London for leadership. At the First Continental Congress, they began relying on themselves. Twelve colonies (all but Georgia) sent delegates. In September 1774, they met at Philadelphia's Carpenters' Hall, a center of artisan strength. They scarcely even debated nonimportation. The southern colonies insisted, and the New Englanders agreed, that nonimportation finally be extended to molasses, which continued to generate revenue under the penny duty of 1766. The delegates were almost unanimous in adopting nonexportation, to be taken as a second step by August 1775, if Britain had not by then redressed colonial grievances. Nonexportation was a much more radical tactic than nonimportation because it contained the implicit threat of repudiating debts to British merchants, which were normally paid off with colonial exports. Joseph Galloway, a Pennsylvania loyalist, submitted a plan of imperial union that would have required all laws affecting the colonies to be passed by both Parliament and an intercolonial congress, but his proposal was tabled by a vote of 6 colonies to 5. The Congress spent three weeks trying to define colonial rights. Everyone (even Galloway) agreed that the Coercive Acts, the Quebec Act, and all surviving revenue acts must be repealed and that infringements on trial by jury must be rejected. The delegates generally agreed on what would break the impasse, but they had trouble finding the precise language for their demands. They finally affirmed the new principle of no *legislation* without consent—but added a saving clause that affirmed colonial assent to the empire's navigation and trade acts, passed as far back as 1650.

Congress petitioned the king rather than Parliament, because patriots no longer recognized Parliament as a legitimate legislature for the colonies. Congress explained its position in separate addresses to the people of the 13 colonies, the people of Quebec, and the people of Great Britain. It took two other radical steps: It agreed to meet again in May 1775 if the British response was unsatisfactory, and it created the Association—with citizen committees in every community—to enforce its trade sanctions against Britain. Most towns and counties heartily embraced the idea, and perhaps 7,000 men served on such committees during the winter of 1774–75. In approving the Association, Congress began to act as a central government for the United Colonies.

TOWARD WAR

The news from Boston and Philadelphia shook the North ministry. "The New England Governments are in a State of Rebellion," George III told North; "blows must decide whether they are to be subject to this Country or independent." Although Franklin kept assuring the British that Congress meant exactly what it said, both North and the opposition assumed that conciliation could be achieved on lesser terms. Edmund Burke, out of office since 1766, urged a return to pre-1763 understandings without explaining how to restore the loyalty that had made them workable. "A great empire and little minds go ill together," he cautioned in an eloquent speech urging conciliation. Lord Chatham (William Pitt) introduced a bill to prohibit Parliament from taxing the colonies, to recognize the Congress, and even to ask Congress to provide revenue for North American defense and to help pay down the national debt. When a spokesman for North's ministry challenged him, Chatham retorted that his plan, if implemented, "must annihilate your power . . . and at once reduce you to that state of insignificance for which God and nature designed you." Neither plan passed.

The initiative lay, of course, with Lord North. An amiable man, he still had vague hopes for a peaceful solution to the crisis. But in January 1775 he took a step that made war inevitable. He ordered Gage to send troops to Concord, destroy the arms stored there, and arrest John Hancock and Samuel Adams. Only after sending this dispatch did he introduce his own Conciliatory Proposition, in which Parliament pledged that it would tax no colony that met its share of the cost of imperial defense and paid proper salaries to its royal officials. Britain would, however, use force against delinquent colonies. To reassure hard-liners that he was not turning soft, he introduced the New England Restraining Act on the same day. It barred New Englanders from the Atlantic fisheries and prohibited all commerce between New England and any place except Britain and the British West Indies, precisely the trade routes that Congress had resolved to block through nonimportation. Both sides were now committed to economic sanctions.

North's orders to Gage arrived before his Conciliatory Proposition reached America, and Gage obeyed. He hoped to surprise Concord with another predawn march, but Boston radicals knew about the expedition almost as soon as the orders were issued. They had already made careful preparations to alert the whole countryside. Their informant, in all likelihood, was Gage's wife, Margaret Kemble Gage, a New Jerseyan by birth. At 2 a.m. on the night of April 18–19, about 700 grenadiers and light infantry began their march toward Concord. Paul Revere, a Boston silversmith who had done as much as anyone to create the information network that he now set in motion, went dashing west with the news that "The redcoats are coming!" When he was captured past Lexington by a British patrol, Dr. Samuel Prescott, returning from a lady friend's house at the awkward hour of 1 a.m., managed to deliver the message to Concord. As the British approached Lexington Green at dawn, they found 60 to 70 militiamen drawn up to face them. The outnumbered militia began to withdraw when somebody—probably a colonial bystander and possibly also a British soldier—fired the first shot. Without orders, the British line opened fire, killing eight and wounding nine. Behind and ahead of them, like angry bees, the whole countryside surged toward them. Secrecy had become pointless, and the British broke out their regimental fifes and drums. Cheered by the tunes, they marched west toward Concord and into another world war.

THE IMPROVISED WAR

In April 1775 neither side had a plan for winning a major war. Gage's soldiers were trying to enforce acts of Parliament. The militia were fighting for a political regime that Parliament was trying to change. They drove the British from Concord Bridge and pursued them all the way to Boston. Suffering only 95 casualties, the militia inflicted 273 on the British. Had a relief force not met the battered British survivors east of Lexington, all of them might have been lost.

Lacking an adequate command or supply structure, the colonists besieged Boston. After two

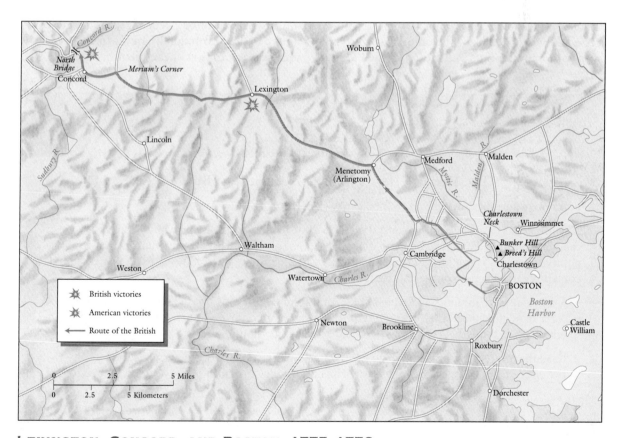

LEXINGTON, CONCORD, AND BOSTON, 1775–1776

months, Gage finally declared that all settlers bearing arms, and those who aided them, were rebels and traitors. He offered to pardon anyone who returned to his allegiance, except John Hancock and Samuel Adams. Instead of complying, the besiegers escalated the struggle two days later. They fortified the high ground on Breed's Hill (next to Bunker Hill) near Charlestown and overlooking Boston. The British sent 2,400 men, one-fifth of the garrison, to take the hills on June 17. Merely by seizing Charlestown Neck, a smaller force could have cut off the Yankee militia at low risk to itself. Instead, to prove that civilians had no chance against a regular army, General William Howe launched three frontal attacks. Secure behind their defenses, the settlers shot more than 1,000 of the attackers, including 92 officers (about one-sixth of those lost in the entire war), before they ran out of ammunition and withdrew. The defenders suffered about 370 casualties, nearly all during the retreat.

For the moment at least, patriotism seemed to make colonial farmers and artisans a match for Britain's professional army. But as the war progressed, "Bunker Hillism" became a dangerous delusion. Time after time, Americans fortified a hill and then waited for the stupid frontal assault that never came. The British got the message at Bunker Hill. A few more such victories, reflected one of them, and no one would be left alive to carry the news to London.

Well into 1776 both sides fought an improvised war. In May 1775 Vermont and Massachusetts militia took Fort Ticonderoga on Lake Champlain and seized the artillery and gunpowder that would be used months later in the siege of Boston. Crown Point also fell. With nearly all of their forces in Boston, the British were too weak to defend other positions or to intervene in the short Indian conflict, Lord Dunmore's War, that broke out in the upper Ohio valley in 1774. The collapse of royal government meant that the rebels now controlled the militia and most of the royal powderhouses.

During the Revolutionary War, the militia became the key to political allegiance. Compulsory service with the militia politicized many waverers, who decided that they really were patriots when a redcoat shot at them or when they drove a loyalist into exile. The militia kept the countryside committed to the Revolution wherever the British army was too weak to overwhelm them.

LINK TO THE PAST

"'The Decisive Day Is Come': The Battle of Bunker Hill"

http://www.masshist.org/bh

This site makes available to the general public a 2001 exhibition on Bunker Hill (June 17, 1775) at the Massachusetts Historical Society. It contains an essay on the battle, a timeline, several contemporary maps and views of Boston and Charlestown, biographies of the major participants, and 10 contemporary accounts of the confrontation.

1. Go to those 10 accounts and compare General John Burgoyne's printed letter, written June 25, eight days after the battle, with the terse diary entry of Nathaniel Ober, a patriot. How important do they think this battle was? Do they agree on its significance?

2. Read the brief American "Address to the [British] Soldiers," an effort to persuade them of the justice of the colonial cause. Did these participants consider the conflict a revolution or a civil war?

THE BATTLE OF LEXINGTON, APRIL 19, 1775 Ralph Earl's painting, which was engraved by Amos Doolittle in 1775, portrays the opening shots of the Revolutionary War. The British are firing a volley into the Lexington militia, who are trying to leave the field without offering resistance. In fact, the first British soldiers who fired did so without orders, possibly in response to a shot from a colonial bystander. The militia was indeed trying to withdraw.

THE SECOND CONTINENTAL CONGRESS

When the Second Continental Congress met in May 1775, it inherited the war. For months it pursued the conflicting strategies of resistance and conciliation. It voted to turn the undisciplined men besieging Boston into a "Continental Army." As in earlier wars, the soldiers were volunteers who expected to serve for only a few months, or a single campaign. In the absence of royal authority, they elected their officers, who tried to win their obedience through persuasion, not command. Supplying the soldiers with food and munitions became a huge problem.

Most of the men were Yankees who would have preferred to serve under their own officers, but Congress realized that a successful war effort would have to engage the other colonies as well. On June 15, at the urging of John Adams of Massachusetts, Congress made George Washington of Virginia commanding general. When Washington took charge of the Continental Army, he was appalled at the poor discipline among the soldiers and their casual familiarity with their officers. He insisted that officers behave with a dignity that would instill obedience, and as the months passed, most of them won his respect.

As the year ended, however, nearly all the men went home, and Washington had to train a new army for 1776. But enthusiasm for the cause remained strong, and fresh volunteers soon filled his camp.

In June 1775, Congress, fearing that the British might recruit French Canadians to attack New York or New England, authorized an invasion of Canada, designed to win over the French before they could side with the British. Two forces of 1,000 men each moved northward. One, under General Richard Montgomery, took Montreal in November. The other, commanded by Colonel Benedict Arnold, advanced on Quebec through the Maine wilderness and laid siege to the city, where Montgomery joined Arnold in December. With enlistments due to expire at year's end, they decided to assault the city, partly to get maximum service out of their men, partly to inspire some of them to reenlist. Their attack on December 31 was a disaster. Nearly half of the 900 men still with them were killed, wounded, or captured. Montgomery was killed and Arnold wounded. Both were hailed as American heroes.

The colonial objective in this fighting was still to restore government by consent under the Crown. After rejecting Lord North's Conciliatory Proposition out of hand, Congress approved an "Olive

Branch Petition" to George III on July 5, 1775, in the hope of ending the bloodshed. Moderates, led by John Dickinson, strongly favored the measure. The petition affirmed the colonists' loyalty to the Crown, did not even mention "rights," and implored the king to take the initiative in devising "a happy and permanent reconciliation." Another document written mostly by Thomas Jefferson, "The Declaration of the Causes and Necessities of Taking Up Arms," set forth the colonies' grievances and justified their armed resistance. "We have counted the cost of this contest," Jefferson proclaimed, "and find nothing so dreadful as voluntary slavery." Like the Olive Branch Petition, the declaration assured the British people "that we mean not to dissolve that Union which has so long and so happily subsisted between us." The king's refusal even to receive this moderate petition strengthened colonial radicals. It reached London along with news of Bunker Hill. George III replied with a formal proclamation of rebellion on August 23.

Congress began to function more and more like a government, but with few exceptions, it assumed royal rather than parliamentary powers, which were taken over by the individual colonies. Congress did not tax or regulate trade, beyond encouraging nonimportation. It passed no laws. It took command of the Continental Army, printed paper money, opened diplomatic relations with Indian nations, took over the postal service, and decided which government was legitimate in individual colonies—all functions previously performed by the Crown. In short, Congress thought of itself as a temporary plural executive for the continent, not as a legislature.

WAR AND LEGITIMACY, 1775–1776

Throughout 1775 the British reacted with fitful displays of violence and grim threats of turning slaves and Indians against the settlers. When the weak British forces could neither restore order nor make good their threats, they conciliated no one, enraged thousands, and undermined British claims to legitimacy. The navy burned Falmouth (now Portland), Maine, in October. On November 7, John Murray, earl of Dunmore and governor of Virginia, offered freedom to any slaves of rebel planters who would join his 200 redcoats. About 800 slaves mustered under his banner only to fall

victim to smallpox after the Virginia militia defeated them in a single action. Dunmore bombarded Norfolk in retaliation on January 1, setting several buildings ablaze. The patriot militia, who considered Norfolk a loyalist bastion, burned the rest of the city and then blamed Dunmore for its destruction. Overall, his campaign undermined whatever loyalist sentiment survived among Virginia planters beyond Norfolk.

The British effort suffered other disasters in Boston and the Carolinas. The greatest colonial victory came at Boston, where most of the British army lay virtually imprisoned. On March 17, 1776, after Washington fortified Dorchester Heights south of the city and brought heavy artillery (from Ticonderoga) to bear on it, the British pulled out and sailed for Nova Scotia. A loyalist uprising by Highland Scots in North Carolina was crushed at Moore's Creek Bridge on February 27, and a British naval expedition sent to take Charleston was repulsed with heavy losses in June. Cherokee attacks against Virginia in 1776 failed because they occurred after Dunmore had left and did not fit into any larger general strategy. Before spring turned to summer, patriot forces had won control of the territory of all 13 colonies. Except in East and West Florida, Quebec, and Nova Scotia, the British had been driven from the continent.

INDEPENDENCE

George III's dismissal of the Olive Branch Petition left moderates no option but to yield or fight. In late 1775, Congress created a committee to correspond with foreign powers. By early 1776 the delegates from New England, Virginia, and Georgia already favored independence, but they knew that unless they won over all 13 colonies, the British would have the leverage to divide them. The British attack on Charleston in June nudged the Carolinas toward independence.

Resistance to independence came mostly from the mid-Atlantic colonies, from New York through Maryland. Elsewhere, provincial congresses had supplanted the colonial assemblies in 1774 and 1775. In the middle colonies, however, both assemblies and congresses met and competed for the loyalties of the people. None of the five legal assemblies in the mid-Atlantic region ever repudiated the Crown. All of them had to be overthrown along with royal (or proprietary) government itself. The last royal governor to be driven from his post was New Jersey's William Franklin, Benjamin's natural son, who was arrested on June 19, 1776, to prevent him from summoning a new session of the regular assembly.

In the struggle for middle colony loyalties, Thomas Paine's pamphlet, *Common Sense*, became a huge success. First published in Philadelphia in January 1776, it sold more than 100,000 copies within a few months and reached more people than any other colonial tract ever had. Paine, a recent immigrant from England who had waged his own contests with the British government, wasted no reverence on Britain's mixed and balanced constitution. To him, George III was "the Pharaoh of England" and "the Royal Brute of Great Britain." Paine attacked monarchy and aristocracy as degenerate institutions and urged Americans to unite under a simple republican government of their own. "Reconciliation and ruin are nearly related," he insisted. "There is something very absurd, in supposing a Continent to be perpetually governed by an island."

The British continued to alienate the colonists. The king named Lord George Germain, a hardliner, as secretary of state for the American colonies, and thus as war minister. Germain tried to hire 20,000 Russian mercenaries who, smirked one British official, would make "charming visitors at New York and civilize that part of America wonderfully." When that effort failed, the British bought 17,000 soldiers from Hesse and other north German states. (The colonists called them all "Hessians.") To Jefferson, that action was "the last stab to [the] agonizing affection" that had once bound together the people of Britain and North America. Disturbing (though false) rumors suggested that Britain and France were about to sign a "partition treaty" dividing the eastern half of North America between them. Many congressmen concluded, some of them sadly, that only independence could counter these dangers by engaging Britain's European enemies on America's side. As long as conciliation was the goal, France would not participate, because American success would mean restoring the British Empire to its former glory. But Louis XVI (1774–93) might well help the colonies win their independence if that meant crippling Britain permanently.

From April to June, about 90 communities issued calls for independence. Most of them looked no further back than 1775 to justify their demand. The king had placed the colonists outside his protection, was waging war against them, and had hired foreigners to kill them. Self-defense demanded a permanent separation.

Congress finally broke the mid-Atlantic stalemate. On May 15, 1776, it voted to suppress "every kind of authority" under the British Crown, thus giving radicals an opportunity to seize power in Pennsylvania and New Jersey. Moderates remained in control in New York, Delaware, and Maryland, but they reluctantly accepted independence as inevitable. In early June, Congress postponed a vote on independence but named a committee of five, including Jefferson, John Adams, and Franklin, to prepare a declaration that would vindicate America's decision to the whole world.

With the necessary votes in place, Congress on July 2 passed Richard Henry Lee's resolution "that these United colonies are, and of right, ought to be, Free and Independent States; . . . and that all political connexion between them, and the state of Great Britain, is, and ought to be, totally dissolved." Two days later, 12 colonies, with New York abstaining for the time being, unanimously approved Jefferson's Declaration of Independence, as amended by Congress.

"We hold these truths to be self-evident, that all men are created equal, that they are endowed by their Creator with certain unalienable Rights, that among these are Life, Liberty, and the pursuit of Happiness," Congress proclaimed in what is perhaps the most famous statement ever made in American public life. Whenever "any Form of Government becomes destructive of these ends, it is the Right of the People to alter or to abolish it, and to institute new Government, laying its foundation on such principles . . . as to them shall seem most likely to effect their Safety and Happiness." The longest section of the Declaration indicted George III as a tyrant.

During the three days that Congress was proclaiming American independence, the first ships of the largest armada yet sent across the Atlantic by any European state began landing British soldiers on Staten Island. Americans celebrated the creation of their new republic at the very moment that they faced a military challenge more ominous than any they had ever confronted before.

1776 (1972)

**Directed by Peter H. Hunt. Starring William Daniels (John Adams),
Virginia Vestoff (Abigail), Ken Howard (Thomas Jefferson),
Howard da Silva (Benjamin Franklin), and Blythe Danner (Martha).**

1776 does not pretend to be a historical re-creation of actual events. It is, rather, an intelligent, off-beat, winning fantasy conceived by Northeasterners at the expense, mostly, of Virginians.

1776 is a screen adaptation of a musical comedy produced on the New York stage by Stuart Ostrow. Some scenes were filmed on location at Independence Hall in Philadelphia. Sherman Edwards's lively music and lyrics carry the drama from May 1776 to the signing of the Declaration of Independence on July 4.

Director Peter Hunt made his motion picture debut with *1776*. He also directed *Give 'Em Hell, Harry* in 1975 and the 1997 Broadway version of *The Scarlet Pimpernel*, along with various films made for television.

The movie opens with John Adams (William Daniels) trying to force the Second Continental Congress into a serious debate on independence. The delegates respond in a fulsome chorus, shouting: "Sit down, John! Sit down, John! For God's sake, John, sit down!" while some of them complain about the flies and the oppressive heat. Adams stalks out and then unburdens himself to his wife, Abigail (Virginia Vestoff), still at home in Massachusetts. Abigail in her reply urges him to "Tell the Congress to declare / independency. / Then sign your name, get out of there / And hurry home to me."

With Benjamin Franklin's help, Adams finally achieves his goal. The film's bite derives from its determination to move Adams to the center of the story, rather than Thomas Jefferson (Ken Howard), whom Adams and Franklin (Howard da Silva) finally maneuver into writing the first draft of the Declaration, much against his will. Adams declines to write the actual Declaration because, as he explains to Franklin and Jefferson, "If I'm the one to do it / They'll run their quill pens through it. / I'm obnoxious and disliked, / You know that, Sir."

Jefferson also declines at first because he pines for Martha (Blythe Danner), his young bride, still in Virginia. "Mr. Adams, damn you Mr. Adams! / . . . once again you stand between me and my lovely bride. / Oh, Mr. Adams you are driving me to homicide!"

This outburst prompts the other members of the drafting committee to chorus: "Homicide! Homicide! We may see murder yet!" But instead, Jefferson accepts the burden. When he is unable to write, Adams and Franklin bring Martha to Philadelphia so that he can concentrate his energies on the Declaration.

Some of the delegates appear as mere caricatures, especially Richard Henry Lee of Virginia and James Wilson of Pennsylvania, two articulate delegates who, in real life, played important roles in creating the new

CONCLUSION

Between 1763 and 1776 Britain and the colonies became trapped in a series of self-fulfilling prophecies. The British feared that without major reforms to guarantee Parliament's control of the empire, the colonies would drift toward independence. Colonial resistance to the new policies convinced the British that a movement for independence was indeed under way, a perception that led to even sterner measures. Until a few months before it happened, nearly all colonists denied that they desired independence, but they began to fear that the British government was determined to deprive them of their rights as Englishmen. Britain's policy drove them toward a closer union with one another and finally provoked armed resistance. With the onset of war, both sides felt vindicated. The thousands of redcoats heading toward America did not bode well for colonial liberties. When the colonists finally did leave the empire, British ministers believed that their predictions had indeed come true.

Both sides were wrong. The British had no systematic plan to destroy liberty in North America,

republic. The film addresses the slavery question by showing South Carolina's fierce opposition to inclusion of an antislavery clause, a point on which Adams, Jefferson, and Franklin reluctantly yield. The film, like the play on which it is based, works well to deliver an articulate, entertaining taste of history.

1776 is a lively musical depicting events from May 1776 to the signing of the Declaration of Independence on July 4.

and until the winter of 1775–76 hardly any colonists favored independence. But the three imperial crises undermined mutual confidence and brought about what no one had desired in 1765, or even 1774—an independent American nation. Unable to govern North America, Britain now faced the grim task of conquering it instead.

Suggested Readings begin on page SR-1.
For Web activities and resources
related to this chapter, go to
http://www.harcourtcollege.com/history.murrin

CHAPTER 6

THE REVOLUTIONARY REPUBLIC

THE PASSAGE OF THE DELAWARE

This painting by Thomas Sully, completed in 1818, celebrates George Washington's attack on the Hessian garrison of Trenton, New Jersey, on December 26, 1776, as a turning point of the Revolutionary War.

The Revolutionary War killed a higher percentage of Americans who fought in it than any other American conflict except the Civil War. It was a civil war in its own right. Neighbors were more likely to shoot at neighbors during the Revolution than during the Civil War, a little less than a hundred years later, when the geographical line separating the two sides would be much sharper. Twice, in 1776 and again in 1780, the British had a chance to win a decisive military victory, but in both campaigns the Americans somehow rallied. The Americans won only by bringing in France as an ally. France brought in Spain.

During the war, more and more Americans began to think in crude racial categories. Ideas about racial inferiority clashed sharply with claims of universal rights and human equality. As settlers and Indians, whites and blacks redefined their differences, they often resorted to racial stereotypes. Most Indians and slaves hoped that Britain would win the war.

Even as the war raged and the economy disintegrated, Americans drafted state constitutions and eloquent bills of rights that reached far beyond the racism many of them felt. They knew they were attempting something daring, something that had never succeeded in the past—the creation of a stable, enduring republic. In the Atlantic world, political stability seemed to require a monarchy. The English monarchy, for example, was about 1,000 years old. No republic had ever lasted that long. Educated people knew a great deal about the city-states of classical Greece and about republican Rome—how they had called forth the noblest sentiments of patriotism for a time and then decayed into despotisms. Still, once Americans broke with Britain, they warmly embraced republicanism and never looked back. They were able to build viable republican governments because they grasped the voluntaristic dynamics of their society. They knew they had to restructure their governments through persuasive means. The use of force against armed fellow citizens would be self-defeating.

The war also demonstrated how weak Congress was, even after ratification of the Articles of Confederation in 1781. Congress could not pay its debts. It could not expel the British from their western military posts or defeat the Indians of the Ohio country. In the Northwest Ordinance of 1787, Congress nevertheless announced plans to create new western states and to admit them to the Union as full equals of the original 13. During that same summer, the Philadelphia Convention drafted

CHRONOLOGY

1769	Spanish found San Diego
1775	Settlement of Kentucky begins
1776	Virginia becomes first state to adopt a permanent constitution and bill of rights • British forces land on Staten Island • Declaration of Independence adopted • Pennsylvania constitution creates unicameral legislature • British win battle of Long Island; New York City falls • Washington wins at Trenton
1777	Washington wins at Princeton • Howe takes Philadelphia • Burgoyne surrenders at Saratoga • Congress completes the Articles of Confederation
1778	Franco-American alliance negotiated
1779	Indians form confederation from the Gulf to the Great Lakes • Spain declares war on Britain • Continental dollar collapses
1780	Massachusetts constitution approved • Pennsylvania adopts gradual emancipation • British take Charleston and overrun South Carolina • Gordon riots in London discredit other reformers • Arnold's treason uncovered • Americans win at King's Mountain
1781	Continental Army mutinies • Americans win at Cowpens • Congress creates executive departments • Articles of Confederation ratified • Cornwallis surrenders at Yorktown
1782	Gnadenhutten massacre leaves 100 unarmed Indians dead
1783	Peace of Paris recognizes American independence
1785	Congress passes Land Ordinance
1786	Virginia passes Statute for Religious Freedom • Annapolis convention meets
1786–87	Shays's Rebellion in Massachusetts protests taxes and economic woes
1787	Congress passes the Northwest Ordinance • Philadelphia Convention drafts a new federal Constitution
1787–88	Eleven states ratify the Constitution
1789	First federal Congress sends Bill of Rights to the states
1799	New York adopts gradual emancipation
1804	New Jersey adopts gradual emancipation

a new Constitution for the United States. After ratification by 11 states in 1787 and 1788, it went into effect in April 1789. The federal system it created was the most distinctive achievement of the Revolutionary generation.

This chapter will focus on the following major questions:

- How did American constitutionalism after 1776 differ from the British constitutional principles that the colonists had accepted and revered before 1776?
- Why, given that the Declaration of Independence proclaimed that all men are created equal, did most Indians and blacks, when given the chance, side with Britain?
- In what ways did the values shared by independent householders limit the reforms that the Revolution could offer to other Americans?
- The Articles of Confederation generally favored small states, especially in giving all states one vote in Congress. Why then did large states ratify quickly while three small states held up final ratification for years? The Constitution shifted power to large states. Why then did most small states ratify quickly while every large state except Pennsylvania came close to rejecting the new government?

HEARTS AND MINDS: THE NORTHERN WAR, 1776–1777

The men who ruled Britain believed that the loss of the colonies would be a fatal blow to British power. Thus, the price of patriotism escalated once independence became the goal. Britain raised more soldiers and larger fleets than ever before and more than doubled its national debt. Americans, too confident after their early successes, staggered under the onslaught.

THE BRITISH OFFENSIVE

The first setback came in Canada. The Americans, devastated by smallpox, had to retreat from Quebec when a fresh British force sailed up the St. Lawrence in May 1776. By July, Sir Guy Carleton drove them back into northern New York, to Fort Ticonderoga on Lake Champlain. Both sides built ships to control that strategic waterway. Largely through Benedict Arnold's efforts, the Americans held, and Carleton returned to Canada for the winter.

Farther south, Richard, viscount Howe, admiral of the British fleet, and his brother General William Howe prepared an awesome striking force on Staten Island. Because both had pro-American reputations in Britain, the Howes also acted as peace commissioners, with power to restore whole colonies to the king's peace and to pardon individual rebels. They hoped to avoid using their huge army, but when they wrote George Washington to open negotiations, he refused to accept the letter because it did not address him as "General." To do so would have recognized the legitimacy of his appointment. Benjamin Franklin, an old friend of the Howes, wrote that "it must give your lordship pain to be sent so far on so hopeless a business." Unable to negotiate, the Howes had to fight.

Since spring, Washington had moved his army from Boston to New York City, where he had about 19,000 men to face more than 30,000 redcoats and Hessians. Early successes had kept morale high among American forces and helped to sustain the *rage militaire* (warlike enthusiasm) that had prompted thousands to volunteer in 1775 and 1776, including 4,000 veterans of 1775 who reenlisted for 1776. Although some served in the Continental Army and others with state militia units, the difference between the two forces was still minimal. Neither of them gave formal military training, and the men in both served only for short terms.

Washington, who knew that civilian morale could be decisive, was reluctant to abandon any large city. Against conventional military wisdom, he divided his inferior force and sent half of it from Manhattan to Long Island. Most of the men dug in on Brooklyn Heights, just two miles from lower Manhattan, and waited for a frontal attack. The British invaded Long Island, a loyalist stronghold, and on August 27, 1776, sent a force around the American left flank through unguarded Jamaica Pass. While Hessians feinted a frontal assault, the flanking force crushed the American left and rear and sent the survivors reeling.

The Howes did nothing to prevent the evacuation of the rest of the American army to Manhattan, even though the navy could have cut them off.

Instead, the British opened informal talks with several members of Congress on Staten Island on September 11, without acknowledging Congress's legality. The talks collapsed when the Americans insisted that the British recognize their independence before discussing substantive issues. Washington evacuated lower Manhattan. The British took New York City, much of which was destroyed by an accidental fire on September 21. The Howes then appealed directly to the people to lay down their arms and return to British allegiance within 60 days in exchange for a full pardon. In southern New York state, thousands complied.

In October, the Howes drove Washington out of Manhattan and Westchester and then turned on two garrisons he had left behind. On November 16, at a cost of 460 casualties, the British forced 3,000 men to surrender at Fort Washington on the Manhattan side of the Hudson River. General Nathanael Greene, a lame Rhode Island Quaker who had given up pacifism for soldiering, saved his men on the New Jersey side by abandoning Fort Lee, including all his supplies.

The Howes probably could have destroyed Washington's army on Long Island or Manhattan, but they knew what they were doing. British victories and the American reliance on short-term volunteers were destroying Washington's army. British success seemed to prove that no American force could stand before a properly organized British army. But to capture Washington's entire army would have been a political embarrassment, leading to massive treason trials, executions, and great bitterness. Instead, Britain's impressive victories demoralized Americans and encouraged them to go home, with or without their muskets. In September, 27,000 Americans stood fit for duty in the northern theater (including the Canadian border); by December, only 6,000 remained, most of whom intended to leave when their enlistments expired on December 31.

The Howes' strategy nearly worked. In December British forces swept across New Jersey as far south as Burlington. They captured Charles Lee, next in command after Washington, and Richard Stockton, a signer of the Declaration of Independence. Several thousand New Jersey residents, including Stockton, took the king's oath. To seal off Long Island Sound from both ends, the Howes also captured Newport, Rhode Island. Many observers

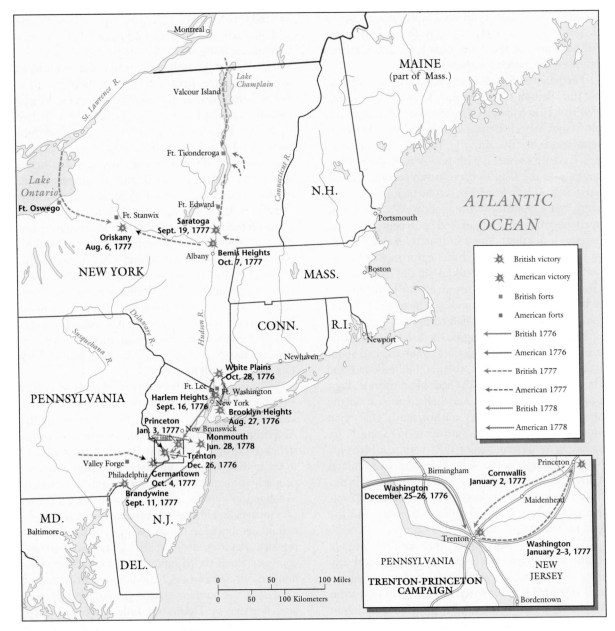

REVOLUTIONARY WAR IN THE NORTHERN STATES

thought the war was all but over as sad remnants of the Continental Army crossed the Delaware River into Pennsylvania, confiscating all boats along the way so that the British could not follow them. One general believed that the time had come to "bargain away the Bubble of Independency for British Liberty well secured." Charles Carroll, another signer of the Declaration, agreed. Even Jefferson began to think about the terms on which a restoration of the monarchy might be acceptable.

THE TRENTON-PRINCETON CAMPAIGN

Washington knew he had to do something dramatic to restore morale and encourage his soldiers to reenlist. On the night of December 25, 1776, he crossed the ice-choked Delaware and marched south, surprising the Trenton garrison at dawn. At almost no cost to the attackers, 1,000 Hessians, suffering from Christmas hangovers, surrendered. The British sent their most energetic general, Charles, earl Cornwallis, south with 8,000 men to "bag the fox"—Washington and the 5,000 Continentals and militia still with him. Cornwallis caught him at Trenton near sunset on January 2 but decided to wait until dawn before attacking. British patrols watched the Delaware to prevent another escape across the river, but Washington tried nothing of the kind. Leaving his campfires burning, he muffled the wheels of his wagons and guns and stole around the British left flank, heading north. At dawn, he met a British regiment just beginning its march from Princeton to Trenton. The Battle of Princeton amounted to a series of sharp clashes in which the Americans, with a five-to-one edge, mauled yet another outpost.

Washington's two quick victories had an enormous impact on the war, although they inspired few reenlistments. The Howes, who until January had shown a firm grasp of revolutionary warfare, blundered in not hounding Washington's remnant of an army to its destruction after Princeton. Instead, afraid that Washington might pick off their outposts one at a time, they called in their garrisons and concentrated the army along the Raritan River from New Brunswick to the sea. As the British departed, the militia returned, asking who had sworn oaths to the king. Those who had taken the oath now groveled, as the price of acceptance, or fled to British lines. The Howes had encouraged loyalists to come forward and then abandoned them to the king's enemies. The Hessians had aroused fierce hatred by looting and raping their way across New Jersey. Together, the British and the Hessians had lost the hearts and minds of the settlers. In Howe's 1777 campaign, few would be willing to declare for the Crown. The Revolution survived.

THE CAMPAIGNS OF 1777 AND FOREIGN INTERVENTION

Britain's thoughtful strategy of 1776 gave way to incoherence in 1777. The Howes again had a plan for winning the war, but it required 20,000 reinforcements that did not exist. Instead, Lord George Germain, Britain's war minister, ordered the Howes to take Philadelphia. He also sent John Burgoyne, a poet and playwright as well as a general, to Canada with orders to march his army south and link up with the garrison of New York City, commanded by Sir Henry Clinton. A small force under Barry St. Leger was to march down the Mohawk valley and threaten Albany from the west. When few reinforcements reached the Howes, they rejected an overland march to Philadelphia as too risky and decided to invade by sea, a decision that allowed Washington to shift men north to oppose Burgoyne.

The British campaign made little sense. If the point of Burgoyne's march was to move his army to New York City, he should have gone by sea. If the point was to force a battle with New Englanders, his army should have been larger. And if Howe's army—Britain's biggest—would not challenge Washington's, who would?

THE LOSS OF PHILADELPHIA

After Trenton and Princeton, Washington recruited a virtually new army in 1777. He demanded stricter discipline and longer terms of enlistment. Congress responded by raising the number of lashes a soldier could receive from 39 to 100, and by promising a cash bonus to anyone enlisting for three years and a land bounty to anyone serving for the duration. Congress never came close to raising the 75,000 men it hoped for, but these new policies did create a solid foundation for the Continental Line, or Army. Longer terms made military training a real possibility, which in turn made the Continentals much more professional than the militia. These improvements took time, however, and did not take hold until 1778 and later, after the first year of service.

The Continental Army acquired its own distinctive character. The men who signed up were often poor. About half of the New Jersey Line came from families not on the tax rolls. Some recruits were British deserters. Short-term militia, by contrast, usually held a secure place in their communities and were more likely than the Continentals to be church members. As the 1777 recruits came in, the two northern armies, swelled by militia, grew to about 28,000 men fit for duty—17,000 in northern New York, and 11,000 under Washington.

The Howes sailed south from New York with 13,000 men. When river pilots could not guarantee a safe ascent up the Delaware against American fire, the fleet sailed on to Chesapeake Bay and landed the troops at Head of Elk, Maryland, on August 24. The British marched toward Philadelphia through southeastern Pennsylvania, a region thickly populated with loyalists and neutral Quakers. Few militia turned out to help Washington, but most residents, aware of the atrocities committed by the Hessians in New Jersey, fled rather than greet the British army as liberators. The British burned many of their abandoned farm houses.

After his experience in New York, Washington was wary of being trapped in a city. Instead of trying to hold Philadelphia, he took up strong posi-

CONGRESS FLEEING PHILADELPHIA BY BALLOON, 1777 This British cartoon mocked Congress as it fled from the British army in the 1777 campaign. Hot air balloon flights, still experimental, were becoming a popular rage in France and Britain. The first flight across the English Channel would occur in 1783.

tions at Brandywine Creek along the British line of march. On September 11, Howe again outmaneuvered him, drove in his right flank, inflicted 1,000 casualties while suffering 500, and forced the Americans to retreat. Congress fled to Lancaster, and the British occupied Philadelphia on September 26. Eight days later, Washington tried to surprise an outpost at Germantown, but the British rallied from early losses and drove him off.

Washington headed west to Valley Forge, where the army endured a miserable winter. There, Frederich Wilhelm, baron von Steuben, a Prussian serving with the Continental Army who would soon become a major general, devised a drill manual based on Prussian standards that he modified for use by the Americans. Through his efforts, the Continentals became far more soldierly. Other European volunteers also helped. From France came the marquis de Lafayette and Johann, baron de Kalb. The Poles sent Thaddeus Kosciuszko (a talented engineer) and Casimir, count Pulaski. De Kalb and Pulaski died in American service. By the last years of the war, perhaps one-fifth of all Continental officers were professional soldiers from Europe, who gave the American officer corps an aristocratic tone that alarmed civilians.

SARATOGA

In northern New York, Fort Ticonderoga fell to Burgoyne on June 2, 1777, but little went right for the British after that. Colonel St. Leger, with 900 soldiers and an equal number of Indians, reached Fort Schuyler in the Mohawk valley in August and defeated 800 militia at Oriskany, but when Benedict Arnold approached with an additional 1,000 men, the Indians fled and St. Leger withdrew to Oswego.

Burgoyne's army of 7,800, advancing from Ticonderoga toward Albany, was overwhelmed in the upper Hudson valley. As his supply line to Canada grew longer, American militia swarmed behind him to cut it. When he detached 700 Hessians to forage in the Green Mountains, they ran into 2,600 militia raised by John Stark of New Hampshire. On August 16 at Bennington, Vermont, Stark killed or captured nearly all of them. A relief force of 650 Hessians was also mauled. By the time Burgoyne's surviving soldiers reached the Hudson and started toward Albany, the Americans under Horatio Gates outnumbered them 3 to 1. The British got as far as Bemis Heights, 30 miles north of Albany, but failed to break through in two costly battles on September 19 and October 7, with Arnold again distinguishing himself. Burgoyne retreated 10 miles to Saratoga, where he surrendered his entire army on October 17.

FRENCH INTERVENTION

Colonial resistance delighted the French court, which was still recovering from its defeats in the Seven Years' War. In May 1776, Louis XVI authorized secret aid to the American rebels. A French dramatist, Pierre-Augustin Caron de Beaumarchais, author of *The Barber of Seville* (1775) and *The Marriage of Figaro* (1784), set up the firm of Roderique Hortalez et Compagnie to smuggle supplies through Britain's weak blockade of the American coast. (The British navy had deployed most of its ships to transport and supply the army and had few left for blockade duty.) About 90 percent of the gunpowder used by Americans from 1775 to 1777 came either from captured British supplies or from abroad. Hortalez et Compagnie's 14 ships brought in most of what arrived from Europe. Without this aid, the Americans could not have continued the war.

In December 1776 Benjamin Franklin arrived in France as an agent of the American Congress. Although the French court could not officially receive him without risking a declaration of war by Britain, the 70-year-old Franklin took Parisian society by storm by adopting simple clothes, replacing his wig with a fur cap, and playing to perfection the role of an innocent man of nature. Through Beaumarchais, he kept the supplies flowing and organized privateering raids on British commerce, which the French court claimed it could not stop.

The fall of Philadelphia and Burgoyne's surrender at Saratoga persuaded the French to intervene openly. The loss of Philadelphia alarmed Foreign Minister Charles Gravier, comte de Vergennes. He feared that Congress might give up unless France entered the war. By contrast Burgoyne's defeat convinced Louis that the Americans could win and that intervention was a good risk. Franklin and Vergennes signed two treaties in February 1778. One, a commercial agreement, granted Americans generous trading terms with France. In the other, France made a perpetual alliance with the United States, recognized American independence, agreed to fight until Britain conceded independence, and disavowed all territorial ambitions on the North American continent. Americans could not have

"THE BALLANCE OF POWER" This cartoon appeared in London in January 1781 when Britain again seemed to be winning the war. Britannia's might outweighs the formidable coalition of European powers arrayed against her.

hoped for more. Vergennes also brought Spain into the war a year later.

The Franco-American treaties stunned London. Lord North tried to resign, but the king would not let him. Lord Chatham, warning that American independence would be a disaster for Britain, collapsed in the House of Lords after finishing his speech and died a month later. North put together a plan of conciliation that conceded virtually everything but independence and sent a distinguished group of commissioners under Frederick Howard, earl of Carlisle, to present it to Congress and block the French alliance. In 1775 such terms would have resolved the imperial crisis, but in June 1778 Congress recognized them as a sign of British desperation and rejected them out of hand.

Americans now expected a quick victory, while the British regrouped. George III declared war on France, recalled the Howe brothers, and ordered General Clinton to abandon Philadelphia. Wary of being caught at sea by the French, Clinton marched overland to New York in June 1778. Washington's newly disciplined army attacked his rear at Monmouth, New Jersey, and almost drove the British from the field, but the redcoats rallied and won a draw. Fearing a French invasion of the British Isles while most of the Royal Navy was in American waters, the British redeployed their forces on a global scale. They stood on the defensive in America through most of 1778 and 1779 and even evacuated Newport, but loyalists often raided Connecticut and New Jersey from their bases in New York City, Staten Island, and Long Island.

SPANISH EXPANSION AND INTERVENTION

Like France, Spain was eager to avenge old defeats against Britain. The Spanish king, Charles III (1759–88), had endured the loss of Florida shortly after ascending the throne but had received Louisiana from France in compensation. Spanish rule there did not begin smoothly. In 1769 Spain suppressed a small revolt against its restrictions on trade, but in later years, when its trade policy became more favorable, Louisiana enjoyed a level of prosperity it had never before known. The province

THE MISSION OF SAN CARLOS BORROMEO The Spanish mission at Carmel, California, was founded in 1770.

attracted 2,000 immigrants from the Canary Islands, perhaps 3,000 Acadian refugees, and other French settlers from the Illinois country, some of whom founded St. Louis in 1764. Louisiana remained heavily French even under Spanish rule.

During this time, Spaniards also moved into California, partly in response to the migration of Russian hunters into Alaska. Spain founded San Diego in 1769. In the next few years, Spaniards explored the Pacific coastline as far north as southern Alaska, set up an outpost at San Francisco Bay, and built a series of Franciscan missions under Junípero Serra. With little danger from other Europeans, Spain sent relatively few soldiers to California. In fact, its California frontier duplicated many aspects of the earlier Florida missions. For the last time in the history of North America, missionaries set the tone for a whole province. As in Florida, the Indians died in appalling numbers from European diseases, and many objected to the harsh discipline of the missions.

Charles III recognized the danger of one imperial power urging the subjects of another to revolt and never made a direct alliance with the United States, but in 1779 he joined France in its war against Britain, hoping to retake Gibraltar and to stabilize Spain's North American borders. Although Spain failed to take Gibraltar, it overran British West Florida. At the end of the war Britain ceded East Florida as well. By 1783, for the first time in a century, Spain once again controlled the entire coastline of the Gulf of Mexico.

THE RECONSTITUTION OF AUTHORITY

In 1776 the prospect of independence touched off an intense debate among Americans on constitutionalism. Now that the British Crown was no longer the source of legitimacy, they had to rebuild their governments along more popular lines. They agreed that every state needed a written constitution to limit the powers of government in terms more explicit than the precedents, statutes, and customs that made up Britain's unwritten constitution. They moved toward ever fuller expressions of popular sovereignty—the theory that all power must be derived from the people themselves. For four years, these lively debates sparked a learning process

until, by 1780, Americans knew what they meant when they insisted that the people of a republic must be their own governors.

JOHN ADAMS AND THE SEPARATION OF POWERS

No one learned more from this process than John Adams. When Thomas Paine advocated a simple, unicameral legislature to carry out the people's will, Adams took alarm. He replied in *Thoughts on Government*, a tract that influenced the men drafting Virginia's constitution, which other states then imitated.

In 1776 Adams was already moving away from the British notion of a "mixed and balanced" constitution, in which government by "King, Lords, and Commons" embodied the distinct social orders of British society. He was groping toward quite a different notion, the separation of powers. Government, he affirmed, should be divided into three branches—an executive armed with veto power, a legislature, and a judiciary independent of both. The legislature, he insisted, must be bicameral, so that each house could expose the failings of the other. A free government need not embody distinct social orders to be stable. It could uphold republican values by being properly balanced within itself.

Governments exist to promote the happiness of the people, Adams declared, and happiness depends on "virtue," both public and private. Public virtue meant "patriotism," the willingness of independent householders to value the common good above their personal interests and even to die for their country. The form of government that rests entirely on virtue, Adams argued, is a republic. Americans must elect legislatures that would mirror the diversity of society. Britain had put the nobility in one house and the commoners in another, but in America, everyone was a commoner. America had no "social orders." In what sense, then, could any government reflect American society? Adams came close to saying that the legislature should represent the "interests" of its citizens, but he did not face the implications of that argument. Should citizens enter politics to pursue selfish interests? What then of selfless patriotism?

In 1776 Adams knew only that the legislature should mirror society and that the structure of a republic should be more complex and balanced than what Paine advocated. Unicameral legislatures, which Georgia, Pennsylvania, and Vermont all adopted, horrified him: "A single assembly, possessed of all the powers of government, would make arbitrary laws for their own interest, execute all laws arbitrarily for their own interest, and adjudge all controversies in their own favor."

Adams had not yet found a way to distinguish between everyday legislation and the power to create a constitution. Nor did his admirers. While struggling to define what a republic ought to be, they could not escape two assumptions on which European politics rested—that government itself must be sovereign, and that it alone could define the rights of the people. A few ordinary settlers had already spotted the dangers of those assumptions. As the citizens of Concord, Massachusetts, warned in October 1776, "A Constitution alterable by the Supreme Legislative [Power] is no Security at all to the Subject against any Encroachment of the Governing part on . . . their Rights and Privileges."

This concern would eventually prompt Americans, including Adams, to invent the embodiment of popular sovereignty in its purest form, the constitutional convention. But meanwhile, in 1776 most Americans still assumed that governments must be sovereign. In the early state constitutions, every state lodged sovereign power in its legislature and let the legislature define the rights of citizens. In 1776 the American reply to Britain's sovereign Parliament was 13 sovereign state legislatures—14, with Vermont.

THE VIRGINIA CONSTITUTION

Only years of struggle exposed the inadequacy of the assumptions that the government possesses supreme authority and that the rights of the people must be defined by the government. In June 1776 Virginia became the first state to adopt a permanent, republican constitution. The provincial congress (called a "convention" in Virginia), which had assumed full legislative powers, affirmed "that the legislative and executive powers . . . should be separate and distinct from the judiciary"—but then wrote a constitution that made the legislature sovereign. The legislature chose the governor, the governor's council, and all judges above the level of justice of the peace. The governor had no veto and hardly any patronage. The lower house faced annual elections, but members of the upper house served four-year terms.

George Mason drafted a declaration of rights that the Virginia delegates passed before approving the constitution itself, on the theory that the people should define their rights before empowering the government. Mason's text affirmed the right to life, liberty, property, and the pursuit of happiness. It condemned hereditary privilege, called for rotation in office, provided strong guarantees for trial by jury and due process, and extolled religious liberty. Legally, Virginia's bill of rights was merely a statute, with no more authority than any other statute, but it was eloquent, and many states copied it.

Other states adopted variations of the Virginia model. Because America had no aristocracy, uncertainty about the proper makeup of the upper house was widespread. Some states imposed higher property qualifications on "senators" than on "representatives." In three states the lower house elected the upper house. Maryland chose state senators through an electoral college, but most states created separate election districts for senators. Most states also increased the number of representatives in the lower house. Inland counties, underrepresented in most colonial assemblies, became better represented, and men of moderate wealth won a majority of seats in most states, displacing the rich who had won most colonial elections. Most states also stripped the governor of patronage and of royal prerogatives, such as the power to dissolve the legislature. At this stage, only New York empowered the governor, in conjunction with a "Council of Revision," to reject bills passed by the legislature.

THE PENNSYLVANIA CONSTITUTION

Many states disagreed sharply on constitutional issues. Pennsylvania learned how troubling these questions could become. Radicals there overthrew Crown, proprietor, and assembly in June 1776, rejected the leadership of both the old Quaker and Proprietary Parties, and elected artisans to office in Philadelphia and ordinary farmers in rural areas. Until 1776 most officeholders had either been Quakers or Anglicans. Now, Scots-Irish Presbyterians and German Lutherans or Calvinists replaced them and drafted a new constitution in their own quest for legitimacy.

In 1776, Pennsylvania came closer than any other state to recognizing the constitutional dangers of resting sovereignty solely in the government—and government's arm, the legislature—rather than in the citizens. The radicals even summoned a special convention whose only task was to write a constitution. That document established a unicameral assembly and a plural executive of 12 men, one of whom would preside and thus be called "president." All freemen who paid taxes, and their adult sons living at home, could vote. Elections were annual, voting was by secret ballot, legislative sessions were open to the public, and no representative could serve for more than four years out of any seven. All bills were to be published before passage for public discussion throughout the state. Only at the next session of the legislature could they be passed into law, except in emergencies. Pennsylvania also created a "Council of Censors" to meet every seven years to determine whether the constitution had been violated. It could also recommend amendments.

The Pennsylvania constitution, however, never worked as planned and generated intense conflict in late 1776 as the British army drew near. In this emergency, the convention that drafted the constitution also began to pass laws, destroying any distinction between itself and the legislature it had created. Likewise, the convention and the legislatures that eventually succeeded it rarely delayed the enactment of a bill until after the voters had had time to discuss it. The war lent a sense of emergency to almost every measure. Even more alarming, many residents condemned the new constitution as illegitimate. The men driven from power in 1776 never consented to it and saw no good reason why they should accept it. The radicals, calling themselves "Constitutionalists," imposed oaths on all citizens obliging them to uphold the constitution and then disfranchised Quakers, German pacifists, and anyone else who refused to support it.

These illiberal measures gave radicals a majority in the legislature into the 1780s and kept voter turnout low in most elections, although some men (mostly leaders of the old Proprietary Party) took the oaths only to form an opposition party. Called "anti-Constitutionalists" at first (that is, opponents of the 1776 constitution), they soon took the name "Republicans." After the war, as the disfranchised regained the right to vote, Republicans won a solid majority in the legislature. In 1787 they won ratification of the federal Constitution, and then, in 1790 they replaced the 1776 state constitution with a new one that created a bicameral legislature and an elective governor with a veto that could be overridden. By then, Massachusetts had created the definitive model of constitution-making.

MASSACHUSETTS REDEFINES CONSTITUTIONALISM

Another bitter struggle occurred in Massachusetts, and it finally generated a new consensus about what a constitution should be. After four years of intense debate, Massachusetts found a way to lodge sovereignty with the people and not with government—that is, a way to distinguish a constitution from simple laws.

In response to the Massachusetts Government Act, passed by Parliament in 1774 (see chapter 5), the colonists had prevented the royal courts from sitting. In the three western counties of Worcester, Hampshire, and Berkshire, they had ousted from office a group of wealthy, intermarried families (called "river gods" in Connecticut valley towns), most of whom became loyalists. The courts remained closed until the British withdrew from Boston in March 1776 and the provincial congress moved into the city and reestablished itself as the General Court under the royal charter of 1691. The legislature then reapportioned itself. Under the old system, most towns elected a single representative. A few (such as Salem) chose two. Only Boston could elect four. The new system let towns choose representatives in proportion to population. It rewarded the older, populous eastern towns at the expense of the lightly settled western towns.

When the General Court also revived royal practice by appointing its own members as county judges and justices of the peace, the western counties exploded. Their hatred of the river gods extended to eastern gentlemen as well. Denouncing the "antient Mode of Government among us which we so much detest and abhor," they attacked the reapportionment act and refused to reopen the courts in Hampshire and Berkshire counties. Most of Berkshire's radicals were Baptists in religion and Lockeans in politics. They insisted on contracts or compacts as the basis of authority in both church and state and continued to use county conventions in place of the courts. To the Berkshire Constitutionalists a "convention" was becoming the purest expression of the will of the people, superior to any legislature. These uneducated farmers set the pace in demanding a formal constitution for the state.

In the fall of 1776 the General Court asked the towns to authorize it to draft a constitution. By a two-to-one margin the voters agreed, a result that reflected growing *distrust* of the legislature. Six months earlier hardly anyone would have questioned such a procedure. The legislature drafted a constitution over the next year and then, in an unusual precaution, asked the towns to ratify it. The voters rejected it by the stunning margin of five to one. Some towns objected to the lack of a bill of rights, and a few insisted that it should have been drafted by a separate convention. Several towns wanted the governor to be directly elected by the people, but most gave no reason for their disapproval. Voters angry with a particular clause were likely to condemn the whole document.

Chastened, the General Court urged the towns to postpone the question until after the war. Hampshire County reopened its courts in April 1778, but Berkshire County threatened to secede from the state unless it summoned a constitutional convention. Drawing upon John Locke, these farmers insisted that they were now in a "state of nature," subject to no legitimate government. They might even join a neighboring state that had a proper constitution. At a time when Vermont was making good its secession from New York, this was no idle threat.

The General Court gave in, and a convention met in Boston in December 1779. John Adams drafted a constitution that the convention used as its starting point. A constitution now had to be drafted by a convention, elected for that specific purpose, and ratified by the people. The people would then be the source of all legitimate authority.

In the four years since 1776, Adams's thoughts on the separation of powers and bicameralism had matured. Like the Virginia constitution, the Massachusetts constitution began with a bill of rights. Both houses would be elected annually. The House of Representatives would be chosen by the towns, as reapportioned in 1776. Senators would be elected by counties and apportioned according to property values, not population. The governor would be elected by the people and would have a veto that two-thirds of both houses could override. Property qualifications rose as a man's civic duties increased. Voters must own £50 of real property or £100 of personal property, representatives must

JOHN ADAMS Mather Brown's London portrait of John Adams, 1788.

have £100 in land or £200 in other property, senators must have £300 in land or £600 in total wealth, respectively, and the governor had to own £1,000 in landed property. He also had to be a Christian. For purposes of ratification only, all free adult males were eligible to vote. In accepting the basic social compact, everyone (that is, all free men) would have a chance to consent. Voters were asked to vote on each article separately, not on the document as a whole.

During the spring of 1780 town meetings began the ratification process. The convention tallied the results and declared that the constitution had received the required two-thirds majority, but it juggled the figures on two articles, both involving religion, to get this result. Those articles provided for the public support of ministers and required the governor to be a Christian. Baptists objected to all taxes for the support of religion, and many Protestants wanted to exclude Catholics from the governorship. The new constitution promptly went into effect and, though it has often been amended, is still in force today, making it the oldest constitution in the world. Starting with New Hampshire in 1784, other states adopted the Massachusetts model.

CONFEDERATION

The states' creativity had no counterpart in the Continental Congress, which met almost continuously during the war. Before independence, hardly anyone had given serious thought to how an American nation ought to be governed. Dozens of colonists had drafted plans of conciliation with Britain, some quite innovative, but through 1775 only Benjamin Franklin and Connecticut's Silas Deane had presented plans for an American union. Franklin's was an updated version of the Albany Plan of 1754 (see chapter 4). Another anonymous proposal appeared in an American newspaper, but none of the three attracted public comment. Colonists passionately debated the empire and their state governments, but not America.

Congress began discussing the American union in the summer of 1776 but did not produce the final text of what became the "Articles of Confederation and perpetual Union" until a year and a half later. Congress had been voting by state since the First Continental Congress in 1774. Delegates from large states favored representation according to population, but no census existed to give precise numbers, and the small states insisted on being treated as equals. As long as Britain was ready to embrace any state that defected, small states had great leverage: The tail could wag the dog. In one early draft of the Articles of Confederation, John Dickinson rejected proportional representation in favor of state equality. He enumerated the powers of Congress, which did not include levying taxes or regulating trade. To raise money, Congress would have to print it or requisition specific amounts from the states. Congress then split over how to apportion these requisitions. Northern states wanted to count slaves in computing the ratios. Southern states wanted to apportion revenues on the basis of each state's free population. Western lands were another tough issue. States with fixed borders pressured states with boundary claims stretching into the Ohio or Mississippi valleys to surrender their claims to Congress. Many speculators favored the land cessions. Congress could not resolve these issues in 1776.

Debate resumed after Washington's victories at Trenton and Princeton. Thomas Burke of North Carolina introduced a resolution that eventually became part of the Articles of Confederation: "Each state retains its sovereignty, freedom and independence, and every power, jurisdiction, and right, which is not by this confederation expressly delegated to the United States in Congress assembled." The acceptance of Burke's resolution, with only Virginia dissenting, ensured that the Articles would contain a firm commitment to state sovereignty. Only after Saratoga, however, was Congress able to complete the Articles. In the final version, Congress was given no power over western land claims, and requisitions would be based on each state's free population. (In 1781 Congress tried to change the formula so that each slave was counted as three-fifths of a person for the purpose of apportioning requisitions, but this amendment was never ratified.)

In November 1777 Congress asked the states to ratify the Articles by March 10, 1778, but only Virginia met the deadline. Most states tried to attach conditions, which Congress rejected, but by midsummer 10 had ratified. The three dissenters were Delaware, New Jersey, and Maryland—all states without western land claims who feared their giant neighbors. Maryland held out for more than three years, until Virginia agreed to cede its land claims north of the Ohio River to Congress. The Articles finally went into force on March 1, 1781.

By then, the Continental Congress had lost most of its power. Some of its most talented members, including Jefferson and Samuel Adams, had returned home to help reshape their state governments. Others, such as Washington, had taken army commands, and some, including Benjamin Franklin, John Adams, and John Jay, had departed on diplomatic assignments. The congressional effort to manage everything through committees created impossible bottlenecks. In 1776 the states had looked to Congress to confer legitimacy on their new governments, especially in the Mid-Atlantic colonies, but as the states adopted their own constitutions, their legitimacy became more obvious than that of Congress. Even more alarming, by the late 1770s Congress simply could not pay its bills.

THE CRISIS OF THE REVOLUTION, 1779–1783

Americans expected a quick victory under the French alliance. Instead, the struggle turned into a grim war of attrition, testing which side would first exhaust its resources or lose the will to fight. Loyalists became much more important to the British war effort, both as a source of manpower and as the main justification for continuing the war. Most settlers, argued Lord North, were still loyal to Britain. They could turn the contest around. To abandon them would be dishonorable and might lead to a bloodbath. The British began to look to the Deep South as the likeliest recruiting ground for armed loyalists. The Carolinas, bitterly divided by the regulator movements and vulnerable to massive slave defections, seemed a promising source.

THE LOYALISTS

Most loyalists were committed to English ideas of liberty. Many of them had objected openly to the Stamp Act and other British measures but doubted that Parliament intended to undermine government by consent in the colonies. They also thought that creating a new American union was a far riskier venture than remaining part of the British Empire. For many, the choice of loyalties was painful. Some waited until the fighting reached their neighborhood before deciding which soldiers to flee from and which to shoot. The loyalists then learned a stark truth: They could not fire at their neighbors

and expect to retain their homes except under the protection of the British army.

The British, in turn, were slow to take advantage of the loyalists. In the early years of the war, British officers regarded the loyalists' military potential with the same disdain that they bestowed on the patriots. As the war continued, however, the loyalists, who stood to lose everything in an American victory, showed that they could be fierce soldiers.

About one-sixth of the white population chose the British side in the war, and 19,000 men joined more than 40 loyalist military units, mostly after 1778 when Britain grew desperate for soldiers. Unlike most patriots, loyalists served long terms, even for the duration, because they could not go home unless they won. By 1780 the number of loyalists under arms exceeded the number of Continentals by almost two to one. State governments retaliated by banishing prominent loyalists under pain of death and by confiscating their property.

LOYALIST REFUGEES, BLACK AND WHITE

When given the choice, most slaves south of New England sided with Britain. In New England, where they sensed that they could gain freedom by joining the rebels, many volunteered for military

---

Extract of a letter from Monmouth county, June 12.
" Ty, with his party of about 20 blacks and whites, last Friday afternoon took and carried off prisoners, Capt. Barns Smock and Gilbert Vanmater; at the same time spiked up the iron four pounder at Capt. Smock's house, but took no ammunition: Two of the artillery horses, and two of Capt. Smock' horses, were likewise taken off."
The above-mentioned Ty is a Negroe, who bears the title of Colonel, and commands a motly crew at Sandy-Hook.

AN OFFER OF FREEDOM An American newspaper reported on British efforts to gain the support of slaves by offering them freedom.

ENCAMPMENT OF LOYALISTS AT JOHNSTON, ONTARIO, JUNE 6, 1784 This painting by James Peachey depicts the arrival of loyalist exiles in Upper Canada.

service. Elsewhere, although some fought for the Revolution, they realized that their best chance of emancipation lay with the British army. During the war, more than 50,000 slaves (about 10 percent) fled their owners; of that total, about 20,000 were evacuated by the British. The decision to flee carried risks. In South Carolina, hundreds reached the sea islands in an effort to join the British during Clinton's 1776 invasion, only to face their owners' wrath when the British failed to rescue them. Others approached British units only to be treated as contraband (property) and to face possible resale. Most slaves who reached British lines won their freedom, however, even though the British army never became an instrument of systematic emancipation. When the British withdrew after the war, blacks went with them, many to Jamaica, some to Nova Scotia, others to London. In the 1780s the British even created a colony for former slaves at Sierra Leone in West Africa.

The war, in short, created an enormous stream of refugees, black and white. In addition to 20,000 former slaves, some 60,000 to 70,000 colonists left the states for other parts of the British Empire. The American Revolution created 30 refugees for every 1,000 people, compared with 5 per 1,000 created by the French Revolution in the 1790s. About 35,000 settlers found their way to Nova Scotia, the western part of which became the province of New Brunswick in the 1780s. Another 6,000 to 10,000 fled to Quebec,

settled upriver from the older French population, and in 1791 became the new province of Upper Canada (later Ontario). A generous land policy, which required an oath of allegiance to George III, attracted thousands of new immigrants to Canada from the United States in the 1780s and 1790s. By the War of 1812, four-fifths of Upper Canada's 100,000 people were American-born. Though only one-fifth of them could be traced to loyalist resettlement, the settlers supported Britain in that war. In a real sense the American Revolution laid the foundation for two new nations—the United States and Canada—and competition between them for settlers and loyalties continued long after the fighting stopped.

THE INDIAN STRUGGLE FOR UNITY AND SURVIVAL

Indians of the eastern woodlands also began to play a more active role in the war. For them the stakes were immense. Most of them saw that an American victory would threaten their survival as a people on their ancestral lands. Nearly all of them sided with Britain in the hope that a British victory might stem the flood of western expansion. In the final years of the war, they achieved a level of unity without precedent in their history.

At first, most Indians tried to remain neutral. The British were rebuffed when they asked the Iroquois to fight against the colonists. The Delawares and the Shawnees, defeated in Lord Dunmore's War in 1774, also stood neutral. Only the Cherokees took up arms in 1776. Short on ammunition and other British supplies, they took heavy losses before making peace and accepting neutrality. The Chickamaugas, a splinter group, continued to resist. In the Deep South, only the Catawbas—by now much reduced in number—fought on the American side.

Burgoyne's invasion brought the Iroquois into the war in 1777. The Mohawks in the east and the Senecas in the west sided with Britain under the leadership of Joseph Brant, a literate and educated Mohawk and a Freemason. His sister, Mary Brant, emerged as a skillful diplomat in the alliance between the Iroquois and the loyalists. A minority of Oneidas and some Tuscaroras fought with the Americans. Most of them were becoming Christians under a patriot Congregational missionary,

JOSEPH BRANT, PORTRAIT BY GILBERT STUART
(1786) Brant, a Mohawk and a Freemason, was one of Britain's ablest commanders of loyalist and Indian forces. After the war he led most of the Six Nations to Canada for resettlement.

Samuel Kirkland. Yet, despite these severe strains during the Revolution, the Iroquois League was not shattered until after the war when those who fought for Britain migrated to Canada.

A minority of Shawnees, led by Cornplanter, and of Delawares, led by White Eyes and Killbuck, also pursued friendly relations with the Americans. They provided intelligence to American forces and served as wilderness guides, but they refused to fight other Indians and did their best to preserve peace along the frontier. Christian Moravian Indians in the Ohio country took a similar stance. The reluctance of Indians to kill other Indians, already evident during the Seven Years' War, became even more obvious during the Revolution. Loyalists and patriots were far more willing than Indians to kill one another.

Frontier racism, already conspicuous in Pontiac's War, became more vicious than ever and made Indian neutrality all but impossible. Backcountry settlers from Carolina through New York refused to accept the neutrals on their own terms. Indian warriors, especially young men strongly influenced by nativist prophets, increasingly believed that the Great Spirit had created whites, Indians, and blacks as separate peoples who ought to remain apart. Their militancy further enraged the settlers. Young white hunters, disdained by many easterners as "near savages," proved their worth as "whites" by killing Indians.

The hatred of Indians grew so extreme that it threatened to undercut the American war effort. In 1777 a Continental officer had Cornplanter murdered. In 1778 American militia killed White Eyes. Four years later Americans massacred 100 unarmed Moravian mission Indians at Gnadenhutten, Ohio. Nearly all of them were women and children, who knelt in prayer as, one by one, their skulls were crushed with mallets. This atrocity brutalized Indians as well as settlers. Until then, most Indians had refrained from the ritual torture of prisoners, but after Gnadenhutten they resumed the custom, not as a general practice, but to punish atrocities. When they captured known leaders of the massacre, they burned them alive.

Faced with hatred, Indians united to protect their lands. They won the frontier war north of the Ohio River. The Iroquois ravaged the Wyoming valley of Pennsylvania in 1778. When an American army

WAR ON THE FRONTIER, 1777–1782

devastated Iroquoia in 1779 and committed many atrocities along the way, the Indians fell back on the British post at Niagara and continued the struggle. In 1779 nearly all Indians, from the Creeks on the Gulf Coast to the nations of the Great Lakes, ex-

changed emissaries and planned an all-out war along the frontier. George Rogers Clark of Virginia thwarted their offensive with a daring winter raid in which he captured Vincennes and cut off the western nations from British supplies. But the Indians regrouped and by 1782 drove the Virginia "Long Knives" out of the Ohio country.

ATTRITION

After 1778, George III's determination to continue the war bitterly divided his kingdom. Much of the British public doubted that the war could be won. Trade was disrupted, thousands of ships were lost to privateers, taxes and the national debt soared, military recruits became harder to find, and a French invasion became a serious threat. Political dissent rose and included widespread demand for the reduction of royal patronage and for electoral reforms. A proposal to abolish Lord George Germain's office, clearly an attack on the American war, failed in the House of Commons by only 208 votes to 201 in March 1780. A resolve condemning the influence of the Crown carried in April, 233 to 215. The king had great difficulty persuading North not to resign.

Desperate for men, the British army had been quietly recruiting Irish Catholics, and North supported a modest degree of toleration for English and Scottish Catholics. This leniency produced a surge of Protestant violence culminating in the Gordon riots, named for an agitator, Lord George Gordon. For a week in June 1780 crowds roared through the streets of London, smashing Catholic chapels attached to foreign embassies, liberating prisoners from city jails, and finally attacking the Bank of England. The army, supported by Lord Mayor John Wilkes, put down the rioters. This spectacular violence discredited the demands for reform that had seemed on the verge of toppling North. The riots gave him one more chance to win the war, this time with strong support from loyalists.

Attrition weakened the United States even more dramatically. The war undermined the American economy. Indian raids reduced harvests, and military levies kept thousands of men away from productive work. Loyalist raids into Connecticut and New Jersey wore down the defenders and destroyed a great deal of property. In a 1779 raid on Virginia, property worth £2 million was either carried off or destroyed. Merchants lost most of their European and West Indian markets, although a few of them made huge profits through blockade running or privateering. Average household income plunged by more than 40 percent. Even some American triumphs came at a high price. Bur-

goyne's surrender left Americans with the burden of feeding his army for the rest of the war. When a French fleet called at Boston, the crews devoured an alarming share of available provisions, as did the French army that landed at Newport in 1780.

Taken together, these heavy demands led to the collapse of the Continental dollar in 1779–80. Congress had been printing money to pay its bills, using the Spanish dollar as its basic monetary unit. With the French alliance bolstering American credit, this practice worked reasonably well into 1778. The money depreciated but without causing widespread dissatisfaction. As the war ground on, though, the value of Continental money fell to less than a penny on the dollar in 1779. Congress agreed to stop the printing presses and to rely instead on requisitions from the states and on foreign and domestic loans, but without paper it could not even pay the army. Congress and the army had to requisition supplies directly from farmers in exchange for certificates geared to an inflation rate of 40 to 1, well below its true rate. Many farmers, rather than lose money on their crops, simply cut back production. William Beadle, a Connecticut shopkeeper, tried to fight inflation by accepting Continental money at face value until he saw the consequences. Rather than leave his wife and children impoverished, he slit their throats and shot himself.

Continental soldiers—unpaid, ill-clothed, and often poorly fed—grew mutinous. As they became more professional through frequent drill, they also became contemptuous of civilians. The winter 1779–80, the worst of the century, marked a low point in morale among the main force of Continentals snowed in with Washington at Morristown, New Jersey. Many deserted. In May 1780 two Connecticut regiments of the Continental Line, without food for three days, threatened to go home, raising the danger that the whole army might dissolve. Their officers barely managed to restore control. On paper, Washington had 16,000 men. His real strength was 3,600 men and not even enough horses to move his artillery.

THE BRITISH OFFENSIVE IN THE SOUTH

Sensing a unique opportunity in 1780, the British attacked in the Deep South with great success. The Revolution entered its most critical phase and almost collapsed. "I have almost ceased to hope," Washington confessed at one point. In December 1778 a small British amphibious force had taken Savannah and had held it through 1779 against an American and French counterthrust. The British even restored royal government with an elective as-

sembly in Georgia between 1780 and 1782. By early 1780 they were ready to move from this enclave and launch a general offensive. Their commander, General Clinton, was a cautious man who had been in charge of Britain's war effort since 1778. He had exasperated the loyalist supporters by

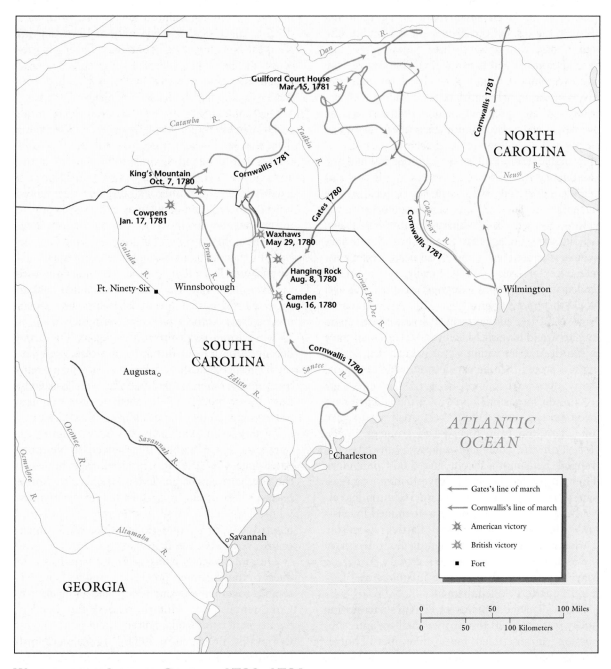

WAR IN THE LOWER SOUTH, 1780–1781

remaining on the defensive in New York City. By the time he took command in Georgia in January 1780, he had finally devised a strategy for winning the war, but he revealed its details to no one.

Clinton's New York army would invade South Carolina, take Charleston, and unleash armed loyalists to pacify the countryside. Part of the regular forces would remain in the Carolinas to deal with any other army the Americans might field. Clinton would sail with the rest back to New York and land on the Jersey coast with a force three times larger than Washington's at Morristown. By dividing this army into two columns, Clinton could break through both passes of the Watchung Mountains leading to Morristown. Washington must either hold fast and be overwhelmed or else abandon his artillery for lack of horses and attack one of the invading columns on unfavorable terms. Either way, Clinton reasoned, the Continental Army would be destroyed. He was also negotiating secretly with Benedict Arnold for the surrender of West Point, which would open the Hudson River to British ships as far north as Albany. Arnold, who thought that Congress had never adequately rewarded his heroism, had begun trading intelligence for cash in 1779. Finally, if the French landed in Newport, as everyone expected, Clinton would then move against them with nearly his entire New York fleet and garrison. If he succeeded there too, he would have smashed every professional force in North America within a year's time. His remaining task would then be pacification, which he could pretty much leave to loyalists.

Clinton's invasion of South Carolina began with awesome successes. While the British navy sealed off Charleston from the sea, an army of 10,000 closed off the land approaches to the city and trapped Benjamin Lincoln and 5,000 defenders. Their surrender on May 12 gave Britain its largest haul of prisoners in the entire war. Clinton had already turned loose his angry, well-trained loyalists under Banastre Tarleton and Patrick Ferguson. Tarleton caught the 350 remaining Continentals at the Waxhaws near the North Carolina border on May 29 and, in what became infamous as "Tarleton's quarter," killed them all.

The calculated brutality of Britain's pacification policy was designed to terrorize civilians into submission. It succeeded for a time, but Thomas Sumter began to fight back after loyalists burned his plantation. His mounted raiders attacked British outposts and terrorized loyalists. At Hanging Rock on August 6, Sumter's 800 men scattered 500 loyalists, killing or wounding nearly half of them before Sumter's own men embarked on an orgy of looting and drinking. All participants on both sides were colonists.

Leaving Cornwallis in command of 8,300 men in South Carolina, Clinton sailed north with one-third of his Carolina army, only to learn that his plans for New Jersey had gone awry. During his absence the leading loyalists, fearing that he never would take the initiative in the north, had persuaded Wilhelm, baron von Knyphausen, the temporary commander, to land in New Jersey with 6,000 men on the night of June 6–7, 1780. Even a force that small would pose a grave threat to Washington unless the militia came to his aid. Most loyalists hoped that the militia was so weary from the harsh winter and numerous raids that they would not turn out. Some companies had even begun to muster women. To the dismay of the British, however, the militia appeared in force on June 7.

Only then, after an inconclusive engagement, did Knyphausen learn that Clinton was on his way with his own plan of attack. The British pulled back to the coast and waited, but they had lost the element of surprise. Clinton attacked at Springfield on June 23 while loyalists set fire to the village. The battle became America's civil war in miniature. New Jersey loyalist regiments attacked the New Jersey regiments of the Continental Line, who were assisted by New Jersey militia. The defense was stout enough to persuade Clinton to withdraw to New York.

With Washington's army still intact, Clinton ignored the French when they landed at Newport. After June 1780 the British put all their hopes on the southern campaign. Even Arnold's attempt to betray West Point was thwarted in September. Clinton's agent, John André, was caught and hanged, but Arnold escaped to British lines and became a general in the British army.

Despite Sumter's harassment, Cornwallis's conquest of the Carolinas proceeded rapidly. Congress scraped together 900 tough Maryland and Delaware Continentals, put Horatio Gates, the hero of Saratoga, in command, and sent them south against Cornwallis. Bolstered by 2,000 Virginia and North Carolina militia, Gates rashly offered battle at

SELF-PORTRAIT OF JOHN ANDRÉ André, a talented amateur artist, sketched this self-portrait after he had been condemned to hang for his role in the treason of Benedict Arnold.

Camden on August 16 even though many of his men had been up all night with diarrhea after eating half-baked bread. The militia, who lacked bayonets, fled in panic at the first British charge. The exposed Continentals fought bravely but were crushed. Gates rode an astonishing 240 miles away from the scene in three days and, from Hillsborough, North Carolina, informed Congress that he had suffered "total Defeat." Two days after Camden, Tarleton surprised Sumter's camp at Fishing Creek, near the Waxhaws, killing 150 men and wounding 300.

In four months the British had destroyed all the Continental forces in the Deep South, mauled Sumter's band of partisans, and left North Carolina open to invasion. These victories seemed to fulfill Clinton's boast that he would strip "three stripes . . . from the detestable thirteen." When the French foreign minister heard the news, he quietly inquired whether Britain would make peace, with each side keeping what it currently possessed. Cornwallis turned the pacification of South Carolina over to his loyalists, many of whom were exiles from other states, and marched confidently on to "liberate" North Carolina.

THE PARTISAN WAR

Resistance continued. Tarleton and Sumter fought one engagement to a draw. Farther west, frontier riflemen, already angered by Britain's alliance with the Indians, crossed the Blue Ridge 1,800 strong to challenge Patrick Ferguson's loyalists at King's Mountain near the North Carolina border on October 7, 1780. Nearly all of the combatants on both sides were Americans. Losing only 88 men, rebel marksmen picked off many defenders, advanced from tree to tree, and finally overwhelmed the loyalists, killing 160 men, including Ferguson, and capturing 860. They shot many prisoners and hanged a dozen, their answer to "Tarleton's quarter." This victory, the first major British setback in the Deep South, stung Cornwallis, who halted his drive into North Carolina.

HISTORY THROUGH FILM

The Patriot (2000)

**Directed by Roland Emmerich. Starring Mel Gibson (Benjamin Martin),
Jason Isaacs (Colonel Tavington), Heath Ledger (Gabriel Martin),
and Joely Richardson (Charlotte Selton).**

Hollywood has a poor record of depicting the American Revolution. First, nearly every screenplay simplifies the issues until the complexities of slavery and abolition disappear altogether. Second, the leading patriots become filiopietistic caricatures of the fascinating men they actually were (the portrayal of George Washington in *Lafayette*, 1962, is an excellent example). *The Patriot* fails on both of these counts. Although the cinematography is superb and the battle scenes are compelling, Robert Rodat's screenplay falls sadly short of his accomplishment in *Saving Private Ryan* (1998).

At the outset, the film shows promise. Mel Gibson portrays Benjamin Martin, a widower with seven children and a prosperous farmer in the South Carolina backcountry. A veteran of the French and Indian War, Martin supports the colonial constitutional position against Great Britain but opposes the resort to arms. His oldest son disagrees and enlists in the Continental Army. Then the war invades Martin's family. After a losing confrontation with the redcoats, some wounded Americans take refuge at the Martin farm. The British find them there, and Col. Tavington (Jason Isaacs) executes another of Martin's sons. With two of his small boys and an armload of muskets, Mar-

tin pursues the British column, ambushes it, and the three Martins kill about 20 redcoats. Up to this point the drama is intense and almost believable, but it soon deteriorates.

In *The Patriot*, South Carolina has almost no loyalists, and Martin owns no slaves but has a free black as a friend and neighbor, all but impossible for that time and place. As the colonists take up arms, they recruit blacks, which in fact South Carolina adamantly refused to do. The film even depicts a free black (or "Maroon") community, presumably of escaped slaves, leading an idyllic life on the Atlantic coast, where it would have had no chance whatever of surviving. In the film's climactic battle, General Nathanael Greene's army smashes the British army of Charles, Earl Cornwallis (Tom Wilkinson) and drives it off the field, something that never happened in the entire southern campaign.

Emmerich, the director, grew up in Germany, where he acquired a laudable hatred for the Nazis. Unfortunately, he also seems to believe that no foe can be credible unless it becomes as loathsome as the Nazis were. In his biggest hit, *Independence Day* (1996), the earth-invading aliens have no redeeming qualities of

In October 1780, Congress sent Nathanael Greene to the Carolinas with a small Continental force. When Sumter withdrew for several months to nurse a wound, Francis Marion took his place. A much abler leader, Marion (who became known as the Swamp Fox) operated from remote bases in the swampy low country. Yet Greene's prospects seemed desperate. The ugliness of the partisan war—the mutilation of corpses, killing of prisoners, and wanton destruction of property—shocked him. The condition of his own soldiers appalled him. Yet Greene and Marion devised a masterful strategy of

partisan warfare that finally wore out the British.

In the face of a greatly superior enemy, Greene ignored a standard maxim of war and split up his force of 1,800 Continentals. In smaller bands they would be easier to feed, but Greene's decision involved more than supplies. He sent 300 men east to bolster Marion and ordered Daniel Morgan and 300 riflemen west to threaten the British outpost of Ninety-Six. Tarleton urged Cornwallis to turn and crush the 1,000 men still with Greene, but Greene had no intention of engaging a superior force. Cornwallis, worried that after King's Mountain Morgan

any kind. They intend to obliterate the human race, loot the planet of all of its resources, and then move on. Emmerich's Col. Tavington, loosely modeled on Banastre Tarleton, is almost as despicable. In one scene, he locks Martin's neighbors, nearly all women and children, in a church and burns them alive, an atrocity familiar to the Nazis in the Russian campaign, but one that had no counterpart in the Revolutionary War. Naturally, Martin must kill Tavington in hand-to-hand combat during the final battle. Such over-exertions make *The Patriot*, for all of its sweeping battle scenes, just another lost opportunity.

The Patriot falls short of portraying the reality and complexity of the American Revolution.

might raise the entire backcountry against the British, divided his own army. He sent Tarleton with a mixed force of 1,100 British and loyalists after Morgan, who decided to stand with his back to a river at a place called Cowpens, where a loyalist kept cattle. Including militia, Morgan had 1,040 men.

Tarleton attacked on January 17, 1781. In another unorthodox move, Morgan sent his militia out front as skirmishers. He ordered them to fire two rounds and then redeploy in his rear as a reserve. Relieved of their fear of a bayonet charge, they obeyed. As they pulled back, the British rushed forward into the Con-tinentals, who also retreated at first, then wheeled and discharged a lethal volley. After Morgan's cavalry charged into the British left flank, the militia returned to the fray. Although Tarleton escaped, Morgan annihilated his army. For the first time in the war, an American force had clearly outfought a British army without an advantage of numbers or terrain.

As Morgan rejoined Greene, Cornwallis staked everything on his ability to find Greene and crush him, precisely what he had failed to do to Washington after Trenton and Princeton four years earlier. But Greene outthought him. He placed flatboats in his rear at major river crossings and then lured Cornwallis into a march of exhaustion. In a race to the Dan River, Cornwallis burned his baggage in order to travel lightly. Greene escaped on his flatboats across the Yadkin River, flooded with spring rains, just ahead of Cornwallis—who had to march to a ford 10 miles upstream, cross the river, and then march back while Greene rested. Greene repeated this stratagem all the way to the Dan until he judged that Cornwallis was so weak that the Americans could offer battle at Guilford Court House on March 15, 1781. With militia, he outnumbered Cornwallis 4,400 to 1,900. Even though the British retained possession of the battlefield, they lost one-quarter of their force along with the strategic initiative.

Cornwallis retreated to the coast at Wilmington to refit. He then marched north into Virginia—the seat of southern resistance, he told Clinton, the one place where Britain could achieve decisive results. Instead of following him, Greene returned to South Carolina, where he and Marion took the surviving British outposts one by one. After the British evacuated Ninety-Six on July 1, 1781, they held only Savannah and Charleston in the Deep South. Against heavy odds, Greene had reclaimed the region for the Revolution.

MUTINY AND REFORM

After the Camden disaster, army officers and state politicians demanded reforms to strengthen Congress and win the war. State legislatures sent their ablest men to Congress. Maryland, the last state to hold out, finally completed the American union by ratifying the Articles of Confederation.

LINK TO THE PAST

Spy Letters of the American Revolution: The Infamous Benedict Arnold

http://www.si.umich.edu/spies/index-main2.html

Maintained by the University of Michigan, this site features spy letters of the American Revolution from the Collections of the Clements Library.

No event of the Revolutionary War made American patriots angrier than the treason of General Benedict Arnold, who attempted to turn over to the British the Hudson River fortress at West Point and possibly George Washington himself. The plot was foiled when American militiamen captured Major John André, the British emissary. André was trying to return to British lines in civilian clothes after his last fateful meeting with Arnold, who barely escaped himself after he learned of André's capture.

1. Follow the "Stories of Spies and Letters" link and, under "The Infamous Benedict Arnold," read the story on "The Death of John André," who was tried as a spy and hanged on September 29, 1780. His American captors greatly admired him, and many of them hoped Washington would commute his sentence. The British begged Washington to spare him. But André was hanged. Why did André have to die when everybody agreed that the real malefactor was Arnold?

2. Read the stories of Ann Bates and Miss Jenny under "Women Spies." What conclusions about contemporary views of women can be drawn from these stories?

Before any reforms could take effect, discontent again erupted in the army. Insisting that their three-year enlistments had expired, 1,500 men of the Pennsylvania Line got drunk on New Year's Day 1781, killed three officers, and marched out of their winter quarters at Morristown. General Clinton sent agents from New York to promise them a pardon and their back pay if they defected to the British, but instead the mutineers marched south toward Princeton and turned Clinton's agents over to Pennsylvania authorities, who executed them. Congress, reassured, negotiated with the soldiers. More than half of them accepted discharges, and those who remained in service got furloughs and bonuses for reenlistment. Encouraged by this treatment, 200 New Jersey soldiers at Pompton also mutinied, but Washington used New England units to disarm them and had two of the leaders executed. The army held together, but well into 1781 more loyalists were still serving with the British than Continentals with Washington.

Civilian violence, such as the "Fort Wilson" riot in Philadelphia, also prompted Congress to change policies. Radical artisans blamed the city's rich merchants for the rampant inflation of 1779 and demanded price controls as a remedy. The merchants blamed paper money. In October, several men were killed when the antagonists exchanged shots near the fortified home of James Wilson, a wealthy lawyer. Spokesmen for the radicals deplored the violence and abandoned the quest for price controls. For city dwellers rich and poor, sound money was becoming the only solution to the devastating inflation.

Congress interpreted these disturbances as a call for reform, for devising better ways to conduct national affairs. While armed partisans were making the war itself more radical, politics veered in a conservative direction, toward the creation of European state forms, such as executive departments and a bank.

Patriot leaders gave up efforts at price control and allowed the market to set prices and the value of money. Congress stopped printing money, abandoned its cumbersome committee system, and created separate executive departments of foreign affairs, finance, war, and marine. Robert Morris, a Philadelphia merchant, became the first secretary of finance, helped to organize the Bank of North America (America's first), and made certain that the Continental Army was clothed and well fed, although it still was not paid. Congress began to requisition revenue from the states. The states began to impose heavy taxes but could never collect enough to meet both their own and national needs. Congress tried to amend the Articles of Confederation in 1781 and asked the states to accept a 5 percent duty on all imports. Most states quickly ratified the "impost" amendment, but Rhode Island rejected it in 1783. Amendments to the Articles needed unanimous approval by the states, and this opposition killed the impost. A new impost proposal in 1783 was defeated by New York in 1786.

The reforms of 1781 just barely kept a smaller army in the field for the rest of the war, but the new executive departments had an unforeseen effect. Congress had been a plural executive, America's answer to the imperial Crown. But once Congress created its own departments, it looked more like a national legislature, and a feeble one at that, for it still had no power to compel obedience. It began to pass, not just "orders" and "resolves," but also "ordinances," intended to be permanent and binding. It still could not punish anyone for noncompliance, which may be why it never passed any "laws."

FROM THE RAVAGING OF VIRGINIA TO YORKTOWN AND PEACE

Both Cornwallis and Washington believed that events in Virginia would decide the war. When a large British force raided the state in late 1780, Governor Thomas Jefferson called up enough militia to keep the British bottled up in Portsmouth, while he continued to ship men and supplies to Greene in the Carolinas. Thereafter, the state's ability to raise men and supplies almost collapsed.

In January 1781, Clinton sent Arnold by sea from New York with 1,600 men, mostly loyalists. They sailed up the James, took the new capital of Richmond almost without resistance, and gutted it. When Jefferson called out the militia, few responded. Virginia had not experienced the partisan struggles that drew men to both sides in New Jersey and the Carolinas. The state provided a different kind of test for American values under stress. The voluntaristic ethic nearly failed to get the state through a long war. Most Virginia freemen had already done service, if only as short-term militia, thousands of them in response to the 1780 raid. In 1781 they thought it was now someone else's turn.

For months, there was no one else. Cornwallis took command in April, and Arnold departed for New York. But the raids continued into summer, sweeping as far west as Charlottesville, where Tarleton, who had recruited a new legion since Cowpens, scattered the Virginia legislature and came within minutes of capturing Jefferson on June 3. Many of Jefferson's slaves greeted the British as liberators. Washington sent Lafayette with 1,200 New England and New Jersey Continentals to contain the damage, while Cornwallis, on Clinton's orders, withdrew to Yorktown.

At last, Washington saw an opportunity to launch a major strike. He learned that a powerful French fleet under François, comte de Grasse, would sail with 3,000 soldiers from Saint-Domingue on August 13 for Chesapeake Bay. Cooperating closely with the French army commander, Jean Baptiste Donatien, comte de Rochambeau, Washington sprang his trap. Rochambeau led his 5,000 soldiers from Newport to the outskirts of New York, where they joined Washington's 5,000 Continentals. After feinting an attack to freeze Clinton in place, Washington led the combined French and American armies 400 miles south to tidewater Virginia, where they linked up with Lafayette's Americans and the other French army brought by de Grasse. After de Grasse's fleet beat off a British relief force at the Battle of the Capes on September 5, Washington cut off all retreat routes and besieged Cornwallis in Yorktown. On October 19, 1781, Cornwallis surrendered his entire army of 8,000 men. Many escaped slaves had died during the siege, most from smallpox, but Virginia planters hovered nearby to reclaim the survivors.

Yorktown brought down the British government in March 1782. Lord North resigned, and George III even drafted an abdication message, although he never released it. The new ministry, committed to American independence as the price of peace, continued to fight the French in the Caribbean and the Spanish at Gibraltar, but the British evacuated Savannah and Charleston and concentrated their remaining forces in New York City.

Contrary to the French Treaty of 1778, and against Franklin's advice, John Jay and John Adams opened secret peace negotiations in Paris with the British. They won British recognition of the Mississippi, though without New Orleans, as the western boundary of the new republic. New Englanders

"THE AMERICAN RATTLE SNAKE" This 1782 cartoon celebrated the victory of Yorktown, the second time in the war that an entire British army had surrendered to the United States.

retained the right to fish off Newfoundland. The treaty recognized the validity of prewar transatlantic debts, and Congress promised to urge the states to restore confiscated loyalist property. These terms gave American diplomats almost everything they could have desired. After the negotiations were far advanced, the Americans told Vergennes, the French foreign minister, what they were doing. He feigned indignation, but the threat of a separate peace gave him the leverage he needed with Spain. Spain stopped demanding that France keep fighting until Gibraltar surrendered. The

Treaty of Paris, though not ratified for months, ended the war in February 1783.

Western Indians were appalled to learn that the treaty gave their lands to the United States. They had not been conquered, whatever European diplomats might say. Their war for survival continued with few breaks into 1795.

Congress still faced ominous problems. In March 1783 many Continental officers threatened a coup d'état unless Congress granted them generous pensions. Washington, confronting them at their encampment at Newburgh, New York, fumbled for

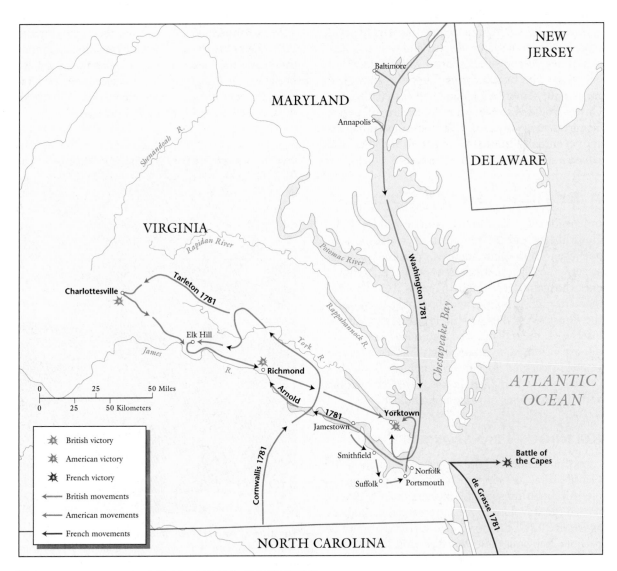

VIRGINIA AND THE YORKTOWN CAMPAIGN

his glasses and remarked, "I have grown old in the service of my country, and now find that I am growing blind." Tears filled the eyes of his comrades in arms, and the threat of a coup vanished.

In Philadelphia two months later, unpaid Pennsylvania soldiers marched on the statehouse where both Congress and the state's executive council sat. Ignoring Congress, they demanded that Pennsylvania redress their grievances. Congress felt insulted and left the city for Princeton, where it reconvened in Nassau Hall. Its archives and administrative departments remained in Philadelphia. "I confess I have great apprehensions for the union of the states," wrote Charles Thomson, secretary to Congress since 1774, "& begin to fear that America will experience internal convulsions, and that the fabrick of her liberty will be stained with the blood of her sons." The British threat, Thomson knew, had created the American Union. He feared that the Union would dissolve with the return of peace. Congress moved on from Princeton to Annapolis and eventually settled in New York, but the Union's survival remained uncertain.

A REVOLUTIONARY SOCIETY

Independence transformed American life. Religious liberty and the pluralism it created became not just tolerated but admired. Within American society, the biggest winners were free householders, who gained enormous benefits from the democratization of politics and the chance to colonize the Great West. Besides the loyalists, the biggest losers were the Indians, who continued to resist settler expansion. Many slaves won their freedom, and women struggled for greater dignity. Both succeeded only when their goals proved compatible with the ambitions of white householders.

RELIGIOUS TRANSFORMATIONS

After independence, the Anglican Church, with George III as its "supreme head," became vulnerable. Although most Anglican clergymen had supported the Revolution or had remained neutral, an aggressive loyalist minority had stirred the wrath of patriots. Religious dissenters disestablished the Anglican Church in every southern state. They deprived it of its tax support and other privileges, such

as the sole right to perform marriages. In 1786 Virginia passed Thomas Jefferson's eloquent Statute for Religious Freedom, which declared that "God hath created the mind free" and that efforts to use coercion in matters of religion "tend only to beget habits of hypocrisy and meanness." In Virginia, church attendance and the support of ministers became voluntary activities.

Other states moved more slowly. In New England (except in Rhode Island), the Congregational churches were established by law. They had strongly supported the Revolution and were less vulnerable to attack. Their ministers' salaries continued to be paid out of public taxes, although lawful dissenters, such as Baptists, could insist that their church taxes go to their own clergy. The Congregational Church exercised other public or quasi-public functions, especially on thanksgiving, fast, and election days. Disestablishment did not become complete until 1818 in Connecticut and 1833 in Massachusetts.

INTERIOR OF TOURO SYNAGOGUE IN NEWPORT, RHODE ISLAND The synagogue shown here presents the best surviving example of Jewish artistic taste in 18th-century America.

Although most states still restricted officeholding to Christians or Protestants, many people were coming to regard the coercion of anyone's conscience as morally wrong. Jews and Catholics both gained from the new atmosphere of tolerance. When Britain recognized the Catholic Church in the Quebec Act of 1774, most colonists had shuddered with anxiety. But in 1790, when John Carroll of Maryland became the first Roman Catholic bishop in the United States, hardly anyone protested. Before independence, an Anglican bishop had been an explosive issue in several colonies, but in the 1780s the Church of England reorganized itself as the Protestant Episcopal Church and quietly began to consecrate its own bishops. Both Episcopalians and Presbyterians paid homage to republican values by adopting written constitutions for their churches.

THE FIRST EMANCIPATION

The Revolution freed tens of thousands of slaves, but it also gave new vitality to slavery in the region that people were beginning to call "the South." Within a generation, slavery was abolished in the emerging "North." Race became a defining factor in both regions. In the South, most blacks remained slaves. In the North, they became free but not equal. The independent householder and his voluntaristic ethic remained almost a white monopoly.

Many slaves freed themselves. The British army enabled more than half the slaves of Georgia and perhaps one-quarter of those in South Carolina to win their freedom. A similar process was under way in Virginia in 1781, only to be cut off at Yorktown. Hundreds of New England slaves won their freedom through military service. They announced what they were fighting for in the surnames they chose. Jeffrey Liberty, Cuff Liberty, Dick Freeman, and Jube Freeman served in one Connecticut regiment. After the Massachusetts bill of rights proclaimed that all people were "born free and equal," Elizabeth (Bett) Freeman sued her master in 1781 and won her liberty. Thereafter, most of the slaves in Massachusetts and New Hampshire simply walked away from their masters.

Elsewhere, legislative action was necessary. Pennsylvania led the way in 1780 with the modern world's first gradual emancipation statute. Instead of freeing current slaves, it declared that all children born to Pennsylvania slaves after a given date would become free at age 28. In other words slaves, not masters or taxpayers, had to pay the costs of their own emancipation. This requirement left them unable to compete on equal terms with free whites, who usually entered adult life with inherited property. Some masters shipped their slaves south before the moment of emancipation, and some whites kidnapped freedmen and sent them south. The Pennsylvania Abolition Society was organized largely to fight these abuses. By 1800 Philadelphia had the largest community of free blacks in America, with their own churches and other voluntary societies.

The Pennsylvania pattern took hold, with variations, in most other northern states until all of them had made provision for emancipation. Where slaves constituted more than 10 percent of the population, as in southern New York and northeastern New Jersey, slaveholders' resistance delayed legislation for years. New York yielded in 1799, and finally so did New Jersey in 1804.

In the upper South, many Methodists and Baptists supported emancipation in the 1780s, only to retreat in later years. Maryland and Virginia authorized the manumission of individual slaves. By 1810 more than one-fifth of Maryland's slaves had been freed, as had 10,000 of Virginia's 300,000 slaves, including more than 300 freed under Washington's will after he died in 1799. But slaves were essential to the plantation economy and were usually their masters' most valuable asset. In the South, emancipation would have amounted to a social revolution and the impoverishment of the planter class. Planters supported the Christianization of their slaves and other humane reforms, but they resisted emancipation, especially with the rise of cotton as a new cash crop after the war. Tragically, the slaves contributed a great deal to the acceptance of cotton as a new staple, which in turn guaranteed that their children and grandchildren would remain in bondage. Cut off from British textiles during the war, South Carolina slaves insisted on growing cotton as a substitute. Their owners quickly recognized the enormous potential of that crop.

Maryland and Virginia, where population growth among the slaves exceeded what the tobacco economy could absorb, banned the Atlantic slave trade, as had all states outside the Deep South. Georgia and South Carolina, to make good their losses during the war and to meet the demand for cotton after 1790, reopened the Atlantic slave trade. South Carolina imported almost 60,000 more Africans before Congress prohibited the Atlantic slave trade in 1808.

THE CHALLENGE TO PATRIARCHY

Nothing as dramatic as emancipation altered relations between the sexes, although subtle changes did occur. With the men away fighting, many women were left in charge of the household, sometimes with interesting consequences. "I hope you will not consider yourself as commander in chief of your own house," Lucy Knox warned her soldier husband, Henry, in 1777, "but be convinced . . . that there is such a thing as equal command." Although some women acquired new authority, nearly all of them had to work harder to keep their households functioning. The war cut them off from most European consumer goods. Household manufactures, mostly the task of women, filled the gap. Women accepted these duties without insisting on broader legal or political rights, but soaring food prices made many women assertive. In numerous food riots through 1779, women often took the lead in trying to make merchants lower prices or stop hoarding grain.

Attitudes toward marriage were also changing. The common-law rule of coverture (see chapter 4) still denied wives any legal personality, but some of them, citing their own support of the Revolution, persuaded state governments not to impoverish them by confiscating the property of their loyalist husbands. Many writers insisted that good marriages rested on mutual affection, not on property settlements. In portraits of wealthy northeastern families, husbands and wives were beginning to appear as equals. Parents were urged to respect the personalities of their children and to avoid severe discipline. Traditional reverence for the elderly was giving way to an idealization of youth and energy.

Esther de Berdt Reed organized the Philadelphia Ladies Association in 1780 to relieve the sufferings of Continental soldiers. It was the first women's society in American history to take on a public role. Although few women demanded equal political rights during the Revolution, the New Jersey Constitution of 1776 let them vote if they headed a household (usually as a widow) and paid taxes. This right was revoked in 1807.

Especially in the Northeast, more women learned to read and write. Philosophers, clergymen, and even popular writers were beginning to treat women as morally superior to men, a sharp reversal of earlier teachings. The first female academies were founded in the 1790s. By 1830 nearly all native-born women in the Northeast had become literate. The ideal of the "republican wife" and the "republican mother" took hold, giving wives and mothers an expanding educational role within the family. They encouraged diligence in their husbands and patriotism in their

> "*I long to hear that you have declared an independancy—and by the way in the new Code of Laws which I suppose it will be necessary for you to make I desire you would Remember the Ladies, and be more generous and favourable to them than your ancestors. Do not put such unlimited power into the hands of the Husbands. Remember all Men would be tyrants if they could. If perticuliar care and attention is not paid to the Laidies we are determined to foment a Rebelion, and will not hold ourselves bound by any Laws in which we have no voice, or Representation.*
> "*That your Sex are Naturally Tyrannical is a Truth so thoroughly established as to admit of no dispute, but such of you as wish to be happy willingly give up the harsh title of Master for the more tender and endearing one of Friend. Why then, not put it out of the power of the vicious and the Lawless to use us with cruelty and indignity.*"
>
> **ABIGAIL ADAMS**
> *discussing women's rights in a letter to John Adams, March 31, 1776*

WOMEN VOTING IN LATE 18TH-CENTURY NEW JERSEY
Alone among the 13 states, the New Jersey constitution
of 1776 permitted women to vote if they were the heads
of their households, a category that included mostly widows. This privilege was revoked in 1807.

sons. The novel became a major cultural form in the
United States. Its main audience was female, as were
many of the authors. Novels cast women as central
characters and warned young women to beware of
suitors motivated only by greed or lust.

WESTERN EXPANSION, DISCONTENT, AND CONFLICT WITH INDIANS

Westward expansion had continued during the
Revolutionary War. With 30 axmen, Daniel
Boone, a North Carolina hunter, hacked out the
Wilderness Road from Cumberland Gap to the
Kentucky bluegrass country in early 1775. The first
settlers to arrive challenged the speculative Tran-
sylvania Company, which claimed title to the land.
They called Kentucky "the best poor-man's country" and claimed it should belong to those who
tilled its soil, not to men with paper titles from governments far to the east in Virginia or London.

Although few Indians lived in Kentucky, it was
the favorite hunting ground of the Shawnees and
other nations. Their raids often prevented the settlers from planting crops. The settlers ate game and
put up log cabins against the inside walls of large
rectangular stockades, 10 feet high and built from
oak logs. At each corner, a blockhouse with a pro-
truding second story permitted the defenders to
fire along the outside walls. Three of these "Ken-

tucky stations" were built—at Boonesborough, St.
Asaph, and Harrodsburg—and they withstood Indian attacks until late in the war.

Because of the constant danger, settlement grew
slowly at first. In 1779, when George Rogers
Clark's victory at Vincennes provided a brief period
of security, thousands of settlers moved in. After
1780, however, the Indians renewed their attacks,
this time with British allies who could smash the
stockades with artillery. Kentucky lived up to its old
Indian reputation as the "dark and bloody ground."
Only a few thousand settlers stuck it out until the
war ended, when they were joined by swarms of
newcomers. Speculators and absentees were already
trying to claim the best bluegrass land. The Federal
Census of 1790 listed 74,000 settlers and slaves in
Kentucky and about half that many in Tennessee,
where the Cherokees had ceded a large tract after
their defeat in 1776. These settlers thrived both because few Indians lived there and because British
and Spanish raiders found it hard to reach them.

To the south and north of this bulge, settlement
was much riskier. After the war, Spain supplied arms
and trade goods to Creeks, Cherokees, Choctaws,
and Chickasaws willing to resist Georgia's attempt
to settle its western lands. North of the Ohio River,
where confederated Indians had won their military
struggle, Britain refused to withdraw its garrisons
and traders from Niagara, Detroit, and a few other
posts, even though, according to the Treaty of Paris,
those forts now lay within the boundaries of the
United States. To justify their refusal, the British
pointed to Congress's failure to honor America's
obligations to loyalists and British creditors under
the treaty. When small groups of Indians sold large
tracts of land to Georgia, Pennsylvania, and New
York, as well as to Congress, the Indian nations repudiated those sales and, supported by either Spain
or Britain, continued to resist into the 1790s.

During the Revolutionary War, many states and
Congress had recruited soldiers with promises of
land after the war ended, and now they needed Indian lands to fulfill these pledges. The few Indian
nations that had supported the United States
suffered the most. In the 1780s, after Joseph Brant
led most of the Iroquois north to Canada, New
York confiscated much of the land of the friendly
Iroquois who stayed. South Carolina dispossessed
the Catawbas of most of their ancestral lands.
The states had a harder time seizing the land of

Toward Equality: The Affectionate Family

Well into the 18th century, family portraits reflected the prevailing patriarchal values of British and colonial society. In Robert Feke's 1741 painting, *Isaac Royall and His Family*, notice that the figure of the New England father is elevated above other members of the household and is dressed more resplendently than anyone else.

This pattern changed dramatically in the Northeast after independence. In the 1849 *Portrait of the Haight Family*, the father and mother share equal elevation, but the mother, the keeper of domestic space, is closer to the viewer and more prominent. The oldest daughter, soon to be of marriageable age, has the

hostile Indians, who usually had Spanish or British allies.

Secessionist movements arose in the 1780s when neither Congress nor eastern state governments seemed able to solve western problems. Some Tennessee settlers seceded from North Carolina and for a time maintained a separate state called Franklin. Separatist sentiment also ran strong in Kentucky. Even the settlers of western Pennsylvania thought of setting up on their own after Spain closed the Mississippi to American traffic in 1784. James Wilkinson explored the possibility of creating an independent republic west of the Appalachians under Spanish protection. When Congress refused to recognize Vermont's independence from New York, even the radical Green Mountain Boys sounded out Canadian officials about readmission to the British Empire as a separate province.

THE NORTHWEST ORDINANCE

Congress did, however, persuade states to cede to it their charter claims to land north of the Ohio River. Virginia's compliance in early 1781 prompted other states to follow suit. Jefferson offered a resolution in 1784 that would have created 10 or more new states in this Northwest Territory. Each state could adopt the constitution and laws of any of the older states and, when its population reached 20,000, could be admitted to the Union on equal terms with the original 13. The possibility that the northwestern states, plus Kentucky, Tennessee, and Vermont, might outvote the old 13

most elevated position in the portrait, which suggests a family strongly oriented toward the welfare of its children. The classical statuary and the portrait in the background indicate taste and refinement.

These new values, however, did not penetrate very deeply into the West. William S. Jewett's *The Promised Land—The Grayson Family* (1850) portrays an armed householder elevated above his wife and child as their protector and provider. His buckskin clothing suggests an egalitarian relationship with other householders in the West, where even ordinary men could become heroes. This theme sometimes ac-

quired strong racist overtones. The 1874 lithograph *Daniel Boone Protects His Family* was copied from an 1852 statue by Horatio Greenough that depicted an unnamed pioneer family and was meant to demonstrate, in Greenough's words, "the superiority of the white man" over all other races. Contemporaries quickly decided that Greenough's hero was really Boone. Here the ordinary man performs heroic deeds while both wife and child cower in fear. Only the dog is not intimidated. But, then, as one commentator remarked, the West was hell for women and horses but heaven for men and dogs.

made Congress hesitate, and Jefferson's resolution was never implemented. In the Land Ordinance of 1785, however, Congress authorized the survey of the Northwest Territory and its division into townships 6 miles square, each composed of 36 "sections" of 640 acres. Surveyed land would be sold at auction starting at a dollar an acre. Alternate townships would be sold in sections or as a whole, to satisfy settlers and speculators, respectively.

In July 1787, while the Constitutional Convention met in Philadelphia, Congress (sitting in New York) returned to the problem of governing the Northwest Territory. By then, Massachusetts veterans were organizing the Ohio Company under Manassah Cutler to obtain a huge land grant from Congress. Cutler joined forces with William Duer, a New York speculator who was organizing the

Scioto Company. Together they pried from Congress 1.5 million acres for the Ohio Company veterans and an option on 5 million more acres, which the Ohio Company assigned to the Scioto Company. The Ohio Company agreed to pay Congress two installments of $500,000 in depreciated securities. To meet the first payment, Duer's backers lent Cutler's $200,000. Once again speculators, rather than settlers, seemed to be winning the West.

In July Congress passed the Northwest Ordinance of 1787 to provide government for the region. Rejecting Jefferson's earlier goal of 10 or more states, the ordinance authorized the creation of from 3 to 5, to be admitted to the Union as full equals of the original 13. The ordinance thus rejected colonialism among white people except as a temporary phase through which a "territory" would pass on its way to

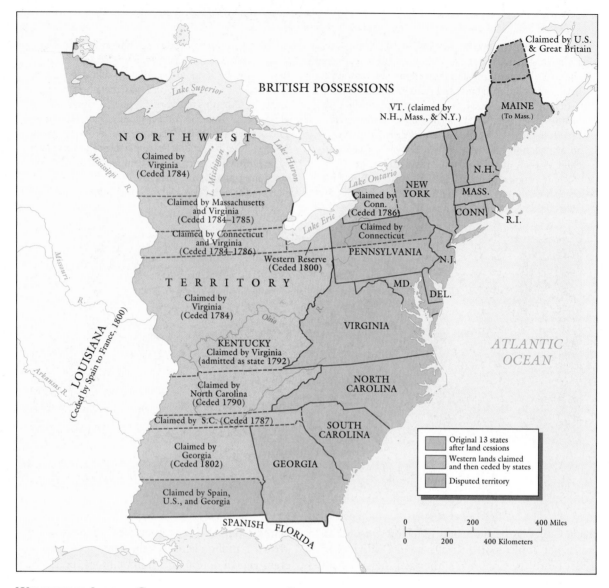

WESTERN LAND CLAIMS DURING THE REVOLUTION

statehood. Congress would appoint a governor and a council to rule until population reached 5,000. At that point, the settlers could elect an assembly empowered to pass laws, although the governor (obviously modeled on earlier royal governors) had an absolute veto. When population reached 60,000, the settlers could adopt their own constitution and petition Congress for statehood. The ordinance protected civil liberties, made provision for public education, and prohibited slavery within the region.

Southern delegates all voted for the Northwest Ordinance despite its antislavery clause. They probably hoped that Ohio would become what Georgia had been in the 1730s, a society of armed free men able to protect vulnerable slave states, such as Kentucky, from hostile invaders. The Ohio valley was the republic's most dangerous frontier. Southern delegates also thought that most settlers would come from Maryland, Virginia, and Kentucky. Even if they could not bring slaves with them, they would

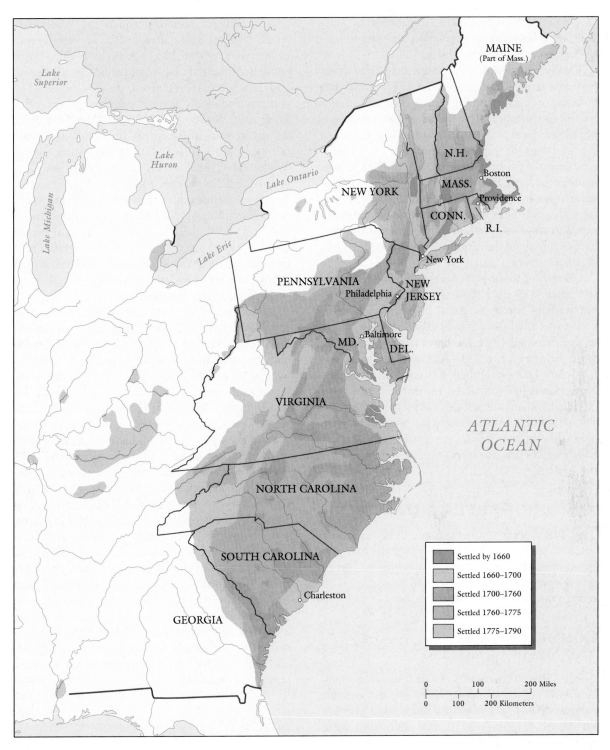

Lake Superior

Lake Huron

Lake Michigan

Lake Ontario

Lake Erie

MAINE
(Part of Mass.)

N.H.

MASS.

Boston

CONN.

Providence

R.I.

NEW YORK

New York

PENNSYLVANIA

NEW JERSEY

Philadelphia

Baltimore

MD.

DEL.

VIRGINIA

ATLANTIC OCEAN

NORTH CAROLINA

SOUTH CAROLINA

Charleston

GEORGIA

	Settled by 1660
	Settled 1660–1700
	Settled 1700–1760
	Settled 1760–1775
	Settled 1775–1790

0   100   200 Miles

0   100   200 Kilometers

ADVANCE OF SETTLEMENT TO 1790

have southern loyalties. New Englanders, by contrast, were counting on the Ohio Company to lure their own veterans to the region.

Finally, the antislavery clause may have been part of a larger "Compromise of 1787," involving both the ordinance and the clauses on slavery in the federal Constitution. The Philadelphia Convention permitted states to count three-fifths of their slaves for purposes of representation. The antislavery concession to northerners in the ordinance was made at the same time that southern states won this concession in Philadelphia. Several congressmen were also delegates to the Constitutional Convention and traveled back and forth between the two cities while these decisions were being made. They may have struck a deal.

Congress had developed a coherent western policy. After 1787 only the Indians, who drove away hundreds of squatters, stood in the way. Federal surveyors risked their lives in Ohio, and few buyers stepped forward when the first townships were offered for sale in late 1787. Yet by 1789, the Ohio Company had established the town of Marietta, Kentuckians had founded a town that would soon be called Cincinnati, and tiny outposts had been set up at Columbia and Gallipolis. But without massive help from the new federal government, the settlers had little chance of defending themselves against the Indians.

A More Perfect Union

The 1780s were difficult times. The economy failed to rebound, debtors fought creditors, and state politics became bitter and contentious. Out of this ferment arose the demand to amend or even replace the Articles of Confederation.

Commerce, Debt, and Shays's Rebellion

In 1784 British merchants flooded American markets with exports worth £3.7 million, the greatest volume since 1771. But Americans could not pay for them. Exports to Britain that year were £750,000—less than 40 percent of the £1.9 million of 1774, the last year of peace. When Britain invoked the Navigation Acts to close the British West Indies to American ships (but not to American goods), indirect returns through this once profitable channel also faltered. Trade with France closed some of the gap, but because the French could not offer the long-term credit that the British had provided, it remained disappointing. The American economy entered a deep depression that lifted only slightly in 1787 and 1788 before the strong recovery of the 1790s. Imports from Britain fell by 40 percent in 1785. Exports rose to almost £900,000 but remained far below prewar levels.

Private debts became a huge social problem that the states, buried under their own war debts, could not easily mitigate. Merchants, dunned by British creditors, sued their customers, many of whom could not even pay their taxes. Farmers, faced with the loss of their crops, livestock, and even their farms, resisted foreclosures and looked to their state governments for relief.

About half of the states issued paper money in the 1780s, and many passed stay laws to postpone the date on which a debt would come due. Massachusetts, which remembered its fierce conflicts over paper money before 1750 (see chapter 4), rejected both options and raised taxes to new highs. In 1786 many farmers in Hampshire County took matters into their own hands. Crowds gathered to prevent the courts from conducting business, much as patriots had done against the British in 1774. Governor James Bowdoin insisted that acts of resistance that had been appropriate against a tyrannical monarch were unacceptable in a government elected by the people. But in early 1787 the protestors, loosely organized under a Continental Army veteran, Captain Daniel Shays, attacked the federal arsenal at Springfield. An army of volunteers under Benjamin Lincoln marched west with artillery and scattered the Shaysites. Even so, Shaysites won enough seats in the May assembly elections to pass a stay law. In Massachusetts, Shays's Rebellion converted into nationalists many gentlemen and artisans who until then had opposed strengthening the central government.

Cosmopolitans versus Localists

The tensions racking Massachusetts surfaced elsewhere as well. Crowds of debtors in other states closed law courts or even besieged the legislature.

State politics reflected a persistent cleavage between "cosmopolitan" and "localist" coalitions. Merchants, professional men, urban artisans, commercial farmers, southern planters, and former Continental Army officers made up the cosmopolitan bloc. They looked to energetic government, both state and continental, to solve their problems. They favored aggressive trade policies, hard money, payment of public debts, good salaries for executive officials and judges, and leniency to returning loyalists. The "localists" were farmers, rural artisans, and militia veterans who distrusted those policies. They demanded paper money and debtor relief. They supported generous salaries for representatives, so that ordinary men could serve, which cosmopolitans resisted.

Localists defeated their opponents most of the time in most states. During and after the war, they destroyed the feudal revival (see chapter 5) by confiscating the gigantic land claims of the Granville District, the Fairfax estate, the Calvert and Penn proprietaries, and the manorial estates of New York loyalists. (Because their owners were patriots, Rensselaerswyck and Livingston Manor survived to become the site of agrarian violence into the 1840s, when the manors were finally abolished.) Except in Vermont, localists were much less adept at blocking the claims of land speculators, some of whom put together enormous tracts. Yet cosmopolitans lost so often that many of them despaired of state politics and looked to a strengthened central government for relief.

Congress faced its own fiscal problems. Between October 1781 and February 1786, it requisitioned $15.7 million from the states but received only $2.4 million. Its annual income had fallen to $400,000 at a time when interest on its debt approached $2.5 million and when the principal on the foreign debt was about to come due. Requisitions were beginning to seem as hopelessly inefficient as George Grenville had proclaimed them to be when he proposed the Stamp Act.

Foreign relations also took an ominous turn. In 1786 Foreign Secretary John Jay negotiated a treaty with Don Diego de Gardoqui, the Spanish minister to the United States, which offered northern merchants trading privileges with Spanish colonies. In exchange, the Mississippi would be closed to American traffic for 25 years. Seven northern states voted for the treaty, but all five southern states in Congress rejected these terms—thus defeating it. Treaties needed nine votes for ratification under the Articles of Confederation. Angry talk of disbanding the Union soon filled Congress. Delegates began haggling over which state would join what union if the breakup occurred. The quarrel became public in February 1787 when a Boston newspaper endorsed a dissolution of the Union.

By the mid-1780s many cosmopolitans were becoming nationalists eager to strengthen the Union. Many of them had served long, frustrating years in the army or in Congress, unable to carry out measures that they considered vital to the Confederation. In 1785 some of them tried to see what could be done outside Congress. To resolve disputes about navigation rights on the Potomac River, George Washington invited Virginia and Maryland delegates to a conference at Mount Vernon, where they drafted an agreement acceptable to both states and to Congress. Prompted by James Madison, a former congressman, the Virginia legislature then urged all the states to participate in a convention at Annapolis to explore ways to improve American trade.

Four states, including Maryland, ignored the call, and the New Englanders had not yet arrived when, in September 1786, the delegates from the four middle states and Virginia accepted a report drafted by Alexander Hamilton of New York. It asked all of the states to send delegates to a convention at Philadelphia the next May "to devise such further provisions as shall appear to them necessary to render the constitution of the Federal Government adequate to the exigencies of the Union." Seven states responded positively before Congress endorsed the convention on February 21, 1787, and five accepted later. Rhode Island refused to participate. Madison used the winter months to study the defects of classical and European confederacies and to draft a plan for a stronger American union.

THE PHILADELPHIA CONVENTION

The convention opened in May 1787 with a plan similar to the Virginia constitution of 1776. It proposed an almost sovereign Parliament for the United States. By September the delegates had produced a document much closer to the Massachusetts constitution of 1780, with a clear separation of powers. The delegates, in four months of secret sessions, repeated the constitutional learning process that had taken four years at the state level after 1776.

With Washington presiding, Governor Edmund Randolph proposed the Virginia, or "large state," plan. Drafted by Madison, it proposed a bicameral legislature, with representation in both houses apportioned according to population. The legislature would choose the executive and the judiciary. It would possess all powers currently lodged in Congress and the power "to legislate in all cases to which the separate States are incompetent." It could "negative all laws passed by the several States, contravening in [its] opinion . . . the articles of Union." Remarkably, the plan did not include specific powers to tax or regulate trade. Madison apparently believed it wiser to be vague and sweeping, rather than explicit. His plan also required ratification by state conventions, not by state legislatures. Within two weeks, the delegates agreed on three-year terms for members of the lower house and seven-year terms for the upper house. The legislature would choose the executive for a single term of seven years.

In mid-June, delegates from the small states struck back. William Paterson proposed the New Jersey Plan, which gave the existing Congress the power to levy import duties and a stamp tax (as in Grenville's imperial reforms of 1764 and 1765), to regulate trade, and to use force to collect delinquent requisitions from the states (as in North's Conciliatory Proposition of 1775). Each state would have one vote.

As another alternative, perhaps designed to terrify the small states into accepting the Virginia Plan, Hamilton suggested a government in which both the senate and the executive would serve "on good behavior"—that is, for life! To him, the British constitution still seemed the best in the world, but he never formally proposed his plan.

All the options before the convention seemed counterrevolutionary at that point. Madison's Parliament for America, Paterson's emulation of Grenville and North, and Hamilton's enthusiasm for the British Empire all challenged in major ways the principles of 1776. As the summer progressed, however, the delegates asked themselves what the voters would or would not accept and relearned the hard lessons of popular sovereignty that the state

constitutions had taught. The result was a federal Constitution that was indeed revolutionary.

Before the Constitution took its final shape, however, the debate grew as hot as the summer weather. The small states warned that their voters would never accept a constitution that let the large states swallow them. The large states insisted on proportional representation in both houses. "The Large States dare not dissolve the Confederation," retorted Delaware's Gunning Bedford in the most inflammatory outburst of the convention. "If they do, the small ones will find some foreign ally of more honor and good faith, who will take them by the hand and do them justice." Then the Connecticut delegates announced that they would be happy with proportional representation in one house and state equality in the other.

In mid-July, the delegates accepted this "Connecticut Compromise" and then completed the document by September. They finally realized that they were creating a government of laws, to be enforced on individuals through federal courts, and were not propping up a system of congressional resolutions to be carried out (or ignored) by the states. Terms for representatives were reduced to two years, and terms for senators to six, with each state legislature choosing two senators. The president would serve four years, could be reelected, and would be chosen by an Electoral College. Each state received as many electors as it had congressmen and senators combined, and the states were free to decide how to choose their electors. Each elector had to vote for two candidates, one of whom had to be from another state. This provision reflected the fear that localist impulses might prevent a majority vote for anyone. The delegates knew that Washington would be the first president, but there was no obvious choice after him.

In other provisions, free and slave states agreed to count only three-fifths of the slaves in apportioning both representation and direct taxes. The enumeration of congressional powers became lengthy and explicit and included taxation, the regulation of foreign and interstate commerce, and the catchall "necessary and proper" clause. Madison's negative on state laws was replaced by the gentler "supreme law of the land" clause. Over George Mason's last-minute objection, the delegates voted not to include a bill of rights.

With little debate, the convention approved a revolutionary proposal for ratifying the Constitution. This clause called for special conventions in

YOUNG JAMES MADISON Charles Willson Peale painted this miniature portrait in 1783, just as Madison was entering the arena of national politics.

> "*Happily for America, happily we trust for the whole human race, [the leaders of the American Revolution] pursued a new and more noble course. They accomplished a revolution which has no parallel in the annals of human society. They reared the fabrics of governments which have no model on the face of the globe. They formed the design of a great Confederacy, which it is incumbent on their successors to improve and perpetuate. If their works betray imperfections, we wonder at the fewness of them. If they erred most in the structure of the Union, this was the work most difficult to be executed; this is the work which has been new modeled by the act of your convention, and it is that act on which you are now to deliberate and decide.*"
>
> **JAMES MADISON**
> *The Federalist, no. 14*

each state and declared that the Constitution would go into force as soon as any nine states had accepted it, even though the Articles of Confederation required unanimous approval for all amendments. The delegates understood that they were proposing an illegal but peaceful overthrow of the existing legal order—that is, a revolution. If all the states approved, it would, they hoped, become both peaceful and legal. The Constitution would then rest on popular sovereignty in a way that the Articles never had. The "Federalists," as supporters of the Constitution now called themselves, were willing to risk destroying the Union in order to save it. But they knew that they would have to use persuasion, not force, to win approval.

RATIFICATION

When the Federalist delegates returned home, they made a powerful case for the Constitution in newspapers, most of which favored a stronger central government. Most "Anti-Federalists," or opponents of the Constitution, were localists with few interstate contacts and only limited access to the press. The Federalists gave them little time to organize. The first ratifying conventions met in December. Delaware ratified unanimously on December 7, Pennsylvania by a 46-to-23 vote five days later, and New Jersey unanimously on December 18. Georgia ratified unanimously on January 2, and Connecticut soon approved, also by a lopsided margin.

Except in Pennsylvania, these victories were in small states. Ironically, although the Constitution was mostly a "large state" document, small states embraced it while large states hesitated. Small states, once they had equality in the senate, saw many advantages in a strong central government. Under the Articles, for example, New Jersey residents had to pay duties to neighboring states on foreign goods imported through New York City or Philadelphia. Under the new Constitution, import duties would go to the federal government, a clear gain for every small state but Rhode Island, which stood to lose import duties at both Providence and Newport.

By contrast, Pennsylvania was the only large state with a solid majority for ratification. But Anti-Federalists there eloquently demanded a federal bill of rights and major changes in the structure of the new government. Large states could consider going it alone. Small states could not—except for Rhode Island with its two cities and its long history of defying its neighbors.

The first hotly contested state was Massachusetts, which set a pattern for struggles in other divided states. Federalists there won by a slim margin (187 to 168) in February 1788. They blocked Anti-Federalist attempts to make ratification conditional on the adoption of specific amendments. Instead the Federalists promised to support a bill of rights by constitutional amendment after ratification. But the Rhode Island legislature voted overwhelmingly not even to summon a ratifying convention. Maryland and South Carolina ratified easily in April and May, bringing the total to eight of the nine states required. Then conventions met almost simultaneously in New Hampshire, Virginia, New York, and North Carolina. In each, a majority at first opposed ratification.

As resistance stiffened, the ratification controversy turned into the first great debate on the American Union, on what kind of a nation the United States should be. By the summer of 1788 Anti-Federalists were eloquent and well organized. They argued that the new government would be too remote from the people to be trusted with the broad powers specified in the Constitution. They warned that in a House of Representatives divided into districts of 30,000 people (twice the size of Boston), only prominent and wealthy men would be elected. The new government would become an aristocracy or oligarchy that would impose heavy taxes and other burdens on the people. The absence of a bill of rights also troubled them.

During the struggle over ratification, Hamilton, Madison, and Jay wrote a series of 85 essays, published first in New York newspapers and widely reprinted elsewhere, in which they defended the Constitution almost clause by clause. Signing themselves "Publius," they later published the col-lected essays as *The Federalist Papers*, the most comprehensive body of political thought produced by the Revolutionary generation. In *Federalist, no. 10*, Madison argued that a large republic would be far more stable than a small one. He challenged 2,000 years of accepted wisdom, which insisted that only small republics could survive. Small republics were inherently unstable, Madison insisted, because majority factions could easily gain power within them, trample upon the rights of minorities, and ignore the common good. In a republic as huge and diverse as the United States, however, factions would seldom be able to forge a majority. "Publius" hoped that the new government would draw on the talents of the wisest and the best-educated citizens. To those who accused him of trying to erect an American aristocracy, he pointed out that the Constitution forbade titles and hereditary rule.

Federalists won a narrow majority (57 to 46) in New Hampshire on June 21, and Madison guided Virginia to ratification (89 to 79) five days later. New York approved, by 30 votes to 27, a month later, bringing 11 states into the Union, enough to launch the new government. North Carolina rejected the Constitution in July 1788 but finally ratified in November 1789 after the first Congress had drafted the Bill of Rights and sent it to the states. Rhode Island, after voting seven times not to call a ratifying convention, finally summoned one that ratified by a vote of only 34 to 32 in May 1790.

CONCLUSION

Americans survived the most devastating war they had yet fought and won their independence, but only with massive aid from France. Most Indians and blacks who could sided with Britain. During the struggle white Americans affirmed liberty and equality for themselves in their new state constitutions and bills of rights, but they rarely applied these values to blacks and Indians, even though every northern state adopted either immediate or gradual emancipation. The discontent of the postwar years created the Federalist coalition, which drafted and ratified a new national Constitution to replace the Articles of Confederation. Federalists endowed the new central government with more power than Parliament had ever successfully exercised over the colonies but insisted that the Constitution was fully compatible with the liberty and equality proclaimed during the Revolution.

Nothing resembling the American federal system had ever been tried before. Under this new system, sovereignty was removed from government and bestowed on the people, who then empowered separate levels of government through their state and federal constitutions. As the Great Seal of the United States proclaimed, it was a *novus ordo seclorum*, a new order for the ages.

Suggested Readings begin on page SR-1. For Web activities and resources related to this chapter, go to http://www.harcourtcollege.com/history.murrin

CHAPTER 7

THE DEMOCRATIC REPUBLIC, 1790–1820

WILLIAM RUSSELL BIRCH, *PREPARATION FOR WAR TO DEFEND COMMERCE*

International commerce made many great fortunes in the early republic, and shipbuilding ranked among the largest and best-developed manufacturing enterprises in America. Yet shipbuilders—like nearly all American craftsmen—continued to perform their work in traditional ways. Workers in this Philadelphia shipyard crafted each ship (and each part of it) individually and by hand—a job that required traditional craft skills, careful cooperation, and heavy physical labor. Large-scale machine industry remained decades in the future.

The Americans who affirmed George Washington as their first president in 1789 were an overwhelmingly rural people. Some, like Washington himself, were planters who sent shiploads of slave-grown crops to world markets. Most, however, owned small farms; they created a subsistence within their own households and neighborhoods, then sent surplus food to Europe and the Caribbean. Whatever their level of prosperity, most households in the American countryside were headed by men who owned land and who enjoyed the liberty and civil equality for which they had fought the Revolution. They also wielded power—both as citizens and as governors of families that included their wives, children, slaves, and other dependents. (The makers of the republic agreed that citizenship was not for everyone; they bestowed power and equal rights upon propertied white fathers, and powerlessness and dependence upon nearly everyone else.)

In the first 30 years of government under the Constitution, the Americans consolidated their republic and seized opportunities to expand their commerce with a war-torn Europe. In these years their population shot from 4 million to 10 million persons; their agrarian republic spilled across the Appalachians and reached the Mississippi River; their exports rose; and their seaport towns became cities. In the midst of this rapid change the revolutionary republic drifted from its moorings in the patriarchal household. Increasing thousands of white men found it hard to maintain their status as propertied citizens or to pass that status on to new generations; others simply grew impatient with the responsibilities and limits of rural patriarchy. The resultant erosion of authority, along with the increasingly equalitarian implications of revolutionary republicanism, encouraged women, slaves, and the growing ranks of propertyless white men to imagine that the revolutionary birthrights of liberty and equality—perhaps even power—might also belong to them. By 1820 the agrarian republic, with its promise of widespread proprietorship and well-ordered paternal authority, was in deep trouble. A more individualistic, democratic, and insecure order was taking its place.

This chapter will focus on the following major questions:

- What was the nature of the American agricultural economy and of agricultural society in the years 1790 through 1815?

- What was the history of slavery in these years? In what areas (and in what ways) did it expand? In what areas (and, again, in what ways) was the slave system called into question?
- In what ways was the spread of evangelical Protestantism in these years beginning to shape American society and culture?
- Which Americans benefited from economic and social change between 1790 and 1815? Which did not?

THE FARMER'S REPUBLIC

In 1782, J. Hector St. John de Crèvecoeur, a French soldier who had settled in rural New York, explained American agrarianism through the words of a fictionalized farmer. First of all, he said, the American farmer owns his own land and bases his claim to dignity and citizenship on that fact. He spoke of "the bright idea of property," and went on: "This formerly rude soil has been converted by my father into a pleasant farm, and in return, it has established all our rights; on it is founded our rank, our freedom, our power as citizens, our importance as inhabitants of [a rural neighborhood]. . . ." Second, farm ownership endows the American farmer with the powers and responsibilities of fatherhood. "Often when I plant my low ground," he said, "I place my little boy on a chair which screws to the beam of the plough—its motion and that of the horses please him; he is perfectly happy and begins to chat. As I lean over the handle, various are the thoughts which crowd into my mind. I am now doing for him, I say, what my father did for me; may God enable him to live that he may perform the same operations for the same purposes when I am worn out and old!"

Crèvecoeur's farmer, musing on liberty and property, working the ancestral fields with his male heir strapped to the plough, evokes a proud citizen of America's revolutionary republic. Few of Crèvecoeur's fellow citizens were as poetic as he, but they shared his concern with propertied independence and its social and political consequences. From New England through the mid-Atlantic and on into the southern Piedmont and backcountry, few farmers in 1790 thought of farming as a business. Their first concern was to provide a subsistence for their households. Their second was to achieve long-term

"*Those who labour in the earth are the chosen people of God, if ever he had a chosen people, whose breasts he has made his peculiar deposit for substantial and genuine virtue. It is the focus in which he keeps alive that sacred fire, which otherwise might escape from the face of the earth. Corruption of morals in the mass of cultivators is a phaenomenon of which no age nor nation has furnished an example. It is the mark set on those, who not looking up to heaven, to their own soil and industry, as does the husbandman, for their subsistence, depend for it on the casualties and caprice of customers. Dependence begets subservience and venality, suffocates the germ of virtue, and prepares fit tools for the designs of ambition. This, the natural progress and consequence of the arts, has sometimes perhaps been retarded by accidental circumstances: but, generally speaking, the proportion which the aggregate of the other classes of citizens bears in any state to that of its husbandmen, is the proportion of its unsound to its healthy parts, and is a good-enough barometer whereby to measure its degree of corruption.*"

THOMAS JEFFERSON
Notes on the State of Virginia

security and the ability to pass their farm on to their sons. The goal was to create what rural folks called a "competence": the ability to live up to neighborhood standards of material decency while protecting the long-term independence of their household—and thus the dignity and political rights of its head. Most of these farmers raised a variety of animals and

CHRONOLOGY

1789 National government under the Constitution begins

1791 Vermont enters the union as the 14th state

1792 Kentucky enters the union as the 15th state

1793 Beginning of Anglo-French War • Eli Whitney invents the cotton gin

1794 Anthony Wayne defeats the northwestern Indians at Fallen Timbers • British abandon their forts in the Old Northwest

1795 Northwestern Indians cede most of Ohio at Treaty of Greenville

1796 Tennessee enters the union as the 16th state

1799 Successful slave revolution in Haiti

1800 Gabriel's Rebellion in Virginia

1801 First camp meeting at Cane Ridge, Kentucky

1803 Jefferson purchases the Louisiana Territory from France • Ohio enters the union as the 17th state

1805 Tenskwatawa's first vision

1810 Nationalist Cherokee chiefs depose old local leaders

1811 Battle of Tippecanoe

1812 Second war with Britain begins

plants, ate most of what they grew, traded much of the rest within their neighborhoods, and sent small surpluses into outside markets.

The world's hunger for American food, however, was growing. West Indian and European markets for American meat and grain had grown since the mid-18th century. They expanded dramatically between 1793 and 1815, when war disrupted farming in Europe. American farmers took advantage of these markets, but few gambled with local food supplies or neighborly relations. They continued to rely on family and neighbors for subsistence, and risked little by sending increased surpluses overseas. Thus they profited from world markets without becoming dependent on them.

HOUSEHOLDS

Production for overseas markets after 1790 did, however, alter relationships within rural house-holds. Farm labor in postrevolutionary America was carefully divided by sex. Men worked in the fields, and production for markets both intensified that labor and made it more exclusively male. In the grain fields, for instance, the long-handled scythe was replacing the sickle as the principal harvest tool. Women could use the sickle efficiently, but the long, heavy scythe was designed to be wielded by men. At the same time, farmers completed the substitution of ploughs for hoes as the principal cultivating tools—not only because ploughs worked better but because rural Americans had developed a prejudice against women working in the fields. By the early 19th century, visitors to the long-settled farming areas (with the exception of some mid-Atlantic German communities) seldom saw women in the fields. In his travels through France, Thomas Jefferson spoke harshly of peasant communities where he saw women doing field labor.

At the same time, household responsibilities multiplied and fell more exclusively to women. It was farm women's labor and ingenuity that helped create a more varied and nutritious rural diet in these years. Bread and salted meat remained staples. The bread was the old mix of Indian corn and coarse wheat ("rye and Injun," the farmers called it), with crust so thick that it was used as a scoop for soups and stews. Though improved brines and pickling techniques augmented the supply of salt meat that could be laid by, farmers' palates doubtless told them that it was the same old salt meat. By the 1790s, however, other foods were becoming available. Improved winter feeding for cattle and better techniques for making and storing butter and cheese kept dairy products on the tables of the more prosperous farm families throughout the year. Chickens became more common, and farm women began to fence and manure their kitchen gardens, planting them with potatoes, turnips, cabbages, squashes, beans, and other vegetables that could be stored in the root cellars that were becoming standard features of farmhouses. By the 1830s a resident of Weymouth, Massachusetts, claimed that "a man who did not have a large garden of potatoes, crooked-necked squashes, and other vegetables . . . was regarded [as] improvident." He might have added poultry and dairy cattle to the list, and he might have noted that all were

A Midwife's Tale
Directed by Richard D. Rodgers (PBS).

The historian Laurel Thatcher Ulrich's *A Midwife's Tale* won the Pulitzer Prize for history and biography in 1991. Shortly thereafter, the Public Broadcasting System turned the book into a documentary movie—a close and imaginative analysis of the diary of Martha Ballard, a Maine farm woman and midwife of the late-eighteenth and early nineteenth century. Events are acted out on screen, and period modes of dress, housing, gardening, washing, coffin-making, spinning and weaving, and other details are reconstructed with labored accuracy.

The viewer hears the sounds of footfalls, horses, handlooms, and dishes, but the only human sounds are an occasional cough, exclamation, or drinking song. The principal narrative is carried by an actress who reads passages from the diary, and Thatcher occasionally breaks in to explain her own experiences with the diary and its interpretation. The result is a documentary film that knows the difference between dramatizing history and making it up. It also drama-

tizes the ways in which a skilled and sensitive historian goes about her work.

Martha Ballard was a midwife in a town on the Kennebec River. She began keeping a daily diary at the age of fifty in 1785, and continued until 1812. Most of the film is about her daily life: delivering babies, nursing the sick, helping neighbors, keeping house, raising and supervising the labor of her daughters and niece, gardening and tending cattle and turkeys. In both the book and the film, the busyness of an ordinary woman's days—and a sense of her possibilities and limits—in the early republic comes through in exhausting detail. The dailiness of her life is interrupted only occasionally by an event: a fire at her husband's sawmill, an epidemic of scarlet fever, a parade organized to honor the death of George Washington, the rape of a minister's wife by his enemies (including the local judge, who is set free), and a neighbor's inexplicable murder of his wife and six children.

more likely to result from the labor of women than from the labor of men.

RURAL INDUSTRY

Industrial outwork provided many farmers with another means of protecting their independence by working their wives and children harder. From the 1790s onwards, city merchants provided country workers with raw materials and paid them for finished shoes, furniture, cloth, brooms, and other handmade goods. In Marple, Pennsylvania, a farming town near Philadelphia, fully one-third of households were engaged in weaving, furniture making, and other household industry in the 1790s. As late as the 1830s, when the rise of the factory system had reduced the demand for household

manufactures, 33,000 New England women were still weaving palm leaf hats at home.

Most of the outwork was taken on by large, relatively poor families, with the work organized in ways that shored up the authority of fathers. When young Caleb Jackson and his brother began making shoes for a Massachusetts merchant in 1803, the account was carried in their father's name. When New Hampshire women and girls fashioned hats, the accounts were kept in the name of the husband or father. In general, household industry was part-time work performed only by the dependent women and children of the household. Even when it was the family's principal means of support, the work was arranged in ways that supported traditional notions of fatherhood and proprietorship. In eastern Massachusetts in the 1790s, for instance, when thousands

There is also the process of getting old. At the beginning, Martha Ballard is the busy wife in a well-run household. As she ages and her children leave to set up households of their own, Ballard hires local girls who—perhaps because an increasingly democratic culture has made them less subservient than Ballard would like, perhaps because Ballard is growing old and impatient, perhaps both—tend to be surly. Her husband, a surveyor who works for merchants speculating in local land, is attacked twice in the woods by squatters, and spends a year and a half in debtor's jail—not for his own debts but because, as tax collector, he failed to collect enough. While the husband is in jail and his aging wife struggles to keep the house going, their son moves his own family into the house and Martha is moved into a single room and is made to feel unwanted—a poignant and unsentimental case of the strained relations between generations that historians have discovered in the early republic.

A Midwife's Tale is a modest film that comes as close as a thorough and imaginative historian and a good filmmaker can to recreating the texture of lived experience in the northeastern countryside at the beginning of the nineteenth century. Students who enjoy the movie should go immediately to the book.

"...a film of almost tactile pleasure and keen intelligence." *The Boston Globe*

The PBS documentary movie *A Midwife's Tale* is based on the Pulitzer Prize–winning book of the same name by historian Laurel Thatcher Ulrich.

of farmers on small plots of worn-out land became household shoemakers, skilled men cut the leather and shaped the uppers, while the more menial tasks of sewing and binding were left to the women. In the town of North Reading, the family of Mayo Greanleaf Patch made shoes throughout the 1790s. Patch was a poor man who drank too much and lived on a small plot of land owned by his father-in-law; the family income came largely from shoemaking. Yet Patch, when asked to name his occupation, described himself as a "yeoman"—a fiction subsidized by the labor of Patch's wife and children.

NEIGHBORS

The struggle to maintain household independence involved most farmers in elaborate networks of neighborly cooperation. Few farmers possessed the tools, the labor, and the food they would have needed to be truly independent. They regularly worked for one another, borrowed oxen and plows, and swapped surpluses of one kind of food for another. Women frequently traded ashes, herbs, butter and eggs, vegetables, seedlings, baby chicks, goose feathers, and the products of their spinning wheels and looms. Such exchanges of goods and services were crucial to the workings of a rural neighborhood. Some cooperative undertakings—house and barn-raisings and husking bees, for example—brought the whole neighborhood together, transforming a chore into a pleasant social event. The gossip, drinking, and dancing that took place on such occasions were welcome rewards for neighborly cooperation.

OLD MRS. HANSMAN KILLING A HOG This Pennsylvania farm wife seldom if ever worked in the fields, but her daily round of work was no dainty business. Along with other arduous and dirty labors, she killed and butchered hogs not only for her family but for some of her neighbors.

Few neighborhood transactions involved money. Indeed, in 1790 the states and federal government had not yet issued paper money, and the widespread use of Spanish, English, and French coins testified to the shortage of specie. In New England, farmers kept careful accounts of neighborhood debts. In the South and West, on the other hand, farmers used a "changing system" in which they simply remembered what they owed; they regarded the New England practice as a sign of Yankee greed and lack of character. Yet farmers everywhere relied more on barter than on cash: "Instead of money going incessantly backwards and forwards into the same hands," observed a French traveler in Massachusetts in 1790, "[Americans] supply their needs in the countryside by direct reciprocal exchanges. The tailor and the bootmaker go and do their work at the home of the farmer . . . who most frequently provides the raw material for it and pays for the work in goods. They write down what they give and receive on both sides, and at the end of the year they settle a large variety of exchanges with a very small quantity of coin." Such a system created an elaborate network of neighborhood debt. In Kent, Connecticut, for instance, the average farmer left 20 creditors when he died. The debts were indicators not of exploitation and class division, however, but of a highly structured and absolutely necessary system of neighborly cooperation.

INHERITANCE

The rural republicanism envisioned by men such as Jefferson and Crèvecoeur rested on widespread farm ownership and on a rough equality among adult male householders. Even as they were formulating that vision, however, its social base was disintegrating. Overcrowding and the growth of markets caused the price of good farmland to rise sharply throughout the older settlements. Most young men could expect to inherit only a few acres of exhausted land, or to move to wilderness land in the backcountry. Failing those, they would quit farming altogether. Crèvecoeur's baby boy—who in fact ended up living in Boston—was in a more precarious position than his seat on his father's plough might have indicated.

In Revolutionary America, fathers had been judged by their ability to support and govern their households, to serve as good neighbors, and to pass land on to their sons. After the war, fewer farm fathers could meet those expectations. Those in the old settlements had small farms and large families, which made it impossible for them to provide a competence for all their offspring. Fathers felt that they had failed as fathers, and their sons, with no prospect of an adequate inheritance, were obliged to leave home. Most fathers tried valiantly to provide for all their heirs (generally by leaving land to their sons and personal property to their daughters). Few left all their land to one son, and many stated in their wills that the sons to whom they left the land must share barns and cider mills—even the house—on farms that could be subdivided no further. Such provisions suited a social system that guaranteed the independence of the household head through complex relations with kin and neighbors. They also indicated that the system had reached the end of the line.

Outside New England, farm tenancy was on the increase. In parts of Pennsylvania and in other areas as well, farmers often bought farms when they became available in the neighborhood, rented them to tenants to augment the household income, and then gave them to their sons when they reached adulthood. The sons of poorer farmers often rented a farm in the hope of saving enough money to buy it.

Some fathers bought tracts of unimproved land in the backcountry—sometimes on speculation, more often to provide their sons with land they could make into a farm. Others paid for their sons' educations or arranged apprenticeships to provide them with an avenue of escape from a declining countryside. As a result, more and more young men left home. The populations of the old farming communities grew older and more female, while the populations of the rising frontier settlements and seaport cities became younger and more male. The young men who stayed home often had nothing to look forward to but a lifetime as tenants or hired hands.

STANDARDS OF LIVING

The rise of markets in the late 18th and early 19th centuries improved living standards for some families but widened the disparity between prosperous farmers and their marginal and disinherited neighbors. Most farmhouses in the older rural areas were small, one-story structures. Few farmers, especially in the South and West, bothered to keep their surroundings clean or attractive. They repaired their fences only when they became too dilapidated to function. They rarely planted trees or shrubs, and

housewives threw out garbage to feed the chickens and pigs that foraged near the house.

Inside, homes had few rooms and many people. Beds stood in every room, and few family members slept alone. Growing up in Bethel, Connecticut, future show business entrepreneur P. T. Barnum shared a bed with his brother and an Irish servant; guests shared beds in New England taverns until the 1820s. The hearth remained the source of heat and light in most farmhouses. In the period from 1790 to 1810, more than half the households in central Massachusetts, an old and relatively prosperous area, owned only one or two candlesticks. One of the great disparities between wealthy families and their less affluent neighbors was that the wealthy families could light their houses at night. Another disparity was in the outward appearance of houses. The wealthier families painted their houses white as a token of pristine republicanism. But their bright houses stood in stark and unrepublican contrast to the weathered gray-brown clapboard siding of their neighbors.

Some improvements emerged in personal comfort. Beds in most houses may have been shared, but as time passed more of them had mattresses stuffed with feathers. At mealtimes, only the poorest

THE DINING ROOM OF DR. WHITBRIDGE, A RHODE ISLAND COUNTRY DOCTOR, CIRCA 1815 It is a comfortable, neatly furnished room, but with little decoration, and the doctor must sit near the fire in layered clothing to ward off the morning chill.

families continued to eat with their fingers or with spoons from a common bowl. By 1800 individual place settings with knives and forks and china plates, along with chairs instead of benches, had become common in rural America. Although only the wealthiest families had upholstered furniture, ready-made chairs were widely available; the number of chairs per household in Massachusetts, for instance, doubled in the first third of the 19th century. Clocks, one of the first items to be mass-produced in the United States, appeared in the more prosperous rural households: As early as the 1790s, fully 35 percent of the families in Chester County, Pennsylvania, owned at least one clock.

FROM BACKCOUNTRY TO FRONTIER

The United States was a huge country in 1790, at least on paper. In the treaty that ended the War of Independence in 1783, the British ignored Indian claims and ceded all the land from the Atlantic Ocean to the Mississippi River to the new republic, with the exceptions of Spanish Florida and New Orleans. The states then surrendered their individual claims to the federal government, and in 1790 George Washington became president of a nation that stretched nearly 1,500 miles inland. Still, most white Americans lived on a thin strips of settlement along the Atlantic coast and along the few navigable rivers that emptied into the Atlantic. Some were pushing their way into the wilds of Maine and northern Vermont, and in New York others set up communities as far west as the Mohawk Valley. Pittsburgh was a struggling new settlement, and two outposts had been established on the Ohio River—at Marietta and at what would become Cincinnati. Farther south, farmers had occupied the Piedmont lands up to the eastern slope of the Appalachians and were spilling through the Cumberland Gap into the new lands of Kentucky and Tennessee. North of the Ohio River, however, the Shawnee, Miami, Delaware, and Potawatomie nations, along with smaller tribes, controlled nearly all the land shown on the Northwest Ordinance's neatly gridded and largely fictitious map. To the south, Indians whom the whites called the "Five Civilized Tribes" still occupied much of their ancestral land: the Cherokees in the Carolinas and northern Georgia, the Creeks in Georgia and Alabama, the Choctaws and Chickasaws in Mississippi, and the Seminoles in southern Georgia and Spanish Florida. Taken together, Indian peoples occupied most of the land that treaties and maps showed as the interior of the United States.

THE DESTRUCTION OF THE WOODLAND INDIANS

Though many of the woodland tribes were still intact and still living on their ancestral lands in 1790, they were in serious trouble. The members of the old Iroquois Federation had been restricted to reservations in New York and Pennsylvania; many had fled to Canada. The once-powerful Cherokees had been severely punished for fighting on the side of the British during the Revolution and by 1790 had ceded three-fourths of their territory to the Americans. Like the Iroquois, by this time they were nearly surrounded by white settlements.

In the Old Northwest, the Shawnee, Miami, and other tribes—with the help of the British who still occupied seven forts within what was formally the United States—continued to trade furs and to impede white settlement. Skirmishes with settlers, however, brought reprisals, and the Indians faced not only hostile pioneers but the United States Army as well. In the Ohio country, punitive expeditions led by General Josiah Harmar and General Arthur St. Clair failed in 1790 and 1791—the second ending in an Indian victory in which 630 soldiers died. In 1794 President Washington sent a third army, under General "Mad Anthony" Wayne, which defeated the Indians at Fallen Timbers, near present-day Toledo. The Treaty of Greenville forced the Native Americans to cede two-thirds of what are now Ohio and southeastern Indiana. It was at this point that the British decided to abandon their forts in the Old Northwest. Following their victory at Fallen Timbers, whites filtered into what remained of Indian lands. In 1796 President Washington threw up his hands and announced that "I believe scarcely any thing, short of a Chinese Wall, or a line of troops, will restrain Land Jobbers and the encroachment of settlers upon the Indian Territory." Five years later Governor William Henry Harrison of Indiana Territory admitted that frontier whites "consider the murdering of the Indians in the highest degree meritorious."

To CREE

To ASSINIBOINE

1808

BRITISH POSSESSIONS

Lake Superior

1808

1807

Sault Ste. Marie

■ Ft. Michilimackinac

IND. TERR.

CHIPPEWA

1808

1807

Saginaw Bay

Lake Huron

Lake Ontario

NEW YORK

DAKOTA

ILLINOIS TERRITORY

Lake Michigan

OTTAWA

MISSISAUGA

MICHIGAN TERR.

Ft. Detroit ■

Lake Erie

PENNSYLVANIA

1807

WINNEBAGO

1808

Fallen Timbers, 1794 ✳

WYANDOT

SAUX AND FOX

Ft. Dearborn ■

Harmar's Defeat, 1790 ✳

Ft. Wayne ■

LENNI LENAPE

MD.

IOWA

POTAWATOMI

1807 *MIAMI*

Tippecanoe, 1811 ✳

✳ St. Clair's Defeat, 1791

1805

Illinois R.

1808

Ft. Madison ■

Prophetstown

INDIANA TERR.

Greenville ○

OHIO

MISSOURI TERRITORY

KICKAPOO

PROPHET'S MOVE, 1808

Chillicothe ○

VIRGINIA

OSAGE

1810

SHAWNEE

Vincennes

ILLINOIS TERRITORY

Ohio R.

KENTUCKY

Arkansas R.

1811

Cumberland R.

TENNESSEE

NORTH CAROLINA

1812 **CHEROKEE**

Mississippi R.

Tennessee R.

SOUTH CAROLINA

QUAPAW

CHICKASAW

MISSISSIPPI TERRITORY

GEORGIA

SPANISH MEXICO

LOUISIANA

CREEK

SPANISH FLORIDA

Gulf of Mexico

SEMINOLE

▨ Ceded before 1784	- - - Treaty of Greenville, 1795
▨ Ceded 1784–1799	- - - Treaty of Fort Wayne, 1809
▨ Ceded 1800–1812	← Spread of Prophet's influence
☐ Unceded Indian lands, 1812	← Tecumseh's travel routes
✳ Battles	*CREEK* Tribes joining movement
■ Forts	

0   100   200 Miles
0 100 200 Kilometers

NATIVE AMERICA, 1783–1812

Relegated to smaller territory but still dependent on the European fur trade, the natives of the Northwest now fell into competition with settlers and other Indians for the diminishing supply of game. The Creeks, Choctaws, and other tribes of the Old Southwest faced the same problem: Even when they chased settlers out of their territory, the settlers managed to kill or scare off the deer and other wildlife, thus ruining the old hunting grounds. When the Shawnee sent hunting parties farther west, they met irate western Indians. The Choctaws also sent hunters across the Mississippi, where they found both new sources of furs and angry warriors of the Osage and other peoples of Louisiana and Arkansas. The Indians of the interior now realized that the days of the fur trade, on which they depended for survival, were numbered.

Faced with shrinking territories, the disappearance of wildlife, and diminished opportunities to be traditional hunters and warriors, many Indian societies sank into despair. Epidemics of European diseases (smallpox, influenza, measles) attacked peoples who were increasingly sedentary and vulnerable. Old internal frictions grew nastier. In the Old Southwest, full-blooded Indians came into conflict with mixed-blood Indians—who often no longer spoke the native language and who wanted their people to adopt white ways. Murder and clan revenge plagued the tribes, and depression and suicide became more common. The use of alcohol, which had been a scourge on Indian societies for two centuries, increased. Indian males spent more time in their villages and less on the hunt, and by most accounts they drank more and grew more violent.

THE FAILURE OF CULTURAL RENEWAL

Out of this cultural wreckage emerged visionary leaders who spoke of a regenerated native society and the expulsion of all whites from the old tribal lands. One of the first was Chief Alexander McGillivray, a mixed-blood Creek who had sided with the British during the Revolution. Between 1783 and 1793, McGillivray tried to unite the Creeks under a national council that could override local chiefs and to form alliances with other tribes and with Spanish Florida. McGillivray's pre-

SEQUOYA The Cherokee linguist Sequoya displays the 86-symbol alphabet that transformed Cherokee into the first written American Indian language.

mature death in 1793 prevented the realization of his vision.

The Cherokees north and east of the Creeks did succeed in making a unified state. Angered by the willingness of village chiefs to be bribed and flattered into selling land, and by the departure of tribe members to remote locations in the Appalachians or to government land in Arkansas, a group of young chiefs staged a revolt between 1808 and 1810. Previously, being a Cherokee had meant loyalty to one's clan and kin group and adherence to the tribe's ancient customs. Now it meant remaining on the tribe's ancestral land (migration across the Mississippi was regarded as treason) and unquestioning acceptance of the laws, courts, and police controlled by the national council. By 1810 the Cherokee had transformed themselves from a defeated and divided tribe into a nation within a nation.

Among the many prophets who emerged during these years, the one who came closest to military success was Tenskwatawa, a fat, one-eyed, alcoholic Shawnee who had failed as a warrior and medicine man. He went into a deep trance in 1805, and the people thought he was dead. During preparations

TENSKWATAWA The Shawnee prophet Tenskwatawa ("The Open Door"), brother of Tecumseh, was painted by George Catlin in 1836—long after the defeat of his prophetic attempt to unify American Indians.

for his funeral he awoke and told them he had visited heaven and hell and had received a prophetic vision. First, all the Indians must stop drinking and fighting among themselves. They must also return to their traditional food, clothing, tools, and hairstyles, and must extinguish all their fires and start new ones without using European tools. All who opposed the new order (including local chiefs, medicine men, shamans, and witches) must be put down by force. When all that had been done, God (a monotheistic, punishing God borrowed from the Christians) would restore the world that Indians had known before the whites came over the mountains.

Tenskwatawa's message soon found its way to the Delawares (who attacked the Christians among their people as witches) and other native peoples of the Northwest. When converts flooded into the prophet's home village, he moved to Prophetstown (Tippecanoe) in what is now Indiana. There, with the help of his brother Tecumseh, he created an army estimated by the whites at anywhere between 650 and 3,000 warriors and pledged to end further encroachment by whites. Tecumseh, who took control of the movement, announced to the whites that he was the sole chief of all the Indians north of the Ohio River; land cessions by anyone else would be invalid. Tenskwatawa's prophecy and Tecumseh's leadership had united the Indians of the Old Northwest in an unprecedented stand against white encroachment.

Tecumseh's confederacy posed a threat to the United States. A second war with England was looming, and Tecumseh was receiving supplies and encouragement from the British in Canada. He was also planning to visit the southern tribes in an attempt to bring them into his confederacy. The prospect of unified resistance by the western tribes in league with the British jeopardized every settler west of the Appalachians. In 1811 William Henry Harrison led an army toward Prophetstown. With Tecumseh away, Tenskwatawa ordered an unwise attack on Harrison's army and was beaten at the Battle of Tippecanoe.

Tecumseh's still-formidable confederacy, joined by the traditionalist wing of the southern Creeks, fought alongside the British in the War of 1812 and lost (see chapter 8). The loss destroyed the military power of the Indians east of the Mississippi River. General Andrew Jackson forced the Creeks (including those who had served as his allies) to cede millions of acres of land in Georgia and Alabama. The other southern tribes, along with the members of Tecumseh's northern confederacy, watched helplessly as new settlers took over their hunting lands. Some of the Indians moved west, and others tried to farm what was left of their old land. All of them had to deal with settlers and government officials who neither feared them nor took their sovereignty seriously. By this time most whites simply assumed that the Indians would have to move on to the barren land west of the Mississippi (see chapter 12).

THE BACKCOUNTRY, 1790–1815

To easterners, the backcountry whites who were displacing the Indians seemed no different from the defeated aborigines. Indeed, in accommodating themselves to a borderless forest used by both Indians and

BACKWOODS BRAWL This backwoods brawl was caricatured in the popular *Crockett Almanac* of 1840. Biting, gouging, and scratching were routine; so was the audience of drunken neighbors.

whites, many settlers—like many Indians—had melded Indian and white ways. To clear the land, backcountry farmers simply girdled the trees and left them to die and fall down by themselves. They plowed the land by navigating between the stumps. Worse, to easterners, women often worked the fields, particularly while their men, as did Indians, spent long periods away on hunting trips for food game and animal skins for trade. The arch-pioneer Daniel Boone, for instance, braided his hair, dressed himself in Indian leggings, and, with only his dogs for company, disappeared for months at a time on "long hunts." When easterners began to "civilize" his neighborhood, Boone moved further west.

Eastern visitors were appalled not only by the poverty, lice, and filth of frontier life but by the drunkenness and violence of the frontiersmen. Americans everywhere drank heavily in the early years of the 19th century. But everyone agreed that frontiersmen drank more and were more violent when drunk than men anywhere else. Travelers told of no-holds-barred fights in which frontiersmen gouged the eyes and bit off the noses and ears of their opponents. No account was complete without a reckoning of the number of one-eyed, one-eared men the traveler had met on the frontier. Stories arose of half-legendary heroes such as Davy Crockett of Tennessee, who wrestled bears and alligators and had a recipe for Indian stew, and Mike Fink, a Pennsylvania boatman who brawled and drank his way along the rivers of the interior until he was shot and killed in a drunken episode that none of the participants could clearly remember. Samuel Holden Parsons, a New Englander serving as a judge in the Northwest Territory, called the frontiersmen "our white savages." Massachusetts conservative Timothy Pickering branded them "the least worthy subjects of the United States. They are little less savage than the Indians."

After 1789 settlers of the western backcountry made two demands of the new national government: protection from the Indians and a guarantee of the right to navigate the Ohio and Mississippi Rivers. The Indians were pushed back in the 1790s and finished off in the War of 1812, and in 1803 Jefferson's Louisiana Purchase (see chapter 8) ended the European presence on the rivers and at the crucial chokepoint at New Orleans. Over these years the pace of settlement quickened. In 1790 only 10,000 settlers lived west of the Appalachians—about 1 American in 40. By 1800 the number of settlers had risen to nearly a million. By 1820, two million Americans were westerners—one in five.

The new settlers bought land from speculators who had acquired tracts under the Northwest Ordinance in the Northwest; from English, Dutch, and American land companies in western New York; and from land dealers in the Southwest and in northern New England. They built frame houses surrounded by cleared fields, planted marketable crops, and settled into the struggle to make farms out of the wilderness and to meet mortgage payments along the way. By 1803 four frontier states had entered the union: Vermont (1791), Kentucky (1792), Tennessee (1796), and Ohio (1803). Louisiana soon followed (1812), and when war ended in 1815 one frontier state after another gained admission: Indiana (1816), Mississippi (1817), Illinois (1818), Alabama (1818), Maine (1820), and Missouri (1821).

As time passed, the term "backcountry," which easterners had used to refer to the wilderness and the dangerous misfits who lived in it, fell into dis-

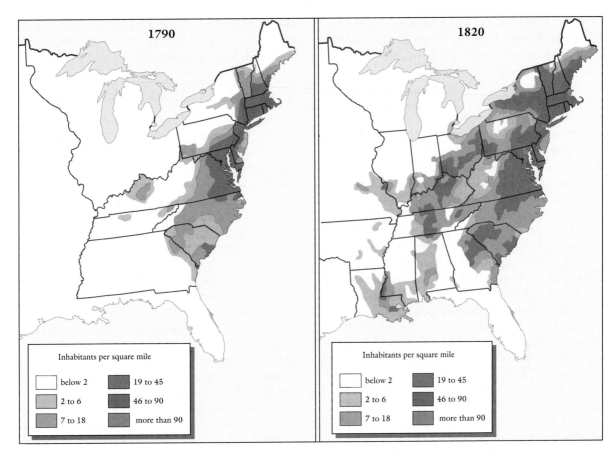

1790

1820

Inhabitants per square mile

below 2	19 to 45
2 to 6	46 to 90
7 to 18	more than 90

POPULATION DENSITY, 1790–1820

use. By 1820 the term "frontier" had replaced it. The new settlements no longer represented the backwash of American civilization. They were its cutting edge.

THE PLANTATION SOUTH, 1790–1820

In 1790 the future of slavery was uncertain in the Chesapeake (the states of Virginia, Maryland, and Delaware, where the institution first took root in North America). The tobacco market had been precarious since before the Revolution, and it continued to decline after 1790. Tobacco depleted the soil, and by the late 18th century tidewater farms and plantations were giving out. As lands west of the Appalachians opened to settlement, white tenants, laborers, and small farmers left the Chesapeake in droves. Many of them moved to Kentucky,

Tennessee, or the western reaches of Virginia. Many others found new homes in nonslave states north of the Ohio River. Faced with declining opportunities within the slave societies of the Chesapeake, thousands of the poorer whites had voted with their feet.

SLAVERY AND THE REPUBLIC

With slave labor becoming less necessary, Chesapeake planters continued to switch to grain and livestock—crops that required less labor than tobacco—and tried to think up new uses for slaves. Some planters divided their land into small plots and rented both the plots and their slaves to white tenant farmers. Others, particularly in Maryland, recruited tenants from the growing ranks of free blacks. Still others hired out their slaves as artisans and urban laborers. None of these solutions, however, could employ the great mass of slaves or repay the planters' huge investment in slave labor.

In this situation many Chesapeake planters (who had, after all, fought a revolution in the name of natural rights) began to manumit their slaves. The farmers of Maryland and Delaware in particular set their slaves free; by the time those states sided with the North in 1861 more than half the blacks in Maryland and nine-tenths of those in Delaware were free. Virginia's economic and cultural commitment to the plantation was stronger, but even the Old Dominion showed a strong movement toward manumitting slaves. George Washington stated that he wished "to liberate a certain species of property," and manumitted his slaves by will. (The manumissions were to take place at the death of his widow—thus, as one wag declared, surrounding Mrs. Washington with 100 people who wanted her dead.) Robert Carter, reputedly the largest slaveholder in Virginia, also freed his slaves, as did many others. The free black population of Virginia stood at 2,000 in 1782, when the state passed a law permitting manumission. The number of free blacks rose to 12,766 in 1790, to 20,124 in 1800, and to 30,570 in 1810. In all, the proportion of Virginia blacks who were free increased from 4 percent in 1790 to 7 percent in 1810.

There were, however, limits on the manumission of Virginia slaves. First, few planters could afford to free their slaves without compensation. Second, white Virginians feared the social consequences of black freedom. Thomas Jefferson, for instance, owned 175 slaves when he penned the phrase that "all men are created equal." He lived off their labor, sold them to pay his debts, gave them as gifts, and sometimes sold them away from their families as a punishment. Through it all he insisted that slavery was wrong. He could imagine emancipation, however, only if freed slaves would be colonized far from Virginia. A society of free blacks and whites, Jefferson insisted, would end in disaster: "Deep rooted prejudices entertained by the whites; ten thousand recollections, by the blacks, of the injuries they have sustained; new provocations; the real distinctions which nature has made . . . [will] produce convulsions which will probably never end but in the extermination of the one or the other race." Near the end of an adult lifetime of condemning slavery but doing nothing to end it, Jefferson cried out that white Virginians held "a wolf by the ears": They could not hold onto slavery forever, and they could never let it go.

THE RECOMMITMENT TO SLAVERY

Jefferson's dilemma eased as cotton cultivation increased further south. British industrialization created a demand for cotton from the 1790s onward, and planters knew they could sell all the cotton they could grow. But long-staple cotton, the only profitable variety, was a delicate plant that thrived only on the Sea Islands off Georgia and South Carolina. The short-staple variety was hardier, but its sticky seeds had to be removed by hand before the cotton could be milled. One adult slave would work an entire day to clean a single pound of short-staple cotton—a profit-killing expenditure of labor. In 1790 the United States produced only 3,000 bales of cotton, nearly all of it on the plantations of the Sea Islands.

In 1793 Eli Whitney, a Connecticut Yankee who had come south to work as a tutor, set his mind to the problem. Within a few days he had made a model of a cotton "gin" (a southern contraction of "engine") that combed the seeds from the fiber with metal pins fitted into rollers. Working with Whitney's machine, a slave could clean 50 pounds of short-staple cotton in a day. At a stroke, cotton became the great American cash crop and plantation agriculture was rejuve-

COTTON GIN The basis for later large-scale milling operations, Eli Whitney's simple, hand-cranked cotton gin made the production of short-staple cotton profitable and revolutionized southern agriculture.

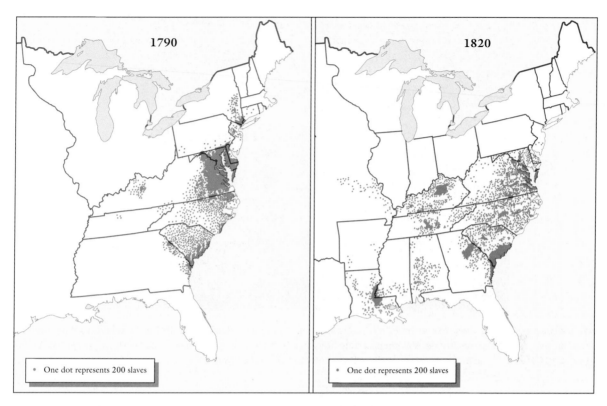

DISTRIBUTION OF SLAVE POPULATION, 1790–1820

nated. Cotton production grew to 73,000 bales in 1800, to 178,000 bales in 1810, and to 334,000 bales in 1820. By 1820, cotton accounted for more than half the value of all agricultural exports.

Short-staple cotton grew well in the hot, humid climate and long growing season of the Lower South (roughly, the land below the southern borders of Virginia and Kentucky), and it grew almost anywhere: in the rolling Piedmont country east of the Appalachians, in the coastal lowlands, and—especially—in the virgin lands of the Old Southwest. It was also a labor-intensive crop that could be grown in either small or large quantities; farmers with few or no slaves could make a decent profit, and planters with extensive land and many slaves could make enormous amounts of money. Best of all, the factories of England and, eventually, of the American Northeast, had a seemingly insatiable appetite for southern cotton.

Plantation slavery, rejuvenated, spread rapidly into the new cotton-growing regions of the South. Meanwhile, Chesapeake planters, who lived too far north to grow cotton, continued to diversify. To fi-

nance the transition to mixed agriculture, they sold their excess slaves at high prices to planters in the cotton frontier. Up until about 1810, most of the slaves who left Virginia had traveled to Kentucky or Tennessee with their masters. Thereafter, most of them left Virginia as commodities in the burgeoning interstate slave trade, headed for the new plantations of Georgia, Alabama, and Mississippi.

The movement of slaves out of the Chesapeake was immense. In the 1790s about 1 in 12 Virginia and Maryland slaves was taken south and west. The figure rose to 1 in 10 between 1800 and 1810, and to 1 in 5 between 1810 and 1820. In 1790 planters in Virginia and Maryland had owned 56 percent of all American slaves; by 1860 they owned only 15 percent. The demand for slaves in the new cotton lands had thus provided many Chesapeake planters with a means of disposing of an endangered investment and with cash to pay for their transition to new crops.

The other center of slavery during the 18th century—coastal South Carolina and Georgia—made a massive recommitment to slave labor in the years

AN OVERSEER DOING HIS DUTY In 1798 the architect and engineer Benjamin Latrobe sketched a white overseer smoking a cigar and supervising slave women as they hoed newly cleared farmland near Fredricksburg, Virginia. A critic of slavery, Latrobe sarcastically entitled the sketch *An Overseer Doing His Duty.*

after the Revolution. There, the principal crop, rice, along with other American foodstuffs, was experiencing a sharp rise in international demand. Most planters in this region were switching from indigo (a source of blue dye) to cotton as a secondary crop, creating an increase in the demand for slaves. Thousands of slaves in this region had either run away or been carried off by the British in the Revolution, and planters knew that the African slave trade was scheduled to end in 1808. With slave prices rising and slave-produced crops becoming steadily more profitable, they rushed to import as many African slaves as they could in the time remaining. Between 1788 and 1808, some 250,000 slaves were brought directly from Africa to the United States—nearly all of them to Charleston and Savannah. That figure equaled the number of Africans who had been brought to North America during the whole colonial period.

RACE, GENDER, AND CHESAPEAKE LABOR

The transition to grain and livestock agriculture in the Chesapeake and the rise of the cotton belt in the Lower South imposed new kinds of labor upon the slaves. The switch to mixed farming in Maryland and Virginia brought about a shift in the chores assigned to male and female slaves. Wheat cultivation, for example, meant a switch from the hoes used for tobacco to the plow and grain cradle—both of which called for the upper-body strength of adult men. The grain economy also required carts, wagons, mills, and good roads, and thus created a need for greater numbers of slave artisans—nearly all of whom were men. Many of these were hired out to urban employers, and lived as a semifree caste in cities and towns. In the diversifying economy of the Chesapeake, male slaves did the plowing, mowing, sowing, ditching, and carting and performed most of the tasks requiring artisan skills. All of this work demanded high levels of training and could be performed by someone working either by himself or in a small group with little need for supervision.

Slave women were left with all the lesser tasks. Contrary to legend, few slave women in the Chesapeake worked as domestic servants in the planter's house. A few of them worked at cloth manufacture, sewing, candle molding, and meat salting, but most female slaves still did farm work—hoeing, weeding, spreading manure, cleaning stables—monotonous work that called for little skill and was closely supervised. This new division of labor was clearly evident during the wheat harvest. On George Washington's farm, for example, male slaves, often working alongside temporary white laborers, moved in a broad line as they mowed the grain. Following them came a gang of children and women bent over and moving along on their hands and knees as they bound wheat into shocks. Similarly Thomas Jefferson, who had been appalled to see French women working in the fields, abandoned his concern for female delicacy when his own slaves were involved. At the grain harvest he instructed his overseers to organize "gangs of half men and half women."

THE LOWLAND TASK SYSTEM

On the rice and cotton plantations of South Carolina and Georgia, planters faced different labor problems. Slaves made up 80 percent of the population in this region, more than 90 percent in many parishes. Farms were large, and the two principal crops demanded skilled, intensive labor. The environment encouraged deadly summer diseases and

kept white owners and overseers out of the fields. Planters solved these problems by organizing slaves according to the so-called "task system." Each morning the owner or overseer assigned a specific task to each slave and allowed him to work at his own pace. When the task was done, the rest of the day belonged to the slave. Slaves who failed to finish their task were punished, and when too many slaves finished early the owners assigned heavier tasks. In the 18th century, each slave had been expected to tend three to four acres of rice each day. In the early 19th century, with the growth of the rice market, the assignment was raised to five acres.

The task system encouraged slaves to work hard without supervision, and they turned the system to their own uses. Often several slaves would work together until all their tasks were completed. Strong young slaves would sometimes help older and weaker slaves after they had finished their own tasks. Once the day's work was done, the slaves would share their hard-earned leisure out of sight of the owner. A Jamaican visitor remarked that South Carolina and Georgia planters were "very particular in employing a negro, without his consent, after his

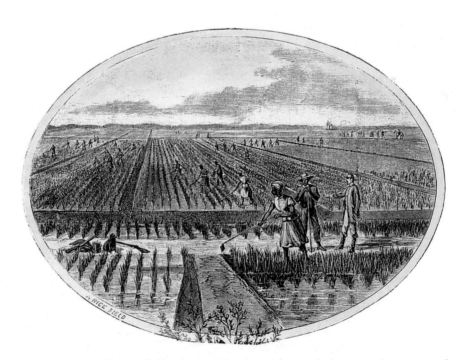

RICE FIELDS OF THE SOUTH The rice fields of coastal South Carolina, with their complex systems of irrigation, often were created by Africans who had done similar work in West Africa before their enslavement.

task is finished, and agreeing with him for the payment which he is to receive." Further west, low-country slaves who were moved onto the cotton frontier often imposed the task system on new plantations, sometimes against the resistance of masters.

Slaves under the task system won the right to cultivate land as "private fields"—not the little garden plots common in the Chesapeake, but farms of up to five acres on which they grew produce and raised livestock for market. A lively trade developed in slave-produced goods, and by the late 1850s slaves in the low-country not only produced and exchanged property but passed it on to their children. The owners tolerated such activity because slaves on the task system worked hard, required minimal supervision, and made money for their owners. The rice and cotton planters in South Carolina and Georgia were among the richest men in the country.

THE SEAPORT CITIES, 1790–1815

When the first federal census takers made their rounds in 1790, they found 94 percent of the population living on farms and in rural villages. The remaining 6 percent lived in the 24 towns that had populations of more than 2,500 (a census definition of "urban" that included many communities that were, by modern standards, tiny). Only five communities had populations over 10,000: Baltimore (13,503), Charleston (16,359), Boston (18,038), New York (33,131), and Philadelphia (42,444). All five were seaport cities—testimony to the key role of international commerce in the economy of the early republic.

COMMERCE

These cities had grown steadily during the 18th century, handling imports from Europe and farm exports from America. With the outbreak of war between Britain and France in 1793—a world war that lasted until 1814—the overseas demand for American foodstuffs and for shipping to carry products from the Caribbean islands to Europe further strengthened the seaport cities. Foreign trade during these years was risky and uneven, subject to the tides of war and the strategies of the belligerents. French seizures of American shipping and the resulting undeclared war of 1798–1800, the 1805 British ban on

America's reexport trade (the carrying of goods from French islands in the Caribbean), Jefferson's importation ban of 1806 and his trade embargo of 1807, and America's entry into the war in 1812 all disrupted the maritime economy and threw the seaports into periods of economic collapse (see chapter 8). But by 1815, it was clear that wartime commerce had transformed the seaports and the institutions of American business. New York City had become the nation's largest city, with a population that had grown from 33,131 in 1790 to 96,373 in 1810. Philadelphia's population had risen to 53,722 by 1810; Boston's to 34,322; and Baltimore's to 46,555. Between 1800 and 1810, for the first time in American history, the growth of the urban population exceeded the growth of the rural population.

Seaport merchants in these years amassed the private fortunes and built the financial infrastructure that would soon take up the task of commercializing and industrializing the northern United States. Old merchants such as the Brown brothers of Providence and Elias Hasket Darby of Salem grew richer, and newcomers such as immigrant John Jacob Astor of New York City built huge personal fortunes. To manage those fortunes, new institutions emerged. Docking and warehousing facilities expanded dramatically. Bookkeepers were replaced by accountants familiar with the new double-entry system of accounting, and insurance and banking companies were formed to handle the risks and rewards of wartime commerce.

The bustle of prosperity was evident on the waterfronts and principal streets of the seaport cities. An Englishman who visited the New York City docks during the wartime boom left this description:

The carters were driving in every direction; and the sailors and labourers upon the wharfs, and onboard the vessels, were moving their ponderous burdens from place to place. The merchants and their clerks were busily engaged in their counting-houses, or upon the piers. The Tontine coffee-house was filled with underwriters, brokers, merchants, traders, and politicians. . . . The steps and balcony of the coffee-house were crowded with people bidding, or listening to the several auctioneers, who had elevated themselves upon a hogshead of sugar, a puncheon of rum, or a bale of cotton; and with Stentorian voices were exclaiming, "Once, twice. Once, twice." "Another cent." "Thank ye, gentlemen. . . ." The coffee-house slip, and the corners of Wall and Pearl Streets were jammed up with carts, drays, and wheelbarrows; horses and men were huddled promiscuously together,

A SCENE NEAR THE NEW YORK CITY DOCKS IN 1798 OR 1799 The large building on the left is the Tontine Coffee House, which housed the Stock Exchange and the principal insurance offices, at the corner of Water and Wall streets.

leaving little or no room for passengers to pass. . . . Everything was in motion; all was life, bustle, and activity.

POVERTY

Away from the waterfront, the main thoroughfares and a few of the side streets were paved with cobblestones and lined with fine shops and townhouses. In other parts of the cities, however, the boom was creating unprecedented poverty as well as wealth. Earlier in the 18th century, seaports had their share of poor people and depressed neighborhoods, but not on the scale that prevailed between 1790 and 1820. A few steps off the handsome avenues were narrow streets crowded with ragged children, browsing dogs, pigs, horses, and cattle, and garbage and waste-filled open sewers. Epidemics had become more frequent and deadly. New York City, for example, experienced six severe epidemics of yellow fever between 1791 and 1822. Each time, the disease entered through the seaport and settled in the slums. Life expectancy in Boston, reputedly the healthiest city in America, was three to five years lower than in the surrounding countryside.

The slums were evidence that money created by commerce was being distributed in undemocratic ways. Per capita wealth in New York rose 60 percent between 1790 and 1825, but the wealthiest 4 percent of the population owned more than half of that wealth. The wages of skilled and unskilled labor rose in these years, but the increase in seasonal and temporary employment, together with the recurring interruptions of foreign commerce, cut deeply into the security and prosperity of ordinary women and men. Added to the old insecurities of sickness, fire, accident, aging, and any number of personal misfortunes, these ate up the gains made by laborers, sailors, and most artisans and their families.

THE STATUS OF LABOR

Meanwhile, the status of artisans in the big cities was undergoing change. In 1790, independent artisans demanded and usually received the respect of their fellow citizens. When a clerk in Boston refused to attend dancing classes that one of the town's master saddlers had joined, a newspaper scolded him (a mere "stockjobber's lackey") for considering himself the social superior of the saddler and other "reputable mechanics." Artisans constituted about half the male workforce of the seaport cities, and their respectability and usefulness, together with the role they had played in the Revolution (see chapter 6), had earned them an honorable status.

That status rested in large part on their independence. In 1790 most artisan workshops were household operations with at most one or two apprentices and hired journeymen, who looked forward to owning their own shops one day. Timothy Dwight, the conservative president of Yale College, observed that few of those "amphibious beings" in America remained journeymen for life. Most master craftsmen lived modestly (on the borderline of poverty in many cases) and aspired only to the ability to support their household in security and decency. They identified their way of life with republican virtue. A doggerel verse dedicated to New York's stonemasons in 1805 reflects their view of themselves:

I pay my debts
I steal from no man; would not cut a throat
To gain admission to a great man's purse
Or a whore's bed. I'd not betray my friend

To get his place of fortune; I scorn to flatter
A blown up fool above me or crush
The wretch beneath me.

This was a classic statement of the republican honesty and virtue that characterized the self-descriptions of skilled workmen. Thomas Jefferson catered to these sensibilities when he pronounced artisans "the yeomanry of the cities."

As in the countryside, however, the patriarchal base of that republicanism was eroding. As the maritime economy grew, changes occurred in the nature of construction work, shipbuilding, the clothing trades, and other specialized crafts. Artisans were replaced by cheaper labor and were undercut by subcontracted "slop work" performed by semiskilled outworkers. Perhaps one in five master craftsmen entered the newly emerging business class. The others took work as laborers or journeymen (the term for wage-earning craftsmen). By 1815 most young craftsmen could no longer hope to own their own shops. About half of New York City's journeymen that year were more than 30 years old; nearly a quarter were more than 40. Most of them were married, and about half of them

PROCESSION OF VICTUALLERS, 1815. The frequent and festive parades in the seaport cities included militia companies, political officials, clergymen, and artisans organized by trade. In this Philadelphia parade celebrating the end of the War of 1812, the victuallers, preceded by militia cavalrymen, carry a penned steer and a craft flag high atop a wagon, while butchers in top hats and clean aprons ride below. Behind them, shipbuilders drag a ship through the streets. Such parades were vivid displays of the system of interlocking labors that made up the city, and of the value of artisans within that system.

headed a household that included four or more dependents. In short, they had become wage earners for life. In the seaport cities between 1790 and 1820, the world of artisans such as Paul Revere, Benjamin Franklin, and Thomas Paine was passing out of existence and was being replaced by wage labor.

The loss of independence undermined the paternal status of artisan husbands and fathers. As wage earners few could support their family unless the wife and children earned money to augment family income. Working-class women took in boarders and did laundry and found work as domestic servants or as peddlers of fruit, candy, vegetables, cakes, or hot corn. They sent their children out to scavenge in the streets. The descent into wage labor and the reliance on the earnings of women and children clashed sharply with the republican, patriarchal assumptions of fathers.

THE ASSAULT ON AUTHORITY

In the 50 years following the Declaration of Independence, the patriarchal republic created by the Founding Fathers became a democracy. The decline of authority and deference and the rise of individualistic, democratic social and political forms had many roots—most obviously in rural overcrowding, the movement of young people west and into the towns, and, more happily, in the increasingly democratic implications of American Revolutionary ideology. Most Americans witnessed the initial stirrings of change as a withering of paternal authority in their own households. Some—slaves and many women in particular—welcomed the decline of patriarchy. Others (the fathers themselves, disinherited sons, and women who looked to the security of old ways) considered it a disaster of unmeasured proportions. Whether they experienced the transformation as a personal rise or fall, Americans by the early 19th century had entered a world where received authority and past experience had lost their power. A new democratic faith emerged, grounded in the experience, intellect, and intuition of ordinary people.

PATERNAL POWER IN DECLINE

The philosopher Ralph Waldo Emerson, who reached adulthood in the 1830s, later mused that he had had the misfortune to be young when age was respected, and to have grown old when youth counted for everything. Arriving in America at about the time Emerson came of age, the French visitor Alexis de Tocqueville observed that paternal power was largely absent in American families. "All that remains of it," he said, "are a few vestiges in the first years of childhood. . . . But as soon as the young American approaches manhood, the ties of filial obedience are relaxed day by day; master of his thoughts, he is soon master of his conduct. . . . At the close of boyhood the man appears and begins to trace out his own path."

From the mid-18th century onward, especially after the Revolution, many young people grew up knowing that their father would be unable to help them and that they would have to make their own way in the world. The consequent decline of parental power became evident in many ways—perhaps most poignantly in changing patterns of courtship and marriage. In the countryside, young men knew that they would not inherit the family farm, and young women knew that their father would be able to provide only a small dowry. As a result, fathers exerted less control over marriage choices than when marriage entailed a significant transfer of property. Young people now courted away from parental scrutiny and made choices based on affection and personal attraction rather than on property or parental pressure. In 18th century America, rural marriages had united families; now they united individuals. One sign of youthful independence (and of young people's lack of faith in their future) was the high number of pregnancies outside of marriage. Such incidents had been few in the 17th-century North, but in the second half of the 18th century and in the first decades of the 19th, the number of first births that occurred within eight months of marriage averaged between 25 and 30 percent—with the rates running much higher among poor couples. Apparently fathers who could not provide for their children could not control them either.

THE ALCOHOLIC REPUBLIC

The erosion of the old family economy was paralleled by a dramatic rise in alcohol consumption. Americans had been drinking alcohol since the time of the first settlements. (The Puritan flagship

Arabella had carried three times as much beer as water.) But drinking, like all other "normal" behaviors, took place within a structure of paternal authority. Americans tippled every day in the course of their ordinary activities: at family meals and around the fireside, at work, and at barn-raisings, militia musters, dances, court days (even judges and juries passed the bottle), weddings, funerals, corn-huskings—even at the ordination of ministers. Under such circumstances, drinking—even drunkenness—seldom posed a threat to authority or to the social order.

That old pattern of communal drinking persisted into the 19th century, but during the 50 years following the Revolution it gradually gave way to a new pattern. Farmers, particularly those in newly settled areas, regularly produced a surplus of grain that they turned into whiskey. In Washington County in western Pennsylvania, for example, 1 family in 10 operated a distillery in the 1790s. Whiskey was safer than water and milk, which often were tainted, and it was cheaper than coffee or tea.

It was also cheaper than imported rum. So Americans embraced whiskey as their national drink and consumed extraordinary quantities of it. Per capita consumption of pure alcohol in all its forms increased by three to four gallons annually between 1790 and 1830. Most of the increase was in consumption of cheap and potent whiskey. By 1830 per capita consumption of distilled spirits was more than five gallons per year—the highest it has ever been, and three times what it is in the United States today. The United States had indeed become, as one historian has said, an "alcoholic republic."

The nation's growing thirst was driven not by conviviality or neighborliness but by a desire to get drunk. Most Americans drank regularly, though with wide variations. Men drank far more than women, the poor and the rich drank more than the emerging middle class, city dwellers drank more than farmers, westerners drank more than easterners, and southerners drank a bit more than northerners. Throughout the nation, the heaviest drinking took place among the increasing numbers of

INTERIOR OF AN AMERICAN INN, 1813 In this democratic, neighborly scene in a country inn in the early republic, men of varying degrees of wealth, status, and inebriety are drinking and talking freely with each other. One man's wife and daughter have invaded this male domain, perhaps to question the time and money spent at the inn.

young men who lived away from their families and outside the old social controls: soldiers and sailors, boatmen and other transport workers, lumberjacks, schoolmasters, journeyman craftsmen, college students. Among such men the controlled tippling of the 18th century gave way to the binge and to solitary drinking. By the 1820s American physicians were learning to diagnose delirium tremens—the trembling and the paranoid delusions brought on by withdrawal from physical addiction to alcohol. By that decade, as we shall see (see chapter 11), social reformers branded alcohol as a threat to individual well-being, to social peace, and to the republic itself.

THE DEMOCRATIZATION OF PRINT

Of course, Americans freed from the comforts and constraints of patriarchal authority did more than fornicate and drink. Many seized more constructive opportunities to think and act for themselves. That tendency was speeded by a rise in literacy and by the emergence of a print culture that catered to popular tastes. The literacy rate in the preindustrial United States was among the highest ever recorded. In 1790 approximately 85 percent of adult men in New England and 60 percent of those in Pennsylvania and the Chesapeake could read and write. The literacy rate was lower among women—about 45 percent in New England—but on the rise. By 1820 all but the poorest white Americans, particularly in the North, could read and write. The rise in literacy was accompanied by an explosive growth in the amount and kinds of reading matter available to the public. At its simplest and most intimate, this took the form of personal letters. Increased mobility separated families and friends and encouraged letter writing. In 1790 only 75 post offices operated in the United States. By 1800 903 were open. The amount of mail increased similarly, and—if what has survived to the present is an indication—the proportion made up of family correspondence, and the proportion of that correspondence written and read by women, both increased dramatically.

Women also were the principal readers of novels, a new form of reading matter that Thomas Jefferson and other authorities denounced as frivolous and aberrant. The first best-selling novel in the United States was *The Power of Sympathy*, a morally ambiguous tale of seduction and betrayal that exposed hypocrisy in male authorities who punished (generally poor and vulnerable) women for their own seductions. Such tales were seen as dangerous not only because they contained questionable subject matter but because girls and women read them silently and in private, without proper surveillance.

The most widely distributed publications, however, were newspapers. In 1790, 90 newspapers were being published in the United States. In 1830, 370 were in publication, and they had grown chattier and more informal. Still, even in New England, only 1 household in 10 or 12 subscribed to a newspaper. The papers were passed from hand to hand, read aloud in groups, and made available at taverns and public houses. Timothy Dwight, conservative president of Yale, hated newspapers and associated them with gambling, tavern-haunting, and drinking.

The increase in literacy and in printed matter accelerated the democratizing process. In the 18th century, when books and newspapers were scarce, most Americans had experienced the written word only as it was read aloud by fathers, ministers, or teachers. Between 1780 and 1820 private, silent reading of new kinds of texts became common—religious tracts, inexpensive Bibles, personal letters, novels, newspapers, and magazines. No longer were authority figures the sole interpreters of the world for families and neighborhoods. The new print culture encouraged Americans to read, think, and interpret information for themselves.

CITIZENSHIP

The transition from republic to democracy—and the relation of that transition to the decline of rural patriarchy—took on formal, institutional shape in a redefinition of republican citizenship.

The revolutionary constitutions of most states retained colonial freehold (property) qualifications for voting. In the yeoman societies of the late 18th century, freehold qualifications granted the vote to between one-half and three-quarters of adult white men. Many of the disenfranchised were dependent sons who expected to inherit citizenship along with land. Some states dropped the freehold clause and gave the vote to all adult men who paid taxes, but with little effect on the voting population. Both the freehold and taxpaying qualifications tended to grant political rights to adult men who headed households, thus reinforcing classical republican notions that granted full citizenship to independent fathers and not to their dependents. Statesmen often defended the qualifications in those terms. Arthur St. Clair, the territorial governor of Ohio, argued for retention of the Northwest Ordinance's 50-acre freehold qualification for voting in territorial elections in set-piece republican language: "I do not count independence and wealth always together," he said, "but I pronounce poverty and dependence inseparable." When Nathaniel Macon, a respected old revolutionary from North Carolina, saw that his state would abolish property qualifications in 1802, he suggested that the suffrage be limited to married men. Like St. Clair's proposition, it was an attempt to maintain the old distinction between citizen-householders and disfranchised dependents.

Between 1790 and 1820 republican notions of citizenship grounded in fatherhood and proprietorship gave way to a democratic insistence on equal rights for all white men. In 1790 only Vermont granted the vote to all free men. Kentucky entered the Union in 1792 without property or taxpaying qualifications; Tennessee followed with a freehold qualification, but only for newcomers who had resided in their counties for less than six months. The federal government dropped the 50-acre freehold qualification in the territories in 1812; of the eight territories that became states between 1796 and 1821 none kept a property qualification, only three maintained a taxpaying qualification, and five explicitly granted the vote to all white men. In the same years, one eastern state after another widened the franchise. By 1840 only Rhode Island retained a propertied electorate—primarily because Yankee farmers in that state wanted to retain power in a society made up more and more of urban, immigrant wage earners. (When Rhode Island finally reformed the franchise in 1843, the new law included a freehold requirement that applied only to the foreign-born.) With that exception, the white men of every state held the vote.

Early 19th century suffrage reform gave political rights to propertyless men, and thus took a long step away from the Founding Fathers' republic and toward mass democracy. At the same time, however, reformers explicitly limited the democratic franchise to those who were white and male. New Jersey's revolutionary constitution, for instance, had granted the vote to "persons" who met a freehold qualification. This loophole enfranchised property-holding widows, many of whom exercised their rights. A law of 1807 abolished property restrictions and gave the vote to all white men; the same law closed the loophole that had allowed propertied women to vote. The question of woman suffrage would not be raised again until women raised it in 1848 (see chapter 11); it would not be settled until well into the 20th century.

New restrictions also applied to African Americans. The revolutionary constitutions of Massachusetts, New Hampshire, Vermont, and Maine—northeastern states with tiny black minorities—granted the vote to free blacks. New York and North Carolina laws gave the vote to "all men" who met the qualifications, and propertied African Americans in many states (a tiny but symbolically crucial minority) routinely exercised the vote. Postrevolutionary laws that extended voting rights to all white men often specifically excluded or severely restricted votes for blacks. Free blacks lost the suffrage in New York, New Jersey, Pennsylvania, Connecticut, Maryland, Tennessee, and North Carolina—all states in which they had previously voted. By 1840 fully 93 percent of blacks in the North lived in states that either banned or severely restricted their right to vote. And the restrictions were explicitly about race. A delegate to the New York constitutional convention of 1821, noting the movement of freed slaves into New York City, argued against allowing them to vote: "The whole host of Africans that now deluge our city (already too impertinent to be borne), would be placed upon an equal with the citizens." A Michigan legislator later confirmed the distinction between "Africans" and "citizens" when he insisted that neither blacks nor Indians belonged to the "great North American Family," and thus could never be citizens of the republic.

Thus the "universal" suffrage of which many Americans boasted was far from universal: New laws dissolved the old republican connections between political rights and property, and thus saved the citizenship of thousands who were becoming propertyless tenants and wage earners; the same laws that gave the vote to all white men, however, explicitly barred other Americans from political participation. Faced with the disintegration of Jefferson's republic of proprietors, the wielders of power had chosen to blur the emerging distinctions of social class while they hardened the boundaries of sex and race. It was a formula that the "democracy" of white men would return to over and over again as the 19th century unfolded.

REPUBLICAN RELIGION

The Founding Fathers had been largely indifferent to organized religion, though a few were pious men. Some, like George Washington, a nominal Episcopalian, attended church out of a sense of obligation. Many of the better educated, including Thomas Jefferson, subscribed to deism, the belief that God had created the universe but did not intervene in its affairs. Many simply did not bother themselves with thoughts about religion. When asked why the Constitution mentioned neither God nor religion, Alexander Hamilton is reported to have smiled and answered, "We forgot."

THE DECLINE OF THE ESTABLISHED CHURCHES

In state after state, postrevolutionary constitutions withdrew government support from religion, and the First Amendment to the U.S. Constitution clearly prescribed the national separation of church and state. Reduced to their own sources of support, the established churches went into decline. The Episcopal Church, which until the Revolution had been the established Church of England in the southern colonies, went into decline. In Virginia, only 40 of the 107 Episcopal parishes supported ministers in the early 19th century. Nor did the Episcopal Church travel west with southern settlers. Of the 408 Episcopal congregations in the South in 1850, 315 were in the old seaboard states.

In New England, the old churches fared little better. The Connecticut Congregationalist Ezra Stiles reported in 1780 that 60 parishes in Vermont and an equal number in New Hampshire were without a minister. In Massachusetts, according to Stiles's reports, 80 parishes lacked a minister. In all, about one-third of New England's Congregational pulpits were vacant in 1780, and the situation was worse to the north and west. In Vermont between 1763 and 1820, the founding of churches followed the incorporation of towns by an average of 15 years, an indication that frontier settlement in that state proceeded almost entirely without the benefit of organized religion. In 1780 nearly all of the 750 Congregational churches in the United States were in New England. In the next 40 years, although the nation's population rose from 4 to 10 million, the number of Congregational churches rose by only 350. Ordinary women and men were leaving the churches that had dominated the religious life of colonial America, sometimes ridiculing the learned clergy as they departed. To Ezra Stiles and other conservatives, it seemed that the republic was plunging into atheism.

THE RISE OF THE DEMOCRATIC SECTS

The collapse of the established churches, the social dislocations of the postrevolutionary years, and the increasingly antiauthoritarian, democratic sensibilities of ordinary Americans provided fertile ground for the growth of new democratic sects. These were the years of camp-meeting revivalism, years in which Methodists and Baptists grew from small, half-organized sects into the great popular denominations they have been ever since. They were also years in which fiercely independent dropouts from older churches were putting together a loosely organized movement that would become the Disciples of Christ. At the same time, ragged, half-educated preachers were spreading the Universalist and Freewill Baptist messages in up-country New England, while in western New York young Joseph Smith was receiving the visions that would lead to Mormonism (see chapter 10).

The result was, first of all, a vast increase in the variety of choices on the American religious landscape. Within that welter of new churches was a roughly uniform democratic style shared by the fastest-growing sects. First, they renounced the need for an educated, formally authorized clergy. Religion was now a matter of the heart and not the head; crisis conversion (understood in most churches as personal transformation that resulted from direct experience of the Holy Spirit) was a necessary credential for preachers; a college degree was not. The new preachers substituted emotionalism and storytelling for Episcopal ritual and Congregational theological lectures; stories attracted listeners, and they were harder for the learned clergy to refute. The new churches also held up the Bible as the one source of religious knowledge, thus undercutting all theological knowledge and placing every literate Christian on a level with the best-educated minister. These tendencies often ended in Restorationism—the belief that all theological and institutional changes since the end of biblical times were man-made mistakes, and that religious organizations must restore themselves to the purity and simplicity of the church of the Apostles. In sum, this loose democratic creed rejected learning and tradition and raised up the priesthood of all believers.

Baptists and Methodists were by far the most successful at preaching to the new populist audience. The United States had only 50 Methodist churches in 1783; by 1820 it had 2,700. Over those same years the number of Baptist churches rose from 400 to 2,700. Together, in 1820, these two denominations outnumbered Episcopalians and Congregationalists by 3 to 1, almost a reversal of their relative standings 40 years earlier. Baptists based much of their appeal in localism and congregational democracy. Methodist success, on the other hand, entailed skillful national organization. Bishop Francis Asbury, the head of the church in its fastest-growing years, built an episcopal bureaucracy that seeded churches throughout the republic and sent circuit-riding preachers to places that had none. These early Methodist missions were grounded in self-sacrifice to the point of martyrdom. Asbury demanded much of his itinerant preachers, and until 1810 he strongly suggested

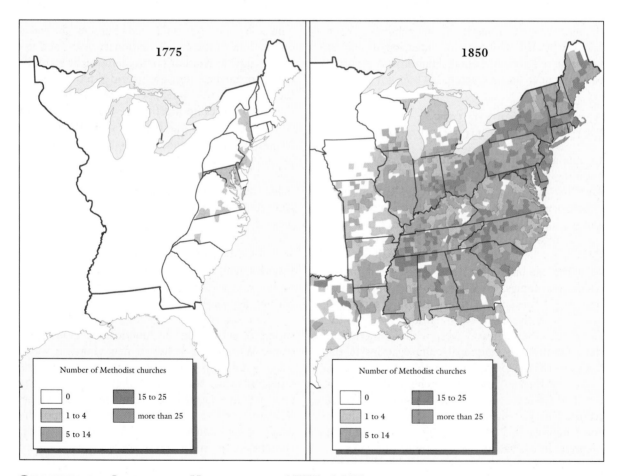

GROWTH OF AMERICAN METHODISM, 1775–1850

that they remain celibate. "To marry," he said, "is to locate." Asbury also knew that married circuit riders would leave many widows and orphans behind, for hundreds of them worked themselves to death. Of the men who served as Methodist itinerants before 1819, at least 60 percent died before the age of 40.

From seaport cities to frontier settlements, few Americans escaped the sound of Methodist preaching in the early 19th century. The Methodist preachers were common men who spoke plainly, listened carefully to others, and carried hymnbooks with simple tunes that anyone could sing. They also, particularly in the early years, shared traditional folk beliefs with their humble flocks. Some of the early circuit riders relied heavily on dreams; some could predict the future; many visited heaven and hell and returned with full descriptions. In the end, however, it was the hopefulness and simplicity of the Methodist message that attracted ordinary

Americans. The Methodists rejected the old terrors of Calvinist determinism and taught that although salvation comes only through God, men and women can decide to open themselves to divine grace and thus play a decisive role in their own salvation. They also taught that a godly life is a gradual, lifetime growth in grace—thus allowing for repentance for minor, and sometimes even major, lapses of faith and behavior. It was by granting responsibility (one might say sovereignty) to the individual believer that the Methodists established their democratic credentials and drew hundreds of thousands of Americans into their fold.

THE CHRISTIANIZATION OF THE WHITE SOUTH

During these same years, evangelical Protestantism became the dominant religion of the white South. That triumph constituted a powerful assault on the

CAMP MEETING Painted in 1839, when camp meetings had become routine, this striking watercolor depicts swooning, crying, and other "exercises" of converts (most of them women) under the sway of revival preachers.

Revival at York, Pennsylvania

The carpenter Lewis Henry Miller sketched scores of events that he witnessed as a child in early 19th-century York, Pennsylvania. York had been founded as a German settlement, and Miller's father served as schoolmaster of the German Lutheran Parochial School, but as a boy Miller saw his father's conservative, liturgical Lutherans outshone by Baptists and Methodists. His sketches aptly caught the evangelicals in their powerful combination of individual piety and public, democratic display. In 1808 the Methodists held a camp meeting near Codorus Creek. Miller remembered their tent city and the shanty from which the evangelists preached. At the center of his sketch, prospective converts (many of them women) revel in public humiliation and spiritual triumph, while a (mostly male) crowd looks on. The Baptists had immersed a Mrs. Stroman in Codorus Creek in 1800 before a huge crowd of onlookers—some of them pious church members, some merely curious. Although much evangelical activity was public and out of doors, the baptisms and mass conversions led ultimately and most importantly to lives of individual dignity through piety and prayer—lives like that of the African servant (probably a slave) Jonne Erven, whom Miller sketched at prayer.

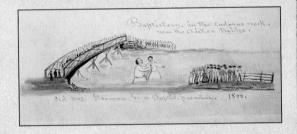

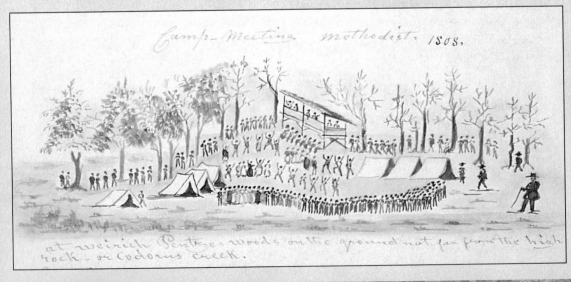

prerevolutionary structure of authority, because the Baptists, Methodists, and evangelical Presbyterians who achieved it saw it as a revolt of poor and middling folk against the cultural dominance of the gentry. The essence of southern evangelicalism was a violent conversion experience followed by a life of piety and a rejection of what evangelicals called "the world." To no small degree, "the world" was the economic, cultural, and political world controlled by the planters. James McGready, who preached in rural North Carolina, openly condemned the gentry: "The world is in all their thoughts day and night. All their talk is of corn and tobacco, of land and stock. The price of merchandise and negroes are inexhaustible themes of conversation. But for them, the name of Jesus has no charms; it is rarely mentioned unless to be profaned." In the 1790s this was dangerous talk, as McGready learned when young rakes rode their horses through one of his outdoor meetings, tipped over the benches, set the altar on fire, and threatened to kill McGready himself.

Southern Baptists, Methodists, and Presbyterians spread their democratic message in the early 19th century through the camp meeting. Though its origins stretched back into the 18th century, the first full-blown camp meeting took place at Cane Ridge, Kentucky, in 1801. Here the annual "Holy Feast," a three-day communion service of Scotch-Irish Presbyterians, was transformed into an outdoor, interdenominational revival at which hundreds experienced conversion under Presbyterian, Methodist, and Baptist preaching. Estimates of the crowd at Cane Ridge ranged from 10,000 to 20,000 persons, and by all accounts the enthusiasm was nearly unprecedented. Some converts fainted; others succumbed to uncontrolled bodily jerkings, while a few barked like dogs—all of them visibly taken by the Holy Spirit. Such exercises fell upon women and men, whites and blacks, rich and poor, momentarily erasing southern social distinctions in moments of profound and very public religious ecstasy. A witness to a later camp meeting recounted that "to see a bold and courageous Kentuckian (undaunted by the horrors of war) turn pale and tremble at the reproof of a weak woman, a little boy, or a poor African; to see him sink down in deep remorse, roll and toss, and gnash his teeth, till black in the face, entreat the prayers of those he

came to devour . . . who can say the change was not supernatural?"

EVANGELICALS AND SLAVERY

Southern evangelicalism was a subversive movement from its origins before the Revolution into the early 19th century. Although it reviled worldliness and its antiauthoritarian emphasis, southern evangelicalism was at bottom conservative, for it seldom questioned the need for social hierarchy. As the 19th century progressed, the Baptists, Methodists, and Presbyterians of the South, though they never stopped railing against greed and pride, learned to live comfortably within a system of fixed hierarchy and God-given social roles.

Slavery became the major case in point. For a brief period after the Revolution, evangelicals included slavery on their list of worldly sins. Methodists and Baptists preached to slaves as well as to whites, and Bishop Francis Asbury, principal architect of American Methodism, was familiar with John Wesley's statement that slavery was against "all the laws of Justice, Mercy, and Truth." In 1780 a conference of Methodist preachers ordered circuit riders to free their slaves and advised all Methodists to do the same. In 1784 the Methodists declared that they would excommunicate members who failed to free their slaves within two years. Lay Methodists took the order seriously: On the Delmarva Peninsula (Delaware and the Eastern Shore of Maryland and Virginia), for instance, Methodist converts freed thousands of slaves in the late 18th century. Other evangelicals shared their views. As early as 1787, southern Presbyterians prayed for "final abolition," and two years later Baptists condemned slavery as "a violent deprivation of the rights of nature and inconsistent with a republican government."

The period of greatest evangelical growth, however, came during the years in which the South was committing irrevocably to plantation slavery. As increasing numbers of both slaves and slave owners came within the evangelical fold, the southern churches had to rethink their position on slavery. The Methodists never carried out their threat to excommunicate slaveholders, confessing in 1816 that southerners were so committed to slavery that "little can be done to abolish the practice so contrary to moral justice." Similarly, the Baptists and Presbyterians never translated their antislavery rhetoric into action. By 1820, evangelicals were coming to terms with slavery. Instead of demanding freedom for slaves, they suggested, as the Methodist James O'Kelly put it, that slave owners remember that slaves were "dear brethren in Christ" who should not be treated cruelly and who should be allowed to attend religious services. By the 1830s, with large numbers of the planter elite converted to the evangelical fold, this evolved into a full-scale effort to Christianize the institution of slavery (see chapter 10).

After 1820 few southern evangelicals spoke out against slavery. Those who held to their antislavery views were concentrated in the up-country, where few whites owned slaves. Many of these were joining the stream of poor and middling whites who were moving to free states north of the Ohio River. A Kentucky farmer and carpenter named Thomas Lincoln, for instance, belonged to a Baptist congregation that had separated from its parent church over the question of slavery. When he moved his family to a site near Pidgeon Creek, Indiana, Lincoln helped build an antislavery Baptist church and served it as trustee. He also arranged a job as church sexton for his young son Abraham.

THE BEGINNINGS OF AFRICAN AMERICAN CHRISTIANITY

Slaves in America who were Christian in the 17th and 18th centuries mostly were converted by Anglican missions. Blacks participated in the revivals of the southern Great Awakening, and the number of Christian slaves increased steadily in the second half of the 18th century. In the slave communities of the Upper South, as well as the burgeoning free and semifree urban black populations of both the North and South, the evangelical revivals of the late 18th and early 19th centuries appealed powerfully to

LINK TO THE PAST

Religion and the Founding of the American Republic

http://lcweb.loc.gov/exhibits/religion/rel07.html

This is an exhibition of paintings, engravings, maps, and lithographs on American religion organized and presented by the Library of Congress. Click to "Religion and the New Republic," and study the items under "The Camp Meeting" and "The Emergence of the African-American Church." Consider the following questions:

1. What can looking at these items tell us about the role of preachers in camp-meeting religion? The role of men? Women? Children? Did these groups occupy the same space on the meeting ground? Do they seem to be experiencing the same things?

2. Do these items reveal differences in the ways in which whites and blacks organized, experienced, and acted out religious enthusiasm?

3. Historians have argued that revival religion in the new republic both democratized society and reinforced its central divisions. Do these items argue for greater democracy or greater division or both? Explain your answer.

African Americans who sensed that the bonds of slavery were loosening. By 1820 most blacks outside the Deep South considered themselves Christians. In the South Carolina and Georgia low country, however, few slaves were Christians before 1830.

During those years from 1780 to 1820, for the first time, thousands of slaves embraced Christianity and began to turn it into a religion of their own. Slaves attended camp meetings (the Cane Ridge revival included a black preacher, probably from the independent church in Lexington), listened to itinerant preachers, and joined the Baptist and Methodist congregations of the southern revival.

Blacks were drawn to revival religion for many of the same reasons as whites. They found the informal, storytelling evangelical preachers more attractive than the old Anglican missionaries. The revivalists, in turn, welcomed slaves and free blacks to their meetings and sometimes recruited them as preachers. Evangelical, emotional preaching, the falling, jerking, and other camp-meeting "exercises," and the revivalists' emphasis on singing and other forms of audience participation were much more attractive than the cold, high-toned preaching of the Anglicans. So were the humility and suffering of the evangelical whites. Slaves respected Methodist missionaries who entered their cabins and talked with them on their own terms; they listened more closely to men such as James McGready than to the slaveholders who rode horses through McGready's meetings. Finally, the slaves gloried in the evangelicals' assault on the slaveholders' culture and in the antislavery sentiments of many white evangelicals. The result was a huge increase in the number of African American Christians. Methodists, who counted converts more carefully than some others, claimed 20,000 black members in 1800—one in three American Methodists.

BETHEL AME CHURCH Founded in 1794 by the Reverend Richard Allen and nine other blacks who resented discrimination at the hands of white Methodists, Philadelphia's Bethel African Methodist Episcopal Church became a cornerstone of the city's free black community.

Neither antislavery beliefs nor openness to black participation, however, persisted long among white evangelicals. Although exceptions existed, most "integrated" congregations in both the North and South were in fact internally segregated, with blacks sitting in the back of the church or upstairs in the gallery, and with only whites serving in positions of authority. Blacks began organizing independent churches. In Philadelphia, black preachers Richard Allen and Absalom Jones rebelled against segregated seating in St. George's Methodist Church and, in 1794, founded two separate black congregations; by 1800, about 40 percent of Philadelphia's blacks belonged to one of those two churches. Similar secessions resulted in new churches farther south: in Baltimore; in Wilmington, Delaware; in Richmond; in Norfolk; and in the cluster of villages that had risen to serve the Chesapeake's new mixed economy. Even Charleston boasted an independent Methodist conference made up of 4,000 slaves and free blacks in 1815. By 1820 roughly 700 independent black churches operated in the United States where there had been none at all 30 years earlier. Only after 1830 did an independent Christian tradition exist among the majority of blacks who remained plantation slaves (see chapter 10). The democratic message of the early southern revival, the brief attempt of white and black Christians to live out the implications of that message, and the independent black churches that rose from the failure of that attempt all left a permanent stamp on southern Protestantism, black and white.

BLACK REPUBLICANISM: GABRIEL'S REBELLION

Masters who talked of liberty and natural rights sometimes worried that slaves might imagine that such language could apply to themselves. The Age of Democratic Revolution took a huge step in that direction in 1789, when the French Revolution—fought in the name of "Liberty, Equality, and Fraternity"—went beyond American notions of restored English liberties and into the heady regions of universal natural rights. Among the first repercussions outside of France was a revolution on the Caribbean island of Hispaniola in the French colony of Saint-Domingue. That island's half-

million slaves fought out a complicated political and military revolt that began with the events in Paris in 1789 and resulted—after the defeats of Spanish, English, and French armies—with the creation of the independent black republic of Haiti on the western one-third of the island. Slave societies throughout the hemisphere heard tales of terror from refugee French planters and stories of hope from the slaves they brought with them (12,000 of these entered South Carolina and Louisiana alone). In 1800 a conservative Virginia white complained that "Liberty and Equality has been infused into the minds of the negroes." A South Carolina congressman agreed that "this new-fangled French philosophy of liberty and equality" was stirring up the slaves. Even Thomas Jefferson, who applauded the spread of French republicanism, conceded that "the West Indies appears to have given considerable impulse to the minds of the slaves . . . in the United States."

Slaves from the 1790s onward whispered of natural rights and imagined themselves as part of the Democratic Revolution. This covert republic of the slaves sometimes came into the open, most ominously in Richmond in 1800, where a slave blacksmith named Gabriel hatched a well-planned conspiracy to overthrow Virginia's slave regime. Gabriel had been hired out to Richmond employers for most of his adult life; he was shaped less by plantation slavery than by the democratic, loosely interracial underworld of urban artisans. In the late 1790s the repressive acts of the Federalist national government and the angry responses of the Jeffersonian opposition (see chapter 8), along with the news from Saint-Domingue (present-day Haiti), drove the democratic sensibilities of that world to new heights. Gabriel's plans took shape within that heated ideological environment.

Gabriel, working with his brother and other hired-out slave artisans, planned his revolt with military precision. Working at religious meetings, barbecues, and the grog shops of Richmond, they recruited soldiers among slave artisans, adding plantation slaves only at the last moment. Gabriel planned to march an army of 1,000 men on Richmond in three columns. The outside columns would set diversionary fires in the warehouse district and prevent the militia from entering the town. The center would seize Capitol Square, including the treasury, the arsenal, and Governor James Monroe.

Although his army would be made up of slaves, and although his victory would end slavery in Virginia, Gabriel hoped to make a republican revolution, not a slave revolt. His chosen enemies were the Richmond "merchants" who had controlled his labor. Later, a co-conspirator divulged the plan: The rebels would hold Governor Monroe hostage and split the state treasury among themselves, and "if the white people agreed to their freedom they would then hoist a white flag, and [Gabriel] would dine and drink with the merchants of the city on the day when it would be agreed to." Gabriel expected what he called "the poor white people" and "the most redoubtable republicans" to join him. He in fact had the shadowy support of two Frenchmen, and rumors indicated that other whites were involved—though never at levels that matched the delusions of the conspirators. Gabriel planned to kill anyone who opposed him, but he would spare Quakers, Methodists, and Frenchmen, for they were "friendly to liberty." Unlike those of earlier slave insurgents, Gabriel's dreams did not center on violent retribution or a return to or reconstruction of West Africa. He was an American revolutionary, and he dreamed of a truly democratic republic for Virginia. His army would march into Richmond under the banner "Death or Liberty."

Gabriel and his co-conspirators recruited at least 150 soldiers who agreed to gather near Richmond on August 30, 1800. The leaders expected to be joined by 500 to 600 more rebels as they marched upon the town. On the appointed day, however, it rained heavily. Rebels could not reach the meeting point, and amid white terror and black betrayals Gabriel and his henchmen were hunted down, tried, and sentenced to death. In all, the state hanged 27 supposed conspirators, while others were sold and transported out of Virginia. The condemned carried their radical republican dreams to their graves. A white Virginian marveled that the rebels on the gallows displayed a "sense of their [natural] rights, [and] a contempt of danger." When asked to explain the revolt, one condemned man replied in terms that could only have disturbed the white republicans of Virginia: "I have nothing more to offer than what General Washington would have had to offer, had he been taken by the British and put to trial by

them. I have adventured my life in endeavoring to obtain the liberty of my countrymen, and am a willing sacrifice in their cause."

CONCLUSION

Between 1790 and 1820 Americans had transformed their new republic—with paradoxical results. The United States more than doubled in both size and population during these years. American trade with Britain, continental Europe, and the Caribbean skyrocketed. Some Americans amassed fortunes; others made more modest gains; others saw their positions deteriorate. Nonwhite Americans experienced the expansion of the republic and the growth of commerce as unmixed catastrophes: Indians between the Appalachians and the Mississippi River lost everything; their hunting grounds became American farmland, much of it worked by slaves who now knew that their masters would never voluntarily free them.

The transformation stemmed both from American independence and from the expansion of agriculture and increased exports of American farm products. When Americans traded plantation staples and surplus food for European (largely British) manufactured goods and financial services, however, they deepened their colonial dependence on the old centers of the world economy—even as they insisted on their independence with a bellicose republican nationalism. This formed the cluttered backdrop of social change, economic and geographic growth, and continuing vulnerability to the whims and needs of the Old World powers against which Federalists and Jeffersonian Republicans fought each other to determine the ultimate outcome of the American Revolution.

> **Suggested Readings begin on page SR-1.**
> **For Web activities and resources**
> **related to this chapter, go to**
> **http://www.harcourtcollege.com/history.murrin**

CHAPTER 8

COMPLETING THE REVOLUTION, 1789–1815

WE OWE ALLEGIANCE TO NO CROWN, A PATRIOTIC PAINTING FROM THE WAR OF 1812

Liberty—portrayed, as always, by a pure and determined woman—holds a Liberty Cap on a staff (the old symbol of international republicanism) and crowns an embattled American seaman with a classical wreath. Here the war is portrayed not only as a conflict between Britain and America but as a contest between monarchy and republicanism.

CHAPTER OUTLINE

Almost by acclamation, George Washington became the first president under the Constitution. Washington and his closest advisers (they would soon call themselves Federalists) believed that the balance between power and liberty had tipped toward anarchy after the Revolution. They had made the Constitution to counter democratic excesses, and they came into office determined to make the national government powerful enough to command respect abroad and to impose order at home. For the most part, they succeeded, but in the process they aroused a determined opposition that swung the balance back toward liberty and limited government. These self-styled Democratic Republicans (led almost from the beginning by Thomas Jefferson) were as firmly tied to revolutionary ideals of limited government and the yeoman republic as the Federalists were tied to visions of an orderly commercial republic with a powerful national state. The fight between Federalists and Democratic Republicans echoed the revolutionary contest between liberty and power—conducted this time against an ominous backdrop of international intrigue and war between France (which entered a republican revolution of its own in 1789) and Britain. Only when this Age of Democratic Revolution ended with the defeat of Napoleon in 1815 could the Americans survey the kind of society and government that their Revolution had made.

This chapter will focus on the following major questions:

- What was the Federalist plan for organizing the national government and its finances? What were the Jeffersonian Republicans' principal objections to those plans?
- What was the nature of the governmental crisis of 1798–1800, and how was it resolved?
- What were the principal reforms of the national government during Thomas Jefferson's administration? What were the implications of those reforms for the nature of republican government?
- What was the situation of the United States within the international politics created by the Napoleonic Wars, and how did that situation degenerate into a second war with Britain?

ESTABLISHING THE GOVERNMENT

George Washington left Mount Vernon for the temporary capital in New York City in April 1789.

The way was lined with the grateful citizens of the new republic. Militia companies and local dignitaries escorted him from town to town, crowds cheered, church bells marked his progress, and lines of girls in white dresses waved demurely as he passed. At Newark Bay he boarded a flower-bedecked barge and, surrounded by scores of boats, crossed to New York City. There he was welcomed by jubilant citizens as he made his way to the president's house. He arrived on April 23 and was inaugurated seven days later.

THE "REPUBLICAN COURT"

Reporting for work, President Washington found the new government embroiled in its first controversy—an argument over the dignity that would attach to his own office. Vice President John Adams had asked the Senate to create a title of honor for the president. Adams, along with many of the senators, wanted a resounding title that would reflect the power of the new executive. They rejected "His Excellency" because that was the term used for ambassadors, colonial governors, and other minor officials. Among the other titles they considered were "His Highness," "His Mightiness," "His Elective Highness," "His Most Benign Highness," "His Majesty," and "His Highness, the President of the United States, and Protector of Their Liberties." The Senate debated the question for a full month, then gave up when it became clear that the more democratic House of Representatives disliked titles. They settled on the austere dignity of "Mr. President." A senator from Pennsylvania expressed relief that the "silly business" was over. Thomas Jefferson, not yet a member of the government, pronounced the whole affair "the most superlatively ridiculous thing I ever heard of."

Jefferson would learn, however, that much was at stake in the argument over titles. Although the Constitution provided a blueprint for the republic, George Washington's administration would translate the blueprint into a working state. Members of the government knew their decisions would set precedents. It mattered very much what citizens called their president, for that was part of the huge constellation of laws, customs, and forms of etiquette that would give the new government either a republican or (as many anti-Federalists feared) a courtly tone. Many of those close to Washington wanted to

"[The president was dressed] in black velvet; his hair in full dress, powdered and gathered behind in a large silk bag; yellow gloves on his hands; holding a cocked hat with cockade in it, and the edges adorned with a black feather about an inch deep. He wore knee and shoe buckles; and a long sword, with a finely wrought and polished steel hilt, which appeared at the left hip; the coat worn over the sword, so that the hilt, and the part below the folds of the coat behind, were in view. The scabbard was white polished leather.

"He stood always in front of the fireplace, with his face towards the door of entrance. . . . He received his visitor with a dignified bow, while his hands were so disposed of as to indicate, that the salutation was not to be accompanied with shaking hands. This ceremony never occurred in these visits. . . ."

WILLIAM SULLIVAN
describing a visit with President Washington

protect presidential power from the localism and democracy that, they believed, had nearly killed the republic in the 1780s. Washington's stately inaugural tour, the high salaries paid to executive appointees, the endless round of formal balls and presidential dinners, the observance of the English custom of celebrating the executive's birthday, the appearance of Washington's profile on some of the nation's coins—all were meant to bolster the power and grandeur of the new government, particularly of its executive. When Jefferson became secretary of state and attended official social functions, he often found himself the only democrat at the dinner table. Aristocratic sentiments prevailed, said Jefferson, "unless there chanced to be some [democrat] from the legislative Houses." Thus the battle over presi-

GEORGE WASHINGTON IN 1796, NEAR THE END OF HIS PRESIDENCY The artist here captured the formal dignity of the first president and surrounded him with gold, red velvet, a presidential throne, and other emblems of kingly office.

dential titles was not "silly business." It was a revealing episode in the argument over how questions of power and liberty that Americans had debated since the 1760s would finally be answered.

THE FIRST CONGRESS

Leadership of the First Congress fell to James Madison, the Virginia congressman who had helped write the Constitution. Under his guidance Congress strengthened the new national government at every turn. First it passed a tariff on imports, which would be the government's chief source of income. Next, it turned to amendments to the Constitution demanded by the state ratifying conventions.

Madison proposed 19 constitutional amendments to the House. The 10 that survived congressional scrutiny and ratification by the states became the Bill of Rights. They reflected fears raised by a generation

of struggle with centralized power. The First Amendment guaranteed the freedoms of speech, press, and religion against federal interference. The Second and Third Amendments, prompted by old fears of a standing army, guaranteed the continuation of a militia of armed citizens and stated the specific conditions under which soldiers could be quartered in citizens' households. The Fourth, Fifth, Sixth, Seventh, and Eighth Amendments protected and defined a citizen's rights in court and when under

CHRONOLOGY

1789 George Washington inaugurated as first president of the United States • Judiciary Act establishes the Supreme Court and federal circuit courts

1790 Hamilton delivers his Report on Public Credit to Congress • Congress drafts the Bill of Rights

1792 Revolutionaries proclaim the French Republic

1793 Anglo-French War begins

1794 Federalists' excise tax triggers Whiskey Rebellion

1796 Jay's Treaty and Pinckney's Treaty ratified • John Adams elected second president

1798 XYZ affair results in undeclared war with France • Alien and Sedition Acts passed by Congress

1799 Slave revolution in Haiti

1800 Thomas Jefferson defeats Adams for the presidency

1803 United States purchases Louisiana Territory from France • *Marbury* v. *Madison* establishes the doctrine of judicial review

1804 Twelfth Amendment to the Constitution passed by Congress

1806 Non-Importation Act forbids importation of many British goods into U.S.

1807 Congress passes Embargo Act • Chesapeake-Leopard affair ignites anti-British sentiment

1810 Congress passes Macon's Bill No. 2

1811 Henry Clay elected Speaker of the House

1812 War of 1812 begins

1814 Federalists call Hartford Convention • Treaty of Ghent ends War of 1812

1815 American victory at the Battle of New Orleans

arrest—rights whose violation had been central to the Revolution's list of grievances. The Ninth Amendment stated that the enumeration of specific rights in the first eight amendments did not imply a denial of other rights; the Tenth stated that powers not assigned to the national government by the Constitution remained with the states and the citizenry.

Madison, a committed nationalist, had performed skillfully. Many doubters at the ratifying conventions had called for amendments that would change the government detailed in the Constitution. By channeling their fears into the relatively innocuous area of civil liberties, Madison soothed their mistrust while preserving the government of the Constitution. The Bill of Rights was an important guarantee of individual liberties. In the context in which it was written and ratified, it was an even more important guarantee of the power of the national government.

To fill out the framework of government outlined in the Constitution, Congress created the executive departments of war, state, and treasury and guaranteed that the heads of those departments and their assistants would be appointed solely by the president, thus removing them from congressional control. Congress next created the federal courts demanded but not specified in the Constitution. The Judiciary Act of 1789 established a Supreme Court with six members, along with 13 district courts and 3 circuit courts of appeal. The act allowed certain cases to be appealed from state courts to federal circuit courts presided over by traveling Supreme Court justices, thus dramatizing federal power. As James Madison and other members of the intensely nationalist First Congress surveyed their handiwork, they could congratulate themselves on having strengthened national authority at every opportunity.

HAMILTONIAN ECONOMICS: THE NATIONAL DEBT

Washington filled posts in what would become the cabinet with familiar faces. As secretary of war he chose Henry Knox, an old comrade from the Revolution. The State Department went to his fellow Virginian, Thomas Jefferson. He chose Alexander Hamilton of New York, his trusted aide-de-camp during the Revolution, to head the Department of the Treasury.

The most single-minded nationalist in the new government, Hamilton was a brilliant economic thinker, an admirer of the British system of centralized government and finance, and a supremely arrogant and ambitious man. More than other cabinet members, and perhaps even more than Washington himself (he later referred to Washington's presidency as "my administration"), Hamilton directed the making of a national government.

In 1789 Congress asked Secretary of the Treasury Hamilton to report on the public debt. The debt fell into three categories, Hamilton reported. The first was the $11 million owed to foreigners—primarily debts to France incurred during the Revolution. The second and third—roughly $24 million each—were debts owed by the national and state governments to American citizens who had supplied food, arms, and other resources to the revolutionary cause. Congress agreed that both justice and the credibility of the new government dictated that the foreign debts be paid in full, but the domestic debts raised troublesome questions. Those debts consisted of notes issued during the Revolution to soldiers, and to merchants, farmers, and others who had helped the war effort. Over the years, speculators had purchased many of these notes at a fraction of their face value; when word spread that the Constitution would create a government likely to pay its debts, speculators and their agents fanned out across the countryside buying up all the notes they could find. By 1790 the government debt was concentrated in the hands of businessmen and speculators—most of them northeasterners—who had bought notes at prices only 10 to 30 percent of their original value. Full payment would bring them enormous windfall profits.

The Revolutionary War debts of the individual states were another source of contention. Nationalists, with Hamilton at their head, wanted to assume the debts of the states as part of a national debt—a move that would concentrate the interests of public creditors, the need for taxation, and an expanded civil service in the national government. The state debts also had been bought up by speculators, and they posed another problem as well: Many states, including all the southern states with the exception of South Carolina, had paid off most of their notes in the 1780s; the other states still had significant outstanding debts. If the federal government assumed the state debts and paid them off at the face value of the notes, money would flow out of the southern, middle, and western states into the

Northeast, whose citizens would hold fully four-fifths of the combined national debt.

That is precisely what Hamilton proposed in his Report on Public Credit, issued in January 1790. He urged Congress to assume the state debts and to combine them with the federal government's foreign and domestic debts into a consolidated national debt. He agreed that the foreign debt should be paid promptly and in full, but he insisted that the domestic debt be a permanent, tax-supported fixture of government. Under his plan, the government would issue securities to its creditors and would pay an annual rate of interest of 4 percent. Hamilton's funding and assumption plans announced to the international community and to actual and potential government creditors that the United States would pay its bills. But Hamilton had domestic plans for the debt as well. A permanent debt would attract the wealthiest financiers in the country as creditors and would render them loyal and dependent on the federal government. It would bring their economic power to the government and at the same time would require a significant enlargement of the federal civil service, national financial institutions, and increased taxes. The national debt, in short, was at the center of Alexander Hamilton's plan for a powerful national state.

HAMILTONIAN ECONOMICS: THE BANK AND THE EXCISE

As part of that plan, Hamilton asked Congress to charter a Bank of the United States. The government would store its funds in the bank and would supervise its operations, but the bank would be controlled by directors representing private stockholders. The Bank of the United States would print and back the national currency and would regulate other banks. Hamilton's proposal also made stock in the bank payable in government securities, thus (1) adding to the value of the securities, (2) giving the bank a powerful interest in the fiscal stability of the government, and (3) binding the holders of the securities even closer to the national government. Those who looked closely saw that

LINK TO THE PAST

Congressional Debates

http://memory.loc.gov/ammem/ammemhome.html

The Library of Congress's American Memory Project has made thousands of documents available on-line. Students of national politics in the early republic may view, for examples, the manuscript papers of George Washington, Thomas Jefferson, and James Madison, the records of Congress, and many, many other items. As an introduction to the riches of this collection, students might click onto the *Annals of Congress* and the records of Senate debates and locate the congressional debates on the Bill of Rights (First Congress, First Session) and the Alien and Sedition Acts (Fifth Congress, First and Second Sessions). Consider these questions:

1. How did Congressmen and Senators argue for and against amendments establishing freedom of speech and the press and a citizen's rights in court in 1790?

2. How did they argue for an against the abridgement of these rights in 1797–98?

3. What had happened in the intervening years?

Hamilton's Bank of the United States was a carbon copy of the Bank of England.

To fund the national debt, Hamilton called for a federal excise tax on wines, coffee, tea, and spirits. The tax on spirits would fall most heavily on the whiskey produced in abundance on the frontier. Its purpose, stated openly by Hamilton, was not only to produce revenue but to establish the government's power to create an internal tax and to collect it in the most remote regions in the republic. The result, as we shall see later in this chapter, was a "Whiskey Rebellion" in the west and an overwhelming display of federal force.

Passed in April 1791, the national bank and the federal excise measures completed Hamilton's organization of government finances. Taken separately, the consolidated government debt, the national bank, and the federal excise tax ably solved discrete problems of government finance. Taken together, however, they constituted a full-scale replica of the treasury-driven government of Great Britain.

THE RISE OF OPPOSITION

In 1789 every branch of government was staffed by supporters of the Constitution. The most radical anti-Federalists took positions in state governments or left politics altogether. Nearly everyone in the national government was committed to making the new government work. In particular, Alexander Hamilton at Treasury and James Madison in the House of Representatives expected to continue the political and personal friendship they had made while writing the Constitution and working to get it ratified. Yet in the debate over the national debt, Madison led congressional opposition to Hamilton's proposals. In 1792 Thomas Jefferson joined the opposition, insisting that Hamilton's schemes would dismantle the Revolution. Within a few short years the consensus of 1789 had degenerated into an angry argument over what sort of government would finally result from the American Revolution. More than 25 years later, Jefferson still insisted that the battles of the 1790s had been "contests of principle between the advocates of republican and those of kingly government."

Hamilton presented his national debt proposal to Congress as a solution to specific problems of government finance, not as part of a blueprint for an English-style state. Madison and other southerners opposed it because they did not want northern speculators—many of whom had received information from government insiders—to reap fortunes from notes bought at rock-bottom prices from soldiers, widows, and orphans. He branded Hamilton's plan "public plunder."

At the urging of Jefferson and others, Madison and members of the congressional opposition compromised with Hamilton. In exchange for accepting his proposals on the debt, they won his promise to locate the permanent capital of the United States at a site on the Potomac River. The compromise went to the heart of American revolutionary republicanism. Hamilton intended to tie northeastern commercial interests to the federal government. If New York or Philadelphia became the permanent capital, political and economic power might be concentrated there as it was in Paris and London—court cities in which power, wealth, and every kind of excellence were in league against a plundered and degraded countryside. Benjamin Rush, a Philadelphian, condemned the "government which has begun so soon to ape the corruption of the British Court, conveyed to it through the impure channel of the City of New York." Madison and other agrarians considered Philadelphia just as bad, and supported Hamilton's debt only on condition that the capital be moved south. The compromise would distance the commercial power of the cities from the federal government and would put an end to the "republican court" that had formed around Washington. This radically republican move ensured that the capital of the United States would be, except for purposes of government, a place of no importance.

JEFFERSON VERSUS HAMILTON

When Hamilton proposed the Bank of the United States, republicans in Congress immediately noted its similarity to the Bank of England and voiced deep suspicion of Hamilton's economic and governmental plans. Thomas Jefferson had joined the opposition, arguing that Congress had no constitutional right to charter a bank, and that allowing Congress to do so would revive the popular fears of centralized despotism that had nearly defeated ratification of the Constitution. Hamilton responded with the first argument for expanded federal power under the clause in the Constitution empowering Congress "to make all laws which shall be necessary and proper" to the performance of its duties. President Washington and a majority in Congress ultimately sided with Hamilton.

Jefferson's strict constructionism (his insistence that the government had no powers beyond those specified in the Constitution) revealed his fears of the de facto constitution that Hamilton's system was making. Jefferson argued that the federal bank was unconstitutional, that a federal excise tax was certain to arouse public opposition, and that funding the debt would reward speculators and penalize ordinary citizens. More importantly, Jefferson argued, Hamilton used government securities and stock in the Bank of the United States to buy the loyalty not only of merchants and speculators but of members of Congress. Thirty congressmen owned stock in the Bank of the United States, and many others held government securities or had close ties to men who did. Jefferson charged that this "corrupt squadron" of "paper men" in Congress was, in the classic fashion of evil ministers, enabling Hamilton to control Congress from his nonelective seat in the executive branch. "The ultimate object of all this," insisted Jefferson, "is to prepare the way for a change, from the present republican form of government, to that of a monarchy, of which the English constitution is to be the model."

For their part, Hamilton and his supporters (who by now were calling themselves Federalists) insisted that the centralization of power and a strong executive were necessary to the survival of the republic. The alternative was a return to the localism and public disorder of the 1780s and ultimately to the failure of the Revolution. The argument drew its urgency from the understanding of both Hamilton and his detractors that the United States was a small revolutionary republic in a world governed by kings and aristocrats, and that republics had a long history of failure. They all knew that Americans might yet lose their Revolution. Until late 1792, however, the argument over Hamilton's centralizing schemes remained mostly among government officials. Hamilton and his supporters tried to mobilize the commercial elite on the side of government, while Madison and Jefferson struggled to hold off the perceived monarchical plot until the citizens could be aroused to defend

their liberties. As both sides began to mobilize popular support, events in Europe came to dominate the politics of the American republican experiment, to place that experiment in even greater jeopardy, and to increase the violence of American politics to the point at which the republic almost failed.

THE REPUBLIC IN A WORLD AT WAR, 1793–1800

Late in 1792 French revolutionaries rejected monarchy and proclaimed the French Republic. They beheaded Louis XVI in January 1793. Eleven days later the French, already at war with Austria and Prussia, declared war on conservative Britain, thus launching a war between French republicanism and British-led reaction that, with periodic outbreaks of peace, would embroil the Atlantic world until the defeat of France in 1815.

AMERICANS AND THE FRENCH REVOLUTION

Americans could not have escaped involvement even had they wanted to. Treaties signed in 1778 allied the United States with France—although Federalists and Jeffersonians would argue whether those treaties applied to the new French Republic or became void with the execution of the monarch who had signed them. Americans had overwhelmingly supported the French Revolution of 1789 and had applauded the progress of French republicanism during its first three years. Both their gratitude for French help during the American Revolution and American hopes for international republicanism faced severe tests in 1793, when the French Republic began to execute thousands of aristocrats, priests, and other "counterrevolutionaries," and when the French threatened the sovereignty of nations by declaring a war of all peoples against all monarchies. The argument between Jeffersonian republicanism and Hamiltonian centralization was no longer a squabble within the United States government. National politics was now caught up and subsumed within the struggle over international republicanism.

As Britain and France went to war in 1793, President Washington declared American neutrality, thereby abrogating obligations made in the 1778 treaties with the French. Washington and most of

The Capital of the Republic

Having determined to build its capital city on the Potomac, Congress commissioned the French architect and engineer Pierre Charles L'Enfant to plan the city. The Americans dismissed L'Enfant's suggestions for ornamentation and for a national church at the center of town, but with these alterations the Frenchman's plan became the plan of Washington, D.C. L'Enfant inscribed the Constitution on the landscape: Congress sat in the Capitol Building, situated on high ground looking down what would become the Capitol Mall; the President's House stood a mile and a half away (neither could be seen from the other), and the Court was equidistant between them.

Most striking to those who had seen European capitals, the city had no function other than republican government. It had no mercantile or financial establishments, no theaters, and no military fortress. Broad, straight streets stretched beyond the built-up areas of the town; visually as well as politically, the capital was dependent upon and vulnerable to the countryside—the opposite of European court cities.

Foreign diplomats complained that Washington was swampy and unpleasant, and that the city provided few amusements. As late as 1842, the English writer Charles Dickens found Washington unfinished and uncivilized: "It is sometimes called the City of Magnificent Distances, but it might with greater propriety be termed the City of Magnificent Intentions. . . . Spacious avenues that begin in nothing, and lead nowhere; streets, mile-long, that only want houses, roads and inhabitants; public buildings that need only a public to be complete." What Dickens and earlier visitors missed, however, was that American republicans had built precisely the capital city that most of them wanted.

his advisers realized that the United States was in no condition to fight a war. They also wanted to stay on good terms with Great Britain. Ninety percent of American imports came from Britain, and 90 percent of the federal revenue came from customs duties on those imports. Thus both the nation's commerce and the financial health of the government depended on good relations with Great Britain. Moreover, Federalists genuinely sympathized with the British in the war with France. They regarded the United States as a "perfected" England and viewed Britain as the defender of hierarchical society and ordered liberty against the homicidal anarchy of the French.

Jefferson and his friends saw things differently. They applauded the French for carrying on the republican revolution Americans had begun in 1776, and they had no affection for the "monarchical" politics of the Federalists or for Americans' continued neocolonial dependence upon British trade. The faction led by Jefferson and Madison wanted to abandon the English mercantile system and trade freely with all nations. They did not care if that course of action hurt commercial interests (most of which supported the Federalists) or impaired the government's ability to centralize power in itself. Although they agreed that the United States should stay out of the war, the Jeffersonians sympathized as openly with the French as the Federalists did with the British.

CITIZEN GENÊT

Throughout the war years from 1793 to 1815, both Great Britain and France, by intervening freely in the internal affairs of the United States, made American isolationism impossible.

In April 1793 the French sent Citizen Edmond Genêt as minister to the United States. Genêt's ruling Girondists were the revolutionary faction that had declared the war on all monarchies; they ordered Genêt to enlist American aid with or without the Washington administration's consent. After the president's proclamation of neutrality, Genêt openly commissioned American privateers to harass British shipping and enlisted Americans in intrigues against the Spanish outpost of New Orleans. Genêt then opened France's Caribbean colonies to American shipping, providing American shippers a choice between French free trade and British mercantilism. Genêt's mission came to an abrupt end in the summer of 1793, when the Girondists fell from power. Learning that he would be guillotined if he returned to France, he accepted the hospitality of Americans, married a daughter of George Clinton, the old anti-Federalist governor of New York, and lived out the rest of his life as an American country gentleman.

The British responded to Genêt's free-trade declaration with a promise to seize any ship trading with French colonies in the Caribbean. Word of these Orders in Council—almost certainly by design—reached the Royal Navy before American merchant seamen had learned of them, with the result that 250 American ships fell into British hands. The Royal Navy also began searching American ships for English sailors who had deserted or who had switched to safer, better-paying work in the American merchant marine. Inevitably, some American sailors were kidnapped into the British navy in a contemptuous and infuriating assault on American sovereignty. Meanwhile the British, operating from Canada and from their still-garrisoned forts in the Northwest, began promising military aid to the Indians north of the Ohio River. Thus, while the French ignored the neutrality of the United States, the English engaged in both overt and covert acts of war.

WESTERN TROUBLES

In the Northwest the situation came to a head in the summer and fall of 1794. The Shawnee and allied tribes, emboldened by two victories over American armies, plotted with the British and talked of driving all settlers out of their territory. At the same time, frontier whites, sometimes with the encouragement of English and Spanish officials, grew increasingly contemptuous of a national government that could neither pacify the Indians nor guarantee their free use of the Mississippi River. President Washington heard that 2,000 Kentuckians were armed and ready to attack New Orleans—a move that would have started a war between the United States and Spain. Settlers in Georgia were making unauthorized forays against the Creeks. Worst of all, settlers up and down the frontier refused to pay the Federalists' excise tax on whiskey—a direct challenge to federal authority. In western Pennsylvania, mobs tarred and feathered excise officers and burned the property of distillers who paid the tax. In July 1794 near Pittsburgh, 500 militiamen marched on the house of General John Neville, one of the most hated of the federal excise collectors. Neville, his family, and a few federal soldiers fought the militiamen, killing two and wounding six before they abandoned the house to be looted and burned. Two weeks later, 6,000 "Whiskey Rebels" met at Braddock's Field near Pittsburgh, threatening to attack the town.

Faced with serious international and domestic threats to his new government, Washington determined to defeat the Indians and the Whiskey Rebels by force—thus securing American control of the Northwest. He sent General "Mad" Anthony Wayne against the northwestern tribes. Wayne's

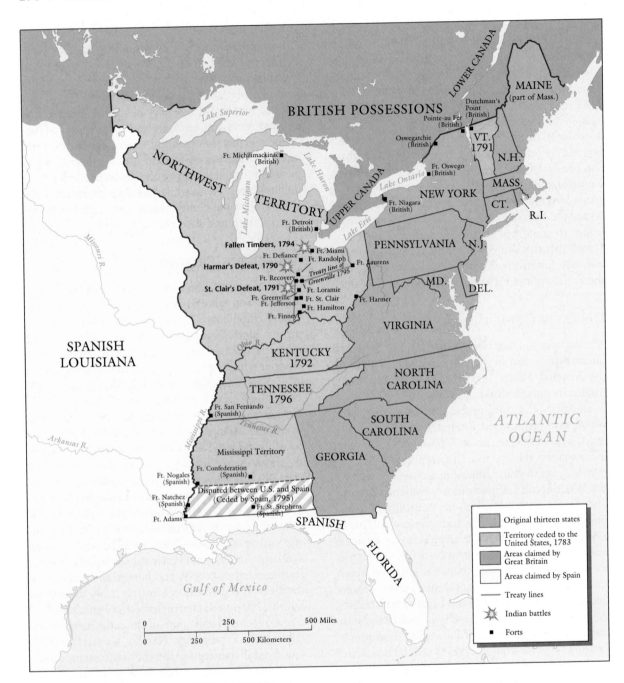

SECURING THE WEST, 1790–1796

decisive victory at Fallen Timbers in August 1794—fought almost in the shadow of a British fort—ended the Indian-British challenge in the Northwest for many years (see chapter 7).

In September, Washington ordered 12,000 federalized militiamen from eastern Pennsylvania, Maryland, Virginia, and New Jersey to quell the Whiskey Rebellion. The president promised amnesty to rebels who pledged to support the government and prison terms to those who did not. As the army marched west from Carlisle, they found defiant liberty poles but no armed resistance. Arriving at Pittsburgh, the army arrested 20 suspected rebels—none of them leaders—and marched them back to Philadelphia for trial. In the end only two "rebels," both of them feeble-minded, were convicted. President Washington pardoned them and the Whiskey Rebellion was over.

THE JAY TREATY

Although he sent armies against Indians and frontiersmen, President Washington capitulated to the British on the high seas. In 1794 he sent John Jay, chief justice of the Supreme Court, to negotiate the conflicts between the United States and Britain. Armed with news of Wayne's victory, Jay extracted a promise from the British to remove their troops from American territory in the Northwest. On every other point of dispute, however, he agreed to British terms. The Jay Treaty made no mention of impressment or other violations of American maritime rights, nor did it refer to the old issue of British payments for slaves carried off during the Revolution. The treaty did allow small American ships back into the West Indies, but only on terms that the Senate would reject. In short, Jay's Treaty granted British trade a most-favored-nation basis in exchange for the agreement of the British to abandon their northwestern forts. Given the power of Great Britain, it was the best that Americans could expect. Washington, obliged to choose between an unpopular treaty and an unwinnable war, passed Jay's Treaty on to the Senate, which in June 1795 ratified it by a bare two-thirds majority.

It was during the fight over Jay's Treaty that dissension within the government was first aired in public. The seaport cities and much of the Northeast reacted favorably to the treaty. It ruled out war with England and cemented an Anglo-American trade relationship that strengthened both Hamilton's national state and the established commercial interests that supported it. Moreover, northeasterners held little enthusiasm for the French Revolution—particularly in New England, with its long history of colonial wars with France. The South, on the other hand, saw Jay's Treaty as a blatant sign of the designs of Britain and the Federalists to subvert republicanism in both France and the United States. The Virginia legislature branded the treaty unconstitutional, and Republican congressmen demanded to see all documents relating to Jay's negotiations. Washington responded by telling them that their request could be

legitimate only if the House was planning to initiate impeachment proceedings—thus tying approval of the treaty to his enormous personal prestige.

Meanwhile, on March 3, 1796, Washington released the details of a treaty that Thomas Pinckney had negotiated with Spain. In this treaty, Spain recognized American neutrality and set the border between the United States and Spanish Florida on American terms. Most important, the Pinckney Treaty put an end to Spanish claims to territory in the Southwest and gave Americans the unrestricted right to navigate the Mississippi River and to transship produce at the Spanish port of New Orleans. Coupled with the victory at Fallen Timbers, the British promise to abandon their posts in the Northwest, and Washington's personal popularity, Pinckney's Treaty helped turn the tide in favor of the unpopular Jay's Treaty. With a diminishing number of hotheads willing to oppose Washington, western representatives joined the Northeast and increasing numbers of southerners to ratify Jay's Treaty.

WASHINGTON'S FAREWELL

George Washington refused to run for reelection in 1796—thus setting a two-term limit observed by every president until Franklin Roosevelt (see chapter 25). Washington could be proud of his accomplishment. He had presided over the creation of a national government. He had secured American control over the western settlements by ending British, Spanish, and Indian military threats and by securing free use of the Mississippi River for western produce. Those policies, together with the federal invasion of western Pennsylvania, had made it evident that the government could and would control its most distant regions. He had also avoided war with Great Britain—though not without overlooking assaults on American sovereignty. As he was about to leave government he wrote, with substantial help from Hamilton, his farewell address. In it he warned against long-term "entangling alliances" with other countries; America, he said, should stay free to operate on its own in international affairs—an ideal that many felt had been betrayed in Jay's Treaty. Washington also warned against internal political divisions. Of course, he did not regard his own Federalists as a "party"—they were simply friends of the government, but he saw the Democratic Republicans (the name by which Jefferson's allies called themselves) as a self-interested, irresponsible "faction," thus branding them, in the language of classical republicanism, as public enemies. Washington's call for national unity and an end to partisanship was in fact a parting shot at the Democratic Republican opposition.

THE ELECTION OF 1796

Washington's retirement opened the way to the fierce competition for public office that he had feared; in 1796 Americans experienced their first contested presidential election. The Federalists chose as their candidate John Adams, an upright conservative from Massachusetts who had served as vice president. The Democratic Republicans nominated Thomas Jefferson. According to the gentlemanly custom of the day, neither candidate campaigned in person. Jefferson stayed home at Monticello and Adams retired to his farm near Boston, while friends of the candidates, the newspaper editors who enjoyed their patronage, and even certain European governments ensured that the election would be intensely partisan.

Adams would certainly carry New England and Jefferson would carry the South, which left the election to be decided in Pennsylvania and New York. Some states, most of them in the South, chose presidential electors by direct vote, but in most states, including the crucial mid-Atlantic states, state legislatures selected the presidential electors. The election of 1796 would be decided in elections to the legislatures of those states, and in subsequent intriguing within those bodies. John Beckley, clerk of the House of Representatives, devised the Republican strategy in Pennsylvania. He secretly circulated a list of well-known and respected candidates for the state legislature who were committed to Jefferson's election as president. Discovering the Republican slate only when it was too late to construct a similar list, the Federalists lost the elections. In December, Beckley delivered all but one of Pennsylvania's electoral votes to Jefferson. New York, however, had no John Beckley. Adams took the state's electoral votes and won the national election. The distribution of electoral votes revealed the bases of Federalist and Republican support: Adams received only 2 electoral votes south of the Potomac, and Jefferson received only 18 (all but 5 of them in Pennsylvania) north of the Potomac.

The voting was over, but the intriguing was not. Alexander Hamilton, who since his retirement from the Treasury in 1795 had directed Federalist affairs from his New York law office, knew that he could not manipulate the independent and almost perversely upright John Adams. So he secretly instructed South Carolina's Federalist electors to withhold their votes from Adams. That would have given the presidency to Adams's running mate, Thomas Pinckney, relegating Adams to the vice presidency. (Prior to the ratification of the Twelfth Amendment in 1804, the candidate with a majority of the electoral votes became president, and the second-place candidate became vice president.) Like some of Hamilton's other schemes, this one backfired. New England electors heard of the plan and angrily withheld their votes from Pinckney. As a result, Adams was elected president and his opponent Thomas Jefferson became vice president. Adams narrowly won the election, but he took office with a justifiable mistrust of many members of his own party, and with the head of the opposition party as his second in command. It was not an auspicious beginning.

TROUBLES WITH FRANCE, 1796–1800

As Adams entered office an international crisis was already in full swing. France, regarding Jay's Treaty as an Anglo-American alliance, had recalled its envoy in 1796 and had broken off relations with the United States. The French hinted that they intended to overthrow the reactionary government of the United States, but would postpone taking action in the hope that a friendlier Thomas Jefferson would replace "old man Washington" in 1797. Then, during the crucial elections in Pennsylvania, they stepped up their seizures of American ships trading with Britain, giving the Americans a taste of what would happen if they did not elect a government friendlier to France. When the election went to John Adams, the French gave up on the United States and set about denying Britain its new de facto ally. In 1797 France expelled the American minister and refused to carry on relations with the United States until it addressed French grievances. The French ordered that American ships carrying "so much as a handkerchief" made in England be

PROPERTY PROTECTED, a la Françoise.

THE XYZ AFFAIR Disclosure of the XYZ affair created a wave of anti-French sentiment in the United States. Here America (depicted as Liberty was usually depicted, as a young woman) is accosted by the five lascivious, money-hungry members of the Directory.

confiscated without compensation and announced that American seamen serving in the British navy would be summarily hanged if captured.

President Adams wanted to protect American commerce from French depredations. But he knew that the United States might not survive a war with France. He also knew that French grievances (including Jay's Treaty and the abrogation of the French-American treaties of 1778) were legitimate. He decided to send a mission to France, made up of three respected statesmen: Charles Cotesworth Pinckney of South Carolina, John Marshall of Virginia, and Elbridge Gerry of Massachusetts. When these prestigious delegates reached Paris, however, they were left cooling their heels in the outer offices of the Directory—the revolutionary committee of five that had replaced France's beheaded king. At last, three French officials (the correspondence identified them only as "X, Y, and Z"—and the incident later became known as the XYZ affair) discreetly hinted that France would receive them if they paid a bribe of $250,000, arranged for the United States to loan $12 million to the French government, and apologized for unpleasant remarks that John Adams had made about France. The delegates refused, saying "No, not a sixpence,"

and returned home. There a journalist transformed their remark into "Millions for defense, but not one cent for tribute."

President Adams asked Congress to prepare for war, and the French responded by seizing more American ships. Thus began, in April 1798, an undeclared war between France and the United States in the Caribbean. While the French navy dealt with the British in the North Atlantic, French privateers inflicted costly blows on American shipping. After nearly a year of fighting, with the British providing powder and shot for American guns, the U.S. Navy chased the French privateers out of the Caribbean.

THE CRISIS AT HOME, 1798–1800

The troubles with France precipitated a crisis at home. Disclosure of the XYZ correspondence, together with the quasi-war in the Caribbean, produced a surge of public hostility toward the French and, to some extent, toward their Republican friends in the United States. Many Federalists, led by Alexander Hamilton, wanted to use the crisis to destroy their political opponents. Without consulting President Adams, the Federalist-dominated Congress passed several wartime measures. The first was a federal property tax—graduated, spread equally between sections of the country, and justified by military necessity—nonetheless a direct federal tax. Congress then passed four laws known as the Alien and Sedition Acts. The first three were directed at immigrants: They extended the naturalization period from 5 to 14 years and empowered the president to detain enemy aliens during wartime and to deport those he deemed dangerous to the United States. The fourth law—the Sedition Act—set jail terms and fines for persons who advocated disobedience to federal law or who wrote, printed, or spoke "false, scandalous, and malicious" statements against "the government of the United States, or the President of the United States [note that Vice President Jefferson was not included], with intent to defame . . . or to bring them or either of them, into contempt or disrepute."

President Adams never used the powers granted under the Alien Acts, but the Sedition Act resulted in the prosecution of 14 Republicans, most of them journalists. William Duane, editor of the *Philadelphia Aurora*, was indicted when he and two Irish friends circulated a petition against the Alien Act on the grounds of a Catholic church. James Callendar, editor of a Jeffersonian newspaper in Richmond, was arrested, while another prominent Republican went to jail for statements made in a private letter. Jedediah Peck, a former Federalist from upstate New York, was arrested when he petitioned Congress to repeal the Alien and Sedition Acts. Matthew Lyon, a scurrilous and uncouth Republican congressman from Vermont, had brawled with a Federalist representative in the House chamber; he went to jail for his criticisms of President Adams, Federalist militarism, and what he called the "ridiculous pomp" of the national administration.

Republicans, charging that the Alien and Sedition Acts violated the First Amendment, turned to the states for help. Southern states, which had provided only 4 of the 44 congressional votes for the Sedition Act, took the lead. Jefferson provided the Kentucky legislature with draft resolutions, and Madison did the same for the Virginia legislature. These so-called Virginia and Kentucky Resolves restated the constitutional fundamentalism that had guided Republican opposition to the Federalists through the 1790s. Jefferson's Kentucky Resolves reminded Congress that the Alien and Sedition Acts

gave the national government powers not mentioned in the Constitution and that the Tenth Amendment reserved such powers to the states. He also argued that the Constitution was a "compact" between sovereign states, and that state legislatures could "nullify" federal laws they deemed unconstitutional—thus anticipating constitutional theories that states'-rights southerners would use after 1830.

The Virginia and Kentucky Resolves demonstrated the extremes to which Jefferson and Madison might go. Beyond that, however, they had few immediate effects. Opposition to the Sedition Act ranged from popular attempts to obstruct the law to fistfights in Congress, and Virginia began calling up its militia. No other states followed the lead of Virginia and Kentucky, however, and talk of armed opposition to Federalist policies was limited to a few areas in the South.

THE POLITICIANS AND THE ARMY

Federalists took another ominous step by implementing President Adams's request that Congress create a military prepared for war. Adams wanted a stronger navy, both because the undeclared war with France was being fought on the ocean and because he agreed with other Federalists that America's future as a commercial nation required a respectable navy. Hamilton and others (who were becoming known as "High Federalists") preferred a standing army. At the urging of Washington and against his own judgment, Adams had appointed Hamilton inspector general. As such, Hamilton would be the de facto commander of the U.S. Army. Congress authorized a 20,000-man army and Hamilton proceeded to raise it. Congress also provided for a much larger army to be called up in the event of a declaration of war. When Hamilton expanded the officer corps in anticipation of such an army, he excluded Republicans and commissioned only his political friends. High Federalists wanted a standing army to enforce the Alien and Sedition Acts and to put down an impending rebellion in the South. Beyond that, there was little need for such a force. The war was being fought at sea, and most Americans believed that the citizen militia could hold off any land invasion until an army was raised. The Republicans, President Adams himself, and many other Federalists now became convinced that Hamilton and his High Federalists were determined to destroy their political opponents, enter into an alliance with Great Britain, and impose Hamilton's statist designs on the nation by force. By 1799 Adams and many of his Federalist friends had come to see Hamilton and his supporters as dangerous, antirepublican militarists.

Adams was both fearful and angry. First the Hamiltonians had tried to rob him of the presidency, then they had passed the Alien and Sedition Acts, the direct tax, and plans for a standing army without consulting him. None of this would have been possible if not for the crisis with France. Adams, who had resisted calls for a declaration of war, began looking for ways to declare peace. In a move that he knew would split his party and probably cost him reelection in 1800, he opened negotiations with France and stalled the creation of Hamilton's army while the talks took place. At first the Senate refused to send an envoy to France. The senators relented when Adams threatened to resign and leave the presidency to Vice President Jefferson. In the agreement that followed, the French canceled the obligations that the United States had assumed under the treaties of 1778. But they refused to pay reparations for attacks on American shipping since 1793—the very point over which many Federalists had wanted to declare war. Peace with France cut the ground from under the more militaristic and repressive Federalists and intensified discord among the Federalists in general. (Hamilton would campaign against Adams in 1800.) It also damaged Adams's chances for reelection.

THE ELECTION OF 1800

Thomas Jefferson and his Democratic Republicans approached the election of 1800 better organized and more determined than they had been four years earlier. Moreover, events in the months preceding the election worked in their favor. The Alien and Sedition Acts, the direct tax of 1798, and the Federalist military buildup were never popular. The army suppressed a minor tax rebellion led by Jacob Fries in Pennsylvania; prosecutions under the Sedition Act revealed its partisan origins; and the Federalists showed no sign of repealing the tax or abandoning the Alien and Sedition Acts and the new military even when peace seemed certain. Taken together,

these events gave credence to the Republicans' allegation that the Federalists were using the crisis with France to increase their power, destroy their opposition, and overthrow the American republic. The Federalists' actions, charged the Republicans, were not only expensive, repressive, unwise, and unconstitutional; they constituted the classic means by which despots destroyed liberty. The Federalists countered by warning that the election of Jefferson and his radical allies would release the worst horrors of the French Revolution onto the streets of American towns. Each side believed that its defeat in the election would mean the end of the republic.

The Democratic Republicans were strong in the South and weak in the Northeast; North Carolina was the one southern state in which Adams had significant support. Jefferson knew that in order to achieve a majority in the electoral college he had to win New York, the state that had cost him the 1796 election. Jefferson's running mate, Aaron Burr, arranged a truce in New York between Republican factions led by the Clinton and Livingston families and chose candidates for the state legislature who were likely to win. In New York City, Burr played skillfully on the interests and resentments of craftsmen and granted favors to merchants who worked outside the British trade, which was dominated by Federalist insiders. The strategy succeeded. The Republicans carried New York City and won a slight majority in the legislature; New York's electoral votes belonged to Jefferson. The election was decided in South Carolina, which after a brisk campaign cast its votes for Jefferson. (When it became clear that Jefferson had won, Hamilton suggested changing the law so that New York's electors would be chosen by popular vote; John Jay, the Federalist governor of New York, rejected the suggestion.)

When the electoral votes were counted, Jefferson and Burr had won with 73 votes each. Adams had 65 votes, and his running mate Charles Cotesworth Pinckney had 64. (In order to distinguish between their presidential and vice presidential candidates—and thus thwart yet another of Hamilton's attempts to rig the election—the Federalists of Rhode Island had withheld one vote from Pinckney.) Congress, which was still controlled by Federalists, would have to decide whether Jefferson or Burr was to be president of the United States.

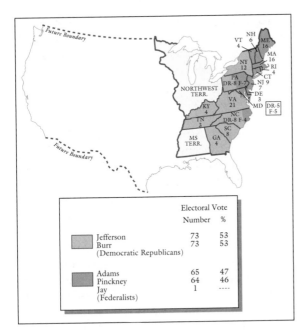

PRESIDENTIAL ELECTION, 1800

After 35 ballots, with most of the Federalists supporting Burr, a compromise was reached whereby the Federalists turned in blank ballots and thus avoided voting for the hated Jefferson. (In 1804, the Twelfth Amendment, which requires electors to vote separately for president and vice president, was ratified to prevent a repetition of this situation.)

THE JEFFERSONIANS IN POWER

On the first Tuesday of March 1801, Thomas Jefferson left his rooms at Conrad and McMunn's boarding house in the half-built capital city of Washington and walked up Pennsylvania Avenue. He received military salutes along the way, but Jefferson forbade the pomp and ceremony that had ushered Washington into office. Jefferson, accompanied by a few friends and a company of artillery from the Maryland militia (and not by the professional military of which Hamilton had dreamed) walked up the street and into the unfinished capitol building. The central tower and the wing that would house Congress were only half completed. Jefferson joined Vice President Burr, other members of the government, and a few foreign diplomats in the newly finished Senate chamber.

THE REPUBLICAN PROGRAM

Jefferson took the oath of office from Chief Justice John Marshall, a distant relative and political opponent from Virginia. Then, in a small voice that was almost inaudible to those at a distance, he delivered his inaugural address. Referring to the political discord that had brought him into office, he began with a plea for unity, insisting that "every difference of opinion is not a difference of principle. We have called by different names brethren of the same principle. We are all Republicans, we are all Federalists."

Jefferson did not mean that he and his opponents should forget their ideological differences. He meant only to invite moderate Federalists into a broad Republican coalition in which there was no room for the statist designs of Alexander Hamilton and his High Federalist friends.

Jefferson went on to outline the kind of government a republic should have. Grateful that the Atlantic Ocean separated the United States from "the exterminating havoc" of Europe and that his countrymen were the possessors of "a chosen country, with room for our descendants to the thousandth and thousandth generation," he declared that Americans were a free people with no need for a national state built on European models. A people blessed with isolation, bountiful resources, and liberty needed only "a wise and frugal Government, which shall restrain men from injuring one another, shall leave them otherwise free to regulate their own pursuits of industry and improvement, and shall not take from the mouth of labor the bread it has earned. This is the sum of good government, and thus is necessary to close the circle of our felicities."

In particular, Jefferson's "wise and frugal" government would respect the powers of the individual states. It would also defend the liberties ensured by the Bill of Rights. It would be made smaller, and it would pay its debts without incurring new ones, thus ending the need for taxation and cutting the ground from beneath the burgeoning Federalist state. It would rely for defense on "a disciplined militia" that would fight invaders while regulars were being trained—thus getting rid of Hamilton's standing army. It would protect republican liberties from enemies at home and from the nations of Europe. And, Jefferson promised, it would ensure "the encouragement of agriculture, and of commerce as its handmaiden." Beyond the fostering of an

> *"Having mentioned Mr. Jefferson, it may be interesting to the reader to have the following description of his person as he appeared to me on my arrival in the United States in the year 1804. He was a tall man with a very red freckled face and grey neglected hair, his manners goodnatured, frank and rather friendly though he had somewhat of a cynical expression of countenance. He wore a blue coat, a thick grey-coloured hairy waistcoat with a red under-waistcoat lapped over it, green velveteen breeches with pearl buttons, yarn stockings and slippers down at the heel, his appearance being very much like that of a tall large-boned farmer. He said he washed his feet as often as he did his hands in order to keep off cold, and appeared to think himself unique in so doing."*
>
> **SIR AUGUSTUS JOHN FOSTER**
> *describing President Jefferson from his perspective as a British diplomat*

PORTRAIT OF JEFFERSON BY REMBRANDT PEALE, 1805 A self-consciously plain President Jefferson posed for this portrait in January 1805, near the end of his first term. He wears an unadorned fur-collared coat, is surrounded by no emblems of office, and gazes calmly and directly at the viewer.

agrarian republic and the maintenance of limited, frugal government, Jefferson promised little. Blessed with peace abroad and the defeat of the High Federalists at home, he believed that the United States could at last enter into its experiment with truly republican government.

The simplicity of Jefferson's inauguration set the social tone of his administration. The new president reduced the number and grandeur of formal balls, levees, and dinners. He sent his annual messages to Congress to be read by a clerk, rather than delivering them in person in the manner of English kings and Federalist presidents. He refused to ride about Washington in a carriage, preferring to carry out his errands on horseback. Abandoning the grand banquets favored by his predecessors, Jefferson entertained senators and congressmen at small dinners— dinners that were served at a round table without

formal seating, thus abandoning the fine-tuned hierarchy of the Federalists' old arrangements. Jefferson presided over the meals without wearing a wig, and dressed in old homespun and a pair of worn bedroom slippers. The casualness (slovenliness, said some of his critics) did not extend to what was served, however. The food was prepared by expert chefs and accompanied by fine wines. And it was followed by brilliant conversation perfected by Jefferson while he was a diplomat and a visitor to the salons of Paris. The president's dinners set examples of the unpretentious excellence through which this cultivated country squire hoped to govern the republic that he claimed to have saved from monarchists.

CLEANSING THE GOVERNMENT

Jefferson's first order of business was to reduce the size and expense of government. The Federalists, despite their elitism and their statist dispositions,

"MAD TOM IN A RAGE" This Federalist cartoon of 1801 portrays Jefferson, with the help of the devil and a bottle of brandy, pulling down the government that Washington and Adams had built.

had left a surprisingly small federal establishment. Jefferson found only 316 employees who were subject to presidential appointment and removal. Those employees, together with 700 clerks and assistants and 3,000 post office workers, made up the entire federal civil service. Jefferson reduced the diplomatic corps and replaced officeholders who were incompetent, corrupt, or avowedly antirepublican. Even so, the rate of turnover was only about 50 percent during his first term. The replacements were not the violent revolutionaries that Federalists had warned against but Republican gentlemen who matched or exceeded the social status of the departed Federalists. Jefferson altered the politics of the civil service, but he left its size and shape intact.

Jefferson made more substantial cuts in the military. The Federalists had built a sizable army and

navy to prepare for war and, if necessary, to put down opposition at home. Legislation passed in March 1802 reduced the army to two regiments of infantry and one of artillery—a total of 3,350 officers and men, most of whom were assigned to western posts far from the centers of white population. Similar cutbacks reduced the navy. The goal, Jefferson explained, was to rely mainly on the militia for national defense but to maintain a small, well-trained professional army as well. (The same legislation that reduced the army created the military academy at West Point.) At Jefferson's urging, Congress also abolished the direct tax of 1798 and repealed the parts of the Alien and Sedition Acts that had not already expired. Jefferson personally pardoned the 10 victims of those acts who were still in jail and repaid with interest the fines that had been levied under them.

Thus with a few deft strokes, Jefferson dismantled the repressive apparatus of the Federalist state. And by reducing government expenditures he reduced the government's debt and the army of civil servants and "paper men" gathered around it. During Jefferson's administration the national debt fell from $80 million to $57 million, and the government built up a treasury surplus, even after paying $15 million in cash for the Louisiana Purchase (discussed later in this chapter). Although some doubted the wisdom of such stringent economy, no one doubted Jefferson's frugality.

THE JEFFERSONIANS AND THE COURTS

Jefferson's demands for a "wise and frugal" government applied to the federal judiciary as well as to other branches. The Constitution had created the Supreme Court but had left the creation of lesser federal courts to Congress. The First Congress had created a system of circuit courts presided over by the justices of the Supreme Court. Only Federalists had served on the Supreme Court under Washington and Adams, and Federalists on the circuit courts had extended federal authority into the hinterland—a fact that their prosecution of Jeffersonians under the Alien and Sedition Acts had made abundantly clear. Thus Jeffersonian Republicans had ample reason to distrust the federal courts. Their distrust was intensified by the Judiciary Act of 1801, which was passed just before Jefferson's inauguration by the lame-duck Federalist Congress. Coupled with President Adams's appointment of Federalist John Marshall as chief justice in January, the Judiciary Act ensured long-term Federalist domination of the federal courts. First, it reduced the number of associate justices of the Supreme Court from six to five when the next vacancy occurred, thus reducing Jefferson's chances of appointing a new member to the Court. The Judiciary Act also took Supreme Court justices off circuit and created a new system of circuit courts. This allowed Adams to appoint 16 new judges, along with a full array of marshals, federal attorneys, clerks, and justices of the peace. He worked until nine o'clock on his last night in office signing commissions for these new officers. All of them were staunch Federalists.

Republicans disagreed on what to do about the Federalists' packing of the courts. A minority distrusted the whole idea of an independent judiciary and wanted judges elected by popular vote. Jefferson and most in his party wanted the courts shielded from democratic control; at the same time, they deeply resented the uniformly Federalist "midnight judges" created by the Judiciary Act of 1801. Jefferson did replace the new federal marshals and attorneys with Republicans and dismissed some of the federal justices of the peace, but judges were appointed for life and could be removed only through impeachment. The Jeffersonians hit on a simple solution: They would get rid of the new judges by abolishing their jobs. Early in 1802, with some of Jefferson's supporters questioning the constitutionality of what they were doing, Congress repealed the Judiciary Act of 1801 and thus did away with the midnight appointees.

THE IMPEACHMENTS OF PICKERING AND CHASE

With the federal courts scaled back to their original size, Republicans in Congress, led by the Virginia agrarian John Randolph, went after High Federalists who were still acting as judges. As a first test of removal by impeachment they chose John Pickering, a federal attorney with the circuit court of New Hampshire. Pickering was a highly partisan Federalist. He was also a notorious alcoholic and clearly insane. The Federalists who had appointed him had

SAMUEL CHASE Samuel Chase was a Supreme Court justice and archenemy of those he considered disturbers of the republic—including Jefferson's Democratic Republicans.

long considered him an embarrassment. The House drew up articles of impeachment and Pickering was tried by the Senate, which, by a strict party vote, removed him from office.

On the same day, Congress went after bigger game: They voted to impeach Supreme Court Justice Samuel Chase. Chase was a much more prominent public figure than Pickering, and his "crimes" were not alcoholism or insanity but mere partisanship. He hated the Jeffersonians, and he had prosecuted sedition cases with real enthusiasm. He had also delivered anti-Jeffersonian diatribes from the bench, and he had used his position and his formidable legal skills to bully young lawyers with whom he disagreed. In short, Chase was an unpleasant, overbearing, and unashamedly partisan member of the Supreme Court. Even so, his faults did not add up to the "high crimes and misdemeanors" that are the constitutional grounds for impeachment.

Moderate Republicans in the government doubted the wisdom of the Chase impeachment, and their uneasiness grew when Congressman John Randolph took over the prosecution. Randolph led a radical states'-rights faction that violently disapproved, among other things, of the way Jefferson had settled a southern land controversy. A corrupt Georgia legislature had sold huge parcels in Mississippi and Alabama to the Yazoo Land Company, which in turn had sold them to private investors—many of them New England speculators. When a new Georgia legislature rescinded the sale and turned the land over to the federal government in 1802, Jefferson agreed to pay off the investors' claims with federal money.

As Randolph led the prosecution of Samuel Chase, he lectured in his annoying, high-pitched voice that Jefferson was double-crossing southern Republicans in an effort to win support in the Northeast. Most of the Republican senators disagreed, and some of them withdrew their support from the impeachment proceedings in order to isolate and humiliate Randolph and his friends. With Jefferson's approval, many Republicans in the Senate joined the Federalists in voting to acquit Samuel Chase.

JUSTICE MARSHALL'S COURT

Chief Justice John Marshall probably cheered the acquittal of Justice Chase, for it was clear that Marshall was next on the list. Secretary of state under John Adams, Marshall was committed to Federalist ideas of national power, as he demonstrated with his decision in the case of *Marbury* v. *Madison*. William Marbury was one of the justices of the peace whom Jefferson had eliminated in his first few days in office. He sued Jefferson's secretary of state, James Madison, for the nondelivery of his commission. Although Marbury never got his job, Marshall used the case to hand down a number of important rulings. The first ruling, which questioned the constitutionality of Jefferson's refusal to deliver Marbury's commission, helped to convince Republican moderates to repeal the Judiciary Act of 1801. The last ruling, delivered in February 1803, laid the basis for the practice of judicial review—that is, the Supreme Court's power to rule on the constitutionality of acts of Congress. In arguing that Congress could not alter the jurisdiction of the

Supreme Court, Marshall stated that the Constitution is "fundamental and paramount law" and that it is "emphatically the province and duty of the judicial department to say what law is."

Some Republicans saw Marshall's ruling as an attempt to arrogate power to the Court. But John Marshall was not a sinister man. As secretary of state under John Adams, he had helped to end the undeclared war with France, and he had expressed doubts about the wisdom and necessity if not the constitutionality of the Alien and Sedition Acts. Of more immediate concern, although he disliked Congress's repeal of the 1801 legislation, he believed in Congress's right to make and unmake laws, and he was determined to accept the situation. The decision in *Marbury* v. *Madison* angered many Republicans, but Jefferson and the moderate Republicans noted that Marshall was less interested in the power of the judiciary than in its independence. Ultimately, they decided they trusted Marshall

JOHN MARSHALL A Virginian and distant relative of Thomas Jefferson, John Marshall became chief justice of the Supreme Court in the last months of John Adams's administration. He used the Court as a conservative, centralizing force until his death in 1835.

more than they trusted the radicals in their own party. With the acquittal of Justice Chase, Jeffersonian attacks on the federal courts ceased.

Justice Marshall demonstrated his strict constructionism (as well as his partisanship) in the treason trial of former Vice President Aaron Burr in 1807. Following his failed attempt at the presidency in 1801, Burr's further intrigues with northern Federalists broke down—a breakdown that helped lead to a duel in which he killed Alexander Hamilton. The disgraced Aaron Burr headed west and organized a cloudy conspiracy that may have involved (according to varying testimonies) an invasion of Mexico or Florida, or the secession of Louisiana. President Jefferson heard that Burr had raised an army and ordered his arrest. He was tried for treason at Richmond, with the Chief Justice, who was riding circuit, on the bench. Kings had frequently used the charge of treason to silence dissent. Marshall stopped what he and other Federalists considered Jefferson's attempt to do the same thing by limiting the definition of treason to overt acts of war against the United States or to adhering to the republic's foreign enemies—and by requiring two witnesses to an overt act of treason. Under these guidelines, Burr went free. At the same time, the United States had formally separated internal dissent from treason.

LOUISIANA

It was Jefferson's good fortune that Europe remained at peace during his first term and stayed out of American affairs. Indeed the one development that posed an international threat to the United States turned into a grand triumph: the purchase of the Louisiana Territory from France in 1803.

By 1801 a half-million Americans lived west of the Appalachians. Although Federalists feared the barbaric westerners, Republicans saw westward expansion as the best hope for the survival of the republic. Social inequality and the erosion of yeoman independence would almost inevitably take root in the East, but in the vast lands west of the mountains the republic could renew itself for many generations to come. To serve that purpose, however, the West needed ready access to markets through the river system that emptied into the Gulf of Mexico at New Orleans. "There is on the globe," wrote President Jefferson, "one single spot, the possessor of which is our natural and habitual enemy. It is New Orleans."

In 1801 Spain owned New Orleans and under Pinckney's Treaty allowed Americans to transship produce from the interior. The year before, however, Spain had secretly ceded the Louisiana Territory (roughly, all the land west of the Mississippi drained by the Missouri and Arkansas rivers) to France. Napoleon Bonaparte had plans for a new French empire in America with the sugar island of Hispaniola (present-day Haiti and Dominican Republic) at its center, and with mainland colonies feeding the islands and thus making the empire self-sufficient. Late in 1802, the Spanish, who had retained control of New Orleans, closed the port to American commerce, giving rise to rumors that they would soon transfer the city to France. To forestall such a move, which would threaten the very existence of American settlements west of the Appalachians, President Jefferson sent a delegation to Paris early in 1803 with authorization to buy New Orleans for the United States.

By the time the delegates reached Paris, events had dissolved French plans for a new American empire. The slaves of Saint-Domingue (the French colony on Hispaniola) had revolted against the French and had defeated their attempts to regain control of the island (see chapter 7). At the same time, another war between Britain and France seemed imminent. Napoleon—reputedly chanting

THE LOUISIANA PURCHASE This panorama of New Orleans celebrates the Louisiana Purchase in 1803. The patriotic caption promises prosperity for the city and (by inference) for the American settlements upriver.

"Damn sugar, damn coffee, damn colonies"—decided to bail out of America and concentrate his resources in Europe. He astonished Jefferson's delegation by announcing that France would sell not only New Orleans but the whole Louisiana Territory—which would roughly double the size of the United States—for the bargain price of $15 million.

Jefferson, who had criticized Federalists whenever they violated the letter of the Constitution, faced a dilemma: The president lacked the constitutional power to buy territory, but the chance to buy Louisiana was too good to refuse. It would ensure Americans access to the rivers of the interior; it would eliminate a serious foreign threat on America's western border; and it would give American farmers enough land to sustain the agrarian republic for a long time to come. Swallowing his constitutional scruples (and at the same time half-heartedly asking for a constitutional amendment to legalize the purchase), Jefferson told the American delegates to buy Louisiana. Republican senators, who shared few of Jefferson's doubts,

quickly ratified the Louisiana treaty over Federalist objections that the purchase would encourage rapid settlement and add to backcountry barbarism and Republican strength. Most Americans agreed that the accidents of French and Haitian history had given the United States a grand opportunity, and Congress's ratification of the Louisiana Purchase met with overwhelming public approval. For his part, Jefferson was certain that the republic had gained the means of renewing itself through time. He had bought, he claimed in his second inaugural address, a great "empire of liberty."

As Jefferson stood for reelection in 1804, he could look back on an astonishingly successful first term. He had dismantled the government's power to coerce its citizens, and he had begun to wipe out the national debt. The Louisiana Purchase had doubled the size of the republic at remarkably little cost. Moreover, by eliminating France from North America it had strengthened the argument for reducing the military and the debts and taxes that went with it. Jefferson was more certain than ever that the repub-

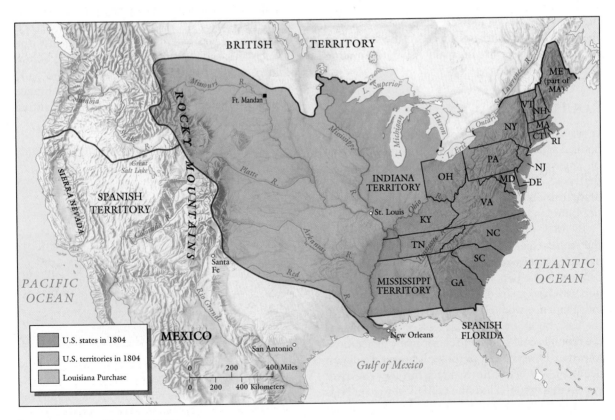

LOUISIANA PURCHASE

lic could preserve itself through peaceful expansion. The "wise and frugal" government he had promised in 1801 was becoming a reality.

The combination of international peace, territorial expansion, and inexpensive, unobtrusive government left the Federalists without an issue in the 1804 election. They went through the motions of nominating Charles Pinckney of South Carolina as their presidential candidate and then watched Jefferson capture the electoral votes of every state but Delaware and Connecticut. As he began his second term in 1805, Jefferson could assume that he had ended the Federalist threat to the republic.

THE REPUBLIC AND THE NAPOLEONIC WARS, 1804–1815

In the spring of 1803, a few weeks after closing the deal for Louisiana, Napoleon Bonaparte declared war on Great Britain. This 11-year war, like the wars of the 1790s, dominated the national politics of the United States. Most Americans wanted to remain neutral. Few Republicans supported Bonaparte as they had supported the French revolutionaries of 1789, and none but the most rabid Federalists wanted to intervene on the side of Great Britain, but neither France nor Britain would permit American neutrality.

THE DILEMMAS OF NEUTRALITY

At the beginning, both Britain and France, whose rural economies were disrupted by war, encouraged the Americans to resume their role as neutral carriers and suppliers of food. For a time, Americans made huge profits. Between 1803 and 1807 U.S. exports—mostly foodstuffs and plantation staples—rose from $66.5 million to $102.2 million. Reexports—goods produced in the British, Spanish, and French islands of the Caribbean, picked up by American vessels and then reloaded in American ports onto American ships bound for Europe—rose even faster, from $13.5 million to $58.4 million.

In 1805 France and Great Britain began systematically to interfere with that trade. Also in 1805 the Royal Navy under Lord Nelson destroyed the French and Spanish fleets at the Battle of Trafalgar. Later that year Napoleon's armies won a decisive victory over Austria and Russia at the Battle of Austerlitz, and won effective control of Europe. The war reached a stalemate: Napoleon's army occupied Europe, the British navy controlled the seas.

Britain decided to use its naval supremacy to blockade Europe and starve the French into submission. In the Essex Decision of 1805, the British ministry dusted off what was known as the Rule of 1756, which stated that a European country could not use a neutral merchant marine to conduct wartime trade with its colonies if its mercantile laws forbade such use during peacetime. Translated into the realities of 1805, the Essex Decision meant that the Royal Navy could seize American ships engaged in the reexport trade with France. In the spring of 1806 Congress, angered by British seizures of American ships, passed the Non-Importation Act forbidding the importation of British goods that could be bought elsewhere or that could be manufactured in the United States. A month after that Britain blockaded long stretches of the European coast. Napoleon responded with the Berlin Decree, which outlawed all trade with the British Isles. The British answered with an Order in Council that demanded that neutral ships trading with Europe stop first for inspection and licensing in a British port. Napoleon responded with the Milan Decree, which stated that any vessel that obeyed the British decrees or allowed itself to be searched by the Royal Navy was subject to seizure by France. Beginning in 1805 and ending with the Milan Decree in December 1807, the barrage of European decrees and counterdecrees meant that virtually all American commerce with Europe had been outlawed by one or the other of the warring powers.

TROUBLE ON THE HIGH SEAS

Given British naval supremacy, French decrees were effective only against American ships that entered ports controlled by France. The Royal Navy, on the other hand, maintained a loose blockade of the North American coast and stopped and searched American ships as they left the major seaports. Hundreds of ships were seized, along with their cargoes and crews. Under British law, the Royal Navy during wartime could impress any British subject into service. The British were certain that many British subjects, including legions of deserters from the Royal Navy, were hiding in the American merchant marine. They were right. The danger, low pay, bad food, and draconian discipline on British warships encouraged many British sailors to jump ship and take jobs on American merchantmen. Many of the British warships that stopped American merchant ships on the high seas were undermanned; the sailors their officers commandeered often included Englishmen who had taken out U.S. citizenship (an act the British did not recognize) and, inevitably, native-born Americans. An estimated 6,000 American citizens were impressed into the Royal Navy between 1803 and 1812.

The kidnapping of American sailors, even more than maritime seizures of American property and other violations of American neutral rights, enraged the citizens of the United States and brought the country close to war in the summer of 1807. In June the American naval frigate *Chesapeake*, which was outfitting in Norfolk, Virginia, signed on four English deserters from the British navy, along with some Americans who had joined the British navy and then deserted. The British warship H.M.S. *Leopard* also was docked at Norfolk, and some of the deserters spotted their old officers and taunted them on the streets. The *Leopard* left port and resumed its patrol of the American coast. Then, on June 21, its officers caught the *Chesapeake* off Hampton Roads and demanded the return of the British deserters. When the captain refused, the British fired on the *Chesapeake*, killing 3 Americans and wounding 18. The British then boarded the *Chesapeake*, seized the four deserters, and later hanged one of them. The Chesapeake limped back into port.

The *Chesapeake* affair set off huge anti-British demonstrations in the seaport towns and angry cries for war throughout the country. President Jefferson responded by barring British ships from American ports and American territorial waters, and by ordering state governors to prepare to call up as many as 100,000 militiamen. The United States in 1807 stood at the brink of full-scale war with the most powerful nation in the world.

EMBARGO

Jefferson wanted to avoid war. War inevitably brought high taxes, government debt, a bloated military and civil service, and the repression of dissent—precisely the evils that Jefferson had vowed to eliminate. Worse, war carried the danger of defeat and thus the possible failure of America's republican experiment.

Jefferson had one more card to play: He could suspend trade with Europe altogether and thus keep American ships out of harm's way. For many years, Jefferson had assumed that U.S. farm products and the U.S. market for imported goods had become crucial to the European economies. He could use trade as a means of "peaceable coercion" that would both ensure respect for American neutral rights and keep the country out of war. "Our commerce," he wrote just before taking office, "is so valuable to them, that they will be glad to purchase it, when the only price we ask is to do us justice." Convinced that America's yeoman republic could survive without European luxuries more easily than Europe could survive without American food, Jefferson decided to give "peaceable coercion" a serious test. Late in 1807 he asked Congress to suspend all U.S. trade with foreign countries.

Congress passed the Embargo Act on December 22. By the following spring, however, it was clear that peaceable coercion would not work. The British found other markets and other sources of food. They encouraged the smuggling of American goods into Canada. And American merchantmen who had been at sea when the embargo went into effect stayed away from their home ports and functioned as part of the British merchant marine. A loophole in the Embargo Act allowed U.S. ships to leave port in order to pick up American property stranded in other countries, and an estimated 6,000 ships set sail under that excuse. Hundreds of others, plying the coastal trade, were "blown off course" and found themselves thrust into international commerce. For his part, Napoleon seized American ships in European ports, explaining that, since the embargo kept all American ships in port, those trading under American flags must be British ships in disguise.

The embargo hurt American commerce badly. Its 1807 exports of $108 million dropped to $22 million in 1808. The economy slowed in every section of the country, but it ground to a halt in the cities of the Northeast. While the ocean-going merchant fleet rotted at anchor, unemployed sailors, dockworkers, and other maritime workers and their families sank to levels of economic despair seldom seen in British North America. Northeastern Federalists branded Jefferson's embargo a "Chinese" (that is, isolationist)

ANTIEMBARGO PROPAGANDA A Federalist cartoonist heard the Embargo Act denounced as a "terrapin policy," and drew a snapping turtle seizing a tobacco smuggler by the seat of the pants. The man cries out "Oh! this cursed Ograbme"—"embargo" spelled backwards.

solution to the problems of commerce and diplomacy. Commerce, they argued, was the great civilizer: "Her victories are over ferocious passions, savage manners, deep rooted prejudices, blind superstition and delusive theory." Federalists accused Jefferson of plotting an end to commerce and a reversion to rural barbarism, and they often took the lead in trying to subvert the embargo through smuggling and other means. In Connecticut, the Federalist governor flatly refused Jefferson's request to mobilize the militia to enforce the embargo.

The Federalists gained ground in the elections of 1808. James Madison, Jefferson's old ally and chosen successor, was elected president with 122 electoral votes to 47 for his Federalist opponent, C. C. Pinckney. And although Republicans retained control of both houses of Congress, Federalists made significant gains in Congress and won control of several state legislatures. Federalist opposition to the embargo, and to the supposed southern, agrarian stranglehold on national power that stood behind it, was clearly gaining ground.

THE ROAD TO WAR

When President Madison took office in the spring of 1809 it was clear that the embargo had failed to coerce the British. On the contrary, the embargo had created misery in the seaport cities, choked off the imports that provided 90 percent of federal revenue, and revived Federalist opposition to Republican dominance. Early in 1809 Congress passed the Non-Intercourse Act, which retained the ban on trade with Britain and France but reopened trade with other nations. It also gave President Madison the power to reopen trade with either Britain or France once they had agreed to respect American rights. Neither complied, and the Non-Intercourse Act proved nearly as ineffective as the embargo.

In 1810 Congress passed Macon's Bill No. 2, a strange piece of legislation that rescinded the ban on trade with France and Britain but also authorized the president to reimpose the Non-Intercourse Act on either belligerent if the other agreed to end its restrictions on U.S. trade. Napoleon decided to test the Americans. In September 1810 the French foreign minister, the Duc de Cadore, promised, with vague conditions, that France would repeal the Berlin and Milan Decrees. Though the proposal was a clear attempt to lead the United States into conflict with Great Britain, Madison saw no choice but to go along with it. He accepted the French promise and proclaimed in November 1810 that the British had three months to follow suit. "It promises us," he said of his proclamation, "at least an extrication from the dilemma, of a mortifying peace, or a war with both the great belligerents."

In the end, Madison's proclamation led to war. The French repealed only those sections of the Berlin and Milan Decrees that applied to the neutral rights of the United States. The British refused to revoke their Orders in Council and told the Americans to withdraw their restrictions on British trade until the French had repealed theirs. The United States would either have to obey British orders (thus making American exports and the American merchant marine a part of the British war effort—a neocolonial situation utterly repugnant to most Americans) or go to war. When Congress reconvened in November 1811, it voted military measures in preparation for war with Great Britain.

THE WAR HAWK CONGRESS, 1811–1812

The Republicans controlled both houses of Congress in the 1811–12 session. However, although 75 percent of the House and 82 percent of the Senate identified themselves as members of President Madison's party, they were a divided majority. The Federalist minority, united against Madison, was joined on many issues by northeastern Republicans who followed the pro-British, Federalist line on international trade, and by Republicans who wanted a more powerful military than other Republicans would allow. Also opposed to Madison were the self-styled Old Republicans of the South, led by John Randolph. Thus it was a deeply divided Congress that met the war crisis.

In this confused situation a group of talented young congressmen took control. Nearly all of them were Republicans from the South or the West: Richard M. Johnson and Henry Clay of Kentucky, John C. Calhoun and William Lowndes of South Carolina, George M. Troup of Georgia, Peter B. Porter from the Niagara district of New York, and others. Called the "War Hawks," these ardent nationalists were more than willing to declare war on England to protect U.S. rights. Through their organizational, oratorical, and intellectual power, they won control of Congress. Henry Clay, only 34 years old and serving his first term in Congress, was elected Speaker of the House. More vigorous than his predecessors, Clay controlled debate, packed key committees, worked tirelessly behind the scenes, and imposed order on his fellow congressmen. When John Randolph, one of the most feared members of the House, brought his dog into the House chamber, Speaker Clay pointedly ordered the dog removed. Earlier speakers had not dared give such an order.

In the winter and spring of 1811–12 the War Hawks led Congress into a declaration of war. In November they voted military preparations, and in April they enacted a 90-day embargo—not to coerce the British but to return American ships safely to port before war began. (As in 1807, the embargo prompted seaport merchants to rush their ships to sea.) On June 1, Madison sent a war message to Congress. This was to be the first war declared under the Constitution, and the president stayed out of congressional territory by not asking explicitly for a declaration of war. He did, however, present a list of British crimes that could be interpreted in no other way: the enforcement of the Orders in Council, even within the territorial waters of the United States; the impressment of American seamen; the use of spies and provocateurs within the United States; and the

HENRY CLAY This portrait of Henry Clay was engraved at about the time the brilliant first-term congressman from Kentucky, as Speaker of the House, helped his fellow War Hawks steer the United States into the War of 1812.

wielding of "a malicious influence over the Indians of the Northwest Territory." Madison concluded that war had in fact begun: "We behold . . . on the side of Great Britain a state of war against the United States; and on the side of the United States, a state of peace toward Great Britain."

Congress declared war on June 18. The vote was far from unanimous: 79 to 49 in the House of Representatives, 19 to 13 in the Senate. All 30 Federalists voted against the declaration, as did one in five Republicans, nearly all of them from the Northeast. Thus the war was declared by the Democratic Republican Party, more particularly by the Republicans of the South and the West. The Northeast, whose commercial rights were supposedly the issue at stake, opposed the declaration.

WAR HAWKS AND THE WAR OF 1812

The War Hawks declared a war to defend the sovereignty, the western territory, and the maritime rights of the United States. The war that they planned and fought, however, bore the stamp of southern and western Republicanism. Federalists and many northeastern Republicans expected a naval war. After all, the British had committed their atrocities on the ocean, and some, remembering U.S. naval successes against France in the quasi-war of 1798–1800 (discussed earlier in this chapter), predicted similar successes against Great Britain. Yet when Madison asked Congress to prepare for war, the War Hawks led a majority that strengthened the U.S. Army and left the navy weak. Reasoning that no U.S. naval force could challenge British control of the seas, they prepared instead for a land invasion of British Canada.

The decision to invade Canada led the Federalists, along with many of Randolph's Old Republicans, to accuse Madison and the congressional majority of planning a war of territorial aggression. Some members of Congress did indeed want to annex Canada to the United States, but most saw the decision to invade Canada as a matter of strategy. Lightly garrisoned and with a population of only one-half million (many of them French, and most of the others American émigrés of doubtful loyalties), Canada seemed the easiest and most logical place in which to damage the British. It was also from bases in Canada that the British armed Tecumseh's formidable Indian confederacy (see chapter 7). The western Republicans were determined to end that threat once and for all. Finally, Canada was a valuable colony of Great Britain. The American embargoes, coupled with Napoleon's control of Europe, had impaired Britain's ability to supply her plantation colonies in the West Indies, and Canadian farmers had begun to fill the gap. Thus Canada was both valuable and vulnerable, and American policymakers reasoned that they could take it and hold it hostage while demanding that the British back down on other issues. Although U.S. military strategy focused on Canada, maritime rights and national honor, along with the British-fed Indian threat west of the Appalachians, were the central issues in 1812. As John C. Calhoun, who was instrumental in taking the nation to war, concluded: "The mad ambition, the lust of power, and commercial avarice of Great Britain have left to neutral nations an alternative only between the base surrender of their rights, and a manly vindication of them."

THE WAR WITH CANADA, 1812–1813

The United States opened its offensive against Canada in 1812, with disastrous results. The plan was to invade Upper Canada (Ontario) from the Northwest, thus cutting off the Shawnee, Potawatomi, and other pro-British Indian tribes from their British support. When General William Hull, governor of Michigan Territory, took a poorly supplied, badly led army of militiamen and volunteers into Canada from a base in Detroit, he found that the British had outguessed him. The area was crawling with British troops and their Indian allies. With detachments of his army overrun and with his supply lines cut, he retreated to the garrison at Detroit. Under siege, he heard that an Indian force had captured the garrison at Fort Dearborn. British General Isaac Brock, who knew that Hull was afraid of Indians, sent a note into the fort telling him that "the numerous body of Indians who have attached themselves to my troops, will be beyond my controul the moment the contest commences." Without consulting his officers, Hull surrendered his army of 2,000 to the smaller British force. Though Hull was later court-martialed for cowardice, the damage had been done: The British and their Indian allies occupied many of the remaining American garrisons in the Northwest and transformed the U.S. invasion of Upper Canada into a British occupation of much of the Northwest.

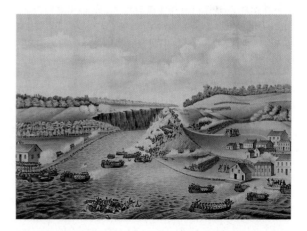

AMERICAN TROOPS INVADE CANADA In this painting, a Canadian artist depicts the failed American invasion at Queenston Heights in October 1812. British troops on the right are rushing to repel the Americans who have occupied the cliffs at center.

The invasion of Canada from the east went no better. In October a U.S. force of 6,000 faced 2,000 British and Indians across the Niagara River separating Ontario from western New York. The U.S. regular army crossed the river, surprised the British, and established a toehold at Queenston Heights. While the British were preparing a counterattack, New York militiamen refused to cross the river to reinforce the regular troops. Ohio militiamen had behaved the same way when Hull invaded Canada, and similar problems had arisen with the New York militia near Lake Champlain. Throughout the war citizen soldiers proved that Jefferson's confidence in the militia could not be extended to the invasion of other countries. The British regrouped and slaughtered the outnumbered, exhausted U.S. regulars at Queenston Heights.

As winter set in, it was clear that Canada would not fall as easily as the Americans had assumed. Indeed the invasion, which U.S. commanders had thought would knife through an apathetic Canadian population, had the opposite effect: The attacks by the United States turned the ragtag assortment of American loyalist émigrés, discharged British soldiers, and American-born settlers into a self-consciously British Canadian people. Years later, an Englishwoman touring Niagara Falls asked a Canadian ferryman if it was true that Canadians had thrown Americans off Queenston Heights to their death on the rocky banks of the Niagara River. "Why yes," he replied, "there was a good many of them; but it was right to show them that there was water between us, and you know it might help to keep the rest of them from coming to trouble us on our own ground."

TECUMSEH'S LAST STAND

Tecumseh's Indian confederacy, bruised but not broken in the Battle of Tippecanoe (see chapter 7), allied itself with the British in 1812. On a trip to the southern tribes Tecumseh found the traditionalist wing of the Creeks—led by prophets who called themselves Red Sticks—willing to join him. The augmented confederacy provided stiff resistance to the United States throughout the war. The Red Sticks chased settlers from much of Tennessee. They then attacked a group of settlers who had taken refuge in a stockade surrounding the house of an Alabama trader named George Mims. In what whites called the Massacre at Fort Mims, the Red Sticks (reputedly with the collusion of black slaves within the fort) killed at least 247 men, women, and children. In the Northwest, Tecumseh's warriors, fighting alongside the British, spread terror throughout the white settlements.

A wiser U.S. army returned to Canada in 1813. They raided and burned the Canadian capital at York (Toronto) in April, and then fought inconclusively through the summer. An autumn offensive toward Montreal failed, but the Americans had better luck on Lake Erie. The barrier of Niagara Falls kept Britain's saltwater navy out of the upper Great Lakes, and on Lake Erie the British and Americans engaged in a frenzied shipbuilding contest through the first year of the war. The Americans won. In September 1813 Commodore Oliver Hazard Perry cornered and destroyed the British fleet at Put-in-Bay. Control of Lake Erie enabled the United States to cut off supplies to the British

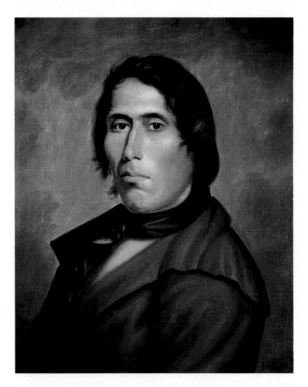

TECUMSEH Tecumseh, military and political leader of the northwestern tribes that sided with the British in 1812, came closer than any other American Indian leader to unifying Indian peoples against white territorial expansion.

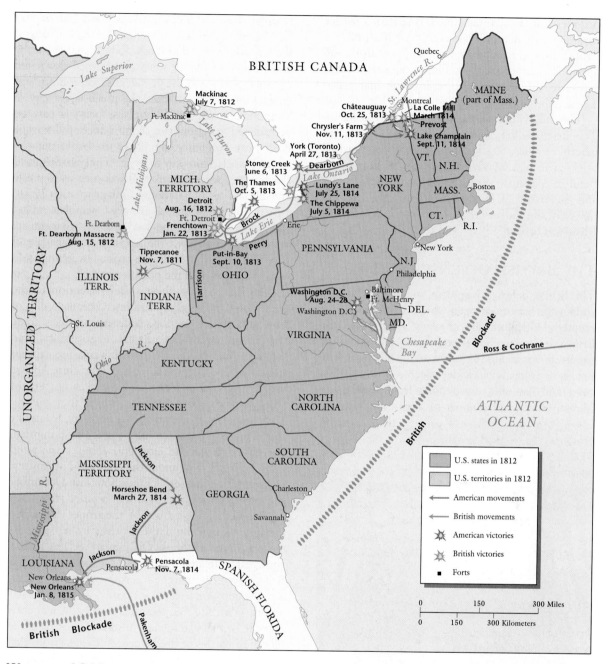

WAR OF 1812

in the Northwest, and a U.S. army under William Henry Harrison retook the area and continued on into Canada. On October 5 Harrison caught up with a force of British and Indians at the Thames River and beat them badly. In the course of that battle Richard M. Johnson, a War Hawk congress-

man acting as commander of the Kentucky militia, killed Tecumseh. Proud militiamen returned to Kentucky with pieces of hair and clothing and even swatches of skin torn from Tecumseh's corpse. Their officers reaped huge political rewards: The Battle of the Thames would eventually produce a president of the United States (Harrison), a vice president (Johnson), 3 governors of Kentucky, 3 lieutenant governors, 4 United States senators, and about 20 congressmen—telling evidence of how seriously the settlers of the interior had taken Tecumseh.

The following spring General Andrew Jackson's Tennessee militia, aided by Choctaw, Creek, and Cherokee allies, attacked and slaughtered the Red Sticks who had fortified themselves at Horseshoe Bend in Alabama. With the Battle of the Thames and the Battle of Horse Shoe Bend, the military power of the Indian peoples east of the Mississippi River was broken.

THE BRITISH OFFENSIVE, 1814

The British defeated Napoleon in April 1814, thus ending the larger war from which the War of 1812 erupted. With both sides thinking about peace, the British decided to concentrate their resources on the American war and in 1814 went on the offensive. The British had already blockaded much of the American coast and had shut down ports from Georgia to Maine. During the summer of 1814 they began to

THE BURNING OF THE CAPITOL The United States suffered one of its greatest military embarrassments ever when British troops burned the Capitol in 1814. This 1974 painting is on an archway in the present-day Capitol building.

raid the shores of Chesapeake Bay and marched on Washington, D.C. As retribution for the torching of the Canadian capital at York, they chased the army and politicians out of town and burned down the capitol building and the president's mansion. In September the British attacked the much larger city of Baltimore, but they could not blast their way past the determined garrison that commanded the harbor from Fort McHenry. This was the battle that inspired Francis Scott Key to write "The Star-Spangled Banner," a doggerel poem that was later set to music and chosen as the national anthem in the 1930s. When a British offensive on Lake Champlain stalled during the autumn, the war reached a stalemate: Britain had prevented the invasion of Canada and had blockaded the American coast, but neither side could take and hold the other's territory.

The British now shifted their attention to the Gulf Coast, particularly to New Orleans, a city of vital importance to U.S. trans-Appalachian trade and communications. Peace negotiations had begun in August, and the British wanted to capture and hold New Orleans as a bargaining chip. A large British amphibious force landed and camped eight miles south of New Orleans. There they met an American army made up of U.S. regulars, Kentucky and Tennessee militiamen, clerks, workingmen, free blacks from the city, and about a thousand French pirates—all under the command of Andrew Jackson of Tennessee. Throughout late December and early January, unaware that a peace treaty had been signed on December 24, the armies exchanged artillery barrages and the British probed and attacked American lines. On January 8, the British launched a frontal assault. A formation of 6,000 British soldiers marched across open ground toward 4,000 Americans concealed behind breastworks. With the first American volley, it was clear that the British had made a mistake. Veterans of the bloodiest battles of the Napoleonic wars swore that they had never seen such withering fire; soldiers in the front ranks who were not cut down threw themselves to the ground and surrendered when the shooting stopped. The charge lasted half an hour. At the end, 2,000 British soldiers lay dead or wounded. American casualties numbered only 70. Fought nearly two weeks after the peace treaty, the Battle of New Orleans had no effect on the outcome of the war or on the peace terms, but it salved the injured pride of Americans and made a national hero and a political power of Andrew Jackson.

THE HARTFORD CONVENTION

While most of the nation celebrated Jackson's victory, events in Federalist New England went otherwise during the closing months of the war. New Englanders had considered themselves the victims of Republican trade policies, and their congressmen had voted overwhelmingly against going to war. The New England states seldom met their quotas of militiamen for the war effort, and some Federalist leaders had openly urged resistance to the war. The British had encouraged that resistance by not extending their naval blockade to the New England coast, and throughout the first two years of the war New England merchants and farmers had traded freely with the enemy. In 1814, after the Royal Navy had extended its blockade northward and had begun to raid the towns of coastal Maine, some Federalists talked openly about seceding and making a separate peace with Britain.

In an attempt to undercut the secessionists, moderate Federalists called a convention at Hartford to air the region's grievances. The Hartford Convention, which met in late December 1814, proposed amendments to the Constitution that indicate New England's position as a self-conscious minority within the Union. First, the convention delegates wanted the "three-fifths" clause, which led to overrepresentation of the South in Congress and the electoral college (see chapter 6), stricken from the Constitution; they wanted to deny naturalized citizens—who were strongly Republican—the right to hold office; they wanted to make it more difficult for new states—all of which sided with the Republicans and their southern leadership—to enter the Union; and finally, they wanted to require a two-thirds majority of both houses for a declaration of war—a requirement that would have prevented the War of 1812.

The Federalist leaders of the Hartford Convention, satisfied that they had headed off the secessionists, took their proposals to Washington in mid-January. They arrived to find the capital celebrating the news of the peace treaty and Jackson's stunning victory at New Orleans. When they aired their sectional complaints and their constitutional proposals, they were branded as negative, selfish, and unpatriotic. Although Federalists continued for a few years to wield power in southern New England, the Hartford debacle ruined any chance of a nationwide Federalist resurgence after the war. Andrew Jackson had stolen control of American history from New England. He would do so again in the years ahead.

THE TREATY OF GHENT

Britain's defeat of Napoleon had spurred British and American efforts to end a war that neither wanted. In August 1814 they opened peace talks in the Belgian city of Ghent. Perhaps waiting for the results of their 1814 offensive, the British opened with proposals that the Americans were certain to reject. They demanded the right to navigate the Mississippi. Moreover, they wanted territorial concessions and the creation of the permanent, independent Indian buffer state in the Northwest that they had promised their Indian allies. The Americans ignored these proposals and talked instead about impressment and maritime rights. As the autumn wore on and the war reached stalemate, both sides began to compromise. The British knew that the Americans would grant concessions in the interior only if they were thoroughly defeated, an outcome that most British commanders thought impossible. For their part, the Americans realized that the British maritime depredations were byproducts of the struggle with Napoleonic France. Faced with peace in Europe and a senseless military stalemate in North America, negotiators on both sides began to withdraw their demands. The Treaty of Ghent, signed on Christmas Eve 1814, simply put an end to the war. The border between Canada and the United States remained where it had been in 1812; Indians south of that border—defeated and without allies—were left to the mercy of the United States; and British maritime violations were not mentioned. The makers of the treaty stopped a war that neither side could win, trusting that a period of peace would resolve the problems created by two decades of world war.

CONCLUSION

In 1816 Thomas Jefferson was in retirement at Monticello, satisfied that he had defended liberty

The Buccaneer (1958)

Directed by Anthony Quinn. Starring Yul Brynner, Charlton Heston, Claire Bloom, Inger Stevens.

Here is one of the enduring legends of American history. Late in 1814 the British had attacked and burned Washington, D.C., and were moving a huge assault force toward the vital gulf port of New Orleans. Perhaps they wished to hold New Orleans as a bargaining chip in the peace negotiations already under way. Or perhaps they wished to conquer the whole Mississippi Valley. With the city in panic, Major General Andrew Jackson, at the head of a band of Tennessee squirrel shooters (the U.S. regulars and the local militia—including two battalions of free blacks—with him are seldom mentioned) rides in to save the day. The privateer Jean Lafitte controls the swamps and river channels that lead from the gulf to New Orleans, and the British try to win his allegiance. He turns them down and—despite an American naval assault on his stronghold and the imprisonment of many of his men—throws his men and munitions into the battle on the side of the victorious Americans. New Orleans is saved, Jackson becomes a national hero, and a pardoned Lafitte sails off into the sunset.

Hollywood took a good legend, added sentimental patriotism and a preposterous love story, and made *The Buccaneer*—with Yul Brynner as Jean Lafitte and Charlton Heston as Andrew Jackson. Brynner's Lafitte is a perfect swashbuckler: a fiery and fair-minded pirate who kills only when he has to, who has agreed not to attack American ships, and who is in love with the governor's daughter (Claire Bloom). Early on, he listens to the Declaration of Independence and wonders aloud if he would not prefer believing in a country to believing in the pirate brotherhood's code. (Another incentive: the governor's daughter refuses to marry him until he becomes respectable.) The dreams of citizenship and domesticity become doubtful, however, when one of Lafitte's (fictional) renegade captains loots and sinks the (fictional) American ship *Corinthian*, killing, along with 79 others, the governor's younger daughter. This remains secret while Lafitte joins Jackson to win the battle—with British automatons in kilts marching to their deaths, bagpipe players falling one by one until their terrifying wail is reduced to one dying note. At the victory ball, Lafitte and his lady love announce their engagement; word of the *Corinthian* spreads through the room. Heston's Jackson (who looks exactly like the older Jackson on the twenty dollar bill) stops a lynching and allows Lafitte and his men an hour to leave town. The mar-

---

against the Federalists' love of power. The High Federalist attempt to militarize government and to jail their enemies had failed. Their direct taxes were repealed. Their debt and their national bank remained in place, but only under the watchful eyes of true republicans. And their attempt to ally the United States with the antirepublican designs of Great Britain had ended in what many called the "Second War of American Independence."

Yet for all his successes, Jefferson in 1816 saw that he must sacrifice his dreams of agrarianism. Throughout his political life, Jefferson envisioned American yeomen trading farm surpluses for European manufactured goods—a relationship that would ensure rural prosperity, prevent the growth of cities and factories, and thus sustain the landed independence on which republican citizenship rested. Westward expansion, he had believed, would ensure the yeoman republic for generations to come. By 1816 that dream was ended. The British and French had "cover[ed] the earth and sea with robberies and piracies," disrupting America's vital export economy whenever it suited their whims. Arguing as Hamilton had argued in 1790, Jefferson insisted that "we must now place the manufacturer by the side of the agriculturalist." As

riage between the French rogue and the blonde American lady—improbable in 1814 and impossible in the movies of the 1950s—is averted. Lafitte sails off to no particular destination (he died in Yucatán a few years later) with a pirate moll (Inger Stevens) at his side, and America has been saved in more ways than one.

The Buccaneer depicts the 1814 British attack on Washington, D.C., with plenty of sentimental patriotism and a love story thrown in for good measure.

he wrote, a Republican congress was taking steps that would help transform the yeoman republic into a market society and a boisterous capitalist democracy.

Suggested Readings begin on page SR-1.
For Web activities and resources
related to this chapter, go to
http://www.harcourtcollege.com/history.murrin

CHAPTER 9

THE MARKET REVOLUTION,
1815–1860

LOCKPORT

The Erie Canal was the first of the great public works projects that helped transform a wilderness continent into a 19th-century commercial society, and early travelers and publicists admired it not only as a feat of engineering but as a work of art. The complex of locks at Lockport in particular became a symbol of the American triumph of civilization over nature. The town itself, filled with boatmen and construction workers, had a reputation for violence.

Jeffersonian Democrats had tied their hopes to the yeoman-artisan republic: Americans, they argued, could trade farm and plantation products for European manufactured goods, thus enjoying material comforts without sacrificing the landed independence on which Jefferson's republic rested. But two decades of world war demonstrated the vulnerability of American dependence on the export economy, and by 1816 Jefferson himself advised his countrymen to build enough factories to serve domestic needs.

The Americans went further than that, and after 1815 a market revolution transformed Jefferson's republic into the market-oriented, capitalist society it has been ever since. Improvements in transportation made that transformation possible, but thousands of farmers, planters, craftsmen, and merchants made the decisions that pulled farms and workshops out of old household and neighborhood arrangements and into production for distant markets. By the 1830s and 1840s the northern United States was experiencing a full-blown market revolution: New cities and towns provided financing, retailing, manufacturing, and markets for food; commercial farms traded food for what the cities made and sold. The South experienced a market revolution as well, but the region remained in its old colonial relationship to the centers of economic power. Away from the plantation belt, most southern farms remained marginal to the national and world economies. The wealthiest southerners, on the other hand, sent mountains of cotton, rice, and other plantation staples onto world markets. They remained provincial grandees who produced for distant markets and purchased shipping, financial services, and manufactured goods from outside the region—increasingly from the Northeast. They increased their wealth and local power and spread their plantation regime into vast new lands, and they maintained their old slaveholder's republic in the southern states. Now, however, they faced an aggressive and expanding capitalist democracy in the North.

This chapter will focus on the following major questions:

• What was the nationalizing dream of the American System, and how did improvements in transportation actually channel commerce within and between regions?

• How did northern farm families experience the transition into commercial agriculture between 1815 and 1850?

- What was the relationship between urban-industrial growth and the commercialization of the northern countryside?
- What were the nature and limits of the Market Revolution in the South? Why?

GOVERNMENT AND MARKETS

The 14th Congress met in the last days of 1815. Made up overwhelmingly of Jeffersonian Republicans, this Congress nevertheless would reverse many of the positions taken by Jefferson's old party. It would charter a national bank, enact a protective tariff, and debate whether or not to build a national system of roads and canals at federal expense. As late as 1811, the Republicans viewed such programs as heresy, but by 1815 the Republican majority in Congress had come to accept it as orthodox. The War of 1812 had demonstrated that the United States was unable to coordinate a fiscal and military effort. It had also convinced many Republicans that reliance on foreign trade rendered the United States dependent on Europe. The nation, they said, must abandon Jefferson's export-oriented agrarianism and encourage national independence through subsidies to commerce and manufactures.

THE AMERICAN SYSTEM: THE BANK OF THE UNITED STATES

Nationalist Henry Clay retained his power in the postwar Congress, and headed the drive for a neo-Federalist program of protective tariffs, internal improvements, and a national bank. He called his program the "American System," arguing that it would foster national economic growth and a salutary interdependence between geographical sections, thus a happy and healthy republic.

In 1816 Congress chartered a Second Bank of the United States, headquartered in Philadelphia and empowered to establish branches wherever it saw fit. The government agreed to deposit its funds in the Bank, to accept the Bank's notes as payment for government land, taxes, and other transactions, and to buy one-fifth of the Bank's stock. The Bank of the United States was more powerful than the one a Republican Congress had rejected as unconstitutional in 1811. The fiscal horrors of the War of 1812, however, had left most representatives in

C H R O N O L O G Y
1790 Samuel Slater builds his first Arkwright spinning mill at Pawtucket, Rhode Island
1801 John Marshall appointed chief justice of the Supreme Court
1807 Robert Fulton launches first steamboat
1813 Boston Associates erect their first textile mill at Waltham, Massachusetts
1815 War of 1812 ends
1816 Congress charters Second Bank of the United States • Congress passes protective tariff • *Dartmouth College* v. *Woodward* defines a private charter as a contract that cannot be altered by a state legislature • *McCulloch* v. *Maryland* affirms Congress's "implied powers" under the Constitution
1818 National Road completed to Ohio River at Wheeling, Virginia
1822 President Monroe vetoes National Road reparations bill
1824 *Gibbons* v. *Ogden* extends power of national government
1825 New York completes the Erie Canal between Buffalo and Albany
1828 Baltimore and Ohio Railroad (America's first) completed
1835 Main Line Canal connects Philadelphia and Pittsburgh

favor of moving toward a national currency and centralized control of money and credit. The alternative was to allow state banks—which had increased in number from 88 to 208 between 1813 and 1815—to issue unregulated and grossly inflated notes that might throw the anticipated postwar boom into chaos.

With no discussion of the constitutionality of what it was doing, Congress chartered the Bank of the United States as the sole banking institution empowered to do business throughout the country. Notes issued by the Bank would be the first semblance of a national currency (they would soon constitute from one-tenth to one-third of the value of notes in circulation). Moreover, the Bank could regulate the currency by demanding that state banknotes used in transactions with the federal government be

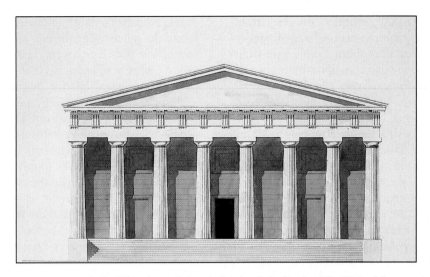

THE BANK OF THE UNITED STATES The classical Greek facade of the Bank of the United States reinforced its image as a conservative, centralizing—but still republican—financial force.

redeemable in gold. In 1816 the Bank set up shop in Philadelphia's Carpenter's Hall, and in 1824 moved around the corner to a Greek Revival edifice modeled after the Parthenon—a marble embodiment of the conservatism that directors of the Bank of the United States adopted as their fiscal stance. From that vantage point they would fight a running battle with state banks and local interests in an effort to impose direction on the transition to a market society.

THE AMERICAN SYSTEM: TARIFFS AND INTERNAL IMPROVEMENTS

In 1816 Congress drew up the first overtly protective tariff in U.S. history. Shepherded through the House by Clay and his fellow nationalist Calhoun, the Tariff of 1816 raised tariffs an average of 25 percent, extending protection to the nation's infant industries at the expense of foreign trade and American consumers. Again, wartime difficulties had paved the way: Because Americans could not depend on imported manufactures, Congress considered the encouragement of domestic manufactures a patriotic necessity. The tariff had strong support in the Northeast and the West and enough southern support to ensure its passage by Congress. Tariffs would rise and fall between 1816 and the Civil War, but the principle of protectionism would persist.

Bills to provide federal money for roads, canals, and other "internal improvements" had a harder time winning approval. The British wartime blockade had hampered coastal shipping and had made Americans dependent on the wretched roads of the interior. Many members of the 14th Congress, after spending days of bruising travel on their way to Washington, were determined to give the United States an efficient transportation network. Consensus was hard to reach. Some urged completion of the National Road linking the Chesapeake with the trans-Appalachian West. Some talked of an inland canal system to link the northern and southern coastal states. Others wanted a federally subsidized turnpike from Maine to Georgia.

Internal improvements, however, were subject to local ambitions and were of doubtful constitutionality as well. Congress agreed to complete the National Road, but President Madison and his Republican successor James Monroe both refused to support further internal improvements without a constitutional amendment. In 1822 Monroe even vetoed a bill authorizing repairs on the National Road, stating once again that the Constitution did not empower the federal government to build roads within the sovereign states.

With a national government squeamish about internal improvements, state governments took up the cause. The resulting transportation network after 1815 reflected the designs of the most ambitious states rather than the nationalizing dreams of men such as Henry Clay. New York's Erie Canal was the most spectacular accomplishment, but the canal systems of Pennsylvania and Ohio were almost as impressive. Before 1830 most toll roads were built and owned by corporations chartered by state governments, with the governments providing $5 million of the $30 million that it cost to build the roads. State expenditures on canals and railroads were even greater. Fully $41.2 million of the $58.6 million spent on the canals before 1834 came from state governments as did more than one-third of the $137 million spend on railroads before 1843. Much of the rest came from foreign investors. Private entrepreneurs could not have built the transportation network that produced the market economy without the active support of state governments. States provided direct funding, bond issues, and corporate charters that gave the turnpike, canal, and railroad companies the privileges and immunities that made them attractive to private investors.

MARKETS AND THE LAW

The Revolution replaced British courts with national and state legal systems based in English common law—systems that made legal action accessible to most white males. Thus many of the disputes generated in the transition to a market society ended up in court. The courts removed social conflicts from the public arena and brought them into a peaceful courtroom. There they dealt with the conflicts in language that only lawyers understood and resolved them in ways that tended to promote the entrepreneurial use of private property, the sanctity of contracts, and the right to do business shielded from neighborhood restraints and the tumult of democratic politics.

John Marshall, who presided over the Supreme Court from 1801 to 1835, took the lead. From the beginning he saw the Court as a conservative hedge against the excesses of democratically elected legislatures. His early decisions protected the independence of the courts and their right to review legislation (see chapter 8). From 1816 onward, his decisions encouraged business and strengthened the national government at the expense of the

states. Marshall's most important decisions protected the sanctity of contracts and corporate charters against state legislatures. For example, in *Dartmouth College* v. *Woodward* (1816), Dartmouth was defending a royal charter granted in the 1760s against changes introduced by a Republican legislature determined to transform Dartmouth from a privileged bastion of Federalism into a state college. Daniel Webster, who was both a Dartmouth alumnus and the school's highly paid lawyer, finished his argument before the Supreme Court on an emotional note: "It is, sir, as I have said, a small college. And yet there are those who love it—." Reputedly moved to tears, Marshall ruled that a state legislature could not alter Dartmouth's corporate charter. Though in this case the Supreme Court was protecting Dartmouth's independence and its chartered privileges, Marshall and Webster knew that the decision also protected the hundreds of turnpike and canal companies, manufacturing corporations, and other ventures that held privileges under corporate charters granted by state governments. Once the charters had been granted, the states could neither regulate the corporations nor cancel their privileges. Thus corporate charters acquired the legal status of contracts, beyond the reach of democratic politics.

Two weeks after the *Dartmouth* decision, Marshall handed down the majority opinion in *McCulloch* v. *Maryland*. The Maryland legislature, nurturing old Jeffersonian doubts about the constitutionality of the Bank of the United States, had attempted to tax the Bank's Baltimore branch, and the Bank had challenged the legislature's right to do so. Marshall decided in favor of the Bank. He stated, first, that the Constitution granted the federal government "implied powers" that included chartering the Bank, and he denied Maryland's right to tax the Bank or any other federal agency: "The power to tax," he said, "involves the power to destroy." It was Marshall's most explicit blow against Jeffersonian strict constructionism. Americans, he said, "did not design to make their government dependent on the states." And yet many, particularly in Marshall's native South, remained certain that that was precisely what the founders had intended.

In *Gibbons* v. *Ogden* (1824) the Marshall Court broke a state-granted steamship monopoly in New

York. The monopoly, Marshall argued, interfered with federal jurisdiction over interstate commerce. Like *Dartmouth College* v. *Woodward* and *McCulloch* v. *Maryland*, this decision empowered the national government in relation to the states. And like them, it encouraged private entrepreneurialism. Agreeing with congressmen who supported the American System, John Marshall's Supreme Court assumed that a natural and beneficial link existed between federal power and market society.

Meanwhile, the state courts were working quieter but equally profound transformations of American law. In the early republic, state courts had often viewed property not only as a private possession but as part of a neighborhood. Thus when a miller built a dam that flooded upriver farms or impaired the fishery, the courts might make him take those interests into account, often in ways that reduced the business uses of his property. By the 1830s, New England courts were routinely granting the owners of industrial mill sites unrestricted water rights, even when the exercise of those rights inflicted damage on their neighbors. As early as 1805, the New York Supreme Court in *Palmer* v. *Mulligan* had asserted that the right to develop property for business purposes was inherent in the ownership of property. A Kentucky court, asked to decide whether a railroad could come into downtown Louisville despite the protests of residents over the noise and the showers of sparks, decided that the public need for transportation outweighed the danger and annoyance to nearby residents. Railroads were necessary, and "private injury and personal damage . . . must be expected." "The onward spirit of the age," concluded the Kentucky court, "must, to a reasonable extent, have its way." In the courts of northern and western states, that "onward spirit" demanded legal protection for the business uses of private property, even when such uses conflicted with old common law restraints.

THE TRANSPORTATION REVOLUTION

After 1815 dramatic improvements in transportation—more and better roads, steamboats, canals, and finally railroads—tied old communities together and penetrated previously isolated neighborhoods. These improvements made the transition to a market society physically possible.

TRANSPORTATION IN 1815

In 1815 the United States was a rural nation stretching from the old settlements on the Atlantic coast to the trans-Appalachian frontier, with transportation facilities that ranged from primitive to nonexistent. Americans despaired of communicating, to say nothing of doing business on a national scale. In 1816 a Senate committee reported that nine dollars would move a ton of goods across the 3,000-mile expanse of the North Atlantic from Britain to the United States; the same nine dollars would move the same ton of goods only 30 miles inland. A year later, the cost of transporting wheat from the new settlement of Buffalo to New York City was three times greater than the selling price of wheat in New York. Farming for profit made sense only for farmers near urban markets or with easy river access to the coast.

West of the Appalachians, transportation was almost entirely undeveloped. Until about 1830, most westerners were southern yeomen who settled near tributaries of the Ohio-Mississippi River system—a network of navigable streams that reached the sea at New Orleans. Frontier farmers floated their produce downriver on jerry-built flatboats; at New Orleans it was transshipped to New York and other eastern ports. Most boatmen knocked down their flatboats, sold the lumber, and walked home to Kentucky or Ohio over the dangerous path known as the Natchez Trace.

Transporting goods to the western settlements was even more difficult. Keelboatmen such as the legendary Mike Fink could navigate upstream—using eddies and back currents, sailing when the wind was right, but usually poling their boat against the current. Skilled crews averaged only 15 miles a day, and the trip from New Orleans to Louisville took three to four months. (The downstream trip took a month.) Looking for better routes, some merchants dragged finished goods across Pennsylvania and into the West at Pittsburgh, but transport costs made these goods prohibitively expensive. Consequently the trans-Appalachian settlements—home to one in five Americans by 1820—remained marginal to the market economy. By 1815 New Orleans was shipping about $5 million of western produce annually—an average of only $15 per farm family in the interior.

IMPROVEMENTS: ROADS AND RIVERS

In 1816 Congress resumed construction of the National Road (first authorized in 1802) that linked the Potomac River with the Ohio River at Wheeling, Virginia. The smooth, crushed-rock thoroughfare reached Wheeling in 1818. At about the same time, Pennsylvania extended the Lancaster Turnpike to make it run from Philadelphia to the Ohio River at Pittsburgh. These ambitious roads into the West, however, had few effects. The National Road made it easier for settlers and a few merchants' wagons to reach the West, but the cost of moving bulky farm produce over the road remained high. Eastbound traffic on the National Road consisted largely of cattle and pigs, which carried themselves to market. Farmers continued to float their corn, cotton, wheat, salt pork, and whiskey south by riverboat and thence to eastern markets.

The steamboat opened the West to commercial agriculture. Tinkerers and mechanics had been experimenting with steam-powered boats for a generation or more when an entrepreneur named Robert Fulton launched the *Clermont* on an upriver trip from New York City to Albany in 1807. Over the next few years Americans developed flat-bottomed steamboats that could navigate rivers even at low water. The first steamboat reached Louisville from New Orleans in 1815. Two years later, with 17 steamboats already working western rivers, the *Washington* made the New Orleans–Louisville run in 25 days, a feat that convinced westerners that two-way river trade was possible. By 1820, 69 steamboats were operating on western rivers. The 60,000 tons of produce that farmers and planters had shipped out of the interior in 1810 grew to 500,000 tons in 1840. By the eve of the Civil War, two million tons of western produce—most of it southwestern cotton—reached the docks at New Orleans. The steamboat had trans-

A RIVER STEAMBOAT IN 1826 By the mid-1820s steamboats regularly plied the river systems of the United States. Businessmen and elite travelers rented nicely appointed cabins on the steamer itself and viewed the scenery as they strolled the comfortable (and usually uncrowded) passenger deck. Poorer passengers bought passage on the "Safety Barge" that was dragged behind the steamer.

formed the interior from an isolated frontier into a busy commercial region that traded farm and plantation products for manufactured goods.

IMPROVEMENTS: CANALS AND RAILROADS

In the East, state governments created rivers where nature had made none. In 1817 Governor DeWitt Clinton talked the New York legislature into building a canal linking the Hudson River with Lake Erie—thus opening a continuous water route between the Northwest and New York City. The Erie Canal was a near-visionary feat of engineering: Designed by self-taught engineers and built by gangs of Irish immigrants, local farm boys, and convict laborers, it stretched 364 miles from Albany to Buffalo. Although "Clinton's Ditch" passed through carefully chosen level ground, it required a complex system of 83 locks, and it passed over 18 rivers on stone aqueducts. Construction began in 1819, and

the canal reached Buffalo in 1825. It was clear even before then that the canal would repay New York state's investment of $7.5 million many times over, and that it would transform the territory it served.

The Erie Canal had its first and most powerful effects on western New York, which had been a raw frontier accessible to the East only over a notoriously bad state road. By 1830 the New York corridor of the Erie Canal, settled largely from hill-country New England, was one of the world's great grain-growing regions, dotted with market towns and new cities such as Syracuse, Rochester, and Buffalo.

The Erie Canal was an immense success, and legislators and entrepreneurs in other states joined a canal boom that lasted for 20 years. When construction began on the Erie Canal there were fewer than 100 miles of canal in the United States. By 1840 there were 3,300 miles, nearly all of them in the Northeast and Northwest. Northwestern states, Ohio in particular, built ambitious canal systems that linked isolated areas to the Great Lakes and

NEAR LOCKPORT ON THE ERIE CANAL This engraving of the Deep Cut through hills near Lockport, New York, was commissioned for the official volume celebrating completion of the Erie Canal in 1825. It gives the canal a scale and an awesome beauty meant to rival and perhaps surpass the works of nature.

thus to the Erie Canal. Northeastern states followed suit: A canal between Worcester and Providence linked the farms of central Massachusetts with Narragansett Bay. Another canal linked the coal mines of northeastern Pennsylvania with the Hudson River at Kingston, New York. In 1835 Pennsylvania completed a canal from Philadelphia to Pittsburgh, although at one point goods were shifted onto an unwieldy railroad that crossed a mountain.

The first American railroads connected burgeoning cities to rivers and canals. The Baltimore and Ohio Railroad, for example, linked Baltimore to the rivers of the West. Although the approximately 3,000 miles of railroads built between the late 1820s and 1840 helped the market positions of some cities, they did not constitute a national or even a regional rail network. A national system developed with the 5,000 miles of track laid in the 1840s and with the flurry of railroad building that gave the United States a rail network of 30,000 miles by 1860—a continuous, integrated system that created massive links between the East and the

RIVERS, ROADS, AND CANALS, 1825–1860

Northwest and that threatened to put canals out of business. In fact, the New York Central, which paralleled the Erie Canal, rendered that canal obsolete. Other railroads, particularly in the northwestern states, replaced canal and river transport almost completely, even though water transport remained cheaper. By 1860 few farmers in the North and West lived more than 20 road miles from railroads, canals, or rivers that could deliver their produce to regional, national, and international markets.

TIME AND MONEY

The transportation revolution brought a dramatic reduction in the time and money it took to move heavy goods. Turnpikes cut the cost of wagon transport in half between 1816 and 1860—from 30 cents per ton-mile to 15 cents. In 1816 freight rates on the Ohio-Mississippi system had been 1.3 cents per ton-mile for downriver travel and 5.8 cents for upriver travel; steamboats cut both costs to a bit more than a third of a cent. The Erie Canal and the Ohio canals reduced the distance between East and West and carried goods at about a cent per ton-mile; the railroads of the 1850s carried freight much faster, although at two to three times the cost. And the longer the haul the greater the per-mile savings: Overall, the cost of moving goods across long distances dropped 95 percent between 1815 and 1860.

Improvements in speed were nearly as dramatic. The overland route from Cincinnati to New York in 1815 (by keelboat upriver to Pittsburgh, then by wagon the rest of the way) had taken a minimum of 52 days. Steamboats traveled from Cincinnati to New Orleans, then passed goods on to coasting ships that finished the trip to New York City in a total of 28 days. By the 1840s, upriver steamboats carried goods to the terminus of the Main Line Canal at Pittsburgh, which delivered them to Philadelphia, which sent them by train to New York City for a total transit time of 18 to 20 days. At about the same time, the Ohio canal system enabled Cincinnati to send goods north through Ohio, across Lake Erie, over the Erie Canal, and down the Hudson to New York City—an all-water route that reduced costs and made the trip in 18 days. By 1852 the Erie Railroad and its connectors could make the Cincinnati–New York City run—though at a higher cost than water routes—in six to eight days. Similar

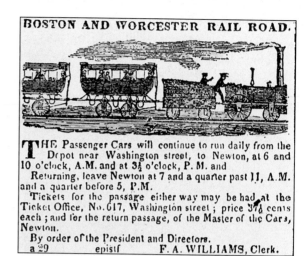

BOSTON AND WORCESTER RAILROAD The Boston and Worcester was typical of the earliest American railroads. It linked Boston with Worcester and, via the Blackstone Canal, with the farming and industrializing communities between Worcester and Providence. Passengers moved reliably and on a fixed schedule, contributing to the speedy and predictable transportation that made the market revolution—and the continuing regional dominance of Boston—possible.

improvements occurred in the densely settled and increasingly urbanized Northeast. By 1840 travel time between the big northeastern cities had been reduced to from one-fourth to one-eleventh of what it had been in 1790—with people, goods, and information traveling at an average of 15 miles an hour. Such improvements in speed and economy made a national market economy possible.

By 1840 improved transportation had made a market revolution. Foreign trade, which had driven American economic growth up to 1815, continued to expand. In 1815 American exports totaled $52.6 million; imports totaled $113 million. Both rose dramatically in the years of the market revolution: Exports (now consisting more of southern cotton than of northern food crops) increased sixfold to $333.6 million by 1860; imports (mostly European manufactured goods) tripled to $353.6 million. Yet the increases in foreign trade represented vast reductions in the proportion of American market activity that involved other countries. Before 1815 Americans had exported about 15 percent of their total national product; by 1830 exports accounted

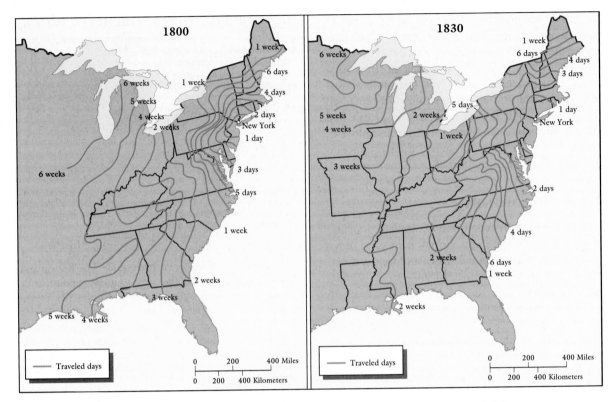

TIME REQUIRED TO TRAVEL FROM NEW YORK CITY, 1800 AND 1830

for only 6 percent of total production. The reason for this shift was that after 1815 the United States developed self-sustaining domestic markets for farm produce and manufactured goods. The great engine of economic growth—particularly in the North and West—was not the old colonial relationship with Europe but a burgeoning internal market.

MARKETS AND REGIONS

Henry Clay and other proponents of the American System dreamed of a market-driven economy that would transcend sectionalism and create a unified United States. Instead, until at least 1840 the market revolution produced greater results within regions than between them. The farmers of New England traded food for finished goods from Boston, Lynn, Lowell, and other towns in what was becoming an urban, industrial region. Philadelphia sold its manufactures to and bought its food from the farmers of the Delaware valley. Although the Erie Canal created a huge potential for interregional trade, until 1839

most of its eastbound tonnage originated in western New York. In the West, market-oriented farmers fed such rapidly growing cities as Rochester, Cleveland, Chicago, and Cincinnati, which in turn supplied the farmers with locally manufactured farm tools, furniture, shoes, and other goods. Farther south, the few plantations that did not produce their own food bought surpluses from farmers in their own region. Thus until about 1840 the market revolution was more a regional than an interregional phenomenon.

In the 1840s and 1850s, however, the new transport networks turned the increasingly industrial Northeast and mid-Atlantic and the commercial farms of the Old Northwest into a unified market society. The earliest settlers in the Northwest were southerners who had carried on a limited trade through the river system that led to New Orleans. From the 1840s onward produce left the Northwest less often by the old Ohio River route than by canal and railroad directly to the Northeast. Of the total produce exported from the Old Northwest in 1853, only 29 percent went by way of the river system,

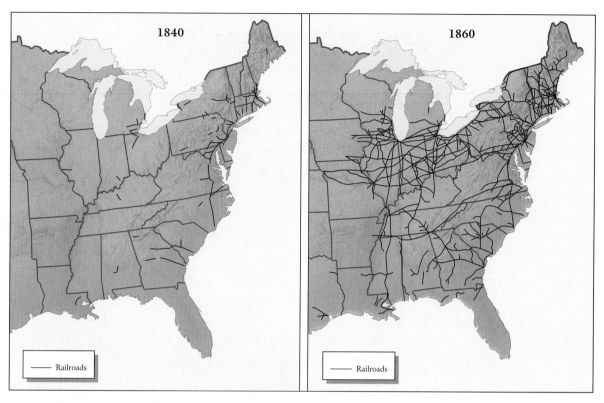

RAILROADS IN THE UNITED STATES, 1840 AND 1860

whereas 60 percent went by way of the Erie Canal alone. At the same time, canals and roads from New York, Philadelphia, and Baltimore became the favored passageways for commodities entering the West. As early as 1835, some 55 percent of the West's imported sugar, salt, iron, and coffee entered the region by the Great Lakes, Pennsylvania, or Wheeling routes. By 1853 that figure stood at 71 percent. In those years the Ohio-Mississippi River system carried vastly increased amounts of goods, but that increase, particularly after 1840, added up to a shrinking share of the expanded total. In short, western farmers and northeastern businessmen and manufacturers were building a national market from which the South was largely excluded.

FROM YEOMAN TO BUSINESSMAN: THE RURAL NORTH AND WEST

In the old communities of the Northeast, the market revolution sent some of the young people off to cities and factory towns and others to the West. Those who remained at home engaged in new forms of agriculture on a transformed rural landscape, while their cousins in the Northwest transformed a wilderness into cash-producing farms.

SHAPING THE NORTHERN LANDSCAPE

An early 19th-century New England farm geared toward family subsistence required only 3 acres of cultivated land, 12 acres of pasture and meadow, another acre for the house, outbuildings, and vegetable garden, and a 30-acre woodlot to stoke the hearth that cooked the food and heated the house. Visitors to even the oldest towns found farmsteads, tilled fields, and pastures scattered across a heavily wooded landscape. In the 18th century, overcrowding had encouraged some farmers to turn woodlots into poor farmland. In the 19th century, however, millions of trees were stripped from the New England countryside and livestock raising replaced

The Making of Rural Respectability

In 1851 a booster's history of the Phelps-Gorham Purchase in western New York published an idealized sequence of rural progress over the previous half century. In the first winter a pioneer farmer sets his cabin in a clearing littered with fresh tree stumps where cattle, sheep, and dogs browse up to the doorstep. The second scene represents the following summer, and it is clear that a particular kind of civilization is being imposed upon the land. The farmer and his neighbors clear and plant a new field, while animals nurse their young in the foreground. The labors of the fields and pastures are separated by a rude fence from the house (now decorated with ornamental plants), a rudimentary vegetable garden, and the farmer's wife. Twenty years later the farm family has achieved respectability. Their new frame house dwarfs the pioneer cabin to which it is attached, and an orchard, a solid barn, walkways, and neat gardens share space with the house behind a white picket fence. A road with a sturdy wooden bridge passes by the front gate, giving the farmer and his neighbors access both to markets and to each other, and thus to economic progress and the pleasures of society. The final view culminates this story of rural progress in ways that mix developmental history and myth. The family now lives in a mansion surrounded by an expensive cast iron fence. The road has been widened and a graceful stone bridge has replaced the old wooden one, the forest has been completely replaced by neat, fenced rectangles of farmland and a village with a high church steeple. A railroad—the surest sign of progress and civilization at midcentury—courses through the completed landscape.

mixed farming. New Englanders who tried to grow grain on their rocky, worn-out soil could not compete with the farmers of western New York and the Old Northwest, who possessed fertile lands and ready access to markets. At the same time, however, the factories and cities of the Northeast provided Yankee farmers with a market for meat and other perishables. Beef became the great New England cash crop. Dairy products were not far behind, and the proximity to city markets encouraged the spread of poultry and egg farms, fruit orchards, and truck gardens. The burgeoning shoe industry bought leather from the farmers, and woolen mills created a demand for wool. In 1840 Vermont held 5.75 times more sheep than people.

The rise of livestock specialization reduced the amount of land under cultivation. Early in the century New Englanders still tilled their few acres in the old three-year rotation: corn the first year, rye the second, fallow the third. By the 1820s and 1830s, as farmers raised more livestock and less grain, the land that remained in cultivation was

A NEW ENGLAND FARM IN THE 1840s Farm households in the 19th century underwent a transformation, as "men's work" became increasingly associated with the cash economy and "women's work" centered in the home. In the scene depicted here, one woman stands in the doorway with a broom and another tends barnyard animals. A man and a boy drive into the farmyard, probably from the outlying fields.

farmed more intensively. Farmers saved manure and ashes for fertilizer, plowed more deeply and systematically, and tended their crops more carefully. These improved techniques, along with cash from the sale of their livestock and the availability of food at stores, encouraged Yankee farmers to allocate less and less land to the growing of food crops. In Concord, Massachusetts—the hometown of the agrarian republic—the portion of town land in tillage dropped from 20 percent to 7 percent between 1771 and 1850.

The transition to livestock raising transformed woodlands into open pastures. As farmers leveled the forests, they sold the wood to fuel-hungry cities. In 1829 a cord of wood sold for $1.50 in Maine and for $7 in Boston. Over the next decade manufacturers began marketing cast-iron stoves that heated houses less expensively and more efficiently than open hearths, and canals brought cheap Pennsylvania anthracite to the Northeast. Farmers who needed pastureland could gain substantial one-time profits from the sale of cut wood. The result was massive deforestation. In 1790, in the central Massachusetts town of Petersham, forest covered 85 percent of the town lands. By 1830 the creation of pastureland through commercial woodcutting had reduced the forested area to 30 percent. By 1850 woods covered only 10 percent of the town, the pasturelands were overgrazed and ruined, and the landscape was dotted with abandoned farms. The pattern was the same throughout New England. At the beginning of European settlement, 95 percent of the region had been covered by forest. By 1850 forest covered only 30 percent of Connecticut, 32 percent of Rhode Island, 40 percent of Massachusetts, 45 percent of Vermont, and 50 percent of New Hampshire.

THE TRANSFORMATION OF RURAL OUTWORK

On that denuded landscape, poor families with many children continued to supplement their income with industrial outwork (see chapter 7). But the quickening of market activity brought new kinds of dependence. Before the 1820s outworkers had used local raw materials such as wool, leather, and flax and had spent only their spare time on such work. Merchants who bought their finished products often complained that outworkers kept their best work for themselves and for exchange with their neighbors. In the 1820s the manufacture of shoes and textiles began to be concentrated in factories, and outworkers who remained were reduced to dependence. Merchants now provided them with raw materials with which to make such items as cloth-covered buttons and palm-leaf hats (imported materials that only merchants could supply), and set the pace of labor and the quality of the finished goods. In the 1830s fully 33,000 New England women were fashioning palm-leaf hats in their homes, far more than the 20,000 who worked in New England's much-publicized cotton mills. Although outwork still helped poor families to maintain their independence, control of their labor had passed to merchants and other agents of the regional economy.

FARMERS AS CONSUMERS

With the shift to specialized market agriculture, New England farmers became customers for necessities that their forebears had produced themselves or had acquired through barter. They heated their houses with coal dug by Pennsylvania miners. They wore cotton cloth made by the factory women at Lowell. New Hampshire farm girls made straw hats for them, and the craftsmen of Lynn made their shoes. By 1830 or so, many farmers were even buying food. The Erie Canal and the western grain belt sent flour from Rochester into eastern neighborhoods where grain no longer grew. Many farmers found it easier to produce specialized crops for market, and to buy butter, cheese, eggs, and vegetables at country stores.

The turning point came in the 1820s. The storekeepers of Northampton, Massachusetts, for instance, had been increasing their stock in trade by about 7 percent per decade since the late 18th century. In the 1820s they increased it 45 percent and now carried not only local farm products and sugar, salt, and coffee, but bolts of New England cloth, sacks of western flour, a variety of necessities and little luxuries from the wholesale houses of New York City and Boston, and pattern samples from which to order silverware, dishes, wallpaper, and

A NEW ENGLAND COUNTRY STORE An 1830s Massachusetts country store was a community gathering place, a market for farm produce, and the source of a growing variety of commodities from the outside world.

other household goods. Those goods were better than what could be made at home and were for the most part cheaper. The price of finished cloth, for instance, declined sixfold between 1815 and 1830; as a result, spinning wheels and handlooms disappeared from the farmhouses of New England. Farm families preferred pies and bread made from western white flour to the old "Rye and Injun" (see chapter 7), and gladly turned their woodlands and unproductive grain fields into cash-producing pastures. Coal and cast-iron stoves replaced the family hearth.

Material standards of living rose, but more and more families "felt" poor, and many more were incapable of feeding, clothing, and warming themselves in years when the market failed. By the 1820s and 1830s northeastern farmers depended on markets in ways that their fathers and grandfathers would have considered dangerous not only to family welfare but to the welfare of the republic itself.

THE NORTHWEST: SOUTHERN MIGRANTS

One reason the market revolution in the Northeast went as smoothly as it did was that young people with little hope of inheriting land in the old settlements moved away to towns and cities or to the new farmlands of the Northwest. Between 1815 and 1840—precisely the years in which northeastern agriculture became a cash-crop business—migrants from the older areas transformed the Northwest Territory into a working agricultural landscape. In 1789 no Americans lived there. When the Treaty of Greenville made southern and eastern Ohio safe, settlers poured into the area. By 1800 the white population of Ohio numbered 45,365. In 1810 the population of Ohio, Indiana, and Illinois numbered 267,562, and settlement skyrocketed after the peace of 1815. By 1830 1,438,379 whites lived in Ohio, Indiana, and Illinois. By 1860 the population of those three states, along with that of the new states of Wisconsin and Michigan, numbered 6,926,884—22 percent of the nation's total population. (With the inclusion of the Old Southwest, nearly half of the population was west of the Appalachians; the geographic center of population was near Chillicothe, Ohio.)

In the Northwest until about 1830 most settlers were yeomen from Kentucky and Tennessee, usually a generation removed from Virginia, the Carolinas, and western Maryland. They moved along the Ohio and up the Muskingum, Miami, Scioto, Wabash, and Illinois Rivers to set up farms in the southern and central counties of Ohio, Indiana, and Illinois. When southerners moved north of the Ohio River into territory that banned slavery, they often did so saying that slavery blocked opportunities for poor whites. The Methodist preacher Peter Cartwright left Kentucky with this thought: "I would get entirely clear of the evil of slavery," and "could raise my children to work where work was not thought a degradation." Similar hopes drew thousands of other southern yeomen north of the Ohio.

But even those who rejected slavery seldom rejected southern folkways. Like their kinfolk in Kentucky and Tennessee, the farmers of southern and central Ohio, Indiana, and Illinois remained tied to the river trade and to a mode of agriculture that favored free-ranging livestock over cultivated fields. The typical farmer fenced in a few acres of corn and left the rest of his land in woods to be roamed by southern hogs known as "razorbacks" and "land sharks." As late as 1860, southern-born farmers in the Northwest averaged 20 hogs apiece. These animals were thin and tough (they seldom grew to more than 200 pounds), and they could run long distances, leap fences, fend for themselves in the woods, and walk to distant markets. They were notoriously fierce; many more settlers were injured by their own hogs than by wild animals. When it was time to gather the hogs for slaughter, settlers often played it safe and hunted them with guns.

The southern-born pioneers of the Northwest, like their cousins across the Ohio River, depended more on their families and neighbors than on distant markets. Newcomers found that they could neither rent tools from their southern neighbors nor present them with "gifts" during hard times. Southerners insisted on repaying debts in kind and on lending tools rather than renting them—thus engaging outsiders in the elaborate network of "neighboring" through which transplanted southerners made their livings. As late as the 1840s, in the bustling town of Springfield, Illinois, barter was the preferred system of exchange. "In no part of the world," said a Scotsman in southern Illinois, "is good neighborship found in greater perfection than in the western territory."

THE NORTHWEST: NORTHERN MIGRANTS

Around 1830 a stream of northeasterners migrated to the Northwest via the Erie Canal and on Great Lakes steamboats. They filled the new lands of Wisconsin and Michigan and the northern counties of the older northwestern states. Most of them were New Englanders who had spent a generation in western New York (such settlers accounted for three-fourths of the early population of Michigan). The rest came directly from New England or— from the 1840s onward—from Germany and Scandinavia. Arriving in the Northwest along the market's busiest arteries, they duplicated the intensive, market-oriented farming they had known at home. They penned their cattle and hogs and fattened them up, making them bigger and worth more than

those farther south. They planted their land in grain and transformed the region—beginning with western New York's Genesee Country in the 1820s and rolling through the Northwest—into one of the world's great wheat-producing regions. In 1820 the Northwest had exported only 12 percent of its agricultural produce. By 1840 that figure had risen to 27 percent, and it stood even higher among northern-born grain farmers. By 1860 the Northwest, intensively commercialized and tied by canals and railways to eastern markets, was exporting 70 percent of its wheat. In that year it produced 46 percent of the nation's wheat crop, nearly all north of the line of southern settlement.

The new settlers were notably receptive to improvements in farming techniques. Even with plenty of southern proponents of "progress" and plenty of "backward" northerners, the line between new and old agricultural ways tended to separate northern grain farmers from corn, hogs, and southern settlers. In breaking new land, for instance, southerners still used the old shovel plow, which dug a shallow fur-

THE MCCORMICK REAPER The boy Abraham Lincoln grew up on Indiana and Illinois farms on which cultivation was haphazard and tools were simple. Later, as a Whig and Republican politician, he rejected that world for the belief that intensive, mechanized farming improved not only crop yields but intellectual, moral, and political standards, "whose course shall be onward and upward, and which, while the earth endures, shall not pass away." As he spoke, this factory in his hometown of Springfield, Illinois, churned out the implements that were bringing that new world into being.

row and skipped over roots. Northerners preferred newer, more expensive cast-iron plows, which cut cleanly through oak roots 4 inches thick. By the 1830s the efficient, expensive grain cradle had become the standard harvest tool in northwestern wheat fields. From the 1840s onward, even this advanced hand tool was replaced by mass-produced machinery such as the McCormick reaper. Instead of threshing their grain by driving cattle and horses over it, farmers bought new horse-powered and treadmill threshers and used hand-cranked fanning mills to speed the process of cleaning the grain.

Most agricultural improvements were tailored to grain and dairy farming, and were taken up most avidly by the northern farmers. Others rejected them as expensive and "unnatural." They thought that cast-iron plows poisoned the soil and that fanning mills made a "wind contrary to nater," and thus offended God. John Chapman, an eccentric Yankee who earned the nickname "Johnny Appleseed" by planting apple tree cuttings in southern Ohio and Indiana before the settlers arrived, planted only low-yield, common trees; he regarded grafting, which farmers farther north and east were using to improve the quality of their apples, as "against nature." Southerners scoffed at the Yankee fondness for mechanical improvements, the systematic breeding of animals and plants, careful bookkeeping, and farm techniques learned from magazines and books. "I reckon," said one, "I know as much about farming as the printers do."

Conflict between intensive agriculture and older, less market-oriented ways reached comic proportions when the Illinois legislature imposed stiff penalties on farmers who allowed their small, poorly bred bulls to run loose and impregnate cows with questionable sperm, thereby depriving the owners of high-bred bulls of their breeding fees and rendering the systematic breeding of cattle impossible. When the poorer farmers refused to pen their bulls, the law was rescinded. A local historian explained that "there was a generous feeling in the hearts of the people in favor of an equality of privileges, even among bulls."

HOUSEHOLDS

The market revolution transformed 18th-century households into 19th-century homes. For one thing, Americans began to limit the size of their families.

White women who married in 1800 gave birth to an average of 6.4 children. Those who married between 1800 and 1849 averaged 4.9 children. The decline was most pronounced in the North, particularly in commercialized areas. Rural birth rates remained at 18th-century levels in the southern uplands, in the poorest and most isolated communities of the North, and on the frontier. (As the New Yorker Washington Irving passed through the Northwest in the 1830s, he noted in his journal: "Illinois—famous for children and dogs—in house with nineteen children and thirty-seven dogs.") These communities practiced the old labor-intensive agriculture and relied on the labor of large families. For farmers who used newer techniques or switched to livestock, large families made less sense. Moreover, large broods hampered the ability of future-minded parents to provide for their children, and conflicted with new notions of privacy and domesticity that were taking shape among an emerging rural middle class.

The commercialization of agriculture was closely associated with the emergence of the concept of housework. Before 1815 farm wives had labored in the house, the barnyard, and the garden while their husbands and sons worked in the fields. With the market revolution came a sharper distinction between "male work" that was part of the cash economy and "female work" that was not. Even such traditional women's tasks as dairying, vegetable gardening, and poultry raising became men's work once they became cash-producing specialties. (A Pennsylvanian who lived among market-oriented New Englanders in the Northwest was appalled at such tampering with hallowed gender roles and wrote the Yankees off as "a shrewd, selfish, enterprising, cow-milking set of men.")

At the same time, new kinds of women's work emerged within households. Although women had fewer children to care for, the culture began to demand forms of child-rearing that were more intensive, individualized, and mother-centered. Store-bought white flour, butter, and eggs and the new iron stoves eased the burdens of food preparation, but they also created demands for pies, cakes, and other fancy foods that earlier generations had only imagined. And while farm women no longer spun and wove their own cloth, the availability of manufactured cloth created the expectation that their families would dress more neatly and with greater variety than they had in the past—at the cost of far

A SOAP ADVERTISEMENT FROM THE 1850s The rigors of "Old Washing Day" lead the mother in this advertisement to abuse the children and house pets, while her husband leaves the house. With American Cream Soap, domestic bliss returns: The children and cats are happy, the husband returns, and the wife has time to sew.

more time spent by women on sewing, washing, and ironing. Similar expectations demanded greater personal and domestic cleanliness, and farm women from the 1830s onward spent time planting flower beds, cleaning and maintaining prized furniture, mirrors, rugs, and ceramics, and scrubbing floors and children. The market and housework grew hand in hand: Among the first mass-produced commodities in the United States was the household broom.

Housework was tied to new notions of privacy, decency, and domestic comfort. Before 1820 farmers cared little about how their houses looked, often tossing trash and garbage out the door for the pigs and chickens that foraged near the house. In the 1820s and 1830s, as farmers began to grow cash crops and adopt middle-class ways, they began to plant shade trees and keep their yards free of trash. They painted their houses and sometimes their

fences and outbuildings, arranged their woodpiles into neat stacks, surrounded their houses with flowers and ornamental shrubs, and tried to hide their privies from view. The new sense of refinement and decorum extended into other aspects of country life. The practice of chewing (and spitting) tobacco was gradually banned in churches and meeting halls, and in 1823 the minister in Shrewsbury, Massachusetts, ordered dogs out of the meetinghouse.

Inside, prosperous farmhouses took on an air of privacy and comfort. Separate kitchens and iron stoves replaced open hearths. Many families used a set of matched dishes for individual place settings, and the availability of finished cloth permitted the regular use of tablecloths, napkins, doilies, curtains, bedspreads, and quilts. Oil lamps replaced homemade candles, and the more comfortable families began to decorate their homes with wallpaper and upholstered furniture. Farm couples moved their beds away from the hearth and (along with the children's beds that had been scattered throughout the house) put them into spaces designated as bedrooms. They took the washstands and basins, which were coming into more common use, out of the kitchen and put them into the bedroom, thus making sleeping, bathing, and sex more private than they had been in the past. At the center of this new house stood the farm wife—apart from the bustling world of commerce, but decorating and caring for the amenities that commerce bought, and demanding that men respect the new domestic world that commerce had made possible.

NEIGHBORHOODS: THE LANDSCAPE OF PRIVACY

By the 1830s and 1840s the market revolution had transformed the rural landscape of the Northeast. The forests had been reduced, the swamps had been drained, and most of the streams and rivers were interrupted by mill dams. Bears, panthers, and wolves had disappeared, along with the beaver and many of the fish. Now English cattle and sheep browsed on extensive pastures of English grasses dotted with English wildflowers such as buttercups, daisies, and dandelions. Next to the pastures lay neatly cultivated croplands that were regularly fertilized and seldom allowed to lie fallow. And at the center stood brightly painted houses and outbuildings surrounded by flowers and shrubs and vegetable gardens. Many towns, particularly in New England, had planted shade trees along the country roads, completing a rural landscape of straight lines and human cultivation—a landscape that made it easy to think of nature as a commodity to be altered and controlled.

Within that landscape, old practices and old forms of neighborliness fell into disuse. Neighbors continued to exchange goods and labor and to contract debts that might be left unpaid for years, but debts were more likely to be owed to profit-minded storekeepers and creditors, and even debts between neighbors often were paid in cash. Traditionally, storekeepers had allowed farmers to bring in produce and have it credited to a neighbor/creditor's account—a practice that made the storekeeper an agent of neighborhood bartering. In 1830 half of the stores in rural Massachusetts carried accounts of this sort; by 1850 that figure had dropped to one in four. Storekeepers began to demand cash payment or to charge lower prices to those who paid cash. The farm newspapers that appeared in these years urged farmers to keep careful records of the amount of fertilizer used, labor costs, and per-acre yields and discouraged them from relying on the old system of neighboring. Neighborly rituals like parties, husking bees, barn-raisings—with their drinking and socializing—were scorned as an inefficient and morally suspect waste of time. The *Farmer's Almanac* of 1833 warned New England farmers: "If you love fun, frolic, and waste and slovenliness more than economy and profit, then make a husking."

Thus the efficient farmer after the 1820s concentrated on producing commodities that could be marketed outside the neighborhood and used his cash income to buy material comforts for his family and to pay debts and provide a cash inheritance for his children. Although much of the old world of household and neighborhood survived, farmers subsisted and maintained the independence of their households not through those spheres but through unprecedented levels of dependence on the outside world.

THE INDUSTRIAL REVOLUTION

In the 50 years following 1820 American cities grew faster than ever before or since. The old sea-ports—New York City in particular—grew rapidly in these years, but the fastest growth was in new cities that served commercial agriculture and in factory towns that produced for a largely rural domestic market. Even in the seaports, growth derived more from commerce with the hinterland than from international trade. Paradoxically, the market revolution in the countryside had produced the beginnings of industry and the greatest period of urban growth in U.S. history.

FACTORY TOWNS: THE RHODE ISLAND SYSTEM

Jeffersonians held that the United States must always remain rural. Americans, they insisted, could expand into the rich new agricultural lands of the West, trade their farm surpluses for European finished goods, and thus avoid creating cities with their dependent social classes. Federalists argued that Americans, in order to retain their independence, must produce their own manufactured goods. Neo-Federalists combined those arguments after the War of 1812. Along with other advocates of industrial expansion, they argued that America's abundant water power—particularly the fast-running streams of the Northeast—would enable Americans to build their factories across the countryside instead of creating great industrial cities. Such a decentralized factory system would provide employment for country women and children and thus subsidize the independence of struggling farmers. It was on those premises that the first American factories were built.

The American textile industry originated in industrial espionage. The key to mass-produced cotton and woolen textiles was a water-powered machine that spun yarn and thread. The machine had been invented and patented by the Englishman Richard Arkwright in 1769. The British government, to protect its lead in industrialization, forbade the machinery or the people who operated it to leave the country. Scores of textile workers, however, defied the law and made their way to North America. One of them was Samuel Slater, who had served an apprenticeship under Jedediah Strutt, a partner of Arkwright who had improved on the original machine. Working from memory while employed by Moses Brown, a Providence merchant,

Slater built the first Arkwright spinning mill in America at Pawtucket, Rhode Island, in 1790.

Slater's first mill was a small frame building tucked among the town's houses and craftsmen's shops. It spun only cotton yarn, providing work for children in the mill and for women who wove yarn into cloth in their homes. Thus this first mill satisfied the neo-Federalists' requirements: It required no factory town, and it supplemented the household incomes of farmers and artisans. As his business grew and he advertised for widows with children, however, Slater encountered families headed by landless, impoverished men. Slater's use of children from these families prompted "respectable" farmers and craftsmen to pull their children out of Slater's growing complex of mills. More poor families arrived to take their places, and during the first years of the 19th century Pawtucket grew rapidly into a disorderly mill town.

Soon Slater and other mill owners built factory villages in the countryside, where they could exert better control over their operations and their workers. The practice became known as the Rhode Island (or "family") system. At Slatersville, Rhode Island, at

SAMUEL SLATER'S MILL AT PAWTUCKET, RHODE ISLAND The first mill was small, painted white, and topped with a cupola. Set among craftsmen's workshops and houses, it looked more like a Baptist meetinghouse than a first step into industrialization.

Oxford, Massachusetts, and at other locations in southern New England, mill owners built whole villages surrounded by company-owned farmland that they rented to the husbands and fathers of their mill workers. The workplace was closely supervised, and drinking and other troublesome practices were forbidden in the villages. Fathers and older sons either worked on rented farms or as laborers at the mills. By the late 1820s Slater and most of the other owners were eliminating outworkers and were buying power looms, thus transforming the villages into disciplined, self-contained factory towns that turned raw cotton into finished cloth—but at great cost to old forms of household independence. When President Andrew Jackson visited Pawtucket in 1829, he remarked to Samuel Slater, "I understand you taught us how to spin, so as to rival Great Britain in her manufactures; you set all these thousands of spindles to work, which I have been delighted in viewing, and which have made so many happy, by a lucrative employment." "Yes sir," replied Slater, "I suppose that I gave out the psalm and they have been singing to the tune ever since."

FACTORY TOWNS: THE WALTHAM SYSTEM

A second act of industrial espionage was committed by a wealthy, cultivated Bostonian named Francis Cabot Lowell. Touring English factory districts in 1811, Lowell asked the plant managers questions and made secret drawings of the machines he saw. He also experienced a genteel distaste for the squalor of the English textile towns. Returning home, Lowell joined with wealthy friends to form the Boston Manufacturing Company—soon known as the Boston Associates. In 1813 they built their first mill at Waltham, Massachusetts, and then expanded into Lowell, Lawrence, and other new towns near Boston during the 1820s. The company, operating under what became known as the Waltham system, built mills that differed from the early Rhode Island mills in two ways: First, they were heavily capitalized and as fully mechanized as possible; they turned raw cotton into finished cloth with little need for skilled workers. Second, the operatives who tended their machines were young, single women recruited from the farms of northern New England—farms that were switching to livestock raising, and thus had little need for the labor of daughters. The company housed the young women in carefully supervised boardinghouses and enforced rules of conduct both on and off the job. The young women worked steadily, never drank, seldom stayed out late, and attended church faithfully. They dressed neatly—often stylishly—and read newspapers and attended lectures. They impressed visitors, particularly those who had seen factory workers in other places, as a dignified and self-respecting workforce.

The brick mills and prim boardinghouses set within landscaped towns and occupied by sober, well-behaved farm girls signified the Boston Asso-ciates' desire to build a profitable textile industry without creating a permanent working class. The women would work for a few years in a carefully controlled environment, send their wages back to their family, and return home to live as country housewives. These young farm women did in fact form an efficient, decorous workforce, but the decorum was imposed less by the owners than by the women themselves. In order to protect their own reputations, they punished misbehavior and shunned fellow workers whose behavior was questionable. Nor did they send their wages home or, as was popularly believed, use them to pay for their brothers' college education. Some saved their money to use as dowries that their fathers could not afford. More, however, spent their wages on themselves—particularly on clothes and books.

The owners of the factories expected that the young women's sojourn would reinforce their own paternalistic position and that of the girls' fathers. Instead, it produced a self-respecting sisterhood of independent, wage-earning women. Twice in the 1830s the women of Lowell went out on strike, proclaiming that they were not wage slaves but "the daughters of freemen"; in the 1840s they were among the leaders of a labor movement in the region. After finishing their stint in the mills, a good many Lowell women entered public life as reformers. Most of them married and became housewives, but not on the same terms their mothers had known. One in three married Lowell men and became city dwellers. Those who returned home to rural neighborhoods remained unmarried longer than their sisters who had stayed at home, and then married men about their own age who worked at something other than farming. Thus through the 1840s the Boston Associates kept their promise to produce cotton cloth profitably without creating a permanent working class, but they failed to shuttle young women from rural to urban paternalism and back again. Wage labor, the ultimate degradation for agrarian-republican men, opened a road out of rural patriarchy for thousands of young women.

WOMEN IN THE MILLS Two female weavers from a Massachusetts textile mill proudly display the tools of their trade. This tintype was made in about 1860, when New England farm women such as these were being replaced by Irish immigrant labor.

URBAN BUSINESSMEN

The market revolution hit American cities—the old seaports as well as the new marketing and manufacturing towns—with particular force. Here was little concern for creating a classless industrial society. Vastly wealthy men of finance, a new middle class that bought and sold an ever-growing range of consumer goods, and the impoverished women and men who produced those goods lived together in communities that unabashedly recognized the reality of social class.

The richest men were seaport merchants who had survived and prospered during the world wars that ended in 1815. They carried on as importers and exporters, took control of banks and insurance companies, and made great fortunes in urban real estate. Those in Boston constituted an elite, urbane, and responsible cluster of families known as the Boston Brahmins. The elite of Philadelphia was somewhat less unified and perhaps less responsible; that of New York even less. These families continued in international commerce, profiting mainly from cotton exports and from a vastly expanded range of imports.

Below the old mercantile elite (or, in the case of the new cities of the interior, at the top of society)

stood a growing middle class of wholesale and retail merchants, master craftsmen who had transformed themselves into manufacturers, and an army of lawyers, salesmen, auctioneers, clerks, bookkeepers, and accountants who took care of the paperwork for the new market society. At the head of this new middle class were the wholesale merchants of the seaports who bought hardware, crockery, and other commodities from importers and then sold them in smaller lots to storekeepers from the interior. The greatest concentration of wholesale firms was on Pearl Street in New York City. Slightly below them were the large processors of farm products, including the meatpackers of Cincinnati and the flour millers of Rochester, and large merchants and real estate dealers in the new cities of the interior. Another step down were specialized retail merchants who dealt in books, furniture, crockery, or some other consumer goods. In Hartford, Connecticut, for instance, the proportion of retailers who specialized in certain commodities rose from

LINK TO THE PAST

Lowell National Historic Park

http://www.nps.gov/lowe/loweweb/Lowell%20History/Millgirls.htm

This is the site for the Lowell National Historic Park, a partial restoration of the mill city of Lowell, Massachusetts. The historical text is by Thomas Dublin, the leading modern historian of Lowell, and it is accompanied by an extensive gallery of photographs and maps. Read the text, study the maps and pictures, and think about these questions:

1. Does Lowell in the period 1825–50 fit what you would expect to find in an early factory town? Why or why not?

2. What does the architecture of Lowell's factories, boarding houses, and churches say about the intentions of the owners? Were they simply putting up buildings to house their machines and workers? Or did they intend their buildings to stand for something more?

3. Why would a young farm woman in the 1820s or 1830s choose to go into the factories at Lowell? Why might she choose to stay away?

24 percent to 60 percent between 1792 and 1845. Alongside the merchants stood master craftsmen who had become manufacturers. With their workers busy in backrooms or in household workshops, they now called themselves shoe dealers and merchant tailors. At the bottom of this new commercial world were hordes of clerks, most of them young men who hoped to rise in the world. Indeed many of them—one study puts the figure at between 25 and 38 percent—did move up in society. Both in numbers and in the nature of the work, this white-collar army formed a new class created by the market revolution—particularly by the emergence of a huge consumer market in the countryside.

In the 1820s and 1830s the commercial classes transformed the look and feel of American cities. As retailing and manufacturing became separate activities (even in firms that did both), the merchants, salesmen, and clerks now worked in quiet offices on downtown business streets. The seaport merchants built counting rooms and decorated their warehouses in the "new countinghouse style." Both in the seaports and the new towns of the interior, impressive brick and glass storefronts appeared on the main streets. Perhaps the most striking monuments of the self-conscious new business society were the handsome retail arcades that began going up in the 1820s. Boston's Quincy Market (1825), a two-story arcade on Philadelphia's Chestnut Street (1827), and Rochester's four-story Reynolds Arcade (1828) provided consumers with comfortable, gracious space in which to shop.

METROPOLITAN INDUSTRIALIZATION

While businessmen were developing a new middle-class ethos, and while their families were flocking to the new retail stores to buy emblems of their status, the people who made the consumer goods were growing more numerous and at the same time disappearing from view. With the exception of textiles and a few other commodities, few goods were made in mechanized factories before the 1850s. Most of the clothes and shoes, brooms, hats, books, furniture, candy, and other goods available in country stores and city shops were made by hand. City merchants and master craftsmen met the growing demand by hiring more workers. The largest handi-

crafts—shoemaking, tailoring, and the building trades—were divided into skilled and semiskilled segments and farmed out to subcontractors who could turn a profit only by cutting labor costs. The result was the creation of an urban working class, not only in the big seaports and factory towns but in scores of milling and manufacturing towns throughout the North and the West.

The rise of New York City's ready-made clothing trade provides an example. In 1815 wealthy Americans wore tailor-made clothing; everyone else wore clothes sewn by women at home. In the 1820s the availability of cheap manufactured cloth and an expanding pool of cheap—largely female—labor, along with the creation of the southern and western markets, transformed New York City into the center of a national market in ready-made clothes. The first big market was in "Negro cottons"—graceless, hastily assembled shirts, pants, and sack dresses with which southern planters clothed their slaves. Within a few years New York manufacturers were sending dungarees and hickory shirts to western farmers and supplying shoddy, inexpensive clothing to the growing ranks of urban workers. By the 1830s many New York tailoring houses, including the storied Brooks Brothers, were offering fancier ready-made clothes to members of the new middle class.

High rents and costly real estate, together with the absence of water power, made it impossible to set up large factories in cities. The nature of the

CHARLES OAKFORD'S HAT STORE IN PHILADELPHIA, CIRCA 1855 Such specialized retail establishments (unlike the craftsmen's shops that preceded them) hid the process of manufacturing from customers' view.

clothing trade and the availability of cheap labor gave rise to a system of subcontracting that transformed needlework into the first "sweated" trade in America. Merchants kept a few skilled male tailors to take care of the custom trade, and to cut cloth into patterned pieces for ready-made clothing. The pieces were sent out, often by way of subcontractors, to needleworkers who sewed them together in their homes. Male tailors continued to do the finishing work on men's suits, but most of the work—on cheap goods destined for the South and West—fell to women who worked long hours for piece rates that ranged from 75 cents to $1.50 per week. In 1860, Brooks Brothers, which concentrated on the high end of the trade, kept 70 workers in its shops and used 2,000 to 3,000 outworkers, most of them women. Along with clothing, women in garrets and tenements manufactured the items with which the middle class decorated itself and its homes: embroidery, doilies, artificial flowers, fringe, tassels, fancy-bound books, and parasols. All provided work for ill-paid legions of female workers. In 1860 25,000 women (about one-fourth of the total workforce) worked in manufacturing jobs in New York City; fully two-thirds of them were in the clothing trades.

Other trades followed similar patterns. For example, northeastern shoes were made in uniform sizes and sent in barrels all over the country. Like tailoring, shoemaking was divided into skilled operations and time-consuming unskilled tasks. The relatively skilled and highly paid work of cutting and shaping the uppers was performed by men; the drudgery of sewing the pieces together went to low-paid women. In the shops of Lynn, Massachusetts, in the shoemakers' boardinghouses in Rochester and other new manufacturing cities of the interior, and in the cellars and garrets of New York City, skilled shoemakers performed the most difficult work for taskmasters who passed the work along to subcontractors who controlled poorly paid, unskilled workers. Skilled craftsmen could earn as much as two dollars a day making custom boots and shoes. Men shaping uppers in boardinghouses earned a little more than half of that; women binders could work a full week and earn as little as 50 cents. In this as in other trades, wage rates and gendered tasks reflected the old family division of labor, which was based on the assumption that female workers lived with an income-earning husband or father. In fact, increasing numbers of them were young women living alone or older women who had been widowed, divorced, or abandoned—often with small children.

In their offices, counting rooms, and shops, members of the new middle class entertained notions of gentility based on the distinction between manual and nonmanual work. Lowly clerks and wealthy merchants prided themselves on the fact that they worked with their heads and not their hands. They fancied that their entrepreneurial and managerial skills were making the market revolution happen, while manual workers simply performed tasks thought up by the middle class. The old distinction between proprietorship and dependence—a distinction that had placed master craftsmen and independent tradesmen, along with farm-owning yeomen, among the respectable "middling sort"—disappeared. The men and women of an emerging working class struggled to create dignity and a sense of public worth in a society that hid them from view and defined them as "hands."

THE MARKET REVOLUTION IN THE SOUTH

With the end of war in 1815, the cotton belt of the South expanded dramatically. The resumption of international trade, the revival of textile production in Britain and on the continent, and the emergence of factory production in the northeastern United States encouraged southern planters to extend the short-staple cotton lands of South Carolina and Georgia into a belt that would stretch across the Old Southwest and beyond the Mississippi into Texas and Arkansas. The speed with which that happened startled contemporaries: By 1834 the new southwestern states of Alabama, Mississippi, and Louisiana grew more than half the U.S. cotton crop. By 1859 these states, along with Georgia, produced fully 79 percent of American cotton.

The southwestern plantation belt produced stupendous amounts of cotton. In 1810 the South produced 178,000 bales of ginned cotton—more than 59 times the 3,000 bales it had produced in 1790. By 1820 production stood at 334,000 bales. As southwestern cotton lands opened, production jumped to 1.35 million bales in 1840 and to 4.8 million on the eve of the Civil War. Over these years cotton accounted for one-half to two-thirds of the value of all U.S. exports. The South produced three-fourths of the world supply of cotton—a commodity that, more than any other, was the raw material of industrialization in Britain and Europe and, increasingly, in the northeastern United States.

THE ORGANIZATION OF SLAVE LABOR

The plantations of the cotton belt were among the most intensely commercialized farms in the world. Although some plantations grew supplementary cash crops and produced their own food, many grew nothing but cotton—a practice that produced huge profits in good years but in bad years sent planters into debt and forced them to sell slaves and land. Nearly all of the plantation owners, from the proudest grandee to the ambitious farmer with a few slaves, organized their labor in ways that maximized production and reinforced the dominance of the white men who owned the farms.

Cotton, which requires a long growing season and a lot of attention, was well suited to slave labor and to the climate of the Deep South. After the land was cleared and plowed, it was set out in individual plants. Laborers weeded the fields with hoes throughout the hot, humid growing season. In the fall, the cotton ripened unevenly. In a harvest season that lasted up to two months, pickers swept through the fields repeatedly, selecting only the ripe bolls. Plantations that grew their own food cultivated large cornfields and vegetable gardens and kept large numbers of hogs. To cope with diverse growing seasons and killing times that overlapped with the cotton cycle, planters created complex labor systems.

On a large plantation in Louisiana in the 1850s, Frederick Law Olmstead, a New York landscape architect, watched a parade of slaves going into the fields. First came the hoe gang: "forty of the largest and strongest women I ever saw together: they were all in a single uniform dress of bluish check stuff, and skirts reaching little below the knee; their legs and feet were bare; they carried themselves loftily, each with a hoe sloping over the shoulder and walking with a free powerful swing, like Zouaves on the march." Following the hoe gang came the "cavalry, thirty strong, mostly men, but some women, two of whom rode astride, on the plow mules."

Although this slave force was larger than most, its organization was familiar to every southerner: Gangs of women wielded the hoes, and men did the plowing, accompanied, especially during the busiest times, by strong women who rode "astride" (and not, like white ladies, sidesaddle). The division of labor by sex was standard: Even at harvest festivals teams of men shucked the corn while women prepared the meal and the after-supper dance. During the harvest, when every slave was in the fields, men tended to work beside men, women beside women. Most of the house slaves were women, and female slaves often worked under the direction of the plantation mistress, seeing to the dairy cattle, chickens and geese, and tending vegetable gardens and orchards.

Although black women routinely worked in southern fields, white women did so only on the poorest farms and only at the busiest times of the year. Like their northern cousins, they took care of the poultry and cattle and the vegetable gardens—and not the profit-oriented fields. As the larger farms grew into plantations, white women took on the task of supervising the household slaves instead of doing the work themselves. According to northern visitors, this association of labor with slavery encouraged laziness among southern whites and robbed work of the dignity it enjoyed in other parts of the country.

PATERNALISM

On the whole, the exploitation of slave labor after 1820 became both more systematic and more humane. An estimated 55 percent of southern slaves spent all their time cultivating cotton, and it was brutal work by any standard. The arduous chore of transforming wilderness into cotton land demanded steady work in gangs, as did the yearly cotton cycle itself. Planters paid close attention to labor discipline: They supervised the work more closely than in the past, tried (often unsuccessfully) to substitute gang labor for the task system, and forcibly "corrected" slaves whose work was slow or sloppy. At the same time, however, planters clothed the new discipline within a larger attempt to make North American slavery into a system that was both

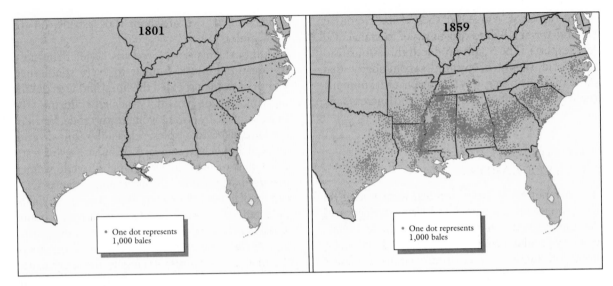

COTTON PRODUCTION, 1801 AND 1859

paternalistic and humane. Food and clothing seem to have improved, and individual cabins for slave families became standard. State laws often forbade the more brutal forms of discipline, and they uniformly demanded that slaves have Sundays off. More and more, the slaves spent that day listening to Christian missionaries provided by the planters.

The systematic paternalism on 19th-century farms and plantations sprang from both planter self-interest and a genuine attempt to exert a kindly, paternal control over slaves that planters uniformly called "our people" or "our family, black and white." The Louisiana planter Bennet H. Barrow insisted that the master must make the slave "as comfortable at home as possible, affording him what is essentially necessary for his happiness—you must provide for him your self and by that means creat[e] in him a habit of perfect dependence on you." On the whole, slaves endured the discipline and accepted the food, clothing, time off, and religious instruction—but used all of them to serve themselves and not the masters (see chapter 10).

HAULING THE WHOLE WEEK'S PICKING William Henry Brown made this collage of a slave harvest crew near Vicksburg, Mississippi, in 1842. The rigors of the harvest put everyone, including small children, into the fields.

In spite of all, slaves' material standards rose. One rough indicator is physical height. On the eve of the Civil War, southern slaves averaged about an inch shorter than northern whites, but they were fully three inches taller than newly imported Africans, two inches taller than slaves on the Caribbean island of Trinidad, and one inch taller than British Marines. Slaves suffered greater infant mortality than whites, but those who survived infancy lived out "normal" life spans. The most telling evidence is that although Brazil, Cuba, and other slave societies had to import Africans to make up for the deaths of slaves, the slave population of the United States increased threefold—from 1,191,354 to 3,953,760—between 1810 and 1860. Imports of new Africans were banned after 1808 (and runaways outnumbered new Africans who were smuggled into the country); the increase reflected that—alone among slave populations of the Western Hemisphere—births outnumbered deaths among North American slaves.

YEOMEN AND PLANTERS

Cotton brought economies of scale: Planters with big farms and many slaves operated more efficiently and more profitably than farmers with fewer resources. And as the price of slaves and good land rose, fewer and fewer owners shared in the profits of the cotton economy, and wealth became more concentrated. Good farmland with ready access to markets was dominated by large plantations. By 1861 only one in four southern white households owned slaves. The market revolution had commercialized southern agriculture, but a shrinking proportion of the region's white population shared in the benefits. The result was not simply an unequal distribution of wealth, but the creation of a dual economy: plantations at the commercial center and a white yeomanry on the fringes.

Some small farmers remained in the plantation counties—most of them on poor, hilly land far from navigable rivers. They tended to be commercial farmers, growing a few bales of cotton with family labor and perhaps a slave or two. Many of them were poor relatives of prosperous plantation owners. They voted the great planters into office, and used their cotton gins and tapped into their marketing networks. Some of them worked as over-seers for their wealthy neighbors, sold them food, and served on local slave patrols. Economic disparities between planters and farmers in the plantation belt continued to widen, but the farmers remained tied to the cotton economy and its economic and social imperatives.

Most small farmers, however, lived away from the plantations in what was called the up-country: the eastern slopes of the Appalachians from the Chesapeake through Georgia, the western slopes of the mountains in Kentucky and Tennessee, the pine-covered hill country of northern Mississippi and Alabama, parts of Texas and Louisiana, most of the Ozark Plateau in Missouri and Arkansas. All of these lands were too high, cold, isolated, and heavily wooded to support plantation crops. Here the farmers built a yeoman society that shared many of the characteristics of the 18th-century countryside, North and South (see chapter 7). But while northern farmers commercialized, their southern cousins continued in a household- and neighborhood-centered agriculture until the Civil War and beyond. Indeed many southern farmers stayed outside the market almost entirely. The mountaineers of the southern Appalachians sent a trickle of livestock and timber out of their neighborhoods, but the mountains remained largely outside the market until the coming of big-business coal mines in the late 19th century. Moreover, farmers in large parts of the up-country South preferred to raise livestock instead of growing cotton or tobacco. They planted cornfields and let their pigs run loose in the woods and on unfenced private land. In late summer and fall they rounded up the animals and sold them to drovers who conducted cross-country drives and sold the animals to flatland merchants and planters. These hill-country yeomen lived off a market with which they had little firsthand experience. It was a way of life that sustained some of the most fiercely independent neighborhoods in the country.

YEOMEN AND THE MARKET

A larger group of southern yeomen practiced mixed farming for household subsistence and neighborhood exchange, with the surplus sent to market. Most of these farmers owned their own land. Indeed the settlement of new lands in the old back-country and the southwestern states reversed the

18th-century growth of white tenancy (see chapter 7). Few of these farmers kept slaves. In the counties of upland Georgia, for instance, only 10 to 30 percent of households had slaves.

These farmers practiced a complicated system of "subsistence plus" agriculture. Northern yeomen before 1815 had grown grain and livestock with which they fed their families and traded with neighbors. Whatever was left over they sent to market, but cotton, like tobacco and other southern cash crops, was not a food; it contributed nothing to family subsistence. Most middling and poor farmers played it safe: They put most of their land into subsistence crops and livestock, cultivating only a few acres of cotton. They devoted more acreage to cotton as transportation made markets more accessible—particularly when railroads penetrated upland neighborhoods in the 1850s—but few southern yeomen allowed themselves to become wholly dependent on the market. The income from a few bales of cotton paid their debts and taxes and bought coffee, tea, sugar, tobacco, cloth, and shoes, but they continued to enter and leave the market at will, for their own purposes. The market served their interests; it seldom dominated them.

This way of life discouraged acquisitiveness and ambition. Because few farms were self-sufficient, the yeomen farmers routinely traded labor and goods with each other. In the plantation counties, such cooperation tended to reinforce the power of planters who put some of their resources at the disposal of their poorer neighbors. In the up-country, cooperation reinforced neighborliness. As one upland Georgian remarked, "Borrowing . . . was neighboring." Debts contracted within the network of kin and neighbors were generally paid in kind or in labor, and creditors often allowed their neighbors' debts to go unpaid for years.

Among southern neighborly restraints on entrepreneurialism, none was more distinctive than the region's attitude toward fences. Northerners never tired of comparing their neatly fenced farms with the dilapidated or absent fences of the South. In the bourgeois North, well-maintained fences were considered a sign of ambitious, hardworking farmers and the poor fences of the South were considered a sign of laziness. Actually, the scarcity of fences in most southern neighborhoods reflected local custom and state law. Georgia, for instance, required farmers to fence their planted fields but not the rest of their land. In country neighborhoods where families fished and hunted for food, and where livestock roamed freely, fences conflicted with a local economy that required neighborhood use of privately owned land. In this sense, the northerners were right: The lack of fences in the South reflected neighborhood constraints on the private use of private property, and thus on individual acquisitiveness and ambition. Such constraints, however, were necessary to the subsistence of families and neighborhoods as they were organized in the upland South.

A BALANCE SHEET: THE PLANTATION AND SOUTHERN DEVELOPMENT

The owners of the South's large farms were among the richest men in the Western Hemisphere. In 1860 the 12 wealthiest counties in the United States were in the South; the wealthiest of all was Adams County, Mississippi, on the Mississippi River. Southern wealth, however, was concentrating in fewer and fewer hands. The slaves whose labor created the wealth owned nothing. As much as one-third of southern white families lived in poverty, and a declining proportion of the others owned slaves. In 1830, some 36 percent of southern white households had owned at least one slave. By 1850 the percentage had dropped to 31 percent; by 1860 to 26 percent. And huge disparities existed even among the slaveholding minority; in 1860 only one-fifth of the slaveholders (1 in 20 white families) owned 20 or more slaves, thus crossing the generally acknowledged line that separated "farmers" from "planters." At the apex of southern society were a few great planters: Between 2 and 3 percent of southern white men owned half of all the southern slaves.

The widening gap between planters and yeomen created a dangerous fault line in southern politics (see chapter 11). In economic terms, the concentration of wealth in the hands of a few planters had profound effects on how the market revolution affected the region. Much of the white population remained marginal to the market economy. A South Carolina yeoman who raised cattle claimed, "I never spent more than ten dollars a year, which was for salt, nails, and the like. Nothing to wear, eat or drink was purchased, as my farm provided all." Whereas in the

A COTTON PRESS Mule-driven presses such as the one shown here packed southern cotton into bales for easier transport to market. The cotton was pressed into a frame by a wooden screw carved from a whole tree.

North the rural demand for credit, banking facilities, farm tools, clothing, and other consumer goods fueled a revolution in commerce, finance, and industry, the South remained a poor market for manufactured goods. The slaves wore cheap cloth made in the Northeast, and the planters furnished themselves and their homes with finery from Europe. In the North the exchange of farm produce for finished goods was creating self-sustaining economic growth by the 1840s, but the South continued to export its plantation staples and to build only those factories, commercial institutions, and cities that served the plantation. In the North the market revolution produced commercial agriculture, a specialized labor force, and technological innovation. In the South it simply produced more slavery.

Not that the South neglected technological innovation and agricultural improvement. Southerners developed Eli Whitney's hand-operated cotton gin into equipment capable of performing complex milling operations; they made many significant improvements in steamboat design as well. They also developed—among other things—the cotton press, a machine with a huge wooden screw powered by horses or mules, used to compress ginned cotton into tight bales for shipping. Jordan Goree, a slave craftsman in Huntsville, Texas, won a reputation for being able to carve whole trees into perfect screws for these machines. Yet the few such innovations had to do with the processing and shipping of cotton rather than with its production. The truth is that cotton was a labor-intensive crop that discouraged innovation. Moreover, plantation slaves often resisted their enslavement by sabotaging expensive tools and draft animals, scattering manure in haphazard ways, and passively resisting innovations that would have added to their drudgery. Cotton fields continued to be cultivated by clumsy, mule-drawn plows that barely scratched the soil, by women wielding hoes, and by gangs who harvested the crop by hand.

Southern state governments spent little on internal improvements. A Virginia canal linked the flour mills at Richmond with inland grain fields, and another connected Chesapeake Bay with the National Road, but planters in the cotton belt had ready access to the South's magnificent system of navigable rivers, while upland whites saw little need for expensive, state-supported internal improvements. Nor did the South build cities. In 1800, about 82 percent of the southern workforce and about 70 percent of the northern workforce were employed in agriculture. By 1860 only 40 percent of the northern workforce was so employed, but in the South the proportion had risen to 84 percent. The South used its canals and railroads mainly to move plantation staples to towns that transshipped them out of the region. Southern cities were located on the periphery of the region and served as transportation depots for plantation crops. River cities such as Louisville, Memphis, and St. Louis were little more than stopping places for steamboats. The great seaports of New Orleans, Charleston, and Baltimore sometimes shipped cotton directly to British and European markets. More often, however, they sent it by coasting vessel to New York City, where it was transshipped to foreign ports.

Thus while the North and the Northwest developed towns and cities throughout their regions, southern cities continued to be few, and to perform the colonial functions of 18th century seaport towns. Southern businessmen turned to New York City for credit, insurance, and coastal and export shipping. From New York they ordered finished goods for the southern market. *DeBow's Review*, the principal business journal of the South, reported that South Carolina storekeepers who bought goods from Charleston wholesalers concealed that fact and claimed they had bought them directly

Gone with the Wind (1939)

Directed by Victor Fleming. Starring Vivian Leigh, Clark Gable, Hattie McDaniel, Butterfly McQueen, Olivia de Haviland, Leslie Howard.

Hollywood filmed Margaret Mitchell's hit novel, *Gone with the Wind*, in 1939. Like the silent *Birth of a Nation* (see chapter 17), it is both a historically silly portrayal of the Old South and a landmark in film history. The love story between Scarlet O'Hara (Vivian Leigh) and Rhett Butler (Clark Gable) is a great and enduring screen romance, and the plantation sets, the re-creation and burning of Atlanta, the great panorama of wounded and dead Confederate soldiers, and much more are rightly admired by students of the movies—though they are a bit less impressive in these days of computer graphics.

Underneath the soap-opera story line and the cinematic triumphs, however, the legend of the Old South sets the tone. The plantation South was, we are told at the beginning, "a land of Cavaliers and Cotton Fields," where "gallantry took its last bow." The whites—with the exception of a philandering, northern-born overseer—are all ladies and gentlemen who spend their time at balls and barbecues. The men are all brave and honorable (or at least committed to being so), and they love the land—"the only thing that lasts." The young women are impatient with politics and interested only in clothes and men (a shallow and gossipy ideal that will affront students born much after 1939), and the mature women help to preserve and preside over, as one of them puts it, "a whole world that wants only to be graceful and beautiful."

The slaves, of course, enjoy all of this. They help the girls prepare for balls, fan them while they take naps, and assume the rightness of the world that holds them in slavery. Scarlet's maid (Hattie McDaniel) is a bossy and caring servant who is proud of her "family" and compares people whom she dislikes to "white trash" and "field hands." The black field boss marches happily with the other male slaves to dig trenches for Confederate troops, telling Scarlet, "We's gonna dig for the South."

In one of the scenes that audiences found most moving, Scarlet delivers a baby during the fall of Atlanta with the hysterical and inept help of a slave girl (Butterfly McQueen). It is in this ordeal that Scarlet begins to grow up, though the film never quite makes the connection between feminine maturity and usefulness and the destruction of the Old South. The slave girl, on the other hand, remains a girl. "But,

from New York City. For it was well known that New York provided better goods at lower prices than any supplier in the South. DeBow himself testified to the superior skill and diversification of the North when, after trying several New Orleans sources, he awarded the contract for his *Review* to a northern printer. That was not surprising in any case, because DeBow received three-fourths of his income from northern advertisers. In all, southerners estimated that 40 cents of every dollar produced by cotton remained in the Northeast.

CONCLUSION

In 1858 James H. Hammond, a slaveholding senator from South Carolina, asked:

What would happen if no cotton was furnished for three years? . . . England would topple headlong and carry the whole civilized world with her save the South. No, you dare not make war on cotton. No power on earth dares to make war on cotton. Cotton is king.

Along with other planter-politicians, Hammond argued, as Jefferson had argued in 1807, that farmers at the fringes of the world market economy could coerce the commercial-industrial center. He was wrong. The commitment to cotton and slavery had not only isolated the South politically, it had also deepened the South's dependence on the world's financial and industrial centers.

The North and West underwent a qualitative market revolution after 1815—a revolution that

Miss Scarlet," she shrieks, "I don' know nuthin' 'bout birthin' no baby!"

Gone with the Wind is both a wondrous movie and a reminder of how long the plantation legend persisted. Indeed, continuing sales of the novel and periodic revivals of the movie suggest that it is not yet dead. Students who view the film and find themselves attracted to the legend might examine their reaction and ask themselves why.

Gone with the Wind (1939) is both a silly portrayal of the Old South and a landmark in film history. It also features one of the great and enduring screen romances, between Rhett Butler and Scarlet O'Hara.

enriched both, and that moved the Northeast from the old colonial periphery (the suppliers of food and raw materials) into the core (the suppliers of manufactured goods and financing) of the world market economy. In contrast, the South, by exporting plantation staples in exchange for imported goods, worked itself deeper and deeper into dependence—now as much upon the American Northeast as upon the old colonial rulers in London.

Suggested Readings begin on page SR-1.
For Web activities and resources
related to this chapter, go to
http://www.harcourtcollege.com/history.murrin

CHAPTER 10

TOWARD AN AMERICAN CULTURE

P. T. BARNUM AND TOM THUMB

Here is Phineas Taylor Barnum, America's greatest showman, together with the sprightly midget Tom Thumb—his first hugely successful attraction. The photograph conveys the combination of chicanery, farce, strangeness, and straight-faced respectability that made Barnum (but not Tom Thumb) a rich man.

Americans after 1815 experienced wave after wave of social and cultural change. Territorial expansion, the market revolution, and the spread of plantation slavery uprooted Americans and broke old social patterns. Americans in these years reinvented family life. They created distinctively American forms of popular literature and art, and they found new ways of having fun. They flocked to evangelical revivals—meetings designed to produce religious conversions and led by preachers who were trained to that task—in which they revived and remade American religious life.

The emerging American culture was more or less uniformly republican, capitalist, and Protestant. Still, different kinds of Americans made different cultures out of the revolutionary inheritance, the market revolution, and revival religion. Southern farmers and their northern cousins thought differently about fatherhood, motherhood, and the proper way to make a family. Northeastern businessmen and southern planters agreed that economic progress was indeed progress, but they differed radically on its moral implications. Slaveholders, slaves, factory hands, rich and poor farmers, and middle-class women all heard the same Bible stories and learned different lessons. The result, visible from the 1830s onward, was an American national culture composed largely of subcultures based on region, class, and race.

This chapter will focus on the following major questions:

- What were the central cultural maxims of the emerging middle class of the North?
- Within the North, what were the alternatives to middle-class culture?
- What was the nature of honor among southern whites, and how did it relate to southern families and southern religion?
- Describe the nature and limits of the cultural life that slaves made for themselves within the confines of slavery.

THE NORTHERN MIDDLE CLASS

"The most valuable class in any community," declared the poet-journalist Walt Whitman in 1858, "is the middle class." At that time, the term "middle class" (and the social group that it described) was no more than 30 or 40 years old. The market revolution since 1815 had created new towns and cities and transformed the old ones, and it had turned the rural North into a landscape of family-owned commercial farms. Those who claimed the title "middle class" were largely the new kinds of proprietors made by the market revolution—city and country merchants, master craftsmen who had turned themselves into manufacturers, and the mass of market-oriented farmers.

A disproportionate number of them were New Englanders. New England was the first center of factory production, and southern New England farms were thoroughly commercialized by the 1830s. Yankee migrants dominated the commercial heartland of western New York and the northern regions of the Northwest. Even in the seaport cities (New York's Pearl Street wholesale houses are a prime example) businessmen from New England were often at the center of economic innovation. This Yankee middle class invented cultural forms that became the core of an emerging business civilization. They upheld the autonomous and morally accountable individual against the claims of traditional neighborhoods and traditional families. They devised an intensely private, mother-centered domestic life. Most of all, they adhered to a reformed Yankee Protestantism whose moral imperatives became the foundation of American middle-class culture.

THE EVANGELICAL BASE

In November 1830 the evangelist Charles Grandison Finney preached in Rochester, New York, to a church full of middle-class men and women. Most of them were transplanted New Englanders, the heirs of what was left of Yankee Calvinism. In their ministers' weekly sermons, in the formal articles of faith drawn up by their churches, and in the set prayers their children memorized, they reaffirmed the old Puritan beliefs in providence and original sin. The earthly social order (the fixed relations of power and submission between men and women, rich and poor, children and parents, and so on) was necessary because humankind was innately sinful and prone to selfishness and disorder. Christians must obey the rules governing their station in life; attempts to rearrange the social order were both sinful and doomed to failure.

Yet while they reaffirmed those conservative Puritan beliefs in church, the men and women in

CHARLES FINNEY The evangelist, pictured here at the height of his preaching power in the 1830s, was remarkably successful at organizing the new middle-class culture into a millennial crusade.

Finney's audience routinely ignored them in their daily lives. The benefits accruing from the market revolution were clearly the result of human effort. Just as clearly, they added up to "improvement" and "progress." And as middle-class Christians increasingly envisioned an improved material and social world, the doctrines of human inability and natural depravity, along with faith in divine providence, made less and less sense.

To such an audience Charles Finney preached the organizing principle of northern middle-class evangelicalism: "God," he insisted, "has made man a moral free agent." Neither the social order, the troubles of this world, nor the spiritual state of individuals were divinely ordained. People would make themselves and the world better by choosing right over wrong, although they would choose right only after an evangelical conversion experience in which they submitted their rebellious wills to the will of God. It was a religion that valued individual holiness over a permanent and sacred social order. It made the spiritual nature of individuals a matter of prayer, submission, and choice. Thus it gave Christians the means—through the spread of revivals—to bring on the thousand-year reign of Christianity that they believed would precede the Second Coming of Christ. As Charles Finney told his Rochester audience, "If [Christians] were united all over the world the Millennium might be brought about in three months."

Charles Finney's Rochester revival—a six-month marathon of preaching and praying—was no isolated event. Yankee evangelists had been moving toward Finney's formulation since the turn of the 19th century. Like Finney, they borrowed revival techniques from the Methodists (weeklong meetings, meetings in which women prayed in public, an "anxious bench" for the most likely converts), but toned them down for their own more "respectable"

and affluent audience. They used democratic methods and preached a message of individualism and free agency, but, middle-class evangelicals retained the Puritans' Old Testament sense of cosmic history: They enlisted personal holiness and spiritual democracy in a fight to the finish between the forces of good and the forces of evil in this world. Building on the imperatives of the new evangelicalism, the entrepreneurial families of the East and Northwest constructed an American middle-class culture after 1825 based, paradoxically, on an intensely private and emotionally loaded family life and an aggressively reformist stance toward the world at large.

DOMESTICITY

The Yankee middle class made crucial distinctions between the home and the world—distinctions that grew from the disintegration of the old patriarchal household economy. Men in cities and towns now went off to work, leaving wives and children to spend the day at home. Even commercializing farmers made a clear distinction between (male) work that was oriented toward markets and (female) work that was tied to household maintenance (see chapter 9). The new middle-class evangelicalism encouraged this division of domestic labor. The public world of politics and economic exchange, said the preachers, was the proper sphere of men; women, on the other hand, were to exercise new kinds of moral influence within households. As one evangelical put it:

> Each has a distinct sphere of duty—the husband to go out into the world—the wife to superintend the household. . . . Man profits from connection with the world, but women never; their constituents [sic] of mind are different. The one is raised and exalted by mingled association. The purity of the other is maintained in silence and seclusion.

The result was a feminization of domestic life. In the old yeoman-artisan republic, the fathers who owned property, headed households, and governed family labor were lawgivers and disciplinarians. They were God's delegated authorities on earth, assigned the task of governing women, children, and other underlings who were mired in original sin. Middle-class evangelicals raised new spiritual possibilities for women and children. Mothers replaced fathers as the principal child-rearers, and they enlisted the doctrines of free agency and individual moral responsibility in that task. Middle-class mothers raised their children with love and reason, not fear. They sought to develop the children's conscience and their capacity to love, to teach them to make good moral choices, and to prepare themselves for conversion and a lifetime of Christian service.

Middle-class mothers could take up these tasks because they could concentrate their efforts on household duties and because they had fewer children than their mothers or grandmothers had had. In Utica, New York, for example, women who entered their childbearing years in the 1830s averaged only 3.6 births apiece; those who had started families only 10 years earlier averaged 5.1. Housewives also spaced their pregnancies differently. Unlike their forebears, who gave birth to a child about once every two years throughout their childbearing years, Utica's middle-class housewives had their children at five-year intervals, which meant that they could give each child close attention. As a result, households were quieter and less crowded; children learned from their mothers how to govern themselves and seldom experienced the rigors of patriarchal family government. Thus mothers assumed responsibility for nurturing the children

who would be carriers of the new middle-class culture—and fathers, ministers, and other authorities recognized the importance of that job. Edward Kirk, a minister in Albany, insisted that "the hopes of human society are to be found in the character, in the views, and in the conduct of mothers."

The new ethos of moral free agency was mirrored in the Sunday schools. When Sunday schools first appeared in the 1790s, their purpose was to teach working-class children to read and write by having them copy long passages from the Bible. Their most heavily publicized accomplishments were feats of memory: In 1823 Jane Wilson, a 13-year-old in Rochester, memorized 1,650 verses of scripture; Pawtucket, Rhode Island, claimed a mill girl who could recite the entire New Testament.

After the revivals of the 1820s and 1830s, the emphasis shifted from promoting feats of memory to preparing children's souls for conversion. Middle-class children were now included in the schools, corporal punishment was forbidden, and Sunday school teachers now tried to develop the moral sensibilities of their charges. They had the children read a few Bible verses each week and led them in a discussion of the moral lessons conveyed by the text. The proudest achievements of the new

A MIDDLE-CLASS NEW ENGLAND FAMILY AT HOME, 1837 The room is carpeted and comfortably furnished. Father reads his newspaper; books rest on the table. Mother entertains their only child, and a kitten joins the family circle. This is the domestic foundation of sentimental culture on display.

schools were children who made good moral choices. Thus Sunday schools became training grounds in free agency and moral accountability—a transformation that made sense only in a sentimental world where children could be trusted to make moral choices.

SENTIMENTALITY

Improvements in the printing, distribution, and marketing of books led to an outpouring of popular literature, much of it directed at the middle class. There were cookbooks, etiquette books, manuals on housekeeping, sermons, and sentimental novels—many of them written, and most of them read, by women. The works of popular religious writers such as Lydia Sigourney, Lydia Maria Child, and Timothy Shay Arthur found their way into thousands of middle-class homes. Sarah Josepha Hale, whose *Godey's Lady's Book* was the first mass-circulation magazine for women, acted as an arbiter of taste not only in furniture, clothing, and food but in sentiments and ideas. Upon reviewing the cloying, sentimental literature read in middle-class homes, Nathaniel Hawthorne was not the only "serious" writer to deplore a literary marketplace dominated by "a damned mob of scribbling women."

Hawthorne certainly had economic reason for complaint. Sentimental novels written by women outsold by wide margins his *Scarlet Letter* and *House of Seven Gables*, Ralph Waldo Emerson's essays, Henry David Thoreau's *Walden*, Herman Melville's *Moby Dick*, Walt Whitman's *Leaves of Grass*, and other works of the "American Renaissance" of the 1850s. Susan Warner's *The Wide, Wide World* broke all sales records when it appeared in 1850. Harriet Beecher Stowe's *Uncle Tom's Cabin* (1852) broke the records set by Warner. In 1854, Maria Cummin's *The Lamplighter* (the direct target of Hawthorne's lament about scribbling women) took its place as the third of the monster best-sellers of the early 1850s.

These sentimental novels upheld the new middle-class domesticity. They sacralized the middle-class home and the trials and triumphs of Christian women. The action in each takes place indoors, usually in the kitchen or parlor, and the heroines are women (in Stowe's book, docile slave Christians are included) who live under worldly patriarchy but who triumph through submission to God. The stories embody spiritual struggle, the renunciation of greed and desire, and mother love. The home is a shrine (and keeping it clean is a sacrament) that is juxtaposed to the marketplace and the world of competition, brutality, and power. Unlike the female characters in British and European novels of the time, the women in these American novels are intelligent, generous persons who grow in strength and independence. (The French visitor Alexis de Tocqueville commented that European women "almost think it a privilege to appear futile, weak, and timid. The women of America never lay claim to rights of that sort.")

In sentimental domestic fiction, women assume the role of evangelical ministers, demonstrating Christian living by precept, example, and moral persuasion. Female moral influence, wielded by women who had given themselves to God, is at war with the male world of politics and the marketplace—areas of power, greed, and moral compromise. Although few sentimental writers shared the views of the feminist Margaret Fuller, they would have agreed with her on the place of religion in women's lives. "I wish women to live first for God's sake," she wrote. "Then she will not make an imperfect man her God, and thus sink to idolatry."

The most successful sentimental novel of the 1850s was Harriet Beecher Stowe's *Uncle Tom's Cabin*. Stowe's book was also the most powerful antislavery tract of these years—in part because it successfully dramatized the moral and political imperatives of the northern middle class. At its core, *Uncle Tom's Cabin* indicts slavery as a system of absolute power at odds with domesticity and Christian love. The novel reverses the power relations of this world: In it, the home, and particularly the kitchen, is the ultimate locus of good, whereas law, politics, and the marketplace—the whole realm of men—are moved to the periphery and defined as unfeeling destroyers. Based solidly in revival Christianity, the novel lambastes the rational calculation, greed, and power hunger of the "real world" that was made and governed by white men, and upholds domestic space filled with women, slaves, and children who gain spiritual power through submission to Christ. The two most telling scenes—the deaths of the Christian slave Uncle Tom and the perfect child Eva

St. Claire—reenact the crucifixion of Jesus. Uncle Tom prays for his tormentors as he is beaten to death, and little Eva extracts promises of Christian behavior from her deathbed. Both are powerless, submissive characters who die in order to redeem a fallen humankind. Their deaths are thus Christian triumphs that convert the powerful and hasten the millennial day when the world will be governed by a feminized Christian love and not by male power.

Thus *Uncle Tom's Cabin* and other popular sentimental novels were not, as Hawthorne and his friends believed, frivolous fairy tales into which housewives retreated from the "real" world. They were subversive depictions of a higher spiritual reality that would move the feminine ethos of the Christian home to the center of civilization. As we shall see in chapter 11, that vision drove an organized public assault on irreligion, drunkenness, prostitution, slavery, and other practices and institutions that substituted passion and force for Christian love, an assault that tried to "domesticate" the world and shape it in the image of the middle-class evangelical home.

FINE ARTS

Educated Americans of the postrevolutionary generation associated the fine arts with the sensuality, extravagance, and artificiality of European courts and European Catholicism. To them, the fine arts were the products of despotism and had nothing to offer the republicans of America. In making government buildings and monuments, building expensive homes, and painting portraits of wealthy and powerful men, American artists copied the classic simplicity of ancient Greece and Rome—republican styles tested by time and free of any hint of sensuality or luxury.

In the 1820s and 1830s, however, educated Americans began to view literature and the arts more favorably. American nationalists began to demand an American art that could compete with the arts of the despotic Old World. At the same time, evangelical Christianity and sentimental culture glorified a romantic cult of feeling that was, within its limits, far more receptive to aesthetic experience than Calvinism and the more spartan forms of republicanism had been. Finally, the more comfort-

able and educated Americans fell into a relationship with nature that called out for aesthetic expression. From the beginnings of English settlement, Americans had known that their civilization would be made in a contest with wilderness—wilderness they saw as dark, filled with demons, and implacably hostile to civilization. After 1815, with the Indians finally broken and scattered, with the agricultural frontier penetrating deep into the interior, and with improvements in transportation and communications annihilating distance, educated northeasterners became certain that Americans would win their age-old contest with nature—that civilization would supplant wilderness on the North American continent. The result was a multivoiced conversation about the relations between nature and civilization—a conversation that occupied a large portion of a new American art and literature that rose between 1830 and the Civil War.

NATURE AND ART

Much of the new American art was practical, to be lived in and used. Andrew Jackson Downing and other landscape designers and architects created beautiful country cottages surrounded by gardens—domestic environments that used art as an avenue to the grand lessons of nature. At the same time, cities began to build cemeteries in the surrounding countryside, replacing the old ill-tended graveyards at the center of town. In 1831 several wealthy Boston families put up the money to build Mount Auburn Cemetery, the first graveyard designed to serve as a cultural institution. Mount Auburn was situated on rolling ground, with footpaths following the contours of the land. Much of the natural vegetation was left untouched, and wildflowers were planted to supplement it. The headstones, which had to be approved by a board of directors, were small and dignified. Mount Auburn became a kind of public park in which nature's annual cycle of death and renewal taught chastening and reassuring lessons to the living. Copied in Brooklyn, Rochester, and other northern cities, the rural cemeteries embodied the faith that nature could teach moral lessons, particularly if nature was shaped and made available to humankind through art.

Not surprisingly, the leading artists of this generation were landscape painters. Thomas Cole, in his "Essay on American Scenery" (1835), reminded readers that the most distinctive feature of America was its wilderness:

> In civilized Europe the primitive features of scenery have long since been destroyed or modified. . . . And to this cultivated state our western world is fast approaching; but nature is still predominant, and there are those who regret that with the improvements of cultivation the sublimity of the wilderness should pass away; for those scenes of solitude from which the hand of nature has never been lifted, affect the mind with a more deep toned emotion than aught which the hand of man has touched. Amid them the consequent associations are of God the creator—they are his undefiled works, and the mind is cast into contemplation of eternal things.

In what became a manifesto of American intellectual and aesthetic life, Cole had found God in nature (previous generations had been taught to see wilderness as the devil's domain), and thus endowed art that depicted nature with religious purpose. Among educated persons, art was no longer subversive of the Protestant republic; done right, it was a bulwark of good citizenship and true religion. American housewives who planted and tended flower gardens were acting on that premise. So were the landscape architects who designed rural cemeteries and public and private gardens; the philosopher Ralph Waldo Emerson, who told Americans that "every natural process is a version of a moral sentence"; and Emerson's friend Henry David Thoreau, who lived in the woods and loved not only nature's beauties but bad weather, wars between insects, and the corpses of horses in an attempt, as he put it, to live "deliberately" in a simple relationship with nature. These and thousands of educated middle- and upper-class northerners after 1830 built a cultural conversation in which Americans defined themselves by talking about American nature—a nature that had become Christianized and benign.

That conversation was strongest among urban northeasterners who benefited from the market revolution and who believed that theirs was an age of progress. Indeed some would argue that the feminization of family life, the rise of sentimentality, and the romantic cult of nature could have appeared only when American civilization had turned the tide in its age-old battle with wilderness. The most sensitive and articulate northeasterners—Emerson, Thoreau, and Thomas Cole among

them—warned that the victory might be too complete, and that the United States could become as "unnatural" and "artificial" as an overcultivated Europe. Similarly, ministers and mothers worried that the marketplace could corrupt the "natural" relations of family life, and middle-class women and men cultivated personal "sincerity" as a badge of moral status and as a hedge against the artificiality and dishonesty that thrived in an anonymous market society. At every level, middle-class culture was balanced, sometimes uncomfortably, between pride in economic and technological progress and veneration of what was "natural."

SCENIC TOURISM: NIAGARA FALLS

In the 1820s rich Americans began to travel for the sole purpose of looking at scenery. Improved transportation and disposable time and money made such journeys possible, but just as important was the determination of the more affluent Americans to re-create themselves not only as a monied class but as a community of sentiment and taste. They stood beside each other on steamboats and admired the picturesque farms and mountains of the Hudson valley; they traveled to the Catskills and the White Mountains; but most of all they descended on what became the most venerated spot in all of North America: Niagara Falls.

Niagara was a new attraction in the 1820s. The falls had become part of the border between the United States and British Canada in 1783, but few Americans visited the place, and even fewer settled there. The falls could be reached only by a difficult and expensive voyage up the St. Lawrence River and across Lake Ontario or, after 1804, over New York's notoriously bad state road. The Niagara frontier remained an unfriendly border, one of the principal battlegrounds of the War of 1812. The few Americans who wrote about Niagara Falls before the 1820s had stressed the power, wildness, and danger of the place along with its stunning beauty. These reactions aped literary convention that demanded terror as part of the apprehension of the sublime in nature; they also repeated old American fears of wilderness. In 1815 Niagara remained part of an unconquered American wilderness.

Completion of the Erie Canal in 1825 brought civilization to Niagara Falls. Every summer crowds

NIAGARA FALLS Frederic Edwin Church, one of the most renowned of American landscape artists, painted Niagara Falls in 1857. Church's Niagara is immense and powerful, yet somehow ordered, benign, and calming.

of genteel tourists traveled the easy water route to Buffalo, then took carriages to the falls, where entrepreneurs had built hotels, paths, and stairways and offered boat rides and guided tours. The falls quickly became surrounded by commerce and were viewed comfortably from various sites by well-dressed tourists. In early paintings of the falls, the foreground figure had usually been an Indian hunter or fisherman; now Indians were replaced by tourist couples, the women carrying parasols. The sublime experience of terror and wonder disappeared. Tourists read travel accounts before their trip and, once they arrived, bought guidebooks and took guided tours, aware that they were sharing their experience with thousands of others. Many of the tourists were women, and many men conceded that women possessed the "genuine emotion" that enabled them to experience Niagara Falls correctly. Niagara had become controlled, orderly, and beautiful, a grand sermon in which God revealed his benign plan to humankind. Young Harriet Beecher Stowe visited Niagara in the early 1830s and gushed, "Oh, it is lovelier than it is great; it is like the Mind that made it: great, but so veiled in beauty that we gaze without terror. I felt as if I could have gone over with the waters; it would be so beautiful a death. . . ." Niagara had be-

come, for Stowe and thousands of others, a part of sentimental culture.

THE PLAIN PEOPLE OF THE NORTH

From the 1830s onward, northern middle-class evangelicals proposed their religious and domestic values as a national culture for the United States, but even in their own region they were surrounded and outnumbered by Americans who rejected their cultural leadership. The plain people of the North were a varied lot: settlers in the lower Northwest who remained culturally southern; hill-country New Englanders, New Yorkers, and Pennsylvanians who had experienced little of what their middle-class cousins called "progress"; refugees from the countryside who had taken up urban wage labor; and increasing thousands of Irish and German immigrants. They did share a cultural conservatism—often grounded in the traditional, father-centered family—that rejected sentimentalism and reformist religion out of hand.

RELIGION AND THE COMMON FOLK

Northern plain folk favored churches as doctrinally varied as the people themselves. These ranged from the voluntaristic "free grace" doctrines of the Methodists to the iron-bound Calvinism of most Baptists, from the fine-tuned hierarchy of the Mormons to the near-anarchy of the Disciples of Christ. They included the most popular faiths (Baptists and Methodists came to contain two-thirds of America's professing Protestants in both the North and the South) as well as such smaller sects as Hicksite Quakers, Universalists, Adventists, Moravians, and Freewill Baptists. Yet for all their diversity, these churches had important points in common. Most shared an evangelical emphasis on individual experience over churchly authority. Most favored democratic, local control of religious life and distrusted outside organization and religious professionalism—not only the declining colonial establishments but the emerging missionary network created by middle-class evangelicals. They also rejected middle-class optimism and reformism, reaffirming God's providence and humankind's duty to accept an imperfect world even while waging war against it.

The most pervasive strain was a belief in providence—the conviction that human history was part of God's vast and unknowable plan, and that all events were willed or allowed by God. Middle-class evangelicals spoke of providence, too, but they seemed to assume that God's plan was manifest in the progress of market society and middle-class religion. Humbler evangelicals held to the older notion that providence was immediate, mysterious, and unknowable. They believed that the events of everyday life were parts of a vast blueprint that existed only in the mind of God—and not in the vain aspirations of women and men. When making plans, they added the caveat "the Lord willing," and they learned to accept misfortune with fortitude. They responded to epidemics, bad crop years, aches and pains, illness, and early death by praying for the strength to endure, asking God to "sanctify" their suffering by making it an opportunity for them to grow in faith. As a minister told the Scots Covenanters of Cambridge, New York, "It is through tribulation that all the saints enter into the kingdom of God. . . . The tempest sometimes ceases, the sky is clear, and the prospect is desirable, but by the by the gathering clouds threaten a new storm; here we must watch, and labor, and fight, expecting rest with Christ in glory, not on the way to it."

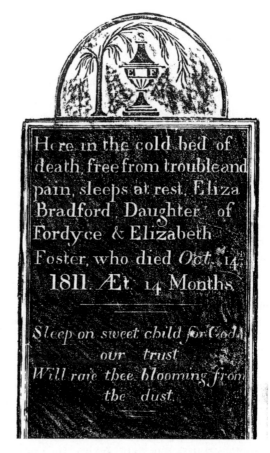

CHILD'S GRAVESTONE Below the weeping willow on this baby girl's gravestone is an inscription affirming that death has set the child "free from trouble and pain" and has ushered her into a better life.

The providential world view, the rejection of this world, and the notion that God granted spiritual progress only through affliction came directly into play when a member of a poor Protestant family died. Country Baptists and working-class Methodists mourned their dead but took care not to "murmur" against God. In a world governed by providence, the death of a loved one was a test of faith. Plain folk considered it a privilege to witness a death in the family, for it released the sufferer from the tribulations of this world and sent him or her to a better place. The death of children in particular called for a heroic act of submission to God's will; parents mourned the loss but stopped short of displaying grief that would suggest selfishness and lack of faith. Poor families washed and dressed the dead body themselves and buried it in a churchyard or on a hilltop plot on the family farm. Whereas the urban middle class preferred formal funerals and carefully tended cemeteries, humbler people regarded death as a lesson in the futility of pursuing worldly goals and in the need to submit to God's will.

POPULAR MILLENNIALISM

The plain Protestants of the North seldom talked about the millennium. Middle-class evangelicals were *postmillennialists:* They believed that Christ's Second Coming would occur at the end of 1,000 years of social perfection that would be brought about by the missionary conversion of the world. Ordinary Baptists, Methodists, and Disciples of Christ, however, assumed that the millennium would arrive with world-destroying violence, followed by 1,000 years of Christ's rule on earth. Few, however, dwelled on this terrifying premillennialism, assuming that God would end the world in his own time. Now and then, however, the ordinary evangelicals of the North predicted the fiery end of the world. Prophets rose and fell, and thousands of people looked for signs of the approaching millennium in thunderstorms, shooting stars, eclipses, economic panics and depressions, and—especially—in hints that God had placed in the Bible.

An avid student of those hints was William Miller, a rural New York Baptist who, after years of systematic study, concluded that God would destroy the world during the year following March 1843. Miller publicized his predictions throughout the 1830s, and near the end of the decade the Millerites (as his followers were called) accumulated thousands of believers—most of them conservative Baptists, Methodists, and Disciples in hill-country New England and in poor neighborhoods in New York, Ohio, and Michigan. As the end approached, the believers read the Bible, prayed, and attended meeting after meeting. A publicist named Henry Jones reported that a shower of meat and blood had fallen on Jersey City, and newspapers published stories alleging that the Millerites were insane and guilty of sexual license. Some of them, the press reported, were busy sewing "ascension robes" in which they would rise straight to heaven without passing through death.

PROPHETIC CHART A fixture at Millerite Adventist meetings, prophetic charts such as the one shown here displayed the succession of Biblical kingdoms and the prophecies of Daniel and John. Millerites revised their charts when the world failed to end in 1843.

When the end of the year—March 23, 1844—came and went, most of the believers quietly returned to their churches. A committed remnant, however, kept the faith and by the 1860s founded the Seventh-Day Adventist Church. The Millerite movement was a reminder that hundreds of thousands of northern Protestants continued to believe that the God of the Old Testament governed everything from bee stings to the course of human history, and that one day he would destroy the world in fire and blood.

FAMILY AND SOCIETY

Baptists, Methodists, Disciples of Christ, and the smaller popular sects evangelized primarily among persons who had been bypassed or hurt by the market revolution. Many had been reduced to dependent, wage-earning status. Others had become market farmers or urban storekeepers or master workmen; few had become rich. Their churches taught them that the attractions and temptations of market society were at the center of the world they must reject.

Often their rhetoric turned to criticism of market society, its institutions, and its centers of power. The Quaker schismatic Elias Hicks, a Long Island farmer who fought the worldliness and pride of wealthy urban Quakers, listed the following among the mistakes of the early 19th century: railroads, the Erie Canal, fancy food and other luxuries, banks and the credit system, the city of Philadelphia, and the study of chemistry. The Baptist millenarian William Miller expressed his hatred of banks, insurance companies, stock-jobbing, chartered monopolies, personal greed, and the city of New York. In short, what the evangelical middle-class identified as the march of progress, poorer and more conservative evangelicals often condemned as a descent into worldliness that would almost certainly provoke God's wrath.

Along with doubts about economic change and the middle-class churches that embraced it, members of the popular sects often held to the patriarchal family form in which they had been raised, and with which both the market revolution and middle-class domesticity seemed at war. Hundreds of thousands of northern Protestants considered the erosion of domestic patriarchy a profound cultural loss and not, as it seemed to the middle-class, an avenue to personal liberation. Their cultural conservatism was apparent in their efforts to sustain the father-centered family of the old rural North, or to revive it in new forms.

For some, religious conversion came at a point of crisis in the traditional family. William Miller, for example, had a strict Calvinist upbringing in a family in which his father, an uncle, and his grandfather were all Baptist ministers. As a young man he rejected his family, set about making money, and became a deist—actions that deeply wounded his parents. When his father died, Miller was stricken with guilt. He moved back to his hometown, took up his family duties, became a leader of the Baptist church, and (after reading a sermon entitled "Parental Duties") began the years of Bible study that resulted in his world-ending prophecies. Alexander Campbell, one of the founders of the Disciples of Christ, dramatized his filial piety when he debated the freethinking socialist Robert Owen before a large audience in the Methodist meetinghouse in Cincinnati in 1828. He insisted that his white-haired father (himself a Scots Presbyterian minister) stand in the pulpit above the debaters.

THE PROPHET JOSEPH SMITH

The weakening patriarchal family and attempts to shore it up were central to the life and work of one of the most unique and successful religious leaders of the period: the Mormon prophet Joseph Smith (see also chapter 13). Smith's father was a landless Vermont Baptist who moved his wife and nine children to seven rented farms within 20 years. Around 1820, when young Joseph was approaching manhood, the family was struggling to make mortgage payments on a small farm outside Palmyra, New York. That farm—Joseph referred to it as "my father's house"—was a desperate token of the Smith family's commitment to yeoman independence and an endangered rural patriarchy. Despite the efforts of Joseph and his brothers, a merchant cheated the Smith family out of the farm. With that, both generations of the Smiths faced lifetimes as propertyless workers. To make matters worse, Joseph's mother and some of his siblings began to attend an evangelical Presbyterian church in Palmyra—apparently against the father's wishes.

Before the loss of the farm, Joseph had received two visions warning him away from existing churches and telling him to wait for further instructions. In 1827 the Angel Moroni appeared to him and led him to golden plates that translated into *The Book of Mormon*. It told of a light-skinned people, descendants of the Hebrews, who had sailed to North America long before Columbus. They had had an epic, violent history, a covenanted relationship with God, and had been visited and evangelized by Jesus following his crucifixion and resurrection.

Joseph Smith later declared that his discovery of *The Book of Mormon* had "brought salvation to my father's house" by unifying the family. It eventually unified thousands of others under a patriarchal faith based on restored theocratic government, male dominance, and a democracy among fathers. The good priests and secular leaders of *The Book of Mormon* are farmers who labor alongside their neighbors; the villains are self-seeking merchants, lawyers, and bad priests. The account alternates between periods when the people obey God's laws and periods when they do not—each period accompanied by the blessings or punishments of a wrathful God. Smith carried that model of brotherly cooperation and patriarchal authority into the Church of Jesus Christ of Latter-day Saints, which he founded in 1830. The new church was ruled, not by professional clergy, but by an elaborate lay hierarchy of adult males. On top sat the father of Joseph Smith, rescued from destitution and shame, who was appointed Patriarch of the Church. Below him were Joseph Smith and his brother Hyrum, who were called First and Second Elders. The hierarchy descended through a succession of male authorities that finally reached the fathers of households. Smith claimed that this hierarchy restored the ancient priesthood that had disappeared over the 18 centuries of greed and error that he labeled the "Great Apostasy" of the Christian churches. Americans who knew the history of the market revolution and the Smith family's travails within it, however, might have noted similarities between the restored ancient order and a poor man's visionary retrieval of the social order of the 18th-century North.

THE RISE OF POPULAR CULTURE

Of course, not all the northern plain folk spent their time in church. Particularly in cities and towns, they became both producers and consumers of a nonreligious (sometimes irreligious) commercial popular culture.

BLOOD SPORTS

Urban working-class neighborhoods were particularly fertile ground for popular amusements. Young working men formed a bachelor subculture that contrasted with the piety and self-restraint of the middle class. They organized volunteer fire companies and militia units that spent more time drinking and fighting rival groups than drilling or putting out fires. Gathering at firehouses, saloons, and street corners, they drank, joked, and boasted, and nurtured notions of manliness based on physical prowess and coolness under pressure.

They also engaged in such "blood sports" as cock fighting, ratting, and dog fighting, even though many states had laws forbidding such activities. In 1823 an English tourist in New York City noted that "it is perfectly common for two or three cockfights to regularly take place every week." Such contests grew increasingly popular during the 1850s and often were staged by saloonkeepers doubling as sports impresarios. One of the best known was Kit Burns of New York City, who ran Sportsman Hall. Sportsman Hall was merely a saloon frequented by prizefighters, criminals, and their hangers-on. Behind the saloon, however, was a space—reached through a narrow doorway that could be defended against the police—with animal pits and a small amphitheater that seated 250 but that regularly held 400 yelling spectators.

Although most of the spectators were working men, a few members of the old aristocracy who rejected middle-class ways also attended these events. In 1861, for instance, 250 spectators paid as much as three dollars each to witness a fight between roosters belonging to the prize fighter John Morrissey and Mr. Genet, president of the New York City board of aldermen. A newspaper estimated bets on the event at $50,000. Frederick Van Wyck, scion of a wealthy old New York family, remembered an evening he had spent at Tommy Norris's livery stable, where he witnessed a fight between billy goats, a rat baiting, a cockfight, and a boxing match between bare-breasted women. "Certainly for a lad of 17, such as I," he recalled, "a night with Tommy Norris and his attraction was quite a night."

BOXING

Prize fighting emerged from the same subterranean culture that sustained cockfights and other blood sports. This sport, imported from Britain, called for an enclosed ring, clear rules, cornermen, a referee, and a paying audience. The early fighters were Irish or English immigrants, as were many of the promoters and spectators. Boxing's popularity rose during the 1840s and 1850s, a time of increasing

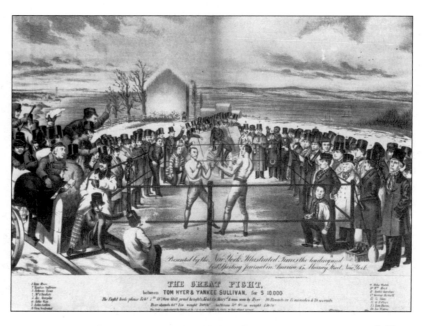

THE MATCH BETWEEN JAMES "YANKEE" SULLIVAN AND TOM HYER, FEBRUARY 1849 Sullivan was an Irish immigrant, Hyer was native-born; both were active in New York street gangs. Hyer defeated Sullivan in 16 rounds.

immigration and violence in poor city neighborhoods. Many of the fighters had close ties with ethnic-based saloons, militia units, fire companies, and street gangs such as New York's (Irish) Dead Rabbits and (native) Bowery B'hoys, and many labored at occupations with a peculiarly ethnic base. Some of the best American-born fighters were New York City butchers—a licensed, privileged trade from which cheap immigrant labor was systematically excluded. Butchers usually finished work by 10 a.m. They could then spend the rest of the day idling at a firehouse or a bar and often were prominent figures in neighborhood gangs. A prizefight between an American-born butcher and an Irish day laborer would attract a spirited audience that understood its class and ethnic meaning.

Prizefighting was a way of rewarding courage and skill and, sometimes, of settling scores through fair contests limited to two combatants. Nonetheless, the fights were brutal. Boxers fought with bare knuckles, and a bout ended only when one of the fighters was unable to continue. In an infamous match in 1842, for instance, the Englishman Christopher Lilly knocked down his Irish opponent Thomas McCoy 80 times; the fight ended with round 119, when McCoy died in his corner.

Although boxing had close ties to ethnic rivalries, the contestants often exhibited a respect for one another that crossed ethnic lines. For example, native-born Tom Hyer, who had defeated Irishman James "Yankee" Sullivan in one of the great early fights, later bailed Sullivan out of jail. And when in 1859 Bill Harrington, a retired native-born boxer, disappeared and left a wife and children, his former Irish-born opponent, John Morrisey, arranged a sparring match and sent the proceeds to Mrs. Harrington.

AN AMERICAN THEATER

In the 18th and early 19th centuries, the only theaters were in the large seaport cities. Those who attended were members of the urban elite, and nearly all the plays, managers, and actors were English. After 1815, however, improvements in transportation and communication, along with the rapid growth of cities, created a much broader audience. Theaters and theater companies sprang up not only in New York and Philadelphia but also in Cincinnati, St. Louis, San Francisco, Rochester, and dozens of other new towns west of the Appalachians, and traveling troupes carried theatrical performances to the smallest hamlets. Most of them catered to male,

THE ASTOR PLACE RIOT The rivalry between English actor William Charles Macready and American actor Edwin Forrest culminated in the bloody Astor Place riot in New York City in May 1849.

largely plebeian audiences. Before 1830 the poorer theatergoers occupied the cheap balcony seats (with the exception of the second balcony, which was reserved for prostitutes); artisans and other working-men filled benches in the ground floor area known as "the pit"; wealthier and more genteel patrons sat in the boxes. Those sitting in the pit and balcony joined in the performance: They ate and drank, talked, and shouted encouragement and threats to the actors. The genteel New Yorker Washington Irving lamented the "discharge of apples, nuts, and gingerbread" flying out of the balconies "on the heads of honest folks" in the pit.

As time passed, however, rowdyism turned into violence. The less genteel members of theater audiences protested the elegant speech, gentlemanly bearing, and understated performances of the English actors, which happened to match the speech, manners, and bearing of the American urban elite. Thus the protests were directed not only at the English actors but also at the ladies and gentlemen in the orchestra who were seen as symbols of English culture unsuitable in a democratic republic.

The first theater riot occurred in 1817 when the English actor Charles Incledon refused a New York audience's demand that he stop what he was doing

and sing "Black-Eyed Susan." Such assaults grew more common during the 1820s. By the 1830s separate theaters offered separate kinds of performances for rich and poor, but violence continued. It culminated in the rivalry between the American actor Edwin Forrest and the English actor William Charles Macready. Macready was a trained Shakespearean actor, and his restrained style and attention to the subtleties of the text had won him acclaim both in Britain and in the United States. Forrest, on the other hand, played to the cheap seats. With his bombast and histrionics he transformed Shakespeare's tragedies into melodramas. Forrest and Macready carried out a well-publicized feud that led to a mob attack on Macready in 1849. Led by E. Z. C. Judson (who, under the pen name Ned Buntline, wrote scores of dime novels), the mob descended on Macready's performance at the exclusive Astor Place Opera House. The militia was waiting for them, and 20 people died in the ensuing riot and gunfight.

Playhouses that catered to working-class audiences continued to feature Shakespearean tragedies (*Richard III*, played broadly and with a lot of sword-play, was the favorite), but they now shared the stage with works written in the American vernacular. The stage "Yankee," rustic but shrewd, appeared at this time and so did Mose the Bowery B'hoy, a New York volunteer fireman who performed feats of derring-do. Both frequently appeared in the company of well-dressed characters with English accents—the Yankee outsmarted them; Mose beat them up.

MINSTRELSY

The most popular form of theater was the blackface minstrel show. Although these shows conveyed blatant racism, they were the preferred entertainment of working men in northern cities from 1840 to 1880. (Few women attended the shows.) The first minstrel show was presented in 1831 when a white showman named Thomas Rice blacked his face and "jumped Jim Crow," imitating a shuffle-dance he had seen on the Cincinnati docks. Within a few years a formula for these shows had emerged that every theatergoer knew by heart.

The minstrel shows lasted an hour and a half and were presented in three sections. The first consisted of songs and dances performed in a walka-round, in which the audience was encouraged to clap and sing along. This was followed by a longer middle section in which the company sat in a row with a character named Tambo at one end and a character named Bones at the other (named for the tambourine and bones, the instruments they played), with an interlocutor in the middle. The Tambo character, often called Uncle Ned, was a simpleminded plantation slave dressed in plain clothing; the Bones character, usually called Zip Coon, was a dandified, oversexed free black dressed in top hat and tails. The interlocutor was the straight man—fashionably dressed, slightly pretentious, with an English accent. This middle portion of the show consisted of a conversation among the three, which included pointed political satire, skits ridiculing the wealthy and the educated, and sexual jokes that bordered on obscenity. The third section featured songs, dances, and jokes—most of them familiar enough so that the audience could sing along and laugh at the right places.

The minstrel shows introduced African American song and dance—in toned-down, Europeanized form—to audiences who would not have permitted black performers onto the stage. They also reinforced racial stereotypes that were near the center of American popular culture. Finally, they

THE VIRGINIA MINSTRELS In the 1840s, the Virginia Minstrels, white entertainers in absurd black masquerade, advertised themselves as "able delineators of the sports and pastimes of the Sable Race of the South."

dealt broadly with aspects of social and political life that other performers avoided.

Minstrel shows and other theatrical entertainments began to travel the new transportation network to rural America. The Grecian Dog Apollo, for example, arrived in New York from London in 1827; he played cards, solved problems in arithmetic "with the celerity of an experienced clerk," and answered questions on astronomy and geography. Apollo traveled the Erie Canal circuit, playing at Albany, Saratoga Springs, Utica, Rochester, Buffalo, and Niagara Falls before returning to Peale's Museum in New York for the 1828 season. Many actors traveled well-established circuits, calling on local amateurs for their supporting casts. Minstrel companies traveled the river system of the interior and played to enthusiastic audiences wherever the riverboats docked. Mark Twain recalled them fondly: "I remember the first Negro musical show I ever saw.

P. T. Barnum's American Museum

Phineas T. Barnum was 32 years old when he purchased New York's American Museum in 1842. He had been a store clerk, a free-thought newspaper editor, and a Bible salesman; he had also traveled with a circus, and had exhibited an aged black woman named Joice Heth (Barnum—and Heth—claimed that she was 161 years old, and had been the nurse of George Washington) and a plate-spinner named Signor Vivalla. At the American Museum, many of Barnum's exhibits were frivolous and some were fraudulent, but he carefully separated his museum from the rough world of blood sports, cheap titillation, and working-class theater. He made the museum a place where respectable persons, including children and women, could enjoy entertainment in a safe, inoffensive place. Patrons passed through a wax museum, a gallery of patriotic portraits, and collections of minerals and stuffed animals to view a caged crocodile (a "living vision of horror and gore") as "The Leviathan of Scripture." In the late 1840s Barnum transformed his lecture room into a theater,

It must have been in the early forties. It was a new institution. In our village of Hannibal [Missouri] . . . it burst upon us as a glad and stunning surprise." Among Americans who had been taught to distrust cities by cultural leaders ranging from Thomas Jefferson to Emerson and Thoreau to the evangelical preachers in their own neighborhoods, minstrel shows and other urban entertainments gave rural folk a sense of the variety and excitement of city life.

NOVELS AND THE PENNY PRESS

Few of the commodities made widely available by the market revolution were more ubiquitous than newspapers and inexpensive books. Improvements in printing and paper making enabled entrepreneurs to sell daily newspapers for a penny. Cheap "story papers" became available in the 1830s, "yellow-back"

fiction in the 1840s, and dime novels from the 1850s onward. Although these offerings were distributed throughout the North and the West, they found their first and largest audience among city workers.

Mass-audience newspapers carried political news and local advertisements, but they were heavily spiced with sensationalism. The *Philadelphia Gazette* in late summer of 1829, for instance, treated its eager readers to the following: "Female Child with Two Heads," "Bats," "Another Shark," "Horrid Murder," "More Stabbing," "Steam Boat Robbery," "Fishes Travelling on Land," "Poisoning by Milk," "Dreadful Steam Boat Disaster," "Picking Pockets," "Raffling for Babies," "Combat with a Bear," "Lake Serpent," "Atrocious Murder," "Frauds on the Revenue," and much, much more. Henry David Thoreau commented on the "startling and monstrous events as fill the family papers," while his

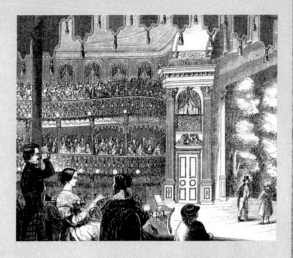

attracting patrons who would never have attended the theaters of either the wine-drinking elite or of the whiskey-soaked rabble into a family-style room in which they enjoyed temperance melodramas, stage renditions of *Uncle Tom's Cabin*, and the same mindless farces that concluded shows at the more disreputable theaters. This fine-tuned combination of frivolity, duplicity, and respectability attracted a huge middle-class audience and established Barnum as America's Greatest Showman.

friend Ralph Waldo Emerson reported that Americans were "reading all day murders & railroad accidents." Even though such sensational stories are most remarkable for their variety, they all portrayed a haunted, often demonic nature that regularly produced monstrosities and ruined the works of humankind, as well as a human nature that, despite appearances, was often deceptive and depraved.

Working-class readers discovered a similarly untrustworthy world in cheap fiction. George Lippard's *Quaker City* (1845) sold 60,000 copies in its first year and 30,000 in each of the next five years, making it the best-selling American book before the sentimental blockbusters of the 1850s. Lippard's book was a fictional "exposé" of the hypocrisy, lust, and cruelty of Philadelphia's outwardly genteel and Christian elite. Lippard and other adventure writers (whose works accounted for 60 percent of all American fic-

tion titles published between 1831 and 1860) indulged in a pornography of violence that included cannibalism, blood drinking, and murder by every imaginable means. They also dealt with sex in unprecedentedly explicit ways. The yellow-back novels of the 1840s introduced readers not only to seduction and rape but to transvestitism, child pornography, necrophilia, miscegenation, group sex, homosexuality, and—perhaps most shocking of all—women with criminal minds and insatiable sexual appetites. The scenes of gore and sexual depravity were presented voyeuristically—as self-righteous exposés of the perversions of the rich and powerful and stories of the Founders' Republic trampled upon by a vicious elite that pretended virtue but lived only for its appetites.

Popular fictions—like most popular plays, Edwin Forrest's Shakespeare, and much of what went on in blood sports, the prize ring, and the

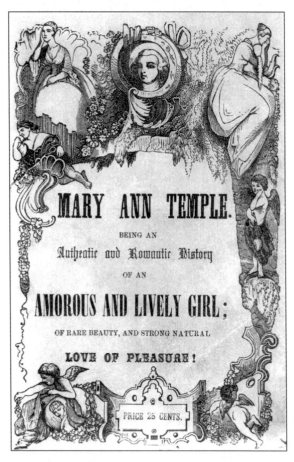

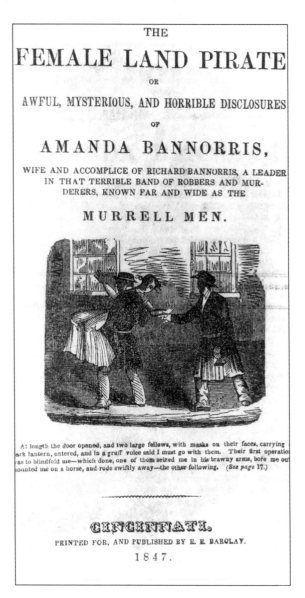

YELLOW-BACK NOVELS Here are two pulp fiction hits of the 1840s: an erotic novel about the "amorous and lively" Mary Ann Temple and a crime story about robberies and murders committed by the "Female Land Pirate"—not the kinds of women encountered in middle-class sentimental fiction.

penny press—were melodramatic contests between good and evil. Evil was described in terms reminiscent of original sin: It provided the background of all human action, and heroes met a demonic and chaotic world with courage and guile without hoping to change it. Indeed, melodramatic heroes frequently acknowledged evil in themselves while claiming moral superiority over the hypocrites and frauds who governed the world. A murderer in Ned Buntline's *G'hals of New York* (1850) remarks, "There isn't no *real* witue [virtue] and honesty nowhere, 'cept among the perfessional *dis*honest." (By contrast, in middle-class sentimental novels, the universe was benign; good could be nurtured, and evil could be defeated

and transformed. Harriet Beecher Stowe's slave driver Simon Legree—the best-known villain in American literature—is evil not because of a natural disposition toward evil, but because he had been deprived of a mother's love during childhood.)

FAMILY, CHURCH, AND NEIGHBORHOOD: THE WHITE SOUTH

Antebellum white southerners remained localistic and culturally conservative. Farm and plantation labor and the routines of family life still centered in the household, and prospects for most whites remained rooted in inherited land and family help. While the new northern middle class nourished a cosmopolitan culture and a domestic sentimentalism that subverted traditional authority, southerners—planters and yeomen alike—distrusted outsiders and defended rural neighborhoods grounded in the authority of fathers and the integrity of families.

SOUTHERN FAMILIES

Most southern whites regarded themselves less as individuals than as representatives of families that extended through time from the distant past to unborn generations. Southern boys often received the family names of heroes as their first names: Jefferson Davis, for example, or Thomas Jefferson (later, "Stonewall") Jackson. More often, however, they took the name of a related family—Peyton Randolph, Preston Brooks, Langdon Cheves—and carried them as proud and often burdensome badges of who they were. Children learned early on that their first duty was to their family's reputation. When young Benjamin Tillman of South Carolina was away at school, his sister wrote, "Don't relax in your efforts to gain a good ed-

ucation. . . . I want you to be an ornament to your family." Two years later, another sister wrote, "Do, Bud, study hard and make good use of your time. . . . I want you to do something for the Tillman name."

In the white South, reputation and the defense of family honor were everything. Boys and girls were taught to act as though everyone were watching them, ready to note any hint of inadequacy. A boy with a reputation for cowardice, for ineptness at riding or fighting, or for failure to control his emotions or hold his liquor, was an embarrassment to his family. Membership in the South's democracy of white men depended less upon wealth than upon the maintenance of personal and family integrity.

An "unsullied reputation," insisted Albert Gallatin Brown of Mississippi, placed a man "on a social level with all his fellows." As John Horry Dent, an Alabama slaveholder and bad amateur poet, put it:

Honor and shame from all conditions rise;
Act well your part and there the honor lies.

Among southern white men, wealth generally counted for less than did maintaining one's personal and family honor and thus winning membership in the democracy of honorable males.

COLONEL AND MRS. WHITESIDE Colonel and Mrs. James Whiteside are pictured at home in their mansion on the heights above Chattanooga. The Colonel, Bible in hand, looks directly at his wife, while she looks shyly and indirectly back at him. Their infant son wears the traditional small child's dress, and the slaves are pictured as both subservient and comfortable. Here is southern patriarchy at its most genteel.

The code of honor, although it forged ties of equality and respect among white men, made rigid distinctions between men and women and whites and blacks. Women and girls who misbehaved—with transgressions ranging from simple gossip to poor housekeeping to adultery—damaged not only their own reputation but also the honor of the fathers, brothers, or husbands who could not control them. Such a charge could mean social death in a rural community made up of patriarchal households and watchful neighbors. In 1813 Bolling Hall of Alabama advised his daughter, "If you learn to restrain every thought, action, and word by virtue and religion, you will become an ornament." A "good man" or a "good woman" was someone who upheld the family by acting within a prescribed social role ("Act well your part. . . ."), and not, as the children of the northern middle class were being taught, by acting as an autonomous, self-governing individual.

The southern code of honor blunted attacks upon social hierarchy and inherited status. When sentimental northerners attacked slavery because it denied the freedom of the individual, one southerner responded in a way that was meant to end the argument: "Do you say that the slave is held to involuntary service? So is the wife, [whose] relation to her husband, in the great majority of cases, is made for her and not by her." Few white southerners would have questioned the good sense of that response. Southern life was not about freedom, individual fulfillment, or social progress; it was about honoring the obligations to which one was born.

SOUTHERN ENTERTAINMENTS

Southerners of all classes and races were leisure-loving people, but the rural character of the South threw them upon their own resources rather than on commercial entertainments. They drank, told stories, engaged in wrestling and boxing matches, and danced. For evangelicals who withdrew from such entertainments, church socials and camp meetings filled the gap. Rural southerners both in and out of the churches engaged in corn-huskings, birthday celebrations, berry-picking expeditions, and so forth. Books were not as readily available as they were in the North. Whereas the big publishing houses produced many titles aimed at northern and western readers and at such specialized constituencies as commercial farmers or middle-class housewives, the southern literary market was too small to justify such special attention. Most southern families owned a Bible, and wealthier families often read histories, religious and political tracts, and English (seldom American) literature—with Shakespeare leading the way and Sir Walter Scott's tales of medieval chivalry not far behind. (Such stories exercised a strong fascination on some southerners; in the last years before the Civil War, jousting tournaments were held in which southern gentlemen clad in armor fought from horseback with lances and broadswords.) Hunting and fishing were passionate pursuits among southern men. Fox and deer hunts provided the gentry with an opportunity to display their skill with horses and guns, while the hunts of poorer whites and slaves both provided sport and enhanced their threatened roles as providers. Although state laws forbade slaves to own guns or dogs, thousands of slave owners found it wise to overlook the laws and to allow slaves to hunt as a favorite recreation.

The commercial entertainments in the South were concentrated in the larger towns and along the major rivers. Showboats brought theatrical troupes, minstrel shows, animal acts, and other entertainment to the river towns. The gentry's love of horses and competition made New Orleans the horse racing capital of the country; New Orleans also was the only southern city where one could watch a professional prizefight. Various violent contests appealed to New Orleans audiences. In 1819 a New Orleans impresario advertised a program that offered a bull versus six "of the strongest dogs in the country"; six bulldogs versus a Canadian bear; a "beautiful Tiger" versus a black bear; and 12 dogs versus a "strong and furious Opeloussas Bull." The advertisement further promised: "If the tiger is not vanquished in his fight with the Bear, he will be sent alone against the last Bull; and if the latter conquers all his enemies, several pieces of fireworks will be placed on his back, which will produce a very entertaining amusement." The impresario also stated that the premises had been inspected by the mayor of New Orleans, and that children would be admitted at half price. Although such events were outlawed in later years, they continued to be held on the sly. In 1852, a crowd of

5,000 gathered outside New Orleans to watch a bull and a grizzly bear fight to the death.

THE CAMP MEETING BECOMES RESPECTABLE

The camp-meeting revivals of the early 19th century had transformed the South into an evangelical Bible belt (see chapter 7), although that label wouldn't be applied for another century. By 1860, 88 percent of southern church members were Methodist, Baptist, Presbyterian, or Disciples of Christ. Revival religion had spread from the frontier and up-country yeomanry into both slave cabins and plantation mansions. Some evangelicals had risen into the slaveholding class, and many of the old families had been converted. As a result, the deist or indifferently Anglican gentry of the 18th century became outnumbered by earnest Baptist and Methodist planters who considered themselves the fathers of an inclusive southern Christian community.

Southern camp meetings continued throughout the antebellum years, but they were no longer the inclusive, ecstatic camp meetings of the past. They were often limited to a single denomination—usually Methodist—and were held on permanent campgrounds maintained by the churches. Conducted with more decorum than in the past, they were routine community events: Women began baking a week ahead of time and looked forward to visiting with neighbors and relatives as much as they did to getting right with God.

The goal of camp meetings was still to induce spiritual crisis and conversion, and sinners still wept and fell on their way to being saved, but such manifestations as the barking exercise and the jerks (see chapter 7) disappeared. Unfriendly observers after the 1820s could find nothing more offensive than simple breaches of decorum among the women. For instance, in 1828 an Englishwoman attended a meeting near Cincinnati at which nearly 100 women came forward to fall at the feet of Christ until "they were soon all lying on the ground in an indescribable confusion of heads and legs." The southern humorist George W. Harris described a fictional camp meeting at which his comic character Sut Lovingood put lizards up the preacher's pant leg. A fat woman fainted in the confusion, rolled down a hill, "tangled her laig an' garters in the top of a huckilberry bush, wif her head in the branch and jis' lay still."

The churches that grew out of southern revivals reinforced localistic neighborhoods and the patriarchal family. Some southern communities began when a whole congregation moved onto new land; others were settled by the chain migration of brothers and cousins, and subsequent revivals spread through family networks. Rural isolation limited most households to their own company during the week, but on Sundays church meetings united the neighborhood's cluster of extended families into a community of believers. In most neighborhoods, social connections seldom extended beyond that. The word "church" referred ultimately to the worldwide community of Christians, and the war between the "church" and the "world" referred to a cosmic history that would end in millennial fire. In the day-to-day understandings of southern evangelicals, however, the "church" was the local congregation and the "world" was local sins and local sinners—many of whom were related to members of the church. Churches disciplined members for such worldly practices as drinking, gambling, dancing, swearing, fornication, and adultery, and even for giving the *impression* of sinful behavior. Mount Olive Baptist Church in North Carolina, for example, expelled Mary Bivens because she was "too thick with young men."

RELIGIOUS CONSERVATISM

Southern evangelicalism based itself, like religious conservatism in the North, on the sovereignty of God, a conviction of human sinfulness, and an acceptance of disappointment and pain as part of God's grand and unknowable design. "Oh man," lamented one slaveholder, "when will thou meekly submit to God without a murmur. . . . His will be done should be your constant prayer." Southern church people continued to interpret misfortune as divine punishment. When yellow fever was killing 1,000 people every week in New Orleans in 1853, the Episcopal bishop (and soon to be Confederate general) Leonidas Polk asked God to "turn us from the ravages of the pestilence, wherewith for our iniquities, thou are visiting us."

The same view held at home. When the young son of a planter family died, the mother was certain that God had killed the child because the parents had loved him more than God: "*But God took* him for he saw he was our idol." A grieving South Carolinian received this consolation from a relative: "Hope you are quite reconciled to the loss of your darling babe. As it was the will of God to take him, we must obey, and He will be angry at us if we go past moderate grief." Francis Pickens, another South Carolinian, wrote after losing his wife and child, "I had almost forgot there was a God, and now I stand the scattered . . . and blasted monument of his just wrath." It was a far cry from the middle-class North's garden cemeteries and the romantic, redemptive deaths of children in sentimental fiction.

Southern cultural conservatism was rooted in religion, in the family, and in a system of fixed social roles. Southern preachers assumed that patriarchal social relations were crucial to Christian living within an irredeemably imperfect and often brutal world. Southerners revered the patriarch and slaveholder Abraham more than any other figure in the Bible, and John C. Calhoun proclaimed "Hebrew Theocracy" the best government ever experienced by humankind. The father must—like Abraham—govern and protect his household; the mother must assist the father; and the women, children, and slaves must faithfully act out the duties of their stations. That meant a Christian must strive to be a good mother, a good father, a good slave; by the same token, a Christian never questioned his or her God-given social role.

PROSLAVERY CHRISTIANITY

In revolutionary and early national America, white southerners had been the most radical of republicans. Jeffersonian planter-politicians led the fights for equal rights and the absolute separation of church and state, and southern evangelicals were the early republic's staunchest opponents of slavery. By 1830, however, the South was an increasingly conscious minority within a democratic and capitalist nation. The northern middle classes proclaimed a link between material and moral progress, identifying both with individual autonomy and universal rights. A radical northern minority was agitating for the immediate abolition of slavery.

Southerners met this challenge with an "intellectual blockade" against outside publications and ideas and with a moral and religious defense of slavery. The Bible provided plenty of ammunition. Proslavery clergymen constantly stated that the Chosen People of the Old Testament had been patriarchs and slaveholders, and that Jesus had lived in a society that sanctioned slavery and never criticized the institution. Some ministers claimed that blacks were the descendants of Ham and thus deserved enslavement. The most common religious argument, however, was that slavery had given millions of heathen Africans the priceless opportunity to become Christians and to live in a Christian society. Thornton Stringfellow, a Virginia Baptist minister, insisted that "their condition . . . is now better than that of any equal number of laborers on earth, and is daily improving."

Like their northern counterparts, southern clergymen applauded the material improvements of the age, but they insisted that moral improvement occurred only when people embraced the timeless truths of the Bible. The South Carolinian William F. Hutson put it simply: "In religion and morals, we doubt all improvements, not known to certain fishermen who lived eighteen hundred years ago." Northern notions of progress through individual liberation, equal rights, and universal Christian love were wrong-headed and dangerous. The Presbyterian John Adger asserted that relations of dominance and submission (and not "barbarism and personal savage independence") were utterly necessary to both social and individual fulfillment, and that the distribution of rights and responsibilities were unequal and God-given. "The rights of the father are natural, but they belong only to the fathers. Rights of property are natural, but they belong only to those who have property"—and such natural rights were coupled with the awesome duties of fatherhood and proprietorship. In the end, southern proslavery intellectuals rejected Jefferson's "self-evident" equality of man; Edmund Ruffin, for instance, branded that passage of the Declaration of Independence as "indefensible" as well as "false and foolish."

THE PRIVATE LIVES OF SLAVES

In law, in the census, and in the minds of planters, slaves were members of a plantation household over which the owner exercised absolute authority, not only as owner but also as paternal protector and lawgiver. Yet both slaveholders and slaves knew that slaves could not be treated like farm animals or little children. Wise slaveholders learned that the success of a plantation depended less on terror and draconian discipline (though whippings—and worse—were common) than on the accommodations by which slaves traded labor and obedience for some measure of privilege and autonomy within the bounds of slavery. After achieving privileges, the slaves called them their own: holidays, garden plots, friendships, and social gatherings both on and off the plantation; hunting and fishing rights; and so on. Together, these privileges provided some of the ground on which they made their own lives within slavery.

THE SLAVE FAMILY

The most precious privilege was the right to make and maintain families. As early as the Revolutionary War era, most Chesapeake slaves lived in units consisting of mother, father, and small children. On Charles Carrol's Maryland farms in 1773, for example, 325 of the 400 slaves lived in such families. At Thomas Jefferson's Monticello, most slave marriages were for life, and small children almost always lived with both parents. The most common exceptions to this practice were fathers who had married away from their own plantations and who visited "broad wives" and children during their off hours. In Louisiana between 1810 and 1864, half the slaves lived in families headed by both parents; another one-fourth lived in single-parent families. Owners encouraged stable marriages because they made farms more peaceful and productive and because they flattered the owners' own religious and paternalistic sensibilities. For their part, slaves demanded families as part of the price of their labor.

Yet slave families were highly vulnerable. Many slaveholders assumed that they had the right to coerce sex from female slaves; some kept slaves as concubines, and a few even moved them into the main house. They tended, however, to stay away from married women. While the slave community—in contrast to the whites—seldom punished sex before marriage, it took adultery seriously. Slaveholders knew that violations of married slave women could be enormously disruptive and strongly discouraged

"Dear Husband   I write you a letter to let you know of my distress   my master has sold Albert to a trader on Monday court day and myself and other child is for sale also and I want you to let [me] hear from you very soon   before next cort if you can   I don't know when   I don't want you to wait till Christmas   I want you to tell Dr. Hamilton your master if either will buy me then can attend to it know and then I can go afterwards

"I don't want a trader to get me   they asked me if I had got any person to buy me and I told them no   they told me to the court house too   they never put me up   A man buy the name of brady bought albert and is gone I don't know whare   they say he lives in scottsville   my things is in several places some is in stanton and if I would be sold I don't know what will become of them   I don't expect to meet with the luck to get that way till I am quite heart sick   nothing more I am and ever will be your kind wife Marie Perkins"

MARIE PERKINS
a slave mother writing to her husband, Richard Perkins, Charlottesville, Virginia, 1852

them. A far more serious threat to slave marriages was the death, bankruptcy, or departure of the slaveholders. Between one-fifth and one-third of slave marriages were broken by such events.

Slaveholders who encouraged slave marriages—even perhaps solemnizing them with a religious ceremony—knew that marriage implied a form of self-ownership that conflicted with the slaves' status as property. Some conducted ceremonies in which couples "married" by jumping over a broomstick; others had the preacher omit the phrases "let no

FIVE GENERATIONS OF A SLAVE FAMILY ON A SOUTH CAROLINA SEA ISLAND PLANTATION, 1862 Complex family ties such as those of the family shown here were among the most hard-won and vulnerable cultural accomplishments of enslaved blacks.

man put asunder" and "till death do you part" from the ceremony. Slaves knew that such ceremonies had no legal force. A Virginia slave remarked, "We slaves knowed that them words wasn't bindin'. Don't mean nothin' lessen you say, 'What God has jined, caint no man pull asunder.' But dey never would say dat. Jus' say 'Now you married.'" A black South Carolina preacher routinely ended the ceremony with "Till death or buckra [whites] part you."

Slaves modified their sense of family and kinship to accommodate such uncertainties. Because separation from father or mother was common, children spread their affection among their adult relatives, treating grandparents, aunts, and uncles almost as though they were parents. In fact, slaves often referred to all their adult relatives as "parents." They also called nonrelatives "brother," "sister," "aunt," and "uncle," thus extending a sense of kinship to the slave community at large. Slaves chose as surnames for themselves the names of former owners, Anglicized versions of African names, or names that simply sounded good. They rarely chose the name of their current owner, however. Families tended to use the same given names from one generation to the next, naming boys after their

father or grandfather—perhaps to preserve the memory of fathers who might be taken away. They seldom named girls after their mother, however. Unlike Southern whites, slaves never married a first cousin—even though many members of their community were close relatives. The origins and functions of some of these customs are unknown. We know only that slaves practiced them consistently, usually without the knowledge of the slaveholders.

WHITE MISSIONS

A powerful aspect of planter paternalism was a widespread Christian mission to the slaves. By the 1820s southern evangelicalism had long since abandoned its hostility toward slavery, and slaveholders commonly attended camp meetings and revivals. These prosperous converts faced conflicting duties. Their churches taught them that slaves had immortal souls and that planters were as responsible for the spiritual welfare of their slaves as they were for the spiritual welfare of their own children. One preacher remarked that it was difficult "to treat them as property, and at the same time render to them that which is just and equal as immortal and accountable beings, and as heirs of the grace of life, equally with our-selves." A planter on his deathbed told his children that humane treatment and religious instruction for slaves was the duty of slave owners; if these were ne-glected, "we will have to answer for the loss of their souls." After Nat Turner's bloody slave revolt in 1831 (to be discussed later in this chapter), missions to the slaves took on new urgency: If the churches were to help create a family-centered, Christian so-ciety in the South, that society would have to include the slaves. The result after 1830 was a concerted at-tempt to Christianize the slaves.

To this end, Charles Colcock Jones, a Presbyter-ian minister from Georgia, spent much of his career writing manuals on how to preach to slaves. He taught that no necessary connection linked social po-sition and spiritual worth—that there were good and bad slaveholders and good and bad slaves. He also taught, preaching from the Epistles of Paul ("Ser-vants, obey your masters"), that slaves must accept the master's authority as God's, and that obedience was their prime religious virtue. Jones warned white preachers never to become personally involved with their slave listeners—to pay no attention to their quarrels, their complaints about their master or about their fellow slaves, or about working conditions on the plantation. "We separate entirely their religious from their civil condition," he said, "and contend that one may be attended to without interfering with the other." The catechism Jones prepared for slaves in-cluded the question, "What did God make you for?" The answer was, "To make a crop."

The evangelical mission to the slaves was not as completely self-serving as it may seem. For to ac-cept one's worldly station, to be obedient and duti-ful within that station, and to seek salvation outside of this world were precisely what the planters de-manded of themselves and their own families. An

LINK TO THE PAST

Africans in America (PBS)

http://www.pbs.org/wgbh/aia/home.html

This is a large Web site tied to a four-part PBS documentary on American slavery. It includes es-says by historians, an activities guide, and substantial excerpts from a wide variety of primary sources. Analyze the documents in Section 2 under "Conspiracy and Rebellion," and in Section 3 under "Antebellum Slavery," and think about these questions:

1. In the rebellions of Denmark Vesey and Nat Turner, what was the role of religion and/or revo-lutionary republicanism?

2. How would you describe the white responses to these rebellions? Why do you think whites re-sponded in those particular ways?

3. The documents in Section 3 concentrate on slavery on the Georgia and South Carolina sea is-lands and on the plantation of Pierce Butler and his wife, Frances Kemble, in particular. What can those documents tell us about the duties, attitudes, and experiences of plantation masters and plantation mistresses? What can they tell us about the experiences of slaves, particularly the ex-perience of being bought and sold?

Beloved (1998)

Directed by Jonathan Demme. Starring Danny Glover, Oprah Winfrey, Beah Richards.

Oprah Winfrey produced and starred in this adaptation of Toni Morrison's Pulitzer Prize–winning novel. It is a story of persisting personal and communal wounds inflicted by slavery, told from within a damaged black household near Cincinnati in 1873.

The action begins when Paul D (Danny Glover) walks up to the house of Sethe (Oprah Winfrey) and her daughter, Denver. As he enters, the house fills with a red glow, and shakes itself into a storm of furniture and kitchen implements. The house is haunted by the ghost of Sethe's baby girl. Paul D is a former slave from Sweet Home, the horrific Kentucky plantation from which Sethe escaped. He moves in, the ghost moves out, and the film follows this household through the next year.

Peace lasts only a short time. A strange young woman named Beloved moves in and becomes Denver's sister, Sethe's daughter, and Paul D's mystical seducer. (The camera pans back from the seduction scene in the red glow that we remember from the initial haunting.) Paul D discovers that Sethe had killed her own baby in 1856 and he leaves. Beloved, now

pregnant, demands (and gets) Sethe's time, money, and affection. Sethe loses her job and runs out of food and money—serving Beloved all the while. Denver begs work from an old teacher, and the community of black women, who have shunned Sethe and her family throughout the movie, begin leaving food. In the climactic scene, Denver waits on the porch for her new white employer (a former abolitionist), when the black women arrive to sing and chant in an effort to exorcise ghosts from the house. Sethe, crazed, followed by naked and pregnant Beloved, comes onto the porch and attacks the employer with an ice pick. The women subdue her, Denver rides off (like her brothers before her) to another life, and Beloved disappears. The film ends with the return of Paul D, and we are left with the hope that Sethe may outlive her ghosts.

Although the action occurs in 1873, the explanation lies in slavery, and in the 1856 escape attempt told—in conversation, dreams, and flashbacks—as memory. Love scenes between Sethe and Paul D display the scars of whippings—particularly on Sethe.

---

important goal of plantation missions was of course to create safe and profitable plantations. Yet that goal was to be achieved by Christianizing both slaveholders and slaves—a lesson that some slaveholders learned when they were expelled from their churches for mistreating their slaves.

SLAVE CHRISTIANS

The white attempt to Christianize slavery, however, depended on the acceptance of slavery by the slaves. But the biblical notion that slavery might be a punishment for sin and the doctrine of divinely ordained social orders never took root among the

slaves. Hannah Scott, a slave in Arkansas, remarked on what she heard a white preacher say: "But all he say is 'bedience to de white folks, and we hears 'nough of dat without him telling us." One slave asked a white preacher, "Is us slaves gonna be free in heaven?" The preacher quickly changed the subject. As one maid boldly told her mistress, *God never made us to be slaves for white people.*

Although the slaves ignored much of what the missionaries taught, they embraced evangelical Christianity and transformed it into an independent African American faith. Some slave owners encouraged them by building "praise houses" on their plantations and by permitting religious meetings.

She saw her mother hanged, she was whipped and beaten while pregnant, and her owner's sons held her down and sucked the milk from her. (Sethe learns later that her husband, whom she thought had abandoned her, witnessed this scene from a hayloft and went hopelessly insane.) Her escape is botched and violent. Sethe secretly sends her two sons ahead to Baby Suggs (Beah Richards), her mother-in-law in Ohio. Sethe sets off alone, gives birth to Denver on the banks of the Ohio, crosses the river, and spends one perfect month tending her children and going to Baby Suggs's church meetings in the woods—meetings at which Suggs demands that her people love themselves. Then the old master arrives to take them back to Kentucky, and Sethe grabs the children, takes them into an outbuilding, and tries to kill them—succeeding only with Denver's infant older sister.

It all works better in Morrison's novel than in Oprah Winfrey's movie, but both are terrible and disturbing dramatizations of the injury slavery inflicted, and of African American attempts to both absorb and transcend the crimes committed against them.

Beloved (1998) stars Danny Glover and Oprah Winfrey and is based on Toni Morrison's Pulitzer Prize–winning novel.

Others tried to resist the trend, but with little success. After 1830 most of the southern states outlawed black preachers, but the laws could not be enforced. James Henry Hammond, a rich South Carolina planter, tried for 20 years to stop his slaves from holding religious meetings, but at night they would slip off to secret gatherings in the woods. Sometimes slaves met in a cabin—preaching, praying, and singing in a whisper. At their meetings they rehearsed a faith that was at variance with the faith of the slaveholders. Reverend Anderson Edwards, a slave preacher from Texas, recalled that he "had to preach what Massa told me. And he say tell them niggers iffen they obeys the Massa they goes to heaven, but I knowed there's something better for them, but daren't tell them 'cept on the sly. That I done lots. I tells 'em iffen they keeps prayin' the Lord will set 'em free."

One way in which slave religion differed from what was preached to them by whites was in the practice of conjuring, folk magic, root medicine, and other occult knowledge—most of it passed down from West Africa. Such practices addressed areas in which Christianity was useless: curing illnesses, making people fall in love, ensuring a good day's fishing, or bringing harm to one's enemies. Sometimes African magic competed with plantation Christianity. Just as often, however, slaves combined the two. For instance, slaves sometimes determined the guilt or innocence of a person accused of stealing by hanging a Bible by a thread, then watching the way it turned. The form was West African; the Bible was not. The slave root doctor George White boasted that he could "cure most anything," but added that "you got to talk wid God an' ask him to help out." "Maum Addie," a slave in coastal South Carolina, dealt with the malevolent African spirits called plat-eyes with a combination of African potions, the Christian God, and a stout stick: "So I totes mah powder en sulphur en I carries mah stick in mah han en puts mah truss in Gawd."

Christianity could not cure sick babies or identify thieves, but it gave slaves something more important: a sense of themselves as a historical people with a role to play in God's cosmic drama. In slave Christianity, Moses the liberator (and not the slaveholders' Abraham) stood beside Jesus. Indeed the slaves' appropriation of the book of Exodus denied the smug assumption of the whites that they were God's chosen people who had escaped the bondage of despotic Europe to enter the promised land of America. To the slaves, America was Egypt, they were the chosen people, and the slaveholders were Pharaoh. Thomas Wentworth Higginson, a Boston abolitionist who went south during the Civil War to lead a Union regiment of freed South Carolina slaves, wrote that his men knew the Old Testament books of Moses and the New Testament book of Revelation. "All that lies between," he said, "even the life of Jesus, they hardly cared to read or to hear." He found their minds "a vast bewildered chaos of Jewish history and biography; and most of the events of the past, down to the period of the American Revolution, they instinctively attribute to Moses." The slaves' religious songs, which became known as "spirituals," told of God's people, their travails, and their ultimate deliverance. In songs and sermons the figures of Jesus and Moses were often blurred, and it was not always clear whether deliverance—accompanied by divine retribution—would take place in this world or the next. In any case, deliverance always meant an end to slavery, with the possibility that it might bring a reversal of relations between slaves and masters. "The idea of a revolution in the conditions of the whites and

PLANTATION BURIAL Slave funerals retained strong West African as well as Christian accents. Burials often took place at night, and mourners were careful to placate the spirits of the dead, who remained temporarily in this world and could torment their enemies.

blacks," said the escaped slave Charles Ball, "is the corner-stone of the religion of the latter."

RELIGION AND REVOLT

Unlike slaves in Cuba, Jamaica, Brazil, and other New World plantation societies, North American slaves seldom went into organized, armed revolt. The environment of the United States was unfriendly to such events. American plantations were relatively small and dispersed, and the southern white population was large, vigilant, and well armed. Whites also enjoyed—until the cataclysm of the Civil War—internal political stability. The slaves encountered few promising opportunities to win their freedom by violent means. Thousands of slaves demonstrated their hatred of the system by running away. Others fought slave owners or overseers, sabotaged equipment and animals, stole from planters, and found other ways to oppose slavery, but most knew that open revolt was suicide.

Christianity convinced slaves that history was headed toward an apocalypse that would result in divine justice and their own deliverance, and thus held out the possibility of revolt. Slave preachers seldom indulged in prophecy and almost never told their congregations to become actively engaged in God's divine plan, for they knew that open resistance was hopeless. Slave Christians believed that God hated slavery and would end it, but that their role was to have faith in God, to take care of one another, to preserve their identity as a people, and to await deliverance. Only occasionally did slaves take retribution and deliverance into their own hands.

The most ambitious conspiracy was hatched by Denmark Vesey, a free black of Charleston, South Carolina. Vesey was a leading member of an African Methodist congregation that had seceded from the white Methodists and had been independent from 1817 to 1821. At its height, the church had 6,000 members—most of them slaves. Vesey and some of the other members read widely in political tracts, including the antislavery arguments in the Missouri debates (see chapter 12) and in the Bible. They talked about their delivery out of Egypt, with all white men, women, and children being cut off. They identified Charleston as Jericho and planned its destruction in 1822: A few dozen

Charleston blacks would take the state armory, then arm rural slaves who would rise up to help them. They would kill the whites, take control of the city, commandeer ships in the harbor, and make their getaway—presumably to black-controlled Haiti. Word of the conspiracy spread secretly into the countryside, largely through the efforts of Gullah Jack, who was both a Methodist and an African conjurer. Jack recruited African-born slaves as soldiers, provided them with charms as protection against whites, and used his spiritual powers to terrify others into keeping silent.

In the end, the Vesey plot was betrayed by slaves. As one coerced confession followed another, white authorities hanged Vesey, Gullah Jack, and 34 other accused conspirators—22 of them in one day. Even so, frightened whites knew that most of the conspirators (estimates ranged from 600 to 9,000) remained at large and unidentified.

NAT TURNER

In August 1831, in a revolt in Southampton County, Virginia, some 60 slaves shot and hacked to death 55 white men, women, and children. Their leader was Nat Turner, a Baptist lay preacher. Turner was neither a conjurer like Gullah Jack (indeed, he violently opposed plantation conjurers) nor a republican revolutionary like Denmark Vesey or the Richmond slave Gabriel (see chapter 7). He was, he told his captors, an Old Testament prophet and an instrument of God's wrath. As a child, he had prayed and fasted often, and the spirit—the same spirit who had spoken to the prophets of the Bible—had spoken directly to him. When he was a young man, he had run away to escape a cruel overseer, but when God told him that he had not chosen Nat merely to have him run away, Nat returned. He justified his return by quoting one of the slave owners' favorite verses of scripture: "He who knoweth his master's will and doeth it not, shall be beaten with many stripes." But Turner made it clear that his Master was God, not a slave owner.

Around 1830, Turner received visions of the final battle in Revelation, recast as a fight between white and black spirits. He saw Christ crucified against the night sky, and the next morning he saw Christ's blood in a cornfield. Convinced by a solar

NAT TURNER This contemporary woodcut depicts scenes from Nat Turner's rebellion. In this bloodiest of all North American slave revolts, 55 whites, most of them women and children, were shot and hacked to death.

eclipse in February 1831 that the time had come, Turner began telling other slaves about his visions, recruited his force, and launched a bloody and hopeless revolt that ended in mass murder, failure, and the execution of Turner and his followers.

The Vesey and Turner revolts, along with scores of more limited conspiracies, deeply troubled southern whites. Paternalistic slaveholders were increasingly committed to making slavery both domestic and Christian. For their part, slaves recognized that they could receive decent treatment and pockets of autonomy in return for outward docility. Vesey and Turner opened wide cracks in that mutual charade. During the Turner revolt, slaves whose masters had been murdered joined the rebels without a second thought. A plantation mistress who survived by hiding in a closet listened to the murders of her husband and children and heard her house servants arguing over possession of her clothes. A Charleston grandee named Elias Horry, upon finding that his coachman was among the Vesey conspirators, asked him, "What were your intentions?" The formerly submissive slave replied that he had intended "to kill you, rip open your belly, and throw your guts in your face."

Such stories sent a chill through the white South—a suspicion that despite the appearance of peace, they were surrounded by people who would kill them in an instant. While northerners patronized plays and cheap fiction that dramatized the trickery and horror beneath placid appearances, the nightmares of slaveholding paternalists were both more savage and closer to home.

CONCLUSION

By the second quarter of the 19th century, Americans had made a patchwork of regional, class, and ethnic cultures. The new middle classes of the North and West compounded their Protestant and republican inheritance with a new entrepreneurial faith in progress. The result was a way of life grounded in the self-made and morally accountable individual and the sentimentalized (often feminized) domestic unit.

Their means of proposing that way of life as a national culture for the United States often offended others. The middle class met resistance, first of all, from poorer urban dwellers and the less prosperous farmers in their own sections—a northern and western majority that remained grimly loyal to the unsentimental, male-dominated families of their fathers and grandfathers, to new and old religious sects that continued to believe in human depravity and the mysterious workings of providence, and to the suspicion that perfidy and disorder lurked behind the smiling moral order of market economics and sentimental culture. They were also people who enjoyed dark and playful popular entertainments that often mocked middle-class sentimentalism. In the South, most white farmers persisted in a neighborhood-based, intensely evangelical, and socially conservative way of life; when asked their opinions, they often talked like classic Jeffersonian yeomen. Southern planters, although they shared in the northern elite's belief in material progress and the magic of the market, were bound by family values, a system of slave labor, and a code of honor that was strikingly at variance with middle-class faith in an orderly universe and perfectible individuals. Slaves in these

years continued to make cultural forms of their own; and despite their exclusion from the white world of liberty and equality, they tied their aspirations to the family (though in broader and more flexible ways than most whites), to an evangelical Protestant God, and to the individual and collective dignity that republics promise to their citizens.

**Suggested Readings begin on page SR-1.
For Web activities and resources
related to this chapter, go to
http://www.harcourtcollege.com/history.murrin**

CHAPTER 11

SOCIETY, CULTURE, AND POLITICS, 1820s–1840s

CANVASSING FOR A VOTE

Electioneering in Jacksonian America was continuous with everyday social and cultural life. Here the Whig artist and politician George Caleb Bingham depicts four men talking outside a Missouri tavern. Although they could be talking about anything, Bingham tells us the man in the top hat at right is a politician, busily canvassing for a vote.

Between 1820 and 1845 Thomas Jefferson's agrarian republic became Andrew Jackson's noisy and deeply divided mass democracy. Politicians who built the Whig and Democratic Parties, which helped to bring about that change, participated in the economic and social transformations of those years as both consumers and producers of new forms of popular culture. In making their political appeals they tapped skillfully into the national patchwork of aspiration, fear, and resentment. John Quincy Adams, Henry Clay, and their National Republican and Whig allies in the states concocted visions of smooth-running, government-sponsored transportation and monetary systems. Such visions echoed the faith in cosmic order, material progress, and moral improvement that had become cultural axioms for the more prosperous and cosmopolitan Americans. Democrats, on the other hand, defended Jefferson's republic of limited government and widespread equality and liberty. They portrayed a haunted political universe in which trickery, deceit, and special privilege lurked behind the promises and power-hunger of the Whigs.

Politicians constructed the Whig and Democratic coalitions largely at the neighborhood and state levels. Their arguments for and against state-supported internal improvements and state-chartered banks and corporations mirrored the ideological wars fought out nationally between Whigs and Jacksonian Democrats (see chapter 12.) At the same time, national debates incorporated Democratic and Whig attitudes on family, religion, race, gender, ethnicity, class, and the proper functions of government that had been shaped by state-level debates. Those local and state issues and the social and cultural constituencies that argued them out are the subjects of this chapter.

This chapter will focus on the following major questions:

- Which Americans were likely to support the Democratic Party in the 1830s and 1840s? Which Americans were likely to support the Whigs?
- What were Whig and Democratic conceptions of the duties and limits of government?
- What were the principal social reform movements of these years, and how did the political parties react to them?
- How did Whigs and Democrats differ on questions of gender and race?

CHRONOLOGY

1816 African Methodist Episcopal denomination founded in Philadelphia • American Colonization Society promises to repatriate blacks to Africa

1819 New York state builds the first prison under the Auburn System

1826 Reformers found the American Society for the Promotion of Temperance

1831 William Lloyd Garrison begins publication of the antislavery *Liberator* • New York Magdalen Society publishes its first annual report

1833 Abolitionists found the American Anti-Slavery Society

1834 Antiabolition mob riots in New York City • First major race riot breaks out in Philadelphia

1840 Working-class drinkers found the Washington Temperance Society

1848 First Women's Rights Convention held in Seneca Falls, New York

1851 Maine becomes the first of 17 states to enact statewide prohibition

1860 New York enacts the Married Women's Property Act

CONSTITUENCIES

By the 1830s support for the Democratic or Whig Party was a matter of personal identity as much as of political preference: A man's vote demonstrated his personal history, his cultural values, and his vision of the good society as clearly as it demonstrated his opinion on any particular political issue. Voters remained loyal to their parties in selecting officeholders ranging from local coroners and school board members to state legislators and presidents of the United States. Thus, political parties reduced the stupendous diversity of American society to two political choices. Of course limiting citizenship to white men narrowed diversity in the electorate, as did the fact that the youngest and poorest white men often failed to vote. But even with the deck stacked in favor of a homogeneous electorate, the Whig and Democratic Parties were national coalitions of ill-matched regional, economic, ethnic, and religious groups. They were united by Whig and Democratic political cultures—consistent attitudes toward government and politics embedded in religion, family, and economic life. For all their patchwork diversity, the Democratic and Whig Parties appealed to coherent constituencies and proposed coherent programs in every corner of the republic.

THE NORTH AND WEST

In the North and West, the makers of what would become the Whig Party found their most loyal support at the centers of the market revolution and the Finneyite revival. The broad band of Yankee commercial farms stretching across southern New England, western New York, and the Old Northwest was the northern Whig heartland. Whigs also enjoyed support in northern cities and towns. The wealthiest men in cities were Whigs; more than 8 in 10 among the merchant elite of Boston and New York supported them. The new urban commercial classes created in the market revolution also supported the Whigs. Factory owners were solidly Whig, and native-born factory workers often joined them—in part because Whigs promised opportunities to rise in the world, in part because Whigs protected their jobs by encouraging domestic markets for what they made, and, increasingly, because Whigs pandered to their fears of immigrant labor. For similar reasons, many skilled urban artisans supported the Whigs, as did smaller numbers of dockworkers, day laborers, and others among the unskilled.

Northern Whiggery was grounded in the market revolution, but the Whig political agenda ranged far beyond economic life. The strongholds of Whiggery and the market were also the strongholds of the Finneyite revival. Among the urban middle class and in the more market-oriented rural neighborhoods, the inheritors of Puritan theocracy translated the spirit of the late 1820s and early 1830s revivals into an avowedly Christian Whig politics. Northern and western Whigs demanded that government actively encourage the transition to market society. At the same time, they called for moral legislation on such issues as Sabbath observance, temperance, and Bible-based public schools. Marching under the banner of activist government,

THE COUNTY ELECTION The Whig artist-politician George Caleb Bingham said this election day scene was "illustrative of the manners of a free people and free institutions." It was a wry comment: Many of the figures are Missouri Democratic politicians who had, Bingham thought, cheated him in a contested election to the state legislature.

economic development, and moral progress, Whigs set the political agenda in most northern states.

They met a determined Democratic opposition. Campaigning as defenders of the Jeffersonian republic, autonomous neighborhoods, and private conscience, Democrats found supporters among cultural traditionalists who had gained little from the expansion of national markets and who had no use for the moral agenda of the Whigs. The "Butternuts" (so named for the yellow vegetable dye with which they colored their homespun clothing) of the southern, river-oriented counties of the Northwest joined the Democratic Party. Farmers in the Allegheny Mountains of southern New York and northern Pennsylvania, in the declining (and non-Yankee) countryside of the Hudson River valley, and in the poor and isolated hill towns of northern and western New England also supported the Democrats.

In cities and towns, Democrats made up substantial minorities among businessmen, master craftsmen, and professionals, but most urban Democrats were wage earners. Perhaps the most overwhelmingly Democratic group in the country were immigrant Irish Catholics, who were filling the lower ranks of the urban workforce. Indeed, their presence in the Democratic Party pushed increasing numbers of native Protestant workers into the Whig ranks—a division that appeared in New York City in the early 1830s, in most cities and towns by the 1840s, and that pervaded the North and West in the 1850s.

When confronted with opposition to evangelical legislation, Whigs labeled the Democratic Party the party of atheism and immorality. Democrats responded that they opposed theocracy, not religion. True, most freethinkers, atheists, and persons who simply did not care about religion supported the Democratic Party. So did immigrant Catholics, who rightfully feared the militant Protestantism of the Whigs. Democrats, however, won the support of hundreds of thousands of evangelical Protestants as well. At least half of Methodists, Baptists, Disciples of Christ, Old School Presbyterians, and members of Reformed churches put their faith in providence and individual piety, and deeply distrusted what they called "church and state" Whiggery and the mixing of politics and religion. "I am myself a candidate," said a Methodist Democrat in 1840, "but it is for eternal life. I aspire to a throne, but I must have one which will not perish." Evangelical Democrats were joined by sectarian Christians who looked to the Democrats for protection: Freewill Baptists, Universalists, Lutherans, Scots Covenanters, many Quakers, Mormons, and others. These Democratic churchgoers rejected Whig moral legislation as antirepublican and as Yankee cultural imperialism. George Washington Bethune, a Dutch Reformed minister and a New York Democrat, put the Democratic creed succinctly: "Religion is not to be advanced by civil power."

THE SOUTH

Throughout the 1830s and 1840s, the southern states divided their votes equally between Whigs and Democrats with most individual southern localities either solidly Democratic or solidly Whig. In the 1844 elections, for instance, the counties of Virginia and Alabama supported their favored candidates by margins of 23 and 27 percent, respectively—landslide margins by the standards of two-party politics. (The comparable figure for New York counties was 9 percent.) Much more than in the North, southern party preferences were tied to differences in economic life.

Isolationist southern neighborhoods tended to support the Democrats. Thus Democrats ran strongest in yeoman neighborhoods with few slaves and relatively little market activity—up-country communities that valued household independence and the society of neighbors and that deeply distrusted intrusions from the outside. The more cosmopolitan southern communities tended to support the Whigs. In general, this meant that Whigs were strongest in plantation counties, where they commanded the votes not only of wealthy planters but of smaller farmers, and of lawyers, storekeepers, and craftsmen in county-seat towns. Upland, nonplantation neighborhoods in which Whigs ran well (eastern Tennessee, western North Carolina, and parts of Virginia are examples) were places where Whigs promised state-sponsored internal improvements that would link ambitious but isolated farmers to outside markets. On the other hand, some plantation districts with easy access to markets, such as the South Carolina low country, opposed expensive Whig projects that would benefit other areas.

Many other southern exceptions to the link between commerce and the Whig Party were grounded in the prestige and power of local leaders. Southern statesmen who broke with the Jacksonians in the 1830s—John C. Calhoun in South Carolina, Hugh Lawson White in Tennessee, and others—took personal and regional followings with them (see chapter 12). Political campaigners also had to contend with southerners such as George Reynolds of Pickens County, Alabama. Reynolds was a half-literate yeoman who fathered 17 children and had 234 direct descendants living in his neighborhood, which he delivered as a bloc to politicians who pleased him. Despite the vagaries of southern kinship and community, Whigs knew that their core constituency in the South was in communities that were or wanted to be linked to commercial society.

In sharp contrast with the North and West, southern political divisions had little to do with religion. The South was thoroughly evangelized by 1830, but southern Baptists, Methodists, and Presbyterians seldom combined religion and politics. The southern evangelical churches had begun as marginal movements that opposed the Anglican establishment; they continued to distrust ties between church and state. Although they enforced morality within their own households and congregations, southern evangelicals seldom asked state legislatures to pass moral legislation. In extreme cases, southern premillennialists rejected politics altogether, insisting that Jesus would soon return to take the reins of government. (One political canvasser faced with that argument responded, "I will bet one hundred dollars he can't carry Kentucky.") Southern evangelicals who embraced the world of the market assumed, along with their northern Whig counterparts, that the new economy encouraged a Christian, civilized life. Other southern churchgoers responded to the Jacksonians' denunciations of greed and the spirit of speculation. Thus, even though many southern communities were bitterly divided over religion, the divisions seldom shaped party politics.

The social, religious, cultural, and economic bases of party divisions formed coherent Whig and Democratic political cultures. Whig voters in the North and South either were or hoped to become beneficiaries of the market revolution and wanted government to subsidize economic development.

In the North, they also demanded that government help shape market society into a prosperous, orderly, and homogeneous Christian republic. Democrats, North and South, demanded a minimal government that kept taxes low and that left citizens, their families, and their neighborhoods alone.

THE POLITICS OF ECONOMIC DEVELOPMENT

Both Whigs and Democrats accepted the transition to market society, but they wanted to direct it into different channels. Whigs wanted to use government and the market to make an economically and morally progressive—albeit hierarchical—republic. Democrats viewed both government and the new institutions of market society with suspicion and vowed to allow neither to subvert the equal rights and rough equality of condition that were, in their view, the preconditions of republican citizenship. In language that echoed their Jeffersonian forebears, Jacksonian Democrats demanded that the market remain subservient to the republic.

GOVERNMENT AND ITS LIMITS

"The government," remarked a New York City Whig in 1848, "is not merely a machine for making wars and punishing felons, but is bound to do all that is within its power to promote the welfare of the People—its legitimate scope is not merely negative, representative, defensive, but also affirmative, creative, constructive, beneficent." *The American Review*, a Whig periodical, agreed: "Forms of government are instituted for the protection and fostering of virtue, and are valuable only as they accomplish this."

The Whigs insisted that economic development, moral progress, and social harmony were linked and that government should foster them. Market society, they argued, opened up opportunities for individual Americans. As long as people developed the work habits and moral discipline required for success, they would be rewarded. To poor farmers and city workers who believed that the market revolution undermined their independence, Whigs promised social mobility within a new system of interdependence—but only to deserving individuals. According to the New York *Herald* in 1836, "The

mechanic who attends quietly to his business—is industrious and attentive—belongs to no club—never visits the porter-house—is always at work or with his family—such a man gradually rises in society and becomes an honor to himself, his friends, and to human nature." The *Herald* editor continued, "On the contrary, look at the Trade Unionist—the pot-house agitator—the stirrer-up of sedition—the clamorer for higher wages—After a short time, he ends his career in the Pen or State Prison." Whigs believed that the United States exhibited a harmony of class interests and an equality of opportunity that every virtuous person would recognize and that only resentful, mean-spirited, unworthy people would doubt. Pointing to self-made Whigs such as Daniel Webster and Abraham Lincoln, they demanded activist government that nurtured the economic, cultural, and moral opportunities provided by market society.

Democrats seldom praised or condemned market society per se. Instead, they argued for the primacy of citizenship: Neither government nor the market, they said, should be allowed to subvert the civil and legal equality among independent men on which the republic rested. Often sharing a view of human nature that was (in contrast to the Whigs' more optimistic views) a grim combination of classical republicanism and gothic romance, Democrats saw government not as a tool of progress but as a dangerous—although regrettably necessary—concentration of power in the hands of imperfect, self-interested men. The only safe course was to limit its power. In 1837, the *United States Magazine and Democratic Review* declared: "The best government is that which governs least," and went on to denounce the "natural imperfection, both in wisdom and judgment and purity of purpose, of all human legislation, exposed constantly to the pressure of partial interest; interests which, at the same time that they are essentially selfish and tyrannical, are ever vigilant, persevering, and subtle in all the arts of deception and corruption."

Democrats argued that the Whig belief in benign government and social harmony was absurd. Corporate charters, privileged banks, and subsidies to turnpike, canal, and railroad companies, they said, benefited privileged insiders and transformed republican government into an engine of inequality. Granting such privileges, warned one Democrat, was sure "to break up that social equality which is the legitimate foundation of our institutions, and the destruction of which would render our boasted freedom a mere phantom." George Bancroft, a radical Democrat from Massachusetts, concurred: "A republican people," he said, "should be in an equality in their social and political condition; . . . pure democracy inculcates equal rights—equal laws—equal means of education—and *equal means* of wealth also." By contrast, the government favored by the Whigs would enrich a favored few. Bancroft and other Democrats demanded limited government that was deaf to the demands of special interests.

BANKS

Andrew Jackson's national administration destroyed the Bank of the United States (see chapter 12). As a result, regulation of banking, credit, and currency fell to the state governments. The proper role of banks emerged as a central political issue in nearly every state, particularly after the widespread bank failures following the crash of 1837. Whigs defended banks as agents of economic progress, arguing that they provided credit for roads and canals, loans to businessmen and commercial farmers, and the banknotes that served as the chief medium of exchange. Democrats, on the other hand, branded banks as agents of inequality dominated by insiders who controlled artificial concentrations of money, who enjoyed chartered privileges, and who issued banknotes and expanded or contracted credit to their own advantage. In short, they regarded banks as government-protected institutions that enabled a privileged few to make themselves rich at the public's expense.

The economic boom of the 1830s and the destruction of the national bank created a dramatic expansion in the number of state-chartered banks—from 329 in 1830 to 788 in 1837. Systems varied from state to state. South Carolina, Georgia, Tennessee, Kentucky, and Arkansas had state-owned banks. Many new banks in the Old Northwest were also partially state-owned. Such banks often operated as public-service institutions. Georgia's Central Bank, for example, served farmers who could not qualify for private loans, as did other state-owned banks in the South. The charter of the Agricultural Bank of Mississippi (1833) stipulated

that at least half of the bank's capital be in long-term loans (farm mortgages) rather than in short-term loans to merchants.

Beginning in the 1820s many states had introduced uniform banking laws to replace the unique charters previously granted to individual banks. The new laws tried to stabilize currency and credit. In New York, the Safety-Fund Law of 1829 required banks to pool a fraction of their resources to protect both bankers and small noteholders in the case of bank failures. The result was a self-regulating and conservative community of state banks. Laws in other states required that banks maintain a high ratio of specie (precious metals) to notes in circulation. Such laws, however, were often evaded. Michigan's bank inspectors, for instance, complained that the same cache of silver and gold was taken from bank to bank one step ahead of them. At one bank, an inspector encountered a bank teller who had 10 metal boxes behind his counter. The teller opened one of the boxes and showed that it was full of federal silver dollars. The wary inspector picked up another one and found that it was full of nails covered with a thin layer of silver dollars. All the other boxes were the same, except for one that was filled with broken glass. Many Americans greeted such stories with a knowing wink until the Panic of 1837, when they presented state banknotes for redemption in specie and were turned down.

"Hard Money" Democrats (those who wanted to get rid of paper money altogether) regarded banks as centers of trickery and privilege and proposed that they be abolished. Banks, they claimed, with their manipulation of credit and currency, encouraged speculation, luxury, inequality, and the separation of wealth from real work. Jackson himself branded banks "a perfect humbug." An Alabama Democrat declared that banking was "in conflict with justice, equity, morality and religion" and that there was "nothing evil that it does not aid—nothing good that it is not averse to." Senator Bedford Brown of North Carolina doubted "whether banking institutions were at all compatible with the existence of a truly republican government," and Richard Swinton of Iowa dismissed banks as "a set of swindling machines." Samuel Medary of Ohio cast banks as the villains of Democratic melodrama. Banks possess, Medary wrote, "every inducement to attract the confidence of the unwary and seduce into

A THREE-DOLLAR BILL This three-dollar bill was no joke. It was one of the small private banknotes that Democrats wanted to take out of circulation.

their grasp the most watchful and shrewd, by the convenience and safety they hold out to the public through a thousand pretenses of being the exclusive friends and engines of trade and commerce."

In state legislatures, Whigs defended what had become a roughly standard system of private banks chartered by state governments. They had the right to circulate banknotes and had limited liability to protect directors and stockholders from debts incurred by their bank. Many Democrats proposed abolishing all banks. Others proposed reforms. They demanded a high ratio of specie reserves to banknotes as a guard against inflationary paper money. They proposed eliminating the issuance of bank notes in small denominations, thus ensuring that day-to-day business would be conducted in hard coin and protecting wage earners and small farmers from speculative ups and downs. Democrats also wanted to hold bank directors and stockholders responsible for corporate debts and bankruptcies; some proposed banning corporate charters altogether.

By these and other means, Democrats in the states protected currency and credit from the government favoritism, dishonesty, and elitism that, they argued, enriched Whig insiders and impoverished honest Democrats. Whigs responded that corporate privileges and immunities and an abundant, elastic currency were keys to economic devel-

opment, and they fought Democrats every step of the way.

INTERNAL IMPROVEMENTS

Democrats in Congress and the White House blocked federally funded roads and canals (see chapter 12). In response, the states launched the transportation revolution themselves, either by taking direct action or by chartering private corporations to do the work (see chapter 9). State legislatures everywhere debated the wisdom of direct state action, of corporate privileges, of subsidies to canals and railroads, and of the accumulation of government debt. Whigs, predictably, favored direct action by state governments. Democrats were lukewarm toward the whole idea of internal improvements, convinced that debt, favoritism, and corruption would inevitably result from government involvement in the economy.

Whigs assumed a connection between market society and moral progress—and used that relationship as a basis of their argument for internal improvements. William H. Seward, the Whig governor of New York, supported transportation projects because they broke down neighborhood isolation and hastened the emergence of a market society with "all the consequent advantages of morality, piety, and knowledge." The historian

Henry Adams, who grew up in a wealthy Whig household in Boston, later recalled that his father had taught him about a strong connection between good roads and good morals. In the minds of Whig legislators, a vote for internal improvements was a vote for moral progress and for individual opportunity within a prosperous and happily interdependent market society.

Democratic state legislators, though with less enthusiasm, supported at least some internal improvements, but they opposed "partial" legislation that would benefit part of their state at the expense of the rest. They also opposed projects that would lead to higher taxes and put state governments into debt—arguments that gathered force after the crash of 1837 bankrupted states that had overextended themselves in the canal boom of the 1830s. The Democrats made the same argument in every state: Beneath Whig plans for extensive improvements lay schemes to create special privilege, inequality, debt, and corruption—all at the expense of a hoodwinked people.

THE POLITICS OF SOCIAL REFORM

In the North, the churchgoing middle class provided the Whig Party with a political culture, a reform-oriented social agenda, and most of its electoral support. Whig evangelicals believed that with God's help they could improve the world by improving the individuals within it, and they enlisted the Whig Party in that campaign. On a variety of issues including prostitution, temperance, public education, and state-supported insane asylums and penitentiaries, Whigs used government to improve individual morality and discipline. Democrats, on the other hand, argued that attempts to dictate morality through legislation were both antirepublican and wrong. Questions of social reform provoked the most angry differences between Democrats and Whigs, particularly in the North.

PUBLIC SCHOOLS

During the second quarter of the 19th century, local and state governments built systems of tax-supported public schools, known as "common" schools. Before that time, most children learned reading, writing, and arithmetic at home, in poorly staffed town schools, in private schools, or in charity schools run by churches or other benevolent organizations. Despite the lack of any "system" of education, most children learned to read and write. That was, however, more likely among boys than among girls, among whites than among blacks, and among northeasterners than among westerners or southerners.

By the 1830s Whigs and Democrats agreed that providing common schools was a proper function of government. And Democrats often agreed with Whigs that schools could equalize opportunity. Massachusetts Democrat Robert Rantoul, for example, believed that rich and poor children should "be brought equally and together up to the starting point at the public expense; after that we must shift for ourselves." More radical Democrats, however, wanted public schooling that would erase snobbery. A newspaper declared in 1828 that "the children of the rich and the poor shall receive a national education, calculated to make republicans and banish aristocrats." Marcus Morton, Democratic governor of Massachusetts, agreed that it was the job of the common schools to democratize children "before the pride of family or wealth, or other adventitious distinction has taken a deep root in the young heart."

The reformers who created the most advanced, expensive, and centralized state school systems were Whigs: Horace Mann of Massachusetts, Henry Barnard of Connecticut, Calvin Stowe (husband of Harriet Beecher) of Ohio, and others. These reformers talked more about character building and Whig Protestant culture than about the three R's, convinced that it was the schools' first duty to train youngsters to respect authority, property, hard work, and social order. They wanted schools that would downplay class divisions, but they were interested less in democratizing wealthy children than in civilizing the poor. Calvin H. Wiley, the Whig superintendent of schools in North Carolina, promised that proper schools would make Americans "homogeneous . . . intelligent, eminently republican, sober, calculating, moral and conservative." A Whig newspaper in Ohio declared in 1836 that character-building schools were essential in a democracy: "Other nations have hereditary sovereigns, and one of the most important duties of their governments is to

THE EUREKA SCHOOLHOUSE IN SPRINGFIELD, VERMONT Mandated by state law and supported by local taxes, such one-room schools taught generations of American children the three R's.

take care of the education of the heir to their throne; these children all about your streets . . . are your future sovereigns." William Seward, the Whig governor of New York, insisted that "education tends to produce equality, not by leveling all to the condition of the base, but by elevating all to the association of the wise and good."

The schools taught a basic Whig axiom: that social questions could be reduced to questions of individual character. A textbook entitled *The Thinker, A Moral Reader* (1855) told children to "remember that all the ignorance, degradation, and misery in the world, is the result of indolence and vice." To teach that lesson, the schools had children read from the King James Bible and recite prayers acceptable to all the Protestant sects. Such texts reaffirmed a common Protestant morality while avoiding divisive doctrinal matters. Until the arrival of significant numbers of Catholic immigrants in the 1840s and 1850s, few parents complained about Protestant religious instruction in the public schools.

Political differences centered less on curriculum than on organization. Whigs wanted state-level centralization and proposed state superintendents and state boards of education, normal schools (state

teachers' colleges), texts chosen at the state level and used throughout the state, and uniform school terms. They also (often with the help of economy-minded Democrats) recruited young women as teachers. In addition to fostering Protestant morality in the schools, these women were a source of cheap labor: Salaries for female teachers in the northern states ranged from 40 to 60 percent lower than the salaries of their male coworkers. Largely as a result, the proportion of women among Massachusetts teachers rose from 56 percent in 1834 to 78 percent in 1860.

Democrats objected to the Whigs' insistence on centralization as elitist, intrusive, and expensive. They preferred to give power to individual school districts, thus enabling local school committees to tailor the curriculum, the length of the school year, and the choice of teachers and texts to local needs. Centralization, they argued, would create a metropolitan educational culture that served the purposes of the rich but ignored the preferences of farmers and working people. It was standard Democratic social policy: inexpensive government and local control. Henry Barnard, Connecticut's superintendent of schools, called his Democratic opponents "ignorant demagogues" and "a set of blockheads."

Horace Mann denounced them as "political mad-men." As early as 1826 Thaddeus Stevens, who would become a prominent Pennsylvania Whig, argued that voters must "learn to dread ignorance more than taxation."

ETHNICITY, RELIGION, AND THE SCHOOLS

The argument between Whig centralism and Democratic parsimony dominated the debate over public education until the children of Irish and German immigrants began to enter schools by the thousands in the mid-1840s. Most immigrant families were poor and relied on their children to work and supplement the family income. Consequently, the children's attendance at school was irregular at best. Moreover, most immigrants were Catholics. The Irish regarded Protestant prayers and the King James Bible as heresies and as hated tools of British oppression. Some of the textbooks were worse. Olney's *Practical System of Modern Geography*, a standard textbook, declared that "the Irish in general are quick of apprehension, active, brave and hospitable; but passionate, ignorant, vain, and superstitious." A nun in Connecticut complained that Irish children in the public schools "see their parents looked upon as an inferior race."

Many Catholic parents simply refused to send their children to school. Others demanded changes in textbooks, the elimination of the King James Bible (perhaps to be replaced by the Douay Bible), tax-supported Catholic schools, or at least tax relief for parents who sent their children to parish schools. Whigs, joined by many native-born Democrats, saw Catholic complaints as popish assaults on the Protestantism that they insisted was at the heart of American republicanism.

Many school districts, particularly in the rural areas to which many Scandinavian and German immigrants found their way, created foreign-language schools and provided bilingual instruction. In other places, state support for church-run charity schools persisted. For example, both Catholic and Protestant schools received such assistance in New York City until 1825, and in Lowell, Massachusetts, Hartford and Middletown, Connecticut, and Milwaukee, Wisconsin, at various times from the 1830s through the 1860s. New Jersey extended state support to Catholic as well as other church schools until 1866. In north-eastern cities, however, where immigrant Catholics often formed militant local majorities, such demands led to violence and to organized nativist (anti-immigrant) politics. In 1844 the Native American Party, with the endorsement of the Whigs, won the New York City elections. That same year in Philadelphia, riots that pitted avowedly Whig Protestants against Catholic immigrants, ostensibly over the issue of Bible reading in schools, killed 13 people. Such conflicts would severely damage the northern Democratic coalition in the 1850s (see chapter 13).

PRISONS

From the 1820s onward, state governments built institutions to house orphans, the dependent poor, the insane, and criminals. The market revolution increased the numbers of such persons and made them more visible, more anonymous, and more separated from family and community resources. Americans in the 18th century (and many in the 19th century as well) had assumed that poverty, crime, insanity, and other social ills were among God's ways of punishing sin and testing the human capacity for both suffering and charity. By the 1820s, however, reformers were arguing that deviance was the result of childhood deprivation. "Normal" people, they suggested, learned discipline and respect for work, property, laws, and other people from their parents. Deviants were the products of brutal, often drunken households devoid of parental love and discipline. The cure was to place them in a controlled setting, teach them work and discipline, and turn them into useful citizens.

In state legislatures, Whigs favored putting deviants in institutions for rehabilitation. Democrats, though they agreed that the states should care for criminals and dependents, regarded attempts at rehabilitation as wrong-headed and expensive; they favored institutions that isolated the insane, ware-housed the dependent poor, and punished criminals. Most state systems were a compromise between the two positions.

Pennsylvania built prisons at Pittsburgh (1826) and Philadelphia (1829) that put solitary prisoners into cells to contemplate their misdeeds and to plot a new life. The results of such solitary confinement included few reformations and numerous attempts

Prisoners at the State Prison at Auburn.

AUBURN PRISON Inmates at New York's Auburn Prison were forbidden to speak and were marched in lockstep between workshops, dining halls, and their cells.

at suicide. Only New Jersey imitated the Pennsylvania system. Far more common were institutions based on the model developed in New York at Auburn (1819) and Sing Sing (1825). In the "Auburn system," prisoners slept in solitary cells and marched in military formation to meals and workshops; they were forbidden to speak to one another at any time. The rule of silence, it was believed, encouraged both discipline and contemplation. The French writer Alexis de Tocqueville, visiting a New York prison in 1830, remarked that "the silence within these vast walls . . . is that of death. . . . There were a thousand living beings, and yet it was a vast desert solitude."

The Auburn system was designed both to reform criminals and to reduce expenses, for the prisons sold workshop products to the outside. Between these two goals Whigs favored rehabilitation. Democrats favored profit-making workshops, and thus lower operating costs and lower taxes. Robert Wiltse, named by the Democrats to run Sing Sing prison in the 1830s, used harsh punishments (including flogging and starving), sparse meals, and forced labor in order to punish criminals and make the prison pay for itself. In 1839 William Seward, as the newly elected Whig governor of New York, fired Wiltse and appointed administrators who substituted privileges and rewards for punishment and emphasized rehabilitation

over profit making. They provided religious instruction; they improved food and working conditions; and they cut back on the use of flogging. When Democrats took back the statehouse in the 1842 elections, they discovered that the Whigs' brief experiment in kindness had produced a $50,000 deficit, so they swiftly reinstated the old regime.

ASYLUMS

The leading advocate of humane treatment for people deemed to be insane was Dorothea Dix, a Boston humanitarian who was shocked by the incarceration and abuse of the insane in common jails. She traveled throughout the country urging citizens to pressure their state legislatures into building asylums committed to what reformers called "moral treatment." The asylums were to be clean and pleasant places, preferably outside the cities, and the inmates were to be treated humanely. Attendants were not to beat inmates or tie them up, although they could use cold showers as a form of discipline. Dix and other reformers wanted the asylums to be safe, nurturing environments in which people with mental illness could be made well.

By 1860 the legislatures of 28 of the 33 states had established state-run insane asylums. Whig legislators, with minimal support from Democrats, approved appropriations for the more expensive and humane moral treatment facilities. Occasionally, however, Dorothea Dix won Democratic support as well. In North Carolina, she befriended the wife of a powerful Democratic legislator as the woman lay on her deathbed; the dying woman convinced her husband to support the building of an asylum. His impassioned speech won the approval of the lower house for a state asylum to be named Dix Hill. In the North Carolina senate, however, the proposal was supported by 91 percent of the Whigs and only 14 percent of the Democrats—a partisan division that was repeated in state after state.

THE SOUTH AND SOCIAL REFORM

On most economic issues, southern state legislatures divided along the same lines as northern legislatures: Whigs wanted government participation in the economy, Democrats did not. On social questions, however, southern Whigs and Democrats responded in distinctly southern ways. The South was a rural, culturally conservative region of patriarchal households that viewed every attempt at government intervention as a threat to independence. Most southern voters, Whigs as well as Democrats, perceived attempts at "social improvement" as expensive and wrong-headed.

The southern states enacted school laws and drew up blueprints for state school systems, but the culturally homogeneous white South had little need for schools to enforce a common culture. Moreover, the South had less money and less faith in government. Consequently southern schools tended to be locally controlled, to be infused with southern evangelical culture, and to have a limited curriculum and a short school year. In 1860 northern children attended school for an average of more than 50 days a year; white children in the South attended school for an average of 10 days annually.

By 1860 every slave state except Florida (which had a tiny population) and the Carolinas operated prisons modeled on the Auburn system. Here, however, prisons stressed punishment and profits over rehabilitation. Though some southerners favored northern-style reforms, they knew that southern voters would reject them. Popular votes in Alabama in 1834 and in North Carolina in 1846 brought in resounding defeats for proposals to

THE WHIPPING POST AND PILLORY AT NEW CASTLE, DELAWARE Delaware was a slave state that continued to inflict public, corporal punishment on lawbreakers. Many of the witnesses to the whipping depicted here are small children, who are supposedly learning a lesson.

build or reform penitentiaries in those states. While northern evangelicals were preaching that criminals could be rescued, southern preachers demanded Old Testament vengeance, arguing that hanging, whipping, and branding were sanctioned by the Bible, inexpensive, and more effective than mere incarceration. Other southerners, defending the code of honor, charged that victims and their relatives would be denied vengeance if criminals were tucked away in prisons. Some southern prisons leased prison labor (and sometimes whole prisons) to private entrepreneurs, and dreams of reforming southern criminals were forgotten.

The South did participate in temperance—the all-consuming reform that will be discussed in the next section. By the 1820s Baptists and Methodists had made deep inroads into southern society. Southern ministers preached against dueling, fighting, dancing, gambling, and drinking, while churchgoing women discouraged their husbands, sons, and suitors from drinking. Many southern men either stopped drinking altogether or sharply reduced their consumption. Accordingly, the South contributed its share to the national drop in alcohol consumption. During the 1840s the Washington Temperance Society and other voluntary temperance groups won a solid footing in southern towns, but southern religious and temperance organizations were based on individual decisions to abstain. Legal prohibition, which became dominant in the North, got nowhere in the South. In the 1850s, when one northern legislature after another passed statewide prohibition, the only slave state to follow was tiny, northern-oriented Delaware.

At bottom, southern resistance to social reform stemmed from a conservative, Bible-based acceptance of suffering and human imperfection and a commitment to the power and independence of white men who headed families. Any proposal that sounded like social tinkering or the invasion of paternal rights was doomed to failure. To make matters worse, many reforms—public schools, Sunday schools, prohibitionism, humane asylums—were seen as the work of well-funded and well-organized missionaries from the Northeast who wanted to fashion society in their own self-righteous image. The southern distrust of reform was powerfully reinforced after 1830, when northern reformers began to call for abolition of slavery and equality of the sexes—reforms most white southerners found unthinkable.

EXCURSUS: THE POLITICS OF ALCOHOL

Central to party formation in the North was the fight between evangelical Whigs who demanded that government regulate public (and often private) morality and Democrats who feared both big government and the Whig cultural agenda. The most persistent issue in the argument was the question of alcohol—so much so that in many places the temperance question defined the differences between Democrats and Whigs.

ARDENT SPIRITS

Drinking had been a part of social life since the beginning of English settlement, but the withering of authority and the disruptions of the market revolution led to increased consumption, increased public drunkenness, and a perceived increase in alcohol-led violence and social problems (see

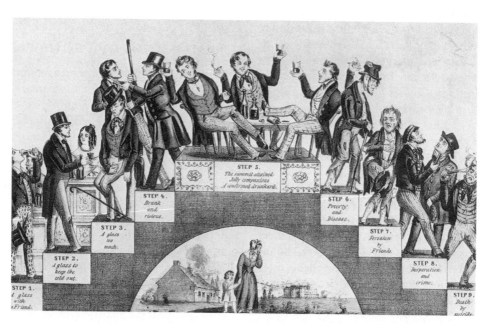

THE DRUNKARD'S PROGRESS This popular print describes the drunkard's progression from social drinking to alcoholism, isolation, crime, and death by suicide. His desolate wife and daughter and his burning house are at bottom.

chapter 7). Beginning in the 1790s, physicians and a few clergymen attacked not only habitual drunkenness but also alcohol itself. And for a short time after 1812, Federalist politicians and Congregational clergymen formed "moral societies" in New England that discouraged strong drink. Their imperious tone and their association with the old seats of authority, however, doomed them to failure.

The temperance crusade began in earnest in 1826, when northeastern evangelicals founded the American Society for the Promotion of Temperance (soon renamed the American Temperance Society). The movement's manifesto was Lyman Beecher's *Six Sermons on the Nature, Occasions, Signs, Evils, and Remedy of Intemperance* (1826). Addressing the churchgoing middle class, Beecher declared alcohol an addictive drug and warned that even moderate drinkers risked becoming hopeless drunkards. Thus temperance, like other evangelical reforms, was presented as a contest between self-control and slavery to one's appetites. By encouraging total abstinence, reformers hoped to halt the creation of new drunkards while the old ones died out. Even though Beecher pinned his hopes on self-discipline, he wanted middle-class abstainers to spread reform through both example and coercion. As middle-class evangelicals eliminated alcohol from their own lives, they would cease to offer it to their guests, buy or sell it, or provide it to their employees, and they would encourage their friends to do the same.

In the atmosphere surrounding the middle-class revivals of the 1820s and 1830s, Beecher's crusade gathered strength. Charles Grandison Finney (see chapter 10), in his revival at Rochester, made total abstinence a condition of conversion. Many other ministers and churches followed suit, and by the mid-1830s members of the middle class had largely disengaged themselves from alcohol and from the people who drank it. Following a temperance lecture by Finney's coworker Theodore Dwight Weld, for instance, Rochester grocers Elijah and Albert Smith rolled their stock of whiskey out on the sidewalk, smashed the barrels, and let the liquor spill into the street. Other merchants threw their liquor into the Erie Canal or sold it off at cost. Hundreds of evangelical businessmen pledged that they would refuse to rent to merchants who sold liquor, sell grain to distillers, or enter a store that sold alcohol. Many of them made abstinence a condition of employment, placing ads that carried the line "None But Temperate Men Need Apply." Abstinence and opposition to the use of distilled spirits (people continued to argue about wine and beer) had become a badge of middle-class respectability.

Among themselves, the reformers achieved considerable success. By 1835 the American Temperance Society claimed 1.5 million members and estimated that 2 million Americans had renounced ardent spirits (whiskey, rum, and other distilled liquors); 250,000 had formally pledged to completely abstain from alcohol. The society further estimated that 4,000 distilleries had gone out of business, and that many of the survivors had cut back their production. Many politicians no longer bought drinks to win voters to their cause. The Kentucky Whig Henry Clay, once known for keeping late hours, began to serve only cold water when he entertained at dinner. And in 1833, members of Congress formed the American Congressional Temperance Society. The U.S. Army put an end to the age-old liquor ration in 1832, and increasing numbers of militia officers stopped supplying their men with whiskey. The annual consumption of alcohol, which had reached an all-time high in the 1820s, dropped by more than half in the 1830s (from 3.9 gallons of pure alcohol per adult in 1830 to 1.8 gallons in 1840).

THE ORIGINS OF PROHIBITION

In the middle 1830s Whigs made temperance a political issue. Realizing that voluntary abstinence would not put an end to drunkenness, Whig evangelicals drafted coercive, prohibitionist legislation. First, they attacked the licenses granting grocery stores and taverns the right to sell liquor by the drink and to permit it to be consumed on the premises. The licenses were important sources of revenue for local governments. They also gave local authorities the power to cancel the licenses of troublesome establishments. Militant temperance advocates, usually in association with local Whigs, demanded that the authorities use that power to outlaw all public drinking places. In communities throughout the North, the licensing issue, always freighted with angry divisions over religion and social class, became the issue around which local parties organized. The question first reached the state level in Massachusetts, when

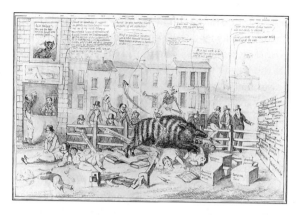

STRIPED PIG This cartoon, filled with the individual sin and misery and the social destruction caused by alcohol, portrays the Boston tavern keeper's notorious striped pig as an instrument of the devil.

in 1838 a Whig legislature passed the "Fifteen-Gallon Law," which decreed that merchants could sell ardent spirits only in quantities of 15 gallons or more—thus outlawing every public drinking place in the state. In 1839 Massachusetts voters sent enough Democrats to the legislature to rescind the law.

The Whig attempt to cancel tavern licenses proved unenforceable, as proprietors simply operated without licenses or found ways to get around the laws. While the Massachusetts Fifteen-Gallon Law was in effect, one Boston tavern keeper painted stripes on a pig and charged patrons an admission fee of six cents (the old price of a drink) to view the "exhibition." He then provided customers—who paid over and over to see the pig—with a "complimentary" glass of whiskey.

Leading Democrats agreed with Whigs that Americans drank too much, but whereas Whigs insisted that regulating morality was a proper function of government, Democrats warned that government intrusion into areas of private choice would violate republican liberties. The Democrats of Rochester, New York, responding to the license issue, made the following declaration:

Anything which savours of restraint in what men deem their natural rights is sure to meet with opposition, and men convinced of error by force will most likely continue all their lives unconvinced in their reason. Whatever shall be done to stay the tide of intemperance, and roll back its destroying wave, must be done by suasive appeals to the reason, the interest, or the pride of men; but not by force.

In many communities, alcohol became the defining difference between Democrats and Whigs. In 1834, for instance, a Whig campaign worker ventured into a poor neighborhood in Rochester and asked a woman how her husband planned to vote. "Why, he has always been Jackson," she said, "and I don't think he's joined the Cold Water."

THE DEMOCRATIZATION OF TEMPERANCE

Democratic voters held ambiguous attitudes toward temperance. Many of them continued to drink, while many others voluntarily abstained or cut down. Yet almost without exception they resented the coercive tactics of the Whigs and supported their party's pledge to protect them from evangelical meddling in their private lives. In 1830, when Lyman Beecher's Hanover Street Church in Boston caught fire, the volunteer fire companies (which doubled as working-class drinking clubs) arrived, noted that it was the hated Beecher's church, and made no effort to put out the fire. Unbeknownst to the Reverend Beecher, the church had rented basement space to a merchant who used it to store barrels of rum. According to a contemporary report, the crowd that gathered to watch the church burn to the ground cheered as the barrels exploded one by one.

Democrats, despite their opposition to prohibition, often spoke out against drunkenness. Many craft unions denied membership to heavy drinkers, and hundreds of thousands of rural and urban Democrats quietly stopped drinking. (The sharp drop in alcohol consumption in the 1830s can be explained in no other way.) In the late 1830s, former antiprohibitionists launched a temperance movement of their own.

One evening in 1840—in the depths of a devastating economic depression—six craftsmen were drinking at Chase's Tavern in Baltimore. More or less as a joke, they sent one of their number to a nearby temperance lecture; he came back a teetotaler and converted the others. They then drew up a total abstinence pledge and promised to devote themselves to the reform of other drinkers. Within months, from this beginning a national movement had emerged, called the Washington Temperance Society. With a core membership of men who had opposed temperance in the 1830s, the Washingtonians differed from older temperance societies in several ways. First, they identified themselves as members of the laboring classes. Second, they were avowedly nonreligious: Although many of them were churchgoers (usually Methodist or Baptist), many were not, and the Washingtonians avoided religious controversy by avoiding religion. Third, the Washingtonians—at least those who called themselves "True Washingtonians"—rejected recourse to politics and legislation and concentrated instead on the conversion of drinkers through compassion and persuasion. Finally, they welcomed "hopeless" drunkards—who accounted for about 10 percent of the membership—and hailed them as heroes when they sobered up.

TEMPERANCE SCHISMS

Even though Whig reformers welcomed the Washingtonians at first, they soon had second thoughts. The nonreligious character of the movement disturbed those who saw temperance as an arm of evangelical reform. Previous advocates of temperance had assumed that sobriety would be accompanied by evangelical decorum. Instead, the meetings, picnics, and parades held by the Washingtonians were continuous with a popular culture that Whig evangelicals opposed. While the temperance regulars read pamphlets and listened to lectures by clergymen, lawyers, and doctors, the Washingtonians enjoyed raucous sing-alongs, comedy routines, barnyard imitations, dramatic skits, and even full-dress minstrel shows geared to temperance themes. Meetings featured experience speeches by reformed drunkards. Speaking extemporaneously, they omitted none of the horrors of an alcoholic life—attempts at suicide, friendships betrayed, fathers and mothers desolated, wives beaten and abandoned, children dead of starvation. Though Washingtonians had given up alcohol, their melodramatic tales, street parades, song books, and minstrel shows—even when presented with a Methodist or Baptist accent—were temperance, but not the temperance Lyman Beecher and the Whigs had had in mind.

Nowhere did the Washingtonians differ more sharply from the temperance regulars than in their visions of the reformed life. The Whig reformers tied abstinence to individual ambition and middle-class domesticity. They expected men who quit drinking to withdraw from the male world in which drinking was common and retreat into the comfort of the newly feminized middle-class family. Washingtonians, on the other hand, translated traditional male sociability into sober forms. Moreover they called former drinkers back to the responsibilities of traditional fatherhood. Their experience stories began with the hurt drunkards had caused their wives and children and ended with their transformation into dependable providers and authoritative fathers. While the Whig temperance regulars tried to extend the ethos of individual ambition and the new middle-class domesticity into society at large, Washingtonians sought to rescue the self-respect and moral authority of working-class fathers.

The Washington Temperance Society collapsed toward the end of the 1840s. Yet its legacy survived. Among former drinkers in the North, it had introduced a new sense of domestic responsibility and a healthy fear of drunkenness. Consumption of pure alcohol dropped from 1.8 to 1.0 gallons annually in the 1840s. Along the way, the Washingtonians and related groups created a self-consciously respectable native Protestant working class in American cities.

ETHNICITY AND ALCOHOL

In the 1840s and 1850s, millions of Irish and German immigrants came pouring into neighborhoods stirred by working-class revivals and temperance agitation. The newcomers had their own time-honored relations to alcohol. The Germans introduced lager beer to the United States, thus providing a wholesome alternative for Americans who wished to give up spirits without joining the teetotalers. The Germans also built old-country beer halls in American cities, complete with sausage counters, oompah bands, group singing, and other family attractions. For their part, the Irish reaffirmed their love of whiskey—a love forged in colonial oppression and in a culture that accepted trouble with resignation—a love that legitimized levels of male drunkenness and violence that Americans, particularly the temperance forces, found appalling. (Differences in immigrant drinking were given architectural expression. German beer halls provided seating arrangements for whole families. Irish bars, on the other hand, provided a bar but no

GERMAN BEER GARDEN A German brewery and beer garden in antebellum Fort Wayne, Indiana. These were pleasant, landscaped establishments where patrons (most of them German immigrants) could bring their families to stroll the grounds, eat, socialize, listen to music—and drink.

tables or chairs. If a drinker had to sit down, they reasoned, it was time for him to go home.)

In the 1850s native resentment of Catholic immigrants drove thousands of Baptist and Methodist "respectables" out of the Democratic coalition and into nativist Whig majorities that—beginning with Maine in 1851—established legal prohibition throughout New England, in the middle states, and in the Old Northwest. These often were the Democrats who became part of the North's Republican majority on the eve of the Civil War (see chapter 14).

THE POLITICS OF RACE

Most whites in antebellum America believed in "natural" differences based on sex and race. God, they said, had given women and men and whites and blacks different mental, emotional, and physical capacities. And, as humankind (female and nonwhite more than others) was innately sinful and prone to disorder, God ordained a fixed social hierarchy in which white men exercised power over others. Slaves and free blacks accepted their subordinate status only as a fact of life, not as something that was natural and just. Some women also questioned patriarchy. But before 1830 hierarchy based on sex and race was seldom questioned in public, particularly by persons who were in a position to change it.

In the antebellum years, as southerners and most northerners stiffened their defense of white paternalism, northern Whig evangelicals began to envision a world based on Christian love and individual worth, not inherited status. They transformed marriage from rank domination into a sentimental partnership—unequal, but a partnership nonetheless. They also questioned the more virulent forms of racism. From among the Whig evangelicals emerged a radical minority that envisioned a world without power. While conservative Christians insisted that relations based on dominance and submission were the lot of a sinful humankind, reformers argued that such relations interposed human power, too often in the form of brute force, between God and the individual spirit. They called for a world that substituted spiritual freedom and Christian love for every form of worldly domination. The result was a community of uncompromising radical reformers who attacked slavery and patriarchy as national sins.

FREE BLACKS

Prior to the American Revolution sizable pockets of slavery existed in the northern states, but revolutionary idealism, and the growing belief that slavery was inefficient and unnecessary, led one northern state after another to abolish it. Vermont, with almost no slaves, outlawed slavery in its revolutionary constitution. By 1804 every northern state had taken some action, usually by passing laws that called for gradual emancipation. The first of such laws, and the model for others, was passed in Pennsylvania in 1780. This law freed slaves born after 1780 when they reached their 28th birthday. Slaves born before 1780 would remain slaves, and slave children would remain slaves through their prime working years. Some northern slave owners, in violation of the laws, sold young slaves into the South as their freedom dates approached. Still, the emancipation laws worked: By 1830 only a handful of aging blacks remained slaves in the North.

The rising population of northern free blacks gravitated to the cities. Most of those who had been slaves in cities stayed there. They were joined by thousands of free blacks who decided to abandon the declining northeastern countryside and move to the city. In many cities—Philadelphia and New York City in particular—they met a stream of free blacks and fugitive slaves from the Upper South, where the bonds of slavery were growing tighter, and where free blacks feared reenslavement. Thus despite the flood of white immigrants from Europe and the American countryside, African Americans constituted a sizable minority in the rapidly expanding cities. New York City's black population, 10.5 percent in 1800, was still 8.8 percent in 1820; Philadelphia, the haven of thousands of southern refugees, was 10.3 percent African American in 1800 and 11.9 percent in 1820.

Blacks in the seaport cities tended to take stable, low-paying jobs. A few became successful (occasionally wealthy) entrepreneurs, and others practiced skilled trades. Many took jobs as waiters or porters in hotels, as barbers, and as butlers, maids, cooks, washerwomen, and coachmen for wealthy families. Others worked as dockworkers, laborers, and sailors. Still others became dealers in used clothing, or draymen with their own carts and horses, or food vendors in the streets and in basement shops (oysters in particular were a black monopoly).

DISCRIMINATION

From the 1820s onward, however, the growing numbers of white wage-workers began to edge blacks out of their jobs by underselling them, by pressuring employers to discriminate, and by outright violence. As a result, African Americans were almost completely eliminated from the skilled trades, and many unskilled and semiskilled blacks lost their jobs on the docks, in warehouses, and in the merchant marine. In 1834 a Philadelphian reported that "colored persons, when engaged in their usual occupations, were repeatedly assailed and maltreated, usually on the [waterfront]. Parties of white men have insisted that no blacks shall be employed in certain departments of labor." And as their old jobs disappeared, blacks were systematically excluded from the new jobs opening up in factories. By the 1830s black workers in Philadelphia were noting "the difficulty of getting places for our sons as apprentices . . . owing to the prejudices with which we have to contend." In 1838 (during a

A BLACK STREET VENDOR, SELLING OYSTERS IN PHILADELPHIA, CIRCA 1814 In early 19th-century New York and Philadelphia, African Americans monopolized the public sale of oysters and clams.

depression that hit blacks first and hardest) an African American newspaper complained that blacks "have ceased to be hackney coachmen and draymen, and they are now almost displaced as stevedores. They are rapidly losing their places as barbers and servants. Ten families employ white servants now, where one did 20 years ago."

The depression was followed by waves of desperately poor Irish immigrants. By accepting low wages, and by rioting, intimidation, gunplay, and even murder, the Irish displaced most of the remaining blacks from their toehold in the economic life of the northeastern cities. An observer of the Philadelphia docks remarked in 1849 that "when a few years ago we saw none but Blacks, we now see none but Irish."

Meanwhile, official discrimination against blacks was on the rise. Political democratization for white men was accompanied by the disfranchisement of blacks (see chapter 7). Cities either excluded black children from public schools or set up segregated schools. In 1845, when Massachusetts passed a law declaring that all children had the right to attend neighborhood schools, the Boston School Committee blithely ruled that the law did not apply to blacks. Blacks were also excluded from white churches or sat in segregated pews; even the Quakers seated blacks and whites separately.

African Americans responded by building institutions of their own. At one end were black-owned gambling houses, saloons, brothels, and dance halls—the only racially integrated institutions to be found in most cities. At the other end were black churches, schools, social clubs, and lodges. The first independent black church was the African Church of Philadelphia, founded in 1790; the African Methodist Episcopal Church, a national denomination still in existence, was founded in Philadelphia in 1816. Schools and relief societies, usually associated with churches, grew quickly. Black Masonic lodges attracted hundreds of members. Many of the churches and social organizations were given names that proudly called up the blacks' African origins. In Philadelphia, for instance, there were African Methodists, Abyssinian Baptists, and the African Dorcas Society, to name only a few.

Northern blacks also organized to fight slavery and discrimination. Perhaps the most radical of them was David Walker, a Boston used-clothing dealer whose *Appeal to the Colored Citizens of the World*

(1829) urged blacks to revolt against slavery. (Soon thereafter, Walker was murdered under mysterious circumstances.) Others, including the escaped slave Harriet Tubman, operated the Underground Railroad, a system of antislavery activists and safe hiding places that smuggled runaway slaves out of the South, through the North, and into Canada. Some worked, like the former New York slave and religious mystic Sojourner Truth, to direct the attention of both black and white religious reformers to the problem of slavery. In Rochester, escaped Maryland slave Frederick Douglass published an antislavery newspaper and forayed throughout the North to lecture black and white audiences on the evils of slavery and discrimination. Thus from within the limited freedom provided by northern society, free blacks—sometimes alone, sometimes in combination with white abolitionists—combated southern slavery and northern discrimination.

DEMOCRATIC RACISM

Neither the Whigs nor the Democrats encouraged the aspirations of slaves or free blacks. But it was the Democrats, from their beginnings in the 1820s, who incorporated racism into their political agenda. Minstrel shows, for example, often reflected the Democratic line on current events, and Democratic cartoonists often featured minstrelsy's bug-eyed, woolly-haired caricatures of blacks. By the time of the Civil War, Democrats mobilized voters almost solely with threats of "amalgamation" and "Negro rule."

Democrats also contributed to the rising tide of antiblack violence. The Whigs had plenty of racists, but Democrats appear to have predominated when mobs moved into black neighborhoods, sometimes burning out whole areas. Indeed many Democrats lumped together evangelical reformers, genteel Whigs, and blacks as a unified threat to the white republic. In July 1834 a New York City mob sacked the house of abolitionist Lewis Tappan, moved on to Charles Finney's Chatham Street Chapel, where abolitionists were said to be meeting, and finished the evening by attacking a British actor at the Bowery Theater. The manager saved his theater by waving two American flags and ordering an American actor to perform popular minstrel routines for the mob. In Jackson, Michigan, in 1839, after the local

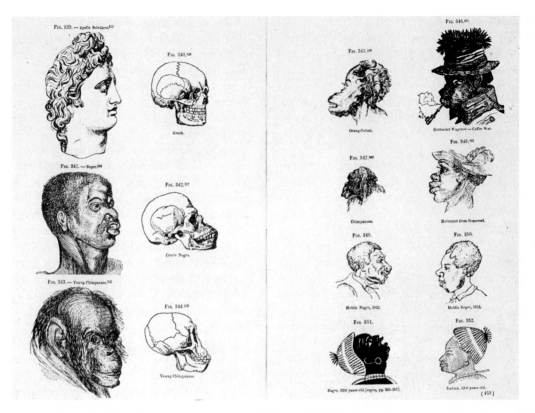

SKULL MEASUREMENTS This illustration is from *Types of Mankind: Or Ethnological Researches* (1845), a "scientific" text that portrayed white men as Greek gods and black men as apes.

Sunday schools announced an outdoor meeting featuring temperance and antislavery speakers, antievangelical rowdies removed the benches from the meeting ground the night before and burned them in the town square. They then dug up the corpse of a black man who had been buried a few days earlier and propped him up in the pulpit of the Presbyterian church, where he greeted the Sunday school the next morning.

The first major American race riot broke out in Philadelphia in 1834 between working-class whites and blacks at a street carnival. Although blacks seemed to have won the first round, the whites refused to accept defeat. Over the next few nights, they wrecked a black-owned tavern; broke into black households to terrorize families and steal property; attacked whites who lived with, socialized with, or operated businesses catering to blacks; wrecked the African Presbyterian Church; and destroyed a black church on Wharton Street by sawing through its timbers and pulling it down. Sporadic racial violence wracked the city throughout the 1830s and 1840s, reaching its height in 1849. That summer a firehouse gang of Irish immigrants calling themselves "the Killers" attacked the California House, a black-owned tavern and gambling hall. The black patrons had anticipated the attack and had armed themselves, and in the melee five Killers were shot. For two months, tempers simmered. Finally the Killers set a fire at the California House that spread to nearby houses. They fought off neighborhood blacks, rival firemen, and the police. The riot ended only when the city sent in four companies of militia.

CONCEPTIONS OF RACIAL DIFFERENCE

Meanwhile, educated whites were being taught to think in racist terms. Among most scientists, biological determinism replaced historical and environmental explanations of racial differences; many argued that whites and blacks were separate species. Democrats welcomed that "discovery." John Van Evrie, a New York doctor and Democratic pamphleteer, declared that "it is a palpable and unavoidable fact that Negroes are a different species," and that the story of Adam and Eve referred only to the origin of white people. In 1850 the *Democratic Review* confided, "Few or none now seriously adhere to the theory of the unity of the races. The whole state of the science at this moment seems to indicate that there are several distinct races of men on the earth, with entirely different capacities, physical and mental."

As whites came to perceive racial differences as God-given and immutable, they changed the nature of those differences as well. In the 18th and early 19th centuries, whites had stereotyped blacks as ignorant and prone to drunkenness and thievery, but they had also maintained a parallel stereotype of blacks as loyal and self-sacrificing servants. From the 1820s onward, racists continued to regard blacks as incompetent, but they found it harder to distinguish mere carelessness from dishonesty. Now they saw all blacks as treacherous, shrewd, and secretive—individuals who only *pretended* to feel loyalty to white families and affection for the white children they took care of, while awaiting the chance to steal from them or poison them. The writer Herman Melville, a lifelong Democrat who shared little of his compatriots' racism but who helped to codify their fascination with duplicity and deceit, dramatized these fears in *Benito Cereno*, a novel about slaves who commandeered a sailing ship and its captain and crew, then (with knives secretly at the throats of their captives) acted out a servile charade for unsuspecting visitors who came aboard.

Above all, Democratic ideologues pronounced blacks unfit to be citizens of the white man's republic. Whigs often supported various forms of black suffrage; Democrats uniformly opposed it. Their insistence that blacks were incapable of citizenship reinforced their concept of an equally natural white male political capacity. This exclusion of blacks (by Democrats whose own political competence was often doubted by wealthier and better-educated Whigs) was designed to protect the republic while extending citizenship to all white men. The most vicious racist assaults were often carried out beneath symbols of the revolutionary republic. Antiblack mobs in Baltimore, Cincinnati, and Toledo called themselves Minute Men and Sons of Liberty. Philadelphia blacks who gathered to hear the Declaration of Independence read on the Fourth of July were attacked for "defiling the government." The antiabolitionist mob that sacked Lewis Tappan's house rescued a portrait of George Washington and carried it as a banner during their later attacks on Finneyite evangelicals and English actors.

THE BEGINNINGS OF ANTISLAVERY

Before 1830 only a few whites considered slavery a moral issue. Quakers, at their annual meeting in 1758, had condemned both the slave trade and slavery, and Methodists and some Baptists had done the same late in the century. Washington, Jefferson, and other Chesapeake gentlemen doubted the wisdom if not the morality of holding slaves; New England Federalists had condemned slavery in the course of condemning Jeffersonian masters. But there were too few Quakers to make a difference, and the movement to free slaves in the Upper South and the antislavery sentiments of southern evangelicals both died out early in the 19th century. Southerners and most northerners—when they bothered to think about it at all—tended to accept slavery as the result of human (read "black") depravity and God's unknowable plan.

Organized opposition to slavery before 1831 was pretty much limited to the American Colonization Society, founded in 1816. Led by wealthy, generally conservative northern churchmen and a contingent of Chesapeake gentlemen, the society proposed the voluntary, gradual, and compensated emancipation of slaves and the "repatriation" of free blacks to West Africa. Although the society transported a few thousand blacks to Liberia, it never posed a serious threat to slavery. Southerners, who owned two million slaves by 1830, opposed emancipation whether compensated or not, and few free blacks were interested in moving to Africa. The society's campaign to deport them so disturbed many free blacks that they substituted "Colored" for "African" in naming their institutions. One black churchman explained that references to Africa provided "an available excuse for a powerful enemy, the American Colonization Society, to use . . . as a weapon of our own make, to expel ourselves from our beloved country."

The Bulwark of the Republic

In the years of peace after 1815, America's citizen militia—the mythic bulwark of the republic—became the butt of jokes. Militia training days, like the one portrayed by Edward Clay as "The Nation's Bulwark: A Well-Disciplined Militia" (1829) were disorderly, often drunken, and decidedly unmilitary gatherings of young men. By the 1820s calls for militia reform arose throughout the political spectrum. Northern evangelicals and other proto-Whig "respectables" decried the drunkenness and disorder (as well as the frequent artillery explosions) associated with citizen militias and called for smaller and less-frequent training days. On the other hand, poorer citizens, particularly in cities and towns, protested the expense and inconvenience of laws that required them to arm and uniform themselves for frequent musters, and that fined them heavily when they failed to do so. The lower-class response was the invention of the Fantastical Parade. Men arrived for training days dressed in ridiculous costumes and mounted on the worst animals they could find, carrying broomsticks, stove pipes, and other improvised "weapons." Workingmen in Philadelphia elected a half-witted dwarf as "Colonel Pluck," provided him with a grandiose mock-military dress uniform, and paraded behind him through the streets. New Yorkers frequently dressed up (some in blackface) to parody military discipline—as in the "Grand Fantastical Parade" of December 1833. In upstate Rochester, a militia "commander" traveled through town riding a bull and brandishing a handsaw. He was followed by a truly fantastical array of citizen soldiers—one of them dressed in hunting attire and green goggles, with a live—and very unhappy—

THE NATION'S BULWARK.

Although few white Americans actively opposed slavery before 1830, the writing was on the wall. Emancipation in the North, though it came about quietly, constituted an implicit condemnation of slavery in the South. So did events outside the United States. Toussaint L'Ouverture's successful slave revolution in Haiti in 1804 threatened slavery everywhere (see chapter 7). The British, whose navy could enforce their dictates on the seas, outlawed the Atlantic slave trade in 1808. Mexico, Peru, Chile, Gran Colombia (present-day Colombia, Venezuela, Ecuador, and Panama), and other new republics carved out of the Spanish empire emancipated their slaves. The most powerful blow came in 1830 when the British Parliament emancipated the slaves of Jamaica, Bermuda, and other Caribbean islands ruled by Britain.

ABOLITIONISTS

Religious revivals during the late 1820s and early 1830s created a reform-minded evangelical culture in the northern United States. Radical abolitionism dates from 1831, when William Lloyd Garrison published the first issue of the *Liberator*. Already a veteran reformer, Garrison condemned slavery as a national sin and demanded immediate emancipation—or at least an immediate start toward emanci-

goose strapped to the top of his head. The message was clear: Although respectables wished to reform and discipline the militia, others were determined to laugh it out of existence. Beginning about 1830, state after state reduced the frequency of training days and stopped punishing those who decided not to participate. The militia became a smaller, more voluntary, and less visible part of neighborhood life.

GRAND FANTASTICAL PARADE, NEW-YORK, DEC 2d 1833
"Come get thee a sword tho' made of a lath"
"Thou's Bots on the tanner and Dick the Butcher and Smith the weaver as ragged as Lazarus No eye
"hath seen such scarecrows I'll not march with them that's flat"

pation. "I am in earnest," he declared in his first editorial; "I will not equivocate—I will not excuse—I will not retreat a single inch—and I will be heard!"

In 1833 Garrison and like-minded abolitionists formed the American Anti-Slavery Society. Some of them—Wendell Phillips, Thomas Wentworth Higginson, Theodore Parker—were Unitarians who opposed slavery as an affront to both humanity and rationality; others—most notably the poet John Greenleaf Whittier—were Quakers who were happy to join the movement. Abolitionists found their greatest support in southern New England, western New York, northern Ohio, and among the new middle classes of the northeastern cities—

ground that Yankee settlement, the market revolution, and Finneyite revivals had turned into the heartland of the northern Whig Party.

Opposition to slavery was a logical extension of middle-class evangelicalism. Charles Finney, Lyman Beecher, and other Whig evangelicals retained a Puritan inheritance that demanded that God's people legislate the behavior of others. The new evangelicalism, however, was grounded in the morally accountable individual, and not in coercive institutions. Whig evangelicals posed a contest between Christian love and moral free agency on the one hand and every kind of passion, brutality, and force on the other. They often promised that their reforms would

Anti-Slavery Almanac.

[25]

[1840.]

"OUR *PECULIAR* DOMESTIC INSTITUTIONS."

AN ABOLITIONIST VIEW OF SLAVE SOCIETY This provocative woodcut appeared in the *Anti-Slavery Almanac for 1840* (Boston, 1839). It pictures the lynching of slaves and their abolitionist allies by a southern mob. Surrounding the hanging tree are men (no women appear in the picture) engaged in other activities that northern reformers insisted grew from the brutal patriarchy of slave society. Men duel with pistols and knives, others engage in an eye-gouging wrestling match, others gamble and drink, and still others cheer for cock fights and horse races. The enemy here is not simply slavery but the debauchery and unbridled passions that abolitionists associated with it.

liberate the individual spirit from "slavery" to alcohol, lust, or ignorance—thus phrasing moral legislation as liberation, not coercion. Before long, some discovered that slavery itself, an institution that obliterated moral choice and encouraged the worst human passions, was America's great national sin.

The American Anti-Slavery Society demanded immediate emancipation of slaves and full civil and legal rights for blacks. Assuming that God had created blacks and whites as members of one human family, abolitionists opposed the "scientific" racism spouted by Democrats and many Whigs. Moderates and latecomers to abolitionism spoke of inherent racial characteristics but still tended to view blacks in benign (if condescending) ways. Harriet Beecher Stowe, for instance, portrayed blacks as simple, innocent, loving people who possessed a capacity for sentiment and emotionalism that most whites had lost. In 1852, Horace Mann told an audience of blacks in

Ohio that "in intellect, the blacks are inferior to the whites, while in sentiment and affections, the whites are inferior to the blacks." Radical abolitionists, however, remained committed environmentalists. Lydia Maria Child of New York City declared, "In the United States, colored persons have scarcely any chance to rise. But if colored persons are well treated, and have the same inducements to industry as others, they [will] work as well and behave as well."

AGITATION

Antislavery, unlike other reforms, was a radical attack on one of the nation's central institutions, and the movement attracted a minority even among middle-class evangelicals. Indeed, both Lyman Beecher and Charles Finney opposed the abolitionists in the 1830s, arguing that emancipation would come about sooner or later as a result of the religious

"What, then, is meant by immediate abolition?

"It means, in the first place, that all title of property in the slaves shall instantly cease, because their Creator has never relinquished his claim of ownership. . . .

"It means . . . that every husband shall have his own wife, and every wife her own husband . . . that parents shall have the control and government of their own children. . . .

"It means . . . that the slaves, instead of being forced to labor for the exclusive benefit of others . . . shall be encouraged to toil for the mutual profit of themselves and their employers, by the infusion of new motives into their hearts, growing out of their recognition and reward as men. . . .

"It means, finally, that right shall take the supremacy over wrong, principle over brute force, humanity over cruelty, honesty over theft, purity over lust, honor over baseness, love over hatred, and religion over heathenism. Is this wrong?

"This is our meaning of Immediate Abolition."

NEW ENGLAND ANTI-SLAVERY SOCIETY
1833

conversion of slave owners; antislavery agitation and the denunciation of slaveholders, they argued, would divide Christians, slow the revival movement, and thus actually delay emancipation. Finney warned his abolitionist friend Theodore Dwight Weld that the logical end of antislavery was civil war.

Savoring its role as a beleaguered minority, the American Anti-Slavery Society staged a series of campaigns to force government and the public at large to confront the question of slavery. In 1835 the society launched its "Postal Campaign," flooding the nation's postal system with abolitionist tracts that southerners and most northerners regarded as "incendiary." From 1836 onward, they petitioned Congress to abolish slavery and the slave trade in the District of Columbia and to deny the slaveholding Republic of Texas admission to the Union. These tactics forced President Andrew Jackson to permit southern postal workers to censor the mails; they also forced Democrats and southern Whigs to abridge the right of petition to avoid discussion of slavery in Congress (see chapter 12).

In these ways, a radical minority forced politicians to demonstrate the complicity of the party system (and the Democrats in particular) in the institution of slavery, brought the slavery question to public attention, and tied it to questions of civil liberties in the North and political power in the South. They were a dangerous minority indeed.

THE POLITICS OF GENDER AND SEX

Whigs valued a reformed masculinity that was lived out in the sentimentalized homes of the northern business classes or in the Christian gentility of the Whig plantation and farm. Jacksonian voters, on the other hand, often defended domestic patriarchy. While most were unimaginative paternalists, Democrats often made heroes of men whose flamboyant, rakish lives directly challenged Whig domesticity. Whigs denounced Andrew Jackson for allegedly stealing his wife from her lawful husband; Democrats often admired him for the same reason. Richard M. Johnson of Kentucky, who was vice president under Martin Van Buren, openly kept a mulatto mistress and had two daughters by her; with his pistols always at hand, he accompanied her openly around Washington, D.C. "Prince" John Van Buren, the president's son and himself a prominent New York Democrat, met a "dark-eyed, well-formed Italian lady" who called herself Amerigo Vespucci and claimed to be a direct descendant of the man for whom America was named. She became young Van Buren's "fancy lady," remaining with him until he lost her in a high-stakes card game.

Whigs made Democratic contempt for sentimental domesticity a political issue. William Crane, a Michigan Whig, claimed that Democrats "despised no man for his sins," and went on to say that "brothel-haunters flocked to this party, because here in all political circles, and political movements, they were treated as nobility." Much of the Whig cultural agenda (and much of Democratic hatred of that agenda) was rooted in contests between Whig and Democratic masculine styles.

APPETITES

Many of the reforms urged by Whig evangelicals had to do with domestic and personal life rather than with politics. Their hopes for the perfection of the world hinged more on the character of individuals than on the role of institutions. Calvinism had taught that because human beings were innately selfish and subject to animal appetites, they must submit to godly authority. Evangelicals, on the other hand, defined original sin as a *tendency* to self-

ishness and sin that could be fought off—with God's help—through prayer and personal discipline. They hoped to perfect the world by filling it with godly, self-governing individuals.

It was not an easy task, for opportunities to indulge in vanity, luxury, and sensuality were on the rise. Charles Finney, for instance, preached long and hard against vanity. "A self-indulgent Christian," he said, "is a contradiction. You might as well write on your clothes 'NO TRUTH IN RELIGION,'" he told fashionably dressed women, for their dress proclaimed "GIVE ME DRESS, GIVE ME FASHION, GIVE ME FLATTERY, AND I AM HAPPY." Finney also worried about the effect of money, leisure time, and cheap novels on middle-class homes. He could not, he said, "believe that a person who has ever known the love of God can relish a secular novel" or open his or her home to "Byron, Scott, Shakespeare, and a host of triflers and blasphemers of God." Evangelicals also disdained

LINK TO THE PAST

Papers of Elizabeth Cady Stanton and Susan B. Anthony (Model Editions Project)

http://adh.csd.sc.edu:80/dynaweb/MEP/sa/@Generic_BookView

The Model Editions Project is in the process of making the papers of important Americans available online. This particular site is a well organized mini-edition of the papers of Stanton and Anthony, combining large selections from the correspondence of these reformers with introductory essays on women's rights, women and temperance, women and antislavery, and relations between these reforms. Read the essays and correspondence, and think about the following questions:

1. Within the women's rights movement, which particular rights received the most attention? Why?

2. With almost no exceptions, women who agitated for women's rights also supported the temperance and antislavery movements. In ideological and political terms, what was the relationship between temperance and women's rights? Between women's rights and antislavery?

3. In broader terms, why did these three movements tend to attract the same groups of middle-class northerners?

luxury in home furnishings; they discouraged the use of silks and velvets and questioned the propriety of decorating the home with mahogany, mirrors, brass furnishings, and upholstered chairs and sofas.

Members of the evangelical middle class tried to define levels of material comfort that would separate them from the indulgences of those above and below them. They made similar attempts in the areas of food and sex. Sylvester Graham (now remembered for the wheat cracker that bears his name) gave up the ministry in 1830 to become a full-time temperance lecturer. Before long, he was lecturing on the danger of excess in diet and sex. He claimed that the consumption of red meat, spiced foods, and alcohol produced bodily excitement that resulted in weakness and disease. Sex—including fornication, fantasizing, masturbation, and bestiality—affected the body in even more destructive ways, and the two appetites reinforced each other. (Graham admitted that marital sex, though it was physiologically no different from other forms of sex, was preferable, for it was the least exciting.)

Acting on Graham's concerns, reformers established a system of Grahamite boardinghouses in which young men who were living away from home were provided with diets that helped them control their other appetites. Oberlin College, when it was founded by evangelicals in 1832, banned "tea and coffee, highly seasoned meats, rich pastries, and all unholsome [sic] and expensive foods." Among others who heeded Graham's advice were such future feminists as Lucy Stone, Susan B. Anthony, and Amelia Bloomer. Reformers who did not actually adopt Graham's system shared his concern over the twin evils of rich food and sexual excess. John R. McDowall, a divinity student who headed a mission to New York City prostitutes, admitted, "Having eaten until I am full, lust gets the control of me." John Humphrey Noyes (another divinity student who turned to reform) set up a community in Oneida, New York, that indulged in plural marriage but at the same time urged sexual self-control; he also believed that a perfect Christian world would not allow meat-eating.

MORAL REFORM

Although most middle-class households failed to embrace Grahamism, simple food and sexual control became badges of class status. Men supposedly had the greatest difficulty taming their appetites. The old image—beginning with Eve and including Delilah and Jezebel and other dangerous women of the Old Testament—of woman as seductress persisted in the more traditionalist churches and in the pulp fiction from which middle-class mothers tried to protect their sons (see chapter 10). Whig evangelicals, on the other hand, had made the discovery that women were naturally free of desire and that only men were subject to the animal passions. "What terrible temptations lie in the way of your sex," wrote Harriet Beecher Stowe to her husband. "Tho I did love you with an almost insane love before I married you, I never knew yet or felt the pulsation which showed me that I could be tempted in that way. I loved you as I now love God." The middle-class ideal combined female purity and male self-control. For the most part it was a private reform, contained within the home. Sometimes, however, evangelical domesticity produced moral crusades to impose that ethos on the world at large. Many of these crusades were led by women.

In 1828 a band of Sunday school teachers—most of them women—initiated an informal mission to prostitutes that grew into the New York Magdalen Society. Taking a novel approach to an age-old question, the society argued that prostitution was created by brutal fathers and husbands who abandoned their young daughters or wives, by dandies who seduced them and turned them into prostitutes, and by lustful men who bought their services. Prostitution, in other words, was not the result of the innate sinfulness of prostitutes; it was the result of the brutality and lust of men. The solution was to remove young prostitutes from their environment, pray with them, and convert them to middle-class morality.

The Magdalen Society's *First Annual Report* (1831) inveighed against male lust and printed shocking life histories of prostitutes. Some men, however, read it as pornography; others used it as a guidebook to the seamier side of New York City. The wealthy male evangelicals who had bankrolled the Magdalen Society withdrew their support, and the organization fell apart. Thereupon many of the women reformers set up the Female Moral Reform Society, with a House of Industry in which prostitutes were taught morality and household skills to prepare them for new lives as domestic servants in pious middle-class homes. This effort also failed, largely because few

Not for Ourselves Alone (PBS, 1999)
Directed by Ken Burns.

In 1999 Ken Burns made a documentary film on the women's rights movement. Part one tells the story from about 1840 through the Civil War. It is vintage Ken Burns: old photographs scanned to give them the appearance of movies, period documents read over the pictures by actors (in this case, Sally Kellerman) modern-day experts speaking with authority, the same period music that Burns used in *The Civil War* and his other forays into the 19th century, and the same undercurrent of sentimentality. The film focuses on the collaboration and friendship between Susan B. Anthony and Elizabeth Cady Stanton, and through that medium and within its limits, it tells its story well.

Elizabeth Cady Stanton was descended, on her mother's side, from one of the great landholding families of colonial New York. Her father was a prosperous lawyer and judge. Young Elizabeth hungered for education, but no American college admitted women. She enrolled at Emma Willard's Female Seminary at Troy, New York, and shared her family's interest in the temperance and antislavery movements. She met lawyer and well-known antislavery speaker Henry B. Stanton through her cousin, wealthy abolitionist Ger-rit Smith, and married Stanton in 1840. (Elizabeth excised the word "obey" from the ceremony.) The Stantons honeymooned at an antislavery convention in London that year. Organizers of the convention segregated women and men and forbade the women to speak. Stanton realized—as legions of women would realize—that the logic of antislavery applied to women as well as slaves, and that rights reform that was less than universal was badly flawed. The Stantons took up housekeeping in Boston, then moved to Seneca Falls in western New York. Henry Stanton was frequently away on lecture tours, and Elizabeth stayed at home, had babies, and grew weary of housework. In 1848, after a visit with her friend and fellow activist Lucretia Mott, she helped organize the first Women's Rights Convention in Seneca Falls. She authored the declaration demanding civil and legal equality for women—including the demand (truly shocking to contemporaries) that women be allowed to vote.

Shortly after the Seneca Falls Convention, Stanton met Susan B. Anthony, another veteran reformer. Anthony, a Quaker, had been born into much humbler circumstances than Stanton, remained unmarried, and

prostitutes were interested in domestic service or evangelical religion. That fact became distressingly clear when in 1836 the society was obliged to close its House of Industry after the residents had taken it over during the caretaker's absence.

The Female Moral Reform Society was more successful with members of its own class. Its newspaper, the *Advocate of Moral Reform*, circulated throughout the evangelical North, eventually reaching 555 auxiliary societies with 20,000 readers. Now evangelical women fought prostitution by publishing the names of customers. They campaigned against pornography, obscenity, lewdness, and seduction and accepted the responsibility of rearing their sons to be pure, even when it meant dragging them out of brothels. Occasionally they prosecuted men who took advantage of servant girls. They also publicized the names of adulterers, and they had seducers brought into court. In the process, women reformers fought the sexual double standard and assumed the power to define what was respectable and what was not.

WOMEN'S RIGHTS

From the late 1820s onward, middle-class women in the North assumed roles that would have been unthinkable to their mothers and grandmothers.

often upbraided other women reformers for marrying and having children. The differences between Stanton and Anthony added up to a lifelong collaboration: the educated and housebound Stanton wrote the manifestos, and the brave and unencumbered Anthony took them into lecture halls and the state legislature. They and their co-workers won some battles (in the area of women's property rights in particular), but could do little more than publicize their radical demands for the legal reform of marriage and for civil and political equality. This became painfully clear during the Civil War, when their fellow reformers told Stanton and Anthony to delay women's rights while slaves were freed and given the same rights for which the women's movement had fought. At the close of Part one, women's civil and legal equality remain far from realization.

Not for Ourselves Alone tells a familiar story clearly and entertainingly. Along the way, it portrays a friendship between women within the antebellum reform community and (intermittently) throws light upon the workings of a reform culture that enlisted much of the zeal and intellect of the antebellum North.

Not for Ourselves Alone is a documentary by Ken Burns about the American woman suffrage movement.

Evangelical domesticity made loving mothers (and not stern fathers) the principal rearers of children. Housewives saw themselves as missionaries to their families, responsible for the choices their children and husband made between salvation or sin. In that role women became arbiters of fashion, diet, and sexual behavior. Many joined the temperance movement and moral reform societies, where they became public reformers while posing as mothers protecting their sons from rum sellers and seducers. Such experiences gave them a sense of spiritual empowerment that led some to question their own subordinate status within a system of gendered social roles. Lydia Maria Child, a writer of sentimental fiction and manuals on household economy as well as a leading abolitionist and moral reformer, proclaimed, "Those who urged women to become missionaries and form tract societies . . . have changed the household utensil to a living, energetic being, and they have no spell to turn it into a broom again."

The antislavery movement turned many women into advocates of women's rights. Abolitionists, following the perfectionist implications of Whig evangelicalism to their logical ends, called for absolute human equality and a near-anarchist rejection of impersonal institutions and prescribed social roles. It became clear to some female abolitionists that the

415

critique of slavery (a root-and-branch denunciation of patriarchy and prescribed hierarchy) applied as well to inequality based on sex.

Radical female abolitionists reached the conclusion that they were human beings first and women second. In 1837 Sarah Grimke announced, "The Lord Jesus defines the duties of his followers in his Sermon on the Mount . . . without any reference to sex or condition . . . never even referring to the distinction now so strenuously insisted upon between masculine and feminine virtues. . . . Men and women are CREATED EQUAL! They are both moral and accountable beings, and whatever is right for a man to do is right for woman." A women's rights convention put it just as bluntly in 1851: "We deny the right of any portion of the species to decide for another portion . . . what is and what is not their 'proper sphere'; that the proper sphere for all human beings is the largest and highest to which they are able to attain."

Beginning about 1840, women lobbied state legislatures and won significant changes in the laws governing women's rights to property, to the wages of their own labor, and to custody of children in cases of divorce. Fourteen states passed such legislation, culminating in New York's Married Women's Property Act in 1860.

The first Woman's Rights Convention met in Seneca Falls, New York, in 1848, and its ties to antislavery were clear. An argument over the right of women to delivery speeches and engage in other forms of public agitation had already split the American Anti-Slavery society in 1840. Feminist abolitionists organized the Seneca Falls Convention. The only male delegate was the black abolitionist Frederick Douglass. Sojourner Truth, another prominent black opponent of slavery, also attended. Nearly all of the other delegates were white women who had worked within the abolition movement. Both as abolitionists and as feminists, they based their demands for equality not only on legal and moral arguments but on the spirit of republican institutions. The principal formal document issued by the convention, a Declaration of Sentiments and Resolutions based on the Declaration of Independence, denounced "the repeated injuries and usurpations on the part of man toward woman."

Most of those "injuries and usurpations" were political. The central issue was the right to vote, for

REPORT

OF THE

WOMAN'S RIGHTS

CONVENTION,

Held at SENECA FALLS, N. Y., July 19th and 20th, 1848.

ROCHESTER:
PRINTED BY JOHN DICK
AT THE NORTH STAR OFFICE.

THE DECLARATION OF SENTIMENTS PUBLISHED BY THE FIRST WOMAN'S RIGHTS CONVENTION IN 1848 This account of the proceedings and list of resolutions announced that there was an organized women's rights movement in the United States. It also announced that women's rights activists knew how to organize a convention and how to publicize their activities in print.

citizenship was central to the "democratic" pattern that granted liberty and equality to white men regardless of class and excluded Americans who were not white and male. Thus female participation in politics was a direct challenge to a male-ordained women's place. A distraught New York legislator agreed: "It is well known that the object of these unsexed women is to overthrow the most sacred of our institutions. . . . Are we to put the stamp of truth upon the libel here set forth, that men and women, in the matrimonial relation, are to be equal?" Later, feminist Elizabeth Cady Stanton recalled such reactions: "Political rights," she said, "involving in their last results equality everywhere, roused all the antagonism of a dominant power, against the self-assertion of a class hitherto subservient."

CONCLUSION

By the 1830s most citizens in every corner of the republic firmly identified with either the Whig or Democratic Party—so much so that party affiliation was recognized as an indicator of personal history and cultural loyalties. In the states and neighborhoods, Whigs embraced commerce and activist government, arguing that both would foster prosperity, social harmony, and moral progress. Faith in progress and improvement led Northern and western Whigs—primarily the more radical evangelicals among them—to entertain the hope that liberty and equality might apply to women and blacks. Democrats, on the other hand, were generally more localistic and culturally conservative. Like the Whigs, they seldom doubted the value of commerce, but they worried that the market revolution and its organization of banking, credit, and monetary supply was creating unprecedented levels of inequality and personal dependence among the republic's white male citizenry; they were certain that Whig public works projects and Whig taxation increased inequality and corrupted the republic. Democrats also looked with angry disbelief at attempts of Whigs (and rebellious members of Whig families) to govern the private and public behavior of their neighbors, and sometimes even to tinker with ancient distinctions of gender and race.

In sum, Whigs reformulated the revolutionary legacy of liberty and equality, moving away from classical notions of citizenship and toward liberty of conscience and equality of opportunity within a market-driven democracy. They often attempted to civilize that new world by using government power to encourage commerce, social interdependence, and cultural homogeneity. When Democrats argued that Whig "interdependence" in fact meant dependence and inequality, Whigs countered with promises of individual success for those who were morally worthy of it. Democrats trusted none of that. Theirs was a Jeffersonian formulation grounded in a fierce defense of the liberty and equality of white men, and in a minimal, inexpensive, decentralized government that protected the liberties of those men without threatening their independence or their power over their households and within their neighborhoods.

Suggested Readings begin on page SR-1.
For Web activities and resources
related to this chapter, go to
http://www.harcourtcollege.com/history.murrin

CHAPTER 12

JACKSONIAN DEMOCRACY

JACKSON AS DEMOCRACY INCARNATE

Andrew Jackson struck a romantic military pose for this portrait painted in 1820. Posing as the embodiment of democracy and as an extravagantly melodramatic hero, Jackson imposed himself upon his times as few Americans have done.

National political leaders from the 1820s until the outbreak of the Civil War faced two persistent questions. First, a deepening rift between slave and free states threatened the very existence of the nation. Second, explosive economic development and territorial expansion made new demands upon the political system—demands that raised the question of government participation in economic life.

The Whig Party proposed the American System as the answer to both questions. The national government, said the Whigs, should subsidize roads and canals, foster industry with protective tariffs, and maintain a national bank capable of exercising centralized control over credit and currency. The result would be a peaceful, prosperous, and truly national market society. If the South, the West, and the Northeast were profiting by doing business with each other, the argument went, sectional fears and jealousies would quiet down. Jacksonian Democrats, on the other hand, argued that the American System was unconstitutional, that it violated the rights of states and localities, and that it would tax honest citizens in order to benefit corrupt and wealthy insiders. Most dangerous of all, argued the Democrats, Whig economic nationalism would create an activist, interventionist national government that would anger and frighten the slaveholding South. To counter both threats, the Jacksonians resurrected Jefferson's agrarian republic of states' rights and inactive, inexpensive government—all of it deeply inflected in the code of white male equality, domestic patriarchy, and racial slavery that was being acted out in families, neighborhoods, and state legislatures.

This chapter will focus on the following major questions:

- In terms of party development, what were the long-term results of the Missouri controversy and the Panic of 1819? Why?
- At the national level, how did Jacksonian Democrats and their opponents deal with widening differences between the northern and southern states during these years?
- How did they address issues raised by economic development?
- What was peculiarly "national" about the Second Party System?

PROLOGUE: 1819

Jacksonian Democracy was rooted in two events that occurred in 1819. First, the angry debate that surrounded Missouri's admission as a slave state revealed the centrality and vulnerability of slavery within the Union. Second, a severe financial collapse led many Americans to doubt the market revolution's compatibility with the Jeffersonian republic. By 1820 politicians were determined to reconstruct the limited-government, states'-rights coalition that had elected Thomas Jefferson. By 1828 they had formed the Democratic Party, with Andrew Jackson at its head.

THE WEST, 1803–1840S

When Jefferson bought the Louisiana Territory in 1803, he knew that he was giving future generations of Americans a huge "Empire for Liberty." He knew almost nothing, however, about the new land itself. Only a few French trappers and traders had traveled the plains between the Mississippi and the Rocky Mountains, and no white person had seen the territory drained by the Columbia River. In 1804 Jefferson sent an expedition under Meriwether Lewis, his private secretary, and William Clark, brother of the Indian fighter George Rogers Clark,

to explore the land he had bought. To prepare for the expedition, Lewis studied astronomy, zoology, and botany; Clark was already an accomplished mapmaker. The two kept meticulous journals of one of the epic adventures in American history.

In May 1804 Lewis and Clark and 41 companions boarded a keelboat and two large canoes at the village of St. Louis. That spring and summer they poled and paddled 1,600 miles up the Missouri River, passing through rolling plains dotted by the farm villages of the Pawnee, Oto, Missouri, Crow, Omaha, Hidatsa, and Mandan peoples. The villages of the lower Missouri had been cut off from the western buffalo herds and reduced to dependence by mounted Sioux warriors who had begun to establish their hegemony over the northern plains.

Lewis and Clark traveled through Sioux territory and stopped for the winter at the prosperous, heavily fortified Mandan villages at the big bend of the Missouri River in Dakota country. In the spring they hired Toussaint Charbonneau, a French fur trader, to guide them to the Pacific. Although Charbonneau turned out to be useless, his wife, a teenaged Shoshone girl named Sacajawea, was an

A BIRDS-EYE VIEW, BY GEORGE CATLIN The Mandan village at the big bend of the Missouri River hosted the Lewis and Clark party in 1804 and 1805. This bird's-eye view of the village was painted by George Catlin in 1832. Within a few years, the Mandan were nearly extinct, victims of smallpox and the Sioux.

CHRONOLOGY

1804–06 Lewis and Clark explore the northern regions of the Louisiana Purchase

1819 Controversy arises over Missouri's admission to the Union as a slave state • Panic of 1819 marks the first failure of the national market economy

1820 Missouri Compromise adopted

1823 Monroe Doctrine written by Secretary of State John Quincy Adams

1824–25 Adams wins the presidency over Andrew Jackson • Adams appoints Henry Clay as secretary of state • Jacksonians charge a "Corrupt Bargain" between Adams and Clay

1827 Cherokees in Georgia declare themselves a republic

1828 Jackson defeats Adams for the presidency • "Tariff of Abominations" passed by Congress • John C. Calhoun's *Exposition and Protest* presents doctrine of nullification

1830 Congress passes the Indian Removal Act

1832 Jackson reelected over Henry Clay • *Worcester* v. *Georgia* exempts the Cherokee from Georgia law • Jackson vetoes recharter of the Bank of the United States

1833 Force Bill and Tariff of 1833 end the nullification crisis

1834 Whig Party formed in opposition to Jacksonians

1836 Congress adopts "gag rule" to table antislavery petitions • Van Buren elected president

1837 Financial panic ushers in a severe economic depression

1838 U.S. Army marches the remaining Cherokee to Indian Territory

1840 Whig William Henry Harrison defeats Van Buren for presidency

indispensable guide, interpreter, and diplomat. With her help, Lewis and Clark navigated the upper Missouri, crossed the Rockies to the Snake River, and followed that stream to the Columbia River. They reached the Pacific in November 1805 and spent the winter at what is now Astoria, Oregon. Retracing their steps the following spring and summer, they returned to St. Louis in September 1806. They brought with them many volumes of drawings and notes, along with assurances that the Louisiana Purchase had been worth many, many times its price.

As time passed, Americans began to settle the southern portions of the Louisiana Purchase. Louisiana itself, strategically crucial and already the site of sugar plantations and the town of New Orleans, entered the Union in 1812. Settlers were also filtering into northern Louisiana and the Arkansas and Missouri territories. Farther north and west, the Sioux extended their control over the northern reaches of the land that Jefferson had bought.

The Sioux were aided in their conquest by the spread of smallpox. The disease moved up the Missouri River periodically from the 1790s onward; by the 1830s, epidemics were ravaging the sedentary peoples of the Missouri. The Mandans, who had been so hospitable to Lewis and Clark, got the worst of it: They were almost completely wiped out. The Sioux and their Cheyenne allies, who lived in small bands and were constantly on the move, fared better. Their horse-raiding parties now grew into armies of mounted invaders numbering as many as 2,000, and they extended their hunting lands south into what is now southern Nebraska and as far west as the Yellowstone River. In the 1840s white settlers began crossing the southern plains, while white politicians entered into a fateful debate on whether these lands would become the site of northern farms or southern plantations. At the same time, the newly victorious Sioux never doubted that the northern plains would be theirs forever.

THE ARGUMENT OVER MISSOURI

Early in 1819 slaveholding Missouri applied for admission to the Union as the first new state to be carved out of the Louisiana Purchase. New York Congressman James Tallmadge, Jr., quickly proposed two amendments to the Missouri statehood bill. The first would bar additional slaves from being brought into Missouri (16 percent of Missouri's people were already slaves). The second would emancipate Missouri slaves born after admission when they reached their 25th birthday. Put simply, the Tallmadge amendments would admit Missouri only if Missouri agreed to become a free state.

The congressional debates on the Missouri question had nothing to do with humanitarian objections to slavery and everything to do with political power. Rufus King of New York, an old Federalist who led the northerners in the Senate, insisted that he opposed the admission of a new slave state "solely in its bearing and effects upon great political interests, and upon the just and equal rights of the freemen of the nation." Northerners had long chafed at the added representation in Congress and in the electoral college that the "three-fifths" rule granted to the slave states (see chapter 6). The rule had, in fact, added significantly to southern power: In 1790 the South, with 40 percent of the white population, controlled 47 percent of the votes in Congress—enough to decide close votes both in Congress and in presidential elections. Federalists pointed out that of the 12 additional electoral votes the three-fifths rule gave to the South, 10 had gone to Thomas Jefferson in 1800 and had given him the election. Without the bogus votes provided by slavery, they argued, Virginia's stranglehold on the presidency would have been broken with Washington's departure in 1796.

In 1819 the North held a majority in the House of Representatives. The South, thanks to the recent admissions of Alabama and southern-oriented Illinois, controlled a bare majority in the Senate. Voting on the Tallmadge amendments was starkly sectional: Northern congressmen voted 86 to 10 for the first amendment, 80 to 14 for the second; southerners rejected both, 66 to 1 and 64 to 2. In the Senate, a unanimous South defeated the Tallmadge amendments with the help of the two Illinois senators and three northerners. Deadlocked between a Senate in favor of admitting Missouri as a slave state and a House dead set against it, Congress broke off one of the angriest sessions in its history and went home.

THE MISSOURI COMPROMISE

The new Congress that convened in the winter of 1819–20 passed the legislative package that became known as the Missouri Compromise. Massachusetts offered its northern counties as the new free state of Maine, thus neutralizing fears that the South would gain votes in the Senate with the admission of Missouri. Senator Jesse Thomas of Illinois proposed the so-called Thomas Proviso: If the North would admit Missouri as a slave state, the South would agree to outlaw slavery in territories above 36°30' N latitude—a line extending from the southern border of Missouri to Spanish (within a year, Mexican) territory. That line would open Arkansas Territory (present-day Arkansas and Oklahoma) to slavery and would close to slavery the remainder of the Louisiana Territory—land that would subsequently become all or part of nine states.

Congress admitted Maine with little debate, but the terms of the Thomas Proviso met northern opposition. A joint Senate-House committee finally decided to separate the two bills. With half of the southern representatives and nearly all of the northerners supporting it, the Thomas Proviso passed. Congress next took up the admission of Missouri. With the votes of a solid South and 14 compromise-minded northerners, Missouri entered the Union as a slave state. President James Monroe applauded the "patriotic devotion" of the northern representatives "who preferr'd the sacrifice of themselves at home" to endangering the Union. His words were prophetic: Nearly all of the 14 were voted out of office when they faced angry northern voters in the next election.

The Missouri crisis brought the South's commitment to slavery and the North's resentment of southern political power into collision, revealing an uncompromisable gulf between slave and free states. While northerners vowed to relinquish no more territory to slavery, southerners talked openly of disunion and civil war. A Georgia politician announced that the Missouri debates had lit a fire that "seas of blood can only extinguish." President Monroe's secretary of state, John Quincy Adams, saw the debates as an omen: Northerners would unanimously oppose the extension of slavery whenever the question came to a vote. Adams confided in his diary:

> Here was a new party ready formed, . . . terrible to the whole Union, but portentiously terrible to the South— threatening in its progress the emancipation of all their slaves, threatening in its immediate effect that Southern domination which has swayed the Union for the last twenty years.

Viewing the crisis from Monticello, the aging Thomas Jefferson was distraught:

> A geographical line, coinciding with a marked principle, moral and political, once conceived and held up to the angry passions of men, will never be obliterated; every new irritation will mark it deeper and deeper. . . . This momentous question, like a fire-bell in the night, awakened and filled me with terror. I considered it at once the knell of the Union.

THE PANIC OF 1819

Politicians debated the Missouri question against a darkening backdrop of economic depression—a downturn that would shape political alignments as much as the slavery question. The origins of the Panic of 1819 were international and numerous: European agriculture was recovering from the Napoleonic wars, thereby reducing the demand for American foodstuffs; war and revolution in the New World had cut off the supply of precious metals (the base of the international money supply) from the mines of Mexico and Peru; debt-ridden European governments hoarded the available specie; and American bankers and businessmen met the situation by expanding credit and issuing banknotes that were mere dreams of real money. Coming in the first years of the market revolution, this speculative boom was encouraged by American bankers who had little experience with corporate charters, promissory notes, bills of exchange, or stocks and bonds.

Congress had in part chartered the Second Bank of the United States in 1816 (see chapter 9) to impose order on this situation, but the Bank itself under the presidency of the genial Republican politician William Jones, became part of the problem. The western branch offices in Cincinnati and Lexington became embroiled in the speculative boom, and insiders at the Baltimore branch hatched criminal schemes to enrich themselves. With matters spinning out of control, Jones resigned early in 1819. The new president, Langdon Cheves of South Carolina, curtailed credit and demanded that state banknotes received by the Bank of the United States be redeemed in specie (precious metals). By doing so, Cheves rescued the Bank from the paper economy created by state-chartered banks, but at huge expense: When the

state banks were forced to redeem their notes in specie, they demanded payment from their own borrowers, and the national money and credit system collapsed.

The depression that followed the Panic of 1819 was the first failure of the market economy. Local ups and downs had occurred since the 1790s, but this collapse was nationwide. Employers who could not meet their debts went out of business, and hundreds of thousands of wage workers lost their jobs. In Philadelphia, unemployment reached 75 percent; 1,800 workers in that city were imprisoned for debt. A tent city of the unemployed sprang up on the outskirts of Baltimore. Other cities and towns were hit as hard, and the situation was no better in the countryside. Thomas Jefferson reported that farms in his neighborhood were selling for what had earlier been a year's rent, and a single session of the county court at Nashville handled over 500 lawsuits for debt.

Faced with a disastrous downturn that none could control and that few understood, many Americans directed their resentment onto the banks, particularly on the Bank of the United States. John Jacob Astor, a New York merchant and possibly the richest man in America at that time, admitted that "there has been too much Speculation and too much assumption of Power on the Part of the Bank Directors which has caused [sic] the institution to become unpopular . . . ." William Gouge, who would become the Jacksonian Democrats' favorite economist, put it more bluntly: When the Bank demanded that state banknotes be redeemed in specie, he said, "the Bank was saved and the people were ruined." By the end of 1819 the Bank of the United States had won the name that it would carry to its death in the 1830s: the Monster.

REPUBLICAN REVIVAL

The crises during 1819 and 1820 prompted demands for a return to Jeffersonian principles. President Monroe's happily proclaimed "Era of Good Feelings"—a new era of partyless politics created by the collapse of Federalism—was, according to worried Republicans, a disaster. Without opposition, Jefferson's dominant Republican Party had lost its way. The nationalist Congress of 1816 had enacted much of the Federalist program under the name of Republicanism; the result, said the old Republicans, was an aggressive government that helped bring on the Panic of 1819. At the same time, the collapse of Republican Party discipline in Congress had allowed the Missouri question to degenerate into a sectional free-for-all. By 1820 many Republicans were calling for a Jeffersonian revival that would limit government power and guarantee southern rights within the Union.

MARTIN VAN BUREN LEADS THE WAY

The busiest and the most astute of those Republicans was Martin Van Buren, leader of New York's Bucktail Republican faction, who took his seat in the Senate in 1821. An immensely talented man with no influential family connections (his father was a Hudson valley tavern keeper) and little formal education, Van Buren had built his political career out of a commitment to Jeffersonian principles, personal charm, and party discipline. Arriving in Washington in the aftermath of the Missouri debates and the Panic of 1819, he hoped to apply his political expertise to what he perceived as a dangerous turning point in national politics.

Van Buren's New York experience, along with his reading of national politics, told him that disciplined political parties were necessary democratic tools. The Founding Fathers—including Jefferson—had denounced parties, claiming that republics rested on civic virtue, not competition. Van Buren, on the other hand, claimed that the Era of Good Feelings had turned public attention away from politics, allowing privileged insiders—many of them unreconstructed Federalists—to create a big national state and to reorganize politics along sectional lines. Van Buren insisted that competition and party divisions were inevitable and good, but that they must be made to serve the republic. He wrote:

> We must always have party distinctions, and the old ones are the best. . . . If the old ones are suppressed, geographical differences founded on local instincts or what is worse, prejudices between free & slave holding states will inevitably take their place.

Working with likeminded politicians, Van Buren reconstructed the coalition of northern and southern agrarians that had elected Thomas Jefferson. The result was the Democratic Party and, ultimately, a national two-party system that persisted until the eve of the Civil War.

THE ELECTION OF 1824

With the approach of the 1824 presidential election, Van Buren and his friends supported William H. Crawford, Monroe's secretary of war and a staunch Georgia Republican. The Van Burenites controlled the Republican congressional caucus, the body that traditionally chose the party's presidential candidates. The public distrusted the caucus as undemocratic, for it represented the only party in government and thus could dictate the choice of a president. Van Buren, however, continued to regard it as a necessary tool of party discipline. With most congressmen fearing their constituents, only a minority showed up for the caucus vote. They dutifully nominated Crawford.

With Republican Party unity broken, the list of sectional candidates grew. John Quincy Adams was the son of a Federalist president, successful secretary of state under Monroe, and one of the northeastern Federalist converts to Republicanism who, according to people like Van Buren and Crawford, had blunted the republican thrust of Jefferson's old party. He entered the contest as New England's favorite son. Henry Clay of Kentucky, a nationalist who claimed as his own the American System of protective tariffs, centralized banking, and government-sponsored internal improvements, expected to carry the West. John C. Calhoun of South Carolina announced his candidacy; but when he saw the swarm of candidates, he dropped out and put himself forth as the sole candidate for vice president.

The wild card was Andrew Jackson of Tennessee, who in 1824 was known only as a military hero—scourge of the southern Indians and victor over the British at New Orleans (see chapter 8). He was also a frontier nabob with a reputation for violence: He had killed a rival in a duel, had engaged in a shoot-out in a Nashville tavern, and had reputedly stolen his wife from her estranged husband. According to Jackson's detractors, such impetuosity marked his public life as well. As commander of U.S. military forces in the South in 1818, Jackson had led an unauthorized invasion of Spanish

JOHN QUINCY ADAMS The politician enjoyed a remarkably productive career as Monroe's Secretary of State, then rode into the presidency in the conflicted and controversial election of 1824. The intelligence and erudition that the picture projects had served him well as a diplomat. As president, it marked him as aloof, aristocratic, and incapable of governing a democratic nation.

Florida, claiming that it was a hideout for Seminole warriors who raided into the United States and a sanctuary for runaway Georgia slaves. During the action he had occupied Spanish forts, summarily executed Seminoles, and hanged two British subjects. Secretary of State John Quincy Adams had belatedly approved the raid, knowing that the show of American force would encourage the Spanish to sell Florida to the United States. Secretary of War Crawford, on the other hand, as an "economy" measure, had reduced the number of major generals in the U.S. Army from two to one, thus eliminating Jackson's job. After being appointed governor of newly acquired Florida in 1821, Jackson retired from public life later that year. In 1824 eastern politicians knew Jackson only as a "military chieftain," "the Napoleon of the woods," a frontier hothead, and, possibly, a robber-bridegroom.

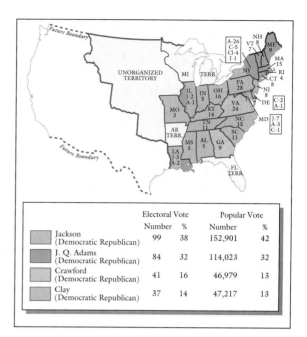

	Electoral Vote		Popular Vote	
	Number	%	Number	%
Jackson (Democratic Republican)	99	38	152,901	42
J. Q. Adams (Democratic Republican)	84	32	114,023	32
Crawford (Democratic Republican)	41	16	46,979	13
Clay (Democratic Republican)	37	14	47,217	13

PRESIDENTIAL ELECTION, 1824

Jackson may have been all those things, but the easterners failed to recognize his immense popularity, particularly in the new states of the South and the West. Thus, in the election of 1824, in the 16 states that chose presidential electors by popular vote (six states still left the choice to their legislatures), Jackson polled 152,901 votes to Adams's 114,023 and Clay's 47,217. Crawford, who suffered a crippling stroke during the campaign, won 46,979 votes. Jackson's support was not only larger but more nearly national than that of his opponents. Adams carried only his native New England and a portion of New York. Clay's meager support was limited to the Northwest, and Crawford's to the Southeast and to the portions of New York that Van Buren was able to deliver. Jackson carried 84 percent of the votes of his own Southwest, and won victories in Pennsylvania, New Jersey, North Carolina, Indiana, and Illinois, and ran a close second in several other states.

"A CORRUPT BARGAIN"

Jackson assumed that he had won the election: He had received 42 percent of the popular vote to his nearest rival's 33 percent, and he was clearly the nation's choice, but his 99 electoral votes were 32 shy of the plurality demanded by the Constitution. And so, acting under the Twelfth Amendment, the House of Representatives would select a president from among the top three candidates. As the candidate with the fewest electoral votes, Henry Clay was eliminated, but he remained Speaker of the House and had enough support to throw the election to either Jackson or Adams. Years later, Jackson told a dinner guest that Clay had offered to support him in exchange for Clay's appointment as secretary of state—an office that traditionally led to the presidency. When Jackson turned him down, according to Jacksonian legend, Clay went to Adams and made the same offer. Adams accepted what became known as the "Corrupt Bargain" in January 1825. A month later, the House of Representatives voted: Clay's supporters, joined by several old Federalists, switched to Adams, giving him a one-vote victory. Soon after becoming president, Adams appointed Henry Clay as his secretary of state.

Reaction to the alleged Corrupt Bargain between John Quincy Adams and Henry Clay dominated the Adams administration and gave rise to a rhetoric of intrigue and betrayal that nourished a rising democratic movement. Before the vote took place in the House of Representatives, Andrew Jackson remarked, "Rumors say that deep intrigue is on foot," and predicted a "bargain & sale" of the presidency. After the election, Jackson declared that the "gamester" Henry Clay has subverted the democratic will to his own purposes, and that "the rights of the people have been bartered for promises of office." "So you see," Jackson said, "The *Judas* of the West has closed the contract and will receive the thirty pieces of silver. His end will be the same." Others in Washington were equally appalled. Robert Y. Hayne of South Carolina denounced the "monstrous union between Clay & Adams," and Louis McLane of Delaware declared the coalition of Clay and Adams utterly "unnatural & preposterous." (Eventually, Clay challenged Virginia Senator John Randolph, one of his nastiest critics, to a duel. Clay's shot passed harmlessly through Randolph's flowing coat, and Randolph fired a gentlemanly shot into the air, but the charge of corruption would follow Clay for the rest of his political life.)

JACKSONIAN MELODRAMA

Andrew Jackson regarded the intrigues that robbed him of the presidency in 1825 as the culmination of

THE ELECTION OF 1824 Cartoonist David Claypoole Johnston portrayed the election of 1824 as a footrace. At left, Adams and Crawford run neck and neck while Jackson has the outside track. At right, Clay has dropped out, but a supporter is helping him to make plans.

a long train of corruption that the nation had suffered over the previous 10 years. Although in the campaign he had made only vague policy statements, he had firm ideas of what had gone wrong with the republic. In 1821, after having been "betrayed" by members of Monroe's cabinet over his raid into Florida, Jackson had retired to his plantation near Nashville to ponder the state of the nation and fill page after page with what he called "memorandums." (This was the kind of gaffe that appalled his educated eastern opponents and pleased nearly everyone else.)

A frontier planter with a deep distrust of banks, Jackson claimed that the Panic of 1819 had been brought on by self-serving miscreants in the Bank of the United States. He insisted that the national debt was another source of corruption; it must be paid off and never allowed to recur. The federal government under James Monroe was filled with swindlers, and in the name of a vague nationalism they were taking power for themselves and scheming against the liberties of the people. The politicians had been bought off, said Jackson, and had attempted—through "King Caucus"—to select a president by backstairs deals rather than by popular election. Finally, in 1825, they had stolen the presidency outright.

Like hundreds of thousands of other Americans, Jackson sensed that something had gone wrong with the republic—that selfishness and intrigue had corrupted the government. In the language of revolutionary republicanism, which Jackson had learned as a boy in the Carolina backwoods and would speak throughout his life, a corrupt power once again threatened to snuff out liberty.

In his "memorandums," Jackson set against the designs of that power the classic republican safeguard: a virtuous citizenry. Unlike most of his revolutionary forebears, however, he believed that government should follow the will of popular majorities. An aroused public, he said, was the republic's best hope: "My fervent prayers are that our republican government may be perpetual, and the people alone by their virtue, and independent exercise of their free suffrage can make it perpetual."

More completely than any of his rivals, Jackson had captured the rhetoric of the revolutionary republic. And, with his fixation on secrecy, corruption, and intrigues, he transformed both that rhetoric and

his own biography into popular melodrama. Finally, with a political alchemy that his rivals never understood, Jackson submerged old notions of republican citizenship into a firm faith in majoritarian democracy: Individuals might become selfish and corrupt, he believed, but a democratic majority was, by its very nature, opposed to corruption and governmental excess. Thus the republic was safe only when governed by the will of the majority. The Corrupt Bargain of 1825 had made that clear: either the people or political schemers would rule.

ADAMS VERSUS JACKSON

While Jackson plotted revenge, John Quincy Adams assumed the duties of the presidency. He was well prepared. The son of a Federalist president, he had been an extraordinarily successful secretary of state under Monroe, guiding American diplomacy in the postwar world.

NATIONALISM IN AN INTERNATIONAL ARENA

In the Rush-Bagot Treaty of 1817 and the British-American Convention of 1818 Secretary of State John Quincy Adams helped pacify the Great Lakes, restore American fishing rights off of Canada, and draw the U.S.-Canadian boundary west to the Rocky Mountains—actions that transformed the Canadian-American frontier from a battleground into the peaceful border that it has been ever since. He pacified the southern border as well. In 1819, following Jackson's raid into Florida, the Adams-Onis Treaty procured Florida for the United States and defined the U.S.-Spanish border west of the Mississippi in ways that gave the Americans claims to the Pacific Coast in the Northwest.

Trickier problems had arisen when Spanish colonies in the Americas declared their independence. Spain could not prevent this, and the powers of Europe, victorious over Napoleon and determined to roll back the republican revolution, talked openly of helping Spain or of annexing South American territory for themselves. Both the Americans and the British opposed such a move, and the British proposed a joint statement outlawing the interference of any outside power (including themselves) in Latin America. Adams had thought it better for the United States to make its own policy than to "come in as cock-boat in the wake of the British man-of-war." In 1823 he wrote what became known as the Monroe Doctrine. Propounded at the same time that the United States recognized the new Latin American republics, it declared American opposition to any European attempt at colonization in the New World without (as the British had wanted) denying the right of the United States to annex new territory. Although the international community knew that the British navy, and not the Monroe Doctrine, kept the European powers out of the Americas, Adams had announced that the United States was determined to become the preeminent power in the Western Hemisphere.

NATIONALISM AT HOME

As president, Adams tried to translate his fervent nationalism into domestic policy. Although the brilliant, genteel Adams had dealt smoothly with European diplomats, as president of a democratic republic he went out of his way to isolate himself and to offend popular democracy. In his first annual message to Congress, Adams outlined an ambitious program for national development under the auspices of the federal government: roads, canals, a national university, a national astronomical observatory ("lighthouses of the skies"), and other costly initiatives:

> The spirit of improvement is abroad upon the earth. . . . While foreign nations less blessed with . . . freedom . . . than ourselves are advancing with gigantic strides in the career of public improvement, were we to slumber in indolence or fold up our arms and proclaim to the world that we are palsied by the will of our constituents, would it not . . . doom ourselves to perpetual inferiority?

Congressmen could not believe their ears as they listened to Adams's extravagant proposals. Here was a president who had received only one in three votes and who had entered office accused of intrigues against the democratic will. And yet at the first opportunity he was telling Congress to pass an ambitious program and not to be "palsied" by the will of the electorate. Even the many members of Congress who favored Adams's program were afraid to vote for it.

Adding to his reputation as an enemy of democracy whenever opportunity presented itself, Adams heaped popular suspicions not only on himself but on his program. Hostile politicians and journalists never tired of joking about Adams's "lighthouses to the skies." More lasting, however, was the connection they drew between federal public works projects and high taxes, intrusive government, the denial of democratic majorities, and expanded opportunities for corruption, secret deals, and special favors. Congress never acted on the president's proposals, and the Adams administration emerged as little more than a long prelude to the election of 1828.

THE BIRTH OF THE DEMOCRATIC PARTY

As early as 1825, it was clear that the election of 1828 would pit Adams against Andrew Jackson. To the consternation of his chief supporters, Adams did nothing to prepare for the contest. He refused to remove even his noisiest enemies from appointive office, and he built no political organization for what promised to be a stiff contest for reelection. The opposition was much more active. Van Buren and like-minded Republicans (with their candidate Crawford hopelessly incapacitated) switched their allegiance to Jackson. They wanted Jackson elected, however, not only as a popular hero but as head of a disciplined and committed Democratic Party that would continue the states'-rights, limited-government positions of the old Jeffersonian Republicans.

The new Democratic Party Richmond *Enquirer* linked popular democracy with the defense of southern slavery. Van Buren began preparations for 1828 with a visit to John C. Calhoun of South Carolina. Calhoun was moving along the road from postwar nationalism to states'-rights conservatism; he also wanted to stay on as vice president and thus keep his presidential hopes alive. After convincing Calhoun to support Jackson and to endorse limited government, Van Buren wrote to Thomas Ritchie, editor of the *Enquirer* and leader of Virginia's Republicans, who could deliver Crawford's southern supporters to Jackson. In his letter, Van Buren proposed to revive the alliance of "the planters of the South and the plain Republicans of the North" that had won Jefferson the presidency. Reminding

Ritchie of how one-party government had allowed the Missouri question to get out of hand, Van Buren insisted that "if the old [party loyalties] are suppressed, prejudices between free and slave holding states will inevitably take their place."

Thus a new Democratic Party, committed to an agrarian program of states' rights and minimal government and dependent on the votes of both slaveholding and non-slaveholding states (beginning, much like Jefferson's old party, with Van Buren's New York and Ritchie's Virginia), would ensure democracy, the continuation of slavery, and the preservation of the Union. The alternative, Van Buren firmly believed, was an expensive and invasive national state (Adams's "lighthouses to the skies"), the isolation of the slaveholding South, and thus mortal danger to the republic.

THE ELECTION OF 1828

The presidential campaign of 1828 was an exercise in slander rather than a debate on public issues. Adhering to custom, neither Adams nor Jackson campaigned directly, but their henchmen viciously personalized the campaign. Jacksonians hammered away at the Corrupt Bargain of 1825 and at the dishonesty and weakness that Adams had supposedly displayed in that affair. The Adams forces attacked Jackson's character. They reminded voters of his duels and tavern brawls and circulated a "coffin handbill" describing Jackson's execution of militiamen during the Creek War. One of Henry Clay's newspaper friends circulated the rumor that Jackson was a bastard and that his mother was a prostitute, but the most egregious slander of the campaign centered on Andrew Jackson's marriage. In 1790 Jackson had married Rachel Donelson, probably aware that she was estranged but not formally divorced from a man named Robards. Branding the marriage an "abduction," the Adams team screamed that Jackson had "torn from a husband the wife of his bosom," and had lived with her in a state of "open and notorious lewdness." They branded Rachel Jackson (now a deeply pious plantation housewife) an "American Jezebel," a "profligate woman," and a "convicted adulteress" whose ungoverned passions made her unfit to be First Lady of a "Christian nation."

RACHEL DONELSON JACKSON AS A MATURE PLANTATION MISTRESS Andrew Jackson supposedly wore this miniature portrait of his beloved Rachel over his heart after her death in 1828.

The Adams strategy ultimately backfired. Many voters did agree that only a man who strictly obeyed the law was fit to be president, and that Jackson's "passionate" and "lawless" nature disqualified him, but many others criticized Adams for making Jackson's private life a public issue. Some claimed that Adams's rigid legalism left no room for privacy or for local notions of justice. Whatever the legality of their marriage, Andrew and Rachel Jackson had lived as models of marital fidelity and romantic love for nearly 40 years; their neighbors had long ago forgiven whatever transgressions they may have committed. Thus on the one hand, Jackson's supporters accused the Adams campaign of a gross violation of privacy and honor. On the other, they defended Jackson's marriage—and his duels, brawls, executions, and unauthorized military ventures—as a triumph of what was right and just over what was narrowly legal. The attempt to brand Jackson as a lawless man, in fact, enhanced his image as a melodramatic hero who battled shrewd,

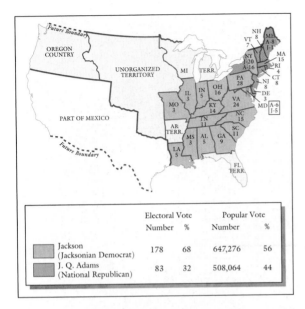

	Electoral Vote		Popular Vote	
	Number	%	Number	%
Jackson (Jacksonian Democrat)	178	68	647,276	56
J. Q. Adams (National Republican)	83	32	508,064	44

PRESIDENTIAL ELECTION, 1828

unscrupulous, legalistic enemies by drawing on his natural nobility and force of will.

The campaign caught the public imagination. Voter turnout was double what it had been in 1824, totaling 56.3 percent. Jackson won the election with 56 percent of the popular vote (a landslide unmatched until the 20th century) and with a margin of 178 to 83 in electoral votes. Adams carried New England, Delaware, and most of Maryland and took 16 of New York's 36 electoral votes. Jackson carried every other state. It was a clear triumph of democracy over genteel statesmanship, of limited government over expansive nationalism, and of the South and the West over New England. Just as clearly, it was a victory of popular melodrama over old forms of cultural gentility.

A PEOPLE'S INAUGURATION

Newspapers estimated that from 15,000 to 20,000 citizens (Duff Green's *United States Telegraph*, a Jackson paper, claimed 30,000) came to Washington to witness Jackson's inauguration on March 4, 1829. They were "like the inundation of the northern barbarians into Rome," remarked Senator Daniel Webster. Many had traveled as much as 500 miles, and "they really seem to think that the coun-

try is rescued from some dreadful danger." As members of the Washington establishment watched uneasily, the crowd filled the open spaces and the streets near the east portico of the Capitol Building, where Jackson was to deliver his inaugural address.

Jackson arrived at the Capitol in deep mourning. In December his wife Rachel had gone to Nashville to shop and had stopped to rest in a newspaper office. There, for the first time, she read the accusations that had been made against her. She fainted on the spot. Although she had been in poor health, no one would ever convince Jackson that her death in January had not been caused by his political enemies. As he arrived to assume the presidency, he wore a black suit and black tie, a black armband, and a black hatband that trailed down his neck in what was called a weeper.

Jackson's inaugural address was vague. He promised "proper respect" for states' rights and a "spirit of equity, caution, and compromise" on the question of the tariff, which was beginning to cause sectional controversy. He promised to reform the civil service by replacing "unfaithful or incompetent" officers, and he vowed to retire the national debt through "a strict and faithful economy." Beyond that, he said little, though he took every opportunity to flatter the popular majority. He had been elected "by the choice of a free people" (and not by King Caucus or Corrupt Bargains), and he pledged "the zealous dedication of my humble abilities to their service and their good." He finished—as he often finished an important statement—by reminding Americans that a benign providence looked over them. He then looked up to a roar of applause.

The new president traveled slowly from the Capitol to the White House, with the throng following and growing noisier along the way. The crowd followed him into the White House, where refreshments had been provided. Soon Jackson's well-wishers were ranging through the mansion, muddying the carpets, tipping things over, breaking dishes, and standing in dirty boots on upholstered chairs. Jackson had to retreat to avoid being crushed. The White House staff lured much of the crowd outside by moving the punch bowls and liquor to the lawn. A wealthy Washington matron who had admired the well-behaved crowd at the inaugural address exclaimed, "What a scene did we witness! *The Majesty of the People* had disappeared,

THE PRESIDENT'S LEVEE Robert Cruikshank drew Jackson's inaugural reception with men and women of all classes, children, dogs, and bucking horses celebrating the Old General's victory. Cruikshank subtitled his lithograph *All Creation Going to the White House.*

and a rabble, a mob, of boys, negros, children, scrambling, fighting, romping. What a pity, what a pity." Another guest pronounced the occasion a "Saturnalia . . . of mud and filth." A Democratic newspaper reported more favorably: "General Jackson is *their own* President. . . . He was greeted by them with an enthusiasm which bespoke him the Hero of a popular triumph."

THE SPOILS SYSTEM

Jackson had begun to assemble his administration months before he took office. Martin Van Buren, who had mobilized much of the support Jackson gained between 1824 and 1828, was the new secretary of state—positioned to succeed Jackson as president. Van Buren quit his newly won post as governor of New York and came to Washington, where he became Jackson's most valued adviser. Other appointments were less promising, for Jackson filled the remaining cabinet posts with old friends and political supporters who in many cases proved unfit for

their jobs. A critic looked at Jackson's cabinet and pronounced it—with the exception of Van Buren— "the Millennium of the Minnows."

Others were more concerned about what Jackson would do to the civil service than about whom he named to his cabinet. During the campaign, Jackson had vowed to fire corrupt officeholders—a term he applied to grafters, incompetents, long-term officeholders who considered their jobs personal property, and those who supported John Quincy Adams. Early in the administration, opponents complained that Jackson was replacing able, educated, patriotic public servants with some dubious appointments. They soon had convincing evidence: Samuel Swarthout, whom Jackson had appointed collector of the Port of New York (an office that handled $15 million dollars in tariff revenue annually), stole $1.2 million and took off for Europe.

Actually, much of the furor over Jackson's "spoils system" was overwrought and misdirected. He aimed, Jackson claimed, only to institute "rotation

Log Cabins and Hard Cider

Sloganeering, torchlight parades, and political theatricality by Whigs in the 1840 "Log Cabin Campaign" overwhelmed all attempts at serious discussion of the issues. Whigs, who had earlier been repelled by the boisterous electioneering techniques of the Democrats, filled the campaign with humor and noise, beating the Democrats at their own game. Whigs covered a great paper ball with slogans and, with music from a brass band and shouts of "Keep the ball rolling!" they rolled the ball through the midwestern and northeastern states. They also hid their

A TIPPECANOE PROCESSION.

in office" and to eject officeholders who expected to hold lifetime appointments. Arguing that most government jobs could be performed by any honest, reasonably intelligent citizen, Jackson proposed ending the long tenures that, he said, turned the civil service into "support of the few at the expense of the many." Jackson removed about 1 in 10 executive appointees during his eight years in office, and his replacements (at least at the level of ambas-

sadors, federal judges and attorneys, and cabinet members) were as wealthy and well-educated as their predecessors. They were, however, most decidedly *political* appointees. Acting out of his own need for personal loyalty and on the advice of Van Buren and other architects of the Democratic Party, Jackson filled vacancies—down to postmasters in the smallest towns—with Democrats who had worked for his election.

distaste for alcohol, tobacco, and other bad (but popular) habits associated with the Democrats. The pewter snuff box shown here (one of thousands of mementos from the campaign) was stamped with the image of a particularly bucolic log cabin—associating the candidate William Henry Harrison not only with the virtues of rural simplicity but with the male, democratic appetite that the contents of the box would satisfy. Another novelty distributed by the Whigs in 1840 was a cardboard picture of President Van Buren smiling at the taste of "White House Champagne." Viewers could pull a tab attached to the card to change the picture to one of Van Buren grimacing at the taste of hard cider from a mug emblazoned with Harrison's initials—thus accomplishing the campaign's transformation of Van Buren into a wine-drinking, extravagant aristocrat with a strong repugnance for the simple virtues and simple pleasures enjoyed by the Whigs.

A BEAUTIFUL GOBLET OF WHITE HOUSE CHAMPAGNE

AN UGLY MUG OF LOG CABIN HARD CIDER

Jackson sought Van Buren's advice on appointments. Van Buren knew the political value of dispensing government jobs; indeed one of his henchmen coined the phrase "To the victor belongs the spoils." In resorting to patronage to build the party, however, Jackson gave his opponents an important issue. Revolutionary republicans feared a government of lackeys dependent on a powerful executive, and congressional opponents argued that Jackson was using appointments to "convert the entire body of those in office into corrupt and supple instruments of power." "A standing army," railed Henry Clay in the Senate, "has been, in all free countries, a just object of jealousy and suspicion. But is not a corps of one hundred thousand dependents upon government, actuated by one spirit, obeying one will, and aiming at one end, more dangerous than a standing army?" It became an anti-Jacksonian

433

axiom that Jackson had made the federal civil service an arm of the Democratic Party and of despotic executive power.

JACKSONIAN DEMOCRACY AND THE SOUTH

In the 1828 election, even though Jackson ran strongly in every region but New England, the base of his support was in the South, where he won 8 of every 10 votes. Southerners had grown wary of an activist government in which they were in the minority. They looked to Jackson not only as a military hero but as a Tennessee planter who talked about returning to republican fundamentals. Although southerners expected Jackson to look after southern interests, disagreement arose within the administration on how those interests should be protected. Some sided with Vice President Calhoun, who believed that any state had the right to veto federal legislation and even in extreme cases to secede from the Union. Others agreed with Secretary of State Van Buren that the Union was inviolable, and that the South's best safeguard was in a political party committed to states' rights within the Union. The differences were fought out in the contest between Calhoun and Van Buren for the right to succeed Jackson as president, a contest that shaped every major issue of Jackson's first term.

SOUTHERNERS AND INDIANS

When Jackson entered office, a final crisis between frontier whites and the native peoples of the eastern woodlands was under way. By the 1820s few Native Americans were left east of the Appalachians. The Iroquois of New York were penned into tiny reservations, and the tribes of the Old Northwest were broken and scattered. But in the Old Southwest 60,000 Cherokees, Creeks, Choctaws, Chickasaws, and Seminoles were still living on their ancestral lands, with tenure guaranteed by federal treaties that (at least implicitly) recognized them as sovereign peoples. Congress had appropriated funds for schools, tools, seeds, and training to help these "Civilized Tribes" make the transition to farming. Most government officials assumed that the tribes would eventually trade their old lands and use their farming skills on new land west of the Mississippi.

Southwestern whites resented federal Indian policy as an affront to both white democracy and states' rights. The poorer farmers coveted the Indians' land, and states'-rights southerners denied that the federal government had the authority to make treaties or to recognize sovereign peoples within their states. Resistance centered in Georgia, where Governor George Troup brought native lands under the state's jurisdiction and then turned them over to poor whites by way of lotteries—thus tying states' rights to white hunger for Indian land. At one point, Troup sent state surveyors onto Creek territory before federal purchase from the Indians was complete, telling President Adams that if he resisted state authority he would be considered a "public enemy." The Cherokees in Georgia pressed the issue in 1827 by declaring themselves a republic with its own constitution, government, courts, and police, but at almost the same time, a gold discovery on their land made it even more attractive to whites. The Georgia legislature promptly declared Cherokee law null and void, extended Georgia's authority into Cherokee country, and began surveying the lands for sale. Hinting at the old connection between state sovereignty and the protection of slavery, Governor Troup warned that the federal "jurisdiction claimed over one portion of our population may very soon be asserted over *another*." Alabama and Mississippi quickly followed Georgia's lead by extending state authority over Indian lands and denying federal jurisdiction.

INDIAN REMOVAL

President Jackson agreed that the federal government lacked the authority to recognize native sovereignty within a state and declared that he could not protect the Cherokees and the other Civilized Tribes from state governments. Instead, he offered to remove them to federal land west of the Mississippi, where they would be under the authority of the benevolent federal government. Congress made that offer official in the Indian Removal Act of 1830.

The Cherokees, with the help of New England missionaries, had taken their claims of sovereignty to court in the late 1820s. In 1830 John Marshall's Supreme Court ruled in *Cherokee Nation* v. *Georgia* that the Cherokees could not sue Georgia because

"Humanity has often wept over the fate of the aborigines of this country, and Philanthropy has been long busily employed in devising means to avert it, but its progress has never for a moment been arrested, and one by one have many powerful tribes disappeared from the earth. . . . Nor is there anything in this which, upon a comprehensive view of the general interests of the human race, is to be regretted. Philanthropy could not wish to see this continent restored to the condition in which it was found by our forefathers. What good man would prefer a country covered with forests and ranged by a few thousand savages to our extensive Republic, studded with cities, towns and prosperous farms, embellished with all the improvements which art can devise or industry execute, occupied by more than 12,000,000 happy people, and filled with all the blessings of liberty, civilization, and religion?"

ANDREW JACKSON
defending Indian removal in his second annual message to Congress, December 6, 1830

"His people melt away; his lands are constantly coveted; millions after millions are ceded. The Indian bears it all meekly; he complains, indeed, as well he may; but suffers on; and now he finds that this neighbor, whom his kindness had nourished, has spread an adverse title over the last remains of his patrimony, barely adequate to his wants, and turns upon him, and says, "Away! We cannot endure you so near us! These forests and rivers, these groves of your fathers, these firesides and hunting grounds, are ours by the right of power, and the force of numbers." Sir, let every treaty be blotted from our records, and in the judgment of natural and unchangeable truth and justice, I ask, who is the injured, and who is the aggressor? Let conscience answer. . . . Do the obligations of justice change with the color of the skin? Is it one of the prerogatives of the white man, that he may disregard the dictates of moral principles, when an Indian shall be concerned? No, sir. In that severe and impartial scrutiny which futurity will cast over this subject, the righteous award will be, that those very causes which are now pleaded for the relaxed enforcement of the rules of equity, urged upon us not only a rigid execution of the highest justice, to the very letter, but claimed at our hands a generous and magnanimous policy."

SENATOR THEODORE FRELINGHUYSEN
a New Jersey anti-Jacksonian, defending the Cherokee, April 9, 1830

they were not a sovereign people but "domestic dependent nations," thus dependents of the federal government, and not of the state of Georgia, though somehow "nations" as well. The Court's decision in *Worcester* v. *Georgia* (1832) declared that Georgia's extension of state law over Cherokee land was unconstitutional. President Jackson ignored the decision, however, reportedly telling a congressman, "John Marshall has made his decision: *now let him enforce it!*" In the end, Jackson sat back as the southwestern states encroached on the Civilized Tribes. In 1838 his successor, Martin Van

TRAIL OF TEARS In 1838 the U.S. Army marched 18,000 Cherokee men, women, and children, along with their animals and whatever they could carry, out of their home territory and into Oklahoma. At least 4,000—most of them old or very young—died on the march.

Buren, sent the army to march the 18,000 remaining Cherokee to Oklahoma. Four thousand of them died along this "Trail of Tears" of exposure, disease, starvation, and white depredation.

Indian removal had profound political consequences. It violated Supreme Court decisions and thus strengthened Jackson's reputation as an enemy of the rule of law and a friend of local, "democratic" solutions; at the same time, it reaffirmed the link between racism and white democracy in the South and announced Jackson's commitment to state sovereignty and limited federal authority.

SOUTHERNERS AND THE TARIFF

In 1828 the Democratic Congress, acting under the direction of Van Buren and his congressional sidekick Silas Wright, set about writing a tariff that would win votes for Jackson in the upcoming presidential election. Assured of support in the South, the creators of the tariff bill fished for votes in the

Middle Atlantic states and in the Old Northwest by including protective levies on raw wool, flax, molasses, hemp, and distilled spirits. The result was a patchwork tariff that pleased northern and western farmers but that worried the South and violated Jackson's own ideas of what a "judicious" tariff should be. Protective tariffs hurt the South by diminishing exports of cotton and other staples and by raising the price of manufactured goods. More ominous, they demonstrated the power of other sections to write laws that helped them and hurt the outnumbered South—a power, as southerners constantly reminded themselves, that might some day be used to attack slavery. Calling the new bill a "Tariff of Abominations," the legislature of one southern state after another denounced it as (this was Virginia's formulation) "unconstitutional, unwise, unjust, unequal, and oppressive."

South Carolina, guided by Vice President Calhoun, took the lead in opposing the Tariff of 1828. During the War of 1812 and the ensuing Era of

Good Feelings, Calhoun's South Carolina—confident of its future and deeply engaged in international markets for its rice and cotton—had favored the economic nationalism of the American System, but the Missouri debates had sent Carolinians looking for ways to safeguard slavery. The Denmark Vesey slave conspiracy of 1822 (see chapter 10) had stirred fears among the outnumbered whites of coastal South Carolina. Their fears grew more intense when federal courts shot down a state law forbidding black merchant seamen from moving about freely while their ships were docked at Charleston. Carolinians were disturbed too by persistent talk of gradual emancipation—at a time when their own commitment to slavery was growing stronger. Finally, southerners noted that in the congressional logrolling that made the Tariff of 1828, many western representatives had abandoned their old Jeffersonian alliance with the South to trade favors with the Northeast. With the growth in the Northeast of urban markets for western produce, the American System's promise of interdependence among regions was beginning to work—but in ways that united the Northwest and Northeast against the export-oriented South. The Tariff of 1828 was the last straw: It benefited the city and commercial food producers at the expense of the plantation, and it demonstrated that the South could do nothing to block the passage of such laws.

NULLIFICATION

As early as 1827 Calhoun concluded that southern states could protect themselves from national majorities only if they possessed the power to veto federal legislation within their boundaries. In 1828, in his anonymously published essay *Exposition and Protest*, he argued that the Constitution was a compact between sovereign states, and that the states (not the federal courts) could decide the constitutionality of federal laws. A state convention (like the conventions that had ratified the Constitution) could nullify any federal law within state borders. "Constitutional government and the government of a majority," Calhoun argued, "are utterly incompatible." *Exposition and Protest* echoed the Virginia and Kentucky Resolves of 1798 and 1799 and anticipated the secessionist arguments of 1861: The Union was a voluntary compact between sovereign states, states were the ultimate judges of the valid-

ity of federal law, and states could break the compact if they wished.

Nullification was a dangerous measure, and Calhoun and his friends tried to avoid it. They knew that President Jackson was a states'-rights slaveholder who disliked the Tariff of 1828, and they assumed that Vice President Calhoun would succeed to the presidency in time and would protect southern interests. They were wrong on both counts. Jackson favored states' rights, but only within a perpetual and inviolable Union. His Indian policy, which had emboldened some southerners, was simply an acknowledgment of state jurisdiction over institutions within state boundaries. A tariff, on the other hand, was ultimately a matter of foreign policy, clearly within the jurisdiction of the federal government. To allow a state to veto a tariff would be to deny the legal existence of the United States.

Jackson revealed his views at a program celebrating Jefferson's birthday on April 13, 1830. Calhoun's southern friends dominated the speechmaking, and Jackson listened quietly as speaker after speaker defended the extreme states-rights position. After the formal speeches were over, the president rose to propose an after-dinner toast. It was a powerful denunciation of what he had just heard: "Our Federal Union," he said in measured tones, "*It must be preserved.*" Isaac Hill, a New Hampshire Democrat and a supporter of Van Buren, reported that "an order to arrest Calhoun where he sat would not have come with more blinding, staggering force." Dumb-struck, the southerners looked to Calhoun, who as vice president was to propose the second toast. Obviously shaken by Jackson's unqualified defense of the Union, Calhoun offered this toast: "The Union. Next to our liberties the most dear." They were strong words, but they had little meaning after Jackson's affirmation of the Union. A few days later, a South Carolina congressman on his way home asked the president if he had any message for him to take back. "Yes, I have," replied Jackson. "Please give my compliments to my friends in your state, and say to them, that if a single drop of blood shall be shed there in opposition to the laws of the United States, I will hang the first man I can lay my hand on engaged in such treasonable conduct, upon the first tree I can reach."

Having reaffirmed the Union and rejected nullification, Jackson asked Congress to reduce the tariff rates in the hope that he could isolate the nullifiers from southerners who simply hated the tariff. The resulting Tariff of 1832 lowered the rates on many items but still affirmed the principle of protectionism. That, along with the Boston abolitionist William Lloyd Garrison's declaration of war on slavery in 1831, followed by Nat Turner's bloody slave uprising in Virginia that same year (see chapter 10), led the whites of South Carolina and Georgia to intensify their distrust of outside authority and their insistence on the right to govern their own neighborhoods. South Carolina, now with Calhoun's open leadership and support, called a state convention that nullified the Tariffs of 1828 and 1832.

In Washington, President Jackson raged that nullification (not to mention the right of secession that followed logically from it) was illegal. Insisting that "Disunion . . . is *treason*," he asked Congress for a Force Bill empowering him to personally lead a federal army into South Carolina. At the same time, however, he supported the rapid reduction of tariffs. When Democratic attempts at reduction bogged down, Henry Clay, now back in the Senate, took on the tricky legislative task of rescuing his beloved protective tariff while quieting southern fears. The result was the Compromise Tariff of 1833, which by lowering tariffs over the course of several years, gave southern planters the relief they demanded while maintaining moderate protectionism and allowing northern manufacturers time to adjust to the lower rates. Congress also passed the Force Bill. Jackson signed both into law on March 2, 1833.

With that, the nullification crisis came to a quiet end. No other southern state had joined South Carolina in nullifying the tariff, though some states had made vague pledges of support in the event that Jackson led his army to Charleston. The Compromise Tariff of 1833 isolated the South Carolina nullifiers. Deprived of their issue and most of their support, they declared victory and disbanded their convention—but not before nullifying the Force Bill. Jackson chose to overlook that last defiant gesture, for he had accomplished what he wanted: he had asserted a perpetual Union, and he had protected southern interests within it.

THE "PETTICOAT WARS"

The spoils system, Indian removal, nullification, and other heated questions of Jackson's first term were fought out against a backdrop of gossip, intrigue, and angry division within the inner circles of Jackson's government. The talk centered on Peggy O'Neal Timberlake, a Washington tavern keeper's daughter who, in January 1829, had married John Henry Eaton, Jackson's old friend and soon to be his secretary of war. Timberlake's former husband, a navy purser, had recently committed suicide; it was rumored that her affair with Eaton was the cause. Eaton was middle-aged; his bride was 29, pretty, flirtatious, and, according to Washington gossip, "frivolous, wayward, [and] passionate." Knowing that his marriage might cause trouble for the new administration, Eaton had asked for and received Jackson's blessings—and, by strong implication, his protection.

The marriage of John and Peggy Eaton came at a turning point in the history of both Washington society and elite sexual mores. Until the 1820s most officeholders had left their families at home. They took lodgings at taverns and boardinghouses and lived in a bachelor world of shirtsleeves, tobacco, card-playing, and occasional liaisons with local women, but in the 1820s the boardinghouse world was giving way to high society. Cabinet members, senators, congressmen, and other officials moved into Washington houses, and their wives presided over the round of dinner parties through which much of the government's business was done. As in other wealthy families, political wives imposed new forms of gentility and politeness upon these affairs, and they assumed the responsibility of drawing up the guest lists. Many of them determined to exclude Peggy Eaton from polite society.

The exclusion of Peggy Eaton split the Jackson administration in half. Jackson himself was committed to protect her. He had met his own beloved Rachel while boarding at her father's Nashville tavern, and their grand romance (as well as the gossip that surrounded it) was a striking parallel to the affair of John and Peggy Eaton. That, coupled with Jackson's honor-bound agreement to the Eaton marriage, ensured that he would protect the Eatons to the bitter end. Always suspicious of intrigues, Jackson labeled the "dark and sly insinuations" about Peggy Eaton part of a "conspiracy" against his presidency. Motivated by chivalry, personal loyalty, grief and rage over Rachel's death, and angry disbelief that political intrigue could sully the private life of a valued friend, Jackson insisted to his cabinet that Peggy Eaton was "as chaste as a virgin!" Jackson noted that the rumor spreaders were not only politicians' wives but prominent clergymen. Most prominent among the latter was Ezra Styles Ely of Philadelphia, who had recently called for an evangelical "Christian Party in politics." Jackson blamed the conspiracy on "females with clergymen at their head."

In fact, Mrs. Eaton's tormentors included most of the cabinet members as well as Jackson's own White House "family." Widowed and without children, Jackson had invited his nephew and private secretary, Andrew Jackson Donelson, along with his wife and her sister, to live in the White House. Donelson's wife, serving as official hostess, resolutely shunned Peggy Eaton. Jackson, who valued domestic harmony and personal loyalty, assumed that schemers had invaded and subverted his own household. Before long, his suspicions centered on Vice President Calhoun, whose wife, Floride Bonneau Calhoun, a haughty and powerful Washington matron, was a leader of the assault on Peggy Eaton. Only Secretary of State Van Buren, a widower and an eminently decent man, included the Eatons in official functions. Sensing that Jackson was losing his patience with Calhoun, Van Buren's friends, soon after the Jefferson birthday banquet in the spring of 1830, showed Jackson a letter from William H. Crawford revealing that while serving in Monroe's cabinet Calhoun, contrary to his protestations, had favored censuring Jackson for his unauthorized invasion of Florida in 1818. An open break with Calhoun became inevitable.

THE FALL OF CALHOUN

Jackson resolved the Peggy Eaton controversy, as he would resolve nullification, in ways that favored Van Buren in his contest with Calhoun. He sent Donelson, his wife, and his sister-in-law back to Tennessee and invited his friend W. B. Lewis and his daughter to take their place, but he pointedly made Peggy Eaton the official hostess at the White House. In the spring of 1831 Van Buren gave Jackson a free hand to reconstruct his tangled administration. He offered to resign his cabinet post and engineered the resignations of nearly all other members of the cabinet—thus allowing Jackson to

remake his administration without firing anyone. Many of those who left were southern supporters of Calhoun. Jackson replaced them with a mixed cabinet that included political allies of Van Buren. Also at this time President Jackson began to consult with an informal "Kitchen Cabinet" that included journalists Amos Kendall and Francis Preston Blair, along with Van Buren and a few others. The Peggy Eaton controversy and the resulting shakeup in the administration were contributing mightily to the success of Van Buren's southern strategy.

Van Buren's victory over Calhoun came to a quick conclusion. As part of his cabinet reorganization, Jackson appointed Van Buren minister to

The Rats leaving a Falling House.

AN OPPOSITION CARTOON ON THE CABINET SHUFFLE OF 1831 The cabinet rats run from the falling house of government, while a bewildered Jackson retains Van Buren by standing on his tail.

Great Britain—an important post that would remove him from the heat of Washington politics. Vice President Calhoun, sitting as president of the Senate, rigged the confirmation so that he cast the deciding vote against Van Buren's appointment—a petty act that turned out to be his last exercise of national power. Jackson replaced Calhoun with Van Buren as the vice presidential candidate in 1832 and let it be known that he wanted Van Buren to succeed him as president.

PETITIONS, THE GAG RULE, AND THE SOUTHERN MAILS

Van Buren and other architects of the Democratic Party promised to protect slavery with a disciplined national coalition committed to states' rights within an inviolable Union. The rise of a northern antislavery movement (see chapter 11) posed a direct challenge to that formulation. Middle-class evangelicals, who were emerging as the reformist core of the northern Whig Party, had learned early on that Jacksonian Democrats wanted to keep moral issues out of politics. In 1828 and 1829, when they petitioned the government to stop movement of the mail on Sundays, Jackson had turned them down. They next petitioned the government for humane treatment of the Civilized Tribes, whose conversion to Christianity had been accomplished largely by New England missionaries; again, the Jackson administration had refused. The evangelicals suspected Jackson of immorality, and they were appalled by his defense of Peggy Eaton and his attack on gentlewomen and preachers. Most of all, reformist evangelicals disliked the Democrats' rigid party discipline, which in each case had kept questions of morality from shaping politics.

In the early 1830s a radical minority of evangelicals formed societies committed to the immediate abolition of slavery, and they devised ways of making the national government confront the slavery question. In 1835 abolitionists launched a "postal campaign," flooding the mail—both North and South—with antislavery tracts that southerners and most northerners considered incendiary. From 1836 onward, they bombarded Congress with petitions—most of them for the abolition of slavery and the slave trade in the District of Columbia (where Congress had undisputed jurisdiction), others against the interstate slave trade, slavery in the federal territories, and the admission of new slave states.

Some Jacksonians, including Jackson himself, wanted to put a stop to the postal campaign with a federal censorship law. Calhoun and other southerners, however, argued that the states had the right to censor mail crossing their borders. Knowing that state censorship of the mail was unconstitutional and that federal censorship of the mail would be a political disaster, Amos Kendall, a Van Burenite who had become postmaster general in the cabinet shuffle, proposed an informal solution. Without changing the law, he would simply look the other way as local postmasters violated postal regulations and removed abolitionist materials from the mail. Almost all such materials were published in New York City and mailed from there. The New York postmaster, a loyal appointee, proceeded to sift them out of the mail and thus cut off the postal campaign at its source. The few tracts that made it to the South were destroyed by local postmasters. Calhoun and his supporters continued to demand that the states be given the power to deal with the mailings, but the Democrats had no intention of relinquishing federal control over the federal mail. They made it clear, however, that no abolitionist literature would reach the South as long as Democrats controlled the U.S. Post Office.

The Democrats dealt in a similar manner with antislavery petitions to Congress. Southern extremists demanded that Congress disavow its power to legislate on slavery in the District of Columbia, but Van Buren, who was preparing to run for president, declared that Congress did indeed have that power but should never use it. In dealing with the petitions, Congress simply voted at each session from 1836 to 1844 to table them without reading them—thus acknowledging that they had been received but sidestepping any debate on them. This procedure, which became known as the "gag rule," was passed by southern Whigs and southern Democrats with the help of most (usually 80 percent or more) of the northern Democrats. Increasingly, abolitionists sent their petitions to ex-President John Quincy Adams, who had returned to Washington as a Whig congressman from Massachusetts. Like other northern Whigs, Adams openly opposed both slavery and the gag rule in Congress. Northern Whigs began calling him "Old Man Eloquent," while Calhoun dubbed him "a mischievous, bad old man." But most southerners saw what the Democrats wanted them to see: that their surest guarantee of safety within the Union was a disciplined Democratic Party determined to avoid sectional arguments.

Thus the Jacksonians answered the question that had arisen with the Missouri debates: how to protect the slaveholding South within the federal Union. Whereas Calhoun and other southern radicals found the answer in nullification and other forms of state sovereignty, Jackson and the Democratic coalition insisted that the Union was inviolable, and that any attempt to dissolve it would be met with force. At the same time, a Democratic Party uniting northern and southern agrarians into a states-rights, limited-government majority could guarantee southern rights within the Union. This answer to the southern question stayed in place until the breakup of the Democratic Party on the eve of the Civil War.

JACKSONIAN DEMOCRACY AND THE MARKET REVOLUTION

Jacksonian Democrats cherished a nostalgic loyalty to the simplicity and naturalness of Jefferson's agrarian republic. They assumed power at the height of the market revolution, and they spent much of the 1830s and 1840s trying to reconcile the market and the republic. Like the Jeffersonians before them, Jacksonian Democrats welcomed commerce as long as it served the independence and rough equality of white men on which republican citizenship rested, but paper currency and the dependence on credit that came with the market revolution posed problems. The so-called "paper economy" separated wealth from "real work" and encouraged an unrepublican spirit of luxury and greed. Worst of all, the new paper economy required government-granted privileges that the Jacksonians, still speaking the language of revolutionary republicanism, branded "corruption." For the same reasons, the protective tariffs and government-sponsored roads and canals of the American System were antirepublican and unacceptable. It was the goal of the Jackson presidency to curtail government involvement in the economy, to end special privilege, and thus to rescue the republic from the "Money Power."

Jacksonians were opposed by those who favored an activist central government—by the mid-1830s they called themselves Whigs—who wished to encourage orderly economic development through the American System of protective tariffs, a federally-subsidized transportation network, and a national bank. This system, they argued, would encourage national prosperity. At the same time, it would create a truly national market economy that would soften sectional divisions. Jacksonian rhetoric about the Money Power and the Old Republic, they argued, was little more than the demagoguery of unqualified, self-seeking politicians.

THE SECOND BANK OF THE UNITED STATES

The argument between Jacksonians and their detractors came to focus on the Second Bank of the United States, a mixed public-private corporation chartered by Congress in 1816 (see chapter 9). The national government deposited its revenue in the Bank, thus giving it an enormous capital base. The government deposits also included state banknotes that had been used to pay customs duties or to buy public land; the Bank of the United States had the power to demand redemption of these notes in specie (gold and silver), thus discouraging state banks from issuing inflationary notes that they could not back up. The Bank also issued notes of its own, and these served as the beginnings of a national paper currency. Thus with powers granted under its federal charter, the Bank of the United States exercised central control over the nation's monetary and credit systems.

Most members of the business community valued the Bank of the United States because it promised a stable, uniform paper currency and competent, centralized control over the banking system. But millions of Americans resented and distrusted the national bank, citing its role in the Panic of 1819 as evidence of the dangers posed by privileged, powerful institutions. President Jackson agreed with the latter. A southwestern agrarian who had lost money in an early speculation, he was leery of paper money, banks, and the credit system. He insisted that both the Bank and paper money were unconstitutional, and that the only safe, natural, republican currencies were gold and silver. Above all, Jackson saw the Bank of the United

States as a government-sponsored concentration of power that threatened the republic.

THE BANK WAR

The charter of the Bank of the United States ran through 1836, but Senators Henry Clay and Daniel Webster encouraged Nicholas Biddle, the Bank's brilliant, aristocratic president, to apply for recharter in 1832. Clay planned to oppose Jackson in the presidential election later that year, and he knew that Jackson hated the Bank. He and his friends hoped to provoke the hot-tempered and supposedly erratic Jackson into a response they could use against him in the election.

Biddle applied to Congress for a recharter of the Bank of the United States in January 1832. Congress passed the recharter bill in early July and sent it on to the president. Jackson understood the early request for recharter as a political ploy. On July 4, Van Buren visited the White House and found Jackson sick in bed; Jackson took Van Buren's hand and said, "The bank, Mr. Van Buren, is trying to kill me, *but I will kill it!*" Jackson vetoed the bill.

Jackson's Bank Veto Message, sent to Congress on July 10, was a manifesto of Jacksonian Democracy. Written by Amos Kendall, Francis Preston Blair, and Roger B. Taney—republican fundamentalists who both hated the Bank and understood the popular culture that shared their hatred—the message combined Jeffersonian verities with appeals to the public's prejudice. Jackson declared that the Bank was "unauthorized by the Constitution, subversive of the rights of the states, and dangerous to the liberties of the people." Its charter, Jackson complained, bestowed special privilege on the Bank and its stockholders—almost all of whom were northeastern businessmen or, worse, British investors. Having made most of its loans to southerners and westerners, the Bank was a huge monster that sucked resources out of the agrarian South and West and poured them into the pockets of wealthy, well-connected northeastern gentlemen and their English friends. The granting of special privilege to such people (or to any others) threatened the system of equal rights that was essential in a republic. Jackson granted that differences in talents and resources inevitably created social distinctions, but he stood firm against "any prostitution of our Government to

the advancement of the few at the expense of the many." He concluded with a call to the civic virtue and the conservative, God-centered Protestantism in which he and most of his agrarian constituency had been raised: "Let us firmly rely on that kind Providence which I am sure watches with peculiar care over the destinies of our Republic, and on the intelligence and wisdom of our countrymen. Through *His* abundant goodness and *their* patriotic devotion our liberty and Union will be preserved."

Henry Clay, Nicholas Biddle, and other anti-Jacksonians had expected the veto. And the Bank Veto Message was a long, rambling attack that, in their opinion, demonstrated Jackson's unfitness for office. "It has all the fury of a chained panther biting the bars of its cage," said Biddle, concluding that "it really is a manifesto of anarchy." So certain were they that the public shared their views that Clay's supporters distributed Jackson's Bank Veto Message as *anti*-Jackson propaganda during the 1832 campaign. They were wrong: A majority of the voters shared Jackson's attachment to a society of virtuous, independent producers and to republican government in its pristine form; they also agreed that the republic was in danger of subversion by parasites who grew rich by manipulating credit, prices, paper money, and

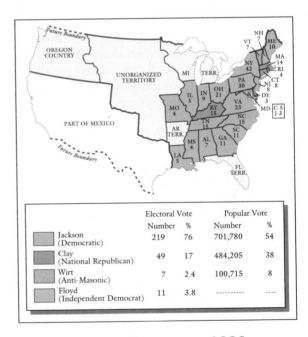

		Electoral Vote		Popular Vote	
		Number	%	Number	%
	Jackson (Democratic)	219	76	701,780	54
	Clay (National Republican)	49	17	484,205	38
	Wirt (Anti-Masonic)	7	2.4	100,715	8
	Floyd (Independent Democrat)	11	3.8	----------	----

PRESIDENTIAL ELECTION, 1832

government-bestowed privileges. Jackson portrayed himself as both the protector of the old republic and a melodramatic hero contending with illegitimate, aristocratic, privileged, secretive powers. With the Bank and Jackson's veto as the principal issues, Jackson won reelection by a landslide in 1832.

Jackson began his second term determined to kill the Bank of the United States before Congress could reverse his veto. The Bank would be able to operate under its old charter until 1836, but Jackson was determined to speed its death by withdrawing government deposits as they were needed and by depositing new government revenues in carefully selected state banks—soon to be called "Pet Banks" by the opposition. By law, the decision to remove the deposits had to be made by the secretary of the treasury, and Treasury Secretary Louis McLane, along with most of the cabinet, doubted the wisdom if not the legality of withdrawing these funds. Jack-son in response transferred McLane to the vacant post of secretary of state and named William J. Duane as treasury secretary. Duane, too, refused to withdraw the deposits. Jackson fired him and appointed Roger B. Taney, the attorney general and a close adviser who had helped write the Bank Veto Message. A loyal Democrat who hated banks as much as Jackson did, Taney withdrew the deposits. In 1835, when the old Federalist John Marshall died, Jackson rewarded Taney by making him Chief Justice of the Supreme Court—a post from which he continued to serve the Democratic Party.

THE BEGINNINGS OF THE WHIG PARTY

Conflict over deposit removal and related questions of presidential power united opposers to the Jacksonian Democrats—most of them committed advocates of

---

LINK TO THE PAST

A Hypertext on American History: Presidents

http://odur.let.rug.nl/~usa/usa.htm

The United States Information Agency created this large Web site on American history and government, and included online transcriptions of many primary documents. The Documents section, under Presidents, provides full texts of the inaugural addresses and other important speeches of the presidents. Read the addresses of Andrew Jackson, Martin Van Buren, and William Henry Harrison, and think about these questions:

1. What were the primary differences between Democratic (Jackson and Van Buren) and Whig (Harrison) conceptions of democracy and majority rule? What were the similarities?

2. What were specific differences between Democrats and Whigs on questions of banking, currency, and internal improvements—and of the proper role of the national government in these areas? Do these specific questions add up to more general differences between Democrats and Whigs on the nature and limits of the federal government?

3. How did Democratic and Whig presidents talk about slavery and Indian removal? How does your answer to this question relate to questions 1 and 2?

the American System—into the Whig Party in 1834. The name of the party, as everyone who knew the language of the republic immediately recognized, stood for legislative opposition to a power-mad executive. Jackson, argued the Whigs, had transformed himself from the limited executive described in the Constitution into "King Andrew I." This had begun with Jackson's arbitrary uses of the executive patronage. It had become worse when Jackson began to veto congressional legislation. Earlier presidents had exercised the veto only nine times, usually on unimportant bills and always on the grounds that the proposed legislation was unconstitutional. Jackson used the veto often— too often, said the Whigs, when a key component of the American System was at stake. In May 1830, for instance, Jackson vetoed an attempt by Congress to buy stock in a turnpike to run from the terminus of the National Road at Louisville to Maysville, Kentucky. Jackson argued that because the road would be entirely in Kentucky it was "partial" legislation that would take money from the whole people to benefit just one locality. He also questioned whether such federal subsidies were constitutional. Most important, however, Jackson announced that he was determined to reduce federal expenditures in order to retire the national debt—hinting strongly that he would oppose all federal public works.

The bank veto conveyed the same message even more strongly, and the withdrawal of the government deposits brought the question of "executive usurpation" to a head in 1834. Withdrawal of the deposits, together with Jackson's high-handed treatment of his treasury secretaries, caused uneasiness even among the president's supporters, and his enemies took extreme measures. Nicholas Biddle, announcing that he must clean up the affairs of the Bank of the United States before closing its doors, demanded that all its loans be repaid—a demand that undermined the credit system and produced a sharp financial panic. No doubt one reason for Biddle's action was to punish Andrew Jackson. While Congress received a well-orchestrated petition campaign to restore the deposits, Henry Clay led an effort in the Senate to censure the president— which it did in March 1834. Daniel Webster, the Bank's best friend in government, and Clay, who had watched as Jackson denied one component after another of his American System, led the old National Republican coalition (the name that anti-

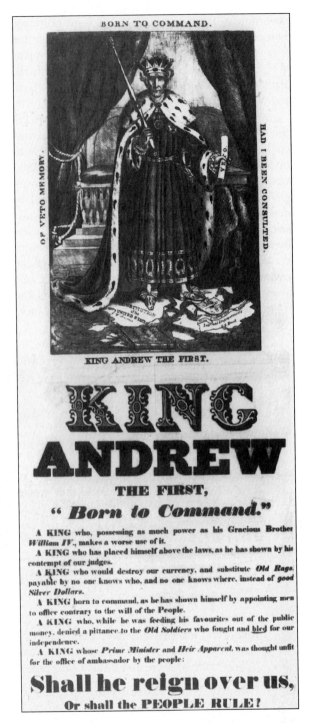

KING ANDREW In this widely distributed opposition cartoon, King Andrew, with a scepter in one hand and a vetoed bill in the other, tramples on internal improvements, the Bank of the United States, and the Constitution.

Jacksonians had assumed since 1824) into the new Whig Party. They were joined by southerners (including Calhoun) who resented Jackson's treatment of the South Carolina nullifiers and Biddle's bank, and who distrusted his assurances on slavery. In any case, Jackson's war on the Bank of the United States did the most to separate parties. His withdrawal of the deposits chased lukewarm supporters into the opposition, while Democrats who closed ranks behind him could point to an increasingly sharp division between the Money Power and the Old Republic. Referring to Biddle's panic of 1834, James K. Polk of Tennessee, who led the Democrats in the House of Representatives, declared that "the question is in fact whether we shall have the Republic without the Bank or the Bank without the Republic."

A BALANCED BUDGET

In part, Jackson removed the deposits because he anticipated a federal surplus revenue that, if handed over to Biddle's Bank of the United States, would have made it stronger than ever. The Tariffs of 1828 and 1832 produced substantial government revenue, and Jackson's frugal administration spent little of it. Even the Compromise Tariff of 1833 left rates temporarily high. And the brisk sale of public lands was adding to the surplus. In 1833, for the only time in history, the United States paid off its national debt. Without Jackson's removal of the deposits, a growing federal treasury would have gone into the Bank and would have found its way into the hated paper economy.

Early in his administration, Jackson had favored distributing surplus revenue to the states to be used for internal improvements, but he came to distrust even that minimal federal intervention in the economy, fearing that redistribution would encourage Congress to keep land prices and tariff rates high. Whigs, who by now despaired of ever creating a federally subsidized, coordinated transportation system, picked up the idea of redistribution. With some help from the Democrats, they passed the Deposit Act of 1836, which increased the number of banks receiving federal deposits (thus removing power from Jackson's "Pet Banks") and distributed any federal surplus to the states to be spent on roads, canals, and schools. Jackson, who distrusted state-chartered banks as much as he distrusted the Bank of the United States, feared that the new deposit banks would use their power

A MOCK BANKNOTE DECRYING THE DEMOCRATS' DESTRUCTION OF THE BANK OF THE UNITED STATES A gang of officeholders pull Van Buren into perdition over the prostrate bodies of honest citizens. At right, Jackson, dressed as an old woman, watches.

Amistad (1997)

Directed by Steven Spielberg. Starring Matthew McConnaughey, Morgan Freeman, Anthony Hopkins, Djimon Hounsou.

In 1839 an American cruiser seized the Cuban slave ship *Amistad* off the shore of Long Island. The ship carried 41 Africans who had revolted, killed the captain and crew, and commandeered the ship—along with two Spanish slave dealers who bargained for their lives by promising to sail the ship east to Africa, then steered for North America. The Africans were imprisoned at New Haven and tried for piracy and murder in federal court. The government of Spain demanded their return, and southern leaders pressured President Van Buren for a "friendly" decision. The legal case centered on whether the Africans were Cuban slaves or kidnapped Africans. (The international slave trade was by then illegal.) The New Haven court acquitted them, the federal government appealed the case, and the Supreme Court freed them again. The Africans were returned to Sierra Leone.

The Africans spend most of the movie in a dark jail or in court, and the film centers on them and their experiences with two groups of Americans: the abolitionists who are trying to free them, and the political and legal officials who want to hang them—largely to keep their own political system intact. Spielberg's abolitionists are Lewis Tappan, a black activist (Morgan Freeman), an obscure young white lawyer (Matthew McConnaughey), and, in the grand finale, Congressman and former President John Quincy Adams (played wonderfully by Anthony Hopkins). In the historical case, the defense was handled by veteran abolitionists, or by persons who had been working with abolitionists for a long time. Spielberg shaped this group to tell his own story, beginning with reluctant and confused reformers and politicians who, along with the audience, gradually realize the moral imperatives of the case.

In one of the film's more powerful sequences the Africans' leader, Cinque (Djimon Hounsou), through a translator, tells his story to the lawyer: his village life in

to issue mountains of new banknotes. He demanded a provision limiting their right to print bank notes. With that provision, he reluctantly signed the Deposit Act.

Jackson and many members of his administration had deep fiscal and moral concerns about the inflationary boom that accompanied the rapid growth of commerce, credit, roads, canals, new farms, and the other manifestations of the market revolution in the 1830s. After insisting that his hard-money, anti-inflationary provision be added to the Deposit Act, Jackson issued a Specie Circular in 1836, which provided that speculators could buy large parcels of public land only with silver and gold coins and settlers could continue to buy farm-sized plots with banknotes. Henceforth, speculators would have to bring wagonloads of coins from eastern banks to frontier land offices. With this provision, Jackson hoped to curtail speculation and to reverse the flow of specie out of the South and West and into the Northeast. The Specie Circular was Jackson's final assault on the paper economy. It repeated familiar themes: It favored hard currency over paper, settlers over speculators, and the South and West over the Northeast.

THE SECOND AMERICAN PARTY SYSTEM

In his farewell address in 1837 Jackson spoke once again of the incompatibility between the republic and the money power. He warned against a revival of the

Sierra Leone (the one scene filmed in bright sunlight), his capture by Africans, his transportation to the slave fort of Lomboko, the horrors of the passage on the Portuguese slaver *Tecora*, the slave market in Havana, and the bloody revolt on the *Amistad*—all of it portrayed wrenchingly on the screen. The Africans' story continues in jail, as they study pictures in a Bible and try to figure out the American legal, political, and moral system. In court, they finally cut through the mumbo-jumbo by standing and chanting "Give Us Free!"

In a fictive interview on the eve of the Supreme Court case, Cinque tells Adams that he is optimistic, for he has called on the spirits of his ancestors to join him in court. This moment, he says, is the whole reason for their having existed at all. Adams, whose own father had helped lead the Revolution, speaks for his and Cinque's ancestors before the Supreme Court: to the prosecution's argument that the Africans are pirates and murderers and to southern arguments that slavery is a natural state he answers that America is founded on the "self-evident truth" that the one natural state is freedom. It is a fine Hollywood courtroom speech: Adams has honored his ancestors, the justices and the audience see the moral rightness of his case, and the Africans are returned to Sierra Leone. (In a subscript, Spielberg tells us that Cinque returns to a village that had been destroyed in civil war, but the final ironic note is overwhelmed by the moral triumphalism of the rest of the movie.)

Amistad (1997) tells the story of 41 Africans who stage a revolt on the slave ship carrying them to Cuba and the trial that follows.

Bank of the United States and against all banks, paper money, the spirit of speculation, and every aspect of the "paper system." That system encouraged greed and luxury, which were at odds with republican virtue, he said. Worse, it thrived on special privilege, creating a world in which insiders meeting in "secret conclaves" could buy and sell elections. The solution, as always, was an arcadian society of small producers, a vigilant democratic electorate, and a chaste republican government that granted no special privileges.

"MARTIN VAN RUIN"

Sitting beside Jackson as he delivered his farewell address was his chosen successor, Martin Van Buren. In the election of 1836 the Whigs had acknowledged that Henry Clay, the leader of their party, could not win a national election. Instead they ran three sectional candidates—Daniel Webster in the Northeast, the old Indian fighter William Henry Harrison in the West, and Hugh Lawson White of Tennessee, a turncoat Jacksonian, in the South. With this ploy the Whigs hoped to deprive Van Buren of a majority and throw the election into the Whig-controlled House of Representatives.

The strategy failed. Van Buren had engineered a national Democratic Party that could avert the dangers of sectionalism, and he questioned the patriotism of the Whigs and their sectional candidates, asserting that "true republicans can never lend their aid and influence in creating geographical parties." That, along with his association with

Jackson's popular presidency, won him the election. Van Buren carried 15 of the 26 states and received 170 electoral votes against 124 for his combined opposition. His popular plurality, however, was just under 51 percent.

Van Buren had barely taken office when the inflationary boom of the mid-1830s collapsed. Economic historians ascribe the Panic of 1837 and the ensuing depression largely to events outside the country. The Bank of England, concerned over the flow of British gold to American speculators, cut off credit to firms that did business in the United States. As a result, British demand for American cotton fell sharply, and the price of cotton dropped by half. With much of the speculative boom tied to cotton grown in the Southwest, the collapse of the economy was inevitable. The first business failures came in March 1837, just as Van Buren took office. By May, New York banks, unable to accommodate people who were demanding hard coin for their notes, suspended specie payments. Other banks followed suit, and soon banks all over the country—including Nicholas Biddle's newly renamed Bank of the United States of Pennsylvania—went out of business. Although few American communities escaped the economic downturn, the commercial and export sectors of the economy suffered most. In the seaport cities, one firm after another closed its doors, and about one-third of the workforce was unemployed. Wages for those who kept their jobs declined by some 30 to 50 percent. It was the deepest, most widespread, and longest economic depression Americans had ever faced.

Whigs blamed the depression on Jackson's hard-money policies—particularly his destruction of the Bank of the United States and his Specie Circular. With economic distress the main issue, Whigs scored huge gains in the midterm elections of 1838, even winning control of Van Buren's New York with a campaign that castigated the president as "Martin Van Ruin." Democrats blamed the crash on speculation, luxury, and Whig paper money. Whigs demanded a new national bank, but Van Buren proposed the complete divorce of government from the banking system through what was known as the "Sub-Treasury," or "Independent Treasury." Under this plan, the federal government would simply hold and dispense its money without depositing it in banks; it would also require that tariffs and land purchases be paid in gold and silver coins or in notes from specie-paying banks, a provision that allowed government to regulate state banknotes without resorting to a central bank. Van Buren asked Congress to set up the Independent Treasury in 1837, and Congress spent the rest of Van Buren's time in office arguing about it. The Independent Treasury Bill finally passed in 1840, completing the Jacksonian separation of bank and state.

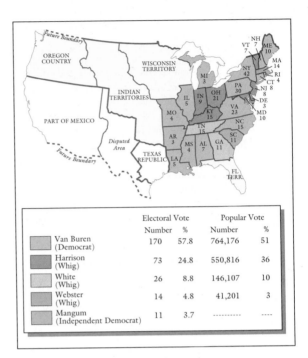

	Electoral Vote		Popular Vote	
	Number	%	Number	%
Van Buren (Democrat)	170	57.8	764,176	51
Harrison (Whig)	73	24.8	550,816	36
White (Whig)	26	8.8	146,107	10
Webster (Whig)	14	4.8	41,201	3
Mangum (Independent Democrat)	11	3.7	----------	----

PRESIDENTIAL ELECTION, 1836

THE ELECTION OF 1840

Whigs were confident that they could blame Van Buren for the country's economic troubles and take the presidency away from him in the election of 1840. Trying to offend as few voters as possible, they passed over their best-known leaders, Senators Henry Clay and Daniel Webster, and nominated William Henry Harrison of Ohio as their presidential candidate. Harrison was the hero of the Battle of Tippecanoe (see chapter 7), and a westerner whose Virginia origins made him palatable in the South. He was also a proven vote-getter: As the Whigs' "western" candidate in 1836 he had carried seven states scattered across the Northwest, the Middle

Atlantic, New England, and the Upper South. Best of all, he was a military hero who had expressed few opinions on national issues and who had no political record to defend. As his running mate, the Whigs chose John Tyler, a states'-rights Virginian who had joined the Whigs out of hatred for Jackson. To promote this baldly pragmatic ticket, the Whigs came up with a catchy slogan: "Tippecanoe and Tyler Too." Philip Hone, a wealthy New York City Whig, admitted that the slogan (and the ticket) had "rhyme, but no reason in it."

Early in the campaign a Democratic journalist, commenting on Harrison's political inexperience and alleged unfitness for the presidency, wrote, "Give [Harrison] a barrel of hard cider, and settle a pension of two thousand a year on him, and my word for it, he will sit out the remainder of his days in his log cabin." Whigs who had been trying to shake their elitist image seized on the statement and launched what was known as the "Log Cabin

Campaign." The log cabin, the cider barrel, and Harrison's folksiness and heroism constituted the entire Whig campaign, while Van Buren was pictured as living in luxury at the public's expense. The Whigs conjured up an image of a nattily dressed President "Van Ruin" sitting on silk chairs and dining on gold and silver dishes while farmers and workingmen struggled to make ends meet. Whig doggerel contrasted Harrison the hero with Van Buren the professional politician:

> The knapsack pillow'd Harry's head
> The hard ground eas'd his toils;
> While Martin on his downy bed
> Could dream of naught but spoils.

Democrats howled that Whigs were peddling lies and refusing to discuss issues, but they knew they had been beaten at their own game. Harrison won only a narrow majority of the popular vote, but a landslide of 234 to 60 votes in the electoral college.

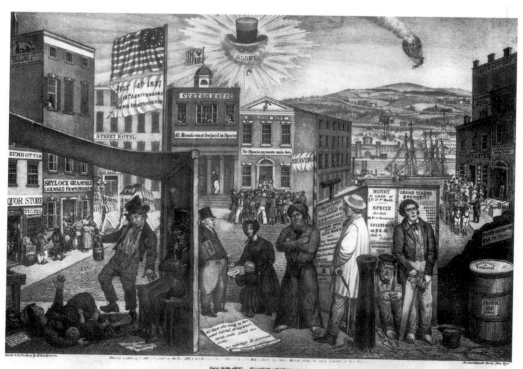

THE TIMES.

1840: SIGNS OF THE TIMES This Whig cartoon from the 1840 campaign blames the Panic of 1837 on the Democrats. The factories are closed, the bank has suspended specie payments, and sailors and craftsmen are out of work, but the sheriff, the prison, the pawnbroker, and the liquor store are doing a booming business.

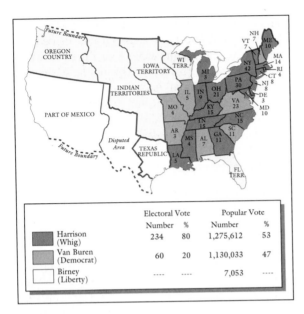

		Electoral Vote		Popular Vote	
		Number	%	Number	%
	Harrison (Whig)	234	80	1,275,612	53
	Van Buren (Democrat)	60	20	1,130,033	47
	Birney (Liberty)	----	----	7,053	----

PRESIDENTIAL ELECTION, 1840

The election of 1840 also witnessed the high-water mark of voter turnout. Whig and Democratic organizations focused on presidential elections, and prospective voters met a quadrennial avalanche of oratory, door-to-door canvassing, torchlight parades, and party propaganda. As the contests became national, Democrats or Whigs could take no state in the Union for granted. (In 1828 winning candidates carried individual states by an average of 36 percent; by 1840 that figure had dropped to 11 percent.) Both Whigs and Democrats maintained organizations and contested elections in nearly every neighborhood in the country, and the result was increased popular interest in politics. In 1824 about one in four adult white men had voted in the presidential election. Jackson's vengeful campaign of 1828 lifted the turnout to 56.3 percent, and it stayed at about that level in 1832 and 1836. The campaign of 1840 brought out 78 percent of the eligible voters, and the turnout remained at that high level throughout the 1840s and 1850s.

TWO PARTIES

The election of 1840 signaled the completion of the second party system—the most fully national alignment of parties in U.S. history. Andrew Jackson had won in 1828 with Jefferson's old southern and western agrarian constituency; in 1832 he had carried his old voters and had won added support in the Middle Atlantic states and in northern New England. In 1836, Whigs capitalized on southern resentment of Jackson's defeat of Calhoun and nullification and on southern mistrust of the New Yorker Van Buren to break the Democratic hold on the South. Whigs came out of their old northeastern strongholds to carry Ohio, Illinois, Kentucky, Georgia, South Carolina, and even Jackson's Tennessee. Jackson had won 8 in 10 southern votes; Van Buren carried barely half but won majorities in old anti-Jackson neighborhoods in New England. The election of 1840 completed the transition: Harrison and Van Buren contested the election in nearly every state; perhaps most significantly, they received nearly equal levels of support in the slave and free states. Van Buren's dream of a national party system was realized. Ironically, the final pieces fell into place in an election that cost him the presidency.

CONCLUSION

By 1840 American politics operated within a stable, national system of two parties—both of which depended on support in every section of the country. Whigs argued for the economic nationalism of the American System. Democrats argued for the limited, inexpensive government that since Jefferson's day had been a bulwark of both republicanism and slavery. The party system provided answers to the questions of sectionalism and economic development that had helped it into being. Democrats successfully fought off the American System: They dismantled the Bank of the United States, refused federal support for roads and canals, and revised the tariff in ways that mollified the export-oriented South. The result, however, was not the return to Jeffersonian agrarianism that many Democrats had wanted but an inadvertent experiment in laissez-faire capitalism. The stupendous growth of the American economy between 1830 and 1860 became a question of state and local—not national—government action. On the growing political problems surrounding slavery, the two-party system did what Van Buren had hoped it would do: Because the Whig and (especially) Democratic Parties needed both northern and southern support, they were careful to focus national political debates on economic development, avoiding any discussion of sectional questions. It worked that way until the party system disintegrated on the eve of the Civil War.

Suggested Readings begin on page SR-1.
For Web activities and resources
related to this chapter, go to
http://www.harcourtcollege.com/history.murrin

CHAPTER 13

MANIFEST DESTINY: AN EMPIRE FOR LIBERTY—OR SLAVERY?

MANIFEST DESTINY

This painting portrays the self-serving symbolism of America's westward expansion in the mid-19th century. White pioneers on foot, on horseback, and in oxen-drawn wagons cross the plains, driving the Indians and buffalo before them while a farmer breaks the sod on the farming frontier. A stagecoach and puffing locomotives follow an ethereal Columbia in flowing raiment bearing a schoolbook and stringing telegraph wire across the continent.

When William Henry Harrison took the oath as the first Whig president on March 4, 1841, the stage seemed set for the enactment of Henry Clay's American System. Instead, Harrison contracted pneumonia after he delivered an interminable inaugural address outdoors in a sleet and snow storm. He died a month later, and John Tyler, a states-rights Virginian, became president. Tyler had become a nominal Whig only because of his hatred of Andrew Jackson. He proceeded to read himself out of the Whig Party by vetoing two bills to create a new national bank. Their domestic program a shambles, the Whigs lost control of the House in the 1842 midterm elections. Thereafter, the political agenda shifted to the Democratic program of territorial expansion. By annexation, negotiation, and war the United States increased its size by 50 percent in the years between 1845 and 1848. But this achievement reopened the issue of slavery's expansion and planted the bitter seeds of civil war.

This chapter will focus on the following major questions:

- What impulses lay behind the "Manifest Destiny" of America's westward expansion?
- How did westward expansion relate to the issue of slavery?
- What were the causes and consequences of the Mexican-American War?
- What issues were at stake in the congressional debates that led to the Compromise of 1850? How successfully did the compromise resolve these issues?

GROWTH AS THE AMERICAN WAY

By 1850, older Americans had seen the area of the United States quadruple in their lifetime. During the 47 years since the Louisiana Purchase of 1803, the American population also had quadrupled. If those rates of growth had continued after 1850, the United States at the end of the 20th century would have contained 1.8 *billion* people and would have occupied every square foot of land on the globe. If the sevenfold increase in the gross national product that Americans enjoyed from 1800 to 1850 had persisted, today's U.S. economy would be larger than that of today's entire world economy.

Many Americans in 1850 took this prodigious growth for granted. They considered it evidence of God's beneficence to this virtuous republic. During the 1840s a group of expansionists affiliated with the Democratic Party began to call themselves the "Young America" movement. They proclaimed that it was the "Manifest Destiny" of the United States "to overspread and to possess the whole of the continent which Providence has given us for the development of the great experiment of liberty," wrote John L. O'Sullivan, editor of the *Democratic Review*, in 1845. "Yes, more, more, more! . . . till our national destiny is fulfilled and . . . the whole boundless continent is ours."

Not all Americans considered this unbridled expansion good. For the earliest Americans, whose ancestors had arrived on the continent thousands of years before the Europeans, it was a story of defeat and contraction rather than of conquest and growth. By 1850 the white man's diseases and guns had reduced the Indian population north of the Rio Grande to fewer than a half million, a fraction of the population of two or three centuries earlier. The relentless westward march of white settlements had pushed all but a few thousand Indians beyond the Mississippi. In the 1840s the U.S. government decided to create a "permanent Indian frontier" at about the 95th meridian (roughly the western borders of Iowa, Missouri, and Arkansas). But white emigrants were already violating that frontier on the overland trails to the Pacific, and settlers were pressing against the borders of Indian territory. In little more than a decade the idea of "one big reservation" in the West would give way to the policy of forcing Indians onto small reservations. The government "negotiated" with Indian chiefs for vast cessions of land in return for annuity payments that were soon spent on the white man's firewater and other purchases from shrewd or corrupt traders. Required to learn the white man's ways or perish, many Indians perished—of disease, malnutrition, and alcohol, and in futile efforts to break out of the reservations and regain their land.

MANIFEST DESTINY AND SLAVERY

If the manifest destiny of white Americans spelled doom for red Americans, it also presaged a crisis in the history of black Americans. By 1846 the Empire for Liberty that Thomas Jefferson had envisioned for the Louisiana Purchase seemed more an empire for slavery: Territorial acquisitions since 1803 had brought into the republic the slave states

CHRONOLOGY	
1844	Senate rejects Texas annexation • James K. Polk elected president
1845	Congress annexes Texas • Mexico spurns U.S. bid to buy California and New Mexico
1846	U.S. declares war on Mexico • U.S. forces under Zachary Taylor win battles of Palo Alto and Resaca de la Palma • U.S. and Britain settle Oregon boundary dispute • U.S. occupies California and New Mexico • House passes Wilmot Proviso • U.S. forces capture Monterrey, Mexico
1847	Americans win battle of Buena Vista • U.S. Army under Winfield Scott lands at Veracruz • Americans win battles of Contreras, Churubusco, Molino del Rey, and Chapultepec • Mexico City falls
1848	Treaty of Guadalupe Hidalgo ends Mexican War, fixes Rio Grande as border, cedes New Mexico and California to U.S. • Gold discovered in California • Spain spurns Polk's offer of $100 million for Cuba • Zachary Taylor elected president
1849	John C. Calhoun pens "Address of the Southern Delegates" • California seeks admission as a free state
1850	Taylor dies, Millard Fillmore becomes president • Bitter sectional debate culminates in Compromise of 1850 • Fugitive Slave Law empowers federal commissioners to recover escaped slaves
1851	Fugitive Slave Law provokes rescues and violent conflict in North • American filibusters executed in Cuba
1852	*Uncle Tom's Cabin* becomes best-seller • Franklin Pierce elected president
1854	Anthony Burns returned from Boston to slavery • William Walker's filibusters invade Nicaragua • Pierce tries to buy Cuba • Ostend Manifesto issued
1856	William Walker legalizes slavery in Nicaragua
1860	William Walker executed in Honduras

of Louisiana, Missouri, Arkansas, Florida, Texas, and parts of Alabama and Mississippi. Only Iowa, admitted in 1846, joined the ranks of the free states.

The division between slavery and freedom in the rest of the Louisiana Purchase had supposedly been settled by the Compromise of 1820. And although

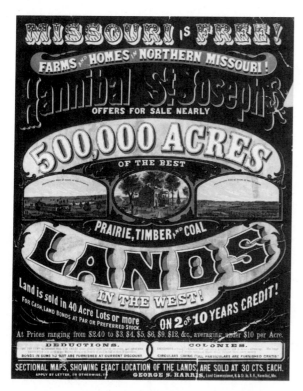

MISSOURI IS FREE!—AN ADVERTISEMENT OF MISSOURI FARMLAND FOR SALE BY THE HANNIBAL AND ST. JOSEPH RAILROAD Railroads received land grants from state governments and later the federal government to help them raise capital for construction. The railroads in turn sold the land to farmers to promote settlement along their lines. The land was not "free," of course, nor was Missouri a "free" state before the abolition of slavery there in 1865.

the issue frequently disturbed public tranquillity for a quarter-century thereafter, as long as the controversy focused on the morality of slavery where it already existed, the two-party system—in which both major parties did their best to evade the issue—managed to contain its explosive potential. However, when the issue became the expansion of slavery into new territories, evasion and containment no longer sufficed. The issue first arose with the annexation of Texas, which helped provoke war with Mexico in 1846—a war that many antislavery northerners considered an ugly effort to expand slavery.

THE WESTERING IMPULSE

Many Americans of European descent saw their future in the West. In the 1840s Horace Greeley urged, "Go west, young man." And to the West they went in unprecedented numbers, driven in part by the depression of 1837–43 that prompted thousands to search for cheap land and better opportunity. "The West is our object, there is no other hope left for us," declared one farmer as he and his family set out on the Oregon trail. "There is nothing like a new country for poor folks."

An earlier wave of migration had populated the region between the Appalachians and the Missouri River, bringing a new state into the Union on an average of every three years. During those years, reports from explorers, fur traders, missionaries, and sailors filtered back from California and the Pacific Northwest, describing the bounteous resources and benign climates of those wondrous regions. Richard Henry Dana's *Two Years before the Mast* (1840), the story of his experience in the cowhide and tallow trade between California and Boston, alerted thousands of Americans to this new Eden on the Pacific. Guidebooks rolled off the presses describing the boundless prospects that awaited settlers who would turn "those wild forests, trackless plains, untrodden valleys" into "one grand scene of continuous improvements, universal enterprise, and unparalleled commerce."

THE HISPANIC SOUTHWEST

Of course, another people of partial European descent already lived in portions of the region west of the 98th meridian. The frontier of New Spain had pushed north of the Rio Grande early in the 17th century. By the time Mexico won its independence from Spain in 1821, some 80,000 Mexicans lived in this region. Three-fourths of them had settled in the Rio Grande Valley of New Mexico, and most of the rest in California. Centuries earlier the Spaniards had introduced horses, cattle, and sheep to the New World. These animals became the economic mainstay of Hispanic society along New Spain's northern frontier. Later, Anglo-Americans would adopt Hispanic ranching methods to invade and subdue the lands of the arid western plains. Spanish words still describe the tools of the trade and the very land itself: *bronco, mustang, lasso, rodeo, stampede, canyon, arroyo, mesa.*

Colonial society on New Spain's northern frontier had centered on the missions and the presidios. Intended to Christianize Indians, the missions also

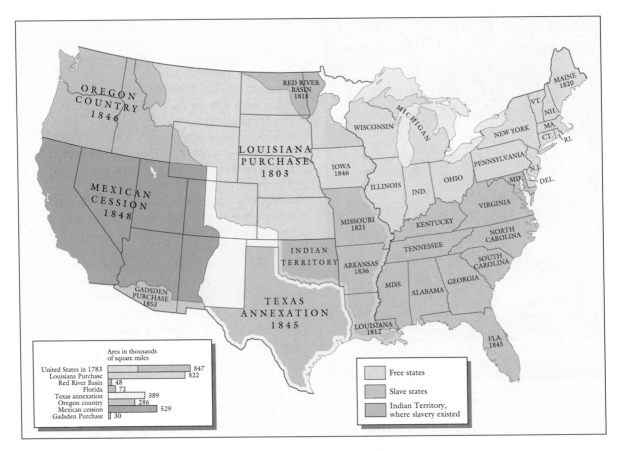

FREE AND SLAVE STATES AND TERRITORIES, 1848

became an instrument to exploit their labor, while the presidios (military posts) protected the settlers from hostile Indians—and foreign nationals hoping to gain a foothold in Spanish territory. By the late 18th century, the mission system had fallen into decline, and a decade and a half after Mexican independence in 1821 it collapsed entirely. The presidios, underfunded and understaffed, also declined after Mexican independence, so that more and more the defense of Mexico's far northern provinces fell to the residents themselves. But by the 1830s, many residents of New Mexico and California were more interested in bringing American traders in than in keeping American settlers out. A flourishing trade over the Santa Fe Trail from Independence, Missouri, brought American manufactured goods to Santa Fe, New Mexico, (and points south) in exchange for Mexican horses, mules, beaver pelts, and silver. New England

ships carried American goods all the way around the horn of South America to San Francisco and other California ports in exchange for tallow and hides produced by *californio* ranchers. This trade linked the economies of New Mexico and California more closely to the United States than to the Mexican heartland. Santa Fe was 600 miles closer to Independence than to Mexico City. The trickle of Americans into California and New Mexico in the 1820s foreshadowed the flood that would engulf these regions two decades later.

THE OREGON AND CALIFORNIA TRAILS

In 1842 and 1843, "Oregon fever" swept the Mississippi Valley. Thousands of farm families sold their land, packed their worldly goods in covered wagons along with supplies for five or six months

EMIGRANTS MAKING CAMP IN THE SNOW This drawing portrays the harsh conditions and dangers faced by many pioneers who crossed plains and mountains. Women often had to do a man's work as well as to cook and take care of children. One can only hope that this family did not suffer the fate of the Donner party, trapped by an early snowfall in the Sierra Nevada Mountains in October 1846. Nearly half of the 87 people in the Donner party died during the subsequent winter.

on the trail, hitched up their oxen, and headed out from Independence or St. Joseph, Missouri, for the trek of almost 2,000 miles to the river valleys of Oregon or California. On the way, they passed through regions claimed by three nations—the United States, Mexico, and Britain—and they settled on land owned by Mexico (California) or claimed jointly by the United States and Britain (Oregon, which then stretched north to the border of Russian Alaska). But no matter who claimed it, the land was occupied mostly by Indians, who viewed this latest intrusion with wary eyes. Few of the emigrants thought about settling down along the way, for this vast reach of arid plains, forbidding mountains, and burning wastelands was then known as "the Great American Desert." White men considered it suitable only for Indians and the disappearing breed of mountain men who had roamed the region trapping beaver.

During the next quarter-century, a half million men, women, and children crossed a half continent in one of the great sagas of American history. After the migration of farm families to Oregon and California came the 1847 exodus of the Mormons to a new Zion in the basin of the Great Salt Lake and the 1849 gold rush to California. The stories of these migrants were of triumph and tragedy, survival and death, courage and despair, success and failure. Most of them reached their destinations; some died on the way—victims of disease, exposure, starvation, suicide, or homicide by Indians or by fellow emigrants. Of those who arrived safely, a few struck it rich, most carved out a modest though hard living, and some drifted on, still looking for the pot of gold that had thus far eluded them. Together, they generated pressures that helped bring a vast new empire—more than a million square miles—into the United States by 1848.

Migration was mostly a male enterprise. Adult men outnumbered women on the Oregon Trail and on the California Trail before the gold rush by more than 2 to 1, and in the gold rush by more than 10 to 1. The quest for new land, a new start, and a chance to make a big strike represented primarily masculine ideals. Women, on the other hand, felt more rooted in family, home, and community, less willing to pull up stakes to march into the wilderness. Yet even on the rough mining frontier of the West, men sought to replicate as soon as possible the homes and communities they had left behind. "We want families," wrote a Californian in 1858, "because their homes and hearth stones everywhere, are the only true and reliable basis of any nation." Except during the gold rush, and the figures for the absolute num-

bers of men and women notwithstanding, family groups predominated on the overland trails. Half of the emigrants were mothers and children, and some of the single men had relatives among the travelers.

Many of the women were reluctant migrants. Though middle-class urban families had made some small beginnings toward equal partnership in marriage, men still ruled the family on the midwestern farms from which most of the migrants came. Men made the decision to go; women obeyed. Diaries kept by women on the trail testify to their unhappiness:

> What had possessed my husband, anyway, that he should have thought of bringing us away out through this God-forsaken country? . . . Oh, how I wish we never had started for the Golden Land. . . . I would make a brave

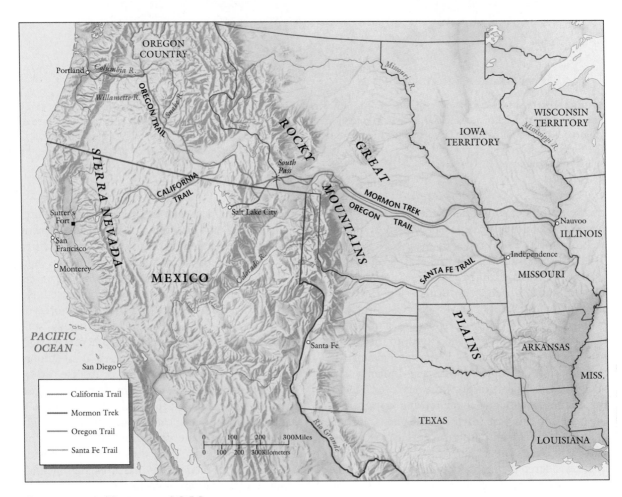

OVERLAND TRAILS, 1846

effort to be cheerful and patient until the camp work was done. Then . . . I would throw myself down on the ground and shed tears, wishing myself back home with my friends and chiding myself for consenting to take this wild goose chase.

For many families it did turn out to be a wild goose chase. But for many of those who stayed the course and settled in the far West, it was a success story, made so in great measure by the women. They turned houses into homes, settlements into communities. The proportionately fewer women may have been more highly prized than they were back East, but the frontier did not break down the separate spheres of men and women. On the contrary, woman's sphere in the West was still the home and the family, the bearing and the nurturing of children, the management of the household economy. Man's sphere

remained the world of public events and economic production.

THE MORMON MIGRATION

Patriarchal rule was strongest among those migrants with the most nearly equal sex ratio—the Mormons. Subjected to persecution that drove them from their original home in western New York to Ohio, Missouri, and eventually to Illinois, the Mormons established Nauvoo, Illinois, a thriving community of 15,000 souls, based on collective economic effort and theocratic discipline imposed by their founder and prophet, Joseph Smith. But the people of Illinois proved no more hospitable to the Mormons than the sect's previous neighbors had been. Smith did not make matters any easier. His insistence that God spoke through him, his

JOSEPH MUSTERING THE NAUVOO LEGION This painting depicts a self-defense force organized by Mormons in Nauvoo, Illinois, in the early 1840s. Beleaguered by neighbors, the Mormons decided to emigrate to Mexican territory in the West after Joseph Smith was murdered in 1844.

The Alamo (1960)
Directed by John Wayne. Starring John Wayne (Davy Crockett), Richard Widmark (Jim Bowie), Laurence Harvey (William Travis).

The legendary actor John Wayne worked a decade to obtain backing for an epic film about the heroic but doomed defense of the Alamo. When the movie was finally released in 1960, Wayne not only played the lead role as Davy Crockett, he was also the producer and director. Out of his depth in this last role, he received advice from the director of Wayne's best movies, John Ford, which helped overcome some but not all of the awkward, sentimental scenes in the film.

Three hours in length, *The Alamo* begins with General Sam Houston, commander of the Texas revolutionary army, ordering Colonel William Travis to delay the Mexican regulars commanded by Santa Anna at the Alamo long enough for Houston to organize his ragtag volunteers in east Texas into an effective fighting force. Colonel Jim Bowie, a rival of Travis for command of the garrison, considers the Alamo (a mission converted into a fort) a trap and wants to pull out, because the Mexican army outnumbers the Texans 20 to 1.

Right away, Hollywood departs from historical reality. Houston had actually ordered Bowie to blow up the Alamo and retreat to join him. But Bowie and Travis agreed to stay and fight, supported by Davy Crockett and his fellow Tennessee volunteers who had come to Texas looking for excitement. The tension between Travis and Bowie (with Crockett as a mediator) was real, and is vividly portrayed if some-

times overdramatized in the film, but the tension concerned their relative authority, not strategy.

In wide-screen splendor, the film depicts the approach of the Mexican army, the artillery duels between the garrison and the Mexicans, and the infantry assaults that finally overpower the garrison after 13 days of resistance, killing them to the last man, sparing only the wife and child of a Texas lieutenant. The combat footage in the final attack is spectacular. Mexican artillery bombard the Alamo, infantry move forward taking heavy casualties, swarm over the wall, and overwhelm the doomed defenders. Bowie is wounded early in the fight and sent to an improvised hospital in the chapel, where he dies fighting from his bed. Travis is killed at the gate after dispatching several Mexicans with his sword. Crockett fights with fury until he is impaled by a Mexican lancer, but lives long enough to throw a torch into the powder magazine, blowing up the fort and hundreds of Mexicans.

In reality, none of it happened this way. Bowie had gone to bed with typhoid fever early in the siege; Travis was killed early in the final assault with a bullet through his head; and Crockett along with a few others surrendered but were executed on Santa Anna's orders. For Hollywood, and indeed perhaps for most Americans, however, history is less important than legend. The Alamo became a heroic legend, a rallying

autocratic suppression of dissent, and his assertion that the Mormons were the only true Christians and would inherit the earth provoked hostility. When a dissident faction of Mormons published Smith's latest revelation, which sanctioned polygamy, he ordered their printing press destroyed. The county sheriff arrested him, and in June 1844 a mob broke into the jail and killed him.

Smith's martyrdom prompted yet another exodus. Under the leadership of Smith's successor,

Brigham Young, the Mormons began the long trek westward that would eventually lead them to the Great Salt Lake basin in a part of Mexican territory that soon was ceded to the United States in the wake of the Mexican War. A man of iron will and administrative genius, Young organized the migration down to the last detail. Arriving with the advance guard of Mormon pioneers at a pass overlooking the Great Basin on July 24, 1847, Young, ill with tick fever, struggled from his wagon and stared

cry for Texans in 1836, and a powerful symbol ever since. The film version dramatizes the legend better than an accurate version could have done.

The movie also reflects the cold-war mentality of the 1950s and Wayne's own full-blooded anti-Communism. Crockett's windy speeches about freedom and individual rights evoke the 1950s rhetoric of "better dead than red." Ironically, the Texans were fighting for an independent republic with slavery, in defiance of Mexico's recent abolition of the institution—an issue that the film virtually ignores.

Although The Alamo might have carried more punch if edited down to two hours, it nevertheless is visually powerful. It received seven Academy Award nominations, including one for Best Picture, but received only one Oscar—for sound.

"THE ALAMO" in TODD - AO
starring JOHN WAYNE   RICHARD WIDMARK   LAURENCE HARVEY
and guest star RICHARD BOONE   Produced and Directed by JOHN WAYNE
TECHNICOLOR® A Batjac Production   Released thru UNITED ARTISTS

©1960, Batjac - United Artists Corporation.
Permission granted for newspaper and Magazine reproduction.   (Made in U.S.A.)

John Wayne and Linda Cristal in an advertising poster for *The Alamo*.

at the barren desert and mountains surrounding the lake. "This is the right place," he declared. Here the Mormons could build their Zion undisturbed.

They built a flourishing community, making the desert bloom with grain and vegetables irrigated by water they ingeniously diverted from mountain streams. Organizing the economy and the civil society as he had organized the exodus, Young reigned as leader of the church, and from 1850 to 1857 as governor of the newly created Utah Territory.

Zion, however, did not remain undisturbed. Relations with the government in Washington and with those sent out as territorial officials were never smooth, especially after Young's proclamation in 1852 that authorized polygamy. (Although Young himself married a total of 55 women, most Mormon men could afford to support no more than one wife and her children; only about one-sixth of Mormon marriages were polygamous.) When conflict between the Mormons and the U.S. Army broke out

462 | CHAPTER 13 MANIFEST DESTINY: AN EMPIRE FOR LIBERTY—OR SLAVERY?

in 1857, Young surrendered his civil authority and made an uneasy peace with the government.

THE REPUBLIC OF TEXAS

As the Mormons were starting west, a crisis between Mexico and the United States was coming to a boil. Although the United States had renounced any claim to Texas in a treaty with Spain negotiated in 1819, many Americans believed that Texas had been part of the Louisiana Purchase. By the time the treaty was ratified in 1821, Mexico had won its independence from Spain. The new Republic of Mexico wanted to develop its northern borderlands in Texas by encouraging immigration and settlement there. Thus, Stephen F. Austin, a Missouri businessman, secured a large land grant from Mexico to settle 300 families from the United States. Despite their pledge to become Roman Catholics and Mexican citizens, these immigrants and many who followed remained Protestants and Americans at heart. They also brought in slaves, in defiance of a recent Mexican law abolishing slavery. Despite Mexican efforts to ban any further immigration, by 1835 30,000 Americans lived in Texas, outnumbering Mexicans 6 to 1.

American settlers, concentrated in east Texas, initially had little contact with Mexican *tejanos* (Texans), whose settlements were further south and west, but political events in Mexico City in 1835 had repercussions on the northern frontier. A new conservative national government seemed intent on consolidating its authority over the northern territories, including Coahuila-Texas. In response, the Anglo-American settlers and the *tejanos* forged a political alliance to protest any further loss of autonomy in their province. When the Mexican government responded militarily, many Texans—both Anglo and Mexican—fought back. Fighting flared fitfully for a year. Then, in March 1836, delegates from across Texas met at a village appropriately called Washington. They declared Texas an independent republic and adopted a constitution based on the U.S. model.

The American Revolution had lasted seven years; it took the Texans less than seven months to win and consolidate their independence. Mexican General Antonio López de Santa Anna led the Mexican army that captured the Alamo (a former mission converted to a fort) in San Antonio on March 6, 1836, killing all 187 of its defenders, in-

cluding the legendary Americans Davy Crockett and Jim Bowie. Rallying to the cry "Remember the Alamo!" Texans swarmed to the revolutionary army commanded by Sam Houston. When the Mexican army slaughtered another force of more than 300 men after they had surrendered at Goliad on March 19, the Texans were further inflamed. A month later, Houston's army, aided by volunteers from southern U.S. states, routed a larger Mexican force on the San Jacinto River (near present-day Houston) and captured Santa Anna himself. Under duress, he signed a treaty granting Texas its independence. The Mexican congress later repudiated the treaty but could not muster enough strength to reestablish its authority north of the Nueces River. The *tejanos*, increasingly marginalized by the Anglo-Americans, now became "foreigners in their native land," as one of their leaders noted. In the succeeding years, conflicts over land titles, slavery, language, and religion would exacerbate ethnic tensions. The victorious Texans, for their part, elected Sam Houston president of their new republic and petitioned for annexation to the United States.

THE ANNEXATION CONTROVERSY

President Andrew Jackson, wary of provoking war with Mexico or quarrels with antislavery northerners who charged that the annexation of Texas was a plot to expand slavery, rebuffed the annexationists. So did his successor, Martin Van Buren. Though disappointed, the Texans turned their energies to building their republic and even talked of extending it all the way to the Pacific by taking more Mexican territory. The British government encouraged the Texans, in the hope that they would stand as a buffer against further U.S. expansion. Abolitionists in England even cherished the notion that Britain might persuade the Texans to abolish slavery. Texas leaders made friendly responses to some of the British overtures, probably in the hope of provoking American annexationists to take action. They did.

Soon after Vice President John Tyler became president on the death of William Henry Harrison in 1841, he broke with the Whig Party that had elected him. Seeking to create a new coalition to reelect him in 1844, Tyler seized on the annexation of Texas as "the only matter that will take sufficient hold of the feelings of the South to rally it on a southern candidate."

Tyler named John C. Calhoun of South Carolina as secretary of state to negotiate a treaty of annexation. The southern press ran scare stories about a British plot to use Texas as a beachhead for an assault on slavery, and annexation became a popular issue in the South. Calhoun concluded a treaty with the eager Texans. But then he made a mistake: He released to the press a letter he had written to the British minister to the United States, informing him that, together with other reasons, Americans wanted to annex Texas in order to protect slavery, an institution "essential to the peace, safety, and prosperity" of the United States. This seemed to confirm abolitionist charges that annexation was a proslavery plot. Northern senators of both parties provided more than enough votes to defeat the treaty in June 1844.

By then, Texas had become the main issue in the forthcoming presidential election. Whig candidate Henry Clay had come out against annexation, as had the leading contender for the Democratic nomination, former president Martin Van Buren. Van Buren's stand ran counter to the rising tide of Manifest Destiny sentiment within the Democratic Party. It also angered southern Democrats, who were determined to have Texas. Through eight ballots at the Democratic national convention they blocked Van Buren's nomination; on the ninth, the southerners broke the stalemate by nominating one of their own, James K. Polk of Tennessee. Polk, a staunch Jacksonian who had served as Speaker of the House of Representatives during Jackson's presidency, was the first "dark horse" candidate (not having been a contender before the convention). Southerners exulted in their victory. "We have triumphed," wrote one of Calhoun's lieutenants. "Polk is nearer to *us* than any public man who was named. He is a large Slave holder and [is for] Texas—States rights *out & out.*" Polk's nomination undercut President Tyler's forlorn hope of being reelected on the Texas issue, so he bowed out of the race.

Polk ran on a platform that called not only for the annexation of Texas but also the acquisition of all of Oregon up to 54°40′ (the Alaskan border). That demand was aimed at voters in the western free states, who believed that bringing Oregon into the Union would balance the expansion of slavery into Texas with the expansion of free territory in the Northwest. Polk was more than comfortable with this platform. In fact, he wanted not only Texas and Oregon, but California and New Mexico as well.

"Texas fever" swept the South during the campaign. So powerful was the issue that Clay began to waver, stating that he would support annexation if it could be done without starting a war with Mexico. This concession won him a few southern votes but angered northern antislavery Whigs. Many of them voted for James G. Birney, candidate of the Liberty Party, which opposed any more slave territory. Birney probably took enough Whig votes from Clay in New York to give Polk victory there and in the electoral college.

ACQUISITION OF TEXAS AND OREGON

Although the election was extremely close (Polk won only a plurality of 49.5 percent of the popular vote), Democrats regarded it as a mandate for annexation. Eager to leave office in triumph, lame-duck President Tyler submitted to Congress a joint resolution of annexation, which required only a simple majority in both houses instead of the two-thirds majority in the Senate that a treaty would have required. Congress passed the resolution in March 1845. Texas thus bypassed the territorial

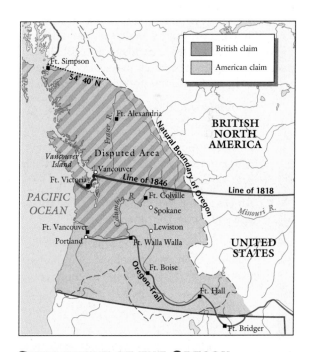

SETTLEMENT OF THE OREGON BOUNDARY DISPUTE, 1846

stage and came in as the fifteenth slave state in December 1845. Backed now by the United States, Texans claimed a southern and western border beyond the Nueces River all the way to the Rio Grande, which nearly tripled the area that Mexico had formerly defined as Texas. Mexico responded by breaking off diplomatic relations with the United States. The stage was set for five years of bitter controversy that included a shooting war with Mexico and political warfare in the United States over the issue of slavery expansion.

Meanwhile, Polk lost no time in addressing his promise to annex Oregon. "Our title to the country of the Oregon is 'clear and unquestionable,'" he said in his inaugural address. "Already our people are preparing to perfect that title by occupying it with their wives and children." The problem was to persuade Britain to recognize the title. Both countries had jointly "occupied" Oregon since 1818, overseeing the fur trade carried on by British and American companies. Chanting the slogan "Fifty-four forty or fight!" many Americans in 1845 demanded all of Oregon, as pledged in the Democratic platform. But Polk proved unwilling to fight for 54°40′. So far, Americans had settled only in the region south of the Columbia River, at roughly the 46th parallel. In June 1846, Polk accepted a compromise treaty that split the Oregon country between the United States and Britain at the 49th parallel. Several Democratic senators from the Old Northwest (states north of the Ohio River and west of Pennsylvania) accused Polk of betrayal and voted against the treaty. They had supported Texas to the Rio Grande, and they had expected

LINK TO THE PAST

The Mexican War

http://www.pbs.org/kera/usmexicanwar/

Based on the superb PBS series on the Mexican War, this site contains a great deal of material not included in the television presentation: primary sources, first person narratives, detailed discussions with Mexican and U.S. historians, timelines, links to other relevant sites, and more. It is a good place to begin a research project on the causes, issues, events, personalities, or consequences of the war, or just to browse among interesting materials.

Choose one of the following questions and analyze it from both the American and Mexican perspectives.

1. Did the Americans provoke the Mexicans to fire the first shots of the war in order to conquer Mexican territory, or did the Mexicans start the conflict to regain all or part of Texas?

2. Why did Americans win all the battles, usually against greater numbers of Mexican troops? Was American superiority a result of better leadership, better weapons, better discipline, better strategy and tactics, or something else?

3. How did the war affect the internal politics of each country? Which country experienced greater destabilization as a consequence of the war? Be careful; although this is not a trick question, the answer may be less obvious and more complicated than it seems.

Polk to support Oregon to 54°40′. A sectional breach had opened in the Democratic Party that would soon grow wider.

THE MEXICAN WAR

Having finessed a war with Britain, Polk provoked one with Mexico in order to gain California and New Mexico. In 1845 he sent a special envoy to Mexico City with an offer to buy California and New Mexico for $30 million. To help Mexico make the right response, he ordered federal troops to the disputed border area between Mexico and Texas, dispatched a naval squadron to patrol the gulf coast of Mexico, and instructed the American consul at Monterey (the Mexican capital of California) to stir up annexation sentiment among settlers there. These strong-arm tactics provoked a political revolt in Mexico City that brought a militant anti-American regime to power.

Polk responded in January 1846 by ordering 4,000 soldiers under General Zachary Taylor to advance all the way to the Rio Grande. Recognizing that he could achieve his goals only through armed conflict, Polk waited for news from Texas that would justify a declaration of war, but none came. His patience having run out, on May 9, 1846, he began to draft a message to Congress asking for a declaration of war on general grounds of Mexican defiance. That evening, word finally arrived that two weeks earlier Mexican troops had crossed the Rio Grande and had attacked an American patrol, killing 11 soldiers. Polk had what he wanted. He quickly revised his message and sent it to Congress on May 11. Most Whigs opposed war with Mexico. But in the end, not wanting to be branded unpatriotic, all but a handful of them voted for the final declaration of war, which passed the House by 174 to 14 and the Senate by 40 to 2. Despite their continuing opposition to what they called "Mr. Polk's War," most Whigs voted supplies for the army. Having witnessed the demise of the Federalist Party after it had opposed the war in 1812, one Whig congressman said sarcastically that from then on he had decided to vote for "war, pestilence, and famine."

The United States went to war with a tiny regular army of fewer than 8,000 men, supplemented by 60,000 volunteers in state regiments, and an efficient navy that quickly established domination of the sea lanes. Mexican soldiers outnumbered American in most of the battles, but the Americans had higher morale, better leadership, better weapons (especially artillery). They also enjoyed the backing of a more determined, stable government and a far richer, stronger economy. The U.S. forces won every battle—and the war—in a fashion that humiliated the proud Mexicans and left a legacy of national hostility and border violence. Especially remarkable was the prominent role played by junior American officers trained at West Point, for whom the Mexican War was a rehearsal for a larger conflict 15 years later: Robert E. Lee, Ulysses S. Grant, Pierre G. T. Beauregard, George B. McClellan, Braxton Bragg, George H. Thomas, Thomas J. Jackson, George G. Meade, Jefferson Davis, and others, whose names would become household words during the Civil War.

MILITARY CAMPAIGNS OF 1846

The Mexican War proceeded through three phases. The first phase was carried out by Zachary Taylor's 4,000 regulars on the Rio Grande. In two small battles on May 8 and 9, at Palo Alto and

AMERICAN FORCES IN SALTILLO, MEXICO This posed photograph of General John E. Wool and his staff of Zachary Taylor's army on its march southward from Monterrey through Saltillo in November 1846 is the earliest known photograph of an American military force. Photography had recently been invented, and pictures such as this one were extremely rare before the 1850s.

Resaca de la Palma, they routed numerically superior Mexican forces even before Congress had declared war. Those victories made "Old Rough and Ready" Taylor a hero, a reputation he rode to the presidency two years later. Reinforced by several thousand volunteers, Taylor pursued the retreating Mexicans 100 miles south of the Rio Grande to the heavily fortified Mexican city of Monterrey. The city was taken after four days of fighting in September 1846. Mexican resistance in the area had crumbled, and Taylor's force settled down as an army of occupation.

Meanwhile, the second phase of American strategy had gone forward in New Mexico and California. In June 1846, General Stephen Watts Kearny led an army of 1,500 tough frontiersmen and regulars west from Fort Leavenworth toward Santa Fe. Kearny bluffed and intimidated the New Mexico governor, who fled southward without ever ordering the local 3,000-man militia into action. Kearny's army occupied Santa Fe on August 18 without firing a shot. With closer economic ties to the United States than to their own country, which taxed them well but governed them poorly, many New Mexicans seemed willing to accept American rule.

After receiving reinforcements, Kearny left a small occupation force and divided his remaining troops into two contingents, one of which he sent under Colonel Alexander Doniphan into the Mexican province of Chihuahua. In the most extraordinary campaign of the war, these 800 Missourians marched 3,000 miles, foraging supplies along the way; fought and beat two much larger enemy forces; and finally linked up with Zachary Taylor's army at Monterrey in the spring of 1847.

Kearny led the other contingent across deserts and mountains to California. Events there had anticipated his arrival. In June 1846 a group of American settlers backed by Captain John C. Frémont, a renowned western explorer with the army topographical corps, captured Sonoma and raised the flag of an independent California, displaying the silhouette of a grizzly bear. Marked by exploits both courageous and comic, this "bear-flag revolt" paved the way for the conquest of California by the *americanos*. The U.S. Pacific fleet seized California's ports and the capital at Monterey; sailors from the fleet and volunteer soldiers under Frémont subdued Mexican resistance. Kearny's

weary and battered force arrived in December 1846, barely in time to help with the mopping up.

MILITARY CAMPAIGNS OF 1847

New Mexico and California had fallen into American hands, and Mexican armies had experienced nothing but defeat, but the Mexican government refused to admit that the war was over. Indeed, a political maneuver by President Polk to secure a more tractable government in Mexico had backfired. In one of Mexico's many palace revolts, Santa Anna had been overthrown and forced into exile in Cuba in 1844. A shadowy intermediary convinced Polk in July 1846 that if Santa Anna returned to power, he would make peace on American terms in return for $30 million. Polk instructed the navy to pass Santa Anna through its blockade of Mexican ports. The wily Mexican general then rode in triumph to Mexico City, where yet another new government named him supreme commander of the army and president of the republic. Breathing fire, Santa Anna spoke no more of peace. Instead, he raised new levies and marched north early in 1847 to attack Taylor's army near Monterrey.

Taylor, 62 years old, was still rough but not as ready to withstand a counteroffensive as he had been a few weeks earlier. After capturing Monterrey in September 1846, he had let the defeated Mexican army go and had granted an eight-week armistice in the hope that it would allow time for peace negotiations. Angry at Taylor's presumption in making such a decision and suspicious of the general's political ambitions, Polk canceled the armistice and named General-in-Chief Winfield Scott to command the third phase of the war, a campaign against Mexico City. A large, punctilious man, Scott acquired the nickname "Old Fuss and Feathers" for a military professionalism that contrasted with the homespun manner of "Rough and Ready" Zach Taylor. Scott decided to lead an invasion of Mexico's heartland from a beachhead at Veracruz and in January 1847 ordered the transfer of more than half of Taylor's troops to his own expeditionary force.

Left with fewer than 5,000 men, most of them untried volunteers, Taylor complained bitterly of political intrigue and military favoritism. Nevertheless, he marched out to meet Santa Anna's

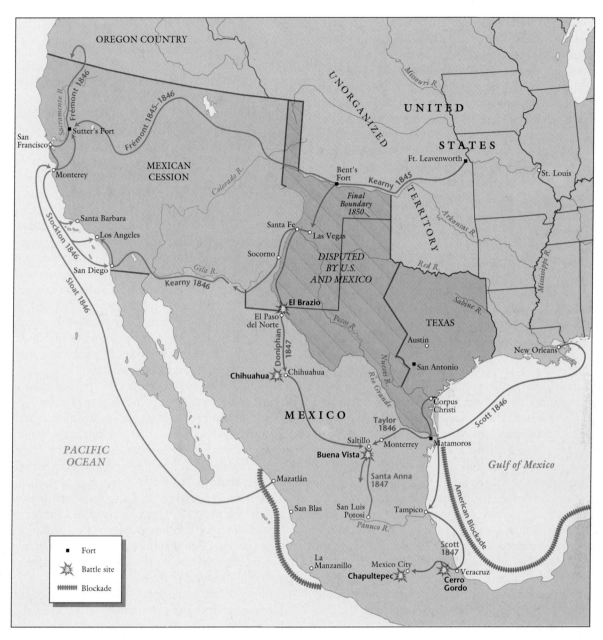

PRINCIPAL CAMPAIGNS OF THE MEXICAN WAR, 1846–1847

army of 18,000. In a two-day battle on February 22 and 23 at Buena Vista, Taylor's little force bent but never broke. They inflicted twice as many casualties as they suffered in a fierce struggle highlighted by the brilliant counterattack of a Mississippi regiment commanded by Jefferson Davis. The bloodied Mexican army retreated toward the capital.

When news of the victory reached the East, Taylor's popularity soared to new heights. If Polk had wanted to quash a political rival by taking away most of his troops—as Taylor believed—he had achieved just the opposite.

But it was Scott who actually won the war. With a combined army-navy force, he took the coastal fortress at Veracruz in March 1847. Over the next five months, his army, which never totaled more than 14,000 men (with considerable turnover because of expiring one-year enlistments), marched and fought its way over more than 200 miles of mountains and plains to Mexico City. It was a bold, high-risk action. When Scott's forces reached the fortifications of Mexico City, held by three times their numbers, the Duke of Wellington, who was following the campaign closely, predicted, "Scott is lost—he cannot capture the city, and he cannot fall back upon his base." But capture it he did, on September 14, after fierce hand-to-hand combat in the battles of Contreras, Churubusco, Molino del Rey, and Chapultepec. It was a brilliant success—even though it owed much to wrangling among Mexican leaders that forced Santa Anna to spend almost as much time facing down his internal enemies as fighting the Americans.

ANTIWAR SENTIMENT

The string of military victories prevented the significant U.S. antiwar sentiment from winning even wider support. The war had enthusiastic support in the South and West and among Democrats, but the Whigs and many people in the Northeast, especially in New England, considered it "a wicked and disgraceful war." Democrats and Whigs had different notions of "progress." Democrats believed in expanding American institutions over *space*—in particular, the space occupied by Mexicans and Indians. Whigs, on the other hand, believed in improving American institutions over *time*. "Opposed to the instinct of boundless acquisition stands that of Internal Improvement," said Horace Greeley. "A nation cannot simultaneously devote its energies to the absorption of others' territories and the improvement of its own."

Antislavery people raised their eyebrows when they heard Manifest Destiny rhetoric about "extending the blessings of American liberty" to benighted regions. They suspected that the real reason was the desire to extend slavery. Hosea Biglow, the rustic Yankee philosopher created by the abolitionist poet James Russell Lowell, observed:

> They jest want this Californy
> So's to lug new slave-states in
> To abuse ye an' to scorn ye,
> And to plunder ye like sin.

THE WILMOT PROVISO

The slavery issue overshadowed all others in the debate over the Mexican War. President Polk could not understand the reason for the fuss. "There is no probability," he wrote in his diary, "that any territory will ever be acquired from Mexico in which slavery would ever exist." But other Americans were less sure. Many southerners hoped that slavery would spread into the fertile lowlands of Mexican territory. Many northerners feared that it might. Their fear was strengthened by an editorial in a Charleston newspaper: "California is peculiarly adapted for slave labor. The right to have [slave] property protected there is not a mere abstraction." The issue came to a head early in the war. On August 8, 1846, Pennsylvania Democratic Congressman David Wilmot offered an amendment to an army appropriations bill: ". . . that, as an express and fundamental condition of the acquisition of any territory from the Republic of Mexico . . . neither slavery nor involuntary servitude shall ever exist in any part of said territory."

This famous "Wilmot Proviso" framed the national debate over slavery for the next 15 years. The House passed the amendment. Nearly all northern Democrats joined all northern Whigs in the majority, while southern Democrats and southern Whigs voted almost unanimously against it. (In the Senate, greater southern strength defeated the proviso.) This outcome marked an ominous wrenching of the party division between Whigs and Democrats into a *sectional* division between free and slave states. It was a sign that the two-party system might not successfully contain the convulsive question of slavery expansion.

Several factors underlay the split of northern Democrats from their own president on this issue. Ever since southern Democrats had blocked Van Buren's nomination in 1844, resentment had been growing in the party's northern wing. Polk's acceptance of 49° latitude for Oregon's northern boundary exacerbated this feeling. "Our rights to Oregon have been shamefully compromised," fumed an Ohio Democrat. "The administration is Southern, Southern, Southern! . . . Since the South have fixed boundaries for free territory, let the North fix boundaries for slave territories." The reduced rates of the Walker tariff in 1846 (sponsored by Robert J. Walker of Mississippi, Polk's secretary of the trea-

SLAVE AUCTION IN ST. LOUIS The public buying and selling of human beings in cities like St. Louis made a mockery of American boasts of liberty and gave a powerful impetus to the drive to prohibit the expansion of slavery into the territories acquired from Mexico. This painting hints at the ugliest dimension of the slave trade, the sale of mothers and children apart from fathers and sometimes apart from each other.

sury) annoyed Democrats from Pennsylvania's industrial districts. Polk further angered Democrats from the Old Northwest by vetoing a rivers and harbors bill that would have provided federal aid for transportation improvements in their districts. The Wilmot Proviso was in part the product of these pent-up frustrations over what more and more northerners—abolitionists, Whigs, and Democrats alike—were calling "the slave power." "The time has come," said a Democratic congressman in 1846, "when the Northern Democracy should make a stand. Every thing has taken a Southern shape and been controlled by Southern caprice for years. . . . We must satisfy the Northern people . . . that we are not to extend the institution of slavery as a result of this war."

The slavery issue hung like the sword of Damocles over Polk's efforts to negotiate peace with Mexico. Polk also came under pressure from expansionist Democrats who, excited by military victory, wanted more Mexican territory, perhaps even "all Mexico." Polk had sent diplomat Nicholas Trist with Scott's army to negotiate the terms of Mexican surrender. Authorized to pay Mexico $15 million for California, New Mexico, and a Texas border on the Rio Grande, Trist worked out such a treaty. In the meantime, though, Polk had succumbed to the "all Mexico" clamor. He ordered Trist back to Washington, intending to replace him with someone who would exact greater concessions from Mexico. Trist ignored the recall, signed the treaty of Guadalupe Hidalgo on

February 2, 1848, and sent it to Washington. Although angered by Trist's defiance, Polk nonetheless decided to end the controversy by submitting the treaty to the Senate, which approved it on March 10 by a vote of 38 to 14. Half the opposition came from Democrats who wanted more Mexican territory and half from Whigs who wanted none. As it was, the treaty sheared off half of Mexico and increased the size of the United States by one-fourth.

THE ELECTION OF 1848

The treaty did nothing to settle the question of slavery in the new territory, however. Mexico had abolished the institution two decades earlier; would the United States reintroduce it? Many Americans looked to the election of 1848 to decide the matter. Four positions on the issue emerged, each identified with a candidate for the presidential nomination.

The Wilmot Proviso represented the position of those determined to bar slavery from all territories. The Liberty Party endorsed the proviso and nominated Senator John P. Hale of New Hampshire for president.

Southern Democrat John C. Calhoun formulated the "southern-rights" position. Directly challenging the Wilmot Proviso, Calhoun introduced resolutions in the Senate in February 1847 affirming the right of slave owners to take their human property into any territory. The Constitution protected the right of property, Calhoun pointed out; Congress could no more prevent a settler from taking his slaves to California than it could prevent him from taking his horses there.

Although most southerners agreed with Calhoun, the Democratic Party sought a middle ground. The Polk administration endorsed the idea of extending the old Missouri Compromise line of 36°30′ to the Pacific. This would have excluded slavery from present-day Washington, Oregon, Idaho, Utah, Nevada, and the northern half of California, but would have allowed it in present-day New Mexico, Arizona, and southern California. Secretary of State James Buchanan, also a candidate for the Democratic presidential nomination (Polk did not seek renomination), embraced this position.

Another compromise position became known as "popular sovereignty." Identified with Senator Lewis Cass of Michigan, yet another contender for the Democratic nomination, this concept proposed to let the settlers of each territory decide for themselves whether to permit slavery. This solution contained a crucial ambiguity: It did not specify *at what stage* the settlers of a territory could decide on slavery. Most northern Democrats assumed that a territorial legislature would make that decision as soon as it was organized. Most southerners assumed that it would not be made until the settlers had drawn up a state constitution. That would normally happen only after several years as a territory, during which time slavery might well have taken deep enough root to be implanted in the state constitution. So long as neither assumption was tested, each faction could support popular sovereignty.

The Democratic convention nominated Cass for president, thereby seeming to endorse popular sovereignty. In an attempt to maintain party unity, however, the platform made no mention of the matter. The attempt was not entirely successful: Two Alabama delegates walked out when the convention refused to endorse Calhoun's "southern-rights" position, and an antislavery faction from New York walked out when it failed to win a credentials fight.

The Whig convention tried to avoid a similar schism by adopting no platform at all. But the slavery issue would not die. In the eyes of many antislavery delegates who styled themselves "Conscience Whigs," the party made itself ridiculous by nominating Zachary Taylor for president. Desperate for victory, the Whigs chose a hero from a war that most of them had opposed. But the fact that Taylor was also a large slaveholder who owned several plantations in Louisiana and Mississippi was too much for the Conscience Whigs. They bolted from the party and formed a coalition with the Liberty Party and antislavery Democrats.

THE FREE SOIL PARTY

The "Free-Soilers" met in convention in August 1848. The meeting resembled a religious camp meeting more than a political gathering. Speakers proclaimed slavery "a great moral, social, and political evil—a relic of barbarism which must necessarily be swept away in the progress of Christian civilization." The convention did not say how that would be done, but it did adopt a platform calling

> "*We inscribe on our banner, 'Free Soil, Free Speech, Free Labor, and Free Men,' and under it we will fight on, and fight ever, until a triumphant victory shall reward our exertions.*"
>
> **FREE SOIL PARTY PLATFORM**
> *excerpt*

for "no more Slave States and no more Slave Territories." The Free Soil Party nominated former president Martin Van Buren, with Charles Francis Adams, the son and grandson of presidents, as his running mate.

The campaign was marked by the futile efforts of both major parties to bury the slavery issue. Free Soil pressure compelled both northern Democrats and Whigs to take a stand against slavery in the territories. Whigs pointed to their earlier support of the Wilmot Proviso, while Democrats said popular sovereignty would keep the territories free. In the South, though, the two parties presented other faces. There, the Democrats pointed with pride to their expansionist record that had brought to the nation hundreds of thousands of square miles of territory—territory into which slavery might expand. But Taylor proved the strongest candidate in the South, because he was a southerner and a slaveholder. "Will the people of [the South] vote for a Southern President or a Northern one?" asked southern newspapers. "We prefer Old Zack with his sugar and cotton plantations and four hundred negroes to all their compromises."

Taylor carried 8 of the 15 slave states and increased the Whig vote in the South by 10 percent over 1844, while the Democratic vote declined by 4 percent. Though he did less well in the north, he carried New York and enough other states to win the election. The Free-Soilers won no electoral votes but polled 14 percent of the popular vote in the north. They also elected nine congressmen along with two senators who would be heard from in the future: Salmon P. Chase of Ohio, architect of the Free Soil coalition in 1848, and Charles Sumner of Massachusetts, leader of the Conscience Whigs.

THE GOLD RUSH AND CALIFORNIA STATEHOOD

About the time Nicholas Trist was putting the finishing touches on the treaty to make California part of the United States, workers building a sawmill on the American River near Sacramento discovered flecks of gold in the riverbed. The news gradually leaked out, reaching the East in August 1848, where a public surfeited with tall tales out of the West greeted it with skepticism. But in December, Polk's final message to Congress confirmed the "extraordinary" discoveries of gold. Two days later, a tea caddy containing 320 ounces of pure gold from California arrived in Washington. Now all doubts disappeared. By the spring of 1849, 100,000 gold-seekers were poised to take off by foot on the overland trail or by ship—either around Cape Horn or to the isthmus of Central America, where after a land crossing, they could board another ship to take them up the Pacific Coast to the new boom town of San Francisco. Eighty thousand actually made it that first year (5,000 succumbed to a cholera epidemic). Some of them struck it rich; most kept hoping to; more came by the scores of thousands every year.

Political organization of California could not be postponed. The mining camps needed law and order; the settlers needed courts, land and water laws, mail service, and other amenities of established government. In New Mexico, the 60,000 former Mexican citizens, now Americans, also needed a governmental structure for their new allegiance. Nor could the growing Mormon community at Salt Lake be ignored.

Still, the slavery question paralyzed Congress. In December 1848 lame-duck president Polk recommended extension of the Missouri Compromise 36°30′ line to the Pacific. The Whig-controlled House defied him, reaffirmed the Wilmot Proviso, drafted a bill to organize California as a free territory, and debated abolishing the slave trade and even slavery itself in the District of Columbia. Fistfights flared in Congress; southerners declared that they would secede if any of those measures became law; the Democratic Senate quashed all the bills. A southern caucus asked Calhoun to draft an "address" setting forth its position. He eagerly complied, producing in January 1849 a document that breathed fire against "unconstitutional" northern efforts to keep slavery out of the territories. Calhoun reminded

The California Gold Rush

Prospectors for gold in the foothills of California's Sierra Nevada came from all over the world, including China. The bottom photograph shows American-born and Chinese miners near Auburn, California, a year or two after the initial gold rush of 1849. It illustrates the original primitive technology of separating gravel from gold by panning or by washing the gravel away in a sluice box, leaving the heavier gold flakes behind. By 1853 most of the gold in streams and accessible gravel beds had been recovered, so gold-seekers turned to hydraulic mining. They dammed a stream at an elevation high enough to create a powerful head of water pressure to blast loose gold-bearing gravel from whole mountainsides, as shown in the photograph at right. Hydraulic mining destroyed or reconfigured thousands of acres of California landscape and left scars still visible today.

southerners that their "property, prosperity, equality, liberty, and safety" were at stake and prophesied secession if the South did not prevail.

But Calhoun's firebomb fizzled. Only two-fifths of the southern congressmen and senators signed it. The Whigs wanted nothing to do with it. They looked forward to good times in the Taylor administration and opposed rocking the boat. "We do not expect an administration which we have brought into power [to] do any act or permit any act to be done [against] our safety," said Robert Toombs of Georgia, a leading Whig congressman. "We feel *secure* under General Taylor," added his fellow Georgian Alexander H. Stephens.

They were in for a rude shock. Taylor viewed matters as a nationalist, not as a southerner. New York's antislavery Senator William H. Seward became one of his principal advisers. A novice in politics, Taylor was willing to be guided by Seward. As a military man, he was attracted to the idea of vanquishing the territorial problem by outflanking it. He proposed to admit California and New Mexico (the latter comprising present-day New Mexico, Arizona, Nevada, Utah, and part of Colorado) immediately as *states*, skipping the territorial stage.

From the South came cries of outrage. Immediate admission would bring in two more free states, for slavery had not existed under Mexican law and most of the forty-niners were Free Soil in sentiment. Indeed, with the administration's support, Californians held a convention in October 1849, drew up a constitution excluding slavery, and applied to Congress for admission as a state. Taylor's end run would tip the existing balance of 15 slave and 15 free states in favor of the North, probably forever. The South would lose its de facto veto in the Senate. "For the first time," said freshman Senator Jefferson Davis of Mississippi, "we are about permanently to destroy the balance of power between the sections." Davis insisted that slave labor was suitable to mining and that slavery should be permitted in California. Southerners vowed never to "consent to be thus degraded and enslaved" by such a "monstrous trick and injustice" as admission of California as a free state.

THE COMPROMISE OF 1850

California and New Mexico became the focal points of a cluster of slavery issues that faced the Congress of 1849–1850. An earlier Supreme Court decision

(*Prigg* v. *Pennsylvania*, 1842) had relieved state officials of any obligation to enforce the return of fugitive slaves who had escaped into free states, declaring that this was a federal responsibility. Southerners therefore demanded a strong national fugitive slave law (in utter disregard of their oft-stated commitment to states' rights). Antislavery northerners, on the other hand, were calling for an end to the disgraceful buying and selling of slaves in the national capital. And in the Southwest, a shooting war threatened to break out between Texas and New Mexico. Having won the Rio Grande as their southern border with Mexico, Texans insisted that the river must also mark their western border with New Mexico. (That would have given Texas more than half of the present state of New Mexico.) This dispute also involved slavery, for the terms of Texas's annexation authorized the state to split into as many as five states, and the territory it carved out of New Mexico would create the potential for still another slave state.

These problems produced both a crisis and an opportunity. The crisis lay in the threat to break up the Union. From Mississippi had gone forth a call for a convention of southern states at Nashville in June 1850 "to devise and adopt some mode of resistance to northern aggression." Few doubted that the mode would be secession unless Congress met southern demands at least halfway. But Congress got off to an unpromising start. Sectional disputes prevented either major party from commanding a majority in electing a Speaker of the House. Through three weeks and 62 ballots, the contest went on while tempers shortened. Northerners and southerners shouted insults at each other, fistfights broke out, and a Mississippian drew a revolver during one heated debate. Southern warnings of secession became a litany: "If, by your legislation, you seek to drive us from the territories of California and New Mexico," thundered Toombs of Georgia, "*I am for disunion.*" On the 63rd ballot, the exhausted legislators finally elected Howell Cobb of Georgia as Speaker by a plurality rather than a majority.

THE SENATE DEBATES

As he had in 1820 and 1833, Henry Clay hoped to turn the crisis into an opportunity. Seventy-two years old, a veteran of 30 years in Congress, three times an unsuccessful candidate for president, Clay was the most respected and still the most magnetic figure in the Senate. A nationalist from the border state of Kentucky, he hoped to unite North and South in a compromise. On January 29, 1850, he presented eight proposals to the Senate and supported them with an eloquent speech, the first of many to be heard in that body during what turned out to be the most famous congressional debate in U.S. history. Clay grouped the first six of his proposals into three pairs, each pair offering one concession to the North and one to the South. The first pair would admit California as a free state but would organize the rest of the Mexican cession without restrictions against slavery. The second would settle the Texas boundary dispute in favor of New Mexico but would compensate Texas to enable the state to pay off bonds it had sold when it was an independent republic. (Many holders of the Texas bonds were southerners.) The third pair of proposals would abolish the slave trade in the District of Columbia but would guarantee the continued existence of slavery there unless both Maryland and Virginia consented to abolition. Of Clay's final two proposals, one affirmed that Congress had no jurisdiction over the interstate slave trade; the other called for a strong national fugitive slave law.

At the end of a long, grueling bargaining process, the final shape of the Compromise of 1850 closely resembled Clay's package. The public face of this process featured set speeches in the Senate, the most notable of which were those of John C. Calhoun, Daniel Webster, and William H. Seward. Calhoun and Webster (along with Clay) represented the grand Senate triumvirate of the previous generation; Seward was the rising star of a new generation, whose speech catapulted him into renown. Each senator spoke for one of the three principal viewpoints on the issues.

Calhoun went first, on March 4. Suffering from consumption (he would die within a month), Calhoun sat shrouded in flannel as a colleague read his speech to a rapt audience. Calhoun's words of gloom seemed almost to come from the grave. Unless northerners returned fugitive slaves in good faith, he warned, unless they consented to the expansion of slavery into the territories and accepted a constitutional amendment "which will restore to the South, in substance, the power she possessed of

protecting herself before the equilibrium between the two sections was destroyed," southern states could not "remain in the Union consistently with their honor and safety."

Webster's famous "seventh of March" speech three days later was both a reply to Calhoun and an appeal to the North for compromise. In words that would be memorized by generations of school-children, Webster announced his theme: "I wish to speak to-day, not as a Massachusetts man, nor as a Northern man, but as an American. I speak to-day for the preservation of the Union. Hear me for my cause." Secession could no more take place "without convulsion," he told the South, than "the heavenly bodies [could] rush from their spheres . . . without causing the wreck of the universe!" But although Webster had himself voted for the Wilmot Proviso, he now urged Yankees to forgo "taunt or reproach" of the South by insisting on the proviso. Nature would exclude slavery from New Mexico. "I would not take pains uselessly to reaffirm an ordinance of nature, nor to reenact the will of God." Believing that God helped those who helped themselves, many of Webster's former antislavery admirers repudiated his leadership—especially because he also endorsed a fugitive slave law.

On March 11 Seward expressed the antislavery position in what came to be known as his "higher law" speech. Both slavery and compromise were "radically wrong and essentially vicious," he said. In reply to Calhoun's arguments for the constitutional protection of slavery in the territories, Seward invoked "a higher law than the Constitution," the law of God in whose sight all persons were equal. Instead of legislating the expansion of slavery or the return of fugitive slaves, the country should be considering how to bring slavery peacefully to an end, for "you cannot roll back the tide of social progress."

PASSAGE OF THE COMPROMISE

While these speeches were being delivered, committee members worked ceaselessly behind the scenes to fashion compromise legislation. They were aided by lobbyists for Texas bondholders and for business interests that wanted an end to this distracting crisis. But, in reaching for a compromise, Clay chose what turned out to be the wrong tactic. He lumped most of his proposals together in a single bill, hoping that supporters of any given part of the compromise would vote for the whole in order to win the part they liked. Instead, most senators and representatives voted against the package in order to defeat the parts they disliked. President Taylor continued to insist on the immediate admission of California (and New Mexico, when it was ready) with no quid pro quo for the South. Exhausted and discouraged, Clay fled Washington's summer heat, leaving a young senator from Illinois, Stephen A. Douglas, to lead the forces of compromise.

Another rising star of the new generation, Douglas reversed Clay's tactics. Starting with a core of supporters made up of Democrats from the Old Northwest and Whigs from the upper South, he built a majority for each part of the compromise by submitting it separately and adding its supporters to his core: northerners for a free California, southerners for a fugitive slave law, and so on. This effort benefited from Taylor's sudden death on July 9 (of gastroenteritis, after consuming large quantities of iced milk and cherries on a hot Fourth of July). The new president, Millard Fillmore, was a conservative Whig from New York who gave his support to the compromise. One after another, in August and September, the separate measures became law: the admission of California as a free state; the organization of the rest of the Mexican cession into the two territories of New Mexico and Utah without restrictions against slavery; the settlement of the Texas–New Mexico border dispute in favor of New Mexico and the compensation of Texas with $10 million; the abolition of the slave trade in the District of Columbia and the guarantee of slavery there; and the passage of a new fugitive slave law. When it was over, most Americans breathed a sigh of relief, the Nashville convention adjourned tamely, and President Fillmore christened the Compromise of 1850 "a final settlement" of all sectional problems. Calhounites in the South and antislavery activists in the North branded the compromise a betrayal of principle. But, for the time being, they seemed to be in a minority.

The compromise produced consequences different from what many anticipated. California came in as the sixteenth free state, but its senators during the 1850s were in fact conservative Democrats who voted with the South on most issues. California law even allowed slave owners to keep their slaves while "sojourning" in the state. The territorial legislatures of Utah and New Mexico legalized slavery, but few slaves were brought there. And the fugitive slave law generated more trouble and controversy than all the other parts of this "final settlement" combined.

THE FUGITIVE SLAVE LAW

The Constitution required that a slave who escaped into a free state must be returned to his or her owner, but failed to specify how that should be done. Under a 1793 law, slave owners could take their recaptured property before any state or federal court to prove ownership. This procedure worked well enough so long as officials in free states were willing to cooperate. As the antislavery movement gained momentum in the 1830s, however, some officials proved uncooperative. And professional slave-catchers sometimes went too far—kidnapping free blacks, forging false affidavits to "prove" they were slaves, and selling them south into bondage. Several northern states responded by passing antikidnapping laws that gave alleged fugitives the right of trial by jury. The laws also prescribed criminal penalties for kidnapping. In *Prigg*

KIDNAPPING AGAIN! This is a typical poster printed by abolitionist opponents of the Fugitive Slave Law. It was intended to rally the citizens of Boston against the recapture and reenslavement of Anthony Burns, a fugitive slave from Virginia seized in Boston in May 1854.

v. *Pennsylvania* (1842) the U.S. Supreme Court declared Pennsylvania's antikidnapping law unconstitutional. But the Court also ruled that enforcing the Constitution's fugitive slave clause was entirely a federal responsibility, thereby absolving the states of any need to cooperate in enforcing it. Nine northern states thereupon passed personal liberty laws prohibiting the use of state facilities (courts, jails, police or sheriffs, and so on) in the recapture of fugitives.

Fugitive slaves dramatized the poignancy and cruelties of bondage more vividly than anything else. A man or a woman risking all for freedom was not an abstract issue but a real human being whose plight invited sympathy and help. Consequently, many northerners not necessarily opposed to slavery in the South nonetheless felt outrage at the idea of fugitives being seized in a land of freedom and returned to slavery. The "underground railroad" that helped spirit slaves out of bondage took on legendary status. Stories of secret chambers where fugitives were hidden, dramatic trips in the dark of the moon between "stations" on the underground, and clever or heroic measures to foil pursuing bloodhounds exaggerated the legend.

Probably fewer than 1,000 of a total 3 million slaves actually escaped to freedom each year. But to southerners the return of those fugitives, like the question of the legality of slavery in California or New Mexico, was a matter of *honor* and *rights.* "Although the loss of property is felt," said Senator James Mason of Virginia, sponsor of the Fugitive Slave Act, "the loss of honor is felt still more." The fugitive slave law, said another southern politician, was "the only measure of the Compromise [of 1850] calculated to secure the rights of the South." Southerners therefore regarded obedience to the law as a test of the North's good faith in carrying out the compromise. President Millard Fillmore vowed to prove that good faith by strictly enforcing the law.

The law's provisions were extraordinary. It created federal commissioners who could issue warrants for arrests of fugitives and before whom a slaveholder would bring a captured fugitive to prove ownership. All the slaveholder needed for proof was an affidavit from a slave-state court or the testimony of white witnesses. The fugitive had no right to testify in his or her own behalf. The com-

missioner received a fee of $10 if he found the owner's claim valid, but only $5 if he let the fugitive go. (The difference was supposedly justified by the larger amount of paperwork required to return the fugitive to slavery.) The federal treasury would pay all costs of enforcement. The commissioner could call on federal marshals to apprehend fugitives, and the marshals in turn could deputize any citizen to help. A citizen who refused could be fined up to $1,000, and anyone who harbored a fugitive or obstructed his or her capture would be subject to imprisonment. Northern senators had tried in vain to weaken some of these provisions and to amend the law to give alleged fugitives the rights to testify, to habeas corpus, and to a jury trial.

Abolitionists denounced the law as draconian, immoral, and unconstitutional. They vowed to resist it. Opportunities soon came, as slave owners sent agents north to recapture fugitives, some of whom had escaped years earlier (the act set no statute of limitations). In February 1851 slave-catchers arrested a black man living with his family in Indiana and returned him to an owner who said he had run away 19 years before. A Maryland man tried to claim ownership of a Philadelphia woman who he said had escaped 22 years earlier; he also wanted her six children, all born in Philadelphia. In this case, the commissioner disallowed his claim to both mother and children. But statistics show that the law was rigged in favor of the claimants. In the first 15 months of its operation, 84 fugitives were returned to slavery and only 5 were released. (For the entire decade of the 1850s the ratio was 332 to 11.)

THE SLAVE-CATCHERS

Unable to protect their freedom through legal means, many blacks, with the support of white allies, resorted to flight and resistance. Thousands of northern blacks fled to Canada—3,000 in the last three months of 1850 alone—sometimes under the very noses of slave-catchers. In February 1851 slave-catchers arrested a fugitive who had taken the name Shadrach when he escaped from Virginia a year earlier. They rushed him to the federal courthouse, where a few deputy marshals held him, pending a hearing. But a group of black men broke into the courtroom, overpowered the deputies, and spirited Shadrach out of the country to Canada.

RETURN OF THOMAS SIMS AND ANTHONY BURNS This symbolic woodcut depicts soldiers and marines returning two of the most famous fugitives to slavery while Bostonians vent their frustration and rage. Although the incidents were real, the Sims and Burns cases occurred three years apart, in 1851 and 1854.

This was too much for the Fillmore administration. In April 1851 another fugitive, Thomas Sims, was arrested in Boston, and the president sent 250 soldiers to help 300 armed deputies enforce the law and return Sims to slavery.

Continued rescues and escapes kept matters at fever pitch for the rest of the decade. In the fall of 1851 a Maryland slave owner and his son accompanied federal marshals to Christiana, Pennsylvania, a Quaker village, where two of the man's slaves had taken refuge. The hunters ran into a fusillade of gunfire from a house where a dozen black men were protecting the fugitives. When the shooting stopped, the slave owner was dead and his son was seriously wounded. Three of the blacks fled to Canada. This time Fillmore sent in the marines. They helped marshals arrest 30 black men and a half dozen whites, who were indicted for treason. But the government's case fell apart, and the U.S.

attorney dropped charges after a jury acquitted the first defendant, a Quaker.

Another white man who aided slaves was not so lucky. Sherman Booth was an abolitionist editor in Wisconsin who led a raid in 1854 to free a fugitive from custody. Convicted in a federal court, Booth appealed for a writ of habeas corpus from the Wisconsin Supreme Court. The court freed him and declared the Fugitive Slave Law unconstitutional. That assertion of states' rights prompted the southern majority on the U.S. Supreme Court to overrule the Wisconsin court, assert the supremacy of federal law, and order Booth back to prison.

Two of the most famous fugitive slave cases of the 1850s ended in deeper tragedy. In the spring of 1854 federal marshals in Boston arrested a Virginia fugitive, Anthony Burns. Angry abolitionists poured into Boston to save him. Some of them tried to attack the federal courthouse, where a deputy was killed in an exchange of gunfire. But the new president, Franklin Pierce, was determined not to back down. "Incur any expense," he wired the district attorney in Boston, "to enforce the law." After every legal move to free Burns had failed, Pierce sent a U.S. revenue cutter to carry Burns back to Virginia. While thousands of angry Yankees lined the streets under American flags hanging upside down to signify the loss of liberty in the cradle of the Revolution, 200 marines and soldiers marched this lone black man back into bondage.

Two years later Margaret Garner escaped from Kentucky to Ohio with her husband and four children. When a posse of marshals and deputies caught up with them, Margaret seized a kitchen knife and tried to kill her children and herself rather than return to slavery. She managed to cut her 3-year-old daughter's throat before she was overpowered. After complicated legal maneuvers, the federal commissioner remanded the fugitives to their Kentucky owner. He promptly sold them down the river to Arkansas, and, in a steamboat accident along the way, one of Margaret Garner's sons drowned in the Mississippi.

Such events had a profound impact on public emotions. Most northerners were not abolitionists, and few of them regarded black people as equals. But millions of them moved closer to an antislavery—or perhaps it would be more accurate to say anti-Southern—position in response to the shock of seeing armed slave-catchers on their streets. "When it was all over," agreed two theretofore conservative Whigs in Boston after the Anthony Burns affair, "I put my face in my hands and wept. I could do nothing less. . . . We went to bed one night old-fashioned, conservative, compromise Union Whigs and waked up stark mad Abolitionists."

Several northern states passed new personal liberty laws in defiance of the South. Although those laws did not make it impossible to recover fugitives, they made it so difficult, expensive, and time consuming that many slave owners gave up trying. The failure of the North to honor the Fugitive Slave Law, part of the Compromise of 1850, was one of the South's bitter grievances in the 1850s. Several southern states cited it as one of their reasons for seceding in 1861.

UNCLE TOM'S CABIN

A novel inspired by the plight of fugitive slaves further intensified public sentiment. Harriet Beecher Stowe, author of *Uncle Tom's Cabin*, was the daughter of Lyman Beecher, the most famous clergyman-theologian of his generation, and the sister of Henry Ward Beecher, the foremost preacher of the next generation. Writing this book made her more famous than either of them. Having grown up in the doctrinal air of New England Calvinist notions of sin, guilt, and atonement, Harriet lived for 18 years in Cincinnati, where she became acquainted with fugitive slaves who had escaped across the Ohio River. During the 1840s, in spare moments that she carved out from the duties of bearing and nurturing seven children, Stowe wrote numerous short stories. Outraged by the Fugitive Slave Law in 1850, she responded to her sister-in-law's suggestion: "Hattie, if I could use a pen as you can, I would write something that will make this nation feel what an accursed thing slavery is."

HARRIET BEECHER STOWE A portrait of Harriet Beecher Stowe painted shortly after the publication of *Uncle Tom's Cabin* made her world famous.

In 1851, writing by candlelight after putting the children to bed, Stowe turned out a chapter a week for serial publication in an antislavery newspaper. When the installments were published as a book in the spring of 1852, *Uncle Tom's Cabin* became a runaway best-seller and was eventually translated into 20 languages. Contrived in plot, didactic in style, steeped in sentiment, *Uncle Tom's Cabin* is nevertheless a powerful novel with unforgettable characters. Uncle Tom himself is not the fawning, servile Sambo of later caricature, but a Christlike figure who bears the sins of white people and carries the salvation of black people on his shoulders. The novel's central theme is the tragedy of the breakup of families by slavery—the theme most likely to pluck at the heartstrings of middle-class Americans of that generation. Few eyes remained dry as they read about Eliza fleeing across the ice-choked Ohio River to save her son from the slave trader, or about Tom grieving for the wife and children he had left behind in Kentucky when he was sold.

Though banned in some parts of the South, *Uncle Tom's Cabin* found a wide but hostile readership there. A measure of the defensiveness of southerners toward the book is the tone of the reviews that appeared in southern journals. The editor of the South's leading literary periodical instructed the reviewer: "I would have the review as hot as hellfire, blasting and searing the reputation of [this] vile wretch in petticoats." Proslavery authors rushed into print with more than a dozen novels challenging Stowe's themes, but all of them together made nothing like the impact of *Uncle Tom's Cabin*. The book helped shape a whole generation's view of slavery. When Abraham Lincoln met Harriet Beecher Stowe a decade after its publication, he reportedly remarked, "So you're the little woman who wrote the book that made this great war."

FILIBUSTERING

If the prospects for slavery in New Mexico appeared unpromising, southerners could contemplate a closer region where slavery already existed—Cuba. Enjoying an economic boom based on slave-grown sugar, this Spanish colony only 90 miles from American shores had nearly 400,000 slaves in 1850—more than any American state except Virginia. President Polk, his appetite for terri-

> "*I want Cuba, and I know that sooner or later we must have it. I want Tamaulipas, Potosi, and one or two other Mexican States: and I want them all for the same reason—for the planting and spreading of slavery.*"
>
> **SENATOR ALBERT G. BROWN, MISSISSIPPI**
> *1858*

tory not yet sated by the acquisition of Texas, Oregon, and half of Mexico, offered Spain $100 million for Cuba in 1848. The Spanish foreign minister spurned the offer, stating that he would rather see the island sunk in the sea than sold.

If money did not work, revolution might. Cuban planters, restive under Spanish rule, intrigued with American expansionists in the hope of fomenting an uprising on the island. Their leader was Narciso López, a Venezuelan-born Cuban soldier-of-fortune. In 1849 López recruited several hundred American adventurers for the first "filibustering" expedition against Cuba (from the Spanish *filibustero*, a freebooter or pirate). When President Taylor ordered the navy to prevent López's ships from leaving New York, López shifted his operations to the friendlier environs of New Orleans, where he raised a new force of filibusters, many of them Mexican War veterans. Port officials in New Orleans looked the other way when the expedition sailed in May 1850, but Spanish troops drove the filibusters into the sea after they had established a beachhead in Cuba.

Undaunted, López escaped and returned to a hero's welcome in the South, where he raised men and money for a third try in 1851. This time, William Crittenden of Kentucky, nephew of the U.S. attorney general, commanded the 420 Americans in the expedition. But the invasion ended in fiasco and tragedy. Spanish soldiers suppressed a local uprising timed to coincide with the invasion and then defeated the filibusters, killing 200 and capturing the rest. López was garroted in the public square of Havana, after which 50 American prisoners, including Crittenden, were lined up and executed by firing squad.

These events dampened southerners' enthusiasm for Cuba, but only for a time. "Cuba must be ours," declared Jefferson Davis, in order to "increase the number of slaveholding constituencies." A southern pamphleteer explained that "the Pearl of the West Indies, with her thirteen or fifteen representatives in Congress, would be a powerful auxiliary to the South." In 1852 the Democrats nominated Franklin Pierce of New Hampshire for president. Though a Yankee, Pierce had a reputation as a "doughface"—a northern man with southern principles. And, indeed, southern Democrats were delighted with his nomination. Pierce was "as reliable as Calhoun himself," wrote one, while another said that "a nomination so favorable to the South had not been anticipated." Especially gratifying was Pierce's support for annexing Cuba, which he made one of the top priorities of his new administration after winning a landslide victory over a demoralized Whig Party weakened by schism between its northern and southern wings.

Pierce covertly encouraged a new filibustering expedition to Cuba. This one was to be led by former Governor John Quitman of Mississippi. While Quitman was recruiting thousands of volunteers, southerners in Congress introduced a resolution to suspend the neutrality law that prohibited American interference in the internal affairs of other countries. But, at the last moment, Pierce backed off, fearful of political damage in the North if his administration became openly identified with filibustering. The Quitman expedition never sailed.

Pierce again tried to buy Cuba, instructing the American minister in Madrid to offer Spain $130 million. The minister was Pierre Soulé, a flamboyant Louisianian who managed to alienate most Spaniards by his clumsy intriguing. Soulé's crowning act came in October 1854 at a meeting with the American ministers to Britain and France in Ostend, Belgium. He persuaded them to sign what came to be known as the Ostend Manifesto. "Cuba is as necessary to the North American republic as any of its present . . . family of states," declared this document. If Spain persisted in refusing to sell, then "by every law, human and divine, we shall be justified in wresting it from Spain."

This "manifesto of the brigands," as antislavery Americans called it, caused an international uproar. The administration repudiated the Ostend Manifesto

and recalled Soulé. Nevertheless, acquisition of Cuba remained an objective of the Democratic Party. The issue played a role in both the 1860 presidential election and the secession controversy during 1860 and 1861. Meanwhile, American filibustering shifted its focus 750 miles south of Havana to Nicaragua. There, the most remarkable of the *filibusteros*, William Walker, had proclaimed himself president and had restored the institution of slavery.

THE GRAY-EYED MAN OF DESTINY

A native of Tennessee and a brilliant, restless man, Walker had earned a medical degree from the University of Pennsylvania and had studied and practiced law in New Orleans before joining the 1849 rush to California. Weighing less than 120 pounds, Walker seemed an unlikely fighter or leader of men. But he fought three duels, and his luminous eyes, which seemed to transfix his fellows, won him the sobriquet "gray-eyed man of destiny."

Walker found his true calling in filibustering. At the time, numerous raids were taking place back and forth across the border with Mexico, some of them staged to seize more of that country for the United States. In 1853 Walker led a ragged "army" of footloose forty-niners into Baja California and Sonora and declared the region an independent republic. Exhaustion and desertion depleted his troops, however, and the Mexicans drove the survivors back to California.

Walker decided to try again, with another goal. Many southerners eyed Nicaragua's potential for growing cotton, sugar, coffee, and other crops. The unstable Nicaraguan government offered a tempting target. In 1854 Walker signed a contract with rebel leaders in the civil war of the moment. The following spring, he led an advance guard of filibusters to Nicaragua and proclaimed himself commander in chief of the rebel forces. At the head of 2,000 American soldiers, he gained control of the country and named himself president in 1856. The Pierce administration extended diplomatic recognition to Walker's regime.

But things soon turned sour. The other Central American republics formed an alliance to invade Nicaragua and overthrow Walker. To win greater support from the southern states, Walker issued a decree in September 1856 reinstituting slavery in Nicaragua. A convention of southern economic promoters meeting in Savannah praised Walker's efforts "to introduce civilization in the States of Central America, and to develop these rich and productive regions by slave labor." Boatloads of new recruits arrived in Nicaragua from New Orleans. But in the spring of 1857 they succumbed to disease and to the Central American armies.

Walker escaped to New Orleans, where he was welcomed as a hero. He had no trouble recruiting men for another attempt, but the navy stopped him in November 1857. Southern congressmen condemned the naval commander and encouraged Walker to try again. He did, in December 1858, after a New Orleans jury refused to convict him of violating the neutrality law. On this third expedition, Walker's ship struck a reef and sank. Undaunted, he tried yet again. He wrote a book to raise funds for another invasion of Nicaragua, urging "the hearts of Southern youth to answer the call of honor. . . . The true field for the expansion of slavery is in tropical America." A few more southern youths answered the call, but they were stopped in Honduras. There, on September 12, 1860, the gray-eyed man met his destiny before a firing squad.

CONCLUSION

Within the three-year period from 1845 to 1848 the annexation of Texas, the settlement of the Oregon boundary dispute with Britain, and the acquisition by force of New Mexico and California from Mexico added 1,150,000 square miles to the United States. This expansion was America's "manifest destiny," according to Senator Stephen A. Douglas of Illinois. "Increase, and multiply, and expand, is the law of this nation's existence," proclaimed Douglas. "You cannot limit this great republic by mere boundary lines. Any one of you gentlemen might as well say to a son twelve years old that he is big enough, and must not grow any larger, and in order to prevent his growth put a hoop around him and keep him to his present size. Either the hoop must burst and be rent asunder, or the child must die. So it would be with this great nation."

But other Americans feared that the country could not absorb such rapid growth without strains that might break it apart. At the outbreak of the war with Mexico, Ralph Waldo Emerson predicted that "the United States will conquer Mexico, but it will be as the man swallows the arsenic, which brings him down in turn. Mexico will poison us."

Emerson proved correct. The poison was the reopening of the question of slavery's expansion, which had supposedly been settled by the Missouri Compromise in 1820. The admission of Texas as a huge new slave state and the possibility that more slave states might be carved out of the territory acquired from Mexico provoked northern congressmen to pass the Wilmot Proviso. Southerners bristled at this attempt to prevent the further expansion of slavery. Threats of secession and civil war poisoned the atmosphere in 1849 and 1850.

The Compromise of 1850 defused the crisis and appeared to settle the issue once again. But events would soon prove that this "compromise" had merely postponed the crisis. The fugitive slave issue and filibustering expeditions to acquire more slave territory kept sectional controversies smoldering. In 1854 the Kansas-Nebraska Act would cause them to burst into a hotter flame than ever.

Suggested Readings begin on page SR-1.
For Web activities and resources
related to this chapter, go to http://
www.harcourtcollege.com/history/murrin

CHAPTER 14

THE GATHERING TEMPEST, 1853–1860

THE 9:45 ACCOMMODATION

The railroad shrank distances and transformed the landscape in antebellum America. The arrival of a train brought much of a town's population to the station to gape at the iron horse belching smoke and sparks like a legendary dragon of old. By 1860, 31,000 miles of railroad track crisscrossed the United States, more than in all of Europe combined.

The wounds caused by the 1850 battle over slavery in the territories had barely healed when they were reopened. This time the strife concerned the question of slavery in the Louisiana Purchase territory, an issue presumably settled 34 years earlier by the Missouri Compromise of 1820. The Compromise of 1820 had admitted Missouri as a slave state but had banned slavery from the rest of the Purchase north of 36°30´. Senator Stephen Douglas, in search of southern support for organizing Kansas and Nebraska as territories, consented to the repeal of this provision of the Missouri Compromise. Northern outrage at this repudiation of a "sacred contract" killed the Whig Party and gave birth to the antislavery Republican Party. In 1857 the Supreme Court added insult to injury with the Dred Scott decision, which denied Congress the power to restrict slavery from the territories. The ominous reorientation of national politics along sectional lines was accompanied by a bloody civil war in Kansas and a raid on the federal arsenal at Harpers Ferry by John Brown and his followers.

This chapter will focus on the following major questions:

- Why did the Whig party die, and why did the Republican rather than the American party emerge as the new majority party in the North?
- What were the origins of Nativism and how did this movement relate to the slavery issue?
- How did economic developments in the 1840s and 1850s widen the breach between North and South?
- What were the "free-labor ideology" and "herrenvolk democracy"? How did these concepts relate to the politics of the 1850s?

KANSAS AND THE RISE OF THE REPUBLICAN PARTY

By 1853 land-hungry settlers had pushed up the Missouri River to its confluence with the Kansas and Platte rivers, and entrepreneurs were talking about a railroad across the continent to San Francisco. But settlement of the country west of Missouri and land surveys for a railroad through it would require its organization as a territory. Accordingly, in 1853 the House passed a bill creating the Nebraska Territory, embracing the area north of Indian Territory (present-day Oklahoma) up to the Canadian border. But the House bill ran into trouble in the Senate. Under the Missouri

Compromise, slavery would be excluded from the new territory. Having lost California, the proslavery forces were determined to salvage something from Nebraska. Missourians were particularly adamant, because a free Nebraska would leave them surrounded on three sides by free soil. "This species of property" (slaves), explained a St. Louis newspaper, "would become insecure, if not valueless in Missouri." Senator David R. Atchison of Missouri vowed to see Nebraska "sink in hell" before having it become free soil.

As president pro tem of the Senate, Atchison wielded great influence. A profane, gregarious man, he had inherited Calhoun's mantle as leader of the southern-rights faction. In the 1853–54 session of Congress, he kept raising the asking price for southern support of a bill to organize the Nebraska Territory.

The sponsor of the Senate bill was Stephen A. Douglas, chairman of the Senate Committee on Territories. Only five feet four inches tall, Douglas had earned the nickname "Little Giant" for his parliamentary skill, which he had demonstrated most dramatically in helping pass the Compromise of 1850 through Congress. In Douglas's opinion, the application of popular sovereignty to the slavery question in New Mexico and Utah had been the centerpiece of the compromise. The initial draft of his Nebraska bill merely repeated the language used for those territories, specifying that when any portion of the Nebraska Territory came in as a state, it could do so "with or without slavery, as its constitution may provide."

This was not good enough for Atchison and his southern colleagues. After talking with them, Douglas announced that because of a "clerical error," a provision calling for the territorial legislature to decide on slavery had been omitted from the draft. But Atchison raised the price once again, insisting on an explicit repeal of the Missouri Compromise. Sighing that this "will raise a hell of a storm," Douglas nevertheless agreed. He further agreed to divide the area in question into two territories: Kansas west of Missouri, and Nebraska west of Iowa and Minnesota. To many northerners this looked suspiciously like a scheme to mark Kansas out for slavery and Nebraska for freedom. Douglas then joined Jefferson Davis, Atchison, and other southern senators on a visit to the White House,

STEPHEN A. DOUGLAS The Little Giant began his meteoric rise to leadership of the Democratic Party with his successful effort to have the Compromise of 1850 enacted by Congress. Having forestalled sectional schism in 1850, he drove a wedge more deeply than ever between North and South with the Kansas-Nebraska bill of 1854. Six years later, Douglas became a victim of sectional schism when the Democratic Party split into northern and southern factions and thereby ruined his chance of winning the presidency.

where they twisted President Pierce's arm to give the revised Kansas-Nebraska bill the administration's support and to make its approval "a test of [Democratic] party orthodoxy."

THE KANSAS-NEBRASKA ACT

The bill did indeed raise a hell of a storm. Contemporaries and historians have speculated endlessly on Douglas's motives. Some thought he wanted to win southern support for the presidential nomination in 1856. Perhaps, but he risked losing northern support. Others point out that Douglas's real estate holdings in Illinois would have risen in value if a transcontinental railroad were to traverse the Nebraska Territory, and that southern opposition could block this route. The most likely reason, however, was Douglas's passionate belief in Manifest Destiny, in filling up the continent with American settlers and institutions. "The tide of immigration and civilization must be permitted to roll onward," he proclaimed. For this, he was willing to pay the South's price for support of his Kansas-Nebraska bill. And despite his earlier "weather forecast," he clearly underestimated the fury of the storm that erupted. He failed to recognize the depth of northern opposition to the "slave power" and to the expansion of slavery. Douglas himself had no firm moral convictions about slavery. He said that he cared not whether the settlers voted slavery up or down; the important thing was to give them a chance to vote.

But millions of Americans did care. They regarded the expansion of slavery as a national question, too important to be left to territorial voters. One of them was an old acquaintance of Douglas, Abraham Lincoln. An antislavery Whig who had served several terms in the Illinois legislature and one term in Congress, Lincoln was propelled back into politics by the shock of the Kansas-Nebraska bill. He acknowledged the constitutional right to hold slave property in the states where it already existed, but he believed slavery was "an unqualified evil to the negro, the white man, and to the state. . . . There can be no moral right in connection with one man's making a slave of another." Lincoln admitted he did not know how to bring this deeply entrenched institution to an end. He understood that race prejudice was a powerful obstacle to emancipation. Still, the country must face up to the problem. It must stop any further expansion of slavery as the first step on the long road to its "ultimate extinction."

Lincoln excoriated Douglas's "care not" attitude toward whether slavery was voted up or down: "I can not but hate" this "*declared* indifference, but as I must think, covert *real* zeal for the spread of" slavery. The assertion that slavery would never be imported into Kansas anyway, because of the region's unsuitable climate, Lincoln branded as a "LULLABY argument." The climate of eastern Kansas was similar to

CHRONOLOGY

1852	Plenary Council of Catholic Church seeks tax support for parochial schools
1853	American Party emerges
1854	Crimean War begins • Congress passes Kansas-Nebraska Act • Republican Party organized • Antebellum immigration reaches peak
1855	Ethnic riots in several cities • "Border Ruffian" legislature in Kansas legalizes slavery
1856	Civil war in Kansas • Preston Brooks canes Charles Sumner on Senate floor • Crimean War ends • Buchanan wins three-way presidential election
1857	Supreme Court issues Dred Scott decision • Lecompton constitution written in Kansas • Congress enacts lower tariff • Panic of 1857 • Helper's Impending Crisis published
1858	Kansas voters reject Lecompton constitution • Lincoln-Douglas debates
1859	Congress defeats federal slave code for territories • John Brown's raid at Harpers Ferry
1860	Shoemakers' strike in New England • Buchanan vetoes Homestead Act

that of the Missouri River Valley in Missouri, where slaves were busily raising hemp and tobacco. Missouri slaveholders were already poised to take their slaves into the Kansas River valley. "Climate will not . . . keep slavery out of these territories," said Lincoln. "Nothing in *nature* will." Many of the founding fathers had looked forward to the day when slavery would no longer exist in republican America. Instead, the United States had become the world's largest slaveholding society, and Douglas's bill would permit slavery to expand even further.

The monstrous injustice of slavery [said Lincoln] deprives our republican example of its just influence in the world—enables the enemies of free institutions, with plausibility, to taunt us as hypocrites. . . . Let us re-adopt the Declaration of Independence, and with it, the practices, and policy, which harmonize with it. . . . If we do this, we shall not only have saved the Union; but we shall have so saved it, as to make, and to keep it, forever worthy of the saving.

Abe Lincoln in Illinois (1940)
Directed by John Cromwell. Starring Raymond Massey (Abraham Lincoln), Gene Lockhard (Stephen Douglas), Ruth Gordon (Mary Todd Lincoln).

Raymond Massey's portrayal of Abraham Lincoln in Robert Sherwood's Broadway play, which opened in 1938 and was made into a movie in 1940, launched this Canadian-born actor as the image and voice of Lincoln on stage, screen, and radio for a generation. Indeed, more people saw or heard Massey as Lincoln than ever saw or heard the real Lincoln. Perhaps that was appropriate, for Sherwood's Lincoln spoke more to the generation of World War II than to the generation of the Civil War.

In one of the film's most dramatic scenes of the Lincoln-Douglas debates, Massey/Lincoln delivers a speech against slavery that applied equally to Fascist totalitarianism and defended democracy in language resonant with the four freedoms that the Allies fought for in World War II. In an interview, Massey said that "If you substitute the word *dictatorship* for the word *slavery* throughout Sherwood's script, it becomes electric for our time." In the final scene, as Lincoln departs from Springfield to take up the burdens of the presidency, Massey's Lincoln sees beyond the challenge of disunion to the challenge to democracy in a world at war.

Sherwood skillfully wove together Lincoln's words with his own script to portray Lincoln's growth from the gawky youth of 1831 to the champion of freedom and democracy in 1861. Sherwood took many liberties—what scriptwriter does not? He combined bits and pieces of several Lincoln speeches into one; he invented incidents and wrenched chronology in some of the twelve scenes from these thirty years of Lincoln's life.

Perhaps the film's sharpest departure from reality is the tension it depicts between "politics," which is bad, and "democracy," which is good. Sherwood's Lincoln doesn't want to play the dirty game of politics; early in the film the homespun youth declares: "I don't want to be no politician." It is Mary Todd Lincoln who is ambitious for her husband and pushes a reluctant Abraham toward his destiny. The real

Lincoln, of course, loved the game of politics and played it masterfully. He was also as ambitious in his own right as Mary was for him; Lincoln's law partner William Herndon said that Abraham's ambition was "a little engine that knew no rest."

Sherwood's Lincoln who transcends politics to become a great statesman could not have existed without the real Lincoln, the ambitious politician.

Raymond Massey as the 23-year-old Abraham Lincoln just elected captain of a New Salem militia company in the Black Hawk War of 1832.

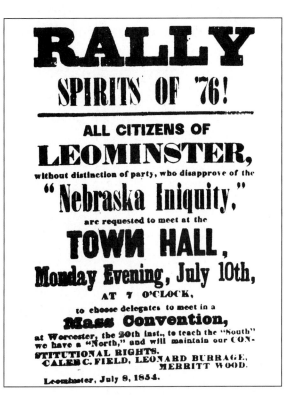

BIRTH OF THE REPUBLICAN PARTY The Kansas-Nebraska Act galvanized antislavery northerners of all parties into new "anti-Nebraska" organizations opposed to the repeal of the Missouri Compromise's ban on slavery in Louisiana Purchase territories north of 36°30′. Appealing to the "spirit of '76," these organizations coalesced into the Republican Party, which held its first convention at Pittsburgh on Washington's birthday in 1856 to organize a national party in preparation for the presidential nominating convention later that year.

With these eloquent words, Lincoln voiced the feelings that fostered an uprising against the Kansas-Nebraska bill. Abolitionists, Free-Soilers, northern Whigs, and even many northern Democrats held impassioned meetings to form "anti-Nebraska" coalitions, but could not stop passage of the bill. It cleared the Senate easily, supported by a solid South and 15 of the 20 northern Democrats. In the House, where all the northern Democrats would have to face the voters in the fall elections, the Pierce administration and the Democratic leadership still managed to wield the whip of patronage and party pressure and force half of them to vote for the bill, which passed by a vote of 113 to 100.

DEATH OF THE WHIG PARTY

These proceedings completed the destruction of the Whigs as a national party. Southern Whigs had been disappearing ever since Zachary Taylor had "betrayed" them on the issue of a free California. After the presidential election of 1852, few Whigs remained in the cotton South. In that year, the Whig Party nominated General Winfield Scott for president. Though a Virginian, Scott, like Taylor, took a national rather than a southern view. He was the candidate of the northern Whigs in the national convention, which nominated him on the 53rd ballot after a bitter contest between the northern and southern wings of the party. A mass exodus of southern Whigs into the Democratic Party enabled Franklin Pierce to carry all but two slave states in the election. The unanimous vote of northern Whigs in Congress against the Kansas-Nebraska bill was the final straw. The Whig Party never recovered its influence in the South.

Whig strength seemed to be on its last legs in the North as well. Antislavery Whig leaders such as Seward and Lincoln hoped to channel the flood of anti-Nebraska sentiment through the Whig Party, an effort akin to containing Niagara Falls. Free-Soilers and antislavery Democrats spurned the Whig label. Political coalitions arose spontaneously in the North under various names: Anti-Nebraska; Fusion; People's; Independent. The name that caught on evoked memories of America's first fight for freedom in 1776: Republican. The first use of this name seems to have occurred at an anti-Nebraska rally in a Congregational church at Ripon, Wisconsin, in May 1854. Soon, most of the congressional candidates fielded by anti-Nebraska coalitions ran their campaigns under the Republican banner.

The 1854 elections were disastrous for northern Democrats. One-fourth of Democratic voters deserted the party. The Democrats lost control of the House of Representatives when 66 of 91 incumbent free-state Democratic congressmen (including 37 of the 44 who had voted for the Kansas-Nebraska bill) went down to defeat. Combined with the increase in the number of Democratic congressmen from the South, where the party had picked up the pieces of the shattered Whig organization, this rout brought the party more than ever under southern domination.

But who would pick up the pieces of old parties in the North? The new Republican Party hoped to, but it suffered a shock in urban areas of the Northeast. Hostility to immigrants created a tidal wave of nativism that threatened to swamp the anti-Nebraska movement. "Nearly everybody appears to have gone deranged on Nativism," reported a Pennsylvania Democrat, while a Whig in upstate New York warned that his district was "very badly infected with Knownothingism." Described as a "tornado," a "hurricane," a "freak of political insanity," the "Know-Nothings" won landslide victories in Massachusetts and Delaware, polled an estimated 40 percent of the vote in Pennsylvania, and did well elsewhere in the Northeast and border states. Who were these mysterious Know-Nothings? What did they stand for? What part did they play in the political upheaval of 1854?

IMMIGRATION AND NATIVISM

During the early 19th century, immigration was less pronounced than in most other periods of U.S. history. The volume of immigration (expressed as the number of immigrants during a decade in proportion to the whole population at its beginning) was little more than 1 percent in the 1820s, increasing to 4 percent in the 1830s. Three-quarters of the newcomers were Protestants, mainly from Britain. Most of them were skilled workers, farmers, or members of white-collar occupations.

In the 1840s a combination of factors abruptly quadrupled the volume of immigration and changed its ethnic and occupational makeup. The pressure of expanding population on limited land in Germany and successive failures of the potato crop in Ireland impelled millions of German and Irish peasants to emigrate. A majority came to the United States, where recovery from the depression of the early 1840s brought an economic boom with its insatiable demand for labor. During the decade after 1845, three million immigrants entered the United States—15 percent of the total American population in 1845, the highest proportional volume of immigration in American history. Many of them, especially the Irish, joined the unskilled and semiskilled labor force in the rapidly growing eastern cities and in the construction of railroads that proliferated to all points of the compass.

IMMIGRATION TO THE UNITED STATES

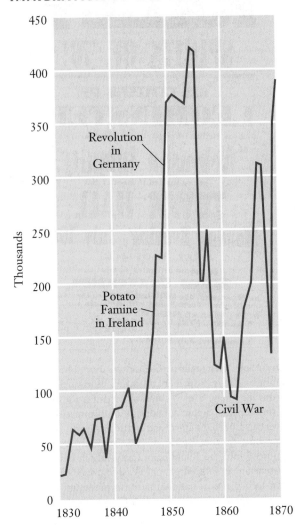

Source: From *Division and the Stresses of Reunion 1845–1876*, by David M. Potter. Copyright © 1973 Scott, Foresman and Company. Reprinted by permission.

Most of them were also Roman Catholics. Anti-Catholicism had centuries-deep roots in Anglo-American Protestantism. Fear of the pope and of the Roman Church as autocratic and antirepublican was never far from the surface of American political culture, and scurrilous anti-Catholic literature circulated during the 1830s. Several ethnic riots between Protestant and Catholic workers over the years culminated in pitched battles and numerous deaths in Philadelphia in 1844. Short-lived nativist political parties that sprang up in several eastern cities in the early 1840s called for curbing the political rights of immigrants. Some of the "nativists" were actually immigrants from Britain and Northern Ireland who brought their anti-Catholicism with them.

Nativism appeared to subside with the revival of prosperity after 1844, but the decline was temporary, as the vast increase of immigration proved too much for the country to absorb. Not only were most of the new immigrants Catholics; many of them also spoke a foreign language and had alien cultural values. The temperance crusade had sharply curtailed drinking among native-born Protestants but had made little impact on the Irish and Germans, much of whose social and political life revolved around taverns and beer parlors (see chapter 11). Established Americans perceived more recent arrivals as responsible for an increase of crime and poverty in the cities. Cincinnati's overall crime rate tripled between 1846 and 1853; its murder rate increased sevenfold. Boston's expenditures for poor relief tripled during the same period.

IMMIGRANTS IN POLITICS

The political power of immigrants also grew. In Boston, for example, the number of foreign-born voters (mostly Irish) increased by 200 percent from 1850 to 1855, whereas the number of native-born voters grew by only 14 percent. Most of the immigrants became Democrats, because that party welcomed or at least tolerated them and many Whigs did not. Foreign-born voters leaned toward the proslavery wing of the Democratic Party, even though seven-eighths of them settled in free states. Mostly working-class and poor, they rubbed shoulders against the small northern black population; Irish American mobs sometimes attacked black neighborhoods and rioted against black workers. They supported the Democratic Party as the best means of keeping blacks in slavery and out of the North. These attitudes sparked hostility toward immigrants among many antislavery people, some of whom equated slavery with Catholicism as a backward, despotic, repressive institution.

The Roman Catholic hierarchy did little to allay that hostility. Pope Pius IX (1846–78) led the Church into a period of reaction against secular liberalism. The Church sided with the counter-

"KNOW-NOTHING" This idealized portrait of a native-born, clean-featured American "citizen" symbolized the opposition to foreign-born voters, especially Irish Catholics, whom the Know-Nothings feared as threats to Protestant American values and institutions.

revolutionary forces that crushed the European uprisings of 1848, which sought greater political and social democracy. In the United States the leading Catholic prelate, Archbishop John Hughes of New York, taking his cue from the pope, attacked abolitionists, Free-Soilers, and various Protestant reform movements as akin to the "Red Republicanism" of Europe. In 1850, in a widely publicized address titled "The Decline of Protestantism and Its Causes," Hughes noted proudly that Catholic Church membership in the United States had grown three times faster than Protestant membership over the previous decade, and he predicted an eventual Catholic majority. "Protestantism is effete, powerless, dying out . . . and conscious that its last moment is come when it is fairly set, face to face, with Catholic truth."

Attitudes toward immigrants had political repercussions. Two of the hottest issues in state and local politics during the early 1850s were temperance and schools. The temperance crusaders had grown confident and aggressive enough to go into politics. The drunkenness and rowdiness they associated with Irish immigrants became one of their particular targets. Beginning with Maine in 1851, 12 states had enacted prohibition laws by 1855. Though several of the laws were soon weakened by the courts or repealed by legislatures, they exacerbated ethnic tensions.

So did battles over public schools versus parochial schools. Catholics resented the Protestant domination of public education and the reading of the King James Bible in schools. Archbishop Hughes flayed the public schools as purveyors of "Socialism, Red Republicanism, Universalism, Infidelity, Deism, Atheism, and Pantheism." The Church began to build parochial schools for the faithful, and in 1852 the first Plenary Council of American bishops decided to seek tax support for these schools or tax relief for Catholic parents who sent their children to them. This effort set off heated election contests in numerous northern cities and states. "Free school" tickets generally won by promising to defend public schools against the "bold effort" of this "despotic faith" to "uproot the tree of Liberty."

THE RISE OF THE "KNOW-NOTHINGS"

It was in this context that the Know-Nothings (their formal name was the American Party) burst onto the political scene. This party was the result of the merger in 1852 of two secret fraternal societies that limited their membership to native-born Protestants: the Order of the Star-Spangled Banner

KNOW-NOTHINGS ON ELECTION DAY In Baltimore, nativist political clubs called "Blood Tubs" and "Plug-Uglies" patrolled the streets at election time to intimidate foreign-born voters. An election riot in 1854 left 17 dead in Baltimore; similar riots in St. Louis and Louisville also resulted in many deaths. This cartoon satirizes Baltimore's Know-Nothing street gangs.

and the Order of United Americans. Recruiting mainly young men in skilled blue-collar and lower white-collar occupations, the merged Order had a membership of one million or more by 1854. The Order supported temperance and opposed tax support for parochial schools. They wanted public office restricted to native-born men and sought to lengthen the naturalization period before immigrants could become citizens and voters from 5 to 21 years. Members were pledged to secrecy about the Order; if asked, they were to reply "I know nothing."

This movement swept through the Northeast in the 1854 elections, doing to the Whig Party in the Northeast what the slavery issue had done to it in the South. Although the American Party drew voters from both major parties, it cut more heavily into the Whig constituency. As a cultural force, nativism had found a more congenial home in the Whig Party than in the Democratic Party. When the American Party raised its banner in 1854, many northern Whigs who had not already gone over to the Republicans flocked to the Know-Nothings.

When the dust of the 1854 elections settled, it was clear that those who opposed the Democrats would control the next House of Representatives. But who would control the opposition—antislavery Republicans or nativist Americans? In truth, some northern voters and the congressmen they elected adhered to both political faiths. A Know-Nothing convention in Massachusetts resolved that "there can exist no real hostility to Roman Catholicism which does not also abhor slavery." In New England, several Know-Nothing leaders were actually Republicans in disguise who had jumped on the nativist bandwagon with the intention of steering it in an antislavery direction.

Many Republicans, however, warned against flirting with religious bigotry. "How can any one who abhors the oppression of negroes, be in favor of degrading classes of white people?" asked Abraham Lincoln in a letter to a friend.

> As a nation, we began by declaring that "all men are created equal." We now practically read it "all men are created equal, except negroes." When the Know Nothings get control, it will read "all men are created equal, except negroes, and foreigners, and catholics." When it comes to this I should prefer emigrating to some country where they make no pretense of loving liberty—to Russia, for instance, where despotism can be taken pure, and without the base alloy of hypocrisy.

Other Republicans echoed Lincoln. Since "we are against Black Slavery, because the slaves are deprived of human rights," they declared, "we are also against . . . [this] system of Northern Slavery to be created by disfranchising the Irish and Germans." Many Republicans also considered nativism a red herring that distracted people's attention from the true danger confronting the country. "Neither the Pope nor the foreigners ever can govern the country or endanger its liberties," wrote the managing editor of the *New York Tribune*, "but the slavebreeders and slavetraders do govern it."

THE DECLINE OF NATIVISM

In 1855 Republican leaders maneuvered skillfully to divert the energies of northern Know-Nothings from their crusade against the pope to a crusade against the slave power. Two developments helped them. The first was turmoil in Kansas, which convinced many northerners that the slave power was indeed a greater threat than the pope. The second was a significant shift southward in the center of nativist gravity. The American Party continued to do well in off-year elections in New England during 1855, but it also won elections in Maryland, Kentucky, and Tennessee and polled at least 45 percent of the votes in five other southern states. Violence in several southern cities with large immigrant populations preceded or accompanied these elections. Riots left 10 dead in St. Louis, 17 in Baltimore, and 22 in Louisville, showing a significant streak of nativism in the South. But the American Party's success there probably owed a great deal to the search by former Whigs for a new political home outside the Democratic Party. Areas of American Party strength in seven or eight southern states more or less coincided with areas of former Whig strength.

These developments had important implications at the national level. Southern Know-Nothings were proslavery, whereas many of their Yankee counterparts were antislavery. Similar to the national Whig Party, so did the American Party founder on the slavery issue during 1855 and 1856. At the party's first national council in June 1855, most of the northern delegates walked out when southerners and northern conservatives joined forces to pass a resolution endorsing the Kansas-Nebraska Act. A similar scene occurred at an American Party convention in 1856. By that time, most northern members of the party had, in effect, become Republicans. When the House of Representatives elected in 1854 convened in December 1855, a protracted fight for the speakership again took place. The Republican candidate was Nathaniel P. Banks of Massachusetts, a former Know-Nothing who now considered himself a Republican. Banks finally won on the 133rd ballot with the support of about 30 Know-Nothings who thereby declared themselves Republicans. This marriage was consummated in the summer of 1856 when the "North Americans" endorsed the Republican candidate for president.

By that time, nativism had faded. The volume of immigration suddenly dropped by more than half in 1855 and stayed low for the next several years.

Ethnic tensions eased, and cultural issues such as temperance and schools receded. Although the Republican Party took on some of the cultural baggage of nativism when it absorbed many northern Know-Nothings, party leaders shoved the baggage into dark corners. The real conflict was not the struggle between native and immigrant, or between Protestant and Catholic, but between North and South over the extension of slavery. That conflict led to civil war—and the war seemed already to have begun in the territory of Kansas.

BLEEDING KANSAS

When it became clear that southerners had the votes to pass the Kansas-Nebraska Act, William H. Seward stood up in the Senate and told his southern colleagues: "Since there is no escaping your

LINK TO THE PAST

The 1850s: An Increasingly Divided Union

http://nac.gmu.edu/mmts/50proto.html

This site focuses on the big issues that polarized North and South in the 1850s: the Fugitive Slave Law, filibustering, the Kansas-Nebraska Act and Bleeding Kansas, the Dred Scott decision, Lecompton, the John Brown raid, the rise of the Republican party, and related matters. The emphasis is on promoting thinking skills to analyze the impact of these events and their interrelationships. It is a multimedia approach: newspapers, speeches, photographs, music, maps, reenactments, and narrative text.

Choose one or more of the following events or issues and describe the role of selected individuals with respect to this event or issue.

1. The Compromise of 1850: Stephen A. Douglas, William H. Seward, John C. Calhoun

2. The Fugitive Slave Law: Millard Fillmore, Frederick Douglass, Theodore Parker

3. The Kansas-Nebraska Act: Franklin Pierce, Jefferson Davis, Abraham Lincoln

4. Violence in Kansas: David R. Atchison, John Brown, James Buchanan

5. The Dred Scott Case: Dred Scott, Roger B. Taney, Benjamin R. Curtis

challenge, I accept it in behalf of the cause of free-dom. We will engage in competition for the virgin soil of Kansas, and God give victory to the side which is stronger in numbers as it is in right." Senator David Atchison of Missouri was ready for the expected influx of Free Soil settlers to the new Kansas Territory. "We are playing for a mighty stake," he wrote. "If we win we carry slavery to the Pacific Ocean; if we fail we lose Missouri, Arkansas, Texas and all the territories; the game must be played boldly."

Atchison did play boldly. At first, Missouri settlers in Kansas posted the stronger numbers. As the year 1854 progressed, however, settlers from the North came pouring in and the scramble for the best lands in Kansas intensified. Alarmed by the growing numbers of northern settlers, bands of Missourians,

labeled "border ruffians" by the Republican press, rode into Kansas prepared to vote as many times as necessary to install a proslavery government. In the fall of 1854 they cast at least 1,700 illegal ballots and sent a proslavery territorial delegate to Congress. The following spring, when the time came to elect a territorial legislature, even greater efforts were needed, for numerous Free Soil settlers had taken up claims during the winter. Atchison was equal to the task. He led a contingent of border ruffians to Kansas for the election. "There are eleven hundred coming over from Platte County to vote," he told his followers, "and if that ain't enough, we can send five thousand—enough to kill every God-damned abolitionist in the Territory."

His count was accurate. Nearly five thousand came—4,968 as determined by a congressional

FREE STATE MEN READY TO DEFEND LAWRENCE, KANSAS, IN 1856 After proslavery forces sacked the free-state capital of Lawrence in 1856, Northern settlers decided they needed more firepower to defend themselves. Somehow they got hold of a six-pound howitzer. This cannon did not fire a shot in anger during the Kansas troubles, but its existence may have deterred the "border ruffians."

investigation—and voted illegally to elect a proslavery territorial legislature. The territorial governor pleaded with President Pierce to nullify the election. Pierce instead listened to Atchison and fired the governor. Meanwhile, the new territorial legislature legalized slavery and adopted a slave code that even authorized the death penalty for helping a slave to escape.

The "free state" party, outraged by these proceedings, had no intention of obeying laws enacted by this "bogus legislature." By the fall of 1855 they constituted a majority of bona fide settlers in Kansas. They called a convention, adopted a free-state constitution, and elected their own legislature and governor. By January 1856, two territorial governments in Kansas stood with their hands at each other's throat.

Kansas now became the leading issue in national politics. The Democratic Senate and President Pierce recognized the proslavery legislature meeting in the town of Lecompton, while the Republican House of Representatives recognized the antislavery legislature in the town of Lawrence. Southerners saw the struggle as crucial to their future. "The admission of Kansas into the Union as a slave state is now a point of honor," wrote Congressman Preston Brooks of South Carolina. "The fate of the South is to be decided with the Kansas issue." On the other side, Charles Sumner of Massachusetts gave a well-publicized speech in the Senate on May 19 and 20 entitled "The Crime against Kansas." "Murderous robbers from Missouri," charged Sumner, "from the drunken spew and vomit of an uneasy civilization" had committed the "rape of a virgin territory, compelling it to the hateful embrace of slavery." Among the southern senators whom Sumner singled out for special condemnation and ridicule was Andrew

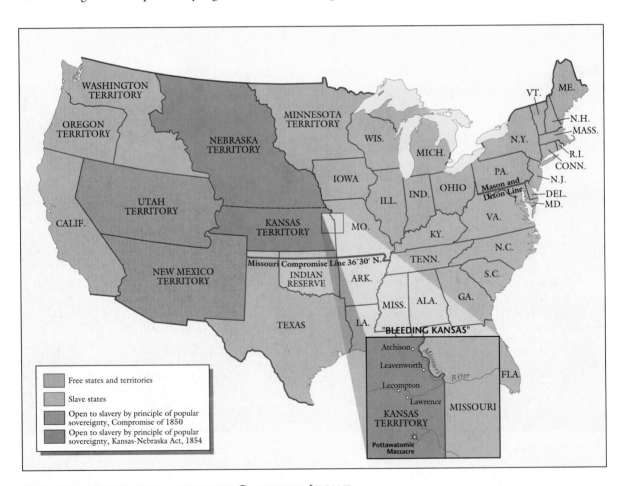

KANSAS-NEBRASKA AND THE SLAVERY ISSUE

Butler of South Carolina, a cousin of Congressman Brooks. Butler was a "Don Quixote," said Sumner, "who had chosen a mistress to whom he has made his vows . . . the harlot, Slavery."

THE CANING OF SUMNER

Sumner's speech incensed southerners, none more than Preston Brooks, who decided to avenge his cousin. He knew that Sumner would never accept a challenge to a duel. Anyway, dueling was for gentlemen, and even horsewhipping was too good for this Yankee blackguard. Two days after the speech, Brooks walked into the Senate chamber, and began beating Sumner with a heavy cane. His legs trapped beneath the desk bolted to the floor, Sumner wrenched it loose as he stood up to try to defend himself, whereupon Brooks clubbed him so ferociously that Sumner slumped forward, bloody and unconscious.

SOUTHERN CHIVALRY — ARGUMENT versus CLUB'S.

THE CANING OF SUMNER This drawing by an antislavery Northerner shows proslavery Congressman Preston Brooks of South Carolina beating Senator Charles Sumner of Massachusetts with a heavy cane on the floor of the Senate on May 22, 1856. It portrays the inability of the South to respond to the power of Northern arguments, symbolized by the pen in Sumner's right hand and a speech in his left hand, except with the unthinking power of the club. Note other Southern senators in the background smiling on the scene or preventing Northern senators from coming to Sumner's aid. The caning of Sumner was the worst of several instances of North-South violence or threatened violence on the floor of Congress in the 1850s, presaging the violence on the battlefields of the 1860s.

News of the incident sent a thrill of pride through the South and a rush of rage through the North. Charleston newspapers praised Brooks for "standing forth so nobly in defense of . . . the honor of South Carolinians." Brooks resigned from Congress after censure by the House and was unanimously reelected. From all over the South came gifts of new canes, some inscribed with such mottoes as "Hit Him Again" and "Use Knock-Down Arguments." But, in the North, the Republicans gained thousands of voters as a result of the affair. It seemed to prove their contentions about "the barbarism of slavery." "Has it come to this," asked the poet William Cullen Bryant, editor of the *New York Evening Post*, "that we must speak with bated breath in the presence of our Southern masters? . . . Are we to be chastised as they chastise their slaves?" A veteran New York politician reported that he had "never before seen anything at all like the present state of deep, determined, & desperate feelings of hatred, & hostility to the further extension of slavery, & its political power."

Republicans were soon able to add "Bleeding Kansas" to "Bleeding Sumner" in their repertory of winning issues. Even as Sumner was delivering his speech in Washington, an "army" of proslavery Missourians, complete with artillery, marched on the free-state capital of Lawrence, Kansas. On May 21 they shelled and sacked the town, burning several buildings. A rival force of free-state men arrived too late to intercept them. One of the free-state "captains" was John Brown, an abolitionist zealot who considered himself anointed by the Lord to avenge the sins of slaveholders. When he learned of the murder of several free-state settlers and the sack of Lawrence, he "went crazy—crazy," according to one of his followers. We must "fight fire with fire," Brown declared. "Something must be done to show these barbarians that we, too, have rights." Leading four of his sons and three other men to a proslavery settlement at Pottawatomie Creek on the night of May 24–25, 1856, Brown dragged five men from their cabins and split open their heads with broadswords.

Here was the Old Testament retribution of an eye for an eye. Brown's murderous act set off a veritable civil war in Kansas. One of Brown's sons was among the estimated 200 men killed in the bushwhackings and raids. Not until President

Pierce sent a tough new territorial governor and 1,300 federal troops to Kansas in September 1856 did the violence subside—just in time to save the Democrats from possible defeat in the presidential election.

THE ELECTION OF 1856

By 1856 the Republicans had become the largest party in the North. With the old Free-Soilers as their radical core, they had recruited about three-fourths of the former Whigs and one-fifth of the Democrats. They were also the first truly sectional party in American history, for they had little prospect of carrying a single county in the slave states. At their first national convention, the Republicans wrote a platform that focused mainly on that "relic of barbarism," slavery. The platform also incorporated the old Whig program of federal aid to internal improvements, including a railroad to California. For its presidential nominee, the party steered away from its most prominent leaders, who were identified with the old parties, and turned instead to John C. Frémont. This "Pathfinder of the West" had a dashing image as an explorer and for his role in the acquisition of California. With little political experience, he had few political enemies and his antislavery credentials were satisfactory.

The Democrats chose as their candidate James Buchanan, a veteran of 30 years in various public offices. He had been minister to Britain during the Kansas-Nebraska controversy and so was not tainted with its unpopularity in the North, as were Pierce and Douglas, the other aspirants for nomination. The Democratic platform endorsed popular sovereignty and condemned the Republicans as a "sectional party" that incited "treason and armed resistance in the Territories."

This would be a three-party election, for the American Party was still in the field. Having become mainly a way station for former southern Whigs, the party nominated ex-Whig Millard Fillmore. The three-party campaign sifted out into a pair of two-party contests: Democrats versus Americans in the South; Democrats versus Republicans in the North. Fillmore, despite a good showing of 44 percent of the popular vote in the South, carried only Maryland. Considering Buchanan colorless but safe, the rest of the South gave him three-fourths of the electoral votes he needed for victory.

The real excitement in this election showed itself in the North. For many Republicans the campaign was a moral cause, an evangelical crusade against the sin of slavery. Republican "Wide Awake" clubs marched in torchlight parades chanting "Free Soil, Free Speech, Free Men, Frémont!" A veteran politician in Indiana marveled: "Men, Women & Children all seemed to be out, with a kind of fervor I have never witnessed before in six Pres. Elections in which I have taken an active part." The turnout of eligible voters in the North was a remarkable 83 percent. One awestruck journalist, anticipating a Republican victory, wrote that "the process now going on in the United States is a *Revolution*."

Not quite. Although the Republicans swept New England and the upper parts of New York state and the Old Northwest—both settled by New Englanders, where evangelical and antislavery reform movements had taken hold—the contest in the lower North was close. Buchanan needed only to carry Pennsylvania and either Indiana or Illinois to win the presidency, and the campaign focused on those states. The immigrant and working-class voters of the eastern cities and the rural voters of the lower Midwest, descendants of upland southerners who had settled there, were antiblack and antiaboli-

POPULAR AND ELECTORAL VOTES IN THE 1856 PRESIDENTIAL ELECTION

Candidate	Free States		Slave States		Total	
	Popular	*Electoral*	*Popular*	*Electoral*	*Popular*	*Electoral*
Buchanan (Democrat)	1,227,000	62	607,000	112	1,833,000	174
Frémont (Republican)	1,338,000	114	0	0	1,338,000	114
Fillmore (American)	396,000	0	476,000	8	872,000	8

tionist in sentiment. They were ripe for Democratic propaganda that accused Republicans of favoring racial equality. "Black Republicans," declared an Ohio Democratic newspaper, intended to "turn loose . . . millions of negroes, to elbow you in the workshops, and compete with you in fields of honest labor." A Democrat in Pennsylvania told voters that "the one aim" of the Republicans was "to elevate the African race in this country to complete equality of political and economic condition with the white man." Indiana Democrats organized parades, with young girls in white dresses carrying banners inscribed "Fathers, save us from nigger husbands."

The Republicans in these areas denied that they favored racial equality. They insisted that the main reason for keeping slavery out of the territories was to enable white farmers and workers to make a living there without competition from black labor. But their denials were in vain. Support for the Republican Party by prominent black leaders, including Frederick Douglass, convinced hundreds of thousands of voters that the "Black Republicans"

Frémont (Republican)

Buchanan (Democrat)

Fillmore (American)

No returns, unsettled, etc.

COUNTIES CARRIED BY CANDIDATES IN THE 1856 PRESIDENTIAL ELECTION

were racial egalitarians. For the next two decades, that sentiment would be one of the most potent weapons in the Democratic arsenal.

In 1856, though, the charge that a Republican victory would destroy the Union was even more effective. Buchanan himself set the tone in his instructions to Democratic Party leaders: "The Black Republicans must be . . . boldly assailed as disunionists, and the charge must be re-iterated again and again." It was. And southerners helped the cause by threatening to secede if Frémont won. We "should not pause," said Senator James Mason of Virginia, "but proceed at once to 'immediate, absolute, and eternal separation.'" Fears of disruption caused many conservative ex-Whigs in the North to support Buchanan. Buchanan carried Pennsylvania, New Jersey, Indiana, Illinois, and California and won the presidency.

But southerners did not intend to let Buchanan forget that he owed his election mainly to the South. "Mr. Buchanan and the Northern Democracy are dependent on the South," wrote a Virginian after the election. "If we can succeed in Kansas . . . and add a little more slave territory, we may yet live free men under the Stars and Stripes."

THE DRED SCOTT CASE

The South took the offensive at the outset of the Buchanan administration. Its instrument was the Supreme Court, which had a majority of five justices from slave states led by Chief Justice Roger B. Taney of Maryland. Those justices saw the Dred Scott case as an opportunity to settle once and for all the question of slavery in the territories.

Dred Scott was a slave whose owner, an army surgeon, had kept him at military posts in Illinois and in Wisconsin Territory for several years before taking him back to Missouri. After the owner's death, Scott sued for his freedom on the grounds of his prolonged stay in Wisconsin Territory, where slavery had been outlawed by the Missouri Compromise. The case worked its way up from Missouri courts through a federal circuit court to the U.S. Supreme Court. There it began to attract attention as a test case of Congress's power to prohibit slavery in the territories.

The southern Supreme Court justices decided to declare that the Missouri Compromise ban on slavery in the territories was unconstitutional. To avoid the appearance of a purely sectional decision, they sought the concurrence of a northern Democratic justice, Robert Grier of Pennsylvania. President-elect Buchanan played an improper role by pressing his fellow Pennsylvanian to go along with the southern majority. Having obtained Justice Grier's concurrence, Chief Justice Taney issued the Court's ruling stating that Congress lacked the power to keep slavery out of a territory, because slaves were property and the Constitution protects the right of property. For good measure, Taney also wrote that the circuit court should not have accepted the Scott case in the first place because black men were not citizens of the United States and therefore had no standing in its courts. Five other justices wrote concurring opinions. The two non-Democratic northern justices (both former Whigs, one of them now a Republican) dissented vigorously. They stated that blacks were legal citizens in several northern states and were therefore citizens of the United States. To buttress their opinion that Congress could prohibit slavery in the territories, they cited Congress's Constitutional power to make "all needful rules and regulations" for the territories.

Modern scholars agree with the dissenters. In 1857, however, Taney had a majority, and his ruling became law. Modern scholars have also demonstrated that Taney was motivated by his passionate commitment "to southern life and values" and by his determination to stop "northern aggression" by cutting the ground from under the hated Republicans. His ruling that their program to exclude slavery from the territories was unconstitutional was designed to do just that.

Republicans denounced Taney's "jesuitical decision" as based on "gross perversion" of the Constitution. The *New York Tribune* sneered that the Dred Scott decision was "entitled to just as much moral weight as would be the judgment of a majority of those congregated in any Washington bar-room." Several Republican state legislatures resolved that the ruling was "not binding in law and conscience." They probably did not mean to advocate civil disobedience, but they did look forward to the election of a Republican president who could "reconstitute" the Court and secure a reversal of the decision. "The remedy," said the *Chicago*

Tribune, "is the ballot box. . . . Let the next President be Republican, and 1860 will mark an era kindred with that of 1776."

THE LECOMPTON CONSTITUTION

Instead of settling the slavery controversy, the Dred Scott decision intensified it. Meanwhile, proslavery advocates, having won legalization of slavery in the territories, moved to ensure that it would remain legal when Kansas became a state. That required deft maneuvering, because legitimate antislavery settlers outnumbered proslavery settlers by more than two to one. In 1857 the proslavery legislature (elected by the fraudulent votes of border ruffians two years earlier) called for a constitutional convention at Lecompton to prepare Kansas for statehood. Because the election for delegates was rigged, Free Soil voters refused to participate. One-fifth of the registered voters thereupon elected convention delegates, who met at Lecompton and wrote a state constitution that made slavery legal.

Then a nagging problem arose. Buchanan had promised that the Lecompton constitution would be presented to the voters in a fair referendum. The problem was how to pass the proslavery constitution given the antislavery majority of voters. The convention came up with an ingenious solution. Instead of a referendum on the whole constitution, it would allow the voters to choose between a constitution "with slavery" and one "with no slavery." The catch was that the constitution "with no slavery" guaranteed slave owners' "inviolable" right of property in the 200 slaves already in Kansas and their progeny. It also did nothing to prevent future smuggling of slaves across the 200-mile border with Missouri. Once in Kansas, they, too, would become "inviolable" property.

Free-state voters branded the referendum a farce and boycotted it. One-quarter of the eligible voters went to the polls in December 1857 and approved the constitution "with slavery." Meanwhile, in a fair election policed by federal troops, the antislavery party won control of the new territorial legislature and promptly submitted both constitutions to a referendum that was boycotted by proslavery voters. This time, 70 percent of the eligible voters went to the polls and overwhelmingly rejected both constitutions.

Which referendum would the federal government recognize? That question proved even more divisive than the Kansas-Nebraska debate four years earlier. President Buchanan faced a dilemma. He had promised a fair referendum. But southerners, who dominated both the Democratic Party and the administration (the vice president and four of the seven cabinet members were from slave states), threatened secession if Kansas was not admitted to statehood under the Lecompton constitution "with slavery." "If Kansas is *driven out of the Union for being a Slave State*," thundered Senator James Hammond of South Carolina, "can any Slave State remain in it with honor?" Buchanan caved in. He explained to a shocked northern Democrat that if he did not accept the Lecompton constitution, southern states would "secede from the Union or take up arms against us." Buchanan sent the Lecompton constitution to Congress with a message recommending statehood. Kansas, said the president, "is at this moment as much a slave state as Georgia or South Carolina."

What would Stephen Douglas do? If he endorsed the Lecompton constitution, he would undoubtedly be defeated in his bid for reelection to the Senate in 1858. And he regarded the Lecompton constitution as a travesty of popular sovereignty. He broke with the administration on the issue. He could not vote to "force this constitution down the throats of the people of Kansas," he told the Senate, "in opposition to their wishes and in violation of our pledges."

The fight in Congress was long and bitter. The South and the administration had the votes they needed in the Senate and won handily there, but the Democratic majority in the House was so small that the defection of even a few northern Democrats would defeat the Lecompton constitution. The House debate at one point got out of hand and a wild fistfight erupted between Republicans and southern Democrats. "There were some fifty middle-aged and elderly gentlemen pitching into each other like so many Tipperary savages," wrote a bemused reporter, "most of them incapable, from want of wind and muscle, from doing each other any serious harm."

When the vote was finally taken, two dozen northern Democrats defected, providing enough votes to defeat Lecompton. Both sides then accepted

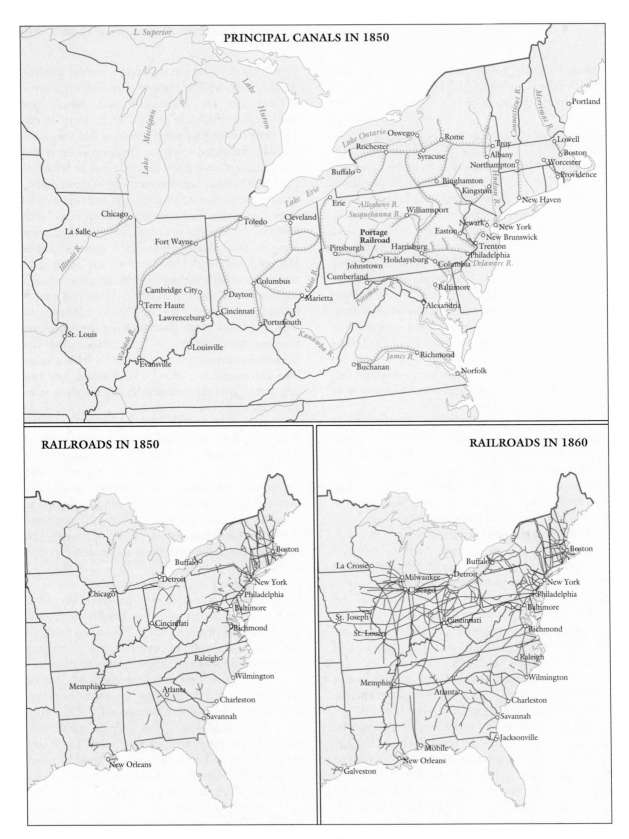

PRINCIPAL CANALS IN 1850

L. Superior

Lake Superior

Lake Michigan

Lake Huron

Lake Ontario

Oswego

Rochester

Rome

Syracuse

Buffalo

Binghamton

Erie

Lake Erie

Allegheny R.

Susquehanna R.

Williamsport

Kingston

Chicago

Toledo

Cleveland

La Salle

Illinois R.

Fort Wayne

Portage Railroad

Pittsburgh

Holidaysburg

Harrisburg

Johnstown

Columbia

Easton

Newark

New York

New Brunswick

Trenton

Philadelphia

Delaware R.

Connecticut R.

Merrimac R.

Portland

Troy

Lowell

Albany

Boston

Northampton

Worcester

Providence

New Haven

Hudson R.

Cambridge City

Columbus

Dayton

Marietta

Cumberland

Baltimore

Terre Haute

Cincinnati

Lawrenceburg

Portsmouth

Ohio R.

Potomac R.

Alexandria

Wabash R.

Louisville

Kanawha R.

James R.

Richmond

St. Louis

Evansville

Buchanan

Norfolk

RAILROADS IN 1850

Buffalo

Detroit

Boston

Chicago

New York

Philadelphia

Baltimore

Cincinnati

Richmond

Raleigh

Wilmington

Memphis

Atlanta

Charleston

Savannah

New Orleans

RAILROADS IN 1860

La Crosse

Buffalo

Detroit

Boston

Milwaukee

Chicago

New York

St. Joseph

Cincinnati

Philadelphia

Baltimore

St. Louis

Richmond

Raleigh

Memphis

Wilmington

Atlanta

Charleston

Savannah

Jacksonville

Mobile

New Orleans

Galveston

MAIN TRANSPORTATION ROUTES IN THE 1850S

a compromise proposal to resubmit the constitution to Kansas voters, who decisively rejected it. This meant that while Kansas would not come in as a slave state, neither would it come in as a free state for some time yet. Nevertheless, the Lecompton debate had split the Democratic Party, leaving a legacy of undying enmity between southerners and Douglas. The election of a Republican president in 1860 was now all but assured.

THE ECONOMY IN THE 1850S

Beginning in the mid-1840s, the American economy enjoyed a dozen years of unprecedented growth and prosperity, particularly for the railroads. The number of miles in operation quintupled during those years. Railroad construction provided employment for many immigrants and spurred growth in industries that produced rails, rolling stock, and other railroad equipment. Most railroad construction took place in the Old Northwest, linking the region more closely to the Northeast and continuing the reorientation of transportation networks from a north-south river pattern to an east-west canal and rail pattern. By the mid-1850s the east-west rail and water routes carried more than twice as much freight tonnage as the north-south river routes. This closer binding of the western and eastern states reinforced the effect of slavery in creating a self-conscious "North" and "South."

Although the Old Northwest remained predominantly agricultural, rapid expansion of railroads there laid the basis for its industrialization. During the 1850s industrial output in the free states west of Pennsylvania grew at twice the rate of Northeast industrial output and three times as great as the rate in the South. The Northwest urban growth rate tripled that of the Northeast and quadrupled that of the South. Chicago became the terminus for 15 rail lines in the 1850s, during which its population grew by 375 percent. In 1847 two companies that contributed to the rapid

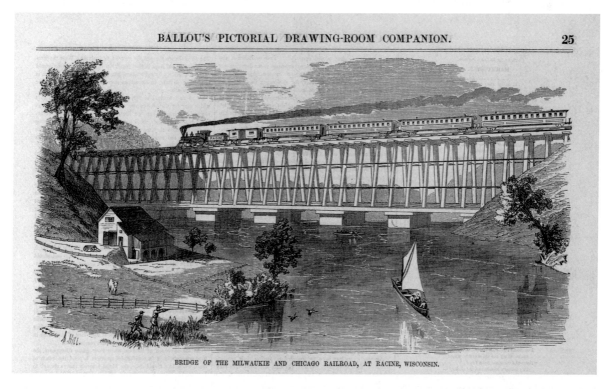

BALLOU'S PICTORIAL DRAWING-ROOM COMPANION.   25

BRIDGE OF THE MILWAUKIE AND CHICAGO RAILROAD, AT RACINE, WISCONSIN.

BRIDGE OF THE MILWAUKIE AND CHICAGO RAILROAD AT RACINE, WISCONSIN By the 1850s, Chicago had become the hub for a dozen or more railroads that tied the fast-growing Midwest to the older South and East. This illustration shows the railroad bridge over the Root River between Chicago and Milwaukee.

growth of agriculture during this era built their plants in Illinois: the McCormick reaper works at Chicago and the John Deere steel-plow works at Moline.

According to almost every statistical index available from that period, economic expansion considerably outstripped even the prodigious pace of population increase. While the number of Americans grew by 44 percent during these 12 years (1844–56), the value of both exports and imports increased by 200 percent; mined coal tonnage by 270 percent; banking capital, industrial capital, and industrial output by approximately 100 percent; farmland value by 100 percent; and cotton, wheat, and corn harvests by about 70 percent. These advances meant a significant increase of per capita production and income, though the distance between rich and poor was widening—a phenomenon that has characterized all capitalist economies during stages of rapid industrial growth.

By the later 1850s the United States had forged ahead of most other countries to become the second-leading industrial producer in the world, behind only Britain. But the country was still in the early stages of industrial development. Agricultural product processing and raw materials still played the dominant role. By 1860, the four leading industries, measured by value added in manufacturing, were cotton textiles, lumber products, boots and shoes, and flour milling. Iron and machinery, industries typical of a more mature manufacturing economy, ranked sixth and seventh.

"THE AMERICAN SYSTEM OF MANUFACTURES"

The United States had pioneered in one crucial feature of modern industry: the mass production of interchangeable parts. This revolutionary concept had begun with the manufacture of firearms earlier in the century and had spread to many products by the 1850s. High wages and a shortage of the skilled craftsmen who had traditionally fashioned guns, furniture, locks, watches, and other products had compelled American entrepreneurs to seek alternative

COLT ARMS PLANT IN HARTFORD, CONNECTICUT Samuel Colt's factory for manufacturing firearms was a showpiece for the American system of manufactures in the 1850s. All of the processes for production of the famous Colt revolver were housed under one roof, with power-driven machinery cutting the metal and shaping the interchangeable parts. Hand filing was necessary, however, for a perfect fit of the parts because the tolerances of machine tools were not yet as finely calibrated as they later became.

methods. "Yankee ingenuity," already world-famous, came up with an answer: special-purpose machine tools that would cut and shape an endless number of parts that could be fitted together with other similarly produced parts to make whole guns, locks, clocks, and sewing machines in mass quantities. These products were less elegant and less durable than products made by skilled craftsmen, but they were also less expensive and thus more widely available to the "middling classes" of a society that professed to be more democratic than Europe in its consumer economy as well as in its politics.

Such American-made products were the hit of the first World's Fair, the Crystal Palace Exhibition at London in 1851. British manufacturers were so impressed by Yankee techniques, which they dubbed "the American system of manufactures," that they sent two commissions to the United States to study them. "The labouring classes are comparatively few," reported one commission in 1854, "and to this very want . . . may be attributed the extraordinary ingenuity displayed in many of these labour-saving machines, whose automatic action so completely supplies the place of the more abundant hand labour of the older manufacturing countries." The British firearms industry imported American experts to help set up the Enfield Armoury in London to manufacture the new British army rifle.

The British also invited Samuel Colt of Connecticut, inventor of the famous six-shooting revolver, to set up a factory in England stocked with machinery from Connecticut. In testimony before a parliamentary committee in 1854, Colt summed up the American system of manufactures in a single sentence: "There is nothing that cannot be produced by machinery." Although the British had a half-century head start over Americans in the industrial revolution, Colt's testimony expressed a philosophy that would enable the United States to surpass Britain as the leading industrial nation by 1880.

The British industrial commissions also cited the American educational system as an important reason for the country's technological proficiency. "Educated up to a far higher standard than those of a much superior grade in the Old World," reported the 1854 commission, "every [American] workman seems to be continually devising some new thing to assist him in his work, and there is a strong desire . . . to be 'posted up' in every new improve-ment." By contrast, the British workman, trained by long apprenticeship "in the trade," rather than in school, lacked "the ductility of mind and the readiness of apprehension for a new thing" and was therefore "unwilling to change the methods he has been used to."

Whether this British commission was right in its belief that American schooling encouraged the "adaptative versatility" of Yankee workers, it was certainly true that public education and literacy were more widespread in the United States than in Europe. Almost 95 percent of adults in the free states were literate in 1860, compared with 65 percent in England and 55 percent in France. The standardization and expansion of public school systems that had begun earlier in New England had spread to the mid-Atlantic states and into the Old Northwest by the 1850s. Nearly all children received a few years of schooling, and most completed at least six or seven years. This improvement in education coincided with the feminization of the teaching profession, which opened up new career opportunities for young women. The notion that "woman's sphere" was in the home, rearing and nurturing children, ironically projected that sphere outside the home into the schoolroom when schools took over part of the responsibility of socializing and educating children. By the 1850s nearly three-quarters of the public school teachers in New England were women (who worked for lower salaries than male teachers), a trend that was spreading to the mid-Atlantic states and the Old Northwest as well.

THE SOUTHERN ECONOMY

The feminization of teaching had not yet reached the South. Nor had the idea of universal public education taken deep root in the slave states. In contrast to the North, where 94 percent of the entire population could read and write, 80 percent of the free population and only 10 percent of the slaves in the South were literate. This was one of several differences between North and South that antislavery people pointed to as evidence of the backward, repressive, and pernicious nature of a slave society.

Still, the South shared in the economy's rapid growth following recovery from the depression of 1837–43. Cotton prices and production both doubled between 1845 and 1855. Similar increases in

THE COUNTRY SCHOOL This famous painting by Winslow Homer portrays the typical one-room rural schoolhouse in which millions of American children learned the three R's in the 19th century. By the 1850s, teaching elementary school was a profession increasingly dominated by women, an important change from earlier generations.

price and output emerged in tobacco and sugar. The price of slaves, a significant index of prosperity in the southern economy, also doubled during this decade. Southern crops provided three-fifths of all U.S. exports, with cotton alone supplying more than half.

But a growing number of southerners deplored the fact that the "colonial" economy of the South was so dependent on the export of agricultural products and the import of manufactured goods. The ships that carried southern cotton were owned by northern or British firms; financial and commercial services were provided mostly by Yankees or Englishmen. In the years of rising sectional tensions around 1850, many southerners began calling for economic independence from the North. How could they obtain their "rights," they asked, if they were "financially more enslaved than our negroes?" Yankees "abuse and denounce slavery and slaveholders," declared a southern newspaper in 1851, yet "we purchase all our luxuries and necessaries from the North. . . . Our slaves are clothed with Northern manufactured goods and work with Northern hoes,

ploughs, and other implements. . . . The slaveholder dresses in Northern goods. . . . In Northern vessels his products are carried to market . . . and on Northern-made paper, with a Northern pen, with Northern ink, he resolves and re-resolves in regard to his rights."

Southerners must "throw off this humiliating dependence," declared James D. B. De Bow, the young champion of economic diversification in the South. In 1846 De Bow had founded in New Orleans a periodical eventually known as *De Bow's Review*. Proclaiming on its cover that "Commerce is King," the *Review* set out to make this slogan a southern reality. De Bow took the lead in organizing annual "commercial conventions" that met in various southern cities during the 1850s. In its early years, this movement encouraged southerners to invest in shipping lines, railroads, textile mills ("bring the spindles to the cotton"), and other enterprises. "Give us factories, machine shops, work shops," declared southern proponents of King Commerce, "and we shall be able ere long to assert our rights."

Economic diversification in the South did make headway during the 1850s. The slave states quadrupled their railroad mileage, increased the amount of capital invested in manufacturing by 77 percent, and boosted their output of cotton textiles by 44 percent. But like Alice in Wonderland, the faster the South ran, the further behind it seemed to fall—for northern industry was growing even faster. The slave states' share of the nation's manufacturing capacity actually dropped from 18 to 16 percent during the decade. In 1860 the North had five times more industrial output per capita than the South, and it had three times the railroad capital and mileage per capita and per thousand square miles. Southerners had a larger percentage of their capital invested in land and slaves in 1860 than they had had 10 years earlier. Some 80 percent of the South's labor force worked in agriculture—the same as 60 years earlier. By contrast, while farming remained, at 40 percent, the largest single occupation in the North, the northern economy developed a strong manufacturing and commercial sector whose combined labor force almost equaled that of agriculture by 1860.

THE SOVEREIGNTY OF KING COTTON

A good many southerners preferred to keep it that way. "That the North does our trading and manufacturing mostly is true," wrote an Alabama planter in 1858. "We are willing that they should. Ours is an agricultural people, and God grant that we may continue so. It is the freest, happiest, most independent, and with us, the most powerful condition on earth." In the later 1850s the drive for economic diversification in the South lost steam. King Cotton reasserted its primacy over King Commerce as cotton output *and* prices continued to rise, suffusing the South in a glow of prosperity. "Our Cotton is the most wonderful talisman on earth," declared a planter. "By its power we are transmuting whatever we choose into whatever we want." In a speech that became famous, James Hammond of South Carolina told his fellow senators in 1858 that "the slaveholding South is now the controlling power of the world. . . . No power on earth dares to make war on cotton. Cotton *is* king."

Even the commercial conventions in the South seem to have embraced this gospel. In 1854 they merged with a parallel series of planters' conventions, and thereafter the delegates heard as much about cotton as they did about commerce. By the later 1850s, one of the main goals of these conventions was to reopen the African slave trade, prohibited by law since 1808. Many southerners rejected that goal, however, partly on moral grounds and partly on economic grounds. Older slave states like Virginia, which profited from the sale of slaves to the booming cotton frontier of the Deep South, objected to any goal that would lower the price of their largest export. The conventions also lobbied for the annexation of Cuba, which would bring a productive agricultural economy and 400,000 more slaves into the United States.

Nowhere in the South, said defenders of slavery, did one see such "scenes of beggary, squalid poverty, and wretchedness" as one could find in any northern city. Black slaves, they insisted, enjoyed a higher standard of living than white "wage slaves" in northern factories. Black slaves never suffered from unemployment or wage cuts; they received free medical care; they were taken care of in old age.

This argument reached its fullest development in the writings of George Fitzhugh, a Virginia farmer-lawyer whose newspaper articles were gathered into two books published in 1854 and 1857, *Sociology for the South* and *Cannibals All*. Free-labor capitalism, said Fitzhugh, was a competition in which the strong exploited and starved the weak. Slavery, by contrast, was a paternal institution that guaranteed protection of the workers. "Capital exercises a more perfect compulsion over free laborers than human masters over slaves," wrote Fitzhugh, "for free laborers must at all times work or starve, and slaves are supported whether they work or not. . . . What a glorious thing is slavery, when want, misfortune, old age, debility, and sickness overtake [the slave]."

LABOR CONDITIONS IN THE NORTH

How true was this portrait of poverty and starvation among northern workers? Some northern labor leaders did complain that the "slavery" of the wage system gave "bosses" control over the

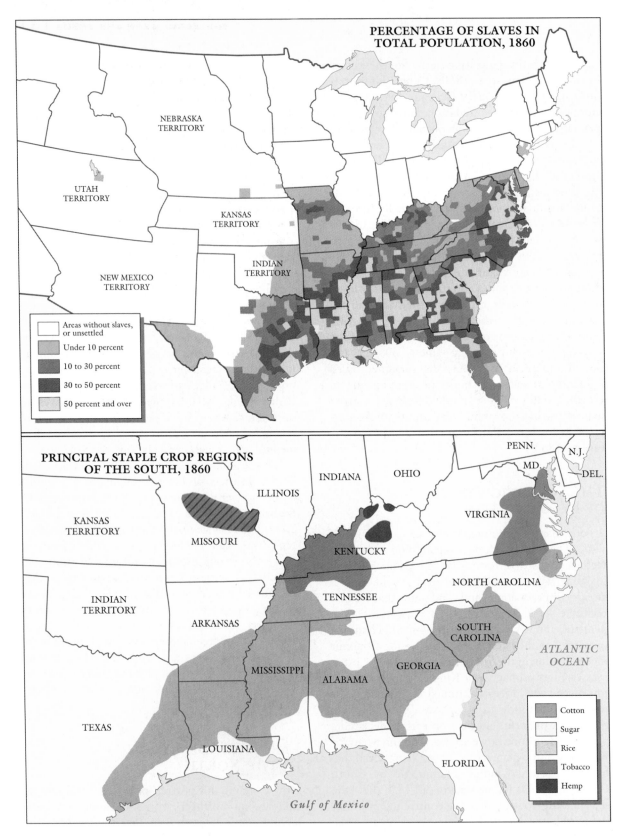

PERCENTAGE OF SLAVES IN TOTAL POPULATION, 1860

Areas without slaves, or unsettled
Under 10 percent
10 to 30 percent
30 to 50 percent
50 percent and over

PRINCIPAL STAPLE CROP REGIONS OF THE SOUTH, 1860

Cotton
Sugar
Rice
Tobacco
Hemp

ATLANTIC OCEAN

Gulf of Mexico

NEBRASKA TERRITORY

UTAH TERRITORY

KANSAS TERRITORY

INDIAN TERRITORY

NEW MEXICO TERRITORY

KANSAS TERRITORY

INDIAN TERRITORY

MISSOURI

ILLINOIS

INDIANA

OHIO

PENN.

N.J.

MD.

DEL.

VIRGINIA

KENTUCKY

TENNESSEE

NORTH CAROLINA

ARKANSAS

SOUTH CAROLINA

MISSISSIPPI

ALABAMA

GEORGIA

TEXAS

LOUISIANA

FLORIDA

SLAVERY AND STAPLE CROPS IN THE SOUTH, 1860

SOUTHERN PORTRAITS OF SLAVERY AND FREE LABOR Romanticized images of happy, well-fed slaves enjoying their work picking cotton were common in proslavery literature. Such images were often contrasted with the supposed harshness of life in Northern tenement districts, as in this illustration of a communal pump that has run dry on a hot summer day in an immigrant neighborhood on New York's lower east side.

hours, conditions, and compensation of labor. Use of this wage-slavery theme in labor rhetoric declined during the prosperous years of the 1850s, and no evidence indicates that a northern working man ever offered to change places with a southern slave. Average per capita income was about 40 percent higher in the North than in the South. Although that average masked large disparities between rich and poor—indeed, between the middle class and the poor—those disparities were no greater, and probably less, in the North than in the South.

To be sure, substantial numbers of recent immigrants, day laborers, and young single women in large northern cities lived on the edge of poverty—or slipped over the edge. Many women seamstresses, shoe binders, milliners, and the like, who worked 60 or 70 hours a week in the outwork system earned less than a living wage. Some of them resorted to prostitution in order to survive. The widespread adoption of the newly invented sewing machine in the 1850s did nothing to make life easier for seamstresses; it only lowered their per-unit piecework wages and forced them to turn out more shirts and trousers than before. Many urban working-class families could not survive on the wages of an unskilled or semiskilled father. The mother had to take in laundry, boarders, or outwork, and one or more children had to work. Much employment was seasonal or intermittent, leaving workers without wages for long periods of time, especially during the winter. The poverty, overcrowding, and disease in the tenement districts of a few large cities—especially New York City—seemed to lend substance to proslavery claims that slaves were better off.

But they were not—even apart from the psychological contrast between being free and being a slave. New York City's poverty, though highly concentrated and visible, was exceptional. In the North, only one-fourth of the people lived in cities or towns of over 2,500 people. Wages and opportunities for workers were greater in the North than anywhere else in the world, including the South. That was why four million immigrants came to the United States from 1845 to 1860 and why seven-eighths of them settled in free states. It was also why twice as many white residents of slave states migrated to free states than vice versa. And it was one

reason why northern farmers and workers wanted to keep slaves *and* free blacks out of the territories, where their cheaper labor would lower wages.

THE PANIC OF 1857

In the fall of 1857 the relative prosperity of the North was interrupted by a financial panic that caused a short-lived but intense depression. When the Crimean War in Europe (1854–56) cut off Russian grain from the European market, U.S. exports had mushroomed to meet the deficiency. After the Crimean War ended, U.S. grain exports slumped. The sharp rise in interest rates in Britain and France, caused by the war, spread to U.S. financial markets in 1857 and dried up sources of credit. Meanwhile, the economic boom of the preceding years had caused the American economy to overheat: Land prices had soared; railroads had built beyond the capacity of earnings to service their debts; banks had made too many risky loans.

This speculative house of cards came crashing down in September 1857. The failure of one banking house sent a wave of panic through the financial community. Banks suspended specie payments, businesses failed, railroads went bankrupt, construction halted, factories shut down. Hundreds of thousands of workers were laid off, and others went on part-time schedules or took wage cuts, just as the cold winter months were arriving. The specter of class conflict such as had occurred during the European revolutions of 1848 haunted the public. Unemployed workers in several northern cities marched in parades carrying banners demanding work or bread. A mob broke into the shops of flour merchants in New York City. On November 10 a crowd gathered in Wall Street and threatened to break into the U.S. customs house and subtreasury vaults, where $20 million was stored. Soldiers and marines had to be called out to disperse the mob.

But the country got through the winter with little violence. No one was killed in the demonstrations—in contrast to the dozens who had been killed in ethnic riots a few years earlier and the hundreds killed in the guerrilla war in Kansas. Class conflict turned out to be the least threatening of the various discords that endangered society in the 1850s. Charity and public works helped tide the poor over the winter, and the panic inspired a

THE PANIC ON WALL STREET This cartoon satirizes the consternation among New York investors and financiers when banks and businesses crashed in the autumn of 1857. Notice the smirk on the faces of two men in the foreground, who undoubtedly stood to benefit from foreclosures on defaulted property. The panic was no laughing matter, for it led to a short but sharp recession in 1857 and 1858.

vigorous religious revival. Spontaneous prayer meetings arose in many northern cities, bringing together bankers and seamstresses, brokers and streetsweepers. They asked God's forgiveness for the greed and materialism that, in a self-flagellating mood, they believed had caused the panic.

Perhaps God heeded their prayers. In any event, the depression was short-lived. By early 1858 banks had resumed specie payments; the stock market rebounded in the spring; factories reopened; railroad construction resumed; and by the spring of 1859 recovery was complete. The modest labor union activities of the 1850s revived after the depression, as workers in some industries went on strike to bring wages back to pre-panic levels. In February 1860 the shoemakers of Lynn, Massachusetts, began the largest strike in U.S. history up to that

time, eventually involving 20,000 workers in the New England shoe industry. Nevertheless, in spite of the organization of several national unions of skilled workers during the 1850s, less than 1 percent of the labor force was unionized in 1860.

SECTIONALISM AND THE PANIC

The Panic of 1857 probably intensified sectional hostility more than it did class conflict. The South largely escaped the depression. Its export-driven economy seemed insulated from domestic downturns. After a brief dip, cotton and tobacco prices returned to high levels and production continued to increase: The cotton crop set new records in 1858 and 1859. Southern boasts about the superiority of the region's economic and labor systems took on added bravado. "Who can doubt, that has looked at recent events, that cotton is supreme?" asked Senator James Hammond in March 1858. "When thousands of the strongest commercial houses in the world were coming down," he told Yankees, "what brought you up? . . . We have poured in upon you one million six hundred thousand bales of cotton. . . . We have sold it for $65,000,000, and saved you."

Northerners were not grateful for their rescue. In fact, many of them actually blamed the South for causing the depression or for blocking measures to ease its effects in the North. Southern congressmen had provided most of the votes for a new tariff in 1857 that brought duties to their lowest levels in 40 years. Some northern Republicans blamed the tariff for causing the panic and wanted to revise certain duties upward to help hard-hit industries, especially Pennsylvania iron, which were being undercut by cheaper imports. They directed their arguments to workers as much as to manufacturers. "We demand that American laborers shall be protected against the pauper labor of Europe," they declared. Tariff revision would "give employment to thousands of mechanics, artisans, laborers, who have languished for months in unwilling idleness." In each session of Congress from 1858 through 1860, however, a combination of southerners and about half of the northern Democrats blocked Republican efforts to raise tariffs. In the words of one bitter Pennsylvania Republican, this was proof that Congress remained "shamelessly prostituted, in a base subserviency to the Slave Power." Republicans made important gains in the Pennsylvania congressional elections of 1858, setting the stage for a strong bid in a state that they had to carry if they were to win the presidency in 1860.

Three other measures acquired additional significance after the Panic of 1857. Republicans supported each of them as a means to promote economic health and to aid farmers and workers. But southerners perceived all of them as aimed at helping *northern* farmers and workers and used their power to defeat them. One was a homestead act to grant 160 acres of public land to each farmer who settled and worked the land. Believing that this bill "would prove a most efficient ally for Abolition by encouraging and stimulating the settlement of free farms with Yankees," southern senators defeated it after the House had passed it in 1859. The following year both houses passed the homestead act, but Buchanan vetoed it and southern senators blocked an effort to pass it over his veto. A similar fate befell bills for land grants to a transcontinental railroad and for building agricultural and mechanical colleges to educate farmers and workers. In the Old Northwest, where these measures were popular, Republican prospects for 1860 were enhanced by southern and Democratic opposition to them.

THE FREE-LABOR IDEOLOGY

By the later 1850s the Republican antislavery argument had become a finely honed philosophy that historians have labeled a "free-labor ideology." It held that all work in a free society was honorable, but that slavery degraded the calling of manual labor by equating it with bondage. Slaves worked inefficiently, by compulsion; free men were stimulated to work hard and efficiently by the desire to get ahead. Social mobility was central to the free-labor ideology. Free workers who practiced the virtues of industry, thrift, self-discipline, and sobriety could move up the ladder of success. "I am not ashamed to confess," Abraham Lincoln told a working-class audience in 1860, "that twenty-five years ago I was a hired laborer, mauling rails, at work on a flat-boat—just what might happen to any poor man's son!" But in the free states, said Lincoln, a man knows that "he can better his condition. . . . There is no such thing as a freeman being fatally fixed for life, in the condition of a hired laborer. . . . The man who labored for another last year, this year labors for himself, and next year will hire others to labor for him. . . . The free labor system opens the way for all—gives hope to all, and energy, and progress, and improvement of condition to all."

Lincoln drew too rosy a picture of northern reality, for large numbers of wage laborers in the North had little hope of advancing beyond that status. Still, he expressed a belief that was widely shared in the antebellum North. "There is not a working boy of average ability in the New England states, at least," observed a visiting British industrialist in 1854, "who has not an idea of some mechanical invention or improvement in manufactures, by which, in good time, he hopes to better his condition, or rise to fortune and social distinction." Americans could point to numerous examples of men who had achieved dramatic upward mobility. Belief in this "American dream" was most strongly held by Protestant farmers, skilled workers, and white-collar workers who had some real hope of getting ahead. These men tended to support the Republican Party and its goal of excluding slavery from the territories.

Slavery was the antithesis of upward mobility. Bondsmen were "fatally fixed in that condition for life," as Lincoln noted. Slaves could not hope to move up the ladder of success, nor could free men who lived in a society where they had to compete with slave labor. "Slavery withers and blights all it touches," insisted the Republicans. "It is a curse upon the poor, free, laboring white men." In the United States, social mobility often depended on geographic mobility. The main reason so many families moved into new territories was to make a new start, move ahead. But, declared a Republican editor, if slavery goes into the territories, "the free labor of all the states will not." "If the free labor of the states goes there, the slave labor of the southern states will not, and in a few years the country will teem with an active and energetic population."

Southerners contended that free labor was prone to unrest and strikes. Of course it was, said Lincoln in a speech to a New England audience during the shoemakers' strike of 1860. "I am glad to see that a system prevails in New England under which laborers *can* strike when they want to (Cheers). . . . I like the system which lets a man quit when he wants to, and wish it might prevail everywhere (Tremendous applause)." Strikes were one of the ways in which free workers could try to improve their prospects. "I want every man," said Lincoln, "to have the chance—and I believe a black man is entitled to it—in which he can better his condition." That was why Republicans were determined to contain the expansion of slavery, for if the South got its way in the territories "free labor that can strike will give way to slave labor that cannot!"

THE IMPENDING CRISIS

From the South came a maverick voice that echoed the Republicans. Hinton Rowan Helper considered himself a spokesman for the non-slaveholding whites of the South. Living in upcountry North Carolina, a region of small farms and few slaves, he had brooded for years over slavery's retarding influence on southern development. In 1857 he poured out his bitterness in a book entitled *The Impending Crisis of the South*. Using selective statistics from the 1850 census, he pictured a South mired in economic backwardness, widespread illiteracy, poverty for the masses, and great wealth for the elite. He contrasted this dismal situation with the bustling, prosperous northern economy and its near-universal literacy, neat farms, and progressive institutions. What was the cause of this startling contrast? "Slavery lies at the root of all the shame, poverty, ignorance, tyranny, and imbecility of the South," he wrote. Slavery monopolized the best land, degraded all labor to the level of bond labor, denied schools to the poor, and impoverished all but "the lords of the lash" who "are not only absolute masters of the blacks [but] of all non-slaveholding whites, whose freedom is merely nominal, and whose unparalleled illiteracy and degradation is purposely and fiendishly perpetrated." The remedy? Non-slaveholding whites must organize and use their votes to overthrow "this entire system of oligarchical despotism."

No southern publisher dared touch this book. Helper lugged his bulky manuscript to New York City, where a printer brought it out in the summer of 1857. *The Impending Crisis* was virtually banned in the South, and few southern whites read it, but it made a huge impact in the North. Republicans welcomed it as confirmation of all they had been saying about the evils of slavery and the virtues of free labor. The Republican Party subsidized an abridged edition and distributed thousands of copies as campaign documents. During the late 1850s, a war of books (Helper's *Impending Crisis* versus Fitzhugh's *Cannibals All*) exacerbated sectional tensions. Fitzhugh's book circulated freely in the North, whereas the sale or possession of Helper's book was a criminal offense in many parts of the South. The New England Antislavery Society even invited Fitzhugh to New Haven to debate the abolitionist Wendell Phillips. Fitzhugh expressed surprise at his courteous reception in the North, aware that Phillips and other abolitionists could not set foot in the South without peril to their life. Northern spokesmen did not hesitate to point the moral: A free society could tolerate free speech and a free press, but a slave society could not.

SOUTHERN NON-SLAVEHOLDERS

How accurate was Helper's portrayal of southern poor whites degraded by slavery and ready to revolt against it? The touchy response of many southern leaders suggested that the planters felt uneasy about that question. After all, slaveholding families constituted less than one-third of the white population in slave states, and the proportion was declining as the price of slaves continued to rise. Open hostility to the planters' domination of society and politics was evident in the mountainous and up-country regions of the South. These would become areas of Unionist sentiment during the Civil War and of Republican strength after it.

But Helper surely exaggerated the disaffection of most non-slaveholders in the South. Three bonds held them to the system: kinship, economic interest, and race. In the Piedmont and the low-country regions of the South, nearly half of the whites were in slaveholding families. Many of the rest were cousins or nephews or in-laws of slave-holders in the South's extensive and tightly knit kinship network. Moreover, many young, ambitious non-slaveholders hoped to buy slaves eventually. Some of them *rented* slaves. And because slaves could be made to do the menial, unskilled labor in the South—the "mudsill" tasks, in Senator Hammond's language—white workers monopolized the more skilled, higher-paying jobs.

Most important, even if they did not own slaves, white people owned the most important asset of all—a white skin. White supremacy was an article of faith in the South (and in most of the North, for that matter). Race was a more important social distinction than class. The southern legal system, politics, and social ideology were based on the concept of "*herrenvolk* democracy" (the equality of all who belonged to the "master race"). Subordination was the Negro's fate, and slavery was the best means of subordination. Emancipation would loose a flood of free blacks on society and would undermine the foundations of white supremacy. Thus, many of the "poor whites" in the South and immigrant workers or poorer farmers in the North supported slavery.

The *herrenvolk* theme permeated proslavery rhetoric. "With us," said John C. Calhoun in 1848, "the two great divisions of society are not the rich and the poor, but white and black; and all the former, the poor as well as the rich, belong to the upper class, and are respected and treated as equals." True freedom as Americans understood it required equality of rights and status (though not of wealth or income). Slavery ensured such freedom for all whites by putting a floor under them, a mudsill of black slaves that kept whites from falling into the mud of inequality. "Break down slavery," said a Virginia congressman, "and you would with the same blow destroy the great Democratic principle of equality among men."

A SOUTHERN YEOMAN FARMER'S HOME This modest log cabin on the edge of a small clearing, with the farmer's wife drawing water from a well in the foreground, was typical of non-slaveholders' farms in the backcountry of the South. Often stigmatized as "poor whites," many of these families were in fact comfortable by the standards of the day. They did not feel the sense of oppression by the planter class that Hinton Rowan Helper believed they should feel.

THE LINCOLN-DOUGLAS DEBATES

Abraham Lincoln believed the opposite. For him, slavery and freedom were incompatible; the one must die that the other might live. This became the central theme of a memorable series of debates between Lincoln and Douglas in 1858, which turned

The Lincoln-Douglas Debates

The Lincoln-Douglas contest for the Senate in 1858 produced the most famous—and fateful—political debates in American history. At stake was nothing less than the future of the nation. Thousands of people crowded into seven towns to listen to these three-hour debates that took place outdoors from August to October in weather ranging from stifling heat to cold rain. Audiences were most friendly to Lincoln in anti-slavery northern Illinois, as portrayed in the upper illustration of the debate in Galesburg, home of Knox College and a hotbed of abolitionism. The lower painting puts Lincoln in the center of the picture because the artist, with hindsight, knew that Lincoln had gone on to become the country's greatest president during its greatest crisis. Douglas, sitting to Lincoln's right, fell by the political wayside and died in June 1861. Note several women in the crowds in both pictures; though women could not then vote, many of them avidly followed political events.

out to be a dress rehearsal for the presidential election of 1860.

The debates were arranged after Lincoln was nominated to oppose Douglas's reelection to the Senate. State legislatures elected U.S. senators at that time, so the campaign was technically for the election of the Illinois legislature. The real issue, however, was the senatorship, and Douglas's prominence gave the contest national significance. Lincoln launched his bid with one of his most notable speeches. "'A house divided against itself cannot stand,'" he said, quoting the words of Jesus recorded in the Gospel of Mark (3:25). "I believe this government cannot endure, permanently half slave and half free. . . . It will become all one thing, or all the other." Under the Dred Scott decision, which Douglas had endorsed, slavery was legal in all the territories. And what, asked Lincoln, would prevent the Supreme Court, using the same reasoning that had led it to interpret the Constitution as protecting property in slaves, from legalizing slavery in free states? (A case based on this question was then before the New York courts.) The advocates of slavery, charged Lincoln, were trying to "push it forward, till it shall become lawful in all the States." But Republicans intended to keep slavery out of the territories, thus stopping its growth and placing it "where the public mind shall rest in the belief that it is in the course of ultimate extinction."

The seven open-air debates between Douglas and Lincoln focused almost entirely on the issue of slavery. Douglas asked: Why could the country not continue to exist half slave and half free as it had for 70 years? Lincoln's talk about the "ultimate extinction" of slavery would provoke the South to secession. Douglas professed himself no friend of slavery—but if people in the southern states or in the territories wanted it, they had the right to have it. Douglas did not want black people—either slave or free—in Illinois. Lincoln's policy would not only free the slaves but would grant them equality. "Are you in favor of conferring upon the negro the rights and privileges of citizenship?" Douglas called out to supporters in the crowd. "No, no!" they shouted back. He continued:

> Do you desire to strike out of our State Constitution that clause which keeps slaves and free negroes out of the State . . . in order that when Missouri abolishes slavery she can send one hundred thousand emancipated slaves into Illinois, to become citizens and voters on an equality with yourselves? ("Never," "no.") . . . If you desire to allow them to come into the State and settle with the white man, if you desire to allow them to vote . . . then support Mr. Lincoln and the Black Republican party, who are in favor of the citizenship of the negro. ("Never, never.")

Douglas's demagoguery put Lincoln on the defensive. He responded with cautious denials that he favored "social and political equality" of the races. The "ultimate extinction" of slavery might take a century. It would require the voluntary cooperation of the South and would perhaps be contingent on the emigration of some freed slaves from the country. But come what may, freedom must prevail. Americans must reaffirm the principles of the founding fathers. In Lincoln's words, a black person was

> entitled to all the natural rights enumerated in the Declaration of Independence, the right to life, liberty and the pursuit of happiness. (Loud cheers.) I hold that he is as much entitled to these as the white man. I agree with Judge Douglas he is not my equal in many respects. . . . But in the right to eat the bread, without leave of anybody else, which his own hand earns, *he is my equal and the equal of Judge Douglas, and the equal of every living man.* (Great applause.)

Lincoln deplored Douglas's "care not" attitude whether slavery was voted up or down. He "looks to no end of the institution of slavery," said Lincoln. Indeed, by endorsing the Dred Scott decision he looks to its "perpetuity and nationalization." Douglas was thus "eradicating the light of reason and liberty in this American people." That was the real issue in the election, insisted Lincoln.

> That is the issue that will continue in this country when these poor tongues of Judge Douglas and myself shall be silent. It is the eternal struggle between these two principles—right and wrong—throughout the world. . . . The one is the common right of humanity and the other the divine right of kings. . . . No matter in what shape it comes, whether from a king who seeks to bestride the people of his own nation and live by the fruit of their labor, or from one race of men as an apology for enslaving another race, it is the same tyrannical principle.

THE FREEPORT DOCTRINE

The popular vote for Republican and Democratic state legislators in Illinois was virtually even in 1858, but because apportionment favored the Democrats, they won a majority of seats and reelected Douglas. Lincoln, however, was the ultimate victor; his performance in the debates lifted him from political obscurity, while Douglas further alienated southern Democrats. In the Freeport debate Lincoln had asked Douglas how he reconciled his support for the Dred Scott decision with his policy of popular sovereignty, which supposedly gave residents of a territory the power to vote slavery down. Douglas replied that even though the Court had legalized slavery in the territories, the enforcement of that right would depend on the people who lived there. This was a popular answer in the North, but it gave added impetus to southern demands for congressional passage of a federal slave code in territories such as Kansas, where the Free Soil majority had by 1859 made slavery virtually null. In the next two sessions of Congress after the 1858 elections, southern Democrats, led by Jefferson Davis, tried to pass a federal slave code for all territories. Douglas and northern Democrats joined with Republicans to defeat it. Consequently, southern hostility toward Douglas mounted as the presidential election of 1860 approached.

The 1859–60 session of Congress was particularly contentious. Once again a fight over the speakership of the House set the tone. Republicans had won a plurality of House seats, but lacking a majority could not elect a Speaker without the support of a few border-state representatives from the American (Know-Nothing) Party. The problem was that the Republican candidate for Speaker was John Sherman, who, along with 67 other congressmen, had signed an endorsement of Hinton Rowan Helper's *The Impending Crisis of the South* (without, Sherman later admitted, having read it). This was a red flag to southerners, even to ex-Whigs from the border states, who refused to vote for Sherman. Through 43 ballots and two months, the House remained deadlocked. Tensions escalated, and members came armed to the floor. One observer commented that "the only persons who do not have a revolver and knife are those who have two revolvers."

As usual, southerners threatened to secede if a Black Republican became Speaker. Several of them wanted a shootout on the floor of Congress. We "are willing to fight the question out," wrote one, "and to settle it right there." The governor of South Carolina told one of his state's congressmen:

"If . . . you upon consultation decide to make the issue of force in Washington, write or telegraph me, and I will have a regiment in or near Washington in the shortest possible time." To avert a crisis, Sherman withdrew his candidacy and the House finally elected a conservative ex-Whig as Speaker on the 44th ballot.

JOHN BROWN AT HARPERS FERRY

Southern tempers were frayed even at the start of this session of Congress because of what had happened at Harpers Ferry, Virginia, the previous October. After his exploits in Kansas, John Brown had disappeared from public view, but had not been idle. Like the Old Testament warriors he admired and resembled, Brown intended to carry his war against slavery into Babylon—the South. His favorite New Testament passage was Hebrews 9:22: "Without shedding of blood there is no remission of sin." Brown worked up a plan to capture the federal arsenal at Harpers Ferry, arm slaves with the muskets he seized there, and move southward along the Appalachian Mountains attracting more slaves to his army along the way until the "whole accursed system of bondage" collapsed.

Brown recruited five black men and seventeen whites, including three of his sons, for this reckless scheme. He also had the secret support of a half-dozen Massachusetts and New York abolitionists who had helped him raise funds. On the night of October 16, 1859, Brown led his men across the Potomac and occupied the sleeping town of Harpers Ferry without resistance. Few slaves flocked to his banner, but the next day state militia units poured into town and drove Brown's band into the fire-engine house. At dawn on October 18 a company of U.S. marines commanded by Colonel Robert E. Lee and Lieutenant J. E. B. Stuart stormed the engine house and captured the surviving members of Brown's party. Four townsmen, one marine, and 10 of Brown's men (including two of his sons) were killed; not a single slave was liberated.

John Brown's raid lasted 36 hours; its repercussions resounded for years. Brown and six of his followers were promptly tried by the state of Virginia, convicted, and hanged. This scarcely ended matters. The raid sent a wave of revulsion and alarm through the South. Though no slaves had risen in

JOHN BROWN This modern mural of John Brown is full of symbolism. Holding an open Bible, Brown bestrides the earth like an Old Testament prophet while dead Union and Confederate soldiers lie at his feet. Other soldiers clash behind him, slaves struggle to break free, and God's wrath at a sinful nation sends a destructive tornado to earth in the background.

revolt, it revived fears of slave insurrection never far beneath the surface of southern consciousness. Exaggerated reports of Brown's network of abolitionist supporters confirmed southern suspicions that a widespread northern conspiracy was afoot, determined to destroy their society. Although Republican leaders denied any connection with Brown and disavowed his actions, few southerners believed them. Had not Lincoln talked of the "extinction" of slavery? And had not William H. Seward, who was expected to be the next Republican presidential nominee, given a campaign speech in 1858 in which he predicted an "irrepressible conflict" between the free and slave societies?

Many northerners, impressed by Brown's dignified bearing and eloquence during his trial, considered him a martyr to freedom. In his final statement to the court, Brown said:

I see a book kissed, which I suppose to be the Bible, which teaches me that all things whatsoever I would that men should do to me, I should do even so to them. It teaches me, further, to remember them that are in bonds as bound with them. I endeavored to act up to that instruction. . . . Now, if it is deemed necessary that I should forfeit my life for the furtherance of the ends of justice, and mingle my blood further with the blood of my children and with the blood of millions in this slave country whose rights are disregarded by wicked, cruel, and unjust enactments, I say, let it be done.

On the day of Brown's execution, bells tolled in hundreds of northern towns, guns fired salutes, ministers preached sermons of commemoration. "The death of no man in America has ever produced so profound a sensation," commented one northerner. Ralph Waldo Emerson declared that Brown had made "the gallows as glorious as the cross."

This outpouring of northern sympathy for Brown shocked and enraged southerners and weakened the already frayed threads of the Union. "The Harper's Ferry invasion has advanced the cause of disunion more than any event that has happened since the formation of the government," observed a Richmond newspaper. "I have always been a fervid Union man," wrote a North Carolinian, but "the endorsement of the Harper's Ferry outrage . . . has shaken my fidelity. . . . I am willing to take the chances of every possible evil that may arise from disunion, sooner than submit any longer to Northern insolence."

Something approaching a reign of terror now descended on the South. Every Yankee seemed to be another John Brown; every slave who acted suspiciously seemed to be an insurrectionist. Hundreds of northerners were run out of the South in 1860, some wearing a coat of tar and feathers. Several "incendiaries," both white and black, were lynched. "Defend yourselves!" Senator Robert Toombs cried out to the southern people. "The enemy is at your door . . . meet him at the doorsill, and drive him from the temple of liberty, or pull down its pillars and involve him in a common ruin."

CONCLUSION

Few decades in American history witnessed a greater disjunction between economic well-being and political upheaval than the 1850s. Despite the recession following the Panic of 1857, the total output of the American economy grew by 62 percent during the decade. Railroad mileage more than tripled, value added by manufacturing nearly doubled, and gross farm product grew by 40 percent. Americans were more prosperous than ever before.

Yet a profound malaise gripped the country. Riots between immigrants and nativists in the mid-1850s left more than 50 people dead. Fighting in Kansas between proslavery and antislavery forces killed at least 200. Fistfights broke out on the floor of Congress. A South Carolina congressman bludgeoned a Massachusetts senator to unconsciousness with a heavy cane. Representatives and senators came to congressional sessions armed with weapons as well as with violent words.

The nation proved capable of absorbing the large influx of immigrants despite the tensions and turmoil of the mid-1850s. It might also have been able to absorb the huge territorial expansion of the late 1840s had not the slavery issue been reopened in an earlier territorial acquisition, the Louisiana Purchase, by the Kansas-Nebraska Act of 1854. This legislation, followed by the Dred Scott decision in 1857, seemed to authorize the unlimited expansion of slavery. Within two years of its founding in 1854, however, the Republican Party emerged as the largest party in the North on a platform of preventing all future expansion of slavery. By 1860 the United States had reached a fateful crossroads. As Lincoln had said, it could not endure permanently half slave and half free. The presidential election of 1860 would decide which road America would take into the future.

Suggested Readings begin on page SR-1. For Web activities and resources related to this chapter, go to http:// www.harcourtcollege.com/history/murrin

CHAPTER 15

SECESSION AND CIVIL WAR, 1860–1862

THE HORNET'S NEST AT SHILOH

In the bloody fighting on April 6 at the Battle of Shiloh, portions of three Union divisions held out along a sunken farm road for several hours. Virtually surrounded by Confederate attackers, the 2,200 Union survivors surrendered in midafternoon. This was a costly Confederate success, for General Albert Sidney Johnston was mortally wounded while directing the attack. The volume of fire from Union defenders was so great that the Confederates called the enemy position the "hornet's nest" because of the angry whizzing bullets coming from it. The stubborn Union fighting at the hornet's nest bought Grant time to establish a defensive line from which he launched a successful counterattack the next day.

As the year 1860 began, the Democratic Party was one of the few national institutions left in the country. The Methodists and Baptists had split into Northern and Southern churches in the 1840s over the issue of slavery; several voluntary associations had done the same; the Whig Party and the nativist American Party had been shattered by sectional antagonism in the mid-1850s. Finally, in April 1860, even the Democratic Party, at its national convention in Charleston, South Carolina, split into Northern and Southern camps. This virtually ensured the election of a Republican president. Such a prospect aroused deep fears among southern whites that a Republican administration might use its power to bring liberty and perhaps even equality to the slaves. When Abraham Lincoln was elected president exclusively by northern votes, the lower-South states seceded from the Union. When Lincoln refused to remove U.S. troops from Fort Sumter, South Carolina, the new Confederate States army opened fire on the fort. Lincoln called out the militia to suppress the insurrection. Four more slave states seceded. In 1861, the country drifted into a civil war whose immense consequences no one could foresee.

This chapter will focus on the following major questions:

- Why did political leaders in the lower South think that Lincoln's election made secession imperative?
- Why did compromise efforts to forestall secession fail, and why did war break out at Fort Sumter?
- What were Northern advantages in the Civil War? What were Southern advantages?
- How did these advantages manifest themselves in the military campaigns and battles in 1861–62?

THE ELECTION OF 1860

A hotbed of southern-rights radicalism, Charleston turned out to be the worst possible place for the Democrats to hold their national convention. Sectional confrontations took place inside the convention hall and on the streets. Since 1836 the Democratic Party had required a two-thirds majority of delegates for a presidential nomination, a rule that in effect gave southerners veto power if they voted together. Although Stephen A. Douglas had the backing of a simple majority of the delegates, southern Democrats were determined to deny him the nomination. His opposition to the Lecompton constitution in Kansas and to a federal slave code for the territories had convinced proslavery southerners that they would be unable to control a Douglas administration.

The first test came in the debate on the platform. Southern delegates insisted on a plank favoring a federal slave code for the territories. Douglas could not run on a platform that contained such a plank, and if the party adopted it, Democrats were sure to lose every state in the North. By a slim majority, the convention rejected the plank and reaffirmed the 1856 platform endorsing popular sovereignty. Fifty southern delegates thereupon walked out of the convention. Even after they left, Douglas could not muster a two-thirds majority, nor could any other candidate. After 57 futile ballots, the convention adjourned to meet in Baltimore six weeks later to try again.

By then the party was too badly shattered to be put back together. That pleased some proslavery radicals, who were convinced that the South would never be secure in a nation dominated by a Northern majority. The election of a "Black Republican" president, they believed, would provide the shock necessary to mobilize a Southern majority for secession. Two of the most prominent secessionists were William L. Yancey and Edmund Ruffin. In 1858, they founded the League of United Southerners to "fire the Southern heart . . . and at the proper moment, by one organized, concerted action, we can precipitate the Cotton States into a revolution." After walking out of the Democratic convention, the eloquent Yancey inspired a huge crowd in Charleston's moonlit courthouse square to give three cheers "for an Independent Southern

THE POLITICAL QUADRILLE This cartoon depicts the four presidential candidates in 1860. Clockwise from the upper left are John C. Breckinridge, Southern Rights Democrat; Abraham Lincoln, Republican; John Bell, Constitutional Union; and Stephen A. Douglas, Democrat. All are dancing to the tune played by Dred Scott, symbolizing the importance of the slavery issue in this campaign. Each candidate's partner represents a political liability: for example, Breckinridge's partner is the disunionist William L. Yancey wearing a devil's horns, while Lincoln's partner is a black woman who supposedly gives color to Democratic accusations that Republicans believed in miscegenation.

C H R O N O L O G Y

1860 Lincoln elected president (November 6)
• South Carolina secedes (December 20)
• Federal troops transfer from Fort Moultrie to Fort Sumter (December 26)

1861 Rest of lower South secedes (January–February) • Crittenden Compromise rejected (February) • Jefferson Davis inaugurated as provisional president of new Confederate States of America (February 18) • Abraham Lincoln inaugurated as president of the United States (March 4) • Fort Sumter falls; Lincoln calls out troops, proclaims blockade (April) • Four more states secede to join Confederacy (April–May) • Battle of Bull Run (Manassas) (July 21) • Battle of Wilson's Creek (August 10) • The *Trent* affair (November–December)

1862 Union captures Forts Henry and Donelson (February 6 and 16) • Congress passes Legal Tender Act (February 25) • Battle of Pea Ridge (March 7–8) • Battle of the *Monitor* and *Merrimac* (*Virginia*) (March 9) • Battle of Glorieta Pass (March 26–28) • Battle of Shiloh (April 6–7) • Union Navy captures New Orleans (April 25) • Stonewall Jackson's Shenandoah Valley campaign (May–June) • Seven Days' battles (June 25–July 1) • Second Battle of Manassas (Bull Run) (August 29–30) • Lee invades Maryland (September) • Battle of Corinth (October 3–4) • Battle of Perryville (October 8)

1863 Congress passes National Banking Act (February 25)

Republic" with his concluding words: "Perhaps even now, the pen of the historian is nibbed to write the story of a new revolution."

The second convention in Baltimore reprised the first at Charleston. This time, an even larger number of delegates from southern states walked out. They formed their own Southern Rights Democratic Party and nominated John C. Breckinridge of Kentucky (the incumbent vice president) for president on a slave-code platform. When regular Democrats nominated Douglas, the stage was set for what would become a four-party election. A coalition of former southern Whigs, who could not bring themselves to vote Democratic, and northern Whigs, who considered the Republican Party too radical, formed the Constitutional Union Party, which nominated John Bell of Tennessee for president. Bell had no chance of winning; the party's purpose was to exercise a conservative influence on a campaign that threatened to polarize the country.

THE REPUBLICANS NOMINATE LINCOLN

From the moment the Democratic Party broke apart, it became clear that 1860 could be the year when the dynamic young Republican Party elected its first president. The Republicans could expect no electoral votes from the 15 slave states. In 1856, however, they had won all but five northern states, and with only two or three of those five they could win the presidency. The crucial states were Pennsylvania, Illinois, and Indiana. Douglas might still carry them and throw the presidential election into the House, where anything could happen. Thus the Republicans had to carry at least two of the swing states to win.

As the Republican delegates poured into Chicago for their convention—held in a huge building nicknamed "the Wigwam" because of its shape—their leading presidential prospect was William H. Seward of New York. An experienced politician who had served as governor and senator, Seward was by all odds the most prominent Republican, but in his long career he had made a good many enemies. His antinativist policies had alienated some former members of the American Party, whose support he would need to carry Pennsylvania. His "Higher Law" speech against the Compromise of 1850 and his "Irrepressible Conflict" speech in 1858, predicting the ultimate overthrow of slavery, had given him a reputation for radicalism that might drive away voters in the vital swing states of the lower North.

Several of the delegates, uneasy about that reputation, staged a stop-Seward movement. The next candidate to the fore was Abraham Lincoln. Though he too had opposed nativism, he had done so less noisily than Seward. His "House Divided"

WIDE-AWAKE PARADE IN NEW YORK, OCTOBER 5, 1860 The Wide-Awakes were an organization of young Republicans who roused political enthusiasm by marching in huge torchlight parades during the political campaign of 1860. A year later, many of these same men would march down the same streets in army uniforms carrying rifles instead of torches on their way to the front.

speech had made essentially the same point as Seward's "Irrepressible Conflict" speech, but his reputation was still that of a more moderate man. He was from one of the lower-North states where the election would be close, and his rise from a poor farm boy and rail-splitter to successful lawyer and political leader perfectly reflected the free-labor theme of social mobility extolled by the Republican Party. By picking up second-choice votes from states that switched from their favorite sons, Lincoln overtook Seward and won the nomination on the third ballot. Seward accepted the outcome gracefully, and the Republicans headed into the campaign as a united, confident party.

Their confidence stemmed in part from their platform, which appealed to many groups in the North. Its main plank pledged exclusion of slavery from the territories. Other planks called for a higher tariff (especially popular in Pennsylvania), a homestead act (popular in the Northwest), and federal aid for construction of a transcontinental railroad and for improvement of river navigation. This was a program designed for a future in which the "house divided" would become a free-labor society modeled on Northern capitalism. Its blend of idealism and materialism proved especially attractive to young people; a large majority of first-time voters in the North voted Republican in 1860. Thousands of them joined "Wide-Awake" clubs and marched in huge torchlight parades through the cities of the North.

SOUTHERN FEARS

Militant enthusiasm in the North was matched by fear and rage in the South. Few people there could see any difference between Lincoln and Seward—or for that matter between Lincoln and William Lloyd Garrison. They were all "Black Republicans" and "Abolitionists." Had not Lincoln branded slavery a moral, social, and political evil? Had he not said that the Declaration of Independence applied to blacks as well as whites? Had he not expressed a hope that excluding slavery from the territories would put it on the road to ultimate extinction? To southerners, the Republican pledge not to interfere with slavery in the states was meaningless.

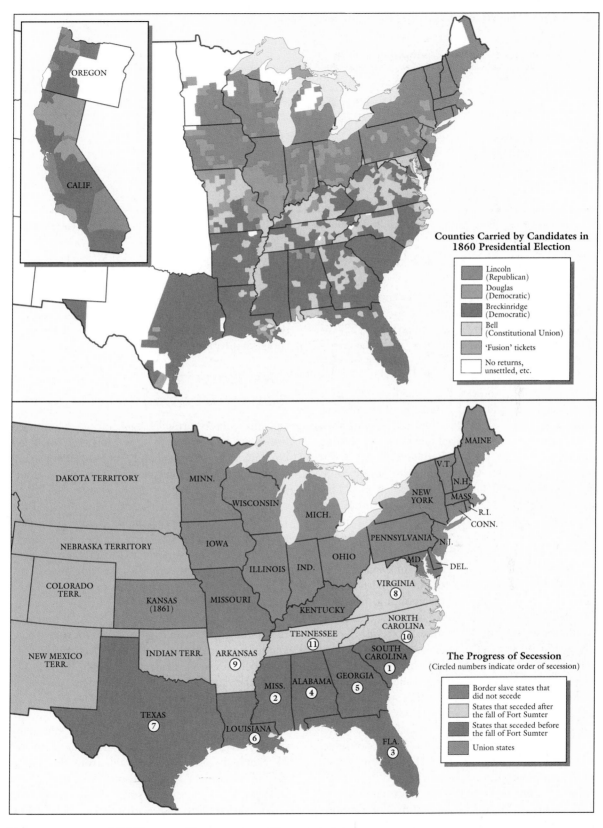

Counties Carried by Candidates in 1860 Presidential Election

OREGON

CALIF.

- Lincoln (Republican)
- Douglas (Democratic)
- Breckinridge (Democratic)
- Bell (Constitutional Union)
- 'Fusion' tickets
- No returns, unsettled, etc.

DAKOTA TERRITORY

MINN.

WISCONSIN

MICH.

MAINE

V.T.

N.H.

NEW YORK

MASS.

R.I.

CONN.

NEBRASKA TERRITORY

IOWA

PENNSYLVANIA

N.J.

MD.

DEL.

COLORADO TERR.

KANSAS (1861)

ILLINOIS

IND.

OHIO

MISSOURI

KENTUCKY

VIRGINIA ⑧

NORTH CAROLINA ⑩

NEW MEXICO TERR.

INDIAN TERR.

ARKANSAS ⑨

TENNESSEE ⑪

SOUTH CAROLINA ①

MISS. ②

ALABAMA ④

GEORGIA ⑤

TEXAS ⑦

LOUISIANA ⑥

FLA. ③

The Progress of Secession
(Circled numbers indicate order of secession)

- Border slave states that did not secede
- States that seceded after the fall of Fort Sumter
- States that seceded before the fall of Fort Sumter
- Union states

ELECTION OF 1860 AND SOUTHERN SECESSION

VOTING IN THE 1860 ELECTION

	All States		Free States (18)		Slave States (15)	
	Popular	*Electoral*	*Popular*	*Electoral*	*Popular*	*Electoral*
Lincoln	1,864,735	180	1,838,347	180	26,388	0
Opposition to Lincoln	2,821,157	123	1,572,637	3	1,248,520	120
"Fusion" Tickets*	595,846	—	580,426	—	15,420	—
Douglas	979,425	12	815,857	3	163,568	9
Breckinridge	669,472	72	99,381	0	570,091	72
Bell	576,414	39	76,973	0	499,441	39

*In several states the two Democratic parties and the Constitutional Union Party arranged a single anti-Lincoln ballot. These "fusion" tickets carried several counties, but failed to win any state.

A Republican victory in the presidential election would put an end to the South's political control of its destiny. Two-thirds of the time from 1789 to 1860, southerners (all slaveholders) had been president of the United States. No northern president had ever won reelection. Two-thirds of the Speakers of the House and presidents pro tem of the Senate had been southerners. Southern justices had been a majority on the Supreme Court since 1791. Lincoln's election would mark an irreversible turning away from this southern ascendancy. Even southern moderates warned that the South could not remain in the Union if Lincoln won. "This Government and Black Republicanism cannot live together," said one of them. "At no period of the world's history have four thousand millions of property [that is, the slave owners] debated whether it ought to submit to the rule of an enemy." And what about the three-quarters of southern whites who did not belong to slaveholding families? Lincoln's election, warned an Alabama secessionist, would show that "the North [means] to free the negroes and force amalgamation between them and the children of the poor men of the South." If Georgia remained in a Union "ruled by Lincoln and his crew," a secessionist in that state told nonslaveholders, "in TEN years or less our CHILDREN will be the *slaves* of negroes."

Most whites in the South voted for Breckinridge, who carried 11 slave states. Bell won the upper-South states of Virginia, Kentucky, and Tennessee. Missouri went to Douglas—the only state he carried, though he came in second in the popular vote. Although Lincoln received less than 40 percent of the popular vote, he won every free state and swept the presidency by a substantial margin in the electoral college (three of New Jersey's seven electoral votes went to Douglas).

THE LOWER SOUTH SECEDES

Lincoln's victory provided the shock that Southern fire-eaters had craved. The tension that had been building up for years suddenly exploded like a string of firecrackers, as seven states seceded one after another. According to the theory of secession, when each state ratified the Constitution and joined the Union, it authorized the national government to act as its agent in the exercise of certain functions of sovereignty—but the states had never given away their fundamental underlying sovereignty itself. Any state, then, by the act of its own convention, could withdraw from its "compact" with the other states and reassert its individual sovereignty. Therefore, the South Carolina legislature called for such a convention and ordered an election of delegates to consider withdrawing from the United States. On December 20, 1860, the South Carolina convention did withdraw, by a vote of 169 to 0.

The outcome was closer in other lower-South states. Unconditional unionism was rare, but many conservatives and former Whigs, including Alexander H. Stephens of Georgia, shrank from the drastic step of secession. At the conventions in each of the next six states to secede, some delegates tried to delay matters with vague proposals for "cooperation" among all southern states, or even with pro-

BANNER OF THE SOUTH CAROLINA SECESSION CONVENTION With its banner featuring a palmetto tree and a snake reminiscent of the American Revolution's "Don't Tread on Me" slogan, the South Carolina secession convention in 1860 looked forward to a grand new Southern republic composed of all 15 slave states and built on the ruins of the old Union. Note the large South Carolina keystone of the arch and the stones of free states lying cracked and broken on the ground.

posals to wait until after Lincoln's inauguration on March 4, 1861, to see what course he would pursue. Those minority factions were overridden by proponents of immediate secession. The conventions followed the example of South Carolina and voted to take their states out of the Union: Mississippi on January 9, 1861, Florida on the 10th, Alabama on the 11th, Georgia on the 19th, Louisiana on the 26th, and Texas on February 1. In those six states as a whole, 20 percent of the delegates voted against secession, but most of these, including Stephens, "went with their states" after the final votes had been tallied. Delegates from the seven seceding states met in Montgomery, Alabama, in February to create a new nation to be called the Confederate States of America.

NORTHERNERS AFFIRM THE UNION

Most people in the North considered secession unconstitutional and treasonable. In his final annual message to Congress, on December 3, 1860, President Buchanan insisted that the Union was not "a mere voluntary association of States, to be dissolved at pleasure by any one of the contracting parties." If secession was consummated, Buchanan warned, it would create a disastrous precedent that would make the United States government "a rope of sand." He continued:

> Our thirty-three States may resolve themselves into as many petty, jarring, and hostile republics. . . . By such a dread catastrophe the hopes of the friends of freedom throughout the world would be destroyed. . . . Our example for more than eighty years would not only be lost, but it would be quoted as proof that man is unfit for self-government.

European monarchists and conservatives were already expressing smug satisfaction at "the great smashup" of the republic in North America. They predicted that other disaffected minorities would also secede and that the United States would ultimately collapse into anarchy and revolution. That was precisely what northerners and even some upper-South Unionists feared. "The doctrine of secession is anarchy," declared a Cincinnati newspaper. "If any minority have the right to break up the Government at pleasure, because they have not had their way, there is an end of all government." Lincoln denied that the states had ever possessed independent sovereignty before becoming part of the United States. Rather, they had been colonies or territories that never would have become part of the United States had they not accepted unconditional sovereignty of the national government. No government, said Lincoln, "ever had provision in its organic law for its own termination. . . . No State, upon its own mere motion, can lawfully get out of the Union. . . . They can only do so against law, and by revolution."

In that case, answered many Southerners, we invoke the right of revolution to justify secession. After all, the United States itself was born of revolution. The secessionists maintained that they were merely following the example of their forefathers in declaring independence from a government that threatened their rights and liberties. An Alabaman asked rhetorically: Were not "the men of 1776, who withdrew their allegiance from George III and set up for themselves . . . Secessionists?"

Northerners could scarcely deny the right of revolution: They too were heirs of 1776. But "the right of revolution, is never a legal right," said Lincoln. "At most, it is but a moral right, when exercised for a morally justifiable cause. When exercised without such a cause revolution is no right, but simply a wicked exercise of physical power." The South, in Lincoln's view, had no morally justifiable cause. In fact, the event that had precipitated secession was his own election by a constitutional majority. For southerners to cast themselves in the mold of 1776 was "a libel upon the whole character and conduct" of the Founding Fathers, said the antislavery poet and journalist William Cullen Bryant. They rebelled "to establish the rights of man . . . and principles of universal liberty," whereas southerners in 1861 were rebelling to protect "a domestic despotism. . . . Their motto is not liberty, but slavery."

COMPROMISE PROPOSALS

Bryant conveniently overlooked the fact that slavery had existed in most parts of the republic founded by the revolutionaries of 1776. In any event, most people in the North agreed with Lincoln that secession was a "wicked exercise of physical power." The question was what to do about it. All kinds of compromise proposals came before Congress when it met in December 1860. To sort them out, the Senate and the House each set up a special committee. The Senate committee came up with a package of compromises sponsored by Senator John J. Crittenden of Kentucky. The Crittenden Compromise consisted of a series of proposed constitutional amendments: to guarantee slavery in the states perpetually against federal interference; to prohibit Congress from abolishing slavery in the District of Columbia or on any federal property (forts, arsenals, naval bases, and so on); to deny Congress the power to interfere with the interstate slave trade; to compensate slaveholders who were prevented from recovering

fugitive slaves who had escaped to the North; and, most important, to protect slavery south of latitude 36°30′ in all territories "now held *or hereafter acquired.*"

Given the appetite of the South for more slave territory in the Caribbean and Central America, that italicized phrase, in the view of most Republicans, might turn the United States into "a great slavebreeding and slavetrading empire." But even though endorsement of the territorial clause in the Crittenden Compromise would require Republicans to repudiate the platform on which they had just won the election, some conservatives in the party were willing to accept it in the interest of peace and conciliation. Their votes, together with those of Democrats and upper-South Unionists whose states had not seceded, might have gotten the compromise through Congress. It is doubtful, however, that the approval of three-quarters of the states required for ratification would have been forthcoming. In any case, word came from Springfield, Illinois, where President-elect Lincoln was preparing for his inaugural trip to Washington, telling key Republican senators and congressmen to stand firm against compromise on the territorial issue. "Entertain no proposition for a compromise in regard to the *extension* of slavery," wrote Lincoln.

> Filibustering for all South of us, and making slave states would follow . . . to put us again on the high-road to a slave empire. . . . We have just carried an election on principles fairly stated to the people. Now we are told in advance, the government shall be broken up, unless we surrender to those we have beaten. . . . If we surrender, it is the end of us. They will repeat the experiment upon us ad libitum. A year will not pass, till we shall have to take Cuba as a condition upon which they will stay in the Union.

Lincoln's advice was decisive. The Republicans voted against the Crittenden Compromise, which therefore failed in Congress. Most Republicans, though, went along with a proposal by Virginia for a "peace convention" of all the states to be held in Washington in February 1861. Although the seven seceded states sent no delegates, hopes that the convention might accomplish something encouraged Unionists in the eight other slave states either to reject secession or to adopt a wait-and-see attitude. In the end, the peace convention produced

"*The new Constitution [of the Confederate States] has put at rest forever all the agitating questions relating to our peculiar institution—African slavery as it exists among us—the proper status of the negro in our form of civilization. This was the immediate cause of the late rupture and present revolution. [Thomas] Jefferson, in his forecast, had anticipated this, as the 'rock upon which the old Union would split.' He was right. . . . But whether he fully comprehended the great truth upon which that rock stood and stands, may be doubted. The prevailing ideas entertained by him and most of the leading statesmen at the time of the formation of the old Constitution were, that the enslavement of the African was in violation of the laws of nature; that it was wrong in principle, socially, morally, and politically. It was an evil they knew not well how to deal with; but the general opinion of the men of that day was, that, somehow or other, in the order of Providence, the institution would be evanescent and pass away. . . . Those ideas, however, were fundamentally wrong. . . . Our new Government is founded upon exactly the opposite ideas; its foundations are laid, its cornerstone rests, upon the great truth that the negro is not equal to the white man; that slavery, subordination to the superior race, is his natural and moral condition. This, our new Government, is the first, in the history of the world, based upon this great physical, philosophical, and moral truth.*"

ALEXANDER H. STEPHENS
*vice president of the Confederate States of America,
March 21, 1861*

nothing better than a modified version of the Crittenden Compromise, which suffered the same fate as the original.

Nothing that happened in Washington would have made any difference to the seven states that had seceded. No compromise could bring them back. "We spit upon every plan to compromise," said one secessionist. No power could "stem the wild torrent of passion that is carrying everything before it," wrote former U.S. Senator Judah P. Benjamin of Louisiana. Secession "is a revolution" that "can no more be checked by human effort . . . than a prairie fire by a gardener's watering pot."

ESTABLISHMENT OF THE CONFEDERACY

While the peace convention deliberated in Washington, the seceded states focused on a convention in Montgomery, Alabama, that drew up a constitution and established a government for the new Confederate States of America. The Confederate constitution contained clauses that guaranteed slavery in both the states and the territories, strengthened the principle of state sovereignty, and prohibited its Congress from enacting a protective (as distinguished from a revenue) tariff and from granting government aid to internal improvements. It limited the president to a single six-year term. The convention delegates constituted themselves a provisional Congress for the new nation until regular elections could be held in November 1861. For provisional president and vice president, the convention turned away from radical secessionists, such as Yancey, and elected Jefferson Davis, a moderate secessionist, and Alexander Stephens, who had originally opposed Georgia's secession but ultimately had supported it.

Davis and Stephens were two of the ablest men in the South, with 25 years of service in the U.S.

Congress between them. A West Point graduate, Davis had commanded a regiment in the Mexican War and had been secretary of war in the Pierce administration—a useful fund of experience if civil war became a reality. But perhaps the main reason they were elected was to present an image of moderation and respectability to the eight upper-South states that remained in the Union. The Confederacy needed those states—at least some of them—if it was to be a viable nation, especially if war came. Without the upper South, the Confederate states would have less than one-fifth of the population (and barely one-tenth of the free population) and only one-twentieth of the industrial capacity of the Union states.

Confederate leaders appealed to the upper South to join them because of the "common origin, pursuits, tastes, manners and customs" that "bind together in one brotherhood the . . . slaveholding states." The principal bond was slavery. In a March 21, 1861, speech at Savannah, aimed in part at the upper South, Vice President Alexander Stephens defined slavery as the "cornerstone" of the Confederacy.

Residents of the upper South were indeed concerned about preserving slavery. But the issue was less salient there. A strong heritage of Unionism competed with the commitment to slavery. Virginia had contributed more men to the pantheon of Founding Fathers than any other state. Tennessee took pride in being the state of Andrew Jackson, famous for his stern warning to John C. Calhoun: "Our Federal Union—It must be preserved." Kentucky was the home of Henry Clay, the "Great Pacificator" who had put together compromises to save the Union on three occasions. These states would not leave the Union without greater cause.

THE FORT SUMTER ISSUE

As each state seceded, it seized the forts, arsenals, customs houses, and other federal property within its borders. Still in federal hands, however, were two remote forts in the Florida keys, another on an island off Pensacola, and Fort Moultrie in the Charleston harbor. Moultrie quickly became a bone of contention. In December 1860 the self-proclaimed republic of South Carolina demanded its evacuation by the 84-man garrison of the United States Army. An obsolete fortification, Moultrie was vulnerable to attack by the South Carolina militia that swarmed into the area. On the day after Christmas 1860, Major Robert Anderson, commander at Moultrie, moved his men to Fort Sumter, an uncompleted but immensely strong bastion on an artificial island in the channel leading into Charleston Bay. A Kentuckian married to a Georgian, Anderson sympathized with the South but remained loyal to the United States. He deplored the possibility of war and hoped that moving the garrison to Sumter would ease tensions by reducing the possibility of an attack. Instead, it lit a fuse that eventually set off the war.

South Carolina sent a delegation to President Buchanan to negotiate the withdrawal of the federal troops. Buchanan, previously pliable, surprised them by saying no. He even tried to reinforce the garrison. On January 9 the unarmed merchant ship *Star of the West*, carrying 200 soldiers for Sumter, tried to enter the bay but was driven away by South Carolina artillery. Loath to start a war, Major Anderson refused to return fire with Sumter's guns. Matters then settled into an uneasy truce. The Confederate government sent General Pierre G. T. Beauregard to take command of the troops ringing Charleston Bay with their cannons pointed at Fort Sumter, and waited to see what the incoming Lincoln administration would do.

When Abraham Lincoln took the oath of office as the 16th—and, some speculated, the last—president of the *United* States, he knew that his inaugural address would be the most important in American history. On his words would hang the issues of union or disunion, peace or war. His goal was to keep the upper South in the Union while cooling passions in the lower South, hoping that, in time, southern loyalty to the Union would reassert itself. In his address, he demonstrated both firmness and forbearance: firmness in purpose to preserve the Union, forbearance in the means of doing so. He repeated his pledge not "to interfere with the institution of slavery where it exists." He assured the Confederate states that "the government

THE BOMBARDMENT OF FORT SUMTER, APRIL 12, 1861 This drawing shows the incoming shells from Confederate batteries at Fort Moultrie and Cummings Point, and Fort Sumter's return fire. Note that Confederate shells have set the fort's interior on fire but the American flag is still flying. It would soon be lowered in surrender as the fire crept toward the powder magazine.

will not assail *you*." His first draft had also included the phrase "unless you *first* assail it," but William H. Seward, whom Lincoln had appointed secretary of state, persuaded him to drop those words as too provocative. Lincoln's first draft had also stated his intention to use "all the powers at my disposal" to "reclaim the public property and places which have fallen." He deleted that as too warlike and said only that he would "hold, occupy, and possess the property, and places belonging to the government," without defining exactly what he meant or how he would do it. In his eloquent peroration, Lincoln appealed to southerners as Americans who shared with other Americans four score and five years of national history. "We are not enemies, but friends," he said.

> Though passion may have strained, it must not break, our bonds of affection. The mystic chords of memory, stretching from every battlefield and patriot grave to every living heart and hearthstone all over this broad land, will yet swell the chorus of the Union when again

touched, as surely they will be, by the better angels of our nature.

Lincoln hoped to buy time with his inaugural address—time to demonstrate his peaceful intentions and to enable southern Unionists (whose numbers Republicans overestimated) to regain the upper hand. But the day after his inauguration, Lincoln learned that time was running out. A dispatch from Major Anderson informed him that provisions for the soldiers at Fort Sumter would soon be exhausted. The garrison must either be resupplied or evacuated. Any attempt to send in supplies by force would undoubtedly provoke a response from Confederate guns at Charleston. And by putting the onus of starting a war on Lincoln's shoulders, such an action would undoubtedly divide the North and unite the South, driving at least four more states into the Confederacy. Thus, most members of Lincoln's cabinet, along with the army's General-in-Chief Winfield Scott, advised Lincoln to withdraw the troops from

Sumter. That, however, would bestow a great moral victory on the Confederacy. It would confer legitimacy on the Confederate government and would probably lead to diplomatic recognition by foreign powers. Having pledged to "hold, occupy, and possess" national property, could Lincoln afford to abandon that policy during his first month in office? If he did, he would go down in history as the president who consented to the dissolution of the United States.

The pressures from all sides caused Lincoln many sleepless nights; one morning he rose from bed and keeled over in a dead faint. Finally he hit upon a solution that evidenced the mastery that would mark his presidency. He decided to send in unarmed ships with supplies but to hold troops and warships outside the harbor with authorization to go into action only if the Confederates used force to stop the supply ships. And he would give South Carolina officials advance notice of his intention. This stroke of genius shifted the decision for war or peace to Jefferson Davis. In effect, Lincoln flipped a coin and said to Davis, "Heads I win; tails you lose." If Confederate troops fired on the supply ships, the South would stand convicted of starting a war by attacking "a mission of humanity" bringing "food for hungry men." If Davis allowed the supplies to go in peacefully, the U.S. flag would continue to fly over Fort Sumter. The Confederacy would lose face at home and abroad, and southern Unionists would take courage.

Davis did not hesitate. He ordered General Beauregard to compel Sumter's surrender before the supply ships got there. At 4:30 a.m. on April 12, 1861, Confederate guns set off the Civil War by firing on Fort Sumter. After a 33-hour bombardment in which the rebels fired 4,000 rounds and the skeleton gun crews in the garrison replied with 1,000—with no one killed on either side—the burning fort lowered the U.S. flag in surrender.

CHOOSING SIDES

News of the attack triggered an outburst of anger and war fever in the North. "The town is in a wild state of excitement," wrote a Philadelphia diarist. "The American flag is to be seen everywhere. . . . Men are enlisting as fast as possible." A Harvard

> *"We must fight now, not because we want to subjugate the South, or because its subjugation would be advisable if it were possible, but because we must. The Nation has been defied. The National Government has been assailed. If either can be done with impunity neither Nation [n]or Government is worth a cent. We are not a Nation, and our Government is a sham. . . . We are fighting therefore, not to subjugate the South, but to maintain over ourselves a Government that we can respect, that can command obedience, and enforce it. In other words, we are fighting for the existence of our own Government, and not for the destruction of that at Montgomery. . . . War is self preservation, if our form of Government is worth preserving. If monarchy would be better, it might be wise to quit fighting, admit that a Republic was too weak to take care of itself, and invite some deposed Duke or Prince of Europe to come over here and rule us. But otherwise, we must fight."*
>
> **INDIANAPOLIS *DAILY JOURNAL***
> *April 27, 1861*

professor born during George Washington's presidency was astounded by the public response. "The heather is on fire," he wrote. "I never knew what a popular excitement can be." A New York woman wrote that the "time before Sumter" seemed like another century. "It seems as if we were never alive till now; never had a country till now."

Because the tiny United States Army—most of whose 16,000 soldiers were stationed at remote frontier posts—was inadequate to quell the "insurrection," Lincoln called on the states for 75,000 militia. The free states filled their quotas immediately. More than twice as many men volunteered as Lincoln had requested. Recognizing that the 90 days' service to which the militia were limited by law would be too short a time, Lincoln, on May 3, issued a call for three-year volunteers. Before the war was over, more than two million men would serve in the Union army and navy.

The eight slave states still in the Union rejected Lincoln's call for troops. Four of them—Virginia, Arkansas, Tennessee, and North Carolina—soon seceded and joined the Confederacy. Forced by the outbreak of actual war to choose between the Union and the Confederacy, most residents of those four states chose the Confederacy. As a former Unionist in North Carolina remarked, "The division must be made on the line of slavery. The South must go with the South. . . . Blood is thicker than Water."

Few found the choice harder to make than Robert E. Lee of Virginia. One of the most promising officers in the United States Army, Lee believed that southern states had no legal right to secede. General-in-Chief Winfield Scott wanted Lee to become field commander of the Union army. Instead, Lee sadly resigned from the army after the

LINK TO THE PAST

The Valley of the Shadow: Two Communities in the Civil War

http://valley.vcdh.virginia.edu

This site contains a wealth of data for two counties from the late 1850s through the end of the war: newspapers, tax lists, manuscript census returns, regimental records, official reports, soldiers' and civilians' letters and diaries, interactive maps, and more. The counties are Augusta County, Virginia, and Franklin County, Pennsylvania. Both are in the same valley (called the Shenandoah Valley in Virginia and Cumberland Valley in Pennsylvania), and their county seats, Staunton, Virginia, and Chambersburg, Pennsylvania, are less than 150 miles apart. Except for slavery, the counties had similar socioeconomic, cultural, ethnic, and political structures, yet their people fought on opposite sides in the war.

1. Analyze the principal newspapers in each county for a selected period (for example, 1860–61) to determine what issues were most important in shaping political allegiances.

2. Using the maps and regimental records, follow the troop movements of three Augusta County Confederate regiments and three Cumberland County Union regiments as they fought in the major campaigns and battles in the Eastern theater, sometimes against each other.

3. In July 1864 Confederate troops burned Chambersburg, and in October of the same year Union troops destroyed crops and other property in Augusta County. Using letters, diaries, newspapers, and other relevant sources, describe how the respective civilian populations reacted to these events.

4. Compare the home-front activities of women in support of the war effort in the two counties.

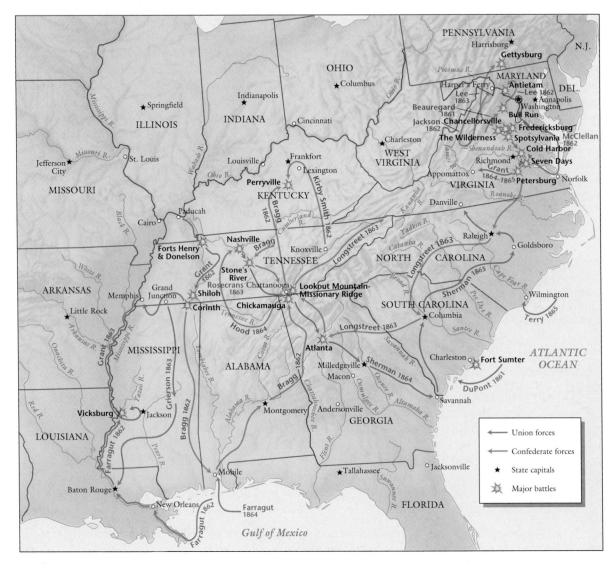

PRINCIPAL MILITARY CAMPAIGNS OF THE CIVIL WAR

Virginia convention passed an ordinance of secession on April 17. "I must side either with or against my section," Lee told a northern friend. "I cannot raise my hand against my birthplace, my home, my children." Along with three sons and a nephew, Lee joined the Confederate army. "I foresee that the country will have to pass through a terrible ordeal," he wrote, "a necessary expiation perhaps for our national sins."

Most southern whites embraced war against the Yankees with less foreboding and with a great deal more enthusiasm. When news of Sumter's surrender reached Richmond, a huge crowd poured into the state capitol square and ran up the Confederate flag. "Everyone is in favor of secession" and "perfectly frantic with delight," wrote a participant. "I never in all my life witnessed such excitement." The London *Times* correspondent described crowds in North Carolina with "flushed faces, wild eyes, screaming mouths, hurrahing for 'Jeff Davis' and 'the Southern Confederacy.'" No one in those cheering crowds could know that before the war ended at least 260,000 Confederate soldiers would lose their lives (along with 365,000 Union soldiers) and that the slave South they fought to defend would be utterly destroyed.

THE BORDER STATES

Except for Delaware, which remained firmly in the Union, the slave states that bordered free states were sharply divided by the outbreak of war. Leaders in these states talked vaguely of "neutrality," but they were to be denied that luxury—Maryland and Missouri immediately, and Kentucky in September 1861 when first Confederate and then Union troops crossed their borders.

The first blood was shed in Maryland on April 19, 1861, when a mob attacked Massachusetts troops traveling through Baltimore to Washington. The soldiers fired back, and, in the end, 12 Baltimoreans and 4 soldiers were dead. Confederate partisans burned bridges and tore down telegraph wires, cutting Washington off from the North for nearly a week until additional troops from Massachusetts and New York reopened communications and seized key points in Maryland. The troops also arrested many Confederate sympathizers, including the mayor and police chief of Baltimore, a judge, and two dozen state legislators. To prevent Washington from becoming surrounded by enemy territory, federal forces turned Maryland into an occupied state. Although thousands of Marylanders slipped into Virginia to join the Confederate army, a substantial majority of Maryland residents remained loyal to the Union.

The same was true of Missouri. Aggressive action by Union commander Nathaniel Lyon provoked a showdown between Unionist and pro-Confederate militia that turned into a riot in St. Louis on May 10 and 11, 1861, in which 36 people died. Lyon then led his troops in a summer campaign that drove the Confederate militia, along with the governor and pro-Southern legislators, into Arkansas, where they formed a Missouri Confederate government in exile. Reinforced by Arkansas regiments, these rebel Missourians invaded their home state, and on August 10 defeated Lyon (who was killed) in the bloody battle of Wilson's Creek in the southwest corner of Missouri. The victorious Confederates marched northward all the way to the Missouri River, capturing a Union garrison at Lexington 40 miles east of Kansas City on September 20. By then, Union forces made up of regiments from Iowa, Illinois, and Kansas as well as Missouri had regrouped and drove the ragged Missouri Confederates back into Arkansas.

From then until the war's end, Unionists maintained political control of Missouri through military power. Even so, continued guerrilla attacks by Confederate "bushwhackers" and counterinsurgency tactics by Unionist "jayhawkers" turned large areas of the state into a no-man's-land of hit-and-run raids, arson, ambush, and murder. During

SLAVERY AND SECESSION *The higher the proportion of slaves and slaveholders in the population of a southern state, the greater the intensity of secessionist sentiment.*

	Percentage of Population Who Were Slaves	Percentage of White Population in Slaveholding Families
Seven states that seceded December 1860–February 1861 (South Carolina, Mississippi, Florida, Alabama, Georgia, Louisiana, Texas)	47%	38%
Four states that seceded after the firing on Fort Sumter (Virginia, Arkansas, Tennessee, North Carolina)	32	24
Four border slave states remaining in Union (Maryland, Delaware, Kentucky, Missouri)	14	15

these years, the famous postwar outlaws Jesse and Frank James and Cole and Jim Younger rode with the notorious rebel guerrilla chieftains William Quantrill and "Bloody Bill" Anderson. More than any other state, Missouri suffered from a civil war within the Civil War, and its bitter legacy persisted for generations.

In elections held during the summer and fall of 1861, Unionists gained firm control of the Kentucky and Maryland legislatures. Kentucky Confederates, like those of Missouri, formed a state government in exile. When the Confederate Congress admitted both Kentucky and Missouri to full representation, the Confederate flag acquired its 13 stars. Nevertheless, two-thirds of the white population in the four border slave states favored the Union—though some of that support was undoubtedly induced by the presence of Union troops.

THE CREATION OF WEST VIRGINIA

The war itself produced a fifth Union border state: West Virginia. Most of the delegates from the portion of Virginia west of the Shenandoah Valley had voted against secession. A region of mountains, small farms, and few slaves, western Virginia's economy was linked more closely to nearby Ohio and Pennsylvania than to the South. Its largest city, Wheeling, was 330 miles from Richmond but only 60 miles from Pittsburgh. Delegates who had opposed Virginia's secession from the Union returned home determined to secede from Virginia. With the help of Union troops, who crossed the Ohio River and won a few small battles against Confederate forces in the area during the summer of 1861, they accomplished their goal. Through a complicated process of conventions and referendums—carried out in the midst of raids and skirmishes—they created the new state of West Virginia, which entered the Union in 1863.

INDIAN TERRITORY AND THE SOUTHWEST

To the south and west of Missouri, civil war raged along a different "border"—between southern

states and territories—for control of the resources of that vast region. In the Indian Territory (present-day Oklahoma), the Native Americans, who had been resettled there from Eastern states in the generation before the war, chose sides and carried on bloody guerrilla warfare against each other as ferocious as the bushwhacking in Missouri. The more prosperous Indians of the five "civilized tribes" (Cherokees, Creeks, Seminoles, Chickasaws, and Choctaws), many of them of mixed blood and some of them slaveholders, tended to side with the Confederacy. Some tribes signed treaties of alliance with the Confederate government. Aided by white and black Union regiments operating out of Kansas and Missouri, the pro-Union Indians gradually gained control of most of the Indian Territory.

In the meantime, Confederates had made their boldest bid to fulfill antebellum Southern ambitions to win the Southwest. A small army composed mostly of Texans pushed up the Rio Grande valley into New Mexico in 1861. The following February they launched a deeper strike to capture Santa Fe. With luck, they hoped to push even farther westward and northward to gain the mineral wealth of California and Colorado gold mines, whose millions were already helping to finance the Union war effort and could do wonders for Confederate finances. A good many Southerners lived in these Western territories and in California.

At first the Confederate drive up the Rio Grande went well. The Texans won a victory over the Unionist New Mexico militia and a handful of regulars at the battle of Valverde, 100 miles south of Albuquerque, on February 21, 1862. They continued up the valley, occupied Albuquerque and Santa Fe, and pushed on toward Fort Union near Santa Fe. But Colorado miners who had organized themselves into Union regiments and had carried out the greatest march of the war, over the rugged Rockies in winter, met the Texans in the battle of Glorieta Pass on March 26–28. The battle was a tactical draw, but a unit of Coloradans destroyed the Confederate wagon train, forcing the Southerners into a disastrous retreat back to Texas. Of the 3,700 who had started out to win the West for the Confederacy, only 2,000 made it back. The Confederates had shot their bolt in this region; the West and Southwest remained safe for the Union.

THE BALANCE SHEET OF WAR

If one counts three-quarters of the border state population (including free blacks) as pro-Union, the total number of people in Union states in 1861 was 22.5 million, compared with 9 million in the Confederate states. The North's military manpower advantage was even greater because the Confederate population total included 3.7 million slaves compared with 300,000 slaves in Union areas. At first, neither side expected to recruit blacks as soldiers. Eventually, the Union did enlist 180,000 black soldiers and at least 10,000 black sailors; the Confederacy held out against that drastic step until the war was virtually over. Altogether, about 2.1 million men fought for the Union and 850,000 for the Confederacy. That was close to half of the North's male population of military age (18 to 40) and three-quarters of the comparable Confederate white population. Because the labor force of the South consisted mainly of slaves, the Confederacy was able to enlist a larger proportion of its white population.

The North's economic superiority was even greater. The Union states possessed nine-tenths of the country's industrial capacity and registered shipping, four-fifths of its bank capital, three-fourths of its railroad mileage and rolling stock, and three-fourths of its taxable wealth.

These statistics gave pause to some Southerners. In a long war that mobilized the total resources of both sides, the North's advantages might prove decisive. But in 1861, few anticipated how long and intense the war would be. Both sides expected a short and victorious conflict. Confederates seemed especially confident, partly because of their vaunted sense of martial superiority over the "blue-bellied" Yankee nation of shopkeepers. Many Southerners really did believe that one of their own could lick three Yankees. "Let brave men advance with flint-locks and old-fashioned bayonets, on the popinjays of Northern cities," said ex-Governor Henry Wise of Virginia, now a Confederate general, and "the Yankees would break and run."

Although this turned out to be a grievous miscalculation, the South did have some reason to believe that its martial qualities were superior. A higher proportion of southerners than northerners had attended West Point and other military schools, had fought in the Mexican War, or had served as officers in the regular army. Volunteer military companies were more prevalent in the antebellum South than in the North. As a rural people, southerners were proficient in hunting, riding, and other outdoor skills useful in military operations. Moreover, the South had begun to prepare for war earlier than the North. As each state seceded, it mobilized militia and volunteer military companies. On March 6, 1861, the Confederate Congress had authorized an army of 100,000 men. By the time Lincoln called for 75,000 militia after the fall of Fort Sumter, the Confederacy already had 60,000 men under arms. Not until the summer of 1861 would the North's greater manpower begin to make itself felt in the form of a larger army.

STRATEGY AND MORALE

Even when fully mobilized, the North's superior resources did not guarantee success. Its military task was much more difficult than that of the South. The Confederacy had come into being in firm control of 750,000 square miles—a vast territory larger than all of western Europe and twice as large as the 13 colonies in 1776. To win the war, Union forces would have to invade, conquer, and occupy much of that territory, cripple its people's ability to sustain a war of independence, and destroy its armies. Britain had been unable to accomplish a similar task in the war for independence, even though it enjoyed a far greater superiority of resources over the United States in 1776 than the Union enjoyed over the Confederacy in 1861. Victory does not always ride with the heaviest battalions.

To "win" the war, the Confederacy need not invade or conquer the Union or even to destroy its armies; it needed only to stand on the defensive and prevent the North from destroying Southern armies—to hold out long enough to convince Northerners that the cost of victory was too high. Most Confederates were confident in 1861 that they were more than equal to the task. Most European

The Red Badge of Courage (1951)
Directed by John Huston. Starring Audie Murphy (The Youth) and Bill Mauldin (The Loud Soldier).

Stephen Crane's short novel *The Red Badge of Courage* became an instant classic when it was published in 1895. Civil War veterans praised its realistic descriptions of the confusion, terror, chaos, courage, despair, and adrenaline-driven rage of men in battle. A story of young Henry Fleming (The Youth) and his buddy Wilson (The Loud Soldier) in their first battle (Chancellorsville), the novel traces Henry's transition from boyhood to manhood, from raw recruit to veteran, over two days of violent combat. Intended by Crane as a portrait of soldiers facing the ultimate moment of truth in combat, the novel strives for universality rather than specificity as a Civil War story. Thus the battle is not actually named (though circumstances make clear that it is Chancellorsville, despite the film misleadingly dating it in 1862). The 304th New York regiment is fictional, and even the fact that it is a Civil War battle is scarcely mentioned. Crane did achieve a sort of universality; the novel is a story of men at war—not simply a story of the Civil War.

The film remains more faithful to the book than most movies based on novels. Most of the dialogue is taken directly from Crane. Henry Fleming's self-doubts, fears, and eventual heroism after he first runs away are brilliantly portrayed on the screen by action and dialogue against a background of a narrator's words. Fleming is played by Audie Murphy, America's most decorated soldier in World War II, and Wilson by Bill Mauldin, whose Willie and Joe cartoons provided the most enduring images of the American infantryman in that war. Virtually unknown as actors before this film, they make the characters come alive with moving performances.

Much of the credit for this success belongs to director John Huston, who brought out the best in his inexperienced actors. One of Hollywood's most prominent directors, Huston had lobbied Louis Mayer of MGM to produce the film. Believing that "Nobody wants to see a Civil War movie," Mayer finally gave in but provided Huston with a skimpy budget. When Huston flew to Africa immediately after the filming was completed to begin directing *The African Queen*, studio executives cut several of Huston's scenes and reduced the movie's length to 69 minutes. The studio also did little to promote the film, and because audiences failed to identify with its grim realism and mostly unknown cast *The Red Badge*

military experts agreed. The military analyst of the London *Times* wrote:

> It is one thing to drive the rebels from the south bank of the Potomac, or even to occupy Richmond, but another to reduce and hold in permanent subjection a tract of country nearly as large as Russia in Europe. . . . No war of independence ever terminated unsuccessfully except where the disparity of force was far greater than it is in this case. . . . Just as England during the revolution had to give up conquering the colonies so the North will have to give up conquering the South.

The important factor of morale also seemed to favor the Confederacy. To be sure, Union soldiers fought for powerful symbols: nation, flag, constitution. "We are fighting to maintain the best government on earth" was a common phrase in their letters and diaries. It is a "grate [sic] struggle for Union, Constitution, and law," wrote a New Jersey soldier. A Chicago newspaper declared that the South had "outraged the Constitution, set at defiance all law, and trampled under foot that flag which has been the glorious and consecrated symbol of American Liberty."

But Confederates, too, fought for nation, flag, constitution, and liberty—of whites. In addition,

of Courage was a box-office failure. Like the novel, however, it has become a classic that is still, a half-century after it was filmed, one of the best cinematic portrayals of the psychology of men in combat.

Audie Murphy (Henry Fleming), Bill Mauldin (The Loud Soldier), and their comrades in *The Red Badge of Courage*.

they fought to defend their land, homes, and families against invading "Yankee vandals" who many southern whites quite literally believed were coming to "free the negroes and force amalgamation between them and the children of the poor men of the South." An army fighting in defense of its homeland generally has the edge in morale. "We shall have the enormous advantage of fighting on our own territory and for our very existence," wrote a Confederate leader. "All the world over, are not one million of men defending themselves at home against invasion stronger in a mere military point of view, than five millions [invading] a foreign country?"

MOBILIZING FOR WAR

More than four-fifths of the soldiers on both sides were volunteers; in the first two years of the war, nearly all of them were. The Confederacy passed a conscription law in April 1862, and the Union followed suit in March 1863, but even afterward, most recruits were volunteers. In both North and South, patriotic rallies with martial music and speeches

UNION RECRUITING POSTER Nearly one-quarter of Union soldiers in the Civil War were foreign-born. Most of them had come to the United States as children during the years of heavy immigration in the 1840s and 1850s. They enlisted for the same motives of patriotism and adventure that actuated native-born Americans. This recruiting poster appeals to these motives in several languages.

motivated local men to enlist in a company (100 men) organized by the area's leading citizens. The recruits elected their own company officers (a captain and two lieutenants), who received their commissions from the state governor. A regiment consisted of 10 infantry companies, and each regiment was commanded by a colonel, with a lieutenant colonel and a major as second and third in command—all of them appointed by the governor.

Cavalry regiments were organized in a similar manner. Field artillery units were known as "batteries," a grouping of four or six cannon with their caissons and limber chests (two-wheeled, horse-drawn vehicles) to carry ammunition; the full complement of a six-gun battery was 155 men and 72 horses.

Volunteer units received a state designation and number in the order of their completion—the 2nd Massachusetts Volunteer Infantry, the 5th Virginia Cavalry, and so on. In most regiments the men in each company generally came from the same town or locality. Some Union regiments were composed of men of a particular ethnic group. By the end of the war, the Union army had raised about 2,000 infantry and cavalry regiments and 700 batteries; the Confederates had organized just under half as many. As the war went on, the original thousand-man complement of a regiment was usually whittled down to half or less by disease, casualties, desertions, and detachments. The states generally preferred to organize new regiments rather than keep the old ones up to full strength.

These were citizen soldiers, not professionals. They carried their peacetime notions of democracy and discipline into the army. That is why, in the tradition of the citizen militia, the men elected their company officers and sometimes their field officers (colonel, lieutenant colonel, and major) as well. Professional military men deplored the egalitarianism and slack discipline that resulted. Political influence often counted for more than military training in the election and appointment of officers. These civilians in uniform were extremely awkward and unmilitary at first, and some regiments suffered battlefield disasters because of inadequate training, discipline, and leadership. Yet this was the price that a democratic society with a tiny professional army had to pay to mobilize large armies almost overnight to meet a crisis. In time, these raw recruits became battle-hardened veterans commanded by experienced officers who had survived the weeding-out process of combat or of examination boards or who had been promoted from the ranks.

As the two sides organized their field armies, both grouped four or more regiments into brigades, and three or more brigades into divisions. By 1862, they began grouping two or more divisions into corps, and two or more corps into armies. Each of

THE RICHMOND GRAYS This photograph depicts a typical volunteer military unit that joined the Confederate army in 1861. Note the determined and confident appearance of these young men. By 1865, one-third of them would be dead and several others maimed for life.

ficers (including generals) *led* their men by example as much as by precept; they commanded from the front, not the rear. Combat casualties were higher among officers than among privates, and highest of all among generals, who died in action at a rate 50 percent higher than enlisted men.

WEAPONS AND TACTICS

In Civil War battles, the infantry rifle was the most lethal weapon. Muskets and rifles caused 80 to 90 percent of the combat casualties. From 1862 on, most of these weapons were "rifled"—that is, they had spiral grooves cut in the barrel to impart a spin to the bullet. This innovation was only a decade old, dating to the perfection in the 1850s of the "minié ball" (named after French army Captain Claude Minié, its principal inventor), a cone-shaped lead bullet with a base that expanded upon firing to "take" the rifling of the barrel. This made it possible to load and fire a muzzle-loading rifle as rapidly (two or three times per minute) as the old smoothbore musket. Moreover, the rifle had greater accuracy and at least four times the effective range (400 yards or more) of the smoothbore.

Civil War infantry tactics adjusted only gradually to the greater lethal range and accuracy of the new rifle, however, for the prescribed massed formations had emerged from experience with the smoothbore musket. Close-order assaults against defenders equipped with rifles resulted in enormous casualties. The defensive power of the rifle became even greater when troops began digging into trenches. Massed frontal assaults became almost suicidal. Soldiers and their officers learned the hard way to adopt skirmishing tactics, taking advantage of cover and working around the enemy flank.

LOGISTICS

Wars are fought not only by men and weapons but by the logistical apparatus that supports and supplies them. The Civil War is often called the world's first "modern" war because of the role played by railroads, steam-powered ships, and the telegraph—which did not exist in earlier wars fought on a similar scale (those of the French Revolution and Napoleon). Railroads and steamboats transported supplies and soldiers with unprecedented speed and efficiency; the

these larger units was commanded by a general appointed by the president. Most of the higher-ranking generals on both sides were West Point graduates, but others were appointed because they represented an important political, regional, or (in the North) ethnic constituency whose support Lincoln or Davis wished to solidify. Some of these "political" generals, like elected regimental officers, were incompetent, but as the war went on, they too either learned their trade or were weeded out. Some outstanding generals emerged from civilian life and were promoted up the ranks during the war. In both the Union and the Confederate armies, the best of-

UNION ARMY WAGON TRAIN IN VIRGINIA, 1863 By 1863, the productive power of farms and factories in the North had made the Union Army the best-fed and best-equipped army in history to that time. This supply wagon train testifies to the logistical efficiency of Union forces.

telegraph provided instantaneous communication between army headquarters and field commanders.

Yet these modern forms of transport and communications were extremely vulnerable. Cavalry raiders and guerrillas could cut telegraph wires, burn railroad bridges, and tear up the tracks. Confederate cavalry became particularly skillful at sundering the supply lines of invading Union armies and thereby neutralizing forces several times larger than their own. The more deeply the Union armies penetrated into the South, the more men they had to detach to guard bridges, depots, and supply dumps.

Once the campaigning armies had moved away from their railhead or wharfside supply base, they returned to dependence on animal-powered transport. Depending on terrain, road conditions, length of supply line, and proportion of artillery and cavalry, Union armies required one horse or mule for every two or three men. Thus a large invading Union army of 100,000 men (the approximate number in Virginia from 1862 to 1865 and in Georgia in 1864) would need about 40,000 draft animals. Confederate armies, operating mostly in friendly territory closer to their bases, needed fewer. The poorly drained dirt roads typical of much of the South turned into a morass of mud in the frequently wet weather.

These logistical problems did much to offset the industrial supremacy of the North, particularly during the first year of the war when bottlenecks, shortages, and inefficiency marked the logistical effort on both sides. By 1862, though, the North's economy had fully geared up for war, making the Union army the best-supplied army in history up to that time.

Confederate officials accomplished impressive feats of improvisation in creating war industries, especially munitions and gunpowder, but the

Southern industrial base was too slender to sustain adequate production. Particularly troublesome for the Confederacy was its inability to replace rails and rolling stock for its railroads. Although the South produced plenty of food, the railroads deteriorated to the point where that food could not reach soldiers or civilians. As the war went into its third and fourth years, the Northern economy grew stronger and the Southern economy grew weaker.

FINANCING THE WAR

One of the greatest defects of the Confederate economy was finance. Of the three methods of paying for a war—taxation, loans, and treasury notes (paper money)—treasury notes are the most inflationary, for they pump new money into the economy. By contrast, taxation and loans (war bonds) soak up money and thus counteract inflation. Though Confederate treasury officials were quite aware of this, the Confederate Congress, wary of dampening patriotic ardor, was slow to raise taxes. And because most capital in the South was tied up in land and slaves, little was available for buying war bonds.

So, expecting a short war, the Confederate Congress in 1861 authorized a limited issue of treasury notes, to be redeemable in specie (gold or silver) within two years after the end of the war. The first modest issue was followed by many more because the notes declined in value from the outset. The rate of decline increased during periods of Confederate military reverses, when people wondered whether the government would survive. At the end of 1861 the Confederate inflation rate was 12 percent every *month*; by early 1863 it took eight dollars to buy what one dollar had bought two years earlier; just before the war's end the Confederate dollar was worth one U.S. cent.

In 1863 the Confederate Congress tried to stem runaway inflation by passing a comprehensive law that taxed income, consumer purchases, and business transactions and included a "tax in kind" on agricultural products, allowing tax officials to seize 10 percent of a farmer's crops. This tax was extremely unpopular among farmers, many of whom hid their crops and livestock or refused to plant, thereby worsening the Confederacy's food shortages. The tax legislation was too little and too late to remedy the South's fiscal chaos. The Confederate

government raised less than 5 percent of its revenue by taxes and less than 40 percent by loans, leaving 60 percent to be created by the printing press. That turned out to be a recipe for disaster.

In contrast, the Union government raised 66 percent of its revenue by selling war bonds, 21 percent by taxes, and only 13 percent by printing treasury notes. The Legal Tender Act authorizing these notes—the famous "greenbacks," the origin of modern paper money in the United States—passed in February 1862. Congress had enacted new taxes in 1861—including the first income tax in American history—and had authorized the sale of war bonds. By early 1862, however, these measures had not yet raised enough revenue to pay for the rapid military buildup. To avert a crisis, Congress created the greenbacks. Instead of promising to redeem them in specie at some future date, as the South had done, Congress made them "legal tender"—that is, it required everyone to accept them as real money at face value. The North's economy suffered inflation during the war—about 80 percent over four years—but that was mild compared with the 9,000 percent inflation in the Confederacy. The greater strength and diversity of the North's economy, together with wiser fiscal legislation, accounted for the contrast.

The Union Congress also passed the National Banking Act of 1863. Before the war, the principal form of money had been notes issued by state-chartered banks. After Andrew Jackson's destruction of the Second Bank of the United States (Chapter 12), the number and variety of bank notes had skyrocketed until 7,000 different kinds of state bank notes were circulating in 1860. Some were virtually worthless; others circulated at a discount from face value. The National Banking Act of 1863 resulted from the desire of Whiggish Republicans to resurrect the centralized banking system and create a more stable bank-note currency, as well as to finance the war. Under the act, chartered national banks could issue bank notes up to 90 percent of the value of the U.S. bonds they held. This provision created a market for the bonds and, in combination with the greenbacks, replaced the glut of state bank notes with a more uniform national currency. To further the cause, Congress in 1865 imposed a tax of 10 percent on state bank notes, thereby taxing them out of existence.

National bank notes would be an important form of money for the next half-century. They had two defects, however: First, because the number of notes that could be issued was tied to each bank's holdings of U.S. bonds, the volume of currency available depended on the amount of federal debt rather than on the economic needs of the country. Second, the bank notes themselves tended to concentrate in the Northeast, where most of the large national banks were located, leaving the South and West short. The creation of the Federal Reserve System in 1913 (Chapter 21) largely remedied these defects, but Civil War legislation established the principle of a uniform national currency issued and regulated by the federal government.

NAVIES, THE BLOCKADE, AND FOREIGN RELATIONS

To sustain its war effort, the Confederacy needed to import large quantities of material from abroad, particularly from Britain. To shut off these imports and the exports of cotton that paid for them, on April 19, 1861, Lincoln proclaimed a blockade of Confederate ports. At first, the blockade was more a policy than a reality, for the navy had only a few ships on hand to enforce it. The task was formidable; the Confederate coastline stretched for 3,500 miles, with two dozen major ports and another 150 bays and coves where cargo could be landed. The United States Navy, which since the 1840s had been converting from sail to steam, recalled its ships from distant seas, took old sailing vessels out of mothballs, and bought or chartered merchant ships and armed them. Eventually the navy placed several hundred warships on blockade duty. But in 1861 the blockade was so thin that nine of every 10 vessels slipped through it on their way to or from Confederate ports.

KING COTTON DIPLOMACY

The Confederacy, however, inadvertently contributed to the blockade's success when it adopted "King Cotton diplomacy." Cotton was vital to the British economy because textiles were at the heart of British industry—and three-fourths of Britain's

supply of raw cotton came from the South. If that supply was cut off, southerners reasoned, British factories would shut down, unemployed workers would starve, and Britain would face the prospect of revolution. Rather than risk such a consequence, people in the South believed that Britain (and other powers) would recognize the Confederacy's independence and then use the powerful British navy to break the blockade.

Southerners were so firmly convinced of cotton's importance to the British economy that they kept the 1861 cotton crop at home rather than try to export it through the blockade, hoping thereby to compel the British to intervene. But the strategy backfired. Bumper crops in 1859 and 1860 had piled up a surplus of cotton in British warehouses and delayed the anticipated "cotton famine" until 1862. In the end, the South's voluntary embargo of cotton cost them dearly. The Confederacy missed its chance to ship out its cotton and store it abroad, where it could be used as collateral for loans to purchase war matériel.

Moreover, the Confederacy's King Cotton diplomacy contradicted its own foreign policy objective: to persuade the British and French governments to refuse to recognize the legality of the blockade. Under international law, a blockade must be "physically effective" to be respected by neutral nations. Confederate diplomats claimed that the Union effort was a mere "paper blockade," yet the dearth of cotton reaching European ports as a result of the South's embargo suggested to British and French diplomats that the blockade was at least partly effective. And indeed, by 1862 it was. Slow-sailing ships with large cargo capacity rarely tried to run the blockade, and the sleek, fast, steam-powered "blockade runners" that became increasingly prominent had a smaller cargo capacity and charged high rates because of the growing risk of capture or sinking by the Union navy. Although most blockade runners got through, by 1862 the blockade had reduced the Confederacy's seaborne commerce enough to convince the British government to recognize it as legitimate. The blockade was also squeezing the South's economy. After lifting its cotton embargo in 1862, the Confederacy had increasing difficulty exporting enough cotton through the blockade to pay for needed imports.

THE CONFEDERATE BLOCKADE RUNNER *ROBERT E. LEE* Confederate armies were heavily dependent upon supplies brought in from abroad on blockade runners, paid for by cotton smuggled out through the Union naval cordon by these same blockade runners. The sleek, narrow-beamed ships with raked masts and smokestacks (which could be telescoped to deck level) were designed for speed and deception to elude the blockade—a feat successfully accomplished on four-fifths of their voyages during the war. One of the most successful runners was the *Robert E. Lee*, photographed here after it had run the blockade fourteen times before being captured on the fifteenth attempt.

Confederate foreign policy also failed to win diplomatic recognition by other nations. That recognition would have conferred international legitimacy on the Confederacy and might even have led to treaties of alliance or of foreign aid. The French Emperor Napoleon III expressed sympathy for the Confederacy, as did influential groups in the British Parliament, but Prime Minister Lord Palmerston and Foreign Minister John Russell refused to recognize the Confederacy while it was engaged in a war it might lose, especially if recognition might jeopardize relations with the United States. The Union foreign policy team of Secretary of State Seward and Minister to England Charles Francis Adams did a superb job. Seward issued blunt warnings against recognizing the Confederacy; Adams softened them with the velvet glove of diplomacy. Other nations followed Britain's lead; by 1862 it had become clear that Britain would withhold recognition until the Confederacy had virtually won its independence—but, of course, such recognition would have come too late to help the Confederacy win.

THE *TRENT* AFFAIR

If anything illustrated the frustrations of Confederate diplomacy, it was the "*Trent* Affair"—which came tantalizingly close to rupturing British–American relations to Confederate advantage, but did not. In October 1861 Southern envoys James Mason and John Slidell slipped through the blockade. Mason hoped to represent the Confederacy in London and Slidell in Paris. On November 8, Captain Charles Wilkes of the U.S.S. *San Jacinto* stopped the British mail steamer *Trent*, with Mason and Slidell on board, near Cuba. Wilkes arrested the two Southerners, took them to Boston, and became an instant hero in the North. When the news reached England, the British government and public were outraged by Wilkes's "high-handed" action. Although the Royal Navy had acted in similar fashion during the centuries when Britannia ruled the waves, John Bull (England) would not take this behavior from his brash American cousin Jonathan (the United States). Britain demanded an apology and the release of Mason and Slidell. The popular press on both sides of the Atlantic stirred up war fever. Soon, however, good sense prevailed and Britain softened its demands. With a philosophy of "one war at a time," the Lincoln administration released Mason and Slidell the day after Christmas 1861, declaring that Captain Wilkes had acted "without instructions." The British accepted this statement in lieu of an apology, and the crisis ended.

THE CONFEDERATE NAVY

Lacking the capacity to build a naval force at home, the Confederacy hoped to use British shipyards for the purpose. Through a loophole in the British neutrality law, two fast commerce raiders built in Liverpool made their way into Confederate hands in 1862. Named the *Florida* and the *Alabama*, they roamed the seas for the next two years, capturing or sinking Union merchant ships and whalers. The *Alabama* was the most feared raider. Commanded by the leading Confederate sea dog, Raphael Semmes, she sank 62 merchant vessels plus a Union warship before another warship, the U.S.S. *Kearsarge* (whose captain, John A. Winslow, had once been Semmes's messmate in the old navy), sank the *Alabama* off Cherbourg, France, on June 19, 1864. Altogether, Confederate privateers and commerce raiders destroyed or captured 257 Union merchant vessels and drove at least 700 others to foreign registry. This Confederate achievement, though spectacular, made only a tiny dent in the Union war effort, especially when compared with the 1,500 blockade runners captured or de-

stroyed by the Union navy, not to mention the thousands of others that decided not even to try to beat the blockade.

THE *MONITOR* AND THE *VIRGINIA*

Its inadequate shipbuilding facilities prevented the Confederate navy from challenging Union seapower where it counted most—along the coasts and rivers of the South. Still, though plagued by shortages on every hand, the Confederate navy department demonstrated great skill at innovation. Southern engineers developed "torpedoes" (mines) that sank or damaged 43 Union warships in southern bays and rivers. Even more innovative (though less successful) was the building of ironclad "rams" to sink the blockade ships. The idea of iron armor for warships was not new—the British and French navies had prototype ironclads in 1861—but the Confederacy built the first one to see action. It was the C.S.S. *Virginia*, commonly called (even in the South) the *Merrimac* because it was rebuilt from the steam frigate U.S.S. *Merrimack*, which had been burned to the waterline by the Union navy at Norfolk when the Confederates seized the naval base there in April 1861. Ready for its trial-by-combat on March 8, 1862, the *Virginia* steamed out to attack the blockade squadron at Hampton Roads. She sank one warship with her iron ram and another with her 10 guns. Other Union ships ran aground trying to escape, to be finished off (Confederates expected) the next day. Union shot and shells bounced off the *Virginia's* armor plate. It was the worst day the United States Navy would have until December 7, 1941.

Panic seized Washington and the whole northeastern seaboard. In almost Hollywood fashion, however, the Union's own ironclad sailed into Hampton Roads in the nick of time and saved the rest of the fleet. This was the U.S.S. *Monitor*, completed just days earlier at the Brooklyn navy yard. Much smaller than the *Virginia*, with two 11-inch guns in a revolving turret (an innovation) set on a deck almost flush with the water, the *Monitor* looked like a "tin can on a shingle." It presented a small target and was capable of concentrating considerable firepower in a given direction with its

THE *MONITOR* AND *MERRIMAC* The black-and-white photograph shows the crew of the Union ironclad *Monitor* standing in front of its revolving two-gun turret. In action, the sun canopy above the turret would be taken down and all sailors would be at their stations inside the turret or the hull, as shown in the color painting of the famed battle, on March 9, 1862, between the *Monitor* and the Confederate *Virginia* (informally called the *Merrimac* because it had been converted from the captured U.S. frigate *Merrimack*). There is no photograph of the *Virginia*, which was blown up by its crew two months later when the Confederates retreated toward Richmond, because its draft was too deep to go up the James River.

revolving turret. Next day, the *Monitor* fought the *Virginia* in history's first battle between ironclads. It was a draw, but the *Virginia* limped home to Norfolk never again to menace the Union fleet. Although the Confederacy built other ironclad rams, some never saw action and none achieved the initial success of the *Virginia*. By the war's end, the Union navy had built or started 58 ships of the *Monitor* class (some of them double-turreted), launching a new age in naval history that ended the classic "heart of oak" era of warships.

CAMPAIGNS AND BATTLES, 1861–1862

Wars can be won only by hard fighting. This was a truth that some leaders on both sides overlooked.

HARVEST OF DEATH This photograph of a Confederate soldier killed in action in Virginia speaks more eloquently than words of the grim reality of war.

One of them was Winfield Scott, General-in-Chief of the United States Army. Scott, a Virginian who had remained loyal to the Union, evolved a military strategy based on his conviction that a great many southerners were eager to be won back to the Union. The main elements of his strategy were a naval blockade and a combined army-navy expedition to take control of the Mississippi, thus sealing off the Confederacy on all sides and enabling the Union to "bring them to terms with less bloodshed than by any other plan." The northern press ridiculed Scott's strategy as "the Anaconda Plan," after the South American snake that squeezes its prey to death.

THE BATTLE OF BULL RUN

Most northerners believed that the South could be overcome only by victory in battle. Virginia emerged as the most likely battleground, especially after the Confederate government moved its capital to Richmond in May 1861. "Forward to Richmond," clamored northern newspapers, and forward toward Richmond moved a Union army of 35,000 men in July, despite Scott's misgivings and those of the army's field commander, Irvin McDowell. McDowell believed his raw, 90-day Union militia were not ready to fight a real battle. They got no farther than Bull Run, a sluggish stream 25 miles southwest of Washington, where a Confederate army commanded by Beauregard had been deployed to defend a key rail junction at Manassas.

Another small Confederate army in the Shenandoah Valley under General Joseph E. Johnston had given a Union force the slip and had traveled to Manassas by rail to reinforce Beauregard. On July 21 the attacking Federals forded Bull Run and hit the rebels on the left flank, driving them back. By early afternoon, the Federals seemed to be on the verge of victory, but a Virginia brigade commanded by Thomas J. Jackson stood "like a stone wall," earning Jackson the nickname he carried ever after. By midafternoon Confederate reinforcements—including one brigade just off the train from the Shenandoah Valley—had grouped for a screaming counterattack (the famed "rebel yell" was first heard here). They drove the exhausted and disorganized Yankees back across Bull Run in a retreat that turned into a rout.

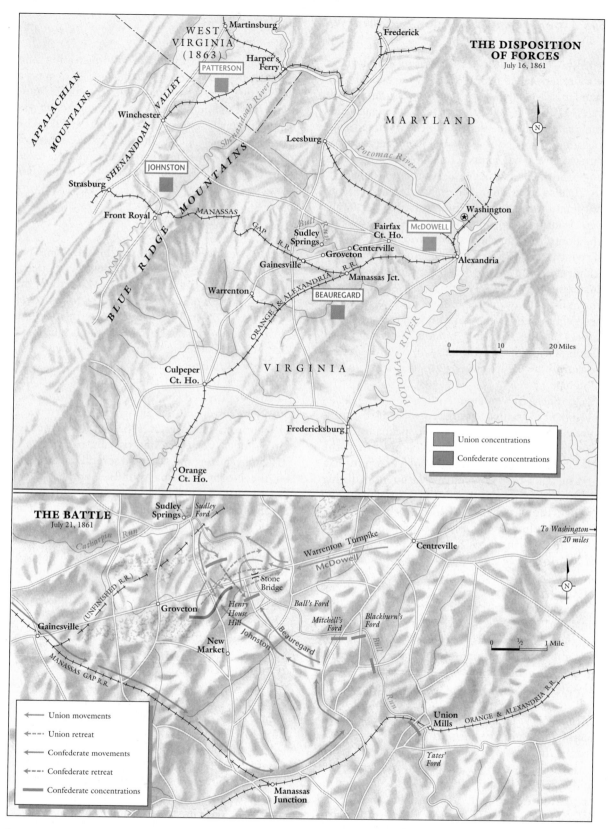

THE DISPOSITION OF FORCES
July 16, 1861

WEST VIRGINIA (1863)

Martinsburg

Frederick

Harper's Ferry

PATTERSON

APPALACHIAN MOUNTAINS

Winchester

Shenandoah River

MARYLAND

Leesburg

Potomac River

JOHNSTON

Strasburg

SHENANDOAH VALLEY

BLUE RIDGE MOUNTAINS

Front Royal

MANASSAS GAP R.R.

Bull Run

Sudley Springs

Fairfax Ct. Ho.

McDOWELL

Washington

Centreville

Groveton

Gainesville

Manassas Jct.

Alexandria

ORANGE & ALEXANDRIA R.R.

Warrenton

BEAUREGARD

VIRGINIA

POTOMAC RIVER

Culpeper Ct. Ho.

0   10   20 Miles

Fredericksburg

Orange Ct. Ho.

| | Union concentrations |
| | Confederate concentrations |

THE BATTLE
July 21, 1861

Sudley Springs

Sudley Ford

Catharpin Run

Warrenton Turnpike

McDowell

Centreville

To Washington
20 miles

UNFINISHED R.R.

Stone Bridge

Groveton

Henry House Hill

Ball's Ford

Mitchell's Ford

Blackburn's Ford

Johnston

Beauregard

New Market

Bull Run

0   ½   1 Mile

Gainesville

MANASSAS GAP R.R.

Union Mills

ORANGE & ALEXANDRIA R.R.

Yates' Ford

← Union movements

←--- Union retreat

← Confederate movements

←--- Confederate retreat

— Confederate concentrations

Manassas Junction

BATTLE OF BULL RUN (MANASSAS), JULY 21, 1861

Although the Battle of Manassas (or Bull Run, as northerners called it) was small by later Civil War standards, it made a profound impression on both sides. Of the 18,000 soldiers actually engaged on each side, Union casualties (killed, wounded, and captured) were about 2,800 and Confederate casualties 2,000. The victory exhilarated Confederates and confirmed their belief in their martial superiority. It also gave them a morale advantage in the Virginia theater that persisted for two years. And yet, Manassas also bred overconfidence. Some in the South thought the war was won. Northerners, by contrast, were jolted out of their expectations of a short war. A new mood of reality and grim determination gripped the North. Congress authorized the enlistment of up to a million three-year volunteers. Hundreds of thousands flocked to recruiting offices in the next few months. Lincoln called General George B. McClellan to Washington to organize the new troops into the Army of the Potomac.

An energetic, talented officer only 34 years old, small of stature but great with an aura of destiny, McClellan soon won the nickname "The Young Napoleon." He had commanded the Union forces that won control of West Virginia, and he took firm control in Washington during the summer and fall of 1861. He organized and trained the Army of the Potomac into a large, well-disciplined, and well-equipped fighting force. He was just what the North needed after its dispiriting defeat at Bull Run. When Scott stepped down as general-in-chief on November 1, McClellan took his place.

As winter approached, however, and McClellan did nothing to advance against the smaller Confederate army whose outposts stood only a few miles from Washington, his failings as a commander began to show. He was a perfectionist in a profession where nothing could ever be perfect. His army was perpetually almost ready to move. McClellan was afraid to take risks; he never learned the military lesson that no victory can be won without risking defeat. He consistently overestimated the strength of enemy forces facing him and used these faulty estimates as a reason for inaction until he could increase his own force. When newspapers began to publish criticism of McClellan from within the administration and among Republicans in Congress (he was a Democrat), he accused his critics of political motives. Having built a fine fighting machine, he was afraid to start it up for fear it might break. The caution that McClellan instilled in the Army of the Potomac's officer corps persisted for more than a year after Lincoln removed him from command in November 1862.

NAVAL OPERATIONS

Because of McClellan, no significant action occurred in the Virginia theater after the Battle of Bull Run until the spring of 1862. Meanwhile, the Union navy won a series of victories over Confederate coastal forts at Hatteras Inlet on the North Carolina coast, Port Royal Sound in South Carolina, and other points along the Atlantic and Gulf coasts. These successes provided new bases from which to expand and tighten the blockade. They also provided small Union armies with take-off points for operations along the southern coast. In February and March 1862, an expeditionary force under General Ambrose Burnside won a string of victories and occupied several crucial ports on the North Carolina sounds. Another Union force captured Fort Pulaski at the mouth of the Savannah River, cutting off that important Confederate port from the sea.

One of the Union navy's most impressive achievements was the capture in April 1862 of New Orleans, the Confederacy's largest city and principal port. Most Confederate troops in the area had been called up the Mississippi to confront a Union invasion of Tennessee, leaving only some militia, an assortment of steamboats converted into gunboats, and two strong forts flanking the river 70 miles below New Orleans. That was not enough to stop Union naval commander David G. Farragut, a native of Tennessee still loyal to the U.S. navy in which he had served for a half century. In a daring action on April 24, 1862, Farragut led his fleet upriver past the forts, scattering the Confederate fleet and fending off fire rafts. He lost four ships, but the rest won through and compelled the surrender of New Orleans with nine-inch naval guns trained on its streets. Fifteen thousand Union

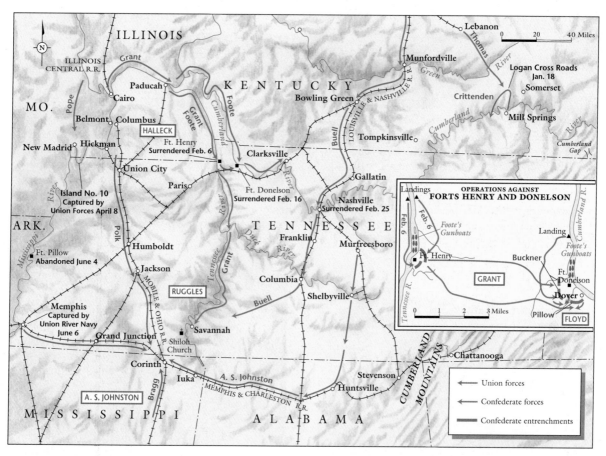

KENTUCKY-TENNESSEE THEATER, WINTER–SPRING 1862

soldiers marched in and occupied the city and its hinterland.

FORT HENRY AND FORT DONELSON

These victories demonstrated the importance of seapower even in a civil war. Even more important were Union victories won by the combined efforts of the army and fleets of river gunboats on the Tennessee and Cumberland rivers, which flow through Tennessee and Kentucky and empty into the Ohio River just before it joins the Mississippi. The unlikely hero of these victories was Ulysses S. Grant, who had failed in several civilian occupations after resigning from the peacetime military in 1854. Grant rejoined when war broke out. His

quiet efficiency and determined will won him promotion from Illinois colonel to brigadier general and the command of a small but growing force based at Cairo, Illinois, in the fall of 1861. When Confederate units entered Kentucky in September, Grant moved quickly to occupy the mouths of the Cumberland and Tennessee rivers. Unlike McClellan, who had known nothing but success in his career and was afraid to jeopardize that record, Grant's experience of failure made him willing to take risks. Having little to lose, he demonstrated that willingness dramatically in the early months of 1862.

Military strategists on both sides understood the importance of these navigable rivers as highways of invasion into the South's heartland. The Confederacy had built forts at strategic points

Confederate Dead on the Battlefield

The technology of photography was two decades old when the Civil War began. Professional photographers, who considered themselves artists, took thousands of pictures of Civil War scenes and soldiers. The most vivid and powerful of these were photographs of soldiers killed in battle. These pictures of Confederate soldiers on the Antietam battlefield conveyed "the terrible reality and suffering of war," as a reporter for the *New York Times* put it. But, he added, "there is one side of the picture that the sun did not catch, one phase that has escaped photographic skill. It is the background of widows and orphans, torn from the bosom of their natural protectors by the red remorseless hand of Battle. . . . All of this desolation imagination must paint—broken hearts cannot be photographed."

along the rivers and had begun to convert a few steamboats into gunboats and rams to back up the forts. The Union also converted steamboats into "timberclad" gunboats—so called because they were armored just enough to protect the engine and the paddle wheels but not enough to impair speed and shallow draft for river operations. The Union also built a new class of ironclad gunboats designed for river warfare. Carrying 13 guns, these flat-bottomed, wide-beamed vessels drew only six feet of water. Their hulls and paddle wheels were protected by a sloping casemate sheathed in iron armor up to 2½ inches thick.

When the first of these strange-looking but formidable craft were ready in February 1862, Grant struck. His objectives were Forts Henry and Donelson on the Tennessee and Cumberland rivers just south of the Kentucky-Tennessee border. The gunboats knocked out Fort Henry on February 6. Fort Donelson proved a tougher nut to crack. Its guns repulsed a gunboat attack on February 14. Next day the 17,000-man Confederate army attacked Grant's besieging army, which had been reinforced to 27,000 men. With the calm decisiveness that became his trademark, Grant directed a counterattack that penned the defenders back up in their fort. Cut off from support by either land or river, the Confederate commander asked for surrender terms on February 16. Grant's reply made him instantly famous when it was published in the North: "No terms except an immediate and unconditional surrender can be accepted. I propose to move immediately upon your works." With no choice, the 13,000 surviving Confederates surrendered (some had escaped), giving Grant the most striking victory in the war thus far.

These victories had far-reaching strategic consequences. Union gunboats now ranged all the way up the Tennessee River to northern Alabama, enabling a Union division to occupy the region, and up the Cumberland to Nashville, which became the first Confederate state capital to surrender to Union forces on February 25. Confederate military units pulled out of Kentucky and most of Tennessee and reassembled at Corinth in northern Mississippi. Jubilation spread through the North and despair through the South. By the end of March 1862, however, the Confederate commander in the western theater, Albert Sidney Johnston (not to be confused with Joseph E. Johnston in Virginia), had built up an army of 40,000 men at Corinth. His plan was to attack Grant's force of 35,000, which had established a base 20 miles away at Pittsburg Landing on the Tennessee River just north of the Mississippi-Tennessee border.

THE BATTLE OF SHILOH

On April 6 the Confederates attacked at dawn near a church called Shiloh, which gave its name to the battle. They caught Grant by surprise and drove his army toward the river. After a day's fighting of unprecedented intensity, with total casualties of 15,000, Grant's men brought the Confederate onslaught to a halt at dusk. One of the Confederate casualties was Johnston, who bled to death when a bullet severed an artery in his leg—the highest-ranking general on either side to be killed in the war. Beauregard, who had been transferred from Virginia to the West, took command after Johnston's death.

Some of Grant's subordinates advised retreat during the dismal night of April 6–7, but Grant would have none of it. Reinforced by fresh troops from a Union army commanded by General Don Carlos Buell, the Union counterattacked next morning (April 7) and, after 9,000 more casualties to the two sides, drove the Confederates back to Corinth. Although Grant had snatched victory from the jaws of defeat, his reputation suffered a decline for a time because of the heavy Union casualties (13,000) and the suspicion that he had been caught napping the first day.

Union triumphs in the western theater continued. The combined armies of Grant and Buell, under the overall command of the top-ranking Union general in the West, Henry W. Halleck, drove the Confederates out of Corinth at the end of May. Meanwhile, the Union gunboat fleet fought its way down the Mississippi to Vicksburg, virtually wiping out the Confederate fleet in a spectacular battle at Memphis on June 6. At Vicksburg the Union gunboats from the north

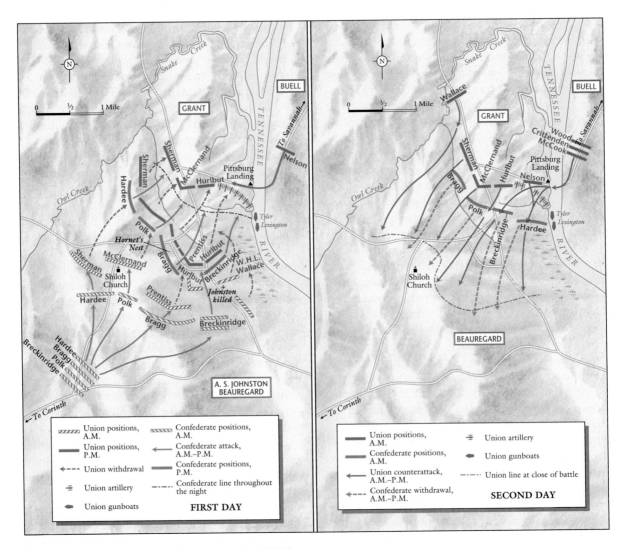

BATTLE OF SHILOH, APRIL 6–7, 1862

connected with part of Farragut's fleet that had come up from New Orleans, taking Baton Rouge and Natchez along the way. The heavily fortified Confederate bastion at Vicksburg, however, proved too strong for Union naval firepower to subdue. Nevertheless, the dramatic succession of Union triumphs in the West from February to June—including a decisive victory at the battle of Pea Ridge in northwest Arkansas on March 7 and 8—convinced the North that the war was nearly won. "Every blow tells fearfully against the rebellion," boasted the leading northern newspaper, the

New York *Tribune*, on May 23, 1862. "The rebels themselves are panic-stricken, or despondent. It now requires no very far reaching prophet to predict the end of this struggle."

THE VIRGINIA THEATER

Even as the editorial writer wrote these words, affairs in Virginia were about to take a sharp turn in favor of the Confederacy. Within three months the Union, so near a knockout victory that spring, was back on the defensive.

In the western theater the broad rivers had facilitated the Union's invasion of the South, but in Virginia a half-dozen small rivers flowing west to east lay athwart the line of operations between Washington and Richmond and provided the Confederates with natural lines of defense. McClellan, still in command of the Army of the Potomac, persuaded a reluctant Lincoln to approve a plan to transport his army down Chesapeake Bay to the tip of the Virginia peninsula, formed by the tidal portions of the York and James rivers. That would shorten the route to Richmond and give the Union army a seaborne supply line secure from harassment by Confederate cavalry and guerrillas.

This was a good plan—in theory. And the logistical achievement of transporting 110,000 men and all their equipment, animals, and supplies by sea to the jump-off point near Yorktown was impressive. But once again, McClellan's failings began to surface. A small Confederate blocking force at Yorktown held him for the entire month of April, as he cautiously dragged up siege guns to blast through defenses that his large army could have punched through in days on foot. McClellan slowly followed the retreating Confederate force up the peninsula to a new defensive line only a few miles east of Richmond, all the while bickering with Lincoln and Secretary of War Edwin M. Stanton over the reinforcements they were withholding to protect Washington against a possible strike by Stonewall Jackson's small Confederate army in the Shenandoah Valley.

Jackson's month-long campaign in the Shenandoah (May 8–June 9), one of the most brilliant of the war, demonstrated what could be accomplished through deception, daring, and mobility. With only 17,000 men, Jackson moved by forced marches so swift that his infantry earned the nickname "Jackson's foot cavalry." Darting here and there through the valley, they marched 350 miles in the course of one month; won four battles against three separate Union armies, whose combined numbers surpassed Jackson's by more than 2 to 1 (but which Jackson's force always outnumbered at the point of contact); and compelled Lincoln to divert to the valley some of the reinforcements McClellan demanded.

Even without those reinforcements, McClellan's army substantially outnumbered the Confederate force defending Richmond, commanded by Joseph E. Johnston. As usual, though, McClellan overestimated Johnston's strength at double what it was and acted accordingly. Even so, by the last week of May, McClellan's army was within six miles of Richmond. A botched Confederate counterattack on May 31 and June 1 (the Battle of Seven Pines) produced no result except 6,000 Confederate and 5,000 Union casualties. One of those casualties was Confederate General Joseph Johnston, who had been wounded in the shoulder. Jefferson Davis named Robert E. Lee to replace him.

THE SEVEN DAYS' BATTLES

That appointment marked a major turning point in the campaign. Lee had done little so far to earn a wartime reputation, having failed in his only field command to dislodge Union forces from control of West Virginia. His qualities as a commander began to manifest themselves when he took over what he renamed "The Army of Northern Virginia." Those qualities were boldness, a willingness to take great risks, an almost uncanny ability to read the enemy commander's mind, and a charisma that won the devotion of his men. While McClellan continued to dawdle, Lee sent his dashing cavalry commander, Jeb Stuart, to lead a reconnaissance around the Union army to discover its weak points. Lee also brought Jackson's army in from the Shenandoah Valley, and launched a June 26 attack on McClellan's right flank in what became known as the Seven Days' battles. Constantly attacking, Lee's army of 88,000 drove McClellan's 100,000 away from Richmond to a new fortified base on the James River. The offensive cost the Confederates 20,000 casualties (compared with 16,000 for the Union) and turned Richmond into one vast hospital. But it reversed the momentum of the war.

CONFEDERATE COUNTEROFFENSIVES

Northern sentiments plunged from the height of euphoria in May to the depths of despair in July.

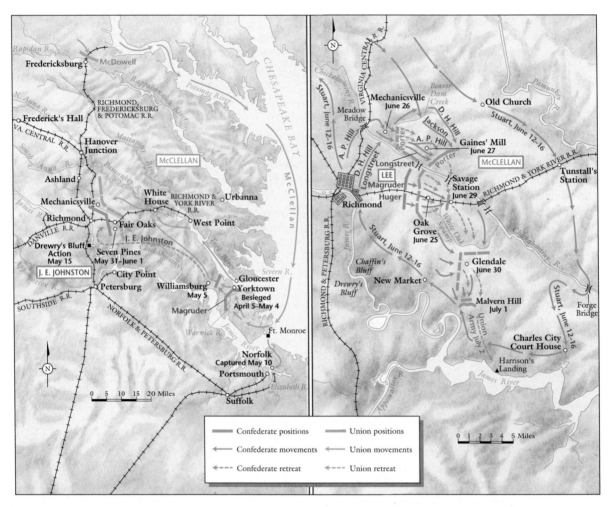

PENINSULA CAMPAIGN,
APRIL–MAY 1862

SEVEN DAYS' BATTLES,
JUNE 25–JULY 1, 1862

"The feeling of despondency here is very great," wrote a New Yorker, while a Southerner exulted that "Lee has turned the tide, and I shall not be surprised if we have a long career of successes." The tide turned in the western theater as well, where Union conquests in the spring had brought 50,000 square miles of Confederate territory under Union control. To occupy and administer this vast area, however, drew many thousands of soldiers from combat forces, which were left depleted and deep in enemy territory, and vulnerable to cavalry raids. During the summer and fall of 1862 the cavalry commands of Tennesseean Nathan Bedford Forrest and Kentuckian John

Hunt Morgan staged repeated raids in which they burned bridges, blew up tunnels, tore up tracks, and captured supply depots and the Union garrisons trying to defend them. By August the once-formidable Union war machine in the West seemed to have broken down.

These raids paved the way for infantry counter-offensives. After recapturing some territory, Earl Van Dorn's Army of West Tennessee got a bloody nose when it failed to retake Corinth on October 3 and 4. At the end of August, Braxton Bragg's Army of Tennessee launched a drive northward from Chattanooga through east Tennessee and Kentucky. It had almost reached the Ohio River in

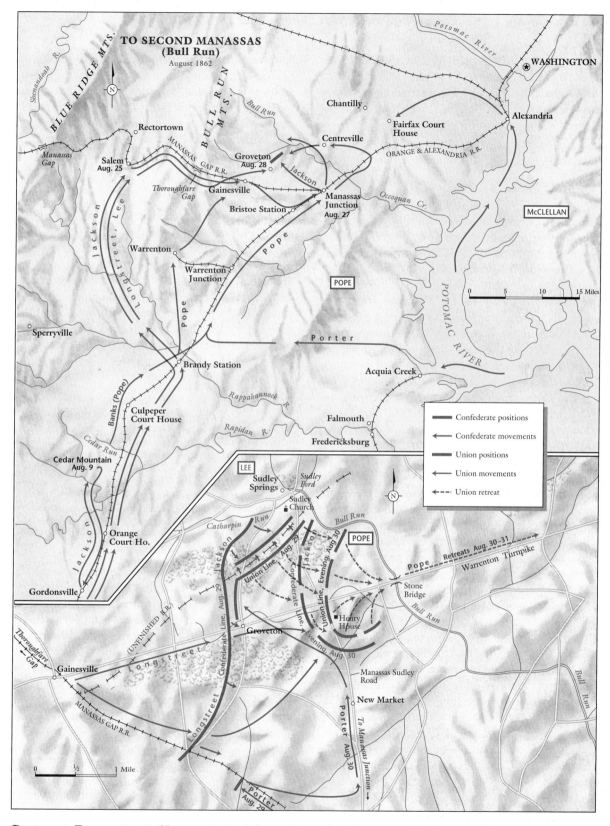

TO SECOND MANASSAS
(Bull Run)

August 1862

BLUE RIDGE MTS.

Shenandoah R.

Manassas Gap

N

BULL RUN MTS.

Bull Run

Rectortown

Salem
Aug. 25

MANASSAS GAP R.R.

Thoroughfare Gap

Gainesville

Bristoe Station

Warrenton

Warrenton
Junction

Jackson, Lee

Longstreet, Lee

Pope

Pope

Chantilly

Centreville

Groveton
Aug. 28

Jackson

Manassas
Junction
Aug. 27

Potomac River

WASHINGTON

Fairfax Court
House

Alexandria

ORANGE & ALEXANDRIA R.R.

Occoquan Cr.

McCLELLAN

POPE

POTOMAC RIVER

0   5   10   15 Miles

Sperryville

Banks (Pope)

Pope

Brandy Station

Porter

Acquia Creek

Culpeper
Court House

Cedar Run

Rappahannock R.

Rapidan R.

Falmouth

Fredericksburg

Cedar Mountain
Aug. 9

Jackson

Orange
Court Ho.

Gordonsville

LEE

Sudley
Springs

Sudley
Ford

Sudley
Church

Catharpin Run

Jackson

Bull Run

N

Union Line, Aug. 29

Confederate Line, Aug. 29

Jackson

Union Line, Evening, Aug. 30

POPE

Pope Retreats Aug. 30–31

Warrenton Turnpike

Stone
Bridge

Bull Run

▬▬	Confederate positions
←	Confederate movements
▬▬	Union positions
←	Union movements
◄--	Union retreat

Thoroughfare
Gap

Gainesville

MANASSAS GAP R.R.

(UNFINISHED R.R.)

Longstreet

Confederate Line, Aug. 29

Longstreet

Groveton

Union Line, Evening, Aug. 30

Henry
House

Manassas Sudley
Road

New Market

Porter Aug. 30

To Manassas
Junction

Bull Run

0   ½   1 Mile

Porter
Aug. 29

SECOND BATTLE OF MANASSAS (BULL RUN), AUGUST 29–30, 1862

September but was turned back at the Battle of Perryville on October 8. Even after these defeats, the Confederate forces in the western theater were in better shape than they had been four months earlier.

THE SECOND BATTLE OF BULL RUN

Most attention, though, focused on Virginia. Lincoln reorganized the Union corps near Washington into the Army of Virginia under General John Pope, who had won minor successes as commander of a small army in Missouri and Tennessee. In August, Lincoln ordered the withdrawal of the Army of the Potomac from the peninsula to reinforce Pope for a drive southward from Washington. Lee quickly seized the opportunity provided by the separation of the two Union armies confronting him, by the ill will between McClellan and Pope and their subordinates, and by the bickering among various factions in Washington. To attack Pope before McClellan could reinforce him, Lee shifted most of his army to northern Virginia, sent Jackson's "foot cavalry" on a deep raid to destroy its supply base at Manassas Junction, and then brought his army back together to defeat Pope's army near Bull Run on August 29 and 30. The demoralized Union forces retreated into the Washington defenses, where Lincoln reluctantly gave McClellan command of the two armies and told him to reorganize them into one.

Lee decided to keep up the pressure by invading Maryland. On September 4, his weary troops began splashing across the Potomac 40 miles upriver from Washington. This move, which took place at the same time Braxton Bragg was invading Kentucky, presented several momentous possibilities: Maryland might be won for the Confederacy. Another victory by Lee might influence the U.S. congressional elections in November and help Democrats gain control of Congress, and might even force the Lincoln administration to negotiate peace with the Confederacy. Successful invasion of Maryland, coming on top of other Confederate successes, might even persuade Britain and France to recognize the Confederacy and offer mediation to end the war—especially since the long-expected cotton famine had finally materialized. In fact, in September 1862 the British and French governments were indeed considering recognition and were awaiting the outcome of Lee's invasion to decide whether to proceed. Great issues rode with the armies as Lee crossed the Potomac and McClellan cautiously moved north to meet him.

CONCLUSION

The election of 1860 had accomplished a national power shift of historic proportions. Through their domination of the Jeffersonian Republican coalition during the first quarter of the 19th century and of the Jacksonian Democrats thereafter, Southern political leaders had maintained effective control of the national government for most of the time before 1860. South Carolina's secession governor Francis Pickens described this leverage of power in a private letter to a fellow South Carolinian in 1857:

We have the Executive [Buchanan] with us, and the Senate & in all probability the H[ouse of] R[epresentatives] too. Besides we have repealed the Missouri line & the Supreme Court in a decision of great power, has declared it . . . unconstitutional null and void. So, that before our enemies can reach us, they must first break down the Supreme Court—change the Senate & seize the Executive & . . . restore the Missouri line, repeal the Fugitive slave law & change the whole govern[men]t. As long as the Govt. is on our side I am for sustaining it, & using its power for our benefit, & placing the screws upon the throats of our opponents.

In 1860 Pickens's worst-case scenario started to come true. With Lincoln's election as the first president of an antislavery party, the South lost control of the executive branch—and perhaps also of the House. They feared that the Senate and Supreme Court would soon follow. The Republicans, Southerners feared, would launch a "revolution" to cripple slavery and, as Lincoln had said in his "House Divided" speech two years earlier, place it "in course of ultimate extinction." The "revolutionary dogmas" of the Republicans, declared a South Carolina newspaper in 1860, were "active and bristling with terrible designs." Worst of all, the Northern "Black Republicans" would force racial equality on the South: "Abolition preachers will be on hand to consummate the marriage of your daughters to black husbands."

Thus the South launched a preemptive counter-revolution of secession to forestall the feared revolution of liberty and equality that would be their fate if they remained in the Union. As the Confederate secretary of state put it in 1861, the southern states had formed a new nation "to preserve their old institutions" from "a revolution [that] threatened to destroy their social system."

Seldom has a preemptive counterrevolution so quickly brought on the very revolution it tried to prevent. If the Confederacy had lost the war in the spring of 1862, as appeared likely after Union victories from February to May of that year, the South might have returned to the Union with slavery intact. Instead, successful Confederate counteroffen-sives in the summer of 1862 convinced Lincoln that the North could not win the war without striking against slavery. Another issue that rode with Lee's troops as they crossed the Potomac into Maryland in September 1862 was the fate of an emancipation proclamation Lincoln had drafted two months earlier and then put aside to await a Union victory.

Suggested Readings begin on page SR-1.
For Web activities and resources related to
this chapter, go to http://
www.harcourtcollege.com/history/murrin

CHAPTER 16

A NEW BIRTH OF FREEDOM,
1862–1865

A RIDE FOR LIBERTY

This splendid painting of a slave family escaping to Union lines during the Civil War dramatizes the experiences of thousands of slaves who thereby became "contrabands" and gained their freedom. Most of them came on foot, but this enterprising family stole a horse as well as themselves from their master.

One of the great issues awaiting resolution as the armies moved into Maryland in September 1862 was emancipation of the slaves. The war had become a "total war," requiring the mobilization of every resource that might bring victory or the destruction of any resource that might inflict defeat. To abolish slavery would strike at a vital Confederate resource (slave labor) and mobilize that resource for the Union along with the moral power of fighting for freedom. Slaves had already made clear their choice by escaping to Union lines by the tens of thousands. Lincoln had made up his mind to issue an emancipation proclamation and was waiting for a Union victory to give it credibility and potency.

This momentous decision would radically enlarge the scope and purpose of the Union war effort. It would also polarize Northern public opinion and political parties. So long as the North fought simply for restoration of the Union, Northern unity was impressive, but the events of 1862 and 1863 raised the divisive question of what kind of Union was to be restored. Would it be a Union without slavery, as abolitionists and radical Republicans hoped? Or "the Union as it was, the Constitution as it is," as Democrats desired? The answer to this question would determine not only the course of the war but also the future of the United States.

This chapter will focus on the following major questions:

- What factors led Lincoln to his decision to issue the Emancipation Proclamation?
- What were the sources of internal dissent and dissension in the Confederacy? In the Union?
- What contribution did women and African Americans made to the war efforts in both North and South?
- Why did Lincoln expect in August 1864 to be defeated for reelection? What changed to enable him to win reelection by a substantial margin?

SLAVERY AND THE WAR

At first, the leaders of both the Union and the Confederacy tried to keep the issue of slavery out of the war. For Southern leaders to proclaim that the defense of slavery was the aim of the war might prompt non-slaveholders to ask why they were risking their lives to protect their rich neighbors' property. Even more important, it might jeopardize

CHRONOLOGY

1862 Confederacy enacts conscription (April 16) • Lincoln informs two cabinet members of intention to issue Emancipation Proclamation (July 13) • Battle of Antietam (September 17) • Lincoln issues preliminary Emancipation Proclamation (September 22) • Battle of Fredericksburg (December 13) • Battle of Stones River (December 31–January 2)

1863 Lincoln issues final Emancipation Proclamation (January 1) • Union enacts conscription (March 3) • Richmond bread riot (April 2) • Battle of Chancellorsville (May 1–5) • Battle of Gettysburg (July 1–3) • Vicksburg surrenders (July 4) • Port Hudson surrenders (July 9) • New York draft riot (July 13–16) • Assault on Fort Wagner (July 18) • Battle of Chickamauga (September 19–20) • Battles of Chattanooga (November 24–25)

1864 Battle of the Wilderness (May 5–6) • Battle of Spotsylvania (May 8–19) • Fighting at Petersburg leads to nine-month siege (June 15–18) • Fall of Atlanta (September 1) • Reelection of Lincoln (November 8) • Battle of Nashville (December 15–16)

1865 Capture of Fort Fisher (January 15) • Confederates evacuate Richmond (April 2) • Lee surrenders at Appomattox (April 9) • Booth assassinates Lincoln (April 14) • Last Confederate army surrenders (June 23) • Thirteenth Amendment abolishing slavery ratified (December 6)

ter two groups served notice that, though they supported a war for the Union, they would not support a war against slavery. In July 1861, with Lincoln's endorsement, Congress passed a resolution affirming that Northern war aims included no intention "of overthrowing or interfering with the rights or established institutions of the States"—in plain words, slavery—but intended only "to defend and maintain the supremacy of the Constitution and to preserve the Union."

Many Northerners saw matters differently. They insisted that a rebellion sustained *by* slavery in defense *of* slavery could be suppressed only by striking *against* slavery. As the black leader Frederick Douglass stated, "To fight against slaveholders, without fighting against slavery, is but a half-hearted business, and paralyzes the hands engaged in it. . . . War for the destruction of liberty must be met with war for the destruction of slavery." A good many Union soldiers began to grumble about protecting the property of traitors in arms against the United States.

Wars tend to develop a logic and momentum that go beyond their original purposes. When Northerners discovered at Bull Run in July 1861 that they were not going to win an easy victory, many of them began to take a harder look at slavery. Slaves constituted the principal labor force in the South. They raised most of the food and fiber, built most of the military fortifications, worked on the railroads and in mines and munitions factories. Southern newspapers boasted that slavery was "a tower of strength to the Confederacy" because it enabled the South "to place in the field a force so much larger in proportion to her white population than the North." Precisely, responded abolitionists. So why not convert this Confederate asset to a Union advantage by confiscating slaves as enemy property and using them to help the Northern war effort? As the war ground on into 1862 and as casualties mounted, this argument began to make sense to many Yankees.

THE "CONTRABANDS"

The slaves themselves entered this debate in a dramatic fashion. As Union armies penetrated the South, a growing number of slaves voted for freedom with their feet. By twos and threes, by families,

Confederate efforts to win recognition and support from Britain. So the Confederates proclaimed liberty rather than slavery as their war aim—the same liberty their ancestors had fought for in 1776. The unspoken corollary of that aim was the liberty of whites to own blacks.

In the North, the issue of slavery was deeply divisive. Lincoln had been elected on a platform pledged to contain the expansion of slavery. But that pledge had provoked most of the southern states to quit the Union. For the administration to take action against slavery in 1861 would be to risk the breakup of the fragile coalition Lincoln had stitched together to fight the war: Republicans, Democrats, and border-state Unionists. Spokesmen for the lat-

eventually by scores, they escaped from their masters and came over to the Union lines. By obliging Union officers either to return them to slavery or accept them, these escaped slaves began to make the conflict a war for freedom.

Although some commanders returned escaped slaves to their masters or prevented them from entering Union camps, most increasingly did not. Their rationale was first expressed by General Benjamin Butler. In May 1861 three slaves who had been working for the Confederate army escaped to Butler's lines near Fortress Monroe at the mouth of the James River in Virginia. Butler refused to return them, on the grounds that they were "contraband of war." The phrase caught on. For the rest of the war, slaves who came within Union lines were known as contrabands. On August 6, 1861, Congress passed a confiscation act that authorized the seizure of all property, including slaves, that was being used for Confederate military purposes. The following March, Congress forbade the return of slaves who entered Union lines—even those belonging to owners loyal to the Union.

THE BORDER STATES

This problem of slavery in the loyal border states preoccupied Lincoln. On August 30, 1861, John C. Frémont, whose political influence had won him a commission as major general and command of Union forces in Missouri, issued an order freeing the slaves of all Confederate sympathizers in Missouri. This caused such a backlash among border-state Unionists, who feared it was a prelude to a general abolition edict, that Lincoln revoked the order, lest it "alarm our Southern Union friends, and turn them against us."

In the spring of 1862, Lincoln tried persuasion instead of force in the border states. At his urging, Congress passed a resolution offering federal compensation to states that voluntarily abolished slavery. Three times, from March to July 1862, Lincoln urged border-state congressmen to accept the offer. He told them that the Confederate hope that their states might join the rebellion was helping to keep the war alive. Adopt the proposal for compensated emancipation, he pleaded, and that hope would die. The pressure for a bold antislavery policy was growing stronger, he warned them in

May. Another Union general had issued an emancipation order; Lincoln had suspended it, but "you cannot," Lincoln told the border-state congressmen, "be blind to the signs of the times."

They did seem to be blind. They complained that they were being coerced, bickered about the amount of compensation, and wrung their hands over the prospects of economic ruin and race war, even if emancipation were to take place gradually over a 30-year period, as Lincoln had suggested. At a final meeting, on July 12, Lincoln, in effect, gave them an ultimatum: Accept compensated emancipation or face the consequences. In fact, thousands of slaves had already run away to Union camps in the border states. "The incidents of the war cannot be avoided," he said. "If the war continue long . . . the institution in your states will be extinguished by mere friction and abrasion . . . and you will have nothing valuable in lieu of it." Again they failed to see the light and by a vote of 20 to 9, they rejected the proposal for compensated emancipation.

THE DECISION FOR EMANCIPATION

That very evening, Lincoln decided to issue an emancipation proclamation in his capacity as commander in chief with power to order the seizure of enemy property. Several factors, in addition to the recalcitrance of the border states, impelled Lincoln to this fateful decision. One was a growing demand from his own party for bolder action: Congress had just passed a second confiscation act calling for seizure of the property of active Confederates. Another was rising sentiment in the Army to "take off the kid gloves" when dealing with "traitors." From General Henry W. Halleck, who had been summoned to Washington as general-in-chief, went orders to General Grant in northern Mississippi instructing him on the treatment of rebel sympathizers inside Union lines: "Handle that class without gloves, and take their property for public use." Grant himself had written several months earlier that if the Confederacy "cannot be whipped in any other way than through a war against slavery, let it come to that." Finally, Lincoln's decision reflected his sentiments about the "unqualified evil" and "monstrous injustice" of slavery.

The military situation, however, rather than his moral convictions, determined the timing and scope of Lincoln's emancipation policy. Northern hopes that the war would soon end had risen after the victories of early 1862 but had then plummeted amid the reverses of that summer.

Three courses of action seemed possible. One, favored by the so-called Peace Democrats, urged an armistice and peace negotiations to patch together some kind of Union, but that would have been tantamount to conceding Confederate victory. Republicans therefore reviled the Peace Democrats as traitorous "Copperheads," after the poisonous snake. A second alternative was to keep on fighting—in the hope that with a few more Union victories, the rebels would lay down their arms and the Union could be restored. Such a policy would leave slavery intact, a course of action that General McClellan strongly advocated. He wrote Lincoln an unsolicited letter of advice on July 7, 1862, warning him that "neither confiscation of property ... [n]or forcible abolition of slavery should be contemplated for a moment." Yet that was precisely what Lincoln was contemplating. This was the third alternative: total war to mobilize all the resources of the North and to destroy all the resources of the South, including slavery—a war not to restore the old Union but to build a new one.

After his meeting with the border-state representatives convinced him that attempts at compromise were futile, Lincoln made his decision. On July 22 he formally notified the whole cabinet of his intention to issue an emancipation proclamation. It was "a military necessity, absolutely essential to the preservation of the Union," said Lincoln. "We must free the slaves or be ourselves subdued. The slaves [are] undeniably an element of strength to those who [have] their service, and we must decide whether that element should be with us or against us. . . . The Administration must set an example, and strike at the heart of the rebellion."

The cabinet agreed, except for Postmaster General Montgomery Blair, a resident of Maryland and a former Democrat, who warned that the border states and the Democrats would rebel against the proclamation and perhaps cost the administration the fall congressional elections as well as vital support for the war. Lincoln might have agreed—two months earlier. Now he believed that the strength gained from an emancipation policy—from the slaves themselves, from the dynamic Republican

segment of Northern opinion, and in the eyes of foreign nations—would more than compensate for the hostility of Democrats and border-state Unionists. Lincoln did, however, accept the advice of Secretary of State Seward to delay the proclamation "until you can give it to the country supported by military success." Otherwise, Seward argued, it might be viewed "as the last measure of an exhausted government, a cry for help . . . our last shriek, on the retreat." Lincoln slipped his proclamation into a desk drawer and waited for a military victory.

NEW CALLS FOR TROOPS

Meanwhile, Lincoln issued a call for 300,000 new three-year volunteers for the army. In July, Congress passed a militia act giving the president greater powers to mobilize the state militias into federal service and to draft men into the militia if the states failed to do so. Although not a national draft law, this was a step in that direction. In August, Lincoln called up 300,000 militia for nine months of service, in addition to the 300,000 three-year volunteers. (These calls eventually yielded 421,000 three-year volunteers and 88,000 nine-month militia.) The Peace Democrats railed against these measures and provoked antidraft riots in some localities. The government responded by arresting rioters and antiwar activists under the president's suspension of the writ of habeas corpus.[1]

Democrats denounced these "arbitrary arrests" as unconstitutional violations of civil liberties—and added this issue to others on which they hoped to gain control of the next House of Representatives in the fall elections. With the decline in Northern

---

[1] A writ of habeas corpus is an order issued by a judge to law enforcement officers requiring them to bring an arrested person before the court to be charged with a crime so that the accused can have a fair trial. The Constitution of the United States, however, permits the suspension of this writ "in cases of rebellion or invasion," so that the government can arrest enemy agents, saboteurs, or any individual who might hinder the defense of the country, and hold such individuals without trial. Lincoln had suspended the writ, but political opponents charged him with usurping a power possessed only by Congress in order to curb freedom of speech of antiwar opponents and political critics guilty of nothing more than speaking out against the war. This issue of "arbitrary arrests" became a controversial matter in both the Union and Confederacy (where the writ was similarly suspended during part of the war).

morale following the defeat at Second Bull Run and the early success of the Confederate invasion of Kentucky, prospects for a Democratic triumph seemed bright. One more military victory by Lee's Army of Northern Virginia might crack the North's will to continue the fight. It would certainly bring diplomatic recognition of the Confederacy by Britain and France. Lee's legions began crossing the Potomac into Maryland on September 4, 1862.

THE BATTLE OF ANTIETAM

The Confederate invasion ran into difficulties from the start. Western Marylanders responded

impassively to Lee's proclamation that he had come "to aid you in throwing off this foreign yoke" of Yankee rule. Lee split his army into five parts. Three of them, under the overall command of Stonewall Jackson, occupied the heights surrounding the Union garrison at Harpers Ferry, which lay athwart the Confederate supply route from the Shenandoah Valley. The other two remained on watch in the South Mountain passes west of Frederick. Then, on September 13, Union commander George B. McClellan had an extraordinary stroke of luck. In a field near Frederick, two of his soldiers found a copy of Lee's orders for these deployments. Wrapped around three cigars, they had apparently been dropped by a careless Southern

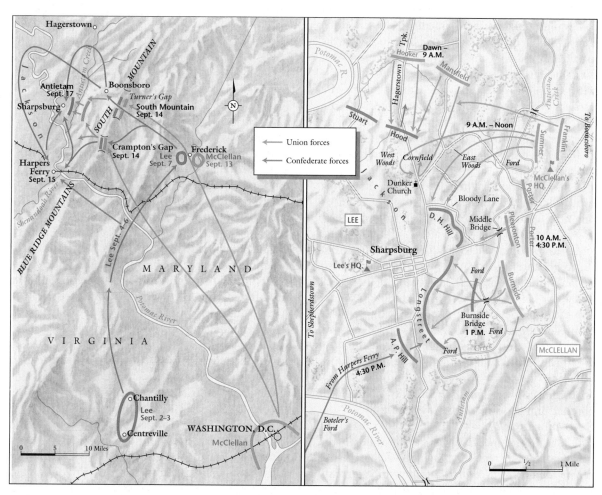

LEE'S INVASION OF MARYLAND, 1862

BATTLE OF ANTIETAM, SEPTEMBER 17, 1862

officer when the Confederate army passed through Frederick four days earlier. With this new information, McClellan planned to pounce on the separated segments of Lee's army before they could reunite. "Here is a paper," he exulted, "with which if I cannot whip 'Bobbie Lee,' I will be willing to go home."

But McClellan moved so cautiously that he lost much of his advantage. Although Union troops overwhelmed the Confederate defenders of the South Mountain passes on September 14, they advanced too slowly to save the garrison at Harpers Ferry, which surrendered 12,000 men to Jackson on September 15. Lee then managed to reunite most of his army near the village of Sharpsburg by September 17, when McClellan finally crossed Antietam Creek to attack. Even so, the Union forces outnumbered the Confederates by almost 2 to 1 (75,000 to 40,000 men), but McClellan, as usual, believed that the enemy outnumbered *him*. Thus he missed several opportunities to inflict a truly crippling defeat on the Confederacy. The battle of Antietam (called Sharpsburg by the Confederates) nevertheless proved to be the single bloodiest day in American history, with more than 23,000 casualties (killed, wounded, and captured) in the two armies.

Attacking from right to left on a four-mile front, McClellan's Army of the Potomac achieved potential breakthroughs at a sunken road northeast of Sharpsburg (known ever after as Bloody Lane) and in the rolling fields southeast of town. But fearing counterattacks from phantom reserves that he was sure Lee possessed, McClellan held back 20,000 of his troops and failed to follow through. Thus the battle ended in a draw. The battered Confederates still clung to their precarious line, with the Potomac at their back, at the end of a day in which more than 6,000 men on both sides were killed or mortally wounded—almost as many Americans as were killed or mortally wounded in combat during the entire seven years of the Revolutionary War.

Even though he received reinforcements the next day and Lee received none, McClellan did not renew the attack. Nor did he follow up vigorously when the Confederates finally retreated across the Potomac on the night of September 18.

> "*Fellow-citizens, we cannot escape history. We of this Congress and this administration, will be remembered in spite of ourselves. . . . The fiery trial through which we pass, will light us down, in honor or dishonor, to the latest generation. . . . In giving freedom to the slave, we assure freedom to the free— honorable alike in what we give, and what we preserve. We shall nobly save, or meanly lose, the last best, hope of earth.*"
>
> **ABRAHAM LINCOLN**
> *from his annual message to Congress,*
> *December 1, 1862*

THE EMANCIPATION PROCLAMATION

Lincoln was not happy with this equivocal Union victory, despite its important consequences. Britain and France decided to withhold diplomatic recognition of the Confederacy. Northern Democrats failed to gain control of the House in the fall elections. And most significant of all, on September 22, Lincoln seized the occasion to issue his preliminary emancipation proclamation. This was less than a total surprise to the public, for the president had already hinted that something of the sort might be in the offing. A month earlier, after Horace Greeley had written a strong editorial in the New York *Tribune* calling for action against slavery, Lincoln had responded with a public letter to Greeley (much as a president today might use a televised news conference). "My paramount object in this struggle," wrote Lincoln, "is to save the Union. . . . If I could save the Union without freeing *any* slave I would do it, and if I could save it by freeing *all* the slaves I would do it; and if I could save it by freeing some and leaving others alone I would also do that." Knowing that the issue of Union united Northerners, while the prospect of emancipation still divided them, Lincoln had crafted these

THE EMANCIPATION PROCLAMATION This famous contemporary painting by Francis Carpenter portrays Lincoln and his cabinet discussing the Emancipation Proclamation, which lies on the desk before Lincoln. The other members of the cabinet, from left to right, are Secretary of War Edwin M. Stanton, Secretary of the Treasury Salmon P. Chase, Secretary of the Navy Gideon Welles, Secretary of the Interior Caleb B. Smith, Secretary of State William H. Seward (seated facing Lincoln), Postmaster General Montgomery Blair, and Attorney General Edward Bates.

phrases carefully to maximize public support for his anticipated proclamation. He portrayed emancipation not as an end in itself—despite his personal convictions to that effect—but only as an instrument, a *means* toward saving the Union.

Lincoln's proclamation of September 22 did not go into effect immediately. Rather, it stipulated that if any state, or part of a state, was still in rebellion on January 1, 1863, the president would proclaim the slaves therein "forever free." Confederate leaders scorned this warning, and by January 1 no Southern state had returned to the Union. After hosting a New Year's Day reception at the White House, Lincoln signed the final proclamation as an "act of justice" as well as "a fit and necessary war measure for suppressing said rebellion."

The Emancipation Proclamation exempted the border states, plus Tennessee and those portions of Louisiana and Virginia already under Union occupation, since these areas were deemed not to be in rebellion, and Lincoln's constitutional authority for the proclamation derived from his power as commander in chief to confiscate enemy property. Although the proclamation could do nothing to liberate slaves in areas under Confederate control, it essentially made the Northern soldiers an army of liberation—however reluctant many of them were to risk their lives for that purpose. The North was now fighting for freedom as well as for Union. If the North won the war, slavery would die. But in the winter and spring of 1862–63 victory was far from assured.

A WINTER OF DISCONTENT

Although Lee's retreat from Maryland and Braxton Bragg's retreat from Kentucky suggested that the Confederate tide might be ebbing, the tide soon turned. The Union could never win the war simply by turning back Confederate invasions. Northern armies would have to invade the South, defeat its armies, and destroy its ability to fight.

Displeased by McClellan's "slows" after Antietam, Lincoln replaced him on November 7 with General Ambrose E. Burnside. An imposing man whose muttonchop whiskers gave the anagram "sideburns" to the language, Burnside proposed to cross the Rappahannock River at Fredericksburg for a move on Richmond before bad weather forced both sides into winter quarters. Although Lee put his men into a strong defensive position on the heights behind Fredericksburg, Burnside nevertheless attacked on December 13. He was repulsed with heavy casualties that shook the morale of both the army and the public. When Lincoln heard the news, he said: "If there is a worse place than hell, I am in it."

News from the western theater did little to dispel the gloom in Washington. The Confederates had fortified Vicksburg on bluffs commanding the Mississippi River. This precaution gave them control of an important stretch of the river and preserved transportation links between the states to the east and west. Grant proposed to sever those links and in November 1862 launched a two-pronged drive against Vicksburg. With 40,000 men, he marched 50 miles southward from Memphis by land, while his principal subordinate William T. Sherman came down the river with 32,000 men accompanied by a gunboat fleet. Confederate cavalry raids destroyed the railroads and supply depots in Grant's rear, however, forcing him to retreat to Memphis. Meanwhile, Sherman attacked the Confederates at Chickasaw Bluffs on December 29 with no more success than Burnside had enjoyed at Fredericksburg.

The only bit of cheer for the North came in central Tennessee at the turn of the year. There, Lincoln had removed General Don Carlos Buell from command of the Army of the Cumberland for the same reason he had removed McClellan—lack of vigor and aggressiveness. Buell's successor, William S. Rosecrans, had proved himself a fighter in subordinate commands. On the Confederate side, Davis stuck with Braxton Bragg as commander of the Army of Tennessee, despite dissension from some subordinate officers within his ranks.

On the day after Christmas 1862, Rosecrans moved from his base at Nashville to attack Bragg's force 30 miles to the south at Murfreesboro. The ensuing three-day battle (called Stones River by the Union and Murfreesboro by the Confederacy) resulted in Confederate success on the first day (December 31) but defeat on the last. Both armies suffered devastating casualties. The Confederate retreat to a new base 40 miles farther south enabled the North to call Stones River a victory. Lincoln expressed his gratitude to Rosecrans: "I can never forget . . . that you gave us a hard-earned victory which, had there been a defeat instead, the nation could scarcely have lived over."

As it was, the nation scarcely lived over the winter of 1862–63. Morale declined, and desertions rose so sharply in the Army of the Potomac that Lincoln replaced Burnside with Joseph Hooker, a controversial general whose nickname "Fighting Joe" seemed to promise a vigorous offensive. Hooker did lift morale in the Army of the Potomac, but elsewhere matters went from bad to worse.

Renewing the campaign against Vicksburg, Grant bogged down in the swamps and rivers that protected that Confederate bastion on three sides. Only on the east, away from the river, did he find high ground suitable for an assault on Vicksburg's defenses. Grant's problem was to get his army across the Mississippi to that high ground, along with supplies and transportation to support an assault. For three months, he floundered in the Mississippi-Yazoo bottomlands, while disease and exposure depleted his troops. False rumors of excessive drinking that had dogged Grant for years broke out anew, but Lincoln resisted pressures to remove him from command. "What I want," Lincoln said, "is generals who will fight battles and win victories. Grant has done this, and I propose to stand by him." Lincoln reportedly added that he would like to know Grant's brand of whiskey so that he could send some to his other generals.

THE RISE OF THE COPPERHEADS

Lincoln's reputation reached a low point during this Northern winter of discontent. A visitor to Washington in February 1863 found that "the lack of respect for the President in all parties is unconcealed. . . . If a Republican convention were to be held tomorrow, he would not get the vote of a State." In this climate, the Copperhead faction of the Democratic Party found a ready audience for its message that the war was a failure and should be abandoned. Having won control of the Illinois and Indiana legislatures the preceding fall, Democrats there called for an armistice and a peace conference. They also demanded retraction of the "wicked, inhuman, and unholy" Emancipation Proclamation.

In Ohio, the foremost Peace Democrat, Congressman Clement L. Vallandigham, was planning to run for governor. What had this wicked war accomplished, Vallandigham asked Northern audiences: "Let the dead at Fredericksburg and Vicksburg answer." The Confederacy could never be conquered; the only trophies of the war were "debt, defeat, sepulchres." The solution was to "stop the fighting. Make an armistice. Withdraw your army from the seceded states." Above all, give up the unconstitutional effort to abolish slavery.

Vallandigham and other Copperhead spokesmen had a powerful effect on Northern morale. Alarmed by a wave of desertions, the army commander in Ohio had Vallandigham arrested in May 1863. A military court convicted him of treason for aiding and abetting the enemy. The court's action raised serious questions of civil liberties. Was the conviction a violation of Vallandigham's First Amendment right of free speech? Could a military court try a civilian under martial law in a state like Ohio where civil courts were functioning?

Lincoln was embarrassed by the swift arrest and trial of Vallandigham, which he learned about from the newspapers. To keep Vallandigham from becoming a martyr, Lincoln commuted his sentence from imprisonment to banishment—to the Confederacy! On May 15, Union cavalry escorted Vallandigham under a flag of truce to Confederate lines in Tennessee, where the Southerners reluctantly accepted their uninvited guest. He soon escaped to Canada on a blockade runner. There, from exile, Vallandigham conducted his campaign for governor of Ohio—an election he lost in October 1863, after the military fortunes of the Union had improved.

ECONOMIC PROBLEMS IN THE SOUTH

Low morale in the North followed military defeat. By contrast, Southerners were buoyed by their mil-itary success but were suffering from food shortages and hyperinflation. The tightening Union blockade, the weaknesses and imbalances of the Confederate economy, the escape of slaves to Union lines, and enemy occupation of some of the South's prime agricultural areas made it increasingly difficult to produce both guns and butter. Despite the conversion of hundreds of thousands of acres from cotton to food production, the deterioration of Southern railroads and the priority given to army shipments made food scarce in some areas. A drought in the summer of 1862 made matters worse. Prices rose much faster than wages. The price of salt—necessary to preserve meat in those days before refrigeration—shot out of sight. Even the middle class suffered, especially in Richmond, whose population had more than doubled since 1861. "The shadow of the gaunt form of famine is upon us," wrote a war department clerk in March 1863. "I have lost twenty pounds, and my wife and children are emaciated." The rats in his kitchen were so hungry that they nibbled bread crumbs from his daughter's hand "as tame as kittens. Perhaps we shall have to eat them!"

WARTIME INFLATION IN THE CONFEDERACY AND THE UNION

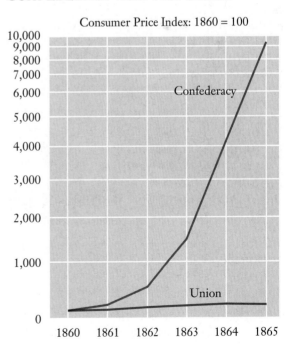

Consumer Price Index: 1860 = 100

Poor people were enough worse off—especially the wives and children of non-slaveholders away in the army. By the spring of 1863, food supplies were virtually gone. Wrote a North Carolina farm woman to the governor in April 1863:"

> A crowd of we Poor women went to Greenesborogh yesterday for something to eat as we had not a mouthful of meet nor bread in my house. What did they do but put us in gail in plase of giveing us aney thing to eat. . . . I have 6 little children and my husband in the armey and what am I to do?

Some women took matters into their own hands. Denouncing "speculators" who allegedly hoarded goods to drive up prices, they marched to stores, asked the price of bacon or cornmeal or salt, denounced such "extortion," took what they wanted without paying. On April 2, 1863, a mob of more than 1,000 women and boys looted several shops in Richmond before the militia, under the personal command of Davis, forced them to disperse. The Confederate government subsequently released some emergency food stocks to civilians, and state and county governments aided the families of soldiers. Better crops in 1863 helped to alleviate the worst shortages, but serious problems persisted.

THE WARTIME DRAFT AND CLASS TENSIONS

In both South and North, the draft intensified social unrest and turned it in the direction of class conflict. The burst of patriotic enthusiasm that had prompted a million men to join the colors in North and South during 1861 had waned by the spring of 1862. That April, the Confederacy enacted a draft that made all white men (with certain occupational exemptions) ages 18 to 35 liable to conscription. A drafted man could hire a substitute, but the price of substitutes soon rose beyond the means of the average Southern farmer or worker, giving rise to the bitter cry that it was "a rich man's war and a poor man's fight."

The cry grew louder in October 1862 when the Confederate Congress raised the draft age to 45 and added a clause exempting one white man from the draft on every plantation with 20 or more slaves. The purpose of this "overseer exemption" was to keep up production and prevent slave uprisings. It had been prompted by the complaints of planters' wives, who had been left alone to manage the slaves after the departure of husbands, sons, and overseers for the army. The so-called Twenty Negro Law was regarded as blatant discrimination by non-slaveholding farm families whose men also were at the front. In addition, raising the age limit to 45 took away many fathers of children too young to work the farm. The law provoked widespread draft-dodging and desertions.

Similar discontent greeted the enactment of a conscription law in the North. In the summer of 1863, some 30,000 Union soldiers—who had enlisted in 1861 for two years rather than the normal three—would be leaving military service, along with 80,000 of the nine-month militia called into service the preceding autumn. To meet the looming shortfall of men, Congress decreed in March that all male citizens ages 20 to 45 must enroll for

THE RICHMOND BREAD RIOT Illustrating the economic problems of the Confederacy and the suffering of poor civilians in overcrowded cities, the bread riot in Richmond involved 1,000 women and boys who broke into shops to take food and other goods on April 2, 1863. The rioters were white, though a few black children may have gotten into the act, as portrayed by the artist of this woodcut.

the draft. Not all of them would necessarily be called (administrative policy exempted married men over 35), but all would be liable.

The law was intended more to encourage volunteers to come forward than to draft men directly into the army. In the president's four calls for troops under this law, the War Department set a quota for every congressional district and allowed 50 days to meet the quota with volunteers before resorting to a draft lottery. Some districts avoided drafting anyone by offering large bounties to volunteers. The bounty system produced glaring abuses, including "bounty jumpers" who enlisted and then deserted as soon as they got their money—often to enlist again under another name somewhere else.

The drafting process itself was also open to abuse. Like the Confederate law, the Union law permitted the hiring of substitutes. To keep the price from skyrocketing as it had in the Confederacy, the law allowed a drafted man the alternative of paying a "commutation fee" of $300 that exempted him from the current draft call (but not necessarily from the next one). That provision raised the cry of "rich man's war, poor man's fight" in the North as well. The Democratic Party nurtured this sense of class resentment and racism intensified it. Democrats in Congress opposed conscription, just as they opposed emancipation. Democratic newspapers told white workers, especially the large Irish American population, that the draft would force them to fight a war to free the slaves, who would then come north to take their jobs. This volatile issue sparked widespread violence when the Northern draft got under way in the summer of 1863. The worst riot occurred in New York City July 13 through 16, where huge mobs consisting mostly of Irish Americans demolished draft offices, lynched several blacks, and destroyed huge areas of the city in four days of looting and burning.

Draft riots in the North and bread riots in the South exposed alarming class fissures that deepened with the strains of full-scale war. Although inflation was much less serious in the North than in the South, Northern wages lagged behind price increases. Labor unions sprang up in several industries and struck for higher wages. In some areas, such as the anthracite coal fields of eastern Pennsylvania, labor organizations dominated by

THE NEW YORK CITY DRAFT RIOT The worst urban violence in all of American history occurred in New York City from July 13 to 16, 1863, when thousands of men and women, mostly poor Irish Americans, attacked draft offices, homes, businesses, and individuals. Black residents of the city were among the mob's victims because they symbolized labor competition to Irish Americans, who did not want to be drafted to fight a war to free the slaves. This illustration shows the burning of the Colored Orphan Asylum, a home for black orphans. More than 100 people were killed in the disturbance, most of them rioters shot down by police and soldiers.

Irish Americans combined resistance to the draft and opposition to emancipation with violent strikes against industries owned by Protestant Republicans. Troops sent in to enforce the draft sometimes suppressed the strikes as well. These class, ethnic, and racial hostilities provided a volatile mixture in several Northern communities.

A POOR MAN'S FIGHT?

The grievance that it was a rich man's war and a poor man's fight was more apparent than real.

Property, excise, and income taxes to sustain the war bore proportionately more heavily on the wealthy than on the poor. In the South, wealthy property owners suffered greater damage and confiscation losses than did non-slaveholders. The war liberated four million slaves, the poorest class in America. Both the Union and Confederate armies fielded men from all strata of society in proportion to their percentage of the population. If anything, among those who volunteered in 1861 and 1862, the planter class was overrepresented in the Confederate army and the middle class in the Union forces, for those privileged groups believed they had more at stake in the war and joined up in larger numbers during the early months of enthusiasm. Those volunteers—especially the officers—suffered the highest percentage of combat casualties.

Nor did conscription itself fall much more heavily on the poor than on the rich. Those who escaped the draft by decamping to the woods, the territories, or Canada were mostly poor. The Confederacy abolished substitution in December 1863 and made men who had previously sent substitutes liable to the draft. In the North, several city councils, political machines, and businesses contributed funds to pay the commutation fees of drafted men who were too poor to pay out of their own pockets. In the end, it was neither a rich man's war nor a poor man's fight. It was an American war.

BLUEPRINT FOR MODERN AMERICA

The 37th Congress (1861–63)—the Congress that enacted conscription, passed measures for confiscation and emancipation, and created the greenbacks and the national banking system (see chapter 15)—also enacted three laws that, together with the war legislation, provided what one historian has called "a blueprint for modern America": the Homestead Act; the Morrill Land-Grant College Act; and the Pacific Railroad Act. For several years before the war, Republicans and some northern Democrats had tried to pass these laws to provide social benefits and to promote economic growth, only to see them defeated by southern opposition or by President Buchanan's veto. The secession of southern states, ironically, enabled Congress to pass all three in 1862.

The Homestead Act granted a farmer 160 acres of land virtually free after he had lived on the land for five years and had made improvements on it. The Morrill Land-Grant College Act gave each state thousands of acres to fund the establishment of colleges to teach "agricultural and mechanical arts." The Pacific Railroad Act granted land and loans to railroad companies to spur the building of a transcontinental railroad from Omaha to Sacramento. Under these laws, the U.S. government ultimately granted 80 million acres to homesteaders, 25 million acres to states for land-grant colleges, and 120 million acres to several transcontinental railroads. Despite waste, corruption, and exploitation of the original Indian owners of this land, these laws helped farmers settle some of the most fertile land in the world, studded the land with state colleges, and spanned it with steel rails in a manner that altered the landscape of the western half of the country.

WOMEN AND THE WAR

The war advanced many other social changes, particularly with respect to women. In factories and on farms, women replaced men who had gone off to war. Explosions in Confederate ordnance plants and arsenals killed at least 100 women, who were as surely war casualties as men killed in battle. The war accelerated the entry of women into the teaching profession, a trend that had already begun in the Northeast and now spread to other parts of the country. It also brought significant numbers of women into the civil service. During the 1850s a few women had worked briefly in the U.S. Patent Office (including Clara Barton, who became a famous wartime nurse and founded the American Red Cross). The huge expansion of government bureaucracies after 1861 and the departure of male clerks to the army provided openings that were filled partly by women. After the war the private sector began hiring women as clerks, bookkeepers, "typewriters" (the machine itself was invented in the 1870s), and telephone operators (the telephone was another postwar invention).

Women's most visible impact was in the field of medicine. The outbreak of war prompted the organization of soldiers' aid societies, hospital societies, and other voluntary associations to provide

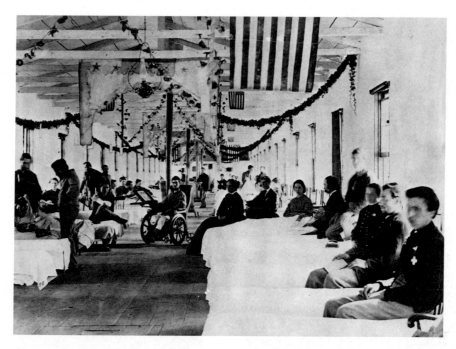

UNION ARMY HOSPITAL The Armory Square military hospital in Washington, with its clean, cheerful wards apparently decorated for the Christmas holidays, showed Union medical care at its best.

home-front support for the soldiers, and women played a leading role. Their most important function was to help—and sometimes to prod—the medical branches of the Union and Confederate armies to provide more efficient, humane care for sick and wounded soldiers. Dr. Elizabeth Blackwell, the first American woman to earn an M.D. (1849), organized a meeting of 3,000 women in New York City on April 29, 1861. They put together the Women's Central Association for Relief, which became the nucleus for the most powerful voluntary association of the war, the United States Sanitary Commission.

Eventually embracing 7,000 local auxiliaries, the Sanitary Commission was an essential adjunct of the Union army's medical bureau. Most of its local volunteers were women, as were most of the nurses it provided to army hospitals. Nursing was not a new profession for women—but it lacked respect as a wartime profession, being classed only slightly above prostitution. The fame won by Florence Nightingale of Britain during the Crimean War a half-dozen years earlier had begun to change that perception. As thousands of

middle- and even upper-class women volunteers flocked to army hospitals, nursing began its transformation from a menial occupation to a respected profession.

The nurses had to overcome the deep-grained suspicions of army surgeons and the opposition of husbands and fathers who shared the cultural sentiment that the shocking, embarrassingly physical atmosphere of an army hospital was no place for a respectable woman. Many thousands of women went to work, winning grudging and then enthusiastic admiration. One Confederate surgeon praised women nurses as far superior to the convalescent soldiers who had formerly done that job, "rough country crackers" who did not "know castor oil from a gun rod nor laudanum from a hole in the ground." In the North, the treasurer of the Sanitary Commission, who at first had disliked the idea of his wife working as a nurse, was converted by her performance as a volunteer for the Sanitary Commission during the summer of 1862. "The little woman has come out amazingly strong during these past two months," he wrote. "Have never given her credit for a tithe of the enterprise, pluck,

FEMALE SPIES AND SOLDIERS In addition to working in war industries and serving as army nurses, some women pursued traditionally male wartime careers as spies and soldiers. One of the most famous Confederate spies was Rose O'Neal Greenhow, a Washington widow and socialite who fed information to officials in Richmond. Federal officers arrested her in August 1861 and deported her to Richmond in the spring of 1862. She was photographed with her daughter in the Old Capitol prison in Washington, D.C., while awaiting trial. In October 1864 she drowned in a lifeboat off Wilmington, North Carolina, after a blockade runner carrying her back from a European mission was run aground by a Union warship.

The second photograph shows a Union soldier who enlisted in the 95th Illinois Infantry under the name of Albert Cashier and fought through the war. Not until a farm accident in 1911 revealed Albert Cashier to be a woman, whose real name was Jennie Hodgers, was her secret disclosed. Most of the other estimated 400 women who evaded the superficial physical exams and passed as men to enlist in the Union and Confederate armies were more quickly discovered and discharged—six of them after they had babies while in the army. A few, however, served long enough to be killed in action.

discretion, and force of character that she has shown."

The war also bolstered the fledgling women's rights movement. It was no coincidence that Elizabeth Cady Stanton and Susan B. Anthony founded the National Woman Suffrage Association in 1869, only four years after the war. Although a half century passed before women won the vote, this movement could not have achieved the mo-

mentum that made it a force in American life without the work of women in the Civil War.

THE CONFEDERATE TIDE CRESTS AND RECEDES

The Army of Northern Virginia and the Army of the Potomac spent the winter of 1862–63 on opposite banks of the Rappahannock River. With the coming of spring, Union commander Joe Hooker resumed the offensive with hopes of redeeming the December disaster at Fredericksburg. On April 30, instead of charging straight across the river, Hooker crossed his men several miles upriver and came in on Lee's rear. Lee quickly faced most of his troops about and confronted the enemy in dense woods, known locally as the Wilderness, near the crossroads hostelry of Chancellorsville. Nonplussed, Hooker lost the initiative.

THE BATTLE OF CHANCELLORSVILLE

Even though the Union forces outnumbered the Confederates by almost two to one, Lee boldly went over to the offensive. On May 2, Stonewall Jackson led 28,000 men on a stealthy march through the woods to attack the Union right flank late in the afternoon. Owing to the negligence of the Union commanders, the surprise was complete.

Jackson's assault crumpled the Union flank as the sun dipped below the horizon. Jackson then rode out to scout the terrain for a moonlight attack but was wounded on his return by jittery Confederates who mistook him and his staff for Union cavalry. Nevertheless, Lee resumed the attack next day. In three more days of fighting that caused 12,800 Confederate and 16,800 Union casualties (the largest number for a single battle in the war so far), Lee drove the Union troops back across the Rappahannock. It was a brilliant victory.

In the North, the gloom grew deeper. "My God!" exclaimed Lincoln when he heard the news of Chancellorsville. "What will the country say?" Copperhead opposition intensified. Southern sympathizers in Britain renewed efforts for diplomatic recognition of the Confederacy. Southern elation, however, was tempered by grief at the death on May 10 of Jackson, who had contracted pneumonia after amputation of his arm. Nevertheless, Lee decided to parlay his tactical victory at Chancellorsville into a

LINK TO THE PAST

The United States Sanitary Commission

http://www.netwalk.com/~jpr/index.htm

This extraordinarily rich site contains all kinds of documents and an explanatory text about the important activities of the Sanitary Commission, especially the crucial role of women in the organization. It also contains many illustrations of ambulances, medical instruments, patterns for making bandages, and the like. This is the best Web site for Civil War medical history.

1. How well did the Sanitary Commission fulfill the initial call signed by more than 100 women in New York City in 1861 to select, train, and employ women nurses in military hospitals?

2. Tensions between the Medical Bureau of the Union army and the Sanitary Commission persisted through much of the war. Analyze the sources and nature of these tensions.

3. What were the "Sanitary Fairs"? Where were they held? How much money did they raise?

4. What long-term impact do you think the Sanitary Commission had on the history of medicine in the United States? The history of nursing?

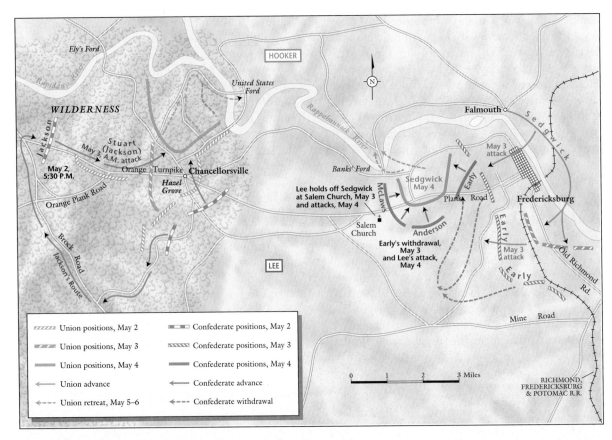

BATTLE OF CHANCELLORSVILLE, MAY 2–6, 1863

strategic offensive by again invading the North. A victory on Union soil would convince Northerners and foreigners alike that the Confederacy was invincible. As his army moved north in June 1863, Lee was confident of success. "There never were such men in an army before," he wrote of his troops. "They will go anywhere and do anything if properly led."

THE GETTYSBURG CAMPAIGN

At first, all went well. The Confederates brushed aside or captured Union forces in the northern Shenandoah Valley and in Pennsylvania. Stuart's cavalry threw a scare into Washington by raiding behind Union lines into Maryland and Pennsylvania. That very success led to trouble. With Stuart's cavalry separated from the rest of the army, Lee lost the vital intelligence that the cavalry garnered as the army's eyes. By June 28 several detachments of Lee's forces were scat-

tered about Pennsylvania, far from their base and vulnerable.

At this point, Lee learned that the Army of the Potomac was moving toward him, now under the command of George Gordon Meade. Lee immediately ordered his own army to reassemble in the vicinity of Gettysburg, an agricultural and college town at the hub of a dozen roads leading in from all directions. There, on the morning of July 1, the vanguard of the two armies met in a clash that grew into the greatest battle in American history.

As the fighting spread west and north of town, couriers pounded up the roads on lathered horses to summon reinforcements to both sides. The Confederates fielded more men and broke the Union lines late that afternoon, driving the survivors to a defensive position on Cemetery Hill south of town. General Richard Ewell, Jackson's successor as commander of the Confederate Second Corps, judging this position too strong to

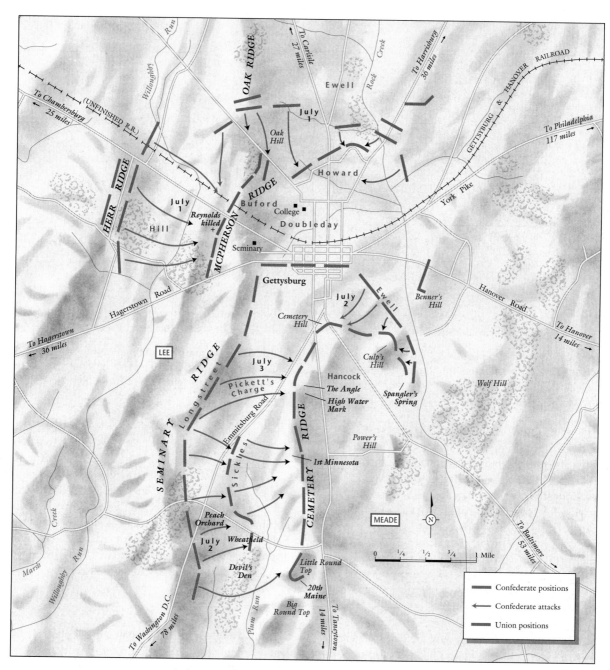

BATTLE OF GETTYSBURG, JULY 1–3, 1863

take with his own troops, chose not to press the attack as the sun went down on what he presumed would be another Confederate victory.

When the sun rose next morning, however, the reinforced Union army was holding a superb defensive position from Culp's Hill and Cemetery Hill south to Little Round Top. Lee's principal subordinate, First Corps commander James Longstreet, advised against attack, urging instead a maneuver to the south, toward Washington, to force the Federals to attack Lee in a strong defensive position. But Lee believed his army invincible. After its victory on

THE BATTLE OF GETTYSBURG This is one of many paintings of Pickett's assault on the Union center on Cemetery Ridge at the climactic moment of the battle on July 3, 1863. The painting depicts "the high tide of the Confederacy" as Virginia and North Carolina troops pierce the Union line only to be shot down or captured—a fate suffered by half of the 13,000 Confederate soldiers who participated in Pickett's Charge.

July 1, a move to the south might look like a retreat. Pointing to the Union lines, he said: "The enemy is there, and I am going to attack him there."

Longstreet reluctantly led the attack on the Union left. Once committed, his men fought with fury. The Union troops fought back with equal fury. As the afternoon passed, peaceful areas with names like Peach Orchard, Wheat Field, Devil's Den, and Little Round Top were turned into killing fields. By the end of the day, Confederate forces had made small gains at great cost, but the main Union line had held firm.

Lee was not yet ready to yield the offensive. Having attacked both Union flanks, he thought the center might be weak. On July 3 he ordered a frontal attack on Cemetery Ridge, led by a fresh division under George Pickett. After a two-hour artillery barrage, Pickett's 5,000 men and 8,000 additional troops moved forward on that sultry afternoon in a picture-book assault that forms our most enduring image of the Civil War. "Pickett's Charge" was shot to pieces; scarcely half of the men returned unwounded to their own lines. It was the final act in an awesome three-day drama that left some 50,000 men killed, wounded, or captured: 23,000 Federals and 25,000 to 28,000 Confederates.

Lee limped back to Virginia pursued by the Union troops. Lincoln was unhappy with Meade for not cutting off the Confederate retreat. Nevertheless, Gettysburg was a great Northern victory, and it came at the same time as other important Union successes in Mississippi, Louisiana, and Tennessee.

THE VICKSBURG CAMPAIGN

In mid-April, Grant had begun a move that would put Vicksburg in a vise. The Union ironclad fleet ran down river past the big guns at Vicksburg with little damage. Grant's troops marched down the Mississippi's west bank and were ferried across the river 40 miles south of Vicksburg. There they kept the Confederate defenders off balance by striking east toward Jackson instead of marching north to Vicksburg. Grant's purpose was to scatter the Confederate forces in central Mississippi and to destroy the rail network so that

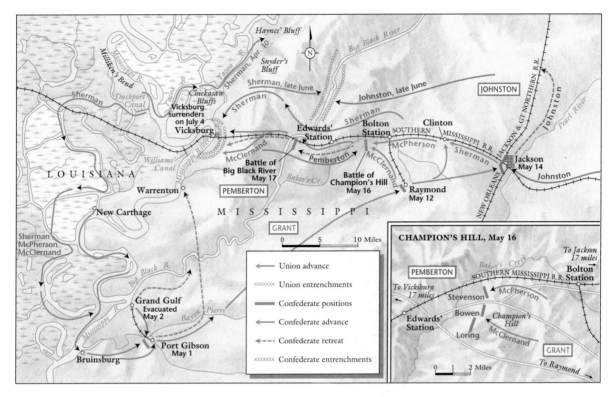

VICKSBURG CAMPAIGN, APRIL–JULY 1863

his rear would be secure when he turned toward Vicksburg. It was a brilliant strategy, flawlessly executed. During the first three weeks of May, Grant's troops marched 180 miles, won five battles, and trapped 32,000 Confederate troops and 3,000 civilians in Vicksburg between the Union army on land and the Union gunboats on the river.

But the Confederate army was still full of fight. Confederate soldiers threw back Union assaults against the Vicksburg trenches on May 19 and 22. Grant then settled down for a siege. By late June he had built up his army to 70,000 men to ward off a Confederate army of 30,000 scraped together by Joseph Johnston to try to rescue Vicksburg. Running out of supplies, the Vicksburg garrison surrendered on July 4. Grant then turned east and drove off Johnston's force. On July 9, the Confederate garrison at Port Hudson, 200 river miles south of Vicksburg, surrendered to a besieging Union army. Northern forces now controlled the entire length of the Mississippi River. "The

Father of Waters again goes unvexed to the sea," said Lincoln. The Confederacy had been torn in two, and Lincoln knew who deserved the credit. "Grant is my man," he said, "and I am his the rest of the war."

CHICKAMAUGA AND CHATTANOOGA

Northerners had scarcely finished celebrating the twin victories of Gettysburg and Vicksburg when they learned of an important—and almost bloodless—triumph in Tennessee. After the traumatic Battle of Stones River at the end of 1862, the Union Army of the Cumberland and the Confederate Army of Tennessee had shadowboxed for nearly six months. On June 24, Union commander Rosecrans finally assaulted the Confederate defenses in the Cumberland foothills of east-central Tennessee. He used his cavalry and a mounted infantry brigade armed with new repeating rifles to get around the Confederate flanks

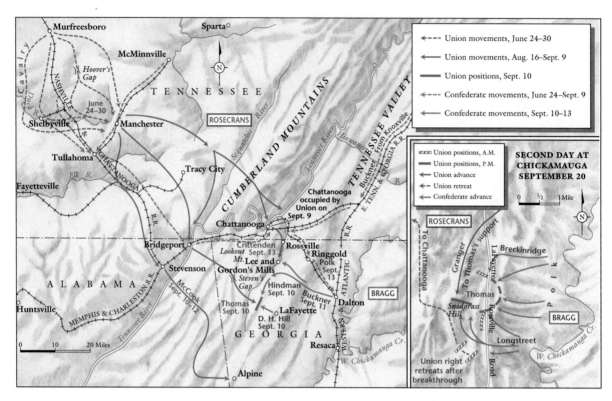

ROAD TO CHICKAMAUGA, JUNE–SEPTEMBER 1863

while his infantry threatened the Confederate front. In the first week of July, the Confederates retreated all the way to Chattanooga.

After a pause for resupply, Rosecrans's army advanced again in August, this time in tandem with a smaller Union army in eastern Tennessee commanded by Burnside, who had come to this theater after being removed from command in Virginia. Again the outnumbered Confederates fell back, evacuating Knoxville on September 2 and Chattanooga on September 9. This action severed the South's only direct east-west rail link. Having sliced the Confederacy in half with the capture of Vicksburg and Port Hudson, Union forces now stood poised for a campaign into Georgia that threatened to slice it into three parts. For the Confederacy it was a stunning reversal of the situation only four months earlier, after Chancellorsville, when the Union cause had appeared hopeless.

Confederate General Braxton Bragg reached into his bag of tricks and sent fake deserters into Union lines with tales of a Confederate retreat to-

ward Atlanta. He then laid a trap for Rosecrans's troops as they advanced through the mountain passes south of Chattanooga. To help him spring it, Davis approved the detachment of Longstreet with two divisions from Lee's army to reinforce Bragg. On September 19, the Confederates turned and counterattacked Rosecrans's now outnumbered army in the valley of Chickamauga Creek.

On that day and the next, in ferocious fighting that produced more casualties (35,000) than any other single battle save Gettysburg, the Confederates finally scored a victory. On September 20, after a confusion of orders left a division-size gap in the Union line, Longstreet's men broke through, sending part of the Union army reeling back to Chattanooga. Only a firm stand by corps commander George H. Thomas—a Virginian who had remained loyal to the Union—prevented a Union rout. For this feat, Thomas earned the nickname "Rock of Chickamauga." Lincoln subsequently appointed Thomas commander of the Army of the

Cumberland to replace Rosecrans, who was, in Lincoln's words, "confused and stunned like a duck hit on the head" after Chickamauga.

Lincoln also sent two army corps from Virginia under Hooker and two from Vicksburg under Sherman to reinforce Thomas, whose troops in Chattanooga were under virtual siege by Bragg's forces, which held most of the surrounding heights. More important, Lincoln put Grant in overall command of the beefed-up Union forces there. When Grant arrived in late October, he welded the various Northern units into a new army and opened a new supply line into Chattanooga. On November 24, Hooker's troops drove Confederate besiegers off massive Lookout Mountain. Next day, an assault on Bragg's main line at Missionary Ridge east of Chattanooga won a smashing success against seemingly greater odds than Pickett had faced at Gettysburg. The Union troops that had been routed at Chickamauga two months earlier redeemed themselves by driving the Confederates off Missionary Ridge and 20 miles south into Georgia.

These battles climaxed a string of Union victories in the second half of 1863, which made that year one of "calamity . . . defeat . . . utter ruin," in the words of a Confederate official. The southern diarist Mary Boykin Chesnut found "gloom and unspoken despondency hang[ing] like a pall everywhere." Jefferson Davis removed the discredited Bragg from command of the Army of Tennessee and reluctantly replaced him with Joseph E. Johnston, in whom Davis had little confidence. Lincoln summoned Grant to Washington and appointed him general-in-chief of all Union armies in March 1864, signifying a relentless fight to the finish.

BLACK MEN IN BLUE

The events of the second half of 1863 also confirmed emancipation as a Union war aim. Northerners had not greeted the Emancipation Proclamation with great enthusiasm. Democrats and border-state Unionists continued to denounce it, and many Union soldiers resented the idea that they would now be risking their lives for black freedom. The Democratic Party had hoped to capitalize on this opposition, and on Union military failures, to win important off-year elections. Northern

military victories knocked one prop out from under the Democratic platform, and the performance of black soldiers fighting for the Union knocked out another.

The enlistment of black soldiers was a logical corollary of emancipation. Free Negroes in the North had tried to enlist in 1861, but they were rejected. Proposals to recruit black soldiers, Democrats said, were part of a Republican plot to establish "the equality of the black and white races." In a way, that charge was correct. One consequence of black men fighting for the Union would be to advance the black race a long way toward equal rights. "Once let the black man get upon his person the brass letters, U.S.," said Frederick Douglass, "and a musket on his shoulder and bullets in his pocket, and there is no power on earth which can deny that he has earned the right to citizenship."

But it was pragmatism more than principle that pushed the North toward black recruitment. One purpose of emancipation was to deprive the Confederacy of black laborers and to use them for the Union. Putting some of those former laborers in uniform was a compelling idea, especially as white enlistments lagged and the North had to enact conscription in 1863. Some Union commanders in occupied portions of Louisiana, South Carolina, and Missouri began to organize black regiments in 1862. The Emancipation Proclamation legitimized this policy with its proposal to enroll able-bodied male contrabands in new black regiments—although these units would serve as labor battalions, supply troops, and garrison forces rather than as combat troops. They would be paid less than white soldiers, and their officers would be white. In other words, black men in blue would be second-class soldiers, just as free blacks in the North were second-class citizens.

BLACK SOLDIERS IN COMBAT

Continuing pressure from abolitionists, as well as military necessity, partly eroded discrimination. Congress enacted equal pay in 1864. Officers worked for better treatment of their men. Above all, the regiments themselves lobbied for the right to fight as combat soldiers. Even some previously hostile white soldiers came around to the notion that black men might just as well stop enemy bullets as white men. In May and June 1863, black regiments in Louisiana fought well in an assault on Port Hudson and in defense of a Union outpost at Milliken's Bend, near Vicksburg. "The bravery of the blacks in the battle of Milliken's Bend completely revolutionized the sentiment of the army with regard to the employment of negro troops," wrote the assistant secretary of war, who had been on the spot with Grant's army. "I heard prominent officers who formerly in private had sneered at the idea of the negroes fighting express themselves after that as heartily in favor of it."

Even more significant was the action of the 54th Massachusetts Infantry, the first black regiment raised in the North. Its officers, headed by Colonel Robert Gould Shaw, came from prominent New England antislavery families. Two sons of Frederick Douglass were in the regiment—one of them as sergeant major. Shaw worked hard to win the right for the regiment to fight. On July 18, 1863, he succeeded: The 54th was assigned to lead an assault on Fort Wagner, part of the network of Confederate defenses protecting Charleston. Though the attack failed, the 54th fought courageously, suffering 50 percent casualties, including Colonel Shaw, who was killed. This battle "made Fort Wagner such a name to the colored race as Bunker Hill had been for ninety years to the white Yankees," declared the New York *Tribune*.

The battle took place just after white mobs of draft rioters in New York had lynched blacks. Abolitionist and Republican commentators drew the moral: Black men who fought for the Union deserved more respect than white men who rioted against it. Lincoln made this point eloquently in a widely published letter to a political meeting in August 1863. When final victory was achieved, he wrote, "there will be some black men who can remember that, with silent tongue, and clenched

PART OF COMPANY E, 4TH U.S. COLORED INFANTRY Organized in July 1863, most of the men were former slaves from North Carolina. The 4th fought in several actions on the Petersburg and Richmond fronts in 1864, helping to capture part of the Petersburg defenses on June 15. Of the 166 black regiments in the Union Army, the 4th suffered the fourth-largest number of combat deaths.

The Fruits of War

The Confederacy held two of the South's foremost cities, Charleston and Richmond, until almost the end of the war. Forced to evacuate these cities in February and April 1865, respectively, Confederate troops blew up or set fire to everything of military value. The fires spread, burning down large parts of the cities. In two of these pictures, photographers who accompanied the Union army when it occupied Charleston posed an aged freedman and several freed slave children amid burnt-out portions of Charleston—to symbolize a new free South rising from the ashes of the old slave South. In the third picture, a photographer posed Northern soldiers in the rubble of Richmond for similar symbolic purposes.

Glory (1989)

**Directed by Edward Zwick. Starring Matthew Broderick (Robert Gould Shaw),
Denzel Washington (Trip), Morgan Freeman (Rawlins).**

Glory was the first feature film to treat the role of black soldiers in the Civil War. It tells the story of the 54th Massachusetts Volunteer Infantry from its organization in early 1863 through its climactic assault on Fort Wagner six months later. When the 54th moved out at dusk on July 18 to lead the attack, the idea of black combat troops still seemed a risky experiment. The New York *Tribune*, a strong supporter of black enlistment, had nevertheless observed in May 1863 that many Northern whites "have no faith" that black soldiers would stand and fight Southern whites who considered themselves a master race. The unflinching behavior of the regiment in the face of an overwhelming hail of lead and iron and its casualties of some 50 percent settled the matter. "Who now asks in doubt and derision 'Will the Negro fight?'" commented one abolitionist. "The answer comes to us from those graves beneath Fort Wagner's walls, which the American people will surely never forget."

Many did forget, but *Glory* revived their collective memory. Its combat scenes, climaxed by the assault on Fort Wagner, are among the most realistic and effective in any war movie. Morgan Freeman and Denzel Washington give memorable performances as a fatherly sergeant and a rebellious private who nevertheless picks up the flag when the color-bearer falls and carries it to the ramparts of Fort Wagner where he too is killed. Matthew Broderick's portrayal of Colonel Robert Gould Shaw is less memorable, for the real Shaw was more assertive and mature than Broderick's Shaw.

Except for Shaw, the principal characters in the film are fictional. There were no real Major Cabot Forbes; no tough Irish Sergeant Mulcahy; no black Sergeant John Rawlins; no brash, hardened Private Trip. Indeed, a larger fiction is involved here. The movie gives the impression that most of the 54th's soldiers were former slaves. In fact, this atypical black regiment was recruited mainly in the North, so most of the men had always been free. The story that screenwriter Kevin Jarre and director Edward Zwick chose to tell is not simply about the 54th Massachusetts but about black soldiers in the Civil War. Most of the 179,000 African Americans in the Union army (and at least 10,000 in the navy) were slaves until a few months, even days, before they joined up. Fighting for the Union bestowed upon former slaves a new dignity, self-respect, and militancy, which helped them achieve equal citizenship and political rights—for a time—after the war.

Many of the events dramatized in *Glory* are also fictional: the incident of the racist quartermaster who initially refuses to distribute shoes to Shaw's men; the whipping Trip receives as punishment for going AWOL; Shaw's threat to expose his superior officer's corruption as a way of securing a combat assignment for the 54th; and the religious meeting the night before the assault on Fort Wagner. All of these scenes point toward a larger truth, however, most vividly portrayed symbolically in a surreal, and at first glance, irrelevant scene. During a training exercise, Shaw gallops his horse along a path flanked by stakes, each holding aloft a watermelon. Shaw slashes right and left with his sword, slicing and smashing every melon. The point becomes clear when we recall the identification of watermelons with the "darky" stereotype. The image of smashed melons drives home the essential message of *Glory*.

A scene from *Glory* showing black soldiers of the 54th Massachusetts ready to fire at the enemy.

teeth, and steady eye, and well-poised bayonet, they have helped mankind on to this great consummation; while, I fear, there will be some white ones, unable to forget that, with malignant heart, and deceitful speech, they have strove to hinder it."

EMANCIPATION CONFIRMED

Lincoln's letter set the tone for Republican campaigns in state elections that fall. The party swept them all, including Ohio, where they buried Vallandigham under a 100,000-vote margin swelled by the soldier vote, which went 94 percent for his opponent. In effect, the elections were a powerful endorsement of the administration's emancipation policy. If the Emancipation Proclamation had been submitted to a referendum a year earlier, observed a newspaper editor in November 1863, "the voice of a majority would have been against it. And yet not a year has passed before it is approved by an overwhelming majority."

Emancipation would not be assured of survival until it had been christened by the Constitution. On April 8, 1864, the Senate passed the Thirteenth Amendment to abolish slavery, but Democrats in the House blocked the required two-thirds majority there. Not until after Lincoln's reelection in 1864 would the House pass the amendment, which became part of the Constitution on December 6, 1865. In the end, though, the fate of slavery depended on the outcome of the war. And despite Confederate defeats in 1863, that outcome was by no means certain. Some of the heaviest fighting lay ahead.

THE YEAR OF DECISION

Many Southerners succumbed to defeatism in the winter of 1863–64. "I have never actually despaired of the cause," wrote a Confederate War Department official in November, but "steadfastness is yielding to a sense of hopelessness." Desertions from Confederate armies increased. Inflation galloped out of control. According to a Richmond diarist, a merchant told a poor woman in October 1863 that the price of a barrel of flour was $70: "'My God!' exclaimed she, 'how can I pay such prices? I have seven children; what shall I do?' 'I don't know, madam,' said he, coolly, 'unless you eat your children.'"

The Davis administration, like the Lincoln administration a year earlier, had to face congressional elections during a time of public discontent, for the Confederate constitution mandated such elections in odd-numbered years. Political parties had ceased to exist in the Confederacy after Democrats and former Whigs had tacitly declared a truce in 1861 to form a united front for the war effort. Many congressmen had been elected without opposition in 1861. By 1863, however, significant hostility to Davis had emerged. Though it was not channeled through any organized party, it took on partisan trappings, as an inchoate anti-Davis faction surfaced in the Confederate Congress and in the election campaign of 1863.

Some antiadministration candidates ran on a quasi-peace platform (analogous to that of the Copperheads in the North) that called for an armistice and peace negotiations. The movement left unresolved the terms of such negotiations—reunion or independence, but any peace overture from a position of weakness was tantamount to conceding defeat. The peace movement was especially strong in North Carolina, where for a time it appeared that the next governor would be elected on a peace platform (in the end, the "peace candidate" was defeated). Still, antiadministration candidates made significant gains in the 1863 Confederate elections, though they fell about 15 seats short of a majority in the House and two seats short in the Senate.

OUT OF THE WILDERNESS

Shortages, inflation, political discontent, military defeat, high casualties, and the loss of thousands of slaves bent but did not break the Southern spirit. As the spring of 1864 came on, a renewed determination infused both home front and battle front. The Confederate armies no longer had the strength to invade the North or to win the war with a knockout blow, but, they could still fight a war of attrition, as the patriots had done in the War of 1775–83 against Britain (chapter 6). If they could hold out long enough and inflict enough casualties on the Union armies, they might weaken the Northern will to continue fighting. And if they could just hold out until the Union presidential election in November, Northern voters might reject Lincoln and elect a Peace Democrat.

Northerners were vulnerable to this strategy of psychological attrition. Military success in 1863 had created a mood of confidence, and people expected a

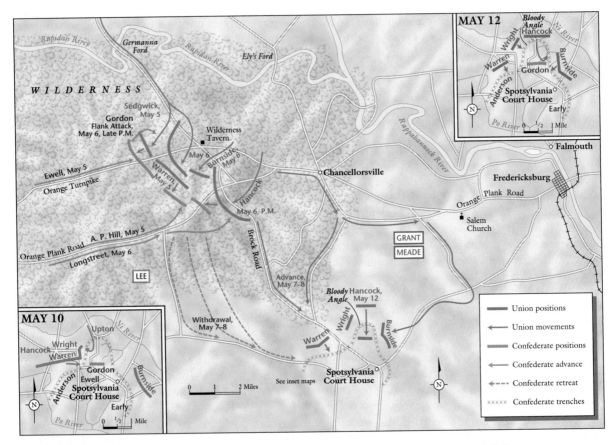

BATTLE OF THE WILDERNESS AND SPOTSYLVANIA, MAY 5–12, 1864

quick, decisive victory in 1864. The mood grew with Grant's appointment as general-in-chief. When Grant decided to remain in Virginia with the Army of the Potomac and to leave Sherman in command of the Union forces in northern Georgia, Northerners expected these two heavyweights to floor the Confederacy with a one-two punch. Lincoln was alarmed by this euphoria. "The people are too sanguine," he told a reporter. "They expect too much at once." Disappointment might trigger despair.

Lincoln was nearly proved right. Grant's strategic plan was elegant in its simplicity. While smaller Union armies in peripheral theaters carried out auxiliary campaigns, the two principal armies in Virginia and Georgia would attack the main Confederate forces under Lee and Johnston. Convinced that in years past Union armies in various theaters had "acted independently and without concert, like a balky team, no two ever pulling to-

gether," Grant ordered simultaneous offensives on all fronts, to prevent the Confederates from shifting reinforcements from one theater to another.

Grant's offensives began the first week of May. The heaviest fighting occurred in Virginia. When the Army of the Potomac crossed the Rapidan River, Lee attacked its flank in the thick scrub forest of the Wilderness, where Union superiority in numbers and artillery would count for little (and where Lee had defeated Hooker a year earlier at Chancellorsville). Lee's action brought on two days (May 5–6) of the most confused, frenzied fighting the war had yet seen. Hundreds of wounded men burned to death in brush fires set off by exploding shells or muzzle flashes. The battle surged back and forth, with the Confederates inflicting 18,000 casualties and suffering 12,000 themselves. Having apparently halted Grant's offensive, they claimed a victory.

SPOTSYLVANIA AND COLD HARBOR

Grant did not admit defeat, nor did he retreat, as other Union commanders in Virginia had done. Instead, he moved toward Spotsylvania Courthouse, a key crossroads 10 miles closer to Richmond. Skillfully, Lee pulled back to cover the road junction. Repeated Union assaults during the next twelve days (May 8–19) left another 18,000 Northerners and 12,000 Southerners killed, wounded, or captured. The Confederates fought from an elaborate network of trenches and log breastworks they had constructed virtually overnight. Civil War soldiers had learned the advantages of trenches, which gave the defense an enormous advantage and made frontal assaults almost suicidal.

Having achieved no better than stalemate around Spotsylvania, Grant again moved south around Lee's right flank in an effort to force the outnumbered Confederates into an open fight. Lee, however, anticipated Grant's moves and confronted him from behind formidable defenses at the North Anna River, Totopotomoy Creek, and near the crossroads inn of Cold Harbor, only 10 miles northeast of Richmond. Believing the Confederates must be exhausted and demoralized by their repeated retreats, Grant decided to attack

TRENCH WARFARE, 1864–1865 During the grueling campaigns of 1864 and 1865, the opposing armies entrenched wherever they paused. By the end of the war, hundreds of square miles in Virginia and Georgia looked like this, especially along a 35-mile line from a point east of Richmond to just southwest of Petersburg, where the armies confronted each other for more than nine months. Note not only the elaborate trench networks but also the absence of trees, cut down to provide firewood and to create open fields of fire for rifles and cannons.

at Cold Harbor on June 3—a costly mistake. Lee's troops were ragged and hungry but far from demoralized. Their withering fire inflicted 7,000 casualties in less than an hour. (By coincidence, this was the same number of casualties suffered during the same length of time by the men in Pickett's Charge at Gettysburg exactly eleven months before.) "I regret this assault more than any other one I have ordered," said Grant.

STALEMATE IN VIRGINIA

Now Grant moved all the way across the James River to strike at Petersburg, an industrial city and rail center 20 miles south of Richmond. If Petersburg fell the Confederates could not hold Richmond. Once more Lee's troops raced southward on the inside track and blocked Grant's troops. Four days of Union assaults (June 15–18) produced another 11,000 Northern casualties but no breakthrough.

Such high Union losses in just six weeks—some 65,000 killed, wounded, and captured, compared with 37,000 Confederate casualties—cost the Army of the Potomac its offensive power. Grant reluctantly settled down for a siege along the Petersburg-Richmond front that would last more than nine grueling months.

Meanwhile, other Union operations in Virginia had achieved little success. Benjamin Butler bungled an attack up the James River against Richmond and was stopped by a scraped-together army under Beauregard. A Union thrust up the Shenandoah Valley was blocked at Lynchburg in June by Jubal Early, commanding Stonewall Jackson's old corps. Early then led a raid all the way to the outskirts of Washington on July 11 and 12 before being driven back to Virginia. Union cavalry under Philip Sheridan inflicted considerable damage on Confederate resources in Virginia—including the mortal wounding of Jeb Stuart in the battle of Yellow Tavern on May 11—but again failed to strike a crippling blow. In the North, frustration set in over failure to win the quick, decisive victory the public had expected in April.

THE ATLANTA CAMPAIGN

In Georgia, Sherman's army seemed to have accomplished more at less cost than Grant had in

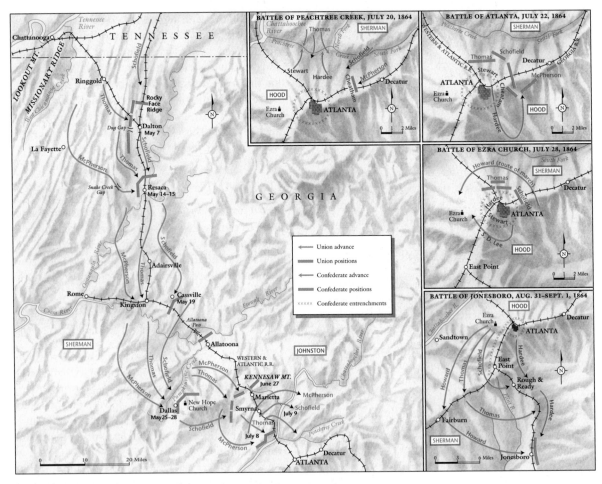

CAMPAIGN FOR ATLANTA, MAY–SEPTEMBER 1864

Virginia, but there too Union efforts had bogged down in apparent stalemate by August. The strategy and tactics of both Sherman and Johnston in Georgia contrasted with those of Grant and Lee in Virginia. Sherman forced Johnston south toward Atlanta by constantly flanking him to the Union right, generally without bloody battles. Grant constantly forced Lee back by flanking moves to the Union left, but only after bloody battles. By the end of June, Sherman had advanced 80 miles at the cost of 17,000 casualties to Johnston's 14,000—only one-third of the combined losses of Grant and Lee.

Davis grew alarmed by Johnston's apparent willingness to yield territory without a fight. Sherman again flanked the Confederate defenses (after a

failed attack) at Kennesaw Mountain in early July. He crossed the Chattahoochee River and drove Johnston back to Peachtree Creek less than five miles from Atlanta. Fearing that Johnston would abandon the city, Davis, on July 17, replaced him with John Bell Hood.

A fighting general from Lee's army who had lost a leg at Chickamauga, Hood immediately prepared to counterattack against the Yankees. He did so three times, in late July. Each time, the Confederates reeled back in defeat, suffering a total of 15,000 casualties to Sherman's 6,000. At last, Hood retreated into the formidable earthworks ringing Atlanta and launched no more attacks, although his army did manage to keep Sherman's cavalry and infantry from taking the two railroads leading into

Atlanta from the south. Like Grant at Petersburg, Sherman seemed to settle down for a siege.

PEACE OVERTURES

By August, the Confederate strategy of attrition seemed to be working. Union casualties on all fronts during the preceding three months totaled a staggering 110,000—double the number for any comparable period of the war. "Who shall revive the withered hopes that bloomed at the opening of Grant's campaign?" asked the leading Democratic newspaper, the *New York World.* "STOP THE WAR!" shouted Democratic headlines. "All are tired of this damnable tragedy."

Even Republicans joined the chorus of despair. "Our bleeding, bankrupt, almost dying country longs for peace," wrote Horace Greeley of the New York *Tribune.* Greeley became involved in abortive "peace negotiations" spawned by Confederate agents in Canada. Those agents convinced Greeley that they carried peace overtures from Davis, but Lincoln, aware that Davis's condition for peace was Confederate independence, was skeptical. Still, given the mood of the North in midsummer 1864, Lincoln could not reject any opportunity to stop the bloodshed. He deputized Greeley to meet with the Confederate agents in Niagara Falls on the Canadian side of the border. At almost the same time (mid-July), two other Northerners met under a flag of truce with Davis in Richmond. Lincoln had carefully instructed them—and Greeley—that his conditions for peace were "restoration of the Union and abandonment of slavery."

Of course, Davis would no more accept those terms than Lincoln would accept his. Although neither of the peace contacts came to anything, the Confederates gained a propaganda victory by claiming that Lincoln's terms had been the only obstacle to peace. Northern Democrats ignored the Southern refusal to accept reunion as a condition of peace and focused on the slavery issue as the sole stumbling block. "Tens of thousands of white men must yet bite the dust to allay the negro mania of the President," ran a typical Democratic editorial. By August, even staunch Republicans such as national party chairman Henry Raymond and his associate Thurlow Weed were convinced that "the

desire for peace" and the impression that Lincoln "is fighting not for the Union but for the abolition of slavery" made his reelection "an impossibility." Lincoln thought so, too. "I am going to be beaten," he told a friend in August, "and unless some great change takes place, *badly* beaten."

Lincoln faced enormous pressure to drop emancipation as a condition of peace so the onus could be shifted to Jefferson Davis's insistence on Confederate independence. Lincoln refused to yield. He would rather lose the election than go back on the promise he had made in the Emancipation Proclamation. "No human power can subdue this rebellion without using the Emancipation lever as I have done," he told weak-kneed Republicans. Some 130,000 black soldiers and sailors were fighting for the Union. They would not do so if they thought the North intended to forsake them:

> If they stake their lives for us they must be prompted by the strongest motive . . . the promise of freedom. And the promise being made, must be kept. . . . There have been men who proposed to me to return to slavery the[se] black warriors. . . . I should be damned in time & eternity for so doing. The world shall know that I will keep my faith to friends and enemies, come what will.

At the end of August, the Democrats nominated McClellan for president. The platform on which he ran declared that "after four years of failure to restore the Union by the experiment of war . . . [we] demand that immediate efforts be made for a cessation of hostilities." Southerners were jubilant. Democratic victory on that platform, said the *Charleston Mercury,* "must lead to peace and our independence" if "for the next two months *we hold our own and prevent military success by our foes.*"

THE PRISONER-EXCHANGE CONTROVERSY

The Democratic platform also condemned the Lincoln administration's "shameful disregard" of prisoners of war in Confederate prison camps. This raised another contentious matter. By midsummer 1864 the plight of Union and Confederate captives had become one of the most bitter issues of the war. The upcoming presidential election and the generally worse conditions in Southern prisons made it mainly a Northern political issue.

In 1862 the Union and Confederate armed forces had signed a cartel for the exchange of prisoners captured in battle. The arrangement had worked reasonably well for a year, making large prison camps unnecessary. When the Union army began to organize regiments of former slaves, however, the Confederate government announced that if they were captured, they and their white officers would be put to death for the crime of fomenting slave insurrections. In practice, the Confederate government did not enforce this policy, for Lincoln threatened retaliation on Confederate prisoners of war if it did so, but Confederate troops sometimes murdered black soldiers and their officers as they tried to surrender—most notably at Fort Pillow, a Union garrison on the Mississippi north of Memphis, where cavalry commanded by Nathan Bedford Forrest slaughtered scores of black (and some white) prisoners on April 12, 1864.

In most cases, Confederate officers returned captured black soldiers to slavery or put them to hard labor on Southern fortifications. Expressing outrage at this treatment of soldiers wearing the United States uniform, the Lincoln administration in 1863 suspended the exchange of prisoners until the Confederacy agreed to treat white and black prisoners alike. The Confederacy refused. The South would "die in the last ditch," said the Confederate exchange agent, before "giving up the right to send slaves back to slavery as property recaptured."

There matters stood as the heavy fighting of 1864 poured many thousands of captured soldiers into hastily contrived prison compounds that quickly became death camps. Prisoners were subjected to overcrowding, poor sanitation, contaminated water, scanty rations, inadequate medical facilities, and exposure to deep-South summer heat and northern winter cold. The suffering of Northern prisoners was especially acute, because the deterioration of the Southern economy made it hard to feed and clothe even Confederate soldiers and civilians, let alone Yankee prisoners. Nearly 16 percent of all Union soldiers held in Southern prison camps died, compared with 12 percent of Confederate soldiers in Northern camps. Andersonville was the most notorious hellhole. A stockade camp of 26 acres with neither huts nor tents, designed to accommodate 15,000 prisoners, it held 33,000 in August 1864. They died at the rate of more than 100 a day. Altogether, 13,000 Union soldiers died at Andersonville.

The suffering of Union prisoners brought heavy pressure on the Lincoln administration to renew exchanges, but the Confederates would not budge on the question of exchanging black soldiers. After a series of battles on the Richmond-Petersburg front in September 1864, Lee proposed an informal exchange of prisoners. Grant agreed, on condition that black soldiers captured in the fighting be included "the same as white soldiers." Lee replied that "negroes belonging to our citizens are not considered subjects of exchange and were not included in my proposition." No exchange, then, responded Grant. The Union government was "bound to secure to all persons received into her armies the rights due to

BURIAL OF UNION POWS AT ANDERSONVILLE On many days during the summer of 1864 at least 100 Union prisoners of war died of disease, malnutrition, or exposure at Andersonville Prison in Georgia. This scene of burial in long trenches became so commonplace as to dull the sense of horror.

soldiers." Lincoln backed this policy. He would not sacrifice the principle of equal treatment of black prisoners, even though local Republican leaders warned that many in the North "will work and vote against the President, because they think sympathy with a few negroes, also captured, is the cause of a refusal" to exchange prisoners.

THE ISSUE OF BLACK SOLDIERS IN THE CONFEDERATE ARMY

During the winter of 1864–65 the Confederate government quietly abandoned its refusal to exchange black prisoners, and exchanges resumed. One reason for this reversal was a Confederate decision to recruit slaves to fight for the South. Two years earlier, Davis had denounced the North's arming of freed slaves as "the most execrable measure recorded in the history of guilty man." Ironically, a few black laborers and body servants with Southern armies had taken up arms in the heat of battle and had unofficially fought alongside their masters against the Yankees. By February 1865, Southern armies were desperate for manpower, and slaves constituted the only remaining reserve. Supported by Lee's powerful influence, Davis pressed the Confederate Congress to enact a bill for recruitment of black soldiers. The assumption that any slaves who fought for the South would have to be granted freedom generated bitter opposition to the measure. "What did we go to war for, if not to protect our property?" asked a Virginia senator. By three votes in the House and one in the Senate, the Confederate Congress finally passed the bill on March 13, 1865. Before any Southern black regiments could be organized, however, the war ended.

LINCOLN'S REELECTION AND THE END OF THE CONFEDERACY

Despite Republican fears, battlefield events, rather than political controversies, had the strongest impact on U.S. voters in 1864. In effect, the election became a referendum on whether to continue fighting for unconditional victory. Within days after the Democratic national convention had declared the war a failure, the military situation changed dramatically.

THE CAPTURE OF ATLANTA

After a month of apparent stalemate on the Atlanta front, Sherman's army again made a large movement by the right flank to attack the last rail link into Atlanta from the south. At the battle of Jonesboro on August 31 and September 1, Sherman's men captured the railroad. Hood abandoned Atlanta to save his army. On September 2, Sherman sent a jaunty telegram to Washington: "Atlanta is ours, and fairly won."

This news had an enormous impact on the election. "VICTORY!" blazoned Republican headlines. "IS THE WAR A FAILURE? OLD ABE'S REPLY TO THE DEMOCRATIC CONVENTION." A New York Republican wrote that the capture of Atlanta, "coming at this political crisis, is the greatest event of the war." The *Richmond Examiner* glumly concurred. The fall of Atlanta, it declared, "came in the very nick of time" to "save the party of Lincoln from irretrievable ruin."

THE SHENANDOAH VALLEY

If Atlanta was not enough to brighten the prospects for Lincoln's reelection, events in Virginia's Shenandoah Valley were. After Early's raid through the valley all the way to Washington in July, Grant put Philip Sheridan in charge of a reinforced Army of the Shenandoah and told him to "go after Early and follow him to the death." Sheridan infused the same spirit into the three infantry corps of the Army of the Shenandoah that he had previously imbued in his cavalry. On September 19 they attacked Early's force near Winchester and after a day-long battle sent the Confederates flying to the south. Sheridan pursued them, attacking again on September 22 at Fisher's Hill 20 miles south of Winchester. Early's line collapsed, and his routed army fled 60 more miles southward.

Early's retreat enabled Sheridan to carry out the second part of his assignment in the Shenandoah Valley, which had twice served as a Confederate route of invasion and whose farms helped feed Confederate armies. Sheridan now set about destroying the valley's crops and mills so thoroughly that "crows flying over it for the balance of the season will have to carry their provender with them." Sheridan boasted that by the time he was through, "the Valley, from Winchester up to Staunton, ninety-two miles, will have little in it for man or beast."

But Jubal Early was not yet willing to give up. Reinforced by a division from Lee, on October 19 he launched a dawn attack across Cedar Creek, 12 miles south of Winchester. He caught the Yankees by surprise and drove them back in disorder. At the time of the attack, Sheridan was at Winchester, returning to his army from Washington, where he had gone to confer on future strategy. He jumped onto his horse and sped to the battlefield in a ride that became celebrated in poetry and legend. By sundown, Sheridan's charisma and tactical leadership had turned the battle from a Union defeat into another Confederate rout. The battle of Cedar Creek ended Confederate power in the valley.

Sherman's and Sheridan's victories ensured Lincoln's reelection on November 8 by a majority of 212 to 21 in the Electoral College. Soldiers played a notable role in the balloting. Every Northern state except three whose legislatures were controlled by Democrats had passed laws allowing absentee voting by soldiers. Seventy-eight percent of the military vote went to Lincoln—compared with 54 percent of the civilian vote. The men who were doing the fighting had sent a clear message that they meant to finish the job.

FROM ATLANTA TO THE SEA

Many Southerners got the message, but not Davis. The Confederacy remained "as erect and defiant as ever," he told his Congress in November 1864. "Nothing has changed in the purpose of its Government, in the indomitable valor of its troops, or in the unquenchable spirit of its people." It was this last-ditch resistance that Sherman set out to break in his famous march from Atlanta to the sea.

Sherman had concluded that "We are not only fighting hostile armies, but a hostile people." Defeat of the Confederate armies was not enough to win the war; the railroads, factories, and farms that supported those armies must also be destroyed. The will of the civilians who sustained the war must be crushed. Sherman expressed more bluntly than anyone else the meaning of total war and was ahead of his time in

SHERMAN'S SOLDIERS TEARING UP THE RAILROAD IN ATLANTA One of the objectives of Sherman's march from Atlanta to the sea was to demolish the railroads so they could not transport supplies to Confederate armies. The soldiers did a thorough job. They tore up the rails and ties, made a bonfire of the ties, heated the rails in the fire, and then wrapped them around trees, creating "Sherman neckties."

his understanding of psychological warfare. "We cannot change the hearts of those people of the South," he said, "but we can make war so terrible and make them so sick of war that generations would pass away before they would again appeal to it."

In Tennessee and Mississippi, Sherman's troops had burned everything of military value within their reach. Now Sherman proposed to do the same in Georgia. He urged Grant to let him march through the heart of Georgia, living off the land and destroying all resources not needed by his army—the same policy Sheridan was carrying out in the Shenandoah Valley. Grant and Lincoln were reluctant to authorize such a risky move, especially with Hood's army of 40,000 men still intact in northern Alabama. Sherman assured them that he would send George Thomas to take command of a force of 60,000 men in Tennessee who would be more than a match for Hood. With another 60,000, Sherman could "move through Georgia, smashing things to the sea. . . . I can make the march, and make Georgia howl!"

Lincoln and Grant finally consented. On November 16, Sherman's avengers marched out of

Atlanta after burning a third of the city, including some nonmilitary property. Southward they marched 280 miles to Savannah, wrecking everything in their path that could by any stretch of the imagination be considered of military value.

THE BATTLES OF FRANKLIN AND NASHVILLE

They encountered little resistance. Instead of chasing Sherman, Hood invaded Tennessee with the hope of recovering that state for the Confederacy, a disastrous campaign that virtually destroyed his army. On November 30, the Confederates attacked part of the

Union force at Franklin, a town 20 miles south of Nashville. The slaughter claimed no fewer than 12 Confederate generals and 54 regimental commanders as casualties. Instead of retreating, Hood moved on to Nashville, where on December 15 and 16 Thomas launched an attack that almost wiped out the Army of Tennessee. Its remnants retreated to Mississippi, where Hood resigned in January 1865.

FORT FISHER AND SHERMAN'S MARCH THROUGH THE CAROLINAS

News of Hood's defeat produced, in the words of a Southern diarist, "the darkest and most dismal day"

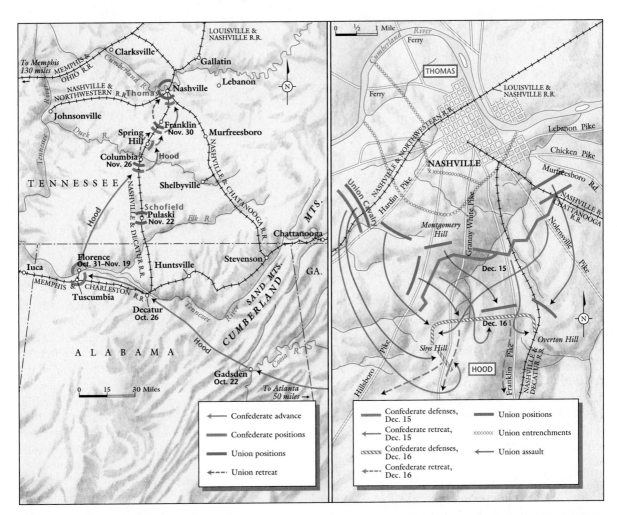

HOOD'S TENNESSEE CAMPAIGN, OCTOBER–NOVEMBER 1864

NASHVILLE, DECEMBER 15–16, 1864

COMPARATIVE STRENGTH OF UNION AND CONFEDERATE ARMIES

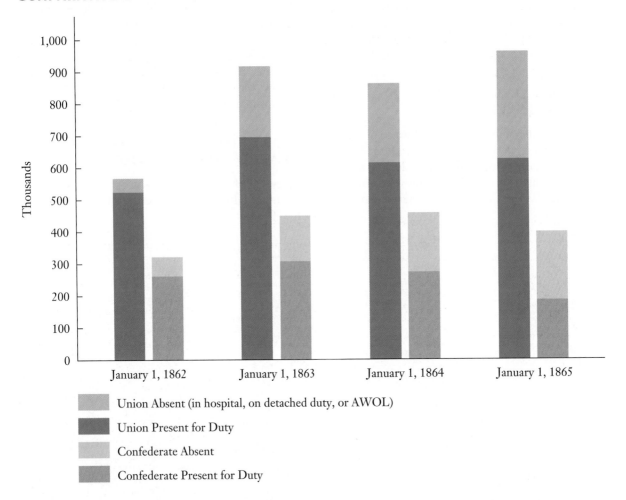

Union Absent (in hospital, on detached duty, or AWOL)

Union Present for Duty

Confederate Absent

Confederate Present for Duty

of the Confederacy's short history, but worse was yet to come. Lee's army in Virginia drew its dwindling supplies overland from the Carolinas and through the port of Wilmington, North Carolina, the only city still accessible to blockade runners. Massive Fort Fisher guarded the mouth of the Cape Fear River below Wilmington, its big guns keeping blockade ships at bay and protecting the runners. The Union navy had long wanted to attack Fort Fisher, but the diversion of ships and troops to the long, futile campaign against Charleston had delayed the effort. In January 1865, though, the largest armada of the war—58 ships with 627 guns— pounded Fort Fisher for two days, disabling most of its big guns. Army troops and marines landed and stormed the fort, capturing it on January 15. That ended the blockade running, and Sherman soon put an end to supplies from the Carolinas as well.

At the end of January, Sherman's soldiers headed north from Savannah, eager to take revenge on South Carolina, which to their mind had started the war. Here, they made even less distinction between civilian and military property than they had in Georgia and left even less of Columbia standing than they had of Atlanta. Seemingly invincible, Sherman's army pushed into North Carolina and brushed aside the force that Joseph E. Johnston had assembled to stop them. The devastation left in their wake appalled Confederates. "All is gloom, despondency, and inactivity," wrote a South Carolinian. "Our army is demoralized and the people panic stricken. To fight longer seems to be madness."

But the war would not end until the Confederate armies surrendered, as Lincoln made clear in his second inaugural address on March 4, 1865. In the best-known words from that address, he urged a binding up of the nation's wounds "with malice toward none" and "charity for all." Even more significant, given that the conflict still raged, were these words:

> American Slavery is one of those offences which, in the providence of God . . . He now wills to remove [through] this terrible war, as the woe due to those by whom the offence came. . . . Fondly do we hope—fervently do we pray—that this mighty scourge of war may speedily pass away. Yet if God wills that it continue, until all the wealth piled by the bondman's two hundred and fifty years of unrequited toil shall be sunk, and until every drop of blood drawn with the lash, shall be paid by another drawn with the sword, as was said three thousand years ago, so still it must be said "the judgments of the Lord, are true and righteous altogether."

THE ROAD TO APPOMATTOX

The Army of Northern Virginia was now the only entity that kept the Confederacy alive, and it was on the verge of disintegration. Scores of its soldiers were deserting every day. On April 1, Sheridan's cavalry and an infantry corps smashed the right flank of Lee's line at Five Forks and cut off the last railroad into Petersburg. Next day, Grant attacked all along the line and forced Lee to abandon both Petersburg and Richmond. As the Confederate government fled its capital, its army set fire to all the military stores it could not carry. The fires spread and destroyed more of Richmond than the Northern troops had destroyed of Atlanta or Columbia.

Lee's starving men limped westward, hoping to turn south and join the remnants of Johnston's army in North Carolina. Sheridan's cavalry raced ahead and cut them off at Appomattox, 90 miles from Petersburg, on April 8. When the weary Confederates tried a breakout attack the next morning, their first probe revealed solid ranks of Union infantry arrayed behind the cavalry. It was the end. "There is nothing left for me to do," said Lee, "but to go and see General Grant, and I would rather die a thousand deaths." Lee met with Grant at the house of Wilmer McLean, who in 1861 had lived near Manassas where a shell had crashed through his kitchen roof during the first battle of

THE SURRENDER AT APPOMATTOX This is one of many paintings of Grant and Lee agreeing to the surrender terms of Lee's army in Wilmer McLean's parlor at Appomattox Court House. No photographer was present to record the scene, but many eyewitnesses provided descriptions to guide artists. Lee was accompanied by a lone aide; Grant was accompanied by nearly a dozen of his generals and staff officers. Standing immediately to the left of the seated Grant is George G. Meade, commander of the Army of the Potomac (who was not actually present), and standing to Meade's left is Philip Sheridan, commander of the army's cavalry.

Bull Run. McLean had moved to the remote village of Appomattox to escape the war, only to have its final drama played out in his parlor. There, the son of an Ohio tanner dictated surrender terms to a scion of one of Virginia's First Families.

The terms were generous. Thirty thousand captured Confederates were allowed to go home on condition that they promise never again to take up arms against the United States. After completing the surrender formalities on April 9, Grant introduced Lee to his staff, which included Colonel Ely Parker, a Seneca Indian. As Lee shook hands with

CASUALTIES IN CIVIL WAR ARMIES AND NAVIES *Confederate records are incomplete; the Confederate data listed here are therefore estimates. The actual Confederate totals were probably higher.*

	Killed and Mortally Wounded in Combat	Died of Disease	Died in Prison	Miscellaneous Deaths	Total Deaths	Wounded, not Mortally*	Total Casualties
Union	111,904	197,388	30,192	24,881	364,345	277,401	641,766
Confederate (estimated)	94,000	140,000	26,000	No Estimates	260,000	195,000	455,000
Both Armies (estimated)	205,904	337,388	56,192	24,881	624,365	472,401	1,096,766

*Accidents, drownings, causes not stated, etc.

Parker, he stared for a moment at Parker's dark features and said: "I am glad to see one real American here." Parker replied solemnly: "We are all Americans." And indeed they now were.

THE ASSASSINATION OF LINCOLN

Wild celebrations broke out in the North at news of the fall of Richmond, followed soon by news of Appomattox. Almost overnight, the celebrations turned to mourning. On the evening of April 14, the careworn Abraham Lincoln sought to relax by attending a comedy at Ford's Theatre. In the middle of the play, John Wilkes Booth broke into Lincoln's box and shot the president fatally in the head. A prominent actor, Booth was a native of Maryland and a frustrated, unstable egotist who hated Lincoln for what he had done to Booth's beloved South. As he jumped from Lincoln's box to the stage and escaped out a back door, he shouted Virginia's state motto at the stunned audience: "Sic semper tyrannis" ("Thus always to tyrants").

Lincoln's death in the early morning of April 15 produced an outpouring of grief throughout the North and among newly freed slaves in the South. The martyred president did not live to see the culmination of his great achievement in leading the nation to a victory that preserved its existence and abolished slavery. Within 10 weeks after Lincoln's death, his assassin was trapped and killed in a burning barn in Virginia (April 26), the remaining Confederate armies surrendered one after another (April 26, May

ABRAHAM LINCOLN IN 1865 This is the last photograph of Lincoln, taken on April 10, 1865, four days before his assassination. Four years of war had left their mark on the 56-year-old president; note the lines of strain, fatigue, and sadness in his face.

4, May 26, June 23), and Union cavalry captured the fleeing Jefferson Davis in Georgia (May 10). The trauma of Civil War was over, but the problems of peace and reconstruction had just begun.

CONCLUSION

Northern victory in the Civil War resolved two fundamental questions of liberty and power left unresolved by the Revolution of 1776 and the Constitution of 1789: whether this fragile republican experiment in federalism called the United States would survive as one nation; and whether that nation, founded on a charter of liberty, would continue to exist as the largest slaveholding country in the world. Before 1861 the question of whether a state could secede from the Union had remained open. Eleven states did secede, but their defeat in a war that cost 625,000 lives resolved the issue: Since 1865 no state has seriously threatened secession. And in 1865 the adoption of the Thirteenth Amendment to the Constitution confirmed the supreme power of the national government to abolish slavery and ensure the liberty of all Americans.

The Civil War also accomplished a regional transfer of power from South to North. From 1800 to 1860 the slave states had used their leverage in the Jeffersonian Republican and Jacksonian Democratic parties to control national politics most of the time.

A southern slaveholder was president of the United States during two-thirds of the years from 1789 to 1861. Most congressional leaders and Supreme Court justices during that period were southerners. In the fifty years after 1861 no native of a southern state was elected president, only one served as Speaker of the House and none as president pro tem of the Senate, and only 5 of the 26 Supreme Court justices appointed during that half-century were from the South. In 1860 the South's share of the national wealth was 30 percent; in 1870 it was 12 percent. The institutions and ideology of a plantation society and a caste system that had dominated half the country before 1861 went down with a great crash in 1865—to be replaced by the institutions and ideology of free-labor capitalism. Once feared as the gravest threat to liberty, the power of the national government sustained by a large army had achieved the greatest triumph of liberty in American history. With victory and peace in 1865, the reunited nation turned its attention to the issue of equality.

Suggested Readings begin on page SR-1. For Web activities and resources related to this chapter, go to http:// www.harcourtcollege.com/history/murrin

CHAPTER 17

RECONSTRUCTION, 1863–1877

SUNDAY MORNING IN VIRGINIA

This painting by Winslow Homer (1877) of four young black people and the grandmother of two of them is full of symbolism that illustrates important themes in both slavery and Reconstruction. The two lighter-skinned children, probably siblings, are reading the Bible while the dark-skinned children on either side—also probably brother and sister—follow along as they too learn to read. The grandmother listens with a wistful look into the distance, perhaps wishing that she was young enough to acquire the powerful tool of literacy denied to slaves. The religiosity of freedpeople, their humble homes, the partly white ancestry of some, and their thirst for education all are portrayed in this splendid painting.

From the beginning of the Civil War, the North fought to "reconstruct" the Union. Lincoln first attempted to restore the Union as it had existed before 1861, but once the abolition of slavery became a Northern war aim, the Union could never be reconstructed on its old foundations. Instead, it must experience a "new birth of freedom," as Lincoln had said at the dedication of the military cemetery at Gettysburg.

But precisely what did "a new birth of freedom" mean? At the very least it meant the end of slavery. The slave states would be reconstructed on a free-labor basis. But what would liberty look like for the four million freed slaves? Would they become citizens equal to their former masters in the eyes of the law? Would they have the right to vote? Should Confederate leaders and soldiers be punished for treason? On what terms should the Confederate states return to the Union? What would be the powers of the states and of the national government in a reconstructed Union?

This chapter will focus on the following major questions:

- What were the positions of Presidents Abraham Lincoln and Andrew Johnson and of moderate and radical Republicans in Congress on the issues of restoring the South to the Union and protecting the rights of freed slaves?
- Why was Andrew Johnson impeached? Why was he acquitted?
- What were the achievements of Reconstruction? What were its failures?
- Why did a majority of the Northern people and their political leaders turn against continued federal involvement in Southern Reconstruction in the 1870s?

WARTIME RECONSTRUCTION

Lincoln pondered the problems of Reconstruction long and hard. At first he feared that whites in the South would never extend equal rights to the freed slaves. After all, even most northern states denied full civil equality to the few black people within their borders. In 1862 and 1863, Lincoln encouraged freedpeople to emigrate to all-black countries such as Haiti, where they would have a chance to get ahead without having to face the racism of whites. Black leaders, abolitionists, and many Republicans objected to that policy. Black people were Americans, they asserted. Why should they not have the rights of American citizens instead of being urged to leave the country?

Lincoln eventually acknowledged the logic and justice of that view, but in beginning the process of reconstruction, he first reached out to southern *whites* whose allegiance to the Confederacy was lukewarm. On December 8, 1863, Lincoln issued his Proclamation of Amnesty and Reconstruction, which offered presidential pardon to southern whites (with the exception of Confederate government officials and high-ranking military officers) who took an oath of allegiance to the United States and accepted the abolition of slavery. In any state where the number of white males aged 21 or older who took this oath equaled 10 percent of the number of voters in 1860, that nucleus could reestablish a state government to which Lincoln promised presidential recognition.

Because the war was still raging, this policy could be carried out only where Union troops controlled substantial portions of a Confederate state: Louisiana, Arkansas, and Tennessee in early 1864. Nevertheless, Lincoln hoped that once the process had begun in those areas, it might snowball as Union military victories convinced more and more Confederates that their cause was hopeless. In the end, those military victories were long delayed, and in most parts of the South reconstruction did not begin until 1865.

Another problem that slowed the process was growing opposition within Lincoln's own party. Many Republicans believed that white men who had fought *against* the Union should not be rewarded with restoration of their political rights while black men who had fought *for* the Union were denied those rights. The Proclamation of Reconstruction had stated that "any provision which may be adopted by [a reconstructed] State government in relation to the freed people of such State, which shall recognize and declare their permanent freedom, provide for their education, and which may yet be consistent, as a temporary arrangement, with their present condition as a laboring, landless, and homeless class, will not be objected to by the national Executive." This seemed to mean that white landowners and former slaveholders could adopt labor regulations and other measures to control former slaves, so long as they recognized their freedom and made minimal provision for their education.

CHRONOLOGY

1863 Lincoln issues Proclamation of Amnesty and Reconstruction

1864 Congress passes Wade-Davis bill; Lincoln kills it by pocket veto

1865 Congress establishes Freedmen's Bureau
• Andrew Johnson becomes president, announces his reconstruction plan
• Southern states enact Black Codes
• Congress refuses to seat southern congressmen elected under Johnson's plan

1866 Congress passes civil rights bill and expands Freedmen's Bureau over Johnson's veto
• Race riots in Memphis and New Orleans
• Congress approves Fourteenth Amendment
• Republicans increase congressional majority in fall elections

1867 Congress passes Reconstruction acts over Johnson's vetoes • Congress passes Tenure of Office Act over Johnson's veto

1868 Most southern senators and representatives readmitted to Congress under congressional plan of Reconstruction • Andrew Johnson impeached but not convicted • Ulysses S. Grant elected president • Fourteenth Amendment is ratified

1870 Fifteenth Amendment is ratified

1871 Congress passes Ku Klux Klan Act

1872 Liberal Republicans defect from party
• Grant wins reelection

1873 Economic depression begins with the Panic

1874 Democrats win control of House of Representatives

1875 Democrats implement Mississippi Plan
• Congress passes civil rights act

1876 Centennial celebration in Philadelphia
• Disputed presidential election causes constitutional crisis

1877 Compromise of 1877 installs Rutherford B. Hayes as president • Hayes withdraws troops from South

1883 Supreme Court declares civil rights act of 1875 unconstitutional

RADICAL REPUBLICANS AND RECONSTRUCTION

These were radical advances over slavery, but for many Republicans they were not radical enough.

LINCOLN'S FUNERAL PROCESSION IN CHICAGO, MAY 1, 1865 After a public funeral in Washington, D.C., on April 19, Lincoln's remains were transported by special train to New York City and then west to their final resting place in Springfield, Illinois, where Lincoln was buried on May 4, 1865. The funeral train stopped in major cities, where grieving citizens paid their last respects. An estimated 7 million people lined the tracks along the train's 1,000-mile journey, which reversed the route Lincoln had taken from Springfield to Washington, D.C., in February 1861.

Led by Thaddeus Stevens in the House and Charles Sumner in the Senate, the radical Republicans wanted to go much further. If the freedpeople were landless, they said, provide them with land by confiscating the plantations of leading Confederates as punishment for treason. Radical Republicans also distrusted oaths of allegiance sworn by ex-Confederates. Rather than simply restoring the old ruling class to power, asked Charles Sumner, why not give freed slaves the vote, to provide a genuinely loyal nucleus of supporters in the South?

These radical positions did not command a majority of Congress in 1864. Yet the experience of Louisiana, the first state to reorganize under Lincoln's more moderate policy, convinced even

nonradical Republicans to block Lincoln's program. With the protection of Union soldiers in the occupied portion of Louisiana (New Orleans and several parishes in the southern half of the state), enough white men took the oath of allegiance to satisfy Lincoln's conditions. They adopted a new state constitution and formed a government that abolished slavery and provided a school system for blacks. But despite Lincoln's private appeal to the new government to grant literate blacks and black Union soldiers the right to vote, the reconstructed Louisiana legislature chose not to do so. It also authorized planters to enforce restrictive labor policies on black plantation workers. Louisiana's actions alienated a majority of congressional Republicans, who refused to admit representatives and senators from the "reconstructed" state.

At the same time, though, Congress failed to enact a reconstruction policy of its own. This was not for lack of trying. In fact, both houses passed the Wade-Davis reconstruction bill (named for Senator Benjamin Wade of Ohio and Representative Henry Winter Davis of Maryland) in July 1864. That bill did not enfranchise blacks, but it did impose such stringent loyalty requirements on southern whites that few of them could take the required oath. Lincoln therefore vetoed it.

Lincoln's action infuriated many Republicans. Wade and Davis published a blistering "manifesto" denouncing the president. This bitter squabble threatened for a time to destroy Lincoln's chances of being reelected. Union military success in the fall of 1864, however, combined with sober second thoughts about the consequences of a Democratic electoral victory, reunited the Republicans behind Lincoln. The collapse of Confederate military resistance the following spring set the stage for compromise between the president and Congress on a policy for the postwar South. Two days after Appomattox, Lincoln promised that he would soon announce such a policy, which probably would have included voting rights for some blacks and stronger measures to protect their civil rights. But three days later, Lincoln was assassinated.

ANDREW JOHNSON AND RECONSTRUCTION

In 1864 Republicans had adopted the name "Union Party" to attract the votes of War Democrats and border-state Unionists who could not bring themselves to vote Republican. For the same reason, they also nominated Andrew Johnson of Tennessee as Lincoln's running mate.

Of "poor white" heritage, Johnson had clawed his way up in the rough-and-tumble politics of east Tennessee. This region of small farms and few slaves held little love for the planters who controlled the state. Andrew Johnson denounced the planters as "stuck-up aristocrats" who had no empathy with the southern yeomen for whom Johnson became a self-appointed spokesman. Johnson,

though a Democrat, was the only senator from a seceding state who refused to support the Confederacy. For this, the Republicans rewarded him with the vice presidential nomination, hoping to attract the votes of pro-war Democrats and upper-South Unionists.

Booth's bullet therefore elevated to the presidency a man who still thought of himself as primarily a Democrat and a southerner. The trouble this might cause in a party that was mostly Republican and northern was not immediately apparent, however. In fact, Johnson's enmity toward the "stuck-up aristocrats" whom he blamed for leading the South into secession prompted him to utter dire threats against "traitors." "Treason is a crime and must be made odious," he said soon after becoming president. "Traitors must be impoverished. . . . They must not only be punished, but their social power must be destroyed."

Radical Republicans liked the sound of this. It seemed to promise the type of reconstruction they favored—one that would deny political power to ex-Confederates and would enfranchise blacks. They envisioned a coalition between these new black voters and the small minority of southern whites who had never supported the Confederacy. These men could be expected to vote Republican. Republican governments in southern states would guarantee freedom and would pass laws to provide civil rights and economic opportunity for freed slaves. Not incidentally, they would also strengthen the Republican Party nationally.

JOHNSON'S POLICY

Radical Republicans, with a combination of pragmatic, partisan, and idealistic motives, prepared to implement a progressive reconstruction policy. Johnson unexpectedly refused to cooperate. Instead of calling Congress into special session, he moved ahead on his own. On May 29, 1865, Johnson issued two proclamations. The first provided for a blanket amnesty for all but the highest-ranking Confederate officials and military officers, and those ex-Confederates with taxable property worth $20,000 or more—the "stuck-up aristocrats." The second named a provisional governor for North Carolina and directed him to call an election of delegates to frame a new state constitu-

ANDREW JOHNSON AND FREDERICK DOUGLASS By 1866 the president and the leading black spokesman for equal rights represented opposite poles in the debate about Reconstruction. Johnson wanted to bring the South back into the Union on the basis of white suffrage; Douglass wanted black men to be granted the right to vote. Johnson's resistance to this policy as Republicans tried to enact it was a factor in his impeachment two years later.

tion. Only white men who had received amnesty and taken an oath of allegiance could vote. Similar proclamations soon followed for other former Confederate states. Johnson's policy was clear. He would exclude both blacks and upper-class whites from the reconstruction process. The backbone of the new South would be yeomen whites who, like himself, had remained steadfastly loyal to the Union, along with those who now proclaimed themselves loyal.

Although at first many Republicans supported Johnson's policy, the radicals were dismayed. They feared that restricting the vote to whites would lead to oppression of the newly freed slaves and restoration of the old power structure in the South. They began to sense that Johnson (who had owned slaves) was as dedicated to white supremacy as any Confederate. "White men alone must govern the South," he told a Democratic

senator. After a tense confrontation with a group of black men led by Frederick Douglass, who had visited the White House to urge black suffrage, Johnson told his private secretary: "Those damned sons of bitches thought they had me in a trap! I know that damned Douglass; he's just like any nigger, and he would sooner cut a white man's throat than not."

Moderate Republicans believed that black men should participate to some degree in the reconstruction process, but in 1865 they were not yet prepared to break with the president. They regarded his policy as an "experiment" that would be modified as time went on. "Loyal negroes must not be put down, while disloyal white men are put up," wrote a moderate Republican. "But I am quite willing to see what will come of Mr. Johnson's experiment." If the new southern state constitutions failed to enfranchise at least literate blacks and those who had fought in the Union army, said another moderate, "the President then will be at liberty to pursue a sterner policy."

SOUTHERN DEFIANCE

As it happened, none of the state conventions enfranchised a single black. Some of them even balked at ratifying the Thirteenth Amendment (which abolished slavery). The rhetoric of some white southerners began to take on a renewed anti-Yankee tone of defiance that sounded like 1861 all over again. Reports from Unionists and army officers in the South told of neo-Confederate violence against blacks and their white sympathizers. Johnson seemed to encourage such activities by his own rhetoric, which sounded increasingly like that of a southern Democrat, and by allowing the organization of white militia units in the South. "What can be hatched from such an egg," asked a Republican newspaper, "but another rebellion?"

Then there was the matter of presidential pardons. After talking fiercely about punishing traitors, and after excluding several classes of them from his amnesty proclamation, Johnson began to issue special pardons to many ex-Confederates, restoring to them all property and political rights. Moreover, under the new state constitutions, southern voters were electing hundreds of ex-Confederates to state offices. Even more alarming to northerners, who thought they had won the war, was the election to Congress of no fewer than nine ex-Confederate congressmen, seven ex-Confederate state officials, four generals, four colonels, and even the former Confederate vice president, Alexander H. Stephens. To apprehensive Republicans, it appeared that the rebels, unable to capture Washington in war, were about to do so in peace.

Somehow the aristocrats and traitors Johnson had denounced in April had taken over the reconstruction process. Instead of weapons, they had resorted to flattering the presidential ego. Thousands of prominent ex-Confederates or their tearful female relatives applied for pardons confessing the error of their ways and appealing for presidential mercy. Reveling in his power over these once-haughty aristocrats who had disdained

him as a humble tailor, Johnson waxed eloquent on his "love, respect, and confidence" toward southern whites, for whom he now felt "forbearing and forgiving."

More effective, perhaps, was the praise and support Johnson received from leading northern Democrats. Though the Republicans had placed him on their presidential ticket in 1864, Johnson was after all a Democrat. That party's leaders enticed Johnson with visions of reelection as a Democrat in 1868 if he could manage to reconstruct the South in a manner that would preserve a Democratic majority there.

THE BLACK CODES

That was just what the Republicans feared. Their concern that state governments devoted to white supremacy would reduce the freedpeople to a condition close to slavery was confirmed in the fall of 1865 when some of those governments enacted "Black Codes."

One of the first tasks of the legislatures of the reconstructed states was to define the rights of four million former slaves. The option of treating them exactly like white citizens was scarcely considered. Instead, the states excluded black people from juries and the ballot box, did not permit them to testify against whites in court, banned interracial marriage, and punished blacks more severely than whites for certain crimes. Some states defined any unemployed black person as a vagrant and hired him out to a planter, forbade blacks to lease land, and provided for the apprenticing to whites of black youths who did not have adequate parental support.

These Black Codes aroused anger among northern Republicans, who saw them as a brazen attempt to reinstate a quasi-slavery. "We tell the white men of Mississippi," declared the *Chicago Tribune*, "that the men of the North will convert the State of Mississippi into a frog pond before they will allow such laws to disgrace one foot of the soil in which the bones of our soldiers sleep and over which the flag of freedom waves." And, in fact, the Union army's occupation forces did suspend the implementation of Black Codes that discriminated on racial grounds.

LAND AND LABOR IN THE POSTWAR SOUTH

The Black Codes, though discriminatory, were designed to address a genuine problem. The end of the war had left black-white relations in the South in a state of limbo. The South's economy was in a shambles. Burned-out plantations, fields growing up in weeds, and railroads without tracks, bridges, or rolling stock marked the trail of war. Nearly half of the livestock in the former Confederacy and most other tangible assets except the land itself had been destroyed. Many people, white as well as black, lived from meal to meal. Law and order broke down in many areas. The war had ended early enough in the spring to allow the planting of at least some food crops, but who would plant and cultivate them? One-quarter of the South's white farmers had been killed in the war; the slaves were slaves no more. "We have nothing left to begin anew with," lamented a South Carolina planter. "I never did a day's work in my life, and I don't know how to begin."

Despite all, life went on. Soldiers' widows and their children plowed and planted. Slaveless planters and their wives calloused their hands for the first time. Confederate veterans drifted home and went to work. Former slave owners asked their former slaves to work the land for wages or shares of the crop, and many did so. Others refused, because for them to leave the old place was an essential part of freedom. In slavery times, the only way to become free was to run away, and the impulse to leave the scene of bondage persisted. "You ain't, none o' you, gwinter feel rale free," said a black preacher to his congregation, "till you shakes de dus' ob de Ole Plantashun offen yore feet" (dialect in original source).

Thus the roads were alive with freedpeople on the move in the summer of 1865. Many of them signed on to work at farms just a few miles from their old homes. Others moved into town. Some looked for relatives who had been sold away during slavery or from whom they had been separated during the war. Some wandered aimlessly. Crime increased as people, both blacks and whites, stole food to survive—and as whites organized vigilante groups to discipline blacks and force them to work.

THE FREEDMEN'S BUREAU

Into this vacuum stepped the United States Army and the Freedmen's Bureau. Tens of thousands of troops remained in the South as an occupation force until civil government could be restored. The Freedmen's Bureau (its official title was Bureau of Refugees, Freedmen, and Abandoned Lands), created by Congress in March 1865, became the principal agency for overseeing relations between former slaves and owners. Staffed by army officers, the bureau established posts throughout the South to supervise free-labor wage contracts between landowners and freedpeople. The Freedmen's Bureau also issued food rations to 150,000 people daily during 1865, one-third of them to whites.

Southern whites viewed the Freedmen's Bureau with hostility. Without it, however, the postwar chaos and devastation in the South would have been much greater—as some whites privately admitted. Bureau agents used their influence with black people to encourage them to sign free-labor contracts and return to work.

In negotiating labor contracts, the bureau tried to establish minimum wages. Lack of money in the

THE FREEDMEN'S BUREAU Created in 1865, the Freedmen's Bureau stood between freed slaves and their former masters in the postwar South, charged with the task of protecting freedpeople from injustice and repression. Staffed by officers of the Union army, the bureau symbolized the military power of the government in its efforts to keep peace in the South.

South, however, caused many contracts to call for share wages—that is, paying workers with shares of the crop. At first, landowners worked their laborers in large groups (called gangs) under direct supervision, but many black workers resented this as reminiscent of slavery. Thus, a new system evolved, called sharecropping, whereby a black family worked a specific piece of land in return for a share of the crop produced on it.

LAND FOR THE LANDLESS

Freedpeople, of course, would have preferred to farm their own land. "What's de use of being free if you don't own land enough to be buried in?" asked one black sharecropper. "Might juss as well stay slave all yo' days" (dialect in original). Some black farmers did manage to save up enough money to buy small plots of land. Demobilized black soldiers purchased land with their bounty payments, sometimes pooling their money to buy an entire plantation on which several black families settled. Northern philanthropists helped some freedmen buy land. Most ex-slaves found the purchase of land impossible. Few of them had money, and even if they did, whites often refused to sell because it would mean losing a source of cheap labor and encouraging notions of black independence.

Several northern radicals proposed legislation to confiscate ex-Confederate land and redistribute it to freedpeople, but those proposals went nowhere. The most promising effort to put thousands of slaves on land of their own also failed. In January 1865, after his march through Georgia, General William T. Sherman had issued a military order setting aside thousands of acres of abandoned plantation land in the Georgia and South Carolina low country for settlement by freed slaves. The army even turned over some of its surplus mules to black farmers. The expectation of "40 acres and a mule" excited freedpeople in 1865, but President Johnson's Amnesty Proclamation and his wholesale issuance of pardons restored most of this property to pardoned ex-Confederates. The same thing happened to white-owned land elsewhere in the South. Placed under the temporary care of the Freedmen's Bureau for subsequent possible distribution to freedpeople, by 1866 nearly all of this land had

SHARECROPPERS WORKING IN THE FIELDS After the war, former planters tried to employ their former slaves in gang labor to grow cotton and tobacco, with the only difference from slavery being the grudging payment of wages. Freedpeople resisted this system as too reminiscent of slavery. They compelled landowners to rent them plots of land on which these black families struggled to raise corn and cotton or tobacco, paying a share of the crop as rent—hence "sharecropping." This posed photograph was intended to depict the family labor of sharecroppers; in reality, most black farmers had a mule to pull their plow.

been restored to its former owners by order of President Johnson.

EDUCATION

Abolitionists were more successful in helping freedpeople obtain an education. During the war, freedmen's aid societies and missionary societies founded by abolitionists had sent teachers to Union-occupied areas of the South to set up schools for freed slaves. After the war, this effort was expanded with the aid of the Freedmen's Bureau. Two thousand northern teachers, three-quarters of them women, fanned out into every

A BLACK SCHOOL DURING RECONSTRUCTION In the antebellum South, teaching slaves to read and write was forbidden. Thus, about 90 percent of the freedpeople were illiterate in 1865. One of their top priorities was education. At first, most of the teachers in the freedmen's schools established by northern missionary societies were northern white women. But as black teachers were trained, they took over the elementary schools, such as this one photographed in the 1870s.

part of the South. There they trained black teachers to staff first the mission schools and later the public schools established by Reconstruction state governments. After 1870 the missionary societies concentrated more heavily on making higher education available to African Americans. Many of the black colleges in the South today were founded and supported by their efforts. This education crusade, which the black leader W. E. B. Du Bois described as "the most wonderful peace-battle of the nineteenth century," reduced the southern black illiteracy rate to 70 percent by 1880 and to 48 percent by 1900.

THE ADVENT OF CONGRESSIONAL RECONSTRUCTION

Political reconstruction shaped the civil and political rights of freedpeople. By the time Congress met in December 1865, the Republican majority was determined to control the process by which former Confederate states would regain full representa-

tion. Congress refused to admit the representatives and senators elected by the former Confederate states under Johnson's reconstruction policy, and set up a special committee to formulate new terms. The committee held hearings at which southern Unionists, freedpeople, and U.S. Army officers testified to abuse and terrorism in the South. Their testimony convinced Republicans of the need for stronger federal intervention to define and protect the civil rights of freedpeople. Many radicals wanted to go further and grant the ballot to black men, who would join with white Unionists and northern settlers in the South to form a southern Republican Party.

Most Republicans realized that northern voters would not support such a radical policy, however. Racism was still strong in the North, where most states denied the right to vote to the few blacks living within their borders. Moderate Republicans feared that Democrats would exploit northern racism in the congressional elections of 1866 if Congress made black suffrage a cornerstone of Reconstruction. Instead, the special committee decided to draft a constitutional amendment that would encourage southern states to enfranchise blacks but would not require them to do so.

SCHISM BETWEEN PRESIDENT AND CONGRESS

Meanwhile, Congress passed two laws to protect the economic and civil rights of freedpeople. The first extended the life of the Freedmen's Bureau and expanded its powers. The second defined freedpeople as citizens with equal legal rights and gave federal courts appellate jurisdiction to enforce those rights. To the dismay of moderates who were trying to heal the widening breach between the president and Congress, Johnson vetoed both measures. He followed this action with an intemperate speech to Democratic supporters in which he denounced Republican leaders as traitors who did not want to restore the Union except on terms that would degrade white southerners. Democratic newspapers applauded the president for vetoing

bills that would "compound our race with niggers, gypsies, and baboons."

THE FOURTEENTH AMENDMENT

Johnson had thrown down the gauntlet to congressional Republicans. They did not hesitate to take it up. With better than a two-thirds majority in both houses, they passed the Freedmen's Bureau and Civil Rights bills over the president's vetoes. Then on April 30, 1866, the special committee submitted to Congress its proposed Fourteenth Amendment to the Constitution. After lengthy debate, the amendment received the required two-thirds majority in Congress on June 13 and went to the states for ratification. Section 1 defined all native-born or naturalized persons, including blacks, as American citizens and prohibited the states from abridging the "privileges and immunities" of citizens, from depriving "any person of life, liberty, or property without due process of law,"

LINK TO THE PAST

African American Odyssey: Quest for Full Citizenship

http://memory.loc.gov/ammem/aaohtm/aohome.html

Part of the Library of Congress's huge American Memory project, this site contains material on slavery and slave resistance but focuses mainly on the transition from slavery to freedom during the Civil War and Reconstruction. Digitized images show black men at voting booths, in state legislatures, and in Congress. Many documents deal with freedpeople's schools. The material, including explanatory texts, is arranged in a chronological narrative, and visitors can proceed through the site as through a museum exhibit.

1. How many African Americans served in Congress during Reconstruction? What was their background? How many had been slaves? How many were college graduates?

2. Describe the leading schools for blacks established during Reconstruction. Who founded them? Where were they located? How well did they fulfill their purpose? How many still exist today?

3. What were the main provisions of the civil rights acts of 1866 and 1875? Of the enforcement acts of 1870 and 1871? How well were these laws enforced and carried out? What was their ultimate fate?

and from denying to any person "the equal protection of the laws." Section 2 gave states the option of either enfranchising black males or losing a proportionate number of congressional seats and electoral votes. Section 3 disqualified a significant number of ex-Confederates from holding federal or state office. Section 4 guaranteed the national debt and repudiated the Confederate debt. Section 5 empowered Congress to enforce the Fourteenth Amendment by "appropriate legislation." The Fourteenth Amendment had far-reaching consequences. Section 1 has become the most important provision in the Constitution for defining and enforcing civil rights.

THE 1866 ELECTIONS

Republicans entered the 1866 congressional elections campaign with the Fourteenth Amendment as their platform. They made clear that any ex-Confederate state that ratified the amendment would be declared "reconstructed" and that its representatives and senators would be seated in Congress. Tennessee ratified the amendment, but Johnson counseled other southern legislatures to reject the amendment, which they did. Johnson then prepared for an all-out campaign to gain a friendly northern majority in the congressional elections.

Johnson began his campaign by creating a "National Union Party" made up of a few conservative Republicans who disagreed with their party, some border-state Unionists who supported the president, and Democrats. The inclusion of Democrats doomed the effort from the start. Many Northern Democrats still carried the taint of having opposed the war effort, and many northern voters did not trust them. The National Union Party was further damaged by race riots in Memphis and New Orleans, where white mobs including former Confederate soldiers killed 80 blacks, among them several former Union soldiers. The riots bolstered Republican arguments that national power was necessary to protect "the fruits of victory" in the South. Perhaps the biggest liability of the National Union Party was Johnson himself. In a whistle-stop tour through the North, he traded insults with hecklers and embarrassed his supporters by comparing himself to Christ and his Republican adversaries to Judas.

Republicans swept the election: They gained a three-to-one majority in the next Congress. Having rejected the Reconstruction terms embodied in the Fourteenth Amendment, southern Democrats now faced far more stringent terms. "They would not cooperate in rebuilding what they destroyed," wrote an exasperated moderate Republican, so "we must remove the rubbish and rebuild from the bottom. Whether they are willing or not, we must compel obedience to the Union and demand protection for its humblest citizen."

THE RECONSTRUCTION ACTS OF 1867

In March 1867 the new Congress enacted over Johnson's vetoes two laws prescribing new procedures for the full restoration of the former Confederate states (except Tennessee, already readmitted) to the Union. These laws represented a complex compromise between radicals and moderates that had been hammered out in a confusing sequence of committee drafts, caucus decisions, all-night debates on the floor, and frayed tempers. The Reconstruction acts of 1867 divided the 10 southern states into five military districts, directed army officers to register voters for the election of delegates to new constitutional conventions, and enfranchised males aged 21 and older (including blacks) to vote in those elections. The acts also disfranchised (for these elections only) those ex-Confederates who were disqualified from holding office under the not-yet-ratified Fourteenth Amendment—fewer than 10 percent of all white voters. When a state had adopted a new constitution that granted equal civil and political rights regardless of race and had ratified the Fourteenth Amendment, it would be declared reconstructed and its newly elected congressmen would be seated.

These measures embodied a true revolution. Just a few years earlier, southerners had been masters of four million slaves and part of an independent Confederate nation. Now they were shorn of political power, with their former slaves not only freed but also politically empowered. To be sure, radical Republicans who warned that the revolution was incomplete as long as the old master class

NEW YORK, SATURDAY, MAY 26, 1866.

THE BURNING OF A FREEDMEN'S SCHOOL Because freedpeople's education symbolized black progress, whites who resented and resisted this progress sometimes attacked and burned freedmen's schools, as in this dramatic illustration of a white mob burning a school during antiblack riots in Memphis in May 1866.

retained economic and social power turned out in the end to be right. In 1867, however, the emancipation and enfranchisement of black Americans seemed, as a sympathetic French journalist described it, "one of the most radical revolutions known in history."

Like most revolutions, the reconstruction process did not go smoothly. Many southern Democrats breathed defiance and refused to cooperate. The presence of the army minimized antiblack violence, but thousands of white southerners who were eligible to vote refused to do so, hoping that their nonparticipation would delay the process long enough for northern voters to come to their senses and elect Democrats to Congress.

Blacks and their white allies organized Union leagues to inform and mobilize the new black voters into the Republican Party. Democrats branded southern white Republicans as "scalawags" and

northern settlers as "carpetbaggers." By September 1867, the 10 states had 735,000 black voters and only 635,000 white voters registered. At least one-third of the registered white voters were Republicans.

President Johnson did everything he could to block Reconstruction. He replaced several Republican generals in command of southern military districts with Democrats. He had his attorney general issue a ruling that interpreted the Reconstruction acts narrowly, thereby forcing a special session of Congress to pass a supplementary act in July 1867. He encouraged southern whites to obstruct the registration of voters and the election of convention delegates.

Johnson's purpose was to slow the process until 1868 in the hope that northern voters would repudiate Reconstruction in the presidential election of that year, when Johnson planned to run as the

Democratic candidate. Off-year state elections in the fall of 1867 encouraged that hope. Republicans suffered setbacks in several northern states, especially where they endorsed referendum measures to enfranchise black men. "I almost pity the radicals," chortled one of President Johnson's aides after the 1867 elections. "After giving ten states to the negroes, to keep the Democrats from getting them, they will have lost the rest."

THE IMPEACHMENT OF ANDREW JOHNSON

Johnson struck even more boldly against Reconstruction after the 1867 elections, despite warnings that he was risking impeachment. "What does Johnson mean to do?" an exasperated Republican asked another. "Does he mean to have another rebellion on the question of Executive powers & duties? . . . I am afraid his doings will make us all favor impeachment." In February 1868, Johnson took a fateful step. He removed from office Secretary of War Edwin M. Stanton, who had administered the War Department in support of the congressional Reconstruction policy. This appeared to violate the Tenure of Office Act, passed the year before over Johnson's veto, which required Senate consent for such removals. By a vote of 126 to 47 along party lines, the House impeached Johnson on February 24. The official reason for

impeachment was that he had violated the Tenure of Office Act (which Johnson considered unconstitutional). The real reason was Johnson's stubborn defiance of Congress on Reconstruction.

Under the U.S. Constitution, impeachment by the House does not remove an official from office. It is more like a grand jury indictment that must be tried by a petit jury—in this case, the Senate, which sat as a court to try Johnson on the impeachment charges brought by the House. If convicted by a two-thirds majority of the Senate, he would be removed from office.

The impeachment trial proved long and complicated, which worked in Johnson's favor by allowing passions to cool. The Constitution specifies the grounds on which a president can be impeached and removed: "Treason, Bribery, or other high Crimes and Misdemeanors." The issue was whether Johnson was guilty of any of these acts. His able defense counsel exposed technical ambiguities in the Tenure of Office Act that raised doubts about whether Johnson had actually violated it. Several moderate Republicans feared that the precedent of impeachment might upset the delicate balance of powers between the executive branch, Congress, and the judiciary that was an essential element of the Constitution. Behind the scenes, Johnson strengthened his case by promising to appoint the respected General John M. Schofield as secretary of war and to stop obstructing the Reconstruction acts. In the end, seven Republican senators voted for acquittal on May 16, and the final tally fell one vote short of the necessary two-thirds majority.

THE COMPLETION OF FORMAL RECONSTRUCTION

The impeachment trial's end cleared the poisonous air in Washington, and Johnson quietly served out his term. Constitutional conventions met in the South during the winter and spring of 1867–68. Hostile whites described them as "Bones and Banjoes Conventions" and the Republican delegates as "ragamuffins and jailbirds." In sober fact, however, the delegates were earnest advocates of a new order and the constitutions they wrote were among the most progressive in the nation. Three-quarters of the delegates to the 10 conventions

FAC-SIMILE OF TICKET OF ADMISSION TO THE IMPEACHMENT TRIAL.

TICKET TO IMPEACHMENT PROCEEDINGS Interest in the impeachment trial of President Andrew Johnson was so great that tickets had to be printed for admission to limited seating in the Senate chamber. Such tickets became the most sought-after items in Washington during the trial.

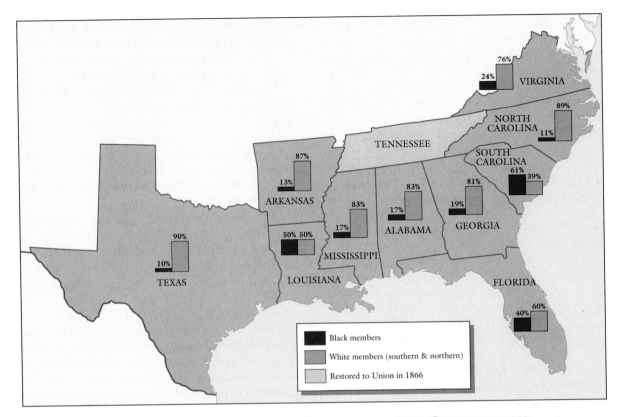

BLACK AND WHITE PARTICIPATION IN CONSTITUTIONAL CONVENTIONS, 1867–1868

were Republicans. About 25 percent of those Republicans were northern whites who had relocated to the South after the war; 45 percent were native southern whites who braved the social ostracism of the white majority to cast their lot with the despised Republicans; and 30 percent were blacks. Only in the South Carolina convention were blacks in the majority.

The new state constitutions enacted universal male suffrage, putting them ahead of most northern states on that score. Some of the constitutions disfranchised certain classes of ex-Confederates for several years, but by 1872 all such disqualifications had been removed. The constitutions mandated statewide public schools for both races for the first time in the South. Most states permitted segregated schools, but schools of any kind for blacks represented a great step forward. Most of the constitutions increased the state's responsibility for social welfare beyond anything previously known in the South.

Violence in some parts of the South marred the voting on ratification of these state constitutions. A night-riding white terrorist organization, the Ku Klux Klan made its first appearance during the elections. Nevertheless, voters in seven states ratified their constitutions and elected new legislatures that ratified the Fourteenth Amendment in the spring of 1868. That amendment became part of the United States Constitution the following summer, and the newly elected representatives and senators from those seven states, nearly all Republicans, took their seats in the House and Senate.

THE FIFTEENTH AMENDMENT

The remaining three southern states completed the reconstruction process in 1869 and 1870. Congress required them to ratify the Fifteenth as well as the Fourteenth Amendment. The Fifteenth Amendment prohibited states from denying the right to vote on grounds of race, color, or previous condition of servitude. Its purpose was not only to prevent the reconstructed states from any future revocation of black suffrage, but also to extend equal suffrage to the border states and to the North. With final ratification of the Fifteenth Amendment in 1870, the Constitution became truly color-blind for the first time in U.S. history.

But the Fifteenth Amendment still left half of the population disfranchised. Many supporters of woman suffrage were embittered by its failure to ban discrimination on the grounds of gender as well as race. The radical wing of the suffragists, led by Elizabeth Cady Stanton and Susan B. Anthony, therefore opposed the Fifteenth Amendment, causing a split in the woman suffrage movement.

This movement had shared the ideological egalitarianism of abolitionism since the Seneca Falls Convention of 1848. In 1866, male and female abolitionists formed the American Equal Rights Association (AERA) to work for both black and woman suffrage. Although some Republicans sympathized with the suffragists, they knew that no strong constituency among male voters favored granting the vote to women. A woman suffrage amendment to the state constitution of Kansas in 1867 suffered a lopsided defeat in a referendum. Most members of the AERA recognized that although Reconstruction politics made black enfranchisement possible, woman suffrage would have to wait until public opinion could be educated up to the standard of gender equality.

Stanton and Anthony refused to accept this reasoning. Why should illiterate Southern blacks have the right to vote, they asked, when educated northern women remained shut out from the polls? It was "infinitely more important to secure the rights of 10 million women than to bring a million more men to the polls," declared Stanton. The Fifteenth Amendment would establish "the most odious form of aristocracy the world has ever seen: an aristocracy of sex." When a majority of delegates at the 1869 convention of the AERA voted to endorse the Fifteenth Amendment, several women led by Stanton and Anthony walked out and founded the National Woman Suffrage Association. The remainder reorganized themselves as the American Woman Suffrage Association. For the next two

decades these rival organizations, working for the same cause, remained at odds with each other.

THE ELECTION OF 1868

Just as the presidential election of 1864 was a referendum on Lincoln's war policies, so the election of 1868 was a referendum on the reconstruction policy of the Republicans. The Republican nominee was General Ulysses S. Grant. Though he had no political experience, Grant commanded greater authority and prestige than anyone else in the country. As general-in-chief of the army, he had opposed Johnson's reconstruction policy in 1866 and had broken openly with the president in January 1868. That spring, Grant agreed to run for the presidency in order to preserve in peace the victory for Union and liberty he had won in war.

The Democrats turned away from Andrew Johnson, who carried too many political liabilities. They nominated Horatio Seymour, the wartime governor of New York, bestowing on him the dubious privilege of running against Grant. Hoping to put together a majority consisting of the South plus New York and two or three other northern states, the Democrats adopted a militant platform denouncing the Reconstruction acts as "a flagrant usurpation of power . . . unconstitutional, revolutionary, and void." The platform also demanded "the abolition of the Freedmen's Bureau, and all political instrumentalities designed to secure negro supremacy."

The vice presidential candidate, Frank Blair of Missouri, became the point man for the Democrats. In a public letter he proclaimed, "There is but one way to restore the Government and the Constitution, and that is for the President-elect to declare these [Reconstruction] acts null and void, compel the army to undo its usurpations at the South, disperse the carpet-bag State Governments, [and] allow the white people to reorganize their own governments."

The only way to achieve this bold counterrevolutionary goal was to suppress Republican voters in the South. This the Ku Klux Klan tried its best to do. Federal troops failed to prevent much of the violence because martial law had been lifted in the states where civilian governments had been restored. In Louisiana, Georgia, Arkansas, and

Tennessee, the Klan or Klan-like groups committed dozens of murders and intimidated thousands of black voters. The violence helped the Democratic cause in the South, but probably hurt it in the North where many voters perceived the Klan as an organization of neo-Confederate paramilitary guerrillas. And indeed they were, for many Klansmen were former soldiers, and such famous Confederate generals as Nathan Bedford Forrest and John B. Gordon held high positions in the Klan.

Seymour did well in the South, carrying five former slave states and coming close in others despite the solid Republican vote of the newly enfranchised blacks. Grant, however, swept the electoral vote 214 to 80. Seymour actually won a slight majority of the white voters nationally; without black enfranchisement, Grant would have had a minority of the popular vote.

THE GRANT ADMINISTRATION

A great military commander, Grant is usually branded a failure as president. That indictment is only partly correct. Grant's inexperience and poor judgment betrayed him into several unwise appointments of officials who were later convicted of corruption, and his back-to-back administrations (1869–77) were plagued by scandals. His secretary of war was impeached for selling appointments to army posts and Indian reservations; and his attor-

THE INAUGURATION OF ULYSSES S. GRANT Throngs of onlookers witnessed the inaugural ceremonies at the east front of the Capitol building on March 4, 1869. With the slogan "Let us have peace," Grant took office amid high hopes that he could achieve the reconstruction of the Union as effectively in peace as he had saved it in war. But the problems of peace proved more intractable than those of war.

ney general and secretary of the interior resigned under suspicion of malfeasance in 1875.

Honest himself, Grant was too trusting of subordinates. He appointed many former members of his military family, as well as several of his wife's relatives, to offices for which they were scarcely qualified. In an era notorious for corruption at all levels of government, many of the scandals were not Grant's fault. The Tammany Hall "Ring" of "Boss" William Marcy Tweed in New York City may have stolen more money from taxpayers than all the federal agencies combined. It was said that the only thing the Standard Oil Company could not do with the Ohio legislature was refine it. In Washington, one of the most widely publicized scandals, the Credit Mobilier affair, concerned Congress rather than the Grant administration. Several congressmen had accepted stock in the Credit Mobilier, a construction company for the Union Pacific Railroad, which received loans and land grants from the government. In return, the company expected lax congressional supervision, thereby permitting financial manipulations by the company.

What accounted for this explosion of corruption in the postwar decade, which one historian has called "The Era of Good Stealings"? During the war, expansion of government contracts and the bureaucracy had created new opportunities for the unscrupulous. Following the intense sacrifices of the war years came a relaxation of tensions and standards. Rapid postwar economic growth, led by an extraordinary rush of railroad construction, further encouraged greed and get-rich-quick schemes of the kind satirized by Mark Twain and Charles Dudley Warner in their 1873 novel *The Gilded Age*, which gave its name to the era.

CIVIL SERVICE REFORM

Some of the apparent increase in corruption during the Gilded Age was more a matter of perception. During a civil service reform movement to purify the government bureaucracy and make it more efficient, reformers focused a harsh light into the dark corners of corruption hitherto unilluminated because of the nation's preoccupation with war and reconstruction. Thus, reformers' publicity may have exaggerated the actual extent of corruption. In reality, during the Grant administration several govern-

ment agencies made real progress in eliminating abuses that had flourished in earlier administrations.

The chief target of civil service reform was the "spoils system." With the slogan "To the victor belongs the spoils," the victorious party in an election rewarded party workers with appointments as postmasters, customs collectors, and the like. The hope of getting appointed to a government post was the glue that kept the faithful together when a party was out of power. An assessment of 2 or 3 percent on the beneficiaries' government salaries kept party coffers filled when in power. The spoils system politicized the bureaucracy and staffed it with unqualified personnel who spent more time working for their party than for the government. It also plagued every incoming president (and other elected officials) with the "swarm of office seekers" that loom so large in contemporary accounts (including those of the humorist Orpheus C. Kerr, whose nom de plume was pronounced "Office Seeker").

Civil service reformers wanted to separate the bureaucracy from politics by requiring competitive examinations for the appointment of civil servants. This movement gathered steam during the 1870s and finally achieved success in 1883 with the passage of the Pendleton Act, which established the modern structure of the civil service. When Grant took office, he seemed to share the sentiments of civil service reformers; several of his cabinet officers inaugurated examinations for certain appointments and promotions in their departments. Grant also named a civil service commission headed by George William Curtis, a leading reformer and editor of *Harper's Weekly*. But many congressmen, senators, and other politicians resisted civil service reform. Patronage greased the political machines that kept them in office and all too often enriched them and their political chums. They managed to subvert reform, sometimes using Grant as an unwitting ally and thus turning many reformers against the president.

FOREIGN POLICY ISSUES

A foreign policy controversy added to Grant's woes. The irregular procedures by which his private secretary had negotiated a treaty to annex Santo Domingo (now the Dominican Republic) alienated leading Republican senators, who defeated ratification of the treaty. Politically inexperienced, Grant acted like a general who needed only to give orders rather than as a president who must cultivate supporters. The fallout from the Santo Domingo affair widened the fissure in the Republican Party between "spoilsmen" and "reformers."

The Grant administration had some solid foreign policy achievements to its credit. Hamilton Fish, the able secretary of state, negotiated the Treaty of Washington in 1871 to settle the vexing "Alabama Claims." These were damage claims against Britain for the destruction of American shipping by the C.S.S. *Alabama* and other Confederate commerce raiders built in British shipyards. The treaty established an international tribunal to arbitrate the U.S. claims, thus creating a precedent for the peaceful settlement of disputes. It resulted in the award of $15.5 million in damages to U.S. shipowners and a British expression of regret.

The events leading to the Treaty of Washington also resolved another long-festering issue between Britain and the United States: the status of Canada. The seven separate British North American colonies were especially vulnerable to U.S. desires for annexation. In fact, many bitter northerners demanded British cession of Canadian colonies to the United States as fair payment for the wartime depredations of the *Alabama* and other commerce raiders. Such demands tended to strengthen the loyalty of many Canadians to Britain as a counterweight to the aggressive Americans. In 1867 Parliament passed the British North America Act, which united most of the Canadian colonies into a new and largely self-governing Dominion of Canada.

Canadian nationalism was further strengthened by the actions of the Irish American Fenian Brotherhood. A secret society organized during the Civil War, the Fenians believed that an invasion of Canada would strike a blow for the independence of Ireland. Three times from 1866 to 1871, small "armies" of Fenians, composed mainly of Irish American veterans of the Union Army, crossed the border into Canada, only to be driven back after comic-opera skirmishes. The Fenian raids intensified Canadian anti-Americanism and complicated the negotiations leading to the Washington Treaty, but after its signing Canadian-American tensions cooled. The treaty also helped resolve disputes over American commercial fishing in Canadian waters. U.S. troops prevented further Fenian raids, and American demands for annexation of Canada faded away. These events gave birth to the modern nation of Canada, whose 3,500-mile border with the United States remains the longest unfortified frontier in the world.

RECONSTRUCTION IN THE SOUTH

During Grant's two administrations, the "Southern Question" was the most intractable issue. A phrase in Grant's acceptance of the presidential nomination in 1868 had struck a responsive chord in the North: "Let us have peace." With the ratification of the Fifteenth Amendment, many people breathed a sigh of relief at this apparent resolution of "the last great point that remained to be settled of the issues of the war." It was time to deal with other matters that had been long neglected. Ever since the annexation of Texas a quarter-century earlier, the nation had known scarcely a moment's respite from sectional strife. "Let us have done with Reconstruction," pleaded the *New York Tribune* in 1870. "LET US HAVE PEACE."

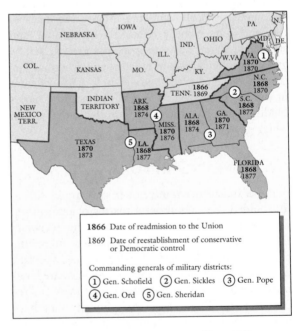

1866 Date of readmission to the Union
1869 Date of reestablishment of conservative or Democratic control

Commanding generals of military districts:
① Gen. Schofield ② Gen. Sickles ③ Gen. Pope
④ Gen. Ord ⑤ Gen. Sheridan

RECONSTRUCTION IN THE SOUTH

But there was no peace. Reconstruction was not over; it had hardly begun. State governments elected by black and white voters were in place in the South, but Democratic violence protesting Reconstruction and the instability of the Republican coalition that sustained it portended trouble.

BLACKS IN OFFICE

Because the Republican Party had no antebellum roots in the South, most southern whites perceived it as a symbol of conquest and humiliation. In the North, the Republican Party represented the most prosperous, educated, and influential elements of the population; but in the South, most of its adherents were poor, illiterate, and landless.

About 80 percent of southern Republican voters were black. Although most black leaders were educated and many had been free before the war, most black voters were illiterate ex-slaves. Neither the leaders nor their constituents, however, were as ignorant or as venal as stereotypes have portrayed them. Of 14 black representatives and two black senators elected in the South between 1868 and 1876, all but three had attended secondary school and four had attended college. Several of the blacks elected to state offices were among the best-educated men of their day. Jonathan Gibbs, secretary of state in Florida from 1868 to 1872 and state superintendent of education from 1872 to 1874, was a graduate of Dartmouth College and Princeton Theological Seminary. Francis L. Cardozo, secretary of state in South Carolina for four years and treasurer for another four, was educated at the University of Glasgow and at theological schools in Edinburgh and London.

It is true that some lower-level black officeholders, as well as their constituents, could not read or write, but the fault for that lay not with them but with the slave regime that had denied them an education. Illiteracy did not preclude an understanding of political issues for them any more than it did for Irish American voters in the North, many of whom also were illiterate. Southern blacks thirsted for education. Participation in the Union League and the experience of voting were themselves forms of education. Black churches and fraternal organizations proliferated during Reconstruction and tutored African Americans in their rights and responsibilities.

Linked to the myth of black incompetence was the legend of the "Africanization" of southern governments during Reconstruction. The theme of "Negro rule"—by which the "barbarous African" exercised "unbridled power" in the 10 southern states—was a staple of Democratic propaganda. It was enshrined in folk memory and in generations of textbooks. In fact, blacks held only 15 to 20 percent of public offices, even at the height of Reconstruction in the early 1870s. No states had black governors (although the black lieutenant governor of Louisiana acted as governor for a month) and only one black man became a state supreme court justice. Nowhere except in South Carolina did blacks hold office in numbers anywhere near their proportion of the population; in that state, they constituted 52 percent of all state and federal elective officials from 1868 to 1876.

"CARPETBAGGERS"

Next to "Negro rule," carpetbagger corruption and scalawag rascality have been the prevailing myths of Reconstruction. "Carpetbaggers" did hold a disproportionate number of high political offices in southern state governments during Reconstruction. More than half of the Republican governors and nearly half of the congressmen and senators were northerners. A few did resemble the proverbial adventurer who came south with nothing but a carpetbag in which to stow the loot plundered from a helpless people. Most of the northerners were Union army officers who stayed on after the war as Freedmen's Bureau agents, teachers in black schools, business investors, pioneers of a new political order—or simply because they liked the climate.

Like others who migrated to the West as a frontier of opportunity, those who settled in the postwar South hoped to rebuild its society in the image of the free-labor North. Many were college graduates at a time when fewer than 2 percent of Americans had attended college. Most brought not empty carpetbags but considerable capital, which they invested in what they hoped would become a new South. They also invested human capital—themselves—in a drive to modernize the region's

The Birth of a Nation (1915)

Directed by D. W. Griffith. Starring Lillian Gish (Elsie Stoneman), Henry B. Walthall (Ben Cameron), Ralph Lewis (Austin Stoneman), George Siegmann (Silas Lynch).

Few if any films have had such a pernicious impact on historical understanding and race relations as *Birth of a Nation*. This movie popularized a version of Reconstruction that portrayed predatory carpetbaggers and stupid, brutish blacks plundering a prostrate South and lusting after white women. It perpetuated vicious stereotypes of rapacious black males. It glorified the Ku Klux Klan of the Reconstruction era, inspiring the founding of the "second Klan" in 1915 that became a powerful force in the 1920s (see chapter 24).

The first half of the film offers a conventional Victorian romance of the Civil War. The two sons and daughter of Austin Stoneman (a malevolent radical Republican who is a thinly disguised Thaddeus Stevens) become friends with the three sons and two daughters of the Cameron family of "Piedmont," South Carolina, through the friendship of Ben Cameron and Phil Stoneman at college. The Civil War tragically separates the families. The Stoneman and Cameron boys enlist in the Union and Confederate armies and—predictably—face each other on the battlefield. Two Camerons and one Stoneman are killed in the war, and Ben Cameron is badly wounded and captured, to be nursed back to health by—you guessed it—Elsie Stoneman.

After the war the younger Camerons and Stonemans renew their friendship. During the Stonemans' visit to South Carolina, Ben Cameron and Elsie Stoneman, and Phil Stoneman and Flora Cameron, fall in love. If the story had stopped there, *Birth of a Nation* would have been just another Hollywood romance. But Austin Stoneman brings south with him Silas Lynch, an ambitious, leering mulatto demagogue who stirs up the animal passions of the ignorant black majority to demand "Equal Rights, Equal Politics, Equal Marriage." A "renegade Negro," Gus, stalks the youngest Cameron daughter, who saves herself from rape by jumping from a cliff to her death. Silas Lynch tries to force Elsie to marry him. "I will build a Black Empire," he tells the beautiful, virginal Elsie (Lillian Gish was the Hollywood beauty queen of silent films), "and you as my queen shall rule by my side."

social structure and democratize its politics. But they underestimated the hostility of southern whites, most of whom regarded them as agents of an alien culture and leaders of an enemy army—as indeed they had been—in a war that for many southerners was not yet over.

"SCALAWAGS"

Most of the native-born whites who joined the southern Republican Party came from the up-country Unionist areas of western North Carolina and Virginia, eastern Tennessee, and elsewhere. Others were former Whigs who saw an opportunity to rebuild the South's economy in partnership with equally Whiggish northern Republicans. Republicans, said a North Carolina scalawag, were the "party of progress, of education, of development. . . . Yankees and Yankee notions are just what we want in this country. We want their capital to build factories and work shops, and railroads."

But Yankees and Yankee notions were just what most southern whites did not want. Democrats saw that the southern Republican Party they abhorred was a fragile coalition of blacks and whites, Yankees and southerners, hill-country yeomen and low-country entrepreneurs, illiterates and college graduates. The party was weakest along the seams where these disparate elements joined—especially the racial seam. Democrats attacked that weakness with every weapon at their command,

Finally provoked beyond endurance, white South Carolinians led by Ben Cameron organize the Ku Klux Klan to save "the Aryan race." Riding to the rescue of embattled whites in stirring scenes that anticipated the heroic actions of the cavalry against Indians in later Hollywood Westerns, the Klan executes Gus, saves Elsie, disperses black soldiers and mobs, and carries the next election for white rule by intimidating black voters. The film ends with a double marriage that unites the Camerons and Stonemans in a symbolic rebirth of a nation that joins whites of the North and South in a new union rightfully based on the supremacy of "the Aryan race."

The son of a Confederate lieutenant colonel, David Wark (D. W.) Griffith was the foremost director of the silent movie era. He pioneered many precedent-setting cinematic techniques and profoundly influenced filmmaking throughout the world. *Birth of a Nation* was the first real full-length feature film, technically and artistically superior to anything before it. Apart from its place in the history of cinema, though, why should anyone today watch a movie that perpetuates such wrongheaded history and noxious racist stereotypes? Precisely *because* it reflects and amplifies an interpretation of Reconstruction that prevailed from the 1890s to the 1950s, and thereby shaped not only historical understanding but also contemporary behavior (as in its inspiration for the Klan of the 1920s). Although *Birth of a Nation* aroused controversy in parts of the North and was picketed by the NAACP, some 200 million people saw the film in the United States and abroad from 1915 to 1946. The story, and director Griffith, demonstrated in dramatic fashion how the South, having lost the Civil War, won the battle for how the War and especially Reconstruction would be remembered for more than half a century.

Henry B. Walthall (Ben Cameron) kissing the hand of Elsie Stoneman (Lillian Gish) in *Birth of a Nation*.

from social ostracism of white Republicans to economic intimidation of black employees and sharecroppers. The most potent Democratic weapon was violence.

THE KU KLUX KLAN

The generic name for the secret groups that terrorized the southern countryside was the Ku Klux Klan. Some went by other names (the Knights of the White Camelia in Louisiana, for example). Part of the Klan's purpose was social control of the black population. Sharecroppers who tried to extract better terms from landowners, or black people who were considered too "uppity," were likely to receive a midnight whipping—or worse—from white-sheeted Klansmen. Scores of black schools, perceived as a particular threat to white supremacy, went up in flames.

The Klan's main purpose was political: to destroy the Republican Party by terrorizing its voters and, if necessary, by murdering its leaders. No one knows how many politically motivated killings took place; certainly hundreds, probably thousands. Nearly all the victims were Republicans; most of them were black. In one notorious incident, the "Colfax Massacre" in Louisiana (April 18, 1873), a clash between black militia and armed whites left three whites and nearly 100 blacks dead. Half of the blacks were killed in cold blood after they had surrendered.

In some places, notably Tennessee and Arkansas, Republican militias formed to suppress and disarm

TWO MEMBERS OF THE KU KLUX KLAN Founded in Pulaski, Tennessee, in 1866 as a social organization similar to a college fraternity, the Klan evolved into a terrorist group whose purpose was intimidation of southern Republicans. The Klan, in which former Confederate soldiers played a prominent part, was responsible for the beating and murder of hundreds of blacks and whites alike from 1868 to 1871.

the Klan, but in most areas the militias were outgunned and outmaneuvered by ex-Confederate veteran Klansmen. Some Republican governors were reluctant to use black militia against white guerrillas for fear of sparking a racial bloodbath—as happened at Colfax.

The answer seemed to be federal troops. In 1870 and 1871 Congress enacted three laws intended to enforce the Fourteenth and Fifteenth Amendments. Interference with voting rights be-

came a federal offense, and any attempt to deprive another person of civil or political rights became a felony. The third law, passed on April 20, 1871, and popularly called the Ku Klux Klan Act, gave the president power to suspend the writ of habeas corpus and send in federal troops to suppress armed resistance to federal law.

Armed with these laws, the Grant administration moved against the Klan. Because Grant was sensitive to charges of "military despotism," he used his powers with restraint. He suspended the writ of habeas corpus in only nine South Carolina counties. Nevertheless, there and elsewhere federal marshals backed by troops arrested thousands of suspected Klansmen. Federal grand juries indicted more than 3,000, and several hundred defendants pleaded guilty in return for suspended sentences. To clear clogged court dockets so that the worst offenders could be tried quickly, the Justice Department dropped charges against nearly 2,000 others. About 600 Klansmen were convicted; most of them received fines or light jail sentences, but 65 went to a federal penitentiary for terms of up to five years.

THE ELECTION OF 1872

These measures broke the back of the Klan in time for the 1872 presidential election. A group of dissident Republicans had emerged to challenge Grant's reelection. They believed that conciliation of southern whites rather than continued military intervention was the only way to achieve peace in the South. Calling themselves Liberal Republicans, these dissidents nominated Horace Greeley, the famous editor of the New York *Tribune*. Under the slogan "Anything to beat Grant," the Democratic Party also endorsed Greeley's nomination, though he had long been their antagonist. On a platform denouncing "bayonet rule" in the South, Greeley urged his fellow northerners to put the issues of the Civil War behind them and to "clasp hands across the bloody chasm which has too long divided" North and South.

This phrase would come back to haunt Greeley. Most voters in the North were still not prepared to trust Democrats or southern whites. Powerful anti-Greeley cartoons by political cartoonist Thomas Nast showed Greeley shaking the hand of a

Klansman dripping with the blood of a murdered black Republican. Nast's most famous cartoon portrayed Greeley as a pirate captain bringing his craft alongside the ship of state, while Confederate leaders, armed to the teeth, hid below waiting to board it.

Grant swamped Greeley on election day. Republicans carried every northern state and 10 of the 16 southern and border states. Blacks in the South enjoyed more freedom in voting than they would enjoy again for a century. This apparent triumph of Republicanism and Reconstruction would soon unravel.

THE PANIC OF 1873

The U.S. economy had grown at an unprecedented pace since recovering from a mild postwar recession. In eight years 35,000 miles of new railroad track were laid down, equal to all the track laid in the preceding 35 years. The first transcontinental railroad had been completed on May 10, 1869, when a golden spike was driven at Promontory Summit, Utah Territory, linking the Union Pacific and the Central Pacific. But the building of a second transcontinental line, the Northern Pacific, precipitated a Wall Street panic in 1873 and plunged the economy into a five-year depression.

Jay Cooke's banking firm, fresh from its triumphant marketing of Union war bonds, took over the Northern Pacific in 1869. Cooke pyramided every conceivable kind of equity and loan financing to raise the money to begin laying rails west from Duluth, Minnesota. Other investment firms did the same as a fever of speculative financing gripped the country. In September 1873 the pyramid of paper collapsed. Cooke's firm was the first to go bankrupt. Like dominoes, thousands of banks and businesses also collapsed. Unemployment rose to 14 percent and hard times set in.

THE RETREAT FROM RECONSTRUCTION

It is an axiom of American politics that the voters will punish the party in power in times of economic depression. That axiom held true in the 1870s. Democrats made large gains in the congressional elections of 1874, winning a majority in the House for the first time in 18 years.

Public opinion also began to turn against Republican policies in the South. The campaign by Liberal Republicans and Democrats against "bayonet rule" and "carpetbag corruption" that left most northern voters unmoved in 1872 found a growing audience in subsequent years. Intraparty battles among Republicans in southern states enabled Democrats to regain control of several state governments. Well-publicized corruption scandals also discredited Republican leaders. Although corruption was probably no worse in southern states than in many parts of the North, southern postwar poverty made waste and extravagance seem worse. White Democrats scored propaganda points by claiming that corruption proved the incompetence of "Negro-carpetbag" regimes.

Northerners grew increasingly weary of what seemed the endless turmoil of southern politics. Most of them had never had a strong commitment to racial equality, and they were growing more and more willing to let white supremacy regain sway in the South. "The truth is," confessed a northern Republican, "our people are tired out with this worn out cry of 'Southern outrages'!!! Hard times & heavy taxes make them wish the 'nigger,' 'everlasting nigger,' were in hell or Africa."

By 1875 only four southern states remained under Republican control: South Carolina, Florida, Mississippi, and Louisiana. In those states, white Democrats had revived paramilitary organizations under various names: White Leagues (Louisiana); Rifle Clubs (Mississippi); and Red Shirts (South Carolina). Unlike the Klan, these groups operated openly. In Louisiana, they fought pitched battles with Republican militias in which scores were killed. When the Grant administration sent large numbers of federal troops to Louisiana, people in both North and South cried out against military rule. The protests grew even louder when soldiers marched onto the floor of the Louisiana legislature in January 1875 and expelled several Democratic legislators after a contested election. Was this America? asked Republican Senator Carl Schurz

Cartoons for Freedom

One of the best political cartoonists in American history, Thomas Nast drew scores of cartoons for *Harper's Weekly* in the 1860s and 1870s advocating the use of federal power to guarantee the liberty and enforce the equal rights of freed slaves. The illustration on the far right (1865) is an eloquent graphic expression of a powerful argument for giving freedmen the right to vote: black men who fought *for* the Union were more deserving of this privilege than white men who fought *against* it. Several of the kneeling figures are recognizable Confederate leaders: Alexander Stephens and Robert E. Lee in the foreground, Jefferson Davis to Lee's left, and John C. Breckinridge, Joseph E. Johnston, and Robert Toombs behind and to Davis's left. The cartoon at right, "Worse than Slavery" (1875), depicts members of the two principal anti-Reconstruction paramilitary groups in the South—the White League and the Ku Klux Klan. Armed to the teeth, they shake hands above a defenseless black family whose rights they seek to overturn by violence. Only the power of the national government, the cartoon suggests, can overcome the unholy alliance and ensure the liberty of freed slaves.

in a widely publicized speech: "If this can be done in Louisiana, how long will it be before it can be done in Massachusetts and Ohio? How long before a soldier may stalk into the national House of Representatives, and, pointing to the Speaker's mace, say 'Take away that bauble!'"

THE MISSISSIPPI ELECTION OF 1875

The backlash against the Grant administration affected the Mississippi state election of 1875. Democrats there devised a strategy called the Mississippi Plan. The first step was to "persuade" the 10 to 15 percent of white voters still calling themselves Republicans to switch to the Democrats. Only a handful of carpetbaggers could resist the economic pressures, social ostracism, and threats that made it "too damned hot for [us] to stay out," wrote one white Republican who changed parties. "No white man can live in the South in the future and act with any other than the Democratic Party unless he is willing and prepared to live a life of social isolation and remain in political oblivion."

The second step in the Mississippi Plan was to intimidate black voters, for even with all whites voting Democratic, the party could still be defeated by the 55 percent black majority. Economic coercion against black sharecroppers and workers kept some of them away from the polls, but vio-

"PARDON, Columbia—'Shall I Trust These Men'?"

"FRANCHISE. 'And Not This Man'?"

lence was the most effective method. Democratic "rifle clubs" showed up at Republican rallies, provoked riots, and shot down dozens of blacks in the ensuing melees. Governor Adelbert Ames—a native of Maine, a Union general who had won a congressional medal of honor in the war, and one of the ablest of southern Republicans—called for federal troops to control the violence. Grant intended to comply, but Ohio Republicans warned him that if he sent troops to Mississippi, the Democrats would exploit the issue of bayonet rule to carry Ohio in that year's state elections. Grant yielded—in effect giving up Mississippi for Ohio. The U.S. attorney general replied to Ames's request for troops:

The whole public are tired out with these annual autumnal outbreaks in the South, and the great majority are now ready to condemn any interference on the part of the government. . . . Preserve the peace by the forces in your own state, and let the country see that the citizens of Mississippi, who are . . . largely Republican, have the courage to fight for their rights.

Governor Ames did try to organize a loyal state militia. But that proved difficult—and in any case, he was reluctant to use a black militia for fear of provoking a race war. "No matter if they are going to carry the State," said Ames with weary resignation, "let them carry it, and let us be at peace and have no more killing." The Mississippi Plan worked like a charm. In five of

621

"The negroes of the South are free—free as air," says the parliamentary Watterson. This is what the *State*, a well-known Democratic organ of Tennessee, says, in huge capitals, on the subject: "Let it be known before the election that the farmers have agreed to spot every leading Radical negro in the county, and treat him as an enemy for all time to come. The rotten ring must and shall be broken at any and all costs. The Democrats have determined to withdraw all employment from their enemies. Let this fact be known."

"OF COURSE HE WANTS TO VOTE THE DEMOCRATIC TICKET."

DEMOCRATIC "REFORMER." "You're as free as air, ain't you? Say you are, or I'll blow yer black head off!"

HOW THE MISSISSIPPI PLAN WORKED This cartoon shows how black counties could report large Democratic majorities in the Mississippi state election of 1875. The black voter holds a Democratic ticket while one of the men, described in the caption as a "Democratic reformer," holds a revolver to his head and says: "You're as free as air, ain't you? Say you are, or I'll blow your black head off!"

the state's counties with large black majorities, the Republicans polled 12, 7, 4, 2, and 0 votes, respectively. What had been a Republican majority of 30,000 in 1874 became a Democratic majority of 30,000 in 1875.

THE SUPREME COURT AND RECONSTRUCTION

Even if Grant had been willing to continue intervening in southern state elections, Congress and the courts would have constricted such efforts. The new Democratic majority in the House threatened to cut any appropriations for the Justice Department and the army intended for use in the South. In 1876 the Supreme Court handed down two decisions that declared parts of the 1870 and 1871 laws for enforcement of the Fourteenth and Fifteenth Amendments unconstitutional. In *U.S. v. Cruikshank* and *U.S. v. Reese*, the Court ruled on cases from Louisiana and Kentucky. Both cases grew out of provisions in these laws authorizing federal officials to prosecute *individuals* (not states) for violations of the civil and voting rights of blacks. But, the Court pointed out, the Fourteenth and Fifteenth Amendments apply to actions by *states*: "No State shall . . . deprive any person of life, liberty, or property . . . nor deny to any person . . . equal protection of the laws": the right to vote "shall not be denied . . . by any State." Therefore,

> "*This decision of the Supreme Court admits that the Fourteenth Amendment is a prohibition of the States. It admits that a State shall not abridge the privileges or immunities of citizens of the United States, but commits the seeming absurdity of allowing the people of a State to do what it prohibits the State itself from doing. . . . It is said that this decision will make no difference in the treatment of colored people; that the Civil Rights Bill was a dead letter, and could not be enforced. There is some truth in all this, but it is not the whole truth. That bill, like all advance legislation, was a banner on the outer wall of American liberty, a noble moral standard, uplifted for the education of the American people. . . . This law, though dead, did speak. It expressed the sentiment of justice and fair play. . . . If it is a bill for social equality, so is the Declaration of Independence, which declares that all men have equal rights; so is the Sermon on the Mount, so is the Golden Rule . . . so is the Constitution of the United States.*"

FREDERICK DOUGLASS
from a speech in Washington, D.C., October 22, 1883, protesting a decision by the Supreme Court that declared the Civil Rights Act of 1875 to be unconstitutional

equal rights. (In the mid-20th century, the Supreme Court would reverse itself and interpret the Fourteenth and Fifteenth Amendments much more broadly.)

Meanwhile, in another ruling, *Civil Rights Cases* (1883), the Court declared unconstitutional a civil rights law passed by Congress in 1875. That law, enacted on the eve of the Democratic takeover of the House elected in 1874, was a crowning achievement of Reconstruction. It banned racial discrimination in all forms of public transportation and public accommodations. If enforced, it would have effected a sweeping transformation of race relations—in the North as well as in the South. Even some of the congressmen who voted for the bill doubted its constitutionality, however, and the Justice Department had made little effort to enforce it. Several cases made their way to the Supreme Court, which in 1883 ruled the law unconstitutional—again on grounds that the Fourteenth Amendment applied only to states, not to individuals. Several states—all in the North—passed their own civil rights laws in the 1870s and 1880s, but less than 10 percent of the black population resided in those states. The mass of African Americans lived a segregated existence.

THE ELECTION OF 1876

In 1876 the remaining southern Republican state governments fell victim to the passion for "reform." The mounting revelations of corruption at all levels of government ensured that reform would be the leading issue in the presidential election. In this centennial year of the birth of the United States, marked by a great exposition in Philadelphia, Americans wanted to put their best foot forward. Both major parties gave their presidential nominations to governors who had earned reform reputations in their states: Democrat Samuel J. Tilden of New York and Republican Rutherford B. Hayes of Ohio.

Democrats entered the campaign as favorites for the first time in two decades. It seemed likely that they would be able to put together an electoral majority from a "solid South" plus New York and two or three other northern states. To ensure a solid South, they looked to the lessons of the Mississippi

the portions of these laws that empowered the federal government to prosecute individuals were unconstitutional.

The Court did not say what could be done when states were controlled by white-supremacy Democrats who had no intention of enforcing

READING THE ELECTION BULLETIN BY GASLIGHT In this drawing, eager voters scan the early returns, which seemed to give Samuel J. Tilden the presidency in 1876.

Plan. In 1876 a new word came into use to describe Democratic techniques of intimidation: "bulldozing." To bulldoze black voters meant to trample them down or keep them away from the polls. In South Carolina and Louisiana, the Red Shirts and the White Leagues mobilized for an all-out bulldozing effort.

The most notorious incident, the "Hamburg Massacre," occurred in the village of Hamburg, South Carolina, where a battle between a black militia unit and 200 Red Shirts resulted in the capture of several militiamen, five of whom were shot "while attempting to escape." This time Grant did send in federal troops. He pronounced the Hamburg Massacre "cruel, blood-thirsty, wanton, unprovoked . . . a repetition of the course that has been pursued in other Southern States."

The federal government also put several thousand deputy marshals and election supervisors on duty in the South. Though they kept an uneasy peace at the polls, they could do little to prevent assaults, threats, and economic coercion in back-country districts, which reduced the potential Republican tally in the former Confederate states by at least 250,000 votes.

DISPUTED RESULTS

When the results were in, Tilden had carried four northern states, including New York with its 35 electoral votes. Tilden also carried all the former slave states except—apparently—Louisiana, South Carolina, and Florida, which produced disputed returns. Because Tilden needed only one of them to win the presidency, while Hayes needed all three, and because Tilden seemed to have carried Louisiana and Florida, it appeared initially that he had won the presidency. But frauds and irregularities reported from several bulldozed districts in the three states clouded the issue. For example, a Louisiana parish that had recorded 1,688 Republican votes in 1874 reported only one in 1876. Many other similar discrepancies appeared. The official returns ultimately sent to Washington gave all three states—and therefore the presidency—to Hayes, but the Democrats refused to recognize the results—and they controlled the House.

The country now faced a serious constitutional crisis. Armed Democrats threatened to march on Washington. Many people feared another civil war. The Constitution offered no clear guidance on how to deal with the matter. A count of the state electoral votes required the concurrence of both houses of Congress, but with a Democratic House and a Republican Senate such concurrence was not forthcoming. To break the deadlock, Congress created a special electoral commission consisting of five representatives, five senators, and five Supreme Court justices split evenly between the two parties, with one member, a Supreme Court justice, supposedly an independent—but in fact a Republican.

Tilden had won a national majority of 252,000 popular votes, and the raw returns gave him a majority in the three disputed states. But an estimated 250,000 southern Republicans had been bulldozed away from the polls. In a genuinely fair and free

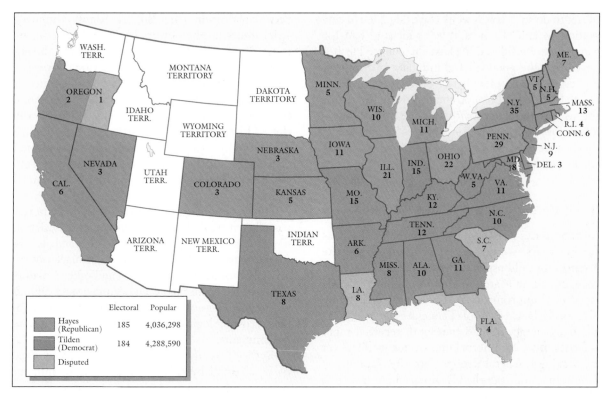

HAYES-TILDEN DISPUTED ELECTION OF 1876

election, the Republicans might have carried Mississippi and North Carolina as well as the three disputed states. While the commission agonized, Democrats and Republicans in Louisiana and South Carolina each inaugurated their own separate governors and legislatures (Republicans in Florida gave up the fight at the state level). Only federal troops in the capitals at New Orleans and Columbia protected the Republican governments in those states.

THE COMPROMISE OF 1877

In February 1877, three months after voters had gone to the polls, the electoral commission issued its ruling. By a partisan vote of 8 to 7—with the "independent" justice voting with the Republicans—it awarded all the disputed states to Hayes. The Democrats cried foul and began a filibuster in the House to delay the final electoral count beyond the inauguration date of March 4, so as to throw the election to the House of

Representatives, an eventuality that threatened to bring total anarchy. But, behind the scenes, a compromise began to take shape. Both northern Republicans and southern Democrats of Whig heritage had similar interests in liquidating the sectional rancor and in getting on with the business of economic recovery and development. Among these neo-Whigs were Hayes and his advisers. To wean southern Whiggish Democrats away from a House filibuster, Hayes promised his support as president for federal appropriations to rebuild war-destroyed levees on the lower Mississippi and federal aid for a southern transcontinental railroad. Hayes's lieutenants also hinted at the appointment of a southerner as postmaster general, who would have a considerable amount of patronage at his disposal—the appointment of thousands of local postmasters.

Most important, southerners wanted to know what Hayes would do about Louisiana and South Carolina. Would he withdraw the troops and allow the Democrats who already governed those states in fact to do so in law as well? Hayes signaled his intention to end "bayonet rule," which he had for some time considered a bankrupt policy. He believed that the goodwill and influence of southern moderates would offer better protection for black rights than federal troops could provide. In return for his commitment to withdraw the troops, Hayes asked for—and received—promises of fair treatment of freedpeople and respect for their constitutional rights.

THE END OF RECONSTRUCTION

Such promises were easier to make than to keep, as future years would reveal. In any case, the Democratic filibuster collapsed and Hayes was inaugurated on March 4. He soon fulfilled his part of the Compromise of 1877: ex-Confederate Democrat David Key of Tennessee became postmaster general; in 1878 the South received more federal money for internal improvements than ever before; and federal troops left the capitals of Louisiana and South Carolina. The last two Republican state governments collapsed. The old abolitionist and radical Republican warhorses denounced Hayes's actions as a sellout of southern blacks. His was a policy "of weakness, of subserviency, of surrender," in the words of the venerable crusader William Lloyd Garrison, a policy that sustained "might against right . . . the rich and powerful against the poor and unprotected."

Voices of protest could scarcely be heard above the sighs of relief that the crisis was over. Most Americans—including even most Republicans—wanted no more military intervention in state affairs. "I have no sort of faith in a local government which can only be propped up by foreign bayonets," wrote the editor of the New York *Tribune* in April 1877. "If negro suffrage means that as a permanency then negro suffrage is a failure."

CONCLUSION

Before the Civil War most Americans had viewed a powerful government as a threat to individual liberties. That is why the first 10 amendments to the Constitution (the Bill of Rights) imposed strict limits on the powers of the federal government. During the Civil War and especially during Reconstruction, however, the national government had to exert an unprecedented amount of power to free the slaves and guarantee their equal rights as free citizens. That is why the Thirteenth, Fourteenth, and Fifteenth Amendments to the Constitution contained clauses stating that "Congress shall have power" to enforce these provisions for liberty and equal rights.

During the post–Civil War decade, Congress passed civil rights laws and enforcement legislation to accomplish this purpose. Federal marshals and troops patrolled the polls to protect black voters, arrested thousands of Klansmen and other violators of black civil rights, and even occupied state capitals to prevent Democratic paramilitary groups from overthrowing legitimately elected Republican state governments.

By 1875 many northerners had grown tired of or alarmed by this continued use of military power to intervene in the internal affairs of states. The Supreme Court stripped the federal government of much of its authority to enforce certain provisions of the Fourteenth and Fifteenth Amendments. Traditional fears of military power as a threat to individual liberties came to the fore again.

The withdrawal of federal troops from the South in 1877 constituted both a symbolic and a substantive end of the 12-year postwar era known as Reconstruction. Reconstruction had achieved the two great objectives inherited from the Civil War: to reincorporate the former Confederate states into the Union, and to accomplish a transition from slavery to freedom in the South. That transition was marred by the economic inequity of sharecropping and the social injustice of white supremacy. A third goal of Reconstruction, enforcement of the equal civil and political rights promised in the Fourteenth and Fifteenth Amendments, was betrayed by the Compromise of 1877. In subsequent decades the freed slaves and their descendants suffered repression into segregated, second-class citizenship. Not until another war hero-turned-president sent troops into Little Rock (chapter 28), 80 years after they had been withdrawn from New Orleans and Columbia, did the federal government launch a second Reconstruction to fulfill the promises of the first.

Suggested Readings begin on page SR-1. For Web activities and resources related to this chapter, go to http:// www.harcourtcollege.com/history/murrin

CHAPTER 18

FRONTIERS OF CHANGE, POLITICS OF STALEMATE, 1865–1898

A DASH FOR TIMBER

Many of our images of the post–Civil War West derive from illustrations by the greatest artist of the Old West, Frederic Remington. In this dramatic painting, Remington combines realism and stereotype in a depiction of the kind of Cowboys-and-Indians conflict that became a staple of Hollywood portrayals of the West.

Despite the nation's preoccupation with the politics of Reconstruction, one of the most remarkable developments in the post–Civil War generation was the accelerating westward expansion of the European-American frontier. From 1865 to 1890 the white population west of the 95th meridian (roughly a line from Galveston, Texas, through Kansas City to Bemidji, Minnesota) increased 400 percent to 8,628,000, a growth rate five times faster than the nation's as a whole. As much new agricultural and grazing land came under cultivation and exploitation by white Americans during these 25 years as during the previous two and a half centuries. Through the Homestead Act, land grants to railroads, the Morrill Act (which turned land over to states to finance "agricultural and mechanical colleges"), and other liberal land laws enacted during and after the Civil War, some 400 million acres passed into private ownership by farmers, ranchers, and other forms of enterprise. The number of American farms more than doubled, from 2.5 million to nearly 6 million. Their output of cattle, hogs, and hay more than doubled while the production of corn, wheat, and oats nearly tripled—considerably outstripping the rate of population increase.

This growth enabled American farmers to increase agricultural exports tenfold during those 25 years thanks also partly to imports—of people. Many of the four million immigrants who during this period came from Germany, the Czech region of the Austro-Hungarian empire, and the Scandinavian countries settled in the Midwest or Far West and became farmers. To younger sons in Norwegian or German farm families who could expect to inherit no land at home, the opportunity to obtain 160 acres in Minnesota or Nebraska seemed miraculous. The power of a generous government to make equality of opportunity available to them, and to other white Americans of both native and foreign birth, underpinned the extraordinary expansion of population and agricultural production after the Civil War.

That growth and opportunity, however, came at great cost. The Indians were despoiled of their remaining open land and herded onto reservations. Buffalo were hunted almost to extinction. Millions of acres of forest and native grasslands were cut down or plowed up, setting the stage for destructive erosion, floods, and dust bowls in future generations. The overproduction of American agriculture drove prices down and contributed to a worldwide agricultural depression by the late 1880s.

This chapter will focus on the following major questions:

- What was the balance between the economic gains and the social and environmental costs of westward expansion after the Civil War?
- How did the Indian peoples of the trans-Mississippi West respond to white settlement and U.S. government policies?
- What were the central themes of economic development and race relations in the post-Reconstruction South?
- What kind of national political structure emerged from the turmoil of war and reconstruction?

AGENCIES OF WESTWARD EXPANSION

One of the main engines of this postwar growth was the railroad. Five transcontinental railroads went into service between 1869 and 1893. At the end of the Civil War, only 3,272 miles of rail ran west of the Mississippi. By 1890 the total was 72,473 miles. Railroad access and mobility spurred settlement and economic development on the high plains and in the mountain valleys.

No longer did this region appear on maps as "The Great American Desert." There was plenty of desert, to be sure, and the average normal rainfall on the plains west of the 98th meridian (a line running roughly from the center of the Dakotas through the center of Texas) was scarcely enough to support farming except in certain river valleys. Unfortunately, precipitation during the 1870s and early 1880s was heavier than normal, giving rise to the erroneous (as it turned out) notion that "rainfall follows the plow"—that settlement and cultivation somehow changed the weather.

This was the age of the "sodbuster," who adapted to the almost treeless prairies and plains by fencing with barbed wire (invented in 1874) and building his first house out of the sod that he broke with his steel plow, cutting deep furrows to bring up subsoil moisture. It was also the era of "bonanza farms" in the Red River Valley of Dakota Territory and the Central Valley of California—huge wheat farms cultivated with heavy machinery and hired labor.

Perhaps even more important to the growth of the West, and surely more prolific of song and

CHRONOLOGY

1862	Sioux uprising in Minnesota; 38 Sioux executed
1864	Colorado militia massacres Cheyenne in village at Sand Creek, Colorado
1866	Cowboys conduct first cattle drive north from Texas
1869	President Grant announces his "peace policy" toward Indians
1876	Sioux and Cheyenne defeat Custer at Little Big Horn
1880	James A. Garfield elected president
1881	Garfield assassinated; Chester A. Arthur becomes president
1883	Pendleton Act begins reform of civil service
1884	Grover Cleveland elected president
1887	Dawes Severalty Act dissolves Indian tribal units and implements individual ownership of tribal lands
1888	Benjamin Harrison elected president
1889	Government opens Indian Territory (Oklahoma) to white settlement
1890	Wounded Knee massacre • New Mississippi constitution pioneers black disfranchisement in South • Republicans try but fail to enact federal elections bill to protect black voting rights • Congress enacts McKinley Tariff
1892	Grover Cleveland again elected president
1895	Booker T. Washington makes his "Atlanta Compromise" address
1896	*Plessy* v. *Ferguson* legalizes "separate but equal" state racial segregation laws
1898	*Williams* v. *Mississippi* condones use of literacy tests and similar measures to restrict voting rights

story, were the mining and ranching frontiers. This was the West of prospectors and boom towns that became ghost towns, of cowboys and cattle drives, of gold rushes and mother lodes, of stagecoach robbers and rustlers. It is a West so celebrated on stage, screen, radio, and television that it is hard to separate myth from reality—a reality in which thousands of black and Mexican American cowboys rode the Goodnight-Loving Trail, eastern capital and railroads came increasingly to control the mines and the grasslands, and gold or silver miners

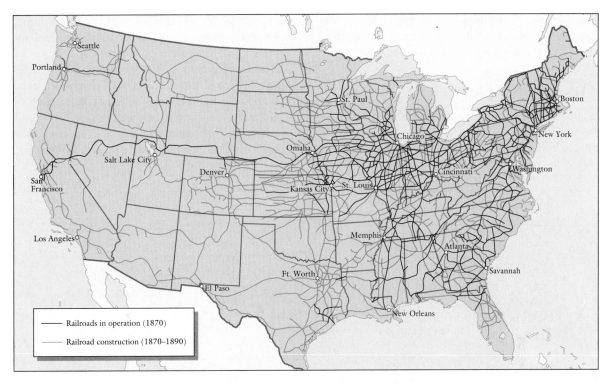

RAILROAD EXPANSION, 1870–1890

THE SOD-HOUSE FRONTIER On the prairies and plains of the regions west of the Mississippi, trees were scarce and the cost of lumber was prohibitive until railroads crisscrossed the land. So the settlers built their first houses from the tough prairie sod, which baked in the sun to almost the hardness of bricks.

and cowboys came to resemble more closely the coal miners and farm laborers of the East than the romanticized independent spirits of legend.

THE MINING FRONTIER

Gold discoveries had propelled the first waves of western settlement, but by the 1870s silver eclipsed gold in volume and some years even in value. Other minerals also increased in value. Rich copper mines opened in Montana in concert with demand for thousands of tons of copper wire brought on by Alexander Graham Bell's invention of the telephone (1876), Thomas A. Edison's invention of the incandescent lightbulb (1879), and construction of a successful electrical generator (1881).

Violence was never far from the surface in the mining frontier. In the early days, claim-jumping,

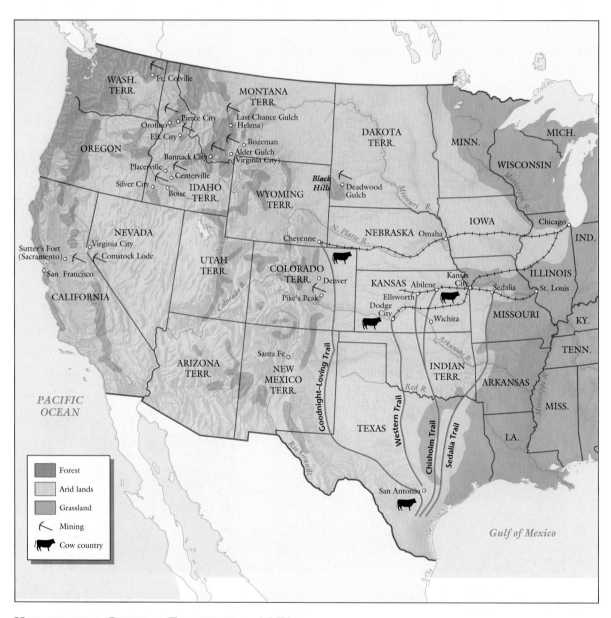

MINING AND CATTLE FRONTIERS, 1870S

robberies, and vigilante justice made life precarious. As placer mining of streams gave out, men ravaged the environment by hydraulic mining, by piling up tons of tailings from deep bores, and (especially in the copper industry) by the creation of strip-mining moonscapes. Mining became a highly capitalized and mechanized industry in which the biggest and richest mines were owned by corporations with headquarters in the East. Capital-labor relations were savage. Violent strikes at Coeur d'Alene, Idaho, in 1892, at Cripple Creek, Colorado, in 1894 and again in 1903, and at other places caused western governors to call out the militia 10 times from 1892 to 1904. From these conflicts emerged the Western Federation of Miners, founded in 1893, which became one of the most militant American labor unions.

THE RANCHING FRONTIER

Of course, the dominant symbol of the Old West is not the prospector or the hard-rock miner: It is the cowboy. The postwar boom in the range cattle industry had its beginnings in southern Texas.

The Spaniards had introduced longhorn cattle there in the 18th century. This hardy breed multiplied rapidly; by the 1850s millions of them roamed freely on the Texas plains. The market for them was limited in this sparsely settled region; the nearest railhead was usually too far distant to make shipping them north and east economically feasible.

The Civil War changed all that. Beef supplies in the older states dropped drastically, and prices rose to the unheard-of sum of $40 a head. The postwar explosion of population and railroads westward brought markets and railheads ever closer to western cattle that were free to anyone who rounded them up and branded them.

Astute Texans quickly saw that the longhorns represented a fortune on the hoof—if they could be driven northward the 800 miles to the railhead at Sedalia, Missouri. In the spring of 1866, cowboys hit the trail with 260,000 cattle in the first of the great drives. Their experiences almost put an end to the range cattle industry before it was born. Disease, stampedes, bad weather, Indians, and irate farmers in Missouri (who were afraid that the

LINK TO THE PAST

Home on the Range: The Cowboy Heritage

http://history.cc.ukans.edu/heritage/old-west/cowboy

This site tells the story of the post–Civil War range cattle industry with a primary focus on the reality and myth of the cowboy. It contains maps and descriptions from primary sources of cattle trails and towns such as Dodge City. Useful links lead to related sites.

1. Who were the cowboys? Where did they come from? Why have they been so romanticized in song and story, film, and television? What is the relationship between image and reality?

2. Using the maps, documents, and text, construct your own narrative of the geographical evolution of cattle ranching from 1865 to the 1890s.

3. What environmental consequences came from replacing buffalo with cattle on the Great Plains?

Texas fever carried by some of the longhorns would infect their own stock) killed or ran off most of the cattle.

Only a few thousand head made it to Sedalia, but the prices they fetched convinced ranchers that the system would work, if only they could find a better route. By 1867 the rails of the Kansas Pacific had reached Abilene, Kansas, 150 miles closer to Texas, making it possible to drive the herds through a sparsely occupied portion of Indian Territory. About 35,000 longhorns reached Abilene that summer, where they were loaded onto cattle cars for the trip to Kansas City or Chicago. This success gave rise to the interlocking institutions of the cattle drive and the Chicago stockyards. The development of refrigerated rail cars in the 1870s enabled Chicago to ship dressed beef all over the country. Abilene mushroomed overnight from a sleepy village whose one bartender spent his spare time catching prairie dogs into a boom town where 25 saloons stayed open all night, and the railroad made almost as much money shipping liquor into town as it did shipping cattle out.

More than a million longhorns bellowed their way north on the Chisholm Trail to Abilene over the next four years while the railhead crept westward to other Kansas towns, chiefly Dodge City, which became the most wide-open and famous of the cow towns. As buffalo and Indians disappeared from the grasslands north of Texas, ranches moved northward to take their place. Cattle drives grew shorter as railroads inched forward. Ranchers grazed their cattle for free on millions of acres of open, unfenced government land. But clashes with "grangers" (the ranchers' contemptuous term for farmers) on the one hand and with a growing army of sheep ranchers on the other—not to mention rustlers—led to several "range wars." Most notable was the Johnson County War in Wyoming in 1892. Grangers and small ranchers there (who had sometimes gotten their start by rustling) defeated the hired guns of the Stock Growers' Association, which represented larger ranchers.

By that time, however, the classic form of open-range grazing was already in decline. The boom years of the early 1880s had overstocked the range and driven down prices. Then came record cold and blizzards on the southern range in the winter of 1884–85, followed by even worse weather on the

BEEF CATTLE IN THE UNITED STATES, 1867–1897

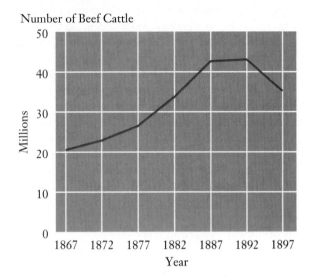

northern plains two years later. Hundreds of thousands of cattle froze or starved to death. These catastrophes spurred reforms that brought an end to open-range grazing. The ranchers who survived turned to growing hay and supplemental feed for the winter. They reduced the size of their herds, started buying or leasing land and fencing in their cattle, and invested in scientific breeding that crossed longhorns with higher-quality stock to produce a better grade of beef.

Ranching and the cowboy survived, but in a form quite different from their Hollywood images. Few cowboys resembled the tall, lean, lantern-jawed, clean-shaven "Marlboro Man." Most of them were small, wiry men; the mustangs they rode could not carry large men. In popular literature and movies, one seldom encounters a Mexican cowboy portrayed in a favorable light and even more rarely a black cowboy, but of the 40,000 cowboys who rode the purple sage during the heyday of the open range (1865–85), several thousand were blacks or Mexicans. Although cowboys were skillful riders, handy with the rope, tough and hardy, hardly any of them became gunfighters. The work was hard, the pay was low, and their life was far from glamorous. Nevertheless, the romantic image of the cowboy, which began with the dime novels of the 19th century, has endured as a central myth of

BLACK COWBOYS Some studies of cowboys estimate that one-quarter of them were black. That estimate is probably too high for all cowboys, but it might be correct for Texas, where this photograph was taken.

American popular culture. The wide-open spaces through which he rode off into the sunset still appeal to urban Americans yearning for a simpler and more heroic past.

THE LAST INDIAN FRONTIER

The westward expansion of the ranching and farming frontiers after 1865 doomed the free range of the Plains Indians and the buffalo. In the 1830s, eastern tribes had been moved to preserves west of the Mississippi to end strife by separating whites and Indians. In scarcely a decade, white settlers had penetrated these lands via the overland trails to the Pacific Coast. In the 1850s, when the Kansas and Nebraska territories opened to white settlement, the government forced a dozen tribes living there to cede 15 million acres, leaving them on reservations totaling less than 1.5 million acres. Thus began what historian Philip Weeks has called the "policy of concentration": No longer were Indians to be pushed west onto the arid plains that early white explorers had christened "The Great American Desert." Rather, as white settlers moved onto and through the plains and mountains, they began to covet these large spaces—which earlier treaties had assigned to the Indians for "as long as waters shall run and the grass shall grow."

Even before the Civil War, the nomadic Plains Indians, whose culture and economy were based on the buffalo, faced pressure not only from the advancing tide of white settlement but also from the forced migration of eastern tribes into their domain. In the aftermath of the Civil War, the process of concentrating Indian tribes on reservations accelerated. Chiefs of the five "civilized tribes"—Cherokees, Creeks, Choctaws, Chickasaws, and Seminoles—had signed treaties of alliance with the Confederacy. At that time they were living in Indian Territory (most of present-day Oklahoma), where their economy was linked to the South. Many of them, especially members of the mixed-blood upper class, were slaveholders. Bitter toward the United States, the leaders of the "civilized tribes," on the principle that "the enemy of my enemy is my friend," cast their lot with the Confederacy. The Cherokee leader Stand Watie rose to brigadier general in the Confederate army and was the last Confederate commander to surrender, on June 23, 1865.

Siding with the Confederacy proved to be a costly mistake for the "civilized tribes." The U.S. government "reconstructed" Indian Territory more quickly and with less contention than it reconstructed the former Confederate states. Treaties with the five tribes in 1866 required them to grant tribal citizenship to their freed slaves and reduced tribal lands by half. The government then settled Indians who had been dispossessed from other areas on the land it had taken from the "civilized tribes."

Fort Apache (1948)

**Directed by John Ford. Starring Henry Fonda (Lt. Col. Owen Thursday),
John Wayne (Capt. Kirby York), Shirley Temple (Philadelphia Thursday).**

With a cast containing some of the most famous actors in Hollywood history, directed by one of the most successful of Hollywood directors, *Fort Apache* lives up to expectations. In a career that spanned a half century from 1917 to 1966, John Ford did more than any other director to fix the images and legends of the Old West in the minds of Americans. He directed both John Wayne and Henry Fonda in some of their best films. In *Fort Apache* he brought them together with a grown-up Shirley Temple in the starkly beautiful Arizona desert. The black-and-white footage resembles old glass-plate photographs from the 1870s.

The film opens with Lieutenant Colonel Owen Thursday traveling by stagecoach with his daughter Philadelphia to Arizona Territory to take command of the frontier outpost of Fort Apache. A Civil War veteran like most of the other soldiers in the film, Thursday had reached the rank of major general of volunteers in that war but reverted to his regular army rank of lieutenant colonel in the downsized postwar army. Resenting his assignment to this remote backwater, the spit-and-polish Thursday is determined to shape up the garrison, which had been under the relaxed temporary command of Captain Kirby York, a veteran Indian fighter, and the Irish-born sergeants who really run the post. Philadelphia Thursday falls in love with Lieutenant Michael O'Rourke, a recent West Point graduate and son of the sergeant major at the fort.

This setting offers Ford and scriptwriter Frank Nugent opportunity to explore class, ethnic, and gender relations as well as social customs in the frontier army of the 1870s. They succeed brilliantly. Thursday opposes his daughter's engagement to the Irish American son of a noncommissioned officer even though the son is a West Pointer and his father won the Medal of Honor in the Civil War. Although many tinges of Hollywood romance creep in, these relationships are sensitively portrayed. So are the efforts by wives of officers and noncoms to create a semblance of stable community and family life at the fort.

Not until halfway through the film does the inevitable conflict with the Indians begin to build. The movie avoids a stereotypical depiction of murderous Indians on the warpath and heroic cavalry coming to the rescue (a stereotype Ford had helped to create in earlier films). A corrupt white Indian agent has been cheating the Mescalero Apaches led by Cochise, who leave the reservation after some of Cochise's hot-headed braves kill two soldiers. Sensing a chance for glory and promotion if he can bring in Cochise, Thursday orders Captain York, whom Cochise trusts, to coax him back from Mexico. York does so, whereupon Thursday defies York's advice, provokes Cochise with impossible conditions, and leads an ill-advised attack against the more numerous Apaches that brings the death of Thursday and all of the men

CONFLICT WITH THE SIOUX

There was no shortage of dispossessed Indians. The Civil War had set in motion a generation of Indian warfare more violent and widespread than anything since the 17th century. During the war, the Union army was forced to pull many units out of frontier posts to fight the Confederacy. Moreover, the drain on the Union treasury to finance the war compounded the usual corruption of Indian agents and delayed annuity payments to tribes that had sold their land to the government. These events had dire consequences on the northern plains.

Herded onto reservations along the Minnesota River by the Treaty of Traverse des Sioux in 1851, the Santee Sioux grew restive when late annuity

636

Two soldiers try to help a dying Henry Fonda (Lt. Col. Owen Thursday) in the climactic battle scene of *Fort Apache*.

with him. In an ironic final twist, the national media make Thursday a heroic martyr and York plays along with this image.

Fort Apache and Cochise were real, but the story in this film is entirely fictional. It is, in fact, a parable of a different conflict in which an entire detachment of U.S. Cavalry was wiped out: the battle of Little Big Horn in Montana Territory on June 26, 1876. The glory-hunting Owen Thursday represents George Armstrong Custer and Cochise is a counterpart of Sitting Bull. Although not obvious, these parallels are clear. In some ways Captain York also seems to be modeled on George Crook, a veteran Indian fighter who came to sympathize with the Native Americans and gained their confidence. In this reading of the film, *Fort Apache* transcends its particular time and place and becomes a broader story of the tragedy of Indian–white conflicts after the Civil War. This movie also represents a long step forward in John Ford's understanding and portrayal of the encounter between whites and Indians as truly tragic rather than as the triumph of Manifest Destiny, as it so often appeared to be in his earlier films.

payments in the summer of 1862 threatened starvation. Angry braves began to speak openly of reclaiming ancestral hunting grounds. Then on August 17, a robbery in which five white settlers were murdered seemed to open the floodgates. The braves persuaded Chief Little Crow to take them on the warpath, and over the next few weeks, at least 500 white Minnesotans were massacred.

Hastily mobilized militia and army units finally suppressed the uprising. A military court convicted 319 Indians of murder and atrocities and sentenced 303 of them to death. Appalled by this ferocious retaliation, Lincoln personally reviewed the trial transcripts and reduced the number of executions to 38—the largest act of executive clemency in American history. Even so, the hanging of 38 Sioux

THE GHOST DANCE This photograph shows a Sioux with a sacred whistle performing the Ghost Dance in 1890. The dance invoked the Great Spirit to restore the buffalo and drive away the whites, thereby revitalizing traditional Sioux culture. Instead, it provoked the U.S. Army into the confrontation that led to the massacre at Wounded Knee, South Dakota.

on December 26, 1862, was the largest mass execution the country has ever witnessed. The government evicted the remaining Sioux from Minnesota to Dakota Territory.

In the meantime, the army's pursuit of fleeing Santee Sioux provoked other Sioux tribes farther west. By 1864 and for a decade afterward, fighting flared between the army and the Sioux across the northern plains. It reached a climax after gold-seekers in 1874 and 1875 poured into the Black Hills of western Dakota, a sacred place to the Sioux. At the battle of Little Big Horn in Montana Territory on June 25, 1876, Sioux warriors led by Sitting Bull and Crazy Horse, along with their Cheyenne allies, wiped out George A. Custer and the 225 men with him in the Seventh Cavalry. In retaliation, General Philip Sheridan carried out a winter campaign in which the Sioux and Cheyenne were crushed.

Largest and most warlike of the Plains tribes, the Sioux were confined to a reservation in Dakota Territory where poverty, disease, apathy, and alcoholism reduced this once proud people to desperation. In 1890 a current of hope arrived at the Sioux reservation in the form of a "Ghost Dance," which

had first appeared among the Paiutes of Nevada and spread quickly to other Indian nations. Similar to earlier revitalization movements among Indian peoples, the Ghost Dance expressed the belief that the Indians' god would destroy the whites and return their land. Alarmed by the frenzy of the dance, federal authorities sent soldiers to the Sioux reservation. A confrontation at Wounded Knee in the Dakota badlands led to a shootout that left 25 soldiers and at least 150 Sioux dead. Wounded Knee symbolized the death of 19th century Plains Indian culture.

SUPPRESSION OF OTHER PLAINS INDIANS

Just as the Sioux uprising in Minnesota had triggered war on the northern plains in 1862, a massacre of Cheyennes in Colorado in 1864 sparked a decade of conflict on the southern plains. The discovery of gold near Pike's Peak set off a rush to Colorado in 1858 and 1859. The government responded by calling several Cheyenne and Arapaho chiefs to a council—and with a combination of threats, promises, and firewater, the agents per-

STUDENTS IN A RESERVATION SCHOOL The government established schools on Indian reservations to teach Indian children the English language and inculcate the elements of Christianity and white culture. These children do not appear happy with the prospect.

suaded the chiefs to sign a treaty giving up all claims to land in this region (guaranteed by an earlier treaty of 1851) in exchange for a reservation at Sand Creek in southeast Colorado.

In 1864 hunger and resentment on the reservation prompted many of the braves to return to their old hunting grounds and to raid white settlements. Skirmishes soon erupted into open warfare. In the fall, Cheyenne Chief Black Kettle, believing that he had concluded peace with the Colorado settlers, returned to the reservation. There, at dawn on November 29, militia commanded by Colonel John Chivington surrounded and attacked Black Kettle's unsuspecting camp, killing 200 Indians, half of them women and children.

The notorious Sand Creek massacre set a pattern for several similar attacks on Indian villages in subsequent years. Ever since the earliest battles between colonists and Indians in the 17th century, whites had followed the strategy of burning Indian crops and villages as a means of destroying or driving off the Indians. Sherman and Sheridan had adopted a similar strategy against the Confederates and followed it again as military commanders responsible for subduing the Plains Indians. Their purpose was to corral all the Indians onto the reservations that were being created throughout the West. In addition to trying to defeat the Indians in battle—which proved to be difficult against the mounted Plains Indians—the army encouraged the extermination of the buffalo herds. Professional hunters slaughtered the large, clumsy animals by the millions for their hides, thus depriving Plains Indians of their principal source of food, shelter, and clothing. By 1883 a scientific expedition counted only 200 buffalo in the West.

The Indians were left with no alternative but to come into the reservations, and by the 1880s nearly all of them had done so. Chief Joseph of the Nez Percé pronounced the epitaph for their way of life

Destruction of the Buffalo

Historians estimate that as many as 30 million bison (popularly called buffalo) once roamed the grasslands of North America. By the mid-19th century, however, the expansion of European American settlement, the demand for buffalo robes in the European and eastern U.S. markets, and competition from Indian horses for grazing lands had reduced the herds by many millions. Such pressures intensified after the Civil War—as railroads penetrated the West and new technology enabled tanners to process buffalo hides for leather. Professional hunters flocked to the range and systematically killed the bison; the hides were then shipped out by rail, as shown in the accompanying photograph. Passengers on trains sometimes shot buffalo from the cars as shown in the magazine illustration. The U.S. Army encouraged this slaughter in order to force the Plains Indians onto reservations by depriving them of their traditional sustenance from hunting bison. By the 1880s the buffalo were almost extinct, leaving behind millions of bones, which were gathered in piles, as in the photograph of buffalo skulls, and shipped to plants that ground them into fertilizer.

THE FAR WEST.—SHOOTING BUFFALO ON THE LINE OF THE KANSAS-PACIFIC RAILROAD.

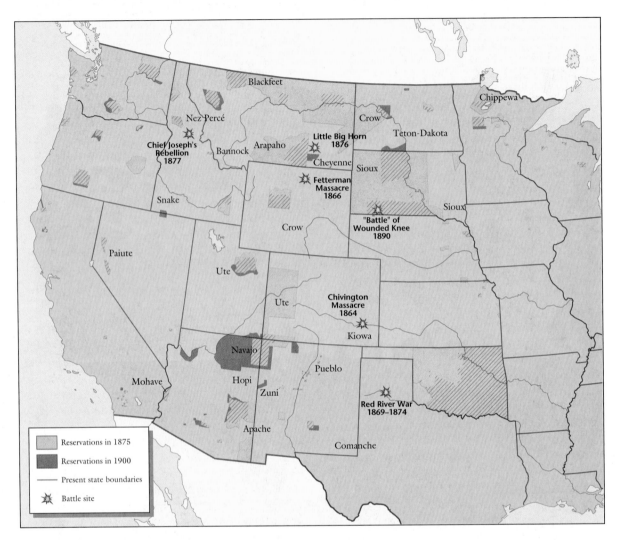

INDIAN RESERVATIONS, 1875 AND 1900

when federal troops blocked the escape of his band from Montana to Canada in 1877:

> I am tired of fighting. Our chiefs are killed. The old men are all dead. It is cold and we have no blankets . . . no food. . . . The little children are freezing to death. . . . Hear me, my chiefs; I am tired; my heart is sick and sad. From where the sun now stands, I will fight no more forever.

THE "PEACE POLICY"

Many eastern reformers condemned America's violent repression of the Indians. One of the most prominent reformers was Helen Hunt Jackson, whose 1881 book, *A Century of Dishonor* summed up their indictment of anti-Indian violence, exploitation, and broken treaties. Jackson may have romanticized Indian culture, especially in her best-selling novel, *Ramona* (1884), but she also helped to humanize them. Nevertheless, most reformers believed that Indians must be compelled to give up their nomadic culture and settle down as the first step toward being assimilated into the American polity as citizens. Just as reformers wanted to reconstruct the South by assimilating emancipated slaves into a free-labor society, so they wished to reconstruct Indian culture into the white man's ways by means of schools and Christian missions.

President Grant, in his inaugural address in 1869, announced this new "Peace Policy" toward Indians. He urged "their civilization and ultimate citizenship." "Civilization" meant acceptance of white culture, including the English language, Christianity, and individual ownership of property. It also meant allegiance to the United States rather than to a tribe. In 1869 Grant established a Board of Indian Commissioners and staffed it with humanitarian reformers. In 1871 the century-long policy of negotiating treaties with Indian "nations" came to an end. From then on, Indians became "wards of the nation," to be civilized and prepared for citizenship, first on reservations and eventually on individually owned parcels of land that were carved out of the reservations.

Some Indians accepted this destruction of their culture as inevitable. Others resisted. That resistance fed the flames of frontier wars for nearly a decade after 1869. "I love the land and the buffalo," said the Kiowa Chief Satanta. "I love to roam over the wide prairie, and when I do, I feel free and happy, but when we settle down we grow pale and die."

With their military power broken and the buffalo gone, most Indians by the 1880s had acquiesced in the "reconstruction" that offered them citizenship. Also in the 1880s, the reformers found themselves in a strange alliance with land-hungry westerners, who greedily eyed the 155 million acres of land tied up in reservations. If part of that land could be allotted directly to individual ownership by Indian families, the remainder would become available for purchase by whites. The Dawes Severalty Act did just that in 1887. This landmark legislation called for the dissolution of Indian tribes as legal entities, offered Indians the opportunity to become citizens, and allotted each head of family 160 acres of farmland or 320 acres of grazing land.

For whites eager to seize reservation land, the Dawes Act brought a bonanza. At noon on April 22, 1889, the government threw open specified parts of the Indian Territory to "Boomers," who descended on the region like locusts and by nightfall had staked claim to nearly 2 million acres. In addition to the reservation lands legally opened for white settlement, many of the Indians who received individual land titles through the Dawes Act lost these lands to unscrupulous whites through fraud and misrepresentation. Eventually, whites gained title to 108 million acres of former reservation land.

For Indians, writes historian Philip Weeks, the Dawes Act "proved an unqualified failure." Private ownership of land was a concept alien to most tribes. And in many Indian cultures, farming was considered woman's work. To "Americanize" Indian males by compelling them to forsake hunting for farming was to strip them of their manhood. Many Indians made a successful transition to the new order, but others slipped further into depression, destitution, and alcoholism.

MEXICAN AMERICANS

Mexican Americans in the West also were forced to adjust to a new order. As with the Indians, some made this transition successfully—but many did not. At the hands of Anglo American settlers, Mexican Americans lost their land, lost political influence, and lost much of their cultural identity. Even as early as 1849 in the northern California gold fields, resentment of "foreigners" provoked violence against Mexican American miners—and the Foreign Miners Tax of 1850 effectively forced Mexican Americans out of the gold fields (even though they were not "foreigners"). As the 19th century progressed, hordes of Anglo American "squatters" invaded the expansive holdings of the Mexican American elite, who were forced to seek relief in the courts. Although their claims were generally upheld, these legal proceedings often stretched on for years. After exorbitant legal fees and other expenses were taken into account, a legal triumph was often a Pyrrhic victory. In the end, most Mexican American landholders in northern California had to sell the very lands they had fought to keep in order to pay their mounting debts. Similarly, ranchers in southern California had to sell their lands to pay outstanding debts after devastating droughts in the 1860s virtually destroyed the ranching industry. Forced off the land, California's Mexican Americans increasingly found themselves concentrated in segregated urban *barrios*.

The migration of Anglos into eastern Texas had played a role in fomenting the war for Texas independence and in bringing about the war with Mexico (see chapter 13). By the latter half of the 19th century, eastern Texas was overwhelmingly Anglo; most Mexican Americans were concentrated in the Rio Grande Valley of southern Texas. As in California, Anglos in Texas used force and intimidation, coupled with exploitative legal maneuvering, to disfranchise the Mexican Americans. The vaunted Texas Rangers often acted as an Anglo vigilante force that exacted retribution for the real or imagined crimes of Mexican Americans. Eventually, Mexican Americans in Texas were reduced to a state of peonage, dependent on their Anglo protectors for political and economic security.

Similar patterns prevailed in New Mexico, but the effects were mitigated somewhat because New Mexicans continued to outnumber Anglo American settlers. Earlier in the 19th century, international trade along the Santa Fe Trail had strengthened the political and economic status of the New Mexican elites. Now these same elites consolidated their position by acting as power brokers between poorer New Mexicans and wealthy Anglos.

Despite all these difficulties, Spanish-speaking peoples in the Southwest and California managed to preserve much of their distinctive culture. Moreover, Anglo American immigrants adopted many Mexican American agricultural methods and mining techniques. Perhaps the most enduring legacy of the Spanish-speaking peoples is to be found in the areas of mining law, community property law, and—most important in the arid West—water law.

THE NEW SOUTH

Southern whites proved more resistant than western Indians to Yankee dominance. Nevertheless, after the North's retreat from Reconstruction, a Yankee presence did remain, in the form of investment and a "New South" ideology.

The Republican Party did not disappear from the South after 1877. Nor was the black vote immediately and totally suppressed. Republican pres-

idential candidates won about 40 percent of the votes in former slave states through the 1880s, and some blacks continued to win elections to state legislatures until the 1890s. Down to 1901, every U.S. Congress but one had at least one black representative from the South. Independent parties occasionally formed coalitions with Republicans to win local or state elections, especially in Virginia.

Even so, "bulldozing" of black voters (chapter 17) continued to keep the southern states solid for the Democrats. In 1880 the Democratic Party hoped to build on this foundation to win the presidency for the first time in a generation. Taking their cue from the Republicans, the Democrats nominated a Civil War hero, General Winfield Scott Hancock. His opponent was another Civil War general, James A. Garfield, who had served in Congress since the war. In an election with the closest popular vote in American history (Garfield had a plurality of only 10,000 votes out of 9 million cast), Hancock carried every southern state, while Garfield won all but three northern states—and the election.

According to legend, Hancock's defeat convinced forward-looking white southerners that the way to salvation was not through politics. They rolled up their sleeves and went to work to build a "New South" of commerce, cotton mills, and steel. The legend embodies some truth. A new spirit of enterprise quickened southern life in the 1880s. Some southerners even went so far as to acknowledge that the Yankees had shown them the way. And they welcomed northern investment. Henry Grady, editor of the Atlanta *Constitution*, was the leading spokesman for the New South ideology. In an 1886 speech to northern businessmen, Grady boasted of the New South's achievements: "We have sown towns and cities in the place of theories, and put business above politics. . . . We have established thrift in city and country. We have fallen in love with work."

SOUTHERN INDUSTRY

Considerable reality underlay this rhetoric. The South's textile industry expanded rapidly during the 1880s. Along the piedmont from Virginia to Alabama, new cotton mills and company towns for their workers sprang up. The labor force was almost entirely white, drawn from farm families on the worn-out red clay soil of the piedmont. About 40 percent of the workers were women, and 25 percent were children aged 16 and younger. These "lintheads," as wealthier whites called them, labored long hours for wages about half the level prevailing in New England's mills. This cheap labor gave southern mill owners a competitive advantage. In 1880 the South had only 5 percent of the country's textile-producing capacity; by 1900 it had 23 percent and was well on its way to surpassing New England a generation later. At first, southerners supplied most of the capital for this expansion. After 1893 an increasing amount came from the North, as New England mill owners came to recognize the benefits of relocating in the low-wage, nonunion South.

Tobacco was another southern industry that developed from a regional crop. Most of the initial capital for this effort also came from the South, and unlike the textile industry, many of the workers in the tobacco factories were black. James B. Duke of North Carolina transformed the tobacco industry when he installed cigarette-making machines at Durham in 1885. In 1890 he created the American Tobacco Company, which controlled 90 percent of the market, with himself at its head. After Duke moved to New York in the 1880s, northern capital played an important role in this regional industry as well.

Railroads and iron were two New South industries even more dependent on outside capital. During the 1880s, railroad construction in the South outpaced the national average. In 1886 southern railroads shifted their 5-foot gauge to the national standard of 4 feet 8½ inches. This change integrated southern lines into the national network and symbolized northern domination of the region's railroads. During those same years, northern capital helped fuel the growth of an iron and steel industry in the South. In 1880 the former slave states produced only 9 percent of the nation's pig iron; by 1890, after a decade of extraordinary expansion for the industry nationwide, that proportion had doubled. Most of the growth was concentrated in northern Alabama, where the proximity of coal, limestone, and ore made the new city of Birmingham the "Pittsburgh of the South."

The heavy northern investment in these industries meant that the South had less control over economic decisions that affected its welfare. Some historians have referred to the South's "colonial" relationship to the North in the late 19th century. The low wages prevailing in the South made for inequitable distribution of the economic benefits of industrial growth. Average southern per capita income remained only two-fifths of the average in the rest of the country well into the 20th century.

SOUTHERN AGRICULTURE

The main reason for the South's relative poverty, however, was its weak agriculture. A crucial reason for this was low-level investment in farming. Although manufacturing capital per capita increased by 300 percent in the ex-Confederate states from 1880 to 1900, the amount per capita invested in agriculture increased by only 29 percent.

One-crop specialization, overproduction, declining prices, and an exploitative credit system all contributed to the problem. The basic institution of the southern rural economy was the crop lien system, which came into being because of the shortage of money and credit in the war-ravaged South. Few banks had survived the war, and land values had plummeted, which left farmers unable to secure a bank loan with their land as collateral. Instead, merchants in the crossroads country stores that sprang up across the South provided farmers with supplies and groceries in return for a lien on their next crop.

This system might have worked well if the merchants had charged reasonable interest rates and if cotton and tobacco prices had remained high enough for the farmer to pay off his debts after harvest with a little left over. But the country storekeeper charged a credit price 50 or 60 percent above the cash price, partly because he had no competition and partly because of the high risk of loss on his loans. And crop prices, especially for cotton, were dropping steadily. Cotton prices declined from an average of 12 cents a pound in the 1870s to 6 cents in the 1890s. As prices fell, many farmers went deeper and deeper into debt to the merchants.

Sharecroppers and tenants incurred a double in-debtedness: to the land-owner whose land they sharecropped or rented, and to the merchant who furnished them supplies on credit. Because many landowners became merchants, and vice versa, that indebtedness was often to the same man. Many sharecroppers, particularly blacks, fell into virtual peonage.

One reason cotton prices fell was overproduction. Britain had encouraged the expansion of cotton growing in Egypt and India during the Civil War to make up for the loss of American cotton. After the war, southern growers had to face international competition. By 1878 the southern crop had reached the output of the best antebellum year, and during the next 20 years output doubled. This overproduction drove prices ever lower. To obtain credit, farmers had to plant every acre with the most marketable cash crop—cotton. This practice exhausted the soil and required ever-increasing amounts of expensive fertilizer, which fed the cycle of overproduction and declining prices.

It also reduced the amount of land that could be used to grow food crops. Farmers who might otherwise have produced their own cornmeal and raised their own hogs for bacon became dependent on merchants for these supplies. Before the Civil War, the cotton states had been nearly self-sufficient in food; by the 1890s they had to import nearly half their food at a price 50 percent higher than it would have cost to grow their own. Many southerners recognized that only diversification could break this dependency, but the crop lien system locked them into it. "We ought to plant less [cotton and tobacco] and more of grain and grasses," said a North Carolina farmer in 1887, "but how are we to do it; the man who furnishes us rations at 50 percent interest won't let us; he wants money crop planted. . . . It is cotton! cotton! cotton! Buy everything and make cotton pay for it."

RACE RELATIONS IN THE NEW SOUTH

The downward spiral of the rural southern economy caused frustration and bitterness in which blacks became the scapegoats of white rage.

BOOKER T. WASHINGTON AT TUSKEGEE The most powerful black leader of his time, Washington built an excellent secondary school and industrial training institute at Tuskegee, Alabama, and gained a great deal of influence with philanthropists and political leaders. But many northern blacks accused him of acquiescing in segregation and second-class citizenship for blacks in return for the crumbs of philanthropy.

Lynching rose to an all-time high in the 1890s, averaging 188 per year. The viciousness of racist propaganda reached an all-time low. Serious antiblack riots broke out at Wilmington, North Carolina, in 1898 and in Atlanta in 1906. Several states adopted new constitutions that disfranchised most black voters by means of literacy or property qualifications (or both), poll taxes, and other clauses implicitly aimed at black voters. The new constitutions contained "understanding clauses" or "grandfather clauses" that enabled registrars to register white voters who were unable to meet the new requirements. In *Williams* v. *Mississippi* (1898), the U.S. Supreme Court upheld these disfranchisement clauses on the grounds that they did not discriminate "on their face" against blacks. Most blacks lost the right to vote, and the Republican Party almost disappeared from most southern states. State Democratic parties then established primary elections in which only whites could vote. For the next 60 years, the primary was the only meaningful election in the South.

It was during these same years that most southern states passed "Jim Crow" laws, which mandated racial segregation in public facilities of all kinds. In the landmark case of *Plessy* v. *Ferguson* (1896), the Supreme Court sanctioned such laws so long as the separate facilities for blacks were equal to those for whites—which, in practice, they never were.

One of the worst features of race relations in the New South was the convict leasing system. Before 1865 most crimes by slaves were punished on the plantations. The southern prison system was therefore inadequate to accommodate the increase in convicted criminals after emancipation. Most states began leasing convicts to private contractors—coal-mining firms, railroad construction companies, planters, and so on. The state not only saved the cost of housing and feeding the prisoners but also received an income for leasing them; the lessees obtained cheap labor whom they could work like slaves. The cruelty and exploitation suffered by the convicts became a national scandal. Ninety percent of the convicts were black, the result in part of discriminatory law enforcement practices. The convicts were ill fed, ill clothed, victimized by sadistic guards, and worked almost to death—sometimes literally to death. Annual mortality rates among convicts in several states ranged up to 25 percent.

Northern reformers condemned what they called "this newest and most revolting form of slavery." Thoughtful southerners agreed; an official investigation in Georgia pronounced convict leasing "barbaric," "worse than slavery," and "a disgrace to civilized people." Reform groups, many of them led by white women, sprang up in the South to work for the abolition of convict leasing. They achieved some success after 1900, though leasing was replaced in some states or counties by the chain gang—a dubious improvement.

At this "nadir" of the black experience in freedom, as one historian has called the 1890s, a new black leader emerged as successor of the abolitionists and Reconstruction politicians who were fading from the scene. Frederick Douglass died in 1895; but in that same year, Booker T. Washington, a 39-year-old educator who had founded Tuskegee Institute in Alabama, gave a speech at the Atlanta Exposition that made him famous. In effect, Washington accepted segregation as a temporary accommodation between the races in return for white support of black efforts for education, social uplift, and economic progress. "In all things that are purely social we can be as separate as the fingers," said Washington, "yet one as the hand in all things essential to mutual progress."

Washington's goal was not permanent second-class citizenship for blacks, but improvement through self-help and uplift until they earned white acceptance as equals. Yet to his black critics, Washington's strategy and rhetoric seemed to play into the hands of white supremacists. The Atlanta Exposition speech of 1895 launched a debate over means and ends in the black struggle for equality that, in one form or another, has continued for more than a century.

THE POLITICS OF STALEMATE

During the twenty years between the Panic of 1873 and the Panic of 1893, serious economic and social issues beset the American polity. As described in the next chapter, the strains of rapid industrialization, an inadequate monetary system, agricultural distress, and labor protest built up to potentially explosive force. The two mainstream political parties, however, seemed indifferent to these problems. Paralysis gripped the national government as the Civil War continued to cast its shadow, preventing political leaders from grappling with new issues facing the country because they remained mired in the passionate partisanship of the past.

KNIFE-EDGE ELECTORAL BALANCE

The five presidential elections from 1876 through 1892, taken together, were the most closely contested elections in American history. No more than 1 percent separated the popular vote of the two major candidates in any of these contests except 1892, when the margin was 3 percent. The Democratic candidate won twice (Grover Cleveland in 1884 and 1892), and in two other elections carried a tiny plurality of popular votes (Tilden in 1876 and Cleveland in 1888) but lost narrowly in the Electoral College. During the 20 years covered by these five administrations, the Democrats controlled the House of Representatives in seven Congresses to the Republicans' three, while the Republicans controlled the Senate in eight Congresses to the Democrats' two. During only six of those 20 years did the same party control the presidency and both houses, and then by razor-thin margins.

The few pieces of major legislation during these years—the Pendleton Civil Service Act of 1883, the Interstate Commerce Act of 1887, and the Sherman Antitrust Act of 1890—could be enacted only by bipartisan majorities, and only after they had been watered down by numerous compromises. Politicians often debated the tariff, but the tariff laws they passed had little real impact on the economy. Tariffs still were the principal source of federal tax revenue, but because the federal budget amounted to less than 3 percent of the gross national product (compared with 20 percent today), federal fiscal policies played only a marginal role in the economy.

Divided government and the even balance between the two major parties accounted for the political stalemate. Neither party had the power to enact a bold legislative program; both parties avoided taking firm stands on controversial issues. Both parties practiced the politics of the past rather than the politics of the present. Individuals voted Republican or Democratic in the 1880s because they or their fathers had done so during the passionate years of the 1860s. Every Republican president from 1869 to 1901 had fought in the Union army; the one Democratic president, Grover Cleveland, had not. At election time,

> *"Every state that seceded from the United States was a Democratic State. . . . Every man that tried to destroy this nation was a Democrat. Every man that loved slavery better than liberty was a Democrat. The man that assassinated Abraham Lincoln was a Democrat. . . . Every man that raised blood-hounds to pursue human beings was a Democrat. . . . Soldiers, every scar you have got on your heroic bodies was given to you by a Democrat."*
>
> **COLONEL ROBERT INGERSOLL**
> *in an 1876 speech to the Grand Army of the Republic (Union veterans organization), reprinted as a Republican campaign document in the election of 1884*

Republican candidates "waved the bloody shirt" to keep alive the memory of the Civil War. They castigated Democrats as former rebels or Copperheads who could not be trusted with the nation's destiny. Democrats, in turn, especially in the South, denounced racial equality and branded Republicans as the party of "Negro rule"—a charge that took on added intensity in 1890 when Republicans tried (and failed by one vote in the Senate) to enact a federal elections law to protect the voting rights of African Americans. From 1876 almost into the 20th century scarcely anyone but a Confederate veteran could be elected governor or senator in the South.

Availability rather than ability or a strong stand on issues became the prime requisite for presidential and vice presidential nominees. Geographical "availability" was particularly important. The solid Democratic South and the rather less solid Republican North gave each party a firm bloc of electoral votes in every election. But in three large northern states—New York, Ohio, and Indiana—the two parties were so closely balanced that the shift of a few thousand votes would determine the margin of victory for one or the other party in the state's electoral votes. These three states alone represented 74 electoral votes, fully one-third of the total necessary for victory. The party that carried New York (36 electoral votes) and either of the other two won the presidency.

It is not surprising that of 20 nominees for president and vice president by the two parties in five elections, 16 were from these three states. Only once did each party nominate a presidential candidate from outside these three states: Democrat Winfield Scott Hancock of Pennsylvania in 1880 and Republican James G. Blaine of Maine in 1884. Both lost.

CIVIL SERVICE REFORM

The most salient issue of national politics in the early 1880s was civil service reform. Old-guard factions in both parties opposed it. Republicans split into three factions known in the colorful parlance of the time as Mugwumps (the reformers), Stalwarts (who opposed reform), and Half-Breeds (who supported halfway reforms). Mugwumps and Half-Breeds combined to nominate James A. Garfield for president in 1880. Stalwarts received a consolation prize with the nomination of Chester A. Arthur for vice president. Four months after Garfield took office, a man named Charles Guiteau approached the president at the railroad station in Washington and shot him. Garfield lingered for two months before dying on September 19, 1881.

Described by psychiatrists as a paranoid schizophrenic, Guiteau was viewed by the public as a symbol of the spoils system at its worst. He had been a government clerk and a supporter of the Stalwart faction of the Republican Party but had lost his job under the new administration. As he shot Garfield he shouted, "I am a Stalwart and Arthur is president now!" This tragedy gave a final impetus to civil service reform. If the spoils system could cause the assassination of a president, it was time to get rid of it.

Though a Stalwart, President Arthur supported reform. In 1883 Congress passed the Pendleton Act, which established a category of civil service jobs that were to be filled by competitive examinations. At first, only a tenth of government positions fell within that category, but a succession of presidential orders gradually expanded the list to about half by 1897. State and local governments began to emulate federal civil service reform in the 1880s and 1890s.

Like the other vice presidents who had succeeded presidents who died in office (John Tyler, Millard Fillmore, and Andrew Johnson), Arthur failed to achieve nomination for president in his own right. The Republicans in 1884 turned instead to their most charismatic figure, James G. Blaine of Maine. His 18 years in the House and Senate had included six years (1869–75) as Speaker of the House. He had made enemies over the years, however, especially among Mugwumps, who believed that his cozy relationship with railroad lobbyists while Speaker and rumors of other shady dealings disqualified him for the presidency.

The Mugwumps, heirs of the old Conscience Whig element of the Republican Party, had a tendency toward elitism and self-righteousness in their self-appointed role as spokesmen for political probity. They were small in number but large in influence. Many were editors, authors, lawyers, college professors, or clergymen. Concentrated in the Northeast, particularly in New York, they admired the Democratic governor of that state, Grover Cleveland, who had gained a reputation as an advocate of reform and "good government." When Blaine won the Republican nomination, the Mugwumps defected to Cleveland.

In such a closely balanced state as New York, that shift could make a decisive difference, but Blaine hoped to neutralize it by shaving a few percentage points from the normal Democratic majority of the Irish vote. He made the most of his Irish ancestry on the maternal side. But that effort was rendered futile late in the campaign when a Protestant clergyman characterized the Democrats as the party of "Rum, Romanism, and Rebellion." Though Blaine was present when the Reverend Samuel Burchard made this remark, he failed to repudiate it. When the incident hit the newspapers, Blaine's hope for Irish support went glimmering. Cleveland carried New York State by 1,149 votes (a margin of one-tenth of 1 percent) and thus became the first Democrat to be elected president in 28 years.

THE TARIFF ISSUE

Ignoring a rising tide of farmer and labor discontent, Cleveland decided to make or break his presidency on the tariff issue. He devoted his annual State of the Union message in December 1887 entirely to the tariff, maintaining that lower duties would help all Americans by reducing the cost of consumer goods and by expanding American exports through reciprocal agreements with other nations. Republicans responded that low tariffs would flood the country with products from low-wage industries abroad, forcing American factories to close and throwing American workers out on the streets. The following year, the Republican nominee for president, Benjamin Harrison, pledged to retain the protective tariff. To reduce the budget surplus that had built up during the 1880s, the Republicans also promised more generous pensions for Union veterans.

The voters' response was ambiguous. Cleveland's popular-vote plurality actually increased from 29,000 in 1884 to 90,000 in 1888 (out of more than 10 million votes cast). Even so, a shift of six-tenths of 1 percent put New York in the Republican column and Harrison in the White House. Republicans also gained control of both houses of Congress. They promptly made good on their campaign pledges by passing legislation that almost doubled Union pensions and by enacting the McKinley Tariff of 1890. Named for Congressman William McKinley of Ohio, this law raised duties on a large range of products to an average of almost 50 percent, the highest since the infamous "Tariff of Abominations" in 1828.

The voters reacted convincingly—and negatively. They handed the Republicans a decisive defeat in midterm congressional elections, converting a House Republican majority of six to a Democratic majority of 147, and a Senate Republican majority of eight to a Democratic majority of six. Nominated for a third time in 1892, Cleveland built on this momentum to win the presidency by the largest margin in 20 years. But this outcome was deceptive. On March 4, 1893, when Cleveland took the oath of office for the second time, he stood atop a social and economic volcano that would soon erupt. When the ashes settled and the lava cooled, the political landscape would be forever altered.

CONCLUSION

In 1890 the superintendent of the U.S. Census made a sober announcement of dramatic import: "Up to and including 1880 the country had a frontier of settlement, but at present the unsettled area has been so broken into by isolated bodies of settlement that there can hardly be said to be a frontier line . . . any longer."

This statement prompted a young historian at the University of Wisconsin, Frederick Jackson Turner, to deliver a paper in 1893 that became the single most influential essay ever published by an American historian. For nearly 300 years, said Turner, the existence of a frontier of European-American settlement advancing relentlessly westward had shaped American character. To the frontier Americans owed their upward mobility, their high standard of living, and the rough equality of opportunity that made liberty and democracy possible. "American social development has been continually beginning over again on the frontier," declared Turner. He continued:

> This perennial rebirth, this fluidity of American life, this expansion westward with its new opportunities . . . furnish the forces dominating American character. . . . Frontier individualism has from the beginning promoted democracy [and] that restless, nervous energy, that dominant individualism . . . and withal that buoyancy and exuberance which comes with freedom—these are traits of the frontier, or traits called out elsewhere because of the existence of the frontier.

For many decades Turner's insight dominated Americans' perceptions of themselves and their history. Today, however, the Turner thesis is largely discredited as failing to explain the experiences of the great majority of people through most of American history who lived and worked in older cities and towns or on farms or plantations hundreds of miles from any frontier, and whose culture and institutions were molded more by their place of origin than by a "frontier." Indeed, the whole concept of a "frontier" as a line of white settlement beyond which lay empty land has been discredited, for other peoples had lived on that land for millennia.

The significance of Turner's remarks is not whether he was right; in the 1890s he expressed a widely shared belief among white Americans. They believed that liberty and equality were at least partly the product of the frontier, of the chance to go west and start a new life. And now that opportunity seemed to be coming to an end at the same time that the Panic of 1893 was launching another depression, the worst that the American economy had yet experienced. This depression caused the social and economic tinder that had been accumulating during the two preceding decades to burst into flame.

Suggested Readings begin on page SR-1. For Web activities and resources related to this chapter, go to http://www.harcourtcollege.com/history/murrin

CHAPTER 19

ECONOMIC CHANGE AND THE CRISIS OF THE 1890s

THE KANSAS LEGISLATURE, 1893

Agricultural depression in wheat and cotton states produced the third-party Populist movement in the 1890s. Populists won the Kansas governorship and state Senate by narrow margins in 1892, but contested returns for the lower House kept Kansas in turmoil for six weeks in early 1893. At one point, gun-toting Populists seized control of the capitol in Topeka, as shown in this dramatic photograph, and a shoot-out on the floor of the legislature seemed possible. A state court finally settled the dispute peacefully by certifying a Republican majority in the House.

Alexis de Tocqueville visited the United States in 1831 and published his famous analysis, *Democracy in America*, in 1835. At that time, more than two-thirds of all Americans lived on farms and only 10 percent lived in towns or cities with populations larger than 2,500. The overwhelming majority of white males owned property and worked for themselves rather than for wages. What impressed Tocqueville most was the relative absence of both great wealth and great poverty; the modest prosperity of the broad middle class created the impression—if not the literal reality—of equality, which Tocqueville made the central theme of *Democracy in America*.

During the next generation the North began to industrialize, cities grew much faster than rural areas, and the inequality of wealth and income grew larger. The country's preoccupation with sectional issues prior to the Civil War and the gnawing problems of Reconstruction after the war diverted attention from the economic and social problems associated with industrialism and class inequality. With the depression that followed the Panic of 1873, however, these problems burst spectacularly into public view. For a time, economic growth promised to deflect class conflict. By the 1890s, however, no American could deny that Tocqueville's republic of equality had long since disappeared.

This chapter will focus on the following major questions:

- What were the main engines of American economic growth in the last third of the 19th century?
- How did post–Civil War economic changes affect working people? How did they respond?
- What provoked the farmer protest movements in the last third of the 19th century?
- What issues were at stake in the contest between "free silver" and the "gold bugs"?

ECONOMIC GROWTH

During the 15 years between recovery from one depression in 1878 and the onset of another in 1893, the American economy grew at one of the fastest rates in its history. The gross national product almost doubled and per capita GNP increased by 35 percent. All sectors of the economy were expanding. The most spectacular growth was in manufacturing, which increased by 180 percent, whereas agriculture grew by 26 percent.

VALUE ADDED BY ECONOMIC SECTOR, 1869–1899 (IN 1879 PRICES)

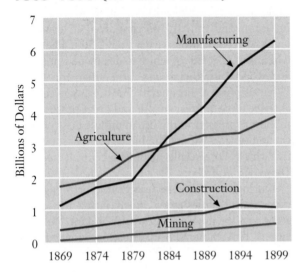

Manufacturing passed agriculture in value added for the first time in the early 1880s, and by 1900 the value added of manufacturing was almost twice that of agriculture.

RAILROADS

The railroad was the single most important agent of economic growth during these years. Track mileage increased by 113 percent, from 103,649 to 221,864 miles; the number of locomotives and revenue cars (freight and passenger) increased by a similar amount. Railroads converted from iron to steel rails and wheels, boosting steel production from 732,000 tons in 1878 to 10,188,000 tons by 1900. Railroads were the largest consumers of coal, the largest carriers of goods and people, the largest single employer of labor.

The power wielded by the railroad companies inevitably aroused hostility. Companies often charged less for long hauls than for short hauls in areas with little or no competition. The rapid proliferation of tracks produced overcapacity in some areas, which led to rate-cutting wars that benefited some shippers at the expense of others—usually large shippers at the expense of small ones. To avoid "ruinous competition" (as the railroads

viewed it), companies formed "pools" by which they divided traffic and fixed their rates. Some of these practices made sound economic sense; others appeared discriminatory and exploitative. Railroads gave credence to farmers' charges of monopoly exploitation by keeping rates higher in areas with no competition (most farmers lived in areas served by only one line) than in regions with competition. Grain elevators, many of which were owned by railroad companies, came under attack for cheating farmers by rigging the classification of their grain.

Farmers responded by organizing cooperatives to sell crops and buy supplies. The umbrella organization for many of these cooperatives was the

1869 Knights of Labor founded

1873 "Crime of 1873" demonetizes silver

1877 Railroad strikes cost 100 lives and millions of dollars in damage

1878 Bland-Allison Act to remonetize silver passed over Hayes's veto

1879 Henry George publishes *Progress and Poverty*

1883 Railroads establish four standard time zones

1886 Knights of Labor membership crests at 700,000 • Haymarket riot causes antilabor backlash • American Federation of Labor founded

1887 Edward Bellamy publishes *Looking Backward* • Interstate Commerce Act creates the first federal regulatory agency

1890 Congress passes Sherman Antitrust Act • Congress passes Sherman Silver Purchase Act

1892 Homestead strike fails • Populists organize the People's Party

1893 Financial panic begins economic depression • Congress repeals Sherman Silver Purchase Act

1894 "Coxey's army" of the unemployed marches on Washington • Pullman strike paralyzes the railroads and provokes federal intervention

1896 William McKinley defeats William Jennings Bryan for the presidency

Patrons of Husbandry, known as the Grange, founded in 1867. But because farmers could not build their own railroads, they organized "antimonopoly" parties and elected state legislators who enacted "Granger laws" in several states. These laws established railroad commissions that fixed maximum freight rates and warehouse charges. Railroads challenged the laws in court. Eight challenges made their way to the U.S. Supreme Court, which in *Munn* v. *Illinois* (1877) ruled that states could regulate businesses clothed with a "public interest"—railroads and other common carriers, millers, innkeepers, and the like. It was a landmark decision.

The welter of different and sometimes conflicting state laws, plus rulings by the U.S. Supreme Court in the 1880s that states could not regulate interstate railroad traffic, brought a drive for federal regulation. After years of discussion, Congress passed the Interstate Commerce Act in 1887. This law, like most such laws, reflected compromise between the varying viewpoints of shippers, railroads, and other pressure groups. It outlawed pools, discriminatory rates, long-haul versus short-haul differentials, and rebates to favored shippers. It required that freight and passenger rates must be "reasonable and just." What that meant was not entirely clear, but the law created the Interstate Commerce Commission (ICC) to define the requirement on a case-by-case basis. Because the ICC had minimal enforcement powers, however, federal courts frequently refused to issue the orders it requested. Staffed by men knowledgeable about railroading, the ICC often sympathized with the viewpoint of the industry it was supposed to regulate. Nevertheless, its powers of publicity had some effect on railroad practices, and freight rates continued to decline during this period as railroad operating efficiency improved.

The outstanding example of the railroads' impact on everyday life was the creation of standard time zones. Before 1883 many localities and cities kept their own time, derived from the sun's meridian in each locality. When it was noon in Chicago, it was 11:27 a.m. in Omaha, 11:56 a.m. in St. Louis, 12:09 p.m. in Louisville, and 12:17 p.m. in Toledo. This played havoc with railroad timeta-

bles. In 1883 a consortium of railroads established four standard time zones—much the same as they exist in the 48 contiguous states today. They put new timetables into effect for these zones on November 18, 1883. Some grumbling followed about the arrogance of railroad presidents changing "God's time." The U.S. attorney general ruled that government agencies need not change their clocks until authorized to do so by Congress; the next day he missed a train by eight minutes because he had not reset his watch to the new Eastern Standard Time. For the most part, however, the public accepted the change, and Congress finally sanctioned standard time zones in 1918.

TECHNOLOGY

Technological advances during this era had an enormous impact: the railroads gained automatic signals, air brakes, and knuckle couplers; steel mills added the Bessemer and then the open-hearth process. The 1870s produced the telephone, electric light, and typewriter; the elevator and structural steel made possible the first "skyscrapers" in the 1880s; and in the 1890s the phonograph and motion pictures provided new forms of entertainment. This era also introduced the electric dynamo (generator), the basis for such household items as refrigerators and washing machines and a new source of industrial power that gradually replaced water power and the steam engine; and the internal combustion engine, which made possible the first automobiles (1890s) and the first airplane flight by the Wright brothers in 1903.

WEALTH AND INEQUALITY

All these wonders of economic growth and technological change came at some human cost. One such cost was a widening gulf between rich and poor. Although the average per capita income of all Americans increased by 35 percent from 1878 to 1893, real wages advanced only 20 percent. That advance masked sharp inequalities of wages by skill, region, race, and gender. Many unskilled and semiskilled workers made barely enough to support themselves, much less a family; many families, especially recent immigrants (who formed a large

"*We meet in the midst of a nation brought to the verge of moral, political, and material ruin. Corruption dominates the ballot-box, the legislatures, the Congress, and touches even the ermine of the bench. The people are demoralized; . . . the newspapers are largely subsidized or muzzled; public opinion silenced; business prostrated; our homes covered with mortgages; labor impoverished; and the land concentrating in the hands of the capitalists. . . . The fruits of the toil of millions are boldly stolen to build up colossal fortunes for a few. . . . From the same prolific womb of governmental injustice we breed the two great classes—tramps and millionaires.*

"*A vast conspiracy against mankind has been organized on two continents, and it is rapidly taking possession of the world. If not met and overthrown at once, it forebodes terrible social convulsions, the destruction of civilization, or the establishment of an absolute despotism.*"

PREAMBLE TO THE POPULIST PLATFORM
1892 presidential election

REAL WAGES OF WORKERS AND PER CAPITA INCOME OF ALL AMERICANS, 1870–1900

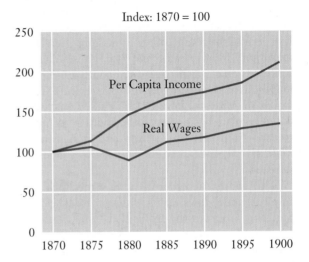

entertained lavishly, sometimes spending on a single party an amount that would have supported a tenement full of immigrant families for a year. These extravagant habits gave substance to the labeling of this era as the Gilded Age. Their well-publicized activities, while millions lived on the edge of poverty, sharpened the growing sense of class consciousness.

Some of the millionaires made their money by methods that critics considered predatory, providing another vivid epithet of the period: "robber barons." Some of the most conspicuous figures who bore this epithet, whether deserved or not, were William Vanderbilt (who once allegedly burst out in response to criticism: "The public be damned!"), Jay Gould, Jim Fisk, and Collis P. Huntington in railroading; John D. Rockefeller in oil; Andrew Carnegie and Henry Clay Frick in steel; James B. Duke in tobacco; and John Pierpont Morgan in banking.

Criticism of the robber barons sometimes focused more on the immense power commanded by their wealth than on the wealth itself. Fisk and Gould bribed legislators, manipulated the stock market, exploited workers, and cheated stockholders in their various schemes to corner the gold market, milk the Erie Railroad for personal profit, and create a railroad empire in the Southwest.

part of the blue-collar workforce), needed two or three wage-earners to survive.

The perception of class inequality was even greater than the reality. The estimated number of "millionaires" (a word that came into use during this era) was 300 in 1860; by 1892 the number was 4,000. Many of them practiced what the eccentric but brilliant economist Thorstein Veblen described in his book *The Theory of the Leisure Class* (1899) as "conspicuous consumption." They sent agents to Europe to buy up paintings and tapestries from impoverished aristocrats. In their mansions on Fifth Avenue and their summer homes at Newport they

The Rise of Sport

Railroads and the telegraph made possible the rise of baseball and football as popular sports after the Civil War. Baseball emerged in the New York City area during the 1840s, caught on with the Union army during the Civil War, and soon spread among ordinary people throughout the North. In 1869 the Cincinnati Red Stockings became the first professional team and, in more than 60 games, defeated all but one of their amateur opponents. In 1876 the National League was organized and thereafter professional athletes set the tone for the sport. Teams traveled by railroad to distant cities for their games, while the telegraphs and newspapers kept "fans" (short for "fanatics") back home informed of the teams' heroics. Baseball appealed to members of the blue-collar working class. In the painting shown here (*Slide, Kelly, Slide*) fans in the 1880s watch one of their heroes, Mike Kelly, stealing second base.

Football, by contrast, took hold in the 1870s among the most privileged young men in the country. Teams at Harvard, Yale, and Princeton flaunted their superiority by destroying all other opponents until well after 1900. The lower illustration depicts the Thanksgiving Day game between Princeton and Yale before 50,000 spectators in New York in 1893. Loyal football fans were willing to pay five dollars per ticket even during the depression that followed the Panic of 1893, at a time when Princeton's annual budget was $500,000. Yale was the powerhouse team during those years—in 1888, for example, Yale outscored all opponents 698 to 0. Not until 1913 when Notre Dame surprised Army (which had recently beaten Yale) with a new offense based on the forward pass did football preeminence begin to pass from the Big Three to the Midwest.

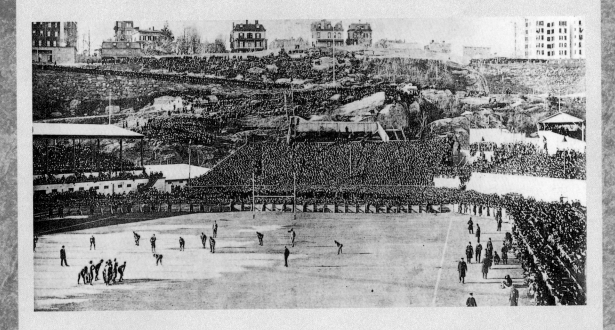

The Molly Maguires (1970)
Directed by Martin Ritt. Starring Richard Harris (James McParlan), Sean Connery (Jack Kehoe), Samantha Eggar (Mary Raines).

The gritty realism of *The Molly Maguires* offers a compelling portrait of labor conditions in 19th-century coal mines. Filmed on location in the anthracite region of eastern Pennsylvania, the film takes the viewer deep into the earth where Irish American miners labored long hours for a pittance at the dangerous, back-breaking, health-destroying job of bringing out the coal that heated American homes and fueled American industry.

These mining communities constituted a microcosm of ethnic and class tensions in American society. Most of the mine owners were Scots-Irish Presbyterians; many foremen, skilled workers, and police were English or Welsh Protestants; most of the unskilled workers were Irish Catholics. This was a volatile mixture, vividly depicted in the movie. The skilled miners had formed the Workingmen's Benevolent Association, which had won modest gains for its members by 1873. Many Irish belonged to the Ancient Order of Hibernians, which aided sick miners and supported the widows and orphans of those who died—and there were many such. The inner circle of this order called itself the Molly Maguires, after an anti-landlord organization in Ireland that resisted the eviction of tenants. In Pennsylvania the Mollies retaliated against exploitative owners, unpopular foremen, and the police with acts of sabotage, violence, intimidation, and murder.

The economic depression following the Panic of 1873 exacerbated tensions and violence. The owners hired the Pinkerton detective agency to infiltrate and gather criminal evidence against the Mollies. Detective James McParlan went to work in the mines, gained the confidence of his fellow Irish Americans, and was eventually admitted to the Molly Maguires. For more than two years he lived a dangerous double existence (foreshortened in the movie) that would have meant instant death if the Mollies had discovered his mole role. In a series of widely publicized trials from 1875 to 1877 in which McParlan was the main witness, dozens of Molly Maguires were convicted and 20 were hanged.

Richard Harris and Sean Connery are superb as McParlan and Jack Kehoe, the Mollies' leader. The real Jamie McParlan courted the sister-in-law of one of the Mollies; the film expands this into a poignant romance between McParlan and a retired miner's beautiful daughter. The love interest fits with the film's effective presentation of McParlan's conflicted conscience and the moral ambiguity of his role as the agent of justice (as defined by the ruling class), which

Rockefeller either bought out or ruined his competitors, obtained rebates and drawbacks on rail shipments of oil, and created a monopoly in his determined efforts to gain control of oil refining—efforts that culminated in the formation of the Standard Oil Trust in 1879. Carnegie and Frick pushed laborers to the limit in 72-hour workweeks, redefined skill levels and changed work rules, and sped up the pace in steel mills in a ceaseless quest for greater efficiency and lower labor costs. Morgan's banking firm built an empire of leveraged financing and interlocking corporate directorates, often using a New Jersey incorporation law passed in 1889 that permitted holding companies to gain control or dominant influence in several firms.

These activities could be—and were—defended on grounds of entrepreneurial innovation and efficiency, and the enterprises these men created did enable the United States to leap ahead of Britain as an industrial power. By 1913 American manufacturing output equaled that of the next three industrial nations combined—Germany, Britain, and France. The robber barons created wealth for all Americans—poorly distributed though it was—as

requires him to betray the men with whom he had lived, sung, plotted, swapped stories, and carried out raids. What were McParlan's real motives? The film does not successfully answer that question; but neither does history. Most viewers, however, will take from this movie a feeling of empathy with the Mollies, whose protest against terrible conditions drove them to desperate acts of violence.

Sean Connery (Jack Kehoe, right) and Art Lund (a fellow Molly Maguire) prepare to dynamite a coal train in *The Molly Maguires*.

well as for themselves, and not all of them practiced conspicuous consumption. Professing a gospel of stewardship, Carnegie, Rockefeller, and others gave away much of their wealth to educational and philanthropic institutions, establishing the basis for modern multibillion-dollar foundations.

THE ANTITRUST MOVEMENT

Nevertheless, many Americans feared the power wielded by these tycoons. Their monopoly or near-monopoly share of the market in oil, steel, tobacco, sugar, transportation, and other products seemed to violate the ideal of fair competition. To curb that power, an "antitrust" movement emerged in the 1880s. The word "trust" derived from an investment strategy pioneered by Rockefeller, in which the stockholders of several refining companies turned over their shares to Standard Oil in return for so-called trust certificates. The term came to be applied to all large corporations that controlled a substantial share of any given market. In response to pressures to curb such "trusts," several states passed antitrust laws in the 1880s.

Because the larger corporations operated across state lines, reformers turned to Congress, which responded in 1890 by passing the Sherman Antitrust Act (named for Senator John Sherman of Ohio, brother of the Civil War general). On the face of it, the Sherman Act seemed to mean business: "Every contract, combination in the form of trust or otherwise, or conspiracy, in restraint of trade or commerce among the several States is hereby declared to be illegal." But what constituted "restraint of trade"? For that matter, what constituted a trust? Did a holding company incorporated under New Jersey's 1889 law violate the Sherman Act? Of eight cases against corporations brought before federal courts from 1890 to 1893, the government lost seven. In 1895 the Supreme Court dealt the Sherman Act a crippling blow in *U.S. v. E. C. Knight Company.* In this case, which concerned a sugar-refining monopoly, the Court ruled that manufacturing was not commerce and therefore did not fall under jurisdiction of the law. For the time being, the Sherman Act was almost a dead letter.

LABOR STRIFE

The drive for even greater speed and productivity on railroads and in factories gave the United States the unhappy distinction of having the world's highest rate of industrial accidents. Workmen's compensation was almost unknown; many families were impoverished by workplace accidents that killed or maimed their chief breadwinner. This was one source of a rising tide of labor discontent. Another was the erosion of worker autonomy in factories, where new machinery took over tasks once performed by skilled workers and where managers made decisions about the procedures and pace of operations once made by workers themselves. Many crafts that had once been a source of pride to those who practiced them became just a job that could be performed by anyone. Labor increasingly became a commodity bartered for wages rather than a craft whereby the worker sold the product of his labor rather than the labor itself. For the first time in American history, the census of 1870 reported that a majority of employed persons worked for wages paid by others rather than working for themselves.

Skilled artisans considered this an alarming trend. Their efforts to preserve or recapture independence from bosses and robber barons fueled much of the labor unrest in the 1870s and 1880s. In 1866 the leaders of several craft unions had formed the National Labor Union. Labor parties sprang up in several states; the Labor Reform candidate for governor of Massachusetts in 1870 won 13 percent of the vote. In response to growing labor political activism, several states established bureaus or departments of labor that had little substantive power but did begin to gather and report data for the first time. These pressures filtered up to Washington, where Congress created the Bureau of Labor in 1884 and elevated it to cabinet rank in 1903. In 1894 Congress also made the first Monday in September an official holiday—Labor Day—to honor working people.

The National Labor Union withered away in the depression of the 1870s, but industrial violence escalated. In the anthracite coal fields of eastern Pennsylvania, the Molly Maguires (an amalgam of a labor union and a secret order of Irish Americans) carried out guerrilla warfare against mine owners. In the later 1870s, the Greenbackers (a group that urged currency expansion to end deflation) and labor reformers formed a coalition that elected several local and state officials plus 14 congressmen in 1878. In 1880 the Greenback-Labor candidate for president won 3 percent of the popular vote.

THE GREAT RAILROAD STRIKE OF 1877

Railroads became an early focal point of labor strife. Citing declining revenues during the depression that followed the Panic of 1873, several railroads cut wages by as much as 35 percent between 1874 and 1877 (during that same period the price index fell only 8 percent). When the Baltimore and Ohio Railroad announced its third 10 percent wage cut on July 16, 1877, workers struck. The strike spread rapidly to other lines. Traffic from St. Louis to the East Coast came to a halt. Ten states called out their militias. Strikers and militia fired on each other, and workers set fire to rolling stock and roundhouses. By the time federal troops gained control in the first week of August, at least 100

THE RAILROAD STRIKES OF 1877 This illustration shows striking workers on the Baltimore and Ohio Railroad forcing the engineer and fireman from a freight train at Martinsburg, West Virginia, on July 17, 1877.

strikers, militiamen, and bystanders had been killed, hundreds more had been injured, and uncounted millions of dollars of property had gone up in smoke. It was the worst labor violence in U.S. history to that time; the specter of class conflict frightened many Americans and gave rise to a desperate view of the future.

THE KNIGHTS OF LABOR

The principal labor organization that emerged in the 1880s was the Knights of Labor. Founded in Philadelphia in 1869, the Knights began as a secret fraternal society. Under the leadership of Terence V. Powderly, a machinist by trade, the Knights abandoned secrecy in 1879 and emerged as a potent national federation of unions—or "assemblies," as they were officially known. The Knights of Labor departed in several respects

from the norm of labor organization at that time. Most of its assemblies were organized by industry rather than by craft, giving many unskilled and semiskilled workers union representation for the first time. Some assemblies admitted women; some also admitted blacks. Despite this inclusiveness, however, tendencies toward exclusivity of craft, gender, and race divided and weakened many assemblies.

A paradox of purpose also plagued the Knights. Most members wanted to improve their lot within the existing system through higher wages, shorter hours, better working conditions—the bread-and-butter goals of working people. This meant collective bargaining with employers; it also meant strikes. The assemblies won some strikes and lost some. Powderly and the Knights' national leadership discouraged strikes, however, partly out of practicality: A losing strike often destroyed an

FIRST LABOR DAY PARADE, SEPTEMBER 5, 1882 One of the goals of the labor movement was greater social recognition of the rights and dignity of working people. Labor unions urged Congress to establish a national holiday for this purpose. Even before Congress acted in 1894, the Knights of Labor sponsored huge "labor day" parades. This illustration depicts the first such parade at Union Square in New York City.

assembly, as employers replaced strikes with strike-breakers, or "scabs."

Another reason for Powderly's antistrike stance was philosophical. Strikes constituted a tacit recognition of the legitimacy of the wage system. In Powderly's view, wages siphoned off to capital a part of the wealth created by labor. The Knights, he said, intended "to secure to the workers the full enjoyment of the wealth they create." This was a goal grounded both in the past independence of skilled workers and in a radical vision of the future—a vision in which workers' cooperatives would own the means of production. "There is no reason," said Powderly, "why labor cannot, through cooperation, own and operate mines, factories, and railroads."

The Knights did sponsor several modest workers' cooperatives. Their success was limited, partly from lack of capital and of management experience

and partly because even the most skilled craftsmen found it difficult to compete with machines in a mass-production economy. Ironically, the Knights gained their greatest triumphs through strikes. In 1884 and 1885 successful strikes against the Union Pacific and Missouri Pacific railroads won enormous prestige and a rush of new members, which by 1886 totaled 700,000. But defeat in a second strike against the Missouri Pacific in the spring of 1886 was a serious blow. Then came the Haymarket bombing in Chicago.

HAYMARKET

Chicago was a hotbed of labor radicalism. In 1878 the newly formed Socialist Labor Party won 14 percent of the vote in the city, electing five aldermen and four members of the Illinois legislature. With recovery from the depression after 1878, the

Socialist Labor Party fell onto lean times. Four-fifths of its members were foreign-born, mostly Germans. Internal squabbles generated several off-shoots of the party in the 1880s. One of these embraced anarchism and called for the violent destruction of the capitalist system so that a new socialist order could be built on its ashes. Anarchists infiltrated some trade unions in Chicago and leaped aboard the bandwagon of a national movement centered in that city for a general strike on May 1, 1886, to achieve the eight-hour workday. Chicago police were notoriously hostile to labor organizers and strikers, so the scene was set for a violent confrontation.

The May 1 showdown coincided with a strike at the McCormick farm machinery plant in Chicago. A fight outside the gates on May 3 brought a police attack on the strikers in which four people were killed. Anarchists then organized a protest meeting at Haymarket Square on May 4. Toward the end of the meeting, when the rain-soaked crowd was already dispersing, the police suddenly arrived in force. When someone threw a bomb into their midst, the police opened fire. When the wild melee was over, 50 people lay wounded and 10 dead—six of them policemen.

This affair set off a wave of hysteria against labor radicals. Police in Chicago rounded up hundreds of labor leaders. Eight anarchists (seven of them German-born) went on trial for conspiracy to commit murder—though no evidence turned up to prove that any of them had thrown the bomb. All eight were convicted; seven were sentenced to hang. One of the men committed suicide; the governor commuted the sentences of two others to life imprisonment; the remaining four were hanged on November 11, 1887. The case became a cause célèbre that bitterly divided the country. Many workers, civil libertarians, and middle-class citizens troubled by the events branded the verdicts judicial murder, but the majority of Americans applauded the summary repression of un-American radicalism.

The Knights of Labor were caught in this anti-labor backlash. Although the Knights had nothing to do with the Haymarket affair and Powderly had repeatedly denounced anarchism, his opposition to the wage system sounded to many Americans suspi-ciously like socialism, perhaps even anarchism. Membership in the Knights plummeted from 700,000 in the spring of 1886 to fewer than 100,000 by 1890.

As the Knights of Labor waned, a new national labor organization waxed. Founded in 1886, the American Federation of Labor (AFL) was a loosely affiliated association of unions organized by trade or craft: cigar-makers, machinists, carpenters, and so on. Under the leadership of Samuel Gompers, an immigrant cigar-maker, the AFL accepted capitalism and the wage system, and worked for better conditions, higher wages, shorter hours, and occupational safety within the system— "pure and simple unionism," as Gompers called it. Most AFL members were skilled workers, and few were women or blacks—a strategy that enabled the AFL to survive and even to prosper in a difficult climate. Its membership grew from 140,000 in 1886 to nearly a million by 1900.

Labor militancy survived Haymarket, however. Two best-selling books helped keep alive the vision of a more equalitarian social order. Although their impact was less powerful than that of *Uncle Tom's Cabin* a generation earlier (see Chapter 13), they nevertheless affected the millions who read them.

HENRY GEORGE

The first, a book on economics titled *Progress and Poverty* (1879), seemed an unlikely candidate for best-seller status. Henry George, a self-educated author, had spent 15 years working as a sailor, printer, and prospector before becoming a newspaper editor in California. In his travels, George had been struck by the appalling contrast between wealth and poverty. He fixed on "land monopoly" as the cause: the control of land and resources by the few at the expense of the many. His solution was 100 percent taxation on the "unearned increment" in the value of land—that is, on the difference between the initial purchase price and the eventual market value (minus improvements), or what today we would call capital gains. Such gains were created by society, he insisted, not by the landowner, and the total amount should be confiscated by taxation for the benefit of society. This would eliminate the need for all other taxes, George maintained; it would free productive capital and labor and would narrow the gulf between rich and poor.

Progress and Poverty achieved astonishing success. By 1905 it had sold two million copies and had been translated into several languages, but few economists endorsed the single tax, and the idea made little headway. The real impact of George's book came from its portrayal of the injustice of poverty in the midst of plenty. George became a hero to labor. He joined the Knights of Labor, moved to New York City, and ran for mayor as the candidate of the United Labor Party in 1886. He narrowly lost, but his campaign dramatized the grievances of labor and alerted the major parties to the power of that constituency. George's influence cast a long shadow into the next century; numerous Progressive leaders were first sensitized to social issues by their reading of *Progress and Poverty*.

EDWARD BELLAMY

The other book that found a wide audience was a novel, *Looking Backward*, by Edward Bellamy. Like Harriet Beecher Stowe, Bellamy was a New England writer imbued with the tenets of Christian reform. *Looking Backward* is a utopian romance that takes place in the year 2000 and contrasts the America of that year with the America of 1887. In 2000 all industry is controlled by the national government, everyone works for equal pay, no one is rich and no one is poor, there are no strikes, no class conflict. Bellamy was not a Marxian socialist—he criticized the Marxian emphasis on class conflict—and he preferred to call his collectivist order "Nationalism," not socialism. His vision of a world without social strife appealed to middle-class Americans, who bought a half million copies of *Looking Backward* every year for several years in the early 1890s. More than 160 Nationalist clubs sprang up to support the idea of public ownership, if not of all industries, at least of public utilities.

Some of Bellamy's followers called themselves Christian Socialists. They formed the left wing of a broader movement, the Social Gospel, that deeply affected mainstream Protestant denominations (and many Catholic leaders as well) in the rapidly growing cities of the Gilded Age. Shocked by poverty and overcrowding in the sprawling tenement districts of urban America, clergymen and laypeople associated with the Social Gospel embraced a theology that considered aiding the poor as important as saving souls. They supported the settlement houses being established in many cities during the 1890s (see Chapter 21) and pressed for legislation to curb the exploitation of the poor and provide them with opportunities for betterment. These efforts gathered strength during the 1890s and contributed to the rise of the Progressive movement after 1900.

THE HOMESTEAD STRIKE

The 1890s provided plenty of evidence to feed middle-class fears that America was falling apart. Strikes occurred with a frequency and a fierceness that made 1877 and 1886 look like mere preludes to the main event. The most dramatic confrontation took place in 1892 at the Homestead plant (near Pittsburgh) of the Carnegie Steel Company. Carnegie and his plant manager, Henry Clay Frick, were determined to break the power of the country's strongest union, the Amalgamated Association of Iron, Steel, and Tin Workers. Frick used a dispute over wages and work rules as an opportunity to close the plant (a "lockout") preparatory to reopening it with nonunion workers. When the union called a strike and refused to leave the plant (a "sitdown"), Frick called in 300 Pinkerton guards to oust them. (The Pinkerton detective agency had evolved since the Civil War era into a private security force that specialized in antiunion activities.) A full-scale gun battle between strikers and Pinkertons erupted on July 6, leaving nine strikers and seven Pinkertons dead and scores wounded. Frick persuaded the governor to send in 8,000 militia to protect the strikebreakers, and the plant reopened. Public sympathy, much of it pro-union at first, shifted when an anarchist tried to murder Frick on July 23. The failed Homestead strike crippled the Amalgamated Association; another strike against U.S. Steel (successor of Carnegie Steel) in 1901 destroyed it.

PENNSYLVANIA MILITIA AT CARNEGIE'S HOMESTEAD STEEL MILL, 1892 After the shoot-out between striking workers and Pinkerton guards, the Pennsylvania militia reopened the mills and protected strikebreakers from striking workers. This photograph shows the militia using steel beams manufactured by the mill as a makeshift barricade.

THE DEPRESSION OF 1893–1897

By the 1890s the use of state militias to protect strikebreakers had become common. Events after 1893 brought an escalation of conflict. The most serious economic crisis since the 1873–78 depression was triggered by the Panic of 1893, a collapse of the stock market that plunged the economy into a severe four-year depression. Its complex origins included an economic slowdown abroad, which caused British banks to call some of their American loans, thereby draining gold from the United States at a time of political controversy about the American monetary system and nervousness in financial circles. Other causes included declining farm prices and attendant rural unrest and the overly rapid expansion of railroad construction and manufacturing capacity after 1885. The bankruptcy of the Reading Railroad and the National Cordage Company in early 1893 set off a process that by the end of the year had caused 491 banks and 15,000 other businesses to fail. By mid-1894 the unemployment rate had risen to more than 15 percent.

An Ohio reformer named Jacob Coxey conceived the idea of sending Congress a "living petition" of unemployed workers to press for appropriations to put them to work on road building and other public works. "Coxey's army," as the press dubbed it, inspired other groups to hit the road and ride the rails to Washington during 1894. This descent of the unemployed on the capital provoked arrests by federal marshals and troops, and ended in anticlimax when Coxey and others were arrested for trespassing on the Capitol grounds. Coxey's idea for using public works to relieve unemployment turned out to be 40 years ahead of its time.

THE PULLMAN STRIKE

Even more alarming to middle-class Americans than Coxey's army was the Pullman strike of 1894.

COXEY'S ARMY ON THE MARCH Reformer Jacob Coxey organized a group of unemployed workers, who traveled to Washington, D.C., as a "petition in boots" to lobby for a public works program to put them back to work in 1894. They failed on this occasion, but their efforts planted a seed that bore fruit during the Great Depression of the 1930s.

George M. Pullman had made a fortune in the manufacture of sleeping cars and other rolling stock for railroads. Workers in his large factory complex lived in the company town of Pullman just south of Chicago, where they enjoyed paved streets, clean parks, and decent houses rented from the company. But Pullman controlled many aspects of their lives, including banning liquor from the town and punishing workers whose behavior did not suit his ideas of decorum. When the Panic of 1893 caused a sharp drop in orders for Pullman cars, the company laid off a third of its workforce and cut wages for the rest by 30 percent, but did not reduce company house rents or company store prices. Pullman refused to negotiate with a workers' committee, which called a strike and appealed to the American Railway Union (ARU) for help.

The Railway Union had been founded the year before by Eugene V. Debs. A native of Indiana, Debs had been elected secretary of the Brotherhood of Locomotive Firemen in 1875 at the age of 20. By 1893 he had become convinced that the conservative stance of the various craft unions in railroading (firemen, engineers, brakemen, and so forth) was divisive and contrary to the best interests of labor. He formed the ARU to include all railroad workers in one union. With 150,000 members, the union won a strike against the Great Northern Railroad in the spring of 1894. When George Pullman refused the ARU's offer to arbitrate the strike of Pullman workers, Debs launched a boycott by which ARU members would refuse to run any trains that included Pullman cars. When the railroads attempted to fire the ARU sympathizers, whole train crews went on strike and quickly paralyzed rail traffic.

Over the protests of Illinois Governor John P. Altgeld, who sympathized with the strikers, President Grover Cleveland sent in federal troops. That action inflamed violence instead of containing it. The U.S. attorney general (a former railroad lawyer) obtained a federal injunction against Debs under the Sherman Antitrust Act on grounds that the boycott and the strike were a conspiracy in restraint of trade. This creative use of the Sherman Act, whose purpose had been to curb corporations, was upheld by the Supreme Court in 1895 and became a powerful weapon against labor unions in the hands of conservative judges.

For a week in July 1894 the Chicago railroad yards resembled a war zone. Millions of dollars of equipment went up in smoke. Thirty-four people, mostly workers, were killed. Finally, 14,000 state militia and federal troops restored order and broke the strike. Debs went to jail (for violation of the federal injunction) for six months. He emerged from prison a socialist.

To many Americans, 1894 was the worst year of crisis since the Civil War. The Pullman strike was only the most dramatic event of a year in which 750,000 workers went on strike and another 3 million were unemployed. But it was a surge of discontent from down on the farm that wrenched American politics off its foundations in the 1890s.

FARMERS' MOVEMENTS

After the Civil War, farmers from the older states and immigrants from northern Europe poured into the territories and states of Dakota, Nebraska, Kansas, Texas, and—after 1889—Indian Territory. Some went on to the Pacific Coast states or stopped in the cattle-grazing and mining territories in between. This wave of settlement brought nine new states into the Union between 1867 and 1896 that almost equaled in total size all the states east of the Mississippi.

The vagaries of nature and weather were magnified in the West. Grasshopper plagues wiped out crops from Minnesota to Kansas several times in the 1870s. Dry, searing summer winds alternated with violent hailstorms to scorch or level whole fields of wheat and corn. Winter blizzards intensified the isolation of farm families and produced loneliness and depression, especially among women. Adding to these woes, the relatively wet years of the 1870s and early 1880s gave way to an abnormally dry cycle the following decade, causing many farmers who had moved beyond the zone of 20 inches of annual precipitation (roughly the 98th meridian) to give up and return east, sometimes with a sign painted on their wagon: "In God we trusted, in Kansas we busted."

Despite these problems, America's soaring grain production increased three times as fast as the American population from 1870 to 1890. Only rising exports could sustain such expansion in farm

RETURNING TO ILLINOIS, 1894 This photograph shows one of the thousands of farm families who had moved into Kansas, Nebraska, and other plains states in the wet years of the 1870s and 1880s, only to give up during the dry years of the 1890s. Their plight added fuel to the fire of rural unrest and protest during those years.

WHOLESALE AND CONSUMER PRICE INDEXES, 1865–1897

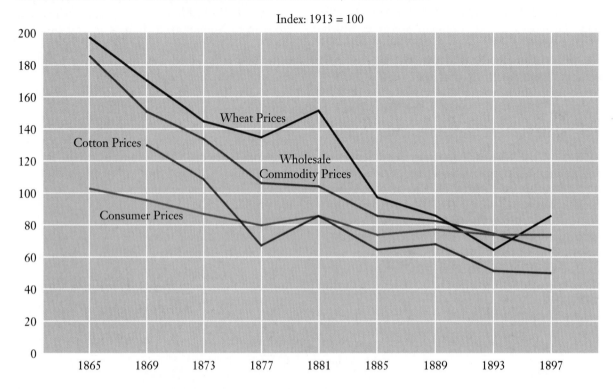

production. But by the 1880s the improved efficiency of large farms in eastern Europe brought intensifying competition and consequent price declines, especially for wheat, just as competition from Egypt and India had eroded prices for American cotton. Prices on the world market for these two staples of American agriculture—wheat and cotton—fell about 60 percent from 1870 to 1895, while the wholesale price index for all commodities (including other farm products) declined by 45 percent during the same period. Not surprisingly, distress was greatest and protest loudest in the wheat-producing West and the cotton-producing South.

CREDIT AND MONEY

Victims of a world market largely beyond their control, farmers lashed out at targets nearer home: banks, commission merchants, railroads, and the monetary system. In truth, these institutions did victimize farmers, though not always intentionally. The long period of price deflation from 1865 to 1897, unique in American history, exacerbated the problem of credit. A price decline of 1 or 2 percent a year added that many points cumulatively to the nominal interest rate. If a farmer's main crop was wheat or cotton, whose prices declined even further, his real interest rate was that much greater. Thus it was not surprising that farmers who denounced banks or country-store merchants for gouging them also attacked a monetary system that brought deflation.

The federal government's monetary policies worsened deflation problems. The 1862 emergency wartime issuance of treasury "greenback" notes (see Chapter 15) had created a dual currency—gold and greenbacks—with the greenback dollar's value relative to gold rising and falling according to Union military fortunes. After the war the Treasury moved to bring the greenback dollar to par with gold by reducing the amount of greenbacks in circulation. This limitation of the money supply produced deflationary pressures. To complicate matters further, national banknotes backed by the banks' holding of government bonds continued to circulate as money. Because national banks were concentrated in the Northeast, the South and West suffered from downward pressures on prices they received for their crops because of money scarcity. Western farmers were particularly vociferous in their protests against this situation, which introduced a new sectional conflict into politics—not North against South, but East against West.

Because parity between greenbacks and gold would not be reached until 1879, a controversy arose in the postwar years over whether Union war bonds should be paid off in greenbacks or in gold. Congress resolved this issue in 1869 by passing the Public Credit Act, which required payment in gold. Because little silver had been coined into money for years, Congress enacted in 1873 a law that ended the coinage of silver dollars, thus putting the United States on the road to joining the international gold standard. In 1874 President Grant vetoed a bill sponsored by antideflation western congressmen to increase the number of greenbacks in circulation, setting the stage for enactment in 1875 of the important Specie Resumption Act. When the provisions of this act went fully into effect on January 1, 1879, the U.S. dollar reached par with the gold dollar on the international market.

Grant's role in bringing about these steps toward "sound money" is more important than generally recognized, but the benefits of his achievement were sharply debated then and remain controversial today. On the one hand, they strengthened the dollar, placed government credit on a firm footing, and helped create a financial structure for the remarkable economic growth that tripled the gross national product during the last quarter of the 19th century. On the other hand, the restraints on money supply hurt the rural economy in the South and West; they hurt debtors who found that deflation enlarged their debts by increasing the value of greenbacks; and they probably worsened the two major depressions of the era (1873–78 and 1893–97) by constraining credit.

THE GREENBACK AND SILVER MOVEMENTS

Many farmers in 1876 and 1880 supported the Greenback Party, whose platform called for the issuance of more U.S. Treasury notes (greenbacks). Even more popular was the movement for "free silver." Until 1873 government mints had coined both silver and gold dollars at a ratio of 16 to 1—that is, 16 ounces of silver were equal in value to one ounce of gold. However, when new discoveries of gold in the West after 1848 placed more gold in circulation relative to silver, that ratio undervalued silver, so that little was being sold for coinage. This was the principal reason for the law of 1873 demonetizing silver, except for small coins. Antideflationists later branded this law as "the Crime of 1873"—a conspiracy to destroy silver, the people's money, in favor of gold, the bankers' money.

Ironically, just when the law of 1873 was enacted, the production of new silver mines began to increase dramatically, which soon brought the price of silver below the old ratio of 16 to 1. Silver miners joined with farmers to demand a return to silver dollars. In 1878 Congress responded by passing, over President Hayes's veto, the Bland-Allison Act requiring the Treasury to purchase and coin not less than $2 million nor more than $4 million of silver monthly. Once again, silver dollars flowed from the mint, but those amounts failed to absorb the increasing production of silver and did little, if anything, to slow deflation. The market price of silver dropped to a ratio of 20 to 1.

Pressure for "free silver"—that is, for government purchase of all silver offered for sale at a price of 16 to 1 and its coinage into silver dollars—continued through the 1880s. The admission of five new western states in 1889 and 1890 contributed to the passage of the Sherman Silver Purchase Act in 1890. That act increased the amount of silver coinage, but not at the 16-to-1 ratio. Even so, it went too far to suit "gold bugs" who wanted to keep the United States on the international gold standard.

President Cleveland blamed the Panic of 1893 on the Sherman Silver Purchase Act, which caused

HE MUST BE KEPT OUT.

UNCLE SAM.—Consarn ye! you 've spoiled my Senate and House of Representatives, but I 'll never let you get into the White House that 's all I 've got left to depend on !

A "GOLD BUG" CARTOON This cartoon shows Uncle Sam guarding the White House from the angry forces of "free silver" bearing plans for "dishonest money"—the demand for unlimited coinage of silver dollars at a ratio of 16 to 1 with gold.

a run on the Treasury's gold reserves triggered by uncertainty over the future of the gold standard. Cleveland called a special session of Congress in 1893 and persuaded it to repeal the Sherman Silver Purchase Act, setting the stage for the most bitter political contest in a generation.

THE FARMERS' ALLIANCE

Agrarian reformers supported the free silver movement, but many had additional grievances concerning problems of credit, railroad rates, and the exploitation of workers and farmers by the "money power." A new farmers' organization emerged in the 1880s, starting in Texas as the Southern Farmers' Alliance and expanding into other southern states and the North. By 1890 it had evolved into the National Farmers' Alliance and Industrial Union, which was affiliated with the Colored Farmers' Alliance, and also with the Knights of Labor.

Reaching out to two million farm families, the Alliance set up marketing cooperatives to eliminate the middlemen who profited as "parasites" on the backs of farmers. The Alliance served the social needs of farm families as well as their economic needs. Alliance farm families came together in what one historian has termed a "movement culture" that helped overcome their isolation, especially in the sparsely settled regions of the West. The Alliance also gave farmers a sense of pride and solidarity to counter the image of "hick" and "hayseed" being purveyed by an increasingly urban American culture.

The Farmers' Alliance developed a comprehensive political agenda. At a national convention in Ocala, Florida, in December 1890, it set forth these objectives: (1) a graduated income tax; (2) direct election of U.S. senators (instead of election by state legislatures); (3) free and unlimited coinage of silver at a ratio of 16 to 1; (4) effective government control and, if necessary, ownership of railroad, telegraph, and telephone companies; and (5) the establishment of "subtreasuries" (federal warehouses) for the storage of crops, with government loans at 2 percent interest on those crops. The most important of these goals, especially for southern farmers, was the subtreasuries. Government storage would allow farmers to hold their crops until market prices were more favorable. Low-interest government loans on the value of these crops would enable farmers to pay their annual debts and thus escape the ruinous interest rates of the crop lien system in the South and bank mortgages in the West.

These were radical demands for the time. Nevertheless, most of them eventually became law: the income tax and the direct election of senators by constitutional amendments in 1913; government control of transportation and communications by various laws in the 20th century; and the subtreasuries in the form of the Commodity Credit Corporation in the 1930s.

Anticipating that the Republicans and the Democrats would resist these demands, many Alliancemen were eager to form a third party. In Kansas they had already done so, launching the People's Party (whose members were known as Populists) in the summer of 1890. Southerners, mostly Democrats, opposed the idea of a third party for fear that it might open the way for the return of the Republican Party to power—with the Reconstruction bogey of "Negro rule." That this antiblack position could coexist alongside the Alliance's affiliation with black farmers suggests the schizophrenic nature of southern politics at the time.

In 1890 farmers helped elect numerous state legislators and congressmen who pledged to support their cause, but the legislative results were thin. By 1892 many Alliance members were ready to take the third-party plunge. The two-party system seemed fossilized and unable to respond to the explosive problems of the 1890s.

THE RISE AND FALL OF THE PEOPLE'S PARTY

By 1892 the discontent of farmers in the West and South had reached the fever stage. Enthusiasm for a third party was particularly strong in the plains and mountain states, five of which had been admitted since the last presidential election: North and South Dakota, Montana, Wyoming, and Idaho. The most prominent leader of the Farmers' Alliance was Leonidas L. Polk of North Carolina. A Confederate veteran, Polk commanded support in the West as well as in the South. He undoubtedly would have been nominated for president by the newly organized People's Party had not death cut short his career at the age of 55 in June 1892.

The first nominating convention of the People's Party met at Omaha a month later. The preamble of their platform expressed the grim mood of delegates. "We meet in the midst of a nation brought to the verge of moral, political, and material ruin," it declared. "The fruits of the toil of millions are boldly stolen to build up colossal fortunes for a few. . . . From the same prolific womb of governmental injustice we breed the two great classes—tramps and millionaires." The platform itself called for unlimited coinage of silver at 16 to 1; creation of the subtreasury program for crop storage and farm loans; government ownership of railroad, telegraph, and telephone companies; a graduated income tax; direct election of senators; and laws to protect labor unions against prosecution for strikes and boycotts. To ease the lingering tension between southern and western farmers, the party nominated Union veteran James B. Weaver of Iowa for president and Confederate veteran James G. Field of Virginia for vice president.

Despite winning 9 percent of the popular vote and 22 electoral votes, Populist leaders were shaken by the outcome. In the South most of the black farmers who were allowed to vote stayed with the Republicans. Democratic bosses in several southern states dusted off the racial demagoguery and intimidation machinery of Reconstruction days to keep white farmers in line for the party of white supremacy. Only in Alabama and Texas, among southern states, did the Populists get more than 20 percent of the vote. They did even worse in the older agricultural states of the Midwest, where their share of the vote ranged from 11 percent in Minnesota down to 2 percent in Ohio. Only in distressed wheat states such as Kansas, Nebraska, and the Dakotas and in the silver states of the West did the Populists do well, carrying Kansas, Colorado, Idaho, and Nevada.

The party remained alive, however, and the anguish caused by the Panic of 1893 seemed to boost its prospects. In several western states, Populists or a Populist-Democratic coalition controlled state governments for a time, and a Populist-Republican coalition won the state elections of 1894 in North Carolina.

President Cleveland's success in getting the Sherman Silver Purchase Act repealed in 1893 drove a wedge into the Democratic Party. Southern and western Democrats turned against Cleveland. In what was surely the most abusive attack on a president ever delivered by a member of his own party, Senator Benjamin Tillman of South Carolina told his constituents in 1894: "When Judas betrayed Christ, his heart was not blacker than this scoundrel, Cleveland, in deceiving the Democracy. He is an old bag of beef and I am going to Washington with a pitchfork and prod him in his fat ribs."

THE SILVER ISSUE

Democratic dissidents stood poised to take over the party in 1896. They adopted free silver as the centerpiece of their program. This stand raised

"*If the gold standard advocates win, this country will be dominated by the financial harpies of Wall Street. I am trying to save the American people from that disaster—which will mean the enslavement of the farmers, merchants, manufacturers, and laboring classes to the most merciless and unscrupulous gang of speculators on earth—the money power. . . . We have petitioned, and our petitions have been scorned; we have entreated, and our entreaties have been disregarded; we have begged, and they have mocked when our calamity came. We beg no longer; we entreat no more; we petition no more. We defy them. . . . If they dare to come out in the open . . . we will fight them to the uttermost. Having behind us the producing masses of this nation and the world, supported by the commercial interests, the laboring interest, and the toilers everywhere, we will answer their demand for a gold standard by saying to them: You shall not press down upon the brow of labor this crown of thorns, you shall not crucify mankind upon a cross of gold.*"

WILLIAM JENNINGS BRYAN
1896 presidential campaign speech

AN ANTI-BRYAN CARTOON, 1896 This cartoon in *Judge* magazine, entitled "The Sacrilegious Candidate," charged William Jennings Bryan with blasphemy in his "Cross of Gold" speech at the Democratic national convention. Bryan grinds his Bible into the dust with his boot while waving a crown of thorns and holding a cross of gold. In the background a bearded caricature of an anarchist dances amid the ruins of a church and other buildings.

possibilities for a fusion with the Populists, who hoped the Democrats would adopt other features of their platform as well. Meanwhile, out of the West came a new and charismatic figure, a silver-tongued orator named William Jennings Bryan, whose shadow would loom large across the political landscape for the next generation. A one-term congressman from Nebraska, Bryan had taken up the cause of free silver. He came to the Democratic convention in 1896 as a young delegate—only 36 years old. Given the opportunity to make the closing speech in the debate on the silver plank in the party's platform, Bryan brought the house to its feet in a frenzy of cheering with his peroration: "You shall not press down upon the brow of labor this crown of thorns, you shall not crucify mankind upon a cross of gold."

This speech catapulted Bryan into the presidential nomination. He ran on a platform that not only endorsed free silver but also embraced the idea of an income tax, condemned trusts, and opposed the use of injunctions against labor. Bryan's nomination created turmoil in the People's Party. Though some Populists wanted to continue as a third party, most of them saw fusion with silver Democrats as the road to victory. At the Populist convention, the fusionists got their way and endorsed Bryan's nomination. In effect, the Democratic whale swallowed the Populist fish in 1896.

THE ELECTION OF 1896

The Republicans nominated William McKinley, who would have preferred to campaign on his specialty, the tariff. Bryan made that impossible. Crisscrossing the country in an unprecedented whistle-stop campaign covering 18,000 miles, Bryan gave as many as 30 speeches a day, focusing almost exclusively on the free silver issue. Republicans responded by denouncing the Democrats as irresponsible inflationists. Free silver, they said, would mean a 57-cent dollar and would demolish the workingman's gains in real wages achieved over the preceding 30 years.

Under the skillful leadership of Ohio businessman Mark Hanna, chairman of the Republican National Committee, McKinley waged a "front-porch campaign" in which various delegations visited his home in Canton, Ohio, to hear carefully crafted speeches that were widely publicized in the mostly Republican press. Hanna sent out an army of speakers and printed pamphlets in more than a dozen languages to reach immigrant voters. His propaganda portrayed Bryan as a wild man from the prairie whose monetary schemes would further wreck an economy that had been plunged into depression during a Democratic administration. McKinley's election, by contrast, would maintain the gold standard, revive business confidence, and end the depression.

The 1896 election was the most impassioned and exciting in a generation. Many Americans believed that the fate of the nation hinged on the outcome. The number of voters jumped by 15 percent

LINK TO THE PAST

The Election of 1896

http://jefferson.village.virginia.edu/seminar/unit8/home.htm

This site contains images, cartoons, text, biographical information, documents, and related links about the pivotal election of 1896.

1. Judging from their platforms, what did the three parties (Republicans, Democrats, and Populists) stand for in this election? In particular, whom did each party blame for the economic depression in which the country was mired at the time of the election?

2. Analyze the cartoons and other illustrations portraying William Jennings Bryan, William McKinley, and Mark Hanna. What kind of image of these men did the media of the time convey?

3. What clues in the documents and other material in this site help to explain why McKinley carried all of the states east of the Mississippi River and north of the Ohio River and Mason-Dixon line? Why did Bryan carry most of the rest?

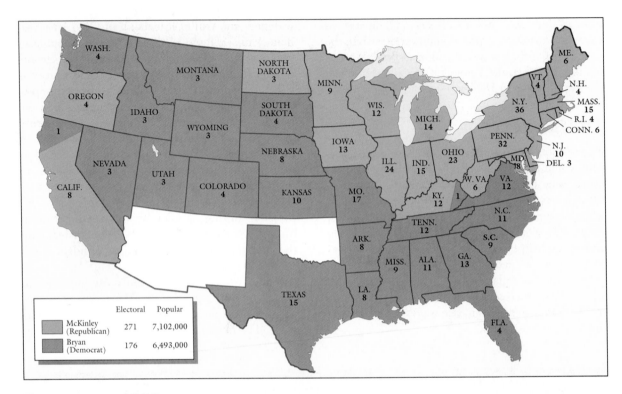

		Electoral	Popular
	McKinley (Republican)	271	7,102,000
	Bryan (Democrat)	176	6,493,000

ELECTION OF 1896

over 1892. The sectional pattern of South and West versus Northeast and North Central was almost as pronounced as the North–South split of 1860. Republicans won a substantial share of the urban, immigrant, and labor vote by arousing fear about the Democratic 57-cent dollar and by inspiring hope with the slogan of McKinley as "the advance agent of prosperity." McKinley rode to a convincing victory by carrying every state in the northeast quadrant of the country. Bryan carried most of the rest. Republicans won decisive control of Congress as well as the presidency. They would maintain control for the next 14 years. The election of 1896 marked a crucial turning point in American political history away from the stalemate of the preceding two decades.

Whether by luck or by design, McKinley did prove to be the advance agent of prosperity. The economy pulled out of the depression during his first year in office and entered into a long period of growth—not because of anything the new administration did (except perhaps to encourage a revival of confidence) but because of the mysterious workings

of the business cycle. With the discovery of rich new gold fields in the Yukon, in Alaska, and in South Africa, the silver issue lost potency and a cascade of gold poured into the world economy. The long deflationary trend since 1865 reversed itself in 1897. Farmers entered a new—and unfamiliar—era of prosperity. Bryan ran against McKinley again in 1900 but lost even more emphatically. The nation seemed embarked on a placid sea of plenty. But below the surface, the currents of protest and reform that had boiled up in the 1890s still ran strong. They would soon surface again.

CONCLUSION

The 1890s were a major watershed in American history. On the past side of that divide lay a largely rural society and agricultural economy, and on the future side lay the cities and a commercial-industrial economy. Before the 1890s most immigrants had come from northern and western Europe, and many became farmers. Later immigrants largely came from eastern and southern

Europe, and nearly all settled in cities. Before the 1890s the old sectional issues associated with slavery, the Civil War, and Reconstruction remained important forces in American politics; after 1900 racial issues would not play an important part in national politics for another 60 years. The election of 1896 ended 20 years of even balance between the two major parties and led to more than a generation of Republican dominance.

Most important of all, the social and political upheavals of the 1890s shocked many people into recognition that the liberty and equality they had taken for granted as part of the American dream was in danger of disappearing before the onslaught of wrenching economic changes that had widened and deepened the gulf between classes. The strikes and violence and third-party protests of the decade were a wake-up call. As the forces of urbanization and industrialism increased during the ensuing two decades, many middle-class Americans supported greater government power to carry out progressive reforms to cure the ills of an industrializing society.

Suggested Readings begin on page SR-1.
For web activities and resources
related to this chapter, go to http://
www.harcourtcollege.com/history/murrin

CHAPTER 20

AN INDUSTRIAL SOCIETY,
1890–1920

THE CITY FROM GREENWICH VILLAGE

This 1922 painting by John Sloan, one of America's foremost early 20th-century painters, captures both the enormous expanse and night-time vitality of New York City. Cities such as New York were the most dynamic centers of business and culture during America's industrial age.

With the collapse of populism in 1896 and the end of the depression in 1897, the American economy embarked on a remarkable stretch of growth. By 1910 America was unquestionably the world's greatest industrial power.

Corporations were changing the face of America. Their railroad and telegraph lines crisscrossed the country. Their factories employed millions. Their production and management techniques became the envy of the industrialized world. A new kind of building—the skyscraper—came to symbolize America's corporate power. These modern towers were made possible by the use of steel rather than stone framework and by the invention of electrically powered elevators. Impelled upward by rising real estate values, they were intended to evoke the same sense of grandeur as Europe's medieval cathedrals. But these monuments celebrated man, not God; material wealth, not spiritual riches; science, not faith; corporations, not the commonweal. Reaching into the sky, dwarfing Europe's cathedrals, they were convincing embodiments of America's worldly might.

This chapter explores how the newly powerful corporations transformed America: how they revolutionized production and management; how the jobs they generated attracted millions of European immigrants, southern blacks, and young single women to northern cities; and how they triggered an urban cultural revolution that made amusement parks, dance halls, vaudeville theater, and movies integral features of American life.

The power of the corporations dwarfed that of individual wage earners, but wage earners sought to limit the power of corporations through labor unions and strikes, and by organizing institutions of collective self-help within their own ethnic or racial communities. Many found opportunities and liberties they had not known before. Immigrant entrepreneurs invented ways to make money through legal and illegal enterprise; young, single, working-class women pioneered a sexual revolution; and radicals dared to imagine building a new society where no one suffered from poverty, inequality, and powerlessness. The power of the new corporations, in other words, did not go unchallenged. Even so, a more egalitarian society would prove difficult to attain.

This chapter will focus on the following major questions:

- How did corporations and workers respond to the social and economic turmoil of the late 19th century?

CHRONOLOGY

1897	Depression ends; prosperity returns
1899	Theodore Roosevelt urges Americans to live the "strenuous life"
1890s	Football becomes the sport of choice in Ivy League • Young women put away their corsets
1900–14	Immigration averages more than one million per year
1901	U.S. Steel is formed from 200 separate companies • Andrew Carnegie devotes himself to philanthropic pursuits • 1 of every 400 railroad workers dies on the job
1904	20 percent of the North's industrial population lives below poverty line
1905	*Lochner* v. *New York:* Supreme Court declares unconstitutional a New York state law limiting the workday of bakery employees • Industrial Workers of World (IWW) founded
1907	Henry Ford unveils his Model T
1907–11	73 of every 100 Italian immigrants return to Italy
1909	Immigrants and their children comprise more than 96 percent of labor force building and maintaining railroads
1910	Black skilled tradesmen in northern cities reduced to 10 percent of total skilled trades workforce • 20,000 nickelodeons dot northern cities
1911	Triangle Shirtwaist Company fire kills 146 workers • Frederick Winslow Taylor publishes *The Principles of Scientific Management*
1913	Henry Ford introduces the first moving assembly line; employee turnover reaches 370 percent a year • 66 men, women, and children killed in "Ludlow massacre" • John D. Rockefeller establishes Rockefeller Foundation
1914	Henry Ford introduces the five-dollar-a-day wage • Theda Bara, movies' first sex symbol, debuts • *The Masses,* a radical journal, begins publication
1919	Japanese farmers in California sell $67 million in agricultural goods, 10 percent of state's total
1920	Nation's urban population outstrips rural population for first time
1921	1,250,000 Model Ts sold, a sixteenfold increase over 1912

- Why did American elites become obsessed with physical and racial fitness? How did this obsession affect attitudes toward immigrants and blacks?
- What hardships and successes did immigrants experience in America? How does the immigrant experience compare to that of African Americans?
- What explains the rise of the New Woman and Feminism?

SOURCES OF ECONOMIC GROWTH

A series of technological innovations in the late 19th century fired up the nation's economic engine, but technological breakthroughs alone do not fully explain the nation's spectacular economic boom. New corporate structures and new management techniques—in combination with the new technology—created the conditions that powered economic growth.

TECHNOLOGY

Two of the most important new technologies were the harnessing of electric power and the invention of the gasoline-powered internal combustion engine. Scientists had long been fascinated by electricity, but only in the late 19th century did they find ways to make it practically useful. The work of Thomas Edison, George Westinghouse, and Nikola Tesla produced the incandescent bulb that brought electric lighting into homes and offices and the alternating current (AC) that made electric transmission possible over long distances. From 1890 to 1920 the proportion of American industry powered by electricity rose from virtually nil to almost one-third. Older industries switched from expensive and cumbersome steam power to more efficient and cleaner electrical power. New sectors of the metalworking and machine-tool industries arose in response to the demand for electric generators and related equipment. Between 1900 and 1920 virtually every major city built electric-powered transit systems to replace horse-drawn trolleys and carriages. By 1912, some 40,000 miles of electric railway and trolley track had been laid. In New

WOOLWORTH BUILDING New York City's 60-story Woolworth Building (1913) was, at the time, the world's tallest and most elegant skyscraper. The shape and ornamentation of the building's spire resembled the Gothic architecture of Europe's medieval churches. Many called Woolworth the "Cathedral of Commerce."

ULM CATHEDRAL Thirteenth-century Ulm Cathedral in Ulm, Germany, is a representative example of a medieval Gothic church. A glance at its vertical lines, intricate detail, and grandeur reveals how the Gothic style influenced the architecture of the Woolworth Building.

York City electricity made possible the construction of the first subways. Electric lighting—on city streets, in department store windows, in brilliantly lit amusement parks such as New York's Coney Island—gave cities a new allure. The public also fell in love with the movies, which depended on electricity to project images onto a screen. Electric power, in short, stimulated capital investment and accelerated economic growth.

The first gasoline engine was patented in the United States in 1878, and the first "horseless carriages" began appearing on European and American roads in the 1890s, but few thought of them as serious rivals to trains and horses. Rather, they were seen as playthings for the wealthy, who liked to race them along country roads.

In 1900 Henry Ford was just an eccentric 37-year-old mechanic who built race cars in Michigan.

In 1909, Ford unveiled his Model T: an unadorned, even homely car, but reliable enough to travel hundreds of miles without servicing and cheap enough to be affordable to most working Americans. Ford had dreamed of creating an automobile civilization with his Model T, and Americans began buying his car by the millions. The stimulus this insatiable demand gave to the economy can scarcely be exaggerated. Millions of cars required millions of pounds of steel alloys, glass, rubber, petroleum, and other material. Millions of jobs in coal and iron-ore mining, oil refining and rubber manufacturing, steelmaking and machine tooling, road construction and service stations came to depend on automobile manufacturing.

Leading Industries

Cotton Goods	Sugar Refining	Marble and Stone Products
Copper Refining	Paper	Woolen Goods
Lumber Products	Shipbuilding	Diversified
Meatpacking	Automobiles	Rubber Products
Brass and Copper Products	Butter	Petroleum Refining
Leather Goods	Clothing	Lead Smelting
Iron and Steel	Products for Railroads	
Flour Mill Products	Tobacco Products	

Distribution of Factory Output, 1919
in thousands

Over $3,000,000
$1,000,000 to $2,999,000
$500,000 to $999,000
$100,000 to $499,000
Less than $99,000

Cities
○ Value of product over $1 billion
• Value of product over $200 million

INDUSTRIAL AMERICA, 1900–1920

CORPORATE GROWTH

Successful inventions such as the automobile required more than the mechanical ingenuity and social vision of inventors like Henry Ford. They relied on corporations with sophisticated organizational and technical know-how to mass-produce and mass-distribute the newly invented products. Corporations had played an important role in the nation's economic life since the 1840s, but in the late 19th and early 20th centuries they underwent significant changes. The most obvious change was

CHANGE IN DISTRIBUTION OF THE AMERICAN WORKFORCE, 1870–1920

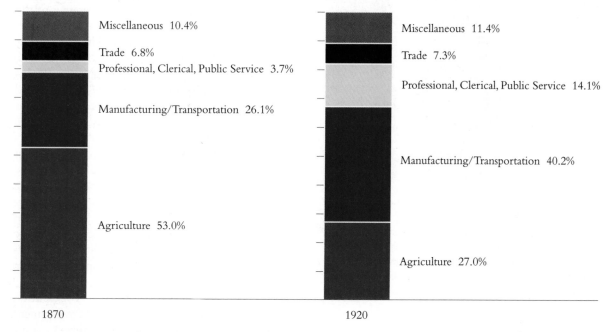

1870

Miscellaneous 10.4%

Trade 6.8%

Professional, Clerical, Public Service 3.7%

Manufacturing/Transportation 26.1%

Agriculture 53.0%

1920

Miscellaneous 11.4%

Trade 7.3%

Professional, Clerical, Public Service 14.1%

Manufacturing/Transportation 40.2%

Agriculture 27.0%

Source: Data from Alba Edwards, *Comparative Occupational Statistics for the United States 1870–1940*, U.S. Bureau of the Census, *Sixteenth Census of the United States, 1940, Population* (Washington, D.C., 1943).

in their size. Employment in Chicago's International Harvester factory, where agricultural implements were built, nearly quadrupled from 4,000 in 1900 to 15,000 in 1916. Delaware's DuPont Corporation, a munitions and chemical manufacturer, employed 1,500 workers in 1902 and 31,000 workers in 1920. Founded with a few hundred employees in 1903, the Ford Motor Company employed 33,000 at its Detroit Highland Park plant by 1916 and 42,000 by 1924. That same year, the 68,000 workers employed at Ford's River Rouge plant (just outside Detroit) made it the largest factory in the world.

This growth in scale was in part a response to the enormous domestic market. By 1900 railroads provided the country with an efficient transportation system that allowed corporations to ship goods virtually anywhere in the United States. A national network of telegraph lines allowed constant communication between buyers and sellers separated by thousands of miles. And the population, which was expanding rapidly, demonstrated an ever-growing appetite for goods and services.

MASS PRODUCTION AND DISTRIBUTION

Manufacturers responded to this burgeoning domestic market by developing mass-production techniques that increased production speed and lowered unit costs. Mass production often meant replacing skilled workers with machines that were coordinated to permit high-speed, uninterrupted production at every stage of the manufacturing process. Mass-production techniques had become widespread in basic steel manufacturing and sugar refining by the 1890s, and they spread to the machine-tool industry and automobile manufacturing in the first two decades of the 20th century.

Such production techniques were profitable only if large quantities of output could be sold. Although the domestic market offered a vast potential for sales, manufacturers often found distribution systems inadequate. This was the case with North Carolina smoking tobacco manufacturer James Buchanan Duke, who almost single-handedly transformed the cigarette into one of the best-selling

AN EARLY CIGARETTE ADVERTISEMENT (1885–1900)
This particular advertisement—including three trading cards, each featuring an attractive female stage star—was aimed at theatergoers, who were encouraged to "light up" between acts. Ads such as this were part of an intensive promotional campaign to generate interest in smoking among a consuming public unaccustomed to the practice.

commodities in American history. In 1885, at a time when relatively few Americans smoked, Duke invested in several Bonsack cigarette machines, each of which manufactured 120,000 cigarettes a day. To create a market for the millions of cigarettes he was producing, Duke advertised his product aggressively throughout the country. He also established regional sales offices so that his sales representatives could keep in touch with local jobbers and retailers. As cigarette sales skyrocketed, more and more corporations sought to emulate Duke's techniques. Over the course of the next 20 years, those corporations that integrated mass production and mass distribution, as Duke did in the 1880s, came to define American "big business."

CORPORATE CONSOLIDATION

Corporate expansion also reflected a desire to avoid market instability. The rapid industrial growth of the late 19th century had proved deeply unsettling to industrialists. As promising economic opportunities arose, more and more industrialists sought to take advantage of them, but overexpansion and increasingly furious competition often turned rosy prospects into less-than-rosy results. Buoyant booms were quickly followed by bankrupting busts.

Soon, corporations began looking for ways to insulate themselves from the harrowing course of the business cycle.

The railroads led the way in tackling this problem. Rather than engaging in ruinous rate wars, railroads began cooperating. They shared information on costs and profits, established standardized rates, and allocated discrete portions of the freight business among themselves. These cooperative arrangements were variously called "pools," "cartels," or "trusts." The 1890 Sherman Antitrust Act declared such cartel-like practices illegal, but the law's enforcement proved to be short-lived (see chapter 19). Still, the railroads' efforts rarely succeeded for long because they depended heavily on voluntary compliance. During difficult economic times, the temptation to lower freight rates and exceed one's market share could become too strong to resist.

Corporations' efforts to restrain competition and inject order into the economic environment continued unabated, however. Mergers now emerged as the favored instrument of control. By the 1890s powerful and sophisticated investment bankers, such as J. P. Morgan, possessed both the capital and the financial skills to engineer the complicated stock transfers and ownership renegotiations that mergers required. James Duke again led the way in 1890 when he and four competitors merged to form the American Tobacco Company. Over the next eight years the quantity of cigarettes produced by Duke-controlled companies quadrupled, from one billion to almost four billion per year. Moreover, American Tobacco used its powerful position in cigarette manufacture to achieve dominance in pipe tobacco, chewing tobacco, and snuff manufacture as well.

The merger movement intensified as the depression of the 1890s lifted. In the years from 1898 to 1904, many of the corporations that would dominate American business throughout most of the 20th century acquired their modern form: Armour and Swift in meatpacking, Standard Oil in petroleum, General Electric and Westinghouse in electrical manufacture, American Telephone and Telegraph in communications, International Harvester in the manufacture of agricultural implements, and DuPont in munitions and chemical processing. The largest merger occurred in steel in 1901, when

Andrew Carnegie and J. P. Morgan together fashioned the U.S. Steel Corporation from 200 separate iron and steel companies. U.S. Steel, with its 112 blast furnaces and 170,000 steelworkers, controlled 60 percent of the country's steelmaking capacity. Moreover, its 78 iron-ore boats and 1,000 miles of railroad gave it substantial control over procuring raw materials and distributing finished steel products.

REVOLUTION IN MANAGEMENT

The dramatic growth in the number and size of corporations revolutionized corporate management. The ranks of managers mushroomed, as elaborate corporate hierarchies defined both the status and the duties of individual managers. Increasingly, senior managers took over from owners the responsibility for long-term planning. Day-to-day operations fell to numerous middle managers who oversaw particular departments (purchasing, research, production, labor) in corporate headquarters, or who supervised regional sales offices or directed particular factories. Middle managers also managed the people—accountants, clerks, foremen, engineers, salesmen—in these departments, offices, or factories. The rapid expansion within corporate managerial ranks created a new middle class, intensely loyal to their employers but at odds both with blue-collar workers and with the older middle class of shopkeepers, small businessmen, and independent craftsmen.

As management techniques grew in importance, companies tried to make them more scientific. Firms introduced rigorous cost-accounting methods into purchasing and other departments charged with controlling the inflow of materials and the outflow of goods. Many corporations began requiring college or university training in science, engineering, or accounting for entry into middle management. Corporations that had built their success on a profitable invention or discovery sought to maintain their competitive edge by creating research departments and hiring professional scientists—those with doctorates from American or European universities—to come up with new technological and scientific breakthroughs. Such departments were modeled on the industrial research laboratory set up by the

inventor-entrepreneur Thomas Edison in Menlo Park, New Jersey, in 1876.

SCIENTIFIC MANAGEMENT ON THE FACTORY FLOOR

The most controversial and, in some respects, the most ambitious effort to introduce scientific practices into management occurred in production. Managers understood that the premium mass production placed on speed and efficiency could be magnified through improvements in factory organization as well as through technological innovation. So, in league with engineers, they sought optimal arrangements of machines and deployments of workers that would achieve the highest speed in production with the fewest human or mechanical interruptions. Some of these managers, such as Frederick Winslow Taylor, the chief engineer at Philadelphia's Midvale Steel Company in the 1880s, styled themselves as the architects of scientific management. They methodically examined every human task and mechanical movement involved in each production process. In "time-and-motion studies," they recorded every distinct movement a worker made in performing his or her job, how long it took, and how often it was performed. They hoped thereby to identify and eliminate wasted human energy. Eliminating waste might mean reorganizing an entire floor of machinery so as to reduce "down time" between production steps; it might mean instructing workers to perform their tasks differently; or it might mean replacing uncooperative skilled workers with machines tended by unskilled, low-wage laborers. Regardless of the method chosen, the goal was the same: to make human labor emulate the smooth and apparently effortless operation of an automatic, perfectly calibrated piece of machinery.

Taylor shared his vision widely in the early 20th century, first through speeches to fellow engineers and managers, and then through his writings. By the time he published *The Principles of Scientific Management* (1911), his ideas had already captivated countless corporate managers and engineers, many of whom sought to introduce "Taylorism" into their own production systems.

Introducing scientific management practices rarely proceeded easily. Time-and-motion studies were costly, and Taylor's formulas for increasing efficiency and reducing waste often were far less scientific than he claimed. Taylor also overestimated workers' willingness to play the mechanical role he assigned them; the skilled workers and general foremen, whom Taylor sought to eliminate, used every available means of resistance. In the end, managers and engineers who persisted in their efforts to apply scientific management invariably modified Taylor's principles.

Henry Ford's engineers initially adopted Taylorism wholeheartedly and with apparent success. By 1910 they had broken down automobile manufacturing into a series of simple, sequential tasks. Each worker performed only one task—adding a carburetor to an engine, inserting a windshield, mounting tires onto wheels. Then, in 1913 Ford's engineers introduced the first moving assembly line, a continuously moving conveyor belt that carried cars in production through each workstation. This innovation eliminated precious time previously wasted in transporting car parts (or partially built cars) by crane or truck from one work area to another. It also sharply limited the time available to workers to perform their assigned tasks. Only the foreman, not the workers, could stop the line or change its speed.

The continuous assembly line helped actualize the potential of the factory's many other organizational and mechanical innovations. By 1913 the Ford Motor Company's new Highland Park plant was the most tightly integrated and continuously moving production system in manufacturing. The pace of production exceeded all expectations. Between 1910 and 1914 production time on Ford Model Ts dropped by 90 percent, from an average

THE WORLD'S FIRST AUTOMOBILE ASSEMBLY LINE Introduced by Henry Ford at his Highland Park plant in 1913, this innovation cut production time on Ford Model Ts by an astounding 90 percent, allowing Ford to reduce the price of his cars by more than half and to double the hourly wages of his workers.

of more than 12 hours per car to 1.5 hours. A thousand Model Ts began rolling off the assembly line each day. This striking increase in the rate of production enabled Ford to slash the price of a Model T from $950 in 1909 to only $295 in 1923, a reduction of 70 percent. The number of Model Ts purchased by Americans increased sixteenfold between 1912 and 1921, from 79,000 to 1,250,000. The assembly line quickly became the most admired—and most feared—symbol of American mass production.

Problems immediately beset the system, however. Repeating a single motion all day long induced mental stupor, and managerial efforts to speed up the line produced physical exhaustion—both of which increased the incidence of error and injury. Some workers tried to organize a union to gain a voice in production matters, but most Ford workers expressed their dissatisfaction simply by quitting. By 1913 employee turnover at Highland

Park had reached the astounding rate of 370 percent a year. At that rate, Ford had to hire 51,800 workers every year just to keep his factory fully staffed at 14,000.

A problem of that magnitude demanded a dramatic solution. Ford provided it in 1914 by raising the wage he paid his assembly-line workers to five dollars a day, double the average manufacturing wage then prevalent in American industry. The result: Workers, especially young and single men, flocked to Detroit. Highland Park's high productivity rate permitted Ford to absorb the wage increase without cutting substantially into profits.

Taylor himself had believed that improved efficiency would lead to dramatic wage gains. With his decision to raise wages, Ford was being true to Taylor's principles, but Ford went even further in his innovations. He set up a sociology department, forerunner of the personnel department, to collect job, family, and other information about his employees. He sent social workers into workers' homes to inquire into (and "improve") their personal lives. For the foreign-born, he instituted Americanization classes. He offered his employees housing subsidies, medical care, and other benefits. In short, Ford recognized that workers were more complex than Taylor had allowed, and that high wages alone would not transform them into the perfectly functioning parts of the mass-production system that Taylor had envisioned.

Although Ford's success impelled others to move in his direction, it would take time for modern management to come of age. Not until the 1920s did a substantial number of corporations establish personnel departments, institute welfare and recreational programs for employees, and hire psychologists to improve human relations in the workplace.

MODEL T PRICES AND SALES, 1909–1923

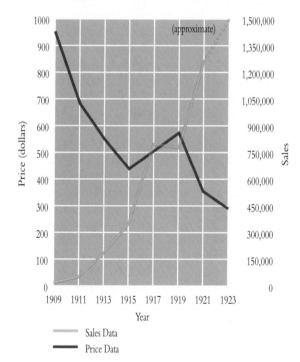

Source: From Alfred D. Chandler, Jr., ed., *Giant Enterprise: Ford, General Motors, and the Automobile Industry* (New York: Harcourt, Brace and World, 1964), pp. 32–33.

"ROBBER BARONS" NO MORE

Innovations in corporate management were part of a broader effort among elite industrialists to shed their "robber baron" image. The swashbuckling entrepreneurs of the 19th century—men such as Cornelius Vanderbilt, Jay Gould, and Leland Stanford—had wielded their economic power brashly

LEADING INDUSTRIALIST PHILANTHROPIC FOUNDATIONS, 1905–1930

Foundation	Date of Origin	Original Endowment
Buhl Foundation	1927	$ 10,951,157
Carnegie Corporation of New York	1911	125,000,000
Carnegie Endowment for International Peace	1910	10,000,000
Carnegie Foundation for the Advancement of Teaching	1905	10,000,000
Carnegie Institution of Washington	1902	10,000,000
Duke Endowment	1924	40,000,000
John Simon Guggenheim Memorial Foundation	1925	3,000,000
W. K. Kellogg Foundation	1930	21,600,000
Rockefeller Foundation	1913	100,000,000
Rosenwald Fund	1917	20,000,000
Russell Sage Foundation	1907	10,000,000

Source: Joseph C. Kiger, *Operating Principles of the Larger Foundations* (New York: Russell Sage Foundation, 1957), p. 122.

and ruthlessly, while lavishing money on European-style palaces, private yachts, personal art collections, and extravagant entertainments. But the depression of the 1890s—along with the populist political movement and labor protests such as the Homestead and Pullman strikes—shook the confidence of members of this elite. Industrialists were terrified when in 1892 anarchist Alexander Berkman marched into the office of Henry Clay Frick, Andrew Carnegie's right-hand man, and shot him at point-blank range (Frick survived). Although such physical assaults were rare, anger over ill-gotten and ill-spent wealth was widespread. In the 1890s, a storm of indignation forced Mrs. Bradley Martin and her husband to flee to England after she spent $370,000 (roughly $3.5 million in 2001 dollars) on an evening of entertainment for her friends in New York's "high society."

Seeking a more favorable image, some industrialists began to restrain their displays of wealth and use their private fortunes to advance the public welfare. As early as 1889 Andrew Carnegie had advocated a "gospel of wealth." The wealthy, he believed, should consider all income in excess of their needs as a "trust fund" for their communities. In 1901, the year in which he formed U.S. Steel, Carnegie withdrew from industry and devoted himself to philanthropic pursuits, especially in art and education. By the time he died in 1919, he had given away or entrusted to several Carnegie foundations 90 percent of his fortune. Among the proj-

ects he funded were New York's Carnegie Hall, Pittsburgh's Carnegie Institute (now Carnegie-Mellon University), and 2,500 public libraries throughout the country.

Other industrialists, including John D. Rockefeller, soon followed Carnegie's lead. Rockefeller, a devout Baptist with an ascetic bent, had never flaunted his wealth (unlike the Vanderbilts and others), but his ruthless business methods in assembling the Standard Oil Company and in crushing his competition made him one of the most reviled of the robber barons. In the wake of journalist Ida Tarbell's stinging 1904 exposé of Standard Oil's business practices, and of the federal government's subsequent prosecution of Standard Oil for monopolistic practices in 1906, Rockefeller transformed himself into a public-spirited philanthropist. Between 1913 and 1919 his Rockefeller Foundation dispersed an estimated $500,000,000. His most significant gifts included money to establish the University of Chicago and the Rockefeller Institute for Medical Research (later renamed Rockefeller University). His charitable efforts did not escape criticism, however; many Americans interpreted them as an attempt to establish control over American universities, scientific research, and public policy. Still, Rockefeller's largesse helped build for the Rockefeller family a reputation for public-spiritedness and good works, a reputation that grew even stronger in the 1920s and 1930s. Many other business leaders, such as Julius Rosenwald of Sears Roebuck, and

Daniel and Simon Guggenheim of the American Smelting and Refining Company, also dedicated themselves to philanthropy during this time.

OBSESSION WITH PHYSICAL AND RACIAL FITNESS

The fractious events of the 1890s also induced many wealthy Americans to engage in what Theodore Roosevelt dubbed "the strenuous life." In an 1899 essay with that title, Roosevelt exhorted Americans to live vigorously, to test their physical strength and endurance in competitive athletics, and to experience nature through hiking, hunting, and mountain climbing. He articulated a way of life

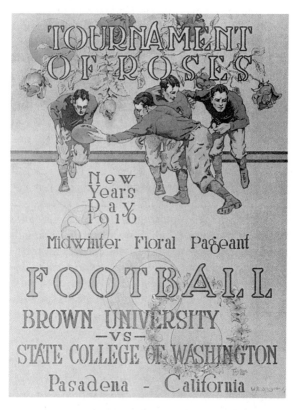

BROWN UNIVERSITY GOES TO THE ROSE BOWL
Seeking to demonstrate their physical prowess and racial fitness, the sons of the nation's elite took up the rough game of football. In the early years of this century, Ivy League schools such as Brown fielded some of the country's best teams.

that influenced countless Americans from a variety of classes and cultures.

The 1890s were indeed a time of heightened enthusiasm for competitive sports, physical fitness, and outdoor recreation. Millions of Americans began riding bicycles and eating healthier foods. A passion for athletic competition gripped American universities. The power and violence of football helped make it the sport of choice at the nation's elite campuses, and for 20 years Ivy League schools were the nation's football powerhouses. In athletic competition, as in nature, one could discover and recapture one's manhood, one's virility. The words "sissy" and "pussyfoot" entered common usage in the 1890s as insults hurled at men whose masculinity was found wanting.

Ironically, this quest for masculinity had a liberating effect on women, who had been barred from strenuous outdoor activity of any sort by Victorian moral codes. In the vigorous new climate of the 1890s, young women began to engage in sports and other activities long considered too manly for "the fragile sex." They put away their corsets and long dresses and began wearing simple skirts, shirtwaists, and other clothing that gave them more comfort and freedom of movement. By the standards of the 1920s, these gentle changes would seem mild, but in the 1890s, they were radical indeed.

In the country at large the new enthusiasm for athletics and the outdoor life reflected a widespread dissatisfaction with the growing regimentation of industrial society. Among wealthy Americans the quest for physical superiority reflected a deeper and more ambiguous anxiety: their *racial* fitness. Most of them were native-born Americans whose families had lived in the United States for several generations and whose ancestors had come from the British Isles, the Netherlands, or some other region of northwestern Europe. They liked to attribute their success and good fortune to their "racial superiority." They saw themselves as "natural" leaders, members of a noble Anglo-Saxon race endowed with uncommon intelligence, imagination, and discipline. But events of the 1890s had challenged the legitimacy of the elite's wealth and authority, and the ensuing depression mocked their ability to exert economic leadership. The immigrant masses laboring in factories, despite their poverty and alleged racial inferiority, seemed to possess a vitality that the "superior" Anglo-Saxons lacked. Immigrant families were overflowing with children. The city neighborhoods where they lived exhibited social and cultural energy (especially apparent in their popular entertainments—vaudeville, amusement parks, nickelodeons, and dance halls) missing in the sedate environs of the wealthy.

Some rich Americans, such as Henry Adams, Henry Cabot Lodge, and other members of Boston's declining political elite, reacted to the immigrants' vigor and industry by calling for a halt to further immigration. Not the ebullient Roosevelt; he argued instead for a return to fitness, superiority, and numerical predominance of the Anglo-Saxon race. He called on American men to live the strenuous life and on women to devote themselves to reproduction. The only way to avoid "race suicide," he declared, was for every American mother to have at least four children.

Such racialist thought was not limited to wealthy elites. Many other Americans, from a variety of classes and regions, also thought that all people demonstrated the characteristics of their race. Racial stereotypes served to describe not only blacks, Asians, and Hispanics, but Italians ("violent"), Jews ("nervous"), and Slavs ("slow"). Such aspersions flowed as easily from the pens of compassionate reformers such as Jacob Riis, who wanted to help the immigrants, as from the pens of bitter reactionaries such as Madison Grant, who argued in *The Passing of the Great Race* (1916) that America should rid itself of inferior races.

SOCIAL DARWINISM

Racialist thinking even received "scientific" sanction from distinguished biologists and anthropologists, who believed that racially inherited traits explained variations in the economic, social, and cultural lives of ethnic and racial groups. Many of the nation's intellectuals believed that human society developed according to the "survival of the fittest" principle articulated by the English naturalist Charles Darwin to describe plant and animal evolution. Human history could be understood in terms of an ongoing struggle among races, with the strongest and the fittest invariably triumphing. The wealth and power of the Anglo-Saxon race was ample testimony, in this view, to its superior fitness.

This view, which would become known as "Social Darwinism," was rooted in two developments of the late 19th century, one intellectual and one socioeconomic. Intellectually, it reflected a widely shared belief that human society operated according to principles every bit as scientific as those governing the natural world. The 19th century had been an age of stunning scientific breakthroughs. The ability of biologists, chemists, and physicists to penetrate the mysteries of the natural world generated great confidence in science, in people's ability to know and control their physical environment. That confidence, in turn, prompted intellectuals to apply the scientific method to the human world. The social sciences—economics, political science, anthropology, sociology, psychology—took shape in the late 19th century, each trying to discover the scientific laws governing individual and group behavior. Awed by the accomplishments of natural scientists, social scientists were prone to exaggerate the degree to which social life mimicked natural life; hence the appeal of Social Darwinism, a philosophy that allegedly showed how closely the history of human beings resembled the history of animal evolution.

Social Darwinism was also rooted in the unprecedented interpenetration of the world's economies and peoples. Cheap and rapid ocean travel had bound together continents as never before. International trade, immigration, and imperial conquest made Americans more conscious of the variety of peoples inhabiting the earth. Although awareness of diversity sometimes encourages tolerance and cooperation, in the economically depressed years of the late 19th century, it encouraged intolerance and suspicion, fertile soil for the cultivation of Social Darwinism.

IMMIGRATION

Perhaps the most dramatic evidence of the nation's growing involvement in the international economy was the high rate of immigration. The United States had always been a nation of immigrants, but never had so many come in so short a time. Between 1880 and 1920, some 23 million immigrants came to a country that numbered only 76 million in 1900. From 1900 to 1914 an average of one million immigrants arrived each year. In many cities of the

*I work, and I work, without rhyme, without
reason—
produce, and produce, and produce without
end.
For what? and for whom? I don't know, I
don't wonder
—since when can a whirling machine
comprehend?
No feelings, no thoughts, not the least
understanding;
this bitter, this murderous drudgery drains
the noblest, the finest, the best and the
richest, the deepest, the highest that living
contains.
Away rush the seconds, the minutes and
hours;
each day and each night like a wind-driven
sail;
I drive the machine, as though eager to catch
them,
I drive without reason—no hope, no avail.*

MORRIS ROSENFELD
*a Jewish immigrant lamenting in poetic form the
"murderous drudgery" of New York sweatshop work,
circa 1890s (translated from the Yiddish)*

IMMIGRANTS AND THEIR CHILDREN AS A PERCENTAGE OF THE POPULATION OF SELECTED CITIES, 1920

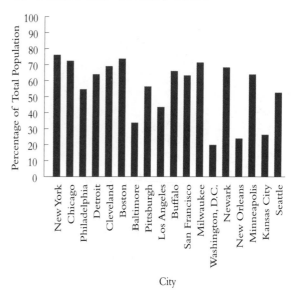

Source: Data from U.S. Department of Commerce, Bureau of the Census, *Fourteenth Census of the United States, 1920, Population* (Washington, D.C.).

Northeast and Midwest, immigrants and their children comprised a majority of the population. In 1920s Boston, New York City, Chicago, and Milwaukee they accounted for more than 70 percent of the total population; in Buffalo, Detroit, and Minneapolis, more than 60 percent; and in Philadelphia, Pittsburgh, and Seattle more than 50 percent. Everywhere in the country, except in the South, the working class was overwhelmingly ethnic.

European immigration accounted for approximately three-fourths of the total. Some states received significant numbers of non-European immigrants—Chinese, Japanese, and Filipinos in California; Mexicans in California and the South-west; and French Canadians in New England. Although their presence profoundly affected regional economies, politics, and culture, their numbers, relative to the number of European immigrants, were small. The U.S. government refused to admit Chinese immigrants after 1882 and Japanese male immigrants after 1907 (see chapter 22). Although immigrants from Latin America were free to enter the United States throughout this period, few did until 1910, when the social disorder caused by the Mexican Revolution propelled a stream of refugees to southwestern parts of the United States. One-half million French Canadians had migrated to New England and the upper Midwest between 1867 and 1901. After that the rate slowed as the pace of industrialization in their Quebec homeland quickened.

Most of the European immigrants who arrived between 1880 and 1914 came from eastern and southern Europe. Among them were three to four million Italians, two million Russian and Polish Jews, two million Hungarians, an estimated four million Slavs (including Poles, Bohemians, Slovaks,

SOURCES OF IMMIGRATION

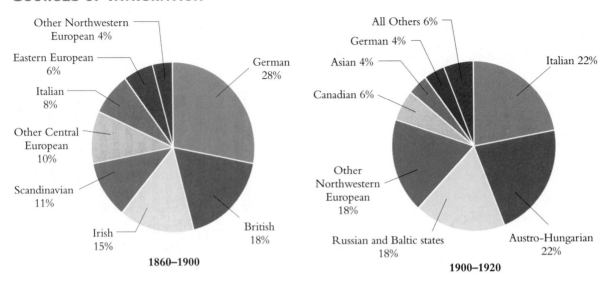

Other Northwestern European 4%
Eastern European 6%
Italian 8%
Other Central European 10%
Scandinavian 11%
Irish 15%
German 28%
British 18%

1860–1900

All Others 6%
German 4%
Asian 4%
Canadian 6%
Other Northwestern European 18%
Russian and Baltic states 18%
Italian 22%
Austro-Hungarian 22%

1900–1920

Source: Data from *Historical Statistics of the United States, Colonial Times to 1970* (White Plains, N.Y.: Kraus International, 1989), pp. 105–109.

Russians, Ukrainians, Bulgarians, Serbians, Croatians, Slovenians, Montenegrins, and Macedonians), and one million from Lithuania, Greece, and Portugal. Hundreds of thousands came as well from Turkey, Armenia, Lebanon, Syria, and other Near Eastern lands abutting the European continent.

These post-1880 arrivals were called "new immigrants" to underscore the cultural gap separating them from the "old immigrants," who had come from northwestern Europe—Great Britain, Scandinavia, and Germany. "Old immigrants" were regarded as racially fit, culturally sophisticated, and politically mature. The "new immigrants," by contrast, were often regarded as racially inferior, culturally impoverished, and incapable of assimilating American values and traditions. This negative view of the "new immigrants" reflected in part a fear of their alien languages, religions, and economic backgrounds. Few spoke English. Most adhered to Catholicism, Greek Orthodoxy, or Judaism rather than Protestantism. Most, with the exception of the Jews, were peasants, unaccustomed to urban industrial life. But they were not as different from the "old immigrants" as the label implied. For example, many of the earlier-arriving Catholic peasants from Ireland and Germany had had no more familiarity

with American values and traditions than did the Italians and Slavs who arrived later.

CAUSES OF IMMIGRATION

In fact, the "old" and "new" European immigrants were more similar than different. Both came to America for the same reasons: either to flee religious or political persecution or to escape economic hardship. It is true that the United States attracted a small but steady stream of political refugees throughout the 19th century: labor militants from England; nationalists from Ireland; socialists and anarchists from Germany, Russia, Finland, and Italy. Many of these people possessed unusual talents as skilled workers, labor organizers, political agitators, and newspaper editors and thus exercised considerable influence in their ethnic communities. However, only the anti-Semitic policies of Russia in the late 19th and early 20th centuries triggered a mass emigration (in this case Jewish) of political refugees.

Most mass immigration was propelled instead by economic hardship. Europe's rural population was growing at a faster rate than the land could support. European factories absorbed some, but not all, of

Chinese and Japanese Immigrants in the West

As many as 300,000 Chinese immigrants arrived in the United States between 1851 and 1882, and more than 200,000 Japanese immigrants journeyed to Hawaii and the western continental United States between 1891 and 1907. The two photos on the right illustrate these groups' contributions to key western industries—railroad building and large-scale commercial agriculture.

Chinese and Japanese newcomers might have formed two of America's largest immigrant groups, but the U.S. government began to exclude Chinese immigrants in 1882 and Japanese immigrants in 1907. The government also interpreted a 1790 law to mean that Chinese and Japanese immigrants were ineligible for citizenship. These exclusions remained in force until the 1940s and 1950s.

Some of the fiercest opponents of Asian immigration were native-born workers, who were angered by an alleged Asian willingness to do any job, irrespective of the conditions or pay. The illustration below depicts one artist's fear that the Chinese would even take over women's jobs and thus undermine the sacred 19th century notion that men and women should not do similar kinds of work. In the West, anti-Asian prejudice rivaled antiblack prejudice in its virulence.

Despite discrimination, Asian immigrants developed economic niches—the Japanese in fruit and vegetable farms and the Chinese in small urban businesses (such as commercial laundries)—that allowed some among them to achieve middle-class status and income.

the rural surplus. And industrialization and urbanization were affecting the European countryside in ways that disrupted rural ways of life. As railroads penetrated the countryside, village artisans found themselves unable to compete with the cheap manufactured goods that arrived from city factories. These handicraftsmen were among the first to emigrate. Meanwhile, rising demand for food in the cities accelerated the growth of commercial agriculture in the hinterland. Some peasant families lost their land. Others turned to producing crops for the market, only to discover that they could not compete with larger, more efficient producers. In addition, by the last third of the 19th century, peasants faced competition from North American farmers. Prices for agricultural commodities plummeted everywhere. The economic squeeze that spread distress among American farmers in the 1880s and 1890s caused even more hardship among Europe's peasantry, and many of them decided to try their luck in the New World.

PATTERNS OF IMMIGRATION

An individual's or family's decision to emigrate often depended on having a contact—a family member, relative, or fellow villager—already established in an American city. These were people who provided immigrants with a destination, with inspiration (they were examples of success in America), with advice about jobs, and with financial aid. Sometimes whole villages in southern Italy or western Russia—or at least all the young men—seemed to disappear, only to reappear in a certain section of Chicago, Pittsburgh, or New York. Villages without contacts in the United States were relatively unaffected by the emigration mania.

A majority of immigrants viewed their trip to the United States as a temporary sojourn. They came not in search of permanent settlement but in search of the high wages that would enable them to improve their economic standing in their homeland. For them, America was a land of economic opportunity, not a land to call home. This attitude explains why men vastly outnumbered women and children in the migration stream. From 1899 to 1910, three-fourths of the immigrants from southern and eastern Europe were adult men. Some had left wives and children behind; more were single. Most wanted merely to make enough money to buy a farm in their native land. And, true to their dream, many did return home. For every 100 Italian immigrants who arrived in the United States between 1907 and 1911, for example, 73 returned to Italy. An estimated 60 to 80 percent of all Slavic immigrants eventually returned to the land of their birth.

The rate of return was negligible among certain groups, however. Jews had little desire to return to the religious persecution they had fled. Most came as families, intending to make America their permanent home. Only 5 percent of them returned to Europe. The rate of return was also low among the Irish, who saw few opportunities in their long-suffering (though much-loved) Emerald Isle. In the early 20th century, however, such groups were exceptional. Most immigrants looked forward to returning to Europe. Not until the First World War shut down transatlantic travel did most immigrants begin to regard their presence in the United States as permanent.

Immigration tended to move in rhythm with the U.S. business cycle. It rose in boom years and fell off during depressions. It remained at a high level during the first 14 years of the new century when the U.S. economy experienced sustained growth broken only by the brief Panic of 1907–1908.

IMMIGRANT LABOR

In the first decade of the 20th century, immigrant men and their male children constituted 70 percent of the workforce in 15 of the 19 leading U.S. industries. They concentrated in industries where work was the most backbreaking. Immigrants built the nation's railroads and tunnels; mined its coal, iron ore, and other minerals; stoked its hot and sometimes deadly steel furnaces; and slaughtered and packed its meat in Chicago's putrid packinghouses. In 1909 first- and second-generation immigrants—especially Greeks, Italians, Japanese, and Mexicans—comprised more than 96 percent of the labor force that built and maintained the nation's railroads. Of the 750,000 Slovaks who arrived in America before 1913, at least 600,000 headed for the coal mines and steel mills of western Pennsylvania. The

CHILD LABOR In addition to immigrant laborers, the American economy made extensive use of child laborers, even ones as young as the little girl photographed by Lewis Hine in this Louisiana oyster factory.

steel mills of Pittsburgh, Buffalo, Cleveland, and Chicago attracted disproportionately large numbers of Poles and other Slavs as well.

Immigrants also performed "lighter" but no less arduous work. Jews and Italians predominated in the garment manufacturing shops of New York City, Chicago, Philadelphia, Baltimore, and Boston. In 1900 French Canadian immigrants and their children held one of every two jobs in New England's cotton textile industry. By 1920 the prosperity of California's rapidly growing agricultural industry depended primarily on Mexican and Filipino labor. In these industries, immigrant women and children, who worked for lower wages than men, formed a large part of the labor force. Few states restricted child labor. More than 25 percent of boys and 10 percent of girls aged 10 to 15 were "gainfully employed."

Immigrants were as essential as fossil fuels to the smooth operation of the American economic machine. Sometimes, however, the "machine" consumed workers as well as coal and oil. Those who

worked in heavy industry, mining, or railroading were especially vulnerable to accident and injury. In 1901, for instance, 1 in every 400 railroad workers died on the job and 1 in every 26 suffered injury. Between the years 1906 and 1911, almost one-quarter of the recent immigrants employed at the U.S. Steel Corporation's South Works (Pittsburgh) were injured or killed on the job. Lax attention to safety rendered even light industry hazardous and sometimes fatal. In 1911 a fire broke out on an upper floor of the Triangle Shirtwaist Company, a New York City garment factory. The building had no fire escapes. The owners of the factory, moreover, had locked the entrances to each floor as a way of keeping their employees at work. A total of 146 workers, mostly young Jewish and Italian women, perished in the fire or from desperate nine-story leaps to the pavement below.

Chronic fatigue and inadequate nourishment increased the risk of accident and injury. Workweeks averaged 60 hours—10 hours every day except Sunday. Workers who were granted Saturday afternoons

TRIANGLE SHIRTWAIST COMPANY FIRE In 1911, a fire at the Triangle Shirtwaist Company in New York City claimed the lives of 146 workers, most of them young Jewish and Italian women. Many died because they could not escape the flames. The building had no fire escapes, and their employer had locked the entrances to each floor. The tragedy spurred the growth of unions and the movement for factory reform in New York.

off—thus reducing their workweek to a "mere" 55 hours—considered themselves fortunate. Steelworkers were not so lucky. They labored from 72 to 89 hours a week, and were required to work one 24-hour shift every two weeks.

Most workers had to labor long hours simply to eke out a meager living. In 1900 the annual earnings of American manufacturing workers averaged only $400 to $500 a year. Skilled jobs offered immigrants far more (as much as $1,500 to $2,000 a year), but most of them were held by Yankees and by the Germans, Irish, Welsh, and other Europeans who had come as part of the "old immigration." Through their unions, workers of northern European extraction also controlled access to new jobs that opened up and usually managed to fill them with a son, relative, or fellow countryman. Consequently, relatively few of the "new immigrants" rose into the prosperous ranks of skilled labor. In any case, employers were replacing many skilled workers with machines operated by cheaply paid operatives.

From the 1870s to 1910 real wages paid to factory workers and common laborers did rise, but not steadily. Wages fell sharply during depressions. And the hope for sharp increases during periods of recovery collapsed under the weight of renewed mass immigration, which brought hundreds of thousands of new job seekers into the labor market. One out of every five industrial workers was unemployed, even during the boom years of the early 20th century.

Most working families required two or three wage earners to survive. If a mother could not go out to work because she had small children at home, she might rent rooms to some of the many single men who had recently immigrated. But economic security was hard to attain. In his book, *Poverty*, published in 1904, social investigator Robert Hunter conservatively estimated that 20 percent of the industrial population of the North lived in poverty.

LIVING CONDITIONS

Strained economic circumstances confined many working-class families to cramped and dilapidated living quarters. Many of them lived in two- or three-room apartments, with several sleeping in each room. To make ends meet, one immigrant New York City family of eight living in a two-room apartment took in six boarders. Some boarders considered themselves lucky to have their own bed. That luxury was denied the 14 Slovaks who shared eight beds in a small Pittsburgh apartment and the New York City printer who slept on a door he unhinged every night and balanced across two chairs. The lack of windows in city tenements allowed little light or air into these apartments, and few had their own toilets or running water. Crowding was endemic. The population density of New York City's Lower East Side—where most of the city's Jewish immigrants settled—reached 700 per acre in 1900, a density greater than that of the poorest sections of Bombay, India. Overcrowding and poor sanitation resulted in high rates of deadly infectious diseases, especially diphtheria, typhoid fever, and pneumonia.

By 1900 this crisis in urban living had begun to yield to the insistence of urban reformers that cities adopt housing codes and improve sanitation. Between 1880 and 1900, housing inspectors condemned the worst of the tenements and ordered landlords to make improvements. City governments built reservoirs, pipes, and sewers to carry clean water to the tenements and to carry away human waste. Newly paved roads lessened the dirt, mud, and stagnant pools of water and thus further curtailed the spread of disease. As a result, urban mortality rates fell in the 1880s and 1890s.

Nevertheless, improvements came far more slowly to the urban poor than they did to the middle and upper classes. Cities such as Pittsburgh built extensive systems of paved roads in wealthy districts but not in working-class areas. Water supplies and pressures were far better in prosperous than in poor neighborhoods. At the outbreak of the First World War, many working-class families still lacked running water in their homes.

BUILDING ETHNIC COMMUNITIES

The immigrants may have been poor, but they were not helpless. Migration itself had required a good deal of resourcefulness, self-help, and mutual aid—assets that survived in the new surroundings of American cities.

A NETWORK OF INSTITUTIONS

Each ethnic group quickly established a network of institutions that supplied a sense of community and multiplied sources of communal assistance. Some people simply reproduced those institutions that had been important to them in the "Old Country." The devout established churches and synagogues. Lithuanian, Jewish, and Italian radicals reestablished Old World socialist and anarchist organizations. Irish nationalists set up clandestine chapters of the Clan Na Gael to keep alive the struggle to free Ireland from the English. Germans felt at home in their traditional *Turnevereins* (athletic clubs) and musical societies.

Immigrants developed new institutions as well. In the larger cities, foreign-language newspapers disseminated news, advice, and culture. Each ethnic group created fraternal societies to bring together immigrants who had known each other in the Old Country, or who shared the same craft, or who had come from the same town or region. Most of these societies provided members with a death benefit (ranging from a few hundred to a thousand dollars) that guaranteed the deceased a decent burial and the family a bit of cash. Some fraternal societies made small loans as well. Among those ethnic groups that prized home ownership, especially the Slavic groups, the fraternal societies also provided mortgage money. And all of them served as centers of sociability—places to have a drink, play cards, or simply relax with fellow countrymen. The joy, solace, and solidarity they generated helped countless immigrants to adjust to American life.

THE EMERGENCE OF AN ETHNIC MIDDLE CLASS

Within each ethnic group, a sizable minority directed their talents and ambitions to economic gain. Some of these entrepreneurs first addressed their communities' needs for basic goods and services. Immigrants preferred to buy from fellow countrymen with whom they shared a language, a history, and presumably a bond of trust. Enterprising individuals responded by opening dry goods stores, food shops, butcher shops, and saloons in their ethnic neighborhoods. Those who could not afford to rent a store hawked their fruit, clothing, or dry goods from portable stands, wagons, or sacks carried on their back. The work was endless, the competition tough. Men often enlisted the entire family—wife, older children, younger children—in their undertakings. Few family members were ever paid for their labor, no matter how long or hard they worked. Although many of these small businesses failed, enough survived to give some immigrants and their children a toehold in the middle class.

Other immigrants turned to small industry, particularly garment manufacture, truck farming, and construction. A clothing manufacturer needed only a few sewing machines to become competitive. Many Jewish immigrants, having been tailors in Russia and Poland, opened such facilities. If a rented space proved beyond their means, they set up shop in their own apartment. Competition among these small manufacturers was fierce, and work environments were condemned by critics as "sweatshops." Workers suffered inadequate lighting, heat, and ventilation; 12-hour workdays and 70-hour workweeks during peak seasons, with every hour spent bent over a sewing machine; and poor pay and no employment security, especially for the women and children who made up a large part of this labor force. Even at this level of exploitation, many small manufacturers failed, but over time, a good many of them managed to firm up their position as manufacturers and to evolve into stable, responsible employers. Their success contributed to the emergence of a Jewish middle class.

The story was much the same in urban construction, where Italians who had established themselves as labor contractors, or *padroni*, went into business for themselves to take advantage of the rapid expansion of American cities. Though few became general contractors on major downtown projects, many of them did well building family residences or serving as subcontractors on larger buildings.

One who did make the leap from small to big business was Amadeo P. Giannini, the son of Italian immigrants, who used his savings from a San Francisco fruit and vegetable stand to launch a career in banking. Determined to make bank loans available and affordable to people of ordinary means, Giannini generated a huge business in small loans. Expanding on this strong base, he eventually made his bank—the Bank of America—into the country's largest financial institution.

In southern California, Japanese immigrants chose agriculture as their route to the middle class. Working as agricultural laborers in the 1890s, they began to acquire their own land in the early years of the 20th century. Altogether, they owned only 1 percent of California's total farm acreage. Their specialization in fresh vegetables and fruits (particularly strawberries), combined with their family-labor-intensive agricultural methods, was yielding $67 million in annual revenues by 1919—one-tenth of the total California agriculture revenue that year. Japanese farmers sold their produce to Japanese fruit and vegetable wholesalers in Los Angeles, who had chosen a mercantile route to middle-class status.

Each ethnic group created its own history of economic success and social mobility. From the emerging middle classes came many leaders who would provide their ethnic groups with identity, legitimacy, and power and would lead the way toward Americanization and assimilation. Their children tended to do better in school than the children of working-class ethnics, and academic success served as a ticket to upward social mobility in a society that depended more and more on university-trained engineers, managers, lawyers, doctors, and other professionals.

POLITICAL MACHINES AND ORGANIZED CRIME

The underside of this success story was the rise of government corruption and organized crime. Many ethnic entrepreneurs operated on the margins of economic failure and bankruptcy, and some accepted the help of those who promised financial assistance. Sometimes the help came from honest unions and upright government officials, but other times it did not. Unions were generally weak, and some government officials, themselves lacking experience and economic security, were susceptible to bribery. Economic necessity became a breeding ground for government corruption and greed. A contractor eager to win a city contract—to build a trolley system, a sewer line, or a new city hall, for example—would find it necessary to "pay off" government officials who could throw the contract his way. By 1900 such payments, referred to as "graft," had become essential to the day-to-day operation of government in most large cities. The graft, in turn, made local officeholding a rich source of economic gain. Politicians began building political organizations called machines to guarantee their success in municipal elections. The machine "bosses" used a variety of legal and illegal means to bring victory on election day. They won the loyalty of urban voters—especially immigrants—by providing poor neighborhoods with paved roads and sewer systems. They helped newly arrived immigrants find jobs (often on city payrolls) and occasionally provided food, fuel, or clothing to families in dire need. Many of their clients were grateful for these services in an age when government itself provided little public assistance.

The bosses who ran the political machines—including "King Richard" Croker in New York, James Michael Curley in Boston, Tom Pendergast in Kansas City, Martin Behrman in New Orleans, and Abe Ruef in San Francisco—served their own needs first. They saw to it that construction contracts went to those who offered the most graft, not to those likely to do the best job. They protected gamblers, pimps, and other purveyors of urban vice who contributed large amounts to their machine coffers. They often required city employees to contribute to their campaign chests, to solicit political contributions, and to get out the vote on election day. And they engaged in widespread election fraud: rounding up truckloads of newly arrived immigrants and paying them to vote a certain way; having their supporters vote two or three times; and stuffing ballot boxes with the votes of phantom citizens who had died, moved away, or never been born.

Big city machines, then, were both positive and negative forces in urban life. Reformers despised them for disregarding election laws and encouraging vice. Many immigrants valued them for providing social welfare services and for creating opportunities for upward mobility.

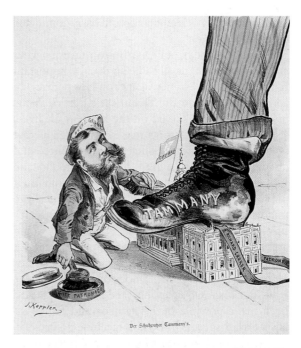

"KEEPING TAMMANY'S BOOTS SHINED" This 1880s cartoon by Joseph Keppler declares that the real boss of New York City was not its elected mayor, Hugh Graham, here depicted as a lowly shoe-shiner, but the Tammany Hall political machine itself. The loose strap underneath the boot, used to control both City Hall and Tammany, belongs to Richard Croker, Tammany's leader from 1886 to 1901.

The history of President John F. Kennedy's family offers a compelling example of the economic and political opportunities opened up by machine politics. Both of Kennedy's grandfathers, John Francis ("Honey Fitz") Fitzgerald and Patrick Joseph Kennedy, were the children of penniless Irish immigrants who arrived in Boston in the 1840s. Fitzgerald was the more talented of the two. He excelled at academics and won a coveted place in Harvard's Medical School, but left Harvard that same year, choosing a career in politics instead. Between 1891 and 1905 Fitzgerald served as a Boston city councilor, Massachusetts state congressman and senator, U.S. congressman, and mayor of Boston. For much of this period, he derived considerable income and power from his position as the North End ward boss, where he supervised the trading of jobs for votes and favors for cash in his section of Boston's Democratic and Irish-dominated political machine.

Patrick Kennedy, an East Boston tavern owner and liquor merchant, became an equally important figure behind the scenes in Boston city politics. In addition to running the Democratic Party's affairs in Ward Two, he served on the Strategy Board, a secret council of Boston's machine politicians that met regularly to devise policies, settle disputes, and divide up the week's graft. Both Fitzgerald and Kennedy derived a substantial income from their political work and used it to lift their families into middle-class prosperity. Kennedy's son (and the future president's father), Joseph P. Kennedy, would go on to make a fortune as a Wall Street speculator and liquor distributor and to groom his sons for Harvard and the highest political offices in the land. But his rapid economic and social ascent had been made possible by his father's and father-in-law's earlier success in Boston machine politics.

Underworld figures, too, influenced urban life. In the early years of the 20th century, gangsterism was a scourge of Italian neighborhoods, where Sicilian immigrants had established outposts of the notorious Mafia, and in Irish, Jewish, Chinese, and other ethnic communities as well. Favorite targets of these gangsters were small-scale manufacturers and contractors, who were threatened with violence and economic ruin if they did not pay a gang for "protection." Gangsters enforced their demands with physical force, beating up or killing those who failed to abide by the "rules." Greedy for money, power, and fame, and willing to use any means necessary, these criminals considered themselves authentic entrepreneurs cut from the American mold. By the 1920s petty extortion had escalated in urban areas, and underworld crime had become big business. Al Capone, the ruthless Chicago mobster who made a fortune from gambling, prostitution, and bootleg liquor during Prohibition, once claimed: "Prohibition is a business. All I do is to supply a public demand. I do it in the best and least harmful way I can." New York City's Arnold Rothstein, whose financial sophistication won him a gambling empire and the power to fix the 1919 World Series, nurtured his reputation as "the J. P. Morgan of the underworld." Mobsters like Rothstein and Capone were charismatic figures, both in their ethnic communities and in the nation at large. Few immigrants, however, followed their criminal path to economic success.

AFRICAN AMERICAN LABOR AND COMMUNITY

Unlike immigrants, African Americans remained a predominately rural and southern people in the early 20th century. Most blacks were sharecroppers and tenant farmers. The markets for cotton and other southern crops had stabilized in the early 20th century, but black farmers remained vulnerable to exploitation. Landowners, most of whom were white, often forced sharecroppers to accept artificially low prices for their crops. At the same time, they charged high prices for seed, tools, and groceries at the local stores that they controlled. Few rural areas generated enough business to support more than one store, or to create a competitive climate that might force prices down. Those sharecroppers who traveled elsewhere to sell their crops or purchase their necessities risked retaliation—either physical assaults by white vigilantes or eviction from their land. Thus, most remained beholden to their landowners, mired in poverty and debt.

Some African Americans sought a better life by migrating to industrial areas of the South and the North. In the South, they worked in iron and coal mines, in furniture and cigarette manufacture, as railroad track layers and longshoremen, and as laborers in the steel mills of Birmingham, Alabama. By the early 20th century, their presence was growing in the urban North as well, where they worked on the fringes of industry as janitors, elevator operators, teamsters, longshoremen, and servants of various kinds. Altogether, about 200,000 blacks left the South for the North and West between 1890 and 1910.

In southern industries, blacks were subjected to hardships and indignities that even the newest immigrants were not expected to endure. Railroad contractors in the South, for example, treated their black track layers like prisoners. Armed guards marched them to work in the morning and back at night. Track layers were paid only once a month and forced to purchase food at the company commissary, where the high prices claimed most of

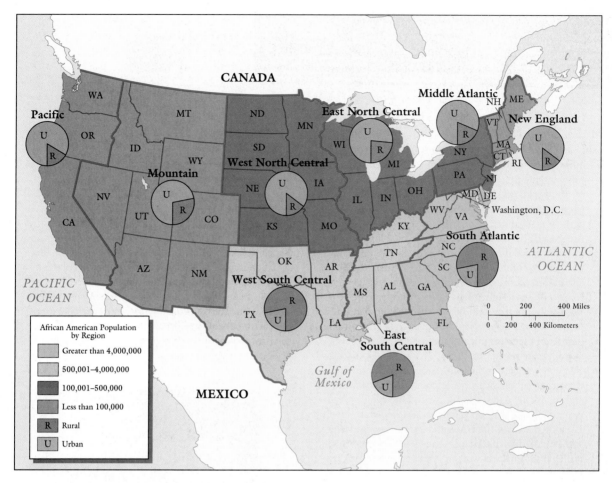

AFRICAN AMERICAN POPULATION, 1910

what they earned. Their belongings were locked up to discourage them from running away. Although discipline usually was less severe among other southern employers of black laborers, blacks often were isolated in the dirtiest and most grueling jobs. The "Jim Crow" laws passed by every southern state legislature in the 1890s legalized this rigid separation of the black and white races (see chapter 18).

Although northern states had no Jim Crow laws, the nation's worsening racial climate adversely affected southern blacks who came north. Industrialists generally refused to hire black migrants for manufacturing jobs, preferring the labor of European immigrants. Only when those immigrants went on strike did employers turn to African Amer-

icans. Black workers first gained a foothold in the Chicago meatpacking industry in 1904, when 28,000 ethnic packinghouse workers walked off their jobs. Employers hoped that the use of black strikebreakers would inflame racial tensions between white and black workers and thus undermine labor unity and strength.

African Americans who had long resided in northern urban areas also experienced intensifying discrimination in the late 19th and early 20th centuries. In 1870 about a third of the black men in many northern cities had been skilled tradesmen: blacksmiths, painters, shoemakers, and carpenters. Serving both black and white clients, these men enjoyed steady work and good pay, but by 1910 only 10 percent of black men made a living in this way.

The Great White Hope (1970)
**Directed by Martin Ritt. Starring James Earl Jones (Jack Jefferson)
and Jane Alexander (Eleanor Backman).**

This movie is a fictional retelling of the life of Jack Johnson, the first black heavyweight boxing champion of the world, and of the furor that his dominance of white boxers, his outspokenness, and his relationships with white women generated in early 20th-century America. The movie opens with white boxing promoters persuading a former white champion (James Bradley) to come out of retirement to battle the black champion, here called Jack Jefferson (rather than Johnson). In a subsequent scene, Jefferson destroys Bradley in the ring, and reacts with defiant cheeriness to the boos and racial epithets that rain down upon him from the predominately white crowd.

Jefferson refuses to accept any of the limitations that white society at the time placed on black men. He is neither submissive nor deferential toward whites, and he openly dates white women. One evening, federal agents burst in on Jefferson and his white lover, Eleanor Backman (Jane Alexander), and accuse Jefferson of violating the Mann Act, a 1910 law that made it illegal to transport women across state lines for sexual purposes (see pages 708 and 716). At Jefferson's trial, prosecutors expected to convince a jury that Backman was coerced into sex, for no white woman, they intended to argue, would have freely chosen to consort with a black man in this way.

Jefferson manages to evade the authorities and flee to Europe, where Backman joins him. The early months abroad are invigorating for both, as Jefferson is celebrated for his fighting prowess and the couple's love for each other flourishes. Soon, however, the opponents dry up, money stops coming in, and a sense of despair between the two of them grows. Their exile ends disastrously in Mexico where Backman kills herself after an argument with Jefferson. Jefferson, his spirit finally broken, agrees to throw a fight against the newest Great White Hope, Jess Willard, in return for an opportunity to end his fugitive status and return to the United States.

Made in 1970, the *Great White Hope* was inspired by the brash and unbowed heavyweight champion of the 1960s, Muhammad Ali. The film is quite faithful to the story of the real Jack Johnson, who dated white women, was arrested for "violating" the Mann Act, fled the country rather than submit to jail, and ultimately lost a heavyweight bout to Jess Willard. The film endows Backman, a fictional character, with more "class" and refinement than the real women who associated with Johnson usually possessed. The film also fictionalizes Johnson's fight against Willard by suggesting that Johnson could have won the fight had he not been required to throw it. Despite these changes, the film successfully recreates the climate of the early years of the 20th century and the white hostility imperiling a black man who dared to assert his pride and independence.

James Earl Jones as Jack Jefferson

In many cities, the number of barber shops and food catering businesses owned by blacks also went into sharp decline, as did black representation in the ranks of restaurant and hotel waiters. These barbers, food caterers, and waiters had formed a black middle class whose livelihood depended on the patronage of white clients. By the early 20th century, this middle class had been dissipated, the victim of growing racism. Whites were no longer willing to engage the services of blacks, preferring to have their hair cut, beards shaved, and food prepared and served by European immigrants. The residential segregation of northern blacks also rose in these years, as whites excluded them from more and more urban neighborhoods.

Although northern blacks at the turn of the 20th century had to cope with a marked deterioration in their working and living conditions, they did not lack for resourcefulness. Urban blacks laced their communities with the same array of institutions—churches, fraternal insurance societies, political organizations—that solidified ethnic neighborhoods. A new black middle class arose, comprised of ministers, professionals, and businesspeople who serviced the needs of their racial group. Black-owned real estate agencies, funeral homes, doctors' offices, newspapers, groceries, restaurants, and bars opened for business on the commercial thoroughfares of African American neighborhoods. Many businessmen had been inspired by the words of black educator Booker T. Washington, and specifically by his argument that blacks should devote themselves to self-help and self-sufficiency. Nevertheless, community-building remained a tougher task among African Americans than among immigrants. Black communities were often smaller and poorer than their white ethnic counterparts; economic opportunities were fewer, and the chance of gaining power or wealth through municipal politics almost nonexistent. Yet, some black entrepreneurs succeeded despite these odds. Madame C. J. Walker, for example, built a lucrative business from the hair and skin lotions she devised and sold to black customers throughout the country. In many cities, African American real estate agents achieved significant wealth and power. Still, most black businessmen could not overcome the obstacles posed by racial prejudice. Finding customers outside their own communities was much more difficult for them than for ethnic businessmen. Thus, the African American middle class remained smaller and more precarious than did its counterpart in ethnic communities, less able to lead the way toward affluence and assimilation.

WORKERS AND UNIONS

Middle-class success eluded most immigrants and blacks in the years prior to the First World War. Even among Jews, whose rate of social mobility was rapid, most immigrants were working class. For most workers, the path toward a better life lay in improving their working conditions, not in escape from the working class. Henry Ford's five-dollars-a-day wage, double the average manufacturing wage, raised the hopes of many. Young immigrant men, in particular, flocked to Detroit to work for Ford. But in the early decades of the century few other manufacturers were prepared to follow Ford's daring lead, and most factory workers remained in a fragile economic state.

SAMUEL F. GOMPERS AND THE AFL

For those workers, the only hope for economic improvement lay in organizing unions powerful enough to wrest wage concessions from reluctant employers. This was not an easy task. The furious, often violent labor protests of the Gilded Age had been put down. Labor organizations, such as the Knights of Labor, that had unified workers had been defeated. Federal and state governments, time and again, had shown themselves ready to use military force to break strikes. The courts, following the lead of the U.S. Supreme Court, repeatedly found unions in violation of the Sherman Antitrust Act, even though that act had been intended to control corporations, not unions. Judges in most states usually granted employer requests for injunctions—court orders that barred striking workers from picketing their place of employment (and thus from obstructing employer efforts to hire replacement workers). And prior to 1916 no federal laws protected the right of workers to organize or required employers to bargain with the unions to which their workers belonged.

MEN AT WORK This photo of male workers stoking a boiler conveys some of the grime and heat associated with much turn-of-the-century blue-collar work as well as the strength and concentration required of workmen.

This hostile legal environment retarded the growth of unions from the 1890s through the 1930s. It also made the major labor organization of those years, the American Federation of Labor (AFL), more timid and conservative than it had been prior to the depression of the 1890s. In the aftermath of that depression, the AFL poured most of its energy into organizing craft, or skilled, workers such as carpenters, typographers, plumbers, painters, and machinists. Because of their skills, these workers commanded more respect from employers than did the unskilled. Employers negotiated contracts, or trade agreements, with craft unions that stipulated the wages workers were to be paid, the hours they were to work, and the rules under which new workers would be accepted into the trade. These agreements were accorded the same legal protection that American law bestowed on other commercial contracts.

As the AFL focused on these "bread-and-butter" issues, it withdrew from the political activism that had once occupied its attention. It no longer agitated for governmental regulation of the economy and the workplace. The AFL had concluded that labor's powerful opponents in the legislatures and the courts would find ways to undermine whatever governmental gains organized labor managed to achieve. That conclusion was reinforced by a 1905 ruling, *Lochner* v. *New York*, in which the U.S. Supreme Court declared unconstitutional a seemingly innocent New York state law limiting bakery employees to a 10-hour day.

The AFL's "business" unionism took its most forceful expression from its president, Samuel F. Gompers. A onetime Marxist and cigarmaker who had helped found the AFL in 1886, Gompers was reelected to the AFL presidency every year from 1896 until his death in 1924. The AFL showed considerable vitality under his leadership, especially in the early years when its membership quadrupled from less than a half million in 1897 to more than two million in 1904. Aware of the AFL's growing significance and conservatism, the National Civic Federation, a newly formed council of corporate executives, agreed to meet periodically with the organization's leaders to discuss the nation's industrial and labor problems.

Nevertheless, the AFL had limited success. Its two million members represented only a small portion of the total industrial workforce. Its concentration among craft workers, moreover, distanced it from the majority of workers, who had no identifiable skill. Unskilled and semiskilled workers could only be organized into an industrial union that offered membership to all workers in a particular industry. Gompers understood the importance of such unions and allowed several of them to participate in the AFL. The most significant in the early 20th century were the United Mine Workers (UMW), the United Textile Workers, and the International Ladies Garment Workers Union (ILGWU). Within the AFL, these unions received support from socialist members, who were trying to make the organization more responsive to the needs of the unskilled

and semiskilled. Members of the conservative craft unions, however, resisted the socialists' efforts. Craftsmen's feelings of superiority over the unskilled were intensified by their ethnic background. Most were from "old immigrant" stock—particularly English, Scottish, German, and Irish—and they shared the common prejudice against immigrants from southern and eastern Europe.

The prejudice demonstrated by AFL members toward black workers was even worse. In the early 20th century, nine AFL unions explicitly excluded African Americans from membership, while several others accomplished the same goal by declaring blacks ineligible for union initiation rituals. National unions that did not officially discriminate often permitted their union locals to segregate African American workers in Jim Crow locals or to

LINK TO THE PAST

Samuel Gompers and the American Federation of Labor

http://www.inform.umd.edu/EdRes/Colleges/ARHU/Depts/History/Gompers/web1.html

The University of Maryland supports the Samuel Gompers Papers project in its efforts to collect and edit primary source material related to Gompers's career and to the union organization, the American Federation of Labor, he led for most of his adult life. The project has published two microfilm series of union papers and seven edited volumes of Gompers's papers. The Samuel Gompers Papers Web site offers sample documents and photos from the project's volumes and archive.

1. Select "Sample Documents" and read the letter Samuel Gompers sent to J. C. Skemp. What does Gompers's letter to Skemp tell you about the difficulties encountered in 1911 by black painters in Georgia who wanted to form a labor union? Why do you think white painters refused to allow black painters to join their union? Who had the power to grant black painters the right to form their own union? What is Gompers's view of the situation, and does he have enough power to enforce his will?

2. Select "Photos" and view "Handbill Re: SG's Visit to Colorado (1899)." What does this handbill reveal about how Americans who favored unions perceived Samuel Gompers?

bar them from membership altogether. The AFL's racist policies partially account for the shrinking numbers of black tradesmen between 1870 and 1910.

Nevertheless, white and black workers sometimes managed to set aside their suspicions of each other and cooperate. The UMW allowed black workers to join and to rise to positions of leadership. In New Orleans, black and white dockworkers constructed a remarkable experiment in biracial unionism that flourished from the 1890s through the early 1920s. Their unity gave them leverage in negotiations with their employers and allowed them to exercise a great deal of control over the conditions of work. But these moments of cooperation were rare.

Although blacks made up too small a percentage of the working class to build alternative labor organizations that would counteract the influence of the AFL, the "new immigrants" from eastern and southern Europe were too numerous to be ignored. Their participation in the UMW enabled that union to grow from only 14,000 in 1897 to more than 300,000 in 1914. In 1909 a strike of 20,000 women workers against the owners of New York City's garment factories inspired tens of thousands of workers, male and female, to join the ILGWU.

"BIG BILL" HAYWOOD AND THE IWW

When the AFL failed to help them organize, immigrants turned to other unions. The most important was the Industrial Workers of the World (IWW), founded by western miners in 1905 and led by the charismatic William "Big Bill" Haywood. The IWW rejected the AFL principle of craft organization, hoping instead to organize all workers into "one big union." It scorned the notion that only a conservative union could survive in American society, declaring its commitment to revolution instead. The IWW refused to sign collective bargaining agreements with employers, arguing that such agreements only trapped workers in capitalist property relations. Capitalism had to be overthrown through struggles between workers and their employers at the point of production.

The IWW was too radical and reckless ever to attract a mass membership. Although hundreds of

THE RADICAL CRITIQUE OF CAPITALISM This "Pyramid of the Capitalist System" humorously illustrates how radicals analyzed capitalism—as an economic system that oppressed workers, rewarded the wealthy, and worshipped money. In this pyramid, the police, political leaders, and clerics are all depicted as the opponents of workers and the servants of capital.

thousands of workers passed through its ranks or participated in its strikes, its regular membership rarely exceeded 20,000. Nevertheless, few organizations inspired as much awe and fear. The IWW organized the poorest and most isolated workers—lumbermen, miners, and trackmen in the West, textile workers and longshoremen in the East. Emboldened by IWW leaders, these workers waged strikes against employers unaccustomed to having their authority challenged. Violence lurked beneath the surface of these strikes and occasionally erupted in bloody skirmishes between strikers and police, National Guardsmen, or the private security forces hired by employers. Some blamed the IWW for the violence, seeing it as a direct outgrowth of calls for a "class war." Others under-

NICKELODEONS IN MAJOR AMERICAN CITIES, 1910

Cities	Population	Nickelodeons (estimate)	Seating Capacity	Population per Seat
New York	4,338,322	450	150,000	29
Chicago	2,000,000	310	93,000	22
Philadelphia	1,491,082	160	57,000	26
St. Louis	824,000	142	50,410	16
Cleveland	600,000	75	22,500	27
Baltimore	600,000	83	24,900	24
San Francisco	400,000	68	32,400	12
Cincinnati	350,000	75	22,500	16
New Orleans	325,000	28	5,600	58

Source: Garth Jowett, *Film: The Democratic Art* (Boston: Little, Brown, 1976), p. 46.

stood that the IWW was not solely responsible. Employers had shown themselves quite willing to resort to violence to enforce their will on employees. In 1913, for example, at Ludlow, Colorado, the Colorado Fuel and Iron Company, a subsidiary of Rockefeller's Standard Oil Company, brought in a private security force and the local militia (which it controlled) to break up a UMW strike. When the company evicted strikers and their families from their homes, the union set up 13 tent colonies to obstruct the entrances to the mines. The standoff came to a bloody conclusion in April 1914 when company police, firing randomly into one colony of tents, killed 66 men, women, and children.

The "Ludlow massacre" outraged the nation. At hearings of the U.S. Commission on Industrial Relations, John D. Rockefeller, Jr., was humiliated by Commissioner Frank Walsh's disclosure of the industrialist's complicity in the events leading up to the violence. The massacre revealed yet again what the IWW strikes had repeatedly demonstrated: that many American workers resented their low wages and poor working conditions; that neither the government nor employers offered workers a mechanism for airing and peacefully resolving their grievances; and that workers, as a result, felt compelled to protest through joining unions and waging strikes, even if it meant risking their lives. On the eve of the First World War, almost 40 years after the anger and destruction unleashed by the Great Railroad Strike of 1877 (chapter 19), industrial conflict still plagued the nation.

THE JOYS OF THE CITY

Industrial workers might be missing their fair share of the nation's prosperity, but they were crowding the dance halls, vaudeville theaters, amusement parks, and ballparks offered by the new world of commercial entertainment. Above all, they were embracing a new technological marvel, the movies.

Movies were well suited to poor city dwellers with little money, little free time, and little English. Initially, they cost only a nickel. The "nickelodeons" where they were shown were usually converted storefronts in working-class neighborhoods. Movies required little leisure time, for at first they lasted only 15 minutes on average. Viewers with more time on their hands could stay for a cycle of two or three films (or for several cycles). And even non-English-speakers could understand what was happening on the "silent screen." By 1910, at least 20,000 nickelodeons dotted northern cities.

These early "moving pictures" were primitive by today's standards, but they were thrilling just the same. The figures appearing on the screen were realistic, yet "larger than life." Moviegoers could transport themselves to parts of the world they would otherwise never see, encounter people they would otherwise never meet, and watch boxing matches they could otherwise not afford to attend. The darkened theater provided a setting in which secret desires, especially sexual ones, could be explored. As one newspaper innocently commented in 1899: "For the first time in the history of the world it is possible to see what a kiss looks like."

THEDA BARA AS CLEOPATRA (1917) Bara was the first movie actress to gain fame for her roles as a "vamp"—a woman whose irresistible sexual charm led men to ruin. Because little effort was made to censor movies prior to the early 1920s, movie directors were able to explore sexual themes and to film their female stars in erotic, and partially nude, poses.

No easy generalizations are possible about the content of these early films, more than half of which came from France, Germany, and Italy. American-made films tended toward slapstick comedies, adventure stories, and romances. Producers did not yet shy away, as they soon would, from the lustier or seedier sides of American life. The Hollywood formula of happy endings had yet to be worked out. In fact, the industry, centered in New York City and Fort Lee, New Jersey, had yet to locate itself in cheery southern California. In 1914 the movies' first sex symbol, Theda Bara, debuted in a movie that showed her tempting an upstanding American ambassador into infidelity and ruin. She would be the first of the big screen's many "vamps," so-called because the characters they portrayed, like vampires, thrived on the blood (and death) of men.

THE NEW SEXUALITY AND THE NEW WOMAN

The introduction of movies was closely bound up with a sexual revolution in American life. For most of the 19th century, the idea of "separate spheres" had dominated relations between the sexes, especially among middle-class Americans. The male sphere was one of work, politics, and sexual passion. The female sphere, by contrast, was one of domesticity, moral education, and sexual reproduction. Men and women were not supposed to intrude into each other's spheres. It was "unnatural" for women to work, or to enter the corrupting world of politics, or to engage in pleasurable sex. It was equally "unnatural" for men to devote themselves to child-rearing, or to "idle" themselves with domestic chores, or to live a life bereft of sexual passion. This doctrine of separate spheres both discriminated against women and also meant that men and women spent substantial portions of their daily lives apart from each other. The ceremonial occasions, meals, and leisure activities that brought them together tended to be closely regulated. The lives of the young, in particular, were closely watched, guided, and supervised by parents, teachers, and ministers.

Although this doctrine, often referred to as Victorianism, never worked as well in practice as it did in theory, throughout the 1880s and 1890s it had a profound influence on gender identity and sexual practice. When the revolt set in it came from many sources: from middle-class men who were tiring of a life devoted to regimented work with no time for play; from middle-class women who, after achieving first-rate educations at elite women's colleges, were told they could not participate in the nation's economic, governmental, or professional enterprises; from immigrants, blacks, and other groups who had never been fully socialized into the Victorian world; and from young people eyeing readily available leisure activities far removed from parental supervision.

Among the most influential rebels in the new century were the young, single, working-class women who were entering the workforce in large numbers. The economy's voracious appetite for labor was drawing women out of the home and into factories and offices. Men who would have preferred to keep their wives and daughters at home were forced, given their own low wages, to allow them to go to work. Women's employment doubled between 1880 and 1900, and increased by 50 percent from 1900 to 1920. Meanwhile, the nature of female employment was undergoing a radical change. Domestic service—women who worked in family households as servants—had been the most common occupation for women during the 19th century. Female servants generally worked alone, or with one or two other servants. They worked long hours cooking, cleaning, and caring for their masters' children and received only part of their wages in cash, the rest being "paid" in the form of room and board. Their jobs offered them little personal or financial independence.

Now, women were taking different kinds of jobs. The jobs tended to be either industrial or clerical. In both cases, women worked both with one another and in proximity to men. Their places of work were distant from their homes and from parental supervision. They received all their pay in the form of wages, which, though low, heightened their sense of economic independence. These were indeed "new women" in what had once been exclusively a man's world. Their ranks, however, included few black women, who, like black men, were largely excluded from the expanding job opportunities in the economy's manufacturing and clerical sectors. Black women's concentration in domestic service jobs actually increased in the early 20th century, as they took the places vacated by white women.

Once the barriers against white women in the workforce had fallen, other barriers also began to weaken—especially the Victorian ban on close associations with men outside of marriage. Young women and men flocked to the dance halls that were opening in every major city. They rejected the stiff formality of earlier ballroom dances like the cotillion or the waltz for the freedom and intimacy of newer forms, like the fox trot, tango, and bunny-hug. They went to movies and to amusement parks together, and they engaged, far more than their parents had, in premarital sex. It is estimated that the proportion of women having sex

before marriage rose from 10 percent to 25 percent in the generation that was coming of age between 1910 and 1920.

THE RISE OF FEMINISM

This movement toward sexual equality was one expression of women's dissatisfaction with their subordinate place in society. By the second decade of the 20th century, eloquent spokeswomen had emerged to make the case for full female equality. The writer Charlotte Perkins Gilman called for the release of women from domestic chores through the collectivization of housekeeping. Social activist Margaret Sanger insisted, in her lectures on birth control, that women should be free to enjoy sexual relations without having to worry about unwanted motherhood. The anarchist Emma Goldman denounced marriage as a kind of prostitution and embraced the ideal of "free love"—love unburdened by contractual commitment. Alice Paul, founder of the National Women's Party, brought a new militancy to the campaign for woman suffrage (see chapter 21).

These women were among the first to use the term "feminism" to describe their desire for complete equality with men. Some of them came together in Greenwich Village, a community of radical artists and writers in lower Manhattan, where they found a supportive environment in which to express and live by their feminist ideals. Crystal Eastman, a leader of the feminist Greenwich Village group called Heterodoxy, defined the feminist challenge as "how to arrange the world so that women can be human beings, with a chance to exercise their infinitely varied gifts in infinitely varied ways, instead of being destined by the accident of their sex to one field of activity."

The movement for sexual and gender equality aroused considerable anxiety in the more conservative sectors of American society. Parents worried about the promiscuity of their children. Conservatives were certain that the "new women" would transform American cities into dens of iniquity. Vice commissions sprang up in every major city to clamp down on prostitution, drunkenness, and pornography. The campaign for prohibition—a ban on the sale of alcoholic beverages—gathered steam. Movie theater owners were pressured into

ELIZABETH GURLEY FLYNN A prominent organizer for the Industrial Workers of the World (IWW), Flynn addressed a rally of striking female textile workers near Paterson, New Jersey, in 1913. The Paterson strike attracted national attention as well as the active involvement of many of Greenwich Village's radical feminists and intellectuals.

excluding "indecent" films from their screens. Many believed the lurid tales of international vice lords scouring foreign lands for innocent girls who could be delivered to American brothel owners. This "white slave trade" inspired passage of the 1910 Mann Act, which made the transportation of women across state lines for immoral purposes a federal crime.

Nor did it escape the attention of conservatives that Greenwich Village was home not only to the dangerous exponents of "free love" but also to equally dangerous advocates of class warfare. Prominent IWW organizer Elizabeth Gurley Flynn

was a member of Heterodoxy; her lover, Carlo Tresca, was a leading IWW theoretician. "Big Bill" Haywood also frequented Greenwich Village, where he was lionized as a working-class hero. When Greenwich Village radicals began publishing an avant-garde artistic journal in 1914, they called it *The Masses;* its editor was Max Eastman, the brother of Crystal. This convergence of labor and feminist militancy intensified conservative feeling that the nation had strayed too far from its roots.

Cultural conservatism was strongest in those areas of the country least involved in the ongoing industrial and sexual revolutions—in farming communities and small towns; in the South, where industrialization and urbanization were proceeding at a slower rate than elsewhere; and among old social elites, who felt pushed aside by the new corporate men of power.

Conservatives and radicals alike shared a conviction that the country could not afford to ignore its social problems—the power of the corporations; the poverty and powerlessness of wage earners; the role of women and African Americans. Conservatives were as determined to restore a Victorian morality as radicals were determined to achieve working-class emancipation and women's equality. But in politics, neither would become the dominant force. That role would fall to the so-called progressives, a diverse group of reformers who confidently and optimistically believed that they could bring both order and justice to the new society.

CONCLUSION

Between 1890 and 1920, corporate power, innovation, and demands had stimulated the growth of cities, attracted millions of immigrants from southern and eastern Europe, enhanced commercial opportunities, and created the conditions for a vibrant urban culture. Many Americans thrived in this new environment, taking advantage of business opportunities or, as in the case of women, discovering liberties in dress, employment, dating, and sex that they had not known. Millions of Americans, however, remained impoverished, unable to rise in the social order or to earn enough in wages to support their families. African Americans who had migrated to the North in search of economic opportunity suffered more than any other single group, as they found themselves shut out of most industrial and commercial employment.

Henry Ford, whose generous five-dollars-a-day wage drew tens of thousands to his Detroit factories, was an exceptional employer. Although other employers had learned to restrain their crass displays of wealth and had turned toward philanthropy in search of a better public image, they remained reluctant to follow Ford's lead in improving the conditions in which their employees labored.

Working-class Americans proved resourceful in creating self-help institutions to serve their own and each other's needs. In some cities, they gained a measure of power through the establishment of political machines. Labor unions arose and fought for a variety of reforms, but their success was limited. How to inject greater equality and opportunity into an industrial society in which the gap between rich and poor had reached alarming proportions remained a daunting challenge.

Suggested Readings begin on page SR-1.
For Web activities and resources
related to this chapter, go to
http://www.harcourtcollege.com/history.murrin

CHAPTER 21

PROGRESSIVISM

"A NEW CAPTAIN IN THE DISTRICT"

This cartoon depicts newly elected President Woodrow Wilson as a police captain who is determined to clean up Washington politics and regulate "crooked business." It illustrates a key belief shared by Wilson, Theodore Roosevelt, and most other progressives: that an activist government was society's best hope for solving the nation's political and economic problems.

CHAPTER OUTLINE

Progressivism was a reform movement that took its name from individuals who left the Republican Party in 1912 to join Theodore Roosevelt's new party, the Progressive Party. The term "progressive," however, refers to a much larger and more varied group of reformers than those who gathered around Roosevelt in 1912.

As early as 1900 these reformers had set out to cleanse and reinvigorate an America whose politics and society they considered in decline. Progressives wanted to rid politics of corruption, tame the power of the "trusts" and, in the process, inject more liberty into American life. They fought against prostitution, gambling, drinking, and other forms of vice. They first appeared in municipal politics, organizing movements to oust crooked mayors and to break up local gas or streetcar monopolies. They carried their fights to the states and finally to the nation. Two presidents, Theodore Roosevelt and Woodrow Wilson, placed themselves at the head of this movement.

Progressivism was popular among a variety of groups who brought to the movement distinct, and often conflicting, aims. On one issue, however, most progressives agreed: the need for an activist government to right political, economic, and social wrongs. Some progressives wanted government to become active only long enough to clean up the political process, end drinking, upgrade the electorate, and break up trusts. These problems were so difficult to solve that many other progressives endorsed the notion of a permanently active government—with the power to tax income, regulate industry, protect consumers from fraud, empower workers, safeguard the environment, and provide social welfare. Progressives, in other words, came to see the federal government as the institution best equipped to solve social problems.

Such positive attitudes toward government power marked an important change in American politics. Americans had long been suspicious of centralized government, viewing it as the enemy of liberty. The Populists had broken with that view (see chapter 19), but they had been defeated. The progressives had to build a new case for strong government as the protector of liberty and equality.

This chapter will focus on the following major questions:

- What was progressivism, and which groups spearheaded the movement?
- What, in your opinion, were the three most important Progressive Era reforms? Be prepared to defend to your choices.
- What was disfranchisement and can it be considered a progressive reform?
- What were the key similarities and differences in the progressive politics of Theodore Roosevelt and Woodrow Wilson?

PROGRESSIVISM AND THE PROTESTANT SPIRIT

Progressivism emerged first and most strongly among young, mainly Protestant, middle-class Americans who felt alienated from their society. Many had been raised in devout Protestant homes in which religious conviction had often been a spur to social action. They were expected to become ministers or missionaries or to serve their church in some other way. They had abandoned this path, but they never lost their zeal for righting moral wrongs and for uplifting the human spirit. They were distressed by the immorality and corruption rampant in American politics, and by the gap that separated rich from poor. They became, in the words of one historian, "ministers of reform."

Other Protestant reformers retained their faith. This was true of William Jennings Bryan, the former Populist leader who became an ardent progressive and evangelical. Throughout his political career, Bryan always insisted that Christian piety and American democracy were integrally related. Billy Sunday, a former major league baseball player who became the most theatrical evangelical preacher of his day, elevated opposition to saloons and the "liquor trust" into a righteous crusade. And Walter Rauschenbusch led a movement known as the Social Gospel, which emphasized the duty of Christians to work for the social good.

Protestants, of course, formed a large and diverse population, sizable sections of which showed little

interest in reform. Thus, it is important to identify smaller and more cohesive groups of reformers. Of the many that arose, three were of particular importance, especially in the early years: investigative journalists, who were called "muckrakers"; the founders and supporters of settlement houses; and socialists.

MUCKRAKERS, MAGAZINES, AND THE TURN TOWARD "REALISM"

The term "muckraker" was coined by Theodore Roosevelt, who had intended it as a criticism of

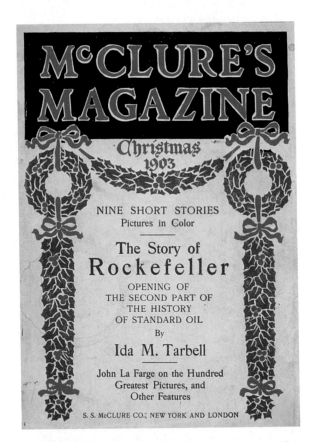

PIONEERING INVESTIGATIVE JOURNALISM This Christmas 1903 issue of *McClure's Magazine* featured the second part of Ida Tarbell's exposé of John D. Rockefeller's business practices. Tarbell's revelations were regarded as sensational, and they convinced many middle-class Americans of the need for economic and political reform.

newspaper and magazine reporters who, for no purpose other than monetary reward, wrote stories about scandalous situations. But it became a badge of honor among journalists committed to exposing the seedy, sordid side of life in the United States. During the first decade of the century they presented the public with one startling revelation after another. Ida Tarbell revealed the shady practices by which John D. Rockefeller had transformed his Standard Oil Company into a monopoly. Lincoln Steffens unraveled the webs of bribery and corruption that were strangling local governments in the nation's great cities. George Kibbe Turner documented the extent of prostitution and family disintegration in the ethnic ghettos of those cities. These muckrakers wanted to shock the public into recognizing the shameful state of political, economic, and social affairs and to prompt "the people" to take action.

The tradition of investigative journalism reached back at least to the 1870s, when newspaper and magazine writers exposed the corrupt practices of New York City's Boss Tweed and his Tammany Hall machine. The 20th-century rise of the muckrakers reflected two factors, one economic—expanded newspaper and magazine circulation—and the other intellectual—increased interest in "realism." Together they transformed investigative reporting into something of national importance.

INCREASED NEWSPAPER AND MAGAZINE CIRCULATION

From 1870 to 1909, daily newspapers rose in number from 574 to 2,600, and their circulation increased from less than 3 million to more than 24 million. During the 1890s magazines also underwent a revolution. Cheap, 10-cent periodicals such as *McClure's Magazine* and *Ladies Home Journal*, with circulations of 400,000 to 1 million, displaced genteel and relatively expensive 35-cent publications such as *Harper's* and *The Atlantic Monthly*. The expanded readership brought journalists considerably more money and prestige and attracted many talented and ambitious men and women to the profession. It also made magazine publishers more receptive to stories, particularly sensational ones about ill-gotten economic power, government corruption, and urban vice, that might appeal to their newly acquired millions of readers.

CIRCULATION OF DAILY NEWSPAPERS AND MAGAZINES, 1880–1919

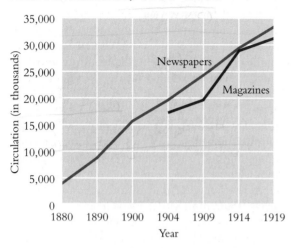

Source: Data from *Historical Statistics of the United States, Colonial Times to 1970* (White Plains, N.Y.: Kraus International, 1989).

CLIFF DWELLERS George Bellows was a member of the "Ashcan School," a group of painters who sought to create a distinctly American and "realist" style. Here Bellows portrays the urban masses sympathetically and in a way that evokes their connection to a group of quintessential Americans, the cliff-dwelling Pueblo Indians.

THE TURN TOWARD "REALISM"

The American middle class's growing intellectual interest in "realism" also favored the muckrakers. "Realism" was a way of thinking that prized detachment, objectivity, and skepticism. Those who embraced it pointed out that constitutional theory, with its emphasis on citizenship, elections, and democratic procedures, had little to do with the way government in the United States actually worked. What could one learn about bosses, machines, and graft from studying the Constitution? There was also a sense that the nation's glorification of the "self-made man" and of "individualism" was preventing Americans from coping effectively with large-scale organizations—corporations, banks, labor unions—and their sudden centrality to the nation's economy and to society. The realists, finally, criticized the tendency, prevalent among American writers and artists, to emulate European styles, and they called on them to pioneer new styles that would be better able to "capture" American life and thought.

By the first decade of the 20th century, intellectuals and artists of all sorts—philosophers John Dewey and William James; social scientists Thorstein Veblen and Charles Beard; novelists Frank Norris, Theodore Dreiser, and Upton Sinclair; painters John Sloan, George Bellows and other members of the "Ashcan school"; photographers Jacob Riis and Lewis Hine; architects Louis Sullivan and Frank Lloyd Wright; jurists Oliver Wendell Holmes and Louis Brandeis—were attempting to create truer, more realistic ways of representing and analyzing American society. Many of them were inspired by the work of investigative journalists; some had themselves been newspapermen. Years of firsthand observation enabled them to describe American society as it "truly was." They brought shadowy figures vividly to life. They pictured for Americans the captain of industry who ruthlessly destroyed his competitors; the con artist who tricked young people new to city life; the innocent immigrant girl who fell prey to the white slave traders; the corrupt policeman under whose protection urban vice flourished.

A vast middle class, uneasy about the state of American society, applauded the muckrakers for telling these stories, and became interested in reform. Members of this class put pressure on city and state governments to send crooked government officials to jail and to stamp out the sources of corruption and vice. Between 1902 and 1916 more than 100 cities launched investigations of the prostitution trade. At the federal level, all three branches of government felt compelled to address the question of "the trusts"—the concentration of power in the hands of a few industrialists and financiers. Progressivism began to crystallize into a political movement centered on the abuses the muckrakers had exposed.

SETTLEMENT HOUSES AND WOMEN'S ACTIVISM

Established by middle-class reformers, settlement houses were intended to help the largely immigrant poor cope with the harsh conditions of city life. Much of the inspiration for settlement houses came from young, college-educated, Protestant women from comfortable but not particularly wealthy backgrounds. Some had imbibed a commitment to social justice from parents and grandparents who had fought to abolish slavery. Highly educated, talented, and sensitive to social injustice, they rebelled against being relegated solely to the roles of wife and mother and sought to assert their independence in socially useful ways.

HULL HOUSE

Jane Addams and Ellen Gates Starr established the nation's first settlement house, in Chicago, in 1889. The two women had been inspired by a visit the year before to London's Toynbee Hall, where a small group of middle-class men had been living and working with that city's poor since 1884. Addams and Starr bought a decaying mansion that had once been the country home of a prominent Chicagoan, Charles J. Hull. By 1889 "Hull House" stood amidst

JANE ADDAMS The founder of the settlement house movement, Addams was the most famous woman reformer of the progressive era. This photograph dates from the 1890s or 1900s, Hull House's formative period.

WOMEN ENROLLED IN INSTITUTIONS OF HIGHER EDUCATION, 1870–1930

Year	Women's Colleges (thousands of students)	Coed Institutions (thousands of students)	Total (thousands of students)	Percentage of All Students Enrolled
1870	6.5	4.6	11.1	21.0%
1880	15.7	23.9	39.6	33.4
1890	16.8	39.5	56.3	35.9
1900	24.4	61.0	85.4	36.8
1910	34.1	106.5	140.6	39.6
1920	52.9	230.0	282.9	47.3
1930	82.1	398.7	480.8	43.7

Source: From Mabel Newcomer, *A Century of Higher Education for American Women* (New York: Harper and Row, 1959), p. 46.

factories, churches, saloons, and tenements inhabited by poor, largely foreign-born working-class families.

Addams quickly emerged as the guiding spirit of Hull House. She moved into the building and demanded that all who worked there do the same. She and Starr enlisted extraordinary women such as Florence Kelley, Alice Hamilton, and Julia Lathrop. They set up a nursery for the children of working mothers, a penny savings bank, and an employment bureau, soon followed by a baby clinic, a neighborhood playground, and social clubs. Determined to minister to cultural as well as economic needs, Hull House sponsored an orchestra, reading groups, and a lecture series. Members of Chicago's widening circle of reform-minded intellectuals, artists, and politicians contributed their energies to the enterprise. John Dewey taught philosophy and Frank Lloyd Wright lectured on architecture. Clarence Darrow, the workingman's lawyer, and Henry Demarest Lloyd, Chicago's radical muckraker, spent considerable time at Hull House. In 1893 Illinois Governor John P. Altgeld named Hull House worker Florence Kelley as the state's chief factory inspector. Her investigations led to Illinois's first factory law, which prohibited child labor, limited the employment of women to eight hours a day, and authorized the state to hire inspectors to enforce the law.

The Hull House principals seemed to have unlimited energy, imagination, and commitment. Julia Lathrop used her appointment to the State Board of Charities to agitate for improvements in the care of the poor, the handicapped, and the delinquent. With Edith Abbott and Sophonisba Breckinridge, she established the Department of Social Research at the University of Chicago (which would evolve into the nation's first school of social work). Alice Hamilton, who had overcome sex discrimination to become a doctor, pioneered in the field of public health.

The Hull House leaders did not command the instant fame accorded the muckrakers. Nevertheless, they were steadily drawn into the public arena. Thousands of women across the country were inspired to build their own settlement houses on the Hull House model (eventually more than 400 settlement houses would open nationwide). By 1910 Jane Addams had become one of the nation's most famous women. She and other settlement house workers played a critical role in fashioning the progressive agenda and in drafting pieces of progressive legislation.

THE CULTURAL CONSERVATISM OF PROGRESSIVE REFORMERS

In general, settlement house workers were much more sympathetic toward the poor, the illiterate, and the downtrodden than the muckrakers were. Jane Addams, though she disapproved of machine politics, saw firsthand the benefits machine politicians delivered to their constituents. She respected the cultural inheritance of the immigrants and admired their resourcefulness. Although she wanted them to become Americans, she encouraged them to preserve their "immigrant gifts" in their new identity. Those attitudes were more liberal than those of other reformers, who considered most immigrants culturally, even racially, inferior.

But there were limits even to Addams's sympathy for the immigrants. In particular, she disapproved of the new working-class entertainments that gave adolescents extensive and unregulated opportunities for intimate association. She was also troubled by the emergence of the "new woman" and her frank sexuality (see chapter 20). Addams tended to equate female sexuality with prostitution, and she joined many other women reformers in a campaign to suppress both. Addams and others had identified a serious problem in American cities, where significant numbers of immigrant and rural women new to urban life were lured into prostitution or chose it as a job preferable to 65 poorly paid hours a week in a sweatshop.

The reformers' zeal on this matter exaggerated the dimensions of the problem and led to some questionable legislation, such as the Mann Act (1910), which made it illegal to transport a woman across state lines "for immoral purposes." If this law permitted the prosecution of true traffickers in women, it also allowed the government to interfere in the private sexual relations of consenting adults. This is what happened in the case of Jack Johnson, the African American heavyweight champion, who was arrested and convicted for "transporting" his white secretary, Lucy Cameron, across state lines (see History Through Film, chapter 20). That Johnson's and Cameron's relationship was consensual and would culminate in marriage did not deter the authorities, who wanted to punish Johnson for his dominance of white boxers and his relationship with a white woman.

The cultural conservatism evident in the attitudes of Jane Addams and others on female sexuality also emerged in their attitudes toward alcohol. Drinking rivaled prostitution as a problem in poor, working-class areas. Many men wasted their hard-earned money on drinks at the local saloon, a drain on meager family resources that created tension between these men and their wives. Domestic fights and family violence sometimes ensued. Settlement house workers were well aware of the ill-effects of alcoholism (250 saloons did business in Chicago's 19th Ward alone) and sought to combat it. They called on working people to refrain from drink and worked for legislation that would shut down the saloons. The progressives joined forces with the Women's Christian Temperance Union (245,000 members strong by 1911), and the Anti-Saloon League. By 1916, through their collective efforts, these groups had won prohibition of the sale and manufacture of alcoholic beverages in 16 states. In 1919 their crowning achievement was the Eighteenth Amendment to the U.S. Constitution, making Prohibition the law of the land (see chapter 23).

In depicting alcohol and saloons as unmitigated evils, however, the prohibition movement ignored the role saloons played in ethnic, working-class communities. On Chicago's South Side, for example, saloons provided tens of thousands of workers with the only decent place to eat lunch. The meatpacking plants where they labored had no cafeterias, and few workers could stomach eating their lunch where animals were slaughtered, dressed, and packed. Some saloons catered to particular ethnic groups: They served traditional foods and drinks, provided meeting space for fraternal organizations, and offered camaraderie to men longing to speak in their native tongue. Saloon-keepers sometimes functioned as informal bankers, cashing checks and making small loans.

Alcohol figured in ethnic life in other ways, too. For Catholics, wine was central to Communion. Jews greeted each Sabbath and religious festival with a blessing over wine. For both groups, the sharing of wine or beer marked the celebration of births, marriages, deaths, and other major family events. Understandably, many immigrants shunned the prohibition movement. They had no interest in being "uplifted" and "reformed" in this way. Here

was a gulf separating the immigrant masses from the Protestant middle class that even compassionate reformers such as Jane Addams could not bridge.

A NATION OF CLUBWOMEN

Settlement house workers comprised only one part of a vast network of female reformers. Hundreds of thousands of women belonged to local women's clubs. Conceived as self-help organizations in which women would be encouraged to sharpen their minds, refine their domestic skills, and strengthen their moral faculties, these clubs began taking on tasks of social reform. Clubwomen typically focused their energies on improving schools, building libraries and playgrounds, expanding educational and vocational opportunities for girls, and securing fire and sanitation codes for tenement houses. In so doing, they made traditional female concerns—the nurturing and education of children, the care of the home—questions of public policy. Clubwomen rose to prominence in black communities, too, and addressed similar sorts of issues; on matters of sexuality and alcohol they often shared the conservative sentiments of their white counterparts. Some groups of black clubwomen ventured into community affairs more boldly than their white counterparts, however, especially in southern states, where black men were being systematically stripped of the right to vote, to serve on juries, and to hold political office. Whites were prepared to punish any African American, male or female, who showed too much initiative or was thought to be challenging the principles of white supremacy. Even so, many black female activists persevered in the face of such threats, determined to provide leadership in their communities and voice their people's concerns.

SOCIALISM AND PROGRESSIVISM

Issues such as women's sexuality and men's alcoholism drew progressives in a conservative direction, but other issues drew them to socialism. In the early 20th century, socialism stood for the transfer of control over industry from a few industrialists to the laboring masses. Socialists believed that such a transfer, usually defined in terms of government ownership and operation of economic institutions, would make it impossible for wealthy elites to control society.

The Socialist Party of America, founded in 1901, became a political force during the first 16 years of the century, and socialist ideas influenced progressivism. In 1912, at the peak of its influence, the Socialist Party enrolled more than 115,000 members. Its presidential candidate, the charismatic Eugene Victor Debs of Terre Haute, Indiana, attracted almost a million votes—6 percent of the total votes cast that year. In that same year, 1,200 Socialists held elective office in 340 different municipalities. Of these, 79 were mayors of cities as geographically and demographically diverse as Schenectady, New York; Milwaukee, Wisconsin; Butte, Montana; and Berkeley, California. More than 300 newspapers and periodicals, with a combined circulation exceeding two million, spread the socialist gospel. The most important socialist publication was *Appeal to Reason*, published by Kansan Julius Wayland and sent out each week to 750,000 subscribers. In 1905 Wayland published, in serial form, a novel by an obscure muckraker named Upton Sinclair, which depicted the scandalous working conditions in Chicago's meatpacking industry. When it was later published in book form in 1906, *The Jungle* created such an outcry that the federal government was forced to regulate the meat industry.

THE MANY FACES OF SOCIALISM

Socialists came in many varieties. In Milwaukee, they consisted of predominantly German working-class immigrants and their descendants; in New York City, their numbers were strongest among Jewish immigrants from eastern Europe. In the Southwest, tens of thousands of disgruntled native-

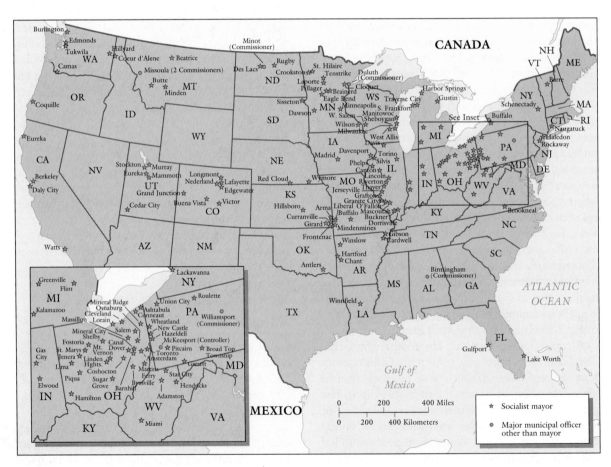

CITIES AND TOWNS ELECTING SOCIALIST MAYORS OR OTHER MAJOR MUNICIPAL OFFICERS, 1911–1920

born farmers who had been Populists in the 1890s now flocked to the socialist banner. In Oklahoma alone, by 1912 these erstwhile Populists were numerous enough to support 11 socialist weeklies. In that same year, Oklahoma voters gave a higher percentage of their votes, over 16 percent, to the Socialist candidate Debs than did the voters of any other state. In the West, socialism was popular among miners, timber cutters, and others who labored in isolated areas where industrialists enjoyed extraordinary power. These radicals gravitated to the militant labor union, the Industrial Workers of the World (IWW) (chapter 20), which from 1905 to 1913 found a home in the Socialist Party.

Socialists differed not only in their occupations and ethnic origins but also in their politics. The IWW was the most radical socialist group, with its incessant calls for revolution. By contrast, mainstream socialism, as articulated by Debs, was more respectful of American political, cultural, and religious traditions. Mainstream socialists saw themselves as the saviors rather than the destroyers of the American republic—as the true heirs of Thomas Jefferson. Their confidence that the nation could be redeemed through conventional politics—through the election of Debs as president—is evidence of their affection for American democracy. And their faith in redemption reveals the degree to which Protestant religious beliefs underlay their quest for social justice and what they called a "cooperative commonwealth." Evolutionary socialists, led by Victor Berger of Milwaukee, abandoned talk of revolution altogether and chose instead an aggressive brand of reform politics. They were dubbed "gas and water socialists" because of their interest in improving city services.

These differences would, after 1912, fragment the socialist movement. For a decade or so, however, all these divergent groups managed to coexist in a single political party thanks, largely, to the eloquence of Debs. When he was released from a Chicago jail in 1895 after serving time for his role in leading the strike against the Pullman Company (see chapter 19), Debs declared to a gathering of 100,000 admirers: "Manifestly the spirit of '76 still survives. The fires of liberty and noble aspirations are not yet extinguished. . . . The vindication and glorification of American principles of government, as proclaimed to the world in the Declaration of Independence, is the high purpose of this convocation."

SOCIALISTS AND PROGRESSIVES

Debs's speeches both attracted and disturbed progressives. On the one hand, he spoke compellingly about the dangers of unregulated capitalism and excessively concentrated wealth, both progressive concerns. His confidence that a strong state could bring the economic system under control mirrored the progressives' own faith in the positive uses of government. Indeed, progressives often worked hand-in-hand with socialists to win economic and political reforms, especially at the municipal and state levels, and many intellectuals and reformers easily moved back and forth between socialism and progressivism. Florence Kelley, Hull House reformer and Illinois factory inspector, was one such person; Clarence Darrow, a Chicago trial lawyer who successfully defended the IWW's William Haywood in 1907 against charges that he had murdered a former Idaho governor, was another. Walter Lippmann, who would become a close adviser to President Wilson during the First World War, began his political career in 1912 as an assistant to the Socialist mayor of Schenectady. Several of the era's outstanding intellectuals, including John Dewey, Richard Ely, and Thorstein Veblen, also traveled back and forth between the socialist and progressive camps. So did Helen Keller, the country's leading spokesperson for the disabled.

THE RISE OF SOCIALISM The socialists hoped to bring economic security and dignity to working men and women. Under the leadership of Eugene V. Debs, pictured on the left in this 1904 campaign poster, they became a significant force in American politics. Their influence crested in the election of 1912, when Debs received nearly a million votes.

On the other hand, Debs's talk of revolution scared progressives, as did his efforts to organize a working-class political movement independent of middle-class involvement or control. Although progressives wanted to tame capitalism, they stopped short of wanting it eliminated. They wanted to improve working and living conditions for the masses but not cede political control to them. The progressives hoped to offer a political program with enough socialist elements to counter the appeal of Debs's more radical movement. In this, they were successful.

MUNICIPAL REFORM

The first reform battles were over control of municipal transportation networks and utilities. Street railways were typically owned and operated by private corporations, as were electrical and gas systems. Many of the corporations used their monopoly power to charge exorbitant fares and rates, and often they won that power by bribing city officials who belonged to one of the political machines. Corporations achieved generous reductions in real estate taxes in the same way.

The assault on private utilities and their protectors in city government gained momentum in the mid-1890s. In Detroit, reform-minded Mayor Hazen S. Pingree led successful fights to control the city's gas, telephone, and trolley companies. In Chicago in 1896 and 1897, a group of middle-class reformers ousted a corrupt city council and elected a mayor, Carter Harrison, Jr., who promised to protect Chicago's streetcar riders from exploitation. In St. Louis in 1900, middle-class consumers and small businessmen joined hands with striking workers to challenge the "streetcar trust." In Cleveland, the crusading reformer Tom Johnson won election as mayor in 1901, curbed the power of the streetcar interests, and brought honest and efficient government to the city.

Occasionally, a reform politician of Johnson's caliber would rise to power through one of the regular political parties. But this path to power was a difficult one, especially in cities where the political parties were controlled by machines. Consequently, progressives worked for reforms that would strip the parties of their power. Two of their favorite reforms were the city commission and the city manager forms of government.

THE CITY COMMISSION PLAN

First introduced in Galveston, Texas, in 1900, in the wake of a devastating tidal wave, the city commission shifted municipal power from the mayor and his aldermen to five city commissioners, each responsible for a different department of city government. In Galveston and elsewhere, the impetus for this reform came from civic-minded businessmen determined to rebuild government on the same principles of efficient and scientific management that had energized the private sector. The results were often impressive. The Galveston commissioners restored the city's credit after a close brush with bankruptcy, improved the city's harbor, and built a massive seawall to protect the city from future floods. All this they accomplished on budgets cut by one-third. In Houston, Texas; Des Moines, Iowa; Dayton, Ohio; Oakland, California; and elsewhere, commissioners similarly improved urban infrastructures, expanded city services, and strengthened the financial health of the cities. Many commissions established publicly owned utilities. By 1913 more than 300 cities, most of them small to middling in size, had adopted the city commission plan.

THE CITY MANAGER PLAN

The city commission system did not always work to perfection, however. Sometimes the commissioners used their position to reward electoral supporters with jobs and contracts; at other times, they pursued power and prestige for their respective departments. The city manager plan was meant to overcome such problems. Under this plan, the commissioners continued to set policy, but policy implementation now rested with a "chief executive." This official, not elected but appointed by the commissioners, would curtail rivalries between commissioners and ensure that no outside influences interfered with the expert, businesslike management of the city. The job of city manager was explicitly modeled after that of a corporation executive. First introduced in Sumter, South Carolina, in 1911 and then in Dayton, Ohio, in 1913, by 1919 the city manager plan had been adopted in 130 cities.

THE COSTS OF REFORM

Although these reforms limited corruption and improved services, they were not universally popular.

Poor and minority voters, in particular, found that their influence in local affairs was weakened by the shift to city commissioners and city managers. Previously, candidates for municipal office (other than the mayor) competed in ward elections rather than in citywide elections. Voters in working-class wards commonly elected workingmen to represent them, and voters in immigrant wards made sure that fellow ethnics represented their interests on city councils. Citywide elections diluted the strength of these constituencies. Candidates from poor districts often lacked the money needed to mount a citywide campaign, and they were further hampered by the nonpartisan nature of such elections. Denied the support of a political party or platform, they had to make themselves personally known to voters throughout the city. That was a much easier task for the city's "leading citizens"—manufacturers, merchants, and lawyers—than it was for workingmen. In Dayton, the resulting tilt of the electoral system toward the city's wealthier citizens prompted a coalition of working-class groups to publish a pamphlet entitled *Dayton's Commission Manager Plan: Why Big Manufacturers, Bond Holders, and Public Franchise Grabbers Favor It, and Workingmen and Common People Oppose.* Dayton's Socialist Party members had good reason to be upset. In the years following the introduction of the commission-manager system, the proportion of Dayton citizens voting Socialist rose from 25 to 44 percent, while the number of Socialists elected to office declined from five to zero. Progressive political reforms thus frequently had the effect of reducing the influence of radicals, minorities, and the poor in elections.

POLITICAL REFORM IN THE STATES

Political reform in the cities quickly spread to the states. As at the local level, political parties at the state level were often dominated by corrupt, incompetent politicians who did the bidding of powerful private lobbies. In New Jersey in 1903, for example, large industrial and financial interests, working through the Republican Party machine, controlled numerous appointments to state government, including the chief justice of the state supreme court, the attorney general, and the commissioner of banking and insurance. Such webs of influence ensured that New Jersey would provide

large corporations such as the railroads with favorable political and economic legislation.

RESTORING SOVEREIGNTY TO "THE PEOPLE"

Progressives introduced reforms designed to undermine the power of party bosses, restore sovereignty to "the people," and encourage honest, talented individuals to enter politics. One such reform was the direct primary, a mechanism that enabled voters themselves, rather than party bosses, to choose party candidates. Mississippi introduced this reform in 1902 and Wisconsin in 1903. By 1916 all but three states had adopted the direct primary. Closely related was a movement to strip state legislatures of their power to choose U.S. senators. State after state enacted legislation that permitted voters to choose Senate candidates in primary elections. In 1912 a reluctant U.S. Senate was obliged to approve the Seventeenth Amendment to the Constitution, mandating the direct election of senators. The state legislatures ratified this amendment in 1913.

Populists had first proposed direct election of U.S. senators in the 1890s; they also proposed the initiative and the referendum, both of which were adopted first by Oregon in 1902 and then by 18 other states between 1902 and 1915. The initiative allowed reformers to put before voters in general elections legislation that state legislatures had yet to approve. The referendum gave voters the right in general elections to repeal an unpopular act that a state legislature had passed. Less widely adopted but important nevertheless was the recall, a device that allowed voters to remove from office any public servant who had betrayed his trust. As a further control over the behavior of elected officials, numerous states enacted laws that regulated corporate campaign contributions and restricted lobbying activities in state legislatures.

These laws neither eliminated corporate privilege nor destroyed the power of machine politicians. Nevertheless, they made politics more honest and strengthened the influence of ordinary voters.

CREATING A VIRTUOUS ELECTORATE

Progressive reformers focused as well on creating a responsible electorate that understood the importance of the vote and that resisted efforts to manipulate elections. To create this ideal electorate, reformers had to see to it that all those citizens who were deemed virtuous could cast their votes free of coercion and intimidation. At the same time, reformers sought to disfranchise all citizens who were considered irresponsible and corruptible. In pursuing these goals, progressives substantially altered the composition of the electorate and strengthened government regulation of voting. The results were contradictory. On the one hand, progressives enlarged the electorate by extending the right to vote to women; on the other hand, they either initiated or tolerated laws that barred large numbers of minority and poor voters from the polls.

THE AUSTRALIAN BALLOT

Government regulation of voting had begun back in the 1890s when virtually every state adopted the Australian, or secret, ballot. This reform required voters to vote in private rather than in public. It also required the government, rather than political parties, to print the ballots and supervise the voting. Prior to this time, each political party had printed its own ballot with only its candidates listed. At election time, each party mobilized its loyal supporters. Party workers offered liquor, free meals, and other bribes to entice voters to the polls and to "persuade" them to cast the party ballot. Because the ballots were cast in public, few voters who had accepted gifts of liquor and food dared to cross watchful party officials. Critics argued that the system corrupted the electoral process. They also pointed out that it made "ticket-splitting"—dividing one's vote between candidates of two or more parties—virtually impossible.

The Australian ballot solved these problems. Although it predated progressivism, it embodied the progressives' determination to use government power to encourage citizens to cast their votes responsibly and wisely.

PERSONAL REGISTRATION LAWS

That same determination was apparent in the progressives' support for the personal registration laws that virtually every state passed between 1890 and 1920. These laws allowed prospective voters to register to vote only if they appeared at a designated government office with proper identification. Frequently, these laws also mandated a certain period of residence in the state prior to registration and a certain interval between registration and actual voting.

Personal registration laws were meant to disfranchise citizens who showed no interest in voting until election day when a party worker arrived with a few dollars and offered a free ride to the polls. However, they also excluded many hardworking, responsible, poor people who wanted to vote but had failed to register, either because their work schedules made it impossible or because they were intimidated by the complex regulations. The laws were particularly frustrating for immigrants with limited knowledge of American government and of the English language.

DISFRANCHISEMENT

Progressives also promoted election laws expressly designed to keep noncitizen immigrants from voting. In the 1880s, 18 states had passed laws allowing immigrants to vote without first becoming citizens. Progressives reversed this trend. At the same time, the newly formed Bureau of Immigration and Naturalization (1906) made it more difficult to become a citizen. Applicants for citizenship now had to appear before a judge who interrogated them, in the English language, on American history and civics. In addition, immigrants were required to provide two witnesses to vouch for their "moral character" and their "attachment to the principles of the Constitution." Finally, immigrants had to swear (and, if necessary, prove) that they were not anarchists or polygamists and that they had resided continuously in the United States for five years.

Most progressives defended the new rigor of the process. U.S. citizenship, they believed, carried responsibilities; it was not to be bestowed lightly. This position was understandable, given the electoral abuses progressives had exposed. Nevertheless, the reforms also had the effect of denying the vote to a large proportion of the population. In cities and towns where immigrants dominated the workforce, the numbers of registered voters fell alarmingly. Nowhere was exclusion more startling than in the South, where between 1890 and 1904 every ex-Confederate state passed laws designed to strip blacks of their right to vote. Because laws explicitly barring blacks from voting would have

VOTER PARTICIPATION IN 13 SOUTHERN STATES, 1876, 1892, 1900, 1912

Source: Data from *Historical Statistics of the United States, Colonial Times to 1970* (White Plains, N.Y.: Kraus International, 1989).

violated the Fifteenth Amendment, this exclusion had to be accomplished indirectly—through literacy tests, property qualifications, and poll taxes. Any citizen who failed a reading test, or who could not sign his name, or who did not own a minimum amount of property, or who could not pay a poll tax, lost his right to vote. The citizens who failed these tests most frequently were blacks, who formed the poorest and least educated segment of the southern population, but a large portion of the region's poor whites also failed the tests. The effects of disfranchisement were stark. In 1900 only 1,300 blacks voted in Mississippi elections, down from 130,000 in the 1870s. Virginia's voter turnout dropped from 60 percent of adult men (white and black) in 1900 to 28 percent in 1904.

Many progressives in the North, such as Governor Robert La Follette of Wisconsin, bitterly criticized southern disfranchisement. Some, including Jane Addams and John Dewey, joined in 1910 with W. E. B. Du Bois and other black reformers to

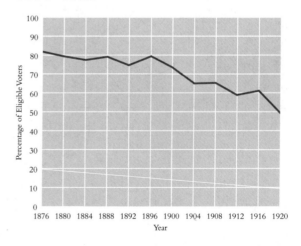

VOTER PARTICIPATION IN PRESIDENTIAL ELECTIONS, 1876–1920

Source: Data from *Historical Statistics of the United States, Colonial Times to 1970* (White Plains, N.Y.: Kraus International, 1989).

found the National Association for the Advancement of Colored People (NAACP), an interracial political organization that made black equality its primary goal. In the South, however, white progressives rarely challenged disfranchisement, and most had little difficulty justifying it with progressive ideology. Because progressives everywhere considered the franchise a precious gift granted only to those who could handle its responsibilities, they equally believed it must be withheld from any deemed racially or culturally unfit. Progressives in the North excluded many immigrants on just those grounds. Progressives in the South saw the disfranchisement of African Americans in the same light.

DISILLUSIONMENT WITH THE ELECTORATE

In the process of identifying those groups "unfit" to hold the franchise, some progressives soured on the electoral process altogether. The more they looked for rational and virtuous voters, the fewer they found. In *Drift and Mastery* (1914), Walter Lippmann developed a theory that ordinary people had been over-

LINK TO THE PAST

Are Women People? A Book of Rhymes for Suffrage Times

http://memory.loc.gov/cgi-bin/query/r?ammem/naw:@field+(SOURCE+@band(rbnawsa+n3348)):@@@REF

The title of this Web exercise is also the title of a book of humorous poems compiled in 1915 by suffrage supporters to counter arguments made by those who opposed giving women the right to vote. The poems from the book have been preserved in the National American Woman Suffrage Association Collection, located in the Rare Books Division of the Library of Congress (LC). The LC has made many of the collection's documents available online as part of its American Memory digitized database. When you access the page, you see that each poem has its own page subhead, which appears immediately below the gray lines that separate the pages. Scroll down past the Contents and look at these four poems:

- "Our Idea of Nothing at All" (subhead: Begin page no. 13)
- "On Not Believing All You Hear" (subhead: Begin page no. 15)
- "The Gallant Sex" (subhead: Begin page no. 19)
- "The Maiden's Vow" (subhead: Begin page no. 27)

1. What do these poems tell us about the arguments put forward by those who opposed giving women the vote?

2. The authors of these poems seem to want rights and opportunities for women beyond the right to vote. What were these rights and opportunities?

3. The supporters of suffrage were often depicted by their contemporaries and by scholars as a serious, humorless group. These poems suggest otherwise. How funny do you find these poems to be, and how effective do you think they might have been in developing support for woman suffrage?

whelmed by industrial and social changes. Because these changes seemed beyond their comprehension or control, they "drifted," unable to "master" the circumstances of modern life or take charge of their own destiny. Lippmann did not suggest that such ordinary people should be barred from voting, but he did argue that more political responsibility should rest with appointed officials with the training and knowledge necessary to make government effective and just. The growing disillusionment with the electorate, in combination with intensifying restrictions on the franchise, created an environment in which fewer and fewer Americans actually went to the polls. Voting participation rates fell from 79 percent in 1896 to only 49 percent in 1920.

WOMAN SUFFRAGE

The major exception to this trend was the enfranchisement of women. This momentous reform was accepted by several states during the 1890s and the first two decades of the 20th century and became federal law with the ratification of the Nineteenth Amendment to the Constitution in 1920.

Launched in 1848 at the famous Seneca Falls convention (see chapter 11), the women's rights movement floundered in the 1870s and 1880s. In 1890 suffragists came together in a new organization, the National American Woman Suffrage Association (NAWSA), led by such venerable figures as Elizabeth Cady Stanton and Susan B. Anthony. Thousands of young, college-educated women campaigned door-to-door, held impromptu rallies, and pressured state legislators.

Wyoming, which attained statehood in 1890, became the first state to grant women the right to vote, followed in 1893 by Colorado and in 1896 by Idaho and Utah. The main reason for success in these sparsely populated western states was not egalitarianism but rather the conviction that women's supposedly gentler and more nurturing nature would tame and civilize the rawness of the frontier.

This notion reflected a subtle but important change in the thrust of the suffrage movement. Earlier generations had insisted that women were fundamentally equal to men, but the new suffragists argued that women were different from men. Women, they stressed, possessed a moral sense and a nurturing quality that men lacked. Consequently, they understood the civic obligations implied by the franchise and could be trusted to vote virtuously. Their votes would hasten to completion the progressive task of cleansing the political process of corruption. Their experience as mothers and household managers, moreover, would enable them to guide local and state governments in efforts to improve education, sanitation, family wholesomeness, and the condition of women and children in the workforce. In other words, the enfranchisement of women would enhance the quality of both public and private life.

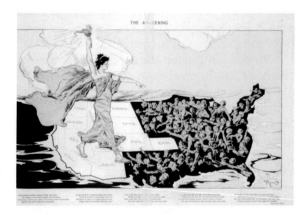

WOMAN SUFFRAGE This confident, torch-bearing suffragist striding across the continent in this 1915 cartoon conveys the conviction of woman suffragists everywhere that their most cherished goal, gaining the vote for women, was within reach. The cartoon also reveals the interesting split among the states: western states had already granted women the vote while eastern states had not.

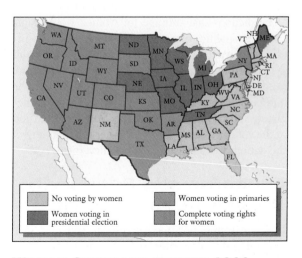

WOMAN SUFFRAGE BEFORE 1920

Suffragists were slow to ally themselves with blacks, Asians, and other disfranchised groups. In fact, many suffragists, especially those in the South and West, vehemently opposed the franchise for Americans of color. They, like their male counterparts, believed that members of these groups lacked moral strength and thus did not deserve the franchise. Unlike the suffrage pioneers of the 1840s and 1850s, many Progressive Era suffragists were little troubled by racial discrimination and injustice.

Washington, California, Kansas, Oregon, and Arizona followed the lead of the other western states by enfranchising women in the years from 1910 to 1912. After a series of setbacks in eastern and midwestern states, the movement regained momentum under the leadership of the strategically astute Carrie Chapman Catt, who became president of NAWSA in 1915, and successfully coordinated myriad grassroots campaigns. Equally important was Alice Paul, a radical who founded the Congressional Union in 1913 and later renamed it the National Woman's Party. Paul and her supporters focused their attention on the White House, picketing President Wilson's home 24 hours a day, unveiling large posters charging him with abandoning his democratic principles, and daring the police to arrest them. Several suffrage demonstrators were jailed, where they continued their protests by going on hunger strikes (refusing to eat). Aided by a heightened enthusiasm for democracy generated by America's participation in the First World War (see chapter 23), which generated a more positive popular response to Paul's tactics than might otherwise have been the case, the suffragists achieved their goal of universal woman suffrage in 1920.

Predictions that suffrage for women would radically alter politics turned out to be false. The political system was neither cleansed of corruption, nor did the government rush headlong to address the private needs of women and their families. Although the numbers of voters increased after 1920, voter participation rates continued to decline. Still, the extension of the vote to women, 144 years after the founding of the nation, was a great political achievement.

ECONOMIC AND SOCIAL REFORM IN THE STATES

In some states, progressive reform extended well beyond political parties and the electorate. Progressives also wanted to limit corporate power, strengthen organized labor, and offer social welfare protection to the weak. State governments were pressured into passing such legislation by progressive alliances of middle-class and working-class reformers, and by dynamic state governors.

ROBERT LA FOLLETTE AND WISCONSIN PROGRESSIVISM

Nowhere else did the progressives' campaign for social reform flourish as it did in Wisconsin. The movement arose first in the 1890s, in hundreds of Wisconsin cities and towns, as citizens began to mobilize against the state's corrupt Republican Party and the special privileges the party had granted to private utilities and railroads. These reform-minded citizens came from varied backgrounds. They were middle class and working class, urban and rural, male and female, intellectual and evangelical, Protestant Scandinavian and German Catholic. Wisconsin progressivism had already gained considerable momentum by 1897, when Robert La Follette assumed its leadership.

La Follette was born into a prosperous farming family in 1855. He entered politics as a Republican in the 1880s and embraced reform in the late 1890s. Elected governor in 1900, he secured for Wisconsin both a direct primary and a tax law that stripped the railroad corporations of tax exemptions they had long enjoyed. In 1905 he pushed through a civil service law mandating that every state employee meet a certain level of competence.

A tireless campaigner and a spellbinding speaker, "Fighting Bob" won election to the U.S. Senate in 1906. Meanwhile, Wisconsin's advancing labor and socialist movements forced progressive reformers to focus their legislative efforts on issues of corporate greed and social welfare. By 1910 reformers had passed state laws that regulated railroad and utility rates, instituted the nation's first state income tax, and provided workers with compensation for injuries, limitations on work hours, restrictions on child labor, and minimum wages for women.

Many of these laws were written by social scientists at the University of Wisconsin, with whom reformers had close ties. In the first decade of the 20th century, John R. Commons, University of Wisconsin economist, drafted Wisconsin's civil service and

ROBERT LA FOLLETTE, WISCONSIN PROGRESSIVE
This cartoon, "Mr. La Follette's Strongest Card," used Robert La Follette's record as governor of Wisconsin (1900–1906) to promote his 1912 campaign for the presidency. During La Follette's governorship, Wisconsin became the nation's leading "laboratory" for social and economic reform—although his accomplishments failed to win him the presidential nomination.

public utilities laws. In 1911 Commons designed and won legislative approval for the Wisconsin Industrial Commission, which brought together employers, trade unionists, and professionals and gave them broad powers to investigate and regulate relations between industry and labor throughout the state. Never before had a state government so plainly committed itself to the cause of industrial justice. For the first time, the rights of labor would be treated with the same respect as the rights of industry. Equally important was the responsibility the commission delegated to nonelected professionals: social scientists, lawyers, engineers, and others. These professionals, Wisconsin reformers believed, would succeed where political parties had failed— namely, in providing the public with expert and honest government.

The "Wisconsin idea" found quick adoption in Ohio, Indiana, New York, and Colorado; and in 1913 the federal government established its own Industrial Relations Commission and hired Commons to direct its investigative staff. In other areas, too, reformers began urging state and federal governments to shift the policymaking initiative away from political parties and toward administrative agencies staffed by professionals.

PROGRESSIVE REFORM IN NEW YORK

New York seemed second only to Wisconsin in the vigor and breadth of its progressive movement. As in Wisconsin, New York progressives focused first on fighting political corruption. Startling revelations of close ties between leading Republican politicians and life insurance companies vaulted reform lawyer Charles Evans Hughes into the governor's mansion in 1907. Hughes immediately established several public service commissions to regulate railroads and utility companies. Also, as in Wisconsin, labor had its effect. New York City garment workers struck and forced state legislators to treat working conditions more seriously. With the establishment of the Factory Investigating Committee, New York, like Wisconsin, became a pioneer in labor and social welfare policy.

New York state legislators also faced pressure from middle-class reformers—settlement house workers such as Lillian Wald of the Henry Street Settlement and lawyers such as Louis Brandeis— whose work with the poor had convinced them that the law must promote social justice. This combined pressure from working-class and middle-class constituencies impelled some state Democrats, including Assemblyman Alfred E. Smith and Senator Robert F. Wagner, to convert from machine to reform politics. Their appearance in the progressive ranks brought a new reform sensibility. Wagner and Smith were both ethnic Catholics (Wagner was born in Germany, and Smith was the grandchild of Irish immigrants). They opposed prohibition, city commissions, voter registration laws, and other reforms whose intent seemed anti-immigrant and anti-Catholic and supported reforms meant to improve the working and living conditions of New York's urban poor. They agitated for a minimum wage, factory safety, workmen's compensation, the right of workers to join unions, and the regulation of excessively powerful corporations. Their participation in progressivism accelerated the movement's shift, first in New York and then elsewhere, away from preoccupation with political parties and electorates and toward questions of economic justice and social welfare.

A RENEWED CAMPAIGN FOR CIVIL RIGHTS

At the same time that politicians such as Smith and Wagner introduced an ethnic sensibility into progressivism, a new generation of African American activists began insisting that the issue of racial equality also be placed on the reform agenda.

THE FAILURE OF ACCOMMODATIONISM

Booker T. Washington's message—that blacks should accept segregation and disfranchisement as unavoidable and focus their energies instead on self-help and self-improvement—faced increasing criticism from black activists such as W. E. B. Du Bois, Ida B. Wells, Monroe Trotter, and others. Washington's accommodationist leadership (see chapter 18), in their eyes, brought southern blacks no reprieve from racism. More than 100 blacks had been lynched in 1900 alone; between 1901 and 1914 at least 1,000 others would be hanged.

Increasingly, unsubstantiated rumors of black assaults on whites became occasions for white mobs to rampage through black neighborhoods and indiscriminately destroy life and property. In 1908 a mob in Springfield, Illinois, attacked black businesses and individuals; a force of 5,000 state militia was required to restore order. The troops were too late, however, to stop the lynching of two innocent black men, one a successful barber and the other an 84-year-old man who had been married to a white woman for more than 30 years. There was a sad irony in the deaths of these African Americans. Murdered in Abraham Lincoln's hometown and within walking distance of his grave, they died just as black and white Americans everywhere were preparing to celebrate the centennial of the Great Emancipator's birth.

Booker T. Washington had long believed that blacks who educated themselves or who succeeded

LYNCHING This grim photo records the death of five of the approximately 1,000 African Americans who were lynched between 1901 and 1914. The increase in lynching was one measure of the virulence of white racism in the early years of the 20th century.

in business should be accepted as equals by whites and welcomed into their society. As Du Bois and other black militants observed, however, white rioters made no distinction between rich blacks and poor, or between solid citizens and petty criminals. All that had seemed to matter was the color of one's skin. Similarly, many black militants knew from personal experience that individual accomplishment was not enough to overcome racial prejudice. DuBois himself was a brilliant scholar who became, in 1899, the first African American to receive a doctorate from Harvard University. Had he been white, Du Bois would have been asked to teach at Harvard or another elite academic institution. No prestigious white university, South or North, ever made him an offer.

FROM THE NIAGARA MOVEMENT TO THE NAACP

Seeing no future in accommodation, Du Bois and other young black activists came together at Niagara Falls in 1905 to fashion their own aggressive political agenda. They demanded that African Americans regain the right to vote in states that had taken it away; that segregation be abolished; and that the many discriminatory barriers to black advancement be removed. They declared their commitment to freedom of speech, the brotherhood of all men, and respect for the working man. Although their numbers were small, the members of the so-called Niagara movement were inspired by the example of the antebellum abolitionists. Meeting in Boston, Oberlin, and Harpers Ferry—all places of special significance to the abolitionist cause—they hoped to rekindle the militant, uncompromising spirit of that earlier crusade (see chapters 12 and 14).

The 1908 Springfield riot had shaken many whites. Some, especially those already working for social and economic reform, now joined in common cause with the Niagara movement. Together, black and white activists planned a conference for Lincoln's birthday in 1909 to revive, in the words of the writer William English Walling, "the spirit of the abolitionists" and to "treat the Negro on a plane of absolute political and social equality." Oswald Garrison Villard, the grandson of William Lloyd Garrison, called on "all believers in democracy to join in a National conference for the discussion of present evils, the voicing of protests, and the renewal of the struggle for civil and political liberty." The conference brought together distinguished progressives, white and black, including Mary White Ovington, Jane Addams, John Dewey, William Dean Howells, Ida B. Wells, and Du Bois. They drew up plans to establish an organization dedicated to fighting racial discrimination and prejudice. In May 1910 the National Association for the Advancement of Colored People (NAACP) was officially launched, with Moorfield Storey of Boston as president, Walling as chairman of the executive committee, and Du Bois as the director of publicity and research.

The formation of the NAACP marked the beginning of the modern civil rights movement. The organization immediately launched a magazine, the *Crisis*, edited by Du Bois, to publicize and protest the lynchings, riots, and other abuses directed against black citizens. Equally important was the Legal Redress Committee, which initiated lawsuits against city and state governments for violating the constitutional rights of African Americans. The committee scored its first major success in 1915, when the U.S. Supreme Court ruled that the so-called "grandfather" clauses of the Oklahoma and Maryland constitutions violated the Fifteenth Amendment. (These clauses allowed poor, uneducated whites—but not poor, uneducated blacks—to vote, even if they failed to pay their state's poll tax or to pass its literacy test, by exempting the descendants of men who had voted prior to 1867.) NAACP lawyers won again in 1917 when the Supreme Court declared unconstitutional a Louisville, Kentucky, law that required all blacks to reside in predetermined parts of the city.

By 1914, the NAACP had enrolled thousands of members in scores of branches throughout the United States. The organization's success generated other civil rights groups. The National Urban League, founded in 1911, worked to improve the economic and social conditions of blacks in cities. It pressured employers to hire blacks, distributed lists of available jobs and housing in African American communities, and developed social programs to ease the adjustment of rural black migrants to city life.

Progress toward racial equality was slow. Attacking segregation and discrimination through lawsuits was, by its nature, a snail-paced strategy that would take decades to complete. The growing membership of the NAACP, although impressive, was not large enough to qualify it as a mass movement. And its interracial character made the organization seem dangerously radical to millions of whites. White NAACP leaders responded to this hostility by limiting the number and power of African Americans who worked for the organization. This conciliatory policy, in turn, outraged black militants who argued that no civil rights organization should be in the business of appeasing white racists.

Despite its limitations, the NAACP made significant strides. The NAACP gave Du Bois the security and visibility he needed to carry on his fight against Booker T. Washington's accommodationist philosophy. Even before his death in 1915, Washington's influence in black and white communities had begun to recede. The NAACP, more than any other organization, helped resurrect the issue of racial equality at a time when many white Americans had accepted as normal the practices of racial segregation and discrimination.

W. E. B. DU BOIS Du Bois was one of the founders of the National Association for the Advancement of Colored People, and the editor of its magazine, the *Crisis*. This photograph shows him in the offices of the *Crisis*. Du Bois would become one of the most important African American intellectuals and activists of the 20th century.

NATIONAL REFORM

The more progressives focused on economic and social matters, the more they sought to increase their influence in national politics. Certain problems demanded national solutions. No patchwork of state regulations, for example, could curtail the power of the trusts, protect workers, or monitor the quality of consumer goods. Moreover, state and federal courts often were hostile toward progressive goals: They repeatedly struck down as unconstitutional reform laws regulating working hours or setting minimum wages, on the grounds that they impinged on the freedom of contract and trade. A national progressive movement could force passage of laws less vulnerable to judicial veto or elect a president who could overhaul the federal judiciary with progressive-minded judges.

National leadership would not emerge from Congress. The Democratic Party had been scarred by the Populist challenge of the 1890s. Divided between the radical Bryanites and the conservative

followers of Grover Cleveland, and consequently unable to speak with one voice on questions of social and economic policy, after 1896 the Democrats seemed incapable of winning a national election or offering a national agenda. The Republican Party was more unified and popular, but it was controlled by a conservative "Old Guard." Led by Senator Nelson Aldrich of Rhode Island and House Speaker Joseph G. Cannon of Illinois, and closely tied to Marcus A. Hanna and other industrialists, the "Grand Old Party" (or GOP, a nickname Republicans gave the party in the 1880s) was pro-business and devoted to a 19th-century style of backroom patronage. It feared insurgency and turned a deaf ear to popular clamor for change. When Robert La Follette arrived in the Senate from Wisconsin in 1907, the Republican Old Guard ostracized him as a dangerous radical.

National progressive leadership came from the executive rather than the legislative branch, and from two presidents in particular, Republican Theodore Roosevelt and Democrat Woodrow

Wilson. These two presidents sponsored reforms that profoundly affected the lives of Americans and altered the nature of the American presidency.

THE ROOSEVELT PRESIDENCY

When the Republican bosses chose Theodore Roosevelt as William McKinley's running mate in 1900, their purpose was more to remove this headstrong, unpredictable character from New York state politics than to groom him for national leadership. As governor of New York, Roosevelt had been a moderate reformer, but even his modest efforts to rid the state's Republican Party of corruption and to institute civil service reform were too much for the state party machine, led by Thomas C. Platt. Consigning Roosevelt to the vice presidency seemed a safe solution. McKinley was a young, vigorous politician, fully in control of his party and his presidency.

Less than a year into his second term, in September 1901, McKinley was shot by an anarchist assassin. The president clung to life for nine days, and then died. Upon succeeding McKinley, Theodore Roosevelt, age 42, became the youngest chief executive in the nation's history.

Born to an aristocratic New York family, Roosevelt nevertheless developed an uncommon affection for "the people." Asthmatic, sickly, and nearsighted as a boy, he remade himself into a vigorous adult. With an insatiable appetite for high-risk adventure—everything from "dude ranching" in the Dakota Territory, to big-game hunting in Africa, to wartime combat—he was also a voracious reader and an accomplished writer. Aggressive and swaggering in his public rhetoric, he was in private a skilled, patient negotiator. A devout believer in the superiority of the English-speaking peoples, he nevertheless appointed members of "inferior" races to important posts in his administration. Rarely has a president's personality so enthralled the American public. He is the only 20th-century president immortalized on Mount Rushmore.

REGULATING THE TRUSTS

Roosevelt quickly revealed his flair for the dramatic. In 1902 he ordered the Justice Department to prosecute the Northern Securities Company, a $400 million monopoly set up by leading financiers and railroad tycoons to control all railroad lines and traffic in the Northwest from Chicago to Washington state. Never before had an American president sought to use the Sherman Antitrust Act to break up a monopoly. The news shocked J. P. Morgan, the banker who had brokered the Northern Securities deal. Morgan rushed to the White House, where he is said to have told Roosevelt, "If we have done anything wrong, send your man to my man and they can fix it up." Roosevelt would have none of this "fixing." In 1903 a federal court ordered Northern Securities dissolved, and the U.S. Supreme Court upheld the decision the next year. Roosevelt was hailed as the nation's "trust-buster."

Roosevelt, however, did not believe in breaking up all, or even most, large corporations. Industrial concentration, he believed, brought the United States wealth, productivity, and a rising standard of living. Government should regulate these industrial giants, punish those that used their power improperly, and protect citizens disadvantaged in their dealings with industry.

This new role would require the federal government to expand its powers. Roosevelt's antitrust campaign aimed to strengthen the federal government, not to return the nation to small-scale industry. And this newly fortified government—the centerpiece of a political program that Roosevelt would later call the "New Nationalism"— was to be led by a forceful president, willing to use all the powers at his disposal to achieve prosperity and justice.

TOWARD A "SQUARE DEAL"

Roosevelt displayed his willingness to use government power to protect the economically weak in a long and bitter 1902 coal miners' strike. Miners in the anthracite fields of eastern Pennsylvania wanted recognition for their union, the United Mine Workers (UMW). They also wanted a 10 to 20 percent increase in wages and an eight-hour day. When their employers, led by the uncompromising George F. Baer of the Reading Railroad, refused to negotiate, they went on strike. In October, the fifth month of the strike, Roosevelt summoned the mine owners and John Mitchell, the UMW president, to the White House. Baer expected Roosevelt to threaten the striking workers with arrest by federal troops if they failed to return to work. Instead, Roosevelt supported Mitchell's request for arbitration and warned the mine owners that if they refused to go along, 10,000 federal troops would seize their property. Stunned, the mine owners agreed to submit the dispute to arbitrators, who awarded the unionists a 10 percent wage increase and a nine-hour day.

The mere fact that the federal government had ordered employers to compromise with their workers carried great symbolic weight. Roosevelt enjoyed a surge of support from ordinary Americans convinced that he shared their dislike for ill-gotten wealth and privilege. He also raised the hopes of African Americans when, only a month into his presidency, he dined with Booker T. Washington at the White House. Rarely had an American president so honored an African American leader. Blacks were impressed, too, by how easily Roosevelt brushed off the protests of white southerners who accused him of striking a blow against segregation.

In his 1904 election campaign, Roosevelt promised that, if reelected, he would offer every American a "square deal." The slogan resonated with voters and helped carry Roosevelt to a victory (57 percent of the popular vote) over the lackluster, conservative Democrat Alton B. Parker. To the surprise of many observers, Roosevelt had aligned the Republican Party with the cause of reform.

EXPANDING GOVERNMENT POWER: THE ECONOMY

Emboldened by his victory, the president intensified his efforts to extend government regulation of economic affairs. His most important proposal was to give the government power to set railroad shipping rates and thereby to eliminate the industry's discriminatory marketing practices. The government, in theory, already possessed this power through the Interstate Commerce Commission (ICC), a national regulatory body established by Congress in 1887, but the courts had so weakened the ICC's oversight and regulatory functions as to render it virtually powerless. Roosevelt achieved his goal in 1906. Congress passed the Hepburn Act, which significantly increased the ICC's powers of rate review and enforcement. Roosevelt supported

> *"The betterment which we seek must be accomplished, I believe, mainly through the national government."*
>
> **THEODORE ROOSEVELT**
> *1910*

the Pure Food and Drug Act, passed by Congress that same year, which protected the public from fraudulently marketed and dangerous foods and medications. The uproar created by the publication of Sinclair's *The Jungle* in 1906 prompted Roosevelt to order a government investigation of conditions in the meatpacking industry. When the investigation corroborated Sinclair's findings, Roosevelt supported the Meat Inspection Act (1906), which committed the government to monitoring the quality and safety of meat being sold to American consumers.

EXPANDING GOVERNMENT POWER: THE ENVIRONMENT

Roosevelt also did more than any previous president to extend federal control over the nation's physical environment. Roosevelt was not a "preservationist" in the manner of John Muir, founder of the Sierra Club, who insisted that the beauty of the land and the well-being of its wildlife should be protected from all human interference. Roosevelt viewed the wilderness as a place to live strenuously, to test oneself against rough natural elements, and to match wits against strong and clever game. Roosevelt further believed that in the West—that land of ancient forests, lofty mountain peaks, and magnificent canyons—Americans could learn something important about their nation's roots and destiny. To preserve this West, Roosevelt oversaw the creation of 5 new national parks, 16 national monuments, and 53 wildlife reserves. The work of his administration led directly to the formation of the National Park Service in 1916.

Roosevelt also emerged a strong supporter of the "conservationist" movement. These conservationists cared little for national parks or grand canyons. They wanted to manage the environment, so as to ensure that the nation's resources were put to the most efficient use for economic development. Roosevelt shared the conservationists' belief that the plundering of western timberlands, grazing areas, water resources, and minerals had reached crisis proportions. Only broad regulatory controls would restore the West's economic potential.

To that end, Roosevelt appointed a Public Lands Commission in 1903 to survey public lands, inventory them, and establish permit systems to regulate the kinds and numbers of users. Soon after, the Departments of Interior and Agriculture placed certain western lands rich in natural resources and waterpower off-limits to agricultural users. Government officials also limited waterpower development by requiring companies to acquire permits and pay fees for the right to generate electricity on their sites. When political favoritism and corruption within the Departments of the Interior and Agriculture threatened these efforts at regulation, Roosevelt authorized the hiring of university-trained bureaucrats to replace state and local politicians. Scientific expertise, rather than political connections, would now determine the distribution and use of western lands.

Gifford Pinchot, a specialist in forestry management and Roosevelt's close friend, led the drive for expert and scientific management of natural resources. In 1905 he persuaded Roosevelt to relocate jurisdiction for the national forests from the Department of the Interior to the Department of Agriculture, which, Pinchot argued, was the most appropriate department to oversee the efficient "harvest" of the nation's forest crop. The newly created National Forest Service, under Pinchot's control, quickly instituted a system of competitive bidding for the right to harvest timber on national forest lands. Pinchot and his expanding staff of college-educated foresters also implemented a new policy that exacted user fees from livestock ranchers who had previously used national forest grazing lands for free. Armed with new legislation and bureaucratic authority, Pinchot and fellow conservationists in the Roosevelt administration also declared vast stretches of federal land in the West off-limits to mining and dam construction.

The Republican Old Guard disliked these initiatives. When Roosevelt recommended prosecution of cattlemen and lumbermen who were illegally using federal land for private gain, congressional conservatives struck back with legislation (in 1907) that curtailed the president's power to create new government land reserves. Roosevelt responded by seizing another 17 million acres for national forest reserves before the new law went into effect. To his conservative opponents, excluding commercial activity from public land—a program they regarded as socialistic—was bad enough, but flouting the will of Congress with a 17-million-acre land grab violated hallowed constitutional principles governing the separation of powers. Yet, to millions of American voters, Roosevelt's willingness to defy western cattle barons, mining tycoons, and other "malefactors of great wealth" added to his popularity.

PROGRESSIVISM: A MOVEMENT FOR THE PEOPLE?

Historians have long debated how much Roosevelt's economic and environmental reforms altered the balance of power between the "interests" and the people. Some have demonstrated that many corporations were eager for federal government regulation—that railroad corporations wanted relief from the ruinous rate wars that were driving them into bankruptcy, for example, and that the larger meatpackers believed that the costs of government food inspections would drive smaller meatpackers out of business. So, too, historians have shown that large agribusinesses, timber companies, and mining corporations in the West believed that government regulation would aid them and hurt smaller competitors. According to this view, government regulation benefited the corporations more than it benefited workers, consumers, and small businessmen.

This view has some validity. These early reforms often curtailed corporate power only to a limited extent. Corporations, working through lobbying organizations such as the National Civic Federation and through Old Guard Republicans in the Senate, fought with some success to turn the final versions of the reform laws to their advantage. That does not mean (as some historians have argued) that the corporations sponsored reform, or that they dictated the content of reform measures.

Popular anger over corporate power and over political corruption remained a driving force of

Origins of the Environmental Movement

An American who visited the Yellowstone River in 1870 was overwhelmed by what he saw: "amid the canyon and falls, the boiling springs and sulphur mountain, and, above all, the mud volcano and the geysers of the Yellowstone, your memory becomes filled and clogged with objects new in experience, wonderful in extent, and possessing unlimited grandeur and beauty." As early as 1872, the awe that this landscape inspired—that would spur Thomas Moran in 1893 to paint the magnificent picture of the Grand Canyon of the

progressivism. After 1906, Senators La Follette, Albert Beveridge of Indiana, and other anticorporate Republicans gave that anger a powerful national voice. Before he left office in 1909, Roosevelt would expand his reform program to include income and inheritance taxes, a national workmen's compensation law, abolition of child labor, and the eight-hour workday. Those proposals widened the rift between Roosevelt and the Old Guard, as did his public attacks on the courts for declaring un-

constitutional important pieces of progressive legislation. In 1907 the progressive program was still evolving. Whether the corporations or the people would benefit most remained unclear.

THE REPUBLICANS: A DIVIDED PARTY

The financial panic of 1907 further strained relations between Roosevelt reformers and Old Guard

Yellowstone that appears on the left—prompted Congress to create Yellowstone National Park and thus to preserve "the wonders within said park" for all time. Concern for the natural environment accelerated in the late 19th and early 20th centuries as economic development in the West, especially mining of the sort depicted below, stripped many landscapes of their natural beauty. Eastern industrialization and urbanization and their associated problems also increased the symbolic importance of a pristine West as a place where individuals could build their character in struggles against nature and partake of a sublime America as yet untrammeled by machines and people.

These sentiments propelled the first environmental movement, which coalesced during the Progressive Era. Among its leaders was John Muir, founder of the Sierra Club, pictured here alongside Theodore Roosevelt and in front of an immense California redwood.

conservatives. When several New York banks failed in a speculative effort to corner the copper market they triggered a run on banks, a short but severe dip in industrial production, and widespread layoffs. Everywhere, people worried that a devastating depression, like that of the 1890s, was in the offing. Indeed, only the timely decision of J. P. Morgan and his fellow bankers to pour huge amounts of private cash into the collapsing banks saved the nation from an economic crisis. Prosperity quickly re-turned, but the panic jitters lingered. Conservatives blamed Roosevelt's "radical" economic policies for the fiasco. To Roosevelt and his fellow progressives, however, the panic merely pointed up how little impact their reforms had actually made on the reign of "speculation, corruption, and fraud."

Roosevelt now committed himself even more strongly to a reform agenda that included an overhaul of the banking system and the stock market. The Republican Old Guard, meanwhile, was more determined than ever to run the "radical" Roosevelt out of the White House. Sensing that he might fail to win his party's nomination, and mindful of a rash promise he had made in 1904 not to run again in 1908, Roosevelt decided not to seek reelection. It was a decision that he would soon regret. Barely 50, he was too young and energetic to end his political career. And much of his reform program had yet to win Congressional approval.

THE TAFT PRESIDENCY

Roosevelt thought he had found in William Howard Taft, his secretary of war, an ideal successor. Taft had worked closely with Roosevelt on foreign and domestic policies. He had supported Roosevelt's progressive reforms and offered him shrewd advice on countless occasions. Roosevelt believed he possessed both the ideas and the skills to complete the reform Republican program.

To reach that conclusion, however, Roosevelt had to ignore some obvious differences between Taft and himself. Taft neither liked nor was particularly adept at politics. With the exception of a judgeship in an Ohio superior court, he had never held elective office. His greatest political asset was an ability to debate thorny constitutional questions. His respect for the Constitution and its separation of powers made him suspicious of the powers that Roosevelt had arrogated to the presidency. He was by nature a cautious and conservative man, qualities that endeared him to the Republican Old Guard. As Roosevelt's anointed successor, Taft easily won the election of 1908, defeating Democrat William Jennings Bryan with 52 percent of the vote. His conservatism soon revealed itself in his choice of staid corporation lawyers, rather than freethinking reformers, for cabinet positions.

TAFT'S BATTLES WITH CONGRESS

Taft's troubles began when he appeared to side with the Old Guard and against progressives in two acrimonious congressional battles. The first was over tariff legislation, the second over the powers of House Speaker "Uncle Joe" Cannon.

Progressives had long desired tariff reduction, believing that competition from foreign manufacturers would benefit American consumers and check the economic power of American manufacturers. Taft himself had raised expectations for tariff reduction when he called Congress into special session to consider a reform bill that called for a modest reduction of tariffs and an inheritance tax. The bill passed the House but was gutted in the Senate when the Old Guard killed the inheritance tax and eliminated most of the tariff reductions. When congressional progressives pleaded with Taft to use his power to whip conservative senators into line, he pressured the Old Guard into including a 2 percent corporate income tax in their version of the bill, but he did not insist on the tariff reductions. As a result, the Payne-Aldrich Tariff he signed into law on August 5, 1909, did nothing to encourage imports. Progressive Republicans, bitterly disappointed, held Taft responsible.

They were further angered when Taft withdrew his support of their efforts to strip Speaker Cannon of his legislative powers, which (they believed) he was putting to improper use. By 1910 Republican insurgents no longer looked to Taft for leadership; instead they entered into an alliance with reform-minded congressional Democrats. This bipartisan coalition of insurgents first curbed Cannon's powers and then, over Taft's objections, diluted the pro-business nature of a railroad regulation bill. Relations between Taft and the progressive Republicans all but collapsed in a bruising controversy over Taft's conservation policies.

THE BALLINGER-PINCHOT CONTROVERSY

Secretary of the Interior Richard A. Ballinger had aroused progressives' suspicions by reopening for private commercial use one million acres of land that the Roosevelt administration had previously brought under federal protection. Gifford Pinchot, still head of the National Forest Service, obtained information implicating Ballinger in the sale of Alaskan coal deposits to a syndicate headed up by J. P. Morgan and mining magnate David Guggenheim. Pinchot showed the information, including an allegation that Ballinger had personally profited from the sale, to Taft. When Taft defended Ballinger, Pinchot leaked the story to the press and publicly called on Congress to investigate the matter. Pinchot's insubordination cost him his job, but it riveted the nation's attention once again on corporate greed and government corruption. Taft's Old Guard allies controlled the investigation that followed, and Congress exonerated Ballinger, but Louis D. Brandeis, lawyer for the congressional reformers, kept the controversy alive by accusing Taft and his attorney general of tampering with information that had been sent to congressional investigators. Whatever hope Taft may have had of escaping political damage disappeared when Roosevelt, returning from an African hunting trip by way of Europe in the spring of 1910, staged a highly publicized rendezvous with Pinchot in England. In so doing, Roosevelt signaled his continuing support for his old friend Pinchot and his sharp displeasure with Taft.

ROOSEVELT'S RETURN

When Roosevelt arrived in the United States later that summer, he quickly returned to politics. In September, Roosevelt embarked on a speaking tour, the high point of which was his elaboration at Osawatomie, Kansas, of his "New Nationalism," a far-reaching reform program that called for a strong federal government to stabilize the economy, protect the weak, and restore social harmony.

THEODORE ROOSEVELT LAUNCHES HIS NEW NATIONALISM CAMPAIGN, 1910 This photograph of Roosevelt at Osawatomie, Kansas, captures some of the strength and exuberance he used to enthrall the public. Roosevelt's appearance at Osawatomie marked his formal return to politics. For the occasion, he unveiled his New Nationalism, a far-reaching program of reform that called on the government to control the powerful corporations in the interests of the commonweal.

The 1910 congressional elections confirmed the popularity of Roosevelt's positions. Insurgent Republicans trounced conservative Republicans in primary after primary, and the Democrats' embrace of reform brought them a majority in the House of Representatives for the first time since 1894. When Robert La Follette, who was challenging Taft for the Republican presidential nomination, seemed to suffer a nervous breakdown in February 1912, Roosevelt announced his own candidacy.

Although La Follette recovered his health and resumed his campaign, he had little chance of beating Roosevelt in the fight for the Republican nomination. Taft, too, would have lost to Roosevelt had the decision been in the hands of rank-and-file Republicans. In the 13 states sponsoring preferential primaries, Roosevelt won nearly 75 percent of the delegates, but the party's national leadership remained in the hands of the Old Guard, and they were determined to deny Roosevelt the Republican nomination. Taft, angered by Roosevelt's behavior, refused to step aside. At the Republican convention in Chicago, Taft won renomination on the first ballot.

THE BULL MOOSE CAMPAIGN

Roosevelt had expected this outcome. The night before the convention opened, he had told a spirited assembly of 5,000 supporters that the party leaders would not succeed in derailing their movement. "We stand at Armageddon," he declared, and "we battle for the Lord." The next day, Roosevelt and his supporters withdrew from the convention and from the Republican Party. In August, the reformers reassembled as the new Progressive Party, nominated Roosevelt for president and California governor Hiram W. Johnson for vice president, and hammered out the reform platform they had long envisioned: sweeping regulation of the corporations, extensive protections for workers (minimum wage, workmen's compensation, the prohibition of child labor), a sharply graduated income tax, and woman suffrage. The new party constituted a remarkable assemblage of reformers—social workers, suffragists, muckrakers, conservationists, and others—all exhilarated by their defiance of party bosses. "I am as strong as a bull moose," Roosevelt roared as he readied for combat; his proud followers took to calling themselves "Bull Moosers."

Some of them, however, probably including Roosevelt himself, knew that their mission was futile. They had failed to enroll many of the Republican insurgents who had supported Roosevelt in the primaries but who now refused to abandon the GOP. Consequently, the Republican vote would be split between Roosevelt and Taft. And Roosevelt could not even guarantee a united progressive vote. The Democrats had nominated a powerful reform candidate of their own.

THE RISE OF WOODROW WILSON

Few would have predicted in 1908 that the distinguished president of Princeton University, Woodrow Wilson, would be the 1912 Democratic nominee for president of the United States. Prior to 1910 Wilson had never run for elective office, nor had he ever held an appointed post in a local, state, or federal administration. The son of a Presbyterian minister from Virginia, Wilson had practiced law for a short time after graduating from Princeton (then still the College of New Jersey) in 1879 before settling on an academic career. Earning his doctorate in political science from Johns Hopkins in 1886, he taught history and political science at Bryn Mawr and Wesleyan (Connecticut) before returning to Princeton in 1890. He became president of Princeton in 1902, a post he held until he successfully ran for the governorship of New Jersey in 1910.

Throughout his almost 30 years in academe, however, Wilson had aspired to a career in politics. As a scholar, he focused largely on the workings of government institutions and on how they might be improved. In 1885 he published *Congressional Government*, a brilliant analysis and critique of Congress that would long remain the most important work in its field. He enjoyed his role as a university president and admired the powerful leadership style of such British parliamentary giants as Benjamin Disraeli and William Gladstone. "I feel like a new prime minister getting ready to address his constituents," he remarked to his wife as he prepared for the Princeton presidency in 1902. The national reputation he won in that office rested less on his originality as an educator than on the leadership he displayed in transforming the humdrum College of New Jersey into a world-class university.

Wilson's public stature as a university president afforded him new opportunities to comment on political as well as educational matters. Identifying himself with the anti-Bryan wing of the Democratic Party, he attracted the attention of wealthy conservatives, such as George Harvey of *Harper's Weekly*, who saw him as a potential presidential candidate. Harvey and his associates convinced the bosses of the New Jersey Democratic machine to nominate Wilson for governor in 1910. Beset by growing opposition to his aggressive style of leadership from trustees and faculty members at Princeton, and eager to test his talents in a new arena, Wilson accepted the nomination and won the governorship handily. He then shocked his conservative backers by declaring his independence from the state's Democratic machine and moving New Jersey into the forefront of reform.

THE UNEXPECTED PROGRESSIVE

Wilson embraced reform partly for expediency. Aspiring to the White House, he sensed that an alliance with reformers rather than with standpatters would best further his political career. But his turn toward progressivism also reflected an impulse that Wilson's conservative supporters had failed to detect. Wilson's Presbyterian upbringing had instilled in him a strong sense that society should be governed by God's moral law. As a young man in the 1880s, he had found the social consequences of unregulated industrialization repugnant to Christian ethical principles. "The modern industrial organization," he wrote at the time, had "so distorted competition as to put it into the power of some to tyrannize over many, as to enable the rich and strong to combine against the poor and weak." And therefore, Wilson asked, "must not government lay aside all timid scruple and boldly make itself an agency for social reform as well as political control?"

As a young man, Wilson had been drawn to socialism because of its plans to build a strong government that would tame the "captains of industry" and reinvigorate American democracy. These early socialist sympathies had dissolved amid the anger, chaos, and violence of the agrarian and labor uprisings of the 1890s. Wilson wanted reform to occur

Wilson (1941)

**Directed by Henry King. Starring Alexander Knox (Wilson),
Thomas Mitchell (Joseph Tumulty), Ruth Nelson (Ellen Wilson—first wife),
Geraldine Fitzgerald (Edith Wilson—second wife), Cedric Hardwicke (Henry Cabot Lodge).**

Hollywood films about presidents are rare, and *Wilson* reveals some of the challenges confronting those willing to undertake such projects: achieving an impartial point of view on a president's political achievements, balancing the president's affairs of state and family affairs, and developing a perspective on the presidential figure himself that is neither fawning nor excessively hostile.

The makers of this movie considered Woodrow Wilson a great man and president: intelligent, principled, courageous, visionary, and devoted to his family. Wilson's greatness lies ultimately, the movie suggests, in his willingness to stand up for what's right—for the common man against wealthy elites; for democracy against the party bosses; for keeping America out of war when some Americans were too eager to fight; and for a new world order of peace, diplomacy, and fairness and against those who wanted to rule through war and conquest. Numerous historians were consulted to assemble this portrait, and no expense was spared in an effort to recreate historically accurate sets.

Nevertheless, the relentless celebration of Wilson's qualities endows the film with a ponderousness, evident in its excessive length, the too frequent efforts to stir the emotions of audiences by playing bars from "My Country 'Tis of Thee," and numbing visual emphasis on the majesty of the White House quarters. The movie, too, makes a great deal of Wilson's love for both of his wives and his three daughters, and of their devotion to him, and too many scenes have the family gathered around the piano, singing songs that express their domestic bliss. The movie would have benefited from exploring Wilson's rigidities and blind spots as well as his strengths and from more fully examining the controversy surrounding his second wife, Edith, especially her role in managing Wilson and the government after his 1919 stroke.

Nevertheless, the movie has significant virtues. It features several lavish sets, such as those for the 1912 Democratic Party convention and for Wilson's appearances before Congress in 1917 and 1918, that impressively re-create the look and feel of contemporary building interiors and political assemblies. Once America enters the war, moreover, the movie acquires the momentum and focus it earlier lacked. Wilson's eloquent speeches for world peace and of his tense interchanges with key political antagonists, such as Senator Henry Cabot Lodge and Premier Georges Clemenceau of France, are brilliantly done; moreover, they are intercut with authentic World War I newsreel footage in effective and illuminating ways. Finally, Wilson's last, and debilitating, campaign to sell the Treaty of Versailles to the American people after opposition had appeared to block its passage in the Senate gives the movie a dramatic climax. For the textbook's analysis of that campaign, see chapter 23, pages 800–806. The film thus retains considerable interest and power.

Alexander Knox as Woodrow Wilson, addressing Congress.

in an orderly, peaceful way; he recoiled from the labor and populist agitators who, in his eyes, showed no respect for existing social and political institutions. The more Wilson stressed the values of order, harmony, and tradition in his public speeches as president of Princeton, the more he attracted the attention of conservatives such as George Harvey.

Wilson's reform impulses had receded by 1910, but they had not disappeared. Their presence in his thought helps to explain his emergence in 1911 and 1912 as one of the most outspoken progressives in the nation.

THE ELECTION OF 1912

At the Democratic convention of 1912, Wilson was something of a dark horse, running a distant second to House Speaker Champ Clark of Missouri. When the New York delegation gave Clark a simple majority of delegates, virtually everyone assumed that he would soon command the two-thirds majority needed to win the nomination. But Wilson's managers held onto Wilson's delegates and began chipping away at Clark's lead. On the fourth day, on the 46th ballot, Wilson finally won the nomination. The exhausted Democrats closed ranks behind a candidate who pledged to renew the national campaign for reform.

The stage was now set for the momentous 1912 election. Given the split in Republican ranks, Democrats had their best chance in 20 years of regaining the White House. A Wilson victory, moreover, would give the country its first southern-born president in almost 50 years. Finally, whatever its outcome, the election promised to deliver a hefty vote for reform. Both Roosevelt and Wilson were running on reform platforms, and the Socialist Party candidate, Eugene V. Debs, was attracting larger crowds and generating greater enthusiasm than had been expected. Taft was so certain of defeat that he barely campaigned.

Debate among the candidates focused on the trusts. All three reform candidates agreed that corporations had acquired too much economic power. Debs argued that the only way to ensure popular control of that power was for the federal government to assume ownership of the trusts. That solu-

tion was anathema to Roosevelt and Wilson. Roosevelt called for the establishment of a powerful government that would regulate and, if necessary, curb the power of the trusts. This was the essence of his New Nationalism, the program he had been advocating since 1910.

Wilson, however, was too suspicious of centralized government to countenance such a program. Rather than regulate the trusts, he wanted to break them up. He wanted to reverse the tendency toward economic concentration and thus restore opportunity to the people. Wilson labeled his philosophy the "New Freedom." He called for a temporary concentration of governmental power in order to dismantle the trusts, but once that was accomplished, Wilson promised, the government would relinquish its power.

Wilson won the November election with 42 percent of the popular vote to Roosevelt's 27 percent and Taft's 23 percent; Debs made a strong showing with 6 percent, the largest in his party's history. The three candidates who had pledged themselves to reform programs—Wilson, Roosevelt, and Debs—together won a remarkable 75 percent of the vote. Never before had a president come into

PRESIDENTIAL ELECTION, 1912

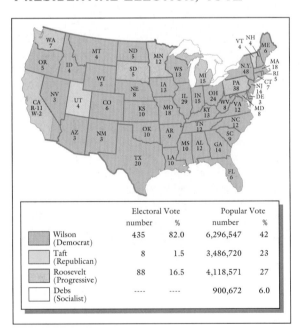

	Electoral Vote		Popular Vote	
	number	%	number	%
Wilson (Democrat)	435	82.0	6,296,547	42
Taft (Republican)	8	1.5	3,486,720	23
Roosevelt (Progressive)	88	16.5	4,118,571	27
Debs (Socialist)	----	----	900,672	6.0

office with such an overwhelming popular mandate for reform. Wilson rose to the challenge.

THE WILSON PRESIDENCY

The new president immediately put into practice the parliamentary-style leadership he had long admired. He assembled a cabinet of talented men who could be counted on for wise counsel, loyalty, and influence over vital Democratic constituencies. He cultivated a public image of himself as a president firmly in charge of his party and as a faithful tribune of the people.

TARIFF REFORM AND A PROGRESSIVE INCOME TAX

Like his predecessor, Wilson first turned his attention to tariff reform. Immediately after his inaugu-

WOODROW WILSON Wilson entered politics after a long career in academia, where he had been a distinguished political scientist, historian, and university president. Here he sits for a full-length seated portrait soon after his election to the presidency.

ration, he called Congress into special session to consider the matter. The House passed a tariff reduction bill within a month, but the bill ran into trouble in the Senate, chiefly because of the pressure that protectionist lobbyists applied to key Democratic senators. Wilson outflanked them by appealing directly to the American people to destroy the influence of private interests on lawmakers. Wilson's plea to the public, together with an ensuing investigation of senator-lobbyist relations, humbled the Senate into complying with the president's wishes. Wilson's display of presidential leadership dazzled Washington.

The resulting Underwood-Simmons Tariff of 1913 achieved the long-sought progressive aim of significantly reducing tariff barriers (from approximately 40 to 25 percent). Then, partly to find new funds to make up for revenue lost to tariff reductions, progressives achieved another ambition with passage of an income tax law. The Sixteenth Amendment to the Constitution, ratified by the states in 1913, had already given the government the right to impose an income tax; the income tax law passed by Congress made good on the progressive pledge to reduce the power and privileges of wealthy Americans by requiring them to pay taxes on a greater *percentage* of their income than the poor.

THE FEDERAL RESERVE ACT

Wilson continued to demonstrate his leadership by keeping Congress in session through the summer to consider various plans to overhaul the nation's financial system. Virtually everyone in both parties agreed on the need for greater federal regulation of banks and currency, but they differed sharply over how to proceed. The banking interests and their congressional supporters wanted the government to give the authority to regulate credit and currency flows either to a single bank or to several regional banks. Bryanite Democrats and Republican progressives opposed the vesting of so much financial power in private hands and insisted that any reformed financial system must be publicly controlled. Wilson worked out a compromise plan that included both private and public controls and marshaled the votes to push it through both the House and the Senate. By the end of 1913, Wilson had signed the Federal Reserve Act, the most important law passed in his first administration.

The Federal Reserve Act established 12 regional banks, each controlled by the private banks in its region. Every private bank in the country was required to deposit an average of 6 percent of its assets in its regional Federal Reserve bank. The reserve would be used to make loans to member banks and to issue paper currency (Federal Reserve notes) to facilitate financial transactions. The regional banks were also instructed to use their funds to shore up member banks in distress and to respond to sudden changes in credit demands by easing or tightening the flow of credit. A Federal Reserve Board appointed by the president and responsible to the public rather than to private bankers would set policy and oversee activities within the 12 reserve banks.

The Federal Reserve system strengthened the nation's financial structure and was in most respects an impressive political achievement for Wilson. In its final form, however, it revealed that Wilson was retreating from his New Freedom pledge. The Federal Reserve Board was a less powerful and less centralized federal authority than a national bank would have been, but it nevertheless represented a substantial increase in government control of banking. Moreover, the bill authorizing the system made no attempt to break up private financial institutions that had grown too powerful or to prohibit the interlocking directorates that large banks used

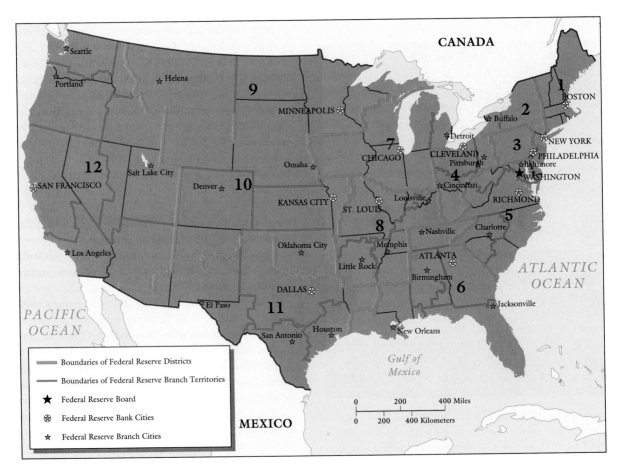

FEDERAL RESERVE DISTRICTS

to augment their power. Because it sought to work with large banks rather than to break them up, the Federal Reserve system seemed more consonant with the principles of Roosevelt's New Nationalism than with those of Wilson's New Freedom.

FROM THE NEW FREEDOM TO THE NEW NATIONALISM

Wilson's failure to mount a vigorous antitrust campaign confirmed his drift toward the New Nationalism. For example, in 1914 Wilson supported the Federal Trade Commission Act, which created a government agency by that name to regulate business practices. The Federal Trade Commission (FTC) had wide powers to collect information on corporate pricing policies and on cooperation and competition among businesses. The FTC might have attacked trusts for "unfair trade practices," but the Senate stripped the FTC Act's companion legislation, the Clayton Antitrust Act, of virtually all provisions that would have allowed the government to prosecute the trusts. Wilson supported this weakening of the Clayton Act, having decided that the breakup of large-scale industry was no longer practical or preferable. The FTC, in Wilson's eyes, would help businesses, large and small, to regulate themselves in ways that contributed to national well-being. In accepting giant industry as an inescapable feature of modern life and in seeking to regulate industrial behavior by means of government agencies such as the FTC, Wilson had become, in effect, a New Nationalist.

But what kind of New Nationalist was he? Would he use government merely to assist businessmen and bankers to regulate themselves? Or would he use government to balance the claims of industry and finance against the claims of labor, farmers, and other disadvantaged groups?

In 1914 and 1915 Wilson favored the first approach: He intended the FTC to become as much a friend to business as a policeman. His nominations to the Federal Reserve Board were generally men who had worked for Wall Street firms and large industrial corporations. At this time, Wilson usually refused to use government powers to aid organized groups of workers and farmers. Court rulings had earlier made worker and farmer organi-

zations vulnerable to prosecution under the terms of the Sherman Antitrust Act of 1890. AFL president Samuel Gompers and other labor leaders tried but failed to convince Wilson to insert into the Clayton Antitrust Act a clause that would unambiguously grant labor and farmer organizations immunity from further antitrust prosecutions.

Nor did Wilson, at this time, view with any greater sympathy the campaign for African Americans' political equality. He supported efforts by white southerners in his cabinet, such as Postmaster General Albert Burleson and Treasury Secretary William McAdoo, to segregate their government departments, and he ignored pleas from the NAACP to involve the federal government in a campaign against lynching.

In late 1915, however, Wilson changed his tune, in part because he feared losing his reelection in 1916. The Bull Moosers of 1912 were retreating back to the Republican Party. Wilson remembered how much his 1912 victory, based on only 42 percent of the popular vote, had depended on the Republican split. To halt the progressives' rapprochement with the GOP, he made a bid for their support. In January 1916 he nominated Louis Brandeis to the Supreme Court. Not only was Brandeis one of the country's most respected progressives, he was also the first Jew nominated to serve on the country's highest court. Congressional conservatives did everything they could to block the confirmation of a man they regarded as dangerously radical, but Wilson, as usual, was better organized, and by June his forces in the Senate had emerged victorious.

Wilson followed up this victory by pushing through Congress the first federal workmen's compensation law (the Kern-McGillicuddy Act, which covered federal employees), the first federal law outlawing child labor (the Keating-Owen Act), and the first federal law guaranteeing workers an eight-hour day (the Adamson Act, which covered the nation's 400,000 railway workers). The number of Americans affected by these acts was rather small. Nevertheless, Wilson had reoriented the Democratic Party to a New Nationalism that cared as much about the interests of the powerless as the interests of the powerful.

Trade unionists flocked to Wilson, as did most of the prominent progressives who had followed the

GROWTH IN FEDERAL EMPLOYMENT, 1891–1917

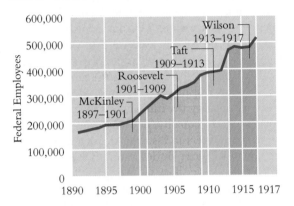

Source: Reprinted by permission from *The Federal Government Service*, ed. W. S. Sayre (Englewood Cliffs, N.J.: Prentice-Hall, 1965), p. 41, The American Assembly.

Bull Moose in 1912. Meanwhile, Wilson had appealed to the supporters of William Jennings Bryan by supporting legislation that made federal credit available to farmers in need. He had put together a reform coalition capable of winning a majority at the polls. In the process, he had transformed the Democratic Party. From 1916 on, the Democrats, rather than the Republicans, became the chief guardians of the American reform tradition.

That Wilson did so is a sign of the strength of the reform and radical forces in American society. By 1916 the ranks of middle-class progressives had grown broad and deep. Working-class protest had also accelerated in scope and intensity. In Lawrence, Massachusetts, in 1912, and in Paterson, New Jersey, in 1913, for example, the IWW organized strikes of textile workers that drew national attention, as did the 1914 strike by Colorado mine workers that ended with the infamous Ludlow massacre (see chapter 20). These protests reflected the mobilization of those working-class constituencies—immigrants, women, the unskilled—long considered inconsequential both to American labor and party politics. Assisted by radicals, these groups had begun to fashion a more inclusive and politically contentious labor movement. Wilson and other Democrats understood the potential strength of this new labor movement, and the president's

pro-labor legislative agenda in 1916 can be understood, in part, as an effort to channel labor's new constituents into the Democratic Party. It was a successful strategy and contributed to Wilson's reelection in 1916.

CONCLUSION

By 1916, the progressives had accomplished a great deal. They demonstrated that traditional American concerns with democracy and liberty could be adapted to an industrial age. They exposed and curbed some of the worst abuses of the American political system. They enfranchised women and took steps to protect the environment. They broke the hold of laissez-faire economic policies on national politics and replaced it with the idea of a strong federal government committed to economic regulation and social justice. They transformed the presidency into a post of legislative and popular leadership. They enlarged the executive branch by establishing new commissions and agencies charged with administering government policies.

The progressives, in short, had presided over the emergence of a new national state, one in which power increasingly flowed away from municipalities and states and toward the federal government. This reorientation followed a compelling logic: A national government stood a better chance of solving the problems of growing economic inequality, mismanagement of natural resources, and consumer fraud than did local and state governments. Although this new state, in 1916, was still small, it offered a blueprint for further reform.

The promise of effective remedies, however, brought new dangers. In particular, the new national state was giving rise to a bureaucratic elite whose power rested on federal authority rather than private wealth or political machines. Progressives argued that the university-educated experts and scientific managers who staffed the new federal agencies would bring to the political process the very qualities that party politicians allegedly lacked: knowledge, dedication, and honesty. Few of these new public servants, however, were entirely disinterested and unassuming. Some had close ties to the corporations and businesses that their agencies were expected to regulate. Others allowed their prejudices against women, immigrants, and minorities to shape social policy. Still others believed that "the people" could not be trusted to evaluate the government's work intelligently. For these reasons, the progressive state sometimes failed to enhance democracy and secure the people's sovereignty. America's involvement in imperial expansion and world war would further demonstrate how a powerful state could serve illiberal ends.

Suggested Readings begin on page SR-1.
For Web activities and resources
related to this chapter, go to
http://www.harcourtcollege.com/history.murrin

CHAPTER 22

BECOMING A WORLD POWER, 1898–1917

UNCLE SAM GETS COCKY, 1901

From 1898 to 1917, the United States broadened its influence in world affairs and especially sought to establish its dominance in Latin America. This cartoon illustrates that dominance through the figure of a giant Uncle Sam rooster that dwarfs both the European chickens (gamely protesting, "you're not the only rooster in South America") and the diminutive Latin American republics.

For much of the 19th century, most Americans were preoccupied by continental expansion. They treasured their distance from European societies, monarchs, and wars. Elections rarely turned on international events, and presidents rarely made their reputations as statesmen in the world arena. The diplomatic corps, like most agencies of the federal government, was small and inexperienced. The government projected its limited military power westward and possessed virtually no capacity or desire for involvement overseas.

The nation's rapid industrial growth in the late 19th century forced a turn away from such continentalism. Technological advances, especially the laying of transoceanic cables and the introduction of steamship travel, diminished America's physical isolation. The babel of languages one could hear in American cities testified to how much the Old World had penetrated the New. Then, too, Americans watched anxiously as England, Germany, Russia, Japan, and other industrial powers intensified their competition for overseas markets and colonies, and some believed America too needed to enter this contest. The voices making this argument grew more insistent and persuasive as the long economic depression of the 1890s stripped the United States of its prosperity and pride.

A war with Spain in 1898 gave the United States an opportunity to upgrade its military and acquire colonies and influence in the Western Hemisphere and Asia. Under Presidents William McKinley and Theodore Roosevelt, the United States pursued these initiatives, with impressive results. But not all Americans supported subjugating the peoples of Cuba, Puerto Rico, and the Philippines, denying them the right to be free and self-governing. The United States seemed to be becoming the kind of nation that many Americans had long despised—one that valued power more than liberty. Roosevelt did not mind exercising imperial power; he wanted to create an international system in which a handful of industrial nations pursued their global economic interests, dominated world trade, and kept the world at peace. Woodrow Wilson, however, did mind. He sought to devise a policy toward postrevolutionary Mexico that restrained American might and respected Mexican desires for liberty. It was a worthy ambition but one that proved exceedingly difficult to achieve.

This chapter will focus on the following major questions:

- What were the causes of the Spanish-American War?

- Over what countries did the United States exert control between 1898 and 1917, and what were the mechanisms of control? How did American expansion compare with that of other industrial powers?
- What were the similarities and differences in the foreign policies of Theodore Roosevelt, William Howard Taft, and Woodrow Wilson?
- What happened on Kettle and San Juan Hills, and why was the prominent role of one group in those battles excised from historical memory?

THE UNITED STATES LOOKS ABROAD

By the late 19th century, sizable numbers of Americans had become interested in extending their country's influence abroad. The most important groups were Protestant missionaries, businessmen, and imperialists.

PROTESTANT MISSIONARIES

Protestant missionaries were among the most active promoters of American interests abroad. Integration of the world economy made evangelical Protestants more conscious of the diversity of the world's peoples. Overseas missionary activity grew quickly between 1870 and 1900, most of it directed toward China. Between 1880 and 1900 the number of women's missionary societies doubled, from 20 to 40; by 1915 these societies enrolled 3 million women. Convinced of the superiority of the Anglo-Saxon race, Protestant missionaries considered it their Christian duty to teach the Gospel to the "ignorant" Asian masses and save their souls. Missionaries also believed that their efforts would free those masses from their racial destiny, enabling them to become "civilized." In this "civilizing" effort, missionaries resembled progressive reformers who sought to uplift America's immigrant masses at home.

BUSINESSMEN

For different reasons, industrialists, traders, and investors also began to look overseas, sensing that they could make fortunes in foreign lands. Exports of American manufactured goods rose substantially after 1880. By 1914 American foreign investment

CHRONOLOGY

1893	Frederick Jackson Turner publishes an essay announcing the end of the frontier
1898	Spanish-American War (April 14–August 12) • Treaty of Paris signed (December 10), giving U.S. control of Philippines, Guam, and Puerto Rico • U.S. annexes Hawaii
1899–1902	American-Filipino War
1899–1900	U.S. pursues Open Door policy toward China
1900	U.S. annexes Puerto Rico • U.S. and other imperial powers put down Chinese Boxer Rebellion
1901	U.S. forces Cuba to adopt constitution favorable to U.S. interests
1903	Hay–Bunau-Varilla Treaty signed, giving U.S. control of Panama Canal Zone
1904	"Roosevelt corollary" to Monroe Doctrine proclaimed
1905	Roosevelt negotiates end to Russo-Japanese War
1906–17	U.S. intervenes in Cuba, Nicaragua, Haiti, Dominican Republic, and Mexico
1907	Roosevelt and Japanese government reach a "gentlemen's agreement" restricting Japanese immigration to U.S. and ending discrimination against Japanese schoolchildren in California
1907–09	Great White Fleet circles the earth
1909–13	William Howard Taft conducts "dollar diplomacy"
1910	Mexican Revolution
1914	Panama Canal opens
1914–17	Wilson struggles to develop a policy toward Mexico
1917	U.S. purchases Virgin Islands from Denmark

already equaled a sizable 7 percent of the nation's gross national product. Companies such as Eastman Kodak (film and cameras), Singer Sewing Machine Company, Standard Oil, American Tobacco, and International Harvester had become multinational corporations with overseas branch offices.

Some industrialists became entranced by the prospect of clothing, feeding, housing, and transporting the 400 million people of China. James B.

SINGER SEWING MACHINE ADVERTISEMENT The Singer Sewing Machine Company was one of the first American multinational corporations. This advertisement, with its maps of the western hemisphere and its description of Singer as "the universal sewing machine," stresses Singer's global orientation.

Duke, who headed American Tobacco, was selling one billion cigarettes a year in East Asian markets. Looking for ways to fill empty boxcars heading west from Minnesota to Tacoma, Washington, the railroad tycoon James J. Hill imagined stuffing them with wheat and steel destined for China and Japan. He actually published and distributed wheat cookbooks throughout East Asia to convince Asians to shift from a rice-based to a bread-based diet. Although export trade with East Asia during this period never fulfilled the expectations of Hill and other industrialists, their talk about the "wealth of the Orient" impressed on politicians its importance to national well-being.

Events of the 1890s only intensified the appeal of foreign markets. First, the 1890 U.S. census announced that the frontier had disappeared; America had completed the task of westward expansion. Then, in 1893 a young historian named Frederick Jackson Turner published an essay, "The Significance of the Frontier in American History," that articulated what many Americans feared: that the frontier had been essential to the growth of the economy and to the cultivation of democracy. Living in the wilderness, Turner argued, had transformed the Europeans who settled the New World into Americans. They shed their European clothing styles, social customs, and political beliefs, and acquired distinctively "American" characteristics—rugged individualism,

egalitarianism, and a democratic faith. How, Turner wondered, could the nation continue to prosper now that the frontier had gone?

In recent years, historians of the American West have criticized Turner's "frontier thesis." They have argued that the very idea of the frontier as uninhabited wilderness overlooked the tens of thousands of Indians who occupied the region and that much else of what Americans believe about the West is based more on myth than on reality. They have also pointed out that it makes little sense to view the 1890s as a decade in which opportunities for economic gain disappeared in the West.

Even though these points are valid, they would have meant little to Americans living in Turner's time. For them, as for Turner, concern about the disappearing frontier expressed a fear that the increasingly urbanized and industrialized nation had lost its way. Turner's essay appeared just as the country was entering the deepest, longest, and most conflict-ridden depression in its history (see chapter 19). What could the republic do to regain its economic prosperity and political stability? Where would it find its new frontiers? One answer to these questions focused on the pursuit of overseas expansion. As Senator Albert J. Beveridge of Indiana declared in 1899: "We are raising more than we can consume. . . . We are making more than we can use. Therefore, we must find new markets for our

LEADING U.S. EXPORTS, 1875 AND 1915

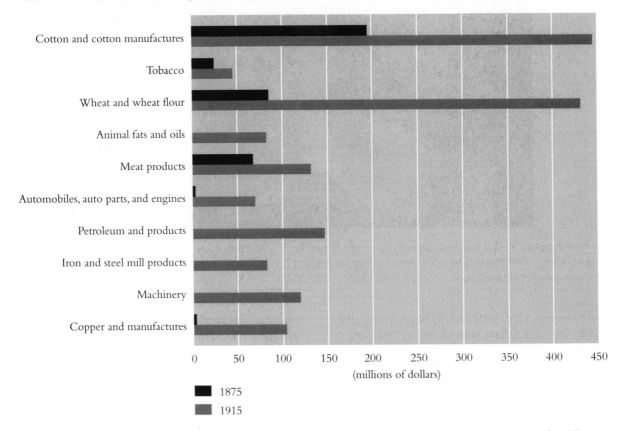

Source: Data from *Historical Statistics of the United States, Colonial Times to 1970* (White Plains, N.Y.: Kraus International, 1989).

produce, new occupation for our capital, new work for our labor."

IMPERIALISTS

Eager to assist in the drive for overseas economic expansion was a group of politicians, intellectuals, and military strategists who viewed such expansion as a key ingredient in the pursuit of world power. They wanted the United States to take its place alongside Britain, France, Germany, and Russia as a great imperial nation. They believed that the United States should build a strong navy, solidify a sphere of influence in the Caribbean, and extend markets into Asia. Their desire to control ports and territories beyond the continental borders of their own country made them imperialists. Many of them were also Social Darwinist who believed that success in international competition and conquest

reflected the laws of nature. America's destiny required that it prove itself the military equal of the strongest European nations and the master of the "lesser" peoples of the world.

Perhaps the most influential imperialist was Admiral Alfred Thayer Mahan. In an influential book, *The Influence of Sea Power upon History, 1660–1783* (1890), Mahan argued that all the world's great empires, beginning with Rome, had relied on their capacity to control the seas. Mahan called for the construction of a U.S. navy with enough ships and firepower to make its presence felt everywhere in the world. To be effective, that global fleet would require a canal across Central America through which U.S. warships could pass swiftly from the Atlantic to the Pacific Oceans. It would also require a string of far-flung service bases from the Caribbean to the southwestern Pacific. Mahan recommended that the U.S. government take possession of Hawaii

"We shall establish trading-posts throughout the world as distributing points for American products. We shall cover the oceans with our merchant marine. We shall build a navy to the measure of our greatness. Great colonies, flying our flag and trading with us, will grow about our posts of trade. Our institutions will follow our flag on the wings of our commerce. And American law, American order, American civilization and the American flag will plant themselves on shores, hitherto bloody and benighted, but, by those agencies of God, henceforth to be made beautiful and bright."

INDIANA SENATOR ALBERT J. BEVERIDGE

in an 1898 speech celebrating the impending worldwide spread of American commerce, power, and civilization

and other strategically located Pacific islands with superior harbor facilities.

Presidents William McKinley and Theodore Roosevelt would eventually make almost the whole of Mahan's vision a reality, but in the early 1890s Mahan doubted that Americans would accept the responsibility and costs of empire. Although the imperialists counted in their ranks such prominent figures as Theodore Roosevelt and Senator Henry Cabot Lodge of Massachusetts, many Americans still insisted that the United States should not aspire to world power by acquiring overseas bases and colonizing foreign peoples.

Mahan underestimated, however, the government's alarm over the scramble of Europeans to extend their imperial control. Every administration from the 1880s on committed itself to a "big navy" policy. By 1898 the U.S. Navy ranked fifth in the world and by 1900 it ranked third. Already in 1878, the United States had secured rights to Pago Pago, a superb deep-water harbor in Samoa (a collection of islands in the southwest Pacific inhabited by Polynesians), and in 1885 it had leased Pearl Harbor from the Hawaiians. Both harbors were expected to serve as fueling stations for the growing U.S. fleet.

These attempts to project U.S. power overseas had already deepened the government's involvement in the affairs of distant lands. In 1889, the United States established a protectorate over part of Samoa, a move meant to forestall German and British efforts to weaken American influence on the islands. In the early 1890s, President Grover Cleveland's administration was increasingly drawn into Hawaiian affairs, as tensions between American sugar plantation owners and native Hawaiians upset the islands' economic and political stability. In 1891, plantation owners succeeded in deposing the Hawaiian king and putting into power Queen Liliuokalani. But when Liliuokalani strove to establish

THE U.S. NAVY, 1890–1914: EXPENDITURES AND BATTLESHIP SIZE

Fiscal Year	Total Federal Expenditures	Naval Expenditures	Naval Expenditures as Percent of Total Federal expenditures	Size of Battleships (average tons displaced)
1890	$318,040,711	$ 22,006,206	6.9%	11,000
1900	520,860,847	55,953,078	10.7	12,000
1901	524,616,925	60,506,978	11.5	16,000
1905	657,278,914	117,550,308	20.7	16,000
1909	693,743,885	115,546,011	16.7	27,000 (1910)
1914	735,081,431	139,682,186	19.0	32,000

Sources: (for expenditures) E. B. Potter, *Sea Power: A Naval History* (Annapolis: Naval Institute Press, 1982), p. 187; (for size of ships) Harold Sprout, *Toward a New Order of Sea Power* (New York: Greenwood Press, 1976), p. 52.

her independence, the planters, assisted by U.S. sailors, overthrew her regime, too. Cleveland declared Hawaii a protectorate in 1893, but he resisted the imperialists in Congress who wanted to annex the islands.

Still, imperialist sentiment in Congress and throughout the nation continued to gain strength, fueled by "jingoism." Jingoists were nationalists who thought that a swaggering foreign policy and a willingness to go to war would enhance their nation's glory. They were constantly on the alert for insults to their country's honor and swift to call for military retaliation. This predatory brand of nationalism emerged not only in Britain and the United States, but in France, Germany, and Japan as well. The anti-imperialist editor of the *Nation*, E. L. Godkin, exclaimed in 1894: "The number of men and officials of this country who are now mad to fight somebody is appalling." Recent feminist scholarship has emphasized the degree to which men of the 1890s saw war as an opportunity to revive frontier-like notions of masculinity—of men as warriors and conquerors—that were proving exceedingly hard to sustain in an increasingly industrialized and bureaucratized American society. Spain's behavior in Cuba in the 1890s gave those men the war they sought.

THE SPANISH-AMERICAN WAR

By the 1890s the islands of Cuba and Puerto Rico were virtually all that remained of the vast Spanish empire in the Americas. Relations between the Cubans and their Spanish rulers had long been deteriorating. The Spanish had taken 10 years to subdue a revolt begun in 1868. In 1895 the Cubans staged another revolt, sparked by their continuing resentment of Spanish control and by a depressed economy caused in part by an 1894 U.S. tariff law that made Cuban sugar too expensive for the U.S. market. The fighting was brutal. Cuban forces destroyed large areas of the island to make it uninhabitable by the Spanish. The Spanish army, led by General Valeriano Weyler, responded in kind, forcing large numbers of Cubans into concentration camps. Denied adequate food, shelter, and sanitation, an estimated 200,000 Cubans—one-eighth of the island's population—died of starvation and disease.

UNCLE SAM The Spanish-American War was tremendously popular among Americans. Here, a proud Uncle Sam salutes the U.S. Navy for its role in winning the "latest, greatest, and shortest war."

Such tactics, especially those ascribed to "Butcher" Weyler (as he was known in much of the U.S. press), inflamed American opinion. Many Americans sympathized with the Cubans, who seemed to be fighting the kind of anticolonial war Americans themselves had waged more than 100 years earlier. Americans stayed well informed about the atrocities by reading the *New York Journal*, owned by William Randolph Hearst, and the *New York World*, owned by Joseph Pulitzer. Hearst and Pulitzer were transforming newspaper publishing in much the same way Sam McClure and others had revolutionized the magazine business (see chapter 21). To boost circulation they sought out sensational and shocking stories and described them in lurid detail. They were accused of engaging in "yellow journalism"—embellishing stories with titillating details when the true reports did not seem dramatic enough.

The sensationalism of the yellow press and its frequently jingoistic accounts failed to bring about American intervention in Cuba, however. In the final days of his administration, President Cleveland resisted mounting pressure to intervene. William McKinley, who succeeded him in 1897, denounced the Spanish even more harshly, with the aim of forcing Spain into concessions that would satisfy the Cuban rebels and bring an end to the conflict. Initially, this strategy seemed to be working: Spain relieved "Butcher" Weyler of his command, stopped incarcerating Cubans in concentration camps, and granted Cuba limited autonomy. Still, Spaniards living on the island refused to be ruled by a Cuban government, and the Cuban rebels continued to demand full independence. Late in 1897, when riots broke out in Havana, McKinley ordered the battleship *Maine* into Havana harbor to protect U.S. citizens and their property. Two unexpected events then set off a war.

The first was the February 9, 1898, publication in Hearst's *New York Journal* of a letter stolen from Depuy de Lôme, the Spanish minister to Washington, in which he described McKinley as "a cheap politician" and a "bidder for the admiration of the crowd." The de Lôme letter also implied that the Spanish cared little about resolving the Cuban crisis through negotiation and reform. The news embarrassed Spanish officials and outraged U.S. public opinion. Then, only six days later, the *Maine* exploded in Havana harbor, killing 260 American sailors. Although subsequent investigations revealed that the most probable cause of the explosion was a malfunctioning boiler, Americans were certain that it had been the work of Spanish agents. "Remember the Maine!" screamed the headlines in the yellow press. On March 8, Congress responded to the clamor for war by authorizing $50 million to mobilize U.S. forces. In the meantime, McKinley notified Spain of his conditions for avoiding war: Spain would pay an indemnity for the *Maine*, abandon its concentration camps, end the fighting with the rebels, and commit itself to Cuban independence. On April 9, Spain accepted all the demands but the last. Nevertheless, on April 11, McKinley

"REMEMBER THE *MAINE*!" The explosion of the battleship *Maine* in Havana harbor on February 15, 1898, killed 260 American sailors and helped drive the United States into war with Spain.

asked Congress for authority to go to war. Three days later Congress approved a war resolution, which included a declaration (spelled out in the Teller Amendment) that the United States would not use the war as an opportunity to acquire territory in Cuba. On April 24, Spain responded with a formal declaration of war against the United States.

"A SPLENDID LITTLE WAR"

Secretary of State John Hay called the fight with Spain "a splendid little war." Begun in April, it ended in August. More than 1 million men volunteered to fight, and fewer than 500 were killed or wounded in combat. The American victory over Spain was complete, not just in Cuba but in the neighboring island of Puerto Rico and in the Philippines, Spain's strategic possession in the Pacific.

Actually, the war was more complicated than it seemed. The main reason for the easy victory was U.S. naval superiority. In the war's first major battle, a naval engagement in Manila harbor in the Philippines on May 1, a U.S. fleet commanded by Commodore George Dewey destroyed an entire Spanish fleet and lost only one sailor (to heat stroke). On land, the story was different. On the eve of war the U.S. Army consisted of only 26,000 troops skilled at skirmishing with Indians but ill-prepared and ill-equipped for all-out war. A force of 80,000 Spanish regulars awaited them in Cuba, with another 50,000 in reserve in Spain. Congress immediately increased the army to 62,000 and called for an additional 125,000 volunteers. The response to this call was astounding, but outfitting, training, and transporting the new recruits overwhelmed the army's capacities. Its standard-issue, blue flannel uniforms proved too heavy for fighting in Cuba. Rations were so poor that soldiers referred to one choice item as "embalmed beef." Most of the volunteers had to make do with ancient Civil War rifles that still used black, rather than smokeless, powder. The invasion force of 16,000 men took more than five days to sail the short distance from Tampa, Florida, to Daiquiri, Cuba. Moreover, the army was unprepared for the effects of malaria and other tropical diseases.

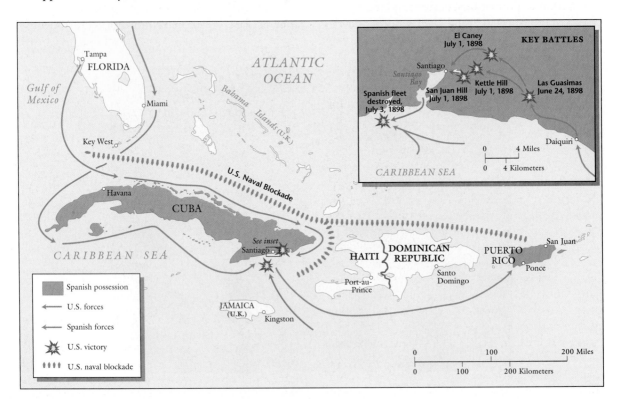

SPANISH-AMERICAN WAR IN CUBA, 1898

That the Cuban revolutionaries were predominantly black also came as a shock to the U.S. forces. In their attempts to arouse support for the Cuban cause, U.S. newspapers had portrayed the Cuban rebels as fundamentally similar to white Americans. They were described as intelligent, civilized, and democratic, possessing an "Anglo-Saxon tenacity of purpose." And, they were "fully nine-tenths" white, according to one report. The Spanish oppressors, by contrast, were depicted as dark complexioned— "dark cruel eyes, dark swaggering men" wrote author Sherwood Anderson—and as possessing the characteristics of their "dark race": barbarism, cruelty, and indolence. The U.S. troops' first encounters with Cuban and Spanish forces dispelled these myths. Their Cuban allies appeared poorly outfitted, rough in their manners, and primarily black-skinned. The Spanish soldiers appeared well disciplined, tough in battle, and light complexioned.

The Cuban rebels were actually skilled guerrilla fighters, but racial prejudice prevented most U.S. soldiers and reporters from crediting their military accomplishments. Instead, they judged the Cubans harshly—as primitive, savage, and incapable of self-control or self-government. White U.S. troops preferred not to fight alongside the Cubans; increasingly, they refused to coordinate strategy with them.

At first, the U.S. Army's ineptitude and its racial misconceptions did little to diminish the soldiers' hunger for a good fight. No one was more eager for battle than Theodore Roosevelt who, along with Colonel Leonard Wood, led a volunteer cavalry unit composed of Ivy League gentlemen, western cowboys, sheriffs, prospectors, Indians, and small numbers of Hispanics and ethnic European Americans. Roosevelt's "Rough Riders," as the unit came to be known, landed with the invasion force and played an active role in the three battles fought in the hills surrounding Santiago. Their most famous action, the one on which Roosevelt would build his lifelong reputation as a military hero, was a furious charge up Kettle Hill into the teeth of Spanish defenses. Roosevelt's bravery was stunning, though his judgment was faulty. Nearly 100 men were killed or wounded in the charge. Reports of Roosevelt's bravery overshadowed the equally brave performance of other troops, notably the 9th and 10th Negro Cavalries, which played a pivotal role in clearing away Spanish fortifications on Kettle Hill and allowing

Roosevelt's Rough Riders to make their charge. One Rough Rider commented: "If it had not been for the Negro cavalry, the Rough Riders would have been exterminated." Another added: "I am a Southerner by birth, and I never thought much of the colored man. But . . . I never saw such fighting as those Tenth Cavalry men did. They didn't seem to know what fear was, and their battle hymn was 'There'll be a hot time in the old town tonight.'" The 24th and 25th Negro Infantry Regiments performed equally vital tasks in the U.S. Army's conquest of the adjacent San Juan Hill.

DEFEAT OF THE SPANISH These scenes illustrate the final two battles of the Spanish-American War. At the bottom, U.S. Navy ships destroy the Spanish fleet as it attempts to escape from Santiago Harbor. In the top scene, U.S. troops bombard Santiago from the trench that they excavated around the city. The Spanish forces surrendered on July 17, 1898.

African American soldiers risked their lives despite the segregationist policies that confined them to all-black regiments. At the time, Roosevelt gave them full credit for what they had done. He praised the black troops as "an excellent breed of Yankee," and declared that no "Rough Rider will ever forget the tie that binds us to the Ninth and Tenth Cavalry." But soon after returning home, he began minimizing their contributions, even to the point of calling their behavior cowardly. Like most white American officers and enlisted men of the time, Roosevelt had difficulty believing that blacks could fight well. By the start of the First World War, the U.S. military had excluded black troops from combat roles altogether.

The taking of Kettle Hill, San Juan Hill, and other high ground surrounding Santiago gave the U.S. forces a substantial advantage over the Spanish defenders. Nevertheless, logistical and medical problems nearly did them in. The troops were short of food, ammunition, and medical facilities. Their ranks were devastated by malaria, typhoid, and dysentery; more than 5,000 soldiers died from disease. Even the normally ebullient Roosevelt was close to despair: "We are within measurable distance of a terrible military disaster," he wrote his friend Henry Cabot Lodge on July 3.

Fortunately, the Spanish had lost the will to fight. On the very day Roosevelt wrote to Lodge, Spain's Atlantic fleet tried to retreat from Santiago harbor and was promptly destroyed by a U.S. fleet. The Spanish army in Santiago surrendered on July 16; on July 18 the Spanish government asked for peace. While negotiations for an armistice proceeded, U.S. forces overran the neighboring island of Puerto Rico. On August 12 the U.S. and Spanish governments agreed to an armistice, but before the news could reach the Philippines, the United States had captured Manila and had taken prisoner 13,000 Spanish soldiers.

The armistice required Spain to relinquish its claim to Cuba, cede Puerto Rico and the Pacific island of Guam to the United States, and tolerate the American occupation of Manila until a peace conference could be convened in Paris on October 1, 1898. At that conference, American diplomats startled their Spanish counterparts by demanding that Spain also cede the Philippines to the United States. After two months of stalling, the Spanish government

agreed to relinquish their coveted Pacific colony for $20 million, and the transaction was sealed by the Treaty of Paris on December 10, 1898.

THE UNITED STATES BECOMES A WORLD POWER

America's initial war aim had been to oust the Spanish from Cuba—an aim that both imperialists and anti-imperialists supported, but for different reasons. Imperialists hoped to incorporate Cuba into a new American empire; anti-imperialists hoped to see the Cubans gain their independence. But only the imperialists condoned the U.S. acquisition of Puerto Rico, Guam, and particularly the Philippines, which they viewed as integral to the extension of American interests into Asia. Soon after the war began, President McKinley had cast his lot with the imperialists. First, he annexed Hawaii, giving the United States permanent control of Pearl Harbor. Next, he set his sights on setting up a U.S. naval base at Manila. Never before had the United States sought such a large military presence outside the Western Hemisphere.

In a departure of equal importance, McKinley announced his intent to administer much of this newly acquired territory as U.S. colonies. Virtually all territory the United States had previously acquired had been settled by Americans, who had eventually petitioned for statehood and been admitted to the Union with the same rights as existing states. In the case of these new territories, however, only Hawaii would be allowed to follow a traditional path toward statehood. There, the powerful American sugar plantation owners prevailed on Congress to pass an act in 1900 extending U.S. citizenship to all Hawaiian citizens and putting Hawaii on the road to statehood. No such influential group of Americans resided in the Philippines. The whole country was made an American colony mainly to prevent other powers, such as Japan and Germany, from gaining a foothold somewhere in the 400-island archipelago and launching attacks on the American naval base in Manila.

The McKinley administration might have taken a different course. The United States might have negotiated a deal with Emilio Aguinaldo, the leader of an anticolonial movement in the Philippines, that would have given the Philippines indepen-

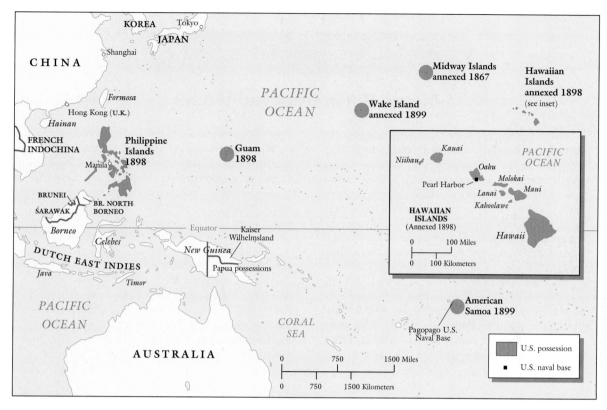

AMERICAN SOUTH PACIFIC EMPIRE, 1900

dence in exchange for a U.S. naval base at Manila. An American fleet stationed there would have been able to protect both American interests and the fledgling Philippine nation from predatory assaults by Japan, Germany, or Britain. Alternatively, the United States might have annexed the Philippines outright and offered Filipinos U.S. citizenship as the first step toward statehood. McKinley, however, believed that the "inferior" Filipino people lacked the capacity for self-government. The United States would undertake a solemn mission to "civilize" the Filipinos and thereby prepare them for independence, but until that mission was complete, the Philippines would submit to rule by presidentially appointed American governors.

THE DEBATE OVER THE TREATY OF PARIS

The proposed acquisition of the Philippines aroused opposition both in the United States and in the Philippines. The northeastern Anti-Imperialist League enlisted the support of several elder statesmen in McKinley's own party, as well as the former Democratic President Grover Cleveland, the industrialist Andrew Carnegie, and the labor leader Samuel Gompers. William Jennings Bryan, meanwhile, marshaled a vigorous anti-imperialist protest among Democrats in the South and West, while Mark Twain, William James, William Dean Howells, and other men of letters lent the cause their prestige. Some anti-imperialists believed that subjugating the Filipinos would violate the nation's most precious principle: the right of all people to independence and self-government. Moreover, they feared that the large military and diplomatic establishment needed to administer the colony would threaten political liberties at home.

Other anti-imperialists were motivated more by self-interest than by democratic ideals. U.S. sugar producers, for example, feared competition from Filipino producers. Trade unionists worried that

Kettle Hill in Black and White

Theodore Roosevelt saw the "Rough Rider" regiment that he commanded in the Spanish-American War (pictured below) as a melting pot, with its mix of southwesterners, Ivy Leaguers, and Indians, with a smattering of Hispanics and ethnic European Americans. Combat, he further believed, would forge these many groups into one, as war had always done in the American past. African Americans and Asian immigrants were the two groups conspicuously absent from this mix.

Yet the success of Roosevelt's charge up Kettle Hill and San Juan Hill had depended on the assistance of four regiments of regular army troops, the 9th and 10th Cavalry and the 24th and 25th Infantry, which happened to be black. Some members of the 10th Cavalry who took part in the battle are pictured at bottom

right. The fury of the fighting so scrambled the different regiments that by the time the troops reached the San Juan summit, they were all intermixed: Ivy Leaguers and southwesterners, Hispanics and European immigrants, even blacks and whites, all fighting side by side. Combat had brought blacks into the great American melting pot, a phenomenon that Roosevelt celebrated at the time by praising the black troops.

But Roosevelt did not truly believe that blacks were the equals of whites, or that they could be absorbed into the American nation. So, over time, he downplayed the role of black troops and questioned their ability to fight. The heroic role of black soldiers not only disappeared from Roosevelt's own memory, but from paintings (such as the illustration at right) and other commemorations of the great charge.

poor Filipinos would flood the U.S. labor market and depress wage rates. Some businessmen warned that the costs of maintaining an imperial outpost would exceed any economic benefits that the colony might produce. Many Democrats, meanwhile, simply wanted to gain partisan advantage by opposing the Republican administration's foreign policy. Still other anti-imperialists feared the contaminating effects of contact with "inferior" Asian races.

The contrasting motivations of the anti-imperialists ultimately weakened their opposition. Even so, they almost dealt McKinley and his fellow imperialists a defeat in the U.S. Senate. On February 6, 1899, the Senate voted 57 to 27 in favor of the Treaty of Paris, only one vote beyond the minimum two-thirds majority required for ratification. Two last-minute developments may have brought victory. First, William Jennings Bryan, in the days just before the vote, abandoned his opposition and announced his support for the treaty. (He would later explain that he had decided for ratification in order to end the war with Spain and that he intended to work for Filipino independence through diplomatic means.) Second, on the eve of the vote, Filipinos rose in revolt against the U.S. army of occupation. With another war looming and the lives of American soldiers imperiled, a few senators who had been reluctant to vote for the treaty may have felt obligated to support the president.

THE AMERICAN-FILIPINO WAR

The acquisition of the Philippines immediately embroiled the United States in a long, brutal war to subdue the Filipino rebels. In four years of fighting, more than 120,000 American soldiers served in the Philippines and more than 4,200 of them died. The war cost $160 million, or eight times what the United States had paid Spain to acquire the archipelago. The war brought Americans face-to-face with an unpleasant truth: that American actions in the Philippines were virtually indistinguishable from Spain's actions in Cuba. Like Spain, the United States refused to acknowledge a people's aspiration for self-rule. Like "Butcher" Weyler, American generals permitted their soldiers to use

Emilio Aguinaldo, Leader of the Filipino Anticolonial Movement, Inspects His Troops Aguinaldo initially welcomed the U.S. invasion of the Philippines, believing that the United States would help Filipinos gain their independence from Spain. But U.S. plans to annex the Philippines angered Aguinaldo and triggered a brutal four-year war between the two countries.

savage tactics. Whole communities suspected of harboring guerrillas were driven into concentration camps, and their houses, farms, and livestock were destroyed. American soldiers executed so many Filipino rebels (whom they called "goo-goos") that the ratio of Filipino dead to wounded reached 15 to 1, a statistic that made the American Civil War, in which one soldier had died for every five wounded, seem relatively humane. One New York infantryman wrote home that his unit had killed 1,000 Filipinos—men, women, and children—in retaliation for the murder of a single American soldier: "I am in my glory when I can sight my gun on some dark skin and pull the trigger," he exclaimed. A total of 15,000 Filipino soldiers died in the fighting. Estimates of total Filipino deaths from gunfire, starvation, and disease range from 50,000 to 200,000.

The United States finally gained the upper hand after General Arthur MacArthur (father of Douglas) was appointed commander of the islands in 1900. MacArthur did not lessen the war's ferocity, but he understood that it could not be won by guns alone. He offered amnesty to Filipino guerrillas who agreed to surrender, and he cultivated close relations with the islands' wealthy elites. McKinley supported this effort to build a Filipino constituency sympathetic to the U.S. presence. To that end, he sent William Howard Taft to the islands in 1900 to establish a civilian government. In 1901 Taft became the colony's first "governor-general" and declared that he intended to prepare the Filipinos for independence. He transferred many governmental functions to Filipino control and sponsored a vigorous program of public works (roads,

LINK TO THE PAST

American-Filipino War

http://www.phil-am-war.org/

The Philippine-American War Centennial Initiative seeks to commemorate the war between the United States and the Philippines through their maintenance of primary source materials on the Web.

1. Select "Treaties, Proclamations and Manifestos" and scroll down to read Felipe Agoncillo's "Memorial to the U.S. Senate" and Emilio Aguinaldo's "Manifesto Recognizing the Opening of Hostilities." Why do Agoncillo and Aguinaldo reject the Treaty of Paris and the United States' sovereignty over the Philippines? What arguments do they make for Filipino independence?

2. Select "Weapons of War" and compare the weapons of the American troops with those of the Filipinos. What conclusions can one draw from such a comparison?

3. Select "Editorial Cartoons of the Day" and browse the cartoons. What do these cartoons reveal about popular American attitudes toward U.S. involvement in the Philippines? What do they reveal about American attitudes toward the Filipinos? Finally, what do the cartoons tell us about European reactions to American acquisition of the Philippines?

bridges, schools) that would give the Philippines the infrastructure necessary for economic development and political independence. By 1902 this dual strategy of ruthless war against those who had taken up arms and concessions to those who were willing to live under benevolent American rule had crushed the revolt. Though sporadic fighting continued until 1913, American had secure control of the Philippines. The explicit commitment of the United States to Philippine independence (a promise that was deferred until 1946), together with an extensive program of internal improvements, eased the nation's conscience.

CONTROLLING CUBA AND PUERTO RICO

Helping the Cubans achieve independence had been a major rationalization for the war against Spain. Even so, in 1900, when General Leonard Wood, now commander of American forces in Cuba, authorized a constitutional convention to write the laws for a Cuban republic, the McKinley administration made clear it would not easily relinquish control of the island. At McKinley's urging, the U.S. Congress attached to a 1901 army appropriations bill the Platt Amendment (Orville Platt was the Republican senator from Connecticut), delineating three conditions for Cuban independence. First, Cuba would not be permitted to make treaties with foreign powers. Second, the United States would have broad authority to intervene in Cuban political and economic affairs. Third, Cuba would sell or lease land to the United States for naval stations. The delegates to Cuba's constitutional convention were so outraged by these conditions that they refused even to vote on them. But the dependence of Cuba's vital sugar industry on the U.S. market and the continuing presence of a U.S. army on Cuban soil rendered resistance futile. In 1901, by a vote of 15 to 11, the delegates reluctantly wrote the Platt conditions into their constitution. "There is, of course, little or no independence left Cuba under the Platt Amendment," Wood candidly admitted to his friend Theodore Roosevelt, who had recently succeeded the assassinated McKinley as president.

Cuba's status, in truth, differed little from that of the Philippines. Both were colonies of the United States. In the case of Cuba, economic dependence closely followed political subjugation. Between 1898 and 1914, American trade with Cuba increased more than tenfold (from $27 million to $300 million), while investments more than quadrupled (from $50 million to $220 million). The United States intervened in Cuban political affairs five times between 1906 and 1921 to protect its economic interests and those of the indigenous ruling class with whom it had become closely allied. The economic, political, and military control that the United States imposed on Cuba would fuel anti-American sentiment there for years to come.

Puerto Rico received somewhat different treatment. The United States did not think independence appropriate, even though under Spanish rule the island had enjoyed a large measure of political autonomy and a parliamentary form of government. Nor did the United States follow its Cuban strategy by granting Puerto Rico nominal independence under informal economic and political controls. Instead, it annexed the island outright with the Foraker Act (1900). This act, unlike every previous annexation authorized by Congress since 1788, contained no provision for making the inhabitants citizens of the United States. Puerto Rico was designated an "unincorporated" territory, which meant that Congress would dictate the island's government and specify the rights of its inhabitants. Puerto Ricans were allowed no role in designing their government, nor was their consent requested. With the Foraker Act, Congress had, in effect, invented a new, imperial mechanism for ensuring sovereignty over lands deemed vital to U.S. economic and military security. The U.S. Supreme Court upheld the constitutionality of this mechanism in a series of historic decisions, known as the Insular Cases, in the years from 1901 to 1904.

In some respects Puerto Rico fared better than "independent" Cuba. Puerto Ricans were granted U.S. citizenship in 1917 and won the right to elect their own governor in 1947. Still, Puerto Ricans enjoyed fewer political rights than Americans in the 48 states. Moreover, throughout the 20th century they endured a poverty rate far exceeding that of the mainland. In 1948, for example, three-fourths of Puerto Rican households subsisted on $1,000 or less annually, a figure below the U.S. poverty line. In its skewed distribution of wealth and its lack of industrial development, Puerto Rico resembled the

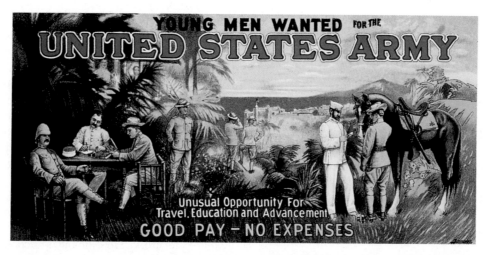

RECRUITING AMERICAN YOUTH FOR MILITARY SERVICE OVERSEAS This U.S. Army advertisement portrays military duty in tropical areas under U.S. control as educational, leisurely, and exotic. The real work of such forces, maintaining social order and defeating anticolonial insurrections, is entirely effaced from this portrait as are the native peoples who inhabited these lands.

poorly developed nations of Central and South America more than it did the affluent country that took over its government in 1900.

The subjugation of Cuba and the annexation of Puerto Rico troubled Americans far less than the U.S. takeover in the Philippines. Since the first articulation of the Monroe Doctrine in 1823, the United States had, in effect, claimed the Western Hemisphere as its sphere of influence. Within that sphere, many Americans believed, the United States possessed the right to act unilaterally to protect its interests. Before 1900 most of its actions (with the exception of the Mexican War) had been designed to limit the influence of European powers—Britain, France, Russia and Spain—on the countries of the hemisphere. After 1900, however, it assumed a more aggressive role, seizing land, overturning governments it did not like, forcing its economic and political policies on weaker neighbors in order to turn the Caribbean Sea into what policymakers called an "American Mediterranean."

CHINA AND THE "OPEN DOOR"

Except for the Philippines and Guam, the United States made no effort to take control of Asian lands. Such a policy might well have triggered war with other world powers already well established in the area. Nor were Americans prepared to tolerate the financial and political costs Asian conquest would have entailed. The United States opted for a diplomatic rather than a military strategy to achieve its foreign policy objectives. In China, in 1899 and 1900, it proposed the policy of the "Open Door."

The United States was concerned that the actions of the other world powers in China would block its own efforts to open up China's markets to American goods. Britain, Germany, Japan, Russia, and France—each coveted their own chunk of China, where they could monopolize trade, exploit cheap labor, and establish military bases. By the 1890s each of these powers was building a sphere of influence, either by wringing economic and territorial concessions from the weak Chinese government or by seizing outright the land and trading privileges they desired.

To prevent China's breakup and to preserve American economic access to the whole of China, McKinley's secretary of state, John Hay, sent "Open Door" notes to the major world powers. The notes asked each power to open its Chinese sphere of influence to the merchants of other nations and to grant them reasonable harbor fees and railroad rates. Hay also asked each power to respect China's sovereignty by enforcing Chinese tariff duties in the territory it controlled.

IS THIS IMPERIALISM?
"NO BLOW HAS BEEN STRUCK EXCEPT FOR LIBERTY AND HUMANITY, AND NONE WILL BE."—WILLIAM McKINLEY

A DEFENSE OF AMERICA'S CHINA OPEN DOOR POLICY
This cartoon portrays a courageous William McKinley and standard bearer Uncle Sam engaging the vicious Chinese Boxers who had risen up to defeat the western imperialists. "Is This Imperialism?" the cartoon asks, answering in McKinley's own words: "No blow has been struck except for liberty and humanity, and none will be."

None of the world powers jumped to endorse either of Hay's requests, though Britain and Japan gave provisional assent. France, Germany, Russia, and Italy responded evasively, indicating their support for the Open Door policy in theory but insisting that they could not implement it until all the other powers had done so. Hay put the best face on their responses by declaring that all the powers had agreed to observe his Open Door principles and that he regarded their assent as "final and definitive." Americans took Hay's bluff as evidence that the United States had triumphed diplomatically over its rivals. The rivals themselves may have been impressed by Hay's diplomacy, but whether they intended to uphold the United States' Open Door policy was not at all clear.

The first challenge to Hay's policy came from the Chinese themselves. In May 1900 a nationalist Chinese organization, colloquially known as the "Box-ers," sparked an uprising to rid China of all "foreign devils" and foreign influences. Hundreds of Europeans were killed, as were many Chinese men and women who had converted to Christianity. When the Boxers laid siege to the foreign legations in Beijing and cut off communication between that city and the outside world, the imperial powers raised an expeditionary force to rescue the diplomats and punish the Chinese rebels. The force, which included 5,000 U.S. soldiers rushed over from the Philippines, broke the Beijing siege in August, and ended the Boxer Rebellion soon thereafter.

Hay feared that other major powers would use the rebellion as a reason to demand greater control over Chinese territory. He sent out a second round of Open Door notes, now asking each power to respect China's political independence and territorial integrity, in addition to guaranteeing unrestricted access to its markets. Impressed by America's show of military strength and worried that the Chinese rebels might strike again, the imperialist rivals responded more favorably to this second round of notes. Britain, France, and Germany endorsed Hay's policy outright. With that support, Hay was able to check Russian and Japanese designs on Chinese territory. Significantly, when the powers decided that the Chinese government should pay them reparations for their property and personnel losses during the Boxer Rebellion, Hay convinced them to accept payment in cash rather than in territory. By keeping China intact and open to free trade, the United States had achieved a major foreign policy victory. Americans began to see themselves as China's savior as well.

THEODORE ROOSEVELT, GEOPOLITICIAN

Roosevelt had been a driving force in the transformation of U.S. foreign policy during the McKinley administration. As assistant secretary of the navy, as a military hero, as a vigorous speaker and writer, and then as vice president, Roosevelt worked tirelessly to remake the country into one of the world's great powers. He believed that the Americans were a racially superior people and destined for supremacy in economic and political affairs. He did not assume, however, that international supremacy would automatically accrue to the United States. A nation, like an individual, must strive for greatness.

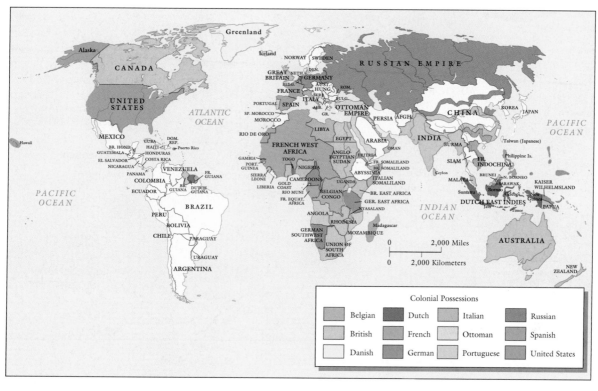

COLONIAL POSSESSIONS, 1900

It must demand of its citizens physical and mental fitness. It must build a military force that could convincingly project power overseas. And it must be prepared to fight. All great nations, Roosevelt declared, ultimately depended on the skill and dedication of their warriors.

Roosevelt's appetite for a good fight caused many people to rue the ascension of this "cowboy" to the White House after McKinley's assassination in 1901. But behind his blustery exterior lay a shrewd analyst of international relations. As much as he craved power for himself and the nation, he understood that the United States could not rule every portion of the globe through military or economic means. Consequently, he sought a balance of power among the great industrial nations through negotiation rather than war. Such a balance would enable each imperial power to safeguard its key interests and contribute to world peace and progress.

Absent from Roosevelt's geopolitical thinking was concern for the interests of less powerful nations. Roosevelt had little patience with the claims

to sovereignty of small countries or the human rights of weak peoples. In his eyes, the peoples of Latin America, Asia (with the exception of Japan), and Africa were racially inferior and thus incapable of self-government or industrial progress. They were better suited to subservience and subsistence than to independence and affluence.

THE ROOSEVELT COROLLARY

Ensuring U.S. dominance in the Western Hemisphere ranked high on Roosevelt's list of foreign policy objectives. In 1904 he issued a "corollary" to the Monroe Doctrine, which had asserted the right of the United States to keep European powers from meddling in hemispheric affairs. In his corollary Roosevelt declared that the United States possessed a further right: the right to intervene in the domestic affairs of hemispheric nations to quell disorder and forestall European intervention. The Roosevelt corollary formalized a policy that the United States had already deployed against Cuba and Puerto Rico

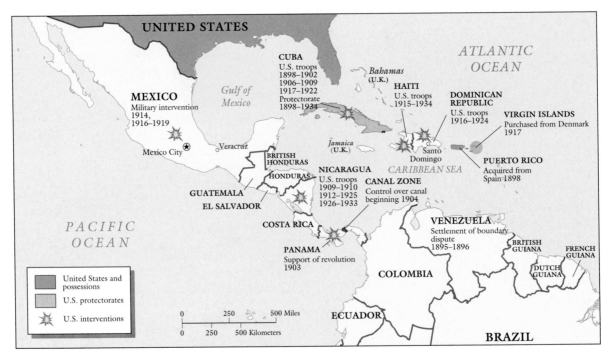

UNITED STATES PRESENCE IN LATIN AMERICA, 1895–1934

in 1900 and 1901. Subsequent events in Venezuela and the Dominican Republic had further convinced Roosevelt of the need to expand the scope of U.S. intervention in hemispheric affairs.

Both Venezuela and the Dominican Republic were controlled by corrupt dictators. Both had defaulted on debts owed to European banks. Their delinquency prompted a German-led European naval blockade and bombardment of Venezuela in 1902 and a threatened invasion of the Dominican Republic by Italy and France in 1903. The United States forced the German navy to retreat from the Venezuelan coast in 1903. In the Dominican Republic, after a revolution had chased the dictator from power, the United States assumed control of the nation's customs collections in 1905 and refinanced the Dominican national debt through U.S. bankers.

The prevalence of corrupt, dictatorial regimes in Latin America and the willingness of European bankers to loan these regimes money had provided ideal conditions for bankruptcy, social turmoil, and foreign intervention. The United States now took aggressive actions to correct those conditions, but rarely in Roosevelt's tenure did the United States show a willingness to help the people who had suffered under these regimes to establish democratic institutions or achieve social justice. When Cubans seeking genuine national independence rebelled against their puppet government in 1906, the United States sent in the Marines to silence them.

THE PANAMA CANAL

Roosevelt's varied interests in Latin America embraced the building of a canal across Central America. The president had long believed, along with Admiral Mahan, that the nation needed a way of moving its ships swiftly from the Pacific Ocean to the Atlantic Ocean, and back again. Central America's narrow width, especially in its southern half, made it the logical place to build a canal. In fact, a French company had obtained land rights and had begun construction of a canal across the Colombian province of Panama in the 1880s. But even though a "mere" 40 miles of land separated the two oceans, the French were stymied by technological difficulties and financial costs of literally moving mountains. Moreover, French doctors found they were unable

Tarzan, the Ape Man (1932)
Directed by W. S. Van Dyke. Starring Johnny Weismuller (Tarzan), Maureen O'Sullivan (Jane Parker), Neil Hamilton (Harry Holt), C. Aubrey Smith (James Parker), and Cheeta the Chimp.

This movie introduced Americans to Tarzan, one of the most popular screen figures of the 1930s, 1940s, and 1950s. Based on the best-selling novels of Edgar Rice Burroughs, this Tarzan movie, like the ones that followed, was meant to puncture the civilized complacency in which Americans and other westernized, imperial peoples had enveloped themselves. The movie opens with an American woman, Jane Parker, arriving in Africa to join her father, James, and the crew he has assembled to search for the mythic elephant graveyard thought to contain untold riches in ivory tusks. Jane is depicted as bright, energetic, attractive, and defiant of female gender conventions. The rest of the white adventurers, however, are depicted as greedy, haughty, contemptuous of the African environment, or just ignorant. The Africans who act as their servants and guides are presented as primitive and superstitious, more like animals than humans. This expedition in search of ivory is destined for disaster, and the movie provides thrills by showing expedition members succumbing to attacks by wild animals and "wild humans" who inhabit this "dark continent."

During one such attack by hippos and pygmies, Tarzan, played by handsome Olympic swimming champion Johnny Weismuller, comes to the rescue, scaring off the attackers by mobilizing a stampede of elephants with a piercing, high-pitched, and unforgettable jungle cry. He takes Jane, who has become separated from the group, to his tree house. Thus begins one of the more unusual and famous screen romances.

Tarzan's origins are not explained, though one infers that he was abandoned by whites as a baby and raised by apes. He has none of the refining features of civilization—decent clothes, language, manners—but he possesses strength, honesty, and virtue. As Jane falls in love with Tarzan and decides to share a jungle life with him, we, the viewers, are asked to contemplate, with Jane, the benefits of peeling off the stultifying features of civilized life (which seem to drop away from Jane along with many of her clothes) and returning to a simpler, more wholesome, and more natural form of existence.

The movie critiques and lampoons the imperial pretensions and smugness of the West, but it never asks viewers to see the indigenous African peoples as anything other than savage. Tarzan may have been ignorant of civilized customs, but he was white and, as such, equipped with the "native" intelligence and character of his race. The movie Africans show no such intelligence or character. They are presented as weak and superstitious or as brutally aggressive and indifferent to human life. Thus *Tarzan, the Ape Man* manages to critique the West without asking Western viewers to challenge the racism that justified the West's domination of non-Western peoples and territories.

Johnny Weismuller and Maureen O'Sullivan as Tarzan and Jane.

to check the spread of malaria and yellow fever among their workers. By the time Roosevelt entered the White House in 1901, the French Panama Company had gone bankrupt.

Roosevelt was not deterred by the French failure. He first presided over the signing of the Hay-Pauncefote Treaty with Great Britain in 1901, releasing the United States from an 1850 agreement that prohibited either country from building a Central American canal without the other's participation. He then instructed his advisers to develop plans for a canal across Nicaragua. The Panamanian route chosen by the French was shorter than the proposed Nicaraguan route and the canal begun by the French was 40 percent complete, but the French company wanted $109 million for it, more than the United States was willing to pay. In 1902, however, the company reduced the price to $40 million, a sum that Congress approved. Secretary of State Hay quickly negotiated an agreement with Tomas Herran, the Colombian chargé d'affaires in Washington. The agreement, formalized in the Hay-Herran Treaty, accorded the United States a six-mile-wide strip across Panama on which to build the canal. Colombia was to receive a onetime $10 million payment and annual rent of $250,000.

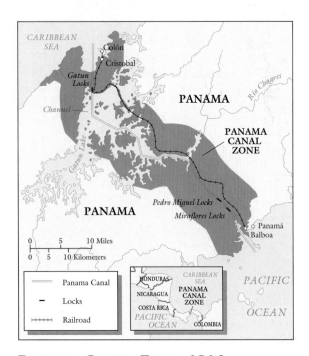

PANAMA CANAL ZONE, 1914

The Colombian legislature, however, rejected the proposed payment as insufficient and sent a new ambassador to the United States with instructions to ask for a onetime payment of $20 million and a share of the $40 million being paid to the French company. Actually, the Colombians (not unreasonably) were hoping to stall negotiations until 1904, when they would regain the rights to the canal zone and consequently to the $40 million sale price promised to the French company.

Although Colombia was acting within its rights, Roosevelt would not tolerate the delay. Failing diplomatic success, he encouraged the Panamanians to revolt against Colombian rule. The Panamanians had staged several rebellions in the previous 25 years, all of which had failed, but the 1903 rebellion succeeded, mainly because a U.S. naval force prevented Colombian troops from landing in Panama. Meanwhile, the U.S.S. *Nashville* put U.S. troops ashore to help the new nation secure its independence. The United States formally recognized Panama as a sovereign state only two days after the rebellion against Colombia began.

Philippe Bunau-Varilla, a director of the French company from which the United States had bought the rights to the canal, declared himself Panama's diplomatic representative, even though he was a French citizen operating out of a Wall Street law firm and hadn't set foot in Panama in 15 years. Even as the duly appointed Panamanian delegation embarked for the United States for negotiations over the canal, Bunau-Varilla rushed to Washington, where he and Secretary of State Hay signed the Hay–Bunau-Varilla Treaty (1903). The treaty granted the United States a 10-mile-wide canal zone in return for the package Colombia had rejected—$10 million down and $250,000 annually. Thus, the United States secured its canal, not by dealing with the newly installed Panamanian government, but with Bunau-Varilla's French company. When the Panamanian delegation arrived in Washington and read the treaty, one of them became so enraged that he knocked Bunau-Varilla cold. Under the circumstances, however, the Panamanian delegation's hands were tied. If it objected to the counterfeit treaty, the United States might withdraw its troops from Panama, leaving the new country at the mercy of Colombia. The instrument through which the United States secured the Canal Zone is known in Panamanian history as "the treaty

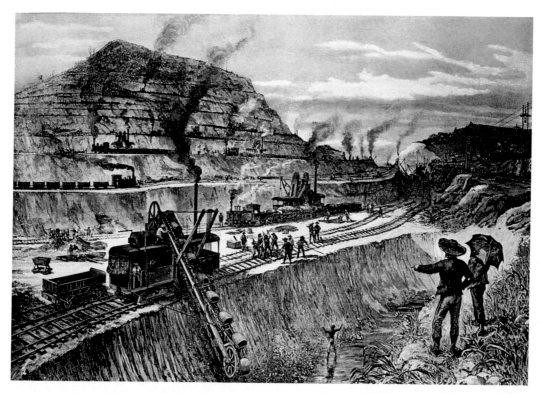

THE PANAMA CANAL UNDER CONSTRUCTION This illustration shows the combination of machine and human labor that moved millions of tons of earth to build the Panama Canal, an undertaking that the British Ambassador James Bryce called "the greatest liberty Man has ever taken with Nature."

which no Panamanian signed" and it bedeviled relations between the two countries for much of the 20th century.

Roosevelt's severing of Panama from Colombia prompted angry protests in Congress. The Hearst newspapers decried the Panama foray as "nefarious" and "a quite unexampled instance of foul play in American politics." Roosevelt was not perturbed. Elihu Root (secretary of state in Roosevelt's second administration), after hearing Roosevelt defend his action before a meeting of his cabinet, jokingly told the president, "You have shown that you were accused of seduction and you have conclusively proved that you were guilty of rape." Roosevelt later gloated, "I took the Canal Zone and let Congress debate!"

Roosevelt turned the building of the canal into a test of American ingenuity and willpower. Engineers overcame every obstacle; doctors developed drugs to combat malaria and yellow fever; armies of construction workers "made the dirt fly." The canal remains a testament to the labor of some 30,000 workers, im-

ported mainly from the West Indies, who, over a 10-year period, labored 10 hours a day, 6 days a week, for 10 cents an hour. Roosevelt visited the canal site in 1906, the first American president to travel overseas while in office. When the canal opened to great fanfare in 1914, the British ambassador James Bryce described it as "the greatest liberty Man has ever taken with Nature." The canal shortened the voyage from San Francisco to New York by more than 8,000 miles and significantly enhanced the international prestige of the United States. Moreover, the strategic importance of the canal further strengthened U.S. resolve to preserve political order in Central America and the Caribbean.

In 1921 the United States paid the Colombian government $25 million as compensation for its loss of Panama. Panama waited more than 70 years, however, to regain control of the 10-mile-wide strip of land that Bunau-Varilla, in connivance with the U.S. government, had bargained away in 1902. President Jimmy Carter signed a treaty in 1977 providing for the reintegration of the Canal Zone into Panama and the canal itself was transferred to Panama in 2000.

KEEPING THE PEACE IN EAST ASIA

In Asia, Roosevelt strove to preserve the Open Door policy in China and the balance of power throughout East Asia. The chief threats came from Russia and Japan, both of whom wanted to seize large chunks of China. At first, Russian expansion into Manchuria and Korea prompted Roosevelt to support Japan's 1904 devastating attack on the Russian Pacific fleet anchored at Port Arthur, China. Once the ruinous effects of the war on Russia became clear, however, Roosevelt entered into secret negotiations to arrange a peace. He invited representatives of Japan and Russia to Portsmouth, New Hampshire, and prevailed on them to negotiate a compromise. The settlement favored Japan by perpetuating its control over most of the territories it had won during the brief Russo-Japanese War. Its chief prize was Korea, which became a protectorate of Japan, but Japan also acquired the southern part of Sakhalin Island, Port Arthur, and the South Manchurian Railroad. Russia avoided paying Japan a huge indemnity and it retained Siberia, thus preserving its role as an East Asian power. Finally, Roosevelt protected China's territorial integrity by inducing the armies of both Russia and Japan to leave Manchuria. Roosevelt's success in ending the Russo-Japanese War won him the Nobel Prize for Peace in 1906; he was the first American to earn that award.

Although Roosevelt succeeded in negotiating a peace between these two world powers, he subsequently ignored, and even encouraged, challenges to the sovereignty of weaker Asian nations. In a secret agreement with Japan (the Taft-Katsura Agreement of 1905), for example, the United States agreed that Japan could dominate Korea in return for a Japanese promise not to attack the Philippines. And in the Root-Takahira Agreement of 1908, the United States tacitly reversed its earlier stand on the inviolability of Chinese borders by recognizing Japanese expansion into southern Manchuria.

In Roosevelt's eyes the overriding need to maintain peace with Japan justified ignoring the claims of Korea and, increasingly, of China. Roosevelt admired Japan's industrial and military might and regarded

ANTI-ASIAN HYSTERIA IN SAN FRANCISCO In 1906, in the midst of a wave of anti-Asian prejudice in California, the San Francisco school board ordered the segregation of all Asian schoolchildren. Here, a 9-year-old Japanese student submits an application for admission to a public primary school and is refused by the principal, Miss M. E. Dean.

Japanese expansion into East Asia as a natural expression of its imperial ambition. The task of American diplomacy, he believed, was first to allow the Japanese to build a secure sphere of influence in East Asia (much as the United States had done in Central America), and second to encourage them to join the United States in pursuing peace rather than war. This was a delicate diplomatic task that required both sensitivity and strength, especially when anti-Japanese agitation broke out in California in 1906.

White Californians had long feared the presence of Asian immigrants. They had pressured Congress into passing the Chinese Exclusion Act of 1882, which ended most Chinese immigration to the United States. They next turned their racism on Japanese immigrants, whose numbers in California had reached 24,000. In 1906 the San Francisco school board ordered the segregation of Asian schoolchildren so that they would not "contaminate" white children. In 1907 the California legislature debated a law to bar any more Japanese immigrants from entering the state. Anti-Asian riots erupted in San Francisco and Los Angeles, encour-

aged in part by hysterical stories in the press about the "Yellow Peril."

Outraged militarists in Japan began talking of a possible war with the United States. Roosevelt assured the Japanese government that he too was appalled by the Californians' behavior. In 1907 he reached a "gentlemen's agreement" with the Japanese, by which the Tokyo government promised to halt the immigration of Japanese adult male laborers to the United States in return for Roosevelt's pledge to end anti-Japanese discrimination. Roosevelt did his part by persuading the San Francisco school board to rescind its segregation ordinance.

At the same time, Roosevelt worried that the Tokyo government would interpret his sensitivity to Japanese honor as weakness. So he ordered the main part of the U.S. fleet, consisting of 16 battleships, to embark on a 45,000-mile world tour, including a splashy stop in Tokyo Bay. Many Americans deplored the cost of the tour and feared that the appearance of the U.S. Navy in a Japanese port would provoke military retaliation. Roosevelt brushed his critics aside, and, true to his prediction,

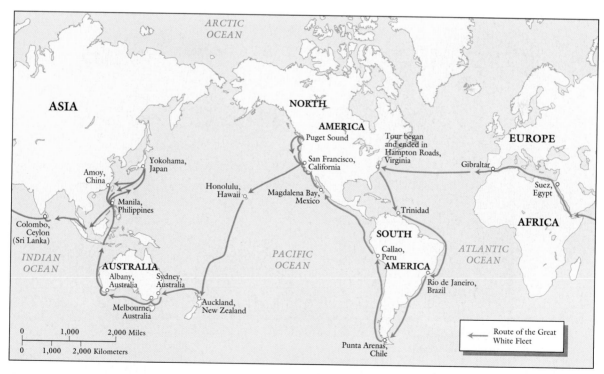

ROUTE OF THE GREAT WHITE FLEET, 1907–1909

the Japanese were impressed by the "Great White Fleet's" show of strength. Their response seemed to lend validity to the African proverb Roosevelt often invoked: "Speak softly and carry a big stick."

In fact, Roosevelt's handling of Japan was the most impressive aspect of his foreign policy. Unlike many other Americans, he refused to let racist attitudes cloud his thinking. He knew when to make concessions and when to stand firm. His policies lessened the prospect of a war with Japan while preserving a strong U.S. presence in East Asia.

WILLIAM HOWARD TAFT, DOLLAR DIPLOMAT

William Howard Taft brought impressive foreign policy credentials to the job of president. He had gained valuable experience in colonial administration as the first governor-general of the Philippines. As Roosevelt's secretary of war and chief negotiator for the delicate Taft-Katsura agreement of 1905, he had learned a great deal about conducting diplomacy with imperialist rivals. Yet Taft lacked Roosevelt's grasp of

balance-of-power politics and capacity for leadership in foreign affairs. Further, Taft's secretary of state, Philander C. Knox, a corporation lawyer from Pittsburgh, lacked diplomatic expertise. Knox's conduct of foreign policy seemed directed almost entirely toward expanding opportunities for corporate investment overseas, a disposition that prompted critics to deride his policies as "dollar diplomacy."

Taft and Knox believed that U.S. investments would effectively substitute "dollars for bullets," and thus offer a more peaceful and less coercive way of maintaining stability and order. Taking a swipe at Roosevelt's "big stick" policy, Taft announced that "modern diplomacy is commercial."

The inability of Taft and Knox to grasp the complexities of power politics led to a diplomatic reversal in East Asia. Knox, prodded by his banker friends, sought to expand American economic activities throughout China—even in Manchuria, where they encroached on the Japanese sphere of influence. In 1911 Knox proposed that a syndicate of European and American bankers buy the Japanese-controlled South Manchurian Railroad to open up

U.S. GLOBAL INVESTMENTS AND INVESTMENTS IN LATIN AMERICA, 1914

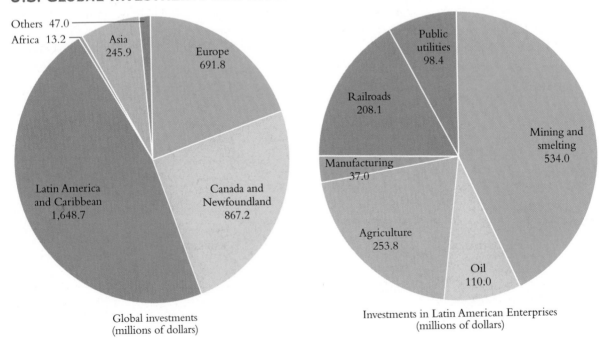

Global investments
(millions of dollars)

Investments in Latin American Enterprises
(millions of dollars)

Source: From Cleona Lewis, *America's Stake in International Investments* (Washington, D.C.: The Brookings Institute, 1938), pp. 576–606.

North China to international trade. Japan reacted by signing a friendship treaty with Russia, its former enemy, which signaled their joint determination to exclude American, British, and French goods from Manchurian markets. Knox's plan to purchase the railroad collapsed, and the United States' Open Door policy suffered a serious blow. Knox's further efforts to increase American trade with Central and South China triggered further hostile responses from the Japanese and the Russians and contributed to the collapse of the Chinese government and the onset of the Chinese Revolution in 1912.

Dollar diplomacy worked better in the Caribbean, where no major power contested U.S. policy. Knox encouraged American investment. Companies such as United Fruit of Boston, which established extensive banana plantations in Costa Rica and Honduras, grew powerful enough to influence both the economies and the governments of Central American countries. When political turmoil threatened their investments, the United States simply sent in its troops. Thus, when Nicaraguan dictator José Santos Zelaya reportedly began negotiating with a European country to build a second trans-Isthmian canal in 1910, a force of U.S. Marines toppled his regime. Marines landed again in 1912 when Zelaya's successor, Adolfo Diaz, angered Nicaraguans with his pro-American policies. This time the Marines were instructed to keep the Diaz regime in power. Except for a brief period in 1925, U.S. troops would remain in Nicaragua continuously from 1912 until 1933. Under Taft, the United States continued to do whatever American policymakers deemed necessary to bolster friendly governments and maintain order in Latin America.

WOODROW WILSON, STRUGGLING IDEALIST

Woodrow Wilson's foreign policy in the Caribbean initially appeared no different from that of his Republican predecessors. In 1915 the United States sent troops to Haiti to put down a revolution; they remained as an army of occupation for 21 years. In 1916, when the people of the Dominican Republic (who shared the island of Hispaniola with the Haitians) refused a treaty making them more or less a protectorate of the United States, Wilson forced them to accept the rule of a U.S. military government. When German influence in the Danish West Indies began to expand, Wilson purchased the islands from Denmark, renamed them the Virgin Islands, and added them to the U.S. Caribbean empire. By the time Wilson left office in 1921, he had intervened militarily in the Caribbean more often than any American president before him.

Wilson's relationship with Mexico in the wake of its revolution, however, reveals that he was troubled by a foreign policy that ignored a less powerful nation's right to determine its own future. He deemed the Mexicans capable of making democracy work and, in general, showed a concern for morality and justice in foreign affairs—matters to which Roosevelt and Taft had paid scant attention. Wilson determined that U.S. foreign policy should help to advance democratic ideals and institutions in Mexico.

Wilson's Mexican dealings were motivated by more than his fondness for democracy. He also feared that political unrest in Mexico could lead to violence, social disorder, and a revolutionary government hostile to U.S. economic interests. With a U.S.-style democratic government in Mexico, property rights would be respected and U.S. investments would remain secure. Wilson's desire both to encourage democracy and to limit the extent of social change made it difficult to devise a consistent foreign policy toward Mexico.

The Mexican Revolution broke out in 1910 when dictator Porfirio Diaz, who had ruled for 34 years, was overthrown by democratic forces led by Francisco Madero. Madero's talk of democratic reform frightened many foreign investors, especially those in the United States and Great Britain, who owned more than half of all Mexican real estate, 90 percent of its oil reserves, and practically all of its railroads. Thus, when Madero himself was overthrown early in 1913 by Victoriano Huerta, a conservative general who promised to protect foreign investments, the dollar diplomatists in the Taft administration and in Great Britain breathed a sigh of relief. Henry Lane Wilson, the U.S. ambassador to Mexico, had helped to engineer Huerta's coup. Before close relations between the United States and Huerta could be worked out, however, Huerta's men murdered Madero.

Woodrow Wilson, who became president shortly after Madero's assassination in 1913, might have overlooked it (as did the European powers) and entered into close ties with Huerta on condition that he protect American property. Instead, Wilson refused to recognize Huerta's "government of butchers" and demanded that Mexico hold democratic elections. Wilson favored Venustiano Carranza and Francisco ("Pancho") Villa, two enemies of Huerta who commanded rebel armies and who claimed to be democrats. In April 1914 Wilson used the arrest of several U.S. sailors by Huerta's troops as a reason to send a fleet into Mexican waters. He ordered the U.S. Marines to occupy the Mexican port city of Veracruz and to prevent a German ship there from unloading munitions meant for Huerta's army. In the resulting action between U.S. and Mexican forces, 19 Americans and 126 Mexicans were killed. The battle brought the two countries dangerously close to war. Eventually, however, American control over Veracruz weakened and embarrassed Huerta's regime to the point where Carranza was able to take power.

Carranza did not behave as Wilson had expected. He rejected Wilson's efforts to shape a new Mexi-can government and announced a bold land reform program. That program called for the distribution of some of Mexico's agricultural land to impoverished peasants and the transfer of developmental rights on oil lands from foreign corporations to the Mexican government. If the program went into effect, U.S. petroleum companies would lose control of their Mexican properties, a loss that Wilson deemed unacceptable. Wilson now threw his support to Pancho Villa, who seemed more willing than Carranza to protect U.S. oil interests. When Carranza's forces defeated Villa's forces in 1915, Wilson reluctantly withdrew his support of Villa and prepared to recognize the Carranza government.

Furious that Wilson had abandoned him, Villa and his soldiers pulled 18 U.S. citizens from a train in northern Mexico and murdered them, along with another 17 in an attack on Columbus, New Mexico. Determined to punish Villa, Wilson got permission from Carranza to send a U.S. expeditionary force under General John J. Pershing into Mexico to hunt down Villa's hated "bandits." Pershing's troops pursued Villa's forces 300 miles into Mexico but failed to catch them. The U.S. troops did, however, clash twice with Mexican

PANCHO VILLA Francisco "Pancho" Villa was the charismatic commander of a rebel Mexican army during the years of the Mexican Revolution (1910–17). Failing to attract the support of President Wilson, Villa became a bitter enemy of the United States. After Villa's forces murdered more than 30 U.S. civilians, Wilson dispatched an army to Mexico to hunt him down. U.S. forces pursued him 300 miles into Mexico but never caught him.

troops under Carranza's command, once again bringing the countries to the brink of war. The United States, about to enter the First World War, could not afford a fight with Mexico; in 1917, Wilson quietly ordered Pershing's troops home and grudgingly recognized the Carranza government.

Wilson's policies toward Mexico in the years from 1913 to 1917 seemed to have produced few concrete results, except to reinforce an already deep antagonism among Mexicans toward the United States. His repeated changes in strategy, moreover, seemed to indicate a lack of skill and decisiveness in foreign affairs. Actually, however, Wilson recognized something that Roosevelt and Taft had not: that more and more peoples of the world were determined to control their own destinies. The United States needed a way to support these peoples' democratic aspirations while also safeguarding its own economic interests. The First World War would make this quest for a balance between democratic principles and national self-interest all the more urgent.

CONCLUSION

We can assess the dramatic turn in U.S. foreign policy after 1898 either in relation to the foreign policies of rival world powers or against America's own democratic ideals. By the first standard, U.S. foreign policy looks impressive. The United States achieved its major objectives in world affairs: It tightened its control over the Western Hemisphere and projected its military and economic power into Asia. It did so while sacrificing relatively few American lives and while constraining the jingoistic appetite for truly extensive military adventure and conquest. The United States added only 125,000 square miles to its empire in the years from 1870 to 1900, while Great Britain, France, and Germany enlarged their empires by 4.7, 3.5, and 1.0 million square miles, respectively. Relatively few foreigners were subjected to American colonial rule. By con-

trast, in 1900 the British Empire extended over 12 million square miles and embraced one-fourth of the world's population. At times, American rule could be brutal, as it was to Filipino soldiers and civilians alike, but on the whole it was no more severe than British rule and significantly less severe than that of the French, German, Belgian, or Japanese imperialists. McKinley, Roosevelt, Taft, and Wilson all placed limits on American expansion and avoided, prior to 1917, extensive foreign entanglements and wars.

If measured against the standard of America's own democratic ideals, however, U.S. foreign policy after 1898 must be judged more harshly. It demeaned the peoples of the Philippines, Puerto Rico, Guam, Cuba, and Colombia as inferior, primitive, and barbaric and denied them the right to govern themselves. In choosing to behave like the imperialist powers of Europe, the United States abandoned its long-standing claim to being a different kind of nation—one that valued liberty more than power.

Many Americans of the time judged their nation by both standards and thus faced a dilemma that would extend throughout the 20th century. On the one hand, they believed with Roosevelt that the size, economic strength, and honor of the United States required it to accept the role of world power and policeman. On the other hand, they continued to believe with Wilson that they had a mission to spread the values of 1776 to the farthest reaches of the earth. The Mexico example demonstrates how hard it was for the United States to reconcile these two very different approaches to world affairs.

Suggested Readings begin on page SR-1.
For Web activities and resources
related to this chapter, go to
http://www.harcourtcollege.com/history.murrin

CHAPTER 23

WAR AND SOCIETY, 1914–1920

THE SINKING OF THE *LUSITANIA*

On May 7, 1915, a German U-boat torpedoed and sank the British passenger liner *Lusitania*, killing 1,198 people, 128 of them Americans. The event turned U.S. opinion sharply against the Germans, especially because the civilians on board had been given no chance to escape or surrender.

The First World War broke out in Europe in August 1914. The Triple Alliance of Germany, Austria-Hungary, and the Ottoman Empire squared off against the Triple Entente of Great Britain, France, and Russia. The United States entered the war on the side of the Entente (the Allies, or Allied Powers, as they came to be called) in 1917. Over the next year and a half, the United States converted its immense and sprawling economy into a disciplined war production machine, raised a five-million-man army, and provided both the war matériel and troops that helped propel the Allies to victory. The United States emerged from the war as the world's mightiest country. In these and other respects, the war was a great triumph.

But the war also convulsed American society more deeply than any event since the Civil War. This was the first "total" war, meaning that combatants devoted virtually all their resources to the fight. Thus the United States government had no choice but to pursue a degree of industrial control and social regimentation unprecedented in American history. Needless to say, this degree of government control was itself a controversial measure in a society that had long distrusted state power. Moreover, significant numbers of Americans from a variety of constituencies opposed the war. To overcome this opposition, Wilson couched American war aims in disinterested and idealistic terms: The United States, he claimed, wanted a "peace without victory," a "war for democracy," and liberty for the world's oppressed peoples. Because these words drew deeply on American political traditions, Wilson believed that Americans would find them inspiring, put aside their suspicions, and support him.

Although many people in the United States and abroad responded enthusiastically to Wilson's ideals, Wilson needed England and France's support to deliver peace without victory, and this support never came. At home, disadvantaged groups stirred up trouble by declaring that American society had failed to live up to its democratic and egalitarian ideals. Wilson supported repressive policies to silence these rebels and to enforce unity and conformity on the American people. In the process, he tarnished the ideals for which America had been fighting. Only a year after the war had triumphantly ended, Wilson's hopes for peace without victory abroad had been destroyed, and America was being torn apart by violent labor disputes and race riots at home.

This chapter will focus on the following major questions:

- Why did the United States become involved in World War I?
- What problems did the U.S. government encounter as it sought to mobilize its people and economy for war, and how were they overcome?
- What were Woodrow Wilson's peace proposals and how did they fare?
- Did World War I enhance or interrupt the pursuit of liberty and equality on the home front?

EUROPE'S DESCENT INTO WAR

Europe began its descent into war on June 28, 1914, in Sarajevo, Bosnia, when a Bosnian nationalist assassinated Archduke Franz Ferdinand, heir to the Austro-Hungarian throne. This act was meant to protest the Austro-Hungarian imperial presence in the Balkans, and to encourage the Bosnians, Croatians, and other Balkan peoples to join the Serbs in establishing independent nations. Austria-Hungary responded to this provocation on July 28 by declaring war on Serbia, holding it responsible for the archduke's murder.

The conflict might have remained local had not an intricate series of treaties divided Europe into two hostile camps. Germany, Austria-Hungary, and Italy, the so-called Triple Alliance, had promised to come to each other's aid if attacked. Italy would soon opt out of this alliance, to be replaced by the Ottoman Empire. Arrayed against the nations of the Triple Alliance were Britain, France, and Russia in the Triple Entente. Russia was obligated by another treaty to defend Serbia against Austria-Hungary, and consequently on July 30 it mobilized its armed forces to go to Serbia's aid. That brought Germany into the conflict to protect Austria-Hungary from Russian attack. On August 3 German troops struck not at Russia itself but at France, Russia's western ally. To reach France, German troops had marched through neutral Belgium. On August 4 Britain reacted by declaring war on Germany. Within the space of only a few weeks, Europe found itself engulfed in war.

Complicated alliances and defense treaties of the European nations undoubtedly hastened the rush toward war. But equally important was the competition among the larger powers to build the strongest economies, the largest armies and navies, and the grandest colonial empires. Britain and Germany, in particular, were engaged in a bitter struggle for European and world supremacy. Few Europeans had any idea that these military buildups might lead to a terrible war that would kill nearly an entire generation of young men and expose the barbarity lurking in their civilization. Historians now believe that several advisers close to the German

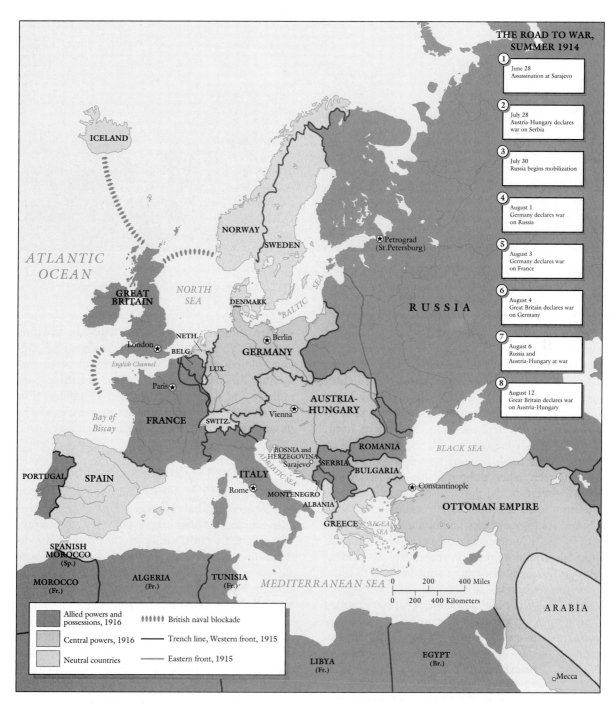

THE ROAD TO WAR, SUMMER 1914

1. June 28
Assassination at Sarajevo

2. July 28
Austria-Hungary declares war on Serbia

3. July 30
Russia begins mobilization

4. August 1
Germany declares war on Russia

5. August 3
Germany declares war on France

6. August 4
Great Britain declares war on Germany

7. August 6
Russia and Austria-Hungary at war

8. August 12
Great Britain declares war on Austria-Hungary

Legend:
- Allied powers and possessions, 1916
- Central powers, 1916
- Neutral countries
- British naval blockade
- Trench line, Western front, 1915
- Eastern front, 1915

EUROPE GOES TO WAR

emperor, Kaiser Wilhelm II, were actually eager to engage Russia and France in a fight for supremacy on the European continent. They expected that a European war would be swift and decisive—in Ger-

many's favor. England and France also believed in their own superiority. Millions of young men, rich and poor, rushed to join the armies on both sides and share in the expected glory.

***GASSED,* BY JOHN SINGER SARGENT** An artist renders the horror of a poison gas attack in the First World War. The Germans were the first to use this new and brutal weapon, which contributed greatly to the terror of war.

Victory was not swift. The two camps were evenly matched. Moreover, the first wartime use of machine guns and barbed wire made defense against attack easier than staging an offensive. (Both tanks and airplanes had also been invented by this time, but military strategists on both sides were slow to put them to offensive use). On the western front, after the initial German attack narrowly failed to take Paris in 1914, the two opposing armies confronted each other along a battle line stretching from Belgium in the north to the Swiss border in the southeast. Troops dug trenches to protect themselves from artillery bombardment and poison gas attacks. Commanders on both sides mounted suicidal ground assaults on the enemy by sending tens of thousands of infantry, armed only with rifles, bayonets, and grenades, out of the trenches and directly into enemy fire. Barbed wire further retarded forward progress, enabling enemy artillery and machine guns to cut down appalling numbers of men. In 1916, during one 10-month German offensive at Verdun (France), 600,000 German troops died; 20,000 British troops were killed during only the first day of an Entente assault on the Somme River (also in France). Many of those who were not killed in combat succumbed to disease that spread rapidly in the cold, wet, and rat-infested trenches. In eastern Europe the armies of Germany and Austria-Hungary squared off against those of Russia and Serbia. Though that front did not employ trench warfare, the combat was no less lethal. By the time the First World War ended, an estimated 8.5 million soldiers had died and more than twice that number had been wounded. Total casualties, both military and civilian, had reached 37 million. Europe had lost a generation of young men, as well as its confidence, stability, and global supremacy.

AMERICAN NEUTRALITY

Soon after the fighting began, Woodrow Wilson told Americans that this was a European war; neither side was threatening a vital American interest. The United States would therefore proclaim its neutrality and maintain normal relations with both sides while seeking to secure a peace. Normal relations meant that the United States would continue trading with both camps. Wilson's neutrality policy met with lively opposition, especially from Theodore Roosevelt, who was convinced that the United States should join the Entente to check German power and expansionism. A majority of Americans, however, applauded Wilson's determination to keep the country out of war.

Neutrality was easier to proclaim than to achieve. Many Americans, especially those with economic and political power, identified culturally more with Britain than with Germany. They shared with the English a language, a common ancestry, and a commitment to liberty. Wilson himself revered the

British parliamentary system of government. His closest foreign policy adviser, Colonel Edward M. House, was pro-British, as was Robert Lansing, a trusted counselor in the State Department. Only William Jennings Bryan, Wilson's secretary of state, was immune to the appeal of the English.

Germany had no such attraction for U.S. policymakers. On the contrary, Germany's acceptance of monarchical rule, the prominence of militarists in German politics, and its lack of democratic traditions inclined U.S. officials to judge Germany harshly.

The United States had strong economic ties to Great Britain as well. In 1914 the United States exported more than $800 million in goods to Britain and its allies, compared with $170 million to Germany and Austria-Hungary (which came to be known as the Central Powers). As soon as the war began, the British and then the French turned to the United States for food, clothing, munitions, and other war supplies. The U.S. economy, which had been languishing in 1914, enjoyed a boom as a result. Bankers began to issue loans to the Allied Powers, further knitting together the American and British economies and giving American investors a direct stake in an Allied victory. Moreover, the British navy had blockaded German ports, which damaged the United States' already limited trade with Germany. By 1916 U.S. exports to the Central Powers had plummeted to barely one million dollars, a fall of more than 99 percent in two years.

The British blockade of German ports clearly violated American neutrality. The Wilson administration protested the British navy's search and occasional seizure of American merchant ships, but it never retaliated by suspending loans or exports to Great Britain. To do so would have plunged the U.S. economy into a severe recession. In failing to protect its right to trade with Germany, however, the United States compromised its neutrality and allowed itself to be drawn into war.

SUBMARINE WARFARE

To combat British control of the seas and to check the flow of U.S. goods to the Allies, Germany unveiled a terrifying new weapon, the *Unterseeboot*, or U-boat, the first militarily effective submarine. Early in 1915 Germany announced its intent to use its U-boats to sink on sight enemy ships en route to the British Isles. On May 7, 1915, without warning, a German U-boat torpedoed the British passenger liner *Lusitania*, en route from New York to London. The ship sank in 22 minutes, killing 1,198 men, women, and children, 128 of them U.S. citizens. Americans were shocked by the sinking. Innocent civilians who had been given no warning of attack, no chance to surrender, had been murdered in cold blood. The attack appeared to confirm what anti-German agitators were saying: that the Germans were by nature barbaric and uncivilized. The circumstances surrounding the sinking of the *Lusitania*, however, were more complicated than most Americans realized.

Prior to its sailing, the Germans had alleged that the *Lusitania* was secretly carrying a large store of munitions to Great Britain (a charge later proved true) and that it therefore was subject to U-boat attack. Germany had warned American passengers not to travel on British passenger ships that carried munitions. Moreover, Germany claimed, with some justification, that the purpose of the U-boat attacks—the disruption of Allied supply lines—was no different from Britain's purpose in blockading German ports. Because its surface ships were outnumbered by the British navy, Germany claimed it had no alternative but to choose the underwater strategy. If a submarine attack seemed more reprehensible than a conventional sea battle, the Germans argued, it was no more so than the British attempt to starve the German people into submission with a blockade.

American political leaders might have used the *Lusitania* incident to denounce both Germany's U-boat strategy and Britain's blockade as actions that violated the rights of citizens of neutral nations. Only Secretary of State Bryan had the courage to say so, however, and his stand proved so unpopular in Washington that he resigned from office; Wilson chose the pro-British Lansing to take his place. Wilson denounced the sinking of the *Lusitania* in harsh, threatening terms and demanded that Germany pledge never to launch another attack on the citizens of neutral nations, even when they were traveling in British or French ships. Germany acquiesced to Wilson's demand.

The resulting lull in submarine warfare was short-lived, however. In early 1916 the Allies began to arm their merchant vessels with guns and depth charges capable of destroying German U-boats.

Considering this a provocation, Germany renewed its campaign of surprise submarine attacks. In March 1916 a German submarine torpedoed the French passenger liner *Sussex*, causing a heavy loss of life and injuring several Americans. Again Wilson demanded that Germany spare civilians from attack. In the so-called *Sussex* pledge, Germany once again relented but warned that it might resume unrestricted submarine warfare if the United States did not prevail upon Great Britain to permit neutral ships to pass through the naval blockade.

The German submarine attacks strengthened the hand of Theodore Roosevelt and others who had been arguing that war with Germany was inevitable and that the United States must prepare itself to fight. By 1916 Wilson could no longer ignore these critics. Between January and September of that year, he sought and won congressional approval for bills to increase the size of the army and navy, tighten federal control over National Guard forces, and authorize the building of a merchant fleet. Although Wilson had conceded ground to the pro-war agitators, he did not share their belief that war with Germany was either inevitable or desirable. To the contrary, he accelerated his diplomatic initiatives to deter American military involvement. He dispatched Colonel House to London in January 1916 to draw up a peace plan with the British foreign secretary, Lord Grey. This initiative resulted in the House-Grey memorandum of February 22, 1916, in which Britain agreed to ask the United States to negotiate a settlement between the Allies and the Central Powers. The British believed that the terms of such a peace settlement would favor the Allies. They were furious when Wilson revealed that he wanted an impartial, honestly negotiated peace in which the claims of the Allies and Central Powers would be treated with equal respect and consideration. Britain now rejected U.S. peace overtures, and relations between the two countries grew unexpectedly tense.

THE PEACE MOVEMENT

Underlying Wilson's 1916 peace initiative was a vision of a new world order in which relations between nations would be governed by negotiation rather than war and in which justice would replace power as the fundamental principle of diplomacy.

ON A MISSION FOR PEACE Members of the American Women's Peace Party pose on a ship taking them to The Hague (The Netherlands) for a 1915 meeting of the International Committee for Permanent Peace. These women were part of a large domestic movement that opposed U.S. involvement in the war. Jane Addams, one of the peace movement's leaders, is third from the right behind the banner.

In a major foreign policy address on May 27, 1916, Wilson formally declared his support for what he later call the League of Nations, an international parliament dedicated to the pursuit of peace, security, and justice for all the world's peoples.

Many Americans supported Wilson's efforts to commit national prestige to the cause of international peace rather than conquest and to keep the United States out of war. Carrie Chapman Catt, president of the National American Woman Suffrage Association, and Jane Addams, founder of the Women's Peace Party, actively opposed the war. In 1915 an international women's peace conference at The Hague (in the Netherlands) had drawn many participants from the United States. A substantial pacifist group emerged among the nation's Protestant clergy. Midwestern progressives such as Robert La Follette, Bryan, and George Norris urged that the United States steer clear of this European conflict, as did leading socialists such as Eugene V. Debs. In April 1916 many of the country's most prominent progressives and socialists joined hands in the American Union Against Militarism and pressured Wilson to continue pursuing the path of peace.

Wilson's peace campaign also attracted support from the country's sizable Irish and German ethnic populations, who were determined to block any formal military alliance with Great Britain. That many German ethnics, who continued to feel affection for their native land and culture, would oppose U.S. entry into the war is hardly surprising. And the Irish viewed England as an arrogant imperial power that kept Ireland subjugated. That view was confirmed when England crushed the "Easter Rebellion" that Irish nationalists had launched on Easter Monday 1916 to win their country's independence. The Irish in America, like those in Ireland, wanted to see Britain's strength sapped (and Ireland's prospects for freedom enhanced) by a long war.

WILSON'S VISION: "PEACE WITHOUT VICTORY"

The 1916 presidential election revealed the breadth of peace sentiment. At the Democratic convention, Governor Martin Glynn of New York, the Irish American speaker who renominated Wilson for a second term, praised the president for keeping the United States out of war. His portrayal of Wilson as the "peace president" electrified the convention and made "He kept us out of war" a campaign slogan. The slogan proved particularly effective against Wilson's Republican opponent, Charles Evans Hughes, whose close ties to Theodore Roosevelt seemed to place him in the pro-war camp. Combining the promise of peace with a pledge to push ahead with progressive reform, Wilson won a narrow victory.

Emboldened by his electoral triumph, Wilson intensified his quest for peace. On December 16, 1916, he sent a peace note to the belligerent governments, entreating them to consider ending the conflict and, to that end, to state their terms for peace. Although Germany refused to specify its terms and Britain and France announced a set of conditions too extreme for Germany ever to accept, Wilson pressed ahead, initiating secret peace negotiations with both sides. To prepare the American people for what he hoped would be a new era of international relations, Wilson appeared before the Senate on January 22, 1917, to outline his plans for peace. In his speech, he reaffirmed his commitment to the League of Nations, but for such a league to succeed, Wilson argued, it would have to be handed a sturdy peace settlement. This entailed a "peace without victory." Only a peace settlement that refused to crown a victor or humiliate a loser would ensure the equality of the combatants, and "only a peace between equals can last."

Wilson listed the crucial principles of a lasting peace: freedom of the seas; disarmament; and the right of every people to self-determination, democratic self-government, and security against aggression. He was proposing a revolutionary change in world order, one that would allow all the earth's peoples, regardless of their size or strength, to achieve political independence and to participate as equals in world affairs. These views, rarely expressed by the leader of a world power, stirred the despairing masses of Europe and elsewhere caught in deadly conflict.

GERMAN ESCALATION

Wilson's oratory came too late to serve the cause of peace. Sensing the imminent collapse of Russian forces on the eastern front, Germany had decided, in early 1917, to throw its full military might at France and Britain. On land it planned to launch a massive assault on the trenches, and at sea it prepared to unleash its submarines to attack all vessels heading for British ports. Germany knew that this last action would compel the United States to enter the war, but it was gambling on being able to strangle the British economy and leave France isolated before significant numbers of American troops could reach European shores.

On February 1, the United States broke off diplomatic relations with Germany. Wilson continued to hope for a negotiated settlement, however, until February 25, when the British intercepted and passed on to the president a telegram from Germany's foreign secretary, Arthur Zimmermann, to the German minister in Mexico. The infamous "Zimmermann telegram" instructed the minister to ask the Mexican government to attack the United States in the event of war between Germany and the United States. In return, Germany would pay the Mexicans a large fee and regain for them the "lost provinces" of Texas, New Mexico, and Arizona. Wilson, Congress, and the American public were outraged by the story.

In March news arrived that Tsar Nicholas II's autocratic regime in Russia had collapsed and had been replaced by a liberal-democratic government under the leadership of Alexander Kerensky. As long as the tsar ruled Russia and stood to benefit from the Central Powers' defeat, Wilson could not honestly claim that America's going to war against Germany would bring democracy to Europe. The fall of the tsar and the need of Russia's fledgling democratic government for support gave Wilson the rationale he needed to justify American intervention.

Appearing before a joint session of Congress on April 2, Wilson declared that the United States must enter the war because "the world must be made safe for democracy." He continued:

> We shall fight for the things which we have always carried nearest our hearts—for democracy, for the right of those who submit to authority to have a voice in their own Governments, for the rights and liberties of small nations, for a universal dominion of right by such a concert of free peoples as shall bring peace and safety to all nations and make the world itself at last free. To such a task we dedicate our lives and our fortunes.

Inspired by his words, Congress broke into thunderous applause. On April 6, Congress voted to declare war by a vote of 373 to 50 in the House and 82 to 6 in the Senate.

The United States thus embarked on a grand experiment to reshape the world. Wilson had given millions of people around the world reason to hope, both that the terrible war would soon end and that their strivings for freedom and social justice would be realized. Although he was taking America to war on the side of the Allies, he stressed that America would fight as an "associated power," a phrase meant to underscore America's determination to keep its war aims separate from and more honest than those of the Allies.

Still, Wilson understood all too well the risks of his undertaking. A few days before his speech to Congress, he had confided to a journalist his worry that the American people, once at war, will "forget there ever was such a thing as tolerance. To fight you must be brutal and ruthless, and the spirit of ruthless brutality will enter into the very fibre of our national life, infecting Congress, the courts, the policeman on the beat, the man in the street."

AMERICAN INTERVENTION

The entry of the United States into the war gave the Allies the muscle they needed to defeat the Central Powers, but it came almost too late. Germany's resumption of unrestricted submarine warfare took a frightful toll on Allied shipping. From February through July 1917, German subs sank almost four million tons of shipping, more than one-third of Britain's entire merchant fleet. One of every four large freighters departing Britain in those months never returned; at one point, the British Isles were down to a mere four weeks of provisions. American intervention ended Britain's vulnerability in dramatic fashion. U.S. and British naval commanders now grouped merchant ships into convoys and provided them with warship escorts through the most dangerous stretches of the North Atlantic. Destroyers armed with depth charges were particularly effective as escorts. Their shallow draft made them invulnerable to torpedoes, and their great acceleration and speed allowed them to pursue slow-moving U-boats. The U.S. and British navies had begun to use sound waves (later called "sonar") to pinpoint the location of underwater craft, and this new technology increased the effectiveness of destroyer attacks. By the end of 1917, the tonnage of Allied shipping lost each month to U-boat attacks had declined by two-thirds, from almost 1 million tons in April to 350,000 tons in December. The increased flow of supplies stiffened the resolve of the exhausted British and French troops.

The French and British armies had bled themselves white by taking the offensive in 1916 and 1917 and had scarcely budged the trench lines. The Germans had been content in those years simply to hold their trench position in the West, for they were engaged in a huge offensive against the Russians in the East. The Germans intended first to defeat Russia and then to shift their eastern armies to the West for a final assault on the weakened British and French lines. Their opportunity came in the winter and spring of 1918.

A second Russian revolution in November 1917 had overthrown Kerensky's liberal-democratic government and had brought to power a revolutionary socialist government under Vladimir Lenin and his Bolshevik Party. Lenin pulled Russia out of the war on the grounds that the war did not serve the best interests of the working classes, that it was a conflict between rival capitalist elites interested only in wealth and power (and indifferent to the slaughter of soldiers in the trenches). In March 1918 Lenin signed a treaty at Brest-Litovsk that added to Germany's territory and resources and enabled Germany to shift its eastern forces to the western front.

Russia's exit from the war hurt the Allies. Not only did it expose French and British troops to a much larger German force, it also challenged the Allied claim that they were fighting a just war against German aggression. Lenin had published the texts of secret Allied treaties showing that Britain and France, like Germany, had plotted to enlarge their nations and empires through war. The revelation that the Allies were fighting for land and riches rather than democratic principles outraged large numbers of people in France and Great Britain, demoralized Allied troops, and threw the French and British governments into disarray.

The treaties also embarrassed Wilson, who had brought America into the war to fight for democracy, not territory. Wilson quickly moved to restore the Allies' credibility by unveiling, in January

THE ROCK OF THE MARNE Mal Thompson's painting shows infantry units of the U.S. 30th and 38th regiments from the Third Division of the American Expeditionary Force engaging German troops in France in July 1918. Although he shows them under fire, Thompson depicts the soldiers as focused, calm, and determined against a landscape desolated by war.

1918, a concrete program for peace. His Fourteen Points reaffirmed America's commitment to an international system governed by laws rather than by might and renounced territorial aggrandizement as a legitimate war aim. This document provided the ideological cement that held the Allies together at a critical moment. (The Fourteen Points are discussed more fully in the section "The Failure of the International Peace.")

In March and April 1918, Germany launched its huge offensive against British and French positions, sending Allied troops reeling. A ferocious assault against French lines on May 27 met with little resistance; German troops advanced 10 miles a day—a faster pace than any on the western front since the earliest days of the war—until they reached the Marne River, within striking distance of Paris. The French government prepared to evacuate the city. At this perilous moment, a large American army—fresh, well-equipped, and oblivious to the horrors of trench warfare—arrived to reinforce what remained of the French lines.

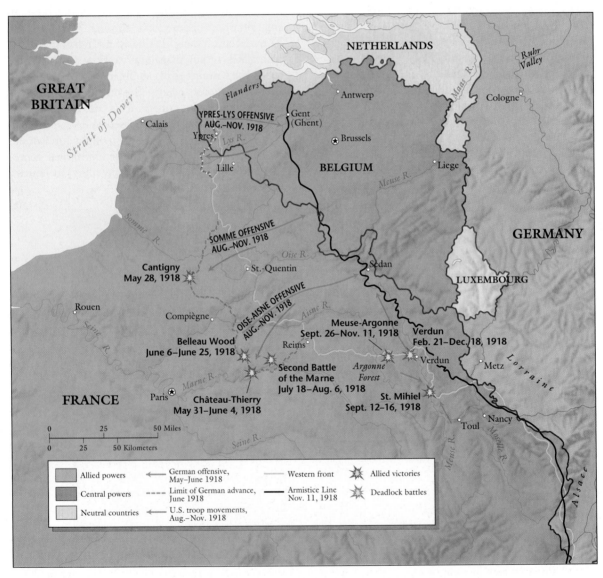

AMERICA IN THE FIRST WORLD WAR: WESTERN FRONT, 1918

In fact, these American troops, part of the American Expeditionary Force (AEF) commanded by General John J. Pershing, had begun landing in France almost a year earlier. During the intervening months, the United States had had to create a modern army from scratch, because its existing force was so small, ranking only 17th in the world. Men had to be drafted, trained, supplied with food and equipment; ships for transporting them to Europe had to be found or built. In France, Pershing put his troops through additional training before committing them to battle. He was determined that the American soldiers—or "doughboys," as they were called—should acquit themselves well on the battlefield. The army he ordered into battle to counter the German spring offensive of 1918 fought well. Many American soldiers fell, but the German offensive ground to a halt. Paris was saved, and Germany's best chance for victory slipped from its grasp.

Buttressed by this show of AEF strength, the Allied troops staged a major offensive of their own in late September. Millions of Allied troops (including more than a million from the AEF) advanced across the 200-mile-wide Argonne forest in France, cutting German supply lines. By late October, they had reached the German border. Faced with an invasion of their homeland and with rapidly mounting popular dissatisfaction with the war, German leaders asked for an armistice, to be followed by peace negotiations based on Wilson's Fourteen Points. Having forced the Germans to agree to numerous concessions, the Allies ended the war on November 11, 1918. The carnage was finally over.

MOBILIZING FOR "TOTAL" WAR

Compared to Europe, the United States suffered little from the war. The deaths of 112,000 American soldiers paled in comparison to European losses: 900,000 by Great Britain, 1.2 million by Austria-Hungary, 1.4 million by France, 1.7 million by Russia, and 2 million by Germany. The U.S. civilian population was spared most of the war's ravages—the destruction of homes and industries, the shortages of food and medicine, the spread of disease—that afflicted millions of Europeans. Only with the flu epidemic that swept across the Atlantic from Europe in 1919 to claim approx-

imately 500,000 American lives did Americans briefly experience wholesale suffering and death.

Still, the war had a profound effect on American society. Every military engagement the United States had fought since the Civil War—the Indian wars, the Spanish-American War, the American-Filipino War, the Boxer Rebellion, the Latin American interventions—had been limited in scope. Even the troop mobilizations that seemed large at the time—the more than 100,000 needed to fight the Spanish and then the Filipinos—failed to tax severely American resources. The First World War was different. It was a "total" war to which every combatant had committed virtually all its resources. The scale of the effort in the United States became apparent early in 1917 when Wilson asked Congress for a conscription law that would permit the federal government to raise a multimillion-man army. The United States would also have to devote much of its agricultural, transportation, industrial, and population resources to the war effort if it wished to end the European stalemate. Who would organize this massive effort? Who would pay for it? Would Americans accept the sacrifice and regimentation it would demand? These were vexing questions for a nation long committed to individual liberty, small government, and a weak military.

ORGANIZING INDUSTRY

The question of how to organize the economy for war reopened a debate that Wilson and Roosevelt had engaged in during the presidential campaign of 1912 (see chapter 21). Southern and midwestern Democrats, fearing the centralization of governmental authority, pushed for a decentralized, or New Freedom, approach to mobilization. Northeastern progressives, on the other hand, saw the war as an opportunity to realize their New Nationalist dream of establishing a strong state to regulate the economy, boost efficiency, and achieve social harmony. Siding at first with the New Freedom faction, Wilson delegated the chore of mobilization to local defense councils throughout the country. When that effort failed, however, Wilson moved to a New Nationalist position and created several centralized federal agencies—the War Industries Board, the National War Labor Board, the Aircraft Production Board, the U.S. Railroad Administration, the Emergency Fleet Corporation, the Fuel Administration, and the Food

Administration—each charged with supervising nationwide activity in its assigned economic sector.

The agencies exhibited varying success. Headed by mining engineer Herbert Hoover, a tireless and innovative administrator, the Food Administration was the federal government's most stunning achievement. The Food Administration used economic incentives to increase substantially production of basic foodstuffs and put in place an efficient distribution system that delivered food to millions of troops and European civilians. Treasury Secretary William McAdoo, as head of the U.S. Railroad Administration, also performed well in shifting the rail system from private to public control, coordinating dense train traffic, and making capital improvements that allowed goods to move rapidly to eastern ports, where they were loaded onto ships and sent to Europe. At the other extreme, the Aircraft Production Board and Emergency Fleet Corporation did a poor job of supplying the Allies with combat aircraft and merchant vessels. On balance, the U.S. economy performed wonders in supplying troops with uniforms, food, rifles, munitions, and other basic items; it failed badly, however, in producing more sophisticated weapons and machines such as artillery, aircraft, and ships.

At the time, many believed that the new government war agencies possessed awesome power over the nation's economy and thus represented a near-revolution in government Most such agencies, however, were more powerful on paper than in fact. Consider, for example, the War Industries Board (WIB), an administrative body established by Wilson in July 1917 to harness manufacturing might to military needs. The WIB floundered for its first nine months without the statutory authority to force manufacturers and the military to adopt its plans. In March 1918, however, Wall Street investment banker Bernard Baruch came on board as WIB chairman and began to turn the agency around. Rather than attempting to force manufacturers to do the government's bidding, Baruch permitted industrialists to charge high prices for their products, thus significantly increasing their profits. He won exemptions from antitrust laws for corporations that complied with his requests, thereby strengthening their economic power. He filled the WIB with investment bankers and corporate lawyers from Wall Street, experienced capitalists whom manufacturers would instinctively trust. Baruch, however, did not hesitate to unleash his wrath upon corpora-

tions that resisted WIB enticements or to expose their recalcitrance to the furies of congressional and public opinion.

Baruch's forceful leadership worked reasonably well throughout his nine months in office. War production increased substantially, and manufacturers discovered the financial benefits of cooperation between the public and private sectors. But Baruch's approach created problems, too. His favoritism toward the large corporations hurt smaller competitors. Moreover, the cozy relationship between government and corporate America violated the progressive pledge to protect the people against the "interests." Achieving cooperation by boosting corporate profits was a costly way for the government to do business. Indeed, the costs of the war soared beyond anyone's expectations. When the United States entered the war, $10 billion was an extravagant war-cost estimate (the federal government's annual budget prior to the war averaged only $700 million). By the time the war ended, its total cost had reached $33 billion.

ORGANIZING CIVILIAN LABOR

The government worried as much about labor's cooperation as about industry's compliance, for the best-laid production plans could be disrupted by a

THE MIGRATION OF THE NEGRO (PANEL I), BY JACOB LAWRENCE Job opportunities in northern industrial plants prompted hundreds of thousands of African American sharecroppers and tenant farmers to leave the South between 1916 and 1920. In this painting, a noted artist shows migrants at a train station preparing to board trains to Chicago, New York, and St. Louis.

Kind Sir:

We have several times read your noted paper and we are delighted with the same because it is a thorough Negro paper. There is a storm of our people toward the North and especially to your city. We have watched your want ad regularly and we are anxious for location with good families (white) where we can be cared for and do domestic work. We want to engage as cook, nurse and maid. We have had some educational advantages, as we have taught in rural schools for few years but our pay so poor we could not continue. We can furnish testimonial of our honesty and integrity and moral standing. Will you please assist us in securing places as we are anxious to come but want jobs before we leave. We want to do any kind of honest labor. Our chance here is so poor.

LETTER WRITTEN BY SEVERAL AFRICAN AMERICAN WOMEN FROM FLORIDA *to the* Chicago Defender, *a leading black newspaper, seeking assistance in joining the "Great Migration" to the North*

labor shortage or an extended strike. The outbreak of war in 1914 had strengthened the market power of workers, because war orders from Europe prompted manufacturers to expand their production facilities and workforces. Meanwhile, the number of European immigrants plummeted—from more than 1 million in 1914, to 200,000 in 1915, to 31,000 in 1918. U.S. industry lost three million potential workers thus and another five million workers to military service in 1917 and 1918.

Manufacturers responded to the shortage by encouraging potential workers around the country to come to their factories in the North. From the rural South, a half million African Americans migrated to the industrial centers of New York, Chicago, Detroit, Cleveland, Philadelphia, and St.

Louis between 1916 and 1920. Another half million white southerners followed the same path during that period. Hundreds of thousands of Mexicans fled their revolution-ridden homeland for agriculture, mining, and railroad jobs in the Southwest; some of them made their way to Kansas City, Chicago, and other manufacturing centers of the Midwest. Approximately 40,000 northern women found work as streetcar conductors, railroad workers, metalworkers, munitions makers, and in other jobs customarily reserved for men. The number of female clerical workers doubled between 1910 and 1920, with many of these women finding work in the government war bureaucracies. Altogether, a million women toiled in war-related industries.

These workers alleviated but did not eliminate the nation's acute labor shortage. Unemployment, which had hovered around 8.5 percent in 1915, plunged to 1.2 percent in 1918. Workers were quick to recognize the benefits of the tight labor market. White male workers quit jobs they did not like, confident that they could do better (opportunities for blacks, Mexicans, and women were more limited). Workers took part in strikes and other collective actions in unprecedented numbers. From 1916 to 1920 more than one million workers went on strike every year. Union membership almost doubled, from 2.6 million in 1915 to 5.1 million in 1920. Workers commonly sought higher wages and shorter hours through strikes and unionization. Wages rose an average of 137 percent from 1915 to 1920, although postwar inflation largely negated these gains. Between 1916 and 1920 the average workweek declined from 55 to 51 hours. Many workers achieved the 48-hour week. Workers also struck in response to managerial attempts to speed up production and tighten discipline. As time passed, increasing numbers of workers began to wonder why the war for democracy in Europe had no counterpart in their factories at home. "Industrial democracy" became the battle cry of an awakened labor movement.

Wilson's willingness to include labor in his 1916 progressive coalition reflected his awareness of labor's potential power (see chapter 21). In 1917 he was the first U.S. president to address a convention of the American Federation of Labor (AFL). And in 1918 he bestowed prestige on the newly formed National War Labor Board (NWLB) by appointing

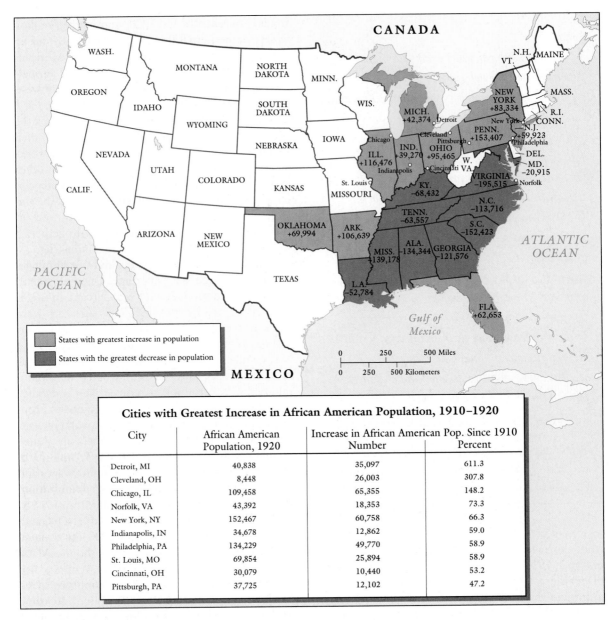

CANADA

WASH.
MONTANA
NORTH DAKOTA
MINN.
N.H. MAINE
VT.
OREGON
IDAHO
WYOMING
SOUTH DAKOTA
WIS.
MICH. +42,374 Detroit
Cleveland
Chicago
NEW YORK +83,334
New York
MASS.
R.I.
CONN.
N.J. +59,923
Philadelphia
NEVADA
UTAH
COLORADO
NEBRASKA
IOWA
ILL. +116,476
IND. +39,270
Indianapolis
Pittsburgh
PENN. +153,407
OHIO +95,465
Cincinnati
DEL.
MD. -20,915
W. VA.
CALIF.
KANSAS
St. Louis
MISSOURI
KY. -68,432
VIRGINIA -195,515
Norfolk
ARIZONA
NEW MEXICO
OKLAHOMA +69,994
ARK. +106,639
TENN. -63,557
N.C. -113,716
S.C. -152,423
ATLANTIC OCEAN
PACIFIC OCEAN
MISS. -139,178
ALA. -134,344
GEORGIA -121,576
TEXAS
L.A. -52,784
Gulf of Mexico
FLA. +62,653

States with greatest increase in population

States with the greatest decrease in population

MEXICO

0   250   500 Miles
0   250   500 Kilometers

Cities with Greatest Increase in African American Population, 1910–1920			
City	African American Population, 1920	Increase in African American Pop. Since 1910	
		Number	Percent
Detroit, MI	40,838	35,097	611.3
Cleveland, OH	8,448	26,003	307.8
Chicago, IL	109,458	65,355	148.2
Norfolk, VA	43,392	18,353	73.3
New York, NY	152,467	60,758	66.3
Indianapolis, IN	34,678	12,862	59.0
Philadelphia, PA	134,229	49,770	58.9
St. Louis, MO	69,854	25,894	58.9
Cincinnati, OH	30,079	10,440	53.2
Pittsburgh, PA	37,725	12,102	47.2

AFRICAN AMERICAN MIGRATION, 1910–1920

former president William Howard Taft as one of its two cochairmen. The NWLB brought together representatives of labor, industry, and the public to resolve labor disputes. The presence of Samuel Gompers, president of the American Federation of Labor, on the board gave unions a national voice in government affairs. In return for his appointment, Gompers was expected to mobilize workers behind Wilson, discredit socialists who criticized the war, and discourage strikes that threatened war production. Although, like most other federal wartime agencies, the NWLB lacked the ability to impose its will, it managed to pressure many manufacturers into improving wages and hours, reducing wage discrimination, and allowing their workers to join unions.

OCCUPATIONS WITH LARGEST INCREASE IN WOMEN, 1910–1920

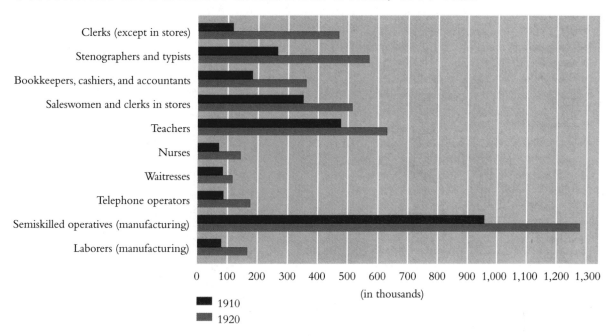

Clerks (except in stores)
Stenographers and typists
Bookkeepers, cashiers, and accountants
Saleswomen and clerks in stores
Teachers
Nurses
Waitresses
Telephone operators
Semiskilled operatives (manufacturing)
Laborers (manufacturing)

0 100 200 300 400 500 600 700 800 900 1,000 1,100 1,200 1,300

(in thousands)

■ 1910
■ 1920

Source: Joseph A. Hill, *Women in Gainful Occupations, 1870–1920*, U.S. Bureau of the Census, Monograph no. 9 (Washington, D.C.: Government Printing Office, 1929), p. 33.

WOMEN DOING "MEN'S" WORK Labor shortages during the war years allowed thousands of women to take industrial jobs customarily reserved for men. The two female lathe operators in this photograph (taken in an industrial plant in Portland, Oregon) had been schoolteachers before the war.

ORGANIZING MILITARY LABOR

When it came to raising an army, the federal government used its full power without hesitation. From the start, the Wilson administration rejected the idea of a volunteer army in favor of conscription—the drafting of most men of a certain age, irrespective of their family's wealth, ethnic background, or social standing. The Selective Service Act of May 1917 empowered the administration to do just that. By war's end, local Selective Service boards had registered 24 million young men age 18 and older, and had drafted nearly 3 million of them into the military; another 2 million volunteered for service.

Relatively few men resisted the draft, even among recently arrived immigrants. Foreign-born men constituted 18 percent of the armed forces—a percentage greater than their share of the total population. Almost 400,000 African Americans served, representing approximately 10 percent, the same as the percentage of African Americans in the total population. Many more would have served had southern draft boards permitted more of them

TOTAL MEMBERSHIP OF AMERICAN TRADE UNIONS, 1900–1920

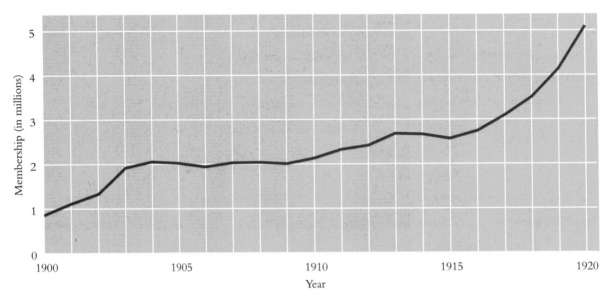

Source: Leo Wolman, *The Growth of American Trade Unions, 1880–1923* (New York: National Bureau of Economic Research, 1924), p. 33.

to register and had the Marines and other service branches been willing to accept African Americans into their ranks.

The U.S. Army, under the command of Chief of Staff Peyton March and General John J. Pershing, faced the difficult task of fashioning these ethnically and racially diverse millions into a professional fighting force. Teaching raw recruits to fight was hard enough, Pershing and March observed; the generals refused the task of teaching them to put aside their prejudices. Rather than integrate the armed forces, they segregated black soldiers from white. Virtually all African Americans were assigned to all-black units and barred from combat. Being stripped of a combat role was particularly galling to blacks, who, in previous wars, had proven themselves to be among the best American fighters. Pershing was fully aware of the African American contribution. He himself had commanded African American troops in the 10th Cavalry, the all-black regiment that had distinguished itself in the Spanish-American War (chapter 22). Pershing's military reputation had depended so heavily on the black troops who fought for him that he had acquired the nickname "Black Jack."

For a time, the military justified its intensified discrimination against blacks by referring to the results of rudimentary "IQ" (intelligence quotient) tests administered by psychologists to two million AEF soldiers. These tests allegedly "proved" that native-born Americans and immigrants from the British Isles, Germany, and Scandinavia were well endowed with intelligence, while African Americans and immigrants from southern and eastern Europe were poorly endowed. The tests were scientifically so ill-conceived, however, that their findings revealed nothing about the true distribution of intelligence in the population. Their most sensational revelation was that more than half of the soldiers in the AEF—white and black—were "morons," men who had failed to reach the mental age of 13. After trying to absorb the apparent news that most U.S. soldiers were feeble-minded, the military sensibly rejected the pseudo-science on which these intelligence findings were based. In 1919 it discontinued the IQ testing program.

Given the sharp racial and ethnic differences among American troops and the short time Pershing and his staff had to train recruits, the performance of the AEF was impressive. The United States increased the army from a mere 100,000 to 5 million in little more than a year. The Germans sank no troop ships, nor were any soldiers killed

RECRUITING POSTER, WORLD WAR I, 1917 The government plastered public institutions with recruiting posters. This one represents navy work as glamorous, masculine, and brave, as a way of enticing more young men to join up.

during the dangerous Atlantic crossing. In combat, U.S. troops became known for their sharpshooting skills. The most decorated soldier in the AEF was Sergeant Alvin C. York of Tennessee, who captured 35 machine guns, took 132 prisoners, and killed 17 German soldiers with 17 bullets. York had learned his marksmanship hunting wild turkeys in the Tennessee hills. "Of course, it weren't no trouble

THE 369TH RETURNS TO NEW YORK Denied the opportunity to fight in the U.S. Army, this unit fought for the French. For the length and distinction of its service in the front lines, this entire unit was awarded the *Croix de Guerre* by the French government.

nohow for me to hit them big [German] army targets," he later commented. "They were so much bigger than turkeys' heads."

One of the most decorated AEF units was New York's 369th Regiment, a black unit recruited in Harlem. Bowing to pressure from civil rights groups, including the NAACP, to allow some black troops to fight, Pershing had offered the 369th to the French army. The 369th entered the French front line, served in the forward Allied trenches for 191 days (longer than any other U.S. regiment), and scored one major success after another. In gratitude for its service, the French government decorated the entire unit with one of its highest honors—the *Croix de Guerre*.

PAYING THE BILLS

The government incurred huge debts buying food, uniforms, munitions, weapons, vehicles, and sundry other items for the U.S. military. To help pay its bills, it sharply increased tax rates. The new taxes hit the wealthiest Americans the hardest: The richest were slapped with a 67 percent income tax and a 25 percent inheritance tax. Corporations were ordered to pay an "excess profits" tax. Proposed by the Wilson administration and backed by Robert La Follette and other congressional progressives who feared that the "interests" would use the war to enrich themselves, these taxes were meant to ensure that all Americans would sacrifice something for the war.

Tax revenues, however, provided only about one-third of the $33 billion that the government ultimately spent on the war. The rest came from the sale of "Liberty Bonds." These 30-year government bonds offered individual purchasers a return of $3\frac{1}{2}$ percent in annual interest. The government offered five bond issues between 1917 and 1920, and all quickly sold out, thanks, in no small measure, to a high-powered sales pitch, orchestrated by Treasury Secretary William G. McAdoo, that equated bond purchases with patriotic duty. McAdoo's agents blanketed the country with posters, sent bond "salesmen" into virtually every American community, enlisted Boy Scouts to go door-to-door, and staged rallies at which movie stars such as Mary Pickford, Douglas Fairbanks, and Charlie Chaplin stumped for the war.

THE FIRST WORLD WAR AND THE FEDERAL BUDGET

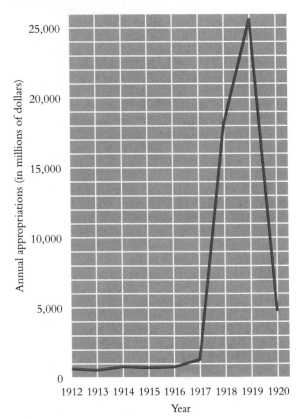

Source: Data from *Statistical Abstract of the United States, 1919* (Washington, D.C.: Government Printing Office, 1920), p. 681.

AROUSING PATRIOTIC ARDOR

The Treasury's bond campaign was only one aspect of an extraordinary government effort to arouse public support for the war. In 1917 Wilson set up a new agency, the Committee on Public Information (CPI), to publicize and popularize the war. Under the chairmanship of George Creel, a midwestern progressive and a muckraker, the CPI conducted an unprecedented propaganda campaign. It distributed 75 million copies of pamphlets explaining U.S. war aims in several languages. It trained a force of 75,000 "Four-Minute Men" to deliver succinct, uplifting war speeches to numerous groups in their home cities and towns. It papered the walls of virtually every public institution (and many private ones) with posters, placed advertisements in mass-circulation magazines, sponsored exhibitions, and peppered newspaper editors with thousands of press releases on the progress of the war.

Faithful to his muckraking past, Creel wanted to give the people "the facts" of the war, believing that well-informed citizens would see the wisdom of Wilson's policies. He also saw his work as an opportunity to achieve the progressive goal of uniting all Americans into a single moral community. Americans everywhere heard that the United States had entered the war "to make the world safe for democracy," to help the world's weaker peoples achieve self-determination, to bring a measure of justice into the conduct of international affairs. Americans were asked to affirm those ideals by doing everything they could to support the war.

This uplifting message had a profound effect on the American people, although not necessarily in ways anticipated by CPI propagandists. It imparted to many a deep love of country and a sense of participation in a grand democratic experiment. Among others, particularly those experiencing poverty and discrimination, it sparked a new spirit of protest. Workers, women, European ethnics, and African Americans began demanding that America live up to its democratic ideals at home as well as abroad. Workers rallied to the cry of "industrial democracy." Women seized upon the democratic fervor to bring their fight for suffrage to a successful conclusion (see chapter 21). African Americans began to dream that the war might deliver them from second-class citizenship. European ethnics believed that Wilson's support of their countrymen's rights abroad would improve their own chances for success in the United States.

Although the CPI had helped to unleash it, this new democratic enthusiasm troubled Creel and others in the Wilson administration. The United States, after all, was still deeply divided along class, ethnic, and racial lines. Workers and industrialists regarded each other with suspicion. Cultural differences compounded this class division, for the working class was overwhelmingly ethnic in composition, and the industrial and political elites consisted mainly of the native-born whose families had been "Americans" for generations. Progressives had fought hard to overcome these divisions. They had tamed the power of capitalists, improved the condition of workers, encouraged the Americanization of immi-

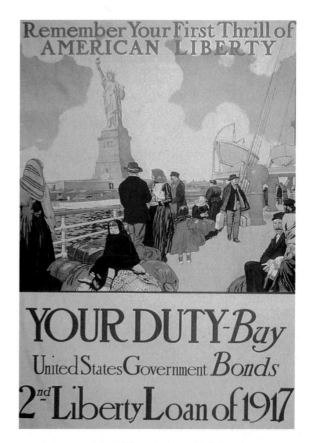

SELLING LIBERTY The government left no stone unturned in its campaign to sell war bonds. In this poster, the government calls on immigrants to make their (cash) contribution toward protecting American liberty. The poster also expresses the government's confidence that immigrants were patriotic and, if kept properly informed, would do their duty. By 1918, this confidence had been eroded.

grants, and articulated a new, more inclusive idea of American nationhood. But their work was far from complete when the war broke out, and the war itself opened up new social and cultural divisions. German immigrants still formed the largest foreign-born population group—2.3 million. Another 2.3 million immigrants came from some part of the Austro-Hungarian Empire. And more than one million Americans—native-born and immigrants—supported the Socialist Party and the Industrial Workers of the World, both of which had opposed the war. The decision to authorize the CPI's massive unity campaign indicates that the progressives understood how widespread the discord was. Still, they had not anticipated that the promotion of democratic ideals at home would exacerbate, rather than lessen, the nation's social and cultural divisions.

WARTIME REPRESSION

By early 1918 the CPI's campaign had developed a darker, more coercive side. Inflammatory advertisements called on patriots to report on neighbors, coworkers, and ethnics whom they suspected of subverting the war effort. Propagandists called on all immigrants, especially those from central, southern, and eastern Europe, to pledge themselves to "100 percent Americanism" and to repudiate all ties to their homeland, native language, and ethnic customs. The CPI aroused hostility to Germans by spreading lurid tales of German atrocities and encouraging the public to see movies such as *The Prussian Cur* and *The Beast of Berlin*. The Justice Department arrested thousands of German and Austrian immigrants whom it suspected of subversive activities. Congress passed the Trading with the Enemy Act, which required foreign-language publications to submit all war-related stories to post office censors for approval.

RENAMED GERMAN AMERICAN WORDS

Original	"Patriotic" Name
hamburger	salisbury steak, liberty steak, liberty sandwich
sauerkraut	liberty cabbage
Hamburg Avenue, Brooklyn, New York	Wilson Avenue, Brooklyn, New York
Germantown, Nebraska	Garland, Nebraska
East Germantown, Indiana	Pershing, Indiana
Berlin, Iowa	Lincoln, Iowa
pinochle	liberty
German shepherd	Alsatian shepherd
Deutsches Hans of Indianapolis	Athenaeum of Indiana
Germania Maennerchor of Chicago	Lincoln Club
Kaiser Street	Maine Way

Source: From La Vern J. Rippley, *The German Americans* (Boston: Twayne, 1976), p. 186; and Robert H. Ferrell, *Woodrow Wilson and World War I, 1917–1921* (New York: Harper and Row, 1985), pp. 205–206.

German Americans became the objects of popular hatred. American patriots sought to expunge every trace of German influence from American culture. In Boston, performances of Beethoven's symphonies were banned, and the German-born conductor of the Boston Symphony Orchestra was forced to resign. Although Americans would not give up the German foods they had grown to love, they would no longer call them by their German names. Sauerkraut was rechristened "liberty cabbage," hamburgers became "liberty sandwiches." Libraries removed works of German literature from their shelves, and Theodore Roosevelt and others urged school districts to prohibit the teaching of the German language. Patriotic school boards in Lima, Ohio, and elsewhere burned the German books in their districts.

German Americans risked being fired from work, losing their businesses, and being assaulted on the street. A St. Louis mob lynched an innocent German immigrant whom they suspected of subversion. After only 25 minutes of deliberation, a St. Louis jury acquitted the mob leaders, who had brazenly defended their crime as an act of patriotism. German Americans began hiding their ethnic identity, changing their names, speaking German only in the privacy of their homes, celebrating their holidays only with trusted friends. This experience devastated the once-proud German American community; many would never recover from the shame and vulnerability they experienced in those years.

The anti-German campaign escalated into a general anti-immigrant crusade. Congress passed the Immigration Restriction Act of 1917, over Wilson's veto, which declared that all adult immigrants who failed a reading test would be denied admission to the United States. The act also banned the immigration of laborers from India, Indochina, Afghanistan, Arabia, the East Indies, and several other countries within an "Asiatic Barred Zone." This legislation marked the beginning of a movement in Congress that, four years later, would close the immigration door to virtually all transoceanic peoples. Congress also passed the Eighteenth Amendment to the Constitution, which prohibited the manufacture and distribution of alcoholic beverages (see chapter 21). The crusade for Prohibition was not new, but anti-immigrant feelings generated by the war gave it added impetus. Prohibitionists pictured the nation's urban ethnic ghettos as scenes of drunkenness, immorality, and disloyalty. They also accused German American brewers of operating a "liquor trust" to sap people's will to fight. The states quickly ratified the Eighteenth Amendment, and in 1919 Prohibition became the law of the land.

More and more, the Wilson administration relied on repression to achieve domestic unity. In the Espionage, Sabotage, and Sedition Acts passed in 1917 and 1918, Congress gave the administration sweeping powers to silence and even imprison dissenters. These acts went far beyond outlawing behavior that no nation at war could be expected to tolerate, such as spying for the enemy, sabotaging war production, and calling for the enemy's victory. They constituted the most drastic restriction of free speech at the national level since enactment of the Alien and Sedition Acts of 1798 (see chapter 8). Now citizens could be prosecuted for writing or uttering any statement that could be construed as profaning the flag, the Constitution, or the military.

Government repression fell most heavily on the IWW and the Socialist Party. Both groups had opposed intervention before 1917. Although they subsequently muted their opposition, they continued to insist that the true enemies of American workers were to be found in the ranks of American employers, not in Germany or Austria-Hungary. The government responded by banning many socialist materials from the mails and by disrupting socialist and IWW meetings. By the spring of 1918 government agents had raided countless IWW offices and had arrested 2,000 IWW members, including its entire executive board. Many of those arrested would be sentenced to long jail terms. William Haywood, the IWW president, fled to Europe and then to the Soviet Union rather than go to jail. Eugene V. Debs, the head of the Socialist Party, received a 10-year jail term for making an antiwar speech in Canton, Ohio, in the summer of 1918.

This federal repression, carried out in an atmosphere of supercharged patriotism, encouraged local governments and private citizens to initiate their own anti-radical crusades. In the mining town of Bisbee, Arizona, a sheriff with an eager force of 2,000 deputized citizens kidnapped 1,200 IWW members, herded them into cattle cars, and dumped them onto the New Mexico desert with hardly any food or water. Vigilantes in Butte, Montana, chained an IWW organizer to a car and let his body scrape the pavement as they drove the vehicle through city streets. Next, they strung him up to a railroad trestle, castrated him, and left him to die. The 250,000 members of the American Protective League, most of them businessmen and professionals, routinely spied on fellow workers and neighbors. They opened mail and tapped phones and otherwise harassed those suspected of disloyalty. Attorney General Thomas Gregory publicly endorsed the group and sought federal funds to support its "police" work.

The spirit of coercion even infected institutions that had long prided themselves on tolerance. In July 1917 Columbia University fired two professors for speaking out against U.S. intervention in the war. The National Americanization Committee, which prior to 1917 had pioneered a humane approach to the problem of integrating immigrants into American life, now supported surveillance, internment, and deportation of aliens suspected of anti-American sentiments.

Wilson himself bore significant responsibility for this climate of repression. On the one hand, he did attempt to block certain pieces of repressive legislation; for example, he vetoed both the Immigration Restriction Act and the Volstead Act (the act passed to enforce Prohibition), only to be overridden by Congress. On the other hand, Wilson did little to halt Attorney General Gregory's prosecution of radicals or Postmaster General Burleson's campaign to exclude Socialist Party publications from the mail. He ignored pleas from progressives that he intervene in the Debs case to prevent the ailing 62-year-old from going to jail. His acquiescence in these matters cost him dearly among progressives and socialists. Wilson believed, however, that once the Allies, with U.S. support, won the war and arranged a just peace in accordance with the Fourteen Points, his administration's wartime actions would be forgiven and the progressive coalition would be restored.

THE FAILURE OF THE INTERNATIONAL PEACE

In the month following Germany's surrender on November 11, 1918, Wilson was confident about

Turning Enemies into Apes

From the mid-19th to the mid-20th century, Americans frequently drew on simian imagery to describe and demean their enemies, both internal and external. Blacks and Asians were the groups most commonly depicted as apelike, a reflection in part of popular and pseudoscientific notions that human beings belonged to a series of distinct and unequal "races" with varying capacities for intelligence, morality, and achievement. Africans and Asians often were categorized as the most primitive human races, closest to the apes, and northwest Europeans the most civilized.

Simian imagery was sometimes used against northwest and west Europeans themselves, as the three images shown here demonstrate: the one at left portrays Germany in the First World War; the center illustration represents Spain as a brute who cruelly sank the battleship *Maine* in 1898; and the one below depicts drunken Irish immigrants in an 1867 New York City

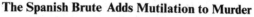

the prospects of achieving a just peace. Both Germany and the Allies had publicly accepted the Fourteen Points as the basis for negotiations. Wilson's international prestige was enormous. People throughout the world were inspired by his dream of a democratic, just, and harmonious world order free of poverty, ignorance, and war. Poles, Lithuanians, and other eastern Europeans whose pursuit of nationhood had been frustrated for 100 years or more now believed that independence might be

riot on St. Patrick's Day. All three enemies appear as "brutes" that possess no self-control, no knowledge of right from wrong, and no respect for human life, pure womanhood, or law and order. Such depictions served to justify America's obligation to use force against its enemies. They implied that brutes, like animals, could only be killed or beaten into submission; they would not respond—as would civilized peoples (such as Americans)—to reason or negotiation. In the case of the Spanish and the Germans, using force meant war; in the case of the Irish, it meant, first, loosing the police on them and, second, continuing to treat them as a lowly, impulsive, and violent people. Depictions of the Spanish and Germans as apes ended soon after the wars against them ended, but not until the late 19th century did the Irish escape simian stereotyping.

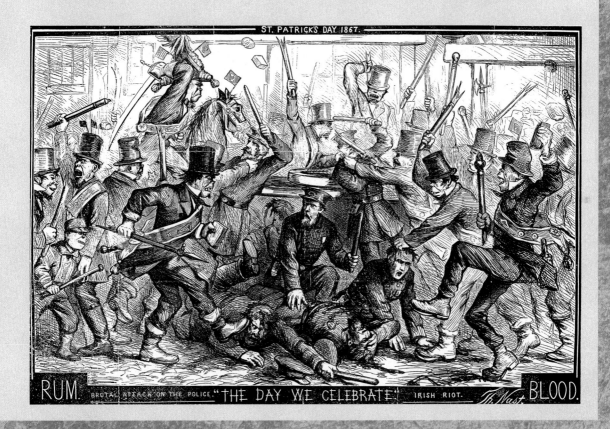

ST. PATRICK'S DAY 1867.

RUM — BRUTAL ATTACK ON THE POLICE. "THE DAY WE CELEBRATE" IRISH RIOT. — BLOOD.

within their reach. Zionist Jews in Europe and the United States dared to dream of a Jewish homeland within their lifetimes. Countless African and Asian peoples imagined achieving their freedom from colonial domination.

To capitalize on his fame and to maximize the chances for a peace settlement based on his Fourteen Points, Wilson broke sharply with diplomatic precedent and decided to head the American delegation to the Paris Peace Conference in January

799

"THE SAVIOR OF HUMANITY" Wherever he went in Europe, Woodrow Wilson was greeted by huge, delirious crowds eager to thank him for ending Europe's terrible war and to endorse his vision of a peaceful, democratic world. Here millions of Italians greet Wilson's arrival in Milan.

1919. Enormous crowds of wildly enthusiastic Europeans turned out to hail Wilson's arrival on the Continent in December. Some two million French citizens—the largest throng ever assembled on French soil—lined the parade route in Paris to catch a glimpse of "Wilson, *le juste* [the just]." In Rome, Milan, and La Scala near-delirious Italians acclaimed him "The Savior of Humanity" and "The Moses from Across the Atlantic."

In the Fourteen Points, Wilson had translated his principles for a new world order into specific proposals for international peace and justice. The first group of points called for all nations to abide by a code of conduct that embraced free trade, freedom of the seas, open diplomacy, disarmament, and the resolution of disputes through mediation. A second group, based on the principle of self-determination, proposed redrawing the map of Europe to give the subjugated peoples of the Austro-Hungarian, Ottoman, and Russian empires national sovereignty. The last point called for establishing the League of Nations, an assembly in which all nations would be represented and in which all international disputes would be given a fair hearing and an opportunity for peaceful solutions.

THE PARIS PEACE CONFERENCE AND THE TREATY OF VERSAILLES

Although representatives of 27 nations began meeting in Paris on January 12, 1919, to discuss Wilson's Fourteen Points, negotiations were controlled by the "Big Four": Wilson, Prime Minister David Lloyd George of Great Britain, Premier Georges Clemenceau of France, and Prime Minister Vittorio Orlando of Italy. When Orlando quit the conference after a dispute with Wilson, the Big Four became the Big Three. Wilson quickly learned that his negotiating partners' support for the Fourteen Points was much weaker than he had believed. The cagey Clemenceau mused: "God gave us the Ten Commandments, and we broke them. Wilson gives us Fourteen Points. We shall see." Indeed, Clemenceau and Lloyd George refused to include most of Wilson's points in the peace treaty. The points having to do with freedom of the seas and free trade were omitted, as were the proposals for open diplomacy and Allied disarmament. Wilson won partial endorsement of the principle of self-determination: Belgian sovereignty was restored, Poland's status as a nation was affirmed, and the new nations of Czechoslovakia, Yugoslavia, Finland, Lithuania, Latvia, and Estonia were created. In addition, some lands of the former Ottoman Empire—Armenia, Palestine, Mesopotamia, and Syria—were to be placed under League of Nations' trusteeships with the understanding that they would some day gain their independence. Wilson failed in his efforts to block a British plan to transfer former German colonies in Asia to Japanese control, an Italian plan to annex territory inhabited by 200,000 Austrians, and a French plan to take from Germany its valuable Saar coal mines.

Nor could Wilson blunt the drive to punish Germany for its wartime aggression. In addition to awarding the Saar basin to France, the Allies gave portions of northern Germany to Denmark and portions of eastern Germany to Poland and Czechoslovakia. Germany was stripped of virtually its entire navy and air force, and forbidden to place soldiers or fortifications in western Germany along the Rhine. It was allowed to keep an army of only 100,000 men. In addition, Germany was forced to admit its responsibility for the war. In accepting this "war guilt," Germany was, in effect, agreeing to compensate the victors in cash ("reparations") for the pain and suffering it had inflicted on them.

PRESIDENT WOODROW WILSON IN PARIS, 1919
Wilson arrives at the Paris Peace Conference to begin negotiations on the treaty that would formally end the First World War and establish the League of Nations as a first step to a new world order.

Lloyd George and Clemenceau brushed off the protests of those who viewed this desire to prostrate Germany as a cruel and vengeful act. That the German people, after their nation's 1918 defeat, had overthrown the monarch (Kaiser Wilhelm II) who had taken them to war, and had reconstituted their nation as a democratic republic—the first in their country's history—won them no leniency. In 1921 an Allied commission notified the Germans that they were to pay the victors $33 billion, a sum well beyond the resources of a defeated and economically ruined Germany. On June 28, 1919, Great Britain, France, the United States, Germany, and other European nations signed the Treaty of Versailles.

THE LEAGUE OF NATIONS

The Allies' single-minded pursuit of self-interest disillusioned many liberals and socialists in the United States, but Wilson seemed undismayed. He had won approval of the most important of his Fourteen Points—the point that called for the creation of the League of Nations. The League, whose structure and responsibilities were set forth in the Covenant attached to the peace treaty, would usher in Wilson's new world order. Drawing its membership from the signatories to the Treaty of Versailles (except, for the time being, Germany), the League would function as an international parliament and judiciary, establishing rules of international behavior and resolving disputes between nations through rational and peaceful means. A nine-member executive council—the United States, Britain, France, Italy, and Japan would have permanent seats on the council, while the other four seats would rotate among the smaller powers—was charged with administering decisions.

The League, Wilson believed, would redeem the failures of the Paris Peace Conference. Under its auspices, free trade and freedom of the seas would be achieved, reparations against Germany would be reduced or eliminated, disarmament of the Allies would proceed, and the principle of self-determination would be extended to peoples outside Europe. Moreover, the Covenant (Article X) would endow the League with the power to punish aggressor nations through economic isolation and military retaliation.

To Great Britain		New states as of 1921	

Legend:
- To Great Britain
- To France
- To Belgium
- To Denmark
- To Romania
- To Greece
- To Italy
- Became independent
- New states as of 1921
- Border of German Empire in 1914
- Border of Austrian-Hungarian Empire in 1914
- Border of Russian Empire in 1914
- Border of Ottoman Empire in 1914
- New boundaries as a result of postwar treaties
- Boundaries as of 1914

EUROPE AND THE NEAR EAST AFTER THE FIRST WORLD WAR

WILSON VERSUS LODGE: THE FIGHT OVER RATIFICATION

The League's success, however, depended on Wilson's ability to convince the U.S. Senate to ratify the Treaty of Versailles. Wilson knew that this would be no easy task. The Republicans had gained a majority in the Senate in 1918, and two groups within their ranks were determined to frustrate Wilson's ambitions. One group was a caucus of 14 midwesterners and westerners known as the "irreconcilables." Most of them were conservative isolationists who wanted the United States to preserve its separation from Europe, but a few were prominent progressives—Robert La Follette, William Borah, and Hiram Johnson—who had voted against the declaration of war in 1917. The self-interest displayed by England and France at the peace conference convinced this progressive group that the Europeans were incapable of decent behavior in international matters.

The second opposition group was led by Senator Henry Cabot Lodge of Massachusetts. The members rejected Wilson's belief that every group of people on earth had a right to form their own nation; that every state, regardless of its size, its economic condition, and the vigor and intelligence of its people, should have a voice in world affairs; and that disputes between nations could be settled in open, democratic forums. They subscribed instead to Theodore Roosevelt's vision of a world controlled by a few great nations, each militarily strong, secure in its own sphere of influence, and determined to avoid war through a carefully negotiated balance of power. These Republicans preferred to let Europe return to the power politics that had prevailed before the war rather than experiment with a new world order that might constrain and compromise U.S. power and autonomy.

This Republican critique was a cogent one that merited extended discussion. Particularly important questions addressed the power given the League by Article X to undertake military actions against aggressor nations. Did Americans want to authorize an international organization to decide when the United States would go to war? Was this not a violation of the Constitution, which vested war-making power solely in the Congress? Even if the constitutional problem could be solved, how could the United States ensure that it would not be forced into a military action that might damage its national interest?

It soon became clear, however, that a number of the Republicans, especially Lodge, were more interested in humiliating Wilson than in engaging in debate. They accused him of promoting socialism through his wartime expansion of government power. They were angry that he had failed to include any distinguished Republicans, such as Lodge, Elihu Root, or William Howard Taft, in the Paris peace delegation. And they were still bitter about the 1918 congressional elections, when Wilson had argued that a Republican victory would embarrass the nation abroad in a critical moment in world affairs. Though Wilson's electioneering had failed to sway the voters (the Republicans won a majority in both Houses), his suggestion that a Republican victory would injure na-

tional honor had infuriated Theodore Roosevelt and his supporters. Roosevelt died in 1919, but his close friend Lodge kept his rage alive. "I never thought I could hate a man as much as I hate Wilson," Lodge conceded in a moment of candor.

As chairman of the Senate Foreign Relations Committee, charged with considering the treaty before reporting it to the Senate floor, Lodge had considerable power, and he did everything possible to obstruct ratification. He packed the committee with senators likely to oppose the treaty. He delayed action by reading every one of the treaty's 300 pages aloud and by subjecting it to endless criticism in six long weeks of public hearings. When his committee finally reported the treaty to the full Senate, it came encumbered with nearly 50 amendments whose adoption Lodge made a precondition of his support. Some of the amendments expressed reasonable concerns—namely, that participation in the League not diminish the role of Congress in determining foreign policy, or compromise the sovereignty of the nation, or involve the nation in an unjust or ill-advised war. But many were meant only to complicate the task of ratification.

Despite Lodge's obstructionism, the treaty's chances for ratification by the required two-thirds majority of the Senate remained good. Many Republicans were prepared to vote for ratification if Wilson indicated his willingness to accept some of the proposed amendments. Wilson possessed the political savvy to salvage the treaty and, along with it, U.S. participation in the League of Nations. At this crucial moment, however, Wilson refused to compromise with the Republicans and announced that he would carry his case directly to the people instead. In September 1919 he undertook a whirlwind cross-country tour that covered more than 8,000 miles with 37 stops. He addressed as many crowds as he could reach, sometimes speaking for an hour at a time, four times a day. However, in thinking that this "appeal to the country" would force Republican senators to change their votes, Wilson had gravely miscalculated. He achieved only his own physical exhaustion.

On September 25, after giving a speech at Pueblo, Colorado, Wilson suffered excruciating headaches throughout the night. His physician ordered him back to Washington, where on October 2 he suffered a near-fatal stroke. Wilson hovered near death for two weeks and remained seriously disabled for another six. His condition improved somewhat in November, but his left side remained paralyzed, his speech was slurred, his energy level low, and his emotions dangerously unstable. Wilson's wife, Edith Bolling Wilson, and his doctor isolated him from Congress and the press, withholding news they thought might upset him and preventing the public from learning how much his body and mind had deteriorated.

Many historians believe that the stroke impaired Wilson's political judgment. If so, that may explain his refusal to consider any of the Republican amendments to the treaty, even after it had become clear that compromise offered the only chance of winning U.S. participation in the League of Nations. When Lodge presented an amended treaty for a ratification vote on November 19, Wilson ordered Senate Democrats to vote against it; 42 (of 47) Democratic senators complied, and with the aid of 13 Republican irreconcilables, the Lodge version was defeated. Only moments later, the unamended version of the treaty—Wilson's version—received only 38 votes.

THE TREATY'S FINAL DEFEAT

As the magnitude of the calamity became apparent, supporters of the League in Congress, the nation, and the world urged the Senate and the president to reconsider. Wilson would not budge. A bipartisan group of senators desperately tried to work out a compromise without consulting him. When that effort failed, the Senate put to a vote, one more time, the Lodge version of the treaty. Because 23 Democrats, most of them southerners, still refused to break with Wilson, this last-ditch effort at ratification failed on March 8, 1920, by a margin of seven votes. Wilson's dream of a new world order died that day. The crumpled figure in the White House seemed to bear little resemblance to the hero who, barely 15 months before, had been greeted in Europe as the world's savior. Wilson filled out his remaining 12 months in office as an invalid, presiding over the interment of progressivism. He died in 1924.

The judgment of history lies heavily upon these events, for many believe that the flawed treaty and the failure of the League contributed to Adolf Hitler's rise and the outbreak of a second world war even more terrifying than the first. It is necessary to ask, then, whether American participation in the League would have significantly altered the course of world history.

The mere fact of U.S. membership in the League would not have magically solved Europe's postwar problems. The U.S. government was inexperienced

---

WOODROW WILSON'S FOURTEEN POINTS, 1918: RECORD OF IMPLEMENTATION

1. Open covenants of peace openly arrived at	Not fulfilled
2. Absolute freedom of navigation upon the seas in peace and war	Not fulfilled
3. Removal of all economic barriers to the equality of trade among nations	Not fulfilled
4. Reduction of armaments to the level needed only for domestic safety	Not fulfilled
5. Impartial adjustments of colonial claims	Not fulfilled
6. Evacuation of all Russian territory; Russia to be welcomed into the society of free nations	Not fulfilled
7. Evacuation and restoration of Belgium	Fulfilled
8. Evacuation and restoration of all French lands; return of Alsace-Lorraine to France	Fulfilled
9. Readjustment of Italy's frontiers along lines of Italian nationality	Compromised
10. Self-determination for the former subjects of the Austro-Hungarian Empire	Compromised
11. Evacuation of Romania, Serbia, and Montenegro; free access to the sea for Serbia	Compromised
12. Self-determination for the former subjects of the Ottoman Empire; secure sovereignty for Turkish portion	Compromised
13. Establishment of an independent Poland with free and secure access to the sea	Fulfilled
14. Establishment of the League of Nations to secure mutual guarantees of independence and territorial integrity	Compromised

Source: From G. M. Gathorne-Hardy, *The Fourteen Points and the Treaty of Versailles*, Oxford Pamphlets on World Affairs, no. 6 (1939), pp. 8–34; and Thomas G. Paterson et al., *American Foreign Policy: A History*, 2nd ed. (Lexington, Mass.: Heath, 1983), vol. 2, pp. 282–93.

in diplomacy and prone to mistakes. Its freedom to negotiate solutions to international disputes would have been limited by the large number of American voters who remained strongly opposed to U.S. entanglement in European affairs. Even if such opposition could have been overcome, the United States would still have confronted European countries determined to go their own way.

Nevertheless, one thing is clear: No stable international order could have arisen after the First World War without the full involvement of the United States. The League of Nations required American authority and prestige in order to operate effectively as an international parliament. We cannot know whether the League, with American involvement, would have offered the Germans a less humiliating peace, allowing them to rehabilitate their economy and salvage their national pride; nor whether an American-led League would have stopped Hitler's expansionism before it escalated into full-scale war in 1939. Still, it seems fair to suggest that American participation would have strengthened the League and improved its ability to bring a lasting peace to Europe.

THE POSTWAR PERIOD: A SOCIETY IN CONVULSION

The end of the war brought no respite from the forces convulsing American society. Workers were determined to regain the purchasing power they had lost to inflation. Employers were determined to halt or reverse the wartime gains labor had made. Radicals saw in this conflict between capital and labor the possibility of a socialist revolution. Conservatives were certain that the revolution had already begun. Returning white servicemen were nervous about regaining their civilian jobs and looked with hostility on the black, Hispanic, and female workers who had been recruited to take their places. Black veterans were in no mood to return to segregation and subordination. The federal government, meanwhile, uneasy over the centralization of power during the war, quickly dismantled such agencies as the War Industries Board and the National War Labor Board. By so doing, it deprived itself of mechanisms that might have enabled it to intervene in

social conflicts and keep them from erupting into rage and violence.

LABOR-CAPITAL CONFLICT

Nowhere was the escalation of conflict more evident than in the workplace. In 1919, four million workers—one-fifth of the nation's manufacturing workforce—went on strike. In January 1919, a general strike paralyzed the city of Seattle when 60,000 workers walked off their jobs. By August, walkouts had been staged by 400,000 eastern and midwestern coal miners, 120,000 New England textile workers, and 50,000 New York City garment workers. Then came two strikes that turned public opinion sharply against labor. In September, Boston policemen walked off their jobs after the police commissioner refused to negotiate with their newly formed union. Rioting and looting soon broke out. Massachusetts Governor Calvin Coolidge, outraged by the policemen's betrayal of their sworn public duty, refused to negotiate with them, called out the National Guard to restore order, and fired the entire police force. His tough stand would bring him national fame and the Republican vice presidential nomination in 1920.

Hard on the heels of the policemen's strike came a strike by more than 300,000 steelworkers in the Midwest. No union had established a footing in the steel industry since the 1890s, when Andrew Carnegie had ousted the ironworkers' union from his Homestead, Pennsylvania, mills. Most steelworkers labored long hours (the 12-hour shift was still standard) for low wages in dangerous workplaces. The organizers of the 1919 strike had somehow managed to persuade steelworkers with varied skill levels and ethnic backgrounds to put aside their differences and demand an eight-hour day and union recognition. When the employers rejected those demands, the workers walked off their jobs. The employers responded by procuring armed guards to beat up the strikers and by hiring nonunion labor to keep the plants running. In many areas, local and state police prohibited union meetings, ran strikers out of town, and opened fire on those who disobeyed orders. In Gary, Indiana, a confrontation between unionists and armed guards left 18 strikers dead. To arouse public support for their antiunion campaign, industry leaders painted

THE 1919 STEEL STRIKE FAILS The steel corporations were united in their opposition to the steelworkers' union and skillful in their use of media to demoralize the strikers. This poster reveals another reason for the strike's failure: a workforce so diverse that strike announcements had to be communicated in eight languages.

the strike leaders as dangerous and violent radicals bent on the destruction of political liberty and economic freedom. They succeeded in arousing public opinion against the steelworkers, and the strike collapsed in January 1920.

RADICALS AND THE RED SCARE

The steel companies succeeded in putting down the strike by fanning the public's fear that revolutionary sentiment was spreading among the workers. Radical sentiment was indeed on the rise. Mine workers and railroad workers had begun calling for the permanent nationalization of coal mines and railroads. Longshoremen in San Francisco and Seattle refused to load ships carrying supplies to the White Russians who had taken up arms against Lenin's Bolshevik government. Socialist trade

unionists mounted the most serious challenge to Gompers's control of the AFL in 25 years. In 1920, nearly a million Americans voted for the Socialist presidential candidate Debs, who ran his campaign from the Atlanta Federal Penitentiary. Small groups of anarchists contemplated, and occasionally carried out, bomb attacks on businessmen and public officials.

This radical surge did not mean, however, that leftists had fashioned themselves into a single movement or political party. On the contrary, the Russian Revolution had split the American Socialist Party. One faction, which would keep the name Socialist and would continue under Debs's leadership, insisted that radicals follow a democratic path to socialism. The other group, which would take the name Communist, wanted to establish a Lenin-style "dictatorship of the proletariat." Small groups of anarchists, some of whom advocated campaigns of terror to speed the revolution, represented yet a third radical tendency.

Few Americans noticed the disarray in the radical camp. Most assumed that radicalism was a single, coordinated movement bent on establishing a communist government on American soil. They saw the nation's vast immigrant communities as breeding grounds for Bolshevism. Beginning in 1919, this perceived "Red Scare" prompted government officials and private citizens to embark on yet another campaign of repression.

The postwar repression of radicalism closely resembled the wartime repression of dissent. Thirty states passed sedition laws to punish people who advocated revolution. Numerous public and private groups intensified Americanization campaigns designed to strip foreigners of their "subversive" ways and remake them into loyal citizens. Universities fired radical professors, and vigilante groups wrecked the offices of socialists and assaulted IWW agitators. A newly formed veterans' organization, the American Legion, took on the American Protective League's role of identifying seditious individuals and organizations and ensuring the public's devotion to "100 percent Americanism."

The Red Scare reached its climax on New Year's Day 1920 when federal agents broke into the homes and meeting places of thousands of suspected revolutionaries in 33 cities. Directed by Attorney General A. Mitchell Palmer, these widely

Reds (1981)

Directed by Warren Beatty. Starring Warren Beatty (John Reed), Diane Keaton (Louise Bryant), Edward Herrmann (Max Eastman), Jerzy Kosinski (Grigory Zinoviev), Jack Nicholson (Eugene O'Neill), and Maureen Stapleton (Emma Goldman).

In this epic film Warren Beatty, producer, director, and screenplay cowriter, attempts to integrate the history of the American Left in the early 20th century, especially as it became intertwined with the Russian Revolution of 1917, with a love story about two radicals of that era, John "Jack" Reed and Louise Bryant. Reed was a well-known radical journalist whose dispatches from Russia during its 1917 revolution were published as a book, *Ten Days That Shook the World*, that brought him fame and notoriety. Bryant never developed the public reputation that Reed enjoyed, but she was an integral member of the radical circles that gathered in apartments and cafes in New York's Bohemian Greenwich Village before and during World War I.

At times, the love principals in this movie seem to resemble Warren Beatty and Diane Keaton more than they do the historical figures they are meant to represent. In general, however, the movie keeps love and politics in balance and thus successfully conveys an important and historically accurate message about the American Left, especially prior to World War I: namely, that its participants wanted to revolutionize the personal as well as the political. Thus equality between men and women, women's right to enjoy the same sexual freedom as men, and marriage's impact on personal growth and adventure were issues debated with the same fervor as building a radical political party and accelerating the transition to socialism. (See chapter 20, The Rise of Feminism.)

Reds is also an exceptionally serious film about political parties and ideologies. The film follows the arc of John Reed's and Louise Bryant's lives from their pre-war days as discontented members of the Portland, Oregon, social elite, through their flight to the freedom and radicalism of Greenwich Village, to the hardening of their radicalism as a result of repression during World War I at home and the excitement engendered by the Russian Revolution and birth of communism in 1917. Beatty has recreated detailed and complex stories about internal fights within the Left both in the United States and Russia, through which he seeks to show how hopes for social transformation went awry. To give this film added historical weight, he introduces "witnesses," individuals who knew Reed and Bryant and who appear on screen periodically to share their memories, both serious and whimsical, about the storied couple and the times in which they lived. *Reds* should be compared to *Wilson*, the movie featured in chapter 22, for the two films offer very different perspectives on the World War I era.

Jack Nicholson as Eugene O'Neill, Diane Keaton as Louise Bryant, and Warren Beatty as Jack Reed, together on the beaches of Provincetown, Massachusetts.

publicized "Palmer raids" were meant to expose the extent of revolutionary activity. Palmer's agents uncovered three pistols, no rifles, and no explosives. Nevertheless, they arrested 6,000 people and kept many of them in jail for weeks without formally charging them with a crime. Finally, those who were not citizens (approximately 500) were deported and the rest were released.

Palmer's failure to expose a revolutionary plot blunted support for him in official circles, but, undeterred, Palmer now alleged that revolutionaries were planning a series of assaults on government

THE PASSION OF SACCO AND VANZETTI, BY BEN SHAHN The 1920 trial and 1927 execution of Nicola Sacco and Bartolomeo Vanzetti became the passion of many immigrants, liberal intellectuals, and artists (such as Ben Shahn) who were convinced that the two anarchists had been unfairly tried and convicted.

officials and government buildings for May 1, 1920. When nothing happened on that date, his credibility suffered another serious blow.

As Palmer's exaggerations of the Red threat became known, many Americans began to reconsider their near-hysterical fear of dissent and subversion Even so, the political atmosphere remained hostile to radicals, as the Sacco and Vanzetti case revealed. In May 1920, two Italian-born anarchists, Nicola Sacco and Bartolomeo Vanzetti, were arrested in Brockton, Massachusetts, and charged with armed robbery and murder. Both men proclaimed their innocence and insisted that they were being punished for their political beliefs. Indeed, their foreign accents and their defiant espousal of anarchist doctrines in the courtroom inclined many Americans, including the judge who presided at their trial, to view them harshly. In spite of the weak case against them, they were convicted of first-degree murder and sentenced to death. Their lawyers attempted numerous appeals, all of which failed. Anger over the verdicts began to build, first among Italian Americans, then among radicals, and finally among liberal intellectuals. Protests compelled the governor of Massachusetts to appoint a commission to review the case, but no new trial was ordered. On August 23, 1927, Sacco and Vanzetti were executed, still insisting that they were innocent.

RACIAL CONFLICT AND THE RISE OF BLACK NATIONALISM

The more than 400,000 blacks who served in the armed forces believed that a victory for democracy abroad would help them achieve democracy for themselves at home. At first, in spite of discrimination they encountered in the military, they maintained their conviction that they would be treated as full-fledged citizens upon their return. Many began to talk about the birth of a "New Negro"—independent and proud. Thousands joined the NAACP, at the forefront of the fight for racial equality. By 1918, 100,000 African Americans subscribed to the NAACP's magazine, the *Crisis*, whose editor, W. E. B. Du Bois, had urged them to support the war.

That wartime optimism made the postwar discrimination and hatred African Americans encountered hard to endure. Many black workers who had found jobs in the North were fired to make way for returning white veterans. Returning black servicemen, meanwhile, had to scrounge for poorly paid jobs as unskilled laborers. In the South, lynch mobs targeted black veterans who now refused to tolerate the usual insults and indignities; 10 of the 70 blacks lynched in the South in 1919 were veterans.

The worst antiblack violence that year occurred in the North, however. Crowded conditions during the war had forced black and white ethnic city dwellers into uncomfortably close proximity. Many white ethnics regarded blacks with a mixture of fear and prejudice. They resented having to share neighborhoods, trolleys, parks, streets, and workplaces with blacks. They also wanted blacks barred from unions, seeing them as threats to their job security rather than as fellow workers.

Racial tensions escalated into race riots. The deadliest explosion occurred in Chicago in July 1919, when a black teenager who had been swimming in Lake Michigan was killed by whites after coming too close to a whites-only beach. Rioting soon broke out, with white mobs invading black neighborhoods, torching homes and stores, and attacking innocent residents. Led by war veterans, some of whom were armed, the blacks fought back, turning the border areas between white and black neighborhoods into battle zones. Fighting raged for five days, leaving 38 dead (23 black, 15 white) and more than 500 injured. Race rioting in other cities pushed the death total to 120 before the summer of 1919 ended.

The riots made it clear to blacks that the North was not the Promised Land. Confined to unskilled jobs and to segregated neighborhoods with substandard housing and exorbitant rents, black migrants in Chicago, New York, and other northern cities suffered severe economic hardship throughout the 1920s. The NAACP carried on its campaign for civil rights and racial equality, but many blacks no longer shared its belief that they would one day be accepted as first-class citizens. They

LINK TO THE PAST

Marcus Garvey

http://www.isop.ucla.edu/mgpp/

The James S. Coleman African Studies Department at the University of California, Los Angeles, maintains a Web site that displays photographs, sound recordings and documents written by and about Marcus Garvey.

1. Select "American Series" and then "Sample documents" under Volume One. Read the entire selection from Marcus Garvey's *The Negro's Greatest Enemy*. How did Garvey come to understand that his race was considered inferior? What steps did he advocate for confronting racism and building a strong international alliance among peoples of African descent? Why did Garvey insist on protecting the racial purity of both whites and blacks?

2. Select "American Series" and then "Sample documents" from Volumes Two and Four. Read all the documents. Why did W. E. B. Du Bois and an African prince object to Garvey, the UNIA, and the Black Star Line? The U.S. government ordered an undercover agent to infiltrate the Garvey movement. What was the agent seeking to uncover?

turned instead to a compelling leader from Jamaica, Marcus Garvey, who gave voice to their bitterness. "The first dying that is to be done by the black man in the future," Garvey declared in 1918, "will be done to make himself free. And then when we are finished, if we have any charity to bestow, we may die for the white man. But as for me, I think I have stopped dying for him."

Garvey called on blacks to give up their hopes for integration and to set about forging a separate black nation. He reminded blacks that they possessed a rich culture stretching back over the centuries that would enable them to achieve greatness as a nation. Garvey's grand vision was to build a black nation in Africa that would bring together all the world's people of African descent. In the short term, he wanted to help American and Caribbean blacks to achieve economic and cultural independence.

Garvey's call for black separatism and self-sufficiency—or black nationalism, as it came to be called—elicited a remarkable response among blacks in the United States. In the early 1920s, the Universal Negro Improvement Association (UNIA), which Garvey had founded, enrolled millions of members in 700 branches in 38 states. His newspaper, the *Negro World*, reached a circulation of 200,000. The New York chapter of UNIA embarked on an ambitious economic de-

velopment program and set up grocery stores, restaurants, and factories. Garvey's most visible economic venture was the Black Star Line, a shipping company with three ships that proudly flew the UNIA flag from their masts.

This black nationalist movement did not endure for long. Garvey entered into bitter disputes with other black leaders, including W. E. B. Du Bois, who regarded him as a flamboyant, self-serving demagogue. Garvey sometimes showed poor judgment, as when he expressed support for the Ku Klux Klan on the grounds that it shared his pessimism about the possibility of racial integration. Inexperienced in economic matters as well, Garvey squandered a great deal of UNIA money on abortive business ventures. The U.S. government regarded his rhetoric as inflammatory and sought to silence him. In 1923 he was convicted of mail fraud involving the sale of Black Star stocks and was sentenced to five years in jail. In 1927 he was deported to Jamaica and the UNIA folded. Nevertheless, Garvey's philosophy of black nationalism endured.

CONCLUSION

The resurgence of racism in 1919 and the consequent turn to black nationalism among African Americans were signs of how the high hopes of the war years had been dashed. Industrial workers, immigrants, and radicals also learned through bitter experience that the fear, intolerance, and repression unleashed by the war interrupted their pursuit of liberty and equality. They came to understand as well that Wilson's commitment to these ideals counted for less than did his administration's and Congress's determination to discipline a people whom they regarded as dangerously heterogeneous and unstable. Of the reform groups, only woman suffragists made enduring gains—especially the right to vote—but, for the feminists in their ranks, these steps forward failed to compensate for the collapse of the progressive movement and, with it, their program of achieving equal rights for women across the board.

A similar disappointment engulfed those who had embraced and fought for Wilson's dream of creating a new and democratic world order. The world in 1919 appeared as volatile as it had been in 1914. More and more Americans—perhaps even a

MARCUS GARVEY, BLACK NATIONALIST Marcus Garvey participates in a black nationalist parade in Harlem. Garvey wears a plumed hat and is seated on the right, in the car's back seat. He often appeared in public as he does here—in a showy military-style uniform complete with epaulets and an admiral's hat.

majority—were coming to believe that U.S. intervention had been a colossal mistake.

In other ways, the United States benefited a great deal from the war. By 1919, the American economy was by far the world's strongest. Many of the nation's leading corporations had improved productivity and management during the war. U.S. banks were poised to supplant those of London as the most influential in international finance. The nation's economic strength triggered an extraordinary burst of growth in the 1920s, and millions of Americans rushed to take advantage of the prosperity that this "people's capitalism" had put within their grasp. But even affluence failed to dissolve the class, ethnic, and racial tensions that the war had exposed. And the failure of the peace process added to Europe's problems, delayed the emergence of the United States as a leader in world affairs, and created the preconditions for another world war.

Suggested Readings begin on page SR-1.
For Web activities and resources
related to this chapter, go to
http://www.harcourtcollege.com/history.murrin

CHAPTER 24

THE 1920S

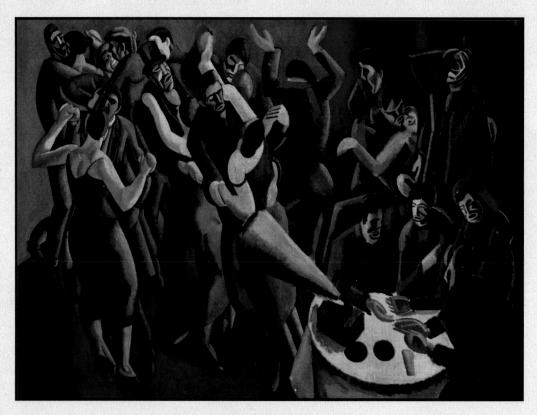

THE JAZZ AGE

This 1923 painting by William Patrick Roberts, entitled "The Dance Club" or "The Jazz Party," captures the dress, dancing, physical intimacy, and emotional intensity associated with modernist impulse of the 1920s.

I n 1920, Americans elected as president Warren G. Harding, who could not have been more different from his predecessor Woodrow Wilson. A Republican, Harding presented himself as a common man with common desires. In his 1920 campaign he called for a "return to normalcy." Although he died in office in 1923, his carefree spirit is thought to characterize the 1920s.

To many Americans, indeed, the decade was one of fun rather than reform, of good times rather than high ideals. It was, in the words of novelist F. Scott Fitzgerald, the "Jazz Age," a time when the quest for personal gratification seemed to replace the quest for public welfare.

Despite Harding's call for a return to a familiar past, America seemed to be rushing headlong into the future. The word "modern" began appearing everywhere: modern times, modern women, modern technology, the modern home, modern marriage. Although the word was rarely defined, it connoted certain beliefs: that science was a better guide to life than religion; that people should be free to choose their own lifestyles; that sex should be a source of pleasure for women as well as men; that women and minorities should be equal to white men and enjoy the same rights.

Many other Americans, however, reaffirmed their belief that God's word transcended science; that people should obey the moral code set forth in the Bible; that women were not equal to men; and that blacks, Mexicans, and eastern European immigrants were inferior to Anglo-Saxon whites. They made their voices heard in a resurgent Ku Klux Klan and the fundamentalist movement, and on issues such as evolution and migration. In seeking to restore an older America, they argued against their nation's commitment to liberty and equality.

Modernists and traditionalists confronted each other in party politics, in legislatures, in courtrooms, and in the press. Their battles belie the vision of the 1920s merely as a time for the pursuit of leisure. Nor were the 1920s free of economic and social problems that had troubled Americans for decades.

This chapter will focus on the following major questions:

- What were the achievements and limitations of "people's capitalism?"
- Why is the 1920s sometimes described as the "age of celebrity culture" and what caused this culture to arise?
- What were the key similarities and differences in the politics of the three Republican presidents

CHRONOLOGY

1920 Prohibition goes into effect • Warren G. Harding defeats James M. Fox for presidency • Census reveals a majority of Americans live in urban areas • eight million cars on road

1922 United States, Britain, Japan, France, and Italy sign Five-Power Treaty, agreeing to reduce size of their navies

1923 Teapot Dome scandal lands Secretary of the Interior Albert Fall in jail • Harding dies in office; Calvin Coolidge becomes president

1924 Dawes Plan to restructure Germany's war debt put in effect • Coolidge defeats John W. Davis for presidency • Ku Klux Klan membership approaches four million • Immigration Restriction Act cuts immigration by 80 percent and discriminates against Asians and southern and eastern Europeans

1925 Scopes trial upholds right of Tennessee to bar teaching of evolution in public schools • *Survey Graphic* publishes a special issue on Harlem announcing the Harlem Renaissance • F. Scott Fitzgerald publishes *The Great Gatsby* • U.S. withdraws Marines from Nicaragua

1926 Revenue Act cuts income and estate taxes • U.S. sends Marines back to Nicaragua to end civil war and protect U.S. property

1927 Coolidge vetoes McNary-Haugen bill, legislation meant to relieve agricultural distress

1928 15 nations sign Kellogg-Briand pact, pledging to avoid war • Coolidge vetoes McNary-Haugen bill again • Herbert Hoover defeats Alfred E. Smith for presidency

1929 Union membership drops to three million • 27 million cars on road • William Faulkner publishes *The Sound and the Fury*

1930 Los Angeles's Mexican population reaches 100,000

of the 1920s, Harding, Coolidge, and Hoover?
• Who were the "traditionalists" of the 1920s and what did they believe? How did traditionalists view cities and urban culture, alcohol, religion?
• How were the experiences of ethnic and racial communities in 1920s America similar to each other and how were they different?

PROSPERITY

On balance, the First World War had been good for the American economy. Its industries had emerged intact, even strengthened, from the war. The war needs of the Allies had created an insatiable demand for American goods and capital. Manufacturers and bankers had exported so many goods and extended so many loans to the Allies that by war's end the United States was the world's leading creditor nation. New York City challenged London as the hub of world finance. At home, the government had helped the large corporations and banks to consolidate their power. Corporate America had responded by lifting productivity and efficiency to new heights through advances in technology and management.

Postwar economic turmoil and depression hampered these advances for a time. From 1919 to 1921, the country struggled to redirect industry from wartime production to civilian production, a process slowed by the government's hasty withdrawal from its wartime role as economic regulator and stabilizer. Workers went on strike to protest wage reductions or increases in the workweek. Farmers were hit by a depression as the overseas demand for American foodstuffs fell from its peak of 1918 and 1919. Disgruntled workers and farmers even joined forces to form statewide farmer-labor parties, which for a time threatened to disrupt the country's two-party system in the upper Midwest. In 1924 the two groups formed a national Farmer-Labor Party. Robert La Follette, their presidential candidate, received an impressive 16 percent of the vote that year. But then the third-party movement fell apart.

Its collapse reflected a rising public awareness of how vigorous and productive the economy had become. Beginning in 1922, the nation embarked on a period of remarkable growth. From 1922 to 1929, gross national product grew at an annual rate of 5.5 percent, rising from $149 billion to $227 billion. The unemployment rate never exceeded 5 percent—and real wages rose about 15 percent.

A CONSUMER SOCIETY

The variety of products being produced matched the rate of economic growth. In the 19th century economic growth had rested primarily on the production of capital goods, such as factory machinery and railroad tracks. In the 1920s, however, growth rested more on consumer goods. Some products, such as cars and telephones, had been available since the early 1900s, but in the 1920s their sales reached new levels. In 1920, just 12 years after Ford introduced the Model T, eight million cars were on the road. By 1929, there were 27 million—one for every five Americans. Other consumer goods became available for the first time—tractors, washing machines, refrigerators, electric irons, radios, and vacuum cleaners. The term "consumer durable" was coined to describe such goods, which, unlike food, clothing, and other "perishables," were meant to last. Even "perishables" took on new allure. Scientists had discovered the importance of vitamins in the diet and began urging Americans to consume more fresh fruits and vegetables. The agricultural economy of southern California grew rapidly as urban demand for the region's fresh fruits and vegetables skyrocketed. Improvements in refrigeration and in packaging, meanwhile, allowed fresh produce to travel long distances and extended its shelf life in grocery stores. And more and more stores were being operated by large grocery chains that could afford the latest refrigeration and packaging technology.

The public responded to these innovations with excitement. American industry had made fresh food and stylish clothes available to the masses. Refrigerators, vacuum cleaners, and washing machines would spare women much of the drudgery of housework. Radios would expand the public's cultural horizons. Automobiles, asphalt roads, service stations, hot dog stands, "tourist cabins" (the forerunners of motels), and traffic lights seemed to herald a wholly new civilization. By the middle of the decade, the country possessed a network of paved roads. City dwellers now had easy access to the country and made a ritual of day-long excursions. Camping trips and long-distance vacations became routine. Farmers and their families could now hop into their cars and head for the nearest town with its stores, movies, amusement parks, and sporting events. Suburbs proliferated, billed as the perfect mix of urban and rural life. Young men and women everywhere discovered that cars were a place where they could "make out," and even make love, without fear of reproach by prudish parents or prying neighbors.

In the 1920s Americans also discovered the benefits of owning stocks. The number of stockholders

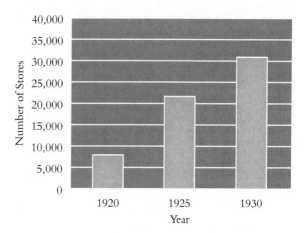

GROWTH OF SIX LEADING GROCERY CHAINS BY NUMBER OF STORES, 1920–1930

Source: From Godfrey M. Labhar, *Chain Stores in America, 1859–1962* (New York: Chain Store Publishing, 1963).

in AT&T, the nation's largest corporation, rose from 140,000 to 568,000. U.S. Steel stockholder numbers increased from 96,000 to 146,000. By 1929, as many as seven million Americans owned stock, most of them people of middle-class means. This spread of stock ownership reflected the need for working capital among the nation's corporations. Because privately held wealth could not satisfy that need, corporations sought to sell their stocks and bonds to the general public. The New York Stock Exchange, first organized in 1792, assisted in processing complicated transactions.

A PEOPLE'S CAPITALISM

Capitalists boasted that they had created a "people's capitalism" in which virtually all Americans could participate. Now, everyone could own a piece of corporate America. Now, everyone could have a share of luxuries and amenities. Poverty, capitalists claimed, was banished and the gap between rich and poor closed. If every American could own a car and house, buy quality clothes, own stock, take vacations, and go to the movies, then clearly no significant inequality existed.

Actually, although wages were rising, millions of Americans still earned too little to partake fully of

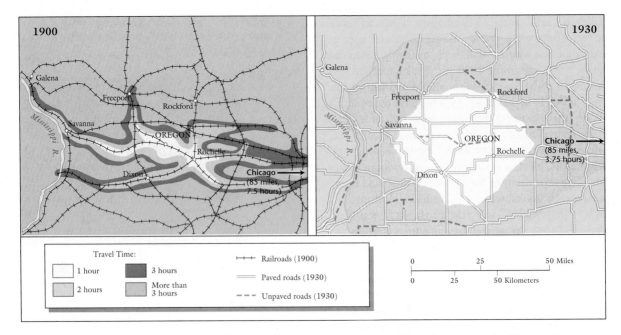

AUTOMOBILE CIVILIZATION: CARS, ROADS, AND THE EXPANSION OF TRAVEL HORIZONS IN OREGON, ILLINOIS

the marketplace. The percentage of Americans owning stocks remained small. Social scientists Robert and Helen Lynd discovered, in their celebrated 1929 study of Muncie, Indiana, that working-class families who bought a car often lacked money for other goods. One housewife admitted, "We don't have no fancy clothes when we have the car to pay for. . . . The car is the only pleasure we have." Another declared, "I'll go without food before I'll see us give up the car." Many industrialists resisted any increase in wages, and workers lacked the organizational strength to force them to pay more.

One solution came with the introduction of consumer credit. Car dealers, home appliance salesmen, and other merchants began to offer installment plans that enabled consumers to purchase a product by making a down payment and promising to pay the rest in installments. By 1930, 15 percent of all purchases—60 percent of all cars and 75 percent of all radios—were made on the installment plan.

Even so, many poor Americans benefited little from the consumer revolution. Middle-class Americans acquired a disproportionate share of consumer durables. They also ate most of the fresh vegetables and bought most of the stock.

THE RISE OF ADVERTISING AND MASS MARKETING

But even middle-class consumers had to be wooed. How could they be persuaded to buy another car only a few years after they had bought their first one? General Motors had the answer. In 1926, it introduced the concept of the annual model change. GM cars took on a different look every year as GM engineers changed headlights and chassis colors, streamlined bodies, and added new features. The strategy worked. GM leaped past Ford and became the world's largest car manufacturer.

Henry Ford reluctantly introduced his Model A in 1927 to provide customers with a colorful alternative to the drab Model T. Having spent his lifetime selling a product renowned for its utility and reliability, Ford rejected the idea that sales could be increased by appealing to the intangible hopes and fears of consumers. He was wrong. The desire to be beautiful, handsome, or sexually attractive; to exercise power and control; to demonstrate competence and success; to escape anonymity, loneliness, and boredom; to experience pleasure—all such desires, once activated, could motivate a consumer to buy a new car even when the old one was still serviceable, or to spend money on goods that might have once seemed frivolous.

Arousing such desires required more than bright colors, sleek lines, and attractive packaging. It called for advertising campaigns intended to make a product seem to be the answer to the consumer's desires. To create those campaigns, corporations turned to a new kind of company: professional advertising firms. The new advertising entrepreneurs, people such as Edward Bernays, Doris Fleischmann, and Bruce Barton—well-educated, sensitive to public taste, and knowledgeable in human psychology— believed that many Americans were bewildered by bureaucratic workplaces and the anonymity of urban living. This modern anomie, they argued, left consumers susceptible to suggestion.

In their campaigns, advertisers played upon the emotions and vulnerabilities of their target audiences. One cosmetics ad decreed: "Unless you are one woman in a thousand, you must use powder and rouge. Modern living has robbed women of much of their natural color." A perfume manufacturer's ad pronounced: "The first duty of woman is to attract. . . . It does not matter how clever or independent you may be, if you fail to influence the men you meet, consciously or unconsciously, you are not fulfilling your fundamental duty as a woman." A mouthwash ad warned about one unsuspecting gentleman's bad breath—"the truth that his friends had been too delicate to mention," while a tobacco ad matter-of-factly declared: "Men at the top are apt to be pipe-smokers. . . . It's no coincidence—pipe-smoking is a calm and deliberate habit—restful, stimulating. His pipe helps a man think straight. A pipe is back of most big ideas."

Advertising professionals believed they were helping people to manage their lives in ways that would increase their satisfaction and pleasure. By enhancing one's appearance and personality with the help of goods to be found in the marketplace, one would have a better chance of achieving success and happiness.

American consumers responded enthusiastically. Their interest in fashion, their eagerness to fill their homes with the latest products, their alacrity to take up the craze of the moment (mah-jongg, crossword puzzles, miniature golf)—all evidenced Americans' preoccupation with self-improvement and personal pleasure. The most enthusiastic of all were middle-class Americans, who could afford to

buy what the advertisers were selling. Many of them were newcomers to middle-class ranks, searching for ways to affirm—or even create—their new identity. The aforementioned ad for pipe tobacco, for example, was certainly targeted at the new middle-class man—who held a salaried position in a corporate office or bank, or worked as a commission salesman, or owned a small business.

As male wage earners moved into the new middle class, their wives were freed from the necessity of outside work. Advertisers appealed to the new middle-class woman, too, as she refocused her attention toward dressing in the latest fashion, managing the household, and raising the children. Vacuum cleaners and other consumer durables would make her more efficient, and books on child-rearing, many imbued with a popularized Freudianism, would enable

SELLING BEAUTY AND HEALTH This advertisement hints at the negative health effects of smoking, but touts "Luckies" as a healthful cigarette more appropriate for the delicate bodies of beautiful women.

EXPENDITURES ON ADVERTISING, 1915–1929

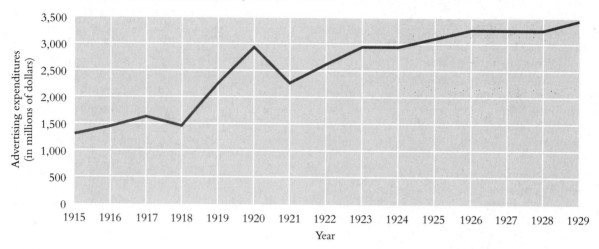

Source: Data from *Historical Statistics of the United States, Colonial Times to 1970* (White Plains, N.Y.: Kraus International, 1989), p. 856.

her to mold her children for future success in work and marriage. Cosmetics would aid women in their "first duty"—to be beautiful for the men in their lives—a beauty that would lead to sexual arousal and fulfillment for both men and women.

CHANGING ATTITUDES TOWARD MARRIAGE AND SEXUALITY

That husbands and wives were encouraged to pursue sexual satisfaction together was one sign of how much prescriptions for married life had changed since the 19th century, when women were thought to lack sexual passion and men were tacitly expected to satisfy their drives through extramarital liaisons. Modern husbands and wives were expected to share other leisure activities as well—dining out, playing cards with friends, going to the movies, attending concerts, and discussing the latest selection from the newly formed Book-of-the-Month Club. Husbands and wives now aspired to a new ideal—to be best friends, full partners in the pursuit of happiness.

The public pursuit of pleasure was also noticeable among young and single middle-class women. The so-called "flappers" of the 1920s donned short dresses, rolled their stockings down, wore red lipstick, and smoked in public. They took their inspiration from depictions of saucy, working-class women of the previous decade, whom moviemakers had popularized and refined. Flappers were signal-

ing their desire for independence and equality; but they had little thought of achieving those goals through politics, as had their middle-class predecessors in the woman suffrage movement. Rather, they aimed to create a new female personality endowed with self-reliance, outspokenness, and a new appreciation for the pleasures of life.

AN AGE OF CELEBRITY

The pursuit of pleasure became both an individual and a group endeavor. Mass marketers began to understand the enormous amount of money that could be made by staging mega-events, mostly connected to sports, that tens of thousands would attend and that radio announcers would broadcast to a radio audience of millions. Newspapers and word-of-mouth would ensure that enthusiasts would discuss these events for days, even weeks and months. Baseball and boxing became the two areas where this trend became most pronounced. When Yankee Stadium opened in 1923, its size dwarfed every other sport amphitheater in the country. Boxing matches began drawing audiences unimaginable twenty years earlier. To succeed on this scale, these sports required not just stirring athletic competitions but individual athletes who seemed larger than life and whose exploits and character could be endlessly promoted. No sports figure achieved greater fame than did George Herman "Babe" Ruth, who overcame the hardships of a poor and orphaned youth to become the slugging star, the "Sultan of Swat," of the New York Yankees. In the 1920s, Ruth hit more home runs than baseball experts had thought humanly possible, culminating in 1927, when he hit a magical 60, a record that would last for 34 years and that would be surpassed only three times in the 20th century. A close second in popularity to Ruth was heavyweight prizefighter Jack Dempsey, whose ruthlessness and efficiency in the ring combined with the gentleness of his character outside to enthrall millions.

Americans also drew their celebrities from the movies, where stars such as comedian Charles Chaplin and the exotically handsome Rudolph Valentino stirred laughter and sexual longings in audiences. These and other figures became so familiar on the silver screen that they created an insatiable appetite among fans for news about their private lives as well, an interest that the movie industry was only too eager to exploit.

The new heroes of the 1920s, then, unlike past heroes, did not earn their status through their accomplishments in politics or war, but through their prowess at a game or their skill at acting in front of a camera. Historians have tended to criticize such celebrity worship, especially when the lionized individual seemed to possess no quality greater than the ability to hit a ball 400 feet or to smash an opponent's face. But such scholarly criticism, perhaps, has been too quick to overlook the human longing to experience the intensity of emotions associated with competition and triumph or to draw close to someone who demonstrates that the impossible—whether in the form of a physical feat, or a love relationship, or an escape from a confining life—can be accomplished.

Some of these sentiments can be discerned in the adulation bestowed on Charles A. Lindbergh, the young pilot who, in 1927, became the first individual to cross the Atlantic in a solo flight. Piloting his single-engine white monoplane, *The Spirit of St. Louis*, he flew nonstop (and without sleep) for thirty-four hours from the time he took off from Long Island until he landed at Le Bourget Airport in Paris. Thousands of Parisians were waiting for him at the airfield and began charging his plane as soon as it landed. When he returned to New York, an estimated four million fans lined the parade route. This shy individual from Minnesota instantly became the most famous and adored man in America, mobbed by crowds everywhere he went.

None of this fame could have happened without the new machinery of celebrity culture—aggressive journalists and radio commentators, promoters and others who understood how fame could make a profit. It mattered, too, that Lindbergh performed his feat in an airplane, one of the newest and most exciting innovations of the time. But Lindbergh's celebrity involved more than hype and technology: He accomplished what others said could not be done, and he did it on his own in a time when corporations and other private institutions of immense power seemed to be shrinking the realm for individual initiative. Some of Lindbergh's popularity no doubt rested on his ability to demonstrate that an individual of conviction and skill could still make a difference in an increasingly industrialized and bureaucratized world.

CELEBRATING BUSINESS CIVILIZATION

Industrialists, advertisers, and merchandisers in the 1920s began to claim that that their accomplishments lay at the heart of American civilization. Business, they argued, made America great, and businessmen provided the nation with its wisest, most vigorous leadership. In 1924 President Calvin Coolidge declared that "the business of America is business." Even religion became a business. Bruce Barton, in his best-seller *The Man Nobody Knows* (1925), depicted Jesus as a business executive "who picked up twelve men from the bottom ranks of business and forged them into an organization that conquered the world." Elsewhere, Barton hailed Jesus as an early "national advertiser," and proclaimed that Peter and Paul were really not so different from Americans who sold vacuum cleaners.

Some corporate leaders adopted benevolent attitudes toward their employees. They set up workplace cafeterias, hired doctors and nurses to staff on-site medical clinics, and engaged psychologists to counsel troubled workers. They built ball fields and encouraged employees to join industry-sponsored leagues. They published employee newsletters and gave awards to employees who did their jobs well and with good spirit. Some employers set up profit-sharing plans and offered stock options to reward employees for their efforts. And some even gave employees a voice in determining working conditions.

The real purpose of these measures—collectively known as welfare capitalism—was to encourage

WELFARE CAPITALISM AT WORK Employees at the Cluett Peabody plant in Troy, New York, eat lunch in a spacious, well-lit, and clean cafeteria. By providing their workforces with first-rate facilities, large corporations hoped to secure the loyalty of their employees.

employee loyalty to the firm and to the capitalist system. Management had an understandable fear of union power arising from the paralyzing strikes of 1919. As the decade proceeded and as prosperity rolled on, however, the programs reflected the confidence that capitalism had indeed become humane.

INDUSTRIAL WORKERS

Many industrial workers benefited from the nation's prosperity. A majority of them enjoyed rising wages and a reasonably steady income. Skilled craftsmen in the older industries of construction, railroad transportation, and printing fared especially well. Their real wages rose by 30 to 50 percent over the decade. The several million workers employed in the large mass-production industries (such as automobile and electrical equipment manufacture) also did well. Their wages were relatively high, and they enjoyed good benefits—paid sick leave, paid vacations, life insurance, stock options, subsidized mortgages, and retirement pensions. Although all workers in companies with these programs were eligible for such benefits, skilled workers were in the best position to claim them.

Semiskilled and unskilled industrial workers had to contend with a labor surplus throughout the decade. As employers replaced workers with machines, the aggregate demand for industrial labor increased at a lower rate than it had in the preced-

ing 20 years. Despite a weakening demand for labor, rural whites, rural blacks, and Mexicans continued their migration to the cities, stiffening the competition for factory jobs. Employers could hire and fire as they saw fit and could therefore keep wage increases lagging behind increases in productivity.

This softening demand for labor helps to explain why many working-class families benefited little from the decade's prosperity or from its consumer revolution. An estimated 40 percent of workers remained mired in poverty, unable to afford a healthy diet or adequate housing, much less any of the more costly consumer goods. In 1930, for instance, only 25 to 40 percent percent of American households owned a washing machine, a vacuum cleaner, and a radio, and only 50 percent had a car.

The million or more workers who labored in the nation's two largest industries, coal and textiles, suffered the most during the 1920s. Throughout the decade, both industries experienced severe overcapacity. By 1926 only half of the coal mined each year was being sold. Many New England textile cities experienced levels of unemployment that sometimes approached 50 percent. One reason was that many textile industrialists had shifted their operations to the South, where taxes and wages were lower. But the southern textile industry also suffered from excess capacity, and prices and wages continued to fall. Plant managers put constant pressure on their workers to speed up production.

VALUE OF REGIONAL COTTON TEXTILE OUTPUT, 1880–1930

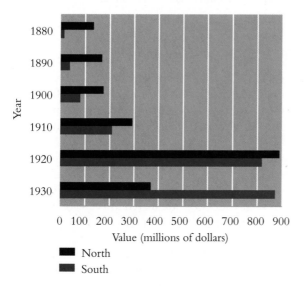

North
South

Source: Data from Nancy F. Kane, *Textiles in Transition: Technology, Wages, and Industry Relocation in the U.S. Textile Industry, 1880–1939* (New York: Greenwood Press, 1988), p. 29.

Workers loathed the frequent "speed-ups" of machines and the "stretch-outs" in the number of spinning or weaving machines each worker was expected to tend. By the late 1920s, labor strife and calls for unionization were rising sharply among disgruntled workers in both the South and the North.

Unionization of textiles and coal, and of more prosperous industries as well, would have brought workers a larger share of the decade's prosperity. Moreover, progressive labor leaders, such as Sidney Hillman of the Amalgamated Clothing Workers, argued that unionization would actually increase corporate profits by compelling employers to observe uniform wage and hour schedules that would restrain ruinous competition. Hillman pointed out—as Henry Ford had in the preceding decade—that rising wages would enable workers to purchase more consumer goods and thus increase corporate sales and revenues, but Hillman's views were ignored outside the garment industry.

Elsewhere, unions lost ground as business and government, backed by middle-class opinion, remained hostile to labor organization. Employers attacked unions as un-American. A conservative Supreme Court whittled away at labor's legal pro-

tections. In 1921 it ruled that lower courts could issue injunctions against union members, prohibiting them from striking or picketing an employer. State courts also enforced what union members called "yellow dog" contracts, written pledges by which employees promised not to join a union while they were employed. Any employee who violated that pledge was subject to immediate dismissal.

These measures crippled efforts to organize trade unions. Membership fell from a high of five million in 1920 to less than three million in 1929, a mere 10 percent of the nation's industrial workforce. Other forces contributed to the decline, too. Many workers, especially those benefiting from welfare capitalist programs, decided they no longer needed trade unions. And the labor movement hurt itself by moving too slowly to open its ranks to semiskilled and unskilled factory workers.

WOMEN AND WORK

Women workers experienced the same hardships as men in the industrial workforce and fewer of the benefits. They were largely excluded from the ranks of the skilled craftsmen and thus missed out on the substantial wage increases that the men in those positions enjoyed. Women also had trouble finding work in the automobile industry, the most glamorous and highest paying of the mass production industries. They had better access to the electrical equipment and meatpacking industries, though often they were segregated in departments given over to "women's" work. Where women could have the same jobs as men, they usually earned less. Thus, a female trimmer in a meatpacking plant typically made 37 cents an hour, only two-thirds what a male trimmer earned. The textile industry had long been a major source of employment for women but, in the 1920s, women and men alike in this ailing manufacturing sector suffered high rates of unemployment and declining wages.

White-collar work established itself, in the 1920s, as a magnet for women. This sector enjoyed rapid growth in a decade in which corporations expanded and refined their managerial and accounting practices. Discrimination prevented women from becoming managers, accountants, or supervisors themselves, but they did dominate the lower level ranks of secretaries, typists, filing clerks, bank tellers, and department store clerks. By the 1930s, two million women, or 20 percent of the female work force, labored in these and related occupations. Initially, these positions had a glamour that factory work lacked. Work environments were cleaner and brighter, and women had the opportunity—indeed were expected—to dress well and fashionably. But wages were low and managerial authority was absolute. Unions had virtually no presence in white-collar places of employment and workers had difficulty finding alternative ways of protesting abusive managers or difficult working conditions.

Women with ambitious work aspirations had to focus their energies on "female" professions, such as teaching, nursing, social work, and librarianship. Opportunities in several of these fields, especially teaching and social work, were growing, and women responded by enrolling in college in substantially greater numbers. Indeed, the number of female college students increased by 50 percent during the 1920s. Some of these college graduates used their new skills in new fields, such as writing for women's magazines. A few, drawing strength from their feminist forebears during the Progressive Era, managed to crack such male bastions of work as mainstream journalism and university research and teaching. In every field of endeavor, even such new and exotic ones as airplane flying, at least one woman arose to demonstrate that her sex had the necessary talent and drive to match or exceed what men had done. Thus in 1932, Amelia Earhart became the first woman to fly the Atlantic solo, matching Lindbergh's feat and inspiring women everywhere. Even so, Earhart's feat failed to improve substantially opportunities for women who wanted to work as pilots in the airline industry. In this industry, as in most lines of work, gender prejudices remained too entrenched. And the women who had broken the gender line remained, by and large, solitary figures.

THE POLITICS OF BUSINESS

Republican presidents governed the country from 1921 to 1933. In some respects, their administrations resembled those of the Gilded Age, a time of mediocre presidents, rampant corruption, and government bent on removing obstacles to capitalist development. In other respects, however, the state-building tradition of Theodore Roosevelt lived on, although in somewhat altered form.

HARDING AND THE POLITICS OF PERSONAL GAIN

Warren Gamaliel Harding defeated Democrat James M. Cox for the presidency in 1920. From modest origins as a newspaper editor in the small town of Marion, Ohio, Harding had risen to the U.S. Senate chiefly because the powerful Ohio Republican machine knew it could count on him to do its bidding. He gained the presidency for the same reason. The Republican Party bosses believed that almost anyone they nominated in 1920 could defeat the Democratic opponent. They chose Harding because they could control him. Harding's good looks and geniality made him a favorite with voters, and he swept into office with 61 percent of the popular vote, the greatest landslide since 1820.

To his credit, Harding released 66-year-old Socialist Party leader Eugene V. Debs from jail and took other measures to cool the passions unleashed by the Red Scare. Aware of his own intellectual limitations, Harding included talented men in his cabinet. Indeed, his choice of Herbert Hoover as secretary of commerce, Charles Evans Hughes as secretary of state, and Andrew Mellon as secretary of the treasury were particularly impressive appointments. Still, Harding lacked the will to alter his ingrained political habits. He had built his political career on a willingness to please the lobbyists who came to his Senate office asking for favors and deals. He had long followed Ohio boss Harry M. Daugherty's advice and would continue to do so with Daugherty as his attorney general. Harding apparently did not consider men such as Daugherty self-serving or corrupt. They were his friends; they had been with him since the beginning of his political career. He made sure the "boys" had jobs in his administration, and he continued to socialize with them. Many a night he could be found drinking (despite Prohibition), gambling, and womanizing with the "Ohio Gang" at its K Street hangout. Sometimes the gang convened in the White House itself. Alice Roosevelt Longworth, Theodore Roosevelt's daughter, once came into the White House study and found the air "heavy with tobacco smoke," its tables cluttered with "bottles containing every imaginable brand of whiskey, . . . [and] cards and poker chips at hand."

It seems that Harding kept himself blind to the widespread use of public office for private gain that characterized his administration. The K Street house was more than a place to carouse. It was a place of business where the Ohio Gang became rich selling government appointments, judicial pardons, and police protection to bootleggers. By 1923 the corruption could no longer be concealed. Journalists and senators began to focus public attention on the actions of Secretary of the Interior Albert Fall, who had persuaded Harding to transfer control of large government oil reserves at Teapot Dome, Wyoming, and Elk Hills, California, from the navy to the Department of the Interior. Fall had immediately leased the deposits to two oil tycoons, Harry F. Sinclair and Edward L. Doheny, who pumped oil from the wells in exchange for providing the navy with a system of fuel tank reserves. Fall had issued the leases secretly, without allowing other oil corporations to compete for them, and he had accepted almost $400,000 from Sinclair and Doheny.

Fall would pay for this shady deal with a year in jail. He was not the only Harding appointee to do so. Charles R. Forbes, head of the Veterans' Bureau, would go to Leavenworth Prison for swindling the government out of $200 million in hospital supplies.

WARREN G. HARDING, CAMPING PARTNER This photo shows President Harding (on the right) participating in the kind of informal male gathering he so enjoyed. His "buddies" on this camping trip were Henry Ford (left) and Thomas Edison (center).

The exposure of Forbes's theft prompted his lawyer, Charles Cramer, to commit suicide; Jesse Smith, Attorney General Daugherty's close friend and housemate, also killed himself, apparently to avoid being indicted and brought to trial. Daugherty managed to escape conviction and incarceration for bribery by burning incriminating documents held by his brother's Ohio bank. Still, Daugherty left government service in disgrace.

Harding grew depressed when he finally realized what had been going on. In the summer of 1923, in poor spirits, he left Washington for a West Coast tour. He fell ill in Seattle and died from a heart attack in San Francisco. The train returning his body to Washington attracted crowds of grief-stricken mourners who little suspected the web of corruption and bribery in which Harding had been caught. Even as the revelations poured forth in 1924 and 1925, few Americans seemed bothered. Some of this insouciance reflected the carefree atmosphere of the 1920s, but much of it had to do with the character of the man who succeeded Harding.

COOLIDGE AND LAISSEZ-FAIRE POLITICS

Calvin Coolidge rarely smiled. At the many dinners he attended as vice president, he said hardly a word. Silence was his public creed, much to the chagrin of Washington's socialites. He was never enticed into carousing with the "boys," nor did he ever stand by as liquor was being served. He believed that the best government was the government that governed least, and he took a nap every afternoon. Coolidge, saying that the welfare of the country hinged on the character of its people—their willingness to work hard, to be honest, to live within their means—quickly put to rest the anxiety aroused by the Harding scandals.

Born in Vermont and raised in Massachusetts, Calvin Coolidge gained national visibility in September 1919, when as governor of Massachusetts he took a firm stand against Boston's striking policemen (see chapter 23). His reputation as a man who battled labor radicals earned him a place on the 1920 national Republican ticket. His image as an ordinary man helped convince voters in 1920 that the Republican Party would return the country to its common-sensical ways after eight years of reckless reforms.

Coolidge won his party's presidential nomination handily in 1924 and easily defeated his Democratic opponent, John W. Davis. Coolidge's popularity remained strong throughout his first full term, and he probably would have been renominated and re-elected in 1928, but he chose not to run.

Coolidge took greatest pride in those measures that reduced the government's control over the economy. The Revenue Act of 1926 slashed the high income and estate taxes that progressives had pushed through Congress during the First World War. Coolidge curtailed the power of the Federal Trade Commission to regulate business affairs and endorsed Supreme Court decisions invalidating Progressive Era laws that had strengthened organized labor and protected children and women from employer exploitation. His strong stand against government meddling in economic affairs prompted a later Republican president, Ronald Reagan, to substitute

A STERN YANKEE In sharp contrast to Harding, President Calvin Coolidge did not enjoy informality, banter, or carousing. Here he fishes alone and in formal attire.

a portrait of the laissez-faire Yankee for one of Harry Truman on a White House wall.

HOOVER AND THE POLITICS OF ASSOCIATIONALISM

Republicans in the 1920s did more than simply lift government restraints and regulations from the economy. Some, led by Secretary of Commerce Herbert Hoover, conceived of government as a dynamic, even progressive, economic force. Hoover wanted government, rather than to control industry, to persuade private corporations to abandon their wasteful, selfish ways and turn to cooperation and public service. Hoover envisioned an economy built on the principle of association. Industrialists, wholesalers, retailers, operators of railroad and shipping lines, small businessmen, farmers, workers, doctors—each of these groups would form a trade association whose members would share economic information, discuss problems of production and distribution, and seek ways of achieving greater efficiency and profit. Hoover believed that the very act of associating in this way—an approach that historian Ellis Hawley has called "associationalism"—would convince participants of the superiority of cooperation over competition, of negotiation over conflict, of public service over selfishness.

Trained as a geologist at Stanford University, Hoover had worked first as a mining engineer and then as a manager of large mining operations in Australia, China, Latin America, and Russia. During the war, he had directed the government's Food Administration and had made it an outstanding example of public management. From that experience, he had come to appreciate the role that government could play in coordinating the activities of thousands of producers and distributors scattered across the country.

Hoover's ambition as secretary of commerce was to make the department the grand orchestrator of economic cooperation. During his eight years in that post, from 1921 to 1929, he organized more than 250 conferences around such themes as unemployment or the problems of a particular industry or economic sector. He brought together government officials, representatives of business, policymakers, and others who had a stake in strengthening the economy.

Hoover achieved some notable successes. He convinced steel executives to abandon the 12-hour day.

HERBERT HOOVER IN GOVERNMENT SERVICE Herbert Hoover poses for an official photograph in 1917 while sitting in the Paris office of the U.S. Food Administration. The success of this venture, especially in terms of getting government and private industry to work together for the common good, would inspire Hoover's work as secretary of commerce and later as president.

His support of labor's right to organize contributed to the passage of the 1926 Railway Labor Act, one of the few acts of the 1920s that endorsed labor's right to bargain collectively. He worked to standardize the size and shape of a great variety of products—everything from nuts and bolts to automobile tires, from toilet paper to pipes—so as to increase their usefulness and strengthen their sales. When the Mississippi River overflowed its banks in 1927, Coolidge turned to Hoover to organize the relief effort. Hoover used this disaster as an opportunity to place credit operations in flood-affected areas on a more secure footing and to organize local banks into associations with adequate resources and expertise.

Hoover's dynamic conception of government brought him into conflict with Republicans whose economic philosophy began and ended with laissez-faire. Hoover found himself increasingly at odds with Coolidge, who declared in 1927: "That man has offered me unsolicited advice for six years, all of it bad."

THE POLITICS OF BUSINESS ABROAD

Republican domestic policy disagreements between laissez-faire and associationalism spilled over into foreign policy as well. Hoover had accepted the post of secretary of commerce thinking he would represent the United States in negotiations with foreign companies and governments. In fact, he intended to apply associationalism to international relations. He wanted the world's leading nations to meet regularly in conferences, to limit military buildups and to foster an international environment in which capitalism could flourish. Aware that the United States must help create such an environment, Hoover hoped to persuade American bankers to adopt investment and loan policies that would aid European recovery. If they refused to do so, he was prepared to urge the government to take an activist, supervisory role in foreign investment.

In 1921 and 1922 Hoover had some influence on the design of the Washington Conference on the Limitation of Armaments. Although he did not serve as a negotiator at the conference—Secretary of State Charles Evans Hughes reserved that role for himself and his subordinates—Hoover did supply Hughes's team with a wealth of economic information. And he helped Hughes to use that information to design forceful, detailed proposals for disarmament. Those proposals gave U.S. negotiators a decided advantage over their European and Asian counterparts and helped them win a stunning accord, the Five-Power Treaty, by which the United States, Britain, Japan, France, and Italy agreed to scrap more than two million tons of warships. Hughes also obtained pledges from all the signatories that they would respect the "Open Door" in China, long a U.S. foreign policy objective (see chapter 22).

These triumphs redounded to Hughes's credit but not to Hoover's, and Hughes used it to consolidate his control over foreign policy. He rebuffed Hoover's efforts to put international economic affairs under the direction of the Commerce Department and rejected Hoover's suggestion to intervene in the international activities of U.S. banks. In so doing, Hughes revealed his affinity for the laissez-faire rather than the associational school of Republican politics. Hughes was willing to urge bankers to participate in Europe's economic recovery, and he was willing to use the power of government to protect their investments once they were made, but the bankers would be free to decide which loans would be appropriate.

Hughes put his policy into action in 1923 to resolve a crisis in Franco-German relations. The victorious Allies had imposed on Germany an obligation to pay $33 billion in war reparations (see chapter 23). In 1923, when the impoverished German government suspended its payments, France sent troops to occupy the Ruhr valley, whose industry was vital to the German economy. German workers retaliated by going on strike, and the crisis threatened to undermine Europe's precarious economic recovery.

Hughes understood that the only way to relieve the situation was to convince the French to reduce German reparations to a reasonable level. To help them come to that decision, he demanded that France repay in full the money it had borrowed from the United States during the First World War. The only way France could pay off those loans was to get additional credit from U.S. bankers, but Hughes made it clear that this would not happen until France had agreed to reduce German reparations. At last France relented and sent representatives to a U.S.-sponsored conference in 1924 to restructure Germany's obligation.

At this point, Hughes withdrew the government from the conference proceedings and turned negotiations over to a group of American bankers. The conference produced the Dawes Plan (after the Chicago banker and chief negotiator, Charles G. Dawes), which sharply reduced German reparations from $542 million to $250 million annually and called on U.S. and foreign banks to stimulate the German economy with a quick infusion of $200 million in loans. Within a matter of days, banker J. P. Morgan, Jr., raised more than one billion dollars from eager American investors. Money poured into German financial markets, and the German economy appeared stabilized.

The Dawes Plan won applause on both sides of the Atlantic, but soon the U.S. money flooding into Germany created its own problems. American investors were so eager to lend to Germany that their investments became speculative and unsound. At this point, a stronger U.S. government effort to direct loans to sound investments might have helped, but Hughes's successor as secretary of state, Frank Kellogg, had no interest in such initiatives; nor did Secretary of the Treasury Mellon. They believed that the market, rather than the U.S. government, should provide the solution to this problem.

Nevertheless, the Republicans were willing to deploy the power of the American state for certain foreign policy objectives. One was in the pursuit of disarmament and world peace. The Five-Power Treaty, negotiated by Hughes in 1921 and 1922, was a major success. Kellogg built on Hughes's achievement, working with Aristide Briand, the French foreign minister, to outlaw war as a tool of national policy. In 1928, representatives of the United States, France, and 13 other nations met in Paris to sign the Kellogg-Briand pact, in which the signatories pledged to avoid war and to settle all international disputes through "pacific means." Hailed as a major stride toward world peace, the pact soon attracted the support of 48 other nations. In the United States, it energized a broad peace movement born of disillusionment with Woodrow Wilson's belief that America could save humanity by going to war. The pact gave these pacifists hope that the United States would never again commit the grievous Wilsonian error.

Coolidge viewed Kellogg-Briand as an opportunity to further reduce the size of the U.S. government. With the threat of war removed, the United States could scale back its military forces and eliminate much of the bureaucracy needed to support a large standing army and navy. Unfortunately, the pact contained no enforcement mechanism. It would do nothing to slow the next decade's descent into militarism and war.

The Republican administrations of the 1920s also adopted a hands-on approach toward Latin America. U.S. investments in the region more than doubled from 1917 to 1929, and the U.S. government continued its policy of intervening in the internal affairs of Latin America to protect U.S. interests. Republican administrations did attempt to curtail American military involvement in the Caribbean. Indeed, the Coolidge administration pulled American troops out of the Dominican Republic in 1924 and Nicaragua in 1925. In the case of Nicaragua, however, U.S. Marines returned in 1926 to end a war between liberal and conservative Nicaraguans and to protect American property; this time they stayed until 1934. U.S. troops, meanwhile, occupied Haiti continuously between 1919 and 1934, keeping in power governments friendly to U.S. interests. Opposition to such heavy-handed tactics continued to build in the United States, but they would not yield a significant change in U.S. policy until the 1930s (see chapter 25).

FARMERS, SMALL-TOWN PROTESTANTS, AND MORAL TRADITIONALISTS

Although many Americans benefited from the prosperity of the 1920s, others did not. Overproduction was impoverishing substantial numbers of farmers. Beyond these economic hardships, many moral-traditionalist white Protestants, especially those in rural areas and small towns, believed that the country was being overrun by racially inferior and morally suspect foreigners.

AGRICULTURAL DEPRESSION

The 1920s brought hard times to the nation's farmers after the boom period of the war years. During the war, domestic demand for farm products had risen steadily and foreign demand had exploded as the war disrupted agricultural production in France, Ukraine, and other European food-producing regions. Herbert Hoover, who through his Food Administration made large quantities of American agricultural commodities available to the Europeans, also ensured that U.S. farmers would reap ample profits. Soon after the war, however, Europe's farmers quickly resumed their customary levels of production. Foreign demand for American foodstuffs fell precipitously, leaving U.S. farmers with an oversupply and depressed prices.

Contributing further to the plight was a rise in agricultural productivity made possible by the tractor, which enabled farmers to increase their cultivated acreage. The number of tractors in use almost quadrupled in the 1920s, and 35 million new acres came under cultivation. Produce flooded the market. Prices fell even further, as did farm incomes. By 1929, the annual per capita income of rural Americans was only $223, one-quarter that of the nonfarm population. Farmers by the hundreds of thousands had to sell their farms and either scrape together a living as tenants or abandon farming altogether. Many chose to abandon the farm life, packed their belongings into jalopies or loaded them onto trains, and headed for the city.

Those who stayed on the land grew increasingly vociferous in their demands. Early in the decade, radical farmers working through such organizations as the Nonpartisan League of North Dakota and

PRICE OF MAJOR CROPS, 1914–1929

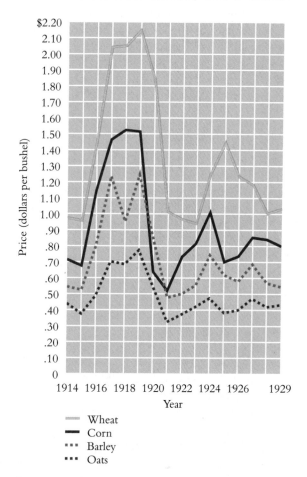

Source: Data from *Historical Statistics of the United States, Colonial Times to 1970* (White Plains, N.Y.: Kraus International, 1989), pp. 511–12.

farmer-labor parties in Minnesota, Wisconsin, and other midwestern states led the movement. By the second half of the decade, however, leadership of the farm movement had passed from farming radicals to farming moderates, and from small farmers in danger of dispossession to larger farmers and agribusinesses seeking to extend their holdings. By lobbying through such organizations as the Farm Bureau Federation, the more powerful agricultural interests brought pressure on Congress to set up economic controls that would protect them from failure. Their proposals, embodied in the McNary-Haugen Bill, called on the government to erect high tariffs on foreign produce and to purchase surplus

U.S. crops. The government would then sell the surplus crops in the world market for whatever prices they fetched. Any money lost in international sales would be absorbed by the government rather than by the farmers. The McNary-Haugen Bill passed Congress in 1927 and in 1928, only to be vetoed by President Coolidge both times.

CULTURAL DISLOCATION

Added to the economic plight of the farmers was a sense of cultural dislocation among the majority who were white, Protestant, and of northwest European descent. These farmers had long perceived themselves as the backbone of the nation—hardworking, honest, God-fearing yeomen, guardians of independence and liberty.

The 1920 census challenged the validity of that view. For the first time, a slight majority of Americans now lived in urban areas. That finding in itself signified little, for the census classified as "urban" those towns with a population as small as 2,500. But the census figures did reinforce the widespread perception that both the economic and cultural vitality of the nation had shifted from the countryside to the metropolis. Industry, the chief engine of prosperity, was an urban phenomenon. Leisure—the world of amusement parks, department stores, professional sports, movies, cabarets, and theaters—was to be enjoyed in cities; so too were flashy fashions and open sexuality. Catholics, Jews, and African Americans, who together outnumbered white Protestants in many cities, seemed to be the principal creators of this new world. They were also thought to be the

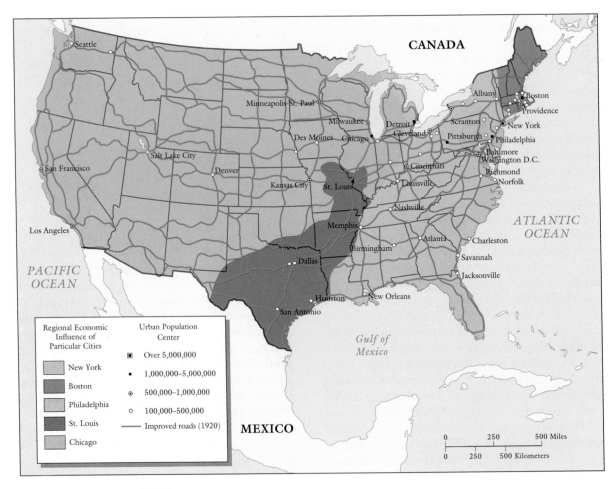

URBANIZATION, 1920

purveyors of Bolshevism, hedonism, and other modes of radicalism. Cities, finally, were the home of secular intellectuals who had scrapped their belief in Scripture and in God and had embraced science as their new, unimpeachable authority.

All through the Progressive Era rural white Americans had believed that the cities could be redeemed, that city dwellers could be reformed, that the Protestant values of rural America would triumph. War had crushed that confidence and had replaced it with the fear that urban culture and urban people would undermine all that "true" Americans held dear.

These fears grew even more intense with the changes brought by prosperity. Urban-industrial America was obviously the most prosperous sector of society; its consumer culture and its commodities were penetrating the countryside as never before. Even small towns now sported movie theaters and automobile dealerships. Radio waves carried news of city life into isolated farmhouses. The growth in the circulation of national magazines also broke down the wall separating country from city. Mail-order catalogs—Sears, Roebuck, and Company and others—invited farmers to fantasize that they too could fill their homes with refrigerators, RCA Victrolas, and Hoover vacuum cleaners.

Rural white Americans showed ambivalence toward this cultural invasion. On the one hand, most of these country dwellers were eager to participate in the consumer marketplace. On the other, many were terrified that by doing so they would expose the countryside to atheism, immorality, and radicalism. Their determination to protect their imperiled way of life was manifested by their support of Prohibition, the Ku Klux Klan, immigration restriction, and religious fundamentalism.

PROHIBITION

The Eighteenth Amendment to the Constitution, which prohibited the manufacture and sale of alcohol, went into effect in January 1920. At its inception it was supported by a large and varied constituency that included farmers, middle-class city dwellers, feminists, and progressive reformers who loathed the powerful "liquor trust" and who saw firsthand the deleterious effects of drink on the urban poor. It soon became apparent, however, that Prohibition was encouraging law-breaking rather than abstinence. With only 1,500 federal agents to enforce the law, the government could not possibly police the drinking habits of 110 million people. With little fear of punishment, those

CONSUMER CULTURE PENETRATES THE COUNTRY-SIDE By the 1920s, cars, Coca-Cola, radios, and other commodities had found their way to the country's smallest towns. Here a farmer tunes his radio as he milks his cow.

EVADING PROHIBITION Prohibition did slow the consumption of alcohol, but most people who wanted a hard drink found one. Here, a customer carrying a mysterious brown bag seeks admittance to a speakeasy (a place where alcohol was illegally sold).

who wanted to drink did so, either brewing liquor at home or buying it from speakeasies and bootleggers. Because the law prevented legitimate businesses from manufacturing liquor, organized crime simply added alcohol to its business portfolio. Mobsters procured much of their liquor from Canadian manufacturers, smuggled it across the border, protected it in warehouses, and distributed it to speakeasies. Al Capone's Chicago-based mob alone employed 1,000 men to protect its liquor trafficking, which was so lucrative that Capone became the richest (and most feared) gangster in America. Blood flowed in the streets of Chicago and other northern cities as rival mobs fought one another to enlarge their share of the market.

These unexpected consequences caused many early advocates of Prohibition, especially in the cities, to withdraw their support. Not so for Prohibition's rural, white Protestant supporters, however. The violence spawned by liquor trafficking confirmed their view of alcohol as an agent of evil to be eradicated. The high-profile participation of Italian, Irish, and Jewish gangsters in the bootleg trade merely reinforced their view that Catholics and Jews were threats to law and morality. Many

rural white Protestants became more, not less, determined to rid the country of liquor once and for all; others resolved to rid the country of Jews and Catholics as well.

THE KU KLUX KLAN

The original Ku Klux Klan, formed in the South in the late 1860s, had died out with the defeat of Reconstruction and the reestablishment of white supremacy (see chapter 17). The new Klan was created in 1915 by William Simmons, a white southerner who had been inspired by D. W. Griffith's racist film, *Birth of a Nation*, in which the early Klan was depicted as having saved the nation (and especially its white women) from predatory blacks. By the 1920s control of the Klan had passed from Simmons to a Texas dentist, Hiram Evans, and its ideological focus had expanded from a loathing of blacks to a hatred of Jews and Catholics as well. Evans's Klan propagated a nativist message that the country should contain—or better yet, eliminate—the influence of Jews and Catholics and restore "Anglo-Saxon" racial purity, Protestant supremacy, and traditional morality to national life. Evans's message

WOMEN OF THE KU KLUX KLAN Women comprised a substantial portion of the Klan's membership in the 1920s. Here a group marches in an "America First" parade in Binghamton, New York.

swelled Klan ranks and expanded its visibility and in-fluence in the North and South alike. By 1924, as many as four million Americans are thought to have belonged to the Klan, including the half-million members of its female auxiliary, Women of the Ku Klux Klan. Not only was the Klan strong in states of the Old Confederacy such as Louisiana and Texas and in border states such as Oklahoma and Kansas; it thrived, too, in such northern states as Indiana, Pennsylvania, Washington, and Oregon. It even drew significant membership from the cities of those states. Indiana, for example, was home to 500,000 Klansmen and women, many of them in the Indi-anapolis area. In 1924 Indiana voters elected a Klansman to the governorship and sent several other Klan members to the statehouse.

In some respects, the Klan functioned just as many other fraternal organizations did. It offered members friendship networks, social services, and conviviality. Its rituals, regalia, and mock-medieval language (the Imperial Wizard, Exalted Cyclops, Grand Dragons, and such) gave initiates the same sense of superiority, valor, and mystery that so many other fraternal societies, from the Masons to the Knights of Columbus, imparted to their members.

The Klan also stirred up hate. It thrived on lurid tales of financial extortion by Jewish bankers and sex-ual exploitation by Catholic priests. The accusations were sometimes general, as in the claim that an in-ternational conspiracy of Jewish bankers had caused the agricultural depression, or allegations that the pope had sent agents to the United States with in-structions to destroy democracy. More common, and more incendiary, however, were the seemingly plau-sible, yet totally manufactured, tales of Jewish or Catholic depravity. Stories circulated of Jewish busi-nessmen who had opened amusement parks and dance halls to which they lured innocent adolescents, tempting them with sexual transgression and profit-ing handsomely from their moral debasement. Like-wise, Catholic priests and nuns were said to prey on Protestant girls and boys who had been forced into convents and Catholic orphanages. These outra-geous stories sometimes provoked attacks on individ-ual Jews and Catholics. More commonly, they prompted campaigns to boycott Jewish businesses and Catholic institutions, and to ruin reputations.

The emphasis on sexual exploitation in these stories reveals the anxiety Klan members felt about modern society's acceptance of sexual openness and sexual gratification. Many Klan supporters lived in towns bursting with modern attitudes. That such attitudes might reflect the yearnings of Protestant children rather than the manipulation of deceitful Jews and Catholics was a truth some Protestant parents found difficult to accept.

IMMIGRATION RESTRICTION

Although the vast majority of white Protestants never joined the Klan, many of them did respond to the Klan's nativist argument that the country and its values would best be served by limiting the entry of outsiders. That was the purpose of the Johnson-Reed Immigration Restriction Act of 1924.

By the early 1920s most Americans believed that the country could no longer accommodate the mil-lion immigrants who had been arriving each year prior to the war and the more than 800,000 who ar-rived in 1921. Industrialists no longer needed un-skilled European laborers to operate their factories, their places having been taken either by machines or by African American and Mexican workers. And most of the leaders of the labor movement were convinced that the influx of workers unfamiliar with English and with trade unions was weakening labor solidarity. Progressive reformers no longer believed that immigrants could be easily American-ized or that harmony between the native-born and the foreign-born could be readily achieved. Con-gress responded to constituents' concerns by pass-ing an immigration restriction act in 1921. In 1924, the more comprehensive Johnson-Reed Act im-posed a yearly quota of 165,000 immigrants from countries outside the Western Hemisphere, effec-tively reducing total immigration to only 20 per-cent of the prewar annual average.

The sponsors of the 1924 act believed that cer-tain groups—British, Germans, and Scandinavians, in particular—were racially superior and that, con-sequently, these groups should be allowed to enter the United States in greater numbers. However, because the Constitution prohibits the enactment of explicitly racist laws, Congress had to achieve this racist aim through subterfuge. Lawmakers es-tablished a formula to determine the annual immi-grant quota for each foreign country, which was to be computed at 2 percent of the total number of

ANNUAL IMMIGRANT QUOTAS UNDER THE JOHNSON-REED ACT, 1925–1927

Northwest Europe and Scandinavia		Eastern and Southern Europe		Other Countries	
Country	*Quota*	*Country*	*Quota*	*Country*	*Quota*
Germany	51,227	Poland	5,982	Africa (other than Egypt)	1,100
Great Britain and Northern Ireland	34,007	Italy	3,845	Armenia	124
Irish Free State (Ireland)	28,567	Czechoslovakia	3,073	Australia	121
Sweden	9,561	Russia	2,248	Palestine	100
Norway	6,453	Yugoslavia	671	Syria	100
France	3,954	Romania	603	Turkey	100
Denmark	2,789	Portugal	503	New Zealand and Pacific Islands	100
Switzerland	2,081	Hungary	473	All others	1,900
Netherlands	1,648	Lithuania	344		
Austria	785	Latvia	142		
Belgium	512	Spain	131		
Finland	471	Estonia	124		
Free City of Danzig	228	Albania	100		
Iceland	100	Bulgaria	100		
Luxembourg	100	Greece	100		
Total (number)	142,483	Total (number)	18,439	Total (number)	3,745
Total (%)	86.5%	Total (%)	11.2%	Total (%)	2.3%

Note: Total annual immigrant quota was 164,667
Source: From *Statistical Abstract of the United States* (Washington, D.C.: Government Printing Office, 1929), p. 100.

immigrants from that country already resident in the United States in the year 1890. In 1890, immigrant ranks had been dominated by the British, Germans, and Scandinavians, so the new quotas would thus allow for a relatively larger cohort of immigrants from those countries. Immigrant groups that were poorly represented in the 1890 population—Italians, Greeks, Poles, Slavs, and eastern European Jews—were effectively locked out. The Johnson-Reed Act also reaffirmed the longstanding policy of excluding Chinese immigrants, and it added Japanese and other Asians to the list of groups that were altogether barred from entry. The act did not officially limit immigration from nations in the Western Hemisphere, chiefly because agribusiness interests in Texas and California had convinced Congress that cheap Mexican labor was indispensable to their industry's prosperity. Still, the establishment of a Border Patrol along the U.S.-Mexican border and the imposition of a

$10 head tax on all prospective Mexican immigrants made entry into the United States more difficult than ever for Mexicans.

The Johnson-Reed Act accomplished Congress's underlying goal. Annual immigration from transoceanic nations fell by 80 percent. The large number of available slots for English and German immigrants regularly went unfilled, while the smaller number of available slots for Italians, Poles, Russian Jews, and others prevented hundreds of thousands of them from entering the country. A "national origins" system put in place in 1927 further reduced the total annual quota to 150,000 and reserved more than 120,000 of these slots for immigrants from northwestern Europe. Except for minor modifications in 1952, the Johnson-Reed Act would dictate U.S. immigration policy until 1965.

Remarkably few Americans, outside of the ethnic groups being discriminated against, objected to these laws at the time they were passed—an indica-

"There is little or no similarity between the clear-thinking, self-governing [racial] stocks that sired the American people and this stream of irresponsible and broken wreckage [eastern and southern Europeans] that is pouring into the lifeblood of America the social and political diseases of the Old World."

INDIANA REPRESENTATIVE FRED S. PURNELL (REPUBLICAN)
in a 1924 speech to Congress supporting immigration restriction

"I stood awhile at the tomb of America's Unknown Soldier, the last resting place of him, whom we know not, nor whence came. Standing there, with a bared head, I wondered if in life he was an Italian, an Irishman, a Jew, a Nordic, a Slav, or what. . . . I thought of what a travesty on American ideals it would be if in passing this bill we would prevent coming to America the unknown mother of our revered unknown soldier."

MASSACHUSETTS REPRESENTATIVE PETER F. TAGUE (DEMOCRAT)
in a 1924 speech to Congress opposing immigration restriction

FUNDAMENTALISM

Of all the forces reacting against urban life, Protestant fundamentalism was perhaps the most enduring. Fundamentalists regard the Bible as God's word and thus the source of all "fundamental" truth. They believe that every event depicted in the Bible, from the creation of the world in six days to the resurrection of Christ, happened exactly as the Bible describes it. For fundamentalists, God is a deity who intervenes directly in the lives of individuals and communities and who makes known both his pleasure and his wrath to those who acknowledge his divinity. Sin must be actively purged, salvation actively sought.

The rise of the fundamentalist movement from the 1870s through the 1920s roughly paralleled the rise of urban-industrial society. Fundamentalists recoiled from the "evils" of the city—from what they perceived as its poverty, its moral degeneracy, its irreligion, and its crass materialism. Fundamentalism took shape in reaction against two additional aspects of urban society: the growth of liberal Protestantism and the revelations of science.

Liberal Protestants believed that religion had to be adapted to the skeptical and scientific temper of the modern age. No biblical story in which a sea opens up, the sun stands still, or a woman springs forth from a man's rib could possibly be true. The Bible was to be mined for its ethical values rather than for its literal truth. Liberal Protestants removed God from his active role in history and refashioned him into a distant and benign deity who watches over the world but does not intervene to punish or to redeem. They turned religion away from the quest for salvation and toward the pursuit of good deeds, social conscience, and love for one's neighbor. Although those with a liberal bent constituted only a minority of Protestants, they were articulate, visible, and influential in social reform movements. Fundamentalism arose in part to counter the "heretical" claims of the liberal Protestants.

Liberal Protestants and fundamentalists both understood that science was the source of most challenges to Christianity. Scientists believed that rational inquiry was a better guide to the past and to the future than prayer and revelation. Scientists even challenged the ideas that God had created the world and had fashioned mankind in his own image. These were

tion of how broadly acceptable racism and nativism had become. In fact, racism and religious bigotry enjoyed a resurgence during the Jazz Age. The pseudoscience of eugenics, based upon the idea that nations could improve the racial quality of their population by pruning away its weaker racial strains, found supporters not only in Congress but among prestigious scientists as well. Universities such as Harvard and Columbia set quotas similar to those of the Johnson-Reed Act to reduce the proportion of Jews among their undergraduates.

assertions that many religious peoples, particularly fundamentalists, simply could not accept. Conflict was inevitable. It came in 1925, in Dayton, Tennessee.

THE SCOPES TRIAL

No aspect of science aroused more anger among fundamentalists than Charles Darwin's theory of evolution. There was no greater blasphemy than to suggest that man emerged from lower forms of life instead of being created by God himself. In Tennessee in 1925, fundamentalists succeeded in passing a law that forbade teaching "any theory that denies the story of the divine creation of man as taught in the Bible."

For Americans who accepted the authority of science, denying the truth of evolution was as ludicrous as insisting that the sun revolved around the earth. They ridiculed the fundamentalists, but they worried that the passage of the Tennessee law might signal the onset of a campaign to undermine First Amendment guarantees of free speech. The American Civil Liberties Union, founded by liberals during the Red Scare of 1919 and 1920, began searching for a teacher who would be willing to challenge the constitutionality of the Tennessee law. They found their man in John T. Scopes, a 24-year-old biology teacher in Dayton, Tennessee. After confessing that he had taught evolution to his students, Scopes was arrested. The case quickly attracted national attention. William Jennings Bryan, the former Populist, progressive, and secretary of state, announced that he would help to prosecute Scopes, and the famous liberal trial lawyer Clarence Darrow rushed to Dayton to lead Scopes's defense. That Bryan and Darrow had once been allies in the progressive movement only heightened the drama. A small army of journalists descended on Dayton, led by H. L. Mencken, a Baltimore-based journalist famous for his savage critiques of the alleged stupidity and prudishness of small-town Americans.

The trial dragged on, and most of the observers expected Scopes to be convicted. He was, but the

LINK TO THE PAST

The Scopes Trial

http://www.law.umkc.edu/faculty/projects/ftrials/scopes/scopes.htm

Professor Doug Linder of the University of Missouri, Kansas City, School of Law maintains a Web site devoted to famous trials in American history. Professor Linder presents trial testimony, evidence, biographies, and historical context regarding the Scopes Trial of 1925, one of many trials he explores.

1. Select and read "H. L. Mencken's Trial Account." What does Mencken's report reveal about the contrasting views of rural and urban dwellers of the 1920s? What are Mencken's attitudes toward the people of Dayton, Tennessee, and toward William Jennings Bryan and Clarence Darrow? Why does Mencken think that a guilty verdict for John Scopes was unavoidable?

2. Select "Excerpts from Scopes Trial Transcript," then select "Day 7: Darrow Examines Bryan" and scroll down to the examination of Bryan in the transcript. How does Bryan defend his interpretation of the Bible? How does Darrow attempt to undermine Bryan's testimony? Is Darrow's questioning relevant to the innocence or guilt of Scopes? If not, why did Darrow question Bryan in this way?

THE SCOPES TRIAL Defense attorney Clarence Darrow (left) and prosecutor William Jennings Bryan take a break from their celebrated courtroom fight to enjoy each other's company. The two men had been allies in the Progressive Era.

hearing took an unexpected turn when Darrow persuaded the judge to let Bryan testify as an "expert on the Bible." Darrow knew that Bryan's testimony would have no bearing on the question of Scopes's innocence or guilt. The jury was not even allowed to hear it. His aim was to expose Bryan as a fool for believing that the Bible was a source of literal truth and thus to embarrass the fundamentalists. In a riveting confrontation, Darrow made Bryan's defense of the Bible look problematic and led Bryan to admit that the "truth" of the Bible was not always easy to determine. But Darrow could not shake Bryan's belief that the Bible was God's word and thus the source of all truth.

In his account of the trial, Mencken portrayed Bryan as a pathetic figure devastated by his humiliating experience on the witness stand, a view popularized in the 1960 movie, *Inherit the Wind.* When Bryan died only a week after the trial ended, Mencken claimed that the trial had broken Bryan's heart.

Bryan deserved a better epitaph than the one Mencken had given him. Diabetes caused his death, not a broken heart. Nor was Bryan the innocent fool that Mencken made him out to be. He remembered when social conservatives had used Darwin's phrase "survival of the fittest" to prove that the wealthy and politically powerful were racially superior to the poor and powerless (see chapter 20). His rejection of Darwinism evidenced his democra-

tic faith that all human beings were creatures of God and thus capable of striving for perfection and equality.

The public ridicule attendant on the Scopes trial took its toll on fundamentalists. Many of them retreated from politics and refocused their attention on purging sin from their own hearts rather than from the hearts of others. In the end, the fundamentalists prevailed on three more states to prohibit the teaching of evolution, but the controversy had even more far-reaching effects. Worried about losing sales, publishers quietly removed references to Darwin from their science textbooks, a policy that would remain in force until the 1960s. In this respect, the fundamentalists had scored a significant victory.

ETHNIC AND RACIAL COMMUNITIES

The 1920s were a decade of change for ethnic and racial minorities. Government policy simultaneously discouraged the continued immigration of "new immigrants" from southern and eastern Europe and encouraged the migration of African Americans from the South to the North and of Mexicans across the Rio Grande and into the American Southwest. Some minorities benefited from the prosperity of the decade; others created and sustained vibrant subcultures. All, however, experienced a surge in religious and racial discrimination that made them uneasy in Jazz Age America.

EUROPEAN AMERICANS

European American immigrants—and especially the southern and eastern European majority among them—were concentrated in the cities of the Northeast and Midwest. Many were semiskilled and unskilled industrial laborers who suffered economic insecurity. In addition, they faced cultural discrimination. Catholic ethnics and Jews were favorite targets of the Klan and its politics of hate. Catholics generally opposed Prohibition, viewing it as a crude attempt by Protestants to control their behavior. Southern and eastern Europeans, particularly Jews and Italians, resented immigration restriction and the implication that they were unworthy of citizenship. Many Italians were outraged by the execution of Nicola Sacco and Bartolomeo Vanzetti in 1927 (chapter 23). Had the two men been native-born white Protestants, Italians argued, their lives would have been spared.

Southern and eastern Europeans everywhere endured intensive Americanization campaigns. State after state passed laws requiring public schools to instruct children in the essentials of citizenship. Several states, including Rhode Island, extended these laws to private schools as well, convinced that immigrants' children who attended Catholic parochial schools were spending too much time

DEMOCRATIC PRESIDENTIAL VOTING IN CHICAGO BY ETHNIC GROUPS, 1924 AND 1928

	Percent Democratic	
	1924	*1928*
Czechoslovaks	40%	73%
Poles	35	71
Lithuanians	48	77
Yugoslavs	20	54
Italians	31	63
Germans	14	58
Jews	19	60

Source: From John M. Allswang, *A House for All Peoples: Ethnic Politics in Chicago, 1890–1936* (Lexington: University Press of Kentucky), p. 42.

learning about their native religion, language, and country. An Oregon law tried to eliminate Catholic schools altogether by ordering all children aged 8 to 16 to enroll in public schools. But attending a public school was no guarantee of acceptance, either—a lesson learned by Jewish children who had excelled in their studies only to be barred from Harvard, Columbia, and other elite universities.

Southern and eastern European Americans responded to these insults and attacks by strengthening the very institutions and customs Americanizers sought to undermine. Ethnic associations flourished in the 1920s—Catholic churches and Jewish synagogues, fraternal and mutual benefit societies, banks and charitable organizations, athletic leagues and youth groups. Children learned their native languages and customs at home and at church if not at school, and joined with their parents to celebrate their ethnic heritage. Among Italians and French Canadians, saints' days were occasions for parades, speeches, band concerts, games, and feasts, all serving to solidify ethnic bonds and affirm ethnic identity.

Many of these immigrants and their children entered into the new consumer culture, however. They flocked to movies and amusement parks, to baseball games and boxing matches. Children usually entered more enthusiastically into the world of American mass culture than did their immigrant parents, a behavior that often set off family conflicts. The famed New York Yankee, Lou Gehrig, had to fight to convince his German-born mother that playing baseball was honorable work. But many ethnics found it possible to reconcile their own culture with American culture. Youngsters who went to the movies did so with friends from within their community. Ethnics also played sandlot baseball, but their leagues were customarily organized around churches or ethnic associations. In these early days of radio, ethnics living in large cities could always find programs in their native language and music from their native lands.

European American ethnics also resolved to develop sufficient political muscle to defeat the forces of nativism and to turn government policy in a more favorable direction. One sign of this determination was a sharp rise in the number of immigrants who became U.S. citizens. Immigrant Poles, Slavs, Italians, Lithuanians, and Hungarians who became naturalized citizens nearly doubled their numbers during the decade; the number of naturalized Greeks almost tripled. Armed with the vote, ethnics turned out on election day to defeat unsympathetic city councilmen, mayors, state representatives, and even an occasional governor. Their growing national strength first became apparent at the Democratic national convention of 1924, when urban-ethnic delegates almost won approval of planks calling for the repeal of Prohibition and condemnation of the Klan. After denying the presidential nomination to William G. McAdoo—Woodrow Wilson's treasury secretary, son-in-law, and heir apparent—they nearly secured it for their

candidate, Alfred E. Smith, the Irish American governor of New York. McAdoo represented the rural and southern constituencies of the Democratic Party. His forces ended up battling Smith's urban-ethnic forces for 103 ballots, until the two men gave up and supporters from each camp switched their votes to a compromise candidate, the corporate lawyer John W. Davis.

The nomination fight devastated the Democratic Party in the short term, and popular Calvin Coolidge easily defeated little-known John Davis. This split between the party's rural Protestant and urban-ethnic constituencies would keep the Democrats from the White House for nearly a decade, but the convention upheaval of 1924 also marked an important milestone in the bid by European ethnics for political power. They would achieve a second milestone at the Democratic national convention of 1928 when, after another bitter nomination struggle, they finally secured the presidential nomination for Al Smith. Never before had a major political party nominated a Catholic for that high office. Herbert Hoover crushed Smith in the general election, as nativists stirred up anti-Catholic prejudice yet again, and as large numbers of southern Democrats either stayed home or voted Republican. Even so, the campaign offered encouraging signs, none more so than Smith's beating Hoover

ALFRED E. SMITH, NEW YORK DEMOCRAT This portrait of Al Smith, the New York-born Irish American politician who became the first Catholic to be nominated for the presidency by either party, originally appeared in the *New Yorker* magazine in 1934. It suggests that his spirit was as buoyant and irrepressible as that of New York City itself. But there is a touch of sadness etched in his eyes and smile, a reflection perhaps of the defeats he had suffered, first in the 1928 presidential election and then in 1932, when the presidential nomination that he hoped would come his way again went instead to his successor as governor of New York, Franklin D. Roosevelt.

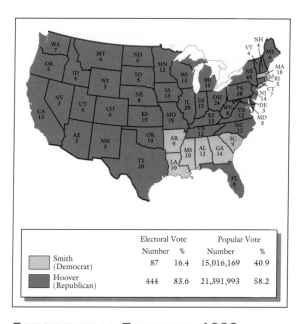

	Electoral Vote		Popular Vote	
	Number	%	Number	%
Smith (Democrat)	87	16.4	15,016,169	40.9
Hoover (Republican)	444	83.6	21,391,993	58.2

PRESIDENTIAL ELECTION, 1928

in the nation's 12 largest cities. European American ethnics would yet have their day.

AFRICAN AMERICANS

Despite the urban race riots of 1919 (see chapter 23), African Americans continued to leave their rural homes for the industrial centers of the South and the North. In the 1920s alone, nearly a million blacks traveled North. In New York City and Chicago, their numbers grew so large—300,000 in New York and 234,000 in Chicago—that they formed cities unto themselves. When word of New York City's urban black enclave reached the Caribbean, thousands of West Indian blacks set off for Harlem. Within these black metropolises emerged complex societies consisting of workers, businessmen, professionals, intellectuals, artists, and entertainers. Social differentiation intensified as various groups—long-resident northerners and newly arrived southerners, religious conservatives and cultural radicals, African Americans and African Caribbeans—found reason to disapprove of one another's ways. Still, the diversity and complexity of urban black America were thrilling, nowhere more so than in Harlem, the "Negro capital." Black writer James Weldon Johnson described Harlem in the 1920s:

> Throughout colored America Harlem is the recognized Negro capital. Indeed, it is Mecca for the sightseer, the pleasure-seeker, the curious, the adventurous, the enterprising, the ambitious, and the talented of the entire Negro world. . . . Not merely a colony or a community or a settlement—not at all a "quarter" or a slum or a fringe—[Harlem is] . . . a black city, located in the heart of white Manhattan, and containing more Negroes to the square mile than any other spot on earth. It strikes the uninformed observer as a phenomenon, a miracle straight out of the skies.

Not even the glamour of Harlem could erase the reality of racial discrimination, however. Most African Americans could find work only in New York City's least-desired and lowest-paying jobs. Because they could rent apartments only in areas that real estate agents and banks had designated as "colored," African Americans suffered the highest rate of residential segregation of any minority group. Although Harlem had its fashionable districts where affluent blacks lived, most of the housing stock was poor and rents were high. Harlem became a black ghetto, an area set apart from the rest of the city by the skin color of its inhabitants, by its higher population density and poverty rate, by its higher incidence of infectious diseases, and by the lower life expectancy of its people.

Blacks did enjoy some important economic breakthroughs in the 1920s. Henry Ford, for example, hired large numbers of African Americans to work in his Detroit auto factories. Even here, however, a racist logic was operating, for Ford believed that black and white workers, divided along racial lines, would not challenge his authority. Until the 1940s, in fact, unions made less headway at Ford plants than at the plants of other major automobile manufacturers.

African Americans grew pessimistic about achieving racial equality. After Marcus Garvey's black nationalist movement collapsed in the mid-1920s (see chapter 23), no comparable organization arose to take

DEATH RATES FROM SELECTED CAUSES FOR NEW YORK CITY RESIDENTS, 1925

Cause of Death	Total Population	African American Population
General death rate (per 1,000 population)	11.4	16.5
Pneumonia	132.8	282.4
Pulmonary tuberculosis	75.5	258.4
Infant mortality (per 1,000 live births)	64.6	118.4
Maternal mortality (per 1,000 total births)	5.3	10.2
Stillbirths (per 1,000 births)	47.6	82.7
Homicide	5.3	19.5
Suicide	14.8	9.7

Note: Rate is per 100,000 population, unless noted
Source: Cheryl Lynn Greenberg, *"Or Does It Explode?" Black Harlem in the Great Depression* (New York: Oxford University Press, 1991), p. 32.

its place. The NAACP continued to fight racial discrimination, and the Urban League carried on quiet negotiations with industrial elites to open up jobs to African Americans. Black socialists led by A. Philip Randolph built a strong all-black union, the Brotherhood of Sleeping Car Porters, but the victories were small; white allies were scarce. The political initiatives emerging among European ethnics had few counterparts in the African American community.

In terms of black culture, however, the 1920s were vigorous and productive. Black musicians coming north to Chicago and New York brought with them their distinctive musical styles, most notably the blues and ragtime. Influenced by the harmonies and techniques of European classical music, which black musicians learned from their European ethnic counterparts, these southern styles metamorphosed into jazz. Urban audiences, first black and then white, found this new music alluring. They responded to its melodies, its sensuality, its creativity, its savvy. In Chicago, Detroit, New York, New Orleans, and elsewhere, jazz musicians came together in cramped apartments, cabarets, and nightclubs to jam, compete, and entertain. Willie Smith, Charles P. Johnson, Count Basie, Fats Waller, Duke Ellington, and Louis Armstrong were among the most famous musicians of the day. By the late 1920s they were being hailed in Europe as well.

JAZZ COMES OF AGE Jazz music became enormously popular in the 1920s in the United States and Europe. Trumpet player Louis Armstrong, third from the left (in rear), became one of the most celebrated and innovative jazz performers.

Jazz seemed to express something quintessentially modern. Jazz musicians broke free of convention, improvised, and produced new sounds that gave rise to new sensations. Both blacks and whites found in jazz an escape from the routine, the predictability, and the conventions of their everyday lives.

THE HARLEM RENAISSANCE

Paralleling the emergence of jazz was a black literary and artistic awakening known as the Harlem Renaissance. Black novelists, poets, painters, sculptors, and playwrights set about creating works rooted in their own culture instead of imitating the styles of white Europeans and Americans. The movement had begun during the war, when blacks sensed that they might at last be advancing to full equality. It was symbolized by the image of the "New Negro," who would no longer be deferential to whites but who would display his or her independence through talent and determination. The "New Negro" would be assertive in every field—at work, in politics, in the military, and in arts and letters. As racial discrimination intensified after the war, cultural activities took on special significance. The world of culture was the one place where blacks could express their racial pride and demonstrate their talent.

Langston Hughes, a young black poet, said of the Harlem Renaissance: "We younger Negro artists who create now intend to express our individual dark-skinned selves without fear or shame. If white people are pleased, we are glad. If they are not, it doesn't matter. We know we are beautiful. And ugly, too." Writers Claude McKay, Jean Toomer, and Zora Neale Hurston; poet Countee Cullen; and painter Aaron Douglas were other prominent Renaissance participants. In 1925, *Survey Graphic*, a white liberal magazine, devoted an entire issue to "Harlem—the Mecca of the New Negro." Alain Locke, an art and literary critic and professor of philosophy at Howard University in Washington, D.C., edited both the issue and the book *The New Negro*, published later that year. Locke became the movement's leading visionary and philosopher.

But even these cultural advances failed to escape white prejudice. The most popular jazz nightclubs in Harlem, most of which were owned and operated by whites, refused to admit black customers. The only African Americans permitted inside were the jazz musicians, singers and dancers, prostitutes,

Major League Baseball in White and Black

The popularity of baseball soared to new heights in the 1920s. New York Yankees slugger George Herman "Babe" Ruth became the biggest star that the sport had ever known. In 1923, his team began playing in the nation's newest and largest sports venue, Yankee Stadium, built to hold the millions who wanted to see the "Babe" play. The 1927 Yankees, with Ruth batting fourth and a younger slugger, Lou Gehrig, batting fifth, established themselves as one of the greatest teams in baseball history, winning 110 games and losing only 44 (both Ruth and Gehrig appear below in the third row of the Yankees' 1927 team photo, Ruth fourth from left, and

Gehrig eighth from right). Ruth set his most famous record that year: 60 home runs. In 1930, the Yankees' home city population was 70 percent European immigrants and their children; many immigrant children came to love America through their love of baseball.

African Americans loved baseball, too, and Ruth enjoyed a large black following. But African Americans were themselves barred from playing in the lily-white major leagues. They formed their own "Negro Leagues" in the United States and played in Mexico and the Caribbean, where they earned extra income and escaped the racial prejudice that met them every-

and kitchen help. Moreover, the musicians had to play what the white patrons wanted to hear. Duke Ellington, for example, featured "jungle music," which for whites revealed the "true" African soul—sensual, innocent, primitive. Such pressures curtailed the artistic freedom of musicians and reinforced racist stereotypes of African Americans as

inferior people who were closer to nature than the "more civilized" white audiences who came to hear their music.

Artists and writers experienced similar pressures. Many of them depended for their sustenance on the support of wealthy white patrons. Those patrons were generous, but they wanted a return on their

where in the United States. Cuba, Puerto Rico, Mexico, and other countries in which African Americans played, did not organize baseball along racial lines.

The greatest team in Negro League history may well have been the Pittsburgh Crawfords, pictured here after winning the 1935 championship of the Negro National League. Its roster included Josh Gibson, "the black Babe Ruth" (fifth from right), who hit more than 70 home runs in 1931 and is thought to have hit 1,000 during his career; and celebrated pitcher Leroy "Satchel" Paige, who claimed to have won 2,000 games. Paige pitched in the major leagues after Jackie Robinson broke the color line in 1947, and won the 1948 Rookie of the Year Award in the American League at the age of 42.

Many years later, these and other black stars would be inducted into the Major League Baseball Hall of Fame, a belated recognition of their achievements during the era of segregated baseball.

investment. Charlotte Mason, the New York City matron who supported Hughes and Hurston, for example, felt free to judge their work and expected them to entertain her friends by demonstrating "authentic Negritude." Hurston accepted this role, but for Hughes it became intolerable. Both Hughes and Hurston paid a price for their patron's support,

including the collapse of their once-close friendship.

MEXICAN AMERICANS

After the Johnson-Reed Act of 1924, Mexicans became the country's chief source of immigrant labor.

HISTORY THROUGH FILM

The Jazz Singer (1927)
**Directed by Alan Crosland. Starring Al Jolson (Jake Rabinowitz/Jack Robin),
May McAvoy (Mary Dale), Warner Oland (Cantor Rabinowitz).**

The Jazz Singer was a sensation when it opened, for it was the first movie to use sound (although relatively few words of dialogue were actually spoken). It also starred Al Jolson, the era's most popular Broadway entertainer, and bravely explored an issue that the film industry usually avoided—the religious culture and generational dynamics of a "new immigrant" family.

The movie focuses on Jake Rabinowitz and his immigrant parents, who are Jewish and devout. Jake's father is a fifth-generation cantor whose job it is to fill his New York City synagogue with ancient and uplifting melodies every Sabbath and Jewish holiday. Cantor Rabinowitz looks upon his work as sacred, and he expects Jake one day to take his place. Jake has other ideas. He loves music but is drawn to the new rhythmic ragtime and sensual jazz melodies emerging from his American surroundings. In an early scene, we encounter Jake at a dance hall, absorbed in playing and singing ragtime tunes and forgetting that he should be at home preparing for Yom Kippur, the holiest day in the Jewish calendar. His distraught father finds him and whips him, and Jake, in anger and pain, runs away.

Jake's break with his family allows him to pursue his passion for American song and to reinvent himself as "Jack Robin," the jazz singer. A relationship with a prominent (and non-Jewish) stage actress, Mary Dale, brings him a starring role in a Broadway show. Jack hopes to use his return to New York to reconcile with his father. This eventually happens when Jake, on the eve of Yom Kippur once again, agrees to skip his show's premiere in order to take his ailing father's place as cantor in the synagogue. Jake's melodies soar to the heavens and reach his bedridden father who, upon thinking that his son has succeeded him as cantor and thus fulfilled his (the father's) deepest wish, peacefully and contentedly dies.

The movie, ultimately, rejects the father's insistence that Jake must choose between the Old World and the New, between Judaism and America. After Yom Kippur ends, Jake returns to his Broadway show and to his non-Jewish lover and, with his approving mother in the audience, delivers an outstanding performance that secures his reputation as the "Jazz Singer."

A total of 500,000 Mexicans came north in the 1920s. Some headed for the steel, auto, and meatpacking plants of the Midwest, but most settled in the Southwest, where they worked on the railroads and in construction, agriculture, and manufacturing. In Texas 3 of every 4 construction workers and 8 of every 10 migrant farm workers were Mexicans. An official of the San Antonio Chamber of Commerce declared: "Mexican farm labor is rapidly proving the making of this State." In California, Mexican immigrants made up 75 percent of the state's agricultural workforce.

Mexican farm laborers in Texas worked long hours for little money. As a rule, they earned 50 cents to a dollar less per day than Anglo workers. They were usually barred from becoming machine operators or assuming other skilled positions. Forced to follow the crops, they had little opportunity to develop settled homes and communities. Mexican farm workers depended for shelter on whatever facilities farm owners offered. Because farm owners rarely required the services of Mexican workers for more than several days or weeks, few were willing to spend the money required to provide decent homes and schools. Houses typically lacked even wooden floors or indoor plumbing. Mexican laborers found it difficult to protest these conditions. Their knowledge of English and

Today, watching the movie raises questions about its optimistic belief that America permits resolution of even the most serious conflicts between immigrant parents and American-born children. Jake's blackface routine—his use of burnt cork to turn his face and neck black and thus to appear to audiences as a "black" performer—also draws attention. In this performance style—minstrelsy—dating from the 19th century and still popular when the movie was made, white entertainers "blacked up" in order both to appropriate and to ridicule expressive aspects of black culture. That it appears in this movie seems puzzling: why would an individual whose change of name (from Jake Rabinowitz to Jack Robin) reveals his desire to hide his own new immigrant past cast himself as a member of a group (African Americans) whose status was lower and more vulnerable than that of new immigrants? There is no easy answer to this question, except to suggest that the minstrel act was so transparent—everyone in the audience knew that the performer was really white and not black—that it became a way for someone who belonged to a group whose "racial fitness" had been challenged to secure his membership in America's white race. By the terms of the minstrel routine, anyone who blacked up was, by definition, white and thus a "good American." Ironically, then, blacking up may have been a way for a Jake Rabinowitz to complete his Americanizing journey from immigrant outsider to white insider.

A German poster advertising *The Jazz Singer*. Al Jolson is shown in blackface.

of American law was limited. Few owned cars or trucks that would have allowed them to escape a bad employer and search for a good one. Many were in debt to employers who had advanced them money and who threatened them with jail if they failed to fulfill the terms of their contract. Others feared deportation; they lacked visas, having slipped into the United States illegally rather than pay the immigrant tax or endure harassment from the Border Patrol.

Increasing numbers of Mexican immigrants, however, found their way to California, where daily wages for agricultural work sometimes exceeded those in Texas by as much as 80 percent. Some escaped agricultural labor altogether for construction and manufacturing jobs in midwestern and southwestern cities. Thousands had worked on building military installations in San Antonio during the war, and by 1920 the 40,000 immigrants who lived there comprised the largest Mexican community in the United States. As the decade progressed, that distinction shifted to Los Angeles, where a rapidly growing Mexican population reached 100,000 by 1930. Mexican men in Los Angeles worked in the city's large railroad yards, at the city's numerous construction sites, as unskilled workers in local factories, and as agricultural workers in the fruit and vegetable fields of Los Angeles County. Mexican

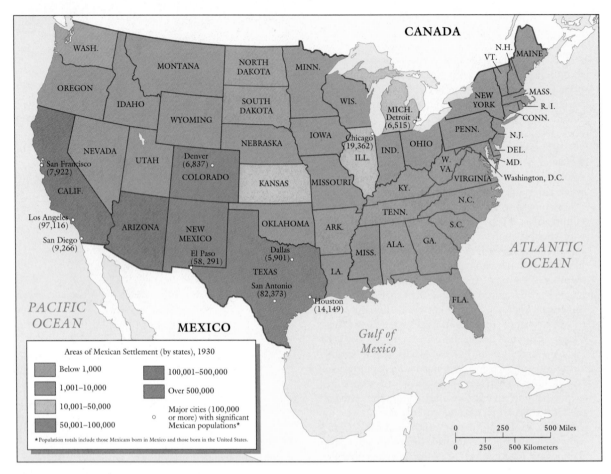

MEXICAN POPULATION IN THE UNITED STATES, 1930

women labored in the city's garment shops, fish canneries, and food processing plants.

The Los Angeles Mexican American community increased in complexity as it grew in size. By the mid-1920s it included a growing professional class, a proud group of *californios* (Spanish-speakers who had been resident in California for generations), many musicians and entertainers, a small but energetic band of entrepreneurs and businessmen, conservative clerics and intellectuals who had fled or been expelled from revolutionary Mexico, and Mexican government officials who had been sent to counter the influence of the conservative exiles and to strengthen the ties of the immigrants to their homeland. This diverse mix gave rise to much internal conflict, but it also generated considerable cultural vitality. Indeed, Los Angeles became the same kind of magnet for Mexican Americans that Harlem had be-

come for African Americans. Mexican musicians flocked to Los Angeles, as did Mexican playwrights. The city supported a vigorous Spanish-language theater. Mexican musicians performed on street corners, at ethnic festivals and weddings, at cabarets, and on the radio. Especially popular were folk ballads, called *corridos*, that spoke to the experiences of Mexican immigrants. Although different in form and melody from the African American blues, *corridos* resembled the blues in their emphasis on the suffering, hope, and frustrations of ordinary folk.

This flowering of Mexican American culture in Los Angeles could not erase the low wages, high rates of infant mortality, racial discrimination, and other hardships Mexicans faced; nor did it encourage Mexicans, in Los Angeles or elsewhere, to mobilize themselves as a political force. Unlike European immigrants, Mexican immigrants showed

"LOS MADRUGADORES" Led by Pedro J. Gonzalez (seated, on left), this popular Mexican group sang corridos in live performances and on KMPC, a Spanish-language radio station in 1920s Los Angeles.

little interest in becoming American citizens and acquiring the vote. Yet, the cultural vibrancy of the Mexican immigrant community did sustain many individuals who were struggling to survive in a strange, and often hostile, environment.

THE "LOST GENERATION" AND DISILLUSIONED INTELLECTUALS

Many native-born white artists and intellectuals also felt uneasy in America in the 1920s. Their unease arose not from poverty or discrimination but from alienation. They despaired of American culture and regarded the average American as anti-intellectual, small-minded, materialistic, and puritanical. Many

fled to Europe, and those who remained walled themselves off from contact with the masses. H. L. Mencken once described the American people as "a timorous, sniveling, poltroonish, ignominious mob." The novelist Sinclair Lewis ridiculed small-town Americans in *Main Street* (1920), "sophisticated" city dwellers in *Babbitt* (1922), physicians in *Arrowsmith* (1925), and evangelicals in *Elmer Gantry* (1927).

Before the First World War intellectuals and artists had been deeply engaged with "the people," some as progressive reformers, some as radicals. Although they were critical of many aspects of American society, they believed that they could help bring about a new politics and improve social conditions. Some of them joined the war effort before the United States had officially intervened. Ernest Hemingway, John Dos Passos, and E. E. Cummings, among others, sailed to Europe and volunteered their services to the Allies, usually as ambulance drivers carrying wounded soldiers from the front. They found little idealism in the trenches, however—only disease and death.

America's intellectuals were shocked by the war's effect on American society. The wartime push for consensus created intolerance of radicals, immigrants, and blacks. Intellectuals had been further dismayed by Prohibition, the rebirth of the Ku Klux Klan, the rise of fundamentalism, and the executions of Sacco and Vanzetti. Not only had many Americans embraced conformity for themselves, but they seemed determined to force conformity on others. The young critic Harold Stearns wrote in 1921 that "the most moving and pathetic fact in the social life of America today is emotional and aesthetic starvation." Before these words were published, Stearns had sailed for France. So many alienated young men like Stearns showed up in Paris that Gertrude Stein, an American writer whose Paris apartment became a gathering place for them, took to calling them the "Lost Generation."

Their indictment of America was not always justified. Most of these writers and intellectuals were young and inexperienced, with little knowledge of how most Americans lived. Few expressed sympathy for the plight of farmers or the working-class poor. Few knew much about the rich cultural heritage of immigrant communities. Still, they managed to convert their disillusionment into a new literary sensibility. The finest works of the decade focused on the psychological toll of living in what the poet T. S. Eliot referred to as *The Waste Land* (1922). F. Scott

THE GREAT GATSBY F. Scott Fitzgerald emerged as a major American novelist with publication of *The Great Gatsby*. Like so much of the best 1920s fiction, *Gatsby* tells the story of a man's disillusionment and ruin.

Fitzgerald's novel *The Great Gatsby* (1925) told of a man destroyed by his desire to be accepted into a world of wealth, fancy cars, and fast women. In the novel *A Farewell to Arms* (1929), Ernest Hemingway wrote of an American soldier overwhelmed by the senselessness and brutality of war who deserts the army for the company of a woman he loves. Playwright Eugene O'Neill created characters haunted by despair, loneliness, and unfulfilled longing. Writers created innovations in style as well as in content. Sherwood Anderson, in his novel *Winesburg, Ohio* (1919), blended fiction and autobiography. John Dos Passos, in *Manhattan Transfer* (1925), mixed journalism with more traditional literary methods. Hemingway wrote in an understated, laconic prose that somehow drew attention to his characters' rage and vulnerability.

White Southern writers found a tragic sensibility surviving from the South's defeat in the Civil War that spoke to their own loss of hope. One group of writers, calling themselves "the Agrarians," argued that the enduring agricultural character of their region offered a more hopeful path to the future than did the mass-production and mass-consumption regime that had overtaken the North. In 1929 William Faulkner published *The Sound and the Fury*, the first in a series of novels set in northern Mississippi's fictional Yoknapatawpha County. Faulkner explored the violence and terror that marked relationships among family members and townspeople, while at the same time maintaining compassion and understanding. Faulkner, Lewis, Hemingway, O'Neill, and Eliot each received the Nobel Prize for Literature.

DEMOCRACY ON THE DEFENSIVE

Their disdain for the masses led many intellectuals to question democracy itself. If ordinary people were as stupid, prejudiced, and easily manipulated as they seemed, how could they be entrusted with the fate of the nation? Although few intellectuals were as frank as Mencken, who dismissed democracy as "the worship of jackals by jackasses," their distrust of democracy ran deep. Walter Lippmann, a former radical and progressive, declared that modern society had rendered democracy obsolete. In his view, average citizens, buffeted by propaganda emanating from powerful opinion makers, could no longer make the kind of informed, rational judgments needed to make democracy work. They were vulnerable to demagogues who played on their emotions and fears. Lippmann's solution, and that of many other political commentators, was to shift government power from the people to educated elites. Those elites, who would be appointed rather than elected, would conduct foreign and domestic policy in an informed, intelligent way. Only then, in Lippmann's view, could government be effective and just.

Mencken and Lippmann enjoyed especially strong influence and prestige among university students, whose ranks and political significance were growing. But their antidemocratic views did not go uncontested. The philosopher John Dewey, who taught at Columbia University but whose reputation and influence extended well beyond academia, was the most articulate spokesman for the "prodemocracy" position. He acknowledged that the concentration of power in a few giant organizations had eroded the authority of Congress, the presidency, and other democratic institutions, but democracy, he insisted, was not doomed. The people could reclaim their freedom by making big business subject to government control. The government could use its power to democratize corporations and to regulate the communications industry to ensure that every citizen had access to the facts needed to make reasonable, informed political decisions.

Dewey's views attracted the support of a wide range of liberal intellectuals and reformers, including Robert and Helen Lynd; Rexford Tugwell, professor of economics at Columbia; and Felix Frankfurter, a rising star at Harvard's law school. Some of these activists had ties to labor leaders and to New York Governor Franklin D. Roosevelt. They formed the vanguard of a new liberal movement committed to taking up the work the progressives had left unfinished.

But these reformers were utterly without power, except in a few states. The Republican Party had driven reformers from its ranks. The Democratic Party was a fallen giant, crippled by a split between its principal constituencies—rural Protestants and urban ethnics—over Prohibition, immigration restriction, and the Ku Klux Klan. The labor movement was moribund. The Socialist Party had never recovered from the trauma of war and Bolshevism. La Follette's Farmer-Labor Party, after a promising debut, had stalled. John Dewey and his friends tried to launch yet another third party, but they failed to raise money or arouse mass support.

Reformers took little comfort in the presidential election of 1928. Hoover's smashing victory suggested that the trends of the 1920s—the dominance of the Republicans, the centrality of Prohibition to political debate, the paralysis of the Democrats, the growing economic might of capitalism, and the pervasive influence of the consumer culture—would continue unabated.

CONCLUSION

Signs abounded in the 1920s that Americans were creating a new and bountiful society. The increased accessibility of cars, radios, vacuum cleaners, and other consumer durables; rising real wages, low unemployment, and installment buying; the widening circle of stock owners; and the spread of welfare capitalism—all these pointed to an economy that had become more prosperous, more consumer-oriented, even somewhat more egalitarian. Moves to greater equality within marriage and to enhanced liberty for single women suggested that economic change was propelling social change as well.

Even so, many working-class and rural Americans benefited little from the decade's prosperity. And the changes aroused resistance, especially from white farmers and small-town Americans who feared that the rapid growth of cities and the large urban settlements of European and Mexican Catholics, Jews, and African Americans were rendering their Protestant America unrecognizable.

In the Democratic Party, farmers, small-town Americans, and moral traditionalists fought bitterly against the growing power of urban, ethnic constituencies. Elsewhere, the traditionalists battled hard to protect religion's authority against the inroads of science and to purge the nation of "inferior" population streams. In the process they arrayed themselves against American traditions of liberty and equality, even as they posed as the defenders of the best that America had to offer.

Their resistance to change caused many of the nation's most talented artists and writers to turn away from their fellow Americans in disgust. Meanwhile, although ethnic and racial minorities experienced high levels of discrimination, they nevertheless found enough freedom to create vibrant ethnic and racial communities and to launch projects—as in the case of African Americans in Harlem and Mexican Americans in Los Angeles—of cultural renaissance.

The Republican Party, having largely shed its reputation for reform, took credit for engineering the new economy of consumer plenty. It looked forward to years of political dominance. A steep and unexpected economic depression, however, would soon dash that expectation, revive the Democratic Party, and destroy Republican political power for a generation.

Suggested Readings begin on page SR-1.
For Web activities and resources
related to this chapter, go to
http://www.harcourtcollege.com/history.murrin

CHAPTER 25

THE GREAT DEPRESSION AND THE NEW DEAL, 1929–1939

Detroit Industry, North Wall, 1932–33, Diego Rivera. Gift of Edsel B. Ford. Photograph © 1991 The Detroit Institute of Arts.

DETROIT INDUSTRY

This picture depicts part of the mural that the Mexican artist Diego Rivera painted for the walls of the Detroit Art Museum in 1932–33. The mural conveys both the awesome size of Detroit's industrial plants and the centrality of workers to their operation. Rivera's work, like that of other 1930s artists, suggested that industrial workers stood at the very heart of American civilization and that they would play a key role in rehabilitating an economy devastated by depression.

The Great Depression began on October 29, 1929—"Black Tuesday"—with a spectacular stock market crash. On that one day, stock values plummeted $14 billion. By the end of that year, stock prices had fallen 50 percent from their September highs. By 1932, the worst year of the depression, they had fallen another 30 percent. In three years, $74 billion of wealth had simply vanished. Meanwhile the unemployment rate had soared to 25 percent.

Many Americans who lived through the Great Depression could never forget the scenes of misery that they saw on every hand. In cities, the poor meekly awaited their turn for a piece of stale bread and thin gruel at ill-funded soup kitchens. Scavengers poked through garbage cans for food, scoured railroad tracks for coal that had fallen from trains, and sometimes ripped up railroad ties for fuel. Hundreds of thousands of Americans built makeshift shelters out of cardboard, scrap metal, and whatever else they could find in the city dump. They called their towns "Hoovervilles," after the president whom they despised for his apparent refusal to help them.

The Great Depression brought cultural crisis as well as economic crisis. In the 1920s American

VICTIMS OF THE DEPRESSION This image evokes the hardship of the 1930s in the form of a strong, able-bodied man in the prime of his life who is unable to find work and must depend on charity.

business leaders had successfully redefined the national culture in business terms, as Americans' values became synonymous with the values of business: economic growth, freedom of enterprise and acquisitiveness. But the swagger and bluster of American businessmen during the 1920s made them vulnerable to attack in the 1930s, as jobs, incomes, and growth all disappeared. With the prestige of business and business values in decline, how could Americans regain their hope and recover their confidence in the future? The first years of the 1930s held no convincing answers.

The gloom broke in early 1933 when Franklin Delano Roosevelt became president and unleashed the power of government to regulate capitalist enterprises, to restore the economy to health, and to guarantee the social welfare of Americans unable to help themselves. Roosevelt called his progovernment program a "new deal for the American people," and it would dominate national politics for the next 40 years. Hailed as a hero, Roosevelt became (and remains) the only president to serve more than two terms. In the short term, the New Deal failed to restore prosperity to America, but the "liberalism" it championed found acceptance among millions, who agreed with Roosevelt that only a large and powerful government could guarantee Americans their liberty.

This chapter will focus on the following major questions:

- What caused the "Crash of 1929," and why did the ensuing depression last so long?
- What were the First and Second New Deals? What were their similarities and differences? When and why did one give way to the other?
- Which groups in American society benefited most from the New Deal and which benefited least?
- In what ways did the New Deal affect American culture?

CAUSES OF THE GREAT DEPRESSION

America had experienced other depressions, or "panics," and no one would have been surprised had the boom of the 1920s been followed by one- or two-year economic downturn. No one was pre-

pared, however, for the economic catastrophe of the 1930s.

STOCK MARKET SPECULATION

In 1928 and 1929 the New York Stock Exchange had undergone a remarkable run-up in prices. In less than two years, the Dow Jones Industrial Average had doubled. Money had poured into the market, but many investors were buying on 10 percent "margin"—putting up only 10 percent of the price of a stock and borrowing the rest from brokers or banks. Few thought they would ever have to repay these loans with money out of their own pockets. Instead, investors expected to resell their shares within a few months at dramatically higher prices, pay back their loans from the proceeds, and still clear a handsome profit. And, for a while, that is exactly what they did. In 1928 alone, for example, RCA stock value soared 400 percent.

The possibility of making a fortune by investing only a few thousand dollars only intensified investors' greed. As speculation became rampant, money flowed indiscriminately into all kinds of risky enterprises. The stock market spiraled upward, out of control. When, in October 1929, confidence in future earnings finally faltered, creditors began demanding that investors who had bought stocks on margin repay their loans. The market crashed from its dizzying heights.

Still, the crash, by itself, fails to explain why the Great Depression lasted as long as it did. Poor decision making by the Federal Reserve Board, an ill-advised tariff that took effect soon after the depression hit, and a lopsided concentration of wealth in the hands of the rich deepened the economic collapse and made recovery more difficult.

MISTAKES BY THE FEDERAL RESERVE BOARD

In 1930 and 1931, the Federal Reserve curtailed the amount of money in circulation and raised interest rates, thereby making credit more difficult for the public to secure. Although employing such a tight money policy during the boom years of 1928 or 1929 might have restrained the stock market and strengthened the economy, it was disastrous once the market had crashed. What the economy needed in 1930 and

1931 was an expanded money supply, lower interest rates, and easier credit. Such a course would have enabled debtors to pay their creditors. Instead, by choosing the opposite course, the Federal Reserve plunged an economy starved for credit deeper into depression. Higher interest rates also triggered an international crisis, as the banks of Germany and Austria, heavily dependent on U.S. loans, went bankrupt. The German-Austrian collapse, in turn, spread financial panic through Europe and ruined many U.S. manufacturers and banks specializing in European trade and investment.

AN ILL-ADVISED TARIFF

The Tariff Act of 1930, also known as the Hawley-Smoot Tariff Act, accelerated economic decline abroad and at home. Throughout the 1920s, agricultural interests had sought higher tariffs to protect American farmers against foreign competition. But Hawley-Smoot not only raised tariffs on 75 agricultural goods from 32 to 40 percent (the highest rate in American history); it also raised tariffs by a similar percentage on 925 manufactured products. Industrialists had convinced their supporters in the Republican-controlled Congress that such protection would give American industry much needed assistance. The legislation was a disaster. Angry foreign governments retaliated by raising their own tariff rates to keep out American goods. International trade, already weakened by the tight credit policies of the Federal Reserve, took another blow at the very moment when it desperately needed a boost. Shortsighted U.S. monetary and trade policies spread economic crisis throughout the western industrialized world.

A MALDISTRIBUTION OF WEALTH

A serious maldistribution in the nation's wealth that had developed in the 1920s also stymied economic recovery. Although average income rose in the 1920s, the incomes of the wealthiest families rose higher than the rest. Between 1918 and 1929 the share of the national income that went to the wealthiest 20 percent of the population rose by more than 10 percent, while the share that went to the poorest 60 percent fell by almost 13 percent. The Coolidge administration contributed to this maldistribution

CHRONOLOGY

1929 Herbert Hoover assumes the presidency • Stock market crashes on "Black Tuesday"

1930 Tariff Act (Hawley-Smoot) raises tariffs

1931 2,000 U.S. banks fail • Austrian bank failure triggers European depression

1932 Unemployment rate reaches 25 percent • Reconstruction Finance Corporation established • Bonus Army marches on Washington • Roosevelt defeats Hoover for presidency

1933 Roosevelt assumes presidency • "Hundred Days" legislation defines First New Deal (March–June) • Roosevelt administration recognizes the Soviet Union • "Good Neighbor Policy" toward Latin America launched • Reciprocal Trade Agreement lowers tariffs

1934 Father Charles Coughlin and Huey Long challenge conservatism of First New Deal • 2,000 strikes staged across country • Democrats overwhelm Republicans in off-year election • Radical political movements emerge in Wisconsin, Minnesota, Washington, and California • Indian Reorganization Act restores tribal land, provides funds, and grants limited right of self-government to Native Americans

1935 Committee for Industrial Organization (CIO) formed • Supreme Court declares NRA unconstitutional • Roosevelt unveils his Second New Deal • Congress passes Social Security Act • National Labor Relations Act (Wagner Act) guarantees workers' right to join unions • Holding Company Act breaks up utilities' near-monopoly • Congress passes Wealth Tax Act • Emergency Relief Administration Act passed; funds Works Progress Administration and other projects • Rural Electrification Administration established • Number of Mexican immigrants returning to Mexico reaches 500,000

1936 Roosevelt defeats Alf Landon for second term • Supreme Court declares AAA unconstitutional • Congress passes Soil Conservation and Domestic Allotment Act to replace AAA • Farm Security Administration established

1937 United Auto Workers defeat General Motors in sit-down strike • Roosevelt attempts to "pack" the Supreme Court • Supreme Court upholds constitutionality of Social Security and National Labor Relations acts • Severe recession hits

1938 Conservative opposition to New Deal does well in off-year election • Superman comic debuts

1939 75,000 gather to hear Marian Anderson sing at Lincoln Memorial

INCOME DISTRIBUTION BEFORE THE GREAT DEPRESSION

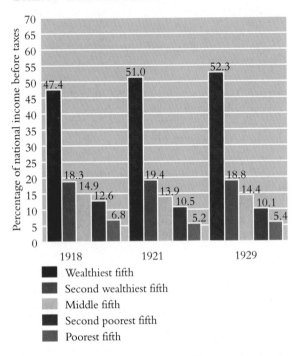

Source: From Gabriel Kolko, *Wealth and Power in America: An Analysis of Social Class and Income Distribution* (New York: Praeger, 1962), p. 14.

by lowering taxes on the wealthy, thereby increasing the proportion of the national wealth concentrated in their hands. The deepening inequality of income distribution slowed consumption and held back the growth of consumer-oriented industries (cars, household appliances, processed and packaged foods, recreation), the most dynamic elements of the U.S. economy. Even when the rich spent their money lavishly—building huge mansions, buying expensive cars, vacationing on the French Riviera— they still spent a smaller proportion of their total incomes on consumption than wage earners did. The average 1920s wage earner might spend one-quarter to one-half of annual earnings to buy a car.

Putting more of the total increase in national income into the pockets of average Americans during the 1920s would have steadied the demand for consumer goods and kept the newer consumer industries correspondingly stronger. Such an economy might have recovered relatively quickly from the stock market crash of 1929. Instead, recovery from

the Great Depression lagged until 1941, more than a decade later.

HOOVER: THE FALL OF A SELF-MADE MAN

In 1928 Herbert Hoover seemed to represent living proof that anyone who was willing to work for it could realize the American dream. Circumstances that would have deterred others—the loss of both parents at an early age, being raised by relatives with little money—seemed only to intensify Hoover's ambition. At Stanford University he majored in geology, and after graduation worked on mining expeditions in many parts of the world. As he rose quickly through corporate ranks, Hoover's managerial skills brought him more demanding and more handsomely rewarded tasks. By the age of 40, he had become a millionaire.

Hoover's government service began during the First World War, when he won an international reputation for his expert management of agricultural production in the United States and his success in feeding millions of European soldiers and civilians. In the 1920s, he served as an active and influential secretary of commerce (see chapters 23 and 24). As the decade wound down, no American seemed better qualified to become president of the United States, an office that Hoover assumed in March 1929. Hoover was certain he could make prosperity a permanent feature of American life. "We in America today are nearer to the final triumph over poverty than ever before in the history of any land," he declared in August 1928. A little more than a year later, the Great Depression struck.

HOOVER'S PROGRAM

Within a short time after the stock market collapse, the depression had spread to nearly every sector of the economy. To cope with the crisis, Hoover first turned to the associational principles he had followed as secretary of commerce (see chapter 24). He encouraged organizations of farmers, industrialists, and bankers to share information, bolster one another's spirits, and devise policies to aid economic recovery. Farmers would restrict output, industrialists would hold wages at predepression levels, and bankers would help each other remain solvent. The federal government would provide them with information, strategies of mutual aid, occasional loans, and morale-boosting speeches.

Hoover, to his credit, pursued a more aggressive set of economic policies once he realized that associationalism had failed to improve economic conditions. To ease the European crisis, Hoover secured a one-year moratorium on loan payments that European governments owed American banks. He steered through Congress the Glass-Steagall Act of 1932, intended to help American banks meet the demands of European depositors who wished to convert their dollars to gold. And to ease the crisis at home he began to expand the government's economic role. The Reconstruction Finance Corporation (RFC), created in 1932, made two billion dollars available in loans to ailing banks and to corporations willing to build low-cost housing, bridges, and other public works. The RFC was the biggest federal peacetime intervention in the economy to that point in American history. The Home Loan Bank Board, set up that same year, offered funds to savings and loans, mortgage companies, and other financial institutions that lent money for home construction.

Despite this new government activism, Hoover was uncomfortable with the idea that the government was responsible for restoring the nation's economic welfare. In 1932 RFC expenditures gave rise to the largest peacetime deficit in U.S. history, prompting Hoover to try to balance the federal budget. He supported the Revenue Act of 1932, which tried to increase government revenues by raising taxes, thus erasing the deficit. He also insisted that the RFC issue loans only to relatively healthy institutions that were capable of repaying them and that it favor public works, such as toll bridges, that were likely to become self-financing. As a result of these constraints, the RFC spent considerably less than Congress had mandated.

Hoover was especially reluctant to engage the government in providing relief to unemployed and homeless Americans. To give money to the poor, he insisted, would destroy their desire to work, undermine their sense of self-worth, and erode their capacity for citizenship.

Hoover saw no similar peril in extending government assistance to ailing banks and businesses. Critics pointed to the seeming hypocrisy of Hoover's policies. For example, in 1930 Hoover refused a request of $25 million to help feed Arkansas farmers and their families but approved $45 million to feed the same farmers' livestock. And in 1932, shortly after rejecting an urgent request from Chicago for aid to help pay its teachers and municipal workers, Hoover approved a $90 million loan to rescue that city's Central Republic Bank.

THE BONUS ARMY

In the spring of 1932 a group of army veterans mounted a particularly emotional challenge to Hoover's policies. In 1924 Congress had authorized a thousand-dollar bonus for First World War veterans in the form of compensation certificates that would mature in 1945. Now the veterans were demanding that the government pay the bonus immediately. A group of Portland, Oregon, veterans decided to take action. Calling themselves the Bonus Expeditionary Force, they hopped onto empty boxcars of freight trains heading east, determined to

THE BONUS ARMY'S ENCAMPMENT SET ABLAZE U.S. troops under the command of General Douglas MacArthur torched the tents and shacks that housed thousands of First World War veterans who had come to Washington to demand financial assistance from the government.

stage a march on Washington. As the impoverished "army" moved eastward, its ranks multiplied, so that by the time it reached Washington its numbers had swelled to 20,000, including wives and children. The so-called Bonus Army set up camp in the Anacostia Flats, southeast of the Capitol, and petitioned Congress for early payment of the promised bonus. The House of Representatives agreed, but the Senate turned them down. Hoover refused to meet with the veterans. In July, federal troops led by Army Chief of Staff Douglas MacArthur and 3rd Cavalry Commander George Patton attacked the veterans' Anacostia encampment, set the tents and shacks ablaze, and dispersed the protestors. In the process, more than 100 veterans were wounded and one infant was killed.

News that veterans and their families had been attacked in the nation's capital served only to harden anti-Hoover opinion. In the 1932 elections, the discredited Republicans were voted out of office after having dominated national politics (excepting Woodrow Wilson's two terms) for 36 years. Hoover received only 39.6 percent of the popular vote and just 59 (of 531) electoral votes. Hoover left the presidency in 1933 a bewildered man, reviled by Americans for his seeming indifference to suffering and ineptitude in dealing with economy's collapse.

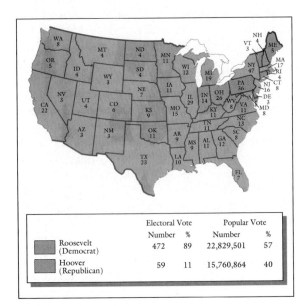

	Electoral Vote		Popular Vote	
	Number	%	Number	%
Roosevelt (Democrat)	472	89	22,829,501	57
Hoover (Republican)	59	11	15,760,864	40

PRESIDENTIAL ELECTION, 1932

THE DEMOCRATIC ROOSEVELT

The voters who swept Franklin D. Roosevelt into office in 1932 were determined to punish Hoover, even though they knew little about the man they were electing or what he would do as president.

AN EARLY LIFE OF PRIVILEGE

Roosevelt was born in 1882 into a patrician family descended, on his father's side, from Dutch gentry who in the 17th century had built large estates on the fertile land along the Hudson River. By the 1880s the Hyde Park manor where Roosevelt grew up had been in the family for more than 200 years. His mother's family—the Delanos—were no less distinguished; several of her ancestors had come over on the Mayflower. In short, Roosevelt was raised among people who were convinced of their superiority. His education at Groton, Harvard College, and Columbia Law School was typical of the path followed by the sons of America's elite.

The Roosevelt family was wealthy, although not spectacularly so by the standards of the late 19th century. His parents' net worth of more than a million dollars was relatively small in comparison to the fortunes being amassed by the rising class of industrialists and railroad tycoons, many of whom commanded fortunes of $50 to $100 million or more. This widening gap in wealth disturbed families like the Roosevelts, who worried that the new industrial elite would dislodge them from their social position. Moreover, they took offense at newcomers' vulgar displays of wealth, lack of taste and etiquette, indifference to the natural environment, and hostility toward those less fortunate than themselves. In 1899 Theodore Roosevelt, an older cousin of Franklin Roosevelt, had remarked that such people were "sunk in a scrambling commercialism, heedless of the higher life." He classified the highest type of man as "a statesman like Lincoln, a soldier like Grant"—men committed to national glory and national well-being. In his career as president and as a progressive, Theodore Roosevelt strove to become such a statesman through his willingness to challenge the trusts, his commitment to national parks, and his sympathies with the poor and powerless (see chapter 21).

Theodore was young Franklin's hero. In 1907, as a 25-year-old law clerk, Franklin imagined a career for himself that would duplicate that of his world-famous cousin. First, he would win a seat in the New York State Assembly, next he would be appointed assistant secretary of the navy, and then he would become governor of New York, vice president, and, finally, president of the United States. Incredibly, this is almost exactly what happened (except that he became a state senator rather than an assemblyman and he lost his 1920 race for the vice presidency).

The New York governorship and the U.S. presidency might have eluded him had he not been transformed by personal calamity. In 1921, at the age of 39, he contracted polio and permanently lost the use of his legs. Before becoming paralyzed, Roosevelt had distinguished himself neither at school nor at law. He could point to few significant political achievements, and owed his political ascent mostly to his famous name. He was charming, gregarious, and popular among his associates in the New York Democratic Party. He enjoyed a good time and devoted a great deal of energy to sailing, partying, and enjoying the company of women other than his wife, Eleanor. Roosevelt spent the two years following his illness bedridden, and he seemed to acquire a new determination and seriousness. He developed a compassion for those suffering misfortune that would later enable him to reach out to the millions caught in the Great Depression.

Roosevelt's physical debilitation also transformed his relationship with Eleanor, with whom he had shared a testy and increasingly loveless marriage. Eleanor's dedication to nursing Franklin back to health forged a new bond between them. More conscious of his dependence on others, he now welcomed her as a partner in his career. Eleanor soon displayed a talent for political organization and public speaking, a talent that surprised those who knew her only as a shy, awkward woman. She would become an active, eloquent First Lady, her husband's trusted ally, and an architect of American liberalism.

ROOSEVELT LIBERALISM

As governor of New York for four years (1929–33), Roosevelt had initiated various reform programs,

and his success made him the front-runner for the 1932 Democratic presidential nomination. Even so, he had little assurance that he would be the party's choice. Since 1924 the Democrats had been sharply divided between southern and midwestern agrarians on the one hand and northeastern ethnics on the other. The agrarians, heirs to William Jennings Bryan and now led by John Nance Garner of Texas and William Gibbs McAdoo of Georgia and California, favored government regulation—both of the nation's economy and of the private affairs of its citizens. Their support of government intervention in the pursuit of social justice marked them as economic progressives, while their advocacy of Prohibition revealed a cultural conservatism as well as a nativistic strain. By contrast, urban ethnics, led by Al Smith, an Irish Catholic, former governor of New York, and the 1928 Democratic presidential candidate, opposed Prohibition and other forms of government interference in the private lives of its citizens. Urban ethnics were divided over whether the government should regulate the economy, with Smith increasingly committed to a laissez-faire policy and Senator Robert Wagner of New York and others supporting more federal control.

Roosevelt understood the need to carve out a middle ground. As governor of New York, and then as a presidential candidate in 1932, he surrounded himself with men and women who embraced the new reform movement called liberalism. Frances Perkins, Harry Hopkins, Raymond Moley, Rexford Tugwell, Adolph Berle, Samuel Rosenman—all were interventionist in economic matters and libertarian on questions of personal behavior. They shared with the agrarians and Wagner's supporters a desire to regulate capitalism, but they agreed with Al Smith that the government had no business telling people how to behave. This was the liberalism that Roosevelt championed.

At the Democratic convention in July, Smith worked to secure the nomination of the more conservative Newton Baker. McAdoo, hoping to deadlock the convention so that he could take the nomination himself, initially supported Speaker of the House Garner. As the balloting entered its third round, Roosevelt began to fall behind. At that point, however, McAdoo and Garner reevaluated their strategy. Recognizing that party unity and a victory in the general election might be more important than their own ambitions, they swung their support to Roosevelt, putting him over the top. Roosevelt, in gratitude, chose Garner as his vice presidential running mate. In a move designed to dramatize the party's new vigor, Roosevelt flew from the governor's mansion in Albany, New York, to Chicago to deliver his acceptance speech in person, the first nominee in party history to do so. In a rousing call to action, he declared: "Ours must be the party of liberal thought, of planned action, of enlightened international outlook, and of the greatest good for the greatest number of citizens." He promised "a new deal for the American people."

In his campaign, Roosevelt sometimes spoke of using government programs to stabilize the economy, but he also spent much of his time wooing conservative Democrats. In point of fact, Roosevelt only made two outright promises during his presidential campaign: to repeal Prohibition and to balance the budget. Thus, the nation had to wait until March 4, 1933—the day Roosevelt was sworn in as president—to learn what the New Deal would bring.

THE FIRST NEW DEAL, 1933–1935

By the time Roosevelt assumed office, the economy lay in shambles. From 1929 to 1932 industrial production fell by 50 percent, while new investment declined from $16 billion to less than a billion dollars. In those same years more than 100,000 businesses went bankrupt. The nation's banking system hung on the verge of collapse; in 1931 alone, more than 2,000 banks with deposits of $1.7 billion had shut their doors. The unemployment rate was soaring. Some Americans feared that the opportunity for reform had already passed.

Not Roosevelt. "This nation asks for action, and action now," Roosevelt declared in his inaugural address. Roosevelt was true to his word. In his first "Hundred Days," from early March through early June 1933, Roosevelt persuaded Congress to pass 15 major pieces of legislation to help bankers, farmers, industrialists, workers, homeowners, the unemployed, and the hungry. He also prevailed on Congress to repeal Prohibition. Not all the new laws helped to relieve distress and promote recovery, but, in the short term, that seemed to matter little. Roosevelt had brought excitement and hope to the

nation. He was confident, decisive, and defiantly cheery. "The only thing we have to fear is fear itself," he declared. He used the radio to reach out to ordinary Americans. On the second Sunday after his inauguration, he launched a series of radio addresses known as "fireside chats," speaking in a plain, friendly, and direct voice to the forlorn and discouraged. In his first chat, he explained the banking crisis in simple terms, but without condescension. "I want to take a few minutes to talk with the people of the United States about banking," he began. An estimated 20 million Americans listened.

To hear the president speaking warmly and conversationally—as though he were actually there in the room—was riveting. An estimated 500,000 Americans wrote letters to Roosevelt within days of his inaugural address. Millions more would write to him and to Eleanor Roosevelt over the next few years. Many of the letters were simply addressed to "Mr. or Mrs. Roosevelt, Washington, D.C." Democrats began to hang portraits of Franklin Roosevelt in their homes, often next to a picture of Jesus or the Madonna.

Roosevelt was never the benign father figure he made himself out to be. He skillfully crafted his

FRANKLIN D. ROOSEVELT A smiling, confident Roosevelt delivering a speech. The man on the left in the first row behind Roosevelt is Interior Secretary Harold Ickes.

LEGISLATION ENACTED DURING THE "HUNDRED DAYS," MARCH 9–JUNE 16, 1933

Date	Legislation	Purpose
March 9	Emergency Banking Act	Provide federal loans to private bankers
March 20	Economy Act	Balance the federal budget
March 22	Beer-Wine Revenue Act	Repeal Prohibition
March 31	Unemployment Relief Act	Create the Civilian Conservation Corps
May 12	Agricultural Adjustment Act	Establish a national agricultural policy
May 12	Emergency Farm Mortgage Act	Provide refinancing of farm mortgages
May 12	Federal Emergency Relief Act	Establish a national relief system, including the Civil Works Administration
May 18	Tennessee Valley Authority Act	Promote economic development of the Tennessee Valley
May 27	Securities Act	Regulate the purchase and sale of new securities
June 5	Gold Repeal Joint Resolution	Cancel the gold clause in public and private contracts
June 13	Home Owners Loan Act	Provide refinancing of home mortgages
June 16	National Industrial Recovery Act	Set up a national system of industrial self-government and establish the Public Works Administration
June 16	Glass-Steagall Banking Act	Create Federal Deposit Insurance Corporation; separate commercial and investment banking
June 16	Farm Credit Act	Reorganize agricultural credit programs
June 16	Railroad Coordination Act	Appoint federal coordinator of transportation

Source: Arthur M. Schlesinger, Jr., *The Coming of the New Deal* (Boston: Houghton Mifflin, 1959), pp. 20–21.

public image. Compliant news photographers agreed not to show him in a wheelchair or struggling with the leg braces and cane he used to take even small steps. His political rhetoric sometimes promised more than he was prepared to deliver in actual legislation. This was not simply a strategy meant to confuse his opponents and to sustain his own appeal. Roosevelt was struggling to keep together a party deeply divided over a variety of issues. At the same time, he was attempting to establish a strong government in a society that had long been hostile to that idea. In America, unlike Great Britain, for example, relatively few individuals were experienced in public service. This lack of administrative expertise created dilemmas for Roosevelt and other New Dealers who often found it difficult to translate ambitious social programs into effective social policy. This has been a chronic problem for American liberals ever since.

SAVING THE BANKS

Roosevelt's first order of business was to save the nation's financial system. By inauguration day, several states had already shut their banks. Roosevelt immediately ordered all the nation's banks closed—

a bold move he brazenly called a "bank holiday." At his request, Congress rushed through the Emergency Banking Act (EBA) that made federal loans available to private bankers, which he followed with

BANK FAILURES, 1929–1933

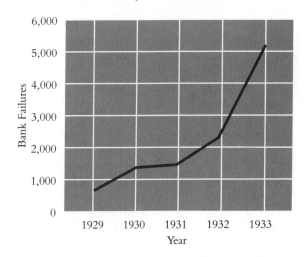

Source: From C. D. Bremer, *American Bank Failures* (New York: Columbia University Press, 1935), p. 42.

the Economy Act (EA) that committed the government to balancing the budget.

Both the EBA and the EA were fiscally conservative programs that Hoover, himself, had proposed. The EBA made it possible for private bankers to retain financial control of their institutions, and the EA announced the government's intention of pursuing a fiscally prudent course. Only after the financial crisis had eased did Roosevelt turn to the structural reform of banking. A second Glass-Steagall Act (1933) separated commercial banking from investment banking. It also created the Federal Deposit Insurance Corporation (FDIC), which assured depositors that the government would protect up to $5,000 of their savings. The Securities Act (1933) and the Securities Exchange Act (1934) imposed long overdue regulation on the New York Stock Exchange, both by reining in buying on the margin and by establishing the Securities and Exchange Commission to enforce federal law.

SAVING THE PEOPLE

Roosevelt understood the need to temper financial prudence with compassion. Congress responded swiftly in 1933 to Roosevelt's request to establish the Federal Emergency Relief Administration (FERA), granting it $500 million for relief to the poor. To head FERA, Roosevelt appointed a brash young reformer, Harry Hopkins, who disbursed two million dollars during his first two hours on the job. Roosevelt next won congressional approval for the Civilian Conservation Corps (CCC), which put more than two million single young men to work planting trees, halting erosion, and otherwise improving the environment. The following winter, Roosevelt launched the Civil Works Administration (CWA), an ambitious work-relief program, also under Harry Hopkins's direction, that hired four million unemployed at $15 a week and put them to work on 400,000 small-scale government projects. For middle-class Americans threatened with the loss of their homes, Roosevelt won Congressional approval for the Homeowners' Loan Corporation (1933) to refinance mortgages. These direct subsidies to millions of jobless and home-owning Americans lent credibility to Roosevelt's claim that the New Deal would set the country on a new course.

REPAIRING THE ECONOMY: AGRICULTURE

In 1933 Roosevelt expected economic recovery to come not from relief, but through agricultural and industrial cooperation. He regarded the Agricultural Adjustment Act, passed in May, and the National Industrial Recovery Act (NIRA), passed in June, as the most important legislation of his Hundred Days. Both were based on the idea that curtailing production would trigger economic recovery. By shrinking the supply of agricultural and manufactured goods, Roosevelt's economists

HELPING DUST BOWL VICTIMS This poster by the artist and New Deal supporter Ben Shahn dramatizes the plight of the Dust Bowl's victims while expressing the belief that relief is forthcoming from a New Deal agency, the Resettlement Administration.

reasoned, they could restore the balance of normal market forces. As demand for scarce goods exceeded supply, prices would rise and revenues would climb. Farmers and industrialists, earning a profit once again, would increase their investment in new technology and hire more workers, and prosperity and full employment would be the final result.

To curtail farm production, the Agricultural Adjustment Administration (AAA), set up by the Agricultural Adjustment Act, began paying farmers to keep a portion of their land out of cultivation and to reduce the size of their herds. The program was controversial; many farmers were skeptical of a government offer to pay more money for working less land and husbanding fewer livestock, but few refused to accept payments. As one young Kansas farmer reported:

> There were mouthy individuals who seized every opportunity to run down the entire program . . . condemning it as useless, crooked, revolutionary, or dictatorial; but . . . when the first AAA payments were made available, shortly before Christmas, these same wordy critics made a beeline for the courthouse. They jostled and fell over each other in their mad scramble to be the first in line to receive allotment money.

The AAA had made no provision, however, for the countless tenant farmers and farm laborers who would be thrown out of work by the reduction in acreage. In the South, the victims were disproportionately black. A Georgia sharecropper wrote Harry Hopkins of his misery: "I have Bin farming all my life But the man I live with Has Turned me loose taking my mule [and] all my feed. . . . I can't get a Job so Some one said Rite you." New Dealers within the Department of Agriculture, such as Rexford Tugwell and Jerome Frank, were sympathetic to the plight of sharecroppers, but they failed during the First New Deal in extending to them the government's helping hand.

The programs of the AAA also proved inadequate to Great Plains farmers, whose economic problems had been compounded by ecological crisis. Just as the depression rolled in, the rain stopped falling on the plains. The land, stripped of its native grasses by decades of excessive plowing, dried up and turned to dust. And then the dust began to blow, sometimes traveling 1,000 miles across open prairie. Dust became a fixed feature of daily life on the plains (which soon became known as the "Dust Bowl"), covering furniture, floors, and stoves, and penetrating people's hair and lungs. The worst dust storm occurred on April 14, 1935, when a great mass of dust, moving at speeds of 45 to 70 miles an hour, roared through Colorado, Kansas, and Oklahoma, blackening the sky, suffocating cattle, and dumping thousands of tons of topsoil and red clay on homes and streets.

The government responded to this calamity by establishing the Soil Conservation Service (SCS) in

COPING WITH DUST STORMS Red Cross volunteers in Liberal, Kansas, don gas masks in preparation for an impending storm.

1935. Recognizing that the soil problems of the Great Plains could not be solved simply by taking land out of production, SCS experts urged plains farmers to plant soil-conserving grasses and legumes in place of wheat. They taught farmers how to plow along contour lines and how to build terraces—techniques that had been proven effective in slowing the runoff of rainwater and improving its absorption into the soil. Plains farmers were open to these suggestions, especially when the government offered to subsidize those willing to implement them. Bolstered by the new assistance, plains agriculture began to recover.

Still, the government offered little to the rural poor—the tenant farmers and sharecroppers. Nearly 1 million had left their homes by 1935, and another 2.5 million would leave after 1935. Most headed west, piling their belongings onto their jalopies, snaking along Route 66 until they reached California. They became known as Okies, because many, although not all, had come from Oklahoma. Their dispossession and forced migration disturbed many Americans, for whom the plight of these once-sturdy yeomen became a symbol of how much had gone wrong with the American dream.

In 1936 the Supreme Court ruled that AAA-mandated limits on farm production constituted illegal restraints of trade. Congress responded by passing the Soil Conservation and Domestic Allotment Act, which justified the removal of land from cultivation for reasons of conservation rather than economics. This new act also called upon landowners to share their government subsidies with sharecroppers and tenant farmers, although many landowners managed to evade this and subsequent laws that required them to share federal funds.

The use of subsidies, begun by the AAA, did eventually bring stability and prosperity to agriculture, but at high cost. Agriculture became the most heavily subsidized sector of the U.S. economy, and the Department of Agriculture grew into one of the government's largest bureaucracies. The rural poor, black and white, never received a fair share of federal benefits. Beginning in the 1930s, and continuing in the 1940s and 1950s, they would be forced off the land and into the cities of the North and West.

REPAIRING THE ECONOMY: INDUSTRY

American industry was so vast that Roosevelt's administration never contemplated paying individual manufacturers direct subsidies to reduce, or even halt, production. Instead, the government decided to limit production through persuasion and association—techniques that Hoover had also favored. To head the National Recovery Administration (NRA), authorized under the National Industrial Recovery Act, Roosevelt chose General Hugh Johnson, a participant in industrial planning experiments during the First World War. Johnson's first task was to persuade industrialists and businessmen to agree to raise employee wages to a minimum of 30 to 40 cents an hour and to limit employee hours to a maximum of 30 to 40 hours a week. The limitation on hours was meant to reduce the quantity of goods that any factory or business could produce.

Johnson launched a high-powered publicity campaign. He distributed pamphlets and pins throughout the country. He used the radio to exhort all Americans to do their part. He staged an

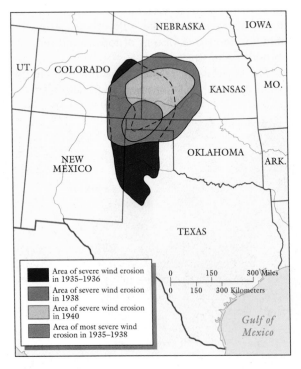

DUST BOWL, 1935–1940

Area of severe wind erosion in 1935–1936
Area of severe wind erosion in 1938
Area of severe wind erosion in 1940
Area of most severe wind erosion in 1935–1938

0   150   300 Miles
0   150   300 Kilometers

NEBRASKA
IOWA
UT.
COLORADO
KANSAS
MO.
NEW MEXICO
OKLAHOMA
ARK.
TEXAS
Gulf of Mexico

SELLING THE NRA THROUGH SEX AND SUNBURN Americans were asked to display their support for the NRA by pasting eagles onto their factory entrances, storefronts, and even clothes. The young women in this photo dispensed with pasting, choosing instead to allow the sun to burn their bare backs around a stenciled blue eagle and NRA lettering, which were being applied by the woman in the white gown. This gimmick attracted attention, no doubt.

elaborate NRA celebration in Yankee Stadium and organized a massive parade down New York City's Fifth Avenue. He sent letters to millions of employers asking them to place a "blue eagle"—the logo of the NRA—on storefronts, at factory entrances, and on company stationery to signal their participation in the campaign to limit production and restore prosperity. Blue eagles soon sprouted everywhere, usually accompanied by the slogan "We Do Our Part."

Johnson understood, however, that his propaganda campaign could not by itself guarantee recovery. So he brought together the largest producers in every sector of manufacturing and asked each group (or conference) to work out a code of fair competition that would specify prices, wages, and hours throughout the sector. He also asked each conference to restrict production.

In the summer and fall of 1933, the NRA codes drawn up for steel, textiles, coal mining, rubber, garment manufacture, and other industries seemed to be working. The economy picked up, and people began to hope for an end to the depression. But in the winter and spring of 1934, economic indicators plunged downward once again and manufacturers began to evade the code provisions. Government committees set up to enforce the codes were powerless to punish violators. By the fall of 1934, it was clear that the NRA had failed. When the Supreme Court declared the NRA codes unconstitutional in May 1935, the Roosevelt administration allowed the agency to die.

REBUILDING THE NATION

In addition to establishing the NRA, the National Industrial Recovery Act launched the Public Works Administration (PWA). The PWA had a $3.3 billion budget to sponsor internal improvements that would strengthen the nation's infrastructure of roads, bridges, sewage systems, hospitals, airports, and schools. The labor needed for these projects would shrink relief rolls and reduce unemployment, but the projects themselves could be justified in terms that conservatives approved: economic investment rather than short-term relief.

The PWA authorized the building of three major dams in the West—the Grand Coulee, Boulder, and Bonneville—that opened up large stretches of Arizona, California, and Washington to industrial and agricultural development. It funded the construction of the Triborough Bridge in New York City and the 100-mile causeway linking Florida to Key West. It also appropriated money for the construction of thousands of new schools between 1933 and 1939.

THE TVA ALTERNATIVE

One piece of legislation passed during Roosevelt's First New Deal specified a strategy for economic recovery significantly different from the one promoted by the NRA. The Tennessee Valley Authority Act (1933) called for the government itself—rather than private corporations—to promote economic development throughout the Tennessee Valley, a vast river basin winding through parts of Kentucky, Tennessee, Mississippi, Alabama, Georgia, and North Carolina. The act created the Tennessee Valley Authority (TVA) to control flooding on the Tennessee River, harness its water power to generate electricity, develop local industry (such as fertilizer production), improve river navigability, and ease the poverty and isolation of the area's inhabitants. In some respects the TVA's mandate resembled that of the PWA, but the TVA enjoyed even greater authority. The extent of its control over economic development reflected the influence of Rexford Tugwell

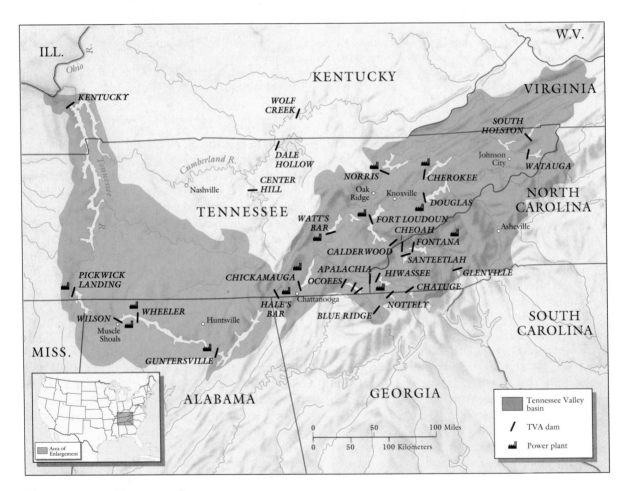

TENNESSEE VALLEY AUTHORITY

and other New Dealers who were committed to a government-planned and government-operated economy. Although they rarely said so, these reformers were drawn to socialism.

The accomplishments of the TVA were many. It built, completed, or improved more than 20 dams, including the huge Wheeler Dam near Muscle Shoals in Alabama. At several of the dam sites, the TVA built hydroelectric generators and soon became the nation's largest producer of electricity. Its low rates compelled private utility companies to reduce their rates as well. The TVA also constructed waterways to bypass non-navigable stretches of the river, reduced the danger of flooding, and taught farmers how to prevent soil erosion and use fertilizers.

Although the TVA was one of the New Deal's most celebrated successes, it generated little support for more ambitious experiments in national planning. For the government to have assumed control of established industries and banks would have been quite a different matter from bringing prosperity to an impoverished region. Like Roosevelt, few members of Congress or the public favored the radical growth of governmental power that such programs would entail. Thus, the thought of replacing the NRA with a nationwide TVA, for instance, made little headway. The New Deal never embraced the idea of the federal government as a substitute for private enterprise.

THE NEW DEAL AND WESTERN DEVELOPMENT

As the TVA showed, New Deal programs could make an enormous difference to a particular region's welfare. Other regional beneficiaries of the New Deal included the New York City area, which prospered from the close links of local politicians to the Roosevelt administration, but the region that most benefited from the New Deal was the West. Between 1933 and 1939, per capita payments for public works projects, welfare, and federal loans in the Rocky Mountain and Pacific Coast states outstripped those of any other region.

Central to this western focus was the program of dam building. Western real estate and agricultural interests wanted to dam the West's major rivers to provide water and electricity for urban and agricultural development. But the costs were prohibitive,

even to the largest capitalists, until the New Deal offered to defray the expenses with federal dollars. Western interests found a government ally in the Bureau of Reclamation, a hitherto small federal agency (in existence since 1902) that became, under the New Deal, a prime dispenser of funds for dam construction, reservoir creation, and the provision of water to western cities and farms. Drawing on PWA monies, the bureau oversaw the building of the Boulder Dam (later renamed Hoover Dam), which provided drinking water for southern California, irrigation water for California's Imperial Valley, and electricity for Los Angeles and southern Arizona. It also authorized the Central Valley Project and the All-American Canal, vast water-harnessing projects in central and southern California meant to provide irrigation, drinking water, and electricity to California farmers and towns. The greatest construction project of all was the Grand Coulee Dam on the Columbia River in Washington, which created a lake 150 miles long. Together with the Bonneville Dam (also on the Columbia), the Grand Coulee gave the Pacific Northwest the

IMPROVING THE NATION'S INFRASTRUCTURE The Public Works Administration built several major dams in the West to boost agricultural and industrial development. This is a picture of the mammoth Boulder Dam (later renamed Hoover Dam) on the Colorado River.

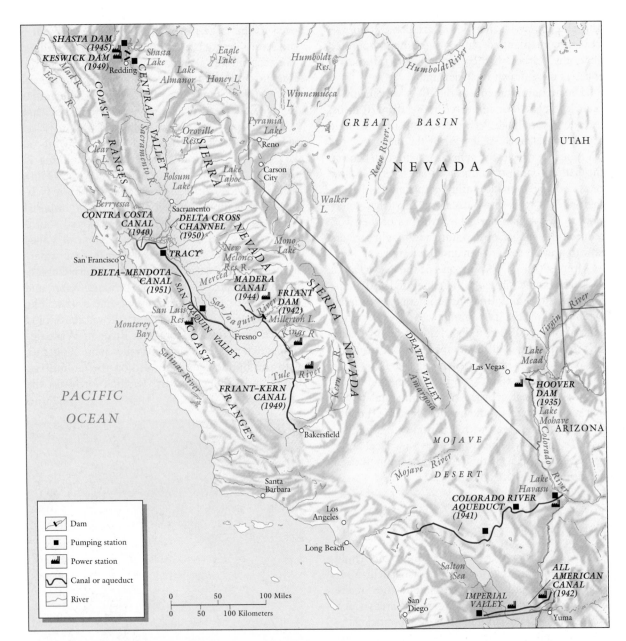

FEDERAL WATER PROJECTS IN CALIFORNIA BUILT OR FUNDED BY THE NEW DEAL

cheapest electricity in the country and created the potential for huge economic and population growth. Not surprisingly, these two dams also made Washington state the largest per capita recipient of New Deal aid.

These developments attracted less attention in the 1930s than the TVA. Their benefits were not fully realized until after the Second World War. Also, dam building in the West was not seen as a radical experiment in government planning and management. Unlike the TVA, the Bureau of Reclamation hired private contractors to do the work and made them rich. Moreover, the benefits of these dams were intended to flow first to large agricultural and real estate interests, not to the poor; they were intended to aid private enterprise, rather than bypass it. In political terms, then, dam building in the West was more conservative than it was in the Tennessee Valley. Even so, this activity made the federal government a key architect of the modern American West.

POLITICAL MOBILIZATION, POLITICAL UNREST, 1934–1935

Although Roosevelt and the New Dealers quickly dismantled the NRA in 1935, they could not stop the political forces it had set it in motion. Ordinary Americans now believed that they themselves could make a difference. If the New Dealers could not achieve economic recovery, the people would find others who could.

POPULIST CRITICS OF THE NEW DEAL

Some critics were disturbed by what they perceived as the conservative character of New Deal programs. Banking reforms, the AAA, and the NRA, they alleged, all seemed to favor large economic interests. Ordinary people had been ignored.

In the South and Midwest, millions listened regularly to the radio addresses of Louisiana Senator Huey Long, a former governor of that state and a spellbinding orator. In attacks on New Deal programs, he alleged that "not a single thin dime of concentrated, bloated, pompous wealth, massed in the hands of a few people has been raked down to relieve the masses." Long offered a simple alternative: "Break up the swollen fortunes of America and . . . spread the wealth among all our people." He called for a redistribution of wealth that would guarantee each American family a $5,000 estate.

Long's rhetoric inspired hundreds of thousands of Americans to join the Share the Wealth clubs his supporters organized. A majority came from middle-class ranks: independent proprietors who operated their own farms, businesses, and shops; self-employed doctors and lawyers; plumbers, carpenters, electricians, and other contractors. Each of these groups worried that the big business orientation of New Deal programs might undermine their eco-

HUEY LONG, POPULIST A spellbinding speaker, Long influenced millions with his calls for redistributing America's wealth in a more equitable manner.

nomic and social status. Substantial numbers of Share the Wealth club members also came from highly skilled and white-collar sections of the working class—railroad workers, bricklayers, postal workers, teachers, department store salesclerks, and others who aspired to a middle-class income and lifestyle. By 1935 Roosevelt regarded Long as the man most likely to unseat him in the presidential election of 1936. Before that campaign began, however, Long was murdered by an assassin.

Meanwhile, in the Midwest, Father Charles Coughlin, the "radio priest," delivered a message similar to Long's. Coughlin had a weekly radio audience in 1933 and 1934 of between 30 and 40 million listeners. Like Long, Coughlin appealed to anxious middle-class Americans and to privileged groups of workers who believed that middle-class status was slipping from their grasp. A devoted Roosevelt supporter at first—he had once called the New Deal

"Christ's Deal"—Coughlin had become a harsh critic. The New Deal was run by bankers, he claimed. The NRA was a program to resuscitate corporate profits. Coughlin called for a strong government to compel capital, labor, agriculture, professionals, and other interest groups to do its bidding. He founded the National Union of Social Justice (NUSJ) in 1934 as a precursor to a political party that would challenge the Democrats in 1936. Coughlin admired leaders, such as Italy's Benito Mussolini, who built strong states through decree rather than through democratic consent. If necessary, he admitted in 1936, he would "'dictate' to preserve democracy."

As Coughlin's disillusionment with the New Deal deepened, his admiration for Hitler and Mussolini grew more pronounced. A strain of anti-Semitism became apparent in his radio talks, as in his accusation that Jewish bankers were masterminding a world conspiracy to dispossess the toiling masses. Although Coughlin was a compelling speaker, he failed to build the NUSJ into an effective force. Its successor, the Union Party, attracted only a tiny percentage of voters in 1936. Embittered, Coughlin moved further and further to the political right. By 1939 his denunciations of democracy and Jews had become so extreme that some radio stations refused to carry his addresses. Even so, millions of ordinary Americans retained their allegiance to the "radio priest." Another popular figure was Francis E. Townsend, a California doctor who claimed that the way to end the depression was to give every senior citizen $200 a month with the stipulation that seniors would spend that money, thus putting more money in circulation and reviving economic demand. The Townsend Plan briefly garnered the support of an estimated 20 million Americans.

None of these self-styled reformers—Long, Coughlin, and Townsend—showed much skill at transforming his popularity into disciplined political parties that could compete in elections. Still, their attacks on New Deal programs deepened popular discontent and helped to legitimize other insurgent movements. The most important of them was the labor movement.

LABOR'S REBIRTH

The ranks of the working class were diverse—immigrant radicals and ethnic conservatives, northerners and southerners, blacks and whites, skilled and unskilled, factory workers and farm workers, men and women—but less diverse than during the Progressive Era. Mass immigration had ended in 1921, and the trend toward Americanization at school, at work, and in popular entertainment had broadened throughout the decade. The Great Depression itself further heightened the sense of shared experience. Few working-class families escaped the distress and despair of the early depression years.

This commonality of working-class sentiment first became apparent in 1932, when many workers voted for Roosevelt. Following his election, the NRA helped to transform their despair into hope. It set guidelines for wages and work hours that, if implemented by employers, would improve working conditions. Moreover, Clause 7(a) of the National Industrial Recovery Act granted workers the right to join labor unions of their own choosing, and obligated employers to recognize unions and bargain with them in good faith.

Millions of workers joined labor unions in 1933 and early 1934, encouraged by John L. Lewis, president of the United Mine Workers, who often declared in his rousing speeches and radio addresses: "The president wants you to join a union." Actually, Roosevelt opposed the rapid growth of unions, but Lewis believed that by repeatedly invoking the president's name he could transform working-class support for Roosevelt into union strength.

Union members made quite modest demands at first. They wanted employers to observe the provisions of the NRA codes. They wanted to be treated fairly by their foremen. And they wanted employers to recognize their unions. Few employers, however, were willing to grant them any say in their working conditions. Many ignored the NRA's wage and hour guidelines altogether and even used their influence over NRA code authorities to thwart worker requests for wage increases and union recognition. Workers flooded Washington with letters addressed to President Roosevelt, Labor Secretary Frances Perkins, and General Hugh Johnson asking them to force employers to comply with the law. A Rhode Island textile worker who had been fired for joining a union asked why the NRA had neither responded to his complaint nor punished the company that had fired him. "If people can be arrested for violating certain laws," he wondered, "why can't this company?"

***CITY LIFE* BY VICTOR ARNAUTOFF** This fresco was done by Arnautoff for the top of Coit Tower, one of the highest points in San Francisco. The city life of San Francisco is depicted as cosmopolitan, attracting many different kinds of people, rich and poor, men and women, sailors and civilians, adults and young people. Arnautoff's radical political sympathies are apparent in the rack of newspapers on the left, which prominently features the *Masses* and the *Daily Worker*. Both newspapers were closely associated with the Communist party.

When their pleas went unanswered, workers began to take matters into their own hands. In 1934 they staged 2,000 strikes in virtually every industry and region of the country. A few of those strikes escalated into armed confrontations between workers and police that shocked the nation. In Toledo, Ohio, in May, 10,000 workers surrounded the Electric Auto-Lite plant, declaring that they would block all exits and entrances until the company agreed to shut down operations and negotiate a union contract. A seven-hour pitched battle between strikers and police waged with water hoses, tear gas, and gunfire failed to dislodge the strikers. Ultimately, the Na-

tional Guard was summoned, and two strikers were killed in an exchange of gunfire. In Minneapolis, unionized truck drivers and warehousemen fought police, private security forces, and the National Guard in a series of street battles from May through July that left four dead and hundreds wounded. In San Francisco in July, longshoremen fought employers and police in street skirmishes in which two were killed and scores wounded. Employers had hoped that the use of force would break a two-month-old strike, but the violence provoked more than 100,000 additional workers in the transportation, construction, and service industries to walk off their jobs in a general strike. From July 5 to July 19, the city of San Francisco was virtually shut down. In both Minneapolis and San Francisco, the intervention of evenhanded municipal and state authorities eventually enabled strikers to win important concessions from employers.

The largest and most violent confrontation began on September 1, 1934, with the strike of 400,000 textile workers at mills from Maine to Alabama. Workers who had never acknowledged a common bond with their fellows—Catholic Euro-Americans in New England and white Protestants in the Southeast—now joined hands. They insisted that they were Americans bound together by class and national loyalties that transcended ethnic and religious differences. In the first two weeks of September, the strikers brought cotton production to a virtual standstill. Employers recruited replacement workers and hired private security forces to protect them. At many of the mills, the arrival of strikebreakers prompted violent confrontations between strikers and police. In northern communities, such as Saylesville and Woonsocket, Rhode Island, full-scale riots erupted. The result was several deaths, hundreds of injuries, and millions of dollars in property damage. Similar confrontations took place throughout the South, where vigilante bands helped local police and National Guardsmen beat up strikers, kill union organizers or run them out of the state, and incarcerate hundreds of strikers in barbed-wire camps.

ANGER AT THE POLLS

By late September, textile union leaders had lost their nerve and called off the strike. Workers took their anger to the polls. In Rhode Island, they broke the Republican Party's 30-year domination of state politics. In the South Carolina gubernatorial race, working-class voters rejected a conservative Democrat, Coleman Blease, and chose instead Olin T. Johnston, a former mill worker and an ardent New Dealer. In the country as a whole, Democrats won 70 percent of the contested seats in the Senate and House. The Democrats increased their majority, from 310 to 319 (out of 432) in the House, and from 60 to 69 (out of 96) in the Senate. No sitting president's party had ever done so well in an off-year election.

The victory was not an unqualified one for Roosevelt and the First New Deal. The 74th Congress would include the largest contingent of radicals ever sent to Washington: Tom Amlie of Wisconsin, Ernest Lundeen of Minnesota, Maury Maverick of Texas, Vito Marcantonio of New York, and some 30 others. Their support for the New Deal depended on whether Roosevelt delivered more relief, more income security, and more political power to farmers, workers, the unemployed, and the poor.

THE RISE OF RADICAL THIRD PARTIES

Radical critics of the New Deal also made an impressive showing in state politics in 1934 and 1936. They were particularly strong in states gripped by labor unrest. In Wisconsin, for example, Philip La Follette, the son of Robert La Follette (see chapter 21), was elected governor in 1934 and 1936 as the candidate of the radical Wisconsin Progressive Party. In Minnesota, discontented agrarians and urban workers organized the Minnesota Farmer-Labor (MFL) Party and elected their candidate to the governorship in 1930, 1932, 1934, and 1936. In Washington, yet another radical third party, the Commonwealth Builders, elected both senators and almost half the state legislators in 1932 and 1934. And in California, the socialist and novelist Upton Sinclair and his organization, End Poverty in California (EPIC), came closer to winning the governorship than anyone had expected.

These impressive showings made it clear that many voters were prepared to abandon Democrats who refused to endorse a more socialist, or at least more comprehensive, program of reform. A widespread movement to form local labor parties offered further evidence of voter volatility, as did the growing appeal of the Communist Party.

The American Communist Party (CP) had emerged in the early 1920s with the support of radicals who wanted to adopt the Soviet Union's path to socialism. The CP began to attract attention in early 1930s. Confident that the Great Depression signaled the death throes of capitalism, party members dedicated themselves to marshaling the forces of socialism.

CP organizers spread out among the poorest and most vulnerable populations in America—homeless urban blacks in the North, black and white sharecroppers in the South, Chicano and Filipino agricultural workers in the West—and mobilized them in unions and unemployment leagues. CP members also played significant roles in strikes described earlier, and they were influential in the Minnesota Farmer-Labor Party and in Washington's Commonwealth Builders. Once they stopped preaching world revolution in 1935 and began calling instead for a "popular front" of democratic forces against fascism (a new form of dictatorship represented in Germany by Hitler and in Italy by Mussolini), their ranks grew even more. By 1938, approximately 80,000 Americans were thought to have been members of the Communist Party.

Although the Communist Party proclaimed its allegiance to democratic principles beginning in 1935, it nevertheless remained a dictatorial organization that took its orders from the Soviet Union. Many Americans feared the growing strength of the CP and began to call for its suppression. Actually, the CP was never strong enough to pose a real political threat. Membership turnover was high, as many left the party after learning about its undemocratic character. Its chief role in 1930s politics was to channel popular discontent into unions and political parties that would, in turn, force New Dealers to respond to the demands of the nation's dispossessed.

THE SECOND NEW DEAL, 1935–1937

The labor unrest of 1934 had taken Roosevelt by surprise. For a time he kept his distance from the masses mobilizing in his name, but in the spring of

Mr. Deeds Goes to Town (1936)

**Directed by Frank Capra. Starring Gary Cooper (Longfellow Deeds),
Jean Arthur (Babe Bennett), Lionel Stander (Cornelius Cobb),
George Bancroft (McWade), and H. B. Warner (Judge Walker).**

Mr. Deeds Goes to Town was one of several films made by Frank Capra, the most popular director of the 1930s, in which he charmed audiences with fables of simple, small-town heroes vanquishing the evil forces of wealth and decadence. (See page 876 regarding another of these movies, *Mr. Smith Goes to Washington*). The heroic ordinary American in *Mr. Deeds* is Longfellow Deeds from Mandrake Falls, Vermont, who goes to New York City to claim a fortune left to him by a deceased uncle. Deciding to give the fortune away, he becomes the laughingstock of slick city lawyers, hardboiled newspapermen and women, cynical literati, and self-styled aristocrats. He also becomes a hero to the unemployed and downtrodden to whom he wishes to give the money. By making the conflict between the wealthy and ordinary Americans central to this story, Capra illuminated convictions popular in 1930s politics, as expressed by the New Deal.

The movie delivers its serious message, however, in an entertaining and often hilarious style. Capra was a master of what became known as "screwball" comedy. Longfellow Deeds slides down banisters, locks his bodyguards in a closet, uses the main hall of his inherited mansion as an echo chamber, punches a famous intellectual in the "kisser" (face), and turns his own trial for insanity into a delightful attack on the pretensions and peculiarities of corporate lawyers, judges, and psychiatrists. Central to the story, too, is an alternately amusing and serious love story between Deeds and a newspaperwoman, Babe Bennett (Jean Arthur). Bennett insinuates herself into Deeds' life by pretending to be a destitute woman without work, shelter, family, or friends. Deeds has long dreamed about rescuing a "lady in distress," and falls for the beautiful Bennett. Bennett, in turn, uses her privileged access to Deeds to learn about his foibles and to mock them (and him) in newspaper stories written for a ruthless and scandal-hungry public. But Deeds's idealism, honesty, and virtue overwhelm Bennett's cynicism and cause her to fall in love

with him. By movie's end, she has proclaimed her love and seems ready to return with Deeds to Mandrake Falls, where she will become his devoted wife and the nurturing mother of his children.

In Babe Bennett's conversion from tough reporter to female romantic we can detect the gender conservatism of 1930s culture. The movie suggests that Bennett's early cruelty toward Deeds arose as a consequence of her inappropriate involvement in the rough, male realm of newspaper work. Only by abandoning this realm and returning to the "natural" female realm of hearth and home can she recover her true and soft womanly soul. Thus this movie is as rich a document for exploring attitudes toward male and female behavior as for examining the relations between the rich and poor.

Gary Cooper as Longfellow Deeds (center of photo with hand on cheek) during his hilarious insanity trial. Cooper's bodyguard, Lionel Stander (Cobb) sits to the left of Cooper, and Cooper is looking at H. B. Warner (Judge Walker), who is presiding at the trial.

1935, with the presidential election coming up in 1936, he decided to place himself at their head. He called for the "abolition of evil holding companies," attacked the wealthy for their profligate ways, and called for new programs to aid the poor and down-trodden. Rather than becoming a socialist, as his critics have charged, Roosevelt sought to reinvigorate his appeal among poorer Americans and turn them away from radical solutions.

PHILOSOPHICAL UNDERPINNINGS

To point the New Deal in a more populist direction, Roosevelt turned increasingly to a relatively new economic theory, underconsumptionism. Advocates of this theory held that a chronic weakness in consumer demand had caused the Great Depression. The path to recovery lay, therefore, not in restricting production, as the architects of the First New Deal had tried to do, but in boosting consumer expenditures through government support for strong labor unions (to force up wages), higher social welfare expenditures (to put more money in the hands of the poor), and vast public works projects (to create hundreds of thousands of new jobs).

Underconsumptionists did not worry that new welfare and public works programs might strain the federal budget. If the government found itself short of revenue, it could always borrow additional funds from private sources. They in fact viewed government borrowing as a crucial antidepression tool. Those who lent the government money would receive a return on their investment; those who received government assistance would have additional income to spend on consumer goods; and manufacturers would profit from increases in consumer spending. Government borrowing, in short, would stimulate the circulation of money throughout the economy and would end the depression. This fiscal policy, a reversal of the conventional wisdom that government should always balance its budget, would in the 1940s come to be known as Keynesianism, after John Maynard Keynes, the British economist who had been its most forceful advocate.

Many politicians and economists rejected the notion that increased government spending and the deliberate buildup of federal deficits would lead to prosperity. Roosevelt himself remained committed to fiscal restraint and balanced budgets. But in 1935, as the nation entered its sixth year of the depression, he was willing to give the new ideas a try. Reform-minded members of the 1934 Congress were themselves eager for a new round of legislation directed more to the needs of ordinary Americans than to the needs of big business.

LEGISLATION OF THE SECOND NEW DEAL

Congress passed much of that legislation in January to June 1935—a period that came to be known as the Second New Deal. Two of the acts were of historic importance. The Social Security Act, passed in May, required the states to set up welfare funds from which money would be disbursed to the elderly poor, the unemployed, unmarried mothers with dependent children, and the disabled. It also enrolled a majority of working Americans in a pension program that guaranteed them a steady income upon retirement. A federal system of employer and employee taxation was set up to fund the pensions. Despite limitations on coverage and inadequate pension levels, the Social Security Act of 1935 provided a sturdy foundation upon which future presidents and congresses would erect the American welfare state.

Equally historic was the passage, in June, of the National Labor Relations Act (NLRA). This act delivered what the NRA had only promised: the right of every worker to join a union of his or her own choosing, and the obligation of employers to bargain with that union in good faith. The NLRA, also called the Wagner Act after its Senate sponsor, Robert Wagner of New York, set up a National Labor Relations Board (NLRB) to supervise union elections and to investigate claims of unfair labor practices. The NLRB was to be staffed by federal appointees, who would have the power to impose fines on employers who violated the law. Never before had the government sided so strongly with labor. Union leaders hailed the act as their "Magna Carta."

Congress also passed the Holding Company Act to break up the 13 utility companies that controlled 75 percent of the nation's electric power. It passed the Wealth Tax Act, which increased tax rates on the wealthy from 59 to 75 percent, and on corporations

SELECTED WPA PROJECTS IN NEW YORK CITY, 1938

Construction and Renovation	Education, Health, and Art	Research and Records
East River Drive	Adult education: homemaking, trade and technical skills, and art and culture	Sewage treatment, community health, labor relations, and employment trends surveys
Henrik Hudson Parkway		
Bronx sewers	Children's education: remedial reading, lip reading, and field trips	Museum and library catalogs and exhibits
Glendale and Queens public libraries		
King's County Hospital	Prisoners' vocational training, recreation, and nutrition	Municipal office clerical support
Williamsburg housing project		Government forms standardization
School buildings, prisons, and firehouses	Dental clinics	
	Tuberculosis examination clinics	
Coney Island and Brighton Beach boardwalks	Syphilis and gonorrhea treatment clinics	
Orchard Beach	City hospital kitchen help, orderlies, laboratory technicians, nurses, doctors	
Swimming pools, playgrounds, parks, drinking fountains	Subsistence gardens	
	Sewing rooms	
	Central Park sculpture shop	

Source: John David Millet, *The Works Progress Administration in New York City* (Chicago: Public Administration Service, 1938), pp. 95–126.

WPA MURAL BY ANTON REFREGIER The WPA funded a vast program of public art that employed thousands of artists and adorned public buildings with murals, paintings, and sculptures. This mural depicts an encounter between a Franciscan monk and Indians at a California mission during the era of Spanish rule.

from 13¾ to 15 percent; and it passed the Banking Act, which strengthened the power of the Federal Reserve Board over its member banks. It created the Rural Electrification Administration (REA) to bring electric power to rural households. Finally, it passed the huge $5 billion Emergency Relief Appropriation Act. Roosevelt funneled part of this sum to the PWA and the CCC and used another part to create the National Youth Administration (NYA), which provided work and guidance to the nation's youth.

Roosevelt directed most of the new relief money, however, to the Works Progress Administration (WPA) under the direction of the irrepressible Harry Hopkins, who was now known as the New Deal's "minister of relief." The WPA built or improved thousands of schools, playgrounds, airports, and hospitals. WPA crews raked leaves, cleaned streets, and landscaped cities. In the process, the WPA provided jobs to approximately 30 percent of the nation's jobless.

By the time the decade ended, the WPA, in association with an expanded Reconstruction Finance Corporation, PWA, and other agencies, had built 500,000 miles of roads, 100,000 bridges, 100,000 public buildings, and 600 airports. The New Deal had transformed America's urban and rural landscapes. The awe generated by these public works projects helped Roosevelt retain popular support at a time when the success of the New Deal's economic policies was uncertain. The WPA also funded a vast program of public art, supporting the work of thousands of painters, architects, writers, playwrights, actors, and intellectuals. Beyond extending relief to struggling artists, it fostered the creation of art that spoke to the concerns of ordinary Americans, adorned public buildings with colorful murals, and boosted public morale.

VICTORY IN 1936: THE NEW DEMOCRATIC COALITION

Roosevelt described his Second New Deal as a program to limit the power and privilege of the wealthy few and to increase the security and welfare of ordinary citizens. In his 1936 reelection campaign, he excoriated the corporations as "economic royalists" who had "concentrated into their own hands an almost complete control over other peo-

ple's property, other people's money, other people's labor—other people's lives." He called on voters to strip the corporations of their power and "save a great and precious form of government for ourselves and the world." American voters responded by handing Roosevelt the greatest landslide victory in the history of American politics. He received 61 percent of the popular vote; Alf Landon of Kansas, his Republican opponent, received only 37 percent. Only two states, Maine and Vermont, representing a mere eight electoral votes, went for Landon.

The 1936 election won the Democratic Party its reputation as the party of reform and the party of the "forgotten American." Of the six million Americans who went to the polls for the first time, many of them European ethnics, five million voted for Roosevelt. Among the poorest Americans, Roosevelt received 80 percent of the vote. Black voters in the North deserted the Republican Party—the "Party of Lincoln"—calculating that their interests would best be served by the "Party of the Common Man." Roosevelt also did well among white middle-class voters, many of whom stood to benefit from the Social Security Act. These constituencies would constitute the "Roosevelt coalition" for most of the next 40

		Electoral Vote		Popular Vote	
		Number	%	Number	%
	Roosevelt (Democrat)	523	98	27,757,333	61
	Landon (Republican)	8	2	16,684,231	37

PRESIDENTIAL ELECTION, 1936

VOTER PARTICIPATION IN
PRESENTIAL ELECTIONS,
1920–1940

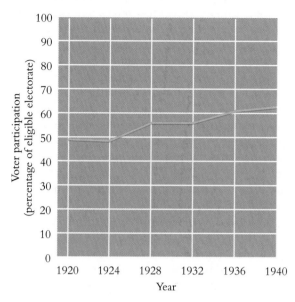

Source: Data from *Historical Statistics of the United States, Colonial Times to 1970* (White Plains, N.Y.: Kraus International, 1989), p. 1071.

GROWTH IN FEDERAL CIVILIAN
EMPLOYMENT, 1920–1940

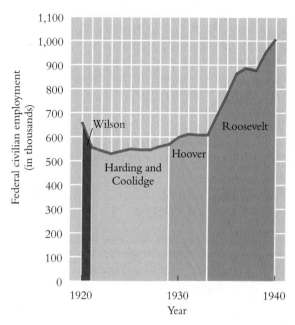

Source: Data from *Historical Statistics of the United States, Colonial Times to 1970* (White Plains, N.Y.: Kraus International, 1989), p. 1102

years, helping to solidify the Democratic Party as the new majority party in American politics.

RHETORIC VERSUS REALITY

Roosevelt's 1935–36 anticorporate rhetoric was more radical than the laws he supported. The Wealth Tax Act took considerably less out of wealthy incomes and estates than was advertised, and the utility companies that the Holding Company Act should have broken up remained largely intact. Moreover, Roosevelt promised more than he delivered to the nation's poor. Farm workers, for example, were not covered by the Social Security Act or by the National Labor Relations Act. Consequently, thousands of African American sharecroppers in the South, along with substantial numbers of Chicano farm workers in the Southwest, missed out on their protections and benefits. The sharecroppers were shut out because southern Democrats would not have voted for an act that was meant to improve the economic or social con-

dition of southern blacks. For the same reason, the New Deal made little effort to restore voting rights to southern blacks or to protect their basic civil rights. White supremacy lived on in New Deal democracy.

Roosevelt's 1935–36 populist stance also obscured the enthusiastic support that some capitalists were according the Second New Deal. In the West, Henry J. Kaiser headed a consortium of six companies that built the Hoover, Bonneville, and Grand Coulee dams; and in Texas, building contractors Herman and George Brown were bankrolling a group of elected officials that included a young Democratic congressman named Lyndon Johnson. In the Midwest and the East, Roosevelt's corporate supporters included real estate developers, mass merchandisers (such as Bambergers and Sears, Roebuck), clothing manufacturers, and the like. These firms, in turn, had financial connections with recently established investment banks such as Lehman Brothers and Goldman Sachs, competitors of the House of Morgan and its allies in the Republican banking establishment, and with consumer-oriented banks such as the Bank of America and the Bowery Savings Bank. They tolerated strong labor unions, welfare programs, and high levels of government spending in the belief that these developments would strengthen consumer spending. But they had no intention of surrendering their wealth or power. The Democratic Party had become, in effect, the party of the masses and one section of big business. The conflicting interests of these two constituencies would create tensions within the Democratic Party throughout all the years of its political domination.

NEW DEAL MEN, NEW DEAL WOMEN

The academics, policymakers, and bureaucrats who designed and administered the rapidly growing roster of New Deal programs and agencies found 1936 and 1937 exciting years. Fired by idealism and dedication, they were confident they could make the New Deal work. They planned and won congressional approval for the Farm Security Administration (FSA), an agency designed to improve the eco-

nomic lot of tenant farmers, sharecroppers, and farm laborers. They drafted and saw passed laws that outlawed child labor, set minimum wages and maximum hours for adult workers, and committed the federal government to building low-cost housing. They investigated and tried to regulate concentrations of corporate power.

Although they worked on behalf of "the people," the New Dealers themselves constituted a new class of technocrats. The prospect of building a strong state committed to prosperity and justice fired their imaginations. They delighted in the intellectual challenge and the technical complexity of social policy. They did not welcome interference from those they regarded as less intelligent or motivated by outworn ideologies.

This was particularly true of the men. Many had earned advanced degrees in law and economics at elite universities such as Harvard, Columbia, and Wisconsin. Not all had been raised among wealth and privilege, however, as was generally the case with earlier generations of reformers. To his credit, Franklin Roosevelt was the first president since his cousin Theodore Roosevelt to

RATES OF UNEMPLOYMENT IN SELECTED MALE AND FEMALE OCCUPATIONS, 1930

Male Occupations	Percentage Male	Percentage Unemployed
Iron and steel	96%	13%
Forestry and fishing	99	10
Mining	99	18
Heavy manufacturing	86	13
Carpentry	100	19
Laborers (road and street)	100	13

Female Occupations	Percentage Female	Percentage Unemployed
Stenographers and typists	96%	5%
Laundresses	99	3
Trained nurses	98	4
Housekeepers	92	3
Telephone operators	95	3
Dressmakers	100	4

Source: U.S. Department of Commerce, Bureau of the Census, *Fifteenth Census of the United States, 1930, Population* (Washington, D.C.: Government Printing Office, 1931).

welcome Jews and Catholics into his administration. Some became members of Roosevelt's inner circle of advisers—men such as Thomas "Tommy the Cork" Corcoran, Jim Farley, Ben Cohen, and Samuel Rosenman. These men had struggled to make their way, first on the streets and then in school and at work. They brought to the New Deal intellectual aggressiveness, quick minds, and mental toughness.

The profile of New Deal women was different. Although a few, notably Eleanor Roosevelt and Secretary of Labor Frances Perkins, were more visible than women in previous administrations had been, many of the female New Dealers worked in relative obscurity, in agencies such as the Women's Bureau or the Children's Bureau (both in the Department of Labor). Women who worked on major legislation, as did Mary Van Kleeck on the Social Security Act, or who directed major programs, as

did Jane Hoey, chief of Social Security's Bureau of Public Assistance, received less credit than men in comparable positions. Moreover, female New Dealers tended to be a generation older than their male colleagues and were more likely to be Protestant than Catholic or Jewish. Many of them had known each other since the days of Progressive Era reform and woman suffrage (see chapter 21).

The New Deal offered these female reformers little opportunity to advance the cause of women's equality. Demands for greater economic opportunity, sexual freedom, and full equality for women and men were put forward less often in the 1930s than they had been in the preceding two decades. One reason was that the women's movement had lost momentum after the achieving the vote in 1920. Another was that prominent New Deal women chose, rather than to vigorously pursue a campaign for equal rights, to concentrate instead

LINK TO THE PAST

Eleanor Roosevelt

http://newdeal.feri.org/index.htm

The New Deal Network Web site is sponsored by the Franklin and Eleanor Roosevelt Institute and the Institute for Learning Technologies at Columbia University. The site covers a wide range of topics on the New Deal and features photographs, cartoons, and documents of interest to students of history.

1. Select "Document Library" and search by subject for Eleanor Roosevelt. After scrolling to the documents written by Eleanor Roosevelt, read "I Want You to Write to Me" and "In Defense of Curiosity." Why was Roosevelt anxious to communicate with the American people? How did she envision her role as first lady? How did she defend that role? Why does she defend curiosity? What do you see as her major concerns about America during the Great Depression?

2. Select "Photo Gallery," then select "Public Figures" under Miscellaneous. Select "Eleanor Roosevelt" and view some of the photographs in the New Deal Network archives. What types of people and places did Eleanor Roosevelt visit? How do the other persons in the photographs appear to react to her visits? What do these pictures suggest about Roosevelt's concerns and beliefs?

Images of Men and Women in the Great Depression

Women played an important role in the New Deal. Eleanor Roosevelt set the tone through her visible involvement in numerous reform activities. She met with many different groups of Americans, including the miners depicted in the first photo, seeking to learn more about their condition and ways that the New Deal might assist them. But women also found their activism limited by a widespread hostility toward working women, who were thought to be taking scarce jobs away from men. In the popular movie, *Mr.*

Smith Goes to Washington (1939), Jefferson Smith (Jimmy Stewart) helps a hardboiled career secretary, Clarissa Saunders (Jean Arthur), to realize that work has damaged her sweet, womanly soul. By movie's end, Saunders is ready to leave her job and become Smith's wife and homemaker. Many other movies of the period also conveyed the sentiment that women belonged in the home.

Men, for their part, responded enthusiastically to the hypermasculinism that characterized much of the

on "protective legislation"—laws that safeguarded female workers, whom they considered more fragile than men. Those who insisted that women needed special protections could not easily argue that women were the equal of men in all respects.

Even so, feminism was hemmed in on all sides by a male hostility that the depression had only intensified. Men had built their male identities on the value of hard work and the ability to provide eco-

nomic security for their families. For them, the loss of work unleashed feelings of inadequacy. Male vulnerability increased as unemployment rates of men—most of whom labored in blue-collar industries—tended to rise higher than those of women, many of whom worked in white-collar occupations less affected by job cutbacks. Many fathers and husbands resented wives and daughters who had taken over their breadwinning roles.

decade's mass culture. Images of strong, muscled workers (such as in the portrait below of a working man in front of the White House) were popular with trade unionists who feared that the Depression would strip them of their manly roles as workers and bread-winners. Boys and male adolescents, meanwhile, found a new hero in Superman, the "man-of-steel" comic-book hero who debuted in 1938. Superman's strength, unlike that of so many men in the 1930s, could not be taken away—except by Kryptonite and Lois Lane, that "dangerous" working woman.

This male anxiety had political and social consequence. Several states passed laws outlawing the hiring of married women. New Deal relief agencies were reluctant to authorize aid for unemployed women. The labor movement made protection of the male wage earner one of its principal goals. The Social Security pension system left out waitresses, domestic servants, and other largely female occupations. Some commentators even proposed ludicrous gender remedies to the problem of unemployment. Norman Cousins of the *Saturday Evening Post*, for example, suggested that the depression could be ended simply by firing 10 million working women and giving their jobs to men. "Presto!" he declared. "No unemployment, no relief roles. No Depression."

Many artists introduced a strident masculinism into their painting and sculpture. Mighty *Superman*, the new comic-strip hero of 1938, reflected the spirit of the times. Superman was depicted as a working-class hero who, on several occasions, saved workers from coal mine explosions and other disasters caused by the greed and negligence of villainous employers.

Superman's greatest vulnerability, however, other than kryptonite, was his attraction to the sexy and aggressive *working* woman, Lois Lane. He could never resolve his dilemma by marrying Lois and tucking her away in a safe domestic sphere, because the continuation of the comic strip demanded that Superman be repeatedly exposed to kryptonite and female danger. But the producers of male and female images in other mass media, like the movies, faced no such technical obstacles. Anxious men could take comfort from the conclusion of the movie *Woman of the Year*, in which Spencer Tracy persuades the ambitious Katharine Hepburn to exchange her successful newspaper career for the bliss of motherhood and homemaking. From a thousand different points, 1930s politics and culture made it clear that woman's proper place was in the home. Faced with such obstacles, it is not surprising that women activists failed to make feminism a part of New Deal reform.

LABOR ASCENDANT

In 1935 John L. Lewis of the United Mine Workers, Sidney Hillman of the Amalgamated Clothing Workers, and the leaders of six other unions that had seceded from the American Federation of Labor (AFL) cobbled together a new labor organization. The Committee for Industrial Organization (CIO—later renamed the Congress of Industrial Organizations) aspired to organize millions of nonunion workers into effective unions that would strengthen labor's influence in politics. In 1936 Lewis and Hillman created a second organization, Labor's Non-Partisan League (LNPL), to develop a labor strategy for the 1936 elections. Although professing the league's nonpartisanship, Lewis intended from the start that LNPL's role would be to channel labor's money, energy, and talent into Roosevelt's reelection campaign. Roosevelt welcomed the league's help, and labor would become one of the most important constituencies of the

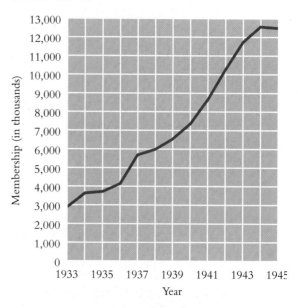

LABOR UNION MEMBERSHIP, 1933–1945

Source: From Christopher Tomlins, "AFL Unions in the 1930s," in Melvyn Dubofsky and Stephen Burwood, eds., *Labor* (New York: Garland, 1990), p. 1023.

new Democratic coalition. The passage of the Wagner Act and the creation of the NLRB in 1935 enhanced the labor movement's status and credibility. Membership in labor unions climbed steadily, and in short order union members began flexing their new muscles.

In late 1936 the United Auto Workers (UAW) took on General Motors, widely regarded as the mightiest corporation in the world. Workers occupied key GM factories in Flint, Michigan, declaring that their "sit-down" strike would continue until GM agreed to recognize the UAW and negotiate a collective bargaining agreement. Frank Murphy, the pro-labor governor of Michigan, refused to use National Guard troops to evict the strikers, and Roosevelt declined to send federal troops. The 50-year-old practice of using soldiers to break strikes came to an end, and General Motors capitulated after a month of resistance. Soon, the U.S. Steel Corporation, which had defeated unionists in the bloody strike of 1919 (see chapter 23), announced that it was ready to negotiate a contract with the newly formed CIO steelworkers union.

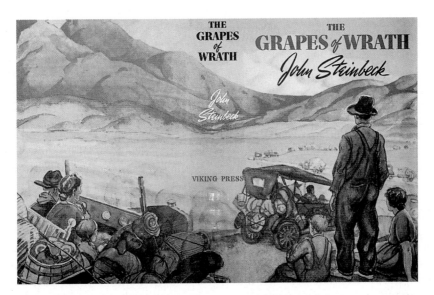

THE GRAPES OF WRATH In this bestselling novel of 1939, John Steinbeck told the epic story of an Oklahoma family's fortitude in the face of misfortune and exploitation.

The labor movement's public stature grew along with its size. Many writers and artists, funded through the WPA, depicted the labor movement as the voice of the people and the embodiment of the nation's values. Murals sprang up in post offices and other public buildings featuring portraits of blue-collar Americans at work. Broadway's most celebrated play in 1935 was Clifford Odets's *Waiting for Lefty*, a raw drama about taxi drivers who confront their bosses and organize an honest union. Audiences were so moved by the play that they often spontaneously joined in the final chorus of "Strike, Strike, Strike," the words that ended the play. *Pins and Needles*, a 1937 musical about the hopes and dreams of garment workers, performed by actual members of the International Ladies Garment Workers Union, became the longest-running play in Broadway history (until *Oklahoma!* broke its record of 1,108 performances in 1943).

Similarly, many of the most popular novels and movies of the 1930s celebrated the decency, honesty, and patriotism of ordinary Americans. In *Mr. Deeds Goes to Town* (1936) and *Mr. Smith Goes to Washington* (1939) Frank Capra delighted movie audiences with fables of simple, small-town heroes vanquishing the evil forces of wealth and decadence. Likewise, in *The Grapes of Wrath*, the best-

selling novel of 1939, John Steinbeck told an epic tale of an Oklahoma family's fortitude in surviving eviction from their land, migrating westward, and suffering exploitation in the "promised land" of California. In 1940 John Ford turned Steinbeck's novel into one of that year's highest grossing and most acclaimed movies. Moviegoers found special meaning in the declaration of one of the story's main characters, Ma Joad: "We'll go on forever . . . 'cause we're the people." In themselves and in one another, Americans seemed to discover the resolve they needed to rebuild a culture that had surrendered its identity to corporations and business.

AMERICA'S MINORITIES AND THE NEW DEAL

Reformers generally believed that issues of capitalism's viability, economic recovery, and the inequality of wealth and power outweighed problems of racial and ethnic discrimination; only in the case of Native Americans did New Dealers pass legislation specifically designed to improve a minority's social and economic position. Because they were disproportionately poor, most minority groups did profit from the populist and pro-labor character of New Deal reforms, but the gains were distributed unevenly. Eastern and southern European ethnics benefited the most, and African Americans and Mexican Americans advanced the least.

EASTERN AND SOUTHERN EUROPEAN ETHNICS

Eastern and southern European immigrants and their children had begun mobilizing politically in the 1920s in response to religious and racial discrimination (see chapter 24). By the early 1930s, they had made themselves into a formidable political force in the Democratic Party. Roosevelt understood their importance well, for he was a product of New York Democratic politics where men such as Robert Wagner and Al Smith had begun to organize the "ethnic vote" even before 1920 (see chapter 21). He made sure that a significant portion of New Deal monies for welfare, building and road construction, and unemployment relief reached the urban areas where most European ethnics lived. As a result, Jewish and Catholic Americans, especially those descended from southern and eastern European immigrants, voted for Roosevelt in overwhelming numbers. The New Deal did not eliminate anti-Semitism and anti-Catholicism from American society, but it did allow millions of European ethnics to believe, for the first time, that they would overcome the second-class status they had long endured.

Southern and eastern European ethnics also benefited from their strong working-class presence. Forming one of the largest groups in the mass-production industries of the Northeast, Midwest, and West, they made crucial contributions to the labor movement's rebirth. Roosevelt accommodated himself to their wishes because he understood and feared the power they wielded through their labor organizations.

AFRICAN AMERICANS

The New Deal did more to reproduce patterns of racial discrimination than to advance the cause of racial equality. African Americans who belonged to CIO unions or who lived in northern cities benefited from New Deal programs, but the vast majority of blacks lived in the rural South where they were barred from voting, largely excluded from AAA programs, and denied federal protection in

their efforts to form agricultural unions. The CCC ran separate camps for black and white youth. The TVA hired few blacks. Those enrolled in the CWA and other work-relief programs frequently received less pay than whites doing the same jobs. Roosevelt consistently refused to support legislation to make lynching a federal crime.

This failure to push a strong civil rights agenda did not mean that New Dealers were themselves racist. Eleanor Roosevelt spoke out frequently against racial injustice. In 1939 she resigned from the Daughters of the American Revolution when the organization refused to allow black opera singer Marian Anderson to perform in its concert hall. She then pressured the federal government into granting Anderson permission to sing from the steps of the Lincoln Memorial. On Easter Sunday, 75,000 people gathered to hear Anderson and to demonstrate their support for racial equality. The president did not attend.

Roosevelt did eliminate segregationist practices in the federal government that had been in place since Woodrow Wilson's presidency. He appointed Mary McLeod Bethune, Robert Weaver, William Hastie, and other African Americans to important second-level posts in his administration. Working closely with each other in what came to be known as the "Black Cabinet," these officials fought hard against discrimination in New Deal programs.

Roosevelt, however, remained unwilling to make the fight for racial justice a priority. He refused to support the Black Cabinet if it meant alienating white southern senators who controlled key congressional committees. This refusal revealed Roosevelt's belief that economic issues were more important than racial ones. It revealed, too, Roosevelt's pragmatism. His decisions to support particular policies often depended on his calculation of their potential political cost or gain. Roosevelt believed that pushing for civil rights would cost him the support of the white South. Meanwhile, African Americans and their supporters were not yet strong enough as an electoral constituency or as a reform movement to force Roosevelt to accede to their wishes.

MEXICAN AMERICANS

The Chicano experience of the Great Depression was particularly harsh. In 1931, Hoover's secretary

> "I worked in the U.S. of A. since 1904 with different companies. I registered in the world war in Johnson, Arizona, Cochise Co. I have never given my services to the Mexican government nor to Mexican capital. I have worked all my life, since I was 19 years of age in the U.S. of A., and that is why I wish to return to the country where I am entitled to live with my children so that they be educated in the schools of your country and not in Mexico."
>
> **PABLO GUERRERO**
> *a Mexican American, in a 1934 letter to the Los Angeles County Board of Supervisors protesting his repatriation to Mexico*

of labor, William N. Doak, announced a plan for repatriating illegal aliens (returning them to their land of origin) and giving their jobs to American citizens. The federal campaign quickly focused on Mexican immigrants in California and the Southwest. The U.S. Immigration Service staged a series of highly publicized raids, rounded up large numbers of Mexicans and Mexican Americans, and demanded that each detainee prove his or her legal status. Those who failed to produce the necessary documentation were deported.

Local governments pressured many more into leaving. Los Angeles County officials, for example, "persuaded" 12,000 unemployed Mexicans to leave by threatening to remove them from the relief rolls and offering them free railroad tickets to Mexico. Colorado officials secured the departure of 20,000 Mexicans through the use of similar techniques. The combined efforts of federal, state, and local governments created a climate of fear in Mexican communities that prompted 500,000 to return to Mexico by 1935. This total equaled the number of Mexicans who had come to the United States in the 1920s. Los Angeles lost one-third of its Mexican population. Included in repatriate ranks were a significant number of legal immigrants who were unable to produce

their immigration papers, the American-born children of illegals, and some Mexican Americans who had lived in the Southwest for generations.

The advent of the New Deal in 1933 eased but did not eliminate pressure on Chicano communities. New Deal agencies made more money available for relief, thereby lightening the burden on state and local governments. Some federal programs, moreover, prohibited the removal of illegal aliens from relief rolls, but federal laws, more often than not, failed to dissuade local officials from continuing their campaign against Mexican immigrants. Where Mexicans gained access to relief rolls, they received payments lower than those given to "Anglos" (whites) or were compelled to accept tough agricultural jobs that paid less than living wages.

Life grew harder for immigrant Mexicans who stayed behind. The Mexican cultural renaissance that had arisen in 1920s Los Angeles (see chapter 24) folded. Hounded by government officials, Mexicans everywhere sought to escape public attention and scrutiny. In Los Angeles, where their influence had been felt throughout the city in the 1920s, they retreated into the separate community of East Los Angeles. To many, they became the "invisible minority."

Mexicans and Mexican Americans who lived in urban areas and worked in blue-collar industries, however, did benefit from New Deal programs. In Los Angeles, for example, Chicanos employed in canneries, in garment and furniture shops, and on the docks responded to the New Deal's pro-labor legislation by joining unions in large numbers and winning concessions from their employers. These Mexicans and Mexican Americans, a minority, shared the belief of southern and eastern Europeans that the New Deal would bring them economic improvement and cultural acceptance. Most Chicanos, however, lived in rural areas and labored in agricultural jobs, and the New Deal offered them little. The National Labor Relations Act did not protect their right to organize unions, and the Social Security Act excluded them from the new federal welfare system.

AMERICAN INDIANS

From the 1880s until the early 1930s, federal policy had contributed to the elimination of American

THE NAVAJO VERSUS THE UNITED STATES In 1940, federal agents seized Navajo horses as part of a longstanding campaign to reduce the size of Navajo livestock herds and thereby halt the erosion of reservation lands. The policy angered the Navajo, who were already at odds with other government policies, including the Indian Reorganization Act of 1934.

Indians as a distinctive population. The Dawes Act of 1887 (see chapter 19) had called for tribal lands to be broken up and allotted to individual owners in the hope that Indians would adopt the work habits of white farmers. But American Indianss had proved stubbornly loyal to their languages, religions, and cultures. Few of them succeeded as farmers, and many of them lost land to white speculators. By 1933, nearly half the Native Americans living on reservations whose land had been allotted were landless, and many who retained allotments held land that was largely desert or semidesert.

The shrinking land base in combination with a growing population deepened American Indian poverty. The assimilationist pressures on Native Americans, meanwhile, reached a climax in the intolerant 1920s when the Bureau of Indian Affairs (BIA), outlawed Indian religious ceremonies, forced children from tribal communities into federal boarding schools, banned polygamy, and imposed limits on the length of men's hair.

Government officials working in the Hoover administration began to question this draconian policy, but its reversal had to await the New Deal and Roosevelt's appointment of John Collier as the commissioner of the BIA. Collier pressured the CCC, AAA, and other New Deal agencies to employ Indians on projects that improved reservation land and trained Indians in land conservation methods. He prevailed on Congress to pass the Pueblo Relief Act of 1933, which compensated Pueblos for land taken from them in the 1920s, and the Johnson-O'Malley Act of 1934, which funded states to provide for Indian health care, welfare, and education. As part of his campaign to make the BIA more responsive to Native Americans needs, Collier increased the number of Indian employees of the BIA from a paltry few hundred in 1933 to a respectable 4,600 in 1940.

Collier also took steps to abolish federal boarding schools, encourage enrollment in local public schools, and establish community day schools. He insisted that Native Americans be allowed to practice their traditional religions, and he created the Indian Arts and Crafts Board in 1935 to nurture traditional Indian artists and to help them market their works.

The centerpiece of Collier's reform strategy was the Indian Reorganization Act (also known as the Wheeler-Howard Act) of 1934, which revoked the allotment provisions of the Dawes Act. The IRA restored land to tribes, granted Indians the right to establish constitutions and bylaws for self-government, and provided support for new tribal corporations that would regulate the use of communal lands. This landmark act signaled the government's recognition that Native American tribes possessed the right to chart their own political, cultural, and economic futures. It reflected Collier's commitment to "cultural pluralism," a doctrine that celebrated the diversity of peoples and cultures in American society and sought to protect that diversity against the pressures of assimilation. Collier hoped that the IRA would invigorate traditional Indian cultures and tribal societies, and sustain both for generations. Cultural pluralism was not a popular creed in America during the depression years, which makes its acceptance as the rationale for the IRA all the more remarkable.

Collier encountered opposition everywhere: from Protestant missionaries and cultural conservatives who wanted to continue an assimilationist policy; from white farmers and businessmen who feared that the new legislation would restrict their access to Native American land; and even from a sizable number of Indian groups, some of which had embraced assimilation and others who viewed the IRA as one more attempt by the federal government to impose "the white man's will" on the Indian peoples. This opposition made the IRA a more modest bill than the one Collier had originally championed.

A vocal minority of Indians continued to oppose the act even after its passage. The most crushing blow came when the Navajo, the nation's largest tribe, voted to reject its terms. They voted as the BIA was forcing them to reduce their livestock herds in order to halt the erosion of reservation land. For a variety of reasons, 76 other tribes joined the Navajo in opposition. Still, 181 tribes, nearly 70 percent of the total, supported Collier's reform and began organizing new governments under the IRA. Although their quest for independence would suffer setbacks, as Congress and the BIA continued to interfere with their economic and political affairs, these tribes gained significant measures of freedom and autonomy. Taken all together, the New Deal showed considerably more sensitivity to the needs and aspirations of American Indians than had previous administrations.

THE NEW DEAL ABROAD

When he first entered office, Roosevelt seemed to favor a nationalist approach to international relations. The United States, he believed, should pursue foreign policies to benefit its domestic affairs, without regard for the effects of those policies on world trade and international stability. Thus, in June 1933, Roosevelt abruptly pulled the United States out of the World Economic Conference in London, a meeting called by leading nations to strengthen the gold standard and thereby stabilize the value of their currencies. Roosevelt feared that the United States would be forced into an agreement designed to keep the gold content of the dollar high and U.S. commodity prices low, which would frustrate New Deal efforts to inflate the prices of agricultural and industrial goods.

Soon after his withdrawal from the London conference, however, Roosevelt put the United States on a more internationalist course. In November 1933, he became the first president to recognize the Soviet Union and to establish diplomatic ties with its Communist rulers. In December 1933, he inaugurated a "Good Neighbor Policy" toward Latin America by formally renouncing U.S. rights to intervene in the affairs of Latin American nations. To back up his pledge, Roosevelt ordered home the Marines stationed in Haiti and Nicaragua, scuttled the Platt Amendment that had given the United States control over the Cuban government since 1901, and granted Panama more political autonomy and a greater administrative role in operating the Panama Canal.

None of this, however, meant that the United States had given up its influence over Latin America. When a 1934 revolution brought a radical government to power in Cuba, the United

States ambassador there worked with conservative Cubans to replace it with a regime more favorable to U.S. interests. The United States did refrain from sending troops to Cuba. It also kept its troops at home in 1936 when a radical government in Mexico nationalized a number of U.S.-owned and British-owned petroleum companies. The United States merely demanded that the new Mexican government compensate the oil companies for their lost property—a demand that Mexico eventually met. Although the United States was still the dominant power in hemispheric affairs, its newfound restraint inspired Latin American hopes that a new era had dawned.

The Roosevelt administration's recognition of the Soviet Union and embrace of the Good Neighbor Policy can be seen as an international expression of the liberal principles that guided its domestic policies. These diplomatic initiatives, however, also reflected Roosevelt's interest in stimulating international trade. American businessmen wanted access to the Soviet Union's market. Latin America was already a huge market for the United States, but one in need of greater stability. To win the support of American traders and investors, Roosevelt stressed how the Good Neighbor Policy would improve the region's business climate.

Roosevelt further expressed his interest in building international trade through his support for the Reciprocal Trade Agreement, passed by Congress in 1934. This act allowed his administration to lower U.S. tariffs by as much as 50 percent in exchange for similar reductions by other nations. By the end of 1935, the United States had negotiated reciprocal trade agreements with 14 countries. Roosevelt's turn to free trade—a move consonant with the Second New Deal's program of increasing the circulation of goods and money through the economy—further solidified support for the New Deal in parts of the business community, especially among those firms, such as United Fruit and Coca-Cola, with large stakes in foreign trade.

Actually increasing the volume of international trade was more difficult than passing legislation to encourage it. The supporters of free trade encountered vociferous opposition to tariff reduction both within the United States and abroad. In Germany and Italy, belligerent nationalists Adolf Hitler and Benito Mussolini told their people that the solution to their ills lay not in trade but in military strength and conquest. Throughout the world, similar appeals to national pride proved more popular than calls for tariff reductions and international trade. In the face of this historical current, the New Deal's internationalist economic policies made little headway.

STALEMATE, 1937–1940

By 1937 and 1938 the New Deal had begun to lose momentum. One reason was an emerging split between working-class and middle-class Democrats. After the UAW's victory over General Motors in 1937, other workers began to imitate the successful tactics pioneered by the Flint militants. The sit-down strike became ubiquitous across the nation. Many middle-class Americans, meanwhile, found labor's growing power disturbing.

THE COURT-PACKING FIASCO

The president's proposal on February 5, 1937, to alter the makeup of the Supreme Court exacerbated middle-class fears. Roosevelt asked Congress to give him the power to appoint one new Supreme Court justice for every member of the court who was over the age of 70 and who had served for at least 10 years. His stated reason was that the current justices were too old and feeble to handle the large volume of cases coming before them. But his real purpose was to prevent the conservative justices on the court—a majority of whom had been appointed by Republican presidents—from dismantling his New Deal. Roosevelt had not minded when, in 1935, the court had declared the NRA unconstitutional, but he was not willing to see the Wagner Act and the Social Security Act invalidated. His proposal, if accepted, would have given him the authority to appoint six additional justices, thereby securing a pro–New Deal majority.

What seems remarkable about this episode is Roosevelt's willingness to tamper with an institution that many Americans considered sacred. The president seemed genuinely surprised by the storm of indignation that greeted his "court-packing" proposal. Roosevelt's political acumen had apparently been dulled by his 1936 victory. His inflated sense of power infuriated many who had previously been New Deal enthusiasts. Although working-class support for Roosevelt remained strong, many middle-class voters turned away from the New Deal. In 1937 and 1938 a conservative opposition took shape, uniting Republicans, conservative Democrats (many of them southerners), and civil libertarians determined to protect private property and government integrity.

Ironically, Roosevelt's court-packing scheme may have been unnecessary. In March 1937, just one month after he proposed his plan, Supreme Court Justice Owen J. Roberts, a former opponent of New Deal programs, decided to support them. In April and May, the Court upheld the constitutionality of the Wagner Act and Social Security Act, both by a 5-to-4 margin. The principal re-

forms of the New Deal would endure. Roosevelt allowed his court-reform proposal to die in Congress that summer. Within three years, five of the aging justices had retired, giving Roosevelt the opportunity to fashion a court more to his liking. Nonetheless, Roosevelt's reputation had suffered.

THE RECESSION OF 1937–1938

Whatever hope Roosevelt may have had for a quick recovery from the court-packing fiasco was dashed by a sharp recession that struck the country in late 1937 and 1938. The New Deal programs of 1935 had stimulated the economy. In 1937 production surpassed the highest level of 1929, and unemployment fell to 14 percent. Believing that the depression was easing at last, Roosevelt began to scale back relief programs. New payroll taxes took two

UNEMPLOYMENT IN THE NONFARM LABOR FORCE, 1929–1945

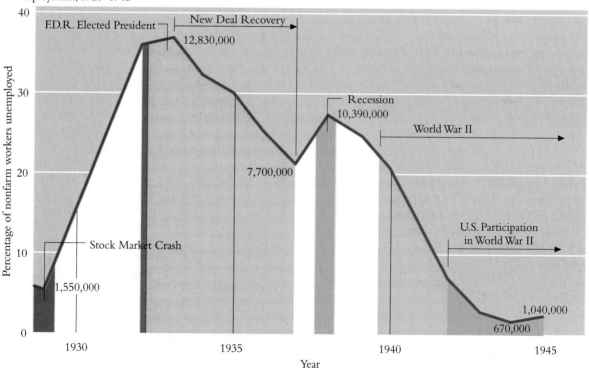

Source: Data from *Historical Statistics of the United States, Colonial Times to 1970* (White Plains, N.Y.: Kraus International, 1989), p. 126.

FEDERAL EXPENDITURES AND SURPLUSES/DEFICITS, 1929–1945

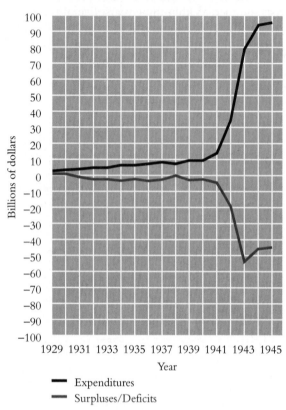

Expenditures

Surpluses/Deficits

Source: Data from *Historical Statistics of the United States, Colonial Times to 1970* (White Plains, N.Y.: Kraus International, 1989), p. 1105.

billion dollars from wage earners' salaries to finance the Social Security pension fund. That withdrawal would not have hurt the economy had the money been returned to circulation as pensions for retirees, but no Social Security pensions were scheduled to be paid until 1941. Once again, the economy became starved for money, and once again the stock market crashed. By October 1937, the market fell by almost 40 percent from its August high. By March 1938, the unemployment rate had soared to 20 percent. In the off-year elections later that year, voters elected many conservative Democrats and Republicans opposed to the New Deal. These conservatives could not dismantle the New Deal reforms already in place, but they did block the passage of new programs. Some liberals,

meanwhile, lost confidence in their ability to use government power to effect far-reaching changes in the American economy.

CONCLUSION

The New Deal reinvigorated American democracy. Roosevelt first assumed the presidency in the same week that Adolf Hitler established a Nazi dictatorship in Germany. Some feared that Roosevelt, by accumulating more power into the hands of the federal government than had ever been held in peacetime, aspired to autocratic rule. Nothing of the sort happened. Roosevelt and the New Dealers not only strengthened democracy, they inspired millions of Americans who had never before voted to go to the polls. Groups that had been marginalized—southern and eastern Europeans, unskilled workers, Native Americans—now believed that their political activism could make a difference.

Not everyone benefited to the same degree from the broadening of American democracy. Northern factory workers, farm owners, European ethnics, and middle-class consumers (especially homeowners) were among the groups who benefited most. In contrast, the socialist and communist elements of the labor movement failed to achieve their radical demands. Southern industrial workers, black and white, benefited little from New Deal reforms; so did farm laborers. Feminists made no headway. African Americans and Mexican Americans gained meager influence over public policy.

Of course, New Deal reforms might not have mattered to any group had not the Second World War rescued the New Deal economic program. With government war orders flooding factories from 1941 on, the economy grew vigorously, unemployment vanished, and prosperity finally returned. The architects of the Second New Deal, who had argued that large government expenditures would stimulate consumer demand and trigger economic recovery, were vindicated.

The war also solidified the political reforms of the 1930s: an increased role for the government in regulating the economy and in ensuring the social welfare of those unable to help themselves; strong state support of unionization, agricultural subsidies, and progressive tax policies; the use of government power and money to develop the West and Southwest. In sharp contrast to progressivism, the reforms of the New Deal endured. Voters returned Roosevelt to office for unprecedented third and fourth terms. And these same voters remained wedded for the next 40 years to Roosevelt's central idea: that a powerful state would enhance the pursuit of liberty and equality.

Suggested Readings begin on page SR-1. For Web activities and resources related to this chapter, go to http://www.harcourtcollege.com/history.murrin

CHAPTER 26

AMERICA DURING THE SECOND WORLD WAR

"UNITED WE WIN"

Government posters during the Second World War attempted to mute class and racial divisions and to offer images of all Americans united against fascism.

The Second World War, a struggle of unprecedented destruction that brought death to some *60 million* people worldwide, vastly changed American life. During a decade-long process, the United States abandoned isolationism, moved toward military engagement on the side of the Allies, and emerged triumphant in a global war in which U.S. forces fought and died in North Africa, Europe, and Asia.

To succeed militarily, the United States greatly expanded the power of its national government. The mobilization for war finally brought the country out of the Great Depression and produced significant economic and social change. The nation's productive capacity—spurred by new technologies and by a new working relationship among government, business, labor, and scientific researchers—dwarfed that of every other nation and provided the economic basis for military victory.

At home, citizens considered the meaning of liberty and equality both in the international order and in their own lives. A massive propaganda effort to bolster popular support for wartime sacrifice heralded the war as a struggle to protect and preserve "the American way of life," but the conflict inevitably raised significant questions about how to define the American way. How would America, while striving for victory, reorder its economy, its culture, and the social patterns that had shaped racial, ethnic, and gender relationships during the 1930s? What process of international reconstruction might be required to build a prosperous and lasting peace?

This chapter will focus on the following major questions:

- How did events in Asia and in Europe affect the domestic debate over isolationism versus intervention in the Second World War?
- What central strategic issues arose in fighting the war in both Europe and Asia?
- Why did mobilization for war produce complex economic and social changes in American life?
- What major institutions and policies shaped the reconstruction of the postwar world?

THE ROAD TO WAR: AGGRESSION AND RESPONSE

The road to the Second World War began at least two decades before it started. Resentments growing out of the First World War, together with the

CHRONOLOGY

1931 Japanese forces seize Manchuria

1933 Hitler takes power in Germany

1936 Spanish Civil War begins • Germany and Italy agree to cooperate as the Axis Powers

1937 Neutrality Act broadens provisions of Neutrality Acts of 1935 and 1936 • Roosevelt makes "Quarantine" speech • Japan invades China

1938 France and Britain appease Hitler at Munich

1939 Hitler and Stalin sign Soviet–German nonaggression pact • Hitler invades Poland; war breaks out in Europe • Congress amends Neutrality Act to assist Allies

1940 Paris falls after German blitzkrieg (June) • Battle of Britain carried to U.S. by radio broadcasts • Roosevelt makes "destroyers-for-bases" deal with Britain • Selective Service Act passed • Roosevelt wins third term

1941 Lend-Lease established • Roosevelt creates Fair Employment Practices Commission • Atlantic Charter proclaimed by Roosevelt and Churchill • U.S. engages in undeclared naval war in North Atlantic • Congress narrowly repeals Neutrality Act • Japanese forces attack Pearl Harbor (December 7)

1942 Rio de Janeiro Conference (January) • President signs Executive Order 9066 for internment of Japanese Americans (February) • General MacArthur driven from Philippines (May) • U.S. victorious in Battle of Midway (June) • German army defeated at Battle of Stalingrad (August) • Operation TORCH begins (November)

1943 Axis armies in North Africa surrender (May) • Allies invade Sicily (July) and Italy (September) • "Zoot suit" incidents in Los Angeles; racial violence in Detroit • Allies begin drive toward Japan through South Pacific islands

1944 Allies land at Normandy (D-Day, June 6) • Allied armies reach Paris (August) • Allies turn back Germans at Battle of the Bulge (September) • Roosevelt reelected to fourth term • Bretton Woods Conference creates IMF and World Banks • Dumbarton Oaks Conference establishes plan for UN

1945 U. S. firebombs Japan • Yalta Conference (February) • Roosevelt dies; Truman becomes president (April) • Germany surrenders (May) • Hiroshima and Nagasaki hit with atomic bombs (August) • Japan surrenders (September) • United Nations established (December)

worldwide depression of the 1930s, set the stage for international political instability. In Japan, Italy, and Germany, economic collapse and rising unemployment created political conditions that nurtured ultranationalist movements promising recovery through military buildup and territorial expansion. Elsewhere in Europe and in the United States itself, economic problems made governments turn inward, concentrating on domestic ills and avoiding expensive foreign entanglements. As international economic and political stability deteriorated, Americans debated how to respond to acts of aggression overseas.

THE RISE OF AGGRESSOR STATES

War began first in the Far East. On September 18, 1931, Japanese military forces seized Manchuria and created a puppet state called Manchukuo. This action violated the League of Nations charter, the Washington treaties, and the Kellogg-Briand Pact (see chapter 24). Japanese military leaders, who had urged their nation to accumulate an empire, won their gamble: The international community was too preoccupied with domestic economic problems to counter Japan's move. In the United States, the Hoover-Stimson Doctrine declared a policy of "nonrecognition" of Manchukuo, and the League of Nations also condemned Japan's action. These stands were not backed by force, however, and Japan first ignored them and then withdrew from the League of Nations in 1935.

Meanwhile, ultranationalist states in Europe also sought to alleviate domestic ills through military aggressiveness. Adolf Hitler's National Socialist (Nazi) Party came to power in Germany in 1933, instituting a fascist regime, a one-party dictatorial state. Hitler denounced the Versailles peace settlement of 1919, blamed Germany's plight on a Jewish conspiracy, claimed a genetic superiority for the "Aryan" race of German-speaking peoples, and promised to build a new empire (the "Third Reich"). The regime withdrew from the League of Nations in 1933 and reinstituted compulsory military service. Nearly doubling Germany's military expenditures (a blatant violation of the Treaty of Versailles), Hitler sought to create an air force and an army that would outnumber those of France, Germany's major European rival. The fascist government of Italy, headed by Benito Mussolini, who had come to power in 1922, also launched a military buildup and dreamed of empire. In October 1935 Mussolini's armies invaded Ethiopia, a proud and independent African kingdom that had never before succumbed to colonialist rule. After meeting fierce resistance, Italy prevailed over Ethiopian forces.

ISOLATIONIST SENTIMENT AND AMERICAN NEUTRALITY

Many Americans wished to isolate their country from these foreign troubles. Revisionist historians, writing after the First World War, had maintained that Woodrow Wilson manipulated the country into a war that had not been in the nation's best interests. Antiwar movies, such as *All Quiet on the Western Front* and *The Big Parade*, popularized the notion that war was a power game played by business and governmental elites who used appeals to nationalism to dupe common people into serving as cannon fodder. Between 1934 and 1936 a Senate investigating committee headed by Republican Gerald P. Nye of North Dakota held well-publicized hearings on U.S. participation in the First World War. The Nye committee emphasized that American bankers and munitions makers had developed a huge financial stake in an Anglo-French victory and claimed that these interests had maneuvered the nation into the First World War to preserve their own profits. By 1935 public opinion polls suggested that Americans overwhelmingly opposed involvement in foreign conflicts and feared being manipulated by what one writer called "merchants of death."

To prevent a repetition of the circumstances that had supposedly drawn the United States into the First World War, Congress enacted neutrality legislation to prohibit the growth of financial or emotional connections to belligerents. The Neutrality Acts of 1935 and 1936 mandated an arms embargo against belligerents, prohibited loans to them, and curtailed Americans' travel on ships belonging to nations at war. The Neutrality Act of 1937 further broadened the embargo to cover all trade with belligerents, unless the nation at war paid in cash and carried the products away in its own ships. This "cash-and-carry" provision mini-

mized damage to America's export sector while it reduced the risk that loans or the presence of American commerce in a war zone might entangle the country in a conflict.

The isolationist mood in the United States, matched by British policies of appeasement, encouraged Hitler's expansionist designs. In March 1936 Nazi troops again violated the Versailles agreement by remilitarizing the Rhineland. A few months later, Hitler and Mussolini extended aid to General Francisco Franco, a fellow fascist who was seeking to overthrow Spain's republican government. By lending Franco sophisticated weaponry and soldiers, Italy and Germany used Spain's civil war as a training ground for fascist forces. Republicans in Spain appealed to antifascist nations for assistance, but only the Soviet Union responded. Britain, France, and the United States, fearing that the conflict would flare into world war if more nations took sides, adopted policies of noninvolvement. The United States even extended its arms embargo to cover civil wars, a move that aided the well-armed fascist forces and crippled republican resistance.

GROWING INTERVENTIONIST SENTIMENT

Although the United States remained officially uninvolved, the Spanish Civil War precipitated a major debate over foreign policy. Many conservative groups in the United States applauded Franco as a strong anticommunist whose fascist state would support religion and a stable social order in Spain. In contrast, the political left, particularly writers and intellectuals, championed the cause of republican Spain and denounced the fascist repression sweeping Europe. Cadres of Americans, including the famed "Abraham Lincoln brigade," crossed the Atlantic and joined Soviet-organized, international brigades, which fought alongside republican forces. American peace groups, strong during the 1920s and early 1930s, now split over how peace could be best maintained. Some continued to advocate neutrality and isolation, but others argued for a strong stand against fascist militarism and aggression. Increasingly, Americans separated into camps of isolationists and interventionists.

The administration of President Franklin Roosevelt, tilting cautiously toward interventionism, tried to influence the debate. In October 1937 Roosevelt called for international cooperation to "quarantine" aggressor states, and he gingerly suggested some modification of America's neutrality legislation. Congressional leaders, however, remained adamant in maintaining the policy of noninvolvement.

JAPAN INVADES CHINA

As Americans debated strict neutrality versus cautious engagement, Japan once again launched an attack, this time on China itself. In the summer of 1937, after an exchange of gunfire between Japanese and Chinese troops at the Marco Polo Bridge southwest of Beijing, Japanese armies invaded and captured Beijing, Shanghai, Nanjing, and Shandong. The Japanese government demanded that China become subservient politically and economically to Tokyo. It also proclaimed Japan's intention to lead a greater East Asia Co-Prosperity Sphere, a self-sufficient economic zone that would supposedly liberate peoples throughout Asia from Western colonialism. Toward the end of 1937 Japanese planes sank the American gunboat *Panay* as it evacuated American officials from Nanjing, but Japan's quick apology defused the potential crisis. Even so, the *Panay* incident and Japanese brutality in occupying Nanjing, where perhaps 300,000 Chinese were killed in a deliberate assault against civilians, alarmed Roosevelt. The president began to consult with Britain about planning for a possible war in Asia.

Further aggression heightened the sense of alarm among interventionists in the United States, especially when the expansionist states began cooperating with each other. In October 1936 Germany and Italy agreed to cooperate as the "Axis Powers," and Japan joined them in alliance against the Soviet Union in November 1936. Italy followed Japan and Germany in withdrawing from the League of Nations. In March 1938 Hitler annexed Austria to the Third Reich and announced his intention to seize the Sudetenland, a portion of Czechoslovakia inhabited by 3.5 million people of German descent. In May, Roosevelt announced a program of naval rearmament that would increase the American navy beyond the treaty limits that Japan had already violated.

THE OUTBREAK OF WAR IN EUROPE

French and British leaders, wishing to avoid a confrontation with Germany, met with Hitler in Munich in September 1938. They acquiesced to Germany's seizure of the Sudetenland in return for Hitler's promise to seek no more territory. Roosevelt expressed relief that the Munich Conference seemed to promise future peace in Europe.

The promise of peace did not last. In March 1939 Germans marched into Prague and, within a few months, annexed the rest of Czechoslovakia. In August 1939 Hitler secured Germany's eastern flank by signing a nonaggression pact with the Soviet Union. The bitterest of enemies, Stalin and Hitler nonetheless agreed to cooperate in carving up territory: In a secret protocol they plotted to divide Poland and the Baltic states. By the fall of 1939 Germany was clearly preparing for an attack on Poland.

Britain and France were finally ready to draw the line. Both countries pledged to defend Poland, and on September 1, 1939, Hitler's invasion forced them into action. Two days after Hitler's armies stormed into Poland, Britain and France declared war on Germany. The Allies, however, were unable to mobilize in time to help the Poles. Outnumbered and outgunned, Polish forces fought valiantly but could not withstand Germany's unrelenting strikes on land and from the air. With Soviet troops moving in simultaneously from the east, Poland fell within weeks. Once the occupation of Poland was completed, Hitler's troops waited out the winter of 1939–40. Some observers dubbed this period a *sitzkrieg*, or "sitting war."

The lull proved only temporary. In April 1940 a German *blitzkrieg*, or "lightning war" of massed tank formations, motorized infantry and artillery, and air support, swiftly overran Denmark, Norway, the Netherlands, Belgium, Luxembourg, and France. The speed with which Hitler's well-trained army moved shocked Allied leaders in Paris and London. Britain barely managed to evacuate its

German submarine attacks in North Atlantic

Denmark and Norway occupied, April 1940 — 5

Belgium, the Netherlands occupied, May 1940 — 6

Poland invaded, September 1939. World War II begins — 4

Battle of Britain Fall, 1940 — 9

Allied evacuation from Dunkirk, May 1940 — 7

Germany demands annexation of Sudetenland, September 1938 — 2

Czechoslovakia seized, August 1939 — 3

Western Soviet Union and Eastern Europe occupied, 1941–1942 — 10

Germany effects *Anschuss* with Austria, March, 1938 — 1

France surrenders, June 1940, and Vichy government installed, June 1940 — 8

Legend:

- Axis Powers, Germany and Italy, 1938
- Axis satellites and areas brought under Axis control
- Areas controlled by Allies, as of November 1942
- Neutral nations
- - - - - German advance up to December 1941
- —— German advance up to November 1942

GERMAN EXPANSION AT ITS HEIGHT

troops, but not its equipment, from the French coastal town of Dunkirk, just before it fell to the German onslaught that began in late May. Early in June, Italy joined Germany by declaring war on the Allies. In June 1940, France fell, and Hitler in-

stalled a pro-Nazi government at Vichy in southern France. French officials were forced to surrender to Hitler in the same railway car used for the German surrender to France at the end of the First World War. In only six weeks, Hitler's army had seized complete control of Europe's Atlantic coastline, from the North Sea south to Spain, where Franco remained officially neutral but decidedly pro-Axis.

AMERICA'S RESPONSE TO WAR IN EUROPE

In a somber, six-minute speech delivered on the day that Britain and France entered the war against Germany, President Roosevelt declared U.S. neutrality. But the tone of his speech was hardly neutral. Unlike Woodrow Wilson when the European war had broken out in 1914, Roosevelt did not urge Americans to be impartial. From 1939 to 1941 Roosevelt tried to mobilize public opinion against Congress's Neutrality Acts and in favor of what he called "measures short of war" that would bolster the Allied fight against the Axis.

At Roosevelt's urging, late in 1939 Congress lifted the Neutrality Act's ban on selling arms to either side and substituted a "cash-and-carry" provision allowing arms sales to belligerents who could pay cash and use their own ships for transport. Because Britain and France controlled the Atlantic sea lanes, they clearly benefited from this change in policy. Congress responded further to Roosevelt's requests, appropriating more funds for rearmament and passing the Selective Training and Service Act of 1940, the first peacetime draft in U.S. history. Abandoning any further pretense of neutrality, the United States began supplying war matériel directly to Great Britain. The appointment of two Republicans to the cabinet—Henry Stimson as secretary of war and Frank Knox as secretary of the navy—gave the new policies bipartisan overtones, if not full bipartisan support.

Meanwhile, Hitler concentrated his attention on Great Britain. From August through October 1940 Germany's *Luftwaffe* subjected British air bases to daily raids, coming close to knocking Britain's Royal Air Force (RAF) out of the war. Just as he was on the verge of success, however, Hitler lost patience with this strategy and ordered instead the bombing of London and other cities—first by day and then by night. In addition to giving the RAF time to recover, Germany's nighttime bombings of Britain's cities also spurred the United States' sense of urgency about the war. The use of airpower against civilians in the Battle of Britain, as it was

called, shocked Americans, who heard the news in dramatic radio broadcasts from London. As writer Archibald MacLeish phrased it, radio journalist Edward R. Murrow had "skillfully burned the city of London in our homes and we felt the flames."

In September 1940 the president ignored any possible constitutional questions about the limits of his authority and transferred 50 First World War–era naval destroyers to the British navy. In return, the United States gained the right to build eight naval bases in British territory in the Western Hemisphere. This "destroyers-for-bases" deal infuriated isolationist members of Congress. Even within the president's own party, opposition was strong. Democratic Senator Burton K. Wheeler of Montana distributed more than a million antiwar postcards, at government expense, an action that Secretary of War Stimson characterized as "very near the line of subversion . . . if not treason."

Resistance to Roosevelt's pro-Allied policies extended beyond Congress. The most formidable opposition came from the America First Committee, organized by General Robert E. Wood, head of Sears, Roebuck, and Company, the giant department store chain. Included among its members was the aviation hero Charles Lindbergh, who campaigned vigorously at mass rallies across the country against aid to the Allies.

Although the people who tried to keep the United States out of the war were generally lumped together as "isolationists," this single term obscures their ideological diversity. Some pacifists, including members of religious groups committed to nonviolence, opposed all wars as immoral, even those against evil regimes. Some political progressives disliked fascism but feared even more the growth of centralized power that the conduct of war would require in the United States; they also distrusted the elites who dominated international decision making. On the other hand, some conservatives sympathized with fascism, viewing Germany not as an enemy but as the future. Finally, some Americans opposed Roosevelt's pro-Allied policies because they shared Hitler's anti-Semitism.

Indeed, a strong current of anti-Semitism existed in the country at large. An organization called the German American Bund, for example, defended Hitler's anti-Semitic policies and denounced

ANTI-INTERVENTIONISTS PICKET THE WHITE HOUSE
Women rally in March 1941 against H.R. 1776, the
Lend-Lease Act, which many isolationists feared would
lead the United States into another world war.

Roosevelt's "Jew Deal," a reference to the presence
of Jewish advisers in FDR's New Deal administration. In 1939 congressional leaders had quashed the
Wagner-Rogers Bill, which would have boosted immigration quotas in order to allow for the entry of
20,000 Jewish children otherwise slated for Hitler's
concentration camps. Bowing to anti-Semitic prejudices, the United States adopted a restrictive
refugee policy that did not permit even the legal
quota of Jewish immigrants from Eastern Europe
to enter the country during the Second World
War. The consequences of these policies became
even graver after June 1941, when Hitler established the death camps that would systematically ex-
terminate millions of Jews, gypsies, homosexuals,
and anyone else whom the Nazis deemed "unfit" for
life in the Third Reich and its occupied territories.

To counteract the isolationists, those who favored supporting the Allies also organized. The
Military Training Camps Association, for example,

lobbied on behalf of the Selective Service Act. The
Committee to Defend America by Aiding the Allies, headed by William Allen White, a well-known
Republican newspaper editor, organized more
than 300 local chapters in just a few weeks. Like
the isolationists, interventionist organizations
drew from an ideologically diverse group of supporters. All, however, sounded alarms about the
dangerous possibility that fascist brutality, militarism, and racism might overrun Europe as Americans stood by.

Presidential election politics in 1940 forced Roosevelt to tone down his pro-Allied rhetoric. The Republicans nominated Wendell Willkie, a lawyer and
business executive with ties to the party's liberal, internationalist wing. Democrats broke with the practice of limiting presidents to two terms in office and
nominated Roosevelt for a third. To overcome the
disadvantages of the third-term issue, and to differ-
entiate his policies from Willkie's, the president
played to the popular opposition to war. He
promised not to send American boys to fight in
"foreign wars." Once he had defeated Willkie and
won an unprecedented third term in November,
however, Roosevelt produced his most ambitious
plan yet to support Britain's war effort.

AN "ARSENAL OF DEMOCRACY"

Britain was nearly out of money, so the president
proposed an additional provision to the Neutrality
Act. The United States would now loan, or "lend-
lease," rather than sell, munitions to the Allies. By
making the United States a "great arsenal of democracy," FDR assured Americans, he would "keep
war away from our country and our people." Not
everyone in Congress shared Roosevelt's opinions.
During bitter debate over the Lend-Lease Act,
Senator Wheeler evoked Roosevelt's unpopular destruction of farm surpluses during the early years of
the New Deal by charging that the act would result
in the "plowing under" of every fourth American
boy. Nevertheless, Congress passed the symbolically numbered House Resolution 1776 on March
11, 1941. When Germany turned its attention away
from Britain and suddenly attacked its recent ally
the Soviet Union in June, Roosevelt extended lend-
lease to Joseph Stalin's communist regime, even
though it had earlier cooperated with Hitler.

Wheeler continued his opposition. In September 1941 he created a special Senate committee to investigate whether Hollywood movies were being used to sway people in a pro-war direction. Some isolationists, pointing out that many Hollywood producers were Jewish, expressed blatantly anti-Semitic opinions.

Still maintaining his stated policy of nonbelligerence, Roosevelt next took steps to coordinate military strategy with Britain. Should the United States be drawn into a two-front war against both Germany and Japan, the president pledged to follow a Europe-first strategy. To back up his promise, Roosevelt deployed thousands of U.S. marines to Greenland and Iceland to relieve British troops, which had occupied these strategic Danish possessions after Germany's seizure of Denmark.

In August 1941, Roosevelt and British Prime Minister Winston Churchill met on the high seas off the coast of Newfoundland to work toward a formal wartime alliance. An eight-point declaration of common principles, the so-called Atlantic Charter, disavowed territorial expansion, endorsed free trade and self-determination, and pledged the postwar creation of a new world organization that would ensure "general security." Roosevelt agreed to Churchill's request that the U.S. Navy convoy American goods as far as Iceland. This step, aimed at ensuring the safe delivery of lend-lease supplies to Britain, inched the United States even closer to belligerence. Soon, in an undeclared naval war, Germany was using its formidable submarine "wolf packs" to attack U.S. ships.

By this time, Roosevelt and his advisers firmly believed that defeating Hitler would require American entry into the war, but public support still lagged. The president urged Congress to repeal the Neutrality Act altogether to allow U.S. merchant ships to carry munitions directly to Britain. Privately, he may have hoped that Germany would commit some provocative act in the North Atlantic that would jar public opinion. The October 1941 sinking of the U.S. destroyer *Reuben James* did just that, and Congress repealed the Neutrality Act. But the vote was so close and the debate so bitter that Roosevelt knew he could not yet seek a formal declaration of war. Roosevelt's insistence that aid to the Allies was an alternative to U.S. involvement in the war rather than a way into it entangled him in a web of his own rhetoric. By avoiding any further provocations at sea, Hitler made Roosevelt's task harder still. In addition, beginning in late June, Hitler now concentrated his attacks on the Soviet Union, a country for which Americans held far less sympathy than they did for Britain.

THE ATTACK AT PEARL HARBOR

As it turned out, America's formal entry into the war stemmed from escalating tensions with Japan rather than Germany. In response to Japan's invasion of China in 1937, the United States sought to bolster China's defense by extending economic credits to China and halting sales of some types of U.S. equipment to Japan. In 1939 the United States abrogated its Treaty of Commerce and Navigation with Japan, an action that allowed for the possible future curtailment or even the outright prohibition of U.S. exports to the island nation.

These measures did little to deter Japanese aggression, and by 1940 Germany's successes in Europe had further raised the stakes in Asia. As the European war sapped their strength, France, Britain, and the Netherlands had more trouble maintaining links with their Southeast Asian colonies. Japan quickly mobilized to exploit the vacuum as Japanese expansionists called for the incorporation of Southeast Asia into their East Asian Co-Prosperity Sphere.

President Roosevelt hoped that a 1940 ban on the sale of aviation fuel and high-grade scrap iron to Japan would slow Japan's imminent military advance into Southeast Asia. Instead, this act only intensified Japanese militancy. After joining the Axis alliance in September 1940, Japan pushed deeper into Indochina to secure strategic positions and access to raw materials it could no longer buy from the United States. When Japan's occupation of French Indochina went unopposed, its military forces prepared to launch attacks on Singapore, the Netherlands East Indies (Indonesia), and the Philippines. Roosevelt expanded the trade embargo against Japan, promised further assistance to China, and accelerated the U.S. military buildup in the Pacific.

In mid-1941, Roosevelt played his most important card. He froze Japanese assets in the United States, effectively bringing under presidential control all commerce between the two countries, including trade in petroleum vital to the Japanese economy. Roosevelt hoped this action would bring Japan to the bargaining table, but, faced with impending economic strangulation, Japanese leaders instead began planning for a preemptive attack on the United States.

On December 7, 1941, Japanese bombers swooped down without warning on Pearl Harbor, Hawaii, to destroy much of the U.S. Pacific fleet. Altogether, 19 ships were sunk or severely damaged; 288 aircraft were destroyed or disabled; and more than 2,200 Americans were killed. The attack could have been worse: the three American carriers and seven heavy cruisers were not in port at the time, and Japan's commander failed to destroy the navy's submarine base, fuel storage tanks, or repair facilities. Still, the damage was severe, and the psychological effect galvanized the nation. In a war message broadcast by radio on December 8, Roosevelt decried the attack and labeled December 7 "a date which will live in infamy," a phrase that served as a rallying cry throughout the war. Secretary of War Stimson remembered: "My first feeling was of relief that the indecision was over and that a crisis had come that would unite all our people."

Japan's attack on Pearl Harbor was an act of desperation. The U.S. embargoes, especially on petroleum, had narrowed Japan's options. Negotiations between the two countries proved fruitless: Japan was unwilling to abandon its designs on China, the only concession that might have ended the embargoes. With limited supplies of raw materials, Japan had little hope of winning a prolonged war. Japanese military strategists gambled that a crippling blow would so weaken U.S. military power as to avoid a long war. Japanese leaders decided to risk a surprise attack. "Sometimes a man has to jump with his eyes closed," remarked General Hideki Tojo, who became Japan's prime minister.

A few Americans charged that Roosevelt had intentionally provoked Japan in order to open a "backdoor" to war. They pointed out that the fleet at Pearl Harbor, the nation's principal Pacific base, lay vulnerable at its docks, not even in a state of full alert. In actuality, the American actions and inactions that led to Pearl Harbor were more confused than devious. Beginning in 1934 the United States had gradually enlarged its Pacific fleet, and Roo-

sevelt had also increased the number of B-17 bombers based in the Philippines. The president hoped that the possibility of aerial attacks would intimidate Japan and slow its expansion. The strategy of deterrence not only failed, but it may also have contributed to the lack of vigilance at Pearl Harbor. American leaders doubted that Japan would risk a direct attack. Intelligence experts, who had broken Japan's secret diplomatic code (the decrypted messages were called MAGIC), expected Japan to move toward Singapore or other British or Dutch possessions. MAGIC intercepts, along with visual sightings of Japanese transports, seemed to confirm preparations for a strike in Southeast Asia (a strike that did occur). An insufficiently urgent warning that Japan might also be targeting Pearl Harbor was lost under a mountain of intelligence reports. Confusion and error, not official duplicity, explain America's lack of preparedness at Pearl Harbor; Roosevelt's priorities had been, and would remain, focused on Europe and Hitler.

On December 8, 1941, Congress declared war against Japan. The lone dissenting vote came from Representative Jeannette Rankin, a longtime peace activist from Montana. Three days later, on December 11, Japan's allies, Germany and Italy, declared war on the United States. Hitler, whose eastern offensive had stalled within sight of Moscow, mistakenly assumed that war with Japan would keep the United States preoccupied in the Pacific. The three Axis Powers drastically underestimated America's ability to mobilize swiftly and effectively. And they utterly failed to perceive how their own actions, more than anything Roosevelt himself could have done, would now unite Americans behind the war.

FIGHTING THE WAR IN EUROPE

The first few months after America's entry into the war proved discouraging. German forces already controlled most of Europe from Norway to Greece and had pushed rapidly eastward into the Soviet Union. Now they were rolling across North Africa, threatening the strategically important Suez Canal and the Middle East, which remained under British control. In the Atlantic, German submarines were sinking hundreds of thousands of tons of Allied

Saving Private Ryan (1998)

**Directed by Stephen Spielberg. Starring Tom Hanks (Captain John Miller);
Matt Damon (Private James Ryan); Harve Presnell (General George Marshall).**

Hollywood marked the 50th anniversary of the Allied effort in the Second World War with a series of films about "the good war." In *Saving Private Ryan*, Stephen Spielberg updated the male-centered, big-budget combat genre with cinematic and thematic trademarks he had used in earlier blockbusters such as *Jaws* (1975), *Raiders of the Lost Ark* (1981), and *Jurassic Park* (1993). In 1993, the director-producer had already received critical acclaim for another Second World War film, *Schindler's List*, an unconventional black-and-white examination of the Nazi campaign against Polish Jews.

Although *Saving Private Ryan* invited comparison with *The Longest Day* (1962) because of its depiction of the D-Day invasion of Normandy, Spielberg's greater battlefield "realism" represented a considerable advance in the arts of waging war on film. His production team employed sophisticated computer graphics and nearly deafening Dolby sound to mount battle scenes so realistic that reviewers felt compelled to caution veterans who might be prone to post-traumatic stress syndrome about watching the film. One graphic, thirty-minute spectacle (which recalled the destruction of the Warsaw ghetto in *Schindler's List*) purported to recreate the first deadly hours of the U.S. assault at Omaha Beach.

The film, however, also suggested the kind of family-centered melodrama that Spielberg had grafted onto the sci-fi genre in *E.T.: The Extra-Terrestrial* (1982). A heroic squad led by Captain John Miller is not fighting to liberate France or even to defeat the Germans. Instead, it is trying to locate a single U.S. soldier, Private James Ryan, whose mother has already lost her three other sons to the war. The film poses the question of whether or not such a family-centered mission is worth the risks involved. Might it be, looking back a half-century later, that the concern for family (with family perhaps also a symbol of nation) legitimates and sanctifies the sacrifices of the Second World War? *Private Ryan* answers "yes" to this question.

The major body of the film carefully justifies the rescue mission. Although Captain Miller wonders if his dangerous assignment is simply a public relations stunt, he quickly drops this idea and pursues his mission with all the gallantry required of a Hollywood-commissioned officer. Later, his platoon members debate the morality of risking eight lives to save one, but the cause of Ryan's mother always seems overriding. General George Marshall cuts off debate over the appropriateness of the Ryan mission by invoking an

shipping, endangering Allied supply lines. Japan seemed unstoppable in the Pacific. Following the attack on Pearl Harbor, Japanese forces overran Malaya, the Dutch East Indies, and the Philippines and drove against the British in Burma and the Australians in New Guinea.

Long before December 7, 1941, the Roosevelt administration had expected war and had tried to prepare for it. The challenge had been to train personnel and mobilize resources without, as Henry Stimson noted, "any declaration of war by Congress and with the country not facing the danger before

it." When war came, army morale was low, industrial production was still on a peacetime footing, and labor–management relations were contentious.

Economic and military mobilization began with new government bureaucracies springing up everywhere. Washington reeled under the proliferation of new agencies, new faces, and new procedures. In March 1943, Stimson confided in his diary: "The president is the poorest administrator I have ever worked under. . . . [H]e has constituted an almost innumerable number of new administrative posts." These positions were filled with generally inexperi-

earlier war leader, Abraham Lincoln, who once faced a similar family-centered dilemma. When Miller's troops finally locate Private Ryan, the film's audience discovers that he is the kind of clean-cut Iowa farm boy who will stay by his would-be saviors rather than retreat to safety. Ryan survives, though most of his comrades perish. Captain Miller, dying, implores young Ryan to lead a "good" life, to justify the sacrifice of so many others.

The film *Private Ryan*, in contrast to its characters, takes few risks. It secures its emotional investment in the rescue mission by enclosing the film's Second World War segments with two brief "framing" sequences in which an aging Ryan, along with his family, returns to Normandy and visits the grave of Captain Miller. Both sequences, the one at the beginning of the film and the one at the end, are shot against the backdrop of a sun-drenched American flag. In the final segment, Ryan's wife provides the final reassurance that the trauma of the Second World War served a good cause, because Private Ryan's own family life has justified Miller's sacrifice. "Tell me I've led a good life. Tell me I'm a good man," he implores his wife. After nearly three hours of Spielberg epic, the question is entirely rhetorical.

Saving Private Ryan, which garnered four Academy Award nominations, celebrated the heroism of what popular historians called America's "greatest generation."

enced people, all of whom now laid claim to the president's time.

Indeed, the wartime expansion of government transformed American foreign policymaking. Military priorities—acquiring naval bases, securing landing rights for aircraft, ensuring points for radio transmissions, and gaining access to raw materials—superseded all other demands. The administration was forced to settle on new policies overnight and implement them on a global scale the following day. The newly formed Joint Chiefs of Staff, consisting of representatives from each of the armed services, became Roosevelt's major source of guidance on military strategy. In Washington, where architecture symbolizes political power, the War Department's new Pentagon complex dwarfed the State Department's cramped quarters at "Foggy Bottom." The giant five-story, five-sided building was completed in January 1943, after 16 months of around-the-clock work.

In the Atlantic, German submarines sank seven million tons of Allied shipping in the first 16 months after Pearl Harbor. Aircraft equipped with radar, a new technology developed with encouragement from the war department and in collaboration with Britain, proved effective against submarines in 1942, but the army and navy engaged in months of bickering over who should conduct the antisubmarine warfare. Finally, the navy received official responsibility, and after developing effective radar strategies, it performed well. During 1943 Germany's submarine capability faded "from menace to problem," in the words of Admiral Ernest King. Radar was one of the most important innovations of the war.

Code-breaking was another. In the 1920s a private company had developed the complex ENIGMA encryption machine to encode radio messages. Realizing that radio communications would be essential to his war strategy, Hitler adapted the machine to military purposes. ENIGMA messages were considered unbreakable because the cipher keys changed once or twice a day and the machine could be configured 150 million million million different ways for any message. But Polish mathematicians, who had obtained an ENIGMA machine, made some key breakthroughs on decryption and escaped from Poland just as German armies overran the country. Their discoveries added to others made by cryptographers assembled at Bletchley Park in England. The massive Allied code-breaking operation, so secret that most records were destroyed after the war and no open mention was allowed before 1974, gradually perfected decryption machines. At its height, Bletchley Park employed some 4,000 people, including many Americans. Decrypted messages, called "Ultra" for "Ultra-secret," helped British defenses during the Battle of Britain and would prove critical in campaigns in North Africa and France. Throughout the war the Germans never discovered that many of their radio communications were being forwarded to Allied commanders—occasionally even before they had made it through to their German recipient. In the postwar world, the code-breaking technologies of Ultra would lead toward the development of computer technology.

CAMPAIGNS IN NORTH AFRICA AND ITALY

Military strategy became a contentious issue among the Allied Powers, now consisting principally of the United States, Britain, and the Soviet Union. All advisers agreed that their primary focus would be the European theater, and Roosevelt and his military strategists immediately established a unified command with the British. The Soviet Union, facing 200 German divisions just west of Moscow and suffering hundreds of thousands of casualties, pleaded with Roosevelt and Churchill to open a second front in western Europe to relieve pressure on the USSR. Many of Roosevelt's advisers, including Stimson and General George C. Marshall, agreed. They feared that if German troops forced the Soviet Union out of the war, Germany would then turn its full attention to defeating Britain.

Churchill, however, urged instead the invasion of French North Africa, which was under the control of Vichy France. Churchill's strategy sought to peck away at the edges of enemy power rather than strike at its heart. At a meeting between Roosevelt and Stalin at Casablanca, Morocco, in January 1943, Roosevelt sided with Churchill, and the promised invasion of France was postponed. The risks of a cross-Channel assault were great, Roosevelt reasoned, and the home front needed some rapid victories. To assuage Stalin's fears that his two allies might sign a separate peace with Hitler, the two leaders did announce that they would stay in the fight until Germany agreed to nothing less than unconditional surrender. Continuing disagreements over the timing of the cross-Channel invasion, however, still strained the alliance.

The North African operation, code-named TORCH, began with Anglo-American landings in Morocco and Algeria in November 1942. To ease resistance against the Allies' North African invasion, U.S. General Dwight D. Eisenhower struck a deal with French Admiral Jean Darlan, a Nazi sympathizer, an anti-Semite, and the Vichy officer who controlled France's colonies in North Africa. Darlan agreed to break with the Vichy regime and stop resisting the Allied operation in return for Eisenhower's pledge that the United States would support him. The deal outraged some Americans who believed that it compromised the moral purpose of the war. Darlan's assassination in December 1942, called an "act of Providence" by one of Eisenhower's deputies, put an end to the embarrassment. Even so, the antagonism that Eisenhower's action had created between Americans and the Free

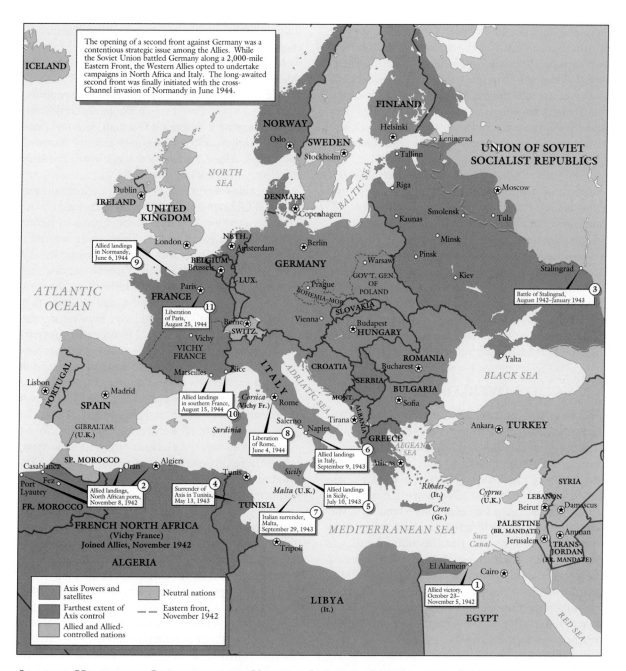

The opening of a second front against Germany was a contentious strategic issue among the Allies. While the Soviet Union battled Germany along a 2,000-mile Eastern Front, the Western Allies opted to undertake campaigns in North Africa and Italy. The long-awaited second front was finally initiated with the cross-Channel invasion of Normandy in June 1944.

ALLIED MILITARY STRATEGY IN NORTH AFRICA, ITALY, AND FRANCE

French movement, led by General Charles de Gaulle, had lasting consequences after the war.

As TORCH progressed, assisted by Ultra intercepts, the Soviets managed to turn the tide of battle at Stalingrad. They cut off and destroyed one German army in the city and sent other German armies reeling backward. Despite this defeat in the East, Hitler poured reinforcements into North Africa but could not stop either TORCH or the British, who were driving west from Egypt. About 200,000 Axis soldiers surrendered to the Allies in April and May 1943.

In the summer of 1943 Allied troops followed up the successful North African campaign by overrunning the island of Sicily and fighting their way slowly north through Italy's mountains. Their successes boosted morale in the United States, but the Italian campaign drained badly needed resources for the upcoming cross-Channel invasion of France, while scarcely denting the German stranglehold on Europe.

Some American officials increasingly worried about the postwar implications of wartime strategy. Stimson, for example, warned that the peripheral campaigns through Africa and Italy might leave the Soviets dominating central Europe. Unless the western democracies confronted Germany in the heart of Europe, he argued, Germany would be left holding "the leg for Stalin to skin the deer and I think that will be dangerous business for us at the end of the war." Acting on such advice, Roosevelt finally agreed to set a date for the cross-Channel invasion that Stalin had long been promised.

OPERATION OVERLORD

Operation OVERLORD, directed by Supreme Allied Commander Dwight Eisenhower, finally began on June 6, 1944, D-Day. During the months preceding D-Day, probably the largest invasion force in history had been assembled in England. Allied double agents and diversionary tactics had tricked the Germans into expecting a landing at the narrowest part of the English Channel rather than in the Normandy region. Just five months earlier, a new decoding machine had dramatically increased the number of Ultra intercepts, and Allied intelligence officers therefore had the advantage of knowing that their deception had worked. After several delays, due to the Channel's unpredictable weather, nervous commanders finally ordered the daring plan to begin. The night before, as naval guns pounded the Normandy shore, three divisions of paratroopers were dropped behind enemy lines to disrupt German communications. Then, at dawn, more than 4,000 Allied ships landed troops and supplies on Normandy's beaches. The first American troops to land at Omaha Beach met especially heavy German fire and took enormous casualties, but the waves of invading troops continued throughout the day and indeed through the weeks that followed. Within three weeks, more than one

million people had landed, secured the Normandy coast, and opened the long-awaited second front.

Just as the Battle of Stalingrad had reversed the tide of the war in the East, so Operation OVERLORD turned the tide in the West. Within three months, U.S., British, and Free French troops entered Paris. After repulsing a desperate German counteroffensive in Belgium, at the December–January Battle of the Bulge, Allied armies swept eastward, crossing the Rhine and heading toward Berlin.

The Allies disagreed on how to orchestrate the defeat of Germany. British strategists favored a swift drive, so as to meet up with Soviet armies in Berlin or even farther east. General Eisenhower favored a strategy that was militarily less risky and politically less provocative to the Soviets. Eisenhower doubted that Allied troops could reach Berlin from the west before the Soviet armies arrived, and he knew that stopping short of Berlin would save lives among the troops under his command. He was also eager to end the war on a note of trust and believed that racing the Soviets to Berlin would undermine the basis for postwar Soviet–American cooperation. In the end, Eisenhower's views prevailed. He moved cautiously along a broad front, halting his troops at the Elbe River, west of Berlin, and allowing Soviet troops to roll into the German capital. The Soviets, who suffered staggering casualties in taking Berlin, worked with the other Allies to establish joint administration of the city.

As the war in Europe drew to a close, the horrors perpetrated by the Third Reich became visible to the world. Almost from the beginning of U.S. participation in the war, many Americans knew that Hitler was bent on genocide against Jews, gypsies, and other targeted groups. Although only a military victory could put an end to German death camps, the Allies might have saved thousands of Jews by encouraging them to emigrate and helping them to escape. Allied leaders, however, worried about the impact of large numbers of Jewish refugees on their countries, and they also were reluctant to use scarce ships to transport Jews to neutral sanctuaries. In 1943, after Romania proposed permitting an evacuation of 70,000 Jews from its territory, Allied leaders avoided any serious discussion of the plan. The United States even refused to relax its strict policy on visas to admit Jews who might have escaped on their own. With no way of crossing the Atlantic and with few places to go in Europe,

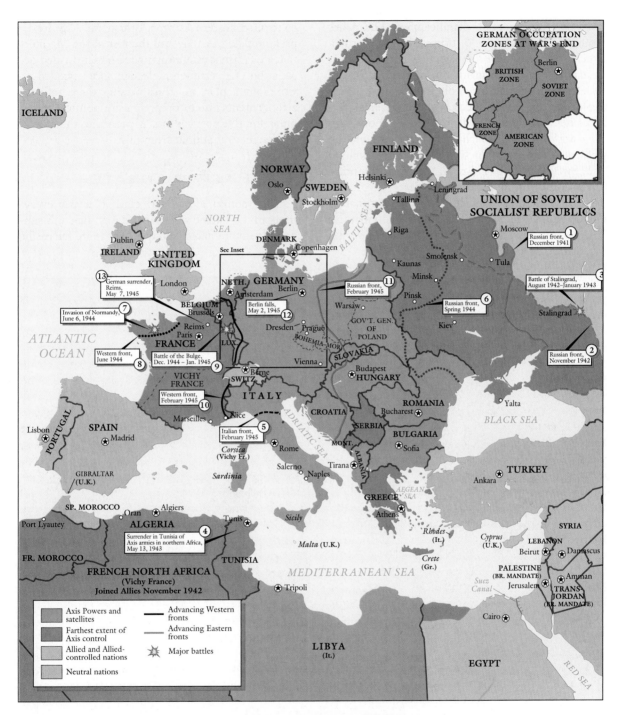

ALLIED ADVANCES AND COLLAPSE OF GERMAN POWER

hundreds of thousands of Jews who might have been saved went to Nazi death camps.

Hitler's campaign of extermination, now called the Holocaust, killed between 5 and 6 million Jews out of Europe's prewar population of 10 million; hundreds of thousands more from various other groups were also murdered, especially gypsies, homosexuals, intellectuals, communists, and the physically and mentally handicapped. The Allies would, in 1945 and 1946, bring 24 high German officials to trial at Nuremberg for "crimes against humanity." Large quantities of money, gold, and jewelry that Nazi leaders stole from victims of the Holocaust and deposited in Swiss banks, however, remained largely hidden from view for more than 50 years. Not until 1997 did Jewish groups and the U.S. government begin to force investigations of the Swiss banking industry, finally prompting some restitution for victim's families.

With Hitler's suicide in April and Germany's surrender on May 8, 1945, the military foundations for peace in Europe were complete. Soviet armies controlled Eastern Europe; British and U.S. forces predominated in Italy and the rest of the Mediterranean; Germany and Austria fell under divided occupation. Governmental leaders now needed to work out a plan for transforming these military arrangements into a comprehensive political settlement for the postwar era. Meanwhile, the war in the Pacific was still far from over.

THE PACIFIC THEATER

For six months after Pearl Harbor, nearly everything in the Pacific went Japan's way. Britain's supposedly impregnable colony at Singapore fell easily.

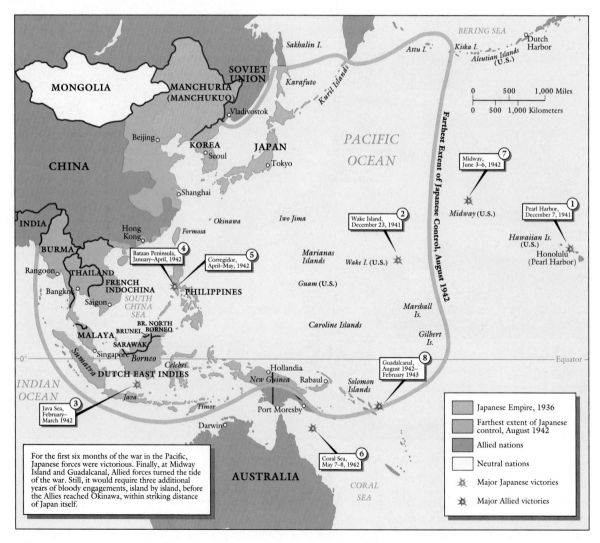

For the first six months of the war in the Pacific, Japanese forces were victorious. Finally, at Midway Island and Guadalcanal, Allied forces turned the tide of the war. Still, it would require three additional years of bloody engagements, island by island, before the Allies reached Okinawa, within striking distance of Japan itself.

JAPANESE EXPANSION AND EARLY BATTLES IN THE PACIFIC

American naval garrisons in the Philippines and on Guam and Wake islands were overwhelmed, and American and Filipino armies were forced to surrender at Bataan and Corregidor in the Philippines. In one of the most notorious incidents of the war, the Bataan Death March, Japanese commanders forced many of their 75,000 American and Filipino captives to walk to a rail line for transport to prison camp. Suffering from disease, hunger, and cruelty, more than 7,000 soldiers died in the forced march. Elsewhere, Japanese forces streamed southward to menace Australia. Then the tide turned.

SEIZING THE INITIATIVE IN THE PACIFIC

When Japan finally suffered its first naval defeat at the Battle of the Coral Sea in May 1942, Japanese naval commanders decided to hit back hard. They amassed 200 ships and 600 planes to destroy what remained of the U.S. Pacific fleet and to take Midway Island, a strategic location for Hawaii's security. U.S. Naval Intelligence, however, was able to break enough of the Japanese code to warn Admiral Chester W. Nimitz of the plan. Surprising the Japanese navy, U.S. planes sank four Japanese carriers, destroyed a total of 322 planes, and preserved American presence at Midway. The U.S. Navy's losses were substantial, but Japan's were so much greater that its offensive capabilities were crippled.

Two months later, American forces splashed ashore at Guadalcanal in the Solomon Islands and successfully relieved the pressure on Australia and its military supply lines. The bloody engagements in the Solomons continued for months on both land and sea, but they accomplished one major objective: seizing the initiative against Japan. This success, combined with the delay in opening a second front in Europe, also affected grand strategy. According to prewar plans, the war in Europe was to have received highest priority, but by 1943 the two theaters were receiving roughly equal resources.

The bloody engagements in the Pacific dramatically illustrated that the war was, in historian John Dower's phrase, a "war without mercy." It was one in which racial prejudice reinforced brutality. For Japan, the Pacific conflict was a war to establish forever the superiority of the divine Yamato race. Prisoners taken by the Japanese, mostly on the Asian mainland, were brutalized in unimaginable ways,

and survival rates were low. The Japanese army's Unit 731 tested bacteriological weapons in China and, like the Nazi doctors, conducted horrifying medical experiments on live subjects. American propaganda images also played upon themes of racial superiority, portraying the Japanese as animalistic subhumans. American troops often rivaled Japan's forces in their disrespect for the enemy dead and sometimes killed the enemy rather than take prisoners. The longer the Pacific war lasted, the more it seemed to loosen the boundaries of acceptable violence against combatants and civilians alike.

CHINA POLICY

U.S. policymakers hoped that China would fight Japan more effectively and emerge after the war as a strong and united nation. Neither hope was realized.

General Joseph W. Stilwell, who had worked with the Chinese armies resisting the Japanese invasion in the late 1930s, undertook the job of turning China into an effective military force. Jiang Jieshi (formerly spelled Chiang Kai-shek) headed China's government and appointed the prickly Stilwell his chief of staff, but frictions between "Vinegar Joe" Stilwell and Jiang, fueled by disputes over military priorities, became so intense that in May 1943 Roosevelt bowed to Jiang's demand for Stilwell's dismissal. Meanwhile, Japan's advance into China continued, and in 1944 its forces captured seven of the principal U.S. air bases in China.

To complicate matters further, China was beset by civil war. Jiang's Nationalist government was incompetent, corrupt, and unpopular. It avoided engaging the Japanese invaders and still made extravagant demands for U.S. assistance. Meanwhile, a growing communist movement led by Mao Zedong was fighting effectively against the Japanese and enjoyed widespread support among Chinese peasants. Stilwell urged Roosevelt to cut off support to Jiang unless he fought with more determination. Roosevelt, however, feared that such actions would create even greater chaos and resisted strengthening Mao's position. He continued to provide moral support and matériel to Jiang's armies and even convinced Stalin to support Jiang rather than Mao. Moreover, pressed by a powerful "China lobby" of domestic conservatives, he insisted that Jiang's China be permitted to stand with the major powers after victory had been won. By tying U.S. policy to

Jiang's leadership and entertaining the myth that China was a stable power, Roosevelt and the "China lobby" prepared the way for great difficulties in forging a China policy in the postwar period.

PACIFIC STRATEGY

In contrast to the war in Europe, no unified command guided the war in the Pacific, and top military commanders continually disagreed on matters of strategy. Consequently, military actions often emerged from compromise. General Douglas MacArthur, commander of the army in the South Pacific, favored an offensive launched from his headquarters in Australia through New Guinea and the Philippines and on to Japan. After Japan drove him out of the Philippines in May 1942, he had promised to return, and he was determined to keep his word. He argued that the United States must be in control of the Philippines at war's end in order to preserve its strategic position in Asia. Admiral

Nimitz disagreed. He favored an advance across the smaller islands of the central Pacific, pointing out that a route that bypassed the Philippines would provide more direct access to Japan. Unable to decide between the two strategies, the Joint Chiefs of Staff authorized both.

Marked by fierce fighting and heavy casualties, both offensives moved forward. MacArthur took New Guinea, and Nimitz's forces liberated the Marshall Islands and the Marianas in 1943 and 1944. An effective radio communication system conducted by a Marine platoon of Navajo Indians made a unique contribution. On hundreds of Pacific beaches Navajo-speaking squads set up radio contact with headquarters and with supporting units. Navajo, a language unfamiliar to Japanese intelligence officers, provided a secure medium for sensitive communications. In late 1944 the fall of Saipan brought American bombers within range of Japan. The capture of the island of Iwo Jima—18 square miles taken at the cost of 27,000 American

NAVAJO SIGNAL CORPS Sending messages in their native language, which neither the Japanese nor the Germans could decipher, Navajo Indians in the Signal Corps made a unique contribution to preserving the secrecy of U.S. intelligence.

casualties—and of Okinawa further shortened that distance during the spring of 1945. Okinawa illustrated the nearly unbelievable ferocity of the island campaigns: 120,000 Japanese soldiers died; 48,000 Americans. U.S. military planners extrapolated from these numbers when considering the dreaded prospect of an invasion of the home islands of Japan itself.

As the seaborne offensive proceeded, the United States brought its airpower into play. Before the war, Roosevelt had become convinced that aerial bombing offered almost magical power. At one time, he even had hoped that the mere threat of bombing would be so frightening that airpower would be a deterrent to war rather than a means of conducting it. The effects of strategic bombing in Europe, however, had been ambiguous. The Nazi bombardment of British cities in 1940 and 1941 did heavy damage but only steeled British resolve, uniting the nation and boosting civilian morale. The Allies' strategic bombing of German cities, including the destruction of such large cities as Hamburg and Dresden, produced equally mixed results. Indeed, military historians continue to debate the relative merits of the strategic bombing in Europe, wondering whether the gains against military targets really offset the huge civilian casualties and the unsustainable losses of American pilots and aircraft. Still, Roosevelt continued to believe that airpower might provide the crucial advantage over the Japanese, and strategic bombing once more became a major tactic.

In February 1944 General Henry Harley ("Hap") Arnold, commander of the newly formed 20th Army Air Force, presented Roosevelt with a plan for strategic air assaults on Japanese cities. His proposal included a systematic campaign of destruction through the firebombing of urban targets, "not only because they are greatly congested but because they contain numerous war industries." Roosevelt approved the plan. In the month before bombing began, the Office of War Information lifted its ban on atrocity stories about Japan's treatment of American prisoners. The effort was designed to prepare the public for expected massive killing of Japanese civilians. Officials expected that, as grisly reports and racist anti-Japanese propaganda swept across the country, the public would become more permissive in accepting the results of

ANTI-JAPANESE PROPAGANDA The Second World War evoked racist hostility toward Japanese Americans who, before the war, had developed a substantial economic stake on the West Coast.

war. Arnold's original air campaign, operating from bases in China, turned out to be cumbersome and ineffective; it was replaced by an even more lethal operation, running from Saipan, under the aegis of General Curtis LeMay.

The official position was that the incendiary raids on Japanese cities constituted "precision" rather than "area" bombing. In actuality, the success of a mission was measured by the number of square miles it left scorched and useless. Destroying Japan's industrial capacity by firebombing the workers who ran the factories sounded like a focused strategy, but the systematic burning of entire cities brought unprecedented civilian casualties. Estimates are that more Japanese civilians were killed in the raids than Japanese soldiers were killed in battle. An attack on Tokyo on the night of March 9–10, 1945, inaugurated the new policy by leveling 16 square miles (one-fourth) of the city, destroying 267,000 buildings and inflicting 185,000 casualties. One by one, LeMay torched other cities. In his memoirs, LeMay summarized his strategy: "Bomb and burn them until they quit."

By the winter of 1944–45, a combined sea and air strategy had emerged: The United States would seek "unconditional surrender" by blockading Japan's seaports, continuing its bombardment of

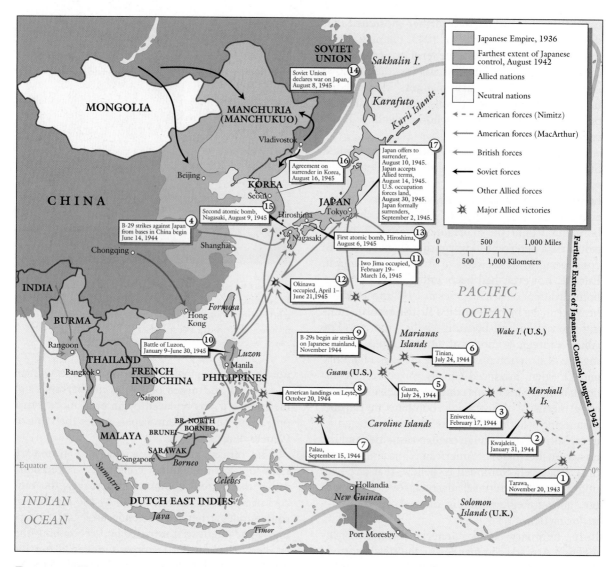

PACIFIC THEATER OFFENSIVE STRATEGY AND FINAL ASSAULT AGAINST JAPAN

Japanese cities from the air, and perhaps invading Japan itself. Later critics of the policy of unconditional surrender have suggested that it may have hardened the determination with which Japan fought the war after its ultimate defeat had become obvious. These critics have pointed out that many Japanese assumed that unconditional surrender would mean the death of the emperor; moreover, the policy prevented U.S. negotiators from vigorously pursuing peace feelers, which some Japanese leaders were trying to send through third parties. With the unconditional surrender policy in place

and Japan's determination to fight even in the face of certain defeat, the strategy of American leaders seemed to require massive destruction to achieve victory.

A NEW PRESIDENT

On April 13, 1945, just one month before Germany's formal surrender and five months before Japan's, newspaper headlines across the country mourned, "President Roosevelt Dead." Profound sorrow and shock spread through the armed forces, where many young men and women had hardly known any other president; through diplomatic conference halls, where Roosevelt's magnetism had often brought unity, if not clarity; and among factory workers, farmers, and bureaucrats, for whom Roosevelt had symbolized optimism and unity through depression and war. Roosevelt had accumulated a host of critics and enemies. Indeed, he had defeated Republican Thomas E. Dewey in the 1944 presidential election by the smallest popular vote margin in nearly 30 years. Still, he had been a very popular president, and he left an enduring imprint on American life. "He was Commander-in-Chief, not only of the Armed Forces, but of our generation," wrote an editor of *Yank* magazine.

Compared with the legacy of Roosevelt, Vice President Harry S. Truman's stature seemed impossibly small. Born on a farm near Independence, Missouri, Harry Truman had served in France during the First World War. After the war, he went into politics under the auspices of Thomas J. Pendergast's Democratic party machine in Kansas City. He was elected to the Senate in 1934, where he made his reputation in the early years of the Second World War, fighting waste in spending programs, and was chosen as Roosevelt's running mate in 1944. In contrast to Roosevelt, who was upper class, elite educated, and worldly, Truman was simply a "little man from Missouri." He prided himself on plain, direct talk. His critics considered him poorly prepared for the job of president. Truman had almost no background in international affairs. Roosevelt had not included him in high-level policy discussions, and he knew little about any informal understandings that Roosevelt may have made with foreign leaders. In fact, during the period between the inauguration following the 1944 election and the president's death, Truman had met with Roosevelt only three times.

ATOMIC POWER AND JAPANESE SURRENDER

At Los Alamos, New Mexico, scientists from all across the United States had been secretly working on a project that gave Truman a weapon of massive destruction. Advances in theoretical physics during the 1930s had suggested that splitting the atom (fission) would release a tremendous amount of energy.

Fearful that Germany was racing ahead in this effort, Albert Einstein, a Jewish refugee from Germany, in 1939 had urged President Roosevelt to launch a secret program to build a bomb based on atomic research. The government subsequently enlisted top scientists in the Manhattan Project, the largest and most secretive military project yet undertaken. On July 16, 1945, after a succession of breakthroughs in physics research, the first atomic weapon was successfully tested at Trinity Site, near Alamagordo, New Mexico. The researchers notified Truman that the terrifying new weapon was ready.

Truman and his top policymakers assumed that it should be put to immediate military use. They were eager to end the war, both because a possible land invasion of Japan might have cost so many American lives and also because the Soviet Union was planning to enter the Pacific theater, and Truman wished to limit Soviet power in that region. Secretary of War Stimson wrote: "It was our common objective, throughout the war, to be the first to produce an atomic weapon and use it. The possible atomic weapon was considered to be a new and tremendously powerful explosive, as legitimate as any other of the deadly explosive weapons of modern war." Churchill called the bomb a "miracle of deliverance" and a peace-giver. Truman later said that he had never lost a night's sleep over its use because it saved lives.

Other advisers had more qualms; disagreement arose over where and how the bomb should be deployed. A commission of atomic scientists, headed by Jerome Franck, recommended a "demonstration" that would impress Japan with the bomb's power yet cause no loss of life. General Marshall suggested using the bomb only on military installations or on some large manufacturing area from which people would be warned away in advance, but most of Truman's advisers agreed that simply demonstrating the bomb's power might not be enough. The purpose of the bomb, Stimson said, was to make "a profound psychological impression on as many inhabitants as possible." They believed that it would take massive destruction to bring unconditional surrender.

In the context of the earlier aerial bombardment of Japanese cities, dropping atomic bombs on the previously unbombed cities of Hiroshima and Nagasaki on August 6 and 9, 1945, seemed simply an

TOTAL WAR: DRESDEN AND HIROSHIMA The effects of "total war" are graphically illustrated in these photographs—of the devastation of Dresden, Germany (top), by the British Bomber Command and the U.S. 8th Air Force on February 13 and 14, 1945, and that of Hiroshima, Japan (bottom), by the U.S. 509th Composite Group on August 6, 1945. In the initial attack on Dresden, 786 aircraft dropped 5,824,000 pounds (2,600 long tons) of bombs on the city, killing an estimated 60,000 people and injuring another 30,000. An area of more than 2.5 square miles in the city center was demolished, and some 37,000 buildings were destroyed. To critics, the bombing of Dresden, a target that many argued was of little strategic value, exemplified the excessive use of airpower.

In sobering comparison, Hiroshima was devastated by one bomb weighing only 10,000 pounds (4.4 long tons)—an atomic bomb—dropped from one aircraft. The single U-235 bomb killed 68,000 people outright, injured another 30,000, and left 10,000 missing. (These figures do not include those who later developed diseases from deadly gamma rays.) The bomb obliterated almost 5 square miles of the city's center and destroyed 40,653 buildings. Truman reported the strike as "an overwhelming success." Many hailed the atomic bomb as a necessary step toward military victory; others worried about the dawn of the "nuclear age."

acceleration of existing policy rather than a departure from it. "Fat Man" and "Little Boy," as the two bombs were nicknamed, were merely viewed as bigger, more effective firebombs. Of course, atomic weapons did produce yet a new level of violence. Colonel Paul Tibbets, who piloted the plane that dropped the first bomb, reported that "the shimmering city became an ugly smudge . . . a pot of bubbling hot tar." Teams of U.S. observers who entered the cities in the aftermath were stunned at the immediate devastation, including the instantaneous incineration of both human beings and manmade structures, as well as the longer-lasting horror of radiation disease.

The mushroom clouds over Hiroshima and Nagasaki inaugurated a new "atomic age" in which dreams of peace were mingled with nightmares of Armageddon. But in those late summer days of 1945, most Americans sighed with relief. Although some of Japan's military leaders wanted to continue the fight, Emperor Hirohito summoned the cabinet and declared that, with the nation on the brink of destruction, "I cannot endure the thought of letting my people suffer any longer." News reports on August 15 proclaimed Japan's defeat. On September 2, V-J Day, Japan formally signed a surrender document aboard the battleship *Missouri* in Tokyo Bay.

THE WAR AT HOME: THE ECONOMY

The success of the U.S. military effort in both Europe and Asia depended on mobilization at home. Ultimately, this mobilization, first to help the Allies and then to support America's own war effort, finally ended the Great Depression of the 1930s and helped Roosevelt to two more terms as president. The war did more than restore prosperity. From 1941 to 1945, as America's people and productivity bent toward the single aim of victory, the war also transformed the nation's political economy—its government, its business and financial institutions, and its labor force.

GOVERNMENT'S ROLE IN THE ECONOMY

The federal bureaucracy nearly quadrupled in size during the war, as new economic agencies prolifer-

ated. The most powerful of these, the War Production Board, oversaw the conversion and expansion of factories, allocated resources, and enforced production priorities and schedules. The War Labor Board had jurisdiction over labor–management disputes, and the War Manpower Commission allocated labor to various industries. The Office of Price Administration regulated prices to control inflation and rationed such scarce commodities as gasoline, rubber, steel, shoes, coffee, sugar, and meat. All these agencies, and others, intruded into the workings of the market economy by imposing government controls on economic decisions, both in business and in the home. Although most of the controls were abandoned after the war, the concept of greater governmental regulation of the economy survived.

From 1940 to 1945 the U.S. economy expanded rapidly, accelerating from a decade of sluggishness to one of full-speed, even force-fed production. In each year of the war, GNP rose by 15 percent or more. According to a War Production Board report, "A country that . . . could produce in 1944 $199,000,000,000 in goods and services was an invincible opponent." When Roosevelt called for the production of 60,000 planes, shortly after Pearl Harbor, skeptics jeered. Yet within the next few years the nation produced nearly 300,000 planes—in a dazzling range of designs. The Maritime Commission oversaw construction of more than 53 million tons of shipping, turning out ships faster than German submarines could sink them. The previously dormant economy spewed out prodigious quantities of other supplies, including 2.5 million trucks and 50 million pairs of shoes. This was a "war of massed machines," as the journalist Hanson Baldwin described it.

Striving to increase production, industry entered into an unprecedented relationship with government to promote scientific and technological research and development (R&D). Government money subsidized new industries, such as electronics, and enabled others, such as rubber and chemicals, to transform their processes and products. Annual expenditures on R&D doubled prewar levels, with the government providing most of the funds. The newly established Office of Scientific Research and Development, headed by Vannevar Bush, entered into contracts for a variety of projects with universities and scientists. Under this program, radar and penicillin (both British breakthroughs), rocket engines, and other new products were rapidly perfected for wartime use. Refugees from Nazi tyranny brought added strength to the scientific and academic establishments, contributing to advances in physics, astronomy, psychiatry, and architecture. In the four decades after 1930, they won no fewer than 24 Nobel Prizes.

The Manhattan Project was perhaps the most dramatic example of the new connections among science, national defense, and the federal government. The project employed nearly 130,000 people by mid-1944 and eventually cost more than two billion dollars. Many of the émigré scientists who had fled Nazi regimes participated.

BUSINESS AND FINANCE

Government war spending rose from $9 billion in 1940 to $98 billion in 1944. In 1941 the national debt stood at $48 billion; by VJ Day it was $280 billion. With few goods to buy, Americans invested in war bonds, turning their savings into tanks and planes. Although war bonds provided a relatively insignificant contribution to the war, they did help drive the level of personal saving up to 25 percent of consumer income. War bond purchases also became an important psychological motivator by giving millions of Americans an even larger stake in victory.

As production shifted from autos to tanks, from refrigerators to guns, many consumer goods became scarce. Essentials such as food, fabrics, and gasoline were rationed and, consequently, were shared more equitably than they had been before the war. Higher taxes on wealthier Americans tended to redistribute income and narrow the gap between the poor and the well-to-do. War bonds, rationing, and progressive taxation gave Americans a sense of shared sacrifice and helped ease the class tensions of the 1930s.

As the war fostered an increase in personal savings and promoted a measure of income redistribution it also facilitated the dismantling of many of the New Deal agencies that most directly aided the poor. A Republican surge in the 1942 off-year elections gained the GOP 44 seats in the House and 7 new senators and helped strengthen a conservative, anti–New Deal coalition in Congress. In 1943 Congress abolished the job-creation programs of

the Works Progress Administration (WPA), the Civilian Conservation Corps (CCC), and the National Youth Administration (NYA) (see chapter 25). It also shut down the Rural Electrification Administration (REA) and Farm Security Administration (FSA), agencies that had assisted impoverished rural areas. The budget was drastically reduced for the National Recovery Planning Board, designed to introduce comprehensive national planning into America's market economy. As "dollar-a-year" business executives virtually donated their time to run the new wartime bureaus, the Roosevelt administration shifted its attitude toward big business from one of guarded hostility to one of cooperation. Although many in the business community never fully trusted Roosevelt, the war nevertheless nudged the president's New Deal to the right.

In win-the-war Washington, social programs withered as big businesses considered essential to victory flourished under government subsidies. What was "essential," of course, became a matter of definition. Coca-Cola and Wrigley's chewing gum won precious sugar allotments by arguing that GIs overseas "needed" to enjoy these products. Both companies prospered. The Kaiser Corporation, whose spectacular growth in the 1930s had been spurred by federal dam contracts, now turned its attention to the building of ships, aircraft, and military vehicles, such as the famous "jeep." By 1943 the company was handling nearly one-third of the nation's military construction, establishing a new industrial base for southern California's previously agricultural economy. Federal subsidies, low-interest loans, and tax breaks enabled factories to expand and retool. A cost-plus formula built into government contracts guaranteed that manufacturers would make a profit.

The war concentrated power in the largest corporations. Roosevelt postponed the enforcement of antitrust laws. Legal challenges that had been years in preparation, such as the case against America's great oil cartel, were tucked away. The renewal of some antitrust activity in 1944, when victory seemed assured, helped keep the concept of trust-busting alive, but it did little to curtail the growing power of giant enterprises. Congressional efforts to investigate alleged collusion in the awarding of government contracts and to increase assistance to small businesses similarly made little progress in Washington's crisis atmosphere. The top 100 companies, which had provided 30 percent of the nation's total manufacturing output in 1940, were providing 70 percent by 1943. Small businesses were left catering mainly to the civilian economy, which was plagued by erratic allocations, shortages, and stagnation.

THE WORKFORCE

During the first two years of military buildup, as factories began to step up production, many workers who had been idled during the Great Depression were called back to work. Employment in heavy industry invariably went to men, and most of the skilled jobs went to whites. Initially, administrators of newly established, government-sponsored vocational training centers focused their efforts on training white males. They refused to set up courses for women or, especially in the South, to admit minority workers. Employers, they said, would never hire from these groups. But as military service drained the supply of white male workers, women and minorities became more attractive candidates for production jobs. Soon, both private employers and government were encouraging women to go to work, southern African Americans to move to northern industrial cities, and Mexicans to enter the United States under the *bracero* guest unskilled worker program. As the country re-

WOMEN JOIN THE WAR EFFORT Women employees at the Convair Company in California use a rivet gun and bucking bar, tools traditionally used only by men.

sponded to labor shortages, the composition of the workforce changed dramatically.

Women were hired for jobs never before open to them. They became welders, shipbuilders, lumberjacks, miners. For the first time, women won places in prestigious symphony orchestras. As major league baseball languished from a lack of players, female teams sprang up to give new life to the national pastime; the owner of the Chicago Cubs organized a woman's league in 1943 that eventually fielded 10 teams. Many employers hired married women, who, before the war, often were banned even from such traditionally female occupations as teaching. Minority women, who before the war had worked mostly on farms or as domestic servants, moved into clerical or secretarial jobs, where they had not previously been welcome. Most workplaces, however, tended to be segregated by sex—women working with other women and men working with other men. Still, the range of jobs open to women grew wider.

The character of unpaid labor, long provided mostly by women, also underwent significant change. Volunteer activities such as Red Cross projects, civil defense work, and recycling drives claimed more and more of the time of women, children, and older people. Government home conservation propaganda exhorted homemakers: "Wear it out, use it up, make it do, or do without." "Work in a garden this summer." "Save waste fats for explosives." Most Depression-era Americans were already used to scarcity and to "getting by," but the war now equated parsimonious lifestyles with patriotism rather than with poverty. Both in the home and in the factory, women's responsibilities and workloads increased.

The new labor market improved the general economic position of African Americans as many moved into labor-scarce cities and into jobs previously reserved for whites. By executive order in June 1941, the president created the Fair Employment Practices Commission (FEPC), which tried to ban discrimination in hiring. In 1943 the government announced that it would not recognize as collective bargaining agents any unions that denied admittance to minorities. The War Labor Board outlawed the practice of paying different wages to whites and nonwhites doing the same job. Before the war, the African American population had been

CHILDREN ENLIST IN THE WAR EFFORT These children, flashing the "V-for-Victory" sign, stand atop a pile of scrap metal. Collecting scrap of all kinds for war production helped to engage millions of Americans young and old on the home front.

mainly southern, rural, and agricultural; within a few years, a substantial percentage of African Americans had become northern, urban, and industrial. Although employment discrimination was hardly eliminated, twice as many African Americans held skilled jobs at the end of the war as at the beginning.

For both men and women, the war brought higher wages and longer work hours. Although in 1943 the government insisted that labor unions limit demands for wage increases to 15 percent, overtime often raised paychecks far more. During the war, average weekly earnings rose nearly 70 percent. Farmers, who had suffered through many years of low prices and overproduction, doubled their income and then doubled it again.

LABOR UNIONS

The scarcity of labor during the war substantially strengthened the labor union movement. Union membership rose by 50 percent. Women and mi-

nority workers joined unions in unprecedented numbers (women accounted for 27 percent of total union membership by 1944), but the main beneficiaries of labor's new power were the white males who still comprised the bulk of union membership.

Especially on the national level, organized labor showed only weak commitment to female workers. Not a single woman served on the executive boards of either the AFL or the CIO. The International Brotherhood of Teamsters even required women to sign a statement that their union membership could be revoked when the war was over. Unions did fight for contracts stipulating equal pay for men and women in the same job, but these benefited women only as long as they held "male" jobs.

The unions' primary purpose in advocating equal pay was to maintain wage levels for the men who would return to their jobs after the war. During the first year of peace, as employers trimmed their workforces, both business and unions gave special consideration to returning veterans and worked to ease both women and minority workers out of their wartime jobs. During the war, women held 25 percent of all jobs in automobile factories; by mid-1946 they held only 7.5 percent of those jobs. Older patterns of segregation based on sex and race returned to the workplace. Unions based their policies on seniority and their wage demands on the goal of securing male workers a "family wage," one that would be sufficient to support an entire family.

Some unions, reflecting the interests of their white male members, supported racial discrimination for fear that hiring lower-paid, nonwhite workers would jeopardize their own, better-paid positions. Early in the war, most AFL affiliates in the aircraft and shipbuilding industries—sources of the highest-paid jobs—had refused to accept African Americans as members. They quarreled with the FEPC over this policy throughout the war, some even claiming that the effort to advance blacks was the work of subversive, procommunist "agitators." As growing numbers of African Americans were hired, racial tensions in the workplace increased. In a Baltimore munitions factory, whites suspended work rather than integrate their washrooms and cafeterias. In Beaumont, Texas, martial law was declared to protect black workers from attacks by whites. All across the country—in a defense plant in Lockland, Ohio, at a transit company in Philadelphia, at a shipbuilding company in Mobile—white workers walked off the job to protest the hiring of African Americans. Beyond revealing deep-seated racism, such incidents reflected the union leaders' fears of losing the economic gains and recognition they had fought so hard to win during the 1930s. They wanted to prevent management from using the war as an excuse to erode their power and their wages.

The labor militancy of the 1930s was muted by a wartime no-strike pledge, but it nonetheless persisted. Despite no-strike assurances, for example, the United Mine Workers union called a strike in the bituminous coal fields in 1943. When the War Labor Board took a hard line against the union's demands, the strike was prolonged, prompting Secretary of the Interior Harold L. Ickes to blast both sides. He called the impasse "a black and stupid chapter in the history of the home front." In Detroit, disgruntled aircraft workers roamed the factory floors, cutting off the neckties of their supervisors; wildcat strikes erupted among St. Louis bus drivers, Dodge assembly-line employees in Detroit, and Philadelphia streetcar conductors. The increasingly conservative Congress responded by passing the Smith-Connally Act of 1943, which empowered the president to seize plants or mines if strikes interrupted war production. Even so, the war helped to strengthen organized labor's place in American life. By the end of the war, union membership was at an all-time high.

ASSESSING ECONOMIC CHANGE

Overall, the impact of the war on America's political economy was varied. During the war, the workplace became more inclusive than ever before in terms of gender and race, and so did labor unions. More people entered the paid labor force, and many of them earned more money than rationing restrictions allowed them to spend. In a remarkable and welcome change from the decade of the Great Depression, jobs were plentiful and savings piled up. Although some of these changes proved short-lived, the new precedents and expectations arising from the wartime experience could not be entirely effaced at war's end.

More than anything else, the institutional scale of American life was transformed. Big government, big business, and big labor all grew even bigger during the war years. Science and technology forged new links of mutual interest among these three sectors. The old America of small farms, small businesses, and small towns did not disappear, but urban-based, bureaucratized institutions, in both the public and private sectors, increasingly organized life in postwar America.

THE WAR AT HOME: SOCIAL ISSUES

Dramatic social changes accompanied the wartime mobilization. By the end of the war, 16 million Americans had served in the military. Ordered by military service or attracted by employment, many people moved away from the communities in which they had grown up. Even on the home front, the war involved constant sacrifice—rationing, recycling, volunteer work. The war, most Americans believed, was being fought to preserve democracy

Norman Rockwell's *Four Freedoms*

Wartime sacrifices were justified as necessary to protect liberty, which often became identified with Franklin Roosevelt's concept of "The Four Freedoms." Norman Rockwell, a master of the storytelling form of artistic illustration, tried to "take the Four Freedoms out of the [President's] noble language and put them in terms everybody can understand." Rockwell's illustrations—conceived during the summer of 1942, published in consecutive issues of *The Saturday Evening Post* in early 1943, and adapted to government-produced war posters—provided familiar images of why Americans needed to fight the Second World War. They tapped deeply held values and prompted more than 60,000 people to write to Rockwell with their reactions.

Some of Rockwell's correspondents, critical of Roosevelt's leadership and suspicious of social changes

and individual freedom against political systems that trampled on both.

Yet America hardly had an unblemished record in according full and equal access to the promise of American life. For many, wartime ideals highlighted everyday inequalities. As mobilization created new economic opportunities and demanded new sacrifices, many groups engaged in defining and redefining the American way of life.

WARTIME PROPAGANDA

During the First World War, government propagandists had asked Americans to fight for a more democratic world and a permanent peace. But such idealistic goals had little appeal for the skeptical generation of the 1930s and 1940s, who had witnessed the failures of Woodrow Wilson's promises. Only 20 years after Wilson's "war to end all wars," Americans were now embroiled in another worldwide conflict. Sensitive to popular cynicism about high-minded goals, the Roosevelt administration asked Americans to fight to preserve the "American way of life"—not to save the world. Artist and illustrator Norman Rockwell and movie director Frank Capra, masters of nostalgia, became the most celebrated and successful of the wartime image-makers.

Hollywood studios and directors eagerly answered the government's call by shaping inspiring

that the war effort seemed to be encouraging, disliked his paintings. One New Yorker complained that only *Freedom of Speech* and *Freedom of Worship* really grew out of the American past, and that *Freedom from Want* and *Freedom from Fear* seemed "the invention" of Roosevelt's New Deal. Another critic wondered how Rockwell "could have gone so completely wrong," especially by including so many "foreign-looking" characters, in his *Freedom of Worship* picture.

Most of the letters, though, praised Rockwell's paintings. "For your noble and human and deeply stir-ring series interpreting the Four Freedoms, I want to send my warmest appreciation," wrote a person with three family members serving in the armed forces. Rockwell's *Freedom of Speech* painting drew special acclaim for its nostalgic depiction of a venerated small-town tradition, the town meeting. "Thank you, Mr. Rockwell, for your reassurance!" wrote a person from Pennsylvania. Rockwell's images seemed to reassure millions of Americans that the Second World War was a struggle to preserve and protect basic American liberties, not a crusade to change the world.

and sentimental representations of American life. "The American film is our most important weapon," proclaimed one Hollywood producer. During the 1930s Frank Capra had become the champion of the self-made man in his box office winners such as *Mr. Deeds Comes to Town* and *Mr. Smith Goes to Washington*. Now called to make a series of government films entitled *Why We Fight*, Capra set Rockwell-type characters in motion and contrasted them with harrowing portrayals of the mass obedience and militarism in Germany, Italy, and Japan. (In this, he used footage from the enemy's own propaganda films.) A hundred or so Hollywood personalities received commissions to make films for the army's Pictorial Division. Commissioned as a lieutenant colonel, Darryl Zanuck, head of Twentieth Century Fox, filmed Allied troops in North Africa and the Aleutian Islands. John Ford produced a gripping combat documentary of the Battle of Midway.

Print advertising also contributed to the wartime propaganda effort. Roosevelt encouraged advertisers to sell the benefits of freedom. Most obliged, and "freedom" often appeared in the guise of new washing machines, ingenious kitchen appliances, improved automobiles, a wider range of lipstick hues, and automation in a hundred forms. As soon as the war was over, the ads promised, American technological know-how would usher in a consumer's paradise. Ads sometimes suggested that

Americans were fighting to restore the consumer society of the 1920s (see chapter 24).

The president initially resisted the creation of an official propaganda bureau, preferring to rely on a newly created Office of Facts and Figures (OFF) to disseminate information to the public. Poet Archibald MacLeish, who headed the OFF, however, acknowledged that his office most often resembled a "Tower of Babel" when it came to setting forth the aims and progress of the war. So, in the spring of 1942, Roosevelt created the Office of War Information (OWI) to coordinate policies related to propaganda and censorship. Liberals charged that the OWI was dominated by advertising professionals who dealt in slogans rather than substance. Conservatives blasted it as a purveyor of crass political advertisements for causes favored by Roosevelt and liberal Democrats. Despite such sniping, the OWI established branches throughout the world; published a magazine called *Victory*; and produced hundreds of films, posters, and radio broadcasts.

GENDER EQUALITY

Paradoxically, nostalgic portraits of an "American way of life" often clashed with the socioeconomic changes that wartime mobilization brought. Nowhere was this more apparent than in matters affecting the lives and status of women. As women took over jobs traditionally held by men, many people began to take more seriously the idea of gender equality. Some 350,000 women volunteered for military duty during the war; more than 1,000 women served as civilian pilots with the WASPs (Women's Airforce Service Pilots). Although they comprised only 2 percent of all military personnel, these women broke gender stereotypes. Not everyone approved. One member of Congress asked: "What has become of the manhood of America, that we have to call on our women?" Still, Congress eventually authorized a women's corps, with full status, for each branch of the military, a step that had been thwarted during the First World War.

The military service of women, together with their new importance in the labor market, strengthened arguments for laws to guarantee equal treatment. Congress seriously considered, but did not

pass, an Equal Rights Amendment (ERA) to the Constitution and a national equal-pay law. Women's organizations themselves, however, disagreed over how to advance women's opportunities. Organizations representing middle-class women strongly backed passage of the ERA, but other groups, more responsive to the problems of poor women, opposed its passage. They saw it as a threat to the protective legislation that regulated hours and hazardous conditions, which women's rights crusaders had struggled to win earlier in the century. The dilemma of whether women should continue to be accorded "protected" status in view of their vulnerability to exploitation in a male-directed workplace or should fight for "equal" status divided women long into the postwar era.

Even as the war temporarily narrowed gender differences in employment, government policies and propaganda frequently framed changes in women's roles in highly traditional terms. Women's expanded participation in the workplace was often portrayed as a short-term sacrifice, necessary to preserve women's "special" responsibilities— hearth and home. Feminine stereotypes abounded. A typical ad suggesting that women take on farm work declared: "A woman can do anything if she knows she looks beautiful doing it." Despite the acceptance of women into the armed services, most were assigned to stateside clerical and supply jobs; only a relatively few women served overseas. Day care programs for mothers working outside their homes received reluctant and inadequate funding. The 3,000 centers set up during the war filled only a fraction of the need and were swiftly shut down after the war. Leading social scientists and welfare experts, mostly male, blamed working mothers for an apparent rise in juvenile delinquency and in the divorce rate during the war years.

The war also widened the symbolic gap between "femininity" and "masculinity." Military culture often fostered a "pin-up" mentality toward women. Service publications contained pin-up sections, and tanks and planes were decorated with symbols of female sexuality. Wartime fiction often associated manliness with brutality and casual sex. After the war, tough-guy fiction with a violent and misogynist edge, like Mickey Spillane's "Mike Hammer"

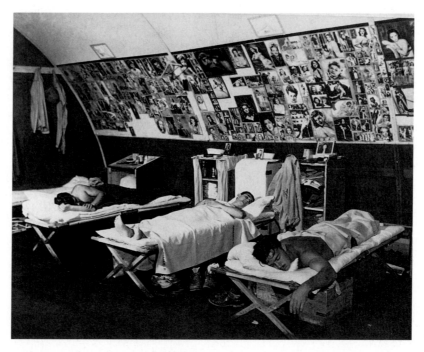

"PIN-UP GIRLS" Male G.I.s often surrounded themselves with "pin-up girls," images very different from the home-front "Rosie-the-Riveter" image.

series of detective novels, became one of the most successful formulas of popular culture.

RACIAL EQUALITY

Messages about race were as ambiguous as those related to gender; wartime culture both propelled yet firmly resisted change. Before the Second World War, America had been a sharply segregated society, with racial inequality enforced by law and custom. African Americans, disfranchised in the South and only beginning to achieve voting power in the North, had only limited access to the political, legal, or economic systems. The fight against fascism, however, challenged this old order.

Nazism, a philosophy based on the idea of racial inequality, exposed the racist underpinnings of much of 20th-century social science theory. "The Huns have wrecked the theories of the master race with which we were so contented so long," Frank Dixon, ex-governor of Alabama, remarked in 1944. The view that racial difference was not a function of biology but a function of culture—a view most

American anthropologists had been advancing for a generation—gained wider popular acceptance during the war. The implication was that a democratic society could accommodate racial difference. This new thinking helped to lay the foundation for the postwar struggle against discrimination.

The northward migration of African Americans accelerated demands for equality. Drawn by the promise of wartime jobs, nearly 750,000 African Americans relocated to northern cities, where many sensed the possibility of political power for the first time in their lives. They found an outspoken advocate of civil rights within the White House itself. First Lady Eleanor Roosevelt repeatedly antagonized southern Democrats and members of her husband's administration (often including the president himself) by her advocacy of civil rights and her participation in integrated social functions. The writer Clare Boothe Luce once remarked that Mrs. Roosevelt "enjoyed comforting the afflicted and afflicting the comfortable." Although the president often ignored her appeals for federal action against discrimination, her advocacy nevertheless dramatized the need for reform.

A SEGREGATED MILITARY This photo of an African American regiment eating in a mess hall during the Second World War illustrates racial segregation in the armed forces.

African Americans understood the irony of fighting for a country that denied them equality and challenged the government to live up to its own rhetoric about freedom and democracy. The *Amsterdam News*, a Harlem newspaper, called for a "Double V" campaign—victory at home as well as abroad. In January 1941, even before the United States entered the war, labor leader A. Philip Randolph threatened to lead tens of thousands of frustrated black workers in a march on Washington to demand more defense jobs and integration of the military forces. With the support of major black organizations and other prestigious African American leaders, Randolph invited Roosevelt to address the planned gathering. The president, however, viewed the march as potentially embarrassing to his administration and urged that it be canceled. Faced with Randolph's persistence, Roosevelt made concessions. In return for Randolph's canceling the march, the president created the FEPC in June 1941. The FEPC initially seemed a victory for equal rights, but Roosevelt gave the agency little power over discriminatory employers, who contin-

ued to argue that integrating the workforce would impair war production. During the war, the agency lost as many antidiscrimination cases as it won. Still, it provided an important precedent for federal action in civil rights.

Roosevelt also let stand the policy of segregation in the armed forces. "A jim crow army cannot fight for a free world," proclaimed the NAACP newspaper *The Crisis*. Yet General Marshall, Secretary of War Stimson, and others remained opposed to change. The army and the Red Cross even went so far as to follow the scientifically absurd practice of segregating donated blood into "white plasma" and "black plasma." African Americans were relegated to inferior jobs in the military and excluded from combat status, practices that Roosevelt supported out of deference to his white southern constituency who feared that participation in combat might give African Americans new claims on full civil rights. Toward the end of the war, when manpower shortages forced the administration to put African American troops into combat, they performed with distinction.

Complaints about discrimination in the military reached a peak in July 1944 when an explosion at a naval ammunition depot at Port Chicago, near San Francisco, killed 300 stevedores, most of them black and untrained in the process of loading ammunition. When the navy assigned another group of black sailors to similar duty nearby, some of them refused, citing the dangerous safety conditions. The resulting court-martial of 50 African American men was the largest mass trial in naval history. All of the sailors were found guilty of disobeying orders and received prison terms ranging from 8 to 15 years. After the war, the men were released on reduced sentences, but their convictions were not overturned, even after Congress requested a special naval review of the incident in 1994. In 1999, one of the men, Freddie Meeks, then 80, requested and received a presidential pardon.

RACIAL TENSIONS

Racial tensions arose, especially in urban centers throughout the country. In industrial cities, the wartime boom threw already overcrowded, working-class neighborhoods into turmoil. Many of the residents of these neighborhoods came from European immigrant backgrounds or had migrated from rural areas. Wartime work provided their first real opportunity to escape from poverty, and they viewed the minority newcomers as unwelcome rivals for jobs and housing. In 1943, for example, it was estimated that between 6,000 and 10,000 African Americans arrived in Los Angeles every month. Once there, their living options were effectively limited to a few overcrowded neighborhoods segregated by landlords' practices and by California's restrictive housing covenants—legal agreements prohibiting the sale of homes to certain religious or racial groups. One official reported: "You will see life as no human is expected to endure it. Conditions are pitiful, and health problems are prevalent." Under such conditions, racial tensions festered.

Around the country, public housing projects presented a particularly explosive dilemma to federal officials charged with administering the supply of desperately needed housing. Should they follow local practice and keep housing segregated, or should they integrate people of color into hostile white neighborhoods? Whites resisted the forced integration of public housing; nonwhites denounced the government for vacillating. In Buffalo, New York, threats of violence caused the cancellation of one housing project. In Detroit in June 1943, when police escorted African American tenants into a new complex, a full-scale race riot erupted. Several cities that attempted integration had to call in federal troops to restore order.

Racial disturbances were not restricted to confrontations between whites and blacks. In Los Angeles, the so-called "zoot suit" incidents of 1943 pitted Anglos against Mexican Americans. Minor incidents between young Mexican American men wearing "zoot suits"—flamboyant outfits that featured oversized coats and trousers—and soldiers and sailors from nearby military bases escalated into virtual warfare between the zoot-suiters and local police. The Los Angeles City Council, recognizing that the zoot suit was becoming a symbol of rebellion for Mexican American youths, even tried to make it a crime to wear one. The Roosevelt administration feared that the zoot suit violence might have a negative effect on the Good Neighbor Policy in Latin America. The president's coordinator of inter–American affairs, therefore, implemented a series of programs to ameliorate conditions contributing to tension. He allocated federal money to train Spanish-speaking Americans for wartime jobs, to improve education in barrios, and to open up more opportunities in colleges throughout the American Southwest.

American Indians comprised a significant group of new migrants to urban areas during the war. Although New Deal Indian policies (see chapter 25) had attempted to restore tribal communities and Indian traditions, the Second World War introduced powerful pressures for migration and assimilation. By the end of the war, approximately 25,000 Indian men and several hundred Indian women had served in the armed forces, where Indians were fully integrated with whites. Some 40,000 other Indians found war work in nearby cities, many leaving their reservation for the first time. For Indians, the white-dominated towns and cities tended to be strange and hostile places. Rapid City, South Dakota, for example, attracted more than 2,000 Sioux from the Pine

Ridge Reservation; most settled in informal camps at the outskirts of the city. Especially in smaller towns near reservations, such as Gallup, New Mexico; Flagstaff, Arizona; or Billings, Montana, established white residents often constructed formalized systems of discrimination against the newcomers. Many Indians moved back and forth between city and reservation, holding their urban jobs for only a few months at a time while seeking to live between two quite different worlds. Economic opportunities continued to be scarce on most reservations.

For African Americans, Latinos, and Indians, fighting for the "American way of life" represented a commitment not to the past but to the future. Demographic trends and a new militancy pointed the way to change. Increasingly, Americans of all backgrounds were realizing that racial grievances

must be addressed. In Detroit, for example, the local chapter of the National Association for the Advancement of Colored People (NAACP) emerged from the wartime years with a strong base from which to fight for jobs and political power. The Committee (later, Congress) on Racial Equality (CORE), an organization founded in 1942 and composed of whites and blacks who advocated nonviolent resistance to segregation, devised new strategies during the war. CORE activists staged sit-ins to integrate restaurants, theaters, and even prison dining halls in Washington, D.C. These same tactics would serve in the 1950s and 1960s to force the desegregation of interstate buses and public accommodations. As the Swedish sociologist Gunnar Myrdal predicted in his influential study of American racial issues, *An American Dilemma*

INTERNMENT Uniformed officials check the baggage of people of Japanese descent as they are being evacuated to internment camps.

"Exclusion of those of Japanese origin was deemed necessary because of the presence of an unascertained number of disloyal members of the group, most of whom we have no doubt were loyal to this country. It was because we could not reject the finding of the military authorities that it was impossible to bring about an immediate segregation of the disloyal from the loyal. . . .

"Compulsory exclusion of large groups of citizens from their homes, except under circumstances of direct emergency and peril, is inconsistent with our basic governmental institutions. But when under conditions of modern warfare our shores are threatened by hostile forces, the power to protect must be commensurate with the threatened danger. . . . To cast this case into outlines of racial prejudice, without reference to the real military dangers which were presented, merely confuses the issue."

JUSTICE HUGO BLACK
from the majority opinion of the Supreme Court in Korematsu v. U.S. *(1944), upholding the constitutionality of Executive Order 9066*

"We must accord great respect and consideration to the judgments of the military authorities who are on the scene and who have full knowledge of the military facts. . . . At the same time, however, it is essential that there be definite limits to military discretion, especially where martial law has not been declared. Individuals must not be left impoverished of their constitutional rights on a plea of military necessity that has neither substance nor support. . . .

"In support of this blanket condemnation of all persons of Japanese descent, however, no reliable evidence is cited to show that such individuals were generally disloyal, or had . . . furnished reasonable ground for their exclusion as a group. . . . No adequate reason is given for the failure to treat these Japanese Americans on an individual basis by holding investigations and hearings to separate the loyal from the disloyal, as was done in the case of persons of German and Italian ancestry. . . . I dissent, therefore, from this legalization of racism."

JUSTICE FRANK MURPHY
from the dissenting opinion in Korematsu v. U.S.

(1944), "fundamental changes" would soon have to come throughout the nation. Prominent African American novelist Richard Wright wrote that America had to do something about its "white problem."

Of all the minority groups in the United States, Japanese Americans suffered most unjustly during the war. In the two months following the attack on Pearl Harbor, West Coast communities became engulfed in hysteria against people of Japanese descent. Fear of saboteurs was widespread. One military report concluded that a "large, unassimilated, tightly knit racial group, bound to an enemy nation

by strong ties of race, culture, custom, and religion . . . constituted a menace" that justified extraordinary action.

Despite lack of evidence of disloyalty, government officials in February 1942 issued Executive Order 9066, directing the relocation and internment of first- and second-generation Japanese Americans (called Issei and Nisei, respectively) at inland camps. Curiously, in Hawaii where the presumed danger of subversion might have been much greater, no such internment took place; there, people of Japanese ancestry comprised 37 percent of the population and were essential to the economy.

Forced to abandon their possessions or sell them for a pittance, nearly 130,000 mainland Japanese Americans were confined in flimsy barracks, enclosed by barbed wire and under armed guard. Two-thirds of the detainees were native-born U.S. citizens. Many had been substantial landowners in California's agricultural industries. In December 1944 a divided Supreme Court upheld the constitutionality of Japanese relocation in *Korematsu* v. *U.S.* (In 1988, however, Congress officially apologized for the injustice, concluding that it was "not justified by military necessity, and . . . not driven by analysis of military conditions." Congress authorized the payment of a cash indemnity to any affected person who was still living.)

Despite the internment, the suffering and sacrifice of Japanese American soldiers became legendary: The 100th Battalion, composed of Nisei

LINK TO THE PAST

The Power of Persuasion: Poster Art from the Second World War

http://www.nara.gov/exhall/powers/powers.html

The National Archives and Records Administration (NARA) in Washington, D.C., is the repository for official U.S. government records. Thousands of historical researchers from around the world use its holdings each year. In 1994–95 NARA presented an exhibit of U.S. government posters from the Second World War. Later, NARA's online "exhibit hall" featured 33 poster images. These war posters employed psychological methods pioneered by American advertisers to mobilize the American people for war. Analyze the various techniques of persuasion exemplified in these posters and consider the following questions.

1. Examine the posters in the sections called "Man the Guns," "It's a Woman's War Too," and "United We Win." How do the images support or complicate the discussion in this chapter of men's and women's gender roles and of wartime racial issues?

2. During the first 21 months of war, military censors withheld all photographs showing dead American soldiers. Later, as the war turned in favor of the Allies, more graphic photos of battlefield deaths were allowed to appear in magazines, newspapers, and war posters. After thinking about the possible emotional impact made by two such posters in the section called "He Knew the Meaning of Sacrifice," advance your ideas about why such a change in policy might have been made.

3. Consider the posters in the section "He's Watching You." Why do you think the government produced so many posters emphasizing the dangers of "careless talk"? What might be the broad repercussions of such messages of fear and distrust?

4. Describe and evaluate the role of government propaganda in the Second World War.

from Hawaii, was nearly wiped out; 57 percent of the famed 442nd Regimental Combat Team were killed or wounded in the mountains of Italy; and 6,000 members of the Military Intelligence Service provided invaluable service in the Pacific theater.

Racial hostilities reflected the underlying strains in America's social fabric, but other tensions pulled at Americans as well. Rifts developed between city dwellers and migrants from rural areas. Californians derided the "Okies," people who had fled the Oklahoma dust bowl, as ignorant. In Chicago, migrants from Appalachia met with similar derision. At the beginning of the war, more than a third of white Americans were still either first- or second-generation immigrants, and many ethnic communities remained closely tied to the language and culture of their homelands.

Despite the underlying fragmentation of American society, the symbol of the "melting pot," together with appeals to nationalism, remained powerful. The war heightened racial and ethnic tensions precisely because the population was becoming less segmented geographically, ethnically, and racially. Wartime propaganda stressed the theme of national unity by calling the Second World War a "people's war" and contrasting America's "melting pot" with German and Japanese obsessions about racial purity. Wartime movies, plays, and music reinforced a sense of national community by building on cultural nationalism and expressing pride in American historical themes. Many foreign-language broadcasts and publications ceased to exist during the war, and naturalization applications nearly doubled from what they had been only five years earlier.

The great movements of population during the war—rural to urban, south to north, east to west—eroded geographical distinctions. Wartime demands for additional labor weakened the barriers to many occupations. As each of America's racial and ethnic minorities established records of distinguished military service, the claim of equality—"Americans All," in the words of a wartime slogan—took on greater moral force. The possibility for more equitable participation in the mainstream of American life, together with rhetoric extolling social solidarity and freedom, provided a foundation for the civil rights movements of the decades

ahead. The war for "the American way of life," it turned out, carried many different meanings.

SHAPING THE PEACE

The end of the war brought difficult questions about demobilization and peace. Despite his inexperience, Truman built on Roosevelt's many wartime conferences and agreements to shape the framework of international relations for the next half-century. Truman participated in the establishment of the United Nations, the creation of new international economic institutions, and the settlement of global political issues involving territory and governance.

INTERNATIONAL ORGANIZATIONS

In the Atlantic Charter of 1941 and at a conference in Moscow in October 1943, the Allies had already pledged to create an international organization to replace the League of Nations. The new United Nations (UN) fulfilled Woodrow Wilson's vision of collective security—his concept of an international body to deter aggressor nations. At the Dumbarton Oaks Conference in Washington in August 1944 and at a subsequent meeting in San Francisco in April 1945, the Allies worked out the UN's organizational structure. Each member nation would be represented and have one vote in a General Assembly. A Security Council would include five permanent members—the United States, Great Britain, the Soviet Union, France, and China—and six rotating members. The Security Council would have primary responsibility for maintaining peace, but any individual member of the council could exercise an absolute veto over any council decision. The inclusion of China in the Security Council was a victory for the United States. It was assumed that Jiang's government would remain in power and would continue to be a close U.S. ally. A UN Secretariat would handle day-to-day business, and an Economic and Social Council would promote social and economic advancement throughout the world.

The U.S. Senate accepted the UN charter in July 1945 with only two dissenting votes. This resounding victory for internationalism contrasted sharply with the Senate's rejection of membership in the League of Nations after the First World War. Americans of an earlier generation had worried that internationalist policies might impinge on their country's ability to follow its own national interests. Following the Second World War, however, U.S. domination of emerging organizations such as the UN, persuaded Americans that decisions of international bodies were unlikely to clash with their nation's own foreign policies. In addition, Americans recognized that the war had partly resulted from the lack of a coordinated, international response to aggression during the 1930s and wanted to avoid the same mistake again. Eleanor Roosevelt, the former first lady and a leading social activist, played a prominent role in building the new postwar internationalist ethos. A delegate to the first meeting of the UN's General Assembly, she also chaired the U.S. Commission on Human Rights and guided the drafting of a Universal Declaration of Human Rights, adopted by the UN in 1948. The Declaration set forth "inalienable" human rights and freedoms as cornerstones of international law.

Postwar economic settlements also illustrated a growing acceptance of new international organizations designed to preclude the currency devaluation and economic protectionism that had unsettled the world economy during the 1930s. U.S. policymakers wanted international institutions that would stabilize exchange rates for currency, provide an international lending authority, and eliminate discriminatory trade practices.

Agreements reached at the Bretton Woods (New Hampshire) Conference of 1944 created two new institutions. The International Monetary Fund (IMF) was to maintain stable exchange by ensuring that each national currency could be converted into any other currency at a fixed rate. Exchange rates could be altered only with the agreement of the fund. (This international system of fixed exchange rates was replaced in 1971 by a system of floating exchange rates.) The International Bank for Reconstruction and Development, later renamed the World Bank, was to provide loans to war-battered countries and promote the resumption of world trade. In the postwar era, American capital and American policies dominated both the IMF and the World Bank, even though they are international bodies financed by member nations throughout the world. The Soviet Union, whose state-directed economic policies challenged the assumptions of western capitalism, did not participate. In 1947 the General Agreement on Tariffs and Trade (GATT) created an institutional structure for breaking up closed trading blocs and implementing free and fair trade agreements.

SPHERES OF INTEREST AND POSTWAR SETTLEMENTS

In wartime conversations, Stalin, Churchill, and Roosevelt all had assumed that powerful nations would have special "spheres of influence" in the postwar world. As early as January 1942 the Soviet ambassador to the United States reported to Stalin that Roosevelt had tacitly assented to Soviet postwar control over the Baltic states of Lithuania, Latvia, and Estonia. The Soviets accepted British and U.S. dominance of Italy's post-fascist government. And in 1944 Stalin and Churchill agreed informally and secretly that Britain would continue its dominance in Greece and that the Soviets could dominate Romania and Bulgaria.

Precisely how Roosevelt intended to handle the issue of Soviet spheres of influence in the postwar world will never be known. Roosevelt had implied to Stalin that he understood the Soviet's need to create friendly states on its vulnerable western border, but, at the same time, he had talked about self-determination for small nations. For example, at the Teheran Conference of November 1943, held just a year before the 1944 presidential election, Roosevelt told Stalin that American voters of Polish, Latvian, Lithuanian, and Estonian descent expected their homelands to be independent after the war. Roosevelt, a master of finesse, probably felt confident that he could improvise and smooth over such contradictions. As long as Soviet armies were essential to Germany's defeat—and the president also wanted the USSR to join the war against Japan—Roosevelt struck a tone of cooperation with Stalin.

Flexibility, holding together unlikely coalitions, and taking contradictory positions simultaneously were Roosevelt's special strengths as a politician. On many critical international issues of the

1930s—the gold standard, tariff policy, and entry into the war—he had managed to straddle both sides of seemingly irreconcilable positions. On postwar issues, for which he seemed to have only vague policy ideas, Roosevelt likely thought he could perform a similar juggling act.

Roosevelt's contradictory policies toward a Soviet sphere of interest became apparent after his death. The military results of the war, particularly the USSR's powerful position in Eastern Europe, strongly influenced postwar settlements regarding territory. On issues of governance—particularly in Germany, Poland, and Korea—splits between U.S. and Soviet interests widened. Germany, especially, became a focus and a symbol of bipolar tensions.

Early in the war, both the United States and the Soviet Union had urged the dismemberment and deindustrialization of Nazi Germany after its defeat. Roosevelt endorsed a controversial plan proposed by Secretary of the Treasury Henry Morgenthau that would have turned Germany into a pastoral, agricultural country. At a conference held at Yalta, in Ukraine, in early February 1945, the three Allied powers agreed to divide Germany into four zones of occupation (with France as the fourth occupation force). Later, as relations among the victors cooled, this temporary division of Germany permanently solidified into a Soviet-dominated zone in the East and the three Allied zones in the West. Berlin, the German capital, also was divided, even though it lay totally within the Soviet zone. As fear of the Soviets began to replace earlier concerns of a revived Germany, Truman abandoned the Morgenthau plan in favor of efforts to rebuild the western zones of Germany.

Postwar rivalries also centered on Poland. During the war, Poland had two governments, a government-in-exile based in London and a communist-backed one in Lublin. At the Yalta Conference, the Soviets agreed to permit free elections in Poland after the war and to create a government "responsible to the will of the people," but Stalin also believed that the other Allied leaders had tacitly accepted Soviet dominance over Poland. The agreement at Yalta was ambiguous at best, as many on the negotiating teams realized at the time. During Yalta, the war was still at a critical stage, and the western Allies chose to sacrifice clarity over the Polish issue in order to encourage cooperation with the Soviets. After Yalta, the Soviets assumed that Poland would be in their sphere of influence, but many Americans charged the Soviets with bad faith for failing to hold free elections and for not relinquishing control.

In Asia, military realities also influenced postwar settlements. Roosevelt had long wanted to bring the USSR into the war against Japan to relieve pressure on U.S. forces fighting in the Pacific. At Teheran in November 1943 and again at Yalta, Stalin pledged to send troops to Asia as soon as Germany was defeated, but when U.S. policymakers learned that the atomic bomb was ready for use against Japan, they became eager to limit Soviet involvement in the Pacific war. The first atomic bomb fell on Hiroshima just one day before the Soviets were to enter the war against Japan, and the United States took sole charge of the occupation and postwar reorganization of Japan. The Soviet Union and the United States split Korea, which had been occupied by Japan, into separate zones of occupation. Here, as in Germany, the zones later emerged as two antagonistic states (see chapter 27).

The fate of the European colonies seized by Japan in Southeast Asia was another unresolved issue. During the war, the United States had declared itself in favor of decolonization. Although the United States would have preferred to see the former British and French colonies become independent nations, with moderate governments friendly to the West and especially to American economic interests, U.S. policymakers also worried about left-leaning anticolonial nationalist movements. As the cold war developed, the United States gradually moved to support Britain and France in their efforts to reassemble their colonial empires. Long struggles would ensue over the independence and political orientation of postwar governments throughout the colonized world.

In its own colony, the Philippines, the United States honored its long-standing pledge to grant independence. A friendly government that agreed to respect U.S. economic interests and military bases took power in 1946 and enlisted American advisers to help suppress leftist rebels. The Mariana, Caroline, and Marshall Islands, all of which had been captured by Japan during the war, were designated

Trust Territories of the Pacific by the United Nations and placed under U.S. administration in 1947.

Although the countries of Latin America had not been very directly involved in the war or the peace settlements, U.S. relations with them were also profoundly affected. During the 1930s the Roosevelt administration had sought to curb Nazi influence in Latin America. The Good Neighbor Policy, building upon a 1928 pledge to carry out no more military interventions in the hemisphere, had helped to improve U.S.–Latin American relations. The Office of Inter-American Affairs (OIAA), created in 1937, began an aggressive and successful policy of expanding cultural and economic ties. Just weeks after the German invasion of Poland in 1939, at a Pan American Conference in Panama City, Latin American leaders showed that the hemisphere was united behind the Allies. The conferees strengthened hemispheric economic cooperation and declared a 300-mile-wide band of neutrality in waters around the hemisphere (excepting Canada). After U.S. entry into the war, at a January 1942 conference in Rio de Janeiro, all the Latin American countries except Chile and Argentina broke off diplomatic ties with the Axis governments. When naval warfare in the Atlantic severed commercial connections between Latin America and Europe, Latin American countries became critical suppliers of raw materials to the United States, to the benefit of all.

Wartime conferences and settlements avoided clear decisions about creating a Jewish homeland in the Middle East, a proposal that England had supported, but not effected, after the First World War. The Second World War prompted survivors of the Holocaust and Jews from around the world to take direct action. Zionism, the movement to found a Jewish state in Palestine, their ancient homeland, attracted thousands of Jews, who began to carve out the new state of Israel. Middle Eastern affairs, which had been of small concern to U.S. policymakers before 1941, would take on greater urgency after 1948, when the Truman administration formally recognized Israel.

CONCLUSION

The world changed dramatically during the era of the Second World War. Wartime mobilization ended the Great Depression and shifted the New Deal's focus away from domestic social issues and toward international concerns. It brought a historic victory over dictatorial, brutal regimes. Afterward, as Europe lay in ruins, with at least 22 million people displaced from their homes, the United States emerged as the world's preeminent power, owning two-thirds of the world's gold reserves and controlling more than half of its manufacturing capacity.

At home, the war brought significant change. A more powerful national government, concerned with preserving national security, assumed nearly complete power over the nation's economy. New, cooperative ties were forged among government, business, labor, and scientific researchers. All sectors worked together to provide the seemingly miraculous growth in productivity that ultimately won the war.

The early 1940s sharpened debates over the nature of liberty and equality. Many Americans saw the Second World War as a struggle to protect and preserve the power and liberties they already enjoyed. Others, inspired by a struggle against racism and injustice abroad, insisted that a war for freedom should help secure equal rights at home.

News of Japan's surrender prompted the largest celebration in the nation's history, but questions remained about postwar policies. International conferences established a structure for the United Nations and for new, global economic institutions. Still, Americans remained uncertain about postwar reconstruction of former enemies and about future relations with wartime allies, particularly the Soviet Union. Domestically, the wrenching dislocations of war—psychic, demographic, and economic—took their toll. Postwar adjustments would be difficult for all Americans. And, of course, the nation now faced the future without the charismatic leadership of Franklin D. Roosevelt, the only president that many Americans had ever known.

For the next fifty years veterans of the Second World War remained relatively quiet about their combat experiences. A former tank commander commented, "The reason they don't talk is they couldn't get the picture over to somebody that wasn't there. He would think that you're making that story up." After the 50th anniversary of the war's end, however, with remaining veterans reaching old age, Americans suddenly rediscovered what journalist

Tom Brokaw called the "greatest generation." Books about the war dominated bestseller lists during the late 1990s; Steven Spielberg's film *Saving Private Ryan* packed theaters; and Congress approved construction of a huge memorial on the grounds of the National Mall in Washington D.C. The Second World War, through these popular representations, continued to stand as a powerful symbol of honor, unity, and common sacrifice.

Suggested Readings begin on page SR-1. For Web activities and resources related to this chapter, go to http://www.harcourtcollege.com/history.murrin

CHAPTER 27

THE AGE OF CONTAINMENT, 1946–1954

HOLLYWOOD IN THE SERVICE OF THE ANTICOMMUNIST CRUSADE

Fears about communist infiltration of the motion picture industry prompted Hollywood studios to display their anticommunist credentials by "blacklisting" left-leaning screenwriters and by making films such as RKO's *I Married a Communist*. These anticommunist films, with their simplistic political messages, tended to bomb at the box office. This particular film did better when rereleased as *The Woman on Pier 13*.

The Second World War, heralded as an effort to preserve and protect the fabric of American life, ended up transforming it. The struggle against fascism brought foreign policy issues to the center of political debate, and the international struggles of the postwar period kept them there. As the Second World War gave way to a "cold war" between the United States and the Soviet Union, Washington adopted global policies to "contain" the Soviet Union and to enhance America's economic and military security. Preoccupation with national security abroad, however, raised calls for limiting dissent at home. To fight communism overseas, might it also be necessary to institute containment policies at home?

The cold war years from 1946 to 1954 also produced questions about government power. Should the activist, New Deal–style national government be scaled back? What role should Washington play in planning the postwar economy? What should be government's relationship to social policymaking, especially efforts to achieve equality? These broad questions first emerged during the 1945–53 presidency of Democrat Harry Truman as he struggled to define his Fair Deal programs. They would remain central concerns during the administration of his Republican successor, Dwight David Eisenhower.

This chapter will focus on the following major questions:

- What were the principal elements of the foreign policy called containment, and what major conflicts shaped the cold war?
- How did the foreign policy of containment affect domestic policy and American life?
- What was the Fair Deal, and what was its impact on American political life?
- How did social changes such as population growth and movement to the suburbs affect Americans?

CREATING A NATIONAL SECURITY STATE, 1945–1949

The wartime alliance between the United States and the Soviet Union had never been more than a marriage of convenience. Defeat of the Axis powers had required the two governments to cooperate, but collaboration scarcely lasted beyond VE Day. Especially after President Franklin Roosevelt's death in April 1945, relations between the United

C H R O N O L O G Y

1946 Baruch plan for atomic energy proposed • Employment Act passed • Republicans gain control of Congress in November elections

1947 Truman Doctrine announced • HUAC begins hearings on communist infiltration of Hollywood • George Kennan's "Mr. X" article published • National Security Act passed (CIA and NSC established) • Marshall Plan adopted • Truman's loyalty order announced • Taft-Hartley Act passed over Truman's veto • Jackie Robinson and Larry Doby break major league baseball's color line

1948 Berlin Airlift begins • Truman wins reelection • The Kinsey Report and Dr. Benjamin Spock's *Baby and Child Care* published

1949 NATO established • China "falls" to communism • NSC-68 drafted • Soviet Union explodes atomic device • Truman unveils his Fair Deal

1950 Korean War begins • Senator Joseph McCarthy charges communist infiltration of State Department • McCarran Internal Security Act passed

1951 Truman removes General MacArthur as commander in Korea

1952 GI Bill of Rights passed • Dwight Eisenhower elected president

1953 Korean War ends • Julius and Ethel Rosenberg executed • *Playboy* magazine debuts

1954 Joseph McCarthy censured by U.S. Senate • Communist Control Act passed

States and the Soviet Union steadily degenerated into a cold war of suspicion and growing tension.

ONSET OF THE COLD WAR

Historians have discussed the origins of the cold war from many different perspectives. The traditional interpretation, which gained new power after the collapse of the Soviet Union in 1989, focuses on Soviet expansionism, stressing a traditional Russian appetite for new territory, an ideological zeal to spread international communism, or some interplay between the two. The United States, proponents of this view still insist, needed to take as hard a line as possible. Other historians—generally called revisionists—argue that the Soviet Union's obsession with securing its borders was an understandable defensive response to the invasion of its territory during both world wars. The United States, in this view, should have tried to reassure the Soviets by seeking accommodation, instead of pursuing policies that intensified Stalin's fears. Still other scholars maintain that assigning blame obscures the clash of deep-seated rival interests that made postwar tensions between the two superpowers inevitable.

In any view, Harry Truman's role proved important. His brusque manner, in sharp contrast to Franklin Roosevelt's urbanity, brought a harsher tone to U.S.–Soviet meetings. Truman initially hoped that he could somehow cut a deal with Soviet Premier Joseph Stalin, much like his old mentor, "Boss" Tom Pendergast, struck bargains with rogue politicians back in Missouri. "I like Stalin," Truman once wrote his wife. "[He] knows what he wants and will compromise when he can't get it." However, as disagreements between the two former allies mounted, Truman came to rely on advisers hostile to Stalin's Soviet Union.

The atomic bomb provided an immediate source of friction. At the July 1945 Potsdam Conference Truman had casually remarked to Stalin, "We have a new weapon of unusual destructive force." Calmly, Stalin had replied that he hoped the United States would make "good use" of it against Japan. Less calmly, Stalin immediately ordered a crash program to develop nuclear weapons of his own. After atomic bombs hit Japan, Stalin reportedly told his scientists that "the equilibrium has been destroyed. Provide the bomb. It will remove a great danger from us." Truman hoped that the bomb would scare the Soviets, and it did. Stalin grew even more concerned about Soviet security. Historians still debate whether "wearing the bomb ostentatiously on our hip," as Secretary of War Henry Stimson put it, frightened the Soviets into more cautious behavior or made them more fearful and aggressive.

In 1946 Truman authorized Bernard Baruch, a presidential adviser and special representative to the United Nations, to offer a proposal for the international control of atomic power. The Baruch Plan called for full disclosure by all UN member nations of nuclear research and materials, creation of an international authority to ensure concurrence, and destruction of all U.S. atomic weapons once these first steps were completed. Andrei A. Gromyko, the Soviet ambassador to the UN, argued that the Baruch plan would require other nations to halt their atomic research and disclose their secrets to the United Nations (dominated by the United States) before the United States itself was required to do anything. He complained that it would allow the United States to scrutinize Soviet progress in atomic research, while it maintained its own nuclear monopoly. Gromyko countered by proposing that the United States unilaterally destroy its atomic weapons first, with international disclosure and control to follow. The United States refused. Both sides used this deadlock to justify a stepped-up arms race.

Other sources of Soviet-American friction involved U.S. loan policies and the Soviet sphere of influence in Eastern Europe. Truman abruptly suspended lend-lease assistance to the Soviet Union in early September 1945, partly to pressure the Soviets into holding elections in Poland. Subsequently, Truman's administration similarly linked extension of U.S. reconstruction loans to its goal of rolling back Soviet power in Eastern Europe. This linkage strategy never worked. Lack of capital and signs of Western hostility provided the Soviets with excuses for tightening their grip on Eastern Europe, a course of action that further discouraged the United States from extending economic assistance to countries dominated by Moscow. A Soviet sphere of influence, which Stalin called defensive and Truman labeled proof of communist expansionism, emerged in Eastern Europe. Suspicion steadily widened into mutual distrust. By 1946, the former allies were well on the way to becoming bitter adversaries.

From 1947 on, Harry Truman placed his personal stamp on the presidency by focusing on the fight against the Soviet Union. Truman used the menace of an "international communist conspiracy" to justify extraordinary measures to ensure U.S. national security. Protecting "national security"—an emotionally powerful term, whose meanings seemed infinitely expandable—provided justification for both foreign and domestic policy

initiatives, which extended the reach and power of the executive branch of government.

CONTAINMENT ABROAD: THE TRUMAN DOCTRINE

In March 1947, the president announced what became known as the Truman Doctrine when he addressed Congress on the civil war in Greece, a conflict in which communist-led insurgents were trying to topple a corrupt but pro-Western government. Historically, Greece had fallen within Great Britain's sphere of influence, but Britain, badly weakened by the Second World War, could no longer maintain its formerly strong presence there or in the Middle East. A leftist victory in Greece, Truman's advisers claimed, would open neighboring Turkey, which they considered crucial to U.S. interests, to Soviet subversion. Truman's policymakers doubted they enjoyed broad support, either among the public or in Congress, for such a move. Seeking to justify U.S. aid to Greece and Turkey, Truman addressed Congress on March 12, 1947, in dramatic terms.

U.S. security interests, according to this Truman Doctrine, were now worldwide. Truman declared that the fate of "free peoples" everywhere, not simply the future of Greece and Turkey, hung in the balance. Unless the United States unilaterally aided countries "who are resisting attempted subversion by armed minorities or by outside pressures," totalitarian communism would spread around the world and threaten the security of the United States itself.

Initially, the Truman Doctrine's global vision of national security encountered skepticism. Henry Wallace, the president's most visible Democratic critic, chided Truman for exaggerating the expansive nature of Soviet foreign policy and its threat to the United States. Conservative Republicans suspected the increase of executive power and the vast expenditures that the Truman Doctrine seemed to foreshadow. If Truman wanted to win support for his position, Republican Senator Arthur Vandenberg had already advised, he would need to "scare hell" out of people, something that Truman proved quite willing to do.

The rhetorical strategy worked. With backing from both Republicans and Democrats, Congress passed Truman's request for $400 million in assistance to Greece and Turkey, most of it in military aid, in the spring of 1947. This vote signaled broad, bipartisan support for a national security policy that came to be called "containment."

The term *containment* first appeared in a 1947 article in the influential journal *Foreign Affairs*, written under the pseudonym "X" by George Kennan, the State Department's leading expert on Soviet affairs. Kennan argued that the "main element" in any U.S. policy "must be that of a long-term, patient but firm and vigilant containment of Russian expansive tendencies." Although Kennan later insisted that he had meant containment to be a series of discrete responses to specific moves by the Soviets and never proposed an open-ended crusade, his broad prose lent itself to different interpretations. Whatever Ken-

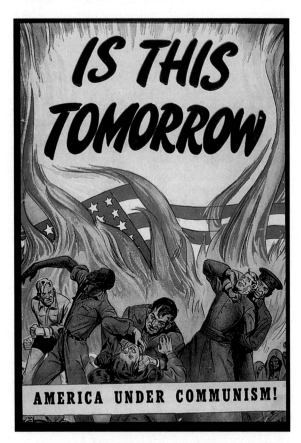

AMERICA UNDER COMMUNISM? The fear of communist subversion became a prominent theme in mass culture in the postwar era. Church groups distributed more than four million copies of this lurid comic book. It warned that communist subversion was the prelude to a direct, violent takeover of the United States.

nan's intent, his "X" article quickly became associated with the alarmist tone of the Truman Doctrine.

Containment thus became the catchphrase for a global, anticommunist, national security policy. In the popular view, containment linked all leftist insurgencies, wherever they occurred, to a totalitarian movement controlled from Moscow that directly threatened, by heinous ideas as much as by military might, the United States. Although foreign policy debates regularly included sharp disagreements over precisely *how* to pursue the goal of containment, few Americans dared to question the basic premise that the country needed a far-flung, activist foreign policy.

TRUMAN'S LOYALTY PROGRAM

Nine days after proclaiming the Truman Doctrine, the president issued Executive Order 9835, which brought the containment of communism to the home front. Truman's order called for a system of loyalty boards empowered to determine if "reasonable grounds" existed for believing that any government employee belonged to an organization or held political ideas that might pose a "security risk" to the United States. People judged to be security risks would lose their government jobs. The Truman loyalty program also authorized the attorney general's office to identify organizations it considered subversive, and in December 1947 the first Attorney General's List was released.

The Truman administration's domestic loyalty program rested on its assessment of the extent of Soviet espionage activity in the United States, an assessment that has generated great controversy over the years. Although few people ever doubted the administration's claim that Soviets were carrying out operations in the United States during the 1940s, sharp disagreement has persisted regarding their scope and success. Were the Soviets operating only at the fringes, or had they penetrated the top levels of the U.S. government? Were they obtaining information available almost anywhere, or were they stealing vital national secrets? Did the administration exaggerate, underestimate, or accurately assess the situation?

Although such debates continue, they now take place in light of recently declassified evidence about Soviet activities in the United States. The U.S. Communist Party (CPUSA) was receiving clandestine financial support from Moscow, and some of its members were actively engaged in collecting classified information for the Soviets. Other governmental officials and employees, who were not CPUSA members, were also in contact with Soviet agents. A super-secret Army counterintelligence unit began intercepting transmissions between Moscow and the United States in 1943. Collected as the "Venona files," these intercepted messages (first decoded in 1946 and not revealed to the public until 1995) show that the USSR had been obtaining information from within governmental agencies, including the Office of War Information and the top-secret Office of Strategic Services (OSS). According to one historical study based on the Venona files and materials in the Soviet archives, several hundred governmental officials had contact with Soviet intelligence during the 1940s. In 1944, Moscow even began obtaining classified information about U.S. atomic work. In short, there may have been legitimate concerns about the activities of some governmental officials and some members of the CPUSA.

Curiously, though, the national security bureaucrats who intercepted the Soviet messages appear to have told neither the president nor his attorney general anything about their own super-secret operation or the intelligence being gathered. The mania for secrecy went so far that when it was discovered that a U.S. government employee working for the Soviet Union had informed Soviet intelligence about Venona, the project's leaders never sought to prosecute him because, in doing so, they would have had to reveal their own operation.

The secrecy of the Venona documents may help to explain Truman's difficulties in defending his loyalty initiative. On the one hand, the president claimed that the government faced relatively few security risks but that their potential to do harm demanded a response unprecedented in peacetime. Framed in this way, the president's program responded to Republican charges that hundreds, perhaps even thousands, of Communist Party members had been infiltrating the federal bureaucracy since the New Deal. On the other hand, the president's program worried civil liberties groups who insisted that a limited internal security threat logically demanded an equally limited governmental response. Should not, for example, civil libertarians

asked, any loyalty investigation distinguish between an atomic scientist with suspicious ties to the Soviet embassy and a clerical worker in the Interior Department with leftist political leanings? Truman's approach angered both fervent anticommunists, who accused the president of doing too little to fight the Red Menace at home, and civil libertarians, who charged him with going too far.

THE NATIONAL SECURITY ACT, THE MARSHALL PLAN, AND THE BERLIN CRISIS

The Truman Doctrine and the loyalty program only began the administration's national security initiatives. The National Security Act of 1947 created several new bureaucracies and began the process that transformed the old Navy and War departments into a new Department of Defense, finally established in 1949. It instituted another new arm of the executive branch, the National Security Council, with broad authority over planning foreign policy. It established the Air Force as a separate service equal to the Army and Navy. And it created the Central Intelligence Agency (CIA) to gather information and to undertake covert activities in support of the nation's newly defined security interests.

The CIA proved the most flexible arm of the national security bureaucracy. Shrouded from public scrutiny, it used its secret funds to finance and encourage anticommunist activities around the globe. Between 1949 and 1952 the CIA's office for covert operations expanded its overseas stations from 7 to 47. The CIA cultivated ties with anti-Soviet groups in Eastern Europe and even within the Soviet Union itself. It helped finance pro-U.S. labor unions in Western Europe to curtail the influence of leftist organizations. It orchestrated covert campaigns to prevent the Italian Communist Party from winning an electoral victory in 1948 and to bolster anticommunist parties in France, Japan, and elsewhere. From the beginning, the Truman administration encouraged the CIA to use its national security mandate broadly and aggressively.

Truman's administration also linked economic policies in Western Europe to the doctrine of containment. Concerned that the region's severe economic problems might embolden leftist, pro-Soviet political movements, Secretary of State George

Marshall sought to strengthen the economies of Western Europe. Shortly after Congress approved funding for the Truman Doctrine, the secretary proposed the Marshall Plan, under which governments in Western Europe would coordinate their plans for postwar economic reconstruction with the help of funds provided by the United States. Between 1946 and 1951, the United States provided nearly $13 billion in assistance to 17 Western European nations. The Soviets were also invited to participate in the Marshall Plan, but American policymakers correctly anticipated that Moscow would avoid any program whose major goal was rebuilding capitalism in Europe. Instead, Stalin responded to the Marshall Plan by further consolidating the Soviet's sphere of influence in Eastern Europe.

The Marshall Plan proved a stunning success. When conservatives called it a "giveaway" program, the administration emphasized how it opened up both markets and investment opportunities in Western Europe to American businesses. Moreover, within its first few years the Marshall Plan helped stabilize the European economy by quadrupling industrial production. Improved standards of living enhanced political stability and, along with the CIA's covert activities, helped undermine left-wing political parties in Western Europe.

American policymakers believed that to revitalize Europe under the Marshall Plan they must first restore the economy of Germany, which was still divided into zones of occupation. In June 1948 the United States, Great Britain, and France announced a plan for currency reform that would be the first step in merging their zones into a federal German republic. Soviet leaders were alarmed by the prospect of a revitalized German state under Western auspices. After twice suffering German invasion during the preceding 35 years, they wanted Germany reunited but weak. Hoping to sidetrack Western plans for Germany, in June 1948 the Soviets cut

TESTING THE ATOMIC BOMB AT BIKINI ATOLL This atomic test, one of 23 detonations at Bikini Atoll in the Marshall Islands during the late 1940s, raised a column of water 5,000 feet high. Although Bikini islanders were evacuated, the radiation from these blasts affected both the people involved, including U.S. service personnel, and the island's ecology for years to come. New "bikini" swimsuits for "bombshell" women became a fashion rage, as nuclear imagery permeated American culture.

off all highways, railroads, and water routes linking West Berlin (which lay wholly within the Soviet sector of East Germany) to West Germany.

This Soviet blockade of Berlin failed. Air routes to the city remained open, and American and British pilots made 250,000 flights, round-the-clock, to deliver a total of two million tons of supplies to the city's beleaguered residents. Truman, hinting at a military response, reinstated the draft and sent two squadrons of B-29 bombers to Britain. Recognizing his defeat, Stalin abandoned the blockade in May 1949. The Soviets then created the German Democratic Republic out of their East German sector, and West Berlin survived as an enclave tied to the West. The "two Germanys" and the divided city of Berlin stood as symbols of cold war tensions.

THE ELECTION OF 1948

Concerns about national security helped Harry Truman win the 1948 presidential election, a victory that capped a remarkable political comeback. Truman had been losing the support of left-leaning Democrats, led by his Secretary of Commerce Henry A. Wallace, who thought his containment policies too militant. In September 1946, after Wallace criticized Truman's policies toward the Soviet Union, Truman had ousted him from the cabinet. Two months later, in the off-year national election of 1946, voters had given the Republicans control of Congress for the first time since 1928. Although his standing in public opinion polls had risen slowly in 1947 and 1948, most political pundits thought Truman had little chance to win the presidency in his own right in 1948. Truman waged a vigorous campaign against challenges from the left by a new Progressive Party, which nominated Wallace, and from the right by both the Republican nominee Thomas E. Dewey and the southern segregationist candidacy of Strom Thurmond (running as the standard-bearer of the States' Rights Party, or "Dixiecrats"). Truman called the Republican-controlled Congress into special session, presented it with domestic policy proposals that were anathema to the GOP, and then denounced the "Republican Eightieth Congress, that do-nothing, good-for-nothing, worst Congress."

Thomas Dewey, who had been defeated by Franklin Roosevelt four years earlier, proved a cautious, lackluster campaigner in 1948. Even Republicans complained about his bland speeches and empty platitudes. A pro-Democratic newspaper caricatured Dewey's standard speech as four "historic sentences: Agriculture is important. Our rivers are full of fish. You cannot have freedom without liberty. The future lies ahead." When Dewey's campaign train, called "The Victory Special," reached Kansas City, Truman's old political base, Dewey was so confident of victory that he booked the hotel suite the president used whenever he was in town.

Truman conducted an energetic campaign. He moved from town to town, stopping to denounce Dewey and Henry Wallace from the back of a railroad car. Dewey was plotting "a real hatchet job on the New Deal," he charged, and the Republican Party was controlled by a cabal of "cunning men" who were planning "a return of the Wall Street economic dictatorship." "Give 'em hell, Harry!" shouted enthusiastic crowds. In November, Truman won only 49.6 percent of the popular vote but gained a solid majority in the electoral college. He, and not Thomas Dewey, would be moving back into the presidential suite in Kansas City—and into the White House in Washington, D.C.

Truman's victory seems less surprising to historians than it did to political analysts in 1948.

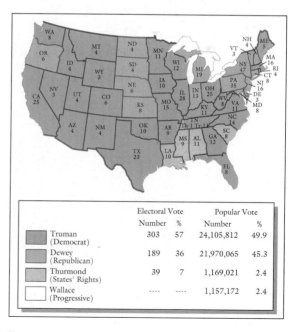

	Electoral Vote		Popular Vote	
	Number	%	Number	%
Truman (Democrat)	303	57	24,105,812	49.9
Dewey (Republican)	189	36	21,970,065	45.3
Thurmond (States' Rights)	39	7	1,169,021	2.4
Wallace (Progressive)	----	----	1,157,172	2.4

PRESIDENTIAL ELECTION, 1948

Despite Republican electoral gains in the congressional elections of 1946, the Democratic Party was hardly enfeebled. Indeed, the Democrats running for Congress in 1948, who identified themselves with Franklin Roosevelt rather than with his successor, generally polled a higher percentage of the popular vote in their districts than did Truman himself. Still, voter loyalty to the memory of Roosevelt and to his New Deal coalition—labor union members, farmers, people of color, and social justice activists—helped Truman.

Truman also attracted a constituency of his own by virtue of his anticommunist policies. In this sense, Truman's presidency established a pattern that would persist for several decades: If Democratic candidates could avoid appearing "soft" or "weak" on national security issues, they stood a good chance of being elected president. The candidacies of both George McGovern in 1972 and Jimmy Carter in 1980 faltered on the issue of national security. Conversely, Harry Truman stood "tough" in 1948. His hard-line national security credentials proved especially effective against Henry Wallace. After the election, Wallace's Progressive Party, which had challenged Truman's national security policies and had promised to revive

DEWEY DEFEATS TRUMAN? Contrary to the predictions that led to this newspaper headline, Harry Truman defeated Thomas Dewey in the close election of 1948. The "little man from Missouri" would continue to pursue containment abroad.

the New Deal at home, lay in shambles. Hampered by his refusal to reject support from members of the CPUSA, Wallace failed to win a single electoral vote and received less than 3 percent of the popular tally.

THE KOREAN WAR ERA, 1949–1952

As the Truman administration marshaled the nation's economic and military resources behind the containment policy, a series of cold war crises in 1949 heightened its anticommunist rhetoric and deepened its focus on national security issues. These crises led ultimately to warfare in Korea.

NATO, CHINA, AND THE BOMB

Building on the Truman Doctrine, the Marshall Plan, the Berlin Airlift, and the 1949 creation of the Federal Republic of Germany (West Germany), the United States set about creating a worldwide system of military alliances. In April 1949 the United States, Canada, and 10 European nations formed the North Atlantic Treaty Organization (NATO). Members of NATO pledged that an attack against one would automatically be considered an attack against all and agreed to cooperate on economic and political, as well as military, matters. Some U.S. leaders worried about the implications of NATO. Republican Senator Robert Taft of Ohio declared that it was a provocation to the Soviet Union and an "entangling alliance" that defied common sense, violated the traditional U.S. foreign policy of nonentanglement, and threatened constitutional government by eclipsing Congress's power to declare war. The nation's use of military force, Taft warned, could be dictated by a response to events in other countries rather than shaped through its own policymaking processes. Even so, the NATO concept prevailed, and the United States expanded the idea of pursuing containment through such "collective security" during the 1950s.

Meanwhile, events in China aggravated cold-war tensions. Between 1945 and 1948 the United States had extended to Jiang Jieshi's government one billion dollars in military aid and another billion in economic assistance. Jiang, however, steadily lost ground to the communist forces of Mao Zedong, who promised land reform and commanded wide support among China's peasantry. Although experi-

The cold war split Europe into two opposing alliances. Germany was divided into two countries: The Federal Republic of Germany (West Germany) and the German Democratic Republic (East Germany). Berlin, the former capital of Germany, was also divided. In 1949 NATO was formed, and in 1955 the Warsaw Pact came into existence.

THE DIVISION OF BERLIN

American Zone
British Zone
French Zone
Soviet Zone

(The American, British, and French zones were consolidated as West Berlin)

NATO Countries
Warsaw Pact Countries
Nonaligned Countries

DIVIDED GERMANY AND THE NATO ALLIANCE

enced U.S. diplomats privately predicted that Jiang's downfall was inevitable, the Truman administration continued publicly to portray Jiang as a respected leader of "free China" and to prop up his regime.

In 1949, when Mao's armies forced Jiang off the mainland to the island of Formosa (Taiwan), many Americans wondered how communist forces could have triumphed. Republican opponents charged the

Truman administration with a "sellout." Financed by conservative business leaders, the powerful "China lobby" excoriated Truman and his new secretary of state, Dean Acheson, for being "soft" on communism. Despite evidence of friction between Stalin and Mao, the detractors spoke of a global communist conspiracy directed from Moscow. Tainted by the "loss" of China, several State Department officials who had criticized Jiang or merely predicted his downfall were dismissed and discredited, depriving the U.S. government of its most knowledgeable experts on China and Southeast Asia. Meanwhile, responding to criticism, Acheson and Truman escalated their anticommunist rhetoric. For more than 20 years, even after friction between China and the Soviet Union became evident, the United States refused to recognize or deal with Mao's "Red China." Jiang's anticommunist island of Taiwan, like Berlin, became a powerful cold-war symbol.

In September 1949 news reached Washington that the Soviets had exploded a crude atomic device, marking the end of the U.S. nuclear monopoly. Already besieged by critics who saw a world filled with Soviet gains and American defeats, Truman issued reassuring public statements but privately took the advice of hard-line advisers and authorized the development of a new bomb based upon the still unproven concept of nuclear fusion. The decision to build this "hydrogen bomb" wedded the doctrine of containment to the creation of ever more deadly nuclear technology.

NSC-68

Prompted by events of 1949, the Truman administration reviewed its foreign policy assumptions. George Kennan, worried that a simplistic and increasingly militaristic version of his containment

LINK TO THE PAST

A Blueprint for National Security in the Cold War: NSC-68

http://www.fas.org/irp/offdocs/nsc-hst/nsc-68.htm

Drafted in the spring of 1950 by Paul Nitze, head of the State Department's policy planning staff, the lengthy document called National Security Council 68 established both a cold-war rhetorical style and a blueprint for policies designed to enlarge U.S. power in the world.

1. The early sections of NSC-68 describe the conflict between "U.S. Purpose" and "Kremlin [Soviet government] Design." Describe the highly emotive language used and discuss why you think a top-secret, classified document might rely upon such language to make its case.

2. How might this language have both reflected and affected the cold-war events outlined in this chapter?

3. Consider each of the recommended actions listed toward the end of the document. Describe the various policies that comprise the "build-up of strength" advocated in the document and discuss their potential effects abroad.

4. How might each of these policies have affected America's domestic politics and society?

concept was emerging, resigned from the State Department's policy planning staff. As a result, the task of conducting this review fell to Paul Nitze, a hard-liner who produced a top-secret policy paper officially identified as National Security Council document number 68 (NSC-68). It provided a blueprint for both the rhetoric and the strategy of future cold-war foreign policy.

NSC-68 opened with an emotional account of a global ideological clash between "freedom," spread by U.S. power, and "slavery," promoted by the Soviet Union as the center of "international communism." Warning against any negotiations with the Soviets, the report urged a full-scale offensive to enlarge U.S. power. It endorsed covert action, economic pressure, more vigorous propaganda efforts, and a massive military buildup. Because Americans might oppose larger military spending and budget deficits, the report warned, U.S. actions should be labeled as "defensive" and be presented as a stimulus to the economy rather than as a drain on national resources. In NSC-68, "freedom" meant simply "anticommunism." Although NSC-68 remained classified for over two decades, the early 1950s public heard its message well. Secretary of State Dean Acheson stumped the country preaching its tenets and elaborating upon its dramatic portrayal of the cold war as a global showdown between good and evil.

THE KOREAN WAR

The dire warnings of NSC-68 seemed confirmed in June 1950 when communist North Korea attacked South Korea. The Truman administration portrayed the move as a simple case of Soviet-inspired aggression against a "free" state. An assistant secretary of state remarked that the relationship of the Soviet Union to North Korea was "the same as that between Walt Disney and Donald Duck." Truman invoked once again the policy of containment: "If aggression is successful in Korea, we can expect it to spread through Asia and Europe to this hemisphere."

The Korean situation, however, defied such simplistic analysis. Korea had been occupied by Japan between 1905 and 1945, and after Japan's defeat in the Second World War, Koreans had expected to establish their own independent state. Instead, the postwar Soviet and U.S. zones of occupation trans-

formed into political entities. Against the desires of both North and South Koreans, Korea became two states, split at the 38th parallel. The Soviet Union supported a North Korean communist government under the dictatorial Kim Il-sung; the United States backed Syngman Rhee, who held a Ph.D. from Princeton University, to head the unsteady and autocratic government in South Korea. Both leaders hoped that the patronage of a superpower might help to bolster their control and advance their respective notions of how Korean society should be organized.

Korea could not be easily split along an arbitrary geographic line. It remained a single society though riven by political factions as well as by ethnic and religious divisions. Rhee's oppressive regime, protective of upper-class landholders, generated opposition in South Korea, a movement that Kim's communist dictatorship encouraged. As discontent spread in South Korea, Kim moved troops across the 38th parallel on June 25, 1950, to attempt unification. Earlier, he had consulted both Soviet and Chinese leaders about his plans and received their support, after assuring them that a U.S. military response was highly unlikely.

The fighting in Korea soon escalated into an international conflict. The Soviets, uninformed about the precise details of Kim's plans, were boycotting the United Nations on the day the invasion was launched. Consequently, they were not present to veto a U.S. proposal to send a peacekeeping force to Korea. Under UN auspices, the United States rushed assistance to the dictatorial Rhee, who moved to eliminate disloyal South Korean civilians as well as to repel the invading North Koreans.

U.S. goals in Korea were unclear. Should the United States seek to "contain" communism by driving the North Koreans back over the 38th parallel? Or should it try to reunify the country under Rhee's leadership? At first, that decision could be postponed because the war was going so badly. North Korean troops pushed their Soviet-made tanks rapidly southward; within three months, they took Seoul and reached the southern tip of the Korean peninsula. American troops seemed unprepared and, unaccustomed to the unusually hot Korean weather during these first months, many fell sick. Fearing the worst, U.S. generals laid contingency plans for a large-scale American evacuation

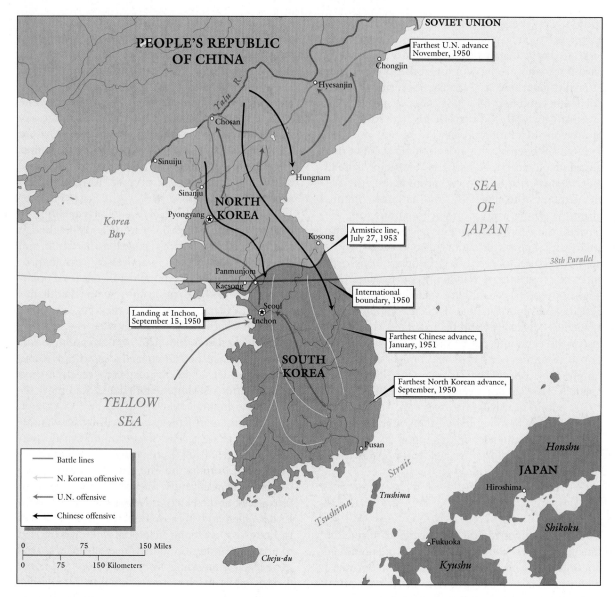

KOREAN WAR

from Pusan. American firepower, however, gradually took its toll on the elite troops who had spearheaded North Korea's rapid move southward. North Korea had to send fresh, untrained recruits to replace seasoned fighters. As supply lines stretched out, the North Korean effort became more vulnerable.

General Douglas MacArthur devised a plan that most other commanders considered crazy: an amphibious landing behind enemy lines at Inchon. MacArthur, now 70 years old, remained as bold and egotistical as he had been both during the Second World War and as head of the occupation government of Japan. Rear Admiral James Doyle remarked, "If MacArthur had gone on the stage you never would have heard of John Barrymore." Those stunned by his risky proposed invasion were even more astounded by its results. On September 15, 1950, the Marines successfully landed 13,000 troops at Inchon, suffered only 21 deaths, and moved back into Seoul within 11 days.

The price of recovering the military offensive was devastation on the ground. The Korean war

MACARTHUR RETURNS After the firing of General Douglas MacArthur by President Truman in April 1951, MacArthur received a huge ticker tape reception on New York's lower Broadway.

was called a "limited" war because the United States did not employ atomic weapons, but intense American bombing proceeded every military move. The number of estimated dead and wounded reached perhaps a tenth of Korea's total population. As armies contested for control of Seoul, the city itself became rubble, with only the Capitol and a train station left standing.

As MacArthur's troops drove northward, Truman faced a crucial decision. MacArthur, emboldened by success, urged moving beyond containment to an all-out war of "liberation" and reunification. Other advisers warned that China would retaliate if U.S. forces approached its border. Cautiously, Truman allowed MacArthur to carry the war into North Korea but ordered him to avoid antagonizing China.

MacArthur pushed too far. Downplaying encounters between his troops and Chinese "volunteers," he continued to advance toward the Yalu River on the Chinese-Korean border. China responded by sending troops into North Korea and driving MacArthur back across the 38th parallel.

With China now in the war, Truman again faced the question of military goals. When MacArthur's troops regained the initiative, Truman ordered his general to negotiate a truce at the 38th parallel. MacArthur challenged the president, arguing instead for all-out victory over North Korea—and over China, too. Truman thereupon relieved him of his command in April 1951, pointing out that the Constitution specified that military commanders must obey the orders of the president, the commander in chief.

MacArthur returned home as a war hero. New York City greeted him with a ticker-tape parade that drew a crowd nearly twice as large as the one that had greeted General Dwight Eisenhower at the end of the Second World War. One poll reported that less than 30 percent of the U.S. public supported Truman's actions. The China lobby portrayed MacArthur as a martyr to Truman's "no-win," containment policy. For a brief but intense moment MacArthur seemed a genuine presidential possibility for 1952, but this outpouring of admiration reflected MacArthur's personal charisma rather than any significant public support for a full-scale land war in Asia. During Senate hearings on the general's dismissal, military strategists expressed their opposition to such a war. And most Americans apparently preferred a negotiated settlement in Korea. Truman now set about convincing North Korea and South Korea to meet at the conference table. Eisenhower, the Republican candidate for president in 1952, promised to go to Korea to hasten the peace process. The negotiations that eventually reestablished the borderline at the 38th parallel emerged as a major foreign policy task for the new Eisenhower administration in 1953.

KOREA AND CONTAINMENT

The Korean War had repercussions elsewhere. It focused American foreign policy ever more narrowly on anticommunism and justified the global offensive that NSC-68 had recommended. The United States announced a plan to rearm West Germany, scarcely five years after Germany's defeat, and increased NATO's military forces. In 1951 the United States signed a formal peace treaty with Japan, and a Japanese-American security pact granted the United States bases on Okinawa and permission to station U.S. troops in Japan. The

Invasion of the Body Snatchers (1956)

**Directed by Don Siegel. Starring Kevin McCarthy (Dr. Miles Bennell)
and Dana Wynter (Becky Driscoll).**

Dr. Miles Bennell, his clothing disheveled, dashes across a Southern California freeway. "You're in danger! Can't you see? They're after you! They're after all of us. . . . They're already here! You're next!" After confirming Miles's bizarre story, a horrified psychiatrist calls for help. "Block all highways and stop all traffic and call in every law enforcement agency in the State. . . . Get me the Federal Bureau of Investigation!" What is terrifying enough to trigger an appeal to the national security bureaucracy? Giant seed pods, which have mysteriously arrived from outer space. Although seeds raining down from the sky might seem a silly threat on which to build a political-social allegory, *Invasion of the Body Snatchers* spawned two remakes—in 1978 and 1993—and itself remains a classic artifact of the cold-war era.

Miles initially fails to diagnose the pod menace. Returning to Santa Mira, California, after a brief vacation, he encounters patients who claim that their relatives are no longer themselves. Little Jimmy Grimaldi insists that his mother is not really his mother. Wilma, another patient, finds that her uncle can still recall every detail about his life, but "there's no emotion. None! Memories or not, he isn't my Uncle Ira," Wilma tells the perplexed physician. General practitioner Miles suggests that Wilma consult an expert, psychiatrist Danny Kaufman, but she assures him that she is perfectly normal.

In time, Miles realizes that nearly everyone in Santa Mira, including Dr. Kaufman himself, has succumbed to the pods, which have the power to lodge themselves in peoples' bodies and to erase their minds, feelings, and individuality. Once taken over by the pods, converts place new seeds near relatives and friends. While these people are sleeping, the plants assume their outer appearance and steal their inner substance. Miles, a few close friends, and his girlfriend Becky Driscoll fight back, but, one by one, they fall

United States also acquired bases in Saudi Arabia and Morocco, bolstering its strategic position in the Middle East. In 1950 direct military aid to Latin American governments, which had been voted down in the past, slid through Congress. By 1952 such aid amounted to nearly $52 million. In French Indochina, Truman provided assistance to strengthen French efforts against a communist-led, independence movement. In the Philippines, the United States stepped up military assistance to suppress the leftist Huk rebels. And in 1951 the ANZUS collective security pact linked the United States strategically to Australia and New Zealand. Throughout the world, economic pressure, CIA covert activities, and propaganda campaigns helped to forge anticommunist alliances. Truman's global "Campaign of Truth," an intensive informational and psychological offensive, used mass media and cultural exchanges to counter Soviet claims with pro-American perspectives.

While the Truman administration fortified America's strategic position throughout the world, U.S. military budgets increased in order to fund ongoing weapons research and production. The Atomic Energy Commission had been created in 1946 to succeed the Manhattan Project in overseeing development of nuclear power; aviation had received special government funding for the first time in the 1946 budget; the army had joined with aircraft manufacturers in an effort to develop surface-to-surface missiles. To coordinate global strategy with the development of long-range weapons, a new "think tank"—RAND, an acronym for Research and Development—was created. Expensive

victim to the pods. Danny Kaufman urges Miles to abandon his resistance and allow the pods to do their work. Once he falls asleep and surrenders, he will be "reborn into an untroubled world." Without emotions such as love and ambition, "life will be so simple," the psychiatrist assures Miles. After Becky finally becomes a "pod person," she urges Miles to "stop acting like a fool . . . and accept us." Fleeing in terror, Miles tries to warn the outside world that Santa Mira has been overrun.

The pods can symbolize any number of "alien" threats that comprised common themes in cold-war culture. Like communist cadres, they attack minds, souls, and individuality. Conversely, as the film's producer Walter Wanger once claimed, the passive condition produced by the pods could equally warn against the kind of conformity, encouraged by extreme anticommunists, that blighted cold-war culture. Cascading from the sky, the pods also might represent the dangers of nuclear fallout. Given their ability to reproduce endlessly, they may symbolize the postwar era's simultaneous fascination with and fear of sexuality.

In much of the cold-war–era public discourse, a vaguely delineated "they"—which could signify such widely varied threats as communists, anticommunists, nuclear danger, and social conformity—were said to be a threat to "us." In this sense, *Invasion of the Body Snatchers* might portray, rather than a warning about any specific danger, more a general symptom of pervasive anxieties that enveloped postwar culture.

Miles and Becky flee from the "pod people."

contracts for manufacturing military materials worried cost-conscious members of Congress, but the prospect that the contracts would create new jobs in their home districts muted their opposition. The cold war, especially after Korea, thus brought what the historian Michael Sherry has called "the militarization of American life": a steady military buildup and an intermingling of military and economic policies, all justified by an emphasis on anticommunism at home and abroad.

As the effort to contain communism intensified, U.S. policymakers became more suspicious of any movement supported by local communists or left-leaning in its political orientation. The U.S. occupation government in Japan, for example, increasingly restricted labor union activities, suspended an antitrust program that American officials had earlier implemented, brought back conservative wartime leaders, and barred communists from government offices and universities. As in Germany, the United States tried to contain communism by strengthening industrial elites and promoting economic growth. U.S. purchases during the Korean conflict stimulated Japan's economy and provided the foundation for the procapitalist, anticommunist Japanese government that succeeded the American occupation in 1952.

In Africa, as well, anticommunism shaped U.S. policies, bringing the United States into an alliance with South Africa. In 1948 the all-white (and militantly anticommunist) Nationalist Party instituted a legal system based on elaborate rules of racial separation and subordination of blacks (apartheid). Some State Department officials warned that supporting apartheid in South Africa would damage U.S. prestige, but the Truman administration decided to cement an alliance with South Africa nonetheless. That country, Truman reasoned, possessed important raw materials (especially, uranium for bombs and manganese for steel) and a large labor force. Moreover, South Africa's Nationalist Party was militantly anticommunist.

From 1947 to the early 1950s, U.S. citizens often felt embattled and insecure in the world. Containment relied on a rhetoric of defensiveness: the term "national security" replaced "national interest"; the War Department became the Department of Defense. Yet the United States during this time extended its power into the former British sphere of influence of Iran, Greece, and Turkey; initiated the Marshall Plan and NATO; and transformed its former enemies—Italy, Germany, and Japan—into anti-Soviet bulwarks. Furthermore, the United States assumed control of hundreds of Pacific islands, launched research to develop the hydrogen bomb, winked at anticommunist ally South Africa's apartheid policies, solidified its sphere of influence in Latin America, acquired bases around the world, and devised a master plan for using military, economic, and covert action to achieve its goals. Beginning with the Truman Doctrine of 1947, the United States staked out a global military and strategic presence.

CONTAINMENT AT HOME

Although containment abroad generally gained bipartisan support, Harry Truman's national security policies at home became increasingly divisive. A strident debate over how best to counter alleged communist influences in the United States raged from the late 1940s through the middle 1950s. Politicians, professional organizations, labor unions, business corporations, and individual citizens all strove to demonstrate their anticommunist credentials. Conservative members of Congress and private watchdog groups, building on Truman's anticommunist rhetoric, launched their own search for evidence of internal communist subversion. Civil libertarians complained of a "witch hunt" against people whose only sins were dissent from the Truman administration's anticommunist measures or support for a leftist political agenda at home. In-

deed, the more extreme red-hunters charged Truman's own anticommunist administration with knowingly harboring people who were disloyal or "soft" on communism. In time, even devoted anticommunists began to complain that wild goose chases after unlikely offenders were hampering the search for authentic Soviet agents. A commission on the role of cold-war intelligence-gathering later concluded that many of the country's most vocal anticommunists "clearly knew little or nothing" about internal security matters. Still, the search for supposed subversives affected many areas of postwar life, and a particularly aggressive group of anticommunists emerged in Congress.

ANTICOMMUNISM AND THE LABOR MOVEMENT

The labor movement became a prominent target for anticommunist legislators. An unprecedented wave of labor strikes had swept across the country after the end of the Second World War. Militant workers had struck for increased wages and for a greater voice in workplace routines and production decisions. Strikes had brought both the auto industry and the electronics industry to a standstill. In Stamford, Connecticut, and Lancaster, Pennsylvania, general strikes had led to massive work stoppages that later spread to Rochester, Pittsburgh,

STEELWORKERS STRIKE Striking steelworkers picket their employer in 1946. During that year, strikes affected millions of American workers.

Oakland, and other large cities. By 1947, however, labor militancy had begun to subside as Truman took a hard line. He warned oil refinery strikers to "cut out all the foolishness." He threatened to seize mines and railroads shut down by strikes and ordered the strikers back to work.

In 1947 congressional opponents of organized labor effectively tapped anticommunist sentiment to help pass the Labor-Management Relations Act, popularly known as the Taft-Hartley Act. The law negated some gains unions had made during the 1930s by limiting a union's power to conduct boycotts, to compel employers to accept "closed shops" in which only union members could be hired, and to conduct any strike that the president judged against the national interest. In addition, as a means of curtailing "wildcat" strikes, the law strengthened the power of union leaders to discipline their own members. Finally, Taft-Hartley required that these same union officials sign affidavits stating that they did not belong to the Communist Party or to any other "subversive" organization. A union that refused to comply was effectively denied protection under national labor laws when engaged in conflict with management. Truman vetoed Taft-Hartley, but Congress swiftly overrode him. Trying to uncover communist infiltration of labor unions became a consistent quest of anticommunists in Congress and within the labor movement itself.

The place of communists in the labor movement, which had long been a contentious issue, was advanced as a national-security matter. Anticommunist unionists had long charged that communists, despite their energetic work in grass-roots organizing campaigns, were more loyal to the CPUSA than to their unions; now, they could cite communists for being disloyal to the nation itself. Differences over whether to support the Democratic Party or Henry Wallace's third-party effort in 1948 heightened tensions within many unions. In the years following Truman's victory the Congress of Industrial Organizations (CIO) expelled 13 unions—and a full third of its membership—for allegedly following pro-Soviet, rather than pro-labor, policies. Meanwhile, many workers found their jobs at risk because of their political ideas, as red-hunters searched for subversives in the workplace. By the end of the Truman era, some type of

loyalty-security check had been conducted on about 20 percent of the American workforce, more than 13 million people.

HUAC AND THE LOYALTY PROGRAM

Anticommunists also scrutinized the entertainment industry. In 1947, only three days after the unveiling of the Truman Doctrine, the House Committee on Un-American Activities (popularly known as HUAC) opened hearings on the CPUSA's activities in Hollywood. Basking in the glare of newsreel cameras, committee members seized on the refusal of 10 screen writers, producers, and directors who had been or still were Party members to testify about their own political affiliations and those of other members of the film community. Known as "the Hollywood Ten," this group claimed that the First Amendment shielded their political activities from official scrutiny. After the federal courts upheld HUAC's power and denied the Hollywood Ten's First Amendment claim, members of the group went to prison for contempt of Congress.

Meanwhile, studio heads secretly drew up a "blacklist" of alleged subversives who could no longer work in Hollywood. Industry leaders denied the existence of such a list, but their disavowals were unconvincing. Actor John Wayne later explained, "The only thing our side did that was anywhere near blacklisting was just running a lot of people out of the business. . . ." By the mid-1950s hundreds of people in Hollywood and in the fledgling television industry—technicians who worked behind the scenes as well as performers who appeared in front of them—were unable to find jobs until they agreed to appear before HUAC and other investigative bodies. There, they were required to name people whom they had seen at some "communist meeting" some time in the past.

Ronald Reagan and Richard Nixon, two future Republican presidents, first attracted the political spotlight through the HUAC hearings. Reagan, who was president of the Screen Actors Guild and also a secret informant for the FBI (identified as "T-10"), decried the presence of subversives in the movie industry. Nixon, then an obscure member of Congress from California, began his political ascent in 1948 when Whittaker Chambers, a journalist who had once been active in the Communist Party, came before HUAC. Chambers charged Alger Hiss, a prominent liberal Democrat who had a long career in government, with having links to the CPUSA and with passing documents to Soviet agents during the 1930s.

The Hiss-Chambers-Nixon affair set off a raging controversy. Hiss immediately claimed that he had been framed in an elaborate FBI plot and alleged that the Bureau had even rigged his typewriter so it would appear to be the source of incriminating evidence. Although the passage of time legally shielded Hiss from prosecution for any acts of espionage that might have occurred during the 1930s, he was charged with committing perjury in his Congressional testimony about his activities. Nixon and his supporters considered the exposure of Hiss, who had been one of Franklin Roosevelt's advisers during the Yalta Conference (see chapter 26), proof that the search for Soviet subversion required greater vigor than the Truman administration could provide. To civil libertarians, however, attacks on Hiss suggested a witch-hunt. Debates over whether the Hiss case was an example of high-level espionage or anticommunist hysteria would continue for decades.

During the mid-1990s, the availability of long-classified documents, such as those in the Venona files, tilted the debate against Hiss. He died in 1996, at the age of 92, still maintaining his innocence and still attracting his defenders. Even so, historians increasingly agreed that the evidence indicated that Hiss (along several other high-ranking public officials and certain lower-level government employees with ties to the CPUSA) had been passing information to agents of the Soviet Union during the 1930s and 1940s.

TARGETING DIFFERENCE

Meanwhile, as controversy swirled around the Hiss case, the Truman administration continued to pursue its own hard-line policies. Under the president's loyalty program, hundreds of government employees

ALGER HISS AND WHITTAKER CHAMBERS The confrontation between Whittaker Chambers and Alger Hiss, before the House Un-American Activities Committee in August 1948, began a controversy that has lasted more than 50 years. Did prominent members of the Roosevelt administration, such as Hiss, secretly provide information to the Soviet Union, as Chambers steadfastly maintained? Or were Chambers and others overzealous in their "red-hunting"?

lost their jobs. Truman's attorneys general allowed J. Edgar Hoover, head of the FBI, to assume broad, discretionary power to uncover subversion. Attorney General Tom Clark (whom Truman appointed to the Supreme Court in 1949) authorized Hoover to draw up his own list of alleged subversives and to detain them, without any legal hearing, in the event of a national security emergency. Clark's successor, Howard McGrath, proclaimed that communist subversives, each carrying "the germs of death for society," were lurking "in factories, offices, butcher stores, on street corners, in private business."

At the same time, the FBI initiated surveillance activities against and accumulated dossiers on many members of the arts and entertainment world. The Bureau compiled secret files on prominent liberals with no ties to the CPUSA, such as writers Ernest Hemingway and John Steinbeck. African American artists and writers became special targets. Richard Wright (author of the novel *Native Son*), W. E. B. Du Bois (a celebrated historian) and Paul Robeson (one of America's best-known entertainer-activists) were singled out by State Department and immigration officials because of their ties to the CPUSA and their frequent overseas travel on behalf of anticolonial movements.

Concern that people with subversive political affiliations and ideas might emigrate to the United States produced a new immigration law. In 1952 Congress passed the McCarran-Walter Act, which placed restrictions on immigration from areas outside northern and western Europe and on the entry of people who immigration officials suspected might threaten national security.

Homosexuals also attracted special attention. During the Second World War, with the disruption of many traditional social patterns, more visible and assertive gay and lesbian subcultures had begun to emerge, even within the armed forces. After the war, Dr. Alfred Kinsey's research on sexual behavior—the first volume, on male sexuality, was published in 1948—claimed that gays and lesbians could be found throughout American society. At about the same time, gays themselves formed the Mattachine Society (in 1950) and lesbians founded the Daughters of Bilitis (in 1955), organizations that began to push for recognition of legal rights for homosexuals. The Kinsey Report's implicit claim that homosexuality was simply another form of sexuality that should be tolerated, together with the discreet militancy among gays and lesbians, produced a backlash that became connected to the broader antisubversion crusade. The fact that several founders of the Mattachine Society had also been members of the Communist Party, coupled with the claim that homosexuals could be blackmailed by Soviet agents more easily than heterosexuals, helped to link homosexuality with subversion.

A connection between antihomosexual and anticommunist rhetoric developed. Radical political ideas and homosexuality were both portrayed as "diseases" that could be spread throughout the body politic by people who often looked no different from "ordinary" Americans. As a report from the U.S. Senate put it, "one homosexual can pollute a Government office" in much the same way as could a person with subversive ideas. According to this logic, homosexuality was an acceptable basis for denying people government employment.

"THE GREAT FEAR"

Harry Truman's final years as president unfolded in an atmosphere of public anxiety about communist subversion that the historian David Caute has called "the Great Fear." With their ceaseless warnings about hidden enemies, at home and abroad, the guardians of national security seemed to have intensified that fear instead of allaying it.

Foreign policy events of 1949 and 1950, especially the Soviets' nuclear tests, highlighted the issue of whether subversives and spy rings were at work in the most sensitive recesses of the U.S. government. How had the Soviets so quickly developed atomic weaponry? Suspicions arose about the loyalty of foreign policy personnel, and stories about Soviet agents having stolen U.S. nuclear secrets spread rapidly. In early 1950, Great Britain released evidence that a spy ring had long been operating in the United States. Shortly afterward, the U.S. Justice Department arrested several alleged members of this ring, including two members of the CPUSA, Julius and Ethel Rosenberg.

The Rosenberg case became a cold war melodrama. The trial, the verdicts of guilty, the sentences of death at Sing Sing prison, the numerous legal appeals, the worldwide protests, and the executions in 1953—all provoked intense controversy.

Were the Rosenbergs party to thefts of important nuclear secrets? And if so, were their death sentences on the charge of espionage the constitutionally appropriate punishment? To their supporters, the Rosenbergs (who steadfastly maintained their innocence) were not spies but left-leaning activists who fell victim to anticommunist hysteria. Many believed that the government seemed more intent on punishing them as scapegoats than in conducting a fair trial. To others, the evidence showed that information had been channeled to the Soviets. The new documents released during the 1990s convinced most historians that Julius Rosenberg had been engaged in espionage and that Ethel Rosenberg, though not directly involved, may have known of his activities. Yet, as the Commission on Protecting and Reducing Government Secrecy noted in 1997, the government declined to prosecute "a fair number of Americans who almost certainly were atomic spies." In some instances, it seems, officials feared a court trial could have compromised ongoing intelligence projects; in other cases, they worried that a formal legal proceeding could have revealed illegal activities by Hoover's FBI and likely ended in a failed prosecution. Of those prosecuted for dealing with the Soviets, only Julius and Ethel Rosenberg were charged with a crime that carried the death penalty.

The courts' response to anticommunist crusading sparked controversy. During the 1949 prosecution of Communist Party leaders for sedition, for example, the trial judge allowed the Justice Department wide latitude to introduce evidence against the defendants. In effect, he accepted the claim that, by definition, the CPUSA was simply the arm of an international conspiracy. Its Marxist ideology and its theoretical publications, even in the absence of any proof of subversive acts, could justify sedition convictions against the party's leaders. In contrast, civil libertarians insisted that the government had produced no evidence that the publications and speeches of Communist Party members, by themselves, posed any "clear and present danger" to national security. In this view of the clear and present danger test, the Communist Party's abstract political beliefs, which should enjoy the protection of the First Amendment, were unconstitutionally put on trial. (The kind of evidence later made public in the Venona files, of course, was unavailable to the courts and civil libertarians during the late 1940s and early 1950s.)

When the convictions of the Communist Party leaders were appealed to the Supreme Court, in the landmark case of *Dennis* v. *U.S.* (1951), civil libertarians renewed their arguments that this prosecution violated constitutional guarantees for the protection of speech. The Supreme Court, however, modified the "clear and present danger" doctrine and upheld the broad definition of sedition used by the lower courts. The defendants, a majority of the Court declared, had been constitutionally convicted.

By 1952, the Democrats who had created the national security state were no longer leading the anticommunist effort. Instead, the Truman administration itself became a primary target of anticommunist zealots. In Congress, Republicans and conservative Democrats condemned the administration's handling of anticommunist initiatives and introduced their own legislation, the McCarran Internal Security Act of 1950. It authorized the detention, during any national emergency, of alleged subversives in special camps, and created the Subversive Activities Control Board (SACB) to investigate organizations suspected of being affiliated with the Communist Party and to administer the registration of organizations allegedly controlled by communists.

The Truman administration responded ambiguously to the McCarran Act. Although the president vetoed the law as too extreme, a gesture that Congress quickly overrode, his administration secretly allowed the FBI's J. Edgar Hoover to devise a covert detention program that offered even fewer legal safeguards than the McCarran Act. No national emergency ever triggered either of these plans, but the administration's anticommunist activities continued. Still, Truman could never defuse the charges leveled at his own administration.

McCARTHYISM

Republican Senator Joseph McCarthy of Wisconsin became Truman's prime accuser. Charging in 1950 that communists were at work in Truman's State Department, a wild allegation that supposedly explained foreign policy "losses" such as China, McCarthy put the administration on the defensive. The nation was in a precarious position, according to McCarthy, "not because our only powerful potential enemy has sent men to invade our shores, but rather because of the traitorous actions of those

> *"Communists always appear before the public as 'Progressives.' Yesterday they were 'Twentieth Century Americans,' last week they were 'defenders of all civil liberties,' tonight they may be 'honest, simple trades unionists.' They are 'liberals' at breakfast, 'defenders of world peace' in the afternoon, and 'the voice of the people' in the evening. These artful dodges and ingenious dissimulations obviously make it difficult for the average trusting citizen to keep up with every new Communist swindle and con game. . . . Many newspapers and other publicity media have secret Communists on their staffs who regularly slip in a neat hypodermic full of Moscow virus."*
>
> **JAMES G. O'NEIL**
> *"How You Can Fight Communism,"* American Legion Magazine, *August, 1948*

who have been treated so well by this Nation." Among those people, McCarthy named Secretary of State Dean Acheson and his predecessor, General George C. Marshall.

Truman's efforts to contain McCarthy failed. Although McCarthy rarely tried to substantiate his charges, he lacked neither imagination nor targets. McCarthy and his imitators targeted former members of the CPUSA and people associated with "communist front" organizations, supposedly legitimate political groups secretly manipulated by communists. In most of the cases McCarthy cited, the affiliations had been perfectly legal. He also made vague charges against the entertainment industry and academic institutions. Despite his claims that hundreds—and, later, dozens—of communist subversives were continuing, in the face of Truman's loyalty program, to work in the State Department, he produced no credible evidence to support his case.

Nevertheless, McCarthy seemed unstoppable. In the summer of 1950, a subcommittee of the Senate Foreign Relations Committee, after examining State Department files in search of the damning material, concluded that McCarthy's charges amounted to "the most nefarious campaign of half-truths and untruths in the history of this republic." McCarthy simply charged that the files had been "raped," and he broadened his mudslinging to include Millard Tydings, the Maryland senator who had chaired the subcommittee and who had called McCarthy's charges "an effort to inflame the American people with a wave of hysteria and fear on an unbelievable scale." In the November 1950 elections, Tydings was defeated, in part, because of a fabricated photograph that linked him to an alleged Communist Party member.

Despite McCarthy's recklessness, influential people tolerated, even supported, him. Conservative, anticommunist leaders of the Roman Catholic Church endorsed McCarthy, himself a Catholic. Leading Republicans—including Senator Robert Taft, chair of the GOP policy committee in the Senate, and Kenneth Wherry, the Republican minority leader in the Senate—welcomed McCarthy's attacks on their Democratic rivals. Wherry, cheering McCarthy on, called for rooting out "the alien-minded radicals and moral perverts" in the Truman administration. As head of a special Senate Subcommittee on Investigations, popularly known as the "McCarthy committee," McCarthy enjoyed broad subpoena power and legal immunity from libel suits. He bullied witnesses and allowed self-styled "experts" to offer exaggerated estimates of a vast Red Menace. Although McCarthy's contemporaries, historians now agree, overestimated his political power and personal appeal, the senator personified the form of demagoguery, "McCarthyism," that continues to bear his name.

In the long run, growing concern about national security subtly altered the nation's constitutional structure. Except for the Twenty-second and the Twenty-third Amendments (adopted in 1951 and 1961, respectively), which barred future presidents from serving more than two terms and allowed the District of Columbia a vote in presidential elections, no formal modifications were made to the written Constitution during these years. But legislative enactments, especially the National Security Act of 1947, and the growing power of the executive branch of government, particularly of agencies such as the CIA and the FBI, brought important informal changes to the nation's unwritten constitution. As the Truman administration sought to contain communism and conduct a global foreign policy, older ideas about a constitutional structure of limited governmental powers gave way to the idea of a "national security constitution" in which the executive branch enjoyed broader authority to safeguard the nation's security. During the 1960s, when Lyndon Johnson waged an undeclared war in Southeast Asia, and the 1970s, when Richard Nixon used claims of national security to cover up his own administration's illegal actions, the view of government power that emerged during the 1940s would come under intense scrutiny.

DOMESTIC POLICY: TRUMAN'S FAIR DEAL

Although the Truman administration placed its greatest priority on constructing a global policy of containment, it also reconstructed the domestic legacy of Franklin Roosevelt. Many supporters of FDR's New Deal still endorsed FDR's "Second Bill of Rights." According to Roosevelt's 1944 vision, all Americans had the "right" to a wide range of substantive liberties, including employment, food and shelter, education, and health care. Whenever people could not obtain these, the national government was responsible for providing access to them. Such governmental largesse required constant economic and social planning—and government spending—for the general welfare.

In post–Second World War Europe, the idea of a "welfare state" that undertook economic planning in order to guarantee certain substantive rights won wide acceptance. However, talk about increased spending for government planning proved highly controversial in the United States. Even before the Second World War, the pace of domestic legislation had begun to slow, and throughout the war itself critics had assailed economic planning as meddlesome interference in private decision making. Attempts to expand the New Deal programs, Republicans charged, threatened unconstitutional intrusion into people's private affairs and posed a threat to individual initiative and responsibility.

During Truman's presidency, opposition to dramatic innovations in social policymaking hardened. The National Association of Manufacturers (NAM) warned that new domestic programs would destroy the private free-enterprise system. Southern Democrats in Congress joined Republicans in blocking new programs they feared might weaken white supremacy in their region. Even before Truman succeeded Roosevelt, these conservative forces had succeeded in abolishing several New Deal agencies that might have contributed to economic planning after the war and had flatly rejected FDR's Second Bill of Rights.

THE EMPLOYMENT ACT OF 1946 AND THE PROMISE OF ECONOMIC GROWTH

Faced with such intense opposition to FDR's old agenda, Truman needed a new approach to domestic policymaking. The 1946 debate over the Full Employment Bill helped identify one. The Full Employment Bill, as initially conceived, would have increased government spending and empowered Washington to intervene aggressively in the job market, so as to ensure employment for all citizens seeking work. To the bill's opponents, these provisions and the phrase "full employment" suggested the European welfare state, even socialism.

As the effort to enact this part of the bill stalled, a scaled-down vision of domestic policymaking gradually emerged. The law that Congress finally passed, renamed the Employment Act of 1946, called for "maximum" (rather than full) employment and specifically acknowledged that private enterprise, not government, bore primary responsibility for economic decision making. The act, though it said nothing about full employment, nonetheless recognized that the national government would play an ongoing role in economic management. Rejecting the idea that government economic involvement was automatically suspect, it created a new executive branch body, the Council of Economic Advisers, to help formulate long-range policy recommendations and signaled that government policymakers would assume some yet to be defined responsibility for the performance of the economy.

A crucial factor in the gradual acceptance of Washington's new role was a growing faith that *advice* from economic experts, as an alternative to government *planning*, could guarantee a constantly expanding economy. An influential group of theorists, many of them disciples of the British economist John Maynard Keynes, insisted that the United States no longer needed to endure the boom-and-bust cycles that had long afflicted its economy. Instead of holding the economy hostage to the largely uncoordinated decisions of private individuals and business firms, policymakers and citizens alike were urged to trust in the theoretical expertise of economists. They would advise government and private business on the policies most likely to produce uninterrupted economic growth.

The promise of economic growth as a permanent condition of American life dazzled postwar leaders. Corporate executives, many of whom had feared that the end of the war would intensify labor unrest and trigger recession, viewed economic growth as a guarantee of social stability. The Truman administration embraced the idea that the government should encourage economic growth by updating, through measures such as the Employment Act of 1946, the cooperative relationship with both big business and organized labor that the Roosevelt administration had been forced to pursue during the Second World War. The president's advisers claimed that such cooperation would actually ease domestic policymaking. Economic growth would produce increased tax revenues and, in turn, finance Washington's domestic programs. "With economic expansion, every problem is capable of solution," insisted George Soule, a celebrant of economic growth. Walter Heller, another leader of the postwar generation of economists, likened the promise of economic growth to finding both the rainbow and its proverbial pot of gold. Using the relatively new measure of "gross national product" (GNP), postwar experts could actually calculate the nation's growing economic bounty. Developed in 1939, GNP—defined as the total dollar value of all goods and services produced in the nation during a given year—became the standard gauge of economic health.

By the end of 1948 Truman and his advisers were preaching the gospel of economic growth. Indeed, that ideal fitted nicely with their foreign policy programs, such as the Marshall Plan, which were designed to create markets and investment opportunities overseas. Economic growth at home was linked to development in the world at large—and to the all-pervasive concern with national security.

TRUMAN'S FAIR DEAL

Convinced of a future marked by constant economic growth, Truman unveiled, in his inaugural address of 1949, a domestic agenda he had outlined during his 1948 presidential campaign: the "Fair Deal." He called for the extension of popular New Deal programs such as Social Security and minimum wage laws; enactment of long-stalled, Democratic-sponsored civil rights and national health care legislation; federal aid for education; and repeal of the Taft-Hartley Act of 1947. Charles Brannan, Truman's secretary of agriculture, proposed an ambitious new plan for supporting farm prices by means of additional governmental subsidies, and the president himself urged substantial spending on public housing projects. The assumption on which Truman built his Fair Deal—that domestic programs could be financed from economic growth—would dominate political discussions for years to come. Through the magic of constant economic growth, all Americans would enjoy progressively bigger pieces of an always expanding economic pie.

Two prominent government programs, both of which predated Truman's administration, suggested the approach to domestic policymaking that dominated the Fair Deal years. The first, the so-called GI Bill (officially entitled the Serviceman's Readjustment Act of 1944), had always enjoyed strong support in Congress. After the First World War, Congress had voted veterans cash pensions or bonuses. This time, Congress worked out a comprehensive program of benefits for the several million men and 40,000 women who had served in the armed forces. The GI Bill encompassed several different programs, including immediate financial assistance for college and job-training programs for veterans of the Second World War. By 1947, the year of peak veteran enrollment, about half of the entire college and university population was receiving government assistance. Other provisions ensured veterans preferential treatment when applying for government jobs; generous terms on loans when purchasing homes or businesses; and, eventually, comprehensive medical care in veterans' hospitals. The Veterans' Readjustment Assistance Act of 1952, popularly known as the "GI Bill of Rights," extended these programs to veterans of the Korean War. In essence, although the Truman administration did not enact FDR's Second Bill of Rights in its entirety, the Fair Deal did grant many of its social and economic protections to veterans.

Meanwhile, Social Security, the most popular part of Roosevelt's New Deal, expanded under Truman's

Fair Deal. When conservatives attacked Social Security as an unwarranted extension of federal power, Social Security officials noted that it included needed support for the disabled and the blind and that older people had themselves earned the "income security" through years of work and monetary contributions withheld from their paychecks.

Under the Social Security Act of 1950, benefit levels increased significantly; the retirement portions of the program were expanded; and coverage was extended to more than 10 million people, including agricultural workers. As subsequent debate would highlight, however, no new financing system accompanied this program expansion—a decision that reflected postwar faith in the ability of steady economic growth to underwrite the cost of domestic programs and that postponed politically divisive adjustments for a later day.

The more expansive (and expensive) Fair Deal proposals either failed or were scaled back. For instance, Truman's plan for a comprehensive national health insurance program ran into strong opposition. The American Medical Association (AMA) and the American Hospital Association (AHA) opposed any government intervention in the traditional fee-for-service medical system and steered Congress toward a less controversial alternative—federal financing of new hospitals under the Hill-Burton Act. Opinion polls suggested that most voters, many of whom were enrolling in private health insurance plans such as Blue Cross and Blue Shield, were either apathetic or confused about Truman's national health proposals.

Continued shortage of affordable housing in urban areas stirred greater support for home-building programs, another part of Truman's Fair Deal. Private construction firms and real estate agents welcomed extension of federal home loan guarantees, such as those established under the GI Bill and through the Federal Housing Administration, but they lobbied against publicly financed housing projects. Yet even conservatives such as Senator Taft recognized the housing shortage and supported the Housing Act of 1949. This law promised "a decent home and a suitable living environment for every American family." It authorized construction of 810,000 public housing units (cutting back Truman's goal of 1.05 million). And, most important in the long run, it provided federal funds for "urban renewal" zones, areas to be

CHILDREN RECEIVE THE FIRST VACCINATION AGAINST POLIO IN 1954 Polio was one of the most fearful diseases of the cold war period because it crippled young children. Its postwar history illustrated differences between the Canadian and U.S. medical systems. The Canadian government, with its national health care system, was heavily involved in funding research, testing, and ultimately distributing the new vaccine. In the United States, a nongovernmental organization called the March of Dimes—famous for its effective solicitation of small donations—took the lead. Dr. Jonas Salk, cooperating with Canadian researchers, developed an effective vaccine that was approved in 1954.

cleared of run-down dwellings and rebuilt with new construction. The Housing Act of 1949 announced bold goals but provided only modest funding for its public housing component.

Domestic policymaking during the Truman era, ultimately focused on specific groups, such as Second World War veterans and older Americans, rather than on more extensive programs for all, such as a national health care plan and a large-scale commitment to government-built, affordable housing projects. Opponents of economic planning and greater government spending considered the broader proposals of the Fair Deal—such as health care—to be "welfare," and the Truman administration found it easier to defend more narrowly targeted programs that could be hailed as economic "security" measures for specific groups. This approach to social policymaking under the Fair Deal significantly narrowed the approach of Roosevelt's Second Bill of Rights, which had envisioned a broad program of constitutionally guaranteed entitlements for all citizens.

CIVIL RIGHTS

Truman, while modifying the New Deal's domestic policy assumptions, actually broadened its commitment to civil rights. In fact, he supported the fight against racial discrimination more strongly than any previous president.

Truman had made a special appeal to African American voters during his 1948 presidential campaign. He had strongly endorsed proposals advanced by a civil rights committee he established in 1946. The committee's report, entitled "To Secure These Rights," called for federal legislation against lynching; a special civil rights division within the Department of Justice; antidiscrimination initiatives in employment, housing, and public facilities; and desegregation of the military. Although these proposals prompted many white southern Democrats to bolt to the short-lived Dixiecrat Party in the 1948 election, they won Truman significant support from African Americans.

The Dixiecrat Party episode of 1948, a reaction to Truman's stance on civil rights, portended significant political change among southern whites who had been voting overwhelmingly Democratic since the late 19th century. Strom Thurmond, the Dixiecrats' presidential candidate, denounced Truman for offering a "civil wrongs" program. Although Thurmond insisted that southern Democrats did not oppose all civil rights measures, he also argued that the Constitution required this kind of legislation to come from state governments and not from Washington. Moreover, white southern Democrats pledged to fight any effort to end the pattern of legally enforced racial segregation. Thurmond carried four states in 1948, and his candidacy showed that the race issue was powerful enough to incite lifelong southern Democrats to desert the party in national presidential elections.

Despite discord within his own party, Truman generally supported the civil rights movement. When successive Congresses failed to enact any civil rights legislation—including a law against lynching

and a ban on the poll taxes that prevented most southern blacks from voting—the movement turned to a sympathetic White House and to the federal courts. After labor leader A. Philip Randolph threatened to organize protests against continued segregation in the military, Truman issued an executive order calling for desegregation of the armed forces, a move that began to be implemented during the Korean War. Truman also endorsed the efforts of the Fair Employment Practices Commission (FEPC) to end racial discrimination in federal hiring.

Meanwhile, Truman's Justice Department regularly appeared in court on behalf of litigants who contested government-backed public school segregation and "restrictive covenants" (legal agreements that prevented racial or religious minorities from acquiring real estate). In 1946, the Supreme Court declared restrictive covenants illegal and began chipping away at the "separate but equal" principle used since *Plessy* v. *Ferguson* (1898) to justify segregated schools. In 1950, the Court ruled that under the Fourteenth Amendment racial segregation in state-financed graduate and law schools was unconstitutional. These decisions seemed to open to a successful challenge to all the traditional legal arguments used since *Plessy* to legitimate racial segregation in public schools. The challenge would finally come in 1954 (see chapter 28).

In summary, the years immediately after the Second World War marked a turning point in domestic policymaking. The New Deal's hope for comprehensive socioeconomic planning gave way to a view of social policy based on the assumption that the nation could now expect uninterrupted economic growth. Henceforth, Washington could reap, through taxation, its own steady share of a growing economy and so finance programs targeted to assist specific groups, such as military veterans and older people. As one supporter of this new approach argued, postwar policymakers were sophisticated enough to embrace "partial remedies," such as the GI Bill, rather than to wait for fanciful "cure-alls," such as FDR's Second Bill of Rights.

SOCIAL CHANGE AND CONTAINMENT

The postwar years brought dramatic changes in the daily life of most Americans. Encouraged by the advertising industry, most people seemed, at one level, to view virtually any kind of change automatically as "progress." Yet, at another level, the pace and scope of social change during these years brought a feeling of uneasiness into American life, prompting many people to try to contain the impact of new developments. Containment abroad sometimes paralleled a similar stance toward containing social innovation at home.

JACKIE ROBINSON AND THE BASEBALL "COLOR LINE"

The interplay between these two forces could be seen in the integration of organized baseball during the 1940s and 1950s. In 1947, major league baseball's policy of racial segregation finally changed when Jackie Robinson, who had played in the Negro National League, became the Brooklyn Dodgers' first baseman. Certain players, including several on Robinson's own club, had talked about a boycott. Baseball's leadership, aware of the need for new sources of players and the steady stream of African American fans coming out to the parks, crushed the opposition by threatening to suspend any player who refused to play with Robinson. (Baseball's moguls, though, did relatively little to protect Robinson himself; he was ordered to endure, without protest, racist insults, flying spikes, and brush-back pitches during his rookie season.)

The pressure to integrate the national pastime became inexorable. Several months after Robinson's debut, the Cleveland Indians signed center fielder Larry Doby, and other African American stars quickly began leaving the Negro leagues for the American and National circuits. Eventually, the talents of Robinson—named Rookie of the Year in 1947 and the National League's Most Valuable Player in 1949—and of the other African American players carried the day. By 1960 every major league team fielded black players, and some had begun extensive recruiting in Puerto Rico and in the Caribbean nations. During the 50th anniversary of Robinson's debut, major league baseball staged elaborate memorial ceremonies for Robinson—and congratulated itself for having led the fight against racial prejudice during the cold war years.

During the late 1940s and early 1950s, though, baseball's leaders had worked to contain the participation of African Americans. Several teams delayed

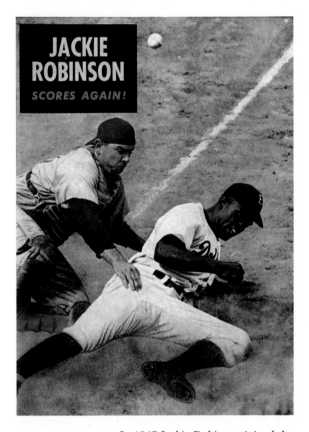

JACKIE ROBINSON In 1947 Jackie Robinson joined the Brooklyn Dodgers and became the first African American since the 19th century to play major league baseball. He had served as a lieutenant in the Army during the Second World War. The racial integration of the national pastime of baseball became a powerful symbol of progress in race relations, and Robinson himself was a favorite of fans, both white and black.

signing any black players, claiming they could find no talented prospects. More commonly, teams restricted the number of nonwhite players they would take on and kept their managers, coaches, and front-office personnel solidly white. Even Jackie Robinson, a successful entrepreneur outside of baseball, never received an offer to return to the game in a management capacity after he retired as a player.

THE POSTWAR SUBURBS

In suburbia, too, the celebration of change and efforts to contain its effects were both constant themes. Suburban living had long been a feature of the "American dream." The new Long Island, New

York, suburb of Levittown, which welcomed its first residents in October 1947, seemed to make that dream a reality, at affordable prices, for middle-income families.

Nearly everything about Levittown seemed unprecedented. A construction company that had mass-produced military barracks during the Second World War, Levitt & Sons could complete a five-room bungalow every 15 minutes. Architectural critics sneered at these "little boxes," but potential buyers stood in long lines hoping to purchase one. By 1950, Levittown consisted of more than 10,000 homes and 40,000 residents, and bulldozers and construction crews were sweeping into other suburban developments across the country. One-quarter of all the houses that existed in 1960 were built after 1949.

To help buyers purchase these homes, the government offered an extensive set of programs. The Federal Housing Administration (FHA), established during the New Deal, helped private lenders extend credit to mass-production builders, who in turn sold the houses on generous financing terms. Typically, people who bought FHA-financed homes needed only 5 percent of the purchase price as a down payment; they could finance the rest with a long-term, government-insured mortgage. Millions of war veterans enjoyed even more favorable terms under the GI loan program operated by the Veterans Administration. These government programs made it cheaper to buy a new house in the average suburb than to rent a comfortable apartment in most cities. Moreover, families could deduct from their federal income tax the interest they paid on their mortgages. This deduction could be seen as a disguised form of governmental subsidy for the building and lending industries and for homeowners. And, because construction never caught up with demand during the 1950s, many suburbanites could sell their first house at a profit and move up to a more spacious, more expensive dwelling.

SUBURBIA Builder William Levitt's opening of Levittown, New York, in the late 1940s set a pattern for mass-produced homes in suburban developments. Assistance from governmental financing programs, such as the GI Bill, and economies gained from standardized production methods brought the cost of such homes within the reach of millions of Americans and hastened the flight, particularly of whites, out of central cities.

ESTIMATED MEDIAN AGE AT FIRST MARRIAGE, 1890–1990

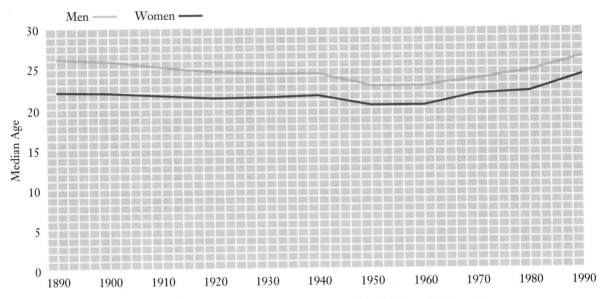

Source: From William Kornblum, *Sociology*, 5th ed. (Fort Worth: Harcourt College Publishers, 2000), p. 506.

Suburban homes promised greater privacy and more amenities than crowded city neighborhoods. Builders, quick to recognize the appeal of the new suburbs, soon began to offer larger houses, including the sprawling, one-level "ranch" model. The joys of "easy and better" living often came with the house. Levitt homes, for example, contained an automatic washer and a built-in television set. Even the television, by being attached to the house itself, qualified as a "structural" component and could be financed under federally guaranteed loan programs.

Suburbs enjoyed the reputation for being ideal places in which to raise children, and many more families were having babies. After the war, a complex set of factors, including early marriages and rising incomes, helped produce a "baby boom" that would last well into the 1950s. With houses generally occupying only about 15 percent of suburban lots, large lawns served as private playgrounds. Nearby schools were as new as the rest of the neighborhood, and suburban school boards used their well-equipped, up-to-date buildings to attract both skilled teachers and middle-income families.

In many respects, the new suburban lifestyle epitomized an optimistic spirit of new possibilities, confidence in the future, and acceptance of change. In other respects, though, it represented an effort to contain some of the effects of rapid change by creating a material and psychological refuge. Most obviously, buying a new suburban home seemed a way of cushioning the impact of social and demographic change. As African American families left the rural South in search of work in northern cities, "white flight" to suburbia quickened. Although Jackie Robinson, Larry Doby, and other talented athletes could find a place in professional baseball during the 1940s, not a single black person could buy a home in Long Island's Levittown until well into the 1960s.

Government and private housing policies helped to structure and maintain the segregationist pattern of white suburbs and increasingly nonwhite urban neighborhoods. Federal laws allowed local groups to veto public housing projects in their communities. Although land and building costs would have been cheaper in the suburbs, public housing projects were concentrated on relatively expensive, high-density urban sites. More important, the lending industry channeled government loan guarantees away from most urban neighborhoods, and private lenders generally denied credit to nonwhites seeking new suburban housing.

No one in the postwar housing industry admitted intentional complicity in these discriminatory patterns. William Levitt might identify his private

THE BABY BOOM

Birth Rate, 1940–1970★

*Based on estimated total live births per 1,000 population.

THE SUBURBAN FAMILY AND GENDER ISSUES

Because the new suburbs generally lacked mass transit facilities, life revolved around the automobile. If the male breadwinner needed the "family" car to commute to work, the wife spent the day at home. Until car ownership expanded in the mid-1950s, even a trip to the supermarket could prove difficult.

Still, wives and mothers found plenty of work at home. New appliances and conveniences—automatic clothes washers, more powerful vacuum cleaners, frozen foods, and home freezers—eased old burdens but created new ones. Contrary to what the ads promised, women were actually spending as much time on housework after the war as their grandmothers had spent at the turn of the century. The time spent on domestic tasks was reallocated but not reduced. Moreover, because child-care facilities were rare in the new suburbs, mothers spent a great deal of time taking care of their children. In contrast to the urban neighborhoods or rural communities where many suburban housewives had grown up, the postwar Levittowns contained few older relatives or younger single women who could help with household and child-care duties.

Daily life in the suburbs fell into a broad pattern of "separate spheres"—a public sphere of work and politics dominated by men and a private sphere of housework and child care reserved for women. Because few jobs of any kind initially were available in postwar suburbia, suburban men commuted farther, and women who wanted to work found nearby job opportunities about as scarce as child-care facilities.

Without mothers and grandmothers living close by, suburban mothers turned elsewhere for child-rearing advice. Local Parent and Teachers Associations (PTAs), connected to a neighborhood school, offered mothers opportunities to exchange information among themselves, as did other women's organizations such as La Leche League. Increasingly, though, parents turned to child-care manuals. Dr. Benjamin Spock's *Baby and Child Care*, first published in 1946, sold millions of copies. Like earlier manuals, Spock's book assigned virtually all child-care duties to women and underscored their nurturing role by stressing the need constantly to oversee a child's psychological growth. The future of the family and the nation itself, Spock implied, depended on the skill with which mothers handled the daily traumas of

housing projects with the public crusade against communism. "No man who owns his house and lot can be a Communist," he remarked in 1948. "He has too much to do." Levitt held himself blameless, however, for racial issues. He could help solve the nation's housing problem—and perhaps even the problem of domestic communism—but he insisted that his "private" construction choices had nothing to do with the public issue of race.

Similarly, the architects of suburbia saw nothing problematic with postwar gender patterns. William Levitt's confident identification of home ownership with men unconsciously reflected the fact that the lending industry generally would not extend loan guarantees to women. Single women simply could not obtain FHA-backed loans, a policy that the agency justified on the grounds that men were the family breadwinners and that women rarely made enough money to qualify as good credit risks. As a result, home ownership in the new suburbs was invariably limited to white males, with wives as co-owners at best.

THE "MRS. AMERICA" GAS KITCHEN In 1959, the American National Exhibition in Moscow featured a "typical housewife" working in this RCA/Whirlpool "Mrs. America" gas kitchen, a symbol of the streamlined material progress of the postwar United States.

THE TYPICAL HOUSEWIFE This photograph depicts a different view of the "typical housewife" in her kitchen.

childhood. Other manuals picked up where Dr. Spock left off and counseled mothers on the care and feeding of teenagers. The alarmist tone of many of these books reflected—and also helped to generate—widespread concern over "juvenile delinquency."

The crusade against an alleged increase in juvenile crime also attracted the attention of government officials. J. Edgar Hoover, director of the FBI, and Attorney General Tom Clark coupled their pleas for containing communism with pleas for containing juvenile delinquency. In a 1953 report, Hoover claimed that the first of the war babies were about to enter their teenage years, "the period in which some of them will inevitably incline toward juvenile delinquency and, later, full-fledged criminal careers."

How could this threat be contained? Many authorities suggested cures that focused on the individual family. Delinquents, according to one study in the early 1950s, sprang from a "family atmosphere not conducive to development of emotionally well-integrated, happy youngsters, conditioned

to obey legitimate authority." It was up to parents, especially mothers, to rear good children. The ideal mother, according to most advice manuals, did not work outside the home but devoted herself to rearing her own segment of the baby boom generation. Women who sought careers outside the home risked being labeled as lost, maladjusted, guilt-ridden, man-hating, or all of the above.

Versions of this message appeared nearly everywhere. Even the nation's prestigious women's colleges offered instruction that was assumed to lead to marriage, not to work or careers. In his 1955 commencement address at Smith, a women's college, Adlai Stevenson, the Democratic Party's urbane presidential candidate in 1952 and 1956, told the graduates that it was the duty of each to keep her husband "truly purposeful, to keep him whole." Postwar magazines, psychology, and popular culture were filled with concerns about the reintegration and stability of returned war veterans. Understanding, supportive wives and mothers seemed the antidote to social turmoil.

Discussions about the ideal postwar family occasionally, however, offered a wider view of gender relationships. When interviewed by researchers, most men claimed not to want a "submissive, stay-at-home" wife. Popular television shows, such as *Father Knows Best* or *Leave It to Beaver*, suggested a hope that middle-class fathers would become more involved in family life than their own fathers had been. And although experts on domestic harmony still envisioned suburban men earning their family's entire income, they also urged them to be "real fathers" at home. A 1947 article in *Parent's Magazine* declared that being a father was "the most important occupation in the world and for the world." Parenting literature emphasized "family togetherness," and institutions such as the YMCA began to offer courses on how to achieve it.

The call for family togetherness, in part, responded to what some cultural historians have seen as an incipient "male revolt" against "family values." Hugh Hefner's *Playboy* magazine, which debuted in 1953, preached that men who neglected their own happiness in order to support a wife and children were not saints but suckers. In *Playboy*'s first issue, Hefner proclaimed: "We aren't a 'family magazine.'" He told women to pass *Playboy* "along to the man in your life and get back to your *Ladies Home Companion*." In Hefner's version of the good life, the man rented a "pad" rather than owned a home; drove a sports car rather than a sedan or a station wagon; and courted the Playmate of the Month rather than the Mother of the Year.

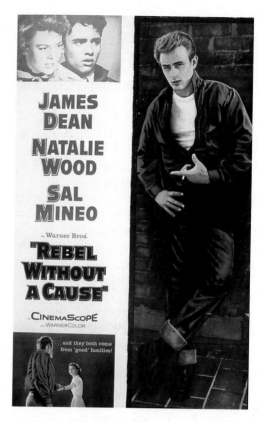

JAMES DEAN James Dean had perished in a car crash just before the release of *Rebel Without a Cause*. The film about misguided kids from "good homes" capitalized on the debate about juvenile delinquency during the 1950s.

WOMEN'S CHANGING ROLES

Despite all of the media images that depicted the average woman as a homebound wife and mother, economic realities were propelling more and more women into the job market. Female employment outside the home rose steadily during the late 1940s and throughout the 1950s. Moreover, increasing numbers of married women were entering the labor force, many of them as part-time workers in the expanding clerical and service sectors. In 1948, about 25 percent of married mothers had jobs outside the home; at the end of the 1950s, nearly 40 percent did.

If more women were holding jobs outside their homes, employment opportunities nevertheless remained largely contained within well-defined, gender-segregated areas. In 1950, for example, more than 90 percent of all nurses, telephone operators, secretaries, and elementary school teachers were women.

Historically, pay scales in these "service" jobs were lower, labor unions were not as active, and chances for advancement were more limited than in male-dominated occupations. As low-paid jobs for women expanded, professional opportunities actually narrowed. Medical and law schools and many professional societies admitted few, if any, women; the number of women on college faculties shrank back even from the low levels of the 1920s and 1930s.

Although the "family wage" ideal was still invoked to explain the disparity of pay and opportunity based on gender, more and more women were trying to support a family on their own paychecks. This was especially true for women of color; by 1960 slightly more than 20 percent of black families were headed by women. Recognizing that stereotypical images of domesticity hardly fit the lives of African American women, a large percentage of whom had always worked outside the home, *Ebony* magazine celebrated women who were able to combine success in parenting and in work. One story, for example, highlighted the only female African American mechanic at American Airlines; many others featured prominent educators and entertainers.

Postwar magazines targeted to white women also carried somewhat ambiguous messages about domesticity. Although pursuing activities outside the home was stigmatized by conservative social commentators as "unnatural," magazines that depended on a broad, popular readership generally gave more positive portrayals of women who were participating in public life, whether in politics or in the job market. Women's magazines, although deferential to the dominant ideal of domesticity, still published articles that chronicled the difficulties of running a home and raising children and often ran stories on prominent career women. The immediate postwar era, in short, was a time of growing diversity in both the roles that women were assuming and the ways in which women were represented in mass culture.

The fear of communism during the years from 1947 to 1954 accentuated pressures for conformity and often made it difficult to advocate significant social change. Yet, despite efforts to contain change at home, demographic shifts, new expectations stemming from the war, and robust prosperity inevitably transformed many social and cultural patterns. The everyday lives of Americans—racial patterns, child-rearing practices, living arrangements, and gender relationships—were inexorably changing.

FROM TRUMAN TO EISENHOWER

Emphasis on anticommunism and containment continued into the presidency of Republican Dwight D. Eisenhower. The 1952 election saw personnel changes in Washington, but it marked few fundamental shifts in either foreign or domestic policies. Containing communism overseas and at home continued to be central issues, especially during the first two years of the Eisenhower presidency.

THE ELECTION OF 1952

By 1952, Harry Truman and the Democrats were on the defensive. Denunciations of the communist threat remained the order of the day, for Democrats as well as for Truman's Republican critics. Adlai Stevenson of Illinois, the Democratic presidential candidate, warned that "Soviet secret agents and their dupes" had "burrowed like moles" into governments throughout the world. "We cannot let our guard drop for even a moment." Stevenson approved of the prosecution of the Communist Party's leaders and the dismissal of schoolteachers who were party members.

A strong anticommunist stance could not save Stevenson or the Democratic Party in 1952. The GOP's vice presidential candidate, Senator Richard Nixon, called Stevenson "Adlai the appeaser" and claimed he held a Ph.D. from "Dean Acheson's Cowardly College of Communist Containment." Republicans criticized Truman's handling of the Korean War and highlighted revelations about favoritism and kickbacks on government contracts. Their successful election formula could be reduced to a simple equation, "K^1C^2": "Korea, corruption, and communism."

For their presidential candidate, Republicans turned to Second World War hero Dwight David Eisenhower, popularly known as "Ike." Eisenhower had neither sought elective office nor even been identified with a political party before 1952, but nearly a half-century of military service had made him a skilled politician. The last president to have been born in the 19th century, Ike grew up in Kansas; won an appointment to, and graduated from, West Point; rose through the army ranks under the patronage of General George Marshall; directed the Normandy invasion of 1944 as supreme Allied commander; served as army chief of staff from 1945 to 1948; and, after an interim period as president of Columbia University, returned to active duty as the commander of NATO, a post he held until May 1952.

Eisenhower seemed an attractive candidate. Although his partisan affiliations had always been vague—at one point, dissident Democrats had even hoped he might challenge Truman for their party's 1948 nomination—Eisenhower finally declared himself a Republican. Initially reluctant to seek the presidency, he became convinced that Robert Taft, his main GOP rival, leaned too far to the right on domestic issues and lacked a firm commitment to containment policies overseas. Positioning himself as a pragmatic moderate, Ike seemed able to lead the nation through a cold war as firmly as he had during

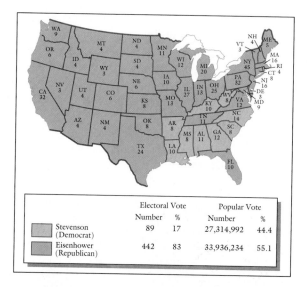

	Electoral Vote		Popular Vote	
	Number	%	Number	%
Stevenson (Democrat)	89	17	27,314,992	44.4
Eisenhower (Republican)	442	83	33,936,234	55.1

PRESIDENTIAL ELECTION, 1952

EISENHOWER PURSUING HIS HOBBY AS A PAINTER
President Eisenhower epitomized the postwar emphasis on leisure time and hobbies. The president was often photographed playing golf, fishing, and painting. Here, he is painting a picture of his grandchildren from a photo.

a hot one. Adlai Stevenson grumbled that the nation's press had embraced the old war hero even before knowing "what his party platform would be" or "what would be the issues of the campaign."

Ike achieved a great personal victory in the 1952 election. The Eisenhower-Nixon ticket received almost seven million more popular votes than the Democrats and won in the Electoral College by a margin of 442 to 89. The Republican Party itself made less spectacular gains. The GOP gained only a one-vote majority in the Senate and an eight-vote majority in the House of Representatives. The electoral coalition Franklin Roosevelt had put together during the 1930s still survived, even though it showed signs of fraying, especially in the South. There, many of the white southern votes that had gone to the Dixiecrats in 1948 began swinging over to the Republicans, and Eisenhower carried four states in the Democratic Party's once "solid South."

EISENHOWER TAKES COMMAND

Eisenhower's "moderate Republicanism" brought few sweeping changes to either foreign or domestic policies. Eisenhower honored his campaign pledge to travel to Korea as a means of bringing an end to U.S. military involvement there. However, armistice talks stalled when an impasse developed over whether prisoners of war (POWs) who had asked to remain in South Korea should be forcibly

returned to North Korea and China. Hoping to end the diplomatic stalemate, Eisenhower began to threaten, in vague messages that quickly reached China and North Korea, the use of nuclear weapons if negotiations failed. Talks resumed, and on July 27, 1953, both sides signed a truce that established a special commission of neutral nations to rule on the POW cases. (The POWs themselves were subsequently allowed to determine whether they wished to be repatriated.) So, finally, ended the fighting in which more than 2 million Asians, mostly noncombatants, and 33,000 Americans had died. A formal peace treaty remained unsigned, however, and the 38th parallel between North and South Korea remained one of the most heavily armed borders in the world.

Eisenhower stood near the center in both foreign and domestic policy. From there he could pursue a bipartisan foreign policy and eventually wrest control over the issue of national security at home from Senator Joseph McCarthy and other extreme anticommunists in Congress. The Republican-controlled Congress did exceed the Eisenhower administration's stance and passed the Communist Control Act of 1954, which barred the Communist Party from entering candidates in elections and extended the registration requirements established by the McCarran Act of 1950. But with a Republican administration now handling surveillance at home and covert operations

Femmes Fatales from Film Noir

During the 1940s and 1950s Hollywood released a cycle of motion pictures that came to be called film noir. These movies, nearly always filmed in black-and-white and often set at night in large cities, peeked into the dark corners of postwar America. They hinted at deep-seated anxieties and fears, especially related to the possibility of men and women living together happily and harmoniously.

Many film noir pictures featured alluring femmes fatales: beautiful but dangerous women who challenged the prevailing social order. The femme fatale represented the opposite of the nurturing, safely contained wife and mother. Usually unmarried and childless, she posed a threat to both men and other women. In *The File on Thelma Jordan* (1949), for instance, the title character, played by Barbara Stanwyck, cynically destroys the marriage of a young, weak-willed district attorney. She initiates an illicit affair with him not because of love, or even lust, but as part of a complicated plot to use him in manipulating the criminal justice system. The postwar era's most prominent female stars—such as Stanwyck, Joan Crawford, Rita Hayworth, and Lana Turner—achieved both popular and critical acclaim playing such roles.

It is of course tempting to view the significance of the many femme fatale characters in postwar film culture as nothing more than negative symbols, part of a cold-war culture that exalted family life and stressed the subordination of women to male heads-of-households. Film noir features, however, developed a loyal audience among women, and some students of Hollywood films have suggested that the femme fatale—seeker of independence and power—might have provided an exaggerated symbol of female filmgoers' dissatisfaction with tightly contained women's roles.

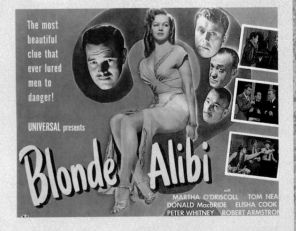

abroad, many GOP members began to see the erratic McCarthy more as a liability than an asset.

McCarthy finally careened completely out of control when he claimed that the U.S. Army was harboring subversives within its ranks. During the spring of 1954, a televised Senate committee investigation into McCarthy's fantastic claim finally brought him down. Under the glare of television lights during the Army-McCarthy hearings, the senator appeared as a crude, desperate bully who was flinging slanders in every direction. In December 1954 a majority of his colleagues, including some who had once shielded him, voted to censure McCarthy for conduct "unbecoming" a member of the Senate. McCarthy faded from the limelight and died in obscurity in 1957, still a Senate member.

With McCarthyism discredited, Eisenhower proceeded with his own expansion of the national security state. Following the excesses of McCarthyism, Ike's low-key approach seemed eminently reasonable. Indeed, the demonstrated unreliability of Congress's anticommunist zealots strengthened Eisenhower's own position when he claimed the constitutional privilege to withhold from Congress secret information on national security matters. Relatively free from congressional oversight, the Eisenhower administration quietly proceeded to extend Truman's earlier programs of domestic surveillance, wiretapping, and covert action overseas.

Many historians now see Eisenhower as a skilled leader who increased the reach of the executive branch while seeming to do the opposite. This revisionist view contrasts with the grandfatherly, slightly befuddled image that Eisenhower himself cultivated during the 1950s. According to one scholar, the crafty Eisenhower conducted a "hidden hand presidency." Mindful of how the mercurial Truman had become personally linked to unpopular policies, Ike often stayed in the background and projected an air of calm steadiness. On matters of foreign policy, he usually let John Foster Dulles take center stage; on domestic issues, he encouraged people to assume that White House policies were being shaped by George Humphrey, his secretary of the treasury, and by Sherman Adams, his chief of staff.

Eisenhower's presidency helped to lower the shrill pitch of the anticommunist crusade that characterized American domestic and international policy from 1946 to 1954. A new sense of calm was settling over life in the United States in the middle 1950s—or so it seemed to the many people who supported Dwight Eisenhower.

CONCLUSION

Efforts at containing communism dominated both domestic and foreign policy during the years after the Second World War. As worsening relations between the United States and the Soviet Union developed into a cold war, the Truman administration pursued policies that expanded the power of the government, particularly the executive branch, to counter the threat. The militarization of foreign policy intensified when the United States went to war in Korea in 1950. At home, anticommunism focused on containing both the activities and ideas of alleged subversives. These initiatives raised difficult issues about how to protect legitimate national security interests while still safeguarding constitutional liberties.

Within this cold-war climate, struggles to achieve greater equality still emerged. Truman's Fair Deal promised that new economic wisdom would be able to guarantee economic growth and thereby provide the tax revenue to expand domestic programs. Truman himself pressed, more strongly than any previous president, for national measures against racial discrimination.

The election of a Republican president, Dwight D. Eisenhower, in 1952 brought few immediate changes in the cold-war climate. A moderate on most issues and a skillful political strategist, Eisenhower projected the image of an elder statesman who kept above day-to-day partisan battles. In time, his style of presidential leadership helped calm the anticommunist rhetoric and offer the prospect of calmer times.

Suggested Readings begin on page SR-1.
For Web activities and resources
related to this chapter, go to
http://www.harcourtcollege.com/history.murrin

CHAPTER 28

AFFLUENCE AND ITS DISCONTENTS, 1954–1963

"THE PROBLEM WE ALL LIVE WITH"

Eighty years after federal troops withdrew from enforcement of Reconstruction in southern states in 1877, they returned to enforce school desegregation against resistance by southern whites. This 1960 painting by Norman Rockwell shows a young black girl being escorted by U.S. marshals to a newly desegregated school in New Orleans, while an unseen mob screams obscenities and threats. Despite the affluence enjoyed by most of U.S. society in the decade following the Korean War, some members of the population were still fighting for their most basic rights.

Beginning in 1954 the cold-war tensions that had prevailed since 1947 began to abate. President Dwight Eisenhower lowered the pitch of superpower rivalry. Yet he and his successor, John F. Kennedy, still directed a determined anticommunist foreign policy.

At home, Eisenhower's relaxed presidential style and Kennedy's youthful charisma helped them cautiously extend some of the domestic programs initiated during the Roosevelt and Truman eras. The economic growth of the late 1950s and early 1960s encouraged talk about an age of affluence. General prosperity, however, also generated apprehension about presumed conformity, the emergence of a "youth culture," and the impact of mass commercial culture. At the same time, a broad-based movement against racial discrimination and new attention to the distribution of the nation's economic bounty prompted renewed debate over the meaning of liberty, how to imagine equality, and the use of governmental power.

This chapter will focus on the following major questions:

- How did the Eisenhower administration change and adapt the foreign policy of containment?
- Why was affluence considered both an opportunity and a problem during the 1950s?
- How did antidiscrimination efforts raise new political issues during the 1950s and early 1960s? How did the Eisenhower and Kennedy administrations respond to these issues?
- What foreign and domestic policies did Kennedy champion during his brief presidency? Why does Kennedy's legacy loom so large in popular memory?

FOREIGN POLICY, 1954–1960

By 1954 the strident anticommunist rhetoric associated with McCarthyism and the Korean War era was beginning to subside. The dominant assumption of cold-war policy—that the United States must protect the "free world" and fight communism everywhere—remained unchanged, but its focus shifted. Bipolar confrontations between the United States and the Soviet Union over European issues gave way to greater reliance on nuclear deterrence and to more subtle and complex power plays in the "Third World"—the Middle East, Asia, Latin America, and Africa.

968 | CHAPTER 28 AFFLUENCE AND ITS DISCONTENTS, 1954–1963

CHRONOLOGY

1954 *Brown* v. *Board of Education of Topeka* decision • SEATO formed • Arbenz government overthrown in Guatemala • Elvis Presley releases first record on Sun label • Geneva Peace Accords in Southeast Asia

1955 Montgomery bus boycott begins • *National Review* founded

1956 Suez Crisis • Anti-Soviet uprisings occur in Poland and Hungary • Federal Highway Act passed • Eisenhower reelected

1957 Eisenhower sends troops to Lebanon • Eisenhower sends troops to Little Rock, Arkansas • Congress passes Civil Rights Act, first civil rights legislation in 80 years • Soviets launch Sputnik • Gaither Report urges more defense spending

1958 National Defense Education Act passed by Congress • *The Affluent Society* published

1959 Khrushchev visits United States

1960 Civil Rights Act passed • U-2 incident ends Paris summit • Kennedy elected president • Sit-in demonstrations begin

1961 Bay of Pigs invasion fails • Berlin Wall erected • Freedom rides begin in the South • Kennedy announces Alliance for Progress

1962 Cuban Missile Crisis • Kennedy sends troops to University of Mississippi to enforce integration

1963 Civil rights activists undertake march on Washington • Betty Friedan's *The Feminine Mystique* published • Kennedy assassinated (November 22); Lyndon Johnson becomes president

THE NEW LOOK AND SUMMITRY

One reason for this shift was a change of leadership in Moscow after the death of Joseph Stalin in 1953. Nikita Khrushchev, the new Soviet leader, talked of "peaceful coexistence" and denounced Stalin's murderous tactics during a speech in 1956. Seeking to free up resources to produce more consumer goods, Khrushchev began reducing Soviet armed forces.

The political climate in the United States also was changing. In December 1953, Admiral Arthur Radford, chairman of the Joint Chiefs of Staff, called for a reduction of the military budget and a revision of defense strategy. Radford's "New Look" reflected Eisenhower's belief that massive military expenditures could eventually impede the nation's economic growth. The new strategy would rely less on expensive ground forces and more on airpower, advanced nuclear capabilities, and covert action.

According to the Eisenhower administration's doctrine of "massive retaliation," the threat of U.S. atomic weaponry would hold communist expansion in check. To make America's nuclear umbrella more effective worldwide, Eisenhower expanded NATO to include West Germany in 1955 and added two other mutual defense pacts with noncommunist nations in Central and Southeast Asia. The Southeast Asia Treaty Organization (SEATO), formed in 1954, was a mutual defense pact among Australia, France, Great Britain, New Zealand, Pakistan, the Philippines, and Thailand. The weakly bonded Central Treaty Organization (CENTO), formed in 1959, linked Pakistan, Iran, Turkey, Iraq, and Britain.

The Eisenhower administration also elevated psychological warfare and "informational" programs into major cold-war weapons. The government-run Voice of America extended its radio broadcasts globally and programmed in more languages. Covertly, the government also funded Radio Free Europe, Radio Liberty (directly to the Soviet Union), and Radio Asia. In 1953 Eisenhower persuaded Congress to create the United States Information Agency (USIA) to coordinate anticommunist informational and propaganda campaigns.

In an effort to improve relations, the United States and the Soviet Union resumed high-level "summit" meetings. In May 1955 negotiators agreed to end the postwar occupation of Austria and to transform that country into a neutral state. Two months later the United States, the Soviet Union, Britain, and France met in Geneva. Making little progress on arms reduction, the future of Germany, and other matters, the meetings nonetheless inaugurated new cultural exchanges. Cold-war tensions eased somewhat, and all sides hailed the conciliatory "spirit of Geneva." In the fall of 1959, to soothe a crisis that had developed over Berlin, Khrushchev toured the United States, met with Eisenhower, and paid well-publicized visits to farmers in Iowa and to Disneyland in California.

Although a 1960 Paris summit meeting was canceled after the Soviets shot down an American U-2 spy plane over their territory, the tone of cold-war rhetoric had calmed.

The superpowers even began to consider arms limitation. In Eisenhower's "open skies" proposal of 1955, the president proposed that the two nations verify disarmament efforts by reconnaissance flights over each other's territory. The Soviets, fearful of opening their land to inspection, refused, but discussions progressed on limiting atomic tests. Responding to worries about the health hazards of atomic fallout, both countries slowed their aboveground testing and discussed some form of test-ban agreement. For many Americans, concerns about the impact of nuclear testing came too late. Government documents declassified in the 1980s finally confirmed what antinuclear activists had long suspected: Many people who had lived "downwind" from rural nuclear test sites during the 1940s and 1950s had suffered an unusual number of atomic-related illnesses. Worse, in the 1990s information surfaced that the federal government had conducted tests with radioactive materials on American citizens who had no knowledge of these experiments.

Events in Eastern Europe accentuated American policymakers' caution about being drawn into a military confrontation with the Soviet Union. Soviet satellite countries were chafing under managed economies and police-state control. Seizing on the post-Stalin thaw, Poland's insurgents staged a three-day rebellion in June 1956 and forced the Soviets to accept Wladyslaw Gomulka, an old foe of Stalin, as head of state. Hungarians began to demonstrate in support of Imre Nagy, another anti-Stalinist communist, who formed a new government and pledged a multiparty democracy. Although the Soviets sought an accommodation that would both preserve their control and allow some reform, armed rebellion spread throughout Hungary.

Taking hope from Secretary of State John Foster Dulles's talk of supporting "liberation" from communism rather than mere containment, Hungarian revolutionaries appealed for American assistance. The United States, however, could hardly launch a military effort so close to the Soviet Union. Soviet armies crushed the uprising and killed thousands of Hungarians, including Nagy. U.S. policymakers learned that although advocating liberation from communism made good political rhetoric at home, it could lead to tragedy abroad.

COVERT ACTION AND ECONOMIC LEVERAGE

Increasingly, the U.S. battle against communism shifted focus from Europe to the Third World, and CIA covert action and economic leverage replaced overt military confrontation as primary foreign policy tools. These proved both less expensive than military action and less visible, and therefore less likely to provoke public controversy.

In 1953 the CIA helped anticommunist leader Ramón Magsaysay's election as president of the Philippines. That same year, it helped execute a coup to overthrow Mohammed Mossadegh's constitutional government in Iran, restoring to power Shah Reza Pahlavi. The increasingly dictatorial Shah remained a firm ally of the United States and a friend of American oil interests in Iran until his ouster by Moslem fundamentalists in 1979. In 1954 the CIA, working closely with the United Fruit Company, helped topple President Jacobo Arbenz Guzmán's elected government in Guatemala. Officials of the Eisenhower administration and officers of the fruit company regarded Arbenz as a communist because he sought to nationalize and redistribute large tracts of land, including some owned by United Fruit itself.

After these covert actions the CIA, under the direction of John Foster Dulles's brother Allen, grew in influence and power. In 1954 the National Security Council widened the CIA's mandate, and by 1960 it had approximately 15,000 agents (compared to about 6,000 when Eisenhower took office) deployed around the world.

Eisenhower also employed economic strategies—trade and aid—to fight communism and win converts in the Third World. Those strategies were aimed at opening more opportunities for American enterprises overseas, discouraging other countries from adopting state-directed economic systems, and encouraging expansion of commerce. U.S. policymakers came to identify "freedom" with the "free market," and they regarded efforts of Third World nations to break old colonial bonds by creating government-directed economies and nationalized industries as a threat to freedom. New governmental assistance programs offered economic aid to friendly nations, and military aid rose sharply as well. Under the Mutual Security Program and the Military Assistance Program, the United States spent three billion dollars a year and trained 225,000 representatives from nations around the world in anticommunism and police tactics. The buildup of military forces in friendly Third World nations strengthened anticommunist forces but also contributed to the development of military dictatorships.

AMERICA AND THE THIRD WORLD

In applying these new anticommunist measures, the Eisenhower administration defined "communist" broadly. In many countries, communist political parties had joined other groups in fighting to bring about changes in labor laws and land ownership that would benefit the poor. Meanwhile, U.S. companies doing business abroad joined forces with local elites to resist the redistribution of power that such programs implied. Often economic elites and dictators abroad won U.S. support against their political opponents simply by whispering the word "communist." Consequently, the United States often found itself supporting "anticommunist" measures that suppressed political and social change.

LATIN AMERICA

In Latin America, Eisenhower talked about expanding freedom but regularly supported dictatorial regimes as long as they welcomed U.S. investment and suppressed leftist movements. Eisenhower awarded the Legion of Merit to unpopular dictators in Peru and Venezuela and privately confessed his admiration for the anticommunism of Paraguay's General Alfredo Stroessner, who sheltered ex-Nazis and ran his country as a private fiefdom. Vice President Richard Nixon toasted Cuban dictator Fulgencio Batista as "Cuba's Abraham Lincoln," and the CIA established a training program for Batista's repressive security forces. Surveying Eisenhower-era policies, America's disgruntled ambassador to democratic Costa Rica complained that Dulles had advised foreign service officers to "do nothing to offend the dictators; they are the only people we can depend on."

Such policies offended many Latin Americans. "Yankeephobia" spread, and events in Cuba dramatized the growing anti-American hostility. After Fidel Castro overthrew Batista in 1959 and tried to curtail Cuba's dependence on the United States, the Eisenhower administration imposed an economic boycott of the island. Castro turned to the Soviet Union, declared himself a communist, and pledged to support leftist insurgencies throughout Latin America. Although the CIA had begun to plot an invasion to unseat Castro, the Eisenhower administration at the same time ordered a review of the policies that had sparked such ill will throughout Latin America. The review recommended that policymakers should place more emphasis on democracy, human rights, and economic growth, recommendations that would soon find articulation in President John Kennedy's Alliance for Progress.

NASSERISM AND THE SUEZ CRISIS OF 1956

In the Middle East, distrust of nationalism, neutralism, and social reform also influenced U.S. policy. In 1954, when Gamal Abdel Nasser overthrew a corrupt monarchy and took power in Egypt, he promised to rescue Arab nations from imperialist domination and guide them toward "positive neutralism." Denouncing Israel and accepting aid from both the United States and the Soviet Union, Nasser strengthened Egypt's economic and military power. He also purchased advanced weapons from communist Czechoslovakia and extended diplomatic recognition to communist China. Those actions prompted the United States to cancel construction loans for the huge Aswan Dam, a project designed to improve agriculture along the Nile River and provide power for new industries. Nasser retaliated in July 1956 by nationalizing the British-controlled Suez Canal, arguing that canal tolls would provide substitute financing for the dam. Suez was of major economic and symbolic importance to Britain, and the British government, joined by France and Israel, attacked Egypt in October to retake the canal.

Although Eisenhower distrusted Nasser, he decried Britain's blatant attempt to retain its imperial position. The Soviets were, at that same time, ruthlessly suppressing the Hungarian revolt, and Eisenhower could not effectively criticize the Soviets for

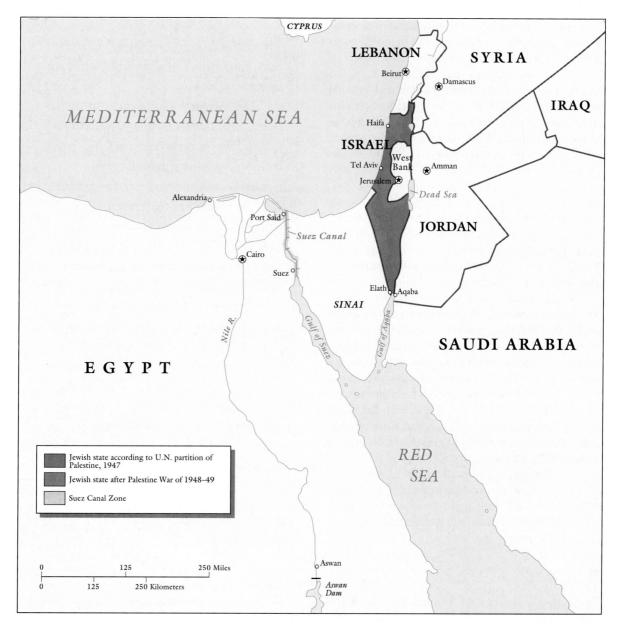

ISRAEL, THE MIDDLE EAST, AND THE SUEZ CRISIS, 1956

maintaining a sphere of influence when Britain was engaged in a similar pursuit. Denouncing the Anglo-French-Israeli action, Eisenhower threatened to destabilize the British currency unless the invasion ended. Eventually, a plan supported by the United States and the United Nations allowed Nasser to retain the Suez Canal, but American prestige and power in the area suffered as the So-

viet Union took over financing of the Aswan Dam and cemented ties with Nasser.

With Nasser-style nationalism now more closely aligned with the Soviets, the Eisenhower administration feared the spread of "Nasserism" throughout the oil-rich Middle East. In the spring of 1957, the "Eisenhower Doctrine" pledged to defend Middle Eastern countries "against overt armed aggression from any nation controlled by international communism." Although designs by "international communism" hardly described the multiple causes of Nasser-style nationalism and civil unrest in the Middle East, anticommunist rhetoric did provide justification for maintaining governments that supported the West's need for oil. When elites in Lebanon and Jordan, fearful of revolts by groups friendly to Nasser, asked the United States and Britain to stabilize their countries, Eisenhower sent U.S. marines to Lebanon to set up an anti-Nasser government in Beirut, and Britain simultaneously restored King Hussein to the throne in Jordan. These actions were part of Eisenhower's policy to support friendly, conservative governments in the Middle East, but Western military intervention also intensified Arab nationalism and anti-Americanism.

The Eisenhower administration tried to thwart revolutionary political movements elsewhere in the world. In 1958 the president approved a plan for the CIA to support an uprising against Achmed Sukarno, the president of Indonesia, who drew support from Indonesia's large Communist Party. When civil war broke out, the CIA furnished planes, pilots, and encouragement to the rebels. But when the rebellion failed, the United States abandoned its Indonesian allies, and Sukarno tightened his grip on power. In the next few years, CIA activities included various schemes to assassinate Fidel Castro (these efforts failed) and Patrice Lumumba, a popular black nationalist in the Congo. (Lumumba was killed in 1961, although scholars still debate the degree of CIA involvement in his death.)

> "*We annually spend on military security more than the net income of all United States corporations.*
>
> "*This conjunction of an immense military establishment and a large arms industry is new in the American experience. The total influence—economic, political, even spiritual—is felt in every city, every State house, every office of the Federal government. We recognize the imperative need for this development. Yet we must not fail to comprehend its grave implications. . . .*
>
> "*In the councils of government, we must guard against the acquisition of unwarranted influence, whether sought or unsought, by the military-industrial complex. The potential for the disastrous rise of misplaced power exists and will persist.*
>
> "*We must never let the weight of this combination endanger our liberties or democratic processes. . . . I confess that I lay down my official responsibilities in this field with a definite sense of disappointment.*"
>
> **PRESIDENT DWIGHT D. EISENHOWER**
> *Farewell address, 1961*

VIETNAM

Eisenhower's strategy of thwarting communism and neutralism in the Third World set the stage for the nation's most fateful foreign policy involvement since the Second World War: Indochina.

There, communist-nationalist forces led by Ho Chi Minh were fighting for independence from France. Ho Chi Minh had studied in France and in the Soviet Union before returning to lead his country's anticolonial insurgency. At the end of the Second World War, as Japan withdrew its occupation armies, Ho Chi Minh appealed in vain to the United States to support independence rather than allow the return of French colonial administration.

U.S. leaders, despite their wartime criticism of colonialism, backed France and its ally, the government of Bao Dai. Ho Chi Minh went to war against the French who, after a major defeat at Dien Bien Phu in 1954, decided to withdraw. The subsequent Geneva Peace Accords of 1954 removed French forces from all of Indochina and divided the region into the countries of Laos, Cambodia, and Vietnam. Vietnam itself was split into two jurisdictions—North Vietnam and South Vietnam—until an election could be held to unify it under one leader.

Eisenhower's advisers believed that Ho Chi Minh's powerful communist-nationalist appeal might set off a geopolitical chain reaction. Using familiar cold-war language, the Eisenhower administration took the position that "the loss of any of the countries of Southeast Asia to Communist aggression" would ultimately "endanger the stability and security of Europe" and of Japan. This formulation became known as the "domino theory." As Ho Chi Minh's government established itself in North Vietnam, Eisenhower supported a noncommunist government in South Vietnam and ordered covert operations and economic programs to prevent Ho Chi Minh from being elected the leader of a unified Vietnam.

Colonel Edward Lansdale, who had directed CIA efforts against a leftist insurgency in the Philippines from 1950 to 1953, arrived in Saigon, capital of South Vietnam, in 1954. Lansdale was to mastermind the building of a pro-U.S. government in South Vietnam under Ngo Dinh Diem, an anticommunist Catholic who had been educated in New Jersey. At first, Lansdale seemed to be succeeding. Diem's government, with U.S. concurrence, denounced the Geneva Peace Accords and refused to take part in elections to create a unified government for Vietnam. It extended control over South Vietnam, redistributed land formerly owned by the French, built up its army, and launched a program of industrialization. Diem alienated much of South Vietnam's predominantly Buddhist population, however, and his narrowing circle of political allies was notoriously corrupt. As time passed, Diem grew more and more isolated from his own people and almost totally dependent on the United States. As early as 1955 the French prime minister had warned the United States of Diem's liabilities, but the Eisenhower administration could see no alternative. By 1960 the United States had sent billions of American dollars and 900 advisers to prop up Diem's government.

Opposition to Diem coalesced in the National Liberation Front (NLF). The NLF, formed in December 1960, was an amalgam of nationalists who resented Diem's dependence on the United States, communists who demanded more extensive land reform, and politicians who decried Diem's corruption and cronyism. It allied itself with the Viet Minh communists of North Vietnam, from whom it gradually received more and more supplies.

Although Eisenhower warned that military intervention in Indochina would be a "tragedy" (and he himself had refused direct military intervention to help the French in 1954), he committed more and more aid and national prestige to South Vietnam and tied America's honor to Diem's diminishing political fortunes. The decision of whether to turn these commitments into a large-scale military intervention would fall to Eisenhower's successors in the White House.

In his farewell address of 1961, Eisenhower warned that the greatest danger to the United States was not communism but the nation's own "military-industrial complex." Despite his desire to limit militarism and reduce cold-war rivalries, however, Eisenhower and Secretary of State Dulles had nevertheless directed a resolutely anticommunist foreign policy that helped fuel the nuclear arms race and aggravated superpower rivalry in the Third World.

AFFLUENCE— A "PEOPLE OF PLENTY"

In 1940 the United States had still teetered on the brink of economic depression. Only a decade and a

STEADY GROWTH OF GROSS NATIONAL PRODUCT, 1940–1970

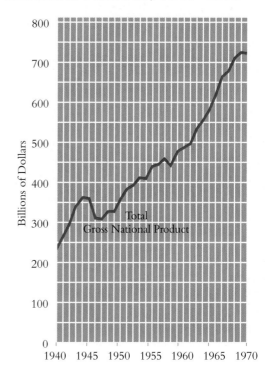

half later, the nation's GNP had soared to more than 5 times that of Great Britain and more than 10 times that of Japan. The output of corporations such as General Motors surpassed the GNP of many nations. Writing in 1954, historian David Potter called Americans a "people of plenty."

The 1950s marked the midpoint of a period of generally steady economic growth that began during the Second World War and continued until the early 1970s. Corporations turned out vast quantities of consumer goods and enjoyed rising profits. Investments and business ventures overseas boosted corporate profits at home. The domestic economy intersected with an international marketplace dominated by U.S.-based firms. The label "Made in America" symbolized both the quality of particular products and the economic power of the nation at large. National security policies helped keep the economy growing by keeping raw materi-als and energy flowing from the Third World. Abundant supplies of inexpensive oil and natural gas lowered production costs and allowed indus-tries to replace domestic coal with less costly, and less polluting, energy sources from abroad.

Newer industries, such as chemicals and elec-tronics, became particularly dominant in the world market. The Corning Glass Company reported that most of its sales in the mid-1950s came from products unknown in 1940. General Electric pro-claimed that "progress is our most important prod-uct." Government spending on national security pumped money into the general economy and stimulated specific industries. In 1955 military ex-penditures accounted for about 10 percent of the GNP. The fact that the business of national secu-rity had become big business was dramatized by President Eisenhower's selection of Charles Wil-son of General Motors in 1953 and Neil McElroy

LINK TO THE PAST

Advertising the New Consumer Products of the Fifties

http://scriptorium.lib.duke.edu/adaccess/browse.html

The John W. Hartman Center for Sales, Advertising, and Marketing History at Duke University maintains an online archive of 7,000 advertising images, divided into categories.

1. Select the category "Television," and browse the advertisements from 1948 and earlier. Browse those from the mid-1950s. What changes do you see in television set design? Why do you think the earliest sets were shaped as they were, and why might manufacturers have rapidly altered the look?

2. Select the category "Beauty and Hygiene" and browse the advertisements from the 1950s for "hair preparations." These ads differ significantly from those of earlier decades in their reliance on the images of Hollywood stars. How and why did these stars become icons of consumption? What implications does this appeal have for standards of physical attractiveness?

3. How do you think the advertising industry may have affected American life in the 1950s?

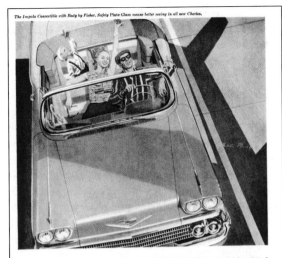

YOU'LL HAVE PLENTY TO SHOW OFF *in the high-spirited performance of your* **NEW CHEVROLET.** *With its radical new Turbo-Thrust V8* and new action in all engines, it's so quick, agile and eager that once you take the wheel, you'll never want to leave it. You've got your hands on something really special!*

Your pride can't help showing just a bit when you slide behind the wheel of this new Chevrolet. You couldn't be sitting prettier—and you know it.

You're in charge of one of the year's most looked at, most longed for cars. Chevy's crisply sculptured contours and downright luxurious interiors are enough to make anybody feel like a celebrity.

Move your foot a fraction on the gas pedal and you feel the instant, silken response of a unique new kind of V8. You ride smoothly and serenely—cushioned by deep coil springs at every wheel. You can even have a real air ride*, if you wish.

See your Chevrolet dealer. . . . Chevrolet Division of General Motors, Detroit 2, Mich. **Optional at extra cost.*

CHEVROLET

AUTOMOBILES SYMBOLIZE A NEW LIFESTYLE This ad for a 1958 pink convertible shows off not only the nation's new economic productivity and consumer lifestyle but also suggests the dominant ideal of family "togetherness."

of Procter and Gamble in 1957 to head the Department of Defense.

HIGHWAYS AND WATERWAYS

Although some experts argued that greater government expenditures for nonmilitary programs would generate even greater economic growth, Eisenhower was a fiscal conservative. Fearing that increased spending would fuel an inflationary spiral of rising prices and destabilize the economy, his administration kept nonmilitary expenditures under tight control. After 1955 even the Pentagon's bud-

AUTO SALES, 1940–1970

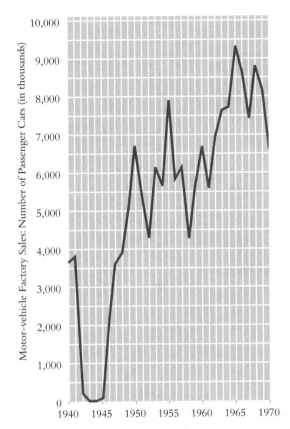

get was reduced; and for several years, the federal government itself ran a balanced budget.

Eisenhower did, however, eventually endorse several costly new domestic programs. He supported the Highway Act of 1956, citing national security considerations as justification. (In a military emergency, supplies and personnel, it was claimed, could speed along the new superhighways.) Financed by a national tax on gasoline and other highway-related products, the Highway Act funded construction of a national system of limited-access expressways. Touted as the largest public works project in the history of the world, the interstate highway program delighted the auto, oil, concrete, and tire industries; provided steady work for construction firms; and boosted the interstate trucking business. It was the first centrally planned transportation system in the nation's history.

By the mid-1950s, U.S. highways were crowded with automobiles that rivaled suburban homes as symbols of abundance. With autos built overseas considered either luxuries or curiosities, shoppers needed no reminders to "buy American." Automakers touted their annual model changes and their increasingly larger engines. Their emphasis was on speed and power, rather than safety and reliability. Detroit's auto industry helped support other domestic industries such as steel. In 1956 the steel industry could boast of being three and a half times more efficient than its fledgling Japanese rival.

The Eisenhower administration also supported costly river-diversion projects in the Far West. The Army Corps of Engineers and the Bureau of Reclamation, agencies with many supporters in business and in Congress, spent billions of dollars on dams, irrigation canals, and reservoirs. Irrigation turned desert into crop land, and elaborate pumping systems even allowed rivers to flow uphill. No society in world history had ever devoted a similar portion of its national treasury to water projects. By 1960, the western

states had access to trillions of gallons of water per year, and the basis for new economic growth in Texas, California, and Arizona was established.

These water projects came at a high price. Technologically complicated and costly, they generated similarly complex and expensive bureaucracies to sustain them. As a consequence, local communities lost power to the government agencies and private entrepreneurs whose decisions came to shape the water-dependent economy of the postwar West. Increasingly, large corporate-style operations pushed out smaller farmers and ranchers. In addition, American Indians found portions of their tribal lands being flooded for large water reservoirs or being purchased by agribusinesses or large ranching interests.

The vast water projects also laid the basis for ecological problems. Plans to divert surface waters, to tap into groundwater tables, and to dot the West with dams and reservoirs began to take their toll upon the land. Worse, the buildup of salt byproducts in the water and the soil, the inevitable

TURNING DESERTS INTO CROP LAND California's 153-mile-long Friant-Kern Canal, one of many projects of the Army Corps of Engineers, allowed farmers to cultivate water-intensive fruit and other crops. Huge irrigation projects, financed by the federal government, turned dry western lands into farming areas but also carried long-term environmental implications for water tables and soil quality.

consequence of massive efforts to harness water resources, was accompanied by the disastrous overuse of pesticides such as DDT.

LABOR–MANAGEMENT ACCORD

Most corporate leaders, having accepted the kind of government involvement required to build interstate highways and water projects, were learning to live with labor unions as well. The auto industry, where management and labor leaders had negotiated a mutually acceptable work contract in 1950, led the way.

Labor leaders reasoned that closer cooperation with corporate management could guarantee employment stability and political influence for their unions. Taking their cue from the United Auto Workers, one of the most militant CIO unions during the 1930s and pioneers of the sit-down strike, labor dropped the demand for greater union involvement in corporate decision making and agreed to bargain in a "responsible, businesslike" manner. In exchange for recognizing "management prerogatives" over crucial issues—such as the organization of the daily work routine, the introduction of new technologies, and investment priorities—union leaders could still bargain aggressively for wages and fringe benefits.

Moreover, union leaders guaranteed management that rank-and-file workers would abide by the terms of their union contracts and disavow the wildcat tactics of the 1930s and 1940s. The impartial umpire in this new labor–management détente would be the federal government's National Labor Relations Board (NLRB). Meanwhile, in 1955, the AFL and the CIO, which had long differed on labor-organizing strategy, merged—another sign of declining militancy within the labor movement. The 1950s thus ended the fierce labor–capital conflicts that had marked the 1930s and had continued through the 1940s.

Business leaders regarded this labor–management accord as a substantial victory. *Fortune* magazine noted that General Motors had paid a price in terms of more costly employee benefit packages and higher wages in the 1950s, but that "it got a bargain" in terms of labor peace. To safeguard their control over decision making, corporations regularly expanded their supervisory staffs, a practice that drove up con-

sumer prices and deprived workers of active participation in planning the work process. This accord may also have helped to divide industrial workers from one another, as those who worked in the more prosperous sectors of the economy, such as the auto industry, were able to bargain more effectively than those who worked in peripheral areas.

Most workers, however, did make economic gains. During the 1950s and early 1960s, real wages (what workers earn after their paychecks are adjusted for inflation) steadily rose; the rate of industrial accidents dropped; fringe benefits (what workers receive in terms of health insurance, paid vacation time, and pension plans) improved; and job security was generally high.

Economic growth, according to celebrants of the 1950s, had made the United States the envy of the world. Widespread ownership of kitchen appliances, television sets, and automobiles supported the claim that American consumers were enjoying a culture of abundance. Theories about class conflict and the limits of capitalism, widely expressed during the 1930s, now seemed outdated. Capitalism worked, and it worked spectacularly well. Indeed, it seemed so successful that only a new vocabulary of superlatives could describe its wonders. In 1955 *Fortune* hailed "The Changing American Market" and highlighted "The Rich Middle-Income Class" and "The Wonderful Ordinary Luxury Market." Harvard's celebrated economist John Kenneth Galbraith had simply entitled his 1952 study of the economy *American Capitalism;* his 1958 follow-up book, *The Affluent Society,* topped the best-seller lists for nearly six months.

Although Galbraith's second study was actually much more critical of economic affairs than his first, the term "affluence" fit nicely with the vision of constant economic growth. It also directed attention away from the deeply rooted inequalities that persisted in American society. Talking about affluence, for example, meant that one could avoid using the word "wealth," which might suggest its opposite, "poverty," a term seldom used in economic analyses of the mid-1950s. And by shifting the focus from what people *actually owned*—their accumulated wealth—to their affluence—what they could, with the aid of generous credit terms, *consume*—observers found that the "American way of life" was constantly improving.

The most buoyant observers even detected a leveling out of living standards between the top and the bottom levels of this consumer society. The gulf was no longer between people with cars and people without cars, they declared, but between people with Cadillacs and Lincolns and those with Chevrolets and Fords. "Luxury has reached the masses," proclaimed *Fortune*.

POLITICAL PLURALISM

Many observers also credited economic affluence with giving rise to a new political structure. Galbraith, for example, suggested that unions, consumer lobbies, farm organizations, and other groups could exert effective "countervailing power" against giant corporations. Only a few mavericks, such as the sociologist C. Wright Mills, disagreed. Mills saw corporate leaders as members of a small "power elite" that dominated American life. He claimed that this elite had made all of the big decisions on foreign and domestic policy in the decade since the Second World War. In Mills's critique, the nation's cold-war policies represented an unwise, potentially disastrous, extension of government power at home and overseas. The vaunted affluent society featured increasingly regimented work and little job satisfaction. Although Mills anticipated and inspired critics of the 1960s and early 1970s, most of his contemporaries dismissed the power elite thesis as a simplistic conspiracy theory.

To those who subscribed to the dominant view, called "pluralism," no power elite could ever dominate the political process. According to pluralist accounts, public policymaking proceeded from wide participation in public debate by a broad range of different interest groups. Short-term conflicts over specific issues would obviously continue to arise, but pluralism's celebrants believed that affluence had effectively moderated political passions and had fostered a set of procedures by which different interests eventually could frame a consensus. As a professor at Harvard Law School put it, constant economic growth meant that "in any conflict of interest," it was "always possible to work out a solution" because affluence guaranteed that all interests would be "better off than before."

Pluralists praised postwar leaders for finding "realistic" solutions to difficult problems. The acid test of political "realism" in the 1950s was whether or not the national government was updating policies from the 1940s: containment of international communism, maintenance of a powerful national security state, and promotion of domestic programs based on the vision of constant economic growth.

A RELIGIOUS PEOPLE

In this anticommunist era the celebration of political pluralism dovetailed with an exaltation of religion's role in American life. Members of Congress, as part of the crusade against "atheistic communism," emphasized religious values. They constructed a non-denominational prayer room on Capitol Hill; added the phrase "under God" to the Pledge of Allegiance; and declared the phrase "In God We Trust," which had been emblazoned on U.S. currency for nearly a century, the national motto.

The emphasis on a pluralistic, transdenominational religious faith was not simply a product of anticommunism. Intense religious commitments, most analysts insisted, no longer divided people as much as in the past. President Eisenhower captured this idea when he urged people to practice their own religious creed, whatever it might be. "Our government makes no sense," he declared "unless it is founded in a deeply felt religious faith—and I don't care what it is." Tommy Sands, a young pop singer, advised his teenage fans that "all religions are the greatest."

Religious leaders echoed this theme. Will Herberg's *Protestant-Catholic-Jew* (1955) argued that these three faiths were really "'saying the same thing' in affirming the 'spiritual ideals' and 'moral values' of the American Way of Life." Rabbi Morris Kretzer, head of the Jewish Chaplain's Organization, reassured Protestants and Catholics that they and their Jewish neighbors shared "the same rich heritage of the Old Testament . . . the sanctity of the Ten Commandments, the wisdom of the prophets, and the brotherhood of man." A 1954 survey indicated that more than 95 percent of the population identified with one of the three major faiths, and religious commentators increasingly talked about the "Judeo-Christian tradition."

Individual religious leaders became national celebrities. Norman Vincent Peale, a Protestant minister who emphasized the relationship between religious faith and peace of mind, sold millions of books declaring that belief in a Higher Power could reinvigorate daily life "with health, happiness, and goodness." His *The Power of Positive Thinking* (1952) remained a best-seller throughout the 1950s. The Catholic Bishop Fulton J. Sheen hosted an Emmy-winning, prime-time television program called *Life Is Worth Living*. Oral Roberts and Billy Graham—two younger, more charismatic television ministers—began to spread their fiery brand of Protestant evangelism during the 1950s.

Peale, Sheen, Roberts, and Graham identified themselves with conservative, anticommunist causes, but an emphasis on religious faith was hardly limited to the political right. Dorothy Day, who had been involved in grassroots activism since the early 1930s, continued to crusade for world peace and for a program aimed at redistributing wealth at home through the pages of the *Catholic Worker*. Church leaders and laypeople from all three major denominations supported the antidiscrimination cause and came to play important roles in the civil rights movement. Even so, the revival of religious faith during the 1950s remained closely identified with the culture of affluence.

DISCONTENTS OF AFFLUENCE

Alongside the celebrations of economic affluence, political pluralism, and religious faith, the 1950s still produced an immense body of social criticism—especially about conformity, youth, mass culture, discrimination, and inequality.

CONFORMITY IN AN AFFLUENT SOCIETY

In *The Organization Man* (1956), sociologist William H. Whyte, Jr., indicted corporate business for contributing to one of the problems of affluence: conformity. Criticizing the social, cultural, psychological (though not the economic) impact of large corporations, Whyte saw middle-class corporate employees accepting the values of their employers at the expense of their own individuality. The security of knowing what the corporate hierarchy wanted—and when it wanted it—outweighed the organization man's concerns about loss of individuality, Whyte argued.

In *The Lonely Crowd* (1950), David Riesman, another sociologist, offered an even broader analysis. He wrote of a shift from an "inner-directed" society, in which people looked to themselves and to their immediate families for a sense of identity and self-worth, to an "other-directed" society, in which people looked to peer groups for approval and measured their worth against mass-mediated models. A nation of other-directed citizens emphasized "adjustment" to the expectations of others rather than the individual "autonomy" displayed by an inner-directed citizenry. Riesman subsequently conceded that his autonomy-to-adjustment thesis might be overly broad but still insisted that he had correctly identified a growing trend toward conformity in American life.

To illustrate the subtle manner in which children were taught conformist values, Riesman pointed to the *Tootle, the Engine*, a popular children's book. When Tootle showed a preference for frolicking in the fields beside the tracks, people exerted peer pressure to make him conform. If Tootle stayed on tracks laid down by others, they assured him, he would grow up to be a powerful and fast-moving streamliner. This message of unprotesting adjustment to peer expectations in this "modern cautionary tale," Riesman argued, contrasted vividly with the conflict-filled fairy tales, such as *Little Red Riding Hood*, on which earlier generations of young people had been reared.

The critique of conformity reached a broader audience through the best-selling books of journalist Vance Packard. *The Hidden Persuaders* (1957) argued that advertising—especially through calculated, subtle appeals to the insecurities of consumers—produced conformity. The book, Packard claimed, showed "how to achieve a creative life in these conforming times" when so many people "are left only with the roles of being consumers or spectators."

Critics such as Whyte, Riesman, and Packard primarily focused on the lives of middle-class men, but writers such as Betty Friedan claimed to find a similar psychological malaise among many women. Corporation managers, for example, were criticized for expecting the wives of their male executives to help their husbands deal with the demands of corporate life, including the need for frequent relocation. The organization man, it was said, found that his ascent up the corporate ladder depended on how well his wife performed her informal corporate duties in an equally conformist social world.

YOUTH CULTURE

Concerns about young people also intensified during the 1950s. Many criminologists linked burgeoning sales of comic books to the alleged rise in juvenile delinquency. Psychologist Frederick Wertham, in *The Seduction of the Innocent* (1954), blamed comics displaying sex and violence for "mass-conditioning" children and for stimulating juvenile unrest. Responding to local legislation and to calls for federal regulation, the comic book industry resorted to self-censorship. Publishers who adhered to new, industry-developed guidelines for the portrayal of violence and deviant behavior could display a seal of approval, and the great comic book scare soon faded away.

Critics of the youth culture, however, easily found other worrisome signs. In 1954 Elvis Presley, a former truck driver from Memphis, rocked the pop music establishment with a string of hits on the tiny Sun record label. Presley's sensual, electric stage presence thrilled his youthful admirers and outraged critics. Presley ("The King") and other youthful rock stars—such as Buddy Holly from West Texas, Richard Valenzuela (Richie Valens) from East Los Angeles, and Frankie Lymon from Spanish Harlem—crossed cultural and ethnic barriers and shaped new musical forms from older ones, especially African American rhythm and blues (R & B) and the "hillbilly" music of southern whites.

The first rock 'n' rollers inspired millions of fans and thousands of imitators. They sang about the joys of "having a ball tonight"; the pain of the "summertime blues"; the torment of being "a teenager in love"; and the hope of deliverance, through the power of rock, from "the days of old." Songs such as "Roll Over Beethoven" by Chuck Berry (a singer-songwriter who merged southern hillbilly music with the blues of his native St. Louis) became powerful teen anthems.

Guardians of older, family-oriented forms of mass culture found rock 'n' roll music even more frightening than comic books. They denounced its sparse lyrics, pulsating guitars, and screeching saxophones as an assault on the very idea of music. Religious groups condemned it as the "devil's music";

ELVIS PRESLEY A former truck driver from Memphis, "Elvis the Pelvis" drew upon blues, gospel, hillbilly, and pop music traditions to become the premier rock 'n' roll star of the 1950s.

red-hunters detected a communist plan to corrupt youth; and segregationists labeled it part of a sinister plot to mix the races. The dangers of rock 'n' roll were abundantly evident in *The Blackboard Jungle* (1955), a film in which a racially mixed gang of high school students terrorized teachers.

Some rock 'n' roll music looked critically at daily life in the 1950s. The satirical song "Charley Brown" contrasted pieties about staying in school with the bleak educational opportunities open to many students. Chuck Berry sang of alienated teenagers riding around "with no particular place to go." This kind of implied social criticism, which most older listeners failed to decode, anticipated the more overtly rebellious rock music of the 1960s.

Rock music and the larger youth culture gradually merged into the mass-consumption economy of the 1950s. Top-40 radio stations and producers of 45-rpm records identified middle-class teenagers, whose average weekly income/allowance reached $10 by 1958, as a market worth targeting. Chuck Berry's "Sweet Little Sixteen" portrayed an affluent teenager eagerly chasing after the latest fashions, the next rock 'n' roll concert, and "about half-a-million famed autographs." By 1960, record companies and disk jockeys promoted songs and performers exalting the pursuit of "fun, fun, fun" with the help of clothes, cars, and rock 'n' roll records. Rock music—and the product-centered culture of youth—had come to celebrate the ethic of a people of plenty.

THE MASS CULTURE DEBATE

Criticism of conformity and of youth culture merged into a wider debate over "mass culture." Much of the anxiety about the decline of individualism and the rise of rock 'n' roll could be traced to fears that "hidden persuaders" were now conditioning millions of people.

Custodians of culture decried mass-marketed products. According to cultural critic Dwight MacDonald, "bad" art—such as rock music and Mickey Spillane's best-selling Mike Hammer novels—was driving "good" art from the marketplace and making it difficult for people to distinguish between them. MacDonald and other critics of mass culture argued that entrepreneurs, by treating millions of consumers as if they were all the same, obscured complicated social issues with a blur of pleasant, superficial imagery. Critics also charged mass culture with destroying the richness of local differences. In a classic study of a small town in upstate New York, a team of sociologists claimed that the mass media were "so overwhelming that little scope is left for the expression of local cultural forms."

Television became a prominent target. Evolving out of network radio, three major corporations (NBC, CBS, and ABC) dominated television and sustained it with advertisers, euphemistically called sponsors. Picturing millions of seemingly passive viewers gathered around "the boob tube," critics decried both the quality of mass-produced programming and its impact on the public. Situation comedies such as *Father Knows Best* generally featured middle-class, consumption-oriented suburban families. At the same time, network television responded to pressure from advertisers and favored programs that, according to television's critics, encouraged retreat into unrealities such as the mythical Old West. Television networks in 1958 were broadcasting 25 prime-time westerns.

Critics also worried about how mass culture, especially television, seemed to be transforming the fabric of everyday life. Architects were calling for the rearrangement of living space within middle-class homes so that the television set could become the new focal point for family life, serving as an electronic substitute for the traditional fireplace hearth. Entire new lines of products—such as the frozen TV dinner, the TV tray, the recliner chair, and the influential magazine *TV Guide*—became extensions of the new televisual culture. And the 1950s television set itself, almost always encased in some kind of substantial wooden cabinet, became an important symbol of postwar affluence.

THE LIMITS OF THE MASS CULTURE DEBATE

Most critics acknowledged that mass culture was closely linked to the economic system they generally celebrated. Was it really possible to cure the ills of mass culture while still enjoying the benefits of affluence? Convinced that the nation, much like "Tootle, the Engine," was on the right track, critics of mass culture invariably refused to join mavericks such as C. Wright Mills and question the distribution of political and economic power in the United States. Radical critiques of industrial capitalism, heard so often during the 1930s, were no longer in vogue during the 1950s.

Moreover, the most obvious cures for the disease of mass culture clashed with the critics' own commitment to an open, pluralistic society. If, on the one hand, Congress were encouraged (as it had been during the comic book scare) to legislate against "dangerous" cultural products, censorship might end up curtailing the freedom of expression to which liberals of the 1950s swore allegiance. On the other hand, if local communities were to step in (as some did in the case of comics), the results might be even worse. The prospect of southern

Icons of Daily Life in the 1950s

The ever-greater array of new consumer products that became part of daily life during the 1950s supported claims about a growing affluence and the benefits of a free society. The frost-free refrigerator and the family television set were just two of the decade's many icons of affluence.

The double-door, frost-free refrigerator offered consumers an elegant, in-home repository for the new prepackaged and frozen food products that became available during the 1950s. As the advertisement suggests, a refrigerator could serve as visual display case that confirmed to neighbors, and to families themselves, that Americans had become "people of plenty."

Like the frost-free refrigerator, the television set, which came into most living rooms during the 1950s, also symbolized more than a new technology. By bringing visual images into homes and apartments, television helped to make the process of looking—and wanting to be looked at—a central cultural preoccupation. It made the art of visual display, highlighting anything from the stylish fins on an automobile to a dour politician's five o'clock shadow, more important than ever before. Looking at life through a television set became an important ritual of daily life during an era in which family-oriented entertainment, such as *Leave It to Beaver*, dominated network programming.

segregationists censoring civil rights literature or of local censorship boards banning movies produced in Hollywood or books published in New York City hardly appealed to the cosmopolitan critics of mass culture. The critique of mass culture, in short, seemed to generate few solutions.

Meanwhile, amid the concern about mass culture, other questions about the direction of postwar life were beginning to emerge. Americans remained especially divided over issues related to racial discrimination and to government's role in confronting it.

THE FIGHT AGAINST DISCRIMINATION, 1954–1960

When Dwight Eisenhower took office, the Supreme Court was slated to rehear a legal challenge to racially segregated school systems spearheaded by the NAACP and its legal strategist, Thurgood Marshall. Following the death in 1953 of Chief Justice Fred Vinson, Eisenhower rejected more conservative candidates to replace him on the Supreme Court and chose Earl Warren, a former governor of California. Under Warren, the Court would come to play an important role in the civil rights struggle, the most significant movement for change in the postwar period.

BROWN V. BOARD OF EDUCATION OF TOPEKA

In 1954 Warren wrote the Court's unanimous opinion in *Brown* v. *Board of Education of Topeka*, which declared that legally enforced segregation of public schools violated the constitutional right of African American students to equal protection of the law. Although it technically applied only to educational facilities, *Brown* implied that all segregated public facilities, not simply schools, were open to legal challenge.

Carrying out the broader implications of *Brown* tested the nation's political and social institutions. The crusade against racial discrimination had long centered on the 16 states that the Census Bureau officially called "the South," but demographic changes meant that national leaders could no longer treat the issue as simply a regional one.

SEGREGATION Dressed in his Air Force uniform, a young man from New York City is faced with a "colored waiting room" in an Atlanta bus terminal in 1956. Before the civil rights revolution of the 1960s, southern states maintained legally enforced segregation in most public facilities, a practice popularly called "Jim Crow" (see chapter 18).

During the 1950s the South was becoming more like the rest of the country. New cultural forces, such as network television, were linking the South more closely with a nationally based culture. Economic forces were also at work. Machines were replacing the region's predominantly black field workers, and the absence of strong labor unions and the presence of favorable tax laws were attracting national chain stores, business franchises, and northern-based industries to the South.

At the same time, the racial composition of cities in the West, Midwest, and Northeast was becoming more like that of the South. In 1940 more than three-quarters of the nation's African Americans lived in the South. Accelerating the pattern begun during the Second World War, African Americans left the rural South and settled in Los Angeles, Chicago, New York, Cleveland, and other big cities

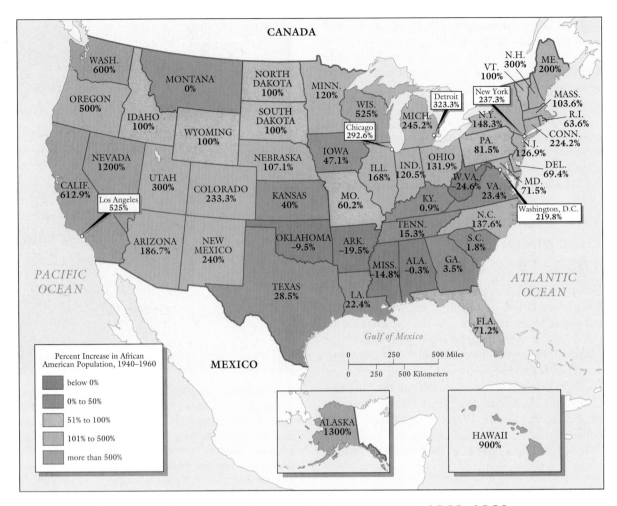

SHIFTS IN AFRICAN AMERICAN POPULATION PATTERNS, 1940–1960

during the late 1940s and early 1950s. In the mid-1950s this demographic shift was accompanied by "white flight" to the new suburbs and by significant changes in political alignments. With African American voters becoming increasingly important in the North, for example, urban Democrats came to support the drive to end racial discrimination. Meanwhile, the Republicans were making small electoral gains in what had long been the Democratic Party's "solid South." Most important, African Americans themselves mounted a new attack on segregation and racial discrimination in the South.

The battle against racial discrimination was coming to dominate domestic politics. Segregationists in the South pledged "massive resistance" to the Supreme Court ruling in *Brown* v. *Board of*

Education. Their lawyers resorted to traditional delaying tactics and invented new ones. This strategy seemed to be succeeding when in 1955 the Supreme Court ruled that school desegregation, although the law of the land, should proceed cautiously—with "all deliberate speed," as the justices put it. In the following year, 100 members of the U.S. House and Senate signed a "Southern Manifesto" in which they promised to support any state that intended "to resist forced integration by any lawful means."

Defiance went beyond the courtroom. Vigilantes unfurled the banners and donned the white robes of the Ku Klux Klan, which was joined by new racist organizations, such as the White Citizens Council. As a result, antidiscrimination activists constantly risked injury and death, and even people only indirectly connected to the struggle fell victim to racist violence. In August 1955 two white Mississippians murdered 14-year-old Emmett Till, a visitor from Chicago, for acting "disrespectful" to a white woman. Mamie Till Bradley demanded that her son's murder not remain a private incident; she insisted that his maimed corpse be displayed publicly for "the whole world to see" and that young Till's killers be punished. When their case came to trial, an all-white jury found the killers—who would subsequently confess their part in the murder—not guilty.

THE MONTGOMERY BUS BOYCOTT AND MARTIN LUTHER KING, JR.

In response to the uncertainty of judicial remedies, African Americans began supplementing legal maneuvering with aggressive campaigns of direct action. In Montgomery, Alabama, Rosa Parks, a member of the local NAACP, was arrested in 1955 for refusing to obey a state segregation law that required black passengers to give up their seats to whites and sit at the back of the bus. Montgomery's black community, which had a long history of civil rights activism, responded to her arrest by boycotting public transportation and by organizing a system of private car pools as alternative transit. The resulting financial losses convinced the city's public transit system to reconsider its segregationist policy. Joining with Rosa Parks, many African American women spearheaded the bus boycott. The Montgomery boycott during 1955 and 1956 thus resulted in the desegregation of city buses and demonstrated to other black communities in the South that they could mobilize against acts of overt discrimination.

The Montgomery boycott vaulted the Reverend Martin Luther King, Jr., one of its leaders, into the national spotlight. Born, raised, and educated in Atlanta, with a doctorate in theology from Boston University, King followed up the victory in Montgomery by joining with other black ministers to form the Southern Christian Leadership Conference (SCLC). In addition to pressing for the desegregation of public facilities, the SCLC launched an effort to register African American voters throughout the South. More activist than the NAACP, the

ROSA PARKS IGNITES DESEGREGATION CAMPAIGN
Rosa Parks's refusal to sit at the back of a segregated bus in 1955 sparked a campaign to integrate public transportation in Montgomery, Alabama. Here, following a successful boycott, Rosa Parks rides in the front seat on the first day of desegregated bus travel.

SCLC spread King's broad vision of social change—integration forced by passive civil disobedience—throughout the nation. The purpose of civil disobedience, according to King, was to persuade people, through both words and deeds, of the moral evil of segregation and racial discrimination. The ultimate goal of the civil rights crusade was to bring "redemption and reconciliation" to American society. Aided by the national media, especially network television, King's powerful presence and religiously rooted rhetoric carried the message of the antidiscrimination movement in the South to the entire nation.

THE POLITICS OF CIVIL RIGHTS

Political institutions in Washington responded slowly. The Supreme Court expanded its definition of civil rights but generally backed away from mandating the sweeping institutional changes needed to make these rights meaningful. Congress, meanwhile, remained deeply divided on racial issues.

With southern segregationists, all of them members of the Democratic majority, holding key posts on Capitol Hill, antidiscrimination legislation faced formidable obstacles.

Even so, Congress passed its first civil rights measures in more than 80 years. The Civil Rights Act of 1957 set up a procedure for expediting lawsuits by African Americans who claimed their right to vote had been illegally abridged. It also created a permanent Commission on Civil Rights, although this was only an advisory body empowered to study alleged violations and recommend new remedies. In 1960, with the support of Lyndon Johnson of Texas, the Democratic leader in the Senate, another act promised additional federal support for blacks who were being barred from voting in the South. These civil rights initiatives, which became law against fierce opposition from southern Democrats, dramatized the difficulty of getting even relatively limited antidiscrimination measures through Congress.

President Eisenhower appeared largely indifferent to the issue of racial discrimination. When liberal Republicans urged him to take action—perhaps through an executive order barring racial discrimination on construction projects financed by federal funds—Ike did nothing. A gradualist on racial issues, he regarded the fight against discrimination as primarily a local matter, and he publicly doubted that any federal civil rights legislation could change the attitudes of people opposed to the integration of public facilities or job sites.

Indeed, Eisenhower's grasp of domestic issues seemed to grow less certain during his second term as president. In the election of 1956, he achieved another landslide victory over Democrat Adlai Stevenson, but his personal appeal did relatively little to help his party. In 1956 the Republicans failed to win back control of Congress from the Democrats. In fact, in this presidential election and in the off-year races of 1958, the GOP lost congressional seats as well as state legislatures and governors' mansions to the Democrats. After the 1958 elections, the Democrats outnumbered Republicans 64 to 34 in the Senate and 282 to 154 in the House. Meanwhile, Eisenhower, who had suffered a mild heart attack prior to the 1956 election, seemed progressively enfeebled, physically as well as politically. He appeared especially weak in his handling of racial issues.

In 1957, however, Eisenhower was forced to act. Orval Faubus, the segregationist governor of Arkansas, ordered his state's National Guard to block enforcement of a federal court order mandating integration of Little Rock's Central High School. Responding to this direct challenge to national authority, Eisenhower put the Arkansas National Guard under federal control and augmented it with members of the U.S. Army. Black students, escorted by armed troops, could then enter the high school.

AMERICAN INDIAN POLICY

The Eisenhower administration also lacked coherent policies on issues affecting American Indians. The government attempted to implement two programs, "termination" and "relocation," that had been developed during the Truman years. The termination policy pledged to end Indians' status as "wards of the United States" and to grant them all the "rights and privileges pertaining to American citizenship." It called for the national government to end its oversight of tribal affairs and to treat American Indians as individuals rather than as members of tribes. Its long-term goals, to be pursued tribe-by-tribe, were to abolish reservations, to liquidate assets of the tribes, and to end federal services offered by the Bureau of Indian Affairs (BIA).

In 1954, one year after this general policy had received congressional approval, six bills of termination were enacted. Immediately at stake was the legal status of more than 8,000 American Indians and more than one million acres of tribal land.

Under the relocation program, which had begun in 1951, Indians were encouraged to leave their rural reservations and take jobs in urban areas. In 1954 the BIA intensified its relocation efforts, with Minneapolis, St. Louis, Dallas, and several other cities joining Denver, Salt Lake City, and Los Angeles as relocation sites. This program, like the termination policy, encouraged American Indians to migrate to urban areas and become assimilated into the social mainstream.

Both programs were flawed. As several more termination bills were enacted during the Eisenhower years, almost 12,000 people lost their status as tribal members, and the bonds of communal life for many Indians grew weaker. At the same time, nearly 1.4

TOTAL URBAN AND RURAL INDIAN POPULATION IN THE UNITED STATES, 1940–1980

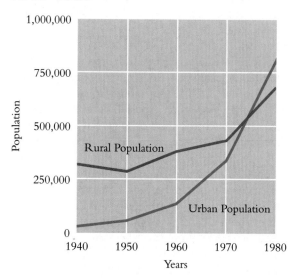

million acres of tribal lands were lost, often falling into the hands of real estate speculators. Indians from terminated tribes lost both their exemptions from state taxation and the social services provided by the BIA and gained almost nothing in return. Most terminated Indians sank into even deeper poverty. Relocation went no better. Most of the people relocated from reservations found only low-paying, dead-end jobs, and racial discrimination. In the mid-1950s, Indian children who had left reservations found it difficult even to enter *segregated*, let alone integrated, public schools in some cities. Despite its problems, the program nevertheless continued throughout the Eisenhower years.

Gradually, however, both Indians and civil rights activists mobilized against the termination and relocation policies. Termination lost legitimacy rather quickly. By 1957 the BIA had scaled back its initial timetable for terminating every tribe within five years, and in 1960 the party platforms of both the Republicans and Democrats repudiated the policy entirely. In 1962 this disastrous policy was itself terminated. Meanwhile, however, the relocation program continued, and by 1967 almost half of the nation's Indians were living in relocation cities. The policy hardly touched the deep-rooted problems that many Indians confronted, including a life expectancy only two-thirds that of whites, nor

did it ever provide significantly better opportunities for employment or education.

THE GROWTH OF SPANISH-SPEAKING POPULATIONS

Millions of Spanish-speaking people, many of whom had recently arrived in the United States, also highlighted discrimination issues. In the 1950s people from Puerto Rico began moving to the mainland in large numbers. Finding only low-paying jobs and settling in older urban neighborhoods, these new arrivals were U.S. citizens but often spoke only Spanish. By 1960 New York City's Puerto Rican community was nearly 100 times greater than it had been before the Second World War.

Meanwhile, large numbers of Spanish-speaking people from Mexico were moving into the Southwest, where they joined already sizable Mexican American communities. Beginning during the Second World War and continuing until 1967, the U.S. government sponsored the *bracero* (or farmhand) program, which brought nearly five million Mexicans northward, theoretically on short-term contracts, to serve as agricultural laborers. Many of the *braceros* remained in the United States after their contracts expired. Joining them were legal immigrants from Mexico and growing numbers of people who illegally filtered across the border. The illegal Mexican immigrants, derisively labeled "wetbacks" because they supposedly swam across the Rio Grande, became the target of an ongoing government dragnet, begun in 1950 and intensified by the Eisenhower administration, called "Operation Wetback." During a five-year period, the government claimed to have rounded up and deported to Mexico nearly four million people, allegedly all illegal immigrants. The well-publicized operation helped to stigmatize all people of Mexican descent and to justify discriminatory treatment by both government and private employers.

Leaders in long-established Mexican American communities mobilized to fight such discrimination. Labor organizers sought higher wages and better working conditions in the factories and fields, although the FBI labeled many of these efforts as "communist-inspired" and harassed unions—such as the United Cannery, Agricultural, Packing and

Allied Workers of America (UCAPAWA)—that had large Mexican American memberships. A lengthy mining strike in New Mexico became the subject of the 1954 motion picture *Salt of the Earth*. Middle-class organizations, such as the League of United Latin American Citizens (LULAC) and the Unity League, also sought to desegregate schools, public facilities, and housing in Southern California and throughout the Southwest. In 1940 Mexican Americans had been the most rural of all the major ethnic groups; by 1950, in contrast, more than 65 percent of Mexican Americans were living in urban areas, a figure that would climb to 85 percent by 1970. As a result of this fundamental demographic shift, Mexican Americans began to gain political clout in many southwestern cities.

URBAN ISSUES

The growth of new, largely white, suburban areas in the 1950s spawned new urban issues, many of them related to race. Throughout the 1950s, both public and private institutions were shifting money and construction projects away from the cities, especially away from neighborhoods in which Latinos and African Americans had settled. Adopting a policy called "redlining," many banks and loan institutions denied funds for home buying and business expansion in neighborhoods that were considered "decaying" or "marginal" because they contained aging buildings, dense populations, and growing numbers of nonwhites. Meanwhile, the Federal Housing Authority and other government agencies channeled most of their funds toward the new suburbs. In 1960, for example, the FHA failed to put up a single dollar for home loans in Camden or Paterson, New Jersey, cities in which nonwhite populations were growing, while it poured millions of dollars into surrounding, largely all-white suburbs.

"Urban renewal" programs, authorized by the Housing Act of 1949 (see chapter 27), often amounted to "urban removal." Although federal housing laws called for "a feasible method for the temporary relocation" of persons displaced by urban renewal projects, developers often ignored the housing needs of the people they displaced. During the 1950s, Robert Moses, who directed New York City's housing policies, routinely manipulated figures in order to conceal the massive dislocations caused by his urban renewal and highway building programs. People with low-income jobs, especially African Americans and Puerto Ricans, were evicted so that their apartments and homes could be replaced by office buildings and freeways.

Public housing projects, supposed to provide affordable housing for low- and moderate-income families who were saving money to purchase their own homes, proved an especially grave disappointment. Although the suburbs, where land was abundant and relatively inexpensive, seemed an obvious place in which to build public housing, middle-income suburbanites blocked such construction. Consequently, public housing had to be built in the cities, where population density was high and land was expensive. At the same time, private housing interests lobbied to limit the units actually built and to ensure that public housing would offer few amenities. Originally conceived as a temporary alternative for families who would rather quickly move out to their own homes, public housing facilities became stigmatized as "the projects," housing of last resort for people with chronically low incomes and little prospect for economic advancement.

PRUITT-IGOE, AS IT APPEARED IN 1964 The vast Pruitt-Igoe public housing complex in St. Louis—completed in 1954 and at one time home to 10,000 people—became a powerful symbol of misguided government social welfare programs. Originally touted as a model of public housing, the complex rapidly deteriorated, and it was razed in 1976.

By the end of the 1950s, the urban policies of both the Fair Deal and the Eisenhower era were widely regarded as failures. Urban renewal projects not only disrupted housing patterns but also helped to dislocate industries that had long provided entry-level jobs for unskilled workers. Both major presidential candidates in 1960 pledged to create a new cabinet office for urban affairs and to expand the federal government's role, a clear rejection of the Eisenhower administration stance.

DEBATES OVER GOVERNMENT'S ROLE IN THE ECONOMY

Controversy over urban issues tied to larger debates over the role that government should play in economic life. Although Eisenhower sometimes hinted to conservative Republicans that he wanted to roll back the New Deal and the Fair Deal, he lacked both the will and the political support to do so. Actually, Eisenhower presided over a modest expansion of those earlier initiatives: an expanded Social Security system, a higher minimum wage, better unemployment benefits, and a new Department of Health, Education, and Welfare (HEW). Still, as his stance on urban and racial issues showed, he took few steps to enlarge governmental power. His popularity seemed to rest on his personality rather than on the specifics of his policies.

EISENHOWER AND THE NEW CONSERVATIVES

As a result of his centrist position on most domestic issues, Eisenhower attracted the ire of a growing group of political conservatives. Eisenhower, of course, was the first Republican president since Herbert Hoover, but did his administration really represent basic GOP principles?

Not to Arizona's Barry Goldwater, the hero of the Republican Party's right wing. A fervent anticommunist elected to the U.S. Senate in 1952, Goldwater demanded a more aggressive military stance than Eisenhower's. In his book *Conscience of a Conservative* (1960), Goldwater criticized postwar U.S. leaders for failing to take stronger military measures against the Soviet Union and for not making "victory the goal of

American policy." At the same time, Goldwater decried almost all domestic programs, especially civil rights legislation, as grave threats to individual liberty and came to criticize the Eisenhower administration for having aped the Democratic Party's "New Deal antics" in domestic policymaking.

While Goldwater was pressing the GOP to abandon Eisenhower's moderate Republicanism, other conservatives, led by William F. Buckley, Jr., were trying to reshape a broader right-wing message for the country at large. Buckley, a devout Roman Catholic, first gained national attention while still in his twenties. His book *God and Man at Yale* (1952) detected a "collectivist" and antireligious tilt in American higher education and defended capitalism and Christianity. In 1955, Buckley helped found the *National Review*, a magazine that attracted a talented group of writers. It avoided extremist positions, particularly the anti-Semitism of some old-line conservatives and the hysterical anticommunism of groups such as the John Birch Society. Although this "new conservatism" began amid considerable doubts about its immediate prospects for success, it confidently sought a long-term strategy for building a right-of-center movement. To that end, conservatives established their own youth movement, Young Americans for Freedom (YAF), in 1960.

ADVOCATES OF A MORE ACTIVE GOVERNMENT

While the new conservatives were criticizing the Eisenhower administration for failing to break decisively with the policies of the Roosevelt and Truman years, liberals were grumbling about the administration's failure to use governmental power to address pressing public issues. They were especially critical of Eisenhower's relatively passive approach to questions involving racial discrimination. Moreover, pointing to a severe economic downturn in 1958–59 when unemployment rose precipitously, critics ridiculed Eisenhower's commitment to a balanced budget as evidence of his 19th-century approach. After Eisenhower suffered a second heart attack and a mild stroke during his second term, many critics talked about the need for more vigorous presidential leadership. Liberal advocates of greater governmental intervention in the economy, confident of their ability to maintain growth and prosperity, urged government deficit spending to stimulate continued economic expansion.

Other critics recommended dramatic increases in spending for national security. The 1957 Gaither Report, prepared by prominent people with close ties to defense industries, claimed that the Soviet Union's GNP was growing even more quickly than that of the United States and that much of this expansion came in the military sector. The Gaither Report urged an immediate increase of about 25 percent in the Pentagon's budget and long-term programs for building fallout shelters, for developing intercontinental ballistic missiles (ICBMs), and for expanding conventional military forces. Another report, written by Henry Kissinger and issued by the Rockefeller Foundation, claimed that Eisenhower's New Look endangered national security because it relied too heavily on massive nuclear retaliation and downplayed nonnuclear options. It, too, called for greater spending on defense.

Eisenhower reacted cautiously to these reports. Although he agreed to accelerate the development of ICBMs, he opposed any massive program for building fallout shelters or for fighting limited, nonnuclear wars around the globe. In fact, he reduced the size of several Army and Air Force units and kept his defense budget well below the levels his critics were proposing. Eisenhower could take such steps confidently because secret U-2 surveillance flights over the USSR, which had begun in 1956, revealed that the Soviets were lagging behind, rather than outpacing, the United States in military capability.

Concerns about national security and calls for greater governmental spending also surfaced in the continuing controversy over education. Throughout the 1950s, some critics complained that schools were emphasizing "life adjustment" skills—getting along with others and accommodating to social change—instead of teaching the traditional academic subjects. Rudolf Flesch's *Why Johnny Can't Read* was a best-selling book of 1955. Other books suggested that Johnny and his classmates couldn't add or subtract well either and that they lagged behind their counterparts in the Soviet Union in their mastery of science. Meanwhile, the nation's leading research universities were seeking greater government funding for higher education. In the summer of 1957, a committee of prominent scientists implored the Defense

Department to expand funding for basic scientific research. "Research is a requisite for survival" in the nuclear age, it declared. Arguments for increased spending on education gained new intensity when, in October 1957, the Soviets launched the world's first artificial satellite, a 22-inch sphere called *Sputnik*.

Using the magical phrase "national security," school administrators and university researchers sought and won more federal dollars. The National Defense Education Act of 1958 funneled money to

COLD WAR COMPETITION REACHES INTO SPACE This "Space Race" card game was manufactured after the Soviet Union orbited its first Sputnik satellite in 1957. The fear that the Soviets were ahead of the United States in space technology prompted the nation to undertake a crash program of upgrading mathematics and science teaching and to accelerate its own space program, run by the newly created National Aeronautics and Space Administration (NASA). A fascination with space technology permeated popular culture in the late 1950s, but the cost implications of this initiative worried Eisenhower.

college-level programs in science, engineering, foreign languages, and the social sciences. This act marked a milestone in the long battle to overcome congressional opposition, especially from southern segregationists who feared any intervention by Washington, to federal aid to education. A growth industry in federally supported research projects put down firm roots during the late 1950s.

Other critics urged the Eisenhower administration to seek increased federal spending for social welfare programs. Writing in 1958, in *The Affluent Society*, John Kenneth Galbraith found a dangerous tilt in the "social balance," away from "public goods." Affluent families could travel in air-conditioned, high-powered automobiles, Galbraith observed, but they must pass "through cities that are badly paved, made hideous by litter, blighted buildings," and billboards. Although the researcher who develops a new carburetor or an improved household cleanser is well rewarded, the "public servant who dreams up a new public service is [labeled] a wastrel."

Galbraith's musings seemed mild in comparison to the jeremiads of Michael Harrington. In 1959, *Commentary*, one of several influential magazines that featured social criticism during the late 1950s, published an article in which Harrington argued that the problem of economic inequality remained as urgent as it had been during the 1930s. At least one-third of the population was barely subsisting in a land of supposed affluence. Avoiding statistics and economic jargon, Harrington told dramatic stories about the ways in which poverty could ravage the bodies and spirits of people who had missed out on the affluence of the 1940s and 1950s.

During the early 1960s, when John F. Kennedy and Lyndon Baines Johnson made domestic policymaking a priority, critics such as Galbraith and Harrington became political celebrities. Their critiques, however, were products of the political culture of the late 1950s. The Kennedy presidency of 1961–63 would in fact be firmly rooted in the critique of both foreign and domestic policymaking that had emerged during the Eisenhower years.

THE KENNEDY YEARS: FOREIGN POLICY

John Fitzgerald Kennedy, the first president to be born in the 20th century, had been groomed for the

JOHN F. KENNEDY AND JACQUELINE BOUVIER John and Jacqueline Kennedy, shown here before their marriage and while he was a senator from Massachusetts, always sought to project images of youth, glamour, and vigor. A naval officer in the Second World War, Kennedy often was pictured sailing with his family. Such images added to the allure of the Kennedy mystique.

White House by his politically ambitious father. After his graduation from Harvard in 1940, Kennedy pursued a life devoted to both private passions (especially for Hollywood movie stars) and public service. After winning military honors while serving in the U.S. Navy during the Second World War, Kennedy entered politics. In 1946 he won election from Massachusetts to the House of Representatives, and in 1952 he captured a seat in the Senate. In Washington, Kennedy was better known for his active social life than for his command of legislative details, but he gradually gained a national political reputation, largely on the basis of his charm and youthful image. He was aided by his 1953 marriage to Jacqueline Bouvier. In 1956, he narrowly missed winning the Democratic vice presidential nomination.

THE ELECTION OF 1960

Between 1956 and 1960, Kennedy barnstormed the country, speaking at party functions and rounding up supporters for a presidential bid. This early campaigning, along with his talented political advisers and his family's vast wealth, helped Kennedy overwhelm his primary rivals, including the more liberal Senator Hubert Humphrey of Minnesota and Lyndon Johnson. By pledging to keep his Catholic religion separate from his politics and by openly confronting those who appealed to anti-Catholic prejudice, Kennedy defused the religious issue that had doomed Al Smith's candidacy in 1928 (see chapter 24).

Richard Nixon, who was obliged to run on Eisenhower's record even though Ike initially seemed lukewarm about Nixon's candidacy, remained on the defensive throughout the campaign of 1960. Nixon seemed notably off balance during the first of several televised debates in which political pundits credited the cool, tanned Kennedy with a stunning victory over the pale, nervous Nixon. Despite chronic and severe health problems, which his loyal staff effectively concealed, Kennedy projected the image of a youthful, vigorous leader.

During the 1960 campaign, Kennedy stressed four issues, firmly associated with critics of the Eisenhower administration, that together made up what he called his "New Frontier" proposals. On civil rights and social programs, he espoused liberal positions that as a senator he had avoided. He pledged support for antidiscrimination efforts, which had been downplayed in the Democratic campaigns of 1952 and 1956. In an important symbolic act, he sent his aides to Georgia to assist Martin Luther King, Jr., who had been sentenced to six months in jail for a minor traffic violation. Although Senator Kennedy's own civil rights record was mixed, he promised to take the kind of presidential action that Eisenhower had rejected and to push for new legislation against racial discrimination. Moreover, Kennedy endorsed the sorts of social programs John Kenneth Galbraith and other liberals had been advocating. Although his proposals remained vague, he did mention greater federal spending to rebuild rural communities, to increase educational opportunities, and to improve urban conditions.

Kennedy also highlighted two other issues that had provoked debate during the 1950s: stimulating greater economic growth and conducting a more aggressive cold-war foreign policy. Dismissing Eisen-

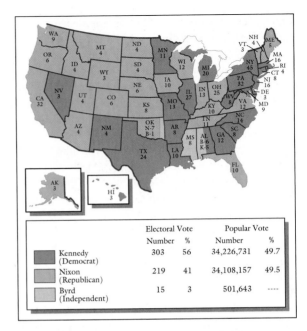

| | | Electoral Vote | | Popular Vote | |
		Number	%	Number	%
	Kennedy (Democrat)	303	56	34,226,731	49.7
	Nixon (Republican)	219	41	34,108,157	49.5
	Byrd (Independent)	15	3	501,643	----

PRESIDENTIAL ELECTION, 1960

hower's cautious economic policies as ineffectual, Kennedy surrounded himself with advisers who spoke of stimulating the economy by means of tax cuts and deficit spending measures. Gradually, Kennedy embraced the promises, though not all of the specific proposals, of these pro-growth economists. And on cold-war issues, he criticized Eisenhower for failing to rid the hemisphere of Castro in Cuba and for allowing a "missile gap" to develop in U.S. defenses against the Soviet Union. By spending heavily on defense, he claimed, he would create a "flexible response" against communism, especially in the Third World. Adlai Stevenson, in his 1956 campaign against Eisenhower, had said Americans could no longer "drift, we must go forward." Using similar rhetoric, Kennedy declared that his campaign rested on "the [single] assumption that the American people are tired of the drift in our national course . . . and that they are ready to move again."

The 1960 election defied easy analysis. Kennedy defeated Nixon by only about 100,000 popular votes and won the electoral votes of several states, including Illinois, by a razor-thin margin. Apparently hurt by his Catholicism, especially in the South, Kennedy won a smaller percentage of the popular vote than most other Democrats running for lesser offices. His victory seemed to owe a great deal to his vice presidential running mate, Lyndon Johnson, whose appeal to southern whites helped the ticket carry the Deep South and Johnson's home state of Texas.

From the outset, the president and his wife Jacqueline focused media attention on the White House. They hobnobbed with movie stars and brought prominent intellectuals into the administration. The Kennedy inaugural featured designer clothing, the aged poet Robert Frost, and a stirring speech in which the new president challenged people to "ask not what your country can do for you; ask what you can do for your country." The "best and the brightest," the hard-driving people who joined Kennedy's New Frontier, promised to launch exciting new crusades, even to the ultimate frontier of outer space. Momentum and change, however, lay more often in rhetoric and style than in action.

KENNEDY'S FOREIGN POLICY GOALS

On foreign policy, Kennedy boasted of making a break with the past to wage the cold war more vigorously. Although Secretary of Defense Robert McNamara discovered that the much-publicized "missile gap" simply did not exist, Kennedy raised the defense budget anyway. Military assistance programs, propaganda agencies, and covert action plans all received strong support from the White House. In one of his most popular initiatives, the president created the Peace Corps, a new program that sent Americans, especially young people, to nations around the world to work on development projects designed to undercut the appeal of communism.

Kennedy, however, also built upon many of Eisenhower's policies. Eisenhower's last-minute efforts to reorient Latin American policies away from reliance on dictators and toward support of more progressive programs were elaborated on and repackaged as Kennedy's "Alliance for Progress." Proposed in the spring of 1961 as a way to prevent the spread of anti-Americanism and communist insurgencies, the Alliance offered $20 billion in loans over a 10-year period to Latin American countries that would undertake land reform and democratic development measures. The Alliance, which under-estimated the obstacles to social and economic change, fell far short of its grandiose goals.

CUBA AND BERLIN

The worst fiasco of the Kennedy presidency, a daring but ill-conceived CIA mission against Cuba, also had its roots in the Eisenhower administration. The CIA, experienced from the covert actions to overthrow leftist governments in Iran and Guatemala, was planning a secret invasion to topple Fidel Castro, Cuba's revolutionary leader. On April 17, 1961, however, when U.S.-backed and trained forces (mainly anticommunist Cuban exiles) landed at the Bahia de Cochinas (the Bay of Pigs) on the southern coast of Cuba, the expected popular uprising against Castro did not occur. Instead, the invaders were quickly surrounded and imprisoned. Kennedy failed to provide the air support that Cuban exiles had been led to expect and at first even tried to deny that the United States had been involved in the invasion, but the CIA's role quickly became public, and anti-Yankee sentiment mounted in Latin America. Castro tightened his grip over Cuba and strengthened his ties with the Soviet Union. "I have made a tragic mistake," Kennedy told Clark Clifford, an adviser. "Not only were our facts in error, but our policy was wrong." Yet, stung by the failed invasion, the Kennedy administration continued to target Castro with a covert program called Operation Mongoose, which consisted of economic destabilization activities and futile assassination plots. In one of many attempts to kill Castro, the CIA worked directly with U.S. crime figures, who also wanted revenge on Castro for shutting down their casinos.

Another dramatic confrontation loomed in Berlin. In June 1961, Nikita Khrushchev and Kennedy met in Vienna, where Khrushchev proposed ending the Western presence in Berlin and reuniting the city as part of East Germany. His proposal was motivated by the steady flow of immigrants from East Germany into West Berlin, a migration that was both embarrassing and economically draining to the German communist regime. Kennedy was forceful in his refusal to abandon West Berlin, but the East German government continued to press Khrushchev to help solve their problems. On August 13, 1961, the

THE CUBAN MISSILE CRISIS During the Cuban Missile Crisis of October 1962, these Cuban refugees, like most people, were riveted to their television sets to obtain the latest update from President Kennedy. This nuclear confrontation seemed to place the fate of the world at stake.

communist regime began to erect first a barbed-wire fence and then a concrete wall to separate East from West Berlin. East Germans attempting to escape into the West were shot. The Berlin Wall became a symbol of the cold war and of communist repression. Kennedy's assertion, *"Ich bin ein Berliner"* ("I am a Berliner"), delivered in front of the wall to a massive crowd, which cheered his pledge to defend West Berlin, became one of the most memorable lines of his presidency.

Superpower confrontation escalated to its most dangerous level during the Cuban Missile Crisis of 1962. The Soviet Union, responding to a request from Fidel Castro, sent sophisticated weapons to Cuba. In October, after spy-plane flights confirmed the existence of Cuban missile-launching sites, the Kennedy administration publicly warned that it would not allow nuclear warheads to be installed so close to American shores. Kennedy demanded that the Soviets dismantle the missile silos they had already prepared and turn back some supply ships heading for Cuba. After dramatic meetings with his top advisers, Kennedy rejected an outright military

strike that might have set off war between the United States and the Soviet Union. Instead, he ordered the U.S. Navy to "quarantine" the island. The Strategic Air Command was put on full alert for possible nuclear war. Meanwhile, both sides engaged in complicated, secret diplomatic maneuvers to prevent a nuclear confrontation.

The maneuvers succeeded. On October 28, 1962, Khrushchev ordered the missiles dismantled and the Soviet supply ships brought home; Kennedy promised not to invade Cuba and secretly assured Khrushchev that he would complete the previously ordered withdrawal of U.S. Jupiter missiles from Turkey.

When some Soviet archives were opened in the mid-1990s Americans learned that the crisis had been even more perilous that they had imagined. Unknown to Kennedy's circle at the time, the Soviets already had tactical nuclear weapons in Cuba that could have been launched.

After the Cuban Missile Crisis, both superpowers seemed to recognize the perils of direct conflict. Secretary of Defense McNamara later recalled leaving a presidential conference during the 13-day crisis, looking up at the sky, and wondering if the world would still be there 24 hours later. A direct phone line was established between Moscow and Washington to ensure the kind of communication that might forestall a nuclear confrontation or an accident in the future. And both nations became a bit more cautious.

SOUTHEAST ASIA AND "FLEXIBLE RESPONSE"

In Southeast Asia, Kennedy followed Eisenhower's policy of supporting the Diem regime and trying to build South Vietnam into a viable, noncommunist state. After the Bay of Pigs disaster, in which the attempt to overthrow an already established procommunist government had failed, Kennedy decided that the U.S. must put down communist-led "wars of national liberation" before they succeeded.

Kennedy viewed Vietnam as a test case for "flexible response," a new policy that relied on a variety of methods to combat the growth of communist movements. Elite U.S. special forces, known as Green Berets, were trained in "counterinsurgency" tactics to use against communist guerrillas; cadres of social scientists charged with "nation building" were sent as advisers; Michigan State University dispatched experts to revamp South Vietnam's police forces. And when all these efforts brought nothing but greater corruption and a deeper sense of isolation to the Diem regime, the CIA gave disgruntled military officers in the South Vietnamese army the green light to orchestrate Diem's overthrow. Just weeks before Kennedy himself would be assassinated, Diem—the man whom both Eisenhower and Kennedy had tried to convert into the founding father of a democratic Vietnam—was run out of his palace and murdered. The coup against Diem brought a military regime to power, but this seemed only to breed even greater political instability in South Vietnam.

THE KENNEDY YEARS: DOMESTIC POLICY

Despite his campaign promises to increase federal spending as a way of stimulating faster economic growth, Kennedy was slow to depart from Eisenhower's cautious fiscal policies. He was fearful of angering fiscal conservatives and business leaders by running federal budget deficits greater than those of the Eisenhower years. Relations with corporate leaders nevertheless turned ugly in 1962, when Kennedy publicly clashed with the president of U.S. Steel over that company's decision to raise prices beyond the guidelines suggested by the administration.

POLICYMAKING UNDER KENNEDY

Eventually, though, Kennedy endorsed tax breaks as a means of promoting economic growth. According to prevailing theory, lower tax rates for everyone and special deductions for corporations that invested in new plants and equipment would free up money for investment that would eventually help all Americans. Kennedy had cautiously suggested such tax breaks on business investments in 1961, and in 1962 he urged Congress to change the complex tax code. Despite opposition from those who thought the breaks would unfairly benefit corporations and the wealthy, the bill seemed headed for passage in the fall of 1963.

On matters of social welfare, the Kennedy administration stuck with policies initiated by the Fair Deal of the 1940s—namely, a higher minimum wage and continuation of urban renewal programs. It also lent its support to the Area Redevelopment Bill of 1961, which called for directing federal grants and loans to areas (such as Appalachia) that had missed out on the general economic prosperity of the postwar years. Meanwhile, under the urban renewal programs begun during the 1940s, bulldozers were still razing large parts of urban America so that construction projects aimed to benefit middle- and upper-income people continued to replace low-income housing. Finally, the Kennedy administration made the fight against organized crime a top priority—much more so (at least initially) than the fight for racial equality.

THE CIVIL RIGHTS CRUSADE, 1960–1963

Although JFK talked about new civil rights legislation, he tried to placate segregationist Democrats by doing little to press the matter during the early months of his presidency. Meanwhile, the president and his brother Robert, the attorney general, listened sympathetically when J. Edgar Hoover, director of the FBI, complained about links between Martin Luther King, Jr., and members of the Communist party. To keep tabs on King's activities and gather information that it might use against him, the FBI intensified surveillance and even illegally wiretapped his private conversations.

Rising dissatisfaction over the slow pace of the campaign against racial discrimination, however, gradually forced the Kennedy administration to consider new initiatives. In early 1960 African American students at North Carolina A & T College in Greensboro defied state segregation laws, sat down at a lunch counter, and asked to be served along with white customers. It was the beginning of the "sit-in" movement, a new phase in the civil rights movement in which groups of young activists risked being arrested under legal segregation laws and demanded equal access to places serving the general public. All across the South, demonstrators staged nonviolent sit-in demonstrations at restaurants, bus and train stations, and other public facilities.

The courage and commitment of these demonstrators gave the antidiscrimination movement new momentum. With songs such as "We Shall Overcome" and "Oh, Freedom" inspiring solidarity, young people pledged their talents, their resources—indeed their lives—to the civil rights struggle. In 1961 interracial activists from the Congress of Racial Equality (CORE) and the Student Nonviolent Coordinating Committee (SNCC), a student group that had grown out of the sit-in movement, risked racist retaliation by boarding interstate buses and conducting "freedom rides" across the South. The freedom riders were determined not to allow southern officials to ignore a series of federal court decisions, which had declared segregation on buses and in waiting rooms to be unconstitutional.

The new grassroots activism forced the Kennedy administration to respond. In 1961 it sent federal marshals into the South in order to protect freedom riders. In 1962 and again the following year, it called on National Guard troops and federal marshals to prevent segregationists from stopping

BERNICE JOHNSON REAGON During the civil rights crusade, "freedom songs" fostered a sense of solidarity and provided outreach to people sympathetic to the cause. The singers pictured here include Bernice Johnson Reagon, a member of the Freedom Singers during the civil rights movement and, later, founder of the all-woman a cappella singing group, Sweet Honey in the Rock.

RACIAL CONFLICT IN BIRMINGHAM Images such as this 1963 photograph of a confrontation in Birmingham, Alabama, in which segregationists turned dogs on youthful demonstrators, helped rally public support for civil rights legislation. Events in Birmingham, however, also presaged the increasingly violent clashes that would punctuate the efforts to end racial discrimination.

racial integration at several educational institutions in the Deep South, including the Universities of Mississippi and Alabama. In November 1962, Kennedy issued a long-promised executive order that banned racial discrimination in federally financed housing. In February 1963, Kennedy sent Congress a moderate civil rights bill that called for faster trial procedures in voting rights cases, in the hope of forestalling future confrontations.

Even so, events were outpacing Kennedy's policies. Racial conflict convulsed Birmingham, Alabama, in 1963. White police officers used dogs and high-pressure water hoses on African Americans who were demanding an end to segregation in the city. Four children were later murdered (and 20 injured) when racists bombed Birmingham's Sixteenth Street Baptist Church, a center of the antisegregation campaign. When thousands of protesters took to the streets—and two more children were killed, this time by police officers—the

Kennedy administration finally took more vigorous action to head off tensions it feared might break into "a "real race war" in Birmingham.

During the final six months of Kennedy's presidency, the issue of civil rights dominated domestic politics. The escalating violence in the South prompted frequent television specials on the major networks. Kennedy himself made an emotional plea on television for a national commitment to the cause of antidiscrimination. Recent events had raised "a moral issue . . . as old as Scriptures and . . . as clear as the Constitution." The time for "patience" and "delay," he declared, had passed.

The administration, however, still hoped to shape the direction and pace of change by passing new laws to get demonstrators "off the streets and into the courts." Thus, it supported stronger civil rights legislation, including a ban on racial discrimination in all public facilities and housing and new

JFK (1991)

**Directed by Oliver Stone. Starring Kevin Costner (Jim Garrison),
Tommy Lee Jones (Clay Shaw), Donald Sutherland ("Mr. X"), and Joe Pesci (David Ferrie).**

JFK addresses two questions that have long intrigued both historians and the general public. Who killed John F. Kennedy? What would have been the course of U.S. history, especially the nation's involvement in the Vietnam War, had not Kennedy's presidency ended in 1963? This film dramatizes the prosecution by Jim Garrison, the district attorney of New Orleans, of Clay Shaw, a local business leader, as a vehicle for suggesting that a shadowy conspiracy—hatched by government officials, military officers, and business executives—ordered JFK's assassination because he planned to withdraw U.S. troops from Vietnam.

JFK marshals a variety of film techniques to articulate its claims. It uses archival sources from the period, such as Dwight Eisenhower's farewell-address warning of the dangers of a "military-industrial complex" and famed CBS newscaster Walter Cronkite's announcement of Kennedy's death. *JFK* supplements the archival record with simulated "documentary" footage. When Garrison is showing jurors the famous Zapruder film, the home movie that provides the only actual film record of Kennedy's shooting, for example, the film inserts black-and-white shots of marksmen catching the president in a cross-fire. Later, it shows someone planting the "magic bullet," which the Warren Commission later claimed came from Oswald's gun, on a hospital gurney.

The film is vintage Oliver Stone. The most prolific filmmaker-historian of the past twenty years, Stone persistently highlights the difficulty of producing clearly delineated narratives (the kind of stories about the past told in traditional history books and in classical Hollywood films) when dealing with recent events such as Kennedy's assassination, the Vietnam War, the 1960s, and Watergate. His films about these events—such as *JFK*, *Platoon* (1986), *Born on the Fourth of July* (1989), *The Doors* (1991), and *Nixon* (1995)—all feature imagery and plot lines that constantly underscore the disjuncture and uncertainty in history. When Jim Garrison decides that he will defy the "lone-gunman theory," the settled narrative of the Kennedy assassination as told in the Warren Commission and in the media, he warns his staff, ". . . we're through the looking glass . . . white is black, and black is white."

In films such as *JFK* and *Natural Born Killers* (1994) Stone focuses less on telling a coherent story than on

federal laws to guarantee the vote to millions of African Americans who were being kept from polls in the South. Later, when the administration discovered that it could not derail a grassroots "March on Washington for Jobs and Freedom," planned for the late summer of 1963, it belatedly endorsed this demonstration.

A massive march on Washington, a dream since the 1940s of such activists as labor leader A. Philip Randolph, finally took place on August 28, 1963. An integrated group of more than 200,000 people marched through the nation's capital. Leaders of the march endorsed Kennedy's new civil rights bill, but they also pressed a broader agenda. In addition to more effective civil rights legislation, the march's formal demands included a higher minimum wage and a federal program to guarantee new jobs. Standing in front of the Lincoln Memorial, Martin Luther King, Jr., delivered his famous "I Have a Dream" speech. The march on Washington, which received favorable coverage from the national media, put considerable pressure on the White House and Congress to offer new legislative initiatives.

WOMEN'S ISSUES

The seeds of a resurgent women's movement were also being sown, although more quietly, during the

contemplating the way in which visual imagery shapes popular perceptions about history and daily life. The beginning of *JFK*, for example, bombards viewers with quick-moving, seemingly disconnected images: Color footage from President Eisenhower's farewell address clashes with black-and-white images of a woman (who later turns out to be associated with Jack Ruby, the killer of alleged Kennedy assassin Lee Harvey Oswald) being thrown from a moving car. Viewers must continue watching, as if they have gone "through the looking glass," if they hope to fit together the pieces in the puzzle that is *JFK*.

JFK, in this sense, provides as a cinematic forum that raises, rather than settles, historical questions. Viewers might compare and contrast, for example, how Kennedy's death is explained through performances of two veteran character actors, Donald Sutherland and Joe Pesci. Sutherland's Mr. X, who portrays an operative in the national security bureaucracy, tells Garrison that Kennedy's death was simply one example in a long line of "dirty tricks" by agents of the military-industrial complex. Filmed against the familiar iconography of the nation's capital—iconography that seems adapted from Frank Capra's classic *Mr. Smith Goes to Washington* (1939)—Sutherland offers Garrison (and film viewers) a logically ordered, tightly packaged explanation. In contrast, Pesci's David Ferrie, a lowly foot soldier who traveled in organized crime and Cuban exile circles, warns Garrison that he will find no simple answers to his inquiry.

Questions raised by *JFK* did prompt Congress to order a massive project to declassify and save all government documents that might relate to Kennedy's assassination. These traditional sources, however, seem to have brought historians no closer to solving the puzzle of Kennedy's death. As Pesci's Ferrie warns in *JFK*, "It's a mystery, inside a riddle, wrapped in an enigma."

Kevin Costner portrays New Orleans District Attorney Jim Garrison.

Kennedy years. Kennedy's own call for young people to enter public service in organizations such as the Peace Corps raised young women's expectations for careers outside of marriage and child rearing.

All across the political spectrum, women were speaking out on contemporary issues. The new conservative movement benefited from the energy of women such as Phyllis Schlafly, whose book *A Choice, Not an Echo* (1964) became one of the leading manifestos of the Republican Party's right wing. African American activists such as Bernice Johnson Reagon (whose career with the Freedom Singers combined music and social activism) and Fannie Lou Hamer (who helped to organize an in-

tegrated Mississippi Freedom Democratic Party) fought discrimination based on both race and gender. Similarly, Chicana farm workers were key figures in the activism that led to the organization of the United Farm Workers of America, a union headed by Cesar Chavez. Women also played an important role in protests by the Committee for a Sane Nuclear Policy (Sane) and the Women's Strike for Peace against the U.S.-Soviet arms race. During Kennedy's final year in office, 1963, Betty Friedan published *The Feminine Mystique*. Generally credited with helping to spark a new phase of the feminist movement, Friedan's book drew on her own social criticism from the late 1950s and articulated the dissatisfactions that many middle-class women felt about the narrow confines of domestic life and the lack of public roles available to them.

To address women's concerns, Kennedy appointed the Presidential Commission on the Status of Women, chaired by Eleanor Roosevelt. Negotiating differences between moderate and more militant members, the commission issued a report that documented discrimination against women in employment opportunities and wages. Kennedy responded with a presidential order designed to eliminate gender discrimination within the federal civil service system. His administration also supported the Equal Pay Act of 1963, which made it a federal crime for employers to pay lower wages to women who were doing the same work as men.

THE ASSASSINATION OF JOHN F. KENNEDY

By the fall of 1963 the Kennedy administration, though still worried about its ability to push legislation through a recalcitrant Congress, was preparing initiatives on civil rights and economic opportunity. Then, on November 22, 1963, John F. Kennedy was shot down as his presidential motorcade moved through Dallas, Texas. Lyndon Johnson, who had accompanied Kennedy to Texas, took the oath of office before hurrying back to Washington. Police quickly arrested Lee Harvey Oswald and accused him of being the assassin. Oswald had ties to the Marcello crime family, had once lived in the Soviet Union, and had a bizarre set of political affiliations, especially with groups interested in Cuba. Oswald declared his innocence, but never faced trial. Jack Ruby, whose Dallas nightclub catered to powerful crime figures, killed Oswald on national television, while the alleged assassin was in the custody of the Dallas police. A lengthy, controversial investigation by a special commission headed by Chief Justice Earl Warren concluded that both Oswald and Ruby had acted alone.

The claims of the Warren Commission came under increasing scrutiny. In 1978 a special panel of the House of Representatives claimed that Kennedy might have been the victim of an assassination plot, perhaps involving organized crime, but produced little supporting evidence. A variety of other theories about Kennedy's assassination, including ones that

pointed toward the CIA and high governmental officials, sprang up. Oliver Stone's film, *JFK* (1991), refocused attention on the limits of the Warren Commission's report. In response, Congress created the Assassinations Records Review Board as a means of preserving all existing evidence about Kennedy's death, such as the famous Zapruder home movie of the assassination, from destruction. Meanwhile, competing theories about the number of shots, the trajectory of the bullets, the nature of the wounds on Kennedy's body, and the identity of his assassins continued to reverberate through public discourse.

CONCLUSION

After 1954, cold-war fears associated with McCarthyism began to abate. Presidents Dwight Eisenhower and John F. Kennedy cautiously eased tensions with the Soviet Union, especially after Kennedy found himself on the brink of nuclear war over the presence of Soviet weapons in Cuba in 1962. Even so, both presidents continued to pursue similar staunchly anticommunist foreign policies that focused on the buildup of nuclear weapons, economic pressure, and covert activities. Developments in the Third World, particularly in Cuba and Southeast Asia, became of growing concern.

At home, 1954–63 were years of generally steady economic growth. A cornucopia of new consumer products encouraged talk about an age of affluence but also produced apprehension about conformity, mass culture, and the problems of youth. At the same time, the concerns of racial minorities and other people who were missing out on this period's general affluence increasingly moved to the center of public debates over the meaning of liberty and equality. The Eisenhower administration, many critics charged, seemed too reluctant to use the power of government to fight segregation or to create economic conditions that would distribute the benefits of affluence more widely. The political initiatives of the early 1960s, associated with John F. Kennedy, grew out of such criticisms.

Although Kennedy did not rush to deal with domestic issues, the press of events gradually forced his administration to use government power to confront racial discrimination and address the issue of equality. When Kennedy was killed in November 1963, a new kind of insurgent politics, growing out of the battle against racial discrimination in the Deep South, was beginning to transform political life in the United States.

In the post-Kennedy era, debates would become riveted around issues related to the government's exercise of power: Was the U.S. spreading liberty in Vietnam? Was it sufficiently active in pursuing equality for racial minorities and the poor? Lyndon Johnson's troubled presidency would grapple with these questions.

Suggested Readings begin on page SR-1.
For Web activities and resources
related to this chapter, go to
http://www.harcourtcollege.com/history.murrin

CHAPTER 29

AMERICA DURING ITS LONGEST WAR, 1963–1974

THE VIETNAM WAR MEMORIAL

This memorial, a kind of wailing wall that bears the names of all Americans who were killed in action in Vietnam, was dedicated on the Mall in Washington, D.C., in 1982.

Lyndon Baines Johnson promised to finish what John F. Kennedy had begun. "Let us continue," he said in his first speech as president. That phrase, which recalled Kennedy's own "Let us begin," did characterize Johnson's first months in office. Ultimately though, Johnson's troubled presidency bore little resemblance to John Kennedy's thousand days of "Camelot."

In Southeast Asia, Johnson faced a crucial decision: Should the United States introduce its own forces and weaponry in order to prop up its South Vietnamese ally? If Johnson did this, what would result?

At home, Johnson enthusiastically mobilized the federal government's power in order to promote equality. But could federal action produce the Great Society that Johnson envisioned?

Many Americans, particularly young people, began to dissent from Johnson's foreign and domestic policies. As a result of a war overseas and opposition at home, the late 1960s and early 1970s became a time of increasingly sharp political and cultural polarization. Richard Nixon's presidency both suffered from—and contributed to—this polarization. By the end of America's longest war and the Watergate crisis that caused Nixon's resignation, the nation's political culture and social fabric differed significantly from what Johnson had inherited from Kennedy in 1963.

This chapter will focus on the following major questions:

- What were the goals of the Great Society? Why did it produce so much controversy?
- Why did the United States become involved in the war in Vietnam? How did the war affect the U.S. economy and its social fabric?
- In addition to the war in Vietnam, what were other the sources of domestic dissent, especially among young people, during the 1960s?
- What new domestic and foreign policies did the Nixon administration initiate? How successful were these policies?
- What was involved in the Watergate controversy? Why did Watergate result in Nixon's resignation from the presidency?

THE GREAT SOCIETY

Lyndon Johnson lacked Kennedy's charisma, but he possessed political assets of his own. As a member of the House of Representatives during the late 1930s and early 1940s, and majority leader of the

THE PRESENCE OF LYNDON B. JOHNSON As both senator and president, Lyndon Johnson employed body language—the "Johnson treatment"—as a favored means of lining up support for his policies.

U.S. Senate during the 1950s, the gangling Texan became the consummate legislative horse trader. He drove himself to a nearly fatal heart attack worrying over legislative details and courting Senate colleagues. Few issues, Johnson believed, defied consensus. Nearly everyone could be flattered, cajoled, even threatened into lending him their support. During his time in Congress, LBJ's wealthy Texas benefactors gained valuable oil and gas concessions and lucrative construction contracts, while Johnson himself acquired a personal fortune. At the same time, the growth of cities such as Dallas and Houston and the economic boom throughout the Southwest owed much to Johnson's skill in pushing measures such as federally funded irrigation and space-exploration projects through Congress.

Kennedy's death gave Johnson the opportunity to fulfill his dreams of transforming the nation, just as he had transformed Dallas and Houston. Confident that he could use his Senate-days tactics to build national consensus for expanding government power, Johnson set to work. He began by urging Congress

to honor JFK's memory by passing legislation that Kennedy's administration had originated.

COMPLETING KENNEDY'S INITIATIVES

More knowledgeable in the ways of Congress than Kennedy, Johnson quickly achieved the major domestic goals of JFK's New Frontier. Working behind the scenes, Johnson secured passage of Kennedy's proposed $10 billion tax cut, a measure intended to stimulate the economy by making more money available for business investment. Although opinions differ on how much this tax cut contributed to the economic boom of the mid-1960s, it *appeared* to work. GNP rose 7 percent in 1964 and 8 percent the following year; unemployment dropped to about 5 percent; and consumer prices rose by less than 3 percent.

Johnson also built on Kennedy-era plans for addressing the problems of people who were not yet sharing in the new economic bounty. In his January 1964 State of the Union address, Johnson announced that his administration was declaring "an unconditional war on poverty in America." With Johnson's constant prodding, in August 1964 Congress created the Office of Economic Opportunity (OEO) to coordinate a multipart program. First headed by R. Sargent Shriver, brother-in-law of John Kennedy, the OEO was to "eliminate the paradox of poverty in the midst of plenty . . . by opening to everyone the opportunity to live in decency and in dignity." The Economic Opportunity Act of 1964, in addition to establishing OEO, mandated loans for rural and small-business development; established a program of work training called the Jobs Corps; created Volunteers in Service to America (VISTA), a domestic version of the Peace Corps program; provided low-wage jobs for young people, primarily in urban areas; began a work-study plan to assist college students; and, most important, authorized the creation of additional federally funded social programs to be planned in concert with local community groups.

Johnson also secured passage of civil rights legislation. Because he was at first distrusted by activists working to end racial discrimination, Johnson took special pride in helping to push an expanded version of Kennedy's civil rights bill through Congress in 1964. Championing the bill as a memorial to Kennedy, he nevertheless recognized that southern segregationists in the Democratic Party would try to delay and dilute the measure. Consequently, he successfully lobbied key Republicans for their support. Passed in July 1964 after lengthy delaying tactics by southerners, the Civil Rights Act of 1964, administered by a new Equal Employment Opportunity Commission (EEOC), strengthened federal remedies for fighting job discrimination. It also prohibited racial discrimination in public accommodations connected with interstate commerce, such as hotels and restaurants. Moreover, Title VII, a provision added to the bill during the legislative debates, barred discrimination based on sex, a provision that became extremely important to the women's movement.

THE ELECTION OF 1964

Civil rights legislation was also a testimony to the moral power of civil rights workers and their faith that local organizing could shape national policy-making. During the summer of 1964, while Lyndon

CHRONOLOGY

1963 Johnson assumes presidency and pledges to continue Kennedy's initiatives

1964 Congress passes Kennedy's tax bill, the Civil Rights Act of 1964, and the Economic Opportunity Act • Gulf of Tonkin Resolution gives Johnson authority to conduct undeclared war • Johnson defeats Barry Goldwater in presidential election

1965 Johnson announces plans for the Great Society • Malcolm X assassinated • U.S. intervenes in Dominican Republic • Johnson announces significant U.S. troop deployments in Vietnam • Congress passes Voting Rights Act • Violence rocks Los Angeles and other urban areas

1966 Black Power movement emerges • *Miranda* v. *Arizona* decision guarantees rights of criminal suspects • Ronald Reagan elected governor of California • U.S. begins massive air strikes in North Vietnam

1967 Large antiwar demonstrations begin • Beatles release *Sgt. Pepper's Lonely Hearts Club Band*

1968 Tet offensive (January) • Martin Luther King, Jr., assassinated (April) • Robert Kennedy assassinated (June) • Violence at Democratic national convention in Chicago • Civil Rights Act of 1968 passed • Vietnam peace talks begin in Paris • Richard Nixon elected president

1969 Nixon announces "Vietnamization" policy • Pictures of My Lai massacre become public

1970 U.S. troops enter Cambodia • Student demonstrators killed at Kent State and Jackson State

1971 "Pentagon Papers" published; White House "plumbers" formed • Military court convicts Lieutenant Calley for My Lai incident

1972 Nixon crushes McGovern in presidential election

1973 Paris peace accords signed • *Roe* v. *Wade* upholds women's right to abortion • Nixon's Watergate troubles begin to escalate

1974 House votes impeachment, and Nixon resigns • Ford assumes presidency

1975 Saigon falls to North Vietnamese forces

Johnson was dominating policymaking in Washington, a coalition of civil rights organizations enlisted young volunteers to help register voters in Mississippi—an operation they called "Freedom Summer." During that violent time, segregationists murdered six civil rights workers, but their fellow activists pressed forward, only to see their political work frustrated at the Democratic national convention. Pressured by Johnson, who used the FBI to gather information on dissidents, party leaders seated Mississippi's "regular" all-white delegates rather than members of the alternative (and racially diverse) "Freedom Democratic Party."

This rebuff prompted civil rights activists such as Fannie Lou Hamer of the Freedom Democratic Party to recall earlier suspicions about Lyndon Johnson and the national Democratic Party. Although Johnson seemed more committed to change than John Kennedy had been, would LBJ—and Hubert Humphrey, his personal choice for vice presidential running mate—continue to press for antidiscrimination measures after the election? This question became all the more important as Johnson appeared more and more likely to win the 1964 presidential race.

The Republicans nominated Senator Barry Goldwater of Arizona, a fervent conservative, to oppose Johnson. Goldwater's strategists, who had captured the nomination by waging a grassroots organizing effort within the Republican Party, predicted that an unabashedly conservative campaign would attract the millions of voters who appeared dissatisfied with both Democratic liberalism and moderate Republicanism. Goldwater denounced Johnson's foreign policies as too timid and his domestic programs as destructive of individual freedom. Goldwater, only one of eight Republican senators who had voted against the Civil Rights Act of 1964, criticized the measure as an unconstitutional extension of national power to address a problem against which only the states could legislate.

Goldwater's blunt pronouncements on controversial issues allowed critics to picture him as a fanatical and unpredictable reactionary. Goldwater suggested that people who feared nuclear war were "silly and sissified." U.S. weapons were so accurate, he once quipped, that the military could target the men's room in the Kremlin. He wondered, out loud, if Social Security might be converted to a voluntary program. When Goldwater's acceptance speech at the 1964 Republican convention proclaimed that "extremism in the pursuit of liberty is no vice" and "moderation in the pursuit of justice is no virtue," critics cited the phrase as another sign of a "radical-right" position.

Even some Republican voters came to view Goldwater as too extreme, and he led the GOP to a crushing defeat in November. Johnson carried 44 states and won more than 60 percent of the popular vote; in addition, Democrats gained 38 new seats in Congress. Most political pundits immediately declared the 1964 election a repudiation of Goldwater's brand of conservatism and a great triumph for Johnson's vision of domestic policymaking.

In retrospect, however, this contest signaled political changes that would eventually erode support for Johnson's vision of domestic policy. During the 1964 Democratic primaries, for example, Alabama's segregationist governor, George Wallace, had run strongly against the president in several northern states. An opponent of civil rights legislation, Wallace attacked federal "meddling" in local affairs, injected the issue of race into politics in both South and North, and demonstrated the appeal of a "white backlash" movement. The 1964 presidential election was the last the Democratic Party would win by adhering to the New Deal–Fair Deal tradition of urging expanded use of governmental power at home.

Goldwater's defeat seemed to invigorate rather than discourage conservatives. His youthful campaign staff had pioneered several innovative stratagems such as direct mail fund-raising. By refining these tactics in future campaigns, conservative strategists helped to make the 1964 election the beginning, not the end, of the Republican Party's movement to the right. Moreover, Goldwater's stand against the Civil Rights Act of 1964 helped him carry five southern states, and these victories convinced Republicans that presidential opposition to antidiscrimination measures would continue to attract white voters in the South who had once been solidly Democratic.

The Goldwater effort also propelled an attractive group of conservative leaders into national politics. Actor and corporate spokesperson Ronald Reagan proved such an effective campaigner in 1964 that conservative Republicans began to

"Ten, nine, eight, seven . . .

six, five, four, three . . .

two, one . . .

These are the stakes, to make a world in which all of god's children can live . . .

or to go into the dark. We must either love each other or we must die . . .

The stakes are too high for you to stay home."

LBJ'S 1964 CAMPAIGN AGAINST BARRY GOLDWATER In this television ad from the 1964 campaign, Lyndon Johnson's supporters exploited Republican Barry Goldwater's image as a far-right extremist who might take the nation into a nuclear war.

groom him for a political career. Other prominent conservatives such as William Rehnquist also entered national politics through the 1964 campaign. In the immediate aftermath of Goldwater's defeat, however, the prospect that a President Ronald Reagan would one day nominate William Rehnquist to be chief justice of the United States seemed beyond any conservative's wildest dream or any liberal's worst nightmare (see chapter 31).

LYNDON JOHNSON'S GREAT SOCIETY

Lyndon Johnson wanted to capitalize quickly on his electoral victory. Shortly after taking the oath of office in January 1965, he ordered his staff to work on an ambitious legislative agenda. Enjoying broad support in Congress, Johnson soon announced plans for a "Great Society," an array of programs, funded by the national government, that were to provide economic opportunity to the people who had missed the prosperity of the 1950s and early 1960s. Johnson called on government to help "en-

rich and elevate our national life" by building a society that was also wealthy "in mind and spirit."

Some of Johnson's Great Society programs fulfilled the dreams of his Democratic predecessors. Nationally funded medical coverage for the elderly (Medicare) and for low-income citizens (Medicaid) culminated efforts begun during the New Deal and revived during the Fair Deal. Similarly, an addition to the president's cabinet, the Department of Housing and Urban Development (HUD), built upon earlier plans for coordinating urban revitalization programs. And the Voting Rights Act of 1965, which mandated federal oversight of elections in the South, seemed to cap federal efforts begun during the 1930s to end racial discrimination in political life.

Other programs sought to build on the prosperity of the 1960s. Roosevelt had to cope with the Great Depression, and Truman had to deal with the economic uncertainties of the postwar years. Johnson, in contrast, launched his Great Society during a time of economic boom. Even a costly war in Southeast Asia could not dampen his faith that continued economic growth would support his boldest initiative: a "War on Poverty."

The sheer array of Johnson-sponsored initiatives that rolled through Congress heartened his liberal supporters and appalled his conservative critics. The "Model Cities Program" encouraged small-scale alternatives to massive urban renewal efforts; rent supplements helped low-income families improve their living conditions; an expanded Food Stamp program boosted nutritional levels; Head Start helped preschool youngsters from low-income families climb the educational ladder; a variety of other federally financed educational programs upgraded classroom instruction, especially in low-income neighborhoods; and a Legal Services program provided legal advice for those who could not afford private attorneys. These programs were designed to offer a broad range of social services, funded by federal tax dollars, that could help people fight their own way out of economic distress and into Johnson's new and greater society. Such a service-based approach, Johnson insisted, would give people a "hand up" rather than a "hand out."

The innovative Community Action Program (CAP) went further by suggesting the possibility of empowering local activists. It encouraged citizens, working through neighborhood organizations, to design community-based projects that would be financed from Washington. By promoting "maximum feasible participation" by citizens themselves, CAP was supposed to use federal funds to spark a kind of community-based democracy that could transform the entire political system.

EVALUATING THE GREAT SOCIETY

Why did the Great Society become so controversial? Most obviously, Johnson's dramatic extension of Washington's power rekindled old debates about the proper role of the national government. In addition, the president's extravagant rhetoric, with its promise of an "unconditional" victory over poverty, raised expectations impossible to meet in one presidency, or even in one generation. Most important, the faith that economic growth would generate the tax revenues needed to fund expanding social programs simply collapsed with the onset of economic problems during the late 1960s. Facing unexpected financial worries of their own, many people who

had initially been inclined to support the Great Society came to accept the argument, first popularized by George Wallace, that bureaucrats in Washington were taking hard-earned dollars from taxpayers and redirecting them in unproductive directions. In 1964 Lyndon Johnson assumed that continued prosperity would allow him to build a consensus for the Great Society; worsening economic conditions, however, made greater federal spending for domestic programs highly divisive.

Historians have evaluated Lyndon Johnson's Great Society programs in a variety of ways. Conservatives have subjected them to harsh criticism. Charles Murray's influential *Losing Ground* (1984) set the tone by charging that massive government expenditures during the Johnson years encouraged antisocial behavior. Lured by welfare payments, this study argued, many people with low incomes abandoned the goals of marrying, settling down, and seeking jobs. According to this view, the Great Society's spending had also created huge government deficits that slowed economic growth. Had Great Society spending not weakened the nation's economic structure, continued growth would have brought virtually everyone in America a middle-class lifestyle. This conservative argument saw Johnson's program as the cause, not the remedy, for persistent economic inequality in America.

Historians more sympathetic to Johnson's approach have vigorously rejected the conservative argument. Where is the evidence that low-income people preferred welfare to meaningful work? Spending on the military sector far outstripped that for social programs and seemed the principal cause of burgeoning government deficits. Moreover, they note, expenditures on Great Society programs neither matched Johnson's promises nor commanded the massive amount of funds claimed by conservatives.

Historians on the left have persistently criticized the Great Society's failure to challenge the prevailing distribution of political and economic power. The Johnson administration, they argue, remained closely wedded to large-scale bureaucratic solutions for problems that had many local variations. Generally, it worked to ensure that people loyal to the Democratic Party machinery, rather than grassroots activists, dominated the planning and execution of new social programs. The CAP model, in other words, was quickly jettisoned. In addition, these critics point out, the Great Society never sought a redistribution of wealth and income. In this view, the Great Society was a flawed project that was never seriously implemented; the War on Poverty was only a series of small skirmishes.

Although historians continue to evaluate the impact of the Great Society in different ways, they generally agree that Johnson's domestic agenda did leave a mark on American life. It represented the first significant new outlay of federal dollars for domestic social programs since the New Deal. Spending on such programs did increase more than 10 percent in every year of Johnson's presidency. In 1960, federal spending on social welfare comprised 28 percent of total government outlays; by 1970, such expenditures had risen to more than 40 percent. Within a decade of the beginning of the Great Society, programs such as Medicaid, legal services, and job training provided low-income individuals with some of the services more affluent Americans had long taken for granted.

The Great Society, by trying to extend the reach of the welfare state that had begun to take shape during the 1930s, ignited increasingly intense public debate over how best to use the power and resources of the national government. In seeking to extend tangible assistance to the poor, how could policymakers follow the distinction, which became increasingly accepted in public discourse, between people who seemed to deserve assistance and those who seemed to be, in Lyndon Johnson's own formulation, seeking a "hand out" rather than a "hand up"?

ESCALATION IN VIETNAM

Johnson's crusade to build a Great Society at home had its counterpart in an ambitious extension of U.S. power abroad. The escalation of the war in Vietnam demanded ever more of the administration's energy and resources. Eventually, it alienated many Americans, especially the young, and divided the entire nation.

THE GULF OF TONKIN RESOLUTION

Immediately after John Kennedy's assassination in November 1963, Johnson had avoided widening the war in Vietnam. He did not wish to be seen as "soft"

on communism, however, and Johnson felt pressure to follow up on Kennedy's public commitments to fight the spread of communism everywhere. Insecure about his knowledge of foreign affairs and surrounded by Kennedy's Ivy League advisers, Johnson saw no alternative to backing the government in South Vietnam. He accepted his military advisers' recommendation to forestall enemy offensives in South Vietnam by staging air strikes against North Vietnam, and he prepared a congressional resolution authorizing such an escalation.

Events in the Gulf of Tonkin, off the coast of North Vietnam, provided him with a rationale for taking the resolution to Congress. On August 1, 1964, the U.S. destroyer *Maddox*, while conducting an intelligence-gathering mission, was fired on by North Vietnamese torpedo boats. Three days later, the *Maddox* returned with the destroyer *Turner Joy* and, amid severe weather conditions, reported another torpedo attack. Although the *Maddox*'s commander radioed that the "attack" might have been a false report and should be confirmed, Johnson proclaimed that U.S. forces had been the target of "unprovoked aggression." He rushed the resolution to Congress, where he received overwhelming approval to take "all necessary measures to repel armed attack." Johnson subsequently used this Gulf of Tonkin Resolution as tantamount to a congressional declaration of war and cited it as legal authorization for all subsequent military action in Vietnam. On the eve of the 1964 election, the president's tough stand dramatically increased his approval ratings in public opinion polls.

Despite his moves in the Gulf of Tonkin, the president still managed to position himself as a cautious moderate during the presidential campaign of 1964. When Goldwater urged stronger measures against North Vietnam and mentioned the possible use of tactical nuclear weapons, Johnson's supporters warned that Goldwater's approach risked a wider war with China and the Soviet Union. His campaign managers portrayed Goldwater as a threat to the survival of civilization. A Democratic television commercial depicted a little girl picking the petals from a daisy as a nuclear bomb exploded onscreen. Although the ad was so controversial that it ran only once, it nonetheless became a familiar icon in the campaign: the implication was that a Goldwater victory would bring nuclear holocaust.

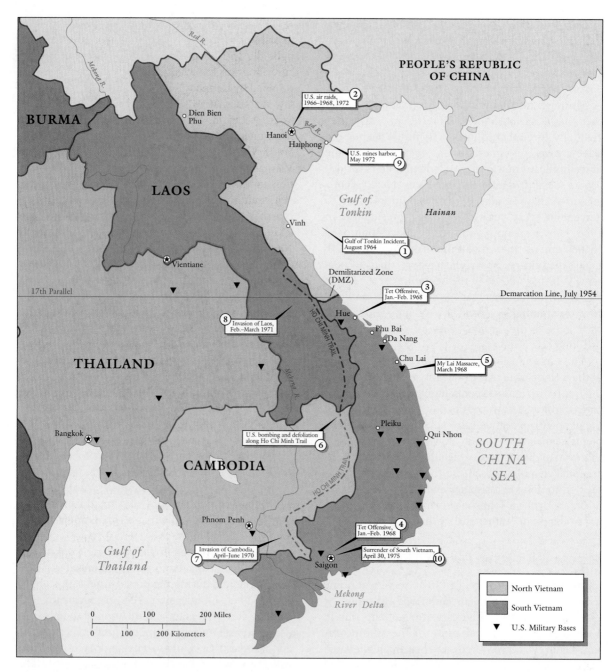

VIETNAM WAR

Johnson promised not to commit American troops to fight a land war in Asia.

Soon after the election, however, Johnson further escalated the war. The 1963 coup against Diem (see chapter 28) had left a political vacuum in South Vietnam, and the National Liberation Front was making rapid gains in several rural provinces. South Vietnam's incompetent new military-led government sparked growing discontent even in the capital city of Saigon, where strikes by workers and students brought widespread civic disorder. Soldiers deserted at an alarming rate. In January 1965, the regime fell, and factionalism prevented any stable government from emerging in its wake.

With no credible or effective government in South Vietnam, Johnson increasingly worried over his options. Should the pursuit of anticommunism turn the Vietnamese struggle into America's war? Were the stakes worth the potential costs? What public backlash would greet a possible communist victory? Could the United States escalate and win the war without provoking a deadly clash with China or even the Soviet Union?

In 1965, Johnson canvassed for advice and weighed his options. His advisers offered conflicting views. National Security Adviser McGeorge Bundy predicted inevitable defeat unless the United States sharply escalated its military role. Walt Rostow assured Johnson that a determined effort would bring a clear-cut victory. "Historically, guerrilla wars have generally been lost or won cleanly," Rostow wrote. If all routes to victory are denied the enemy, he advised, they will give up. Undersecretary of State George Ball, by contrast, warned that greater Americanization of the war would bring defeat, not victory. "The South Vietnamese are losing the war," he wrote, and "no one has demonstrated that a white ground force of whatever size can win a guerrilla war . . . in jungle terrain in the midst of a population that refuses cooperation to the white forces." Senate Majority Leader Mike Mansfield urged the president to devise some plan that would reunite Vietnam as a neutral country. The Joint Chiefs of Staff, afflicted by interservice rivalries, provided differing military assessments and no clear advice.

Although privately questioning the long-term prospects for success, Johnson nonetheless feared the immediate political hazards of a U.S. pullout. Domestic criticism of a communist victory in South Vietnam, he believed, would certainly endanger his Great Society programs and, perhaps, end the effectiveness of his presidency. Moreover, to those who argued that Vietnam had little strategic importance to the United States, Johnson countered that U.S. withdrawal would set off a "domino effect": encouraging Castro-style insurgencies in Latin America, increasing pressure on West Berlin, and damaging American credibility around the world. Both Eisenhower and Kennedy, after all, had staked American prestige on preserving a noncommunist South Vietnam. Johnson now either had to retract that commitment or face—as his predecessors had avoided—the uncertain course of ordering a massive infusion of America's own troops.

Swayed by political calculations and trapped within the cold-war mentality of the times, Johnson gambled that escalation of the U.S. offensive would somehow strengthen the weak and unpopular government in Saigon. He decided on a sustained campaign of bombing in North Vietnam, code-named "Rolling Thunder." During the bombing he deployed U.S. ground forces to regain South Vietnamese territory, expanded covert operations, and stepped up economic aid to the beleaguered Saigon government. Only six months into his new term, with both civilian and military advisers divided in their recommendations, Johnson committed the United States to full-scale war against North Vietnam and risked the nation's prestige on the rescue of a tottering ally in Saigon.

THE WAR WIDENS

The war grew more intense throughout 1965. Trying to break the enemy's will, U.S. military commanders called for an all-out effort to inflict more casualties. Accordingly, the administration authorized the use of napalm, a chemical that charred both foliage and people, and allowed the Air Force to bomb new North Vietnamese targets. Additional combat troops arrived to secure South Vietnamese enclaves, converting the struggle into the kind of far-away ground war that most military strategists (including Dwight Eisenhower) had once warned against. Each escalation seemed to make further escalation inevitable. When North Vietnam rejected an unrealistic "peace plan," outlined by Johnson in a speech in April 1965, U.S. military spending and action rose once more. North Vietnam's leader, Ho Chi Minh, played the same game of escalation and attrition. Convinced that Johnson commanded meager public and congressional support for continuing the costly war, Ho Chi Minh increased the southward flow of North Vietnamese troops and supplies.

In April 1965, Johnson brought his anticommunist crusade closer to home. Prompted by exaggerated reports of a communist threat in the Dominican

Republic, Johnson sent American troops to unseat a left-leaning elected president and to install a government favorable to U.S. economic interests. This U.S. incursion violated a longstanding, "good neighbor" pledge not to intervene militarily in the western hemisphere. Although the action raised criticism throughout Latin America, the successful military ouster of a leftist regime boosted the administration's determination to hold the line against communism in Vietnam.

During the spring of 1965, as the fifth government since Diem's death took office in Saigon, U.S. strategists were still puzzling over how to prop up South Vietnam. The commander in charge of the American effort, General William Westmoreland, recommended moving U.S. forces out of their enclaves and sending them on "search and destroy" missions. In July, Johnson dispatched 50,000 additional troops to Vietnam, privately agreed to send an additional 50,000, and left open the possibility of sending even more. He also approved saturation bombing of the South Vietnamese countryside and intensified bombing in North Vietnam.

Some of his advisers urged Johnson to publicly admit that the scope of the war was being steadily enlarged. They also recommended either an outright declaration of war or emergency legislation that would formally put the United States on a wartime footing so that the president could wield the economic and informational controls that past administrations had used in conflicts of this magnitude. But Johnson feared that assuming the formal status of a belligerent would provoke the Soviet Union or China. He also worried about arousing greater protests from Congress and the public. Although Congress had approved $400 million for military expenditures in May 1965, many legislators expressed grave doubts about the war. Rather than risk open debate that might reveal his shallow political support, Johnson decided to stress the administration's efforts to negotiate and to pretend that the war was not a war. As the president talked about seeing "light at the end of the tunnel," the public remained in the dark as to exactly what its government was doing and why.

Over the next three years, American troop numbers in Vietnam increased from 50,000 to 535,000. By 1967, the United States was spending more than $2 billion a month on the war and was subjecting

the Vietnamese landscape to widespread devastation. Operation RANCHHAND scorched South Vietnam's crop lands and defoliated half its forests in an effort to eliminate the natural cover for enemy troop movements. One and a half million tons of bombs—more than all the tonnage dropped in the Second World War—leveled North Vietnamese cities and pummeled the villages and inhabitants of "free-fire zones" (designated areas in which anything was considered a fair target) in the South. Still, Johnson was careful to avoid bombing too close to the Chinese border or doing anything else that might provoke either Chinese or Soviet entry into the war. Despite the escalating violence, Vietnam would remain a "limited" war.

The strategy was attrition. The weekly body count of enemy dead became the measure by which the Johnson administration gauged the war's progress. Estimates that a kill ratio of 10 to 1 would force the North to surrender encouraged the military to inflate body count figures and to engage in indiscriminate killing. Johnson, whose notorious temper flared whenever he received bad news, welcomed figures suggesting that "victory was around the corner." Actually, North Vietnam was matching each American escalation and controlling its losses by concealing troops under the jungle canopy that remained. The North Vietnamese channeled a constant flow of supplies south through a shifting network of jungle paths called the Ho Chi Minh Trail. The war had reached a stalemate, but few members of Johnson's administration would admit it.

The massive destruction wreaked by the U.S. effort gave North Vietnamese leaders a decided propaganda advantage. Critics around the world condemned the escalation of American attacks. The Soviet Union and China increased their aid to Ho Chi Minh and helped foment anti-Americanism elsewhere. Both at home and abroad, Johnson administration officials were hounded by protesters almost everywhere they went.

Meanwhile, the government in Saigon was reeling under the devastation of its countryside, the destabilizing effect of the flood of U.S. dollars on its economy, and the corruption of its politicians. So-called "pacification" and "strategic hamlet" programs, which brought Vietnamese farmers together in tightly guarded villages, sounded viable in Washington but caused further chaos by uprooting one in four South Vietnamese from their villages and ancestral lands. Buddhist priests persistently demonstrated against foreign influence. When Generals Nguyen Van Thieu and Nguyen Cao Ky, who had led the government since 1965, held elections in 1967 to legitimate their regime, their narrow margin of victory merely highlighted their weakness.

THE MEDIA AND THE WAR

Johnson lectured the American public about upholding national honor and standing by commitments, but antiwar criticism continued to mount. In most earlier wars, Congress had imposed strict controls on what journalists could report to the public. Because the Vietnam War was undeclared, Johnson had to resort to informal, though at first effective, ways of managing information. With television coverage making Vietnam a "living room war," Johnson kept three television sets playing in his office in order to monitor the major networks. Sometimes he would phone the news anchors after their broadcasts and castigate them for their stories. The "Johnson treatment," some called it. After one CBS report, the network's president, Frank Stanton, reportedly received this call: "Frank, are you trying to f— me? . . . This is your president, and yesterday your boys shat on the American flag." Increasingly sensitive to criticism, Johnson equated any question or doubt about his policy in Vietnam with a lack of patriotism.

Antiwar activists were equally disturbed by what they regarded as the media's uncritical reporting on the war. Most of the reporters, they claimed, relied on official handouts for their stories, spent their time in Saigon's best hotels, and took pains to avoid offending anyone at the White House. Indeed, especially in the early years, few reporters filed hard-hitting stories. Though the press corps did not invite Americans to love the war, as it had during the two world wars, neither did it encourage much criticism.

In time, however, the effect of the news coverage became less ambiguous. The unrelenting images of destruction on the nightly news and in *Life* magazine's photos, whatever their intent, turned people against the war. In addition, a few journalists forthrightly expressed their opposition. Harrison Salisbury of the *New York Times* sent reports from Viet-

nam that dramatized the destructiveness of U.S. bombing missions. Gloria Emerson's grim and widely read reports portrayed the war as a class-based effort in which the United States used poor and disproportionately nonwhite fighting forces, while rich men with draft-exempt sons raked in war profits.

As the war dragged on, Americans became polarized into "hawks" and "doves." Johnson insisted that he was merely following the containment policy favored by Eisenhower and Kennedy. Secretary of State Dean Rusk spoke of the dangers of "appeasement." But influential senators—including J. William Fulbright of Arkansas, chair of the powerful Foreign Relations Committee, and Eugene McCarthy of Minnesota—warned of misplaced priorities and an "arrogance of power." Meanwhile, antiwar protestors began to challenge the structure of American society itself.

THE WAR AT HOME

Millions came to oppose the war in Southeast Asia, and support eroded for the Great Society at home. By 1968, the recent years of slowly building tensions appeared to reach a critical point.

A NEW LEFT

During the early 1960s small groups of people, many of them college students, came to reject the welfare-state policies of the postwar years. In 1962, two years after conservative activists had formed Young Americans for Freedom (YAF), insurgents on the left established an organization called Students for a Democratic Society (SDS). While YAF worked quietly to build a "New Right," SDS captured the media's attention. Although SDS endorsed familiar political causes, especially the fight against racial discrimination, its founding "Port Huron Statement" also spoke of new, more spiritual and personal issues. SDS pledged to attack the "loneliness, estrangement, isolation" of postwar society.

SDS became an important part of a "New Left," a political insurgency that tried to distance itself from both the welfare-state policies of the Great Society and the "old" communist-inspired Left. By charging that the dominant culture valued bureaucratic expertise over citizen engagement and conspicuous consumption over meaningful work,

ANTIWAR DEMONSTRATION IN WASHINGTON, D.C.
Mass rallies against U.S. involvement in the Vietnam War became an important part of antiwar politics during the late 1960s and early 1970s.

this New Left sought to create an alternative vision. It called for "participatory democracy," grassroots politics responsive to the wishes of local communities rather than the preferences of national elites. "We felt that we were different, and that we were going to do things differently," recalled one early SDS member. "It felt like the dawn of a new age."

During the early 1960s, many young white college students found inspiration from the antidiscrimination movement in the Deep South. Risking racist violence, they went to the South where they forged bonds of community with African American activists. Some remained in the South or migrated to political projects in northern neighborhoods. Others returned to their college campuses and joined New Left protests against both the war in Southeast Asia and social conditions at home.

The New Left denounced the nation's prestigious colleges and universities as part of a vast "establishment" that resisted significant change. Giant universities, sustained by funds from government and corporations, seemed oblivious to the social and moral implications of their war-related research, dissenting students claimed. They charged the curriculum of the early 1960s with ignoring the relevant issues of the day and administrators with muzzling political dissent on campus. Moreover, traditional restrictions on a student's personal choices, such as dress codes and mandatory dormitory hours, seemed relics of an authoritarian past in which colleges and universities acted *in loco parentis* (in place of parents). In 1964 and 1965, students and sympathetic faculty from the prestigious University of California at Berkeley came out of the classroom to protest both campuswide restrictions on political activity and lifestyle choices and broader issues such as Vietnam and racial discrimination. This "Berkeley student revolt," which disrupted classes and polarized campus politics, ushered in nearly a decade of turmoil among college students.

By 1966, the war in Vietnam dominated the agenda of student protesters. For young men, who were required by federal law to register for possible military service at age eighteen, a draft card signified their personal connection to American involvement in Southeast Asia. Local draft boards usually granted men who were attending college a student deferment, but these expired upon graduation and could, in some instances, be revoked or denied. The burning of draft cards, as a symbolic protest against both the war and universal military service for men, became a central feature of many antiwar demonstrations.

Many campuses became embroiled in bitter strife. At "teach-ins," supporters and opponents of the war presented their positions and debated the morality of the involvement of universities in national security policies. Teach-ins soon gave way to less-structured demonstrations. As controversy over the war intensified, campus supporters of Johnson's policies claimed that protestors were curtailing *their* right to free speech. Conservatives, along with many moderates, pressured college administrators to crack down on "troublemakers" and return "civility" to the campus. As the debate broadened, conservatives—including

AMERICAN ATTITUDES TOWARD THE VIETNAM WAR *Responses to the question: "Do you think that the United States made a mistake in sending troops to fight there?"*

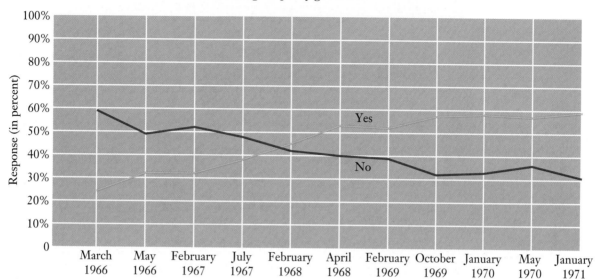

THE COUNTERCULTURE

Ronald Reagan, who was elected governor of California in 1966—made opposition to campus protests a prominent part of their new agenda.

Accompanying the spread of New Left politics was the rise of a much-publicized "counterculture." Only a relatively small percentage of young people fully embraced countercultural values, but the mass media immediately portrayed devotees of cultural insurgency, caricatured as "hippies," as representatives of a broad-based "youth revolt." Rejecting traditional attitudes on such matters as clothing, hair styling, and sexuality, spokespeople for the counterculture espoused an open, experimental approach to daily life. Members of the counterculture often championed causes such as environmentalism and sparked interest in "natural" foods. The media highlighted the counterculture's association with drugs such as marijuana and LSD, communal living arrangements, and new forms of folk-rock music. Bob Dylan, who had been a central figure in the revival of acoustical folk music in the early 1960s, suddenly "went electric" in 1965. Reworking musical idioms used by African American blues artists such as Muddy Waters, Dylan's "Like a Rolling Stone" (1965) exploded onto both the Top 40 charts of AM radio and the freewheeling play lists of the new, alternative FM stations. The media hailed Dylan, who shunned the role, as the prophet for an entire generation.

Images and products connected to the counterculture soon found a ready market among middle-class consumers. The mass-culture industry, recognizing the appeal of countercultural bands such as San Francisco's Grateful Dead and the Jefferson Airplane, welcomed the youth rebellion. The Rolling Stones made big money with their ode to a "Street Fighting Man" (1968) and their pledge of "Sympathy for the Devil" (1968). The Beatles made even more money and attracted critical acclaim with *Sgt. Pepper's Lonely Hearts Club Band* (1967) and *The Beatles* (popularly known as *The White Album*) (1968). Hollywood tapped the youth culture market with *The Graduate* (1967) and *Bonnie and Clyde* (1967) and followed up with a brief cycle of films, such as *Easy Rider* (1969) and *Wild in the Streets* (1968), which portrayed adult authority figures as vampire-like ravagers of youth. Further commercializing the idea of a "new generation," automobile manufacturers embraced a "youth rebellion" theme to sell their latest models.

A much-publicized march on the Pentagon in 1967 crystallized growing controversy over the counterculture. Moving beyond burning draft cards as a symbol of antiwar protest, some of the marchers

Malcolm X (1992)

**Directed by Spike Lee. Starring Denzel Washington (Malcolm X),
Angela Bassett (Betty Shabbaz), Al Freeman, Jr. (Elijah Muhammad).**

Spike Lee, the U.S. film industry's best-known African American director, enjoys a formidable multimedia reputation. His resume is impressive: award-winning commercials for Nike; books about the filmmaking art; acting roles in his own movies; a visiting professorship at Harvard; frequent appearances on television talk shows, and a starring role, albeit as a courtside celebrity-fan, for the New York Knicks basketball team.

Lee campaigned actively in order to become the director of the long-delayed film about *Malcolm X*. For nearly twenty-five years, Hollywood film moguls had been discussing a movie about the charismatic leader who was gunned down in 1965 and whose *Autobiography*, published in 1963, had become a literary classic. Debates over obtaining financing, crafting a suitable script, and finding an appropriate director always stymied production plans. Lee, who had protested vigorously when the Hollywood establishment passed over his celebrated, and controversial, *Do The Right Thing* (1989) for an Academy Award nomination, insisted that only he could do justice to the life of Malcolm X. Initially buoyed by a $34 million budget, Lee soon encountered a series of problems, including the insistence that only a three-hour film could capture his historical vision. He called *Malcolm X* "my interpretation of the man. It is nobody else's."

Certainly, the finished film displays Lee's desire to emphasize the presence of the past in the present. Produced by Lee's own independent production—whose name, "Forty Acres and a Mule," recalls the land-distribution program advanced by radical Reconstructionists after the Civil War—the film, particularly in its opening and closing segments, argues for the continuing relevance of Malcolm X's ideas.

The segments that begin and end the film feature a collage of iconic images. Against the backdrop of the Warner Brothers logo, the soundtrack features the voice of Malcolm X decrying American history as the continuing story of racist actions. Malcolm's accusations continue as a giant American flag, perhaps a reference to the popular film *Patton* (1970), appears on screen. Then, the image of the flag is cut into pieces by jagged images from the videotape of the controversial 1991 incident in which Los Angeles police officers beat an African American named Rodney King. Next, the flag itself begins to burn until, revealed behind it, the screen becomes filled with a giant "X," adorned with remnants of the flag, as if to provide a counterpoint to a history in which racists burned

chanted mystical incantations and claimed they hoped to levitate the Pentagon. In a similar vein, Abbie Hoffman, self-proclaimed leader of the fictitious Youth International Party (the "Yippies"), facetiously urged "loot-ins at department stores to strike at the property fetish that underlies genocidal war" in Vietnam. The Pentagon march played well as a media spectacle and won novelist Norman Mailer, who had participated in it, a National Book Award for *Armies of the Night*, his account of the event.

Extensive media coverage of countercultural happenings such as this—and their relationship to political and social change—sparked a lively, ongoing debate. Did the counterculture offer a viable alternative vision of how to imagine liberty, equality and power? Or did it simply provide the media and corporate marketers an appealing set of images? Were political and cultural insurgency complementary or antagonistic movements? Conservative critics of the youth culture charged the media with spreading dangerous, antisocial images. In their view, the media's focus on demonstrations in which young radicals and countercultural musicians joined with older opponents of the war only exaggerated

crosses as a symbol of white supremacy. The ending uses substantial archival footage of Malcolm X, along with images of South African freedom fighter Nelson Mandela, while the soundtrack features the voice of Ozzie Davis, the celebrated African American actor, giving a eulogy to Malcolm.

The body of the lengthy film, borrowing its organizational structure from Malcolm's *Autobiography* and its historical imagery from a 1972 documentary by Marvin Worth, breaks into three parts. Denzel Washington, an Academy-Award winner for his role in *Glory* (1986), plays the title role. The film first traces how the young man, born Malcolm Little and later known as "Detroit Red," financed a gaudy lifestyle through small-time criminal schemes. The second part covers how, following his imprisonment and his acceptance of the religious-social creed of the Nation of Islam (a group popularly known as the "Black Muslims"), the flamboyant hustler became the almost ascetic rebel, Malcolm X. The final portion of the film, which takes roughly 90 minutes, races through the rest of Malcolm's private and public life. Reviewers and filmgoers unfamiliar with Malcolm's career found this portion of the film difficult to follow.

Released near Thanksgiving, the film opened to packed houses and, early on, took in considerably more money than Oliver Stone's *JFK* had garnered when released during the same time period only a year earlier. But, despite a multimedia publicity blitz, *Malcolm X*'s box-office revenues steadily declined. Reviewers and industry spokespeople reported that the lengthy, episodic film seemed to tax many filmgoers' patience and attention spans.

Watching *Malcolm X* on video or DVD, however, allows the luxury of concentrating on its many stunning sequences, speeding by ones that seem to drag, and returning to scenes that may at first viewing have seemed unclear. *Malcolm X* remains a fascinating attempt to represent on film the development of the Black Power movement and, more generally, the social turmoil that engulfed the nation at the beginning of its longest war.

Denzel Washington stars as Malcolm X.

the strength of the antiwar movement. Conversely, some veterans of the early New Left claimed that media attention on the counterculture actually undercut antiwar politics. The media's insatiable need for spectacular demonstrations and more exciting celebrities from the youth culture, they charged, trivialized issues that insurgents were trying to articulate in new, more powerful ways. Other activists suggested, however, that any attempt to draw a clear line between political and cultural dissent created artificial distinctions. Movements concerned about environmentalism, feminism, and racial discrimina-

tion, for example, cut across political-cultural divides and drew on values articulated by people associated with the counterculture. Moreover, innovative ways of using mass-mediated imagery seemed to offer insurgents their best hope for building viable alternative movements.

FROM CIVIL RIGHTS TO BLACK POWER

Sharp debate over the role of the media and its relationship to political and cultural insurgency also accompanied the new directions in the campaign against racial discrimination that emerged in the mid-1960s. Early on, leaders in the fight against discrimination, notably Dr. Martin Luther King, Jr., had recognized the benefits to be derived from media coverage. During King's 1965 drive to win access to the ballot box for African Americans, television pictures of the violence in Selma, Alabama, helped to galvanize support for federal legislation. At one point, ABC television interrupted the anti-Nazi film *Judgment at Nuremberg* in order to show white Alabama state troopers beating peaceful, mostly African American, civil rights marchers. President Johnson used television to dramatize his support for voting-rights legislation and to promise that "we shall overcome" the nation's "crippling legacy of bigotry and injustice."

At the same time, the media became the forum for debate over what was increasingly being called a "racial crisis." Conservatives argued that subversive agitators were provoking conflict and violence and that only a firm commitment to law and order would ease racial tensions. Social activists argued that a complex mix of racism, lack of educational and employment opportunities, and inadequate government responses were producing the frustration and despair that burst forth in sporadic racial violence. This debate intensified in 1965 in the wake of a devastating racial conflict in Los Angeles. A confrontation between a white highway patrol officer and a black motorist escalated into six days of urban violence, centered in the largely African American community of Watts in South-Central Los Angeles. Thirty-four people died; hundreds of businesses and homes were burned; the National Guard patrolled the streets; and television cameras framed the conflagration as an ongoing media spectacle.

Meanwhile, a new "Black Power" movement was emerging, heralded by charismatic minister Malcolm X. A member of the Nation of Islam, Malcolm X differed with leaders of the civil rights movement. He considered King's gradualist, nonviolent approach to political change as irrelevant to the social and economic problems of most African Americans and proclaimed that integration was unworkable. Although he never called for violent confrontation,

VIOLENCE IN DETROIT, 1967 Outbreaks of violence, rooted in economic inequality and racial tension, swept through many U.S. cities between 1965 and 1969. The 1967 violence in Detroit, which federal troops had to quell, left many African American neighborhoods in ruin.

he did endorse self-defense "by any means necessary." Malcolm X, a growing group of followers argued, was simply "telling it like it is."

Malcolm X offered more than sharp rhetoric. He called for renewed pride in the African American cultural heritage and for vigorous efforts at community reconstruction. In order to revitalize their contemporary institutions, he urged African Americans to "recapture our heritage and identity" and "launch a cultural revolution to unbrainwash an entire people." Seeking to forge a broader movement, Malcolm X eventually broke from the Nation of Islam, established his own Organization of Afro-American Unity, and explored alliances with other insurgent groups. Murdered in 1965 by enemies from the Nation of Islam, Malcolm X remained a powerful symbol of both militant politics and a renewed pride in African American culture.

While demonstrations against discrimination in politics, jobs, and housing continued in both the North and South, younger African Americans picked up the mantle of Malcolm X. Refashioning the integrationist agenda into a broader cultural crusade, they embraced the identity "black." As "Black Power" replaced the old civil rights call for "Freedom Now," advocates soon caught the media's attention and began to gain support within African American communities. "Black Is Beautiful" became a watchword. James Brown, the "Godfather of Soul," captured this new cultural spirit with his 1965 hit song, "Papa's Got a Brand New Bag," which announced a defiant refusal to abide by old rules and restrictions. Later, Brown's "Say It Loud, I'm Black and Proud" encapsulated the cultural message of the Black Power movement.

Black Power raised a philosophical and tactical challenge to the antidiscrimination movement. Frustrated by the slow pace of civil rights litigation, some younger African Americans, including Stokely Carmichael, who became head of the Student Nonviolent Coordinating Committee (SNCC) in 1966, and members of the Black Panther Party, criticized the gradualist approach of organizations such as King's Southern Christian Leadership Conference. A Black Panther manifesto, for example, called for community "self-defense" groups as protection against police harassment, the release from jail of all African American prisoners (on the assumption that none had re-

ceived fair trials in racist courts), and guaranteed employment for all citizens. Although opinion surveys suggested that the vast majority of African Americans still supported the integrationist agenda, the new modes of insurgency challenged the established, black–white civil rights alliance on which Martin Luther King, Jr., and Lyndon Johnson had relied.

Within this context, the Civil Rights Act of 1968 passed Congress. One provision of this omnibus law finally extended the constitutional guarantees of the Bill of Rights to American Indians (see chapter 30). Another, popularly known as the Fair Housing Act, addressed racial discrimination in housing. In response to complaints that its provisions infringed on the rights of landlords and real estate agents, however, the act included exemptions that made it cumbersome to enforce. Moreover, the Civil Rights Act included another section that declared it a crime to move from one state to another in order to incite a "riot." Supporters of the provision hailed it as an effort to reestablish "law and order." Civil libertarians countered that it unconstitutionally invoked the power of the federal government against activists, especially those preaching Black Power.

1968: THE VIOLENCE OVERSEAS

In 1968, a series of shocking events further polarized American life. The first came in Vietnam. At the end of January, during a truce in observance of Tet, the lunar new year celebration, troops of the National Liberation Front (NLF) joined North Vietnamese forces in a series of coordinated surprise attacks throughout South Vietnam. After sweeping into eight provincial capitals, they even seized the grounds of the U.S. embassy in Saigon for a few hours. Militarily, this so-called "Tet offensive" was a defeat for the NLF and the North; during two weeks of intense fighting, they suffered heavy casualties and made no significant territorial gains. Even so, Tet proved in fact a serious psychological defeat for the United States because it suggested the unreliability of Johnson's claims about an imminent South Vietnamese–United States victory. When General Westmoreland asked for 206,000 additional troops, most of Johnson's closest advisers, led by his new secretary of state, Clark

Clifford, criticized his request and urged that South Vietnamese troops be required to assume more of the military burden. Johnson accepted these arguments, realizing that such a large troop increase would have fanned antiwar opposition at home. Tet contributed to the beginning of a policy that would later be referred to as the "Vietnamization" of the war.

The Tet offensive destroyed much of whatever political support Johnson still commanded among antiwar Democrats and threw his strategic planners into confusion. Supporters of the war blamed the media for exaggerating the effect of the early attacks and ignoring the heavy losses to the NLF and North Vietnamese and thereby turning a "victory" into a "defeat;" critics countered that the Tet offensive had caught the U.S. military off guard and ill prepared to take advantage of enemy losses. Faced with revolt in his own party, led by Senator Eugene McCarthy of Minnesota, Johnson suddenly declared on March 31, 1968, that he would not run for reelection. He halted the bombing of North Vietnam and promised to devote his remaining time in office to seeking an end to the war. McCarthy, campaigning on a peace platform, continued his election bid against Johnson's vice president and party stalwart, Hubert H. Humphrey.

1968: THE VIOLENCE AT HOME

One person who rejoiced at Johnson's withdrawal was Martin Luther King, Jr. He hoped that the Democratic Party would now turn to an antiwar liberal, preferably Senator Robert Kennedy of New York, who might embrace King's new program for economic transformation. But on April 4, 1968, during a trip to Memphis, Tennessee, in support of a strike by African American sanitation workers, King was assassinated. Allegedly, a lone gunman named James Earl Ray was the assassin. Ray quickly pleaded guilty and was sentenced to 99 years. He subsequently recanted and crusaded unsuccessfully for a new trial. When he died in 1998, Ray still insisted that he had been nothing more than a pawn of a racist conspiracy.

As news of King's assassination spread, the kind of violence that had engulfed Watts in 1965 swept through urban neighborhoods around the country. More than 100 cities and towns witnessed out-

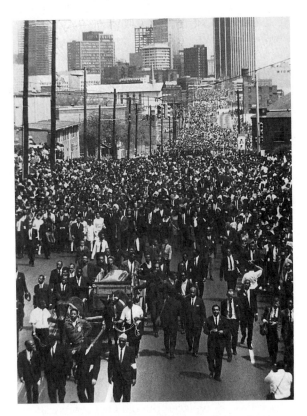

MARTIN LUTHER KING, JR.'S, FUNERAL CORTEGE
Martin Luther King, Jr.'s, assassination in 1968 sparked both violent protests and solemn mourning for the slain civil rights leader. Thousands of his grieving supporters followed the cart, drawn by mules, which carried King's body through the streets of his native Atlanta.

breaks; 39 people died; 75,000 regular and National Guard troops were called to duty. When Johnson proclaimed Sunday, April 7, as a day of national mourning for the slain civil rights leader, parts of Washington, D.C., were still ablaze.

Meanwhile, Robert Kennedy had challenged Hubert Humphrey and Eugene McCarthy for the Democratic presidential nomination. His campaign brought together veterans of John Kennedy's New Frontier, youthful activists, and media celebrities. Campaigning at a feverish pace, Kennedy battled McCarthy in a series of primaries, hoping to gain a majority of those convention delegates not already pledged to Humphrey by the party's old-line bosses such as Richard J. Daley, mayor of Chicago. Then, on June 5, only minutes after winning California's primary, Kennedy, too, fell victim to an assassin.

ROBERT F. KENNEDY'S FUNERAL An elaborately staged funeral also followed the 1968 assassination of Robert Kennedy. The shootings of the two beloved leaders—King and Kennedy—prompted widespread concern about the stability of America's social and political fabric and added to the tensions of this tumultuous year.

"*The line of cops moved forward to clear the street. Here and there an individual resisted, or stumbled—and in an instant the cops were lunging forward and clubbing heads with all their might. . . . People ran up to plead with cops beating kids on the ground and the cops turned around and clubbed them. They clubbed men in white who knelt to carry off the fallen and clubbed anyone with a camera on his neck. . . . All at once I was angrier than I would ever have believed. Down in the street I saw what we'd been waiting for all summer. The same violence that burnt villages, the violence that smashed up anything it couldn't understand. I was raging.*"

JEREMY LARNER
on protests and policy response outside the 1968 Democratic convention in Chicago (from Nobody Knows: Reflections on the McCarthy Campaign of 1968*)*

His nationally televised funeral was a disturbing reminder of King's recent murder and that of his own brother five years earlier.

The violence continued throughout 1968. During the Republican national convention in Miami, as presidential candidate Richard Nixon was promising to restore "law and order," racial violence, in which four people died, wracked that city. Later that summer thousands of antiwar demonstrators converged on the Democratic Party's Chicago convention to protest the nomination of Humphrey, who was still supporting Johnson's policy in Vietnam. Mayor Richard Daley ordered police to crush the demonstration. Some protestors seemed to welcome confrontation, and some Chicago police officers responded with indiscriminate attacks on demonstrators and mere bystanders alike. Antiwar delegates to the convention denounced Mayor Daley, their host, for presiding

over a "police state." Although an official report later characterized the violence in Chicago as a "police riot," opinion polls showed that a majority of Americans supported police efforts. Hubert Humphrey left the Chicago convention with the Democratic presidential nomination, but controversy over Johnson's Vietnam policies and over the response to antiwar demonstrations left his party badly divided.

THE ELECTION OF 1968

Both Humphrey and Nixon faced a serious challenge from the political right, spearheaded by Alabama's George Wallace. After his strong showing in several 1964 Democratic primaries, Wallace decided to seek nationwide support as a third-party candidate in 1968. A grassroots campaign eventually placed his American Independent Party on the presidential ballot in every state. Because Wallace's opposition to racial integration was well established, he could concentrate his fire on other controversial targets, particularly the counterculture and the antiwar movement. He bragged that if any "hippie" tried to block his motorcade, "it'll be the last car he'll ever lay down in front of." Wallace also recognized that many voters were beginning to lose faith in welfare-state programs and to see themselves as victims of an aloof, tax-and-spend bureaucracy in Washington.

Wallace's candidacy exacerbated the political polarization of 1968. If he prevented either major-party candidate from winning a majority of the electoral votes, the choice of the nation's president would rest with the House of Representatives and Wallace himself might act as a power broker between Democrats and Republicans. (A president had last been selected by the House in 1824.) Hoping to court voters who wanted a U.S. victory in Vietnam, Wallace chose the hawkish General Curtis LeMay, as his running mate. The former head of the Strategic Air Command quickly self-destructed by complaining that too many Americans had a "phobia" against using nuclear weapons, and critical pundits labeled Wallace and LeMay the "Bombsey Twins."

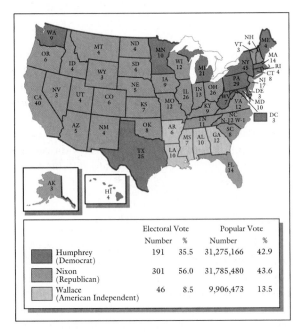

	Electoral Vote		Popular Vote	
	Number	%	Number	%
Humphrey (Democrat)	191	35.5	31,275,166	42.9
Nixon (Republican)	301	56.0	31,785,480	43.6
Wallace (American Independent)	46	8.5	9,906,473	13.5

PRESIDENTIAL ELECTION, 1968

Nixon narrowly prevailed in November. Although he won 56 percent of the electoral vote, he out-polled Humphrey in the popular vote by less than 1 percent. Humphrey had benefited when Johnson ordered a pause in the bombing of North Vietnam and pledged to begin peace talks in Paris, and he had helped his own cause with a belated decision to distance himself from the president's Vietnam policies. Still, Humphrey carried only Texas in the South, losing the grip the Democratic Party had held there since Reconstruction. George Wallace picked up 46 electoral votes, all from the Deep South, and 13.5 percent of the popular vote nationwide. Nixon won five key southern states and attracted, all across the country, those whom he called "the forgotten Americans, the nonshouters, the nondemonstrators." Hinting at a plan for ending the war in Vietnam, he predicted he would restore tranquillity to the domestic front. But soon after taking office, Nixon's policies proved every bit as divisive as those of Lyndon Johnson.

THE NIXON YEARS, 1969–1974

Raised in a modest Quaker home in southern California, Richard Nixon graduated from Whittier College, a small Quaker school near his hometown. Three years at Duke Law School, a hitch in the navy during the Second World War, and a job in Franklin Roosevelt's wartime bureaucracy gave Nixon a taste of new, more cosmopolitan worlds. After the war, however, he returned to his small-town California law practice before beginning a meteoric political career that took him to the House of Representatives in 1946, the Senate in 1950, and the vice presidency in 1952.

Nixon seemed to thrive on seeking out enemies, at home and abroad, and on confronting a constant series of personal challenges. He titled an early memoir of his political life *Six Crises*. Devastated by his narrow loss to Kennedy in 1960, Nixon seemed crushed politically when, in 1962, he failed to win the governorship of California. At a post-election press conference, a bitter Nixon denounced the press for distorting his record and announced his retirement from politics.

Barry Goldwater's 1964 defeat and Johnson's problems helped to revive Nixon's political prospects. During his presidency (1969–74) this self-proclaimed "new Nixon" seemed little different from the old one in his ability to inflame, rather than to calm, political passions.

THE ECONOMY

Nixon's presidency coincided with a series of economic problems unthinkable only a decade earlier. No simple cause can account for these difficulties, but analysis usually begins with the war in Vietnam. This expensive military commitment, along with fundamental changes in the world economy, brought an end to the economic growth of the previous two decades.

Lyndon Johnson, determined to stave off defeat in Indochina without cutting Great Society programs, had concealed the rising costs of the war even from his own advisers. Johnson bequeathed Nixon a deteriorating (though still favorable) trade balance and rising inflation rate. Between 1960 and 1965, consumer prices had risen an average of only about 1 percent a year; by 1968, the rate exceeded 4 percent.

Nixon hoped to check inflation by cutting government expenditures. He cut some costs by reducing U.S. troop levels and expanding bombing, but this strategy still drained economic resources. Moreover, although Nixon spoke of reducing domestic spending, he lacked the ability to slash programs that still enjoyed support in the Democrat-controlled Congress and among voters. During his first years in office, the percentage of federal funds spent on domestic programs increased steadily.

Meanwhile, the unemployment rate soared, topping 6 percent by 1971. According to conventional wisdom, expressed in a technical economic concept called "the Phillips curve," when unemployment rises, prices should remain constant or even decline. Yet *both* unemployment and inflation were rising, as if in tandem. Economists coined the term "stagflation" to describe this puzzling, unprecedented convergence of economic stagnation and price inflation. Along with stagflation, U.S. exports were becoming less competitive in international markets, and in 1971, for the first time in the 20th century, the United States ran a trade deficit, importing more products than it exported.

Long identified as an opponent of economic management by government but fearful of the political consequences of stagflation and the trade deficit, Nixon sought a cure for the economy's ills. In a reversal that one media commentator likened to a religious conversion, Nixon suddenly proclaimed himself a believer in governmental remedies. Hoping to cool down inflationary pressures before the 1972 election, he announced a "new economic policy" in August 1971 that mandated a 90-day freeze on any increase in wages and prices, to be followed by government monitoring to detect "excessive" increases in either.

To try to reverse the trade deficit, Nixon also revised the U.S. relationship to the world monetary structure. Dating from the 1944 Bretton Woods agreement (see chapter 26), the value of the U.S. dollar had been tied to the value of gold at $35 for every ounce. This meant that the United States, in order to provide an anchor for world currencies, was prepared to exchange its dollars for gold at that rate if any other nation's central bank requested it to do so. Other countries had fixed their own exchange rates against the dollar. But U.S. trade deficits undermined the value of the American dollar, enabling foreign banks to exchange U.S. dollars for gold at highly favorable rates. Consequently, in August 1971 the Nixon administration abandoned the fixed gold-to-dollar ratio, announcing that the dollar soon would be free to "float" against the prevailing market price of gold and against all other currencies. In 1973, the Nixon administration devalued the dollar, cheapening the price of American goods in foreign markets in order to make them more competitive. The strategy fundamentally altered the international economic order but had little immediate impact on the deterioration of U.S. trade balances. Over the next decade, U.S. exports more than tripled in value, but imports more than quadrupled.

SOCIAL POLICY

At the urging of Daniel Patrick Moynihan, a Democrat who became Nixon's chief adviser on domestic policy, the president began to consider a drastic revision of the nation's welfare programs. Moynihan insisted that Nixon, while still identifying himself as a conservative Republican, could bring about significant change in domestic social policy. After heated debates within his inner circle,

Nixon unveiled his Family Assistance Plan (FAP) during a television address in August 1969. The centerpiece of this complex policy package was the replacement of most welfare programs, including the controversial Aid to Families with Dependent Children (AFDC), with a guaranteed annual income for all families. AFDC provided government payments to cover basic costs of care for low-income children who had lost the support of a bread-winning parent. By 1970, half of all persons in families headed by women were receiving AFDC payments.

Under Nixon's proposal, the government would guarantee a family of four an annual income of $1,600, with the possibility of further assistance depending on how much income the family earned. In one bold stroke, FAP would replace the post–New Deal welfare system, which provided services and assistance *only* to those in particular circumstances, such as low-income mothers with small children or people who were unemployed, with a system that offered government aid to *all* low-income families. Even a family with an annual income of nearly twice Nixon's $1,600 level, according to one projection, would still benefit from FAP because of its tax refund and food stamp provisions.

FAP attracted tepid support in Congress and among the citizenry. Conservatives blasted it, especially the idea of supplementing the income of families that had a regularly employed, though low-paid, wage earner. In contrast, proponents of more generous government assistance programs criticized a guaranteed income of $1,600 as too miserly. The House of Representatives approved a modified version of FAP in 1970, but an unusual alliance among senators to the right and to the left of Nixon blocked its passage. Beset by economic issues and the lingering war in Vietnam, Nixon simply let FAP drop. A comprehensive overhaul of the nation's welfare system would not come until the 1990s.

Some changes in domestic programs did occur during the Nixon years, however. For example, Congress passed the president's revenue-sharing plan, part of his "new federalism," which returned a certain percentage of federal tax dollars to state and local governments in the form of "block grants." Instead of Washington specifying how these funds were to be used, the block grant concept left the state and local governments free, within broad limits, to spend the funds as they saw fit.

SOCIAL WELFARE SPENDING, 1960–1990

As a Percentage of Total Spending

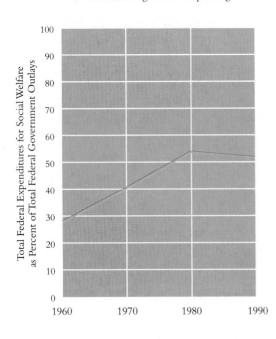

Total Expenditures

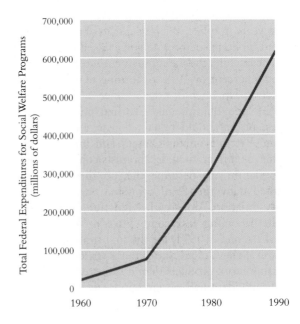

The Democratic-controlled Congress also cobbled together a revised welfare program during the early 1970s. This patchwork plan included rent subsidies for people at the lowest income levels and Supplementary Security Insurance (SSI) payments for those who were elderly, blind, or disabled. The Medicare and Medicaid programs, established under Johnson's Great Society, gradually expanded during Nixon's presidency. In 1972 Social Security benefits were "indexed," which meant they would rise with the rate of inflation. More cautious than Nixon's FAP proposals, these congressional initiatives, though they attracted relatively little attention when passed, substantially extended the nation's income-support programs, albeit only for specific groups, especially older Americans. Between 1970 and 1980 the federal government's spending for social welfare rose from 40.1 percent of total government outlays to slightly over 53 percent.

CONTROVERSIES OVER RIGHTS

These legislative changes came against the backdrop of a much broader debate over how to define the federal government's responsibility to protect basic constitutional rights. The struggle to define these rights embroiled the U.S. Supreme Court in controversy. An "activist" majority devoted to recognizing a broad range of constitutionally protected rights had come to dominate the Court's agenda during the 1960s

LINK TO THE PAST

Documents from the Women's Liberation Movement

http://scriptorium.lib.duke.edu/wlm/

Duke University's digitalized Special Collections include an archive of writings from the early "women's liberation" movement. These documents show women challenging traditional structures of power and thought in all aspects of their lives—work, sexuality, politics, race relations, music, and reproduction. They suggest the diversity of concerns of the emerging women's movement.

1. Read the documents under the section "Women of Color." What might have been some relationships between the civil rights movement and the women's liberation movement? How might these movements for change have both reinforced and also undermined each other?

2. Read "The Hand that Rocks the Cradle Should Be Paid" under the section "Work and Roles." How does this argument address issues of liberty, equality, and power in people's personal lives? Explain what might have been meant by the slogan of the women's movement: "the personal is political."

3. Read "Women of the World Unite; We Have Nothing to Lose But Our Men" and "Woman as Child," both under "Notes from the First Year" in the section "General and Theoretical." Compare and contrast these conversations and responses from the year 1968 to conversations and responses you might hear on your campus today.

4. Referring to these writings, describe what you consider the central concerns motivating women who built this liberation movement.

under the leadership of Eisenhower appointees Chief Justice Earl Warren and Associate Justice William Brennan. Although nearly all the Warren Court's rights-related decisions, especially those involving school desegregation, drew critical fire, perhaps the most emotional cases involved the rights of persons accused of violent crime. In *Miranda* v. *Arizona* (1966), the Court's activists held that the Constitution required police officers to advise people arrested for a felony offense of their constitutional rights to remain silent and to consult an attorney. While civil libertarians defended decisions such as *Miranda* as the logical extension of settled judicial precedents, the Court's numerous critics attacked the activist justices for allegedly inventing new rights not found in the text of the Constitution. Amid rising public concern over crime, conservatives made *Miranda* a symbol of the judicial "coddling" of criminals.

Richard Nixon, who had campaigned for president as an opponent of the Warren Court, promised to appoint judges who would "apply" rather than "make" the law. Before the 1968 election, Chief Justice Warren had announced his resignation, and the victorious Nixon was therefore able to appoint a moderately conservative Republican, Warren Burger, as chief justice. Later, he appointed three new associate justices to the Supreme Court—Harry Blackmun, William Rehnquist, and Lewis Powell.

Considerable discussion focused on how this new "Burger Court" would address the relationship between social welfare programs and the issue of constitutionally protected rights. Seeking to extend Warren Court decisions on equal protection of the laws, activist lawyers argued that access to adequate economic assistance from the federal government should be recognized as a national right every bit as fundamental as, say, the right to vote. Many observers predicted that the Court might soon take this step. In 1970, however, in *Dandridge* v. *Williams*, the Court rejected the argument that laws capping the amount a state would pay to welfare recipients violated the constitutional requirement that the government cannot deny equal protection of the laws to all citizens. The Court drew a sharp distinction between the government's responsibility to respect the individual liberties of all citizens, such as the right to vote and freedom of speech, and its discretionary ability to make distinctions in the administration of spending programs such as AFDC. In short, the Court refused to hold, as a matter of constitutional law, that welfare was a national right.

Another controversial aspect of the rights debate involved issues of health and safety. A vigorous consumer rights movement, which had initially drawn inspiration from Ralph Nader's exposé about auto safety (*Unsafe at Any Speed*, 1965) and Rachel Carson's warnings about environmental and food safety (*Silent Spring*, 1962), continued to build support during the late 1960s and early 1970s. Consumer advocates lobbied for federal legislation to protect the right to safety in the workplace, the right to safe consumer products, and the right to a healthy environment. This effort, despite strong opposition from many business groups, found expression in such legislation as the Occupational Safety Act of 1973, stronger consumer protection laws, and measures to protect the environment (see chapter 30). The Burger Court invariably ruled laws of this type to be constitutional.

At the same time, a newly energized women's rights movement pushed its own set of rights-related issues. The National Organization for Women (NOW), founded in 1966, backed a constitutional change, an Equal Rights Amendment (ERA) that would explicitly guarantee women the same legal rights as men. After having been passed by Congress in 1972 and quickly ratified by more than half the states, the ERA suddenly became a controversial issue. Conservative women's groups, such as Phyllis Schlafly's "Stop ERA," charged that equal rights for women (including the right to equality within the military) would undermine traditional "family values." Anti-ERA rallies featured children carrying signs that read "Please Don't Send My Mommy to War." As a result of such opposition, the ERA, which once seemed assured of passage, failed to attain approval from the three-quarters of states needed for ratification. Ultimately, women's groups abandoned the ERA effort in favor of urging the courts to recognize equal rights on a case-by-case, issue-by-issue basis.

One of these specific issues, whether or not a woman could claim a constitutional right to terminate a pregnancy, became even more controversial than the ERA. In *Roe* v. *Wade* (1973), the Supreme Court ruled that a state law making abortion a criminal offense violated a woman's right of privacy. This decision outraged conservatives. Rally-

MARCH FOR WOMEN'S RIGHTS Massive demonstrations, especially in the nation's capital, became a familiar part of politics during the 1960s and early 1970s. Modeled on earlier civil rights and antiwar rallies, this 1970 march on Washington on behalf of women's rights helped give greater visibility to the issue of gender inequality.

ing under the "Right to Life" banner and focusing on the rights of the unborn fetus, antiabortion groups showed that political conservatives, as well as liberals and the left, could make powerful rights-based claims. Antiabortion forces labeled *Roe* v. *Wade* another threat to family values, and in 1976 they scored their first victory when Congress voted to ban the use of federal funds to finance abortions for women with low incomes. Standing behind the right to privacy—and behind the right of a woman to have access to a safe, medically supervised abortion—feminist groups made the issue of individual choice in reproductive decisions a principal rallying point.

Richard Nixon had promised an administration that, in contrast to Lyndon Johnson's, would "bring us together." Instead, bitter divisions over economic policies, government spending programs, and the meaning of constitutional rights made the Nixon presidency a period of increasing, rather than decreasing, polarization.

FOREIGN POLICY UNDER NIXON AND KISSINGER

Even as it wrestled with divisive domestic concerns, the Nixon administration was far more preoccupied with international affairs. Nixon appointed Henry Kissinger, a political scientist from Harvard, as his national security adviser. Under Kissinger, the National Security Council (NSC) emerged as the most powerful shaper of foreign policy within the government, eclipsing the State Department and its head, William Rogers. In 1973 Kissinger himself became secretary of state, a position that he continued to hold until 1977. Kissinger was the dominant personality of the Nixon and Gerald Ford administrations and one of the few top advisers who managed to remain unscathed by the scandals that ended Nixon's presidency. With Nixon, Kissinger orchestrated a grand strategy for foreign policy: détente with the Soviet Union, normalization of relations with China, and disengagement from direct military involvement in Southeast Asia and other parts of the world.

DÉTENTE

Although Nixon had built his political career on hard-line anticommunism, the Nixon-Kissinger team mapped a foreign policy that aimed at easing tensions with the two major communist nations, the Soviet Union and China. Kissinger surmised that, as both nations began to seek favor with the

United States, they might ease up on their support for North Vietnam, facilitating America's ability to withdraw from a divisive war.

Arms-control talks took top priority in U.S.–Soviet relations. In 1969 the two superpowers opened the Strategic Arms Limitation Talks (SALT). After several years of high-level diplomacy they signed an agreement (SALT I) that limited further development of both antiballistic missiles (ABMs) and offensive intercontinental ballistic missiles (ICBMs), although it failed to limit the number of warheads each missile could carry. Despite SALT I's dubious overall impact on the arms race, the very fact that the Soviet Union and the United States had concluded high-level discussions on arms control signaled a shift. Moreover, to promote an agreement on arms control, the Nixon administration took another step toward accommodation by offering the faltering Soviet economy greater access to U.S. trade and technology.

Nixon's overtures toward the People's Republic of China brought an even more dramatic break with the cold-war past. Nixon had been one of the most vocal critics of the communist regime established in China in 1949. Now, tentative conversations arranged through the embassies of both countries in Poland led to a slight easing of U.S. trade restrictions against China in early 1971 and to China's invitation for Americans to compete in a table tennis tournament. This celebrated exhibition prefaced more significant exchange. In 1972 Nixon himself visited China, posing for photos with Mao Zedong and strolling along the Great Wall. Relations between the two countries remained difficult, especially over the status of Taiwan, which the United States still recognized as the legitimate government of China. A few months after Nixon's visit, however, the United Nations admitted the People's Republic as the representative of China, and in 1973 the United States and China exchanged informal diplomatic missions.

VIETNAMIZATION

In Vietnam, Nixon and Kissinger decided to start the withdrawal of U.S. ground forces (the policy called "Vietnamization") while stepping up the air war and intensifying diplomatic efforts to reach a settlement. In July 1969, the president publicly announced the "Nixon Doctrine," which pledged that

> "*It is time for the preponderant majority, the responsible citizens of this country, to assert their rights. It is time to stop dignifying the immature actions of arrogant, reckless, inexperienced elements within our society. The reason is compelling. It is simply that their tantrums are insidiously destroying the fabric of American democracy.*
>
> *By accepting unbridled protest as a way of life, we have tacitly suggested that the great issues of our times are best decided by posturing and shouting matches in the streets. . . . If, in challenging, we polarize the American people, I say it is time for a positive polarization. . . . It is time to rip away the rhetoric and to divide on authentic lines. It is time to discard the fiction that in a country of 200 million people, everyone is qualified to quarterback the government. . . . The mature and sensitive people of this country must realize that their freedom of protest is being exploited by avowed anarchists and communists who detest everything about this country and want to destroy it.*"
>
> **VICE PRESIDENT SPIRO T. AGNEW**
> *in a 1969 dinner speech to fellow Republicans*

the United States would provide military assistance to anticommunist governments in Asia but would leave it to them to provide their own military forces.

The goal of Vietnamization was to withdraw U.S. ground troops without accepting compromise or defeat. Like Johnson before him, Nixon hoped that U.S. technology could bring military victory. While officially adhering to Johnson's 1968 bombing halt over the North, Nixon and Kissinger accelerated both the ground war and the air war by launching new offensives in South Vietnam and, in April 1970, by approving a military incursion into Cambodia, an ostensibly neutral country. Extending the war into Cambodia revealed how powerful Kissinger had become in shaping the nation's foreign policy. Both Secretary of State William Rogers and Secretary of Defense Melvin Laird had advised against such a drastic step.

The move set off a new wave of protest at home. Campuses exploded in anger, and bomb threats led many colleges to close early for the 1970 summer recess. White police officers fatally shot two students at the all-black Jackson State College in Mississippi, and National Guard troops at Kent State University in Ohio fired on demonstrators and killed four students. As growing numbers of protestors took to the streets, moderate business and political leaders became alarmed by how war issues were dividing the country. Further disillusionment with the war grew from revelations that, a month after Tet, troops led by U.S. Lieutenant William Calley had entered a small hamlet called My Lai and shot more than 200 people, mostly women and children. This massacre of South Vietnamese civilians became public in 1969; in 1971 a military court convicted Calley and, in a controversial decision, sentenced him to life imprisonment.

The Cambodian incursion of 1970 was part of a widening secret war in Cambodia and Laos. Although U.S. leaders denied that they were waging any such war, large areas of these agricultural countries came under American bombing. As the number of Cambodian refugees swelled and food supplies dwindled, the communist guerrilla force in Cambodia—the Khmer Rouge—grew into a well-disciplined army. The Khmer Rouge would later seize the government and, in a murderous attempt to eliminate potential dissent, turn Cambodia into a "killing field." While Nixon continued to talk about U.S. troop withdrawals and while peace negotiations with North Vietnam proceeded in Paris, the Vietnam War actually broadened into a war that destabilized all of Indochina.

Even greater violence was yet to come. In the spring of 1972 a North Vietnamese offensive approached within 30 miles of Saigon. U.S. generals warned of imminent defeat. Nixon responded by resuming the bombing of North Vietnam and by mining its harbors. Just weeks before the 1972 elec-

JACKSON STATE In 1970 the violence associated with America's longest war came home. In May, police gunfire killed 2 students and wounded 15 others at Jackson State University in Mississippi. This picture was taken through a bullet-riddled window in a women's dorm.

tion, Kissinger again promised peace and announced a cease-fire. After the election, however, the United States unleashed even greater firepower. In the so-called Christmas bombing of December 1972, the heaviest bombardment in history, B-52 bombers pounded North Vietnamese military and civilian targets around the clock.

By this time, however, much of the media, Congress, and the public had become sickened by the violence and apprehensive over the extent of government secrecy and surveillance at home. Low morale among some U.S. troops in the field began to threaten the military's combat effectiveness. In response, Nixon proceeded with full-scale Vietnamization of the war. In January 1973 North Vietnam and

Images That Shocked

The war in Indochina produced a spiral of violence that found its way back to the United States. Because the Vietnam conflict was fought without the kind of rigorous media censorship that had accompanied earlier wars, this violence became engraved in visual images more quickly than during any previous hostility. With camera crews and photojournalists filming nearly every aspect, Vietnam became a "living room war."

These three photos capture some of the most shocking images of violence from the era. In one, a military officer in the South Vietnamese army summarily executes a prisoner whom he suspects of being a member of the Viet Cong. This image made it more difficult for Washington to argue that America was fighting on the side of democracy and helped to stimulate doubts about the nation's moral stance in the war.

Similarly, the picture of small children, including a naked girl with terrible burns fleeing from a napalm attack, provided a particularly horrifying image of

the United States signed peace accords in Paris stipulating the withdrawal of U.S. troops. As American ground forces departed, the South Vietnamese government, headed by Nguyen Van Thieu, continued to fight, though it was growing increasingly demoralized and disorganized.

In the spring of 1975, nearly two years after the Paris accords, South Vietnam's army could no longer withstand the forces of North Vietnam's skilled general Nguyen Giap. Thieu's government collapsed, North Vietnamese armies entered Saigon, and U.S. helicopters scrambled to airlift the last remaining officials out of the besieged U.S. embassy. America's longest war ended in defeat.

THE AFTERMATH OF WAR

Between 1960 and 1973, approximately 3.5 million American men and women served in Vietnam:

58,000 died; 150,000 were wounded; 2,000 remained missing. In the aftermath of the long, costly war, many Americans struggled to understand why their country failed to prevail over a small, barely industrialized nation. Conservatives, arguing that the war had been lost at home, blamed the uncensored and irresponsible media, the coddling of dissenters, and the "failure of will" in Congress. The goals of the war, they believed, were laudable; politicians, afraid of domestic dissent and possible Chinese involvement, had set unrealistic limits on the war and thereby denied the military the means to attain victory. By contrast, those who had opposed the war stressed the overextension of American power, the misguided belief that the United States was unbeatable, the deceitfulness of governmental leaders, and the incompetence of bureaucratic processes. For them, the war had been in the wrong place and waged for the wrong reasons; and

how the war was being fought. The 9-year-old girl, Kim Phuc, suffered burns over 75 percent of her body, and an American doctor later performed plastic surgery. Now a Christian peace activist, she lives in Canada.

Among the many images of "the war at home," the third picture is easily the most famous. In it, a young woman, a teenage runaway who had become caught up in the antiwar movement, bends in anguish over the body of a college student killed by Ohio National Guard troops at Kent State University in 1970. The photo seemed to symbolize the feelings of distress and helplessness that many people experienced in confronting America's longest war.

the human costs to Indochina outweighed any possible gain.

Regardless of their positions on the war, most Americans could agree on one proposition: "No more Vietnams." Within the Pentagon, especially, the lesson of Vietnam was clear. The United States should avoid future military involvements lacking clear and compelling political objectives, demonstrable public support, and the provision of adequate means to accomplish the goal.

THE NIXON DOCTRINE

Although the Nixon Doctrine received its fullest articulation in the Vietnamization of the war in Indochina, Nixon and Kissinger extended its basic premise to other areas of the world. In molding foreign policy, Kissinger relied increasingly on pro-U.S. anticommunist allies to police their own regions of the world. Kissinger made it clear that the United States would not dispatch troops to oppose revolutionary insurgencies but would give generous assistance to anticommunist regimes or factions willing to fight the battle themselves.

During the early 1970s, America's cold-war strategy came to rely on supporting staunchly anticommunist regional powers: nations such as Iran under Shah Reza Pahlavi, South Africa with its apartheid regime, and Brazil with its repressive military dictatorship. All of these states built large military establishments trained by the United States. U.S. military assistance, together with covert CIA operations, also incubated and protected anticommunist dictatorships in South Korea, the Philippines, and much of Latin America. U.S. arms sales to the rest of the world skyrocketed from $1.8 billion in 1970 to $15.2 billion six years later. In one of its most controversial foreign policies, the Nixon administration employed covert action against the elected socialist government of Salvador Allende Gossens in Chile in 1970. After Allende took office, Kissinger gave top priority to encouraging destabilization of his government, and in 1973 Allende was overthrown by the Chilean military, who immediately suspended democratic rule and announced that Allende had committed suicide.

Critics charged that the United States, in the name of anticommunism, too often wedded its diplomatic fortunes to such questionable covert actions and unpopular military governments. In 1975 Senator Frank Church conducted widely publicized Senate hearings into possible abuses by the CIA (including the action in Chile). Supporters of the Nixon Doctrine, however, applauded the administration for strengthening a system of allies and for its tough anticommunism. In many circles, Nixon received high marks for a pragmatic foreign policy that combined détente toward the communist giants with containment directed toward the spread of revolutionary regimes.

THE WARS OF WATERGATE

Nixon's presidency ultimately collapsed as a result of a series of fateful decisions made in the president's own Oval Office. From the time Nixon entered the White House, he had been deeply suspicious of nearly every person and institution in Washington. He pressed the Internal Revenue Service to harass prominent Democrats with expensive audits and suspected the IRS of disloyalty when it seemed to be moving too slowly. Nixon's suspicions centered on antiwar activists and old political opponents but even extended to likely allies, such as J. Edgar Hoover, the staunchly conservative director of the FBI. Isolated behind a close-knit group of advisers, Nixon ultimately set up his own secret intelligence unit, which operated out of the White House.

During the summer of 1971 Daniel Ellsberg, a dissident member of the national security bureaucracy, leaked to the press a top-secret history of U.S. involvement in the Vietnam War, subsequently known as the "Pentagon Papers." Nixon responded by seeking, unsuccessfully, a court injunction to stop publication of the study and, more ominously, by unleashing his secret intelligence unit, now dubbed "the plumbers," to stop informa-

tion leaks to the media. Looking for materials that might discredit Ellsberg, the plumbers burglarized his psychiatrist's office. Thus began a series of "dirty tricks" and outright crimes, often financed by funds illegally solicited for Nixon's 1972 reelection campaign, that would culminate in the political scandal and constitutional crisis known as "Watergate."

THE ELECTION OF 1972

As the 1972 election approached, Nixon's political strategists worried that economic troubles and the war in Vietnam might deny the president reelection. Creating a campaign organization separate from that of the Republican Party, with the ironic acronym of CREEP (Committee to Re-Elect the President), they secretly raised millions of dollars, much of it from illegal contributions.

As the 1972 campaign proceeded, Nixon's chances of reelection dramatically improved. An assassination attempt crippled George Wallace, thereby preventing a possible drain of conservative voters. Meanwhile, Democratic Senator Edmund Muskie of Maine, hoping to translate his impressive showing as Hubert Humphrey's running mate in 1968 into a presidential bid of his own, made a series of blunders (some of them, perhaps, precipitated by Republican "dirty tricksters") that derailed his campaign. Eventually, Senator George McGovern of South Dakota, an outspoken opponent of the Vietnam War, won the Democratic nomination.

McGovern never seriously challenged Nixon. McGovern called for higher taxes on the wealthy, a guaranteed minimum income for all Americans, amnesty for Vietnam War draft resisters, and the decriminalization of marijuana—positions significantly to the left of the views of many traditional Democrats. In foreign policy, McGovern called for deep cuts in defense spending and for vigorous efforts to achieve peace in Vietnam—positions that Nixon successfully portrayed as signs of weakness.

Nixon won an easy victory in November. McGovern lost traditional Democrats without attracting a significant number of new or disaffected voters. The president received the electoral college votes of all but one state and the District of Columbia, won more than 60 percent of the popular vote, and carried virtually every traditional Democratic bloc except the African American vote. His margin of victory was one

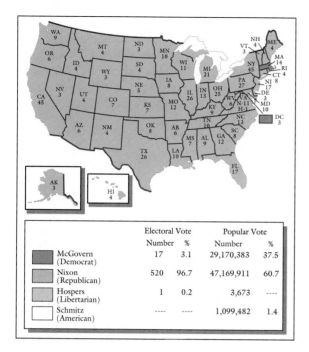

	Electoral Vote		Popular Vote	
	Number	%	Number	%
McGovern (Democrat)	17	3.1	29,170,383	37.5
Nixon (Republican)	520	96.7	47,169,911	60.7
Hospers (Libertarian)	1	0.2	3,673	----
Schmitz (American)	----	----	1,099,482	1.4

PRESIDENTIAL ELECTION, 1972

of the largest in U.S. history, only slightly below that of Johnson's 1964 landslide. Although the Twenty-sixth Amendment, ratified a year before the election, had lowered the voting age to 18, relatively few of the newly enfranchised voters cast ballots.

NIXON PURSUED

In achieving victory, however, the president's team left a trail of corruption that helped to cut short Nixon's second term. In June 1972 a surveillance team with links to both CREEP and the White House had been arrested while fine-tuning eavesdropping equipment that it had earlier installed in the Democratic Party's headquarters in Washington's Watergate office complex. Nixon's spokespeople dismissed the Watergate break-in as an insignificant "third-rate burglary"; in private, the president and his inner circle immediately launched a cover-up. They paid hush money to the Watergate burglars and had the CIA falsely warn the FBI that any investigation into the break-in would jeopardize national security.

While reporters from the *Washington Post* pursued the taint of scandal around the White House,

Congress and the federal judiciary sought evidence of possible violations of the law. In January 1973 Judge John Sirica, a Republican appointee who was presiding over the trial of the Watergate burglars, refused to accept their claim that neither CREEP nor the White House had been involved in the break-in. While Sirica pushed for more information, Senate leaders convened a special Watergate Committee, headed by North Carolina's conservative Democratic Senator Sam Ervin, to investigate the 1972 campaign. Meanwhile, federal prosecutors uncovered evidence that seemed to link key administration and White House figures, including John Mitchell, Nixon's former attorney general and later the head of CREEP, to illegal activities.

Nixon's political and legal difficulties grew steadily worse during 1973. Under unyielding pressure from Judge Sirica in March, one of the Watergate burglars, a former CIA operative working for CREEP, finally broke his silence. By May, he joined other witnesses who testified before the Senate's Watergate Committee about various illegal activities committed by CREEP and the White House. Nixon's closest aides were soon called before the committee, and the hearings became the biggest political soap opera since the Army-McCarthy hearings of 1954. John Dean, who had been Nixon's chief legal counsel, gave testimony that linked the president himself to an attempt to cover-up Watergate and to other illegal activities.

Along the way, Senate investigators discovered that a voice-activated taping machine had recorded every conversation held in Nixon's Oval Office. Now it was possible to determine whether the president or Dean, Nixon's primary accuser, was lying. Nixon claimed an "executive privilege" to keep these tapes from being released to other branches of government, but Judge Sirica, Archibald Cox (who had been appointed as a special, independent prosecutor in the Watergate case), and Congress all launched legal moves to gain access to them.

If Nixon's own problems were not enough, his vice president, Spiro Agnew, resigned in October 1973 after pleading "no contest" to income tax evasion. He agreed to a plea-bargain arrangement in order to avoid prosecution for having accepted illegal kickbacks while he was in Maryland politics. Acting under the Twenty-fifth Amendment (ratified in 1967), Nixon appointed—and both houses of Congress confirmed—Representative Gerald Ford of Michigan, a Republican Party stalwart, as the new vice president.

NIXON'S FINAL DAYS

By early summer of 1974, the nation's legal-constitutional system was closing in on Nixon, and the president's attempts to sidetrack his pursuers only rebounded against him. During the previous autumn, for example, Nixon had clumsily orchestrated the firing of Archibald Cox, hoping to prevent the special prosecutor from gaining access to the White House tapes. When this rash action raised a public outcry—the affair came to be known as Nixon's "Saturday Night Massacre"—the president was obliged to appoint another independent prosecutor, Leon Jaworski, who proved as tenacious as Cox. Similarly, Nixon's own release of edited, and occasionally garbled, transcripts of a series of Watergate-related conversations only helped to increase demands for the original tape recordings. Finally, by announcing that he would only obey a "definitive" Supreme Court decision on the tapes' legal status, Nixon all but invited the justices to deliver a unanimous ruling. And on July 24, 1974, the Court did just that in the case of *U.S.* v. *Nixon.* By this time, Nixon was in desperate straits. The Supreme Court unanimously ruled that Nixon's claim of "executive privilege" over the tapes could not justify his refusal to release evidence needed in a criminal investigation, and the Judiciary Committee of the House of Representatives prepared for a vote on impeachment.

At the end of July, only a few loyalists supported Nixon. After nearly a full week of televised deliberations, a majority of the House Judiciary Committee voted three formal articles of impeachment against the president for obstruction of justice, violation of constitutional liberties, and refusal to produce evidence requested during the impeachment process. Nixon boasted that he would fight these accusations before the Senate, the body authorized by the Constitution (Article I, Section 3) to render a verdict of guilty or innocent after the House votes impeachment.

Nixon's aides, however, were already orchestrating his departure. One of his own attorneys had discovered that a tape Nixon had been withholding contained the long-sought "smoking gun." It confirmed that during a 1972 conversation Nixon himself had agreed to a plan by which the CIA would advance the fraudulent claim of national security in order to stop the FBI from investigating the Watergate burglary. At this point, Nixon's secretary of defense ordered military commanders to ignore any order from the president, their titular commander in chief, unless the secretary had countersigned it. Abandoned by almost every prominent Republican and confronted by a Senate prepared to vote him guilty on the impeachment charges, Nixon went on television on August 8, 1974, to announce that he would resign from office. On August 9, Gerald Ford became the nation's 38th president.

In 1974, most people told pollsters that Watergate was one of the gravest crises in the history of the republic and that the Nixon administration had posed a serious threat to constitutional government. As time passed, though, the public's recollection and knowledge of the Watergate illegalities and Nixon's forced resignation faded. Opinion polls conducted on the 20th anniversary of Nixon's resignation suggested that most Americans retained only a dim memory of Watergate.

One reason for the fading memory of Watergate may be that although nearly a dozen members of the Nixon administration—including its chief law enforcement officer, John Mitchell—were convicted of criminal activities, the president himself escaped punishment. Only a month after Nixon's resignation, Gerald Ford granted Nixon an unconditional presidential pardon. The nation was spared the spectacle of witnessing a former president undergoing a lengthy, perhaps divisive trial; but it was also denied an authoritative accounting, in a court of law, of the full range of Nixon's misdeeds.

Another reason may be the popular penchant for linking the Watergate label to nearly every political scandal of the post-Nixon era. The suffix *–gate* became attached to grave constitutional episodes (such as Ronald Reagan's "Iran-Contragate" affair) and to the most trivial of political events (such as the brief "Nannygate" controversy that eliminated one of Bill Clinton's nominees for attorney general in 1993). And in light of the impeachment trial of Bill Clinton in 1998, the Watergate events of 1973 and 1974 could seem, to many people, as just another example of partisan political warfare rather than as a uniquely serious constitutional crisis.

Finally, what the historian Stanley Kutler calls the "wars of Watergate" increasingly seem part of the broader upheaval and loss that grew out of America's longest war. In this sense, the Watergate episode tends to blend into a broader picture of political, social, economic, and cultural turmoil that emerged during the lengthy, increasingly divisive war in Southeast Asia.

CONCLUSION

The national government expanded its powers during the 1960s. Lyndon Johnson's Great Society created a blueprint for an expanding welfare state and his War on Poverty. The Great Society, however, was quickly overshadowed by Johnson's escalation of the war in Vietnam, a struggle that consumed increasingly more of the nation's wealth in order to prevent a communist victory in Southeast Asia.

This growth of domestic social programs and the waging of war abroad prompted debates about governmental power that polarized the country. During Johnson's term, both the war effort and the economy faltered, top leaders became discredited, and his once promising presidency collapsed. His Republican successor, Richard Nixon, in trying to control the divisions at home, prompted a constitutional crisis that forced him to resign from office. The exalted hopes of the early 1960s—that the U.S. government would be able to promote liberty and equality both in America and throughout the rest of the world—ended in frustration and defeat.

The era of America's longest war was a time of high political passion, of generational and racial conflict, of differing definitions of patriotism. It saw the growth of an antiwar movement, along with the emergence of youthful dissent, of Black Power, of "women's liberation," and of contests over what should constitute the basic rights of citizenship. Different people invoked different explanations of the failures of both the Great Society and the war effort, and the divisions from these years shaped the fault lines of politics for years to come. Most Americans, however, became much more skeptical, many even cynical, about the possibility of further enlarging the power of the federal government in the name of expanding liberty and equality.

Suggested Readings begin on page SR-1.
For Web activities and resources
related to this chapter, go to
http://www.harcourtcollege.com/history.murrin

CHAPTER 30

ECONOMIC AND SOCIAL CHANGE IN THE LATE 20TH CENTURY

STAYING CONNECTED

Cafes featuring access to the Internet became another sign of the technological revolution.

At the beginning of the 21st century, historians tried to assess several decades of remarkable economic and cultural changes. The 1960s—marked by political assassinations, a lengthy foreign war, and domestic turmoil—had once seemed a period peculiar for its upheavals. In fact, the decades that followed brought even more far-reaching, although less violent, changes. Increasing immigration, urbanization, and movement of people southward and westward altered the demographics of American life. A transformation from manufacturing to postindustrial employment swept the economy. A digital revolution transfigured systems of information and entertainment. Social movements associated with environmentalism, women's rights, gay pride, racial and ethnic solidarity, and the New Right affected both politics and how Americans defined themselves.

This chapter will focus on the following major questions:

- What major demographic changes characterized the last three decades of the twentieth century, and how did they change American life?
- What were the most important technological and economic trends, and why did these create both new problems and new possibilities?
- How did new forms of media change the ways in which people received information and entertainment?
- How have the various social movements of the post-1960s era affected society, culture, and the ways in which people see their own personal identity?

A CHANGING PEOPLE

In demographic terms, the post-1970 period marked a watershed in American life. The population was becoming older, more urban, and more ethnically and racially diverse. Moreover, the nation's center of power was shifting away from the Northeast and toward the South and West.

AN AGING POPULATION

After about 1970 the birthrate slowed dramatically. During the 1950s, the height of the baby boom, the population had grown by 1.8 percent a year; during the 1970s and 1980s, even with a new wave of immigration and longer life expectancy, the growth rate slowed to about 1 percent a year. Birthrates sank

CHRONOLOGY

1965 Congress passes Immigration Act of 1965

1968 Indian Bill of Rights enacted by Congress

1969 The Stonewall Inn raid inaugurates new phase in gay and lesbian activism

1970 First Earth Day observed • Environmental Protection Act passed • Clean Air Act passed • Congressional Black Caucus organized

1973 *Roe* v. *Wade* decision upholds women's right to abortion • Endangered Species Act passed • Sudden rise in oil prices as result of OPEC influence

1975 National Conservative Action Political Committee formed

1980 Microsoft licenses its first personal computer software

1981 MTV and CNN debut

1985 Supreme Court rules that home taping of TV programs does not violate copyright law

1986 Immigration Reform and Control Act toughens laws against employing undocumented immigrants • Supreme Court holds that sexual harassment qualifies as discrimination

1987 Alan Bloom's *Closing of the American Mind* published

1988 Congress enacts Indian Gaming Regulation Act • Fox television network debuts

1990 Immigration Act revises conditions for admittance • Census designates "Asian or Pacific Islanders" as single, pan-Asian category

1991 Clarence Thomas confirmation hearings highlight issue of sexual harassment • Catch-phrase "surfing the Internet" is coined

1992 "Earth Summit" held in Brazil

1993 Cesar Chavez dies • Number of Internet sites passes the 100,000 mark

1995 Million Man March takes place in Washington, D.C. • Federal Building in Oklahoma City bombed • Dial-in Internet services begin

1996 O. J. Simpson acquitted of murder • Opponents of affirmative action pass Proposition 209 in California

1997 Golfer Tiger Woods wins Masters

1998 E-commerce begins in earnest • Chrysler and Daimler merge

1999 E-commerce and dot-com stocks surge

2000 Last census of 20th century conducted • Elian Gonzalez controversy highlights immigration issues • Many dot-com enterprises collapse

2001 People classified as "non-Hispanic whites" no longer a majority of California's population • America Online merges with Time-Warner

to their lowest levels in U.S. history, except for the Great Depression decade of the 1930s. Most young people were delaying marriage until well into their twenties, and the number of women in their mid-thirties who had never married tripled between 1970 and 1990 to 16 percent.

As a result of declining birthrates, rising life expectancy, and the aging of the baby boom generation, the median age of the population rose steadily. In 1970, at the height of student protests and the youth culture, the median age of Americans was 28; by 2000 it had risen to 34. Advertising agencies and television serials turned to midlife appeals. As aging baby boomers pondered retirement, policymakers grew concerned that the projected Social Security and Medicare payouts would bequeath a staggering cost burden to the smaller post–baby boom generation of workers. Trend-watchers of the 1960s had talked of a "youth revolt"; at the turn of the century they talked about the "graying of America."

THE RISE OF THE SUNBELT

Not only did population growth slow, but the regional pattern of population distribution began to shift political and economic power within the country. Historically, European settlement had proceeded from east to west. The nation's political capital was in the East, and so were its financial, industrial, and cultural centers. Between 1970 and 2000, however, 90 percent of the nation's population growth occurred in the South and the West. The 1980 census reported for the first time that more Americans lived in the South and the West than in the North and the East. From 1940 on, Nevada, California, Florida, Arizona, and (after 1959) Alaska were the fastest-growing states, and by 1990 more than 1 in 10 Americans lived in California. During the 1990s, Nevada enlarged its population by an astonishing 66 percent.

The population shift tilted the regional balance of national political power. In 1990 and 2000 California gained eight seats in the House of Representatives, Florida added six, New York lost five, and several other northeastern states lost two or three. The focus of electoral politics shifted from the northeastern states to Florida, Texas, and California.

Many reasons accounted for this demographic shift. One was the availability of affordable air-conditioning for homes and offices. Another was the rise of tourism and the proliferation of new retirement communities in Nevada, California, Arizona, and Florida. Also, lower labor costs and the absence of strong unions prompted manufacturers to build new plants and relocate old ones in the Sunbelt. Equally important was the growth of high-tech industries, initially tied to cold war military-industrial spending and to the computer revolution. Santa Clara County, a rural area near San Francisco, exemplified the trend. Experiencing spectacular growth of its new semiconductor industry and its network of electronics-related suppliers, this area came to be called "Silicon Valley." It doubled its population each decade after 1940 and boasted one of the highest median family incomes in the country.

Government spending on the space program also helped shift research and technology to the Sunbelt. After the Soviet Union launched its Sputnik satellite in 1957, the United States stepped up its own space program under the newly formed National Aeronautics and Space Administration (NASA). In 1961 President Kennedy announced plans for the Apollo program, promising a manned mission to the moon by 1970. In July 1969 astronauts Neil Armstrong and Edwin ("Buzz") Aldrin stepped from their spacecraft onto the moon, planted the American flag, and gathered 47 pounds of lunar rocks for later study. Apollo flights continued until 1972, when NASA turned to the development of a space station, an earth-orbiting platform from which to conduct experiments and research. In the 1980s NASA began launching a series of "space shuttles," manned craft that served as scientific laboratories and could be flown back to earth for reuse. This progression of ever more innovative advances in space technology, led from NASA's operations in Texas and Florida, spurred economic development in the Sunbelt states.

LINK TO THE PAST

Who Are We Americans?

http://www.census.gov

Every 10 years, the U.S. Census Bureau conducts a count of all Americans and compiles statistical data about their lives. The Internet makes this array of demographic, social, and economic information easily accessible to all.

Browse the site to see what kind of information you can find here and consider the following questions.

1. Detailed information from the 2000 Census will be issued between 2001 and 2003. Go to "News-Releases" to discover the most recently released data. How does this data confirm or alter the various demographic trends described in this chapter?

2. Type in the name of your state under "Quick Facts." How does your state compare to the national average in population growth, racial and ethnic composition, education, homeownership, median income, and poverty?

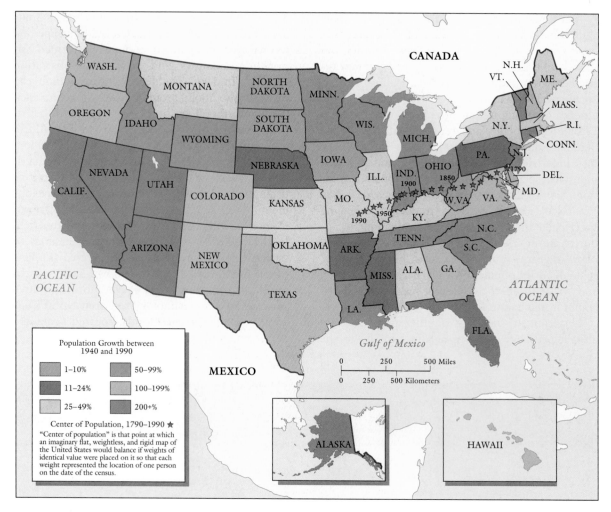

POPULATION SHIFTS TOWARD THE "SUNBELT"

NEW IMMIGRATION

Another reason for the sharp rise in the Sunbelt population was a dramatic increase in immigration. Before 1960, most immigrants had come from Europe and entered the country through the cities of the Northeast. During the 1970s and 1980s, however, 10 million immigrants from Asia and Latin America arrived in the United States, six times the number of European immigrants arriving over the same period. (If illegal immigrants were included, the count would be far higher.) Preliminary estimates from the 2000 census indicated that during the decade of the 1990s alone, both immigration and natural increase raised the nation's Asian and Pacific Islander population 43 percent to 10.8 million and its Hispanic population nearly 39 percent to 31.3 million. These new first- and second-generation immigrants rapidly changed the face of America.

The largest number of non-European immigrants came from Mexico. Many Americans of Mexican ancestry, of course, were not recent immigrants; perhaps 80,000 Mexicans were living in the Southwest when the United States annexed northern Mexico in 1848. Immigration into the United States, however, became significant in the 20th century, spurred by the Mexican revolution after 1910 (see chapter 24) and responding to U.S. labor

REGIONAL SHIFTS IN CONGRESS

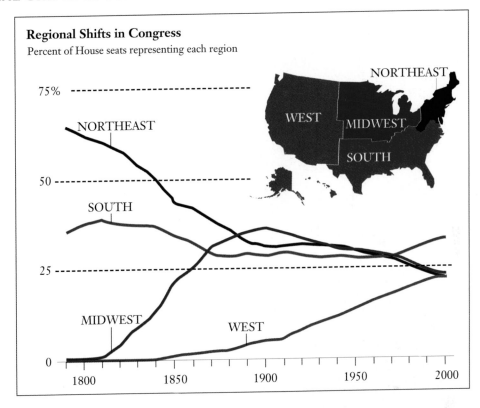

Regional Shifts in Congress
Percent of House seats representing each region

Source: Clerk of the House.

shortages during the First World War, the Second World War, and the Korean War. In every decade of the postwar period, both legal and illegal immigration from Mexico rose substantially. Many migrants came as seasonal agricultural workers; many others formed permanent communities. Ninety percent of all Mexican Americans lived in the Southwest, primarily in Texas and California.

Although Mexican Americans comprised the majority of the Spanish-speaking population across the country in the late 20th century, Puerto Ricans were more numerous on the East Coast. The United States annexed Puerto Rico after the Spanish-American War of 1898 (see chapter 22) and in 1917 granted U.S. citizenship to its inhabitants. Puerto Ricans, therefore, were not really immigrants but could come and go freely from island to mainland. Before the Second World War, the Puerto Rican population in the United States was small and centered in New York City. After the war, however, ingress rose significantly (see chapter 28). By the 1970s, more Puerto Ricans were living in New York City than in San Juan, Puerto Rico's capital. Sizable Puerto Rican communities also developed in Chicago and in industrial cities in New England and Ohio. U.S. economic problems during the 1970s decreased migration from Puerto Rico and increased the number of people who returned to the island, but trends reversed during the 1980s and 1990s. By 2000, the Puerto Rican population on the U.S. mainland had grown to about three million, compared to a population of nearly four million in Puerto Rico itself.

Cubans began immigrating in large numbers as a result of Fidel Castro's revolution. In 1962 the U.S. Congress designated the upper- and middle-class

LITTLE HAVANA Vibrant ethnic neighborhoods, such as Miami's "Little Havana," offered tangible evidence of the nation's new, multicultural composition at the end of the 20th century.

Cubans who were fleeing from Castro's regime to South Florida as refugees eligible for admittance. Over the next 30 years, 800,000 Cubans from every strata of society came to the United States. In 1995, an agreement with Castro brought the first U.S. restrictions on the flow of immigrants from Cuba. Although immigrants began settling outside of South Florida, particularly in New Jersey, the Miami metropolitan area remained the center of Cuban American life. Sociologists called Miami a "true ethnic enclave," a community that provided cradle-to-grave Cuban-owned services for residents of Cuban origin. By 2000, about half of all Miamians were of Cuban descent.

By the beginning of the 21st century, the number of Spanish-speaking people in the United States totaled more than in all but four countries of Latin America. Los Angeles was the second largest "Mexican city," after Mexico City; its Salvadoran population was about the same as that of San Salvador. More Puerto Ricans lived in New York City as in San Juan, and the Big Apple's Dominican population equaled that of Santo Domingo. The most popular name for baby boys in California and Texas was José.

The Immigration Act of 1965, one of the least controversial but ultimately most important pieces of President Lyndon Johnson's Great Society legislation, sharply altered national immigration policy. Since the 1920s, rates of immigration had been determined by quotas based on national origins (see chapter 24). The 1965 act ended these quotas and, although largely unforeseen at the time, laid the basis not only for a resumption of high-volume immigration but also for a substantial shift in region of origin. The law placed a ceiling of 20,000 immigrants for every country, gave preference to those with close family ties in the United States, and accorded priority to those with special skills and those classified as "refugees." Under the new act, large numbers of people immigrated from Korea, China, the Philippines, the Dominican Republic, Colombia, and the Middle East. In the aftermath of the Vietnam War, Presidents Ford and Carter ordered the admittance of many Vietnamese, Cambodians, Laotians, and Hmong (an ethnically distinct people who inhabited lands extending across the borders of all three countries) who had assisted the United States during the war and whose families were consequently in peril.

In response to the growing number of refugees, Congress passed the Refugee Act of 1980. It specified that political refugees, "those fleeing overt persecution," would be admitted but that refugees who were seeking simply to improve their economic lot would be denied entry. In practice, the terms "political" and "economic" tended to be interpreted so that people fleeing communist regimes were admitted but those fleeing right-wing oppression were turned away or deported. For example, Cubans and Soviet Jews were admitted, but Haitians were often denied immigrant status. (The number of Haitians

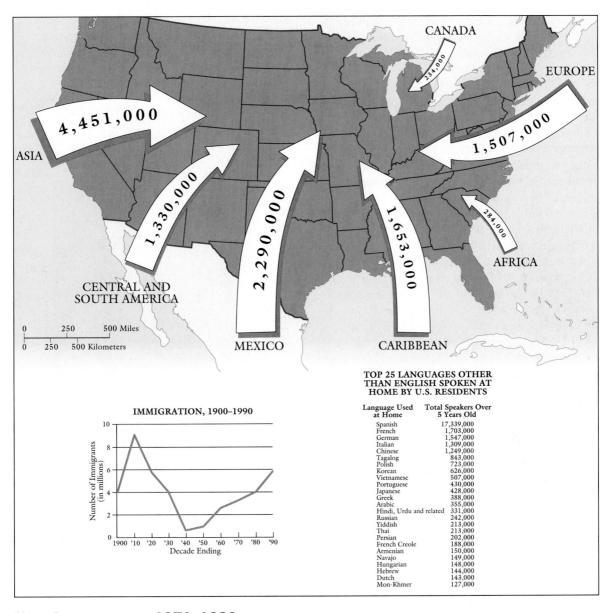

TOP 25 LANGUAGES OTHER
THAN ENGLISH SPOKEN AT
HOME BY U.S. RESIDENTS

Language Used at Home	Total Speakers Over 5 Years Old
Spanish	17,339,000
French	1,703,000
German	1,547,000
Italian	1,309,000
Chinese	1,249,000
Tagalog	843,000
Polish	723,000
Korean	626,000
Vietnamese	507,000
Portuguese	430,000
Japanese	428,000
Greek	388,000
Arabic	355,000
Hindi, Urdu and related	331,000
Russian	242,000
Yiddish	213,000
Thai	213,000
Persian	202,000
French Creole	188,000
Armenian	150,000
Navajo	149,000
Hungarian	148,000
Hebrew	144,000
Dutch	143,000
Mon-Khmer	127,000

NEW IMMIGRANTS, 1970–1990

entering the United States illegally, however, rose rapidly.) Many Guatemalans and Salvadorans, leaving repressive military governments backed by the United States during the 1980s, stood little chance of being admitted as legal immigrants. Thousands, however, entered illegally, some helped by a church-based "sanctuary movement" that opposed U.S. policies in Central America.

Illegal immigration became a major political issue during the mid-1980s, and Congress passed an immigration law designed to tighten enforcement. The Immigration Reform and Control Act of 1986 imposed stricter penalties on businesses employing illegal aliens, while granting residency to workers who could prove that they had been living in the United States since 1982. Although this law may have temporarily reduced the number of undocumented immigrants entering the country, its effectiveness soon dwindled.

The booming economy of the 1990s acted as a magnet for new immigrants and, with prosperity and labor shortages, fear of newcomers abated along with political pressures for stronger controls. Old sources of illegal immigration from Latin America and new ones, especially from China, continued to transform the American population. The Immigration Act of 1990 raised the number of immigrants legally admitted on the basis of special job skills or investment capital.

California, especially, became a microcosm of world cultures. In 1980, eight of every ten Californians were classified as non-Hispanic whites. By 2001, however, this group no longer constituted a majority. Fewer than half of Los Angeles schoolchildren were proficient in English, and some 80 different languages were spoken in L.A. homes.

In 1990 a new museum opened in the former immigrant reception center on Ellis Island in New York harbor. It celebrated America's immigrant origins at the same time that the nation was once again being reshaped by newcomers. Like the wave of immigration that had peaked shortly after 1900, the immigration of the late 20th century roused not only ethnic rivalries and tensions but also hope and cooperation.

DECREASING NUMBER OF FARMERS, 1940–1990 *During the late 20th century, Americans continued to leave farms and small towns for cities and suburbs. In 1990 only a few states retained a preponderance of rural population.*

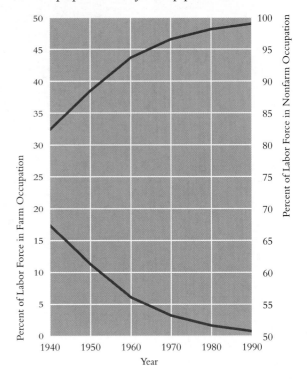

URBANIZATION AND SUBURBANIZATION

Urban-suburban demographics, too, were in a state of flux. In 1990 nearly 80 percent of Americans were living in metropolitan areas. As those areas continued to expand, the relationship between central city and adjacent suburbs changed. The suburbs melded into "urban corridors," metropolitan strips often running between older cities, as between Los Angeles and San Diego, Washington and Baltimore, Seattle and Tacoma, or into "edge cities," former suburban areas such as the Galleria area west of Houston, the Perimeter Center south of Atlanta, and Tysons Corner near Washington, D.C. They came to rival the cities themselves as centers of business and population.

Meanwhile, central cities transformed. As retail shopping fled to suburban malls, central cities became primarily financial, administrative, and enter-

tainment centers. During the 1970s and 1980s, the percentage of upper- and middle-income residents within city boundaries fell, and tax bases declined at the same time that an influx of low-income populations placed greater demands on public services. Higher rates of homelessness and crime, together with deteriorating schools and urban infrastructures (such as sewer and water systems), plagued most large cities. Big-city mayors complained about the decline of federal funding, which decreased from $64 per urban resident in 1980 to less than $30 per resident by 1993.

The dramatic economic boom of the 1990s helped revive many central cities. Crime rates and policing improved, building boomed, and more and more people seemed to desire the amenities of an urban lifestyle with shorter commutes. Still, the population growth of urban corridors continued to outpace that of traditional cities. Urban sprawl,

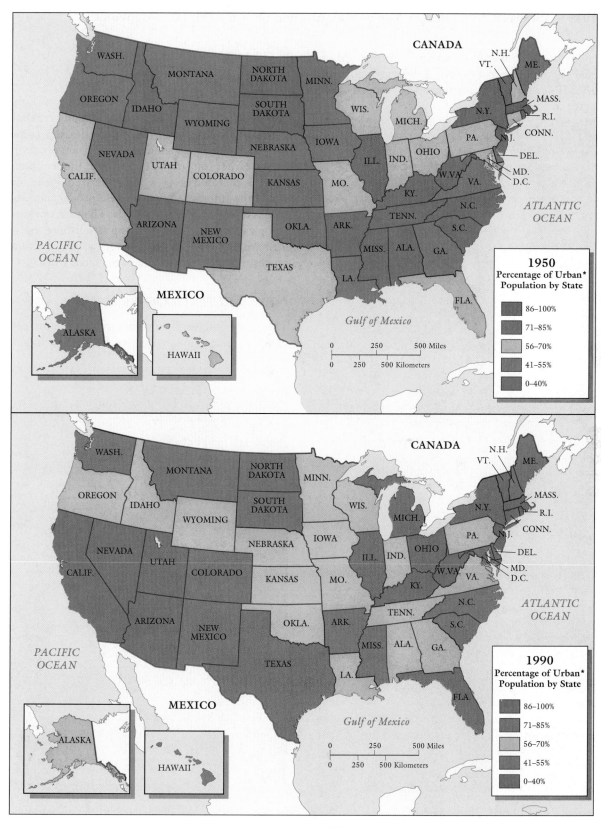

URBANIZATION OF AMERICAN LIFE, 1950–1990

1950
Percentage of Urban*
Population by State

86–100%
71–85%
56–70%
41–55%
0–40%

1990
Percentage of Urban*
Population by State

86–100%
71–85%
56–70%
41–55%
0–40%

traffic, and affordable housing remained major challenges. Between 1997 and 1999 the number of affordable apartments in urban areas dropped by 13 percent.

ECONOMIC TRANSFORMATIONS

An American adult of the early 21st century would likely awake to a digital alarm clock, pop breakfast into a microwave oven, work at a desktop computer, and relax with a movie or television program taped earlier on the VCR, while the children amused themselves at a computerized game or surfed the Internet. None of these products or activities existed in the early 1960s. The pace of technological change had brought an astonishing transformation in consumer products, production processes, and the structure of the labor force.

NEW TECHNOLOGIES

The most noteworthy technological advances occurred in biotechnology, high-performance comput-

URBAN CORRIDORS These official California road maps from the 1940s and the 1990s show urbanization and the development of urban corridors in the Los Angeles area.

ing, and communications systems. After one of the most important research projects of the late twentieth century, scientists announced in June 2000 that they had successfully mapped the entire human genetic code. This Human Genome Project deepened scientists' understanding of genetic engineering and paved the way for new techniques of gene transfer, embryo manipulation, tissue regeneration, and even cloning. Such biotechnology promised new approaches to the treatment of cancer and genetically inherited diseases. Genetic manipulation in plants led to new experiments affecting farming, waste conversion, and toxic cleanup. At the same time, biotechnology advances contributed to fears about a decline in biodiversity, the variety of biological organisms. New ethical questions also arose about the role of science in manipulating reproduction.

The computer revolution, which began after the Second World War, entered a new phase during the 1970s, when the availability of microchips boosted computer hardware capability and reduced computer size and cost. Sales of home computers soared, led by a fledgling company, Apple, and by its formidable rival, IBM. High-performance computers with powerful memory capabilities and "parallel processors," which allow many operations to run simultaneously, began to transform both industry and information systems. Computerized factories and robotics heightened efficiency by lowering labor costs, making production schedules more flexible, and rendering obsolete the giant warehouses that had once held goods until they were shipped. "Artificial intelligence" capabilities emerged, along with voice interaction between people and machines.

Enhanced by new communications technologies such as fiber-optic networks and satellite transmission, the computer revolution fueled an "information revolution." Libraries replaced card catalogs with computer networks that easily link users to specialized national and international databases. Electronic mail, fax transmissions, voice mail, and the World Wide Web rapidly came to supplement posted (sometimes called "snail") mail and telephone conversations. Cellular phones became widespread. The variety of ways in which people could speedily communicate with other people or with information-bearing machines changed patterns of human interaction and work. "Telecommuting" from home became common as electronic networks made it less necessary for workers to appear in person at an office.

BIG BUSINESS

Computerized communications helped transform ways of doing business by enabling the growth of electronic banking, far-flung business franchising, and huge globalized industries. Although buying on credit had been widespread in the United States since the 1920s, Bank of America's Visa credit card lifted credit-buying to new levels. From the 1970s on, use of bank-issued credit cards efficiently organized through computer systems mounted; by 1990, 4,000 bankcard issuers served 75 million cardholding customers. Private debt and personal bankruptcies also soared, and the rate of personal savings fell to the lowest in the industrialized world. Other innovations in electronic banking—automated teller machines (ATMs), checking (or debit) cards, automatic depositing, and electronic bill payment—moved Americans closer to a cashless economy where electronic codes substituted for currency. Sweeping deregulation of financial industries in the 1980s and 1990s permitted banking institutions and brokerage houses to offer similar financial services, which accelerated competition and innovation.

Franchising and "chain" stores also changed the way consumer products were bought and sold. McDonald's and Holiday Inn pioneered nationwide standardization in the fast-food and travel industries during the 1950s. Other chain restaurants soon copied the McDonald's model. Starbuck's parlayed a simple beverage, coffee, into a pricey designer commodity. And Sam Walton's successful Wal-Mart chain symbolized the transformation engulfing the entire retailing industry. Books, videotapes, records, electronics equipment, shoes, groceries, travel accommodations, and just about every other consumer item became available in nationwide or regional chains that brought a greater array of merchandise and lower prices but often crushed independent retailers in thousands of midsize towns across the country.

American chain businesses expanded overseas as well as at home. Especially after the collapse of communist regimes in the Soviet Union and Eastern Europe, chains rushed to supply consumers with long-denied, American-style goods and services.

MCDONALD'S IN MOSCOW Changes in the former Soviet Union and Eastern Europe created new opportunities for U.S.-based corporations. Hamburger lovers in Moscow quickly flocked to the golden arches of McDonald's.

McDonald's opened to great fanfare in Moscow and Budapest, while the Hilton chain quickly opened new hotels in Eastern European capitals. Pepsi and Coke carried their "cola wars" into foreign markets. Starbucks created a controversy when it opened a branch in Beijing's imposing Forbidden City.

Amazon.com led another branch of innovation—e-commerce (buying over the Internet). In 1999 a wave of new "dot-com" businesses promised to move more and more purchasing to the Internet, and the extravagant claims of their often-youthful entrepreneurs fueled a short-term bubble in dot-com stocks. In 2000 stock prices collapsed as dramatically as they had risen for most of these Internet retailers, and many of the new companies folded. Still, buying and selling on the Web, often within a global market, had become an important new feature of consumer culture.

Production, as well as consumption, turned global. U.S. automakers, for example, moved much of their production and assembly outside of the United States; by 1990 well over 50 percent of the sticker price on most "American" models went to foreign businesses and workers. Moreover, the trend toward privatization (the sale of government-owned industries to private business) in many economies worldwide provided American companies with new opportunities for acquisition. Foreign interests also purchased many U.S. companies and real estate holdings. In the early 1990s foreign corporations owned RCA, Doubleday, Mack Truck, Goodyear, and Pillsbury, among many other traditionally "American" brands. In the late 1990s German automaker Daimler merged with the venerable Chrysler Corporation. Even the entertainment industry, which the United States had dominated for decades, attracted significant foreign investment. A Japanese conglomerate, for example, temporarily owned Columbia Pictures during the early 1990s, and Mexico's Televiso took over U.S.-owned Univision in 1993. So many industrial giants had become global by the late 20th century that it was often difficult to define what constituted an American company or a foreign one. Drinking the most prominent brands of "Mexican" beer, after an acquisition in 1997, actually meant drinking a product of Anheuser-Busch. Assembling a Honda may have employed more U.S. workers than assembling a Pontiac.

POSTINDUSTRIAL RESTRUCTURING

New technologies and economic globalization brought structural changes to American business and the workforce. In the 1970s, citing pressure from international competition and declining profits, many companies cut their work forces and trimmed their management staffs in efforts to "downsize." More than a dozen major steel plants closed, and the auto industry laid off thousands of workers. In the 1980s and 1990s, the steel and auto industries regained profitability, but other sectors took their turn at downsizing. Business restructuring, together with the government's deregulation of major industries, touched off a merger boom. In the prosperity of the late 1990s, huge mergers, with acquisitions totaling more than 1.6 trillion dollars a year, brought a concentration in corporate power unseen since the 1890s. The 2001 merger of America Online with Time Warner, a company that had earlier acquired CNN, exemplified the new environment in which bigger seemed better.

As employment in traditional manufacturing and extractive sectors decreased, jobs in service, high technology, and information and entertainment sectors increased. By the end of the 1990s, unemployment fell to its lowest point in several decades, but the kinds of jobs Americans held had shifted. Computing and other high-tech jobs brought high salaries, but jobs in the expanding service sector—clerks, servers, cleaners—were largely low paid, part time, and nonunionized.

Union membership, always highest in the manufacturing occupations that comprised a decreasing proportion of jobs in the restructuring economy, fell to less than 15 percent of the labor force by the late 1990s. While union membership rolls and political power steadily slipped, efforts to expand the union movement into new sectors of the economy initially met with little success. For example, some union locals around the country attempted to organize clerical, restaurant, and hotel workers, sectors that employed many women, but businesses adamantly fought unionization, claiming that it would raise labor costs, and the AFL-CIO initially gave weak support to such organizing efforts, which they considered unlikely to succeed.

During the late 1960s and early 1970s Cesar Chavez's efforts to organize agricultural workers, who were largely of Mexican and Filipino descent, also dramatized the difficulties of expanding the union movement. Chavez, a charismatic leader who emulated the nonviolent tactics of Martin Luther King, Jr., vaulted the United Farm Workers (UFW) into public attention. As the union president, Chavez undertook a series of personal hunger strikes and instituted several well-publicized consumer boycotts of lettuce and grapes as means of pressuring growers to bargain with the UFW. He also established close ties with liberal Democrats in California and nationally and won a major contract victory in 1970. During the late 1970s and the 1980s, however, the UFW steadily lost ground. Strong stands by growers to keep out union organizers and the continued influx of new immigrants eager for work undercut the UFW's efforts. When Chavez died in April 1993, the UFW was struggling to rebuild its membership and regain bargaining power.

The major growth for organized labor came among government employees and workers in the health care industry. These gains, however, failed to offset union membership losses in the old industrial sectors.

Some economists warned that the shift to a "postindustrial" economy was "de-skilling" the labor force and putting people out of work because the jobs for which they were trained no longer existed. Might a globalized economy erode the living standards in America? Critics of the new trends expressed alarm over statistical evidence that well over half the new jobs created in the U.S. economy during the 1980s paid less than $7,000 per year. Moreover, the firms that provided temporary

PERCENTAGES OF GOODS-PRODUCING AND SERVICE-PRODUCING U.S. JOBS, 1920–2000

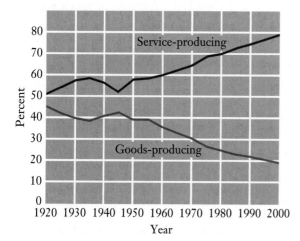

Source: U.S. Census Bureau.

workers to other businesses were among the largest employers in the country. Some analysts warned that the widening gulf between highly paid, highly skilled positions and minimum-wage jobs might ultimately undermine the middle-class nature of American society. By the late 1990s, the labor movement was trying to revitalize itself by making part-time work and improvement in real wages the centerpieces of new organizing efforts.

Other economists pointed out that internationalization and corporate downsizing might temporarily mean lost jobs for some people but that gains in productivity would eventually translate into lower consumer prices and rising living standards. Indeed, real wages did begin to rise in the 1990s. Moreover, new technologies created business opportunities for future generations. Celebrants of change could point to many success stories, especially in high-tech industries where innovation paved a broad avenue of upward economic mobility for those with computer-age skills.

In 1980, for example, a small company called Microsoft, headed by a young engineer named Bill Gates, licensed the software for a computer operating system called MS-DOS to IBM and to hundreds of companies who were manufacturing clones of IBM personal computers (PCs). MS-DOS became the standard operating system for PCs and, together with a succession of other software products, transformed Microsoft into one of America's most profitable corporations. In 1995 Bill Gates, with his boyish grin and shrewd business instincts, became the richest person in the world. Business analysts marveled at the meteoric growth of a company whose product had only been invented in 1980; one comic suggested that MS-DOS stood for "Microsoft Seeks Dominion Over Society." Although the Microsoft story clearly was exceptional, new high-tech businesses turned many computer mavens into millionaires and created more new jobs than the workforce could fill.

These revolutionary changes in technology and the economy had profound effects on the lives of Americans. Skilled workers of earlier generations had tended to stick to one profession or place of employment throughout their working life, but by the end of the 20th century, even middle-income professionals were likely to switch occupations several times before retiring. The need for training and retraining programs that served all ages of peo-

ple transformed ideas about education, as well as ideas about work.

THE ENVIRONMENT

The modern environmental movement began during the 1970s, but its roots reached back to earlier conservation and preservation movements. During the first four decades of the 20th century, the conservation movement promoted "wise use" of water, forests, and farmlands by urging government to promote scientific resource management and to designate areas as national parks and forests (see chapter 21). A preservation movement—led by the Sierra Club, the Audubon Society, the Wilderness Society, and others—was primarily concerned with the aesthetics of nature and wanted to protect and enjoy the natural environment in a state as pristine as possible. Landmark legislation during the 1960s—the Wilderness Act of 1964, the National Wild and Scenic Rivers Act of 1968, and the National Trails Act of 1968—set aside new areas, protecting them from development. Lady Bird Johnson, President Johnson's wife, championed a Commission on Natural Beauty that spurred the nation's growing interest in its natural habitat.

ENVIRONMENTAL ACTIVISM AND GOVERNMENT POLICY

The earlier conservation and preservation movements broadened into an "environmental movement" that focused on improving people's health and on maintaining ecological balances. In 1962 Rachel Carson had published *Silent Spring*, which warned that the pesticides used in agriculture, especially DDT, threatened bird populations. Air pollution in major cities such as Los Angeles became so bad that simply breathing urban air was equivalent to smoking several packs of cigarettes a day. Industrial processes polluted water systems, and atomic weapons testing and the proliferation of nuclear power plants increased fears of overexposure to radiation. In response to these concerns, environmentalists tried to focus national attention on toxic chemicals and the adverse impact of industrial development on air, water, and soil quality. The Environmental Defense Fund, a private organization formed in 1967, took the crusade against DDT and other dangerous toxins to the courts. And in 1970 activists came together for

AIR QUALITY IN LOS ANGELES: GOOD DAYS AND BAD During the 1960s, before the introduction of federal air-quality laws, a layer of thick smog that endangered public health hung over the Los Angeles basin 80 percent of the time. By the late 1990s, left, the bad old days seemed to be over. Yet, enough bad days still occurred, right, that during two of every five days the air quality level failed to meet minimum safety levels, despite the existence of pollution controls.

Earth Day, organized largely by college students, to raise awareness about environmental degradation and to popularize the science of ecology, a branch of biology that studies the interrelationships between living organisms and their physical environments.

During the early 1970s President Richard Nixon established the Environmental Protection Agency (EPA) and signed major pieces of environmental legislation: the Resources Recovery Act of 1970 (dealing with waste management), the Clean Air Act of 1970, the Water Pollution Control Act of 1972, the Pesticides Control Act of 1972, and the Endangered Species Act of 1973. National parks and wilderness areas were further expanded, and a new law required that "environmental impact statements" be prepared in advance of any major government project.

New standards brought some significant improvements. The Clean Air Act's restrictions on auto and smokestack emissions, for example, reduced six major airborne pollutants by one-third in a single decade. Lead emissions into the atmosphere declined by 95 percent. Still, the remedies could also create new problems. For example, requiring higher smokestacks helped clear smog out of city skies but also moved pollutants higher into the atmosphere, where they produced damaging "acid rain."

In the late 1970s families living at Love Canal, a housing development near Buffalo, New York, learned that the soil under their homes was contaminated by chemical wastes produced 30 years earlier. The finding explained why residents of the area

suffered from high levels of cancer and gave birth to children with genetic defects. The struggle to exact payment for the costs of resettlement and cleanup of such wastes from now-defunct companies prompted

DECLINING AIR POLLUTANT EMISSIONS, 1970–1991

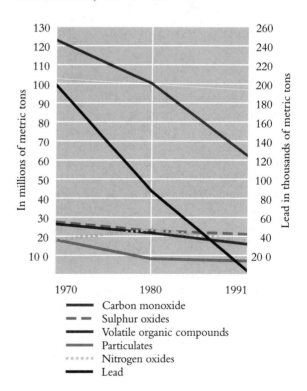

In millions of metric tons
130
120
110
100
90
80
70
60
50
40
30
20
10 0

Lead in thousands of metric tons
260
240
220
200
180
160
140
120
100
80
60
40
20 0

1970   1980   1991

— Carbon monoxide
- - Sulphur oxides
— Volatile organic compounds
— Particulates
···· Nitrogen oxides
— Lead

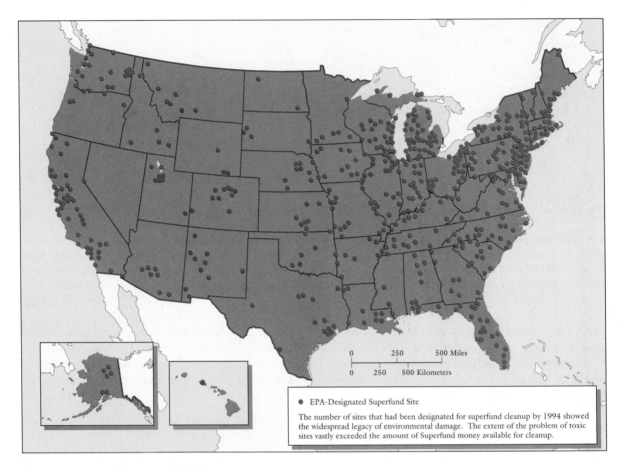

0   250   500 Miles

0   250   500 Kilometers

● EPA-Designated Superfund Site

The number of sites that had been designated for superfund cleanup by 1994 showed the widespread legacy of environmental damage. The extent of the problem of toxic sites vastly exceeded the amount of Superfund money available for cleanup.

SUPERFUND SITES, 1994

Congress to create a cleanup "Superfund" to be financed by taxes imposed on polluting industries. The most heavily contaminated areas in the country were designated as Superfund sites and slated for special cleanup efforts. Superfund money, however, hardly touched anticipated costs, and, once awareness had been aroused, additional evidence of toxic dumping rapidly multiplied the number of potential Superfund sites.

Administering environmental policies, which substantially expanded the power of government, became a complex task requiring sophisticated research and negotiations among conflicting interest groups. Heated public debates erupted as environmentalist groups grew in size, resources, and expertise. Businesses attacked government regulation and branded environmentalism an elitist cause that destroyed jobs and impeded economic growth.

President Ronald Reagan, who campaigned in 1980 on a promise to halt the growth of government power, denounced the environmental regulations of the 1970s and tried to weaken the EPA. James Watt, Reagan's first secretary of the interior, angered environmentalists by supporting the "sagebrush rebellion," in which western states demanded fewer restrictions on the use of public land within their borders. Emotional battles broke out during the 1980s over private use of resources in federal wilderness areas. Particularly in the timber states of the Pacific Northwest, people hotly debated whether endangered species, such as rare bird populations, should be protected to the detriment of economic activities such as timber cutting.

The acrimony of environmental debates lessened somewhat during the 1990s, as all sides became more accustomed to negotiating differences.

President Bill Clinton's administration, for example, negotiated plans to manage and protect old-growth forests in the Pacific Northwest, to implement a conservation framework in nine national forests in the Sierra Nevada, and to handle the crowds of tourists in Yosemite National Park. In more controversial moves, Clinton's secretary of the interior, Bruce Babbitt, set aside 16 new national monuments, blocked road construction and logging in 58 million acres of wild areas in national forests, and placed 5.6 million new surface and underwater acres under federal protection. New approaches to environmental management often sought to promote change through incentives rather than penalties. In 1997, for example, the Conservation Reserve Program, a farm subsidy program that previously paid farmers to remove land from tillage, now extended payment to farmers who would restore wetlands on their properties in order to decrease polluted runoff into streams and preserve wildlife habitat.

The U.S. government itself, however, turned out to be one of the country's most flagrant polluters. In 1988 the secretary of energy admitted that the government's nuclear facilities had been lax on safety measures and estimated that cleanup would cost more than one billion dollars. The revelation of hazardous conditions at sites where atomic weapons had been produced shocked nearby residents, who feared they might have been victims of radiation poisoning. Workers at the sites had been inadequately warned about radiation, even though government officials knew of its dangers. Moreover, medical records, long suppressed by the government, revealed that people living downwind of nuclear test sites in the 1940s and 1950s had experienced an abnormally high incidence of cancer, leukemia, and thyroid disorders. In 1993, Clinton's energy secretary, Hazel O'Leary, finally released records relating to radiation testing and experimentation and promised programs to inform and compensate victims. The legacy of other kinds of military-related toxic pollutants also became evident as many of the nation's bases were closed down during the 1990s.

The environmental movement increasingly focused on international, as well as national, ecological dangers. Those hazards included global warming (the "greenhouse effect"); holes in the ozone layer caused by chlorofluorocarbons (CFCs); massive deforestation and desertification with accompanying climatic changes; pollution of the oceans; and the rapid decline of biological diversity among both plant and animal species. Solutions to these global problems required worldwide cooperation toward "sustainable development," and international meetings on environmental issues became more frequent. Conventions in Vienna in 1985, Montreal in 1987, London in 1990, Kyoto in 1997, and The Hague in 2000 worked toward establishing international standards on emissions of CFCs and greenhouse gases. A so-called Earth Summit was held in Brazil in 1992, and a conference in Cairo in 1994 took up global population issues. Fear that environmental restrictions could harm economic growth and disagreements over mechanisms to measure and enforce agreed-on targets, however, slowed the progress of the international environmental movement.

ENERGY

Environmental problems stemmed partly from patterns of energy use. The United States obtained 90 percent of its energy from the burning of fossil fuels, a major source of the carbon dioxide that creates the greenhouse effect. The nation's dependence on fossil fuels, especially on petroleum imported from abroad, aroused serious public concern during the 1970s. Part of the concern was economic. In 1973 and again in 1976 the Organization of Petroleum Exporting Countries (OPEC), a cartel dominated by the oil-rich nations of the Middle East, sharply raised the price of oil by precipitating acute shortages in the industrialized world. As Americans wearied of high prices and long lines at gas stations, President Jimmy Carter (1977–81) promised to make the United States less dependent on imported fossil fuel. He created a new cabinet-level Department of Energy in 1977 and gave some support to conservation efforts and to the development of renewable sources such as solar and wind-generated energy.

Carter also continued to support the use of nuclear power generated by giant reactors, a source of energy that became increasingly controversial. Boosters of the nation's atomic research program during the early days of the cold war had

Star Wars (1977)

Directed by George Lucas. Starring Mark Hamill (Luke Skywalker), Alec Guinness (Obi-Wan Kenobi), Harrison Ford (Han Solo), Carrie Fisher (Princess Leia), James Earl Jones (Voice of Darth Vader).

During the fall of 1998, filmgoers stood in line and bought tickets to motion pictures they had no intention of seeing. They were buying their way into theaters in order to see a two-minute preview of the fourth entry in the popular science fiction series, *Star Wars Episode I: The Phantom Menace* (1999). During the more than twenty years that had followed the release of the first *Star Wars* film in 1977, the series had attracted a vast, almost cult-like following. Not only did the initial *Star Wars* break all previous box-office records, it launched literally thousands of merchandising tie-ins. The marketing campaign began in the era of low-tech products, such as Luke Skywalker lunch boxes, and extended into the age of interactive computer games and screen-savers. The film's creator, George Lucas, earned even more money from licensing images from *Star Wars* to marketers than he made from the unprecedented box-office receipts for the film itself.

Star Wars, which took three years and a then-astronomical sum of $30 million to produce, immediately generated a similarly outsized popular response. Within three years, it returned a nearly 2000 percent profit. It also gained ten Academy Award nominations, seven Oscars, and three Grammies. The film financed Lucas's own private film empire, Lucasfilm Ltd; introduced six-track Dolby stereo to motion-picture theaters; helped to make viewers in their teens and twenties Hollywood's primary target audience; and pioneered breakthroughs in the use of computer-assisted graphics and computer-controlled camera work. The economics of the movie industry increasingly came to turn less on producing a steady supply of successful films than on releasing a few "blockbusters" modeled on *Star Wars*. These films were designed to attract huge initial audiences, to create the expectation of sequels, to sustain a variety of ancillary products, to boost sales in foreign markets, and to sell briskly in VCR and DVD formats.

promised that nuclear reactors would provide a cheap, almost limitless supply of energy. The cost of building and maintaining the reactors, however, far exceeded the original estimates, and critics charged that the reactors posed a grave safety risk. A 1979 incident offered a graphic illustration of the danger when a reactor malfunction at Three Mile Island, Pennsylvania, nearly produced a nuclear meltdown. In response to growing public alarm, power companies canceled orders for new reactors, and nuclear power industry expansion halted. The power company that served the state of Washington, once a leader in the use of nuclear energy, went into bankruptcy.

Meanwhile, OPEC oil prices skyrocketed from $1.80 a barrel in 1971 to nearly $30 a decade later, helping to boost U.S. inflation rates during Carter's presidency. On taking office as president in 1981, Ronald Reagan promised to break OPEC's oil monopoly by encouraging the development of new sources of supply. Ignoring environmentalists' calls to break U.S. dependence on fossil fuels by promotion of renewable sources, Reagan and his successor George Bush followed a "cheap oil" energy policy throughout the 1980s. The tapping of new supplies of oil, together with rivalries among OPEC members, weakened OPEC's hold over the world market and reduced energy costs, which remained moderate during the economic boom of the 1990s.

MEDIA AND CULTURE

Innovations in electronic technologies transformed America's culture as well as its economy. By 2000

In one sense, *Star Wars* tells a simple upbeat, allegorical story that responds to the cynicism and divisions of the Vietnam era. Young Luke Skywalker, aided by the wizened Obi-Wan Kenobi and the independent Han Solo, joins the fight to defeat the evil "Empire" and to rescue the virginal Princess Leah from the villainous Darth Vader. The film skillfully embellishes this sparse tale with elaborate imagery borrowed from a wide range of Hollywood film genres, including science fiction, combat films, westerns, and the Saturday morning serials of the 1930s and 1940s.

The film's major event, the triumph of old-fashioned individual effort and resourcefulness—not sophisticated technology—over an evil enemy is arguably an attempt to counter the traumatic history of U.S. involvement in Southeast Asia with a more heroic folk tale. Similarly, the alliance between youthful Skywalker and aging Obi-Wan Kenobi can be viewed as parable about the need to repudiate the "generation gap" that had emerged during the cultural conflicts of the 1960s and early 1970s.

Seen another way, though, the logic that shaped a movie such as *Star Wars* focused less and less on crafting stories, even the kind of political-historical allegories found in earlier films such as *Invasion of the Body Snatchers* (1956). Instead, a successful blockbuster primarily needed to create opportunities for inserting eye-filling special effects (often involving considerable violence and mayhem) and for devising imagery (such as cute robots and cuddly creatures) that could be re-marketed in various off-screen products. Indeed, film spectacles such as *Star Wars* merit attention less as representations of specific historical events than as historical events in their own right—something that the filmgoers who paid full price just to see a *Star Wars* preview implicitly acknowledged.

Star War's C3PO and R2D2, a droid and a robot with personalities, generated considerable nonfilm revenue from product tie-ins.

virtually every residential unit had at least one television and a VCR, and about 80 percent had a personal computer. More than one-third of the population used a computer in their daily work, and more than half of all schoolchildren used one in the classroom. Magazines and books were being published on line, and rock concerts were carried over the Internet. The omnipresent video screen seemed the preeminent symbol of the nation's mass culture. Visitors to museums and historical sites could access information about a particular display simply by touching an interactive video screen. Television screens sometimes replaced last year's magazines in doctors' waiting rooms and auto repair shops. Sports bars lined their walls with video monitors, enabling patrons to follow favorite teams or to scan several sporting events simultaneously. Air travelers could catch the latest news updates and weather conditions by glancing at the airport channel.

THE VIDEO REVOLUTION

The kind of specially targeted programming found in airports highlighted the increasingly fragmented nature of cultural production, especially television programming. At the beginning of the 1970s, television networks still followed the network radio "broadcasting" practice of offering a range of general-interest programming designed to attract a mass audience. A typical 30-minute television situation comedy (sitcom) episode might draw more viewers in a single evening than a hit motion picture attracted over an entire year. The three networks could promise advertisers that a cross section of the American public would be watching their sales pitches and then prove their claim as one of several ratings devices, including the venerable Nielsen system, tracked the number of viewers tuning in.

During the 1970s, the networks began to modify this broadcasting strategy through "narrowcasting." Early in the decade, CBS replaced certain highly rated programs popular among older and rural viewers with ones targeted to younger urban and suburban viewers. (*The Beverly Hillbillies* was an early casualty.) This shift in strategy, CBS assured advertisers, would allow them concentrate on the viewers most likely to spend money on new products. CBS also introduced more controversial programming into its comedy lineup. *All in the Family*, a sitcom that highlighted intergenerational conflict within a blue-collar family from Queens, allowed Archie Bunker, the show's bigoted protagonist, to serve as a lightning rod for controversial issues involving race and gender. Although *The Mary Tyler Moore Show* rarely took overtly "feminist" positions, it did address the personal politics of working women and broke the male-dominated sitcom formula established in the 1950s. Even television's harshest critics applauded new CBS shows, such as *M*A*S*H*, for integrating comedy with social commentary. NBC soon joined the trend; in 1975, it brought the barbed humor of the 1960s counterculture to network television by introducing *Saturday Night Live*.

Adopting a different approach to narrowcasting, ABC cultivated an audience among high-schoolers and college-age viewers. Aware that young people generally controlled at least one of the family's television sets, ABC boosted its ratings with sex-and-action programs (*Charlie's Angels*), mildly risqué sitcoms (*Three's Company*), and series about teen life (*Happy Days*). ABC used its soaring ratings to lure local affiliates away from its larger rivals. All three networks enjoyed rising profits during the 1970s, and some media analysts likened operating a local television affiliate to owning a press that could legally print money. At the end of the decade, 9 of every 10 television sets were tuned to a network program during prime-time viewing hours.

During the 1980s, however, programmers found it increasingly difficult to create successful prime-time offerings, and the networks began to confront a slow, yet steady, loss of viewers. NBC, for instance, could claim *The Bill Cosby Show*, which featured an affluent African American family, and *Cheers*, a sitcom set in a Boston tavern where "everybody knows your name." Its other programs, though, attracted significantly smaller audiences, and NBC adjusted by slashing budgets and staff, especially in the news division.

Meanwhile, independent stations began to compete effectively in local markets. During the 1980s, even as the number of daily newspapers was steadily shrinking, 200 independent television stations went on the air. During the middle of the decade, earnings for UHF independents (channels between 14 and 81 on the standard television dial) more than doubled. Lacking access to new network programs, these independents targeted small but lucrative markets by strategically scheduling Hollywood films, sporting events, and reruns of canceled network programs.

Building on the rise of the independents, the Fox television network debuted in 1988. Fox broke new ground by offering a limited, though sometimes highly rated, schedule to previously independent stations. One of its first hit series, *The Simpsons*, an animated send-up of the venerable family sitcom, became a mass-marketing bonanza. Fox gradually expanded its nightly offerings and in 1993 shocked the television industry by outbidding CBS for the rights to carry the National Football League's NFC conference games. During the 1990s, two other communication conglomerates, Universal-Paramount and Time-Warner, built networks based on the Fox model and aimed much of their programming at younger, urban viewers with offerings such as *Buffy the Vampire Slayer* and *The Jamie Foxx Show*.

New technologies also undermined the hold of the major networks. At the simplest level, the remote-control, which had been introduced in the 1960s but not widely marketed until the 1980s, gave rise to a television aesthetic, called "zapping" or "channel surfing," in which viewers rapidly switched from program to program, usually during commercial breaks. The mass-marketing of videocassette recorders (VCRs) also gave people new control over their television viewing habits.

The greatest challenge to the networks came from cable television (CATV). By 2000, more than

OPRAH Both the obscure and the famous appeared on Oprah Winfrey's talk show, one of the most successful in television history.

65 percent of the nation's homes were wired for CATV. Carrying scores of different programs for specific audiences, CATV further fragmented television viewing. Ted Turner, one of the first to recognize the potential of CATV, introduced the Cable News Network (CNN), several movie channels, and an all-cartoon network before his communications empire merged with that of Time-Warner. Cable operations—whether they featured news, cartoons, sports, public affairs, commercial-free movies, round-the-clock weather, or home shopping programs—steadily expanded. During the 1990s, companies touting direct satellite transmission challenged both the networks and CATV, but the lack of a standard reception format slowed the expansion of this competing medium. By 2000 the percentage of television viewers watching network programs had fallen from 90 to about 60 per-

cent, and the corporations that owned them had themselves expanded into the cable industry.

THE CHANGING MEDIA ENVIRONMENT

The new media environment affected nearly every aspect of mass culture. With movie ticket sales remaining about the same in 1980 as they had been in 1960, Hollywood studios raised the price of each ticket and concentrated on turning out a handful of blockbuster films, such as the *Star Wars* series (1977–99), while hoping for an occasional surprise hit, such as *The Blair Witch Project* (1999). But for every *Star Wars*, Hollywood moguls could produce at least one expensive dud such as *Judge Dredd* (1995). Thus, the new Hollywood system encouraged filmmakers to play it safe and recycle the story lines and special effects that had made money in the past. Television staples, such as *The Grinch Who Stole Christmas*, also became motion pictures (2000), while mega-hits such as *Mission Impossible* (1996) and *The Matrix* (1999) automatically spawned sequels. Following another television strategy, Hollywood targeted younger viewers with films such as *Ferris Bueller's Day Off* (1986), *Clueless* (1995), and *Save the Last Dance* (2000).

The new Hollywood became intertwined with the television industry, once its feared rival. CATV and VCRs provided Hollywood with new sources of revenue from theatrical films and from those that had been relegated to the storage vaults. Although huge multiplex movie theaters opened in suburban shopping areas throughout the 1980s and 1990s, video rental stores surpassed them in number, and VCR sales soared. Digital video disk (DVD) technology gave home viewers improved visual imagery and bonus attractions, such as footage cut from the theatrical release and running commentary by a film's director. People increasingly used VCRs, DVDs, and all-movie channels from CATV and satellite transmission to convert their television sets, with ever-larger screens and digital technology, into home movie theaters. The Internet became an outlet for filmmakers who, pioneering the use of digital technology, were specializing in short, offbeat fare.

CATV, VCRs, and digital technology also transformed the pop music industry. The Music Television (MTV) channel, initially offering a 24-hour supply of rock videos, was launched in 1981. Critics charged it with portraying women as sex objects and with excluding artists of color. Eventually, however, MTV defused complaints—especially after featuring Michael Jackson's 29-minute video based on his hit single "Thriller" (1983). By the end of the 20th century, CATV provided a home for a wide range of videos that represented the increasingly multiethnic nature of the American music industry.

Performers such as Madonna used MTV to create a new relationship between music and visual image, the "MTV aesthetic." This aesthetic emphasized fast-paced visual imagery. It played with traditional ideas about time and space, recycled images from older films and television programs, and often carried a satirical edge. The MTV aesthetic crossed over between video, television, and motion pictures. MTV itself abandoned its original all-video format and developed a wide range of youth-oriented programming. Its hit, *The Real World*, presaged a run of controversial "reality" shows such as *Survivor* and *Temptation Island* on network television.

Companies such as Sony began marketing musical packages in a variety of different, constantly updated formats. The 45-rpm record and the long-play (LP) record, which had been at the heart of the musical revolutions of the 1950s and 1960s, disappeared or became collector's items for those who claimed that the new digital technologies failed to match the rich, analog sound of music recorded on vinyl. Introduction of digital compact disks (CDs) not only changed the technology through which pop music was delivered but the nature of the product and the listening experience. The classic LPs of the 1960s and early 1970s, such as the Beatles *Abbey Road* (1969) or Willie Nelson's *The Red-Headed Stranger* (1975), ideally contained a relatively coherent set of 10 to 12 songs, split between the two sides, organized around a core theme or concept. The CD of the 1990s, able to hold 15 or 20 minutes more music than an LP, was rarely structured thematically and often contained a hodge-podge of songs, several tossed in as "bonus tracks." Thematic coherence in a single CD became increasingly irrelevant with the introduction of players that could shuffle back and forth between the tracks on a hundred different CDs. Listeners could program their players according to their own whims or simply let songs play randomly.

The Internet also promised to change the ways in which people listened to music. Most obvious, the Internet allowed access to commercial and noncommercial stations far beyond the range of the most powerful FM receiver. More important, the Internet and the versatile MP3 technology allowed people to hear, preserve, and exchange music in entirely new ways. Its celebrants proclaimed that the Internet would break the hold of the commercial music companies and make a wide array of sounds instantly available to consumers, but the industry and artists such as Metallica complained that people were using the Internet, and services such as Napster, to "pirate" copyrighted material. Although the U.S. Supreme Court had, in 1985, ruled that home copying of television programs on VCRs did not violate the law, copyright experts debated how this decision applied to the home copying of music through MP3 technology and the Internet.

THE NEW MASS CULTURE DEBATE

New trends in mass commercial culture generated other legal controversies. In 1975 the Federal Communications Commission (FCC) ordered the television networks to dedicate the first 60 minutes of prime time each evening to "family" programming free of violence or "mature" themes. Several television production companies challenged this family-hour requirement as government censorship, and a federal court ruled that it was a violation of the First Amendment's guarantee of free speech. Demands that the government regulate rock lyrics and album covers also ran afoul of complaints that this amounted to unconstitutional censorship. Although governmental efforts faltered, private organizations were more successful in pressing media companies to practice self-censorship. In 1992, pressure on Time-Warner resulted in the withdrawal of a song titled "Cop Killer" by rap artist Ice-T, and television networks adopted a rating system designed to inform parents about the amount of violence and sexual content in prime-time programs during the 1990s.

Meanwhile, a new generation of writers, reviewers, and university professors were paying serious attention to mass culture. Unlike the critics of the 1950s, who dismissed mass culture as trivial and condemned its effects on American life, the critics of the 1980s and 1990s often seemed fans of the cultural products they were reviewing. Instead of comparing mass culture to "high" culture (the so-called classical works of Western civilization), this new generation of cultural critics increasingly abandoned the distinction between lowbrow and highbrow. They insisted that music of the Beatles should be studied along with that of Beethoven and argued that the lyrics of Chuck Berry and Bob Dylan merited academic analysis. Observers of contemporary culture debated the meaning of the MTV aesthetic and wrote scholarly essays and books about celebrities such as Madonna.

These new analysts also studied the ways in which consumers integrated the products of mass culture into their daily lives. Again rejecting the cultural criticism of the 1950s—which saw the consumers of mass culture as dupes who passively soaked up worthless products—they stressed ordinary people's creative interaction with commercial culture. Much of this analysis came from professors in the new academic field of "cultural studies," who focused on how people reworked images from the mass media. Scholarly studies of *Star Trek*, for example, explored the ways in which loyal fans had kept this popular 1960s television series alive in syndication and had subsequently prompted a succession of Hollywood motion pictures and several new *Star Trek* television series. Moreover, through conventions, self-produced magazines (called "fanzines"), and Web sites, fans of *Star Trek* ("Trekkies") and of shows such as *Xena* created a grassroots subculture that used television programs as vehicles for discussing social and political issues, especially ones that touched on race, gender, and sexuality. Those who advocated cultural studies generally embraced "multiculturalism" and insisted that students should study works by women, political outsiders, and non-Western writers and artists. Over the complaints of traditionalists, they also urged students to see traditional texts, such as those of Shakespeare, in light of their political and historical contexts rather than study them as timeless works.

SOCIAL ACTIVISM

The legacy of 1960s activism became embedded in American political life and rippled through the decades that followed. The mass demonstration remained a familiar protest and advocacy tool. Wash-ington, D.C., continued to provide a favorite stage for rallies that could attract the attention of national lawmakers and the media, but activists also mounted smaller protests. In the early 1980s the Clamshell Alliance conducted a campaign of civil disobedience against a nuclear reactor being built in Seabrook, New Hampshire, and a broad coalition of West Coast activists waged an unsuccessful three-year struggle to close the University of California's Lawrence Livermore National Laboratory, which was developing nuclear weapons. Women's groups staged annual "Take Back the Night" marches in major cities to protest the rising tide of sexual assaults, and both prochoice and antiabortion groups sponsored demonstrations in Washington, D.C., and in local communities. In October 1995, the "Million Man March" in Washington, D.C., sought to mobilize African American men behind a campaign of social reconstruction in black communities; two years later an evangelical men's group called the "Promise Keepers" filled Washington's Mall. In 1999, thousands of people representing worker-rights and environmental causes tried to disrupt an international meeting of the World Trade Organization (WTO) in Seattle.

Mass demonstrations, however, gradually lost their power to attract media attention. During a period of violence in May 1991 in Los Angeles, 30,000 Korean Americans staged a march for peace. Although it was the largest demonstration ever conducted by any Asian American group, even the local media ignored it. And few people learned from the media that 75,000 California high school students staged a walkout in 1994 to denounce a state measure aimed at curtailing education, welfare, and medical care for undocumented immigrants.

WOMEN'S ISSUES

Old ideologies of domesticity increasingly clashed with the situations in which millions of women found themselves. More and more women were working outside the home, postponing marriage, remaining single, and divorcing. Moreover, the birth control pill gave women greater control over reproduction and significantly changed sexual behavior. In this environment many women questioned gender-based divisions in both the public and private sectors.

"The purpose of NOW is to take action to bring women into full participation in the mainstream of American society now, exercising all the privileges and responsibilities thereof in truly equal partnership with men. . . . We reject the current assumptions that a man must carry the sole burden of supporting himself, his wife, and family, and that a woman is automatically entitled to lifelong support by a man upon her marriage, or that marriage, home and family are primarily woman's world and responsibility. . . . We believe that a true partnership between the sexes demands a different concept of marriage, an equitable sharing of the responsibilities of home and children and of the economic burdens of their support. . . . We will strive to ensure that no party, candidate, president, senator, governor, congressman, or any public official who betrays or ignores the principle of full equality between the sexes is elected or appointed to office."

**NATIONAL ORGANIZATION
FOR WOMEN (NOW)**
Statement of Purpose, 1966

Struggles over gender issues emerged within older civil rights and antiwar movements, where men often saw no contradiction between women's second-class status and their own egalitarian beliefs. Some male leaders of these movements expected women to provide secretarial or sexual services and complained that raising issues of sexual equality interfered with the movements' more important tasks of redirecting racial and foreign policies. African American women, such as the cultural critic bell hooks, advocated black feminism; Chicana groups coalesced within the United Farm Workers movement and Mexican American organizations; radical feminists split off from the antiwar movement; other women formed new, female-directed cooperatives.

Throughout the 1970s groups of women came together in "consciousness-raising" sessions to discuss issues and share perspectives. These discussions produced a growing conviction that women's concerns about the distribution of *political* power in the United States were inseparable from *personal* power relationships involving housework, child-rearing, sexuality, and economic independence. Although this new generation of feminists recognized traditional public issues, such as fighting discrimination, "the personal is political" became its watchword.

Economic self-sufficiency became a pressing issue for many women. During the 1960s, social welfare benefits for single mothers with children had been boosted by higher AFDC payments and by the Food Stamp program, but during the economic dislocations of the 1970s and early 1980s, the real monetary value of these benefits, measured in constant dollars, steadily decreased. In 1972 a family of four, headed by a woman, received welfare benefits that, on average, were worth about $577 per month; by 1990, the monthly value of the same benefits had fallen to about $430. Homeless shelters, which once catered primarily to single men, increasingly coped with the particular needs of women and children. Throughout the 1970s and 1980s, activists campaigned against the "feminization of poverty" and urged greater public assistance for the growing number of children reared in low-income, female-headed families. Political proposals to reshape welfare sought to limit entitlements and create assistance for women moving into the workforce, but the workforce itself was laced with inequalities. Although women increasingly entered the professions and gained unionized positions (by 1990, fully 37 percent of union members were women, compared with about 18 percent in 1960), the average female worker throughout the 1970s and 1980s continued to earn about 60 cents for every dollar earned by the average male worker. "Glass ceilings" limited women's chances for promotion, and child-care expenses often fell disproportionately on women who worked outside the home.

With so many issues to address, and with agendas often varying along lines of class, race, ethnicity, and region, the women's movement became highly diverse. Women from all sectors of society built institutions and networks to address needs that had long been ignored: battered-women's shelters, health and birthing clinics specializing in women's medicine, rape crisis centers, economic development counseling for women-owned businesses, union-organizing efforts led by women, organizations of women in specific businesses or professions, women's studies programs in colleges and universities, and academic journals devoted to research on women.

Pressure to end gender discrimination changed existing institutions as well. Previously all-male bastions, such as country clubs and service organizations, were pressured into admitting women. Most mainline Protestant churches and Reform Jewish congregations were challenged to accept women into the ministry. Educational institutions began to adopt "gender-fair" hiring practices and curricula. American women by the beginning of the 21st century lived in an institutional environment significantly different from that of their mothers.

Sexual harassment, to take only one of the new concerns, became a significant issue among women. A few activists, such as Camille Paglia, argued that to focus on sexual harassment—or on the related issue of pornography—would tend to identify feminism with a kind of sexual puritanism that the women's movement had once promised to end. Others, however, pressed government and private employers to regulate behavior that demeaned women and exploited their lack of power vis-à-vis male supervisors and coworkers. In 1986 the U.S. Supreme Court ruled that sexual harassment constituted a form of discrimination covered under the 1964 Civil Rights Act.

In 1991 the issue of sexual harassment attracted national attention when Anita Hill, an African American law professor, accused Clarence Thomas, an African American nominee for the Supreme Court, of having sexually harassed her when both had worked for the Office of Economic Opportunity. Feminists were angered when the all-male Senate Judiciary Committee, which was responsible for considering Thomas's qualifications for the Supreme Court, seemed unable to understand the issues raised by Hill's charges. When the Senate confirmed Thomas's nomination, women's groups gained new converts to their views on sexual harassment. Political observers credited anger over the Thomas-Hill hearings with helping to mobilize female voters to elect four women to the U.S. Senate in 1992. The numbers of women in public office continued to rise slowly, as a political "gender gap"—a difference in the way men and women voted—also widened.

Sexual harassment became a controversial issue within the U.S. military, too, which began to recruit women more actively during the 1980s and 1990s. The service academies began accepting female cadets, and women seemed to be finding places within the military establishment. Soon, however, front-page revelations about harassment and even sexual assaults against female naval officers by their male comrades at the 1991 "Tailhook" convention, revealed problems. Attempts by navy officials to cover up the incident provoked outrage, and several high-ranking officers were forced to step down.

SEXUAL POLITICS

Debates over gender and sexuality became extremely divisive over issues involving gays and lesbians. Some homosexuals, especially gay men affiliated with the left-leaning Mattachine Society and lesbians who organized the Daughters of Bilitis, had already begun to claim rights on the basis of their sexuality during the 1950s (see chapter 27). A new spirit of insurgence and self-assurance emerged toward the end of the 1960s. In 1969, New York City police raided the Stonewall Inn, a gay bar in Greenwich Village. Patrons resisted arrest, and the confrontation pitted homosexuals, who claimed the right to be free from police harassment, against law enforcement officials.

"Stonewall" marked a turning point in homosexual politics. New York City's Gay Liberation Front (GLF) provided a model for similar groups across the country, which also borrowed ideas and rhetoric from the civil rights and feminist movements. During the decades after Stonewall, thousands of gay and lesbian advocacy groups sprang up to fight homophobia, and many homosexuals "came out of the closet," proudly proclaiming their sexual orientation. A group called Act Up became a leader of new, in-your-face protests.

Soon, newspapers, theaters, nightspots, and religious groups identifying themselves with the homosexual community became part of daily life, particularly in larger cities. Specific forms of popular entertainment, such as the disco era of the 1970s, became closely identified with the gay and lesbian subcultures, which benefited significantly from a general relaxation of legal and cultural controls over the portrayal and practice of all forms of explicit sexuality.

Homosexuals joined civil-liberties groups in pressuring state and local governments to enact laws prohibiting discrimination in housing and jobs on the basis of sexual preference. Moreover, they demanded that the police treat attacks on homosexuals no less seriously than they treated other forms

of violent crime. As gays and lesbians gained political voice, however, their activism often met with either indifference or determined opposition from conservatives.

One issue especially dominated debate during the 1980s and early 1990s: acquired immunodeficiency syndrome (AIDS), a fatal and contagious condition that attacks the body's immune system. First identified in the early 1980s, AIDS quickly became an intensely emotional and often misunderstood medical and political issue. Epidemiologists correctly recognized AIDS as a health problem for the general public. The disease could be transmitted through the careless use of intravenous drugs, tainted blood supplies, and unprotected heterosexual intercourse. At first, however, its incidence in the United States was limited almost solely to gay men. Gay activists charged that, as a consequence of this association,

AIDS "ACT UP" CAMPAIGN Health care issues increasingly galvanized grassroots activists in the late 20th century. In 1989, members of Act Up, a group that represented militant homosexuals, protested the federal government's inattention to the issue of AIDS during the presidencies of Ronald Reagan and George Bush.

the Reagan and Bush administrations placed a low priority on medical efforts to check its spread. The controversy over medical funding galvanized gay and lesbian activists to assert their concerns more forcefully.

Another hotly contested issue involved gays and lesbians serving in the military. During the 1992 campaign, Bill Clinton promised to end the military's ban on homosexuals. Faced with opposition from the Pentagon, however, Clinton accepted a "don't ask, don't tell" policy, which left the ban in place but stipulated that, because the military would "not ask," homosexuals who "didn't tell" could have military careers. This solution satisfied neither the military establishment nor gay and lesbian activists and continued to promote controversy.

RACE, ETHNICITY, AND SOCIAL ACTIVISM

The increasing emphasis on group identity as the basis for social activism grew especially strong among various racial and ethnic communities in the late 20th century. In movements that grew out of 1960s activism, groups emphasized pride in their distinctive traditions and declared that cultural differences among Americans should be affirmed rather than feared, celebrated rather than simply tolerated. Especially with the influx of new immigrants (by 2000 one of every ten Americans was foreign born), issues related to identity politics and multiculturalism took on growing importance in American life.

AFRICAN AMERICAN ACTIVISM

African Americans had developed a strong sense of cultural identity during the civil rights and black power struggles of the 1960s (see chapters 28 and 29). Battles against discrimination and for cultural pride continued in the post-Vietnam era. Controversies over future directions, however, also emerged.

Much of the activism looked inward and stressed pride in the African American heritage. A trend that one African American writer called "Malcolmania" accelerated with the appearance of Spike Lee's film *Malcolm X* (1991). The emphasis on racial pride also showed in rap, hip-hop, and in the hundreds of schools established in order to offer an

RAPPER DR. DRE OF NWA Rap music became a staple of the pop music scene.

"Afrocentric" curriculum. The Black Entertainment Network (BET) catered specifically to African American viewers.

African American scholars such as Henry Lewis Gates, Jr., who became head of Harvard's Afro-American studies department in 1991, made pride in the black experience one part of the larger multicultural project in colleges and universities. In 1999, Gates and Kwame Anthony Appiah brought out *Africana: The Encyclopedia of the African and African American Experience*. This project, which had been started by W. E. B. DuBois, brought together more than 200 contributors who offered the latest scholarly perspective on thousands of issues and individuals. African American culture, in Gates's view, was not "a thing apart, separate from the whole, having no influence on the shape and shaping of American culture." Gates urged that African American authors, such as Toni Morrison (who won the Nobel Prize for Literature in 1993) and Alice Walker, be viewed as writers who take "the blackness of the culture for granted, as a springboard to write about those human emotions that we share with everyone else, and that we have always shared with each other." Although African American cultures could be seen as unique and different, Gates argued, they should not be considered apart from their interaction with other cultures.

Pride in racial heritage could be a contested proposition. African American women who identified with feminist issues tended to view some male rap music as infected with misogyny. Queen Latifah, one of the first rappers to incorporate feminist themes in her music, sang songs like "Ladies First," which criticized what she saw as gender stereotyping and romanticizing a mythical African past in many rap lyrics. African American women's groups organized to pressure record companies and radio stations to censor rap songs and videos that they considered misogynistic.

African Americans expressed a broad spectrum of views. Controversy over the appointment of Clarence Thomas to the U.S. Supreme Court divided African Americans, just as it divided whites. Some, especially African American feminists, saw Anita Hill's testimony against Thomas as evidence of pervasive sexism within black culture, but many other African Americans remained focused on race. No white nominee, they argued, would ever have faced the kind of personal scrutiny that Thomas confronted. Opinion polls also suggested that a majority of African Americans thought protecting Thomas's position as a successful male professional was more important than attacking his conservative politics or pressing any of the gender issues raised by Hill.

The 1996 trial of sports star O. J. Simpson, which became a media spectacle for nearly a year, raised another important debate about the place of African Americans in American life. On this issue, African Americans were less divided. In the "trial of the century," Simpson was prosecuted for two brutal murders, including that of his former wife. Simpson's defense team, headed by Johnnie Cochran, Jr., a prominent African American civil rights attorney, successfully refocused the trial on alleged misconduct by racist officers within the Los Angeles police department, and a largely black jury returned a verdict of not guilty. Polls indicated a significant division in public opinion along racial lines: Whites were solidly convinced of Simpson's guilt, and African Americans overwhelmingly believed he was

innocent. (Simpson was subsequently found liable for the murders in a civil trial for monetary damages, a judicial proceeding in which the laws of evidence and burden of proof differ from those required in criminal prosecution.) Quite apart from whatever the criminal trial proved about Simpson's guilt or innocence, it indicated a significant gulf between whites and African Americans stemming from distrust of the police and the legal system in African American communities, a distrust that efforts to develop "community policing" and more racially diverse police forces had yet to overcome.

Issues of equal treatment in the legal and criminal justice systems remained a major agenda for African American activists. A post-Simpson investigation of the Los Angeles police department featured allegations that officers regularly manufactured evidence against criminal defendants who were African American. Ethnic differences in the sentencing of convicted felons also become an important issue to activists. They pointed out that courts generally imposed harsher sentences for crimes involving crack cocaine, a drug consumed in African American neighborhoods, than for those involving the more expensive varieties of cocaine favored by white users. The fact that, by the 1990s, more African American men were in jails and prisons than were in colleges and universities, activists claimed, could partly be explained by sentencing disparities such as the one involving cocaine. In addition, statistical evidence also indicated that African Americans convicted of potential capital crimes were more likely to receive the death penalty than nonblack convicts.

"Racial profiling," a practice that could touch anyone of African descent, became a prominent issue in many communities during the 1990s. Statistics showed that police detained African Americans as criminal suspects and stopped black motorists far more often than members of any other ethnic group. Activists called this practice "DWB," or "driving while black." Some law-enforcement officials claimed that such statistics merely reflected probabilities based on crime data, but most recognized that the practice raised questions about equal protection and hardly engendered respect for the criminal justice system. Even if someone were released immediately, the mere fact of having been detained, critics of racial profiling argued, represented a serious, race-related affront to a person's dignity. Profiling seemed a symbolic reminder of the days of slavery and legally sanctioned discrimination.

Other practices that symbolized racism of the past also became activist targets. At the beginning of the 1990s, several southern states and many institutions, such as colleges and private clubs, still flew the flag of the Confederacy. The battle over the flags, and over other memorials relating to the Civil War, could become highly charged. Groups that defended memorials to the Confederacy argued that symbols such as the Confederate flag honored the people who had fought "the War Between the States" and not the system of chattel slavery. Civil libertarians wondered how campaigns to remove forms of expression that carried multiple meanings could be squared with the First Amendment's guarantee of free speech. Activists and their legal supporters, however, countered that the cause of the Confederacy was inseparable from that of preserving slavery and that the Confederate flag, as recently as the 1950s, had provided a powerful symbol of massive, racist resistance to the Supreme Court's decisions striking down legal segregation.

By the early 1970s, African American activists no longer worked from outside of the country's dominant institutions. In 1970, thirteen African American members of Congress established the Congressional Black Caucus (CBC) as a means of providing a common front on a wide range of foreign and domestic issues. By 2001, nearly 40 members of the House, all Democrats, supported the CBC. (Congress's African American Republicans did not join the CBC.) It issued an "Alternative Budget," which targeted much more money toward social programs than the one presented by the White House and considered by Congress; campaigned on behalf of better relations with African nations and other countries with large populations of African descent, such as Cuba and Haiti; and pressed for changes in domestic programs that addressed issues, such as racial profiling and drug sentencing, that particularly affected African Americans.

AMERICAN INDIAN ACTIVISM

American Indians conducted their political and social activism along two broad fronts. Indians had, of course, long-standing identities based on their tribal affiliation, and many issues, particularly those involving land and treaty disputes, turned on specific tribal-based claims. Other issues were generally identified as "pan-Indian" and seemed to require more nationally visible strategies that extended beyond a single tribe. In 1969 activists began a two-year sit-in, designed to dramatize a history of broken treaty promises, at the former federal prison on Alcatraz Island in San Francisco harbor. Expanding on this tactic, the American Indian Movement (AIM), created in 1968 by young activists from several Northern Plains tribes, adopted a confrontational approach. Clashes, with both federal officials and more conservative American Indian leaders, eventually erupted in early 1973 on the Pine Ridge Reservation in South Dakota. In response, the FBI and federal prosecutors targeted members of AIM for illegal surveillance and controversial criminal prosecutions.

Meanwhile, important legal changes were taking place. The omnibus Civil Rights Act of 1968 contained six sections that became known as the "Indian Bill of Rights." In these, Congress finally extended most of the provisions of the constitutional Bill of Rights to American Indians on reservations while still upholding the legitimacy of tribal laws. Federal legislation and several Supreme Court decisions in the 1970s subsequently reinforced the broad principle of tribal self-determination. In 1978 Congress passed the Tribally Controlled College Assistance Act that supported educational institutions designed to impart job skills and preserve tribal cultures. Tribal identification itself required legal action. By the beginning of the 21st century, the federal government officially recognized about 560 separate tribes and bands and about another 150 were seeking such recognition; 30 others had secured recognition from states. Tribes were not always geographical entities. Three-quarters of American Indians lived in urban areas, and about half of the people residing on reservations were not officially identified as Indians.

Following the suggestion of American Indian lawyers and tapping the expertise of the Native American Rights Fund (NARF), tribes used the courts aggressively to press legal demands that derived from old treaties with the U.S. government and the unique status of tribal nations. Some tribal representatives sought restoration of traditional fishing and agricultural rights, a campaign that often provoked resentment among non–American Indians, who complained that such special claims should not take precedence over state and local laws. At the same time, American Indians also sued to protect tribal water rights and traditional religious ceremonies (some of which include ritualistic use of drugs such as peyote) and to secure repatriation of Indian skeletal remains that were being displayed or stored in museums across the country. (At one point, the Smithsonian Institution was housing the remains of more than 18,000 Indians, supposedly for historical and scientific purposes.) Pressure from American Indian rights groups led Congress in 1990 to pass the Native American Graves Protection and Repatriation Act, requiring universities and museums to return human remains and sacred objects to tribes that requested them.

Tribes also used the courts to press claims related to Las Vegas-style gaming. Claiming exemption from state gaming laws, American Indians first opened bingo halls, then full-blown casinos. In 1988 the Supreme Court ruled that states could not prohibit gaming operations on tribal land, and Congress soon passed the Indian Gaming Regulatory Act, which gave a seal of approval to their casino operations. By the mid-1990s gambling had become one of the most lucrative sectors of the nation's entertainment business, and American Indian–owned casinos had become a major part of this phenomenon. In states such as Connecticut, Minnesota, and Wisconsin, American Indian gaming establishments became a major source of employment for Indians and non-Indians alike. Tribes vied with one another to establish casinos in prime locations and became entangled in political and legal squabbles. Tribes in California worked with the state government to devise a unique solution: the larger tribes with substantial gaming operations would share profits with smaller ones whose location and resources prevented them from establishing their own casinos.

Vividly underscoring the contradictions within American Indian culture, the glitzy postmodernism of tribal-owned casinos existed alongside tribal

GAMING AT MYSTIC LAKE CASINO IN MINNESOTA By the mid-1990s, legal gambling had become one of the nation's leading recreational enterprises. Native Americans saw casinos as an important way to generate jobs and capital on Indian reservations.

LOS ANGELES POWWOW Tribal dancers participate in a powwow in Los Angeles. Many Native Americans in the late 20th century embraced the rediscovery of traditional ways.

powwows and efforts to revive older cultural practices. Indeed, the Mashantucket Pequot tribe in Connecticut used the profits from its Foxwoods casino to finance one the nation's largest powwows, which offered nearly one million dollars in prizes for entrants in its American Indian dance contests.

Powwows were only one part of the attempt to build a stronger sense of identity through the reviving traditional cultural practices. To forestall the disappearance of their languages, American Indian activists urged bilingualism and the renewal of traditional rituals. At the millennium, only about 175 native languages were spoken at all, and only about 20 were used between parents and children. Activists forged links with aboriginal peoples throughout the Americas and the South Pacific and organized trips to Central and South America to draw international attention to the problems facing aboriginal peoples as a broad group. Many denounced the use of stereotypical Indian-style names in amateur and professional sports and pressured teams with names such as "Chiefs" or "Redskins" to seek new names. The federal government assisted this cultural pride movement by appropriating funds in 1989 for two National Museums of the American Indian, one established in New York and off the Mall in the heart of the nation's capitol. In 1991 the National Park Service changed the name of "Custer Battlefield" in Montana to "Little Bighorn Battlefield," shifting the historical emphasis and redesigning the interpretive exhibits to help celebrate, not denigrate, American Indian traditions.

ACTIVISM IN SPANISH-SPEAKING COMMUNITIES

Spanish-speaking Americans comprise the country's the fastest-growing ethnic group. The matter of ethnic identity, however, is complex. Many Spanish-speaking people, especially in the Southwest, prefer the umbrella term "Latino," while others, particularly in Florida, use the term "Hispanic." At the same time, people whom the U.S. Census began (in 1980) labeling Hispanic more frequently identified themselves according to the Spanish-speaking country or commonwealth from which they or their ancestors had immigrated. Beneath these general designations and a common Spanish language lay further diversity. For example, the Cuban Americans who came to South Florida during the 1960s generally enjoyed greater access to education and higher incomes than did most Latinos who came later, even from Cuba. The initial wave of Cuban immigrants also tended to be more politically conservative than other Latinos; they espoused a hard-line stance against the communist government of Cuba's Fidel Castro. Émigrés from Puerto Rico were already U.S. citizens, yet they focused some of their political energies on the persistent "status" question—that is, whether Puerto Rico should hope for independence, strive for statehood, or retain a "commonwealth" connection to the mainland. Immigrants from the Dominican Republic and Central America (both legal and undocumented) generally were the most recent and most impoverished newcomers.

Mexican Americans, who comprised the oldest and most numerous Spanish-speaking group in the United States, could tap a long tradition of social activism. The 1960s saw an emerging spirit of *Chicanismo*, a populistic pride in a heritage that could be traced back to the ancient civilizations of Middle America. Young activists made "Chicano/a," once terms of derision that most Mexican Americans avoided, a rallying cry. In cities in the Southwest, advocates of *Chicanismo*, though still a minority force within Mexican American life, gained considerable cultural influence. Attempts by the police to crack down on Chicano activism during the 1970s backfired, especially in Los Angeles, and increasing numbers of young Mexican Americans came to identify with the new insurgent spirit.

Cities in the Southwest with large Mexican American populations experienced considerable ferment during the 1970s. La Raza Unida, a movement founded in 1967, began to win local elections during the early 1970s. At the same time, *Chicanismo* continued to stimulate a cultural flowering. Although Catholic priests generally avoided militancy, many of them opened their churches to groups devoted to ethnic dancing, mural painting, poetry, and literature. Spanish-language newspapers and journals, too, reinforced the growing sense of pride. Mexican Americans pushed for Chicano studies at colleges and universities.

Developments in San Antonio, a city with a large Mexican American population, suggested the potential fruits of grassroots political organizing. In the 1970s Ernesto Cortes, Jr., took the lead in founding COPS (Communities Organized for Public Service), a group that focused on achieving concrete, tangible changes that touched the everyday lives of ordinary citizens. In San Antonio this strategy meant that Mexican American activists worked with Anglo business leaders and with Democratic politicians such as Henry Cisneros, who became the city's mayor in 1981. (In 1993 Cisneros and Federico Peña, a former mayor of Denver, both joined President Clinton's cabinet.) COPS brought many Mexican Americans, particularly women, into the public arena for the first time.

By the 1990s Mexican American activism was becoming increasingly diverse. La Raza Unida continued its activities during the 1980s but never became a national force. Instead, the Mexican American Legal Defense and Educational Fund (MALDEF), established in 1968 with funding from the Ford Foundation, emerged as the most visible national group ready to lobby or litigate on behalf of Mexican Americans. At the local level, organizations formed on the model of COPS, such as UNO (United Neighborhood Organization) in Los Angeles, continued to work on community concerns. Mexican Americans spearheaded labor-organizing efforts, particularly in the service industries and won several celebrated victories for custodial workers in 2000. Meanwhile, the U.S. economy of the 1990s offered expanding employment and educational opportunities, especially for women. Most of the new jobs, Mexican-American advocacy groups complained, offered only low wages and few benefits. Even so, some Mexican Americans did well, and women continued to join organizations such as the National Network of Hispanic Women, which represented Chicanas who had been successful in professional and business life. Conservatives such as Linda Chavez—a Republican activist who moved among the worlds of business, politics, and public policy—joined Democrats such as Henry Cisneros as of symbols of Mexican American mobility.

Social activism among Puerto Ricans in the United States emerged more slowly than among Mexican Americans. Much of the effort during the 1960s went toward strengthening community-based institutions and building new ones. New York City's Puerto Rican Day Parade, an important focus of cultural pride that had begun during the 1950s, became the city's largest ethnic celebration, but despite the formation of activist groups, such as the Young Lords, the social programs of the Great Society often bypassed Puerto Ricans. A 1976 report by the U.S. Commission on Civil Rights concluded that Puerto Ricans remained "the last in line" for whatever benefits and opportunities had become available during the sixties. During the late 1970s and 1980s, activists focused on legal and political issues; the Puerto Rican Legal Defense

CINCO DE MAYO Cinco de Mayo, a Mexican festival that commemorates the military defeat of French forces that tried to occupy Mexico in 1862, has become a tradition in many American cities. This photo shows a 1988 celebration in San Francisco.

and Education Fund and allied groups succeeded in obtaining court victories that helped Puerto Ricans surmount obstacles to voting and to political office-holding. Puerto Rican voters provided important support for insurgent, grassroots politics in Chicago and many cities on the East Coast.

Even after leaving the Caribbean, Puerto Ricans continued to address issues there as well. In 2000, the Puerto Rican Legal Defense and Education Fund, among other groups, organized a well-publicized protest against the U.S. Navy for using the small island of Vieques as a target range, thereby creating health and ecological hazards.

People of Cuban origin increasingly wrestled with how much activism they should devote toward affairs in their homeland. Although Cuban Americans became active in southern Florida politics and civic affairs, critics noted the persistent "exile mentality" that revolved around anti-Castro activities. The issue of how to focus activism emerged most vividly in 2000 over a familial struggle involving Elián González, a Cuban boy whom U.S. authorities had picked up in the Atlantic after his mother, fleeing from the island, had drowned. Although most people in Miami's Little Havana seemed to rally behind the effort of Elián's U.S. relatives to contest the Clinton's administration's decision to return him to his father in Cuba, some Cuban Americans argued that this media-saturated episode presented a one-dimensional view of a community in which diversity and involvement in American life transcended an obsession with the fate of Castro's regime.

ASIAN AMERICAN ACTIVISM

Diverse people with ancestral roots in Asia increasingly adopted the term "Asian American" as a way of signifying a new identity consciousness. During the 1970s Asian American studies programs took shape at colleges and universities on the West Coast. By the early 1980s political activists were gaining influence, especially within the Democratic Party, and more Asian American politicians won election to offices during the late 1980s and 1990s. During the 1970s, older Japanese Americans finally began to talk about what had long been unspoken—their experiences in internment camps during the Second World War (see chapter 26). Talk eventually turned to political agitation, and in 1988

Congress issued a formal apology and voted a reparations payment of $20,000 to every living Japanese American who had been confined in the camps.

The new Asian American vision encouraged Americans of Chinese, Japanese, Korean, Filipino, and other backgrounds to join together in a single pan-Asian movement. Organizations such as the Asian Pacific Planning Council (APPCON), founded in 1976, lobbied to obtain government funding for projects that benefited Asian American communities. The Asian Law Caucus, founded in the early 1970s by opponents of U.S. intervention in Vietnam, and the Committee Against Anti-Asian Violence, created a decade later in response to a wave of racist attacks, mobilized to fight a wide range of legal battles. And in 1997, the National Asian Pacific American Network Council, the first civil rights group to be formed by Asian Americans, began to lobby on issues related to immigration and education.

Emphasis on this broad, pan-Asian identity, however, raised problems of inclusion and exclusion. Filipino American activists, part of the second largest Asian American group in the United States in 1990, often resisted the Asian American label because they believed that Chinese Americans or Japanese Americans dominated groups such as APPCON. Many Filipinos focused on specific goals, particularly an effort to obtain citizenship and veteran's benefits for former soldiers of the Second World War who had fought against Japan in the Philippines. Similarly, Hmong groups often focused on issues specific to their own particular concerns. In 2000, for instance, they and their allies succeeded in obtaining the Hmong Veterans Naturalization Act, which allowed Hmong immigrants (and their spouses and widows) to use an interpreter when taking the test to obtain U.S. citizenship. At the same time, as new arrivals continued to come from Asia, groups such as Filipinos for Affirmative Action agreed to cooperate with non-Filipino organizations in opposing efforts to deny social services to legal immigrants.

As a result of complex pressures from different ethnic groups, the federal government finally decided to designate "Asian or Pacific Islanders" (API) as a single pan-ethnic category in the 1990 census. It also provided, however, nine specifically enumerated subcategories (such as Hawaiian or Filipino) and allowed other API groups (such as

ASIAN AMERICAN VEGETABLE MARKET The cultural influence of recent immigrants, particularly those from Latin America and Asia, became increasingly evident in U.S. cities during the 1980s. This grocery store serves a Chinese American community in New York City.

Hmong or Samoan) to write in their respective ethnic identifications.

Socioeconomic differences also made it difficult to frame a single Asian American agenda. Although in the late 1980s and early 1990s many Asian American groups showed remarkable upward mobility, demonstrating both economic and educational achievement, others such as Hmong immigrants and Chinese American garment workers, struggled to find jobs that paid more than the minimum wage. Thus, the term "Asian American"—which, by the end of the 20th century, applied to more than 10 million people and dozens of different ethnicities—both reflected and was challenged by the new emphasis on ethnic identity.

DILEMMAS OF ANTIDISCRIMINATION EFFORTS

How can governmental power best advance the cause of equality? Between the end of the Second

World War and about 1970, the antidiscrimination movement had demanded that the government not categorize people according to group identities based on race or ethnicity. On matters such as education, housing, or employment, the law must remain "color-blind" and treat people equally. The courts stood ready to strike down discriminatory laws and practices and to guarantee equality for all individuals.

Gradually, ideas about how to achieve equality began to change. With people placing new importance on the recognition of group identities, there was a shift of emphasis in social policymaking. By the 1970s a new agenda envisioned that governmental power could do more than simply eliminate discriminatory barriers to *individual* opportunity. Social justice, according to this new antidiscrimination credo, required government to take "affirmative action" so that *groups* that had historically faced discrimination could begin to receive an equitable share of the nation's jobs, public spending, and educational programs. It was not enough, in short, that individual members of ethnic minorities theoretically be permitted to compete for jobs and educational opportunities; government needed to make sure that a representative number of people from different groups had a reasonable chance of acceptance. Affirmative action, supporters argued, would help compensate for historic discrimination and hidden racial attitudes that continued to thwart members of minority groups.

Affirmative action sparked controversy. Some people, generally in the Republican party, found the idea of affirmative action a dangerous form of interest-group politics. Any program that set aside jobs or openings in educational institutions for certain racial or ethnic groups, they charged, smacked of racist "quotas." And was not affirmative action *on behalf of* some groups inevitably also "reverse discrimination" *against* others? The issue of reverse discrimination became particularly emotional when members of one ethnic group received jobs or entry to educational institutions despite lower scores on admissions exams. Even some beneficiaries of affirmative action programs began to claim that the "affirmative action" label devalued their individual talents and accomplishments.

Courts found it difficult to square affirmative action programs with traditional laws against discrimination. They tended to strike down as unconstitutional affirmative action plans that seemed to contain inflexible quotas and to uphold plans designed to remedy past patterns of discrimination and to make ethnicity only one of several criteria in hiring or educational decisions. Neither proponents nor opponents of affirmative action were fully satisfied with the pattern of judicial decisions in this new area of law.

A movement to eliminate or radically scale back affirmative action plans gained momentum during the 1990s. In 1996, after a hotly contested referendum campaign, voters in California passed Proposition 209, which aimed at ending most affirmative action measures in California by abolishing racial or gender preference in state hiring, contracting,

RACIAL TENSION IN BROOKLYN, 1990 In 1990, African American demonstrators staged a four-month boycott of a Brooklyn grocery store, owned by Korean Americans, after a black customer allegedly was assaulted by the store's employees. Tensions among racial and ethnic groups were part of the new diversity in American life during the late 20th century.

Television's Family Values

Television sitcoms have always provided visual representations of the "typical" family. During the 1940s, when most viewers resided in urban areas, television families also lived in cities and often held blue-collar jobs. Chester A. Riley, played by Jackie Gleason and later William Bendix, worked in an aircraft factory on *The Life of Riley*. Ralph Kramden, also portrayed by Gleason, drove a bus on *The Honeymooners*. By the mid-1950s, sitcom families were moving out to suburbia and up the socioeconomic scale. Ward Cleaver of *Leave It to Beaver* and Jim Anderson of *Father Knows Best* were prosperous professionals who provided their families with all of the amenities appropriate to the age of affluence. Other sitcom families—such as those portrayed on *I Love Lucy*, *The Adventures of Ozzie and Harriet*, and *Make Room for Daddy*—featured a husband who worked in show business and a wife who dominated home life from her command post in the kitchen.

Although most of these classic sitcoms continued to appear on television through syndication to local stations or on cable channels such as Nick-at-Nite, they were joined by a new and different generation of television families. The Huxtables (Bill Cosby and Phylicia Rashad), although as middle-class and affluent as the Andersons or the Cleavers, represented a

and college admissions. The number of African Americans and Latinos admitted to the state's most prestigious law and medical schools temporarily dropped as most of those who were admitted chose to go elsewhere.

Proponents of affirmative action challenged Proposition 209 as discriminatory. New programs that boosted ethnic diversity were subsequently devised, in California and elsewhere, but these emphasized income or high school ranking, rather than race or ethnicity.

Ironically, the late 20th-century debates over identity politics and affirmative action coincided with a rise in racial and ethnic intermarriage—a movement that might, in time, change the entire basis of discussion about equality. The 2000 census confirmed that growing numbers of people identified themselves as "mixed race" and either could not or would not claim a single ethnic-racial identity. In 1997, the media hailed Eldrick ("Tiger") Woods as the first African American golfer to win the prestigious Masters tournament, but Woods, whose mother was from Thailand, fiercely resisted being assigned any particular ethnic identification. In an official statement to the media, he said he was "EQUALLY PROUD" to be "both African American and Asian!" But he hoped that he could also "be just a golfer and a human being."

successful African American family co-headed by two well-educated professionals. The title character of *Murphy Brown* (Candice Bergen) worked in the media, but her family was composed of coworkers rather than a spouse. When the unmarried Murphy gave birth, Dan Quayle, then vice president of the United States, condemned her for endangering family values. The resultant flap only increased *Murphy Brown*'s ratings.

The *Simpsons* also survived the ire of conservative cultural critics. Although Homer and Marge were married with children, *The Simpsons*, especially during its early years, drew humor by portraying a dysfunctional family. Bart was "an underachiever—and proud of it," and Homer spent more time at Moe's Tavern than with his children. Gradually, the show gained cult status, particularly as viewers came to appreciate the subtle ways in which it playfully parodied television and movie conventions.

THE NEW RIGHT

Beginning in the mid-1970s, a diverse coalition called "the New Right" mobilized for a conservative reconstruction of American life. By the 1980s and 1990s its conservative vision had captured the imagination of millions.

Several different constituencies comprised the New Right. Older activists, who had rallied around William F. Buckley's *National Review* during the 1950s and Barry Goldwater during the mid-1960s, contributed continuity (see chapter 28). Espousing anticommunism and denouncing domestic spending programs, they also spoke out on a widening range of social issues. Phyllis Schlafly assumed a prominent role in mobilizing opposition to ratification of the Equal Rights Amendment, and Buckley's broad-ranging *Firing Line* became one of public television's most successful programs during the 1970s and 1980s.

NEW CONSERVATIVE INSTITUTIONS

These established activists teamed up with a group of intellectuals called the "neoconservatives" or "neocons." Neoconservatives such as Norman Podhoretz and Gertrude Himmelfarb had been anticommunist liberals during the 1950s and early

1960s. Unsettled by the insurgencies of the sixties, they claimed that the Democratic Party was retreating from an anticommunist foreign policy and catering to social activists. Although in 1968 most had supported Democrat Hubert Humphrey over Republican Richard Nixon, they moved increasingly rightward during the 1970s and supported the Republicans during the 1980s.

Neoconservatives remained true to their cold war–era roots. Their lively essays, written for established organs of conservatism such as *National Review* and the *Wall Street Journal* and for neoconservative publications such as *Commentary* and the *New Criterion*, denounced any movement associated with the 1960s, especially affirmative action. Neoconservatives offered intellectual sustenance to a new generation of conservative thinkers who worked to reinvigorate the nation's anticommunist foreign policy and celebrate its capitalist economic system.

A new militancy among conservative business leaders contributed to the emergence of the New Right. Denouncing the Great Society and even criticizing Richard Nixon's Republican administration, many business people claimed that health and safety regulations and environmental legislation endangered "economic freedom." They urged a rededication to the idea of limited government. Generous funding by corporations and philanthropic organizations helped to staff conservative research institutions (such as the American Enterprise Institute and Heritage Foundation) and to finance new lobbying organizations (such as the Committee on the Present Danger). Conservatism also gained considerable ground on college campuses, the birthplace of the New Left and the counterculture during the sixties.

THE NEW RELIGIOUS RIGHT

The New Right of the 1970s also attracted important grassroots support from Protestants in fundamentalist and evangelical churches. (Fundamentalists preach the necessity of fidelity to a strict moral code, of an individual commitment to Christ, and of a faith in the literal truth of the Bible. Evangelicals generally espouse the same doctrinal tenets as fundamentalists but place more

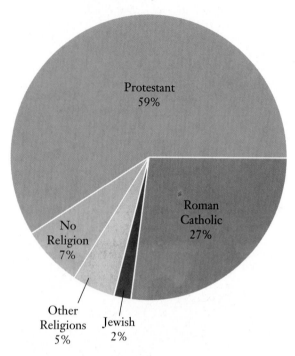

RELIGIOUS PREFERENCES IN THE UNITED STATES (PERSONS 18 YEARS OF AGE AND OLDER)

Source: *Statistical Abstract*, 1998

emphasis on converting non-Christians and less on defending the literal truth of the Bible.) Since the 1920s, fundamentalist and evangelical Protestants had generally stayed clear of partisan politics, but the Supreme Court's abortion decision in *Roe* v. *Wade* (1973) mobilized fundamentalist and evangelical leaders. They joined with Catholic conservatives in opposing abortion. Reverend Jerry Falwell of the Thomas Road Baptist Church and the *Old Time Gospel Hour* television ministry declared that *Roe* v. *Wade* showed that it was time to fight back on the political front because "liberals have been imposing morality on us for the last fifty years." Leaders of the New Religious Right, particularly in the South, also embarked on a lengthy legal battle to prevent the Internal Revenue Service from denying tax-exempt status to private Christian colleges and academies that opposed racial integration.

> "*I believe that at the foundation of the women's liberation movement there is a minority core of women who were once bored with life, whose real problems are spiritual problems. Many women have never accepted their God-given roles. . . . God Almighty created men and women biologically different and with differing needs and roles. He made men and women to complement each other and to love each other. Not all the women involved in the feminist movement are radicals. Some are misinformed, and some are lonely. . . . I believe that women deserve more than equal rights. . . . Men and women have differing strengths. . . . Because a woman is weaker does not mean that she is less important.*"
>
> **JERRY FALWELL**
> *calling for a "Moral Majority" in his 1980 book,* Listen America!

THE CONSERVATIVE SOCIAL AGENDA

Political developments of the 1970s also contributed to the emergence of the New Right. The declining political fortunes of George Wallace, who was badly wounded in a 1972 attempt on his life, left many conservatives, especially southerners, looking for new leadership. Similarly, many on the right had ultimately judged Richard Nixon more of an Eisenhower-style moderate than a Goldwater-style conservative. The end of Nixon's presidency in 1974 only intensified the desire for a "real" conservative leader. This desire became a crusade after Nixon's successor, Gerald Ford, selected the standard-bearer of Republican liberalism, Nelson Rockefeller, as his vice president. "I could hardly have been more upset if Ford had selected Teddy Kennedy," one disappointed conservative lamented (see chapter 31).

George Wallace had shown that conservative politics, especially when focused on social and cultural issues, could excite millions of voters. In 1975, activists organized the National Conservative Political Action Committee (NCPAC), the first of many right-oriented organizations, including the Conservative Caucus, The Committee for the Survival of a Free Congress, and Jerry Falwell's Moral Majority. Although these organizations initially focused on lobbying in Washington and electing conservative Republicans, they had broader cultural and social goals. As one architect of the New Right coalition put it, they fervently believed that "God's truth ought to be manifest politically."

Increasingly, their political crusade became phrased in terms of defending "family values" by opposing abortion and what the religious right called "degenerate lifestyles," particularly those espoused by feminists and homosexuals. Jerry Falwell's *Listen America!* (1980) suggested that the nation's military establishment was "under the complete control of avid supporters of the women's liberation movement." Because homosexuality was "one of the gravest sins condemned in the Scriptures," argued Paul Weyrich of NCPAC, the issue of gay and lesbian rights was not a matter of private lifestyles but a "question of morality which . . . affects the society as a whole." American institutions, particularly the male-headed nuclear family, needed protection. Similarly, parents needed to protect their children from educational "experiments." School boards and liberal educators, religious conservatives argued, were not only challenging Biblical precepts by teaching evolution but were advancing dangerous new ideas such as multiculturalism and feminism. Such conservatives believed that educational bureaucrats were forcing students to accept values that violated their personal religious values.

The New Right especially condemned innovations in college curricula associated with the sixties as evidence of "the closing of the American mind" (the title of a best-selling 1987 book by Allan Bloom) and of the "opening" of students' minds only to what was trendy and "politically correct" (or "PC"). The new attention to multicultural works, traditionalists charged, represented a debasement of intellectual life. During the late 1970s, the government-funded National Endowment for the Humanities (NEH) and the National Endowment for the Arts (NEA) had begun to fund projects that focused on America's cultural diversity and on politically sensitive reinterpretations of traditional works. During the 1980s the New Right launched a counterattack. Secretary of Education William Bennett crusaded against multicultural education, and Lynn Cheney, head of the NEH, championed traditional cultural values. During the early 1990s, conservatives successfully pressured the NEA to reject grants to controversial artistic projects, especially those relating to feminism or homosexuality. Supporters of these programs insisted that the NEA's action amounted to censorship and violated the First Amendment, a position that the U.S. Supreme Court rejected in a 1998 lawsuit involving performance artist Karen Finley.

The New Right adeptly publicized its positions. Conservative foundations funded conferences and radio and television programs. The New Religious Right embraced the electronic media, and preachers such as Pat Robertson capitalized on the expansion of CATV in the 1970s and early 1980s. Robertson built a multimedia empire that included the 24-hour Christian Broadcasting Network. During the 1980s, scandals and financial problems overtook some religious broadcasters, but Robertson's *700 Club*, a program that adapted his conservative evangelicalism to the talk-show and morning-news formats, continued to flourish through the 1990s. At the same time, broadcasters associated with the New Right used talk-radio programs at both the local and national levels to spread the conservative message. Representative Newt Gingrich of Georgia, a former history professor, mounted a state-of-the-art television course on conservative values, and other New Right leaders eagerly embraced the Internet. With the advent of 24-hour cable news channels, New Right activists such as Pat Buchanan and Mary Matalin became prominent political commentators.

The New Right struggled to separate itself from radical paramilitary groups who shared some of its broad values such as opposition to gun control laws, high taxes, and abortion. Deadly confrontations between several paramilitary groups and federal authorities, especially the Clinton administration's ill-conceived and poorly managed assault on the Branch Davidians group in Texas (in which 78 people, including many children, were killed), left their supporters feeling besieged and retaliatory. Any symbol of the federal government, one paramilitary leader claimed, could become a "strategic military target." In April 1995, on the second anniversary of the government's attack on the Branch Davidians, the Alfred P. Murrah Federal Building in Oklahoma City became such a target. A powerful bomb ripped through the building and killed 168 people, many of them children who were playing in a day care center. This bombing, for which a paramilitary sympathizer named Timothy McVeigh was convicted in 1997 and sentenced to death, helped to isolate the extremist, antigovernment movement from the New Right, which denounced the violent tendencies of the paramilitary fringe.

The New Right, a coalition of disparate parts, became a powerful force in both American politics and culture. It successfully challenged the Democratic party's liberalism; propelled the Republican party rightward; and, more generally, remapped the nation's political culture (chapter 31).

CONCLUSION

Sweeping changes occurred in demographics, economics, culture, and society during the last quarter of the 20th century. The nation aged, and more of its people gravitated to the Sunbelt. Sprawling "urban corridors" and "edge cities" challenged older central cities as sites for commercial, as well as residential, development. Rapid technological change fueled the growth of globalized industries, restructuring the labor force to fit a postindustrial economy. Americans also developed a new environmental consciousness.

The most prominent development in American mass culture was the proliferation of the video screen. Television, motion pictures, and the Internet increasingly targeted specific audiences, and the fragmented nature of cultural reception was exemplified by the rise of new, particularistic media ventures.

Meanwhile, American society itself also seemed to fragment into specialized identifications. Social activism often organized around sexual, ethnic, and racial identities. Multiculturalists celebrated this fragmentation, while another activist movement, the New Right, argued that identity politics was dividing the nation. The New Right's stress on limiting the power of government and promoting conservative values increasingly set the terms for political debate during the 1980s and 1990s, reconfiguring discussions about whether government power advanced, or worked against, greater liberty and equality in American life.

Suggested Readings begin on page SR-1.
For Web activities and resources
related to this chapter, go to
http://www.harcourtcollege.com/history.murrin

CHAPTER 31

POWER AND POLITICS SINCE 1974

RINGING IN A NEW MILLENNIUM

Revelers in Times Square at midnight joined a sequence of celebrations throughout the world to welcome the new century.

The national government continually expanded its powers during the three decades after the Second World War. Most people supported augmenting the government's military and intelligence capabilities to maintain the United States' dominant role in world affairs. They also endorsed the use of government power to cushion against economic downturns and to assist needy families.

The Vietnam War and the Watergate scandals (see chapter 29), however, shook faith in government. Disillusionment with secrecy, corruption, budget deficits, and failed crusades (especially the intervention in Vietnam and the War on Poverty) bred considerable popular distrust of power located in Washington. In this environment, divisive debates punctuated political life. During the 1970s and 1980s, questions focused on how to respond to an aging industrial economy, a ballooning federal deficit, and a beleaguered welfare system. Did the country need more governmental activism in addressing persistent problems of poverty and inequality, or would conditions improve if the national government reduced its role? Other debates centered on highly emotional issues such as abortion, environmental regulation, and tax policy.

When the U.S. economy began to expand during the mid-1980s and entered a period of unprecedented growth during the 1990s, public cynicism about government seemed to wane a bit. The overhaul of the nation's social-welfare programs, plus unexpected budget surpluses and declining crime, suggested that government power could work effectively. Still, partisan political debates remained divisive and culminated in the only impeachment trial of a president in the twentieth century.

Disagreements also focused on foreign policy. Should the United States set aside anticommunism to pursue other goals, as President Jimmy Carter initially urged, or should it wage the cold war even more vigorously, as his successor Ronald Reagan advocated? After 1989, when the cold war ended unexpectedly, the United States faced the task of reorienting its foreign policy in a new post–cold war world.

This chapter will focus on the following major questions:

- How were the Ford and Carter presidencies shaped by the legacies of Watergate and the Vietnam War?
- What conservative agenda, in both domestic and foreign policy, did President Ronald Reagan's administration construct?

- What forces and events contributed to the end of the cold war?
- Around what policies and appeals did President Bill Clinton reorient the Democratic party, and what was his post–cold war agenda in foreign policy?

FORD'S CARETAKER PRESIDENCY

When Richard Nixon resigned in August 1974, Gerald Ford became the first person to serve as vice president and then as president without having been elected to either office. Ford promised to mend the divisions that had split the nation during the 1960s and early 1970s. He hoped to draw on political ties he had forged during many years in the House of Representatives to reestablish the presidency as a focus of national unity. But Ford's ability to "heal the land," as he put it, proved limited. A genial, unpretentious former football star who asked to enter public events to the fight song of his alma mater, the University of Michigan, rather than to "Hail to the Chief," Ford failed to shake the impression that he was a weak, indecisive chief executive.

TRYING TO WHIP STAGFLATION

Ford's plan to rebuild his party around an updated version of the moderate Republicanism of the 1950s (chapter 27) quickly foundered. He infuriated conservative Republicans by appointing New York liberal Nelson Rockefeller as vice president (subject to congressional approval). His presidential pardon to former President Nixon, in September 1974, proved even more controversial. Ford's approval rating plummeted.

Economic problems soon dominated the domestic side of Ford's 865-day presidency. Focusing on rising prices, rather than on increasing unemployment, Ford touted a program called "Whip Inflation Now" (WIN). It offered a one-year income tax surcharge and cuts in federal spending as solutions to inflation. Prices, however, defied the predictions of prevailing economic wisdom and rose, accompanied by a sharp recession. Both prices and unemployment continued to rise—creating the condition known during Nixon's presidency as "stagflation"—and Ford abandoned WIN. In 1975, unemployment reached 8.5 percent and the inflation rate topped 9 percent.

Meanwhile, Ford and the Democratic-controlled Congress differed over how to deal with stagflation. Ford vetoed 39 spending bills during his brief presidency. He eventually acquiesced to a congressional economic program that included a tax cut, an increase in unemployment benefits, an unbalanced federal budget, and a limited set of controls over oil prices. Democrats charged that Ford could not implement coherent programs of his own, and Republicans feared that he could not stand up to Congress.

FOREIGN POLICY

As he struggled with economic problems at home, Ford steered the nation through its final involvement in the war in Southeast Asia. Upon assuming office, Ford assured South Vietnam that the United States would renew its military support if the government in Saigon ever became directly menaced by North Vietnamese troops. The antiwar mood in Congress and throughout the country, however, made fulfilling this commitment impossible. North Vietnam's armies, sensing final victory, moved rapidly through the South in March 1975, and Congress, relieved that American troops had finally been withdrawn following the 1973 Paris peace accords, refused to reintroduce U.S. military power.

The spring of 1975 brought communist victories. In early April, Khmer Rouge forces in Cambodia drove the American-backed government from the capital of Phnom Penh, and on April 30, 1975, North Vietnamese troops overran the South Vietnamese capital of Saigon, renaming it Ho Chi Minh City. The final defeat reignited debate over U.S. policy in Indochina: Former "doves" lamented the lives lost and money wasted, while former "hawks" derided their country's "failure of will."

Within this charged atmosphere, Ford immediately sought to demonstrate that the United States could still conduct an assertive foreign policy. In May 1975, the Khmer Rouge boarded a U.S. ship, the *Mayaguez*, and seized its crew. Secretary of State Henry Kissinger, declaring that it was time to "look ferocious," convinced Ford to order a rescue mission for the *Mayaguez*'s crew and bombing strikes against Cambodia. This military response,

CHRONOLOGY

1974 Nixon resigns and Ford becomes president; Ford soon pardons Nixon

1975 South Vietnam falls to North Vietnam • Ford asserts U.S. power in *Mayaquez* incident

1976 Jimmy Carter elected president

1978 Carter helps negotiate Camp David peace accords on Middle East

1979 Soviet Union invades Afghanistan
• Sandinista party comes to power in Nicaragua
• U.S. hostages seized in Iran

1980 Reagan elected president • U.S. hostages in Iran released

1981 Reagan tax cut passed

1983 U.S. troops removed from Lebanon • U.S. troops invade Grenada • Reagan announces SDI ("Star Wars") program

1984 Reagan defeats Walter Mondale

1986 Reagan administration rocked by revelation of Iran-*Contra* affair

1988 George Bush defeats Michael Dukakis in presidential election

1989 Communist regimes in Eastern Europe collapse; Berlin Wall falls • Cold war, in effect, ends

1990 Bush angers conservative Republicans by agreeing to a tax increase

1991 Bush orchestrates Persian Gulf War against Iraq

1992 Bill Clinton defeats Bush and third-party candidate Ross Perot in presidential race

1993 Congress approves North American Free Trade Agreement (NAFTA)

1994 Republicans gain control of both houses of Congress and pledge to enact their "Contract with America"

1995 Special prosecutor Kenneth Starr takes over the investigation of "Whitewater" allegations • World Trade Organization (WTO) created

1996 Personal Responsibility and Work Opportunity Reconciliation Act becomes first major overhaul of the national welfare system since the 1930s • Clinton defeats Robert Dole in the presidential race

1997 Congress and the White House agree on legislation aimed at reducing taxes and rolling back the federal deficit

1998 Republicans lose House seats in off-year election • Republican-controlled House impeaches Clinton

1999 Senate fails to convict Clinton on impeachment charges • Clinton orders bombing campaign against Serbia

2000 Longest economic expansion in U.S. history continues • Bush defeats Gore in close, disputed election

along with pressure on the Khmer Rouge from China, secured the release of the *Mayaguez* and its crew. The president's approval ratings briefly shot up, but the incident did little to allay growing doubts about Ford's effectiveness. The White House seemed primarily interested in looking tough, and more U.S. troops were lost than people rescued during the *Mayaguez* incident. Meanwhile, the president's other foreign policy initiatives, which included extending Nixon's policy of détente with the Soviet Union and pursuing a peace treaty for the Middle East, achieved little. Gerald Ford increasingly appeared a caretaker president.

THE ELECTION OF 1976

Conservative Republicans rallied behind Ronald Reagan, the former governor of California, and nearly denied Ford the GOP presidential nomination in 1976. Reagan's campaign caught fire when his advisers urged him to forgo specific policy proposals and simply highlight his image as a true conservative who, unlike Ford, was not beholden to Washington insiders. By this time, however, Ford had already won just enough delegates in the early primaries to eke out a narrow, first-ballot victory at the Republican Party's national convention.

RONALD REAGAN AS GOVERNOR OF CALIFORNIA IN 1968 A latecomer to politics, the former motion picture star often used cowboy imagery to overcome charges that he was too old for national leadership.

The Democrats did turn to an outsider, James Earl (Jimmy) Carter, the former governor of Georgia. Carter had graduated from the naval academy with a degree in nuclear engineering and, as a young officer, had worked on the nuclear submarine program. He cut short his military career in the early 1950s to return to Plains, Georgia, to run his family's peanut farming business. Later, Carter entered state politics, gaining the reputation of being a moderate on social issues and a fiscal conservative. When he announced his intention to run for the presidency in 1976, few people took him seriously; no governor, after all, had captured the White House since Franklin Roosevelt in 1932.

Carter campaigned as a person of many virtues. With Watergate still a vivid memory, he emphasized his personal character and the fact that he had spent most of his life outside of politics. Highlighting his small-town roots, he pledged to "give the government of this country back to the people of this country." A devout Baptist, Carter campaigned as a born-again Christian. Touting his record as a successful governor, he asked people to "help me evolve an efficient, economical, purposeful, and manageable government for our nation." In order to counterbalance his own status as a Washington outsider, he picked Minnesota senator Walter Mondale as his running mate. In November, Carter won a narrow victory over Ford.

Carter's triumph rested on a diverse, transitory coalition. Capitalizing on his regional appeal, Carter carried every southern state except Virginia. Although he ran well among southern white members of fundamentalist and evangelical churches, his victory in the South depended on a strong turnout among African Americans, the beneficiaries of federal voter protection laws enacted during the 1960s. Carter courted the youth vote by promising to pardon most of the young men who had resisted the draft during the Vietnam War. With the poor economy a major issue, Mondale's appeal to traditional Democrats helped Carter narrowly capture three key states that had long been Democratic strongholds—New York, Pennsylvania, and Ohio. Even so, Carter won by less than 2 million popular ballots and by only 56 electoral votes. Voter turnout in 1976 hit its lowest mark since the end of the Second World War; only about 54 percent of eligible voters went to the polls.

CARTER'S ONE-TERM PRESIDENCY

Jimmy Carter's lack of a popular mandate and his image as an outsider posed serious handicaps. Powerful constituencies, including both labor unions and corporations, feared that Carter might prove an unpredictable leader. Moreover, many Democratic members of Congress, especially those first elected in 1974 in the immediate aftermath of Watergate, stressed their independence from the White House. In 1976 most of these Democrats had, after all, rolled up higher vote totals in their states than Carter had. Carter also lacked the image of a national leader. Although he brought some people with long experience in government into his cabinet, he relied on the Georgians on his White House staff, a small cadre of advisers that the Washington press corps dubbed the "Georgia Mafia." After leaving government, Carter reflected on his difficulties: "I had a different way of governing. . . . I was a southerner, a born-again Christian, a Baptist, a newcomer. . . . As an engineer and a

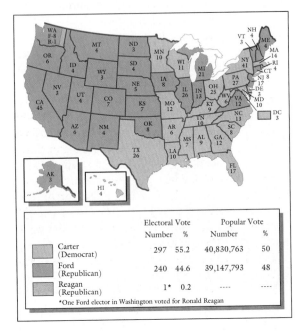

	Electoral Vote		Popular Vote	
	Number	%	Number	%
Carter (Democrat)	297	55.2	40,830,763	50
Ford (Republican)	240	44.6	39,147,793	48
Reagan (Republican)	1*	0.2	----	----

*One Ford elector in Washington voted for Ronald Reagan

PRESIDENTIAL ELECTION, 1976

governor I was more inclined to move rapidly and without equivocation."

WELFARE AND ENERGY INITIATIVES

In trying to frame his agenda, Carter seemed caught between those who claimed that the national government had assumed too much power and those who argued that Washington did too little to address social and economic problems. Unlike Richard Nixon, who had unveiled a bold Family Assistance Plan (FAP) in 1969 (chapter 29), Carter temporized on what to do about welfare policy. His advisers were divided between those who favored a more complicated version of FAP, which would have granted greater monetary assistance to low-income families, and those who thought the national government should create several million new public service jobs. Carter, while opposing any increase in the federal budget, asked Congress for a program that included both additional cash assistance and more jobs. He presented his proposal to Congress in 1977, where it quickly died in committee, and the effort to change the welfare system stalled for nearly a decade.

Carter pushed harder on energy issues. In response to soaring Middle East oil prices (see chapter 30), he delegated James Schlesinger, a veteran of both the Nixon and the Ford administrations, to develop a sweeping energy plan. Schlesinger, Carter's secretary of energy, came up with a set of ambitious goals: (1) decrease U.S. reliance on foreign oil and natural gas; (2) expand domestic energy production through new tax incentives and deregulation of natural gas production; (3) levy new taxes to discourage gasoline use; (4) foster conservation by encouraging energy-saving measures; and (5) promote nonpetroleum energy sources, especially coal and nuclear power. Neither Carter nor Schlesinger consulted Congress or even some members of the president's own administration. Instead, Carter went on national television, in April 1977, and suddenly announced a complicated energy proposal that included more than 100 interrelated provisions.

Congress quickly rejected the plan. Legislators from oil-producing states opposed higher taxes on gasoline, and critics of the big oil companies blocked rapid deregulation of oil and natural gas

production. Meanwhile, environmentalists opposed any increase in coal production because of coal's contribution to air pollution. Most Americans simply ignored Carter's claim that the nation's struggle with its energy problems amounted to "the moral equivalent of war."

A FALTERING ECONOMY

Carter had no greater success with economic policy. He inherited the economic problems—especially stagflation—that had bedeviled Nixon and Ford. He pledged to lower both unemployment and inflation, to stimulate greater economic growth, and to balance the federal budget (which showed a deficit of about $70 billion in 1976). Instead, by 1980 the economy had almost stopped expanding, unemployment (after dipping below 6 percent in 1979) was beginning to rise again, and inflation topped 13 percent. Most voters told opinion pollsters that their own economic conditions had dramatically deteriorated during Carter's presidency.

The economic difficulties of the 1970s spread beyond individuals. New York City, beset by long-term economic and social problems and short-term fiscal mismanagement, faced bankruptcy. It could neither meet its financial obligations nor borrow money through the usual channels. Finally, private bankers and public officials collaborated on congressional legislation to provide the nation's largest city with federal loan guarantees. New York's troubles reflected a broader urban crisis. According to one estimate, New York City lost 600,000 manufacturing jobs in the 1970s; Chicago lost 200,000. Bricks from demolished, industrial-era buildings became a leading export of St. Louis, Missouri. Increasing numbers of people living in central cities could find only low-paying, short-term jobs with no fringe benefits. Many found no jobs at all. Rising crime rates and deteriorating downtown neighborhoods afflicted most urban areas, even as inflation further eroded city budgets.

What explains the economic dislocations of the late 1970s? Tax cuts and increased spending on public works projects had temporarily lowered the unemployment rate. The Federal Reserve Board, hoping to add its own economic stimulus, had permitted the money supply to grow. These very

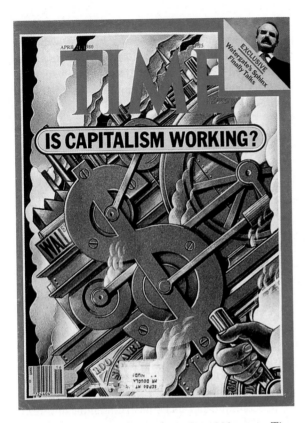

"IS CAPITALISM WORKING?" In 1980 even *Time* magazine wondered about the future of the United States. Persistent economic problems—in particular, high rates of inflation and unemployment—dominated the Ford and Carter presidencies.

measures intended to stimulate recovery, drove price inflation. Meanwhile, ever-rising international oil prices triggered a series of gasoline and home heating fuel price increases that rippled through the economy. Inflation and high interest rates choked off productivity and economic growth.

Conservative economists and business groups charged that the favored domestic programs of most congressional Democrats had contributed to rising prices. Conservatives argued that increasing the minimum wage and vigorously enforcing safety and antipollution regulations had driven up the cost of doing business and had forced companies to pass on this increase to consumers in the form of higher prices. During the last two years of his presidency, Carter himself seemed to agree with some of this analysis when, over the protests of members of his own party, he reduced spending for a variety of social programs, supported a law that reduced capital gains taxes for wealthier citizens, and began a process of deregulating transportation industries.

NEGOTIATING FOREIGN DISPUTES

In foreign policy, as in domestic policy, Carter promised a significant change of direction. On his first day in office, he extended amnesty to those who had resisted the draft during the Vietnam War. He also declared that he would not be afflicted by an "inordinate fear of communism" and would put a concern for human rights at the center of U.S. foreign policy. After four years, however, his foreign policy initiatives were in disarray. Ronald Reagan's "get-tough-again" presidential campaign of 1980 would make Carter a symbol of foreign policy ineptitude.

Although skillful in handling small-group negotiations, Carter had little experience working with long-term foreign policy issues. Furthermore, his top policy advisers—Cyrus Vance as secretary of state and Zbigniew Brzezinski as national security adviser—often pursued contradictory approaches to policymaking. Brzezinski favored a hard-line, anti-Soviet policy with an emphasis on military muscle; Vance preferred avoiding public confrontations and emphasized the virtues of quiet diplomacy. Pulled in divergent directions, Carter's policy often seemed to waffle. Still, Carter set some important new directions, emphasizing negotiation in particular trouble spots of the world and making human rights a priority.

One of Carter's first concerns involved the Panama Canal treaties. The status of the Panama Canal Zone had been under negotiation for 13 years. U.S. ownership of the canal, a legacy of turn-of-the-century imperialism, had sparked growing anti-Yankee sentiment throughout Latin America. Moreover, Carter argued, the canal was no longer the economic and strategic necessity it had once been. Despite strong opposition, Carter adroitly managed public and congressional relations to secure treaties that granted Panama increasing jurisdiction over the canal, culminating in full control in the year 2000.

Carter's faith in negotiations, and in his personal skill as a facilitator, again emerged in the Camp

David peace accords of 1978. Egypt and Israel had endured strained relations since the Yom Kippur War of 1973, when Israel repelled an Egyptian attack and seized the Sinai Peninsula and territory along the West Bank (of the Jordan River). Reviving Henry Kissinger's earlier efforts to mediate Arab-Israeli conflicts, Carter brought Menachem Begin and Anwar Sadat, leaders of Israel and Egypt, respectively, to the Camp David presidential retreat. After 13 days of bargaining, the three leaders announced the framework for a negotiating process and a peace treaty. Although Middle East tensions hardly vanished, the Camp David accords kept high-level discussions alive, lowered the level of acrimony between Egypt and Israel, and bound both sides to the United States through its promises of economic aid.

In Asia and Africa, the Carter administration also emphasized accommodation. Building on Nixon's initiative, Carter expanded economic and cultural relations with China and finally established formal diplomatic ties with the People's Republic on New Year's Day 1979. In Africa, Carter abandoned Kissinger's reliance on white colonial regimes and supported the transition of Zimbabwe (formerly Rhodesia) to a government run by the black majority.

CAMPAIGNING FOR HUMAN RIGHTS ABROAD

Carter's foreign policy became best known for its emphasis on human rights. Cold war alliances with anticommunist dictatorships, Carter believed, were undermining U.S. influence in the world. In his 1976 campaign he had criticized Nixon for supporting repressive regimes. In the long run, Carter's policy helped to raise worldwide consciousness of human rights issues and tied the extension of U.S. foreign aid to a regime's behavior. The trend toward democratization that occurred in many nations during the 1980s and 1990s was partially triggered by the rising awareness associated with Carter's stress on human rights.

The immediate impact of the human rights policy, however, was ambiguous. Because Carter applied the policy inconsistently, many of America's most repressive allies, such as Ferdinand Marcos in the Philippines, felt little pressure to change their

ways. Moreover, Carter's rhetoric about human rights helped spark revolutionary movements against America's long-standing dictator-allies in Nicaragua and Iran. These revolutions, fueled by old resentments against the United States, brought anti-American regimes to power and presented Carter with thorny policy dilemmas. In Nicaragua, for example, the Sandinista revolution toppled dictator Anastasio Somoza, whom the United States had long supported. The Sandinistas, initially a coalition of moderate democrats and communists, quickly drifted toward a more militant Marxism and began to expropriate private property. Carter opposed Nicaragua's movement to the left but could not change the revolution's course. The president's Republican critics charged that his policies had given a green light to communism in Central America and pledged that they would work to oust the Sandinista government.

CONFRONTING A HOSTAGE CRISIS IN IRAN

Events in Iran dramatically eroded Carter's standing. Shah Reza Pahlavi had regained his throne with the help of Western intelligence agencies in a 1953 coup, and the United States had subsequently provided him with a steady supply of military hardware. The overthrow of the Shah by an Islamic fundamentalist revolution in January 1979 thus signaled a massive rejection of U.S. influence in Iran. When the Carter administration bowed to political pressure and allowed the deposed and ailing Shah to enter the United States for medical treatment in November 1979, a group of Iranians took 66 Americans hostage at the U.S. embassy compound in Tehran. They demanded the return of the Shah in exchange for the release of the hostages.

As the hostage incident gripped the country, Carter's critics cited it as evidence of how weak and impotent the United States had become. Carter talked tough; levied economic reprisals against Iran; and, over Vance's objections, sent a military mission to rescue the hostages. (Vance subsequently resigned.) The mission proved an embarrassing failure, and Carter never managed to resolve the situation. After his defeat in the 1980 election, diplomatic efforts finally brought the hostages home, but the United States and Iran remained at odds.

Meanwhile, criticism of Carter intensified when the Soviet Union invaded Afghanistan in December 1979, a move that may have been sparked by Soviet fear of the growing influence of Islamic fundamentalists along its borders. Many Americans interpreted the invasion as a simple sign that the Soviets now dismissed the United States as too weak to contain their expansionism. Carter never shook the charge that he suffered from "post-Vietnam syndrome," a failure to act strongly in foreign affairs. He halted grain exports to the Soviet Union (angering his farm constituency), organized a boycott of the 1980 Olympic Games in Moscow, withdrew a new Strategic Arms Limitation Treaty (SALT) from the Senate, and revived registration for the military draft. Still, conservatives charged Carter with presiding over a decline of American power and prestige, and Ronald Reagan made constant reference to Iran and Afghanistan as he prepared for the 1980 elections.

THE ELECTION OF 1980

For a time, when Senator Edward Kennedy of Massachusetts entered the party's 1980 presidential primaries, it seemed that Democrats themselves might deny Carter a second term. Although Kennedy's challenge fizzled, it did underscore Carter's vulnerability. Kennedy popularized anti-Carter themes that Republicans gleefully embraced. "It's time to say no more hostages, no more high interest rates, no more high inflation, and no more Jimmy Carter," went one of Kennedy's stump speeches. More than one-third of the people who supported Kennedy in the final eight Democratic primaries (five of which Kennedy won) were conservative Democrats who told pollsters they probably would vote Republican in the general election. As Carter entered the fall campaign against the Republicans, he seemed a likely loser.

Republican Ronald Reagan exuded confidence. He stressed his opposition to many domestic social programs and his support for a stronger national defense. His successful primary campaign glossed over specific details, especially those related to his promise of massive tax cuts, and highlighted an optimistic vision of a rejuvenated America and a supply of movie-inspired quips. To remind voters of the economic problems associated with the Carter presidency, he asked repeatedly, "Are you better off now than you were four years ago?" He would quickly answer his own question by invoking what he called a "misery index," which added the rate of inflation to the rate of unemployment.

Reagan seized an issue that Democrats had long regarded as their own: economic growth. In 1979 one of Jimmy Carter's economic advisers had gloomily portrayed the nation's economic problems as so severe that there was "no way we can avoid a decline in our standard of living. All we can do is adapt to it." In contrast, Reagan optimistically promised sharp tax cuts to bring back the kind of economic expansion the nation had enjoyed during the 1950s and 1960s. During a crucial television debate, when Carter tried to criticize Reagan's economic proposals for their lack of specificity, a smiling Reagan spotlighted Carter's apparent pessimism by repeatedly quipping, "There you go again!"

Reagan won the November presidential election with only slightly more than 50 percent of the popular vote. (Moderate Republican John Anderson, who ran an independent campaign for the White House, won about 7 percent.) Reagan's vote total in the electoral college overwhelmed Carter's: 489 to 49. Moreover, Republicans took 12 Senate seats

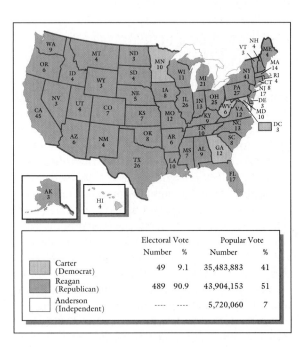

	Electoral Vote		Popular Vote	
	Number	%	Number	%
Carter (Democrat)	49	9.1	35,483,883	41
Reagan (Republican)	489	90.9	43,904,153	51
Anderson (Independent)	----	----	5,720,060	7

PRESIDENTIAL ELECTION, 1980

away from Democrats, gaining control of the Senate for the first time since 1954.

Noting Reagan's slim majority in the popular vote, old-line Democrats portrayed 1980 as more of a defeat for Carter than a victory for the Republicans. By reducing expenditures for domestic programs and lowering taxes on capital gains, according to this analysis, Carter had alienated traditional Democratic voters. Moreover, they accused Reagan's sophisticated media campaign of temporarily misleading voters; in due course, they claimed, Reagan would be unmasked as a media-manufactured president.

These Democrats, however, failed to recognize that their party's domestic agenda had been steadily losing support for more than a decade. In 1980 voters ousted seven prominent liberal Democratic senators, including former presidential candidate George McGovern. The real income of the average American family, which had risen at an annual rate of nearly 3 percent per year between 1950 and 1965, rose only 1.7 percent a year between 1965 and 1980, with the worst times coming after 1973. In such an economic climate, middle-income taxpayers, themselves struggling to make ends meet, found Democratic social welfare programs far less palatable than during more prosperous times.

The 1970s had produced a new, more conservative era in social policymaking. Liberal Democrats continued to talk about how to improve, and even expand, welfare-state initiatives. Conservatives, on the other hand, advocated a significant reduction in government spending programs, decrying public housing as a waste of tax dollars and denouncing AFDC (Aid to Families with Dependent Children) and food stamps as socially debilitating for their recipients and a drag on the nation's economy. More and more voters came to identify with Reagan's antigovernment rhetoric.

REAGAN'S "NEW MORNING IN AMERICA"

Reagan's advisers set about crafting a bold conservative agenda. Tapping concerns about declining national power and eroding living standards, Reagan promised a "new morning in America," especially in the area of taxation. A taxpayer revolt that had swept California during the late 1970s pro-

vided a model for Reagan's attack on federal domestic spending. (The situation was ironic: California's tax revolt had emerged in response to increases while Reagan himself had been the state's governor.) Across the country, people responded to Reagan's tax-reduction message.

In addition, Reagan courted the New Right with opposition to abortion, support for prayer in school, and the endorsement of traditional "family values." Conservative religious figures, including Jerry Falwell and Pat Robertson, former Democrats, joined Reagan's new Republican coalition. Even Carter's own Southern Baptists, who had rallied behind him in 1976, along with born-again Christians across the country, flocked to Reagan in 1980. Reagan also found a way to reach white (especially male) voters, who were upset over affirmative action, while avoiding being charged with making racial appeals. Reagan embraced the cause of "color-blind" social policies and brought conservative African American and Hispanic leaders into his administration. "Guaranteeing equality of treatment is the government's proper function," Reagan proclaimed at one of his first presidential press conferences.

PURSUING SUPPLY-SIDE ECONOMICS

To justify cutting taxes, Reagan touted "supply-side economics." This theory held that sizable tax reductions would stimulate the economy by putting more money in the hands of both producers and consumers, thereby reversing the economic stagnation of the 1970s. Reagan pushed his tax plan through Congress during the summer of 1981. The new law significantly reduced taxes for people who earned high incomes and already possessed significant wealth. Taxes on businesses also were slashed to encourage investment in new facilities and equipment. Most Democrats, who had supported tax reductions under Carter in 1978, endorsed Reagan's plan. At the same time, the Federal Reserve Board under Paul Volcker, a Carter appointee, kept interest rates high in order to drive down inflation.

After a severe economic downturn in 1981 and 1982, the worst since the Great Depression of the 1930s, the economy rebounded and entered a period of noninflationary growth. Between 1982 and 1986, more than 11 million new jobs were added to

The First Movie-Star President

Ronald Wilson Reagan began his presidency in Hollywood, where he lived and worked before entering national politics during the turbulent 1960s. The political career of the "great communicator" built on, rather than broke with, his early days as a screen idol. Reagan's media advisers could count on directing a seasoned professional. Instinctively, Reagan knew where to stand; how to deliver lines flawlessly; how to convey emotions through body language as well as dialogue; and when to melt into the background so that supporting players on his presidential team might carry a crucial scene.

Reagan's films provided a rehearsal for the roles that he would play in the White House. Initially, Reagan's opponents hoped that his old film parts, particularly *Bedtime for Bonzo* (1947), in which he co-starred with a chimpanzee, would become political liabilities. Reagan himself, however, never tried to disavow his Hollywood days. Instead, he accentuated his fluency with film-related references. His efforts to cheer on the nation during the 1980s, for example, deliberately recalled his favorite film role, that of the 1920s Notre Dame football star, George Gipp, whom Reagan played in *Knute Rockne, All American* (1940). Throughout his political career, Reagan eagerly identified with "the Gipper," whose upbeat attitude in the face of death had allegedly inspired the Fighting Irish to football victories. Similarly, when tilting with a Democratic-controlled Congress over tax policy, Reagan invoked Clint Eastwood's famous screen character "Dirty Harry" and promised to veto any tax increase. "Go ahead, make my day," he taunted. On another occasion, he cited Sylvester Stallone's *Rambo* films as possible blueprints for dealing with countries that had seized American hostages. Sometimes, as he freely attributed lines from motion pictures to real-world situations, Reagan seemed to have difficulty separating "reel" from "real" life. During one session with reporters, he even referred to his own dog as "Lassie," the canine performer who had been Reagan's Hollywood contemporary during the 1940s and 1950s.

Life in Hollywood also appeared to provide a prologue to President Reagan's conservative policies. Early in his film career, Reagan appeared in four films as the same character, a government agent named Brass Bancroft. In these B-grade thrillers Reagan defined a popular image that he later deployed in politics: that of a confident leader who maintained a clear distinction, especially in foreign policy, between (good) friends and (evil) foes. One of the Brass Bancroft series, entitled *Murder in the Air* (1940), even featured a

the economy. By 1986, the GNP was steadily climbing, and the inflation rate had plunged to less than 2 percent; unemployment figures, however, stubbornly refused to drop. Reagan's supporters called the turnaround an "economic miracle" and hailed the "Reagan revolution."

The economic revival sparked new debates over the cumulative impact of annual federal budget deficits and the consequences of the economic expansion. On the first issue—budget deficits—Reagan's critics complained that he had not matched tax cuts with budget reductions. Although Reagan constantly inveighed against budget deficits and big spenders, his administration rolled up the most extraordinary record of deficits and spending in U.S. history. During his presidency, annual deficits tripled to nearly $300 billion. To finance such spending, the United States borrowed abroad and piled up the largest foreign debt in the world. Reagan's "revolution," critics charged, brought short-term recovery for some people by courting a long-term budget crisis that would harm low-income people who relied on government programs. Future generations would pay for the soaring government debt.

science-fiction-style "death ray" that resembled the Strategic Defense Initiative armaments that President Reagan would champion more than forty years later.

Reagan's subsequent film roles refined this early Hollywood image. Although poor eyesight prevented him from replicating the fictional Brass Bancroft's combat experience during the Second World War, Reagan served long hours as an Army Air Corps officer, making films in support of the war effort. He appeared as a military hero in films such as *For God and Country* (1943) but more often provided upbeat voice-overs, once even sharing the soundtrack with President Franklin Roosevelt. He also starred, on loan from the Air Corps, in *This Is the Army* (1943), one of the most successful of Hollywood's uplifting military-backdrop musicals produced during the Second World War.

After the war, Reagan never regained the star status that he had enjoyed earlier, and he devoted more and more of his time to Hollywood's own cold-war politics. His tenure as the communist-fighting president of the Screen Actors Guild, historians often speculate, likely speeded his conversion from New Deal Democrat to right-leaning Republican. In his final on-screen roles, Reagan usually portrayed the kind of independent, rugged individualist—often in westerns such as *Law and Order* (1953)—whom he would later lionize in his political speeches.

Nancy Reagan, who co-starred with her husband in *Hellcats of the Navy* (1957) and later as the nation's First Lady, perceptively summed up the integral relationship between Reagan the actor and Reagan the political leader. "There are not two Ronald Reagans," she observed. In 1980s America, movie culture and political culture became intertwined and embodied in the same charismatic leader.

Ronald Reagan as the "Gipper" in *Knute Rockne, All American*.

On the second issue—the soundness of the U.S. economy—critics charged that the new economic growth was unevenly distributed. Reagan's policies, they said, produced a "Swiss-cheese" economy full of holes. Farmers in the Midwest were especially battered during the 1981–82 recession as falling crop prices hampered their efforts to pay off high-interest loans contracted during the inflation-ridden 1970s. The value of land, a farmer's primary asset, plummeted. A series of mortgage foreclosures, reminiscent of the 1930s, hit farm states, and the ripple effect decimated many small-town businesses. At the same time, urban families struggling to survive on low-paying jobs and declining welfare benefits also were puzzled by talk of a "Reagan boom." Many jobs created in the 1980s were nonunionized service jobs that offered relatively low wages and few, if any, fringe benefits. In 1981 the average weekly paycheck was $270; measured in constant dollars, the same check was worth only $254 in 1991. The minimum wage, when measured in constant dollars, fell throughout Reagan's presidency.

The economic changes of the Reagan era fell especially hard on what was called a new "underclass."

FARM FORECLOSURES During the early 1980s many Midwest farmers endured hard times. Farm foreclosures—followed by auctions of land, equipment, and personal property—swept across the Farm Belt during Ronald Reagan's first term as president.

From the late 1960s on, people with educational credentials and marketable skills had made significant economic gains. The number of African American families earning a solid middle-class income more than doubled between 1970 and 1990. African American college graduates could expect incomes comparable to those of white college graduates, partly as a result of affirmative action hiring plans put in place by the Carter administration. Many people, therefore, could afford to leave the problem-plagued inner-city neighborhoods. The story of mobility looked seriously different, however, for people who remained persistently unemployed and trapped in declining urban centers. At the end of the 1980s, one-third of all black families lived in poverty and the number earning less than $15,000 per year had doubled since 1970. In inner cities, less than half of African American children were completing high school, and more than 60 percent were unemployed. Throughout America, the gap between rich and poor widened significantly.

CONSTRUCTING A CONSERVATIVE AGENDA

Meanwhile, Reagan made changes in other areas. In 1981 he summarily fired the nation's air traffic controllers when their union refused to halt a nationwide strike. Overall, union membership continued to decline, as both the Reagan administration and many large businesses pursued aggressive antiunion strategies during the 1980s. The percentage of workers not employed on farms who were unionized, which had been declining since the 1960s, fell to just 16 percent by the end of Reagan's presidency. Workers recognized that the balance of power was tilting against them and increasingly turned away from strikes as an economic weapon.

Reagan also placed a conservative stamp on the federal court system. Almost immediately, he nominated a Supreme Court justice, Sandra Day O'Connor, the first woman to sit on the Court. Justice O'Connor initially seemed a staunch conservative, particularly in addressing social issues or criminal justice matters. During Reagan's first term, when the Republican Party controlled the Senate, Reagan also named prominent conservative jurists, such as Robert Bork and Antonin Scalia, to lower federal courts. Conservatives, who had long decried the decisions of the Court under Earl Warren and even many of those handed down under Warren Burger, welcomed the influx of judges from the political right. Civil libertarians complained that the federal courts were becoming less hospitable to legal claims made by criminal defendants, labor unions, and political dissenters. Because of retirements, by 1990 about 50 percent of the federal judiciary had been nominated and confirmed during Ronald Reagan's presidency.

Reagan also looked for staunch conservatives to fill his nonjudicial appointments. He filled the Justice Department with lawyers who were eager to end the "rights revolution" and—in line with the "color-blind" approach to racial issues—to sidetrack affirmative action programs. Reagan appointed James Watt, an outspoken critic of environmental legislation, as secretary of the interior, the department that guides the nation's conservation policy. Reagan's first two appointees to the Department of Energy actually proposed eliminating the cabinet office they headed—an idea that Congress blocked. Reagan himself mused about abolishing the Department of Education and often criticized programs espoused by his own secretary of education. Finally, having staffed most of the administrative agencies with conservatives, Reagan sought to ease regulations on businesses by relaxing enforcement of the safety and environmental laws that conservative economists had blamed for escalating the "cost of doing business."

In addition, Reagan eliminated some social welfare programs, most notably the Comprehensive Employment and Training Act (CETA), established during Richard Nixon's first term. He reduced funding for others, such as food stamps. Reagan proved to be much more conservative on domestic issues than Nixon, who had allowed social expenditures to increase, had courted some labor union leaders, and had advanced his guaranteed-income program, FAP. Nevertheless, Reagan pledged that Washington would maintain a "safety net" for those who in true need of governmental assistance.

Critics complained, however, about the rising number of people whose total package of income and government benefits still fell below what economists considered the poverty level. Conditions would have been worse if the nation's most popular welfare program, Social Security, had not been redesigned in the 1970s. Social Security benefits now automatically increased along with the rate of inflation (an arrangement called "indexing"). Rising Social Security payments, along with Medicare benefits, enabled millions of older Americans who might otherwise have fallen below the official poverty line to hold their own economically during the Reagan years. The burden of poverty, then, fell disproportionately on female-headed households and especially on children. By the end of the 1980s, one of every five children was being raised in a household whose total income fell below the official poverty line.

Amid controversies over the growing budget deficit and the inequalities in wealth, Reagan became known as the "Teflon president." No matter what problems beset his administration, nothing negative ever seemed to stick to Reagan himself. His genial optimism seemed unshakable. He even appeared to rebound quickly after being shot by a would-be assassin in March 1981.

ROUTING THE DEMOCRATS, 1984

Democrats continued to underestimate Reagan's popular appeal—a miscalculation that doomed their 1984 presidential campaign. Walter Mondale, Jimmy Carter's vice president, ran on a platform calling for "the eradication of discrimination in all aspects of American life" and for an expansion of national social-welfare programs. Mondale even proposed higher taxes to pay for his proposals. Convinced that Reagan's "economic miracle" would eventually self-destruct, Mondale insisted that Reagan must soon raise taxes to cover the burgeoning federal deficit. And "so will I," Mondale bravely declared. "He won't tell you; I just did."

Republicans ran a textbook-perfect campaign. They labeled Mondale's support by labor and civil rights groups as a vestige of the old politics of "special interests" and denounced his tax proposal as a reminder of the "wasteful tax-and-spend policies" popularly associated with 1970s stagflation. Mondale's running-mate, Representative Geraldine Ferraro of New York, the first woman to run for president or vice president on a major party ticket, became another symbol of kowtowing to special interests—in this case, feminist and pro-choice groups. Reagan himself continued to sketch the picture of a bright, conservative future for America. His campaign films pictured the United States as a glowing landscape of bustling small towns and lush farmland. His campaign slogan was "It's Morning Again in America," and his campaign song was "I'm Proud to Be an

American." The 1984 presidential election ended with Mondale carrying only his home state of Minnesota and the District of Columbia. In 1964, the Republican Party had hit bottom with Barry Goldwater's defeat; 20 years later, Ronald Reagan's victory capped a remarkable revival for the GOP.

REAGAN'S SECOND TERM

During Reagan's second term, the White House and Congress addressed two long-term domestic issues: federal budget reduction and welfare reform. First, the Gramm-Rudman-Hollings Act of 1985 mandated a balanced federal budget by 1991, but neither Congress nor the Reagan administration seemed eager to implement either that goal or the larger one of reducing the soaring government deficit. Second, the Family Support Act of 1988 required states to inaugurate work training programs and to move people, even mothers receiving AFDC, off the welfare rolls. This law, its critics noted, did little to guarantee that its work training provision would actually result in people finding— and keeping—jobs. Without a plan to create new employment opportunities, the Family Support Act seemed more aimed at allowing politicians of both parties to cut domestic programs and less aimed at finding actual welfare alternatives. Yet, despite their limitations, Gramm-Rudman-Hollings and the Family Support Act set policymakers in the White House and in Congress on a course that would eventually culminate in a comprehensive budget-reduction and welfare-overhaul package nearly a decade later.

Even some of Reagan's own supporters became disappointed by domestic developments. In 1986, following the resignation of Warren Burger, the Senate confirmed William Rehnquist as chief justice of the United States, and Antonin Scalia, another staunch conservative, to replace Rehnquist as associate justice of the Supreme Court. In 1987, however, the Senate rebuffed Reagan's attempt to elevate Robert Bork, another prominent conservative, to the Court. Bork's rejection angered the New Right, which blamed Reagan himself for not working hard enough to support his nominee. Meanwhile, the Religious Right chafed at what it considered Reagan's tepid support for the antiabortion crusade. Reagan also showed little interest in

overhauling the Social Security system and his massive military spending undermined the conservative dream of decreasing the federal budget and reducing the long-term federal debt.

Reagan's second term was also marked by charges of mismanagement and corruption. The process of banking deregulation became linked to malfeasance in financial circles and to risky speculation that critics called "casino capitalism." Problems in the savings and loan industry reached crisis proportions. During a period of lax oversight by federal regulators, many savings and loan institutions (S&Ls) had overextended loans to risky ventures, particularly in the overbuilt real estate market, and had incurred financial obligations far beyond their means. As hundreds of S&Ls fell insolvent, the people and the businesses to which they had lent money also faced financial disaster. The agency that regulated S&Ls predicted an impending crisis as early as the spring of 1985, but the Reagan administration and most members of Congress, hoping to delay any decisive response until after the 1988 election, dismissed the warning as unduly alarmist.

Finally, in 1989 Congress had to act. It enacted an expensive bailout plan, designed to save some institutions and to provide a means of transferring the assets of failed S&Ls to those still solvent. Even as taxpayers began paying for this bailout plan, corruption plagued its execution; large, well-connected commercial banks, for instance, purchased the assets of bankrupt S&Ls at bargain prices. By the time the Treasury Department stepped in, early in 1994, most of the larger S&Ls had already been sold. As a consequence, some shareholders had been defrauded, and the banking industry had undergone a sudden, unplanned consolidation.

Despite criticism, the Reagan revolution changed American political life. Ronald Reagan's presidency altered the meaning of many traditional political terms. "Liberal" no longer meant a set of government programs that would stimulate the economy and help people buy new homes and more consumer goods. Instead, Republicans made "liberalism" a code word for supposedly wasteful social programs devised by a bloated federal government that gouged hardworking people and squandered their dollars on undeserving people. The term "conservative," as used by Republicans, came to mean economic growth, curtailment of government, and support for traditional sociocultural values. The once-dominant Democratic Party lay in disarray.

RENEWING THE COLD WAR

Reagan quickly established foreign policy themes that dominated both of his terms in office. Under Carter, he claimed, the nation's power had been eroded by the "Vietnam syndrome" of passivity and "loss of will." Reagan promised to reverse that trend. In contrast to Carter's amnesty for Vietnam War resisters, Reagan declared that the war had been a "noble cause" that the government had refused to win. Although he did not repudiate

LINK TO THE PAST

History Through Presidential Libraries

www.nara.gov/

The National Archives and Records Administration (NARA) oversees 10 presidential libraries. Not traditional libraries, these repositories hold the papers and other historical materials of every president since Herbert Hoover. Each also contains a museum and conducts public programs. After a president leaves office, NARA establishes a presidential "project" until a new library is built.

Although the libraries implicitly focus on history related to presidential officeholders, the exhibits and programs nonetheless often engage broader trends that characterize the era during which a president served. The libraries and their exhibits, therefore, may provide a useful place to begin an examination of recent American history.

From NARA's opening page, click on "Presidential Libraries" and visit the Internet site of each library, considering the following questions.

1. How well have these presidential libraries, conceived as "brick-and-mortar" sites until the 1990s, adapted to the Internet? What kinds of cybertools do they employ? How would you compare these sites' adaptation of Internet technology to other historically oriented sites highlighted in Links to the Past?

2. How, in terms of their approach to the past, do these library sites differ from each other? Do some sites, for example, primarily offer a memorial to the achievements of a previous president? Find two or more sites that differ and compare and contrast both their content and style.

3. How do these sites deal with the controversial aspects of a presidential administration? (Nixon's Watergate problems, Reagan's Iran-*Contra* episode, and Clinton's impeachment offer obvious examples.)

4. What types of Internet historical sources do these different libraries offer? Can you determine how often the sites are updated to provide new sources? Which libraries do the best job of including materials that go beyond a narrow focus on political history?

5. Have you visited any of the actual presidential libraries in person? If so, reflect on your reactions.

Carter's human rights policy, he employed it in a renewed cold war, highlighting the Soviet Union's mistreatment of its Jewish population and ethnic minorities.

THE DEFENSE BUILDUP

The United States, Reagan claimed, had "unilaterally disarmed" during the 1970s, while the Soviets had staged a massive military buildup. He called for a new battle against the "evil empire" of the Soviet Union. He dismissed critics of his foreign policy as the "Blame-America-First Crowd" and as "the strangest collection of misfits, loony tunes, and squalid criminals since the advent of the Third Reich."

Closing what Reagan called America's "window of vulnerability" against Soviet military power was expensive. Even though his tax cuts would inevitably reduce government revenues, Reagan asked Congress for dramatic increases in military spending. The Pentagon launched programs to enlarge the navy and to modernize strategic nuclear forces. It also deployed new missiles throughout Western Europe. At the height of Reagan's military buildup, the Pentagon was purchasing about 20 percent of the nation's manufacturing output.

In 1984 Reagan surprised even his closest advisers by proposing the most expensive defense system in history—a space-based shield against incoming missiles. Although it began as a nebulous idea, the Strategic Defense Initiative (SDI) soon had its own agency in the Pentagon that projected a need for $26 billion over five years, just for start-up research. Controversy swirled around the SDI program. Critics dubbed it "Star Wars," and many members of Congress shuddered at its astronomical costs. Although most scientists considered the project impractical, Congress voted appropriations for SDI, and throughout his presidency Reagan clung to the idea of a defensive shield. SDI dominated both the strategic debate at home and arms talks with the Soviet Union.

Greater defense spending had another strategic dimension. Secretary of Defense Caspar Weinberger predicted that, as the Soviets increased the burden on their own faltering economy in order to compete in the accelerating arms race, the Soviet Union itself might collapse under the economic strain. This had been an implicit goal of the containment policy since NSC-68 (1950).

Reagan's foreign policy included initiatives other than military incursions. In a new "informational" offensive, the administration funded a variety of conservative groups around the world and established Radio Martí, a Florida station beamed at Cuba and designed to discredit Fidel Castro. When the United Nations agency UNESCO adopted an anti-American tone and called for a "New World Information Order" that would reduce the influence of U.S.-originated news and information, Reagan cut off U.S. contributions to UNESCO and demanded changes in UN operations. Reagan also championed free markets, urging other nations to minimize tariffs and restrictions on foreign investment. His Caribbean Basin Initiative, for example, rewarded with U.S. aid those small nations in the Caribbean region that adhered to free-market principles.

The CIA, under Director William Casey, stepped up covert activities, some of which became so obvious that they were hardly "covert." It was no secret, for example, that the United States was aiding anticommunist forces in Afghanistan and the *contras* in Nicaragua, but the U.S. government acknowledged neither the extent nor the nature of that aid. The Reagan administration's zeal for covert action gave rise to its most controversial legacy: the Iran-*Contra* affair.

DEPLOYING MILITARY POWER

In waging the renewed cold war, Reagan promised vigorous support to "democratic" revolutions around the globe, a move designed to constrain the Soviet Union's sphere of influence. Reagan's UN representative, Jeane Kirkpatrick, wrote that "democratic" forces included almost any movement, no matter how autocratic, that was noncommunist. The United States thus funded opposition movements in countries aligned with the Soviet Union: Ethiopia, Angola, South Yemen, Cambodia, Grenada, Cuba, Nicaragua, and Afghanistan. Reagan called the participants in such movements "freedom fighters," although few had any visible commitment to democratic processes.

The Reagan administration also displayed a new willingness to unleash U.S. military power. The first occasion was in southern Lebanon, where Israeli troops were facing off against Lebanese Muslims supported by Syria and the Soviet Union. Alarmed by Muslims gains, the Reagan administration in 1982 convinced Israel to withdraw and sent 1,600 American marines as part of a "peacekeeping force" to restore stability. Muslim fighters, however, turned their wrath against the Americans. After a suicide commando mission into a U.S. military compound killed 241 marines, Reagan decided that this ill-defined undertaking could never win public support. He subsequently pulled out U.S. troops and disengaged from the conflict.

Although the debacle in Lebanon raised questions about Reagan's policies, another military intervention restored his popularity. In October 1983 Reagan sent 2,000 U.S. troops to the tiny Caribbean island of Grenada, whose socialist leader was forging ties with Castro's Cuba. U.S. troops overthrew the government and installed one friendly to American interests.

Buoyed by Grenada, the Reagan administration fixed its sights on Nicaragua in Central America, where the Marxist Sandinista party was building ties with Cuba and trying to break its country's historic dependence on the United States. The United States augmented its military forces in neighboring Honduras, conducted training exercises throughout the region, stepped up economic pressure, and launched a psychological offensive to discredit the Sandinistas. Most importantly, the United States trained and equipped an opposition military force of Nicaraguans, the *contras*. Meanwhile, the administration supported murderous dictatorships in nearby El Salvador and Guatemala to prevent other leftist insurgencies from gaining ground in Central America.

U.S. initiatives in Central America became the most controversial aspect of Reagan's foreign policy. U.S.-backed regimes were clearly implicated in human-rights abuses, not only against their own people but also against American nuns, journalists, and humanitarian-aid workers. Mounting evidence of brutality and corruption among the Nicaraguan *contras*—Reagan's so-called "freedom fighters"— brought growing public criticism. In 1984, the Democratic-controlled Congress broke with the president's policy and denied further military aid to the *contras*.

The Reagan administration quickly sought ways around the congressional ban. One solution was to encourage wealthy U.S. conservatives and other governments to donate money to the *contras*. In June 1984, at a top secret meeting of the National Security Planning Group, Reagan and his top advisers discussed the legality of pressing "third parties" to contribute to the *contra* cause. Reagan ended the meeting with a bid for secrecy: "If such a story gets out, we'll all be hanging by our thumbs in front of the White House."

Meanwhile, violence continued to escalate throughout the Middle East. Militant Islamic groups increased terrorism against Israel and Western powers; bombings and the kidnapping of Western hostages became more frequent. Apparently, both Libyan leader Muammar al-Qaddafi and Iran were encouraging such activities. In spring 1986, the United States launched an air strike into Libya aimed at Qaddafi's personal compound. The bombs did serious damage and killed Qaddafi's young daughter, but Qaddafi and his government survived. Despite some public criticism of this action, which looked like a long-range assassination attempt against a foreign leader (an action outlawed by Congress), Americans generally approved of using strong measures against sponsors of terrorism and hostage-taking.

THE IRAN-*CONTRA* AFFAIR

In November 1986, a magazine in Lebanon reported that the Reagan administration was selling arms to Iran as part of a secret deal to secure the release of Americans being held hostage by Islamic militants. The story quickly became front-page news in the United States because such a deal stood in clear conflict with the Reagan administration's stated position that it would not sell arms to Iran and that it would not reward hostage-taking by negotiating for the release of captives.

Six years earlier, during the 1980 campaign, Reagan had made hostages a symbol of U.S. weakness under Carter. When Iranian-backed groups continued to kidnap Americans under his presidency, Reagan, increasingly worried about the hostage issue, had sought a way to bring them home. As Congress began to investigate the arms-for-hostages charge, matters turned even more bizarre.

IRAN-CONTRA Ronald Reagan's presidency lost some of its luster after the public learned of the Iran-*Contra* affair. At press conferences such as this one in 1986, President Reagan seemed confused about how his key aides had been conducting foreign policy.

The Reagan administration itself confirmed the arms sales to Iran and further revealed that profits had been channeled to the *contra* forces in Nicaragua as a means of circumventing the congressional ban on U.S. military aid. Oliver North, a lieutenant colonel who served in the office of the national security adviser, had directed the effort, working with a secret unit in the National Security Council, shadowy international arms dealers, and private go-betweens. It became clear that North had been running a covert operation that violated both the stated policy of the White House and the congressional ban.

In the end, critics failed to establish the Iran-*Contra* affair as a serious constitutional episode comparable to Watergate. Ronald Reagan successfully maintained that he could remember no details about either the hostages' release or funding the *contras*. His management style might deserve criticism, he admitted, but no legal-constitutional issues were involved. Vice President George Bush also claimed ignorance of any deal. Oliver North, who became a right-wing celebrity as a result of his artful dodging during televised hearings into the affair, destroyed so many documents and left so many false trails that congressional investigators

struggled to compile even a simple narrative of events. North and National Security Adviser John Poindexter were convicted of felonies, including falsification of documents and lying to Congress, but their convictions were overturned on appeal. In 1992, just a few days before the end of his presidency, George Bush pardoned six former officials linked to the Iran-*Contra* affair.

THE BEGINNING OF THE END OF THE COLD WAR

Although Reagan's first six years in office had revived the cold war confrontation, his last two years saw a sudden thaw in U.S.–Soviet relations. The economic cost of superpower rivalry was burdening both nations. Moreover, changes within the Soviet Union were eliminating the reasons for confrontation. Mikhail Gorbachev, who became general secretary of the Communist Party in 1985, was a new style of Soviet leader. Gorbachev understood the pace of technological change in Western democracies as economies and communications became globally integrated. He also realized that his isolated country faced economic stagnation and an environmental crisis brought on by decades of poorly planned industrial development. To redirect the Soviet Union's course, he withdrew Soviet troops from Afghanistan, reduced commitments to Cuba and Nicaragua, proclaimed a policy of *glasnost* ("openness"), and began to implement *perestroika* ("economic liberalization") at home.

Gorbachev's policies brought him acclaim throughout the West and stirred winds of change. He began summit meetings with the United States to discuss arms control. At Reykjavik, Iceland, in October 1986, Reagan shocked both Gorbachev and his own advisers by proposing a wholesale ban on nuclear weapons. Although negotiations at Reykjavik stumbled over Gorbachev's insistence that the United States abandon its "Star Wars" program, the next year Gorbachev dropped that condition. In December 1987 Reagan and Gorbachev signed a major arms treaty that reduced each nation's supply of intermediate-range missiles and allowed for on-site verification, which the Soviets had never before permitted. The next year, Gorbachev scrapped the policy that forbade any nation under Soviet influence from renouncing communism. In effect, Gorbachev declared an end to the cold war. Within the next few years, the Soviet sphere of influence—and the Soviet Union itself—would cease to exist.

THE FIRST BUSH PRESIDENCY

During his first term, Ronald Reagan became America's most popular president since Franklin Roosevelt, but even before the Iran-*Contra* affair, his presidential image and influence were beginning to fade. Members of the New Right came to criticize the president for failing to support their agendas vigorously enough. Economic problems—especially the growing federal deficit and disarray in the financial sector—sparked broader-based calls for more assured leadership from the White House. Despite criticism of Reagan's leadership at home, cold war détente boosted the 1988 presidential prospects of his heir-apparent, Vice President George Bush.

THE ELECTION OF 1988

Bush easily gained the Republican nomination. Born into a prominent Connecticut Republican family, Bush had moved to Texas and entered the oil business as a young man. His lengthy political resume included a time in the House of Representatives and a stint as director of the CIA. He was both a less charismatic and a more establishment-style politician than Reagan. Bush chose as his running mate Senator J. Danforth Quayle, a staunch conservative better known for golfing prowess than his legislative skills. Choosing Quayle pleased the New Right—and delighted political comedians, who found the bumbling Quayle a rich source for new comic material.

Governor Michael Dukakis of Massachusetts emerged as the Democratic presidential candidate. In an effort to distance himself from the disastrous Democratic effort in 1984, Dukakis avoided talk of new domestic programs and higher taxes. Instead, he pledged to bring competence and honesty to the White House and boasted of how he had mobilized private experts to help streamline the Massachusetts government and stimulate that state's economy. By running a cautious campaign and avoiding controversial domestic issues, Dukakis gambled that he could defeat Bush, who lacked Reagan's charisma.

The election of 1988, the last of the cold-war era, featured negative campaigning. Pro-Bush television commercials usually presented Dukakis bathed in shadows and always showed him with a frown on his face. The campaign's most infamous ad linked Dukakis to Willie Horton, an African American inmate who had committed a rape while on furlough from a Massachusetts prison. Playing on racial fears, the ad implied that Dukakis, whom Bush identified as a "card-carrying member of the American Civil Liberties Union," was soft on crime. Rising rates of violent crime during the late 1980s, much of it stemming from the spread of crack cocaine, alarmed Americans across the country. As one pundit put it, the Bush campaign made it seem that Willie Horton was Dukakis's running mate.

At first glance, Bush appeared to sweep both the popular vote and the electoral college. Yet, he carried so many states by such small margins that relatively minor shifts in voter turnouts, especially among black and Latino voters who failed to support Dukakis as enthusiastically as they had backed Mondale four years earlier, could have given the victory to the Democrats. Dukakis bested Mondale's 1984 performance with 111 electoral votes. Outside the South, which Bush swept, Dukakis carried more than 500 counties that had supported Reagan in 1984. Overall, voter turnout was the lowest of any national election since 1924, and polls suggested that a majority of voters considered neither Bush nor Dukakis worthy of being president.

Although the New Right wanted Bush to build on the Reagan presidency, many doubted his commitment to their cause. Had not his campaign pledge of a "kinder, gentler America" seemed a veiled criticism of Reagan's domestic policies? Bush angered conservatives by agreeing to an increase in the minimum wage and by failing to veto the Civil Rights Act of 1991, a law they claimed set up quotas for the preferential hiring of women and people of color in business and government. Most important, in 1990 he broke his campaign promise of "no new taxes," the issue on which most conservatives came to judge his worthiness as Reagan's successor, and accepted a tax increase as a means of dealing with the rising federal deficit. Although Bush's move began the process that would dramatically shrink the deficit, the Republican Right bitterly denounced his decision.

BERLINERS CELEBRATE THE SYMBOLIC END OF THE COLD WAR The dismantling of the Berlin Wall, which the communists had erected in 1962 to separate East from West Berlin, symbolized the reunification of a divided Germany and the victory over communism.

GEORGE BUSH PLEDGES "NO NEW TAXES" During his acceptance speech at the 1988 Republican national convention, nominee George Bush tried to placate his party's New Right. His pledge that he would permit "no new taxes"—a promise that he could not keep once elected—severely undermined his credibility, particularly among conservatives.

Meanwhile, the national government, divided between a Democratic-controlled Congress and a Republican-occupied White House, appeared more and more to suffer from "gridlock." Action on domestic issues lagged, especially reorganization of the health care and welfare systems. Moreover, the economic growth of the Reagan years began slowing, and the budget deficit continued expanding. George Bush's chances for a second term seemed to depend on his record in foreign, rather than domestic, policy.

THE END OF THE COLD WAR

During Bush's presidency Soviet communism collapsed. As communist states fell like dominoes, the international order underwent its greatest transformation since the end of the Second World War.

Beginning in 1989, political change swept through Eastern and Central Europe. In Poland, the anticommunist labor party, Solidarity, ousted the pro-Soviet regime. The pro-Soviet government in East Germany fell in November 1989, and both West and East Germans hacked down the Berlin Wall. Divided since the Second World War, Germany began the difficult process of reunification. In Czechoslovakia, Hungary, Romania, and Bulgaria, public demonstrations forced out communist governments. Yugoslavia disintegrated, and warfare ensued as some ethnic groups tried to re-create separate states in Slovenia, Serbia, Bosnia, and Croatia. The Baltic countries of Latvia, Lithuania, and Estonia, under Soviet control since the Second World War, declared their independence. And most dramatic, the major provinces that had comprised the Soviet Union itself assumed self-government. The president of the new state of Russia, Boris Yeltsin, put down a coup by hard-line communists in August 1991, and his popularity rapidly eclipsed that of Mikhail Gorbachev. In December 1991, the Russian Parliament ratified Yeltsin's plan to abolish the Soviet Union and replace it with 11 republics, loosely joined in a commonwealth.

As the map of Europe changed, the United States faced the task of establishing diplomatic relations with many new regimes and countries. In December 1991 Congress authorized $400 million to help the

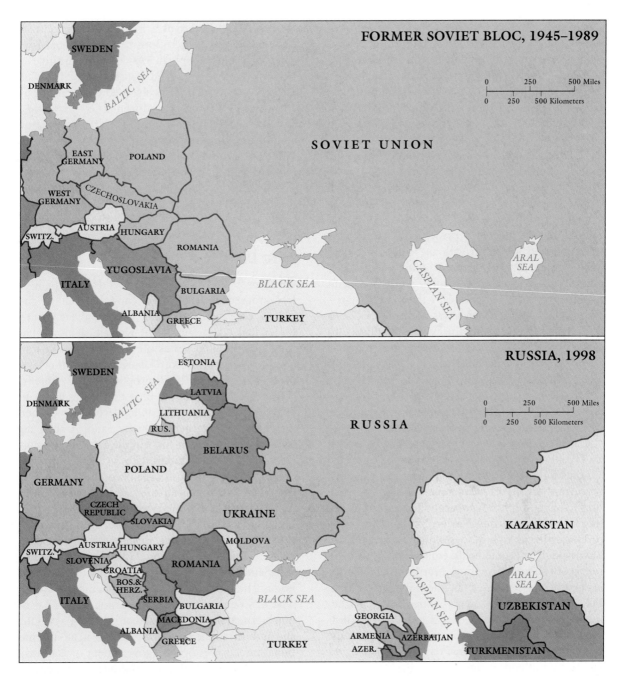

FORMER SOVIET BLOC, 1945–1989

SWEDEN

DENMARK

BALTIC SEA

SOVIET UNION

EAST GERMANY

POLAND

WEST GERMANY

CZECHOSLOVAKIA

SWITZ.

AUSTRIA HUNGARY

ROMANIA

CASPIAN SEA

ARAL SEA

YUGOSLAVIA

BLACK SEA

ITALY

BULGARIA

ALBANIA GREECE

TURKEY

0   250   500 Miles

0   250   500 Kilometers

RUSSIA, 1998

SWEDEN

ESTONIA

DENMARK

BALTIC SEA

LATVIA

LITHUANIA

RUS.

RUSSIA

BELARUS

GERMANY

POLAND

CZECH REPUBLIC

SLOVAKIA

UKRAINE

KAZAKSTAN

AUSTRIA HUNGARY

MOLDOVA

SWITZ.

SLOVENIA

CROATIA

BOS.& HERZ.

ROMANIA

CASPIAN SEA

ARAL SEA

ITALY

SERBIA

BULGARIA

UZBEKISTAN

MACEDONIA

ALBANIA

GREECE

BLACK SEA

GEORGIA

ARMENIA AZERBAIJAN

AZER.

TURKEY

TURKMENISTAN

0   250   500 Miles

0   250   500 Kilometers

COLLAPSE OF THE SOVIET BLOC

Soviet Union's successor states, especially Ukraine, dismantle their nuclear weaponry, and it allotted an equivalent amount the next year for promoting democracy in the new European republics.

Meanwhile, the Bush administration successfully promoted economic liberalization within an improving international economy. In the mid-1980s, huge debts that Third World nations owed to U.S. banks had threatened to shake the international banking system, but by the end of the decade most of these obligations had been renegotiated. Free-market economies began to emerge in the former communist states, and Western Europe moved toward economic integration. The nations of the Pacific Rim prospered, and Bush pressed for the North American Free Trade Agreement (NAFTA), which would bring Canada, the United States, and Mexico together to form the largest free-market zone in the world.

As the likelihood of armed conflict with the Soviet Union faded, the Bush administration set about redefining "national security." The leftist threats in Central America that had preoccupied the Reagan administration weakened with the end of the cold war. The Sandinistas were voted out of office in Nicaragua and became just another political party in a multiparty state. Supported by the United States, the United Nations began to assist both El Salvador and Guatemala in turning their armed conflicts into electoral ones. The Pentagon pondered new missions for its military forces. Future action, its planners predicted, would take the form of rapid, sharply targeted strikes rather than lengthy campaigns. The military might even serve in the "war against drugs" that Bush had promised during his 1988 presidential campaign.

Panamanian president General Manuel Noriega was deeply involved in the drug trade. The Reagan administration had secured an indictment against Noriega for drug trafficking and had tried to force him from power through economic pressure, but this had only deepened Noriega's reliance on drug revenues. Deciding how to deal with Noriega posed a significant and potentially embarrassing problem for the Bush administration. Noriega had been recruited as a CIA "asset" in the mid-1970s, when Bush himself was the agency's director. Nevertheless, the United States needed a friendly, responsible government in Panama in order to complete the transfer of the Panama Canal to Panamanian sovereignty by the end of the century. Bush finally decided to topple Noriega. In a military incursion called "Operation Just Cause" and broadcast live on television throughout the world, U.S. Marines landed in Panama in December 1989, pinpointed Noriega's whereabouts, and put him under siege. Noriega soon surrendered and was extradited to stand trial in Florida. In April 1992 he was convicted of cocaine trafficking and imprisoned.

Seizing the leader of a foreign government in this manner raised questions of international law, and using military force in a region long sensitive to U.S. intervention sparked controversy. Still, this military action, which involved 25,000 troops but caused only about two dozen U.S. casualties, boosted Bush's popularity at home. It also provided a new model for post–cold war military action. The Pentagon firmed up plans to phase out its older military bases, particularly in Germany and the Philippines, and to create highly mobile, rapid-deployment forces. A test of this new strategy came in the Persian Gulf War.

THE PERSIAN GULF WAR

On August 2, 1990, President Saddam Hussein of Iraq ordered his troops to occupy the small neighboring emirate of Kuwait. Within a day, Iraq's forces had taken control of Kuwait, a move that caught the United States off guard. Although Iraq had been massing troops on Kuwait's border and denouncing Kuwaiti oil producers, U.S. intelligence forecasters had doubted that it was about to take over the country. Now, however, they warned that Iraq's next target might be Saudi Arabia, the largest oil exporter in the Middle East and a longtime friend of the United States.

Moving swiftly, Bush organized an international response. He convinced the Saudi government, at first reluctant to harbor Western troops on its soil, to accept a U.S. military presence. Four days after Iraq's invasion of Kuwait, Bush launched operation "Desert Shield" by sending 230,000 troops to protect Saudi Arabia. After consulting with European leaders, he took the matter to the United Nations. The UN denounced Iraqi aggression, ordered economic sanctions against Saddam Hussein's regime, and authorized the United States to lead an international force to restore the government of Kuwait if Saddam Hussein had not withdrawn his troops by January 15, 1991. Bush assembled a massive force, ultimately deploying nearly one half million American troops and some 200,000 from other countries, and he persuaded Congress to approve a resolution backing the use of force. Although Bush claimed a moral obligation to rescue Kuwait, his policymakers spoke frankly about the economic peril Hussein's aggression posed for the United States and other oil-dependent economies. Secretary of State James Baker summed up the danger in one word: "Jobs."

Just after the January 15 deadline passed, the United States launched an air war on Iraq. "Pools" of journalists, whose movements were carefully controlled by the military, focused mainly on new military technology, especially the antimissile missile called the "Patriot." Television networks showed Patriots, in video game fashion, intercepting and downing Iraqi "Scud" missiles. (Later, careful studies significantly reduced claims about the success rate of the Patriot missiles.) The media also highlighted the new role of women in America's modernized military. After six weeks of devas-

tating aerial bombardment and economic sanctions against Iraq, General Colin Powell ordered a ground offensive on February 24. Over the next four days Saddam Hussein's armies were shattered. The United States controlled the skies and kept its casualties relatively light (148 deaths in battle). Estimates of Iraq's casualties ranged from 25,000 to 100,000 deaths. Although the conflict had lasted scarcely six weeks, the damage to highways, bridges, communications, and other infrastructure in both Iraq and Kuwait was enormous.

In a controversial decision, Bush decided not to force Saddam Hussein's ouster, an ambitious goal that the UN had never approved and that military

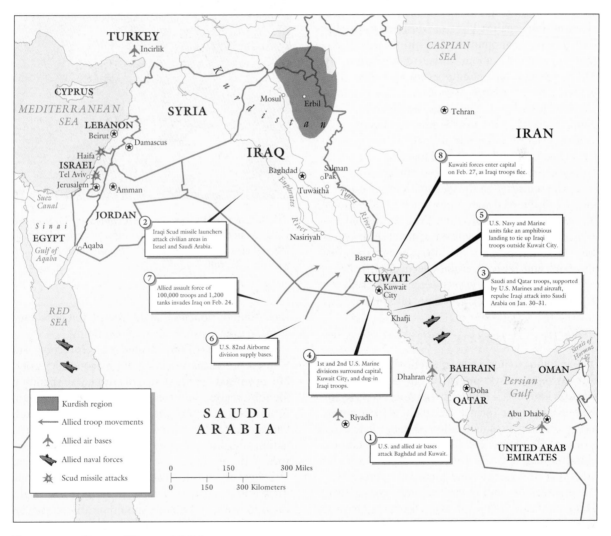

PERSIAN GULF WAR, 1991

advisers had considered costly to achieve. Instead, the United States, backed by the UN, maintained its economic pressure, worked to dismantle Iraq's nuclear and bacteriological capabilities, and enforced a "no-fly" zone over northern Iraq to protect the Kurdish population from Hussein's continued persecution.

The Persian Gulf War temporarily boosted George Bush's popularity, but the president proved less adept in articulating long-term diplomatic goals for a post–cold war world. Turmoil broke out in some of the former Soviet provinces, and Russia struggled to develop a private-property, free-market economy. Full-scale warfare erupted among the states of the former Yugoslavia, with Serbs launching a brutal campaign of aggrandizement and "ethnic cleansing" against Bosnian Muslims. In the Far East, Japan's economic strength prompted Americans to grumble about unfair competition. In Africa, when severe famine struck the country of Somalia, Bush ordered American troops to establish humanitarian supply lines, but the American public remained wary of this military mission.

Overall, Bush left a mixed legacy in foreign policy. He had assembled and held together an international coalition against Iraq, had constructively assisted the transition in Russia and Eastern Europe at the end of the cold war, and had advanced a global process of trade liberalization. Even so, the old reference points that had defined national security, especially containment of the Soviet enemy, had disappeared, and Bush never did effectively articulate a new vision that could inspire people and firmly establish his reputation as a foreign policy leader.

THE ELECTION OF 1992

The inability to portray a coherent vision of either foreign or domestic policy threatened Bush's re-election and forced him to make concessions to the New Right. Dan Quayle returned as his running mate, and the president allowed conservative activists to dominate the 1992 Republican national convention. They talked about "a religious war" for "the soul of America" and pictured Democrats as the enemies of "family values." Still, conservative Democrats and independents, who had supported Ronald Reagan and George Bush in the previous three presidential elections, found this rhetoric no

BILL CLINTON PLAYS THE SAXOPHONE During the 1992 presidential campaign, Clinton eagerly identified himself as a "New Democrat," one who had grown up with rock 'n' roll.

substitute for policies that addressed domestic concerns, particularly the sluggish economy.

Bush's Democratic challenger, Governor Bill Clinton of Arkansas, zeroed in on economic issues. He promised to increase governmental spending for job creation and long-term economic growth. Addressing a concern that cut across partisan lines, Clinton promised a comprehensive revision of the nation's health care system. On other domestic issues, Clinton almost sounded like a Republican. "It's time to end this [welfare] system as we know it," Clinton insisted. "People who can work ought to go to work, and no one should be able to stay on welfare forever." He campaigned as a "new Democrat" who would reduce taxes for middle-class

Americans, cut the federal deficit, and shrink the size of government. Clinton, in short, made it difficult for Bush to label him as a "big government" liberal.

A focus on economic questions also helped to deflect attention from sociocultural issues on which Clinton was vulnerable. As a college student in the 1960s, he had not only avoided service in Vietnam but also had participated in antiwar demonstrations while in England as a Rhodes scholar. When Bush, a decorated veteran of the Second World War, challenged Clinton's patriotism, Clinton countered by emphasizing, rather than repudiating, his roots in the rock 'n' roll and Vietnam War generation. He became the first presidential candidate to appear on MTV. In addition, he chose Senator Albert Gore of Tennessee, a Vietnam veteran, as his running mate. When Clinton's personal life became an issue, Bill and Hillary Rodham Clinton acknowledged past problems but defended their marriage as an effective, ongoing partnership. Hillary Rodham Clinton's career as a lawyer and advocate for children's issues, the couple insisted, would be an asset to a Clinton presidency.

The 1992 presidential campaign was enlivened by the third-party candidacy of Ross Perot, a bil-lionaire from Texas who spent $60 million of his own money on a quixotic run for the White House. A blunt, folksy speaker, Perot entered politics by appearing on television and radio talk shows to expound a quasi-conspiratorial view of recent U.S. history: Political insiders in Washington, both Republicans and Democrats, had created a "mess" that insulted the common sense of the American people and satisfied only special interests. If people would only come together as they had done during the Second World War, he claimed, they could "take back our country." The unpredictable Perot's $37 million media blitz likely hurt Bush more than Clinton.

Clinton won by a comfortable margin. He garnered 43 percent of the popular vote and won 370 electoral votes by carrying 32 states and the District of Columbia. Perot gained no electoral votes but did attract 19 million popular votes. For George Bush the 1992 election was a crushing defeat. He won a majority only among white Protestants in the South. In contrast, Clinton carried the Jewish, African American, and Latino vote by large margins, and he even gained a plurality among people who had served in the Vietnam War. He also ran well among independents, voters whom Reagan and Bush had carried during the 1980s and on whom Perot had counted in 1992. Perhaps most surprising, about 55 percent of eligible voters went to the polls, a turnout that reversed 32 years of steady decline in voter participation.

THE CLINTON PRESIDENCY: "NEW DEMOCRATS" COME TO WASHINGTON

Bill Clinton, the first Democratic president in 12 years and the first chief executive from the baby boom generation, brought an emphasis on youth, vitality, and cultural diversity to Washington. Inaugural celebrations included different inaugural balls for different musical tastes; one (broadcast live on MTV) featured rock 'n' roll from the Vietnam War era. Clinton's initial cabinet included three African Americans and two Latinos; three cabinet posts went to women. His first nominee to the Supreme Court was Ruth Bader Ginsburg, only the second woman to sit on the Court. As representative to the United

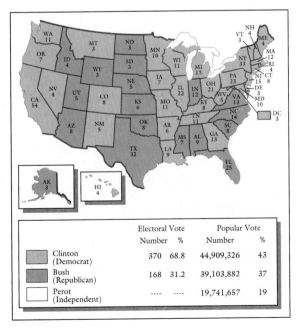

	Electoral Vote		Popular Vote	
	Number	%	Number	%
Clinton (Democrat)	370	68.8	44,909,326	43
Bush (Republican)	168	31.2	39,103,882	37
Perot (Independent)	----	----	19,741,657	19

PRESIDENTIAL ELECTION, 1992

Nations, Clinton named Madeleine Albright, who would become the country's first female secretary of state during his second term.

Clinton claimed several victories on domestic issues during his first term. He ended the Reagan era's ban on abortion counseling in family planning clinics; pushed through Congress a family leave program for working parents; established the Americorps program, which allowed students to repay their college loans through community service; and secured passage of the Brady Bill, which instituted a five-day waiting period on handgun purchases. Limited college-loan and youth training programs also received funding. An anti-crime bill, passed in 1994, provided federal funds to put more police officers on the streets; it also contained more money for prison construction and a controversial "three strikes and you're out" provision, which mandated a lifetime prison sentence for a third felony conviction.

Most important, Clinton obtained new economic legislation. His 1993 deficit-reduction plan, which required a tie-breaking vote of Vice President Al Gore to pass the Senate, featured a tax-increase and spending-cut package aimed at reducing the federal deficit and eventually lowering interest rates as a means of stimulating economic growth. The plan also included a provision that expanded an existing governmental program, called the earned tax credit, that provided annual cash bonuses to low-income workers with children.

White House efforts to reshape the health care system collapsed. Hillary Rodham Clinton led a task force that produced a plan so complex that few understood it; even worse, it pleased virtually no one. Republicans used the health care fiasco to paint Clinton as an advocate of big government, and his health care proposal died in Congress. Talk-radio shows featured nonstop criticism of the Clinton White House for bungling the health care issue and for raising taxes. As the welfare rolls soared to an all-time high of 14.4 million people in 1994, Clinton delayed any effort to overhaul that system.

Clinton also faced personal problems. Hillary Rodham Clinton's prominent role in the failed heath care effort fueled criticism of her public activities. The Clintons' joint involvement in financial dealings in Arkansas—particularly those connected to a bankrupt savings and loan institution and to a failed land development called "Whitewater"—drew criticism. In August 1994, a three-judge panel appointed Kenneth Starr, a conservative Republican, to replace the independent prosecutor

WORK AND FAMILY

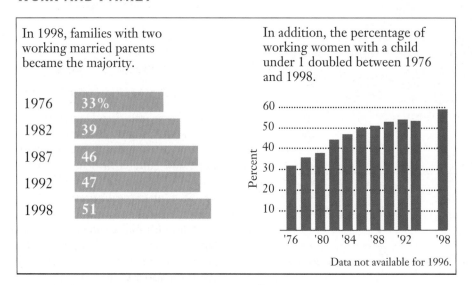

In 1998, families with two working married parents became the majority.

1976	33%
1982	39
1987	46
1992	47
1998	51

In addition, the percentage of working women with a child under 1 doubled between 1976 and 1998.

Data not available for 1996.

Source: U.S. Census Bureau

INCOME AND POVERTY IN THE LATE 20TH CENTURY *Two new reports by the Census Bureau show the economic expansion reaching all racial and ethnic groups.*

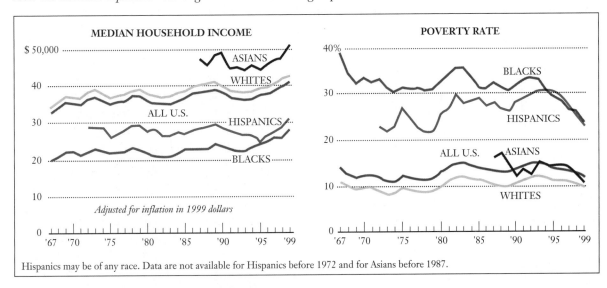

Hispanics may be of any race. Data are not available for Hispanics before 1972 and for Asians before 1987.

appointed in January. Charged with investigating the Whitewater affair, Starr moved aggressively to expand his inquiry into new allegations and seemed intent on securing an indictment against at least one of the Clintons.

A REPUBLICAN CONGRESS, A DEMOCRATIC WHITE HOUSE

The November 1994 elections brought a dramatic, unexpected GOP victory. Republicans secured control of both houses of Congress for the first time in 40 years; they won several new governorships; gained ground in most state legislatures; and made significant headway in many city and county elections, particularly across the South. Led by Representative Newt Gingrich of Georgia, the Republican Right hailed these gains as a mandate for their new agenda called the "Contract with America," which aimed at rolling back federal spending and a variety of governmental programs and regulations.

Congressional Republicans, however, overplayed their hand. Opinion polls suggested that people found Gingrich, who became Speaker of the House of Representatives, less trustworthy than the president. Moreover, surveys also showed little support for the kind of "revolution" against federal programs that congressional conservatives were

seeking. When conflict between the Democratic president and GOP Congress over budget issues led to two brief shutdowns of many government agencies (November 14–20, 1995, and December 16, 1995, through January 4, 1996), most people blamed the Republicans in Congress, rather than the White House, for the impasse.

Most important, a revived U.S. economy buoyed Clinton's presidency. Alan Greenspan, chairman of the Federal Reserve Board, gained a reputation for economic wizardry, particularly for his ability to keep inflation in check through adroit management of interest rates. Low rates of inflation, accompanied by steady economic growth, spurred millions of new jobs. The stock market, led by investment in technology companies, soared to new heights in what some called a speculative "bubble." Traditional Democrats often complained that benefits of this general expansion were distributed unequally. The agricultural economy continued to push smaller farmers off the land; the gap between earnings of corporate executives and ordinary workers grew steadily larger; and the wealthiest 10 percent of households still owned 90 percent of the nation's stock holdings. Yet, most people did see their economic fortunes improve. Unemployment figures steadily fell, and real income began to grow for the first time in nearly fifteen years.

THE LONGEST ECONOMIC EXPANSION IN U.S. HISTORY BEGAN IN 1991 *As the federal budget deficit turned to a surplus and inflation declined, the nation's employment figures, productivity, stock index, and GDP soared.* **Note:** Green vertical shading indicates recessions.

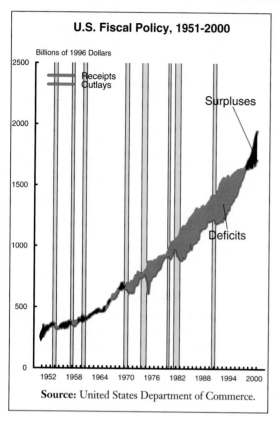

U.S. Fiscal Policy, 1951-2000

Billions of 1996 Dollars

Receipts
Outlays

Surpluses

Deficits

Source: United States Department of Commerce.

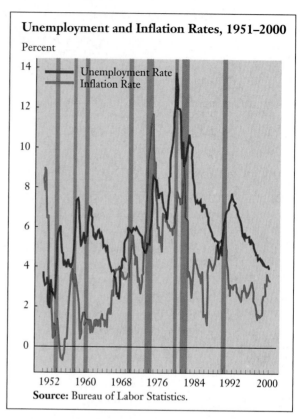

Unemployment and Inflation Rates, 1951–2000

Percent

Unemployment Rate
Inflation Rate

Source: Bureau of Labor Statistics.

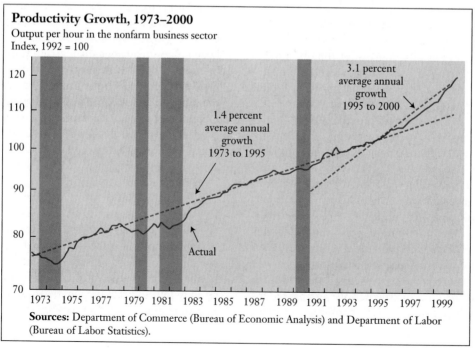

Productivity Growth, 1973–2000

Output per hour in the nonfarm business sector
Index, 1992 = 100

3.1 percent average annual growth 1995 to 2000

1.4 percent average annual growth 1973 to 1995

Actual

Sources: Department of Commerce (Bureau of Economic Analysis) and Department of Labor (Bureau of Labor Statistics).

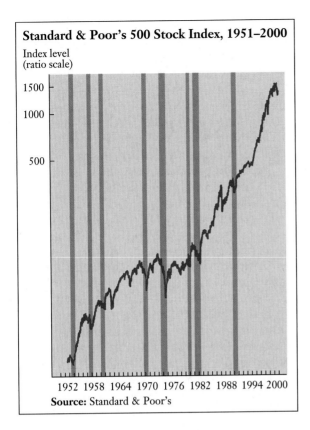

Standard & Poor's 500 Stock Index, 1951–2000

Index level
(ratio scale)

1500

1000

500

1952 1958 1964 1970 1976 1982 1988 1994 2000

Source: Standard & Poor's

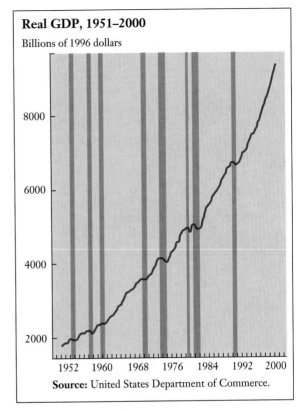

Real GDP, 1951–2000

Billions of 1996 dollars

8000

6000

4000

2000

1952   1960   1968   1976   1984   1992   2000

Source: United States Department of Commerce.

Clinton's political stock rose with the overhaul of the welfare system. The backlash against the budget gridlock, together with the continued economic growth, inclined the president (whose 1996 state of the union address declared that "the era of big government is over") and Congress to cooperate on the long-delayed welfare issue. The Personal Responsibility and Work Opportunity Reconciliation Act of 1996 represented a series of compromises that pleased conservatives more than liberals. Relatively noncontroversial sections of the law tightened collection of child support payments and reorganized nutrition and child care programs. Clinton, while voicing concern about provisions that cut the food stamp program and benefits for recent immigrants, embraced the law's central feature. It replaced the AFDC program, which provided funds and basic social services to poor families headed by single unemployed women, with a flexible system of block grants to individual states. Under the new program, entitled Temporary Assistance to Needy Families (TANF), the 50 states

were to design, under broad federal guidelines, their own welfare-to-work programs.

TANF, which effectively ended the national welfare system created in the New Deal and Great Society, provoked bitter controversy. Its proponents claimed it would encourage states to experiment with new programs that would reduce their welfare costs and create job opportunities. Critics worried that its provisions, including those that limited a person to five years of government assistance during his or her lifetime and authorized states to cut off support if recipients failed to find employment within two years, underestimated the difficulty that people without job skills faced. They also feared the impact that TANF might have on daily lives of children, especially if states provided inadequate child care, nutritional, and medical care programs. By pushing debate over these difficult issues into the future, however, the new welfare law helped to remove several potential domestic issues from the political campaign of 1996, a turn that especially helped Bill Clinton.

VICTORY AND IMPEACHMENT

The election of 1996 capped Clinton's political comeback. Independent prosecutor Kenneth Starr secured no new indictments, and White House "corruption" never became a major issue during the campaign. Clinton and Gore, riding the economic expansion, defeated Republicans Robert Dole and Jack Kemp by about the same margin that they had beaten George Bush and Dan Quayle in 1992. Clinton, the first Democratic president since Franklin Roosevelt to win back-to-back terms, ran particularly well among African Americans, women, and Hispanic voters. Republicans did retain control of Congress and gained several new governorships, but Democrats still held a majority of the seats in the 50 state legislatures, a sign that many voters believed that ticket-splitting (voting for both Democrats and Republicans) need not produce gridlock.

After the election, Clinton and congressional Republicans cooperated by passing legislation that established a timetable for reducing the federal deficit. In his 1998 State of the Union address, Clinton proudly proclaimed that the budget deficit would inevitably disappear, and he began to nego-

tiate with congressional Republicans about what to do with potential surpluses. He also launched a "national conversation" about racial issues, pressed for programs to improve education, and secured a measure extending health care coverage to several million children from low-income families. The White House even seemed poised, in early 1998, to work with congressional Republicans on reshaping Social Security and Medicare programs.

The nation's political life during 1998 and early 1999, however, revolved not around new legislative initiatives but around new charges about the president's personal behavior. Kenneth Starr's inquiry finally centered on claims that the president was concealing sexual encounters with female employees, including a young White House intern named Monica Lewinsky. Clinton unequivocally denied wrongdoing, including any relationship with Lewinsky. Republicans charged the Clinton White House with impeding Starr's investigation and the president himself with committing perjury and with pressuring others to testify falsely. In response, the president's defenders charged Starr with pursing a partisan vendetta against Clinton and leaking information to the media. They further accused Starr of conspiring with conservative activists financing a civil lawsuit against the president by Paula Corbin Jones for sexual harassment that had allegedly occurred during Clinton's governorship of Arkansas. Political Internet sites and 24-hour cable news channels, relatively new additions to the informational matrix, competed to provide the latest tidbits on the Clinton-Starr battle. Meanwhile, with economic statistics continuing to show improvement, Clinton's approval rating rose, while Starr's plummeted.

Clinton's denials crumbled after Starr obtained evidence, including a stained blue dress, of the president's involvement with Monica Lewinsky. Faced with both Starr's criminal investigation and the civil lawsuit involving Paula Jones, the president's problems went beyond personal embarrassment. Clinton had seemingly denied, while under oath in the Jones lawsuit, any sexual relationship such as the one with Lewinsky. The president's Republican opponents insisted that his conduct, particularly his deposition in the Jones case (which a federal judge had actually dismissed in April 1998), justified his ouster from the White House. Even as

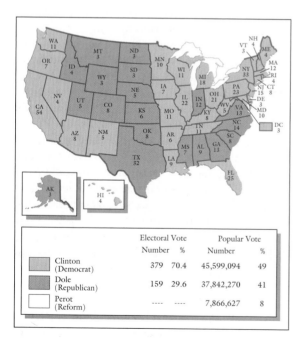

		Electoral Vote		Popular Vote	
		Number	%	Number	%
	Clinton (Democrat)	379	70.4	45,599,094	49
	Dole (Republican)	159	29.6	37,842,270	41
	Perot (Reform)	----	----	7,866,627	8

PRESIDENTIAL ELECTION, 1996

Democrats denounced Clinton's behavior, they insisted that his personal failings did not merit his impeachment. Partisan passions, both inside Congress and in the media, intensified as political invective mingled with legal debate over what constituted the kind of "high crime or misdemeanors" that the Constitution required for impeachment.

Through all of the controversy, Clinton's approval ratings, which remained higher than those of any of his Republican critics, provided a formidable barrier against his removal from office. After making the president their target during off-year election of 1998, Clinton's GOP opponents actually lost five seats in the House of Representatives. (It was the first time since 1934 that the opposition party had not gained House seats in an off-year election.) Even worse for the GOP, Clinton's main antagonist, House Speaker Newt Gingrich, soon resigned from Congress when a long-term extramarital affair became public, and a similar affair forced his successor to step down almost immediately. Undeterred, the Republican majority in the lame-duck House of Representatives sent two articles of impeachment (one for perjury and another for obstruction of justice involving the Lewinsky affair) against Clinton to the Senate on December 19, 1998. Although no one expected that Republicans could attract enough Democratic senators to secure the two-thirds vote required by the Constitution to remove Clinton, only the second president in U.S. history to face an impeachment trial, bipartisan attempts to find an alternative sanction failed. After a month-long trial, which concluded on February 12, 1999, Republicans failed to muster even a bare majority on either article of impeachment.

The impeachment imbroglio damaged Clinton's personal reputation, but his popularity actually grew during the final two years of his presidency. Economic growth, carefully watched over by Alan Greenspan, continued. Unemployment dropped under 4 percent for the first time in more than 30 years, and the economic expansion that began during the Bush presidency and lasted more than eight years ranked as the longest in U.S. history. Crime statistics dropped dramatically, and the welfare rolls shrank to one-seventh of their 1994 high, or 2.2 million families. The earned income tax credit, whose expansion the president had obtained in 1993, provided more than $30 billion in federal assistance to low-income workers with families. On the eve of Clinton's departure from office, nearly 70 percent of poll respondents believed he had been an effective political leader.

More broadly, the national political climate changed between 1992 and 2000. Clinton and other New Democrats succeeded in reviving their party's fortunes. Once reviled by Ronald Reagan as the party of the "misery index," the Democrats became associated with economic growth, full employment, low inflation, and fiscal responsibility. A person who generated bitter enemies, Clinton also engendered equally fervent support, particularly from African Americans. Writer Toni Morrison joked that Clinton, who had grown up in a multiracial community, might be considered the nation's first "black president." The success of the earned income tax credit allowed Clinton to retain a strong base among low-income families. As the White House and congressional Republicans found common ground on issues such as overhauling the welfare system and reducing federal deficit, the Clinton years undercut some of the previous cynicism about government action making a difference in people's lives.

Meanwhile, partisan rancor marked postimpeachment politics, as both major parties prepared for the election of 2000. The political stalemate was broken only by a few minor measures (such as a new law providing federal funds to support the hiring of additional school teachers) and by repeal of New Deal-era regulations that had barred banks from entering the insurance and securities businesses. Otherwise, the two parties failed to fulfill their promises to address problems in the Social Security and Medicare programs. Congress rejected Clinton-backed legislation dealing with gun control, changes in the financing of political campaigns, and a "bill of rights" for medical patients. It passed several tax-cutting measures but could not override presidential vetoes. Leaders of both parties charged the other with holding the legislative agenda hostage to partisan advantages in the upcoming elections of 2000.

POST–COLD WAR FOREIGN POLICY

For nearly a half century, anticommunism and rivalry with the Soviet Union had shaped policymaking.

Cityscapes

During the mid-1970s New York City's South Bronx became a symbol of urban decay and of America's neglected cities. Over a four-year period, 40,000 arson fires reduced block after block of deteriorated apartment buildings to charred rubble. During the 1977 World Series, an ABC sportscaster noted the plumes of smoke drifting toward Yankee Stadium and reported, "There it is again, ladies and gentlemen. The Bronx is burning."

Americans had often shown a distrust of cities. The myth of the virtuous "yeoman farmer" captivated the nation's founding generation, who warned that the old cities of Europe had bred corruption and social inequality. America's strength, many 19th-century commentators claimed, sprang from the moral values of rural life and the egalitarian impulses of its vast frontier. America did have its great cities, which became centers of commerce and industry, but affluent city-dwellers increasingly escaped to the fringes. During the late 19th century, "street-car suburbs" sprouted on the urban outskirts, and in the 20th century the car culture pushed the suburban ring out farther and farther. These suburbs, initially inhabited mostly by whites, implicitly expressed a widespread preference for individual, detached homes, spaced off and surrounded by lawns. By the 1970s, the older neighborhoods of many cities had become impoverished. Retail businesses closed down; apartment buildings, parks, and streets fell prey to disrepair and crime; the quality of education and health care declined. The old fears about urban life seemed fulfilled.

Another American tradition, however, glorified cities. Poets celebrated their noise, power, and ethnic diversity. Writers and artists often portrayed cities as attractive alternatives to the narrow and intellectually stifling atmosphere of small-town life. Painters, photographers, and filmmakers used urban skylines, with their silhouetted skyscrapers, to symbolize America's

Freeway artistry in Atlanta.

vitality and global power. During the closing years of the 20th century, a resurgence of urban pride accompanied a stunning transformation in most cities. A building boom brought new office towers, residential buildings, and sports and arts complexes to downtowns across the country.

This 1990s urban revival sprang from many sources. A booming national economy and improved air and

The United States now began to redefine national security. During both of his presidential campaigns Clinton focused primarily on domestic issues, and the public seemed suspicious of new international commitments. Still, throughout his presidency, Clinton articulated an expansive, internationalist vision: promoting free-market policies, improving relations with the UN, expanding NATO, advancing

New affordable housing in Oakland.

Water park and skyscrapers in Houston.

water quality helped. Innovative urban design plans skillfully integrated architectural styles with new green spaces and revitalized river and lakefronts. Community development corporations (CDCs), grassroots agencies first seen in the 1960s, helped low-income neighborhoods create more affordable housing, child care, and employment opportunities. The Community Reinvestment Act, which obliged banks to invest in low-income neighborhoods, stimulated economic activity. Retailers moved in and found new markets. Community policing and an aging population dramatically lowered crime rates during the 1990s.

As sprawling suburban developments continued to grow around most American cities, frustrated commuters increasingly clogged freeways. The conges-

tion, in turn, assisted urban revival. In Atlanta and Houston, cities with perhaps the worst traffic problems, approximately 22 percent of household budgets were spent on transportation. Some people found that they could save both time and money by living downtown.

In addition, new immigrants repopulated many once-declining neighborhoods. African newcomers in the South Bronx, Salvadorans and Vietnamese in Los Angeles, Cubans in Miami, all refurbished and revived urban life. Home-ownership rates climbed. Along with these diverse new populations came new flavors and rhythms, making many American cities exciting, transnational spaces that paralleled the growing globalization of the world itself.

human rights and democracy abroad, reducing nuclear threats, and working on global environmental and health concerns. Critics charged that his administration lacked any overall vision or framework; de-

fenders claimed that such flexibility was a virtue in the fragmented post–cold war world.

One of the most perplexing issues involved when, and under what conditions, to use U.S. military power in localized conflicts. Several trouble spots sparked debate. In the African country of Somalia, U.S. troops, under the umbrella of a UN mission, had been assisting a humanitarian effort to provide food and relief supplies since May 1992. The effort, however, cost the lives of 18 American servicemen killed in factional fighting. Under heavy domestic criticism for undertaking an ill-defined mission, Clinton ordered a pullout during the spring of 1994. The next year, recalling criticism over Somalia, Clinton withheld support from a UN peacekeeping effort in Rwanda, where a half million Tutsis died in a genocidal civil war.

In Haiti, closer to home, U.S. interests seemed clearer, and Clinton vowed to help reestablish the ousted president, Jean-Bertrand Aristide. In September 1994, the first 3,000 of a projected force of 15,000 troops landed in Haiti, in cooperation with the UN. Last-minute negotiations by former president Jimmy Carter persuaded the Haitian military to step aside. After six months, with Aristide in power, U.S. soldiers handed over the responsibility for keeping civil order to UN forces.

The United States, through NATO, also sent troops into former Yugoslavia to stop Bosnian Serbs from massacring Bosnian Muslims. The troops remained to oversee a cease-fire and peace-building process in the U.S.-brokered Dayton (Ohio) accords of 1995.

In March 1999, Clinton supported a NATO bombing campaign in Kosovo, a province of Serbia. NATO leaders and Clinton insisted that this controversial use of military force was necessary to protect ethnic Albanian Muslims, who comprised nearly 90 percent of Kosovo's population, from an "ethnic cleansing" program directed by Serbia's president Slobodan Milosevic. As NATO's bombs systematically decimated Serbia's economic infrastructure, Milosevic stepped up his campaign and forced hundreds of thousands of ethnic Albanians to flee from Kosovo into neighboring countries. Finally, in June 1999, after 78 days of bombardment, Serbia withdrew its forces and, watched over by NATO troops, ethnic Albanians returned to Kosovo. In the fall of 2000, Serbs repudiated Milosevic, turned him out of office, and elected a president more friendly to multiethnic democracy and the West. As in Bosnia, however, American and other allied troops remained as peacekeepers.

In the controversies surrounding these military involvements, critics accused Clinton of an erratic policy with no clear guiding principles about when and how to employ force. Many critics were especially suspicious of cooperation with UN forces and sought clearer exit strategies. Defenders argued that flexibility and working with allied forces were strengths, not weaknesses, in the post–cold war world. In 2000, a large program of military assistance called Plan Colombia, undertaken to combat drug cartels and guerrilla fighters in that country, suggested that the issue of when and how to organize military intervention would remain a contentious one.

Meanwhile, other post–cold war concerns also drew Clinton's attention. In February 1994, a high-ranking CIA official, Aldrich Ames, pled guilty to selling information to the Soviet Union and Russia over the preceding decade and contributing to the deaths of several CIA agents. A year later, information surfaced that the CIA had maintained connections to death squads in Guatemala that had murdered American citizens in that country. Following calls for reform, the CIA charted new, post–cold war missions against international drug traffickers and other criminal syndicates. The CIA also pursued international terrorists such as those involved in bombings of the World Trade Center in New York City in 1993, the U.S. embassies in Kenya and Tanzania in 1998, and a U.S. battleship docked in Yemen in 2000. For Clinton, the new post–cold war agenda also included working to promote accords among antagonists in the trouble spots of Northern Ireland and the Middle East. In the summer of 2000 Clinton brought Israeli and Palestinian heads of state to Camp David in an unsuccessful effort to broker a peace, an issue to which he devoted his energy into the closing hours of his administration.

Clinton also shaped new policies on weapons of mass destruction. He dismantled some of the U.S. nuclear arsenal and tried to curtail the potential danger from other nuclear powers. When the Soviet Union collapsed and its nuclear weapons became dispersed among several independent states, the Clinton administration feared these might find their way onto the black market and to terrorists. In early 1994 Clinton increased economic aid for Ukraine, then the third greatest nuclear power in the world, in return for promises to disarm its 1,600 warheads. In the same year, highly secret "Project Sapphire" transferred enriched uranium stocks from Kazakhstan to storage facilities in the United States. Jimmy Carter helped negotiate a complicated agreement with North Korea over nuclear weapons, signed in 1994. North Korea agreed to begin dismantling its nuclear program and permit international inspections in return for American help in constructing safe, light-water nuclear reactors for its energy needs. Throughout the rest of the world, the United States successfully pressed many nations to sign a new Nuclear Nonproliferation Treaty in the spring of 1995. In early 1998, Clinton went to the brink of war with Iraq to maintain international inspections of Saddam Hussein's weapons programs, but after enduring punishing air strikes, Iraq still expelled the investigators.

GLOBALIZATION

The highest priority of Clinton's foreign policy was to lower trade barriers and expand global markets—a process called "globalization." Building on the Reagan-Bush legacy, Clinton argued that globalization would boost prosperity and foster democracy around the world. His administration frequently used economic enticements to persuade other nations to embrace globalization and democracy. He signed more than 300 trade agreements during his presidency.

Clinton strongly backed the North American Free Trade Agreement (NAFTA), which projected cutting tariffs and eliminating other trade barriers between the United States, Canada, and Mexico over a 15-year period. After adding new provisions on labor and environmental issues, in December 1993 he muscled NAFTA through Congress in a close vote that depended on Republican support and faced fierce opposition from labor unions. Then, in early 1995, Mexico's severe debt crisis and a dramatic devaluation of its peso prompted Clinton to extend a $20 billion loan from America's Exchange Stabilization Fund. This unprecedented and controversial loan stabilized the Mexican economy and, within a few years, had been paid back with one billion dollars in interest.

Clinton's trade negotiators also completed the so-called "Uruguay Round" of the General Agreement on Trade and Tariffs (GATT) in late 1993, and in early 1995 GATT was replaced by a more powerful World Trade Organization (WTO), created to enlarge world trade by implementing new agreements and mediating disputes.

Clinton particularly emphasized efforts to move China toward capitalism. He reversed his election-year position and granted China, despite its dismal record on human rights, equal trading status with other nations. In October 1999 the Clinton administration agreed to back China's entry into the WTO in exchange for a promise to liberalize its policies toward the United States and other potential trading partners. Clinton argued that increased trade with China would contribute to long-term pressures for democratization there. Similarly, in February 1994, the United States had ended its 19-year-old trade embargo against Vietnam.

Clinton claimed that all of these efforts to expand trade, along with the emerging free-market economies in Eastern Europe and Latin America, provided the framework for a new era of global prosperity. When Asian economies faltered during 1998, the president strongly supported acting with the International Monetary Fund to provide huge emergency credits to reform and restore financial systems from Korea to Indonesia. Everywhere he went, Clinton extolled the "new century" in which "liberty will spread by cell phone and cable modem."

THE LONG ELECTION

The election of 2000 had a retro quality. Al Gore, once again, was on the ballot. This time he headed the ticket, with Connecticut senator Joseph Lieberman, an Orthodox Jew, as his running mate. The Republican presidential candidate was, as eight years earlier, named George Bush, but this was the son of the chief executive ousted by the Clinton-Gore team in 1992. George W. Bush chose his father's former defense secretary, Richard Cheney, for the vice-presidential slot. The ballot also included a well-known third-party candidate: Ralph Nader, the consumer activist, ran for the Green Party and as a left-wing alternative to Gore's New Democrat stance.

The campaign stirred few passions. Bush claimed that his record as governor of Texas

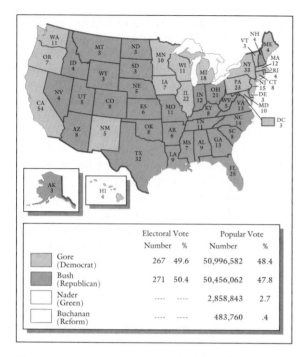

		Electoral Vote		Popular Vote	
		Number	%	Number	%
	Gore (Democrat)	267	49.6	50,996,582	48.4
	Bush (Republican)	271	50.4	50,456,062	47.8
	Nader (Green)	----	----	2,858,843	2.7
	Buchanan (Reform)	----	----	483,760	.4

PRESIDENTIAL ELECTION, 2000

showed that he could work with Democrats and pursue policies grounded in "compassionate conservatism." In stark contrast to the "Willie Horton strategy" of 1992, George W. Bush energetically courted African American and Hispanic voters. Gore tried to craft a political appeal to "working families," but political strategists faulted him for running a disorganized campaign that never capitalized on its main asset, the economic successes of the eight-year Clinton presidency. The election-day turnout on November 7, 2000, was relatively light (51 percent of voters); Nader's candidacy drew less than 3 percent of the popular vote; and Bush and Gore finished nearly tied.

Following the pattern in place since the Reagan era, the popular vote highlighted the gender, racial, and ethnic imbalances between the two parties. According exit polls, Bush attracted 54 percent of the votes cast by men but only 43 percent of those from women. He received 38 percent of his popular votes from Latinos, 37 percent from Asian Americans, and 9 percent from African Americans. Gore won the popular vote by about 500,000 ballots.

The only vote that mattered, however, was in the electoral college, and there the result hinged on

GEORGE W. SHOWS TEXAS STYLE The son of former president George Bush, George W. emerged victorious despite losing the popular vote to Democrat Al Gore.

who had won Florida, where the Republican candidate's brother, Jeb Bush, was governor. For a month, the outcome of the election remained uncertain. When all the absentee votes were finally counted, more than 10 days after election day, Bush led in Florida by 930 votes. Gore and individual supporters, however, filed lawsuits alleging that Florida's antiquated voting machines prevented a fair count of all of the ballots. They asked for hand recounts in Gore-leaning counties where vote totals seemed especially irregular. Meanwhile, African Americans charged that they had faced numerous obstacles to voting in Florida.

The partisan passion absent from the campaign suddenly flared. Lawsuits by both political parties rebounded through the Florida and federal court systems; several local canvassing boards, following an order from the state's supreme court, began manual recounts of contested ballots; both candidates flooded Florida with cadres of lawyers and demonstrators; the Florida secretary of state, a Republican, declared Bush the winner by a revised total of 537 votes; and the Republican-controlled legislature prepared to select a slate of presidential electors pledged to Bush. Finally, on December 9, 2000, the U.S. Supreme Court, by a five-to-four vote, issued a temporary injunction halting manual recounts in Florida until their legality could be adjudicated. Three days later, after receiving briefs and hearing oral arguments, the Court's conservative majority, in another five-to-four decision, declared that conducting manual recounts only in the contested counties violated the Constitution. At this point, Gore conceded defeat, and George W. Bush began assembling a cabinet and a White House staff. The new Bush presidency would be working with a narrow Republican margin in Congress. Republicans still held a slim majority in the House, and the Senate was divided 50–50.

CONCLUSION

Two outsized personalities dominated American political life in the late 20th century: Ronald Reagan and Bill Clinton. The "Reagan revolution" of the 1980s saw the emergence of a new conservative movement that had been born in the shadow of Lyndon Johnson's Great Society. Reagan Republicans distrusted extending federal government power, advocated sharp tax cuts, and stressed a so-ciocultural agenda emphasizing "traditional" values. The dozen years of Republican dominance in the White House from 1980 to 1992 significantly shifted the terms of political debate to the right. The once-proud label of "liberal" became a term that politicians of both parties sought to avoid.

During the 1990s, however, the Republican agenda met its match in Bill Clinton, a "New Democrat." Clinton blunted the Republican surge by adopting a conservative economic agenda (slashing the federal deficit, reshaping the welfare system, and downsizing the federal bureaucracy). At the same time, he supported other issues heatedly opposed by most Republicans: abortion rights, gun control, affirmative action, and environmental protection. In doing so, he moved the Democratic Party away from its big-government agenda of the 1960s and 1970s. Reagan's military build-up coincided with the last years of the cold war; Clinton's emphasis on economic globalization addressed the post–cold war environment.

Reagan and Clinton, both charismatic, media-savvy, two-term presidents, inspired intense adoration and passionate dislike. Together, their administrations redrew the political landscape. In their shadow, Americans continued to negotiate the difficult balances among liberty, equality, and power.

Suggested Readings begin on page SR-1.
For Web activities and resources
related to this chapter, go to
http://www.harcourtcollege.com/history.murrin

Appendix

CANADA

Mt. Olympus
2424 m
(7954 ft)

Olympia ★

Mt. Rainier ▲
4392 m
(14,410 ft)   WASHINGTON

Salem ★   Columbia R.

Cascade   Range

Blue
Mts.

Bitterroot

Range

ROCKY

Missouri   R.

Helena ●

MONTANA

G
R
E
A
T

Badlands

NORTH DAKOTA

Bismarck ★

OREGON

Columbia

Plateau

Snake R.

Boise ★

IDAHO

Absaroka Range

Bighorn Mts.

Black   Hills

SOUTH DAKOTA

Pierre ★

Ranges

Klamath
Mts.

Coast

Sacramento R.

Central

Sierra

Sacramento ★

Lake
Tahoe

San Francisco ○

Carson City ★

Great
Basin

NEVADA

Nevada

San Joaquin

Valley

R.

Coast

Mt. Whitney ▲
4418 m
(14,494 ft)

Death Valley

Great
Salt
Lake

Salt
Lake City ★

Wind River

Range

Uinta Mts.

Wyoming   Basin

WYOMING

Cheyenne ★

Colorado R.

UTAH

Lake
Powell

Lake
Mead

M
O
U
N
T
A
I
N
S

Denver ★

COLORADO

Mt. Elbert ▲
4399 m
(14,433 ft)

▲ Pikes Peak
4301 m
(14,110 ft)

P
L
A
I
N
S

Sand   Hills

NEBRASKA

Platte R.

Smoky Hills

KANSAS

Arkansas R.

Point
Conception

Channel
Islands

Los Angeles ○

CALIFORNIA

Ranges

Mojave

Desert

Salton
Sea

Colorado R.

Grand
Canyon

Colorado
Plateau

Black
Mesa

Painted   Desert

Sangre de   Cristo Mts.

Santa Fe ★

Phoenix ●

Sonoran
Desert

ARIZONA

NEW MEXICO

Oklahoma
City

OKLAHO

PACIFIC

OCEAN

Llano   Estacado

Guadalupe   Mts.

Red R.

Rio   Grande

Stockton
Plateau

TEXA

Austin ★

Austin Cho
Cliffs

HAWAII

Kauai
Niihau

Oahu

Honolulu ★

Molokai

Lanai   Maui
Kahoolawe

Hawaii

PACIFIC
OCEAN

0   75   150 Miles

0   75   150 Kilometers

ARCTIC   OCEAN

Chukchi
Sea

RUSSIA

Beaufort Sea

Brooks   Range

ALASKA

MacKenzie R.

Yukon R.

CANADA

Bering Strait

St.
Lawrence I.

Yukon R.

Mt. McKinley
6194 m
(20,320 ft)

▲ Range

Alaska

Kuskokwim

Bering
Sea

Aleutian Islands

Alaska   Peninsula

Kodiak
I.

Gulf of
Alaska

0   150   300 Miles

0   150   300 Kilometers

Juneau ★

Alexander
Archipelago

MEXICO

Rio   Grande

UNITED STATES
Physical

Lake of the Woods

Mesabi Range

Lake Superior

Upper Peninsula

Lake Huron

MINNESOTA

WISCONSIN

St. Paul

Madison

Lower Peninsula

Lake Michigan

MICHIGAN

Lansing

Mississippi R.

IOWA

Des Moines

Chicago

ILLINOIS

INDIANA

OHIO

Springfield

Indianapolis

Columbus

Kansas City

Jefferson City

St. Louis

MISSOURI

Missouri R.

Ozark Plateau

KENTUCKY

Frankfort

Ohio R.

Kentucky Lake

Nashville

Boston Mts.

Arkansas R.

Little Rock

ARKANSAS

Ouachita Mts.

TENNESSEE

Cumberland Plateau

Great Smoky Mts.

Mt. Mitchell 2037 m (6684 ft)

Yazoo Basin

Mississippi R.

Tennessee R.

LOUISIANA

MISSISSIPPI

ALABAMA

Jackson

Montgomery

GEORGIA

Red R.

Baton Rouge

New Orleans

GULF COASTAL PLAIN

Houston

Tallahassee

FLORIDA

Gulf of Mexico

Cape Canaveral

L. Okeechobee

Miami

Florida Keys

Straits of Florida

CUBA

BAHAMAS

St. Lawrence R.

Lake Champlain

Adirondack Mts.

Green Mts.

White Mts.

MAINE

Augusta

Montpelier

N.H.

VT.

Concord

Boston

Lake Ontario

NEW YORK

Albany

MASS.

Cape Cod

Gulf of Maine

Niagara Falls

Finger Lakes

Hartford

CONN.

Providence

R.I.

Connecticut R.

APPALACHIAN MOUNTAINS

Allegheny Front

Susquehanna R.

Long Island

Lake Erie

PENN.

Harrisburg

N.J.

New York

Trenton

Dover

DEL.

Delaware Bay

WEST VIRGINIA

VIRGINIA

MD.

Annapolis

Washington, D.C.

Chesapeake Bay

Charleston

Richmond

Blue Ridge

Piedmont

ATLANTIC COASTAL PLAIN

NORTH CAROLINA

Raleigh

SOUTH CAROLINA

Columbia

Piedmont

Atlanta

ATLANTIC OCEAN

PUERTO RICO
San Juan

ATLANTIC OCEAN

Charlotte Amalie

VIRGIN ISLANDS

| 0 | 50 | 100 Miles |
| 0 | 50 | 100 Kilometers |

Elevation in feet	Elevation in meters
Over 13,100	Over 4,000
6,600–13,100	2,000–4,000
1,600–6,600	500–2,000
700–1,600	200–500
0–700	0–200
Below sea level	Below sea level

| 0 | 150 | 300 Miles |
| 0 | 150 | 300 Kilometers |

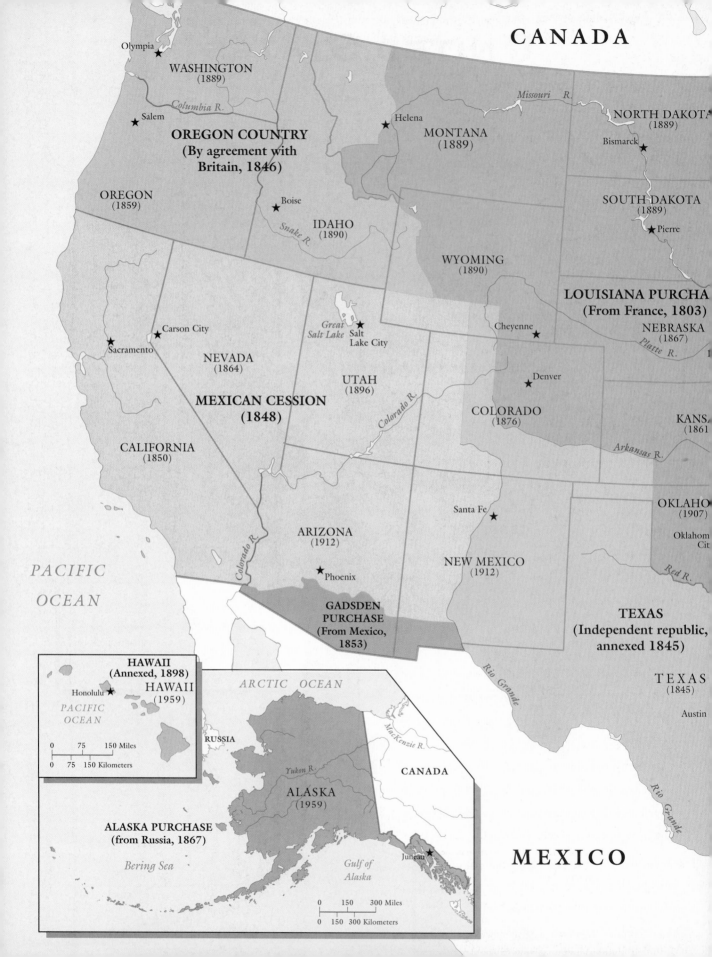

CANADA

Olympia ★
WASHINGTON
(1889)

★ Salem
Columbia R.

OREGON COUNTRY
(By agreement with
Britain, 1846)

OREGON
(1859)

Boise ★

Snake R.

IDAHO
(1890)

Helena ★
MONTANA
(1889)

Missouri R.

NORTH DAKOTA
(1889)

Bismarck ★

SOUTH DAKOTA
(1889)

Pierre ★

WYOMING
(1890)

LOUISIANA PURCHA
(From France, 1803)

NEBRASKA
(1867)

Platte R.

Carson City ★
Sacramento ★

NEVADA
(1864)

*Great
Salt Lake*

Salt ★
Lake City

UTAH
(1896)

Colorado R.

Cheyenne ★

Denver ★

COLORADO
(1876)

KANS
(1861

Arkansas R.

MEXICAN CESSION
(1848)

CALIFORNIA
(1850)

Colorado R.

ARIZONA
(1912)

Phoenix ★

Santa Fe ★

NEW MEXICO
(1912)

OKLAHO
(1907)

Oklahoi
Cit

Red R.

GADSDEN
PURCHASE
(From Mexico,
1853)

TEXAS
(Independent republic,
annexed 1845)

PACIFIC
OCEAN

TEXAS
(1845)

Austin

HAWAII
(Annexed, 1898)
HAWAII
(1959)

Honolulu ★

PACIFIC
OCEAN

| 0 | 75 | 150 Miles |
| 0 | 75 | 150 Kilometers |

ARCTIC OCEAN

RUSSIA

MacKenzie R.

Yukon R.

CANADA

ALASKA
(1959)

Rio Grande

ALASKA PURCHASE
(from Russia, 1867)

Bering Sea

*Gulf of
Alaska*

Juneau ★

MEXICO

Rio Grande

| 0 | 150 | 300 Miles |
| 0 | 150 | 300 Kilometers |

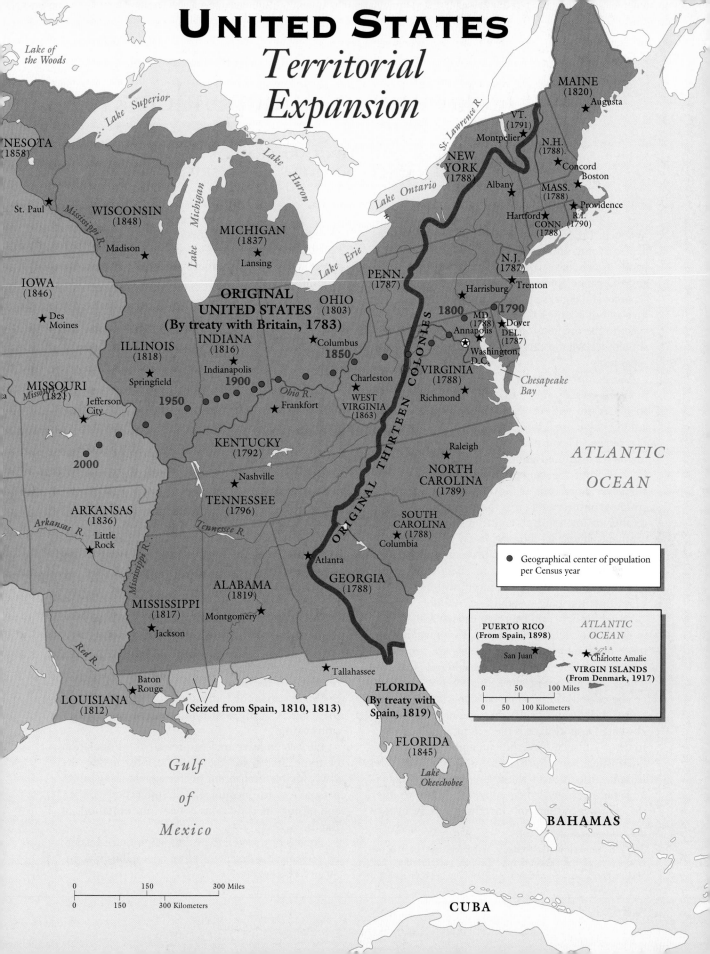

UNITED STATES
Territorial Expansion

Lake of the Woods

Lake Superior

NESOTA
(1858)

St. Paul

WISCONSIN
(1848)

Madison

Lake Michigan

Lake Huron

MICHIGAN
(1837)

Lansing

IOWA
(1846)

Des Moines

ILLINOIS
(1818)

Springfield

MISSOURI
(1821)

Jefferson City

Missouri R.
Mississippi R.

2000

1950

ARKANSAS
(1836)

Little Rock

Arkansas R.

Red R.

Mississippi R.

LOUISIANA
(1812)

Baton Rouge

(Seized from Spain, 1810, 1813)

MISSISSIPPI
(1817)

Jackson

ALABAMA
(1819)

Montgomery

**ORIGINAL
UNITED STATES
(By treaty with Britain, 1783)**

OHIO
(1803)

INDIANA
(1816)

Indianapolis

1900

Columbus

1850

Ohio R.

KENTUCKY
(1792)

Frankfort

Nashville

TENNESSEE
(1796)

Tennessee R.

Atlanta

GEORGIA
(1788)

Tallahassee

FLORIDA
(By treaty with
Spain, 1819)

FLORIDA
(1845)

Lake Okeechobee

Charleston

WEST
VIRGINIA
(1863)

SOUTH
CAROLINA
(1788)

Columbia

NORTH
CAROLINA
(1789)

Raleigh

Richmond

VIRGINIA
(1788)

Lake Erie

Lake Ontario

St. Lawrence R.

ORIGINAL THIRTEEN COLONIES

PENN.
(1787)

Harrisburg

1800

1790

MD.
(1788)

Annapolis

Washington, D.C.

Chesapeake Bay

Dover

DEL.
(1787)

N.J.
(1787)

Trenton

NEW
YORK
(1788)

Albany

VT.
(1791)

Montpelier

N.H.
(1788)

Concord

MASS.
(1788)

Hartford

CONN.
(1788)

Providence

R.I.
(1790)

Boston

MAINE
(1820)

Augusta

*ATLANTIC
OCEAN*

Gulf

of

Mexico

BAHAMAS

CUBA

● Geographical center of population per Census year

PUERTO RICO
(From Spain, 1898)

*ATLANTIC
OCEAN*

San Juan

Charlotte Amalie

VIRGIN ISLANDS
(From Denmark, 1917)

0   50   100 Miles

0   50   100 Kilometers

0   150   300 Miles

0   150   300 Kilometers

The Declaration of Independence

THE UNANIMOUS DECLARATION OF
THE THIRTEEN UNITED STATES OF AMERICA,

When in the Course of human events it becomes necessary for one people to dissolve the political bands which have connected them with another, and to assume among the Powers of the earth, the separate and equal station to which the Laws of Nature and of Nature's God entitle them, a decent respect to the opinions of mankind requires that they should declare the causes which impel them to the separation.

We hold these truths to be self-evident, that all men are created equal, that they are endowed by their Creator with certain unalienable Rights, that among these are Life, Liberty and the pursuit of Happiness. That to secure these rights, Governments are instituted among Men, deriving their just Powers from the consent of the governed. That whenever any Form of Government becomes destructive of these ends, it is the Right of the People to alter or to abolish it, and to institute new Government, laying its foundation on such principles and organizing its Powers in such form, as to them shall seem most likely to effect their Safety and Happiness. Prudence, indeed, will dictate that Governments long established should not be changed for light and transient causes; and accordingly all experience hath shewn, that mankind are more disposed to suffer, while evils are sufferable, than to right themselves by abolishing the forms to which they are accustomed. But when a long train of abuses and usurpations, pursuing invariably the same Object evinces a design to reduce them under absolute Despotism, it is their right, it is their duty, to throw off such Government, and to provide new Guards for their future security. Such has been the patient sufferance of these Colonies; and such is now the necessity which constrains them to alter their former Systems of Government. The history

of the present King of Great Britain is a history of repeated injuries and usurpations, all having in direct object the establishment of an absolute Tyranny over these States. To prove this, let Facts be submitted to a candid world.

He has refused his Assent to Laws, the most wholesome and necessary for the public good.

He has forbidden his Governors to pass Laws of immediate and pressing importance, unless suspended in their operation till his Assent should be obtained; and when so suspended, he has utterly neglected to attend to them.

He has refused to pass other Laws for the accommodation of large districts of people, unless those people would relinquish the right of Representation in the Legislature, a right inestimable to them and formidable to tyrants only.

He has called together legislative bodies at places unusual, uncomfortable, and distant from the depository of their Public Records, for the sole Purpose of fatiguing them into compliance with his measures.

He has dissolved Representative Houses repeatedly, for opposing with manly firmness his invasions on the rights of the People.

He has refused for a long time, after such dissolutions, to cause others to be elected; whereby the Legislative Powers, incapable of Annihilation, have returned to the People at large for their exercise; the State remaining in the mean time exposed to all the dangers of invasion from without, and convulsions within.

He has endeavoured to prevent the Population of these States; for that purpose obstructing the Laws for Naturalization of Foreigners; refusing to pass others to encourage their migrations hither, and raising the conditions of new Appropriations of Lands.

He has obstructed the Administration of Justice, by refusing his Assent to Laws for establishing Judiciary Powers.

Text is reprinted from the facsimile of the engrossed copy in the National Archives. The original spelling, capitalization, and punctuation have been retained. Paragraphing has been added.

He has made Judges dependent on his Will alone, for the tenure of their offices, and the amount and payment of their salaries.

He has erected a multitude of New Offices, and sent hither swarms of Officers to harass our People, and eat out their substance.

He has kept among us, in times of peace, Standing Armies without the Consent of our legislatures.

He has affected to render the Military independent of and superior to the Civil Power.

He has combined with others to subject us to a jurisdiction foreign to our constitution, and unacknowledged by our laws; giving his Assent to their Acts of pretended Legislation:

For Quartering large bodies of armed troops among us:

For protecting them, by a mock Trial, from Punishment for any Murders which they should commit on the Inhabitants of these States:

For cutting off our Trade with all parts of the world:

For imposing Taxes on us without our Consent:

For depriving us in many cases, of the benefits of Trial by Jury:

For transporting us beyond Seas to be tried for pretended offences:

For abolishing the free System of English Laws in a neighbouring Province, establishing therein an Arbitrary government, and enlarging its Boundaries so as to render it at once an example and fit instrument for introducing the same absolute rule into these Colonies:

For taking away our Charters, abolishing our most valuable Laws, and altering fundamentally the Forms of our Governments:

For suspending our own Legislatures, and declaring themselves invested with Power to legislate for us in all cases whatsoever.

He has abdicated Government here, by declaring us out of his Protection, and waging War against us.

He has plundered our seas, ravaged our Coasts, burnt our towns, and destroyed the lives of our people.

He is at this time transporting large Armies of foreign Mercenaries to compleat the works of death, desolation and tyranny, already begun with circumstances of Cruelty and perfidy scarcely paralleled in the most barbarous ages, and totally unworthy the Head of a civilized nation.

He has constrained our fellow Citizens taken Captive on the high Seas to bear Arms against their Country, to become the executioners of their friends and Brethren, or to fall themselves by their Hands.

He has excited domestic insurrections amongst us, and has endeavoured to bring on the inhabitants of our frontiers, the merciless Indian Savages, whose known rule of warfare, is an undistinguished destruction of all ages, sexes and conditions.

In every stage of these Oppressions We have Petitioned for Redress in the most humble terms: Our repeated Petitions have been answered only by repeated injury. A Prince, whose character is thus marked by every act which may define a Tyrant, is unfit to be the ruler of a free People.

Nor have We been wanting in attentions to our British brethren. We have warned them from time to time of attempts by their legislature to extend an unwarrantable jurisdiction over us. We have reminded them of the circumstances of our emigration and settlement here. We have appealed to their native justice and magnanimity, and we have conjured them by the ties of our common kindred to disavow thee usurpations, which, would inevitably interrupt our connections and correspondence. They too have been deaf to the voice of justice and of consanguinity. We must, therefore, acquiesce in the necessity, which denounces our Separation, and hold them, as we hold the rest of mankind, Enemies in War, in Peace Friends.

WE, THEREFORE, the Representatives of the UNITED STATES OF AMERICA, in General Congress, Assembled, appealing to the Supreme Judge of the world for the rectitude of our intentions, do, in the Name, and by Authority of the good People of these Colonies, solemnly publish and declare, That these United Colonies are, and of Right ought to be FREE AND INDEPENDENT STATES; that they are Absolved from all Allegiance to the British Crown, and that all political connection between them and the State of Great Britain, is and ought to be totally dissolved; and that, as Free and Independent States, they have full Power to levy War, conclude Peace, contract Alliances, establish Commerce, and to do all other Acts and Things which Independent States may of right do. And for the support of this Declaration, with a firm reliance on the protection of divine Providence, we mutually pledge to each other our Lives, our Fortunes and our sacred Honor.

The Constitution of the United States of America

We the People of the United States, in Order to form a more perfect Union, establish Justice, insure domestic Tranquility, provide for the common defence, promote the general Welfare, and secure the Blessings of Liberty to ourselves and our Posterity, do ordain and establish this Constitution for the United States of America.

ARTICLE I.

SECTION 1. All legislative Powers herein granted shall be vested in a Congress of the United States, which shall consist of a Senate and House of Representatives.

SECTION 2. The House of Representatives shall be composed of Members chosen every second Year by the People of the several States, and the Electors in each State shall have the Qualifications requisite for Electors of the most numerous Branch of the State Legislature.

No Person shall be a Representative who shall not have attained to the Age of twenty five Years, and been seven Years a Citizen of the United States, and who shall not, when elected, be an Inhabitant of that State in which he shall be chosen.

Representatives and direct Taxes[1] shall be apportioned among the several States which may be included within this Union, according to their respective Numbers, which shall be determined by adding to the whole Number of free Persons, including those bound to Service for a Term of Years, and excluding Indians not taxed, three fifths of all other Persons.[2] The actual Enumeration shall be made within three Years after the first Meeting of the Congress of the United States, and within every subsequent Term of ten Years, in such Manner as they shall by Law direct. The Number of Representatives shall not exceed one for every thirty Thousand, but each State shall have at Least one Representative; and until such enumeration shall be made, the State

of New Hampshire shall be entitled to chuse three; Massachusetts eight; Rhode Island and Providence Plantations one; Connecticut five; New York six; New Jersey four; Pennsylvania eight; Delaware one; Maryland six; Virginia ten; North Carolina five; South Carolina five; and Georgia three.

When vacancies happen in the Representation from any State, the Executive Authority thereof shall issue Writs of Election to fill such Vacancies.

The House of Representatives shall chuse their Speaker and other Officers; and shall have the sole Power of Impeachment.

SECTION 3. The Senate of the United States shall be composed of two Senators from each State, chosen by the Legislature thereof, for six Years; and each Senator shall have one Vote.[3]

Immediately after they shall be assembled in Consequence of the first Election, they shall be divided as equally as may be into three Classes. The Seats of the Senators of the first Class shall be vacated at the Expiration of the second Year, of the second Class at the Expiration of the fourth Year, and of the third Class at the Expiration of the sixth Year, so that one third may be chosen every second Year; and if Vacancies happen by Resignation, or otherwise, during the Recess of the Legislature of any State, the Executive thereof may make temporary Appointments until the next Meeting of the Legislature, which shall then fill such Vacancies.[4]

No Person shall be a Senator who shall not have attained to the Age of thirty Years, and been nine Years a Citizen of the United States, and who shall not, when elected, be an Inhabitant of that State for which he shall be chosen.

The Vice President of the United States shall be President of the Senate, but shall have no Vote, unless they be equally divided.

The Senate shall chuse their other Officers, and also a President pro tempore, in the Absence of the Vice President, or when he shall exercise the Office of President of the United States.

Text is from the engrossed copy in the National Archives. Original spelling, capitalization, and punctuation have been retained.

[1]Modified by the Sixteenth Amendment.

[2]Replaced by the Fourteenth Amendment.

---

[3]Superseded by the Seventeenth Amendment.

[4]Modified by the Seventeenth Amendment.

The Senate shall have the sole Power to try all Impeachments. When sitting for that Purpose, they shall be on Oath or Affirmation. When the President of the United States is tried, the Chief Justice shall preside: And no Person shall be convicted without the Concurrence of two thirds of the Members present.

Judgment in Cases of Impeachment shall not extend further than to removal from Office, and disqualification to hold and enjoy any Office of honor, Trust or Profit under the United States: but the Party convicted shall nevertheless be liable and subject to Indictment, Trial, Judgment and Punishment, according to Law.

SECTION 4. The Times, Places and Manner of holding Elections for Senators and Representatives, shall be prescribed in each State by the Legislature thereof, but the Congress may at any time by Law make or alter such Regulation, except as to the Places of chusing Senators.

The Congress shall assemble at least once in every Year, and such Meeting shall be on the first Monday in December, unless they shall by Law appoint a different Day.[5]

SECTION 5. Each House shall be the Judge of the Elections, Returns and Qualifications of its own Members, and a Majority of each shall constitute a Quorum to do Business; but a smaller Number may adjourn from day to day, and may be authorized to compel the Attendance of absent Members, in such Manner, and under such Penalties as each House may provide.

Each House may determine the Rules of its Proceedings, punish its Members for disorderly Behaviour, and, with the Concurrence of two thirds, expel a Member.

Each House shall keep a Journal of its Proceedings, and from time to time publish the same, excepting such Parts as may in their Judgment require Secrecy; and the Yeas and Nays of the Members of either House on any question shall, at the Desire of one fifth of those Present, be entered on the Journal.

Neither House, during the Session of Congress, shall, without the Consent of the other, adjourn for more than three days, nor to any other Place than that in which the two Houses shall be sitting.

SECTION 6. The Senators and Representatives shall receive a Compensation for their Services, to be ascertained by Law, and paid out of the Treasury of the United States. They shall in all Cases, except Treason, Felony and Breach of the Peace, be privileged from Arrest during their Attendance at the Session of their respective Houses, and in going to and returning from the same; and for any Speech or Debate in either House, they shall not be questioned in any other Place.

No Senator or Representative shall, during the Time for which he was elected, be appointed to any civil Office under the Authority of the United States, which shall have been created, or the Emoluments whereof shall have been encreased during such time; and no Person holding any Office under the United States, shall be a Member of either House during his Continuance in Office.

SECTION 7. All Bills for raising Revenue shall originate in the House of Representatives; but the Senate may propose or concur with Amendments as on other Bills.

Every Bill which shall have passed the House of Representatives and the Senate shall, before it become a Law, be presented to the President of the United States; If he approve he shall sign it, but if not he shall return it, with his Objections to that House in which it shall have originated, who shall enter the Objections at large on their Journal, and proceed to reconsider it. If after such Reconsideration two thirds of that House shall agree to pass the Bill, it shall be sent, together with the Objections, to the other House, by which it shall likewise be reconsidered, and if approved by two thirds of that House, it shall become a Law. But in all such Cases the Votes of both Houses shall be determined by yeas and Nays, and the Names of the Persons voting for and against the Bill shall be entered on the Journal of each House respectively. If any Bill shall not be returned by the President within ten Days (Sundays excepted) after it shall have been presented to him, the Same shall be a Law, in like Manner as if he had signed it, unless the Congress by their Adjournment prevent its Return, in which Case it shall not be a Law.

Every Order, Resolution, or Vote to which the Concurrence of the Senate and House of Representatives may be necessary (except on a question of Adjournment) shall be presented to the President of the United States; and before the Same shall take Effect, shall be approved by him, or being disapproved by him shall be repassed by two thirds of the Senate and House of Representatives,

---

[5]Superseded by the Twentieth Amendment.

according to the Rules and Limitations prescribed in the Case of a Bill.

SECTION 8. The Congress shall have power To lay and collect Taxes, Duties, Imposts and Excises, to pay the Debts and provide for the common Defence and general Welfare of the United States; but all Duties, Imposts and Excises shall be uniform throughout the United States;

To borrow Money on the credit of the United States;

To regulate Commerce with foreign Nations, and among the several States, and with the Indian Tribes;

To establish an uniform Rule of Naturalization, and uniform Laws on the subject of Bankruptcies throughout the United States;

To coin Money, regulate the Value thereof, and of foreign Coin, and fix the Standard of Weights and Measures;

To provide for the Punishment of counterfeiting the Securities and current Coin of the United States;

To establish Post Offices and post Roads;

To promote the Progress of Science and useful Arts, by securing for limited Times to Authors and Inventors the exclusive Right to their respective Writings and Discoveries;

To constitute Tribunals inferior to the supreme Court;

To define and punish Piracies and Felonies committed on the high Seas, and Offences against the Law of Nations;

To declare War, grant Letters of Marque and Reprisal, and make Rules concerning Captures on Land and Water;

To raise and support Armies, but no Appropriation of Money to that Use shall be for a longer Term than two Years;

To provide and maintain a Navy;

To make Rules for the Government and Regulation of the land and naval Forces;

To provide for calling forth the Militia to execute the Laws of the Union, suppress Insurrections and repel Invasions;

To provide for organizing, arming, and disciplining, the Militia, and for governing such Part of them as may be employed in the Service of the United States, reserving to the States respectively, the Appointment of the Officers, and the Authority of training the Militia according to the discipline prescribed by Congress;

To exercise exclusive Legislation in all Cases whatsoever, over such District (not exceeding ten Miles square) as may, by Cession of particular States, and the Acceptance of Congress, become the Seat of the Government of the United States, and to exercise like Authority over all Places purchased by the Consent of the Legislature of the State in which the Same shall be, for the Erection of Forts, Magazines, Arsenals, dock-Yards, and other needful Buildings;—And

To make all Laws which shall be necessary and proper for carrying into Execution the foregoing Powers, and all other Powers vested by this Constitution in the Government of the United States, or in any Department or Officer thereof.

SECTION 9. The Migration or Importation of such Persons as any of the States now existing shall think proper to admit, shall not be prohibited by the Congress prior to the Year one thousand eight hundred and eight, but a Tax or duty may be imposed on such Importation, not exceeding ten dollars for each Person.

The Privilege of the Writ of Habeas Corpus shall not be suspended, unless when in Cases of Rebellion or Invasion the public Safety may require it.

No Bill of Attainder or ex post facto Law shall be passed.

No Capitation, or other direct, Tax shall be laid, unless in Proportion to the Census or Enumeration herein before directed to be taken.

No Tax or Duty shall be laid on Articles exported from any State.

No Preference shall be given by any Regulation of Commerce or Revenue to the Ports of one State over those of another: nor shall Vessels bound to, or from, one State, be obliged to enter, clear, or pay Duties in another.

No Money shall be drawn from the Treasury, but in Consequence of Appropriations made by Law, and a regular Statement and Account of the Receipts and Expenditures of all public Money shall be published from time to time.

No Title of Nobility shall be granted by the United States: And no Person holding any Office of Profit or Trust under them, shall, without the Consent of the Congress, accept of any present, Emolument, Office, or Title, of any kind whatever, from any King, Prince, or foreign State.

SECTION 10. No State shall enter into any Treaty, Alliance, or Confederation; grant Letters of

Marque and Reprisal; coin Money; emit Bills of Credit; make any Thing but gold and silver Coin a Tender in Payment of Debts; pass any Bill of Attainder, ex post facto Law, or Law impairing the Obligation of Contracts, or grant any Title of Nobility.

No State shall, without the Consent of the Congress, lay any Imposts or Duties on Imports or Exports, except what may be absolutely necessary for executing its inspection Laws: and the net Produce of all Duties and Imposts, laid by any State on Imports or Exports, shall be for the Use of the Treasury of the United States; and all such Laws shall be subject to the Revision and Controul of the Congress.

No State shall, without the Consent of Congress, lay any Duty of Tonnage, keep Troops, or Ships of War in time of Peace, enter into any Agreement or Compact with another State, or with a foreign Power, or engage in War, unless actually invaded, or in such imminent Danger as will not admit of delay.

ARTICLE II.

SECTION 1. The executive Power shall be vested in a President of the United States of America. He shall hold his Office during the Term of four Years, and, together with the Vice President, chosen for the same Term, be elected, as follows:

Each State shall appoint, in such Manner as the Legislature thereof may direct, a Number of Electors, equal to the whole Number of Senators and Representatives to which the State may be entitled in the Congress: but no Senator or Representative, or Person holding an Office of Trust or Profit under the United States, shall be appointed an Elector.

The Electors shall meet in their respective States, and vote by Ballot for two Persons, of whom one at least shall not be an Inhabitant of the same State with themselves. And they shall make a List of all the Persons voted for, and of the Number of Votes for each; which List they shall sign and certify, and transmit sealed to the Seat of the Government of the United States, directed to the President of the Senate. The President of the Senate shall, in the Presence of the Senate and House of Representatives, open all the Certificates, and the Votes shall then be counted. The Person having the greatest Number of Votes shall be the President, if such Number be a Majority of the whole Number of Electors appointed; and if there be more than one who have such Majority, and have an equal Number of Votes,

then the House of Representatives shall immediately chuse by Ballot one of them for President; and if no Person have a Majority, then from the five highest on the List the said House shall in like Manner chuse the President. But in chusing the President, the Votes shall be taken by States, the Representation from each State having one Vote; A quorum for this Purpose shall consist of a Member or Members from two thirds of the States, and a Majority of all the States shall be necessary to a Choice. In every Case, after the Choice of the President, the Person having the greatest Number of Votes of the Electors shall be the Vice President. But if there should remain two or more who have equal Votes, the Senate shall chuse from them by Ballot the Vice President.[6]

The Congress may determine the Time of chusing the Electors, and the Day on which they shall give their Votes; which Day shall be the same throughout the United States.

No Person except a natural born Citizen, or a Citizen of the United States, at the time of the Adoption of this Constitution, shall be eligible to the Office of President, neither shall any Person be eligible to that Office who shall not have attained to the Age of thirty five Years, and been fourteen Years a Resident within the United States.

In Case of the Removal of the President from Office, or of his Death, Resignation, or Inability to discharge the Powers and Duties of the said Office, the Same shall devolve on the Vice President, and the Congress may by Law provide for the Case of Removal, Death, Resignation or Inability, both of the President and Vice President, declaring what Officer shall then act as President, and such Officer shall act accordingly, until the Disability be removed, or a President shall be elected.[7]

The President shall, at stated Times, receive for his Services, a Compensation, which shall neither be encreased nor diminished during the Period for which he shall have been elected, and he shall not receive within that Period any other Emolument from the United States, or any of them.

Before he enter on the Execution of his Office, he shall take the following Oath or Affirmation:—"I do solemnly swear (or affirm) that I will faithfully execute the Office of President of the United States,

---

[6]Superseded by the Twelfth Amendment.

[7]Modified by the Twenty-fifth Amendment.

and will to the best of my Ability, preserve, protect and defend the Constitution of the United States."

SECTION 2. The President shall be Commander in Chief of the Army and Navy of the United States, and of the Militia of the several States, when called into the actual Service of the United States; he may require the Opinion, in writing, of the principal Officer in each of the executive Departments, upon any Subject relating to the Duties of their respective Offices, and he shall have Power to grant Reprieves and Pardons for Offences against the United States, except in Cases of Impeachment.

He shall have Power, by and with the Advice and Consent of the Senate, to make Treaties, provided two thirds of the Senators present concur; and he shall nominate, and by and with the Advice and Consent of the Senate, shall appoint Ambassadors, other public Ministers and Consuls, Judges of the supreme Court, and all other Officers of the United States, whose Appointments are not herein otherwise provided for, and which shall be established by Law; but the Congress may by Law vest the Appointment of such inferior Officers, as they think proper, in the President alone, in the Courts of Law, or in the Heads of Departments.

The President shall have Power to fill up all Vacancies that may happen during the Recess of the Senate, by granting Commissions which shall expire at the End of their next Session.

SECTION 3. He shall from time to time give the Congress Information of the State of the Union, and recommend to their Consideration such Measures as he shall judge necessary and expedient; he may, on extraordinary Occasions, convene both Houses, or either of them, and in Case of Disagreement between them, with Respect to the Time of Adjournment, he may adjourn them to such Time as he shall think proper; he shall receive Ambassadors and other public Ministers; he shall take Care that the Laws be faithfully executed, and shall Commission all the Officers of the United States.

SECTION 4. The President, Vice President and all civil Officers of the United States, shall be removed from Office on Impeachment for, and Conviction of, Treason, Bribery, or other high Crimes and Misdemeanors.

ARTICLE III.

SECTION 1. The judicial Power of the United States, shall be vested in one supreme Court, and in such inferior Courts as the Congress may from time to time ordain and establish. The Judges, both of the supreme and inferior Courts, shall hold their Offices during good Behaviour, and shall, at stated Times, receive for their Services, a Compensation, which shall not be diminished during their Continuance in Office.

SECTION 2. The judicial Power shall extend to all Cases, in Law and Equity, arising under this Constitution, the Laws of the United States, and Treaties made, or which shall be made, under their Authority;—to all Cases affecting Ambassadors, other public Ministers and Consuls;—to all Cases of admiralty and maritime Jurisdiction;—to Controversies to which the United States shall be a Party;—to Controversies between two or more States;—between a State and Citizens of another State;[8]—between Citizens of different States,—between Citizens of the same State claiming Lands under Grants of different States, and between a State, or the Citizens thereof, and foreign States, Citizens or Subjects.

In all Cases affecting Ambassadors, other public Ministers and Consuls, and those in which a State shall be Party, the supreme Court shall have original Jurisdiction. In all the other Cases before mentioned, the supreme Court shall have appellate Jurisdiction, both as to Law and Fact, with such Exceptions, and under such Regulations as the Congress shall make.

The Trial of all Crimes, except in Cases of Impeachment, shall be by Jury; and such Trial shall be held in the State where the said Crimes shall have been committed; but when not committed within any State, the Trial shall be at such Place or Places as the Congress may by Law have directed.

SECTION 3. Treason against the United States, shall consist only in levying War against them, or in adhering to their Enemies, giving them Aid and Comfort. No Person shall be convicted of Treason unless on the Testimony of two Witnesses to the same overt Act, or on Confession in open Court.

The Congress shall have Power to declare the Punishment of Treason, but no Attainder of Treason shall work Corruption of Blood, or Forfeiture except during the Life of the Person attainted.

ARTICLE IV.

SECTION 1. Full Faith and Credit shall be given in each State to the public Acts, Records, and judicial

---

[8]Modified by the Eleventh Amendment.

Proceedings of every other State. And the Congress may by general Laws prescribe the Manner in which such Acts, Records and Proceedings shall be proved, and the Effect thereof.

SECTION 2. The Citizens of each State shall be entitled to all Privileges and Immunities of Citizens in the several States.

A Person charged in any State with Treason, Felony, or other Crime, who shall flee from Justice, and be found in another State, shall on Demand of the executive Authority of the State from which he fled, be delivered up, to be removed to the State having Jurisdiction of the Crime.

No Person held to Service or Labour in one State, under the Laws thereof, escaping into another, shall, in Consequence of any Law or Regulation therein, be discharged from such Service or Labour, but shall be delivered up on Claim of the Party to whom such Service or Labour may be due.

SECTION 3. New States may be admitted by the Congress into this Union; but no new State shall be formed or erected within the Jurisdiction of any other State, nor any State be formed by the Junction of two or more States, or Parts of States, without the Consent of the Legislatures of the States concerned as well as of the Congress.

The Congress shall have Power to dispose of and make all needful Rules and Regulations respecting the Territory or other Property belonging to the United States; and nothing in this Constitution shall be so construed as to Prejudice any Claims of the United States, or of any particular State.

SECTION 4. The United States shall guarantee to every State in this Union a Republican Form of Government, and shall protect each of them against Invasion; and on Application of the Legislature, or of the Executive (when the Legislature cannot be convened) against domestic Violence.

ARTICLE V.

The Congress, whenever two thirds of both Houses shall deem it necessary, shall propose Amendments to this Constitution, or, on the Application of the Legislatures of two thirds of the several States, shall call a Convention for proposing Amendments, which, in either Case, shall be valid to all Intents and Purposes, as Part of this Constitution, when ratified by the Legislatures of three fourths of the several States, or by Conventions in three fourths thereof, as the one or the other Mode

of Ratification may be proposed by the Congress; Provided that no Amendment which may be made prior to the Year One thousand eight hundred and eight shall in any Manner affect the first and fourth Clauses in the Ninth Section of the first Article; and that no State, without its Consent, shall be deprived of its equal Suffrage in the Senate.

ARTICLE VI.

All Debts contracted and Engagements entered into, before the Adoption of this Constitution, shall be as valid against the United States under this Constitution, as under the Confederation.

This Constitution, and the Laws of the United States which shall be made in Pursuance thereof; and all Treaties made, or which shall be made, under the Authority of the United States, shall be the supreme Law of the Land; and the Judges in every State shall be bound thereby, any Thing in the Constitution or Laws of any State to the Contrary notwithstanding.

The Senators and Representatives before mentioned, and the Members of the several State Legislatures, and all executive and judicial Officers, both of the United States and of the several States, shall be bound by Oath or Affirmation, to support this Constitution; but no religious Test shall ever be required as a Qualification to any Office or public Trust under the United States.

ARTICLE VII.

The Ratification of the Conventions of nine States, shall be sufficient for the Establishment of this Constitution between the States so ratifying the Same.

Done in Convention by the Unanimous Consent of the States present the Seventeenth Day of September in the Year of our Lord one thousand seven hundred and Eighty seven and of the Independence of the United States of America the Twelfth. In witness whereof We have hereunto subscribed our Names,

Articles in Addition to, and Amendment of, the Constitution of the United States of America, Proposed by Congress, and Ratified by the Legislatures of the Several States, Pursuant to the Fifth Article of the Original Constitution.

AMENDMENT I[9]

Congress shall make no law respecting an establishment of religion, or prohibiting the free exercise thereof; or abridging the freedom of speech, or of the press; or the right of the people peaceably to assemble, and to petition the Government for a redress of grievances.

AMENDMENT II

A well regulated Militia, being necessary to the security of a free State, the right of the people to keep and bear Arms shall not be infringed.

AMENDMENT III

No Soldier shall, in time of peace, be quartered in any house, without the consent of the Owner, nor in time of war, but in a manner to be prescribed by law.

AMENDMENT IV

The right of the people to be secure in their persons, houses, papers, and effects, against unreasonable searches and seizures, shall not be violated, and no Warrants shall issue, but upon probable cause, supported by Oath or affirmation, and particularly describing the place to be searched, and the persons or things to be seized.

AMENDMENT V

No person shall be held to answer for a capital or otherwise infamous crime, unless on a presentment or indictment of a Grand Jury, except in cases arising in the land or naval forces, or in the Militia, when in actual service in time of War or public danger; nor shall any person be subject for the same offence to be twice put in jeopardy of life or limb; nor shall be compelled in any criminal case to be a witness against himself, nor be deprived of life, liberty, or property, without due process of law; nor shall private property be taken for public use, without just compensation.

AMENDMENT VI

In all criminal prosecutions, the accused shall enjoy the right to a speedy and public trial, by an impartial jury of the State and district wherein the crime shall have been committed, which district shall have been previously ascertained by law, and to be informed of the nature and cause of the accusation; to be confronted with the witnesses against him; to have compulsory process for obtaining witnesses in his favor, and to have the Assistance of Counsel for his defence.

AMENDMENT VII

In suits at common law, where the value in controversy shall exceed twenty dollars, the right of trial by jury shall be preserved, and no fact tried by a jury, shall be otherwise reexamined in any Court of the United States, than according to the rules of the common law.

AMENDMENT VIII

Excessive bail shall not be required, nor excessive fines imposed, nor cruel and unusual punishments inflicted.

AMENDMENT IX

The enumeration in the Constitution, of certain rights, shall not be construed to deny or disparage others retained by the people.

AMENDMENT X

The powers not delegated to the United States by the Constitution; nor prohibited by it to the States, are reserved to the States respectively, or to the people.

AMENDMENT XI[10]

The Judicial power of the United States shall not be construed to extend to any suit in law or equity, commenced or prosecuted against one of the United States by Citizens of another State, or by Citizens or Subjects of any Foreign State.

AMENDMENT XII[11]

The Electors shall meet in their respective States and vote by ballot for President and Vice-President, one of whom, at least, shall not be an inhabitant of

---

[9]The first ten amendments were passed by Congress September 25, 1789. They were ratified by three-fourths of the states December 15, 1791.

[10]Passed March 4, 1794. Ratified January 23, 1795.

[11]Passed December 9, 1803. Ratified June 15, 1804.

the same State with themselves; they shall name in their ballots the person voted for as President, and in distinct ballots the person voted for as Vice-President, and they shall make distinct lists of all persons voted for as President, and of all persons voted for as Vice-President, and of the number of votes for each, which lists they shall sign and certify, and transmit sealed to the seat of the government of the United States, directed to the President of the Senate;—The President of the Senate shall, in the presence of the Senate and House of Representatives, open all the certificates and the votes shall then be counted;—The person having the greatest number of votes for President, shall be the President, if such number be a majority of the whole number of Electors appointed; and if no person have such majority, then from the persons having the highest numbers not exceeding three on the list of those voted for as President, the House of Representatives shall choose immediately, by ballot, the President. But in choosing the President, the votes shall be taken by states, the representation from each state having one vote; a quorum for this purpose shall consist of a member or members from two-thirds of the states, and a majority of all the states shall be necessary to a choice. And if the House of Representatives shall not choose a President whenever the right of choice shall devolve upon them, before the fourth day of March next following, then the Vice-President shall act as President, as in the case of the death or other constitutional disability of the President.—The person having the greatest number of votes as Vice-President, shall be the Vice-President, if such number be a majority of the whole number of Electors appointed, and if no person have a majority, then from the two highest numbers on the list, the Senate shall choose the Vice-President; a quorum for the purpose shall consist of two-thirds of the whole number of Senators, and a majority of the whole number shall be necessary to a choice. But no person constitutionally ineligible to the office of President shall be eligible to that of Vice-President of the United States.

AMENDMENT XIII[12]

SECTION 1. Neither slavery nor involuntary servitude, except as a punishment for crime whereof

the party shall have been duly convicted, shall exist within the United States, or any place subject to their jurisdiction.

SECTION 2. Congress shall have power to enforce this article by appropriate legislation.

AMENDMENT XIV[13]

SECTION 1. All persons born or naturalized in the United States, and subject to the jurisdiction thereof, are citizens of the United States and of the State wherein they reside. No State shall make or enforce any law which shall abridge the privileges or immunities of citizens of the United States; nor shall any State deprive any person of life, liberty, or property, without due process of law; nor deny to any person within its jurisdiction the equal protection of the laws.

SECTION 2. Representatives shall be apportioned among the several States according to their respective numbers, counting the whole number of persons in each State, excluding Indians not taxed. But when the right to vote at any election for the choice of electors for President and Vice-President of the United States, Representatives in Congress, the Executive and Judicial officers of a State, or the members of the Legislature thereof, is denied to any of the male inhabitants of such State, being twenty-one years of age, and citizens of the United States, or in any way abridged, except for participation in rebellion, or other crime, the basis of representation therein shall be reduced in the proportion which the number of such male citizens shall bear to the whole number of male citizens twenty-one years of age in such State.

SECTION 3. No person shall be a Senator or Representative in Congress, or elector of President and Vice-President, or hold any office, civil or military, under the United States, or under any State, who, having previously taken an oath, as a member of Congress, or as an officer of the United States, or as a member of any State legislature, or as an executive or judicial officer of any State, to support the Constitution of the United States, shall have engaged in insurrection or rebellion against the same, or given aid or comfort to the enemies thereof. But Congress may by a vote of two-thirds of each House, remove such disability.

---

[12]Passed January 31, 1865. Ratified December 6, 1865.

[13]Passed June 13, 1866. Ratified July 9, 1868.

SECTION 4. The validity of the public debt of the United States, authorized by law, including debts incurred for payment of pensions and bounties for services in suppressing insurrection or rebellion, shall not be questioned. But neither the United States nor any State shall assume or pay any debt or obligation incurred in aid of insurrection or rebellion against the United States, or any claim for the loss or emancipation of any slave; but all such debts, obligations, and claims shall be held illegal and void.

SECTION 5. The Congress shall have the power to enforce, by appropriate legislation, the provisions of this article.

AMENDMENT XV[14]

SECTION 1. The right of citizens of the United States to vote shall not be denied or abridged by the United States or by any State on account of race, color, or previous conditions of servitude—

SECTION 2. The Congress shall have power to enforce this article by appropriate legislation.

AMENDMENT XVI

The Congress shall have power to lay and collect taxes on incomes, from whatever source derived, without apportionment among the several States, and without regard to any census or enumeration.

AMENDMENT XVII[15]

The Senate of the United States shall be composed of two Senators from each State, elected by the people thereof, for six years; and each Senator shall have one vote. The electors in each State shall have the qualifications requisite for electors of the most numerous branch of the State legislatures.

When vacancies happen in the representation of any State in the Senate, the executive authority of such State shall issue writs of election to fill such vacancies: *Provided*, That the legislature of any State may empower the executive thereof to make temporary appointments until the people fill the vacancies by election as the legislature may direct.

This amendment shall not be so construed as to affect the election or term of any Senator chosen before it becomes valid as part of the Constitution.

AMENDMENT XVIII[16]

SECTION 1. After one year from the ratification of this article the manufacture, sale, or transportation of intoxicating liquors within, the importation thereof into, or the exportation thereof from the United States and all territory subject to the jurisdiction thereof for beverage purposes is hereby prohibited.

SECTION 2. The Congress and the several States shall have concurrent power to enforce this article by appropriate legislation.

SECTION 3. This article shall be inoperative unless it shall have been ratified as an amendment to the Constitution by the legislatures of the several States, as provided in the Constitution, within seven years from the date of the submission hereof to the States by the Congress.

AMENDMENT XIX[17]

The right of citizens of the United States to vote shall not be denied or abridged by the United States or by any State on account of sex.

Congress shall have power to enforce this article by appropriate legislation.

AMENDMENT XX[18]

SECTION 1. The terms of the President and Vice-President shall end at noon on the 20th day of January, and the terms of Senators and Representatives at noon on the 3d day of January, of the years in which such terms would have ended if this article had not been ratified; and the terms of their successors shall then begin.

SECTION 2. The Congress shall assemble at least once in every year, and such meeting shall begin at noon on the 3d day of January, unless they shall by law appoint a different day.

SECTION 3. If, at the time fixed for the beginning of the term of the President, the President elect

---

[14]Passed February 26, 1869. Ratified February 2, 1870.

[15]Passed May 13, 1912. Ratified April 8, 1913.

[16]Passed December 18, 1917. Ratified January 16, 1919.

[17]Passed June 4, 1919. Ratified August 18, 1920.

[18]Passed March 2, 1932. Ratified January 23, 1933.

shall have died, the Vice-President elect shall become President. If a President shall not have been chosen before the time fixed for the beginning of his term, or if the President elect shall have failed to qualify, then the Vice-President elect shall act as President until a President shall have qualified; and the Congress may by law provide for the case wherein neither a President elect nor a Vice-President elect shall have qualified, declaring who shall then act as President, or the manner in which one who is to act shall be selected, and such person shall act accordingly until a President or Vice-President shall have qualified.

SECTION 4. The Congress may by law provide for the case of the death of any of the persons from whom the House of Representatives may choose a President whenever the right of choice shall have devolved upon them, and for the case of the death of any of the persons from whom the Senate may choose a Vice-President whenever the right of choice shall have devolved upon them.

SECTION 5. Sections 1 and 2 shall take effect on the 15th day of October following the ratification of this article.

SECTION 6. This article shall be inoperative unless it shall have been ratified as an amendment to the Constitution by the legislatures of three-fourths of the several States within seven years from the date of its submission.

AMENDMENT XXI[19]

SECTION 1. The eighteenth article of amendment to the Constitution of the United States is hereby repealed.

SECTION 2. The transportation or importation into any State, Territory, or possession of the United States for delivery or use therein of intoxicating liquors, in violation of the laws thereof, is hereby prohibited.

SECTION 3. This article shall be inoperative unless it shall have been ratified as an amendment to the Constitution by conventions in the several States, as provided in the Constitution, within seven years from the date of the submission hereof to the States by the Congress.

AMENDMENT XXII[20]

No person shall be elected to the office of the President more than twice, and no person who has held the office of President, or acted as President, for more than two years of a term to which some other person was elected President shall be elected to the office of the President more than once.

But this Article shall not apply to any person holding the office of President when this Article was proposed by the Congress, and shall not prevent any person who may be holding the office of President, or acting as President, during the term within which this Article becomes operative from holding the office of President or acting as President during the remainder of such term.

AMENDMENT XXIII[21]

SECTION 1. The District constituting the seat of Government of the United States shall appoint in such manner as the Congress may direct:

A number of electors of President and Vice President equal to the whole number of Senators and Representatives in Congress to which the District would be entitled if it were a State, but in no event more than the least populous State; they shall be in addition to those appointed by the States, but they shall be considered, for the purposes of the election of President and Vice President, to be electors appointed by the State; and they shall meet in the District and perform such duties as provided by the twelfth article of amendment.

SECTION 2. The Congress shall have power to enforce this article by appropriate legislation.

AMENDMENT XXIV[22]

SECTION 1. The right of citizens of the United States to vote in any primary or other election for President or Vice President, or for Senator or Representative in Congress, shall not be denied or abridged by the United States or any State by reason of failure to pay any poll tax or other tax.

SECTION 2. The Congress shall have power to enforce this article by appropriate legislation.

---

[19]Passed February 20, 1933. Ratified December 5, 1933.

[20]Passed March 12, 1947. Ratified March 1, 1951.

[21]Passed June 16, 1960. Ratified April 3, 1961.

[22]Passed August 27, 1962. Ratified January 23, 1964.

AMENDMENT XXV[23]

SECTION 1. In case of the removal of the President from office or of his death or resignation, the Vice President shall become President.

SECTION 2. Whenever there is a vacancy in the office of the Vice President, the President shall nominate a Vice President who shall take office upon confirmation by a majority vote of both Houses of Congress.

SECTION 3. Whenever the President transmits to the President pro tempore of the Senate and the Speaker of the House of Representatives his written declaration that he is unable to discharge the powers and duties of his office, and until he transmits them a written declaration to the contrary, such powers and duties shall be discharged by the Vice President as Acting President.

SECTION 4. Whenever the Vice President and a majority of either the principal officers of the executive department or of such other body as Congress may by law provide, transmit to the President pro tempore of the Senate and the Speaker of the House of Representatives their written declaration that the President is unable to discharge the powers and duties of his office, the Vice President shall immediately assume the powers and duties of the office of Acting President

Thereafter, when the President transmits to the President pro tempore of the Senate and the Speaker of the House of Representatives his written declaration that no inability exists, he shall resume the powers and duties of his office unless the Vice President and a majority of either the principal officers of the executive department or of such other body as Congress may by law provide, transmit within four days to the President pro tempore of the Senate and the Speaker of the House of Representatives their written declaration that the President is unable to discharge the powers and duties of his office. Thereupon Congress shall decide the issue, assembling within forty-eight hours for that purpose if not in session. If the Congress, within twenty-one days after receipt of the latter written declaration, or, if Congress is not in session, within twenty-one days after Congress is required to assemble, determines by two-thirds vote of both Houses that the President is unable to discharge the powers and duties of his office, the Vice President shall continue to discharge the same as Acting President; otherwise, the President shall resume the powers and duties of his office.

AMENDMENT XXVI[24]

SECTION 1. The right of citizens of the United States, who are eighteen years of age or older, to vote shall not be denied or abridged by the United States or by any State on account of age.

SECTION 2. The Congress shall have power to enforce this article by appropriate legislation.

AMENDMENT XXVII[25]

No law, varying the compensation for the service of the Senators and Representatives, shall take effect, until an election of Representatives shall have intervened.

---

[23]Passed July 6, 1965. Ratified February 11, 1967.

[24]Passed March 23, 1971. Ratified July 5, 1971.

[25]Passed September 25, 1789. Ratified May 7, 1992.

ADMISSION OF STATES

Order of admission	State	Date of admission	Order of admission	State	Date of admission
1	Delaware	December 7, 1787	26	Michigan	January 26, 1837
2	Pennsylvania	December 12, 1787	27	Florida	March 3, 1845
3	New Jersey	December 18, 1787	28	Texas	December 29, 1845
4	Georgia	January 2, 1788	29	Iowa	December 28, 1846
5	Connecticut	January 9, 1788	30	Wisconsin	May 29, 1848
6	Massachusetts	February 6, 1788	31	California	September 9, 1850
7	Maryland	April 28, 1788	32	Minnesota	May 11, 1858
8	South Carolina	May 23, 1788	33	Oregon	February 14, 1859
9	New Hampshire	June 21, 1788	34	Kansas	January 29, 1861
10	Virginia	June 25, 1788	35	West Virginia	June 20, 1863
11	New York	July 26, 1788	36	Nevada	October 31, 1864
12	North Carolina	November 21, 1789	37	Nebraska	March 1, 1867
13	Rhode Island	May 29, 1790	38	Colorado	August 1, 1876
14	Vermont	March 4, 1791	39	North Dakota	November 2, 1889
15	Kentucky	June 1, 1792	40	South Dakota	November 2, 1889
16	Tennessee	June 1, 1796	41	Montana	November 8, 1889
17	Ohio	March 1, 1803	42	Washington	November 11, 1889
18	Louisiana	April 30, 1812	43	Idaho	July 3, 1890
19	Indiana	December 11, 1816	44	Wyoming	July 10, 1890
20	Mississippi	December 10, 1817	45	Utah	January 4, 1896
21	Illinois	December 3, 1818	46	Oklahoma	November 16, 1907
22	Alabama	December 14, 1819	47	New Mexico	January 6, 1912
23	Maine	March 15, 1820	48	Arizona	February 14, 1912
24	Missouri	August 10, 1821	49	Alaska	January 3, 1959
25	Arkansas	June 15, 1836	50	Hawaii	August 21, 1959

POPULATION OF THE UNITED STATES

Year	Total population	Number per square mile	Year	Total population	Number per square mile	Year	Total population	Number per square mile
1790	3,929	4.5	1808	6,838		1826	11,580	
1791	4,056		1809	7,031		1827	11,909	
1792	4,194		1810	7,224	4.3	1828	12,237	
1793	4,332		1811	7,460		1829	12,565	
1794	4,469		1812	7,700		1830	12,901	7.4
1795	4,607		1813	7,939		1831	13,321	
1796	4,745		1814	8,179		1832	13,742	
1797	4,883		1815	8,419		1833	14,162	
1798	5,021		1816	8,659		1834	14,582	
1799	5,159		1817	8,899		1835	15,003	
1800	5,297	6.1	1818	9,139		1836	15,423	
1801	5,486		1819	9,379		1837	15,843	
1802	5,679		1820	9,618	5.6	1838	16,264	
1803	5,872		1821	9,939		1839	16,684	
1804	5,065		1822	10,268		1840	17,120	9.8
1805	6,258		1823	10,596		1841	17,733	
1806	6,451		1824	10,924		1842	18,345	
1807	6,644		1825	11,252		1843	18,957	

Figures are from *Historical Statistics of the United States, Colonial Times to 1957* (1961), pp. 7, 8; *Statistical Abstract of the United States: 1974*, p. 5, Census Bureau for 1974 and 1975; and *Statistical Abstract of the United States: 1988*, p. 7.

Note: Population figures are in thousands. Density figures are for land area of continental United States.

(continued)

Year	Total population	Number per square mile	Year	Total population[1]	Number per square mile	Year	Total population[1]	Number per square mile
1844	19,569		1897	72,189		1950	150,697	50.7
1845	20,182		1898	73,494		1951	154,878	
1846	20,794		1899	74,799		1952	157,553	
1847	21,406		1900	76,094	25.6	1953	160,184	
1848	22,018		1901	77,585		1954	163,026	
1849	22,631		1902	79,160		1955	165,931	
1850	23,261	7.9	1903	80,632		1956	168,903	
1851	24,086		1904	82,165		1957	171,984	
1852	24,911		1905	83,820		1958	174,882	
1853	25,736		1906	85,437		1959	177,830	
1854	26,561		1907	87,000		1960	178,464	60.1
1855	27,386		1908	88,709		1961	183,672	
1856	28,212		1909	90,492		1962	186,504	
1857	29,037		1910	92,407	31.0	1963	189,197	
1858	29,862		1911	93,868		1964	191,833	
1859	30,687		1912	95,331		1965	194,237	
1860	31,513	10.6	1913	97,227		1966	196,485	
1861	32,351		1914	99,118		1967	198,629	
1862	33,188		1915	100,549		1968	200,619	
1863	34,026		1916	101,966		1969	202,599	
1864	34,863		1917	103,414		1970	203,875	57.5[2]
1865	35,701		1918	104,550		1971	207,045	
1866	36,538		1919	105,063		1972	208,842	
1867	37,376		1920	106,466	35.6	1973	210,396	
1868	38,213		1921	108,541		1974	211,894	
1869	39,051		1922	110,055		1975	213,631	
1870	39,905	13.4	1923	111,950		1976	215,152	
1871	40,938		1924	114,113		1977	216,880	
1872	41,972		1925	115,832		1978	218,717	
1873	43,006		1926	117,399		1979	220,584	
1874	44,040		1927	119,038		1980	226,546	64.0
1875	45,073		1928	120,501		1981	230,138	
1876	46,107		1929	121,700		1982	232,520	
1877	47,141		1930	122,775	41.2	1983	234,799	
1878	48,174		1931	124,040		1984	237,001	
1879	49,208		1932	124,840		1985	239,283	
1880	50,262	16.9	1933	125,579		1986	241,596	
1881	51,542		1934	126,374		1987	234,773	
1882	52,821		1935	127,250		1988	245,051	
1883	54,100		1936	128,053		1989	247,350	
1884	55,379		1937	128,825		1990	250,122	70.3
1885	56,658		1938	129,825		1991	254,521	
1886	57,938		1939	130,880		1992	245,908	
1887	59,217		1940	131,669	44.2	1993	257,908	
1888	60,496		1941	133,894		1994	261,875	
1889	61,775		1942	135,361		1995	263,434	
1890	63,056	21.2	1943	137,250		1996	266,096	
1891	64,361		1944	138,916		1997	267,901	
1892	65,666		1945	140,468		1998	269,501	
1893	66,970		1946	141,936		1999	272,700	
1894	68,275		1947	144,698		2000	281,400	
1895	69,580		1948	147,208				
1896	70,885		1949	149,767				

[1]Figures after 1940 represent total population including armed forces abroad, except in official census years.

[2]Figure includes Alaska and Hawaii.

PRESIDENTIAL ELECTIONS

Year	Number of states	Candidates[1]	Parties	Popular vote	Electoral vote	Percentage of popular vote[2]
1789	11	**George Washington**	No party designations		69	
		John Adams			34	
		Minor Candidates			35	
1792	15	**George Washington**	No party designations		132	
		John Adams			77	
		George Clinton			50	
		Minor Candidates			5	
1796	16	**John Adams**	Federalist		71	
		Thomas Jefferson	Democratic-Republican		68	
		Thomas Pinckney	Federalist		59	
		Aaron Burr	Democratic-Republican		30	
		Minor Candidates			48	
1800	16	**Thomas Jefferson**	Democratic-Republican		73	
		Aaron Burr	Democratic-Republican		73	
		John Adams	Federalist		65	
		Charles C. Pinckney	Federalist		64	
		John Jay	Federalist		1	
1804	17	**Thomas Jefferson**	Democratic-Republican		162	
		Charles C. Pinckney	Federalist		14	
1808	17	**James Madison**	Democratic-Republican		122	
		Charles C. Pinckney	Federalist		47	
		George Clinton	Democratic-Republican		6	
1812	18	**James Madison**	Democratic-Republican		128	
		DeWitt Clinton	Federalist		89	
1816	19	**James Monroe**	Democratic-Republican		183	
		Rufus King	Federalist		34	
1820	24	**James Monroe**	Democratic-Republican		231	
		John Quincy Adams	Independent Republican		1	
1824	24	**John Quincy Adams**	Democratic-Republican	108,740	84	30.5
		Andrew Jackson	Democratic-Republican	153,544	99	43.1
		William H. Crawford	Democratic-Republican	46,618	41	13.1
		Henry Clay	Democratic-Republican	47,136	37	13.2
1828	24	**Andrew Jackson**	Democratic	647,286	178	56.0
		John Quincy Adams	National Republican	508,064	83	44.0
1832	24	**Andrew Jackson**	Democratic	687,502	219	55.0
		Henry Clay	National Republican	530,189	49	42.4
		William Wirt	Anti-Masonic ⎫	33,108	7	
		John Floyd	National Republican ⎭		11	2.6

[1] Before the passage of the Twelfth Amendment in 1804, the Electoral College voted for two presidential candidates; the runner-up became vice president. Figures are from *Historical Statistics of the United States, Colonial Times to 1957* (1961), pp. 682–83; and the U.S. Department of Justice.

[2] Candidates receiving less than 1 percent of the popular vote have been omitted. For that reason the percentage of popular vote given for any election year may not total 100 percent.

(continued)

Year	Number of states	Candidates	Parties	Popular vote	Electoral vote	Percentage of popular vote[1]
1836	26	**Martin Van Buren**	Democratic	765,483	170	50.9
		William H. Harrison	Whig		73	
		Hugh L. White	Whig	739,795	26	
		Daniel Webster	Whig		14	
		W. P. Mangum	Whig		11	
1840	26	**William H. Harrison**	Whig	1,274,624	234	53.1
		Martin Van Buren	Democratic	1,127,781	60	46.9
1844	26	**James K. Polk**	Democratic	1,338,464	170	49.6
		Henry Clay	Whig	1,300,097	105	48.1
		James G. Birney	Liberty	62,300		2.3
1848	30	**Zachary Taylor**	Whig	1,360,967	163	47.4
		Lewis Cass	Democratic	1,222,342	127	42.5
		Martin Van Buren	Free Soil	291,263		10.1
1852	31	**Franklin Pierce**	Democratic	1,601,117	254	50.9
		Winfield Scott	Whig	1,385,453	42	44.1
		John P. Hale	Free Soil	155,825		5.0
1856	31	**James Buchanan**	Democratic	1,832,955	174	45.3
		John C. Frémont	Republican	1,339,932	114	33.1
		Millard Fillmore	American	871,731	8	21.6
1860	33	**Abraham Lincoln**	Republican	1,865,593	180	39.8
		Stephen A. Douglas	Democratic	1,382,713	12	29.5
		John C. Breckinridge	Democratic	848,356	72	18.1
		John Bell	Constitutional Union	592,906	39	12.6
1864	36	**Abraham Lincoln**	Republican	2,206,938	212	55.0
		George B. McClellan	Democratic	1,803,787	21	45.0
1868	37	**Ulysses S. Grant**	Republican	3,013,421	214	52.7
		Horatio Seymour	Democratic	2,706,829	80	47.3
1872	37	**Ulysses S. Grant**	Republican	3,596,745	286	55.6
		Horace Greeley	Democratic	2,843,446	[2]	43.9
1876	38	**Rutherford B. Hayes**	Republican	4,036,572	185	48.0
		Samuel J. Tilden	Democratic	4,284,020	184	51.0
1880	38	**James A. Garfield**	Republican	4,453,295	214	48.5
		Winfield S. Hancock	Democratic	4,414,082	155	48.1
		James B. Weaver	Greenback-Labor	308,578		3.4
1884	38	**Grover Cleveland**	Democratic	4,879,507	219	48.5
		James G. Blaine	Republican	4,850,293	182	48.2
		Benjamin F. Butler	Greenback-Labor	175,370		1.8
		John P. St. John	Prohibition	150,369		1.5
1888	38	**Benjamin Harrison**	Republican	5,477,129	233	47.9
		Grover Cleveland	Democratic	5,537,857	168	48.6
		Clinton B. Fisk	Prohibition	249,506		2.2
		Anson J. Streeter	Union Labor	146,935		1.3

[1]Candidates receiving less than 1 percent of the popular vote have been omitted. For that reason the percentage of popular vote given for any election year may not total 100 percent.

[2]Greeley died shortly after the election; the electors supporting him then divided their votes among minor candidates.

Year	Number of states	Candidates	Parties	Popular vote	Electoral vote	Percentage of popular vote[1]
1892	44	**Grover Cleveland**	Democratic	5,555,426	277	46.1
		Benjamin Harrison	Republican	5,182,690	145	43.0
		James B. Weaver	People's	1,029,846	22	8.5
		John Bidwell	Prohibition	264,133		2.2
1896	45	**William McKinley**	Republican	7,102,246	271	51.1
		William J. Bryan	Democratic	6,492,559	176	47.7
1900	45	**William McKinley**	Republican	7,218,491	292	51.7
		William J. Bryan	Democratic; Populist	6,356,734	155	45.5
		John C. Wooley	Prohibition	208,914		1.5
1904	45	**Theodore Roosevelt**	Republican	7,628,461	336	57.4
		Alton B. Parker	Democratic	5,084,223	140	37.6
		Eugene V. Debs	Socialist	402,283		3.0
		Silas C. Swallow	Prohibition	258,536		1.9
1908	46	**William H. Taft**	Republican	7,675,320	321	51.6
		William J. Bryan	Democratic	6,412,294	162	43.1
		Eugene V. Debs	Socialist	420,793		2.8
		Eugene W. Chafin	Prohibition	253,840		1.7
1912	48	**Woodrow Wilson**	Democratic	6,296,547	435	41.9
		Theodore Roosevelt	Progressive	4,118,571	88	27.4
		William H. Taft	Republican	3,486,720	8	23.2
		Eugene V. Debs	Socialist	900,672		6.0
		Eugene W. Chafin	Prohibition	206,275		1.4
1916	48	**Woodrow Wilson**	Democratic	9,127,695	277	49.4
		Charles E. Hughes	Republican	8,533,507	254	46.2
		A. L. Benson	Socialist	585,113		3.2
		J. Frank Hanly	Prohibition	220,506		1.2
1920	48	**Warren G. Harding**	Republican	16,143,407	404	60.4
		James N. Cox	Democratic	9,130,328	127	34.2
		Eugene V. Debs	Socialist	919,799		3.4
		P. P. Christensen	Farmer-Labor	265,411		1.0
1924	48	**Calvin Coolidge**	Republican	15,718,211	382	54.0
		John W. Davis	Democratic	8,385,283	136	28.8
		Robert M. La Follette	Progressive	4,831,289	13	16.6
1928	48	**Herbert C. Hoover**	Republican	21,391,993	444	58.2
		Alfred E. Smith	Democratic	15,016,169	87	40.9
1932	48	**Franklin D. Roosevelt**	Democratic	22,809,638	472	57.4
		Herbert C. Hoover	Republican	15,758,901	59	39.7
		Norman Thomas	Socialist	881,951		2.2

[1]Candidates receiving less than 1 percent of the popular vote have been omitted. For that reason the percentage of popular vote given for any election year may not total 100 percent.

(continued)

Year	Number of states	Candidates	Parties	Popular vote	Electoral vote	Percentage of popular vote[1]
1936	48	**Franklin D. Roosevelt**	Democratic	27,752,869	523	60.8
		Alfred M. Landon	Republican	16,674,665	8	36.5
		William Lemke	Union	882,479		1.9
1940	48	**Franklin D. Roosevelt**	Democratic	27,307,819	449	54.8
		Wendell L. Willkie	Republican	22,321,018	82	44.8
1944	48	**Franklin D. Roosevelt**	Democratic	25,606,585	432	53.5
		Thomas E. Dewey	Republican	22,014,745	99	46.0
1948	48	**Harry S Truman**	Democratic	24,105,812	303	49.5
		Thomas E. Dewey	Republican	21,970,065	189	45.1
		J. Strom Thurmond	States' Rights	1,169,063	39	2.4
		Henry A. Wallace	Progressive	1,157,172		2.4
1952	48	**Dwight D. Eisenhower**	Republican	33,936,234	442	55.1
		Adlai E. Stevenson	Democratic	27,314,992	89	44.4
1956	48	**Dwight D. Eisenhower**	Republican	35,590,472	457	57.6
		Adlai E. Stevenson	Democratic	26,022,752	73	42.1
1960	50	**John F. Kennedy**	Democratic	34,227,096	303	49.9
		Richard M. Nixon	Republican	34,108,546	219	49.6
1964	50	**Lyndon B. Johnson**	Democratic	43,126,506	486	61.1
		Barry M. Goldwater	Republican	27,176,799	52	38.5
1968	50	**Richard M. Nixon**	Republican	31,785,480	301	43.4
		Hubert H. Humphrey	Democratic	31,275,165	191	42.7
		George C. Wallace	American Independent	9,906,473	46	13.5
1972	50	**Richard M. Nixon**	Republican	47,169,911	520	60.7
		George S. McGovern	Democratic	29,170,383	17	37.5
1976	50	**Jimmy Carter**	Democratic	40,827,394	297	50.0
		Gerald R. Ford	Republican	39,145,977	240	47.9
1980	50	**Ronald W. Reagan**	Republican	43,899,248	489	50.8
		Jimmy Carter	Democratic	35,481,435	49	41.0
		John B. Anderson	Independent	5,719,437		6.6
		Ed Clark	Libertarian	920,859		1.0
1984	50	**Ronald W. Reagan**	Republican	54,281,858	525	59.2
		Walter F. Mondale	Democratic	37,457,215	13	40.8
1988	50	**George H. Bush**	Republican	47,917,341	426	54
		Michael Dukakis	Democratic	41,013,030	112	46
1992	50	**William Clinton**	Democratic	44,908,254	370	43.0
		George H. Bush	Republican	39,102,343	168	37.4
		Ross Perot	Independent	19,741,065		18.9
1996	50	**William Clinton**	Democratic	45,628,667	379	49.2
		Robert Dole	Republican	37,869,435	159	40.8
		Ross Perot	Reform	7,874,283		8.5
2000	50	**George W. Bush**	Republican	50,456,141	271	47.87
		Albert Gore	Democratic	50,996,039	266	48.38
		Ralph Nader	Green	2,882,807		2.73

[1]Candidates receiving less than 1 percent of the popular vote have been omitted. For that reason the percentage of popular vote given for any election year may not total 100 percent.

PRESIDENTIAL ADMINISTRATIONS

President	Vice President	Secretary of State	Secretary of Treasury	Secretary of War	Secretary of Navy	Postmaster General	Attorney General
George Washington 1789–1797	John Adams 1789–1797	Thomas Jefferson 1789–1794 Edmund Randolph 1794–1795 Timothy Pickering 1795–1797	Alexander Hamilton 1789–1795 Oliver Wolcott 1795–1797	Henry Knox 1789–1795 Timothy Pickering 1795–1796 James McHenry 1796–1797		Samuel Osgood 1789–1791 Timothy Pickering 1791–1795 Joseph Habersham 1795–1797	Edmund Randolph 1789–1794 William Bradford 1794–1795 Charles Lee 1795–1797
John Adams 1797–1801	Thomas Jefferson 1797–1801	Timothy Pickering 1797–1800 John Marshall 1800–1801	Oliver Wolcott 1797–1801 Samuel Dexter 1801	James McHenry 1797–1800 Samuel Dexter 1800–1801	Benjamin Stoddert 1798–1801	Joseph Habersham 1797–1801	Charles Lee 1797–1801
Thomas Jefferson 1801–1809	Aaron Burr 1801–1805 George Clinton 1805–1809	James Madison 1801–1809	Samuel Dexter 1801 Albert Gallatin 1801–1809	Henry Dearborn 1801–1809	Benjamin Stoddert 1801 Robert Smith 1801–1809	Joseph Habersham 1801 Gideon Granger 1801–1809	Levi Lincoln 1801–1805 John Breckinridge 1805–1807 Caesar Rodney 1807–1809
James Madison 1809–1817	George Clinton 1809–1813 Elbridge Gerry 1813–1817	Robert Smith 1809–1811 James Monroe 1811–1817	Albert Gallatin 1809–1814 George Campbell 1814 Alexander Dallas 1814–1816 William Crawford 1816–1817	William Eustis 1809–1813 John Armstrong 1813–1814 James Monroe 1814–1815 William Crawford 1815–1817	Paul Hamilton 1809–1813 William Jones 1813–1814 Benjamin Crowninshield 1814–1817	Gideon Granger 1809–1814 Return Meigs 1814–1817	Caesar Rodney 1809–1811 William Pinkney 1811–1814 Richard Rush 1814–1817
James Monroe 1817–1825	Daniel D. Tompkins 1817–1825	John Quincy Adams 1817–1825	William Crawford 1817–1825	George Graham 1817 John C. Calhoun 1817–1825	Benjamin Crowninshield 1817–1818 Smith Thompson 1818–1823 Samuel Southard 1823–1825	Return Meigs 1817–1823 John McLean 1823–1825	Richard Rush 1817 William Wirt 1817–1825
John Quincy Adams 1825–1829	John C. Calhoun 1825–1829	Henry Clay 1825–1829	Richard Rush 1825–1829	James Barbour 1825–1828 Peter B. Porter 1828–1829	Samuel Southard 1825–1829	John McLean 1825–1829	William Wirt 1825–1829
Andrew Jackson 1829–1837	John C. Calhoun 1829–1833 Martin Van Buren 1833–1837	Martin Van Buren 1829–1831 Edward Livingston 1831–1833 Louis McLane 1833–1834 John Forsyth 1834–1837	Samuel Ingham 1829–1831 Louis McLane 1831–1833 William Duane 1833 Roger B. Taney 1833–1834 Levi Woodbury 1834–1837	John H. Eaton 1829–1831 Lewis Cass 1831–1837 Benjamin Butler 1837	John Branch 1829–1831 Levi Woodbury 1831–1834 Mahlon Dickerson 1834–1837	William Barry 1829–1835 Amos Kendall 1835–1837	John M. Berrien 1829–1831 Roger B. Taney 1831–1833 Benjamin Butler 1833–1837
Martin Van Buren 1837–1841	Richard M. Johnson 1837–1841	John Forsyth 1837–1841	Levi Woodbury 1837–1841	Joel R. Poinsett 1837–1841	Mahlon Dickerson 1837–1838 James K. Paulding 1838–1841	Amos Kendall 1837–1840 John M. Niles 1840–1841	Benjamin Butler 1837–1838 Felix Grundy 1838–1840 Henry D. Gilpin 1840–1841

(continued)

President	Vice President	Secretary of State	Secretary of Treasury	Secretary of War
William H. Harrison 1841	John Tyler 1841	Daniel Webster 1841	Thomas Ewing 1841	John Bell 1841
John Tyler 1841–1845		Daniel Webster 1841–1843 Hugh S. Legaré 1843 Abel P. Upshur 1843–1844 John C. Calhoun 1844–1845	Thomas Ewing 1841 Walter Forward 1841–1843 John C. Spencer 1843–1844 George M. Bibb 1844–1845	John Bell 1841 John C. Spencer 1841–1843 James M. Porter 1843–1844 William Wilkins 1844–1845
James K. Polk 1845–1849	George M. Dallas 1845–1849	James Buchanan 1845–1849	Robert J. Walker 1845–1849	William L. Marcy 1845–1849
Zachary Taylor 1849–1850	Millard Fillmore 1849–1850	John M. Clayton 1849–1850	William M.Meredith 1849–1850	George W. Crawford 1849–1850
Millard Fillmore 1850–1853		Daniel Webster 1850–1852 Edward Everett 1852–1853	Thomas Corwin 1850–1853	Charles M. Conrad 1850–1853
Franklin Pierce 1853–1857	William R. King 1853–1857	William L. Marcy 1853–1857	James Guthrie 1853–1857	Jefferson Davis 1853–1857
James Buchanan 1857–1861	John C. Breckinridge 1857–1861	Lewis Cass 1857–1860 Jeremiah S. Black 1860–1861	Howell Cobb 1857–1860 Philip F. Thomas 1860–1861 John A. Dix 1861	John B. Floyd 1857–1861 Joseph Holt 1861
Abraham Lincoln 1861–1865	Hannibal Hamlin 1861–1865 Andrew Johnson 1865	William H. Seward 1861–1865	Salmon P. Chase 1861–1864 William P. Fessenden 1864–1865 Hugh McCulloch 1865	Simon Cameron 1861–1862 Edwin M. Stanton 1862–1865
Andrew Johnson 1865–1869		William H. Seward 1865–1869	Hugh McCulloch 1865–1869	Edwin M. Stanton 1865–1867 Ulysses S. Grant 1867–1868 John M. Schofield 1868–1869
Ulysses S. Grant 1869–1877	Schuyler Colfax 1869–1873 Henry Wilson 1873–1877	Elihu B. Washburne 1869 Hamilton Fish 1869–1877	George S. Boutwell 1869–1873 William A. Richardson 1873–1874 Benjamin H. Bristow 1874–1876 Lot M. Morrill 1876–1877	John A. Rawlins 1869 William T. Sherman 1869 William W. Belknap 1869–1876 Alphonso Taft 1876 James D. Cameron 1876–1877

Secretary of Navy	Postmaster General	Attorney General	Secretary of Interior
George E. Badger 1841	Francis Granger 1841	John J. Crittenden 1841	
George E. Badger 1841 Abel P. Upshur 1841–1843 David Henshaw 1843–1844 Thomas Gilmer 1844 John Y. Mason 1844–1845	Francis Granger 1841 Charles A. Wickliffe 1841–1845	John J. Crittenden 1841 Hugh S. Legaré 1841–1843 John Nelson 1843–1845	
George Bancroft 1845–1846 John Y. Mason 1846–1849	Cave Johnson 1845–1849	John Y. Mason 1845–1846 Nathan Clifford 1846–1848 Isaac Toucey 1848–1849	
William B. Preston 1849–1850	Jacob Collamer 1849–1850	Reverdy Johnson 1849–1850	Thomas Ewing 1849–1850
William A. Graham 1850–1852 John P. Kennedy 1852–1853	Nathan K. Hall 1850–1852 Sam D. Hubbard 1852–1853	John J. Crittenden 1850–1853	Thomas McKennan 1850 A. H. H. Stuart 1850–1853
James C. Dobbin 1853–1857	James Campbell 1853–1857	Caleb Cushing 1853–1857	Robert McClelland 1853–1857
Isaac Toucey 1857–1861	Aaron V. Brown 1857–1859 Joseph Holt 1859–1861 Horatio King 1861	Jeremiah S. Black 1857–1860 Edwin M. Stanton 1860–1861	Jacob Thompson 1857–1861
Gideon Welles 1861–1865	Horatio King 1861 Montgomery Blair 1861–1864 William Dennison 1864–1865	Edward Bates 1861–1864 James Speed 1864–1865	Caleb B. Smith 1861–1863 John P. Usher 1863–1865
Gideon Welles 1865–1869	William Dennison 1865–1866 Alexander Randall 1866–1869 William M. Evarts 1868–1869	James Speed 1865–1866 Henry Stanbery 1866–1868 O. H. Browning 1866–1869	John P. Usher 1865 James Harlan 1865–1866
Adolph E. Borie 1869 George M. Robeson 1869–1877	John A. J. Creswell 1869–1874 James W. Marshall 1874 Marshall Jewell 1874–1876 James N. Tyner 1876–1877	Ebenezer R. Hoar 1869–1870 Amos T. Akerman 1870–1871 G. H. Williams 1871–1875 Edwards Pierrepont 1875–1876 Alphonso Taft 1876–1877	Jacob D. Cox 1869–1870 Columbus Delano 1870–1875 Zachariah Chandler 1875–1877

(continued)

President	Vice President	Secretary of State	Secretary of Treasury	Secretary of War	Secretary of Navy
Rutherford B. Hayes 1877–1881	William A. Wheeler 1877–1881	William M. Evarts 1877–1881	John Sherman 1877–1881	George W. McCrary 1877–1879 Alexander Ramsey 1879–1881	R. W. Thompson 1877–1881 Nathan Goff, Jr. 1881
James A. Garfield 1881	Chester A. Arthur 1881	James G. Blaine 1881	William Windom 1881	Robert T. Lincoln 1881	William H. Hunt 1881
Chester A. Arthur 1881–1885		F. T. Frelinghuysen 1881–1885	Charles J. Folger 1881–1884 Walter Q. Gresham 1884 Hugh McCulloch 1884–1885	Robert T. Lincoln 1881–1885	William E. Chandler 1881–1885
Grover Cleveland 1885–1889	T. A. Hendricks 1885	Thomas F. Bayard 1885–1889	Daniel Manning 1885–1887 Charles S. Fairchild 1887–1889	William C. Endicott 1885–1889	William C. Whitney 1885–1889
Benjamin Harrison 1889–1893	Levi P. Morton 1889–1893	James G. Blaine 1889–1892 John W. Foster 1892–1893	William Windom 1889–1891 Charles Foster 1892–1893	Redfield Procter 1889–1891 Stephen B. Elkins 1891–1893	Benjamin F. Tracy 1889–1893
Grover Cleveland 1893–1897	Adlai E. Stevenson 1893–1897	Walter Q. Gresham 1893–1895 Richard Olney 1895–1897	John G. Carlisle 1893–1897	Daniel S. Lamont 1893–1897	Hilary A. Herbert 1893–1897
William McKinley 1897–1901	Garret A. Hobart 1897–1899 Theodore Roosevelt 1901	John Sherman 1897–1898 William R. Day 1898 John Hay 1898–1901	Lyman J. Gage 1897–1901	Russell A. Alger 1897–1899 Elihu Root 1899–1901	John D. Long 1897–1901
Theodore Roosevelt 1901–1909	Charles Fairbanks 1905–1909	John Hay 1901–1905 Elihu Root 1905–1909 Robert Bacon 1909	Lyman J. Gage 1901–1902 Leslie M. Shaw 1902–1907 George B. Cortelyou 1907–1909	Elihu Root 1901–1904 William H. Taft 1904–1908 Luke E. Wright 1908–1909	John D. Long 1901–1902 William H. Moody 1902–1904 Paul Morton 1904–1905 Charles J. Bonaparte 1905–1906 Victor H. Metcalf 1906–1908 T. H. Newberry 1908–1909
William H. Taft 1909–1913	James S. Sherman 1909–1913	Philander C. Knox 1909–1913	Franklin MacVeagh 1909–1913	Jacob M. Dickinson 1909–1911 Henry L. Stimson 1911–1913	George von L. Meyer 1909–1913
Woodrow Wilson 1913–1921	Thomas R. Marshall 1913–1921	William J. Bryan 1913–1915 Robert Lansing 1915–1920 Bainbridge Colby 1920–1921	William G. McAdoo 1913–1918 Carter Glass 1918–1920 David F. Houston 1920–1921	Lindley M. Garrison 1913–1916 Newton D. Baker 1916–1921	Josephus Daniels 1913–1921

Postmaster General	Attorney General	Secretary of Interior	Secretary of Agriculture	Secretary of Commerce and Labor	
David M. Key 1877–1880 Horace Maynard 1880–1881	Charles Devens 1877–1881	Carl Schurz 1877–1881			
Thomas L. James 1881	Wayne MacVeagh 1881	S. J. Kirkwood 1881			
Thomas L. James 1881 Timothy O. Howe 1881–1883 Walter Q. Gresham 1883–1884 Frank Hatton 1884–1885	B. H. Brewster 1881–1885	Henry M. Teller 1881–1885			
William F. Vilas 1885–1888 Don M. Dickinson 1888–1889	A. H. Garland 1885–1889	L. Q. C. Lamar 1885–1888 William F. Vilas 1888–1889	Norman J. Colman 1889		
John Wanamaker 1889–1893	W. H. H. Miller 1889–1893	John W. Noble 1889–1893	Jeremiah M. Rusk 1889–1893		
Wilson S. Bissel 1893–1895 William L. Wilson 1895–1897	Richard Olney 1893–1895 Judson Harmon 1895–1897	Hoke Smith 1893–1896 David R. Francis 1896–1897	J. Sterling Morton 1893–1897		
James A. Gary 1897–1898 Charles E. Smith 1898–1901	Joseph McKenna 1897–1898 John W. Griggs 1898–1901 Philander C. Knox 1901	Cornelius N. Bliss 1897–1898 E. A. Hitchcock 1898–1901	James Wilson 1897–1901		
Charles E. Smith 1901–1902 Henry C. Payne 1902–1904 Robert J. Wynne 1904–1905 George B. Cortelyou 1905—1907 George von L. Meyer 1907–1909	Philander C. Knox 1901–1904 William H. Moody 1904–1906 Charles J. Bonaparte 1906–1909	E. A. Hitchcock 1901–1907 James R. Garfield 1907–1909	James Wilson 1901–1909	George B. Cortelyou 1903–1904 Victor H. Metcalf 1904–1906 Oscar S. Straus 1906–1909	
Frank H. Hitchcock 1909–1913	G. W. Wickersham 1909–1913	R. A. Ballinger 1909–1911 Walter L. Fisher 1911–1913	James Wilson 1909–1913	Charles Nagel 1909–1913	

				Secretary of Commerce	Secretary of Labor
Albert S. Burleson 1913–1921	J. C. McReynolds 1913–1914 T. W. Gregory 1914–1919 A. Mitchell Palmer 1919–1921	Franklin K. Lane 1913–1920 John B. Payne 1920–1921	David F. Houston 1913–1920 E. T. Meredith 1920–1921	W. C. Redfield 1913–1919 J. W. Alexander 1919–1921	William B. Wilson 1913–1921

(continued)

President	Vice President	Secretary of State	Secretary of Treasury	Secretary of War	Secretary of Navy	Postmaster General	Attorney General
Warren G. Harding 1921–1923	Calvin Coolidge 1921–1923	Charles E. Hughes 1921–1923	Andrew W. Mellon 1921–1923	John W. Weeks 1921–1923	Edwin Denby 1921–1923	Will H. Hays 1921–1922 Hubert Work 1922–1923 Harry S. New 1923	H. M. Daugherty 1921–1923
Calvin Coolidge 1923–1929	Charles G. Dawes 1925–1929	Charles E. Hughes 1923–1925 Frank B. Kellogg 1925–1929	Andrew W. Mellon 1923–1929	John W. Weeks 1923–1925 Dwight F. Davis 1925–1929	Edwin Denby 1923–1924 Curtis D. Wilbur 1924–1929	Harry S. New 1923–1929	H. M. Daugherty 1923–1924 Harlan F. Stone 1924–1925 John G. Sargent 1925–1929
Herbert C. Hoover 1929–1933	Charles Curtis 1929–1933	Henry L. Stimson 1929–1933	Andrew W. Mellon 1929–1932 Ogden L. Mills 1932–1933	James W. Good 1929 Patrick J. Hurley 1929–1933	Charles F. Adams 1929–1933	Walter F. Brown 1929–1933	J. D. Mitchell 1929–1933
Franklin Delano Roosevelt 1933–1945	John Nance Garner 1933–1941 Henry A. Wallace 1941–1945 Harry S Truman 1945	Cordell Hull 1933–1944 E. R. Stettinius, Jr. 1944–1945	William H. Woodin 1933–1934 Henry Morgenthau, Jr. 1934–1945	George H. Dern 1933–1936 Harry H. Woodring 1936–1940 Henry L. Stimson 1940–1945	Claude A. Swanson 1933–1940 Charles Edison 1940 Frank Knox 1940–1944 James V. Forrestal 1944–1945	James A. Farley 1933–1940 Frank C. Walker 1940–1945	H. S. Cummings 1933–1939 Frank Murphy 1939–1940 Robert Jackson 1940–1941 Francis Biddel 1941–1945
Harry S Truman 1945–1953	Alben W. Barkley 1949–1953	James F. Byrnes 1945–1947 George C. Marshall 1947–1949 Dean G. Acheson 1949–1953	Fred M. Vinson 1945–1946 John W. Snyder 1946–1953	Robert P. Patterson 1945–1947 Kenneth C. Royall 1947 **Secretary of Defense** James V. Forrestal 1947–1949 Louis A. Johnson 1949–1950 George C. Marshall 1950–1951 Robert A. Lovett 1951–1953	James V. Forrestal 1945–1947	R. E. Hannegan 1945–1947 Jesse M. Donaldson 1947–1953	Tom C. Clark 1945–1949 J. H. McGrath 1949–1952 James P. McGranery 1952–1953
Dwight D. Eisenhower 1953–1961	Richard M. Nixon 1953–1961	John Foster Dulles 1953–1959 Christian A. Herter 1957–1961	George M. Humphrey 1953–1957 Robert B. Anderson 1957–1961	Charles E. Wilson 1953–1957 Neil H. McElroy 1957–1961 Thomas S. Gates 1959–1961		A. E. Summerfield 1953–1961	H. Brownell, Jr. 1953–1957 William P. Rogers 1957–1961
John F. Kennedy 1961–1963	Lyndon B. Johnson 1961–1963	Dean Rusk 1961–1963	C. Douglas Dillon 1961–1963	Robert S. McNamara 1961–1963		J. Edward Day 1961–1963 John A. Gronouski 1961–1963	Robert F. Kennedy 1961–1963
Lyndon B. Johnson 1963–1969	Hubert H. Humphrey 1965–1969	Dean Rusk 1963–1969	C. Douglas Dillon 1963–1965 Henry H. Fowler 1965–1968 Joseph W. Barr 1968–1969	Robert S. McNamara 1963–1968 Clark M. Clifford 1968–1969		John A. Gronouski 1963–1965 Lawrence F. O'Brien 1965–1968 W. Marvin Watson 1968–1969	Robert F. Kennedy 1963–1965 N. deB. Katzenbach 1965–1967 Ramsey Clark 1967–1969

Secretary of Interior	Secretary of Agriculture	Secretary of Commerce	Secretary of Labor	Secretary of Health, Education and Welfare	Secretary of Housing and Urban Development	Secretary of Transportation
Albert B. Fall 1921–1923 Hubert Work 1923	Henry C. Wallace 1921–1923	Herbert C. Hoover 1921–1923	James J. Davis 1921–1923			
Hubert Work 1923–1928 Roy O. West 1928–1929	Henry C. Wallace 1923–1924 Howard M. Gore 1924–1925 W. J. Jardine 1925–1929	Herbert C. Hoover 1923–1928 William F. Whiting 1928–1929	James J. Davis 1923–1929			
Ray L. Wilbur 1929–1933	Arthur M. Hyde 1929–1933 Roy D. Chapin 1932–1933	Robert P. Lamont 1929–1932 William N. Doak 1930–1933	James J. Davis 1929–1930			
Harold L. Ickes 1933–1945	Henry A. Wallace 1933–1940 Claude R. Wickard 1940–1945	Daniel C. Roper 1933–1939 Harry L. Hopkins 1939–1940 Jesse Jones 1940–1945 Henry A. Wallace 1945	Frances Perkins 1933–1945			
Harold L. Ickes 1945–1946 Julius A. Krug 1946–1949 Oscar L. Chapman 1949–1953	C. P. Anderson 1945–1948 C. F. Brannan 1948–1953	W. A. Harriman 1946–1948 Charles Sawyer 1948–1953	L. B. Schwellenbach 1945–1948 Maurice J. Tobin 1948–1953			
Douglas McKay 1953–1956 Fred Seaton 1956–1961	Ezra T. Benson 1953–1961	Sinclair Weeks 1953–1958 Lewis L. Strauss 1958–1961	Martin P. Durkin 1953 James P. Mitchell 1953–1961	Oveta Culp Hobby 1953–1955 Marion B. Folsom 1955–1958 Arthur S. Flemming 1958–1961		
Stewart L. Udall 1961–1963	Orville L. Freeman 1961–1963	Luther H. Hodges 1961–1963	Arthur J. Goldberg 1961–1963 W. Willard Wirtz 1962–1963	A. H. Ribicoff 1961–1963 Anthony J. Celebrezze 1962–1963		
Stewart L. Udall 1963–1969	Orville L. Freeman 1963–1969	Luther H. Hodges 1963–1965 John T. Connor 1965–1967 Alexander B. Trowbridge 1967–1968 C. R. Smith 1968–1969	W. Willard Wirtz 1963–1969	Anthony J. Celebrezze 1963–1965 John W. Gardner 1965–1968 Wilbur J. Cohen 1968–1969	Robert C. Weaver 1966–1968 Robert C. Wood 1968–1969	Alan S. Boyd 1966–1969

(continued)

President	Vice President	Secretary of State	Secretary of Treasury	Secretary of Defense	Postmaster General[1]	Attorney General	Secretary of Interior	Secretary of Agriculture
Richard M. Nixon 1969–1974	Spiro T. Agnew 1969–1973 Gerald R. Ford 1973–1974	William P. Rogers 1969–1973 Henry A. Kissinger 1973–1974	David M. Kennedy 1969–1970 John B. Connally 1970–1972 George P. Schultz 1972–1974 William E. Simon 1974	Melvin R. Laird 1969–1973 Elliot L. Richardson 1973 James R. Schlesinger 1973–1974	Winton M. Blount 1969–1971	John M. Mitchell 1969–1972 Richard G. Kleindienst 1972–1973 Elliot L. Richardson 1973 William B. Saxbe 1974	Walter J. Hickel 1969–1971 Rogers C. B. Morton 1971–1974	Clifford M. Hardin 1969–1971 Earl L. Butz 1971–1974
Gerald R. Ford 1974–1977	Nelson A. Rockefeller 1974–1977	Henry A. Kissinger 1974–1977	William E. Simon 1974–1977	James R. Schlesinger 1974–1975 Donald H. Rumsfeld 1975–1977		William B. Saxbe 1974–1975 Edward H. Levi 1975–1977	Rogers C. B. Morton 1974–1975 Stanley K. Hathaway 1975 Thomas D. Kleppe 1975–1977	Earl L. Butz 1974–1976
Jimmy Carter 1977–1981	Walter F. Mondale 1977–1981	Cyrus R. Vance 1977–1980 Edmund S. Muskie 1980–1981	W. Michael Blumenthal 1977–1979 G. William Miller 1979–1981	Harold Brown 1977–1981		Griffin Bell 1977–1979 Benjamin R. Civiletti 1979–1981	Cecil D. Andrus 1977–1981	Robert Bergland 1977–1981
Ronald W. Reagan 1981–1989	George H. Bush 1981–1989	Alexander M. Haig, Jr. 1981–1982 George P. Shultz 1982–1989	Donald T. Regan 1981–1985 James A. Baker 1985–1988 Nicholas F. Brady 1988–1989	Caspar W. Weinberger 1981–1987 Frank C. Carlucci 1987–1989		William French Smith 1981–1985 Edwin Meese 1985–1988 Richard Thornburgh 1988–1989	James G. Watt 1981–1983 William P. Clark 1983–1985 Donald P. Hodel 1985–1989	John R. Block 1981–1986 Richard E. Lyng 1986–1989
George H. Bush 1989–1993	J. Danforth Quayle 1989–1993	James A. Baker 1989–1992 Lawrence S. Eagleburger 1992–1993	Nicholas F. Brady 1989–1993	Richard Cheney 1989–1993		Richard Thornburgh 1989–1990 William Barr 1990–1993	Manuel Lujan 1989–1993	Clayton Yeutter 1989–1990 Edward Madigan 1990–1993
William Clinton 1993–2001	Albert Gore 1993–2001	Warren M. Christopher 1993–1996 Madeleine K. Albright 1997–2001	Lloyd Bentsen 1993–1994 Robert E. Rubin 1994–1999 Lawrence H. Summers 1999–2001	Les Aspin 1993–1994 William J. Perry 1994–1996 William S. Cohen 1997–2001		Janet Reno 1993–2001	Bruce Babbitt 1993–2001	Mike Espy 1993–1994 Dan Glickman 1995–2001
George W. Bush 2001–	Richard B. Cheney 2001–	Gen. Colin L. Powell 2001–	Paul H. O'Neill 2001–	Donald H. Rumsfeld 2001–		John Ashcroft 2001–	Gale A. Norton 2001–	Ann M. Veneman 2001–

[1]On July 1, 1971, the Post Office became an independent agency. After that date, the postmaster general was no longer a member of the Cabinet.

[2]Acting secretary.

Secretary of Commerce	Secretary of Labor	Secretary of Health, Education and Welfare / Health and Human Services	Secretary of Education	Secretary of Housing and Urban Development	Secretary of Transportation	Secretary of Energy	Secretary of Veterans Affairs
Maurice H. Stans 1969–1972 Peter G. Peterson 1972 Frederick B. Dent 1972–1974	George P. Shultz 1969–1970 James D. Hodgson 1970–1973 Peter J. Brennan 1973–1974	Robert H. Finch 1969–1970 Elliot L. Richardson 1970–1973 Caspar W. Weinberger 1973–1974		George W. Romney 1969–1973 James T. Lynn 1973–1974	John A. Volpe 1969–1973 Claude S. Brinegar 1973–1974		
Frederick B. Dent 1974–1975 Rogers C. B. Morton 1975 Elliot L. Richardson 1975–1977	Peter J. Brennan 1974–1975 John T. Dunlop 1975–1976 W. J. Usery 1976–1977	Caspar W. Weinberger 1974–1975 Forrest D. Matthews 1975–1977		James T. Lynn 1974–1975 Carla A. Hills 1975–1977	Claude S. Brinegar 1974–1975 William T. Coleman 1975–1977		
Juanita Kreps 1977–1981	F. Ray Marshall 1977–1981	Joseph Califano 1977–1979 Patricia Roberts Harris 1979–1980		Patricia Roberts Harris 1977–1979 Moon Landrieu 1979–1981	Brock Adams 1977–1979 Neil E. Goldschmidt 1979–1981	James R. Schlesinger 1977–1979 Charles W. Duncan, Jr. 1979–1981	
		Secretary of Health and Human Services Patricia Roberts Harris 1980–1981	*Secretary of Education* Shirley M. Hufstedler 1980–1981				
Malcolm Baldridge 1981–1987 C. William Verity, Jr. 1987–1989	Raymond J. Donovan 1981–1985 William E. Brock 1985–1987 Ann Dore McLaughlin 1987–1989	Richard S. Schweiker 1981–1983 Margaret M. Heckler 1983–1985 Otis R. Bowen 1985–1989	Terrell H. Bell 1981–1985 William J. Bennett 1985–1988 Lauro Fred Cavazos 1988–1989	Samuel R. Pierce, Jr. 1981–1989	Drew Lewis 1981–1983 Elizabeth H. Dole 1983–1987 James H. Burnley 1987–1989	James B. Edwards 1981–1982 Donald P. Hodel 1982–1985 John S. Harrington 1985–1989	
Robert Mosbacher 1989–1991 Barbara Franklin 1991–1993	Elizabeth Dole 1989–1990 Lynn Martin 1992–1993	Louis Sullivan 1989–1993	Lamar Alexander 1990–1993	Jack Kemp 1989–1993	Samuel Skinner 1989–1990 Andrew Card 1990–1993	James Watkins 1989–1993	Edward J. Derwinski 1989–1993
Ronald H. Brown 1993–1996 William M. Daley 1997–2000 Norman Y. Mineta 2000–2001	Robert B. Reich 1993–1996 Alexis M. Herman 1997–2001	Donna E. Shalala 1993–2001	Richard W. Riley 1993–2001	Henry G. Cisneros 1993–1996 Andrew M. Cuomo 1997–2001	Federico F. Peña 1993–1996 Rodney E. Slater 1997–2001	Hazel O'Leary 1993–1996 Federico F. Peña 1997–1998 Bill Richardson 1998–2001	Jesse Brown 1993–1997 Togo D. West, Jr.[2] 1998–2001
Donald L. Evans 2001–	Elaine L. Chao 2001–	Tommy G. Thompson 2001–	Roderick R. Paige 2001–	Melquiades R. Martinez 2001–	Norman Y. Mineta 2001–	Spencer Abraham 2001–	Anthony Principi 2001–

JUSTICES OF THE U.S. SUPREME COURT

Name	Term of Service	Years of Service	Appointed By	Name	Term of Service	Years of Service	Appointed By
John Jay	1789–1795	5	Washington	Rufus W. Peckham	1895–1909	14	Cleveland
John Rutledge	1789–1791	1	Washington	Joseph McKenna	1898–1925	26	McKinley
William Cushing	1789–1810	20	Washington	Oliver W. Holmes, Jr.	1902–1932	30	T. Roosevelt
James Wilson	1789–1798	8	Washington	William R. Day	1903–1922	19	T. Roosevelt
John Blair	1789–1796	6	Washington	William H. Moody	1906–1910	3	T. Roosevelt
Robert H. Harrison	1789–1790	—	Washington	Horace H. Lurton	1910–1914	4	Taft
James Iredell	1790–1799	9	Washington	Charles E. Hughes	1910–1916	5	Taft
Thomas Johnson	1791–1793	1	Washington	Willis Van Devanter	1911–1937	26	Taft
William Paterson	1793–1806	13	Washington	Joseph R. Lamar	1911–1916	5	Taft
John Rutledge[1]	1795	—	Washington	**Edward D. White**	1910–1921	11	Taft
Samuel Chase	1796–1811	15	Washington	Mahlon Pitney	1912–1922	10	Taft
Oliver Ellsworth	1796–1800	4	Washington	James C. McReynolds	1914–1941	26	Wilson
Bushrod Washington	1798–1829	31	J. Adams	Louis D. Brandeis	1916–1939	22	Wilson
Alfred Moore	1799–1804	4	J. Adams	John H. Clarke	1916–1922	6	Wilson
John Marshall	1801–1835	34	J. Adams	**William H. Taft**	1921–1930	8	Harding
William Johnson	1804–1834	30	Jefferson	George Sutherland	1922–1938	15	Harding
H. Brockholst Livingston	1806–1823	16	Jefferson	Pierce Butler	1922–1939	16	Harding
Thomas Todd	1807–1826	18	Jefferson	Edward T. Sanford	1923–1930	7	Harding
Joseph Story	1811–1845	33	Madison	Harlan F. Stone	1925–1941	16	Coolidge
Gabriel Duval	1811–1835	24	Madison	**Charles E. Hughes**	1930–1941	11	Hoover
Smith Thompson	1823–1843	20	Monroe	Owen J. Roberts	1930–1945	15	Hoover
Robert Trimble	1826–1828	2	J. Q. Adams	Benjamin N. Cardozo	1932–1938	6	Hoover
John McLean	1829–1861	32	Jackson	Hugo L. Black	1937–1971	34	F. Roosevelt
Henry Baldwin	1830–1844	14	Jackson	Stanley F. Reed	1938–1957	19	F. Roosevelt
James M. Wayne	1835–1867	32	Jackson	Felix Frankfurter	1939–1962	23	F. Roosevelt
Roger B. Taney	1836–1864	28	Jackson	William O. Douglas	1939–1975	36	F. Roosevelt
Philip P. Barbour	1836–1841	4	Jackson	Frank Murphy	1940–1949	9	F. Roosevelt
John Catron	1837–1865	28	Van Buren	**Harlan F. Stone**	1941–1946	5	F. Roosevelt
John McKinley	1837–1852	15	Van Buren	James F. Byrnes	1941–1942	1	F. Roosevelt
Peter V. Daniel	1841–1860	19	Van Buren	Robert H. Jackson	1941–1954	13	F. Roosevelt
Samuel Nelson	1845–1872	27	Tyler	Wiley B. Rutledge	1943–1949	6	F. Roosevelt
Levi Woodbury	1845–1851	5	Polk	Harold H. Burton	1945–1958	13	Truman
Robert C. Grier	1846–1870	23	Polk	**Fred M. Vinson**	1946–1953	7	Truman
Benjamin R. Curtis	1851–1857	6	Fillmore	Tom C. Clark	1949–1967	18	Truman
John A. Campbell	1853–1861	8	Pierce	Sherman Minton	1949–1956	7	Truman
Nathan Clifford	1858–1881	23	Buchanan	**Earl Warren**	1953–1969	16	Eisenhower
Noah H. Swayne	1862–1881	18	Lincoln	John Marshall Harlan	1955–1971	16	Eisenhower
Samuel F. Miller	1862–1890	28	Lincoln	William J. Brennan, Jr.	1956–1990	34	Eisenhower
David Davis	1862–1877	14	Lincoln	Charles E. Whittaker	1957–1962	5	Eisenhower
Stephen J. Field	1863–1897	34	Lincoln	Potter Stewart	1958–1981	23	Eisenhower
Salmon P. Chase	1864–1873	8	Lincoln	Byron R. White	1962–1993	31	Kennedy
William Strong	1870–1880	10	Grant	Arthur J. Goldberg	1962–1965	3	Kennedy
Joseph P. Bradley	1870–1892	22	Grant	Abe Fortas	1965–1969	4	Johnson
Ward Hunt	1873–1882	9	Grant	Thurgood Marshall	1967–1994	24	Johnson
Morrison R. Waite	1874–1888	14	Grant	**Warren E. Burger**	1969–1986	18	Nixon
John M. Harlan	1877–1911	34	Hayes	Harry A. Blackmun	1970–1994	24	Nixon
William B. Woods	1880–1887	7	Hayes	Lewis F. Powell, Jr.	1971–1987	15	Nixon
Stanley Matthews	1881–1889	7	Garfield	**William H. Rehnquist**[2]	1971–	—	Nixon
Horace Gray	1882–1902	20	Arthur	John P. Stevens III	1975–	—	Ford
Samuel Blatchford	1882–1893	11	Arthur	Sandra Day O'Connor	1981–	—	Reagan
Lucius Q. C. Lamar	1888–1893	5	Cleveland	Antonin Scalia	1986–	—	Reagan
Melville W. Fuller	1888–1910	21	Cleveland	Anthony M. Kennedy	1988–	—	Reagan
David J. Brewer	1890–1910	20	B. Harrison	David Souter	1990–	—	Bush
Henry B. Brown	1890–1906	16	B. Harrison	Clarence Thomas	1991–	—	Bush
George Shiras, Jr.	1892–1903	10	B. Harrison	Ruth Bader Ginsburg	1993–	—	Clinton
Howell E. Jackson	1893–1895	2	B. Harrison	Stephen G. Breyer	1994–	—	Clinton
Edward D. White	1894–1910	16	Cleveland				

Note: Chief justices appear in bold type.

[1] Acting chief justice; Senate refused to confirm appointment.

[2] Chief justice from 1986 on (Reagan administration).

CHAPTER 1 WHEN OLD WORLDS COLLIDE: CONTACT, CONQUEST, CATASTROPHE

Pre-Columbian America

General discussions of pre-Columbian America are found in Brian M. Fagan, *The Great Journey: The Peopling of Ancient America* (1987); Alfred M. Josephy, ed., *America in 1492: The World of the Indian Peoples before the Arrival of Columbus* (1993); and Francis Jennings, *The Founders of America: How Indians Discovered the Land, Pioneered in It, and Created Great Classical Civilizations . . .* (1993). Joseph H. Greenberg, *Language in the Americas* (1987), and William M. Denevan, ed., *The Native Population of the Americas in 1492* (1976), are standard. Philip Kopper, *The Smithsonian Book of North American Indians before the Coming of the Europeans* (1986), is accurate, accessible, and wonderfully illustrated. Michael Coe, Dean Snow, and Elizabeth Benson, *Atlas of Ancient America* (1986), provides a narrative and maps for the major cultures of North and South America. Lynda Norene Shaffer, *Native Americans before 1492: The Moundbuilding Centers of the Eastern Woodlands* (1992), provides a brief survey that covers thousands of years, while Thomas E. Emerson and R. Barry Lewis, eds., *Cahokia and the Hinterlands: Middle Mississippian Cultures of the Midwest* (1991), gives a series of detailed studies of the last cycle of mound building. Some important continuities between the pre-Columbian and post-Columbian eras are established in Neal Salisbury, "The Indians' Old World: Native Americans and the Coming of Europeans," *William and Mary Quarterly*, 3rd ser., 53 (1996): 435–458. Frederich Katz, *The Ancient American Civilizations* (1972), remains an excellent introduction. Michael D. Coe, *The Olmec World: Ritual and Rulership* (1995), is superb. Esther Pasztory's *Teotihuacan: An Experiment in Living* (1997), provides a bold and original interpretation of the Classic era's greatest metropolis. The complex cultures of Mesoamerica are covered in Norman Hammond, *Ancient Maya Civilization* (1982); Michael D. Coe, *The Maya*, 3rd ed. (1984); Linda Schele and Mary Ellen Miller, *The Blood of Kings: Dynasty and Ritual in Maya Art* (1986); Linda Schele and David Freidel, *A Forest of Kings: The Untold Story of the Ancient Maya* (1990); and Inga Clendinnen, *Aztecs: An Interpretation* (1991). For a comprehensive coverage of Andean cultures, compare Richard L. Burger, *Chavin and the Origins of Andean Civilization* (1992); Alan L. Kolata, *The Tiwanaku: Portrait of an Andean Civilization* (1993); Evan Hadingham, *Lines to the Mountain Gods: Nazca and the Mysteries of Peru* (1987); Thomas C. Patterson, *The Inca Empire: The Formation and Disintegration of a Pre-Capitalist State* (1991); and Nigel Davies, *The Incas* (1995). For the prehistory of the Pacific and Hawaii, see Peter Bellwood, *The Polynesians: Prehistory of an Island People*, rev. ed. (1987); and David E. Stannard, *Before the Horror: The Population of Hawai'i on the Eve of Western Contact* (1989).

The Expansion of Europe

Works that trace the early expansion of Europe are G. V. Scammell, *The First Imperial Age: European Overseas Expansion c. 1400–1715* (1989); Carlo M. Cipolla, *Guns, Sails, and Empire: Technological Innovation and the Early Phases of European Expansion 1400–1700* (1965); Charles Verlinden, *The Beginnings of Modern Colonization: Eleven Essays with an Introduction* (1970); and Samuel Eliot Morison, *The European Discovery of America: The Northern Voyages, A.D. 500–1600* (1971), and *The European Discovery of America: The Southern Voyages, A.D. 1492–1616* (1974). P. E. Russell's elegant lecture, *Prince Henry the Navigator* (1960), greatly reduces Henry's importance. William D. Phillips Jr. and Carla Rahn Phillips, *The Worlds of Christopher Columbus* (1992), is a strong, recent biography. The religious motives of Columbus are explored in Pauline Moffitt Watts, "Prophecy and Discovery: On the Spiritual Origins of Christopher Columbus's 'Enterprise of the Indies,'" *American Historical Review* 90 (1985): 73–102, while Arthur Davies argues that Columbus scuttled his flagship in "The Loss of the *Santa Maria*, Christmas Day, 1492," *American Historical Review* 58 (1952–53): 854–865. Alfred W. Crosby analyzes the long-term consequences of expansion in *The Columbian Exchange: Biological and Cultural Consequences of 1492* (1972) and in *Ecological Imperialism: The Biological Expansion of Europe, 900–1900* (1986).

Africa and the Atlantic Slave Trade

J. D. Fage, *A History of West Africa: An Introductory Survey*, 4th ed. (1969), although aging, is still useful. John Thornton, *Africa and Africans in the Making of the Modern World, 1400–1680* (1992), insists that Africans retained control of their affairs, including the slave trade, before 1700. Patrick Manning, *Slavery and African Life: Occidental, Oriental, and African Slave Trades* (1990), emphasizes the devastating impact of the slave trade in the 18th and 19th centuries. Philip D. Curtin, *The Atlantic Slave Trade: A Census* (1969), is a classic, although it is modified by Paul E. Lovejoy, "The Volume of the Atlantic Slave Trade: A Synthesis," *Journal of African History* 23 (1982): 473–501. For a strong introduction to this topic, also see Lovejoy, "The Impact of the African Slave Trade on Africa: A Review of the Literature," *Journal of African History* 30 (1989): 365–394. Hugh Thomas, *The Slave Trade: The Story of the Atlantic Slave Trade, 1440–1870* (1997), is comprehensive and detailed. Robin Blackburn, *The Making of New World Slavery: From the Baroque to the Modern, 1492–1800* (1997), is a lucid and comprehensive synthesis, the best yet written. David Brion Davis, *Slavery and Human Progress* (1984), is a meditation on the changing significance of slavery between the onset of European expansion and the abolition of the institution.

The Iberian Empires

James Lockhart and Stuart B. Schwartz, *Early Latin America: A History of Colonial Spanish America and Brazil* (1983), is a superb survey. Charles R. Boxer, *The Portuguese Seaborne Empire: 1415–1825* (1969), is excellent. David E. Stannard, *American Holocaust: Columbus and the Conquest of the New World* (1992), is an angry account of the European conquest. Major studies of the early Spanish empire include J. H. Parry, *The Spanish Seaborne Empire* (1966); Carl O. Sauer, *The Early Spanish Main* (1966); Tzvetan Todorov, *The Conquest of America* (1984); Charles Gibson, *The Aztecs under Spanish Rule: A History of the Indians of the Valley of Mexico, 1519–1810* (1964); John Hemming, *The Conquest of the Incas* (1970); James Lockhart, *Spanish Peru, 1532–1560: A Colonial Society* (1968); David Noble Cook, *Demographic Collapse: Indian Peru, 1520–1620* (1981); and James Lockhart, "Encomienda and Hacienda: The Evolution of the Great Estate in the Spanish Indies," *Hispanic American Historical Review* 49 (1969): 411–29. David J. Weber, *The Spanish Frontier in North America* (1992), is excellent on the Franciscan missions in Florida and New Mexico. John Hemming, *Red Gold: The Conquest of the Brazilian Indians, 1500–1760* (1978), is careful and sobering.

The First Global Economy

Immanuel Wallerstein, *The Modern World System: Capitalist Agriculture and the Origins of the European World Economy in the Sixteenth Century* (1974), and Fernand Braudel, *Capitalism and Material Life, 1400–1800* (1967), both explore the emergence of a global economy. Charles A. Levinson, ed., *Circa 1492: Art in the Age of Exploration* (1991), provides a global view of art in the same era.

Videos

The *Nova* series on PBS has produced two outstanding documentaries on pre-Columbian America. *Search for the First Americans* (1992) assembles evidence for early occupancy of the Americas. *Secrets of the Lost Red Paint People* (1987) is a fascinating example of how archaeologists reconstruct the distant past and the surprises that this process creates. Another challenging program is *The Sun Dagger* (1982), narrated by Robert Redford, on Anasazi astronomy, available through Pacific Arts Publishing.

CHAPTER 2 THE CHALLENGE TO SPAIN AND THE SETTLEMENT OF NORTH AMERICA

French and Dutch Expansion

W. J. Eccles, *The French in North America, 1500–1783*, rev. ed. (1998), is a concise and authoritative survey. Also helpful are Peter N. Moogk, "Reluctant Exiles: The Problem of Colonization in French North America," *William and Mary Quarterly* 3rd ser., 46 (1989): 463–505; Morris Altman, "Economic Growth in Canada: Estimates and Analysis," *William and Mary Quarterly*, 3rd ser., 45 (1988): 684–711; and Winstanley Briggs, "Le Pays des Illinois," *William and Mary Quarterly*, 3rd ser., 47 (1990): 30–56. Superb overviews are found in Jonathan I. Israel, *The Dutch Republic: Its Rise, Greatness, and Fall* (1995); Simon Schama, *The Embarrassment of Riches: An Interpretation of Dutch Culture in the Golden Age* (1987); and Charles R. Boxer, *The Dutch Seaborne Empire: 1600–1800* (1965). George Masselman, *The Cradle of Colonialism* (1963), and Jonathan I. Israel, *Dutch Primacy in World Trade, 1585–1740* (1989), are more specialized. Oliver A. Rink, *Holland on the Hudson: An Economic and Social History of Dutch New York* (1986), and S. G. Nissenson, *The Patroon's Domain* (1937), cover New Netherland.

Elizabethan Expansion

David B. Quinn, *England and the Discovery of America, 1481–1620* (1974), and Kenneth R. Andrews, *Trade, Plunder, and Settlement: Maritime Enterprise and the Genesis of the British Empire, 1480–1630* (1984), offer fine narratives. Karen O. Kupperman's *Roanoke: The Abandoned Colony* (1984) is briefer than David B. Quinn's *Set Fair for Roanoke: Voyages and Colonies, 1584–1606* (1985); both are excellent. Nicholas P. Canny places the conquest of Ireland in a broad, Atlantic context in *The Elizabethan Conquest of Ireland: A Pattern Established, 1565–76* (1976) and *Kingdom and Colony: Ireland in the Atlantic World, 1560–1800* (1988).

The 13 Colonies: General Studies

Jack P. Greene, *Pursuits of Happiness: The Social Development of Early Modern British Colonies and the Formation of American Culture* (1988), surveys all 13 colonies within the context of Britain's other Atlantic provinces, including Ireland and the West Indies. David Hackett Fischer, *Albion's Seed: Four British Folkways in America* (1989), traces the regional identities of New England, the upper South, the Mid-Atlantic, and the early backcountry to specific subcultures within the British Isles. Bernard Bailyn, *The Peopling of British North America: An Introduction* (1985), is a broadly conceived overview of the settlement process. Mary Beth Norton, *Founding Mothers and Fathers: Gendered Power and the Forming of American Society* (1996), sees gender relationships taking shape in the early Chesapeake colonies markedly different from those she finds in early New England. Some major interpretive essays are found in Stanley N. Katz, John M. Murrin, and Douglas Greenberg, eds., *Colonial America: Essays in Politics and Social Development*, 5th ed. (2000), and Jack P. Greene and J. R. Pole, eds., *Colonial British America: Essays in the New History of the Early Modern Era* (1984).

The Chesapeake and West Indian Colonies

Edmund S. Morgan, *American Slavery, American Freedom: The Ordeal of Colonial Virginia* (1975), remains the best history of any American colony. For a sobering essay, see J. Frederick Fausz, "An 'Abundance of Blood Shed on Both

Sides': England's First Indian War, 1609–1614," *Virginia Magazine of History and Biography* 98 (1990): 3–56. For perspectives on the social history of the Chesapeake colonies, see Thad W. Tate and David L. Ammerman, eds., *The Chesapeake in the Seventeenth Century: Essays on Anglo-American Society* (1979); Lois Green Carr, Philip D. Morgan, and Jean B. Russo, eds., *Colonial Chesapeake Society* (1988); and Aubrey Land, Lois Green Carr, and Edward C. Papenfuse, eds., *Law, Society, and Politics in Early Maryland* (1977). Kathleen M. Brown, *Good Wives, Nasty Wenches, and Anxious Patriarchs: Gender, Race, and Power in Colonial Virginia* (1996), is fresh and imaginative. Darrett and Anita Rutman, *A Place in Time* (1984), is a community study of Middlesex County, Virginia. On the role of younger sons in shaping cultural values, see Martin H. Quitt, "Immigrant Origins of the Virginia Gentry: A Study of Cultural Transmission and Innovation," *William and Mary Quarterly*, 3rd ser., 45 (1988): 629–655. Strong studies of Maryland include Gloria L. Main, *Tobacco Colony: Life in Early Maryland, 1650–1720* (1982); Russell R. Menard, *Economy and Society in Early Colonial Maryland* (1985); and David W. Jordan, *Foundations of Representative Government in Maryland, 1632–1715* (1987). On the West Indies, see Carl and Roberta Bridenbaugh, *No Peace beyond the Line: The English in the Caribbean, 1624–1690* (1972), and Richard S. Dunn, *Sugar and Slaves: The Rise of the Planter Class in the English West Indies, 1624–1713* (1972). Karen O. Kupperman, *Providence Island, 1630–1641: The Other Puritan Colony* (1993), tells the story of Puritan colonization in the tropics. Winthrop Jordan, *White over Black: American Attitudes toward the Negro, 1550–1812* (1968), and Orlando Patterson, *Slavery and Social Death: A Comparative Study* (1982), are classics. Ira Berlin, *Many Thousands Gone: The First Two Centuries of Slavery in North America* (1998), is essential.

New England
Three indispensable studies of New England Puritanism are Perry Miller, *The New England Mind: The Seventeenth Century* (1939); Edmund S. Morgan, *Visible Saints: The History of a Puritan Idea* (1963); and David D. Hall, *Worlds of Wonder, Days of Judgment: Popular Religious Belief in Early New England* (1989). Other major contributions include Sacvan Bercovitch, *The Puritan Origins of the American Self* (1975); Charles L. Cohen, *God's Caress: The Psychology of Puritan Religious Experience* (1986); Harry S. Stout, *The New England Soul: Preaching and Religious Culture in Colonial New England* (1986); and Andrew Delbanco, *The Puritan Ordeal* (1989). Darren Stoloff, *The Making of an American Thinking Class: Intellectuals and Intelligentsia in Puritan Massachusetts* (1998), is original and provocative. The best edition of an American classic is William Bradford, *Of Plymouth Plantation, 1620–1647*, edited by Samuel Eliot Morison (1959).

David Hall, John M. Murrin, and Thad W. Tate, eds., *Saints and Revolutionaries: Essays on Early American History* (1984), contains several important contributions on early New England. Virginia D. Anderson, *New England's Generation: The Great Migration and the Formation of Society and Culture in the Seventeenth Century* (1991), is the best study of the migration process. Major community and demographic studies include Darrett B. Rutman, *Winthrop's Boston: A Portrait of a Puritan Town, 1630–1649* (1965); John Demos, *A Little Commonwealth: Family Life in Plymouth Colony* (1970); Philip J. Greven Jr., *Four Generations: Population, Land and Family in Colonial Andover, Massachusetts* (1970); Kenneth A. Lockridge, *A New England Town, the First Hundred Years: Dedham, Massachusetts, 1636–1736*, rev. ed. (1985); and Stephen Innes, *Labor in a New Land: Economy and Society in Seventeenth-Century Springfield* (1983). Laurel T. Ulrich, *Good Wives: Images and Reality in the Lives of Women in Northern New England, 1650–1750* (1982), has been pathbreaking. Another important study is Amanda Porterfield, *Female Piety in Puritan New England: The Emergence of Religious Humanism* (1992).

Major studies of the New England economy include Bernard Bailyn, *The New England Merchants in the Seventeenth Century* (1955); Elaine Forman Crane, *Ebb Tide in New England: Women, Seaports, and Social Change, 1630–1800* (1998); Stephen Innes, *Creating the Commonwealth: The Economic Culture of Puritan New England* (1995); and Daniel Vickers, *Farmers and Fishermen: Two Centuries of Work in Essex County, Massachusetts, 1630–1850* (1994). John Frederick Martin, *Profits in the Wilderness: Entrepreneurship and the Founding of New England Towns in the Seventeenth Century* (1991), tries to integrate economic history with community studies.

Studies of dissent in New England include Edmund S. Morgan, *Roger Williams: The Church and the State* (1967); Emery Battis, *Saints and Sectaries: Anne Hutchinson and the Antinomian Controversy in the Massachusetts Bay Colony* (1962); and Carla G. Pestana, *Quakers and Baptists in Colonial Massachusetts* (1991). Robert E. Wall shows how the political and legal systems of Massachusetts took shape in response to dissent and controversy in *Massachusetts Bay: The Crucial Decade, 1640–1650* (1972). Robert G. Pope, *The Half-Way Covenant: Church Membership in Puritan New England* (1969), is insightful and thorough.

The Lower South
Peter H. Wood, *Black Majority: Negroes in Colonial South Carolina from 1670 through the Stono Rebellion* (1974), remains the best book on early South Carolina. Charles Hudson, *The Southeastern Indians* (1976), and James H. Merrell, *The Indians' New World: Catawbas and Their Neighbors from European Contact through the Era of Removal* (1989), are superb studies of southern Indians. Other contributions on South Carolina include Peter A. Coclanis, *The Shadow of a Dream: Economic Life and Death in the South Carolina Low Country, 1670–1920* (1989); Richard Waterhouse, *A New World Gentry: The Making of a Merchant and Planter Class in South Carolina, 1670–1770* (1989); David C. Littlefield, *Rice and Slaves: Ethnicity and the Slave Trade in Colonial South Carolina* (1981); and M. Eugene Sirmans, *Colonial South Carolina: A Political History, 1663–1763* (1966).

England's Mid-Atlantic Colonies
For a look at Restoration New York, see Robert C. Ritchie, *The Duke's Province: A Study of New York Politics and Society,*

1664–1691 (1977); Joyce D. Goodfriend, *Before the Melting Pot: Society and Culture in Colonial New York City, 1664–1730* (1992); and Donna Merwick, *Possessing Albany, 1630–1710: The Dutch and English Experiences* (1990). Still standard are John E. Pomfret's *The Province of East New Jersey, 1609–1702* (1962) and *The Province of West New Jersey, 1609–1702* (1956). Melvin B. Endy, *William Penn and Early Quakerism* (1973), and the essays in Richard S. Dunn and Mary Maples Dunn, eds., *The World of William Penn* (1986), are comprehensive. Barry J. Levy, *Quakers and the American Family: British Settlement in the Delaware Valley* (1988), is strong on family life, while Gary B. Nash, *Quakers and Politics: Pennsylvania, 1681–1726* (1968), is one of the best political histories of any American colony.

Videos
Black Robe, a 1991 Canadian film based on Brian Manning's novel of the same name, is a powerful evocation of the early Jesuit missions in New France. The PBS miniseries *Roanoak* (1986) explores tensions between settlers and Indians in England's first sustained attempt to colonize North America.

CHAPTER 3 ENGLAND DISCOVERS ITS COLONIES: EMPIRE, LIBERTY, AND EXPANSION

Two strong overviews of public events in England during these years are Derek Hirst, *Authority and Conflict: England, 1603–1658* (1986), and J. R. Jones, *Country and Court: England, 1658–1714* (1978). Wesley F. Craven, *The Colonies in Transition, 1660–1713* (1968), remains a strong survey of colonial developments. Edmund S. Morgan, *Inventing the People: The Rise of Popular Sovereignty in England and America* (1988), connects political thought in the English civil wars with the American Revolution more than a century later. Another influential work is J. G. A. Pocock, "Machiavelli, Harrington, and English Political Ideologies in the Eighteenth Century," *William and Mary Quarterly*, 3rd ser., 22 (1965): 549–583. Pocock's *The Machiavellian Moment: Florentine Political Thought and the Atlantic Republican Tradition* (1975) is difficult but essential.

Mercantilism
Albert O. Hirschman, *The Passions and the Interests: Political Arguments for Capitalism before Its Triumph* (1977), is brief and brilliant. Important studies of trade wars and the Navigation Acts include Charles Wilson, *Profit and Power: A Study of England and the Dutch Wars* (1957); Charles M. Andrews, *The Colonial Period of American History*, vol. 4 (1938); Lawrence A. Harper, *The English Navigation Acts: A Seventeenth-Century Experiment in Social Engineering* (1939); and Michael Kammen's brief *Empire and Interest: The American Colonies and the Politics of Mercantilism* (1969).

Indians and Settlers
Colin G. Calloway, *New Worlds for All: Indians, Europeans, and the Remaking of Early America* (1997), surveys settler–Indian relations to about 1800. Daniel K. Richer, *The Ordeal of the Longhouse: The Peoples of the Iroquois League in the Era of European Colonization* (1992); Matthew Dennis, *Cultivating a Landscape of Peace: Iroquois-European Encounters in Seventeenth-Century America* (1993); and Francis Jennings, *The Ambiguous Iroquois Empire: The Covenant Chain Confederation of Indian Tribes with English Colonies from Its Beginnings to the Lancaster Treaty of 1744* (1984), are all essential. A brief and up-to-date account of Puritan missions is Richard W. Cogley, *John Eliot's Mission to the Indians before King Philip's War* (1999). Jill Lepore, *The Name of War: King Philip's War and the Origins of American Identity* (1998), Patrick M. Malone, *The Skulking Way of War: Technology and Tactics among the New England Indians* (1991), and Richard I. Melvoin, *New England Outpost: War and Society in Colonial Deerfield* (1989), are transforming the way that historians approach Metacom's War. Edmund S. Morgan, *American Slavery, American Freedom: The Ordeal of Colonial Virginia* (1975), provides the strongest analysis of Bacon's Rebellion, but also useful is Wilcomb Washburn, *The Governor and the Rebel: A History of Bacon's Rebellion in Virginia* (1957).

Royal Government
Stephen S. Webb analyzes the origins of royal government through the Glorious Revolution in *The Governors General: The English Army and the Definition of Empire, 1569–1681* (1979) and in his *Lord Churchill's Coup: The Anglo-American Empire and the Glorious Revolution Reconsidered* (1995). Still impressive is Winfred T. Root, "The Lords of Trade, 1675–1696," *American Historical Review* 23 (1917–18): 20–41.

The Glorious Revolution and Its Aftermath
The following works lay out various aspects of the transformation of English politics between 1660 and 1720: John Miller, *Popery and Politics in England, 1660–1688* (1973); Robert Willman, "The Origins of 'Whig' and 'Tory' in English Political Language," *Historical Journal* 17 (1974): 247–64; Clayton Roberts, *The Growth of Responsible Government in Stuart England* (1966); W. A. Speck, *Reluctant Revolutionaries: Englishmen and the Revolution of 1688* (1989); J. H. Plumb, *The Growth of Political Stability in England, 1675–1725* (1967); John Brewer, *The Sinews of Power: War, Money, and the English State, 1688–1783* (1989); P. G. M. Dickson, *The Financial Revolution in England: A Study in the Development of Public Credit, 1688–1756* (1967); Geoffrey Holmes, *The Electorate and the National Will in the First Age of Party* (1976); and Isaac Kramnick, *Bolingbroke and his Circle: The Politics of Nostalgia in the Age of Walpole* (1968). For an unusually thoughtful essay, consult Peter Laslett, "John Locke, the Great Recoinage, and the Origins of the Board of Trade: 1695–1698," *William and Mary Quarterly*, 3rd ser., 14 (1957): 370–402. Ian K. Steele, *The English Atlantic, 1675–1740: An Exploration of Communication and Community* (1986), is careful and original. John M. Murrin looks for similarities and differences in the English and American Revolutions in "The Great Inversion, or Court versus Country: A Comparison of the Revolution Settlements in England (1688–1721) and America

(1776–1816)," in J. G. A. Pocock, ed., *Three British Revolutions: 1641, 1688, 1776* (1980), pp. 368–453.

David S. Lovejoy, *The Glorious Revolution in America* (1972), covers all the colonies. For more specific studies of the Glorious Revolution in New England, New York, and Maryland, see Richard R. Johnson, *Adjustment to Empire: The New England Colonies, 1675–1715* (1981); John M. Murrin, "The Menacing Shadow of Louis XIV and the Rage of Jacob Leisler: The Constitutional Ordeal of Seventeenth Century New York," in Stephen L. Schechter and Richard B. Bernstein, eds., *New York and the Union: Contributions to the American Constitutional Experience* (1990), pp. 29–71; and Lois G. Carr and David W. Jordan, *Maryland's Revolution of Government, 1689–1692* (1974). Imaginative and distinctive perspectives on the Salem witch trials are found in Paul Boyer and Stephen Nissenbaum, *Salem Possessed: The Social Origins of Witchcraft* (1974); John P. Demos, *Entertaining Satan: Witchcraft and the Culture of Early New England* (1982); Richard Weisman, *Witchcraft, Magic, and Religion in 17th Century Massachusetts* (1984); and Bernard Rosenthal, *Salem Story: Reading the Witch Trials of 1692* (1993); but Carol F. Karlsen, *The Devil in the Shape of a Woman: Witchcraft in Colonial New England* (1987), and Elizabeth Reis, *Damned Women: Sinners and Witches in Puritan New England* (1997), are conceptual breakthroughs.

The Spanish and French Colonies
Ramón A. Gutiérrez, *When Jesus Came, the Corn Mothers Went Away: Marriage, Sexuality, and Power in New Mexico, 1500–1846* (1991), has a strong account of the Pueblo revolt. David J. Weber, *The Spanish Frontier in North America* (1992), treats the Florida missions and Texas. Richard White, *The Middle Ground: Indians, Empires, and Republics in the Great Lakes Region, 1650–1815* (1991), and Eric Hinderaker, *Elusive Empires: Constructing Colonialism in the Ohio Valley, 1673–1800* (1997), are both superb. Daniel H. Usner, *Indians, Settlers, and Slaves in a Frontier Exchange Economy: The Lower Mississippi Valley before 1783* (1992), nicely covers Louisiana.

The Householder Economy
Important studies of the 18th-century household are James A. Henretta, "Families and Farms: Mentalite in Pre-Industrial America," *William and Mary Quarterly*, 3rd ser., 35 (1978): 3–32; Daniel Vickers, "Competency and Competition: Economic Culture in Early America," *William and Mary Quarterly*, 3rd ser., 47 (1990): 3–27; Mary M. Schweitzer, *Custom and Contract: Household, Government, and the Economy in Colonial Pennsylvania* (1987); and Laurel Thatcher Ulrich, *Good Wives: Images and Reality in the Lives of Women in Northern New England* (1982).

Videos
The PBS miniseries *Three Sovereigns for Sarah* (1986), starring Vanessa Redgrave, is a superb dramatization of the Salem witch trials.

CHAPTER 4 PROVINCIAL AMERICA AND THE STRUGGLE FOR A CONTINENT

Immigration and Economic Change
The best studies of immigration during the 18th century are Bernard Bailyn, *Voyagers to the West: A Passage in the Peopling of America on the Eve of the Revolution* (1986); A. G. Roeber, *Palatines, Liberty, and Property: German Lutherans in Colonial British America* (1993); Aaron S. Fogleman, *Hopeful Journeys: German Immigration, Settlement, and Political Culture in Colonial America, 1717–1775* (1996); R. J. Dickson, *Ulster Emigration to Colonial America, 1718–1775* (1966); Alan L. Karras, *Sojourners in the Sun: Scottish Migrants in Jamaica and the Chesapeake, 1740–1800* (1992); and A. Roger Ekirch, *Bound for America: The Transportation of British Convicts to the Colonies, 1718–1775* (1987).

Ian K. Steele, *The English Atlantic, 1675–1740: An Exploration of Communication and Community* (1986), discusses the quickening pace of Atlantic commerce. Richard L. Bushman, *The Refinement of America: Persons, Houses, Cities* (1992), and Rhys Isaac, *The Transformation of Virginia* (1982), explore the rise of elegance and of gentry culture. Three works that deal with the decline of opportunity for 18th-century householders are Toby L. Ditz, "Ownership and Obligation: Inheritance and Patriarchal Households in Connecticut, 1750–1820," *William and Mary Quarterly*, 3rd ser., 47 (1990): 235–265; Lucy Simler, "The Landless Worker: An Index of Economic and Social Change in Chester County, Pennsylvania, 1750–1820," *Pennsylvania Magazine of History and Biography* 94 (1990): 163–99; and Allan Kulikoff, *Tobacco and Slaves: The Development of Southern Culture in the Chesapeake, 1680–1800* (1986). John J. McCusker and Russell R. Menard, *The Economy of British America, 1607–1789* (1985), covers most economic patterns and questions. Joyce E. Chaplin, *An Anxious Pursuit: Agricultural Innovation and Modernity in the Lower South, 1730–1815* (1993), is thoughtful and important.

The Enlightenment and the Great Awakening
Henry F. May, *The Enlightenment in America* (1976), needs to be supplemented by Norman Fiering, "The First American Enlightenment: Tillotson, Leverett, and Philosophical Anglicanism," *New England Quarterly* 54 (1981): 307–44; and by Charles E. Clark, *The Public Prints: The Newspaper in Anglo-American Culture, 1665–1740* (1994); Michael Warner, *The Letters of the Republic: Publication and the Public Sphere in Eighteenth-Century America* (1990); David S. Shields, *Civil Tongues & Polite Letters in British America* (1997); and Ned Landsman, *From Colonials to Provincials: Thought and Culture in America, 1680–1760* (1998). On the rise of the professions, contrast Daniel J. Boorstin, *The Americans: The Colonial Experience* (1958), with John M. Murrin, "The Legal Transformation: The Bench and Bar in Eighteenth-Century Massachusetts," in Stanley N. Katz and John M. Murrin, eds., *Colonial America: Essays in Politics and Social Development*, 3rd ed. (1983), pp. 540–72. Phinzey Spalding, *Oglethorpe in*

America (1977), and Harold E. Davis, *The Fledgling Province: Social and Cultural Life in Colonial Georgia, 1733–1776* (1976), are standard.

Indispensable studies of the Great Awakening include John Walsh, "Origins of the Evangelical Revival," in G. V. Bennett and J. D. Walsh, eds., *Essays in Modern English Church History in Honor of Norman Sykes* (1966), pp. 132–62; W. R. Ward, *The Protestant Evangelical Awakening* (1992); Susan O'Brien, "A Transatlantic Community of Saints: The Great Awakening and the First Evangelical Network, 1735–1755," *American Historical Review* 91 (1986): 811–32; and Frank J. Lambert, *"Pedlar in Divinity": George Whitefield and the Transatlantic Revivals* (1994). Perry Miller, *Jonathan Edwards* (1949), is brilliant and controversial. Other important studies are Richard Warch, "The Shephard's Tent: Education and Enthusiasm in the Great Awakening," *American Quarterly* 30 (1978): 177–198; Martin E. Lodge, "The Crisis of the Churches in the Middle Colonies, 1720–1750," *Pennsylvania Magazine of History and Biography* 95 (1971): 195–220; Milton J Coalter, *Gilbert Tennent, Son of Thunder* (1986); Leigh Eric Schmidt, "'The Grand Prophet,' Hugh Bryan: Early Evangelicalism's Challenge to the Establishment and Slavery in the Colonial South," *South Carolina Historical Magazine* 87 (1986): 238–50; and Mark A. Noll, *Princeton and the Republic, 1768–1822: The Quest for a Christian Enlightenment in the Era of Samuel Stanhope Smith* (1989). To explore links between revivalism and revolution, see Harry S. Stout, "Religion, Communications, and the Ideological Origins of the American Revolution," *William and Mary Quarterly*, 3rd ser., 34 (1977): 519–41; and Nathan O. Hatch, *The Sacred Cause of Liberty: Republican Thought and the Millennium in Revolutionary New England* (1977).

Colonial Politics

For two views that clash sharply over provincial politics, compare Bernard Bailyn, *The Origins of American Politics* (1968), and Jack P. Greene, "Political Mimesis: A Consideration of the Historical and Cultural Roots of Legislative Behavior in the British Colonies in the Eighteenth Century," *American Historical Review* 75 (1969): 337–67. Greene elaborates his position in *Peripheries and Center: Constitutional Development in the Extended Polities of the British Empire and the United States, 1607–1788* (1987). More specialized studies include David Alan Williams, *Political Alignments in Colonial Virginia Politics* (1989); Robert M. Weir, "'The Harmony We Were Famous For': An Interpretation of Pre-Revolutionary South Carolina Politics," *William and Mary Quarterly*, 3rd ser., 26 (1969): 473–501; W. W. Abbot, *The Royal Governors of Georgia, 1754–1775* (1959); Alan Tully, *William Penn's Legacy: Politics and Social Structure in Provincial Pennsylvania, 1726–1755* (1977); Patricia U. Bonomi, *A Factious People: Politics and Society in Colonial New York* (1971); Stanley N. Katz, *Newcastle's New York: Anglo-American Politics, 1732–1753* (1968); William Pencak, *War, Politics, and Revolution in Provincial Massachusetts* (1981); Richard L. Bushman, *King and People in Provincial Massachusetts* (1985); and Jere R. Daniell, "Politics in New Hampshire under Governor Benning Wentworth," *William and Mary Quarterly*, 3rd

ser., 23 (1966): 76–105. Two recent studies examine middle-colony politics on a regional scale. They are Alan Tully, *Forming American Politics: Ideals, Interests, and Institutions in Colonial New York and Pennsylvania* (1994); and Benjamin H. Newcombe, *Political Partisanship in the American Middle Colonies, 1700–1776* (1995).

The Renewal of Imperial Conflict

Richard Harding, *Amphibious Warfare in the Eighteenth Century: The British Expeditions to the West Indies* (1991), is the best account of the Caribbean theater during the War of Jenkins's Ear. For important perspectives on the crisis in the Deep South from 1739 to 1742, see Jane Landers, "Gracia Real de Santa Teresa de Mose: A Free Black Town in Spanish Colonial Florida," *American Historical Review* 95 (1990): 9–30; John Thornton, "African Dimensions of the Stono Rebellion," *American Historical Review* 96 (1991): 1101–113; and Larry E. Ivers, *British Drums on the Southern Frontier: The Military Colonization of Georgia, 1733–1749* (1974). T. J. Davis, *A Rumor of Revolt: The "Great Negro Plot" in Colonial New York* (1985), is standard. John A. Schutz, *William Shirley, King's Governor of Massachusetts* (1961), is a good introduction to King George's War. Strong specialized studies include Robert E. Wall Jr., "Louisbourg, 1745," *New England Quarterly* 37 (1964): 64–83; and John Lax and William Pencak, "The Knowles Riot and the Crisis of the 1740s in Massachusetts," *Perspectives in American History* 10 (1976): 163–214.

The War for North America

Fred Anderson, *Crucible of War: The Seven Years' War and the Fate of Empire in British North America, 1754–1766* (2000) is a brilliant narrative and compelling synthesis. Lawrence H. Gipson, *The British Empire before the American Revolution*, 15 vols. (1936–1972), is the most detailed narrative ever written for the period 1748–1776 and is ardently pro-empire. Volumes four and five cover the background to the fourth Anglo-French war, which Gipson calls "the Great War for the Empire." Volumes six and seven cover the war in North America. Three other standard works are Robert C. Newbold, *The Albany Congress and Plan of Union of 1754* (1955); Alison G. Olson, "The British Government and Colonial Union in 1754," *William and Mary Quarterly*, 3rd ser., 17 (1960): 22–34; and Paul E. Kopperman, *Braddock at the Monongahela* (1977). Francis Jennings, *Empire of Fortune: Crowns, Colonies, and Tribes in the Seven Years War in America* (1988), tries to put Indians at the center of the conflict, not on the margins, as do earlier narratives. Two much-needed Canadian perspectives, both of which are highly critical of Montcalm, can be found in Guy Frégault, *Canada: The War of the Conquest* (1968), and D. Peter MacLeod, "The Canadians against the French: The Struggle for Control of the Expedition to Oswego in 1756," *Ontario History* 80 (1988): 143–57. Ian K. Steele, *Betrayals: Fort William Henry and the "Massacre"* (1990), is innovative and persuasive. Victor L. Johnson explores some of the dilemmas of smuggling in "Fair Traders and Smugglers in Philadelphia, 1754–1763," *Pennsylvania Magazine of History and Biography*

83 (1959): 125–49. Fred Anderson, *A People's Army: Massachusetts Soldiers and Society in the Seven Years' War* (1984), emphasizes the contractual principles of colonial soldiers at the outset of the war. In *Empire and Liberty: American Resistance to British Authority, 1755–1763* (1974), Alan Rogers overstates the confrontation between colonists and imperial officials by failing to notice that it had largely been resolved by 1758. Harold E. Selesky, *War and Society in Colonial Connecticut* (1990), argues that the colonists became more soldierly as the war progressed. Tom Hatley, *The Dividing Paths: Cherokees and South Carolinians through the Era of Revolution* (1993), covers the Cherokee War.

CHAPTER 5 REFORM, RESISTANCE, REVOLUTION

General Histories

Good general histories of the American Revolution include Robert M. Calhoon's moderate *Revolutionary America: An Interpretive Overview* (1976), Edward Countryman's more radical *The American Revolution* (1985), and Colin Bonwick's recent British perspective in *The American Revolution* (1991). Major attempts to understand the broader significance of the Revolution include Robert R. Palmer, *The Age of the Democratic Revolution, 1760–1800*, 2 vols. (1959–1964), which sees a close affinity between the American and French Revolutions; Lester D. Langley, *The Americas in the Age of Revolution, 1750–1850* (1996), which compares the American Revolution with Haiti's successful slave revolt and with the Latin American struggles for independence; Marc Egnal, *A Mighty Empire: The Origins of the American Revolution* (1988), which argues that westward expansion provided the underlying thrust for independence; and Gordon S. Wood, *The Radicalism of the American Revolution* (1992), which insists that the Revolution was the most important defining event in American history and the most successful revolution in world history. Merrill Jensen's *The Founding of a Nation: A History of the American Revolution, 1763–1776* (1968) remains the best one-volume history of the coming of the Revolution. Robert W. Tucker and David C. Hendrickson, *The Fall of the First British Empire: Origins of the War of American Independence* (1982), is intelligent but argumentative. Bernard Bailyn's *The Ideological Origins of the American Revolution* (1967) has had an enormous impact on studies of the Revolution and the early republic.

Pontiac's War

Howard H. Peckham, *Pontiac and the Indian Uprising* (1947), although aging badly, remains the standard narrative. Gregory E. Dowd, *A Spirited Resistance: The North American Indian Struggle for Unity, 1745–1815* (1992), explores the religious roots of pan-Native American identity; and Dowd offers a fresh perspective on the goals of the uprising in "The French King Wakes Up in Detroit: 'Pontiac's War' in Rumor and History," *Ethnohistory* 37 (1990): 254–78. Bernhard Knollenberg sets out to refute the allegation of germ warfare but ends up affirming it in "General Amherst and Germ Warfare," *Mississippi Valley Historical Review* 41 (1954–1955): 489–94, 762–63. Alden T. Vaughan describes the murderous violence that followed the war in "Frontier Banditti and the Indians: The Paxton Boys' Legacy, 1763–1775," *Pennsylvania History*, 51 (1984): 1–29.

British Politics and the Revolution

Important recent studies of British politics and policy beginning in the late 1750s include Marie Peters, *Pitt and Popularity: The Patriot Minister and London Opinion during the Seven Years' War* (1981); Richard Middleton, *The Bells of Victory: The Pitt-Newcastle Ministry and the Conduct of the Seven Years' War, 1757–1762* (1985); John Brewer, *Party, Ideology, and Popular Politics at the Accession of George III* (1976); John L. Bullion, *A Great and Necessary Measure: George Grenville and the Genesis of the Stamp Act, 1763–1765* (1982); Paul Langford, *The First Rockingham Administration, 1765–1766* (1973); George F. E. Rudé, *Wilkes and Liberty: A Social Study of 1763 to 1774* (1962); Peter D. G. Thomas, *British Politics and the Stamp Act Crisis: The First Phase of the American Revolution, 1763–1767* (1975); Thomas, *John Wilkes: A Friend to Liberty* (1996); Thomas, *The Townshend Duties Crisis: The Second Phase of the American Revolution, 1767–1773* (1987); and Thomas, *Tea Party to Independence: The Third Phase of the American Revolution, 1773–1776* (1991).

The First Two Imperial Crises

Alison G. Olson, *Making the Empire Work: London and American Interest Groups, 1690–1790* (1992), is perceptive on the breakdown of imperial authority after 1760. Edmund S. and Helen M. Morgan, *The Stamp Act Crisis, Prologue to Revolution*, 3rd ed. (1953, 1995), has become a classic. Pauline Maier, *From Resistance to Revolution: Colonial Radicals and the Development of American Opposition to Britain, 1765–1776* (1972), emphasizes the links between the Sons of Liberty and the English Wilkite movement. The best studies of merchants and the resistance movement are John W. Tyler, *Smugglers and Patriots: Boston Merchants and the Advent of the American Revolution* (1986), and Thomas H. Doerflinger, *A Vigorous Spirit of Enterprise: Merchants and Economic Development in Revolutionary Philadelphia* (1986). Hiller Zobel's *The Boston Massacre* (1970) is the standard study, but Jesse Lemisch's review in *The Harvard Law Review* 84 (1970–71) makes some telling criticisms. Richard D. Brown, *Revolutionary Politics in Massachusetts: The Boston Committee of Correspondence and the Towns* (1970), is a fine study of the growth of disaffection. John Shy's *Toward Lexington: The Role of the British Army in the Coming of the American Revolution* (1965) remains indispensable.

Internal Discontent

Gary B. Nash, *The Urban Crucible: Social Change, Political Consciousness, and the Origins of the American Revolution* (1979), is a superb study of social tensions in Boston, New York, and Philadelphia. Rowland Berthoff and John M. Murrin, "Feudalism, Communalism, and the Yeoman Freeholder: The American Revolution considered as a Social

Accident," in Stephen G. Kurtz and James H. Hutson, eds., *Essays on the American Revolution* (1973), pp. 256–88, lays out the feudal revival. Conflicting views about the New York manor lords emerge from Sung Bok Kim's favorable portrait in *Landlord and Tenant in Colonial New York: Manorial Society, 1664–1775* (1978) and from Edward Countryman's more negative analysis in *A People in Revolution: The American Revolution and Political Society in New York, 1760–1790* (1981). An excellent study of the New Jersey riots is Thomas L. Purvis, "Origins and Patterns of Agrarian Unrest in New Jersey," *William and Mary Quarterly*, 3rd ser., 39 (1982): 600–627. James H. Hutson, *Pennsylvania Politics, 1746–1770: The Movement for Royal Government and Its Consequences* (1972), explores the Quaker Party's assault on Pennsylvania's proprietary regime. Ronald Hoffman's *A Spirit of Dissension: Economics, Politics, and the Revolution in Maryland* (1973) is the best study of internal tensions in revolutionary Maryland. Woody Holton imaginatively explores the onset of revolution in Virginia in his *Forced Founders: Indians, Debtors, Slaves, and the Making of the American Revolution in Virginia* (1999). On North Carolina's internal tensions, see A. Roger Ekirch, *"Poor Carolina": Politics and Society in Colonial North Carolina, 1729–1776* (1981); James P. Whittenburg, "Planters, Merchants, and Lawyers: Social Change and the Origins of the North Carolina Regulation," *William and Mary Quarterly*, 3rd ser., 34 (1977): 214–38; and E. Merton Coulter, "The Granville District," *James Sprunt Historical Studies* 13 (1913): 33–56. Three excellent South Carolina studies are Richard M. Brown, *The South Carolina Regulators* (1963); Rachel N. Klein, *Unification of a Slave State: The Rise of the Planter Class in the South Carolina Backcountry, 1760–1808* (1990); and Jack P. Greene, "Bridge to Revolution: The Wilkes Fund Controversy in South Carolina, 1769–1775," *Journal of Southern History* 29 (1963): 19–52. Alan Taylor, *Liberty Men and Great Proprietors: The Revolutionary Settlement on the Frontier, 1760–1820* (1990), finds strong backcountry resentments in Maine, although they peaked rather later.

David Grimsted, "Anglo-American Racism and Phillis Wheatley's 'Sable Veil,' 'Length'ned Chain,' and 'Knitted Heart,'" in Ronald Hoffman and Peter J. Albert, eds., *Women in the Age of the American Revolution* (1989), pp. 338–444, is a superb study of the emerging antislavery movement and the role of women in it.

The Third Imperial Crisis

Benjamin W. Labaree's *The Boston Tea Party* (1964) is the fullest study of that event. David Ammerman's *In the Common Cause: American Response to the Coercive Acts of 1774* (1974) carefully traces the aftermath. Philip Lawson, *The Imperial Challenge: Quebec and Britain in the Age of the American Revolution* (1989), ends with the Quebec Act. David Hackett Fischer, *Paul Revere's Ride* (1994), is a brilliant study of how the Revolutionary War began. Jerrilyn Greene Marston, *King and Congress: The Transfer of Political Legitimacy from the King to the Continental Congress, 1774–76* (1987), is fresh and insightful. Together, Richard A. Ryerson's *The Revolution Is Now Begun: The Radical Committees of*

Philadelphia, 1765–1776 (1978); Larry R. Gerlach's *Prologue to Revolution: New Jersey in the Coming of the American Revolution* (1976); and Joseph S. Tiedemann's *Reluctant Revolutionaries: New York City and the Road to Independence, 1763–1776* (1997) analyze the radicalization of politics in three critical colonies. Explorations of other aspects of the movement toward independence can be found in Eric Foner's *Tom Paine and Revolutionary America* (1976), Jack N. Rakove's *The Beginnings of National Politics: An Interpretive History of the Continental Congress* (1979), and James H. Hutson's "The Partition Treaty and the Declaration of American Independence," *Journal of American History* 58 (1971–1972): 877–896. Garry Wills, *Inventing America: Jefferson's Declaration of Independence* (1978), and Jay Fliegelman, *Declaring Independence: Jefferson, Natural Language, and the Culture of Performance* (1993), are imaginative studies by literary scholars. Pauline Maier, *American Scripture: Making the Declaration of Independence* (1997), uses 90 local declarations in the spring of 1776 to give context to Jefferson's famous text.

Videos

The musical *1776* (1972), while it makes no claim to serious historical reconstruction of events, has many delightful scenes, even if it burlesques Richard Henry Lee and gives John Adams more credit than Thomas Jefferson for American independence.

CHAPTER 6 THE REVOLUTIONARY REPUBLIC

The Revolutionary War

Major histories of the Revolutionary War include Piers Mackesy, *The War for America, 1775–1783* (1964), which argues that Britain could have won; Don Higginbotham, *The War of American Independence: Military Attitudes, Policies, and Practices, 1763–1789* (1971); Marshall Smelser, *The Winning of Independence* (1972); Jeremy Black, *War for America: The Fight for Independence, 1775–1783* (1991), which is nicely illustrated; and Stephen Conway, *The War of American Independence* (1995). For differing views on the Continental Army, compare Charles Royster, *A Revolutionary People at War: The Continental Army and American Character, 1775–1783* (1979), and James Kirby Martin and Mark E. Lender, *A Respectable Army: The Military Origins of the Republic, 1763–1789* (1982). John Shy, *A People Numerous and Armed: Reflections on the Military Struggle for American Independence*, rev. ed. (1990), contains several provocative essays, especially on the political role of the militia. Mark V. Kwasny, *Washington's Partisan War, 1775–1783* (1996), argues that effective use of the militia became a major component of Washington's strategy. Howard H. Peckham, ed., *The Toll of Independence: Engagements and Battle Casualties of the American Revolution* (1974), documents the war's high mortality rate. Outstanding studies of the wartime experience of particular states include John E. Selby, *The Revolu-*

tion in Virginia, 1775–1783 (1988), Richard Buel, *Dear Liberty: Connecticut's Mobilization for the Revolutionary War* (1981), and Buel *In Irons: Britain's Naval Supremacy and the American Revolutionary Economy* (1998).

Strong studies of major campaigns include Ira D. Gruber, *The Howe Brothers and the American Revolution* (1972); Thomas Fleming, *1776: Year of Illusions* (1975); Alfred H. Bill, *The Campaign of Princeton, 1776–1777* (1948); John S. Pancake, *1777: The Year of the Hangman* (1977); Pancake, *This Destructive War: The British Campaign in the Carolinas, 1780–1782* (1985); Max M. Mintz, *The Generals of Saratoga: John Burgoyne and Horatio Gates* (1990); David G. Martin, *The Philadelphia Campaign, June 1777–July 1778* (1993); Thomas Fleming, *The Forgotten Victory: The Battle for New Jersey* (1975), on Springfield in 1780; Russell F. Weigley, *The Partisan War: The South Carolina Campaign of 1780–1782* (1970), which is brief but brilliant; and Thomas Fleming, *Beat the Last Drum: The Siege of Yorktown, 1781* (1963). The essays in Ronald Hoffman, Thad W. Tate, and Peter J. Albert, eds., *An Uncivil War: The Southern Backcountry during the American Revolution* (1985), offer a variety of perspectives on the region most fiercely divided by the Revolution. Diplomacy is well covered in Jonathan R. Dull, *A Diplomatic History of the American Revolution* (1985), and Richard B. Morris, *The Peacemakers: The Great Powers and American Independence* (1965). Lee Kennett, *The French Forces in America, 1780–1783* (1977), is standard. Still offering the fullest studies of army discontent are Carl Van Doren, *Mutiny in January: The Story of a Crisis in the Continental Army* (1943), and Richard H. Kohn, "The Inside History of the Newburgh Conspiracy: America and the Coup d'État," *William and Mary Quarterly*, 3rd ser., 27 (1970): 187–220.

Biographies
Most major men of the Revolutionary Era have attracted multiple and often multivolume biographies. Among the more accessible are John Ferling, *John Adams: A Life* (1992); James T. Flexner, *The Traitor and the Spy: Benedict Arnold and John André* (1953, or 1975 illustrated ed.); Isabel T. Kelsay, *Joseph Brant, 1743–1807: Man of Two Worlds* (1984); John Mack Faragher, *Daniel Boone: The Life and Legend of an American Pioneer* (1992); Theodore Thayer, *Nathanael Greene: Strategist of the American Revolution* (1960); John C. Miller, *Alexander Hamilton, Portrait in Paradox* (1959); Joseph J. Ellis, *American Sphinx: The Character of Thomas Jefferson* (1997); Lance Banning, *The Sacred Fire of Liberty: James Madison and the Founding of the Federal Republic* (1995); Marcus Cunliffe, *George Washington: Man and Monument* (1958); and Garry Wills, *George Washington and the Enlightenment: Images of Power in Early America* (1984).

Loyalism
Robert M. Calhoon's *The Loyalists in Revolutionary America* (1973) is comprehensive, while Wallace Brown's *The Good Americans: Loyalists in the American Revolution* (1969) is briefer. Important specialized studies include Paul H. Smith, "The American Loyalists: Notes on Their Organization and Numerical Strength," *William and Mary Quarterly*, 3rd ser.,

25 (1968): 259–277; Smith, *Loyalists and Redcoats: A Study in British Revolutionary Policy* (1964); Mary Beth Norton, *The British Americans: Loyalist Exiles in England, 1774–1789* (1972); Norton, "The Fate of Some Black Loyalists of the American Revolution," *Journal of Negro History* 58 (1973): 202–226; Charles Royster, "'The Nature of Treason': Revolutionary Virtue and American Reactions to Benedict Arnold," *William and Mary Quarterly*, 3rd ser., 36 (1979): 163–193; Janice Potter, *The Liberty We Seek: Loyalist Ideology in Colonial New York and Massachusetts* (1983); Ann G. Condon, *The Envy of the American States: The Loyalist Dream for New Brunswick* (1984); and Jane Errington, *The Lion, the Eagle, and Upper Canada: A Developing Colonial Ideology* (1987).

Republicanism and Constitutionalism
The fullest study of an emerging American identity is David Waldstreicher, *In the Midst of Perpetual Fetes: The Making of American Nationalism, 1776–1820* (1997). Gordon S. Wood, *The Creation of the American Republic, 1776–1787* (1969), has been the most influential study of early American republicanism and constitutionalism. Thomas L. Pangle dissents sharply from Wood in *The Spirit of Modern Republicanism: The Moral Vision of the American Founders and the Philosophy of Locke* (1988). Other important contributions include Willi Paul Adams, *The First American Constitutions: Republican Ideology and the Making of the State Constitutions in the Revolutionary Era* (1980), and H. James Henderson, *Party Politics in the Continental Congress* (1974). Two standard works on hyperinflation and its consequences during the revolutionary era are E. James Ferguson, *The Power of the Purse: A History of American Public Finance, 1776–1790* (1961), and John K. Alexander, "The Fort Wilson Incident of 1779: A Study of the Revolutionary Crowd," *William and Mary Quarterly*, 3rd ser., 31 (1974): 589–612.

Indians, the West, and the Revolution
On the eastern woodland Indian nations during the Revolution, see Gregory E. Dowd, *A Spirited Resistance: The North American Indian Struggle for Unity, 1745–1815* (1992); Colin B. Calloway, *The American Revolution in Indian Country: Crisis and Diversity in Native American Communities* (1995); and Barbara Graymont, *The Iroquois in the American Revolution* (1972). Stephen Aron, *How the West Was Lost: The Transformation of Kentucky from Daniel Boone to Henry Clay* (1995), and R. Douglas Hurt, *The Ohio Frontier: Crucible of the Old Northwest* (1996), are fresh and challenging.

Social Transformations
John F. Jameson, *The American Revolution Considered as a Social Movement* (1925), remains provocative. Other indispensable studies of slavery and emancipation include Benjamin Quarles, *The Negro in the American Revolution* (1961, 1996); Ira Berlin and Ronald Hoffman, eds., *Slavery and Freedom in the Age of the American Revolution* (1983); Sylvia R. Frey, *Water from the Rock: Black Resistance in a Revolutionary Age* (1991); Arthur Zilversmit, *The First Emancipation: The Abolition of Slavery in the North* (1967); Gary B. Nash, *Forging Freedom:*

The Formation of Philadelphia's Black Community, 1720–1840 (1988); and Shane White, *Somewhat More Independent: The End of Slavery in New York City, 1770–1810* (1991).

For comprehensive studies of gender and age relations in the era, see Mary Beth Norton, *Liberty's Daughters: The Revolutionary Experience of American Women, 1750–1800* (1979); Linda Kerber, *Women of the Republic: Intellect and Ideology in Revolutionary America* (1980); Rosemarie Zagarrie, "Morals, Manners, and the Republican Mother," *American Quarterly* 44 (1992): 192–215; Ronald Hoffman and Peter J. Albert, eds., *Women in the Age of the American Revolution* (1989); and David Hackett Fischer, *Growing Old in America* (1978). More specialized but highly significant studies include Laurel Thatcher Ulrich, *A Midwife's Tale: The Life of Martha Ballard, Based on Her Diary, 1785–1812* (1990); Barbara Clark Smith, "Food Rioters and the American Revolution," *William and Mary Quarterly*, 3rd ser., 51 (1994): 3–38; Judith A. Klinghoffer and Lois Elkis, "The Petticoat Electors: Women's Suffrage in New Jersey, 1776–1807," *Journal of the Early Republic* 12 (1992): 159–93; Cathy N. Davidson, *Revolution and the Word: The Rise of the Novel in America* (1986); and Joel Perlman and Dennis Shirley, "When Did New England Women Acquire Literacy?" *William and Mary Quarterly*, 3rd ser., 48 (1991): 50–67.

For religious changes, see Ronald Hoffman and Peter J. Albert, eds., *Religion in a Revolutionary Age* (1994); Hamilton J. Eckenrode, *Separation of Church and State in Virginia: A Study in the Development of the Revolution* (1910); Thomas O. Hanley, *Their Rights and Liberties: The Beginnings of Religious and Political Freedom in Maryland* (1959); Frank Baker, *From Wesley to Asbury: Studies in Early American Methodism* (1976); Stephen A. Marini, *Radical Sects of Revolutionary New England* (1982); and Susan Juster, *Disorderly Women: Sexual Politics and Evangelicalism in Revolutionary New England* (1994).

Confederation and Constitution

General histories of the Confederation era include Merrill Jensen, *The New Nation: A History of the United States during the Articles of Confederation* (1950); Forrest McDonald, *E Pluribus Unum: The Formation of the American Republic* (1965); and Richard B. Morris, *The Forging of the Union, 1781–1789* (1987). Jackson Turner Main, *Political Parties before the Constitution* (1973), is a comprehensive study of state politics; also essential is his "Government by the People: The American Revolution and the Democratization of the Legislatures," *William and Mary Quarterly*, 3rd ser., 23 (1966): 354–67. On events from the rise of the Berkshire Constitutionalists through Shays's Rebellion, consult Robert J. Taylor, *Western Massachusetts in the Revolution* (1954), and John L. Brooke, "To the Quiet of the People: Revolutionary Settlements and Civil Unrest in Western Massachusetts, 1774–1789," *William and Mary Quarterly*, 3rd ser., 46 (1989): 425–62. For challenging perspectives on the Northwest Ordinance, see Peter S. Onuf, *Statehood and Union: A History of the Northwest Ordinance* (1987), and Staughton Lynd, "The Compromise of 1787," *Political Science Quarterly* 71 (1966): 225–50.

Jack N. Rakove, *Original Meanings: Politics and Ideas in the Making of the Constitution* (1996), won a Pulitzer Prize. Robert A. Rutland's *The Ordeal of the Constitution: The Antifederalists and the Ratification Struggle of 1787–1788* (1966) is still the fullest history of the ratification struggle, but two other works with telling points to make are Saul Cornell, *The Other Founders: Anti-Federalism and the Dissenting Tradition in America* (1999); and Kenneth R. Bowling, "'A Tub to the Whale': The Founding Fathers and the Adoption of the Federal Bill of Rights," *Journal of the Early Republic* 8 (1988): 223–51.

CHAPTER 7 THE DEMOCRATIC REPUBLIC, 1790–1820

For good introductions to social and economic trends in these years, see Melvyn Stokes and Stephen Conway, eds., *The Market Revolution in America* (1996), and the *Journal of the Early Republic* 16 (Summer 1996). James A. Henretta, *The Origins of American Capitalism: Collected Essays* (1991), and Alan Kulikoff, *The Agrarian Origins of American Capitalism* (1992), are theoretically sophisticated social histories of the American economy in these years. Still essential is Douglas C. North, *The Economic Growth of the United States, 1790–1860* (1961).

The Northeast

On rural society after the Revolution, the most thorough regional study is Christopher Clark, *The Roots of Rural Capitalism: Western Massachusetts, 1780–1860* (1990). Laurel Thatcher Ulrich, *A Midwife's Tale: The Life of Martha Ballard, Based on Her Diary, 1785–1812* (1990), is a beautiful and insightful account. Jack Larkin, *The Reshaping of Everyday Life, 1790–1840* (1988), is a valuable synthesis of scholarship on material culture, particularly in the Northeast. Also valuable are Winifred Barr Rothenberg, *From Market-Places to Market Economy: The Transformation of Rural Massachusetts, 1750–1850* (1994); Thomas Dublin, *Transforming Women's Work: New England Lives in the Industrial Revolution* (1994); Joan M. Jensen, *Loosening the Bonds: Mid-Atlantic Farm Women, 1750–1850* (1986); Toby L. Ditz, *Property and Kinship: Inheritance in Early Connecticut, 1750–1820* (1986); and the essays in Stephen Innes, ed., *Work and Labor in Early America* (1988). Other relevant studies are cited in the suggested readings for Chapter 9.

The West

Study of the postrevolutionary frontier begins with the final chapters of Richard White's magisterial *The Middle Ground: Indians, Empires, and Republics in the Great Lakes Region, 1650–1815* (1991). Other graceful and thoughtful accounts of Native Americans in these years include R. David Edmunds, *The Shawnee Prophet* (1983); Anthony F. C. Wallace, *The Death and Rebirth of the Seneca* (1969); William G. McLoughlin, *Cherokee Renaissance in the New Republic* (1986); Joel W. Martin, *Sacred Revolt: The Muskogees' Struggle for a New World* (1991); and Gregory Evans Dowd, *A Spirited Resistance: The North American Indian Struggle for Unity, 1745–1815* (1992).

White settler societies are ably treated in John Mack Faragher, *Daniel Boone: The Life and Legend of an American Pioneer* (1992); Stephen Aron, *How the West was Lost: The Transformation of Kentucky from Daniel Boone to Henry Clay* (1996); Andrew R. L. Cayton, *The Frontier Republic: Ideology and Politics in the Ohio Country, 1780–1825* (1986); Alan Taylor, *Liberty Men and Great Proprietors: The Revolutionary Settlement on the Maine Frontier, 1760–1820* (1990); William Cooper's *Town: Power and Persuasion on the Frontier of the Early American Republic* (1995); and Thomas P. Slaughter, *The Whiskey Rebellion: Frontier Epilogue to the American Revolution* (1986).

The South

The best introduction to the slave South in these years is the final section of Ira Berlin, *Many Thousands Gone: The First Two Centuries of Slavery in America* (1998). Economic and demographic change is traced in Robert William Fogel and Stanley L. Engerman, *Time on the Cross: The Economics of American Negro Slavery*, 2 vols. (1974); Robert William Fogel, *Without Consent or Contract: The Rise and Fall of American Slavery* (1989); and Peter A. Coclanis, *The Shadow of a Dream: Economic Life and Death in the South Carolina Lowcountry, 1670–1920* (1989). The essays in Ira Berlin and Ronald Hoffman, eds., *Slavery and Freedom in the Age of the American Revolution* (1983), are essential, as are Barbara Jeane Fields, *Slavery and Freedom on the Middle Ground: Maryland during the Nineteenth Century* (1985); Ira Berlin, *Slaves without Masters: The Free Negro in the Antebellum South* (1974); Robert McColley, *Slavery and Jeffersonian Virginia*, 2nd ed. (1973). The limits of southern antislavery in these years are traced in David Brion Davis, *The Problem of Slavery in the Age of Revolution, 1770–1823* (1975), and in the relevant essays in Peter S. Onuf, ed., *Jeffersonian Legacies* (1993). On Gabriel's Rebellion, see James Sidbury, *Ploughshares into Swords: Race, Rebellion, and Identity in Gabriel's Virginia, 1730-1810* (1997), and Douglas R. Egerton, *Gabriel's Rebellion: The Virginia Slave Conspiracies of 1800 & 1802* (1993). Further studies of economic and social life in the South are listed in the suggested readings for Chapter 9.

Cities

David T. Gilchrist, ed., *The Growth of the Seaport Cities, 1790–1825* (1967), ably treats its subject. Thomas C. Cochran, *Frontiers of Change: Early Industrialization in America* (1981), synthesizes urban economic development. For the social history of cities in these years, see Howard B. Rock, *Artisans of the New Republic: The Tradesmen of New York City in the Age of Jefferson* (1979); Charles G. Steffen, *The Mechanics of Baltimore: Workers and Politics in the Age of Revolution, 1763–1812* (1984); the early chapters of Sean Wilentz, *Chants Democratic: New York City and the Rise of the American Working Class* (1984), and Christine Stansell, *City of Women: Sex and Class in New York, 1789–1860* (1986); Stuart M. Blumin, *The Emergence of the Middle Class: Social Experience in the American City, 1760–1900* (1989); and Elizabeth Blackmar, *Manhattan for Rent, 1785–1850* (1989). For other relevant studies, see the suggested readings for Chapter 9.

Cultural Trends

A stirring introduction to the "democratization of mind" in these years is the concluding section of Gordon S. Wood, *The Radicalism of the American Revolution* (1992). On suffrage, see Chilton Williamson, *American Suffrage from Property to Democracy* (1960). On print culture, see Cathy N. Davidson, *Revolution and the Word: The Rise of the Novel in America* (1986); Davidson, ed., *Reading in America: Literature and Social History* (1989); and William J. Gilmore, *Reading Becomes a Necessity of Life: Material and Cultural Life in Rural New England, 1780–1835* (1989). On drinking, W. J. Rorabaugh, *The Alcoholic Republic: An American Tradition* (1979).

Religion

The study of American religion in the postrevolutionary years begins with two books: Nathan O. Hatch, *The Democratization of American Christianity* (1989), and Jon Butler, *Awash in a Sea of Faith: Christianizing the American People* (1990). More specialized accounts include Christine Leigh Heyrman, *Southern Cross: The Beginnings of the Bible Belt* (1997); Paul K. Conkin, *Cane Ridge: America's Pentecost* (1990); John B. Boles, *The Great Revival, 1787–1805* (1972); and Stephen A. Marini, *Radical Sects of Revolutionary America* (1982). Religious developments among slaves and free blacks are treated in Sylvia R. Frey, *Water from the Rock: Black Resistance in a Revolutionary Age* (1991); Albert J. Raboteau, *Slave Religion: The 'Invisible Institution' in the Antebellum South* (1978); and the early essays in Paul E. Johnson, ed., *African-American Christianity: Essays in History* (1994). The "republicanization" of slave resistance is described in Eugene D. Genovese, *From Rebellion to Revolution: Afro-American Slave Revolts in the Making of the Modern World* (1979). Other works on early 19th century religion are listed in the suggested readings for Chapter 10.

CHAPTER 8 COMPLETING THE REVOLUTION, 1789–1815

Stanley Elkins and Eric McKitrick, *The Age of Federalism: The Early American Republic, 1788–1800* (1993), is the best study of politics in the 1790s. James Roger Sharp, *American Politics in the Early Republic: The New Nation in Crisis* (1993), is an extended interpretive essay; John C. Miller, *The Federalist Era, 1789–1801* (1960), remains the best brief account. Stephen G. Kurtz, *The Presidency of John Adams* (1957), is a valuable study of the second Federalist presidency.

Politics, 1790–1800

Federalist approaches to government and administration are the subjects of Ralph Ketcham, *Presidents above Party: The First American Presidency, 1789–1829* (1984); Leonard D. White, *The Federalists: A Study in Administrative History* (1948); and Carl E. Prince, *The Federalists and the Origins of the U.S. Civil Service* (1977). Specific issues are handled ably in Robert A. Rutland, *The Birth of the Bill of Rights, 1776–1791* (1955); Thomas G. Slaughter, *The Whiskey Rebellion: Frontier Epilogue* to the American Revolution (1986); Richard H. Kohn, *Eagle and Sword: The Federalists and the Creation of the Military Establishment in America, 1783–1802* (1975); and James M. Smith, *Freedom's Fetters: The Alien and Sedition Laws and American Civil Liberties*, rev. ed. (1967). The rise of Jeffersonian opposition is treated in Richard Hostadter, *The Idea of a Party System: The Rise of Legitimate Opposition in the United States, 1780–1840* (1970); Lance Banning, *The Jeffersonian Persuasion: Evolution of a Party Ideology* (1980); and Joyce Appleby, *Capitalism and a New Social Order: The Republican Vision of the 1790s* (1984). David Waldstreicher, *In the Midst of Perpetual Fetes: The Making of American Nationalism, 1776-1820* (1997) is a fascinating account of how Federalists and Republicans made and celebrated American nationhood in these and subsequent years.

Politics, 1800–1815

The classic work on national politics from 1801 to 1815 is Henry Adams, *History of the United States of America during the Administrations of Thomas Jefferson and of James Madison*, 9 vols. (1889–91; reprint, 2 vols., 1986). Marshall Smelser, *The Democratic Republic, 1801–1815* (1968), is a solid modern account, and Forrest McDonald, *The Presidency of Thomas Jefferson* (1976), is both critical and thoughtful. Drew R. McCoy, *The Elusive Republic: Political Economy in Jeffersonian America* (1980), is a stimulating essay on Jeffersonian economic policy. See also John R. Nelson Jr., *Liberty and Property: Political Economy and Policymaking in the New Nation, 1789–1812* (1987). The court controversies are treated in Richard E. Ellis, *The Jeffersonian Crisis: Courts and Politics in the Young Republic* (1971); Mary K. B. Tachau, *Federal Courts in the Early Republic: Kentucky, 1789–1816* (1978); Robert Lowry Clinton, *Marbury vs. Madison and Judicial Review* (1989); and R. Kent Newmyer, *The Supreme Court under Marshall and Taney* (1968). Other studies of domestic questions during the Jefferson and Madison administrations include Leonard B. White, *The Jeffersonians: A Study in Administrative History, 1801–1829* (1951); R. M. Johnstone, *Jefferson and the Presidency* (1978); and Robert W. Tucker and David C. Hendrickson, *Empire of Liberty: The Statecraft of Thomas Jefferson* (1990). Opposition to the Jeffersonians is treated in Norman K. Risjord, *The Old Republicans: Southern Conservatism in the Age of Jefferson* (1965); Robert E. Shalhope, *John Taylor of Caroline: Pastoral Republican* (1980); Linda K. Kerber, *Federalists in Dissent: Imagery and Ideology in Jeffersonian America* (1970); and James M. Banner Jr., *To the Hartford Convention: The Federalists and the Origins of Party Politics in Massachusetts, 1789–1815* (1969).

Foreign Affairs

A convenient introduction to foreign policy under the Federalists and Jeffersonians is Bradford Perkins, *The Creation of a Republican Empire, 1776–1860*, vol. 1 of *The Cambridge History of American Foreign Relations* (1993). Also helpful is Reginald Horsman, *The Diplomacy of the New Republic, 1776–1815* (1985). More specialized accounts include Harry Ammon, *The Genêt Mission* (1973); Samuel F. Bemis's classic studies, *Jay's Treaty*, 2nd ed. (1962), and *Pinckney's Treaty*, 2nd ed. (1960); Jerald A. Combs, *The Jay Treaty* (1970); Wiley Sword,

President Washington's Indian War: The Struggle for the Old Northwest, 1790–1795 (1985); Alexander DeConde, *The Quasi-War: Politics and Diplomacy of the Undeclared War with France, 1797–1801* (1966), and *This Affair of Louisiana* (1976); William Stinchcombe, *The XYZ Affair* (1981); Lawrence Kaplan, *"Entangling Alliances with None": American Foreign Policy in the Age of Jefferson* (1987); and Bradford Perkins, *The First Rapprochement: England and the United States, 1795–1805* (1967). On the diplomatic, political, and military history of the War of 1812, the essential accounts are Bradford Perkins, *Prologue to War: England and the United States, 1805–1812* (1961); Clifford L. Egan, *Neither Peace nor War: Franco-American Relations, 1803–1812* (1983); J. C. A. Stagg, *Mr. Madison's War: Politics, Diplomacy, and Warfare in the Early Republic, 1783–1830* (1983); and Donald R. Hickey, *The War of 1812: A Forgotten Conflict* (1989).

Biographies

National politics under the Federalists and Jeffersonians can be approached through several excellent biographies. The multivolume works of Douglas Southall Freeman on Washington, Dumas Malone on Jefferson, and Irving Brant on Madison are definitive. The following are good single-volume studies of individuals: John R. Alden, *George Washington: A Biography* (1984); Marcus Cunliffe, *George Washington: Man and Monument* (1958); Gerald Stourzh, *Alexander Hamilton and the Idea of a Republican Government* (1970); Forrest McDonald, *Alexander Hamilton: A Biography* (1979); Peter Shaw, *The Character of John Adams* (1976); Joseph J. Ellis, *American Sphinx: The Character of Thomas Jefferson* (1997); Merrill Peterson, *Thomas Jefferson and the New Nation* (1960); Nobel E. Cunningham, *In Pursuit of Reason: The Life of Thomas Jefferson* (1987); Ralph Ketcham, *James Madison: A Biography* (1971); and Drew R. McCoy, *The Last of the Fathers: James Madison and the Republican Legacy* (1989).

CHAPTER 9 THE MARKET REVOLUTION, 1815–1860

Works on the earlier phases of most questions covered in this chapter are included in the suggested readings for Chapter 7.

The American Economy

Charles G. Sellers, *The Market Revolution: Jacksonian America, 1815–1848* (1991), is a broad synthesis of economic, cultural, and political development. More narrowly economic surveys include Douglass C. North, *The Economic Growth of the United States, 1790–1860* (1961); George Rogers Taylor, *The Transportation Revolution, 1815–1860* (1951); Allan R. Pred, *Urban Growth and the Circulation of Information: The United States System of Cities, 1790–1840* (1973); Harry N. Scheiber, *Ohio Canal Era: A Case Study of Government and the Economy, 1820–1861*, 2nd ed. (1987); Ronald E. Shaw, *Erie Water West* (1966); Albert Fishlow, *American Railroads and the Transformation of the Ante-Bellum Economy* (1965); and Erik F. Haites, James Mak, and Gary M. Walton, *Western River Transportation: The Era of Early Internal Development, 1810–1860* (1975). On the role of federal and state courts, see R. Kent Newmeyer, *The Supreme Court under Marshall and Taney* (1968); Francis N. Stites, *John Marshall: Defender of the Constitution* (1981); and, especially, Morton J. Horwitz, *The Transformation of American Law, 1780–1860* (1977).

Farmers

The market revolution in northern and western agriculture is treated in Christopher Clark, *The Roots of Rural Capitalism: Western Massachusetts, 1780–1860* (1990); Carolyn Merchant, *Ecological Revolutions: Nature, Gender, and Science in New England* (1989); John Mack Faragher, *Sugar Creek: Life on the Illinois Prairie* (1986); Joan M. Jensen, *Loosening the Bonds: Mid-Atlantic Farm Women, 1750–1850* (1986); and Jack Larkin, *The Reshaping of Everyday Life, 1790–1840* (1988). Still useful is R. Carlyle Buley, *The Old Northwest: Pioneer Period, 1815–1840*, 2 vols. (1950).

Industry

Solid studies of early industrial communities include Thomas Dublin, *Women at Work: The Transformation of Work and Community in Lowell, Massachusetts, 1826–1860* (1979); Jonathan Prude, *The Coming of Industrial Order: Town and Factory Life in Rural Massachusetts, 1810–1860* (1983); Anthony F. C. Wallace, *Rockdale: The Growth of an American Village in the Early Industrial Revolution* (1978); Alan Dawley, *Class and Community: The Industrial Revolution in Lynn* (1976); and Mary H. Blewett, *Men, Women, and Work: Class, Gender, and Protest in the New England Shoe Industry, 1780–1910* (1990). On the transformation of cities, see Stuart M. Blumin, *The Emergence of the Middle Class: Social Experience in the American City, 1760–1900* (1989); Edward Pessen, *Riches, Class, and Power before the Civil War* (1973); Bruce Laurie, *Working People of Philadelphia, 1800–1850* (1980); Sean Wilentz, *Chants Democratic: New York City & the Rise of the American Working Class, 1788–1850* (1984); and Christine Stansell, *City of Women: Sex and Class in New York, 1789–1860* (1986).

The Slave South

Mark M. Smith, *Debating Slavery: Economy and Society in the Antebellum American South* (1998) provides a solid introductory overview of the economics of the plantation South. Students should also consult Robert William Fogel and Stanley Engerman's controversial *Time on the Cross: The Economics of American Negro Slavery*, 2 vols. (1974), and R. W. Fogel, *Without Consent or Contract: The Rise and Fall of American Slavery* (1989). Other useful studies include Orville Vernon Burton, *In My Father's House Are Many Mansions: Family and Community in Edgefield, South Carolina* (1985); Eugene D. Genovese, *The Political Economy of Slavery: Studies in the Economy and Society of the Slave South*, 2nd ed. (1989); James Oakes, *The Ruling Race: A History of American Slaveholders* (1982); Gavin Wright, *The Political Economy of the Cotton South: Households, Markets, and Wealth in the Nineteenth Century* (1978); and Elizabeth Fox-Genovese, *Within the Plantation Household: Black and White Women of the Old South* (1988). On the southern yeomanry, see Stephanie McCurry,

Masters of Small Worlds: Yeoman Households, Gender Relations, & the Political Culture of the Antebellum South Carolina Lowcountry (1995); Steven Hahn, *The Roots of Southern Populism: Yeomen Farmers and the Transformation of the Georgia Upcountry, 1850–1890* (1983); J. William Harris, *Plain Folk and Gentry in a Slave Society: White Liberty and Black Slavery in Augusta's Hinterlands* (1985); and Grady McWhiney, *Cracker Culture: Celtic Folkways in the Old South* (1988).

CHAPTER 10 TOWARD AN AMERICAN CULTURE

The Middle Classes

Stuart M. Blumin, *The Emergence of the Middle Class: Social Experience in the American City, 1760–1900* (1989), is a thorough study of work and material life among the urban middle class. Studies that treat religion, family, and sentimental culture include Paul E. Johnson, *A Shopkeeper's Millennium: Society and Revivals in Rochester, New York, 1815–1837* (1978); Mary P. Ryan, *Cradle of the Middle Class: The Family in Oneida County, New York, 1790–1865* (1981); Carroll Smith-Rosenberg, *Disorderly Conduct: Visions of Gender in Victorian America* (1985); Karen Halttunen, *Confidence Men and Painted Women: A Study of Middle-Class Culture in America, 1830–1870* (1982); and Jane Tompkins, *Sensational Designs: The Cultural Work of American Fiction, 1790–1860* (1985). On art and artists, see Neil Harris, *The Artist in American Society: The Formative Years, 1790–1860* (1966); Barbara Novak, *Nature and Culture: American Landscape and Painting, 1825–1875* (1980); Angela Miller, *The Empire of the Eye: Landscape Representation and American Cultural Politics, 1825–1875* (1993); and Elizabeth McKinsey, *Niagara Falls: Icon of the American Sublime* (1985).

Popular Religion

Lewis O. Saum, *The Popular Mood of Pre–Civil War America* (1980), is a valuable study of the unsentimental culture of antebellum plain folk. The most thorough treatments of popular evangelicalism are the works of Jon Butler and Nathan Hatch listed in the suggested readings for Chapter 7. See also Curtis D. Johnson, *Redeeming America: Evangelicals and the Road to Civil War* (1993); Michael Barkun, *Crucible of the Millennium: The Burned-Over District of New York in the 1840s* (1986); David L. Rowe, *Thunder and Trumpets: Millerites and Dissenting Religion in Upstate New York, 1800–1850* (1985); Paul E. Johnson and Sean Wilentz, *The Kingdom of Matthias: A Story of Sex and Salvation in 19th-Century America* (1994); and John L. Brooke, *The Refiner's Fire: The Making of Mormon Cosmology, 1644–1844* (1994).

Popular Entertainments

Studies of popular literature and entertainments in these years include Elliott J. Gorn, *The Manly Art: Bare-Knuckle Prize Fighting in America* (1986); Melvin L. Adelman, *A Sporting Time: New York City and the Rise of Modern Athletics* (1986); Alexander P. Saxton, *The Rise and Fall of the White*

Republic: Class Politics and Mass Culture in Nineteenth-Century America (1990); Eric Lott, *Love & Theft: Blackface Minstrelsy and the American Working Class* (1993); Michael Denning, *Mechanic Accents: Dime Novels and Working-Class Culture in America* (1987); David S. Reynolds, *Beneath the American Renaissance: The Subversive Imagination in the Age of Emerson and Melville* (1988); and Walt Whitman's *America: A Cultural Biography* (1995). New directions in literary criticism in these years can be sampled in Sacvan Bercovitch and Myra Jehlen, eds., *Ideology and Classic American Literature* (1986).

Southern Whites

Peter Kolchin's *American Slavery, 1619–1877* (1993), is a brilliant synthesis of recent scholarship on the Old South. On the family culture of southern whites, see Bertram Wyatt-Brown, *Southern Honor: Ethics & Behavior in the Old South* (1982); Elizabeth Fox-Genovese, *Within the Plantation Household: Black and White Women in the Old South* (1988); Kenneth S. Greenberg, *Honor & Slavery* (1996); and Steven W. Stowe, *Intimacy and Power in the Old South* (1987). Eugene D. Genovese, *The Slaveholder's Dilemma: Southern Conservative Thought, 1820–1860* (1992), demonstrates the pervasive paternalism of southern social thought. Donald G. Matthews, *Religion in the Old South* (1977), is a valuable introduction to its subject. Other studies of southern religion are listed in the suggested readings to Chapter 7.

Slave Culture

A now-classic overview of slave culture is Eugene D. Genovese, *Roll, Jordan, Roll: The World the Slaves Made* (1974). Also essential are Lawrence W. Levine, *Black Culture and Black Consciousness: Afro-American Folk Thought from Slavery to Freedom* (1977), and Charles Joyner, *Down by the Riverside: A South Carolina Slave Community* (1984). Study of the slave family begins with Herbert G. Gutman, *The Black Family in Slavery and Freedom, 1750–1925* (1976), which can be supplemented with Ann Patton Malone, *Sweet Chariot: Slave Family and Household Structure in Nineteenth-Century Louisiana* (1992). John Michael Vlach, *Back of the Big House: The Architecture of Plantation Slavery* (1993), is a valuable cultural study. Slave religion is treated in Mechal Sobel, *Travelin' On: The Slave Journey to an Afro-Baptist Faith* (1979), and Margaret Washington Creel, *"A Peculiar People": Slave Religion and Community-Culture among the Gullahs* (1988). Other essential studies on these and related topics are cited in the suggested readings for Chapters 7 and 9.

CHAPTER 11 SOCIETY, CULTURE, AND POLITICS, 1820S–1840S

Constituencies

A choice of studies provide careful examinations of constituencies and issues at the state and local levels during the Jacksonian era. Students should consult Lee Benson, *The Concept of Jacksonian Democracy: New York as a Test Case*

(1961); John L. Hammond, *The Politics of Benevolence: Revival Religion and American Voting Behavior* (1979); Ronald P. Formisano, *The Transformation of Political Culture: Massachusetts Parties, 1790s–1840s* (1983), and *The Birth of Mass Political Parties: Michigan, 1827–1861* (1971); John L. Brooke, *The Heart of the Commonwealth: Society and Political Culture in Worcester County, Massachusetts, 1713–1861* (1989); Amy Bridges, *A City in the Republic: Antebellum New York and the Origins of Machine Politics* (1984); Paul Bourke and Donald DeBats, *Washington County: Politics and Community in Antebellum America* (1995); Harry L. Watson, *Jacksonian Politics and Community Conflict: The Emergence of the Second American Party System in Cumberland County, North Carolina* (1981); Lacy K. Ford Jr., *Origins of Southern Radicalism: The South Carolina Upcountry, 1800–1860* (1988); and David W. Crofts, *Old Southampton: Politics and Society in a Virginia County, 1834–1869* (1992). Richard J. Carwardine, *Evangelicals and Politics in Antebellum America* (1993), is a good study of relations between religion and politics in these years.

Ideologies

On party ideologies and political culture, see John Ashworth, *"Agrarians & Aristocrats": Party Political Ideology in the United States, 1837–1846* (1983); Daniel Walker Howe, *The Political Culture of the American Whigs* (1979); Anne Norton, *Alternative Americas: A Reading of Antebellum Political Culture* (1986); and Jean H. Baker, *Affairs of Party: The Political Culture of Northern Democrats in the Mid-Nineteenth Century* (1983). Aging but still valuable are John William Ward, *Andrew Jackson: Symbol for an Age* (1953), and Marvin Meyers, *The Jacksonian Persuasion: Politics and Belief* (1957).

Economic Issues

Party debates on banking and internal improvements are discussed in James Roger Sharp, *The Jacksonians versus the Banks: Politics in the States after the Panic of 1837* (1970); Harry N. Scheiber, *Ohio Canal Era: A Case Study of Government and the Economy, 1820–1861*, 2nd ed. (1987); L. Ray Gunn, *The Decline of Authority: Public Economic Policy and Political Development in New York, 1800–1860* (1988); and Oscar Handlin's now-classic *Commonwealth: A Study of the Role of Government in the American Economy: Massachusetts, 1774–1861*, rev. ed. (1969).

Social Questions

Political controversies surrounding schools are the subject of Carl F. Kaestle, *Pillars of the Republic: Common Schools and American Society, 1780–1860* (1983), and Kaestle's *The Evolution of an Urban School System: New York City, 1750–1850* (1973). An influential study of prisons and asylums is David J. Rothman, *The Discovery of the Asylum: Social Order and Disorder in the New Republic* (1971). It should be supplemented with W. David Lewis, *From Newgate to Dannemora: The Rise of the Penitentiary in New York, 1796–1848* (1965), Michael Meranze, *Laboratories of Virtue: Punishment, Revolution, and Authority in Philadelphia, 1760–1835* (1996), and Edward L.

Ayers, *Vengeance and Justice: Crime and Punishment in the 19th-Century South* (1984). Drinking and temperance are the subjects of W. J. Rorabaugh, *The Alcoholic Republic: An American Tradition* (1979), and Ian Tyrrell, *Sobering Up: From Temperance to Prohibition in Ante-Bellum America, 1800–1860* (1979). The best discussion of Washingtonianism is in Teresa Anne Murphy, *Ten Hours' Labor: Religion, Reform, and Gender in Early New England* (1992).

Race and Gender

The standard study of northern free blacks is Leon F. Litwack, *North of Slavery: The Negro in the Free States, 1790–1860* (1960). It can be supplemented by Gary B. Nash, *Forging Freedom: The Formation of Philadelphia's Black Community, 1720–1840* (1988). James Brewer Stewart, *Holy Warriors: The Abolitionists and American Slavery* (1976), is a graceful overview of the crusade against slavery. Black abolitionists are treated in R. J. M. Blackett, *Building and Antislavery Wall: Black Americans in the Abolitionist Movement, 1830-1860* (1983) and Nell Irvin Painter, *Sojourner Truth: A Life, A Symbol* (1996). Students should also consult Robert H. Abzug, *Cosmos Crumbling: American Reform and the Religious Imagination* (1994); Thomas Bender, ed., *The Antislavery Debate: Capitalism and Abolitionism as a Problem in Historical Interpretation* (1992); and Lewis Perry, *Radical Abolitionism: Anarchy and the Government of God in Antislavery Thought* (1973).

On the origins of the women's rights movement, students should consult Ellen Carol DuBois, *Feminism and Suffrage: The Emergence of an Independent Women's Movement in America, 1848–1869* (1978); Jean Fagan Yellin, *Women & Sisters: The Antislavery Feminists in American Culture* (1989); and Lori D. Ginzberg, *Women and the Work of Benevolence: Morality, Politics, and Class in the 19th-Century United States* (1990).

CHAPTER 12 JACKSONIAN DEMOCRACY

General

Arthur M. Schlesinger, Jr., *The Age of Jackson* (1945), is a now-classic overview of politics from the 1820s to the 1840s. Charles Sellers, *The Market Revolution: Jacksonian America, 1815–1846* (1991), synthesizes social, economic, and cultural history, while Harry L. Watson, *Liberty and Power: The Politics of Jacksonian America* (1990), is an excellent account of politics. Aging but still valuable (and friendlier to the Whigs) is Glyndon G. Van Deusen, *The Jacksonian Era, 1828–1848* (1959). A full study of the Whigs is Michael F. Holt, *The Rise and Fall of the American Whig Party* (1991). This period has been particularly well served by biographers. See especially Robert V. Remini's *Andrew Jackson and the Course of American Freedom, 1822–1833* (1981), *Andrew Jackson and the Course of American Democracy, 1833–1845* (1984), and *Henry Clay: Statesman for the Union* (1991). Also valuable are Merrill D. Peterson, *The Great Triumvirate: Webster, Clay, and Calhoun* (1987); John Niven, *Martin Van Buren: The Roman-*

tic Age of American Politics (1983), and *John C. Calhoun and the Price of Union* (1988); Irving H. Bartlett, *Daniel Webster* (1978); and Samuel Flagg Bemis, *John Quincy Adams and the Foundations of American Foreign Policy* (1949), and *John Quincy Adams and the Union* (1956).

Government

On presidential elections in these years, the best place to start is with the essays in Arthur M. Schlesinger, Jr., and Fred J. Israels, eds., *History of American Presidential Elections, 1789–1968*, 3 vols. (1971). George Dangerfield, *The Era of Good Feelings* (1953), and Glover Moore, *The Missouri Controversy, 1819–1821* (1953), are the standard treatments of their subjects. On Jacksonian administrative policies and the spoils system, see Leonard D. White, *The Jacksonians: A Study in Administrative History, 1829–1861* (1954); Sidney H. Aronson, *Status and Kinship in the Higher Civil Service* (1964); and Matthew A. Crenson, *The Federal Machine: Beginnings of Bureaucracy in Jacksonian America* (1975).

The South and National Politics

William W. Freehling, *The Road to Disunion: Secessionists at Bay, 1776–1854* (1990), provides an interpretive overview of the South and slavery in national politics. On nullification, see Freehling, *Prelude to Civil War: The Nullification Controversy in South Carolina, 1816–1836* (1965); Richard E. Ellis, *The Union at Risk: Jacksonian Democracy, States' Rights and the Nullification Crisis* (1987); and Merrill D. Peterson, *Olive Branch and Sword: The Compromise of 1833* (1982). Michael Paul Rogin, *Fathers and Children: Andrew Jackson and the Subjugation of the American Indian* (1975), is an imaginative essay, although students should also consult the works in Native American history cited in the suggested readings for Chapter 7. The fullest account of Congress's dealings with the abolitionists is William Lee Miller, *Arguing about Slavery: The Great Battle in the United States Congress* (1995). Students should also consult Leonard L. Richards, *The Life and Times of Congressman John Quincy Adams* (1986).

The Bank War

Study of the bank war still begins and ends with Bray Hammond, *Banks and Politics in America from the Revolution to the Civil War* (1957). Students should also consult Peter Temin, *The Jacksonian Economy* (1969), and Robert V. Remini, *Andrew Jackson and the Bank War* (1967).

The Party System

On party development, see Richard Hofstadter, *The Idea of a Party System: The Rise of Legitimate Opposition in the United States, 1780–1840* (1969); Richard P. McCormick, *The Second American Party System: Party Formation in the Jacksonian Era* (1966), and *The Presidential Game: The Origins of American Presidential Politics* (1982); and Joel H. Silbey, *The Partisan Imperative: The Dynamics of American Politics before the Civil War* (1985), and *The American Political Nation, 1838–1893* (1991).

CHAPTER 13 MANIFEST DESTINY: AN EMPIRE FOR LIBERTY—OR SLAVERY?

Manifest Destiny

For the West and the rise of Manifest Destiny, the best introductions are Malcolm J. Rohrbough, *The Trans-Appalachian Frontier: People, Societies, and Institutions 1775–1850* (1978), and Ray Allen Billington, *The Far Western Frontier, 1830–1860* (1956). Two books by Frederick Merk, *Manifest Destiny and Mission in American History* (1963) and *The Monroe Doctrine and American Expansion 1843–1849* (1967), explore the expansionism of the 1840s, while Norman A. Graebner, *Empire on the Pacific: A Study of American Continental Expansionism* (1955) traces its results.

California and Oregon

Westward migration on the overland trails is chronicled and analyzed in John D. Unruh, Jr., *The Plains Across: The Overland Emigrants and the Trans-Mississippi West, 1840–1860* (1979); John Mack Faragher, *Women and Men on the Overland Trail* (1978); and Julie Roy Jeffries, *Frontier Women: The Trans-Mississippi West, 1840–1860* (1979). Migration to Oregon is treated in Malcolm Clark, *Eden Seekers: The Settlement of Oregon, 1812–1862* (1981), while the California gold rush and its consequences are described by Malcolm J. Rohrbough, *Days of Gold: The California Gold Rush and the American Nation* (1997). For the harrowing story of the Donner Party, see George R. Stewart, *Ordeal by Hunger: The Story of the Donner Party* (1960).

Mormons

For the Mormon migration and the creation of their Zion in Utah, see Wallace Stegner, *The Gathering of Zion: The Story of the Mormon Trail* (1964); Leonard J. Arrington, *Brigham Young: American Moses* (1985); and Leonard J. Arrington and Davis Bitton, *The Mormon Experience: A History of the Latter-Day Saints* (1979).

Indians

A fine introduction to the impact of American expansion westward on the Native American residents of this region is Philip Weeks, *Farewell, My Nation: The American Indian and the United States, 1820–1890* (1990). Other important studies include Ronald M. Satz, *American Indian Policy in the Jacksonian Era* (1975); Robert A. Trennert Jr., *Alternatives to Extinction: Federal Indian Policy and the Beginnings of the Reservation System, 1846–1851* (1975); and Robert M. Utley, *The Indian Frontier of the American West, 1846–1890* (1984).

Texas

For Texas and the northern frontier of Mexico that became part of the United States in 1848, see David J. Weber, *The Mexican Frontier, 1821–1846: The American Southwest under Mexico* (1982). American settlement in Texas and its annexation by the United States are described in Frederick Merk, *Slavery and the Annexation of Texas* (1972); Marshall De Bruhl, *Sword of San Jacinto: A Life of Sam Houston* (1993); and John Hoyt Williams, *Sam Houston* (1993). The impact of settlement of these regions by Anglo-Americans and the absorption of the region into the United States are analyzed by Leonard Pitts, *The Decline of the Californios: A Social History of the Spanish-Speaking Californians, 1846–1890* (1970), and Arnoldo De Léon, *The Tejano Community, 1836–1900* (1982).

Mexican War

Two good studies of the relationship between American expansion and the coming of the war with Mexico are David Pletcher, *The Diplomacy of Annexation: Texas, Oregon, and the Mexican War* (1973) and Dean B. Mahin, *Sword and Olive Branch: The United States and Mexico, 1845–1848* (1997). Mexican viewpoints are described in Gene M. Brack, *Mexico Views Manifest Destiny: An Essay on the Origins of the Mexican War* (1975). Glen M. Price, *Origins of the War with Mexico: The Polk-Stockton Intrigue* (1967), charges Polk with deliberately provoking Mexico to war, while Charles G. Sellers, *James K. Polk, Continentalist 1843–1846* (1966), is more sympathetic to the American president. The most detailed study of the Mexican War is still Justin H. Smith, *The War with Mexico*, 2 vols. (1919). Modern studies include Seymour V. Connor and Odie B. Faulk, *North America Divided: The Mexican War, 1846–1848* (1971); K. Jack Bauer, *The Mexican War* (1974); and John S. D. Eisenhower, *So Far from God: The U.S. War with Mexico 1846–1848* (1989). John H. Schroeder, *Mr. Polk's War: American Opposition and Dissent, 1846–1848* (1973), documents antislavery and Whig opposition, while Robert W. Johannsen, *To the Halls of the Montezumas: The Mexican War in the American Imagination* (1985), focuses on the popularity of the war among Democrats and expansionists. For the experiences of American soldiers in the Mexican War, see James M. McCaffrey, *Army of Manifest Destiny: The American Soldier in the Mexican War* (1992) and Richard Bruce Winders, *Mr. Polk's Army: The American Military Experience in the Mexican War* (1997).

Slavery and Expansion

A huge literature addresses the sectional conflict provoked by the issue of slavery's expansion into the territory acquired from Mexico. For an introduction, consult David M. Potter, *The Impending Crisis 1848–1861* (1976), and Allan Nevins, *Ordeal of the Union*, 2 vols. (1947). Michael A. Morrison, *Slavery and the American West: The Eclipse of Manifest Destiny and the Coming of the Civil War* (1997) shows how the slavery-expansion issue emerged as the dominant one in American politics. The best single study of antislavery politics in this era is Richard H. Sewell, *Ballots for Freedom: Antislavery Politics in the United States 1837–1860* (1976). For northern Democrats and the Wilmot Proviso, see Chaplain Morrison, *Democratic Politics and Sectionalism: The Wilmot Proviso Controversy* (1967). The divisive impact of the slavery issue on Whigs is treated in Kinley J. Brauer, *Cotton versus Conscience: Massachusetts Whig Politics and Southwestern Expansion 1843–1848* (1967). The Free Soil Party and the 1848 presidential election are treated in Joseph Rayback, *Free Soil: The*

Election of 1848 (1970), and Frederick J. Blue, *The Free Soilers: Third Party Politics 1848–1854* (1973). For the South and the sectional controversy over slavery's expansion, see William J. Cooper Jr., *The South and the Politics of Slavery, 1828–1856* (1978); William W. Freehling, *The Road to Disunion: Secessionists at Bay, 1776–1854* (1990); John Barnwell, *Love of Order: South Carolina's First Secession Crisis* (1982); and a study of nine Southern nationalists, Eric H. Walther, *The Fire-Eaters* (1992).

Compromise of 1850
The fullest studies of the Compromise of 1850 are Holman Hamilton, *Prologue to Conflict: The Crisis and Compromise of 1850* (1964), and Mark J. Stegmaier, *Texas, New Mexico, and the Compromise of 1850* (1996). The careers of the three great senators who played such an important part in the compromise debate are portrayed in Merrill Peterson, *The Great Triumvirate: Webster, Clay, and Calhoun* (1987). For these and other key figures, see the following biographies: Robert F. Dalzell, *Daniel Webster and the Trial of American Nationalism 1843–1852* (1972); Robert V. Remini, *Henry Clay: Statesman for the Union* (1991); John Niven, *John C. Calhoun and the Price of Union* (1988); Robert W. Johannsen, *Stephen A. Douglas* (1973); Glyndon G. Van Deusen, *William Henry Seward* (1967); and K. Jack Bauer, *Zachary Taylor: Soldier, Planter, Statesman of the Old Southwest* (1985). The failed efforts of fire-eaters to capitalize on resentment of events that surrounded the compromise are treated in Thelma Jennings, *The Nashville Convention: Southern Movement for Unity 1848–1850* (1980), while the destructive impact of these events on the southern Whigs is narrated in Arthur C. Cole, *The Whig Party in the South* (1913).

Fugitive Slaves
The basic study of the passage and enforcement of the Fugitive Slave Act is Stanley W. Campbell, *The Slave Catchers* (1970). See also Paul Finkelman, *An Imperfect Union: Slavery, Federalism, and Comity* (1980). For northern personal liberty laws, see Thomas D. Morris, *Free Men All: The Personal Liberty Laws of the North 1780–1861* (1974). A scholarly study of the underground railroad is Larry Gara, *Liberty Line: The Legend of the Underground Railroad* (1961). One of the most dramatic fugitive slave confrontations is treated in Thomas P. Slaughter, *Bloody Dawn: The Christiana Riot and Racial Violence in the North* (1991). The tragedy of Margaret Garner is chronicled in Steven Weisenburger, *Modern Medea: A Family Story of Slavery and Child-Murder in the Old South* (1998). The powerful impact of Harriet Beecher Stowe's novel is measured by Thomas F. Gossett, *Uncle Tom's Cabin and American Literature* (1985).

Filibustering
The best accounts of southern expansionism and filibustering in the 1850s are Robert E. May, *The Southern Dream of a Caribbean Empire 1854–1861* (1971), and Charles H. Brown, *Agents of Manifest Destiny: The Lives and Times of the Filibusterers* (1979). For licit as well as illicit attempts to obtain

Cuba, see Basil Rauch, *American Interest in Cuba 1848–1855* (1948), and Tom Chaffin, *Fatal Glory: Narciso Lopez and the First Clandestine U.S. War against Cuba* (1996). The remarkable career of William Walker is chronicled in William O. Scroggs, *Filibusters and Financiers: The Story of William Walker and His Associates* (1916), and Albert Z. Carr, *The World and William Walker* (1963).

CHAPTER 14 THE GATHERING TEMPEST, 1853–1860
For general studies of the mounting sectional conflict during the 1850s, see David M. Potter, *The Impending Crisis 1848–1861* (1976); Allan Nevins, *Ordeal of the Union*, 2 vols. (1947) and *The Emergence of Lincoln*, 2 vols. (1950); Avery Craven, *The Coming of the Civil War*, 2nd ed. (1957); Michael F. Holt, *The Political Crisis of the 1850s* (1978); James M. McPherson, *Battle Cry of Freedom: The Civil War Era* (1988); and Gabor S. Borritt, ed., *Why the Civil War Came* (1996).

The Kansas Controversy
The Kansas-Nebraska Act and the ensuing conflict in Kansas are treated in Gerald W. Wolff, *The Kansas-Nebraska Bill: Party, Section, and the Coming of the Civil War* (1977); James A. Rawley, *Race and Politics: "Bleeding Kansas" and the Coming of the Civil War* (1969); and Thomas Goodrich, *War to the Knife: Bleeding Kansas, 1854-1861* (1999). Biographies of key figures in this controversy include Robert W. Johannsen, *Stephen A. Douglas* (1973), and Larry Gara, *The Presidency of Franklin Pierce* (1991).

Nativism and Immigration
The foregoing books contain a great deal of material about the relationship between the Kansas conflict and the origins of the Republican Party. For the crosscutting issue of nativism and the Know-Nothings, see especially William E. Gienapp, *The Origins of the Republican Party, 1852–1856* (1987), and Tyler Anbinder, *Nativism and Slavery: The Northern Know Nothings and the Politics of the 1850s* (1992). Other important studies of immigration and the nativist response include Oscar Handlin, *Boston's Immigrants* (1941); Robert Ernst, *Immigrant Life in New York City, 1825–1863* (1949); Jay P. Dolan, *The Immigrant Church: New York's Irish and German Catholics 1815–1865* (1975); and Dale T. Knobel, *Paddy and the Republic: Ethnicity and Nationality in Antebellum America* (1985). The best general narrative of nativism is still Ray Allen Billington, *The Protestant Crusade 1800–1861* (1938). See also Ira M. Leonard and Robert D. Parmet, *American Nativism, 1830–1860* (1971).

Politics and Sectionalism
Three of the numerous state studies of the political transformation in northern states are Mark L. Berger, *The Revolution in the New York Party Systems, 1840–1860* (1973); Steven E. Maizlish, *The Triumph of Sectionalism: The Transformation of Ohio Politics, 1844–1856* (1983); and Dale Baum, *The Civil*

War Party System: The Case of Massachusetts, 1848–1876 (1984). The Kansas-Nebraska Act brought Abraham Lincoln back into the political arena; for a fine study of Lincoln's role in the rise of the Republican Party, see Don E. Fehrenbacher, Prelude to Greatness: Lincoln in the 1850's (1962). A somewhat different interpretation is provided by Robert W. Johannsen, Lincoln, the South, and Slavery (1991). Two other valuable biographical studies are David Donald, Charles Sumner and the Coming of the Civil War (1960), and Frederick Blue, Salmon P. Chase: A Life in Politics (1987).

The southern response to these events in the North is chronicled in Avery Craven, The Growth of Southern Nationalism 1848–1861 (1953); John McCardell, The Idea of a Southern Nation (1979); William L. Barney, The Road to Secession: A New Perspective on the Old South (1972); William J. Cooper Jr., The South and the Politics of Slavery 1828–1856 (1978); and Eric H. Walther, The Fire-Eaters (1992). The widening North-South fissure in the Democratic Party is treated in Philip S. Klein, President James Buchanan (1962); Elbert B. Smith, The Presidency of James Buchanan (1975); and Roy F. Nichols, The Disruption of American Democracy (1948). The year 1857 witnessed a convergence of many of these events; for a stimulating book that pulls together the threads of that year of crisis, see Kenneth M. Stampp, America in 1857: A Nation on the Brink (1990). Another account of an important issue during this period is Mark W. Summers, The Plundering Generation: Corruption and the Crisis of the Union, 1849–1861 (1987).

The Economy and Education

For economic developments during this era, a still valuable classic is George Rogers Taylor, The Transportation Revolution, 1815–1860 (1951). Agriculture is treated in Paul W. Gates, The Farmer's Age: Agriculture, 1815–1860 (1960). Important studies of railroads include Albert Fishlow, American Railroads and the Transformation of the Antebellum Economy (1965), and John F. Stover, Iron Road to the West: American Railroads in the 1850s (1978). For the "American System of Manufactures," see Nathan Rosenberg, ed., The American System of Manufactures (1969); David A. Hounshell, From the American System to Mass Production, 1800–1932 (1983); and Donald R. Hoke, Ingenious Yankees: The Rise of the American System of Manufactures in the Private Sector (1990). For the relationship of education to social and economic change, see Frederick M. Binder, The Age of the Common School 1830–1865 (1974); Lee Soltow and Edward Stevens, The Rise of Literacy and the Common School in the United States (1981); Carl F. Kaestle, Pillars of the Republic: Common Schooling and American Society, 1780–1860 (1983); and Carl F. Kaestle and Maris A. Vinovskis, Education and Social Change in Nineteenth-Century Massachusetts (1980).

The Southern Economy

For the southern economy in these years, see Gavin Wright, The Political Economy of the Cotton South (1978), and Fred Bateman and Thomas Weiss, A Deplorable Scarcity: The Failure of Industrialization in the Slave Economy (1981). Vicki Vaughn Johnson, The Men and the Vision of the Southern Commercial Conventions, 1845-1871 (1992) chronicles the efforts of southerners to promote economic diversification. Other important studies include Harold D. Woodman, King Cotton and His Retainers: Financing and Marketing the Cotton Crop of the South (1968), and Laurence Shore, Southern Capitalists: The Ideological Leadership of an Elite, 1832–1885 (1986). The Panic of 1857 and its sectional and political consequences are treated in James L. Huston, The Panic of 1857 and the Coming of the Civil War (1987).

Antislavery and Proslavery Ideology

The best study of the Republican free-labor ideology is Eric Foner, Free Soil, Free Labor, Free Men: The Ideology of the Republican Party before the Civil War (1970). Susan-Mary Grant, North Over South: Northern Nationalism and American Identity in the Antebellum Era (2000) shows how this ideology created a sense of nationalism in the North. Still the fullest account of the southern defense of slavery and its way of life is William S. Jenkins, Pro-Slavery Thought in the Old South (1935), which should be supplemented by Drew Gilpin Faust, ed., The Ideology of Slavery: Proslavery Thought in the Antebellum South (1981).

Southern Yeomen

The numerous studies of white social structure and non-slaveholders in the South include Frank L. Owsley, Plain Folk of the Old South (1949); Bruce Collins, White Society in the Antebellum South (1985); Steven Hahn, The Roots of Southern Populism: Yeoman Farmers and the Transformation of the Georgia Upcountry, 1850–1890 (1983); Paul D. Escott, Many Excellent People: Power and Privilege in North Carolina, 1850–1900 (1985); J. William Harris, Plain Folk and Gentry in a Slave Society: White Liberty and Black Slavery in Augusta's Hinterlands (1985); Bill Cecil-Fronsman, Common Whites: Class and Culture in Antebellum North Carolina (1992); and Stephanie McCurry, Masters of Small Worlds: Yeoman Households, Gender Relations, and the Political Culture of the Antebellum South Carolina Low Country (1995).

Dred Scott, the Lincoln-Douglas Debates, and John Brown

The best single study of the Dred Scott case is Don E. Fehrenbacher, The Dred Scott Case: Its Significance in American Law and Politics (1978), which was published in an abridged version with the title Slavery, Law, and Politics: The Dred Scott Case in Historical Perspective (1981). Among several editions of the Lincoln-Douglas debates the fullest is Paul M. Angle, ed., Created Equal? The Complete Lincoln-Douglas Debates of 1858 (1958). For analyses of the debates, see Harry F. Jaffa, Crisis of the House Divided (1959), and David Zarefsky, Lincoln, Douglas and Slavery in the Crucible of Public Debate (1990). See also Damon Wells, Stephen Douglas: The Last Years, 1857–1861 (1971), and William E. Baringer, Lincoln's Rise to Power (1937). For John Brown's raid on Harpers Ferry, see Stephen B. Oates, To Purge This Land with Blood: A Biography of John Brown (1970); Jeffrey S. Rossback, Ambivalent Conspirators: John Brown, the Secret Six, and a Theory of *Slave Violence* (1982); and Benjamin Quarles, *Allies for Freedom: Blacks and John Brown* (1974).

CHAPTER 15 SECESSION AND CIVIL WAR, 1860–1862

The most comprehensive one-volume study of the Civil War years is James M. McPherson, *Battle Cry of Freedom: The Civil War Era* (1988). The same ground is covered in greater detail by Allan Nevins, *The War for the Union*, 4 vols. (1959–1971). For single-volume accounts of the Confederacy and the Union that emphasize the home fronts, see Emory M. Thomas, *The Confederate Nation, 1861–1865* (1979); George C. Rable, *The Confederate Republic* (1994); and Phillip Shaw Paludan, *"A People's Contest": The Union and Civil War, 1861–1865* (1988). Two multivolume classics that concentrate mainly on military campaigns and battles are Bruce Catton, *The Centennial History of the Civil War, vol. 1: The Coming Fury* (1961), *vol. 2: Terrible Swift Sword* (1963), *vol. 3: Never Call Retreat* (1965); and Shelby Foote, *The Civil War: A Narrative*, 3 vols. (1958–1974). Russell F. Weighley, *A Great Civil War: A Military and Political History* (2000), offers a systematic analysis of strategy and command.

Women and the War

The important roles of women in many facets of the war effort are described by Mary Elizabeth Masset, *Bonnet Brigades* (1966); Agatha Young, *Women and the Crisis: Women of the North in the Civil War* (1959); Elizabeth D. Leonard, *Yankee Women: Gender Battles in the Civil War* (1994) and the same author's *All the Daring of the Soldier: Women of the Civil War Armies* (1999); George C. Rable, *Civil Wars: Women and the Crisis of Southern Nationalism* (1989); and Drew Gilpin Faust, *Mothers of Invention: Women of the Slaveholding South in the American Civil War* (1996). Social history is the main focus of two collections of essays: Maris A. Vinovskis, ed., *Toward a Social History of the American Civil War* (1990), and Catherine Clinton and Nina Silber, eds., *Divided Houses: Gender and the Civil War* (1992).

Armies and Soldiers

For penetrating studies of the officers and men in three of the Civil War's most famous armies, see Bruce Catton's three volumes on the *Army of the Potomac: Mr. Lincoln's Army* (1951), *Glory Road* (1952), and *A Stillness at Appomattox* (1953); Douglass Southall Freeman's study of officers in the Army of Northern Virginia, *Lee's Lieutenants: A Study in Command*, 3 vols. (1942–44); Thomas L. Connelly's two works on the *Army of Tennessee: Army of the Heartland* (1967) and *Autumn of Glory* (1971); and Larry J. Daniel's *Soldiering in the Army of Tennessee: A Portrait of Life in the Confederate Army* (1991). The classic studies of Civil War soldiers by Bell Irvin Wiley are *The Life of Johnny Reb* (1943) and *The Life of Billy Yank* (1952). For additional insights into the character and experience of soldiers, see Reid Mitchell, *Civil War Soldiers* (1988) and *The Vacant Chair: The Northern Soldier Leaves Home* (1993); James M. McPherson, *What They Fought For, 1861–1865* (1994) and *For Cause and Comrades: Why Men Fought in the Civil War* (1997); and Earl J. Hess, *The Union Soldier in Battle: Enduring the Ordeal of Combat* (1997).

Biographies

Biographies of leading Civil War figures are of great value for understanding the period. For Abraham Lincoln, see especially Benjamin P. Thomas, *Abraham Lincoln* (1952); Stephen B. Oates, *With Malice Toward None: The Life of Abraham Lincoln* (1977); Mark E. Neely Jr., *The Last Best Hope of Earth: Abraham Lincoln and the Promise of America* (1993); James G. Randall, *Lincoln the President*, 4 vols. (1945–1955; vol. 4 completed by Richard N. Current); James M. McPherson, *Abraham Lincoln and the Second American Revolution* (1991); Philip S. Paludan, *The Presidency of Abraham Lincoln* (1994); and David Herbert Donald, *Lincoln* (1995). For Jefferson Davis, the best one-volume biography is William J. Cooper, *Jefferson Davis, American* (2000). See also Hudson Strode, *Jefferson Davis*, 3 vols. (1955–1964). The classic biography of Robert E. Lee is Douglas Southall Freeman, *R. E. Lee: A Biography*, 3 vols. (1934–1935), which has been condensed into a one-volume abridgement by Richard Harwell, *Lee* (1961). For revisionist interpretations of Lee, see Thomas L. Connelly, *The Marble Man: Robert E. Lee and His Image in American Society* (1977); Alan T. Nolan, *Lee Considered: General Robert E. Lee and Civil War History* (1991); and Emory M. Thomas, *Robert E. Lee: A Biography* (1995). Biographies of two other leading Confederate generals are Grady McWhiney, *Braxton Bragg and Confederate Defeat* (1969); Judith Lee Hallock, *Braxton Bragg and Confederate Defeat* (1991); and Craig L. Symonds, *Joseph E. Johnston: A Civil War Biography* (1992). On the Union side, two biographies of Ulysses S. Grant are Brooks D. Simpson, *Ulysses S. Grant: Triumph Over Adversity, 1822-1865* (2000) and Jean Edward Smith, *Ulysses S. Grant* (2001). For a fuller account of Grant during the war, see Bruce Catton, *Grant Moves South* (1960) and *Grant Takes Command* (1969), and Brooks D. Simpson, *Let Us Have Peace: Ulysses S. Grant and the Politics of War and Reconstruction, 1861–1868* (1991). Of the many biographies of William T. Sherman, two of the most valuable are Basil H. Liddell Hart, *Sherman: Soldier, Realist, American* (1929), and John F. Marszalek, *Sherman: A Soldier's Passion for Order* (1993). For George B. McClellan, the best biography is Stephen W. Sears, *George B. McClellan: The Young Napoleon* (1988).

Election of 1860 and Secession

The election of 1860 and the crisis of secession have been the subject of numerous studies: Emerson D. Fite, *The Presidential Campaign of 1860* (1911); Reinhard H. Luthin, *The First Lincoln Campaign* (1944); Ollinger Crenshaw, *The Slave States in the Presidential Election of 1860* (1945); William E. Baringer, *Lincoln's Rise to Power* (1937); Dwight L. Dumond, *The Secession Movement 1860–1861* (1931); Ralph Wooster, *The Secession Conventions of the South* (1962); Donald E. Reynolds, *Editors Make War: Southern Newspapers in the Secession Crisis* (1970); Steven A. Channing, *A Crisis of Fear:*

Secession in South Carolina (1970); William L. Barney, *The Secessionist Impulse: Alabama and Mississippi in 1860* (1974); Michael P. Johnson, *Toward a Patriarchal Republic: The Secession of Georgia* (1977); Daniel W. Crofts, *Reluctant Confederates: Upper South Unionists in the Secession Crisis* (1989); David M. Potter, *Lincoln and His Party in the Secession Crisis* (1942; new ed. 1962); and Kenneth M. Stampp, *And the War Came: The North and the Secession Crisis, 1860–1861* (1950). The best accounts of the standoff at Fort Sumter that led to war are Richard N. Current, *Lincoln and the First Shot* (1963), and Maury Klein, *Days of Defiance: Sumter, Secession, and the Coming of the Civil War* (1997).

The Border States

The bitter experiences of the border states in the war are chronicled by William E. Parrish, *Turbulent Partnership: Missouri and the Union 1861–1865* (1963); Jean H. Baker, *The Politics of Continuity: Maryland Political Parties from 1858 to 1870* (1973); William H. Townsend, *Lincoln and the Bluegrass: Slavery and Civil War in Kentucky* (1955); and Lowell Harrison, *The Civil War and Kentucky* (1975). For guerrilla warfare along the border, particularly in Missouri, the best studies are Jay Monaghan, *Civil War on the Western Border 1854–1865* (1955), and Michael Fellman, *Inside War: The Guerrilla Conflict in Missouri during the Civil War* (1989). For the creation of West Virginia, see Richard O. Curry, *A House Divided: A Study of Statehood Politics and the Copperhead Movement in West Virginia* (1964).

War and Finance

The problem of Confederate war finance is treated in Richard C. Todd, *Confederate Finance* (1954), and Douglas B. Ball, *Financial Failure and Confederate Defeat* (1990). For Union war finance, see Bray Hammond, *Sovereignty and an Empty Purse: Banks and Politics in the Civil War Era* (1970), and Heather Cox Richardson, *The Greatest Nation of the Earth: Republican Economic Policies during the Civil War* (1997).

The Naval War

A large literature treats Civil War navies and the blockade. Perhaps the best place to begin is with William M. Fowler Jr., *Under Two Flags: The American Navy in the Civil War* (1990), and Ivan Musicant, *Divided Waters: The Naval History of the Civil War* (1995). The fullest account of naval warfare is Virgil C. Jones, *The Civil War at Sea*, 3 vols. (1960–62). For the river war, see H. Allen Gosnell, *Guns on the Western Waters: The Story of River Gunboats in the Civil War* (1949); John D. Milligan, *Gunboats down the Mississippi* (1965); and James M. Merrill, *Battle Flags South: The Story of the Civil War Navies on Western Waters* (1970). A good general history of the Confederate navy is Raimundo Luraghi, *A History of the Confederate Navy* (1996). For the blockade and blockade running, see Robert Carse, *Blockade: The Civil War at Sea* (1958), and Stephen R. Wise, *Lifeline of the Confederacy: Blockade Running during the Civil War* (1988). The story of Confederate commerce raiding is told in George W.

Dalzell, *The Flight from the Flag* (1943), and Edward C. Boykin, *Ghost Ship of the Confederacy: The Story of the "Alabama" and Her Captain* (1957).

Foreign Policy

Foreign policy complications caused by Confederate shipbuilding in Britain are treated in Frank J. Merli, *Great Britain and the Confederate Navy* (1970). The most concise account of Civil War diplomacy is David P. Crook, *The North, the South, and the Powers 1861–1865* (1974), an abridged version of which was published with the title *Diplomacy during the Civil War* (1975). The classic study of Confederate diplomacy is Frank L. Owsley, *King Cotton Diplomacy* (1931; rev. ed. 1959). British-American and British-Confederate relations have received exhaustive attention; the fullest studies are Ephraim D. Adams, *Great Britain and the American Civil War*, 2 vols. (1925); Brian Jenkins, *Britain and the War for the Union*, 2 vols. (1974–80); and Howard Jones, *The Union in Peril: The Crisis over British Intervention in the Civil War* (1992). For the Trent Affair, consult Gordon H. Warren, *Fountains of Discontent: The "Trent" Affair and the Freedom of the Seas* (1981). For relations between France and the two warring parties, see Lynn M. Case and Warren F. Spencer, *The United States and France: Civil War Diplomacy* (1970).

CHAPTER 16 A NEW BIRTH OF FREEDOM, 1862–1865

For works that cover the entire Civil War period, including the years encompassed by this chapter, see the books cited in the first four paragraphs of suggested readings for Chapter 15. In addition, for analyses of military strategy and leadership that focus mainly on the period 1862–65, consult T. Harry Williams, *Lincoln and His Generals* (1952); Archer Jones, *Civil War Command and Strategy* (1992); Joseph T. Glatthaar, *Partners in Command: The Relationships between Leaders in the Civil War* (1993); Steven E. Woodworth, *Jefferson Davis and His Generals* (1990); and *Davis and Lee at War* (1995). Richard M. McMurry, *Two Great Rebel Armies* (1989), analyzes the reasons for the success of the Army of Northern Virginia and the relative failure of the Army of Tennessee, while Michael C. Adams, *Our Masters the Rebels: A Speculation on Union Military Defeat in the East, 1861–1865* (1978), reissued under the title *Fighting for Defeat* (1992), offers an interpretation of the Army of the Potomac's problems. Charles W. Royster, *The Destructive War: William Tecumseh Sherman, Stonewall Jackson, and the Americans* (1991), and Mark Grimsley, *The Hard Hand of War: Union Military Policy toward Southern Civilians, 1981–1865* (1995), focus on the escalating destructiveness of the war. Six studies canvass various explanations for Union victory: David Donald, ed., *Why the North Won the Civil War* (1960); Herman Hattaway and Archer Jones, *How the North Won: A Military History of the Civil War* (1983); Richard E. Beringer, Herman Hattaway, Archer Jones, and William N. Still, Jr., *Why the South Lost the Civil War* (1986), an abridged version of which was published with the title *The Elements of Confederate Defeat* (1988); Grady

McWhiney and Perry D. Jamieson, *Attack and Die: Civil War Military Tactics and the Southern Heritage* (1982); Gabor S. Boritt, ed., *Why the Confederacy Lost* (1992); and Gary W. Gallagher, *The Confederate War* (1997). See also Drew Gilpin Faust, *The Creation of Confederate Nationalism* (1988).

Slavery and Emancipation
On the issues of slavery and emancipation in the war, the best place to begin is Ira Berlin, Barbara J. Fields, Steven F. Miller, Joseph P. Reidy, and Leslie S. Rowland, *Slaves No More: Three Essays on Emancipation and the Civil War* (1992). An older but still useful study is Bell I. Wiley, *Southern Negroes 1861–1865* (1938). A superb study of one Confederate state is Clarence L. Mohr, *On the Threshold of Freedom: Masters and Slaves in Civil War Georgia* (1986), while a classic account of the experience of emancipation on the South Carolina sea islands is Willie Lee Rose, *Rehearsal for Reconstruction: The Port Royal Experiment* (1964). Two books on Maryland provide the best studies of slavery and emancipation in a border state: Charles L. Wagandt, *The Mighty Revolution: Negro Emancipation in Maryland 1862–1864* (1964), and Barbara Jeanne Fields, *Slavery and Freedom on the Middle Ground: Maryland during the Nineteenth Century* (1985). See also Victor B. Howard, *Black Liberation in Kentucky: Emancipation and Freedom, 1862–1884* (1983). For the hopes and realities of freedom as experienced by the slaves, see Leon F. Litwack, *Been in the Storm So Long: The Aftermath of Slavery* (1979). A fine study of the Emancipation Proclamation is John Hope Franklin, *The Emancipation Proclamation* (1963). Two books by James M. McPherson analyze the role of Northern abolitionists and black leaders in the achievement of emancipation: *The Struggle for Equality: Abolitionists and the Negro in the Civil War and Reconstruction* (1964), and *The Negro's Civil War* (1965; new ed. 1991). The impact of the loss of slavery on the slaveholding class is chronicled by James L. Roark, *Masters without Slaves: Southern Planters in the Civil War and Reconstruction* (1977).

Black Soldiers
For black soldiers in the Union army, the best studies are Dudley T. Cornish, *The Sable Arm: Negro Troops in the Union Army* (1956); Joseph T. Glatthaar, *Forged in Battle: The Civil War Alliance of Black Soldiers and White Officers* (1990); and Noah Andre Trudeau, *Like Men of War: Black Troops in the Civil War 1862-1865* (1998). A classic account by a white officer of a black regiment is Thomas Wentworth Higginson, *Army Life in a Black Regiment* (1869; reprinted 1961). For the Confederate debate about arming and freeing slaves, see Robert Durden, *The Gray and the Black: The Confederate Debate on Emancipation* (1972).

Copperheads and Democrats
Antiblack and antiemancipation sentiments in the North are the focus of V. Jacque Voegeli, *Free but Not Equal: The Midwest and the Negro during the Civil War* (1967), and Forrest G. Wood, *Black Scare: The Racist Response to Emancipation and Reconstruction* (1968). Hostility to emancipation was at the core of Copperheadism in the North, a phenomenon provocatively interpreted in three books by Frank L. Klement: *The Copperheads in the Middle West* (1960); *The Limits of Dissent: Clement L. Vallandigham and the Civil War* (1970); and *Dark Lanterns: Secret Political Societies, Conspiracies, and Treason Trials in the Civil War* (1984). See also Wood Gray, *The Hidden Civil War: The Story of the Copperheads* (1942). For the Northern Democrats, one should also consult Joel Silbey, *A Respectable Minority: The Democratic Party in the Civil War Era* (1977).

Politics and the Constitution
Three studies of the Lincoln administration's record on civil liberties and related constitutional issues are important: Mark E. Neely Jr., *The Fate of Liberty: Abraham Lincoln and Civil Liberties* (1990); Dean Sprague, *Freedom under Lincoln* (1965); and James G. Randall, *Constitutional Problems under Lincoln* (rev. ed., 1951). Other studies of constitutional issues during the war include Harold M. Hyman, *A More Perfect Union: The Impact of the Civil War and Reconstruction on the Constitution* (1973), and Phillip S. Paludan, *A Covenant with Death: The Constitution, Law, and Equality in the Civil War Era* (1975). For civil liberties in the South, see Mark E. Neely Jr., *Southern Rights: Political Prisoners and the Myth of Confederate Constitutionalism* (1999).

Economics and Logistics
Still a useful book on the Confederate economy is Charles W. Ramsdell, *Behind the Lines in the Southern Confederacy* (1944), while for the Union, the same can be said of Emerson D. Fite, *Social and Economic Conditions in the North during the Civil War* (1910). Railroads in North and South are treated in George E. Turner, *Victory Rode the Rails* (1953); Thomas Weber, *The Northern Railroads in the Civil War* (1952); and Robert C. Black, *The Railroads of the Confederacy* (1952). Robert V. Bruce, *Lincoln and the Tools of War* (1956), is a fascinating study of Northern technology in the war, while Edward Hagerman, *The American Civil War and the Origins of Modern Warfare* (1988), and Richard Goff, *Confederate Supply* (1969), are the best studies of logistics.

Dissent and Class Conflict
Class conflict and political dissent in the Confederacy are discussed in Paul D. Escott, *After Secession: Jefferson Davis and the Failure of Confederate Nationalism* (1978); Bell I. Wiley, *The Plain People of the Confederacy* (1943); Fred Arthur Bailey, *Class and Tennessee's Confederate Generation* (1987); Wayne K. Durrill, *War of Another Kind: A Southern Community in the Great Rebellion* (1990); and Frank L. Owsley, *State Rights in the Confederacy* (1966). The most dramatic manifestation of class conflict in the North was the New York draft riot. Two important studies of it are Adrian Cook, *The Armies of the Streets: The New York City Draft Riots of 1863* (1974), and Iver Bernstein, *The New York City Draft Riots: Their Significance for American Society and Politics in the Age of the Civil War* (1990). For the conflict in the Pennsylvania coal fields, see Grace Palladino, *Another Civil War: Labor,*

Capital, and the State in the Anthracite Regions of Pennsylvania (1990).

Conscription

Controversies about conscription lay at the root of much wartime class conflict. For studies of the draft in South and North, see Albert B. Moore, *Conscription and Conflict in the Confederacy* (1924); Eugene C. Murdock, *One Million Men: The Civil War Draft in the North* (1971); and James W. Geary, *We Need Men: The Union Draft in the Civil War* (1991). The modernizing legislation of the Union Congress that drafted a "blueprint for modern America" is analyzed by Leonard P. Curry, *Blueprint for Modern America: Non-Military Legislation of the First Civil War Congress* (1968). For a provocative interpretation of the Confederacy's attempted crash program of modernization and industrialization, see Emory M. Thomas, *The Confederacy as a Revolutionary Experience* (1971; new ed. 1991).

Civil War Medicine

For Civil War medicine, in addition to the books about women in the war cited in the suggested readings for Chapter 15, see Paul E. Steiner, *Disease in the Civil War* (1968); George W. Adams, *Doctors in Blue: The Medical History of the Union Army in the Civil War* (1952); Horace H. Cunningham, *Doctors in Gray: The Confederate Medical Service* (1958); and Frank R. Freemon, *Gangrene and Glory: Medical Care During the Civil War* (1999). The basic history of the U.S. Sanitary Commission is William Q. Maxwell, *Lincoln's Fifth Wheel: The Political History of the United States Sanitary Commission* (1956). A stimulating interpretation of the Sanitary Commission in the context of wartime transformations in northern attitudes toward other social and cultural issues is George M. Fredrickson, *The Inner Civil War: Northern Intellectuals and the Crisis of the Union* (1965).

The Peace Issue

The complex relationships between peace negotiations and the Union presidential election of 1864 are discussed in Edward C. Kirkland, *The Peacemakers of 1864* (1927); William F. Zornow, *Lincoln and the Party Divided* (1954); David E. Long, *The Jewel of Liberty: Abraham Lincoln's Re-Election and the End of Slavery* (1994); and Larry E. Nelson, *Bullets, Ballots, and Rhetoric: Confederate Policy for the United States Presidential Contest of 1864* (1980). The best analysis of Lincoln's assassination and of the many unsubstantiated conspiracy theories to explain it is William Hanchett, *The Lincoln Murder Conspiracies* (1983). See also William A. Tidwell, James O. Hall, and David Winfred Gaddy, *Come Retribution: The Confederate Secret Service and the Assassination of Lincoln* (1988).

Women in the Sanitary Commission

The vital activities of women in the Sanitary Commission are the subject of Jeanie Attie, *Patriotic Toil: Northern Women and the American Civil War* (1998).

CHAPTER 17 RECONSTRUCTION, 1863–1877

The most comprehensive and incisive general history of Reconstruction is Eric Foner, *Reconstruction: America's Unfinished Revolution 1863–1877* (1988). For a skillful abridgement of this book, see Eric Foner, *A Short History of Reconstruction* (1990). A more concise survey of this era can be found in James M. McPherson, *Ordeal by Fire: The Civil War and Reconstruction*, 3rd ed. (2000), Part 3. Still valuable are Kenneth M. Stampp, *The Era of Reconstruction, 1865–1877* (1965), and John Hope Franklin, *Reconstruction: After the Civil War* (1961). The essays in Eric Anderson and Alfred A. Moss Jr., eds., *The Facts of Reconstruction: Essays in Honor of John Hope Franklin* (1991), offer important insights. The constitutional issues involved in the era are analyzed by Harold M. Hyman, *A More Perfect Union: The Impact of the Civil War and Reconstruction on the Constitution* (1973). Brooks D. Simpson, *The Reconstruction Presidents* (1998) offers insights on presidential policies from Lincoln through Hayes.

For the evolution of federal Reconstruction policies during the war and early postwar years, see three books by Herman Belz: *Reconstructing the Union: Theory and Policy during the Civil War* (1969), *A New Birth of Freedom: The Republican Party and Freedmen's Rights* (1976), and *Emancipation and Equal Rights: Politics and Constitutionalism in the Civil War Era* (1978). Also valuable is David Donald, *The Politics of Reconstruction 1863–1867* (1965). Important for their insights on Lincoln and the Reconstruction question are Peyton McCrary, *Abraham Lincoln and Reconstruction: The Louisiana Experiment* (1978), and LaWanda Cox, *Lincoln and Black Freedom: A Study in Presidential Leadership* (1981). A superb study of the South Carolina Sea Islands as a laboratory of Reconstruction is Willie Lee Rose, *Rehearsal for Reconstruction: The Port Royal Experiment* (1964).

Johnson versus Congress

For the vexed issues of Andrew Johnson, Congress, and Reconstruction from 1865 to 1868, the following are essential: Eric L. McKitrick, *Andrew Johnson and Reconstruction* (1960); LaWanda Cox and John H. Cox, *Politics, Principle, and Prejudice 1865–1866* (1963); William R. Brock, *An American Crisis: Congress and Reconstruction 1865–1867* (1963); Michael Les Benedict, *A Compromise of Principle: Congressional Republicans and Reconstruction* (1974); David Warren Bowen, *Andrew Johnson and the Negro* (1989); and Hans L. Trefousse, *The Radical Republicans: Lincoln's Vanguard for Racial Justice* (1969), *Thaddeus Stevens: Nineteenth-Century Egalitarian* (1997), and *Andrew Johnson: A Biography* (1989). The two best studies of Johnson's impeachment are Michael Les Benedict, *The Impeachment and Trial of Andrew Johnson* (1973), and Hans L. Trefousse, *Impeachment of a President: Andrew Johnson, the Blacks, and Reconstruction* (1975).

The Fourteenth and Fifteenth Amendments

For the political and judicial dimensions of the Fourteenth and Fifteenth Amendments and their enforcement, see

Joseph B. James, *The Framing of the Fourteenth Amendment* (1956), and *The Ratification of the Fourteenth Amendment* (1984); Michael Kent Curtis, *No State Shall Abridge: The Fourteenth Amendment and the Bill of Rights* (1986); William E. Nelson, *The Fourteenth Amendment: From Political Principle to Judicial Doctrine* (1988); James E. Bond, *No Easy Walk to Freedom: Reconstruction and the Ratification of the Fourteenth Amendment* (1997); William Gillette, *The Right to Vote: Politics and Passage of the Fifteenth Amendment* (1965); and Robert J. Kaczorowski, *The Politics of Judicial Interpretation: The Federal Courts, Department of Justice and Civil Rights, 1866–1876* (1985).

Reconstruction Society, Politics, and Economics

For the social and political scene in the South during Reconstruction, a good introduction is Howard N. Rabinowitz, *The First New South, 1865–1920* (1991). Dan T. Carter, *When the War Was Over: The Failure of Self-Reconstruction in the South, 1865–1867* (1985), and Michael Perman, *Reunion without Compromise: The South and Reconstruction, 1865–1868* (1973), portray the early postwar years, while Michael Perman, *The Road to Redemption: Southern Politics, 1868–1879* (1984), is a provocative interpretation. Otto H. Olsen, ed., *Reconstruction and Redemption in the South* (1980), contains essays on the Reconstruction process in a half dozen states. For the role of the Ku Klux Klan and other white paramilitary organizations, see Allen W. Trelease, *White Terror: The Ku Klux Klan Conspiracy and Southern Reconstruction* (1974), and George C. Rable, *But There Was No Peace: The Role of Violence in the Politics of Reconstruction* (1984). For a fresh and intelligent look at the carpetbaggers, see Richard Nelson Current, *Those Terrible Carpetbaggers: A Reinterpretation* (1988). Economic issues are the subject of Mark W. Summers, *Railroads, Reconstruction, and the Gospel of Prosperity: Aid under the Radical Republicans, 1865–1877* (1984), and Terry L. Seip, *The South Returns to Congress: Men, Economic Measures, and Intersectional Relationships, 1868–1879* (1983). Daniel Stowell, *Rebuilding Zion: The Religious Reconstruction of the South, 1863-1877* (1998) deals with both black and white churches.

Freedpeople during Reconstruction

Two classics that portray sympathetically the activities of freedpeople during Reconstruction are W. E. Burghardt DuBois, *Black Reconstruction* (1935), and Leon F. Litwack, *Been in the Storm So Long: The Aftermath of Slavery* (1979). A challenging brief interpretation is provided by Eric Foner, *Nothing But Freedom: Emancipation and Its Legacy* (1983). Howard N. Rabinowitz, *Race Relations in the Urban South, 1865–1890* (1978), and Howard N. Rabinowitz, ed., *Southern Black Leaders of the Reconstruction Era* (1982), add important dimensions to the subject. There are many good studies of black social and political life in various states during Reconstruction; three of the best deal with the state in which African Americans played the most active part: Joel Williamson, *After Slavery: The Negro in South Carolina during Reconstruction 1861–1877* (1965); Thomas Holt, *Black over White: Negro Political Leadership in South Carolina during Reconstruction* (1977); and Laura F. Edwards, *Gendered Strife and Confusion: The Political Culture of Reconstruction* (1997). See also Eric Foner, *Freedom's Lawmakers: A Directory of Black Officeholders during Reconstruction* (1993).

For the evolution of sharecropping and other aspects of freedpeople's economic status, see Roger L. Ransom and Richard Sutch, *One Kind of Freedom: The Economic Consequences of Emancipation* (1977), and William Cohen, *At Freedom's Edge: Black Mobility and the Southern White Quest for Racial Control, 1861–1915* (1991). Two sound studies of the Freedmen's Bureau are George R. Bentley, *A History of the Freedmen's Bureau* (1955), and Donald G. Nieman, *To Set the Law in Motion: The Freedmen's Bureau and the Legal Rights of Blacks 1865–1868* (1979). See also Paul A. Cimbala and Randall Miller, eds., *The Freedmen's Bureau and Reconstruction* (1999). For the education of freedpeople, see especially William Preston Vaughan, *Schools for All: The Blacks & Public Education in the South 1865–1877* (1974); Joe M. Richardson, *Christian Reconstruction, The American Missionary Association and Southern Blacks, 1861–1890* (1986); and James M. McPherson, *The Abolitionist Legacy: From Reconstruction to the NAACP* (1975).

The End of Reconstruction

The national political scene in the 1870s and the retreat from Reconstruction are the subject of William Gillette, *Retreat from Reconstruction: A Political History 1867–1878* (1979). The issues of corruption and civil service reform receive exhaustive treatment in Mark Wahlgren Summers, *The Era of Good Stealings* (1993). The classic analysis of the disputed election of 1876 and the Compromise of 1877 is C. Vann Woodward, *Reunion and Reaction: The Compromise of 1877 and the End of Reconstruction*, rev. ed., (1956); for challenges to aspects of Woodward's thesis see Keith I. Polakoff, *The Politics of Inertia: The Election of 1876 and the End of Reconstruction* (1973), and Michael Les Benedict, "Southern Democrats in the Crisis of 1876–1877: A Reconsideration of Reunion and Reaction," *Journal of Southern History* 46 (1980): 489–524. Xi Wang, *The Trial of Democracy: Black Suffrage and Northern Republicans, 1860-1910* (1997), shows the difficulty of enforcing the Fifteenth Amendment in the South.

CHAPTER 18 FRONTIERS OF CHANGE, POLITICS OF STALEMATE, 1865–1898

Westward Expansion

Classic accounts of the post–Civil War West can be found in Walter Prescott Webb, *The Great Plains* (1931), and Wallace Stegner, *Beyond the Hundredth Meridian* (1954). Also valuable are Rodman Paul, *The Far West and the Great Plains in Transition* (1988), and Howard Lamar, *The Far Southwest, 1846–1912* (1970). The best modern general study of the history of the West from the first contact between Europeans and Indians down to the present is Richard White, *"It's Your Misfortune and None of My Own": A History of the American West* (1991).

Railroads

The role of railroads in westward expansion is treated in Robert R. Riegel, *The Story of the Western Railroads* (1926), and Stephen E. Ambrose, *Nothing Like It in the World: The Men Who Built the Transcontinental Railroad 1863-1869* (2000).

The Farming Frontier

The farmers' frontier is chronicled in Gilbert C. Fite, *The Farmer's Frontier, 1865–1900* (1966), and Fred Shannon, *The Farmers' Last Frontier, 1860–1897* (1945). The important part played by immigrants in western settlement is treated in Frederick C. Luebke, *Ethnicity on the Great Plains* (1980). Farmers' wives and other frontier women are the subject of Sandra Myres, *Western Women and the Frontier Experience, 1880–1915* (1982); Julie Roy Jeffrey, *Frontier Women: The Trans-Mississippi West, 1840–1880* (1979); and Christiane Fischer, *Let Them Speak for Themselves: Women in the American West, 1849–90* (1977). The experience of children is discussed in Elliott West, *Growing Up with the Country: Childhood on the Far Western Frontier* (1989).

The Mining Frontier

For the mining frontier, the following are valuable: William Greever, *The Bonanza West: The Story of the Western Mining Rushes* (1963); Rodman Paul, *Mining Frontiers of the Far West, 1848–1880* (1963); Richard Lingenfelter, *The Hardrock Miners: A History of the Mining Labor Movement in the American West, 1863–1893* (1974); and Mark Wyman, *Hard Rock Epic: Western Miners and the Industrial Revolution, 1860–1910* (1979). The conflicts generated by the Colorado gold rush are described in Elliott West, *The Contested Plains: Indians, Goldseekers, and the Rush to Colorado* (1998).

The Ranching Frontier

The saga of the ranching frontier and the cowboy is the subject of many books, including Lewis Atherton, *The Cattle Kings* (1961); Edward E. Dale, *The Range Cattle Industry*, rev. ed., (1969); Robert Dykstra, *The Cattle Towns* (1968); Ernest S. Osgood, *The Day of the Cattleman* (1929); Joe B. Frantz and Julian Choate, *The American Cowboy: The Myth and Reality* (1955); and William Savage, *The Cowboy Hero: His Image in American History and Culture* (1979). For black cowboys, see William L. Katz, *The Black West* (1971).

Indians and the West

The best brief survey of Indians and Indian-white relations in this period is Philip Weeks, *Farewell, My Nation: The American Indian and the United States, 1820–1890* (1990). Other valuable works include Ralph K. Andrist, *The Long Death: The Last Day of the Plains Indians* (1964); Paul H. Carlson, *The Plains Indians* (1998); and Robert M. Utley, *The Indian Frontier of the American West 1846–1890* (1984), and *The Last Days of the Sioux Nation* (1963). For the reformers and the Dawes Act, see Robert Mardock, *Reformers and the American Indian* (1971), and Leonard A. Carlson, *Indians, Bureaucrats, and Land* (1981). Two books by Francis Paul Prucha contain valuable material on this period: *The Great Father: The United States Government and the American Indians* (1984), and *The Indians in American Society from the Revolutionary War to the Present* (1985). For the fate of the buffalo, see Andrew Isenberg, *The Destruction of the Bison: An Environmental History, 1750-1920* (2000).

The New South

The classic study of the New South is C. Vann Woodward, *Origins of the New South, 1877–1913* (1951). It can be supplemented by Paul M. Gaston, *The New South Creed: A Study in Southern Mythmaking* (1970), and Edward L. Ayres, *The Promise of the New South: Life after Reconstruction* (1992). For the economy of the New South, see Gavin Wright, *Old South, New South: Revolutions in the Southern Economy Since the Civil War* (1986); Pete Daniel, *Breaking the Land: The Transformation of Cotton, Tobacco, and Rice Cultures Since 1880* (1985); John F. Stover, *The Railroads of the South, 1865–1900* (1955); Patrick H. Hearden, *Independence and Empire: The New South's Cotton Mill Campaign, 1865–1901* (1982); and David L. Carlton, *Mill and Town in South Carolina, 1880–1920* (1982).

Race Relations

The politics of race in the New South is the subject of Vincent P. DeSantis, *Republicans Face the Southern Question . . . 1877–1897* (1959); Stanley P. Hirshson, *Farewell to the Bloody Shirt: Northern Republicans and the Southern Negro 1877–1893* (1962); and J. Morgan Kousser, *The Shaping of Southern Politics: Suffrage Restriction and the Establishment of the One-Party South 1880–1910* (1974). The rising tide of racism and segregation is treated in C. Vann Woodward, *The Strange Career of Jim Crow*, 3rd rev. ed., (1974); Joel Williamson, *The Crucible of Race: Black-White Relations in the American South Since Emancipation* (1984), which was also published in an abridged edition with the title *A Rage for Order: Black-White Relations in the American South Since Emancipation* (1986); Howard B. Rabinowitz, *Race Relations in the Urban South 1865–1890* (1978); and Leon F. Litwack, *Trouble in Mind: Black Southerners in the Age of Jim Crow* (1998). The horrors of lynching and the convict lease system are analyzed in Fitzhugh Brundage, *Lynching in the New South: Georgia and Virginia, 1880–1930* (1993), and Matthew J. Mancini, *One Dies, Get Another: Convict Leasing in the American South, 1866–1928* (1996). For responses by black leaders to these developments, see August Meier, *Negro Thought in America, 1880–1915* (1963), and Louis R. Harlan, *Booker T. Washington: The Making of a Black Leader, 1856–1901* (1972).

The Politics of Stalemate

Two useful political narratives of this period are John A. Garraty, *The New Commonwealth, 1877–1890* (1968), and John M. Dobson, *Politics in the Gilded Age* (1972). For the continuing impact of Civil War issues and memories in politics, see Mary R. Dearing, *Veterans in Politics: The Story of the G.A.R.* (1952); Stuart McConnell, *Glorious Contentment: The Grand Army of the Republic, 1865–1900* (1992); and Gaines

M. Foster, *Ghosts of the Confederacy: Defeat, the Lost Cause, and the Emergence of the New South* (1987). Other useful studies include Paul Kleppner, *The Third Electoral System, 1853–1892* (1979); Robert Marcus, *Grand Old Party: Political Structure in the Gilded Age* (1971); H. Wayne Morgan, *From Hayes to McKinley* (1969); Ari Hoogenboom, *Outlawing the Spoils: A History of the Civil Service Reform Movement* (1961); and David M. Tucker, *Mugwumps: Public Moralists of the Gilded Age* (1998).

CHAPTER 19 ECONOMIC CHANGE AND THE CRISIS OF THE 1890s

For stimulating overviews of this period and the Progressive era that followed, consult Richard Hofstadter, *The Age of Reform* (1955); Robert H. Wiebe, *The Search for Order 1877–1920* (1967); and Nell Irvin Painter, *Standing at Armageddon: The United States, 1877–1919* (1987).

Railroads and Industrial Growth

For the impact of the railroad on the Gilded Age economy and culture, see George R. Taylor and Irene D. Neu, *The American Railroad Network, 1861–1890* (1956); Albro Martin, *Railroads Triumphant: The Growth, Rejection, and Rebirth of a Vital American Force* (1992); and Alfred D. Chandler, Jr., *The Railroads: The Nation's First Big Business* (1965). For the rise of industry and "big business," the following are useful: Glen Porter, *The Rise of Big Business, 1860–1910* (1973); Edward C. Kirkland, *Industry Comes of Age . . . 1860–1897* (1961); Harold G. Vatter, *The Drive to Industrial Maturity: The U.S. Economy, 1865–1914* (1975); Robert Higgs, *The Transformation of the American Economy, 1865–1914* (1971); and Alfred D. Chandler, *The Visible Hand: The Managerial Revolution in American Business* (1977). An old and entertaining (although biased and outmoded) portrait of the financial and industrial leaders of the era is Matthew Josephson, *The Robber Barons: The Great American Capitalists 1861–1901* (1934).

The Response to Industrialism

The response to industrialism and the rise of a regulatory antitrust movement are treated in Samuel P. Hays, *The Response to Industrialism, 1885–1914* (1957); Sidney Fine, *Laissez Faire and the General Welfare State: A Study of Conflict in American Thought, 1865–1900* (1956); George H. Miller, *Railroads and the Granger Laws* (1971); Gabriel Kolko, *Railroads and Regulation, 1877–1915* (1965); and Ari and Olive Hoogenboom, *A History of the ICC* (1976).

Labor

For the labor movement and labor strife, the following are particularly useful: Melvin Dubofsky, *Industrialism and the American Worker, 1865–1920* (1975); Walter Licht, *Working for the Railroad* (1983); Herbert G. Gutman, *Work, Culture, and Society in Industrializing America* (1976); Bruce Laurie, *Artisans into Workers: Labor in Nineteenth-Century America* (1989); David Montgomery, *The Fall of the House of Labor . . . 1865–1925* (1987); David Montgomery, *Workers' Control in*

America: Studies in the History of Work, Technology, and Labor Struggles (1979); Kevin Kenny, *Making Sense of the Molly Maguires* (1998); Leon Fink, *Workingmen's Democracy: The Knights of Labor and American Politics* (1983); Robert E. Weir, *Beyond Labor's Veil: The Culture of the Knights of Labor* (1996); Stuart Kaufman, *Samuel Gompers and the Origins of the American Federation of Labor* (1973); David Brody, *Steelworkers in America: The Nonunion Era* (1960); Robert V. Bruce, *1877: Year of Violence* (1959); Paul Avrich, *The Haymarket Tragedy* (1984); Leon Wolff, *Lockout, the Story of the Homestead Strike of 1892* (1965); and Almont Lindsey, *The Pullman Strike* (1971).

Populism and the Election of 1896

The classic history of the Populist movement, still valuable as a narrative, is John D. Hicks, *The Populist Revolt* (1931). The best modern survey of the movement is Lawrence Goodwyn, *Democratic Promise: The Populist Moment in America* (1976), which was published in an abridged edition with the title *The Populist Moment* (1978). Among the many other fine books about Populism, the following are especially useful: C. Vann Woodward, *Tom Watson, Agrarian Rebel* (1938); Peter Argersinger, *Populism and Politics* (1974); Steven Hahn, *The Roots of Southern Populism* (1983); Sheldon Hackney, *Populism to Progressivism in Alabama* (1969); Robert McMath, *Populist Vanguard: A History of the Southern Farmers' Alliance* (1975); and Gerald H. Gaither, *Blacks and the Populist Revolt* (1977). The complexities of the silver issue are unraveled in Allen Weinstein, *Prelude to Populism: Origins of the Silver Issue* (1970) and Gretchen Ritter, *Goldbugs and Greenbacks: The Antimonopoly Tradition and the Politics of Finance in America, 1865-1896* (1997).

The politics of the 1890s culminating in the climactic election of 1896 are treated in J. Rogers Hollingsworth, *The Whirligig of Politics: The Democracy of Cleveland and Bryan* (1963); Richard J. Jensen, *The Winning of the Midwest: Social and Political Conflict, 1888–1896* (1971); R. Hal Williams, *Years of Decision: American Politics in the 1890s* (1978); Paul W. Glad, *McKinley, Bryan, and the People* (1964); Stanley Jones, *The Presidential Election of 1896* (1964); and Robert F. Durden, *The Climax of Populism: The Election of 1896* (1965).

CHAPTER 20 AN INDUSTRIAL SOCIETY, 1890–1920

For a general overview of the period, Alan Dawley, *Struggles for Justice: Social Responsibility and the Liberal State* (1991), and Nell Irvin Painter, *Standing at Armageddon: The United States, 1877–1919* (1987), are excellent accounts and are particularly strong on issues of social history.

Economic Growth and Technological Innovation

On economic growth in the late 19th and early 20th centuries, see Harold G. Vatter, *The Drive to Industrial Maturity: The United States Economy, 1860–1914* (1975); Elliot Brownlee, *Dynamics of Ascent: A History of the American Economy*, 2nd ed. (1979); David Hounshell, *From the American System* to Mass Production, 1800–1932: The Development of Manufacturing Technology in the United States (1984); Nathan Rosenberg, Technology and American Economic Growth (1972); Charles Singer et al., eds., History of Technology, vol. 5: The Late Nineteenth Century (1958); and Harold I. Sharlin, The Making of the Electrical Age (1963). David Nye, Electrifying America: Social Meanings of a New Technology, 1890–1940 (1990), is a fascinating account of the social consequences of technological change. For an older but lively history on this theme, see Frederick Lewis Allen, The Big Change: America Transforms Itself, 1900–1950 (1952). Robert Conot, A Streak of Luck (1979), and Matthew Josephson, Edison (1959), assess Thomas Edison's contributions to the electrical revolution.

The Rise of the Modern Corporation

Alfred D. Chandler Jr., The Visible Hand: The Managerial Revolution in American Business (1977), is the classic work. See also Richard Tedlow, The Rise of the American Business Corporation (1991); Naomi Lamoreaux, The Great Merger Movement in American Business, 1895–1904 (1985); and Glenn Porter, The Rise of Big Business, 1860–1910 (1973). On the emerging alliance between corporations and science, see David F. Noble, America by Design: Science, Technology and the Rise of Corporate Capitalism (1977); Frederick A. White, American Industrial Research Laboratories (1961); and Leonard S. Reich, The Making of Industrial Research: Science and Business at GE and Bell, 1876–1926 (1985). On the legal and political changes that undergirded the corporation's triumph, see Martin J. Sklar, The Corporate Reconstruction of American Capitalism, 1890–1916: The Market, the Law and Politics (1988). Olivier Zunz, Making America Corporate, 1870–1920 (1990), is one of the first social histories to focus on the middle managers who comprised the new corporate middle class. A provocative exploration of the paths to economic development shut off by the triumph of mass production is found in Michael J. Piore and Charles F. Sabel, The Second Industrial Divide: Possibilities for Prosperity (1984). For an equally provocative critique of this interpretation, consult Philip Scranton, Endless Novelty: Specialty Production and American Industrialization, 1865–1925 (1997).

Scientific Management

Any examination of this topic must start with Frederick Winslow Taylor, The Principles of Scientific Management (1911), and Robert Kanigel, The One Best Way: Frederick Winslow Taylor and the Enigma of Efficiency (1997). Daniel Nelson, Frederick W. Taylor and the Rise of Scientific Management (1980), and David Montgomery, The Fall of the House of Labor: The Workplace, the State, and American Labor Activism, 1865–1925 (1987), are important. For its broader political ramifications, see Samuel Haber, Efficiency and Uplift: Scientific Management in the Progressive Era (1964). Allan Nevins and Frank E. Hill, Ford (1954–1963), is still the best biography of Henry Ford, but on Ford's labor policies, Stephen Meyer III, The Five Dollar Day: Labor Management and Social Control in the Ford Motor Company, 1908–1921 (1981), and Nelson Lichtenstein and Stephen Meyer III, eds., On the Line: Essays in the History of Auto Work (1989), are essential reading. For a general perspective on the changes in work and management in this period, consult Sanford M. Jacoby, Employing Bureaucracy: Managers, Unions, and the Transformation of Work in American Industry, 1900–1945 (1985).

Robber Barons and the Turn to Philanthropy

The classic work on the robber barons themselves is Matthew Josephson, The Robber Barons (1934). On the industrialists' turn to philanthropy, see Andrew Carnegie, The Gospel of Wealth (1889), and Autobiography (1920); Robert H. Bremner, American Philanthropy (1988); George E. Pozzetta, ed., Americanization, Social Control and Philanthropy (1991); Barry D. Karl and Stanley N. Katz, "The American Private Philanthropic Foundation and the Public Sphere, 1890–1930," Minerva 19 (Summer 1981): 236–70; and Ellen Condliffe Lagemann, The Politics of Knowledge: The Carnegie Corporation, Philanthropy, and Public Policy (1989).

"Racial Fitness" and Social Darwinism

On America's growing obsession with physical and racial fitness during this period, see John Higham, "The Reorientation of American Culture in the 1890s," in John Horace Weiss, ed., The Origins of Modern Consciousness, pp. 25–48 (1965), and Higham, Strangers in the Land: Patterns of American Nativism, rev. ed. (1992). For an assessment of the influence of Darwinist thinking on American culture, see Richard Hofstadter, Social Darwinism in American Thought, rev. ed. (1955); Robert Bannister, Social Darwinism: Science and Myth in Anglo-American Social Thought (1979); and Carl N. Degler, In Search of Human Nature: The Decline and Revival of Darwinism in American Social Thought (1991).

Immigration: General Histories

The best single-volume history of European immigrants is John Bodnar, The Transplanted: A History of Immigrants in Urban America (1985). Maldwyn Allen Jones, American Immigration (1974), and Alan M. Kraut, The Huddled Masses: The Immigrant in American Society, 1880–1921 (1982), are also useful. Ronald Takaki, A Different Mirror: A History of Multicultural America (1993), Roger Daniels, Coming to America: A History of Immigration and Ethnicity in American Life (1990), and Leonard Dinnerstein, Roger L. Nichols, and David Reimers, Natives and Strangers: Ethnic Groups and the Building of America (1979), integrate the story of European immigrants with that of African, Asian, and Latin American newcomers. Stephan Thernstrom, ed., Harvard Encyclopedia of American Ethnic Groups (1980), is indispensable on virtually all questions pertaining to immigration and ethnicity. Frank Thistlewaite, "Migration from Europe Overseas," in Stanley N. Katz and Stanley I. Kutler, eds., New Perspectives on the American Past (1969), vol. 2, pp. 152–81, is a pioneering article on patterns of European migration. On European immigrants' encounters with racial patterns in the United States, see Matthew Frye Jacobson, Whiteness of a Different Color: European Americans and the Alchemy of Race (1998).

Histories of Particular Immigrant Groups

Irving Howe, *World of Our Fathers: The Journey of the East European Jews to America and the Life They Found and Made* (1976), is the best work on Jewish immigration, although it must be supplemented by Susan A. Glenn, *Daughters of the Shtetl: Life and Labor in the Immigrant Generation* (1990). For work on the Irish, see Kerby A. Miller, *Emigrants and Exiles: Ireland and the Irish Exodus to North America* (1985), and Hasia A. Diner, *Erin's Daughters in America: Irish Immigrant Women in the Nineteenth Century* (1983). Other excellent works on particular ethnic groups include Ewa Morawska, *For Bread with Butter: The Life-Worlds of East Central Europeans in Johnstown, Pennsylvania, 1890–1940* (1985); John J. Bukowczyk, *And My Children Did Not Know Me: A History of Polish Americans* (1987); Virginia Yans-McLaughlin, *Family and Community: Italian Immigrants in Buffalo, 1880–1930* (1977); Yuji Ichioka, *The Issei: The World of the First Japanese Immigrants, 1895–1924* (1988); Sucheng Chan, *Asian Americans: An Interpretive History* (1991); and Mario T. Garcia, *Desert Immigrants: The Mexicans of El Paso, 1880–1920* (1981). Olivier Zunz, *The Changing Face of Inequality: Urbanization, Industrial Development and Immigrants in Detroit, 1880–1920* (1982), and S. J. Kleinberg, *The Shadow of the Mills: Working-Class Families in Pittsburgh, 1870–1907* (1989), compare the experiences of several European American groups in one city.

Immigrant Labor

Essential sources on both immigrant and nonimmigrant labor are Herbert Gutman, *Work, Culture and Society in Industrializing America* (1976); Montgomery, *The Fall of the House of Labor* (previously cited); and Alice Kessler-Harris, *Out of Work: A History of Wage-Earning Women in the United States* (1982). For a brief but incisive survey of working conditions in this period, consult Melvyn Dubofsky, *Industrialism and the American Worker, 1865–1920*, 2nd ed. (1985). Tamara Hareven, *Family Time and Historical Time: The Relationship between the Family and Work in a New England Industrial Community* (1982), and James R. Barrett, *Work and Community in the Jungle: Chicago's Packinghouse Workers, 1894–1922* (1990), are excellent local studies. Leon Stein, *The Triangle Fire* (1962), and John F. McClymer, *The Triangle Strike and Fire* (1998), chronicle that industrial disaster; and Alexander Keyssar, *Out of Work: The First Century of Unemployment in Massachusetts* (1986), offers the best analysis of unemployment in this period.

Immigrants, African Americans, and Social Mobility

Good sources on this topic include Stephan Thernstrom, *The Other Bostonians: Poverty and Progress in the American Metropolis* (1973); Joel Perlman, *Ethnic Differences: Schooling and Social Structure among the Irish, Italians, Jews, and Blacks in an American City, 1880–1935* (1988); Thomas Kessner, *The Golden Door: Italian and Jewish Mobility in New York City, 1880–1915* (1977); Edna Bonacich and John Modell, *The Economic Basis of Ethnic Solidarity: Small Businessmen in the Japanese-American Community* (1980); Stephen Steinberg, *The Ethnic Myth: Race, Ethnicity, and Class in America* (1981); Thomas Sowell, *Ethnic America: A History* (1981); and Stanley Lieberson, *A Piece of the Pie: Blacks and White Immigrants Since 1880* (1980).

Immigrants, Political Machines, and Organized Crime

Steven P. Erie, *Rainbow's End: Irish Americans and the Dilemmas of Urban Machine Politics, 1840–1945* (1988), insightfully examines the benefits and costs of big city machines. See also Harold Zink, *City Bosses in the United States: A Study of Twenty Municipal Bosses* (1930); M. Craig Brown and Charles N. Halaby, "Machine Politics in America, 1870–1945," *Journal of Interdisciplinary History* 8 (1987): 587–612; John M. Allswang, *Bosses, Machines, and Urban Voters* (1977); Alexander B. Callow, ed., *The City Boss in America* (1976); and William L. Riordon, *Plunkitt of Tammany Hall: A Series of Very Plain Talks on Very Practical Politics* (1994). On organized crime, consult Joseph Albini, *The American Mafia* (1971); Humbert Nelli, *The Business of Crime* (1976); and Jenna Weissman Joselit, *Our Gang: Jewish Crime and the New York Jewish Community* (1983). Doris Kearns Goodwin, *The Fitzgeralds and the Kennedys* (1987), chronicles the history of President John F. Kennedy's family.

African Americans

John Hope Franklin and Alfred A. Moss Jr., *From Slavery to Freedom: A History of Negro Americans*, 7th ed. (1994), offers a masterful overview. Gavin Wright, *Old South, New South: Revolutions in the Southern Economy since the Civil War* (1986), analyzes the southern sharecropping economy, while William H. Harris, *The Harder We Run: Black Workers since the Civil War* (1982), assesses the experiences of black industrial workers, South and North. On black female workers, consult Jacqueline Jones, *Labor of Love, Labor of Sorrow: Black Women, Work and the Family from Slavery to the Present* (1985). Kenneth L. Kusmer, *A Ghetto Takes Shape: Black Cleveland, 1870–1930* (1978), is the best work on the formation of urban black communities in the North prior to the Great Migration (1916–1920), but it should be supplemented with Elizabeth Hafkin Pleck, *Black Migration and Poverty: Boston, 1865–1900* (1979); Allan H. Spear, *Black Chicago: The Making of a Negro Ghetto, 1890–1920* (1967); and Theodore Hershberg et al., *Philadelphia: Work, Space, Family, and Group Experience in the Nineteenth Century* (1981). On the rise of a new black middle class, see Evelyn Brooks Higginbotham, *Righteous Discontent: The Women's Movement in the Black Baptist Church, 1880–1920* (1993), and Kevin K. Gaines, *Uplifting the Race: Black Leadership, Politics, and Culture in the Twentieth Century* (1996).

Workers and Unions

Indispensable sources are Montgomery, *The Fall of the House of Labor* (previously cited); David Brody, *Workers in Industrial America: Essays on the Twentieth Century Struggle* (1980); and Melvyn Dubofsky, *We Shall Be All: A History of the Industrial Workers of the World* (1969). Samuel Gompers's career can be traced through Stuart Kaufman, *Samuel Gompers and the Origins of the American Federation of Labor* (1973), and Gompers's own *Seventy Years of Life and Labor: An Autobiography*, ed.

Nick Salvatore (1984). Michael Kazin, *Barons of Labor: The San Francisco Building Trades and Union Power in the Progressive Era* (1987), is a sterling study of AFL craftsmen at work and in local politics; and Gwendolyn Mink, *Old Labor and New Immigrants in American Political Development: Union, Party, and State, 1875–1920* (1986), offers a provocative interpretation of the AFL's role in national politics. Christopher Tomlins, *The State and the Unions: Labor Relations, Law, and the Organized Labor Movement in America, 1880–1960* (1985), carefully analyzes the effect of law on the labor movement's development.

David A. Corbin, *Life, Work, and Rebellion in the Coal Fields: The Southern West Virginia Miners, 1880–1922* (1981), examines the rise of the United Mine Workers; and Howe, *World of Our Fathers* (previously cited), treats the early years of the ILGWU in New York City. Sterling D. Spero and Abram L. Harris, *The Black Worker: The Negro and the Labor Movement* (1931), and James R. Grossman, *Land of Hope: Chicago, Black Southerners, and the Great Migration* (1989), analyze AFL attitudes toward black workers. Eric Arnesen, *Waterfront Workers of New Orleans: Race, Class and Politics, 1863–1923* (1991), probes that city's remarkable experiment in biracial unionism. Graham Adams Jr., *Age of Industrial Violence, 1910–1915: The Activities and Findings of the United States Commission on Industrial Relations* (1966), chronicles the Ludlow massacre and other labor–capital confrontations in these years. See also J. Anthony Lukas, *Big Trouble: A Murder in a Small Western Town Sets Off a Struggle for the Soul of America* (1997), a remarkable study of class conflict in the West during the early years of the 20th century.

The Rise of Mass Culture

On the rise of mass culture, see David Nasaw, *Going Out: The Rise and Fall of Public Amusements* (1993); William Leach, *Land of Desire: Merchants, Power, and the Rise of a New American Culture* (1993); Roy Rosenzweig, *Eight Hours for What We Will: Workers and Leisure in an Industrial City, 1870–1920* (1983); and Lewis A. Erenberg, *Steppin' Out: New York Nightlife and the Transformation of American Culture, 1890–1930* (1981). Warren I. Susman, *Culture as History: The Transformation of American Society in the Twentieth Century* (1984), is essential reading for any student of this subject. Excellent studies of the rise of movies are Rosenzweig, *Eight Hours for What We Will* (previously cited); Lary May, *Screening Out the Past: The Birth of Mass Culture and the Motion Picture Industry* (1980); Robert Sklar, *Movie-Made America: A Social History of the American Movies* (1975); and Steven J. Ross, *Working-Class Hollywood: Silent Film and the Shaping of Class in America* (1998).

The "New Woman"

On the emergence of the "new woman," see Kathy Peiss, *Cheap Amusements: Working Women and Leisure in Turn-of-the-Century New York* (1986); Elaine Tyler May, *Great Expectations: Marriage and Divorce in Post-Victorian America* (1980); Leslie Woodcock Tentler, *Wage-Earning Women: Industrial Work and Family Life in the United States, 1900–1930* (1979); Joanne Meyerowitz, *Women Adrift: Inde-* *pendent Wage-Earners in Chicago, 1870–1930* (1988); and Elizabeth Lunbeck, *The Psychiatric Persuasion: Knowledge, Gender and Politics in Modern America* (1994).

Feminism

Nancy F. Cott, *The Grounding of Modern Feminism* (1987), is the most important study of the movement's origins. Linda Gordon, *Woman's Body, Woman's Right: A Social History of Birth Control in America* (1976), and James Reed, *The Birth Control Movement and American Society: From Private Vice to Public Virtue* (1983), are important works on the history of birth control. Also see the following first-rate biographies: David M. Kennedy, *Birth Control in America: The Career of Margaret Sanger* (1970); Alice Wexler, *Emma Goldman: An Intimate Life* (1984); and Christine A. Lunardini, *From Equal Suffrage to Equal Rights: Alice Paul and the National Women's Party, 1912–1928* (1986). For a brief biography of Charlotte Perkins Gilman, see Gary Scharnhorst, *Charlotte Perkins Gilman* (1985). Leslie Fishbein, *Rebels in Bohemia: The Radicals of "The Masses," 1911–1917* (1982), deftly recreates the politics and culture of Greenwich Village.

CHAPTER 21 PROGRESSIVISM

No topic in 20th-century American history has generated as large and rapidly changing a scholarship as has progressivism. Today, few scholars treat this political movement in the terms set forth by the Progressives themselves: as a movement of "the people" against the "special interests." In *The Age of Reform: From Bryan to FDR* (1955), Richard Hofstadter argues that progressivism was the expression of a declining Protestant middle class at odds with the new industrial order. In *The Search for Order, 1877–1920* (1967), Robert Wiebe finds the movement's core in a rising middle class, closely allied to the corporations and bureaucratic imperatives that were defining this new order. Gabriel Kolko, *The Triumph of Conservatism: A Reinterpretation of American History* (1963), and James Weinstein, *The Corporate Ideal in the Liberal State, 1900–1918* (1969), both argue that progressivism was the work of industrialists themselves, who were eager to ensure corporate stability and profitability in a dangerously unstable capitalist economy. Without denying the importance of this corporate search for order, Nell Irvin Painter, *Standing at Armageddon: The United States, 1877–1919* (1987), and Alan Dawley, *Struggles for Justice: Social Responsibility and the Liberal State* (1991), insist on the role of the working class, men and women, whites and blacks, in shaping the progressive agenda. James T. Kloppenberg, *Uncertain Victory: Social Democracy and Progressivism in European and American Thought, 1870–1920* (1986), and Thomas J. Knock, *To End All Wars: Woodrow Wilson and the Quest for a New World Order* (1992), emphasize the influence of socialism on progressive thought, while Martin J. Sklar, *The Corporate Reconstruction of American Capitalism, 1900–1916: The Market, the Law and Politics* (1988), stresses the role of progressivism in "containing" or taming socialism. Paul Boyer, *Urban Masses and Moral Order in America, 1820–1920* (1978), treats progressivism as a cultural movement to enforce middle-class norms on an unruly urban and immigrant population. Theda Skocpol, *Protecting Soldiers and Mothers: The Political Origins of Social Policy in the United States* (1992), reconstructs the central role of middle-class Protestant women in shaping progressive social policy, while Robert M. Crunden, *Ministers of Reform: The Progressives' Achievement in American Civilization, 1889–1920* (1982), stresses the religious roots of Progressive reform. Summaries of some of these various interpretations of progressivism—but by no means all—can be found in Arthur S. Link and Richard L. McCormick, *Progressivism* (1983).

Muckrakers, Settlement Houses, and Women Reformers

On the muckrakers, see Walter M. Brasch, *Forerunners of Revolution: Muckrakers and the American Social Conscience* (1990); Harold S. Wilson, *McClure's Magazine and the Muckrakers* (1970); and Justin Kaplan, *Lincoln Steffens* (1974). On the settlement houses and women reformers, consult Jane Addams, *Twenty Years at Hull House* (1910); Kathryn Kish Sklar, *Florence Kelley and the Nation's Work: The Rise of Women's Political Culture, 1830–1900* (1995); Allen F. Davis, *Spearheads for Reform: The Social Settlements and the Progressive Movement, 1890–1914* (1967); Mina Julia Carson, *Settlement Folk: Social Thought and the American Settlement Movement, 1885–1930* (1990); and Rivka Shpak Lissak, *Pluralism and the Progressives: Hull House and the New Immigrants, 1890–1919* (1989). Ruth Borden, *Women and Temperance* (1980), is useful on the role of women in the prohibition movement. Paula Baker, "The Domestication of Politics: Women and American Political Society, 1780–1920," *American Historical Review* 89 (June 1984): 620–47, and Robyn Muncy, *Creating a Female Dominion in American Reform, 1890–1935* (1991), are important for understanding women's political activism in the years before they gained the vote.

Socialism

For general histories, see James Weinstein, *The Decline of Socialism in America, 1912–1925* (1967), and Irving Howe, *Socialism in America* (1985). Mari Jo Buhle, *Women and American Socialism, 1870–1920* (1981), expertly analyzes the experiences of women who became socialists. Nick Salvatore, *Eugene V. Debs: Citizen and Socialist* (1982), is a superb biography of the charismatic Debs; Melvyn Dubofsky, *We Shall Be All: A History of the Industrial Workers of the World* (1969), offers the most thorough treatment of the IWW. James R. Green, *Grass-Roots Socialism: Radical Movements in the Southwest, 1895–1943* (1978), and Elliott Shore, *Talkin' Socialism: J. A. Wayland and the Role of the Press in American Radicalism, 1890–1912* (1988), analyze socialist movements in the Southwest.

Political Reform in the Cities

Melvin Holli, *Reform in Detroit: Hazen S. Pingree and Urban Politics* (1969), is an exemplary study of a progressive mayor. On efforts to reform municipal governments, see David C. Hammack, *Power and Society: Greater New York at the Turn of the Century* (1982); Bradley R. Rice, *Progressive Cities: The Commission Government Movement in America, 1901–1920* (1977); and Martin J. Schiesl, *The Politics of Efficiency: Municipal Administration and Reform in America* (1977).

Reform in the States

Richard L. McCormick, *The Party Period and Public Policy* (1986), is indispensable on the roots of state reform. Thomas E. Cronin, *Direct Democracy: The Politics of Initiative, Referendum and Recall* (1989), examines the various movements to limit the power of party bosses and private interests in state politics. David P. Thelen, *The New Citizenship: Origins of Progressivism in Wisconsin, 1885–1900* (1972) and *Robert M. La Follette and the Insurgent Spirit* (1976), offer the best introduction to Wisconsin progressivism. For New York progressivism, consult Richard L. McCormick, *From Realignment to Reform: Political Change in New York State, 1893–1910* (1981); J. Joseph Huthmacher, *Senator Robert F. Wagner and the Rise of Urban Liberalism* (1971); Oscar Handlin, *Al Smith and His America* (1958); and Irvin Yellowitz, *Labor and the Progressive Movement in New York State* (1965). On social and economic reform movements more generally, see John D. Buenker, *Urban Liberalism and Progressive Reform* (1973). George E. Mowry, *The California Progressives* (1951), and Michael Kazin, *Barons of Labor: The San Francisco Building Trades and Union Power in the Progressive Era* (1987), examine the complexities of progressivism in California. On progressivism in the South, consult Sheldon Hackney, *Populism to Progressivism in Alabama* (1969); Jack Temple Kirby, *Darkness at the Dawning: Race and Reform in the Progressive South* (1972); and Dewey Grantham, *Southern Progressivism: The Reconciliation of Progress and Tradition* (1983).

Reconfiguring the Electorate and the Regulation of Voting

On progressive efforts to reform and reconfigure the electorate, see Michael E. McGerr, *The Decline of Popular Politics: The American North, 1865–1928* (1986); L. E. Fredman, *The Australian Ballot: The Story of an American Reform* (1968); Paul Kleppner, *Who Voted? The Dynamics of Electoral Turnout, 1870–1980* (1982); and John Francis Reynolds, *Testing Democracy: Electoral Behavior and Progressive Reform in New Jersey, 1880–1920* (1988). J. Morgan Kousser, *The Shaping of Southern Politics: Suffrage Restriction and the Establishment of the One-Party South, 1880–1910* (1974), is indispensable on black disfranchisement. On the campaign for woman suffrage, see Anne Firor Scott and Andrew MacKay Scott, *One Half the People: The Fight for Woman Suffrage* (1982); Aileen Kraditor, *Ideas of the Woman Suffrage Movement* (1965); David Morgan, *The Suffragists and Democrats: The Politics of Woman's Suffrage in America* (1972); and Christine Lunardini, *From Equal Suffrage to Equal Rights: Alice Paul and the National Women's Party, 1912–1920* (1986).

Civil Rights

On the renewed campaign for black civil rights, see Charles F. Kellogg, *NAACP: The History of the National Association for* the *Advancement of Colored People* (1967); Louis R. Harlan, *Booker T. Washington: Wizard of Tuskegee, 1901–1915* (1983); David Levering Lewis, *W. E. B. DuBois: Biography of a Race, 1868–1919* (1993); and Nancy Weiss, *The National Urban League, 1910–1940* (1974).

National Reform
George E. Mowry, *The Era of Theodore Roosevelt* (1958), and Arthur Link, *Woodrow Wilson and the Progressive Era* (1954), are comprehensive overviews of progressivism at the national level. On the conservation movement, see Samuel P. Hays, *The Gospel of Efficiency: The Progressive Conservation Movement, 1890–1920* (1962); Stephen R. Fox, *The American Conservation Movement: John Muir and His Legacy* (1981); and Alfred Runte, *National Parks: The American Experience* (1979). On conflicts within the Republican Party, consult Horace S. Merrill and Marion G. Merrill, *The Republican High Command* (1971). On the Federal Reserve Act, see Robert T. McCulley, *Banks and Politics during the Progressive Era: The Origins of the Federal Reserve System* (1992), and James Livingston, *Origins of the Federal Reserve System: Money, Class and Corporate Capitalism, 1890–1913* (1986). On Louis Brandeis, consult Phillippa Strum, *Louis D. Brandeis* (1984), and Melvin Urofsky, *Louis D. Brandeis and the Progressive Tradition* (1981).

Theodore Roosevelt
Good biographies of Roosevelt include Henry F. Pringle, *Theodore Roosevelt* (1931); William H. Harbaugh, *The Life and Times of Theodore Roosevelt* (1975); G. Wallace Chessman, *Theodore Roosevelt and the Politics of Power* (1969); Robert V. Friedenberg, *Theodore Roosevelt and the Rhetoric of Militant Decency* (1990); and H. W. Brands, *TR: The Last Romantic* (1997). John M. Blum, *The Republican Roosevelt* (1954), is a brief but significant interpretive account of Roosevelt's career, and Edmund Morris, *The Rise of Theodore Roosevelt* (1979), is a lively account of Roosevelt's early years.

William Howard Taft
The fullest biography is still Henry F. Pringle, *The Life and Times of William Howard Taft*, 2 vols. (1939). For more critical views of Taft, see Paolo E. Coletta, *The Presidency of Taft* (1973), and Donald E. Anderson, *William Howard Taft* (1973). On the Pinchot-Ballinger affair, consult James Penich Jr., *Progressive Politics and Conservation: The Ballinger-Pinchot Affair* (1968), and Harold T. Pinkett, *Gifford Pinchot: Private and Public Forester* (1970).

Woodrow Wilson
The premier biography and chronicle of Wilson's life from birth until the First World War is Arthur S. Link, *Woodrow Wilson*, 5 vols. (1947–65). Other important biographies include Arthur Walworth, *Woodrow Wilson*, 2 vols. (1958); John M. Blum, *Woodrow Wilson and the Politics of Morality* (1962); August Heckscher, *Woodrow Wilson* (1991); Kendrick A. Clements, *The Presidency of Woodrow Wilson* (1992); and John Milton Cooper Jr., *The Warrior and the Priest: Woodrow Wilson and Theodore Roosevelt* (1983).

CHAPTER 22 BECOMING A WORLD POWER, 1898–1917
General works on America's imperialist turn in the 1890s and early years of the 20th century include John Dobson, *America's Ascent: The United States Becomes a Great Power, 1880–1914* (1978); H. Wayne Morgan, *America's Road to Empire* (1965); David F. Healy, *U.S. Expansionism: Imperialist Urge in the 1890s* (1970); Ernest R. May, *Imperial Democracy: The Emergence of America as a Great Power* (1961); Robert L. Beisner, *From the Old Diplomacy to the New, 1865–1900* (1986); and Walter LaFeber, *The Cambridge History of Foreign Relations: The Search for Opportunity, 1865–1913* (1993).

Motives for Expansion
Patricia Hill, *The World Their Household: The American Woman's Foreign Mission Movement and Cultural Transformation, 1870–1920* (1984), and Jane Hunter, *The Gospel of Gentility: American Women Missionaries in Turn-of-the-Century China* (1984), are excellent on the overseas work of female Protestant missionaries. William Appleman Williams, *The Tragedy of American Diplomacy*, rev. ed. (1972), is still indispensable on the economic motives behind imperialism, but it should be supplemented with Emily Rosenberg, *Spreading the American Dream: American Economic and Cultural Expansion, 1890–1945* (1982). For an important critique of Frederick Jackson Turner's notion that the year 1890 marked the end of the frontier, consult Patricia Nelson Limerick, *The Legacy of Conquest: The Unbroken Past of the American West* (1987). William E. Livezey, *Mahan on Sea Power* (1981), analyzes Admiral Mahan's strategy for transforming the United States into a world power, and Walter R. Herrick, *The American Naval Revolution* (1966), examines the emergence of a "Big Navy" policy. Julius W. Pratt, *Expansionists of 1898* (1936), is an important account of mounting jingoist fever in the 1890s.

The Spanish-American War
David F. Trask, *The War with Spain in 1898* (1981), is a comprehensive study of the Spanish-American War, but it should be supplemented with Philip S. Foner, *The Spanish-Cuban-American War and the Birth of American Imperialism*, 2 vols. (1972). See also James E. Bradford, *Crucible of Empire: The Spanish-American War and Its Aftermath* (1993). Joyce Milton, *The Yellow Journalists* (1989), discusses the role of the press in whipping up war fever, and Michael Blow, *A Ship to Remember: The Maine and the Spanish-American War* (1992), analyzes the battleship sinking that became the war's catalyst. Graham A. Cosmas, *An Army for Empire: The United States Army in the Spanish-American War* (1971), examines the achievements and failures of the army. Edmund Morris, *The Rise of Theodore Roosevelt* (1979), captures the daring of Roosevelt's Rough Riders and their charge up Kettle Hill, while William B. Gatewood Jr., *"Smoked Yankees": Letters from Negro Soldiers, 1898–1902* (1971), examines the important and unappreciated contributions of black soldiers. Gerald F. Linderman, *The Mirror of War: American Society and the Spanish-American War* (1974), brilliantly recaptures the

shock that overtook Americans who discovered that their Cuban allies were black and the Spanish enemies were white.

Building an Empire

Julius W. Pratt, *America's Colonial Empire* (1950), analyzes steps the United States took to build itself an empire in the wake of the Spanish-American War. The annexation of Hawaii can be followed in Merze Tate, *The United States and the Hawaiian Kingdom* (1965), and William A. Russ, Jr., *The Hawaiian Republic, 1894–1898, and Its Struggle to Win Annexation* (1961). The acquisition of Guam and Samoa is examined in Paul Carano and Pedro Sanchez, *A Complete History of Guam* (1964), and Paul M. Kennedy, *The Samoan Tangle* (1974). The anti-imperialist movement is analyzed in E. Berkeley Tompkins, *Anti-Imperialism in the United States, 1890–1920: The Great Debate* (1970); Robert L. Beisner, *Twelve against Empire: The Anti-Imperialists, 1898–1900* (1968); and Daniel B. Schirmer, *Republic or Empire? American Resistance to the Philippine War* (1972). Richard E. Welch, Jr., *Response to Imperialism: The United States and the Philippine War, 1899–1902* (1979), and Stuart Creighton Miller, *"Benevolent Assimilation": The American Conquest of the Philippines, 1899–1903* (1982), analyze the Filipino-American war, while Peter Stanley, *A Nation in the Making: The Philippines and the United States, 1899–1921* (1974), examines the fate of the Philippines under the first 20 years of U.S. rule. James H. Hitchman, *Leonard Wood and Cuban Independence, 1898–1902* (1971), and Louis A. Perez, *Cuba under the Platt Amendment, 1902–1934* (1986), analyze the extension of U.S. control over Cuba, while Raymond Carr, *Puerto Rico: A Colonial Experiment* (1984), examines the history of Puerto Rico following its annexation by the United States. For the unfolding of the Open Door policy toward China, consult Marilyn B. Young, *The Rhetoric of Empire: American China Policy, 1895–1901* (1968); Warren I. Cohen, *America's Response to China* (1971); and Thomas J. McCormick, *China Market: America's Quest for Informal Empire, 1890–1915* (1971).

Theodore Roosevelt

Howard K. Beale, *Theodore Roosevelt and the Rise of America to World Power* (1956), is still a crucial work on Roosevelt's foreign policy, although it should be supplemented with David H. Burton, *Theodore Roosevelt: Confident Imperialist* (1968), and Frederick Marks III, *Velvet on Iron: The Diplomacy of Theodore Roosevelt* (1979). Richard H. Collin, *Theodore Roosevelt's Caribbean: The Panama Canal, the Monroe Doctrine and the Latin American Context* (1990), examines Roosevelt's Caribbean policy. Of the many books written on the Panama Canal, two stand out: Walter LaFeber, *The Panama Canal* (1978), and David McCullough, *The Path between the Seas* (1977), a lively account of the canal's construction. See also Michael L. Conniff, *Black Labor on a White Canal: Panama, 1904–1981* (1985). For Roosevelt's policy in East Asia, consult Akira Iriye, *Pacific Estrangement: Japanese and American Expansion, 1897–1911* (1972); Charles Neu, *An Uncertain Friendship: Theodore Roosevelt and Japan, 1906–1909* (1967); and Charles Neu, *The Troubled Encounter* (1975). On the

treatment of the Japanese in California, see Jules Becker, *The Course of Exclusion, 1882–1924: San Francisco Newspaper Coverage of the Chinese and Japanese in the United States* (1991).

William Howard Taft

Ralph E. Minger, *William Howard Taft and American Foreign Policy* (1975), and Walter V. Scholes and Marie V. Scholes, *The Foreign Policies of the Taft Administration* (1970), are the standard works on William Howard Taft's foreign policies. For a comprehensive look at his "dollar diplomacy" and its effects on the Caribbean, see Dana G. Munro, *Intervention and Dollar Diplomacy in the Caribbean, 1900–1920* (1964). See also Emily Rosenberg, *Financial Missionaries to the World: The Politics and Culture of Dollar Diplomacy, 1900–1930* (1999).

Woodrow Wilson

Two books by Arthur Link, *Wilson the Diplomatist* (1957) and *Woodrow Wilson: Revolution, War, and Peace* (1979), sympathetically treat Wilson's struggle to fashion an idealistic foreign policy. These works must be supplemented with Thomas J. Knock, *To End All Wars: Woodrow Wilson and the Quest for a New World Order* (1992). Lloyd C. Gardner, *Safe for Democracy: The Anglo-American Response to Revolution, 1913–1923* (1984), offers a more critical appraisal of Wilson's policies. On U.S. responses to the Mexican Revolution, see John S. D. Eisenhower, *Intervention: The United States and the Mexican Revolution, 1913–1917* (1993); Peter Calvert, *The Mexican Revolution, 1910–1914* (1968); Kenneth J. Grieb, *The United States and Huerta* (1969); and Robert E. Quirk, *An Affair of Honor: Woodrow Wilson and the Occupation of Veracruz* (1962).

CHAPTER 23 WAR AND SOCIETY, 1914–1920

On the factors leading to the outbreak of war in Europe in 1914, see James Joll, *The Origins of the First World War* (1984), and Fritz Fisher, *Germany's War Aims in the First World War* (1972). On the horrors of trench warfare, see John Keegan, *The Face of Battle* (1976), and Erich Maria Remarque's classic novel, *All Quiet on the Western Front* (1929). Paul Fussell, *The Great War and Modern Memory* (1973), is indispensable for understanding the effects of the First World War on European culture.

American Neutrality and Intervention

On American neutrality, see Arthur S. Link, *Woodrow Wilson: Revolution, War and Peace* (1979); John Milton Cooper Jr., *The Vanity of Power: American Isolationism and the First World War, 1914–1917* (1969); and Ernest R. May, *The World War and American Isolation, 1914–1917* (1959). Roland C. Marchand, *The American Peace Movement and Social Reform, 1898–1918* (1972), reconstructs the large and influential antiwar movement, while Ross Gregory, *The Origins of American Intervention in the First World War* (1971), analyzes the events that triggered America's intervention. Daniel R.

Beaver, *Newton D. Baker and the American War Effort, 1917–1919* (1966), and John W. Chambers, *To Raise an Army: The Draft Comes to Modern America* (1987), analyze efforts to raise a multimillion-man fighting machine. Russell Weigley, *The American Way of War* (1973), examines the combat experiences of the American Expeditionary Force, while David F. Trask, *The AEF and Coalition Warmaking, 1917–1918* (1973), looks at relations between the AEF and the Allied armies. On the soldiers themselves, consult J. Garry Clifford, *The Citizen Soldiers* (1972), and A. E. Barbeau and Florette Henri, *The Unknown Soldiers: Black American Troops in World War I* (1974). Frank E. Vandiver, *Black Jack: The Life and Times of John J. Pershing* (1977), chronicles the life of the AEF's commander. Daniel H. Kevles, "Testing the Army's Intelligence: Psychologists and the Military in World War I," *Journal of American History* 55 (December 1968): 565–82, examines the military's use and misuse of IQ tests.

The Home Front

David Kennedy, *Over Here: The First World War and American Society* (1980), is a superb account of the effects of war on American society, but it should be supplemented with Robert H. Ferrell, *Woodrow Wilson and World War I, 1917–1921* (1985), and Ronald Schaffer, *America in the Great War: The Rise of the War Welfare State* (1991). On industrial mobilization, see Robert D. Cuff, *The War Industries Board: Business-Government Relations during World War I* (1973), and the pertinent sections of Jordan Schwarz, *The Speculator* (1981), an excellent biography of Bernard Baruch. Efforts to secure labor's cooperation are examined in Valerie J. Connor, *The National War Labor Board* (1983); Keith Grieves, *The Politics of Manpower, 1914–1918* (1988); and Frank L. Grubb, *Samuel Gompers and the Great War* (1982). On the migration of African Americans to northern industrial centers and the movement of women into war production, see Florette Henri, *Black Migration: Movement North, 1900–1920* (1975); Joe William Trotter Jr., ed., *The Great Migration in Historical Perspective: New Dimensions of Race, Class, and Gender* (1991); James R. Grossman, *Land of Hope: Chicago, Black Southerners, and the Great Migration* (1989); and Maurine W. Greenwald, *Women, War and Work* (1980). David Montgomery, *The Fall of the House of Labor: The Workplace, the State, and American Labor Activism, 1865–1925* (1987), expertly reconstructs the escalation of labor-management tensions during the war, but it should be read alongside Joseph A. McCartin, *Labor's Great War: The Struggle for Industrial Democracy and the Origins of Modern Labor Relations, 1912–1921* (1997). Charles Gilbert, *American Financing of World War I* (1970), is indispensable on wartime tax and bond policies. See also Sidney Ratner, *Taxation and Democracy in America* (1967), and Dale N. Shook, *William G. McAdoo and the Development of National Economic Policy, 1913–1918* (1987).

Government Propaganda and Repression

Stephen Vaughn, *Holding Fast the Inner Lines: Democracy, Nationalism, and the Committee on Public Information* (1980), is an important account of the CPI, the government's central propaganda agency. See also George Creel, *How We Advertised America* (1920); John A. Thompson, *Reformers and War: Progressive Publicists and the First World War* (1987); and Walton Rawls, *Wake Up, America! World War I and the American Poster* (1987). The government's turn to repression as a way of achieving social unity can be followed in Zechariah Chafee Jr., *Free Speech in the United States* (1941); Harry N. Scheiber, *The Wilson Administration and Civil Liberties, 1917–1921* (1960); Harold C. Peterson and Gilbert Fite, *Opponents of War, 1917–1918* (1968); and William Preston Jr., *Aliens and Dissenters: Federal Suppression of Radicals, 1903–1933* (1966). John Higham, *Strangers in the Land: Patterns of American Nativism, 1865–1925* (1955), and Frederick C. Luebke, *Bonds of Loyalty: German-Americans and World War I* (1974), analyze the effects of this repression on European ethnic communities. Carol S. Gruber, *Mars and Minerva: World War I and the Uses of Higher Learning in America* (1975), discusses the effects of war on universities.

Woodrow Wilson and the League of Nations

The best introduction is Thomas J. Knock, *To End All Wars: Woodrow Wilson and the Quest for a New World Order* (1992). For a more critical view of Wilson's motives, however, consult Arno Mayer, *The Politics and Diplomacy of Peacemaking: Containment and Counterrevolution at Versailles, 1918–1919* (1967); N. Gordon Levin Jr., *Woodrow Wilson and World Politics: America's Response to War and Revolution* (1968); and Lloyd C. Gardner, *Safe for Democracy: The Anglo-American Response to Revolution, 1913–1923* (1984). On Republican opposition to the League of Nations, see Ralph Stone, *The Irreconcilables: The Fight against the League of Nations* (1970), and William C. Widenor, *Henry Cabot Lodge and the Search for an American Foreign Policy* (1980).

Postwar Strikes and Radicalism

Nell Irvin Painter, *Standing at Armageddon: The United States, 1877–1919* (1987), offers a good overview of the class and racial divisions that convulsed American society in 1919. Consult Dana Frank, *Purchasing Power: Consumer Organizing, Gender, and the Seattle Labor Movement, 1919–1929* (1994), on the Seattle general strike; Francis Russell, *A City in Terror* (1975), on the Boston police strike; and David Brody, *Labor in Crisis: The Steel Strike of 1919* (1965), on the steel strike. James Weinstein, *The Decline of Socialism in America, 1912–1925* (1967), and Theodore Draper, *The Roots of American Communism* (1957), analyze the effects of the Bolshevik Revolution on American socialism. On the Red Scare, consult Robert K. Murray, *Red Scare: A Study in National Hysteria* (1955); Stanley Coben, *A. Mitchell Palmer: Politician* (1963); and Richard Polenberg, *Fighting Faiths: The Abrams Case, the Supreme Court, and Free Speech* (1987). Roberta Strauss Feuerlicht, *Justice Crucified* (1977), and Francis Russell, *Tragedy in Dedham* (1962), offer divergent interpretations of the Sacco-Vanzetti affair. Paul Avrich, *Sacco-Vanzetti: The Anarchist Background* (1991), reconstructs the anarchist milieu from which Sacco and Vanzetti emerged.

Race Riots and Black Nationalism

William Tuttle Jr., *Race Riot: Chicago in the Red Summer of 1919* (1970), and Elliott M. Rudwick, *Race Riot at East St. Louis* (1964), examine the two most notorious race riots of 1919. On the emergence of Marcus Garvey and the Universal Negro Improvement Association, see Judith Stein, *The World of Marcus Garvey: Race and Class in Modern Society* (1986), and David Cronon, *Black Moses* (1955).

CHAPTER 24 THE 1920s

Overviews

See William Leuchtenberg, *The Perils of Prosperity, 1914–1932* (1958); Geoffrey Perrett, *America in the Twenties* (1982); and Ellis Hawley, *The Great War and the Search for a Modern Order: A History of the American People and Their Institutions, 1917–1933* (1979). Frederick Lewis Allen, *Only Yesterday* (1931), remains the most entertaining account of the Jazz Age.

Prosperity and a Consumer Society

George Soule, *Prosperity Decade: From War to Depression, 1917–1929* (1947), offers a thorough analysis of the decade's principal economic developments. Alfred D. Chandler, Jr., *Strategy and Structure: Chapters in the History of the American Enterprise* (1962), and Adolph A. Berle, Jr., and Gardiner F. Means, *The Modern Corporation and Private Property* (1932), examine changes in the structure and management of corporations. Important works on the consumer revolution include Robert S. Lynd and Helen Merrell Lynd, *Middletown: A Study in Modern American Culture* (1929); Warren I. Susman, *Culture as History: The Transformation of American Society in the Twentieth Century* (1984); Stewart Ewen, *Captains of Consciousness: Advertising and the Social Roots of the Consumer Culture* (1976); Roland Marchand, *Advertising the American Dream: Making Way for Modernity, 1920–1940* (1985); Richard Wightman Fox and T. J. Jackson Lears, eds., *The Culture of Consumption: Critical Essays in American History, 1880–1980* (1983); Kathy Lee Peiss, *Hope in a Jar: The Making of America's Beauty Culture* (1998); and Jackson Lears, *Fables of Abundance: A Cultural History of Advertising in America* (1994). The ways in which consumer ideals reshaped gender roles and family life can be followed in Ruth Schwartz Cowan, *More Work for Mother* (1982); William Chafe, *The American Woman: Her Changing Social, Economic, and Political Role* (1972); Dorothy M. Brown, *Setting a Course: American Women in the 1920s* (1987); Paula S. Fass, *The Damned and the Beautiful: American Youth in the 1920s* (1977); and Ben B. Lindsay and Wainright Evans, *The Companionate Marriage* (1927).

Republican Politics

John D. Hicks, *Republican Ascendancy, 1921–1933* (1960), and Arthur M. Schlesinger Jr., *The Crisis of the Old Order* (1957), are excellent introductions to national politics during the 1920s. On Harding, see Robert K. Murray, *The Politics of Normalcy: Governmental Theory and Practice in the Harding-Coolidge Era* (1973), and Eugene Trani and David Wilson, *The Presidency of Warren G. Harding* (1977). William Allen White, *A Puritan in Babylon* (1939), is a colorful portrait of Calvin Coolidge; but see also Donald McCoy, *Calvin Coolidge: The Quiet President* (1967), and Thomas B. Silver, *Coolidge and the Historians* (1982). On Hoover's efforts to substitute "associational" politics for laissez-faire, two indispensable sources are Ellis Hawley, ed., *Herbert Hoover as Secretary of Commerce: Studies in New Era Thought and Practice* (1974), and Joan Hoff Wilson, *Herbert Hoover: Forgotten Progressive* (1975); see also David Burner, *Herbert Hoover: A Public Life* (1979). On Republican foreign policy, see Thomas Buckley, *The United States and the Washington Conference* (1970); Dexter Perkins, *Charles Evans Hughes and American Democratic Statesmanship* (1953); Joan Hoff Wilson, *American Business and Foreign Policy, 1920–1933* (1971); Warren I. Cohen, *Empire without Tears* (1987); Derek A. Aldcroft, *From Versailles to Wall Street, 1919–1929* (1977); and Robert H. Ferrell, *Peace in Their Time* (1952).

Agricultural Distress and Prohibition

On agricultural distress and protest, see Gilbert Fite, *George Peek and the Fight for Farm Parity* (1954), and Theodore Saloutos and John D. Hicks, *Twentieth Century Populism: Agricultural Discontent in the Middle West, 1900–1939* (1951). For an examination of the economic and social effects of Prohibition, consult Andrew Sinclair, *The Era of Excess* (1962); Norman Clark, *Deliver Us from Evil: An Interpretation of American Prohibition* (1976); Mark Thornton, *The Economics of Prohibition* (1991); and John C. Burnham, *Bad Habits: Drinking, Smoking, Taking Drugs, Gambling, Sexual Misbehavior, and Swearing in American History* (1993).

Nativism, Ku Klux Klan, and Immigration Restriction

John Higham, *Strangers in the Land: Patterns of American Nativism, 1865–1925* (1955), remains the best work on the spirit of intolerance that gripped America in the 1920s. On the 1920s resurgence of the Ku Klux Klan, consult David Chalmers, *Hooded Americanism: The History of the Ku Klux Klan* (1965); Kenneth Jackson, *The Ku Klux Klan in the City* (1965); Nancy MacLean, *Behind the Mask of Chivalry: The Making of the Second Ku Klux Klan* (1994); Leonard J. Moore, *Citizen Klansmen: The Ku Klux Klan in Indiana, 1921–1928* (1991); Katherine M. Blee, *Women of the Klan: Racism and Gender in the 1920s* (1991); and Shawn Lay, ed., *The Invisible Empire in the West: Toward a New Historical Appraisal of the Ku Klux Klan of the 1920s* (1992). The movement for immigration restriction is examined in William S. Bernard, *American Immigration Policy: A Reappraisal* (1950); Robert A. Divine, *American Immigration Policy* (1957); and Henry B. Leonard, *The Open Gates: The Protest Against the Movement to Restrict Immigration, 1896–1924* (1980).

Liberal and Fundamentalist Protestantism

Ferenc Morton Szasz, *The Divided Mind of Protestant America, 1880–1930* (1982), expertly analyzes the split in Protestant ranks between liberals and fundamentalists. On the fundamentalist movement itself, consult George S. Marsden, *Fundamentalism in American Culture* (1980); Norman Furniss, *The Fundamentalist Controversy, 1918–1931* (1954); and William G. McLoughlin, *Modern Revivalism* (1959). Ray Ginger, *Six Days or Forever? Tennessee versus John Thomas Scopes* (1958), is a colorful account of the Scopes trial, while Lawrence Levine, *Defender of the Faith: William Jennings Bryan: The Last Decade, 1915–1925* (1965), offers a sympathetic portrait of Bryan during his final years. For a provocative reading of the Scopes trial, see Garry Wills, *Under God: Religion and American Politics* (1990).

Industrial Workers

Irving Bernstein, *The Lean Years: A History of the American Worker, 1920–1933* (1960), remains the most thorough examination of 1920s workers, but it should be supplemented with Robert H. Zeiger, *American Workers, American Unions, 1920–1985* (1986); Melvyn Dubofsky and Warren Van Tine, *John L. Lewis: A Biography* (1977); Leslie Tentler, *Wage-Earning Women* (1979); and Jacquelyn Hall et al., *Like a Family: The Making of a Southern Cotton Mill World* (1987). Siegfried Giedion, *Mechanization Takes Command: A Contribution to Anonymous History* (1948), is an insightful account of the effects of mechanization.

European American Ethnic Communities

On ethnic communities and Americanization in the 1920s, see Gary Gerstle, *Working-Class Americanism: The Politics of Labor in a Textile City, 1914–1960* (1989); Lizabeth Cohen, *Making a New Deal: Industrial Workers in Chicago, 1919–1939* (1990); and Stephen J. Shaw, *The Catholic Parish as a Way-Station of Ethnicity and Americanization: Chicago's Germans and Italians, 1903–1939* (1991). Leonard Dinnerstein, *Anti-semitism in America* (1994), analyzes the resurgence of anti-semitism in the 1920s and the use of quotas by universities to limit the enrollment of Jews. On the growing political strength of European American ethnics, see David Burner, *The Politics of Provincialism* (1967); Oscar Handlin, *Al Smith and His America* (1958); Paula Elder, *Governor Alfred E. Smith: The Politician as Reformer* (1983); and Kristi Andersen, *The Creation of a Democratic Majority, 1928–1936* (1979).

African Americans

Good studies of the African American experience in the 1920s include Gilbert Osofsky, *Harlem: The Making of a Ghetto: Negro New York, 1890–1930* (1963); Kenneth L. Kusmer, *A Ghetto Takes Shape: Black Cleveland, 1870–1930*; Joe William Trotter Jr., *Black Milwaukee: The Making of an Industrial Proletariat, 1915–1945* (1985); and August Meier and Elliott Rudwick, *Black Detroit and the Rise of the UAW* (1979). Kathy H. Ogren, *The Jazz Revolution: Twenties America and the Meaning of Jazz* (1989), offers a probing analysis of jazz's place in 1920s culture. On the Harlem Renaissance, see Nathan Huggins, *Harlem Renaissance* (1971); Cary D. Mintz, *Black Culture and the Harlem Renaissance* (1988); and Jervis Anderson, *This Was Harlem: A Cultural Portrait, 1900–1950* (1981). Arnold Rampersand, *The Life of Langston Hughes*, 2 vols. (1986–88), and Robert E. Hemenway, *Zora Neale Hurston: A Literary Biography* (1977), are important biographical works on two leading African American literary figures.

Mexican Americans

On the 1920s experience of Mexican immigrants and Mexican Americans, see George J. Sánchez, *Becoming Mexican American: Ethnicity, Culture and Identity in Chicano Los Angeles, 1900–1945* (1993); David Montejano, *Anglos and Mexicans in the Making of Texas, 1836–1986* (1987); Ricardo Romo, *East Los Angeles: History of a Barrio* (1983); Mark Reisler, *By the Sweat of Their Brow: Mexican Immigrant Labor in the United States, 1900–1940* (1976); and Manuel Gamio, *The Life Story of the Mexican Immigrant* (1931).

The "Lost Generation" and Disillusioned Intellectuals

Malcolm Cowley, *Exiles Return* (1934), is a marvelous account of the writers and artists who comprised the "lost generation." See also Arlen J. Hansen, *Expatriate Paris* (1990), and William Wiser, *The Great Good Place: American Expatriate Women in Paris* (1991). On the southern "Agrarians," see John Stewart, *The Burden of Time* (1965), and Paul K. Conkin, *Southern Agrarians* (1988). Frederick J. Hoffman, *The Twenties: American Writing in the Postwar Decade*, rev. ed. (1962), is a fine sampler of the decade's best fiction. For biographical treatments of some of the decade's notable writers, consult Cleanth Brooks, *William Faulkner: The Yoknapatawpha County* (1963); Joel Williamson, *William Faulkner and Southern History* (1993); Carlos Baker, *Hemingway: The Writer as Artist* (1965); Kim Townshend, *Sherwood Anderson* (1987); and Virginia S. Carr, *Dos Passos: A Life* (1984). For a provocative interpretation of the intertwined character of white and black literary cultures in 1920s New York, see Ann Douglas, *Terrible Honesty: Mongrel Manhattan in the 1920s* (1995).

Political Thought

Robert Crunden, *From Self to Society: Transition in American Thought, 1919–1941* (1972), and Roderick Nash, *The Nervous Generation: American Thought, 1917–1930* (1969), are superior analyses of intellectual thought during the decade. On Mencken, see George H. Douglas, *H. L. Mencken* (1978), and Edward A. Martin, *H. L. Mencken and the Debunkers* (1984). Ronald Steel, *Walter Lippmann and the American Century* (1980), and Robert Westbrook, *John Dewey and American Democracy* (1991), are the best biographies of these two critical thinkers. On the new reform vanguard that began to form around Sidney Hillman, Franklin Roosevelt, and others, see Steven Fraser, *Labor Will Rule: Sidney Hillman and the Rise of American Labor* (1991), and Kenneth S. Davis, *FDR: The New York Years, 1928–1933* (1985).

CHAPTER 25 THE GREAT DEPRESSION AND THE NEW DEAL, 1929–1939

T. H. Watkins, *The Great Depression: America in the 1930s* (1993), provides a broad overview of society and politics during the 1930s. No work better conveys the tumult and drama of that era than Arthur M. Schlesinger, Jr.,'s three-volume *The Age of Roosevelt: The Crisis of the Old Order* (1957), *The Coming of the New Deal* (1958), and *The Politics of Upheaval* (1960).

Causes of the Great Depression

On causes of the depression, consult John Kenneth Galbraith, *The Great Crash* (1955); Milton Friedman and Anna J. Schwartz, *The Great Contraction, 1929–1933* (1965); Michael A. Bernstein, *The Great Depression: Delayed Recovery and Economic Change in America, 1929–1939* (1987); Charles Kindelberger, *The World in Depression* (1973); and John A. Garraty, *The Great Depression* (1986).

Herbert Hoover

On Hoover's failure to restore prosperity and popular morale, see Albert U. Romasco, *The Poverty of Abundance: Hoover, the Nation, the Depression* (1965), and David Burner, *Herbert Hoover: A Public Life* (1979). Roger Daniels, *The Bonus March* (1971), analyzes the event that became a symbol of Hoover's indifference to the depression's victims. More sympathetic treatments of Hoover's efforts to cope with the depression can be found in Harris G. Warren, *Herbert Hoover and the Great Depression* (1959); Joan Hoff Wilson, *Herbert Hoover: Forgotten Progressive* (1975); and Martin L. Fausold, *The Presidency of Herbert C. Hoover* (1985). Hoover offered his own spirited defense of his policies and a critique of the New Deal in his *Memoirs: The Great Depression* (1952).

Franklin D. Roosevelt and Eleanor Roosevelt

No 20th-century president has attracted more scholarly attention than Franklin Roosevelt. The most detailed biography is Frank Freidel, *Franklin D. Roosevelt* (1952–73), four volumes that cover Roosevelt's life from birth through the Hundred Days of 1933. The most complete biography, and one that is remarkably good at balancing Roosevelt's life and times, is Kenneth S. Davis, *FDR* (1972–93), also in four volumes. Anyone interested in Roosevelt's youth and prepresidential career should consult Geoffrey Ward's *Before the Trumpet: Young Franklin Roosevelt, 1882–1905* (1985) and *A First-Class Temperament: The Emergence of Franklin Roosevelt* (1989). James McGregor Burns, *Roosevelt: The Lion and the Fox* (1956), offers an intriguing portrait of Roosevelt as president.

On Eleanor Roosevelt, see Lois Scharf, *Eleanor Roosevelt: First Lady of American Liberalism* (1987); Joseph P. Lash, *Eleanor and Franklin* (1981); and, most importantly, Blanche Wiesen Cook, *Eleanor Roosevelt*, vol. 1 (1992), which chronicles her life from birth until she moved into the White House in 1933.

New Deal Overviews

William E. Leuchtenberg, *Franklin D. Roosevelt and the New Deal, 1932–1940* (1963), is still an authoritative account of the New Deal, although it should be supplemented with Robert S. McElvaine, *The Great Depression* (1984). Both books treat the New Deal as a transformative moment in American politics and economics. For more critical interpretations of the New Deal, stressing the limited nature of the era's reforms, see Barton J. Bernstein, "The New Deal: The Conservative Achievements of Liberal Reform," in Barton J. Bernstein, ed., *Toward a New Past: Dissenting Essays in American History* (1968); Paul K. Conkin, *The New Deal* (1975); and Anthony J. Badger, *The New Deal: The Depression Years, 1933–1940* (1989). Barry D. Karl, *The Uneasy State: The United States from 1915–1945* (1983), and the essays in Steve Fraser and Gary Gerstle, eds., *The Rise and Fall of the New Deal Order, 1930–1980* (1989), offer new perspectives on the achievements and limitations of the New Deal.

First New Deal

See Susan E. Kennedy, *The Banking Crisis of 1933* (1973), and Michael Parrish, *Securities Regulation and the New Deal* (1970), on the First New Deal's efforts to restructure the nation's financial institutions. On New Deal relief efforts, consult George T. McJimsey, *Harry Hopkins: Ally of the Poor and Defender of Democracy* (1987); John Salmond, *The Civilian Conservation Corps, 1933–42* (1967); Percy H. Merrill, *Roosevelt's Forest Army: A History of the Civilian Conservation Corps, 1933–1942* (1981); and Bonnie Fox Schwartz, *The Civilian Works Administration: The Business of Emergency Employment in the New Deal 1933–1934* (1984). James T. Patterson, *America's Struggle against Poverty, 1900–1980* (1981), contains a substantial section on New Deal poor relief. For the New Deal's role in rebuilding the nation's infrastructure, see T. H. Watkins, *Righteous Pilgrim: The Life and Times of Harold Ickes, 1874–1952* (1990), and James S. Olson, *Saving Capitalism: The Reconstruction Finance Corporation and the New Deal, 1933–1940* (1988). Albert V. Romasco, *The Politics of Recovery: Roosevelt's New Deal* (1983), provides a useful overview of the First New Deal's efforts to restore prosperity.

First New Deal, Agricultural Policy

Van Perkins, *Crisis in Agriculture* (1969), and Theodore M. Saloutos, *The American Farmer and the New Deal* (1982), examine efforts to revive agriculture; David E. Conrad, *The Forgotten Farmers: The Story of Sharecroppers in the New Deal* (1965), and Paul Mertz, *The New Deal and Southern Rural Poverty* (1978), focus on groups ignored by New Deal programs. Donald Worster, *Dust Bowl: The Southern Plains in the 1930s* (1979), and James N. Gregory, *American Exodus: The Dust Bowl Migration and Okie Culture in California* (1989), are indispensable on the crisis in plains agriculture and the ensuing "Okie" migration.

First New Deal, Industrial Policy

Ellis Hawley, *The New Deal and the Problem of Monopoly* (1966), is essential to understand the First New Deal's industrial policy. See also Bernard Bellush, *The Failure of the NRA* (1975); Michael Weinstein, *Recovery and Redistribution under the NRA* (1980); and Donald R. Brand, *Corporatism and the Rule of Law: A Study of the National Recovery Administration* (1988). On the TVA alternative, see Thomas K. McCraw, *TVA and the Power Fight, 1933–1939* (1971), and Walter L. Creese, *TVA's Public Planning: The Vision, the Reality* (1990).

Popular Unrest

On populist critics of the New Deal, see Alan Brinkley, *Voices of Protest: Huey Long, Father Coughlin and the Great Depression* (1982); Michael Kazin, *The Populist Persuasion: An American History* (1995); and Abraham Holtzman, *The Townsend Movement* (1963). For the rebirth of the labor movement, consult Irving Bernstein, *The Turbulent Years: A History of the American Worker, 1933–1941* (1969); Lizabeth Cohen, *Making a New Deal: Industrial Workers in Chicago, 1919–1939* (1990); Gary Gerstle, *Working-Class Americanism: The Politics of Labor in a Textile City, 1914–1960* (1989); Jacquelyn Hall et al., *Like a Family: The Making of a Southern Cotton Mill World* (1987); Bruce Nelson, *Workers on the Waterfront: Seamen, Longshoremen, and Unionism in the 1930s* (1988); and Joshua B. Freeman, *In Transit: The Transport Workers Union in New York City, 1933–1966* (1989).

Radical Politics

Richard M. Vallely, *Radicalism in the States: The Minnesota Farmer-Labor Party and the American Political Economy* (1989), and Greg Mitchell, *The Campaign of the Century: Upton Sinclair's EPIC Race for Governor of California and the Birth of Media Politics* (1992), analyze the upheaval in state politics that followed closely upon labor's resurgence. Irving Howe and Lewis Coser, *The American Communist Party: A Critical History, 1919–1957* (1957), is still the best single-volume history of the Communist Party during the 1930s. On the work of communists among the nation's dispossessed, see Mark Naison, *Communists in Harlem during the Depression* (1983); Robin D. G. Kelley, *Hammer and Hoe: Alabama Communists during the Great Depression* (1990); Dorothy Ray Healey and Maurice Isserman, *California Red: A Life in the American Communist Party* (1990); and Vicki Ruiz, *Cannery Women/Cannery Lives: Mexican Women, Unionization, and the California Food Processing Industry, 1930–1950* (1987).

The Second New Deal

Steven Fraser, *Labor Will Rule: Sidney Hillman and the Rise of American Labor* (1991), is indispensable for understanding the ideology, programs, and personalities of the Second New Deal. On the forging of the 1936 Democratic coalition, see Kristi Andersen, *The Creation of a Democratic Majority, 1928–1936* (1979), and Nancy J. Weiss, *Farewell to the Party of Lincoln: Black Politics in the Age of FDR* (1983). Roy Lubove, *The Struggle for Social Security* (1968), and J. Joseph Huthmacher, *Senator Robert Wagner and the Rise of Urban Liberalism* (1968), provide in-depth analyses of the Social Security Act, Wagner Act, and other crucial pieces of Second New Deal legislation. For critical perspectives on these reforms that stress their limitations as well as their achievements, consult Christopher Tomlins, *The State and the Unions: Labor Relations, Law and the Organized Labor Movement in America, 1880–1960* (1985), and Mark Leff, *The Limits of Symbolic Reform: The New Deal and Taxation, 1933–1939* (1984). Important for understanding the role of capitalists and money in the New Deal coalition are Jordan A. Schwarz, *The New Dealers: Power Politics in the Age of Roosevelt* (1993); Robert A. Caro, *The Years of Lyndon Johnson: The Path to Power* (1981); and Colin Gordon, *New Deals: Business, Labor, and Politics in America, 1920–1935* (1994).

New Deal Men, New Deal Women

On the political and cultural style of New Deal men, see Peter H. Irons, *The New Deal Lawyers* (1982); Samuel I. Rosenman, *Working with Roosevelt* (1952); Joseph P. Lash, *Dealers and Dreamers: A New Look at the New Deal* (1988); and Katie Louchheim, ed., *The Making of the New Deal: The Insiders Speak* (1983). On New Deal women, consult Susan Ware, *Beyond Suffrage: Women in the New Deal* (1981), and *Partner and I: Molly Dewson, Feminism and New Deal Politics* (1987); also see Linda Gordon, *Pitied but Not Entitled: Single Mothers and the History of Welfare, 1890–1935* (1994). On feminist weakness and male anxiety during the depression, see Lois Scharf, *To Work and to Wed: Female Employment, Feminism, and the Great Depression* (1980); Winifred Wandersee, *Women's Work and Family Values, 1920–1940* (1981); and Alice Kessler-Harris, *Out to Work: A History of Wage-Earning Women in the United States* (1982). Elizabeth Faue, *Community of Suffering and Struggle: Women, Men, and the Labor Movement in Minneapolis, 1915–1945* (1991), is illuminating on the strident masculinism that dominated 1930s labor and popular culture.

Labor and the CIO

Melvyn Dubofsky and Warren Van Tine, *John L. Lewis: A Biography* (1977), is important on the birth of the CIO and labor's growing power in 1936 and 1937. Sidney Fine, *Sit-Down: The General Motors Strike of 1936–1937* (1967), is the most complete study of that pivotal event, but Nelson Lichtenstein, *"The Most Dangerous Man in Detroit": Walter Reuther and the Fate of American Labor* (1995), should be consulted for the broader industrial and union context in which it occurred. The best work on the centrality of labor and the "common man" to literary and popular culture in the 1930s is that of Michael Denning, *The Cultural Front: The Laboring of American Culture in the Twentieth Century* (1996); see also Richard H. Pells, *Radical Visions and American Dreams: Culture and Social Thought in the Depression Years* (1973). On the government's role in supporting public art through the WPA and other federal agencies, see William F. McDonald, *Federal Relief Administration and the Arts* (1968); Richard D. McKinzie, *The New Deal for Artists* (1973); and Barbara Melosh, *Engendering Culture: Manhood and Womanhood in New Deal Public Art and Theater* (1991).

Minorities and the New Deal
Harvard Sitkoff, *A New Deal for Blacks* (1978), is a wide-ranging examination of the place of African Americans in New Deal reform. See also John B. Kirby, *Black Americans in the Roosevelt Era: Liberalism and Race* (1980); Robert L. Zangrando, *The NAACP Crusade against Lynching, 1909–1950* (1980); and James Goodman, *Stories of Scottsboro* (1994). Abraham Hoffman, *Unwanted Mexican Americans in the Great Depression: Repatriation Pressures, 1929–1939* (1974), is the best introduction to the repatriation campaign. George J. Sánchez, *Becoming Mexican American: Ethnicity, Culture and Identity in Chicano Los Angeles, 1900–1945* (1993), reconstructs the experience of the largest Mexican urban settlement in 1930s America; and Cletus E. Daniel, *Bitter Harvest: A History of California Farmworkers, 1870–1941* (1981), shows how little Chicanos and other groups of agricultural laborers benefited from New Deal reform. On Native Americans, consult Francis Paul Prucha, *The Great Father: The United States Government and the American Indians* (1984), and Christine Bolt, *American Indian Policy and American Reform* (1987). The importance of John Collier and the Indian Reorganization Act are treated well in Lawrence C. Kelly, *The Assault on Assimilation: John Collier and the Origins of Indian Policy Reform* (1983), and Graham D. Taylor, *The New Deal and American Indian Tribalism: The Administration of the Indian Reorganization Act, 1934–1945* (1980). For more detailed examinations of particular tribes' encounters with the New Deal, see Donald L. Parman, *The Navajos and the New Deal* (1976), and Harry A. Kersey Jr., *The Florida Seminoles and the New Deal, 1933–1942* (1989).

Ebbing of New Deal
James T. Patterson, *Congressional Conservatism and the New Deal* (1967), expertly analyzes the growing congressional opposition to the New Deal in the late 1930s. See also Frank Freidel, *FDR and the South* (1965). Leonard Baker, *Back to Back: The Duel between FDR and the Supreme Court* (1967), chronicles the court-packing fight. Alan Brinkley, *The End of Reform: New Deal Liberalism in Recession and War* (1995), provocatively examines the efforts of New Dealers to adjust their beliefs and programs as they lost support, momentum, and confidence in the late 1930s.

CHAPTER 26 AMERICA DURING THE SECOND WORLD WAR

U.S. Entry into World War II
The U.S. entry into World War II is analyzed in Arnold A. Offner, *The Origins of the Second World War: American Foreign Policy and World Politics, 1917–1941* (1975); Waldo H. Heinrichs, *Threshold of War: Franklin D. Roosevelt and American Entry into World War II* (1988); Michael A. Barnhart, *Japan Prepares for Total War: The Search for Economic Security* (1987); Robert Dallek, *Franklin D. Roosevelt and American Foreign Policy, 1932–1945* (1979); Robert Divine, *The Reluctant Belligerent: American Entry into World War II* (1965); Akira Iriye,

The Origins of the Second World War in Asia and the Pacific (1987); Ralph E. Schaffer, ed., *Towards Pearl Harbor: The Diplomatic Interchange between Japan and the United States, 1899–1941* (1991); and Sabura Ienaga, *The Pacific War: World War II and the Japanese* (1978). On isolationism, see Manfred Jonas, *Isolationism in America, 1935–1941* (1966); Wayne S. Cole, *Roosevelt and the Isolationists, 1932–45* (1983); and Geoffrey S. Smith, *To Save a Nation: American "Extremism," the New Deal, and the Coming of World War II* (1992).

Pearl Harbor
Pearl Harbor is the subject of several books by Gordon N. Prange, including *At Dawn We Slept: The Untold Story of Pearl Harbor* (1981) and *December 7, 1941: The Day the Japanese Attacked Pearl Harbor* (1988). See also John Toland, *Infamy: Pearl Harbor and its Aftermath* (1982), and Michael Slackman, *Target–Pearl Harbor* (1990).

Conduct and Diplomacy of the War
The conduct and diplomacy of the war can be surveyed in Alistair Parker, *The Second World War: A Short History* (1997); Gerhard L. Weinberg, *A World at Arms: A Global History of World War II* (1994); and Stephen E. Ambrose, *The American Heritage New History of World War II* (rev. ed., 1997) and *Citizen Soldiers* (1997). Other important studies include Martin Gilbert, *The Second World War: A Complete History* (1989); John Ellis, *Brute Force: Allied Strategy and Tactics in the Second World War* (1990); Michael J. Lyons, *World War II: A Short History* (1989); Gary R. Hess, *The United States at War, 1941–1945* (1986); Gaddis Smith, *American Diplomacy during the Second World War* (2nd ed., 1985); John Keegan, *The Second World War* (1989); Robert A. Divine, *Roosevelt and World War II* (1969) and *Second Chance: The Triumph of Internationalism in America during World War II* (1967); Mark Stoler, *The Politics of the Second Front: American Military Planning and Diplomacy in Coalition Warfare, 1941–1943* (1977) and his *Allies and Adversaries: The Joint Chiefs of Staff, the Grand Alliance, and U.S. Strategy in World War II* (2000); Warren Kimball, *Forged in War: Roosevelt, Churchill, and the Second World War* (1997); Ronald Schaffer, *Wings of Judgment: American Bombing in World War II* (1985); Michael S. Sherry, *The Rise of American Air Power: The Creation of Armageddon* (1987); D. Clayton James, *A Time for Giants: Politics of the American High Command in World War II* (1987); and Nathan Miller, *War at Sea: A Naval History of World War II* (1995).

On soldiers themselves, see Gerald F Linderman, *The World Within War: America's Combat Experience in World War II* (1997); Peter Schrijvers, *The Crash of Ruin: American Combat Soldiers in Europe* (1998); Paul Fussell, *Wartime: Understanding and Behavior in the Second World War* (1989); and David R. Segal, *Recruiting for Uncle Sam: Citizenship and Military Manpower Policy* (1989). Tom Brokaw, *The Greatest Generation* (1998) and *The Greatest Generation Speaks: Letters and Reflections* (1999) have attracted a broad, popular audience.

On intelligence-gathering activities, see Stephen Budiansky, Thomas Parrish, *The American Codebreakers: The U.S.*

Role in Ultra (1991), and Bradley F. Smith, *Sharing Secrets with Stalin: How the Allies Traded Intelligence, 1941-1945* (l996).

David Wyman, *The Abandonment of the Jews: America and the Holocaust, 1941–1945* (1984) and William B. Rubinstein, *The Myth of Rescue: Why the Democracies Could Not Have Saved More Jews from the Nazis* (1997) offer different views of U.S. policy toward the Holocaust. See also Eric Markusen and David Kopf, *The Holocaust and Strategic Bombing: Genocide and Total War in the Twentieth Century* (1995) and Verne W. Newton, ed., *FDR and the Holocaust* (1996).

War in the Pacific
On the war in the Pacific, see Christopher Thorne, *Allies of a Kind: The United States, Britain, and the War against Japan, 1941–1945* (1978); Ronald Lewin, *The American Magic: Codes, Ciphers, and the Defeat of Japan* (1983); Ronald H. Spector, *Eagle against the Sun: The American War with Japan* (1985); John Dower, *War without Mercy: Race and Power in the Pacific War* (1986); Akira Iriye, *Power and Culture: The Japanese-American War, 1941–1945* (1981); Michael Schaller, *The U.S. Crusade in China, 1938–1945* (1979) and *Douglas MacArthur, The Far Eastern General* (1989); Sheldon H. Harris, *Factories of Death: Japan's Biological Warfare 1932–45 and the American Cover-Up* (1994); Edward J. Drea, *MacArthur's ULTRA: Code Breaking and the War against Japan* (1992); Bartlett E. Kerr, *Flames over Tokyo* (1991); Kenneth P. Werrell, *Blankets of Fire: U.S. Bombers over Japan During World War II* (1996); John D. Chappell, *Before the Bomb: How America Approached the End of the Pacific War* (1997); and Gunter Bischof and Robert L. Dupont, eds., *The Pacific War Revisited* (1997).

Individual Policymakers
Individual policymakers are treated in Warren Kimball, *The Juggler: Franklin Roosevelt as Wartime Statesman* (1991); Forrest C. Pogue, *George C. Marshall*, vols. II and III, (1966, 1973); Stephen E. Ambrose, *Eisenhower* (1983); Michael Schaller, *Douglas MacArthur: The Far Eastern General* (1989); James Hershberg, *James B. Conant: Harvard to Hiroshima and the Making of the Nuclear Age* (1993); and Keith E. Eiler, *Mobilizing America: Robert P. Patterson and the War Effort, 1940-1945* (1997).

The Home Front
The home front receives attention in John Morton Blum's *V Was for Victory: Politics and American Culture during World War II* (1976); William L. O'Neill, *A Democracy at War: America's Fight at Home and Abroad in World War II* (1993); Richard Polenberg's *War and Society: The United States, 1941–1945* (1972); Allan M. Winkler, *Home Front U.S.A.: America during World War II* (1986); Gerald D. Nash, *The Great Depression and World War II: Organizing America, 1933–1945* (1979); William Tuttle, *Daddy's Gone to War: The Second World War in the Lives of America's Children* (1993); Michael C. C. Adams, *The Best War Ever: America and World War II* (1994); and John W. Jeffries, *Wartime America: The World War II Home Front* (1996). Geoffrey Perret, *Days of Sadness, Years of Triumph: The American People, 1939–1945* (1973) remains good reading; Studs Terkel, *"The Good War": An Oral History of World War II* (1984) is a classic.

Helpful works on the economy and labor include Paul A. C. Koistinen, *The Military-Industrial Complex: A Historical Perspective* (1980); Stephen B. Adams, *Mr. Kaiser Goes to War* (1998); and James B. Atleson, *Labor and the Wartime State: Labor Relations and Law during World War II* (1998). Nelson Lichtenstein, *Labor's War at Home: The CIO in World War II* (1982); Bartholomew H. Sparrow, *From the Outside In: World War II and the American State* (1996); David Palmer, *Organizing the Shipyards: Union Strategy in Three Northeast Ports, 1933-1945* (1998); and George Lipsitz, *Rainbow at Midnight: Labor and Culture in the 1940s* (rev. ed., 1994). David M. Hart, *Forged Consensus: Science, Technology, and Economic Policy in the United States, 1921-1951* (1998) is a broad study.

Changing Gender Relations on the Home Front
Major studies on the changing gender relations on the home front include Leila J. Rupp, *Mobilizing Women for War: German and American Propaganda, 1939–1945* (1978), a comparative study of the United States and Germany; Karen Anderson, *Wartime Women: Sex Roles, Family Relations, and the Status of Women During World War II* (1981); D'Ann Campbell, *Women at War with America: Private Lives in a Patriotic Era* (1984); Susan Hartman *The Home Front and Beyond: American Women in the 1940s* (1982); Ruth Milkman, *Gender at Work: The Dynamics of Job Segregation during World War II* (1987); and Sherna Berger Gluck, *Rosie the Riveter Revisited: Women, the War, and Social Change* (1988). See also Glen Jeansonne, *Women of the Far Right: The Mothers' Movement and World War II* (1996); Leisa D. Meyer, *Creating G.I. Jane: Sexuality and Power in the Women's Army Corp during World War II* (1996); and Amy Bentley, *Eating for Victory: Food Rationing and the Politics of Domesticity* (1998). Judy Barrett Litoff and David C. Smith, eds., *Since You Went Away: World War II Letters from American Women on the Home Front* (1991) is a moving compilation. John Costello, *Virtue Under Fire: How World War II Changed Our Social and Sexual Attitudes* (1985), and Allan Berube, *Coming Out Under Fire: The History of Gay Men and Women in World War II* (1990) discuss changing sexual politics.

Race and the Home Front
On issues of race and the home front, see Ronald Takaki, *Double Victory: A Multicultural History of American in World War II* (2000). More specific studies include Peter Irons, *Justice at War* (1993); Roger Daniels, *Concentration Camps U.S.A.: Japanese Americans and World War II* (1989); Gary Y. Okihiro, *Storied Lives: Japanese American Students and World War II* (1999); Mauricio Mazon, *The Zoot-Suit Riots: The Psychology of Symbolic Annihilation* (1984); Clete Daniel, *Chicano Workers and the Politics of Fairness* (1991); Neil Wynn, *The Afro-American and the Second World War* (1993); Dominic J. Capeci Jr.; Martha Wilkerson, *Layered Violence: The Detroit Rioters of 1943* (1991); Alison Bernstein, *American Indians and World War II: Toward a New Era in Indian Affairs* (1991);

Merl E. Reed, *Seedtime for the Modern Civil Rights Movement: The President's Committee on Fair Employment Practice, 1941–1946* (1991); and Andrew Edmund Kerston, *Race, Jobs, and the War: The FEPC in the Midwest, 1941-46* (2000). Frank Füredi, *The Silent War: Imperialism and the Changing Perception of Race* (1998) shows how race relations became an international issue during WWII.

The Peace Movement and Pacifism
The peace movement and pacifism are examined in Lawrence Wittner, *Rebels against War: The American Peace Movement, 1941-1960* (1969); Cynthia Eller, *Conscientious Objectors and the Second World War: Moral and Religious Arguments in Support of Pacifism* (1991); Heather T. Frazier and John O'Sullivan, *"We Have Just Begun to Not Fight": An Oral History of Conscientious Objectors in Civilian Public Service during World War II* (1996); and Rachel Waltner Goosen, *Women against the Good War* (1998).

Culture during the War
On culture during the war, see Lewis A. Erenberg and Susan E. Hirsch, eds., *The War in American Culture: Society and Consciousness during World War II* (1996); Lawrence Samuel, *Pledging Allegiance: American Identity and the Bond Drive of World War II* (1997); Gerald I. Sittset, *A Cautious Patriotism: The American Churches & the Second World War* (1997); and Michael Denning, *The Cultural Front: The Laboring of American Culture in the Twentieth Century* (1996).

Thomas Patrick Doherty, *Projections of War: Hollywood, American Culture, and World War II* (1993); Clayton Koppes and Gregory D. Black, *Hollywood Goes to War: How Politics, Profits & Propaganda Shaped World War II Movies* (1987); and John Whiteclay Chambers II and David Culbert, *World War II, Film, and History* (1996) concentrate on film. Allan M. Winkler, *The Politics of Propaganda: The Office of War Information, 1942–1945* (1978) covers propaganda; Frank W. Fox, *Madison Avenue Goes to War* (1975), describes wartime advertising; and Robin Winks, *Cloak and Gown: Scholars in the Secret War, 1939–1961* (1987) and Frank A. Warren, *Noble Extractions: American Liberal Intellectuals and World War II* (1999) describe the ties of scholars to government policy. Karl Ann Marling and John Wetenhall, *Iwo Jima: Monuments, Memory, and the American Hero* (1991), and George H. Roeder Jr., *The Censored War: American Visual Experience during World War II* (1993) both deal with the popular memory of the war. Richard W. Steele, *Free Speech and the Good War* (1999) examines governmental efforts to regulate dissent.

Wartime Diplomacy and Postwar Settlements
On wartime diplomacy and postwar settlements, see Gabriel Kolko, *The Politics of War: The World and the United States Foreign Policy, 1943–1945* (1990); Remi Nadeau, *Stalin, Churchill, and Roosevelt Divide Europe* (1990); Randall B. Woods and Howard Jones, *Dawning of the Cold War: The United States' Quest for Order* (1991); Diane S. Clemens, *Yalta* (1970); Randall B. Woods, *A Changing of the Guard:*

Anglo-American Relations, 1941–1946 (1990); Gary B. Ostrower, *The United States and the United Nations* (1998); Michael Schaller, *The American Occupation of Japan: The Origins of the Cold War in Asia* (1985); and John Dower, *Embracing Defeat: Japan in the Wake of World War II* (2000).

Dropping the Atomic Bomb
The dropping of the atomic bomb has attracted a large literature. Good starting places for understanding the various controversies are Michael J. Hogan, ed., *Hiroshima in History and Memory* (1996); Edward J. Linenthal and Tom Engelhardt, *History Wars: The* Enola Gay *and Other Battles for the American Past* (1996); and J. Samuel Walker, *Prompt and Utter Destruction: Truman and the Use of Atomic Bombs against Japan* (1997). Other major works that address this topic from various perspectives include Martin Sherwin, *A World Destroyed: The Atomic Bomb and the Grand Alliance* (1975); Barton J. Bernstein, *The Atomic Bomb: The Critical Issues* (1976); Michael Mandelbaum, *The Nuclear Revolution: International Politics before and after Hiroshima* (1981); John Ray Skates, *The Invasion of Japan: Alternative to the Bomb* (1994); Peter Wyden, *Day One: Before Hiroshima and After* (1984); Richard Rhodes, *The Making of the Atomic Bomb* (1986); Gar Alperowitz, *The Decision to Use the Bomb and the Architecture of an American Myth* (1995); Robert Jay Lifton, *Hiroshima in America: Fifty Years of Denial* (1995); and Ronald Takaki, *Hiroshima: Why America Dropped the Atomic Bomb* (1995).

Videos
Many video sources address World War II. *How Hitler Lost the War* (1990) and *The Call to Glory* (1991) are useful. The original *Why We Fight* series, produced by Frank Capra during the war, remains an important primary source. "WW II—The Propaganda Battle" is a fascinating entry in the *Walk Through the 20th Century* series hosted by Bill Moyers. *Rosie the Riveter* (1980) is a documentary of women workers during the war. *Without Due Process* (1991) is a video account of the evacuation of Japanese Americans. On the development of the atomic bomb, see *Day After Trinity* (1980) and *J. Robert Oppenheimer: Father of the Atomic Bomb* (1995). *The Promised Land* (1995) is a three-part documentary on the African American migration from the Deep South to Chicago.

CHAPTER 27 THE AGE OF CONTAINMENT, 1946–1954

U.S. Foreign Policy and the Origins of the Cold War
For overviews of U.S. foreign policy and the origins of the cold war, see David Reynolds, *One World Divisible* (2001); Melvin Leffler, *The Specter of Communism* (1994); Thomas G. Paterson, *Meeting the Communist Threat: Truman to Reagan* (1988) and his *On Every Front: The Making and Unmaking of the Cold War* (rev. ed., 1992); Thomas J. McCormick, *America's Half-Century: United States Foreign Policy in the Cold War and After* (2nd ed., 1995); Warren I.

Cohen, *America in the Age of Soviet Power* (1993); Fraser J. Harbutt, *The Iron Curtain: Churchill, America, and the Origins of the Cold War* (1986); John Lewis Gaddis has contributed important studies such as *Strategies of Containment: A Critical Appraisal of Postwar American National Security Policy* (1982), *The Long Peace: Inquiries into the History of the Cold War* (1987); and *We Now Know: Rethinking Cold War History* (1997). Other important overviews include Walter LaFeber, *America, Russia, and the Cold War, 1945–1992* (7th ed., 1993); Allen Hunter, ed., *Rethinking the Cold War* (1998); Stephen Ambrose, *Rise to Globalism: American Foreign Policy Since 1938* (8th ed., 1997); H. W. Brands, *The Devil We Knew: Americans and the Cold War* (1993); Deborah Welch Larson, *Anatomy of Mistrust: U.S.-Soviet Relations during the Cold War* (1997); and Ronald E. Powaksi, *The Cold War: The United States and the Soviet Union, 1917–1991* (1998);

Specific Regions and Cold War–Era Policy

For regional histories of the cold war, see Bruce R. Kuniholm, *The Origins of the Cold War in the Near East: Great Power Conflict and Diplomacy in Iran, Turkey, and Greece* (1980); Howard Jones, *"A New Kind of War:" America's Global Strategy and the Truman Doctrine in Greece* (1989); Steven Hugh Lee, *Outposts of Empire: Korea, Vietnam, and the Origins of the Cold War in Asia, 1949–84* (1995); Robert Accinelli, *Crisis and Commitment: United States Policy toward Taiwan, 1950–55* (1996); Michael Schaller, *The American Occupation of Japan: The Origins of the Cold War in Asia* (1985); John Dower, *Embracing Defeat: Japan in the Wake of World War II* (2000); and Michael L. Krenn, *The Chains of Interdependence: U.S. Policy toward Central America, 1945–1954* (1996).

On issues related to European integration see Alan Milward, *The European Rescue of the Nation State* (1993), and contrast this study with Geir Lundestad, *"Empire" by Integration: The United States and European Integration, 1945–1997* (1998) and John Killick, *The United States and European Reconstruction, 1945–1960* (1997). Other major books on Europe include Marc Trachtenberg, *A Constructed Peace: The Making of the European Settlement, 1945–1963* (1999); Michael J. Hogan, *The Marshall Plan: America, Britain, and the Reconstruction of Western Europe, 1949–52* (1987); Frank Ninkovich, *Germany and the United States: The Transformation of the German Question since 1945* (1988); Frank Costigliola, *France and the United States: The Cold Alliance since World War II* (1996); Sallie Pisani, *The CIA and the Marshall Plan* (1991); and Lawrence S. Kaplan, *The Long Entanglement: NATOs First Fifty Years* (1999).

On international economic issues see especially Robert A. Pollard, *Economic Security and the Origins of the Cold War, 1945–1950* (1985) and Thomas W. Zeiler, *Free Trade, Free World: The Advent of GATT* (1999).

A superb political history of the early cold war years is James T. Patterson, *Grand Expectations: The United States, 1945–74* (1996). See also Louis Liebovich, *The Press and the Origins of the Cold War, 1944–1947* (1988); and Justus D. Doenecke, *Not to the Swift: The Old Isolationists in the Cold War Era* (1979).

National Security Policy

On national security policy during the late 1940s and early 1950s consult Michael J. Hogan, *A Cross of Iron and the Origins of the National Security State, 1945–1954* (1998); Daniel Yergin, *Shattered Peace: The Origins of the Cold War and the National Security State* (1977); Melvyn Leffler, *A Preponderance of Power: National Security, the Truman Administration, and the Cold War* (1992); and Michael S. Sherry, *In the Shadow of War: The United States Since the 1930s* (1995). See also Walter Isaacson and Evan Thomas, *The Wise Men: Six Friends and the World They Made: Acheson, Bohlen, Harriman, Kennan, Lovett, McCloy* (1986); Evan Thomas, *The Very Best Men: Four Who Dared; The Early Years of the CIA* (1995); Walter Hixson and George F. Kennan, *Cold War Iconoclast* (1989); and James Chace, *Acheson: The Secretary of State Who Created the American World* (1988).

On atomic weapons, see Gregg Herken, *The Winning Weapon: The Atomic Bomb in the Cold War, 1945–1950* (1980); Paul Boyer, *By the Bomb's Early Light* (1985); Richard Rhodes, *Dark Sun: The Making of the Hydrogen Bomb* (1995); and Lawrence S. Wittner, *One World or None: A History of the World Nuclear Disarmament Movement through 1953* (1993)

Cultural Interpretations of National Security Policies

For cultural interpretations of national security policies see the relevant chapters of Richard Slotkin, *Gunfighter Nation: The Myth of the Frontier in Twentieth-Century America* (1992) and Robert J. Corber, *In the Name of National Security: Hitchcock, Homophobia, and the Political Construction of Gender in Postwar America* (1993). For broader views of the cultural climate see Lary May, ed., *Recasting America: Culture and Politics in the Age of the Cold War* (1989); Stephen J. Whitfield, *The Culture of the Cold War* (2nd ed., 1996); William Graebner, *The Age of Doubt: American Thought and Culture in the 1940s* (1991); Tom Englehardt, *The End of Victory Culture: Cold War America and the Disillusioning of a Generation* (1994); Guy Oakes, *The Imaginary War: Civil Defense and American Cold War Culture* (1994); Mark Jancovich, *Rational Fears: American Horror in the 1950s* (1996); Alan Nadel, *Containment Culture: American Narrative, Postmodernism, and the Atomic Age* (1995); and Margot A. Henriksen, *Dr. Strangelove's America: Society and Culture in the Atomic Age* (1997).

President Truman

Harry Truman enjoys a number of good biographical treatments. See Robert H. Ferrell, *Harry S. Truman and the Modern American Presidency* (1983) and *Harry S. Truman: A Life* (1994); Donald R. McCoy, *The Presidency of Harry S. Truman* (1984); William E. Pemberton, *Harry S. Truman: Fair Dealer and Cold Warrior* (1988); David G. McCullough, *Truman* (1992); Alonzo L. Hamby, *Man of the People: A Life of Harry S. Truman* (1995); and Sean J. Savage, *Truman and the Democratic Party* (1998). Michael J. Lacey, ed., *The Truman Presidency* (1989) offers interpretive essays, while Alonso L. Hamby, *Beyond the New Deal: Harry S Truman and American Liberalism* (1973) remains a useful look at Truman's Fair Deal that can be supplemented by the relevant chapter of the same author's *Liberalism and Its Challengers: Liberalism from*

FDR to Bush (2nd ed., 1992). Steve Fraser and Gary Gerstle, eds., *The Rise and Fall of the New Deal Order, 1930–1980* (1989) takes a longer view of postwar themes. On the election of 1948, see Gary A. Donaldson, *Truman Defeats Dewey* (1998) and Harold I. Gullan, *The Upset that Wasn't: Harry S. Truman and the Crucial Election of 1948* (1998).

Domestic Policymaking during the Fair Deal
On domestic policymaking during the Fair Deal, see R. Alton Lee, *Truman and Taft-Hartley: A Question of Mandate* (1966); Kevin Boyle, *The UAW and the Heyday of American Liberalism, 1945–1968* (1997). Allen J. Matusow, *Farm Policies and Politics in the Truman Years* (1967); Richard O. Davies, *Housing Reform during the Truman Administration* (1966); Susan M. Hartmann, *Truman and the 80th Congress* (1971); Monte M. Poen, *Harry S. Truman versus the Medical Lobby: The Genesis of Medicare* (1979); Andrew J. Dunar, *The Truman Scandals and the Politics of Morality* (1984); the relevant chapters of Edward D. Berkowitz, *America's Welfare State: From Roosevelt to Reagan* (1991); and Sheryl R. Tynes, *Turning Points in Social Security: From "Cruel Hoax" to "Sacred Entitlement"* (1996).

Anticommunism
Anticommunism is the subject of M. J. Heale, *American Anticommunism: Combating the Enemy Within, 1880–1970* (1990) and Richard Gid Powers, *Not without Honor: The History of American Anticommunism* (1995), both of which take a long view. Fred Inglis, *The Cruel Peace: Everyday Life in the Cold War* (1991) offers an international perspective. Richard M. Fried, *Nightmare in Red: The McCarthy Era in Perspective* (1990) and Ellen Schrecker, *The Age of McCarthyism: A Brief History with Documents* (1994) and her *Many are the Crimes: McCarthyism in America* (1998) are important syntheses, but David Caute's *The Great Fear: The Anti-Communist Purge under Truman and Eisenhower* (1978) remains the most detailed account. See also Michael R. Belknap, *Cold War Political Justice: The Smith Act, the Communist Party, and American Civil Liberties* (1977); Stanley I. Kutler, *The American Inquisition: Justice and Injustice in the Cold War* (1982); Marjorie Garber and Rebecca L. Walkowitz, eds., *Secret Agents: The Rosenberg Case, McCarthyism, and Fifties America* (1995); and John F. Neville, *The Press, the Rosenbergs, and the Cold War* (1995). Allen Weinstein's *Perjury: The Hiss Chambers Case* (rev. ed., 1997) is now bolstered by, among other recent works, Joseph Albright and Marcia Kunstel, *Bombshell: The Secret Story of America's Unknown Atomic Spy Conspiracy* (1997); Sam Tanenhaus, *Whittaker Chambers: A Biography* (1997); Daniel Patrick Moynihan, *Secrecy: The American Experience* (1998); Allen Weinstein and Alexander Vassiliev, *The Haunted Wood: Soviet Espionage in America: the Stalin Era* (1999); Harvey Klehr, *The Secret World of American Communism* (1995); and Harvey Klehr and John Earl Haynes, *Venona: Decoding Soviet Espionage in America* (1999). Jessica Wang, *American Science in an Age of Anxiety: Scientists, Anticommunism, and the Cold War* (1999) stresses FBI pressure on scientists to support the cold war. Philip Jenkins, *The Cold War at Home: The Red Scare in Pennsylvania, 1945–1960*

(1999) is a good local study showing bipartisan support for the red scare.

Social Changes of the Early Cold War Years
The social changes of the early cold war years are highlighted in Wendy Kozol, *Life's America: Family and Nation in Postwar Photojournalism* (1994). The baby boom is the focus of Richard A. Easterlin, *Birth and Fortune: The Impact of Numbers on Personal Welfare* (2nd ed., 1987) and Landon Y. Jones, *Great Expectations: America and the Baby Boom Generation* (1980). See also the relevant chapters of John Modell, *Into One's Own: From Youth to Adulthood in the United States, 1920–1975* (1989). On women's issues, see the final chapters of Susan Strasser, *Never Done: A History of American Housework* (1982); Alice Kessler-Harris, *Out to Work: A History of Wage-Earning Women in the United States* (1982); Jacqueline Jones, *Labor of Love, Labor of Sorrow: Black Women, Work and the Family, From Slavery to the Present* (1985); Eugenia Kaledin, *Mothers and More: American Women in the 1950s* (1984); Leila Rupp and Verta Taylor, *Survival in the Doldrums: The American Women's Rights Movement, 1945 to the 1960s* (1990); Cynthia Harrison, *On Account of Sex: The Politics of Women's Issues, 1945–68* (1988). Family and gender issues are nicely tied to cold war culture in Elaine Tyler May's *Homeward Bound: American Families in the Cold War Era* (1989) and in Stephanie Coontz, *The Way We Never Were: American Families and the Nostalgia Trip* (1992); and Elizabeth Siegel Watkings, *On the Pill: A Social History of Oral Contraceptives, 1950-1970* (1998). On issues related to sexuality and gender, see the relevant chapters of John D'Emilio and Estelle B. Freedman, *Intimate Matters: A History of Sexuality in America* (1988); Wini Breines, *Young, White, and Miserable: Growing Up Female in the Fifties* (1992); Graham McCann, *Rebel Males: Clift, Brando and Dean* (1993); and Joanne Meyerowitz, ed., *Not June Cleaver: Women and Gender in Postwar America, 1945–1960* (1994). On health care see Robert Cunningham III and Robert M. Cunningham Jr., *The Blues: A History of the Blue Cross and Blue Shield System* (1997).

Suburban and Urban Issues
On suburban and urban issues, see Robert A. Caro, *The Power Broker: Robert Moses and the Fall of New York* (1974); Mark Gelfand, *A Nation of Cities: The Federalist Government and Urban America, 1933–1945* (1975); Herbert Gans, *The Levittowners: Ways of Life and Politics in a New Suburban Community* (2nd ed., 1982); the relevant chapters of Kenneth T. Jackson, *Crabgrass Frontier: The Suburbanization of the United States* (1985); Barbara M. Kelly, *Expanding the American Dream: Building and Rebuilding Levittown* (1993); Rob Kling, Spencer Olin, and Mark Poster, *Postsuburban California: The Transformation of Orange County Since World War II* (1991). See also John M. Findlay, *Magic Lands: Western City Scapes and American Culture after 1940* (1992); David L. Kirp, John P. Dwyer, and Larry A. Rosenthal, *Our Town: Race, Housing and the Soul of Suburbia* (1995); John R., Gillis, *A World of their Own: Myth, Ritual, and the Quest for Family Values* (1996); Jon C. Teaford, *The Rough Road to Renaissance: Urban*

Revitalization in America, 1940–85 (1990) and *Post-Suburbia: Government and the Politics in the Edge Cities* (1997); Alan Ehrenhalt, *The Lost City: Discovering the Forgotten Virtues of Community in the Chicago of the 1950s* (1995); Michael F. Logan, *Fighting Sprawl and City Hall: Resistance to Urban Growth in the Southwest* (1995); James Hudnut-Beumler, *Looking for God in the Suburbs: the Religion of the American Dream and Its Critics, 1945–1965* (1994). Thomas J. Sugrue, *The Origins of the Urban Crisis: Race and Inequality in Postwar Detroit* (1996) is an award-winning study.

The Korean War
On the Korean War, Burton I. Kaufman, *The Korean War: Challenges in Crisis, Credibility, and Command* (1986) is a brief synthesis. More detailed analyses may be found in several volumes by Bruce Cumings, *The Origins of the Korean War* (1981); *Child of Conflict: The Korean-American Relationship, 1943–53* (1983), a series of essays that he edited; and *Korea: The Unknown War* (coauthored with Jon Halliday) (1988); William Stueck, *The Korean War: An International History* (1995); Chen Jian, *China's Road to the Korean War: The Making of the Sino-American Confrontation* (1994); Shu Guang Zhang, *Mao's Military Romanticism: China and the Korean War, 1950–1953* (1995). On more specific topics, see William T. Bowers, William M. Hammond, and George L. MacGarrigle, *Black Soldier, White Army: The 24th Infantry Regiment in Korea* (1996); Paul G. Pierpaoli Jr., *Truman and Korea: The Political Culture of the Early Cold War* (1999); Katharine H. S. Moon, *Sex Among Allies: Military Prostitution in U.S.-Korea Relations* (1997); and Sherie Mershon and Steven Schlossman, *Foxholes and Color Lines: Desegregating the U.S. Armed Forces* (1998).

The Eisenhower Years
The Eisenhower years received an early scholarly synthesis in Charles C. Alexander, *Holding the Line: The Eisenhower Era, 1952–1960* (1975), which can be updated with Chester Pach Jr. and Elmo Richardson, *The Presidency of Dwight D. Eisenhower* (rev. ed., 1991); Robert F. Burk, *Dwight David Eisenhower* (1986); William B. Pickett, *Dwight David Eisenhower and American Power* (1995); the relevant chapter of Hamby, *Liberalism and Its Challengers* (2nd ed., 1992); and Jeff Broadwater, *Eisenhower and the Anti-Communist Crusade* (1992). Stephen E. Ambrose's massive two-volume study *Eisenhower* (1983, 1984) contains a wealth of information. Jeff Broadwater, *Adlai Stevenson and American Politics: The Odyssey of a Cold War Liberal* (1994) is a solid biography of the man twice defeated by Eisenhower for the presidency. Fred I. Greenstein, *The Hidden-Hand Presidency: Eisenhower as Leader* (rev. ed., 1994) helped to bring about the reappraisal of Eisenhower's presidency.

Videos
March of Time: American Lifestyles (1987) is a five-video compilation taken from newscasts of the period. "Post-War Hopes, Cold War Fears," from the *Walk Through the 20th Century* series, offers an interesting overview, and *The G.I.*

Bill: The Law that Changed America (PBS, 1997) addresses important social changes. For a visual recounting of the beginning of U.S. involvement in the Vietnam War, see "The First Vietnam War (1946–1954)," a one-hour video documentary in the series *Vietnam: A Television History.* "The Rise of J. Edgar Hoover" (1991) is a superb video documentary in the *American Experience* series. *The Forgotten War* (1987) is a three-part video documentary on Korea. "Truman" (1997) and "Ike," formally titled "Eisenhower" (1993), are solid entries in PBS's *The White House Collection. George Marshall and the American Century* (1993) offers a sweeping overview of Eisenhower's important military benefactor, while *The Marshall Plan: Against All Odds* (1997) covers Marshall's most important cold war initiative and A&E's *George C. Marshall, Soldier and Statesman* (1996) provides a biography.

Adlai Stevenson: The Man from Libertyville (1992) is a video portrait of the Democrat who was twice defeated by Eisenhower for the presidency. *Seeing Red* (1993) looks, with considerable compassion, on the people who supported the Communist Party. The anti-communist crusade in Hollywood is the subject of *Hollywood on Trial* (1976) and *Legacy of the Hollywood Blacklist* (1987). *Point of Order: A Documentary of the Army-McCarthy Hearings* (1964) is a classic account of the congressional hearings that marked the beginning of McCarthy's demise. *The Race for the Superbomb* (PBS, 1999) is excellent on the link between science and the cold war.

CHAPTER 28 AFFLUENCE AND ITS DISCONTENTS, 1954–1963

Eisenhower's Foreign Policy
Robert Divine, *Eisenhower and the Cold War* (1981) and Blanche Wiesen Cook, *The Declassified Eisenhower* (1981) offer differing interpretations of Eisenhower's foreign policies. See also Joann P. Krieg, ed., *Dwight D. Eisenhower: Soldier, President and Statesman* (1987); H. W. Brands, *Cold Warriors: Eisenhower's Generation and American Foreign Policy* (1988); and Robert R. Bowie and Richard H. Immerman, *Waging Peace: How Eisenhower Shaped an Enduring Cold War Strategy* (1998). See also the many works on Eisenhower cited in Chapter 27.

Specialized Studies on Foreign Policy
More specialized studies on foreign policy include Robert Divine, *Blowing In the Wind: The Nuclear Test-Ban Debate* (1978) and *The Sputnik Challenge: Eisenhower's Response to the Soviet Satellite* (1993); Allan M. Winkler, *Life Under a Cloud: American Anxiety About the Atom* (1993); Campbell Craig, *Destroying the Village: Eisenhower and Thermonuclear War* (NY, 1998); Stuart W. Leslie, *The Cold War and American Science: The Military-Industrial-Academic Complex at MIT and Stanford* (1993); and Caroline Pruden, *Conditional Partners: Eisenhower, The United Nations, and the Search for a Permanent Peace* (1998). Saki Dockrill, *Eisenhower's New Look: National Security Policy, 1953-1961* (1996) presents a positive look; Peter J. Roman, *Eisenhower and the Missile Gap* (1995) is

more critical. See also Richard H. Immerman, *John Foster Dulles: Piety, Pragmatism, and Power in U.S. Foreign Policy* (1999) and David L. Snead, *The Gaither Committee, Eisenhower, and the Cold War* (1999).

Regional studies include Stephen G. Rabe, *Eisenhower and Latin America: The Foreign Policy of Anticommunism* (1988); Thomas G. Paterson, *Contesting Castro: The United States and the Triumph of the Cuban Revolution* (1994); Zachary Karabell, *Architects of Intervention: The United States, the Third World, and the Cold War, 1946–1962* (1999); David F. Schmitz, *Thank God They're On Our Side: The United States and Right-Wing Dictatorships, 1921–1965* (1999); Zhang Shu Guang, *Deterrence and Strategic Culture Culture: Chinese-American Confrontations, 1949–1958* (1992); Robert J. McMahon, *The Cold War on the Periphery: The United States, India and Pakistan* (1994); Kenton J. Clymer, *Quest for Freedom: The United States and India's Independence* (1995); Isaac Alteras, *Eisenhower and Israel: U.S.-Israeli Relations, 1953–1960* (1993); Abraham Ben-Zvi, *Decade of Transition: Eisenhower, Kennedy, and the Origins of the American-Israeli Alliance* (1998); Irene L. Grendzier, *Notes from the Mine Field: United States Intervention in Lebanon and the Middle East, 1945–1958* (1997); Bonnie F. Saunders, *The United States and Arab Nationalism: The Syrian Case, 1953–1960* (1996); James F. Goode, *The United States and Iran: In the Shadow of Mussaddiq* (1997); Cole C. Kingseed, *Eisenhower and Suez Crisis of 1956* (1995). Deborah Welch Larson, *Anatomy of Mistrust: U.S.-Soviet Relations during the Cold War* (1997); and G. Wyn Rees, *Anglo-American Approaches to Alliance Security, 1955–60* (1996).

The growing importance of intelligence agencies in foreign policy is examined in Stephen Ambrose and Richard H. Immerman, *Ike's Spies: Eisenhower and the Espionage Establishment* (1981) and *The CIA in Guatemala: The Foreign Policy of Intervention* (1982); Michael R. Beschloss, *Mayday: Eisenhower, Khrushchev, and the U-2 Affair* (1986); Rhodri Jeffreys-Jones, *The CIA and American Democracy* (1989); Loch K. Johnson, *America's Secret Power: The CIA in a Democratic Society* (1989); Thomas F. Troy, *Donovan and the CIA: A History of the Establishment of the Central Intelligence Agency* (1981); John Prados, *President's Secret Wars: CIA and Pentagon Covert Operations since World War II* (1986); Audrey R. Kahin and George McT. Kahin, *Subversion as Foreign Policy: The Secret Eisenhower and Dulles Debacle in Indonesia* (1995); and Nicholas Cullather, *Operation PSSUCCESS: The United States and Guatemala 1952–54* (1997). African Americans and foreign policy are discussed in Brenda Gayle Plummer, *Rising Wind: Black Americans and U.S. Foreign Affairs, 1935–1960* (1996); Penny M. Von Eschen, *Race Against Empire: Black Americans and Anticolonialism, 1937–1957* (1997), and Mary L. Dudziak, *Cold War and Civil Rights* (2001). On cultural diplomacy, see especially Walter L. Hixson, *Parting the Curtain: Propaganda, Culture, and the Cold War, 1945–1961* (1997); Robert H. Haddow, *Pavilions of Plenty: Exhibiting American Culture Abroad in the 1950s* (1997); Richard Pells, *Not Like Us: How Americans Have Loved, Hated, and Transformed American Culture Since World War II* (1997); Naima Prebots, *Dance for Export: Cultural Diplomacy*

and the Cold War (1998); and Arch Puddington, *Broadcasting Freedom: The Cold War Triumph of Radio Free Europe and Radio Liberty* (2000).

U.S. Involvement in Vietnam

On the deepening U.S. involvement in Vietnam, see David L. Anderson, *Trapped by Success: The Eisenhower Administration and Vietnam, 1953–1961* (1991); George Herring, *America's Longest War: The United States and Vietnam, 1950–1975* (1986); Andrew J. Rotter, *The Path to Vietnam: Origins of the American Commitment to Southeast Asia* (1987); Lloyd C. Gardner, *Approaching Vietnam: From World War II through Dien Bien Phu* (1988); James Arnold, *The First Domino: Eisenhower, the Military, and America's Intervention in Vietnam* (1991); Melanie Billings-Yun, *Decision against War: Eisenhower and Dien Bien Phu, 1954* (1988); Lloyd C. Gardner and Ted Gittinger, eds., *Vietnam: The Early Decisions* (1997); and Mark Philip Bradley, *Imagining Vietnam and America: The Making of Postcolonial Vietnam, 1919–1950* (2000).

Domestic Politics

The politics of the 1950s are treated in Mark Rose, *Interstate: Express Highway Politics, 1941–1956* (1979); Tom Lewis, *Divided Highways: Building the Interstate Highways, Transforming American Life* (1997); R. Alton Lee, *Eisenhower and Landrum Griffin: A Study in Labor-Management Politics* (1990); Richard Kluger, *Simple Justice: The History of* Brown v. Board of Education *and Black America's Struggle for Equality* (1975); Arthur J. Sabin, *In Calmer Times: The Supreme Court and Red Monday* (1999); Clarence G. Lasby, *Eisenhower's Heart Attack: How Ike Beat Heart Disease and Held on to the Presidency* (1996).

Postwar Mass Culture

For overviews of postwar mass culture, see Andrew Ross, *No Respect: Intellectuals and Popular Culture* (1989); W. T. Lhamon Jr., *Deliberate Speed: The Origins of a Cultural Style in the American 1950s* (1990); Karal Ann Marling, *As Seen on TV: The Visual Culture of Everyday Life in the 1950s* (1994); and James L. Baughman, *The Republic of Mass Culture: Journalism, Filmmaking, and Broadcasting in America Since 1941* (2nd ed., 1996). The debates over mass culture in the 1950s can be sampled in Bernard Rosenberg and David Manning White, *Mass Culture* (1957) and *Mass Culture Revisited* (1971). James Gilbert, *A Cycle of Outrage: America's Reaction to the Juvenile Delinquent in the 1950s* (1986) critiques this debate and relates it to an emerging youth culture. On television, see Cecelia Tichi, *The Electronic Hearth* (1991); Michael Curtin, *Redeeming the Wasteland: Television Documentary and Cold War Politics* (1995). On rock music, see Greil Marcus, *Mystery Train: Images of America in Rock n' Roll* (3rd ed., 1990); Charley Gillet, *Sound of the City: The Rise of Rock and Roll* (rev. ed., 1984); and Nelson George, *The Death of Rhythm and Blues* (1988). On the diversity of the youth culture, see William Graebner, *Coming of Age in Buffalo: Youth and Authority in the Postwar Era* (1989). On Hollywood, see Lary

May, *The Big Tomorrow: Hollywood and the Politics of the American Way* (2000) and Michael Coyne, *The Crowded Prairie: American National Identity in the Hollywood Western* (1997). Murray Sperber, *Unward to Victory: The Crises That Shaped College Sports* (1998) traces the rise of commercialism in sports, and Bruce Adelson, *Brushing Back Jim Crow: The Integration of Minor League Baseball in the American South* (1999) discusses integration of sports. On arts and culture generally, see Daniel Belgrad, *The Culture of Spontaneity: Improvisation and the Arts in Cold War America* (1998); Pete Daniel, *Lost Revolutions: The South in the 1950s* (2000); and John Fousek, *The Leader of the Free World: American Nationalism and the Cultural Roots of the Cold War* (2000).

On religious trends, see Christopher Owen Lynch, *Selling Catholicism: Bishop Sheen and the Power of Television* (1998); Robert Wuthnow, *After Heaven: Spirituality in America since the 1950s* (1998); James Gilbert, *Redeeming Culture: American Religion in an Age of Science* (1997); John R. Stone, *On the Boundaries of American Evangelicalism: The Postwar Evangelical Coalition* (1997); Douglas Jacobsen and William Trollinger, ed., *Reforming the Center: American Protestantism from 1900 to the Present* (1998); and Joel A. Carpenter, *Revive Us Again: The Reawakening of American Fundamentalism* (1997).

Social Issues

On poverty, see Michael Harrington's classic *The Other America: Poverty in the United States* (1962); James T. Patterson, *America's Struggle against Poverty, 1900–1980* (1981).

On gender and childrearing, see Thomas Maier, *Dr. Spock* (1998); Julia Grant, *Raising Baby by the Book: The Education of American Mothers,* (1998); Daniel Horowitz, *Betty Friedan and the Making of the Feminine Mystique: The American Left, the Cold War, and Modern Feminism* (1998); and Jonathan Gathorn-Hardy, *Sex the Measure of All Things: A Life of Alfred C. Kinsey* (2000).

On civil rights, see Doug McAdam, *Political Process and the Development of Black Insurgency, 1930–1970* (1982); Harvard Sitkoff, *The Struggle for Black Equality, 1954–1992* (1993); Larry Burt, *Tribalism in Crisis: Federal Indian Policy, 1953–1961;* (1982); Donald L. Fixico, *Termination and Relocation: Federal Indian Policy, 1945–1960* (1986); Manuel Alers-Montalvo, *The Puerto Rican Migrants of New York* (1985); David Garrow, *Bearing the Cross: Martin Luther King, Jr., and the Southern Christian Leadership Conference* (1986); Joseph P. Fitzpatrick, *Puerto Rican Americans: The Meaning of Migration to the Mainland* (2nd ed., 1987); Taylor Branch, *Parting the Waters: America in the King Years, 1954–1963* (1988); Steven J. Whitfield, *A Death in the Delta: The Story of Emmett Till* (1988); Mario Garcia, *Mexican-Americans: Leadership, Ideology, Identity, 1930–1960* (1989); Ricardo Romo, *East Los Angeles: History of a Barrio* (1989); Armstead L. Robinson and Patricia Sullivan, eds., *New Directions in Civil Rights Studies* (1991); the relevant chapters of Jacqueline Jones, *The Dispossessed: America's Underclass from the Civil War to the Present* (1992); Mark V. Tushnet, *Making Civil Rights Law: Thurgood Marshall and the Supreme Court, 1936–1961* (1993); James F. Findlay, *Church People in the Struggle: The National Council of Churches and the Black Freedom Movement, 1950–1970* (1993); Maria

Cristina Garcia, *Havana USA: Cuban Exiles and Cuban Americans in South Florida, 1959–1994* (1996); and David G. Gutierrez, *Walls and Mirrors: Mexican Americans, Mexican Immigrants, and the Politics of Ethnicity* (1995). Claybourne Carson, ed., *The Papers of Martin Luther King, Jr.* (Vol III., 1997) focuses on struggles during the Montgomery bus boycott; see also Richard Lischer, *The Preacher King: Martin Luther King, Jr. and the Words that Moved America* (1995); and Glenn T. Eskew, *But for Birmingham: The Local and National Movements in the Civil Rights Struggle* (1997). On civil rights issues during the Kennedy years, see Howard Zinn, *SNCC: The New Abolitionists* (1965); William Chafe, *Civilities and Civil Rights: Greensboro, North Carolina and the Black Struggle for Freedom* (1980); John Walton Cotman, *Birmingham, JFK, and the Civil Rights Act of 1963* (1989); Kenneth O'Reilly, *Racial Matters: The FBI's Secret Files on Black America, 1960–72* (1989); and Mark Stern, *Calculating Visions: Kennedy, Johnson, and Civil Rights* (1992). In addition, consult the many other works that are listed in readings for Chapter 29.

John F. Kennedy

Garry Wills, *Nixon Agonistes: The Crisis of the Self-Made Man* (rev. ed., 1980) and *The Kennedy Imprisonment: A Meditation on Power* (1983) offer critical viewpoints on John F. Kennedy, as does Thomas C. Reeves, *A Question of Character: A Life of John F. Kennedy* (1991). Seymour M. Hersh, *The Dark Side of Camelot* (1997) attempts to obliterate the Kennedy mystique. More favorable, though not uncritical, is David Burner, *John F. Kennedy and a New Generation* (1988). James N. Giglio's *The Presidency of John F. Kennedy* (1991) and Mark J. White, ed, *Kennedy: The New Frontier Revisited* (1998) provide overviews. For more detail, see Herbert J. Parmet's two volumes: *Jack: The Struggle of John F. Kennedy* (1980) and *JFK: The Presidency of John F. Kennedy* (1983). Close associates have produced many sympathetic accounts of Kennedy's presidency; by far the best is Arthur Schlesinger, Jr., *A Thousand Days* (1965). Specific policy decisions and people are the subject of Jim F. Heath, *John Kennedy and the Business Community* (1969); Victor Navasky, *Kennedy Justice* (1971); Carl M. Brauer, *John F. Kennedy and the Second Reconstruction* (1977); James R. Williamson, *Federal Antitrust Policy during the Kennedy-Johnson Years* (1995); and Kai Bird, *The Color of Truth: McGeorge Bundy and William Bundy, Brothers in Arms: A Biography* (1998); Jeff Shesol, *Mutual Contempt: Lyndon Johnson, Robert Kennedy, and the Feud that Defined the Decade* (1997); and James W. Hilty, *Robert Kennedy: Brother Protector* (1997).

Kennedy's Foreign Policy

On Kennedy's foreign policy, see Thomas G. Paterson, ed., *Kennedy's Quest for Victory: American Foreign Policy, 1961–1963* (1989); Michael R. Beschloss, *The Crisis Years: Kennedy and Khrushchev, 1960–1963* (1991); and Noam Chomsky, *Rethinking Camelot: JFK, the Vietnam War, and U.S. Political Culture* (1993). A huge literature on the missile crisis in Cuba includes Graham T. Allison, *Essence of Decision: Explaining the Cuban Missile Crisis* (1971); Trumbell Higgins, *The Perfect Failure: Kennedy, Eisenhower, and the CIA at the*

Bay of Pigs (1989); Dino A. Brugioni, *Eyeball to Eyeball: The Inside Story of the Cuban Missile Crisis* (1991); James Blight, *Cuba on the Brink: Castro, the Missile Crisis, and the Soviet Challenge* (1993); Mark J. White, *The Cuban Missile Crisis* (1996); John C. Ausland, *Kennedy, Khrushchev, and the Berlin-Cuba Crisis, 1961–1964* (1996); Timothy Naftali and Aleksandr Fursenko, *"One Hell of a Gamble": Khrushchev, Castro, and Kennedy, 1958–1964* (1997); Ernest R. May and Philip D. Zelikow, eds., *The Kennedy Tapes: Inside the White House during the Cuban Missile Crisis* (1997), and Philip Nash, *The Other Missiles of October: Eisenhower, Kennedy, and the Jupiters, 1957–1963*.

On other specific issues, see Lawrence Freedman, *Kennedy's Wars: Berlin, Cuba, Laos, and Vietnam* (2000); Michael E. Latham, *Modernization as Ideology: American Social Science and 'Nation Building' in the Kennedy Era* (2000); Stephen G. Rabe, *The Most Dangerous Area in the World: John F. Kennedy Confronts Communist Revolution in Latin America* (1999); Elizabeth Cobbs-Hoffman, *All You Need Is Love: The Peace Corps and the Spirit of the 1960s* (1998); and Fritz Fischer, *Making Them Like Us: Peace Corps Volunteers in the 1960s* (1998).

Kennedy's Death
Events surrounding Kennedy's death have attracted almost as much attention as his life. Michael J. Kurtz, *The Crime of the Century: The Kennedy Assassination from an Historian's Perspective* (1982) tries to offer historical grounding, while Barbie Zelizer, *Covering the Body: The Kennedy Assassination, the Media, and the Shaping of Collective Memory* (1992) is a superb cultural study. Theories of the assassination itself include Peter Dale Scott, *Deep Politics and the Death of JFK* (1993), which is critical of the Warren Commission's findings, and Gerald L. Posner, *Case Closed: Lee Harvey Oswald and the Assassination of JFK* (1993), which defends them. See also John Newman, *Oswald and the CIA* (1995).

Videos
"Eisenhower" (1993) is an excellent documentary in the *American Experience* series. *America's Mandarin (1954–1967)* is a one-hour video documentary of U.S. involvement in Vietnam, from Eisenhower to Johnson, in the series *Vietnam: A Television History* (1983). "The Quiz Show Scandal" (1991) and "That Rhythm, Those Blues" (1988) are solid entries in the *American Experience* series. The multipart documentary series *Eyes on the Prize* (1987) provides a dramatic, visual representation of the struggle for African American civil rights. *The Road to Brown* (1990) offers a more limited, but still important, view. See also, *Dr. Martin Luther King Jr.: A Historical Perspective* (1993) and *Southern Justice: The Murder of Medger Evers* (1994). "The Kennedys" (1992) is a four-hour video documentary in the *American Experience* series. *Spy in the Sky* (1996) is the story of the U.S. reconnaissance program during the Eisenhower years. *Crisis: Missiles in Cuba* (1989) offers a brief, 30-minute overview. *Thirteen Days* (2001) is a thought-provoking feature film. *Divided Highways: The Interstates and the Transformation of American Life* (1997) focuses on the new interstate system.

CHAPTER 29 AMERICA DURING ITS LONGEST WAR, 1963–1974

Lyndon Johnson
On Lyndon Johnson see Paul K. Conkin, *Big Daddy from the Pedernales: Lyndon Baines Johnson* (1986); Robert Caro, *The Path to Power* (1982) and *Means of Ascent* (1990); Robert J. Dallek, *Lone Star Rising: Lyndon Johnson and His Times, 1908–1960* (1991) and *Flawed Giant: Lyndon Johnson and His Times, 1961-1973* (1998) Other titles include Vaughn Davis Bornet, *The Presidency of Lyndon Baines Johnson* (1993), which is relatively sympathetic, and Doris Kearns Goodwin, *Lyndon Johnson and the American Dream* (1976). Joseph A. Califano Jr., *The Triumph and Tragedy of Lyndon Johnson: The White House Years* (1991), is an interesting memoir, and Michael R. Beschloss, ed., *Taking Charge: The Johnson White House Tapes, 1963–1964* (1997), offers fascinating insights. Irving Bernstein, *Guns or Butter: The Presidency of Lyndon Johnson* (1996), is a detailed synthesis.

Civil Rights
Civil rights issues are treated in David Garrow, *Protest at Selma: Martin Luther King, Jr., and the Voting Rights Act of 1965* (1980); Clayborne Carson, *In Struggle: SNCC and the Black Awakening of the 1960s* (1981); Doug McAdam, *Freedom Summer* (1988); Emily Stoper, *The Student Non-Violent Coordinating Committee: The Growth of Radicalism in a Civil Rights Organization* (1989); Mark Stern, *Calculating Visions: Kennedy, Johnson, and Civil Rights* (1992); William L. Van Deburg, *New Day in Babylon: The Black Power Movement and American Culture, 1965–1975* (1992); Gerald Horne, *Fire This Time: The Watts Uprising and the 1960s* (1995); David J. Armor, *Forced Justice: School Desegregation and the Law* (1995); Louis A. DeCaro, Jr., *On the Side of My People: A Religious Life of Malcolm X* (1996); Michael Eric Dyson, *Making Malcolm: the Myth and Meaning of Malcolm X* (1995); Charles M. Payne, *I've Got the Light of Freedom: The Organizing Tradition and the Mississippi Freedom Struggle* (1995); Taylor Branch, *Pillar of Fire: America in the King Years, 1963–65* (1998); Brian Ward, *Just My Soul Responding: Rhythm and Blues, Black Consciousness, and Race Relations* (1998); Belinda Robnett, *How Long? How Long? African American Women in the Struggle for Civil Rights* (1997); Gerald D. McKnight, *The Last Crusade: Martin Luther King, Jr., the FBI, and the Poor People's Campaign.* (1998); Timothy J. Minchin, *Hiring the Black Worker: The Racial Integration of the Southern Textile Industry, 1960–1980* (1999); Timothy N. Thurber, *The Politics of Equality: Hubert H. Humphrey and the African American Freedom Struggle* (1999); and William L. Van Deburg, *Black Camelot: African American Cultural Heroes in Their Times, 1960–1980* (1997). Komozi Woodard, *A Nation within a Nation: Amiri Baraka (LeRoy Jones) and Black Power Politics* (1999) illuminates the local black power movement in Newark. See also Richard Griswold del Castillo and Richard A. Garcia, *Cesar Chavez: A Triumph of Spirit* (1995); Mario T. García, *The Making of a Mexican American Mayor: Raymond L. Telles of El Paso* (1998); George Pierre Castile, *To Show Heart: Native American Self-Determination and Federal*

Indian Policy, 1960–1975 (1998). On the women's movement, see Lauri Umansky, *Motherhood Reconceived: Feminism and the Legacies of the 1960s* (1996); Beth Bailey, *Sex in the Heartland* (1999); Susan M. Hartmann, *The Other Feminists: Activists in the Liberal Establishment* (1998); Dennis A. Deslippe, *"Rights, Not Roses": Unions and the Rise of Working-Class Feminism, 1945–80* (2000).

On the legal issues, see Morton J. Horwitz, *The Warren Court and the Pursuit of Justice* (1998); Laura Kalman, *The Strange Career of Legal Liberalism* (1996); Charles R. Epp, *The Rights Revolution: Lawyers, Activists, and Supreme Courts in Comparative Perspective* (1998).

The Great Society and the War on Poverty
The Great Society and the War on Poverty receive a critical assessment in Alan J. Matusow, *The Unraveling of America: A History of Liberalism in the 1960s* (1984). The most influential analysis from the right of Great Society liberalism has been Charles Murray's *Losing Ground: American Social Policy, 1950–1980* (1984), which can be compared with Christopher Jencks, *Rethinking Social Policy: Race, Poverty and the Underclass* (1992). A recent overview is Gareth Davies, *From Opportunity to Entitlement: The Transformation and Decline of Great Society Liberalism* (1996). See also Michael L. Gillette, *Launching the War on Poverty: An Oral History* (1996); Robert C. Lieberman, *Shifting the Color Line: Race and the American Welfare State* (1998); and Michael K. Brown, *Race, Money, and the American Welfare State* (1999).

Johnson's Foreign Policies
Johnson's foreign policies are treated in Bernard Firestone and Robert C. Vogt, eds., *Lyndon Baines Johnson and the Uses of Power* (1988); Warren I. Cohen and Nancy Bernkopf Tucker, eds., *Lyndon Johnson Confronts the World: American Foreign Policy, 1963–1968* (1994); Diane Kunz, ed., *The Diplomacy of the Crucial Decade: American Foreign Relations during the 1960s* (1994). On the Dominican intervention see Bruce Palmer Jr., *Intervention in the Caribbean: The Dominican Crisis of 1965* (1989); and Abraham F. Lowenthal, *The Dominican Intervention* (1995).

Johnson's Policies in Vietnam
Johnson's policies in Vietnam have attracted an immense literature. Overviews include George Herring, *America's Longest War: The United States and Vietnam, 1950–1975* (1986); Marilyn Blatt Young, *The Vietnam-American Wars, 1945–1990* (1991); and Robert D. Schulzinger, *A Time for War: The United States and Vietnam, 1941–1975* (1997). More specific studies include David L. DiLeo, *George Ball, Vietnam, and the Rethinking of Containment* (1991); Melvin Small, *Johnson, Nixon, and the Doves* (1988); Larry Berman, *Lyndon Johnson's War: The Road to Stalemate in Vietnam* (1989); Marilyn Young and Jon Livingston, *The Vietnam War: How the United States Intervened in the History of Southeast Asia* (1990); Gabriel Kolko, *Anatomy of War: Vietnam, The United States, and the Modern Historical Experience* (1994); Lloyd C. Gardner, *Approaching Vietnam: From World War II*

through Dien Bien Phu (1988); George McT. Kahin, *Intervention: How America Became Involved in Vietnam* (1986); R. B. Smith, *An International History of the Vietnam War* (1983); James J. Wirtz, *The Tet Offensive: Intelligence Failure in War* (1991); Ronald Spector, *After Tet: The Bloodiest Year in Vietnam* (1993); David M. Barrett, *Uncertain Warriors: Lyndon Johnson and His Vietnam Advisors* (1993); James A. Bill, *George Ball: Behind the Scenes in U.S. Foreign Policy* (1998); David L. Anderson, ed., *Facing My Lai: Moving Beyond the Massacre* (1997); Michael Hunt, *Lyndon Johnson's War: America's Cold War Crusade in Vietnam, 1945–1968* (1996); Joseph G. Morgan, *The Vietnam Lobby: The American Friends of Vietnam, 1955–1975* (1997); Orrin Schwab, *Defending the Free World: John F. Kennedy, Lyndon Johnson, and the Vietnam War, 1961–1965* (1998); Robert Buzzanco, *Masters of War: Military Dissent and Politics in the Vietnam Era* (1996); Richard A. Hunt, *Pacification: The American Struggle for Vietnam's Hearts and Minds* (1995); Edwin Moise, *Tonkin Gulf and the Escalation of the Vietnam War* (1996); Roger Warner, *Back Fire: The CIA's Secret War in Laos and Its Link to the Vietnam War* (1995); Robert J. McMahon, *The Limits of Empire: The United States and Southeast Asia since World War II* (1999); William M. Hammond. *Reporting Vietnam: Media and Military at War* (1998); William H. Hammond, *Reporting Vietnam: Media and Military at War* (1998); and Charles E. Neu, eds., *After Vietnam: Legacies of a Lost War* (2000).

Cultural Debates Generated by the War in Vietnam
For cultural debates generated by the war in Vietnam, see Loren Baritz, *Backfire: A History of How American Culture Led Us into Vietnam and Made Us Fight the Way We Did* (1985); Kathleen Turner, *Lyndon Johnson's Dual War: Vietnam and the Press* (1985); Susan Jeffords, *The Remasculinization of America: Gender and the Vietnam War* (1989); Albert Auster and Leonard Quart, *How the War Was Remembered: Hollywood and Vietnam* (1988); John Carlos Rowe and Rick Berg, eds., *The Vietnam War and American Culture* (1991); Michael Gregg, ed., *Inventing Vietnam: The War in Film and Television* (1991); David W. Levy, *The Debate over Vietnam* (2nd ed., 1995); Fred Turner, *Echoes of Combat: The Vietnam War in American Memory* (1996); Robert R. Tomes, *Apocalypse Then: American Intellectuals and the Vietnam War, 1954–1975* (1998); and Donald Alexander Downs, *Cornell '69: Liberalism and the Crisis of the American University* (1999). Keith Beattie, *The Scar that Binds: American Culture and the Vietnam War* (1998) deals with movies and fiction.

Political Insurgency of the 1960s
On the political insurgency of the 1960s see W. J. Rorbaugh, *Berkeley at War: The 1960s* (1989); Barbara Tischler, ed., *Sights on the Sixties* (1992); David Chalmers, *And the Crooked Place Made Straight: The Struggle for Social Change in the 1960s* (1996); Timothy Miller, *The Hippies and American Values* (1991); Peter Collier and David Horowitz, *Destructive Generation: Second Thoughts about the Sixties* (1996); Paul Berman, *A Tale of Two Utopias: The Political Journey of the Generation of 1968* (1998); David Farber, ed., *The Sixties: From Memory to History* (1994); Alexander Bloom and Wini

Breines, eds., *"Takin it to the Streets": A Sixties Reader* (1995); Paul Lyons, *New Left, New Right, and the Legacy of the Sixties* (1996); Jonah Raskin, *For the Hell of It: The Life and Times of Abbie Hoffman* (1996); David Burner, *Making Peace with the Sixties* (1996); Ron Jacobs, *The Way the Wind Blew: A History of the Weather Underground* (1997); Thomas Frank, *The Conquest of Cool: Business Culture, Counterculture, and the Rise of Hip Consumerism* (1997); and Doug Rossinow, *The Politics of Authenticity: Liberalism, Christianity, and the New Left in America* (1998).

The conservative insurgency is the subject of Mary C. Brennan, *Turning Right in the Sixties: The Conservative Capture of the GOP* (1995); Robert Alan Goldberg, *Barry Goldwater* (1995); John A. Andrew III, *The Other Side of the Sixties: Young Americans for Freedom and the Rise of Conservative Politics* (1997); and Gregory L. Schneider, *Cadres for Conservatism: Young Americans for Freedom and the Rise of the Contemporary Right* (1999).

Opposition to the War

On opposition to the war, see Charles De Benedetti, *An American Ordeal: The Anti-War Movement of the Vietnam Era* (1990); Melvin Small and William D. Hoover, eds., *Give Peace a Chance* (1992); Kenneth J. Heineman, *Campus Wars: The Peace Movement at American State Universities in the Vietnam Era* (1993); Amy Swerdlow, *Women Strike for Peace: Traditional Motherhood and Radical Politics in the 1960s* (1993); Tom Wells, *The War Within: America's Battle Over Vietnam* (1993); Adam Garfinkle, *Telltale Hearts: The Origins and Impact of the Vietnam Antiwar Movement* (1995). Todd Gitlin indicts the media for speeding the fall of opposition efforts in *The Whole World is Watching: Mass Media in the Making and Unmaking of the New Left* (1980), while Maurice Isserman's *If I Had a Hammer: The Death of the Old Left and the Birth of the New Left* (1987) looks at the general conflict among radicals. See also Wini Breines, *Community and Organization in the New Left, 1962–1968* (1982); Jim Miller, *Democracy Is in the Streets: From Port Huron to the Siege of Chicago* (1987); Todd Gitlin, *The Sixties: Years of Hope, Days of Rage* (1987); Michael B. Friedland, *Lift Up Your Voice Like a Trumpet: White Clergy and the Civil Rights and Antiwar Movements, 1954–1973* (1998); and Douglas Knight, *Streets of Dreams: The Nature and Legacy of the 1960s* (1989). On the politics of 1968 see Lewis Gould, *1968: The Election That Changed America* (1993).

Richard Nixon and His Policies

For various perspectives on Richard Nixon and his policies, see Garry Wills, *Nixon Agonistes* (rev. ed., 1980); Bruce Odes, ed., *From the President: Richard Nixon's Secret Files* (1989); Stephen Ambrose, *Nixon* (1989); Roger Morris, *Richard Milhous Nixon: The Rise of an American Politician* (1990); Joan Hoff, *Nixon Reconsidered* (1994); and Anthony Summers, *The Arrogance of Power: The Secret World of Richard Nixon* (2000). On foreign policy, in addition to the works on Vietnam cited above, see Seycom Brown, *The Crisis of Power: An Interpretation of United States Foreign Policy during the Kissinger Years* (1979); Terry Terriff, *The Nixon Administration and the Making of U.S. Nuclear Strategy* (1995); William Bundy, *A Tangled Web: The Making of Foreign Policy in the Nixon Presidency* (1998). On Kissinger, see Walter Isaacson, *Kissinger: A Biography (1993). On economic policy see Diane B. Kunz, Butter and Guns: America's Cold War Economic Policy (1997); and Allen J. Matusow, Nixon's Economy: Booms, Busts, Dollars, and Votes* (1997).

Watergate

On Watergate and the broader ethos of secret government, see Peter Schrag, *Test of Loyalty: Daniel Ellsberg and the Rituals of Secret Government* (1974); Theodore White, *Breach of Faith: The Fall of Richard Nixon* (1975); Athan Theoharis, *Spying on Americans: Political Surveillance from Hoover to the Huston Plan* (1978); Frank J. Donner, *The Age of Surveillance: The Aims and Methods of America's Surveillance System* (1980); L. H. LaRue, *Political Discourse: A Case Study of the Watergate Affair* (1988); Stanley I. Kutler, *The Wars of Watergate: The Last Crisis of Richard Nixon* (1990) and *Abuse of Power: The New Nixon Tapes* (1998); Angus Mackenzie, *Secrets: The CIA's War at Home* (1997); Michael Schudson, *Watergate in American Memory: How We Remember, Forget, and Reconstruct the Past* (1992); and Bob Woodward, *Shadow: Five Presidents and the Legacy of Watergate* (1999).

Videos

"LBJ" (1991) is a four-hour video documentary in the *American Experience* series; "Chicago, 1968" (1995) is a solid, one-hour entry in the same series. Video accounts of Malcolm X, include *Malcolm X: Make It Plain* (1993) and *The Real Malcolm X: An Intimate Portrait of the Man* (1992). On civil rights, also consult the appropriate one-hour segments in the longer *Eyes on the Prize* series. On the political insurgency of the 1960s, see *Making Peace with the Sixties* (1991), a three-part series and the more limited, but more insightful, *Berkeley in the Sixties* (1990). *Watergate* (1994) is a multipart documentary produced in Great Britain.

CHAPTER 30 ECONOMIC AND SOCIAL CHANGE IN THE LATE 20TH CENTURY

Social, Economic, and Demographic Developments

On social, economic, and demographic developments, see Wendy F. Katkin, Ned Landsman, Andrea Tyree, eds., *Beyond Pluralism: The Conception of Groups and Group Identities in America* (1998); David Hollinger, *Post-Ethnic America* (1995); Raymond Mohl, ed., *Searching for the Sunbelt: Historical Perspectives on a Region* (1990); Mike Davis, *City of Quartz: Excavating the Future in Los Angeles* (1990); Alejandro Portes and Alex Stepick, *City on the Edge: The Transformation of Miami* (1993); Merry Ovnick, *Los Angeles: The End of the Rainbow* (1994); Nathan Glazer, ed., *Clamor at the Gates: The New American Immigration* (1985); Michael D'Innocenzo and Josef P. Sirefman, eds., *Immigration and Ethnicity* (1992); Alejandro Portes and Ruben G. Rumbaut, *Immigrant America: A Portrait* (1996); Norman L. Zucker and Naomi Flink Zucker, *Desperate Crossings: Seeking Refuge in America* (1996); David M. Reimers, *Unwelcome Strangers: American Identity* and the Turn against Immigration (1998); Howard Kohn, We Had a Dream: A Tale of the Struggle for Integration in America (1998); Stephen Steinberg, Turning Back: The Retreat from Racial Justice in American Thought and Policy (1995); Howard Ball, The Bakke Case: Race, Education, and Affirmative Action (2000); and Allen J. Scott and Edward W. Soja, eds., The City: Los Angeles and Urban Theory at the End of the Twentieth Century (1996).

Specific studies include, on American Indians, Nancy Shoemaker, American Indian Population Recovery in the Twentieth Century (1999); Joy A. Bilharz, The Allegany Senecas and Kinzua Dam: Forced Relocation through Two Generations (1998); Joane Nagel, American Indian Ethnic Renewal: Red Power and the Resurgence of Identity and Culture (1996); John Williams Sayers, Ghost Dancing the Law: The Wounded Knee Trials (1997). On Latinos, see Manuel G. Gonzales, Mexicanos: A History of Mexicans in the United States (1999); Juan Gonzalez, Harvest of Empire: A History of Latinos in America (2000); John R. Chávez, East Side Landmark: A History of the East Los Angeles Community Union, 1968–1993 (1998); Michael Jones-Correa, Between Two Nations: The Political Predicament of Latinos in New York City (1998); José E. Cruz, Identity and Power: Puerto Rican Politics and the Challenge of Ethnicity (1998); Roberto Suro, Strangers Among Us: How Latino Immigration Is Transforming America (1998); Mark Davis, Magical Urbanism: Latinos Reinvent the US City (2000); María Cristina García, Havana USA: Cuban Exiles and Cuban Americans in South Florida, 1959–1994 (1996); Vicki L. Ruiz, From Out of the Shadows: Mexican Women in Twentieth-Century America (1998); Mary Patrice Erdmans, Opposite Poles: Immigrants and Ethnics in Polish Chicago, 1976–1990 (1998); Barbara Posadas, The Filipino Americans (1999); and Benson Tong, The Chinese Americans (2000).

Changes in Technology, Business, and the Environment

On changes in technology, work, and business see Robert Reich, The Work of Nations: Preparing Ourselves for 21st Century Capitalism (1991); Daniel Yergin, The Prize: The Epic Quest for Oil, Money, and Power (1991) and The Commanding Heights: The Battle between Government and the Marketplace That is Remaking the Modern World (1998); Thomas I. Palley, Plenty of Nothing: The Downsizing of the American Dream and the Case for Structural Keynesianism (1998); Kathleen Barker and Kathleen Christensen, Contingent Work: American Employment Relations in Transition (1998); Jefferson Cowie, Capital Moves: RCA's Seventy-Year Quest for Cheap Labor (1999); Robert J. Samuelson, The American Dream in the Age of Entitlement, 1945–1995 (1996); Steven P. Dandaneau, A Town Abandoned: Flint, Michigan, Confronts Deindustrialization (1996); Ruth Milkman, Farewell to the Factory: Auto Workers in the Late Twentieth Century (1997); Judith Stein, Running Steel, Running America: Race, Economic Policy, and the Decline of Liberalism (1998); and Charles Noble, Welfare as We Knew It: A Political History of the American Welfare State (1997).

On the computer revolution see James W. Cortada, The Computer in the United States: From Laboratory to Market, 1930–1960 (1993); Paul N. Edwards, The Closed World: Computers and the Politics of Discourse in Cold War America (1996); Arthur L. Norberg and July O'Neill, Transforming Computer Technology: Information Processing for the Pentagon, 1962–1986; and Janet Abbate, Inventing the Internet (1999).

On environment, see Samuel P. Hays, Beauty, Health, and Permanence: Environmental Politics in the United States, 1955–1985 (1987) and Explorations in Environmental History (1998); Kirkpatrick Sale, The Green Revolution; The Environmental Movement (1993); Craig E. Coltren and Peter N. Skinner, The Road to Love Canal: Managing Industrial Waste before the EPA (1996); Michele Stenehjem Gerber, On the Home Front: The Cold War Legacy of the Hanford Nuclear Site (1992); Terence Kehoe, Cleaning Up the Great Lakes: From Cooperation to Confrontation (1997); (1987); Ann Markusen et al., The Rise of the Gunbelt: The Military Remapping of Industrial America (1991); and Philip Shabecoff, A Fierce Green Fire: The American Environmental Movement (1993).

Changes in the Media Environment and Mass Culture

On changes in the media environment and mass culture, see Todd Gitlin, Inside Prime Time (1983); John Fiske, Television Culture (1987); Mark Crispin Miller, Boxed-In: The Culture of TV (1988); Robert Kolker, Cinema of Loneliness: Penn, Kubrick, Scorcese, Spielberg, Altman (rev. ed., 2000); Marsha Kinder, Playing with Power in Movies, Television, and Video Games (1991); Elizabeth G. Traube, Dreaming Identities: Class, Gender, and Generation in the 1980s Hollywood Movies (1992); Andrew Goodwin, Dancing in the Distraction Factory: Music Television and Popular Culture (1992); Henry Jenkins, Textual Poachers: Television Fans & Participatory Culture (1992); Anne Friedberg, Window Shopping: Cinema and the Postmodern (1993); Jane Feuer, Seeing Through the Eighties: Television and Reaganism (1995); Alan Nadel, Flatlining on the Field of Dreams: Cultural Narratives in the Films of President Reagan's America (1997); Daniel Wojcik, The End of the World as We Know It: Faith, Fatalism, and Apocalypse in America (1997); Henry A. Giroux, Channel Surfing: Race Talk and the Destruction of Today's Youth (1997); Joseph Turow, Breaking Up America: Advertisers and the New Media World (1997); Jim Cullen, Born in the U.S.A.: Bruce Springsteen and the American Tradition (1997).

Continuation of Political Insurgency

On the continuation of political insurgency, begin with Barbara Epstein, Political Protest and Cultural Revolution: Non-Violent Direct Action in the 1970s (1991); and Thomas Raymond Wellock, Critical Masses: Opposition to Nuclear Power in California, 1958–1978 (1998).

On women's movements, see Sara Evans, Personal Politics: The Roots of Women's Liberation in the Civil Rights Movement and the New Left (1979); Alice Echols, Daring to Be Bad: Radical Feminism in America, 1967–1975 (1989); Nancy Whittier, Feminist Generations: the Persistence of the Radical Women's Movement (1995); Jane J. Mansbridge, Why We Lost the ERA (1986); Mary Frances Berry, Why ERA Failed: Politics, Women's Rights, and the Amending Process of the Constitution (1986); Johnnetta B. Cole, ed., All American Women: Lines That Divide, Ties That Bind (1986); Catherine MacKinnon,

Feminism Unmodified: Discourses on Life and Law (1988); Susan Staggenborg, *The Pro-Choice Movement: Organization and Activism in the Abortion Conflict* (1991); and the relevant chapters of Leslie Reagan, *When Abortion Was a Crime: Women, Medicine, and Law in the United States, 1867–1973* (1997); Amy Erdman Farrell, *Yours in Sisterhood: Ms. Magazine and the Promise of Popular Feminism* (1998); Kate Weigand, *Red Feminism: American Communism and the Making of Women's Liberation* (2001); Marilyn Jacoby Boxer, *When Women Ask the Questions: Creating Women's Studies in America* (1998); Ruth Rosen, *The World Split Open: How the Modern Women's Movement Changed America* (2000).

On the gay and lesbian rights movement, see the relevant chapters of John D'Emilio and Estelle B. Freedman, *Intimate Matters: A History of Sexuality in America* (1988); Randy Shilts, *And the Band Played On: Politics, People, and the AIDS Epidemic* (1987); Steven Epstein, *Impure Science: AIDS, AIDS Activism, and the Politics of Science* (1996); Jeffrey Escoffier, *American Homo: Community and Perversity* (1998); Rodger Streitmatter, *Unspeakable: The Rise of the Gay and Lesbian Press in America* (1995); Paul Robinson, *Gay Lives: Homosexual Autobiography from John Addington Symonds to Paul Monette* (1999); Leila J. Rupp, *A Desired Past: A Short History of Same-Sex Love in America* (1999); Lillian Faderman, *To Believe in Women: What Lesbians Have Done for America* (1999); and David A. J. Richards, *Women, Gays, and the Constitution: The Grounds for Feminism and Gay Rights in Culture and Law* (1998).

Race and Multiculturalism
On the dilemmas of race and multiculturalism see Russell Ferguson et al., eds., *Out There: Marginalization and Contemporary Cultures* (1990); Toni Morrison, ed., *Race-ing Justice, En-Gendering Power: Essays on Anita Hill, Clarence Thomas, and the Construction of Social Reality* (1992); Andrew Hacker, *Two Nations: Black and White, Separate, Hostile, and Unequal* (1992); bell hooks, *Black Looks: Race and Representation* (1992); Michael Eric Dyson, *Reflecting Black: African-American Cultural Criticism* (1993); Cornel West, *Race Matters* (1993) and *Beyond Eurocentrism and Multiculturalism* (1993); James Davison Hunter, *Culture Wars: The Struggle to Define America* (1991); Henry Louis Gates Jr., *Loose Canons: Notes on the Culture Wars* (1992); Patricia Turner, *I Heard it Through the Grapevine: Rumor in African-American Culture* (1993); Russell A. Potter, *Spectacular Vernaculars: Hip-Hop and the Politics of Postmodernism* (1995); David A. Hollinger, *Post-Ethnic America: Beyond Multiculturalism* (1995); Robert C. Smith, *Racism in the Post–Civil Rights Era: Now You See It, Now You Don't* (1995); Roger Waldinger, *Still the Promised City? African-Americans and New Immigrants in Postindustrial New York* (1996); Mattias Gardell, *In the Name of Elijah Muhammed: Louis Farrakhan and the Nation of Islam* (1996); Michael Eric Dyson, *Between God and Gangsta Rap: Bearing Witness to Black Culture* (1996); Jennifer L. Hochschild, *Facing Up to the American Dream: Race, Class, and the Soul of the Nation* (1995); Toni Morrison, ed., *Birth of a Nation 'Hood: Gaze, Script, and Spectacle in the O. J. Simpson Case* (1997); Elaine Bell Kaplan, *Not Our Kind of Girl: Unraveling the Myths of Black Teenage Motherhood* (1997); Pyong Gap, *Min, Caught in the Middle: Korean Merchants in America's Multiethnic Cities* (1996); Raymond Tatalovich, *Nativism Reborn? The Official English Language Movement and the American States* (1995); Gary Y. Okihiro, *Margins and Mainstreams: Asians in American History and Culture* (1994); John William Sayer, *Ghost Dancing and the Law: The Wounded Knee Trials* (1997); Joane Nagel, *American Indian Ethnic Revival: Red Power and the Resurgence of Identity and Culture* (1996); Paul Chaat Smith and Robert Allen Warrior, *Like a Hurricane: The Indian Movement from Alcatraz to Wounded Knee* (1996); Fergus M. Bordewich, *Killing the White Man's Indian: Reinventing Native Americans at the End of the Twentieth Century* (1996); Ambrose I. Lane Sr., *Return of the Buffalo: the Story Behind America's Indian Gaming Explosion* (1995); Rennard Strickland, *Tonto's Revenge: Reflections on American Indian Culture and Policy* (1997); Pierrette Hondagneu-Sotelo, *Gendered Transitions: Mexican Experiences of Immigration* (1994); Alan Klein, *Baseball on the Border: A Tale of Two Laredos* (1997) offers a unique look, through the American pastime, of multiculturalism.

Conservative Politics
The growth of the "new conservatism" may be traced in Jerome Himmelstein, *To the Right: The Transformation of American Conservatism* (1990); Walter Capps, *The New Religious Right: Piety, Patriotism, and Politics* (1990); Walter Hixson, *Searching for the American Right* (1992); Michael Lienesch, *Redeeming America: Piety and Politics in the New Christian Right* (1993); Mary C. Brennan, *Turning Right in the Sixties: The Conservative Capture of the GOP* (1995); Robert Alan Goldberg, *Barry Goldwater* (1995); Dan T. Carter, *The Politics of Rage: George C. Wallace, the Origins of the New Conservatism, and the Transformation of American Politics* (1995); Catherine McNicol Stock, *Rural Radicals: Righteous Rage in the American Grain Belt* (1996); Mark J. Rozell and Clyde Wilcox, *Second Coming: The New Christian Right in Virginia Politics* (1996); Raymond Wolters, *Right Turn: William Bradford Reynolds, the Reagan Administration, and Black Civil Rights* (1996); and Didi Herman, *The Antigay Agenda: Orthodox Vision and the Christian Right* (1997). On extremist movements, see Sara Diamond, *Roads to Dominion: Right-Wing Power and Political Power in the United States* (1995); James D. Tabor and Eugene V. Gallagher, *Why Waco? Cults and the Battle for Religious Freedom in America* (1995); Betty A. Dobrats and Stephanie L. Shanks-Neili, *"White Power, White Pride!" The White Separatist Movement in the United States* (1997); and James Gibson, *Warrior Dreams: Paramilitary Culture in Post Vietnam America* (1994).

Videos
Dream Worlds II: Desire, Sex, and Power in Music Video (1996) is an award-winning critique of the images in rock videos, while Michael Eric Dyson, *Material Witness: Race, Identity and the Politics of Gangsta Rap* (1996) offers a more complex view. The Myth of the Liberal Media (1994) is a three-part critique, by Noam Chomsky and Edward Herman, of how U.S. media shape popular understandings.

CHAPTER 31 POWER AND POLITICS SINCE 1974

General Surveys of Recent Political Trends

General surveys of political trends include Martin T. Wattenberg, *The Decline of American Political Parties, 1952–1980* (1984); Ryan Barilleaux, *The Post-Modern Presidency: The Office After Ronald Reagan* (1988); Kathleen Hall Jamieson, *Packaging the Presidency: A History and Criticism of Presidential Campaign Advertising* (3rd ed., 1996); William Greider, *Who Will Tell the People: The Betrayal of American Democracy* (1992); Thomas Byrne and Mary D. Edsall, *Chain Reaction: The Impact of Race, Rights, and Taxes on American Politics* (1992); Kevin Phillips, *Boiling Point: Republicans, Democrats, and the Decline of Middle Class Prosperity* (1993); William C. Berman *America's Right Turn: From Nixon to Bush* (1994); Ronald Radosh, *Divided They Fell: The Demise of the Democratic Party, 1964–1996* (1996); Philip John Davies, *An American Quarter Century: U.S. Politics from Vietnam to Clinton* (1995); Robert W. Speel, *Changing Patterns of Voting in the Northern United States: Electoral Realignment, 1952–1996* (l998); and Kenneth S. Baer, *Reinventing Democrats: The Politics of Liberalism from Reagan to Clinton* (2000).

Foreign Policy

On general trends and specific episodes in foreign policy, see Paul Kennedy, *The Rise and Fall of the Great Powers: Economic Change and Military Conflict from 1500 to 2000* (1987); Eric Alterman, *Who Speaks for America? Why Democracy Matters in Foreign Policy* (l998); Raymond Garthoff, *Detente and Confrontation: American-Soviet Relations from Nixon to Reagan* (1985); Gaddis Smith, *Morality Reason, and Power: American Diplomacy in the Carter Years* (1986) and *The Last Years of the Monroe Doctrine, 1945–1993*; Herbert D. Rosenbaum and Alexej Ugrinsky, eds., *Jimmy Carter: Foreign Policy and Post-Presidential Years* (1994); Richard C. Thornton, *The Carter Years: Toward a New Global Order* (1991); David Skidmore, *Reversing Course: Carter's Foreign Policy, Domestic Politics, and the Failure of Reform* (1996); Timothy P. Maga, *The World of Jimmy Carter: U.S. Foreign Policy, 1977–1981* (1994); Joanna Spear, *Carter and Arms: Implementing the Carter Administration's Arms Transfer Restraint Policy* (1995); John Dumbrell, *American Foreign Policy: Carter to Clinton* (1996); Robert A. Pastor, *Whirlpool: U.S. Foreign Policy Toward Latin America and the Caribbean* (1992); William M. LeoGrande, *Our Own Backyard: The United States and Central America, 1977-1992* (1998); Walter LaFeber, *Inevitable Revolutions: The United States in Central America* (1983); Keith L. Nelson, *The Making of Detente: Soviet-American Relations in the Shadow of Vietnam* (1995); Theodore Draper, *A Very Thin Line: The Iran-Contra Affairs* (1991); Gary Sick, *October Surprise: America's Hostages in Iran and the Election of Ronald Reagan* (1991); Morris H. Morley, ed., *Crisis and Confrontation: Ronald Reagan's Foreign Policy* (1988); H. Bruce Franklin, *War Stars: The Superweapon and the American Imagination* (1988).

On the end of the cold war, see Raymond Garthoff, *The Great Transition: America-Soviet Relations and the End of the Cold War* (1994); Michael R. Beschloss and Strobe Talbott, *At the Highest Levels: The Inside Story of the End of the Cold War* (1993); John Lewis Gaddis, *The United States and the End of the Cold War: Implications, Reconsiderations, Provocations* (1991) and *We Now Know* (1997); and Michael Hogan, ed., *The End of the Cold War: Its Meaning and Implications* (1992). Dana H. Allin, *Cold War Illusions: America, Europe, and Soviet Power, 1969–1989* (1998), downplays Bush's role; George Bush and Brent Scowcroft, *A World Transformed* (1998), and Philip Zelikow and Condoleezza Rice, *Germany Unified and Europe Transformed: A Study in Statecraft* (1995), accentuate it.

The Gulf War

For the Gulf War, specifically, see Lawrence Freedman and Efraim Karsh, *The Gulf Conflict, 1990–1991: Diplomacy and War in the New World Order* (1993); Dilip Hiro, *Desert Shield to Desert Storm: The Second Gulf War* (1992); Douglas Kellner, *The Persian Gulf TV War* (1992); Richard Hallion, *Storm Over Iraq: Air Power and the Gulf War* (1992); Susan Jeffords and Lauren Rabinovitz, eds., *Seeing Through the Media: The Persian Gulf War* (1994); and Frank N. Schubert and Theresa L. Kraus, *The Whirlwind War: The United States Army in Operations Desert Shield and Desert Storm* (1995).

The Ford Presidency

On the brief Ford presidency, see Edward L. and Frederick H. Schapsmeier, *Gerald R. Ford's Date with Destiny: A Political Biography* (1989); James Cannon, *Time and Chance: Gerald Ford's Appointment with History* (1994); John R. Greene, *The Presidency of Gerald R. Ford* (1995); and John F. Guilmartin Jr., *A Very Short War: The* Mayaguez *and the Battle of Koh Tang* (1995).

The Carter Years

On the Carter years, see Burton I. Kaufman, *The Presidency of James Earl Carter Jr.* (1993); Betty Glad, *Jimmy Carter: In Search of the Great White House* (1980); Erwin C. Hargrove, *Jimmy Carter as President* (1988); Garland Haas, *Jimmy Carter and the Politics of Frustration* (1992); Kenneth Morris, *Jimmy Carter: American Moralist* (1996); Anthony S. Campagna, *Economic Policy in the Carter Administration* (1995); and Gary M. Fink and Hugh Davis Graham, eds., *The Carter Presidency: Policy Choices in the Post–New Deal Era* (1998). Douglas Brinkley, *The Unfinished Presidency: Jimmy Carter's Journey beyond the White House* (1998) details post-presidential years.

The Reagan Era

On the Reagan era, see Sidney Blumenthal and Thomas Byrne Edsall, eds., *The Reagan Legacy* (1988); Robert Dallek, *Ronald Reagan: The Politics of Symbolism* (1984); Garry Wills, *Reagan's America: Innocents at Home* (1987); Robert E. Denton Jr., *The Primetime Presidency of Ronald Reagan* (1988); Michael Schaller, *Reckoning with Reagan* (1992); James E. Combs, *The Reagan Range: The Nostalgic Myth in American Politics* (1993); William Pemberton, *Exit with Honor: The Life and Presidency of Ronald Reagan* (1997); John Lofland, *Polite Protesters: The American Peace Movement of the 1980s* (1993);

Raymond Wolters, *Right Turn: William Bradford Reynolds, the Reagan Administration, and Black Civil Rights* (1996); Diane Vaughan, *The* Challenger *Launch Decision: Risky Technology, Culture and Deviance at NASA* (1997); Beth A. Fischer, *The Reagan Reversal: Foreign Policy at the End of the Cold War* (1998); and John W. Sloan, *The Reagan Effect: Economics and Presidential Leadership* (1999).

The Bush Presidency

On the Bush presidency see Michael Duffy and Dan Goodgame, *Marching in Place: The Status Quo Presidency of George Bush* (1992); David Mervin, *George Bush and the Guardian Presidency* (1996); John Podhoretz, *Hell of a Ride: Backstage at the White House Follies 1989–1993* (1993); Charles Kolb, *White House Daze: The Unmaking of Domestic Policy in the Bush Years* (1994); and Herbert S. Parmet, *George Bush: The Life of a Lone Star Yankee* (1997).

The Clinton Presidency and the Politics of the 1990s

On the politics of the 1990s, see Kenneth Baer, *Reinventing Democrats: The Politics of Liberalism from Reagan to Clinton* (2000); Jack W. Germond and Jules Witcover, *Mad as Hell: Revolt at the Ballot Box 1992* (1993); David Maraniss, *First in His Class: A Biography of Bill Clinton* (1995); Bob Woodward, *The Agenda: Inside the Clinton White House* (1994); Kathryn S. Olmsted, *Challenging the Secret Government: The Post-Watergate Investigations of the CIA and the FBI* (1996); Gwendolyn Mink, *Welfare's End* (1998); David J. Rothman, *Beginnings Count: The Technological Imperative in American Health Care* (1997); Theda Skocpol, *Boomerang: Clinton's Health Security Effort and the Turn against Government in U.S. Politics* (1996); Jacob S. Hacker, *The Road to Nowhere: The Genesis of President Clinton's Plan for Health Security* (1997); John Hohenberg, *Reelecting Bill Clinton: Why America Chose a "New" Democrat* (1997); and Robert Reich, *Locked in the Cabinet* (1997). Bruce Cumings, *Parallax Visions: Making Sense of American-East Asian Relations at the End of the Century* (1999); Frederick W. Mayer, *Interpreting NAFTA: The Science and Art of Political Analysis* (1998), look at politics and foreign policy. Bob Woodward, *Maestro: Greenspan's Fed and the American Boom* (2000), provides a view of economic policy.

Videos

The A & E *Biography* series contains videos appropriate for these years, including *Jimmy Carter: To the White House and Beyond* (1995). *Reagan* (PBS, 1998) is an effective introduction. The Gulf War is covered in *A Line in the Sand* (1990), three-part series *Desert Triumph* (1991), and *The Gulf War* (1997), also a three-part series. *Rush to Judgment: The Anita Hill Story* (1997) offers interviews with both advocates and critics of Justice Clarence Thomas's chief accuser. *The War Room* (1994) provides a candid, behind-the-scenes look at the 1992 Clinton campaign. *An American Journey: The Great Society to the Reagan Revolution* (1998) is a five-part overview of the period.

PHOTO CREDITS

Images not referenced below are in the public domain.

CHAPTER 1

xlviii (left) © Bettmann / Corbis. **xlviii (right)** Bibliotheque Nationale de France. **p. 3** © John Maier, Jr. / JB Pictures. **p. 6** © Werner Forman / Art Resource, NY. **p. 8** © Erich Lessing / Art Resource, NY. **p. 10** © Jon Adkins / National Geographic Society. **p. 13 (left)** © Werner Forman / Art Resource, NY. **p. 13 (right)** Werner Forman / Art Resource, NY. **p. 18** Folding Screen: The Encounter of Cortes and Moctezuma (obverse); The Four Continents (reverse) Collection Banco Nacional de Mexico, Mexico City. **p. 19 (top, right)** © Stock Montage, Inc. **p. 19 (top, left)** © Bettmann / Corbis **p. 20** Courtesy of the John Carter Brown Library at Brown University. **p. 22** © Ancient Art & Architecture Collection. **p. 23 (right)** © Boltin Picture Library. **p. 24** © Werner Forman / Art Resource, NY. **p. 25** © Boltin Picture Library. **p. 26** Image taken from exhibit produced by the Florida Museum of Natural History. **p. 27** © Boltin Picture Library. **p. 28 (left)** © Ancient Art & Architecture Collection. **p. 30 (left)** Readers Digest, Mysteries of the Ancient Americas, art by Lloyd Kenneth Townsend. **p. 30 (right)** © David Muench. **p. 32** Moctezuma's Mexico, by David Carrasco and Eduardo Mato Moctezuma, © 1992 University Press of Colorado. Photographs by Salvador Guil'liem Arroyo. **p. 34** Fray Bernardinode Sahagun, General History of the Things of New Spain. **p. 35** New York Public Library. Astor, Lenox and Tilden Foundations, Rare book Division. **p. 38** Kobal Collection / Warner Bros. **p. 39** © Macduff Everton / Corbis. **p. 43** Courtesy, New York State Library, Albany.

CHAPTER 2

p. 44 (left) North Wind Picture Archives. **p. 44 (right)** © SEF / Art Reource, NY. **p. 47** Theodore DeBry. **p. 49** Kobal Collection / Alliance/ Goldwyn. **p. 50** New York Public Library. Astor, Lenox and Tilden Foundations, Rare book Division. **p. 56** Theodore De Bry. **p. 58** From the Collections of the Library of Congress. **p. 59** William C. Clements Library, University of Michigan, Ann Arbor. **p. 61** Courtesy of the John Carter Brown Library at Brown University. **p. 62** Courtesy of the John Carter Brown Library at Brown University. **p. 66** The Library Company of Philadelphia. **p. 73** New York Public Library. Astor, Lenox and Tilden Foundations, Rare book Division. **p. 74** Copyright © 1965 by Edwin Tunis. Copyright renewed 1993 by David Hutton, Executor for the Estate of Edwin Tunis. Illustrations from Colonial Craftsmen and the beginnings of American Industry, now published by Johns Hopkins University Press. Reprinted by permission of Curtis Brown, Ltd. **p. 76** From the Collections of the Library of Congress. **p. 77 (left)** Hans Oswald Wild / TimePix. **p. 77 (right)** The Granger Collection. **p. 84** North Wind Picture Archives. **p. 85** © Bettmann / Corbis.

CHAPTER 3

p. 88 © The Granger Collection, New York. **p. 97** © The British Museum. **p. 101** Patrick M. Malone, The Skulking Way of War, Madison Books © 1991. **p. 104** © Wendell Metzen / Bruce Coleman Inc. **p. 105** The Virginia Journals of Benjamin Henry Latrobe (2 vols., New Haven, 1977) I, 181-82, 247, plate 21. **p. 108** Thomas B. Macaulay, History of England from the Accession of James II, ed. by Charles H. Firth (London: Macmillan, 1914). **p. 109 (left)** Thomas B. Macaulay, History of England from the Accession of James II, ed. by Charles H. Firth (London: Macmillan, 1914). **p. 109 (right)** Thomas B. Macaulay, History of England from the Accession of James II, ed. by Charles H. Firth (London: Macmillan, 1914). **p. 112** PBS Home Video. **p. 117 (left)** Hampton Court Palace"A View of Hampton Court" by Leonard Knyff, c.1703 (detail). The Royal Collection © 1998 Her Majesty The Queen. The Royal Picture Library, Windsor Castle. **p. 117 (right)** Dixon Harvesters, c.1725. by English School, (18th century) Cheltenham Art Gallery & Museums, Gloucestershire, U.K. / The Bridgeman Art Lirbrary. **p. 119** Archives Nationales. **p. 121** © Bettmann / Corbis. **p. 124 (top)** Courtesy Massachusetts Historical Society. **p. 124 (bottom)** National Park Service, Historic Photographic Collections, Harpers Ferry. **p. 125** Illustrated London News.

CHAPTER 4

p. 126 1963.6.1 (1904)/PA: Copley, John Singelton, "Watson and the Shark", Ferdinand Lammot Belin Fund © 1998 Board of Trustees, National Gallery of Art, Washington, 1778, oil on canvas, 1.82 x 2.297 (71 3/4 x 90 1/2); framed: 2.413 x 2.642 x .101 (95 x 104 x 4). **p. 131** after John Barbot, from Churchill's Vogages. **p. 132** Colonial Williamsburg. **p. 136** Copyright © 1965 by Edwin Tunis. Copyright renewed 1993 by David Hutton, Executor for the Estate of Edwin Tunis. Illustrations from Colonial Craftsmen and the beginnings of American Industry, now published by Johns Hopkins University Press. Reprinted by permission of Curtis Brown, Ltd. **p. 137** Copyright © 1965 by Edwin Tunis. Copyright renewed 1993 by David Hutton, Executor for the Estate of Edwin Tunis. Illustrations from Colonial Craftsmen and the beginnings of American Industry, now published by Johns Hopkins University Press. Reprinted by permission of Curtis Brown, Ltd. **p. 139** from the Collections of the Library of Congress. **p. 141** Hargrett Rare Book and Manuscript Library / University of Georgia Libraries, Athens. **p. 142 (left)** Courtesy of The Harvard University Portrait Collection. Bequest of Dr. John Collins Warren, 1856. **p. 142 (right)** The Metropolitan Museum of Art, Purchase, The Sylmaris Collection, Gift of George Coe Graves, by exchange, 1940. (40.127) Photograph by Richard Cheek. **p. 143** The Saint Louis Museum Purchase. **p. 147** © Bettmann / Corbis. **p. 149** Colonial Williamsburg Foundation. **p. 153** New Jersey State Museum Collection. **p. 155** Peabody Museum, Harvard University. Photograph by Hillel Burger. **p. 157** Courtesy of the Massachusetts Historical Society. **p. 158** Collection of The New-York Historical Society. **p. 160** North Wind Picture Archives. **p. 163** Courtesy Derby Museums and Art Gallery. **p. 167** Kobal Collection / 20th Century Fox / Morgan Creek.

CHAPTER 5

p. 172 Engraving, hand colored, "Plate UV. A View of South Part of Lexington," engraved by Amos Doolittle after a drawing by Ralph Earl; New Haven, Conn., 1775. Chicago Historical Society. **p. 175** © 2000. Museum of Fine Arts, Boston. **p. 178** Colonial Williamsburg Foundation. **p. 182** New York Public Library. **pp. 183 and 185** Courtesy of the

John Carter Brown Library at Brown University. **p. 188** The Granger Collection, New York. **p. 190** Colonial Williamsburg Foundation. **p. 197** From the Collections of the Library of Congress. **p. 198** American Antiquarian Society. **p. 199** Courtesy of the John Carter Brown Library at Brown University. **p. 200** Clements Library, University of Michigan, Ann Arbor. **p. 201 (left)** © Tate Gallery, London / Art Resource, NY **p. 201 (right)** Yale University Art Gallery. Trumbull Collection. **p. 202** © Bettmann / Corbis. **p. 203** Colonial Williamsburg Foundation. **p. 207** The Granger Collection, New York. **p. 211** Kobal Collection / Columbia.

CHAPTER 6
p. 212 Gift of the Owners of the Old Boston Museum Courtesy, Museum of Fine Arts, Boston © 2002 / All Rights Reserved. **p. 218** Lewis Walpole Library, Yale University. **p. 219** Colonial Williamsburg Foundation. **p. 220** © Alon Reininger / Woodfin Camp. **p. 224** Boston Athenaeum. **p. 226** Courtesy, American Antiquarian Society. **p. 227** National Archives of Canada / C-002001. **p. 228** New York State Historical Association, Cooperstown, New York. **p. 233** Yale University Art Gallery, Gift of Ebenezer Baldwin, B.A. 1808. **p. 235** Kobal Collection / Cooper, Andrew / Columbia Tristar. **p. 238** From the Collections of the Library of Congress. **p. 240** © J. Gilbert Harrington. **p. 244 (left)** Harvard Law Art Collection. Oil on canvas, 56-3/16 x 77-3/4. Gift of Dr. George Stevens Jones, Mar. 31, 1879. **p. 244 (right)** Nicolino Calyo The Richard K. Haight Family, ca. 1848. Museum of the City of New York. Gift of Elizabeth Cushing Iselin. **p. 245 (left)** Berry-Hill Galleries, New York. **p. 245 (right)** Missouri Historical Society. **p. 251** From the Collections of the Library of Congress.

CHAPTER 7
p. 254 The Historical Society of Pennsylvania, Preparation for War to Defend Commerce, by William Russell Birch (BD61B531.2pl.29). **p. 259** PBS Home Video. **p. 260** Lewis Miller (1796-1882). The Historical Society of York County, PA. **p. 261** Old Dartmouth Historical Society / New Bedford Whaling Museum. **p. 264** The Granger Collection, New York. **p. 265** The Granger Collection, New York. **p. 266** The Crockett Almanac, 1840. **p. 268** National Museum of American History, The Smithsonian Institution. **p. 270** Collection of the Maryland Historical Society, Baltimore. **p. 271** The Granger Collection, New York. **p. 273** from the Collection of the New-York Historical Society. **p. 274** The Historical Society of Pennsylvania, Procession of the Victuallers, by John Lewis Krimmel (Bc85 K89). **p. 276** John Lewis Krimmel, American, 1786-1821 Village Tavern, 1813-14, oil on canvas, 16 7/8 x 22 1/2 in. (42.8 x 56.9 cm) The Toledo Museum of Art, Toledo, Ohio; Purchased with funds from the Florence Scott Libbey Bequest in Memory of he Father, Maurice A. Scott. **p. 281** Old Dartmouth Historical Society / New Bedford Whaling Museum. **p. 282 (top)** Lewis Miller (1796-1882). The Historical Society of York County, PA. **p. 282 (middle)** Lewis Miller (1796-1882). The Historical Society of York County, PA. **p. 282 (bottom)** Lewis Miller (1796-1882). The Historical Society of York County, PA. **p. 285** Historical Commission, Mother Bethel AME Church, Philadelphia, PA.

CHAPTER 8
p. 288 collections of Davenport West, Jr. **p. 291** © National Portrait Gallery, Smithsonian Institution / Art Resource, NY. **p. 296 (both)** North Wind Picture Archives. **p. 301** Courtesy of the Lilly Library, Indiana University, Bloomington, Indiana. **p. 305** © Bettmann / Corbis. **p. 306** The Granger Collection, New York. **p. 307** National Portrait Gallery, Smithsonian Institution / Art Resource, NY. **p. 308** Architect of the Capitol. **p. 309** A View of New Orleans Taken from the Plantation of Marigny, Novermber, 1803 by Boqueto de Woiserie, Chicago Historical Society. **p. 313** North Wind Picture Archives. **p. 314** North Wind Picture Archives. **p. 315** Courtesy of the Royal Ontario Museum, Toronto, Canada. **p. 316** The Field Museum, Neg.#A93581c. **p. 318** Allyn Cox, 19741 Architect of the Capitol. **p. 321** Kobal Collection / Paramount.

CHAPTER 9
p. 322 from the Collections of the Library of Congress. **p. 325** The Library Company of Philadelphia. **p. 328** North Wind Picture Archives. **p. 329** The Granger Collection. **p. 331** © North Wind Picture Archives. **p. 334 (all)** Smithsonian Institution. **p. 335** New England Farmstead, 1849. by Samuel Gerry 1813-1891. Old Sturbridge Village, photo by Henry E. Peach. #20.1.106-B23486. **p. 336** Old Sturbridge Village, Photo by: Thomas Neill, #25.K74if.1994.2.1. **p. 338** Chicago Historical Society. **p. 340** © Bettmann / Corbis. **p. 342** The Granger Collection, New York. **p. 343** American Textile History Museum. Lowell, Mass. **p. 345** The Library Company of Philadelphia. **p. 348** The Historic New Orleans Collection, Accension #1975.931 & 2. **p. 351** The Historic New Orleans Collection, Accension # 1977.13734311. **p. 353** Kobal Collection / Selznick / MGM.

CHAPTER 10
p. 354 National Portrait Gallery, Smithsonian Institution / Art Resource, NY. **p. 356** © Bettmann / Corbis. **p. 358** Abby Aldrich Rockefeller Folk Art Center, Williamsburg, VA. **p. 362** Frederic Edwin Church NIAGARA, 1857. oil on canvas, 42 1/2 x 90 1/2 in. (107.95 x 229.87 cm) In the Collection of the Corcoran Gallery of Art, Museum Purchase, Gallery Fund. 76.15. **p. 364** Courtesy American Antiquarian Society. **p. 367** © Bettmann / Corbis. **p. 368** The Granger Collection, New York. **p. 369** The Granger Collection, NY. **p. 370** Drawn by J. W. Hill, engraved by Henry Papprill, Papprill View of New York, 1855. Museum of the City of New York. Gift of Mrs. Louis J. Hector, 82.116. **p. 371 (left)** © Collection of The New-York Historical Society. **p. 371 (right)** North Wind Picture Archives. **p. 372 (both)** Courtesy, American Antiquarian Society. **p. 373** Hunter Museum of American Art, Chattanooga, Tennessee, Gift of Mr. and Mrs. Thomas B. Whiteside. **p. 378** Reproduced form the collection of the Library of Congress, B811 152. **p. 381** Kobal Collection / Regan, Ken / Touchstone. **p. 382** The Historic New Orleans Collection, accession # 1960.46.

CHAPTER 11

p. 386 The Nelson-Atkins Museum of Art, Kansas City, Missouri (Purchase: Nelson Trust). **p. 389** The Saint Louis Art Museum, Purchase. **p. 395** North Wind Picture Archives. **p. 397** The Granger Collection, New York. **p. 398** North Wind Picture Archives. **p. 401** © 2002 All Rights Reserved. The Rhode Island Historical Society. **p. 403** Reproduced from the Collections of the Library of Congress. **p. 404** A Black Oyster Seller in Philadelphia, 1814, Watercolor by John Lewis Krimmel. The Metropolitan Museum of Art, Rogers Fund, 1942. (42.95.18). **p. 406** from J.C. Nott and George R. Gliddon, types of Mankind; or, Ethnological Researches (1845). **p. 408** Library Company of Philadelphia. **p. 409** Reproduced from the Collections of the Library of Congress, #LC-USZ62-5567-80/005. **p. 410** Old Sturbridge Village, photo by Henry E. Peach. **p. 415** PBS Home Video.

CHAPTER 12

p. 418 National Portrait Gallery, Smithsonian Institution / Art Resource, NY. **p. 420** National Museum of American Art, Washington DC / Art Resource, NY. **p. 425** The Granger Collection. **p. 426** Collection of The New-York Historical Society. **p. 429** The Hermitage: Home of President Andrew Jackson, Nashville, TN. **p. 431** White House Collection. **p. 432 (left)** The Smithsonian Institution, Division of Political History. **p. 432 (right)** Reproduced from the collections of the Library of Congress. **p. 433 (both)** The Smithsonian Institution, Division of Political History **p. 436** Woolaroc Museum. **p. 439** The Historical Society of Pennsylvania. **p. 444** Collection of The New-York Historical Society. **p. 445** North Wind Picture Archives. **p. 447** Kobal Collection / Cooper, Andrew / Dreamworks LLC. **p. 449** Collection of The New-York Historical Society.

CHAPTER 13

p. 452 From the collections of the Library of Congress. **p. 455** © Bettmann / Corbis. **p. 457** North Wind Picture Archives. **p. 459** Joseph Mustering the Nauvoo Legion, C.C.A. Christensen. © Courtesy Museum of Art, Brigham Young University. All Rights reserved. Photographer: David W. Hawkinson. **p. 461** © John Springer Collection / Corbis. **p. 465** Yale Collection of Western Americana, Beinecke Rare Book and Manuscript Library. **p. 469** Missouri Historical Society. MHS art acc# 1939.3.1. **p. 472 (top)** The Granger Collection, New York. **p. 472 (bottom)** Courtesy of the California History Room, California State Library, Sacramento, California. **p. 475** Courtesy of The Trustees of Boston Public Library. **p. 477** North Wind Picture Archives. **p. 478** The Granger Collection, New York.

CHAPTER 14

p. 482 The Granger Collection, New York. **p. 484** Reproduced from the Collections of the Library of Congress. **p. 486** © Bettmann / Corbis. **p. 487** © Bettmann / Corbis. **p. 489** Reproduced from the Collections of the Library of Congress. **p. 490** Maryland Historical Society, Baltimore. **p. 493** Kansas State Historical Society, Topeka. **p. 495** Prints Division, The New York Public Library. Astor, Lenox and Tilden Foundations. **p. 501** © Corbis. **p. 502** Reproduced from the Collections of the Library of Congress. **p. 504** © Bettmann / Corbis. **p. 507 (top)** © Bettmann / Corbis. **p. 507 (bottom)** The Granger Collection. **p. 509** © Bettmann / Corbis. **p. 512** North Wind Picture Archives. **p. 513 (top)** Courtesy of the Illinois State Historical Library. **p. 513 (bottom)** North Wind Picture Archives. **p. 516** Kansas State Historical Society.

CHAPTER 15

p. 518 Thomas C. Linday, Hornet's Nest, Cincinnati Historical Society. **p. 520** Reproduced from the Collections of the Library of Congress. **p. 522** From the Ralph E. Becker Colleciton of Political Americana, The Smithsonian Institution. **p. 525** Courtesy of The South Carolina Historical Society. **p. 529** from the Collection of the Library of Congress. **p. 537** © Springer / Corbis. **p. 538** Collection of The New-York Historical Society. **p. 539** Cook Collection, Valentine Museum, Richmond, Virginia. **p. 540** Photo by Timothy O'Sullivan, Chicago Historical Society, ICHi-08091. **p. 543** Reproduced from the Collections of the Library of Congress. **p. 545 (both)** © Bettmann / Corbis. **p. 546** Reproduced from the Collections of the Library of Congress. **p. 550 (top, both)** Reproduced for the Collections of the Library of Congress. **p. 550 (bottom)** © Bettmann / Corbis.

CHAPTER 16

p. 558 Eastman Johnson 1824-1906 A RIDE FOR LIBERTY—THE FUGITIVE SLAVES, circa 1862. Oil on board The Brooklyn Museum 40.59. A Gift of Miss Gwendolyn O.L. Conkling. **p. 565** Architect of the Capitol. **p. 568** The Library of Virginia. **p. 569** New-York Historical Society. **p. 571** Reproduced from the Collections of the Library of Congress. **p. 572 (left)** Reproduced from the Collections of the Library of Congress. **p. 572 (right)** Courtesy of the Illinois State Historical Library. **p. 576** National Park Service, Harpers Ferry Center. **p. 580** Reproduced from the Collections of the Library of Congress. **p. 581 (top, left)** Reproduced from the Collections of the Library of Congress, LC-B8171-872-801004. **p. 581 (top, right)** Reproduced from the Collections of the Library of Congress, LC-B8171-3078LC. **p. 581 (bottom)** Reproduced from the Collections of the Library of Congress. **p. 582** Kobal Collection/ Tri Star. **p. 585** Brown Brothers. **p. 588** Reproduced from the Collections of the Library of Congress #LCB8171-8221/412312. **p. 590** Reproduced from the Collections of the Library of Congress. **p. 593** © Bettmann / Corbis. **p. 594** Reproduced from the Collections of the Library of Congress.17299-3479.

CHAPTER 17

p. 596 Winslow Homer, *Sunday Morning in Virginia*, 1877. Cincinnati Art Museum John J. Emery Fund. Acc.#1924.247. **p. 599** Courtesy Chicago Historical Society. **p. 603** Reproduced from the Collections of the Library of Congress. **p. 604** © Bettmann / Corbis. **p. 605** Reproduced from the Collections of the Library of Congress #LCUSZ26229112/412312. **p. 609** North Wind Picture Archives. **p. 612** © Bettmann / Corbis. **p. 617** © Bettmann / Corbis. **p. 618** © Bettmann / Corbis. **p. 620** Reproduced from the Collections of the Library of Congress #LCUSZ262-18094/413325. **p. 621 (both)** © Stock Montage, Inc. **p. 622** © Bettmann / Corbis. **p. 624** The Granger Collection, New York.

CHAPTER 18

p. 628 Frederic Remington, "A Dash for Timber" oil on canvas, 1889. 1961.381. © Amon Carter Museum, Fort Worth, Texas. **p. 631** Nebraska State Historical Society. **p. 635** Erwin E. Smith Collection of the Library of Congress on deposit at the Amon Carter Museum, Fort Worth. **p. 637** © John Springer Collection / Corbis. **p. 638** Smithsonian Institution, Bureau of American Ethnology. **p. 639** Sophia Smith Collection, Smith College. **p. 640** Kansas State Historical Society, Topeka, Kansas. **p. 641 (top)** Burton Historical Collection, Detroit Public Library. **p. 641 (bottom)** The Granger Collection, New York. **p. 646** © Bettmann / Corbis.

CHAPTER 19

p. 652 The Kansas State Historical Society Topeka, Kansas. **p. 657 (top)** Boston Public Library. **p. 657 (bottom)** Archives of the University, Department of Rare Books and Special Collections. Princeton University Library. **p. 659** © Bettmann / Corbis. **p. 661** © Bettmann / Corbis. **p. 662** The Granger Collection, New York. **p. 665** North Wind Picture Archives. **p. 666** © Bettmann / Corbis. **p. 667** Kansas State Historical Society. **p. 670** © Bettmann / Corbis. **p. 672** The Granger Collection, New York.

CHAPTER 20

p. 676 John Sloan, The City from Greenwich Village, 1922. National Gallery of Art. Gift of Helen Farr Sloan, 1970.I. I. **pp. 679 (both), 682, and 684** © Bettmann / Corbis. **p. 687** Brown University Archives. **p. 691 (top and bottom)** The Granger Collection, New York. **p. 691 (middle)** Brown Brothers. **p. 693** Lewis Hine, Louisiana Oyster Company, 1911. Museum of the City of New York. The Jacob A. Riis Collection (UN2) 90.13.2.23. **p. 694** Victor Joseph Gatto Triangle Fire, March 25, 1911. Oil on canvas, 19 x 28 inches. Museum of the City of New York, 54.75, Gift of Mrs. Henry L. Moses. **p. 697** © Bettmann / Corbis. **p. 700** Kobal Collection / 20th Century Fox. **p. 702** Underwood Photo Archives. **p. 704** The Granger Collection, New York. **p. 706** © Bettmann / Corbis. **p. 708** Brown Brothers.

CHAPTER 21

p. 710 Culver Pictures. **p. 712** Culver Pictures. **p. 714** George Bellows, "Cliff Dwellers" 1913. oil on canvas. Los Angeles County Museum of Art, Los Angeles County Fund. **p. 715** Brown Brothers. **p. 719** The Granger Collection, New York. **p. 725** Reproduced from the Collections of the Library of Congress. **p. 727** © Bettmann / Corbis. **p. 728** The Granger Collection, New York. **p. 730** © Bettmann / Corbis. **p. 734** National Museum of American Art, Washington DC / Art Resource, NY. **p. 735 (left)** Idaho State Historical Society. Acc. #349. **p. 735 (right)** © Bettmann / Corbis. **p. 737** Brown Brothers. **p. 739** Kobal Collection / 20th Century Fox. **p. 741** Reproduced from the Collections of the Library of Congress.

CHAPTER 22

p. 746 Culver Pictures. **p. 749** Smithsonian Institution Photo No. 85-14366. **p. 752** The Granger Collection, New York. **p. 753** Chicago Historical Society. **p. 755** © Bettmann / Corbis. **p. 758** © Bettmann / Corbis. **p. 759 (both)** The Granger Collection. **p. 760** © UPI-Bettmann / Corbis. **p. 763** The Granger Collection, New York. **p. 764** The Granger Collection, New York. **p. 767** © Bettmann / Corbis. **p. 769** The Granger Collection, New York. **p. 770** North Wind Picture Archives. **p. 774** Brown Brothers.

CHAPTER 23

p. 776 Mary Evans Picture Library. **p. 780** Imperial War Museum, London. **p. 782** Records of the Women's International League for peace and Freedom, U.S. Section, Swarthmore College Peace Collection. **p. 785** The Granger Collections, New York. **p. 788** © The Phillips Collection, Washington, D.C. Photo Edward Owen. / Francine Seders Gallery Ltd., Seattle, Washington. **p. 791** Brown Brothers. **p. 793 (top)** Reproduced from the Collections of the Library of Congress. **p. 793 (bottom)** National Archives. **p. 795** National Archives #45-WP-115. **p. 798 (left)** Imperial War Museum. **p. 798 (right)** Grant Hamilton. Judge, 1898. **p. 799** The Granger Collection, New York. **p. 800** New York Times, 1919. **p. 801** © UPI-Bettmann / Corbis. **p. 806** Library & Archives Division, Historical Society of Western Pennsylvania, Pittsburgh, Pa. **p. 807** Kobal Collection / Paramount. **p. 808** © 1995 Estate of Ben Shahn / VAGA, New York . Collection of Whitney Museum of American Art. **p. 810** Stock Montage, Inc.

CHAPTER 24

p. 812 *The Dance Club*, or *The Jazz Party*, 1923 (oil on cansvas) by Roberts, William Patrick (1895–1980) Leeds Museums and Galleries (City Art Gallery) / The Bridgeman Art Library. Reproduced by permission of the Treasury Solicitor (administrator of the estate of John David Roberts). **p. 817** The Granger Collection, New York. **p. 820** © Bettmann / Corbis. **p. 823** Brown Brothers. **p. 824** Brown Brothers. **p. 825** © Bettmann / Corbis. **p. 829 (left)** Brown Brothers. **p. 829 (right)** © Bettmann / Corbis. **p. 830** © Bettmann / Corbis. **p. 835** Brown Brothers. **p. 837** National Portrait Gallery, Smithsonian Institution / Art Resource, NY. **p. 839** © Archive Photos / Frank Driggs Collection. **p. 840** © Bettmann / Corbis. **p. 841 (top)** *Pitchin' Man*, by Satchel Paige, published by Alfred A. Knopf. **p. 841 (bottom)** National Baseball Hall of Fame Library. Cooperstown, N.Y. **p. 843** The Granger Collection. **p. 845** Chicano Studies Reseach Library, University of California, Los Angeles. **p. 846** The Granger Collection, New York.

CHAPTER 25

p. 848 Detroit Industry, North Wall, 1932-1933., Diego Rivera. Gift of Edsel B. Ford. Photograph © 1991 The Detroit Institute of Arts. **p. 849** The Granger Collection, New York. **p. 853** © Bettmann / Corbis. **pp. 856 and 858** from the Collections of the Library of Congress. **p. 859** Kansas State Historical Society. **p. 861** © Bettmann / Corbis. **pp. 863 and 865** © UPI-Bettmann / Corbis. **p. 867** The

Congress of Industrial Organizations
(CIO), 878. *See also* AFL-CIO
anticommunism and, 922
in Second World War, 914
Congress of Racial Equality (CORE),
996
in Second World War, 924
Connecticut, 72
charter for, 99
Pequot Indians and, 73–74
Connecticut Compromise, 250
Conquest, patterns of, 42–43
Conquistadores, 34–39
in Mexico, 34
in North America, 35–39
in Peru, 34–35
Conscience Whigs, 470, 471, 649
Consciousness-raising, for women,
1060
Conscription. *See also* Draft (military)
law (1863), 568–569
Conservationist movement, 732–733
Conservation Reserve Program, 1053
Conservatism
cultural, 376, 716–717
election of 1964 and, 1006–1007
election of 1980 and, 1086–1087
of New Right, 1073–1076
"new woman" and, 707–708
of Reagan, 1090–1091
religious, 375–376
Republican use of term, 1092–1093
social agenda of, 1075–1076
Consolidation, of corporations,
682–683
Constitution(s)
British, 116–117
citizenship rights in states and,
278
Confederate, 527
for ex-Confederate states,
600–601, 607, 609–610
free-state in Kansas, 494
Lecompton, 499–501
of New South states, 646–647
in South, 150
Constitution (U.S.), 222
as compact between sovereign
states, 437
drafting of, 214, 249–251
national security concerns and,
951–952
New Jersey Plan and, 250
Pennsylvania model and, 222–223
Virginia and Kentucky Resolves
and, 302
Virginia model and, 222
Virginia Plan and, 250
Constitutional Convention, 214, 245,
248, 249–251
Constitutional convention(s)
black and white participation in
(1867-1868), 610 (map)
in ex-Confederate states, 609–610
Constitutionalism, in Massachusetts,
223–225

Constitutional rule, in colonies, 108
Constitutional Union Party, 521
Consumer credit, 816
Consumer price index (1865-1897),
668
Consumers and consumerism
advertising and, 816–818
durables vs. perishables, 815
on farms, 336–337
in Fifties, 974
mass culture and, 1059
product safety and, 1026
retail shopping and, 345
in rural areas, 829
in Twenties, 814–815
Consumption
globalization of, 1047–1048
Second New Deal and, 870
Containment policy, 931
at home, 945–952
intensification of, 944–945
Korea and, 943
in Korean War, 941
social change and, 955–956
Truman Doctrine and, 933–934
use of term, 934
Continental Army, 217–218. *See also*
Armed forces; Revolutionary
War
conditions in, 230
Delaware River crossing by, 216
New Jersey Line and, 217
professional European soldiers in,
218
after Revolution, 239–240
Washington and, 207
Continental Congress, 173, 225
First (1774), 203–204
Second (1775), 207–208
Continental dollar, collapse of, 230
Contrabands (slaves), 558, 560–561
in Union army, 579
Contracts
in Second World War, 912–913
Supreme Court on, 326
Contract with America, 1105
Contras. See also Iran-*Contra* affair
in Nicaragua, 1095
Convention(s), for secession, 473,
475, 524–525
Convention of towns (Massachusetts),
187
Conversion
among northern common people,
365
Sunday schools and, 358–359
Conversion of Indians, 33, 36–39,
100. *See also* Christianity; Mis-
sions and missionaries
by Jesuits, 51
in New England, 72
Puritans and, 47, 100–101
Convict leasing system, 647
Cooke, Jay, 619
Coolidge, Calvin, 805, 823–824
on business, 819

maldistribution of wealth and,
851–852
troops removed by, 826
Cooper, James Fenimore, *Last of the
Mohicans*, 166–167
Cooperatives
Farmers' Alliance and, 670
farming, 654–655
Grange and, 655
Copernicus, Nicolas, 8
Copley, John Singleton, 126, 201
Copper
Indians and, 20
inventions and demand for, 632
Copperheads, 562, 566–567
COPS (Communities Organized for
Public Service), 1068
Coral Sea, Battle of, 905
Corcoran, Thomas "Tommy the
Cork," 875
CORE. *See* Congress of Racial
Equality (CORE)
Corinth, battle at, 551
Corn, as crop, 62
Corning Glass Company, 974
Cornplanter, 228
Cornwallis, Charles, earl, 217, 232,
233, 235–236, 238
surrender at Yorktown, 238
Coronado, Francisco Vasquez de, 36
Corporate form of government, in
New England, 94
Corporations, 387, 677
antitrust movement and, 660
consolidation of, 682–683
First World War taxation and, 794
foreign, 1048
growth of, 680–681
Roosevelt, Franklin D., and,
873–874
Roosevelt, Theodore, and, 733
in Second World War, 912
Supreme Court on contract rights,
326
Correa, Juan, 18
Corregidor, 905
Corridos, 844
Corrupt Bargain, election of 1824
and, 425–426, 427, 429
Corruption
election of 1824 and, 426
during Grant administration, 612,
613, 619
Jackson and, 431–432
popular anger over, 733–734
Cortes, Ernesto, Jr., 1068
Cortés, Hernán, 17
Mesoamerican culture and, 25
Cortés Scuttles Ship (Graeff), xlviii
Cosby, William, 137
Cosmopolitans, vs. localists, 248–249
Cost-accounting methods, 683
Costa Rica, 773, 970
Costs. *See also* Budget
of First World War, 788
of government, 108–109

I-64 | INDEX

UNO (United Neighborhood Organization), 1068
Unsafe at Any Speed (Nader), 1026
Unterseeboot (U-boat), 781. *See also* Submarine warfare
Upper Canada. *See also* Ontario
invasion of, 315
Upper house, 222
Upper South, 130
Confederacy's appeal to, 528
slaves in, 130
Urban areas, 1044–1046. *See also* Cities and towns
barrios in, 643
black communities in, 701–702
business in, 343–345
changes in (1950-1990), 1045 (map)
immigrant living conditions in, 695
issues in, 988–989
mass transit in, 679
population of (1790), 272
revival of, 1110–1111
sprawl in, 1044–1046
suburban growth and, 956–959
Urban commercial classes, Whig support from, 388
Urban corridors, 1046 (map)
Urbanization, in Twenties, 828–829
Urban League. *See* National Urban League
Urban middle class, Christian Whig politics of, 388
Urban renewal, 954
programs, 988
Urban societies, in Americas, 20
Ursuline nuns, 124
Uruguay Round, 1113
Ury, John, 155
Utah Territory, Mormons in, 461
Utopia, in Georgia, 140–141
Utrecht, Treaty of, 123
U-2 surveillance flights, 990

V
Vacations, 815
Vaccination, for polio, 954
Valentino, Rudolph, 819
Vallandigham, Clement L., 567, 583
Valley Forge, Washington at, 218
Valley of Mexico, 17–19, 20
Aztecs in, 27–28
in 1519, 27 (map)
Mayan trade with, 26
"Vamps," in movies, 706
Van Buren, Martin, 442
appointment as minister to Great Britain, 439–440
Democratic Party development and, 424
Eaton controversy and, 439
election of 1828 and, 428–429
election of 1836 and, 447–448
election of 1840 and, 448–449, 450

election of 1844 and, 463
election of 1848 and, 471
Lob Cabin Campaign and, 433
Panic of 1837 and, 447
political appointments and, 432–433
as secretary of state, 431, 434
Texas annexation and, 462
Trail of Tears and, 435–436
as vice presidential candidate, 439
Van Buren, "Prince" John, 411
Vance, Cyrus, 1084, 1085
Vandenberg, Arthur, 933
Vanderbilt, Cornelius, 685
Vanderbilt, William, 656
Van de Velde, Willem, the Younger, 88
Van Dorn, Earl, 554
Van Evrie, John, 407
Van Kleeck, Mary, 875
Van Rensselaer family, 193
Vanzetti, Bartolomeo, 808, 836
Vaudreuil, Pierre de Rigaud de, 164
VCRs, 1055, 1056
Veblen, Thorstein, 656, 714, 719
VE Day, 931
Venezuela, 766, 970
Venona files, 935, 948, 950
Veracruz, 17
Battle of, 468
occupation of, 774
Verdun, battle at, 780
Vergennes, comte de (Charles Gravier), 219–220 239
Vermont
Green Mountain Boys and, 244
as state, 266
Vernon, Edward, 154
Verplanck family, 143
Verrazano, Giovanni da, 47
Versailles Treaty, 800–801
U.S. ratification battle, 801–805
Wilson and, 739
Vesey, Denmark, 383, 437
Vespucci, Amerigo, 17
Veterans
African American, 799
Bonus Army and, 853–854
after First World War, 805
GI Bill and, 953
GI loans and, 957
pensions for Union, 650
Veterans Administration, housing loans and, 957
Veterans' Readjustment Assistance Act (1952). *See* GI Bill of Rights
"V-for-Victory" sign, 914
Vice admiralty courts, 114
Vice president. *See also* specific vice presidents
appointment of Ford, 1033–1034
resignation of Agnew, 1033
Viceroyalties, Spanish, 40
Vichy France, 893, 900
North African campaign and, 900

Vicksburg
Battle of, 551–552
campaign, 576–577, 577 (map)
during Civil War, 566
Victorianism, 706
Victuallers, 274
Video revolution, 1055–1057
Vieques, protests in, 1069
Viet Minh, 973
Vietnam. *See also* Vietnam War
Eisenhower and, 972–973
flexible response program and, 995
Ford and, 1080
immigrants from, 1042
Vietnamization policy, 1020
Nixon and, 1029–1030
Vietnam War, 1010 (map)
aftermath of, 1030–1031
American attitudes toward, 1015
antiwar movement and, 1013–1015
Christmas bombing and, 1029
escalation of, 1009–1013
images of, 1030–1031
media coverage of, 1013
in 1968, 1019–1020
Nixon and, 1028–1030
Paris peace accord and, 1030
Vietnam War Memorial, 1002
Vigilantism
in First World War, 799
on mining frontier, 633
regulators and, 195
Vikings, 6–7
Villa, Francisco ("Pancho"), 774
Villages. *See also* Cities and towns; Urban areas
farming, 5
Vinland colony, 6
Violence. *See also* Race riots; Riot(s)
against abolitionists, 405–406
antiblack, 809
at Democratic Convention (1968), 1021
in ex-Confederate states, 610
Haymarket bombing and, 662–663
in mining frontier, 632–633
against slaves, 132
against southern black voters, 611–612
in Vietnam War (1968), 1019–1020
Virginia, 193. *See also* Bacon's Rebellion (1676); Chesapeake region; Civil War (U.S.)
cession of land claims by, 244
Gabriel's Rebellion in, 286–287
government of, 63
headright system in, 62
Indian wars and, 100, 103–104
manumission in, 241, 268
militia in, 237–238
Powhatan chiefdom and, 100
in Revolutionary War, 236, 237–238, 239 (map)
royal charter for, 62

Wives. *See also* Families and family
    life; Women
    political, in 1820s Washington,
      438
Wolfe, James, 164, 165, 168–169,
    200–201
Woman of the Year (film), 878
Woman's sphere. *See also* Separate
    spheres
    teaching profession and, 503, 504
Woman suffrage, 707, 725–726
    Fifteenth Amendment and, 611
    film documentary on movement,
      414–415
    First World War and, 795
    before 1920, 725 (map)
Women
    activism of, 714–717
    Addams and, 716
    advertising to, 817
    African American, 1064
    anglicizing role of, 129–130
    changing roles of, 961–962
    in Chesapeake region, 65
    cigarette smoking and, 682
    during Civil War, 570–572
    clubwomen and, 717
    in cotton mills of New South, 645
    crops and, 5
    domesticity and, 357–359
    economic independence of, 707
    economic self-sufficiency of, 1060
    farm work and, 19, 257–258,
      339–340
    "female" professions and, 822
    feminine stereotypes and, 918
    as femmes fatales, 964
    in First World War, 789, 790
    as flappers, 818
    glass ceiling and, 1060
    in higher education (1870-1930),
      715
    historical resources on, 412, 724
    household responsibilities of, 257
    housing built by, 19
    in Indian societies, 33–34
    in Knights of Labor, 661
    in labor unions, 914
    liberties in Massachusetts, 75
    Lincoln-Douglas debates and, 513
    literacy of, 277
    loans and home ownership by, 959
    in medicine during Civil War,
      570–572
    as midwives, 258
    migration to West and, 458–459
    in ministry, 1061
    moral crusades and, 413–414
    in New Deal, 875–878
    in New France, 51
    occupations of, 791
    in outwork system, 508
    prostitution and, 508
    among Quakers, 84
    revivalism and, 145–146, 147
    after Revolution, 242

    in Second World War, 913, 914
    in sentimental fiction, 359
    sex ratio in colonies, 91
    slavery and, 196–197, 270–271,
      347
    as soldiers in Civil War, 572
    in South, 374
    as spies during Civil War, 572
    sports and, 687
    suburban family life and, 959–961
    on Supreme Court, 1090, 1103
    teaching and, 395, 503, 504
    in textile mills, 343
    voting rights in New Jersey, 242,
      243
    voting rights of, 278
    in westward movement, 457
    white vs. black laborers and, 347
    workday limits for, 716
    in workforce, 821–822, 913, 914,
      961–962
Women of the Ku Klux Klan, 830,
    831
Women's Bureau, 875
Women's Central Association for Re-
    lief, 571
Women's Christian Temperance
    Union (WCTU), 717
Women's issues, activism in,
    1059–1061
Women's liberation movement, doc-
    uments from, 1025
Women's rights, 414–416
    Civil War and, 572
    Kennedy and, 999–1000
    march for, 1027
    after Revolution, 242–243
    right to vote and, 426
    state legislation for, 416
    woman suffrage and, 725–726
Women's Rights Convention, 414,
    416
Wood, as fuel, 335
Wood, Leonard, 755, 762
Wood, Robert E., 894
Woodland Indians, destruction of,
    262–264
Woods, Eldrick ("Tiger"), 1072
Wool, John E., 465
Woolens Act (1699), 116
Woolman, John, 196
Woolworth Building, 678
Worcester v. *Georgia*, 435
Workday
    courts and, 703
    eight-hour, 743
    Hoover and, 824
    of women, 716
Workers
    at Ford, 685
    inequality of wealth and, 655–656
    labor conditions in North,
      505–508
Workforce
    distribution of (1870-1920), 681
    in Fifties, 977

    in First World War, 789
    industrial, 820–821
    in Second World War, 913–915
    skilled, 703
    in South, 351
    unions and, 702–705
    welfare capitalism and, 819–820
    white women in, 707
    women in, 789, 791, 821–822,
      961–962
Working class. *See also* Immigrants
    and immigration
    families in, 508
    living conditions of, 694–695
    novels and penny press for,
      371–372
Workmen's compensation law, 743
Workplace
    Ford and, 685
    safety in, 693, 694
    sexual harassment and, 1061
Works Progress Administration
    (WPA), 872, 912
    arts and, 879
    New York City projects, 1938,
      871
Workweek, 860
    in First World War, 789
    length of, 693–694
World Bank, 926
World Economic Conference, Roo-
    sevelt, Franklin D., and, 883
World power, United States as, 746,
    747, 756–764
World's Fair (1851), 503
World Trade Center, 1112
World Trade Organization (WTO),
    protests against, 1059
World War I. *See* First World War
World War II. *See* Second World
    War
World War II Memorial, 929
World Wide Web, 1047
Wounded Knee, confrontation at,
    638
WPA. *See* Works Progress Adminis-
    tration (WPA)
Wrangel Island, 4
Wright, Frank Lloyd, 714, 716
Wright, Richard, 922, 949
Wright, Silas, 436
Wright brothers, 655
Wrigley, 912
Writers. *See also* Literature; Lost
    Generation; specific writers
    adventure, 371
    black, 1063–1064
    in England, 117
    FBI files on, 949
    mass culture and, 1058–1059
    sentimentality of, 359–360
    white southern, 846
Writ of habeas corpus. *See* Habeas
    corpus, writ of
Written language
    Aztec, 34

**Sidney Silverman Library
and Learning Resource Center
Bergen Community College
400 Paramus Road
Paramus, NJ 07652-1595**

www.bergen.cc.nj.us

Return Postage Guaranteed

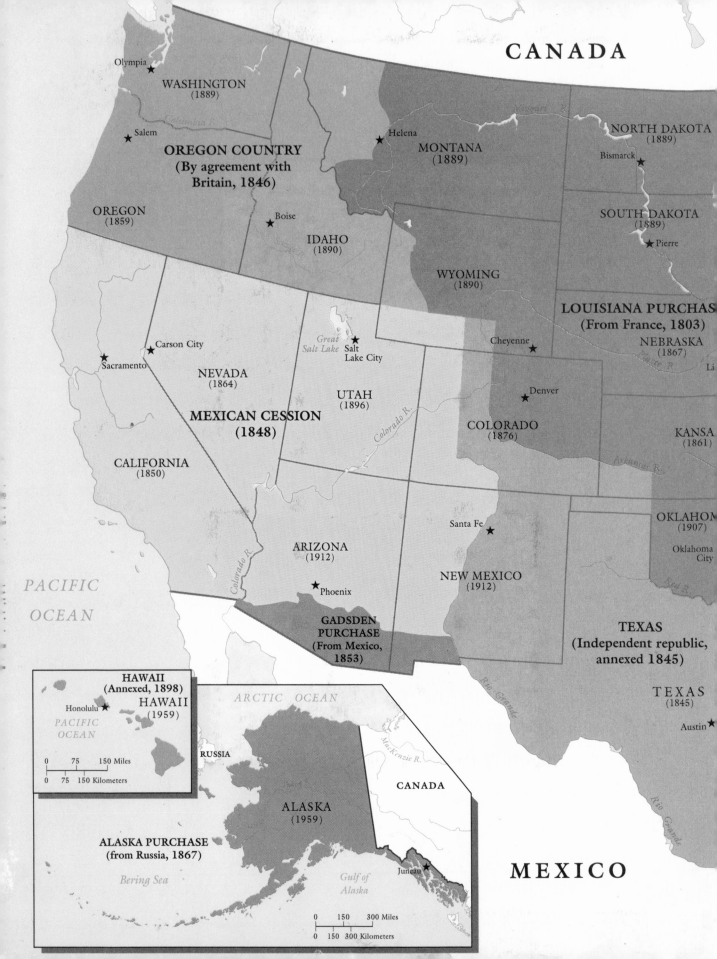

CANADA

Olympia ★
WASHINGTON
(1889)

Salem ★

OREGON COUNTRY
(By agreement with
Britain, 1846)

OREGON
(1859)

Boise ★
IDAHO
(1890)

Helena ★
MONTANA
(1889)

NORTH DAKOTA
(1889)

Bismarck ★

SOUTH DAKOTA
(1889)

Pierre ★

WYOMING
(1890)

LOUISIANA PURCHASE
(From France, 1803)

NEBRASKA
(1867)

Carson City ★

Sacramento ★

NEVADA
(1864)

Great
Salt Lake ★ Salt
Lake City

UTAH
(1896)

Cheyenne ★

Denver ★
COLORADO
(1876)

KANSAS
(1861)

MEXICAN CESSION
(1848)

CALIFORNIA
(1850)

Colorado R.

Colorado R.

ARIZONA
(1912)

Phoenix ★

Santa Fe ★

NEW MEXICO
(1912)

OKLAHOMA
(1907)

Oklahoma
City

PACIFIC

OCEAN

GADSDEN
PURCHASE
(From Mexico,
1853)

TEXAS
(Independent republic,
annexed 1845)

TEXAS
(1845)

Austin ★

HAWAII
(Annexed, 1898)
HAWAII
(1959)

Honolulu ★

PACIFIC
OCEAN

0   75   150 Miles

0   75   150 Kilometers

ARCTIC OCEAN

RUSSIA

MacKenzie R.

CANADA

ALASKA
(1959)

ALASKA PURCHASE
(from Russia, 1867)

Bering Sea

Juneau ★

Gulf of
Alaska

MEXICO

Rio Grande

Rio Grande

0   150   300 Miles

0   150   300 Kilometers